W9-BVH-919

Dear West Customer:

West Academic Publishing has changed the look of its American Casebook Series®.

In keeping with our efforts to promote sustainability, we have replaced our former covers with book covers that are more environmentally friendly. Our casebooks will now be covered in a 100% renewable natural fiber. In addition, we have migrated to an ink supplier that favors vegetable-based materials, such as soy.

Using soy inks and natural fibers to print our textbooks reduces VOC emissions. Moreover, our primary paper supplier is certified by the Forest Stewardship Council, which is testament to our commitment to conservation and responsible business management.

The new cover design has migrated from the long-standing brown cover to a contemporary charcoal fabric cover with silver-stamped lettering and black accents. Please know that inside the cover, our books continue to provide the same trusted content that you've come to expect from West.

We've retained the ample margins that you have told us you appreciate in our texts while moving to a new, larger font, improving readability. We hope that you will find these books a pleasing addition to your bookshelf.

Another visible change is that you will no longer see the brand name Thomson West on our print products. With the recent merger of Thomson and Reuters, I am pleased to announce that books published under the West Academic Publishing imprint will once again display the West brand.

It will likely be several years before all of our casebooks are published with the new cover and interior design. We ask for your patience as the new covers are rolled out on new and revised books knowing that behind both the new and old covers, you will find the finest in legal education materials for teaching and learning.

Thank you for your continued patronage of the West brand, which is both rooted in history and forward looking towards future innovations in legal education. We invite you to be a part of our next evolution.

Best regards,

Louis H. Higgins
Editor in Chief, West Academic Publishing

West's Law School Advisory Board

CIVIL PROCEDURE
CASES AND MATERIALS

Tenth Edition

▪ ▪ ▪

By

Jack H. Friedenthal
Edward F. Howrey Professor of Law
George Washington University

Arthur R. Miller
University Professor
New York University
Formerly Bruce Bromley Professor of Law
Harvard University

John E. Sexton
President and Benjamin Butler Professor of Law
New York University

Helen Hershkoff
Anne and Joel Ehrenkranz Professor of Law
New York University

AMERICAN CASEBOOK SERIES®

WEST®
A Thomson Reuters business

Mat #40635232

610 Opperman Drive
St. Paul, MN 55123
1–800–313–9378

Printed in the United States of America

ISBN: 978–0–314–18402–3

For Jo Anne

—Jack

In Ellen's Memory

—Arthur

For Lisa

—John

For my family

—Helen

*

PREFACE

This Tenth Edition offers an up-to-date and accessible approach to the study of civil procedure. Students tend to find Civil Procedure the most mysterious of their law school courses. Our goal in this edition is to present the material in a clear and simple environment, yet one that challenges and stimulates the student toward increasing critical understanding. Moreover, because courses in civil procedure vary greatly as to the hours allotted, the extent to which they are mandatory or optional, and the law school year or years when students are expected to enroll in them, we have designed this edition for maximum flexibility in terms of an individual classroom's coverage, depth, sensibility, and emphasis.

This revised edition reflects the restyled Federal Rules of Civil Procedure and covers important new Supreme Court cases on pleading, federal jurisdiction, summary judgment, due process, and res judicata. The edition addresses not simply doctrinal change, but also the still uncertain effects of new technology, globalism, and privatization on the system of civil justice. The edition also responds to the many helpful comments from judges, practitioners, colleagues, and students at the large number of schools in which earlier editions have been used. Our conversations confirm our own conclusion that the book is and continues to be a highly successful teaching tool, and we have preserved the basic format and much of the material in the earlier edition. When we have deleted earlier material, our preference has been to substitute contemporary cases in which the facts are interesting, in which the conflicting policies seem to be in a state of equilibrium, or in which the context has extrinsic fascination, rather than materials that offer a tight monograph on various aspects of procedure. In addition, we have streamlined some earlier notes and cases to make room for cutting-edge issues—including the effect of the Internet on personal jurisdiction, the federalization of interstate, state law class actions, the relation between human rights litigation and forum non conveniens doctrine, the effect of pleading rules on corporate accountability and civil rights enforcement, and the incorporation of alternative dispute resolution techniques into judicial practice—that we believe will contribute in positive ways to a lively and engaged classroom discussion.

As has been the practice with all of the past editions, we offer substantial emphasis on the operation of the Federal Rules of Civil Procedure and also draw comparisons with state and international practice. The materials in this volume refer to and are augmented by a Supplement, which contains not only the federal statutes and rules governing procedure, but also selected state provisions for comparison. A number of other materials, such as Advisory Committee notes, proposed rule alterations, and local court rules, also are included. The Supplement contains a litigation timechart and an illustrative litigation problem, showing how a case develops in practice and samples of the documents that actually might have formed a portion of the record. These samples are not designed as models to be emulated. To the contrary, they often contain defects intended to encourage students to criticize them in light of knowledge they have obtained from the cases and classroom discussion. The Supplement also includes the complaint from a principal leading case and an important note case.

The cases and excerpts from other materials have been edited carefully in order to shorten them and clarify issues for discussion. With regard to footnotes, the same numbering appears in the casebook as appears in the original sources; our footnotes are indicated by letters. Omissions are indicated with asterisks.

The authors are deeply grateful to a host of people who have assisted us in the preparation of this volume, the earlier editions, and the Supplements. Among our students deserving special mention for the aid they have provided in preparing earlier editions of the book are Judge Prudence C. Beatty, Sam L. Abram, Kim Barry, James J. Beha, Jeffrey A. Benjamin, (Professor) Richard B. Bernstein, Michael Blasie, (Professor) Barry B. Boyer, (Professor) Michael Broyde, William M. Burns, Bertram Carp, (Professor) Sanford Caust–Ellenbogen, Anna L. Cavnar, Jeffrey J. Chapman, Daniel Chazin, Tan Yee Cheung, Caroline P. Cincotta, Adam S. Cohen, Stephanie Cohen, Steven Cohen, Diane Costa, Russell C. Crane, David Drueding, Gary Eisenberg, Seth K. Endo, Lisa Fair, David E. Firestone, (Judge) Raymond Fisher, Grant H. Franks, Kelly A. Frawley, Patrick P. Garlinger, Stacy Gershwind, Lisa E. Goldberg, Robert H. Goldman, Steven F. Goldman, Ashley K. Goodale, Amanda W. Goodin, Susanna R. Greenberg, Debra L. Greenberger, Kimberly M. Greene, Kevin A. Griffin, Edward Hartnett, Daniel M. Hennefeld, Nancy Louise Hoffman, Wendy B. Jacobs, (Professor) Joe J. Kalo, (Dean) Mary Kay Kane, Lonnie Keene, Christopher D. Kercher, Tarek M. Khanachet, Amy Kimpel, Jessica M. Kumm, Pearline M. Kyi, Daniel Laguardia, Fredrick W. Lambert, Judyann M. Lee, Susan S. Lee, Kevin J. Lynch, Alexandra A. Magness, Christopher Mahon, Shirin Malkani, Maureen P. Manning, (Professor) John J. McGonagle, Matthew McGrath, Kiran H. Mehta, Lisabeth C. Meletta, Franklin N. Meyer, Gary Meyerhoff, Tara Mikkilineni, Joy E. Milligan, Jennifer Nevins, John Nichols, Greg G. Oehler, Marcy Oppenheimer, Jennifer Pariser, Dawn A. Pederson, Avi Perry, Kate Elizabeth Phillips, Norman A. Platt, Martin C. Recchuite, Christopher Reich, James E. Rossman, Beth A. Rotman, Gregory S. Schmolka, Marc Schuback, (Professor) Linda J. Silberman, Donna Silverberg, Robert Silvers, (Professor) William Slomanson, Roger D. Smith, David A. Stein, Brian A. Stern, Christopher M. Straw, Reuben B. Teague, Eva A. Temkin, Mara E. Trager, Lee Turner–Dodge, Jacqueline Veit, (Professor) Michael Vitiello, and Gail Zweig. For their help in preparing the Tenth Edition, we thank the following students of New York University School of Law: Brandon Adoni, Gabriel Bedoya, Lina Bensman, John M. Bentil, Matt Brown, Stavan Shivraj Desai, Drew Johnson–Skinner, Xiang Li, Jeanette E. Markle, Claire Martirosian, Christen M. Martosella, Chris C. Morley, Benjamin M. Stoll, Robert M. Swan, Gregory Tuttle, Christopher R. Utecht, Ellison S. Ward, and Nir Zicherman. We also thank Nancy Louise Hoffman, a student at The George Washington University Law School, for her help on this volume and earlier editions. Roxanne Birkel and Louis Higgins of Thomson–West deserve special mention. We also extend deep thanks to Jo Anne Friedenthal and Stephen Loffredo for personal encouragement and intellectual support; to Dan Evans, Stephen Wagner, Erica Tate, Michael Malavarca, and Kristin Silberman for important work on this volume or prior editions; to Gretchen Feltes and Linda Ramsingh for exemplary library support; and to John Easterbrook and Silah Karim for invaluable assistance on this volume and prior editions.

Finally, we sincerely thank our many colleagues and students across the legal community for the countless excellent suggestions they have offered. Their contributions have been instrumental in the preparation of this Tenth Edition.

J.H.F.

A.R.M.

J.E.S.

H.H.

June 2009

*

Summary of Contents

TABLE OF CONTENTS

TABLE OF CASES

The principal cases are in bold type. Cases cited or discussed in the text are in roman type. References are to pages. Cases cited in principal cases and within other quoted materials are not included.

*

Table of Authorities

References are to Pages

Grant, The Domestic Relations Exception to Diversity Jurisdiction: Spousal Support Enforcement in the Federal Courts, 14 J. Contemp. Legal Issues 15 (2004), 293

Graves, Marshall v. Marshall: The Past, Present, and Future of the Probate Exception to Federal Jurisdiction, 59 Ala.L.Rev. 1643 (2008), 294

Green & Bornstein, Determining Damages: The Psychology of Jury Awards (2003), 1044

Green & Matasar, The Supreme Court and the Products Liability Crisis: Lessons from Boyle's Government Contractor Defense, 63 S.Calif.L.Rev. 637 (1989–1990), 492

Green, Justice Scalia and Ancillary Jurisdiction: Teaching a Lame Duck New Tricks in Kokkonen v. Guardian Life Insurance Company of America, 81 Va.L.Rev. 631 (1995), 349

Green, Repressing Erie's Myth, 96 Calif.L.Rev. 595 (2008), 415

Greenbaum, Jacks or Better to Open: Procedural Limitations on Co–Party and Third–Party Claims, 74 Minn.L.Rev. 507 (1990), 656

Greenbaum, The Postman Never Rings Twice: The Constitutionality of Service of Process by Posting After Greene v. Lindsey, 33 Am. U.L.Rev. 601 (1984), 209

Greenberger, Justice Scalia's Due Process Traditionalism Applied to Territorial Jurisdiction: The Illusion of Adjudication Without Judgment, 33 B.C.L.Rev. 981 (1992), 185

Grenig, The Civil Jury in America: Improving the Jury's Understanding of a Case, 24 Am.J. Trial Advoc. 93 (2000), 1095

Grimm, Berman, Crowley & Wharton, Proportionality in the Post-hoc Analysis of Pre–Litigation Preservation Decisions, 37 U.Balt.L.Rev. 381 (2008), 877

Gross, Settling for a Judge: A Comment on Clermont & Eisenberg, 77 Cornell L.Rev. 1178 (1992), 1045

Gross, When Perception Changes Reality: An Empirical Study of Investors' Views of the Fairness of Securities Arbitration, 2008 J.Disp.Resol. 349 (2008), 1377

Hadfield, Framing the Choice between Cash and the Courthouse: Experiences with the 9/11 Victim Compensation Fund, 42 Law & Soc'y Rev. 645 (2008), 1361

Haiber, Removing the Bias Against Removal, 53 Cath.U.L.Rev. 609 (2004), 350

Hamabe, Functions of Rule 12(b)(6) in the Federal Rules of Civil Procedure: A Categorization Approach, 15 Campbell L.Rev. 119 (1993), 584

Hannaford–Agor, Judicial Nullification? Judicial Compliance and Non–Compliance with Jury Improvement Efforts, 28 N.Ill. U.L.Rev. 407 (2008), 1106

Hannon, Note—How Much Ado About Twombly? A Study on the Impact of Bell Atlantic Corp. v. Twombly on 12(b)(6) Motions, 83 Notre Dame L.Rev. 1811 (2008), 609

Hans & Albertson, Empirical Research and Civil Jury Reform, 78 Notre Dame L.Rev. 1497 (2003), 1043

Hans & Jehle, Avoid Bald Men and People with Green Socks? Other Ways To Improve the Voie Dire Process in Jury Selection, 78 Chi.-Kent L.Rev. 1179 (2003), 1061

Hans, Empowering the Active Jury: A Genuine Tort Reform, 13 Roger Williams U.L.Rev. 39 (2008), 1107

Hans, Hannaford & Munsterman, The Arizona Jury Reform Permitting Civil Jury Trial Discussions: The Views of Trial Participants, Judges, and Jurors, 32 U.Mich.J.L.F. 349 (1999), 1107

Hans, Judges, Juries, and Scientific Evidence, 16 J.L. & Pol'y 19 (2007), 1015

Hanson & Rottman, United States: So Many States, So Many Reforms, 20 Just.Sys.J. 121 (1999), 930

Harrington, The Law–Finding Function of the American Jury, Wis.L.Rev. 377 (1999), 1036

Hart, And the Chill Goes On—Federal Civil Rights Plaintiffs Beware: Rule 11 vis-à-vis 28 U.S.C. '1927 and the Court's Inherent Power, 37 Loy.L.A.L.Rev. 645 (2004), 651

Hart, Still Chilling After All These Years: Rule 11 of the Federal Rules of Civil Procedure and Its Impact on Federal Civil Rights Plaintiffs After the 1993 Amendments, 37 Val.U.L.Rev. 1 (2002), 651

Hart, The Relations Between State and Federal Law, 54 Colum.L.Rev. 489 (1954), 499

Hartnett, A New Trick from an Old and Abused Dog: Section 1441(c) Lives and Now Permits the Remand of Federal Question Cases, 63 Fordham L.Rev. 1099 (1995), 361

Hasday, Federalism and the Family Reconstructed, 45 UCLA L.Rev. 1297 (1998), 294

Hay, Civil Discovery: Its Effects and Optimal Scope, 23 J. Legal Stud. 481 (1994), 828

Hay, Transient Jurisdiction Especially Over International Defendants: Critical Comments on Burnham v. Superior Court of California, U.Ill.L.Rev. 593 (1990), 185

Hayes, Crogate's Case: A Dialogue in Ye Shades on Special Pleading, in 9 Holdsworth, A History of English Law 417 (2d ed. 1938), 513

Hayes, That Pernicious Pop–Up, the Prima Facie Case, 39 Suffolk U.L.Rev. 343 (2006), 1091

Hazard & Moskovitz, An Historical and Critical Analysis of Interpleader, 52 Calif.L.Rev. 706 (1964), 718

Hazard, From Whom No Secrets Are Hid, 76 Texas L.Rev. 1665 (1998), 826

Hazard, Has the Erie Doctrine Been Repealed by Congress?, 156 U.Pa.L.Rev. 1629 (2008), 493

Hazard, Indispensable Party: The Historical Origin of a Procedural Phantom, 61 Colum.L.Rev. 1254 (1961), 693

Hazard, Preclusion as to Issues of Law: The Legal System's Interest, 70 Iowa L.Rev. 81 (1984), 1289

Ides, The Supreme Court and the Law To Be Applied in Diversity Cases: A Critical Guide to the Development and Application of the Erie Doctrine and Related Problems, 163 F.R.D. 19 (1995), 416

Ieyoub & Eisenberg, Class Actions in the Gulf South Symposium: State Attorney General Actions, the Tobacco Litigation, and the Doctrine of Parens Patriae, 74 Tul.L.Rev. 1859 (2000), 764

Interpleader in the United States Courts, 41 Yale L.J. 1134 (1932), 42 Yale L.J. 41 (1932), 721

Issacharoff & Loewenstein, Second Thoughts About Summary Judgment, 100 Yale L.J. 73 (1990), 973

Issacharoff & Loewenstein, Unintended Consequences of Mandatory Disclosure, 73 Texas L.Rev. 753 (1995), 852

Issacharoff, Governance and Legitimacy in the Law of Class Actions, 1999 Sup.Ct.Rev. 337 (1999), 741

Issacharoff, Settled Expectations in a World of Unsettled Law: Choice of Law After the Class Action Fairness Act, 106 Colum.L.Rev. 1839 (2006), 795

Jacob, The Elusive Shadow of the Law, 26 L. & Soc'y Rev. 565 (1992), 1364

James, Functions of Judge and Jury in Negligence Cases, 58 Yale L.J. 667 (1949), 1100

James, Sufficiency of the Evidence and Jury–Control Devices Available Before Verdict, 47 Va.L.Rev. 218 (1961), 1143

Johnson, Why Alienage Jurisdiction? Historical Foundations and Modern Justifications for Federal Jurisdiction Over Disputes Involving Noncitizens, 21 Yale J.Int'l L. 1 (1996), 282

Johnston & Johnston, Contention Interrogatories in Federal Court, 148 F.R.D. 441 (1993), 865

Jones, Finishing a Friendly Argument: The Jury and the Historical Origins of Diversity Jurisdiction, 82 N.Y.U.L.Rev. 997 (2007), 273

Jones, Judge–Versus Attorney–Conducted Voir Dire: An Empirical Investigation of Juror Candor, 11 Law & Human Behav. 131 (1987), 1061

Juenger, Judicial Jurisdiction in the United States and in the European Communities: A Comparison, 82 Mich.L.Rev. 1195 (1984), 81

Juror Impeachment of Verdicts, 101 Harv. L.Rev. 250 (1987), 1133

Kahan & Silberman, Matsushita and Beyond: The Role of State Courts in Class Actions Involving Exclusive Federal Claims, 1996 Sup.Ct.Rev. 219 (1996), 1347

Kahan, Hoffman & Braman, Whose Eyes Are You Going To Believe? Scott v. Harris and the Perils of Cognitive Illiberalism, 122 Harv.L.Rev. 837 (2009), 983

Kakalik, Dunworth, Hill, McCaffrey, Oshiro, Pace & Vaiana, Just, Speedy, and Inexpensive? An Evaluation of Judicial Case Management under the Civil Justice Reform Act, 49 Ala.L.Rev. 17 (1997), 930

Kakalik, Dunworth, Hill, McCaffrey, Oshiro, Pace & Vaiana, An Evaluation of Mediation and Early Neutral Evaluation Under the Civil Justice Reform Act (1996), 1386

Kalo, Jurisdiction as an Evolutionary Process: The Development of Quasi In Rem and In Personam Principles, Duke L.J. 1147 (1978), 101

Kalven & Rosenfield, The Contemporary Function of a Class Suit, 8 U.Chi.L.Rev. 684 (1941), 743

Kalven, The Dignity of the Civil Jury, 50 Va. L.Rev. 1055 (1964), 1100

Kamp, The History Behind Hansberry v. Lee, 20 U.C. Davis L.Rev. 481 (1987), 781

Kane, Civil Jury Trial: The Case for Reasoned Iconoclasm, 28 Hastings L.J. 1 (1976), 1013

Kane, Of Carrots and Sticks: Evaluating the Role of the Class Action Lawyer, 66 Texas L.Rev. 385 (1987), 771

Kane, Original Sin and the Transaction in Federal Civil Procedure, 76 Texas L.Rev. 1723 (1998), 663

Kane, Relief from Federal Judgments: A Morass Unrelieved by a Rule, 30 Hastings L.J. 41 (1978), 1154

Kaplan, Amendments of the Federal Rules of Civil Procedure, 1961–1963 (II), 77 Harv. L.Rev. 801 (1964), 711

Kaplan, Continuing Work of the Civil Committee: 1966 Amendments of the Federal Rules of Civil Procedure (I), 81 Harv.L.Rev. 356 (1967), 702

Kaplan, Paddling Up the Wrong Stream: Why the Stream of Commerce Theory Is Not Part of the Minimum Contacts Doctrine, 55 Baylor L.Rev. 503 (2003), 138

Kaufman, Masters in the Federal Courts: Rule 53, 58 Colum.L.Rev. 452 (1958), 948

Kay & Lubin, Making Sense of the Prejudgment Seizure Cases, 64 Ky.L.J. 705 (1976), 254

Kaye & Weissman, Interactive Judicial Federalism: Certified Questions in New York, 69 Fordham L.Rev. 373 (2000), 471

Keefe & Roscia, Immunity and Sentimentality, 47 Cornell L.Q. 471 (1947), 236

Keeton, Time Limits as Incentives in an Adversary System, 137 U.Pa.L.Rev. 2053 (1989), 930

Kelleher, The December 1993 Amendments to the Federal Rules of Civil Procedure—A Critical Analysis, 12 Touro L.Rev. 7 (1995), 931

Kelner, Note—"Adrift on an Unchartered Sea": A Survey of Section 1404(a) Transfer in the Federal System, 67 N.Y.U.L.Rev. 612 (1992), 389

Kelso, A Report on the California Appellate System, 45 Hastings L.J. 433 (1994), 1192

Kennedy, Counterclaims Under Federal Rule 13, 11 Houston L.Rev. 255 (1974), 658

Kennedy, Federal Summary Judgment: Reconciling Celotex v. Catrett with Adickes v.

Martin, Rationalizing the Irrational, The Treatment of Untenable Federal Civil Jury Verdicts, 28 Creighton L.Rev. 683 (1995), 1132

Massey, The Excessive Fines Clause and Punitive Damages: Some Lessons from History, 40 Vand.L.Rev. 1233 (1987), 1172

Maull, ADR in the Federal Courts: Would Uniformity Be Better?, 34 Duq.L.Rev. 245 (1996), 1386

McClintock, Equity (2d ed. 1948), 718, 1169

McCoid, Procedural Reform and the Right to Jury Trial, 116 U.Pa.L.Rev. 1 (1967), 1009

McDaniel, Jr., Case Note—First National Bank of Dewitt v. Cruthis: An Analysis of the Right to a Jury Trial in Arkansas after the Merger of Law and Equity, 60 Ark.L.Rev. 563 (2007), 1036

McDonald, Alternative Pleading: I, 48 Mich. L.Rev. 311 (1950), 594

McFarland, In Search of the Transaction or Occurrence: Counterclaims, 40 Creighton L.Rev. 699 (2007), 662

McFarland, The Unconstitutional Stub of Section 1441(c), 54 Ohio St. L.J. 1059 (1993), 356

McGovern, Appointing Special Masters and Other Judicial Adjuncts: A Handbook for Judges (ALI–ABA, 2007), 949

McInnis, The $75,000.01 Question: What is the Value of Injunctive Relief, 6 Geo.Mason L.Rev. 1013 (1998), 292

Mckelway, Profiles—Place and Leave With, New Yorker, August 24, 1935, 217

McMahon, The Law of Unintended Consequences: Shockwaves in the Lower Courts After Bell Atlantic Corp. v. Twombly, 41 Suffolk U.L.Rev. 851 (2008), 579

McManamon, Dispelling the Myths of Pendent and Ancillary Jurisdiction: The Ramifications of a Revised History, 46 Wash. & Lee L.Rev. 863 (1989), 330

Meadows, Rule 60(b)(6): Whether "Tapping the Grand Reservoir of Equitable Power" Is Appropriate To Right an Attorney's Wrong, 88 Marq.L.Rev. 997 (2005), 1154

Melilli, Succeeding in the Opening Statement, 28 Am.J.Trial Advoc. 525 (2006), 1066

Meltzer, State Court Forfeitures of Federal Rights, 99 Harv.L.Rev. 1128 (1986), 476

Menkel–Meadow, Pursuing Settlement in an Adversary Culture: A Tale of Innovation Co-opted or "The Law of ADR," 19 Fla.St. U.L.Rev. 1 (1990), 1371

Menkel–Meadow, The Lawyer as Problem Solver and Third–Party Neutral: Creativity and Non–Partisanship in Lawyering, 72 Temple L.Rev. 785 (1999), 1360

Menkel–Meadow, Whose Dispute Is It Anyway?: A Philosophical and Democratic Defense of Settlement (In Some Cases), 83 Geo.L.J. 2663 (1995), 1382

Merrigan, Erie to York to Ragan—A Triple Play on the Federal Rules, 3 Vand.L.Rev. 711 (1950), 424

Michael, The Basic Rules of Pleading, 5 Record of N.Y.C.B.A. 175 (1950), 1079

Michelman, The Supreme Court and Litigation Access Fees: The Right to Protect One's Rights, 1973 Duke L.J. 1153 (1973), 213

Michels, Case Management Techniques Work, 18 Just.Sys.J. 75 (1995), 1062

Mickum, Guise, Contrivance, or Artful Dodging? The Discovery Rules Governing Testifying Employee Experts, 24 Rev.Litig. 301 (2005), 920

Millar, Civil Procedure of the Trial Court in Historical Perspective (1952), 1163

Millar, Counterclaim Against Counterclaim, 48 Nw.U.L.Rev. 671 (1954), 667

Millar, The Joinder of Actions in Continental Civil Procedure, 28 Ill.L.Rev. 26 (1933), 679

Millar, Three American Ventures in Summary Civil Procedure, 38 Yale L.J. 193 (1928), 959

Miller & Crump, Jurisdiction and Choice of Law in Multistate Class Actions After Phillips Petroleum Co. v. Shutts, 96 Yale L.J. 1 (1986), 277, 794

Miller & Kazmar, Psychology Research and Public Opinion Do Not Support Proposed Changes to the Jury System, 30 Hamline L.Rev. 285 (2007), 1049

Miller, An Economic Analysis of Rule 68, 15 J.Legal Studies 93 (1986), 1382

Miller, An Empirical Study of Forum Choices in Removal Cases Under Diversity and Federal Question Jurisdiction, 41 Am.U.L.Rev. 369 (1992), 273

Miller, Artful Pleading: A Doctrine in Search of Definition, 76 Texas L.Rev. 1781 (1998), 303, 1263

Miller, Confidentiality, Protective Orders, and Public Access to the Courts, 105 Harv. L.Rev. 428 (1991), 848

Miller, International Cooperation in Litigation Between the United States and Switzerland: Unilateral Procedural Accommodation in a Test Tube, 49 Minn.L.Rev. 1069 (1965), 228

Miller, Of Frankenstein Monsters and Shining Knights: Myth, Reality, and the "Class Action Problem," 92 Harv.L.Rev. 664 (1979), 744

Miller, Overlapping Class Actions, 71 N.Y.U.L.Rev. 514 (1996), 1169

Miller, Reliving and Reflecting on Shutts, 74 UMKC L.Rev. 505 (2006), 795

Miller, Six of One Is Not a Dozen of the Other: A Reexamination of Williams v. Florida and the Size of State Criminal Juries, 146 U.Pa. L.Rev. 621 (1998), 1047

Miller, The Adversary System: Dinosaur or Phoenix, 69 Minn.L.Rev. 1 (1984), 929

Miller, The August 1983 Amendments to the Federal Rules of Civil Procedure: Promoting Effective Case Management and Lawyer Responsibility (Fed.Jud.Center 1984), 608, 837

Miller, The Pretrial Rush to Judgment: Are the "Litigation Explosion," "Liability Crisis,"

Civil Procedure, 61 Wash.L.Rev. 1367 (1986), 553

Oakley, A Fresh Look at the Federal Rules in State Courts, 3 Nev.L.J. 354 (2003), 25, 553, 836, 930

Oakley, Joinder and Jurisdiction in the Federal District Courts: The State of the Union of Rules and Statutes, 69 Tenn.L.Rev. 35 (2001), 688

Oakley, Kroger Redux, 51 Duke L.J. 663 (2001), 337, 711

Oakley, Recent Statutory Changes in the Law of Federal Jurisdiction and Venue: The Judicial Improvements Acts of 1988 and 1990, 24 U.C.Davis L.Rev. 735 (1991), 382

Oakley, The Story of Owen Equipment v. Kroger: A Change in the Weather of Federal Jurisdiction, in Civil Procedure Stories (Clermont ed. 2008), 332

Oestreicher, "We're on a Road to Nowhere"—Reasons for the Continuing Failure to Regulate Recognition and Enforcement of Foreign Judgments, 42 Int'l Law. 59 (2008), 81

Offenbacher, Note—The Multiparty, Multiforum Trial Jurisdiction Act: Opening the Door to Class Action Reform, 23 Rev. Litig. 177 (2004), 354

Oldham, Origins of the Special Jury, 50 U.Chi. L.Rev. 137 (1983), 1051

Omnibus Consolidated Rescissions and Appropriations Act of 1996, Pub. L. No. 104–134, § 504(a)(7), 110 Stat. 1321–53, 747

Paetty, Classless Not Clueless: A Comparison of Case Management Mechanisms for Non–Class–Based Complex Litigation in California and Federal Courts, 41 Loy.L.A.L.Rev. 845 (2008), 930

Page, After the Judicial Improvements Act of 1990: Does the General Federal Venue Statute Survive as a Protection for Defendants?, 74 U.Colo.L.Rev. 1153 (2002), 383

Parness & Walker, Thinking Outside the Civil Case Box: Reformulating Pretrial Conference Laws, 50 U.Kan. L.Rev. 347 (2002), 939

Parness, Civil Claim Settlement Talks Involving Third Parties and Insurance Company Adjusters: When Should Lawyer Conduct Standards Apply?, 77 St. John's L. Rev. 603 (2003), 939

Peckham, The Federal Judge as Case Manager: The New Role in Guiding a Case from Filing to Disposition, 69 Calif.L.Rev. 770 (1981), 929, 957

Percy, Making a Federal Case of It: Removing Civil Cases to Federal Court Based on Fraudulent Joinder, 91 Iowa L.Rev. 189 (2005), 352

Perdue, Sin, Scandal and Substantive Due Process: Personal Jurisdiction and Pennoyer Reconsidered, 62 Wash.L.Rev. 479 (1987), 79

Perino, Did the Private Securities Litigation Reform Act Work?, 2003 U.Ill.L.Rev. 913 (2003), 593

Peterson, In re AIU Insurance Company, 41 Tex.J.Bus.L. 101 (2005), 374

Peterson, Note—Exemption Stacking in Montana Bankruptcies—"Windfall" or "Fresh Start"?, 64 Mont.L.Rev. 543 (2003), 1179

Peterson, The Misguided Law of Compulsory Counterclaims in Default Cases, 50 Ariz. L.Rev. 1107 (2008), 664, 1269

Pfander, Protective Jurisdiction, Aggregate Litigation, and the Limits of Article III, 95 Calif.L.Rev. 1423 (2007), 299

Phillips & Christenson, The Historical and Legal Background of the Diversity Jurisdiction, 46 A.B.A.J. 959 (1960), 273

Pielemeier, Due Process Limitations on the Application of Collateral Estoppel Against Nonparties to Prior Litigation, 63 B.U.L.Rev. 383 (1983), 1326

Pike, Objections to Pleadings Under the New Federal Rules of Civil Procedure, 47 Yale L.J. 50 (1937), 603

Player, Note—After the Fall: The Cigarette Papers, the Global Settlement, and the Future of Tobacco Litigation, 49 S.C.L.Rev. 311 (1998), 764

Plucknett, A Concise History of the Common Law (5th ed. 1956), 509, 529

Polasky, Collateral Estoppel—Effects of Prior Litigation, 39 Iowa L.Rev. 217 (1954), 1290

1 Pollock & Maitland, The History of English Law (2d ed. 1911), 999

4 Pomeroy, Equity Jurisprudence (5th ed. 1941), 714

Posner, Economic Analysis of Law (4th ed. 1992), 213

Posner, The Federal Courts: Crisis and Reform (1985), 1359

Posner, The Summary Jury Trial and Other Alternative Methods of Alternative Dispute Resolution: Some Cautionary Observations, 53 U.Chi.L.Rev. 366 (1986), 1367

Poulos & Varner, Review of Intermediate Appellate Court Decisions in California, 15 Hastings L.J. 11 (1963), 1246

Powell & Leiferman, Results Most Embarrassing: Discovery and Admissibility of Net Worth of the Defendant, 40 Baylor L.Rev. 527 (1988), 853

Powell, Opening Statements: The Art of Storytelling, 31 Stetson L.Rev. 89 (2001), 1066

Preis, Reassessing the Purposes of Federal Question Jurisdiction, 42 Wake Forest L.Rev. 247 (2007), 295

Priest, Private Litigants and the Court Congestion Problem, 69 B.U.L.Rev. 527 (1989), 1359

Pritchard & Sale, What Counts as Fraud? An Empirical Study of Motions to Dismiss Under the Private Securities Litigation Reform Act, 2 J. Empirical Legal Stud. 125 (2005), 590

Procedural History of the Agent Orange Product Liability Litigation, 52 Brook.L.Rev. 335 (1986), 492

Purcell, Litigation and Inequality: Federal Diversity Jurisdiction in Industrial America, 1870–1958 (1992), 276, 289

Purcell, The Story of Erie: How Litigants, Lawyers, Judges, Politics, and Social Change Reshape the Law, in Civil Procedure Stories: Second Edition (Clermont ed. 2008), 416

Radin, The Authenticated Full Faith and Credit Clause: Its History, 39 Ill.L.Rev. 1 (1994), 1336

Ragazzo, Reconsidering the Artful Pleading Doctrine, 44 Hastings L.J. 273 (1993), 303

Ratner & Schwartz, The Impact of Shaffer v. Heitner on the Substantive Law of Corporations, 45 Brooklyn L.Rev. 641 (1979), 173

Rave, Note—Questioning the Efficiency of Summary Judgment, 81 N.Y.U.L.Rev. 875 (2006), 959

Recent Developments in Alternative Forms of Dispute Resolution, 100 F.R.D. 512 (1984), 1367

Redish & Kastanek, Settlement Class Actions, The Case-or-Controversy Requirement, and the Nature of the Adjudicatory Process, 73 U.Chi.L.Rev. 545 (2006), 817

Redish & Larsen, Class Actions, Litigant Autonomy, and the Foundations of Procedural Due Process, 95 Calif.L.Rev. 1573 (2007), 742

Redish, Class Actions and the Democratic Difficulty: Rethinking the Intersection of Private Litigation and Public Goals, 2003 U.Chi. Legal F. 71 (2003), 744

Redish, Reassessing the Allocation of Judicial Business Between State and Federal Courts: Federal Jurisdiction and "The Martian Chronicles," 78 Va.L.Rev. 1769 (1992), 276

Redish, Seventh Amendment Right to Jury Trial: A Study in the Irrationality of Rational Decision Making, 70 Nw.U.L.Rev. 486 (1975), 1013

Redish, The Pragmatic Approach to Appealability in the Federal Courts, 75 Colum.L.Rev. 89 (1975), 1204

Reggio, Removal and Remand: A Guide to Navigating Between the State and Federal Courts, 23 Miss.L.Rev. 97 (2004), 351

Reich, The New Property, 73 Yale L.J. 733 (1964), 240

Rendleman, Beyond Contempt: Obligors to Injunctions, 53 Texas L.Rev. 873 (1975), 1169

Rendleman, Inadequate Remedy at Law Prerequisite for an Injunction, 33 U.Fla.L.Rev. 346 (1981), 1167

Report of the Committee on Rules of Practice and Procedure of the Judicial Conference of the United States (2006), 1152

Report of the Federal Courts Study Committee (April 2, 1990), 274

Resnik, "Naturally" Without Gender: Women, Jurisdiction, and the Federal Courts, 66 N.Y.U.L.Rev. 1682 (1991), 294

Resnik, Aggregation, Settlement, and Dismay, 80 Cornell L.Rev. 918 (1995), 743

Resnik, Changing Practices, Changing Rules: Judicial and Congressional Rulemaking on Civil Juries, Civil Justice, and Civil Judging, 49 Ala.L.Rev. 133 (1997), 1049

Resnik, Class Action Lessons in Federalism, 156 U.Pa.L.Rev. 1929 (2008), 277

Resnik, Curtis & Hensler, Individuals within the Aggregate: Relationships, Representation, and Fees, 71 N.Y.U.L.Rev. 296 (1996), 777

Resnik, Failing Faith: Adjudicatory Procedure in Decline, 53 U.Chi.L.Rev. 494 (1986), 1362

Resnik, Managerial Judges, 96 Harv.L.Rev. 374 (1982), 929

Resnik, Many Doors? Closing Doors? Alternative Dispute Resolution and Adjudication, 10 Ohio St.J. on Disp.Resol. 211 (1995), 1372

Resnik, Mediating Preferences: Litigant Preferences for Process and Judicial Preferences for Settlement, 2002 J.Disp.Resol. 155 (2002), 939

Resnik, Procedure as Contract, 80 Notre Dame L.Rev. 593 (2005), 190

Resnik, Processes of the Law: Understanding Courts and Their Alternatives (2004), 1356, 1362

Resnik, Trial as Error, Jurisdiction as Injury, Transforming the Meaning of Article III, 113 Harv.L.Rev. 924 (2000), 945

Resnik, Whose Judgment? Vacating Judgments, Preferences for Settlement, and the Role of Adjudication at the Close of the Twentieth Century, 41 UCLA L.Rev. 1471 (1994), 1297

Reuben, Democracy and Dispute Resolution: The Problem of Arbitration, 67 Law & Contemp.Probs. 279 (Spring 2004), 1372

Reuben, Public Justice: Toward a State Action Theory of Alternative Dispute Resolution, 85 Calif.L.Rev. 579 (1997), 1371

Rhode, Class Conflicts in Class Actions, 34 Stan.L.Rev. 1183 (1982), 769

Rice, Enforceable or Not: Class Action Waivers in Mandatory Arbitration Clauses and the Need for a Judicial Standard, 45 Hous. L.Rev. 215 (2008), 1377

Richardson, Shifting the Burden of Production Under Rule 4(k)(2): A Cost-Minimizing Approach, 69 U.Chi.L.Rev. 1427 (2002), 193

Richey, Rule 16 Revised, and Related Rules: Analysis of Recent Developments for the Benefit of Bench and Bar, 157 F.R.D. 69 (1994), 931

Richey, Rule 16 Revisited: Reflections for the Benefit of Bench and Bar, 139 F.R.D. 525 (1991), 929

Richman, Lively & Mell, The Pleading of Fraud: Rhymes Without Reason, 60 S.Calif.L.Rev. 959 (1987), 589

Richman, Review Essay, Part II: A Sliding Scale to Supplement the Distinction Between General and Specific Jurisdiction, 72 Calif.L.Rev. 1328 (1984), 149

tion Survive?, 42 Wm. & Mary L.Rev. 1 (2000), 1377
Sternlight, Is Alternative Dispute Resolution Consistent with the Rule of Law? Lessons from Abroad, 56 DePaul L.Rev. 569 (2007), 1387
Sternlight, Is Binding Arbitration a Form of ADR?: An Argument that the Term "ADR" Has Begun To Outlive Its Usefulness, J.Disp.Resol. 97 (2000), 1363
Sternlight, Mandatory Binding Arbitration and the Demise of the Seventh Amendment Right to a Jury Trial, 16 Ohio St J.Disp.Resol. 669 (2001), 1047
Sternlight, Rethinking the Constitutionality of the Supreme Court's Preference for Binding Arbitration: A Fresh Assessment of Jury Trial, Separation of Powers, and Due Process Concerns, 72 Tul.L.Rev. 1 (1997), 1372
Sternlight, Separate and Not Equal: Integrating Civil Procedure and ADR in Legal Academia, 80 Notre Dame L.Rev. 681 (2005), 1360
Stevens, Venue Statutes: Diagnosis and Proposed Cure, 49 Mich.L.Rev. 307 (1951), 369
Stewart & Sunstein, Public Programs and Private Rights, 95 Harv.L.Rev. 1193 (1982), 307
Stier, Now It's Personal: Punishment and Mass Tort Litigation after Philip Morris v. Williams, 2 Charleston L.Rev. 433 (2008), 765
Stramondo & Goodspeed, Defendant's Presentation, 57 Mass.L.Q. 179 (1972), 1065
Stravitz, Personal Jurisdiction in Cyberspace: Something More Is Required on the Electronic Stream of Commerce, 49 S.C.L.Rev. 925 (1998), 155
Strier, Making Jury Trials More Truthful, 30 U.C. Davis L.Rev. 95 (1996), 1107
Strier, The Educated Jury: A Proposal for Complex Litigation, 47 DePaul L.Rev. 49 (1997), 1051
Subrin & Main, The Integration of Law and Fact in an Uncharted Parallel Procedural Universe, 79 Notre Dame L.Rev. 1981 (2004), 829
Subrin, A Traditionalist Looks at Mediation: It's Here to Stay and Much Better than I Thought, 3 Nev.L.J. 196 (2002–03), 1386
Subrin, Discovery in Global Perspective: Are We Nuts?, 52 DePaul L. Rev 299 (2002), 826
Subrin, Fishing Expeditions Allowed: The Historical Background of the 1938 Federal Discovery Rules, 39 B.C.L.Rev. 691 (1998), 826
Subrin, Fudge Points and Thin Ice in Discovery Reform and the Case for Selective Substance–Specific Procedure, 46 Fla.L.Rev. 27 (1994), 578
Subrin, Uniformity in Procedural Rules and the Attributes of a Sound Procedural System: The Case for Presumptive Limits, 49 Ala.L.Rev. 79 (1997), 852
Suggs & Sales, Using Communication Clues To Evaluate Prospective Jurors During the Voir Dire, 20 Ariz.L.Rev. 629 (1978), 1053
Sullivan, Enforcement of Government Antitrust Decrees by Private Parties: Third Party Beneficiary Rights and Intervenor Status, 123 U.Pa.L.Rev. 822 (1975), 740
Sunderland, Joinder of Actions, 18 Mich.L.Rev. 571 (1920), 652
Sunderland, Problems Connected with the Operation of a State Court System, Wis.L.Rev. 585 (1950), 267
Sutton, Personal Actions at Common Law (1929), 510
Swank, Das Boot! A National Survey of Booting Programs' Impact on Child Support Compliance, 4 J.L. & Fam.Stud. 265 (2002), 264
Swank, The National Child Non–Support Epidemic, Mich.St. DCL L.Rev. 357 (2003), 1181
Sward, Appellate Review of Judicial Fact–Finding, 40 U.Kan. L.Rev. 1 (1991), 1241
Sward, Values, Ideology and the Evolution of the Adversary System, 64 Ind.L.J. 301 (1988/1989), 4
Symposium on Shaffer v. Heitner, 45 Brooklyn L.Rev. 493 (1979), 174
Symposium on Shaffer v. Heitner, Wash. U.L.Q. 273 (1973), 174
Symposium, Personal Jurisdiction in the Internet Age, 98 Nw.U.L.Rev. 409 (2004), 157
Symposium: Secrecy in Litigation, 81 Chi.-Kent L.Rev. 305 (2006), 848
Szalai, The New ADR: Aggregate Dispute Resolution and Green Tree Financial Corp. v. Bazzle, 41 Cal.W.L.Rev. 1 (2004), 1378
Tamayo, Catch Me If You Can: Serving United States Process on an Elusive Defendant Abroad, 17 Harv.J.L. & Tech. 211 (2003), 228
Tarpley, ADR, Jurisprudence, and Myth, 17 Ohio St.J. on Disp.Resol. 113 (2001), 1365
Taylor, Registration Statutes, Personal Jurisdiction, and the Problem of Predictability, 103 Colum.L.Rev. 1163 (2003), 188
Teitz, Both Sides of the Coin: A Decade of Parallel Proceedings and Enforcement of Foreign Judgments in Transnational Litigation, 10 Roger Williams U.L.Rev. 1 (2004), 1169
Tew, Electronic Discovery Misconduct in Ligation: Letting the Punishment Fit the Crime, 61 U. Miami L.Rev. 289 (2007), 878
Thayer, The Jury and Its Development, 5 Harv.L.Rev. 249 (1892), 999
The Federal Interpleader Act of 1936, 45 Yale L.J. 963 (1936), 721
The Federal Judicial Center's "Illustrative" Forms of Class Action Notices, SJ069 ALI–ABA 73 (2003), 769
The Future of Personal Jurisdiction: A Symposium on Burnham v. Superior Court, 22 Rutgers L.J. 559 (1991), 186
The Sedona Principles: Best Practices Recommendations & Principles for Addressing

5A Wright, Miller & Cooper, Federal Practice and Procedure: Jurisdiction and Related Matters 2d § 3902.1, 1228
13E Wright, Miller & Cooper, Federal Practice and Procedure: Jurisdiction and Related Matters 3d §§ 3609–10, 292; § 3612, 281
14 Wright, Miller & Cooper, Federal Practice and Procedure: Jurisdiction and Related Matters 3d § 3636, 732
14B Wright, Miller & Cooper, Federal Practice and Procedure: Jurisdiction and Related Matters 3d § 3721, 351, 354
14C Wright, Miller & Cooper, Federal Practice and Procedure: Jurisdiction and Related Matters 3d § 3725, 353
14D Wright, Miller & Cooper, Federal Practice and Procedure: Jurisdiction and Related Matters 3d § 3801, 372; § 3803.1, 373; § 3805, 381; § 3806.2, 382; § 3811.1, 382; § 3828.2, 401
15 Wright, Miller & Cooper, Federal Practice and Procedure: Jurisdiction and Related Matters 3d § 3861, 391
15A Wright, Miller & Cooper, Federal Practice and Procedure: Jurisdiction and Related Matters 2d § 3905, 1192
18 Wright, Miller & Cooper, Federal Practice and Procedure: Jurisdiction and Related Matters 2d §§ 4401–15, 1250; § 4406, 1251; § 4409, 1266; § 4414, 1267, 1271; § 4420, 1278; § 4424, 1292
18A Wright, Miller & Cooper, Federal Practice and Procedure: Jurisdiction and Related Matters § 4428, 368; § 4433, 1262; § 4449, 1304; § 4463, 1305; § 4464, 1312
18B Wright, Miller & Cooper, Federal Practice and Procedure: Federal Jurisdiction and Related Matters § 4467, 1335; § 4468, 494, 1348; § 4469, 1335; § 4472, 1348
19 Wright, Miller & Cooper, Federal Practice and Procedure: Jurisdiction and Related Matters 2d § 4510, 430
17A Wright, Miller, Cooper & Amar, Federal Practice and Procedure: Jurisdiction and Related Matters 3d § 4211, 1169; § 4221, 1169
17B Wright, Miller, Cooper & Amar, Federal Practice and Procedure: Jurisdiction & Related Matters 3d § 4251, 1169
16A Wright, Miller, Cooper & Struve, Federal Practice and Procedure: Jurisdiction and Related Matters 4th § 3949.6, 1221
6 Wright, Miller & Kane, Federal Practice and Procedure: Civil 2d § 1401, 1270; § 1410, 663; § 1414, 663; § 1435, 674; § 1443, 710, 711; § 1445, 712; § 1471, 623
6A Wright, Miller & Kane, Federal Practice and Procedure: Civil 2d § 1504, 635; § 1582, 656
7 Wright, Miller & Kane, Federal Practice and Procedure: Civil 3d § 1611, 703; § 1651, 679; § 1653, 684; § 1654, 688; § 1701, 721; § 1702, 713; § 1715, 732
7A Wright, Miller & Kane, Federal Practice & Procedure: Civil 3d § 1752, 743; § 1753, 802; § 1755, 784; § 1756.2, 354, 785; § 1757, 796; § 1760, 749; § 1763, 750; § 1765, 781; § 1767, 754, 755; § 1777, 802
7AA Wright, Miller & Kane, Federal Practice and Procedure: Civil 3d § 1772, 758; § 1784.1, 767; § 1785.4, 767
7B Wright, Miller & Kane, Federal Practice and Procedure: Civil 3d § 1789, 823; § 1793, 768; § 1802.3, 772; § 1806, 757
7C Wright, Miller & Kane, Federal Practice and Procedure: Civil 3d § 1901, 733; § 1906, 739; § 1917, 740
10 Wright, Miller & Kane, Federal Practice and Procedure: Civil 3d § 2663, 601
10A Wright, Miller & Kane, Federal Practice and Procedure: Civil 3d § 2712, 958
10B Wright, Miller & Kane, Federal Practice and Procedure: Civil 3d § 2737, 987
11A Wright, Miller & Kane, Federal Practice and Procedure: Civil 2d §§ 2931–36, 1163; § 2947, 1166; §§ 2947–50, 1167; §§ 2951–53, 1167, § 2960, 364
8 Wright, Miller & Marcus, Federal Practice and Procedure: Civil 2d § 2008.1, 837; § 2010, 853; § 2028, 907; §§ 2045–47, 857; § 2050, 888
8A Wright, Miller & Marcus, Federal Practice and Procedure: Civil 2d § 2131, 859; § 2201, 871; § 2204, 871; § 2210, 871; § 2213, 871; §§ 2254–56, 887
12 Wright, Miller & Marcus, Federal Practice and Procedure: Civil 2d §§ 2981–86, 1169; §§ 3066–73, 945; §§ 3077.1–80, 945
Wright, Book Review—Justice Rutledge and the Bright Constellation, 79 Harv.L.Rev. 212 (1965), 424
Wright, Estoppel by Rule: The Compulsory Counterclaim Under Modern Pleading, 38 Minn.L.Rev. 423 (1954), 664, 1270
Wright, Instructions to the Jury: Summary Without Comment, Wash.U.L.Q. 177 (1954), 1102
Wright, The Doubtful Omniscience of Appellate Courts, 41 Minn.L.Rev. 751 (1957), 1232, 1233
Wyatt & Bales, The Presence of Third Parties at Rule 35 Examinations, 71 Temp. L.Rev. 103 (1998), 885
Yablon, Hindsight, Regret, and Safe Harbors in Rule 11 Litigation, 37 Loy.L.A.L.Rev. 599 (2004), 642
Yablon, Stupid Lawyer Tricks: An Essay on Discovery Abuse, 96 Colum.L.Rev. 1618 (1996), 828
Yackle, Federal Courts (3d ed. 2009), 355
Yeazell, From Medieval Group Litigation to the Modern Class Action (1987), 742
Yoo, Rule 33(a)'s Interrogatory Limitation: By Party or by Side?, 75 U.Chi.L.Rev. 911 (2008), 865
Young & McIntyre, Developments Under the Fair Debt Collection Practices Act (FDCPA), 27(2) Banking & Fin. Services Pol'y Rep. 18 (2008), 1185
Young, Vanishing Trials, Vanishing Juries, Vanishing Constitution, 40 Suffolk U.L.Rev. 67 (2006), 1062

CIVIL PROCEDURE
CASES AND MATERIALS

Tenth Edition

*

CHAPTER 1

A SURVEY OF THE CIVIL ACTION

■ ■ ■

In this Chapter, we provide a thematic and doctrinal framework for studying civil procedure. Civil disputes in the United States typically are resolved by courts according to adversarial principles of justice—the idea that individual litigants should have autonomy in shaping lawsuits and in moving claims to their ultimate resolution. The materials examine how adversarial assumptions shape judicial procedures and also explore the ways in which adversarial decision making differs from other methods of resolving disputes. Another theme we consider is that of federalism: the relation between the federal government and the states. Federalism is important because the civil justice system in the United States comprises not a single set, but rather a multiplicity, of court systems. Civil procedure helps to coordinate the work of these courts and also to ensure that laws are developed and enforced in ways that are democratic. With these concepts in hand, the materials then offer a nuts-and-bolts picture of a civil action, tracing a lawsuit from the commencement of the suit and the service of the summons, to the entry of judgment and subsequent appeals. As you read these materials, it is important to be alert to the historical context of your studies. Procedural doctrine has developed a great deal over the centuries, corresponding, in part, to changes in social attitudes toward such matters as fairness, efficiency, participation, and justice. The materials invite you to take a critical view of civil procedure and to ask how the rules and doctrine that you study can be improved.

SECTION A. THE CONCERN AND CHARACTER OF CIVIL PROCEDURE

Courts exist to provide a decision "by an agent of state power, [of] a controversy existing between two individuals (or the State and an individual), by rational (not merely personal) considerations, purporting to rest on justice and law (i.e. the community's general sense of order)." Wigmore, The Judicial Function, in Science of Legal Method xxvi, xxviii (1917). Although this definition contains some question-begging elements that need definition themselves, it provides a starting point for understanding the judicial system in the United States. For now, it will suffice to recognize the following points about courts:

(1) The judicial process deals with actual controversies between real parties and also helps to express abstract values for the society.

(2) Courts draw on public power to resolve controversies.

(3) This resolution proceeds not arbitrarily but according to some standards of general application.

(4) These standards are applied in a proceeding that follows some fixed lines set out by a system of rules known as procedure.

In resolving the legal disputes they are presented, courts apply two types of law—*substantive* and *procedural.* Your other courses (such as Torts and Contracts) deal with the substantive rights and duties that regulate the everyday relationships among individuals and between individuals and institutions. The substantive law also defines the standard of liability in a particular case. This course, by contrast, will explore the procedures used by the courts to resolve the disputes that are brought before them. Our focus will be on how attorneys frame their cases in order to bring them properly before a particular court, and how the case proceeds from its commencement until a judgment is reached and enforced. The materials also provide opportunities to compare court-based dispute resolution with alternative and less formal mechanisms, such as mediation and arbitration.

It is interesting but sometimes frustrating that the line separating the substantive law from the procedural law is not clear in every instance. Certainly a requirement that all papers filed with a particular court be on 8 1/2 by 14-inch paper is a procedural rule. Equally certain is that the elements of the law of assault and battery are substantive. But not every legal rule can be so easily classified. For example, a statute of limitations (which determines the length of time a party has to sue on a claim) may appear at first glance to be purely procedural. But upon closer examination, it becomes clear that the length of a jurisdiction's statute of limitations is as much a product of public policy, and will affect the plaintiff's ability to recover, as any purely "substantive" provision of the jurisdiction's law. As a student of civil procedure, keep your eye on the substance-procedure dichotomy, but also remain wary of its rigid application.

This course deals with the procedural questions presented in *civil* suits; the aspects of *criminal* suits will not concern us. In analyzing questions of civil procedure, however, you should bear in mind the societal goals of civil suits as compared with those of criminal suits. The principal difference is that civil suits generally are initiated and litigated by private parties attempting to vindicate their legal rights vis-à-vis other private parties. The community thus is seeking to provide a method for resolving the disputes that arise out of the everyday interactions of private parties. Criminal suits, by contrast, are instituted and prosecuted by the government (on behalf of "the People") in an effort to punish those individuals whose conduct has violated the community's moral judgments as expressed in its penal law. Government involvement, however, is not always an indicator of a criminal suit since the government often is a party to civil suits, and can be either a plaintiff or a defendant.

The most distinctive element of our procedure for resolving legal controversies is the *adversary system.* The central feature of this system is the almost total responsibility placed on the parties to the controversy for beginning suit, for shaping the issues, and for producing evidence. By contrast, the judicial systems in civil law countries employ what often is called the *inquisitorial system.* Under this model, the court conducts an active and independent inquiry into the merits of each case, which may include having the judge question and examine witnesses, as well as order certain fact-finding.

The trend in this country is toward increasing the affirmative or active functions of the court. This is evidenced, for example, by the participation of judges in the settlement process, their active involvement during the pretrial conference stage, and their use of techniques to supervise discovery. Nonetheless, primary responsibility and control over almost all phases of the judicial process continue to reside in the parties.

Despite criticisms of the adversary system, this mode of decision making persists in many parts of the world. Four explanations typically are put forward to explain its perseverance:

(1) A truer decision is reached as the result of a contest directed by interested parties.

(2) The parties, who after all are the ones principally interested in the controversy's resolution, should bear the major burden of the time and energy required.

(3) Although impartial investigation may be better when no final decision need be reached, setting up sides makes easier the type of yes-or-no decision that is thought to be necessary in most lawsuits.

(4) Since resort to law has replaced the resort to force that characterized primitive ages, the atavistic instinct to do battle is better satisfied by a means of settling disputes that is very much in the hands of the parties.

When one reflects on the fact that the adversary system often means that victory will turn on considerations other than the justice or true merits of the cause, there is reason to believe that we have permitted it to assume an exaggerated place in our civil dispute resolution scheme. But the system remains and its presence will color every facet of this course. Full understanding of the materials in this book will require your constant attention to its existence, as well as critical analysis of its shortcomings.

What is the test of a good system of procedure? One answer is: *Does it tend to lead to the just and efficient determination of legal controversies?* In this regard, recognize that although this course is only an introduction to procedure, you are not to assume that your function simply is to digest uncritically the law you read. Instead, this course will play an integral part in your process of learning to examine, to question, "to wash in cynical acid," each rule, each form, each principle you learn. But while doing so, keep in mind that many, diverse, and complex are the aspects of both justice and efficiency.

NOTES AND QUESTIONS

1. Commentators offer differing perspectives on the goals and values of civil procedure. Professor Solum posits that concepts of procedural justice build on two principles:

> The Participation Principle requires that the arrangements for the resolution of civil disputes be structured to provide each interested party with a right to adequate participation. The Accuracy Principle requires that the arrangements for the resolution of civil disputes be structured to maximize the chances of achieving the legally correct outcome in each proceeding. Together, the two principles provide guidance where guidance is needed, both for the architects of procedural design and reform and for judges who apply general procedural rules to particular cases.

Solum, *Procedural Justice*, 78 S. Cal. L. Rev. 181, 321 (2004). As your study of civil procedure proceeds, consider the importance of additional criteria for assessing the quality of a procedural system.

2. Professor Scott identifies courts with two different social goals. According to the Conflict Resolution Model, "[I]n the interests of preserving the peace, society offers through the courts a mechanism for the impartial judgment of personal grievances, as an alternative to retaliation or forcible self-help." Courts do more, however, than simply resolve disputes. "A Behavior Modification Model * * * sees the courts and civil process as a way of altering behavior by imposing costs on a person. Not the resolution of the immediate dispute but its effect on the future conduct of others is the heart of the matter." Scott, *Two Models of the Civil Process*, 27 Stan.L.Rev. 937, 937–38 (1975). Courts also are associated with rulemaking, a function that is shared with legislatures and administrative agencies. See Sward, *Values, Ideology and the Evolution of the Adversary System*, 64 Ind. L.J. 301, 303 (1988/1989). What are the implications of each of these models for the design of a civil procedure system?

SECTION B. AN OUTLINE OF THE PROCEDURE IN A CIVIL ACTION

Lawsuits do not begin themselves. Someone must first decide to sue someone else. If this decision is made intelligently, the person choosing to sue must have weighed several matters, among which at least three are basic.

A potential litigant obviously feels aggrieved or would not be thinking of a lawsuit. But he or she must further consider whether the grievance is one for which the law furnishes relief. There are a great many harms a person may feel that the law will not redress. She is offended by the paint on her neighbor's house; he has worked for weeks to persuade a distributor to buy his brand of digital recorder, and sees the sale go to a competitor; she has been holding a plot of ground for speculation, expecting industry to move in, and the area is zoned for residential use; he slips on a spot of grease in the county courthouse but the county is immune from suit. A potential litigant often must consult an attorney before deciding whether he or she "has a case."

Even if she concludes that the grievance is one for which the courts will grant relief, a potential litigant must consider the probability of winning a lawsuit. She must ask whether the person who has caused the injury can be found and brought into court; whether witnesses and documents will be available to support the claims being sued on; whether this proof will be believed; whether the potential adversary can justify its conduct or establish any defenses to the action; and whether an accurate assessment of the law can be made ahead of time.

Then, and perhaps most important of all, a potential litigant must consider whether what is won will be worth the time, the effort, and the expense it will cost, which most significantly includes the payment of fees to an attorney providing representation in the case. In the United States, each litigating party typically bears the full costs of these attorney's fees. These fees are calculated in several ways: by time (at an hourly rate); fixed (the attorney sets the fee prior to providing the services); task-based (the attorney charges a fee based on the nature of the tasks she must provide for the client); and on contingency (the attorney is paid a portion of the ultimate judgment or settlement). Although it may seem natural that litigants pay their own way, the so-called "American Rule" stands in contrast to the more widely accepted "English Rule," which requires the losing party to pay the attorney's fees of the prevailing party. In certain kinds of cases, such as antitrust and civil rights, Congress has enacted statutes that mandate fee-shifting from the losing to the prevailing party.

A prospective litigant must weigh these costs against the alternatives to suit, among them settlement, arbitration, self-help, and letting matters rest. What form will the relief take? Most frequently it will be restricted to a judgment for damages. If this is true, the potential litigant must decide whether the injury is one for which a monetary payment will be satisfactory. Assuming it is, will defendant be rich enough to pay? How difficult will a judgment be to collect? How expensive? Will the recovery be enough to pay the lawyer's fees and the other litigation expenses that undoubtedly will be incurred? Even in a context in which the court may grant specific relief—for example, an order directing the opposing party to do something or to stop doing something—will compliance by defendant be possible? Worthwhile? Sufficient? In the same vein, a potential litigant also must consider whether there are risks not directly tied to the suit. Will he antagonize people whose goodwill he needs? Will the action publicize an error of judgment on her part or open her private affairs to public gaze?

Only after considerable thought has resolved questions about the utility and expense of litigation will the prospective plaintiff be ready for the steps that a litigant must take to bring a lawsuit. Let us now consider these steps in the light of a relatively uncluttered hypothetical case:

> Aikin, while crossing the street in front of her private home, was struck and seriously injured by an automobile driven by Beasley. On inquiry, Aikin found that the automobile was owned by Cecil and that Beasley apparently had been in Cecil's employ. Beasley was predictably without substantial assets and a judgment against him for Aikin's injuries promised little material compensation. But Cecil was wealthy, and Aikin was advised that if she could establish that Beasley had indeed been working for Cecil and had been negligent, she then could recover from Cecil. Aikin decided to sue Cecil for $500,000.

1. SELECTING A PROPER COURT

Aikin initially must determine in which court to bring the action. She might have some choice between filing her lawsuit in a state or a federal court, but her choice is not open-ended. This is because the court selected must have *jurisdiction over the subject matter* (that is, the constitution and statutes under which the court operates must have conferred upon it power to decide this type of case) and must also have *jurisdiction over the person* of Cecil (that is, Cecil must be subject or amenable to suit in the state in which the court is located so that a judgment may be entered against him).

Aikin probably will bring suit in a state court, for as we shall shortly see the subject-matter jurisdiction of the federal courts is severely limited. If the court organization of Aikin's state is typical, there will be courts of *original jurisdiction* in which cases are brought and tried, and one court of *appellate jurisdiction* that sits, with rare exceptions, only to review the decisions of lower courts. (In most states there also will be a group of intermediate courts of appellate jurisdiction.) The courts of original jurisdiction probably consist of one set of courts of *general jurisdiction* and several sets of courts of *inferior jurisdiction*. The courts of general jurisdiction are organized into districts comprising for the most part several counties, although the largest or most populous counties each may constitute single districts. These district courts hear cases of many kinds and are competent to grant every kind of relief, but are usually authorized to hear claims for which the relief requested exceeds a statutorily fixed dollar amount. The courts of inferior jurisdiction will include municipal courts, whose jurisdiction resembles that of the district courts except that the claims are of smaller financial significance; justice-of-the-peace courts, which hear very minor matters; and specialized tribunals such as traffic courts. Since Aikin's injuries are quite serious and her claim correspondingly large, she will, if she sues in a state court, bring the action in one of the district courts.

The federal government also operates a system of courts. The principal federal courts are the United States District Courts, courts of original jurisdiction of which there is at least one in every state; the thirteen United States Courts of Appeals, each of which reviews the decisions of federal district courts in the several states within its circuit (with the exception of the Courts of Appeals for the District of Columbia Circuit and the Federal Circuit); and the Supreme Court of the United States, which reviews not only the decisions of federal courts but also those of state courts that involve an issue of federal law.

The jurisdiction over the subject matter of the United States District Courts extends to many, but by no means all, cases involving federal law, and also to many cases, similar to Aikin's, that do not involve federal law; the latter are cases in which there is *diversity of citizenship* (the parties are citizens of different states or one of them is a citizen of a foreign country) and the required *amount in controversy* (currently more than $75,000) is at stake. Diversity jurisdiction, in common with most of the federal courts' jurisdiction, is not *exclusive;* the state courts also are competent to hear these cases and have concurrent jurisdiction with the United States District Courts. If Cecil is not a citizen of Aikin's state, Aikin may bring an action for $500,000 in a federal court even though it asserts only state law claims. Indeed, in these circumstances, if Aikin sued Cecil in a state court in Aikin's home state, Cecil could *remove* the action from the state court in which it was commenced to the federal district court in that state.[a]

It is not enough that the court selected by Aikin has jurisdiction over the subject matter, however. That court, whether state or federal, must be one in which Cecil can be required to appear so that it is appropriate for the legal system to enter a judgment against him. Traditionally, a court could enter a judgment only against a defendant who resides in the state or is physically in the state, even if temporarily. However, constitutional restrictions on a court's jurisdiction over the person have diminished in recent decades, and if Cecil is not present in Aikin's state but he directed Beasley to drive there, Aikin probably will be able to bring the action in that state because of Cecil's prior contact with the state and the benefits that those contacts have brought him, assuming that a statute authorizes the court to exercise personal jurisdiction in these circumstances.

---

a. If Cecil is not a citizen of Aikin's state and Beasley is, then one of the considerations Aikin will have in deciding to join Beasley as a defendant is the effect on the availability of subject-matter jurisdiction in the federal courts. If Aikin wants to be in the federal court, she should not join Beasley; if Aikin wants to begin and stay in a state court, she should join him. In the latter case, there will not be complete diversity of citizenship between plaintiff on the one side and defendants on the other.

Not every court that has jurisdiction over the subject matter and jurisdiction over the person of defendant will hear a case. It also is necessary that an action be brought in a court having proper *venue*. Thus, although every court in Aikin's state could assert personal jurisdiction over Cecil if he was within its boundaries, that state's statutes typically will provide that the case should be brought in a court whose district includes the county in which either Aikin or Cecil lives. Similarly, if Aikin decides to sue in federal court based on diversity of citizenship, she must bring suit in a district that has venue as defined by federal statute (currently, the district in which Cecil resides, or in a district where a substantial part of the events giving rise to the claim occurred, or in a district where Cecil is subject to personal jurisdiction, if there is no district in which the action otherwise may be brought).

Jurisdiction over the subject matter cannot be waived by the parties. If Aikin and Cecil are both citizens of the same state, a federal court will refuse to hear the action even though both are anxious that it do so. Jurisdiction over the person and venue, on the other hand, essentially are protections for defendant, who may waive them if he wishes.

2. COMMENCING THE ACTION

Aikin must give Cecil notice of the commencement of the action by *service of process*. The process typically consists of a *summons,* which directs defendant to appear and defend under penalty of *default;* that is, unless defendant answers the summons, a judgment will be entered against him. Service of process generally is achieved by *personal service;* the summons is physically delivered to defendant or is left at his home, sometimes by plaintiff or her attorney, sometimes by a public official such as a sheriff or a United States marshal. If Cecil lives in another state, but the circumstances are such that a court in Aikin's state may assert jurisdiction over Cecil, the summons may be personally delivered to him, or some form of *substituted service,* such as sending the papers by registered mail or delivering the summons to his agent within Aikin's state, may be employed. Even if Cecil cannot be located, service in yet another form, usually by *publication* in a newspaper for a certain length of time, may be allowed, although the validity of this kind of service in the type of case Aikin is bringing against Cecil is unlikely to be upheld. The United States Supreme Court repeatedly has emphasized that service must be of a kind reasonably calculated to bring the action to defendant's notice.

3. PLEADING AND PARTIES

With the summons, Aikin usually will serve on Cecil the first of the *pleadings,* commonly called the *complaint*. This is a written statement that will contain Aikin's claim against Cecil. What should be required of such a statement? Obviously it may vary from a simple assertion that

Cecil owes her $500,000, to a second-by-second narration of the accident, closely describing the scene and the conduct of each party, followed by a gruesome recital of Aikin's medical treatment and her prognosis for recovery. No procedural system insists upon either of these extremes, but systems do vary greatly in the detail required in the pleadings. The degree of detail required largely reflects the purposes that the pleadings are expected to serve. These purposes are many, but three objectives are particularly relevant and to the extent that a procedural system regards one rather than another as crucial, we may expect to find differing amounts of detail required.

First, the system may desire the pleadings to furnish a basis for identifying and separating the legal and factual contentions involved so that the legal issues—and hopefully through them the entire case—may be disposed of at an early stage. Thus, suppose that Cecil's liability for Beasley's driving depends upon the degree of independence with which Beasley was working at the time of the accident. A dispute on this issue might exist on either or both of two elements. The parties might disagree as to what Beasley's duties were, and they might disagree as to whether those duties put Beasley so much under the control of Cecil that the law will impose liability on Cecil for Beasley's actions. The first disagreement would be a question of fact, and there would be no alternative to trying the suit and letting the finder of fact (usually the jury) decide the truth. But if there was agreement on that first element, a question of law would be presented by the second issue, which could be determined by the judge without a trial. The objective of identifying the legal questions is served in such a case only if the pleadings set forth exactly what Beasley's job required him to do. It would be served very inadequately if the complaint stated only that "Beasley was driving the car on Cecil's business."

Second, the pleadings may be intended to establish in advance what a party proposes to prove at trial so that his opponent will know what contentions he must prepare to meet. If this objective is regarded as very important it will not be enough for the complaint to state that Beasley was negligent, or that Aikin suffered serious bodily injuries. It must say that Beasley was speeding, or was not keeping a proper look-out, or had inadequate brakes, or describe some other act of negligence and say that Aikin suffered a concussion, or a broken neck, or fractures of three ribs, or other injuries.

Third, the pleadings may be intended to give each party only a general notice of his opponent's contentions, in which event the system would rely upon subsequent stages of the lawsuit to identify the legal and factual contentions of the parties and to enable each to prepare to meet the opponent's case. In such a case a complaint similar to that in Form 11 of the Federal Rules of Civil Procedure should be sufficient.

Obviously each of the first two objectives is desirable. It is a waste of everybody's time to try lawsuits when the underlying legal claim is inadequate to support a judgment, and it is only fair that a person called upon to defend a judicial proceeding should know what he is alleged to have done. But to achieve the first objective fully may require pleading after pleading in order to expose and sharpen the issues; if detail is insisted upon, a long time may be consumed in producing it. Moreover, a single pleading oversight may eliminate a contention necessary to one party's case that easily could have been proven, but that will be held to have been waived. To achieve the second objective through the pleadings will mean that the parties must take rigid positions as to their factual contentions at the very beginning when they do not know what they will learn about their cases by the time trial begins. Either the first or second objective, if fully pursued, requires that the parties adhere to the positions taken in the pleadings. They could not be permitted to introduce evidence in conflict with the pleadings or to change them. For to the extent that *variances* between pleading and proof or *amendments* to the pleadings are permitted, the objectives will be lost. The court frequently will find itself forced either to depart from these objectives or to tolerate cases turning on the skill of the lawyers rather than on the merits of the controversy.

The third objective, insofar as it allows the parties to use the later stages of the lawsuit to identify and flesh out the issues in the case, avoids the delays and potential injustices created by trying to decide the case based only on the pleadings. However, simple notice pleading may be used to harass defendant when plaintiff has no real claim. More often, though, plaintiff will use notice pleading to subject defendant to pretrial discovery (discussed more fully below), and in the process to reveal information so that plaintiff can determine whether a bona fide claim actually exists. Discovery may be essential if defendant controls access to the information that plaintiff needs to establish her claim. Lawyers often refer to such use of the pleadings as a "fishing expedition," or alternatively as a "springboard into litigation." One way that courts have dealt with these problems is to sanction parties and lawyers who bring baseless claims.

4. THE RESPONSE

Following the service of Aikin's complaint, Cecil must respond. He may challenge the complaint by a *motion to dismiss*. This motion may challenge the court's jurisdiction over the subject matter or Cecil's person, the service of process, or venue. It also may be a *motion to dismiss for failure to state a claim or cause of action* (the older term for this motion is a *demurrer*). For the purpose of this motion, the facts alleged in the complaint are accepted as true, and the court considers whether, on this assumption, plaintiff has shown that the pleader is entitled to legal relief.

There are three general situations in which such a motion might be granted. First, the complaint may clearly show that the injury is one for which the law furnishes no redress; for example, when plaintiff simply alleges that "defendant has made faces at me." Second, plaintiff may have failed to include an allegation on a necessary part of the case; for example,

Aikin might have alleged the accident, her injuries, and Beasley's negligence, and have forgotten to allege that Beasley was Cecil's servant. Third, the complaint may be so general or so confused that the court finds that it does not give adequate notice of what plaintiff's claim is; this would be true, for example, of a complaint in which Aikin merely said, "Cecil injured me and owes me $500,000," although complaints far more specific have fallen on this ground. Obviously, the extent to which motions to dismiss will be granted on the second and third grounds will vary with the degree of detail that the particular system requires of its pleadings. A court generally has power to allow the plaintiff an opportunity to amend her pleading to cure certain kinds of defects.

If the motion to dismiss is denied, or if none is made, Cecil must file an *answer*. In this pleading, he must admit or deny the factual allegations made by Aikin in the complaint. Moreover, if Cecil wishes to rely on certain legal contentions called *affirmative defenses,* he must plead them in the answer. Thus, if he wishes to contend that Aikin was negligent in the manner in which she tried to cross the street and that this negligence was also a cause of the accident, he must in many states plead this in the answer; if the answer only denied the allegations in Aikin's complaint, Cecil may not advance at trial the contention that Aikin's negligence caused the accident.

There may be further pleadings, particularly a *reply* by Aikin. But the tendency today is to close the pleadings after the answer, and if Cecil has raised new matters in his answer, they automatically are taken as denied by Aikin. There is one major exception: if Cecil has a claim against Aikin, particularly one that arises out of the same occurrence being sued upon by Aikin, Cecil may plead this claim as a *counterclaim* as part of the answer. This is in essence a complaint by Cecil, and Aikin will have to respond to it just as Cecil had to respond to the original complaint.

The original action between Aikin and Cecil may expand in terms of the number of parties, and this frequently will occur at the pleading stage. For example, although Aikin decided not to sue Beasley, Cecil might *implead* Beasley, asking that Beasley be held liable to him for whatever amount he may be found liable to Aikin, since his liability depends upon Beasley having been at fault. Cecil will decide whether to do this in light of a number of practical concerns, including the effect Beasley's presence will have on the jury in the Aikin v. Cecil suit.

5. OBTAINING INFORMATION PRIOR TO TRIAL

Pretrial discovery is the procedure currently designed to allow the parties to exchange information about their claims and defenses and to prepare for trial. At earlier periods, the pleadings served this purpose.

The chief method is to take *depositions* of parties and witnesses. In this procedure, the person whose deposition is to be taken is questioned by lawyers for each side through direct and cross-examination; the *deponent's* statements are taken down and transcribed. The device is useful in finding information that is relevant to the case, including unearthing leads as to other witnesses or documents; it also is useful in laying a basis for impeaching a witness who attempts to change his story at trial. The two parties almost certainly will want depositions taken of each other, as well as of Beasley; the depositions of Aikin and Cecil will be particularly important because they are treated as admissions, and can be used by their adversaries as evidence at trial. In some circumstances, even the deposition of a nonparty witness who will be unavailable at trial may be used in place of live testimony.

Another device especially adapted to probing the content of an opponent's case is *written interrogatories,* which usually may be addressed only to a party to the suit. (The availability of interrogatories may be one reason why Aikin might join Beasley as a defendant with Cecil or why Cecil might implead Beasley.) These interrogatories are answered by the party with counsel's aid, and the answers will not be as spontaneous as they would be on a deposition; on the other hand, interrogatories will require him to supply some information that he does not carry in his head but can get, and may be even more valuable than the deposition in finding out what he will try to prove. Thus, information regarding Beasley's employment that Cecil cannot be expected to have in his mind may best be exposed in this way.

Other discovery devices include *the production of documents,* such as the service record of Cecil's automobile, and *requests for admissions,* which will remove uncontested issues from the case. A particularly useful device for Cecil will be a court order directing Aikin to submit to a *physical examination* by a physician of Cecil's choice to determine the real extent of Aikin's alleged injuries.

The availability of discovery, which is now common throughout the country, has had its effect on our attitude toward the pleadings. This is not simply because it enables parties to prepare for trial better than pleadings ever did. Of more significance perhaps is the fact that if broad discovery is allowed, it is senseless to make parties take rigid positions with respect to the issues at the very beginning of the lawsuit before they have had the chance to utilize these very useful devices for obtaining information. In addition, the availability of discovery does much to make summary judgment, which is discussed below, a viable and fair procedure, since it enables a party to ascertain those issues on which the opposing party has no evidence, and it also gives the opponent a real chance to develop such evidence. On the other hand, if the costs of discovery are excessive, a defendant may be motivated to settle a lawsuit that satisfies a weak pleading standard yet would lack sufficient proof at trial.

Amendments to the Federal Rules of Civil Procedure were promulgated in recent years that, in time, may revolutionize the way in which litigants conduct pretrial discovery. They require both parties—automatically in most cases—to identify individuals "likely to have discoverable information" and to provide copies of documents "that the disclosing party may use to support its claims or defenses." See Federal Rule 26(a). This mandatory self-disclosure procedure theoretically should decrease considerably the amount of time and the amount of resources that the judicial system expends in overseeing the discovery process, but in practice courts sometimes are called upon to define the scope of mandatory disclosure and to enforce its terms, undermining the efficiency of the procedure.

6. SUMMARY JUDGMENT

One of the basic difficulties with attempting to resolve cases at the pleading stage is that the allegations of the parties must be accepted as true for the purpose of ruling on a motion to dismiss. Thus, if the plaintiff tells a highly unlikely but plausible story in the complaint, the court cannot dismiss the action even though it does not believe the allegations or think that the plaintiff will be able to prove the tale. The judge is not the decision maker and the pleading stage is not the time to resolve questions of fact.

But in some cases it will be possible to supplement the pleadings with additional documents to show that an apparent decisive issue is spurious. This is done by a motion for *summary judgment*. This motion can be supported by demonstrating that the crucial issue will have to be resolved in the mover's favor at trial, because the opposing party will be unable to produce any admissible evidence in support of her position on the issue. For example, suppose that it is Cecil's position that prior to the accident he had fired Beasley, but that Beasley had secreted keys to Cecil's automobile and had taken Cecil's car without permission shortly before the accident. On the face of the pleadings, we have only an allegation that Beasley was Cecil's employee and a denial of that allegation; thus, the pleadings seem to present a question of credibility that cannot be resolved at this stage. Cecil now moves for summary judgment, alleging that this issue is not a genuine one; he accompanies his motion with affidavits of his own and two other witnesses that he had fired Beasley; a deposition of the garage attendant indicating that he had been instructed not to allow Beasley to have the car, and that it was taken without Cecil's knowledge; and a deposition of Beasley to the effect that he had been fired, but wanted to use the car once more for his own purposes. It is now incumbent upon Aikin to show that the issue is genuine; Aikin cannot rely simply upon her own assertion that all this is not so; after all, she has no personal knowledge of the facts. Aikin must convince the court that she has admissible evidence that Beasley still was acting as Cecil's employee in driving the car at the time of the accident. If Aikin fails to do so, judgment will be entered against her.

It should be noted that in ruling on a summary judgment motion the judge does not decide which side is telling the truth. If Aikin presents an affidavit of a witness who claims to have been present when Cecil allegedly fired Beasley, and says that Cecil told Beasley that this was only a subterfuge and that he wanted him to continue to work for him but to pretend to steal the car, summary judgment will not be appropriate even though the judge is firmly convinced that Aikin's affiant is lying.

7. SETTING THE CASE FOR TRIAL

After discovery is completed, and if the case has not been terminated by dismissal, summary judgment, or settlement, it must be set for *trial.* Most cases already will have been disposed of prior to trial. If Aikin's lawsuit has not yet been resolved, typically either party may file a *note of issue,* at which time the case will be given a number and placed on a *trial calendar.* These calendars have become extremely long in many courts, and the case may have to wait a year, three years, or more before it is called for trial, especially if a jury trial has been requested.

8. THE JURY AND ITS SELECTION

In most actions for damages, the parties have a right to have the facts tried by a *jury.* This right is assured in the federal courts by the Seventh Amendment to the Constitution, and is protected in the courts of most states by similar state constitutional provisions. If there is a right to a trial by jury, either party may assert it, but if neither wishes to do so, a judge will try the facts as well as the law. Largely for historical reasons growing out of a division of authority in the English court structure, there are many civil actions in which neither party has a right to a jury trial; these include most cases in which plaintiff wants an order directing or prohibiting specified action by defendant rather than a judgment for damages—a so-called *equitable* remedy.

If a jury has been demanded, the first order of business at trial will be to impanel the jurors. A large number of people, selected in an impartial manner from various lists, tax rolls, or street directories, will have been ordered to report to the courthouse for jury duty at a given term of court. The prospective jurors will be questioned—usually by the judge but sometimes by the lawyers—as to their possible biases. If one of the persons called has prior knowledge of the case or is a personal friend of one of the parties, he or she probably will be successfully *challenged for cause* and excused. But suppose Aikin is an architect and her lawyer finds that one of the jury panel has recently constructed a house and believes that he was greatly overcharged for its design and construction; this will likely not be enough to persuade the judge to excuse him, but fearing the juror may be prejudiced against her client, Aikin's lawyer probably will exercise one of the small number of *peremptory challenges* allowed for which no reason need be given. Ultimately, a panel of between six and twelve hopefully unbiased jurors will be selected.

9. THE TRIAL

After the jurors have been sworn, plaintiff's lawyer will make an *opening statement,* in which she will describe for the jury what the case is about, what contentions she will make, and how she will prove them. Defendant's lawyer also may make an opening statement at this time, but he may reserve the right to do so until he is ready to present his own case. Following the opening statement, plaintiff's lawyer calls her witnesses one by one. Each witness is first questioned by the lawyer who has called that witness—this is the *direct examination;* then the lawyer for the other side has the opportunity to *cross-examine* the same witness; this may be followed by *re-direct* and *re-cross* examination, and even further stages. The judge maintains some control over the length and tenor of the examination, and in particular will see to it that the stages beyond cross-examination are not prolonged.

Just as the primary responsibility for introducing evidence is on the lawyers, so too is the responsibility for objecting to evidence that is thought to be inadmissible under the rules of evidence. Suppose that Aikin's lawyer asks: "What happened while you were lying on the ground after the accident?" To which Aikin replies: "The driver of the car came over and said that he had been going too fast and he was sorry." Aikin's answer is objectionable because it contains *hearsay evidence;* that is, it repeats what someone else has said for the purpose of proving the truth of what was said. The judge will not raise this issue herself, however; it is up to Cecil's counsel to object, and then the judge must rule on the objection. This particular issue is not an easy one, for Aikin's answer may well come within one of the exceptions to the rule excluding hearsay evidence. This kind of issue will recur continually throughout the trial and the judge must be prepared to make instantaneous rulings if the trial is to proceed with dispatch. Small wonder that evidentiary rulings form a major source of the errors raised on appeal, but at the same time appellate courts are very reluctant to disturb the trial judge's determination. What happens if the judge rules that Aikin's answer is inadmissible? She will instruct the jury to disregard it. Can a juror who has heard such an important confession totally drive it from his or her mind?

Documents, pictures, and other tangible items may be put into evidence, but unless their admissibility has been stipulated in advance, they will be introduced through witnesses. For example, if Aikin's lawyer has had pictures taken of the accident scene and wishes to get them to the jury, she will call the photographer as a witness, have him testify that he took pictures of the scene, and then show them to the photographer who will identify them as the pictures he took. At this point they may be formally introduced into evidence.

When plaintiff's lawyer has called all of her witnesses, and their examinations are over, plaintiff will *rest.* At this point, defendant's lawyer may ask for a *directed verdict* (now called a judgment as a matter of law in federal practice) for defendant on the ground that plaintiff has not established a prima facie case; the thrust of the motion is that plaintiff has not introduced enough evidence to permit the jury to find in her favor. If the motion is denied, defendant may rest and choose to rely on the jury's agreeing with him, but in almost all cases he will proceed to present witnesses of his own and these witnesses will be exposed to the same process of direct and cross-examination. When defendant has rested, plaintiff may present additional evidence to meet any new matter raised by defendant's witnesses. In turn, defendant, after plaintiff rests, may meet any new matter presented by plaintiff. This procedure will continue until both parties rest. Again, the trial judge will maintain considerable control to prevent the protraction of these latter stages.

When both parties have rested, either or both may move for a directed verdict. Again, this motion asks the trial judge to rule that under the evidence presented, viewed most favorably to the nonmoving party, the jury cannot reasonably find in his or her favor. If these motions are denied, the case must be submitted to the jury.

10. SUBMITTING THE CASE TO THE JURY

At this stage the judge and the lawyers will confer out of the jury's hearing with regard to the content of the judge's *instructions* or *charge* to the jury. Each lawyer may submit proposed instructions, which the trial judge will grant or deny, but the judge is under a duty to charge the jury on the basic aspects of the case in any event. If a party's lawyer has neither requested a particular instruction nor objected to the judge's charge, however, a claim that the charge was erroneous generally will not be upheld on appeal.

Ordinarily the lawyers will make their final arguments to the jury before the judge delivers the charge. The lawyers will review the evidence from their own points of view, and may suggest how the jury should weigh certain items and resolve specific issues, but it is improper for the lawyers to discuss a matter that has been excluded or has never been introduced. In other words, they are arguing, not testifying.

In the instructions the judge will summarize the facts and issues, tell the jury about the substantive law to be applied on each issue, give general information on determining the credibility of witnesses, and state who has the *burden of persuasion* on each issue of fact. The burden of persuasion in a civil case ordinarily requires that one party prove her contention on a given issue by a preponderance of the evidence. On most issues Aikin will carry this burden, but on an affirmative defense such as contributory negligence, the burden probably will be on Cecil. What the burden means is that if a juror is unable to resolve an issue in his mind, he should find on that issue against the party who has the burden. In the federal courts and in some states, the judge may comment on the evidence, as long as she emphasizes that her comments represent her own opinion and that the jurors should not feel bound by it; judicial comment is rare, however, and in many states it is not permitted at all.

Following the charge, the jury retires to reach its *verdict.* The verdict, the jury's decision, will be of a type chosen by the judge. There are three types, of which by far the most common is the *general verdict.* This verdict permits the jurors to determine the facts and apply the law on which they have been charged to those facts; it is simple in form in that only the conclusion as to who prevails, and the amount of the damages, if that party is a claimant, is stated. A second type is the *general verdict with interrogatories,* which combines the form of the general verdict with several key questions that are designed to test the jury's understanding of the issues. Suppose that the accident occurred five miles away from Beasley's appointed route. Aikin's evidence is that Beasley detoured to have the vehicle's brakes fixed; Cecil's is that Beasley was going to visit his friend. The judge might charge the jury that in the former event, but not in the latter, Beasley was acting within the scope of his employment and Cecil would be liable for his negligence, and she might direct the jury, in addition to rendering a verdict for Aikin or for Cecil, to answer the question, "Why did Beasley depart from his route?" If the general verdict was for Aikin, but the jury's answer was that Beasley was driving to his friend's home, the judge would order judgment for Cecil, for if the answer is inconsistent with the verdict, the answer controls. The third type of verdict is the *special verdict,* in which all of the factual issues in the case are submitted to the jury as questions without instructions as to their legal effect; the judge applies the law to the jury's answers and determines which party prevails.

Traditionally, only a unanimous jury verdict has been effective. In many states, and by consent of the parties in the federal courts, a nonunanimous verdict by the jurors may stand in a civil action. If the minimum number of jurors required for a verdict are unable to reach agreement, the jury is said to be *hung,* and a new trial before a different jury is necessary.

11. POST-TRIAL MOTIONS

After the jury has returned its verdict, judgment will be entered thereon, but the losing party will have an opportunity to make certain post-trial motions. There may be a motion for a *judgment notwithstanding the verdict* (commonly called a motion for a *judgment n.o.v.,* from the Latin non obstante veredicto, but now called a renewed motion for judgment as a matter of law in federal practice); this motion raises the same question as a motion for a directed verdict. The losing party also may move for a *new trial;* the grounds for this motion are many, and may include assertions that the judge erred in admitting certain evidence, that the charge was defective, that attorneys, parties, or jurors have been guilty of misconduct, that the damages awarded are excessive, or that the jury's verdict is against the clear weight of the evidence. Should these motions fail, it is sometimes possible to reopen a judgment, even several months after the trial, on the grounds of clerical mistake, newly discovered evidence, or fraud, but the occasions on which relief is granted are very rare.

12. THE JUDGMENT AND ITS ENFORCEMENT

The *judgment* is the final determination of the lawsuit, absent an appeal. Judgment may be rendered on default when the defendant does not appear; or following the granting of a demurrer, a motion to dismiss, or a motion for summary judgment; or based on a settlement agreement of the parties; or upon the jury's verdict, or the findings of fact and conclusions of law of the trial judge in a nonjury case. The judgment may be in the form of an award of money to plaintiff, a declaration of rights between the parties, specific recovery of property, or an order requiring or prohibiting some future activity. When defendant has prevailed, the judgment generally will not be "for" anything nor will it order anything; it simply will provide that plaintiff takes nothing by her complaint.

In most cases a judgment for plaintiff will not order defendant to do anything; typically it will simply state that plaintiff shall recover a sum of money from defendant. This does not necessarily mean that defendant will pay. It is up to plaintiff to collect the money. *Execution* is the common method of forcing the losing party to satisfy a money judgment, if the loser does not do so voluntarily. A *writ of execution* is issued by the court commanding an officer—usually the sheriff—to seize property of the losing party and, if necessary, to sell it at public sale and use the proceeds to satisfy plaintiff's judgment.

When plaintiff's recovery takes the form of an *injunction* requiring defendant to do something or to stop doing something, the judgment (in this context typically called the *decree*) is said to operate against defendant's person (in personam). Its sanction is direct, and if defendant fails to obey, he may be held in *contempt of court* and punished by fine or imprisonment.

Costs provided by statute and certain out-of-pocket disbursements are awarded to the prevailing party and included in the judgment. Usually these costs are nominal in relation to the total expense of litigation and include only such items as the clerk's fee and witnesses' mileage. As previously mentioned, in the United States, in contrast to England, attorney's fees are not recoverable as costs in ordinary litigation.

13. APPEAL

Every judicial system provides for review by an appellate court of the decisions of the trial court. Generally a party has the right to appeal any judgment to at least one higher court. When the system contains two levels of appellate courts, appeal usually lies initially to one of the intermediate courts; review at the highest level is only at the discretion of that court except in certain classes of cases. Thus, in the federal courts, district-court decisions are reviewed by the courts of appeals, but review in the United States Supreme Court currently must be sought in most cases by a *petition for a writ of certiorari,* which that Court may deny as a matter of discretion without reaching any conclusion as to the merits of the case. (In a few cases, a direct appeal lies from the district court to the Supreme Court.) The discretion of a higher-level appellate court generally is exercised so that only cases with legal issues of broad importance are taken.

The *record* on appeal will contain the pleadings, at least a portion of the *transcript of the trial* (the court reporter's verbatim record of the trial), and the orders and rulings relevant to the appeal. The parties present their contentions to the appellate court by written *briefs* and in addition, in most cases, by *oral argument.* The appellate court may review any ruling of law by the trial judge, although frequently it will limit the scope of its review by holding that particular matters were within the trial judge's discretion or that the error if any was not prejudicial, that is, it did not substantially affect the outcome of the case. There are constitutional limits to the review of a jury's verdict, but even when these limits do not apply—for example, when the judge has tried the case without a jury—an appellate court rarely will re-examine a question of fact, because a cold record does not convey the nuances of what the trier observed, notably the demeanor of the witnesses.

The appellate court has the power to *affirm, reverse,* or *modify* the judgment of the trial court. If it reverses, it may order that judgment be entered or it may *remand* the case to the trial court for a new trial or other proceedings not inconsistent with its decision. The decision of an appellate court usually is accompanied by a written *opinion,* signed by one of the judges hearing the appeal, there always being more than one judge deciding an appeal. Concurring and dissenting opinions also may be filed. The opinions of a court are designed to set forth the reasons for a decision and to furnish guidance to lower courts, lawyers, and the public. You will spend much of your time in law school—and afterwards—reading the opinions of appellate courts. Although trial courts frequently deliver opinions when ruling on motions or sitting without a jury, they are rarely published except for decisions by the federal trial courts.

There is an important distinction between the *reviewability* of a particular ruling of a trial judge and its *appealability.* For example, a trial judge's ruling excluding certain evidence at trial as hearsay is reviewable; that is, when the judgment is appealed, that ruling may be assigned as error and the appellate court will consider whether it was correct. But trial would be impossible if an appeal could be taken from every ruling. Thus, appeals lie only from judgments and from certain orders made in the course of litigation when immediate review is deemed so important that a delay in the action during appeal can be tolerated. Judicial systems differ in the extent to which *interlocutory orders* can be appealed. In the federal system, very little other than a final judgment can be taken to the courts of appeals; in some states, on the other hand, many kinds of orders can be appealed even before a final judgment is entered.

A good example of the contrast between the two approaches can be seen by looking at the consequences of an order denying a motion to dismiss. Suppose that Cecil moves to dismiss Aikin's complaint on the grounds that even on Aikin's view of the facts Cecil is not responsible for the conduct of Beasley, and this motion is denied. In the federal courts such an order would not be appealable, since it does not terminate the lawsuit. Indeed, the disposition of the motion means that the action will continue. In some states, however, this question could be taken immediately to a higher court for a ruling, while the other stages of the litigation wait.

The question as to which system is better is not easy to answer. One may argue in favor of the federal practice that everything should be done at one level before going to the next, that too much time is taken in waiting for appellate courts to decide these questions serially, and that no appeal may ever be necessary, since Cecil may prevail anyway. But on the other hand, if the appellate court holds at this early stage that Aikin has no claim against Cecil, we will save the time necessary for discovery and trial.

One point worth noting is that the resolution of the question of the appealability of interlocutory orders has an important bearing on the procedural developments within a given system. In the case of motions to dismiss, for example, if denials are not appealable, the law on this subject will be made largely in the trial courts. The trial judge who is in doubt may tend to deny such motions rather than to grant them, and her decision generally will not be disturbed; even though the ruling theoretically is reviewable after final judgment, by that time the significance of the ruling on the pleadings may have been displaced by more substantive questions. If the denial is appealable, a tactical consideration is added and such motions will be resorted to more frequently, inasmuch as they will afford defendant an additional opportunity to delay trial and thus to wear down his opponent. With respect to other procedural rulings—as in the discovery area—the absence of an interlocutory appeal will strengthen the hand of the trial judge; she will in fact, if not in theory, be given a wider discretion because fewer of her rulings will come before the appellate courts and when they do they will be enmeshed in a final judgment, which will make it easy to conclude that any error was not prejudicial.

14. THE CONCLUSIVENESS OF JUDGMENTS

After the appeal and whatever further proceedings may take place, or, if no appeal is taken, when the time for appeal expires, the judgment is final. With very rare exceptions, the judgment cannot be challenged in another proceeding. It is *res judicata*, a thing decided, and now at rest. Defining the scope and effect of this finality principle is one of the most complex tasks in the entire law of procedure.

SECTION C. A NOTE ON MOTION PRACTICE

Throughout the previous Section the term "motion" is used frequently, and for good reason. What a motion is, how one makes a motion, and when one should make a motion are all questions of "motion practice." A motion is the procedural device by which a litigant asks a court for an order. For example, a request for an order to dismiss a complaint for failure to state a claim, a request for an order granting a summary judgment, and a request for an order granting a new trial all are formally made to a court through a motion.

A litigant generally must make a motion in writing. Two exceptions to this rule are when the court is recording a hearing verbatim or when a trial is taking place. A motion generally must state with particularity the reasons or grounds supporting the motion and the relief sought. The written motion also must appear in a proper form, which usually is determined by local court rules.

The litigant also must serve the motion on her adversary. In addition, a notice of hearing regarding the motion, a brief or memorandum of law in support of the motion, a proposed order, and affidavits, if necessary, generally accompany a motion. Briefs usually have a maximum page limit (and quite often are not brief). Not all courts require the movant to submit a proposed order. Only certain motions require affidavits.

All motions in federal court require the signature of the litigant's attorney or the litigant. The signature attests that the attorney or litigant has read the motion papers and that the motion has sufficient grounds and is made in good faith. If a court decides that any of these are not true, the court may sanction the attorney or the litigant. Sanctions have been imposed more frequently in recent years.

A party served with a motion may answer and usually must do so within a time period specified by the rules. A party also may move for an extension of time, either to make a cross-motion, to extend the time to respond to the motion, or both. In addition, making a motion may defer the next stage of litigation. Finally, making a particular motion may preserve other legal rights.

It is the interrelationship among motions, their intended effects, their secondary effects, and their effects on the opposing party that determine how a party utilizes motion practice. A motion such as summary judgment is usually designed to win the lawsuit. A successful motion to exclude certain material from discovery may convince an adversary that he cannot obtain the information necessary to establish his case and thus may induce him to end the lawsuit early without an unfavorable judgment. A motion to bring a third party into the lawsuit may help convince an adversary that the lawsuit will be more time consuming and costly than expected. A lawyer deciding to make a motion must consider carefully what benefits will accrue to the movant and what obstacles will be imposed on her adversary as a result of the motion.

But a motion may have negative aspects. One of the drawbacks may be the time and expense of making the motion, including drafting and serving multiple copies of papers, spending hours preparing the brief in support of the motion, and taking resources from other more fruitful pursuits. Repeated, unsuccessful motions will result in expense and delay that may reduce client satisfaction.

In addition, poor motion practice may leave the judge with the impression that the lawyer is sloppy, shoddy, and disorganized. Arguing motions at a hearing that the attorneys could have settled without a hearing may convince the judge that the movant is contentious by nature. In short, an unwise use of a motion may do more harm in the long run than not making the motion at all, even if the motion is granted.

In sum, motion practice is a central part of a litigator's arsenal. When a particular motion can be made, how it must be made, and what its effect will be are questions that can be answered by studying the applicable procedural rules. When a motion *should* be made and how it can affect the course of the lawsuit are matters of judgment and experience.

SECTION D. A NOTE ON REMEDIES

The remedies that may be obtained in a modern civil action should principally be viewed as a part of the substantive law: contract law, tort law, commercial law, labor law, and so forth. Yet because the goal of a lawsuit is the remedy and the means of securing it is procedural, there necessarily is a close relationship between them. For example, the range of available remedies in a case may be limited by the manner in which plaintiff has pleaded, and on the other hand, certain procedural aspects of the case, such as whether it is tried to a judge or a jury, may be determined by the remedy that is being sought; again, whether a person may be joined as a party may depend on the relief that is being sought, and conversely certain remedies may be available only if all interested persons can be joined.

Without question, the most important relationship between procedure and remedies grows out of the existence in English law of two great branches of jurisprudence administered in different courts: common law and equity; the latter was envisioned as complementary to the former. There are two special facts about equity that are important for our purpose. First, already alluded to, it had no jury. Second, the injunction was a creature of equity and remained in its sole custody so long as the two branches remained distinct.

From this heritage, two consequences of immense significance for the law of procedure result. One, the right of a trial by jury in the United States today, especially in the federal courts, is determined by inquiring whether the matter in question was a subject of a legal or equitable cognizance in 1791—the date of the Seventh Amendment—and to some extent this question depends on the remedy sought, since the availability of injunctive relief was one form of equity's jurisdiction. Two, just as equity was regarded as a special kind of law to be resorted to only when the common law was inadequate, so too the injunction—and most forms of specific relief, even in those limited circumstances in which it is available at law—has been and still is regarded as a form of exceptional relief, to be allowed only when the ordinary remedy of damages is inadequate.

The most important types of relief that a court may award in a civil action fall into three categories: *declarative, specific,* and *compensatory*. Declarative relief consists simply in a court's defining the rights and duties of the parties in a particular legal context. Suppose a person believes that an agreement she has entered into is not a valid contract and that she is under no obligation to perform it; however, she is afraid to act on this belief in the face of another's insistence that she perform, because if the contract is enforceable the damages for the nonperformance will be great. In these circumstances she may seek a declaratory judgment asking the court to determine whether she is under a duty to perform. This type of relief is not as common as those discussed below and its availability often is limited by statute. In numerous situations, however, it is invaluable.

Specific relief consists generally of an order directing conduct. Defendant may be commanded to return a jewel he has taken from plaintiff, to stop operating a pig farm in a residential neighborhood, to deliver a car she has contracted to sell, or to refrain from opening a barbershop next door to a person to whom he has just sold his former barbershop. Obviously, specific relief is not possible in all cases. For example, no kind of specific relief will compensate or cure Aikin in our hypothetical case; Beasley cannot retroactively be ordered not to run into her. On the other hand, in some kinds of cases specific relief is available almost as a matter of course. A person who has contracted to sell a house or a piece of land ordinarily will be ordered to perform the agreement, for the law regards each bit of real property as unique. But beyond the real-property context, specific relief will be given only if damages would be completely inadequate. Thus, if you order a tuxedo from a tailor who fails to perform his promise to deliver it, it is unlikely that any remedy except damages will be forthcoming. The reasons for this are not purely historical. There is a burden on the court in ordering and supervising performance of a decree of specific performance that is avoided if a simple judgment for money damages is entered; moreover, specific performance might impose a hardship or at least an indignity on the tailor not commensurate with the advantage to be gained by your receiving this tailor's garment rather than one from another tailor. But it may well be asked whether our courts today are not being too reluctant to grant that form of relief that will most adequately redress plaintiff's grievance.

Compensatory relief calls for a judgment that defendant pay plaintiff a certain sum of money. But you should recognize that when we speak of compensation—of the remedy of damages—although we are speaking of one form of relief, it can be computed in accordance with many measures. In your action against the tailor, for example, if you had struck a good bargain, you might claim the difference between the price you agreed to pay and the value the tuxedo would have had if the tailor had performed the promise; or you might claim only the money you had advanced as a down payment; or you might claim the amount you paid for opera tickets you were unable to use without the tuxedo. The difference in amount that could be collected under these theories might be very substantial.

There is a final point to be considered in evaluating the adequacy of any judicial remedy: how much of it will be consumed by the cost of litigation? As we have noted, the costs awarded to a successful plaintiff will not, in most cases, reimburse her for the fees of her lawyer or for many other substantial costs of a suit, such as the expense of investigation or the fees of expert witnesses. It is not possible to give any meaningful figure for the cost of an average trial, but it can be assumed that as the stakes rise the fees will be correspondingly higher and indeed, some top attorneys charge upward of $600 (maybe as high as $800 or $1000) an hour for their services.

In most personal-injury and in many other types of damages actions plaintiff's cost of recovery must be computed differently because the attorney will be litigating the case under a contingent-fee agreement; that is, the attorney will receive a percentage—one-third is common—of plaintiff's judgment. Thus, in a real sense, an adequate legal remedy is not one that simply compensates plaintiff for a loss but is one that covers both the loss and the cost of recovering it. This distinction has not been ignored by many triers of fact. Indeed, it has been suggested that if damages for pain and suffering ever are abolished, defendants should be required explicitly to pay plaintiffs' legal fees.

SECTION E. A NOTE ON PROCEDURAL RULES IN THE FEDERAL AND STATE COURTS

Throughout this Chapter we have referred to federal and state rules of procedure. Rules of procedure derive from constitutional authority, statute, and judicial decision. The Federal Rules of Civil Procedure owe their genesis to the Rules Enabling Act, 28 U.S.C. § 2072, enacted in 1934, which vests power in the United States Supreme Court to promulgate rules of procedure for the district courts and to combine law and equity into one civil action. In 1935, the Supreme Court appointed an Advisory Committee composed of lawyers and law professors to draft federal procedural rules. The Advisory Committee proposed rules that the Court approved in 1937, and the Federal Rules of Civil Procedure became law on September 16, 1938. See Burbank, *The Rules Enabling Act of 1934*, 130 U. Pa. L. Rev. 1015 (1982). Amending the Federal Rules follows a seven-step process that usually runs between two and three years. The process requires giving notice to the public and allowing individuals an opportunity to comment; approval by multiple committees; and final review by the Court and Congress.

An important hallmark of the Federal Rules is their transsubstantivity: The Rules apply to all causes of action no matter how complex or simple. Some commentators regard transsubstantivity as essential to maintaining the neutrality and impartiality of civil process. See, e.g., Carrington, *Making Rules to Dispose of Manifestly Unfounded Assertions: An Exorcism of the Bogy of Non–Trans–Substantive Rules of Civil Procedure*, 137 U. Pa. L. Rev. 2067, 2068 (1989). Others question whether transsubstantivity is practical or even desirable, arguing, for example, that a large antitrust case requires different procedural treatment than that of a simple negligence case. See, e.g., Cover, *For James Wm. Moore: Some Reflections on a Reading of the Rules*, 84 Yale L.J. 718, 732, 739–40 (1975). As your study of procedure goes forward, consider whether procedural developments such as the adoption of local court rules, the negotiation of customized procedural rules, and the enactment of statutory "carve-outs" for discrete areas of the law are compatible with the principle of transsubstantivity. See Tobias, *The Transformation of Trans–Substantivity*, 49 Wash. & Lee L. Rev. 1501 (1992).

The Federal Rules generally do not bind state judicial systems, and currently no state has a set of procedures that completely tracks the federal, although some come close. See Oakley, *A Fresh Look at the Federal Rules in State Courts*, 3 Nev. L.J. 354, 354–55 (2003). States typically use one of two models to adopt procedural rules: in the first, the state constitution grants exclusive rule making power to the state judiciary; in the second, state courts exercise inherent rule making authority but share authority with the legislature. For a collection of state constitutional provisions as they bear on state rulemaking authority, see Main, *Reconsidering Procedural Conformity Statutes*, 35 W. St. U. L. Rev. 75, 84–85 (2007).

SECTION F. ILLUSTRATIVE CASES

The cases that follow have been selected to illustrate many of the basic concepts, doctrines, and devices about which you have just read. The selection is designed to furnish examples of a broad spectrum of procedural problems, and it has been arranged for the most part to present these problems in the order in which they were discussed in the preceding text. Three factors have dominated the choice of the cases. First, each focuses on a specific issue that is typical of a range of problems involving a particular principle and at the same time throws some light on the policies that underlie the principle itself. Second, none of the cases is a "sitting duck"; in each instance strong reasons can be advanced for and against the court's result. Third, each case arises in a context that you can understand and presents an issue about which you should be able to form an opinion, however hesitant it may be. Another purpose of these cases is to help you develop a familiarity with procedural language and a feeling for procedural problems. You must, of course, consider the cases from the perspective of the courts that decided them, seeking to understand not only their rulings but also why they were made, asking what other options were before them, and thinking through the consequences of those possibilities. If the full pedagogical objectives of these cases are to be achieved, you also must regard each of them as a practical lawyer's problem—or rather a problem presenting difficulties and opportunities to the lawyers on the opposite sides. You must inquire why they acted as they did and what else they might have done; finally, you must ask in what position the decision has left them and what if anything they should do next.

1. THE AUTHORITY OF THE COURT TO PROCEED WITH THE ACTION

Plaintiff, having decided to sue, must determine in what court to bring the action. A court must be chosen that has jurisdiction over the subject matter of the suit and in which jurisdiction over the person of the defendant may be obtained. In the following case, consider which of these two types of jurisdiction the Supreme Court is addressing in the context of a lawsuit filed in federal court. In reading the case, notice that the word "jurisdiction" is used without a modifier. But from the context and from the information you have been given above, you should be able to identify the kind of jurisdiction involved.

CAPRON v. VAN NOORDEN

Supreme Court of the United States, 1804.
6 U.S. (2 Cranch) 126, 2 L.Ed. 229.

Error to the [United States] circuit court of North Carolina. The proceedings stated Van Noorden to be late of Pitt county [in North Carolina], but did not allege Capron, the plaintiff, to be an alien, nor a citizen of any state, nor the place of his residence.

Upon the general issue, in an action of trespass on the case, a verdict was found for the defendant, Van Noorden, upon which judgment was rendered.

The writ of error was sued out by Capron, the plaintiff below, who assigned for error, among other things, first, "that the circuit court aforesaid is a court of limited jurisdiction, and that by the record aforesaid it doth not appear, as it ought to have done, that either the said George Capron, or the said Hadrianus Van Noorden, was an alien at the time of the commencement of said suit, or at any other time, or that one of the said parties was at that or any other time, a citizen of the state of North Carolina where the suit was brought, and the other a citizen of another state; or that they the said George and Hadrianus were, for any cause whatever, persons within the jurisdiction of the said court, and capable of suing and being sued there." And, secondly, "that by the record aforesaid it manifestly appeareth that the said circuit court had not any jurisdiction of the cause aforesaid, nor ought to have held plea thereof or given judgment therein, but ought to have dismissed the same, whereas the said court hath proceeded to final judgment therein."

Harper, for the plaintiff in error, stated the only question to be whether the plaintiff had a right to assign for error the want of jurisdiction in that court to which he had chosen to resort. * * *

Here it was the duty of the Court to see that they had jurisdiction, for the consent of parties could not give it. * * *

The defendant in error did not appear, but the citation having been duly served, the judgment was reversed.

NOTES AND QUESTIONS

1. The Supreme Court regarded the defect in this case as extremely serious. Does the fact that it was the plaintiff who brought the case to the Supreme Court make this particularly clear? Why? Why is such significance attached to this error?

2. Read Article III, Section 2, of the United States Constitution, which is set out in the Supplement. What specific language in that Section is pertinent to the Supreme Court's opinion in *Capron?*

3. The Supreme Court reversed the judgment of the lower court. What was the effect of this reversal? Does it mean that Capron wins the lawsuit? If not, why had he sought review in the appellate court?

Unlike the federal courts, which exercise only the limited subject-matter jurisdiction bestowed by the Constitution, as further restricted by acts of Congress, state courts of general jurisdiction have jurisdiction over the subject matter of a very broad spectrum of lawsuits. Indeed, questions of the competence of those courts to decide a particular kind of case rarely arise. But before any court may proceed, it also must have the power to require the defendant to appear in the action. In the next case, the court must decide whether it has that power, and whether it will exercise it.

TICKLE v. BARTON

Supreme Court of Appeals of West Virginia, 1956.
142 W.Va. 188, 95 S.E.2d 427.

HAYMOND, JUDGE. The plaintiff, Richard Tickle, an infant, who sues by his next friend, instituted this action of trespass on the case in the Circuit Court of McDowell County in March, 1955, to recover damages from the defendants, Raymond Barton, a resident of Austinville, Virginia, and Lawrence Coleman, for personal injuries inflicted upon him by a motor vehicle, owned by the defendant Raymond Barton and operated by his agent the defendant Lawrence Coleman, on private property instead of a public highway, in that county which the plaintiff alleges were caused by the negligence of the defendants.

* * * [A first attempt to serve Barton had been made under a statute relating to actions by or against nonresident drivers involved in accidents on a public highway, and the validity of this service was still undecided at the time the instant decision was rendered.]

On December 5, 1955, one of the attorneys for the plaintiff caused an alias process to be issued against the defendants * * * and delivered it to a deputy sheriff for service upon the defendant Barton in McDowell County; and in the evening of December 6, 1955, that process was served by the deputy upon the defendant Barton in person at the War Junior High School in the town of War in that county where he appeared to attend a banquet which was held there at that time.

By his amended plea in abatement No. 2, the defendant Barton challenged the validity of the service of the alias process upon him on the ground that he had been induced to come to that place in McDowell County by trickery, artifice and deceit practiced upon him by the attorney for the plaintiff.

The circuit court overruled the demurrer of the plaintiff to the amended plea in abatement and * * * certified its ruling upon the demurrer to this Court on the joint application of the plaintiff and the defendant Barton.

* * * [T]he amended plea in abatement alleges in substance that after procuring alias process for the purpose of causing it to be served upon the defendant Barton in McDowell County, and inducing him to come to the Junior High School in the town of War in that county, an attorney representing the plaintiff in this action, in the evening of December 5, 1955, called by telephone the defendant Barton at his home in Austinville, Virginia, and wrongfully and deceitfully represented that, in behalf of the sponsors of a banquet honoring a championship high school football team to be held at the Junior High School in the town of War, in McDowell County * * *, he extended an invitation to the defendant Barton, whose son had been a member of an earlier football team of that school, to attend the banquet; that during that telephone conversation between them the attorney, though requested to do so by the defendant Barton, did not disclose his identity except to say that he called him in behalf of the sponsors to extend the defendant Barton a special invitation to attend the banquet; that the defendant Barton before being so invited did not know that the banquet would be held and did not intend to attend it; that he did not know or suspect the identity of the attorney, or realize that the telephone call was a trick or device to entice, induce and inveigle him to come into McDowell County to be served with process in this action; that the attorney was not connected with any of the sponsors of the banquet and was not authorized by them to invite the defendant Barton to attend it; that the attorney called the defendant

Barton and invited him to the banquet solely for the purpose of tricking, deceiving and inveigling him to come to the town of War in order to obtain personal service * * * upon him * * *; that the defendant Barton, believing that the invitation was extended in good faith, by a person authorized to extend it, and not suspecting the real purpose of the telephone call, accepted the invitation and informed the attorney that he would be present at the banquet and on December 6, 1955, left Austinville, Virginia, and went to the town of War with the intention of attending it; that, when he entered the high school where the banquet was held * * * he was served by the deputy sheriff with the alias process * * *; that the service of the alias process upon the defendant Barton, having been procured by trickery, deceit and subterfuge which was not realized or suspected by him, is, for that reason, null and void and of no force or effect and does not confer upon the Circuit Court of McDowell County jurisdiction of the person of the defendant Barton in this action.

The amended plea in abatement also alleges, on information and belief, that after the defendant Barton had left his home * * * the attorney for the plaintiff * * * made a telephone call to the residence of the defendant Barton, or caused some other person to make such call, and inquired of the wife of the defendant Barton if he intended to attend the banquet and was informed by her that he had left his home to attend it and was then on his way to the town of War for that purpose.

The amended plea in abatement further avers that after the defendant Barton had been served with the alias process his attorney inquired of the attorney for the plaintiff if he had made either of the two telephone calls or had procured some person to make the second telephone call and that the attorney for the plaintiff denied that he had made, or procured any person to make, either of the foregoing telephone calls, and denied that he had any knowledge whatsoever of either of them.

The question certified to this Court for decision is whether the allegations of the amended plea in abatement, which insofar as they are material and are well pleaded must be considered as true upon demurrer, are sufficient to render invalid the personal service of process upon the defendant Barton in McDowell County because his presence in that county at the time of such service of process was induced or procured by trickery, artifice, or deceit practiced upon him by an attorney representing the plaintiff in this action.

* * * In 42 Am.Jur., Process, Section 35, the general principle is stated thus:

> * * * "[I]f a person resident outside the jurisdiction of the court and the reach of its process is inveigled, enticed, or induced, by any false representation, deceitful contrivance, or wrongful device for which the plaintiff is responsible, to come within the jurisdiction of the court for the purpose of obtaining service of process on him in an action brought against him in such court, process served upon him through

such improper means is invalid, and upon proof of such fact the court will, on motion, set it aside." * * *

The foregoing principle applies to the party when such service is procured by his agent or by someone acting for and in his behalf. * * *

In Economy Electric Company v. Automatic Electric Power and Light Plant, 185 N.C. 534, 118 S.E. 3, the court, discussing service of process by fraudulent means, used this language: "Where service of process is procured by fraud, that fact may be shown, and, if shown seasonably, the court will refuse to exercise its jurisdiction and turn the plaintiff out of court. The law will not lend its sanction or support to an act, otherwise lawful, which is accomplished by unlawful means. * * * Such a fraud is one affecting the court itself and the integrity of its process. * * * The objection, strictly, is not that the court is without jurisdiction, but that it ought not, by reason of the alleged fraud, to take or to hold jurisdiction of the action. * * * "

Under the material allegations of the amended plea in abatement which, as already indicated, must be considered as true upon demurrer, the defendant Barton was induced or enticed to come into McDowell County by the unauthorized invitation extended to him by the attorney for the plaintiff whose purpose at the time was to obtain personal service upon the defendant Barton * * *; the defendant Barton knew that the present action against him was pending in the circuit court by reason of the service of the original process upon him * * * but he did not suspect or realize that he would be served with process while present in McDowell County to attend the banquet; he was induced to come into that county by the invitation to the banquet; and he would not have come into that jurisdiction if the attorney for the plaintiff had disclosed his identity and his real purpose in extending the invitation, all of which he concealed from the defendant Barton.

* * *

The amended plea in abatement is sufficient on demurrer and the action of the circuit court in overruling the demurrer was correct.

It should perhaps be emphasized that, as the factual allegations of the amended plea in abatement have not been denied at this stage of this action by any pleading filed by the plaintiff, the question of the truth or the falsity of those allegations is not before this Court * * *.

Ruling affirmed.

GIVEN, JUDGE (dissenting).

My disagreement with the majority is not as to the rule of law laid down. I think the rule a salutary one, and masterfully stated. I do not believe, however, that the facts properly pleaded, and the inferences which may be rationally drawn therefrom, bring the facts of this case within the influence of the rule.

Stripped of all explanatory language, and of many allegations of conclusions of fact, * * * the plea in abatement charges no more than that the attorney, by telephone, inquired at defendant's home whether defendant intended to attend a certain social function to be held in McDowell County, to which defendant was then invited by the attorney; that the attorney, though requested to give his name, did not do so; that the attorney later, or someone for him, again by telephone, inquired whether defendant had decided to attend the social function, and was advised that defendant had made arrangements to attend; and that the attorney caused process to be served on defendant while attending the social function. * * * The principal, if not only, fact of wrongdoing, if wrongdoing, alleged against the attorney was his failure to inform defendant of the identity of the telephone caller. * * * It seems to me that the facts properly alleged can not be held to establish fraud or wrongdoing. At most, they would simply show that the attorney took advantage of an opportunity, the holding of the social function in McDowell County and the interest of defendant's son in the holding of the function, to try to obtain proper service of process, which was no more than a duty owed his client. In considering the questions arising, it should be kept in mind that defendant had full knowledge of the institution of the action against him in McDowell County, of the fact that he had questioned the validity of the service of other process issued in that action, and of the fact that the alleged cause of action arose in McDowell County, where ordinarily it would have been triable.

* * *

NOTES AND QUESTIONS

1. Did the court in this case decide that West Virginia courts did not have jurisdiction over the person of defendant (assuming his story were true), or that those courts should not exercise jurisdiction in these circumstances even though they had it?

2. When should a court be able to demand that a person appear before it and defend an action? In what circumstances should this demand be permitted against a nonresident? Why should a nonresident be subject to suit if he is served with process within the state? Insofar as these reasons are concerned, should it make any difference why he is present in the state?

3. In thinking about the cases you read, try to consider how the court might approach the problem presented by a particular case with certain facts changed. For example, should service in West Virginia in the following situations be treated in the same way as it was under the facts alleged in the principal case?

(a) Tickle had asked Barton to appear as a witness in a suit against a third party involved in the accident;

(b) Tickle had asked Barton to come to West Virginia to discuss settling the case;

(c) Tickle had telephoned Barton and falsely told him that his son lay critically injured in a West Virginia hospital;

(d) Tickle (like the Sheriff of Nottingham) had scheduled a football banquet in West Virginia that he knew Barton (like Robin Hood) would be unable to resist attending, although he did not personally invite him.

4. When the case is reconsidered by the West Virginia Circuit Court on remand, Barton's lawyer must prove his allegations if Barton is to avoid trial in West Virginia. What problems do you foresee in his being able to prove them, and how should he proceed to do so?

5. You will later become familiar with state statutes that confer upon their courts power to summon out-of-state motorists to defend actions arising out of their operating automobiles within the state. Tickle had first sought to serve Barton under a statute of this type, but because the accident had occurred on private property rather than a West Virginia public highway, a serious question as to the statute's application existed; this uncertainty prompted the second attempt at service discussed in the case.

2. DEFINING AND DETERMINING THE CASE BEFORE TRIAL

At this point, it will be helpful to reread the part of the Outline of a Civil Action that deals with pleading, especially the portion that discusses the "three general situations" in which a motion to dismiss for failure to state a claim might be granted. Is the court in the following case saying that plaintiff has not properly pleaded its case or that it has no case at all?

CASE v. STATE FARM MUTUAL AUTOMOBILE INSURANCE CO.

United States Court of Appeals, Fifth Circuit, 1961.
294 F.2d 676.

CAMERON, CIRCUIT JUDGE. Appellant Case filed this action against the three insurance companies named as appellees for damages growing out of the termination of his representation of the three Companies as local agent. He charged in his complaint that he was appointed agent by a written contract attached as an exhibit to his complaint, which he charged, and the parties agree, constituted him an independent contractor for all purposes and provided that he was not required to "devote all of his working time to any one of the Companies;" that he represented the three Companies "through the years 1954, 1955, 1956, 1957 and 1958, and up until March 28, 1959," on which date the appellees "began to and did meddle and interfere with the plaintiff's work as agent of (the three Companies) in disregard of the agreement between the defendants and the plaintiff."[1]

1. The meddling and interference upon which appellant lays so much stress before us is stated in the complaint in these words:

Properly construed in connection with the remaining allegations of the complaint,[2] appellant stated nothing in his pleading except an action based upon what he conceived to be the malicious and wrongful cancellation of the written contract between him and appellees, and on that alone. So construed, every word in the complaint related to the alleged wrongful termination of the written contract between the parties. That writing gave either party the right to terminate it with or without cause, and the charges in the complaint relating to meddling and interference make sense only when construed in the light of the allegations that the appellees expressed the purpose not to continue the contractual relationship with appellant unless he would agree to abjure the seeking and holding of the public office of county supervisor. Their efforts to induce him to follow the course which alone would permit the continuation of that contractual relationship related manifestly to the termination which finally took place. The contract gave the appellees the right to cancellation "with or without cause," and in terminating it the appellees acted entirely within their rights.

Appellant argues the case as if it were one in tort for interference with his civil rights. The allegations of the pleadings do not support such an argument. * * *

It is clear also that the complaint does not set forth an independent claim for damages based upon meddling and interference by appellees with

---

"That on or about March 1, 1959, that he, the Plaintiff, publicly announced his candidacy for the office of Supervisor of District Five (5) of Adams County, Mississippi, and Plaintiff shows further that on or about March 28, 1959, the Defendants * * * [began] to and did meddle and interfere with the Plaintiff's work as agent of the State Farm Insurance Companies in disregard of the agreement between the Defendants and the Plaintiff. The Plaintiff was informed orally and by letter by representatives of his principals that his agency would have to be handled in a particular manner and he was directed as to when, how and why his work should be done in a certain manner and was orally informed as well as by letter that he would have to submit his decision as to whether he would be a candidate for the office of supervisor or have his contract or appointment with State Farm Insurance Companies terminated as of May 1, 1959, all of which was done wrongfully in malicious and wanton disregard of the Plaintiff's rights according to his appointment as agent of the Defendants, State Farm Insurance Companies, with the intention of coercing the Plaintiff into withdrawing from the political race and devoting his full time as an employee in the master and servant relationship to the performance of his service for said Defendants.

"Plaintiff charges and avers that the malicious intentional and wrongful direction as to his activities as agent of the Defendants was such a breach and repudiation of his contract or agreement with him as set out in Exhibit I as to entitle him, the Plaintiff to damages for the loss due to the breach or repudiation of the said agreement listed as Exhibit I."

2. E.g., immediately following the language quoted in Footnote 1, supra, the complaint charges the following:

"Plaintiff further shows unto the Court that at the time of the said repudiation or breach of contract by the Defendants, that the Plaintiff's income from the Defendants for the previous year was nine thousand seventy-three ($9,073.00) dollars and that the Plaintiff's life expectancy at his present age of 45 was 25.21 years according to the C.S.O. Mortality table, and that but for the wrongful breach, repudiation and termination of the Plaintiff's contract of agency with the Defendants, the Plaintiff would have been entitled to continued remuneration from the Defendants for the sum of two hundred twenty-six thousand, seven hundred twenty-five ($226,725.00) dollars and that but for the malicious, wanton meddling and interfering and wrongful breach, repudiation and cancellation of the Plaintiff's contract the Plaintiff is entitled to punitive damages in the sum of two hundred thousand ($200,000) dollars."

The judgment demanded against the three defendants, appellees, was the sum of the two figures mentioned above.

appellant's performance of the contract. Appellant invokes the oft repeated statement of the courts that a complaint should not be dismissed if it charges facts upon which a court could possibly grant relief. * * * What the courts have said does not mean that it is the duty of the trial court or the appellate court to create a claim which appellant has not spelled out in his pleading.

The court below was faced with a complaint and a motion to dismiss. Its duty was to judge the complaint by the language used in it. The only damages claimed by the appellant were those based entirely upon his claim that the written contract was wrongfully terminated, and the language concerning the meddling and interference is reasonably construed as referring to appellees' indication to appellant that he would have to give up his quest of public office if he desired to retain his contractual relationship with appellees. We are called upon here merely to test whether the court below erred in interpreting the meaning of language which was, viewed as a whole, clear and unambiguous. We do not think that it did.

If appellant had desired to pursue a charge that appellees had wrongfully interfered with the running of his business in violation of the terms of the written contract, it would have been quite simple for him to file an amended complaint. Doubtless the court below would have permitted this even after the order of dismissal had been granted. But aside from that, appellant had an absolute right to amend his complaint once, no responsive pleading having been filed. * * *

It is apparent that the complaint charged that appellees did nothing more than to exercise the right of termination given them by the explicit terms of the contract exhibited with appellant's complaint. * * * This being true, and since appellant claims no damages whatever except such as would flow from the wrongful termination of the contract, we think the court below correctly granted the motion to dismiss. Its judgment is

Affirmed.

NOTES AND QUESTIONS

1. Can you identify the different claims that Case alleged in his complaint?

2. Which of the three objectives of pleading discussed in the Outline of a Civil Action, pp. 9–10, supra, was most significantly involved in this case?

3. Suppose a valid legal theory did exist that would have entitled Case to some relief, but that Case neglected to invoke it in his pleading. Would the court have been justified in dismissing the complaint on the principle that "it is [not] the duty of the trial court or the appellate court to create a claim which appellant has not spelled out in his pleading"? Would dismissal be appropriate if the complaint "charges facts upon which a court could possibly grant relief"? Wouldn't dismissal in that circumstance simply punish Case for his lawyer's sloppy pleading?

4. What was the effect of the dismissal in *Case?* Should plaintiff have been permitted to amend the complaint and start again? Could plaintiff interpose a new and slightly altered complaint that would survive another motion to dismiss?

5. Suppose that after the motion to dismiss had been granted Case discovered a letter agreement dated after the contract and signed by all of the parties stipulating that the insurance agency agreement could be terminated only for "good cause." Should he be able to amend his complaint and sue again in federal court? In state court?

Disputes often involve more than two people. Procedural rules allow parties to join multiple parties and multiple claims in one lawsuit. Joinder may promote efficiency and sometimes also may be essential for fairness. The following case explores whether all those who are interested in a controversy must always be made parties to a single lawsuit.

TEMPLE v. SYNTHES CORP.

Supreme Court of the United States, 1990.
498 U.S. 5, 111 S.Ct. 315, 112 L.Ed.2d 263.

Certiorari to the United States Court of Appeals for the Fifth Circuit.

PER CURIAM. Petitioner Temple, a Mississippi resident, underwent surgery in October 1986 in which a "plate and screw device" was implanted in his lower spine. The device was manufactured by respondent Synthes, Ltd. (U.S.A.) (Synthes), a Pennsylvania corporation. Dr. S. Henry LaRocca performed the surgery at St. Charles General Hospital in New Orleans, Louisiana. Following surgery, the device's screws broke off inside Temple's back.

Temple filed suit against Synthes in the United States District Court for the Eastern District of Louisiana. The suit, which rested on diversity jurisdiction, alleged defective design and manufacture of the device. At the same time, Temple filed a state administrative proceeding against Dr. LaRocca and the hospital for malpractice and negligence. At the conclusion of the administrative proceeding, Temple filed suit against the doctor and the hospital in Louisiana state court.

Synthes did not attempt to bring the doctor and the hospital into the federal action by means of a third-party complaint, as provided in Federal Rule * * * 14(a). Instead, Synthes filed a motion to dismiss Temple's federal suit for failure to join necessary parties pursuant to Federal Rule * * * 19. Following a hearing, the District Court ordered Temple to join the doctor and the hospital as defendants within twenty days or risk dismissal of the lawsuit. According to the court, the most significant reason for requiring joinder was the interest of judicial economy. The court relied on this Court's decision in Provident Tradesmens Bank & Trust Co. v. Patterson, 390 U.S. 102, 88 S.Ct. 733, 19 L.Ed.2d 936 (1968), wherein we recognized that one focus of Rule 19 is "the interest of the courts and the public in complete, consistent, and efficient settlement of controversies." When Temple failed to join the doctor and the hospital, the court dismissed the suit with prejudice.

Temple appealed, and the United States Court of Appeals for the Fifth Circuit affirmed. The court deemed it "obviously prejudicial to the defendants to have the separate litigations being carried on," because Synthes' defense might be that the plate was not defective but that the doctor and the hospital were negligent, while the doctor and hospital, on the other hand, might claim that they were not negligent but that the plate was defective. The Court of Appeals found that the claims overlapped and that the District Court therefore had not abused its discretion in ordering joinder under Rule 19. * * *

* * * Temple contends that it was error to label joint tortfeasors as indispensable parties under Rule 19(b) and to dismiss the lawsuit with prejudice for failure to join those parties. [In 2007 the term "indispensable party" was deleted from Rule 19(b) and the term "required party" was substituted.] We agree. Synthes does not deny that it, the doctor, and the hospital are potential joint tortfeasors. It has long been the rule that it is not necessary for all joint tortfeasors to be named as defendants in a single lawsuit. * * * The Advisory Committee Notes to Rule 19(a) explicitly state that "a tortfeasor with the usual 'joint-and-several' liability is merely a permissive party to an action against another with like liability." * * * There is nothing in Louisiana tort law to the contrary. * * *

The opinion in *Provident Bank* does speak of the public interest in limiting multiple litigation, but that case is not controlling here. There, the estate of a tort victim brought a declaratory judgment action against an insurance company [for the alleged tortfeasor. The total claims of the persons harmed in the accident exceeded the insurance policy monetary limits, and the purpose of the suit was to determine to which persons the insurance proceeds would be paid]. We assumed that the policyholder was a person "who, under [Rule 19] (a), should be joined if 'feasible' " * * *, and went on to discuss the appropriate analysis under Rule 19(b), because the policyholder could not be joined without destroying diversity. After examining the factors set forth in Rule 19(b), we determined that the action could proceed without the policyholder; he therefore was not an indispensable party whose absence required dismissal of the suit.

Here, no inquiry under Rule 19(b) is necessary, because the threshold requirements of Rule 19(a) have not been satisfied. As potential joint tortfeasors with Synthes, Dr. LaRocca and the hospital were merely permissive parties. The Court of Appeals erred by failing to hold that the District Court abused its discretion in ordering them joined as defendants and in dismissing the action when Temple failed to comply with the court's order. For these reasons, we grant the petition for certiorari, reverse the judgment of the Court of Appeals for the Fifth Circuit, and remand for further proceedings consistent with this opinion.

It is so ordered.

NOTES AND QUESTIONS

1. Why do you think Temple did not name Dr. LaRocca and the hospital as defendants in his federal suit? Why would Temple seek to duplicate his time and effort by litigating a suit in federal court at the same time that he is litigating one in state court with respect to precisely the same injury?

2. Although the Supreme Court failed to specify the citizenship of Dr. LaRocca and the hospital, they were in fact citizens of Louisiana, meaning that complete diversity existed between Temple and the three defendants. See Temple v. Synthes Corp., 130 F.R.D. 68, 69 n.1 (E.D.La.1989). Does this information change your answers to the questions in Note 1, supra?

3. What do you make of the Fifth Circuit's concern with the potential for inconsistent judgments? Does the Supreme Court find that this concern is not warranted? Or does it find that there are other more important considerations? If so, what are they?

4. When this case returns to the district court, could the court order Synthes to file a third-party complaint against the doctor and the hospital under Federal Rule 14(a)? Should a court ever have the power to order parties added to a lawsuit? Why?

5. Suppose that both Temple and Synthes do not want the doctor and the hospital to be added as parties and the court does not order that they be added. Could the doctor and the hospital join the federal suit of their own accord? See Federal Rule 24. Should Temple and/or Synthes be able to stop them from intervening?

The purposes of discovery are many. The most important are obtaining evidence for one's own case and identifying weaknesses in the opposition's. The party seeking discovery usually is asking about something of which he is ignorant or uncertain, but sometimes he seeks information about a matter within his own knowledge. In reading the next case, consider why plaintiff is so determined to obtain the evidence and why defendant is equally determined that he shall not have it.

DiMICHEL v. SOUTH BUFFALO RY. CO.[b]

Court of Appeals of New York, 1992.
80 N.Y.2d 184, 590 N.Y.S.2d 1, 604 N.E.2d 63.

WACHTLER, CHIEF JUDGE. * * * [W]e consider whether surveillance films prepared by a defendant in a personal injury action are discoverable

---

b. The court's treatment of the companion case, Poole v. Consolidated Rail Corp., has been omitted.

by the plaintiff before trial. * * * The Appellate Division held * * * that the defendants would be obligated to disclose only those tapes which they planned to use at trial. Under the facts present here, we find this balance to be an appropriate one. Accordingly, * * * we affirm. * * *

Plaintiff Anthony DiMichel commenced this action against South Buffalo Railway Company (South Buffalo) in Supreme Court, Erie County, by service of summons and complaint dated January 16, 1986. Plaintiff alleged that on June 6, 1984, while employed by South Buffalo, he sustained injuries in a fall. DiMichel charged South Buffalo with violations of the Federal Employers' Liability Act, the Safety Appliance Act and the Boiler Inspection Act and asked for $500,000 in damages.

In the course of pre-trial discovery, plaintiff asked for disclosure of all videotapes or surveillance films that defendant may have taken of plaintiff. Without conceding that it in fact possessed surveillance materials, South Buffalo contended that any such material was not discoverable. Plaintiff then moved to compel disclosure. * * * [T]he motion to compel disclosure was granted and defendant was ordered "to turn over to plaintiff for inspection and copying any and all videotapes and/or surveillance films of the plaintiff," but stayed this order pending appeal to the Appellate Division. The Appellate Division modified, * * * holding that the defendant was obligated to turn over those surveillance materials it intended to use at trial, and that the defendant would be precluded from using any surveillance material it did not supply to plaintiff within 60 days of its order. * * *

* * *

* * * [W]e now turn to the unique problems posed by surveillance films. Personal injury defendants secure surveillance materials in order to verify the extent of a plaintiff's purported injuries and introduce them because they are powerful and immediate images that cast doubt upon the plaintiff's claims. And indeed, if accurate and authentic, a surveillance film that undercuts a plaintiff's claims of injury may be devastatingly probative. At the same time, however, film and videotape are extraordinarily manipulable media. Artful splicing and deceptive lighting are but two ways that an image can be skewed and perception altered. As one court has noted, "[t]he camera may be an instrument of deception. It can be misused. Distances may be minimized or exaggerated. Lighting, focal lengths, and camera angles all make a difference. Action may be slowed down or speeded up. The editing and splicing of films may change the chronology of events. An emergency situation may be made to appear commonplace. That which has occurred once, can be described as an example of an event which recurs frequently. * * * Thus, that which purports to be a means to reach the truth may be distorted, misleading and false." Snead v. American Export–Isbrandtsen Lines, 59 F.R.D. 148, 150 [(E.D.Pa.1973)].

Thus, while an accurate surveillance film may indeed prove to be a bombshell, the possibility of inaccuracy, given the nature of the medium, is very real. In resolving the question now before us, then, it is important to note that New York has long favored open and far-reaching pre-trial discovery. To a large extent, New York's open disclosure policy was intended to mark an end to the presentation of totally unexpected evidence and to substitute honesty and forthrightness for gamesmanship. * * *

* * *

This is clearly an issue that has fragmented the four departments of the Appellate Division. * * * [T]he First Department would treat surveillance films as discoverable in their entirety * * * [as] party statements. The Second Department followed the lead of the Fourth Department in [this case] by treating surveillance films as material prepared for litigation and by holding that substantial need and undue hardship inhered in the nature of the films themselves. Finally, the Third Department, while also treating these films as material prepared for litigation, held that such films were discoverable only upon a showing of substantial need and undue hardship.

Having considered the different approaches, we agree with the Second, Third and Fourth Departments that surveillance films should be treated as material prepared in anticipation of litigation, and as such, are subject to a qualified privilege that can be overcome only by a factual showing of substantial need and undue hardship.

That the plaintiffs * * * have a substantial need to view surveillance films before trial is manifest. Because films are so easily altered, there is a very real danger that deceptive tapes, inadequately authenticated, could contaminate the trial process. The question that remains, therefore, is whether plaintiffs confronted with surveillance films for the first time at trial would have an adequate opportunity to ascertain the films' accuracy and authenticity. * * * Authentication of surveillance films can be a slow and painstaking process, and because of the potentially devastating effects of such evidence, it would be improper to curtail a plaintiff's efforts to do so. Thus, a plaintiff, confronted with a surveillance film at trial, would certainly be entitled to a continuance to examine the video evidence. Indeed, it would appear to be well within the discretion of a Trial Judge, under certain circumstances, to give plaintiff an extended continuance in order to retain an expert who could ascertain the authenticity of proffered video evidence. Thus, if defendants were allowed to withhold surveillance evidence until trial, personal injury trials could be routinely disrupted and delayed.

Further, a plaintiff confronted with altered video evidence for the first time at trial would likely be prejudiced by the apparent weight and authority of such evidence. Even if after careful examination plaintiff was able to demonstrate that the evidence had indeed been distorted, it would be difficult to undo its initial impact and to erase the impression left in the minds of the jury members.

Defendants dispute plaintiffs' claims of substantial need, arguing that the real reason they seek to obtain the tapes prior to trial is to learn what evidence the defendants intend to produce at trial so that they may tailor their trial testimony accordingly. This, defendants argue, would greatly impair the truth-finding function of cross-examination. This argument, however, is flawed for at least two reasons. First, it runs counter to New York's open pre-trial disclosure policy, as discussed earlier. Clearly, to permit defendants to withhold this evidence until trial, even for the ostensible purpose of promoting vigorous cross-examination, would be to return to an earlier time, when subterfuge and surprise were common trial strategies. Second, it is persuasive only if we assume that surveillance tapes are always accurate and plaintiffs always dishonest. As noted above, however, surveillance films are extraordinarily susceptible to manipulation, and, once altered, are peculiarly dangerous. Thus, we cannot fashion a rule that is premised upon their authenticity, as defendants urge. However, the danger identified by defendants is a real one. We believe that it can be largely eliminated by providing that surveillance films should be turned over only after a plaintiff has been deposed.

We further find that plaintiffs have established that they cannot without undue hardship obtain the substantial equivalent of surveillance materials by other means. Although plaintiffs are aware of their own physical ailments and the nature of their disabilities, this is no substitute for viewing the surveillance materials taken by the defendants. It is only by viewing the surveillance film that plaintiffs can determine when it was made and whether the activities depicted were typical of that time or were the product of an emergency situation. Visual evidence of this kind is unique because it memorializes a particular set of conditions that can likely never be replicated. Only by observing the conditions as they appear on film can the plaintiffs respond to possible distortions or prepare to explain seeming inconsistencies to the jury. * * *

* * * Having concluded that the plaintiff was entitled to view those tapes that the defendant intended to use at trial, if indeed any such tapes exist, our analysis * * * is at an end. Accordingly, the order of the Appellate Division should be affirmed * * *.

* * *

NOTES AND QUESTIONS

1. Modern discovery systems prevent trial by surprise. The practice was quite different at common law:

> * * * [T]he common law * * * *recognized no rule requiring prior notice* of intended evidence to be given to the opponent or furnishing legal process for obtaining such information * * *.
>
> It might be supposed that, in the court of Chancery, a bill for discovery served as a means of evading the strict common-law rule, and that thereby a notice could be compulsorily obtained of the evidence intended

> to be produced by the opponent. But there was here no radical departure from the established doctrine of the common law; it was a policy, not of one Court rather than another Court, but of the whole legal system * * * [of England].
>
> * * * It is true that, to a limited extent * * * the result of a bill of discovery would usually be the revelation of some portion of information not before known to the applicant. But the general theory remained, and the rule was strictly enforced, that the adversary's own evidence was not to be revealed on a bill for discovery.
>
> In short, equitable discovery involved no more than the negation of the party's privilege at common-law trials not to testify *against* his own cause, and was not intended to give relief against the common-law principle which refused to exact before trial a disclosure of the tenor of the evidence intended to be given *for* his cause.

6 Wigmore, Evidence §§ 1845, 1846, at 378, 380 (3d ed. 1940).

2. The court in *DiMichel* held that materials prepared in anticipation of trial normally are exempt from discovery, unless a party can show a substantial need and an undue hardship. Do you agree that surveillance videotapes present such a situation? In general, why are materials prepared for trial exempt from discovery at all?

3. Is the holding in *DiMichel* limited to videotaped evidence or does it apply to other types of impeachment evidence as well? Suppose plaintiff is deposed and testifies that prior to the accident being sued on she had never suffered a disabling injury. Plaintiff then attempts to have defendant answer an interrogatory as to what information defendant has regarding plaintiff's prior medical history. What result?

4. Is the court in *DiMichel* correct in not allowing videotapes to be disclosed until after plaintiff has been deposed? If the court is truly following a policy of open discovery, why does it matter when the videotapes are disclosed?

In ruling on a motion to dismiss for failure to state a claim as in Case v. State Farm Mutual Automobile Ins. Co., p. 32, supra, the judge must accept as true the allegations in the complaint. If defendant files an answer denying those allegations, the denials are only assertions of defendant and do not demonstrate whose story is correct. The motion for summary judgment enables a party to show that there is admissible evidence to support the allegations made and to call for a similar showing by the opposing party. The judge will not try to decide a factual dispute when each party has presented competent evidence on an issue and there is a conflict. But if it becomes clear that one party cannot possibly prove his allegations, there is no "genuine issue" and a futile trial may be avoided by granting the motion.

ALDERMAN v. BALTIMORE & OHIO R. CO.

United States District Court, Southern District of West Virginia, 1953.
113 F.Supp. 881.

MOORE, CHIEF JUDGE. Plaintiff * * * brings this action against defendant, * * * to recover for personal injuries sustained by her as a result of the derailment of one of defendant's trains near Adrian, West Virginia, on February 14, 1952.

Plaintiff was not a fare-paying passenger. She was traveling on a trip pass, which afforded her free transportation * * *. The following conditions were printed on the pass: "In consideration of the issuance of this free pass, I hereby assume all risk of personal injury and loss of or of damage to property from whatever causes arising, and release the company from liability therefore, and I hereby declare that I am not prohibited by law from receiving free transportation and that this pass will be lawfully used."

Plaintiff in her original complaint charged defendant with negligence in the maintenance of its tracks and the operation of its train. After a pre-trial conference, at which the legal effect of the release from liability contained in the pass was discussed, plaintiff filed an amended complaint charging defendant with wilful or wanton conduct.

On the basis of the amended pleadings and supporting affidavits filed by defendant, defendant moved for summary judgment under Rule 56 * * *.

It is undisputed that the derailment was caused by a break in one of the rails as the train was passing over the track. It is also shown by defendant's affidavits, and not denied, that the break in the rail was due to a transverse fissure inside the cap of the rail, which broke vertically under the weight of the train; that such a fissure is not visible upon inspection; that such defects occur in both new and old rails; and that a visual inspection was in fact made of this particular rail the day preceding the accident and the defect was not discovered.

Since plaintiff was an intrastate passenger, and since the accident occurred in West Virginia, the law of West Virginia governs both the effect to be given to the release and the degree of care which defendant owed plaintiff. * * *

However, counsel have been unable to direct the Court's attention to, and the Court has not found, any West Virginia decision which has determined the effect which a release from liability contained in a pass has upon the carrier's duty to the holder of such a pass. * * *

Since the Federal statute and the West Virginia statute authorizing the issuance of free passes are similar, 49 U.S.C.A. § 1(7), and W.Va.Code, Ch. 24, Art. 3, § 4, it is pertinent to examine the United States Supreme Court decisions construing the Federal statute. The Supreme Court has held that a carrier may contract against liability for negligent injury to one who accepts a free pass * * *; but that for reasons of public policy it cannot relieve itself of liability for wilful or wanton acts. * * *

I am therefore of [the] opinion that the sole duty imposed upon defendant under the facts of this case was to refrain from wilfully or wantonly injuring plaintiff.

In Kelly v. Checker White Cab, Inc., 131 W.Va. 816 at page 822; 50 S.E.2d 888 at page 892, the West Virginia court, quoting from 29 Cyc. 510 said:

"In order that one may be held guilty of wilful or wanton conduct, it must be shown that he was conscious of his conduct, and conscious, from his knowledge of existing conditions, that injury would likely or probably result from his conduct, and that with reckless indifference to consequences he consciously and intentionally did some wrongful act or omitted some known duty which produced the injurious result. * * *"

The substance of plaintiff's contention that defendant wilfully injured her is that defendant used old and obsolescent rails in its tracks, knowing that the use of these rails made derailments reasonably probable. It is charged that defendant used old rails because the cost of derailments was less than the cost of replacing the old rails, and that for this reason defendant was willing to take the risk of derailments.

I am of opinion that the complaint fails to state sufficient facts to substantiate a charge of wilfulness, as that term is defined by the West Virginia court. It is clear that plaintiff has stated a charge of negligence; but that is not the test in this case. To establish wilfulness it would be necessary to charge that defendant knew of this particular defect in the rail; that the defect would probably result in a break in the rail if the train were run over it, causing a derailment of the train; and that defendant, with this knowledge of existing conditions, and the likelihood or probability of an injury resulting from its conduct, intentionally drove its train over the defective rail with an indifference to the consequences. The undenied affidavits of defendant show clearly that plaintiff cannot establish these facts.

At the hearing of this motion, counsel for plaintiff moved for a continuance of the hearing to enable him to substantiate a newspaper report to the effect that defendant was using old and obsolescent rails in its tracks because the cost of derailments was cheaper than the cost of replacing the rails. The motion was denied since this contention, even if it were true, merely has a bearing on an issue of negligence, and not upon the question of wilful conduct. Plaintiff does not contend that she can establish that defendant knew of the particular defect in the rail that caused the derailment.

For the reasons stated above, defendant's motion for summary judgment will be sustained. * * *

NOTES AND QUESTIONS

1. If very specific allegations of all of the facts giving rise to plaintiff's cause of action were required to be set forth in the complaint, would it have been possible to handle the *Alderman* case by a motion to dismiss or a demurrer rather than waiting for the summary judgment phase? To the extent that this would have been possible, does the case present a strong argument for more specific pleading of facts? Consider whether the court should have ruled as it did if the motion for summary judgment had been made immediately upon the service of the complaint and before plaintiff had an opportunity to utilize the discovery process. Analytically, the motion for summary judgment can be thought of as a demurrer-plus. You should not forget, however, that if summary judgment is to be a fair and effective device, it must frequently be preceded by discovery, so that each party will have an opportunity to disclose the gaps in her opponent's case and to cure any defects in her own.

2. What advantage did defendant gain in *Alderman* by moving for summary judgment, rather than moving to dismiss? Reread the third paragraph of the case. Should plaintiff be able to amend a complaint in this situation? Was her amendment made merely to prolong litigation in the hope of forcing a settlement?

3. Must a court always grant a motion for summary judgment if the requirements of Rule 56 are met? In KENNEDY v. SILAS MASON CO., 334 U.S. 249, 256–57, 68 S.Ct. 1031, 1034, 92 L.Ed. 1347, 1350–51 (1948), Justice Jackson, speaking for the Court, said: "* * * [S]ummary procedures, however salutary where issues are clear-cut and simple, present a treacherous record for deciding issues of far-flung import, on which the Court should draw inferences with caution from complicated courses of legislation, contracting and practice." He stated it would be "good judicial administration to withhold decision of the ultimate questions" absent a record presenting "a more solid basis of findings based on litigation or on a comprehensive statement of agreed facts." See Shannon, *Should Summary Judgment be Granted?*, 58 Am. U. L. Rev. 85 (2008).

4. A motion for summary judgment may be useful even though the moving party believes it will be unsuccessful. For what reasons, other than a hope of obtaining judgment, might defendant in a case like *Alderman* make such a motion?

3. JUDGE AND JURY

You probably will be surprised (and perhaps dismayed) by the comparatively small part of a Civil Procedure course devoted to the actual process of trial. It is true that the trial, if one occurs, is the most important and most interesting stage of a lawsuit. But most of the "law" about trials is the subject matter of a course in Evidence. The most important aspect of trial with which this course is concerned is the division of functions between judge and jury and the various ways in which the judge acts to insure that the jury performs its proper function. In this section, we look at four of those ways: the instruction of the jury as to the law it shall apply, the form that the verdict takes, judicial control over the matters the jury may consider, and the taking from the jury of its power to decide a case when the evidence is inadequate.

A. INSTRUCTING THE JURY

Broadly stated, it is a function of the judge to decide questions of law and a function of the jury to decide questions of fact. But in most cases the jury's final decision will have the effect that one or the other party is entitled to judgment and to do so the jury must apply the law to the facts. Therefore the jury must be told what the law is. The vehicle for this is the judge's charge to the jury, which comes at the end of the trial, immediately before the jury retires to consider its verdict.

An important issue concerning these instructions is how far the adversary system should extend to this stage of the lawsuit. Counsel for both parties may request that particular instructions be given to the jury, and when there is a dispute between them as to the law, they ordinarily will submit conflicting requests. The judge must resolve such conflicts, and it is the court's duty in any event to instruct the jury whether or not the parties make specific requests. The judge, even though an expert on the law, may err. To what extent is it the responsibility of counsel to attempt to correct the trial judge? The next case not only involves this question, but also introduces you to the question of allocating the burden of proof (or burden of persuasion). Why is there no rule that says one party or the other has this burden?

ALEXANDER v. KRAMER BROS. FREIGHT LINES, INC.

United States Court of Appeals, Second Circuit, 1959.
273 F.2d 373.

SWAN, CIRCUIT JUDGE. The present action is a sequel to a collision between two tractor-trailer trucks on the Pennsylvania Turnpike in or near Somerset, Pennsylvania. It occurred * * * about six o'clock in the morning, when there was spotty fog on the Turnpike. The corporate plaintiff owned one of the trucks. It was badly damaged and its operator, the plaintiff Alexander, sustained serious injuries. The other truck was owned by the defendant corporation. Its answer to the complaint denied any negligence on its part and set up the defense of contributory negligence on the part of the plaintiffs. The jury found a verdict for the plaintiffs. * * *

Because of the character of the questions raised, a very brief statement concerning the testimony will suffice. The only eye witnesses to the accident were drivers of the two trucks. The drivers' stories were contradictory and raised issues as to the exact location of the accident and the manner in which it occurred. Both trucks were proceeding westerly. Alexander testified that the collision occurred where there was an entrance to the Turnpike from the right, that defendant's truck cut in ahead of him, and that the fog was such that he could not see the entering truck in time to avoid hitting it. Holman, defendant's driver, denied that he entered from the right and claimed that plaintiff's truck had been following for some time before it ran into the rear end of his truck. Thus the issues of negligence and contributory negligence raised questions of credibility for the jury.

The first question for consideration is whether the judgment should be reversed because of the court's erroneous charge as to the burden of proof of contributory negligence, despite defendant's failure to request a charge on that subject or to object or take exception to the charge given, as required by Rule 51 * * *. Appellant contends that he is excused from complying with the Rule by what occurred in colloquy with the court near the close of the plaintiffs' case. In the colloquy, the court stated that "the burden of proof of contributory negligence is on the defendant." Counsel for plaintiffs expressed agreement with the statement, and counsel for defendant said, "I take an exception," to which the court replied, "Yes, I give you that exception." The plaintiff then rested, and defendant proceeded to put in its case.

* * * Under the [applicable law] the plaintiffs in an action where death has not resulted * * * carry the burden of proving freedom from contributory negligence. The cases now relied upon by appellant to prove the charge wrong were never brought to the trial court's attention either in the colloquy or at the time when counsel submitted numerous requests to charge on other matters. Had they been, it seems probable that Judge Inch would have changed the view he expressed in colloquy. The obvious purpose of the requirement in Rule 51 that objection must be made to matters in the charge in order to assign them as error, is to permit the trial judge to evaluate the objection and correct his charge if further thought persuades him of its error. This purpose is not fulfilled by taking an exception to a statement made by the judge several days prior to the time for charging the jury when nothing was before the judge requiring a ruling in respect to the statement made in colloquy. Certainly an exception under such circumstances does not meet the literal requirement of Rule 51 and, in our opinion, it is an insufficient excuse for failure to object or except to the charge.

The cases relied upon by the appellant deal either with situations where an exception was taken at the time of the charge and the question is whether the exception was sufficiently explicit, or to cases involving evidentiary rulings where exception was taken at the time of the ruling but no further exception was taken at the time of the charge. * * * Nor do we think the instant case of the exceptional character in which an appellate court will sometimes correct an error in the charge in the absence of objection or exception. See Troupe v. Chicago, D. & G. Bay Transit Co., 2 Cir., 234 F.2d 253, 260 [1956].

* * *

Judgment affirmed.

NOTES AND QUESTIONS

1. The opinion in this case speaks of the "burden of proof of contributory negligence." In this book, we use the term "burden of persuasion" when we are referring to the kind of burden involved in *Alexander.* There is another kind of burden—the burden of initially putting in evidence on an issue, without which the issue is not in the case at all. This kind of burden we call the "burden of production." The two burdens are distinct, but the term "burden of proof" often is used to mean either of them. For this reason we avoid it. Ordinarily the burden of production and the burden of persuasion on an issue are placed on the same party. But not always. For example, when a defense is one that is seldom raised, it might be a waste of time to require plaintiff in every case to introduce evidence refuting it; the burden of production would be placed on defendant. But once there is enough evidence on the issue to go to the jury, the court might rule that plaintiff should have the burden of persuasion—that is, establishing that the defense is not valid—as plaintiff does on most aspects of her case.

2. What factors should be considered in determining whether the burden of persuasion on the issue of contributory negligence should be placed on plaintiff or defendant? Are these the same factors that should be involved in deciding who shall be required to plead on the issue of contributory negligence? Why might the two burdens be placed differently?

3. In *Troupe*, cited at the end of the principal case, Judge Frank, in a concurring opinion, said, at 234 F.2d at 260–61:

> On the negligence issue, the judge, at defendant's request, charged, "It is enough if the steps and paint are commonly used and accepted in the industry at the time." This was as obvious an error, on a material matter, as one can imagine. For the Supreme Court, this court and others have often held that usual practices, by others in the same industry or trade, similar to a defendant's practices, do not constitute a defense in a negligence action. * * *
>
> My colleagues indicate that, were it not for our reversal on the unseaworthiness issue, they would probably have disregarded this error. I cannot agree. My colleagues refer to Rule 51 and the fact that, before the jury retired, plaintiffs' counsel did not state distinctly that he objected and the grounds of the objection. My colleagues concede that, in an exceptional case, we may review errors not "saved" by a proper objection. They suggest this is not an exceptional case, relying on a statement in United States v. Atkinson, 297 U.S. 157, 160, 56 S.Ct. 391, 392, 80 L.Ed. 555. There the Supreme Court, set forth, in the disjunctive, two grounds for reviewing such errors:
>
> (1) "the errors are obvious
>
> *or*
>
> (2) they otherwise seriously affect the fairness, integrity, or public reputation of judicial proceedings."

> My colleagues stress the second ground. But the first ground alone suffices, as the cases make clear. And here, as observed above, the error was magnificently obvious. A litigant surely has the right to assume that a federal trial judge knows the elementary substantive legal rules, long established by the precedents, and that therefore the judge will act accordingly, without prompting by the litigant's lawyer.

Was the trial judge's error in *Alexander* "obvious"? What factors are relevant in answering this question?

B. THE FORM OF THE VERDICT

In most cases, the jury is asked to return a "general verdict." In substance, the jury simply says, "We find for plaintiff and fix damages at *x* dollars" or "We find for defendant." But as previously discussed in the Outline, p. 17, supra, there are two variations on the general verdict. One is the special verdict, in which the jury is asked to answer questions as to the facts; the judge then applies the law to the facts as found by the jury. The other is the general verdict with interrogatories; the jury is told to return a verdict in the same form as a general verdict, but in addition it is told to answer certain questions about the facts of the case. If those answers are not consistent with the general verdict, the answers control. There are a number of reasons for using the special verdict or the general verdict with interrogatories. For example, in a complicated case, the special verdict obviates the necessity of instructing the jury about the law and permits it to concentrate on determining the facts. But you should bear in mind that both of these verdict forms also are devices for controlling the jury—for preventing the jury from ignoring the law and simply deciding the case for the party the jurors want to win.

DINIERO v. UNITED STATES LINES CO.

United States Court of Appeals, Second Circuit, 1961.
288 F.2d 595, certiorari denied 368 U.S. 831, 82 S.Ct. 54, 7 L.Ed.2d 34.

MEDINA, CIRCUIT JUDGE.

* * * Julio Diniero, a Junior Third Assistant Engineer aboard the S.S. Pioneer Land, owned by United States Lines Company, claimed to have suffered such repeated strains in his back in the performance of his duties as to cause a ruptured disc with resultant pain and suffering, culminating some years later in a fusion operation and the removal of the disc. According to Diniero's testimony, there was a blow-down valve located below a floor plate * * *. There was a slot in the floor plate and normally the valve could be opened or closed as circumstances required by using a reach rod. For a variety of reasons * * * which include the absence of a reach rod and defects in the valve, Diniero said the only way he could operate the valve was by removing the deck plate, crouching down and moving the wheel of the valve by the use of a wrench. He claimed the injuries to his back were the effect of repeatedly operating the valve under these difficult conditions. The shipowner * * * claimed there

was nothing wrong with the valve, nor any necessity to remove the floor plate or to use a wrench. The eight day trial was devoted to * * * the controverted issue of liability, and there was also considerable medical proof on the general subject of whether Diniero's trouble was due to a long continued condition caused by a degenerative disc disease and having no relation whatever to the operation of the blow-down valve * * *.

At the close of the evidence the trial judge submitted the case to the jury in a wholly unexceptionable charge. In an endeavor to assist the jury in its deliberations, however, * * * he submitted eight questions to be signed and returned as the verdict of the jury. The last two were in the form of a general verdict for plaintiff or defendant, questions 2 to 6 [related] * * * to unseaworthiness, negligence, contributory negligence and proximate cause. The trouble was caused by question number 1, as follows:

> Did the plaintiff injure himself aboard the Pioneer Land because in operating the blow-down valve he had to remove the floor plates, then crouch and exert physical effort with a wrench and not his hand to stop it from leaking?
>
> Answer yes or no.

After some hours of deliberation and the receipt of a number of communications from the jury, the trial judge withdrew all the questions, told the jury to disregard them and bring in a general verdict in the usual form; and, after further deliberations the jury brought in a verdict in favor of the seaman for $46,150. * * *

The position of the shipowner is that * * * Rule 49(b) authorizes the submission of written interrogatories but does not authorize the withdrawal of such interrogatories, after they have once been submitted and the jury has commenced its deliberations thereon. The shipowner further argues that question number 1 related to "one or more issues of fact the decision of which is necessary to a verdict," and that * * * it was a clear abuse of discretion to withdraw a proper and material interrogatory, relating to an issue that must necessarily be decided in plaintiff's favor, if plaintiff was to recover any damages whatever. To permit such withdrawal, the shipowner claims, would defeat the very purpose of * * * Rule 49(b), and smooth the way for a reluctant jury, unable to agree on the facts basic to recovery, to do "popular justice" through the medium of "an old-fashioned verdict."

* * *

The jury commenced their deliberations at 2:45 p.m. At 5:40 p.m. the trial judge received a note from the jury reading: "Your Honor, could we ask for your interpretation of the word 'had' in the second line, first question? Did the plaintiff injure himself?"

Appellant's counsel assures us that the question and the explanation given by the trial judge is just as simple as * * * whether he was injured in the manner described by him in his testimony. What the trial judge said, however, is as follows:

> "What I was trying to find out by the first question was whether or not plaintiff injured himself on board this ship, assuming that he had to remove the plates, assuming that he had to crouch down, and assuming he exerted this pressure with the wrench instead of his hand?
>
> "So in answer to your specific question as to the interpretation of the word 'had' it means that I assumed that he had to remove the plates, and he had to do this, and he had to do that. I didn't mean to take away from you the question as to whether he did in fact have to do that. In other words, the purpose of the question is to find out whether the plaintiff injured himself on board the ship in the manner that he described. The defendant claims that he did not. So the first question that I wanted answered was did he injure himself aboard the ship by doing what he said he did?
>
> "If you find that he didn't remove the plates or he didn't bend down, or he didn't crouch, or he didn't have to, or he didn't do it, those questions will be answered as you go on further down by your answers to the other questions.
>
> "But in my first question I assumed as a fact, accepted the plaintiff's testimony, that he had to bend down, that he had to crouch, that he had to remove the plates.
>
> "What I wanted to find out was, assuming all of that, did he injure himself on board the Pioneer Land.
>
> "Now I hope that is clear. If it isn't you can write me another note."

The jury retired again at 5:50 p.m. and returned with another note at 6:40 p.m. * * * as follows: "Your Honor, we cannot agree on question one. It appears there is no chance for agreement." Thereupon the trial judge withdrew all the questions from the consideration of the jury and asked them to see if they could not agree on a general verdict.

* * * [T]he jury still could not soon reach agreement. At 9:22 p.m. the jury informed the trial judge that "it finds it impossible to arrive at a unanimous agreement in this case." The trial judge thereupon read a quotation from Allen v. United States, 1896, 164 U.S. 492, 501, 17 S.Ct. 154, 41 L.Ed. 528, and returned the jury for further deliberations at 9:30 p.m. * * * At 10:30 p.m. the verdict was announced and the jury polled.

There was an inherent ambiguity in question one, and it is plain enough that the explanation failed to remove the ambiguity. Under these circumstances we think it was not an abuse of discretion to withdraw the questions and give the jury an opportunity to agree upon a general verdict. * * * It was a matter of judgment whether to attempt some further elucidation of the question, or to declare a mistrial, or to withdraw all the questions and authorize a general verdict. We cannot say the decision made here under the circumstances of this case was wrong, particularly as the jury continued its deliberations from about 6:45 p.m. until 10:30 p.m., after the withdrawal of the questions.

* * *

Other cases present the problem in its simplest form. After the submission of material and proper interrogatories, there is a delay of a few hours and the trial judge of his own motion, or on the application of plaintiff's counsel, calls in the jury, withdraws the questions, tells the jury to bring in a general verdict over the objection of defendant's counsel, and shortly thereafter the jury returns a verdict for the plaintiff. This has been held to be an abuse of discretion and ground for reversal. * * * The reason is that the action of the trial judge would probably be prejudicial to defendant. * * * This is a good general rule, and we agree with it. But it has no application to the case before us now, as the interrogatory causing all the difficulty here was unclear and ambiguous. The withdrawal of all the questions was for the purpose of eliminating the confusion caused by the formulation of an improper question. And it is to be noted that a confusing and improperly worded interrogatory cannot fairly be considered a "material" question, or one the answer to which "is necessary to a verdict." Under the circumstances it was, we think, good judgment to withdraw all the questions. Certainly we cannot say to do so was an abuse of discretion.

Affirmed.

NOTES AND QUESTIONS

1. Do you believe the interrogatory as first given to the jury was ambiguous? What are the possible meanings of the question? Could the jury answer the question "No" under any of these meanings and still find for plaintiff? If the jury had answered the interrogatory "No," and a reviewing court found that there was no evidence at all to support a finding that Diniero was *not* required to remove the plate, crouch down, and turn the valve with a wrench, but that a genuine issue existed on the question whether his condition was caused by this work, would the reviewing court be required to reverse a verdict for defendant that was based on the answer to the first interrogatory?

2. Could the judge simply have rewritten the interrogatory in clearer language and resubmitted it? What reasons mitigate against allowing that practice?

3. Could the jury have properly reached a decision for plaintiff without resolving the issue that the judge said in his explanation he intended the interrogatory to present? If it could not, was it proper to withdraw the interrogatory altogether and say to the jury: "What I am going to do, in an effort to see whether you can agree, I am going to ask you to forget all of the questions I gave you and see whether you can't agree on a general verdict. * * * I think that might relieve the situation some. I hope you can come to some agreement." (Judge's Instruction, quoted from the Petition for a Writ of Certiorari, p. 11.)

4. Do you think the judge's explanation of the interrogatory was clear? Read it again very carefully before you decide. Then reflect upon the fact that it was delivered orally to the jurors, even though the interrogatories themselves were in writing. When the jury is asked to return a general verdict, the charge, frequently including very complex instructions on the law, is given orally, and although the jurors may ask to have parts of it repeated, they sometimes are not even given a copy. From the experience in this case do you think written instructions would be a better idea?

5. The use of special verdicts and general verdicts with interrogatories is sometimes criticized as atomizing the jury's deliberations and making a unanimous result more difficult to reach. Assume that in an ordinary automobile accident case, three members of the jury believe that defendant was going too fast but the other three believe that he was not; moreover, the latter group of jurors believes that defendant was not looking where he was going, but the first group believes that defendant was. Could the jury return a unanimous verdict for plaintiff? For defendant? Would the problem be aggravated by the use of a special verdict or a general verdict with interrogatories?

6. ALLEN v. UNITED STATES, 164 U.S. 492, 17 S.Ct. 154, 41 L.Ed. 528 (1896), which the trial court in *Diniero* quoted to the jury, involved a variation on what has come to be called the "dynamite charge," an instruction that is sometimes given in the principal charge but more frequently is given only to a jury that has been unable to reach a unanimous verdict for either party after a substantial period of time. In *Allen* this charge was given some time after the main charge. Its content was,

> * * * in substance, that in a large proportion of cases absolute certainty could not be expected; that, although the verdict must be the verdict of each individual juror, and not a mere acquiescence in the conclusion of his fellows, yet they should examine the question submitted with candor, and with a proper regard and deference to the opinions of each other; that it was their duty to decide the case if they could conscientiously do so; that they should listen, with a disposition to be convinced, to each other's arguments; that, if much the larger number were for conviction, a dissenting juror should consider whether his doubt was a reasonable one which made no impression upon the minds of so many men, equally honest, equally intelligent with himself. If, upon the other hand, the majority were for acquittal, the minority ought to ask themselves whether they might not reasonably doubt the correctness of a judgment which was not concurred in by the majority.

Id. at 501, 17 S.Ct. at 157, 41 L.Ed. at 530–31. The Court found no error in the instruction:

> While, undoubtedly, the verdict of the jury should represent the opinion of each individual juror, it by no means follows that opinions may not be changed by conference in the jury room. The very object of the jury system is to secure unanimity by a comparison of views, and by arguments among the jurors themselves. It certainly cannot be the law that each juror should not listen with deference to the arguments, and with a distrust of his own judgment, if he finds a large majority of the jury taking a different view of the case from what he does himself. It cannot

> be that each juror should go to the jury room with a blind determination that the verdict shall represent his opinion of the case at that moment, or that he should close his ears to the arguments of men who are equally honest and intelligent as himself.

Id. at 501, 17 S.Ct. at 157, 41 L.Ed. at 530. Does this opinion adequately answer the objections that may be made to such a charge?

C. THE JURY'S DELIBERATION

After the judge completes the charge, the jury retires to deliberate in private. Extensive precautions are taken to insure that the jury is undisturbed and unheard during this period. The jury will have been instructed to decide the case in accordance with the law as explained by the judge and only on the basis of the evidence that has been brought forward in the trial. It is improper for the jury to ignore what the judge has said about the law or to speculate about what evidence that was not introduced might have proved. It also is improper for the jurors to decide the case on the basis of their own personal knowledge of matters not in evidence. Indeed, if a juror has specific knowledge of the facts, it should be disclosed at the beginning of the trial, and that person probably will be excused from serving. But a more difficult question is presented by a juror's more general knowledge and experience as it relates to the case. A strength of the jury system is thought to be that it brings together a cross-section of community standards and experienced judgments. At the same time, the parties are not able to meet the special knowledge of jurors of which they are unaware. How should the line between general experience and special knowledge be drawn?

TEXAS EMPLOYERS' INSURANCE ASSOCIATION v. PRICE

Court of Civil Appeals of Texas, Eastland, 1960.
336 S.W.2d 304.

COLLINGS, JUSTICE.

Loyal Grant Price brought suit * * * to set aside an award of the Industrial Accident Board * * *. The defendant Texas Employers' Insurance Association answered by general denial and specifically pleaded that plaintiff's alleged injury did not result in total or permanent incapacity, but that any injury plaintiff may have received resulted only in partial and temporary incapacity, or resulted from other injuries and diseases or a combination thereof. * * *

The case was tried before a jury which found that plaintiff received an accidental injury while working for the Port Houston Iron Works, Inc.; * * * that such injury was the producing cause of total disability; that total disability began November 27, 1957; that such disability was permanent and was not partial * * *. Judgment was entered for the plaintiff for $13,415.96 in a lump sum with interest thereon at the legal rate. * * *

In appellant's first four points it is contended that there was no evidence, and in the alternative that the evidence was insufficient to support the findings that any total incapacity sustained by appellee was permanent and the finding that appellee sustained total and permanent incapacity was so against the great weight and preponderance of the evidence as to be clearly wrong and unjust. * * *

In support of its contention in this respect, appellant further urges that appellee's own doctor testified that his back had been improved by the operation and stated that he "would estimate his (appellee's) partial permanent disability as approximately twenty percent as applied to general deficiency." This testimony is not consistent with the finding of the jury and the testimony of appellee to the effect that he has sustained total and permanent incapacity. It is the province of the jury, however, to determine the weight to be given evidence and to reconcile conflicts or inconsistencies therein. * * * The matter under consideration was not one for experts and skilled witnesses alone. Appellee testified that he could not work without pain, that his back was getting worse, that he was having to wear a brace with which he had previously been fitted by Dr. Brelsford. Dr. Brelsford testified that appellee had sustained permanent incapacity although not total, but that he would not pass him to follow his trade. The fact that appellee's testimony was in conflict with expert opinion testimony concerning the extent of his disability did not, under the circumstances, render it insufficient to support the verdict. * * *

Appellant further urges that the court erred in refusing to grant a new trial on the ground of jury misconduct. The evidence concerning some of the alleged jury misconduct was conflicting and would support a finding that such misconduct did not occur. The implied findings of the court in support of the order overruling appellant's motion for a new trial, which findings have support in the evidence, are binding on us. * * *

The existence of one of the alleged acts of jury misconduct is shown conclusively and in our opinion constitutes reversible error. The question whether the incapacity of appellee was total and permanent or only permanent partial was close, as already indicated. It is our opinion that the evidence supports the finding of total permanent incapacity and that such finding is not against the great weight and preponderance of the evidence. But it is further noted that appellee's own doctor testified, in effect, that his disability was approximately twenty percent partial. It is undisputed that one of the jurors related his personal experiences to persuade the jury that appellee was totally and permanently incapacitated. The witness stated to the jury as follows:

> I said it has been my experience that in employment that if a man has an injury and it is obvious, such as, a scar on his back if he is being examined by a doctor for employment that he would want a statement from that man concerning that injury, and if he mentioned a back injury I doubted very much if he would get employment. The reason

that came out was we were discussing whether or not the injury was partial or total.

The juror testified that he got this experience in union work; that he had read a letter from his company concerning back injuries showing that the company wanted to be more careful in hiring people with such injuries and that he told the jury about this experience. He testified that, in making the above statements to the jury, he was attempting to persuade a juror to come over to his side of the case; that he felt it was proper to give the jury the benefit of his personal knowledge and experience; and that was what he did. He further stated that he knew from experience that appellee could not get a job with Rohm and Haas, Shell Oil Company, Sinclair, or any other company that has a union contract or employee benefits and so advised the jury. He stated his opinion to the jury that appellee should receive total and permanent disability because he could not pass the physical examination he would be required to take; that it had been his experience that companies were very strict about whom they hire and that prospective employees were required to pass a most rigid physical examination. In this connection the juror testified that he also stated to the jury that there might be some jobs that appellee could handle but that he had a doubt whether appellee "could compete favorably on the labor market." The above evidence is undisputed. It shows that a juror related his personal experiences to the jury concerning the practice of company employers in hiring and employing workmen, and that the purpose and effect of such statements was to show that appellee was totally incapacitated. It was misconduct for the juror to relate to the other jurors his own personal experience as original evidence of material facts to be considered in their deliberation. * * * Considered in connection with the entire record, we are of the opinion that the misconduct shown was material and that it reasonably appears that injury probably resulted to appellant. * * *

For the reasons stated the judgment of the trial court is reversed and the cause is remanded.

NOTES AND QUESTIONS

1. Why is it misconduct for a juror "to relate to the other jurors his own personal experience as original evidence of material facts to be considered in their deliberation"? In HEAD v. HARGRAVE, 105 U.S. (15 Otto) 45, 49–50, 26 L.Ed. 1028, 1030 (1881), a case involving the value of legal services, Justice Field said:

> It was the province of the jury to weigh the testimony of the attorneys as to the value of the services, by reference to their nature, the time occupied in their performance, and other attending circumstances, and by applying to it their own experience and knowledge of the character of such services. To direct them to find the value of the services from the testimony of the experts alone, was to say to them that the issue should be determined by the opinions of the attorneys, and not by the exercise of

> their own judgment of the facts on which those opinions were given. * * * So far from laying aside their own general knowledge and ideas, the jury should have applied that knowledge and those ideas to the matters of fact in evidence in determining the weight to be given to the opinions expressed * * *. While they cannot act in any case upon particular facts material to its disposition resting in their private knowledge, but should be governed by the evidence adduced, they may, and to act intelligently they must, judge of the weight and force of that evidence by their own general knowledge of the subject of inquiry. If, for example, the question were as to the damages sustained by a plaintiff from a fracture of his leg by the carelessness of a defendant, the jury would ill perform their duty and probably come to a wrong conclusion, if, controlled by the testimony of the surgeons, not merely as to the injury inflicted, but as to the damages sustained, they should ignore their own knowledge and experience of the value of a sound limb. Other persons besides professional men have knowledge of the value of professional services; and, while great weight should always be given to the opinions of those familiar with the subject, they are not to be blindly received * * *.

Can the principal case be reconciled with this language?

2. The issue of jury misconduct is complicated by the doctrine, recognized in most jurisdictions but enforced with varying strictness, that a jury verdict may not be impeached by evidence that comes from the jurors themselves. In Kilgore v. Greyhound Corp., 30 F.R.D. 385, 388 (E.D.Tenn. 1962), in which a juror conducted an unsupervised and unauthorized study of the accident scene and reported thereon to his fellow jurors, it was said:

> Any time a new trial is sought on the basis of the misconduct of a juror, or the receipt and consideration by a jury of improper evidence which may have had prejudicial effect on the jurors, the Court is forced to choose between the possibility that a party litigant may have been done an injustice, and, on the other hand, the possibility that the Court will inflict a public injury which will result if jurors are permitted to testify regarding what happened in the jury room.

What is the possible "public injury" of which this court speaks? Why are jurors generally prohibited from impeaching their verdict? Notice that although the *Price* court allowed the jurors to impeach their verdict, Texas has amended its rules of evidence and no longer permits this practice. See Texas Rules of Evidence, Rule 606(b) ("Competency of Juror as Witness").

D. TAKING THE CASE FROM THE JURY

The most direct and drastic example of jury control occurs in those cases in which it is held that there is no evidence on which a reasonable jury could find for a particular party (usually plaintiff, but sometimes defendant). If the judge makes this determination at the close of the evidence, she will direct the jury to return a verdict for the other party. Even after the jury has returned a verdict for one party, the judge in most systems may order that judgment be entered for the other party "notwithstanding the verdict," if she decides that the case should not have been submitted to the jury. The judge also has the power to set aside the verdict and order a new trial on the ground that the verdict is against the great weight of the evidence or because of mistakes or erroneous rulings during trial.

So also, an appellate court may determine, even in the face of a jury verdict, that no reasonable jury could have reached the result announced. Clearly when these devices are used, the jury is more than "controlled"; it is eliminated from the process. If such devices were not available, the jury could decide a case any way it wanted without respect to the evidence or the law. But if the devices are not very severely restricted, the right to a jury trial can be negated.

LAVENDER v. KURN

Supreme Court of the United States, 1946.
327 U.S. 645, 66 S.Ct. 740, 90 L.Ed. 916.

On Writ of Certiorari to the Supreme Court of the State of Missouri.

MR. JUSTICE MURPHY delivered the opinion of the Court.

* * *

Petitioner, the administrator of the estate of L.E. Haney, brought this suit under the [Federal Employers' Liability] Act against the respondent trustees of the St. Louis–San Francisco Railway Company (Frisco) and the respondent Illinois Central Railroad Company. It was charged that Haney, while employed as a switch-tender by the respondents in the switchyard of the Grand Central Station in Memphis, Tennessee, was killed as a result of respondents' negligence. Following a trial * * *, the jury returned a verdict in favor of petitioner and awarded damages in the amount of $30,000. * * * On appeal, however, the Supreme Court of Missouri reversed the judgment, holding that there was no substantial evidence of negligence to support the submission of the case to the jury. * * *

[Haney was employed by the Illinois Central which owned the yards; Frisco's trains used the yards, and part of Haney's wages were paid by Frisco.]

The Illinois Central tracks run north and south directly past and into the Grand Central Station. About 2700 feet south of the station the Frisco tracks cross at right angles to the Illinois Central tracks. A westbound Frisco train wishing to use the station must stop some 250 feet or more west of this crossing and back into the station over a switchline curving east and north. The events in issue center about the switch several feet north of the main Frisco tracks at the point where the switch line branches off. This switch controls the tracks at this point.

It was very dark on the evening of December 21, 1939. At about 7:30 p.m. a westbound interstate Frisco passenger train stopped on the Frisco main line, its rear some 20 or 30 feet west of the switch. Haney, in the performance of his duties, threw or opened the switch to permit the train to back into the station. The respondents claimed that Haney was then required to cross to the south side of the track before the train passed the switch; and the conductor of the train testified that he saw Haney so cross. But there was also evidence that Haney's duties required him to wait at the switch north of the track until the train had cleared, close the switch, return to his shanty near the crossing and change the signals from red to green to permit trains on the Illinois Central tracks to use the crossing. The Frisco train cleared the switch, backing at the rate of 8 or 10 miles per hour. But the switch remained open and the signals still were red. Upon investigation Haney was found north of the track near the switch lying face down on the ground, unconscious. An ambulance was called, but he was dead upon arrival at the hospital.

Haney had been struck in the back of the head, causing a fractured skull from which he died. There were no known eye-witnesses to the fatal blow. Although it is not clear there is evidence that his body was extended north and south, the head to the south. Apparently he had fallen forward to the south; his face was bruised on the left side from hitting the ground and there were marks indicating that his toes had dragged a few inches southward as he fell. His head was about 5½ feet north of the Frisco tracks. Estimates ranged from 2 feet to 14 feet as to how far west of the switch he lay.

The injury to Haney's head was evidenced by a gash about two inches long from which blood flowed. The back of Haney's white cap had a corresponding black mark about an inch and a half long and an inch wide, running at an angle downward to the right of the center of the back of the head. A spot of blood was later found at a point 3 or 4 feet north of the tracks. The conclusion following an autopsy was that Haney's skull was fractured by "some fast moving small round object." One of the examining doctors testified that such an object might have been attached to a train backing at the rate of 8 or 10 miles per hour. But he also admitted that the fracture might have resulted from a blow from a pipe or club or some similar round object in the hands of an individual.

Petitioner's theory is that Haney was struck by the curled end or tip of a mail hook hanging down loosely on the outside of the mail car of the backing train. This curled end was 73 inches above the top of the rail, which was 7 inches high. The overhang of the mail car in relation to the rails was about 2 to 2½ feet. The evidence indicated that when the mail car swayed or moved around a curve the mail hook might pivot, its curled end swinging out as much as 12 to 14 inches. The curled end could thus be swung out to a point 3 to 3½ feet from the rail and about 73 inches above the top of the rail. Both east and west of the switch, however, was an uneven mound of cinders and dirt rising at its highest points 18 to 24 inches above the top of the rails. Witnesses differed as to how close the mound approached the rails, the estimates varying from 3 to 15 feet. But taking the figures most favorable to the petitioner, the mound extended to a point 6 to 12 inches north of the overhanging side of the mail car. If the mail hook end swung out 12 to 14 inches it would be 49 to 55 inches above the highest parts of the mound. Haney was 67½ inches tall. If he had been standing on the mound about a foot from the side of the mail car he could have been hit by the end of the mail hook, the exact point of contact depending upon the height of the mound at the particular point. His wound was about 4 inches below the top of his head, or 63½ inches above the point where he stood on the mound—well within the possible range of the mail hook end.

Respondents' theory is that Haney was murdered. They point to the estimates that the mound was 10 to 15 feet north of the rail, making it impossible for the mail hook end to reach a point of contact with Haney's head. Photographs were placed in the record to support the claim that the ground was level north of the rail for at least 10 feet. * * * It also appears that many hoboes and tramps frequented the area at night in order to get rides on freight trains. Haney carried a pistol to protect himself. This pistol was found loose under his body by those who came to his rescue. It was testified, however that the pistol had apparently slipped out of his pocket or scabbard as he fell. Haney's clothes were not disarranged and there was no evidence of a struggle or fight. No rods, pipes or weapons of any kind, except Haney's own pistol, were found near the scene. Moreover, his gold watch and diamond ring were still on him after he was struck. Six days later his unsoiled billfold was found on a high board fence about a block from the place where Haney was struck and near the point where he had been placed in an ambulance. It contained his social security card and other effects, but no money. His wife testified that he "never carried much money, not very much more than $10." Such were the facts in relation to respondents' theory of murder.

Finally, one of the Frisco foremen testified that he arrived at the scene shortly after Haney was found injured. He later examined the fireman's side of the train very carefully and found nothing sticking out or in disorder. In explaining why he examined this side of the train so carefully he stated that while he was at the scene of the accident "someone said they thought that train No. 106 backing in to Grand Central Station is what struck this man" and that Haney "was supposed to have been struck by something protruding on the side of the train." The foreman testified that these statements were made by an unknown Illinois Central switchman standing near the fallen body of Haney. The foreman admitted that the switchman "didn't see the accident." This testimony was admitted by the trial court over the strenuous objections of respondents' counsel that it was mere hearsay falling outside the *res gestae* rule.

The jury was instructed that Frisco's trustees were liable if it was found that they negligently permitted a rod or other object to extend out from the side of the train as it backed past Haney and that Haney was killed as the direct result of such negligence, if any. The jury was further told that Illinois Central was liable if it was found that the company negligently maintained an unsafe and dangerous place for Haney to work, in that the ground was high and uneven and the light insufficient and inadequate, and that Haney was injured and killed as a direct result of the said place being unsafe and dangerous. This latter instruction as to Illinois Central did not require the jury to find that Haney was killed by something protruding from the train.

The Supreme Court, in upsetting the jury's verdict against both the Frisco trustees and the Illinois Central, admitted that "It could be inferred from the facts that Haney could have been struck by the mail hook knob *if* he were standing on the south side of the mound and the mail hook extended out as far as 12 or 14 inches." * * * But it held that "all reasonable minds would agree that it would be mere speculation and conjecture to say that Haney was struck by the mail hook" and that "plaintiff failed to make a submissible case on that question." It also ruled that there "was no substantial evidence that the uneven ground and insufficient light were causes or contributing causes of the death of Haney." Finally, the Supreme Court held that the testimony of the foreman as to the statement made to him by the unknown switchman was inadmissible under the *res gestae* rule since the switchman spoke from what he had heard rather than from his own knowledge.

* * *

The evidence we have already detailed demonstrates that there was evidence from which it might be inferred that the end of the mail hook struck Haney in the back of the head, an inference that the Supreme Court admitted could be drawn. That inference is not rendered unreasonable by the fact that Haney apparently fell forward toward the main Frisco track so that his head was 5½ feet north of the rail. He may well have been struck and then wandered in a daze to the point where he fell forward. The testimony as to blood marks some distance away from his head lends credence to that possibility, indicating that he did not fall immediately upon being hit. When that is added to the evidence most favorable to the petitioner as to the height and swing-out of the hook, the height and location of the mound and the nature of Haney's duties, the inference that Haney was killed by the hook cannot be said to be unsupported by probative facts or to be so unreasonable as to warrant taking the case from the jury.

It is true that there is evidence tending to show that it was physically and mathematically impossible for the hook to strike Haney. And there are facts from which it might reasonably be inferred that Haney was murdered. But such evidence has become irrelevant upon appeal, there being a reasonable basis in the record for inferring that the hook struck Haney. The jury having made that inference, the respondents were not free to relitigate the factual dispute in a reviewing court. Under these circumstances it would be an undue invasion of the jury's historic function for an appellate court to weigh the conflicting evidence, judge the credibility of witnesses and arrive at a conclusion opposite from the one reached by the jury. * * *

It is no answer to say that the jury's verdict involved speculation and conjecture. Whenever facts are in dispute or the evidence is such that fair-minded men may draw different inferences, a measure of speculation and conjecture is required on the part of those whose duty it is to settle the dispute by choosing what seems to them to be the most reasonable inference. Only when there is a complete absence of probative facts to support the conclusion reached does a reversible error appear. But where, as here, there is an evidentiary basis for the jury's verdict, the jury is free to discard or disbelieve whatever facts are inconsistent with its conclusion. And the appellate court's function is exhausted when that evidentiary basis becomes apparent. * * *

We are unable, therefore, to sanction a reversal of the jury's verdict against Frisco's trustees. Nor can we approve any disturbance in the verdict as to Illinois Central. The evidence was uncontradicted that it was very dark at the place where Haney was working and the surrounding ground was high and uneven. The evidence also showed that this area was entirely within the domination and control of Illinois Central * * *. It was not unreasonable to conclude that these conditions constituted an unsafe and dangerous working place * * *.

In view of the foregoing disposition of the case, it is unnecessary to decide whether the allegedly hearsay testimony was admissible under the *res gestae* rule. Rulings on the admissibility of evidence must normally be left to the sound discretion of the trial judge in actions under the Federal Employers' Liability Act. But inasmuch as there is adequate support in the record for the jury's verdict apart from the hearsay testimony, we need not determine whether that discretion was abused in this instance.

The judgment of the Supreme Court of Missouri is reversed and the case is remanded for whatever further proceedings may be necessary not inconsistent with this opinion.

THE CHIEF JUSTICE and MR. JUSTICE FRANKFURTER concur in the result.

MR. JUSTICE REED dissents.

NOTES AND QUESTIONS

1. Why does a trial judge or an appellate court have the power to take a case away from the jury or to set aside its verdict? Does the existence of this power necessarily mean that a jury cannot properly refer to its members' own knowledge? See Texas Employers' Ins. Ass'n v. Price, p. 53, supra. Why?

2. In PENNSYLVANIA R. CO. v. CHAMBERLAIN, 288 U.S. 333, 339, 53 S.Ct. 391, 393, 77 L.Ed. 819, 822–23 (1933), the Supreme Court, in approving a directed verdict for defendant, said:

> * * * At most there was an inference to that effect drawn from observed facts which gave equal support to the opposite inference * * *.
>
> We, therefore, have a case belonging to that class of cases where proven facts give equal support to each of two inconsistent inferences; in which event, neither of them being established, judgment, as a matter of law, must go against the party upon whom rests the necessity of sustaining

one of these inferences as against the other, before he is entitled to recover.

Is this language consistent with the opinion of the Court in the principal case? Is there a difference between cases in which the evidence simply fails to point one way or the other, and cases in which the evidence on one side is overwhelming, in terms of taking a case away from the jury? Would *Lavender* have been decided the same way if stronger evidence was presented that Haney had been murdered?

3. When *Lavender* is remanded to the Missouri Supreme Court, what should that court do? In this connection, do you agree with the United States Supreme Court that it was unnecessary to determine whether evidence of the statement of the unknown switchman was improperly admitted?

4. APPEAL

The grounds for appeal are chiefly mistakes of law—for example, an erroneous ruling that the court had jurisdiction, an improper admission of evidence, or an incorrect instruction to the jury. Even if an error of law has been committed, the appellate court must be convinced that the error was prejudicial, and that the case probably would not have come out the same if the error had not occurred. In the event of an erroneous ruling on jurisdiction, the prejudice is obvious. But appellate courts are reluctant to reverse merely because an error has been committed during the trial.

An appellate court rarely will reverse a decision on the ground that a question of fact was decided improperly. If there has been a jury, the constitutional right to jury trial itself is involved in such a ruling by an appellate court. See Amendment VII to the United States Constitution in the Supplement. When there has been no jury, no constitutional problem is involved, but it may be asked whether a broad scope of review of the trial judge's findings of fact will not encourage needless appeals and denigrate the function of the trial judge.

HICKS v. UNITED STATES

United States Court of Appeals, Fourth Circuit, 1966.
368 F.2d 626.

SOBELOFF, CIRCUIT JUDGE. This action was brought under the Federal Tort Claims Act, 28 U.S.C. § 1346, to recover damages for the death of Carol Greitens. The plaintiff, administrator of her estate, alleges that death was due to the negligence of the doctor on duty at the dispensary of the United States Naval Amphibious Base, Little Creek, Virginia, in diagnosing and treating her illness. The District Court, concluding that the evidence was insufficient to establish that the doctor was negligent, or that his concededly erroneous diagnosis and treatment was the proximate cause of her death, dismissed the complaint. * * *

The decedent, 25 years of age, had been a diabetic since the age of 13, although the condition was under control. * * * Mrs. Greitens' husband brought her to the dispensary at about 4 a.m. on August 25, 1963, suffering from intense abdominal pain and continual vomiting which had begun suddenly an hour before. The corpsman on duty in the examining room procured her medical records, obtained a brief history, took her blood pressure, pulse, temperature, and respiration and summoned the doctor on duty, then asleep in his room at the dispensary. The doctor arrived 15 or 20 minutes later and after questioning the patient concerning her symptoms, felt her abdomen and listened to her bowel sounds with the aid of a stethoscope. Recording his diagnosis on the chart as gastroenteritis, he told Mrs. Greitens that she had a "bug" in her stomach, prescribed some drugs for the relief of pain, and released her with instructions to return in eight hours. The examination took approximately ten minutes.

The patient returned to her home, and after another episode of vomiting, took the prescribed medicine and lay down. At about noon, she arose and drank a glass of water, vomited immediately thereafter and fell to the floor unconscious. She was rushed to the dispensary, but efforts to revive her were unsuccessful. She was pronounced dead at 12:48 p.m. and an autopsy revealed that she had a high obstruction, diagnosed formally as an abnormal congenital peritoneal hiatus with internal herniation into this malformation of some of the loops of the small intestine. Death was due to a massive hemorrhagic infarction of the intestine resulting from its strangulation.

I

The plaintiff contends that the doctor at the dispensary did not meet the requisite standard of care and skill demanded of him by the law of Virginia. Compliance with this standard, the plaintiff maintains, would have required a more extended examination and immediate hospitalization. More specifically, plaintiff's expert witnesses, two general practitioners in the Norfolk–Virginia Beach area, testified that, according to prevailing practice in the community, the doctor should have inquired whether the patient had had diarrhea and should have made a rectal examination to determine whether the patient was suffering from an obstruction rather than from gastroenteritis. While the latter condition does not ordinarily require immediate radical treatment, a high obstruction is almost invariably lethal unless promptly operated upon. Plaintiff's experts further testified that on observing the symptoms manifested by Mrs. Greitens, the procedure of general practitioners in the community would have been to order immediate hospitalization. * * *

The standard of care which Virginia law exacts from a physician, in this case a general practitioner, is * * * [such that] if he uses ordinary care in reaching his diagnosis, and thereafter acts upon it, he incurs no liability, even if the diagnosis proves to be a mistake in judgment.

It is undisputed that the symptoms of high obstruction and of gastroenteritis are quite similar. The District Court placed great emphasis on this fact as an indication that the doctor's erroneous diagnosis was not negligent, but was merely an error of judgment. It would seem, however, that where the symptoms are consistent with either of two possible conditions, one lethal if not attended to promptly, due care demands that a doctor do more than make a cursory examination and then release the patient. * * * The fact that an intestinal obstruction is a rare occurrence, and that some form of gastroenteritis is the more likely of the two conditions, does not excuse the failure to make inquiries and perform recognized additional tests that might have served to distinguish the one condition from the other. The dispensary doctor himself, as well as the experts for both sides, agreed that an inquiry as to diarrhea and a rectal examination were the "proper procedure" and "the accepted standard" in order to be able to rule out gastroenteritis and to make a definite diagnosis of high intestinal obstruction. If he had made the inquiry which he admits was the accepted standard, he would at least have been alerted to the fact that the case was one calling for close observation with a view to immediate surgical intervention if the graver diagnosis were confirmed. In these circumstances, failure to make this investigation constitutes a lack of due care on the part of the physician. * * * Only if a patient is adequately examined, is there no liability for an erroneous diagnosis.

Our conclusion that the physician was negligent in his diagnosis and treatment of the patient is not inconsistent with * * * [Rule] 52(a), which declares that the trial judge's findings of fact are not to be disturbed unless clearly erroneous. [This provision has been renumbered as Rule 52(a)(6).] This Rule comes into play primarily where the trial judge as fact finder has had to reconcile conflicting testimony. Where the veracity of witnesses is in issue, the decision is for the judge who has had the opportunity to see and evaluate the witnesses' demeanor. * * * But we are dealing here with the testimony of expert witnesses who are not in controversy as to the basic facts; thus, the opportunity of the trial court to observe the witnesses is of limited significance. It has often been held that where the trial court's conclusions are based on undisputed facts, they are not entitled to the finality customarily accorded basic factual findings under Rule 52(a). * * *

The question before us is not one of fact in the usual sense, but rather whether the undisputed facts manifest negligence. Although the absence of a factual dispute does not *always* mean that the conclusion is a question of law, it becomes so *here* since the ultimate conclusion to be drawn from the basic facts, i.e., the existence or absence of negligence, is actually a question of law. For this reason, the general rule has been that when a judge sitting without a jury makes a determination of negligence his conclusion, as distinguished from the evidentiary findings leading to it, is freely reviewable on appeal. * * * The determination of negligence involves not only the formulation of the legal standard, but more particularly in this case, its application to the evidentiary facts as established; and since these are uncontested, there is no basis for applying the "clearly erroneous" rule. * * *

The government's expert opined that the dispensary physician exercised "average judgment," but analysis of his entire testimony points unavoidably to the opposite conclusion. Revealing are his statements that it was wrong not to inquire about diarrhea, conceding that "that is one question that one usually asks," and that given a patient with abdominal pain of one hour's duration, it is too soon "to expect anybody to come up with a proper diagnosis." Furthermore, his opinion was predicated upon a factual assumption not permissible in this case. His assumption was that the dispensary physician had made only a "working" or "tentative" diagnosis * * *. However, the uncontradicted evidence indicates that this was not a "tentative" diagnosis.

The examining doctor himself testified that he had already considered and ruled out at the beginning of his examination the possibility of an obstruction without making the additional differentiating diagnostic tests. He said that his only reason for asking the patient to return eight hours later was because her diabetic condition could become complicated by a case of gastroenteritis. * * * By releasing the patient, the dispensary physician made his diagnosis final, allowing no further opportunity for revision * * *.

On careful scrutiny, therefore, the government's expert is seen to have demonstrated that the examiner did *not* conform to the required standard of care. Coupled with the explicit testimony of the plaintiff's experts, the government's testimony leads us inevitably to the conclusion that the doctor was negligent as a matter of law. We think that the District Court gave undue weight to the purely conclusory opinion of the government witness. The District Court is not bound by his statement that "average judgment" had been exercised, nor are we bound by it. Only the standard of care is to be established by the testimony of experts. If under the undisputed facts the defendant failed to meet that standard it is not for the expert but for the court to decide whether there was negligence.

* * *

Judgment reversed and cause remanded for the determination of damages.

NOTES AND QUESTIONS

1. Would the Court of Appeals have reached the same result if the judgment appealed from had been based on the verdict of a jury rather than the findings of a judge? Why is there any difference between the standard enunciated in Lavender v. Kurn and that in Federal Rule 52(a)(6)?

2. Is the question whether certain conduct is negligent one of law or of fact? Legal scholars have long debated the issue without resolution. In any event, the issue ordinarily is left to the jury. Why? Are the reasons for giving the issue to the jury any less persuasive when the finder of fact is a judge sitting without a jury? Is there a difference if the standard of care to be

applied by the judge sitting without a jury must be derived from the testimony of experts? Why?

3. In ANDERSON v. CITY OF BESSEMER CITY, 470 U.S. 564, 105 S.Ct. 1504, 84 L.Ed.2d 518 (1985), the Supreme Court, in interpreting Rule 52(a), said: "Where there are two permissible views of the evidence, the factfinder's choice between them cannot be clearly erroneous." The Court added:

> This is so even when the district court's findings do not rest on credibility determinations, but are based instead on physical or documentary evidence or inferences from other facts. To be sure, various Courts of Appeals have on occasion asserted the theory that an appellate court may exercise *de novo* review over findings not based on credibility determinations * * *.
>
> The rationale for deference to the original finder of fact is not limited to the superiority of the trial judge's position to make determinations of credibility. The trial judge's major role is the determination of fact, and with experience in fulfilling that role comes expertise. Duplication of the trial judge's efforts in the court of appeals would very likely contribute only negligibly to the accuracy of fact determination at a huge cost in diversion of judicial resources * * *. As the Court has stated in a different context, the trial on the merits should be "the 'main event' * * * rather than a 'tryout on the road.' "

Id. at 574, 105 S.Ct. at 1511–12, 84 L.Ed.2d at 528–29. Does *Anderson* undermine the basis of the Fourth Circuit's holding in *Hicks*? Does *Anderson* overrule *Hicks*?

5. CONCLUSIVENESS OF JUDGMENTS

Lawsuits are designed to settle disputes. An idealist might argue that nothing should be considered settled until it is settled *correctly*. A pragmatist could counter that nothing is settled at all unless it is settled *finally*. Cosmic questions may be debated endlessly, but controversies between individuals that are expected to result in enforceable judgments for damages or orders that must be obeyed under penalty of contempt must come to an end if the judicial process is to work at all. Res judicata requires that occasionally we let a judgment stand even when we become convinced that it was wrongly decided. A doctrine that only correct decisions have res judicata effect would furnish no finality at all.

The following case decided almost 300 years ago raises the same doubts that the res judicata doctrine raises today: Is the decision fair to plaintiff? Would an opposite decision be fair to defendant?

FETTER v. BEAL, 1 Ld.Raym. 339, 91 Eng.Rep. 1122 (King's Bench 1697). Plaintiff had brought an action for battery against defendant and recovered £11. Subsequently "part of his skull by reason of the said battery came out of his head," and plaintiff brought another action. Plaintiff's counsel argued that "this action differed from the nature of the former * * * because the recovery in the former action was only for the bruise and battery, but here there is a maihem by the loss of the skull."

> And per totam Curiam, the jury in the former action considered the nature of the wound, and gave damages for all the damages that it had done to the plaintiff; and therefore a recovery in the said action is good here. And it is the plaintiff's fault, for if he had not been so hasty, he might have been satisfied for this loss of the skull also. Judgment for the defendant * * *.

A particularly difficult question of res judicata is presented when it is alleged that the first decision—now advanced as conclusive—was rendered by a court that lacked jurisdiction over the subject matter. This group of Illustrative Cases began with a decision that demonstrated the grave concern of the United States Supreme Court to keep the federal courts from deciding cases outside their constitutional and statutory jurisdiction. Res judicata was not involved in Capron v. Van Noorden, p. 26, supra; the trial court's decision was reversed in the ordinary course of appellate review. What if plaintiff in that case had not sought a writ of error but had permitted the decision to become final and then instituted another action?

DES MOINES NAVIGATION & RAILROAD CO. v. IOWA HOMESTEAD CO.

Supreme Court of the United States, 1887.
123 U.S. 552, 8 S.Ct. 217, 31 L.Ed. 202.

Error to the Supreme Court of the State of Iowa.

MR. CHIEF JUSTICE WAITE delivered the opinion of the court.

This suit was brought by the Iowa Homestead Company against the Des Moines Navigation and Railroad Company to recover the same taxes for the years 1864 to 1871, both inclusive, which formed part of the subject matter of the litigation between the same parties in Homestead Co. v. Valley Railroad, 17 Wall. 153 * * *. The Railroad Company set up the decree in its favor in that suit as a bar to the present action, and to this the Homestead Company replied "that the decree or judgment referred to is null and void, for the reason that the courts of the United States had no jurisdiction of said suit, and no legal power or authority to render said decree or judgment."

* * * It must be conceded that the Homestead Company and the Navigation and Railroad Company were both Iowa corporations, and, therefore, in law, citizens of the same State; but the defendants * * * who caused the removal to be made [from the Iowa state court to the United States Circuit Court], were citizens of the State of New York. After the

removal was effected, all the above named defendants, as well as * * * the Navigation and Railroad Company, appeared, filed answers, and defended the action. The Homestead Company took issue on all the answers, and actually contested the matters in dispute with the Navigation and Railroad Company, as well as the other defendants, in the Circuit Court, and in this court on appeal, without taking any objection to the jurisdiction.

The precise question we have now to determine is whether the adjudication by this court, under such circumstances, of the matters then and now at issue between the Homestead Company and the Navigation and Railroad Company was absolutely void for want of jurisdiction. The point is not whether it was error in the Circuit Court to take jurisdiction of the suit, or of so much of it as related to the Navigation and Railroad Company, originally, but as to the binding effect of the decree of this court so long as it remains in force, and is not judicially annulled, vacated, or set aside.

* * *

It was settled by this court at a very early day, that, although the judgments and decrees of the Circuit Courts might be erroneous, if the records failed to show the facts on which the jurisdiction of the court rested, such as that the plaintiffs were citizens of different States from the defendants, yet that they were not nullities, and would bind the parties until reversed or otherwise set aside. * * * In * * * McCormick v. Sullivant, 10 Wheat. 192 [(1825)] * * * this court held on appeal that "the courts of the United States are courts of *limited,* but not of *inferior,* jurisdiction. If the jurisdiction be not alleged in the proceedings, their judgments and decrees may be reversed for that cause on a writ of error or appeal; but until reversed they are conclusive between the parties and their privies." "But they are not nullities." There has never been any departure from this rule.

It is said, however, that these decisions apply only to cases where the record simply fails to show jurisdiction. Here it is claimed that the record shows there could be no jurisdiction, because it appears affirmatively that the Navigation and Railroad Company, one of the defendants, was a citizen of the same State with the plaintiff. But the record shows, with equal distinctness, that all the parties were actually before the court, and made no objection to its jurisdiction. The act of 1867, under which the removal was had, provided that when a suit was pending in a state court "in which there is a controversy between a citizen of the State in which the suit is brought and a citizen of another State, * * * such citizen of another State, * * * if he will make and file an affidavit stating that he has reason to and does believe that, from prejudice or local influence, he will not be able to obtain justice in such state court, may * * * file a petition in such state court for the removal of the suit" into the Circuit Court of the United States, and, when all things have been done that the act requires, "it shall be * * * the duty of the state court to * * * proceed no further with the suit," and, after the record is entered in the Circuit

Court, "the suit shall then proceed in the same manner as if it had been brought there by original process."[c]

In the suit now under consideration there was a separate and distinct controversy between the plaintiff, a citizen of Iowa, and each of the citizens of New York, who were defendants. Each controversy related to the several tracts of land claimed by each defendant individually, and not as joint owner with the other defendants. Three of the citizens of New York caused to be made and filed the necessary affidavit and petition for removal, and thereupon, by common consent apparently, the suit as an entirety was transferred to the Circuit Court for final adjudication as to all the parties. * * * Whether in such a case the suit could be removed was a question for the Circuit Court to decide when it was called on to take jurisdiction. If it kept the case when it ought to have been remanded, or if it proceeded to adjudicate upon matters in dispute between two citizens of Iowa, when it ought to have confined itself to those between the citizens of Iowa and the citizens of New York, its final decree in the suit could have been reversed, on appeal, as erroneous, but the decree would not have been a nullity. To determine whether the suit was removable in whole or in part or not, was certainly within the power of the Circuit Court. The decision of that question was the exercise and the rightful exercise of jurisdiction, no matter whether in favor of or against taking the cause. Whether its decision was right, in this or any other respect, was to be finally determined by this court on appeal. As the Circuit Court entertained the suit, and this court, on appeal, impliedly recognized its right to do so, and proceeded to dispose of the case finally on its merits, certainly our decree cannot, in the light of prior adjudications on the same general question, be deemed a nullity. It was, at the time of the trial in the present case in the court below, a valid and subsisting prior adjudication of the matters in controversy, binding on these parties, and a bar to this action. In refusing so to decide, the court failed to give full faith and credit to the decree of this court * * * and this was error.

* * *

NOTES AND QUESTIONS

1. When a court has rendered a judgment in a contested action, the judgment precludes the parties from litigating the question of the court's subject-matter jurisdiction in subsequent litigation except if:

(1) The subject matter of the action was so plainly beyond the court's jurisdiction that its entertaining the action was a manifest abuse of authority; or

---

c. The Judiciary Act of 1789 had been interpreted by the Supreme Court to require complete diversity of citizenship (all the plaintiffs being of a citizenship different from that of any defendant) for removal. It was widely argued that the 1867 statute referred to in the *Des Moines* case, because of a difference in language, did not have the same requirement. The Supreme Court held that the 1867 statute did require complete diversity, Case of the Sewing Machine Cos., 85 U.S. (18 Wall.) 553, 21 L.Ed. 914 (1874), but this decision came a year *after* the Court's decision in the Homestead Company's first suit in which the issue had not been raised.

(2) Allowing the judgment to stand would substantially infringe upon the authority of another tribunal or agency of government; or

(3) The judgment was rendered by a court lacking capability to make an adequately informed determination of a question concerning its own jurisdiction and as a matter of procedural fairness the party seeking to avoid the judgment should have opportunity belatedly to attack the court's subject-matter jurisdiction.

Restatement (Second), Judgments § 12 (1982). What factors should a court regard as important in deciding such questions as what is "a manifest abuse of authority," or when a judgment "substantially" infringes a tribunal's authority, or when a court lacks "capability to make an adequately informed determination"?

2. Was it critical to the Supreme Court's opinion in *Des Moines* that the first case had been heard and determined by the Supreme Court itself? Would the case have been decided differently if no review had been sought in the first action at all?

3. Was the fact that the question of jurisdiction was a doubtful one at the time the first *Homestead Company* case arose relevant to the Supreme Court's decision in the second case?

4. Suppose that the issue of jurisdiction is raised in a case and erroneously decided. Is this a factor arguing for or against the application of res judicata in a second action?

5. Since it is clear in the principal case that in the suit before the Court there was no diversity of citizenship and the writ of error was to the Supreme Court of Iowa, what was the basis for appellate jurisdiction in the United States Supreme Court?

CHAPTER 2

JURISDICTION OVER THE PARTIES OR THEIR PROPERTY

■ ■ ■

In this Chapter, we explore the doctrine of personal jurisdiction: the power of a court to enter a judgment against a specific defendant. A court can assert personal jurisdiction only if its power is authorized by statute and does not exceed the limitations of the Due Process Clause of the United States Constitution. The earliest basis for a court's assertion of personal jurisdiction over a person or a thing was the presence of the defendant within the territory of the tribunal. As the national economy developed and technology fostered the movement of goods and people across state boundaries, severe pressures were placed on this territorial theory and the doctrine of personal jurisdiction underwent evolution and change. Under contemporary doctrine, the question of a court's power is analyzed in functional terms, "based upon a review of the relationship that exists among the place where the underlying transaction took place, the parties, and the territory of the state where suit is brought." Friedenthal, Kane & Miller, Civil Procedure § 3.1 (4th ed. 2005). The Digital Revolution, with its virtual world of emails, hyperlinks, and software, is creating new issues for personal jurisdiction doctrine, which is continuing to develop in significant ways. The materials covered in this Chapter are important and complex—one federal court has gone so far as to call personal jurisdiction "a riddle wrapped in a mystery inside an enigma." Donatelli v. National Hockey League, 893 F.2d 459, 462 (1st Cir.1990).

SECTION A. THE TRADITIONAL BASES FOR JURISDICTION

PENNOYER v. NEFF

Supreme Court of the United States, 1877.
95 U.S. (5 Otto) 714, 24 L.Ed. 565.

Error to the Circuit Court of the United States for the District of Oregon.

MR. JUSTICE FIELD delivered the opinion of the court.

This is an action to recover the possession of a tract of land, of the alleged value of $15,000, situated in the State of Oregon. The plaintiff asserts title to the premises by a patent of the United States issued to him in [March] 1866, under the Act of Congress of September 27th, 1850, 9 Stat. at L., 496, usually known as the Donation Law of Oregon. The defendant claims to have acquired the premises under a sheriff's deed, made upon a sale of the property on execution issued upon a judgment recovered against the plaintiff in one of the circuit courts of the State. The case turns upon the validity of this judgment.

It appears from the record that the judgment was rendered in February, 1866, in favor of J.H. Mitchell, for less than $300, including costs, in an action brought by him upon a demand for services as an attorney; that, at the time the action was commenced and the judgment rendered, the defendant therein, the plaintiff here, was a non-resident of the State; that he was not personally served with process, and did not appear therein; and that the judgment was entered upon his default in not answering the complaint, upon a constructive service of summons by publication.

The Code of Oregon provides for such service when an action is brought against a non-resident and absent defendant, who has property within the State. It also provides, where the action is for the recovery of money or damages, for the attachment of the property of the non-resident. And it also declares that no natural person is subject to the jurisdiction of a court of the State, "unless he appear in the court, or be found within the State, or be a resident thereof, or have property therein; and in the last case, only to the extent of such property at the time the jurisdiction attached." Construing this latter provision to mean that, in an action for money or damages where a defendant does not appear in the court, and is not found within the State, and is not a resident thereof, but has property therein, the jurisdiction of the court extends only over such property, the declaration expresses a principle of general, if not universal, law. The authority of every tribunal is necessarily restricted by the territorial limits of the State in which it is established. Any attempt to exercise authority beyond those limits would be deemed in every other forum, as has been said by this court, an illegitimate assumption of power, and be resisted as mere abuse. * * * In the case against the plaintiff, the property here in controversy sold under the judgment rendered was not attached, nor in any way brought under the jurisdiction of the court. Its first connection with the case was caused by a levy of the execution. It was not, therefore, disposed of pursuant to any adjudication, but only in enforcement of a personal judgment, having no relation to the property, rendered against a non-resident without service of process upon him in the action, or his appearance therein. The court below did not consider that an attachment of the property was essential to its jurisdiction or to the validity of the sale, but held that the judgment was invalid from defects in the affidavit upon which the order of publication was obtained, and in the affidavit by which the publication was proved.

There is some difference of opinion among the members of this court as to the rulings upon these alleged defects. The majority are of opinion that, inasmuch as the statute requires, for an order of publication, that certain facts shall appear by affidavit *to the satisfaction of the court or judge,* defects in such affidavit can only be taken advantage of on appeal, or by some other direct proceeding, and cannot be urged to impeach the judgment collaterally. The majority of the court are also of opinion that the provision of the statute requiring proof of the publication in a newspaper to be made by the "affidavit of the printer, or his foreman, or his principal clerk," is satisfied when the affidavit is made by the editor of the paper. * * *

If, therefore, we were confined to the rulings of the court below upon the defects in the affidavits mentioned, we should be unable to uphold its decision. But it was also contended in that court, and is insisted upon here, that the judgment in the State Court against the plaintiff was void for want of personal service of process on him, or of his appearance in the action in which it was rendered, and that the premises in controversy could not be subjected to the payment of the demand of a resident creditor except by a proceeding *in rem;* that is, by a direct proceeding against the property for that purpose. If these positions are sound, the ruling of the Circuit Court as to the invalidity of that judgment must be sustained, notwithstanding our dissent from the reasons upon which it was made. And that they are sound would seem to follow from two well established principles of public law respecting the jurisdiction of an independent State over persons and property. The several States of the Union are not, it is true, in every respect independent, many of the rights and powers which originally belonged to them being now vested in the government created by the Constitution. But, except as restrained and limited by that instrument, they possess and exercise the authority of independent States, and the principles of public law to which we have referred are applicable to them. One of these principles is, that every State possesses exclusive jurisdiction and sovereignty over persons and property within its territory. As a consequence, every State has the power to determine for itself the civil *status* and capacities of its inhabitants; to prescribe the subjects upon which they may contract, the forms and solemnities with which their contracts shall be executed, the rights and obligations arising from them, and the mode in which their validity shall be determined and their obligations enforced; and also to regulate the manner and conditions upon which property situated within such territory, both personal and real, may be acquired, enjoyed and transferred. The other principle of public law referred to follows from the one mentioned; that is, that no State can exercise direct jurisdiction and authority over persons or property without its territory. * * * The several States are of equal dignity and authority, and the independence of one implies the exclusion of power from all others. And so it is laid down by jurists, as an elementary principle, that the laws of one State have no operation outside of its territory, except so far as is allowed by comity; and that no tribunal established by it can extend its process beyond that territory so as to subject either persons or property to its decisions. * * *

But as contracts made in one State may be enforceable only in another State, and property may be held by non-residents, the exercise of the jurisdiction which every State is admitted to possess over persons and property within its own territory will often affect persons and property without it. To any influence exerted in this way by a State affecting persons resident or property situated elsewhere, no objection can be justly taken; whilst any direct exertion of authority upon them, in an attempt to give ex-territorial operation to its laws, or to enforce an ex-territorial jurisdiction by its tribunals, would be deemed an encroachment upon the independence of the State in which the persons are domiciled or the property is situated, and be resisted as usurpation.

Thus the State, through its tribunals, may compel persons domiciled within its limits to execute, in pursuance of their contracts respecting property elsewhere situated, instruments in such form and with such solemnities as to transfer the title, so far as such formalities can be complied with; and the exercise of this jurisdiction in no manner interferes with the supreme control over the property by the State within which it is situated. * * *

So the State, through its tribunals, may subject property situated within its limits owned by non-residents to the payment of the demand of its own citizens against them; and the exercise of this jurisdiction in no respect infringes upon the sovereignty of the State where the owners are domiciled. Every State owes protection to its own citizens; and, when non-residents deal with them, it is a legitimate and just exercise of authority to hold and appropriate any property owned by such non-residents to satisfy the claims of its citizens. It is in virtue of the State's jurisdiction over the property of the non-resident situated within its limits that its tribunals can inquire into that non-resident's obligations to its own citizens, and the inquiry can then be carried only to the extent necessary to control the disposition of the property. If the non-resident have no property in the State, there is nothing upon which the tribunals can adjudicate.

* * * If, without personal service, judgments *in personam,* obtained *ex parte* against non-residents and absent parties, upon mere publication of process, which, in the great majority of cases, would never be seen by the parties interested, could be upheld and enforced, they would be the constant instruments of fraud and oppression. Judgments for all sorts of claims upon contracts and for torts, real or pretended, would be thus obtained, under which property would be seized, when the evidence of the transactions upon which they were founded, if they ever had any existence, had perished.

Substituted service by publication, or in any other authorized form, may be sufficient to inform parties of the object of proceedings taken where property is once brought under the control of the court by seizure or some equivalent act. The law assumes that property is always in the possession of its owner, in person or by agent; and it proceeds upon the theory that its seizure will inform him, not only that it is taken into the custody of the court, but that he must look to any proceedings authorized by law upon such seizure for its condemnation and sale. * * * In other words, such service may answer in all actions which are substantially proceedings *in rem*. But where the entire object of the action is to determine the personal rights and obligations of the defendants, that is, where the suit is merely *in personam*, constructive service in this form upon a non-resident is ineffectual for any purpose. Process from the tribunals of one State cannot run into another State, and summon parties there domiciled to leave its territory and respond to proceedings against them. Publication of process or notice within the State where the tribunal sits cannot create any greater obligation upon the non-resident to appear. Process sent to him out of the State, and process published within it, are equally unavailing in proceedings to establish his personal liability.

The want of authority of the tribunals of a State to adjudicate upon the obligations of non-residents, where they have no property within its limits, is not denied by the court below; but the position is assumed that, where they have property within the State, it is immaterial whether the property is in the first instance brought under the control of the court by attachment or some other equivalent act, and afterwards applied by its judgment to the satisfaction of demands against its owner; or such demands be first established in a personal action, and the property of the non-resident be afterwards seized and sold on execution. But the answer to this position has already been given in the statement, that the jurisdiction of the court to inquire into and determine his obligations at all is only incidental to its jurisdiction over the property. Its jurisdiction in that respect cannot be made to depend upon facts to be ascertained after it has tried the cause and rendered the judgment. If the judgment be previously void, it will not become valid by the subsequent discovery of property of the defendant, or by his subsequent acquisition of it. The judgment, if void when rendered, will always remain void; it cannot occupy the doubtful position of being valid if property be found, and void if there be none. Even if the position assumed were confined to cases where the non-resident defendant possessed property in the State at the commencement of the action, it would still make the validity of the proceedings and judgment depend upon the question whether, before the levy of the execution, the defendant had or had not disposed of the property. If, before the levy, the property should be sold, then, according to this position, the judgment would not be binding. This doctrine would introduce a new element of uncertainty in judicial proceedings. The contrary is the law; the validity of every judgment depends upon the jurisdiction of the court before it is rendered, not upon what may occur subsequently. * * *

The force and effect of judgments rendered against non-residents without personal service of process upon them, or their voluntary appearance, have been the subject of frequent consideration in the courts of the United States and of the several States, as attempts have been made to enforce such judgments in States other than those in which they were rendered, under the provision of the Constitution requiring that "Full faith and credit shall be given in each State to the public Acts, records and judicial proceedings of every other State;" and the Act of Congress providing for the mode of authenticating such Acts, records and proceedings, and declaring that, when thus authenticated, "They shall have such faith and credit given to them in every court within the United States as they have by law or usage in the courts of the State from which they are or shall be taken." In the earlier cases, it was supposed that the Act gave to all judgments the same effect in other States which they had by law in the State where rendered. But this view was afterwards qualified so as to make the Act applicable only when the court rendering the judgment had jurisdiction of the parties and of the subject-matter, and not to preclude an inquiry into the jurisdiction of the court in which the judgment was rendered, or the right of the State itself to exercise authority over the person or the subject-matter. * * *

Since the adoption of the 14th Amendment to the Federal Constitution, the validity of such judgments may be directly questioned, and their enforcement in the State resisted, on the ground that proceedings in a court of justice to determine the personal rights and obligations of parties over whom that court has no jurisdiction do not constitute due process of law. Whatever difficulty may be experienced in giving to those terms a definition which will embrace every permissible exertion of power affecting private rights, and exclude such as is forbidden, there can be no doubt of their meaning when applied to judicial proceedings. They then mean a course of legal proceedings according to those rules and principles which have been established in our systems of jurisprudence for the protection and enforcement of private rights. To give such proceedings any validity, there must be a tribunal competent by its constitution—that is, by the law of its creation—to pass upon the subject-matter of the suit; and, if that involves merely a determination of the personal liability of the defendant, he must be brought within its jurisdiction by service of process within the State, or his voluntary appearance.

Except in cases affecting the personal *status* of the plaintiff, and cases in which that mode of service may be considered to have been assented to in advance as hereinafter mentioned, the substituted service of process by publication allowed by the law of Oregon and by similar laws in other States, where actions are brought against non-residents, is effectual only where, in connection with process against the person for commencing the action, property in the State is brought under the control of the court, and subjected to its disposition by process adapted to that purpose, or where the judgment is sought as a means of reaching such property or affecting some interest therein; in other words, where the action is in the nature of a proceeding *in rem*. * * *

It is true that, in a strict sense, a proceeding *in rem* is one taken directly against property, and has for its object the disposition of the property, without reference to the title of individual claimants; but, in a larger and more general sense, the terms are applied to actions between parties, where the direct object is to reach and dispose of property owned by them, or of some interest therein. Such are cases commenced by attachment against the property of debtors, or instituted to partition real estate, foreclose a mortgage, or enforce a lien. So far as they affect property in the State, they are substantially proceedings *in rem* in the broader sense which we have mentioned.

* * *

It follows from the views expressed that the personal judgment recovered in the State Court of Oregon against the plaintiff herein, then a non-resident of the State, was without any validity, and did not authorize a sale of the property in controversy.

To prevent any misapplication of the views expressed in this opinion, it is proper to observe that we do not mean to assert, by anything we have said, that a State may not authorize proceedings to determine the *status* of one of its citizens towards a non-resident, which would be binding within the State, though made without service of process or personal notice to the non-resident. The jurisdiction which every State possesses to determine the civil *status* and capacities of all its inhabitants involves authority to prescribe the conditions on which proceedings affecting them may be commenced and carried on within its territory. The State, for example, has absolute right to prescribe the conditions upon which the marriage relation between its own citizens shall be created, and the causes for which it may be dissolved. One of the parties guilty of acts for which, by the law of the State, a dissolution may be granted, may have removed to a State where no dissolution is permitted. The complaining party would, therefore, fail if a divorce were sought in the State of the defendant; and if application could not be made to the tribunals of the complainant's domicile in such case, and proceedings be there instituted without personal service of process or personal notice to the offending party, the injured citizen would be without redress. * * *

Neither do we mean to assert that a State may not require a non-resident entering into a partnership or association within its limits, or making contracts enforceable there, to appoint an agent or representative in the State to receive service of process and notice in legal proceedings instituted with respect to such partnership, association or contracts, or to designate a place where such service may be made and notice given, and provide, upon their failure, to make such appointment or to designate such place that service may be made upon a public officer designated for that purpose, or in some other prescribed way, and that judgments rendered upon such service may not be binding upon the non-residents both within and without the State. * * * Nor do we doubt that a State, on creating corporations or other institutions for pecuniary or charitable purposes, may provide a mode in which their conduct may be investigated, their obligations enforced, or their charters revoked, which shall require other than personal service upon their officers or members. * * *

In the present case, there is no feature of this kind and, consequently, no consideration of what would be the effect of such legislation in enforcing the contract of a non-resident can arise. * * *

Judgment affirmed.

[The dissenting opinion of JUSTICE HUNT is omitted.]

NOTES AND QUESTIONS

1. The colorful characters and scandalous facts surrounding Pennoyer v. Neff have been chronicled by Professor Perdue:

> Our story begins with a young man, Marcus Neff, heading across the country by covered wagon train, presumably to seek his fortune. Neff left Iowa in early 1848 * * * [and] was one of the earliest settlers to claim land under the Oregon Donation Act. * * *
>
> Early in 1862 Neff made the unfortunate decision to consult a local Portland attorney, J.H. Mitchell. * * * Neff may have consulted Mitchell in an attempt to expedite the paperwork concerning his land patent. * * * "J.H. Mitchell" was actually the Oregon alias of one John Hipple. Hipple had been a teacher in Pennsylvania who, after being forced to marry the 15–year–old student whom he seduced, left teaching and took up law. * * * [I]n 1860 Hipple headed west taking with him four thousand dollars of client money and his then current paramour, a local school teacher. They made their way to California where Hipple abandoned the teacher, * * * and moved on to Portland, Oregon. There, using the name John H. Mitchell, he quickly established himself as a successful lawyer, specializing in land litigation and railroad right-of-way cases. He also remarried without bothering to divorce his first wife. * * *
>
> On November 3, 1865, Mitchell filed suit against Neff in Oregon state court [seeking payment for the legal services that had been rendered]. * * * A default judgment * * * was entered against Neff on February 19, 1866. Although Mitchell had an immediate right to execute on the judgment, he waited until early June 1866 to seek a writ of execution, possibly waiting for the arrival of Neff's land patent. * * * On August 7, 1866, the property was sold at a sheriff's auction * * *. Notably, the buyer was not Sylvester Pennoyer, as the Supreme Court opinion and commentators have implied. The property was purchased by none other than J.H. Mitchell, who three days later assigned the property to Sylvester Pennoyer. * * *
>
> Following the litigation, Neff disappeared into obscurity; not so Pennoyer and Mitchell. Pennoyer went on to be Governor of Oregon * * *. Mitchell * * * was elected to the United States Senate in 1872, [but] lost his senate seat in 1879 * * *. * * * Shortly before the 1885 election, Judge Deady, the lower court judge in *Pennoyer v. Neff,* came into possession of a set of love letters which Mitchell had written to Mitchell's second wife's younger sister during the five years that he carried on an affair with her. Deady turned the love letters over to a newspaper, the *Oregonian* * * *. [However, in spite of] the scandal, Mitchell was [re]elected four days later

> * * *. In July of 1905, while still serving in the United States Senate, Mitchell was convicted [of land fraud] and sentenced to six months in jail, a $1,000 fine, and complete disbarment from public office.

Perdue, *Sin, Scandal and Substantive Due Process: Personal Jurisdiction and Pennoyer Reconsidered*, 62 Wash.L.Rev. 479, 481–90 (1987).

2. Traditional analysis distinguishes three types of jurisdiction. In a proceeding in personam, the court exercises its power to render a judgment for or against a person by virtue of his presence within the state's territory or his citizenship there. In a proceeding in rem, the court exercises its power to determine the status of property located within its territory, and the determination of the court is binding with respect to all possible interest holders in that property. In a proceeding quasi-in-rem, the court renders a judgment for or against a person but recovery is limited to the value of property that is within the jurisdiction and thus subject to the court's authority. The dispute that gives rise to an action quasi-in-rem may be related to the property or unrelated to it. In an action quasi-in-rem, the property may be used to satisfy any judgment assessed in the action.

3. The concepts of jurisdiction found in the *Pennoyer* opinion were derived from nineteenth-century international law. In the traditional international model, a citizen of Country A might have been injured by a citizen of Country B in Country A. The citizen of Country A seeking relief had three options: proceed against the citizen of Country B in personam in Country A (with the likelihood that the paper called a judgment would be worthless because the courts of Country B would not enforce it against citizens of Country B); proceed against the citizen of Country B quasi-in-rem in Country A (with the advantage that the property of the citizen of Country B in Country A would be available to satisfy at least part (possibly all) of the judgment); or proceed against the citizen of Country B in the courts of Country B (in the hope of winning a judgment enforceable in Country B). Given these choices, it is understandable that the citizen of Country A probably would prefer the courts of Country A to the courts of Country B, the latter being farther away and possibly more disposed to find in favor of its own citizens, or to sue quasi-in-rem in Country A, so at least partial payment would be assured.

Do the same factors warrant applying these distinctions in jurisdiction in the context of the American federal system? Does the Full Faith and Credit Clause of the Constitution require states to recognize and enforce valid judgments by other states? Do the states have the same kind of interest in adjudicating claims brought by their citizens when the stake is state sovereignty rather than national sovereignty? Are there analogous grounds for concern that state courts may be unduly disposed to find in favor of citizens of their own state?

4. According to the territorial principle identified in *Pennoyer*, does the length of time the defendant is in the jurisdiction matter in an in personam action? Does the reason why the person is in the jurisdiction make a difference? In GRACE v. MacARTHUR, 170 F.Supp. 442 (E.D.Ark.1959), service of the complaint was made on the defendant while he was a passenger on a commercial flight from Tennessee to Texas when the plane was over

Arkansas. The court upheld the exercise of jurisdiction by the federal district court sitting in Arkansas. This Chapter later considers "transient" jurisdiction, see p. 175, infra.

5. Can a court assert jurisdiction over a citizen who is absent from the jurisdiction? In BLACKMER v. UNITED STATES, 284 U.S. 421, 438–39, 52 S.Ct. 252, 255, 76 L.Ed. 375, 383 (1932), petitioner, an American citizen, sought reversal of a contempt conviction resulting from his refusal to comply with a subpoena issued by an American court and served upon him in France in connection with a proceeding that grew out of the Teapot Dome Scandal during President Harding's administration. Service was authorized by federal statute. The Supreme Court concluded that no violation of due process had taken place because

> the jurisdiction of the United States over its absent citizen, so far as the binding effect of its legislation is concerned, is a jurisdiction in personam, as he is personally bound to take notice of the laws that are applicable to him and to obey them. * * * The question of the validity of the provision for actual service of the subpoena in a foreign country is one that arises solely between the * * * United States and the citizen. The mere giving of such a notice to the citizen in the foreign country of the requirement of his government that he shall return is in no sense an invasion of any right of the foreign government and the citizen has no standing to invoke any such supposed right.

The *Blackmer* principle was applied to state-court litigation in MILLIKEN v. MEYER, 311 U.S. 457, 462–63, 61 S.Ct. 339, 342–43, 85 L.Ed. 278, 283 (1940). Milliken sued Meyer, a Wyoming resident, in a Wyoming state court. Personal service was effected in Colorado under a Wyoming statute that permitted such service, in lieu of service by publication, on absent residents. Meyer did not appear and an in personam judgment was entered against him. Four years later Meyer asked a Colorado court to restrain Milliken's enforcement of the Wyoming judgment. The United States Supreme Court held the Wyoming judgment valid and entitled to full faith and credit. According to the Court:

> * * * Domicile in the state is alone sufficient to bring an absent defendant within the reach of the state's jurisdiction for purposes of a personal judgment by means of appropriate substituted service. * * * [T]he authority of a state over one of its citizens is not terminated by the mere fact of his absence from the state. The state which accords him privileges and affords protection to him and his property by virtue of his domicile may also exact reciprocal duties.

The Court's opinion made no attempt to distinguish among "resident," "domicile," and "citizen." What factors are relevant in deciding whether defendant's relationship with the forum state is sufficient to invoke the *Milliken* doctrine? Does Section 1 of the Fourteenth Amendment help answer the question by defining what it means to be a citizen of a state? Do *Blackmer* and *Milliken* fall within the scope of the statement in *Pennoyer* that "every State has the power to determine for itself the civil *status* and capacities of its inhabitants," or do they involve a different basis of jurisdiction?

6. Suppose a plaintiff brings suit in a forum with which she has no other connection. Should that forum be able to entertain a suit *against* the plaintiff if the claim is asserted as a part of the same proceeding? Consider ADAM v. SAENGER, 303 U.S. 59, 67–68, 58 S.Ct. 454, 458, 82 L.Ed. 649, 654–55 (1938).

> There is nothing in the Fourteenth Amendment to prevent a state from adopting a procedure by which a judgment *in personam* may be rendered in a cross-action against a plaintiff in its courts, upon service of process or of appropriate pleading upon his attorney of record. The plaintiff having, by his voluntary act in demanding justice from the defendant, submitted himself to the jurisdiction of the court, there is nothing arbitrary or unreasonable in treating him as being there for all purposes for which justice to the defendant requires his presence. It is the price which the state may exact as the condition of opening its courts to the plaintiff.

Would it matter whether or not the action is between the same two parties? Suppose a third party had instituted suit in California against the plaintiff in an action unrelated to the pending suit. Would the California court have had jurisdiction? If there was jurisdiction, would it be based on plaintiff's presence in the state or on some other notion? Should a state be permitted to condition the use of its courts on consent to the jurisdiction of those courts for purposes unrelated to the initial lawsuit? See generally 4 Wright & Miller, Federal Practice and Procedure: Civil 3d § 1064.

7. The expanding global economy has encouraged efforts to define an international law of jurisdiction, but agreement has proved difficult to reach. See Oestreicher, *"We're on a Road to Nowhere"—Reasons for the Continuing Failure to Regulate Recognition and Enforcement of Foreign Judgments*, 42 Int'l Law. 59 (2008). Although the cornerstone of the common law's concept of jurisdiction historically has been defendant's presence, domicile has been the key in the Netherlands and Switzerland, plaintiff's nationality has been of great importance in France, and domicile and the situs of property have been of major significance in Germany. See Juenger, *Judicial Jurisdiction in the United States and in the European Communities: A Comparison*, 82 Mich. L.Rev. 1195 (1984). Commentators emphasize that, "[i]n this area of law, differences among civil-law countries are as great as differences between given civil-law and common-law countries." de Vries & Lowenfeld, *Jurisdiction in Personal Actions—A Comparison of Civil Law Views*, 44 Iowa L.Rev. 306, 344 (1959).

SECTION B. EXPANDING THE BASES OF PERSONAL JURISDICTION

Increased interstate travel in the early twentieth century, particularly as a result of the growing popularity of the automobile, brought with it increased interstate litigation. In order to ensure that transient drivers not be beyond jurisdiction when they drove into another state, some states came to condition the use of their roads by out-of-state drivers on consent to the jurisdiction of the state's courts over matters arising from a party's activity within the state. In KANE v. NEW JERSEY, 242 U.S. 160, 37

S.Ct. 30, 61 L.Ed. 222 (1916), the Supreme Court held that New Jersey could require an out-of-state motorist to file a formal instrument appointing a New Jersey agent to receive process prior to using the state's highways. Eventually, some states moved beyond express consent as a basis for asserting jurisdiction.

HESS v. PAWLOSKI

Supreme Court of the United States, 1927.
274 U.S. 352, 47 S.Ct. 632, 71 L.Ed. 1091.

In Error to the Superior Court of Worcester County, Massachusetts.

MR. JUSTICE BUTLER delivered the opinion of the Court.

This action was brought by defendant in error to recover damages for personal injuries. The declaration alleged that plaintiff in error negligently and wantonly drove a motor vehicle on a public highway in Massachusetts, and that by reason thereof the vehicle struck and injured defendant in error. Plaintiff in error is a resident of Pennsylvania. No personal service was made on him, and no property belonging to him was attached. The service of process was made in compliance with chapter 90, General Laws of Massachusetts, as amended by Stat.1923, c. 431, § 2, the material parts of which follow:

> The acceptance by a nonresident of the rights and privileges conferred by section three or four, as evidenced by his operating a motor vehicle thereunder, or the operation by a nonresident of a motor vehicle on a public way in the commonwealth other than under said sections, shall be deemed equivalent to an appointment by such nonresident of the registrar or his successor in office, to be his true and lawful attorney upon whom may be served all lawful processes in any action or proceeding against him, growing out of any accident or collision in which said nonresident may be involved while operating a motor vehicle on such a way, and said acceptance or operation shall be a signification of his agreement that any such process against him which is so served shall be of the same legal force and validity as if served on him personally. Service of such process shall be made by leaving a copy of the process with a fee of two dollars in the hands of the registrar, or in his office, and such service shall be sufficient service upon the said nonresident: Provided, that notice of such service and a copy of the process are forthwith sent by registered mail by the plaintiff to the defendant, and the defendant's return receipt and the plaintiff's affidavit of compliance herewith are appended to the writ and entered with the declaration. * * *

Plaintiff in error appeared specially for the purpose of contesting jurisdiction, and filed an answer in abatement and moved to dismiss on the ground that the service of process, if sustained, would deprive him of his property without due process of law, in violation of the Fourteenth Amendment. The court overruled the answer in abatement and denied the motion. The Supreme Judicial Court held the statute to be a valid exercise of the police power, and affirmed the order. * * * At the trial the contention was renewed and again denied. Plaintiff in error excepted. The jury returned a verdict for defendant in error. The exceptions were overruled by the Supreme Judicial Court. * * * Thereupon the superior court entered judgment. The writ of error was allowed by the Chief Justice of that court.

The question is whether the Massachusetts enactment contravenes the due process clause of the Fourteenth Amendment.

The process of a court of one state cannot run into another and summon a party there domiciled to respond to proceedings against him. Notice sent outside the state to a nonresident is unavailing to give jurisdiction in an action against him personally for money recovery. Pennoyer v. Neff * * *. There must be actual service within the state of notice upon him or upon some one authorized to accept service for him. * * * A personal judgment rendered against a nonresident, who has neither been served with process nor appeared in the suit, is without validity. McDonald v. Mabee, 243 U.S. 90, 37 S.Ct. 343, 61 L.Ed. 608, L.R.A.1917F, 458. The mere transaction of business in a state by nonresident natural persons does not imply consent to be bound by the process of its courts. Flexner v. Farson, 248 U.S. 289, 39 S.Ct. 97, 63 L.Ed. 250. The power of a state to exclude foreign corporations, although not absolute, but qualified, is the ground on which such an implication is supported as to them. * * * But a state may not withhold from nonresident individuals the right of doing business therein. The privileges and immunities clause of the Constitution (section 2, art. 4), safeguards to the citizens of one state the right "to pass through, or to reside in any other state for purposes of trade, agriculture, professional pursuits, or otherwise." And it prohibits state legislation discriminating against citizens of other states. * * *

Motor vehicles are dangerous machines, and, even when skillfully and carefully operated, their use is attended by serious dangers to persons and property. In the public interest the state may make and enforce regulations reasonably calculated to promote care on the part of all, residents and nonresidents alike, who use its highways. The measure in question operates to require a nonresident to answer for his conduct in the state where arise causes of action alleged against him, as well as to provide for a claimant a convenient method by which he may sue to enforce his rights. Under the statute the implied consent is limited to proceedings growing out of accidents or collisions on a highway in which the nonresident may be involved. It is required that he shall actually receive and receipt for notice of the service and a copy of the process. And it contemplates such continuances as may be found necessary to give reasonable time and opportunity for defense. It makes no hostile discrimination against nonresidents, but tends to put them on the same footing as residents. Literal and precise equality in respect of this matter is not attainable; it is not required. * * * The state's power to regulate the use of its highways extends to their use by nonresidents as well as by residents. * * * And, in advance of the operation of a motor vehicle on its highway by a nonresident, the state may require him to appoint one of its officials as his agent on whom process may be served in proceedings growing out of such use. Kane v. New Jersey * * *. That case recognizes power of the state to exclude a nonresident until the formal appointment is made. And, having the power so to exclude, the state may declare that the use of the highway by the nonresident is the equivalent of the appointment of the registrar as agent on whom process may be served. * * * The difference between the formal and implied appointment is not substantial, so far as concerns the application of the due process clause of the Fourteenth Amendment.

Judgment affirmed.

NOTE AND QUESTION

What are the limits to the theory of jurisdiction expressed in *Hess*? Would a nonresident-motorist statute that purported to assert jurisdiction over any cause of action that arises out of the presence of defendant's vehicle within the state, or over people other than the driver of the vehicle, be constitutional? Could the implied consent to jurisdiction created by driving within a state be employed to support jurisdiction over a nonresident in a matter unrelated to her conduct within the state?

SECTION C. A NEW THEORY OF JURISDICTION

The jurisdictional bases developed in *Pennoyer* were not easily applied to corporations. A corporation is, after all, a fiction (an artificial legal entity). It exists on paper and acts through its employees, directors, and shareholders. It generally was accepted well into the nineteenth century that a "corporation can have no legal existence out of the boundaries of the sovereignty by which it is created." Bank of Augusta v. Earle, 38 U.S. (13 Pet.) 519, 588, 10 L.Ed. 274, 308 (1839) (Taney, J.). Nonetheless, as corporate activity grew beyond those boundaries, and technology facilitated interstate transport, courts were forced to adapt the jurisdictional principles of *Pennoyer* to reach corporate defendants.

The courts first developed the "consent" theory, which presupposed that a foreign corporation could transact business in a state only with that state's consent. Under this theory, a foreign corporation could be required to consent to service of process in the state by appointing an agent to receive process within the state, as a condition of obtaining permission to do business there. The courts soon began to apply this principle both when the corporation actually designated an agent to receive process and when it did not appoint an agent and, thus, could be said only to have granted implied consent.

As the courts became increasingly disenchanted with the unrealistic nature of the "consent" theory, they developed the "presence" theory premised on the notion that: "A foreign corporation is amenable to process * * * if it is doing business within the State in such manner and to such extent as to warrant the inference that it is present there." Philadelphia & Reading Ry. Co. v. McKibbin, 243 U.S. 264, 265, 37 S.Ct. 280, 61 L.Ed. 710, 711–12 (1917) (Brandeis, J.). This doctrine measured the propriety of a state's assertion of jurisdiction over a foreign corporation in terms of the actual activities of the corporation in the state. Under the presence theory, however, a court lost its adjudicatory authority over a corporation once it ceased doing business in the state. In addition, "presence" is a conclusory term, and all too often was used by the courts without any meaningful analysis.

Under both the presence theory and the implied consent theory, the first question to be asked was whether the corporation was "doing business" within the state. As the number of cases making this factual inquiry multiplied, "doing business" gradually came to be a test in and of itself. The cases became cluttered with refined and often senseless distinctions that sought to measure the quantity of defendant's activities within the state but paid little or no attention to the burden imposed on the corporation of asserting jurisdiction over it or the overall desirability of litigating in the particular forum.

> With doctrine in so bad a state of disrepair, the time had long since passed for the Supreme Court to acknowledge the truth of Holmes' dictum that "[t]he Constitution is not to be satisfied with a fiction." International Shoe Co. v. Washington afforded the Court an opportunity to begin to set its house in order in this field.

Kurland, *The Supreme Court, the Due Process Clause and the In Personam Jurisdiction of State Courts—From* Pennoyer *to* Denckla: *A Review,* 25 U.Chi.L.Rev. 569, 586 (1958).

INTERNATIONAL SHOE CO. v. WASHINGTON

Supreme Court of the United States, 1945.
326 U.S. 310, 66 S.Ct. 154, 90 L.Ed. 95.

Appeal from the Supreme Court of the State of Washington.

MR. CHIEF JUSTICE STONE delivered the opinion of the Court.

The questions for decision are (1) whether, within the limitations of the due process clause of the Fourteenth Amendment, appellant, a Delaware corporation, has by its activities in the State of Washington rendered itself amenable to proceedings in the courts of that state to recover unpaid contributions to the state unemployment compensation fund exacted by state statutes, * * * and (2) whether the state can exact those contributions consistently with the due process clause of the Fourteenth Amendment.

The statutes in question set up a comprehensive scheme of unemployment compensation, the costs of which are defrayed by contributions required to be made by employers to a state unemployment compensation fund. The contributions are a specified percentage of the wages payable annually by each employer for his employees' services in the state. The assessment and collection of the contributions and the fund are administered by respondents. Section 14(c) of the Act, Wash.Rev.Stat.1941 Supp., § 9998–114c, authorizes respondent Commissioner to issue an order and notice of assessment of delinquent contributions upon prescribed personal service of the notice upon the employer if found within the state, or, if not so found, by mailing the notice to the employer by registered mail at his last known address. That section also authorizes the Commissioner to collect the assessment by distraint if it is not paid within ten days after service of the notice. * * *

In this case notice of assessment for the years in question was personally served upon a sales solicitor employed by appellant in the State of Washington, and a copy of the notice was mailed by registered mail to appellant at its address in St. Louis, Missouri. Appellant appeared specially before the office of unemployment and moved to set aside the order and notice of assessment on the ground that the service upon appellant's salesman was not proper service upon appellant; that appellant was not a corporation of the State of Washington and was not doing business within the state; that it had no agent within the state upon whom service could be made; and that appellant is not an employer and does not furnish employment within the meaning of the statute.

The motion was heard on evidence and a stipulation of facts by the appeal tribunal which denied the motion and ruled that respondent Commissioner was entitled to recover the unpaid contributions. That action was affirmed by the Commissioner; both the Superior Court and the Supreme Court affirmed. * * * Appellant in each of these courts assailed the statute as applied, as a violation of the due process clause of the Fourteenth Amendment, and as imposing a constitutionally prohibited burden on interstate commerce.

* * * Appellant is a Delaware corporation, having its principal place of business in St. Louis, Missouri, and is engaged in the manufacture and sale of shoes and other footwear. It maintains places of business in several states, other than Washington, at which its manufacturing is carried on and from which its merchandise is distributed interstate through several sales units or branches located outside the State of Washington.

Appellant has no office in Washington and makes no contracts either for sale or purchase of merchandise there. It maintains no stock of merchandise in that state and makes there no deliveries of goods in intrastate commerce. During the years from 1937 to 1940, now in question, appellant employed eleven to thirteen salesmen under direct supervision and control of sales managers located in St. Louis. These salesmen resided in Washington; their principal activities were confined to that state; and they were compensated by commissions based upon the amount of their sales. The commissions for each year totaled more than $31,000. Appellant supplies its salesmen with a line of samples, each consisting of one shoe of a pair, which they display to prospective purchasers. On occasion they rent permanent sample rooms, for exhibiting samples, in business buildings, or rent rooms in hotels or business buildings temporarily for that purpose. The cost of such rentals is reimbursed by appellant.

The authority of the salesmen is limited to exhibiting their samples and soliciting orders from prospective buyers, at prices and on terms fixed by appellant. The salesmen transmit the orders to appellant's office in St. Louis for acceptance or rejection, and when accepted the merchandise for filling the orders is shipped f.o.b. from points outside Washington to the purchasers within the state. All the merchandise shipped into Washington is invoiced at the place of shipment from which collections are made. No salesman has authority to enter into contracts or to make collections.

The Supreme Court of Washington was of opinion that the regular and systematic solicitation of orders in the state by appellant's salesmen, resulting in a continuous flow of appellant's product into the state, was sufficient to constitute doing business in the state so as to make appellant amenable to suit in its courts. But it was also of opinion that there were sufficient additional activities shown to bring the case within the rule frequently stated, that solicitation within a state by the agents of a foreign corporation plus some additional activities there are sufficient to render the corporation amenable to suit brought in the courts of the state to enforce an obligation arising out of its activities there. * * * The court found such additional activities in the salesmen's display of samples sometimes in permanent display rooms, and the salesmen's residence within the state, continued over a period of years, all resulting in a substantial volume of merchandise regularly shipped by appellant to purchasers within the state. * * *

Appellant * * * insists that its activities within the state were not sufficient to manifest its "presence" there and that in its absence the state courts were without jurisdiction, that consequently it was a denial of due process for the state to subject appellant to suit. It refers to those cases in which it was said that the mere solicitation of orders for the purchase of goods within a state, to be accepted without the state and filled by shipment of the purchased goods interstate, does not render the corporation seller amenable to suit within the state. * * * And appellant further argues that since it was not present within the state, it is a denial of due process to subject it to taxation or other money exaction. It thus denies the power of the state to lay the tax or to subject appellant to a suit for its collection.

Historically the jurisdiction of courts to render judgment in personam is grounded on their de facto power over the defendant's person. Hence his presence within the territorial jurisdiction of a court was prerequisite to its rendition of a judgment personally binding him. Pennoyer v. Neff * * *. But now that the capias ad respondendum has given way to personal service of summons or other form of notice, due process requires only that in order to subject a defendant to a judgment in personam, if he be not present within the territory of the forum, he have certain minimum contacts with it such that the maintenance of the suit does not offend "traditional notions of fair play and substantial justice." Milliken v. Meyer * * *. See Holmes, J., in McDonald v. Mabee, 243 U.S. 90, 91, 37 S.Ct. 343, 61 L.Ed. 608, L.R.A.1917F, 458. * * *

Since the corporate personality is a fiction, although a fiction intended to be acted upon as though it were a fact * * *, it is clear that unlike an individual its "presence" without, as well as within, the state of its origin can be manifested only by activities carried on in its behalf by those who are authorized to act for it. To say that the corporation is so far "present" there as to satisfy due process requirements, for purposes of taxation or the maintenance of suits against it in the courts of the state, is to beg the question to be decided. For the terms "present" or "presence" are used merely to symbolize those activities of the corporation's agent within the state which courts will deem to be sufficient to satisfy the demands of due process. L. Hand, J., in Hutchinson v. Chase & Gilbert * * *. Those demands may be met by such contacts of the corporation with the state of the forum as make it reasonable, in the context of our federal system of government, to require the corporation to defend the particular suit which is brought there. An "estimate of the inconveniences" which would result to the corporation from a trial away from its "home" or principal place of business is relevant in this connection. * * *

"Presence" in the state in this sense has never been doubted when the activities of the corporation there have not only been continuous and systematic, but also give rise to the liabilities sued on, even though no consent to be sued or authorization to an agent to accept service of process has been given. * * * Conversely it has been generally recognized that the casual presence of the corporate agent or even his conduct of single or isolated items of activities in a state in the corporation's behalf are not enough to subject it to suit on causes of action unconnected with the activities there. * * * To require the corporation in such circumstances to defend the suit away from its home or other jurisdiction where it carries on more substantial activities has been thought to lay too great and unreasonable a burden on the corporation to comport with due process.

While it has been held in cases on which appellant relies that continuous activity of some sorts within a state is not enough to support the demand that the corporation be amenable to suits unrelated to that activity * * *, there have been instances in which the continuous corporate operations within a state were thought so substantial and of such a nature as to justify suit against it on causes of action arising from dealings entirely distinct from those activities. * * *

Finally, although the commission of some single or occasional acts of the corporate agent in a state sufficient to impose an obligation or liability on the corporation has not been thought to confer upon the state authority to enforce it, Rosenberg Bros. & Co. v. Curtis Brown Co., 260 U.S. 516, 43 S.Ct. 170, 67 L.Ed. 372, other such acts, because of their nature and quality and the circumstances of their commission, may be deemed sufficient to render the corporation liable to suit. Cf. Kane v. New Jersey * * *; Hess v. Pawloski * * *. True, some of the decisions holding the corporation amenable to suit have been supported by resort to the legal fiction that it has given its consent to service and suit, consent being implied from its presence in the state through the acts of its authorized agents. * * * But more realistically it may be said that those authorized acts were of such a nature as to justify the fiction. * * *

It is evident that the criteria by which we mark the boundary line between those activities which justify the subjection of a corporation to suit, and those which do not, cannot be simply mechanical or quantitative. The test is not merely, as has sometimes been suggested, whether the activity, which the corporation has seen fit to procure through its agents in another state, is a little more or a little less. * * * Whether due process is satisfied must depend rather upon the quality and nature of the activity in relation to the fair and orderly administration of the laws which it was the purpose of the due process clause to insure. That clause does not contemplate that a state may make binding a judgment in personam against an individual or corporate defendant with which the state has no contacts, ties, or relations. * * *

But to the extent that a corporation exercises the privilege of conducting activities within a state, it enjoys the benefits and protection of the laws of that state. The exercise of that privilege may give rise to obligations; and, so far as those obligations arise out of or are connected with the activities within the state, a procedure which requires the corporation to respond to a suit brought to enforce them can, in most instances, hardly be said to be undue. * * *

Applying these standards, the activities carried on in behalf of appellant in the State of Washington were neither irregular nor casual. They were systematic and continuous throughout the years in question. They resulted in a large volume of interstate business, in the course of which appellant received the benefits and protection of the laws of the state, including the right to resort to the courts for the enforcement of its rights. The obligation which is here sued upon arose out of those very activities. It is evident that these operations establish sufficient contacts or ties with the state of the forum to make it reasonable and just according to our traditional conception of fair play and substantial justice to permit the state to enforce the obligations which appellant has incurred there. Hence we cannot say that the maintenance of the present suit in the State of Washington involves an unreasonable or undue procedure.

We are likewise unable to conclude that the service of the process within the state upon an agent whose activities establish appellant's "presence" there was not sufficient notice of the suit, or that the suit was so unrelated to those activities as to make the agent an inappropriate vehicle for communicating the notice. It is enough that appellant has established such contacts with the state that the particular form of substituted service adopted there gives reasonable assurance that the notice will be actual. * * *

Appellant having rendered itself amenable to suit upon obligations arising out of the activities of its salesmen in Washington, the state may maintain the present suit in personam to collect the tax laid upon the exercise of the privilege of employing appellant's salesmen within the state. For Washington has made one of those activities, which taken together establish appellant's "presence" there for purposes of suit, the taxable event by which the state brings appellant within the reach of its taxing power. The state thus has constitutional power to lay the tax and to subject appellant to a suit to recover it. The activities which establish its "presence" subject it alike to taxation by the state and to suit to recover the tax. * * *

Affirmed.

MR. JUSTICE JACKSON took no part in the consideration or decision of this case.

MR. JUSTICE BLACK delivered the following opinion.

* * *

I believe that the Federal Constitution leaves to each State, without any "ifs" or "buts," a power to tax and to open the doors of its courts for its citizens to sue corporations whose agents do business in those States. Believing that the Constitution gave the States that power, I think it a judicial deprivation to condition its exercise upon this Court's notion of "fair play," however appealing that term may be. Nor can I stretch the meaning of due process so far as to authorize this Court to deprive a State of the right to afford judicial protection to its citizens on the ground that it would be more "convenient" for the corporation to be sued somewhere else.

There is a strong emotional appeal in the words "fair play," "justice," and "reasonableness." But they were not chosen by those who wrote the original Constitution or the Fourteenth Amendment as a measuring rod for this Court to use in invalidating State or Federal laws passed by elected legislative representatives. No one, not even those who most feared a democratic government, ever formally proposed that courts should be given power to invalidate legislation under any such elastic standards. Express prohibitions against certain types of legislation are found in the Constitution, and under the long settled practice, courts invalidate laws found to conflict with them. This requires interpretation, and interpretation, it is true, may result in extension of the Constitution's purpose. But that is no reason for reading the due process clause so as to restrict a State's power to tax and sue those whose activities affect persons and businesses within the State, provided proper service can be had. * * *

NOTES AND QUESTIONS

1. In its argument before the United States Supreme Court, International Shoe contended, in part, that it would be imprudent to link the company's amenability to suit with service on mere salesmen: "It would be manifestly impolitic to uphold service upon a salesman in a case not involving a sale. It would require of mere soliciting salesmen, notoriously happy-go-lucky fellows, good mixers, a higher degree of judgment and responsibility than that for which they are selected." For more of the facts of *International Shoe* and a discussion of how the company litigated the question of personal jurisdiction, see Cameron & Johnson, *Death of a Salesman? Forum Shopping and Outcome Determination Under International Shoe,* 28 U.C.Davis L.Rev. 769 (1995).

2. *International Shoe* uses contacts with the forum in two different ways. First, a defendant may have sufficient contact with the forum to warrant asserting jurisdiction over it for all matters. This is termed "general jurisdiction," and we will return to study it in more detail later in this Chapter. Second, a defendant may have sufficient contact with the forum to warrant asserting jurisdiction over it for matters related to its activity with the forum without having sufficient contact with the forum to warrant general jurisdiction. In such a case, the jurisdiction is termed "specific jurisdiction." Whether a corporation is subject to specific or general jurisdiction, however, depends on the nature and number of contacts it has with the forum. Determining what constitutes sufficient business within the state, or what matters are related to activity within it, often are uncertain questions that may blur the distinction between general and specific jurisdiction. See Brilmayer, *Related Contacts and Personal Jurisdiction,* 101 Harv.L.Rev. 1444 (1988).

3. Do you notice any differences between Justice Stone's style of argument in *International Shoe* and that of Justice Field in *Pennoyer*, p. 71, supra? Commentators associate *International Shoe* with the philosophy of Legal Realism, which takes a functional approach to questions of judicial decision making, while Justice Field is associated with that of Classical Formalism. See Rutherglen, *International Shoe and the Legacy of Legal Realism*, 2001 Sup.Ct. Rev. 347 (2001). Is there a benefit to setting bright-line jurisdictional rules? On the other hand, is it important for courts to use flexible standards so the exercise of jurisdiction can easily adapt to changing social circumstances? As you read the cases that follow, consider the relative merits of each approach.

SECTION D. SPECIFIC JURISDICTION AND STATE LONG-ARM LAWS

1. THE DEVELOPMENT OF LONG-ARM LAWS

The Supreme Court's decision in Hess v. Pawloski, p. 82, supra, encouraged states to utilize their police powers to enact a number of statutes asserting jurisdiction based not only on the operation of automobiles within a state but also on engaging in a variety of other hazardous activities or enterprises. As time progressed and liberal judicial construction and emboldened state legislatures gave broader scope to these statutes, the usefulness of the technique suggested by the nonresident motorist statutes became even more apparent.

The Court's decision in *International Shoe*—with its emphasis on contacts with the forum state—further encouraged states to expand their jurisdictional reach and led to efforts on the part of many state legislatures to conform their statutory pattern to the Supreme Court's latest view as to when personal jurisdiction could be asserted consistently with the Constitution. This spate of legislative activity came largely in the form of "long-arm" or "single-act" statutes, which seek to provide personal jurisdiction over nonresidents who cannot be found and served in the forum. These statutes predicate jurisdiction over nonresidents upon the defendant's general activity in the state, or the commission of any one of a series of enumerated acts within the jurisdiction, or, in some cases, the commission of a certain act outside the jurisdiction causing consequences within it. The theory supporting the assertion of jurisdiction in these circumstances flows naturally from the *International Shoe* decision and its emphasis on the quantum and quality of the defendant's activity in the forum state.

The first truly comprehensive long-arm statute was enacted in Illinois and it was used as a model by a number of states. Under the Illinois act an individual or a corporation, whether a citizen or noncitizen of Illinois, is said to be amenable to the jurisdiction of the state's courts if he transacts any business within the state; commits a tort within the state; owns, uses, or possesses any real estate within the state; or contracts to insure any person, property, or risk located within the state. Several years after its enactment, the Illinois statute was amended to include jurisdiction over claims involving alimony, support, and property division against former residents. Other states soon followed Illinois's lead in expanding the jurisdictional reach of their courts.

Contemporary long-arm statutes run the gamut from very broad ones that permit states to assert jurisdiction up to the limits allowed by the Constitution, to narrow ones that only carve out small parts of their constitutionally permitted authority. Long-arm statutes are set out in the supplement. Which of the statutes are most limited in application? In what ways? As you read the following case, consider whether the state court could exercise personal jurisdiction, assuming the same facts, if the applicable long-arm statute were that of New York or California. One limitation that generally is placed on the use of long-arm statutes is that they apply only to suits brought in the courts of the state in which the jurisdictional act occurs or in the federal courts sitting in that state. Despite the textual similarities of many of these statutes, judicial construction of them often differs.

Read the selected state jurisdiction statutes in the Supplement.

GRAY v. AMERICAN RADIATOR & STANDARD SANITARY CORP.

Supreme Court of Illinois, 1961.
22 Ill.2d 432, 176 N.E.2d 761.

KLINGBIEL, JUSTICE. Phyllis Gray appeals from a judgment of the circuit court of Cook County dismissing her action for damages. The issues are concerned with the construction and validity of our statute providing for substituted service of process on nonresidents. Since a constitutional question is involved, the appeal is direct to this court.

The suit was brought against the Titan Valve Manufacturing Company and others, on the ground that a certain water heater had exploded and injured the plaintiff. The complaint charges, *inter alia*, that the Titan company, a foreign corporation, had negligently constructed the safety valve; and that the injuries were suffered as a proximate result thereof. Summons issued and was duly served on Titan's registered agent in Cleveland, Ohio. The corporation appeared specially, filing a motion to quash on the ground that it had not committed a tortious act in Illinois. Its affidavit stated that it does no business here; that it has no agent physically present in Illinois; and that it sells the completed valves to defendant, American Radiator & Standard Sanitary Corporation, outside Illinois. The American Radiator & Standard Sanitary Corporation (also made a defendant) filed an answer in which it set up a cross claim against Titan, alleging that Titan made certain warranties to American Radiator, and that if the latter is held liable to the plaintiff it should be indemnified and held harmless by Titan. The court granted Titan's motion, dismissing both the complaint and the cross claim.

Section 16 of the Civil Practice Act provides that summons may be personally served upon any party outside the State; and that as to nonresidents who have submitted to the jurisdiction of our courts, such service has the force and effect of personal service within Illinois. (Ill.Rev. Stat.1959, chap. 110, par. 16.) Under section 17(1)(b) a nonresident who, either in person or through an agent, commits a tortious act within this State submits to jurisdiction. * * * The questions in this case are (1) whether a tortious act was committed here, within the meaning of the statute, despite the fact that the Titan corporation had no agent in Illinois; and (2) whether the statute, if so construed, violates due process of law.

The first aspect to which we must direct our attention is one of statutory construction. Under section 17(1)(b) jurisdiction is predicated on the committing of a tortious act in this State. It is not disputed, for the purpose of this appeal, that a tortious act was committed. The issue depends on whether it was committed in Illinois, so as to warrant the assertion of personal jurisdiction by service of summons in Ohio.

The wrong in the case at bar did not originate in the conduct of a servant physically present here, but arose instead from acts performed at the place of manufacture. Only the consequences occurred in Illinois. It is well established, however, that in law the place of a wrong is where the last event takes place which is necessary to render the actor liable. Restatement, Conflict of Laws, sec. 377. A second indication that the place of injury is the determining factor is found in rules governing the time within which an action must be brought. In applying statutes of limitation our court has computed the period from the time when the injury is done. * * * We think it is clear that the alleged negligence in manufacturing the valve cannot be separated from the resulting injury; and that for present purposes, like those of liability and limitations, the tort was committed in Illinois.

Titan seeks to avoid this result by arguing that instead of using the word "tort," the legislature employed the term "tortious act"; and that the latter refers only to the act or conduct, separate and apart from any consequences thereof. We cannot accept the argument. To be tortious an act must cause injury. The concept of injury is an inseparable part of the phrase. In determining legislative intention courts will read words in their ordinary and popularly understood sense. * * * We think the intent should be determined less from technicalities of definition than from considerations of general purpose and effect. To adopt the criteria urged by defendant would tend to promote litigation over extraneous issues concerning the elements of a tort and the territorial incidence of each, whereas the test should be concerned more with those substantial elements of convenience and justice presumably contemplated by the legislature. As we observed in Nelson v. Miller, 11 Ill.2d 378, 143 N.E.2d 673, the statute contemplates the exertion of jurisdiction over nonresident defendants to the extent permitted by the due-process clause.

The Titan company contends that if the statute is applied so as to confer jurisdiction in this case it violates the requirement of due process of law. The precise constitutional question thus presented has not heretofore been considered by this court. * * *

Under modern doctrine the power of a State court to enter a binding judgment against one not served with process within the State depends upon two questions: first, whether he has certain minimum contacts with the State * * * and second, whether there has been a reasonable method of notification. See International Shoe Co. v. State of Washington * * *. In the case at bar there is no contention that section 16 provides for inadequate notice or that its provisions were not followed. Defendant's argument on constitutionality is confined to the proposition that applying section 17(1)(b), where the injury is defendant's only contact with the State, would exceed the limits of due process.

A proper determination of the question presented requires analysis of those cases which have dealt with the quantum of contact sufficient to warrant jurisdiction. Since the decision in Pennoyer v. Neff * * * the power of a State to exert jurisdiction over nonresidents has been greatly expanded, particularly with respect to foreign corporations. * * * [In International Shoe Co. v. Washington,] the court pointed out that the activities of the corporation in Washington were not only continuous and systematic but also gave rise to the liability sued on. It was observed that such operations, which resulted in a large volume of business, established "sufficient contacts or ties with the state of the forum to make it reasonable and just according to our traditional conception of fair play and substantial justice to permit the state to enforce the obligations which appellant has incurred there." * * *

Where the business done by a foreign corporation in the State of the forum is of a sufficiently substantial nature, it has been held permissible for the State to entertain a suit against it even though the cause of action arose from activities entirely distinct from its conduct within the State. Perkins v. Benguet Consolidated Mining Co. * * *. But where such business or other activity is not substantial, the particular act or transaction having no connection with the State of the forum, the requirement of "contact" is not satisfied. * * *

In the case at bar the defendant's only contact with this State is found in the fact that a product manufactured in Ohio was incorporated in Pennsylvania, into a hot water heater which in the course of commerce was sold to an Illinois consumer. The record fails to disclose whether defendant has done any other business in Illinois, either directly or indirectly; and it is argued, in reliance on the International Shoe test, that since a course of business here has not been shown there are no "minimum contacts" sufficient to support jurisdiction. We do not think, however, that doing a given volume of business is the only way in which a nonresident can form the required connection with this State. Since the International Shoe case was decided the requirements for jurisdiction have been further relaxed, so that at the present time it is sufficient if the act or transaction itself has a substantial connection with the State of the forum.

In McGee v. International Life Insurance Co., 355 U.S. 220, 78 S.Ct. 199, 201, 2 L.Ed.2d 223 (1957), suit was brought in California against a foreign insurance company on a policy issued to a resident of California. The defendant was not served with process in that State but was notified by registered mail at its place of business in Texas, pursuant to a statute permitting such service in suits on insurance contracts. The contract in question was delivered in California, the premiums were mailed from there and the insured was a resident of that State when he died, but defendant had no office or agent in California nor did it solicit any business there apart from the policy sued on. After referring briefly to the International Shoe case the court held that "it is sufficient for purposes of due process that the suit was based on *a contract* which had substantial connection'' with California. (Emphasis supplied.)

In Smyth v. Twin State Improvement Corp. * * * the court discussed the principal authorities on the question and concluded, *inter alia,* that ''continuous activity within the state is not necessary as a prerequisite to jurisdiction.''

In Nelson v. Miller * * * the commission of a single tort within this State was held sufficient to sustain jurisdiction under the present statute. The defendant in that case, a resident of Wisconsin, was engaged in the business of selling appliances. It was alleged that in the process of delivering a stove in Illinois, an employee of the defendant negligently caused injury to the plaintiff. In holding that the defendant was not denied due process by being required to defend in Illinois, this court observed * * *: ''The defendant sent his employee into Illinois in the advancement of his own interests. While he was here, the employee and the defendant enjoyed the benefit and protection of the laws of Illinois, including the right to resort to our courts. In the course of his stay here the employee performed acts that gave rise to an injury. The law of Illinois will govern the substantive rights and duties stemming from the incident. Witnesses, other than the defendant's employee, are likely to be found here, and not in Wisconsin. In such circumstances, it is not unreasonable to require the defendant to make his defense here.''

Whether the type of activity conducted within the State is adequate to satisfy the requirement depends upon the facts in the particular case. * * * The question cannot be answered by applying a mechanical formula or rule of thumb but by ascertaining what is fair and reasonable in the circumstances. In the application of this flexible test the relevant inquiry is whether defendant engaged in some act or conduct by which he may be said to have invoked the benefits and protections of the law of the forum. * * * The relevant decisions since Pennoyer v. Neff show a development of the concept of personal jurisdiction from one which requires service of process within the State to one which is satisfied either if the act or transaction sued on occurs there or if defendant has engaged in a sufficiently substantial course of activity in the State, provided always that reasonable notice and opportunity to be heard are afforded. * * * [T]he trend in defining due process of law is away from the emphasis on territorial limitations and toward emphasis on providing adequate notice and opportunity to be heard: from the court with immediate power over the defendant, toward the court in which both parties can most conveniently settle their dispute.

In the McGee case the court commented on the trend toward expanding State jurisdiction over nonresidents, observing that: ''In part this is attributable to the fundamental transformation of our national economy over the years. Today many commercial transactions touch two or more States and may involve parties separated by the full continent. With this increasing nationalization of commerce has come a great increase in the amount of business conducted by mail across state lines. At the same time modern transportation and communication have made it much less burdensome for a party sued to defend himself in a State where he engages in economic activity."

It is true that courts cannot "assume that this trend heralds the eventual demise of all restrictions on the personal jurisdiction of state courts." Hanson v. Denckla * * *. An orderly and fair administration of the law throughout the nation requires protection against being compelled to answer claims brought in distant States with which the defendant has little or no association and in which he would be faced with an undue burden or disadvantage in making his defense. It must be remembered that lawsuits can be brought on frivolous demands or groundless claims as well as on legitimate ones, and that procedural rules must be designed and appraised in the light of what is fair and just to both sides in the dispute. * * *

In the case at bar defendant does not claim that the present use of its product in Illinois is an isolated instance. While the record does not disclose the volume of Titan's business or the territory in which appliances incorporating its valves are marketed, it is a reasonable inference that its commercial transactions, like those of other manufacturers, result in substantial use and consumption in this State. To the extent that its business may be directly affected by transactions occurring here it enjoys benefits from the laws of this State, and it has undoubtedly benefited, to a degree, from the protection which our law has given to the marketing of hot water heaters containing its valves. Where the alleged liability arises, as in this case, from the manufacture of products presumably sold in contemplation of use here, it should not matter that the purchase was made from an independent middleman or that someone other than the defendant shipped the product into this State.

With the increasing specialization of commercial activity and the growing interdependence of business enterprises it is seldom that a manufacturer deals directly with consumers in other States. The fact that the benefit he derives from its laws is an indirect one, however, does not make it any the less essential to the conduct of his business; and it is not unreasonable, where a cause of action arises from alleged defects in his product, to say that the use of such products in the ordinary course of commerce is sufficient contact with this State to justify a requirement that he defend here.

As a general proposition, if a corporation elects to sell its products for ultimate use in another State, it is not unjust to hold it answerable there for any damage caused by defects in those products. Advanced means of distribution and other commercial activity have made possible these modern methods of doing business, and have largely effaced the economic significance of State lines. By the same token, today's facilities for transportation and communication have removed much of the difficulty and inconvenience formerly encountered in defending lawsuits brought in other States.

* * *

The principles of due process relevant to the issue in this case support jurisdiction in the court where both parties can most conveniently settle their dispute. The facts show that the plaintiff, an Illinois resident, was injured in Illinois. The law of Illinois will govern the substantive questions, and witnesses on the issues of injury, damages and other elements relating to the occurrence are most likely to be found here. Under such circumstances the courts of the place of injury usually provide the most convenient forum for trial. * * * In Travelers Health Association v. Commonwealth of Virginia, 339 U.S. 643, 70 S.Ct. 927, 94 L.Ed. 1154, a Nebraska insurance corporation was held subject to the jurisdiction of a Virginia regulatory commission although it had no paid agents within the State and its only contact there was a mail-order business operated from its Omaha office. The court observed, by way of *dictum,* that "suits on alleged losses can be more conveniently tried in Virginia where witnesses would most likely live and where claims for losses would presumably be investigated. Such factors have been given great weight in applying the doctrine of *forum non conveniens.* * * * And prior decisions of this Court have referred to the unwisdom, unfairness and injustice of permitting policyholders to seek redress only in some distant state where the insurer is incorporated. The Due Process Clause does not forbid a state to protect its citizens from such injustice." 339 U.S. at page 649, 70 S.Ct. at page 930, 94 L.Ed. at 1161–1162. * * *

* * * We conclude accordingly that defendant's association with this State is sufficient to support the exercise of jurisdiction.

* * *

Reversed and remanded, with directions.

NOTE AND QUESTION

As *Gray* illustrates, the application of long-arm statutes often entails difficult questions of statutory construction. In GREEN v. ADVANCE ROSS ELECTRONICS CORP., 86 Ill.2d 431, 437–38, 439–40, 56 Ill.Dec. 657, 660–62, 427 N.E.2d 1203, 1206–08 (1981), the issue was whether Advance Ross, a Delaware corporation with headquarters in Illinois, in an action claiming breach of fiduciary duty, could assert jurisdiction over Green, a Texas resident, who once served as president of two of its affiliates. All of Green's corporate responsibilities, including the acts that allegedly injured the corporation, were performed outside Illinois. Nonetheless, Advance Ross argued that, under Section 17(1)(b) of Illinois' long-arm statute, an out-of-state resident submits to the jurisdiction of the Illinois courts when he commits a tort that causes a diminution of the funds of a corporation organized or headquartered in Illinois. The Illinois Supreme Court, distinguishing *Gray*, refused to read Section 17(1)(b) to establish jurisdiction:

As in *Gray* * * *, for the purpose of disposing of the propriety of long-arm jurisdiction there is no dispute that tortious acts were committed. To be resolved is whether their commission was "within this State" as those words are used in section 17(1)(b).

* * * [Advance Ross's] theory is that although the misconduct of Green, Sr., took place outside Illinois, the consequences of his misconduct were felt in Illinois. They * * * contend that the misconduct alleged resulted in a drain upon those assets in Illinois. But the consequences upon which [Advance Ross relies] are too remote from the misconduct of Green, Sr., to support the conclusion that the tortious acts complained of were committed in Illinois. The situs of the last event whose happening was necessary to hold Green, Sr., liable was in Texas.

In support of its conclusion, the Illinois court noted:

[A]cceptance of the theory of long-arm jurisdiction advanced by [Advance Ross] would be tantamount to permitting a corporation operating nation-wide to sue employees, suppliers, customers and perhaps others, at the company's State of incorporation or at its headquarters no matter how far away they lived and worked or their contact with the corporation was. Any interpretation of the Illinois long-arm statute which would permit that result is neither fair nor wise as a matter of policy. The meaning [which Advance Ross] ask[s] us to give the words "within this State" takes us too easily out of this State to be acceptable. * * *

Illinois' long-arm statute, 735 ILCS 5/2–209, formerly cited as Ill.Rev.Stat. ch. 110, ¶ 2–209(a), was amended in 1989 to give the Illinois state courts jurisdiction over any cause of action arising out of:

* * *

(7) The making or performance of any contract or promise substantially connected with this State; * * *

(11) The breach of any fiduciary duty within this State;

(12) The performance of duties as a director or officer of a corporation organized under the laws of this State or having its principal place of business within this State * * *.

If these provisions had been in effect, would the Illinois Supreme Court have decided *Advance Ross* the same way? In this regard, consider whether *Gray* and *Advance Ross* are applicable only to cases asserting jurisdiction based on a "tortious act within this State," or whether they apply equally to all assertions of jurisdiction under Illinois's long-arm statute.

2. DUE PROCESS AND LONG–ARM STATUTES

As is illustrated by the decision of the Illinois Supreme Court in *Gray,* interpreting the relevant long-arm statute is only half of the job. Once the meaning of the statute has been determined, it must be asked whether the statute, as interpreted, is consistent with the Due Process Clause of the Constitution.

———

McGEE v. INTERNATIONAL LIFE INSURANCE CO., 355 U.S. 220, 222–24, 78 S.Ct. 199, 200–01, 2 L.Ed.2d 223, 225–26 (1957). The plaintiff, McGee, was the beneficiary of a life insurance policy issued by the Empire Mutual Insurance Co., an Arizona corporation, to one Lowell Franklin, a resident of California. In 1948, the defendant, International Life Insurance Co., assumed Empire Mutual's insurance obligations. Franklin and International Life transacted business by mail until Franklin's death in 1950. Neither Empire Mutual nor International Life ever had any office or agent in California, and, as far as the record disclosed, International Life had never solicited or done any insurance business in California other than the policy with Franklin.

When International Life refused to pay McGee upon Franklin's death, she sued in a California state court, basing jurisdiction on the California Unauthorized Insurer's Process Act. The Act subjects foreign corporations to suit on insurance contracts with in-state residents. After recovering a judgment in California, McGee sought to enforce the judgment in Texas. The Texas court refused to enforce the judgment, holding it to be void under the Fourteenth Amendment on the ground that the California courts could not assume jurisdiction over International Life without service of process within its boundaries. The Supreme Court held that the exercise of jurisdiction by California was proper.

The Court noted that, with increased "nationalization of commerce," the tremendous growth "in the amount of business conducted by mail across state lines" and the frequency with which "commercial transactions touch two or more States," there had developed "a trend * * * clearly discernible toward expanding the permissible scope of state jurisdiction over foreign corporations and other nonresidents."

> * * * [W]e think it apparent that the Due Process Clause did not preclude the California court from entering a judgment binding on respondent. It is sufficient * * * that the suit was based on a contract which had substantial connection with that State. * * * The contract was delivered in California, the premiums were mailed from there and the insured was a resident of that State when he died. * * * California has a manifest interest in providing effective means of redress for its residents when their insurers refuse to pay claims. These residents would be at a severe disadvantage if they were forced to follow the insurance company to a distant State in order to hold it legally accountable. When claims were small or moderate individual claimants frequently could not afford the cost of bringing an action in a foreign forum—thus in effect making the company judgment proof. Often the crucial witnesses—as here on the company's defense of suicide—will be found in the insured's locality. Of course there may be inconvenience to the insurer if it is held amenable to suit in California * * * but certainly nothing which amounts to a denial of due process. * * * There is no contention that respondent did not have adequate notice of the suit or sufficient time to prepare its defenses and appear.

NOTES AND QUESTIONS

1. Did the *McGee* Court modify the *International Shoe* test? Is *McGee* consistent with *International Shoe*?

2. Is it appropriate to characterize the *McGee* Court as using a two-step approach to the question of whether a court can exercise personal jurisdiction over a non-resident defendant? The first is to determine whether sufficient minimum contacts exist so as to make the exercise of personal jurisdiction permissible. The second is to balance the interests of the plaintiff, defendant, and the forum to determine if exercising jurisdiction is desirable. Or is the thrust of *McGee* that the number of contacts between the defendant and the forum that normally would be required for jurisdiction are reduced when the interests of the forum state and plaintiff strongly support jurisdiction?

3. Do you agree that *McGee* supports the exercise of jurisdiction in *Gray*, p. 93, supra? Why or why not?

4. The Court said in *McGee* that improvements in transportation and communication make it less burdensome for out-of-state litigants to defend suits. Does this observation sufficiently justify making the defendant travel to the forum chosen by the plaintiff? Don't advances in transportation and communication also make it easier for plaintiffs to sue out of state? For a discussion of the impact of social change on jurisdictional doctrine, see Kalo, *Jurisdiction as an Evolutionary Process: The Development of Quasi In Rem and In Personam Principles*, 1978 Duke L.J. 1147.

HANSON v. DENCKLA, 357 U.S. 235, 78 S.Ct. 1228, 2 L.Ed.2d 1283 (1958). Dora Donner, a resident of Pennsylvania, established a trust in Delaware, naming a Delaware bank as trustee. By the terms of the trust, during her lifetime the income from the trust would go to her and, upon her death, the remainder would pass to whomever she had appointed as beneficiaries. Mrs. Donner retained the power to change the appointed beneficiaries at any time.

Later, Mrs. Donner moved to Florida, and, several years before her death, she executed her last will and testament, leaving most of her estate to two of her daughters, Katherine and Dorothy. On the same day, she executed (for the last time) her power to change the appointed beneficiaries under the Delaware trust—this time, she designated two of her grandchildren (the children of a third daughter, Elizabeth) beneficiaries of a significant portion of the trust's assets, with the remainder going to her estate.

After Mrs. Donner's death, Katherine and Dorothy, the two daughters named in the will, brought an action in Florida claiming that the appointment of their sister's children as beneficiaries of the trust had been ineffective. If that were true, the assets of the trust would pass under the will to the two daughters, as legatees.

The defendants argued that the suit could not go forward because the Florida court could not assert jurisdiction over the Delaware trustee, an indispensable party under Florida law.

The Florida court found that it had jurisdiction over the trustee, concluded that the trust was invalid and that the exercise of the power of appointment was ineffective to pass title, and held that the trust property therefore passed under the will. Before the Florida judgment was rendered, an action was commenced in Delaware by Elizabeth, as executrix of the estate, to determine who was entitled to share the trust assets, which were situated in Delaware. With minor exceptions, the parties were the same as in the Florida action. When the Florida judgment was rendered, the legatees under the will unsuccessfully urged it as res judicata of the Delaware action. The Delaware court ultimately held the trust and the exercise of the power of appointment valid under Delaware law.

Accepting both cases for review, a divided Supreme Court found that because the trustee's contacts with Florida had been less than minimal, that state could not assert personal jurisdiction over it. Since Florida had not obtained personal jurisdiction over an indispensable party to the action, the trustee, Delaware was justified in refusing full faith and credit to the Florida decree. Writing for a majority of five, Chief Justice Warren explained that:

> * * * [T]he requirements for personal jurisdiction over nonresidents have evolved from the rigid rule of Pennoyer v. Neff * * * to the flexible standard of International Shoe Co. v. State of Washington * * *. But it is a mistake to assume that this trend heralds the eventual demise of all restrictions on the personal jurisdiction of state courts. * * * Those restrictions are more than a guarantee of immunity from inconvenient or distant litigation. They are a consequence of territorial limitations on the power of the respective States. However minimal the burden of defending in a foreign tribunal, a defendant may not be called upon to do so unless he has had the "minimal contacts" with that State that are a prerequisite to its exercise of power over him. * * *
>
> We fail to find such contacts in the circumstances of this case. The defendant trust company has no office in Florida, and transacts no business there. None of the trust assets has ever been held or administered in Florida, and the record discloses no solicitation of business in that State either in person or by mail. * * *
>
> The cause of action in this case is not one that arises out of an act done or transaction consummated in the forum State. * * * From Florida Mrs. Donner carried on several bits of trust administration that may be compared to the mailing of premiums in *McGee*. But the record discloses no instance in which the trustee performed any acts in Florida that bear the same relationship to the agreement as the solicitation in *McGee*. Consequently, this suit cannot be said to be one

> to enforce an obligation that arose from a privilege the defendant exercised in Florida. * * *
>
> * * * The unilateral activity of those who claim some relationship with a nonresident defendant cannot satisfy the requirement of contact with the forum State. The application of that rule will vary with the quality and nature of the defendant's activity, but it is essential in each case that there be some act by which the defendant purposefully avails itself of the privilege of conducting activities within the forum State, thus invoking the benefits and protections of its laws. * * *
>
> * * * As we understand [Florida's] law, the trustee is an indispensable party over whom the court must acquire jurisdiction before it is empowered to enter judgment in a proceeding affecting the validity of a trust. It does not acquire that jurisdiction by being the "center of gravity" of the controversy, or the most convenient location for litigation. The issue is personal jurisdiction, not choice of law. * * *

Id. at 251–54, 78 S.Ct. at 1238–40, 2 L.Ed.2d at 1296–98.

Justice Black's dissent stands in sharp contrast to the Chief Justice's perception of personal jurisdiction.

> In light of the * * * circumstances it seems quite clear to me that there is nothing in the Due Process Clause which denies Florida the right to determine whether [the] appointment was valid as against its statute of wills. * * * Not only was the appointment made in Florida by a domiciliary of Florida, but the primary beneficiaries also lived in that State. In my view it could hardly be denied that Florida had sufficient interest so that a court with jurisdiction might properly apply Florida law, if it chose, to determine whether the appointment was effectual. * * * True, the question whether the law of a State can be applied to a transaction is different from the question whether the courts of that State have jurisdiction to enter a judgment, but the two are often closely related and to a substantial degree depend upon similar considerations. It seems to me that where a transaction has as much relationship to a State as * * * [this] appointment had to Florida its courts ought to have power to adjudicate controversies arising out of that transaction, unless litigation there would impose such a heavy and disproportionate burden on a nonresident defendant that it would offend what this Court has referred to as "traditional notions of fair play and substantial justice." * * * Florida, the home of the principal contenders * * *, was a reasonably convenient forum for all. Certainly there is nothing fundamentally unfair in subjecting the corporate trustee to the jurisdiction of the Florida courts. It chose to maintain business relations with [the settlor] in that State for eight years, regularly communicating with her with respect to the business of the trust including the very appointment in question.
>
> Florida's interest in the validity of [the] appointment is made more emphatic by the fact that her will is being administered in that State. It has traditionally been the rule that the State where a person is

> domiciled at the time of his death is the proper place to determine the validity of his will, to construe its provisions and to marshal and distribute his personal property. Here Florida was seriously concerned with winding up [this] estate and with finally determining what property was to be distributed under her will. * * *

Id. at 258–59, 78 S.Ct. at 1242–43, 2 L.Ed.2d at 1300–01.

NOTES AND QUESTIONS

1. Under the last appointment of the trust, the children of Mrs. Donner's third daughter Elizabeth would have received about $400,000 from the trust. Mrs. Donner's other two daughters, the residual legatees under the will, would have received over $1,000,000 from the estate. The Florida decision would have invalidated the last appointment over the trust, defeated Mrs. Donner's estate plan, and added $400,000 to the amount received by Elizabeth's sisters at the expense of Elizabeth's family.

2. Could the *Hanson* decision be justified on the ground that Delaware, as the state where the trust was validly established (at least under Delaware law), had a stronger interest in the disposition of the trust's funds than Florida? Delaware's interest certainly is sufficient to support jurisdiction in Delaware, but was it sufficient to preclude jurisdiction in Florida? Could it be that the result in this case is a function of the fact that the Court had before it two conflicting judgments and that it could not accord full faith and credit to both? How much of an interest must the forum state have to justify a court's exercising personal jurisdiction over an out-of-state resident? Compare California's interests in *McGee*, in which jurisdiction was upheld, with Florida's interests in *Hanson*, in which jurisdiction was denied. What defines a state "interest" sufficient to support jurisdiction?

3. In their opinions in *Hanson,* the Chief Justice and Justice Black agree that the question whether a court may apply its own law to a controversy is to be decided by a standard that differs from that used to decide the question whether the court can adjudicate the controversy at all. That is, the constitutional power to apply local law is of a different dimension from the constitutional power to assert jurisdiction. Professor Silberman questions the *Hanson* Court's implication "that more contacts with the forum state are needed for jurisdiction than for choice of law":

> The impact of a conflict of laws decision more seriously affects the rights of the parties than a decision on jurisdiction, which merely directs the parties to an appropriate forum in which to litigate their case. * * * I am confident that, given the choice, the Florida plaintiffs would rather have litigated in a Delaware Court applying Florida law than in a Florida court applying Delaware law.

Silberman, Shaffer v. Heitner: *The End of an Era,* 53 N.Y.U. L. Rev. 33, 82–83 (1978).

4. Do you think it appropriate to allow a court to adjudicate any controversy to which it might apply local law under the applicable choice-of-law rule? In ALLSTATE INS. CO. v. HAGUE, 449 U.S. 302, 312–13, 101 S.Ct.

633, 640, 66 L.Ed.2d 521, 531 (1981), the plurality opinion held that "for a State's substantive law to be selected in a constitutionally permissible manner, that State must have a significant contact or significant aggregation of contacts, creating state interests, such that choice of its law is neither arbitrary nor fundamentally unfair." Under this test, the plurality upheld Minnesota's decision to apply its own law in an action by a former Wisconsin resident who moved to Minnesota just prior to filing suit to collect proceeds under an automobile insurance policy made in Wisconsin covering vehicles owned by a Wisconsin resident who had been killed in an accident in Wisconsin. After *Hague* it seems clear that the Due Process Clause allows states extraordinary latitude in developing and applying choice-of-law rules. The due process restrictions on state jurisdiction are considerably greater than those on choice of law.

WORLD-WIDE VOLKSWAGEN CORP. v. WOODSON

Supreme Court of the United States, 1980.
444 U.S. 286, 100 S.Ct. 559, 62 L.Ed.2d 490.

Certiorari to the Supreme Court of Oklahoma.

MR. JUSTICE WHITE delivered the opinion of the Court.

The issue before us is whether, consistently with the Due Process Clause of the Fourteenth Amendment, an Oklahoma court may exercise *in personam* jurisdiction over a nonresident automobile retailer and its wholesale distributor in a products liability action, when the defendants' only connection with Oklahoma is the fact that an automobile sold in New York to New York residents became involved in an accident in Oklahoma.

I

Respondents Harry and Kay Robinson purchased a new Audi automobile from petitioner Seaway Volkswagen, Inc. (Seaway) in Massena, N.Y., in 1976. The following year the Robinson family, who resided in New York, left that State for a new home in Arizona. As they passed through the State of Oklahoma, another car struck their Audi in the rear, causing a fire which severely burned Kay Robinson and her two children.

The Robinsons subsequently brought a products liability action in the District Court for Creek County, Okla., claiming that their injuries resulted from defective design and placement of the Audi's gas tank and fuel system. They joined as defendants the automobile's manufacturer, Audi NSU Auto Union Aktiengesellschaft (Audi); its importer, Volkswagen of America, Inc. (Volkswagen); its regional distributor, petitioner World-Wide Volkswagen Corporation (World-Wide); and its retail dealer, petitioner Seaway. Seaway and World-Wide entered special appearances, claiming that Oklahoma's exercise of jurisdiction over them would offend the limitations on the State's jurisdiction imposed by the Due Process Clause of the Fourteenth Amendment.

The facts presented to the District Court showed that World-Wide is incorporated and has its business office in New York. It distributes vehicles, parts, and accessories, under contract with Volkswagen, to retail dealers in New York, New Jersey, and Connecticut. Seaway, one of these retail dealers, is incorporated and has its place of business in New York. Insofar as the record reveals, Seaway and World–Wide are fully independent corporations whose relations with each other and with Volkswagen and Audi are contractual only. Respondents adduced no evidence that either World–Wide or Seaway does any business in Oklahoma, ships or sells any products to or in that State, has an agent to receive process there, or purchases advertisements in any media calculated to reach Oklahoma. In fact, * * * there was no showing that any automobile sold by World–Wide or Seaway has ever entered Oklahoma with the single exception of the vehicle involved in the present case.

Despite the apparent paucity of contacts between petitioners and Oklahoma, the District Court rejected their constitutional claim and reaffirmed that ruling in denying petitioners' motion for reconsideration. Petitioners then sought a writ of prohibition in the Supreme Court of Oklahoma to restrain the District Judge, respondent Charles S. Woodson, from exercising *in personam* jurisdiction over them. They renewed their contention that, because they had no "minimal contacts" * * * with the State of Oklahoma, the actions of the District Judge were in violation of their rights under the Due Process Clause.

The Supreme Court of Oklahoma denied the writ, * * * holding that personal jurisdiction over petitioners was authorized by Oklahoma's "long-arm" statute, Okla.Stat., Tit. 12, § 1701.03(a)(4) (1971).[7] Although the court noted that the proper approach was to test jurisdiction against both statutory and constitutional standards, its analysis did not distinguish these questions, probably because § 1701.03(a)(4) has been interpreted as conferring jurisdiction to the limits permitted by the United States Constitution. The court's rationale was contained in the following paragraph * * *:

> In the case before us, the product being sold and distributed by the petitioners is by its very design and purpose so mobile that petitioners can foresee its possible use in Oklahoma. This is especially true of the distributor, who has the exclusive right to distribute such automobile in New York, New Jersey and Connecticut. The evidence presented below demonstrated that goods sold and distributed by the petitioners were used in the State of Oklahoma, and under the facts we believe it reasonable to infer, given the retail value of the automobile, that the petitioners derive substantial income from automobiles which from time to time are used in the State of Oklahoma. This being the case, we hold that under the facts presented, the trial court was justified in

---

7. This subsection provides:

"A court may exercise personal jurisdiction over a person, who acts directly or by an agent, as to a cause of action or claim for relief arising from the person's * * * causing tortious injury in this state by an act or omission outside this state if he regularly does or solicits business or engages in any other persistent course of conduct, or derives substantial revenue from goods used or consumed or services rendered, in this state * * *." * * *

concluding that the petitioners derive substantial revenue from goods used or consumed in this State.

We granted certiorari * * * to consider an important constitutional question with respect to state-court jurisdiction and to resolve a conflict between the Supreme Court of Oklahoma and the highest courts of at least four other States. We reverse.

II

* * *

As has long been settled, and as we reaffirm today, a state court may exercise personal jurisdiction over a nonresident defendant only so long as there exist "minimum contacts" between the defendant and the forum State. International Shoe Co. v. Washington * * *. The concept of minimum contacts, in turn, can be seen to perform two related, but distinguishable, functions. It protects the defendant against the burdens of litigating in a distant or inconvenient forum. And it acts to ensure that the States, through their courts, do not reach out beyond the limits imposed on them by their status as coequal sovereigns in a federal system.

The protection against inconvenient litigation is typically described in terms of "reasonableness" or "fairness." We have said that the defendant's contacts with the forum State must be such that maintenance of the suit "does not offend 'traditional notions of fair play and substantial justice.'" * * * The relationship between the defendant and the forum must be such that it is "reasonable * * * to require the corporation to defend the particular suit which is brought there." * * * Implicit in this emphasis on reasonableness is the understanding that the burden on the defendant, while always a primary concern, will in an appropriate case be considered in light of other relevant factors, including the forum State's interest in adjudicating the dispute * * *; the plaintiff's interest in obtaining convenient and effective relief, * * * at least when that interest is not adequately protected by the plaintiff's power to choose the forum * * *; the interstate judicial system's interest in obtaining the most efficient resolution of controversies; and the shared interest of the several States in furthering fundamental substantive social policies * * *.

The limits imposed on state jurisdiction by the Due Process Clause, in its role as a guarantor against inconvenient litigation, have been substantially relaxed over the years. As we noted in McGee v. International Life Ins. Co., * * * this trend is largely attributable to a fundamental transformation in the American economy:

> Today many commercial transactions touch two or more States and may involve parties separated by the full continent. With this increasing nationalization of commerce has come a great increase in the amount of business conducted by mail across state lines. At the same time modern transportation and communication have made it much less burdensome for a party sued to defend himself in a State where he engages in economic activity.

The historical developments noted in *McGee,* of course, have only accelerated in the generation since that case was decided.

Nevertheless, we have never accepted the proposition that state lines are irrelevant for jurisdictional purposes, nor could we, and remain faithful to the principles of interstate federalism embodied in the Constitution. * * * [T]he Framers * * * intended that the States retain many essential attributes of sovereignty, including, in particular, the sovereign power to try causes in their courts. The sovereignty of each State, in turn, implied a limitation on the sovereignty of all of its sister States—a limitation express or implicit in both the original scheme of the Constitution and the Fourteenth Amendment.

Hence, even while abandoning the shibboleth that "[t]he authority of every tribunal is necessarily restricted by the territorial limits of the State in which it is established," Pennoyer v. Neff, * * * we emphasized that the reasonableness of asserting jurisdiction over the defendant must be assessed "in the context of our federal system of government," International Shoe Co. v. Washington, * * * and stressed that the Due Process Clause ensures not only fairness, but also the "orderly administration of the laws," id. * * *

Thus, the Due Process Clause "does not contemplate that a state may make binding a judgment *in personam* against an individual or corporate defendant with which the state has no contacts, ties, or relations." International Shoe Co. v. Washington * * *. Even if the defendant would suffer minimal or no inconvenience from being forced to litigate before the tribunals of another State; even if the forum State has a strong interest in applying its law to the controversy; even if the forum State is the most convenient location for litigation, the Due Process Clause, acting as an instrument of interstate federalism, may sometimes act to divest the State of its power to render a valid judgment. Hanson v. Denckla * * *.

III

Applying these principles to the case at hand, we find in the record before us a total absence of those affiliating circumstances that are a necessary predicate to any exercise of state-court jurisdiction. Petitioners carry on no activity whatsoever in Oklahoma. They close no sales and perform no services there. They avail themselves of none of the privileges and benefits of Oklahoma law. They solicit no business there either through salespersons or through advertising reasonably calculated to reach the State. Nor does the record show that they regularly sell cars at wholesale or retail to Oklahoma customers or residents or that they indirectly, through others, serve or seek to serve the Oklahoma market. In short, respondents seek to base jurisdiction on one, isolated occurrence and whatever inferences can be drawn therefrom: the fortuitous circumstance that a single Audi automobile, sold in New York to New York residents, happened to suffer an accident while passing through Oklahoma.

It is argued, however, that because an automobile is mobile by its very design and purpose it was "foreseeable" that the Robinsons' Audi would cause injury in Oklahoma. Yet "foreseeability" alone has never been a sufficient benchmark for personal jurisdiction under the Due Process Clause. In Hanson v. Denckla * * * it was no doubt foreseeable that the settlor of a Delaware trust would subsequently move to Florida and seek to exercise a power of appointment there; yet we held that Florida courts could not constitutionally exercise jurisdiction over a Delaware trustee that had no other contacts with the forum State. * * *

If foreseeability were the criterion, a local California tire retailer could be forced to defend in Pennsylvania when a blowout occurs there, * * * a Wisconsin seller of a defective automobile jack could be haled before a distant court for damage caused in New Jersey, * * * or a Florida soft-drink concessionaire could be summoned to Alaska to account for injuries happening there * * *. Every seller of chattels would in effect appoint the chattel his agent for service of process. His amenability to suit would travel with the chattel. * * *

This is not to say, of course, that foreseeability is wholly irrelevant. But the foreseeability that is critical to due process analysis is not the mere likelihood that a product will find its way into the forum State. Rather, it is that the defendant's conduct and connection with the forum State are such that he should reasonably anticipate being haled into court there. * * * The Due Process Clause, by ensuring the "orderly administration of the laws," * * * gives a degree of predictability to the legal system that allows potential defendants to structure their primary conduct with some minimum assurance as to where that conduct will and will not render them liable to suit.

When a corporation "purposefully avails itself of the privilege of conducting activities within the forum State," * * * it has clear notice that it is subject to suit there, and can act to alleviate the risk of burdensome litigation by procuring insurance, passing the expected costs on to customers, or, if the risks are too great, severing its connection with the State. Hence if the sale of a product of a manufacturer or distributor such as Audi or Volkswagen is not simply an isolated occurrence, but arises from the efforts of the manufacturer or distributor to serve, directly or indirectly, the market for its product in other States, it is not unreasonable to subject it to suit in one of those States if its allegedly defective merchandise has there been the source of injury to its owner or to others. The forum State does not exceed its powers under the Due Process Clause if it asserts personal jurisdiction over a corporation that delivers its products into the stream of commerce with the expectation that they will be purchased by consumers in the forum State. Cf. Gray v. American Radiator & Standard Sanitary Corp. * * *.

But there is no such or similar basis for Oklahoma jurisdiction over World–Wide or Seaway in this case. Seaway's sales are made in Massena, N.Y. World–Wide's market, although substantially larger, is limited to dealers in New York, New Jersey, and Connecticut. There is no evidence of record that any automobiles distributed by World–Wide are sold to retail customers outside this tristate area. It is foreseeable that the purchasers of automobiles sold by World–Wide and Seaway may take them to Oklahoma. But the mere "unilateral activity of those who claim some relationship with a nonresident defendant cannot satisfy the requirement of contact with the forum State." Hanson v. Denckla * * *.

In a variant on the previous argument, it is contended that jurisdiction can be supported by the fact that petitioners earn substantial revenue from goods used in Oklahoma. * * * While this inference seems less than compelling on the facts of the instant case, we need not question the court's factual findings in order to reject its reasoning.

This argument seems to make the point that the purchase of automobiles in New York, from which the petitioners earn substantial revenue, would not occur *but for* the fact that the automobiles are capable of use in distant States like Oklahoma. Respondents observe that the very purpose of an automobile is to travel, and that travel of automobiles sold by petitioners is facilitated by an extensive chain of Volkswagen service centers throughout the country, including some in Oklahoma. However, financial benefits accruing to the defendant from a collateral relation to the forum State will not support jurisdiction if they do not stem from a constitutionally cognizable contact with that State. * * * In our view, whatever marginal revenues petitioners may receive by virtue of the fact that their products are capable of use in Oklahoma is far too attenuated a contact to justify that State's exercise of *in personam* jurisdiction over them.

Because we find that petitioners have no "contacts, ties, or relations" with the State of Oklahoma, International Shoe Co. v. Washington, * * * the judgment of the Supreme Court of Oklahoma is

Reversed.

[The dissenting opinions of JUSTICE MARSHALL and JUSTICE BLACKMUN are omitted.]

MR. JUSTICE BRENNAN, dissenting.

* * *

I

The Court's opinions focus tightly on the existence of contacts between the forum and the defendant. In so doing, they accord too little weight to the strength of the forum State's interest in the case and fail to explore whether there would be any actual inconvenience to the defendant. The essential inquiry in locating the constitutional limits on state-court jurisdiction over absent defendants is whether the particular exercise of jurisdiction offends " 'traditional notions of fair play and substantial justice.' " * * * The clear focus in *International Shoe* was on fairness and reasonableness. * * * The Court specifically declined to establish a mechanical test based on the quantum of contacts between a State and the defendant * * *. The existence of contacts, so long as there were some, was merely one way of giving content to the determination of fairness and reasonableness.

Surely *International Shoe* contemplated that the significance of the contacts necessary to support jurisdiction would diminish if some other consideration helped establish that jurisdiction would be fair and reasonable. The interests of the State and other parties in proceeding with the case in a particular forum are such considerations. McGee v. International Life Ins. Co., * * * for instance, accorded great importance to a State's "manifest interest in providing effective means of redress" for its citizens. * * *

Another consideration is the actual burden a defendant must bear in defending the suit in the forum. * * * Because lesser burdens reduce the unfairness to the defendant, jurisdiction may be justified despite less significant contacts. The burden, of course, must be of constitutional dimension. Due process limits on jurisdiction do not protect a defendant from all inconvenience of travel * * *. Instead, the constitutionally significant "burden" to be analyzed relates to the mobility of the defendant's defense. For instance, if having to travel to a foreign forum would hamper the defense because witnesses or evidence or the defendant himself were immobile, or if there were a disproportionately large number of witnesses or amount of evidence that would have to be transported at the defendant's expense, or if being away from home for the duration of the trial would work some special hardship on the defendant, then the Constitution would require special consideration for the defendant's interests.

That considerations other than contacts between the forum and the defendant are relevant necessarily means that the Constitution does not require that trial be held in the State which has the "best contacts" with the defendant. * * * The defendant has no constitutional entitlement to the best forum or, for that matter, to any particular forum. Under even the most restrictive view of *International Shoe,* several States could have jurisdiction over a particular cause of action. We need only determine whether the forum States in these cases satisfy the constitutional minimum.

II

* * * I would find that the forum State has an interest in permitting the litigation to go forward, the litigation is connected to the forum, the defendant is linked to the forum, and the burden of defending is not unreasonable. Accordingly, I would hold that it is neither unfair nor unreasonable to require these defendants to defend in the forum State.

* * *

* * * [T]he interest of the forum State and its connection to the litigation is strong. The automobile accident underlying the litigation occurred in Oklahoma. The plaintiffs were hospitalized in Oklahoma when

they brought suit. Essential witnesses and evidence were in Oklahoma. * * * The State has a legitimate interest in enforcing its laws designed to keep its highway system safe, and the trial can proceed at least as efficiently in Oklahoma as anywhere else.

The petitioners are not unconnected with the forum. Although both sell automobiles within limited sales territories, each sold the automobile which in fact was driven to Oklahoma where it was involved in an accident. It may be true, as the Court suggests, that each sincerely intended to limit its commercial impact to the limited territory, and that each intended to accept the benefits and protection of the laws only of those States within the territory. But obviously these were unrealistic hopes that cannot be treated as an automatic constitutional shield.

An automobile simply is not a stationary item or one designed to be used in one place. An automobile is *intended* to be moved around. Someone in the business of selling large numbers of automobiles can hardly plead ignorance of their mobility or pretend that the automobiles stay put after they are sold. It is not merely that a dealer in automobiles foresees that they will move. * * * The dealer actually intends that the purchasers will use the automobiles to travel to distant States where the dealer does not directly "do business." The sale of an automobile does *purposefully* inject the vehicle into the stream of interstate commerce so that it can travel to distant States. * * *

The Court accepts that a State may exercise jurisdiction over a distributor which "serves" that State "indirectly" by "deliver[ing] its products into the stream of commerce with the expectation that they will be purchased by consumers in the forum State." * * * It is difficult to see why the Constitution should distinguish between a case involving goods which reach a distant State through a chain of distribution and a case involving goods which reach the same State because a consumer, using them as the dealer knew the customer would, took them there. In each case the seller purposefully injects the goods into the stream of commerce and those goods predictably are used in the forum State. The manufacturer in the case cited by the Court, *Gray v. American Radiator & Standard Sanitary Corp.* [p. 93, supra] * * *, had no more control over which States its goods would reach than did the petitioners in this case.

* * *

III

It may be that affirmance of the judgments in these cases would approach the outer limits of *International Shoe*'s jurisdictional principle. But that principle, with its almost exclusive focus on the rights of defendants, may be outdated. * * *

International Shoe inherited its defendant focus from Pennoyer v. Neff * * * and represented the last major step this Court has taken in the long process of liberalizing the doctrine of personal jurisdiction. Though its flexible approach represented a major advance, the structure of our society has changed in many significant ways since *International Shoe* was decided in 1945. * * * As the Court acknowledges, * * * both the nationalization of commerce and the ease of transportation and communication have accelerated in the generation since 1957. The model of society on which the *International Shoe* Court based its opinion is no longer accurate. Business people, no matter how local their businesses, cannot assume that goods remain in the business' locality. Customers and goods can be anywhere else in the country usually in a matter of hours and always in a matter of a very few days.

In answering the question whether or not it is fair and reasonable to allow a particular forum to hold a trial binding on a particular defendant, the interests of the forum State and other parties loom large in today's world and surely are entitled to as much weight as are the interests of the defendant. The "orderly administration of the laws" provides a firm basis for according some protection to the interests of plaintiffs and States as well as of defendants. Certainly, I cannot see how a defendant's right to due process is violated if the defendant suffers no inconvenience. * * *

The conclusion I draw is that constitutional concepts of fairness no longer require the extreme concern for defendants that was once necessary. Rather, * * * minimum contacts must exist "among the *parties,* the contested transaction, and the forum State."[15] The contacts between any two of these should not be determinative. * * *

In effect the Court is allowing defendants to assert the sovereign rights of their home States. The expressed fear is that otherwise all limits on personal jurisdiction would disappear. But the argument's premise is wrong. I would not abolish limits on jurisdiction or strip state boundaries of all significance * * *; I would still require the plaintiff to demonstrate sufficient contacts among the parties, the forum, and the litigation to make the forum a reasonable State in which to hold the trial.

I would also, however, strip the defendant of an unjustified veto power over certain very appropriate fora—a power the defendant justifiably enjoyed long ago when communication and travel over long distances were slow and unpredictable and when notions of state sovereignty were impractical and exaggerated. * * *

NOTES AND QUESTIONS

1. Neither Audi nor Volkswagen of America objected to jurisdiction. How would they have fared had they contested it? Is it likely that specific jurisdiction would exist with regard to them? Considering the deep pockets of Audi and Volkswagen, why were the plaintiffs so interested in gaining jurisdiction over Seaway and World-Wide? Recall that a plaintiff sometimes can choose between filing her lawsuit in state or federal court, pp. 6–8, supra.

---

15. In some cases, the inquiry will resemble the inquiry commonly undertaken in determining which State's law to apply. That it is fair to apply a State's law to a nonresident defendant is clearly relevant in determining whether it is fair to subject the defendant to jurisdiction in that State. * * *

Both Seaway and World–Wide were incorporated and had their places of business in New York; the Robinsons technically were also New York citizens at the time the action was commenced. Given the requirement of "complete diversity" for subject-matter jurisdiction, see p. 272, infra, joining Seaway and World–Wide as defendants would block the possibility of having a federal court hear the lawsuit. At the time, federal juries in Oklahoma were often finding for defendant or awarding smaller damages on claims like the Robinsons' than were their state counterparts. Is it possible that the jurisdictional fight really was about whether the case would be tried in state court or federal court in Oklahoma? Professor Lowenfeld reports:

> In the end, the forum shopping calculations of both sides proved accurate. Once the Supreme Court decided that World–Wide and Seaway could not be sued in Oklahoma, the principal defendants * * * removed the case to the U.S. Court for the Northern District of Oklahoma. Following discovery under the federal rules, the case was tried to a jury, which in January 1982 returned a verdict for defendants.

Lowenfeld, Conflict of Laws 565 (1986).

2. As you consider litigation strategy with respect to forum choice, do not lose sight of the human dimension of the lawsuit. At the time the suit was filed, Kay Robinson and her two children, Sam and Eva, were hospitalized with severe burns:

> Since Kay Robinson had been trapped in the burning car the longest, her burns were the most horrible of all. She had burns on forty-eight percent of her body—thirty-five percent of which were third degree. Kay was in the intensive care unit for seventy-seven days and was hospitalized in Tulsa for another several months. She underwent thirty-four operations, all but two of which were under general anesthetic, for skin grafts and other reconstructive surgery. Most of her fingers were amputated, and she had severe scarring over the entire part of her body. Eva and Kay also suffered severe psychological trauma both from the ordeal and from their permanent disfigurement.

See Adams, World-Wide Volkswagen v. Woodson—*The Rest of the Story*, 72 Neb.L.Rev. 1122, 1127 (1993).

3. In the course of its *World–Wide Volkswagen* opinion, the Court employs notions of sovereignty (like those emphasized in *Hanson*) and of convenience (like those emphasized in *McGee*). Is there a tension between these two notions? Is the Court promulgating a two-part test with a "sovereignty branch" and a "convenience branch"? Is this a new test or a refinement of the "minimum contacts" test announced in *International Shoe*?

In INSURANCE CORP. OF IRELAND v. COMPAGNIE DES BAUXITES DE GUINEE, 456 U.S. 694, 102 S.Ct. 2099, 72 L.Ed.2d 492 (1982), Justice White, the author of *World–Wide Volkswagen,* wrote for eight Justices. He described the personal jurisdiction requirement imposed by the Due Process Clause as one that "recognizes and protects an individual liberty interest." His opinion further elaborated this thought in a footnote that expressly addressed his opinion in *World–Wide Volkswagen*:

> It is true that we have stated that the requirement of personal jurisdiction, as applied to state courts, reflects an element of federalism and the character of state sovereignty vis-à-vis other states. [Justice White then quoted from *World–Wide Volkswagen*] * * *. The restriction on state sovereign power described in *World–Wide Volkswagen Corp.*, however, must be seen as ultimately a function of the individual liberty interest preserved by the Due Process Clause. That clause is the only source of the personal jurisdiction requirement and the clause itself makes no mention of federalism concerns. Furthermore, if the federalism concept operated as an independent restriction on the sovereign power of the court, it would not be possible to waive the personal jurisdiction requirement: Individual actions cannot change the powers of sovereignty, although the individual can subject himself to powers from which he may otherwise be protected.

Id. at 702 n.10, 102 S.Ct. at 2104–05 n.10, 72 L.Ed.2d at 501 n.10. Does this footnote transform the "sovereignty branch" of the *World–Wide Volkswagen* test? Is it possible to say that the Court's opinion in *World–Wide Volkswagen* demonstrates that protection of interstate federalism is a reason for including in the test for personal jurisdiction a requirement of pre-litigation contact with the forum, but that the Court's use of its test shows that the protection of federalism is not an independent component of the test? How could a defendant waive the requirement of minimum contacts (as he can) if the protection of federalism created an independent restriction on the power of a court? For thoughtful discussions of this issue, see Stein, *Styles of Argument and Interstate Federalism in the Law of Personal Jurisdiction*, 65 Texas L.Rev. 689, 725 (1987), and Knudsen, Keeton, Calder, Helicopteros *and* Burger King—International Shoe*'s Most Recent Progeny*, 39 U.Miami L.Rev. 809 (1985).

4. How would *World–Wide Volkswagen* have been decided if the Robinsons had been Oklahoma residents and had purchased the ill-fated car while in New York on vacation? Would the Justices in the majority have given more weight to plaintiff's foreseeability argument? What if the driver of the other car sued World–Wide and Seaway for injuries resulting from the exploding gas tank? What if that driver never had been outside the state of Oklahoma?

5. In KEETON v. HUSTLER MAGAZINE, INC., 465 U.S. 770, 104 S.Ct. 1473, 79 L.Ed.2d 790 (1984), Kathy Keeton, a resident of New York, brought a libel suit against Hustler Magazine, an Ohio corporation, in federal court in New Hampshire. Keeton chose the New Hampshire court because New Hampshire was the only state where the action was not time-barred when it was filed. She argued that jurisdiction existed under New Hampshire's long-arm statute because Hustler sold 10,000 to 15,000 magazines a month in the state. Keeton herself had only one connection to New Hampshire: a magazine that she helped to produce was circulated there.

The District Court dismissed Keeton's suit for lack of jurisdiction, and the First Circuit affirmed, holding that Keeton's lack of contacts with New Hampshire rendered the state's interest in redressing the libel to the plaintiff too attenuated to support jurisdiction over a suit necessarily involving nationwide damages. In the Circuit Court's words, "the New Hampshire tail is too small to wag so large an out-of-state dog."

The Supreme Court unanimously reversed, saying:

> [R]egular monthly sales of thousands of magazines cannot by any stretch of the imagination be characterized as random, isolated, or fortuitous. It is, therefore, unquestionable that New Hampshire jurisdiction over a complaint based on those contacts could ordinarily satisfy the requirement of the Due Process Clause that a State's assertion of personal jurisdiction over a nonresident defendant be predicated on "minimum contacts" between the defendant and the State. And, as the Court of Appeals acknowledged, New Hampshire has adopted a "long-arm" statute authorizing service of process on nonresident corporations whenever permitted by the Due Process Clause. Thus, all the requisites for personal jurisdiction over Hustler Magazine, Inc., in New Hampshire are present.

Id. at 774–75, 104 S.Ct. at 1478, 79 L.Ed.2d at 797. Is the key to the Court's decision in *Keeton* that the defendants intentionally acted in the forum? What of Hustler's argument that the plaintiff's contacts with New Hampshire were minimal? Is that argument relevant to the sovereignty branch? Or the convenience branch? In discussing the argument, the Supreme Court said:

> * * * [I]mplicit in the Court of Appeals' analysis of New Hampshire's interest is an emphasis on the extremely limited contacts of the *plaintiff* with New Hampshire. But we have not to date required a plaintiff to have "minimum contacts" with the forum State before permitting that State to assert personal jurisdiction over a nonresident defendant. On the contrary, we have upheld the assertion of jurisdiction where such contacts were entirely lacking. * * *

Id. at 779, 104 S.Ct. at 1480–81, 79 L.Ed.2d at 800. The Court went on to say, however, that "[t]he plaintiff's residence is not, of course, completely irrelevant to the jurisdiction inquiry." The Court noted, for example, that a plaintiff's residence in the forum, because of the defendant's relationship with the plaintiff, may enhance the defendant's forum contacts.

What of the argument that it was unfair to allow suit to be brought in the only state where it was not time-barred? Is that relevant to the jurisdictional inquiry? The Court did not believe that it was:

> * * * [A]ny potential unfairness in applying New Hampshire's statute of limitations to all aspects of this nationwide suit has nothing to do with the jurisdiction of the Court to adjudicate the claims. "The issue is personal jurisdiction, not choice of law." Hanson v. Denckla * * *. The question of the applicability of New Hampshire's statute of limitations to claims for out-of-state damages presents itself in the course of litigation only after jurisdiction over respondent is established, and we do not think that such choice of law concerns should complicate or distort the jurisdictional inquiry.

Id. at 778, 104 S.Ct. at 1480, 79 L.Ed.2d at 800.

6. In determining whether personal jurisdiction may be exercised under the Fourteenth Amendment, what weight ought the court give to an out-of-state defendant's forum contacts that are unrelated to plaintiff's claim? For

example, suppose that World–Wide Volkswagen had maintained an agent in Oklahoma and had advertised there. These contacts with Oklahoma arguably are unrelated to the Robinsons' accident in that state, since they bought their car in New York. Reconsider this question when you reach the discussion of general jurisdiction, p. 138, infra.

KULKO v. SUPERIOR COURT, 436 U.S. 84, 98 S.Ct. 1690, 56 L.Ed.2d 132 (1978), was a suit for modification of a child support agreement by a California citizen against her ex-husband, a New Yorker. The couple's two children lived with their father in New York under the original separation agreement. However, when the daughter told defendant that she wanted to live with her mother, he assented and bought her a one-way plane ticket to California. The other child also joined his mother in California, after receiving a one-way ticket from her, without defendant's knowledge.

The California Supreme Court upheld jurisdiction over the defendant husband under the California long-arm statute, which authorized the exercise of jurisdiction "on any basis not inconsistent with the Constitution." The court concluded that it was "fair and reasonable" for the New York defendant to be subject to personal jurisdiction in California because by purchasing his daughter's airline ticket, he had committed a "purposeful act" outside the state that caused an effect within the state. The United States Supreme Court reversed:

> * * * We cannot accept the proposition that appellant's acquiescence in Ilsa's desire to live with her mother conferred jurisdiction over appellant in the California courts in this action. A father who agrees, in the interests of family harmony and his children's preferences, to allow them to spend more time in California than was required under a separation agreement can hardly be said to have "purposefully availed himself" of the "benefits and protections" of California's laws. * * *
>
> Nor can we agree with the assertion of the court below that the exercise of *in personam* jurisdiction here was warranted by the financial benefit appellant derived from his daughter's presence in California for nine months of the year. * * * [T]his circumstance, even if true, does not support California's assertion of jurisdiction here. Any diminution in appellant's household costs resulted, not from the child's presence in California, but rather from her absence from appellant's home.

Id. at 94–95, 98 S.Ct. at 1698, 56 L.Ed.2d at 142–43.

The Court also noted that the California court's reliance on the "effects" test was misplaced because that approach applies only to wrongful activity without the state causing injury within it or to commercial activity affecting state residents, when that application would not be "unreasonable." Merely causing an effect within the forum state without purposeful availment will not support jurisdiction.

> * * * There is no claim that appellant has visited physical injury on either property or persons within the State of California. The cause of action herein asserted arises, not from the defendant's commercial transactions in interstate commerce, but rather from his personal, domestic relations. * * * Furthermore, the controversy between the parties arises from a separation that occurred in the State of New York * * *.
>
> Finally, basic considerations of fairness point decisively in favor of appellant's State of domicile as the proper forum for adjudication of this case, whatever the merits of appellee's underlying claim. It is appellant who has remained in the State of the marital domicile, whereas it is appellee who has moved across the continent. * * * [Exercising jurisdiction] would impose an unreasonable burden on family relations, and one wholly unjustified by the "quality and nature" of appellant's activities in or relating to the State of California. * * *

Id. at 96–98, 98 S.Ct. at 1699–1700, 56 L.Ed.2d at 144–45.

NOTES AND QUESTIONS

1. The Court considered the "effects" test in CALDER v. JONES, 465 U.S. 783, 104 S.Ct. 1482, 79 L.Ed.2d 804 (1984). Shirley Jones, an actress who lived and worked in California, brought suit in California Superior Court, claiming that she had been libeled in an article published in the National Enquirer, a national magazine having its largest circulation in California. The plaintiff sued the writer and editor of the article, both residents of Florida, as well as the magazine. The writer and the editor moved to quash service of process for lack of personal jurisdiction, and the Superior Court granted the motion on the ground that First Amendment concerns weighed against an assertion of jurisdiction otherwise proper under the Due Process Clause. Ultimately, the United States Supreme Court disagreed, explaining:

> The allegedly libelous story concerned the California activities of a California resident. It impugned the professionalism of an entertainer whose television career was centered in California. The article was drawn from California sources, and the brunt of the harm, in terms both of respondent's emotional distress and the injury to her professional reputation, was suffered in California. In sum, California, is the focal point both of the story and of the harm suffered. Jurisdiction over petitioners is therefore proper in California based on the "effects" of their Florida conduct in California.

Id. at 788–89, 104 S.Ct. at 1486–87, 79 L.Ed.2d at 812. Given that the writer and editor had acted intentionally to produce an article for dissemination in California, the Court had no trouble finding that they could foresee being haled into court there. In addition, the Court rejected any role for the First Amendment in the jurisdictional analysis: "The infusion of such concerns would needlessly complicate an already imprecise inquiry." Id. at 789, 104 S.Ct. at 1487–88, 79 L.Ed.2d at 813. That same term the Court underscored this approach in KEETON v. HUSTLER MAGAZINE, INC., 465 U.S. 770, 780 n.12, 104 S.Ct. 1473, 1481 n.12, 79 L.Ed.2d 790, 801 n.12 (1984) ("[W]e reject categorically the suggestion that invisible radiations from the First Amendment may defeat jurisdiction otherwise proper under the Due Process Clause."). See Note 5, p. 115, supra.

2. Can you reconcile the "effects" test with the requirement of purposeful availment as elaborated in *World-Wide Volkswagen*? In HARRIS RUTSKY & CO. INSURANCE SERVICES, INC. v. BELL & CLEMENTS LTD., 328 F.3d 1122 (9th Cir.2003), a California insurance broker sued an England-based insurance broker and its parent company alleging that defendants had interfered with plaintiff's business opportunities through activity done outside the forum state. In assessing whether defendants had purposefully availed themselves of the benefits of California law, the Ninth Circuit applied a three-prong "effects" test, under which purposeful availment may be present "if the defendant is alleged to have (1) committed an intentional act; (2) expressly aimed at the forum state; (3) causing harm, the brunt of which is suffered—and which the defendant knows is likely to be suffered—in the forum state." See 4 Wright & Miller, Federal Practice and Procedure: Civil 3d § 1067.1 (explaining that the effects test "continues to have viability, but only when the defendant's conduct both has an effect in the forum state and was directed at the forum state by the defendant * * * ").

BURGER KING CORP. v. RUDZEWICZ

Supreme Court of the United States, 1985.
471 U.S. 462, 105 S.Ct. 2174, 85 L.Ed.2d 528.

[Burger King is a Florida corporation whose principal offices are in Miami. Franchisees are licensed to use its trademarks and service marks in leased standardized restaurant facilities for a period of twenty years. The governing contracts provide that the franchise relationship is established in Miami and governed by Florida law, and call for payment of all required monthly fees and forwarding of all relevant notices to the Miami headquarters. The Miami headquarters sets policy and works directly with the franchisees in attempting to resolve major problems. Day-to-day monitoring of franchisees, however, is conducted through district offices that in turn report to the Miami headquarters. John Rudzewicz is a Michigan resident who, along with another Michigan resident (Brian MacShara), entered into a twenty-year franchise contract with Burger King to operate a restaurant in Michigan. Subsequently, when the restaurant's patronage declined, the franchisees fell behind in their monthly payments. Burger King then brought a diversity action in federal District Court in Florida, alleging that the franchisees had breached their franchise obligations and requesting damages and injunctive relief. The franchisees claimed that, because they were Michigan residents and because Burger King's claim did not "arise" within Florida, the District Court lacked personal jurisdiction over them. But the court held that the franchisees were subject to personal jurisdiction pursuant to Florida's long-arm statute, which extends jurisdiction to any person, whether or not a citizen or resident of the State, who breaches a contract in the State by failing to perform acts that the contract requires to be performed there. Thereafter, the court entered judgment against the franchisees on the merits. The Court of Appeals reversed, holding that "[j]urisdiction under these circumstances would offend the fundamental fairness which is the touchstone of due process," but the Supreme Court disagreed.]

Appeal from the United States Court of Appeals for the Eleventh Circuit.

JUSTICE BRENNAN delivered the opinion of the Court.

[After a lengthy presentation of the facts, Justice Brennan began Part II of his opinion by rehearsing the basic jurisdictional rules. In that context, he turned to the requirement that the defendant "purposefully direct" his activity toward the forum state.]

* * *

We have noted several reasons why a forum legitimately may exercise personal jurisdiction over a nonresident who "purposefully directs" his activities toward forum residents. A State generally has a "manifest interest" in providing its residents with a convenient forum for redressing injuries inflicted by out-of-state actors. * * * Moreover, where individuals "purposefully derive benefit" from their interstate activities, * * * it may well be unfair to allow them to escape having to account in other States for consequences that arise proximately from such activities; the Due Process Clause may not readily be wielded as a territorial shield to avoid interstate obligations that have been voluntarily assumed. And because "modern transportation and communications have made it much less burdensome for a party sued to defend himself in a State where he engages in economic activity," it usually will not be unfair to subject him to the burdens of litigating in another forum for disputes relating to such activity. McGee v. International Life Insurance Co., * * * [p. 100, supra].

Notwithstanding these considerations, the constitutional touchstone remains whether the defendant purposefully established "minimum contacts" in the forum State. * * * Although it has been argued that foreseeability of causing *injury* in another State should be sufficient to establish such contacts there when policy considerations so require, the Court has consistently held that this kind of foreseeability is not a "sufficient benchmark" for exercising personal jurisdiction. * * * Instead, "the foreseeability that is critical to due process analysis * * * is that the defendant's conduct and connection with the forum State are such that he should reasonably anticipate being haled into court there." * * *

This "purposeful availment" requirement ensures that a defendant will not be haled into a jurisdiction solely as a result of "random," "fortuitous," or "attenuated" contacts, * * * or of the "unilateral activity of another party or a third person" * * *. Jurisdiction is proper, however, where the contacts proximately result from actions by the defendant *himself* that create a "substantial connection" with the forum State. * * * Thus where the defendant "deliberately" has engaged in significant activities within a State, * * * or has created "continuing obligations" between himself and residents of the forum, * * * he manifestly has availed himself of the privilege of conducting business there, and because his activities are shielded by "the benefits and protections" of the forum's laws it is presumptively not unreasonable to require him to submit to the burdens of litigation in that forum as well. * * *

Once it has been decided that a defendant purposefully established minimum contacts within the forum State, these contacts may be considered in light of other factors to determine whether the assertion of personal jurisdiction would comport with "fair play and substantial justice." * * * Thus courts in "appropriate case[s]" may evaluate "the burden on the defendant," "the forum State's interest in adjudicating the dispute," "the plaintiff's interest in obtaining convenient and effective relief," "the interstate judicial system's interest in obtaining the most efficient resolution of controversies," and the "shared interest of the several States in furthering fundamental substantive social policies." * * * These considerations sometimes serve to establish the reasonableness of jurisdiction upon a lesser showing of minimum contacts than would otherwise be required. * * * On the other hand, where a defendant who purposefully has directed his activities at forum residents seeks to defeat jurisdiction, he must present a compelling case that the presence of some other considerations would render jurisdiction unreasonable. Most such considerations usually may be accommodated through means short of finding jurisdiction unconstitutional. For example, the potential clash of the forum's law with the "fundamental substantive social policies" of another State may be accommodated through application of the forum's choice-of-law rules. Similarly, a defendant claiming substantial inconvenience may seek a change of venue. Nevertheless, minimum requirements inherent in the concept of "fair play and substantial justice" may defeat the reasonableness of jurisdiction even if the defendant has purposefully engaged in forum activities. * * * As we previously have noted, jurisdictional rules may not be employed in such a way as to make litigation "so gravely difficult and inconvenient" that a party unfairly is at a "severe disadvantage" in comparison to his opponent. * * *

B

(1)

Applying these principles to the case at hand, we believe there is substantial record evidence supporting the District Court's conclusion that the assertion of personal jurisdiction over Rudzewicz in Florida for the alleged breach of his franchise agreement did not offend due process. At the outset, we note a continued division among lower courts respecting whether and to what extent a contract can constitute a "contact" for purposes of due process analysis. If the question is whether an individual's contract with an out-of-state party *alone* can automatically establish sufficient minimum contacts in the other party's home forum, we believe the answer clearly is that it cannot. The Court long ago rejected the notion that personal jurisdiction might turn on "mechanical" tests, or on "conceptualistic * * * theories of the place of contracting or of performance" * * *. Instead, we have emphasized the need for a "highly realistic" approach that recognizes that a "contract" is "ordinarily but an intermediate step serving to tie up prior business negotiations with future consequences which themselves are the real object of the business transaction." * * * It is these factors—prior negotiations and contemplated future consequences, along with the terms of the contract and the parties' actual course of dealing—that must be evaluated in determining whether the defendant purposefully established minimum contacts within the forum.

In this case, no physical ties to Florida can be attributed to Rudzewicz other than MacShara's brief training course in Miami.[22] Rudzewicz did not maintain offices in Florida and, for all that appears from the record, has never even visited there. Yet this franchise dispute grew directly out of "a contract which had a *substantial* connection with that State." McGee v. International Life Insurance Co. * * *. Eschewing the option of operating an independent local enterprise, Rudzewicz deliberately "reach[ed] out beyond" Michigan and negotiated with a Florida corporation for the purchase of a long-term franchise and the manifold benefits that would derive from affiliation with a nationwide organization. * * * Upon approval, he entered into a carefully structured 20-year relationship that envisioned continuing and wide-reaching contacts with Burger King in Florida. In light of Rudzewicz's voluntary acceptance of the long-term and exacting regulation of his business from Burger King's Miami headquarters, the "quality and nature" of his relationship to the company in Florida can in no sense be viewed as "random," "fortuitous," or "attenuated." * * * Rudzewicz's refusal to make the contractually required payments in Miami, and his continued use of Burger King's trademarks and confidential business information after his termination, caused foreseeable injuries to the corporation in Florida. For these reasons it was, at the very least, presumptively reasonable for Rudzewicz to be called to account there for such injuries.

The Court of Appeals concluded, however, that in light of the supervision emanating from Burger King's district office in Birmingham [Michi-

---

22. The Eleventh Circuit held that MacShara's presence in Florida was irrelevant to the question of Rudzewicz's minimum contacts with that forum, reasoning that "Rudzewicz and MacShara never formed a partnership" and "signed the agreements in their individual capacities." * * * The two did jointly form a corporation through which they were seeking to conduct the franchise, however. * * * They were required to decide which one of them would travel to Florida to satisfy the training requirements so that they could commence business, and Rudzewicz participated in the decision that MacShara would go there. We have previously noted that when commercial activities are "carried on in behalf of" an out-of-state party those activities may sometimes be ascribed to the party, * * * at least where he is a "primary participan[t]" in the enterprise and has acted purposefully in directing those activities. * * * Because MacShara's matriculation at Burger King University is not pivotal to the disposition of this case, we need not resolve the permissible bounds of such attribution.

gan], Rudzewicz reasonably believed that "the Michigan office was for all intents and purposes the embodiment of Burger King" and that he therefore had no "reason to anticipate a Burger King suit outside of Michigan." * * * This reasoning overlooks substantial record evidence indicating that Rudzewicz most certainly knew that he was affiliating himself with an enterprise based primarily in Florida. The contract documents themselves emphasize that Burger King's operations are conducted and supervised from the Miami headquarters, that all relevant notices and payments must be sent there, and that the agreements were made in and enforced from Miami. * * * Moreover, the parties' actual course of dealing repeatedly confirmed that decisionmaking authority was vested in the Miami headquarters and that the district office served largely as an intermediate link between the headquarters and the franchisees. When problems arose over building design, site development fees, rent computation, and the defaulted payments, Rudzewicz and MacShara learned that the Michigan office was powerless to resolve their disputes and could only channel their communications to Miami. Throughout these disputes, the Miami headquarters and the Michigan franchisees carried on a continuous course of direct communications by mail and by telephone, and it was the Miami headquarters that made the key negotiating decisions out of which the instant litigation arose.

Moreover, we believe the Court of Appeals gave insufficient weight to provisions in the various franchise documents providing that all disputes would be governed by Florida law. The franchise agreement, for example, stated:

> This Agreement shall become valid when executed and accepted by BKC at Miami, Florida, it shall be deemed made and entered into in the State of Florida and shall be governed and construed under and in accordance with the laws of the State of Florida. The choice of law designation does not require that all suits concerning this Agreement be filed in Florida.

* * * The Court of Appeals reasoned that choice-of-law provisions are irrelevant to the question of personal jurisdiction, relying on Hanson v. Denckla for the proposition that "the center of gravity for choice-of-law purposes does not necessarily confer the sovereign prerogative to assert jurisdiction." * * * This reasoning misperceives the import of the quoted proposition. The Court in *Hanson* and subsequent cases has emphasized that choice-of-law *analysis*—which focuses on all elements of a transaction, and not simply on the defendant's conduct—is distinct from minimum-contacts jurisdictional analysis—which focuses at the threshold solely on the defendant's purposeful connection to the forum. Nothing in our cases, however, suggests that a choice-of-law *provision* should be ignored in considering whether a defendant has "purposefully invoked the benefits and protections of a State's laws" for jurisdictional purposes. Although such a provision standing alone would be insufficient to confer jurisdiction, we believe that, when combined with the 20-year interdependent relationship Rudzewicz established with Burger King's Miami headquar-

ters, it reinforced his deliberate affiliation with the forum State and the reasonable foreseeability of possible litigation there. * * * Rudzewicz "purposefully availed himself of the benefits and protections of Florida's laws" by entering into contracts expressly providing that those laws would govern franchise disputes. * * *

(2)

Nor has Rudzewicz pointed to other factors that can be said persuasively to outweigh the considerations discussed above and to establish the *unconstitutionality* of Florida's assertion of jurisdiction. We cannot conclude that Florida had no "legitimate interest in holding [Rudzewicz] answerable on a claim related to" the contacts he had established in that State. [See] McGee v. International Life Insurance Co. * * * (noting that the State frequently will have a "manifest interest in providing effective means of redress for its residents").[25] Moreover, although Rudzewicz has argued at some length that Michigan's Franchise Investment Law * * * governs many aspects of this franchise relationship, he has not demonstrated how Michigan's acknowledged interest might possibly render jurisdiction in Florida *unconstitutional.*[26] Finally, the Court of Appeals' assertion that the Florida litigation "severely impaired [Rudzewicz's] ability to call Michigan witnesses who might be essential to his defense and counterclaim" * * * is wholly without support in the record. And even to the extent that it is inconvenient for a party who has minimum contacts with a forum to litigate there, such considerations most frequently can be accommodated through a change of venue. * * * Although the Court has suggested that inconvenience may at some point become so substantial as to achieve *constitutional* magnitude, McGee v. International Life Insurance Co., * * * this is not such a case.

The Court of Appeals also concluded, however, that the parties' dealings involved "a characteristic disparity of bargaining power" and "elements of surprise," and that Rudzewicz "lacked fair notice" of the potential for litigation in Florida because the contractual provisions suggesting to the contrary were merely "boilerplate declarations in a lengthy printed contract." * * * Rudzewicz presented many of these arguments to the District Court, contending that Burger King was guilty of misrepresentation, fraud, and duress; that it gave insufficient notice in its dealings with him; and that the contract was one of adhesion. * * * After a 3–day

25. Complaining that "when Burger King is the plaintiff, you won't 'have it your way' because it sues all franchisees in Miami," * * * Rudzewicz contends that Florida's interest in providing a convenient forum is negligible given the company's size and ability to conduct litigation anywhere in the country. We disagree. Absent compelling considerations, cf. McGee v. International Life Insurance Co., * * * a defendant who has purposefully derived commercial benefit from his affiliations in a forum may not defeat jurisdiction there simply because of his adversary's greater net wealth.

26. Rudzewicz has failed to show how the District Court's exercise of jurisdiction in this case might have been at all inconsistent with Michigan's interests. * * * In any event, minimum-contacts analysis presupposes that two or more States may be interested in the outcome of a dispute, and the process of resolving potentially conflicting "fundamental substantive social policies" * * * can usually be accommodated through choice-of-law rules rather than through outright preclusion of jurisdiction in one forum. * * *

bench trial, the District Court found that Burger King had made no misrepresentations, that Rudzewicz and MacShara "were and are experienced and sophisticated businessmen," and that "at no time" did they "ac[t] under economic duress or disadvantage imposed by" Burger King. * * * Federal Rule of Civil Procedure 52(a) [now Rule 52(a)(6)] requires that "[f]indings of fact shall not be set aside unless clearly erroneous," and neither Rudzewicz nor the Court of Appeals have pointed to record evidence that would support a "definite and firm conviction" that the District Court's findings are mistaken. * * *

III

Notwithstanding these considerations, the Court of Appeals apparently believed that it was necessary to reject jurisdiction in this case as a prophylactic measure, reasoning that an affirmance of the District Court's judgment would result in the exercise of jurisdiction over "out-of-state consumers to collect payments due on modest personal purchases" and would "sow the seeds of default judgments against franchisees owing smaller debts." * * * We share the Court of Appeals' broader concerns and therefore reject any talismanic jurisdictional formulas; "the facts of each case must [always] be weighed" in determining whether personal jurisdiction would comport with "fair play and substantial justice." * * * The "quality and nature" of an interstate transaction may sometimes be so "random," "fortuitous," or "attenuated" that it cannot fairly be said that the potential defendant "should reasonably anticipate being haled into court" in another jurisdiction. * * * We also have emphasized that jurisdiction may not be grounded on a contract whose terms have been obtained through "fraud, undue influence, or overweening bargaining power" and whose application would render litigation "so gravely difficult and inconvenient that [a party] will for all practical purposes be deprived of his day in court." * * * Just as the Due Process Clause allows flexibility in ensuring that commercial actors are not effectively "judgment proof" for the consequences of obligations they voluntarily assume in other States, McGee v. International Life Insurance Co., * * * so too does it prevent rules that would unfairly enable them to obtain default judgments against unwitting customers. * * *

For the reasons set forth above, however, these dangers are not present in the instant case. Because Rudzewicz established a substantial and continuing relationship with Burger King's Miami headquarters, received fair notice from the contract documents and the course of dealing that he might be subject to suit in Florida, and has failed to demonstrate how jurisdiction in that forum would otherwise be fundamentally unfair, we conclude that the District Court's exercise of jurisdiction * * * did not offend due process. The judgment of the Court of Appeals is accordingly reversed, and the case is remanded for further proceedings consistent with this opinion.

JUSTICE POWELL took no part in the consideration or decision of this case.

JUSTICE STEVENS, with whom JUSTICE WHITE joins, dissenting.

In my opinion there is a significant element of unfairness in requiring a franchisee to defend a case of this kind in the forum chosen by the franchisor. It is undisputed that respondent maintained no place of business in Florida, that he had no employees in that State, and that he was not licensed to do business there. Respondent did not prepare his french fries, shakes, and hamburgers in Michigan, and then deliver them into the stream of commerce "with the expectation that they [would] be purchased by consumers in" Florida. * * * To the contrary, respondent did business only in Michigan, his business, property, and payroll taxes were payable in that State, and he sold all of his products there.

Throughout the business relationship, respondent's principal contacts with petitioner were with its Michigan office. Notwithstanding its disclaimer, * * * the Court seems ultimately to rely on nothing more than standard boilerplate language contained in various documents * * * to establish that respondent " 'purposefully availed himself of the benefits and protections of Florida's laws.' " * * * Such superficial analysis creates a potential for unfairness not only in negotiations between franchisors and their franchisees but, more significantly, in the resolution of the disputes that inevitably arise from time to time in such relationships.

JUDGE VANCE'S opinion for the Court of Appeals for the Eleventh Circuit adequately explains why I would affirm the judgment of that court. I particularly find the following more persuasive than what this Court has written today:

> "Nothing in the course of negotiations gave Rudzewicz reason to anticipate a Burger King suit outside of Michigan. The only face-to-face or even oral contact Rudzewicz had with Burger King throughout months of protracted negotiations was with representatives of the Michigan office. Burger King had the Michigan office interview Rudzewicz and MacShara, appraise their application, discuss price terms, recommend the site which the defendants finally agreed to, and attend the final closing ceremony. There is no evidence that Rudzewicz ever negotiated with anyone in Miami or even sent mail there during negotiations. He maintained no staff in the state of Florida, and as far as the record reveals, he has never even visited the state.
>
> "The contracts contemplated the startup of a local Michigan restaurant whose profits would derive solely from food sales made to customers in Drayton Plains. The sale, which involved the use of an intangible trademark in Michigan and occupancy of a Burger King facility there, required no performance in the state of Florida. Under the contract, the local Michigan district office was responsible for providing all of the services due Rudzewicz, including advertising and management consultation. Supervision, moreover, emanated from that office alone. To Rudzewicz, the Michigan office was for all intents and purposes the embodiment of Burger King. He had reason to believe that his working relationship with Burger King began and

ended in Michigan, not at the distant and anonymous Florida headquarters. * * *

"Given that the office in Rudzewicz' home state conducted all of the negotiations and wholly supervised the contract, we believe that he had reason to assume that the state of the supervisory office would be the same state in which Burger King would file suit. Rudzewicz lacked fair notice that the distant corporate headquarters which insulated itself from direct dealings with him would later seek to assert jurisdiction over him in the courts of its own home state. * * *

"Just as Rudzewicz lacked notice of the possibility of suit in Florida, he was financially unprepared to meet its added costs. The franchise relationship in particular is fraught with potential for financial surprise. The device of the franchise gives local retailers the access to national trademark recognition which enables them to compete with better-financed, more efficient chain stores. This national affiliation, however, does not alter the fact that the typical franchise store is a local concern serving at best a neighborhood or community. Neither the revenues of a local business nor the geographical range of its market prepares the average franchise owner for the cost of distant litigation. * * *

"The particular distribution of bargaining power in the franchise relationship further impairs the franchisee's financial preparedness. In a franchise contract, 'the franchisor normally occupies [the] dominant role'. . . .

"We discern a characteristic disparity of bargaining power in the facts of this case. There is no indication that Rudzewicz had any latitude to negotiate a reduced rent or franchise fee in exchange for the added risk of suit in Florida. He signed a standard form contract whose terms were non-negotiable and which appeared in some respects to vary from the more favorable terms agreed to in earlier discussions. In fact, the final contract required a minimum monthly rent computed on a base far in excess of that discussed in oral negotiations. Burger King resisted price concessions, only to sue Rudzewicz far from home. In doing so, it severely impaired his ability to call Michigan witnesses who might be essential to his defense and counterclaim.

"In sum, we hold that the circumstances of the Drayton Plains franchise and the negotiations which led to it left Rudzewicz bereft of reasonable notice and financially unprepared for the prospect of franchise litigation in Florida. Jurisdiction under these circumstances would offend the fundamental fairness which is the touchstone of due process. * * *"

Accordingly, I respectfully dissent.

NOTES AND QUESTIONS

1. Is the Supreme Court's decision in *Burger King* consistent with its decision in *World–Wide Volkswagen?* In what way were Rudzewicz's contacts with Florida quantitatively or qualitatively different from Seaway's contacts with Oklahoma? Which measuring rod should be more important?

2. The First Circuit has described the Supreme Court's decision in *Burger King* as mandating a "contract-plus" analysis: "[A] court is to look at all of the communications and transactions between the parties, before, during and after the consummation of the contract, to determine the degree and type of contacts the defendant has with the forum, apart from the contract alone." Ganis Corp. of California v. Jackson, 822 F.2d 194, 197–98 (1st Cir.1987). What purpose is served by this "plus" analysis? Is it constitutionally compelled? Does the relative bargaining position of the parties affect your answer to this question?

3. How important to the decision in *Burger King* was the inclusion of the choice-of-law provision in the franchise agreement? Is that type of provision appropriately considered a "contact" with the chosen forum? Is it a "plus" factor? What if the forum has no interest in the contract other than the parties' agreement to be bound by the law of that state?

4. Before *Burger King*, some courts had concluded that a single sale contract could be sufficient to support long-arm jurisdiction (usually under a "transaction of business" provision) over a nonresident seller. For example, in ALCHEMIE INTERNATIONAL, INC. v. METAL WORLD, INC., 523 F.Supp. 1039, 1050 (D.N.J.1981), the court upheld jurisdiction over the defendant, even though Metal World maintained no office in New Jersey and had sent no personnel into the state; it was enough that Metal World, by numerous mail and telephone contacts had solicited a substantial contract with Alchemie, a New Jersey corporation, even assuming that the contract was executed in Illinois. The goods never entered New Jersey; and there was no evidence indicating the parties anticipated that the goods were to be taken into New Jersey. Nor was there any evidence of other contacts with the forum unrelated to the contract at issue. Nonetheless, the district judge ruled that the assertion of jurisdiction was consistent with due process.

> I see little to distinguish a corporation's using the telephone and mail to solicit or negotiate a contract the size of that at issue here from that same corporation sending an agent into the state in pursuit of the identical contract from the identical buyer. * * * Indeed, a refusal to acknowledge the fashion in which modern business is conducted and the increasingly dominant role played in that conduct by mail and telephone communications is as much a return to the shibboleths of Pennoyer v. Neff, * * * long abandoned by the Court, * * * and the "magical and medieval concepts of presence and power" that typified that era as would resurrection of the notion that a defendant must be present within the territorial jurisdiction of a court before its judgment will bind him. I therefore count defendant's calls and mail communications to plaintiff as significant contacts with the State of New Jersey.

Other courts, however, have declined to exercise jurisdiction in these circumstances. See, e.g., CPC–Rexcell, Inc. v. La Corona Foods, Inc., 912 F.2d 241 (8th Cir.1990).

ASAHI METAL INDUSTRY CO. v. SUPERIOR COURT

Supreme Court of the United States, 1987.
480 U.S. 102, 107 S.Ct. 1026, 94 L.Ed.2d 92.

Certiorari to the Supreme Court of California.

JUSTICE O'CONNOR announced the judgment of the Court and delivered the unanimous opinion of the Court with respect to Part I, the opinion of the Court with respect to Part II–B, in which THE CHIEF JUSTICE, JUSTICE BRENNAN, JUSTICE WHITE, JUSTICE MARSHALL, JUSTICE BLACKMUN, JUSTICE POWELL, and JUSTICE STEVENS join, and an opinion with respect to Parts II–A and III, in which THE CHIEF JUSTICE, JUSTICE POWELL, and JUSTICE SCALIA join.

This case presents the question whether the mere awareness on the part of a foreign defendant that the component it manufactured, sold, and delivered outside the United States would reach the forum state in the stream of commerce constitutes "minimum contacts" between the defendant and the forum state such that the exercise of jurisdiction "does not offend 'traditional notions of fair play and substantial justice.' " * * *

I

On September 23, 1978, on Interstate Highway 80 in Solano County, California, Gary Zurcher lost control of his Honda motorcycle and collided with a tractor. Zurcher was severely injured, and his passenger and wife, Ruth Ann Moreno, was killed. In September 1979, Zurcher filed a product liability action in the Superior Court of the State of California in and for the County of Solano. Zurcher alleged that the 1978 accident was caused by a sudden loss of air and an explosion in the rear tire of the motorcycle, and alleged that the motorcycle tire, tube, and sealant were defective. Zurcher's complaint named, *inter alia,* Cheng Shin Rubber Industrial Co., Ltd. (Cheng Shin), the Taiwanese manufacturer of the tube. Cheng Shin in turn filed a cross-complaint seeking indemnification from its codefendants and from petitioner, Asahi Metal Industry Co., Ltd. (Asahi), the manufacturer of the tube's valve assembly. Zurcher's claims against Cheng Shin and the other defendants were eventually settled and dismissed, leaving only Cheng Shin's indemnity action against Asahi.

California's long-arm statute authorizes the exercise of jurisdiction "on any basis not inconsistent with the Constitution of this state or of the United States." * * * Asahi moved to quash Cheng Shin's service of summons arguing the State could not exert jurisdiction over it consistent with the Due Process Clause of the Fourteenth Amendment.

In relation to the motion, the following information was submitted by Asahi and Cheng Shin. Asahi is a Japanese corporation. It manufactures tire valve assemblies in Japan and sells the assemblies to Cheng Shin, and to several other tire manufacturers, for use as components in finished tire tubes. Asahi's sales to Cheng Shin took place in Taiwan. The shipments from Asahi to Cheng Shin were sent from Japan to Taiwan. Cheng Shin bought and incorporated into its tire tubes 150,000 Asahi valve assemblies in 1978; 500,000 in 1979; 500,000 in 1980; 100,000 in 1981; and 100,000 in 1982. Sales to Cheng Shin accounted for 1.24 percent of Asahi's income in 1981 and 0.44 percent in 1982. Cheng Shin alleged that approximately 20 percent of its sales in the United States are in California. Cheng Shin purchases valve assemblies from other suppliers as well, and sells finished tubes throughout the world.

In 1983 an attorney for Cheng Shin conducted an informal examination of the valve stems of the tire tubes sold in one cyclery in Solano County. The attorney declared that of the approximately 115 tire tubes in the store, 97 were purportedly manufactured in Japan or Taiwan, and of those 97, 21 valve stems were marked with the circled letter "A", apparently Asahi's trademark. Of the 21 Asahi valve stems, 12 were incorporated into Cheng Shin tire tubes. The store contained 41 other Cheng Shin tubes that incorporated the valve assemblies of other manufacturers. * * * An affidavit of a manager of Cheng Shin whose duties included the purchasing of component parts stated: " 'In discussions with Asahi regarding the purchase of valve stem assemblies the fact that my Company sells tubes throughout the world and specifically the United States has been discussed. I am informed and believe that Asahi was fully aware that valve stem assemblies sold to my Company and to others would end up throughout the United States and in California.' " * * * An affidavit of the president of Asahi, on the other hand, declared that Asahi " 'has never contemplated that its limited sales of tire valves to Cheng Shin in Taiwan would subject it to lawsuits in California.' " * * * The record does not include any contract between Cheng Shin and Asahi. * * *

Primarily on the basis of the above information, the Superior Court denied the motion to quash summons, stating that "Asahi obviously does business on an international scale. It is not unreasonable that they defend claims of defect in their product on an international scale." Order Denying Motion to Quash Summons * * *.

The Court of Appeal of the State of California issued a peremptory writ of mandate commanding the Superior Court to quash service of summons. The court concluded that "it would be unreasonable to require Asahi to respond in California solely on the basis of ultimately realized foreseeability that the product into which its component was embodied would be sold all over the world including California." * * *

The Supreme Court of the State of California reversed and discharged the writ issued by the Court of Appeal. * * * The court observed that

"Asahi has no offices, property or agents in California. It solicits no business in California and has made no direct sales [in California]." * * * Moreover, "Asahi did not design or control the system of distribution that carried its valve assemblies into California." * * * Nevertheless, the court found the exercise of jurisdiction over Asahi to be consistent with the Due Process Clause. It concluded that Asahi knew that some of the valve assemblies sold to Cheng Shin would be incorporated into tire tubes sold in California, and that Asahi benefited indirectly from the sale in California of products incorporating its components. The court considered Asahi's intentional act of placing its components into the stream of commerce—that is, by delivering the components to Cheng Shin in Taiwan—coupled with Asahi's awareness that some of the components would eventually find their way into California, sufficient to form the basis for state court jurisdiction under the Due Process Clause.

We granted certiorari * * * and now reverse.

II

A

* * *

Applying the principle that minimum contacts must be based on an act of the defendant, the Court in World–Wide Volkswagen Corp. v. Woodson * * * rejected the assertion that a *consumer's* unilateral act of bringing the defendant's product into the forum State was a sufficient constitutional basis for personal jurisdiction over the defendant. It had been argued in *World–Wide Volkswagen* that because an automobile retailer and its wholesale distributor sold a product mobile by design and purpose, they could foresee being haled into court in the distant States into which their customers might drive. The Court rejected this concept of foreseeability as an insufficient basis for jurisdiction under the Due Process Clause. * * * The Court disclaimed, however, the idea that "foreseeability is wholly irrelevant" to personal jurisdiction, concluding that "[t]he forum State does not exceed its powers under the Due Process Clause if it asserts personal jurisdiction over a corporation that delivers its products into the stream of commerce with the expectation that they will be purchased by consumers in the forum State." * * *

* * *

In *World–Wide Volkswagen* itself, the state court sought to base jurisdiction not on any act of the defendant, but on the foreseeable unilateral actions of the consumer. Since *World–Wide Volkswagen,* lower courts have been confronted with cases in which the defendant acted by placing a product in the stream of commerce, and the stream eventually swept defendant's product into the forum State, but the defendant did nothing else to purposefully avail itself of the market in the forum state. Some courts have understood the Due Process Clause, as interpreted in *World–Wide Volkswagen,* to allow an exercise of personal jurisdiction to be based on no more than the defendant's act of placing the product in the stream of commerce. Other courts have understood the Due Process Clause and the above-quoted language in *World–Wide Volkswagen* to require the action of the defendant to be more purposefully directed at the forum State than the mere act of placing a product in the stream of commerce.

The reasoning of the Supreme Court of California in the present case illustrates the former interpretation of *World–Wide Volkswagen.* The Supreme Court of California held that, because the stream of commerce eventually brought some valves Asahi sold Cheng Shin into California, Asahi's awareness that its valves would be sold in California was sufficient to permit California to exercise jurisdiction over Asahi consistent with the requirements of the Due Process Clause. The Supreme Court of California's position was consistent with those courts that have held that mere foreseeability or awareness was a constitutionally sufficient basis for personal jurisdiction if the defendant's product made its way into the forum State while still in the stream of commerce. * * *

Other courts, however, have understood the Due Process Clause to require something more than that the defendant was aware of its product's entry into the forum State through the stream of commerce in order for the state to exert jurisdiction over the defendant. In the present case, for example, the State Court of Appeal did not read the Due Process Clause, as interpreted by *World–Wide Volkswagen,* to allow "mere foreseeability that the product will enter the forum state [to] be enough by itself to establish jurisdiction over the distributor and retailer." * * *

We now find this latter position to be consonant with the requirements of due process. The "substantial connection" * * * between the defendant and the forum State necessary for a finding of minimum contacts must come about by *an action of the defendant purposefully directed toward the forum State.* * * * The placement of a product into the stream of commerce, without more, is not an act of the defendant purposefully directed toward the forum State. Additional conduct of the defendant may indicate an intent or purpose to serve the market in the forum State, for example, designing the product for the market in the forum State, advertising in the forum State, establishing channels for providing regular advice to customers in the forum State, or marketing the product through a distributor who has agreed to serve as the sales agent in the forum State. But a defendant's awareness that the stream of commerce may or will sweep the product into the forum State does not convert the mere act of placing the product into the stream into an act purposefully directed toward the forum State.

Assuming, *arguendo,* that respondents have established Asahi's awareness that some of the valves sold to Cheng Shin would be incorporated into tire tubes sold in California, respondents have not demonstrated any action by Asahi to purposefully avail itself of the California market. Asahi does not do business in California. It has no office, agents, employees, or property in California. It does not advertise or otherwise solicit business in California. It did not create, control, or employ the distribution system that brought its valves to California. * * * There is no evidence that Asahi designed its product in anticipation of sales in California. * * * On the basis of these facts, the exertion of personal jurisdiction over Asahi by the Superior Court of California exceeds the limits of due process.

B

* * *

We have previously explained that the determination of the reasonableness of the exercise of jurisdiction in each case will depend on an evaluation of several factors. A court must consider the burden on the defendant, the interests of the forum state, and the plaintiff's interest in obtaining relief. It must also weigh in its determination "the interstate judicial system's interest in obtaining the most efficient resolution of controversies; and the shared interest of the several States in furthering fundamental substantive social policies." * * *

A consideration of these factors in the present case clearly reveals the unreasonableness of the assertion of jurisdiction over Asahi, even apart from the question of the placement of goods in the stream of commerce.

Certainly the burden on the defendant in this case is severe. Asahi has been commanded by the Supreme Court of California not only to traverse the distance between Asahi's headquarters in Japan and the Superior Court of California in and for the County of Solano, but also to submit its dispute with Cheng Shin to a foreign nation's judicial system. The unique burdens placed upon one who must defend oneself in a foreign legal system should have significant weight in assessing the reasonableness of stretching the long arm of personal jurisdiction over national borders.

When minimum contacts have been established, often the interests of the plaintiff and the forum in the exercise of jurisdiction will justify even the serious burdens placed on the alien defendant. In the present case, however, the interests of the plaintiff and the forum in California's assertion of jurisdiction over Asahi are slight. All that remains is a claim for indemnification asserted by Cheng Shin, a Taiwanese corporation, against Asahi. The transaction on which the indemnification claim is based took place in Taiwan; Asahi's components were shipped from Japan to Taiwan. Cheng Shin has not demonstrated that it is more convenient for it to litigate its indemnification claim against Asahi in California rather than in Taiwan or Japan.

Because the plaintiff is not a California resident, California's legitimate interests in the dispute have considerably diminished. The Supreme Court of California argued that the State had an interest in "protecting its consumers by ensuring that foreign manufacturers comply with the state's safety standards." * * * The State Supreme Court's definition of California's interest, however, was overly broad. The dispute between Cheng Shin and Asahi is primarily about indemnification rather than safety standards. Moreover, it is not at all clear at this point that California law should govern the question whether a Japanese corporation should indemnify a Taiwanese corporation on the basis of a sale made in Taiwan and a shipment of goods from Japan to Taiwan. * * * The possibility of being haled into a California court as a result of an accident involving Asahi's components undoubtedly creates an additional deterrent to the manufacture of unsafe components; however, similar pressures will be placed on Asahi by the purchasers of its components as long as those who use Asahi components in their final products, and sell those products in California, are subject to the application of California tort law.

World–Wide Volkswagen also admonished courts to take into consideration the interests of the "several States," in addition to the forum state, in the efficient judicial resolution of the dispute and the advancement of substantive policies. In the present case, this advice calls for a court to consider the procedural and substantive policies of other *nations* whose interests are affected by the assertion of jurisdiction by the California court. The procedural and substantive interests of other nations in a state court's assertion of jurisdiction over an alien defendant will differ from case to case. In every case, however, those interests, as well as the Federal interest in its foreign relations policies, will be best served by a careful inquiry into the reasonableness of the assertion of jurisdiction in the particular case, and an unwillingness to find the serious burdens on an alien defendant outweighed by minimal interests on the part of the plaintiff or the forum State. "Great care and reserve should be exercised when extending our notions of personal jurisdiction into the international field." * * *

Considering the international context, the heavy burden on the alien defendant, and the slight interests of the plaintiff and the forum State, the exercise of personal jurisdiction by a California court over Asahi in this instance would be unreasonable and unfair.

III

Because the facts of this case do not establish minimum contacts such that the exercise of personal jurisdiction is consistent with fair play and substantial justice, the judgment of Supreme Court of California is reversed, and the case is remanded for further proceedings not inconsistent with this opinion.

It is so ordered.

JUSTICE BRENNAN, with whom JUSTICE WHITE, JUSTICE MARSHALL, and JUSTICE BLACKMUN join, concurring in part and concurring in the judgment.

I do not agree with the interpretation in Part II–A of the stream-of-commerce theory, nor with the conclusion that Asahi did not "purposely avail itself of the California market." * * * I do agree, however, with the Court's conclusion in Part II–B that the exercise of personal jurisdiction over Asahi in this case would not comport with "fair play and substantial justice" * * *. This is one of those rare cases in which "minimum requirements inherent in the concept of 'fair play and substantial justice' ... defeat the reasonableness of jurisdiction even [though] the defendant has purposefully engaged in forum activities." * * * I therefore join Parts I and II–B of the Court's opinion, and write separately to explain my disagreement with Part II–A.

Part II–A states that "a defendant's awareness that the stream of commerce may or will sweep the product into the forum State does not convert the mere act of placing the product into the stream into an act purposefully directed toward the forum State." * * * Under this view, a plaintiff would be required to show "[a]dditional conduct" directed toward the forum before finding the exercise of jurisdiction over the defendant to be consistent with the Due Process Clause. * * * I see no need for such a showing, however. The stream of commerce refers not to unpredictable currents or eddies, but to the regular and anticipated flow of products from manufacture to distribution to retail sale. As long as a participant in this process is aware that the final product is being marketed in the forum State, the possibility of a lawsuit there cannot come as a surprise. Nor will the litigation present a burden for which there is no corresponding benefit. A defendant who has placed goods in the stream of commerce benefits economically from the retail sale of the final product in the forum State, and indirectly benefits from the State's laws that regulate and facilitate commercial activity. These benefits accrue regardless of whether that participant directly conducts business in the forum State, or engages in additional conduct directed toward that State. Accordingly, most courts and commentators have found that jurisdiction premised on the placement of a product into the stream of commerce is consistent with the Due Process Clause, and have not required a showing of additional conduct.

* * *

JUSTICE STEVENS, with whom JUSTICE WHITE and JUSTICE BLACKMUN join, concurring in part and concurring in the judgment.

The judgment of the Supreme Court of California should be reversed for the reasons stated in Part II–B of the Court's opinion. While I join Parts I and II–B, I do not join Part II–A for two reasons. First, it is not necessary to the Court's decision. An examination of minimum contacts is not always necessary to determine whether a state court's assertion of personal jurisdiction is constitutional. See Burger King Corp. v. Rudzewicz * * *. Part II–B establishes, after considering the factors set forth in World–Wide Volkswagen Corp. v. Woodson, * * * that California's exercise of jurisdiction over Asahi in this case would be "unreasonable and unfair." * * * This finding alone requires reversal; this case fits within the rule that "minimum requirements inherent in the concept of 'fair play and substantial justice' may defeat the reasonableness of jurisdiction even if the defendant has purposefully engaged in forum activities." *Burger King* * * *. Accordingly, I see no reason in this case for the plurality to articulate "purposeful direction" or any other test as the nexus between an act of a defendant and the forum State that is necessary to establish minimum contacts.

Second, even assuming that the test ought to be formulated here, Part II–A misapplies it to the facts of this case. The plurality seems to assume that an unwavering line can be drawn between "mere awareness" that a component will find its way into the forum State and "purposeful availment" of the forum's market. * * *. Over the course of its dealings with Cheng Shin, Asahi has arguably engaged in a higher quantum of conduct than "[t]he placement of a product into the stream of commerce, without more.* * *." * * * Whether or not this conduct rises to the level of purposeful availment requires a constitutional determination that is affected by the volume, the value, and the hazardous character of the components. In most circumstances I would be inclined to conclude that a regular course of dealing that results in deliveries of over 100,000 units annually over a period of several years would constitute "purposeful availment" even though the item delivered to the forum State was a standard product marketed throughout the world.

NOTES AND QUESTIONS

1. Notice that there was no majority opinion in *Asahi*. Given the division among the Justices, which opinion states the law as it now stands? For a comprehensive discussion of *Asahi*, see Dessem, *Personal Jurisdiction After* Asahi*: The Other (International) Shoe Drops*, 55 Tenn. L. Rev. 41 (1987).

2. The Supreme Court did not disturb the California court's finding that "Asahi knew that some of the valve assemblies sold to Cheng Shin would be incorporated into tire tubes sold in California." Under Part II–A of Justice O'Connor's opinion, this knowledge, alone, could not serve as a basis for jurisdiction unless Asahi had taken some further action "purposefully directed toward the forum state." In RODRIGUEZ v. FULLERTON TIRES CORP. v. CUSTOM METAL SPINNING CORP., 115 F.3d 81, 85 (1st Cir.1997), the First Circuit adopted Justice O'Connor's view that mere awareness that a product will pass through the stream of commerce into the forum state does not satisfy the requirement of purposeful availment, stating: "Even assuming that [defendant] had specific knowledge that the stream of commerce would move its tire rims into Puerto Rico—and there is neither evidence nor allegation to that effect—this awareness alone would not be enough to constitute the purposeful availment which is necessary for a showing of minimum contacts."

3. What did Justice O'Connor mean by suggesting that "designing the product for the market in the forum State" is an example of "additional conduct"? In PARRY v. ERNST HOME CENTER CORP., 779 P.2d 659 (Utah 1989), plaintiff was injured in Utah while splitting logs with a maul manufactured by Hirota, a Japanese manufacturer. The maul had been sold by Hirota to Okada Hardware in Japan for export to the United States. Okada sold it to Mansour, a California corporation, who then sold it to Pacific Marine Schwabacher, its regional distributor. Schwabacher distributed and sold the mauls

to retailers throughout the western portion of the United States, including defendant Ernst Home Center Corp. The Ernst Home Center in Twin Falls, Idaho, sold the maul to Linda Thayne in 1979. She then gave it to her father in Utah. Plaintiff borrowed it from him and was injured while using it.

Both Hirota and Okada had been informed that the maul would be sold in the United States, but there was no evidence that either company directly sold or advertised any of their products in Utah. Plaintiff contended that Utah had personal jurisdiction over Hirota and Okada under the stream-of-commerce theory. In analyzing whether the assertion of jurisdiction over the foreign defendants would violate the Due Process Clause, the Utah Supreme Court relied on *Asahi* and reasoned that:

> * * * Hirota and Okada * * * were informed of potential sales to the western United States, but they neither came to Utah nor sent sales representatives to Utah to facilitate the marketing and purchase of their product. Further, the record does not provide the number or percentage of mauls manufactured which were actually sold in Utah. Finally, * * * although plaintiff was injured and resides in Utah, an advertising effort in Utah had not occurred sufficient to link the Japanese defendants to this forum.
>
> Of the following examples of "additional conduct" outlined in *Asahi,* Hirota and Okada had not engaged in even one. The record does not show special designing for Utah's market, advertising in Utah, establishing channels for providing regular advice to customers in Utah, or marketing the product through a distributor who has agreed to act as a sales agent in Utah. * * *.
>
> The record does not reveal any further knowledge or intent by Hirota and Okada to specifically sell the product in Utah or in any other given state. True, the Japanese defendants have not placed any restrictions upon the sale of their products in any particular section of the United States. But an intentional and knowing distribution of the product in the western United States is not necessarily sufficient to satisfy the "minimum contacts" requirement. Further, Hirota and Okada have their principal place of business in Japan; neither has an office in Utah. They have no sales representatives or other agents, no bank account, and no personal property in Utah. They do not own, lease, or rent real property in Utah. Hirota and Okada have not solicited, directly or indirectly, the sale of any of its products in Utah. They have not provided brochures or sent any sales representatives to Utah. They do not render services in Utah and do not give advice to anyone in Utah with regard to the * * * maul. Without a showing of "additional conduct," we are unable to find that the eventual sale of a product in Utah justifies personal jurisdiction.

Id. at 666–67. Was it proper for the Utah Supreme Court to apply the "additional conduct" test? Did the court apply the test correctly? What is the rationale for requiring "additional conduct"? Will the effect be to allow manufacturers to organize their operations so as to avoid the safety standards of a particular state? By organizing their business as they have, are Hirota and Okada effectively immune from suit in the United States? See Note, Parry v. Ernst Home Center Corp.: *The "Mauling" of Personal Jurisdiction*

Theory, 1990 Utah L.Rev. 479. Some courts have declined to follow the plurality's approach, see, e.g., Juelich v. Yamazaki Mazak Optonics Corp., 682 N.W.2d 565 (Minn. 2004), and others have applied Justice Brennan's "stream of commerce" test, see, e.g., Barone v. Rich Brothers Interstate Display Fireworks Co., 25 F.3d 610, 613–15 (8th Cir.1994).

4. Is *Asahi* limited in its application to assertions of jurisdiction over foreign defendants? The Supreme Court made clear that: "The unique burdens placed upon one who must defend oneself in a foreign legal system should have significant weight in assessing the reasonableness of stretching the long arm of personal jurisdiction over national borders." Some courts have held that the weight accorded to this factor decreases for defendants who are located closer to the forum state or who are more familiar with the American legal system. Compare Theunissen v. Matthews, 935 F.2d 1454, 1462 (6th Cir.1991) (burdens on defendant are "slight" since Windsor, Ontario is only ten miles from Detroit and "Canada and the United States are rooted in the same common law tradition"), with Hardy v. Ford Motor Car, 20 F.Supp.2d 339, 343 (D.Conn.1998) ("the burden on the defendant is assessed in terms of the significant distance between Connecticut and Korea, the existence of dissimilar legal systems * * *, and the interest of the forum state in insuring remedy for its citizen by injury caused by tort-feasors"). As you consider whether *Asahi* ought to be limited to foreign defendants, what significance ought to be given to differences between American rules of personal jurisdiction and those of some nations abroad? See p. 81, supra. Does it affect your view that some American bases of jurisdiction are regarded as "exorbitant" from an international perspective? See Clermont & Palmer, *Exorbitant Jurisdiction*, 58 Me. L. Rev. 474 (2006).

5. For further discussions of *Asahi*, see Kaplan, *Paddling Up the Wrong Stream: Why the Stream of Commerce Theory Is Not Part of the Minimum Contacts Doctrine*, 55 Baylor L. Rev. 503, 570–71 (2003); Stephens, *Sovereignty and Personal Jurisdiction Doctrine: Up the Stream of Commerce Without a Paddle*, 19 Fla.St.L.Rev. 105 (1991); Maltz, *Unraveling the Conundrum of the Law of Personal Jurisdiction: A Comment on* Asahi Metal Industry Co. v. Superior Ct. of California, 1987 Duke L.J. 669.

SECTION E. GENERAL JURISDICTION AND STATE LONG-ARM LAWS

PERKINS v. BENGUET CONSOLIDATED MINING CO., 342 U.S. 437, 445–48, 72 S.Ct. 413, 418–20, 96 L.Ed. 485, 492–94 (1952). The defendant, a Philippine corporation, was sued by a nonresident of Ohio in an Ohio state court on two causes of action arising from activities conducted by defendant outside of Ohio. Plaintiff claimed $68,400 in dividends due her as a stockholder, and $2,500,000 in damages due to defendant's failure to issue to her certificates for 120,000 shares of its stock. The Ohio state courts granted defendant's motion to quash the service of summons. The Supreme Court addressed the issue of whether or not the Due Process Clause of the Fourteenth Amendment prohibited Ohio from exercising jurisdiction:

> * * * The corporate activities of a foreign corporation which, under state statute, make it necessary for it to secure a license and to

designate a statutory agent upon whom process may be served provide a helpful but not a conclusive test. * * * [I]f the same corporation carries on, in that state, other continuous and systematic corporate activities as it did here—consisting of directors' meetings, business correspondence, banking, stock transfers, payment of salaries, purchasing of machinery, etc.—those activities are enough to make it fair and reasonable to subject that corporation to proceedings *in personam* in that state, at least insofar as the proceedings *in personam* seek to enforce causes of action relating to those very activities or to other activities of the corporation within the state.

The instant case takes us one step further to a proceeding *in personam* to enforce a cause of action not arising out of the corporation's activities in the state of the forum. * * * [W]e find no requirement of federal due process that either *prohibits* Ohio from opening its courts to the cause of action here presented or *compels* Ohio to do so. * * *

It remains only to consider * * * whether, as a matter of federal due process, the business done in Ohio by the respondent mining company was sufficiently substantial and of such a nature to *permit* Ohio to entertain a cause of action against a foreign corporation, where the cause of action arose from activities entirely distinct from its activities in Ohio. * * *

* * * [T]he following facts are substantially beyond controversy: The company's mining properties were in the Philippine Islands. Its operations there were completely halted during the occupation of the Islands by the Japanese. During that interim the president, who was also the general manager and principal stockholder of the company, returned to his home in Clermont County, Ohio. There he maintained an office in which he conducted his personal affairs and did many things on behalf of the company. He kept there office files of the company. He carried on there correspondence relating to the business of the company and to its employees. He drew and distributed there salary checks on behalf of the company, both in his own favor as president and in favor of two company secretaries who worked there with him. He used and maintained in Clermont County, Ohio, two active bank accounts carrying substantial balances of company funds. A bank in Hamilton County, Ohio, acted as transfer agent for the stock of the company. Several directors' meetings were held at his office or home in Clermont County. From that office he supervised policies dealing with the rehabilitation of the corporation's properties in the Philippines and he dispatched funds to cover purchases of machinery for such rehabilitation. Thus he carried on in Ohio a continuous and systematic supervision of the necessarily limited wartime activities of the company. * * * While no mining properties in Ohio were owned or operated by the company, many of its wartime activities were directed from Ohio and were being given the personal

> attention of its president in that State at the time he was served with summons. * * * [W]e conclude that, under the circumstances above recited, it would not violate federal due process for Ohio either to take or decline jurisdiction of the corporation in this proceeding.

On remand the Ohio courts refused to quash the summons. 158 Ohio St. 145, 107 N.E.2d 203 (1952).

NOTES AND QUESTIONS

1. The dispute in *Perkins* can be traced back to the marriage of Eugene and Idonah Slade Perkins in Manila under authority granted by the United States Military Occupation of the Philippines. Husband and wife were both United States citizens. Beginning in 1916, the wife used her personal funds to purchase stock in the Benguet Consolidated Mining Co., a Philippine corporation. Later, the husband also purchased stock in the company and gave the shares to his wife as a Christmas present. In 1930, the couple separated and a messy divorce followed. The husband claimed a right to his wife's stock under the community property laws of the Philippines, and lawsuits followed in the courts of the Philippines, New York, and California. By the time the United States Supreme Court entered the picture, a New York court had declared the wife the owner of the stock, and she had recovered some of the cash dividends from the Benguet company. However, the company refused to deliver the stock dividends that she claimed to be owed, and in 1947 she sued the company in state court in Ohio, where the company had relocated temporarily during World War II. Does this procedural history help to explain why the Supreme Court said that the cause of action in *Perkins* did not arise "out of the corporation's activities in the state of the forum"?

2. In the wake of *Perkins*, lower courts expressed difficulty in determining when contacts with the forum were "continuous and systematic" and so "sufficiently substantial" to permit the exercise of personal jurisdiction over a cause of action not arising out of the defendant's "activities in the state of the forum." E.g., Aquascutum of London, Inc. v. S.S. American Champion, 426 F.2d 205, 211 (2d Cir. 1970) ("The problem of what contacts with the forum state will suffice to subject a foreign corporation to suit there on an unrelated cause of action is such that the formulation of useful general standards is almost impossible and even an examination of the multitude of decided cases can give little assistance."). Consider the following cases in light of the Supreme Court's decision in *Perkins*.

In FISHER GOVERNOR CO. v. SUPERIOR COURT, 53 Cal.2d 222, 225, 1 Cal.Rptr. 1, 3, 347 P.2d 1, 3 (1959), a wrongful death action growing out of an explosion in Idaho, plaintiffs served defendant, an Iowa corporation, by delivering the papers to a California manufacturers' agent who sold defendant's products. The California Supreme Court ordered the process quashed. In his opinion for the court, Justice Traynor said:

> Although a foreign corporation may have sufficient contacts with a state to justify an assumption of jurisdiction over it to enforce causes of action having no relation to its activities in that state * * *, more contacts are required for the assumption of such extensive jurisdiction than sales and

sales promotion within the state by independent nonexclusive sales representatives. * * * To hold otherwise would subject any corporation that promotes the sales of its goods on a nationwide basis to suit anywhere in the United States without regard to other considerations bearing on "the fair and orderly administration of the laws which it was the purpose of the due process clause to insure." * * * Accordingly, we must look beyond defendant's sales activities in this state to determine whether jurisdiction may constitutionally be assumed.

In FRUMMER v. HILTON HOTELS INTERNATIONAL, INC., 19 N.Y.2d 533, 281 N.Y.S.2d 41, 227 N.E.2d 851, certiorari denied 389 U.S. 923, 88 S.Ct. 241, 19 L.Ed.2d 266 (1967), a New York tourist who fell and injured himself while taking a shower in the London Hilton brought a personal injury action against the hotel (an English corporation) in New York. Jurisdiction was upheld on the basis of the activities of the Hilton Reservation Service, a separate corporation. Although separate, the interlocking ownership of the two corporations and other facts persuaded New York's highest court that an agency relationship existed between them. It thus held that London Hilton did business in New York by "do[ing] all the business which [the principal] could do were it [in New York] by its own officials."

In RATLIFF v. COOPER LABORATORIES, INC., 444 F.2d 745 (4th Cir.), certiorari denied 404 U.S. 948, 92 S.Ct. 271, 30 L.Ed.2d 265 (1971), the court held that South Carolina could not assert personal jurisdiction over the defendants, two drug manufacturing companies incorporated in Delaware with principal places of business in Connecticut and New York, because their contacts with South Carolina were insufficient to satisfy due process requirements. The court placed great significance on the facts that the plaintiffs were nonresidents of South Carolina who chose the forum for its long statute of limitations, that the allegedly defective drugs were both manufactured and consumed outside the forum, and that the cause of action was unrelated to defendants' activities in the forum.

3. The *Perkins* Court did not use the term "general jurisdiction" or distinguish this basis of power from that of "specific jurisdiction." The distinction between the two concepts was first put forward by Professors von Mehren and Trautman. See von Mehren & Trautman, *Jurisdiction to Adjudicate: A Suggested Analysis*, 79 Harv. L. Rev. 1121 (1966).

> [A]ffiliations between the forum and the underlying controversy normally support only the power to adjudicate * * * issues deriving from, or connected with, the very controversy that establishes jurisdiction * * *. This we call specific jurisdiction. On the other hand, American practice for the most part is to exercise power to adjudicate any kind of controversy when jurisdiction is based on relationships, direct or indirect, between the forum, and the person or persons whose legal rights are to be affected. This we call general jurisdiction.

Id. at 1136. Which of the traditional bases of jurisdiction already examined in this Chapter ought to support a court's exercise of general jurisdiction?

HELICOPTEROS NACIONALES DE COLOMBIA, S.A. v. HALL

Supreme Court of the United States, 1984.
466 U.S. 408, 104 S.Ct. 1868, 80 L.Ed.2d 404.

Certiorari to the Supreme Court of Texas.

JUSTICE BLACKMUN delivered the opinion of the Court.

We granted certiorari in this case * * * to decide whether the Supreme Court of Texas correctly ruled that the contacts of a foreign corporation with the State of Texas were sufficient to allow a Texas state court to assert jurisdiction over the corporation in a cause of action not arising out of or related to the corporation's activities within the State.

I

Petitioner Helicopteros Nacionales de Colombia, S.A., (Helicol) is a Colombian corporation with its principal place of business in the city of Bogota in that country. It is engaged in the business of providing helicopter transportation for oil and construction companies in South America. On January 26, 1976, a helicopter owned by Helicol crashed in Peru. Four United States citizens were among those who lost their lives in the accident. Respondents are the survivors and representatives of the four decedents.

At the time of the crash, respondents' decedents were employed by Consorcio, a Peruvian consortium, and were working on a pipeline in Peru. Consorcio is the alter-ego of a joint venture named Williams–Sedco–Horn (WSH). The venture had its headquarters in Houston, Texas. Consorcio had been formed to enable the venturers to enter into a contract with Petro Peru, the Peruvian state-owned oil company. Consorcio was to construct a pipeline for Petro Peru running from the interior of Peru westward to the Pacific Ocean. Peruvian law forbade construction of the pipeline by any non-Peruvian entity.

Consorcio/WSH needed helicopters to move personnel, materials, and equipment into and out of the construction area. In 1974, upon request of Consorcio/WSH, the chief executive officer of Helicol, Francisco Restrepo, flew to the United States and conferred in Houston with representatives of the three joint venturers. At that meeting, there was a discussion of prices, availability, working conditions, fuel, supplies, and housing. Restrepo represented that Helicol could have the first helicopter on the job in 15 days. The Consorcio/WSH representatives decided to accept the contract proposed by Restrepo. Helicol began performing before the agreement was formally signed in Peru on November 11, 1974. The contract was written in Spanish on official government stationery and provided that the residence of all the parties would be Lima, Peru. It further stated that controversies arising out of the contract would be submitted to the jurisdiction of Peruvian courts. In addition, it provided that Consorcio/WSH would make payments to Helicol's account with the Bank of America in New York City. * * *

Aside from the negotiation session in Houston between Restrepo and the representatives of Consorcio/WSH, Helicol had other contacts with Texas. During the years 1970–1977, it purchased helicopters (approximately 80% of its fleet), spare parts, and accessories for more than $4 million from Bell Helicopter Company in Fort Worth. In that period, Helicol sent prospective pilots to Fort Worth for training and to ferry the aircraft to South America. It also sent management and maintenance personnel to visit Bell Helicopter in Fort Worth during the same period in order to receive "plant familiarization" and for technical consultation. Helicol received into its New York City and Panama City, Florida, bank accounts over $5 million in payments from Consorcio/WSH drawn upon First City National Bank of Houston.

Beyond the foregoing, there have been no other business contacts between Helicol and the State of Texas. Helicol never has been authorized to do business in Texas and never has had an agent for the service of process within the State. It never has performed helicopter operations in Texas or sold any product that reached Texas, never solicited business in Texas, never signed any contract in Texas, never had any employee based there, and never recruited an employee in Texas. In addition, Helicol never has owned real or personal property in Texas and never has maintained an office or establishment there. Helicol has maintained no records in Texas and has no shareholders in that State. None of the respondents or their decedents were domiciled in Texas, * * *[5] but all of the decedents were hired in Houston by Consorcio/WSH to work on the Petro Peru pipeline project.

Respondents instituted wrongful-death actions in the District Court of Harris County, Texas, against Consorcio/WSH, Bell Helicopter Company, and Helicol. Helicol filed special appearances and moved to dismiss the actions for lack of *in personam* jurisdiction over it. The motion was denied. After a consolidated jury trial, judgment was entered against Helicol on a jury verdict of $1,141,200 in favor of respondents.[6] * * *

The Texas Court of Civil Appeals, Houston, First District, reversed the judgment of the District Court, holding that *in personam* jurisdiction over Helicol was lacking. * * * The Supreme Court of Texas * * * reversed the judgment of the intermediate court. * * * In ruling that the Texas courts had *in personam* jurisdiction, the Texas Supreme Court first held that the State's long-arm statute reaches as far as the Due Process

5. Respondents' lack of residential or other contacts with Texas of itself does not defeat otherwise proper jurisdiction. * * * We mention respondents' lack of contacts merely to show that nothing in the nature of the relationship between respondents and Helicol could possibly enhance Helicol's contacts with Texas. The harm suffered by respondents did not occur in Texas. Nor is it alleged that any negligence on the part of Helicol took place in Texas.

6. Defendants Consorcio/WSH and Bell Helicopter Company were granted directed verdicts with respect to respondents' claims against them. Bell Helicopter was granted a directed verdict on Helicol's cross-claim against it. * * * Consorcio/WSH, as cross-plaintiff in a claim against Helicol, obtained a judgment in the amount of $70,000. * * *

Clause of the Fourteenth Amendment permits. * * *[7] Thus, the only question remaining for the court to decide was whether it was consistent with the Due Process Clause for Texas courts to assert *in personam* jurisdiction over Helicol. * * *

II

* * *

Even when the cause of action does not arise out of or relate to the foreign corporation's activities in the forum State, due process is not offended by a State's subjecting the corporation to its *in personam* jurisdiction when there are sufficient contacts between the State and the foreign corporation. * * *

All parties to the present case concede that respondents' claims against Helicol did not "arise out of," and are not related to, Helicol's activities within Texas.[10] We thus must explore the nature of Helicol's contacts with the State of Texas to determine whether they constitute the kind of continuous and systematic general business contacts the Court found to exist in *Perkins*. We hold that they do not.

It is undisputed that Helicol does not have a place of business in Texas and never has been licensed to do business in the State. Basically, Helicol's contacts with Texas consisted of sending its chief executive officer to Houston for a contract-negotiation session; accepting into its New York bank account checks drawn on a Houston bank; purchasing helicopters, equipment, and training services from Bell Helicopter for substantial sums; and sending personnel to Bell's facilities in Fort Worth for training.

The one trip to Houston by Helicol's chief executive officer for the purpose of negotiating the transportation-services contract with Consorcio/WSH cannot be described or regarded as a contact of a "continuous

---

7. * * * It is not within our province, of course, to determine whether the Texas Supreme Court correctly interpreted the State's long-arm statute. We therefore accept that court's holding that the limits of the Texas statute are coextensive with those of the Due Process Clause.

10. * * * Because the parties have not argued any relationship between the cause of action and Helicol's contacts with the State of Texas, we, contrary to the dissent's implication, * * * assert no "view" with respect to that issue.

The dissent suggests that we have erred in drawing no distinction between controversies that "relate to" a defendant's contacts with a forum and those that "arise out of" such contacts. * * * This criticism is somewhat puzzling, for the dissent goes on to urge that, for purposes of determining the constitutional validity of an assertion of specific jurisdiction, there really should be no distinction between the two. * * *

We do not address the validity or consequences of such a distinction because the issue has not been presented in this case. Respondents have made no argument that their cause of action either arose out of or is related to Helicol's contacts with the State of Texas. Absent any briefing on the issue, we decline to reach the questions (1) whether the terms "arising out of" and "related to" describe different connections between a cause of action and a defendant's contacts with a forum, and (2) what sort of tie between a cause of action and a defendant's contacts with a forum is necessary to a determination that either connection exists. Nor do we reach the question whether, if the two types of relationship differ, a forum's exercise of personal jurisdiction in a situation where the cause of action "relates to," but does not "arise out of," the defendant's contacts with the forum should be analyzed as an assertion of specific jurisdiction.

and systematic" nature, as *Perkins* described it, * * * and thus cannot support an assertion of *in personam* jurisdiction over Helicol by a Texas court. Similarly, Helicol's acceptance from Consorcio/WSH of checks drawn on a Texas bank is of negligible significance for purposes of determining whether Helicol had sufficient contacts in Texas. There is no indication that Helicol ever requested that the checks be drawn on a Texas bank or that there was any negotiation between Helicol and Consorcio/WSH with respect to the location or identity of the bank on which checks would be drawn. Common sense and everyday experience suggest that, absent unusual circumstances, the bank on which a check is drawn is generally of little consequence to the payee and is a matter left to the discretion of the drawer. Such unilateral activity of another party or a third person is not an appropriate consideration when determining whether a defendant has sufficient contacts with a forum State to justify an assertion of jurisdiction. * * *

The Texas Supreme Court focused on the purchases and the related training trips in finding contacts sufficient to support an assertion of jurisdiction. We do not agree with that assessment, for the Court's opinion in Rosenberg Bros. & Co. v. Curtis Brown Co., 260 U.S. 516 (1923) (Brandeis, J., for a unanimous tribunal), makes clear that purchases and related trips, standing alone, are not a sufficient basis for a State's assertion of jurisdiction.

* * *

* * * In accordance with *Rosenberg,* we hold that mere purchases, even if occurring at regular intervals, are not enough to warrant a State's assertion of *in personam* jurisdiction over a nonresident corporation in a cause of action not related to those purchase transactions. Nor can we conclude that the fact that Helicol sent personnel into Texas for training in connection with the purchase of helicopters and equipment in that State in any way enhanced the nature of Helicol's contacts with Texas. The training was a part of the package of goods and services purchased by Helicol from Bell Helicopter. The brief presence of Helicol employees in Texas for the purpose of attending the training sessions is no more a significant contact than were the trips to New York made by the buyer for the [Oklahoma] retail store in *Rosenberg.* * * *

III

We hold that Helicol's contacts with the State of Texas were insufficient to satisfy the requirements of the Due Process Clause of the Fourteenth Amendment. Accordingly, we reverse the judgment of the Supreme Court of Texas.

It is so ordered.

JUSTICE BRENNAN, dissenting.

* * *

What is troubling about the Court's opinion * * * are the implications that might be drawn from the way in which the Court approaches the constitutional issue it addresses. * * * I believe that the undisputed contacts in this case between petitioner Helicol and the State of Texas are sufficiently important, and sufficiently related to the underlying cause of action, to make it fair and reasonable for the State to assert personal jurisdiction over Helicol for the wrongful-death actions filed by the respondents. Given that Helicol has purposefully availed itself of the benefits and obligations of the forum, and given the direct relationship between the underlying cause of action and Helicol's contacts with the forum, maintenance of this suit in the Texas courts "does not offend [the] 'traditional notions of fair play and substantial justice,'" * * * that are the touchstone of jurisdictional analysis under the Due Process Clause. I therefore dissent.

I

* * * As active participants in interstate and foreign commerce take advantage of the economic benefits and opportunities offered by the various States, it is only fair and reasonable to subject them to the obligations that may be imposed by those jurisdictions. And chief among the obligations that a nonresident corporation should expect to fulfill is amenability to suit in any forum that is significantly affected by the corporation's commercial activities.

As a foreign corporation that has actively and purposefully engaged in numerous and frequent commercial transactions in the State of Texas, Helicol clearly falls within the category of nonresident defendants that may be subject to the forum's general jurisdiction. Helicol not only purchased helicopters and other equipment in the State for many years, but also sent pilots and management personnel into Texas to be trained in the use of this equipment and to consult with the seller on technical matters. Moreover, negotiations for the contract under which Helicol provided transportation services to the joint venture that employed the respondents' decedents also took place in the State of Texas. Taken together, these contacts demonstrate that Helicol obtained numerous benefits from its transaction of business in Texas. In turn, it is eminently fair and reasonable to expect Helicol to face the obligations that attach to its participation in such commercial transactions. Accordingly, on the basis of continuous commercial contacts with the forum, I would conclude that the Due Process Clause allows the State of Texas to assert general jurisdiction over petitioner Helicol.

II

The Court also fails to distinguish the legal principles that controlled our prior decisions in *Perkins* and *Rosenberg*. In particular, the contacts between petitioner Helicol and the State of Texas, unlike the contacts between the defendant and the forum in each of those cases, are significantly related to the cause of action alleged in the original suit filed by the respondents. Accordingly, in my view, it is both fair and reasonable for the Texas courts to assert specific jurisdiction over Helicol in this case.

By asserting that the present case does not implicate the specific jurisdiction of the Texas courts, * * * the Court necessarily removes its decision from the reality of the actual facts presented for our consideration. Moreover, the Court refuses to consider any distinction between contacts that are "related to" the underlying cause of action and contacts that "give rise" to the underlying cause of action. In my view, however, there is a substantial difference between these two standards for asserting specific jurisdiction. Thus, although I agree that the respondents' cause of action did not formally "arise out of" specific activities initiated by Helicol in the State of Texas, I believe that the wrongful-death claim filed by the respondents is significantly related to the undisputed contacts between Helicol and the forum. On that basis, I would conclude that the Due Process Clause allows the Texas courts to assert specific jurisdiction over this particular action.

The wrongful-death actions filed by the respondents were premised on a fatal helicopter crash that occurred in Peru. Helicol was joined as a defendant in the lawsuits because it provided transportation services, including the particular helicopter and pilot involved in the crash, to the joint venture that employed the decedents. Specifically, the respondents claimed in their original complaint that "Helicol is * * * legally responsible for its own negligence through its pilot employee." * * * Viewed in light of these allegations, the contacts between Helicol and the State of Texas are directly and significantly related to the underlying claim filed by the respondents. The negotiations that took place in Texas led to the contract in which Helicol agreed to provide the precise transportation services that were being used at the time of the crash. Moreover, the helicopter involved in the crash was purchased by Helicol in Texas, and the pilot whose negligence was alleged to have caused the crash was actually trained in Texas. * * * This is simply not a case, therefore, in which a state court has asserted jurisdiction over a nonresident defendant on the basis of wholly unrelated contacts with the forum. Rather, the contacts between Helicol and the forum are directly related to the negligence that was alleged in the respondent Hall's original complaint.[4] * * *

Despite this substantial relationship between the contacts and the cause of action, the Court declines to consider whether the courts of Texas may assert specific jurisdiction over this suit. Apparently, this simply reflects a narrow interpretation of the question presented for review. * * * It is nonetheless possible that the Court's opinion may be read to imply that the specific jurisdiction of the Texas courts is inapplicable because the cause of action did not formally "arise out of" the contacts between Helicol and the forum. In my view, however, such a rule would

4. The jury specifically found that "the pilot failed to keep the helicopter under proper control," that "the helicopter was flown into a treetop fog condition, whereby the vision of the pilot was impaired," that "such flying was negligence," and that "such negligence * * * was a proximate cause of the crash." * * *

place unjustifiable limits on the bases under which Texas may assert its jurisdictional power.

Limiting the specific jurisdiction of a forum to cases in which the cause of action formally arose out of the defendant's contacts with the State would subject constitutional standards under the Due Process Clause to the vagaries of the substantive law or pleading requirements of each State. For example, the complaint filed against Helicol in this case alleged negligence based on pilot error. Even though the pilot was trained in Texas, the Court assumes that the Texas courts may not assert jurisdiction over the suit because the cause of action "did not 'arise out of,' and [is] not related to," that training. * * * If, however, the applicable substantive law required that negligent training of the pilot was a necessary element of a cause of action for pilot error, or if the respondents had simply added an allegation of negligence in the training provided for the Helicol pilot, then presumably the Court would concede that the specific jurisdiction of the Texas courts was applicable.

Our interpretation of the Due Process Clause has never been so dependent upon the applicable substantive law or the State's formal pleading requirements. * * * [T]he principal focus when determining whether a forum may constitutionally assert jurisdiction over a nonresident defendant has been on fairness and reasonableness to the defendant. To this extent, a court's specific jurisdiction should be applicable whenever the cause of action arises out of *or* relates to the contacts between the defendant and the forum. It is eminently fair and reasonable, in my view, to subject a defendant to suit in a forum with which it has significant contacts directly related to the underlying cause of action. Because Helicol's contacts with the State of Texas meet this standard, I would affirm the judgment of the Supreme Court of Texas.

NOTES AND QUESTIONS

1. *Helicopteros* addressed the distinction between general and specific jurisdiction, a terminology that the Court first used in Calder v. Jones, Note 1, p. 118, supra. What purpose does the distinction serve? Has the expansion of specific jurisdiction rendered the concept of general jurisdiction obsolete? See Nichols v. G.D. Searle & Co., 991 F.2d 1195, 1200 (4th Cir.1993) (noting that expansion of specific jurisdiction has enabled plaintiffs to bring suit in fora in which claims arise and concluding that "broad constructions of general jurisdiction should be generally disfavored"). Some commentators have argued that the concept of general jurisdiction ensures the availability of at least one state in which "a defendant may be sued on any cause of action." Twitchell, *The Myth of General Jurisdiction,* 101 Harv. L. Rev. 610, 632, 667 (1988). See also Borchers, *The Problem with General Jurisdiction*, 2001 U. Chi. Legal F. 119, 139 (describing general jurisdiction as "an imperfect safety valve that sometimes allows plaintiffs access to a reasonable forum in a case when specific jurisdiction would deny it").

2. Justice Brennan's concurrence in *Helicopteros* argued that specific jurisdiction is implicated whenever the defendant's contacts with the forum

"relate to" the cause of action; he expressed concern that the Court had defined specific jurisdiction to require the cause of action to "arise out of" the defendant's forum contacts and, as such, to entangle personal jurisdiction with the substantive law of the case. Professor Brilmayer has proposed just such a "substantive relevance" standard:

> Substantive relevance provides a natural test. A contact is related to the controversy if it is the geographical qualification of a fact relevant to the merits. A forum occurrence which would ordinarily be alleged as part of a comparable domestic complaint is a related contact. In contrast, an occurrence in the forum State of no relevance to a totally domestic cause of action is an unrelated contact, a purely jurisdictional allegation with no substantive purpose. If a fact is irrelevant in a purely domestic dispute, it does not suddenly become related to the controversy simply because there are multistate elements.

Brilmayer, *How Contacts Count: Due Process Limitations on State Court Jurisdiction*, 1980 Sup.Ct.Rev. 77, 82–83. Professor Brilmayer later defended the test of "substantive relevance" on the view that it helps to identify cases in which the exercise of jurisdiction "would further the state's legitimate interests in local regulation." Brilmayer, Haverkamp & Logan, *A General Look at General Jurisdiction*, 66 Texas L. Rev. 721, 740 (1988). Do you agree with that analysis?

3. Are general and specific jurisdiction two separate categories or are they two ends of a continuum? Professor Richman has urged replacing the binary distinction with a "sliding scale model" that looks at "the extent of the defendant's forum contacts on the one hand and the proximity of the connection between those contacts and the plaintiff's claim on the other." According to this view, "As the quantity and quality of the defendant's forum contacts increase, a weaker connection between the plaintiff's claim and those contacts is permissible; as the quantity and quality of the defendant's forum contacts decrease, a strong connection between the plaintiff's claim and those contacts is required." Richman, *Review Essay, Part II: A Sliding Scale to Supplement the Distinction Between General and Specific Jurisdiction*, 72 Calif.L.Rev. 1328, 1345 (1984).

4. The *Helicopteros* decision provided the lower courts with little guidance in applying general jurisdiction in the individual case and left many questions unanswered. For example, are assertions of general jurisdiction subject to the reasonableness factors developed by *International Shoe* and its progeny in the context of specific jurisdiction? In METROPOLITAN LIFE INSURANCE CO. v. ROBERTSON–CECO CORP., 84 F.3d 560 (2d Cir.), certiorari denied 519 U.S. 1006, 117 S.Ct. 508, 136 L.Ed.2d 398 (1996), the Second Circuit held that the exercise of general jurisdiction over the defendant was unreasonable in light of the five-factor *Asahi* test, but other courts have not applied this approach consistently. See Cebik, *"A Riddle Wrapped in a Mystery Inside an Enigma": General Personal Jurisdiction and Notions of Sovereignty*, 1998 Ann. Surv. Am. L. 1, 10 (1998).

SECTION F. INTERNET AND OTHER TECHNOLOGICAL CONTACTS

As technology has changed, courts have expanded the field of contacts that satisfy the *International Shoe* test. Telephone calls, faxes, and emails sent by businesses or individuals and directed at a recipient in a forum state today clearly count as contacts for personal jurisdiction purposes. Questions still arise, however, in applying traditional personal jurisdiction doctrine when the alleged contacts arise from widely available Internet websites. Websites often are not targeted at a particular state, but rather at all online users. Do the operators of those websites have contacts wherever the Internet is available, i.e., everywhere? As you read this Section, ask yourself what factors should matter in assessing a website as a contact with a forum. Should the answer depend on what kind of harm is alleged? Do you agree that trying to apply traditional personal jurisdiction doctrine to the Internet is "like trying to board a moving bus"? Millennium Enterprises, Inc. v. Millennium Music, LP, 33 F.Supp.2d 907, 914 (D.Ore.1999).

PEBBLE BEACH CO. v. CADDY

United States Court of Appeals, Ninth Circuit, 2006.
453 F.3d 1151.

TROTT, CIRCUIT JUDGE.

Pebble Beach Company ("Pebble Beach"), a golf course resort in California, appeals the dismissal for lack of jurisdiction of its complaint against Michael Caddy ("Caddy"), a small-business owner located in southern England. * * * Because Caddy did not expressly aim his conduct at California * * *, we hold that the district court determined correctly that it lacked personal jurisdiction. * * * Thus, we affirm.

I

Pebble Beach is a well-known golf course and resort located in Monterey County, California. The golf resort has used "Pebble Beach" as its trade name for 50 years. Pebble Beach contends that the trade name has acquired secondary meaning in the United States and the United Kingdom. Pebble Beach operates a website located at *www.pebblebeach.com.*

Caddy, a dual citizen of the United States and the United Kingdom[,] occupies and runs a three-room bed and breakfast, restaurant, and bar located in southern England. Caddy's business operation is located on a cliff overlooking the pebbly beaches of England's south shore, in a town called Barton-on-Sea. The name of Caddy's operation is "Pebble Beach," which, given its location, is no surprise. Caddy advertises his services, which do not include a golf course, at his website, *www.pebblebeach-uk.com.* Caddy's website includes general information about the accommodations he provides, including lodging rates in pounds sterling, a menu, and a wine list. The website is not interactive. Visitors to the website who have questions about Caddy's services may fill out an on-line inquiry form. However, the website does not have a reservation system, nor does it allow potential guests to book rooms or pay for services on-line.

Except for a brief time when Caddy worked at a restaurant in Carmel, California, his domicile has been in the United Kingdom.

On October 8, 2003, Pebble Beach sued Caddy under the Lanham Act [a federal statute prohibiting trademark infringement] and the California Business and Professions Code for intentional infringement and dilution of its "Pebble Beach" mark. Caddy moved to dismiss the complaint for lack of personal jurisdiction * * *. On March 1, 2004, the district court granted Caddy's motion on personal jurisdiction grounds * * *. * * * Pebble Beach timely appealed to the Ninth Circuit.

II

* * *

A. Personal Jurisdiction

The arguments are straight forward. Caddy contends that the district court may not assert personal jurisdiction over him, and, consequently, that the complaint against him was properly dismissed. Pebble Beach argues in return that Caddy is subject to specific personal jurisdiction in California * * * because he has expressly aimed tortious conduct at California * * *.[1] * * *

* * *

In this circuit, we employ the following three-part test to analyze whether a party's "minimum contacts" meet the Supreme Court's * * * [due process requirements]. This "minimum contacts" test is satisfied when,

> (1) the defendant has performed some act or consummated some transaction within the forum or otherwise purposefully availed himself of the privileges of conducting activities in the forum, (2) the claim arises out of or results from the defendant's forum-related activities, and (3) the exercise of jurisdiction is reasonable.

* * * "If any of the three requirements is not satisfied, jurisdiction in the forum would deprive the defendant of due process of law." * * * Here, Pebble Beach's arguments fail under the first prong. Accordingly, we need not address whether the claim arose out of or resulted from Caddy's forum-related activities or whether an exercise of jurisdiction is reasonable per the factors outlined by the Supreme Court in *Burger King Corp. v. Rudzewicz*, * * * [, p. 119, supra].

---

1. Caddy's contacts with California * * * are not continuous or substantial enough to establish general jurisdiction. * * * Thus, we consider only the question of whether Caddy's contacts are sufficient to establish specific jurisdiction.

Under the first prong of the "minimum contacts" test, Pebble Beach has the burden of establishing that Caddy "has performed some act or consummated some transaction within the forum or otherwise purposefully availed himself of the privileges of conducting activities in the forum." * * * We have refined this to mean whether Caddy has either (1) "purposefully availed" himself of the privilege of conducting activities in the forum, or (2) "purposefully directed" his activities toward the forum. * * * Although we sometimes use the phrase "purposeful availment" to include both purposeful availment and direction, "availment and direction are, in fact, two distinct concepts." * * *

* * *

1. *Purposeful Availment*

Pebble Beach fails to identify any conduct by Caddy that took place in California * * * that adequately supports the availment concept. Evidence of availment is typically action taking place in the forum that invokes the benefits and protections of the laws in the forum. * * * Evidence of direction generally consists of action taking place outside the forum that is directed at the forum. * * * All of Caddy's action identified by Pebble Beach is action taking place outside the forum. Thus, if anything, it is the type of evidence that supports a purposeful direction analysis. Accordingly, we reject Pebble Beach's assertion that Caddy has availed himself of the jurisdiction of the district court under both concepts and proceed only to determine whether Caddy has purposefully directed his action toward * * * [California].

2. *Purposeful Direction: California*

In *Calder v. Jones,* * * * [Note 1, p. 118, supra,] the Supreme Court held that a foreign act that is both aimed at and has effect in the forum satisfies the first prong of the specific jurisdiction analysis. * * * We have commonly referred to this holding as the "*Calder* effects test." * * * To satisfy this test the defendant "must have (1) committed an intentional act, which was (2) expressly aimed at the forum state, and (3) caused harm, the brunt of which is suffered and which the defendant knows is likely to be suffered in the forum state." * * * However, referring to the *Calder* test as an "effects" test can be misleading. For this reason, we have warned courts not to focus too narrowly on the test's third prong—the effects prong—holding that "something more" is needed in addition to a mere foreseeable effect. * * *

* * *

We conclude that Caddy's actions were not expressly aimed at California. The only acts identified by Pebble Beach as being directed at California are the website and the use of the name "Pebble Beach" in the domain name. These acts were not aimed at California and, regardless of foreseeable effect, are insufficient to establish jurisdiction.

In support of its contention that Caddy has expressly aimed conduct at California, Pebble Beach identifies a list of cases where we have found that a defendant's actions have been expressly aimed at the forum state sufficient to establish jurisdiction over the defendant. Pebble Beach asserts that these cases show that Caddy's website and domain name, coupled by his knowledge of the golf resort as a result of his working in California, are sufficient to satisfy the express aiming standard that it is required to meet. We disagree. If anything, these cases establish that "something more"—the express aiming requirement—has not been met by Pebble Beach.

* * *

In *Metropolitan Life Insurance Co. v. Neaves*, [912 F.2d 1062 (9th Cir.1990),] * * * the defendant's alleged plan to defraud the insurance company involved direct interaction with the forum state. * * * We held that the action at issue satisfied *Calder's* "effects test" because the defendant sent a letter to the forum state addressed to the plaintiff, thereby defrauding a forum state entity. * * *

In *Bancroft & Masters, Inc. v. Augusta National Inc.*, [223 F.3d 1082 (9th Cir.2000),] a dispute over the domain name *www.masters.org* was triggered by a letter sent by Augusta that required Bancroft & Masters, a computer corporation in California, to sue or lose the domain name. * * * We stated that the "expressly aiming" standard was satisfied when "individualized targeting was present." * * * We reasoned that specific jurisdiction was proper and that the expressly aiming requirement was satisfied because the letter sent by Augusta constituted "individualized targeting." * * *

The defendant in both *Bancroft* and *Metropolitan Life* did "something more" than commit a "foreign act with foreseeable effects in the forum state." * * * In both cases this "individualized targeting" was correspondence that was a clear attempt to force the plaintiff to act. Here, Caddy engaged in no "individualized targeting." There is no letter written by Caddy forcing Pebble Beach to act. The only substantial action is a domain name and non-interactive informative web site along with the extraneous fact that Caddy had worked, at some point in his past, in California. This does not constitute "individualized targeting." Indeed, to hold otherwise would be contrary to what we have suggested in earlier case law.

In *Rio Properties, Inc. v. Rio Int'l Interlink,* 284 F.3d 1007, 1020 (9th Cir.2000), we cited *Cybersell, Inc. v. Cybersell, Inc.*, 130 F.3d 414, 418–20 (9th Cir.1997), for the proposition that when a "website advertiser [does] nothing other than register a domain name and post an essentially passive website" and nothing else is done "to encourage residents of the forum state," there is no personal jurisdiction. Similarly, * * * we stated, "We agree that simply registering someone else's trademark as a domain name and posting a web site on the Internet is not sufficient to subject a party domiciled in one state to jurisdiction in another." * * * Why? Because "the objectionable webpage simply was not aimed intentionally at the [forum state] knowing that harm was likely to be caused there," and "[u]nder the effects doctrine, 'something more' was required to indicate that the defendant purposefully directed its activity in a substantial way to the forum state." * * *

These cases establish two salient points. First, there can be no doubt that we still require "something more" than just a foreseeable effect to conclude that personal jurisdiction is proper. * * * Second, an internet domain name and passive website alone are not "something more," and, therefore, alone are not enough to subject a party to jurisdiction. * * *

In contrast to those cases where jurisdiction was proper because "something more" existed, the circumstances here are more analogous to *Schwarzenegger v. Fred Martin Motor Co.*, 374 F.3d 797 (9th Cir.2004). In *Schwarzenegger,* we determined that personal jurisdiction based solely on a non-interactive print advertisement would be improper. * * * In *Schwarzenegger,* the former movie star and current California governor, brought an action in California alleging that an Ohio car dealership used impermissibly his "Terminator" image in a newspaper advertisement in Akron, Ohio. * * * The federal district court in California dismissed the complaint for lack of personal jurisdiction. * * * Applying the *Calder* "effects test," we affirmed, concluding that even though the advertisement might lead to eventual harm in California this "foreseeable effect" was not enough because the advertisement was expressly aimed at Ohio rather than California. * * * We concluded that, without "something more" than possible effect, there was simply no individualized targeting of California, or the type of wrongful conduct, that could be construed as being directed at the forum state. * * * We held that Schwarzenegger had not established jurisdiction over the car dealership.

Pebble Beach, like Schwarzenegger, relies almost exclusively on the possible foreseeable effects. Like Schwarzenegger, Pebble Beach's arguments depend on the possible effects of a non-interactive advertisement—here, Caddy's passive website. Notably absent in both circumstances is action that can be construed as being expressly aimed at California. The fact that Caddy once lived in California and therefore has knowledge of the Pebble Beach golf resort goes to the foreseeable effect prong of the "effects test" and is not an independent act that can be interpreted as being expressly aimed at California. * * * [W]e reject * * * any contention that a passive website constitutes expressed aiming. Thus, today, we extend the holding of *Schwarzenegger* to * * * situations * * * where the sole basis for asserting jurisdiction is a non-interactive passive website. As with * * * print advertisement * * *, the fact that Caddy's website is not directed at California is controlling.

* * *

Affirmed.

NOTE ON THE INTERNET

The Supreme Court has yet to consider the issue of personal jurisdiction based upon Internet contacts. As a result, lower courts have been left to face the problem on their own, leading to what one commentator has called a "hodgepodge of case law [that] is inconsistent, irrational, and irreconcilable." Stravitz, *Personal Jurisdiction in Cyberspace: Something More Is Required on the Electronic Stream of Commerce*, 49 S.C. L. Rev. 925, 939 (1998). One proposed solution is to shift the emphasis in the due process analysis from a focus on the defendant's individual interest in not litigating in a particular forum to an assessment of "whether a state is acting within its legitimate sphere of sovereign authority" in regulating Internet activity. See Stein, *Personal Jurisdiction and the Internet: Seeking Due Process Through the Lens of Regulatory Precision*, 98 Nw. U. L. Rev. 411 (2004). What difficulties do you anticipate with this approach?

One of the first cases to deal with the question of personal jurisdiction and the Internet was INSET SYSTEMS, INC. v. INSTRUCTION SET, INC., 937 F.Supp. 161 (D.Conn.1996), in which the court found that an Internet website advertisement operated by a nonresident, although not directed at any state in particular, was sufficient to establish personal jurisdiction in Connecticut under the purposeful availment test. In CYBERSELL, INC. v. CYBERSELL, INC., 130 F.3d 414, 418 (9th Cir.1997), mentioned in *Pebble Beach*, the court held that "something more" than the mere maintenance of a website is required to show that the defendant purposefully directed its activities at the forum. A district court expanded upon this notion in ZIPPO MANUFACTURING CO. v. ZIPPO DOT COM, INC., 952 F.Supp. 1119, 1124 (W.D.Pa.1997). In *Zippo* the court articulated a "sliding scale" test, which places at one end of the scale "active" websites that businesses use to carry out transactions with residents of a forum state. At the other end of the scale are "passive" websites, which do little more than make information available to those who choose to visit the website. The "active" websites almost always provide for an exercise of personal jurisdiction; the "passive" websites rarely can be used alone to establish personal jurisdiction. In the middle are "interactive" websites, which permit a user to exchange information with the business; it is in these cases that the sliding scale of commercial activity becomes relevant.

Courts almost immediately recognized *Zippo* as a leading case, but applied it in an inconsistent manner. Some courts found that an interactive website alone is sufficient to establish minimum contacts; others required additional non-Internet activity in the forum, regardless of whether it was related to the underlying claim. Finally, some courts looked for additional conduct in the forum that is related to the plaintiff's cause of action. Courts and commentators increasingly criticize the *Zippo* test. In HY CITE CORP. v. BADBUSINESSBUREAU.COM, L.L.C., 297 F.Supp.2d 1154, 1160 (W.D.Wis. 2004), the District Court declined to follow *Zippo*:

> First, it is not clear why a website's level of interactivity should be determinative on the issue of personal jurisdiction. As even courts adopting the *Zippo* test have recognized, a court cannot determine whether

> personal jurisdiction is appropriate simply by deciding whether a website is "passive" or "interactive" (assuming that websites can be readily classified into one category or the other). * * *
>
> Second, * * * [t]he Supreme Court has never held that courts should apply different standards for personal jurisdiction depending on the type of contact involved.

Many courts today have begun to move away from *Zippo*, either replacing it entirely with *Calder*'s "effects test," Note 1, p. 118, supra, relied on by the Ninth Circuit in *Pebble Beach*, or combining the two standards. In ALS SCAN, INC. v. DIGITAL SERVICE CONSULTANTS, INC., 293 F.3d 707 (4th Cir.2002), the Fourth Circuit declined to base personal jurisdiction on "passive" Internet activity alone, and required additional conduct directed at the forum. In BEST VAN LINES, INC. v. WALKER, 490 F.3d 239, 252 (2d Cir.2007), the Second Circuit used *Zippo*'s interactivity scale to assess the defendant's contacts under both due process and the state long-arm statute, but noted that it is not "a separate framework for analyzing internet-based jurisdiction"; traditional principles "remain the touchstone of the inquiry" (internal quotations omitted). Some commentators have urged that courts abandon the *Zippo* test. E.g., Floyd & Baradaran–Robison, *Toward a Unified Test of Personal Jurisdiction in an Era of Widely Diffused Wrongs: The Relevance of Purpose and Effects*, 81 Ind. L.J. 601 (2006).

NOTES AND QUESTIONS

1. In BELLINO v. SIMON, 1999 WL 1059753, at *5 (E.D.La.1999), a sports memorabilia dealer claimed that two defendants hurt his sales of autographed baseballs on eBay by defaming him in emails and telephone calls with a potential buyer. The court found personal jurisdiction over defendant Simon who had e-mailed and called the buyer in the forum state, and no jurisdiction over defendant Spence, who had received one unsolicited telephone call from the buyer. In finding jurisdiction over Simon, the court pointed to his website, which provided a form visitors could fill out to contact him about sports memorabilia. The court applied traditional principles of personal jurisdiction in evaluating all of the defendants' contacts:

> With regard to Mr. Spence, * * * this Court will not exercise personal jurisdiction based on one unsolicited telephone call from the forum state to a nonresident defendant.
>
> * * * It is uncontested that allegedly defamatory comments made by Mr. Simon first occurred during a telephone call made by * * * [the buyer]. * * * However, this telephone call resulted from several e-mail communications which began when * * * [the buyer] took advantage of a visitor form on Mr. Simon's company website allowing readers to contact Mr. Simon directly. In a broad sense, Mr. Simon solicited this communication. Moreover, it is undisputed that Mr. Simon initiated several subsequent e-mails relating to plaintiffs' defamation charge. * * * Mr. Simon affirmatively directed the allegedly tortious e-mails to Louisiana. That allegedly defamatory comments are made over the Internet does not alter the jurisdictional analysis. * * * Mr. Simon purposefully established mini-

mum contacts with Louisiana such that he could reasonably anticipate being haled into court here.

In CONSULTING ENGINEERS CORP. v. GEOMETRIC LTD., 561 F.3d 273 (4th Cir.2009), the Court of Appeals affirmed the District Court's holding that specific jurisdiction could not be exercised against a Colorado company that had contacts with the forum consisting of four telephone conversations and twenty-four emails (only eight of which were sent by defendant). The Fourth Circuit emphasized that "the mere fact that emails, telephone calls, and faxes were employed does not, of itself, alter the minimum contacts analysis." Id. at 279 n.5. Do you agree that technological contacts should be assessed under traditional personal jurisdiction principles? Or do they present questions that cannot be resolved within the existing *International Shoe* framework? For discussions of the issue, see Symposium, *Personal Jurisdiction in the Internet Age*, 98 Nw. U. L. Rev. 409 (2004).

2. What if defendant does not direct an email to a user in the forum state, but the email is instead forwarded through a chain of other email users? In HEADSTRONG CORP. v. JHA, 2007 WL 1238621, *4 (E.D.Va.2007), the plaintiff attempted to assert personal jurisdiction over the defendant, a resident of India, based on emails that were forwarded to recipients in Virginia and "broadly and globally republished." The court, citing *ALS Scan*, p. 156, supra, held that the "act of placing information on the Internet" does not subject the sender to personal jurisdiction solely because the email might be accessed in the forum state. Similarly, in GTE NEW MEDIA SERVICES INC. v. BELLSOUTH CORP., 199 F.3d 1343, 1350 (D.C.Cir.2000), the District of Columbia Circuit Court declined to find that a non-resident company did business in the forum simply because District residents accessed defendant's websites, explaining that using an Internet search engine is "akin to searching a telephone book." Id. at 1350.

3. How would you treat sales that are made through Internet sites such as eBay? For a discussion of this issue that compares judicial approaches in the United States, Canada, and the European Union, see Neumueller, *Are We "There" Yet? An Analysis of Canadian and European Adjudicatory Jurisdiction Principles in the Context of Electronic Commerce Consumer Protection and Policy Issues*, 3 U. Ottawa L. & Tech. J. 421 (2006).

4. What weight ought to be given to the *Zippo* factors in determining assertions of general jurisdiction? *Zippo*'s focus on "passive" and "active" websites should have little value alone for the question whether the defendant has systematic and continuous contacts with a forum state. See 4A Wright & Miller, Federal Practice and Procedure: Civil 3d § 1073.1. Note that *Pebble Beach* rejected any assertion of general jurisdiction over the English website operator, see p. 151, footnote 1, supra. Would it ever be appropriate to base general jurisdiction solely on Internet contacts? See Nemeyer, *Don't Hate the Player, Hate the Game: Applying the Traditional Concepts of General Jurisdiction to Internet Concepts*, 52 Loyola L. Rev. 147, 148 (2006).

SECTION G. JURISDICTION BASED UPON POWER OVER PROPERTY

Reread Pennoyer v. Neff, p. 71, supra.

TYLER v. JUDGES OF THE COURT OF REGISTRATION, 175 Mass. 71, 55 N.E. 812, writ of error dismissed 179 U.S. 405, 21 S.Ct. 206, 45 L.Ed. 252 (1900). Petitioner sought a writ of prohibition against the judges of the Court of Registration, to prevent their passing upon an application to register title to a parcel of land in which petitioner claimed an interest. The basis of the petition was that the act establishing the court violated due process because it deprived all persons except the registered owner of any interest in the land, and it provided for insufficient notice to persons having adverse claims.

The statute in question established a procedure and court for registering and confirming titles to land. It provided that the decree of registration "shall bind the land and quiet the title thereto," and "shall be conclusive upon and against all persons" whether named in the proceedings or not. It further required that notice of the proposed registration be published in a newspaper, posted on the land, and mailed to adjoining owners and all persons known to have an adverse interest. Chief Justice Holmes, writing for the majority, denied the petition and upheld the act as constitutional, but cautioned that it ought to be amended to insure actual notice:

> If it does not satisfy the constitution, a judicial proceeding to clear titles against all the world hardly is possible; for the very meaning of such a proceeding is to get rid of unknown as well as known claims,—indeed, certainty against the unknown may be said to be its chief end,—and unknown claims cannot be dealt with by personal service upon the claimant. * * *
>
> Looked at either from the point of view of history or of the necessary requirements of justice, a proceeding in rem, dealing with a tangible res, may be instituted and carried to judgment without personal service upon claimants within the state, or notice by name to those outside of it, and not encounter any provision of either constitution. Jurisdiction is secured by the power of the court over the res. * * *
>
> But it is said that this is not a proceeding "in rem." It is certain that no phrase has been more misused. * * * If the technical object of the suit is to establish a claim against some particular person, with a judgment which generally in theory, at least, binds his body, or to bar some individual claim or objection, so that only certain persons are entitled to be heard in defense, the action is in personam, although it may concern the right to, or possession of, a tangible thing. * * * If,

> on the other hand, the object is to bar indifferently all who might be minded to make an objection of any sort against the right sought to be established, and if any one in the world has a right to be heard on the strength of alleging facts which, if true, show an inconsistent interest, the proceeding is in rem. * * * All proceedings, like all rights, are really against persons. Whether they are proceedings or rights in rem depends on the number of persons affected. Hence the res need not be personified, and made a party defendant * * *. It need not even be a tangible thing at all * * *. Personification and naming the res as defendant are mere symbols, not the essential matter. They are fictions, conveniently expressing the nature of the process and the result; nothing more. * * *

Id. at 73, 75–76, 55 N.E. at 813–14.

PENNINGTON v. FOURTH NATIONAL BANK, 243 U.S. 269, 271–72, 37 S.Ct. 282, 282–83, 61 L.Ed. 713, 714–15 (1917). Petitioner challenged the garnishment of his bank account to pay alimony. Although petitioner did not reside in the forum state, the Court held that attachment of his in-state bank account satisfied due process. Justice Brandeis explained in his opinion for the Court:

> The 14th Amendment did not, in guarantying due process of law, abridge the jurisdiction which a state possessed over property within its borders, regardless of the residence or presence of the owner. That jurisdiction extends alike to tangible and to intangible property. Indebtedness due from a resident to a nonresident—of which bank deposits are an example—is property within the state. * * * It is, indeed, the species of property which courts of the several states have most frequently applied in satisfaction of the obligations of absent debtors. * * * Substituted service on a nonresident by publication furnishes no legal basis for a judgment in personam. * * * But garnishment or foreign attachment is a proceeding quasi in rem. * * * The thing belonging to the absent defendant is seized and applied to the satisfaction of his obligation. The Federal Constitution presents no obstacle to the full exercise of this power.
>
> * * * The power of the state to proceed against the property of an absent defendant is the same whether the obligation sought to be enforced is an admitted indebtedness or a contested claim. * * * It is likewise immaterial that the claim is, at the commencement of the suit, inchoate, to be perfected only by time or the action of the court. The only essentials to the exercise of the state's power are presence of the res within its borders, its seizure at the commencement of proceedings, and the opportunity of the owner to be heard.

NOTE AND QUESTION

What is the situs of corporate stock for purposes of attachment—the corporation's place of incorporation, the domicile of the shareholder, or the state in which the stock certificates actually are located? See generally Note, *Attachment of Corporate Stock: The Conflicting Approaches of Delaware and the Uniform Stock Transfer Act*, 73 Harv.L.Rev. 1579 (1960).

HARRIS v. BALK, 198 U.S. 215, 25 S.Ct. 625, 49 L.Ed. 1023 (1905). Harris, a citizen of North Carolina, owed Balk, also of North Carolina, $180. Epstein, a Maryland citizen, claimed that Balk owed him $344. On August 6, 1896, while Harris was visiting Baltimore, Epstein instituted a garnishee proceeding in a Maryland court, attaching the debt due Balk from Harris. Harris was personally served with the writ of attachment and summons, and notice of the suit was posted at the courthouse door, as required by Maryland law. Harris consented to the entry of judgment against him and paid the $180 to Epstein. On August 11, 1896, Balk commenced an action against Harris in a North Carolina court to recover the $180. Harris asserted that he no longer owed Balk the $180, having paid that sum to Epstein in partial satisfaction of Balk's debt to Epstein, since the Maryland judgment and his payment thereof was valid in Maryland, and was therefore entitled to full faith and credit in the courts of North Carolina. The trial court ruled in favor of Balk, and the North Carolina Supreme Court affirmed on the ground that the Maryland court had no jurisdiction over Harris to attach the debt because Harris was only temporarily in the state, and the situs of the debt was in North Carolina. The Supreme Court reversed:

> * * * We do not see how the question of jurisdiction *vel non* can properly be made to depend upon the so-called original situs of the debt, or upon the character of the stay of the garnishee, whether temporary or permanent, in the state where the attachment is issued. Power over the person of the garnishee confers jurisdiction on the courts of the state where the writ issues. * * * If, while temporarily there, his creditor might sue him there and recover the debt, then he is liable to process of garnishment, no matter where the situs of the debt was originally. We do not see the materiality of the expression "situs of the debt," when used in connection with attachment proceedings. If by situs is meant the place of the creation of the debt, that fact is immaterial. If it be meant that the obligation to pay the debt can only be enforced at the situs thus fixed, we think it plainly untrue. The obligation of the debtor to pay his debt clings to and accompanies him wherever he goes. He is as much bound to pay his debt in a foreign state when therein sued upon his obligation by his creditor, as he was in the state where the debt was contracted. * * * It would be no defense to such suit for the debtor to plead that he was

> only in the foreign state casually or temporarily. * * * It is nothing but the obligation to pay which is garnished or attached. This obligation can be enforced by the courts of the foreign state after personal service of process therein, just as well as by the courts of the domicil of the debtor. * * *

Id. at 222, 25 S.Ct. at 626, 49 L.Ed. at 1026. The Court indicated in dictum that the result might have been different if Balk had not been given notice of the attachment and an opportunity to defend in the Maryland action.

NOTES AND QUESTIONS

1. Professor Lowenfeld provides the following interesting information concerning Harris, Balk, and Epstein. Epstein was an importer of goods who regularly did business with Balk, a retailer. The $344 debt was for money owed on shipments of goods by Epstein to Balk. Harris was a dry goods merchant from the same town as Balk, and had borrowed money from Balk on several occasions, including a $10 loan just before the fateful trip to Baltimore. Harris carried with him on that trip a message from Balk to Epstein saying that Balk would be coming to Baltimore soon. See Lowenfeld, *In Search of the Intangible: A Comment on* Shaffer v. Heitner, 53 N.Y.U. L. Rev. 102, 104–06 (1978).

If this case were to occur today, could Epstein have sued Balk in personam, assuming a long-arm statute similar to Rhode Island's? Could Epstein have served Harris as Balk's agent?

SHAFFER v. HEITNER

Supreme Court of the United States, 1977.
433 U.S. 186, 97 S.Ct. 2569, 53 L.Ed.2d 683.

On Appeal from the Supreme Court of Delaware.

MR. JUSTICE MARSHALL delivered the opinion of the Court.

* * *

I

Appellee Heitner, a nonresident of Delaware, is the owner of one share of stock in the Greyhound Corp., a business incorporated under the laws of Delaware with its principal place of business in Phoenix, Ariz. On May 22, 1974, he filed a shareholder's derivative suit in the Court of Chancery for New Castle County, Del., in which he named as defendants Greyhound, its wholly owned subsidiary Greyhound Lines, Inc.,[1] and 28 present or former officers or directors of one or both of the corporations. In essence, Heitner alleged that the individual defendants had violated their duties to Greyhound by causing it and its subsidiary to engage in

1. Greyhound Lines, Inc., is incorporated in California and has its principal place of business in Phoenix, Ariz.

actions that resulted in the corporations being held liable for substantial damages in a private antitrust suit and a large fine in a criminal contempt action. The activities which led to these penalties took place in Oregon.

A WRIT AUTHORIZING SEIZURE OF PROPERTY

Simultaneously with his complaint, Heitner filed a motion for an order of sequestration of the Delaware property of the individual defendants pursuant to Del.Code Ann., Tit. 10, § 366 (1975). This motion was accompanied by a supporting affidavit of counsel which stated that the individual defendants were nonresidents of Delaware. The affidavit identified the property to be sequestered as [shares of Greyhound Corporation stock and stock options] * * *. The requested sequestration order was signed the day the motion was filed. Pursuant to that order, the sequestrator "seized" approximately 82,000 shares of Greyhound common stock belonging to 19 of the defendants, and options belonging to another 2 defendants. These seizures were accomplished by placing "stop transfer" orders or their equivalents on the books of the Greyhound Corp. So far as the record shows, none of the certificates representing the seized property was physically present in Delaware. The stock was considered to be in Delaware, and so subject to seizure, by virtue of Del.Code Ann., Tit. 8, § 169 (1975), which makes Delaware the situs of ownership of all stock in Delaware corporations.

All 28 defendants were notified of the initiation of the suit by certified mail directed to their last known addresses and by publication in a New Castle County newspaper. The 21 defendants whose property was seized (hereafter referred to as appellants) responded by entering a special appearance for the purpose of moving to quash service of process and to vacate the sequestration order. They contended that the *ex parte* sequestration procedure did not accord them due process of law and that the property seized was not capable of attachment in Delaware. In addition, appellants asserted that under the rule of International Shoe Co. v. Washington, * * * [p. 85, supra], they did not have sufficient contacts with Delaware to sustain the jurisdiction of that State's courts.

The Court of Chancery rejected these arguments * * *.

On appeal, the Delaware Supreme Court affirmed the judgment of the Court of Chancery. * * * Most of the Supreme Court's opinion was devoted to rejecting appellants' contention that the sequestration procedure is inconsistent with the due process analysis developed in the *Sniadach* [v. Family Finance Corp., 395 U.S. 337, 89 S.Ct. 1820, 23 L.Ed.2d 349 (1969), see Note 1, p. 249, infra,] line of cases. The court based its rejection of that argument in part on its agreement with the Court of Chancery that the purpose of the sequestration procedure is to compel the appearance of the defendant, a purpose not involved in the *Sniadach* cases. The court also relied on what it considered the ancient origins of the sequestration procedure and approval of that procedure in the opinions of this Court, * * * Delaware's interest in asserting jurisdiction to adjudicate claims of mismanagement of a Delaware corporation, and the safeguards for defendants that it found in the Delaware statute. * * *

* * *

Appellants' claim that the Delaware courts did not have jurisdiction to adjudicate this action received much more cursory treatment. * * *[12] We reverse.

II

The Delaware courts rejected appellants' jurisdictional challenge by noting that this suit was brought as a *quasi in rem* proceeding. Since *quasi in rem* jurisdiction is traditionally based on attachment or seizure of property present in the jurisdiction, not on contacts between the defendant and the State, the courts considered appellants' claimed lack of contacts with Delaware to be unimportant. This categorical analysis assumes the continued soundness of the conceptual structure founded on the century-old case of Pennoyer v. Neff, * * * [p. 71, supra].

[The Court's description of *Pennoyer* is omitted.] * * *

From our perspective, the importance of *Pennoyer* is not its result, but the fact that its principles and corollaries derived from them became the basic elements of the constitutional doctrine governing state-court jurisdiction. * * * As we have noted, under *Pennoyer* state authority to adjudicate was based on the jurisdiction's power over either persons or property. This fundamental concept is embodied in the very vocabulary which we use to describe judgments. If a court's jurisdiction is based on its authority over the defendant's person, the action and judgment are denominated "*in personam*" and can impose a personal obligation on the defendant in favor of the plaintiff. If jurisdiction is based on the court's power over property within its territory, the action is called "*in rem*" or "*quasi in rem*." The effect of a judgment in such a case is limited to the property that supports jurisdiction and does not impose a personal liability on the property owner, since he is not before the court. * * * In *Pennoyer*'s terms, the owner is affected only "indirectly" by an *in rem* judgment adverse to his interest in the property subject to the court's disposition.

[JUSTICE MARSHALL'S historical analysis of the expansion of *in personam* jurisdiction is omitted.] * * *

No equally dramatic change has occurred in the law governing jurisdiction *in rem*. There have, however, been intimations that the collapse of the *in personam* wing of *Pennoyer* has not left that decision unweakened as a foundation for *in rem* jurisdiction. Well-reasoned lower court opinions have questioned the proposition that the presence of property in a State gives that State jurisdiction to adjudicate rights to the property regardless of the relationship of the underlying dispute and the property owner to

12. Under Delaware law, defendants whose property has been sequestered must enter a general appearance, thus subjecting themselves to *in personam* liability, before they can defend on the merits. * * *

the forum. * * * The overwhelming majority of commentators have also rejected *Pennoyer*'s premise that a proceeding "against" property is not a proceeding against the owners of that property. Accordingly, they urge that the "traditional notions of fair play and substantial justice" that govern a State's power to adjudicate *in personam* should also govern its power to adjudicate personal rights to property located in the State. * * *

Although this Court has not addressed this argument directly, we have held that property cannot be subjected to a court's judgment unless reasonable and appropriate efforts have been made to give the property owners actual notice of the action. * * * Mullane v. Central Hanover Bank & Trust Co., 339 U.S. 306 (1950) [, p. 199, infra]. This conclusion recognizes, contrary to *Pennoyer,* that an adverse judgment *in rem* directly affects the property owner by divesting him of his rights in the property before the court. * * * Moreover, in *Mullane* we held that Fourteenth Amendment rights cannot depend on the classification of an action as *in rem* or *in personam* * * *.

It is clear, therefore, that the law of state-court jurisdiction no longer stands securely on the foundation established in *Pennoyer.* We think that the time is ripe to consider whether the standard of fairness and substantial justice set forth in *International Shoe* should be held to govern actions *in rem* as well as *in personam.*

III

The case for applying to jurisdiction *in rem* the same test of "fair play and substantial justice" as governs assertions of jurisdiction *in personam* is simple and straightforward. It is premised on recognition that "[t]he phrase, 'judicial jurisdiction over a thing', is a customary elliptical way of referring to jurisdiction over the interests of persons in a thing." Restatement (Second) of Conflict of Laws § 56, Introductory Note * * *. This recognition leads to the conclusion that in order to justify an exercise of jurisdiction *in rem,* the basis for jurisdiction must be sufficient to justify exercising "jurisdiction over the interests of persons in a thing." The standard for determining whether an exercise of jurisdiction over the interests of persons is consistent with the Due Process Clause is the minimum-contacts standard elucidated in *International Shoe.*

This argument, of course, does not ignore the fact that the presence of property in a State may bear on the existence of jurisdiction by providing contacts among the forum State, the defendant, and the litigation. For example, when claims to the property itself are the source of the underlying controversy between the plaintiff and the defendant, it would be unusual for the State where the property is located not to have jurisdiction. In such cases, the defendant's claim to property located in the State would normally indicate that he expected to benefit from the State's protection of his interest. The State's strong interests in assuring the marketability of property within its borders and in providing a procedure for peaceful resolution of disputes about the possession of that property would also support jurisdiction, as would the likelihood that important records and witnesses will be found in the State. The presence of property may also favor jurisdiction in cases, such as suits for injury suffered on the land of an absentee owner, where the defendant's ownership of the property is conceded but the cause of action is otherwise related to rights and duties growing out of that ownership.

It appears, therefore, that jurisdiction over many types of actions which now are or might be brought *in rem* would not be affected by a holding that any assertion of state-court jurisdiction must satisfy the *International Shoe* standard. For the type of *quasi in rem* action typified by Harris v. Balk and the present case, however, accepting the proposed analysis would result in significant change. These are cases where the property which now serves as the basis for state-court jurisdiction is completely unrelated to the plaintiff's cause of action. Thus, although the presence of the defendant's property in a State might suggest the existence of other ties among the defendant, the State, and the litigation, the presence of the property alone would not support the State's jurisdiction. If those other ties did not exist, cases over which the State is now thought to have jurisdiction could not be brought in that forum.

Since acceptance of the *International Shoe* test would most affect this class of cases, we examine the arguments against adopting that standard as they relate to this category of litigation. Before doing so, however, we note that this type of case also presents the clearest illustration of the argument in favor of assessing assertions of jurisdiction by a single standard. For in cases such as *Harris* and this one, the only role played by the property is to provide the basis for bringing the defendant into court. Indeed, the express purpose of the Delaware sequestration procedure is to compel the defendant to enter a personal appearance. In such cases, if a direct assertion of personal jurisdiction over the defendant would violate the Constitution, it would seem that an indirect assertion of that jurisdiction should be equally impermissible.

The primary rationale for treating the presence of property as a sufficient basis for jurisdiction to adjudicate claims over which the State would not have jurisdiction if *International Shoe* applied is that a wrongdoer

> should not be able to avoid payment of his obligations by the expedient of removing his assets to a place where he is not subject to an in personam suit. Restatement [(Second) of Conflicts] § 66, Comment a.

* * * This justification, however, does not explain why jurisdiction should be recognized without regard to whether the property is present in the State because of an effort to avoid the owner's obligations. Nor does it support jurisdiction to adjudicate the underlying claim. At most, it suggests that a State in which property is located should have jurisdiction to attach that property, by use of proper procedures, as security for a judgment being sought in a forum where the litigation can be maintained consistently with *International Shoe*. * * * Moreover, we know of nothing to justify the assumption that a debtor can avoid paying his obligations by

removing his property to a State in which his creditor cannot obtain personal jurisdiction over him. The Full Faith and Credit Clause, after all, makes the valid *in personam* judgment of one State enforceable in all other States.

It might also be suggested that allowing *in rem* jurisdiction avoids the uncertainty inherent in the *International Shoe* standard and assures a plaintiff of a forum.[37] * * * We believe, however, that the fairness standard of *International Shoe* can be easily applied in the vast majority of cases. Moreover, when the existence of jurisdiction in a particular forum under *International Shoe* is unclear, the cost of simplifying the litigation by avoiding the jurisdictional question may be the sacrifice of "fair play and substantial justice." That cost is too high.

We are left, then, to consider the significance of the long history of jurisdiction based solely on the presence of property in a State. Although the theory that territorial power is both essential to and sufficient for jurisdiction has been undermined, we have never held that the presence of property in a State does not automatically confer jurisdiction over the owner's interest in that property. This history must be considered as supporting the proposition that jurisdiction based solely on the presence of property satisfies the demands of due process * * *, but it is not decisive. * * * The fiction that an assertion of jurisdiction over property is anything but an assertion of jurisdiction over the owner of the property supports an ancient form without substantial modern justification. Its continued acceptance would serve only to allow state-court jurisdiction that is fundamentally unfair to the defendant.

We therefore conclude that all assertions of state-court jurisdiction must be evaluated according to the standards set forth in *International Shoe* and its progeny.

IV

The Delaware courts based their assertion of jurisdiction in this case solely on the statutory presence of appellants' property in Delaware. Yet that property is not the subject matter of this litigation, nor is the underlying cause of action related to the property. Appellants' holdings in Greyhound do not, therefore, provide contacts with Delaware sufficient to support the jurisdiction of that State's courts over appellants. If it exists, that jurisdiction must have some other foundation.[40]

---

37. This case does not raise, and we therefore do not consider, the question whether the presence of a defendant's property in a State is a sufficient basis for jurisdiction when no other forum is available to the plaintiff.

40. Appellants argue that our determination that the minimum contacts standard of *International Shoe* governs jurisdiction here makes unnecessary any consideration of the existence of such contacts. * * * They point out that they were never personally served with a summons, that Delaware has no long-arm statute which would authorize such service, and that the Delaware Supreme Court has authoritatively held that the existence of contacts is irrelevant to jurisdiction under Del.Code Ann., Tit. 10, § 366 (1975). As part of its sequestration order, however, the Court of Chancery directed its clerk to send each appellant a copy of the summons and complaint by certified mail. The record indicates that those mailings were made and contains return receipts from at least 19 of the appellants. None of the appellants has suggested that he did not actually

Appellee Heitner did not allege and does not now claim that appellants have ever set foot in Delaware. Nor does he identify any act related to his cause of action as having taken place in Delaware. Nevertheless, he contends that appellants' positions as directors and officers of a corporation chartered in Delaware provide sufficient "contacts, ties, or relations" * * * with that State to give its courts jurisdiction over appellants in this stockholder's derivative action. This argument is based primarily on what Heitner asserts to be the strong interest of Delaware in supervising the management of a Delaware corporation. That interest is said to derive from the role of Delaware law in establishing the corporation and defining the obligations owed to it by its officers and directors. In order to protect this interest, appellee concludes, Delaware's courts must have jurisdiction over corporate fiduciaries such as appellants.

REJECTS THIS ARGUMENT

This argument is undercut by the failure of the Delaware Legislature to assert the state interest appellee finds so compelling. Delaware law bases jurisdiction, not on appellants' status as corporate fiduciaries, but rather on the presence of their property in the State. Although the sequestration procedure used here may be most frequently used in derivative suits against officers and directors, * * * the authorizing statute evinces no specific concern with such actions. Sequestration can be used in any suit against a nonresident * * * and reaches corporate fiduciaries only if they happen to own interests in a Delaware corporation, or other property in the State. But as Heitner's failure to secure jurisdiction over seven of the defendants named in his complaint demonstrates, there is no necessary relationship between holding a position as a corporate fiduciary and owning stock or other interests in the corporation. If Delaware perceived its interest in securing jurisdiction over corporate fiduciaries to be as great as Heitner suggests, we would expect it to have enacted a statute more clearly designed to protect that interest.

Moreover, even if Heitner's assessment of the importance of Delaware's interest is accepted, his argument fails to demonstrate that Delaware is a fair forum for this litigation. The interest appellee has identified may support the application of Delaware law to resolve any controversy over appellants' actions in their capacities as officers and directors. But we have rejected the argument that if a State's law can properly be applied to a dispute, its courts necessarily have jurisdiction over the parties to that dispute. * * *

Appellee suggests that by accepting positions as officers or directors of a Delaware corporation, appellants performed the acts [sufficient to justify the assertion of jurisdiction by Delaware courts under] Hanson v. Denckla. He notes that Delaware law provides substantial benefits to corporate officers and directors, and that these benefits were at least in part the incentive for appellants to assume their positions. It is, he says, "only fair

receive the summons which was directed to him in compliance with a Delaware statute designed to provide jurisdiction over non-residents. In these circumstances, we will assume that the procedures followed would be sufficient to bring appellants before the Delaware courts, if minimum contacts existed.

and just" to require appellants, in return for these benefits, to respond in the State of Delaware when they are accused of misusing their power. * * *

But like Heitner's first argument, this line of reasoning establishes only that it is appropriate for Delaware law to govern the obligations of appellants to Greyhound and its stockholders. It does not demonstrate that appellants have "purposefully avail[ed themselves] of the privilege of conducting activities within the forum State," Hanson v. Denckla * * *, in a way that would justify bringing them before a Delaware tribunal. Appellants have simply had nothing to do with the State of Delaware. Moreover, appellants had no reason to expect to be haled before a Delaware court. Delaware, unlike some States, has not enacted a statute that treats acceptance of a directorship as consent to jurisdiction in the State. And "[i]t strains reason * * * to suggest that anyone buying securities in a corporation formed in Delaware 'impliedly consents' to subject himself to Delaware's * * * jurisdiction on any cause of action." Folk & Moyer, [*Sequestration in Delaware: A Constitutional Analysis*, 73 Colum.L.Rev. 749, 785 (1973)] * * *. Appellants, who were not required to acquire interests in Greyhound in order to hold their positions, did not by acquiring those interests surrender their right to be brought to judgment only in States with which they had had "minimum contacts."

* * * Delaware's assertion of jurisdiction over appellants in this case is inconsistent with that constitutional limitation on state power. The judgment of the Delaware Supreme Court must, therefore, be reversed.

It is so ordered.

MR. JUSTICE REHNQUIST took no part in the consideration or decision of this case.

MR. JUSTICE POWELL, concurring.

* * *

I would explicitly reserve judgment * * * on whether the ownership of some forms of property whose situs is indisputably and permanently located within a State may, without more, provide the contacts necessary to subject a defendant to jurisdiction within the State to the extent of the value of the property. In the case of real property, in particular, preservation of the common law concept of *quasi in rem* jurisdiction arguably would avoid the uncertainty of the general *International Shoe* standard without significant cost to " 'traditional notions of fair play and substantial justice.' " * * *

Subject to the foregoing reservation, I join the opinion of the Court.

MR. JUSTICE STEVENS, concurring in the judgment.

* * *

One who purchases shares of stock on the open market can hardly be expected to know that he has thereby become subject to suit in a forum remote from his residence and unrelated to the transaction. As a practical matter, the Delaware sequestration statute creates an unacceptable risk of judgment without notice. Unlike the 49 other States, Delaware treats the place of incorporation as the situs of the stock, even though both the owner and the custodian of the shares are elsewhere. Moreover, Delaware denies the defendant the opportunity to defend the merits of the suit unless he subjects himself to the unlimited jurisdiction of the court. Thus, it coerces a defendant either to submit to personal jurisdiction in a forum which could not otherwise obtain such jurisdiction or to lose the securities which have been attached. If its procedure were upheld, Delaware would, in effect, impose a duty of inquiry on every purchaser of securities in the national market. For unless the purchaser ascertains both the State of incorporation of the company whose shares he is buying, and also the idiosyncrasies of its law, he may be assuming an unknown risk of litigation. I therefore agree with the Court that on the record before us no adequate basis for jurisdiction exists and that the Delaware statute is unconstitutional on its face.

How the Court's opinion may be applied in other contexts is not entirely clear to me. I agree with MR. JUSTICE POWELL that it should not be read to invalidate *in rem* jurisdiction where real estate is involved. I would also not read it as invalidating other long-accepted methods of acquiring jurisdiction over persons with adequate notice of both the particular controversy and the fact that their local activities might subject them to suit. My uncertainty as to the reach of the opinion, and my fear that it purports to decide a great deal more than is necessary to dispose of this case, persuade me merely to concur in the judgment.

MR. JUSTICE BRENNAN, concurring in part and dissenting in part.

I join Parts I–III of the Court's opinion. I fully agree that the minimum-contacts analysis * * * represents a far more sensible construct for the exercise of state-court jurisdiction than the patchwork of legal and factual fictions that has been generated from the decision in Pennoyer v. Neff * * *. It is precisely because the inquiry into minimum contacts is now of such overriding importance, however, that I must respectfully dissent from Part IV of the Court's opinion.

I

The primary teaching of Parts I–III of today's decision is that a State, in seeking to assert jurisdiction over a person located outside its borders, may only do so on the basis of minimum contacts among the parties, the contested transaction, and the forum state. The Delaware Supreme Court could not have made plainer, however, that its sequestration statute * * * does not operate on this basis, but instead is strictly an embodiment of *quasi in rem* jurisdiction, a jurisdictional predicate no longer constitutionally viable * * *. This state-court ruling obviously comports with the understanding of the parties, for the issue of the existence of minimum contacts was never pleaded by appellee, made the subject of discovery, or ruled upon by the Delaware courts. These facts notwithstanding, the Court in Part IV reaches the minimum-contacts question and finds such contacts lacking as applied to appellants. Succinctly stated, once having properly and persuasively decided that the *quasi in rem* statute that Delaware admits to having enacted is invalid, the Court then proceeds to find that a minimum-contacts law that Delaware expressly *denies* having enacted also could not be constitutionally applied in this case.

In my view, a purer example of an advisory opinion is not to be found. True, appellants do not deny having received actual notice of the action in question. * * * But notice is but one ingredient of a proper assertion of state-court jurisdiction. The other is a statute authorizing the exercise of the State's judicial power along constitutionally permissible grounds—which henceforth means minimum contacts. As of today, § 366 is not such a law.[1] Recognizing that today's decision fundamentally alters the relevant jurisdictional ground rules, I certainly would not want to rule out the possibility that Delaware's courts might decide that the legislature's overriding purpose of securing the personal appearance in state courts of defendants would best be served by reinterpreting its statute to permit state jurisdiction of the basis of constitutionally permissible contacts rather than stock ownership. Were the state courts to take this step, it would then become necessary to address the question of whether minimum contacts exist here. But in the present posture of this case, the Court's decision of this important issue is purely an abstract ruling.

My concern with the inappropriateness of the Court's action is highlighted by two other considerations. First, an inquiry into minimum contacts inevitably is highly dependent on creating a proper factual foundation detailing the contacts between the forum state and the controversy in question. Because neither the plaintiff-appellee nor the state courts viewed such an inquiry as germane in this instance, the Court today is unable to draw upon a proper factual record in reaching its conclusion; moreover, its disposition denies appellee the normal opportunity to seek discovery on the contacts issue. Second, it must be remembered that the Court's ruling is a constitutional one and necessarily will affect the reach of the jurisdictional laws of all 50 States. Ordinarily this would counsel restraint in constitutional pronouncements. * * * Certainly it should have cautioned the Court against reaching out to decide a question that, as here, has yet to emerge from the state courts ripened for review on the federal issue.

II

Nonetheless, because the Court rules on the minimum-contacts question, I feel impelled to express my view. While evidence derived through discovery might satisfy me that minimum contacts are lacking in a given case, I am convinced that as a general rule a state forum has jurisdiction to adjudicate a shareholder derivative action centering on the conduct and

1. Indeed, the Court's decision to proceed to the minimum-contacts issue treats Delaware's sequestration statute as if it were the equivalent of Rhode Island's long-arm law, which specifically authorizes its courts to assume jurisdiction to the limit permitted by the Constitution, R.I.Gen.Laws Ann. § 9–5–33 (1970), thereby necessitating judicial consideration of the frontiers of minimum contacts in every case arising under that statute.

policies of the directors and officers of a corporation chartered by that State. Unlike the Court, I therefore would not foreclose Delaware from asserting jurisdiction over appellants were it persuaded to do so on the basis of minimum contacts.

It is well settled that a derivative lawsuit as presented here does not inure primarily to the benefit of the named plaintiff. Rather, the primary beneficiaries are the corporation and its owners, the shareholders. * * *

Viewed in this light, the chartering State has an unusually powerful interest in insuring the availability of a convenient forum for litigating claims involving a possible multiplicity of defendant fiduciaries and for vindicating the State's substantive policies regarding the management of its domestic corporations. I believe that our cases fairly establish that the State's valid substantive interests are important considerations in assessing whether it constitutionally may claim jurisdiction over a given cause of action.

In this instance, Delaware can point to at least three interrelated public policies that are furthered by its assertion of jurisdiction. First, the State has a substantial interest in providing restitution for its local corporations that allegedly have been victimized by fiduciary misconduct, even if the managerial decisions occurred outside the State. The importance of this general state interest in assuring restitution for its own residents previously found expression in cases that went outside the then-prevailing due process framework to authorize state-court jurisdiction over nonresident motorists who injure others within the State. * * * More recently, it has led States to seek and to acquire jurisdiction over nonresident tortfeasors whose purely out-of-state activities produce domestic consequences. * * * Second, state courts have legitimately read their jurisdiction expansively when a cause of action centers in an area in which the forum State possesses a manifest regulatory interest. * * * Only this Term we reiterated that the conduct of corporate fiduciaries is just such a matter in which the policies and interests of a domestic forum are paramount. * * * Finally, a State like Delaware has a recognized interest in affording a convenient forum for supervising and overseeing the affairs of an entity that is purely the creation of that State's law. For example, even following our decision in *International Shoe,* New York courts were permitted to exercise complete judicial authority over nonresident beneficiaries of a trust created under state law, even though, unlike appellants here, the beneficiaries personally entered into no association whatsoever with New York. Mullane v. Central Hanover Bank & Trust Co., [p. 199, infra] * * *.

To be sure, the Court is not blind to these considerations. It notes that the State's interests "may support the application of Delaware law to resolve any controversy over appellants' actions in their capacities as officers and directors." * * * But this, the Court argues, pertains to choice of law, not jurisdiction. I recognize that the jurisdictional and choice-of-law inquiries are not identical. * * * But I would not compartmentalize thinking in this area quite so rigidly as it seems to me the Court does today, for both inquiries "are often closely related and to a substantial degree depend upon similar considerations." [Hanson v. Denckla, 357 U.S.] at 258, 78 S.Ct. at 1242 (Black, J., dissenting). * * * At the minimum, the decision that it is fair to bind a defendant by a State's laws and rules should prove to be highly relevant to the fairness of permitting that same State to accept jurisdiction for adjudicating the controversy.

Furthermore, I believe that practical considerations argue in favor of seeking to bridge the distance between the choice-of-law and jurisdictional inquiries. Even when a court would apply the law of a different forum, as a general rule it will feel less knowledgeable and comfortable in interpretation, and less interested in fostering the policies of that foreign jurisdiction, than would the courts established by the State that provides the applicable law. * * * Obviously, such choice-of-law problems cannot entirely be avoided in a diverse legal system such as our own. Nonetheless, when a suitor seeks to lodge a suit in a State with a substantial interest in seeing its own law applied to the transaction in question, we could wisely act to minimize conflicts, confusion, and uncertainty by adopting a liberal view of jurisdiction, unless considerations of fairness or efficiency strongly point in the opposite direction.

This case is not one where, in my judgment, this preference for jurisdiction is adequately answered. Certainly nothing said by the Court persuades me that it would be unfair to subject appellants to suit in Delaware. The fact that the record does not reveal whether they "set foot" or committed "acts related to [the] cause of action" in Delaware * * * is not decisive, for jurisdiction can be based strictly on out-of-state acts having foreseeable effects in the forum State. * * * I have little difficulty in applying this principle to nonresident fiduciaries whose alleged breaches of trust are said to have substantial damaging effect on the financial posture of a resident corporation. Further, I cannot understand how the existence of minimum contacts in a constitutional sense is at all affected by Delaware's failure statutorily to express an interest in controlling corporate fiduciaries. * * * To me this simply demonstrates that Delaware did not elect to assert jurisdiction to the extent the Constitution would allow. Nor would I view as controlling or even especially meaningful Delaware's failure to exact from appellants their consent to be sued. * * * Once we have rejected the jurisdictional framework created in Pennoyer v. Neff, I see no reason to rest jurisdiction on a fictional outgrowth of that system such as the existence of a consent statute, expressed or implied.

I, therefore, would approach the minimum-contacts analysis differently than does the Court. Crucial to me is the fact that appellants voluntarily associated themselves with the State of Delaware, "invoking the benefits and protections of its laws," * * * by entering into a long-term and fragile relationship with one of its domestic corporations. They thereby elected to assume powers and to undertake responsibilities wholly derived from that State's rules and regulations, and to become eligible for those benefits that Delaware law makes available to its corporations' officials.

E.g., Del.Code Ann., Tit. 8, § 143 (1975) (interest-free loans); § 145 (1975 ed. and Supp.1976) (indemnification). While it is possible that countervailing issues of judicial efficiency and the like might clearly favor a different forum, they do not appear on the meager record before us; and, of course, we are concerned solely with "minimum" contacts, not the "best" contacts. * * *

NOTES AND QUESTIONS

1. Within thirteen days after the decision in *Shaffer,* the Delaware legislature amended its laws to provide that every nonresident who is elected or appointed a director of a Delaware corporation after September 1, 1977, shall "be deemed" to have consented to the appointment of the corporation's registered agent in Delaware, or, if there is no registered agent, of the Secretary of State of Delaware, as his agent for service of process in any Delaware action based on violation of the director's duties as director after September 1, 1977. 10 Del.Code § 3114. The constitutionality of the section was upheld by the Supreme Court of Delaware in Armstrong v. Pomerance, 423 A.2d 174 (Del.1980), a suit against nonresidents whose sole contact with Delaware was their status as directors of a Delaware corporation. See also Stearn v. Malloy, 89 F.R.D. 421 (E.D.Wis.1981) (reaching the same conclusion under a similar Wisconsin statute). See Comment, *Constitutional Analysis of the New Delaware Director–Consent-to-Service Statute,* 70 Geo.L.J. 1209 (1983).

Shortly after enactment of the Delaware director consent-to-service statute, Greyhound Corporation sought and obtained the approval of its shareholders to reincorporate in Arizona, where Greyhound also has its principal headquarters. A stated reason was that "it would be an unreasonable burden upon directors, not resident in Delaware, several of whom reside in Arizona and California, to be required to journey to Delaware to defend a case there when they have no contact with that state." Ratner & Schwartz, *The Impact of* Shaffer v. Heitner *on the Substantive Law of Corporations,* 45 Brooklyn L.Rev. 641, 653–54 (1979). In 2004, the Delaware consent-to-service statute was extended to high officers of Delaware corporations (such as the president, treasurer, or CEO).

2. Does *Shaffer* preclude a state from rendering a judgment in a pure in rem action that is binding against the world? In this regard, is footnote 37 of Justice Marshall's opinion relevant? See p. 165, supra.

3. In RHOADES v. WRIGHT, 622 P.2d 343 (Utah 1980), certiorari denied 454 U.S. 897, 102 S.Ct. 397, 70 L.Ed.2d 212 (1981), the Supreme Court of Utah upheld the attachment for jurisdictional purposes of farm land in Utah owned by the defendant, a resident of Colorado, who was being sued for the wrongful death of a Utah resident killed outside Utah. The court considered the presence of the land (as distinguished from the kind of intangible and movable property involved in *Shaffer*), together with the fact that the Colorado defendant actively used the land, sufficient contact with Utah to satisfy due process requirements for the exercise of quasi-in-rem jurisdiction.

4. Does *Shaffer* overturn Harris v. Balk? In FEDER v. TURKISH AIRLINES, 441 F.Supp. 1273 (S.D.N.Y.1977), decided after *Shaffer*, the court upheld quasi-in-rem jurisdiction based on the attachment of defendant's New York bank account. The bank account, established by the airline to pay for aircraft parts and components, was the airline's only contact with the forum. The action was a wrongful-death suit stemming from an accident that occurred in Turkey. The plaintiffs were New York residents. Is the result in *Feder* consistent with *Shaffer*?

5. In RUSH v. SAVCHUK, 444 U.S. 320, 100 S.Ct. 571, 62 L.Ed.2d 516 (1980), the Supreme Court settled the question of whether an insurance obligation can be attached to effect quasi-in-rem jurisdiction. In finding such an attachment unconstitutional, the Court separated the contacts between the defendant and the forum from the contacts between the insurer and the forum. Having done so, the Court held that sufficient contacts between the defendant and the forum did not exist and that the Due Process Clause forbade assertion of jurisdiction.

6. For an excellent discussion of *Shaffer,* see Silberman, Shaffer v. Heitner: *The End of an Era*, 53 N.Y.U.L.Rev. 33 (1978). Further commentary is found in symposia on the impact of *Shaffer* in 45 Brooklyn L.Rev. 493 (1979); and 1978 Wash.U.L.Q. 273. See also Smit, *The Enduring Utility of In Rem Rules: A Lasting Legacy of* Pennoyer v. Neff, 43 Brooklyn L.Rev. 600 (1977).

NOTE ON "CYBERSQUATTING" AND IN REM JURISDICTION

The Internet's exploding popularity has generated novel problems for traditional businesses that seek to establish an on-line presence. One such problem is "cybersquatting," which "consists of registering, trafficking in, or using Internet addresses that are identical or confusingly similar to protected trademarks." Callen, *Asserting In Personam Jurisdiction Over Foreign Cybersquatters*, 69 U. Chi. L. Rev. 1837, 1837 (2002). Consider this problem:

> Imagine Mr. Blofeld, a foreign entrepreneur, who discovered the perfect way to make a fast buck. * * * He registered the Internet domain name "pentium3.com" with Verisign, a domain registry based in Virginia, and then set up a pornographic website at that address. Around the world, Internet users seeking information on Intel, the manufacturer of the Pentium computer processor, were diverted to Blofeld's site. Blofeld could either continue to profit from the Internet traffic intended for the Intel website or offer to sell advertising space on his webpage to Intel's competitors. Even though these activities confused consumers and tarnished the value of Intel's protected mark, Intel could do little to stop him. Blofeld had not directly attempted to extort money from Intel. Since Blofeld's only contact in the United States was the registration of the domain name with the Virginia registry, he seems beyond the jurisdictional reach of the United States courts.

Id. One court has referred to such activity as "the Internet version of a land grab," Interstellar Starship Servs., Ltd. v. Epix, Inc., 304 F.3d 936, 946 (9th Cir.2002), and a commentator calls it "a new form of piracy." Sherry, *Haste*

Makes Waste: Congress and the Common Law in Cyberspace, 55 Vand. L. Rev. 309, 317 (2002).

Congress responded to the problem with legislation creating a cause of action by a trademark owner against anyone who "registers, traffics in, or uses" the trademark as a domain name with "a bad faith intent to profit from" the trademark. The statute further provides that in cases in which in personam jurisdiction is not available (typically because the defendant is based overseas), the court has authority to exercise in rem jurisdiction in the judicial district in which the domain name is registered. See Anticybersquatting Consumer Protection Act (ACPA), 15 U.S.C. § 1125(d)(2)(A). In HARRODS LTD. v. SIXTY INTERNET DOMAIN NAMES, 302 F.3d 214 (4th Cir. 2002), Harrods, the famous British retailer, brought suit against an Argentine concern that had registered with a Virginia company sixty domain names that were all variants of the Harrods name, such as cyberharrods.com and harrodsshopping.com. The Court of Appeals upheld the constitutionality of conferring in rem jurisdiction in the judicial district where the domain names had been registered. Relying on Shaffer v. Heitner, p. 161, supra, the court emphasized the state's sovereign interest in protecting property registered within its borders and also the relation of the dispute to the property itself. Id. at 225. For a discussion of the constitutionality of exercising in rem jurisdiction on the basis of domain-name registration, see Magier, *Note—Tick, Tock, Time Is Running Out To Nab Cybersquatters: The Dwindling Utility of the Anticybersquatting Consumer Protection Act*, 46 IDEA 415 (2006).

SECTION H. A REFRAIN: JURISDICTION BASED UPON PHYSICAL PRESENCE

BURNHAM v. SUPERIOR COURT

Supreme Court of the United States, 1990.
495 U.S. 604, 110 S.Ct. 2105, 109 L.Ed.2d 631.

Certiorari to the Court of Appeal of California, First Appellate District.

JUSTICE SCALIA announced the judgment of the Court and delivered an opinion in which THE CHIEF JUSTICE and JUSTICE KENNEDY join, and in which JUSTICE WHITE joins with respect to Parts I, II–A, II–B, and II–C.

The question presented is whether the Due Process Clause of the Fourteenth Amendment denies California courts jurisdiction over a nonresident, who was personally served with process while temporarily in that State, in a suit unrelated to his activities in the State.

I

Petitioner Dennis Burnham married Francie Burnham in 1976 in West Virginia. In 1977 the couple moved to New Jersey, where their two children were born. In July 1987 the Burnhams decided to separate. They agreed that Mrs. Burnham, who intended to move to California, would take custody of the children. Shortly before Mrs. Burnham departed for

California that same month, she and petitioner agreed that she would file for divorce on grounds of "irreconcilable differences."

In October 1987, petitioner filed for divorce in New Jersey state court on grounds of "desertion." Petitioner did not, however, obtain an issuance of summons against his wife and did not attempt to serve her with process. Mrs. Burnham, after unsuccessfully demanding that petitioner adhere to their prior agreement to submit to an "irreconcilable differences" divorce, brought suit for divorce in California state court in early January 1988.

In late January, petitioner visited southern California on business, after which he went north to visit his children in the San Francisco Bay area, where his wife resided. He took the older child to San Francisco for the weekend. Upon returning the child to Mrs. Burnham's home on January 24, 1988, petitioner was served with a California court summons and a copy of Mrs. Burnham's divorce petition. He then returned to New Jersey.

Later that year, petitioner made a special appearance in the California Superior Court, moving to quash the service of process on the ground that the court lacked personal jurisdiction over him because his only contacts with California were a few short visits to the State for the purposes of conducting business and visiting his children. The Superior Court denied the motion, and the California Court of Appeal denied mandamus relief, rejecting petitioner's contention that the Due Process Clause prohibited California courts from asserting jurisdiction over him because he lacked "minimum contacts" with the State. The court held it to be "a valid jurisdictional predicate for *in personam* jurisdiction" that the "defendant [was] present in the forum state and personally served with process." * * * We granted certiorari. * * *

II

A

The proposition that the judgment of a court lacking jurisdiction is void traces back to the English Year Books, * * * and was made settled law by Lord Coke * * * [in 1612]. Traditionally that proposition was embodied in the phrase *coram non judice,* "before a person not a judge"—meaning, in effect, that the proceeding in question was not a *judicial* proceeding because lawful judicial authority was not present, and could therefore not yield a *judgment.* American courts invalidated, or denied recognition to, judgments that violated this common-law principle long before the Fourteenth Amendment was adopted. * * * In Pennoyer v. Neff, * * * we announced that the judgment of a court lacking personal jurisdiction violated the Due Process Clause of the Fourteenth Amendment as well.

To determine whether the assertion of personal jurisdiction is consistent with due process, we have long relied on the principles traditionally followed by American courts in marking out the territorial limits of each

State's authority. * * * In what has become the classic expression of the criterion, we said in International Shoe Co. v. Washington, * * * that a state court's assertion of personal jurisdiction satisfies the Due Process Clause if it does not violate " 'traditional notions of fair play and substantial justice.' " * * * Since *International Shoe,* we have only been called upon to decide whether these "traditional notions" permit States to exercise jurisdiction over absent defendants in a manner that deviates from the rules of jurisdiction applied in the 19th century. We have held such deviations permissible, but only with respect to suits arising out of the absent defendant's contacts with the State. * * * The question we must decide today is whether due process requires a similar connection between the litigation and the defendant's contacts with the State in cases where the defendant is physically present in the State at the time process is served upon him.

B

Among the most firmly established principles of personal jurisdiction in American tradition is that the courts of a State have jurisdiction over nonresidents who are physically present in the State. The view developed early that each State had the power to hale before its courts any individual who could be found within its borders, and that once having acquired jurisdiction over such a person by properly serving him with process, the State could retain jurisdiction to enter judgment against him, no matter how fleeting his visit. * * * That view had antecedents in English common-law practice, which sometimes allowed "transitory" actions, arising out of events outside the country, to be maintained against seemingly nonresident defendants who were present in England. * * * Justice Story believed the principle, which he traced to Roman origins, to be firmly grounded in English tradition * * *.

Recent scholarship has suggested that English tradition was not as clear as Story thought * * *. Accurate or not, however, judging by the evidence of contemporaneous or near-contemporaneous decisions, one must conclude that Story's understanding was shared by American courts at the crucial time for present purposes: 1868, when the Fourteenth Amendment was adopted. * * *

Decisions in the courts of many States in the 19th and early 20th centuries held that personal service upon a physically present defendant sufficed to confer jurisdiction, without regard to whether the defendant was only briefly in the State or whether the cause of action was related to his activities there. * * * Although research has not revealed a case deciding the issue in every State's courts, that appears to be because the issue was so well settled that it went unlitigated. * * * Particularly striking is the fact that, as far as we have been able to determine, *not one* American case from the period (or, for that matter, not one American case until 1978) held, or even suggested, that in-state personal service on an individual was insufficient to confer personal jurisdiction. Commentators were also seemingly unanimous on the rule. * * *

This American jurisdictional practice is, moreover, not merely old; it is continuing. It remains the practice of, not only a substantial number of the States, but as far as we are aware *all* the States and the Federal Government—if one disregards (as one must for this purpose) the few opinions since 1978 that have erroneously said, on grounds similar to those that petitioner presses here, that this Court's due process decisions render the practice unconstitutional. * * * We do not know of a single state or federal statute, or a single judicial decision resting upon state law, that has abandoned in-state service as a basis of jurisdiction. Many recent cases reaffirm it. * * *

C

Despite this formidable body of precedent, petitioner contends, in reliance on our decisions applying the *International Shoe* standard, that in the absence of "continuous and systematic" contacts with the forum, * * * a nonresident defendant can be subjected to judgment only as to matters that arise out of or relate to his contacts with the forum. This argument rests on a thorough misunderstanding of our cases.

The view of most courts in the 19th century was that a court simply could not exercise *in personam* jurisdiction over a nonresident who had not been personally served with process in the forum. * * *

* * * In the late 19th and early 20th centuries, changes in the technology of transportation and communication, and the tremendous growth of interstate business activity, led to an "inevitable relaxation of the strict limits on state jurisdiction" over nonresident individuals and corporations. * * * States required, for example, that nonresident corporations appoint an in-state agent upon whom process could be served as a condition of transacting business within their borders, * * * and provided in-state "substituted service" for nonresident motorists who caused injury in the State and left before personal service could be accomplished * * *. We initially upheld these laws under the Due Process Clause on grounds that they complied with *Pennoyer*'s rigid requirement of either "consent," * * * or "presence" * * * As many observed, however, the consent and presence were purely fictional. * * * Our opinion in *International Shoe* cast those fictions aside and made explicit the underlying basis of these decisions: Due process does not necessarily *require* the States to adhere to the unbending territorial limits on jurisdiction set forth in *Pennoyer*. The validity of assertion of jurisdiction over a nonconsenting defendant who is not present in the forum depends upon whether "the quality and nature of [his] activity" in relation to the forum * * * renders such jurisdiction consistent with " 'traditional notions of fair play and substantial justice.' " * * * Subsequent cases have derived from the *International Shoe* standard the general rule that a State may dispense with in-forum personal service on nonresident defendants in suits arising out of their activities in the State. * * *

Nothing in *International Shoe* or the cases that have followed it, however, offers support for the very different proposition petitioner seeks to establish today: that a defendant's presence in the forum is not only unnecessary to validate novel, nontraditional assertions of jurisdiction, but is itself no longer sufficient to establish jurisdiction. That proposition is unfaithful to both elementary logic and the foundations of our due process jurisprudence. The distinction between what is needed to support novel procedures and what is needed to sustain traditional ones is fundamental * * *. The short of the matter is that jurisdiction based on physical presence alone constitutes due process because it is one of the continuing traditions of our legal system that define the due process standard of "traditional notions of fair play and substantial justice." That standard was developed by *analogy* to "physical presence," and it would be perverse to say it could now be turned against that touchstone of jurisdiction.

D

Petitioner's strongest argument, though we ultimately reject it, relies upon our decision in Shaffer v. Heitner * * *.

It goes too far to say, as petitioner contends, that *Shaffer* compels the conclusion that a State lacks jurisdiction over an individual unless the litigation arises out of his activities in the State. *Shaffer,* like *International Shoe,* involved jurisdiction over an *absent defendant,* and it stands for nothing more than the proposition that when the "minimum contact" that is a substitute for physical presence consists of property ownership it must, like other minimum contacts, be related to the litigation. Petitioner wrenches out of its context our statement in *Shaffer* that "all assertions of state-court jurisdiction must be evaluated according to the standards set forth in *International Shoe* and its progeny" * * *. When read together with the two sentences that preceded it, the meaning of this statement becomes clear * * *. *Shaffer* was saying * * * not that all bases for the assertion of *in personam* jurisdiction (including, presumably, in-state service) must be treated alike and subjected to the "minimum contacts" analysis of *International Shoe,* but rather that *quasi in rem* jurisdiction, that fictional "ancient form," and *in personam* jurisdiction, are really one and the same and must be treated alike—leading to the conclusion that *quasi in rem* jurisdiction, *i.e.,* that form of *in personam* jurisdiction based upon a "property ownership" contact and by definition unaccompanied by personal, in-state service, must satisfy the litigation-relatedness requirement of *International Shoe.* The logic of *Shaffer*'s holding—which places all suits against absent nonresidents on the same constitutional footing, regardless of whether a separate Latin label is attached to one particular basis of contact—does not compel the conclusion that physically present defendants must be treated identically to absent ones. As we have demonstrated at length, our tradition has treated the two classes of defendants quite differently, and it is unreasonable to read *Shaffer* as casually obliterating that distinction. *International Shoe* confined its "minimum contacts" requirement to situations in which the defendant "be not present within the territory of the forum," * * * and nothing in *Shaffer* expands that requirement beyond that.

It is fair to say, however, that while our holding today does not contradict *Shaffer,* our basic approach to the due process question is different. We have conducted no independent inquiry into the desirability or fairness of the prevailing in-state service rule, leaving that judgment to the legislatures that are free to amend it; for our purposes, its validation is its pedigree, as the phrase "*traditional notions* of fair play and substantial justice" makes clear. *Shaffer* did conduct such an independent inquiry, asserting that " 'traditional notions of fair play and substantial justice' can be as readily offended by the perpetuation of ancient forms that are no longer justified as by the adoption of new procedures that are inconsistent with the basic values of our constitutional heritage." * * * Perhaps that assertion can be sustained when the "perpetuation of ancient forms" is engaged in by only a very small minority of the States. Where, however, as in the present case, a jurisdictional principle is both firmly approved by tradition and still favored, it is impossible to imagine what standard we could appeal to for the judgment that it is "no longer justified." * * * For new procedures, hitherto unknown, the Due Process Clause requires analysis to determine whether "traditional notions of fair play and substantial justice" have been offended. * * * But a doctrine of personal jurisdiction that dates back to the adoption of the Fourteenth Amendment and is still generally observed unquestionably meets that standard.

III

A few words in response to Justice Brennan's opinion concurring in the judgment: It insists that we apply "contemporary notions of due process" to determine the constitutionality of California's assertion of jurisdiction. * * * The "contemporary notions of due process" applicable to personal jurisdiction are the enduring "*traditional* notions of fair play and substantial justice" established as the test by *International Shoe.* By its very language, that test is satisfied if a state court adheres to jurisdictional rules that are generally applied and have always been applied in the United States.

But the concurrence's proposed standard of "contemporary notions of due process" requires more: It measures state-court jurisdiction not only against traditional doctrines in this country, including current state-court practice, but also against each Justice's subjective assessment of what is fair and just. Authority for that seductive standard is not to be found in any of our personal jurisdiction cases. It is, indeed, an outright break with the test of "traditional notions of fair play and substantial justice," which would have to be reformulated "*our* notions of fair play and substantial justice."

The subjectivity, and hence inadequacy, of this approach becomes apparent when the concurrence tries to explain *why* the assertion of jurisdiction in the present case meets its standard of continuing-American-tradition-*plus*-innate-fairness. Justice Brennan lists the "benefits" Mr. Burnham derived from the State of California—the fact that, during the few days he was there, "[h]is health and safety [were] guaranteed by the

State's police, fire, and emergency medical services; he [was] free to travel on the State's roads and waterways; he likely enjoy[ed] [in original] the fruits of the State's economy." * * * Three days' worth of these benefits strike us as powerfully inadequate to establish, as an abstract matter, that it is "fair" for California to decree the ownership of all Mr. Burnham's worldly goods acquired during the 10 years of his marriage, and the custody over his children. * * * It would create "an asymmetry," we are told, if Burnham were *permitted* (as he is) to appear in California courts as a plaintiff, but were not *compelled* to appear in California courts as defendant; and travel being as easy as it is nowadays, and modern procedural devices being so convenient, it is no great hardship to appear in California courts. * * * The problem with these assertions is that they justify the exercise of jurisdiction over *everyone, whether or not* he ever comes to California. The only "fairness" elements setting Mr. Burnham apart from the rest of the world are the three days' "benefits" referred to above—and even those do not set him apart from many other people who have enjoyed three days in the Golden State * * * but who were fortunate enough not to be served with process while they were there and thus are not (simply by reason of that savoring) subject to the general jurisdiction of California's courts. * * * In other words, even if one agreed with Justice Brennan's conception of an equitable bargain, the "benefits" we have been discussing would explain why it is "fair" to assert general jurisdiction over Burnham-returned-to-New–Jersey-after-service only at the expense of proving that it is also "fair" to assert general jurisdiction over Burnham-returned-to-New-Jersey-*without*-service—which we *know* does not conform with "contemporary notions of due process."

There is, we must acknowledge, one factor mentioned by Justice Brennan that *both* relates distinctively to the assertion of jurisdiction on the basis of personal in-state service *and* is fully persuasive—namely, the fact that a defendant voluntarily present in a particular State has a "reasonable expectatio[n]" that he is subject to suit there. * * * By formulating it as a "reasonable expectation" Justice Brennan makes that seem like a "fairness" factor; but in reality, of course, it is just tradition masquerading as "fairness." The only reason for charging Mr. Burnham with the reasonable expectation of being subject to suit is that the States of the Union assert adjudicatory jurisdiction over the person, and have always asserted adjudicatory jurisdiction over the person, by serving him with process during his temporary physical presence in their territory. That continuing tradition, which anyone entering California should have known about, renders it "fair" for Mr. Burnham, who voluntarily entered California, to be sued there for divorce—at least "fair" in the limited sense that he has no one but himself to blame. Justice Brennan's long journey is a circular one, leaving him, at the end of the day, in complete reliance upon the very factor he sought to avoid: The existence of a continuing tradition is not enough, fairness also must be considered; fairness exists here because there is a continuing tradition.

* * * Suppose, for example, that a defendant in Mr. Burnham's situation enjoys not three days' worth of California's "benefits," but 15 minutes' worth. Or suppose we remove one of those "benefits"—"enjoy[ment of] the fruits of the State's economy"—by positing that Mr. Burnham had not come to California on business, but only to visit his children. Or suppose that Mr. Burnham were demonstrably so impecunious as to be unable to take advantage of the modern means of transportation and communication that Justice Brennan finds so relevant. Or suppose, finally, that the California courts lacked the "variety of procedural devices" * * * that Justice Brennan says can reduce the burden upon out-of-state litigants. One may also make additional suppositions, relating not to the absence of the factors that Justice Brennan discusses, but to the presence of additional factors bearing upon the ultimate criterion of "fairness." What if, for example, Mr. Burnham were visiting a sick child? Or a dying child? * * * Since, so far as one can tell, Justice Brennan's approval of applying the in-state service rule in the present case rests on the presence of *all* the factors he lists, and on the absence of any others, every different case will present a different litigable issue. Thus, despite the fact that he manages to work the word "rule" into his formulation, Justice Brennan's approach does not establish a rule of law at all, but only a "totality of the circumstances" test, guaranteeing what traditional territorial rules of jurisdiction were designed precisely to avoid: uncertainty and litigation over the preliminary issue of the forum's competence. It may be that those evils, necessarily accompanying a freestanding "reasonableness" inquiry, must be accepted at the margins, when we evaluate *non*traditional forms of jurisdiction newly adopted by the States * * *. But that is no reason for injecting them into the core of our American practice, exposing to such a "reasonableness" inquiry the ground of jurisdiction that has hitherto been considered the very *baseline* of reasonableness, physical presence.

The difference between us and Justice Brennan has nothing to do with whether "further progress [is] to be made" in the "evolution of our legal system." * * * It has to do with whether changes are to be adopted as progressive by the American people or decreed as progressive by the Justices of this Court. Nothing we say today prevents individual States from limiting or entirely abandoning the in-state-service basis of jurisdiction. And nothing prevents an overwhelming majority of them from doing so, with the consequence that the "traditional notions of fairness" that this Court applies may change. But the States have overwhelmingly declined to adopt such limitation or abandonment, evidently not considering it to be progress. The question is whether, armed with no authority other than individual Justices' perceptions of fairness that conflict with both past and current practice, this Court can compel the States to make such a change on the ground that "due process" requires it. We hold that it cannot.

Because the Due Process Clause does not prohibit the California courts from exercising jurisdiction over petitioner based on the fact of in-state service of process, the judgment is

Affirmed.

JUSTICE WHITE, concurring in part and concurring in the judgment.

I join Parts I, II–A, II–B, and II–C of Justice Scalia's opinion and concur in the judgment of affirmance. The rule allowing jurisdiction to be obtained over a nonresident by personal service in the forum State, without more, has been and is so widely accepted throughout this country that I could not possibly strike it down, either on its face or as applied in this case, on the ground that it denies due process of law guaranteed by the Fourteenth Amendment. * * *

JUSTICE BRENNAN, with whom JUSTICE MARSHALL, JUSTICE BLACKMUN, and JUSTICE O'CONNOR join, concurring in the judgment.

I agree with Justice Scalia that the Due Process Clause of the Fourteenth Amendment generally permits a state court to exercise jurisdiction over a defendant if he is served with process while voluntarily present in the forum State. I do not perceive the need, however, to decide that a jurisdictional rule that " 'has been immemorially the actual law of the land,' " * * * automatically comports with due process simply by virtue of its "pedigree." * * * Unlike Justice Scalia, I would undertake an "independent inquiry into the * * * fairness of the prevailing in-state service rule." * * * I therefore concur only in the judgment.

I

I believe that the approach adopted by Justice Scalia's opinion today—reliance solely on historical pedigree—is foreclosed by our decisions in International Shoe Co. v. Washington * * * and Shaffer v. Heitner * * *. * * * The critical insight of *Shaffer* is that all rules of jurisdiction, even ancient ones, must satisfy contemporary notions of due process. * * * I agree with this approach and continue to believe that "the minimum-contacts analysis developed in *International Shoe* . . . [in original] represents a far more sensible construct for the exercise of state-court jurisdiction than the patchwork of legal and factual fictions that has been generated from the decision in Pennoyer v. Neff," * * * [Shaffer v. Heitner, p. 169, supra].

While our *holding* in *Shaffer* may have been limited to *quasi in rem* jurisdiction, our mode of analysis was not. Indeed, that we were willing in *Shaffer* to examine anew the appropriateness of the *quasi in rem* rule—until that time dutifully accepted by American courts for at least a century—demonstrates that we did not believe that the "pedigree" of a jurisdictional practice was dispositive in deciding whether it was consistent with due process. * * * If we could discard an "ancient form without substantial modern justification" in *Shaffer,* * * * we can do so again. Lower courts, commentators, and the American Law Institute all have interpreted *International Shoe* and *Shaffer* to mean that *every* assertion of state-court jurisdiction, even one pursuant to a "traditional" rule such as transient jurisdiction, must comport with contemporary notions of due process. Notwithstanding the nimble gymnastics of JUSTICE SCALIA's opinion today, it is not faithful to our decision in *Shaffer*.

II

Tradition, though alone not dispositive, is of course *relevant* to the question whether the rule of transient jurisdiction is consistent with due process. * * * Tradition is salient not in the sense that practices of the past are automatically reasonable today; indeed, under such a standard, the legitimacy of transient jurisdiction would be called into question because the rule's historical "pedigree" is a matter of intense debate. The rule was a stranger to the common law and was rather weakly implanted in American jurisprudence "at the crucial time for present purposes: 1868, when the Fourteenth Amendment was adopted." * * * For much of the 19th century, American courts did not uniformly recognize the concept of transient jurisdiction, and it appears that the transient rule did not receive wide currency until well after our decision in Pennoyer v. Neff * * *.

Rather, I find the historical background relevant because, however murky the jurisprudential origins of transient jurisdiction, the fact that American courts have announced the rule for perhaps a century * * * provides a defendant voluntarily present in a particular State *today* "clear notice that [he] is subject to suit" in the forum. * * * [Thus, t]he transient rule is consistent with reasonable expectations and is entitled to a strong presumption that it comports with due process. * * *

By visiting the forum State, a transient defendant actually "avail[s]" himself * * * of significant benefits provided by the State. His health and safety are guaranteed by the State's police, fire, and emergency medical services; he is free to travel on the State's roads and waterways; he likely enjoys the fruits of the State's economy as well. Moreover, the Privileges and Immunities Clause of Article IV prevents a state government from discriminating against a transient defendant by denying him the protections of its law or the right of access to its courts. * * * Without transient jurisdiction, an asymmetry would arise: A transient would have the full benefit of the power of the forum State's courts as a plaintiff while retaining immunity from their authority as a defendant. * * *

The potential burdens on a transient defendant are slight. " '[M]odern transportation and communications have made it much less burdensome for a party sued to defend himself' " in a State outside his place of residence. * * * That the defendant has already journeyed at least once before to the forum—as evidenced by the fact that he was served with process there—is an indication that suit in the forum likely would not be prohibitively inconvenient. Finally, any burdens that do arise can be ameliorated by a variety of procedural devices. For these reasons, as a rule the exercise of personal jurisdiction over a defendant based on his voluntary presence in the forum will satisfy the requirements of due process. * * *

In this case, it is undisputed that petitioner was served with process while voluntarily and knowingly in the State of California. I therefore concur in the judgment.

JUSTICE STEVENS, concurring in the judgment.

As I explained in my separate writing, I did not join the Court's opinion in Shaffer v. Heitner * * * because I was concerned by its unnecessarily broad reach. * * * The same concern prevents me from joining either Justice Scalia's or Justice Brennan's opinion in this case. For me, it is sufficient to note that the historical evidence and consensus identified by Justice Scalia, the considerations of fairness identified by Justice Brennan, and the common sense displayed by Justice White, all combine to demonstrate that this is, indeed, a very easy case.* Accordingly, I agree that the judgment should be affirmed.

NOTES AND QUESTIONS

1. The Justices agreed on the result in *Burnham*, but could not agree on its theoretical underpinnings. Which opinion states the law of transient personal jurisdiction as it now stands? Which approach do you find to be more persuasive? Is the intense debate in *Burnham* evidence of a deeper disagreement between Justice Scalia and Justice Brennan? If so, what is it?

2. Has Justice Scalia correctly interpreted the word "traditional" in the phrase "traditional notions of fair play and substantial justice"? See Greenberger, *Justice Scalia's Due Process Traditionalism Applied to Territorial Jurisdiction: The Illusion of Adjudication Without Judgment*, 33 B.C. L. Rev. 981 (1992). If he has not, what is its intended meaning? Similarly, what significance ought to attach to the statement in Shaffer v. Heitner to the effect that: "all assertions of state-court jurisdiction must be evaluated according to the standards set forth in *International Shoe* and its progeny"?

3. What effect does the decision in *Burnham* have on cases like Grace v. MacArthur, Note 4, p. 79, supra, in which the defendant is served while passing over the state in an airplane? Could an astronaut orbiting the Earth be similarly served?

4. Does *Burnham* signal a retreat from the flexible notions of due process developed in *International Shoe* and its progeny, and a return to a strictly territorial approach to personal jurisdiction? Professor Borchers contends that the Supreme Court should "abandon the notion that state court personal jurisdiction is a matter of constitutional law, and relinquish its role as the final authority on the general ability of state courts to reach beyond their borders." See Borchers, *The Death of the Constitutional Law of Personal Jurisdiction: From* Pennoyer *to* Burnham *and Back Again*, 24 U.C. Davis L.Rev. 19 (1990). Would such a constitutional retreat be desirable?

5. Are there special factors in a case brought against a foreign defendant that would argue in favor of adopting Justice Brennan's, rather than Justice Scalia's, approach? See Hay, *Transient Jurisdiction Especially Over Interna-*

---

* Perhaps the adage about hard cases making bad law should be revised to cover easy cases.

tional Defendants: Critical Comments on Burnham v. Superior Court of California, 1990 U.Ill.L.Rev. 593.

6. Should a "virtual" contact with the forum be treated as transient presence for jurisdictional purposes? See p. 155, supra. If so, what types of virtual contacts would qualify?

7. For further discussions, see *The Future of Personal Jurisdiction: A Symposium on Burnham v. Superior Court*, 22 Rutgers L.J. 559 (1991).

SECTION I. ANOTHER BASIS OF JURISDICTION: CONSENT

Earlier we saw that even under the regime of Pennoyer v. Neff, p. 71, supra, a defendant could consent to personal jurisdiction. In the simplest case, a defendant consents to personal jurisdiction either by expressly agreeing to submit to the court or by performing certain acts that constitute a waiver of objections to personal jurisdiction or by failing to assert a defense of lack of jurisdiction. For example, Rule 12(h)(1) of the Federal Rules provides that a defendant who fails to raise an objection to personal jurisdiction in the answer or in an initial motion under Rule 12 is precluded from raising the issue subsequently. Not all consent cases are "simple," however. As you read the following case, consider whether a defendant can consent to varying levels of involvement in a lawsuit.

INSURANCE CORP. OF IRELAND v. COMPAGNIE DES BAUXITES DE GUINEE, 456 U.S. 694, 102 S.Ct. 2099, 72 L.Ed.2d 492 (1982). The plaintiff, Compagnie des Bauxites de Guinee (CBG), a bauxite producer incorporated in Delaware but doing business only in the Republic of Guinea, purchased business-interruption insurance from a domestic insurer in Pennsylvania and from a group of foreign insurance companies through a London brokerage house. When a mechanical failure forced a halt in production, CBG filed a multi-million dollar claim, which the insurers refused to pay. CBG then sued in federal court in Pennsylvania, but most of the foreign insurance companies contested personal jurisdiction. CBG attempted to use discovery to establish the essential jurisdictional facts. After the companies failed to comply with the court's orders for production of the requested information and after repeated warnings, the District Court, pursuant to Federal Rule 37(b)(2)(A)(i), imposed a sanction consisting of a presumptive finding that the insurers were subject to the jurisdiction of the court because of their business contacts in Pennsylvania. The Supreme Court upheld the sanction in an opinion by Justice White.

> * * * The requirement that a court have personal jurisdiction flows not from Art. III, but from the Due Process Clause. * * *

> Because the requirement of personal jurisdiction represents first of all an individual right, it can, like other such rights, be waived. * * *
>
> * * * By submitting to the jurisdiction of the court for the limited purpose of challenging jurisdiction, the defendant agrees to abide by that court's determination on the issue of jurisdiction * * *, [and] the manner in which the court determines whether it has personal jurisdiction may include a variety of legal rules and presumptions, as well as straightforward factfinding. * * *
>
> CBG was seeking through discovery to respond to [the insurers'] contention that the District Court did not have personal jurisdiction. Having put the issue in question, [the insurers] did not have the option of blocking the reasonable attempt of CBG to meet its burden of proof. * * * [They] surely did not have this option once the court had overruled [their] objections. Because of [the insurers'] failure to comply with the discovery orders, CBG was unable to establish the full extent of the contacts between [the insurers] and Pennsylvania, the critical issue in proving personal jurisdiction. * * * [Their] failure to supply the requested information as to [their] contacts with Pennsylvania supports "the presumption that the refusal to produce evidence * * * was but an admission of the want of merit in the asserted defense." * * * The sanction took as established the facts—contacts with Pennsylvania—that CBG was seeking to establish through discovery.

Id. at 702–09, 102 S.Ct. at 2104–08, 72 L.Ed.2d at 501–05.

NOTES AND QUESTIONS

1. In *Ireland*, the defendants appeared in the action to contest jurisdiction. Is it not clear that by making the special appearance they at least consented to the adjudication of that issue by the district court? Does that obligate them to abide by the rules—including the discovery rules—laid down by the court to govern determination of the issue? Was it necessary to base the holding in *Ireland* on concepts of waiver and consent? Isn't the authority of a federal court to determine its jurisdiction implicit in the grant of limited jurisdiction? And, if a court always has jurisdiction to determine whether it has jurisdiction, doesn't that mean that it has authority to force the parties, including the defendant, to cooperate in helping it to resolve that question?

2. Most states have statutes that require a foreign corporation to register as a condition of doing business in the forum state. Would it be constitutional for a court to exercise general jurisdiction based solely on a non-resident company's compliance with a registration statute? Should it be relevant that a registration statute also requires appointment of an in-state agent for service of process? Compare Knowlton v. Allied Van Lines, Inc., 900 F.2d 1196, 1200 (8th Cir.1990) ("appointment of an agent for service of process * * * gives consent to the jurisdiction of Minnesota courts for any cause of action, whether or not arising out of activities within the state"), with Wenche Siemer v. Learjet Acquisition Corp., 966 F.2d 179, 183 (5th

Cir.1992) ("the mere act of registering an agent * * * does not act as consent").

Why isn't this "consent," as Justice Holmes observed, a "mere fiction," Flexner v. Farson, 248 U.S. 289, 39 S.Ct. 97, 63 L.Ed. 250 (1919), that should not be invoked unless the requisite "minimum contacts" exist? In RATLIFF v. COOPER LABORATORIES, INC., 444 F.2d 745 (4th Cir.), certiorari denied 404 U.S. 948, 92 S.Ct. 271, 30 L.Ed.2d 265 (1971), see p. 141, supra, the Court of Appeals held that a foreign corporation that had qualified to do business in South Carolina and regularly sent salesmen into the state could not be sued in South Carolina by plaintiffs from Florida and Indiana who had purchased and consumed in their home states drugs manufactured by the defendant, and who sued in South Carolina because of that state's relatively long statute of limitations: "Applying for the privilege of doing business is one thing, but the actual exercise of that privilege is quite another. * * * The principles of due process require a firmer foundation than mere compliance with state domestication statutes." For a discussion consent jurisdiction and of registration statutes, see Taylor, *Registration Statutes, Personal Jurisdiction, and the Problem of Predictability*, 103 Colum. L. Rev. 1163 (2003).

The possibility of jurisdiction by consent is not limited to situations in which a defendant, in one form or another, consents to jurisdiction to resolve an existing dispute. Frequently, in forming a contract, the parties will draft an express agreement to submit to personal jurisdiction even before a dispute has taken shape. Sometimes they will agree to submit to the jurisdiction of a designated court for any action arising out of the transaction. Sometimes they will agree to submit to the jurisdiction of a designated court—to the exclusion of all others—for any action arising out of the transaction. And, sometimes they will agree to submit to the jurisdiction of *any* court for any action arising out of the transaction. Consider the agreements and resulting disputes in the cases that follow. Although courts traditionally did not give effect to "forum-selection" clauses, a series of Supreme Court cases has given new life to the parties' ability to contract for a jurisdiction they prefer.

M/S BREMEN v. ZAPATA OFF-SHORE CO., 407 U.S. 1, 92 S.Ct. 1907, 32 L.Ed.2d 513 (1972). Plaintiff Zapata, a Houston-based American corporation, contracted with Unterweser, a German corporation, to tow Zapata's drilling rig from Louisiana to Italy. The contract contained a provision that all disputes were to be litigated before the "London Court of Justice." In the course of the towing, the rig was damaged in a storm off Florida, and was towed to Tampa. Zapata commenced suit against Unterweser in a federal court in Florida. Unterweser, citing the forum-selection clause in the contract, moved to dismiss, or, alternatively, to stay the action pending the submission of the dispute to the High Court of Justice in London. Simultaneously, Unterweser sued Zapata for breach of contract in the English court.

The District Court refused to dismiss or stay the American action, and the Court of Appeals affirmed. But the Supreme Court reversed:

> We hold * * * that far too little weight and effect were given to the forum clause in resolving this controversy. * * * The expansion of American business and industry will hardly be encouraged if, notwithstanding solemn contracts, we insist on a parochial concept that all disputes must be resolved under our laws and in our courts. * * * We cannot have trade and commerce in world markets and international waters exclusively on our terms, governed by our laws, and resolved in our courts.

Id. at 8–9, 92 S.Ct. at 1912–13, 32 L.Ed.2d at 519–20.

CARNIVAL CRUISE LINES, INC. v. SHUTE, 499 U.S. 585, 111 S.Ct. 1522, 113 L.Ed.2d 622 (1991). Plaintiffs, Eulala and Russel Shute, purchased passage for a seven-day cruise on defendant's ship, the Tropicale, through a Washington State travel agent. Plaintiffs paid the fare to the agent who forwarded the payment to defendant's headquarters in Florida. Defendant then prepared the tickets and sent them to plaintiffs in Washington. The ticket included a provision stating that:

> 8. It is agreed by and between the passenger and the Carrier that all disputes and matters whatsoever arising under, in connection with or incident to this Contract shall be litigated, if at all, in and before a Court located in the State of Florida, U.S.A., to the exclusion of the Courts of any other state or country.

Plaintiffs boarded the Tropicale in Los Angeles, California and sailed for Puerto Vallarta, Mexico. Off the coast of Mexico, Mrs. Shute slipped on a deck mat and was injured. Plaintiffs filed suit in federal district court in Washington, claiming that the negligence of defendant and its employees had caused Mrs. Shute's injuries. The District Court held that defendant's contacts with Washington were constitutionally insufficient to exercise personal jurisdiction; the Ninth Circuit Court of Appeals declined to enforce the forum-selection clause, but concluded that defendant did have sufficient contacts with Washington, and reversed the lower court.

The Supreme Court did not consider defendant's "minimum contacts" argument; instead, it addressed the enforceability of the forum-selection clause. Rejecting the argument that *Zapata* was limited to contracts between two business corporations, the Court stated:

> * * * Including a reasonable forum clause in a form contract of this kind well may be permissible for several reasons: First, a cruise line has a special interest in limiting the fora in which it potentially could be subject to suit. Because a cruise ship typically carries passengers from many locales, it is not unlikely that a mishap on a cruise could subject the cruise line to litigation in several different fora. * * * Additionally, a clause establishing *ex ante* the forum for dispute resolution has the salutary effect of dispelling any confusion about where suits arising from the contract must be brought and defended,

> sparing litigants the time and expense of pretrial motions to determine the correct forum, and conserving judicial resources that otherwise would be devoted to deciding those motions. * * * Finally, it stands to reason that passengers who purchase tickets containing a forum clause like that at issue in this case benefit in the form of reduced fares reflecting the savings that the cruise line enjoys by limiting the fora in which it may be sued. * * *

Id. at 593, 111 S.Ct. at 1527, 113 L.Ed.2d at 632.

NOTES AND QUESTIONS

1. *The Bremen* held that forum-selection clauses "are prima facie valid" and "should be enforced" by federal courts sitting in admiralty "unless enforcement is shown by the resisting party to be 'unreasonable' under the circumstances." 407 U.S. at 9, 92 S.Ct. at 1913, 32 L.Ed.2d at 520. Applying this test, *Carnival Cruise* emphasized that "forum-selection clauses contained in form passage contracts are subject to judicial scrutiny for fundamental fairness." 499 U.S. at 595, 111 S.Ct. at 1528, 113 L.Ed.2d at 633. What factors are relevant in determining whether a forum-selection clause is "unreasonable" or meets "fundamental fairness"? Are you convinced that the *Carnival Cruise* Court engaged in the appropriate level of scrutiny?

2. *The Bremen* Court evaluated the forum-selection clause under contract, and not due process, principles. For provocative discussions of how this approach might affect the fairness and quality of judicial process, see Marcus, *The Perils of Contract Procedure: A Revised History of Forum Selection Clauses in the Federal Courts*, 82 Tul. L. Rev. 973 (2008); Resnik, *Procedure as Contract*, 80 Notre Dame L. Rev. 593 (2005); Solimine, *Forum-Selection Clauses and the Privatization of Procedure*, 25 Cornell Int'l L.J. 51, 66–69 (1992).

3. Suppose that the Shutes purchased tickets for a pleasure cruise in the Mediterranean Sea from a company based in Greece, and that their ticket contained a forum-selection clause specifying that all litigation was to take place before the courts in Athens. Do you think the Supreme Court would have reached a different result? In this context, consider the following:

> Forum-selection clauses radically change and upset the traditional calculus of personal jurisdiction by shifting the forum advantage in favor of defendants. Here, the usual personal jurisdiction dilemma is reversed: these provisions enable the defendant to hale an unwilling and unsuspecting plaintiff into a distant, foreign forum (or forfeit the plaintiff's cause of action). Yet, because personal jurisdiction jurisprudence has always been defendant-oriented, even to the exclusion of the plaintiff's role in the litigation, no due process rights or review attach to the assertion of personal jurisdiction over a plaintiff.

Mullenix, *Another Easy Case, Some More Bad Law:* Carnival Cruise Lines *and Contractual Personal Jurisdiction*, 27 Texas Int'l L.J. 323, 363 (1992).

4. How should courts analyze forum-selection clauses used in online contracting—so-called "clickwrap" and "browsewrap" agreements:

> Clickwrap agreements typically consist of a window containing the terms of the agreement that "pops up" on the computer screen when a user tries to download or install software. * * * The user has to click on a button labeled "I AGREE" or "I ACCEPT" to continue. * * * Browsewrap agreements appear in the form of a hyperlink on the vendor's website. Unlike clickwrap agreements, the terms of a browsewrap agreement are not displayed on the computer screen unless the user clicks on the hyperlink.

Das, *Forum–Selection Clauses in Consumer Clickwrap and Browsewrap Agreements and the "Reasonably Communicated" Test*, 77 Wash. L. Rev. 481, 482 (2002). Should electronic forum-selection clauses enjoy the same presumption of reasonableness given to clauses in other form contracts? Why or why not?

SECTION J. JURISDICTIONAL REACH OF THE FEDERAL DISTRICT COURTS

Read Federal Rule of Civil Procedure 4 and the accompanying materials in the Supplement.

A federal court, like any court in the United States, can exercise personal jurisdiction over a defendant only if that power is authorized by statute and comports with due process. Conventionally, discussions about personal jurisdiction in the federal courts focus on Rule 4, but it is important to remember that Rule 4 is a service-of-process rule. "The court's jurisdictional power comes from the legal sources that are incorporated by reference in Rule 4." 4 Wright & Miller, Federal Practice and Procedure: Civil 3d § 1063.

When studying Rule 4, distinguish among the different service rules that it sets forth:

> Rule 4(k)(1)(A) is a general service rule that the federal court may use when a federal statute does not otherwise authorize jurisdiction. Under the Rule, the federal court "piggy-backs" on the long-arm statute of the state in which it sits.
>
> Rule 4(k)(1)(B) is a special service rule that applies to parties joined under Rules 14 and 19 and allows for service "within a judicial district of the United States and not more than 100 miles from where the summons was issued." (The topic of the joinder of claims and parties is covered in Chapter 9, infra.)
>
> Rule 4(k)(1)(C) permits service when authorized by a federal statute (for example, the Anti–Terrorism Act allows for service "in any

district where the defendant resides, is found, or has an agent," 18 U.S.C. §§ 2300, 2334(a)).

Rule 4(k)(2) is a limited federal long-arm provision that establishes personal jurisdiction "for a claim that arises under federal law" if the defendant "is not subject to jurisdiction in any state's courts of general jurisdiction" and "exercising jurisdiction is consistent with the United States Constitution and laws."

What are the constitutional limitations on the exercise of adjudicatory authority by a federal court? The Fourteenth Amendment applies only to the states; the Fifth Amendment, which also contains a Due Process Clause, applies to the federal government. To what extent, if any, does the Fifth Amendment require the application of the "minimum contacts" standard developed in *International Shoe?* Is there a difference between the concept of due process as applied to the states and that concept as applied to the federal government? Does the underlying source of the federal courts' jurisdiction affect the constitutional analysis?

NOTES AND QUESTIONS

1. Do you agree that the "minimum contacts" standard of *International Shoe* applies when a federal court, pursuant to Rule 4(k)(1)(A), resorts to the law of the forum state to serve process on an out-of-state defendant? This means that a federal court can use the forum state's long-arm statute only to reach those parties whom a court of the state also could reach.

2. Rule 4(k)(2) was promulgated partly in response to the Supreme Court's decision in OMNI CAPITAL INTERNATIONAL v. RUDOLF WOLFF & CO., 484 U.S. 97, 108 S.Ct. 404, 98 L.Ed.2d 415 (1987). In that case, an investor brought a private action in a Louisiana federal District Court against Omni Capital International, Ltd. and Omni Capital Corp. (collectively "Omni") under the Commodity Exchange Act. Omni was a New York corporation that marketed a commodities futures investment program. Omni impleaded Rudolf Wolff & Co., a British corporation employed by Omni to handle trades in London, and James Gourlay, a British citizen, who, as Wolff's representative, solicited Omni's business. Wolff and Gourlay were not present in Louisiana, and the Louisiana long-arm statute did not reach them. They moved to dismiss for lack of personal jurisdiction. The Supreme Court upheld both lower federal courts' findings that jurisdiction was unobtainable over the foreign defendants. Essentially this meant that foreign defendants doing business in the United States might not be amenable to service of process in any particular state and thus would be unaccountable in the United States for alleged violations of federal law. The Court was well aware of the consequences of its ruling, but insisted that it was for the legislature, not the courts, to fashion a rule authorizing service of process in this situation.

3. When plaintiff alleges Rule 4(k)(2) as the basis for service, does she carry the burden of establishing defendant's lack of amenability to suit in any single state? See BP Chemicals Ltd. v. Formosa Chemical & Fibre Corp., 229 F.3d 254 (3d Cir.2000). Would it be appropriate, once plaintiff has made a prima facie case for application of the rule, to shift the burden to defendant to

establish amenability to suit in a single state? See UNITED STATES v. SWISS AMERICAN BANK, LTD., 191 F.3d 30, 41 (1st Cir.1999), on remand 116 F.Supp.2d 217 (D.Mass.2000), affirmed 274 F.3d 610 (1st Cir.2001). Must the party with the burden canvas the jurisdictional provisions of all fifty states? The Seventh Circuit has offered a streamlined approach:

> * * * A defendant who wants to preclude use of Rule 4(k)(2) has only to name some other state in which the suit could proceed. Naming a more appropriate state would amount to a consent to personal jurisdiction there. * * * If, however, the defendant contends that he cannot be sued in the forum state and refuses to identify any other where suit is possible, then the federal court is entitled to use Rule 4(k)(2). * * *

ISI International, Inc. v. Borden Ladner Gervais LLP, 256 F.3d 548, 551 (7th Cir. 2001). See Richardson, *Shifting the Burden of Production Under Rule 4(k)(2): A Cost–Minimizing Approach*, 69 U.Chi. L. Rev. 1427 (2002).

4. In STAFFORD v. BRIGGS, 444 U.S. 527, 100 S.Ct. 774, 63 L.Ed.2d 1 (1980), Justice Stewart, in dissent, expressed approval of a theory of "national contacts" under the Due Process Clause of the Fifth Amendment.

> The petitioners concede that previous cases in this area have involved the Fourteenth Amendment requirement that a state court may acquire personal jurisdiction only if there exist "minimum contacts" between the defendant and the forum State. Reasoning by analogy, however, the petitioners argue that traditional notions of fair play and substantial justice inherent in the Due Process Clause of the Fifth Amendment similarly limit the exercise of congressional power to provide for nationwide *in personam* jurisdiction.
>
> The short answer to this argument is that due process requires only certain minimum contacts between the defendant and the sovereign that has created the court. * * * The issue is not whether it is unfair to require a defendant to assume the burden of litigating in an inconvenient forum, but rather whether the court of a particular sovereign has power to exercise personal jurisdiction over a named defendant. The cases before us involve suits against residents of the United States in the courts of the United States. No due process problem exists.

Id. at 553–54, 100 S.Ct. at 789, 63 L.Ed.2d at 21. Has Justice Stewart disregarded the fairness concerns developed in *International Shoe* and its progeny? Or is fairness simply irrelevant when the defendant is found within the boundaries of the sovereign asserting jurisdiction? See Fullerton, *Constitutional Limits on Nationwide Jurisdiction in the Federal Courts*, 79 Nw. U. L. Rev. 1 (1984); Lusardi, *Nationwide Service of Process: Due Process Limitations on the Power of the Sovereign*, 33 Vill. L. Rev. 1 (1988).

5. In a thoughtful opinion by Judge Becker in OXFORD FIRST CORP. v. PNC LIQUIDATING CORP., 372 F.Supp. 191 (E.D.Pa.1974), the court concluded that, although federal statutes authorizing extra-district service of process are not constrained by the constitutional strictures defined in *International Shoe,* their application is limited by fundamental notions of "fairness" derived from the Due Process Clause of the Fifth Amendment. Among the factors identified as being relevant to the "fairness" inquiry were: (1) the

extent of the defendant's contacts with the place where the action was brought, (2) the inconvenience of defending in a distant forum, (3) judicial economy, (4) the probable locus of discovery, and (5) the interstate character and impact of defendant's activities. Applying these standards to the case, the court upheld the exercise of jurisdiction. The federal appellate courts are divided on this issue.

6. How should technological contacts affect a court's assessment of nationwide contacts under Rule 4(k)(2)? In *Pebble Beach*, p. 150, supra, the court declined to exercise nationwide service of process based on the non-resident defendant's Internet presence. The court explained:

> * * * [T]he selection of a particular domain name is insufficient by itself to confer jurisdiction over a non-resident defendant, even under Rule 4(k)(2), where the forum is the United States. The fact that the name "Pebble Beach" is a famous mark known world-wide is of little practical consequence when deciding whether action is directed at a particular forum via the world wide web. Also of minimal importance is Caddy's selection of a ".com" domain name instead of a more specific United Kingdom or European Union domain. * * *
>
> This leaves Pebble Beach's arguments that because Caddy's business is located in an area frequented by Americans, and because he occasionally services Americans, jurisdiction is proper. These arguments fail * * *; they go to effects rather than express aiming. * * * [A]lthough Caddy may serve vacationing Americans, there is not a scintilla of evidence indicating that this patronage is related to either Caddy's choice of a domain name or the posting of a passive website. Accordingly, we find no action on the part of Caddy expressly directed at the United States and conclude that an exercise of personal jurisdiction over Caddy would offend due process.

453 F.3d at 1159–60.

7. Prior to 1963, the federal courts had no general original quasi-in-rem jurisdiction. This was a curious limitation since the federal courts permitted the removal of actions initially commenced in a state court by attachment. See Rorick v. Devon Syndicate, Ltd., 307 U.S. 299, 59 S.Ct. 877, 83 L.Ed. 1303 (1939). In 1963 this inconsistency was eliminated by the amendment of Federal Rule 4. Authorization is currently found in Rule 4(n)(2). Full discussions of this topic are found in Carrington, *The Modern Utility of Quasi in Rem Jurisdiction*, 76 Harv.L.Rev. 303 (1962); Currie, *Attachment and Garnishment in the Federal Courts*, 59 Mich.L.Rev. 337 (1961). Quasi-in-rem jurisdiction in the federal courts also is specifically provided for in 28 U.S.C. § 1655 in connection with certain types of claims to land when defendant cannot be served personally within the state. See Blume, *Actions Quasi in Rem Under Section 1655, Title 28, U.S.C.*, 50 Mich.L.Rev. 1 (1951).

NOTE ON PENDENT PERSONAL JURISDICTION

Increasingly, federal courts are recognizing a doctrine of "pendent personal jurisdiction"—the idea that "once a district court has personal jurisdiction over a defendant for one claim, it may 'piggyback' onto that claim other claims over which it lacks independent personal jurisdiction, provided that all the claims arise from the same facts as the claim over which it has proper personal jurisdiction." UNITED STATES v. BOTEFUHR, 309 F.3d 1263 (10th Cir.2002). Cases in which courts exercise pendent personal jurisdiction typically involve a federal claim arising under a statute that authorizes nationwide service of process, joined with state-law claims. E.g., Rubinbaum LLP v. Related Corporate Partners V, 154 F.Supp.2d 481 (S.D.N.Y. 2001); Allen v. Byrne, 2008 WL 1869237 (N.D. Tex. 2008). Courts justify the exercise of pendent personal jurisdiction on the basis of "convenience, judicial economy, and fairness to the litigants." Hofmann, *Blurring Lines: How Supplemental Jurisdiction Unknowingly Gave the World Ancillary Personal Jurisdiction*, 38 U.S.F. L. Rev. 809, 822 (2004). Is this approach constitutional? A leading commentary argues that the exercise of pendent party jurisdiction violates the Due Process Clause:

> * * * [A] district court may not reach beyond the forum state's long-arm statute merely because doing so would promote efficiency. The court first must find that the additional claim is within the same common nucleus of operative fact as a claim that already falls within the ambit of the forum state's long-arm statute. This articulation closely mirrors the approach that most federal courts have followed in the relatively modest number of cases that exist on the subject.

4A Wright & Miller, Federal Practice and Procedure: Civil 3d § 1069.7. In Chapter 4, we will consider the related topic of pendent subject-matter jurisdiction.

SECTION K. CHALLENGING A COURT'S EXERCISE OF JURISDICTION OVER THE PERSON OR PROPERTY

1. RAISING THE JURISDICTIONAL ISSUE DIRECTLY

Read Federal Rules of Civil Procedure 12(b), (g), and (h) and the accompanying material in the Supplement.

The term "special appearance" refers to the procedure at common law by which a defendant presented a challenge to the court's exercise of personal jurisdiction without submitting to the court's jurisdiction for any other purpose. The rules varied from state to state on the technical requirements for making a special appearance. A defendant generally had to designate the appearance "special" and limit himself to raising the jurisdictional defense. If he did anything else, such as argue the merits in any way, the defendant would be deemed to have made a "general appearance," constituting a voluntary submission to the court's jurisdiction and a waiver of any defects in the court's jurisdiction. Although substantial variation still may be encountered among different systems of state procedure, the general rules regarding objections to personal jurisdiction are illustrated by the federal scheme.

Assuming that the jurisdictional issue is timely raised, what procedures should a trial court follow to resolve the issue when the relevant facts are sharply disputed by the parties? Consider the discussion in DATA DISC, INC. v. SYSTEMS TECHNOLOGY ASSOCIATES, INC., 557 F.2d 1280, 1285–86 and n.2 (9th Cir.1977), which recognized that the method of determination is up to the trial court:

> * * * The limits which the district judge imposes on the pre-trial proceedings will affect the burden which the plaintiff is required to meet.
>
> If the court determines that it will receive only affidavits or affidavits plus discovery materials, these very limitations dictate that a plaintiff must make only a prima facie showing of jurisdictional facts through the submitted materials in order to avoid a defendant's motion to dismiss. Any greater burden—such as proof by a preponderance of the evidence—would permit a defendant to obtain a dismissal simply by controverting the facts established by a plaintiff through his own affidavits and supporting materials. * * *
>
> * * * If the pleadings and other submitted materials raise issues of credibility or disputed questions of fact with regard to jurisdiction, the district court has the discretion to take evidence at a preliminary hearing in order to resolve the contested issues. * * * In this situation, where plaintiff is put to his full proof, plaintiff must establish the jurisdictional facts by a preponderance of the evidence, just as he would have to do at trial. * * *
>
> In a footnote, the court observed:
>
> Where the jurisdictional facts are intertwined with the merits, a decision on the jurisdictional issues is dependent on a decision of the merits. In such a case, the district court could determine its jurisdiction in a plenary pretrial proceeding. * * * However, it is preferable that this determination be made at trial, where a plaintiff may present his case in a coherent, orderly fashion and without the risk of prejudicing his case on the merits. * * * [T]he district court may decide that the plaintiff should not be required in a Rule 12(d) [now Rule 12(i)] preliminary proceeding to meet the higher burden of proof which is associated with the presentation of evidence at a hearing, but rather should be required only to establish a prima facie showing of jurisdictional facts with affidavits and perhaps discovery materials. * * * Of course, at any time when the plaintiff avoids a preliminary motion to dismiss by making a prima facie showing of jurisdictional

facts, he must still prove the jurisdictional facts at trial by a preponderance of the evidence.

Data Disc suggests that trial courts have broad leeway in determining the procedures they will follow in resolving the jurisdictional issue. Is this degree of discretion consistent with due process considerations? Should a court have to determine the jurisdictional issue at the earliest possible stage of the proceeding by the most expeditious means? Is early resolution of the jurisdictional issue required to protect the defendant's constitutional right not to have to defend in a forum that does not have jurisdiction over her?

2. COLLATERAL ATTACK ON PERSONAL JURISDICTION

If a defendant contests a court's exercise of personal jurisdiction and loses, may he challenge jurisdiction again in a later action to enforce the judgment? Consider BALDWIN v. IOWA STATE TRAVELING MEN'S ASS'N, 283 U.S. 522, 51 S.Ct. 517, 75 L.Ed. 1244 (1931), in which respondent attempted to attack a judgment rendered against it in a Missouri federal District Court. The company had made a special appearance in the prior suit and had moved to set aside service and dismiss the case for a lack of personal jurisdiction, alleging that (1) it was an Iowa corporation, (2) it never had been present in Missouri, and (3) the person who had been served was not a proper agent for receiving process. The motion was overruled after a full hearing on affidavits and briefs. The company failed to plead on the merits, and judgment was entered against it. No appeal was taken. Suit then was brought in Iowa to enforce the judgment. In rejecting the respondent's attempt to attack the first judgment collaterally, the Supreme Court stated:

> * * * It is of no moment that the appearance was a special one expressly saving any submission to such jurisdiction. That fact would be important upon appeal from the judgment, and would save the question of the propriety of the court's decision on the matter, even though, after the motion had been overruled, the respondent had proceeded, subject to a reserved objection and exception, to a trial on the merits. * * * The special appearance gives point to the fact that the respondent entered the Missouri court for the very purpose of litigating the question of jurisdiction over its person. It had the election not to appear at all. * * * It had also the right to appeal from the decision of the Missouri District Court. * * *
>
> Public policy dictates that there be an end of litigation; that those who have contested an issue shall be bound by the result of the contest; and that matters once tried shall be considered forever settled as between parties. We see no reason why this doctrine should not apply in every case where one voluntarily appears, presents his case and is fully heard, and why he should not, in the absence of

fraud, be thereafter concluded by the judgment of the tribunal to which he has submitted his cause.

Id. at 524–26, 51 S.Ct. at 517–18, 75 L.Ed. at 1245.

The *Baldwin* opinion repeats the established rule that a defendant who makes no appearance whatsoever remains free to challenge a default judgment for want of personal jurisdiction. The principle that a court has power to determine its own personal jurisdiction is limited to defendants who submit the question for resolution in that court. Would it be unthinkable to require a defendant to raise the jurisdictional objection in the initial forum or lose the opportunity to contest personal jurisdiction?

3. THE LIMITED-APPEARANCE PROBLEM

A "limited appearance" allows a defendant in an action commenced on a quasi-in-rem basis to appear for the limited purpose of defending his interest in the attached property without submitting to the full in personam jurisdiction of the court. See, e.g., Dry Clime Lamp Corp. v. Edwards, 389 F.2d 590 (5th Cir.1968); Harvard Trust Co. v. Bray, 138 Vt. 199, 413 A.2d 1213 (1980). Without provision for such a limited appearance, a defendant must choose between appearing, and thereby risking the possibility of an in personam judgment in excess of the value of the attached property, or not appearing, thereby, as a practical matter, suffering the forfeiture of his property. See *Developments in the Law—State Court Jurisdiction,* 73 Harv.L.Rev. 909, 954 (1960). In U.S. INDUSTRIES, INC. v. GREGG, 58 F.R.D. 469, 479–80 (D.Del.1973), a Florida resident whose property had been sequestered in Delaware was refused the right to make a limited appearance and told that any judgment the court might enter in favor of the plaintiff would be an in personam one. Does the limited appearance have a constitutional basis after Shaffer v. Heitner, p. 161, supra? Even after *Shaffer*, in a state in which the long-arm statute does not permit the exercise of personal jurisdiction to the full extent of the Due Process Clause, would the lack of a limited-appearance provision force a defendant to forego litigation on the merits or to accept full in personam liability?

Chapter 3

Providing Notice and an Opportunity to Be Heard

■ ■ ■

In this Chapter, we continue to examine the Due Process Clause and the several conditions it defines that must exist before a court may render a valid judgment. We already have seen that the court must have jurisdiction over the parties and issues before it. In addition, the parties must have adequate notice of the commencement of the action and the issues involved in it. Yet another condition imposed by the Due Process Clause is that the parties must have an adequate opportunity to present their side of the case to the court. These requirements, which are of a constitutional dimension, are essential to the well-functioning of an adversarial system. They also raise basic questions about fairness, efficiency, and the different values that due process is intended to serve.

SECTION A. THE REQUIREMENT OF REASONABLE NOTICE

MULLANE v. CENTRAL HANOVER BANK & TRUST CO.

Supreme Court of the United States, 1950.
339 U.S. 306, 70 S.Ct. 652, 94 L.Ed. 865.

Appeal from the Court of Appeals of New York.

MR. JUSTICE JACKSON delivered the opinion of the Court.

This controversy questions the constitutional sufficiency of notice to beneficiaries on judicial settlement of accounts by the trustee of a common trust fund established under the New York Banking Law * * *. The New York Court of Appeals considered and overruled objections that the statutory notice contravenes requirements of the Fourteenth Amendment * * *. The case is here on appeal * * *.

Common trust fund legislation is addressed to a problem appropriate for state action. Mounting overheads have made administration of small trusts undesirable to corporate trustees. In order that donors and testators of moderately sized trusts may not be denied the service of corporate fiduciaries, the District of Columbia and some thirty states other than

New York have permitted pooling small trust estates into one fund for investment administration. The income, capital gains, losses and expenses of the collective trust are shared by the constituent trusts in proportion to their contribution. By this plan, diversification of risk and economy of management can be extended to those whose capital standing alone would not obtain such advantage.

Statutory authorization for the establishment of such common trust funds is provided in the New York Banking Law, § 100–c * * *. Under this Act a trust company may, with approval of the State Banking Board, establish a common fund and, within prescribed limits, invest therein the assets of an unlimited number of estates, trusts or other funds of which it is trustee. Each participating trust shares ratably in the common fund, but exclusive management and control is in the trust company as trustee, and neither a fiduciary nor any beneficiary of a participating trust is deemed to have ownership in any particular asset or investment of this common fund. The trust company must keep fund assets separate from its own, and in its fiduciary capacity may not deal with itself or any affiliate. Provisions are made for accountings twelve to fifteen months after the establishment of a fund and triennially thereafter. The decree in each such judicial settlement of accounts is made binding and conclusive as to any matter set forth in the account upon everyone having any interest in the common fund or in any participating estate, trust or fund.

In January, 1946, Central Hanover Bank and Trust Company established a common trust fund in accordance with these provisions, and in March, 1947, it petitioned the Surrogate's Court for settlement of its first account as common trustee. During the accounting period a total of 113 trusts, approximately half *inter vivos* and half testamentary, participated in the common trust fund, the gross capital of which was nearly three million dollars. The record does not show the number or residence of the beneficiaries, but they were many and it is clear that some of them were not residents of the State of New York.

The only notice given beneficiaries of this specific application [for judicial settlement of the account] was by publication in a local newspaper [for four successive weeks] in strict compliance with the minimum requirements of N.Y. Banking Law § 100–c(12) * * *. Thus the only notice required, and the only one given, was by newspaper publication setting forth merely the name and address of the trust company, the name and the date of establishment of the common trust fund, and a list of all participating estates, trusts or funds.

At the time the first investment in the common fund was made on behalf of each participating estate, however, the trust company, pursuant to the requirements of § 100–c(9), had notified by mail each person of full age and sound mind whose name and address was then known to it and who was "entitled to share in the income therefrom * * * [or] * * * who would be entitled to share in the principal if the event upon which such estate, trust or fund will become distributable should have occurred at the time of sending such notice." Included in the notice was a copy of those provisions of the Act relating to the sending of the notice itself and to the judicial settlement of common trust fund accounts.

Upon the filing of the petition for the settlement of accounts, appellant was, by order of the court pursuant to § 100–c(12), appointed special guardian and attorney for all persons known or unknown not otherwise appearing who had or might thereafter have any interest in the income of the common trust fund; and appellee Vaughan was appointed to represent those similarly interested in the principal. There were no other appearances on behalf of any one interested in either interest or principal.

Appellant appeared specially, objecting that notice and the statutory provisions for notice to beneficiaries were inadequate to afford due process under the Fourteenth Amendment, and therefore that the court was without jurisdiction to render a final and binding decree. Appellant's objections were entertained and overruled [by] the Surrogate * * *. A final decree accepting the accounts has been entered, affirmed by the Appellate Division of the Supreme Court * * * and by the Court of Appeals of the State of New York * * *.

The effect of this decree, as held below, is to settle "all questions respecting the management of the common fund." We understand that every right which beneficiaries would otherwise have against the trust company, either as trustee of the common fund or as trustee of any individual trust, for improper management of the common trust fund during the period covered by the accounting is sealed and wholly terminated by the decree. * * *

We are met at the outset with a challenge to the power of the State—the right of its courts to adjudicate at all as against those beneficiaries who reside without the State of New York. It is contended that the proceeding is one *in personam* in that the decree affects neither title to nor possession of any *res,* but adjudges only personal rights of the beneficiaries to surcharge their trustee for negligence or breach of trust. Accordingly, it is said, under the strict doctrine of Pennoyer v. Neff, [p. 71, supra], * * * the Surrogate is without jurisdiction as to nonresidents upon whom personal service of process was not made.

Distinctions between actions *in rem* and those *in personam* are ancient and originally expressed in procedural terms what seems really to have been a distinction in the substantive law of property under a system quite unlike our own. * * * The legal recognition and rise in economic importance of incorporeal or intangible forms of property have upset the ancient simplicity of property law and the clarity of its distinctions, while new forms of proceedings have confused the old procedural classification. American courts have sometimes classed certain actions as *in rem* because personal service of process was not required, and at other times have held personal service of process not required because the action was *in rem.* * * *

Judicial proceedings to settle fiduciary accounts have been sometimes termed *in rem,* or more indefinitely *quasi in rem,* or more vaguely still, "in the nature of a proceeding *in rem.*" It is not readily apparent how the courts of New York did or would classify the present proceeding, which has some characteristics and is wanting in some features of proceedings both *in rem* and *in personam.* But in any event we think that the requirements of the Fourteenth Amendment to the Federal Constitution do not depend upon a classification for which the standards are so elusive and confused generally and which, being primarily for state courts to define, may and do vary from state to state. Without disparaging the usefulness of distinctions between actions *in rem* and those *in personam* in many branches of law, or on other issues, or the reasoning which underlies them, we do not rest the power of the State to resort to constructive service in this proceeding upon how its courts or this Court may regard this historic antithesis. It is sufficient to observe that, whatever the technical definition of its chosen procedure, the interest of each state in providing means to close trusts that exist by the grace of its laws and are administered under the supervision of its courts is so insistent and rooted in custom as to establish beyond doubt the right of its courts to determine the interests of all claimants, resident or nonresident, provided its procedure accords full opportunity to appear and be heard.

Quite different from the question of a state's power to discharge trustees is that of the opportunity it must give beneficiaries to contest. Many controversies have raged about the cryptic and abstract words of the Due Process Clause but there can be no doubt that at a minimum they require that deprivation of life, liberty or property by adjudication be preceded by notice and opportunity for hearing appropriate to the nature of the case.

In two ways this proceeding does or may deprive beneficiaries of property. It may cut off their rights to have the trustee answer for negligent or illegal impairments of their interests. Also, their interests are presumably subject to diminution in the proceeding by allowance of fees and expenses to one who, in their names but without their knowledge, may conduct a fruitless or uncompensatory contest. Certainly the proceeding is one in which they may be deprived of property rights and hence notice and hearing must measure up to the standards of due process.

Personal service of written notice within the jurisdiction is the classic form of notice always adequate in any type of proceeding. But the vital interest of the State in bringing any issues as to its fiduciaries to a final settlement can be served only if interests or claims of individuals who are outside of the State can somehow be determined. A construction of the Due Process Clause which would place impossible or impractical obstacles in the way could not be justified.

Against this interest of the State we must balance the individual interest sought to be protected by the Fourteenth Amendment. This is defined by our holding that "The fundamental requisite of due process of law is the opportunity to be heard." Grannis v. Ordean, 234 U.S. 385, 394, 34 S.Ct. 779, 783, 58 L.Ed. 1363 [(1914)]. This right to be heard has little reality or worth unless one is informed that the matter is pending and can choose for himself whether to appear or default, acquiesce or contest.

The Court has not committed itself to any formula achieving a balance between these interests in a particular proceeding or determining when constructive notice may be utilized or what test it must meet. Personal service has not in all circumstances been regarded as indispensable to the process due to residents, and it has more often been held unnecessary as to nonresidents. * * *

An elementary and fundamental requirement of due process in any proceeding which is to be accorded finality is notice reasonably calculated, under all the circumstances, to apprise interested parties of the pendency of the action and afford them an opportunity to present their objections. * * * The notice must be of such nature as reasonably to convey the required information * * * and it must afford a reasonable time for those interested to make their appearance * * *. But if with due regard for the practicalities and peculiarities of the case these conditions are reasonably met the constitutional requirements are satisfied. * * *

But when notice is a person's due, process which is a mere gesture is not due process. The means employed must be such as one desirous of actually informing the absentee might reasonably adopt to accomplish it. The reasonableness and hence the constitutional validity of any chosen method may be defended on the ground that it is in itself reasonably certain to inform those affected * * *, or, where conditions do not reasonably permit such notice, that the form chosen is not substantially less likely to bring home notice than other of the feasible and customary substitutes.

It would be idle to pretend that publication alone, as prescribed here, is a reliable means of acquainting interested parties of the fact that their rights are before the courts. It is not an accident that the greater number of cases reaching this Court on the question of adequacy of notice have been concerned with actions founded on process constructively served through local newspapers. Chance alone brings to the attention of even a local resident an advertisement in small type inserted in the back pages of a newspaper, and if he makes his home outside the area of the newspaper's normal circulation the odds that the information will never reach him are large indeed. The chance of actual notice is further reduced when as here the notice required does not even name those whose attention it is supposed to attract, and does not inform acquaintances who might call it to attention. In weighing its sufficiency on the basis of equivalence with actual notice we are unable to regard this as more than a feint.

Nor is publication here reinforced by steps likely to attract the parties' attention to the proceeding. It is true that publication traditionally has been acceptable as notification supplemental to other action which in itself may reasonably be expected to convey a warning. The ways of an owner with tangible property are such that he usually arranges means to learn of any direct attack upon his possessory or proprietary rights. Hence, libel of a ship, attachment of a chattel or entry upon real estate in the name of law may reasonably be expected to come promptly to the owner's attention. When the state within which the owner has located such property seizes it for some reason, publication or posting affords an additional measure of notification. A state may indulge the assumption that one who has left tangible property in the state either has abandoned it, in which case proceedings against it deprive him of nothing * * *, or that he has left some caretaker under a duty to let him know that it is being jeopardized. * * *

In the case before us there is, of course, no abandonment. On the other hand these beneficiaries do have a resident fiduciary as caretaker of their interest in this property. But it is their caretaker who in the accounting becomes their adversary. Their trustee is released from giving notice of jeopardy, and no one else is expected to do so. Not even the special guardian is required or apparently expected to communicate with his ward and client, and, of course, if such a duty were merely transferred from the trustee to the guardian, economy would not be served and more likely the cost would be increased.

This Court has not hesitated to approve of resort to publication as a customary substitute in another class of cases where it is not reasonably possible or practicable to give more adequate warning. Thus it has been recognized that, in the case of persons missing or unknown, employment of an indirect and even a probably futile means of notification is all that the situation permits and creates no constitutional bar to a final decree foreclosing their rights. * * *

Those beneficiaries represented by appellant whose interests or whereabouts could not with due diligence be ascertained come clearly within this category. As to them the statutory notice is sufficient. However great the odds that publication will never reach the eyes of such unknown parties, it is not in the typical case much more likely to fail than any of the choices open to legislators endeavoring to prescribe the best notice practicable.

Nor do we consider it unreasonable for the State to dispense with more certain notice to those beneficiaries whose interests are either conjectural or future or, although they could be discovered upon investigation, do not in due course of business come to knowledge of the common trustee. Whatever searches might be required in another situation under ordinary standards of diligence, in view of the character of the proceedings and the nature of the interests here involved we think them unnecessary. We recognize the practical difficulties and costs that would be attendant on frequent investigations into the status of great numbers of beneficiaries, many of whose interests in the common fund are so remote as to be ephemeral; and we have no doubt that such impracticable and extended searches are not required in the name of due process. The expense of keeping informed from day to day of substitutions among even current income beneficiaries and presumptive remaindermen, to say nothing of the far greater number of contingent beneficiaries, would impose a severe burden on the plan, and would likely dissipate its advantages. These are practical matters in which we should be reluctant to disturb the judgment of the state authorities.

Accordingly we overrule appellant's constitutional objections to published notice insofar as they are urged on behalf of any beneficiaries whose interests or addresses are unknown to the trustee.

As to known present beneficiaries of known place of residence, however, notice by publication stands on a different footing. Exceptions in the name of necessity do not sweep away the rule that within the limits of practicability notice must be such as is reasonably calculated to reach interested parties. Where the names and post office addresses of those affected by a proceeding are at hand, the reasons disappear for resort to means less likely than the mails to apprise them of its pendency.

The trustee has on its books the names and addresses of the income beneficiaries represented by appellant, and we find no tenable ground for dispensing with a serious effort to inform them personally of the accounting, at least by ordinary mail to the record addresses. * * * Certainly sending them a copy of the statute months and perhaps years in advance does not answer this purpose. The trustee periodically remits their income to them, and we think that they might reasonably expect that with or apart from their remittances word might come to them personally that steps were being taken affecting their interests.

We need not weigh contentions that a requirement of personal service of citation on even the large number of known resident or nonresident beneficiaries would, by reasons of delay if not of expense, seriously interfere with the proper administration of the fund. Of course personal service even without the jurisdiction of the issuing authority serves the end of actual and personal notice, whatever power of compulsion it might lack. However, no such service is required under the circumstances. This type of trust presupposes a large number of small interests. The individual interest does not stand alone but is identical with that of a class. The rights of each in the integrity of the fund and the fidelity of the trustee are shared by many other beneficiaries. Therefore notice reasonably certain to reach most of those interested in objecting is likely to safeguard the interests of all, since any objections sustained would inure to the benefit of all. We think that under such circumstances reasonable risks that notice might not actually reach every beneficiary are justifiable. * * *

The statutory notice to known beneficiaries is inadequate, not because in fact it fails to reach everyone, but because under the circumstances it is not reasonably calculated to reach those who could easily be informed by other means at hand. However it may have been in former times, the mails today are recognized as an efficient and inexpensive means of communication. Moreover, the fact that the trust company has been able to give mailed notice to known beneficiaries at the time the common trust fund was established is persuasive that postal notification at the time of accounting would not seriously burden the plan.

We hold the notice of judicial settlement of accounts required by the New York Banking Law § 100–c(12) is incompatible with the requirements of the Fourteenth Amendment as a basis for adjudication depriving known persons whose whereabouts are also known of substantial property rights. * * *

Reversed.

MR. JUSTICE DOUGLAS took no part in the consideration or decision of this case.

[The dissenting opinion of JUSTICE BURTON is omitted.]

NOTES AND QUESTIONS

1. *Mullane* seems to require notice that is reasonably calculated to succeed. Does this mean that the method *most likely* to succeed is not required? How does *Mullane* justify this? What role should cost play in determining what is reasonable? Does *Mullane* justify applying different notice requirements for small claims than for large claims?

2. In McDONALD v. MABEE, 243 U.S. 90, 92, 37 S.Ct. 343, 344, 61 L.Ed. 608, 609–10 (1917), suit was brought against Mabee, a domiciliary of Texas, upon a promissory note. Although his family was residing in the state, he had left Texas to establish a domicile elsewhere. Service was attempted through publication in a local newspaper once a week for four successive weeks after Mabee's departure from the state. Mabee never appeared in the action. The United States Supreme Court, reversing the Texas Supreme Court, held that the Texas judgment was void under the Fourteenth Amendment: "To dispense with personal service the substitute that is most likely to reach the defendant is the least that ought to be required if substantial justice is to be done." How does *Mullane* affect *Mabee*? Would service at the last and usual place of abode be reasonably calculated to succeed? Would publication in a local newspaper be sufficient if Mabee were still in Texas? What if Mabee had moved to a different part of Texas?

3. In WUCHTER v. PIZZUTTI, 276 U.S. 13, 48 S.Ct. 259, 72 L.Ed. 446 (1928), the Supreme Court invalidated a New Jersey nonresident-motorist statute similar to the one involved in Hess v. Pawloski, p. 82, supra, because it did not expressly require the Secretary of State to communicate notice of the commencement of the action to the nonresident. In fact, notice actually was given by the Secretary of State. According to the Supreme Court: "Every statute of this kind * * * should require the plaintiff bringing the suit to show in the summons to be served the post office address or residence of the defendant being sued, and should impose either on the plaintiff himself or upon the official receiving service or some other, the duty of communication by mail or otherwise with the defendant."

Why would the Supreme Court have invalidated service even though the defendant received actual notice of the action? One commentator has suggested the following explanation: "Apart from the defendant's personal constitutional right to notice, the due process clause also imposes restrictions on how a state must act when it imposes unique burdens on persons. One such restriction, *Wuchter* seems to say, is that the steps that can lead to the imposition of such a burden must be formally and officially predetermined and declared rather than determined ad hoc." Casad, *Book Review*, 80 Mich.L.Rev. 664, 670 (1982). Does this explanation convince you? Would the result of *Wuchter* be the same after *Mullane*?

4. What role ought the historic distinctions of in personam, quasi-in-rem, and in rem jurisdiction play in assessing the adequacy of notice to the defendant? *Mullane* states that attachment of a chattel or real estate, together with publication, may provide adequate notice, under the theory that property owners usually are aware of and concerned about the status of their property. Is this consistent with Justice Jackson's insistence that jurisdiction labels, such as in personam and in rem, should not be considered significant? Should there be more stringent requirements when jurisdiction is asserted pursuant to a long-arm statute? Do the improvements in transportation and communication highlighted in *McGee*, p. 100, supra, suggest that we need to worry less about notice?

5. The Court has held repeatedly that constructive notice does not satisfy *Mullane*'s due process mandate if the name and address of the defendant is known or available from public records. For example, the Court has held that notice by publication in a local newspaper does not meet due process requirements in state condemnation proceedings. E.g., Walker v. City of Hutchinson, 352 U.S. 112, 77 S.Ct. 200, 1 L.Ed.2d 178 (1956). In this setting, the Court also has rejected publication coupled with signs posted on trees, see Schroeder v. City of New York, 371 U.S. 208, 83 S.Ct. 279, 9 L.Ed.2d 255 (1962).

In MENNONITE BOARD OF MISSIONS v. ADAMS, 462 U.S. 791, 103 S.Ct. 2706, 77 L.Ed.2d 180 (1983), the Court held that notice by publication and posting did not provide a mortgagee of real property with adequate notice of a proceeding to sell the mortgaged property for nonpayment of taxes. The Court emphasized that personal service or mailed notice is required even though a mortgagee may have known of the delinquency in the payment of taxes, or as a sophisticated creditor had the means to discover that the taxes had not been paid and that a tax sale proceeding was therefore likely to be initiated.

The Court also found constructive notice constitutionally deficient in TULSA PROFESSIONAL COLLECTION SERVICES, INC. v. POPE, 485 U.S. 478, 108 S.Ct. 1340, 99 L.Ed.2d 565 (1988). Under the nonclaim provision of Oklahoma's probate code, creditors' claims against an estate generally are barred unless presented to the executor or executrix within two months of the publication of notice of the commencement of probate proceedings. Jeanne Pope, an executrix, published the required notice in compliance with the terms of the nonclaim statute and a probate court order, but Tulsa Professional Collection Services, Inc., failed to file a timely claim, and application for payment was rejected. The United States Supreme Court reversed, holding that if Tulsa Professional's identity as a creditor was known or "reasonably ascertainable" by Pope (a fact the Court said could not be determined from the record before it), due process required the creditor be given notice by mail or such other means as is certain to ensure actual notice. See Waterbury, *Notice to Decedents' Creditors*, 73 Minn.L.Rev. 763 (1989); Note, *New Requirements of Creditor Notice in Probate Proceedings*, 54 Mo.L.Rev. 189 (1989).

6. In GREENE v. LINDSEY, 456 U.S. 444, 102 S.Ct. 1874, 72 L.Ed.2d 249 (1982), the Supreme Court held that posting notice of eviction on a tenant's door does not satisfy due process. Plaintiffs, tenants in public housing who had been sued in forcible entry and detainer actions, brought a declaratory judgment suit challenging the application of a Kentucky statute that permitted service by the posting of a summons on the door of a tenant's apartment. Plaintiffs claimed never to have seen the posted summonses, and that they did not learn of the eviction proceedings until served with writs of possession, executed after default judgments had been entered against them, and after their opportunity for appeal had lapsed. The District Court granted summary judgment for defendants, and the Court of Appeals reversed. The Supreme Court affirmed in an opinion written by Justice Brennan:

> The empirical basis of the presumption that notice posted upon property is adequate to alert the owner or occupant of property of the pendency of legal proceedings would appear to make the presumption particularly well-founded where notice is posted at a residence. * * *
>
> But whatever the efficacy of posting in many cases, it is clear that, in the circumstances of this case, merely posting notice on an apartment door does not satisfy minimum standards of due process. In a significant number of instances, reliance on posting pursuant to the provisions of * * * [the statute] results in a failure to provide actual notice to the tenant concerned. Indeed, appellees claim to have suffered precisely such a failure of actual notice. As the process servers were well aware, notices posted on apartment doors in the area where these tenants lived were "not infrequently" removed by children or other tenants before they could have their intended effect. Under these conditions, notice by posting on the apartment door cannot be considered a "reliable means of acquainting interested parties of the fact that their rights are before the courts."

Id. at 452–54, 102 S.Ct. at 1879–80, 72 L.Ed.2d at 257–58. Justice Brennan concluded that, in these circumstances, the Due Process Clause required that the posting be supplemented by notice through the mails. Justice O'Connor, joined by Chief Justice Burger and Justice Rehnquist, dissented:

> The Court * * * holds that notice via the mails is so far superior to posted notice that the difference is of constitutional dimension. How the Court reaches this judgment remains a mystery, especially since the Court is unable, on the present record, to evaluate the risks that notice mailed to public housing projects might fail due to loss, misdelivery, lengthy delay, or theft. Furthermore, the advantages of the mails over posting, if any, are far from obvious. It is no secret, after all, that unattended mailboxes are subject to plunder by thieves. Moreover, unlike the use of the mails, posting notices at least gives assurance that the notice has gotten as far as the tenant's door.

Id. at 459–60, 102 S.Ct. at 1883, 72 L.Ed.2d at 261. See Greenbaum, *The Postman Never Rings Twice: The Constitutionality of Service of Process by Posting After Greene v. Lindsey*, 33 Am.U.L.Rev. 601 (1984).

7. When is the government's use of mail service sufficient to provide notice under the Due Process Clause? The United States Supreme Court has addressed this question in a pair of recent decisions.

DUSENBERY v. UNITED STATES, 534 U.S. 161, 122 S.Ct. 694, 151 L.Ed.2d 597 (2002), involved the adequacy of notice given to a prisoner by the Federal Bureau of Investigation prior to forfeiting property seized under the Controlled Substances Act, 21 U.S.C. § 801. The property consisted of about $30,000 and a car registered in petitioner's step-mother's name. The FBI had published notice in a newspaper, and also sent letters by certified mail addressed to petitioner in care of the federal prison where he was incarcerated; to his residence at the time of arrest; and to an address where his step-mother lived. In challenging the forfeiture, Dusenbery claimed he had never received notice. A prison mailroom officer testified by telephone deposition that the officer had signed the certified mail receipt and that "the procedure would have been for him to log the mail in, for petitioner's 'Unit Team' to sign for it, and for it then to be given to petitioner." However, "a paper trail no longer existed because the Bureau of Prisons * * * had a policy of holding prison logbooks for only one year after they were closed." Applying *Mullane*, the Court held that the government's use of certified mail satisfied the Due Process Clause, and that additional steps were not required and would demand "heroic efforts." 534 U.S. at 170–71, 122 S.Ct. at 701, 151 L.Ed.2d at 606–07. Justice Ginsburg in a dissent, joined by Justices Stevens, Souter, and Breyer, criticized the prison's mail-delivery procedure as "too lax to reliably ensure that a prisoner will receive a legal notice sent to him," and emphasized "the evident feasibility of tightening the notice procedure 'as [would] one desirous of actually informing [the prisoner].' " Id. at 173, 122 S.Ct. at 702, 151 L.Ed.2d at 608.

JONES v. FLOWERS, 547 U.S. 220, 126 S.Ct. 1708, 164 L.Ed.2d 415 (2006), addressed whether the government's sending of notice by mail satisfies the Due Process Clause, this time in a case involving a homeowner who had failed to pay property taxes. The government used certified mail to notify the taxpayer of an impending sale of his property, but made no further effort to contact the taxpayer when the notice was returned unclaimed. The Court held that in these circumstances, the government was required to have taken "additional reasonable steps * * *, if it is practicable to do so," id. at 225, 126 S.Ct. at 1713, 164 L.Ed.2d at 425, to ensure that the taxpayer receives notice before forfeiture of his property. Writing for the Court, Chief Justice Roberts explained:

> We do not think that a person who actually desired to inform a real property owner of an impending tax sale of a house he owns would do nothing when a certified letter sent to the owner is returned unclaimed. If the Commissioner prepared a stack of letters to mail to delinquent taxpayers, handed them to the postman, and then watched as the departing postman accidentally dropped the letters down a storm drain, one would certainly expect the Commissioner's office to prepare a new stack

> of letters and send them again. No one "desirous of actually informing" the owners would simply shrug his shoulders as the letters disappeared and say "I tried." Failure to follow up would be unreasonable, despite the fact that the letters were reasonably calculated to reach their intended recipients when delivered to the postman.

Id. at 229, 126 S.Ct. at 1716, 164 L.Ed.2d at 427–28. The Court identified a number of "reasonable additional steps" that the government could have taken once it knew that the notice had been returned unclaimed:

> The return of the certified letter marked "unclaimed" meant either that Jones still lived at 717 North Bryan Street, but was not home when the postman called and did not retrieve the letter at the post office, or that Jones no longer resided at that address. One reasonable step primarily addressed to the former possibility would be for the State to resend the notice by regular mail, so that a signature was not required. The Commissioner says that use of certified mail makes actual notice more likely, because requiring the recipient's signature protects against misdelivery. But that is only true, of course, when someone is home to sign for the letter, or to inform the mail carrier that he has arrived at the wrong address. * * * [T]he use of certified mail might make actual notice less likely in some cases—the letter cannot be left like regular mail to be examined at the end of the day, and it can only be retrieved from the post office for a specified period of time. * * * Even occupants who ignored certified mail notice slips addressed to the owner (if any had been left) might scrawl the owner's new address on the notice packet and leave it for the postman to retrieve, or notify Jones directly.

Id. at 234–35, 126 S.Ct. at 1718–19, 164 L.Ed.2d at 431. The Court found it would be unjustified, however, to require the government to search the phonebook or public records, such as the tax rolls, to locate the taxpayer's new address.

Justice Thomas in a dissent, joined by Justices Scalia and Kennedy, emphasized that the meaning of the Due Process Clause "should not turn on the antics of tax evaders and scofflaws." Id. at 248, 126 S.Ct. at 1727, 164 L.Ed.2d at 440. Justice Thomas insisted that the government's sending notice by certified mail to the taxpayer's "record address" is constitutionally sufficient and that the state had exceeded due process requirements by publishing additional notice in a local newspaper. Underscoring "the well-established presumption that individuals, especially those owning property, act in their own interest" to guard that interest, the dissent criticized the Court for assessing the government's method of notice from an ex post, and not from an ex ante perspective:

> First, whether a method of notice is reasonably calculated to notify the interested party is determined *ex ante, i.e.*, from the viewpoint of the government agency at the time its notice is sent. * * * [In] *Mullane*, * * * this Court rested its analysis on the information the sender had "at hand" when its notice was sent. * * * Relatedly, we have refused to evaluate the reasonableness of a particular method of notice by comparing it to alternative methods that are identified after the fact. * * *

> Second, implicit in our holding that due process does not require "actual notice," * * * is that when the "government becomes aware . . . that its attempt at notice has failed," * * * it is not required to take additional steps to ensure that notice has been received. * * * Under the majority's logic, each time a doubt is raised with respect to whether notice has reached an interested party, the State will have to consider additional means better calculated to achieve notice. Because this rule turns on speculative, newly acquired information, it has no natural end point, and, in effect, requires the States to achieve something close to actual notice.

Id. at 243–44, 126 S.Ct. at 1723–24, 164 L.Ed.2d at 436–37.

What do you think is more significant about *Flowers*: that the Court required the government to take additional reasonable steps to ensure notice, or that the Court looked to regular mail as an acceptable method of providing notice? See Note, *Tax Sales of Real Property-Notice and Opportunity to Be Heard*, 120 Harv. L. Rev. 233 (2006).

8. *Dusenbery* involved the adequacy of notice given to an incarcerated individual whose access to mail is carefully regulated by the government. One commentator raises concerns that *Dusenbery* "could impact any group of people whose location, travel, and mail are controlled by the government," and includes in this category members of the military, certain law enforcement agents, and some federal employees. Burnett, *Dusenbery v. United States: Setting the Standard for Adequate Notice*, 37 U. Rich. L. Rev. 613, 635 (2003). How does *Flowers* affect this concern?

9. If personal service is impossible or impractical, what methods of service become reasonable? In DOBKIN v. CHAPMAN, 21 N.Y.2d 490, 289 N.Y.S.2d 161, 236 N.E.2d 451 (1968), the New York Court of Appeals upheld court-ordered service in three automobile accident cases by ordinary mail to the defendant's last known address and publication in a local newspaper, when the whereabouts of the defendants were unknown and service in the manner attempted was the best the plaintiffs could do, explaining that these were "situations in which insistence on actual notice, or even on the high probability of actual notice, would be both unfair to plaintiffs and harmful to the public interest." The court stressed that if the defendants failed to get notice it was their fault since they either had failed to furnish the plaintiff a correct address at the scene of the accident, as required by New York law, or had failed to leave a forwarding address.

10. Should defendant's special circumstances affect whether notice satisfies the Due Process Clause? In COVEY v. TOWN OF SOMERS, 351 U.S. 141, 146–47, 76 S.Ct. 724, 727, 100 L.Ed. 1021, 1026 (1956), the Court held that notice by mail of a proceeding to foreclose a lien for delinquent taxes on real property, although ordinarily sufficient, would not satisfy due process requirements when it was mailed to someone known to have been adjudged insane and committed to a hospital, and who is without the protection of a guardian. Would notice by mail have been sufficient if the town authorities were unaware of the defendant's disability?

11. What method of notice is reasonable when the government needs to contact homeless individuals who lack a permanent residence or a fixed address? Cash v. Hamilton County Department of Adult Probation, 388 F.3d

539 (6th Cir.2004), involved a municipality's practice of destroying the property of homeless individuals that it seized during community service clean-up activities. Plaintiffs challenged "the destruction of property without notice." The City defended on the ground that "it published a notice in the local newspaper which was available for anyone in the Cincinnati area to pick up and read." The Court of Appeals held that the question of the adequacy of the proffered notice raised a material issue of fact for the District Court to resolve on remand.

12. The question of what methods for communicating notice are acceptable is different from the question of what the content of the notice should be. In AGUCHAK v. MONTGOMERY WARD CO., 520 P.2d 1352 (Alaska 1974), Montgomery Ward, the plaintiff, sold a snowmobile and freezer to the Aguchaks, which they took to a remote area where they lived. When the Aguchaks allegedly did not pay, Montgomery Ward sent a summons to which the Aguchaks did not respond and a default judgment of $988.22 plus costs was entered against them. The summons did not inform the Aguchaks that they could appear by a written pleading, nor did it inform them that they had a right to request a change of venue. In order to appear in person at the court, the defendants would have had to fly at a cost of $186 with at least one night stopover. On appeal, the Supreme Court of Alaska held that the summons in small claims cases had to include this information and set aside the default judgment.

The content of the government's method of communicating notice is implicated in the administration of a broad range of benefit programs. For examples, see Hershkoff & Loffredo, The Rights of the Poor 94 (Supplemental Security Income benefits), 252 (public housing) (1997). In FINBERG v. SULLIVAN, 634 F.2d 50 (3d Cir.1980), the court, sitting en banc, held that Pennsylvania's post-judgment garnishment procedure violated the Due Process Clause. Beatrice Finberg was a sixty-eight year old widow entirely dependent on Social Security for her income. A discount company obtained a default judgment against her and sought to execute the judgment pursuant to Pennsylvania practice permitting the seizure of assets, without notice or opportunity for a hearing, upon a judgment creditor's petition (to a clerk or magistrate) for a writ of execution. Under this procedure, the plaintiff garnished Finberg's bank accounts, which contained the proceeds of her Social Security benefits. The critical fact was that all of the garnished money was exempt from seizure because federal law proscribes the seizure of Social Security benefits and Pennsylvania law provides a $300 cash exemption to debtors in Finberg's position. The *Finberg* court held the Pennsylvania practice unconstitutional, among other reasons, because it failed to require the creditor to inform the debtor of existing exemptions. Other courts also have found notice to be unconstitutional if it lacks "a detailed individualized explanation of the reason(s) for the action being taken * * * in terms comprehensible to the claimant." Ortiz v. Eichler, 794 F.2d 889, 892 (3d Cir.1986). See also Reynolds v. Giuliani, 35 F. Supp.2d 331 (S.D.N.Y.1999) (adequate notice includes information that specifies the basis for the government's decision to terminate public assistance benefits).

13. What values does the due process notice requirement serve? Professor Michelman contends that process values generally implicate "four dis-

crete, though interrelated, types'' of values, which he calls ''dignity values, participation values, deterrence values, and * * * effectuation values'':

> *Dignity values* reflect concern for the humiliation or loss of self-respect which a person might suffer if denied an opportunity to litigate. *Participation values* reflect an appreciation of litigation as one of the modes in which persons exert influence, or have their wills ''counted,'' in societal decisions they care about. *Deterrence values* recognize the instrumentality of litigation as a mechanism for influencing or constraining individual behavior in ways thought socially desirable. *Effectuation values* see litigation as an important means through which persons are enabled to get, or are given assurances of having, whatever we are pleased to regard as rightfully theirs.

Michelman, *The Supreme Court and Litigation Access Fees: The Right to Protect One's Rights*, 1973 Duke L.J. 1153, 1172 (1973). How do the identified values relate to *Mullane*'s approach to notice? What values compete with those identified by Professor Michelman? Judge Posner characterizes ''the goal of procedure as being the minimization of the sum of error and direct costs.'' Posner, Economic Analysis of Law § 21.1, at 549 (4th ed. 1992). How do the costs of running a litigation system affect your view of how much notice is required as a matter of the Due Process Clause?

SECTION B. THE MECHANICS OF GIVING NOTICE

Read Federal Rule of Civil Procedure 4 and the comparable state statutes set out in the Supplement.

---

1. INTRODUCTION

Notice of a suit is given by the service of process upon the defendant. Each jurisdiction has a set of rules governing the correct methods of making service. Traditionally, process consists of a copy of the plaintiff's complaint, together with a summons directing the defendant to answer. Service of process is made by personal delivery of the summons and complaint to the defendant. Other methods of service, such as delivery by mail, have assumed greater importance since the advent of long-arm statutes.

The procedure governing service of process in federal actions was changed significantly in 1983, and again in 1993. In 1982, the Supreme Court proposed but Congress rejected an amendment to the Rules that would have permitted service by registered or certified mail, return receipt, with delivery restricted to the addressee. It was asserted that the use of certified mail causes problems when, for example, the signature on the return receipt is illegible or the name signed differs somewhat from that of the defendant, or when it is difficult to determine whether mail has been "refused" or "unclaimed." It also was argued that the result of relying on the mail for service of process would be the entry of many more unnecessary and unfair default judgments, which would have to be reopened when challenged. Another objection raised the concern that mail carriers might misdeliver process to the wrong person or fail to make the necessary inquiries to find the proper person. See 128 Cong. Rec. H9848, H9856 (daily ed. Dec. 15, 1982). In 1983, Congress chose a system of service by mail modeled after the one used in California. See Cal.Code Civ.Pro. § 415.30. The summons and complaint could be sent by ordinary first class mail, together with a form for acknowledging receipt of service. If the acknowledgment form was not returned, plaintiff had to effect service through some other means authorized by the Rules. In order to encourage defendants to execute and return the form, the Rule directed the court to order a defendant who did not cooperate to pay the costs incurred by the plaintiff in making personal service, unless the defendant could show good cause for failing to return the acknowledgment form.

This system was not always successful because it relied on the defendant's cooperation in returning the acknowledgment form. Thus, after a decade of use, Rule 4 was revised again in 1993. The most significant change was that the "service by mail" provision was replaced by Rule 4(d), which strongly encourages waiver of formal service. Under this modification, an action commences when the plaintiff sends a form (Official Form 5) entitled "Notice of a Lawsuit and Request to Waive Service of a Summons," or similar document, by mail or some other "reliable" means. Domestic defendants have thirty days from the date on which the waiver was sent to return the waiver; otherwise they will be charged with the costs associated with providing formal service. Along with the threat of paying for the costs of service, defendants receive a positive incentive in that they are allowed sixty days after the date on which the waiver was sent to answer the complaint if the waiver is returned in a timely fashion. Note that even under the new rule, if a plaintiff is confronting a statute of limitations deadline in a state in which the statute continues to run until a defendant is served, formal service sometimes still may be the wisest course of action, because the defendant may refuse to waive service.

Rule 4, in several subdivisions, sets forth specific means of making personal service on, among others, individuals, corporations, partnerships, and other associations subject to suit under a common name. In addition, Rule 4(e)(1) provides an alternative to these methods by broadly authorizing the use in federal courts of the procedures governing the manner of service prescribed by the law of the state in which the District Court is sitting. And Rule 4(e) specifically provides that state procedures to serve a party "may be served in a judicial district of the United States," thus enabling federal courts to take advantage of the reach of state long-arm statutes. See 4B Wright & Miller, Federal Practice and Procedure: Civil 3d §§ 1112–16, 1119–23; Foster, *Long–Arm Jurisdiction in Federal Courts,* 1969 Wis.L.Rev. 9; Foster, *Judicial Economy; Fairness and Convenience of Place of Trial: Long–Arm Jurisdiction in District Courts,* 47 F.R.D. 73 (1969).

2. SPECIFIC APPLICATIONS OF THE SERVICE PROVISIONS

A. FEDERAL RULE 4(d): "WAIVING SERVICE"

MARYLAND STATE FIREMEN'S ASSOCIATION v. CHAVES

United States District Court, District of Maryland, 1996.
166 F.R.D. 353.

MESSITTE, DISTRICT JUDGE.

I.

The Maryland State Firemen's Association ("MSFA") has sued John Chaves, President of the FireFighters Association of America ("FFA"), alleging that Chaves illegally solicited charitable contributions that MSFA has the right to recover. The Complaint was filed on January 2, 1996. On March 4, MSFA filed a Motion for Judgment by Default. On March 11, based on MSFA's attorney's affidavit of service, the Clerk entered default against Chaves for failure to plead.

On April 9, the Court sent a letter to MSFA's counsel questioning the validity of the service and requesting a more detailed affidavit describing the type of service employed and a brief legal memorandum indicating why counsel believed service was effective. * * * Because the Court judges service of process invalid in this case, the Court will SET ASIDE the Clerk's Entry of Default and DENY MSFA's Motion for Default Judgment.

II.

It is axiomatic that service of process must be effective under the Federal Rules of Civil Procedure before a default or a default judgment may be entered against a defendant. * * *

III.

The affidavits submitted by MSFA's counsel posit these facts: MSFA served Chaves with the summons and complaint by first class mail on or about January 3, 1996. These were sent to the address on Chaves's letterhead, which MSFA's attorney was in possession of by reason of prior correspondence with Chaves. Between January 9 and January 15, MSFA's attorney received three phone calls from one Mitchell Gold, purportedly speaking on behalf of FFA. According to Gold, the defense of the instant action was being referred to an attorney in New York named Seth

Pearlman. Since the three phone calls, however, MSFA's attorney has not heard from anyone on behalf of Chaves or FFA.

IV.

MSFA contends that service was effective under Federal Rule * * * 4(c)(2)(C)(ii). That rule, however, has been superseded by Rule 4(d) via the 1993 Amendments. Nonetheless, under either the old rule or the new rule, service was invalid. * * *.

* * *

A. THE OLD RULE 4(c)(2)(C)(ii)

[The court discussed service under old Rule 4(c)(2)(C)(ii) and emphasized that "strict compliance" with the Rule was required.]

* * *

B. THE NEW RULE 4(d)

For cases pending on or after December 1, 1993, including the present case, Rule 4(d) replaces the old Rule 4(c)(2)(C)(ii). * * * The Committee Notes to Rule 4(d) state: "Unless the addressee consents, receipt of the request under the revised rule does not give rise to any obligation to answer the lawsuit [and] does not provide a basis for default judgment." * * * While the Fourth Circuit has yet to interpret this aspect of Rule 4(d), its requirement of strict compliance with old Rule 4(c)(2)(C)(ii) strongly suggests that Rule 4(d) will also be strictly enforced, even where a defendant has actual notice of the pendency of a lawsuit.

C. Maryland Rules

Under the federal rules, a plaintiff may serve process "pursuant to the law of the state in which the district court is located, or in which service is effected." Fed.R.Civ.P. 4(e) [now Rule 4(e)(1)]. The closest fit to the facts of the present case is Maryland Rule of Procedure 2–121, which allows service of process by certified mail. MSFA, however, sent the complaint and summons to Chaves by first class, not certified, mail. Thus it did not meet the requirements of Rule 2–121. MSFA also cites Maryland Rule 2–122, which allows service by posting or publication, but only in in rem or quasi in rem proceedings and then only upon court order. The rule has no bearing. The present proceeding is neither in rem nor quasi in rem, and this Court has never authorized any form of service.

V.

Since service of process was invalid, the Clerk's Entry of Default was improper and the Court will set it aside. See Fed.R.Civ.P. 55(c). MSFA's Motion for Default Judgment will be denied.

NOTES AND QUESTIONS

1. It is apparent that the defendant in *Chaves* received actual notice since the MSFA attorney spoke to Chaves' attorney three times before a default judgment was entered. Does it make sense that service nonetheless was held invalid? Why should defendants who have actual notice be able to claim that they were not served properly?

2. In AUDIO ENTERPRISES v. B & W LOUDSPEAKERS, 957 F.2d 406, 409 (7th Cir.1992), the court rejected service of a summons by private delivery, reasoning that "rule 4(c)(2)(C)(ii) [now Rule 4(d)] specifies first class mail, postage prepaid. Federal Express is not first class mail." However, delivery by Federal Express has been accepted as a valid means of service under Federal Rule 5(b), which calls for "mailing" to the recipient's last known address. See United States v. Certain Real Property & Premises Known as 63–29 Trimble Road, 812 F.Supp. 332, 334 (E.D.N.Y.1992). Do the rules support this distinction?

3. Service-of-process rules have adapted to changes in technology. The Advisory Committee that drafted the 1993 revisions to Rule 4 emphasized that facsimile may be the most efficient and economical means of serving process, especially in certain foreign countries, but the commentaries of the drafters did not address the apparently irreconcilable requirement that the defendants be provided with a "prepaid means of compliance in writing." Rule 5(b)(2)(E), amended in 2001, now allows service by "electronic means if the person consented in writing." See Murphy, *From Snail Mail to E–Mail: The Steady Evolution of Service of Process*, 19 St. John's J. Legal Comment. 73, 75 (2004). In addition, Rule 5(d)(3) permits courts to adopt local rules allowing "papers to be filed, signed, or verified by electronic means." E.g., Local Civil Rule 5.2 Electronic Service and Filing of Documents (S.D.N.Y. Feb. 26, 2003) (exempting Social Security cases from electronic filing requirements). For a discussion of recent developments in electronic service of process, see Colby, *E–SOP's Fables: Recent Developments in Electronic Service of Process*, 9 J. Internet L. 3 (2006).

B. FEDERAL RULE 4(e): PERSONAL DELIVERY ON NATURAL PERSONS

McKELWAY, PROFILES—PLACE AND LEAVE WITH, New Yorker, August 24, 1935, at 23–26:

* * * In a little frame house near the intersection of Rogers and Flatbush Avenues in Brooklyn there lived until a few years ago an old lady named Mrs. Katherina Schnible. She was seventy-two and a little lame. She owned the house and rented out the first two floors as apartments, but there were mortgages and she had not met the payments. She knew the bank that held the mortgages was about to foreclose * * *. Her son, who lived with her, went out to work at eight in the morning and did not return until six, so from eight till six every day, except Sunday, Mrs. Schnible stayed in her room on the third floor and refused to open the door, no matter who knocked. Came a day when she heard a heavy footfall

on the first landing, heard somebody running frantically up the first flight of stairs, heard a man's voice shouting something. Then the footsteps came closer, up the second flight of stairs, and right outside her door she heard yelled the word "Fire!" Mrs. Schnible opened her door and hobbled hurriedly into the hall. "Hello, Mrs. Schnible," said a man standing there. "Here's a summons for you." He handed her the papers, and the proceedings were begun which eventually put Mrs. Schnible out of her house.

Harry Grossman, who was the man in the hall, is regarded by those who employ him as the champion process-server of the day. He is an instrument of justice and his profession is a corner-stone of civil law, but not many of the people he serves appreciate that. * * * Grossman has been cursed by hundreds of defendants, many of them distinguished citizens. Defendants have thrown him down flights of stairs and shoved him off porches. He has been pinched, slapped, punched, and kicked by scores of individuals, and he was beaten up one time by a family of seven.

* * *

"Place and leave with" is the legal phrase for what a process-server must do with a summons when he goes out to serve papers on a defendant, but the courts never have explained precisely what that means. Where the process-server must place the papers is still a nice legal question. A process-server once threw a summons-and-complaint at James Gordon Bennett and hit him in the chest with it, but the courts held that this was not a proper service. Another famous case in the lawbooks tells of a defendant named Martin, who in 1893 hid himself under his wife's petticoats and refused to receive the papers. The process-server saw him crouching there, so he put the papers on what seemed to be the defendant's shoulder, and went away. The Supreme Court rendered a decision which held that "where a person, to avoid service of summons, shelters himself in his wife's petticoats, the laying of the papers on his shoulder will be a sufficient service." * * *

Grossman has never bothered to look up legal precedents for his actions; he simply places the papers in the hands of the defendant and leaves them there. On innumerable occasions he has had to use ingenuity in order to get close enough to the defendant to do this, and only once has he been forced to depart from a literal interpretation of the legal phrase. That was in the case of an elderly lady, who, like Mrs. Schnible, was trying to hide from him. This lady, whose name was Mrs. Mahoney, refused to leave her apartment in the East Side tenement she owned, and Grossman's routine tricks * * * failed to budge her. He knew she was there, because he had wheedled his way into a flat across the court from her and had seen her sitting at her kitchen table in front of an open window, peeling potatoes. Grossman went home to his own apartment in Brooklyn and thought for a while, and then began to practice throwing the summons. He put rubber bands around the paper to make it compact, placed a salad bowl on the dining-room table, and practiced all that afternoon, throwing the subpoena into the bowl from the middle of the living-room. He went back next morning to the flat across the court from Mrs. Mahoney's kitchen. She came into the kitchen a little before noon, puttered around for a while, and then sat down at the table with a bowl of potatoes in front of her and began placidly to peel them. Grossman leaned out of his window and tossed the subpoena. The papers landed in the bowl just as the old lady reached into it. "There you are, Mrs. Mahoney!" Grossman shouted. "There's a foreclosure paper for you!" The courts never questioned his method of placing these papers, and Mrs. Mahoney lost her property.

Tens of thousands of papers have to be served in the course of a year in this city, and the majority of them are handled for the law firms by process-serving agencies, which rely for their profits on quantity and a quick turnover. * * * Cases involving expert dodgers or stubborn hug-the-hearths usually are turned over to private detective agencies, and the detective agencies usually hire Grossman to serve the papers. When the Electrical Research Product Institute sued the Fox Film Corporation for $15,000,000 in 1930, the lawyers for the plaintiff, naturally, surmised that it would be difficult to "place and leave with" William Fox, Winfield Sheehan, and other defendants, the papers summoning them to come to court. Grossman received the assignment through a detective agency. He got in to see Fox by having a telegram sent from Boston saying that Mr. Grossman had "closed the theatre deal" and would call on Fox at eleven o'clock the next morning. When Grossman reached Fox's office, the film executive's secretary told him Mr. Fox had received the wire but was not sure what deal it was that had been closed. "My God," said Grossman, "the theatre deal—that's what deal! If this is the way I am to be received, never mind—to hell with it!" He started out, and the secretary called him back. "Just wait one moment," she said. "I'll tell Mr. Fox." She opened a door marked "Private" and went into an inner office. Grossman followed her and handed Fox the subpoena. Fox started up from his desk indignantly, but Grossman's indignation expressed itself first. "You, a multi-millionaire!" Grossman shouted. "Is it decent, is it nice, for a multi-millionaire who can be sued for fifteen million dollars to hide from me? Why don't you take the papers like a man?" This so flabbergasted Fox that he sank back in his chair, and Grossman went through the corporation's offices unimpeded and served papers on Sheehan, two vice-presidents, the secretary, and the treasurer.

Harry established a reputation as an adroit private detective before he was old enough to serve subpoenas. * * * But after he had passed his eighteenth birthday and had begun to serve summonses and subpoenas, it was evident to his employer, and to everybody else who knew him, that he had found a vocation in which he might expect to excel. During his first year he served Maude Adams by posing as a youthful adorer. When she came out of the stage entrance at the Empire Theatre after a performance one evening, Grossman stepped in front of her holding in his left hand a bouquet of jonquils. "Are you Maude Adams?" he asked. "Oh, are those really for me?" she exclaimed, reaching for the flowers, "No, but this is," said Grossman, jerking back the bouquet. With his right hand he served her with a summons. He still remembers that he had paid fifty cents for the jonquils and that he was able to sell them back to the florist for twenty.

His ability to become more indignant at the attitude of defendants than defendants are at his actions has saved Grossman from bodily injury on many occasions. One of his early triumphs involved Gutzon Borglum. The sculptor was at that time modeling life-size figures in a studio in the Gramercy Park section. Grossman entered by means of what he calls the rush act. A maid opened the door and Grossman rushed past her, saying perfunctorily "Is Mr. Borglum in?" Borglum was chipping stone on a nearly completed nude. "Here's a summons for you, Mr. Borglum," said Grossman. "Of all the effrontery," began the sculptor. "You * * * you * * * you ought to be * * *." Then Grossman began to shout. "How about you?" he asked. "Shouldn't you maybe be ashamed of yourself? You and your naked women!" He went out spluttering with indignation, leaving Borglum speechless, clutching the summons in his hand.

C. RULE 4(e)(2)(B): SERVICE ON A PERSON RESIDING IN DEFENDANT'S DWELLING OR USUAL PLACE OF ABODE

As an alternative to personal delivery, Rule 4(e)(2)(B) permits service of process to be made upon an individual by leaving a copy of the summons and complaint at his "dwelling or usual place of abode with someone of suitable age and discretion who resides there." The facts of a particular case often prove to be crucial.

NOTES AND QUESTIONS

1. In NATIONAL DEVELOPMENT CO. v. TRIAD HOLDING CORP., 930 F.2d 253, 258 (2d Cir. 1990), certiorari denied 502 U.S. 968, 112 S.Ct. 440, 116 L.Ed.2d 459 (1991), defendant moved to vacate a default judgment for lack of personal jurisdiction because of improper service. Defendant, "a wealthy man and a frequent intercontinental traveler," was a Saudi Arabian citizen with twelve homes around the world. Id. at 257. Service was effected by delivering papers to defendant's housekeeper at defendant's New York apartment, which was valued at $20–$25 million and contained 23,000 square feet. The Second Circuit upheld service, holding that "a person can have two or more 'dwelling houses or usual places of abode,' " id. at 25, and that because defendant was "actually living" in the apartment on the day of service, "service there on that day was, if not the most likely method of ensuring that he received the summons and complaint, reasonably calculated to provide actual notice of the action." Id. at 258.

2. To what extent should it be relevant that a defendant actually received the summons and complaint at the particular place where it was served? In KARLSSON v. RABINOWITZ, 318 F.2d 666, 668 (4th Cir.1963), the Fourth Circuit validated service that was left with the defendant's wife in

Maryland even though the family was in the process of moving and the defendant already had left for Arizona, with no intent ever to return. On facts similar to *Karlsson,* the District of Columbia Circuit held that service was invalid because the papers were left with defendant's estranged wife and he did not receive the summons and complaint until three years after a default judgment was entered against him. WILLIAMS v. CAPITAL TRANSIT CO., 215 F.2d 487 (D.C.Cir.1954). Does this insistence on actual receipt of service create a "double" standard for construing the language of Rule 4(e)(2)(B)? Does this make sense?

D. RULE 4(e)(2)(C): DELIVERY TO AN AGENT AUTHORIZED BY APPOINTMENT

A third method of effecting personal service on an individual under Rule 4(e)(2)(C) is by delivering a copy of the summons and complaint to an agent of the defendant who is "authorized by appointment or by law" to receive process. The cases dealing with agency by appointment indicate that an actual appointment for the specific purpose of receiving process normally is expected. Consistent with this judicial construction of "appointment," the courts have held that claims by an agent that he has authority to receive process or the fact that an agent actually accepts process is not enough to bind defendant; there must be evidence that defendant himself intended to confer such authority upon the agent.

NATIONAL EQUIPMENT RENTAL, LTD. v. SZUKHENT

Supreme Court of the United States, 1964.
375 U.S. 311, 84 S.Ct. 411, 11 L.Ed.2d 354.

Certiorari to the United States Court of Appeals for the Second Circuit.

MR. JUSTICE STEWART delivered the opinion of the Court.

* * * The petitioner is a corporation with its principal place of business in New York. It sued the respondents, residents of Michigan, in a New York federal court, claiming that the respondents had defaulted under a farm equipment lease. The only question now before us is whether the person upon whom the summons and complaint were served was "an agent authorized by appointment" to receive the same, so as to subject the respondents to the jurisdiction of the federal court in New York.

The respondents obtained certain farm equipment from the petitioner under a lease executed in 1961. The lease was on a printed form less than a page and a half in length, and consisted of 18 numbered paragraphs. The last numbered paragraph, appearing just above the respondents' signatures and printed in the same type used in the remainder of the instrument, provided that "the Lessee hereby designates Florence Weinberg, 47–21 Forty-first Street, Long Island City, N.Y., as agent for the purpose of accepting service of any process within the State of New York." The respondents were not acquainted with Florence Weinberg.

In 1962 the petitioner commenced the present action by filing in the federal court in New York a complaint which alleged that the respondents had failed to make any of the periodic payments specified by the lease. The Marshal delivered two copies of the summons and complaint to Florence Weinberg. That same day she mailed the summons and complaint to the respondents, together with a letter stating that the documents had been served upon her as the respondents' agent for the purpose of accepting service of process in New York, in accordance with the agreement contained in the lease. The petitioner itself also notified the respondents by certified mail of the service of process upon Florence Weinberg.

Upon motion of the respondents, the District Court quashed service of the summons and complaint, holding that, although Florence Weinberg had promptly notified the respondents of the service of process and mailed copies of the summons and complaint to them, the lease agreement itself had not explicitly required her to do so, and there was therefore a "failure of the agency arrangement to achieve intrinsic and continuing reality." * * * The Court of Appeals affirmed * * * and we granted certiorari * * *.

We need not and do not in this case reach the situation where no personal notice has been given to the defendant. Since the respondents did in fact receive complete and timely notice of the lawsuit pending against them, no due process claim has been made. The case before us is therefore quite different from cases where there was no actual notice * * *. Similarly, as the Court of Appeals recognized, this Court's decision in Wuchter v. Pizzutti, [p. 206, supra,] * * * is inapposite here. * * * *Wuchter* dealt with the limitations imposed by the Fourteenth Amendment upon a statutory scheme by which a State attempts to subject nonresident individuals to the jurisdiction of its courts. The question presented here, on the other hand, is whether a party to a private contract may appoint an agent to receive service of process within the meaning of Federal Rule * * * [4(e)(2)(C)], where the agent is not personally known to the party, and where the agent has not expressly undertaken to transmit notice to the party.

The purpose underlying the contractual provision here at issue seems clear. The clause was inserted by the petitioner and agreed to by the respondents in order to assure that any litigation under the lease should be conducted in the State of New York. The contract specifically provided that "This agreement shall be deemed to have been made in Nassau County, New York, regardless of the order in which the signatures of the parties shall be affixed hereto, and shall be interpreted, and the rights and liabilities of the parties here determined, in accordance with the laws of the State of New York." And it is settled, as the courts below recognized, that parties to a contract may agree in advance to submit to the jurisdiction of a given court, to permit notice to be served by the opposing party, or even to waive notice altogether. * * *

Under well-settled general principles of the law of agency, Florence Weinberg's prompt acceptance and transmittal to the respondents of the summons and complaint pursuant to the authorization was itself sufficient to validate the agency, even though there was no explicit previous promise on her part to do so. * * *

We deal here with a Federal Rule, applicable to federal courts in all 50 States. But even if we were to assume that this uniform federal standard should give way to contrary local policies, there is no relevant concept of state law which would invalidate the agency here at issue. In Michigan, where the respondents reside, the statute which validates service of process under the circumstances present in this case contains no provision requiring that the appointed agent expressly undertake to notify the principal of the service of process. Similarly, New York law, which it was agreed should be applicable to the lease provisions, does not require any such express promise by the agent in order to create a valid agency for receipt of process. * * *

It is argued, finally, that the agency sought to be created in this case was invalid because Florence Weinberg may have had a conflict of interest. This argument is based upon the fact that she was not personally known to the respondents at the time of her appointment and upon a suggestion in the record that she may be related to an officer of the petitioner corporation. But such a contention ignores the narrowly limited nature of the agency here involved. Florence Weinberg was appointed the respondents' agent for the single purpose of receiving service of process. An agent with authority so limited can in no meaningful sense be deemed to have had an interest antagonistic to the respondents, since both the petitioner and the respondents had an equal interest in assuring that, in the event of litigation, the latter be given that adequate and timely notice which is a prerequisite to a valid judgment.

A different case would be presented if Florence Weinberg had not given prompt notice to the respondents, for then the claim might well be made that her failure to do so had operated to invalidate the agency. We hold only that, prompt notice to the respondents having been given, Florence Weinberg was their "agent authorized by appointment" to receive process within the meaning of Federal Rule * * * [4(e)(2)(C)].

* * *

Judgment of Court of Appeals reversed and case remanded.

MR. JUSTICE BLACK, dissenting.

* * * I disagree with * * * [the Court's] holding, believing that (1) whether Mrs. Weinberg was a valid agent upon whom service could validly be effected under Rule * * * [4(e)(2)(C)] should be determined under New York law and that we should accept the holdings of the federal district judge and the Court of Appeals sitting in New York that under that State's law the purported appointment of Mrs. Weinberg was invalid and ineffective; (2) if however, Rule * * * [4(e)(2)(C)] is to be read as calling

upon us to formulate a new federal definition of agency for purposes of service of process, I think our formulation should exclude Mrs. Weinberg from the category of an "agent authorized by appointment * * * to receive service of process"; and (3) upholding service of process in this case raises serious questions as to whether these Michigan farmers have been denied due process of law in violation of the Fifth and Fourteenth Amendments.

* * *

The end result of today's holding is not difficult to foresee. Clauses like the one used against the Szukhents—clauses which companies have not inserted, I suspect, because they never dreamed a court would uphold them—will soon find their way into the "boilerplate" of everything from an equipment lease to a conditional sales contract. Today's holding gives a green light to every large company in this country to contrive contracts which declare with force of law that when such a company wants to sue someone with whom it does business, that individual must go and try to defend himself in some place, no matter how distant, where big business enterprises are concentrated, like, for example, New York, Connecticut, or Illinois, or else suffer a default judgment. In this very case the Court holds that by this company's carefully prepared contractual clause the Szukhents must, to avoid a judgment rendered without a fair and full hearing, travel hundreds of miles across the continent, probably crippling their defense and certainly depleting what savings they may have, to try to defend themselves in a court sitting in New York City. I simply cannot believe that Congress, when by its silence it let Rule * * * [4(e)(2)(C)] go into effect, meant for that rule to be used as a means to achieve such a far-reaching, burdensome, and unjust result. Heretofore judicial good common sense has, on one ground or another, disregarded contractual provisions like this one, not encouraged them. It is a long trip from San Francisco—or from Honolulu or Anchorage—to New York, Boston, or Wilmington. And the trip can be very expensive, often costing more than it would simply to pay what is demanded. The very threat of such a suit can be used to force payment of alleged claims, even though they be wholly without merit. This fact will not be news to companies exerting their economic power to wangle such contracts. * * *

MR. JUSTICE BRENNAN, with whom THE CHIEF JUSTICE and MR. JUSTICE GOLDBERG join, dissenting.

I would affirm. In my view, federal standards and not state law must define who is "an agent authorized by appointment" within the meaning of Rule * * * [4(e)(2)(C)]. * * * In formulating these standards I would, *first,* construe Rule * * * [4(e)(2)(C)] to deny validity to the appointment of a purported agent whose interests conflict with those of his supposed principal * * *. *Second,* I would require that the appointment include an explicit condition that the agent after service transmit the process forthwith to the principal. Although our decision in Wuchter v. Pizzutti * * * dealt with the constitutionality of a state statute, the reasoning of that case is persuasive that, in fashioning a federal agency rule, we should engraft the same requirement upon Rule * * * [4(e)(2)(C)]. *Third,* since the corporate plaintiff prepared the printed form contract, I would not hold the individual purchaser bound by the appointment without proof, in addition to his mere signature on the form, that the individual understandingly consented to be sued in a State not that of his residence. * * * It offends common sense to treat a printed form which closes an installment sale as embodying terms to all of which the individual knowingly assented. The sales pitch aims solely at getting the signature on the form and wastes no time explaining or even mentioning the print. * * *

NOTES AND QUESTIONS

1. Like personal jurisdiction, notice and service of process requirements may be waived by a party at trial or even in advance of litigation. For example, under the provisions of a cognovit note, a debtor may agree to submit to the jurisdiction of any court chosen by the creditor for an action to collect the debt and may even empower the creditor or any attorney to appear in the suit and confess judgment, typically waiving any objection to jurisdiction, notice, or service of process. In D.H. OVERMYER CO. v. FRICK CO., 405 U.S. 174, 92 S.Ct. 775, 31 L.Ed.2d 124 (1972), the Supreme Court considered the constitutionality of cognovit provisions and ruled that they were not per se violative of the Due Process Clause. Such agreements must be judged on a case-by-case basis, with particular sensitivity to whether there was inequality of bargaining power or lack of consideration. See, e.g., Atlantic Leasing & Financial, Inc. v. IPM Technology, Inc., 885 F.2d 188 (4th Cir. 1989) (holding that guarantor's assent to confessed-judgment provision was voluntarily, knowingly, and intelligently made). Many state courts have invalidated cognovit notes and other "consent to judgment" provisions. See, e.g., Isbell v. County of Sonoma, 21 Cal.3d 61, 145 Cal.Rptr. 368, 577 P.2d 188, certiorari denied 439 U.S. 996, 99 S.Ct. 597, 58 L.Ed.2d 669 (1978).

2. The rise of electronic commerce has generated new forms of agreement, known as "shrinkwrap," "clickwrap," and "browsewrap" contracts, in which waivers of jurisdiction, notice, and service of process objections may be embedded and assented to through the click of a mouse. See p. 190, supra. Are such waivers per se violative of the Due Process Clause? Should they be treated as unenforceable as a contract of adhesion? Should courts assess their propriety on a case-by-case basis?

E. FEDERAL RULE 4(h): SERVING A CORPORATION, PARTNERSHIP, OR ASSOCIATION

Rule 4(h) authorizes service upon corporations, partnerships, and unincorporated associations that are subject to suit under a common name. The most frequently invoked portion of the rule is the part permitting service by delivery of process to an officer, a managing agent, or a general agent.

In INSURANCE CO. OF NORTH AMERICA v. S/S "HELLENIC CHALLENGER," 88 F.R.D. 545 (S.D.N.Y.1980), a United States Marshal deposited the summons and complaint with a claims adjuster at the office of defendant. The complaint stated an admiralty and maritime claim for nondelivery, shortage, loss, and damage relating to pickled sheepskins shipped to New York aboard defendant's vessel.

The adjuster who had accepted service of the summons and complaint was not expressly authorized by defendant to accept process; the only employees endowed with express authority to do so on behalf of defendant were all titled officers and the claims manager. At the time of service of the summons and complaint, the claims manager was absent due to illness and the adjuster, an assistant to the claims manager, accepted service.

Since the adjuster misplaced the summons and complaint, defendant remained unaware of the pendency of the lawsuit until its bank informed it that its account had been attached by the plaintiff. Only then did the defendant learn that the plaintiff's counsel had filed a default judgment and that a writ of execution had been issued. The court denied the defendant's motion to set aside the judgment on the basis of improper service of process:

> Rule * * * [4(h)] has been liberally construed by the courts and, as interpreted, does not require rigid formalism. To be valid, service of process is not limited solely to officially designated officers, managing agents or agents appointed by law for the receipt of process. Rather, "[r]ules governing service of process [are] to be construed in a manner reasonably calculated to effectuate their primary purpose: to give the defendant adequate notice that an action is pending. * * * [T]he rule does not require that service be made solely on a restricted class of formally titled officials, but rather permits it to be made 'upon a representative so integrated with the organization that he will know what to do with the papers. Generally, service is sufficient when made upon an individual who stands in such a position as to render it fair, reasonable and just to imply the authority on his part to receive services.' " * * *
>
> Plaintiff's method of service of the summons and complaint was indeed "reasonably calculated" to alert defendants to the initiation of the suit. * * * [T]he adjuster served with the summons and complaint, can be categorized as a representative of defendant "well-integrated" into the organization and quite familiar with the formalities associated with the receipt of service of summonses and complaints. He had accepted service of summonses and complaints on behalf of defendant on at least two previous occasions * * * in connection with his ordinary duties of receiving and investigating new claims against defendant. Furthermore, it may be inferred from the facts presented on this motion that [the adjuster] had easy access to * * * the claims manager officially authorized to accept service of process, since the two men are separated from each other only by [the claims manager's] glass-walled office. [The adjuster's] familiarity with service of process negates any and all suspicion that the U.S. Marshal

> delivered the summons and complaint to a representative of defendant who had infrequent contact with summonses and complaints and whose unfamiliarity with service of process increased the risk of careless or improper handling. * * *
>
> In the case at hand, the * * * adjuster's loss of the summons and complaint is a mistake in the ordinary course of the internal operations of defendant's business and thus does not merit remedial relief * * *.

Id. at 547–48.

NOTES AND QUESTIONS

1. Is the court's willingness to disregard labels and conclusory terms such as "general" and "managing" agent consistent with the clear requirements of Rule 4(h)(1)(B)? Should the court simply have held that the claims adjuster could be regarded as a "managing agent" of the defendant? See also Direct Mail Specialists, Inc. v. Eclat Computerized Technologies, Inc., 840 F.2d 685, 688 (9th Cir.1988) (service of process on receptionist of shared office of defendant corporation and another corporation was sufficient to create personal jurisdiction under the circumstances). But see American Institute of Certified Public Accountants v. Affinity Card, Inc., 8 F.Supp.2d 372 (S.D.N.Y. 1998) (service on vice president of one corporation sharing office with defendant corporation insufficient to create personal jurisdiction despite fact that both corporations were owned by the same individual who had received actual notice). Does the distinction make sense?

2. Could the court reasonably have reached the same result by finding that the claims adjuster was an agent authorized by appointment to receive process? In FASHION PAGE, LTD. v. ZURICH INS. CO., 50 N.Y.2d 265, 270–73, 428 N.Y.S.2d 890, 892–94, 406 N.E.2d 747, 749–51 (1980), the process-server went to the defendant's office where he was greeted by a receptionist. The receptionist told him to proceed down a certain corridor and to "see the girl sitting down there." Following instructions, the process-server went to the executive secretary of the vice president in charge of the New York office. She asked to see the papers and after perusing them said: "Okay, leave it with me. * * * I'll take it." When the process-server questioned her authority, she responded: "I can take it."

There was doubt that the executive secretary possessed sufficient discretionary authority to be a "managing agent" for purposes of service. The New York Court of Appeals, however, refused to be drawn into that issue, finding instead that the executive secretary was an "agent authorized by appointment * * * to receive service." The executive secretary testified that she had regularly accepted summonses for at least five years whenever the vice president was not in the office. During that period about half of the summonses brought to his office had been accepted by her.

> Thus a corporation may assign the task of accepting process and may establish procedures for insuring that the papers are directed to those ultimately responsible for defending its interests. * * * The corporation however cannot escape the consequences of establishing alternative proce-

> dures which it may prefer. * * * Reliance may be based on the corporate employees to identify the proper person to accept service. * * *

See also M. Prusman, Ltd. v. Ariel Maritime Group, Inc., 719 F.Supp. 214, 220 (S.D.N.Y.1989).

F. RULE 4(f): SERVING AN INDIVIDUAL IN A FOREIGN COUNTRY

Federal Rule 4(f) makes provision for service of process in a foreign country, affording American attorneys with a flexible framework to permit accommodation of the widely divergent procedures for service of process employed by the various nations of the world. This accommodation is necessary in order to avoid violating the sovereignty of other countries by committing acts within their borders that they may consider to be "official" and to maximize the likelihood that the judgment rendered in the action in this country will be recognized and enforced abroad. Service of process in a foreign country and other procedural aspects of civil litigation having multi-national incidents are discussed in Baumgartner, *Is Transnational Litigation Different?*, 25 U. Pa. J. Int'l Econ. L. 1297 (2004). See also Miller, *International Cooperation in Litigation Between the United States and Switzerland: Unilateral Procedural Accommodation in a Test Tube*, 49 Minn.L.Rev. 1069, 1075–86 (1965).

Rule 4(f)(1) now expressly provides that "any internationally agreed means of service that is reasonably calculated to give notice, such as those authorized by the Hague Convention on the Service Abroad of Judicial and Extrajudicial Documents" may be used to effect service on those outside the United States. The Hague Convention contains the most important internationally agreed means of service of process, and so far has been adopted by 59 countries. See Convention on the Service Abroad of Judicial and Extrajudicial Documents in Civil or Commercial Matters, The Hague, 1965, 20 U.S.T. 361, T.I.A.S. No. 6638, 658 U.N.T.S. 163, reproduced (with declarations by the contracting states) in 28 U.S.C.A. following Fed.R.Civ.P. 4; see also Status Table, available at http://www.hcch.net (site last visited May 10, 2009). The heart of the Convention is a requirement that each Contracting State establish a Central Authority, which will receive and execute requests for service from judicial authorities in other Contracting States, and will see that a certification that service has been effected is returned to the court of origin. Service may be made either in accordance with the law of the nation in which service is to be made or (unless incompatible with that law) by a particular method requested by the applicant. 1 Ristau, *International Judicial Assistance (Civil and Commercial)* § 4–3–1 (rev. ed. 1990). See Tamayo, *Catch Me If You Can: Serving United States Process on an Elusive Defendant Abroad*, 17 Harv. J.L. & Tech. 211 (2003).

There are, however, several circumstances involving foreign defendants not governed by the Hague Convention. Most significantly, the Convention does not govern in those countries that are not Contracting States. Furthermore, the United States Supreme Court held in VOLKS-

WAGENWERK AKTIENGESELLSCHAFT v. SCHLUNK, 486 U.S. 694, 108 S.Ct. 2104, 100 L.Ed.2d 722 (1988), that the Convention applies only if service actually is made *abroad,* rather than on the domestic subsidiary of a foreign corporation deemed to be the corporation's involuntary agent for service of process. Moreover, as a result of the 1993 change in Rule 4(d), see p. 215, supra, from "service by agreement" to "waiver of service" (renamed "waiving service" in 2007), the Hague Convention appears to be inapplicable when the defendant takes advantage of the waiver procedure. Because the Convention is only invoked by "service" abroad, an agreement to waive service, if voluntary and private, may be regarded as not implicating the Convention, although some other nations might well take a contrary position. Foreign defendants, like domestic defendants, are given incentives by Rule 4(d) to waive service in the form of longer times to respond, but they are not to be charged with the costs for formal service should they refuse to return the waiver; otherwise the waiver could be deemed compulsory and thus might violate the Convention. See Born & Vollmer, *The Effect of the Revised Federal Rules of Civil Procedure on Personal Jurisdiction, Service and Discovery in International Cases,* 150 F.R.D. 221, 230–41 (1994).

Rule 4(f)(3) authorizes forms of service "by other means not prohibited by international agreement, as the court orders." Rule 4(f)(3) is regarded as a flexible provision so that the "use of a court-directed means for service of process under Rule 4(f)(3) is not a disfavored process and should not be considered extraordinary relief." 4B Wright & Miller, Federal Practice and Procedure: Civil 3d § 1134. Trial courts have authorized "a wide variety of alternative methods of service including publication, ordinary mail, mail to the defendant's last known address, delivery to the defendant's attorney, telex, and most recently, email." Rio Properties, Inc. v. Rio International Interlink, 284 F.3d 1007, 1016 (9th Cir.2002). In approving the use of email, the Ninth Circuit has explained that "when faced with an international e-business scofflaw, playing hide-and-seek with the federal court, email may be the only means of effecting service of process." Id. at 1018.

New forms of technology continue to affect the forms of process that are considered permissible. In MKM Capital Pty Ltd. v. Corbo, A.C.T. Sup. Ct. No. SC608–2008 (Dec. 16, 2008), a loan default case, plaintiffs repeatedly but unsuccessfully attempted to serve defendants. The Supreme Court of the Australian Capital Territory finally allowed plaintiffs to effect service through the sending of "a private message via computer to the Facebook page" of the named defendants. What kind of showing should be required before granting permission to effect service by means of Facebook? What problems do you see with this form of service?

3. RETURN OF SERVICE

After the process-server has delivered the papers, she must file a return, which should disclose enough facts to demonstrate that defendant actually has been served and given notice that he is required to appear in court. Thus, although the actual service of process and not the proof of that act is a prerequisite to the court assuming jurisdiction, it has been held that a proper return ordinarily is necessary to enable the trial court to conclude it has jurisdiction. The specific form that proof of service must take varies from state to state, as well as according to the method of service used. An affidavit executed by the person who performed the acts constituting service, or the sworn statement of the officer—the marshal, sheriff, or deputy—who made the service, is the usual proof.

Should the process-server's return of service be considered conclusive or merely presumptive evidence that service has been effected? In MIEDREICH v. LAUENSTEIN, 232 U.S. 236, 34 S.Ct. 309, 58 L.Ed. 584 (1914), plaintiff sought to vacate a mortgage foreclosure judgment rendered in a prior suit. She was not a resident of the county in which the action was brought, was not served with process, and had no knowledge of the prior proceeding; the sheriff had made a false return of summons. The Supreme Court upheld the prior judgment:

> In the present case the * * * original party in the foreclosure proceeding did all that the law required in the issue of and attempt to serve process; and, without fraud or collusion, the sheriff made a return to the court that service had been duly made. * * * [A]lthough contrary to the fact, in the absence of any attack upon it, the court was justified in acting upon such return as upon a true return. If the return is false the law of the State * * * permitted a recovery against the sheriff upon his bond. We are of the opinion that this system of jurisprudence, with its provisions for safeguarding the rights of litigants, is due process of law.

Id. at 246, 34 S.Ct. at 312, 58 L.Ed. at 591. Would *Mullane*, p. 199, supra, affect the result? Is it significant that *Miedreich* involved a collateral attack on the sheriff's return? Would the result have been the same if a direct attack in the original proceeding had been involved?

In most American jurisdictions, the return of service is considered strong evidence of the facts stated, but it is not conclusive and may be controverted by proof that the return is inaccurate. However, the defendant's own testimony generally will not be sufficient to impeach the return unless it is corroborated by other evidence. See, e.g., Trustees of Local Union No. 727 Pension Fund v. Perfect Parking, Inc., 126 F.R.D. 48 (N.D.Ill.1989) (retaining "strong and convincing evidence" standard to overcome return of a private process server); FROF, Inc. v. Harris, 695 F.Supp. 827 (E.D.Pa.1988) (suggesting, but not holding, that the creation of a rebuttable presumption as to the facts of service might be appropriate for the return of a private process server). See generally 4B Wright & Miller, Federal Practice and Procedure: Civil 3d § 1130.

NOTE ON "SEWER" SERVICE

In UNITED STATES v. BRAND JEWELERS, INC., 318 F.Supp. 1293 (S.D.N.Y.1970), noted in 37 Brooklyn L.Rev. 426, 84 Harv.L.Rev. 1930, 46 N.Y.U. L. Rev. 367, 20 J.Pub.L. 337, 24 Vand.L.Rev. 829, 17 Wayne L.Rev. 1287, 1971 Wis.L.Rev. 665, it was held that the United States had standing to seek an injunction preventing defendant from systematically obtaining default judgments against economically disadvantaged people by utilizing so-called "sewer" service techniques, by which the process-server simply disposes of the papers and makes a false affidavit of service. The actions were for the purchase price of consumer goods sold on "easy credit terms" by door-to-door salesmen. The court reasoned that continuously failing to make proper service of process or preparing false affidavits of service imposed "a burden on interstate commerce." Moreover, defendants' alleged conduct was held to be "state action" so that the United States had standing to sue to end a widespread unconstitutional deprivation of property without due process of law.

In 1972, the case was settled, and a consent decree issued. It vacated the default judgments obtained by Brand Jewelers from 1969 to 1971, established procedures to notify those who were not properly served that they could proceed to a trial on the merits, and placed upon Brand Jewelers' attorney the duty of ensuring that future service of process would be fair and in good faith. What are the advantages and disadvantages of placing that duty on an attorney? See Federal Rule 11 for an example of relying on an attorney's good faith in a different context.

Responding to the mounting criticism of "sewer service," in 1970 New York radically changed the requirements of personal service. Until then, delivery of a summons to a person other than the defendant was not permitted unless the process-server had first exercised due diligence to locate the defendant. The burden of this requirement was viewed as the single most important cause of "sewer service." The revision adopted by the legislature allows service by leaving one copy of the summons with a person of suitable age and discretion at the place where the defendant actually works, dwells, or usually abides and by mailing a second copy to defendant's last known address. N.Y.C.P.L.R. § 308(2). In 1973, the legislature took the additional step of requiring process-servers to make more detailed statements relating to how the process was served; and, in 1991, the legislature mandated that a copy of the summons be filed with the return of service. N.Y.C.P.L.R. §§ 306, 306–a.

4. SERVICE OF PROCESS AND STATUTES OF LIMITATIONS

All states have statutes of limitations that fix specific time limits within which various categories of actions must be brought. They are supplemented by bodies of law that define when various causes of action are said to "accrue"—the point when the limitations clock begins to run on an action, and the circumstances in which the running of the clock is suspended or "tolled" because a plaintiff for some reason has been prevented from timely assertion of her rights. See generally *Developments in the Law—Statutes of Limitations,* 63 Harv.L.Rev. 1177 (1950). Although statutes of limitations generally are deemed "procedural," their impact decidedly is "substantive"—a plaintiff loses the opportunity to invoke the assistance of the courts to obtain relief for an otherwise valid claim. Almost the first duty of a lawyer for a potential plaintiff is to determine, by the most conservative estimates, the latest possible day for commencing an action.

When is a suit "commenced" for purposes of a statute of limitations? In some states, an action is not deemed "commenced" until process is served on the defendant. In these states, a defect in service can be fatal to the plaintiff's claim, because the statute of limitations may run before the plaintiff has a chance to correct his error. In federal court, when the underlying cause of action is based on federal law, Rule 3 governs when the action is commenced. Thus, the suit is commenced when a copy of the complaint is filed with the district court. West v. Conrail, 481 U.S. 35, 107 S.Ct. 1538, 95 L.Ed.2d 32 (1987). However, when the underlying cause of action is based on state law, state law will govern when the action is commenced. See Walker v. Armco Steel Corp., 446 U.S. 740, 100 S.Ct. 1978, 64 L.Ed.2d 659 (1980), p. 442, infra.

As a separate matter, it is noteworthy that Rule 4(m) requires a federal court to dismiss without prejudice an action when the defendant has not been served within 120 days of the filing of the complaint, if the plaintiff fails to show "good cause" for not completing service within that time. If the statute of limitations expires during that period, and if the plaintiff's action is dismissed, can the plaintiff refile the complaint and thus still maintain the action? See Burks v. Griffith, 100 F.R.D. 491 (N.D.N.Y.1984) (attempt at refiling civil rights action met with a successful statute of limitations challenge; court observed that the problem could have been avoided had plaintiff utilized Rule 6(b) and requested an extension of time to serve her summons and complaint).

If service is attempted promptly but improperly made, should a federal court dismiss the action without prejudice, or should it merely quash service and order the plaintiff to re-serve? The general view has been that the court has discretion in this matter—discretion that is exercised with an eye toward the circumstances of the case. Courts dismiss when the plaintiff has little likelihood of effecting proper service. In cases in which the plaintiff cannot hope to acquire jurisdiction over the defendant through proper service, keeping the action alive unnecessarily burdens the courts. On the other hand, when the plaintiff can make proper service quickly, courts generally quash the faulty service without prejudice to the plaintiff to serve again. See, e.g., Romandette v. Weetabix Co., 807 F.2d 309, 311 (2d Cir.1986) (describing "a case in which proper service could be yet obtained").

SECTION C. IMMUNITY FROM PROCESS AND ETIQUETTE OF SERVICE

1. IMMUNITY FROM PROCESS

A court sometimes will immunize a party from service of process, despite the fact that the constitutional and statutory conditions governing personal jurisdiction and service of process have been met. In such cases, the grant of immunity usually is justified as promoting the administration of justice. Thus, although the doctrine may help a party avoid suit, it does so not for the benefit of the party, but for the benefit of the court. For example, witnesses, parties, and attorneys who come to a state to participate in a lawsuit often are granted immunity from service of process in other suits.

STATE EX REL. SIVNKSTY v. DUFFIELD

Supreme Court of Appeals of West Virginia, 1952.
137 W.Va. 112, 71 S.E.2d 113.

[On June 30, 1951, while vacationing in Gilmer County, West Virginia, petitioner Sivnksty's automobile struck and injured two children who were walking along the highway. He was arrested on charges of reckless driving, and, being unable to post bond, was incarcerated in the county jail until his trial on July 2. While he was in jail awaiting trial, Sivnksty was served with process in a tort action brought by one of the children in the Circuit Court of Gilmer County. Sivnksty was found guilty of the criminal charge and his appeals from that conviction failed.

Sivnksty made a special appearance in the civil action and filed a plea in abatement, alleging that the court was without jurisdiction because at the time of service he was a nonresident of the county and a prisoner in the county jail. The court sustained a demurrer to the plea in abatement, whereupon Sivnksty petitioned the Supreme Court of Appeals of West Virginia for a writ of prohibition against the judge of the trial court. A stipulation was filed with the appellate court stating that Sivnksty had entered Gilmer County on June 30, 1951, with the intention of remaining there through the Fourth of July holiday and that he left the county immediately upon his release on appeal bond following his conviction on July 2, 1951.]

RILEY, PRESIDENT. * * *

The sole question presented by this record is: In the circumstances of this case was the petitioner immune from civil process at the time he was served with process in the civil action? Petitioner asserts here that the mere fact that he intended, when he came into Gilmer County, to remain for a period of a few days could not render his continuing presence in Gilmer County, after he was arrested, one of a voluntary status, when he was, in fact, incarcerated in the county jail there against his will.

The original and prime purpose for which the privilege of immunity from civil process on nonresidents of a county or state charged with crime therein was the protection of the court itself from interference with its judicial processes. Thus, originally the rule was asserted as the privilege of the court to secure the administration of justice free from outside interference or influence. Later the rule was enlarged for the protection of suitors, witnesses, jurors, and court officials from process, both in civil and criminal cases. Whited v. Phillips, 98 W.Va. 204, 205, 206, 126 S.E. 916, 917, 40 A.L.R. 83. In the Whited case the Court said: "It is well said that, if there is ever a time when a man should be relieved of all other concerns, and when he should be permitted to use unhampered his every faculty, it is when he is on trial under charge of a crime. Judicial reasoning also recognizes the right of a man, ordinarily, to be tried by a jury in the vicinity in which he resides, so that he may have such advantage and safeguard there as his conduct and character shall merit."

In addition the privilege of immunity from civil process of a nonresident of a county or state, charged with crime therein, has underlying it the public policy that a person charged with crime in a county of which he is a nonresident will not be deterred from appearing before the courts of that county or state by the threat of civil or other process; and thus a person so charged with crime because of the immunity extended will be encouraged to return to the county or state in which he is charged with crime to respond to the criminal process.

* * *

In the syllabus to Whited v. Phillips, supra, perhaps the leading case in this jurisdiction, bearing on the instant subject matter, this Court held: "A non-resident of West Virginia, who voluntarily and without compulsion of law, submits himself to the jurisdiction of a state court, in answer to an indictment therein against him, and who is not at the time a fugitive from justice, is privileged while attending court from service of process in a civil suit." In this jurisdiction the immunity rule has been applied to a case in which a defendant in a civil action was served with process while he was in a county, of which he was not a resident, in obedience to a citation from a member of the Department of Public Safety to answer a criminal charge. Morris v. Calhoun, 119 W.Va. 603, pt. 3 syl., 195 S.E. 341. It has also been applied to a case in which a person charged with a criminal offense in a county of which he was a nonresident, was arrested therefore in that county and later released on bond on his own recognizance, and who, in pursuance of such recognizance, returned to the county to answer the charge on the day set for trial. Lang v. Shaw, 113 W.Va. 628, syl., 169 S.E. 444. But in the case of State ex rel. Godby v. Chambers, 130 W.Va. 115, pt. 2 syl., 42 S.E.2d 255, 256, * * * the Court refused the writ of prohibition on the ground that after petitioner's conviction, sentence, and incarceration on a misdemeanor charge, the reason for the application of the immunity rule was not present, and that in that case there was no criminal process within the meaning of the immunity rule. * * *

In the instant case the petitioner went to Gilmer County of his own volition: he did not enter the county in response to a criminal process, because at the time of his entry therein he had committed no crime, and there was pending against him no criminal case. * * * In Crusco v. Strunk Steel Co., 365 Pa. 326, 74 A.2d 142, 20 A.L.R.2d 160, the Pennsylvania Supreme Court held that a defendant residing outside of a county in which a civil action had been commenced, and who was arrested on a warrant issued on an information of the plaintiff in the civil action and brought within the county, was not immune from civil process merely because of his status as a criminal defendant. * * * In 72 C.J.S., Process, § 82, the rule is well stated as follows: "A person confined in jail on a criminal charge or imprisoned on conviction for such charge is subject to service of civil process, irrespective of the question of residence, at least if he was voluntarily in the jurisdiction at the time of the arrest and confinement." * * *

As the petitioner did not come and was not brought into Gilmer County under criminal process, the reason for the application of the immunity rule is not present, and he is not entitled to the writ of prohibition prayed for.

Writ denied.

LOVINS, JUDGE (dissenting).

* * * This court in the Whited case used the following language: "Judicial reasoning also recognizes the right of a man, ordinarily, to be tried by a jury in the vicinity in which he resides, so that he may have such advantage and safeguard there as his conduct and character shall merit. An additional argument for the extension of the rule is that a person should not ordinarily be drawn into a foreign jurisdiction 'and there be exposed to entanglements in litigation far from home, which means he shall be attended with augmented expense.' " * * *

The specific question here considered is: May a defendant in a criminal charge, confined in jail on such charge and unable to furnish bail bond, be served with process commencing a civil action based on the same facts as those involved in the criminal prosecution?

An examination of the various authorities will disclose that the courts of last resort which have considered this question are not in accord and that the authorities are in confusion with respect to the same. * * *

In the instant case, Sivnksty came into Gilmer County voluntarily for the purpose of fishing. While there, he had an accident and thereafter was incarcerated in the jail. His presence in Gilmer County, originally voluntary, became involuntary. * * * I think whether Sivnksty came into Gilmer County voluntarily or otherwise has no pertinency to the question here presented.

Sivnksty will be forced to trial in a county far from his residence, among strangers. Even though he may have led an exemplary life and may have had a good reputation in the county of his residence, he would derive little or no benefit from those factors. In addition, he was harassed in his defense of the criminal charge by the institution of the civil suit against him while the criminal charge was still pending. This case is dissimilar from State ex rel. Godby v. Chambers, supra. In that case, the defendant had already been convicted.

Another element enters into this case. It is a matter of common knowledge that in this day and age there is much travel by motor vehicles. Under the rule laid down in the majority opinion, the luckless motorist, who has the misfortune to have an accident injuring persons or property in a county or state far from his residence, may be arrested and incarcerated in jail on a criminal charge, based on a real or fancied violation of an ordinance or statute having no connection with the accident, and while so incarcerated, the person suffering the injury would immediately commence an action in his own home county for the recovery of alleged damages. This could and may lead to widespread abuse of judicial process.

* * *

NOTES AND QUESTIONS

1. Although immunity from process serves legitimate goals, when carried to extremes it ignores the resident plaintiff's desire to litigate in a local forum. What limitations could be imposed on a witness's immunity from process in order to reach some form of balance between the competing interests? Should immunity be denied when the witness furthers some personal goal by entering the state to testify, or would such a test be too evanescent to enforce? Should a nonresident attorney be exempt from process while in a state representing a client on a matter unrelated to the suit in which he is served? What if it is related? Should immunity depend upon whether the forum is a "convenient" one for defendant? What would be the ingredients of such a standard? See Note, *Immunity of Non–Resident Participants in a Judicial Proceeding from Service of Process—A Proposal for Renovation,* 26 Ind.L.J. 459 (1951). Under what circumstances should a court deny immunity to a witness or governmental official as a matter of discretion? See Lamb v. Schmitt, 285 U.S. 222, 52 S.Ct. 317, 76 L.Ed. 720 (1932); Keefe & Roscia, *Immunity and Sentimentality*, 47 Cornell L.Q. 471 (1947). See generally 4A Wright & Miller, Federal Practice and Procedure: Civil 3d §§ 1076–81.

2. In many instances immunity from process is governed by statute. For example, federal law grants immunity to certain representatives of foreign governments, their families, and members of their households. What justification is there for giving these people immunity? KADIC v. KARADZIC, 70 F.3d 232 (2d Cir.1995), involved whether defendant Karadzic, president of the break-away Bosnian–Serb republic, was entitled to immunity from service in a federal court action by Croat and Muslim citizens of Bosnia–Herzegovina alleging genocide, torture, rape, and other atrocities. Plaintiffs served defendant while he was in the United States as an invitee of the United Nations. The question of immunity under the United Nations "Headquarters Agreement" turned, in part, on whether service was effected in an area "bounded by Franklin D. Roosevelt Drive, 1st Avenue, 42nd Street, and 48th Street."

> In the *Doe* action, the affidavits detail that on February 11, 1993, process servers approached Karadzic in the lobby of the Hotel Intercontinental at 111 East 48th St. in Manhattan, called his name and identified their purpose, and attempted to hand him the complaint from a distance of two feet, that security guards seized the complaint papers, and that the papers fell to the floor. * * * In the *Kadic* action, the plaintiffs obtained from Judge Owen an order for alternative means of service, directing service by delivering the complaint to a member of defendant's State Department security detail, who was ordered to hand the complaint to the defendant. The security officer's affidavit states that he received the complaint and handed it to Karadzic outside the Russian Embassy in Manhattan. * * * Appellants also allege that during his visits to New York City, Karadzic stayed at hotels outside the "headquarters district" of the United Nations and engaged in non-United Nations-related activities such as fundraising.

Id. at 246–47. The court held that immunity from service is confined to the headquarters district itself, and also declined to treat Karadzic as an accredited diplomatic envoy because he was not a designated representative, only an invitee, of the United Nations. Defendant argued that the court's approach would undermine the important work of the United Nations. Do you agree or not?

3. Does it make any sense to grant a defendant, who can be reached outside the state under a long-arm statute, immunity from process when she is within the state for a purpose that otherwise would qualify for immunity? California and New York cases have abrogated immunity in these cases. See, e.g., Silverman v. Superior Court, 203 Cal.App.3d 145, 249 Cal.Rptr. 724 (2d Dist.1988); Waterman S.S. Corp. v. Ranis, 141 Misc.2d 772, 534 N.Y.S.2d 321 (Sup.Ct.1988).

2. ETIQUETTE OF SERVICE

WYMAN v. NEWHOUSE

United States Court of Appeals, Second Circuit, 1937.
93 F.2d 313, certiorari denied 303 U.S. 664, 58 S.Ct. 831, 82 L.Ed. 1122 (1938).

MANTON, CIRCUIT JUDGE. This appeal is from a judgment entered dismissing the complaint on motion before trial. The action is on a judgment entered by default in a Florida state court, a jury having assessed the damages. The recovery there was for money loaned, money advanced for appellee, and for seduction under promise of marriage.

* * *

Appellant and appellee were both married, but before this suit appellant's husband died. They had known each other for some years and had engaged in meretricious relations.

The affidavits submitted by the appellee * * * established that he was a resident of New York and never lived in Florida. On October 25, 1935, while appellee was in Salt Lake City, Utah, he received a telegram from the appellant, which read: "Account illness home planning leaving. Please come on way back. Must see you." Upon appellee's return to New York he received a letter from appellant stating that her mother was dying in Ireland; that she was leaving the United States for good to go to her mother; that she could not go without seeing the appellee once more; and that she wanted to discuss her affairs with him before she left. Shortly after the receipt of this letter, they spoke to each other on the telephone, whereupon the appellant repeated, in a hysterical and distressed voice, the substance of her letter. Appellee promised to go to Florida in a week or ten days and agreed to notify her when he would arrive. This he did, but before leaving New York by plane he received a letter couched in endearing terms and expressing love and affection for him, as well as her delight at his coming. Before leaving New York, appellee telegraphed appellant, suggesting arrangements for their accommodations together while in Miami, Fla. She telegraphed him at a hotel in Washington, D.C., where he was to stop en route, advising him that the arrangements requested had been made. Appellee arrived at 6 o'clock in the morning at the Miami Airport and saw the appellant standing with her sister some 75 feet distant. He was met by a deputy sheriff who, upon identifying appellee, served him with process in a suit for $500,000. A photographer was present who attempted to take his picture. Thereupon a stranger introduced himself and offered to take appellee to his home, stating that he knew a lawyer who was acquainted with the appellant's attorney. The attorney whom appellee was advised to consult came to the stranger's home and seemed to know about the case. The attorney invited appellee to his office, and upon his arrival he found one of the lawyers for the appellant there. Appellee did not retain the Florida attorney to represent him. He returned to New York by plane that evening and consulted his New York counsel, who advised him to ignore the summons served in Florida. He did so, and judgment was entered by default. * * *

These facts and reasonable deductions therefrom convincingly establish that the appellee was induced to enter the jurisdiction of the state of Florida by a fraud perpetrated upon him by the appellant in falsely representing her mother's illness, her intention to leave the United States, and her love and affection for him, when her sole purpose and apparent thought was to induce him to come within the Florida jurisdiction so as to serve him in an action for damages. * * *

This judgment is attacked for fraud perpetrated upon the appellee which goes to the jurisdiction of the Florida court over his person. A judgment procured fraudulently, as here, lacks jurisdiction and is null and void. * * * A fraud affecting the jurisdiction is equivalent to a lack of jurisdiction. * * * The appellee was not required to proceed against the judgment in Florida. His equitable defense in answer to a suit on the judgment is sufficient. A judgment recovered in a sister state, through the fraud of the party procuring the appearance of another, is not binding on the latter when an attempt is made to enforce such judgment in another state. * * *

The appellee was not required to make out a defense on the merits to the suit in Florida. * * * An error made in entering judgment against a party over whom the court had no jurisdiction permits a consideration of the jurisdictional question collaterally. The complaint was properly dismissed.

Judgment affirmed.

NOTES AND QUESTIONS

1. Reread Tickle v. Barton, p. 27, supra. Which case presents a stronger situation for quashing service—*Wyman* or *Tickle?* Why? Would the result have been the same in *Wyman* if Mr. Newhouse had been in Florida and the trickery had been used to "flush him out of hiding"? In GUMPERZ v. HOFMANN, 245 App.Div. 622, 283 N.Y.S. 823 (1st Dep't 1935), affirmed 271 N.Y. 544, 2 N.E.2d 687 (1936), the court distinguished between actions designed to induce a party into a jurisdiction and actions calculated to facilitate service on a party already in the jurisdiction. In upholding service obtained by using trickery on a party who voluntarily was in New York, the court found a duty on the part of the party to accept service of process. The trickery, although reprehensible, did not lead to a quashing of service, since it merely was used to enforce a duty.

2. Instances in which a plaintiff will resort to tactics such as fraud, force, and artifice surely must be rare in an age when legitimate means of obtaining jurisdiction and serving process readily are available under long-arm statutes. Are the doctrines just examined obsolete? Are these rules justified simply because, even in the rare case, they will deter plaintiffs from doing such things? See, e.g., Shaw v. Hughes, 303 S.C. 337, 400 S.E.2d 501 (Ct.App.1991) (court did not have jurisdiction since service of process was procured by fraud and trickery); Terlizzi v. Brodie, 38 A.D.2d 762, 329 N.Y.S.2d 589 (2d Dep't 1972) (when New Jersey defendants were told that they had been chosen to receive two tickets to Broadway show in New York as a promotion to get their opinion as to new curtain time, service of process after show was invalid).

SECTION D. OPPORTUNITY TO BE HEARD

The Due Process Clause requires that parties have a "right to be heard" before the government effects a deprivation of their liberty or property. In simple terms, a defendant has an adequate opportunity to be heard when—in light of the interests at stake in the litigation—she is able to develop the facts and legal issues in the case. Depending on the interests involved, a proper hearing may suffice, or a full trial may be required, or something in between may pass muster. One common requirement is that the defendant must be informed of the action (that is, must receive notice) long enough in advance of the time when she is required to respond so as to allow her to obtain counsel and prepare a defense. Thus, when, in ROLLER v. HOLLY, 176 U.S. 398, 20 S.Ct. 410, 44 L.Ed. 520 (1900), the defendant had been served in Virginia with process requiring him to defend an action in Texas only five days after the service was made, the Supreme Court held that the Due Process Clause had been violated. Federal Rule 12(a) and state statutes generally allow defendants twenty days or more after service in which to respond.

The Warren Supreme Court extended due process protection to "New Property" created by modern regulatory statutes that did not exist at common law. These forms of property include licenses, Social Security benefits, and government jobs. See Reich, *The New Property*, 73 Yale L.J. 733 (1964). A landmark case GOLDBERG v. KELLY, 397 U.S. 254, 90 S.Ct. 1011, 25 L.Ed.2d 287 (1970), held that the recipient of government-funded public assistance is entitled under the Due Process Clause to "the opportunity for an evidentiary hearing prior to termination" of benefits. Acknowledging that the pre-termination hearing does not require a full-scale judicial trial, the Court nevertheless urged that the hearing "must be tailored to the capacities and circumstances of those who are to be heard."

The *Goldberg* Court emphasized that a pre-termination hearing was required given the importance of the plaintiff's private interest: "termination of aid pending resolution of a controversy over eligibility may deprive an *eligible* recipient of the very means by which to live while he waits." Id. at 264, 90 S.Ct. at 1018, 25 L.Ed.2d 297. See Law, *Some Reflections on Goldberg v. Kelly at Twenty Years*, 56 Brooklyn L. Rev. 805 (1990). The question of the "kind of hearing" that the Due Process Clause requires thus was linked to the nature of the plaintiff's interest. See Friendly, *"Some Kind of Hearing,"* 123 U. Pa. L. Rev. 1267 (1975). Subsequent cases raised due process challenges to the use of "provisional remedies"—temporary restraining orders, preliminary injunctions, pre-action attachments, and the like—that play an important role in consumer and other commercial disputes. At common law, provisional remedies represented important exceptions to the ordinary requirements associated with the constitutionally mandated opportunity to be heard and were justified by the need for expedition and summary action. The following cases examine the extent to which the Due Process Clause imposes limitations on the use of provisional remedies because they do not provide an adequate opportunity to be heard.

FUENTES v. SHEVIN

Supreme Court of the United States, 1972.
407 U.S. 67, 92 S.Ct. 1983, 32 L.Ed.2d 556, rehearing denied
409 U.S. 902, 93 S.Ct. 177, 34 L.Ed.2d 165.

Appeal from the United States District Court for the Southern District of Florida.

MR. JUSTICE STEWART delivered the opinion of the Court.

* * *

I

The appellant in No. 5039, Margarita Fuentes, is a resident of Florida. She purchased a gas stove and service policy from the Firestone Tire and Rubber Company (Firestone) under a conditional sales contract calling for monthly payments over a period of time. A few months later, she purchased a stereophonic phonograph from the same company under the same sort of contract. The total cost of the stove and stereo was about $500, plus an additional financing charge of over $100. Under the contracts, Firestone retained title to the merchandise, but Mrs. Fuentes was entitled to possession unless and until she should default on her installment payments.

For more than a year, Mrs. Fuentes made her installment payments. But then, with only about $200 remaining to be paid, a dispute developed between her and Firestone over the servicing of the stove. Firestone instituted an action in a small claims court for repossession of both the stove and the stereo, claiming that Mrs. Fuentes had refused to make her remaining payments. Simultaneously with the filing of that action and before Mrs. Fuentes had even received a summons to answer its complaint, Firestone obtained a writ of replevin ordering a sheriff to seize the disputed goods at once.

* * *

Shortly thereafter, Mrs. Fuentes instituted the present action in a federal district court, challenging the constitutionality of the Florida prejudgment replevin procedures under the Due Process Clause of the Fourteenth Amendment. She sought declaratory and injunctive relief against continued enforcement of the procedural provisions of the state statutes that authorize prejudgment replevin.

The appellants in No. 5138 filed a very similar action in a federal district court in Pennsylvania, challenging the constitutionality of that State's prejudgment replevin process. Like Mrs. Fuentes, they had had possessions seized under writs of replevin. Three of the appellants had purchased personal property—a bed, a table, and other household goods—under installment sales contracts like the one signed by Mrs. Fuentes; and the sellers of the property had obtained and executed summary writs of replevin, claiming that the appellants had fallen behind in their installment payments. The experience of the fourth appellant, Rosa Washington, had been more bizarre. She had been divorced from a local deputy sheriff and was engaged in a dispute with him over the custody of their son. Her former husband, being familiar with the routine forms used in the replevin process, had obtained a writ that ordered the seizure of the boy's clothes, furniture, and toys.

In both No. 5039 and No. 5138, three-judge district courts were convened to consider the appellants' challenges to the constitutional validity of the Florida and Pennsylvania statutes. The courts in both cases upheld the constitutionality of the statutes. * * *

II

Under the Florida statute challenged here, "[a]ny person whose goods or chattels are wrongfully detained by any other person * * * may have a writ of replevin to recover them * * *." Fla.Stats. § 78.01, F.S.A. There is no requirement that the applicant make a convincing showing before the seizure that the goods are, in fact, "wrongfully detained." Rather, Florida law * * * requires only that the applicant file a complaint, initiating a court action for repossession and reciting in conclusory fashion that he is "lawfully entitled to the possession" of the property, and that he file a security bond * * *. On the sole basis of the complaint and bond, a writ is issued "command[ing] the officer to whom it may be directed to replevy the goods and chattels in possession of defendant * * * and to summon the defendant to answer the complaint." Fla.Stats. § 78.08. If the goods are "in any dwelling house or other building or enclosure," the officer is required to demand their delivery; but if they are not delivered, "he shall cause such house, building or enclosure to be broken open and shall make replevin according to the writ * * *." Fla.Stats. § 78.10, F.S.A.

Thus, at the same moment that the defendant receives the complaint seeking repossession of property through court action, the property is seized from him. He is provided no prior notice and allowed no opportunity whatever to challenge the issuance of the writ. *After* the property has been seized, he will eventually have an opportunity for a hearing, as the defendant in the trial of the court action for repossession, which the plaintiff is required to pursue. And he is also not wholly without recourse in the meantime. For under the Florida statute, the officer who seizes the property must keep it for three days, and during that period the defendant may reclaim possession of the property by posting his own security bond in double its value. But if he does not post such a bond, the property is transferred to the party who sought the writ, pending a final judgment in the underlying action for repossession. * * *

The Pennsylvania law differs, though not in its essential nature, from that of Florida. As in Florida, a private party may obtain a prejudgment writ of replevin through a summary process of *ex parte* application, although a prothonotary rather than a court clerk issues the writ. As in Florida, the party seeking the writ may simply post with his application a bond in double the value of the property to be seized. * * * There is no opportunity for a prior hearing and no prior notice to the other party. On this basis, a sheriff is required to execute the writ by seizing the specified property. Unlike the Florida statute, however, the Pennsylvania law does not require that there *ever* be opportunity for a hearing on the merits of the conflicting claims to possession of the replevied property. The party seeking the writ is not obliged to initiate a court action for repossession. Indeed, he need not even formally allege that he is lawfully entitled to the property. * * * If the party who loses property through replevin seizure is to get even a postseizure hearing, he must initiate a lawsuit himself. He may also, as under Florida law, post his own counterbond within three days after the seizure to regain possession. * * *

III

* * * [Prejudgment replevin statutes] are most commonly used by creditors to seize goods allegedly wrongfully detained—not wrongfully taken—by debtors. At common law, if a creditor wished to invoke state power to recover goods wrongfully detained, he had to proceed through the action of debt or detinue. These actions, however, did not provide for a return of property before final judgment. And, more importantly, on the occasions when the common law did allow prejudgment seizure by state power, it provided some kind of notice and opportunity to be heard to the party then in possession of the property, and a state official made at least a summary determination of the relative rights of the disputing parties before stepping into the dispute and taking goods from one of them.

IV

* * *

The primary question in the present cases is whether these state statutes are constitutionally defective in failing to provide for hearings "at a meaningful time." The Florida replevin process guarantees an opportunity for a hearing after the seizure of goods, and the Pennsylvania process allows a post-seizure hearing if the aggrieved party shoulders the burden of initiating one. But neither the Florida nor Pennsylvania statute provides for notice or an opportunity to be heard *before* the seizure. * * *

The constitutional right to be heard is a basic aspect of the duty of government to follow a fair process of decisionmaking when it acts to deprive a person of his possessions. The purpose of this requirement is not only to ensure abstract fair play to the individual. Its purpose, more particularly, is to protect his use and possession of property from arbitrary encroachment—to minimize substantively unfair or mistaken deprivations of property, a danger that is especially great when the State seizes goods simply upon the application of and for the benefit of a private party. So viewed, the prohibition against the deprivation of property without due process of law reflects the high value, embedded in our constitutional and political history, that we place on a person's right to enjoy what is his, free of governmental interference. * * *

The requirement of notice and an opportunity to be heard raises no impenetrable barrier to the taking of a person's possessions. But the fair process of decision-making that it guarantees works, by itself, to protect against arbitrary deprivation of property. For when a person has an opportunity to speak up in his own defense, and when the State must listen to what he has to say, substantively unfair and simply mistaken deprivations of property interests can be prevented. It has long been recognized that "fairness can rarely be obtained by secret, one-sided determination of facts decisive of rights. * * * [And n]o better instrument has been devised for arriving at truth than to give a person in jeopardy of serious loss notice of the case against him and opportunity to meet it."

Joint Anti–Fascist Refugee Committee v. McGrath, 341 U.S. 123, 170–172, 71 S.Ct. 624, 647, 95 L.Ed. 817 (Frankfurter, J., concurring).

If the right to notice and a hearing is to serve its full purpose, then, it is clear that it must be granted at a time when the deprivation can still be prevented. At a later hearing, an individual's possessions can be returned to him if they were unfairly or mistakenly taken in the first place. Damages may even be awarded to him for the wrongful deprivation. But no later hearing and no damage award can undo the fact that the arbitrary taking that was subject to the right of procedural due process has already occurred. * * *

This is no new principle of constitutional law. The right to a prior hearing has long been recognized by this Court under the Fourteenth and Fifth Amendments. * * *

The Florida and Pennsylvania prejudgment replevin statutes fly in the face of this principle. To be sure, the requirements that a party seeking a writ must first post a bond, allege conclusorily that he is entitled to specific goods, and open himself to possible liability in damages if he is wrong, serve to deter wholly unfounded applications for a writ. But those requirements are hardly a substitute for a prior hearing, for they test no more than the strength of the applicant's own belief in his rights.[13] Since his private gain is at stake, the danger is all too great that his confidence in his cause will be misplaced. * * *

The minimal deterrent effect of a bond requirement is, in a practical sense, no substitute for an informed evaluation by a neutral official. More specifically, as a matter of constitutional principle, it is no replacement for the right to a prior hearing that is the only truly effective safeguard against arbitrary deprivation of property. While the existence of these other, less effective, safeguards may be among the considerations that affect the form of hearing demanded by due process, they are far from enough by themselves to obviate the right to a prior hearing of some kind.

V

The right to a prior hearing, of course, attaches only to the deprivation of an interest encompassed within the Fourteenth Amendment's protection. In the present cases, the Florida and Pennsylvania statutes were applied to replevy chattels in the appellants' possession. The replevin was not cast as a final judgment; most, if not all, of the appellants lacked full title to the chattels; and their claim even to continued possession was a matter in dispute. Moreover, the chattels at stake were nothing more than an assortment of household goods. Nonetheless, it is clear that the appellants were deprived of possessory interests in those chattels that were within the protection of the Fourteenth Amendment.

13. They may not even test that much. For if an applicant for the writ knows that he is dealing with an uneducated, uninformed consumer with little access to legal help and little familiarity with legal procedures, there may be a substantial possibility that a summary seizure of property—however unwarranted—may go unchallenged, and the applicant may feel that he can act with impunity.

A

* * * The Florida and Pennsylvania statutes do not require a person to wait until a post-seizure hearing and final judgment to recover what has been replevied. Within three days after the seizure, the statutes allow him to recover the goods if he, in return, surrenders other property—a payment necessary to secure a bond in double the value of the goods seized from him.[14] But it is now well settled that a temporary, nonfinal deprivation of property is nonetheless a "deprivation" in the terms of the Fourteenth Amendment. * * *

* * * The Fourteenth Amendment draws no bright lines around three-day, 10–day or 50–day deprivations of property. Any significant taking of property by the State is within the purview of the Due Process Clause. While the length and consequent severity of a deprivation may be another factor to weigh in determining the appropriate form of hearing, it is not decisive of the basic right to a prior hearing of some kind.

B

The appellants who signed conditional sales contracts lacked full legal title to the replevied goods. The Fourteenth Amendment's protection of "property," however, has never been interpreted to safeguard only the rights of undisputed ownership. Rather, it has been read broadly to extend protection to "any significant property interest" * * *.

The appellants were deprived of such an interest in the replevied goods—the interest in continued possession and use of the goods. * * * They had acquired this interest under the conditional sales contracts that entitled them to possession and use of the chattels before transfer of title. * * *

Their ultimate right to continued possession was, of course, in dispute. If it were shown at a hearing that the appellants had defaulted on their contractual obligations, it might well be that the sellers of the goods would be entitled to repossession. But even assuming that the appellants had fallen behind in their installment payments, and that they had no other valid defenses, that is immaterial here. The right to be heard does not depend upon an advance showing that one will surely prevail at the hearing. * * *

C

* * *

14. The appellants argue that this opportunity for quick recovery exists only in theory. They allege that very few people in their position are able to obtain a recovery bond, even if they know of the possibility. Appellant Fuentes says that in her case she was never told that she could recover the stove and stereo and that the deputy sheriff seizing them gave them at once to the Firestone agent, rather than holding them for three days. She further asserts that of 442 cases of prejudgment replevin in small claims courts in Dade County, Florida, in 1969, there was not one case in which the defendant took advantage of the recovery provision.

VI

There are "extraordinary situations" that justify postponing notice and opportunity for a hearing. Boddie v. Connecticut, supra, 401 U.S., at 379, 91 S.Ct., at 786. These situations, however, must be truly unusual. Only in a few limited situations has this Court allowed outright seizure[23] without opportunity for a prior hearing. First, in each case, the seizure has been directly necessary to secure an important governmental or general public interest. Second, there has been a special need for very prompt action. Third, the State has kept strict control over its monopoly of legitimate force; the person initiating the seizure has been a government official responsible for determining, under the standards of a narrowly drawn statute, that it was necessary and justified in the particular instance. Thus, the Court has allowed summary seizure of property to collect the internal revenue of the United States, to meet the needs of a national war effort, to protect against the economic disaster of a bank failure, and to protect the public from misbranded drugs and contaminated food.

The Florida and Pennsylvania prejudgment replevin statutes serve no such important governmental or general public interest. They allow summary seizure of a person's possessions when no more than private gain is directly at stake.[29] * * *

Nor do the broadly drawn Florida and Pennsylvania statutes limit the summary seizure of goods to special situations demanding prompt action. There may be cases in which a creditor could make a showing of immediate danger that a debtor will destroy or conceal disputed goods. But the statutes before us are not "narrowly drawn to meet any such unusual condition." Sniadach v. Family Finance Corp., supra, 395 U.S. at 339, 89 S.Ct. at 1821. And no such unusual situation is presented by the facts of these cases.

---

23. * * * In three cases, the Court has allowed the attachment of property without a prior hearing. In one, the attachment was necessary to protect the public against the same sort of immediate harm involved in the seizure cases—a bank failure. Coffin Bros. & Co. v. Bennett, 277 U.S. 29, 48 S.Ct. 422, 72 L.Ed. 768. Another case involved attachment necessary to secure jurisdiction in state court—clearly a most basic and important public interest. Ownbey v. Morgan, 256 U.S. 94, 41 S.Ct. 433, 65 L.Ed. 837. It is much less clear what interests were involved in the third case, decided with an unexplicated *per curiam* opinion simply citing *Coffin Bros.* and *Ownbey*. McKay v. McInnes, 279 U.S. 820, 49 S.Ct. 344, 73 L.Ed. 975. As far as essential procedural due process doctrine goes, *McKay* cannot stand for any more than was established in the *Coffin Bros.* and *Ownbey* cases on which it relied completely. * * *

29. By allowing repossession without an opportunity for a prior hearing, the Florida and Pennsylvania statutes may be intended specifically to reduce the costs for the private party seeking to seize goods in another party's possession. Even if the private gain at stake in repossession actions were equal to the great public interests recognized in this Court's past decisions, * * * the Court has made clear that the avoidance of the ordinary costs imposed by the opportunity for a hearing is not sufficient to override the constitutional right. * * *

[The] * * * cost of an opportunity to be heard before repossession should not be exaggerated. For we deal here only with the right to an *opportunity* to be heard. Since the issues and facts decisive of rights in repossession suits may very often be quite simple, there is a likelihood that many defendants would forgo their opportunity, sensing the futility of the exercise in the particular case. And, of course, no hearing need be held unless the defendant, having received notice of his opportunity, takes advantage of it.

The statutes, moreover, abdicate effective state control over state power. Private parties, serving their own private advantage, may unilaterally invoke state power to replevy goods from another. No state official participates in the decision to seek a writ; no state official reviews the basis for the claim to repossession; and no state official evaluates the need for immediate seizure. There is not even a requirement that the plaintiff provide any information to the court on these matters. The State acts largely in the dark.

VII

Finally, we must consider the contention that the appellants who signed conditional sales contracts thereby waived their basic procedural due process rights. The contract signed by Mrs. Fuentes provided that "in the event of default of any payment or payments, Seller at its option may take back the merchandise * * *." The contracts signed by the Pennsylvania appellants similarly provided that the seller "may retake" or "repossess" the merchandise in the event of a "default in any payment." These terms were parts of printed form contracts, appearing in relatively small type and unaccompanied by any explanations clarifying their meaning.

* * * For a waiver of constitutional rights in any context must, at the very least, be clear. We need not concern ourselves with the involuntariness or unintelligence of a waiver when the contractual language relied upon does not, on its face, even amount to a waiver.

The conditional sales contracts here simply provided that upon a default the seller "may take back," "may retake" or "may repossess" merchandise. The contracts included nothing about the waiver of a prior hearing. They did not indicate *how* or *through what process*—a final judgment, self-help, prejudgment replevin with a prior hearing, or prejudgment replevin without a prior hearing—the seller could take back the goods. Rather, the purported waiver provisions here are no more than a statement of the seller's right to repossession upon occurrence of certain events. * * *

VIII

We hold that the Florida and Pennsylvania prejudgment replevin provisions work a deprivation of property without due process of law insofar as they deny the right to a prior opportunity to be heard before chattels are taken from their possessor. Our holding, however, is a narrow one. We do not question the power of a State to seize goods before a final judgment in order to protect the security interests of creditors so long as those creditors have tested their claim to the goods through the process of a fair prior hearing. The nature and form of such prior hearings, moreover, are legitimately open to many potential variations and are a subject, at this point, for legislation—not adjudication. * * *

Vacated and remanded.

MR. JUSTICE POWELL and MR. JUSTICE REHNQUIST did not participate in the consideration or decision of these cases.

MR. JUSTICE WHITE, with whom THE CHIEF JUSTICE and MR. JUSTICE BLACKMUN join, dissenting.

* * * [The dissenters first noted that state proceedings were in progress when these actions were commenced so that jurisdiction should have been refused because there was an adequate remedy at law.]

Second: * * *

* * * The Court holds it constitutionally essential to afford opportunity for a probable cause hearing prior to repossession. Its stated purpose is "to prevent unfair and mistaken deprivations of the property." But in these typical situations, the buyer-debtor has either defaulted or he has not. If there is a default, it would seem not only "fair," but essential, that the creditor be allowed to repossess; and I cannot say that the likelihood of a mistaken claim of default is sufficiently real or recurring to justify a broad constitutional requirement that a creditor do more than the typical state law requires and permits him to do. Sellers are normally in the business of selling and collecting the price for their merchandise. I could be quite wrong, but it would not seem in the creditor's interest for a default occasioning repossession to occur; as a practical matter it would much better serve his interests if the transaction goes forward and is completed as planned. Dollar and cents considerations weigh heavily against false claims of default as well as against precipitate action that would allow no opportunity for mistakes to surface and be corrected. Nor does it seem to me that creditors would lightly undertake the expense of instituting replevin actions and putting up bonds.

* * * Viewing the issue before us in this light, I would not construe the Due Process Clause to require the creditors to do more than they have done in these cases to secure possession pending final hearing. Certainly, I would not ignore, as the Court does, the creditor's interest in preventing further use and deterioration of the property in which he has substantial interest. Surely under the Court's own definition, the creditor has a "property" interest as deserving of protection as that of the debtor. At least the debtor, who is very likely uninterested in a speedy resolution that could terminate his use of the property, should be required to make those payments, into court or otherwise, upon which his right to possession is conditioned. * * *

Third: The Court's rhetoric is seductive, but in end analysis, the result it reaches will have little impact and represents no more than ideological tinkering with state law. It would appear that creditors could withstand attack under today's opinion simply by making clear in the controlling credit instruments that they may retake possession without a hearing, or, for that matter, without resort to judicial process at all. Alternatively, they need only give a few days' notice of a hearing, take possession if hearing is waived or if there is default; and if hearing is necessary merely establish probable cause for asserting that default has occurred. It is very doubtful in my mind that such a hearing would in fact result in protections for the debtor substantially different from those the present laws provide. On the contrary, the availability of credit may well be diminished or, in any event, the expense of securing it increased.

None of this seems worth the candle to me. The procedure which the Court strikes down is not some barbaric hangover from bygone days. The respective rights of the parties in secured transactions have undergone the most intensive analysis in recent years. * * *

NOTES AND QUESTIONS

1. The holding in *Fuentes* as to replevin statutes was an application of the earlier decision in SNIADACH v. FAMILY FINANCE CORP., 395 U.S. 337, 89 S.Ct. 1820, 23 L.Ed.2d 349 (1969), which struck down a Wisconsin prejudgment wage garnishment procedure as violative of due process guarantees:

> A prejudgment garnishment of the Wisconsin type is a taking which may impose tremendous hardship on wage earners with families to support. Until a recent act of Congress, * * * which forbids discharge of employees on the ground that their wages have been garnished, garnishment often meant the loss of a job. Over and beyond that was the great drain on family income.

Id. at 340–42, 89 S.Ct. at 1822–23, 23 L.Ed.2d at 353–54.

2. How sound is the dissent's argument that creditors can avoid the restrictions of *Fuentes* by providing in their financing contracts that they may retake possession of property without a hearing? Reconsider D.H. Overmyer Co. v. Frick Co., Note 1, p. 225, supra, in which the Court held that a clause authorizing a creditor upon default to use a confession-of-judgment procedure and secure the entry of judgment against a debtor without service of process or notice was not per se violative of the Fourteenth Amendment requirements of prejudgment notice and a hearing. Then, consider KOSCHES v. NICHOLS, 68 Misc.2d 795, 327 N.Y.S.2d 968 (N.Y.City Civ.Ct.1971), in which the court stated:

> * * * The court also recognizes that, in these adhesion agreements where the buyer has no alternative but to purchase on credit, the parties are not in equal bargaining position. The era of the company store where the purchaser had no place else to go may not be dead. * * * Needless to say, the clauses giving the seller the right to enter a debtor's residence and seize the goods without a court order are unconscionable.

Id. at 797, 327 N.Y.S.2d at 970.

MITCHELL v. W.T. GRANT CO., 416 U.S. 600, 601, 604–07, 611, 614–15, 617–20, 94 S.Ct. 1895, 1897–1900, 1902, 1904–06, 40 L.Ed.2d 406, 410, 412–13, 415, 418–20 (1974) (White, J.):

In this case, a state trial judge in Louisiana ordered the sequestration of personal property on the application of a creditor who had made an installment sale of the goods to petitioner and whose affidavit asserted delinquency and prayed for sequestration to enforce a vendor's lien under state law. The issue is whether the sequestration violated the Due Process Clause of the Fourteenth Amendment because it was ordered *ex parte,* without prior notice or opportunity for a hearing. * * *

Plainly enough, this is not a case where the property sequestered by the court is exclusively the property of the defendant debtor. The question is not whether a debtor's property may be seized by his creditors, *pendente lite,* where they hold no present interest in the property sought to be seized. The reality is that both seller and buyer had current, real interests in the property, and the definition of property rights is a matter of state law. Resolution of the due process question must take account not only of the interests of the buyer of the property but those of the seller as well.

* * *

Louisiana statutes provide for sequestration where "one claims the ownership or right to possession of property, or a mortgage, lien, or privilege thereon * * * if it is within the power of the defendant to conceal, dispose of, or waste the property or the revenues therefrom, or remove the property from the parish, during the pendency of the action." Art. 3571. The writ, however, will not issue on the conclusory allegation of ownership or possessory rights. Article 3501 provides that the writ of sequestration shall issue "only when the nature of the claim and the amount thereof, if any, and the grounds relied upon for the issuance of the writ clearly appear from specific facts" shown by a verified petition or affidavit. In the parish where this case arose, the clear showing required must be made to a judge, and the writ will issue only upon his authorization and only after the creditor seeking the writ has filed a sufficient bond to protect the vendee against all damages in the event the sequestration is shown to have been improvident. Arts. 3501 and 3574.

The writ is obtainable on the creditor's *ex parte* application, without notice to the debtor or opportunity for a hearing, but the statute entitles the debtor immediately to seek dissolution of the writ, which must be ordered unless the creditor "proves the grounds upon which the writ was issued," Art. 3506, the existence of the debt, lien, and delinquency, failing which the court may order return of the property and assess damages in favor of the debtor, including attorney's fees.

The debtor, with or without moving to dissolve the sequestration, may also regain possession by filing his own bond to protect the creditor against interim damage to him should he ultimately win his case and have judgment against the debtor for the unpaid balance of the purchase price which was the object of the suit and of the sequestration. Arts. 3507 and 3508.

* * *

Petitioner asserts that his right to a hearing before his possession is in any way disturbed is nonetheless mandated by a long line of cases in this Court * * *.

* * * The suing creditor in *Sniadach* had no prior interest in the property attached, and the opinion did not purport to govern the typical case of the installment seller who brings a suit to collect an unpaid balance and who does not seek to attach wages pending the outcome of the suit but to repossess the sold property on which he had retained a lien to secure the purchase price. * * * [The *Fuentes*] holding is the mainstay of petitioner's submission here. But we are convinced that *Fuentes* was decided against a factual and legal background sufficiently different from that now before us and that it does not require the invalidation of the Louisiana sequestration statute, either on its face or as applied in this case.

* * * In Florida and Pennsylvania property was only to be replevied in accord with state policy if it had been "wrongfully detained." This broad "fault" standard is inherently subject to factual determination and adversarial input. * * * [I]n *Fuentes* this fault standard for replevin was thought ill-suited for preliminary *ex parte* determination. In Louisiana, on the other hand, the facts relevant to obtaining a writ of sequestration are narrowly confined. As we have indicated, documentary proof is particularly suited for questions of the existence of a vendor's lien and the issue of default. There is thus far less danger here that the seizure will be mistaken and a corresponding decrease in the utility of an adversary hearing which will be immediately available in any event.

* * * Our conclusion is that the Louisiana standards regulating the use of the writ of sequestration are constitutional. * * *

NOTES AND QUESTIONS

1. Justice Powell joined the majority opinion, but would have decided the case on narrower grounds. Justices Stewart, Douglas, and Marshall dissented arguing that (1) the Louisiana affidavit requirement was little more than a standardized form that only tested the creditor-applicant's own belief in his rights, (2) replacing the court clerk with a judge would have no effect on the assessment of the affidavit or the issuance of the writ, (3) the factual issues in *Mitchell* were no different from those in *Fuentes,* and (4) the majority unjustifiably had disregarded *stare decisis* in overruling *Fuentes.* Justice Brennan agreed with the other dissenters that *Fuentes* required the reversal of the judgment of the Supreme Court of Louisiana.

2. In the majority opinion, Justice White wrote: "In our view, this statutory procedure effects a constitutional accommodation of the conflicting interests of the parties." Id. at 607, 94 S.Ct. at 1900, 40 L.Ed.2d at 413. Although the Louisiana statute required the creditor to make more specific allegations than did the Florida and Pennsylvania statutes, can this requirement adequately replace the debtor's opportunity for a prior hearing? Is it of

constitutional significance that the official who signs the writ after the ex parte application is a judge rather than a court clerk?

3. Are you, as was the *Mitchell* majority, "convinced that *Fuentes* was decided against a factual and legal background sufficiently different" to justify the result in *Mitchell*? Id. at 615, 94 S.Ct. at 1904, 40 L.Ed.2d at 418. Can *Fuentes* and *Mitchell* be reconciled or was Justice Stewart's dissenting opinion correct in its assessment that *Mitchell* "has unmistakably overruled a considered decision of this Court that is barely two years old, without pointing to any change in either societal perceptions or basic constitutional understandings that might justify this total disregard of *stare decisis*"? Id. at 635, 94 S.Ct. at 1913, 40 L.Ed.2d at 429.

4. When, as in *Mitchell,* a pre-action attachment is sought to secure property pending a disposition, what should the focus of the inquiry be? Should the party seeking attachment be required to show a likelihood that the property to be attached will be removed from the jurisdiction, sold, or destroyed? Should she be required to show a likelihood of prevailing on the merits? If the party seeking attachment is not required to demonstrate a need to secure the property and a likelihood of success on the merits, wouldn't there be a serious danger that the pre-action attachment procedure would be used to harass?

When an attachment is sought, not for security purposes, but to establish jurisdiction, should the substantive focus of the inquiry be the same as for security attachments? When a jurisdictional attachment is sought, is there any reason why the need for security should militate for or against an attachment? Aren't the only relevant concerns in assessing the propriety of a jurisdictional attachment the likelihood that the plaintiff will prevail on the merits and the existence or non-existence of minimum contacts sufficient to satisfy *Shaffer*, see p. 161, supra?

NORTH GEORGIA FINISHING, INC. v. DI–CHEM, INC., 419 U.S. 601, 601–08, 95 S.Ct. 719, 720–23, 42 L.Ed.2d 751, 754–58 (1975) (White, J.):

Under the statutes of the State of Georgia, plaintiffs in pending suits are "entitled to the process of garnishment." Ga.Code Ann. § 46–101. To employ the process, plaintiff or his attorney must make an affidavit before "some officer authorized to issue an attachment, or the clerk of any court of record in which the said garnishment is being filed or in which the main case is filed, stating the amount claimed to be due in such action * * * and that he has reason to apprehend the loss of the same or some part thereof unless process of garnishment shall issue." § 46–102. To protect defendant against loss or damage in the event plaintiff fails to recover, that section also requires plaintiff to file a bond in a sum double the amount sworn to be due. Section 46–401 permits the defendant to dissolve the garnishment by filing a bond "conditioned for the payment of any judgment that shall be rendered on said garnishment." Whether these provisions satisfy the Due Process Clause of the Fourteenth Amendment is the issue before us in this case.

* * * [The Court proceeded to explain the background of the case. Respondent had filed suit against petitioner, alleging that petitioner owed it $51,279 for goods sold and delivered. Before petitioner received service of the complaint, respondent filed an affidavit and bond for garnishing petitioner's bank account. Petitioner responded first by filing its own bond to discharge the bank as garnishee and then by filing a motion to discharge its bond on the ground that the statute unconstitutionally failed to provide notice and hearing prior to the garnishment. The Georgia Supreme Court upheld the constitutionality of the statute.]

The Georgia court recognized that Sniadach v. Family Finance Corp. * * * had invalidated a statute permitting the garnishment of wages without notice and opportunity for hearing, but considered that case to have done nothing more than to carve out an exception, in favor of wage earners, "to the general rule of legality of garnishment statutes." * * * The garnishment of other assets or properties pending the outcome of the main action * * * was apparently thought not to implicate the Due Process Clause.

This approach failed to take account of Fuentes v. Shevin * * *. Because the official seizures had been carried out without notice and without opportunity for a hearing or other safeguard against mistaken repossession, they were held to be in violation of the Fourteenth Amendment.

The Georgia statute is vulnerable for the same reasons. Here, a bank account, surely a form of property, was impounded and, absent a bond, put totally beyond use during the pendency of the litigation on the alleged debt, all by a writ of garnishment issued by a court clerk without notice or opportunity for an early hearing and without participation by a judicial officer.

Nor is the statute saved by the more recent decision in Mitchell v. W.T. Grant Co. * * *.

The Georgia garnishment statute has none of the saving characteristics of the Louisiana statute. The writ of garnishment is issuable on the affidavit of the creditor or his attorney, and the latter need not have personal knowledge of the facts. § 46–103. The affidavit, like the one filed in this case, need contain only conclusory allegations. The writ is issuable, as this one was, by the court clerk, without participation by a judge. Upon service of the writ, the debtor is deprived of the use of the property in the hands of the garnishee. Here a sizable bank account was frozen, and the only method discernible on the face of the statute to dissolve the garnishment was to file a bond to protect the plaintiff creditor. There is no provision for an early hearing at which the creditor would be required to demonstrate at least probable cause for the garnishment. Indeed, it would appear that without the filing of a bond the defendant debtor's challenge to the garnishment will not be entertained, whatever the grounds may be.

Respondent also argues that neither *Fuentes* nor *Mitchell* is apposite here because each of those cases dealt with the application of due process protections to consumers who are victims of contracts of adhesion and who might be irreparably damaged by temporary deprivation of household necessities, whereas this case deals with its application in the commercial setting to a case involving parties of equal bargaining power. * * * It is asserted in addition that the double bond posted here gives assurance to petitioner that it will be made whole in the event the garnishment turns out to be unjustified. It may be that consumers deprived of household appliances will more likely suffer irreparably than corporations deprived of bank accounts, but the probability of irreparable injury in the latter case is sufficiently great so that some procedures are necessary to guard against the risk of initial error. We are no more inclined now than we have been in the past to distinguish among different kinds of property in applying the Due Process Clause. * * *

Enough has been said, we think, to require the reversal of the judgment of the Georgia Supreme Court. * * *

NOTES AND QUESTIONS

1. Although the Court in *Di–Chem* claimed to have relied on *Fuentes* in declaring the Georgia garnishment statute unconstitutional, did the Court actually insist that the Georgia statute provide an opportunity for a pre-seizure hearing? Would the Georgia statute have been acceptable if it had provided for an immediate post-seizure hearing, as did the Louisiana statute in *Mitchell?* What did the Court in *Di–Chem* mean by the words "or other safeguard against mistaken repossession," p. 253, supra?

2. Might the result in *Di–Chem* have been different if the creditor had a pre-existing interest in the garnished bank account, as did the creditor in *Mitchell?* See generally Kay & Lubin, *Making Sense of the Prejudgment Seizure Cases*, 64 Ky.L.J. 705 (1976).

CONNECTICUT v. DOEHR

Supreme Court of the United States, 1991.
501 U.S. 1, 111 S.Ct. 2105, 115 L.Ed.2d 1.

Certiorari to the United States Court of Appeals for the Second Circuit.

JUSTICE WHITE delivered an opinion, Parts I, II, and III of which are the opinion of the Court.*

This case requires us to determine whether a state statute that authorizes prejudgment attachment of real estate without prior notice or hearing, without a showing of extraordinary circumstances, and without a requirement that the person seeking the attachment post a bond, satisfies

* The Chief Justice, Justice Blackmun, Justice Kennedy, and Justice Souter join Parts I, II, and III of this opinion, and Justice Scalia joins Parts I and III.

the Due Process Clause of the Fourteenth Amendment. We hold that, as applied to this case, it does not.

I

On March 15, 1988, Petitioner John F. DiGiovanni submitted an application to the Connecticut Superior Court for an attachment in the amount of $75,000 on respondent Brian K. Doehr's home in Meridan, Connecticut. DiGiovanni took this step in conjunction with a civil action for assault and battery that he was seeking to institute against Doehr in the same court. The suit did not involve Doehr's real estate nor did DiGiovanni have any pre-existing interest either in Doehr's home or any of his other property.

Connecticut law authorizes prejudgment attachment of real estate without affording prior notice or the opportunity for a prior hearing to the individual whose property is subject to the attachment. The State's prejudgment remedy statute provides, in relevant part:

> "The court or a judge of the court may allow the prejudgment remedy to be issued by an attorney without hearing * * * upon verification by oath of the plaintiff or of some competent affiant, that there is probable cause to sustain the validity of the plaintiff's claims and (1) that the prejudgment remedy requested is for an attachment of real property * * *." Conn.Gen.Stat. § 52–278e (1991).

The statute does not require the plaintiff to post a bond to insure the payment of damages that the defendant may suffer should the attachment prove wrongfully issued or the claim prove unsuccessful.

As required, DiGiovanni submitted an affidavit in support of his application. In five one-sentence paragraphs, DiGiovanni stated that the facts set forth in his previously submitted complaint were true; that "I was willfully, wantonly and maliciously assaulted by the defendant, Brian K. Doehr"; that "[s]aid assault and battery broke my left wrist and further caused an ecchymosis to my right eye, as well as other injuries"; and that "I have further expended sums of money for medical care and treatment." The affidavit concluded with the statement, "In my opinion, the foregoing facts are sufficient to show that there is probable cause that judgment will be rendered for the plaintiff."

On the strength of these submissions the Superior Court judge * * * found "probable cause to sustain the validity of the plaintiff's claim" and ordered the attachment on Doehr's home "to the value of $75,000." The sheriff attached the property four days later * * *. Only after this did Doehr receive notice of the attachment. He also had yet to be served with the complaint * * *. As the statute further required, the attachment notice informed Doehr that he had the right to a hearing: (1) to claim that no probable cause existed to sustain the claim; (2) to request that the attachment be vacated, modified, or that a bond be substituted; or (3) to claim that some portion of the property was exempt from execution. * * *

Rather than pursue these options, Doehr filed suit against DiGiovanni in Federal District Court, claiming that [the statute] was unconstitutional under the Due Process Clause of the Fourteenth Amendment. The District Court upheld the statute and granted summary judgment in favor of DiGiovanni. * * * On appeal, a divided panel of the United States Court of Appeals for the Second Circuit reversed. * * * Judge Pratt, who wrote the opinion for the court, concluded that the Connecticut statute violated due process in permitting *ex parte* attachment absent a showing of extraordinary circumstances. "The rule to be derived from Sniadach v. Family Finance Corp. * * * and its progeny * * * is not that postattachment hearings are generally acceptable provided that the plaintiff files a factual affidavit and that a judicial officer supervises the process, but that a prior hearing may be postponed where exceptional circumstances justify such a delay, *and where* sufficient additional safeguards are present." * * *

A further reason to invalidate the statute, the court ruled, was the highly factual nature of the issues in this case. In [Mitchell v. W.T. Grant Co.] there were "uncomplicated matters that len[t] themselves to documentary proof" and "[t]he nature of the issues at stake minimize[d] the risk that the writ [would] be wrongfully issued by a judge." * * * Judge Pratt observed that in contrast the present case involved the fact-specific event of a fist fight and the issue of assault. He doubted that the judge could reliably determine probable cause when presented with only the plaintiff's version of the altercation. * * * Judge Pratt went on to conclude that in his view, the statute was also constitutionally infirm for its failure to require the plaintiff to post a bond for the protection of the defendant in the event the attachment was ultimately found to have been improvident.

* * *

II

With this case we return to the question of what process must be afforded by a state statute enabling an individual to enlist the aid of the State to deprive another of his or her property by means of the prejudgment attachment or similar procedure. Our cases reflect the numerous variations this type of remedy can entail. [See, e.g., *Sniadach, Fuentes, Mitchell,* and *Di–Chem.*] * * * In [Mathews v. Eldridge, 424 U.S. 319, 96 S.Ct. 893, 47 L.Ed.2d 18 (1976)], we drew upon * * * [these] decisions to determine what process is due when the government itself seeks to effect a deprivation on its own initiative. * * * That analysis resulted in * * * [a] threefold inquiry requiring consideration of "the private interest that will be affected by the official action"; "the risk of an erroneous deprivation of such interest through the procedures used, and the probable value, if any, of additional or substitute safeguards"; and lastly "the Government's interest, including the function involved and the fiscal and administrative burdens that the additional or substitute procedural requirement would entail." Id. at 335, 96 S.Ct. at 903.

Here the inquiry is similar but the focus is different. Prejudgment remedy statutes ordinarily apply to disputes between private parties rather than between an individual and the government. * * * For this type of case, therefore, the relevant inquiry requires, as in *Mathews,* first, consideration of the private interest that will be affected by the prejudgment measure; second, an examination of the risk of erroneous deprivation through the procedures under attack and the probable value of additional or alternative safeguards; and third, in contrast to *Mathews,* principal attention to the interest of the party seeking the prejudgment remedy, with, nonetheless, due regard for any ancillary interest the government may have in providing the procedure or forgoing the added burden of providing greater protections.

We now consider the *Mathews* factors in determining the adequacy of the procedures before us, first with regard to the safeguards of notice and a prior hearing, and then in relation to the protection of a bond.

III

We agree with the Court of Appeals that the property interests that attachment affects are significant. For a property owner like Doehr, attachment ordinarily clouds title; impairs the ability to sell or otherwise alienate the property; taints any credit rating; reduces the chance of obtaining a home equity loan or additional mortgage; and can even place an existing mortgage in technical default where there is an insecurity clause. * * *

* * * [Connecticut] correctly points out that these effects do not amount to a complete, physical, or permanent deprivation of real property; their impact is less than the perhaps temporary total deprivation of household goods or wages. * * * But the Court has never held that only such extreme deprivations trigger due process concern. * * * To the contrary, our cases show that even the temporary or partial impairments to property rights that attachments, liens, and similar encumbrances entail are sufficient to merit due process protection. * * *

We also agree with the Court of Appeals that the risk of erroneous deprivation that the State permits here is substantial. By definition, attachment statutes premise a deprivation of property on one ultimate factual contingency—the award of damages to the plaintiff which the defendant may not be able to satisfy. * * * For attachments before judgment, Connecticut mandates that this determination be made by means of a procedural inquiry that asks whether "there is probable cause to sustain the validity of the plaintiff's claim." Conn.Gen.Stat. § 52–278e(a). * * * What probable cause means in this context, however, remains obscure. The State initially took the position * * * that the statute requires a plaintiff to show the objective likelihood of the suit's success. * * * DiGiovanni * * * reads the provision as requiring no more than that a plaintiff demonstrate a subjective good faith belief that the suit will succeed. * * * At oral argument, the State shifted its position to argue that the statute requires something akin to the plaintiff stating a claim with sufficient facts to survive a motion to dismiss.

We need not resolve this confusion since the statute presents too great a risk of erroneous deprivation under any of these interpretations. If the statute demands inquiry into the sufficiency of the complaint, or, still less, the plaintiff's good-faith belief that the complaint is sufficient, requirement of a complaint and a factual affidavit would permit a court to make these minimal determinations. But neither inquiry adequately reduces the risk of erroneous deprivation. Permitting a court to authorize attachment merely because the plaintiff believes the defendant is liable, or because the plaintiff can make out a facially valid complaint, would permit the deprivation of the defendant's property when the claim would fail to convince a jury, when it rested on factual allegations that were sufficient to state a cause of action but which the defendant would dispute, or in the case of a mere good-faith standard, even when the complaint failed to state a claim upon which relief could be granted. The potential for unwarranted attachment in these situations is self-evident and too great to satisfy the requirements of due process absent any countervailing consideration.

Even if the provision requires the plaintiff to demonstrate, and the judge to find, probable cause to believe that judgment will be rendered in favor of the plaintiff, the risk of error was substantial in this case. As the record shows, and as the State concedes, only a skeletal affidavit need be and was filed. The State urges that the reviewing judge normally reviews the complaint as well, but concedes that the complaint may also be conclusory. It is self-evident that the judge could make no realistic assessment concerning the likelihood of an action's success based upon these one-sided, self-serving, and conclusory submissions. And as the Court of Appeals said, in a case like this involving an alleged assault, even a detailed affidavit would give only the plaintiff's version of the confrontation. Unlike determining the existence of a debt or delinquent payments, the issue does not concern "ordinarily uncomplicated matters that lend themselves to documentary proof." * * *

What safeguards the State does afford do not adequately reduce this risk. Connecticut points out that the statute also provides an "expeditiou[s]" postattachment adversary hearing * * *; notice for such a hearing * * *; judicial review of an adverse decision * * *; and a double damages action if the original suit is commenced without probable cause * * *. Similar considerations were present in *Mitchell* * * *. But in *Mitchell,* the plaintiff had a vendor's lien to protect, the risk of error was minimal because the likelihood of recovery involved uncomplicated matters that lent themselves to documentary proof, * * * and plaintiff was required to put up a bond. None of these factors diminishing the need for a predeprivation hearing is present in this case. It is true that a later hearing might negate the presence of probable cause, but this would not cure the temporary deprivation that an earlier hearing might have prevented. * * *

Finally, we conclude that the interests in favor of an *ex parte* attachment, particularly the interests of the plaintiff, are too minimal to supply such a consideration here. Plaintiff had no existing interest in Doehr's real estate when he sought the attachment. His only interest in attaching the property was to ensure the availability of assets to satisfy his judgment if he prevailed on the merits of his action. Yet there was no allegation that Doehr was about to transfer or encumber his real estate or take any other action during the pendency of the action that would render his real estate unavailable to satisfy a judgment. Our cases have recognized such a properly supported claim would be an exigent circumstance permitting postponing any notice or hearing until after the attachment is effected. * * * Absent such allegations, however, the plaintiff's interest in attaching the property does not justify the burdening of Doehr's ownership rights without a hearing to determine the likelihood of recovery.

No interest the government may have affects the analysis. The State's substantive interest in protecting any rights of the plaintiff cannot be any more weighty than those rights themselves. Here the plaintiff's interest is *de minimis*. Moreover, the State cannot seriously plead additional financial or administrative burdens involving predeprivation hearings when it already claims to provide an immediate post-deprivation hearing. * * *

* * *

IV

A

Although a majority of the Court does not reach the issue, Justices Marshall, Stevens, O'Connor, and I deem it appropriate to consider whether due process also requires the plaintiff to post a bond or other security in addition to requiring a hearing or showing of some exigency.

As noted, the impairments to property rights that attachments affect merit due process protection. Several consequences can be severe, such as the default of a homeowner's mortgage. In the present context, it need only be added that we have repeatedly recognized the utility of a bond in protecting property rights affected by the mistaken award of prejudgment remedies. * * *

Without a bond, at the time of attachment, the danger that these property rights may be wrongfully deprived remains unacceptably high even with such safeguards as a hearing or exigency requirement. The need for a bond is especially apparent where extraordinary circumstances justify an attachment with no more than the plaintiff's *ex parte* assertion of a claim. * * * Until a postattachment hearing * * *, a defendant has no protection against damages sustained where no extraordinary circumstance in fact existed or the plaintiff's likelihood of recovery was nil. Such protection is what a bond can supply. Both the Court and its individual members have repeatedly found the requirement of a bond to play an essential role in reducing what would have been too great a degree of risk in precisely this type of circumstance. * * *

But the need for a bond does not end here. A defendant's property rights remain at undue risk even when there has been an adversarial hearing to determine the plaintiff's likelihood of recovery. At best, a court's initial assessment of each party's case cannot produce more than an educated prediction as to who will win. This is especially true when, as here, the nature of the claim makes any accurate prediction elusive. * * * In consequence, even a full hearing under a proper probable-cause standard would not prevent many defendants from having title to their homes impaired during the pendency of suits that never result in the contingency that ultimately justifies such impairment, namely, an award to the plaintiff. Attachment measures currently on the books reflect this concern. All but a handful of States require a plaintiff's bond despite also affording a hearing either before, or (for the vast majority, only under extraordinary circumstances) soon after, an attachment takes place. * * *

The State stresses its double damages remedy for suits that are commenced without probable cause. * * * This remedy, however, fails to make up for the lack of a bond. As an initial matter, the meaning of "probable cause" in this provision is no more clear here than it was in the attachment provision itself. Should the term mean the plaintiff's good faith or the facial adequacy of the complaint, the remedy is clearly insufficient. A defendant who was deprived where there was little or no likelihood that the plaintiff would obtain a judgment could nonetheless recover only by proving some type of fraud or malice or by showing that the plaintiff had failed to state a claim. * * *

Nor is there any appreciable interest against a bond requirement. * * * [A] plaintiff [is not required] to show exigent circumstances nor any pre-existing interest in the property facing attachment. A party must show more than the mere existence of a claim before subjecting an opponent to prejudgment proceedings that carry a significant risk of erroneous deprivation. * * *

B

Our foregoing discussion compels the four of us to consider whether a bond excuses the need for a hearing or other safeguards altogether. If a bond is needed to augment the protections afforded by preattachment and postattachment hearings, it arguably follows that a bond renders these safeguards unnecessary. That conclusion is unconvincing, however, for it ignores certain harms that bonds could not undo but that hearings would prevent. The law concerning attachments has rarely, if ever, required defendants to suffer an encumbered title until the case is concluded without any prior opportunity to show that the attachment was unwarranted. Our cases have repeatedly emphasized the importance of providing a prompt postdeprivation hearing at the very least. * * *

The necessity for at least a prompt postattachment hearing is self-evident because the right to be compensated at the end of the case, if the plaintiff loses, for all provable injuries caused by the attachment is inadequate to redress the harm inflicted, harm that could have been avoided had an early hearing been held. An individual with an immediate need or opportunity to sell a property can neither do so, nor otherwise satisfy that need or recreate the opportunity. The same applies to a parent in need of a home equity loan for a child's education, an entrepreneur seeking to start a business on the strength of an otherwise strong credit rating, or simply a homeowner who might face the disruption of having a mortgage placed in technical default. * * * [It should be clear that r]eliance on a bond does not sufficiently account for the harms that flow from an erroneous attachment to excuse a State from reducing that risk by means of a timely hearing.

If a bond cannot serve to dispense with a hearing immediately after attachment, neither is it sufficient basis for not providing a preattachment hearing in the absence of exigent circumstances even if in any event a hearing would be provided a few days later. The reasons are the same: a wrongful attachment can inflict injury that will not fully be redressed by recovery on the bond after a prompt postattachment hearing determines that the attachment was invalid.

* * *

V

Because Connecticut's prejudgment remedy provision * * * violates the requirements of due process * * *, the judgment of the Court of Appeals is affirmed, and the case is remanded to that court for further proceedings consistent with this opinion.

It is so ordered.

CHIEF JUSTICE REHNQUIST with whom JUSTICE BLACKMUN joins, concurring.

I agree with the Court that the Connecticut attachment statute, "as applied in this case," * * * fails to satisfy the Due Process Clause of the Fourteenth Amendment. I therefore join Parts I, II and III of its opinion. Unfortunately, the remainder of the Court's opinion does not confine itself to the facts of this case, but enters upon a lengthy disquisition as to what combination of safeguards are required to satisfy Due Process in hypothetical cases not before the Court. I therefore do not join Part IV.

* * * The Court's opinion is, in my view, ultimately correct when it bases its holding of unconstitutionality of the Connecticut statute as applied here on [*Sniadach, Fuentes, Mitchell,* and *Di–Chem*] * * *. But I do not believe that the result follows so inexorably as the Court's opinion suggests. All of the cited cases dealt with personalty—bank deposits or chattels—and each involved the physical seizure of the property itself, so that the defendant was deprived of its use. * * * [I]n all of them the debtor was deprived of the use and possession of the property. In the present case, on the other hand, Connecticut's prejudgment attachment on real property statute, which secures an incipient lien for the plaintiff, does not deprive the defendant of the use or possession of the property.

The Court's opinion therefore breaks new ground * * *. * * * I agree with the Court, however, that upon analysis the deprivation here is a significant one, even though the owner remains in undisturbed possession. * * *

* * *

It is both unwise and unnecessary, I believe, for the Court to proceed, as it does in Part IV, from its decision of the case before it to discuss abstract and hypothetical situations not before it. * * * The two elements of due process with which the Court concerns itself in Part IV—the requirement of a bond, and of "exigent circumstances"—prove to be upon analysis so vague that the discussion is not only unnecessary, but not particularly useful. Unless one knows what the terms and conditions of a bond are to be, the requirement of a "bond" in the abstract means little. The amount to be secured by the bond and the conditions of the bond are left unaddressed—is there to be liability on the part of a plaintiff if he is ultimately unsuccessful in the underlying lawsuit, or is it instead to be conditioned on some sort of good faith test? The "exigent circumstances" referred to by the Court are admittedly equally vague; non-residency appears to be enough in some states, an attempt to conceal assets is required in others, an effort to flee the jurisdiction in still others. We should await concrete cases which present questions involving bonds and exigent circumstances before we attempt to decide when and if the Due Process Clause of the Fourteenth Amendment requires them as prerequisites for a lawful attachment.

[The concurring opinion of JUSTICE SCALIA is omitted.]

NOTES AND QUESTIONS

1. In MATHEWS v. ELDRIDGE, 424 U.S. 319, 96 S.Ct. 893, 47 L.Ed.2d 18 (1976), the Court held that the Due Process Clause does not require the government to hold a hearing before terminating a recipient's Social Security disability benefits. A post-termination hearing is constitutionally sufficient, the Court explained, given the balance of three factors:

> First, the private interest that will be affected by the official action; second, the risk of an erroneous deprivation of such interest through the procedures used, and the probable value, if any, of additional or substitute procedural safeguards; and finally, the Government's interest, including the function involved and the fiscal and administrative burdens that the additional or substitute procedural requirement would entail.

Id. at 335, 96 S.Ct. at 903, 47 L.Ed.2d at 33. In *Doehr,* the Supreme Court adapted the *Mathews* factors to a dispute between two private parties. Would application of the *Mathews* factors have changed the outcome in *Mitchell*?

2. Can you reconcile *Doehr* with earlier precedent on the right to be heard? By not overruling *Mitchell,* has the Court effectively made the constitutionally required opportunity to be heard dependent on the underlying substantive law claim? On whether the plaintiff has a pre-existing interest in

the attached property? Given the contextual nature of the due-process inquiry, do you agree with the Court's case-specific approach?

3. SHAUMYAN v. O'NEILL, 987 F.2d 122 (2d Cir.1993), a challenge to the application of the same statute at issue in *Doehr,* involved a contract dispute between a homeowner and a contractor hired to do repairs. The homeowner questioned the quality of the repair work, and refused to pay the remainder of the bill. The contractor, ex parte, obtained a prejudgment attachment against the owner's home. While the state court action was pending, the homeowner sued in federal court to enjoin application of the attachment statute, and the District Court upheld the constitutionality of the statute as applied. Relying on *Mathews*, the Court of Appeals affirmed. Although the homeowner had a strong private interest, the likelihood of an erroneous deprivation was not high because the evidence largely involved written documentation; moreover, the contractor "had a substantial pre-existing interest" in the property once his labor and materials had been incorporated into plaintiff's home. Id. at 127. See Alquist, *Balancing the Checklist: Connecticut's Legislative Response to Connecticut v. Doehr*, 26 Conn. L. Rev. 721 (1994).

4. In *Doehr*, defendant continued to possess, and in fact reside, in his home, even after the court's entry of the prejudgment attachment. Although the attachment caused only a "temporary or partial" impairment of Doehr's property right, the Court held that the Due Process Clause afforded protection. In the wake of *Doehr*, questions were raised about the constitutionality of lis pendens statutes, which permit a plaintiff who claims an interest in real property to file a "notice of pendency," see p. 1173, infra, that alerts potential buyers of the claim. See Levy, *Lis Pendens and Procedural Due Process: A Closer Look After Connecticut v. Doehr,* 51 Md.L.Rev. 1054 (1992). In DIAZ v. PATERSON, 547 F.3d 88 (2d Cir. 2008), a federal appeals court upheld the constitutionality of New York's lis pendens statute applying the *Mathews* factors as construed in *Doehr*.

5. In RICHMOND TENANTS ORGANIZATION, INC. v. KEMP, 956 F.2d 1300 (4thCir.1992), a public housing tenants' organization brought a nationwide class action challenging the federal practice of using civil forfeiture procedures to evict drug offenders from public housing immediately without notice and without a hearing. The government argued that drug activity "constitutes in every case an extraordinary situation which requires prompt governmental action to protect other innocent tenants from dangerous drug activities in their buildings." The court disagreed and held that:

> While the level and type of drug trafficking in a particular location might amount to exigent circumstances warranting a summary eviction, the mere use or possession of narcotics would not in every case constitute an extraordinary situation permitting federal law enforcement officers to summarily remove all persons occupying the housing unit where the activity had occurred.

Id. at 1308. Do you agree? In UNITED STATES v. JAMES DANIEL GOOD REAL PROPERTY, 510 U.S. 43, 114 S.Ct. 492, 126 L.Ed.2d 490 (1993), the government filed an in rem action seeking civil forfeiture of a property owner's home four years after he had pled guilty to drug charges under state law. Pursuant to the seizure warrant, the government seized the home and ordered tenants living in the property to pay rent to the government rather than to the homeowner. The Supreme Court held that in the absence of exigent circumstances, the government was required to afford the homeowner notice and an opportunity to be heard before seizing real property that may be subject to civil forfeiture.

6. The first prong of the *Mathews* test, as interpreted in *Doehr,* concerns "the private interest that will be affected by the official action." Note 1, p. 262, supra. Of what significance is the private interest when the government tows, immobilizes, or destroys an automobile driver's car? In BENNIS v. MICHIGAN, 516 U.S. 442, 116 S.Ct. 994, 134 L.Ed.2d 68 (1996), the state of Michigan forfeited a family's automobile as a public nuisance, following the husband's use of the car for sex acts with a prostitute and his conviction for gross indecency. The government provided the wife with notice and an opportunity to contest the forfeiture, but refused to make an offset for the wife's joint interest in the property, and she challenged the forfeiture on due process grounds. The Court rejected her challenge, explaining that "a long and unbroken line of cases holds that an owner's interest in property may be forfeited by reason of the use to which the property is put even though the owner did not know that it was to be put to such use." Id. at 446, 116 S.Ct. at 998, 134 L.Ed.2d at 74.

In an earlier case, PATTERSON v. CRONIN, 650 P.2d 531 (Colo.1982), plaintiff's car had been illegally parked on seven separate occasions before the city of Denver ordered it to be immobilized with a "Denver boot." (The boot is a huge clamp applied to a car's wheel.) Plaintiff argued that the city's failure to provide a hearing before immobilizing his auto violated due process. Applying the *Mathews* factors, the court found that the governmental interest in enforcing parking ordinances was important enough that a hearing prior to immobilization was not constitutionally mandated but due process did require a post-deprivation hearing. Because Denver failed to provide such a post-deprivation hearing the court concluded that the immobilization of plaintiff's vehicle violated his due process rights. See Rosenthal, *Does Due Process Have an Original Meaning? On Originalism, Due Process, Procedural Innovation . . . and Parking Tickets*, 60 Okla. L. Rev. 1 (2007). Some states now use "the boot" to sanction non-custodial parents who have fallen behind in their child support payments. See Swank, *Das Boot! A National Survey of Booting Programs' Impact on Child Support Compliance*, 4 J. L. & Fam. Stud. 265 (2002). Does this use of "the boot" affect how you weigh the private interest that is at stake?

7. In PERALTA v. HEIGHTS MEDICAL CENTER, INC., 485 U.S. 80, 108 S.Ct. 896, 99 L.Ed.2d 75 (1988), the Supreme Court considered attachment in another context. In *Peralta,* a default judgment was entered in a suit by a hospital against Peralta to recover a medical bill owed by one of Peralta's employees and guaranteed by him. A writ of attachment was issued and Peralta's property was sold to satisfy the judgment.

Later, Peralta brought an action to set aside the default judgment and void the sale alleging that the return of service in the first action showed that it was not timely, and that he in fact had not been served personally. The

Texas courts denied his requests, holding that in order to have a default judgment reversed a meritorious defense must be shown. But the Supreme Court held that requiring a party seeking to vacate a judgment to show a meritorious defense violated the Due Process Clause. Justice White wrote:

> The Texas courts * * * held * * * that * * * appellant was required to show that he had a meritorious defense, apparently on the ground that without a defense, the same judgment would again be entered on retrial and hence appellant had suffered no harm from the judgment entered without notice. But this reasoning is untenable. As appellant asserts, had he had notice of the suit, he might have impleaded the employee whose debt had been guaranteed, worked out a settlement, or paid the debt. He would also have preferred to sell his property himself in order to raise funds rather than to suffer it sold at a constable's auction.
>
> Nor is there any doubt that the entry of the judgment itself had serious consequences. It is not denied that the judgment was entered on the county records, became a lien on appellant's property, and was the basis for issuance of a writ of execution under which appellant's property was promptly sold, without notice. Even if no execution sale had yet occurred, the lien encumbered the property and impaired appellant's ability to mortgage or alienate it; and state procedures for creating and enforcing such liens are subject to the strictures of due process. * * * Here, we assume that the judgment against him and the ensuing consequences occurred without notice to appellant, notice at a meaningful time and in a meaningful manner that would have given him an opportunity to be heard.

Id. at 85–86, 108 S.Ct. at 899, 99 L.Ed.2d at 81.

8. To what other types of situations might the *Sniadach* line of cases apply? Consider, for example, the provisions of Federal Rule 65(b)(1) authorizing issuance of temporary restraining orders (TROs) without notice or a hearing. Rule 65(b)(2) provides that a TRO is effective only for a period of ten days. During that time, a hearing may be held to determine whether or not a preliminary injunction should issue. If a preliminary injunction is granted, it remains in effect until a final judgment is rendered. See p. 1166, infra. Do the procedures outlined in Rule 65(b)(1) and (b)(2) satisfy the Due Process Clause as interpreted in *Sniadach* and its progeny? Which of those procedures are constitutionally required?

CHAPTER 4

JURISDICTION OVER THE SUBJECT MATTER OF THE ACTION—THE COURT'S COMPETENCY

■ ■ ■

In this Chapter, we will consider subject-matter jurisdiction: the court's power to hear a case because of the nature of the dispute, as distinct from its power to enter a judgment against a particular defendant. In thinking about this topic, keep in mind that the United States judicial system is really comprised of multiple systems. "Each of the fifty states and the District of Columbia has its own judicial system. In addition, there is a separate federal court system, as well as courts for each of the United States territories and possessions." Friedenthal, Kane & Miller, Civil Procedure § 1.2 (4th ed. 2005). Subject-matter jurisdiction in the state courts is determined by the state constitution, state statutes, and judicial decisions; in the federal system, it is governed by Article III of the federal Constitution, federal statutes, and judicial decisions. State and federal courts have overlapping jurisdiction in certain areas and this concurrent authority allows a plaintiff, when commencing a lawsuit, to choose from among courts of different systems. Removal jurisdiction, which allows the defendant a limited right to transfer a case from state to federal court, creates additional possibilities. These opportunities to "forum shop" help to promote litigant autonomy, but also may conflict with important public concerns.

As was described briefly in Chapter One, pp. 6–8, supra, most Anglo–American jurisdictions have distributed judicial power to hear disputes among a variety of courts. In many instances this is accomplished by segregating certain types of controversies from the mainstream of litigation and giving special courts subject-matter jurisdiction over them, as usually is done with domestic relations and probate matters, and formerly was true of "actions at law" and "suits in equity." As described by one commentator:

> * * * In practically all states * * * there are separate courts for large and small cases with an arbitrary line of division between them.

> There are usually separate courts of first instance and of review. Separate courts of probate, criminal courts, courts of equity, and courts for causes arising in certain localities are common. Jurisdiction of the same kind is often apportioned among several different courts, each exercising only a designated and restricted part of it, as where certain appeals must be taken to one reviewing court and other appeals to another. Sometimes different courts with concurrent jurisdiction in certain classes of cases and exclusive jurisdiction in others are established. It is not uncommon to find a large number of municipal courts in the various cities of the same state, no two of which exercise the same jurisdiction. And as a final complication, the legislature is constantly shifting and changing the jurisdiction of the various courts, practically every change involving litigation to construe the meaning and ascertain the effect of the legislative act.

Sunderland, *Problems Connected with the Operation of a State Court System,* 1950 Wis.L.Rev. 585, 585–86.

Probably the most common method of limiting judicial power is by providing that the court only can adjudicate controversies involving more than a certain minimum or less than a stated maximum amount of money, or its equivalent. These rules often are designed to direct the quantitative and qualitative flow of litigation into the various courts within a jurisdiction. Thus, for example, it is provided by statute, 28 U.S.C. § 1332, that cases in the federal courts based solely on diversity of citizenship must involve more than $75,000. If such a dispute does not, it must be brought in a state court. Amount-in-controversy restrictions also are common in state systems. These often provide that a plaintiff cannot bring his action in a particular court—typically called a court of inferior, limited, or special jurisdiction—if the amount involved exceeds a statutorily established jurisdictional maximum. What factors are relevant in choosing appropriate jurisdictional amount figures? Are the same factors relevant for both the state and federal courts?

SECTION A. SUBJECT-MATTER JURISDICTION IN STATE COURTS

LACKS v. LACKS

New York Court of Appeals, 1976.
41 N.Y.2d 71, 390 N.Y.S.2d 875, 359 N.E.2d 384.

BREITEL, CHIEF JUDGE. * * * The parties were married in New York in 1938. After an apparently turbulent marriage, marked since 1953 by a series of bitter litigations, the husband, on August 10, 1965, began this action for a separation on the ground of cruelty. After nonjury trial, Supreme Court, on June 28, 1967, dismissed the complaint, but, on March 26, 1968, the Appellate Division reversed, and ordered a new trial. At the second trial, plaintiff husband, in reliance upon the then recent liberalizing changes in the divorce law, added a prayer for a judgment of absolute divorce, on the same allegations and proof as the earlier cause for separation. The husband was granted a judgment of divorce on March 16, 1970, and, after modifications not now relevant, the judgment was affirmed by the Appellate Division on October 26, 1972. Leave to appeal to the Court of Appeals was denied by both the Appellate Division and this court. The final judgment was thus beyond further review.

Then, nearly two years later, defendant, through her most recently retained lawyer, moved to vacate the judgment, contending that the court had been without subject matter jurisdiction to entertain the divorce action. She argued that the husband had not been a resident of New York for a full year preceding the commencement of the original action, and that the court had thus erroneously granted a divorce judgment in violation of the provisions of section 230. This defect, she urged, deprived the court of subject matter jurisdiction, and all the proceedings and the judgment were a nullity.

* * *

A statement that a court lacks "jurisdiction" to decide a case may, in reality, mean that elements of a cause of action are absent * * *. Similarly, questions of mootness and standing of parties may be characterized as raising questions of subject matter jurisdiction * * *. But these are not the kinds of judicial infirmities to which CPLR 5015 * * * is addressed. That provision is designed to preserve objections so fundamental to the power of adjudication of a court that they survive even a final judgment or order * * *.[a]

In Thrasher v. United States Liab. Ins. Co. (19 NY2d 159, 166), this court, in discussing subject matter jurisdiction, drew a clear distinction between a court's competence to entertain an action and its power to render a judgment on the merits * * *. Absence of competence to entertain an action deprives the court of "subject matter jurisdiction"; absence of power to reach the merits does not.

The implications of this distinction are serious. It is blackletter law that a judgment rendered without subject matter jurisdiction is void, and that the defect may be raised at any time and may not be waived * * *. Thus stated, the rule is grossly oversimple. * * * Nevertheless, the breadth with which the rule is often stated indicates the importance traditionally attached to so-called subject matter jurisdiction * * *. Beyond the confusion engendered by a misapplication of the * * * concept of subject matter jurisdiction, there is more created by the locution that in this State the courts' power in matrimonial actions is exclusively statutory. Yet in counterpoint, it has often been said: "the Supreme Court [i.e., the New York general trial court] is a court of original, unlimited and unqualified jurisdiction" and "competent to entertain all causes of action unless its jurisdiction has been specifically proscribed" * * *.

---

a. Rule 5015 of the New York Civil Practice Law and Rules allows a party to move for relief from an order that was entered without jurisdiction.

Against the State Constitution's broad grant of jurisdiction to the Supreme Court, defendant offers the language of section 230 of the Domestic Relations Law. It provides merely that "[a]n action * * * for divorce on separation may be maintained only when" the residence requirements are met. Not even the catchall word "jurisdiction" appears in the statute, much less an explicit limitation on the court's competence to entertain the action. In no way do these limitations on the cause of action circumscribe the power of the court in the sense of competence to adjudicate causes in the matrimonial categories. That a court has no "right" to adjudicate erroneously is no circumscription of its power to decide, rightly or wrongly.

* * *

The court has never before considered the unlikely question, until this case, whether the judicial error on an essential element of the cause of action was so fundamental as to permit vacatur of a final judgment, collaterally or after final judgment beyond ordinary appellate review. Had that ever been the problem unlikely until this case, perhaps the need for a less elastic and encompassing term than the word "jurisdiction" would have been apparent.

* * *

Hence, any error of law or fact which might have been committed in the divorce action did not deprive the court of jurisdiction to adjudicate the case, CPLR 5015 * * * is inapplicable, and Special Term erroneously vacated the final judgment.

In sum, the overly stated principle that lack of subject matter jurisdiction makes a final judgment absolutely void is not applicable to cases which, upon analysis, do not involve jurisdiction, but merely substantive elements of a cause for relief. To do so would be to undermine significantly the doctrine of *res judicata,* and to eliminate the certainty and finality in the law and in litigation which the doctrine is designed to protect.

In concluding the jurisdiction-competence issue it is not assumed that the courts in the action made any error of law or fact in determining the durational or initial residence requirements to maintain an action for a separation or a divorce. Nor is it assumed that the same courts did not consider and determine the issues of residence, whether or not raised by the wife. On the contrary, there was considerable evidence of residence by the husband, and the court obviously determined that the husband had some residence even if not of the duration to satisfy the matrimonial statutes. The point is that the litigation having gone to final judgment, the right to review by appeal having been exhausted, that is and should be the end of the matter.

On the foregoing analysis it has been unnecessary to dissect the elements of subject matter jurisdiction, because it turns out that the contentions of the wife are not addressed to bases for subject matter jurisdiction. Rather, despite her characterization of subject matter jurisdiction in order to invoke CPLR 5015 * * * to undo a final judgment of four years' standing, the defects to which she points relate only to substantive elements in a cause of action adjudicable by the Supreme Court, a court competent to decide all the substantive issues.

Accordingly, the order of the Appellate Division should be affirmed, without costs.

NOTES AND QUESTIONS

1. In *Lacks*, the husband won a judgment of divorce even though he apparently failed to meet the residence requirement of the New York divorce law. Despite this defect, the Court of Appeals refused to allow the wife to vacate the judgment for lack of subject-matter jurisdiction. Can you explain the distinction that the court drew between "the jurisdiction-competence issue" and the "substantive elements in a cause of action"? Professor Wasserman argues that jurisdiction statutes are tied to a court's "raw" authority, but merits issues concern "who can sue whom." Wasserman, *Jurisdiction, Merits, and Procedure: Thoughts on a Trichotomy*, 102 Nw. U. L. Rev. 1547, 1547–48 (2008). Does this distinction explain the result in *Lacks*?

2. In a recent pair of cases, the Supreme Court has elaborated on the distinction between jurisdiction and issues that go to the merits. ARBAUGH v. Y & H CORP., 546 U.S. 500, 126 S.Ct. 1235, 163 L.Ed.2d 1097 (2006), involved a discrimination claim under a federal civil rights statute that imposes liability for violations of the act on employers whose workplaces employ fifteen or more employees. Two weeks after the trial court entered a judgment, defendant successfully moved to dismiss for lack of subject-matter jurisdiction, contending that his workplace did not meet the employee-numerosity requirement. The Court of Appeals for the Fifth Circuit affirmed, but the Supreme Court reversed. The Court characterized the employee-numerosity requirement as an element of the claim, rather than as jurisdictional, and so found defendant's challenge to be untimely. JOHN R. SAND & GRAVEL CO. v. UNITED STATES, 552 U.S. 130, 128 S.Ct. 750, 169 L.Ed.2d 591 (2008), involved a claim against the United States filed in the Court of Federal Claims (the special court that hears certain claims against the federal government). The United States had waived objections to the statute of limitations, but the federal appellate court, *sua sponte*, addressed whether plaintiff's suit was timely, found that it was not, and vacated and remanded. The Supreme Court affirmed, 7–2, holding that the limitations period served "a broader system-related goal, such as facilitating the administration of claims, * * * limiting the scope of governmental waiver of sovereign immunity, * * * or promoting judicial efficiency," and so was "more absolute" than a timeliness provision that bars the defense of stale claims and may be waived. Id. at ___, 128 S.Ct. at 753, 169 L.Ed.2d at 596. Do you agree that these two cases can be distinguished?

3. A state court of general jurisdiction is permitted and may be under a constitutional duty to hear a cause of action arising under the laws of another state. In HUGHES v. FETTER, 341 U.S. 609, 71 S.Ct. 980, 95 L.Ed. 1212 (1951), the Supreme Court held that the Full Faith and Credit Clause, U.S.

Const. Art. IV, § 1, precluded Wisconsin from closing its courts to a suit under the Illinois wrongful-death act in the absence of a valid Wisconsin policy to weigh against the national interest favoring the availability of a Wisconsin forum. "[A state] * * * cannot escape [its] constitutional obligation to enforce the rights and duties validly created under the laws of other states by the simple device of removing jurisdiction from courts otherwise competent." *Hughes* has not been construed as a bar to a state applying its own procedural law to vindicate policies related to the conduct of litigation in its courts. For example, a state may apply its own statute of limitations even though the claim would be timely under the law of the state under which the cause of action arose. See Wells v. Simonds Abrasive Co., 345 U.S. 514, 73 S.Ct. 856, 97 L.Ed. 1211 (1953). Conversely, a state may apply its own longer statute of limitations even though the claim would have been time-barred under the law of the state under which the cause of action arose. See Sun Oil Co. v. Wortman, 486 U.S. 717, 108 S.Ct. 2117, 100 L.Ed.2d 743 (1988).

4. Unless Congress allocates jurisdiction to hear a claim exclusively to the federal courts, a state court is presumed to have concurrent jurisdiction and may entertain the action even though it is based entirely on federal law. The presumption of concurrent jurisdiction is rooted in a "system of dual sovereignty":

> * * * This deeply rooted presumption in favor of concurrent state court jurisdiction is, of course, rebutted if Congress affirmatively ousts the state courts of jurisdiction over a particular claim. * * * Thus, the presumption of concurrent jurisdiction can be rebutted by an explicit statutory directive, by unmistakable implication from legislative history, or by a clear incompatibility between state-court jurisdiction and federal interests. * * *

TAFFLIN v. LEVITT, 493 U.S. 455, 458–59, 110 S.Ct. 792, 795, 107 L.Ed.2d 887, 894 (1990) (internal quotation omitted). See Solimine, *Rethinking Exclusive Federal Jurisdiction*, 52 U. Pitt. L. Rev. 383 (1991).

5. If a state court can hear a case arising under federal law, must it do so? In HOWLETT v. ROSE, 496 U.S. 356, 110 S.Ct. 2430, 110 L.Ed.2d 332 (1990), a unanimous Supreme Court found that the Florida court could not decline to hear a federal civil rights claim under 42 U.S.C. § 1983 on the ground of sovereign immunity, when that defense would not bar a similar state-law claim. Noting that the Florida court's holding "raises the concern that the state court may be evading federal law and discriminating against federal causes of action," the Court explained:

> A state policy that permits actions against state agencies for the failure of their officials to adequately police a parking lot and for the negligence of such officers in arresting a person on a roadside, but yet declines jurisdiction over federal actions for constitutional violations by the same persons can be based only on the rationale that such persons should not be liable for § 1983 violations in the courts of the State. That reason,

> whether presented in terms of direct disagreement with substantive federal law or simple refusal to take cognizance of the federal cause of action, flatly violates the Supremacy Clause.

Id. at 380–81, 110 S.Ct. at 2445, 110 L.Ed.2d at 356.

SECTION B. THE SUBJECT-MATTER JURISDICTION OF THE FEDERAL COURTS—DIVERSITY OF CITIZENSHIP

Read Art. III, § 2 and 28 U.S.C. §§ 1332, 1359, and 1369 in the Supplement.

Article III, Section 2 of the United States Constitution extends the judicial power of the United States to controversies "between Citizens of different States * * * and between a State, or the Citizens thereof, and Foreign States, Citizens or Subjects." The current scope of the diversity jurisdiction that Congress has granted to the federal courts is set out in 28 U.S.C. § 1332. The practical implications of diversity jurisdiction are significant: "diversity" jurisdiction allows the federal courts to hear cases in which the claims arise solely under *state* law, so long as constitutional and statutory requirements are satisfied.[b] Diversity jurisdiction thus raises important theoretical questions about federalism and the appropriate relation between unelected federal judges and the states.

One of the most important limitations on federal diversity jurisdiction is the rule of "complete diversity" announced by Chief Justice Marshall in STRAWBRIDGE v. CURTISS, 7 U.S. (3 Cranch) 267, 2 L.Ed. 435 (1806). The rule provides in effect that there is no diversity jurisdiction if any plaintiff is a citizen of the same state as any defendant, no matter how many parties are involved in the litigation. The precise status of the complete diversity doctrine has been a subject of considerable debate because until quite recently it was not clear that the *Strawbridge* decision was intended by Chief Justice Marshall merely as a construction of the diversity statute then in force rather than as a constitutional limitation on federal-court jurisdiction.

The origin and purposes of diversity-of-citizenship jurisdiction have long been the subject of vigorous debate. The most widely accepted rationale—the desire to avoid discrimination against out-of-state residents in state courts—was offered by Chief Justice Marshall in BANK OF THE UNITED STATES v. DEVEAUX, 9 U.S. (5 Cranch) 61, 87, 3 L.Ed. 38, 45 (1809):

---

b. Controversies between a citizen of a state and an alien technically are denominated "alienage cases," but may be considered as diversity cases for purposes of this Section.

> However true the fact may be, that the tribunals of the states will administer justice as impartially as those of the nation, * * * it is not less true that the constitution itself either entertains apprehensions on this subject, or views with such indulgence the possible fears and apprehensions of suitors, that it has established national tribunals for the decision of controversies * * * between citizens of different states.

Another argument of longstanding vintage is that the availability of a federal tribunal during our nation's formative period afforded some measure of security to investors developing the southern and western portions of the country. Analyses of the historical origins of diversity jurisdiction can be found in Frank, *Historical Bases of the Federal Judicial System,* 13 Law & Contemp.Prob. 1 (1948); Friendly, *The Historic Basis of the Diversity Jurisdiction,* 41 Harv.L.Rev. 483 (1928); and Phillips & Christenson, *The Historical and Legal Background of the Diversity Jurisdiction,* 46 A.B.A.J. 959 (1960). Recent research suggests that the grant of diversity jurisdiction protected creditors because federal officials could channel important litigation into the federal courts, where they were able to control the composition of federal juries. See Jones, *Finishing a Friendly Argument: The Jury and the Historical Origins of Diversity Jurisdiction,* 82 N.Y.U. L. Rev. 997 (2007).

Assuming that diversity jurisdiction was created to protect out-of-state litigants against local prejudice and that it has helped speed the economic growth of the country, are these meaningful bases for continuing diversity jurisdiction today? Statistical data on the actual existence of local prejudice against out-of-state parties, or whether an attorney's belief in the existence of such prejudice is a factor influencing forum choice, is sparse and inconclusive. See Miller, *An Empirical Study of Forum Choices in Removal Cases Under Diversity and Federal Question Jurisdiction,* 41 Am.U.L.Rev. 369 (1992); see also Flango, *Litigant Choice Between State and Federal Courts*, 46 S. C. L.Rev. 961, 965 (1995).

More than 72,000 diversity cases were filed in the federal district courts in 2007. This figure represents approximately 28 percent of the total number of federal civil cases filed during that year. (Although the absolute and relative number of diversity cases filed in the district courts declined more than ten percent from 2006 to 2007, the drop reflects an exceptional increase of 29 percent in the earlier year, mainly due to the filing of more than 14,000 asbestos cases filed in the Eastern District of Pennsylvania.) By contrast, only about 57,000 diversity cases were filed in the federal district courts in 1990, representing about 26 percent of the total cases filed.

U.S. District Courts. Civil Cases Filed, by Jurisdiction

Fiscal Year	Total	Federal Question	Diversity
1990	217,013	104,307	57,435
2006	259,541	134,877	80,370
2007	257,507	139,424	72,619

See Annual Report of the Director: Judicial Business of the United States Courts, Table C–2.

Some commentators have questioned whether the current utility of diversity jurisdiction justifies the federal resources devoted to the diversity docket. Indeed, proposals to curtail or abolish diversity jurisdiction have been made in Congress since the 1920s. The Federal Courts Study Committee in 1990 recommended limiting diversity jurisdiction in four ways: (1) prohibiting plaintiffs from invoking diversity jurisdiction in the federal courts of their home states; (2) treating corporations as citizens of every state in which they are licensed to do business; (3) excluding non-economic damages, such as punitive damages, from calculation of the amount in controversy; and (4) raising the amount in controversy and indexing it to inflation. See *Report of the Federal Courts Study Committee* 38–43 (April 2, 1990). See also Kramer, *Diversity Jurisdiction,* 1990 B.Y.U.L.Rev. 97. The first and fourth recommendations were incorporated into the initial version of the Federal Courts Improvement Act of 1996. However, Congress ultimately approved only the raising of the amount in controversy from exceeds $50,000 to exceeds $75,000.

Diversity jurisdiction also has its ardent supporters. See Underwood, *The Late, Great Diversity Jurisdiction*, 57 Case W. Res. L. Rev. 179, 216 (2006). Those favoring an expansion of diversity jurisdiction argue that it is an important institutional tool for solving problems of national significance in areas that traditionally are governed by state law. Diversity jurisdiction is thus associated with national debates about consumer protection, medical malpractice, and corporate accountability, areas of tort law that typically are regulated by the states. In addition, supporters see jurisdictional reform as a way to deal with large or complex disputes that straddle multiple states, comprise multiple state-law claims, and include multiple parties residing in different states. See Rowe & Sibley, *Beyond Diversity: Federal Multiparty, Multiforum Jurisdiction*, 135 U. Pa. L. Rev. 7 (1986). In considering proposals to reform the grant of diversity jurisdiction, an important question to ask is what goals diversity jurisdiction is expected to serve *today*?

The Terms of the Debate

Critics of diversity jurisdiction concentrate primarily on five problems. The first, often noted by Justice Frankfurter, is the congestion diversity cases allegedly cause in the federal courts. Second, the rule of Erie Railroad Co. v. Tompkins, p. 408, infra, which requires the application of state law to substantive issues in diversity cases, has been thought by many to make the handling of diversity cases by federal judges unnecessary, wasteful, and inappropriate. The reasoning behind this argument is that only the state courts are considered to be authoritative on matters of substantive law and the federal courts therefore are unable to exercise their creative function and are performing an unneeded service in avowedly aiming to follow state-court decisions. Third, it is argued that judicial and legislative authority should be coextensive, and that for federal courts to decide cases arising under state law is an undesirable interference with state autonomy. A fourth and related problem is the effect that the diversion of litigation to federal courts may have in retarding the development of state law. Fifth, and finally, it is said that the continuation of diversity jurisdiction diminishes the incentives for state court reform by those influential professional groups who, by virtue of diversity jurisdiction, are able to avoid litigation in the state courts.

Those who seek to retain diversity jurisdiction contend that state-court prejudice against out-of-state parties still exists and that provincial attitudes, especially among jurors, can interfere with the administration of justice. Opponents counter that in today's mobile and wired society, such fears are unfounded. State judges and jurors alike are much more likely to have been exposed to citizens of other states, and indeed, to have visited those states themselves. In our nation today, is prejudice attributable to race, gender, or sexual orientation likely to be more significant than state citizenship?

Another argument in favor of the status quo is that diversity jurisdiction implements the constitutional guarantee that the citizens of each state shall be entitled to all the privileges and immunities of citizens of the several states. See U.S. CONST. Art. IV, § 2. However, abridgement of the Privileges and Immunities Clause is in itself sufficient for federal question jurisdiction under 28 U.S.C. § 1331, and therefore diversity jurisdiction is not needed to provide a federal forum for this purpose.

A further argument in favor of diversity jurisdiction focuses on the purported institutional superiority of the federal courts and contends that it is desirable to channel as many cases as possible away from the state courts, or at least that out-of-state litigants, who have no opportunity to work for the improvement of the state courts, should be spared exposure to them. This argument builds, in part, on structural distinctions between the federal and state courts. Federal judges enjoy life tenure and sit with juries selected from a broader geographical area than most state tribunals. Most importantly, federal judges are appointed; since many state judges are elected, state judges are thought to be more susceptible to political pressure and local biases than federal judges. The idea of federal court superiority also rests on empirical factors, such as court resources, procedural rules, and judicial background, which change over time. Not all lawyers would agree that differences between the state and federal systems inevitably lead to better justice in the federal courts. See Hershkoff, *State Courts and the "Passive Virtues": Rethinking the Judicial Function,*

114 Harv.L.Rev. 1833 (2001). Although the prestige of the federal courts generally has been high, there have been long periods when federal courts were perceived to be rich people's courts or defendants' courts.

A related argument in favor of diversity jurisdiction posits that the existence of concurrent state and federal jurisdiction to resolve state-law disputes creates a competition between the two systems that acts as a spur to higher standards of justice in terms of substantive law and procedural improvement. The metaphor typically used to express this rationale is that of the "cross-pollination" of ideas across courts. See Redish, *Reassessing the Allocation of Judicial Business Between State and Federal Courts: Federal Jurisdiction and "The Martian Chronicles,"* 78 Va. L. Rev. 1769, 1785 (1992).

Critics further argue that parties use the choice of forum made available through the grant of diversity jurisdiction for tactical purposes in order to gain an advantage from one forum or another in a particular case. To the extent that forum shopping exists, as it surely does, how much should it impact our consideration of a grant of power that is authorized by Article III of the federal Constitution? Professor Purcell documents the extreme forum-shopping tactics of large corporations at the end of the nineteenth-century and early twentieth-century, a period in which federal courts were perceived to be partial to commercial interests. See Purcell, Litigation and Inequality: Federal Diversity Jurisdiction in Industrial America, 1870–1958 (1992).

Finally, some commentators justify diversity jurisdiction by pointing to the fear of investors that local prejudice may exist. This argument at one time was endorsed by the Judicial Conference of the United States. In considering this argument, the key question is not whether out-of-state investors in fact will receive fair treatment from state courts, but whether they *think* they will. If the abolition, or significant curtailment, of diversity jurisdiction would inhibit the willingness of investors to enter markets in different parts of the country, then diversity may serve a useful purpose. However, United States investors may now be sufficiently national-minded, and accustomed enough to investing abroad where they enjoy no protection from the federal courts, that they no longer have fears of state courts.

New Developments

Congress recently has expanded the reach of diversity jurisdiction to provide a federal forum to certain large scale, state law, multiparty actions in which one plaintiff is a citizen of a state different from that of one defendant—the basis of so-called "minimal diversity." See Class Action Fairness Act of 2005, 28 U.S.C. §§ 1332(d), 1453; Multiparty, Multiforum Trial Jurisdiction Act of 2002, §§ 1369, 1441(e)(5). Supporters of these statutes have argued that a federal forum is appropriate because the cases that will be heard are of interstate importance, involve interstate commerce, and should be determined from a national perspective. Critics have warned that opening the federal courthouse to complex state law cases will increase judicial workloads dramatically, unnecessarily nationalize local concerns, and undermine democracy by permitting unelected federal judges to decide state law issues. For an overview of these arguments, see Marcus, *Assessing CAFA's Stated Jurisdictional Policy,* 156 U. Pa. L. Rev. 1765 (2008). Other commentators have criticized this use of minimal diversity as result-driven and reflecting a pro-business bias. See Lind, *"Procedural Swift": Complex Litigation Reform, State Tort Law, and Democratic Values*, 37 Akron L. Rev. 717, 718 (2004). Still others have acknowledged the special problems of multistate class actions, in which the law of a single state "can bind the nation," but urge a solution drawn from choice-of-law principles. Miller & Crump, *Jurisdiction and Choice of Law in Multistate Class Actions After Phillips Petroleum Co. v. Shutts*, 96 Yale L.J. 1, 57 (1986).

The Multiparty, Multiforum Act, or Section 1369, deals with the problem of catastrophic mass accidents that involve the deaths of many people. Section 1369 authorizes original federal jurisdiction in any civil action arising "from a single accident, when at least 75 natural persons have died in the accident at a discrete location" provided "minimal diversity exists between adverse parties" and other conditions are satisfied. The statute reflects the view that consolidation of mass accident cases in a single forum will reduce expenses and avoid inconsistent judgments. Other jurisdictional conditions that must be met include the requirement that "any two defendants reside in different States"; "substantial parts of the accident took place in different States"; and "a defendant resides in a State and substantial part of the accident took place in another State." 28 U.S.C. § 1369 (a)(1)–(3). Why do you think Congress imposed these additional conditions?

The Class Action Fairness Act, or CAFA, deals with big dollar class actions (although the individual claims may be small). CAFA makes federal district courts available for any class action in which the aggregate amount in controversy exceeds $5 million and in which any plaintiff "is a citizen of a State different from any defendant." CAFA gives the district court discretion, "in the interests of justice and looking at the totality of the circumstances," to decline jurisdiction over any lawsuit "in which greater than one-third but less than two-thirds of the members of all proposed plaintiff classes and the primary defendants are citizens of the State in which the action was originally filed," based on a consideration of listed factors, such as the national importance of the asserted claims and the "distinct nexus" between the forum and the parties or injuries. CAFA also provides for two jurisdictional exceptions. The district court "shall decline to exercise jurisdiction" over an action in which more than two-thirds of the putative class members are citizens of the state in which the action originally was filed, and over cases involving federal securities claims or claims related to corporate governance. Why do you think Congress included these exceptions? See Resnik, *Class Action Lessons in Federalism*, 156 U. Pa. L. Rev. 1929 (2008).

Some commentators have raised questions about these dual statutory uses of minimal diversity and urge developing limits on the scope of this jurisdictional grant. See Floyd, *The Limits of Minimal Diversity*, 55 Hastings L.J. 613 (2004). Should Congress develop these limits? What statistics and empirical data do you think are relevant to the reform process? How much weight should be given to federalism? To the differing interests of plaintiffs and defendants? What role should the federal courts have in the process? To what extent should the judiciary retain discretion to interpret jurisdictional provisions in the light of changing conditions and evolving social needs? For a discussion of these and other issues, see Burbank, *The Class Action Fairness Act of 2005 in Historical Context: A Preliminary View*, 156 U. Pa. L. Rev. 1439 (2008).

1. DETERMINING CITIZENSHIP

MAS v. PERRY

United States Court of Appeals, Fifth Circuit, 1974.
489 F.2d 1396, certiorari denied 419 U.S. 842, 95 S.Ct. 74, 42 L.Ed.2d 70.

AINSWORTH, CIRCUIT JUDGE.

* * *

Appellees Jean Paul Mas, a citizen of France, and Judy Mas were married at her home in Jackson, Mississippi. Prior to their marriage, Mr. and Mrs. Mas were graduate assistants, pursuing coursework as well as performing teaching duties, for approximately nine months and one year, respectively, at Louisiana State University in Baton Rouge, Louisiana. Shortly after their marriage, they returned to Baton Rouge to resume their duties as graduate assistants at LSU. They remained in Baton Rouge for approximately two more years, after which they moved to Park Ridge, Illinois. At the time of the trial in this case, it was their intention to return to Baton Rouge while Mr. Mas finished his studies for the degree of Doctor of Philosophy. Mr. and Mrs. Mas were undecided as to where they would reside after that.

Upon their return to Baton Rouge after their marriage, appellees rented an apartment from appellant Oliver H. Perry, a citizen of Louisiana. This appeal arises from a final judgment entered on a jury verdict awarding $5,000 to Mr. Mas and $15,000 to Mrs. Mas for damages incurred by them as a result of the discovery that their bedroom and bathroom contained "two-way" mirrors and that they had been watched through them by the appellant during three of the first four months of their marriage.

At the close of the appellees' case at trial, appellant made an oral motion to dismiss for lack of jurisdiction. The motion was denied by the district court. Before this Court, appellant challenges the final judgment below solely on jurisdictional grounds, contending that appellees failed to prove diversity of citizenship among the parties and that the requisite jurisdictional amount is lacking with respect to Mr. Mas. Finding no merit to these contentions, we affirm. Under section 1332(a)(2), the federal judicial power extends to the claim of Mr. Mas, a citizen of France, against the appellant, a citizen of Louisiana. Since we conclude that Mrs. Mas is a citizen of Mississippi for diversity purposes, the district court also properly had jurisdiction under section 1332(a)(1) of her claim.

It has long been the general rule that complete diversity of parties is required in order that diversity jurisdiction obtain; that is, no party on one side may be a citizen of the same State as any party on the other side. Strawbridge v. Curtiss * * *. This determination of one's State citizenship for diversity purposes is controlled by federal law, not by the law of any State. * * * As is the case in other areas of federal jurisdiction, the diverse citizenship among adverse parties must be present at the time the complaint is filed. * * * Jurisdiction is unaffected by subsequent changes in the citizenship of the parties. * * * The burden of pleading the diverse citizenship is upon the party invoking federal jurisdiction * * * and if the diversity jurisdiction is properly challenged, that party also bears the burden of proof.

To be a citizen of a State within the meaning of section 1332, a natural person must be both a citizen of the United States * * * and a domiciliary of that State. * * * For diversity purposes, citizenship means domicile; mere residence in the State is not sufficient. * * *

A person's domicile is the place of "his true, fixed, and permanent home and principal establishment, and to which he has the intention of returning whenever he is absent therefrom * * *." * * * A change of domicile may be effected only by a combination of two elements: (a) taking up residence in a different domicile with (b) the intention to remain there. * * *

It is clear that at the time of her marriage, Mrs. Mas was a domiciliary of the State of Mississippi. While it is generally the case that the domicile of the wife—and, consequently, her State citizenship for purposes of diversity jurisdiction—is deemed to be that of her husband, * * * we find no precedent for extending this concept to the situation here, in which the husband is a citizen of a foreign state but resides in the United States. Indeed, such a fiction would work absurd results on the facts before us. If Mr. Mas were considered a domiciliary of France—as he would be since he had lived in Louisiana as a student-teaching assistant prior to filing this suit * * *—then Mrs. Mas would also be deemed a domiciliary, and thus, fictionally at least, a citizen of France. She would not be a citizen of any State and could not sue in a federal court on that basis; nor could she invoke the alienage jurisdiction to bring her claim in federal court, since she is not an alien. * * * On the other hand, if Mrs. Mas's domicile were Louisiana, she would become a Louisiana citizen for diversity purposes and could not bring suit with her husband against appellant, also a Louisiana citizen, on the basis of diversity jurisdiction.

These are curious results under a rule arising from the theoretical identity of person and interest of the married couple. * * *

An American woman is not deemed to have lost her United States citizenship solely by reason of her marriage to an alien. 8 U.S.C. § 1489. Similarly, we conclude that for diversity purposes a woman does not have her domicile or State citizenship changed solely by reason of her marriage to an alien.

Mrs. Mas's Mississippi domicile was disturbed neither by her year in Louisiana prior to her marriage nor as a result of the time she and her husband spent at LSU after their marriage, since for both periods she was a graduate assistant at LSU. * * * Though she testified that after her marriage she had no intention of returning to her parents' home in Mississippi, Mrs. Mas did not effect a change of domicile since she and Mr. Mas were in Louisiana only as students and lacked the requisite intention to remain there. Until she acquires a new domicile, she remains a domiciliary, and thus a citizen of Mississippi. * * *

[The court's discussion of the jurisdictional amount is omitted.]

Thus the power of the federal district court to entertain the claims of appellees in this case stands on two separate legs of diversity jurisdiction: a claim by an alien against a State citizen; and an action between citizens of different States. We also note, however, the propriety of having the federal district court entertain a spouse's action against a defendant, where the district court already has jurisdiction over a claim, arising from the same transaction, by the other spouse against the same defendant. * * * In the case before us, such a result is particularly desirable. The claims of Mr. and Mrs. Mas arise from the same operative facts, and there was almost complete interdependence between their claims with respect to the proof required and the issues raised at trial. Thus, since the district court had jurisdiction of Mr. Mas's action, sound judicial administration militates strongly in favor of federal jurisdiction of Mrs. Mas's claim.

Affirmed.

NOTES AND QUESTIONS

1. In DRED SCOTT v. SANDFORD, 60 U.S. (19 How.) 393, 15 L.Ed. 691 (1856), the Supreme Court held that persons descended from African slaves were excluded from citizenship and could not invoke the diversity jurisdiction. For a discussion of this aspect of the decision, see Krauss, *New Evidence that* Dred Scott *Was Wrong About Whether Free Blacks Could Count for the Purposes of Federal Diversity Jurisdiction*, 37 Conn. L. Rev. 25 (2004). The Citizenship Clause of the Fourteenth Amendment overruled this holding in *Dred Scott*. See U.S. Constitution Amendment XIV, § 1. How would you treat for diversity jurisdiction purposes a United States citizen who is domiciled abroad? See Cresswell v. Sullivan & Cromwell, 922 F.2d 60, 68 (2d Cir. 1990).

2. The *Mas* court equates state citizenship with state domicile for purposes of diversity jurisdiction, but distinguishes domicile from residence. If

the goal of diversity jurisdiction is to protect out-of-staters from bias in suits against in-staters, does it make sense to disregard residence in defining citizenship for diversity purposes?

3. The party asserting diversity jurisdiction has the burden of proving its existence. How could a party prove citizenship for diversity purposes? What factors ought the court to consider? See 13E Wright, Miller & Cooper, Federal Practice and Procedure: Jurisdiction and Related Matters 3d § 3612. The fact-intensive nature of the court's inquiry is illustrated by CONNECTU LLC v. ZUCKERBERG, 482 F.Supp.2d 3 (D.Mass.2007), involving whether defendant, the founder of Facebook, remained domiciled in New York even after establishing his company in California. The evidence showed he was born in New York, graduated from a high school in New Hampshire, attended college in Massachusetts, and lived in California the summer after his sophomore year. After taking a leave of absence from college, defendant returned to California, where his company was incorporated. He planned to return to college and continued to use his parents' New York address as a permanent residence. On these facts, the District Court held that defendant remained domiciled in New York for purposes of diversity jurisdiction.

4. Under Section 1332, a corporation, unlike a natural person, can be a citizen of more than one state. A corporation is a citizen of (1) the state(s) in which it is incorporated and (2) the state in which it has its principal place of business. It generally is accepted that a corporation can have only one principal place of business for purposes of diversity jurisdiction. How should a court determine where that is? What factors might be relevant? Currently, three different tests are used to locate a corporation's principal place of business:

> The first test is the "nerve center" test. * * * Under this test, "the locus of corporate decision-making authority and overall control constitutes a corporation's principal place of business for diversity purposes." * * *
>
> The second test is referred to as the "corporate activities" or "operating assets" test. Greater weight is attached to the location of a corporation's production or service activities in determining the principal place of business under this test. * * *
>
> The third test is known as the "total activity" test. This test is a hybrid of the "nerve center" and "corporate activities" tests and considers all the circumstances surrounding a corporation's business to discern its principal place of business. "The 'total activity' test provides a realistic, flexible and nonformalistic approach to determining a corporation's principal place of business through a balancing of all relevant factors." * * *

WHITE v. HALSTEAD INDUSTRIES, INC., 750 F.Supp. 395, 397 (E.D.Ark. 1990). Is any one of these tests significantly more reasonable than the others? Or should the circumstances of the individual case dictate which test is applied? See 13F Wright & Miller, Federal Practice and Procedure: Jurisdiction and Related Matters 3d § 3625.

5. In determining the citizenship of an unincorporated association for diversity jurisdiction, courts look to the citizenship of each of the association's members. See United Steelworkers of America v. R.H. Bouligny, Inc., 382 U.S.

145, 86 S.Ct. 272, 15 L.Ed.2d 217 (1965). Unincorporated associations include such entities as partnerships, labor unions, and charitable organizations. Consistent with this approach, the Supreme Court has held that for purposes of diversity jurisdiction, a limited partnership is not a citizen of the state under whose laws it is created. Instead, its citizenship is determined by the citizenship of each of its partners. See Carden v. Arkoma Assocs., 494 U.S. 185, 110 S.Ct. 1015, 108 L.Ed.2d 157 (1990). HOAGLAND v. SANDBERG, PHOENIX & VON GONTARD, P.C., 385 F.3d 737 (7th Cir.2004), raised the question of whether a professional corporation should be treated as a corporation or as a limited partnership for diversity purposes. The Court of Appeals, rejecting "a functional approach," instead drew "a bright line between corporations and all other associations." How is the citizenship of an unincorporated association determined under the Class Action Fairness Act, see 28 U.S.C. § 1332(d)(10)?

6. In addition to conferring jurisdiction over controversies between "citizens of different states," Section 1332(a) authorizes jurisdiction over controversies between state citizens and "citizens or subjects of a foreign state"—often referred to as "alienage" jurisdiction. In JPMORGAN CHASE BANK v. TRAFFIC STREAM (BVI) INFRASTRUCTURE LIMITED, 536 U.S. 88, 122 S.Ct. 2054, 153 L.Ed.2d 95 (2002), the Supreme Court, in a unanimous opinion by Justice Souter, held that citizens of the Overseas Territories of the United Kingdom, such as the British Virgin Islands, are "citizens or subjects of a foreign state" for purposes of Section 1332(a)(2). The Court explained that alienage jurisdiction was enacted to deal with the "penchant of the state courts to disrupt international relations and discourage foreign investment * * *." Id. at 94, 122 S.Ct. at 2058, 153 L.Ed.2d at 101. Does this threat or the threat of prejudice against foreigners continue to justify the existence of alienage jurisdiction? Professor Johnson warns that although technology has "made the world a smaller place * * * there is every reason to worry about whether foreigners can obtain an impartial resolution of these disputes in the United States." Johnson, *Why Alienage Jurisdiction? Historical Foundations and Modern Justifications for Federal Jurisdiction Over Disputes Involving Noncitizens*, 21 Yale J. Int'l L. 1, 2 (1996). Compare Clermont & Eisenberg, *Xenophilia in American Courts*, 109 Harv.L.Rev. 1120 (1996), with Moore, *Xenophobia in American Courts*, 97 Nw. U. L. Rev. 1497 (2003).

7. "Stateless" sometimes refers to an individual who is not a citizen of any country. How should a "stateless" alien be treated for purposes of determining whether jurisdiction exists under Section 1332? In BLAIR HOLDINGS CORP. v. RUBINSTEIN, 133 F.Supp. 496 (S.D.N.Y.1955), the defendant was described in the complaint as "not [being] a citizen of the United States." The court interpreted 28 U.S.C. § 1332(a)(2) to require a showing that the defendant was a citizen of a foreign state. Since that showing had not been made, suit could not be maintained in federal court. One reason that the plaintiff had not made the required showing was that the defendant, Serge Rubinstein, had been issued a so-called "Nansen" passport (a passport given to stateless persons) by the League of Nations and had registered as a stateless person with the United States Department of Justice. Professor Chemerinsky has questioned this result, emphasizing that "individ-

uals who are not citizens of any state seem to be the most vulnerable to potential discrimination." Chemerinsky, Federal Jurisdiction § 5.3 (5th ed. 2007). See Bernheim, *Note—Putting the "Alien" Back into Alienage Jurisdiction: Alienage Jurisdiction and "Stateless" Persons and Corporations after* Traffic Stream, 47 Ariz. L. Rev. 1003 (2005).

8. In 1988, as part of the Judicial Improvements and Access to Justice Act, Pub.L. No. 100–702, 102 Stat. 4642 (1988), Congress amended Section 1332(a) to provide that for purposes of diversity jurisdiction "an alien admitted to the United States for permanent residence shall be deemed a citizen of the State in which such alien is domiciled." See Bassett, *Statutory Interpretation in the Context of Federal Jurisdiction*, 76 Geo. Wash. L. Rev. 52 (2007). Would this provision have changed the outcome in Mas v. Perry?

Does the deeming provision authorize federal jurisdiction in an action involving an alien and a permanent-resident alien? Would this reading of the statute go beyond the limits of Article III? In SINGH v. DAIMLER–BENZ AG, 9 F.3d 303 (3d Cir.1993), the Court of Appeals held that jurisdiction under Section 1332 was available in a state-law action by a permanent resident alien residing in Virginia against a nonresident alien and citizen of a state other than Virginia, reading the 1988 amendment to apply to actions under Section 1332(a)(3). The Court explained: "At a minimum, Congress's deeming provision falls within its power to invest the federal courts with jurisdiction when there is minimal diversity," emphasizing that "the potential unconstitutional application of the deeming provision as to the citizenship of permanent residents is limited to situations in which a permanent resident alien sues as the sole defendant either a permanent resident alien domiciled in another state or a nonresident alien." Id. at 311.

The District of Columbia Circuit rejected this reasoning in SAADEH v. FAROUKI, 107 F.3d 52 (D.C. Cir.1997), holding that "Congress intended to contract diversity jurisdiction through the 1988 amendment to § 1332(a), not to expand it by abrogating the longstanding rule that complete diversity is destroyed in lawsuits between aliens." Id. at 52. In CHINA NUCLEAR ENERGY INDUSTRY CORP. v. ARTHUR ANDERSEN, LLP, 11 F. Supp. 2d 1256 (D.Colo.1998), the District Court followed the approach in *Saadeh* and dismissed a federal-court action by an alien corporation against a partnership made up of both United States citizens and permanent-resident aliens. It is worth noting dictum in a footnote by the Supreme Court in RUHRGAS AG v. MARATHON OIL CO., 526 U.S. 574, 580 n.2, 119 S.Ct. 1563, 1568 n.2, 143 L.Ed.2d 760, 768 n.2 (1999), to the effect that aliens on both sides of the action "rendered diversity incomplete."

The Seventh Circuit addressed the effect of the deeming provision of Section 1332(a) in INTEC USA, LLC v. ENGLE, 467 F.3d 1038 (7th Cir. 2006), rejecting *Singh*'s holding that a permanent-resident alien should be deemed a citizen only of the state of domicile, but questioning *Saadeh*'s suggestion that a permanent resident alien retains only foreign citizenship. Instead, Judge Easterbrook concluded "that permanent-resident aliens have both state and foreign citizenship," and that this "dual citizenship" sometimes will defeat, but sometimes support, diversity jurisdiction depending on the citizenship of the other parties to the litigation. Id. at 1043. Plaintiff, a limited liability company, had one member who was alleged to be a North Carolina citizen under the "deeming" provision, but also was a citizen of New Zealand. The individual defendant and three of the seven corporate defendants were citizens of New Zealand. Under Judge Easterbrook's reasoning, did the District Court properly exercise diversity jurisdiction over the action?

9. Plaintiffs who prefer to litigate in federal court as opposed to state court may attempt to create diversity of citizenship to accomplish their goal. In KRAMER v. CARIBBEAN MILLS, INC., 394 U.S. 823, 89 S.Ct. 1487, 23 L.Ed.2d 9 (1969), a Panamanian corporation assigned its interest under a contract with a Haitian corporation to Kramer, a Texas attorney, for $1. By a separate agreement, Kramer reassigned 95% of any net recovery on the assigned cause of action to the Panamanian company. Kramer then commenced suit against the Haitian company on the basis of diversity of citizenship. The District Court denied defendant's motion to dismiss for want of jurisdiction. The Court of Appeals reversed, holding that the assignment was "improperly or collusively made" within the meaning of 28 U.S.C. § 1359. The Supreme Court affirmed, holding that:

> If federal jurisdiction could be created by assignments of this kind, which are easy to arrange and involve few disadvantages for the assignor, then a vast quantity of ordinary contract and tort litigation could be channeled into the federal courts at the will of one of the parties. Such "manufacture of Federal jurisdiction" was the very thing which Congress intended to prevent when it enacted § 1359 and its predecessors.

Id. at 828–29, 89 S.Ct. at 1490, 23 L.Ed.2d at 14. Would it have made a difference if the assignment had been made for a valid business reason? Note that Section 1359 prohibits only the creation of diversity jurisdiction and says nothing about its destruction. Is such a "one-way street" consistent with the purposes that diversity jurisdiction is intended to serve? See Grassi v. Ciba–Geigy, Ltd., 894 F.2d 181 (5th Cir.1990) (assignments that destroy diversity and those that create diversity should be analyzed under the same standard).

10. In 1988, Congress added to Section 1332(c) a provision that "the legal representative of the estate of a decedent shall be deemed to be a citizen only of the same State as the decedent, and the legal representative of an infant or incompetent shall be deemed to be a citizen only of the same State as the infant or incompetent." How does this change affect the parties' ability to create or to destroy diversity jurisdiction? See Mullenix, *Creative Manipulation of Federal Jurisdiction: Is There Diversity After Death?*, 70 Cornell L.Rev. 1011 (1985). Could the courts have used Section 1359 to solve the problem? Why wasn't it used?

11. Plaintiffs who prefer to litigate in state court rather than in federal court may attempt to destroy diversity of citizenship to make it impossible for defendant to remove the action to federal court. In ROSE v. GIAMATTI, 721 F.Supp. 906 (S.D.Ohio 1989), plaintiff, Pete Rose, was the manager of the Cincinnati Reds baseball team. The Commissioner of Baseball, A. Bartlett Giamatti, was conducting an investigation into allegations that Rose had wagered on major league baseball games in violation of the Rules of Major League Baseball. Rose filed suit in an Ohio state court seeking a temporary restraining order and preliminary injunction against pending disciplinary

proceedings on the ground that he was being denied his right to a fair hearing because Giamatti was a biased decisionmaker. Rose named Giamatti, Major League Baseball, and the Cincinnati Reds as defendants. Giamatti removed the action to federal district court in Ohio. Rose, a citizen of Ohio, sought to have the case remanded to the Ohio state court arguing that diversity was lacking between himself, and both the Cincinnati Reds and Major League Baseball (an unincorporated association), who he alleged were also citizens of Ohio. Giamatti, a citizen of New York, argued that the citizenship of the other defendants should be ignored. The District Court noted:

> * * * [I]t is * * * a long-established doctrine that a federal court in its determination of whether there is diversity of citizenship between the parties, must disregard nominal or formal parties to the action, and determine jurisdiction based solely upon the citizenship of the real parties to the controversy. * * * A real party in interest defendant is one who, by the substantive law, has the duty sought to be enforced or enjoined. * * * [A] formal or nominal party is one who, in a genuine legal sense, has no interest in the result of the suit, * * * or no actual interest or control over the subject matter of the litigation. * * *
>
> The court then concluded:
>
> [T]he controversy in this case is between plaintiff Rose and defendant Giamatti; that they are the real parties in interest in this case; that the Cincinnati Reds and Major League Baseball, are, at best, nominal parties in this controversy; and that, consequently, the citizenship of the Cincinnati Reds and Major League Baseball may be disregarded for diversity of citizenship purposes. The Court determines that diversity of citizenship exists between Rose, * * * and Commissioner Giamatti, * * * and that the Court has diversity subject matter jurisdiction over this action.

Id. at 914, 923–24. Is it right for a court to disregard parties it determines to be "formal or nominal"? Do you agree that the Cincinnati Reds and Major League Baseball were "nominal" parties? Why was Rose so anxious to keep the case in state court? Is *Rose* the prototypical case in which diversity jurisdiction serves to protect an out-of-state defendant against local prejudice? See Case Note, *"Root, Root, Root for the Home Team": Pete Rose, Nominal Parties and Diversity Jurisdiction*, 66 N.Y.U. L. Rev. 148 (1991).

2. AMOUNT IN CONTROVERSY

A.F.A. TOURS, INC. v. WHITCHURCH

United States Court of Appeals, Second Circuit, 1991.
937 F.2d 82.

KEARSE, CIRCUIT JUDGE. Plaintiff A.F.A. Tours, Inc., doing business as Alumni Flights Abroad ("AFA"), appeals from a final judgment of the United States District Court for the Southern District of New York * * * dismissing for lack of subject matter jurisdiction this diversity action against defendant Desmond Whitchurch for misappropriation of trade secrets. The district court summarily dismissed the complaint on the ground that it would not be possible for AFA to prove damages amounting to more than $50,000. For the reasons below, we vacate and remand for further proceedings.

* * * AFA operates a travel and tour business, specializing in deluxe tours for United States residents to overseas destinations including Australia, New Zealand, and New Guinea. It expended large sums of money and invested significant time and labor to develop, *inter alia,* a client and customer list, marketing information, and tour information. It regarded this information as confidential trade secrets.

From 1972 through 1989, Whitchurch was employed by AFA as its exclusive tour escort in the above areas. In that position, Whitchurch was privy to certain of the above confidential information. The complaint alleged that in or about October 1989, Whitchurch resigned from AFA, misappropriated the confidential information known to him, and organized his own tour business. Since that time, he has offered or intends to offer tours that compete with those offered by AFA; in connection with his own tours, he has solicited or intends to solicit participants from AFA's customer list.

AFA commenced the present diversity action in the district court for misappropriation of its trade secrets, seeking an injunction against any use by Whitchurch of confidential AFA information, and damages "in an amount which is not presently ascertainable, but which is believed to exceed the sum of $50,000.00." It also sought punitive damages of "no less than $250,000.00."

* * *

At the oral argument of Whitchurch's motion, Whitchurch's attorney began by characterizing the motion as "turn[ing] on a very narrow issue" of whether the AFA information constituted trade secrets * * *, and stating that the case was important to Whitchurch because "he may one day in the future wish to organize a tour, and write letters to individuals again" * * *. The court, however, asked whether it even had to reach the question of trade secrets, raising sua sponte the question of whether the value of AFA's claims exceeded $50,000, a jurisdictional prerequisite for a diversity action. In response to the court's jurisdictional question, Whitchurch's attorney stated that Whitchurch, in soliciting for his planned tour, had written to 100–200 former AFA tour participants but had received favorable responses from only two. * * *

AFA's attorney argued that Whitchurch's lack of success on his first effort was hardly dispositive of the issue of the amount of damages AFA might suffer, in light of Whitchurch's desire to conduct other tours in the future. * * * AFA's attorney, noting that over the years Whitchurch had escorted some 1,500 AFA clients on tours and had indicated that he would conduct a number of tours, argued that AFA's damages would be substantial. He stated that a single 10–customer tour to the area in question would easily generate more than $50,000 * * *. * * *

At the close of this hearing, the court granted summary judgment in favor of Whitchurch * * *. * * * On appeal, AFA contends that the dismissal for lack of jurisdiction was improper because the court (1) failed to give AFA an appropriate opportunity to show that it satisfied the jurisdictional amount, and (2) failed to apply the proper standard to AFA's requests for (a) damages and (b) injunctive relief. * * * For the reasons below, we conclude that the dismissal on the jurisdictional ground was improper. * * *

The district courts have jurisdiction over civil diversity suits "where the matter in controversy exceeds the sum or value of $50,000, exclusive of interest and costs." 28 U.S.C. § 1332 (1988). The test for determining whether a plaintiff meets the jurisdictional amount, established by the Supreme Court in St. Paul Mercury Indemnity Co. v. Red Cab Co., 303 U.S. 283, 58 S.Ct. 586, 82 L.Ed. 845 (1938), is as follows:

> The rule governing dismissal for want of jurisdiction in cases brought in the federal court is that, unless the law gives a different rule, the sum claimed by the plaintiff controls if the claim is apparently made in good faith. It must appear *to a legal certainty* that the claim is really for less than the jurisdictional amount to justify a dismissal.

303 U.S. at 288–89, 58 S.Ct. at 590 (emphasis added).

The amount of damages recoverable in an action for misappropriation of trade secrets may be measured either by the plaintiff's losses, * * * or by the profits unjustly received by the defendant * * *. In addition, if punitive damages are permitted under the controlling law, the demand for such damages may be included in determining whether the jurisdictional amount is satisfied. * * * New York law apparently allows the recovery of punitive damages in a trade secrets case if the defendant's conduct has been sufficiently "gross and wanton." * * *

Further, in appropriate circumstances, the owner of trade secrets may obtain an injunction against their use or disclosure by another in breach of his confidential relationship with the owner. * * * Where the plaintiff seeks injunctive relief, the value of his claim is generally assessed with reference to the right he seeks to protect and measured by the extent of the impairment to be prevented by the injunction. * * * In calculating that impairment, the court may look not only at past losses but also at potential harm. * * *

Before making a determination that the plaintiff's claim does not meet the jurisdictional minimum, the court must afford the plaintiff an "appropriate and reasonable opportunity to show good faith in believing that a recovery in excess of [the jurisdictional amount] is reasonably possible." * * * Under these substantive and procedural principles, although the record indicates that AFA has not yet suffered actual damages even approaching $50,000, we have difficulty with the district court's decision.

First, though AFA did not make an evidentiary showing in support of its contention that the value of its claims exceeded $50,000, it was not afforded a proper opportunity to do so. The issue of the jurisdictional amount was first raised by the district court sua sponte at the argument on the summary judgment motion, and the court rendered its decision at the end of that argument. To the extent that the court thought AFA could not meet the jurisdictional minimum, it should not have dismissed without giving AFA an opportunity to present substantiation directed toward that issue.

Second, despite AFA's lack of an opportunity to present evidence addressed directly to the jurisdictional question, there was evidence in the record to suggest that the matter could not be conclusively resolved against it, for the oral arguments made by AFA's attorney to show that its claims were worth more than $50,000 had some support from documents already before the court. For example, he said Whitchurch had the names of some 1,500 AFA customers; this was consistent with (a) Whitchurch's own statement that in the 17 years he was employed by AFA he had led approximately seven tours each year (thus totaling some 119 tours) and (b) his attorney's statement that there were usually 10–15 people per tour. * * * As to AFA's attorney's estimate that a single tour of this type "[i]s about seven to ten thousand dollars per customer," the evidence in the record as to the destination and deluxe nature of the tours, including evidence that some participants traveled first class and reserved preferred hotel accommodations, supports an inference that a 28–day tour could well cost $10,000 per person.

What this means in terms of loss of earnings to a tour operator, however, is not revealed by the present record. AFA's suggestion that the tour operator himself would earn $10,000 per tourist * * * does not have the same record support and seems questionable. The district court was also undoubtedly correct in its assumption that many of the persons who traveled to the South Pacific with Whitchurch during the 17 years he was with AFA are not likely to travel to that area again. But it could not be said to a legal certainty that no one would return to that area. There was ample support in the record for the proposition that AFA has the prospects for repeat customers. For example, AFA had submitted from one of its brochures two pages excerpting comments from participants in a recent AFA tour * * *; nearly one-third of those quoted indicated that they either had been on other AFA tours or would hope to go on future AFA tours. * * * If a tour operator could earn 17% of the price of a tour, and if Whitchurch were eventually successful in soliciting even 30 of the approximately 1,500 AFA participants he has escorted (*i.e.*, 2%, which may reflect the ratio of his success on his first attempt), the profit he could siphon from AFA would total $51,000. Thus, on the present record, the court could not conclude to a legal certainty that the value of AFA's claims did not exceed the jurisdictional minimum.

Further, AFA requested injunctive relief not just against Whitchurch's solicitation of its customers but also against any use of the information. Presumably such an injunction would include a prohibition against Whitchurch's sale or disclosure of the names and addresses of AFA's customers to other tour operators who might be better equipped than Whitchurch to exploit the information and attract more than 2% of the persons whose names Whitchurch could provide them. In addition, AFA's request for punitive damages in the amount of $250,000 might provide a basis for satisfaction of the jurisdictional amount. Whether or not AFA will be able to prove that Whitchurch's conduct was "gross and wanton" and warrants the recovery of such damages under New York law is an open question. But the present record does not foreclose that possibility.

In all the circumstances, we conclude that the record as it existed in the district court did not permit the court to find with legal certainty that the value of AFA's claims did not exceed $50,000.

* * *

NOTES AND QUESTIONS

1. An amount-in-controversy requirement currently applies to diversity jurisdiction and to federal claims that arise under a federal statute that expressly imposes such a jurisdictional requirement (for example, actions brought under the Consumer Product Safety Act). Congress otherwise deleted an amount-in-controversy requirement for federal question cases in 1980. Why do you think Congress did not eliminate this requirement in diversity actions? What function does the current amount-in-controversy requirement serve? For a historical perspective on the social impact of the amount-in-controversy requirement in diversity jurisdiction cases, see Purcell, Litigation and Inequality: Federal Diversity Jurisdiction in Industrial America, 1870–1958, 97 (1992).

2. The test for determining whether the plaintiff has met the amount-in-controversy requirement is well settled: "The rule * * * is that * * * the sum claimed by the plaintiff controls if the claim is apparently made in good faith. It must appear to a legal certainty that the claim is really for less than the jurisdictional amount to justify dismissal." ST. PAUL MERCURY INDEMNITY CO. v. RED CAB CO., 303 U.S. 283, 288–89, 58 S.Ct. 586, 589, 82 L.Ed. 845, 848 (1938) (footnotes omitted). "When applying this test, a court must look at the circumstances at the time the complaint is filed." Stewart v. Tupperware Corp., 356 F.3d 335, 338 (1st Cir. 2004). In HALL v. EARTHLINK NETWORK, INC., 396 F.3d 500 (2d Cir. 2005), the Court of Appeals said that it would look to post-filing events when they "suggest that the amount in controversy allegation in the complaint was made in bad faith" or that the complaint contained "a mistake." Id. at 507. Do you agree that post-filing changes generally ought not to affect the court's power to hear a lawsuit? Why or why not?

3. Congress raised the jurisdictional amount in diversity cases to more than $75,000 in 1996. Commentators see the increase as a compromise between those who wished to abolish diversity jurisdiction and those who

wished to maintain the option of federal court for some litigants with state law claims. However, just as litigants may try to create or eliminate diversity jurisdiction by manipulating state citizenship, so some litigants may try to engage in "jurisdictional amount gamesmanship." Baker, *The History and Tradition of the Amount in Controversy Requirement: A Proposal to "Up the Ante" in Diversity Jurisdiction*, 102 F.R.D. 299, 323–24 (1984).

ARNOLD v. TROCCOLI, 344 F.2d 842 (2d Cir.1965), concerned the sequential filing of a personal injury action, first in state court and then in federal court. In state court, plaintiff alleged damages of $6,000. In federal court, plaintiff alleged $15,000 (at a time when the amount for diversity jurisdiction required more than $10,000). There appeared to be no justification for the increase in claimed damages, and plaintiff's counsel admitted that the switch from state to federal court was made because of the congested condition of the state courts. The District Court dismissed the action, and the federal appellate court affirmed, making clear, however, that in such circumstances, "plaintiffs and their counsel should be afforded appropriate and reasonable opportunity to show good faith in believing that a recovery in excess of $10,000 is reasonably possible." Id. at 846. What if plaintiff discovers new facts during pretrial proceedings showing that any possible recovery cannot reach the jurisdictional amount, and his attorney files a written stipulation to that effect? Must the action be dismissed or is it saved by the fact that the original claim was made in "good faith"? See National Sur. Corp. v. City of Excelsior Springs, 123 F.2d 573 (8th Cir.1941).

4. The Federal Rules allow parties to join together as plaintiffs or as defendants in a single lawsuit. See Chapter 9, infra. As a result, a plaintiff who asserts a claim for $40,000 might wish to join in the same lawsuit as another plaintiff who asserts a claim for $50,000. Each plaintiff alone would not satisfy the amount-in-controversy requirement of Section 1332(a). Should the parties be permitted to "aggregate" the amounts of their claims to meet the jurisdictional requirement? See Friedenthal, Kane & Miller, Civil Procedure § 2.9 (4th ed. 2005). Courts have developed a number of rules to govern the variety of situations that typically arise.

Generally, one plaintiff can aggregate all of her claims against one defendant to meet the amount-in-controversy requirement, "even when those claims share nothing in common besides the identity of the parties." Everett v. Verizon Wireless, Inc., 460 F.3d 818, 822 (6th Cir.2006). Thus, a plaintiff can satisfy the amount-in-controversy requirement by alleging a number of small claims against one defendant, assuming the total value satisfies the statutory condition and citizenship is diverse. By contrast, multiple plaintiffs who join together in one lawsuit may not aggregate their claims to meet the jurisdictional requirement if the claims are separate and distinct. Rather, multiple plaintiffs may aggregate their claims only when they seek "to enforce a single title or right, in which they have a common and undivided interest." TROY BANK v. G.A. WHITEHEAD & CO., 222 U.S. 39, 40–41, 32 S.Ct. 9, 9, 56 L.Ed. 81, 82 (1911). "An identifying trait of a common and undivided interest is that if one plaintiff were to fail to collect his share, the remaining plaintiffs would collect a larger share." Durant v. Servicemaster Co. Trugreen, Inc., 147 F.Supp.2d 744, 749 (E.D.Mich.2001).

Given the current amount-in-controversy requirement of more than $75,000, and assuming citizenship is satisfied, consider whether diversity jurisdiction is available in the following cases:

(a) One plaintiff sues one defendant, claiming $40,000 in property damage and $45,000 for personal injury resulting from the same accident.

(b) One plaintiff sues one defendant on two unrelated claims, one for $40,000 and the other for $45,000.

(c) Two plaintiffs sue one defendant, each seeking $40,000 in damages.

(d) Two plaintiffs sue one defendant, jointly seeking $80,000 in damages.

(e) One plaintiff sues two defendants, seeking $40,000 from each defendant.

(f) Two plaintiffs sue one defendant on the same issue. One plaintiff seeks $45,000 in damages; the other seeks $35,000.

5. Federal Rule 23 permits a named plaintiff to file suit on behalf of a class and represent the interests of the unnamed class members. How should the district court determine whether the case satisfies the amount-in-controversy requirement for diversity purposes? In ZAHN v. INTERNATIONAL PAPER CO., 414 U.S. 291, 94 S.Ct. 505, 38 L.Ed.2d 511 (1973), four owners of Vermont lakefront property brought a diversity action on behalf of a class consisting of themselves and 200 other lakefront property owners seeking damages from a New York corporation alleged to have polluted the waters of Lake Champlain and, as a result, to have damaged the value and utility of the surrounding property. The Supreme Court held that only those plaintiffs whose claims individually exceeded the then-applicable $10,000 jurisdictional amount requirement could be members of the class. The Supreme Court overturned *Zahn* in EXXON MOBIL CORP. v. ALLAPATTAH SERVICES, INC., 545 U.S. 546, 125 S.Ct. 2611, 162 L.Ed.2d 502 (2005), holding, 5–4, that when the named representative satisfies the amount-in-controversy requirement, "a federal court in a diversity action may exercise supplemental jurisdiction over additional plaintiffs whose claims do not satisfy the minimum amount-in-controversy requirement, provided the claims are part of the same case or controversy as the claims of plaintiffs who do allege a sufficient amount in controversy." This Chapter revisits this issue, p. 338, infra.

6. The Class Action Fairness Act of 2005 (CAFA), see p. 276, supra, specifically rejects *Zahn*'s non-aggregation rule, providing that "the claims of the individual class members shall be aggregated to determine whether the matter in controversy exceeds the sum or value of $5,000,000, exclusive of interest and costs." See 28 U.S.C. § 1332(d)(6). LOWDERMILK v. UNITED STATES BANK NATIONAL ASS'N, 479 F.3d 994 (9th Cir.2007), raised the question of whether a class action may be removed to federal court under CAFA "when the plaintiff has pled damages *less* than the jurisdictional amount." In this employment-compensation case, plaintiff alleged that damages, penalty wages, and other relief were "in total, less than five million dollars." The employer removed under CAFA, and the Ninth Circuit affirmed the District Court's order remanding the action to state court, relying on the legal certainty standard.

7. Determining the amount in controversy in diversity cases seeking injunctive relief poses a difficult problem for federal courts. At least three different approaches are available. As explained in McCARTY v. AMOCO PIPELINE CO., 595 F.2d 389, 392–93 (7th Cir.1979):

> * * * Some courts have resolved the difficulty by adopting the rule that only the value to the plaintiff may be used to determine the jurisdictional amount. Support for this interpretation is principally garnered from the Supreme Court's opinion in Glenwood Light & Water Co. v. Mutual Light, Heat & Power Co., 239 U.S. 121, 36 S.Ct. 30, 60 L.Ed. 174 (1915) * * *.
>
> Although supportive of the "plaintiff viewpoint" rule, the holding in *Glenwood* is only that jurisdiction is present if the value to the plaintiff exceeds the required amount regardless of the value to the defendant. The *Glenwood* case does not exclude the possibility that jurisdiction would be present in a case where the value required was present from the defendant's viewpoint but not from the plaintiff's. * * *
>
> Another approach taken by some courts is to view the amount in controversy from the point of view of the party seeking to invoke federal jurisdiction. Under this rule, the court would look to the plaintiff's viewpoint in a case brought originally in federal court and to the defendant's viewpoint in a case removed to federal court from a state court.
>
> Although this rule has certain attractive features such as tying the controlling viewpoint to the burden of proof as to jurisdiction, two problems with it arise. The first is the possibility of anomalous results. Under the rule, if a case originally brought in federal court were dismissed for failure to meet the jurisdictional amount from the plaintiff's viewpoint, it could yet end up in federal court if the plaintiff reinstituted the case in state court and the defendant—from whose point of view the required amount was present—then removed it. * * *
>
> There is yet a third rule which a number of courts have adopted and which may be termed the "either viewpoint" rule. Under this rule, * * *:
>
> In determining the matter in controversy, we may look to the object sought to be accomplished by the plaintiffs' complaint; the test for determining the amount in controversy is the pecuniary result to either party which the judgment would directly produce.

See McInnis, *The $75,000.01 Question: What is the Value of Injunctive Relief?*, 6 Geo. Mason L.Rev. 1013 (1998).

NOTE ON JUDICIALLY CREATED EXCEPTIONS TO DIVERSITY JURISDICTION

Even if the requirements of diversity jurisdiction are met, a federal court generally will decline to hear probate matters and domestic-relations cases and instead dismiss for lack of subject-matter jurisdiction. See 13E Wright, Miller, & Cooper, Federal Practice and Procedure: Jurisdiction and Related Matters 3d §§ 3609–10. These judicially created exceptions to diversity jurisdiction were first developed at a time when the diversity statute granted jurisdiction of "suits of a civil nature in law or in equity," and it was thought that probate and domestic-relations cases, being matters that would have been heard in the ecclesiastical courts, did not fit this description. The 1948 Judicial Code substituted the term "civil action" for the phrase used in the older statutes, but the exceptions have persisted.

The Supreme Court addressed the domestic-relations exception in ANKENBRANDT v. RICHARDS, 504 U.S. 689, 112 S.Ct. 2206, 119 L.Ed.2d 468 (1992), in which plaintiff invoked diversity jurisdiction to assert claims of physical and sexual abuse on behalf of her daughters against the children's father and his female companion. The Court found that a domestic-relations exception does exist, but the exception reaches only cases involving the issuance of a divorce, alimony, or a child custody decree. As a result, the Supreme Court upheld the District Court's jurisdiction over this tort action and ordered it to proceed. Is this distinction reasonable? Appropriate? See Grant, *The Domestic Relations Exception to Diversity Jurisdiction: Spousal Support Enforcement in the Federal Courts*, 14 J. Contemp. Legal Issues 15 (2004).

Ankenbrandt treated the domestic-relations exception as a matter of statutory interpretation, not constitutional prohibition. Professor Cahn observes, "[B]ecause the Exception is located in the diversity statute, not the Constitution, Congress can modify or entirely eliminate the restriction." Cahn, *Family Law, Federalism, and the Federal Courts*, 79 Iowa L. Rev. 1073, 1087 (1994). What factors should be considered in determining whether a particular family-law issue would benefit from a federal forum? See Saylor, *Federalism and the Family after* Morrison*: An Examination of the Child Support Recovery Act, the Freedom of Access to Clinic Entrances Act, and a Federal Law Outlawing Gun Possession by Domestic Violence Abusers*, 25 Harv. Women's L.J. 57 (2002).

The *Ankenbrandt* Court also stated: "As a matter of judicial economy, state courts are eminently more suited to work of this type than are federal courts, which lack the close association with the state and local government organizations dedicated to handling issues that arise out of conflict over divorce, alimony, and child custody decrees." 504 U.S. at 704, 112 S.Ct. at 2215, 119 L.Ed.2d at 482. Does this rationale apply to all issues on which a state agency represents the primarily responsible government institution, as is true of subjects such as education, fire safety, water management, public transportation, and recreation? If so, what justification is there for having federal courts hear these cases? Should state courts resolve cases when a "close association" is desirable?

Consider another argument by the *Ankenbrandt* Court in favor of the domestic-relations exception: "[A]s a matter of judicial expertise, it makes far more sense to retain the rule that federal courts lack power to issue these types of decrees because of the special proficiency developed by state tribunals over the past century and a half in handling issues that arise in the granting of such decrees." Id. at 704, 112 S.Ct. at 2215, 119 L.Ed.2d at 482–83. Does this prove too much?

Professor Resnik posits that the exclusion of domestic-relations cases from the grant of diversity jurisdiction reflects "the usually unstated and widely shared assumption that women are not relevant to the federal courts" and "that women's role in the family are not much a part of the national issues to which federal court resources should be dedicated." Resnik, *"Naturally" Without Gender: Women, Jurisdiction, and the Federal Courts*, 66 N.Y.U. L. Rev. 1682, 1685, 1687 (1991). Recall that one justification for diversity jurisdiction is the possibility of a "cross-pollination" of ideas between the state and federal courts. In what ways might a national perspective on domestic-relations cases educate the states and the federal system on issues that affect the family? What is the federal interest in this area? See Hasday, *Federalism and the Family Reconstructed*, 45 UCLA L. Rev. 1297 (1998). How would the availability of diversity jurisdiction for domestic-relations cases contribute to a national dialogue on issues affecting women, children, and the family?

The Supreme Court clarified the limited nature of the probate exception in MARSHALL v. MARSHALL, 547 U.S. 293, 126 S.Ct. 1735, 164 L.Ed.2d 480 (2006), a bankruptcy proceeding concerning the estate of J. Howard Marshall II. Marshall died in 1994, leaving his entire estate to a son and nothing to his widow, who was not the son's mother and was significantly younger than decedent. Two years later, while the estate was subject to proceedings in a Texas probate court, the widow filed for bankruptcy in the Federal Bankruptcy Court of Central California. In that latter case, the son filed a claim, asserting that the widow had defamed him. The widow counterclaimed, alleging that the son had tortiously interfered to prevent her husband from making her a promised substantial gift of money. The Bankruptcy Judge, finding it had authority to enter a final judgment on these claims, dismissed the son's claim and found for the widow, awarding her nearly $500 million. The son filed a post-trial motion, alleging that the widow's claim could only be heard in the Texas probate matter. After review in the District Court, the Ninth Circuit held that under the "probate exception" to federal-court jurisdiction, federal courts cannot take subject-matter jurisdiction over claims that involve the validity of a decedent's estate planning instrument, and that this exception also includes tort claims that do not directly involve any probate issues. The Supreme Court granted certiorari and reversed. Justice Ginsburg, writing for a unanimous Court, held that the widow's claim, seeking damages for a "widely recognized tort," id. at 312, 126 S. Ct. at 1748, 164 L. Ed. 2d at 498, did not interfere with the state probate proceeding and was within the subject-matter jurisdiction of the Bankruptcy Court. She explained: "[N]o 'sound policy considerations' militate in favor of extending the probate exception to cover the case at hand. Trial courts, both federal and state, often address conduct of the kind * * * [the widow] alleges. State probate courts possess no 'special proficiency . . . in handling [such] issues.' " Id. at 312, 126 S. Ct. at 1748–49, 164 L. Ed. 2d at 498 (citations omitted). Justice Stevens concurred in a separate opinion advocating the elimination of the probate exception as historically unjustified. For a discussion of the jurisdictional questions left open by the Court in *Marshall*, see Graves, *Marshall v. Marshall: The Past, Present, and Future of the Probate Exception to Federal Jurisdiction*, 59 Ala. L. Rev. 1643 (2008).

SECTION C. THE SUBJECT-MATTER JURISDICTION OF THE FEDERAL COURTS—FEDERAL QUESTIONS

Read Art. III, § 2 and 28 U.S.C. §§ 1331, 1334, 1337, 1338, 1343, 1345, and 1346 in the Supplement.

Article III, § 2 of the United States Constitution extends the judicial power of the United States "to all Cases, in Law and Equity, arising under this Constitution, the Laws of the United States, and Treaties made, or which shall be made under their Authority." The current grant of "federal question" jurisdiction is set out in 28 U.S.C. § 1331. Although the grant of diversity jurisdiction dates to the Judiciary Act of 1789, Congress did not enact federal question jurisdiction until the Midnight Judges Act of 1801, which was repealed the next year when the Federalists lost power and Thomas Jefferson became President. The current statute traces to the jurisdictional grant made in 1875. "Federal question jurisdiction is premised on the principle that the federal judiciary should have authority to interpret and apply federal law." Friedenthal, Kane & Miller, Civil Procedure § 2.3 (4th ed. 2005). Commentators believe that Section 1331 serves three purposes: to promote the uniformity of federal law; to encourage judicial expertise in interpreting federal law; and to protect against possible state-court hostility to claims arising under federal law. See Preis, *Reassessing the Purposes of Federal Question Jurisdiction*, 42 Wake Forest L. Rev. 247, 248–60 (2007). In applying the grant of jurisdiction, courts also consider the federal interest that is at stake in the lawsuit. See Shapiro, *Reflections on the Allocation of Jurisdiction Between State and Federal Courts: A Response to "Reassessing the Allocation of Judicial Business Between State and Federal Courts,"* 78 Va. L. Rev. 1839, 1842 (1992). Congress also has conferred jurisdiction on the federal courts to hear claims arising under specific federal statutes. E.g., 28 U.S.C. § 1338 (patent, trademark, and unfair competition claims).

MISHKIN, THE FEDERAL "QUESTION" IN THE DISTRICT COURTS, 53 Colum.L.Rev. 157, 157–59 (1953):

Although the framers of our Constitution could not agree upon whether there should be any federal trial courts at all, it was generally conceded at the Convention that the national judicial power should, in some form, extend to cases arising under the laws of the new government. However, though the first Congress did exercise its option to establish a system of "inferior" national tribunals, it did not assign to them general jurisdiction over cases of that type. With the exception of an extremely shortlived statute enacted just after the end of the eighteenth century, it was not until 1875 that the federal courts were given initial cognizance of all types of federal question cases. * * *

Whatever may have been the circumstances and needs during the first century of our country's history, there seems to be little doubt that today, with the expanding scope of federal legislation, the exercise of power over cases of this sort constitutes one of the major purposes of a full independent system of national trial courts. The alternative would be to rely entirely upon United States Supreme Court review of state court decisions. But, at least in our present judicial system, Supreme Court pronouncements as to any particular segment of national law are comparatively few. Consequently, sympathetic handling of the available Supreme Court rulings assumes a role of substantial importance in achieving widespread, uniform effectuation of federal law. Presumably judges selected and paid by the central government, with tenure during good behavior—and that determined by the Congress—and probably even somewhat insulated by a separate building, are more likely to give full scope to any given Supreme Court decision, and particularly ones unpopular locally, than are their state counterparts. By the same token, should a district judge fail, or err, a more sympathetic treatment of Supreme Court precedents can be expected from federal circuit judges than from state appellate courts.

Thus, the exercise of federal question jurisdiction by lower federal tribunals presumably permits the Supreme Court to confine itself (insofar as any such distinction can be drawn) to the solving of new problems rather than the policing of old solutions, without the loss that might otherwise be entailed in the effectuation of national rights. Further, the fact that the lower federal bench is chosen by officials of the national government under the same procedure as the members of the high Court suggests a greater similarity in the interpretation of national law, even on first impression, among the several parts of the national system than between the Supreme Court and any state system, or among the various state tribunals themselves. Insofar as this is true, it also promotes a more uniform, correct application of federal law in that significant group of cases where, either because of the novelty of the question, disproportionate expense or for other reasons, recourse to the Supreme Court has previously either not been attempted or been precluded. Finally, it might even be argued that the very existence of an alternative forum stimulates state courts to give a more attentive treatment to claims of federal right.

These factors suggest that it is desirable that Congress be competent to bring to an initial national forum all cases in which the vindication of federal policy may be at stake. However, it does not follow from this that at any given time all such cases should in fact be brought before the federal courts. There are other considerations which must enter into any decision as to the actual use of the national judiciary. For example, there are limits on the volume of litigation which they can handle without an expansion which might not be warranted by the advantages to be gained; the hardships which the geographic location of these courts may impose on the litigants and a willingness to trust that a party's self-interest will lead him to bring or remove an appropriate case to the federal courts might well justify the current rule that federal question jurisdiction is, for the most part, shared by the local courts; in some circumstances, such as where the validity of state action may be at issue, it may avoid friction and wasted effort, without sacrificing national authority, to allow the initial adjudication to be made by the state's tribunals subject to ultimate review by the United States Supreme Court. Other factors could easily be added. * * *

OSBORN v. BANK OF THE UNITED STATES, 22 U.S. (9 Wheat.) 738, 6 L.Ed. 204 (1824). The Bank of the United States brought suit in federal court to enjoin the state auditor of Ohio from collecting from it a tax alleged to be unconstitutional. The court granted a temporary injunction restraining the state auditor from collecting the tax. The state auditor, however, forcibly entered the bank and took the money he claimed the state was owed. The court ordered the state officials to return the money that had been taken from the bank. The officials appealed on the grounds that the federal court lacked subject-matter jurisdiction over the case.

The congressional act chartering the bank authorized it "to sue and be sued * * * in any Circuit Court of the United States." First, Chief Justice Marshall held that this authorization was a grant by Congress to the federal courts of jurisdiction in all cases to which the bank was a party. He then considered whether Congress had the constitutional power to confer jurisdiction over these cases pursuant to the "arising under" language of Article III, § 2. That power clearly existed in the actual case, since the bank was alleging that Ohio's attempt to tax it violated the federal Constitution. The Chief Justice, however, undertook to support the validity of the jurisdictional grant in all cases to which the bank was a party. In particular, he discussed the situation presented if the bank asserted a claim under state law arising out of a contract:

> When [the] Bank sues, the first question which presents itself, and which lies at the foundation of the cause, is, has this legal entity a right to sue? Has it a right to come, not into this Court particularly, but into any Court? This depends on a law of the United States. The next question is, has this being a right to make this particular contract? If this question be decided in the negative, the cause is determined against the plaintiff; and this question, too, depends entirely on a law of the United States. These are important questions, and they exist in every possible case. The right to sue, if decided once, is decided for ever; but the power of Congress was exercised anteced-

ently to the first decision on that right, and if it was constitutional then, it cannot cease to be so, because the particular question is decided. It may be revived at the will of the party, and most probably would be renewed, were the tribunal to be changed. But the question respecting the right to make a particular contract, or to acquire a particular property, or to sue on account of a particular injury, belongs to every particular case, and may be renewed in every case. The question forms an original ingredient in every cause. Whether it be in fact relied on or not, in the defence, it is still a part of the cause, and may be relied on. The right of the plaintiff to sue, cannot depend on the defence which the defendant may choose to set up. His right to sue is anterior to that defence, and must depend on the state of things when the action is brought. The questions which the case involves, then, must determine its character, whether those questions be made in the cause or not.

The appellants say, that the case arises on the contract; but the validity of the contract depends on a law of the United States, and the plaintiff is compelled, in every case, to show its validity. The case arises emphatically under the law. The act of Congress is its foundation. The contract could never have been made, but under the authority of that act. The act itself is the first ingredient in the case, is its origin, is that from which every other part arises. That other questions may also arise, as the execution of the contract, or its performance, cannot change the case, or give it any other origin than the charter of incorporation. The action still originates in, and is sustained by, that charter.

Id. at 823–25, 6 L.Ed. at 224–25.

NOTES AND QUESTIONS

1. The contract case discussed in *Osborn* in fact was presented by the companion case of BANK OF THE UNITED STATES v. PLANTERS' BANK OF GEORGIA, 22 U.S. (9 Wheat.) 904, 6 L.Ed. 244 (1824). The Bank of the United States had purchased notes issued by a state bank, which refused to honor them. The Bank of the United States sued for payment, and the state bank contested the federal court's jurisdiction. The Supreme Court held that the question had been "fully considered" in *Osborn,* and that it was "unnecessary to repeat the reasoning used in that case." In what respect is the jurisdictional issue in *Planters' Bank* different from that in *Osborn*?

2. Justice Frankfurter has stated, although critically, that *Osborn* could be read to permit the conferring of federal jurisdiction "whenever there exists in the background some federal proposition that might be challenged, despite the remoteness of the likelihood of actual presentation of such a federal question." TEXTILE WORKERS UNION v. LINCOLN MILLS, 353 U.S. 448, 471, 77 S.Ct. 912, 928–29, 1 L.Ed.2d 972, 989 (1957) (Frankfurter, J., dissenting). In VERLINDEN B.V. v. CENTRAL BANK OF NIGERIA, 461 U.S. 480, 103 S.Ct. 1962, 76 L.Ed.2d 81 (1983), the Supreme Court, in a

unanimous opinion by Chief Justice Burger, observed that *Osborn* "reflects a broad conception of 'arising under' jurisdiction, according to which Congress may confer on the federal courts jurisdiction over any case or controversy that might call for the application of federal law," but declined to identify "the precise boundaries of Art. III jurisdiction." Id. at 492, 103 S.Ct. at 1971, 76 L.Ed.2d at 91–92. Do you see any advantages to retaining a broad reading of Article III?

3. Some commentators read *Osborn* as permitting federal jurisdiction in "all cases where issues of federal law might possibly be an issue." Cohen, *The Broken Compass: The Requirement that a Case Arise "Directly" Under Federal Law*, 115 U. Pa. L. Rev. 890, 891 (1967). Consistent with this broad reading, *Osborn* is said to support the exercise of "protective jurisdiction," a species of federal question jurisdiction that permits "federal courts to hear state law claims, even though the claims themselves neither incorporate an original federal ingredient nor seek to enforce rights conferred by federal law." Pfander, *Protective Jurisdiction, Aggregate Litigation, and the Limits of Article III*, 95 Cal. L. Rev. 1423 (2007). Why might this expansive form of federal jurisdiction be needed to protect federal interests?

The *Osborn* decision took on added importance after an 1875 statute (the predecessor to 28 U.S.C. § 1331) gave the federal courts jurisdiction over cases arising under federal law. Although Section 1331 uses the same language as Article III, § 2, "the statutory language * * * has been more narrowly construed than its constitutional counterpart." Currie, *The Federal Courts and the American Law Institute, Part II*, 36 U. Chi. L. Rev. 268, 268–69 (1969). As you read the cases that follow, be clear when the court is interpreting Article III and when it is construing the statutory grant of jurisdiction under Section 1331.

LOUISVILLE & NASHVILLE R. CO. v. MOTTLEY

Supreme Court of the United States, 1908.
211 U.S. 149, 29 S.Ct. 42, 53 L.Ed. 126.

Appeal from the Circuit Court of the United States for the Western District of Kentucky * * *.

The appellees (husband and wife), being residents and citizens of Kentucky, brought this suit in equity in the circuit court of the United States for the western district of Kentucky against the appellant, a railroad company and a citizen of the same state. * * *

The bill alleged that in September, 1871, plaintiffs, while passengers upon the defendant railroad, were injured by the defendant's negligence, and released their respective claims for damages in consideration of the agreement for transportation during their lives, expressed in the contract. It is alleged that the contract was performed by the defendant up to January 1, 1907, when the defendant declined to renew the passes. The bill then alleges that the refusal to comply with the contract was based solely upon that part of the act of Congress of June 29, 1906 (34 Stat. at L. 584, chap. 3591, U.S.Comp.Stat.Supp.1907, p. 892), which forbids the giving of free passes or free transportation. The bill further alleges: First, that the act of Congress referred to does not prohibit the giving of passes under the circumstances of this case; and, second, that, if the law is to be construed as prohibiting such passes, it is in conflict with the 5th Amendment of the Constitution, because it deprives the plaintiffs of their property without due process of law. The defendant demurred to the bill. The judge of the circuit court overruled the demurrer, entered a decree for the relief prayed for, and the defendant appealed directly to this court.

MR. JUSTICE MOODY, after making the foregoing statement, delivered the opinion of the court:

Two questions of law were raised by the demurrer to the bill, were brought here by appeal, and have been argued before us. They are, first, whether * * * the act of Congress of June 29, 1906 * * * makes it unlawful to perform a contract for transportation of persons who, in good faith, before the passage of the act, had accepted such contract in satisfaction of a valid cause of action against the railroad; and, second, whether the statute, if it should be construed to render such a contract unlawful, is in violation of the 5th Amendment of the Constitution of the United States. We do not deem it necessary, however, to consider either of these questions, because, in our opinion, the court below was without jurisdiction of the cause. Neither party has questioned that jurisdiction, but it is the duty of this court to see to it that the jurisdiction of the circuit court, which is defined and limited by statute, is not exceeded. * * *

There was no diversity of citizenship, and it is not and cannot be suggested that there was any ground of jurisdiction, except that the case was a "suit * * * arising under the Constitution or laws of the United States." 25 Stat. at L. 434, chap. 866, U.S.Comp.Stat.1901, p. 509. It is the settled interpretation of these words, as used in this statute, conferring jurisdiction, that a suit arises under the Constitution and laws of the United States only when the plaintiff's statement of his own cause of action shows that it is based upon those laws or that Constitution. It is not enough that the plaintiff alleges some anticipated defense to his cause of action, and asserts that the defense is invalidated by some provision of the Constitution of the United States. Although such allegations show that very likely, in the course of the litigation, a question under the Constitution would arise, they do not show that the suit, that is, the plaintiff's original cause of action, arises under the Constitution. In Tennessee v. Union & Planters' Bank, 152 U.S. 454, 38 L.Ed. 511, 14 S.Ct.Rep. 654, the plaintiff, the state of Tennessee, brought suit in the circuit court of the United States to recover from the defendant certain taxes alleged to be due under the laws of the state. The plaintiff alleged that the defendant claimed an immunity from the taxation by virtue of its charter, and that therefore the tax was void, because in violation of the provision of the Constitution of the United States, which forbids any state from passing a law impairing the obligation of contracts. The cause was held to be beyond the jurisdiction of the circuit court, the court saying, by Mr. Justice Gray (p. 464): "A suggestion of one party, that the other will or may set up a claim under the Constitution or laws of the United States, does not make the suit one arising under that Constitution or those laws." Again, in Boston & M. Consol. Copper & S. Min. Co. v. Montana Ore Purchasing Co., 188 U.S. 632, 47 L.Ed. 626, 23 S.Ct.Rep. 434, the plaintiff brought suit in the circuit court of the United States for the conversion of copper ore and for an injunction against its continuance. The plaintiff then alleged, for the purpose of showing jurisdiction, in substance, that the defendant would set up in defense certain laws of the United States. The cause was held to be beyond the jurisdiction of the circuit court, the court saying, by Mr. Justice Peckham (pp. 638, 639):

> It would be wholly unnecessary and improper, in order to prove complainant's cause of action, to go into any matters of defense which the defendants might possibly set up, and then attempt to reply to such defense, and thus, if possible, to show that a Federal question might or probably would arise in the course of the trial of the case. To allege such defense and then make an answer to it before the defendant has the opportunity to itself plead or prove its own defense is inconsistent with any known rule of pleading, so far as we are aware, and is improper.
>
> The rule is a reasonable and just one that the complainant in the first instance shall be confined to a statement of its cause of action, leaving to the defendant to set up in his answer what his defense is, and, if anything more than a denial of complainant's cause of action, imposing upon the defendant the burden of proving such defense.
>
> Conforming itself to that rule, the complainant would not, in the assertion or proof of its cause of action, bring up a single Federal question. The presentation of its cause of action would not show that it was one arising under the Constitution or laws of the United States.

* * *

* * * The application of this rule to the case at bar is decisive against the jurisdiction of the circuit court.

It is ordered that the judgment be reversed and the case remitted to the circuit court with instructions to dismiss the suit for want of jurisdiction.

NOTES AND QUESTIONS

1. Some commentators question the Court's narrowing interpretation of Section 1331, pointing to the fact that the statutory language is identical to that of Article III. Moreover, the legislative history to Section 1331, although characterized as "skimpy," appears to support a reading of the statute that runs the full length of the Article III provision. Chemerinsky, Federal Jurisdiction § 5.2.1 (5th ed. 2007) (quoting the floor manager of the bill in the

Senate as stating that "[t]he act of 1789 did not confer the whole power which the Constitution conferred.... This bill does.... This bill gives precisely the power which the Constitution confers—nothing more, nothing less.") (omission in original).

2. To what extent is *Mottley* a reaction to *Osborn*'s broad reading of the "arising under" language in the Constitution? After the Civil War, the number of lawsuits filed in the federal courts dramatically increased, but Congress was slow to address the mounting problems of court congestion and docket overload. *Mottley* helped deal with the problem by turning away cases that satisfied Article III but did not meet the more stringent statutory test. Is it appropriate for federal courts to control the size of their dockets by narrowly construing jurisdictional statutes?

3. What policy considerations ought to affect the Court's interpretation of the statutory grant? Why should subject-matter jurisdiction depend on technical pleading rules and the content of the complaint? Following the Court's decision, the Mottleys commenced an action in a Kentucky state court. The case ultimately was brought to the United States Supreme Court by appeal from the highest court in Kentucky on the question of the validity and construction of the 1906 Act; three years after the Supreme Court dismissed the federal action it examined the merits of the Mottleys' contentions and decided in favor of the railroad. In light of this history, what was gained by the original dismissal?

4. Should a federal forum be available for lawsuits in which a defendant raises a federal issue as a defense or as a counterclaim? Consider the proposal of the American Law Institute, Study of the Division of Jurisdiction Between State and Federal Courts § 1312(d) (1969), which provides that a federal court may retain subject-matter jurisdiction even when the complaint does not present a claim within its original jurisdiction if defendant introduces a federal defense or counterclaim. Do you see any advantages to this reform? See Doernberg, *There's No Reason for It; It's Just Our Policy: Why the Well–Pleaded Complaint Rule Sabotages the Purposes of Federal Question Jurisdiction*, 38 Hastings L.J. 597 (1987). In HOLMES GROUP, INC. v. VORNADO AIR CIRCULATION SYSTEMS, INC., 535 U.S. 826, 122 S.Ct. 1889, 153 L.Ed.2d 13 (2002), the Court held that the Federal Circuit Court, which has exclusive appellate jurisdiction over patent claims, lacked jurisdiction to hear a case in which the patent issue was raised by defendant's counterclaim. Professor Cotropia identifies "the core of the Court's decision * * * [as the view] that federal law counterclaims cannot form the sole basis for federal question jurisdiction." Cotropia, *Counterclaims, the Well–Pleaded Complaint, and Federal Jurisdiction*, 33 Hofstra L.Rev. 1, 2–3 (2004).

5. The Declaratory Judgment Act, 28 U.S.C. §§ 2201–02, allows the federal court to issue a declaration of "rights and other legal relations" to an "interested party" in "a case of actual controversy within its jurisdiction." Would there have been jurisdiction in the principal case if the railroad had sought, as it can today, a judicial declaration that the 1906 Act had rendered the passes invalid? See SKELLY OIL CO. v. PHILLIPS PETROLEUM CO., 339 U.S. 667, 673–74, 70 S.Ct. 876, 880, 94 L.Ed. 1194, 1200–01 (1950), in which suit was brought under the Declaratory Judgment Act for a declaration

that certain contracts had not been terminated. Had the plaintiff (who also was the party who initiated the declaratory action) simply sued to enforce the contract, the complaint would not have raised a federal question; in defending against the breach of contract complaint, however, the defendant would have argued termination, and the effectiveness of an attempted termination turned on a federal question. The Court denied jurisdiction, writing, "[t]o sanction suits for declaratory relief as within the jurisdiction of the District Courts merely because, as in this case, artful pleading anticipates a defense based on federal law would contravene the whole trend of jurisdictional legislation by Congress, disregard the effective functioning of the federal judicial system and distort the limited procedural purposes of the Declaratory Judgment Act." How would the assertion of jurisdiction in *Skelly* have done all of these things?

6. A party wanting to litigate in federal court might attempt to create federal question jurisdiction through "artful pleading." "The term 'artful pleading' * * * describe[s] an attempt by the plaintiff to create federal question jurisdiction through the anticipation and inclusion of a federal defense on the face of its complaint in an action brought under the Declaratory Judgment Act." Miller, *Artful Pleading: A Doctrine in Search of Definition*, 76 Texas L.Rev. 1781, 1783 (1998). In BRIGHT v. BECHTEL PETROLEUM, INC., 780 F.2d 766 (9th Cir.1986), plaintiff brought suit against his employer in state court alleging that the employer had breached his employment contract by paying him less than the contract required because the employer withheld state and federal income taxes. The employer removed the case to federal court arguing that plaintiff had artfully pleaded what really was a challenge to the employer's compliance with federal law. The Ninth Circuit, allowing an exception to the "well-pleaded complaint" rule, found that federal question jurisdiction existed: "Although the plaintiff is generally considered the 'master of his complaint' and is free to choose the forum for his action, this principle is not without limitation. * * * A plaintiff will not be allowed to conceal the true nature of a complaint through 'artful pleading.' " Id. at 769. See also Ragazzo, *Reconsidering the Artful Pleading Doctrine*, 44 Hastings L.J. 273 (1993).

T.B. HARMS CO. v. ELISCU

United States Court of Appeals, Second Circuit, 1964.
339 F.2d 823, certiorari denied 381 U.S. 915, 85 S.Ct. 1534, 14 L.Ed.2d 435 (1965).

FRIENDLY, CIRCUIT JUDGE. A layman would doubtless be surprised to learn that an action wherein the purported sole owner of a copyright alleged that persons claiming partial ownership had recorded their claim in the Copyright Office and had warned his licensees against disregarding their interests was not one "arising under any Act of Congress relating to * * * copyrights" over which 28 U.S.C. § 1338 gives the federal courts exclusive jurisdiction. Yet precedents going back for more than a century teach that lesson and lead us to affirm Judge Weinfeld's dismissal of the complaint.

The litigation concerns four copyrighted songs. * * * The music for the songs was composed by Vincent Youmans for use in a motion picture,

"Flying Down to Rio," pursuant to a contract made in 1933 with RKO Studios, Inc. He agreed to assign to RKO the recordation and certain other rights relating to the picture during the existence of the copyrights and any renewals. RKO was to employ a writer of the lyrics and to procure the publishing rights in these for Youmans, who was "to pay said lyric writer the usual and customary royalties on sheet music and mechanical records." Subject to this, Youmans could assign the publication and small performing rights to the music and lyrics as he saw fit. In fact RKO employed two lyric writers, Gus Kahn and the defendant Edward Eliscu, who agreed to assign to RKO certain rights described in a contract dated as of May 25, 1933. Max Dreyfus, principal stockholder of the plaintiff Harms, which has succeeded to his rights, acquired Youmans' reserved rights to the music and was his designee for the assignment with respect to the lyrics. Allegedly—and his denial of this is a prime subject of dispute—Eliscu then entered into an agreement dated June 30, 1933, assigning his rights to the existing and renewal copyrights to Dreyfus in return for certain royalties.

When the copyrights were about to expire, proper renewal applications were made by the children of Youmans, by the widow and children of Kahn, and by Eliscu. The two former groups executed assignments of their rights in the renewal copyrights to Harms. But Eliscu, by an instrument dated February 19, 1962, recorded in the Copyright Office, assigned his rights in the renewal copyrights to defendant Ross Jungnickel, Inc., subject to a judicial determination of his ownership. Thereafter Eliscu's lawyer advised ASCAP and one Harry Fox—respectively the agents for the small performing rights and the mechanical recording license fees—that Eliscu had become vested with a half interest in the renewal copyrights and that any future payments which failed to reflect his interest would be made at their own risk; at the same time he demanded an accounting from Harms. Finally, Eliscu brought an action in the New York Supreme Court for a declaration that he owned a one-third interest in the renewal copyrights and for an accounting.

Harms then began the instant action in the District Court for the Southern District of New York for equitable and declaratory relief against Eliscu and Jungnickel. Jurisdiction was predicated on 28 U.S.C. § 1338; plaintiff alleged its own New York incorporation and did not allege the citizenship of the defendants, which concededly is in New York. Defendants moved to dismiss the complaint for failure to state a claim on which relief can be granted and for lack of federal jurisdiction; voluminous affidavits were submitted. The district court dismissed the complaint for want of federal jurisdiction * * *.

In line with what apparently were the arguments of the parties, Judge Weinfeld treated the jurisdictional issue as turning solely on whether the complaint alleged any act or threat of copyright infringement. He was right in concluding it did not. Infringement, as used in copyright law, does not include everything that may impair the value of the copyright; it is doing one or more of those things which * * * the Act * * * reserves exclusively to the copyright owner. * * *

Although Chief Justice Marshall, construing the "arising under" language in the context of Article III of the Constitution, indicated in Osborn v. Bank of the United States * * * that the grant extended to every case in which federal law furnished a necessary ingredient of the claim even though this was antecedent and uncontested, the Supreme Court has long given a narrower meaning to the "arising under" language in statutes defining the jurisdiction of the lower federal courts. * * * If the ingredient theory of Article III had been carried over to the general grant of federal question jurisdiction now contained in 28 U.S.C. § 1331, there would have been no basis—to take a well-known example—why federal courts should not have jurisdiction as to all disputes over the many western land titles originating in a federal patent, even though the controverted questions normally are of fact or of local land law. Quite sensibly, such extensive jurisdiction has been denied. * * *

The cases dealing with statutory jurisdiction over patents and copyrights have taken the same conservative line. * * * Just as with western land titles, the federal grant of a patent or copyright has not been thought to infuse with any national interest a dispute as to ownership or contractual enforcement turning on the facts or on ordinary principles of contract law. Indeed, the case for an unexpansive reading of the provision conferring exclusive jurisdiction with respect to patents and copyrights has been especially strong since expansion would entail depriving the state courts of any jurisdiction over matters having so little federal significance.

In an endeavor to explain precisely what suits arose under the patent and copyright laws, Mr. Justice Holmes stated that "[a] suit arises under the law that creates the cause of action"; in the case *sub judice,* injury to a business involving slander of a patent, he said, "whether it is a wrong or not depends upon the law of the State where the act is done" so that the suit did not arise under the patent laws. American Well Works Co. v. Layne & Bowler Co. * * * The Holmes "creation" test explains the taking of federal jurisdiction in a great many cases, notably copyright and patent infringement actions, both clearly authorized by the respective federal acts, * * * and thus unquestionably within the scope of 28 U.S.C. § 1338; indeed, in the many infringement suits that depend only on some point of fact and require no construction of federal law, no other explanation may exist.

Harms' claim is not within Holmes' definition. The relevant statutes create no explicit right of action to enforce or rescind assignments of copyrights, nor does any copyright statute specify a cause of action to fix the locus of ownership. To be sure, not every federal cause of action springs from an express mandate of Congress; federal civil claims have been "inferred" from federal statutes making behavior criminal or otherwise regulating it. * * * Such statutes invariably impose a federal duty and usually create some express remedy as well, while the relevant copyright provision merely authorizes an assignment by written instrument, 17 U.S.C. § 28. * * *

It has come to be realized that Mr. Justice Holmes' formula is more useful for inclusion than for the exclusion for which it was intended. Even though the claim is created by state law, a case may "arise under" a law of the United States if the complaint discloses a need for determining the meaning or application of such a law. * * * But Harms likewise does not meet this test. The crucial issue is whether or not Eliscu executed the assignment to Dreyfus; possibly the interpretation of the initial May, 1933, contract is also relevant, but if any aspect of the suit requires an interpretation of the Copyright Act, the complaint does not reveal it.

* * *

Mindful of the hazards of formulation in this treacherous area, we think that an action "arises under" the Copyright Act if and only if the complaint is for a remedy expressly granted by the Act, e.g., a suit for infringement or for the statutory royalties for record reproduction, * * * or asserts a claim requiring construction of the Act, * * * or, at the very least and perhaps more doubtfully, presents a case where a distinctive policy of the Act requires that federal principles control the disposition of the claim. The general interest that copyrights, like all other forms of property, should be enjoyed by their true owner is not enough to meet this last test.

* * *

Affirmed.

NOTES AND QUESTIONS

1. Would a congressional statute conferring federal question jurisdiction over a case like *Harms* be constitutional under *Osborn*'s ingredient test?

2. Areas in which Congress has given the federal courts exclusive jurisdiction include, *inter alia,* certain securities-law class actions, 15 U.S.C. § 77p(b) and (c); bankruptcy, 28 U.S.C. § 1334; patents and copyrights, 28 U.S.C. § 1338(a); actions against foreign consuls and vice-consuls, 28 U.S.C. § 1351; actions to recover a fine, penalty, or forfeiture under federal law, 28 U.S.C. § 1355; and actions involving certain seizures, 28 U.S.C. § 1356. What factors should motivate Congress in choosing between a grant of concurrent or exclusive jurisdiction? See Note, *Exclusive Jurisdiction of the Federal Courts in Private Civil Actions*, 70 Harv. L. Rev. 509 (1957).

3. As suggested in *Harms,* the notion that a federal court has exclusive jurisdiction often means less than it seems to say. Consider disputes involving patents. In LUCKETT v. DELPARK, INC., 270 U.S. 496, 46 S.Ct. 397 70 L.Ed. 703 (1926), the patentee apparently could have sued for infringement of his patent but chose instead to sue for breach of contract. The District Court dismissed for want of jurisdiction, and the Supreme Court affirmed.

> [W]here a patentee complainant makes his suit one for recovery of royalties under a contract of license or assignment, or for damages for a

> breach of its covenants, or for a specific performance thereof, or asks the aid of the Court in declaring a forfeiture of the license or in restoring an unclouded title to the patent, he does not give the federal district court jurisdiction of the cause as one arising under the patent laws.

Id. at 510–11, 46 S.Ct. at 402, 70 L.Ed. at 708–09. What is the point of the grant of exclusive jurisdiction if a plaintiff by artful pleading can choose whether the claim is to be heard in state or federal court?

NOTE ON PRIVATE RIGHTS OF ACTION

Private rights of action refer to "suits brought by private litigants against private persons allegedly acting in violation of a statute." Stewart & Sunstein, *Public Programs and Private Rights*, 95 Harv. L. Rev. 1193, 1196 (1982). Legislation creating an enforceable private right of action may do so either expressly or by implication. "At common law, courts created private rights of action either by relying upon statutes to give specific content to the open-textured 'reasonable man' standard of negligence, or by creating an action in damages for statutory wrongs." Id. at 1206. In CORT v. ASH, 422 U.S. 66, 95 S.Ct. 2080, 45 L.Ed.2d 26 (1975), the Supreme Court announced a four-part test for determining whether a private right of action should be implied from a federal statute that does not expressly provide for a private remedy.

> * * * First, is the plaintiff "one of the class for whose *especial* benefit the statute was enacted," * * *—that is, does the statute create a federal right in favor of the plaintiff? Second, is there any indication of legislative intent, explicit or implicit, either to create such a remedy or to deny one? * * * Third, is it consistent with the underlying purposes of the legislative scheme to imply a remedy for the plaintiff? * * * And finally, is the cause of action one traditionally relegated to state law, in an area basically the concern of the States, so that it would be inappropriate to infer a cause of action based solely on federal law? * * *

Id. at 78, 95 S.Ct. at 2088, 45 L.Ed.2d at 36–37. In TRANSAMERICA MORTGAGE ADVISORS, INC. v. LEWIS, 444 U.S. 11, 100 S.Ct. 242, 62 L.Ed.2d 146 (1979), the Court retreated from the Cort v. Ash test, explaining that the question "whether a statute creates a cause of action, either expressly or by implication, is basically a matter of statutory construction." Id. at 15, 100 S.Ct. at 245, 62 L.Ed.2d at 152.

In BIVENS v. SIX UNKNOWN NAMED AGENTS OF THE FEDERAL BUREAU OF NARCOTICS, 403 U.S. 388, 91 S.Ct. 1999, 29 L.Ed.2d 619 (1971), the Court recognized a damage action against a federal official for a violation of the Fourth Amendment despite the absence of any congressional authorization of such a remedy. The Court directed the Court of Appeals to develop the details of the implied remedy on remand. Is it appropriate for the Court to enforce the Constitution when Congress has failed to enact a remedy? Should the standard for enforcing the Constitution be the same as for implying a right of action to enforce a federal statute?

Should all causes of action created by federal law confer federal question jurisdiction? Consider this question in light of SHOSHONE MINING CO. v. RUTTER, 177 U.S. 505, 20 S.Ct. 726, 44 L.Ed. 864 (1900). Congress established a system allowing miners to file land patents on claims and to settle conflicting claims. The federal statute provided that the right to possession was to be determined by the "local customs or rules of miners in the several mining districts, so far as the same are applicable and not inconsistent with the laws of the United States." The Court determined:

> Inasmuch * * * as the "adverse suit" to determine the right of possession may not involve any question as to the construction or effect of the Constitution or laws of the United States, but may present simply a question of fact as to the time of the discovery of mineral, the location of the claim on the ground, or a determination of the meaning and effect of certain local rules and customs prescribed by the miners of the district, or the effect of state statutes, it would seem to follow that it is not one which necessarily arises under the Constitution and laws of the United States.

Id. at 509, 20 S.Ct. at 727, 44 L.Ed. at 866.

Conversely, should all causes of action created by state law be outside Section 1331? SMITH v. KANSAS CITY TITLE & TRUST CO., 255 U.S. 180, 41 S.Ct. 243, 65 L.Ed. 577 (1921), provides an example of a claim that, although created by state law, was found to arise under a law of the United States. In *Smith*, a shareholder sued to enjoin the Trust Company, a Missouri corporation, from investing in certain federal bonds on the ground that the Act of Congress authorizing their issuance was unconstitutional. The plaintiff claimed that under Missouri law an investment in securities the issuance of which had not been authorized by a valid law was *ultra vires* and enjoinable. The cause of action was thus created by the state. Nonetheless, the Supreme Court held that the action arose under federal law.

> The general rule is that where it appears from the bill or statement of the plaintiff that the right to relief depends upon the construction or application of the Constitution or laws of the United States, and that such federal claim is not merely colorable, and rests upon a reasonable foundation, the District Court has jurisdiction. * * *

Id. at 199, 41 S.Ct. at 245, 65 L.Ed. at 585. Justice Holmes dissented on the ground that because state and not federal law created the cause of action, the case did not arise under the federal law for purposes of Section 1331.

> It is evident that the cause of action arises not under any law of the United States but wholly under Missouri law. The defendant is a Missouri corporation and the right claimed is that of a stockholder to prevent the directors from doing an act, that is, making an investment, alleged to be contrary to their duty. But the scope of their duty depends upon the charter of their corporation and other laws of

> Missouri. If those laws had authorized the investment in terms the plaintiff would have no case, and this seems to me to make manifest what I am unable to deem even debatable, that, as I have said, the cause of action arises wholly under Missouri law. If the Missouri law authorizes or forbids the investment according to the determination of this Court upon a point under the Constitution or acts of Congress, still that point is material only because the Missouri law saw fit to make it so. The whole foundation of the duty is Missouri law, which at its sole will incorporated the other law as it might incorporate a document. The other law or document depends for its relevance and effect not on its own force but upon the law that took it up, so I repeat once more the cause of action arises wholly from the law of the State.

Id. at 214, 41 S.Ct. at 250, 65 L.Ed. at 591 (Holmes, J., dissenting).

The holding of *Smith* appears to be contradicted by the Court's later decision in MOORE v. CHESAPEAKE & OHIO RAILWAY CO., 291 U.S. 205, 54 S.Ct. 402, 78 L.Ed. 755 (1934). In *Moore,* plaintiff brought an action under Kentucky's Employer Liability Act, which provided that a plaintiff could not be held responsible for contributory negligence or assumption of risk if the defendant had violated state or federal employee-safety laws. Plaintiff alleged defendant's failure to comply with the Federal Safety Appliance Act. Although the cause of action was created by the state, an important issue was whether the terms of the federal statute had been violated. The Supreme Court found that federal question jurisdiction did not exist, holding that:

> [A] suit brought under the state statute which defines liability to employees who are injured while engaged in intrastate commerce, and brings within the purview of the statute a breach of the duty imposed by the federal statute, should [not] be regarded as a suit arising under the laws of the United States and cognizable in the federal court in the absence of diversity of citizenship.

Id. at 214–15, 54 S.Ct. at 406, 78 L.Ed. at 762. Professor Freer points out that plaintiff "raised the federal issue as a way to rebut an anticipated defense." Freer, *Of Rules and Standards: Reconciling Statutory Limitations on "Arising Under" Jurisdiction*, 82 Ind. L.J. 309, 326 (2007). If that is the case, could the Supreme Court have rejected federal jurisdiction under the *Mottley* rule?

MERRELL DOW PHARMACEUTICALS INC. v. THOMPSON

Supreme Court of the United States, 1986.
478 U.S. 804, 106 S.Ct. 3229, 92 L.Ed.2d 650.

Certiorari to the United States Court of Appeals for the Sixth Circuit.

JUSTICE STEVENS delivered the opinion of the Court.

The question presented is whether the incorporation of a federal standard in a state-law private action, when Congress has intended that there not be a federal private action for violations of that federal standard, makes the action one "arising under the Constitution, laws, or treaties of the United States," 28 U.S.C. § 1331.

I

The Thompson respondents are residents of Canada and the MacTavishes reside in Scotland. They filed virtually identical complaints against petitioner, a corporation, that manufactures and distributes the drug Bendectin in the Court of Common Pleas in Hamilton County, Ohio. Each complaint alleged that a child was born with multiple deformities as a result of the mother's ingestion of Bendectin during pregnancy. In five of the six counts, the recovery of substantial damages was requested on common-law theories of negligence, breach of warranty, strict liability, fraud, and gross negligence. In Count IV, respondents alleged that the drug Bendectin was "misbranded" in violation of the Federal Food, Drug, and Cosmetic Act (FDCA), * * * because its labeling did not provide adequate warning that its use was potentially dangerous. Paragraph 26 alleged that the violation of the FDCA "in the promotion" of Bendectin "constitutes a rebuttable presumption of negligence." Paragraph 27 alleged that the "violation of said federal statutes directly and proximately caused the injuries suffered" by the two infants. * * *

Petitioner filed a timely petition for removal * * * alleging that the action was "founded, in part, on an alleged claim arising under the laws of the United States." * * * Respondents filed a motion to remand to the state forum on the ground that the federal court lacked subject matter jurisdiction. Relying on our decision in Smith v. Kansas City Title & Trust Co., * * * the District Court held that Count IV of the complaint alleged a cause of action arising under federal law and denied the motion to remand. It then granted petitioner's motion to dismiss on *forum non conveniens* grounds.

The Court of Appeals for the Sixth Circuit reversed. * * * [N]oting "that the FDCA does not create or imply a private right of action for individuals injured as a result of violations of the Act," it explained:

> "Federal question jurisdiction would, thus, exist only if plaintiffs' right to relief *depended necessarily* on a substantial question of federal law. Plaintiffs' causes of action referred to the FDCA merely as one available criterion for determining whether Merrell Dow was negligent. Because the jury could find negligence on the part of Merrell Dow without finding a violation of the FDCA, the plaintiffs' causes of action did not depend necessarily upon a question of federal law. Consequently, the causes of action did not arise under federal law and, therefore, were improperly removed to federal court." * * *

We granted certiorari, * * * and we now affirm.

II

* * *

* * * [T]he propriety of the removal in this case * * * turns on whether the case falls within the original "federal question" jurisdiction of the federal courts. There is no "single, precise definition" of that concept * * *. * * * This much, however, is clear. The "vast majority" of cases that come within this grant of jurisdiction are covered by Justice Holmes' statement that a " 'suit arises under the law that creates the cause of action.' " * * * American Well Works Co. v. Layne & Bowler Co. * * *. Thus, the vast majority of cases brought under the general federal-question jurisdiction of the federal courts are those in which federal law creates the cause of action. * * * We have, however, also noted that a case may arise under federal law "where the vindication of a right under state law necessarily turned on some construction of federal law."

This case does not pose a federal question of the first kind; respondents do not allege that federal law creates any of the causes of action that they have asserted. This case thus poses what Justice Frankfurter called the "litigation-provoking problem," * * *—the presence of a federal issue in a state-created cause of action.

* * *

In this case, both parties agree with the Court of Appeals' conclusion that there is no federal cause of action for FDCA violations. For purposes of our decision, we assume that this is a correct interpretation of the FDCA. * * * In short, Congress did not intend a private federal remedy for violations of the statute that it enacted.

* * *

The significance of the necessary assumption that there is no federal private cause of action * * * cannot be overstated. For the ultimate import of such a conclusion, as we have repeatedly emphasized, is that it would flout congressional intent to provide a private federal remedy for the violation of the federal statute. We think it would similarly flout, or at least undermine, congressional intent to conclude that the federal courts might nevertheless exercise federal-question jurisdiction and provide remedies for violations of that federal statute solely because the violation of the federal statute is said to be a "rebuttable presumption" or a "proximate cause" under state law, rather than a federal action under federal law.

III

* * *

[The Court considered and rejected three arguments to support the finding of jurisdiction despite the absence of a federal cause of action to enforce an alleged violation of the federal statute: that under *Smith*, federal-question jurisdiction is present if a "substantial, disputed question of federal law is a necessary element of one of the well-pleaded state claims"; that a federal forum is warranted to ensure uniform interpretation of the federal statute; and that "special circumstances" relating to the extraterritorial effect of the statute warrant affording a federal forum.]

* * * Given the significance of the assumed congressional determination to preclude federal private remedies, the presence of the federal issue as an element of the state tort is not the kind of adjudication for which jurisdiction would serve congressional purposes and the federal system. * * * We simply conclude that the congressional determination that there should be no federal remedy for the violation of this federal statute is tantamount to a congressional conclusion that the presence of a claimed violation of the statute as an element of a state cause of action is insufficiently "substantial" to confer federal-question jurisdiction.[12]

* * *

IV

We conclude that a complaint alleging a violation of a federal statute as an element of a state cause of action, when Congress has determined that there should be no private, federal cause of action for the violation, does not state a claim "arising under the Constitution, laws, or treaties of the United States." 28 U.S.C. § 1331.

The judgment of the Court of Appeals is affirmed.

It is so ordered.

JUSTICE BRENNAN, with whom JUSTICE WHITE, JUSTICE MARSHALL, and JUSTICE BLACKMUN join, dissenting.

* * *

I

While the majority of cases covered by § 1331 may well be described by Justice Holmes' adage that "[a] suit arises under the law that creates the cause of action," * * * it is firmly settled that there may be federal-question jurisdiction even though both the right asserted and the remedy sought by the plaintiff are state created. * * *

12. Several commentators have suggested that our § 1331 decisions can best be understood as an evaluation of the *nature* of the federal interest at stake. * * *

Focusing on the nature of the federal interest, moreover, suggests that the widely perceived "irreconcilable" conflict between the finding of federal jurisdiction in Smith v. Kansas City Title & Trust Co., * * * and the finding of no jurisdiction in Moore v. Chesapeake & Ohio R. Co. * * * is far from clear. For the difference in result can be seen as manifestations of the differences in the nature of the federal issues at stake. In *Smith*, as the Court emphasized, the issue was the constitutionality of an important federal statute. * * * In *Moore*, in contrast, the Court emphasized that the violation of the federal standard as an element of state tort recovery did not fundamentally change the state tort nature of the action. * * *

The importance of the nature of the federal issue in federal-question jurisdiction is highlighted by the fact that, despite the usual reliability of the Holmes test as an inclusionary principle, this Court has sometimes found that formally federal causes of action were not properly brought under federal-question jurisdiction because of the overwhelming predominance of state-law issues. See * * * Shoshone Mining Co. v. Rutter * * *.

The continuing vitality of *Smith* is beyond challenge. We have cited it approvingly on numerous occasions, and reaffirmed its holding several times * * *.[1]

There is, to my mind, no question that there is federal jurisdiction over the respondents' fourth cause of action under the rule set forth in *Smith* * * *. Respondents pleaded that petitioner's labeling of the drug Bendectin constituted "misbranding" in violation of * * * the Federal Food, Drug, and Cosmetic Act (FDCA), * * * and that this violation "directly and proximately caused" their injuries. * * * Respondents asserted in the complaint that this violation established petitioner's negligence *per se* and entitled them to recover damages without more. * * * As pleaded, then, respondents' "right to relief depend[ed] upon the construction or application of the Constitution or laws of the United States." *Smith* * * *. * * * [Furthermore, p]etitioner's principal defense is that the Act does not govern the branding of drugs that are sold in foreign countries. It is certainly not immediately obvious whether this argument is correct. Thus, the statutory question is one which "discloses a need for determining the meaning or application of [the FDCA]," T.B. Harms Co. v. Eliscu, * * * and the claim raised by the fourth cause of action is one "arising under" federal law within the meaning of § 1331.

II

* * * According to the Court, if we assume that Congress did not intend that there be a private federal cause of action under a particular federal law (and, presumably, *a fortiori* if Congress' decision not to create a private remedy is express), we must also assume that Congress did not intend that there be federal jurisdiction over a state cause of action that is determined by that federal law. Therefore, assuming—only because the parties have made a similar assumption—that there is no private cause of action under the FDCA, the Court holds that there is no federal jurisdiction over the plaintiffs' claim * * *. * * *

The Court nowhere explains the basis for this conclusion. Yet it is hardly self-evident. Why should the fact that Congress chose not to create a private federal *remedy* mean that Congress would not want there to be

---

1. * * * In one sense, the Court is correct in asserting that we can reconcile *Smith* and *Moore* on the ground that the "nature" of the federal interest was more significant in *Smith* than in *Moore*. Indeed, as the Court appears to believe, * * * we could reconcile many of the seemingly inconsistent results that have been reached under § 1331 with such a test. But this is so only because a test based upon an ad hoc evaluation of the importance of the federal issue is infinitely malleable: at what point does a federal interest become strong enough to create jurisdiction? What principles guide the determination whether a statute is "important" or not? * * * The point is that if one makes the test sufficiently vague and general, virtually any set of results can be "reconciled." * * *

My own view is in accord with those commentators who view the results in *Smith* and *Moore* as irreconcilable. * * * That fact does not trouble me greatly, however, for I view *Moore* as having been a "sport" at the time it was decided and having long been in a state of innocuous desuetude. Unlike the jurisdictional holding in *Smith,* the jurisdictional holding in *Moore* has never been relied upon or even cited by this Court. * * * *Moore* simply has not survived the test of time; it is presently moribund, and, to the extent that it is inconsistent with the well-established rule of the *Smith* case, it ought to be overruled.

federal *jurisdiction* to adjudicate a state claim that imposes liability for violating the federal law? Clearly, the decision not to provide a private federal remedy should not affect federal jurisdiction unless the reasons Congress withholds a federal remedy are also reasons for withholding federal jurisdiction. * * *

A

In the early days of our Republic, Congress was content to leave the task of interpreting and applying federal laws in the first instance to the state courts; with one short-lived exception, Congress did not grant the inferior federal courts original jurisdiction over cases arising under federal law until 1875. * * * The reasons Congress found it necessary to add this jurisdiction to the district courts are well known. First, Congress recognized "the importance, and even necessity of *uniformity* of decisions throughout the whole United States, upon all subjects within the purview of the constitution." Martin v. Hunter's Lessee, [1 Wheat. 304, 347–48 (1816)] (Story, J.) (emphasis in original). * * * Concededly, because federal jurisdiction is not always exclusive and because federal courts may disagree with one another, absolute uniformity has not been obtained even under § 1331. However, while perfect uniformity may not have been achieved, experience indicates that the availability of a federal forum in federal-question cases has done much to advance that goal. * * *

In addition, § 1331 has provided for adjudication in a forum that specializes in federal law and that is therefore more likely to apply that law correctly. Because federal-question cases constitute the basic grist for federal tribunals, "[t]he federal courts have acquired a considerable expertness in the interpretation and application of federal law." * * * As a result, the federal courts are comparatively more skilled at interpreting and applying federal law, and are much more likely correctly to divine Congress' intent in enacting legislation.[6] * * *

These reasons for having original federal-question jurisdiction explain why cases like this one and *Smith—i.e.,* cases where the cause of action is a creature of state law, but an essential element of the claim is federal—"arise under" federal law within the meaning of § 1331. Congress passes laws in order to shape behavior; a federal law expresses Congress' determination that there is a federal interest in having individuals or other entities conform their actions to a particular norm established by that law. Because all laws are imprecise to some degree, disputes inevitably arise over what specifically Congress intended to require or permit. It is the duty of courts to interpret these laws and apply them in such a way that the congressional purpose is realized. * * *

6. * * * One might argue that this Court's appellate jurisdiction over state-court judgments in cases arising under federal law can be depended upon to correct erroneous state-court decisions and to insure that federal law is interpreted and applied uniformly. However, * * * having served on this Court for 30 years, it is clear to me that, realistically, it cannot even come close to "doing the whole job" and that § 1331 is essential if federal rights are to be adequately protected.

B

The only remaining question is whether the assumption that Congress decided not to create a private cause of action alters this analysis in a way that makes it inappropriate to exercise original federal jurisdiction. According to the Court, * * * " 'the increased complexity of federal legislation,' " " 'the increased volume of federal litigation,' " and " 'the desirability of a more careful scrutiny of legislative intent' " [argue against finding federal-question jurisdiction] * * *.

These reasons simply do not justify the Court's holding. Given the relative expertise of the federal courts in interpreting federal law, * * * the increased complexity of federal legislation argues rather strongly in *favor* of recognizing federal jurisdiction. And, while the increased volume of litigation may appropriately be considered in connection with reasoned arguments that justify limiting the reach of § 1331, I do not believe that the day has yet arrived when this Court may trim a statute solely because it thinks that Congress made it too broad.

This leaves only the third reason: " 'the desirability of a more careful scrutiny of legislative intent.' " * * * I certainly subscribe to the proposition that the Court should consider legislative intent in determining whether or not there is jurisdiction under § 1331. But the Court has not examined the purposes underlying either the FDCA or § 1331 in reaching its conclusion that Congress' presumed decision not to provide a private federal remedy under the FDCA must be taken to withdraw federal jurisdiction over a private state remedy that imposes liability for violating the FDCA. Moreover, such an examination demonstrates not only that it is consistent with legislative intent to find that there is federal jurisdiction over such a claim, but, indeed, that it is the Court's contrary conclusion that is inconsistent with congressional intent.

* * * Congress has provided the [Food and Drug Administration ("FDA")] with a wide-ranging arsenal of weapons to combat violations of the FDCA * * *. Significantly, [however,] the FDA has no independent enforcement authority; final enforcement must come from the federal courts, which have exclusive jurisdiction over actions under the FDCA. * * * Thus, while the initial interpretive function has been delegated to an expert administrative body whose interpretations are entitled to considerable deference, final responsibility for interpreting the statute in order to carry out the legislative mandate belongs to the federal courts. * * *

* * *

It may be that a decision by Congress not to create a private remedy is intended to preclude all private enforcement. If that is so, then a state cause of action that makes relief available to private individuals for violations of the FDCA is pre-empted. But if Congress' decision not to provide a private federal remedy does *not* pre-empt such a state remedy, then, in light of the FDCA's clear policy of relying on the federal courts for enforcement, it also should not foreclose federal jurisdiction over that state remedy. * * *

The Court's contrary conclusion requires inferring from Congress' decision not to create a private federal remedy that, while some private enforcement is permissible in state courts, it is "bad" if that enforcement comes from the *federal* courts. But that is simply illogical. * * * [I]f anything, Congress' decision not to create a private remedy *strengthens* the argument in favor of finding federal jurisdiction over a state remedy that is not pre-empted.

NOTES AND QUESTIONS

1. Both Justice Stevens and Justice Brennan attempt to "fit" their *Merrell Dow* opinions within the Court's earlier decisions in *Smith* and *Moore*. Does either succeed? How would you have decided *Merrell Dow* in light of these earlier decisions? In light of the *Shoshone* decision? Have all three cases been overruled to the extent that they express categorical rules, and affirmed to the extent that they turn on a weighing of the federal interests involved?

2. Justice Stevens argues that it would be inconsistent for the Court to find that Congress did not intend for an implied private right of action to exist and, at the same time, to allow the federal court to hear a state-created cause of action addressing the same issue. On this view, the only way the federal court in *Merrell Dow* would have jurisdiction is if Congress had created an express cause of action. How does this differ, if at all, from Justice Holmes' test?

3. Justice Brennan argues that *Merrell Dow* is a case in which federal jurisdiction should exist even though the cause of action is state created. Consider anew whether a state-created claim ever can be said to arise under federal law in light of Justice Holmes' dissent in *Smith*.

> It is evident that the cause of action arises not under any law of the United States but wholly under Missouri law. The defendant is a Missouri corporation and the right claimed is that of a stockholder to prevent the directors from doing an act, that is, making an investment, alleged to be contrary to their duty. But the scope of their duty depends upon the charter of their corporation and other laws of Missouri. If those laws had authorized the investment in terms the plaintiff would have no case, and this seems to me to make manifest what I am unable to deem even debatable, that, as I have said, the cause of action arises wholly under Missouri law. If the Missouri law authorizes or forbids the investment according to the determination of this Court upon a point under the Constitution or acts of Congress, still that point is material only because the Missouri law saw fit to make it so. The whole foundation of the duty is Missouri law, which at its sole will incorporated the other law as it might incorporate a document. The other law or document depends for its relevance and effect not on its own force but upon the law that took it up, so I repeat once more the cause of action arises wholly from the law of the State.

Smith v. Kansas City Title & Trust Co., 255 U.S. at 214, 41 S.Ct. at 250, 65 L.Ed. at 591 (Holmes, J., dissenting).

4. *Merrell Dow* generated a split in the circuits as to whether Section 1331 requires a federal private right of action for the exercise of federal question jurisdiction or whether the presence of a substantial federal issue, embedded in a state cause of action, suffices. The Supreme Court addressed this question in the pair of cases that follow.

GRABLE & SONS METAL PRODUCTS, INC. v. DARUE ENGINEERING & MANUFACTURING

Supreme Court of the United States, 2005.
545 U.S. 308, 125 S.Ct. 2363, 162 L.Ed.2d 257.

Certiorari to the United States Court of Appeals for the Sixth Circuit.

JUSTICE SOUTER delivered the opinion of the Court.

The question is whether want of a federal cause of action to try claims of title to land obtained at a federal tax sale precludes removal to federal court of a state action with nondiverse parties raising a disputed issue of federal title law. We answer no, and hold that the national interest in providing a federal forum for federal tax litigation is sufficiently substantial to support the exercise of federal question jurisdiction over the disputed issue on removal, which would not distort any division of labor between the state and federal courts, provided or assumed by Congress.

I

In 1994, the Internal Revenue Service seized Michigan real property belonging to petitioner Grable & Sons Metal Products, Inc., to satisfy Grable's federal tax delinquency. Title 26 U.S.C. § 6335 required the IRS to give notice of the seizure, and there is no dispute that Grable received actual notice by certified mail before the IRS sold the property to respondent Darue Engineering & Manufacturing. Although Grable also received notice of the sale itself, it did not exercise its statutory right to redeem the property within 180 days of the sale, § 6337(b)(1), and after that period had passed, the Government gave Darue a quitclaim deed, § 6339.

Five years later, Grable brought a quiet title action in state court, claiming that Darue's record title was invalid because the IRS had failed to notify Grable of its seizure of the property in the exact manner required by § 6335(a), which provides that written notice must be "given by the Secretary to the owner of the property [or] left at his usual place of abode or business." Grable said that the statute required personal service, not service by certified mail.

Darue removed the case to Federal District Court as presenting a federal question, because the claim of title depended on the interpretation of the notice statute in the federal tax law. The District Court declined to remand the case at Grable's behest after finding that the "claim does pose a 'significant question of federal law,' " * * * and ruling that Grable's lack of a federal right of action to enforce its claim against Darue did not bar the exercise of federal jurisdiction. On the merits, the court granted summary judgment to Darue, holding that although § 6335 by its terms required personal service, substantial compliance with the statute was enough. * * *

The Court of Appeals for the Sixth Circuit affirmed. * * * On the jurisdictional question, the panel thought it sufficed that the title claim raised an issue of federal law that had to be resolved, and implicated a substantial federal interest (in construing federal tax law). The court went on to affirm the District Court's judgment on the merits. We granted certiorari on the jurisdictional question alone * * * to resolve a split within the Courts of Appeals on whether *Merrell Dow* * * *, [p. 309, supra,] always requires * * * a federal cause of action as a condition for exercising federal-question jurisdiction. We now affirm.

II

Darue was entitled to remove the quiet title action if Grable could have brought it in federal district court originally, 28 U.S.C. § 1441(a), as a civil action "arising under the Constitution, laws, or treaties of the United States," § 1331. This provision for federal-question jurisdiction is invoked by and large by plaintiffs pleading a cause of action created by federal law (e.g., claims under 42 U.S.C. § 1983). There is, however, another longstanding, if less frequently encountered, variety of federal "arising under" jurisdiction, this Court having recognized for nearly 100 years that in certain cases federal-question jurisdiction will lie over state-law claims that implicate significant federal issues. * * * The doctrine captures the commonsense notion that a federal court ought to be able to hear claims recognized under state law that nonetheless turn on substantial questions of federal law, and thus justify resort to the experience, solicitude, and hope of uniformity that a federal forum offers on federal issues, see ALI, Study of the Division of Jurisdiction Between State and Federal Courts 164–166 (1968).

The classic example is *Smith* * * *, [p. 308, supra]. Although Missouri law provided the cause of action, the Court recognized federal-question jurisdiction because the principal issue in the case was the federal constitutionality of the bond issue. * * *

* * * *Smith* * * * has been subject to some trimming to fit earlier and later cases recognizing the vitality of the basic doctrine, but shying away from the expansive view that mere need to apply federal law in a state-law claim will suffice to open the "arising under" door. * * * [Justice Cardozo later explained] that a request to exercise federal-question jurisdiction over a state action calls for a "common-sense accommodation of judgment to [the] kaleidoscopic situations" that present a federal issue, in "a selective process which picks the substantial causes out of the web and lays the other ones aside." *Gully v. First Nat. Bank in Meridian*, 299 U.S. 109, 117–118, 81 L. Ed. 70, 57 S. Ct. 96 (1936). It has in fact become a constant refrain in such cases that federal jurisdiction demands

not only a contested federal issue, but a substantial one, indicating a serious federal interest in claiming the advantages thought to be inherent in a federal forum. [Citations omitted.]

But even when the state action discloses a contested and substantial federal question, the exercise of federal jurisdiction is subject to a possible veto. For the federal issue will ultimately qualify for a federal forum only if federal jurisdiction is consistent with congressional judgment about the sound division of labor between state and federal courts governing the application of § 1331. * * * Because arising-under jurisdiction to hear a state-law claim always raises the possibility of upsetting the state-federal line drawn (or at least assumed) by Congress, the presence of a disputed federal issue and the ostensible importance of a federal forum are never necessarily dispositive; there must always be an assessment of any disruptive portent in exercising federal jurisdiction. * * *

These considerations have kept us from stating a "single, precise, all-embracing" test for jurisdiction over federal issues embedded in state-law claims between nondiverse parties. *Christianson v. Colt Industries Operating Corp.*, 486 U.S. 800, 821, 100 L. Ed. 2d 811, 108 S. Ct. 2166 (1988) (Stevens, J., concurring). We have not kept them out simply because they appeared in state raiment, as Justice Holmes would have done * * * [dissenting in *Smith*, pp. 316–17, supra], but neither have we treated "federal issue" as a password opening federal courts to any state action embracing a point of federal law. Instead, the question is, does a state-law claim necessarily raise a stated federal issue, actually disputed and substantial, which a federal forum may entertain without disturbing any congressionally approved balance of federal and state judicial responsibilities.

III

A

This case warrants federal jurisdiction. Grable's state complaint must specify "the facts establishing the superiority of [its] claim," Mich. Ct. Rule 3.411(B)(2)(c) (West 2005), and Grable has premised its superior title claim on a failure by the IRS to give it adequate notice, as defined by federal law. Whether Grable was given notice within the meaning of the federal statute is thus an essential element of its quiet title claim, and the meaning of the federal statute is actually in dispute; it appears to be the only legal or factual issue contested in the case. The meaning of the federal tax provision is an important issue of federal law that sensibly belongs in a federal court. The Government has a strong interest in the "prompt and certain collection of delinquent taxes," *United States v. Rodgers*, * * * and the ability of the IRS to satisfy its claims from the property of delinquents requires clear terms of notice to allow buyers like Darue to satisfy themselves that the Service has touched the bases necessary for good title. The Government thus has a direct interest in the availability of a federal forum to vindicate its own administrative action, and buyers (as well as tax delinquents) may find it valuable to come before judges used to federal tax matters. Finally, because it will be the rare state title case that raises a contested matter of federal law, federal jurisdiction to resolve genuine disagreement over federal tax title provisions will portend only a microscopic effect on the federal-state division of labor. * * *

* * *

B

Merrell Dow * * *, on which Grable rests its position, is not to the contrary. * * * The Court assumed that federal law would have to be applied to resolve the claim, but after closely examining the strength of the federal interest at stake and the implications of opening the federal forum, held federal jurisdiction unavailable. * * *

Because federal law provides for no quiet title action that could be brought against Darue, Grable argues that there can be no federal jurisdiction here, stressing some broad language in *Merrell Dow* * * * that on its face supports Grable's position * * *. But an opinion is to be read as a whole, and *Merrell Dow* cannot be read whole as overturning decades of precedent, as it would have done by effectively adopting the Holmes dissent in *Smith* * * * and converting a federal cause of action from a sufficient condition for federal-question jurisdiction into a necessary one.

In the first place, *Merrell Dow* disclaimed the adoption of any bright-line rule, as when the Court reiterated that "in exploring the outer reaches of § 1331, determinations about federal jurisdiction require sensitive judgments about congressional intent, judicial power, and the federal system." * * * The opinion included a lengthy footnote explaining that questions of jurisdiction over state-law claims require "careful judgments," * * * about the "nature of the federal interest at stake," * * * (emphasis deleted). And as a final indication that it did not mean to make a federal right of action mandatory, it expressly approved the exercise of jurisdiction sustained in *Smith*, despite the want of any federal cause of action available to *Smith*'s shareholder plaintiff. * * * *Merrell Dow* then, did not toss out, but specifically retained, the contextual enquiry that had been *Smith*'s hallmark for over 60 years. At the end of *Merrell Dow*, Justice Holmes was still dissenting.

Accordingly, *Merrell Dow* should be read in its entirety as treating the absence of a federal private right of action as evidence relevant to, but not dispositive of, the "sensitive judgments about congressional intent" that § 1331 requires. The absence of any federal cause of action affected *Merrell Dow*'s result two ways. The Court saw the fact as worth some consideration in the assessment of substantiality. But its primary importance emerged when the Court treated the combination of no federal cause of action and no preemption of state remedies for misbranding as an important clue to Congress's conception of the scope of jurisdiction to be exercised under § 1331. The Court saw the missing cause of action not as a missing federal door key, always required, but as a missing welcome mat, required in the circumstances, when exercising federal jurisdiction over a state misbranding action would have attracted a horde of original filings and removal cases raising other state claims with embedded federal issues. For if the federal labeling standard without a federal cause of action could get a state claim into federal court, so could any other federal standard without a federal cause of action. And that would have meant a tremendous number of cases.

One only needed to consider the treatment of federal violations generally in garden variety state tort law. "The violation of federal statutes and regulations is commonly given negligence per se effect in state tort proceedings." Restatement (Third) of Torts § 14 Reporters' Note, Comment *a*, p. 195 (Tent. Draft No. 1, March 28, 2001) (hereinafter Restatement). * * * A general rule of exercising federal jurisdiction over state claims resting on federal mislabeling and other statutory violations would thus have heralded a potentially enormous shift of traditionally state cases into federal courts. Expressing concern over the "increased volume of federal litigation," and noting the importance of adhering to "legislative intent," *Merrell Dow* thought it improbable that the Congress, having made no provision for a federal cause of action, would have meant to welcome any state-law tort case implicating federal law "solely because the violation of the federal statute is said to [create] a rebuttable presumption [of negligence] . . . under state law." * * * (internal quotation marks omitted). In this situation, no welcome mat meant keep out. *Merrell Dow*'s analysis thus fits within the framework of examining the importance of having a federal forum for the issue, and the consistency of such a forum with Congress's intended division of labor between state and federal courts.

As already indicated, however, a comparable analysis yields a different jurisdictional conclusion in this case. Although Congress also indicated ambivalence in this case by providing no private right of action to Grable, it is the rare state quiet title action that involves contested issues of federal law * * *. * * * Consequently, jurisdiction over actions like Grable's would not materially affect, or threaten to affect, the normal currents of litigation. Given the absence of threatening structural consequences and the clear interest the Government, its buyers, and its delinquents have in the availability of a federal forum, there is no good reason to shirk from federal jurisdiction over the dispositive and contested federal issue at the heart of the state-law title claim. * * *

IV

The judgment of the Court of Appeals * * * is affirmed.

It is so ordered.

[A concurring opinion by JUSTICE THOMAS stated that "[i]n an appropriate case, I would be willing to consider * * * limiting § 1331 jurisdiction to cases in which federal law creates the cause of action pleaded on the face of the plaintiff's complaint * * *."]

———

EMPIRE HEALTHCHOICE ASSURANCE, INC. v. McVEIGH, 547 U.S. 677, 126 S.Ct. 2121, 165 L.Ed.2d 131 (2006). Joseph McVeigh, a federal employee, was injured and eventually died, allegedly as a result of acts of a third party. Empire Healthchoice Assurance, McVeigh's private insurance carrier, paid substantial sums for McVeigh's medical care. After McVeigh's death, the administrator of McVeigh's estate sued the third party and received a large monetary settlement. Empire then sued McVeigh's estate in federal court to recoup amounts Empire had paid for McVeigh's medical expenses. Empire is under contract with the federal Office of Personnel Management (OPM) to provide insurance coverage to federal workers like McVeigh. The Federal Employees Health Benefits Act of 1959, the federal statute regulating health-benefit plans for federal employees, is silent on whether private carriers can recoup third-party medical payments. However, OPM's contract with Empire requires the carrier to take reasonable steps to make such recoupment, and enrolled employees are informed that if they recover medical expenses from an outside party, they must reimburse the private carrier. The District Court dismissed the case for lack of federal question jurisdiction, and the Court of Appeals for the Second Circuit, by divided vote, affirmed. The Supreme Court granted certiorari on the subject-matter jurisdiction question, and affirmed.

Justice Ginsburg, writing for the Court, observed that Congress had not created a federal right of action allowing insurance carriers to seek reimbursement from beneficiaries in federal court. The Court declined to characterize the insurer's claim as federal, despite "distinctly federal interests," such as negotiation of the OPM master contract by a federal agency; the effect of the contract on the interests of federal employees; and the crediting of reimbursements to a federal fund. Nevertheless, the Court wrote, "countervailing considerations control"—in particular, Congress's conferring of federal jurisdiction over suits involving benefits against the United States, but not over carrier reimbursement claims. "Had Congress found it necessary or proper to extend federal jurisdiction * * *," the Court explained, "it would have been easy enough for Congress to say so." Id. at 696, 126 S.Ct. at 2134–35, 165 L.Ed.2d at 147.

The Court further declined to characterize the claim as arising under federal law simply because federal law forms a necessary element of the claim for relief. To the contrary, the Court emphasized, Empire's claim "does not fit within the special and small category" of state-law claims cognizable in federal court under *Grable*. First, the dispute in *Grable* "centered on the action of a federal agency (IRS) and its compatibility with a federal statute, the question qualified as 'substantial,' and its resolution was both dispositive of the case and would be controlling in numerous other cases." By contrast, Empire's "reimbursement claim was triggered, not by the action of any federal department, agency, or service, but by the settlement of a personal-injury action launched in state court." Second, "*Grable* presented a nearly 'pure issue of law,' one 'that could be settled once and for all and thereafter would govern numerous tax sale cases.'" Empire's claim "is fact-bound and situation-specific," involving such matters as whether there were overcharges or duplicative charges. Finally, even if Empire's claim might raise the legal issue of whether to account for the beneficiary's attorney's fees expended for recovery, "it is hardly apparent why a proper 'federal-state balance' * * * would place such a nonstatutory issue under the complete governance of federal law, to be declared in a federal forum." Id. at 700–01, 126 S.Ct. at 2137, 165 L.Ed.2d at 150.

Justice Breyer's dissent, in which Justices Kennedy, Souter, and Alito joined, emphasized that Empire's claim, because it "is based on the interpretation of a federal contract, * * * should be governed by federal common law," and "federal common law means federal jurisdiction where Congress so intends." Id. at 707–08, 126 S.Ct. at 2141, 165 L.Ed.2d at 154–55. The dissent pointed to three factors indicating that intention. First, the United States is the real party in interest because amounts recovered are credited to a federal fund; second, the need for uniform interpretation is strong because the benefits are provided under a federal program; and third, the reimbursement provision is one of a number of federal contract provisions, "all of which federal courts will interpret and apply (when reviewing the federal agency's resolution of disputes regarding benefits)." The absence of an explicit conferral of jurisdiction over reimbursement claims, Justice Breyer explained, "may reflect inadvertence. Or it may reflect a belief that § 1331 covered such cases regardless." Id. at 709–10, 126 S.Ct. at 2142, 165 L.Ed.2d at 156.

NOTES AND QUESTIONS

1. *Grable* upholds federal jurisdiction over a state cause of action that involves an important issue of federal law and affects the interests of the United States. The carrier's reimbursement claim in *Empire Healthchoice* likewise affects significant federal interests, including the treatment of federal employees and protection of the federal fisc. Why did the Court nevertheless withhold federal question jurisdiction from the reimbursement claim?

2. The dissent in *Empire Healthchoice* emphasizes the role of federal common law in resolving the carrier's reimbursement claim. The topic of federal common law is a complex one and is taken up in Chapter 6, infra.

3. What types of cases should be heard in the federal courts? In formulating your thoughts on the subject, keep in mind that the character of federal litigation has changed dramatically in the past few decades. To a large degree, this stems from a fundamental rethinking of the role of the federal government in assuring justice, allocating judicial resources, and protecting individual rights. Some of these changes have been reflected in legislation

authorizing public or private rights of actions to vindicate statutory policies. For example, the Civil Rights Act of 1964 and the Voting Rights Act of 1965 have spawned a multitude of cases challenging racial and sex-based discrimination; similarly, the Truth in Lending and Fair Credit Reporting Acts exemplify federal statutes that have led to the growth of consumer protection litigation. Other incentives to sue have been generated by judicially recognized private rights of action to enforce federal statutes, and increased sensitivity to due process concerns. Should these developments affect the Court's interpretation of Section 1331?

4. Professor Cohen has argued that the search for "a single, all-purpose, neutral analytical concept which marks out federal question jurisdiction" is futile. He suggests a "pragmatic" test that would include consideration of the extent of the effect on judicial caseload if jurisdiction is recognized, the extent to which a class of cases is likely to turn on issues of state or federal law, the extent to which the federal courts would have expertise in the area, and the extent to which a sympathetic tribunal is necessary. Cohen, *The Broken Compass: The Requirement that a Case Arise "Directly" Under Federal Law*, 115 U. Pa. L. Rev. 890 (1967). See also Shapiro, *Jurisdiction and Discretion*, 60 N.Y.U. L. Rev. 543 (1985). Is this approach consistent with the Court's approach in *Grable* and *Empire Healthchoice*?

SECTION D. THE SUBJECT-MATTER JURISDICTION OF THE FEDERAL COURTS—SUPPLEMENTAL CLAIMS AND PARTIES

Read Art. III, § 2 and 28 U.S.C. § 1367 in the Supplement.

Sometimes a federal court may be asked to decide matters that, if presented independently, would not provide a basis for federal subject-matter jurisdiction. This situation may arise when a plaintiff has multiple claims against a defendant, some of which are federal claims within the federal question jurisdictional grant and others are state-law claims outside the grant. In addition, a plaintiff may have multiple claims against different defendants, all related to the same disputed transaction, but only some have an independent basis for federal jurisdiction. To complicate matters even more, multiple plaintiffs may have multiple claims against multiple defendants, all related to the same disputed transaction, but only some of the claims may have an independent basis for federal jurisdiction. The judicially created doctrines of pendent and ancillary jurisdiction were developed to deal with the jurisdictional issues posed by these different situations (Chapter 9 addresses the procedural rules that allow claims and parties to be joined in one lawsuit). The term "pendent jurisdiction" has been used when the plaintiff, in her complaint, appends a claim lacking an independent basis for federal jurisdiction to a claim possessing such a basis. The term "ancillary jurisdiction" has been used when either a plaintiff or a defendant injects a claim lacking an independent basis for federal jurisdiction by way of a counterclaim, cross-claim, or third-party complaint.

Although the doctrines of ancillary and pendent jurisdiction were spawned from two separate lines of authorities, they became two species of the same generic phenomenon. In 1990, when Congress undertook to codify these doctrines, it gave them the collective name of "supplemental jurisdiction." 28 U.S.C. § 1367. In analyzing these doctrines, consider how Article III limits the scope of supplemental jurisdiction and the policies that ought to govern its exercise.

UNITED MINE WORKERS OF AMERICA v. GIBBS

Supreme Court of the United States, 1966.
383 U.S. 715, 86 S.Ct. 1130, 16 L.Ed.2d 218.

Certiorari to the United States Court of Appeals for the Sixth Circuit.

MR. JUSTICE BRENNAN delivered the opinion of the Court.

Respondent Paul Gibbs was awarded compensatory and punitive damages in this action against petitioner United Mine Workers of America (UMW) for alleged violations of § 303 of the Labor Management Relations Act, 1947, and of the common law of Tennessee. The case grew out of the rivalry between the United Mine Workers and the Southern Labor Union over representation of workers in the southern Appalachian coal fields. Tennessee Consolidated Coal Company, not a party here, laid off 100 miners of the UMW's Local 5881 when it closed one of its mines in southern Tennessee during the spring of 1960. Late that summer, Grundy Company, a wholly owned subsidiary of Consolidated, hired respondent as mine superintendent to attempt to open a new mine on Consolidated's property at nearby Gray's Creek through use of members of the Southern Labor Union. As part of the arrangement, Grundy also gave respondent a contract to haul the mine's coal to the nearest railroad loading point.

On August 15 and 16, 1960, armed members of Local 5881 forcibly prevented the opening of the mine, threatening respondent and beating an organizer for the rival union. The members of the local believed Consolidated had promised them the jobs at the new mine; they insisted that if anyone would do the work, they would. * * * George Gilbert, the UMW's field representative for the area including Local 5881, * * * [had] explicit instructions from his international union superiors to establish a limited picket line, to prevent any further violence, and to see to it that the strike did not spread to neighboring mines. There was no further violence at the mine site * * *.

Respondent lost his job as superintendent, and never entered into performance of his haulage contract. He testified that he soon began to lose other trucking contracts and mine leases he held in nearby areas. Claiming these effects to be the result of a concerted union plan against him, he sought recovery not against Local 5881 or its members, but only against petitioner, the International. The suit was brought in the United States District Court for the Eastern District of Tennessee, and jurisdiction was premised on allegations of secondary boycotts under § 303. The state law claim, for which jurisdiction was based upon the doctrine of pendent jurisdiction, asserted "an unlawful conspiracy and an unlawful boycott aimed at him and [Grundy] to maliciously, wantonly and willfully interfere with his contract of employment and with his contract of haulage."

* * * The jury's verdict was that the UMW had violated both § 303 and state law. Gibbs was awarded $60,000 as damages under the employment contract and $14,500 under the haulage contract; he was also awarded $100,000 punitive damages. On motion, the trial court set aside the award of damages with respect to the haulage contract on the ground that damage was unproved. It also held that union pressure on Grundy to discharge respondent as supervisor would constitute only a primary dispute with Grundy, as respondent's employer, and hence was not cognizable under § 303. Interference with employment was cognizable as a state claim, however, and a remitted award was sustained on the state law claim. * * * The Court of Appeals for the Sixth Circuit affirmed. * * * We granted certiorari. * * *

I

A threshold question is whether the District Court properly entertained jurisdiction of the claim based on Tennessee law. * * *

* * * The Court held in Hurn v. Oursler, 289 U.S. 238, 53 S.Ct. 586, 77 L.Ed. 1148, that state law claims are appropriate for federal court determination if they form a separate but parallel ground for relief also sought in a substantial claim based on federal law. The Court distinguished permissible from non-permissible exercises of federal judicial power over state law claims by contrasting "a case where two distinct grounds in support of a single cause of action are alleged, one only of which presents a federal question, and a case where two separate and distinct causes of action are alleged, one only of which is federal in character. In the former, where the federal question averred is not plainly wanting in substance, the federal court, even though the federal ground be not established, may nevertheless retain and dispose of the case upon the nonfederal *ground;* in the latter it may not do so upon the nonfederal *cause of action.*" 289 U.S., at 246, 53 S.Ct., at 589. The question is into which category the present action fell.

Hurn was decided in 1933, before the unification of law and equity by the Federal Rules of Civil Procedure. At the time, the meaning of "cause of action" was a subject of serious dispute * * *. The Court in *Hurn* identified what it meant by the term by citation of Baltimore S.S. Co. v. Phillips, 274 U.S. 316, 47 S.Ct. 600, 71 L.Ed. 1069, a case in which "cause of action" had been used to identify the operative scope of the doctrine of *res judicata.* In that case the Court had noted that " 'the whole tendency of our decisions is to require a plaintiff to try his whole cause of action and his whole case at one time,' " 274 U.S., at 320, 47 S.Ct., at 602, and stated its holding in the following language, quoted in part in the *Hurn* opinion:

> Upon principle, it is perfectly plain that the respondent [a seaman suing for an injury sustained while working aboard ship] suffered but one actionable wrong, and was entitled to but one recovery, whether his injury was due to one or the other of several distinct acts of alleged negligence, or to a combination of some or all of them. In either view, there would be but a single wrongful invasion of a single primary right of the plaintiff, namely, the right of bodily safety, whether the acts constituting such invasion were one or many, simple or complex.
>
> A cause of action does not consist of facts, but of the unlawful violation of a right which the facts show. The number and variety of the facts alleged do not establish more than one cause of action so long as their result, whether they be considered severally or in combination, is the violation of but one right by a single legal wrong. The mere multiplication of grounds of negligence alleged as causing the same injury does not result in multiplying the causes of action. "The facts are merely the means, and not the end. They do not constitute the cause of action, but they show its existence by making the wrong appear." Id., at 321.

Had the Court found a jurisdictional bar to reaching the state claim in *Hurn,* we assume that the doctrine of *res judicata* would not have been applicable in any subsequent state suit. But the citation of *Baltimore S.S. Co.* shows that the Court found that the weighty policies of judicial economy and fairness to parties reflected in *res judicata* doctrine were in themselves strong counsel for the adoption of a rule which would permit federal courts to dispose of the state as well as the federal claims.

With the adoption of the Federal Rules of Civil Procedure and the unified form of action * * * much of the controversy over "cause of action" abated. The phrase remained as the keystone of the *Hurn* test, however, and * * * has been the source of considerable confusion. Under the Rules, the impulse is toward entertaining the broadest possible scope of action consistent with fairness to the parties; joinder of claims, parties and remedies are strongly encouraged. Yet because the *Hurn* question involves issues of jurisdiction as well as convenience, there has been some tendency to limit its application to cases in which the state and federal claims are, as in *Hurn,* "little more than the equivalent of different epithets to characterize the same group of circumstances." 289 U.S., at 246, 53 S.Ct. at 590.

This limited approach is unnecessarily grudging. Pendent jurisdiction, in the sense of judicial *power,* exists whenever there is a claim "arising under [the] Constitution, the Laws of the United States, and Treaties made, or which shall be made, under their Authority * * *," U.S. Const., Art. III, § 2, and the relationship between that claim and the state claims made in the complaint permits the conclusion that the entire action before the court comprises but one constitutional "case." The federal claim must have substance sufficient to confer subject matter jurisdiction on the court. * * * The state and federal claims must derive from a common nucleus of operative fact. But if, considered without regard for their federal or state character, a plaintiff's claims are such that he would ordinarily be expected to try them all in one judicial proceeding, then, assuming substantiality of the federal issues, there is *power* in federal courts to hear the whole.

That power need not be exercised in every case in which it is found to exist. It has consistently been recognized that pendent jurisdiction is a doctrine of discretion, not of plaintiff's right. Its justification lies in considerations of judicial economy, convenience and fairness to litigants; if these are not present a federal court should hesitate to exercise jurisdiction over state claims, even though bound to apply state law to them, Erie R. Co. v. Tompkins * * * [p. 408, infra]. Needless decisions of state law should be avoided both as a matter of comity and to promote justice between the parties, by procuring for them a surer-footed reading of applicable law. Certainly, if the federal claims are dismissed before trial, even though not insubstantial in a jurisdictional sense, the state claims should be dismissed as well. Similarly, if it appears that the state issues substantially predominate, whether in terms of proof, of the scope of the issues raised, or of the comprehensiveness of the remedy sought, the state claims may be dismissed without prejudice and left for resolution to state tribunals. There may, on the other hand, be situations in which the state claim is so closely tied to questions of federal policy that the argument for exercise of pendent jurisdiction is particularly strong. In the present case, for example, the allowable scope of the state claim implicates the federal doctrine of pre-emption; while this interrelationship does not create statutory federal question jurisdiction, Louisville & N.R. Co. v. Mottley, [p. 299, supra.] * * * its existence is relevant to the exercise of discretion. Finally, there may be reasons independent of jurisdictional considerations, such as the likelihood of jury confusion in treating divergent legal theories of relief, that would justify separating state and federal claims for trial, Fed.Rule Civ.Proc. 42(b). If so, jurisdiction should ordinarily be refused.

The question of power will ordinarily be resolved on the pleadings. But the issue whether pendent jurisdiction has been properly assumed is one which remains open throughout the litigation. Pretrial procedures or even the trial may reveal a substantial hegemony of state law claims, or likelihood of jury confusion, which could not have been anticipated at the pleading stage. Although it will of course be appropriate to take account in this circumstance of the already completed course of the litigation, dismissal of the state claim might even then be merited. For example, it may appear that the plaintiff was well aware of the nature of his proofs and the relative importance of his claims; recognition of a federal court's wide latitude to decide ancillary questions of state law does not imply that it must tolerate a litigant's effort to impose upon it what is in effect only a state law case. Once it appears that a state claim constitutes the real body of a case, to which the federal claim is only an appendage, the state claim may fairly be dismissed.

We are not prepared to say that in the present case the District Court exceeded its discretion in proceeding to judgment on the state claim. * * *

It is true that the § 303 claims ultimately failed and that the only recovery allowed respondent was on the state claim. We cannot confidently say, however, that the federal issues were so remote or played such a minor role at the trial that in effect the state claim only was tried. Although the District Court dismissed as unproved the claims that petitioner's secondary activities included attempts to induce coal operators other than Grundy to cease doing business with respondent, the court submitted the § 303 claims relating to Grundy to the jury. The jury returned verdicts against petitioner on those § 303 claims, and it was only on petitioner's motion for a directed verdict and a judgment *n.o.v.* that the verdicts on those claims were set aside. * * * Although there was some risk of confusing the jury in joining the state and federal claims—especially since, as will be developed, differing standards of proof of UMW involvement applied—the possibility of confusion could be lessened by employing a special verdict form, as the District Court did. * * *

[The Court went on to hold that the plaintiff could not recover damages for conspiracy under Tennessee common law on the basis of the record.]

Reversed.

THE CHIEF JUSTICE took no part in the decision of this case.

[A concurring opinion by JUSTICE HARLAN, joined by JUSTICE CLARK, is omitted.]

NOTES AND QUESTIONS

1. To what extent are Hurn v. Oursler and United Mine Workers of America v. Gibbs inconsistent with the notion that the subject-matter jurisdiction of the federal courts is limited by Article III of the Constitution and whatever enabling legislation Congress chooses to enact?

2. Convenience and judicial administration, although admirable goals, do not inevitably override basic tenets regarding the distribution of judicial business in a federal system. Are pendent and ancillary jurisdiction necessary to ensure the integrity of the federal courts? Consider the following:

> * * * [T]he exercise of pendent jurisdiction must be judged by whether it furthers some federal policy. Measured by that test pendent jurisdiction serves two purposes. First, it ensures that litigants will not be dissuaded from maintaining their federal rights in a federal court solely because they can dispose of all claims by one litigation in the state but not the federal forum. When jurisdiction over the federal claim is exclusive in the federal judiciary, only pendent jurisdiction makes possible a complete remedy for vindication of the plaintiff's rights. Second, assuming that the

litigants are in a federal forum, pendent jurisdiction serves the interest of avoiding piecemeal litigation, thus promoting judicial economy and greater expedition for the litigants.

Note, *The Evolution and Scope of the Doctrine of Pendent Jurisdiction in the Federal Courts*, 62 Colum.L.Rev. 1018, 1044 (1962). See also McManamon, *Dispelling the Myths of Pendent and Ancillary Jurisdiction: The Ramifications of a Revised History*, 46 Wash. & Lee L.Rev. 863 (1989). Are you convinced by these arguments?

3. *Gibbs* confirmed a species of federal jurisdiction already recognized in *Hurn*. The aspect of *Hurn* that caused the most interpretive difficulty was the requirement that the state and federal claims merely be two distinct grounds of a "single cause of action" rather than "two separate and distinct causes of action." "Gibbs confirmed that 'causes of action' are unimportant and established the correct inquiry to be simply whether in a broad sense there is fact relatedness." Note, *UMW v. Gibbs and Pendent Jurisdiction*, 81 Harv.L.Rev. 657, 659 (1968).

4. Should the considerations of judicial economy and party convenience underlying pendent subject-matter jurisdiction also allow the court to assert "pendent" personal jurisdiction over the defendant for the purposes of adjudicating a nonfederal claim in circumstances in which the court would not have adjudicative authority over the defendant on that claim standing alone? See p. 195 supra. For example, if jurisdiction over defendant has been effected pursuant to a federal statute providing for nationwide service of process, but defendant would not be subject to process in the forum state for purposes of the joined state claim, must the court dismiss the latter? See Rice v. Nova Biomedical Corp., 763 F.Supp. 961 (N.D.Ill.1991). See also Note, *Pendent Personal Jurisdiction and Nationwide Service of Process,* 64 N.Y.U. L. Rev. 113 (1989).

NOTE ON PENDENT AND ANCILLARY JURISDICTION FOLLOWING GIBBS

In the years following *Gibbs*, the expansion of federal substantive law placed similar pressures on pendent and ancillary jurisdiction. In *Gibbs,* plaintiff joined related federal and state claims against a single nondiverse defendant, and pendent jurisdiction was exercised over the state-law claim. Courts also began to consider whether pendent jurisdiction could be justified in cases in which plaintiff files a federal claim against one defendant and a state-law claim against a different nondiverse defendant. In a series of cases, the Supreme Court considered whether "pendent party" jurisdiction is constitutionally permissible given the absence of an explicit statutory grant of such power.

1. ALDINGER v. HOWARD, 427 U.S. 1, 96 S.Ct. 2413, 49 L.Ed.2d 276 (1976), involved a suit by a citizen of Washington against several officers of Spokane County, Washington, alleging violations of the federal Civil Rights Act, 42 U.S.C. § 1983. Plaintiff sought to join the county itself as an additional defendant, but under the construction given the federal statute at

the time, counties were not considered to be subject to it.[c] Therefore, plaintiff was forced to sue the county under state law and argue that a federal court could hear her claim under its pendent jurisdiction, despite the absence of diversity, since her two claims met the *Gibbs* "common nucleus of operative fact" test. The Supreme Court rejected the argument and distinguished *Gibbs* on two grounds:

> * * * From a purely factual point of view, it is one thing to authorize two parties, already present in federal court by virtue of a case over which the court has jurisdiction, to litigate in addition to their federal claim a state-law claim over which there is no independent basis of federal jurisdiction. But it is quite another thing to permit a plaintiff, who has asserted a claim against one defendant with respect to which there is federal jurisdiction, to join an entirely different defendant on the basis of a state-law claim over which there is no independent basis of federal jurisdiction, simply because his claim against the first defendant and his claim against the second defendant "derive from a common nucleus of operative fact." * * * True, the same considerations of judicial economy would be served * * *. But the addition of a completely new party would run counter to the well-established principle that federal courts, as opposed to state trial courts of general jurisdiction, are courts of limited jurisdiction marked out by Congress. * * *
>
> There is also a significant legal difference. In * * * *Gibbs* Congress was silent on the extent to which the defendant, already properly in federal court under a statute, might be called upon to answer nonfederal questions or claims; the way was thus left open for the Court to fashion its own rules under the general language of Art. III. But the extension of *Gibbs* to this kind of "pendent party" jurisdiction—bringing in an additional defendant at the behest of the plaintiff—presents rather different statutory jurisdictional considerations. Petitioner's contention that she should be entitled to sue Spokane County as a new third party, and then to try a wholly state-law claim against the county, all of which would be "pendent" to her federal claim against respondent county treasurer, must be decided, not in the context of congressional silence or tacit encouragement, but in quite the opposite context. The question here, which it was not necessary to address in *Gibbs* * * *, is whether by virtue of the statutory grant of subject matter jurisdiction, upon which petitioner's principal claim against the treasurer rests, Congress has addressed itself to the *party* as to whom jurisdiction pendent to the principal claim is sought. And it undoubtedly has done so.
>
> * * *
>
> Resolution of a claim of pendent-party jurisdiction, therefore, calls for careful attention to the relevant statutory language. As we have indicated, we think a fair reading of the language used in [the relevant statutes] * * * requires a holding that the joinder of a municipal corporation, like the county here, for purposes of asserting a state-law claim not within

---

c. Municipalities and other governmental units have since been held to be amenable to suit under the Civil Rights Act. See Monell v. Dep't of Soc. Servs., 436 U.S. 658, 98 S.Ct. 2018, 56 L.Ed.2d 611 (1978).

federal diversity jurisdiction, is without the statutory jurisdiction of the district court.

Id. at 14–17, 96 S.Ct. at 2420–22, 49 L.Ed.2d at 286–88.

The Court in *Aldinger* carefully refused to lay down any "sweeping pronouncement upon the existence or exercise of [pendent party] jurisdiction":

> * * * Other statutory grants and other alignments of parties and claims might call for a different result. When the grant of jurisdiction to a federal court is exclusive, for example, as in the prosecution of tort claims against the United States * * *, the argument of judicial economy and convenience can be coupled with the additional argument that *only* in a federal court may all of the claims be tried together. * * *

Id. at 18, 96 S.Ct. at 2422, 49 L.Ed.2d at 288–89. District courts also were instructed that before they can conclude that pendent party jurisdiction existed, they must ask if "Congress in the statutes conferring jurisdiction has not expressly or by implication negated its existence." Id. at 18, 96 S.Ct. at 2422, 49 L.Ed.2d at 289.

2. OWEN EQUIPMENT & ERECTION CO. v. KROGER, 437 U.S. 365, 98 S.Ct. 2396, 57 L.Ed.2d 274 (1978), concerned the availability of federal jurisdiction in a case in which one of the asserted claims was within the district court's diversity jurisdiction and the other was not. Kroger, a citizen of Iowa, sued Omaha Public Power District (OPPD), a Nebraska corporation, for the wrongful death of her husband, who had been electrocuted when the beam of a steel crane, next to which he was walking, came too close to a high-tension electric line. Kroger brought the action in federal district court in Nebraska based on diversity of citizenship, alleging that OPPD's negligent operation of the power line had caused her husband's death. OPPD, in turn, filed a third-party complaint pursuant to Federal Rule 14(a) against Owen Equipment and Erection Company, alleging that the crane was owned and operated by Owen, and that it was Owen's negligence that had been the proximate cause of the decedent's death.

Plaintiff was allowed to amend her complaint to name Owen as a defendant, which she alleged was a Nebraska corporation with its principal place of business in Nebraska. OPPD requested, and was granted, summary judgment, leaving Owen as the sole defendant. During the course of the trial, it was discovered that Owen's principal place of business actually was in Iowa.[d] As a result, Owen moved to dismiss the case based on a lack of subject-matter jurisdiction. The District Court denied the motion and the Court of Appeals affirmed. The Supreme Court, however, reversed in an opinion by Justice Stewart:

> It is apparent that *Gibbs* delineated the constitutional limits of judicial power. * * * Constitutional power[, however,] is merely the first hurdle

d. The problem concerned the Missouri River, which generally marks the boundary between Iowa and Nebraska. Carter Lake, Iowa, where the accident occurred and where Owen had its main office, lies west of the river, adjacent to Omaha, Nebraska. Apparently, the river had avulsed at one of its bends, cutting Carter Lake off from the rest of Iowa. See Oakley, *The Story of* Owen Equipment v. Kroger: *A Change in the Weather of Federal Jurisdiction*, in Civil Procedure Stories 81–134 (Clermont ed.)(2d ed. 2008).

that must be overcome in determining that a federal court has jurisdiction over a particular controversy. For the jurisdiction of the federal courts is limited not only by the provisions of Art. III of the Constitution, but by Acts of Congress. * * *

That statutory law as well as the Constitution may limit a federal court's jurisdiction over nonfederal claims is well illustrated by * * * Aldinger v. Howard * * *. * * * The *Aldinger* * * * [case] make[s] clear that a finding that federal and nonfederal claims arise from a "common nucleus of operative fact," the test of *Gibbs,* does not end the inquiry into whether a federal court has power to hear the nonfederal claims along with the federal ones. Beyond this constitutional minimum, there must be an examination of the posture in which the nonfederal claim is asserted and of the specific statute that confers jurisdiction over the federal claim, in order to determine whether "Congress in [that statute] has * * * expressly or by implication negated" the exercise of jurisdiction over the particular nonfederal claim. * * *

The relevant statute in this case, 28 U.S.C. § 1332(a)(1), * * * and its predecessors have consistently been held to require complete diversity of citizenship. * * * Over the years Congress has repeatedly re-enacted or amended the statute conferring diversity jurisdiction, leaving intact this rule of complete diversity. Whatever may have been the original purposes of diversity-of-citizenship jurisdiction, this subsequent history clearly demonstrates a congressional mandate that diversity jurisdiction is not to be available when any plaintiff is a citizen of the same State as any defendant. * * *

Thus it is clear that the respondent could not originally have brought suit in federal court naming Owen and OPPD as codefendants, since citizens of Iowa would have been on both sides of the litigation. Yet the identical lawsuit resulted when she amended her complaint. Complete diversity was destroyed just as surely as if she had sued Owen initially. * * * [U]nder the reasoning of the Court of Appeals in this case, a plaintiff could defeat the statutory requirement of complete diversity by the simple expedient of suing only those defendants who were of diverse citizenship and waiting for them to implead nondiverse defendants. * * *

* * *

It is not unreasonable to assume that, in generally requiring complete diversity, Congress did not intend to confine the jurisdiction of federal courts so inflexibly that they are unable to protect legal rights or effectively to resolve an entire, logically entwined lawsuit. Those practical needs are the basis of the doctrine of ancillary jurisdiction. But neither the convenience of litigants nor considerations of judicial economy can suffice to justify extension of the doctrine of ancillary jurisdiction to a plaintiff's cause of action against a citizen of the same State in a diversity case. Congress has established the basic rule that diversity jurisdiction exists * * * only when there is complete diversity of citizenship. * * * To allow the requirement of complete diversity to be circumvented as it was in this case would simply flout the congressional command.

Id. at 371–74, 377, 98 S.Ct. at 2401–03, 2404, 57 L.Ed.2d at 280–82, 284.

3. FINLEY v. UNITED STATES, 490 U.S. 545, 109 S.Ct. 2003, 104 L.Ed.2d 593 (1989), addressed the availability of pendent party jurisdiction when one of the claims was within the exclusive jurisdiction of the federal court and the other was a state-law claim against a nondiverse defendant. Plaintiff's husband and two of her children were killed when their plane struck electric power lines on its approach to a city-run airfield in San Diego, California. Plaintiff alleged that the Federal Aviation Administration had been negligent in its operation and maintenance of the runway lights and in its performance of air traffic control functions, and invoked jurisdiction under 28 U.S.C. § 1346(b). Later, plaintiff was allowed to amend her complaint to include state-law tort claims against both the city of San Diego and the utility company that maintained the power lines. The Court of Appeals reversed the District Court's decision to allow the amendment, and the Supreme Court affirmed:

> * * * It remains rudimentary law that "[a]s regards all courts of the United States inferior to this tribunal, two things are necessary to create jurisdiction, whether original or appellate. The Constitution must have given to the court the capacity to take it, *and an act of Congress must have supplied it* * * *. To the extent that such action is not taken, the power lies dormant." The Mayor v. Cooper, 73 U.S. (6 Wall.) 247, 252, 18 L.Ed. 851 (1868) (emphasis added) * * *.
>
> Despite this principle, in a line of cases by now no less well established we have held, without specific examination of jurisdictional statutes, that federal courts have "pendent" claim jurisdiction * * * to the full extent permitted by the Constitution. Mine Workers v. Gibbs * * *. * * * Analytically, petitioner's case is fundamentally different from *Gibbs* in that it brings into question what has become known as pendent-*party* jurisdiction, that is, jurisdiction over parties not named in any claim that is independently cognizable by the federal court. We may assume, without deciding, that the constitutional criterion for pendent-party jurisdiction is analogous to the constitutional criterion for pendent-claim jurisdiction, and that petitioner's state-law claims pass that test. Our cases show, however, that with respect to the addition of parties, as opposed to the addition of only claims, we will not assume that the full constitutional power has been congressionally authorized, and will not read jurisdictional statutes broadly. * * *
>
> * * *
>
> * * * The FTCA, § 1346(b), confers jurisdiction over "civil actions on claims against the United States." It does not say "civil actions on claims that include requested relief against the United States," nor "civil actions in which there is a claim against the United States"—formulations one might expect if the presence of a claim against the United States constituted merely a minimum jurisdiction requirement, rather than a definition of the permissible scope of FTCA actions. Just as the statutory provision "between * * * citizens of different States" has been held to mean citizens of different States and no one else, * * * so also here we

conclude that "against the United States" means against the United States and no one else. * * *

* * *

As we noted at the outset, our cases do not display an entirely consistent approach with respect to the necessity that jurisdiction be explicitly conferred. The *Gibbs* line of cases was a departure from prior practice, and a departure that we have no intent to limit or impair. But *Aldinger* indicated that the *Gibbs* approach would not be extended to the pendent-party field, and we decide today to retain that line. Whatever we say regarding the scope of jurisdiction conferred by a particular statute can of course be changed by Congress. What is of paramount importance is that Congress be able to legislate against a background of clear interpretive rules, so that it may know the effect of the language it adopts. All our cases * * * have held that a grant of jurisdiction over claims involving particular parties does not itself confer jurisdiction over additional claims by or against different parties. Our decision today reaffirms that interpretive rule; the opposite would sow confusion.

Id. at 547–49, 552, 556, 109 S.Ct. at 2005–07, 2008, 2010, 104 L.Ed.2d at 600–01, 603–04, 606.

In dissent, Justice Stevens characterized the Court's holding as a major departure from its earlier decision in Aldinger v. Howard:

In *Aldinger,* we adopted a rule of construction that assumed the existence of pendent jurisdiction unless "Congress in the statutes conferring jurisdiction has * * * expressly or by implication negated its existence" * * *. We rejected the assertion of pendent-party jurisdiction there because it arose "not in the context of congressional silence or tacit encouragement, but in quite the opposite context." * * * Congress' exclusion of municipal corporations from the definition of persons under § 1983, we concluded, evinced an intent to preclude the exercise of federal-court jurisdiction over them. If congressional silence were sufficient to defeat pendent jurisdiction, the careful reasoning in our *Aldinger* opinion was wholly unnecessary, for obviously the civil rights statutes do not affirmatively authorize the joinder of any state-law claims.

* * *

The Court today adopts a sharply different approach. Without even so much as acknowledging our statement in *Aldinger* that before a federal court may exercise pendent party jurisdiction it must satisfy itself that Congress "has not expressly or by implication negated its existence," * * * it now instructs that "a grant of jurisdiction over claims involving particular parties does not itself confer jurisdiction over additional claims by or against different parties." * * *

Id. at 573, 574–75, 109 S.Ct. at 2019–20, 104 L.Ed.2d at 617, 618 (Stevens, J., dissenting).

Read 28 U.S.C. § 1367 in the Supplement.

Consider whether the District Court has power to exercise supplemental jurisdiction in the following circumstances:

> J.E. Dunn Construction Co. hired Sunset Security, Inc. to provide security for one of its construction sites. Sunset Security employed Susanne Massey as a security guard. While on duty, Massey contacted the Kansas City, Missouri Policy Department and reported that she had been assaulted at the site. A month later, the police showed Massey a photographic lineup of possible assailants, and she chose Fentress Wilson as the person who had assaulted her. Wilson was subsequently arrested and incarcerated for 311 days before being released. He was never tried. Wilson sued the Kansas City Police in federal district court under 28 U.S.C. § 1983 for a violation of his civil rights and also asserted a state law claim for malicious prosecution. Wilson included in his complaint a state law claim against J.E. Dunn, alleging that defendant was negligent in hiring Sunset Security. Wilson is a citizen of Missouri; J.E. Dunn is incorporated in Texas and has its principal place of business in Missouri.

Adapted from: Wilson v. Massey, 2009 WL 537559 (W.D.Mo. 2009).

> Rebuffed by his insurance company when a landowner sued him for cutting down her trees, David Yates, a logger, and various insurance entities filed suits in state and federal courts. State National Insurance Co. filed a diversity action in federal district court seeking a declaratory judgment that Yates's liability insurance policy did not provide Yates with coverage. Yates counterclaimed against State National for breach of contract and bad faith breach of contract and also asserted claims against an additional party, the local agent, Bruce Insurance Agency, for professional negligence and negligent misrepresentation. All parties agree that Bruce is a necessary party required to be joined under Federal Rule 19. State National is a Texas citizen, and Yates and Bruce are both citizens of Mississippi.

Adapted from: State National Ins. Co. v. Yates, 391 F.3d 577, 578–79 (5th Cir. 2004).

NOTES AND QUESTIONS

1. Section 1367(a) defines supplemental jurisdiction as including claims that "form part of the same case or controversy." It generally is accepted that Congress intended the *Gibbs* test to define what constitutes a "case or controversy" under the statute. Section 1367, however, does not refer to "common nucleus of operative fact" and instead uses the term "related."

Professor Fletcher contends "that the constitutional test for supplemental jurisdiction is broader than the 'common nucleus of operative fact' test" and uses "the example of an unrelated claim for defensive set-off" to test his argument. See Fletcher, *"Common Nucleus of Operative Fact" and Defensive Set–Off: Beyond the* Gibbs *Test*, 74 Ind. L.J. 171 (1998).

2. Does supplemental jurisdiction extend to a permissive counterclaim? As you will learn in Chapter 9, infra, a permissive counterclaim is not transactionally related to plaintiff's claim and so probably does not share with it a "common nucleus of operative fact." Before the enactment of Section 1367, a permissive counterclaim was assumed to require an independent basis of subject-matter jurisdiction in federal court, and at least some circuits have applied this same limitation to Section 1367. The Court of Appeals for the First Circuit in IGLESIAS v. MUTUAL LIFE INSURANCE, CO. OF NEW YORK, 156 F.3d 237, 241 (1st Cir.1998), emphasized that "[o]nly compulsory counterclaims can rely upon supplemental jurisdiction; permissive counterclaims require their own jurisdictional basis." However, in JONES v. FORD MOTOR CREDIT CO., 358 F.3d 205 (2d Cir.2004), the Court of Appeals for the Second Circuit held that Section 1367 "displaced, rather than codified, * * * the earlier view * * * that a permissive counterclaim requires independent jurisdiction (in the sense of federal question or diversity jurisdiction)." Id. at 213–14. In *Jones*, the complaint alleged racially discriminatory lending practices in violation of federal law. Defendant counterclaimed to recover the plaintiffs' unpaid state-law loans. The Court of Appeals found that Section 1367(a) was satisfied, but remanded to let the District Court decide whether to exercise its discretion under Section 1367(c). Are you convinced that the jurisdictional concept of "so related" completely overlaps with the test for permissive counterclaims? See Floyd, *Three Faces of Supplemental Jurisdiction After the Demise of United Mine Workers v. Gibbs*, 60 Fla.L.Rev. 277 (2008).

3. Section 1367(b) restricts supplemental jurisdiction in diversity cases when plaintiff seeks to assert claims against nondiverse parties. If P, from Virginia, sues D, from Texas, can D implead a third-party defendant from Texas? From Virginia? Can P assert claims against a third-party defendant from Virginia? See Oakley, Kroger *Redux*, 51 Duke L.J. 663 (2001).

4. Section 1367 allows a federal court to exercise discretion in deciding to retain or to dismiss state-law claims when the federal basis for an action drops away. Does that discretion also apply to diversity cases in which the amount in controversy drops below the jurisdictional requirement? In SHANAGHAN v. CAHILL, 58 F.3d 106 (4th Cir.1995), plaintiff brought a diversity action to recover from defendant three separate debts, in the amounts of $40,000, $23,696, and $14,700. The District Court granted summary judgment for defendant on the $40,000 claim and dismissed the remaining claims, noting that the amount in controversy had fallen below $50,000, the then-applicable requirement. On appeal, the Fourth Circuit ruled that, when the federal basis for an action disappears, a court is free to decide whether to assert jurisdiction over the remaining claims, in accordance with Section 1367. It went on to hold that similar discretion exists when the amount in controversy falls below the statutory minimum. How does this ruling compare to the *St. Paul Mercury* test, discussed p. 289, supra? See Wolde–Meskel v.

Vocational Instruction Project Community Services, Inc., 166 F.3d 59, 64–65 (2d Cir.1999) (rejecting *Shanaghan* for confusing "(i) state-law claims that are supplemental to claims within the court's original jurisdiction (which are covered by 28 U.S.C. § 1367 and heard at the court's discretion), with (ii) state-law claims that are aggregated to satisfy the amount-in-controversy requirement for diversity (which are within the court's original jurisdiction)").

Section 1367(b), which applies when the District Court exercises original jurisdiction under the diversity jurisdiction statute, 28 U.S.C. § 1332, generated a number of questions involving application of the amount-in-controversy requirement to supplemental claims and parties. In particular, courts and commentators disagreed as to whether Section 1367(b) codified or changed the judicial rules that had developed governing the aggregation of claims for diversity jurisdiction, see pp. 290–91, supra, and whether *Zahn*, barring aggregation of claims by unnamed class members, continued in force, see p. 291, supra. The Supreme Court resolved this issue in the following case.

EXXON MOBIL CORP. v. ALLAPATTAH SERVICES, INC.

Supreme Court of the United States, 2005.
545 U.S. 546, 125 S.Ct. 2611, 162 L.Ed.2d 502.

Certiorari to the United States Courts of Appeals for the First and Eleventh Circuits.

JUSTICE KENNEDY delivered the opinion of the Court.

These consolidated cases present the question whether a federal court in a diversity action may exercise supplemental jurisdiction over additional plaintiffs whose claims do not satisfy the minimum amount-in-controversy requirement, provided the claims are part of the same case or controversy as the claims of plaintiffs who do allege a sufficient amount in controversy. Our decision turns on the correct interpretation of 28 U.S.C. § 1367. The question has divided the Courts of Appeals, and we granted certiorari to resolve the conflict. * * *

We hold that, where the other elements of jurisdiction are present and at least one named plaintiff in the action satisfies the amount-in-controversy requirement, § 1367 does authorize supplemental jurisdiction over the claims of other plaintiffs in the same Article III case or controversy, even if those claims are for less than the jurisdictional amount specified in the statute setting forth the requirements for diversity jurisdiction. We affirm the judgment of the Court of Appeals for the Eleventh Circuit in [*Allapattah Services, Inc. v. Exxon Corp.*, 333 F.3d 1248 (11th Cir.2003)] * * *, and we reverse the judgment of the Court of Appeals for the First Circuit in *Ortega v. Star–Kist Foods, Inc.*, 370 F.3d 124 (1st Cir.2004) * * *.

I

* * * [Allapattah, a diversity action filed in the Northern District of Florida, involved claims by a class of about 10,000 car dealers that they had been systematically overcharged by defendant for fuel purchases. Following a unanimous jury verdict in favor of the plaintiffs, the District Court certified the case for interlocutory review on the question of whether supplemental jurisdiction was appropriately exercised over the claims of class members who did not meet the amount-in-controversy requirement of diversity jurisdiction. The Court of Appeals for the Eleventh Circuit upheld the exercise of jurisdiction under Section 1367, emphasizing that original jurisdiction existed over the claims of at least one of the class representatives.

Ortega, a diversity action filed in the District of Puerto Rico, involved a personal injury claim by a child. Plaintiff's family joined the action seeking damages for emotional distress and certain medical expenses. The District Court dismissed the action. The Court of Appeals for the First Circuit found that the injured child had alleged jurisdictionally sufficient damages, but that supplemental jurisdiction could be exercised] "only when the district court has original jurisdiction over the action, and that in a diversity case original jurisdiction is lacking if one plaintiff fails to satisfy the amount-in-controversy requirement. Although the Court of Appeals claimed to 'express no view' on whether the result would be the same in a class action, * * * its analysis is inconsistent with that of the Court of Appeals for the Eleventh Circuit. * * *

II

* * *

All parties to this litigation and all courts to consider the question agree that § 1367 overturned the result in *Finley* [, p. 334, supra]. There is no warrant, however, for assuming that § 1367 did no more than to overrule *Finley* and otherwise to codify the existing state of the law of supplemental jurisdiction. * * *

* * * The single question before us * * * is whether a diversity case in which the claims of some plaintiffs satisfy the amount-in-controversy requirement, but the claims of other plaintiffs do not, presents a "civil action of which the district courts have original jurisdiction." If the answer is yes, § 1367(a) confers supplemental jurisdiction over all claims, including those that do not independently satisfy the amount-in-controversy requirement, if the claims are part of the same Article III case or controversy. If the answer is no, § 1367(a) is inapplicable and * * * the district court has no statutory basis for exercising supplemental jurisdiction over the additional claims.

We now conclude the answer must be yes. When the well-pleaded complaint contains at least one claim that satisfies the amount-in-controversy requirement, and there are no other relevant jurisdictional defects, the district court, beyond all question, has original jurisdiction over that claim. The presence of other claims in the complaint, over which the district court may lack original jurisdiction, is of no moment. If the court has original jurisdiction over a single claim in the complaint, it has original jurisdiction over a "civil action" within the meaning of § 1367(a), even if the civil action over which it has jurisdiction comprises fewer claims than were included in the complaint. Once the court determines it has original jurisdiction over the civil action, it can turn to the question whether it has a constitutional and statutory basis for exercising supplemental jurisdiction over the other claims in the action.

* * *

If § 1367(a) were the sum total of the relevant statutory language, our holding would rest on that language alone. The statute, of course, instructs us to examine § 1367(b) to determine if any of its exceptions apply, so we proceed to that section. While § 1367(b) qualifies the broad rule of § 1367(a), it does not withdraw supplemental jurisdiction over the claims of the additional parties at issue here. * * * The natural, indeed the necessary, inference is that § 1367 confers supplemental jurisdiction over claims by Rule 20 and Rule 23 plaintiffs. This inference, at least with respect to Rule 20 plaintiffs, is strengthened by the fact that § 1367(b) explicitly excludes supplemental jurisdiction over claims against defendants joined under Rule 20.

We cannot accept the view * * * that a district court lacks original jurisdiction over a civil action unless the court has original jurisdiction over every claim in the complaint. As we understand this position, it requires assuming either that all claims in the complaint must stand or fall as a single, indivisible "civil action" as a matter of definitional necessity—what we will refer to as the "indivisibility theory"—or else that the inclusion of a claim or party falling outside the district court's original jurisdiction somehow contaminates every other claim in the complaint, depriving the court of original jurisdiction over any of these claims—what we will refer to as the "contamination theory."

The indivisibility theory is easily dismissed, as it is inconsistent with the whole notion of supplemental jurisdiction. If a district court must have original jurisdiction over every claim in the complaint in order to have "original jurisdiction" over a "civil action," then in *Gibbs* there was no civil action of which the district court could assume original jurisdiction under § 1331, and so no basis for exercising supplemental jurisdiction over any of the claims. The indivisibility theory is further belied by our practice—in both federal-question and diversity cases—of allowing federal courts to cure jurisdictional defects by dismissing the offending parties rather than dismissing the entire action. * * * If the presence of jurisdictionally problematic claims in the complaint meant the district court was without original jurisdiction over the single, indivisible civil action before it, then the district court would have to dismiss the whole action rather than particular parties.

* * *

The contamination theory * * * can make some sense in the special context of the complete diversity requirement because the presence of nondiverse parties on both sides of a lawsuit eliminates the justification for providing a federal forum. The theory, however, makes little sense with respect to the amount-in-controversy requirement, which is meant to ensure that a dispute is sufficiently important to warrant federal-court attention. The presence of a single nondiverse party may eliminate the fear of bias with respect to all claims, but the presence of a claim that falls short of the minimum amount in controversy does nothing to reduce the importance of the claims that do meet this requirement.

It is fallacious to suppose, simply from the proposition that § 1332 imposes both the diversity requirement and the amount-in-controversy requirement, that the contamination theory germane to the former is also relevant to the latter. There is no inherent logical connection between the amount-in-controversy requirement and § 1332 diversity jurisdiction. After all, federal-question jurisdiction once had an amount-in-controversy requirement as well. If such a requirement were revived under § 1331, it is clear beyond peradventure that § 1367(a) provides supplemental jurisdiction over federal-question cases where some, but not all, of the federal-law claims involve a sufficient amount in controversy. * * *

* * *

We also reject the argument * * * that while the presence of additional claims over which the district court lacks jurisdiction does not mean the civil action is outside the purview of § 1367(a), the presence of additional parties does. * * * Section 1367(a) applies by its terms to any civil action of which the district courts have original jurisdiction, and the last sentence of § 1367(a) expressly contemplates that the court may have supplemental jurisdiction over additional parties. So it cannot be the case that the presence of those parties destroys the court's original jurisdiction, within the meaning of § 1367(a), over a civil action otherwise properly before it. Also, § 1367(b) expressly withholds supplemental jurisdiction in diversity cases over claims by plaintiffs joined * * * under Rule 19. If joinder of such parties were sufficient to deprive the district court of original jurisdiction over the civil action within the meaning of § 1367(a), this specific limitation on supplemental jurisdiction in § 1367(b) would be superfluous. The argument that the presence of additional parties removes the civil action from the scope of § 1367(a) also would mean that § 1367 left the *Finley* result undisturbed. * * * Yet all concede that one purpose of § 1367 was to change the result reached in *Finley*.

Finally, it is suggested that our interpretation of § 1367(a) creates an anomaly regarding the exceptions listed in § 1367(b): It is not immediately obvious why Congress would withhold supplemental jurisdiction over plaintiffs joined as parties "needed for just adjudication" under Rule 19 but would allow supplemental jurisdiction over plaintiffs permissively joined under Rule 20. [Rule 19 now refers to a "required party."] The omission of Rule 20 plaintiffs from the list of exceptions in § 1367(b) may have been * * * [unintentional]. If that is the case, it is up to Congress rather than the courts to fix it. An alternative explanation for the different treatment of Rule 19 and Rule 20 is that Congress was concerned that extending supplemental jurisdiction to Rule 19 plaintiffs would allow circumvention of the complete diversity rule: A nondiverse plaintiff might be omitted intentionally from the original action, but joined later under Rule 19 * * *. * * * The contamination theory described above, if applicable, means this ruse would fail, but Congress may have wanted to make assurance double sure. More generally, Congress may have concluded that federal jurisdiction is only appropriate if the district court would have original jurisdiction over the claims of all those plaintiffs who are so essential to the action that they could be joined under Rule 19.

* * *

And so we circle back to the original question. When the well-pleaded complaint in district court includes multiple claims, all part of the same case or controversy, and some, but not all, of the claims are within the court's original jurisdiction, does the court have before it "any civil action of which the district courts have original jurisdiction"? It does. Under § 1367, the court has original jurisdiction over the civil action comprising the claims for which there is no jurisdictional defect. * * * Though the special nature and purpose of the diversity requirement mean that a single nondiverse party can contaminate every other claim in the lawsuit, the contamination does not occur with respect to jurisdictional defects that go only to the substantive importance of individual claims.

* * * We hold that § 1367 by its plain text overruled * * * *Zahn* [, p. 291, supra,] and authorized supplemental jurisdiction over all claims by diverse parties arising out of the same Article III case or controversy * * *.

* * *

D

* * *

The judgment of the Court of Appeals for the Eleventh Circuit is affirmed. The judgment of the Court of Appeals for the First Circuit is reversed, and the case is remanded for proceedings consistent with this opinion.

It is so ordered.

[A dissenting opinion by JUSTICE STEVENS is omitted.]

JUSTICE GINSBURG dissented, joined by JUSTICE STEVENS, JUSTICE O'CONNOR, and JUSTICE BREYER.

[The dissent rejected the view that Section 1367 overruled *Zahn* and abrogated the nonaggregation rule for determining the amount in controversy under Section 1332. Rather, a district court has "original jurisdiction" under Section 1367(a) only if the complaint meets both the complete diversity rule and "the decisions restricting aggregation to arrive at the amount in controversy." If original jurisdiction is not present, supplemental jurisdiction is not authorized. This view, the dissent maintained, "accounts for the omission of Rule 20 plaintiffs and Rule 23 class actions in § 1367(b)'s text":

> * * * [I]f one recognizes that the nonaggregation rule * * * forms part of the determination whether "original jurisdiction" exists in a diversity case, * * * then plaintiffs who do not meet the amount-in-controversy requirement would fail at the § 1367(a) threshold. Congress would have no reason to resort to a § 1367(b) exception to turn such plaintiffs away from federal court * * *.

Id. at 589–92, 125 S.Ct. at 2638–39, 162 L.Ed.2d at 539–42.]

EXECUTIVE SOFTWARE NORTH AMERICA, INC. v. UNITED STATES DISTRICT COURT FOR THE CENTRAL DISTRICT OF CALIFORNIA

United States Court of Appeals, Ninth Circuit, 1994.
24 F.3d 1545.

D.W. NELSON, CIRCUIT JUDGE.

Executive Software North America, Inc., Craig Jensen, and Sally Jensen ("Petitioners") petition this court for a writ of mandamus to compel the United States District Court for the Central District of California to retain jurisdiction over certain pendent state law claims filed in an employment discrimination suit against them by the plaintiff-real-party-in-interest, Donna Page. * * * For the reasons stated below, we grant the writ, but on narrower grounds than urged by the parties.

Factual and Procedural Background

On April 8, 1993, Donna Page filed a complaint in state court against the petitioners. She claimed to have experienced several acts of discrimination during her employment with Executive Software. Specifically, Page, a black female, alleged that the company required all of its employees to study the teachings of the Church of Scientology written by L. Ron Hubbard. Page contends that when she refused to comply, she was charged with having made a number of errors in her work, and that when she attempted to contest the charges she was denied an opportunity to do so and was terminated. Page further asserts that the charges and subsequent termination were a mere "subterfuge for illegal discrimination against non believers in the Church of Scientology, women and racial minorities."

In her complaint, Page alleged two federal causes of action, (1) a claim under Title VII, 42 U.S.C. § 2000(e) *et seq.* (1988), and (2) a claim under 42 U.S.C. § 1983 (1988), as well as three state-law causes of action, including (1) a claim for unlawful religious and racial discrimination under the California Fair Employment and Housing Act ("FEHA"), * * * (2) a claim of wrongful termination in violation of the California Constitution, Art. I § 7(a), and (3) a claim for negligent supervision.

Based on the two federal claims, the defendants removed the action to federal court. Subsequently, on May 20, 1993, the district court issued an order *sua sponte* to show cause why the three state-law claims should not be remanded to state court. The court stated that "jurisdiction over the state claims depends upon whether this Court exercises its discretion to retain [them]," and admonished the parties to consider that "the Supreme Court defined the parameters of a federal court's supplemental jurisdiction in *United Mine Workers v. Gibbs* * * *." After noting the requirements set forth in *Gibbs* for exercising supplemental jurisdiction, the Court added:

> Even if [the *Gibbs* test is] met, however, a federal court has discretion to decline jurisdiction over state law claims if, for instance, the state claims substantially predominate, the state claims involve novel or complex issues of state law, trial of the state and federal claims together is likely to result in jury confusion, or retention of the state claims requires the expenditure of substantial additional judicial time and effort. * * *
>
> The Removing Party(ies) [in original] should also be aware that this Court does not interpret the 1990 enactment of Section 1367 as restricting the discretionary factors set forth in *Gibbs*. Rather, this Court interprets Section 1367 as merely allowing this Court, at its discretion, to exercise jurisdiction over supplemental parties, which was previously foreclosed by *Finley v. United States* * * *.

The district court thereafter remanded the three state law claims, but provided no reasons.

* * *

A. *Did the District Court Commit Clear Error?*

The district court provided no reasons for its remand. However, in its Show Cause Order, the court stated that it did not "interpret Section 1367 as restricting the discretionary factors set forth in *Gibbs*. * * * "

We find this interpretation of section 1367 erroneous. It is clear that, once it is determined that the assertion of supplemental jurisdiction is permissible under sections 1367(a) and (b), section 1367(c) provides the only valid basis upon which the district court may decline jurisdiction and remand pendent claims. Moreover, we conclude that although subsections (c)(1)–(3) appear to codify most preexisting applications of the *Gibbs* doctrine, subsection (c)(4), which also permits a court to decline jurisdiction when, "in exceptional circumstances, there are other compelling reasons," channels the district court's discretion to identify new grounds for declining jurisdiction more particularly than did preexisting doctrine.

Accordingly, we conclude the district court erred to the extent that it relied on a basis for remanding pendent claims not permitted under section 1367(c). Finally, we conclude that, because the district court failed to articulate reasons for its remand of the pendent claims, we cannot determine whether the district court relied on a statutory ground and exercised its discretion in a permissible manner. Consequently, we conclude that the district court clearly erred.

* * *

[The court's historical discussion is omitted.]

2. The Relationship of Section 1367(c) to Gibbs

* * *

a.

Section 1367 retains the basic division, reflected in *Gibbs,* between the power of a court to entertain a pendent claim and the authority of a court, in its discretion, to decline to exercise that power. However, Congress, in codifying supplemental jurisdiction, has chosen to codify as well the discretionary factors that warrant declining jurisdiction. Section 1367(a) * * * confers power to entertain supplemental jurisdiction in mandatory terms. By use of the word "shall," the statute makes clear that if power is conferred under section 1367(a), and its exercise is not prohibited by section 1367(b), a court can decline to assert supplemental jurisdiction over a pendent claim only if one of the four categories specifically enumerated in section 1367(c) applies. * * *

By selecting this statutory structure, it is clear that Congress intended section 1367(c) to provide the exclusive means by which supplemental jurisdiction can be declined by a court. Not only is this conclusion supported by the legislative history, * * * but a contrary reading of the statute would appear to render section 1367(c) superfluous. Accordingly, unless a court properly invokes a section 1367(c) category in exercising its discretion to decline to entertain pendent claims, supplemental jurisdiction must be asserted. * * *

b.

A consequence of the statutory structure chosen by Congress is that section 1367(c) somewhat changes the nature of the *Gibbs* discretionary inquiry. Although * * * *Gibbs* and its progeny identified a number of concrete instances in which declining pendent jurisdiction normally would be appropriate, the ultimate inquiry for the courts remained whether the assertion of pendent jurisdiction "[best accommodates] the values of economy convenience, fairness and comity." * * * Application of these underlying values to circumstances not identified in prior cases was not only contemplated, but demanded. * * *

The statute, however, channels the application of the underlying values to a greater degree than the *Gibbs* regime, although section 1367(c) continues to recognize the doctrine's dynamic aspects. Subsections (c)(1)–(c)(3) appear to codify concrete applications of the underlying *Gibbs* values recognized in preexisting case law. * * *

By codifying preexisting applications of *Gibbs* in subsections (c)(1)–(3), however, it is clear that Congress intended the exercise of discretion to be triggered by the court's identification of a factual predicate that corresponds to one of the section 1367(c) categories. Once that factual predicate is identified, the exercise of discretion, of course, still is informed by whether remanding the pendent state claims comports with the underlying objective of "most sensibly accommodat[ing]" the values of "economy, convenience, fairness, and comity." * * *

We believe that the "catchall" * * * provided by subsection (c)(4) should be interpreted in a similar manner. Subsection (c)(4) permits a discretionary remand of pendent claims when "*in exceptional circumstances,* there are *other compelling reasons* for declining jurisdiction." * * * Congress's use of the word "other" to modify "compelling reasons" indicates that what ought to qualify as "compelling reasons" for declining jurisdiction under subsection (c)(4) should be of the same nature as the reasons that gave rise to the categories listed in subsections (c)(1)–(3). Because, as discussed above, the subsection (c)(1)–(3) fact patterns constitute situations in which the underlying *Gibbs* values ordinarily will "point toward" declining jurisdiction, * * * we believe that "compelling reasons" for the purposes of subsection (c)(4) similarly should be those that lead a court to conclude that declining jurisdiction "best accommodate[s] the values of economy, convenience, fairness, and comity." * * *

By providing that an exercise of discretion under subsection 1367(c)(4) ought to be made only in "exceptional circumstances" Congress has sounded a note of caution that the bases for declining jurisdiction should be extended beyond the circumstances identified in subsections (c)(1)–(3) only if the circumstances are quite unusual. In short, although we find that "other compelling reasons" clearly refers the district court back to the subsection (c)(1)–(3) categories, and thus requires the court to balance the underlying values that they embody, we think "exceptional circumstances" requires an additional inquiry.

Of course, when the balance of the *Gibbs* values indicates that there are "compelling reasons" to decline jurisdiction, the underlying circumstances that inform this calculus usually will demonstrate how the circumstances confronted are "exceptional." We do not believe, however, this always will be the case. Even when a court's balancing of the *Gibbs* values provides, in its judgment, "compelling reasons" for declining jurisdiction, it might still be the case that the differences between the case it is confronting and the case in which supplemental jurisdiction is appropriate are not sufficient to justify the conclusion that the court would, in fact, be applying subsection (c)(4) properly. We think that it clear from the language chosen by Congress, however, that declining jurisdiction outside of subsection (c)(1)–(3) should be the exception, rather than the rule. Courts therefore must ensure that the reasons identified as "compelling" are not deployed in circumstances that threaten this principle. The inquiry is not particularly burdensome. A court simply must articulate why the circumstances of the case are exceptional in addition to inquiring whether the balance of the *Gibbs* values provide compelling reasons for declining jurisdiction in such circumstances.

We think this interpretation is compelled not only by our understanding of the meaning of the term "other" in subsection (c)(4) and a commonsense understanding of "exceptional," but also by the statutory structure of section 1367(c). As discussed above, the subsection (c)(1)–(3) categories require both the presence of a factual predicate that triggers the exercise of discretion and a case-specific analysis of whether the *Gibbs* values would be best served by declining jurisdiction. Our interpretation of subsection (c)(4) carries forward this structure into that subsection: the court must identify the predicate that triggers the applicability of the category (the exceptional circumstances), and then determine whether, in its judgment, the underlying *Gibbs* values are best served by declining jurisdiction in the particular case (the compelling reasons).

* * *

Therefore, to the extent that *Gibbs* and [its progeny] were interpreted as permitting courts to extend the doctrine's underlying values beyond previously recognized applications *whenever* doing so was consistent with those values, * * * we believe that section 1367(c)(4) more carefully channels courts' discretion by requiring the court to identify how the circumstances that it confronts, and in which it believes the balance of the *Gibbs* values provides "compelling reasons" for declining jurisdiction, are "exceptional."

* * *

c.

With the above analysis providing the necessary conceptual foundation, we conclude that the district court clearly erred. The court, although acknowledging section 1367(c), stated that it did not rely on the statute, but *Gibbs*. Although this might be insignificant if the Show Cause Order indicated that the court considered only the codified applications of *Gibbs* enumerated therein, the court further intimated that *Gibbs* permitted it to decline jurisdiction when "retention of the state claims [would] require[ ] the expenditure of substantial judicial time and effort." If this statement was intended to go beyond preexisting applications of *Gibbs* by invoking its underlying values, it was an impermissible attempt. More fundamentally, as discussed above, subsection (c)(4) requires the district court not only to determine if consideration of the *Gibbs* values provides compelling reasons for a remand, but also to articulate how the circumstances that warrant declining jurisdiction are exceptional. * * *

* * *

For the above reasons, the writ of mandamus is granted, and the remand order entered by the district court shall be vacated.

LEAVY, CIRCUIT JUDGE, dissenting:

* * *

The record does not suggest that the court relied on any ground or factor not mentioned in its order to show cause. Because the court made no findings, we do not know which one or more of the grounds it relied on. On that basis alone, however, the majority concludes that the district court may have relied on a ground not enumerated in section 1367(c); that this was in error, and not only error, but *clear error* for the purpose of mandamus. I cannot join the majority's reasoning to the effect that our inability to find that the court did not err puts it in *clear error*.

Grounds one and two, suggested in the order to show cause, are mentioned in section 1367(c)(1) and (2). Ground three, jury confusion, in my view would be a sufficiently compelling reason for remand, as would the fourth ground, "the expenditure of substantial additional judicial time and effort."

The district court committed no error unless it relied on an unauthorized ground in exercising its discretion to remand. The court did not say that it relied on an unauthorized ground nor does the record tell us that it did, unless the majority means to hold that likely jury confusion or the expenditure of substantial additional judicial time are not exceptional circumstances in which compelling reasons for declining jurisdiction can be found. The fact that the district court does not interpret the 1990 enactment of section 1367 as restricting the discretionary factors set forth in *Gibbs* is of no moment unless we can say that the trial court exceeded its lawful authority wherever it may be found.

* * *

According to *Gibbs,* the justification for pendent jurisdiction lies in considerations of judicial economy, convenience, and fairness to litigants. Congress chose to except from section 1367(a) those cases that were to be remanded under section 1367(c). * * * The sentence that Congress used to confer jurisdiction excepts from its scope those claims over which the district court may decline to exercise jurisdiction. The statute does not say that the court shall "exercise" jurisdiction. * * *

Just as the doctrine of supplemental jurisdiction itself is justified by considerations of judicial economy, convenience, and fairness to litigants, * * * so should a federal court "consider and weigh in each case, and at every stage of the litigation, the values of judicial economy, convenience, fairness, and comity in order to decide whether to exercise jurisdiction over a case brought in that court involving pendent state-law claims." * * *

NOTES AND QUESTIONS

1. On what basis may a district court decline to exercise jurisdiction under Section 1367 and remand supplemental claims? Do you agree with the statement in *Executive Software* that "section 1367(c) provides the only valid basis upon which a district court may decline jurisdiction and remand pendent claims," p. 344, supra? The federal courts have not spoken consistently on this point.

> One group of appellate courts gives the district courts unlimited discretion to decline supplemental jurisdiction despite the mandatory grant of supplemental jurisdiction in § 1367(a). This group views § 1367 as a codification of Gibbs with no change to the law occurring with the enactment of the statute. * * *
>
> The other group of appellate courts fall into the category of severely constrained discretion. This group views § 1367 as narrowing the district courts' discretion from the Gibbs standard.

Hinkle, *The Revision of 28 U.S.C. § 1367(c) and the Debate over the District Court's Discretion To Decline Supplemental Jurisdiction*, 69 Tenn. L. Rev. 111, 120 (2001). One commentator recommends that Congress amend Section 1367 to establish a strong presumption in favor of supplemental jurisdiction "whenever Article III requirements are met." Bone, *Revisiting the Policy Case for Supplemental Jurisdiction*, 74 Ind. L.J. 139, 150 (1998).

2. Does the enactment of Section 1367 mean that there no longer can be any judicially created jurisdiction not provided for by statute? In KOKKONEN v. GUARDIAN LIFE INSURANCE CO. OF AMERICA, 511 U.S. 375, 114 S.Ct. 1673, 128 L.Ed.2d 391 (1994), plaintiff sued in federal court to enforce a settlement agreement that resolved a prior federal action. Defendant challenged jurisdiction on the ground that the District Court lost jurisdiction after it entered an order dismissing the prior litigation. The Supreme Court, without citing Section 1367, held that federal courts have "ancillary jurisdiction" to enforce their decrees and orders; however, in this particular case, the Court agreed with defendant that jurisdiction was lacking because the District Court had not made compliance with the settlement agreement a condition of dismissal. A number of lower courts have followed *Kokkonen* in locating an equitable, common-law ancillary enforcement jurisdiction. See Alexandria Resident Council, Inc. v. Alexandria Redevelopment & Housing Authority, 218 F.3d 307 (4th Cir.2000) (discussing the distinction between statutory supplemental jurisdiction and equitable ancillary jurisdiction); United States v. Alpine Land & Reservoir Co., 174 F.3d 1007 (9th Cir.1999). For a discussion of *Kokkonen*, see Green, *Justice Scalia and Ancillary Jurisdiction: Teaching a Lame Duck New Tricks in Kokkonen v. Guardian Life Insurance Company of America*, 81 Va.L.Rev. 1631 (1995).

3. Section 1367 has generated criticism and suggested revisions. In 2004, the American Law Institute, as part of the Federal Judicial Code Project, approved a final draft of an amendment to the statute. See ALI,

Federal Code Revision Project, Tent. Draft No. 2. Professor Shapiro has argued that the scope of supplemental jurisdiction is "a matter best left to 'common law' development" and that Congress simply should "enact a statute establishing the principle of supplemental jurisdiction, and then * * * leave all or most of the details to be worked out by the courts." See Shapiro, *Supplemental Jurisdiction: A Confession, An Avoidance, and a Proposal*, 74 Ind. L.J. 211, 218 (1998). What are the advantages and disadvantages of this approach?

SECTION E. THE SUBJECT-MATTER JURISDICTION OF THE FEDERAL COURTS—REMOVAL

Read 28 U.S.C. §§ 1441, 1442, 1443, 1445, 1453, 1446, and 1447 in the Supplement.

Removal jurisdiction gives a defendant who has been sued in a state court the right to veto plaintiff's forum choice by transferring the action to federal court, but generally "only if the federal court would have had jurisdiction to entertain the case if the plaintiff had chosen to go there originally." Yackle, Federal Courts 155 (3d ed. 2009). One commentator argues that removal "serves as a necessary device to ensure that plaintiffs alone do not decide which cases federal courts hear." See Haiber, *Removing the Bias Against Removal*, 53 Cath. U.L. Rev. 609, 611 (2004). Other commentators, however, refer to removal as an "anomalous jurisdiction, giving a defendant, sued in a court of competent jurisdiction, the right to elect a forum of its own choosing." Wright & Kane, Law of Federal Courts § 38 (6th ed. 2002).

Although Article III of the Constitution does not explicitly refer to removal jurisdiction, Congress has authorized this power since the Judiciary Act of 1789. The justification for removal jurisdiction is in part rooted in equality concerns:

> In a case involving parties of diverse citizenship, removal protects a nonresident defendant against any local bias that might be encountered in the state court because of the defendant being a "foreigner." In a case involving a claim raising an issue of federal law, removal equalizes the ability of both parties to have a federal question litigated in its "natural" forum.

Friedenthal, Kane & Miller, Civil Procedure § 2.11 (4th ed. 2005). Removal jurisdiction also serves the parties' strategic goals:

> While fear of local prejudice and the notion that state judges are not competent to adjudicate federal questions originally drove defendants

> to remove cases, in modern times, removal is driven more by strategic concerns. Defendants assess things such as jury verdicts, trial rules and procedure, and the availability, caseload and personality of federal judges in making the decision of whether to remove a case to federal court.

Reggio, *Removal and Remand: A Guide to Navigating Between the State and Federal Courts*, 23 Miss. L. Rev. 97, 98 (2004).

The current removal statute, 28 U.S.C. § 1441, traces to the Judiciary Act of 1875 and amendments enacted in 1887. See Collins, *The Unhappy History of Federal Question Removal*, 71 Iowa L. Rev. 717 (1986). In addition to the general removal statute, Congress has enacted specific removal statutes to deal with particular federal claims or federal parties. See, e.g., 28 U.S.C. § 1442 (removal of actions by federal officers); 28 U.S.C. § 1443 (removal of civil rights cases); 28 U.S.C. § 1453 (removal of interstate class actions). Congress also has provided that certain claims may not be removed to the federal courts. See, e.g., 28 U.S.C. § 1445 (actions against railroads under the Federal Employers' Liability Act). For an extensive discussion of removal jurisdiction, see 14B Wright, Miller & Cooper, Federal Practice and Procedure: Jurisdiction and Related Matters 3d § 3721.

SHAMROCK OIL & GAS CORP. v. SHEETS, 313 U.S. 100, 105–09, 61 S.Ct. 868, 871–72, 85 L.Ed. 1214, 1217–19 (1941), presented the question whether a plaintiff could remove a state court action to the federal courts because defendant had interposed a counterclaim. Justice Stone, writing for a unanimous Court, held no:

> Section 12 of the Judiciary Act of 1789 * * * declared that "if a suit be commenced in any state court against an alien * * * or * * * against a citizen of another state, and the matter in dispute exceeds" the jurisdictional amount "and the defendant shall, at the time of entering his appearance in such state court, file a petition for the removal of the cause," it shall be removable to the circuit court. In West v. Aurora City, 6 Wall. 139, 18 L.Ed. 819, this Court held that removal of a cause from a state to a federal court could be effected under § 12 only by a defendant against whom the suit is brought by process served upon him. Consequently a non-citizen plaintiff in the state court, against whom the citizen-defendant had asserted in the suit a claim by way of counterclaim which, under state law, had the character of an original suit, was not entitled to remove the cause. The Court ruled that the plaintiff, having submitted himself to the jurisdiction of the state court, was not entitled to avail himself of a right of removal conferred only on a defendant who has not submitted himself to the jurisdiction.

> By § 3 of the Act of 1875 * * * the practice on removal was greatly liberalized. It authorized "either party, or any one or more of the plaintiffs or defendants entitled to remove any suit" from the state court to do so upon petition in such suit to the state court "before or at the term at which said cause could be first tried and before the trial thereof." These provisions were continued until the adoption of the provisions of the present statute so far as now material by the Act of 1887 * * *.
>
> We cannot assume that Congress, in thus revising the statute, was unaware of the history which we have just detailed, or certainly that it regarded as without significance the omission from the earlier act of the phrase "either party," and the substitution for it of the phrase authorizing removal by the "defendant or defendants" in the suit, or the like omission of the provision for removal at any time before the trial, and the substitution for it of the requirement that the removal petition be filed by the "defendant" at or before the time he is required to plead in the state court.
>
> * * *
>
> Not only does the language of the Act of 1887 evidence the Congressional purpose to restrict the jurisdiction of the federal courts on removal, but the policy of the successive acts of Congress regulating the jurisdiction of federal courts is one calling for the strict construction of such legislation. * * *

NOTES AND QUESTIONS

1. A plaintiff generally is considered to be the master of his complaint, and may choose to avoid removal from state court to federal court by pleading only state law claims or by joining parties who will destroy diversity jurisdiction. However, this rule is subject to exceptions. Recall that the "artful pleading" doctrine prevents a plaintiff from disguising a federal cause of action as a state law claim. See p. 303, supra. In addition, certain causes of action are so exclusively federal in character that even if the plaintiff does not plead them, they will completely preempt any state cause of action that the plaintiff does plead and will provide a basis for removal. See Avco Corp. v. Aero Lodge No. 735, 390 U.S. 557, 88 S.Ct. 1235, 20 L.Ed.2d 126 (1968). Similarly, a plaintiff cannot defeat diversity jurisdiction by fraudulently joining a defendant against whom the plaintiff has no cause of action. See Percy, *Making a Federal Case of It: Removing Civil Cases to Federal Court Based on Fraudulent Joinder*, 91 Iowa L. Rev. 189 (2005).

2. Section 1441(b) permits a defendant to remove a federal-question action when plaintiff has commenced it in a state court of competent jurisdiction and presumably is content to have it adjudicated in a local forum. What public interest does this removal option serve? Is defendant's right of removal consistent with the denial of original or removal jurisdiction when plaintiff anticipates or defendant raises a federal defense, as in the *Mottley* case, p. 299,

supra? Should the filing of a counterclaim that raises a federal law question against a plaintiff in a state court action give that plaintiff a right to remove?

The same provision also prevents a defendant from removing an action that could be filed as an original matter in federal court under the diversity statute if that party is "a citizen of the State in which such action is brought." What is the rationale for this limitation? Is it consistent with the fact that plaintiffs are allowed to file diversity cases in federal courts in states where they are citizens?

3. After defendant removes an action that could have been filed as an original matter in federal court under the diversity statute, can plaintiff amend her complaint to ask for less than the jurisdictional amount in an attempt to destroy the federal court's jurisdiction? See St. Paul Mercury Indem. Co. v. Red Cab Co., 303 U.S. 283, 58 S.Ct. 586, 82 L.Ed. 845 (1938). Is it permissible for plaintiff to seek recovery for "no more than $75,000" in order to defeat defendant's right of removal? See Capps v. New Jellico Coal Co., 87 F.Supp. 369 (E.D.Tenn.1950). Is removal precluded if the amount in controversy is not apparent from the face of the plaintiff's complaint? For a discussion of the jurisdictional amount in the context of removal, see 14C Wright, Miller & Cooper, Federal Practice and Procedure: Jurisdiction and Related Matters 3d § 3725.

4. What motivates defendants to remove cases? Do you think that removal affects a party's likelihood of success? An empirical study by Professors Clermont and Eisenberg finds that plaintiffs win less often in cases that are removed to federal court than in cases that are filed in federal court as an original matter. These commentators observe: "Removal of civil cases from state to federal court results in a precipitous drop in the plaintiffs' win rate. * * * [T]he overall win rate in federal civil cases in 57.97%, but in the subset of those cases that have been removed the win rate is only 36.77%." Clermont & Eisenberg, *Do Case Outcomes Really Reveal Anything About the Legal System? Win Rates and Removal Jurisdiction*, 83 Cornell L. Rev. 581, 581 (1998). What factors other than forum selection might explain this win-loss disparity?

5. Generally, all defendants, other than nominal parties, must join in the petition for removal. See Chicago, R.I. & P. Ry. Co. v. Martin, 178 U.S. 245, 20 S.Ct. 854, 44 L.Ed. 1055 (1900). The exception is when removal is on the basis of a separate and independent claim, see p. 356, infra. Why should removal otherwise require consent of all defendants?

6. Section 1441(e) provides special removal rules for multiparty "single accident" actions that can be heard in federal court under the minimal-diversity jurisdiction of Section 1369. See Adomeit, *The Station Nightclub Fire and Federal Jurisdictional Reach: The Multidistrict, Multiparty, Multiforum Jurisdiction Act of 2002*, 25 W. New Eng. L. Rev. 243, 250–51 (2003). The removal provision is designed to encourage consolidation of all related claims arising from an accident in which at least 75 individuals die:

> The removal amendment permits a defendant to remove an action to federal court if the action could have been brought originally in federal district court under § 1369. The second part of the measure provides an exception to the traditional removal rule by permitting removal if the

> action could have been brought under § 1369 "in whole or in part" and arises from the same accident, even if the action could not have been brought in federal district court as an original matter. * * * The legislative history reveals that the removal amendment is meant to allow parties to join actions currently in state courts to cases pending in federal court. In addition, the removal amendment exempts § 1369 removal actions from the traditional requirements, which include the consent of all defendants and, in diversity cases, restrictions on defendants' citizenship.

Offenbacher, Note—*The Multiparty, Multiforum Trial Jurisdiction Act: Opening the Door to Class Action Reform*, 23 Rev. Litig. 177, 194–95 (2004).

Special removal procedures also now exist for "interstate class actions" that can be heard in federal court under the minimal-diversity, $5 million amount-in-controversy requirements of Section 1332(d)(1). Section 1453, enacted as part of the Class Action Fairness Act of 2005 ("CAFA"), see p. 276, supra, provides for the removal of interstate class actions to federal court "without regard to whether any defendant is a citizen of the State in which the action is brought, except that such action may be removed by any defendant without the consent of all defendants." Like the new diversity jurisdiction provision itself, "[t]hese new provisions are very complicated and detailed and undoubtedly it will be some time before some of the ambiguities are resolved." 7A Wright, Miller & Kane, Federal Practice & Procedure: Civil 3d § 1756.2. See Lee & Willging, *The Impact of the Class Action Fairness Act on the Federal Courts: An Empirical Analysis of Filings and Removals*, 156 U. Pa. L. Rev. 1723, 1762 (2008) (describing empirical findings that "provide strong support for the conclusion that CAFA has caused the number of diversity class actions filed in and removed to the federal courts to increase appreciably").

7. Can a defendant remove if the case is within the exclusive jurisdiction of the federal court so that the state court lacks subject-matter jurisdiction? Under the "derivative jurisdiction" principle, removal was not permitted because "there was, legally speaking, no action pending in the state court and hence no action which could be removed to the federal court." Bee Mach. Co. v. Freeman, 131 F.2d 190, 194 (1st Cir.1942), affirmed 319 U.S. 448, 63 S.Ct. 1146, 87 L.Ed. 1509 (1943). In 1986, Congress adopted Section 1441(e), which rejects this limitation and makes clear "that a federal court's removal jurisdiction over a claim is not predicated upon the state court having subject matter jurisdiction over that claim." 14B Wright, Miller, & Cooper, Federal Practice and Procedure: Jurisdiction and Related Matters 3d § 3721. In 2002, this provision was recodified as Section 1441(f) and "for no apparent policy reason, new § 1441(f) limits the abrogation of the derivative jurisdiction doctrine to cases removed under 28 U.S.C.A. § 1441." Id. at § 3721.

8. If a case is removed erroneously, a federal court must remand it to the state court. 28 U.S.C. § 1447(c). As amended in 1996, the statute provides a 30-day window for a remand motion made "on the basis of any defect other than lack of subject matter jurisdiction." For a discussion of how the amended statute affects earlier remand practice, see Hrdlick, *Appellate Review of Remand Orders in Removed Cases: Are They Losing a Certain Appeal?*, 82 Marq. L. Rev. 535 (1999).

9. A federal trial court's decision to remand an action to state court raises complicated questions of appellate review. Section 1447(d) states that an "order remanding a case to the State court from which it was removed is not reviewable on appeal or otherwise," except in civil rights cases removed pursuant to Section 1443. The Supreme Court has emphasized that Section 1447(d) "must be read *in pari materia* with § 1447(c), so that only remands based on grounds specified in § 1447(c) are immune from [appellate] review." Quackenbush v. Allstate Insurance Co., 517 U.S. 706, 711–12, 116 S.Ct. 1712, 1717, 135 L.Ed.2d 1, 10 (1996) (internal citation omitted). Moreover, in Powerex Corp. v. Reliant Energy Services, Inc., 551 U.S. 224, 127 S.Ct. 2411, 168 L.Ed.2d 112 (2007), the Court held that a remand order "is immunized from review only if it was based on a lack of subject-matter jurisdiction." Id. at ___, 127 S.Ct. at 2416, 168 L.Ed.2d at 120.

10. When Section 1367 was first enacted, there were some doubts as to its applicability to cases removed from state courts to federal courts. In City of Chicago v. International College of Surgeons, 522 U.S. 156, 118 S.Ct. 523, 139 L.Ed.2d 525 (1997), the Supreme Court laid these doubts to rest and held that Section 1367 applies equally in removed cases. See Steinman, *Removal, Remand, and Review in Pendent Claim and Pendent Party Cases*, 41 Vand. L.Rev. 923 (1988); Steinman, *Crosscurrents: Supplemental Jurisdiction, Removal, and the ALI Revision Project*, 74 Ind. L.J. 75 (1998). The Court subsequently held that a district court has discretion to remand supplemental state claims after determining that retaining jurisdiction over the case would be inappropriate. See Carnegie–Mellon Univ. v. Cohill, 484 U.S. 343, 108 S.Ct. 614, 98 L.Ed.2d 720 (1988). In Carlsbad Technology, Inc. v. HIF Bio, Inc., ___ U.S. ___, 129 S.Ct. 1862 (2009) the Court held that a district court's order remanding a case to state court after declining to exercise supplemental jurisdiction over state-law claims is not a remand for lack of subject-matter jurisdiction for which appellate review is barred under 28 U.S.C.A. § 1447(c) and (d).

11. What if a district court erroneously denies remand of an action when grounds for federal jurisdiction do not exist and later the defect is remedied—for example, by dropping a nondiverse party—prior to the time a final judgment is rendered? In Caterpillar Inc. v. Lewis, 519 U.S. 61, 117 S.Ct. 467, 136 L.Ed.2d 437 (1996), a unanimous Supreme Court, citing practical concerns about judicial efficiency, reversed the decision of the Sixth Circuit and upheld the trial court judgment. Could the Supreme Court ruling result in game playing by litigants? See Mills, *Caterpillar Inc. v. Lewis: Harmless Error Applied to Removal Jurisdiction*, 35 Hous. L. Rev. 601 (1998). However, in Grupo Dataflux v. Atlas Global Group, L.P., 541 U.S. 567, 124 S.Ct. 1920, 158 L.Ed.2d 866 (2004), the Supreme Court, in a 5–4 vote, declined to extend *Caterpillar* when the jurisdictional "cure" involved a party's change in citizenship. See p. 365, infra.

12. What if plaintiff seeks to defeat federal court jurisdiction by dismissing her federal law claims after removal? To what extent should the determination of federal jurisdiction be different in the original and removal context?

Read 28 U.S.C. § 1441(c) in the Supplement.

Section 1441(c) has provoked considerable discussion among courts and commentators. AMERICAN FIRE & CAS. CO. v. FINN, 341 U.S. 6, 71 S.Ct. 534, 95 L.Ed. 702 (1951), an insurance dispute, involved the assertion of state law claims against multiple defendants. Some of the defendants were diverse from plaintiff, but others were not. The requirement of complete diversity barred diversity jurisdiction as an original matter. However, two of the "diverse" defendants successfully removed to federal court. One of the defendants lost and moved to vacate the judgment on the ground that the matter should not have been removed because original jurisdiction was lacking. The Supreme Court agreed. Looking to an earlier version of Section 1441(c), the Court first found that the claim against the losing defendant was not "separate and independent." The Court found only a "single wrong": "the failure to pay compensation for the loss on the property." The Court thus concluded that removal was improper, explaining that "where there is a single wrong to plaintiffs, for which relief is sought, arising from an interlocked series of transactions, there is no separate and independent claim or cause of action under § 1441(c)." Id. at 14, 71 S.Ct. at 540, 95 L.Ed. at 708–09. This statement has been applied by many courts to determine whether Section 1441(c) is applicable. See McFarland, *The Unconstitutional Stub of Section 1441(c)*, 54 Ohio St. L.J. 1059 (1993).

BOROUGH OF WEST MIFFLIN v. LANCASTER

United States Court of Appeals, Third Circuit, 1995.
45 F.3d 780.

[Allan D. Lindsey and Randall Coughanour alleged that security guards at a mall in West Mifflin Borough "harassed, threatened, and assaulted" them. When they requested help from the West Mifflin Police Department, Officer Evan responded to the call. However, he refused to admonish the guards, and told Lindsey and Coughanour that if they ever returned to the mall, he would arrest them. For three weeks Lindsey unsuccessfully attempted to contact somebody from the DeBartolo organization, which owned the mall, to find out why Coughanour and he had been accosted and banned from the mall. On September 27, 1991, Lindsey and Coughanour returned to the mall and were accosted by security guards and arrested by Officer Evan. They subsequently were convicted on charges stemming from the incidents on the mall; however, a three judge panel of the Superior Court of Pennsylvania vacated the convictions and discharged them.

Lindsey and Coughanour then filed a seven-count complaint in the Court of Common Pleas of Allegheny County alleging that they had been maliciously abused and prosecuted. Among other claims, they brought a federal civil rights claim under 42 U.S.C. § 1983, against the municipal defendants (the Borough of West Mifflin and Officer Evan) and the DeBartolo defendants (the mall owners, supervisors, and security officers).

The municipal defendants relied on the Section 1983 claim to remove the case to the United States District Court for the Western District of Pennsylvania. Lindsey and Coughanour moved to remand. The Magistrate Judge recommended a remand of the entire case, including the Section 1983 claim. He found that, "[t]he issues of state law clearly predominate in this matter." District Judge Lancaster adopted the recommendation and granted the motion to remand the entire case.

The municipal defendants sought a writ of mandamus claiming the District Judge had exceeded his authority when he remanded the entire case under Section 1441(c).]

PRATT, CIRCUIT JUDGE.

* * *

* * * Congress has demonstrated a special concern to preserve our power to review remand orders in civil rights cases.

* * *

C. APPLICATION OF § 1441(c).

The dispute on this mandamus application focuses on the effect of subdivision (c) of § 1441. That provision, prior to 1990, read:

> Whenever a separate and independent claim or cause of action, which would have been removable if sued upon alone, is joined with one or more otherwise nonremovable claims or causes of action, the entire case may be removed and the district court may determine all issues therein, or, in its discretion, remand all matters not otherwise within its original jurisdiction.

In 1990, Congress amended § 1441(c) in a manner which the parties contend affects our decision in this case. See Judicial Improvements Act of 1990, Pub.L. No. 101–650 § 312, 104 Stat. 5089, 5114 (1990). Section 1441(c) now reads:

> Whenever a separate and independent claim or cause of action within the jurisdiction of [Section] 1331 of this title is joined with one or more otherwise non-removable claims or causes of action, the entire case may be removed and the district court may determine all issues therein, or, in its discretion, may remand all matters in which State law predominates.

In enacting the amendment to § 1441(c), Congress altered two provisions of the statute. First, it replaced the phrase "a separate and independent claim or cause of action, *which would have been removable if sued upon alone*" with "a separate and independent claim or cause of action *within the jurisdiction of 1331 of this title*". Second, it replaced the phrase "the district court may . . . remand all matters not otherwise in its original jurisdiction" with "the district court may ... remand all matters *in which State law predominates*."

A fair reading of the Congressional intent in enacting the amendment to § 1441(c) is that it was designed to restrict removal to only those cases falling within the court's federal question jurisdiction and to bring the remand provisions into harmony with 28 U.S.C. § 1367, thereby possibly avoiding piecemeal litigation. * * *

In the present case, the district court relied upon the addition which reads "the district court may ... remand all matters in which State law predominates" to remand the entire case, including the § 1983 claim, to state court. It did so without regard for the requirement, which the Congress left unchanged when it amended § 1441(c), that the federal cause of action removed by the municipal defendants had to be "separate and independent" from the state causes of action.

Thus, § 1441(c) provides for removal or remand only where the federal question claims are "separate and independent" from the state law claims with which they are joined in the complaint. However, where there is a single injury to plaintiff for which relief is sought, arising from an interrelated series of events or transactions, there is no separate or independent claim or cause of action under § 1441(c). American Fire & Casualty Co. v. Finn * * *. Suits involving pendent (now "supplemental") state claims that "derive from a common nucleus of operative fact", see United Mine Workers v. Gibbs, * * * do not fall within the scope of § 1441(c), since pendent claims are not "separate and independent". * * *

* * *

* * * Other district courts have apparently read the 1990 amendments as broadening rather than narrowing the scope of their discretion to remand. We cannot agree.

* * * [U]nless the federal question claims removed by the defendant were "separate and independent" from the state law claims, § 1441(c) cannot apply and the district court must retain the federal claim. Hence, the district court's discretion to remand under § 1441(c) can pertain only to those *state law claims* which the district court could decline to hear under 28 U.S.C. § 1367. * * *

Similarly in the present case, Lindsey and Coughanour rely on the same series of events for all counts of their complaint, including the federal § 1983 count; therefore, the federal claim is not separate and independent under § 1441(c), and the district court had no authority to remand the case under that section.

D. APPLICATION OF § 1367(c)

The plaintiffs insist that, even if the district court was not authorized to remand this entire case under § 1441(c), its action should be sustained under the authority of 28 U.S.C. § 1367(c) which gives a district court discretion to decline to hear certain state claims it would have supplemental jurisdiction to entertain under § 1367(a). We disagree for two reasons. First, nothing in § 1367(c) authorizes a district court to decline to entertain a claim over which it has original jurisdiction and, accordingly, that section clearly does not sanction the district court's remand of this entire case, including the civil rights claims, to the state court.

Further, § 1367(c) cannot legitimately be invoked to affirm even the district court's remand of the state claims to the state court. While we agree with plaintiffs that the discretion bestowed by § 1367(c) exists with respect to removed claims as well as claims filed initially in the district court, it is apparent that the district court has not exercised that discretion in this case. The magistrate judge's opinion, adopted by the district court, refers only to § 1441(c) and it is apparent from that opinion that the court remanded the entire case based solely on the authority of that section. Moreover, the result of an exercise of discretion under § 1367(c) in circumstances like those before the district court would have been two parallel proceedings, one in federal court and one in the state system, and a district court cannot properly exercise its discretion under § 1367(c) without taking that fact into account. * * *

As we have indicated, § 1367(c) is potentially applicable in a removed case involving federal claims and state claims over which the district court has supplemental jurisdiction. A district court may thus be called upon to exercise its discretion at any time during the course of such a proceeding in light of the circumstances that then exist. Gibbs * * *. Because the district court in this case may hereafter be called upon to exercise its discretion under § 1367(c), we offer the following guidance.

* * *

While § 1367(c) does not specify what disposition the district court is to make of state claims it decides not to hear, * * * we believe that in a case that has been removed from a state court, a remand to that court is a viable alternative to a dismissal without prejudice. * * *

* * *

Under Gibbs jurisprudence, where the claim over which the district court has original jurisdiction is dismissed before trial, the district court must decline to decide the pendent state claims unless considerations of judicial economy, convenience, and fairness to the parties provide an affirmative justification for doing so. * * * Where the original federal jurisdiction claim is proceeding to trial, however, such considerations will normally counsel an exercise of district court jurisdiction over state claims based on the same nucleus of operative facts unless the district court can point to some substantial countervailing consideration. * * *

Plaintiffs do not suggest that subparagraphs (1), (3), or (4) of § 1367(c) are applicable here. They do maintain that their state claims substantially predominate over their federal claims and, accordingly, that this case falls within subparagraph (2). The district court is in a better position than we to pass upon this contention. Moreover, even if § 1367(c) does not authorize a refusal to hear the state claims based on the current record, it might provide that authority at some later stage in the proceeding. Accordingly, the following observations concerning § 1367(c)(2) are offered solely by way of guidance and are not intended to foreclose the district court from hereafter exercising its discretion under § 1367(c) upon appropriate application.

As we have noted, the "substantially predominates" standard of § 1367(c)(2) comes from Gibbs. It is important to recognize that this standard was fashioned as a limited exception to the operation of the doctrine of pendent jurisdiction * * *. When a district court exercises its discretion not to hear state claims under § 1367(c)(2), the advantages of a single suit are lost. For that reason, § 1367(c)(2)'s authority should be invoked only where there is an important countervailing interest to be served by relegating state claims to the state court. This will normally be the case only where "a state claim constitutes the real body of a case, to which the federal claim is only an appendage," Gibbs, * * *—only where permitting litigation of all claims in the district court can accurately be described as allowing a federal tail to wag what is in substance a state dog.

Given the origin of the "substantially predominate" standard, a district court's analysis under § 1367(c)(2) should track the Supreme Court's explication of that standard in Gibbs. We do not understand plaintiffs to suggest that there is a substantial quantity of evidence supporting their state claims that would not be relevant to the federal claims that the defendants, acting under color of state law, conspired to violate plaintiffs' constitutional rights by assaulting, wrongfully arresting, and maliciously prosecuting them. Thus, in the terminology of Gibbs, the state issues would not appear to "substantially predominate ... in terms of proof." * * * Nor would they appear to "substantially predominate ... in terms of ... the comprehensiveness of the remedy sought." * * * The remedy sought based on the state claims is the same remedy sought based on the federal claims—damages for the same set of injuries to the plaintiffs. * * *

This leaves the issue of whether the state claims can be said to "substantially predominate ... in terms of ... the scope of the issues raised." Id. It is true that the state claims here outnumber the federal claims. The "substantially predominate" standard, however, is not satisfied simply by a numerical count of the state and federal claims the plaintiff has chosen to assert on the basis of the same set of facts. An analysis more sensitive to the relevant interests is required.

While federal constitutional tort law under § 1983 derives much of its content from the general common law of torts, plaintiffs' civil rights claims based on the alleged assault, arrest, and prosecution are nevertheless governed exclusively by federal law. * * * While the claims based upon the arrest and the prosecution may require an inquiry into whether the defendants had probable cause to believe a crime had been committed and this may in part require some reference to the state criminal law, the probable cause issue and the other issues raised by these claims are nevertheless issues of federal law and concern. * * *

There are, to be sure, a complementary set of state law issues arising out of the state claims based on the alleged assault, arrest, and prosecution. But these state issues do not appear from our vantage point to substantially predominate over the comparable but distinct federal issues. Plaintiffs do not suggest that these state issues are more important, more complex, more time consuming to resolve, or in any other way more significant than their federal counterparts.

The only other state issues are those which may arise from the plaintiffs' negligence claims against the municipal defendants and the DeBartolo defendants. The dimensions of those claims are not clear at this stage of the case, but it seems unlikely to us that they will cause the state issues to "substantially predominate" within the meaning of § 1367(c)(2). If the factual allegations of the complaint are accepted at face value, as we are required to do at this point, this case involves several substantial claims that the plaintiffs' constitutional rights have been infringed. In such circumstances, we believe it will be the rare case, at least, where the addition of straightforward negligence claims based on the same facts as the constitutional claims will cause the state issues to substantially predominate.

* * *

Accordingly, the petition for a writ of mandamus is granted.

NOTES AND QUESTIONS

1. What is the relation between the requirement of a "separate and independent" claim under Section 1441(c) and the requirement that claims be "related" for purposes of supplemental jurisdiction? Courts and commentators offer two alternative readings: (1) since a separate and independent claim under Section 1441(c) does not satisfy the "same case or controversy" requirement of Section 1367, Section 1441(c) is unconstitutional, as it grants federal courts jurisdiction over claims beyond the scope of Article III; (2) if Section 1367 merely codifies the *Gibbs* common nucleus test and does not define the boundaries of Article III, there may be a category of separate and independent claims which, although insufficient to meet Section 1367's requirements, nevertheless fall within the scope of Article III. See Hartnett, *A New Trick from an Old and Abused Dog: Section 1441(c) Lives and Now Permits the Remand of Federal Question Cases*, 63 Fordham L. Rev. 1099 (1995).

2. IN RE CITY OF MOBILE, 75 F.3d 605 (11th Cir.1996), involved a collision between a car and a vehicle under high-speed pursuit by city police. Plaintiff filed suit in state court against the speeding motorist, the police officer, and the City of Mobile, alleging federal civil rights violations as well as state-law claims. All defendants, other than the speeding motorist, removed

the case to federal court. Plaintiff then moved to remand the entire case to state court, and the District Court granted the motion. Reversing the District Court, the Eleventh Circuit cited approvingly the Third Circuit's decision in *Borough of West Mifflin*, noting that Section 1367(c) does not expressly authorize the remand of a properly removed federal claim. The court further held that the District Court had no discretion to remand a case with both federal and state claims, because Section 1441(c) requires that the federal and state claims be separate and independent. Since the federal and state claims arose out of a single accident, the claims were not separate and independent.

In dissent, Circuit Judge Birch agreed that Section 1367(c) accords a district court discretion to remand only state law claims, but disagreed with the majority's interpretation of Section 1441(c):

> * * * Congress recognized that the "separate and independent claim" problem arose in diversity cases, where the "plaintiff could easily bring a single action on a federal claim and a *completely unrelated state claim*." * * * In contrast, Congress acknowledged that federal question jurisdiction, associated with the former doctrine of pendent jurisdiction, involves related claims. * * *
>
> Since amended section 1441(c) concerns only federal question jurisdiction and deletes diversity jurisdiction, now covered by section 1441(b), Congress undertook to relieve federal judges from determining whether the state and federal causes of action are related or unrelated. * * * "[S]eparate and independent claim or cause of action" in section 1441(c) means a legitimate basis of federal jurisdiction apart from jurisdiction under state law claims.

* * *

Id. at 609–11. Under the dissent's reading of Section 1441(c), the District Court appropriately exercised its discretion to remand the entire underlying case to state court.

SECTION F. CHALLENGING THE SUBJECT-MATTER JURISDICTION OF THE COURT

1. DIRECT ATTACK ON A COURT'S LACK OF SUBJECT-MATTER JURISDICTION

Read Federal Rules of Civil Procedure 8(a)(1), 12(b)(1) and (h)(3), and 60(b)(4), Official Form 40, and 28 U.S.C. § 1653 in the Supplement.

A lack of subject-matter jurisdiction may be asserted at any time by any interested party, either in the answer, or in the form of a suggestion to the court prior to final judgment, or on appeal, and also may be raised by the court sua sponte. Moreover, the parties may not create the jurisdiction of a federal court by agreement or by consent. See, e.g., Mansfield, C. & L. M. Ry. Co. v. Swan, 111 U.S. 379, 4 S.Ct. 510, 28 L.Ed. 462 (1884).

NOTES AND QUESTIONS

1. In RUHRGAS AG v. MARATHON OIL CO., 526 U.S. 574, 119 S.Ct. 1563, 143 L.Ed.2d 760 (1999), the defendant removed the case to federal court, and the plaintiff moved to remand for lack of subject-matter jurisdiction. The defendant then moved to dismiss for lack of personal jurisdiction, and the District Court dismissed for lack of personal jurisdiction without deciding the subject-matter jurisdiction question. The Supreme Court unanimously held that because both subject-matter and personal jurisdiction are required by the Constitution and affect a federal court's power to adjudicate a case, there is no reason to require a district court to decide subject-matter jurisdiction first:

> Where * * * a district court has before it a straightforward personal jurisdiction issue presenting no complex question of state law, and the alleged defect in subject matter jurisdiction raises a difficult and novel question, the court does not abuse its discretion by turning directly to personal jurisdiction.

Id. at 588, 119 S.Ct. at 1572, 143 L.Ed.2d at 773. How far does the Supreme Court's approach go? May a court decide a statute of limitations issue or some aspect of the merits when the case may be disposed more efficiently of on one of those grounds than by grappling with a difficult question of jurisdiction? See Friedenthal, *The Crack in the Steel Case*, 68 Geo. Wash. L. Rev. 258 (2000). We revisit this issue in Chapter 5, see Note 9, p. 403, infra.

2. Are there situations in which defects in subject-matter jurisdiction should be immune from direct attack? In DI FRISCHIA v. NEW YORK CENTRAL RAILROAD CO., 279 F.2d 141 (3d Cir.1960), defendant initially objected to the jurisdiction of the court, asserting lack of diversity, but then filed a stipulation withdrawing the objection. After the statute of limitations had run on any state court action, defendant reasserted its jurisdictional objection. The District Court dismissed the action, but the Third Circuit reversed, refusing to permit defendant to "play fast and loose with the judicial machinery and deceive the courts." Id. at 144. The Third Circuit has since reversed *Di Frischia*—a case with virtually no progeny and implicitly rejected by the Supreme Court in *Kroger*, p. 332, supra.

3. In UNITED STATES v. UNITED MINE WORKERS, 330 U.S. 258, 67 S.Ct. 677, 91 L.Ed. 884 (1947), the District Court issued a temporary restraining order to prevent a strike in mines that earlier had been seized by the government. The union and its officers disobeyed the order, and subsequently were held in contempt of court, notwithstanding the defendants' contention that under the Norris–LaGuardia Act the District Court lacked jurisdiction to issue injunctions in labor disputes. A divided Supreme Court held that the order had to be obeyed until set aside, and that the defendants could not raise the asserted lack of jurisdiction as a defense to the contempt

charges. Justice Frankfurter, concurring in the result only, emphasized the power of a federal court to determine its jurisdiction:

> Only when a court is so obviously traveling outside its orbit as to be merely usurping judicial forms and facilities, may an order issued by a court be disobeyed and treated as though it were a letter to a newspaper. Short of an indisputable want of authority on the part of a court, the very existence of a court presupposes its power to entertain a controversy, if only to decide, after deliberation, that it has no power over the particular controversy.

Id. at 309–10, 67 S.Ct. at 704, 91 L.Ed. at 921. Subsequent decisions suggest a general principle that obedience to a temporary restraining order is required, even though the issuing court may lack subject-matter jurisdiction or otherwise may have based its decision on an incorrect view of the law, unless there is no opportunity for effective appellate review of the decree. See 11A Wright, Miller & Kane, Federal Practice and Procedure: Civil 2d § 2960.

4. In WILLY v. COASTAL CORP., 503 U.S. 131, 112 S.Ct. 1076, 117 L.Ed.2d 280 (1992), plaintiff brought a wrongful discharge action against his former employer, who removed the action to federal court. The District Court dismissed the case for failure to state a claim, and imposed sanctions on the plaintiff pursuant to Federal Rule 11. Plaintiff appealed, arguing that the District Court had no authority to impose sanctions since it lacked subject-matter jurisdiction. The Supreme Court upheld the ability of the District Court to impose sanctions:

> The District Court order which the petitioner seeks to upset is one that is collateral to the merits. * * * Such an order implicates no constitutional concern because it "does not signify a district court's assessment of the legal merits of the complaint." * * * It therefore does not raise the issue of a district court adjudicating the merits of a "case or controversy" over which it lacks jurisdiction.

Id. at 137, 112 S.Ct. at 1080, 117 L.Ed.2d at 289.

Does the *Willy* principle extend to cases in which a federal court, although lacking subject-matter jurisdiction, imposes the sanction of dismissal with prejudice? Some federal appellate courts have held that it does not. See, e.g., Hernandez v. Conriv Realty Associates, 182 F.3d 121 (2d Cir.1999); In re Orthopedic "Bone Screw" Products Liability Litig., 132 F.3d 152 (3d Cir. 1997). These courts have reasoned that unlike a Rule 11 sanction, dismissal with prejudice is not collateral to the merits, as its preclusive effect bars further consideration of a case on the merits.

5. In GRUPO DATAFLUX v. ATLAS GLOBAL GROUP, L.P., 541 U.S. 567, 124 S.Ct. 1920, 158 L.Ed.2d 866 (2004), a partnership sued a Mexican corporation in federal district court under diversity jurisdiction. After three years of pretrial motions and discovery, followed by a six-day trial, the jury returned a verdict in favor of the partnership. Before entry of judgment, however, defendant filed a motion to dismiss for lack of subject-matter jurisdiction. At the time the complaint was filed, the parties were not diverse, because two of plaintiff's partners were Mexican citizens. Yet for all practical purposes, diversity did exist during the trial because the Mexican partners

had left the partnership a month before the trial's commencement. In a 5–4 decision, with Justice Scalia writing for the majority, the Court held that in a diversity action, a party's post-filing change in citizenship cannot cure a lack of subject-matter jurisdiction which existed at the time of the filing. *Grupo* has been criticized for not affording due consideration to the values of judicial economy and efficiency, and for tolerating defendants' carelessness when they fail to raise the absence of subject-matter jurisdiction at early stages of the lawsuit. See Simpson–Wood, *Has the Seductive Siren of Judicial Frugality Ceased to Sing?:* Dataflux *and Its Family Tree*, 53 Drake L. Rev. 281 (2005); Gao, Note—*"Salvage Operations Are Ordinarily Preferable to the Wrecking Ball": Barring Challenges to Subject Matter Jurisdiction*, 105 Colum. L. Rev. 2369 (2005).

2. COLLATERAL ATTACK ON A JUDGMENT FOR LACK OF SUBJECT-MATTER JURISDICTION

If both the parties and the court fail to notice the absence of subject-matter jurisdiction at any time during the original proceeding, can defendant successfully raise the lack of jurisdiction as a defense to a subsequent proceeding by plaintiff to enforce the decree? Would it make any difference for purposes of collateral attack if the issue of jurisdiction had been raised and litigated in the original action and it had been decided that the court did have power to proceed? In grappling with this problem, reconsider Capron v. Van Noorden, p. 26, supra, and Des Moines Navigation & R. Co. v. Iowa Homestead Co., p. 67, supra, and recall that one of the oldest pieces of jurisdiction dogma is the maxim that a judgment rendered by a court that lacked jurisdiction over the subject matter (or the "cause," to use the older terminology) is void and a nullity. See, e.g., The Case of the Marshalsea, 10 Co.Rep. 68b, 77 Eng.Rep. 1027 (K.B. 1613); Elliott v. Peirsol's Lessee, 26 U.S. (1 Pet.) 328, 7 L.Ed. 164 (1828). Of course, the subject is considerably more complex than the dogma would indicate, and *Des Moines* demonstrates that collateral attack is not always an available technique for challenging a judgment on the ground that the rendering court lacked subject-matter jurisdiction.

Section 10 of the first Restatement of Judgments analyzed the question of the availability of collateral attack in terms of balancing the policies underlying res judicata and finality of judgments, which are treated in detail in Chapter Seventeen, against the policy of prohibiting a court from exceeding the powers conferred upon it by the legislature or the jurisdiction's organic law. It stated that if the court in the original action determined that it had subject-matter jurisdiction, the permissibility of collateral attack depended on weighing a non-exclusive list of factors:

(a) the lack of jurisdiction over the subject matter was clear;

(b) the determination as to jurisdiction depended upon a question of law rather than of fact;

(c) the court was one of limited and not of general jurisdiction;

(d) the question of jurisdiction was not actually litigated;

(e) the policy against the court's acting beyond its jurisdiction is strong.

The Restatement (Second), Judgments §§ 12, 69 (1982) takes the approach that the judgment in a contested action, whether or not the question of subject-matter jurisdiction actually was litigated, is beyond collateral attack unless there are no justifiable interests of reliance that must be protected, and:

(1) The subject matter of the action was so plainly beyond the court's jurisdiction that its entertaining the action was a manifest abuse of authority; or

(2) Allowing the judgment to stand would substantially infringe the authority of another tribunal or agency of government; or

(3) The judgment was rendered by a court lacking capability to make an adequately informed determination of a question concerning its own jurisdiction and as a matter of procedural fairness the party seeking to avoid the judgment should have opportunity belatedly to attack the court's subject matter jurisdiction.

In addition, the Restatement (Second) of Judgments generally permits collateral attack on the original court's subject-matter jurisdiction, as well as on personal jurisdiction and inadequate notice, in default judgment situations. Id. § 65. Does this approach go far enough, or too far, toward giving preclusive effect to the original court's judgment? See generally Moore, *Collateral Attack on Subject-Matter Jurisdiction: A Critique of the Restatement (Second) of Judgments,* 66 Cornell L.Rev. 534 (1981).

The Supreme Court has had to deal with problems of collateral attack on numerous occasions. In CHICOT COUNTY DRAINAGE DISTRICT v. BAXTER STATE BANK, 308 U.S. 371, 60 S.Ct. 317, 84 L.Ed. 329 (1940), parties who had notice but chose not to appear in the original action attempted to attack collaterally a judgment rendered by a district court sitting as a court of bankruptcy under a statute that was later declared unconstitutional. The Supreme Court refused to allow the attack:

> * * * If the general principles governing the defense of *res judicata* are applicable, [respondents], having the opportunity to raise the question of invalidity, were not the less bound by the decree because they failed to raise it. * * *
>
> * * * The lower federal courts are all courts of limited jurisdiction, that is, with only the jurisdiction which Congress has prescribed. But nonetheless they are courts with authority * * * to determine whether or not they have jurisdiction to entertain the cause and for this purpose to construe and apply the statute under which they are asked to act. Their determinations of such questions, while open to direct review, may not be assailed collaterally.

Id. at 375–76, 60 S.Ct. at 319, 84 L.Ed. at 333.

But collateral attack was allowed by the Court in KALB v. FEUERSTEIN, 308 U.S. 433, 60 S.Ct. 343, 84 L.Ed. 370 (1940), decided the same day as *Chicot*. The questions for decision in *Kalb* were whether a state court had jurisdiction to render a judgment confirming a foreclosure sale while the mortgagor's petition under the Bankruptcy Act was pending in a bankruptcy court, and, if not, whether the mortgagor was prohibited from attacking the state-court judgment collaterally. The Court answered both questions in the negative:

> It is generally true that a judgment by a court of competent jurisdiction bears a presumption of regularity and is not thereafter subject to collateral attack. But Congress, because its power over the subject of bankruptcy is plenary, may by specific bankruptcy legislation create an exception to that principle and render judicial acts taken with respect to the person or property of a debtor whom the bankruptcy law protects nullities and vulnerable collaterally. * * *
>
> We think the language and broad policy of the * * * Act conclusively demonstrate that Congress intended to, and did deprive the Wisconsin County Court of the power and jurisdiction to continue or maintain in any manner the foreclosure proceedings against appellants without the consent * * * of the bankruptcy court * * *.

Id. at 438–40, 60 S.Ct. at 346, 84 L.Ed. at 374–75.

Which of the categories in the two *Restatements* seems determinative of the *Kalb* case? Are *Chicot* and *Kalb* reconcilable? A fuller discussion of *Chicot* and *Kalb* can be found in Boskey & Braucher, *Jurisdiction and Collateral Attack: October Term, 1939,* 40 Colum.L.Rev. 1006 (1940).

DURFEE v. DUKE, 375 U.S. 106, 84 S.Ct. 242, 11 L.Ed.2d 186 (1963), involved a dispute over title to a tract of bottom land on the Missouri River, which forms the boundary between Nebraska and Missouri. A Missouri federal district court allowed collateral attack on a Nebraska judgment quieting title, on the ground that considerations of territorial sovereignty outweighed the policies of res judicata. The Nebraska court's subject matter jurisdiction depended on whether the land was within Nebraska, which "depended entirely upon a factual question—whether a shift in the river's course had been caused by avulsion or accretion." The question had been fully litigated in the Nebraska action. The Supreme Court reversed:

> * * * [W]hile it is established that a court in one State, when asked to give effect to the judgment of a court in another State, may constitutionally inquire into the foreign court's jurisdiction to render that judgment, the modern decisions of this Court have carefully delineated the permissible scope of such an inquiry. From these decisions there emerges the general rule that a judgment is entitled to full faith and credit—even as to questions of jurisdiction—when the second court's inquiry discloses that those questions have been fully and fairly litigated and finally decided in the court which rendered the original judgment. * * *

> To be sure, the general rule of finality of jurisdictional determinations is not without exceptions. Doctrines of federal preemption or sovereign immunity may in some contexts be controlling. Kalb v. Feuerstein * * *. But no such overriding considerations are present here.

Id. at 111–14, 84 S.Ct. at 245–47, 11 L.Ed.2d at 191–93. The decision in *Durfee* was followed in Underwriters National Assurance Co. v. North Carolina Life & Acc. & Health Ins. Guar. Ass'n, 455 U.S. 691, 102 S.Ct. 1357, 71 L.Ed.2d 558 (1982).

A more recent example of the Supreme Court's attitude toward collateral attack can be found in UNITED STATES CATHOLIC CONFERENCE v. ABORTION RIGHTS MOBILIZATION, INC., 487 U.S. 72, 108 S.Ct. 2268, 101 L.Ed.2d 69 (1988). In the underlying action, Abortion Rights Mobilization (ARM) sued to revoke the tax-exempt status of the Roman Catholic Church because of the church's intervention in favor of political candidates who supported the church's position on abortion. ARM served the Conference with a subpoena seeking extensive documentary evidence to support its claims. The Conference refused to comply with the subpoena and was held in civil contempt with a fine of $50,000 per day for further noncompliance. The Supreme Court held that a nonparty witness, the Conference, could challenge the court's lack of subject matter jurisdiction in defense of a civil contempt citation. The Court reasoned:

> * * * The distinction between subject matter jurisdiction and waivable defenses is not a mere nicety of legal metaphysics. It rests instead on the central principle of a free society that courts have finite bounds of authority, some of constitutional origin, which exist to protect citizens from the very wrong asserted here, the excessive use of judicial power. The courts, no less than the political branches of the government, must respect the limits of their authority.

Id. at 77, 108 S.Ct. at 2271, 101 L.Ed.2d at 77.

See generally 18A Wright, Miller & Cooper, Federal Practice and Procedure: Jurisdiction and Related Matters § 4428; Dobbs, *The Validation of Void Judgments: The Bootstrap Principle, Part I,* 53 Va.L.Rev. 1003 (1967); Note, *Filling the Void: Judicial Power and Jurisdictional Attacks on Judgments,* 87 Yale L.J. 164 (1977).

CHAPTER 5

VENUE, TRANSFER, AND FORUM NON CONVENIENS

■ ■ ■

In this Chapter, we consider another principle that affects where a lawsuit can be filed and entertained: venue. Venue is a doctrine that serves to "allocate cases among the same type of courts within a given judicial system." Friedenthal, Kane & Miller, Civil Procedure § 2.1 (4th ed. 2005). Unlike personal jurisdiction and subject-matter jurisdiction, the venue of a civil action is not a constitutional question, as it relates primarily to the convenience of the parties and to concerns of judicial economy.

SECTION A. VENUE

1. GENERAL PRINCIPLES

STEVENS, VENUE STATUTES: DIAGNOSIS AND PROPOSED CURE, 49 Mich.L.Rev. 307, 307–15 (1951):

Venue * * * means the place of trial in an action within a state. Given a cause of action, and having decided what court has jurisdiction over the subject matter, the lawyer must lay the venue, that is, select the place of trial. In making this decision, the lawyer in every state of the United States turns in the first instance, not to common law, but to statute, constitutional provision or rule of court. And he finds that the "proper" venue of his action depends upon the theory of his claim, the subject matter of his claim, the parties involved, or a combination of these factors.

Most codes make provision for the place of trial in local actions, and all codes provide in one way or another for venue in transitory actions arising both within and without the state. Many states make special provision for divorce actions, actions against executors, and actions for the specific recovery of personal property. Most states also provide for venue in actions against residents, against nonresidents, against corporations, domestic and foreign, against partnerships, associations and individuals doing business in the state, and against the state, or a county, or a city or public officers generally or specifically. The nature of the plaintiff, as a resident or nonresident, corporation, domestic or foreign, or political entity, is another factor frequently considered and provided for. * * *

A comparative study of contemporary venue provisions reveals some thirteen different fact situations upon which venue statutes are predicated.

A. *Where the subject of action or part thereof is situated.* The common law concept of actions which were local because the facts could have occurred only in a particular place still persists. As might well be expected, the proper venue for such actions is the county where the subject of the action is situated. There is, however, considerable variation from state to state as to what types of cases are local and fall into this category. * * *

This type of venue * * * is based upon the idea that the court of the county in which the res, which is the subject matter of the suit, is located is best able to deal with the problem. The local sheriff can attach, deliver or execute upon the property. The local clerk can make the necessary entries with a minimum of red tape where title to land is affected. Trial convenience is served where "a view" is necessary or of value in reaching a determination. Third parties can readily ascertain, at a logical point of inquiry, the status of a res in which they may be interested.

It is submitted that these factors are of sufficient importance in this type of case to outweigh other considerations such as convenience of parties or witnesses in the selection of place of trial. * * *

B. *Where the cause of action, or part thereof, arose or accrued.* Convenience of witnesses is the most logical reason for venue provisions allowing the action to be brought in the county where the cause of action, or part thereof, arose or accrued. And since convenience of witnesses is a very practical problem in the trial of a law suit, one would expect to find venue based upon the place where the cause of action arose or accrued a rather common, and general, provision. * * *

The idea behind this type of venue provision * * * is sound and popular. * * * However, its usefulness has been somewhat impaired by difficulties arising out of problems of statutory interpretation. First, what do the words "arose" and "accrued" mean? Second, what is the difference, if any, between "arose" and "accrued"? And, third, what is the meaning of the phrase "or part thereof"? * * *

C. *Where some fact is present or happened.* There is a sizeable group of statutes which provide for trial of the action in the county where some particular fact or fact situation related to, but no part of, the cause of action is present or happened. * * *

If the purpose of venue is trial convenience, either of parties, or witnesses, or the court or court officials, then it is hard to find any real justification for this group of venue provisions. Most if not all of them are examples of singling out certain specific types of actions for special treatment where a need for special treatment is not or at least no longer [is] apparent. * * *

D. *Where the defendant resides.* Convenience of the defendant is the reason usually given for venue statutes which provide for the place of trial in the county where the defendant resides—the theory probably being, as suggested by Professor E.R. Sunderland, "that since the plaintiff controls the institution of the suit he might behave oppressively toward the defendant unless restrained." * * *

E. *Where the defendant is doing business.* * * * Convenience of the defendant, and of witnesses, appears to be the reason behind such provisions where they are tied to causes of action arising out of the doing of business in the state. Convenience of the defendant, and even more clearly, convenience of the plaintiff, by providing a county in which to lay the venue against a nonresident individual, partnership, company or corporation without undue inconvenience to defendant, is served by the broader type of provision—against certain classes of defendants generally. * * *

F. *Where defendant has an office or place of business, or an agent, or representative, or where an agent or officer of defendant resides.* [These venue statutes] * * * are quite common where a corporation, company or some other type of business organization is the defendant. Convenience of the plaintiff, rather than the defendant, is the moving consideration behind such statutes in most instances. * * *

G. *Where the plaintiff resides.* * * *

Convenience of the plaintiff is the obvious reason behind venue statutes of this nature. Convenience of plaintiff's witnesses may or may not be served, depending upon the nature of the action. * * * In certain types of cases against certain classes of defendants—such as an action on a foreign cause of action against a nonresident—this type of provision is both logical and practical. * * *

H. *Where the plaintiff is doing business.* * * * Obviously the convenience of the plaintiff is the sole consideration behind such a provision. It is submitted that other factors of trial convenience such as convenience of witnesses and of the defendant are more important, and that in view of the number of adherents to this ground of venue, it would be wise to advocate its abandonment. * * *

I. *Where the defendant may be found.* Venue based upon the county where the defendant may be found is in accord with the common law doctrine that the right of action follows the person. * * *

It is difficult to find any sound reason for venue based upon where the defendant may be found. It serves no useful purpose—no trial convenience of either witnesses or parties. It is a good example of a historical hangover—a type of provision which has long since outlived its usefulness. The problem which this type of provision was designed to solve was and is not one of venue but of service of process. * * *

J. *Where the defendant may be summoned or served.* Another group of statutes, also based upon the common law doctrine that the right of action follows the person, provides that venue may be laid in the county where the defendant may be summoned, or served with process. * * *

The comments which were made with respect to venue based upon where the defendant may be found apply with equal force to this type of provision. * * *

K. *In the county designated in the plaintiff's complaint.* * * *

Venue provisions of this type give the plaintiff an unnecessary economic advantage not warranted by convenience of parties or witnesses. In the interests of justice and trial convenience they should be eliminated.

L. *In any county.* The broadest venue provision on the books is that which provides that the plaintiff may lay the venue in any county. * * *

M. *Where the seat of government is located.* * * *

Statutes of this sort have a sound and practical reason behind them. With one exception, this type of provision is reserved for actions by or against governmental units or agencies. Convenience of the government appears to be the controlling factor. * * *

NOTES AND QUESTIONS

1. Venue refers to "the place where a lawsuit should be heard" and is distinct from a court's authority to adjudicate a case. See 14D Wright, Miller & Cooper, Federal Practice and Procedure: Jurisdiction and Related Matters 3d § 3801. A state venue rule allocates judicial business within a state. A federal venue rule allocates judicial business within the nation. What should be the underlying goals of a venue system? In what ways should the venue system for the federal courts differ from how a state allocates business among its courts?

2. Is it really necessary to superimpose notions of venue on a soundly conceived jurisdictional system, especially one with a long-arm statute? Indeed, do we need venue provisions at all, given the kind of convenience analysis that *World–Wide Volkswagen*, p. 105, supra, constitutionally requires for making personal jurisdiction decisions? See Clermont, *Refuting Territorial Jurisdiction and Venue for State and Federal Courts*, 66 Cornell L.Rev. 411 (1981). What additional protection is provided through well-considered venue rules? See, e.g., Clardy, *Nonresident Defendants Don't Deserve Convenience or Justice in South Carolina*?, 55 S.C. L. Rev. 443 (2004).

3. What data are relevant for deciding where contract, tort, and property actions should be brought? One author has suggested that juries in some regions or cities give higher damage awards in comparable tort cases than in other regions or cities. See Zeisel, Social Research on the Law: The Ideal and the Practical, in Law and Sociology 130–32 (Evan ed. 1962) (stating general rule derived from empirical data: "add 10 percent to the average if the trial takes place on the East or West coast; add another 10 percent if it is conducted in a large metropolitan city; subtract 10 percent if it is conducted in the South or the Midwest; and another 10 percent if it takes place in a rural area"). Recent commentary, however, cautions against drawing broad

conclusions from studies of jury awards. See, e.g., Nockleby, *How to Manufacture a Crisis: Evaluating Empirical Claims Behind "Tort Reform,"* 86 Or. L. Rev. 533 (2008).

4. In BURLINGTON NORTHERN R.R. CO. v. FORD, 504 U.S. 648, 112 S.Ct. 2184, 119 L.Ed.2d 432 (1992), defendant raised a challenge to Montana's venue rules on the ground that they violated the Equal Protection Clause of the Fourteenth Amendment. Montana's venue rules permit a plaintiff to sue a corporation incorporated in Montana only in the county of its principal place of business, but permit suit in any county against a corporation, like the defendant, that is incorporated elsewhere. The Supreme Court upheld the constitutionality of the state's venue rules in a unanimous opinion by Justice Souter:

> Venue rules generally reflect equity or expediency in resolving disparate interests of parties to a lawsuit in the place of trial. * * * The forum preferable to one party may be undesirable to another, and the adjustment of such warring interests is a valid state concern. * * * In striking the balance between them, a State may have a number of choices, any of which would survive scrutiny, each of them passable under the standard tolerating some play in the joints of governmental machinery. * * * Thus, we have no doubt that a State would act within its constitutional prerogatives if it were to give so much weight to the interest of plaintiffs as to allow them to sue in the counties of their choice under all circumstances. It is equally clear that a State might temper such an "any county" rule to the extent a reasonable assessment of defendants' interest so justified.
>
> Here, Montana has decided that the any-county rule should give way to a single-county rule where a defendant resides in Montana, arguably on the reasonable ground that a defendant should not be subjected to a plaintiff's tactical advantage of forcing a trial far from the defendant's residence. At the same time, Montana has weighed the interest of a defendant who does not reside in Montana differently, arguably on the equally reasonable ground that for most nonresident defendants the inconvenience will be great whether they have to defend in, say, Billings or Havre. * * * Montana could thus have decided that a nonresident defendant's interest in convenience is too slight to outweigh the plaintiff's interest in suing in the forum of his choice.

Id. at 651–52, 112 S.Ct. at 2186–87, 119 L.Ed.2d at 438.

5. Courts traditionally have refused to enforce forum-selection clauses as void and against public policy. See 14D Wright, Miller & Cooper, Federal Practice and Procedure: Jurisdiction and Related Matters 3d § 3803.1. Judicial disfavor extended to venue clauses. However, since its decision in M/S Bremen v. Zapata Off–Shore Co., 407 U.S. 1, 13–15, 92 S.Ct. 1907, 1915–16, 32 L.Ed.2d 513, 522–23 (1972), p. 188, supra, the Supreme Court has abandoned the historical rule, emphasizing instead that forum-selection clauses "should be given full effect" unless "enforcement would be unreasonable and unjust, or that the clause was invalid for such reasons as fraud or overreaching." Even after *The Bremen*, some state courts have continued to refuse to enforce venue clauses, which designate a forum within the state,

although they will give effect to advance agreements that designate a forum outside of a state. See Peterson, *In re AIU Insurance Company*, 41 Texas J. Bus. L. 101, 103–04 (2005). Do different considerations come into play when the venue clause involves a dispute that is litigated in federal court?

2. LOCAL AND TRANSITORY ACTIONS

REASOR–HILL CORP. v. HARRISON

Supreme Court of Arkansas, 1952.
220 Ark. 521, 249 S.W.2d 994.

GEORGE ROSE SMITH, JUSTICE. Petitioner asks us to prohibit the circuit court of Mississippi County from taking jurisdiction of a cross-complaint filed by D.M. Barton. In the court below the petitioner moved to dismiss the cross-complaint for the reason that it stated a cause of action for injury to real property in the state of Missouri. When the motion to dismiss was overruled the present application for prohibition was filed in this court.

The suit below was brought by the Planters Flying Service to collect an account for having sprayed insecticide upon Barton's cotton crop in Missouri. In his answer Barton charged that the flying service had damaged his growing crop by using an adulterated insecticide, and by cross-complaint he sought damages from the petitioner for its negligence in putting on the market a chemical unsuited to spraying cotton. The petitioner is an Arkansas corporation engaged in manufacturing insecticides and is not authorized to do business in Missouri.

The question presented is one of first impression: May the Arkansas courts entertain a suit for injuries to real property situated in another State? For the respondent it is rightly pointed out that if the suit is not maintainable Barton has no remedy whatever. The petitioner cannot be served with summons in Missouri; so unless it is subject to suit in Arkansas it can escape liability entirely by staying out of Missouri until the statute of limitations has run. * * * The petitioner answers this argument by showing that with the exception of the Supreme Court of Minnesota every American court that has passed upon the question (and there have been about twenty) has held that jurisdiction does not exist.

We agree that the weight of authority is almost unanimously against the respondent, although in some States the rule has been changed by statute and in others it has been criticized by the courts and restricted as narrowly as possible. But before mechanically following the majority view we think it worthwhile to examine the origin of the rule and the reasons for its existence.

The distinction between local and transitory actions was recognized at the beginning of the fourteenth century in the common law of England. Before then all actions had to be brought where the cause of action arose, because the members of the jury were required to be neighbors who would know something of the litigants and of the dispute as well. But when cases were presented that involved separate incidents occurring in different communities the reason for localizing the action disappeared, for it was then impossible to obtain a jury who knew all the facts. Consequently the courts developed the distinction between a case that might have arisen anywhere, which was held to be transitory, and one that involved a particular piece of land, which was held to be local. * * *

As between judicial districts under the same sovereign the rule has many advantages and has been followed in America. As between counties our statutes in Arkansas require that actions for injury to real estate be brought where the land lies. * * * But we permit the defendant to be served anywhere in the State * * *; so the plaintiff is not denied a remedy even though the defendant is a resident of another county.

The English courts, in developing the law of local and transitory actions, applied it also to suits for injuries to real property lying outside England. If, for example, there had been a trespass upon land in France, the courts would not permit the plaintiff to bring suit in England, even though the defendant lived in England and could not be subjected to liability in France. The American courts, treating the separate States as independent sovereigns, have followed the English decisions.

In the United States the leading case is unquestionably Livingston v. Jefferson * * *. That suit was a part of the famous litigation between Edward Livingston and Thomas Jefferson * * *. The case was heard by Marshall as circuit justice and Tyler as district judge. Both agreed that the suit, which was for a wrongful entry upon land in Louisiana, could not be maintained in Virginia. In Marshall's concurring opinion he examined the English precedents and concluded that the law was so firmly established that the court was bound to follow it, though Marshall expressed his dissatisfaction with a rule which produced "the inconvenience of a clear right without a remedy."

Since then the American courts have relied almost uniformly upon the Livingston case in applying the rule to interstate litigation in this country. At least three reasons have been offered to justify the rule, but it is easy to show that each reason is more applicable to international controversies than to interstate disputes.

First, the ground most frequently relied upon is that the courts are not in a position to pass upon the title to land outside the jurisdiction. As between nations this reasoning may be sound. The members of this court have neither the training nor the facilities to investigate questions involving the ownership of land in France, in Russia, or in China. But the same difficulties do not exist with respect to land in another State. In our library we have the statutes and decisions of every other State, and it seldom takes more than a few hours to find the answer to a particular question. Furthermore, the American courts do not hesitate to pass upon an out-of-state title when the issue arises in a transitory action. If, for example, Barton had charged that this petitioner converted a mature crop in Missouri and carried it to Arkansas, our courts would decide the case even though it became necessary to pass upon conflicting claims of title to the land in Missouri. Again, a suit for damages for nonperformance of a contract to purchase land is transitory and may be maintained in another State, even though the sole issue is the validity of the seller's title. To put an extreme example, suppose that two companion suits, one local and one transitory, were presented to the same court together. In those States where the courts disclaim the ability to pass upon questions of title in local actions it might be necessary for the court to dismiss the local action for that reason and yet to decide the identical question in the allied transitory case.

Second, it has been argued that since the tort must take place where the land is situated the plaintiff should pursue his remedy before the defendant leaves the jurisdiction. This argument, too, has merit when nations are concerned. A sovereign, by its control of passports and ports of entry, may detain those who wish to cross its borders. But the citizens of the various States have a constitutional right to pass freely from one jurisdiction to another. * * * In the case at bar * * * Barton could hardly be expected to discover the damage and file an attachment suit before the pilot returned to his landing field in Arkansas.

Third, there is an understandable reluctance to subject one's own citizens to suits by aliens, especially if the other jurisdiction would provide no redress if the situation were reversed. * * * One may have some sympathy for this position in international disputes, but it has no persuasive effect when the States are involved. We do not feel compelled to provide a sanctuary in Arkansas for those who have willfully and wrongfully destroyed property, torn down houses, uprooted crops, polluted streams, and inflicted other injuries upon innocent landowners in our sister States. Yet every jurisdiction which follows the rule of the Livingston case affords that refuge to any person—whether one of its citizens or not—who is successful in fleeing from the scene of such misdeeds.

The truth is that the majority rule has no basis in logic or equity and rests solely upon English cases that were decided before America was discovered and in circumstances that are not even comparable to those existing in our Union. Basic principles of justice demand that wrongs should not go unredressed. * * * Under the majority rule we should have to tell Barton that he would have been much better off had the petitioner stolen his cotton outright instead of merely damaging it. And the only reason we could give for this unfortunate situation would be that English juries in the thirteenth century were expected to have personal knowledge of the disputes presented to them. We prefer to afford this litigant his day in court.

Writ denied.

GRIFFIN SMITH, C.J., concurs.

MCFADDIN and WARD, JJ., dissent.

MCFADDIN, JUSTICE (dissenting).

* * *

In the first place, the majority says that we have ample facilities to determine the land laws of other States in the United States. * * * This statement about the size of the law library seems rather weak, because land actions are tried in lower courts and not in the Supreme Court library. Just because we have a fine law library does not mean that we are prepared to determine the title to lands in Texas,[4] Missouri, Vermont, or any other State. But if we have the jurisdiction which the majority claims, then we could determine ejectment actions involving ownership of lands in other States. We might undertake to do this, but the Full Faith and Credit clause of the U.S. Constitution would not require the Sister State to recognize our judgment. * * *

Secondly, the majority says that the rule, requiring that an action be brought in the jurisdiction in which the land is situated, is a good rule between Nations, but is not good as between States in the American Union. For answer to this, I say: I have always understood that each of the American States is Sovereign; that the Federal Government is a government of delegated powers; and that all powers not delegated to the Federal Government are retained by the States and the People. Surely the majority is not attempting to reduce our American States to the level of mere local administrative units. Yet such, unfortunately, is the natural conclusion to which the majority opinion would carry us, when it concedes one rule for Nations and another for States.

Thirdly, the majority says that it does not desire to afford Arkansas Citizens a sanctuary from damage actions by citizens of other States. This is an argument that should be made—if at all—in the Legislative branch of Government, rather than in a judicial opinion. It is for the Legislative Department to determine when and where actions may be prosecuted. * * *

* * * [M]any, many cases * * * have considered the question here involved; and each Court—with the sole exception of Minnesota—has seen fit to follow the great weight of authority which has come down to us from the common law. In matters affecting real property particularly, we should leave undisturbed the ancient landmarks. * * *

NOTES AND QUESTIONS

1. In LIVINGSTON v. JEFFERSON, 15 F. Cas. 660 (C.C.D. Va. 1811), Chief Justice Marshall, sitting as a Circuit Judge, first recognized the local action doctrine. "Actions are deemed transitory," the court explained, "where transactions on which they are founded, might have taken place anywhere, but are local where their cause is in its nature necessarily local." Id. at 664. The lack of clarity in this definition led to its inconsistent application in the

4. The writer knows by experience that only one skilled in Texas Land Law can successfully handle an action of Trespass to Try Title in the State of Texas.

majority of American jurisdictions that adopted the rule, turning on formal distinctions such as whether the complaint alleged trespass to land or a dispute over title to land.

The *Livingston* decision concerned rights to land in what was then the territory of Louisiana. Edward Livingston, a New Yorker, claimed to own a sandbank that he had partially developed. Residents of the territory believed that the public ought to have free use of the sandbank. The Governor persuaded the United States to claim the sandbank as national property, and President Jefferson ordered the United States marshall to evict Livingston from the property. After Jefferson left office, Livingston filed a diversity action for damages against the former President in federal court in Virginia (the state in which Jefferson resided). The circuit court dismissed the action on the basis of the local action rule. Livingston eventually regained the sandbank through an action filed in Louisiana federal court against the marshall who had forced him off the land. For a history of the lawsuit, see Degnan, *Livingston v. Jefferson—A Freestanding Footnote*, 75 Cal.L.Rev. 115 (1987).

2. In those jurisdictions following the "majority" or "local action" rule, can the parties consent to a waiver of the venue objection in actions involving foreign land? See, e.g., Taylor v. Sommers Bros. Match Co., 35 Idaho 30, 204 P. 472 (1922). Parties can waive a defect in venue, but not of subject-matter jurisdiction. Is this why the dissenting opinion in *Reasor–Hill* says that a judgment in ejectment rendered by the Arkansas courts involving lands in other states would not be entitled to full faith and credit? "To this day it is unclear whether the local action rule is jurisdictional or merely a venue rule." Friedenthal, Miller & Kane, Civil Procedure § 2.16 (4th ed. 2005).

3. Have the justifications for the local action rule, discussed in *Reasor–Hill*, eroded over time? Should the doctrine be limited to in rem and quasi-in-rem I actions, where the dispute centers on rights to the property on which venue would be based? In 2001, the American Law Institute recommended eliminating the local action concept from federal venue statutes. For an argument favoring abolition, see Entman, *Abolishing Local Action Rules: A First Step Toward Modernizing Jurisdiction and Venue in Tennessee*, 34 U. Mem. L. Rev. 251 (2004).

3. VENUE IN THE FEDERAL COURTS

Read 28 U.S.C. § 1391 in the Supplement.

BATES v. C & S ADJUSTERS, INC.

United States Court of Appeals, Second Circuit, 1992.
980 F.2d 865.

NEWMAN, CIRCUIT JUDGE. This appeal concerns venue in an action brought under the Fair Debt Collection Practices Act * * *. Specifically, the issue is whether venue exists in a district in which the debtor resides and to which a bill collector's demand for payment was forwarded. The issue arises on an appeal by Phillip E. Bates from the May 21, 1992, judgment of the District Court for the Western District of New York, dismissing his complaint because of improper venue. We conclude that venue was proper under 28 U.S.C. § 1391(b)(2) and therefore reverse and remand.

Bates commenced this action in the Western District of New York upon receipt of a collection notice from C & S Adjusters, Inc. ("C & S"). Bates alleged violations of the Fair Debt Collection Practices Act, and demanded statutory damages, costs, and attorney's fees. The facts relevant to venue are not in dispute. Bates incurred the debt in question while he was a resident of the Western District of Pennsylvania. The creditor, a corporation with its principal place of business in that District, referred the account to C & S, a local collection agency which transacts no regular business in New York. Bates had meanwhile moved to the Western District of New York. When C & S mailed a collection notice to Bates at his Pennsylvania address, the Postal Service forwarded the notice to Bates' new address in New York.

In its answer, C & S asserted two affirmative defenses and also counterclaimed for costs, alleging that the action was instituted in bad faith and for purposes of harassment. C & S subsequently filed a motion to dismiss for improper venue, which the District Court granted.

Bates concedes that the only plausible venue provision for this action is 28 U.S.C. § 1391(b)(2), which allows an action to be brought in "a judicial district in which a substantial part of the events or omissions giving rise to the claim occurred." Prior to 1990, section 1391 allowed for venue in "the judicial district * * * in which the claim arose." * * * This case represents our first opportunity to consider the significance of the 1990 amendments.

Prior to 1966, venue was proper in federal question cases, absent a special venue statute, only in the defendant's state of citizenship. If a plaintiff sought to sue multiple defendants who were citizens of different states, there might be no district where the entire action could be brought. * * * Congress closed this "venue gap" by adding a provision allowing suit in the district "in which the claim arose." This phrase gave rise to a variety of conflicting interpretations. Some courts thought it meant that there could be only one such district; others believed there could be several. Different tests developed, with courts looking for "substantial contacts," the "weight of contacts," the place of injury or performance, or even to the boundaries of personal jurisdiction under state law. * * *

The Supreme Court gave detailed attention to section 1391(b) in Leroy v. Great Western United Corp., 443 U.S. 173, 99 S.Ct. 2710, 61 L.Ed.2d 464 (1979). The specific holding of *Leroy* was that Great Western, a Texas corporation, which had attempted to take over an Idaho corporation, could not bring suit in Texas against Idaho officials who sought to enforce a state anti-takeover law. Although the effect of the Idaho officials' action might be felt in Texas, the Court rejected this factor as a basis for venue, since it would allow the Idaho officials to be sued anywhere a shareholder of the target corporation could allege that he wanted to accept Great Western's tender offer. * * * The Court made several further observations: (1) the purpose of the 1966 statute was to close venue gaps and should not be read more broadly than necessary to close those gaps * * *; (2) the general purpose of the venue statute was to protect defendants against an unfair or inconvenient trial location * * *; (3) location of evidence and witnesses was a relevant factor * * *; (4) familiarity of the Idaho federal judges with the Idaho anti-takeover statute was a relevant factor * * *; (5) plaintiff's convenience was not a relevant factor * * *; and (6) in only rare cases should there be more than one district in which a claim can be said to arise * * *.

Subsequent to *Leroy* and prior to the 1990 amendment to section 1391(b), most courts have applied at least a form of the "weight of contacts" test * * *. Courts continued to have difficulty in determining whether more than one district could be proper. * * *

Against this background, we understand Congress' 1990 amendment to be at most a marginal expansion of the venue provision. * * *

Thus it seems clear that *Leroy*'s strong admonition against recognizing multiple venues has been disapproved. Many of the factors in *Leroy*—for instance, the convenience of defendants and the location of evidence and witnesses—are most useful in distinguishing between two or more plausible venues. Since the new statute does not, as a general matter, require the District Court to determine the best venue, these factors will be of less significance. * * * Apart from this point, however, *Leroy* and other precedents remain important sources of guidance. * * *

Under the version of the venue statute in force from 1966 to 1990, at least three District Courts held that venue was proper under the Fair Debt Collection Practices Act in the plaintiff's home district if a collection agency had mailed a collection notice to an address in that district or placed a phone call to a number in that district. * * * None of these cases involved the unusual fact, present in this case, that the defendant did not deliberately direct a communication to the plaintiff's district.

We conclude, however, that this difference is inconsequential, at least under the current venue statute. The statutory standard for venue focuses not on whether a defendant has made a deliberate contact—a factor relevant in the analysis of personal jurisdiction—but on the location where events occurred. Under the new version of section 1391(b)(2), we must determine only whether a "substantial part of the events * * * giving rise to the claim" occurred in the Western District of New York.

In adopting this statute, Congress was concerned about the harmful effect of abusive debt practices on consumers. See 15 U.S.C. § 1692(a) ("Abusive debt collection practices contribute to the number of personal bankruptcies, to marital instability, to the loss of jobs, and to invasions of individual privacy."). This harm does not occur until receipt of the collection notice. Indeed, if the notice were lost in the mail, it is unlikely that a violation of the Act would have occurred. Moreover, a debt collection agency sends its dunning letters so that they will be received. Forwarding such letters to the district to which a debtor has moved is an important step in the collection process. If the bill collector prefers not to be challenged for its collection practices outside the district of a debtor's original residence, the envelope can be marked "do not forward." We conclude that receipt of a collection notice is a substantial part of the events giving rise to a claim under the Fair Debt Collection Practices Act.

The relevant factors identified in *Leroy* add support to our conclusion. Although "bona fide error" can be a defense to liability under the Act, * * * the alleged violations of the Act turn largely not on the collection agency's intent, but on the content of the collection notice. The most relevant evidence—the collection notice—is located in the Western District of New York. Because the collection agency appears not to have marked the notice with instructions not to forward, and has not objected to the assertion of personal jurisdiction, trial in the Western District of New York would not be unfair.

* * *

NOTES AND QUESTIONS

1. Venue in the federal system is governed by a general venue statute, 28 U.S.C. § 1391, which was extensively amended in 1990 and then modestly revised in 1992 and 1995. Venue also is governed by specialized statutes that apply to particular federal claims such as antitrust, bankruptcy, employment discrimination, and patent. E.g., 28 U.S.C. § 1400 (copyright and patent litigation).

2. The general federal venue statute relies on two important criteria: the residence of the defendants and the location of the transaction that gives rise to the dispute. The majority of courts treat an individual's citizenship for determining diversity jurisdiction the same as residence for venue purposes. See 14D Wright, Miller & Cooper, Federal Practice and Procedure: Jurisdiction and Related Matters 3d § 3805. However, the residence of an unincorporated association for venue purposes differs from its citizenship under the diversity statute, and is "determined by looking to the residence of the association itself rather than that of its individual members." DENVER & R.G.W.R. CO. v. BROTHERHOOD OF RAILROAD TRAINMEN, 387 U.S. 556, 559–62, 87 S.Ct. 1746, 1748–50, 18 L.Ed.2d 954, 958–59 (1967). As the Court explained:

> Otherwise, § 1391(b) would seem to require either holding the association not suable at all where its members are residents of different States, or holding that the association "resides" in any State in which any of its members resides. The first alternative * * * removes federal-question litigation from the federal courts unnecessarily; the second is patently

unfair to the association when it is remembered that venue is primarily a matter of convenience of litigants and witnesses.

To complicate matters more, Section 1391(c) places corporate residence for venue purposes "in any judicial district in which it is subject to personal jurisdiction at the time the action is commenced." See 14D Wright, Miller & Cooper, Federal Practice and Procedure: Jurisdiction and Related Matters 3d § 3811.1. In a state with more than one judicial district, a corporation is deemed to reside in any district within which its contacts would be sufficient to subject it to personal jurisdiction if that district were a separate state. Do the considerations that justify the "minimum contacts" test for personal jurisdiction apply with equal force for venue?

3. Congress amended the transactional-venue provision of Section 1391 to make clear that venue may be proper in more than one district. See, e.g., Gulf Insurance Co. v. Glasbrenner, 417 F.3d 353 (2d Cir.2005). Moreover, as *Bates* emphasizes, p. 378, supra, transactional-venue does not simply fill a venue "gap," but rather may be used in any appropriate case.

4. Section 1391 contains a "fallback" provision that makes venue appropriate in any district in which the defendant is subject to personal jurisdiction. Note, however, the linguistic distinction between the fallback provision of Section 1391(a)(3), for federal-question cases, which permits venue in a judicial district in which "any defendant may be found," and that of Section 1391(b)(3), for diversity cases, which permits venue in a judicial district in which "any defendant is subject to personal jurisdiction at the time the action is commenced." What is the difference between these two default rules? An important commentary characterizes the distinction as one that "seems to be a clear act of drafting inadvertence," without "logical or policy justification." 14D Wright, Miller & Cooper, Federal Practice and Procedure: Jurisdiction and Related Matters 3d § 3806.2.

5. Cases involving multiple claims or multiple parties can raise complicated venue questions. What if one of the claims arises under a federal statute that has a special venue provision narrower than Section 1391? In some circumstances, courts recognize a doctrine of "pendent venue," defined as "discretion to hear claims as to which venue may be lacking if those claims arise out of a common nucleus of operative facts with claims as to which venue is proper." Wilson v. United States, 2006 WL 3431895, at *3 (E.D. Ark. 2006); see Bredberg v. Long, 778 F.2d 1285, 1288 (8th Cir.1985). Do the same considerations of party convenience and judicial efficiency that apply with respect to supplemental federal subject-matter jurisdiction, see p. 325, supra, apply to venue? For an argument urging limits on the concept of pendent venue, see Corn, *Pendent Venue: A Doctrine in Search of a Theory*, 68 U. Chi. L. Rev. 931 (2001); see also Underwood, *Reconsidering Derivative–Venue in Cases Involving Multiple Parties and Multiple Claims*, 56 Baylor L. Rev. 579, 582 (2004).

6. Professor Oakley has argued that the amended federal venue provisions effectively eliminated venue "as a significant independent constraint on choice of a federal forum." Oakley, *Recent Statutory Changes in the Law of Federal Jurisdiction and Venue: The Judicial Improvements Acts of 1988 and 1990*, 24 U.C.Davis L.Rev. 735, 769–82 (1991). Other commentators similarly

have expressed concern that the current venue statute affords insufficient protection to defendants. See Page, *After the Judicial Improvements Act of 1990: Does the General Federal Venue Statute Survive as a Protection for Defendants?*, 74 U. Colo. L. Rev. 1153 (2002). Keep these criticisms in mind when you study federal transfer provisions.

7. How should the local action doctrine affect venue in federal court? 28 U.S.C. § 1392 applies to actions "of a local nature" and Section 1391 establishes the situs of property "a substantial part" of which "is the subject of the action" as a ground for venue in both diversity and federal-question cases. 28 U.S.C. § 1391(a)(2), (b)(2). Should the local action doctrine be treated in the federal system as a rule of venue or of subject-matter jurisdiction? Compare Hayes v. Gulf Oil Corp., 821 F.2d 285, 287 (5th Cir. 1987) ("federal and state courts lack jurisdiction over the subject matter of claims to land located outside the state in which the court sits"), with Hallaba v. Worldcom Network Servs., Inc., 196 F.R.D. 630, 650 (N.D. Okla. 2000) (treating "the local action doctrine as a rule of venue" that is waivable).

8. Transnational litigation may involve property or other commercial assets located outside the United States. Does the local action doctrine apply to these cases? Mann v. Hanil Bank, 900 F.Supp. 1077 (E.D. Wis. 1995), involved failed efforts to distribute "the widely-popular Grip Ball game" in the United States. Id. at 1080. After a third party refused to comply with an attachment order in the underlying distribution litigation, plaintiff sought an order in federal court directing Korean banks to foreclose on $8 million of property in Korea. Finding the local action doctrine to be an alternative ground for dismissal, the court explained that "in cases such as this which involve international jurisdiction, matters of comity make us take the most prudent approach. The plaintiffs' remedy as to the foreclosure of Korean property lies in Korean courts * * *."

SECTION B. TRANSFER OF VENUE IN FEDERAL COURTS

HOFFMAN v. BLASKI

Supreme Court of the United States, 1960.
363 U.S. 335, 80 S.Ct. 1084, 4 L.Ed.2d 1254.

Certiorari to the United States Court of Appeals for the Seventh Circuit.

MR. JUSTICE WHITTAKER delivered the opinion of the Court.

* * *

The instant cases present the question whether a District Court, in which a civil action has been properly brought, is empowered by § 1404(a) to transfer the action, on the motion of the defendant, to a district in which the plaintiff did not have a *right* to bring it.

Respondents, Blaski and others, residents of Illinois, brought this patent infringement action in the United States District Court for the

Northern District of Texas against one Howell and a Texas corporation controlled by him, alleging that the defendants are residents of, and maintain their only place of business in, the City of Dallas, in the Northern District of Texas, where they are infringing respondents' patents. After being served with process and filing their answer, the defendants moved, under § 1404(a), to transfer the action to the United States District Court for the Northern District of Illinois. Respondents objected to the transfer on the ground that, inasmuch as the defendants did not reside, maintain a place of business, or infringe the patents in, and could not have been served with process in, the Illinois district, the courts of that district lacked venue over the action and ability to command jurisdiction over the defendants; that therefore that district was not a forum in which the respondents had a right to bring the action, and, hence, the court was without power to transfer it to that district. Without mentioning that objection or the question it raised, the District Court found that "the motion should be granted for the convenience of the parties and witnesses in the interest of justice," and ordered the case transferred to the Illinois district. Thereupon, respondents moved in the Fifth Circuit for leave to file a petition for a writ of mandamus directing the vacation of that order. That court, holding that "[t]he purposes for which § 1404(a) was enacted would be unduly circumscribed if a transfer could not be made 'in the interest of justice' to a district where the defendants not only waive venue but to which they seek the transfer," denied the motion. * * *

Upon receipt of a certified copy of the pleadings and record, the Illinois District Court assigned the action to Judge Hoffman's calendar. Respondents promptly moved for an order remanding the action on the ground that the Texas District Court did not have power to make the transfer order and, hence, the Illinois District Court was not thereby vested with jurisdiction of the action. After expressing his view that the "weight of reason and logic" favored "retransfer of this case to Texas," Judge Hoffman, with misgivings, denied the motion. Respondents then filed in the Seventh Circuit a petition for a writ of mandamus directing Judge Hoffman to reverse his order. After hearing and rehearing, the Seventh Circuit, holding that "[w]hen Congress provided [in § 1404(a)] for transfer [of a civil action] to a district 'where it might have been brought,' it is hardly open to doubt but that it referred to a district where the plaintiff * * * had a right to bring the case," and that respondents did not have a *right* to bring this action in the Illinois district, granted the writ, one judge dissenting. * * *

Petitioners' "thesis" and sole claim is that § 1404(a), being remedial, * * * should be broadly construed, and, when so construed, the phrase "where it might have been brought" should be held to relate not only to the time of the bringing of the action but also to the time of the transfer; and that "if at such time the transferee forum has the power to adjudicate the issues of the action, it is a forum in which the action might *then* have been brought." (Emphasis added.) They argue that in the interim between the bringing of the action and the filing of a motion to transfer it, the defendants may move their residence to, or, if corporations, may begin the transaction of business in, some other district, and, if such is done, the phrase "where it might have been brought" should be construed to empower the District Court to transfer the action, on motion of the defendants, to such other district; and that, similarly, if, as here, the defendants move to transfer the action to some other district and consent to submit to the jurisdiction of such other district, the latter district should be held one "in which the action might *then* have been brought." (Emphasis added.)

We do not agree. * * *

It is not to be doubted that the transferee courts, like every District Court, had jurisdiction to entertain actions of the character involved, but it is obvious that they did not acquire jurisdiction over these particular actions when they were brought in the transferor courts. The transferee courts could have acquired jurisdiction over these actions only if properly brought in those courts, or if validly transferred thereto under § 1404(a). Of course, venue, like jurisdiction over the person, may be waived. A defendant, properly served with process by a court having subject matter jurisdiction, waives venue by failing seasonably to assert it, or even simply by making default. * * * But the power of a District Court under § 1404(a) to transfer an action to another district is made to depend not upon the wish or waiver of the defendant but, rather, upon whether the transferee district was one in which the action "might have been brought" by the plaintiff.

The thesis urged by petitioners would not only do violence to the plain words of § 1404(a), but would also inject gross discrimination. That thesis, if adopted, would empower a District Court, upon a finding of convenience, to transfer an action to any district desired by the *defendants* and in which they were willing to waive their statutory defenses as to venue and jurisdiction over their persons, regardless of the fact that such transferee district was not one in which the action "might have been brought" by the plaintiff. Conversely, that thesis would not permit the court, upon motion of the *plaintiffs* and a like showing of convenience, to transfer the action to the same district, without the consent and waiver of venue and personal jurisdiction defenses by the defendants. Nothing in § 1404(a), or in its legislative history, suggests such a unilateral objective and we should not, under the guise of interpretation, ascribe to Congress any such discriminatory purpose.

* * *

Affirmed.

[A concurring opinion by JUSTICE STEWART has been omitted. This opinion pertained only to Hoffman v. Blaski.]

MR. JUSTICE FRANKFURTER, whom MR. JUSTICE HARLAN and MR. JUSTICE BRENNAN join, dissenting.*

* * *

The part of § 1404(a) the meaning of which is at issue here is its last phrase * * *. The significance of this phrase is this: even though a place be found to be an overwhelmingly more appropriate forum from the standpoint of "convenience" and "justice," the litigation may not be sent to go forward there unless it is a place where the action "might have been brought." Upon the scope to be given this phrase thus depends almost entirely the effectiveness of § 1404(a) to insure an appropriate place of trial, when the action is begun in an oppressive forum.

One would have to be singularly unmindful of the treachery and versatility of our language to deny that as a mere matter of English the words "where it might have been brought" may carry more than one meaning. * * * On the face of its words alone, the phrase may refer to * * * venue, amenability to service, or period of limitations, to all of them or to none of them, or to others as well. * * *

Surely, the Court creates its own verbal prison in holding that "the plain words" of § 1404(a) dictate that transfer may not be made in this case although transfer concededly was in the interest of "convenience" and "justice." Moreover, the Court, while finding the statutory words "plain," decides the case by applying, not the statutory language, but a formula of words found nowhere in the statute, namely, whether plaintiffs had "a right to bring these actions in the respective transferee districts." This is the Court's language, not that of Congress. * * * There can be expected to be very few, if any, alternative forums in a given case where the plaintiff has a "right" to sue, considering that that means places of unobjectionable venue where the defendant is amenable to service of process and where there are no other impediments such as a statute of limitations which the defendant can rely on to defeat the action.

* * * At the crux of the business, as I see it, is the realization that we are concerned here not with a question of a limitation upon the power of a federal court but with the place in which that court may exercise its power. We are dealing, that is, not with the jurisdiction of the federal courts, which is beyond the power of litigants to confer, but with the locality of a lawsuit, the rules regulating which are designed mainly for the convenience of the litigants. * * *

In light of the nature of rules governing the place of trial in the federal system * * *, what are the competing considerations here? The transferee court in this case plainly had and has jurisdiction to adjudicate this action with the defendant's acquiescence. As the defendant, whose privilege it is to object to the place of trial, has moved for transfer, and has acquiesced to going forward with the litigation in the transferee court, it

* This opinion applies only to [the companion case of] Sullivan v. Behimer [which raised the same question as Hoffman v. Blaski]. [Footnote by the Court.]

would appear presumptively, unless there are strong considerations otherwise, that there is no impediment to effecting the transfer so long as "convenience" and "justice" dictate that it be made. It does not counsel otherwise that here the plaintiff is to be sent to a venue to which he objects, whereas ordinarily, when the defendant waives his privilege to object to the place of trial, it is to acquiesce in the plaintiff's choice of forum. This would be a powerful argument if, under § 1404(a), a transfer were to be made whenever requested by the defendant. Such is not the case, and this bears emphasis. A transfer can be made under § 1404(a) to a place where the action "might have been brought" only when "convenience" and "justice" so dictate, not whenever the defendant so moves. A legitimate objection by the plaintiff to proceeding in the transferee forum will presumably be reflected in a decision that the interest of justice does not require the transfer, and so it becomes irrelevant that the proposed place of transfer is deemed one where the action "might have been brought." * * *

On the other hand, the Court's view restricts transfer, when concededly warranted in the interest of justice, to protect no legitimate interest on the part of the plaintiff. And by making transfer turn on whether the defendant could have been served with process in the transferee district on the day the action was brought, the Court's view may create difficult problems in ascertaining that fact, especially in the case of non-corporate defendants. These are problems which have no conceivable relation to the proper administration of a provision meant to assure the most convenient and just place for trial.

* * *

The relevant legislative history of § 1404(a) is found in the statement in the Reviser's Notes, accompanying the 1948 Judicial Code, that § 1404(a) "was drafted in accordance with the doctrine of forum non conveniens." Under that doctrine, the remedy for an inconvenient forum was not to transfer the action, but to dismiss it. In Gulf Oil Corp. v. Gilbert, [p. 391, infra,] * * * we held that "[i]n all cases in which the doctrine of *forum non conveniens* comes into play, it presupposes at least two forums in which the defendant is amenable to process; the doctrine furnishes criteria for choice between them." It is entirely "in accordance" with this view of the doctrine of *forum non conveniens* to hold that transfer may be made at the instance of the defendant regardless of the plaintiff's right as an original matter to sue him in the transferee court, so long as the defendant stipulates to going forward with the litigation there. Indeed, to hold otherwise as the Court does is to limit § 1404(a) to a much narrower operation than the nonstatutory doctrine of *forum non conveniens*. * * *

The only consideration of the Court not resting on the "plain meaning" of § 1404(a) is that it would constitute "gross discrimination" to permit transfer to be made with the defendant's consent and over the plaintiff's objection to a district to which the plaintiff could not similarly obtain transfer over the defendant's objection. * * * Transfer cannot be made under this statute unless it is found to be in the interest of "convenience" and in the interest of "justice." Whether a party is in any sense being "discriminated" against through a transfer is certainly relevant to whether the interest of justice is being served. If the interest of justice is being served, as it must be for a transfer to be made, how can it be said that there is "discrimination" in any meaningful sense? Moreover, the transfer provision cannot be viewed in isolation in finding "discrimination." It, after all, operates to temper only to a slight degree the enormous "discrimination" inherent in our system of litigation, whereby the sole choice of forum, from among those where service is possible and venue unobjectionable, is placed with the plaintiff. * * *

NOTES AND QUESTIONS

1. On what grounds does Section 1404(a) authorize transfer of venue in the federal courts? In deciding a motion to transfer, the settled view is that "the plaintiff's choice of forum should rarely be disturbed. * * * Rarely, however, is not never." In re National Presto Industries, Inc., 347 F.3d 662, 664 (7th Cir.2003). What factors ought to guide a judge in deciding whether to order the transfer of an action to a more convenient forum? Some commentators have argued that the present transfer system is costly and should be abolished. See Kitch, *Section 1404(a) of the Judicial Code: In the Interest of Justice or Injustice?*, 40 Ind.L.J. 99 (1965); Steinberg, *The Motion To Transfer and the Interests of Justice*, 66 Notre Dame L. Rev. 443 (1990).

2. Why do parties care about where a lawsuit is tried? According to an empirical study, "[T]he plaintiff wins in 58% of the nontransferred cases that go to judgment for one side or the other, but wins in only 29% of such cases in which a transfer occurred." Clermont & Eisenberg, *Exorcising the Evil of Forum–Shopping*, 80 Cornell L. Rev. 1507 (1995). Can you think of reasons other than venue that might explain difference in win rates?

3. *Blaski*, construing the statutory language "where it might have been brought," is typically interpreted to bar the transfer of a case to a district that lacks personal jurisdiction over the defendant. See Friedenthal, Kane & Miller, Civil Procedure § 2.17 (4th ed. 2005). How does the transferor court determine whether defendant is amenable to service in the transferee district? Does *Blaski* require the movant to demonstrate conclusively that defendant was amenable to process in the transferee district court at the time the action was commenced, or should a lesser showing be sufficient? See Dill v. Scuka, 198 F.Supp. 808 (E.D.Pa.1961); Comment, *The Requirement of Personal Jurisdiction When Transferring an Action Under Section 1404(a)*, 57 Nw. U.L.Rev. 456 (1962). The Ninth Circuit upheld a transfer from California to Delaware on the ground that the action could have been brought as a permissive counterclaim in an action between the parties already underway in Delaware. See A.J. Industries, Inc. v. United States District Court, 503 F.2d 384 (9th Cir.1974). The court stated that Hoffman v. Blaski has been widely criticized, and that there was no reason to "extend it unnecessarily." Id. at 387. Commentary suggests that courts are giving uneven treatment to the

"where it might have been brought" standard interpreted in *Blaski*. See Kelner, *Note—"Adrift on an Unchartered Sea": A Survey of Section 1404(a) Transfer in the Federal System*, 67 N.Y.U. L. Rev. 612 (1992).

4. To what extent should the transferee court attempt to reach the same result on the merits that would have been reached by the transferor court? Must the transferee court apply the law of the transferor court? Is the fact that an action would be barred by the statute of limitations in the transferee district relevant to the decision of a motion under Section 1404(a)? In VAN DUSEN v. BARRACK, 376 U.S. 612, 639, 84 S.Ct. 805, 821, 11 L.Ed.2d 945, 962–63 (1964), the Supreme Court held that, in diversity cases, the law applicable in the transferor forum follows the transfer.

Professor Marcus argues that the *Van Dusen* rule should not be applied to federal claims. See Marcus, *Conflict Among Circuits and Transfers Within the Federal Judicial System*, 93 Yale L.J. 677 (1984). Accepting this view, the District of Columbia Circuit has held that the law of the transferor forum on federal questions merits close consideration but does not have *stare decisis* effect in a transferee forum situated in another circuit. See In re Korean Air Lines Disaster of Sept. 1, 1983, 829 F.2d 1171 (D.C.Cir.1987), affirmed on other grounds sub nom. Chan v. Korean Air Lines, Ltd., 490 U.S. 122, 109 S.Ct. 1676, 104 L.Ed.2d 113 (1989). But see In re Dow Co. "Sarabond" Products Liability Litig., 666 F.Supp. 1466, 1468 (D.Colo.1987) (applying law of transferor court). Other commentators, pointing to inter-circuit disagreements, argue that the *Van Dusen* rule is important because it prevents litigants from using transfer motions to shop for favorable interpretations of federal law. See Levy, *The Myth of a Uniform Federal Law and the Reality of CERCLA: Arguments for Application of the Law of the Transferor Court Following a Section 1404(a) Transfer of Venue*, 6 Hastings W.–Nw. J. Envtl. L. & Pol'y 95, 95 (1999).

5. Can a clever plaintiff intentionally bring suit in an inconvenient forum with favorable law and then move for transfer under Section 1404(a), ending up with both the forum and law of her choice?

In FERENS v. JOHN DEERE CO., 494 U.S. 516, 110 S.Ct. 1274, 108 L.Ed.2d 443 (1990), plaintiff, a citizen of Pennsylvania, lost a hand when it allegedly became caught in a harvester manufactured by defendant, a Delaware corporation. Plaintiff failed to file suit within Pennsylvania's two-year tort limitations period. But, in the third year, plaintiff filed one suit in federal court in Pennsylvania, raising contract and warranty claims that were not yet time-barred, and a second suit in federal court in Mississippi, alleging tort claims. Mississippi had a six-year tort statute of limitations, which the federal court was required to apply. The federal court in Mississippi then granted plaintiff's motion to transfer the tort action to the Pennsylvania court under Section 1404(a). The Pennsylvania court, however, refused to apply Mississippi's statute of limitations and dismissed the tort claims as time-barred under Pennsylvania's statute of limitations, and the Court of Appeals affirmed. Relying on *Van Dusen,* the Supreme Court reversed, holding that, in a diversity suit, the transferee forum is required to apply the law of the transferor court, regardless of who initiates the transfer. Is this a sound result? See Bassett, *The Forum Game*, 84 N.C. L. Rev. 333, 352–70 (2006).

6. Section 1404(a) applies to cases in which plaintiff's original venue choice is proper. Section 1406(a) applies to cases in which the original venue choice is improper, and permits the district court to dismiss "or if it be in the interest of justice" to transfer a case to any district in which it could have been brought. Should the *Ferens* doctrine apply if a case is transferred pursuant to Section 1406(a)? In GOLDLAWR, INC. v. HEIMAN, 369 U.S. 463, 82 S.Ct. 913, 8 L.Ed.2d 39 (1962), a treble-damage action under the antitrust laws commenced in the Eastern District of Pennsylvania against a number of defendants, the Supreme Court held that Section 1406 authorizes the transfer of an action even if the transferor court lacks personal jurisdiction. The Court explained: "The filing itself shows the proper diligence on the part of the plaintiff which such statutes of limitation were intended to insure. If by reason of the uncertainties of proper venue a mistake is made, Congress, by the enactment of § 1406(a), recognized that 'the interest of justice' may require that the complaint not be dismissed but rather that it be transferred in order that the plaintiff not be penalized * * *. Id. at 466–67, 82 S.Ct. at 915–16, 8 L.Ed.2d at 42. Justice Harlan and Justice Stewart dissented, finding it "incongruous to consider, as the Court's holding would seem to imply, that in the 'interest of justice' Congress sought in § 1406(a) to deal with the transfer of cases where *both* venue and jurisdiction are lacking in the district where the action is commenced, while neglecting to provide any comparable alleviative measures for the plaintiff who selects a district where venue is proper but where personal jurisdiction cannot be obtained." Id. at 467–68, 82 S.Ct. at 916, 8 L.Ed.2d at 43.

The *Goldlawr* decision leaves open a number of questions that raise doubts as to its soundness. Suppose that plaintiff commences an action in a district court that patently lacks personal jurisdiction one day before the expiration of the applicable statute of limitations and ten days later moves to transfer the action to a district in which venue and jurisdiction are proper. If plaintiff is permitted to transfer, hasn't defendant lost the benefit of the statute of limitations? Put another way, shouldn't plaintiff be required to institute an action in a district having personal jurisdiction over defendant prior to the end of the limitations period? Furthermore, shouldn't defendant be guaranteed an opportunity to contest the transfer motion? If the court lacks personal jurisdiction over her, how will defendant know that the action has been instituted and a transfer motion made? An even broader question is to what extent *Goldlawr* results in plaintiff's abdicating the obligation to choose an appropriate forum in which defendant is amenable to suit and foisting that task upon the federal courts. See Note, *Change of Venue in Absence of Personal Jurisdiction Under 28 U.S.C. §§ 1404(a) and 1406(a)*, 30 U.Chi.L.Rev. 735 (1963); Comment, *Personal Jurisdiction Requirements Under Federal Change of Venue Statutes*, 1962 Wis.L.Rev. 342.

7. Notice that under Section 1404, as interpreted in *Van Dusen*, the law of the transferor court applies to the action; under Section 1406, the law of the transferee court applies. When a case is transferred under Section 1631, to cure a lack of personal jurisdiction, the law of the transferee court applies, as if the action were started there as an initial matter. E.g., Ross v. Colorado Outward Bound School Inc., 822 F.2d 1524 (10th Cir. 1987). See Butler, *Note—Venue Transfers When a Court Lacks Personal Jurisdiction: Where Are*

Courts Going with 28 U.S.C. § 1631?, 40 Val.U.L. Rev. 789 (2006). Do these differences make sense? Why?

8. One significant development in federal venue procedure has been the enactment of 28 U.S.C. § 1407, which provides for the temporary transfer to one district of related complex cases such as multidistrict antitrust actions. Transfer is appropriate when the cases involve common questions of fact and law and when it would be for the convenience of the parties and witnesses and in the interests of justice. This provision has been used frequently to take advantage of coordinated pretrial discovery, for example. A Panel on Multidistrict Litigation, composed of seven Court of Appeals and District Court judges appointed by the Chief Justice, makes decisions on whether or not cases should be transferred. The statute authorizes consolidation of cases for pretrial purposes only. In LEXECON INC. v. MILBERG WEISS BERSHAD HYNES & LERACH, 523 U.S. 26, 118 S.Ct. 956, 140 L.Ed.2d 62 (1998), the Supreme Court held that the panel on multidistrict litigation is required to remand cases consolidated under Section 1407 to their original courts for trial. Prior to this ruling, it was common practice for transferee courts to transfer cases to themselves for trial under Section 1404(a). Given that the intent of Section 1407 is to allow federal courts to handle complex cases more efficiently, what purposes are served by returning cases to their original districts for trial? Should the parties to the litigation be allowed to consent to having the case tried in the transferee court? Does the Court's reading of the statute properly balance efficiency concerns with traditional deference for plaintiff's choice of forum? Should Congress amend Section 1407 and overrule *Lexecon*? See 15 Wright, Miller & Cooper, Federal Practice and Procedure: Jurisdiction and Related Matters 3d § 3861; Marcus, *Cure–All For an Era of Dispersed Litigation? Toward a Maximalist Use of the Multidistrict Litigation Panel's Transfer Power*, 82 Tul. L. Rev. 2245 (2008).

SECTION C. FORUM NON CONVENIENS

GULF OIL CORP. v. GILBERT, 330 U.S. 501, 67 S.Ct. 839, 91 L.Ed. 1055 (1947), delineated the factors to be considered in deciding a motion based upon the principle of forum non conveniens:

> The principle of *forum non conveniens* is simply that a court may resist imposition upon its jurisdiction even when jurisdiction is authorized by the letter of a general venue statute. These statutes are drawn with a necessary generality and usually give a plaintiff a choice of courts, so that he may be quite sure of some place in which to pursue his remedy. But the open door may admit those who seek not simply justice but perhaps justice blended with some harassment. A plaintiff sometimes is under temptation to resort to a strategy of forcing the trial at a most inconvenient place for an adversary, even at some inconvenience to himself.
>
> Many of the states have met misuse of venue by investing courts with a discretion to change the place of trial on various grounds, such as the convenience of witnesses and the ends of justice. The federal law contains no such express criteria to guide the district court in exercis-

ing its power. But the problem is a very old one affecting the administration of the courts as well as the rights of litigants, and both in England and in this country the common law worked out techniques and criteria for dealing with it.

* * *

If the combination and weight of factors requisite to given results are difficult to forecast or state, those to be considered are not difficult to name. An interest to be considered, and the one likely to be most pressed, is the private interest of the litigant. Important considerations are the relative ease of access to sources of proof; availability of compulsory process for attendance of unwilling, and the cost of obtaining attendance of willing witnesses; possibility of view of premises, if view would be appropriate to the action; and all other practical problems that make trial of a case easy, expeditious and inexpensive. There may also be questions as to the enforceability [sic] of a judgment if one is obtained. The court will weigh relative advantages and obstacles to fair trial. It is often said that the plaintiff may not, by choice of an inconvenient forum, "vex," "harass," or "oppress" the defendant by inflicting upon him expense or trouble not necessary to his own right to pursue his remedy. But unless the balance is strongly in favor of the defendant, the plaintiff's choice of forum should rarely be disturbed.

Factors of public interest also have place in applying the doctrine. Administrative difficulties follow for courts when litigation is piled up in congested centers instead of being handled at its origin. Jury duty is a burden that ought not to be imposed upon the people of a community which has no relation to the litigation. In cases which touch the affairs of many persons, there is reason for holding the trial in their view and reach rather than in remote parts of the country where they can learn of it by report only. There is a local interest in having localized controversies decided at home. There is an appropriateness, too, in having the trial of a diversity case in a forum that is at home with the state law that must govern the case, rather than having a court in some other forum untangle problems in conflict of laws, and in law foreign to itself.

Id. at 507–09, 67 S.Ct. at 842–43, 91 L.Ed. at 1062–63.

PIPER AIRCRAFT CO. v. REYNO

Supreme Court of the United States, 1981.
454 U.S. 235, 102 S.Ct. 252, 70 L.Ed.2d 419.

Certiorari to the United States Court of Appeals for the Third Circuit.

JUSTICE MARSHALL delivered the opinion of the Court.

* * *

I

A

In July 1976, a small commercial aircraft crashed in the Scottish highlands during the course of a charter flight from Blackpool to Perth. The pilot and five passengers were killed instantly. The decedents were all Scottish subjects and residents, as are their heirs and next of kin. There were no eyewitnesses to the accident. At the time of the crash the plane was subject to Scottish air traffic control.

The aircraft, a twin-engine Piper Aztec, was manufactured in Pennsylvania by petitioner Piper Aircraft Co. (Piper). The propellers were manufactured in Ohio by petitioner Hartzell Propeller, Inc. (Hartzell). At the time of the crash the aircraft was registered in Great Britain and was owned and maintained by Air Navigation and Trading Co., Ltd. (Air Navigation). It was operated by McDonald Aviation, Ltd. (McDonald), a Scottish air taxi service. Both Air Navigation and McDonald were organized in the United Kingdom. The wreckage of the plane is now in a hangar in Farnsborough, England.

The British Department of Trade investigated the accident several months after it occurred. A preliminary report found that the plane crashed after developing a spin, and suggested that mechanical failure in the plane or the propeller was responsible. At Hartzell's request, this report was reviewed by a three-member Review Board, which held a 9–day adversary hearing attended by all interested parties. The Review Board found no evidence of defective equipment and indicated that pilot error may have contributed to the accident. The pilot, who had obtained his commercial pilot's license only three months earlier, was flying over high ground at an altitude considerably lower than the minimum height required by his company's operations manual.

In July 1977, a California probate court appointed respondent Gaynell Reyno administratrix of the estates of the five passengers. Reyno is not related to and does not know any of the decedents or their survivors; she was a legal secretary to the attorney who filed this lawsuit. Several days after her appointment, Reyno commenced separate wrongful death actions against Piper and Hartzell in the Superior Court of California, claiming negligence and strict liability. Air Navigation, McDonald, and the estate of the pilot are not parties to this litigation. The survivors of the five passengers whose estates are represented by Reyno filed a separate action in the United Kingdom against Air Navigation, McDonald, and the pilot's estate. Reyno candidly admits that the action against Piper and Hartzell was filed in the United States because its laws regarding liability, capacity to sue, and damages are more favorable to her position than are those of Scotland. Scottish law does not recognize strict liability in tort. Moreover, it permits wrongful death actions only when brought by a decedent's relatives. The relatives may sue only for "loss of support and society."

On petitioners' motion, the suit was removed to the United States District Court for the Central District of California. Piper then moved for transfer to the United States District Court for the Middle District of Pennsylvania, pursuant to 28 U.S.C. § 1404(a). Hartzell moved to dismiss for lack of personal jurisdiction, or in the alternative, to transfer.[5] In December 1977, the District Court quashed service on Hartzell and transferred the case to the Middle District of Pennsylvania. Respondent then properly served process on Hartzell.

B

In May 1978, after the suit had been transferred, both Hartzell and Piper moved to dismiss the action on the ground of *forum non conveniens*. The District Court granted these motions in October 1979. It relied on the balancing test set forth by this Court in Gulf Oil Corp. v. Gilbert, [p. 391, supra] * * *.

* * * [T]he District Court analyzed the facts of [this case]. It began by observing that an alternative forum existed in Scotland; Piper and Hartzell had agreed to submit to the jurisdiction of the Scottish courts and to waive any statute of limitations defense that might be available. It then stated that plaintiff's choice of forum was entitled to little weight. The court recognized that a plaintiff's choice ordinarily deserves substantial deference. It noted, however, that Reyno "is a representative of foreign citizens and residents seeking a forum in the United States because of the more liberal rules concerning products liability law," and that "the courts have been less solicitous when the plaintiff is not an American citizen or resident, and particularly when the foreign citizens seek to benefit from the more liberal tort rules provided for the protection of citizens and residents of the United States." * * *

The District Court next examined several factors relating to the private interests of the litigants, and determined that these factors strongly pointed towards Scotland as the appropriate forum. Although evidence concerning the design, manufacture, and testing of the plane and propeller is located in the United States, the connections with Scotland are otherwise "overwhelming." * * * The real parties in interest are citizens of Scotland, as were all the decedents. Witnesses who could testify regarding the maintenance of the aircraft, the training of the pilot, and the investigation of the accident—all essential to the defense—are in Great Britain. Moreover, all witnesses to damages are located in Scotland. Trial would be aided by familiarity with Scottish topography, and by easy access to the wreckage.

The District Court reasoned that because crucial witnesses and evidence were beyond the reach of compulsory process, and because the defendants would not be able to implead potential Scottish third-party defendants, it would be "unfair to make Piper and Hartzell proceed to trial in this forum." * * * The survivors had brought separate actions in Scotland against the pilot, McDonald, and Air Navigation. "[I]t would be

5. The District Court concluded that it could not assert personal jurisdiction over Hartzell consistent with due process. However, it decided not to dismiss Hartzell because the corporation would be amenable to process in Pennsylvania.

fairer to all parties and less costly if the entire case was presented to one jury with available testimony from all relevant witnesses." * * * Although the court recognized that if trial were held in the United States, Piper and Hartzell could file indemnity or contribution actions against the Scottish defendants, it believed that there was a significant risk of inconsistent verdicts.

The District Court concluded that the relevant public interests also pointed strongly towards dismissal. The court determined that Pennsylvania law would apply to Piper and Scottish law to Hartzell if the case were tried in the Middle District of Pennsylvania.[8] As a result, "trial in this forum would be hopelessly complex and confusing for a jury." * * * In addition, the court noted that it was unfamiliar with Scottish law and thus would have to rely upon experts from that country. The court also found that the trial would be enormously costly and time-consuming; that it would be unfair to burden citizens with jury duty when the Middle District of Pennsylvania has little connection with the controversy; and that Scotland has a substantial interest in the outcome of the litigation.

In opposing the motions to dismiss, respondent contended that dismissal would be unfair because Scottish law was less favorable. The District Court explicitly rejected this claim. * * *

C

On appeal, the * * * Third Circuit reversed and remanded for trial. The decision to reverse appears to be based on two alternative grounds. First, the Court held that the District Court abused its discretion in conducting the *Gilbert* analysis. Second, the Court held that dismissal is never appropriate where the law of the alternative forum is less favorable to the plaintiff.

The Court of Appeals began its review of the District Court's *Gilbert* analysis by noting that the plaintiff's choice of forum deserved substantial weight, even though the real parties in interest are nonresidents. It then rejected the District Court's balancing of the private interests. It found that Piper and Hartzell had failed adequately to support their claim that key witnesses would be unavailable if trial were held in the United States: they had never specified the witnesses they would call and the testimony these witnesses would provide. The Court of Appeals gave little weight to the fact that Piper and Hartzell would not be able to implead potential Scottish third-party defendants, reasoning that this difficulty would be

---

8. Under Klaxon v. Stentor Electric Mfg. Co., 313 U.S. 487, 61 S.Ct. 1020, 85 L.Ed. 1477 (1941), [p. 466, infra], a court ordinarily must apply the choice-of-law rules of the State in which it sits. However, where a case is transferred pursuant to 28 U.S.C. § 1404(a), it must apply the choice-of-law rules of the State from which the case was transferred. Van Dusen v. Barrack, [Note 4, p. 389, supra] * * *. Relying on these two cases, the District Court concluded that California choice-of-law rules would apply to Piper, and Pennsylvania choice-of-law rules would apply to Hartzell. It further concluded that California applied a "governmental interests" analysis in resolving choice-of-law problems, and that Pennsylvania employed a "significant contacts" analysis. The court used the "governmental interests" analysis to determine that Pennsylvania liability rules would apply to Piper, and the "significant contacts" analysis to determine that Scottish liability rules would apply to Hartzell.

"burdensome" but not "unfair" * * *. Finally, the court stated that resolution of the suit would not be significantly aided by familiarity with Scottish topography, or by viewing the wreckage.

The Court of Appeals also rejected the District Court's analysis of the public interest factors. It found that the District Court gave undue emphasis to the application of Scottish law: "the fact that the court is called upon to determine and apply foreign law does not present a legal problem of the sort which would justify the dismissal of a case otherwise properly before the court." * * * In any event, it believed that Scottish law need not be applied. After conducting its own choice-of-law analysis, the Court of Appeals determined that American law would govern the actions against both Piper and Hartzell. The same choice-of-law analysis apparently led it to conclude that Pennsylvania and Ohio, rather than Scotland, are the jurisdictions with the greatest policy interests in the dispute, and that all other public interest factors favored trial in the United States.

In any event, it appears that the Court of Appeals would have reversed even if the District Court had properly balanced the public and private interests. * * * [T]he court decided that dismissal is automatically barred if it would lead to a change in the applicable law unfavorable to the plaintiff.

We granted certiorari * * *.

II

The Court of Appeals erred in holding that plaintiffs may defeat a motion to dismiss on the ground of *forum non conveniens* merely by showing that the substantive law that would be applied in the alternative forum is less favorable to the plaintiffs than that of the present forum. The possibility of a change in substantive law should ordinarily not be given conclusive or even substantial weight in the *forum non conveniens* inquiry.

* * *

In fact, if conclusive or substantial weight were given to the possibility of a change in law, the *forum non conveniens* doctrine would become virtually useless. Jurisdiction and venue requirements are often easily satisfied. As a result, many plaintiffs are able to choose from among several forums. Ordinarily, these plaintiffs will select that forum whose choice-of-law rules are most advantageous. Thus, if the possibility of an unfavorable change in substantive law is given substantial weight in the *forum non conveniens* inquiry, dismissal would rarely be proper.

* * *

The Court of Appeals' approach is not only inconsistent with the purpose of the *forum non conveniens* doctrine, but also poses substantial practical problems. If the possibility of a change in law were given substantial weight, deciding motions to dismiss on the ground of *forum* *non conveniens* would become quite difficult. Choice-of-law analysis would become extremely important, and the courts would frequently be required to interpret the law of foreign jurisdictions. First, the trial court would have to determine what law would apply if the case were tried in the chosen forum, and what law would apply if the case were tried in the alternative forum. It would then have to compare the rights, remedies, and procedures available under the law that would be applied in each forum. Dismissal would be appropriate only if the court concluded that the law applied by the alternative forum is as favorable to the plaintiff as that of the chosen forum. The doctrine of *forum non conveniens,* however, is designed in part to help courts avoid conducting complex exercises in comparative law. As we stated in *Gilbert,* the public interest factors point towards dismissal where the court would be required to "untangle problems in conflict of laws, and in law foreign to itself." * * *

Upholding the decision of the Court of Appeals would result in other practical problems. At least where the foreign plaintiff named an American manufacturer as defendant, a court could not dismiss the case on grounds of *forum non conveniens* where dismissal might lead to an unfavorable change in law. The American courts, which are already extremely attractive to foreign plaintiffs, would become even more attractive. The flow of litigation into the United States would increase and further congest already crowded courts.

* * *

We do not hold that the possibility of an unfavorable change in law should *never* be a relevant consideration in a *forum non conveniens* inquiry. Of course, if the remedy provided by the alternative forum is so clearly inadequate or unsatisfactory that it is no remedy at all, the unfavorable change in law may be given substantial weight; the district court may conclude that dismissal would not be in the interests of justice.[22] In these cases, however, the remedies that would be provided by the Scottish courts do not fall within this category. Although the relatives of the decedents may not be able to rely on a strict liability theory, and although their potential damages award may be smaller, there is no danger that they will be deprived of any remedy or treated unfairly.

III

The Court of Appeals also erred in rejecting the District Court's *Gilbert* analysis. The Court of Appeals stated that more weight should have been given to the plaintiff's choice of forum, and criticized the District Court's analysis of the private and public interests. However, the

22. At the outset of any *forum non conveniens* inquiry, the court must determine whether there exists an alternative forum. Ordinarily, this requirement will be satisfied when the defendant is "amenable to process" in the other jurisdiction. *Gilbert* * * *. In rare circumstances, however, where the remedy offered by the other forum is clearly unsatisfactory, the other forum may not be an adequate alternative, and the initial requirement may not be satisfied. Thus, for example, dismissal would not be appropriate where the alternative forum does not permit litigation of the subject matter of the dispute. * * *

District Court's decision regarding the deference due plaintiff's choice of forum was appropriate. Furthermore, we do not believe that the District Court abused its discretion in weighing the private and public interests.

A

The District Court acknowledged that there is ordinarily a strong presumption in favor of the plaintiff's choice of forum, which may be overcome only when the private and public interest factors clearly point towards trial in the alternative forum. It held, however, that the presumption applies with less force when the plaintiff or real parties in interest are foreign.

The District Court's distinction between resident or citizen plaintiffs and foreign plaintiffs is fully justified. * * * When the home forum has been chosen, it is reasonable to assume that this choice is convenient. When the plaintiff is foreign, however, this assumption is much less reasonable. Because the central purpose of any *forum non conveniens* inquiry is to ensure that the trial is convenient, a foreign plaintiff's choice deserves less deference.

B

The *forum non conveniens* determination is committed to the sound discretion of the trial court. It may be reversed only when there has been a clear abuse of discretion; where the court has considered all relevant public and private interest factors, and where its balancing of these factors is reasonable, its decision deserves substantial deference. * * * Here, the Court of Appeals expressly acknowledged that the standard of review was one of abuse of discretion. In examining the District Court's analysis of the public and private interests, however, the Court of Appeals seems to have lost sight of this rule, and substituted its own judgment for that of the District Court.

(1)

In analyzing the private interest factors, the District Court stated that the connections with Scotland are "overwhelming." * * * This characterization may be somewhat exaggerated. Particularly with respect to the question of relative ease of access to sources of proof, the private interests point in both directions. As respondent emphasizes, records concerning the design, manufacture, and testing of the propeller and plane are located in the United States. She would have greater access to sources of proof relevant to her strict liability and negligence theories if trial were held here. However, the District Court did not act unreasonably in concluding that fewer evidentiary problems would be posed if the trial were held in Scotland. A large proportion of the relevant evidence is located in Great Britain.

The Court of Appeals found that the problems of proof could not be given any weight because Piper and Hartzell failed to describe with specificity the evidence they would not be able to obtain if trial were held in the United States. It suggested that defendants seeking *forum non conveniens* dismissal must submit affidavits identifying the witnesses they would call and the testimony these witnesses would provide if the trial were held in the alternative forum. Such detail is not necessary. Piper and Hartzell have moved for dismissal precisely because many crucial witnesses are located beyond the reach of compulsory process, and thus are difficult to identify or interview. Requiring extensive investigation would defeat the purpose of their motion. Of course, defendants must provide enough information to enable the District Court to balance the parties' interests. Our examination of the record convinces us that sufficient information was provided here. Both Piper and Hartzell submitted affidavits describing the evidentiary problems they would face if the trial were held in the United States.

The District Court correctly concluded that the problems posed by the inability to implead potential third party defendants clearly supported holding the trial in Scotland. Joinder of the pilot's estate, Air Navigation, and McDonald is crucial to the presentation of petitioners' defense. If Piper and Hartzell can show that the accident was caused not by a design defect, but rather by the negligence of the pilot, the plane's owners, or the charter company, they will be relieved of all liability. It is true, of course, that if Hartzell and Piper were found liable after a trial in the United States, they could institute an action for indemnity or contribution against these parties in Scotland. It would be far more convenient, however, to resolve all claims in one trial. The Court of Appeals rejected this argument. Forcing petitioners to rely on actions for indemnity or contributions would be "burdensome" but not "unfair." * * * Finding that trial in the plaintiff's chosen forum would be burdensome, however, is sufficient to support dismissal on grounds of *forum non conveniens*.

(2)

The District Court's review of the factors relating to the public interest was also reasonable. On the basis of its choice-of-law analysis, it concluded that if the case were tried in the Middle District of Pennsylvania, Pennsylvania law would apply to Piper and Scottish law to Hartzell. It stated that a trial involving two sets of laws would be confusing to the jury. It also noted its own lack of familiarity with Scottish law. Consideration of these problems was clearly appropriate under *Gilbert*; in that case we explicitly held that the need to apply foreign law pointed towards dismissal. The Court of Appeals found that the District Court's choice-of-law analysis was incorrect, and that American law would apply to both Hartzell and Piper. Thus, lack of familiarity with foreign law would not be a problem. Even if the Court of Appeals' conclusion is correct, however, all other public interest factors favored trial in Scotland.

Scotland has a very strong interest in this litigation. The accident occurred in its airspace. All of the decedents were Scottish. Apart from Piper and Hartzell, all potential plaintiffs and defendants are either Scottish or English. As we stated in *Gilbert,* there is "a local interest in having localized controversies decided at home." * * * Respondent argues that American citizens have an interest in ensuring that American manufacturers are deterred from producing defective products, and that additional deterrence might be obtained if Piper and Hartzell were tried in the United States, where they could be sued on the basis of both negligence and strict liability. However, the incremental deterrence that would be gained if this trial were held in an American court is likely to be insignificant. The American interest in this accident is simply not sufficient to justify the enormous commitment of judicial time and resources that would inevitably be required if the case were to be tried here.

* * *

Reversed.

[JUSTICE POWELL and JUSTICE O'CONNOR took no part in the decision of this case. JUSTICE WHITE concurred in part and dissented in part. JUSTICE STEVENS, with whom JUSTICE BRENNAN joined, dissented.]

NOTES AND QUESTIONS

1. The number of motions for dismissal on forum non conveniens grounds has increased considerably since the Supreme Court addressed the issue in *Gilbert*. Federal district courts heard seven motions for forum non conveniens dismissal in 1947 (the year *Gilbert* was decided), and all were for dismissal based on an alternative forum in the United States. In 2001, courts heard ninety-seven motions and all involved alternative fora outside the United States. See Davies, *Time to Change the Federal Forum Non Conveniens Analysis*, 77 Tul. L. Rev. 309, 386 & n. 335 (2002).

2. Lord Denning famously said: "As a moth is drawn to the light, so is a litigant drawn to the United States." Smith Kline & French Labs. Ltd. v. Bloch, [1983] 2 All E.R. 72, 72 (Eng. C.A. 1982). Why is the American legal system so attractive to foreign litigants?

One commentator emphasizes that courts in the United States offer plaintiffs a "wealth of procedural advantages that may not otherwise be available: extensive pretrial discovery, plaintiff-friendly juries, increased measures of damages, class action capabilities, the 'American rule' of litigation costs (as opposed to the 'loser pays' model), contingency fee arrangements, and more." Muttreja, Note—*How to Fix the Inconsistent Application of Forum Non Conveniens to Latin American Jurisdiction—and Why Consistency May Not Be Enough*, 83 N.Y.U. L. Rev. 1607, 1608 (2008).

In addition, United States law may provide relief for injuries (such as human rights violations) that is not available in a foreign litigant's home country. See Short, *Is the Alien Tort Statute Sacrosanct? Retaining Forum Non Conveniens in Human Rights Litigation*, 33 N.Y.U. J. Int'l L. & Pol. 1001, 1024 (2001).

Finally, increased numbers of foreign plaintiffs may be drawn to United States courts because they have been injured by United States companies doing business abroad. See Van Detta, *The Irony of Instrumentalism: Using Dworkin's Principle–Rule Distinction to Reconceptualize Metaphorically a*

Substance–Procedure Dissonance Exemplified by Forum Non Conveniens Dismissals in International Product Injury Cases, 87 Marq. L. Rev. 425, 429 (2004).

3. Should changed social conditions cause us to rethink the *Gilbert–Piper* approach? "Courts have acknowledged that modern modes of transportation, multilateral treaties providing for service abroad and other procedural mechanisms for international litigation, render *Gilbert*'s private interest analysis, virtually obsolete." Boyd, *The Inconvenience of Victims: Abolishing Forum Non Conveniens in U.S. Human Rights Litigation*, 39 Va. J. Int'l L. 41, 70 (1998). Other commentary argues that *Gilbert's* public interest analysis ought to be jettisoned. See Lear, *National Interests, Foreign Injuries, and Federal Forum Non Conveniens*, 41 U.C. Davis L. Rev. 559 (2007).

4. If the injured parties in *Piper Aircraft* had been United States citizens or residents, would the United States still be an inappropriate forum? In WIWA v. ROYAL DUTCH PETROLEUM CO., 226 F.3d 88 (2d Cir.2000), three Nigerian émigrés living in the United States brought suit alleging that opponents of defendant's oil exploration activities suffered human rights violations. The Second Circuit reversed the District Court's forum non conveniens dismissal and held that the forum choice of a United States resident is entitled to deference. "[T]he greater the plaintiff's ties to the plaintiff's chosen forum, the more likely it is that the plaintiff would be inconvenienced by a requirement to bring the claim in a foreign jurisdiction." Id. at 101–02. But see Carey v. Bayerische Hypo–Und Vereinsbank AG, 370 F.3d 234, 238 (2d Cir. 2004) (granting defendant German bank's motion to dismiss under forum non conveniens, overcoming "deference" due to plaintiff U.S. citizen's choice of home forum).

5. What factors might affect the scope of a court's discretion to order dismissal under the forum non conveniens doctrine? Some federal statutes include special venue provisions. Should these statutes be read to eliminate such discretion? See Hoffman & Rowley, *Forum Non Conveniens in Federal Statutory Cases*, 49 Emory L.J. 1137 (2000). What weight ought to be given to international treaties that require signatories to afford litigants "equal access to courts"? See 14D Wright, Miller & Cooper, Federal Practice and Procedure 3d § 3828.2. Similarly, consider the effect of jurisdictional statutes that confer federal power to hear suits by non-United States citizens. For example, the Alien Tort Claims Act, 28 U.S.C. § 1350, provides, "The district courts shall have original jurisdiction of any civil action by an alien for a tort only, committed in violation of the law of nations or a treaty of the United States." Does a court nevertheless have discretion to dismiss such an action on grounds of forum non conveniens? See Blumberg, *Asserting Human Rights Against Multinational Corporations under United States Law: Conceptual and Procedural Problems*, 50 Am. J. Comp. L. 493, 501–06 (2002).

6. One important requirement of the application of the doctrine of forum non conveniens is that there must be another more convenient forum where the plaintiff can obtain adequate relief. See Annot., 57 A.L.R.4th 973 (1987). In ISLAMIC REPUBLIC OF IRAN v. PAHLAVI, 62 N.Y.2d 474, 478 N.Y.S.2d 597, 467 N.E.2d 245 (1984), certiorari denied 469 U.S. 1108, 105 S.Ct. 783, 83 L.Ed.2d 778 (1985), the Islamic Republic of Iran sued the former

ruler of Iran, Shah Mohammed Reza Pahlavi, and his wife to recover $35 billion dollars in Iranian funds that the couple were alleged to have had misappropriated. The Shah and his wife withdrew these assets from Iran after a fundamental Islamist revolution deposed the Shah in 1979. The plaintiff served the couple in New York while the Shah was undergoing medical treatment at a New York hospital. The New York Court of Appeals affirmed the lower courts' dismissal on forum non conveniens grounds even though it appeared no alternative forum was available to the plaintiff since the Shah would not return to Iran. The New York court held that it was not required to entertain litigation that had no connection with the state.

7. Is an international tribunal—such as the International Court of Justice, the World Trade Organization, or the United Nations Compensation Commission—an acceptable alternative forum for purposes of forum non conveniens? See Alford, *The Proliferation of International Courts and Tribunals: International Adjudication in Ascendance*, 94 Am. Soc'y Int'l L. Proc. 160, 160 (2000). In NEMARIAM v. FEDERAL DEMOCRATIC REPUBLIC OF ETHIOPIA, 315 F.3d 390 (D.C. Cir.2003), certiorari denied 540 U.S. 877, 124 S.Ct. 278, 157 L.Ed.2d 141 (2003), the D.C. Circuit rejected a forum non conveniens dismissal to a Claims Commission designed to resolve war-related suits in Ethiopia and Eritrea. Relief in the Claims Commission was subject to being offset by amounts due from one nation to the other. The court found that "it would be peculiar indeed to dismiss Nemarian's claim in the United States District Court—a forum in which * * * she is certain to be awarded full relief if she wins on the merits of her claim—in favor of a forum in which she has no certainty of getting relief for a meritorious claim." Id. at 395.

8. Courts may choose to condition forum non conveniens dismissals on a defendant's waiver of a defense to being sued in the foreign forum. For example, a court may require a defendant to waive an objection to personal jurisdiction, or waive a defense that the statute of limitations in the foreign forum has run. E.g., In re Union Carbide Corp. Gas Plant Disaster at Bhopal, India in Dec., 1984, 809 F.2d 195 (2d Cir.1987), certiorari denied 484 U.S. 871, 108 S.Ct. 199, 98 L.Ed.2d 150 (1987). Are these conditions sufficient to ensure that the foreign plaintiff has an adequate remedy abroad? What weight should be given to plaintiff's concerns about political pressure or corruption in the alternative forum? In TUAZON v. R.J. REYNOLDS TOBACCO CO., 433 F.3d 1163 (9th Cir.2006), plaintiff, a Philippine citizen, filed a federal action in Washington State against a United States tobacco company, alleging defendant's "participation in a world-wide conspiracy to deny the addictive and harmful effects of smoking." Id. at 1167. The Ninth Circuit affirmed the District Court's denial of defendant's motion to dismiss on forum non conveniens grounds, but rejected plaintiff's contention that the Philippines judicial system would be inadequate because of corruption, delay, or potential influence by wealthy corporate defendants. Plaintiff's only evidence on this issue consisted of a State Department Country Report that focused on human rights criminal litigation in Philippine courts, and did not include "a single episode that * * * [plaintiff] directly observed or of which he has personal knowledge" concerning civil litigation. Id. at 1179. Why would personal information be more probative than a State Department report?

9. The Supreme Court recently addressed whether a district court must first determine that it can assert personal jurisdiction over the parties before dismissing the action on forum non conveniens grounds. In SINOCHEM INTERNATIONAL CO. LTD. v. MALAYSIA INTERNATIONAL SHIPPING CORP., 549 U.S. 422, 127 S.Ct. 1184, 167 L.Ed.2d 15 (2007), Malaysia International brought suit in federal district court against Sinochem, a Chinese company, alleging fraudulent misrepresentation in connection with the shipment of steel coils from a United States port to China. The District Court dismissed the case on forum non conveniens grounds without first establishing personal jurisdiction over Sinochem. The District Court noted that even if, after lengthy and costly discovery, it found that Sinochem had minimum contacts with the United States, the case ultimately would be dismissed on forum non conveniens grounds because China was undoubtedly the more convenient forum for litigation. The Supreme Court held that a district court has the authority "to respond at once to a defendant's *forum non conveniens* plea, and need not take up first any other threshold objection." Id. at 425, 127 S.Ct. at 1188, 167 L.Ed.2d at 22.

CHAPTER 6

ASCERTAINING THE APPLICABLE LAW

■ ■ ■

This Chapter focuses on the ways in which federalism and separation of powers affect choice of law in United States courts. The questions raised implicate some of the most profound issues in the first-year curriculum, involving the nature of law, the distinction between substantive and procedural rules, and the scope of the judicial function.

Civil actions involving citizens of a single state and a transaction that occurred entirely within the boundaries of that state do not present any problems of choosing the proper body of substantive law to be applied in determining the rights and liabilities of the parties. However, as soon as the litigation touches two or more states, one is likely to be confronted with the serious question of choosing between two or more sources of law. For example, suppose plaintiff and defendant, both citizens of State X, are involved in an automobile accident or agree to perform a contract or engage in a sale of property in State Y. Should questions pertaining to defendant's alleged negligence or failure to perform the contract or transfer the ownership of the property be decided under the law of State X or the law of State Y? Should the choice be made in the same way in tort, contract, and property actions? The complexity of these questions increases if plaintiff and defendant are citizens of different states and the event, relationship, or property that forms the predicate of the controversy can be traced to a third, and perhaps a fourth or fifth, state. You will be exposed to problems of this type on numerous occasions. Formal education in the philosophy of choosing among the laws of two or more states is the focus of a course in Conflict of Laws.

This Chapter is devoted to choice-of-law problems of a somewhat different dimension. Let us suppose that plaintiff is a citizen of State X and defendant is a citizen of State Y and that plaintiff has decided to litigate a tort or contract claim against defendant in a federal district court in State Y. What law should the federal court apply to adjudicate this action? The law of State X? Of State Y? Federal law? Would the answer be different if, assuming personal jurisdiction could be acquired, the action was commenced in a federal district court in State X? The problem of choosing between federal and state law also is present when a state court is called upon to decide cases arising under federal statutes or cases in which federal rights and liabilities are in issue. As one might surmise, the process of choosing between the law of two states and that of choosing between federal and state law are analogous, but also involve important differences. This Chapter will explore some of the problems created by the application of state law in the federal courts and the role of federal law in the state courts.

A final observation before beginning: If the law applied by one court differs materially from that applied by another, an attorney interested in achieving a particular result for a client obviously may wish to steer the lawsuit, if the jurisdiction and venue rules permit, to a particular tribunal. To what extent should a court take account of this type of forum manipulation in choosing the law to be applied?

SECTION A. STATE LAW IN THE FEDERAL COURTS

1. THE RULE OF SWIFT v. TYSON

Although Article III of the Constitution sets limits on the jurisdiction of the federal court system, it does not establish any lower federal courts. The power to establish those "inferior" courts was left to Congress, which quickly used it. The Judiciary Act of 1789 established a lower federal court system and promulgated rules governing its jurisdiction and operation. Among those rules, in Section 34 of the Judiciary Act, was the so-called Rules of Decision Act. The modern version of this Act is found in 28 U.S.C. § 1652 and reads:

> The laws of the several states, except where the Constitution or treaties of the United States or Acts of Congress otherwise require or provide, shall be regarded as rules of decision in civil actions in the courts of the United States, in cases where they apply.

For nearly one hundred years, the Supreme Court's decision in SWIFT v. TYSON, 41 U.S. (16 Pet.) 1, 10 L.Ed. 865 (1842), provided the basic interpretation of the language of the Rules of Decision Act. In *Swift,* some Maine land speculators sold land that they did not own to some New Yorkers. Although the speculators planned to use the New Yorkers' money to purchase the land, the New Yorkers thought that the speculators already owned the land. Some New Yorkers, including George W. Tyson, gave the speculators negotiable instruments instead of money to pay for their investments. Tyson "accepted" a bill of exchange in return for a six-month postponement in his payments on the land contract.

One of the speculators gave Tyson's note to Joseph Swift, a Maine banker, in satisfaction of a preexisting debt. When Swift sought payment from Tyson, Tyson refused to pay on the ground that his obligation was unenforceable since he had been induced to "accept" the bill by the speculator's fraud. Swift sued Tyson in federal court in New York based upon diversity jurisdiction. The principal question before the court was whether the case should be governed by New York contract law, under which the fraud tainting the transaction provided a defense for Tyson, or by the new law of negotiable instruments that was developing in recent English decisions, under which Tyson would have to pay Swift if Swift had accepted the instrument without notice of the fraud.

Whether New York law applied or not turned upon the meaning of the phrase "laws of the several states" in the Rules of Decision Act. If the phrase encompassed both the statutory and the decisional law of the states (that is, if the Act commanded federal courts to follow both state statutes and state court decisions in cases in which they covered the controversy), then the New York rule (which was judge-made, not part of a statute) had to be applied. If, on the other hand, the phrase encompassed only statutory law (that is, if the Act commanded federal courts to follow the state rule *only* if it was in a state statute), then the federal court in *Swift* was free to use the emerging rule or any other it felt was best. Justice Story, writing for a unanimous Court, concluded that the Act commanded federal courts to follow only the statutory law of the states:

> It is observable that the courts of New York do not found their decisions upon this point upon any local statute, or positive, fixed, or ancient local usage: but they deduce the doctrine from the general principles of commercial law. It is, however, contended, that the thirty-fourth section of the judiciary act of 1789, ch. 20, furnishes a rule obligatory upon this court to follow the decisions of the state tribunals in all cases to which they apply. * * * In order to maintain the argument, it is essential, therefore, to hold, that the word "laws," in this section, includes within the scope of its meaning the decisions of the local tribunals. In the ordinary use of language it will hardly be contended that the decisions of courts constitute laws. They are, at most, only evidence of what the laws are, and are not of themselves laws. They are often reexamined, reversed, and qualified by the courts themselves, whenever they are found to be either defective, or ill-founded, or otherwise incorrect. The laws of a state are more usually understood to mean the rules and enactments promulgated by the legislative authority thereof, or long established local customs having the force of laws. In all the various cases, which have hitherto come before us for decision, this court have uniformly supposed, that the true interpretation of the thirty-fourth section limited its application to state laws strictly local, that is to say, to the positive statutes of the state, and the construction thereof adopted by the local tribunals, and to rights and titles to things having a permanent locality, such as the rights and titles to real estate, and other matters immovable and intraterritorial in their nature and character. It never has been supposed by us, that the section did apply, or was designed to apply, to questions of a more general nature, not at all dependent upon local statutes or local usages of a fixed and permanent operation, as, for example, to the construction of ordinary contracts or other written instruments and especially to questions of general commercial law,

where the state tribunals are called upon to perform the like functions as ourselves, that is, to ascertain upon general reasoning and legal analogies, what is the true exposition of the contract or instrument, or what is the just rule furnished by the principles of commercial law to govern the case. And we have not now the slightest difficulty in holding, that this section, upon its true intendment and construction, is strictly limited to local statutes and local usages of the character before stated, and does not extend to contracts and other instruments of a commercial nature, the true interpretation and effect whereof are to be sought, not in the decisions of the local tribunals, but in the general principles and doctrines of commercial jurisprudence. * * *

Id. at 18–19, 10 L.Ed. at 871.

Is Justice Story correct when he asserts that "[i]n the ordinary use of language it will hardly be contended that the decisions of courts constitute laws"? Does it make sense to have the federal courts promulgate general, uniformly applied commercial laws? Why should a person suing in federal court in Oklahoma not receive the same remedy as a person suing in federal court in Vermont? On the other hand, if a federal court sitting in diversity is forced to apply the forum state's court decisions, what advantage would a party have in going to federal court?

The *Swift* decision must be evaluated in the context in which it was decided. First, *Swift* was decided in the heyday of "the common law." Justice Story believed that judges were responsible for finding "the truth" by examining all of the available authorities. In commercial matters, such as contracts, Story saw no need to adhere to the decisions of a single jurisdiction. Since the nature of commercial contracts is universal, the principles that should guide them are universal and are to be found by tapping the wisdom and experience of humankind.

Second, the federal government, including the judiciary, was seeking greater uniformity and stability in interstate commerce and, in this specific context, wanted to encourage businessmen to trust out-of-state negotiable instruments. On the other hand, the states' attitudes were guided by provincial concerns, such as trying to protect local debtors from foreign creditors. Thus, the *Swift* decision helped simplify commercial law and simultaneously encouraged the nationalist goals of the federal government.

2. THE *ERIE* DOCTRINE: THE RULES OF DECISION ACT AND THE RULES ENABLING ACT

ERIE R. CO. v. TOMPKINS

Supreme Court of the United States, 1938.
304 U.S. 64, 58 S.Ct. 817, 82 L.Ed. 1188.

[Slightly after midnight on July 27, 1934, Harry James Tompkins was walking home along a well-trodden footpath running parallel to the Erie Railroad tracks in Hughestown, Pennsylvania, when he was struck by "a black object that looked like a door" protruding from a passing train. Tompkins' right arm was severed.

Under Pennsylvania law, a traveler like Tompkins on a parallel (or "longitudinal") path was regarded as a trespasser to whom the railroad merely owes a duty to avoid wanton negligence. The majority rule in most states, however, was that a railroad owes a duty of ordinary care to a traveler on a parallel footpath.

Tompkins' lawyers were well aware of the rule in *Swift* that, absent state statutory law, federal courts apply "general law," and thus they tried to avoid the harsh Pennsylvania rule by suing the New York-based railroad in federal court. As anticipated, the District Court applied "general law," the majority rule, and the jury awarded Tompkins $30,000 in damages.

The Court of Appeals affirmed, holding that:

> [U]pon questions of general law the federal courts are free, in absence of a local statute, to exercise their independent judgment as to what the law is; and it is well settled that the question of the responsibility of a railroad for injuries caused by its servants is one of general law. * * * Where the public has made open and notorious use of a railroad right of way for a long period of time and without objection, the company owes to persons on such permissive pathway a duty of care in the operation of its trains. * * * It is likewise generally recognized law that a jury may find that negligence exists toward a pedestrian using a permissive path on the railroad right of way if he is hit by some object projecting from the side of the train.

The Supreme Court granted certiorari. After hearing the opening arguments, Chief Justice Hughes declared: "If we wish to overrule Swift v. Tyson, here is our opportunity."]

Certiorari to the Circuit Court of Appeals for the Second Circuit.

MR. JUSTICE BRANDEIS delivered the opinion of the Court.

* * *

First. Swift v. Tyson * * * held that federal courts exercising jurisdiction on the ground of diversity of citizenship need not, in matters of general jurisprudence, apply the unwritten law of the state as declared by its highest court; that they are free to exercise an independent judgment as to what the common law of the state is—or should be * * *.

* * * The federal courts assumed, in the broad field of "general law," the power to declare rules of decision which Congress was confessedly without power to enact as statutes. Doubt was repeatedly expressed as to the correctness of the construction given section 34, and as to the soundness of the rule which it introduced. But it was the more recent research of a competent scholar, who examined the original document, which established that the construction given to it by the Court was erroneous; and that the purpose of the section was merely to make certain that, in all matters except those in which some federal law is controlling, the federal courts exercising jurisdiction in diversity of citizenship cases would apply as their rules of decision the law of the state, unwritten as well as written.[5]

Criticism of the doctrine became widespread after the decision of Black & White Taxicab & Transfer Co. v. Brown & Yellow Taxicab & Transfer Co., 276 U.S. 518, 48 S.Ct. 404, 72 L.Ed. 681, 57 A.L.R. 426. There, Brown & Yellow, a Kentucky corporation owned by Kentuckians, and the Louisville & Nashville Railroad, also a Kentucky corporation, wished that the former should have the exclusive privilege of soliciting passenger and baggage transportation at the Bowling Green, Ky., railroad station; and that the Black & White, a competing Kentucky corporation, should be prevented from interfering with that privilege. Knowing that such a contract would be void under the common law of Kentucky, it was arranged that the Brown & Yellow reincorporate under the law of Tennessee, and that the contract with the railroad should be executed there. The suit was then brought by the Tennessee corporation in the federal court for Western Kentucky to enjoin competition by the Black & White; an injunction issued by the District Court was sustained by the Court of Appeals; and this Court, citing many decisions in which the doctrine of Swift v. Tyson had been applied, affirmed the decree.

Second. Experience in applying the doctrine of Swift v. Tyson, had revealed its defects, political and social; and the benefits expected to flow from the rule did not accrue. Persistence of state courts in their own opinions on questions of common law prevented uniformity; and the impossibility of discovering a satisfactory line of demarcation between the province of general law and that of local law developed a new well of uncertainties.

On the other hand, the mischievous results of the doctrine had become apparent. Diversity of citizenship jurisdiction was conferred in order to prevent apprehended discrimination in state courts against those not citizens of the state. Swift v. Tyson introduced grave discrimination by noncitizens against citizens. It made rights enjoyed under the unwritten

5. Charles Warren, New Light on the History of the Federal Judiciary Act of 1789 (1923) 37 Harv.L.Rev. 49, 51–52, 81–88, 108.

"general law" vary according to whether enforcement was sought in the state or in the federal court; and the privilege of selecting the court in which the right should be determined was conferred upon the noncitizen. Thus, the doctrine rendered impossible equal protection of the law. In attempting to promote uniformity of law throughout the United States, the doctrine had prevented uniformity in the administration of the law of the state.

The discrimination resulting became in practice far-reaching. This resulted in part from the broad province accorded to the so-called "general law" as to which federal courts exercised an independent judgment. In addition to questions of purely commercial law, "general law" was held to include the obligations under contracts entered into and to be performed within the state, the extent to which a carrier operating within a state may stipulate for exemption from liability for his own negligence or that of his employee; the liability for torts committed within the state upon persons resident or property located there, even where the question of liability depended upon the scope of a property right conferred by the state; and the right to exemplary or punitive damages. Furthermore, state decisions construing local deeds, mineral conveyances, and even devises of real estate, were disregarded.

In part the discrimination resulted from the wide range of persons held entitled to avail themselves of the federal rule by resort to the diversity of citizenship jurisdiction. Through this jurisdiction individual citizens willing to remove from their own state and become citizens of another might avail themselves of the federal rule. And, without even change of residence, a corporate citizen of the state could avail itself of the federal rule by reincorporating under the laws of another state, as was done in the Taxicab Case.

The injustice and confusion incident to the doctrine of Swift v. Tyson have been repeatedly urged as reasons for abolishing or limiting diversity of citizenship jurisdiction. Other legislative relief has been proposed. If only a question of statutory construction were involved, we should not be prepared to abandon a doctrine so widely applied throughout nearly a century. But the unconstitutionality of the course pursued has now been made clear, and compels us to do so.

Third. Except in matters governed by the Federal Constitution or by acts of Congress, the law to be applied in any case is the law of the state. And whether the law of the state shall be declared by its Legislature in a statute or by its highest court in a decision is not a matter of federal concern. There is no federal general common law. Congress has no power to declare substantive rules of common law applicable in a state whether they be local in their nature or "general," be they commercial law or a part of the law of torts. And no clause in the Constitution purports to confer such a power upon the federal courts. As stated by Mr. Justice Field when protesting in Baltimore & Ohio R.R. Co. v. Baugh, 149 U.S. 368, 401, 13 S.Ct. 914, 927, 37 L.Ed. 772, against ignoring the Ohio common law of fellow-servant liability: "I am aware that what has been termed the general law of the country—which is often little less than what the judge advancing the doctrine thinks at the time should be the general law on a particular subject—has been often advanced in judicial opinions of this court to control a conflicting law of a state. I admit that learned judges have fallen into the habit of repeating this doctrine as a convenient mode of brushing aside the law of a state in conflict with their views. And I confess that, moved and governed by the authority of the great names of those judges, I have, myself, in many instances, unhesitatingly and confidently, but I think now erroneously, repeated the same doctrine. But, notwithstanding the great names which may be cited in favor of the doctrine, and notwithstanding the frequency with which the doctrine has been reiterated, there stands, as a perpetual protest against its repetition, the constitution of the United States, which recognizes and preserves the autonomy and independence of the states,—independence in their legislative and independence in their judicial departments. Supervision over either the legislative or the judicial action of the states is in no case permissible except as to matters by the constitution specifically authorized or delegated to the United States. Any interference with either, except as thus permitted, is an invasion of the authority of the state, and, to that extent, a denial of its independence."

The fallacy underlying the rule declared in Swift v. Tyson is made clear by Mr. Justice Holmes.[23] The doctrine rests upon the assumption that there is "a transcendental body of law outside of any particular State but obligatory within it unless and until changed by statute," that federal courts have the power to use their judgment as to what the rules of common law are; and that in the federal courts "the parties are entitled to an independent judgment on matters of general law":

> But law in the sense in which courts speak of it today does not exist without some definite authority behind it. The common law so far as it is enforced in a State, whether called common law or not, is not the common law generally but the law of that State existing by the authority of that State without regard to what it may have been in England or anywhere else. * * *
>
> The authority and only authority is the State, and if that be so, the voice adopted by the State as its own [whether it be of its Legislature or of its Supreme Court] should utter the last word.

Thus the doctrine of Swift v. Tyson is, as Mr. Justice Holmes said, "an unconstitutional assumption of powers by the Courts of the United States which no lapse of time or respectable array of opinion should make us hesitate to correct." In disapproving that doctrine we do not hold unconstitutional section 34 of the Federal Judiciary Act of 1789 or any other act of Congress. We merely declare that in applying the doctrine this

23. Kuhn v. Fairmont Coal Co., 215 U.S. 349, 370–372, 30 S.Ct. 140, 54 L.Ed. 228; Black & White Taxicab, etc., Co. v. Brown & Yellow Taxicab, etc., Co., 276 U.S. 518, 532–536, 48 S.Ct. 404, 408, 409, 72 L.Ed. 681, 57 A.L.R. 426.

Court and the lower courts have invaded rights which in our opinion are reserved by the Constitution to the several states.

Fourth. The defendant contended that by the common law of Pennsylvania * * * the only duty owed to the plaintiff was to refrain from willful or wanton injury. The plaintiff denied that such is the Pennsylvania law. In support of their respective contentions the parties discussed and cited many decisions of the Supreme Court of the State. The Circuit Court of Appeals ruled that the question of liability is one of general law; and on that ground declined to decide the issue of state law. As we hold this was error, the judgment is reversed and the case remanded to it for further proceedings in conformity with our opinion.

Reversed.

MR. JUSTICE CARDOZO took no part in the consideration or decision of this case.

MR. JUSTICE BUTLER (dissenting).

* * *

Defendant's petition for writ of certiorari presented two questions: Whether its duty toward plaintiff should have been determined in accordance with the law as found by the highest court of Pennsylvania, and whether the evidence conclusively showed plaintiff guilty of contributory negligence. Plaintiff contends that, as always heretofore held by this Court, the issues of negligence and contributory negligence are to be determined by general law against which local decisions may not be held conclusive * * *.

No constitutional question was suggested or argued below or here. And as a general rule, this Court will not consider any question not raised below and presented by the petition. * * * Here it does not decide either of the questions presented, but, changing the rule of decision in force since the foundation of the government, remands the case to be adjudged according to a standard never before deemed permissible.

* * *

The doctrine of * * * [Swift v. Tyson] has been followed by this Court in an unbroken line of decisions. So far as appears, it was not questioned until more than 50 years later, and then by a single judge.[1] Baltimore & O. Railroad Co. v. Baugh * * *.

And since that decision, the division of opinion in this Court has been of the same character as it was before. In 1910, Mr. Justice Holmes, speaking for himself and two other Justices, dissented from the holding that a court of the United States was bound to exercise its own independent judgment in the construction of a conveyance made before the state courts had rendered an authoritative decision as to its meaning and effect. Kuhn v. Fairmont Coal Co. * * *. But that dissent accepted * * * as

1. Mr. Justice Field filed a dissenting opinion.

"settled" the doctrine of Swift v. Tyson, and insisted * * * merely that the case under consideration was by nature and necessity peculiarly local.

* * *

So far as appears, no litigant has ever challenged the power of Congress to establish the rule as construed. It has so long endured that its destruction now without appropriate deliberation cannot be justified. There is nothing in the opinion to suggest that consideration of any constitutional question is necessary to a decision of the case. * * * Against the protest of those joining in this opinion, the Court declines to assign the case for reargument. It may not justly be assumed that the labor and argument of counsel for the parties would not disclose the right conclusion and aid the Court in the statement of reasons to support it. Indeed, it would have been appropriate to give Congress opportunity to be heard before divesting it of power to prescribe rules of decision to be followed in the courts of the United States. * * *

The course pursued by the Court in this case is repugnant to the Act of Congress of August 24, 1937, 50 Stat. 751, 28 U.S.C.A. §§ 17 and note, 349a, 380a and note, 401. It declares that: "Whenever the constitutionality of any Act of Congress affecting the public interest is drawn in question in any court of the United States in any suit or proceeding to which the United States, or any agency thereof, or any officer or employee thereof, as such officer or employee, is not a party, the court having jurisdiction of the suit or proceeding shall certify such fact to the Attorney General. In any such case the court shall permit the United States to intervene and become a party for presentation of evidence * * * and argument upon the question of the constitutionality of such Act." * * * If defendant had applied for and obtained the writ of certiorari upon the claim that, as now held, Congress has no power to prescribe the rule of decision, section 34 as construed, it would have been the duty of this Court to issue the prescribed certificate to the Attorney General in order that the United States might intervene and be heard on the constitutional question. * * * Congress intended to give the United States the right to be heard in every case involving constitutionality of an act affecting the public interest. In view of the rule that, in the absence of challenge of constitutionality, statutes will not here be invalidated on that ground, the Act of August 24, 1937 extends to cases where constitutionality is first "drawn in question" by the Court. * * *

I am of opinion that the constitutional validity of the rule need not be considered, because under the law, as found by the courts of Pennsylvania and generally throughout the country, it is plain that the evidence required a finding that plaintiff was guilty of negligence that contributed to cause his injuries, and that the judgment below should be reversed upon that ground.

MR. JUSTICE MCREYNOLDS concurs in this opinion.

MR. JUSTICE REED (concurring in part).

I concur in the conclusion reached in this case, in the disapproval of the doctrine of Swift v. Tyson, and in the reasoning of the majority opinion, except in so far as it relies upon the unconstitutionality of the "course pursued" by the federal courts.

The "doctrine of Swift v. Tyson," as I understand it, is that the words "the laws," as used in section 34 of the Federal Judiciary Act of September 24, 1789, do not include in their meaning "the decisions of the local tribunals." * * *

To decide the case now before us and to "disapprove" the doctrine of Swift v. Tyson requires only that we say that the words "the laws" include in their meaning the decisions of the local tribunals. As the majority opinion shows, by its reference to Mr. Warren's researches and the first quotation from Mr. Justice Holmes, that this Court is now of the view that "laws" includes "decisions," it is unnecessary to go further and declare that the "course pursued" was "unconstitutional," instead of merely erroneous.

The "unconstitutional" course referred to in the majority opinion is apparently the ruling in Swift v. Tyson that the supposed omission of Congress to legislate as to the effect of decisions leaves federal courts free to interpret general law for themselves. I am not at all sure whether, in the absence of federal statutory direction, federal courts would be compelled to follow state decisions. There was sufficient doubt about the matter in 1789 to induce the first Congress to legislate. No former opinions of this Court have passed upon it. * * * If the opinion commits this Court to the position that the Congress is without power to declare what rules of substantive law shall govern the federal courts, that conclusion also seems questionable. The line between procedural and substantive law is hazy, but no one doubts federal power over procedure. * * * The Judiciary Article, 3, and the "necessary and proper" clause of article 1, § 8, may fully authorize legislation, such as this section of the Judiciary Act.

* * *

NOTES AND QUESTIONS

1. Is *Erie* really a constitutional decision or does it rest on other grounds? What constitutional provision could provide the basis for Justice Brandeis's opinion? Does it matter that at the time of the decision the Fifth Amendment "was not interpreted to have an equal protection component"? Rutherglen, *Reconstructing* Erie: *A Comment on the Perils of Legal Positivism*, 10 Const. Comment. 285, 286 (1993). Must the Constitution specifically authorize a regime of federal common law making? The Commerce Clause of the Constitution, Article I, Section 8, certainly allows Congress to regulate interstate railroads. If Congress can legislate in this area, why can't the courts act as well? Professor Clark has argued that *Erie* "is best understood as resting on the Supremacy Clause and the associated political and procedural

safeguards of federalism built into constitutionally prescribed lawmaking procedures." Clark, *Federal Lawmaking and the Role of Structure in Constitutional Interpretation*, 96 Cal. L. Rev. 699, 699 (2008). What are the limits of that argument? For a skeptical view of *Erie*'s constitutional foundation, see Green, *Repressing* Erie's *Myth*, 96 Cal.L.Rev. 595 (2008).

2. The constitutional discussion in *Erie* is sometimes referred to as "dicta." Is Justice Brandeis's reference to the Constitution merely a way of bolstering his interpretation of the Rules of Decision Act? See Clark, *State Law in the Federal Courts: The Brooding Omnipresence of Erie v. Tompkins*, 55 Yale L.J. 267, 278 (1946).

3. If discrimination against in-state defendants really is a problem, could it not be solved by allowing in-state defendants to remove to federal court? Does it make sense to require federal courts to apply state law in diversity cases simply out of a desire for parity between in-state defendants who cannot remove and out-of-state defendants who can? Justice Brandeis uses the *Black & White Taxicab* case to illustrate the evils resulting from *Swift*. But could not the problem presented in that case be handled without overruling *Swift* by preventing reincorporation solely to assert diversity jurisdiction? Reread 28 U.S.C. § 1359, set out in the Supplement. Would application of Section 1359 have alleviated the problem?

4. The *Erie* decision relied on research that revealed a previously unknown draft of what became the Rules of Decision Act of 1789. The draft read:

> And be it further enacted, That the Statute law of the several States in force for the time being and their unwritten or common law now in use, whether by adoption from the common law of England, the ancient statutes of the same or otherwise, except where the Constitution, treaties or statutes of the United States shall otherwise require or provide, shall be regarded as rules of decision in the trials at common law in the courts of the United States in cases where they apply.

Warren, *New Light on the History of the Federal Judiciary Act of 1789*, 37 Harv.L.Rev. 86 (1923). Did Justice Brandeis properly interpret the Rules of Decision Act given this legislative history? Or, did the shorter final version reflect congressional intent to limit the definition of "laws of the several states" to statutory laws, thus expanding the federal common law making power of the federal courts in diversity cases? Subsequent scholarship casts doubt on the Warren interpretation of the Judiciary Act of 1789. See Ritz, Holt, & Larue eds., Rewriting the History of the Judiciary Act of 1789: Exposing Myths, Challenging Premises, and Using New Evidence (1990). Does this debate suggest some of the difficulties of determining legislative intent?

5. *Erie* raises important questions about law and its relation to background concepts such as justice, fairness, and custom. Justice Holmes's statement that "law in the sense in which courts speak of it today does not exist without some definite authority behind it," quoted by Justice Brandeis in *Erie*, p. 408, supra, reflects a view that some commentators associate with the jurisprudence of legal positivism. Compare Lessig, Erie-*Effects of Volume 110: An Essay on Context in Interpretive Theory*, 110 Harv.L.Rev. 1785, 1793 (1997), with Goldsmith & Walt, Erie *and the Irrelevance of Legal Positivism*,

84 Va.L.Rev. 673 (1998). By contrast, *Swift* is said to have reflected "a natural law philosophy that places the judiciary at the forefront of discovery of the transcendent principles of an omnipresent and omniscient common law." Ides, *The Supreme Court and the Law To Be Applied in Diversity Cases: A Critical Guide to the Development and Application of the* Erie *Doctrine and Related Problems*, 163 F.R.D. 19, 23 (1995). Does *Erie* banish "general" law principles from federal court decision making, or rather limit the situations in which a diversity court may exercise independent judgment about those principles? See Nelson, *The Persistence of General Law*, 106 Colum. L. Rev. 503 (2006).

6. Professors Wright and Kane have said: "It is impossible to overstate the importance of the *Erie* decision." Wright & Kane, Law of Federal Courts § 55 (6th ed. 2002). As you read the cases that follow, consider why this might be so. Reactions to the *Erie* decision voiced shortly after it was handed down include Shulman, *The Demise of Swift v. Tyson*, 47 Yale L.J. 1336 (1938); and Tunks, *Categorization and Federalism: "Substance" and "Procedure" After Erie Railroad v. Tompkins*, 34 Ill.L.Rev. 271 (1939). Since then, *Erie* has continued to generate a large and lively discussion. For an analysis of the social and political context of the decision, as well as its jurisprudential underpinnings, see Purcell, The Story of *Erie*: How Litigants, Lawyers, Judges, Politics, and Social Change Reshape the Law, in Civil Procedure Stories 21 (Clermont ed.) (2d ed. 2008).

GUARANTY TRUST CO. v. YORK

Supreme Court of the United States, 1945.
326 U.S. 99, 65 S.Ct. 1464, 89 L.Ed. 2079.

[The Guaranty Trust Company served as trustee for some of the noteholders of Van Sweringen Corporation. In October 1930, Guaranty loaned money to corporations affiliated with and controlled by Van Sweringen. By October 1931, it was evident that the corporation was having trouble meeting its financial obligations. Guaranty and several other banks worked out a plan by which Guaranty would offer to purchase the notes by paying $500 and twenty shares of Van Sweringen stock for each $1,000 note.

Respondent York received $6,000 of the notes from a donor who had not accepted Guaranty's offer. York brought a diversity suit alleging that Guaranty had breached its fiduciary duties. York's complaint involved allegations of fraud and misrepresentation, relief for which was governed by equitable principles. On appeal, the Circuit Court of Appeals, one judge dissenting, found that in a suit brought on the equity side of a federal district court the court was not required to apply the state statute of limitations that would govern similar suits in state courts, even though the exclusive basis of federal jurisdiction was diversity of citizenship. The Supreme Court granted review in order to decide whether federal courts should apply state statutes of limitations in such cases.]

Certiorari to the Circuit Court of Appeals for the Second Circuit.

MR. JUSTICE FRANKFURTER delivered the opinion of the Court.

* * *

Our starting point must be the policy of federal jurisdiction which Erie R. Co. v. Tompkins * * * embodies. In overruling Swift v. Tyson * * * Erie R. Co. v. Tompkins did not merely overrule a venerable case. It overruled a particular way of looking at law which dominated the judicial process long after its inadequacies had been laid bare. * * * Law was conceived as a "brooding omnipresence" of Reason, of which decisions were merely evidence and not themselves the controlling formulations. Accordingly, federal courts deemed themselves free to ascertain what Reason, and therefore Law, required wholly independent of authoritatively declared State law, even in cases where a legal right as the basis for relief was created by State authority and could not be created by federal authority and the case got into a federal court merely because it was "between Citizens of different States" under Art. III, § 2 of the Constitution * * *.

In exercising their jurisdiction on the ground of diversity of citizenship, the federal courts, in the long course of their history, have not differentiated in their regard for State law between actions at law and suits in equity. Although § 34 of the Judiciary Act of 1789 * * * directed that the "laws of the several states * * * shall be regarded as rules of decision in trials of common law * * *," this was deemed, consistently for over a hundred years, to be merely declaratory of what would in any event have governed the federal courts and therefore was equally applicable to equity suits. * * * Indeed, it may fairly be said that the federal courts gave greater respect to State-created "substantive rights," Pusey & Jones Co. v. Hanssen, 261 U.S. 491, 498, 43 S.Ct. 454, 456, 67 L.Ed. 763, in equity than they gave them on the law side, because rights at law were usually declared by State courts and as such increasingly flouted by extension of the doctrine of Swift v. Tyson, while rights in equity were frequently defined by legislative enactment and as such known and respected by the federal courts. * * *

Partly because the States in the early days varied greatly in the manner in which equitable relief was afforded and in the extent to which it was available, * * * Congress provided that "the forms and modes of proceeding in suits * * * of equity" would conform to the settled uses of courts of equity. * * * But this enactment gave the federal courts no power that they would not have had in any event when courts were given "cognizance," by the first Judiciary Act, of suits "in equity." From the beginning there has been a good deal of talk in the cases that federal equity is a separate legal system. And so it is, properly understood. The suits in equity of which the federal courts have had "cognizance" ever since 1789 constituted the body of law which had been transplanted to this country from the English Court of Chancery. * * * In giving federal courts "cognizance" of equity suits in cases of diversity jurisdiction,

Congress never gave, nor did the federal courts ever claim, the power to deny substantive rights created by State law or to create substantive rights denied by State law.

This does not mean that whatever equitable remedy is available in a State court must be available in a diversity suit in a federal court, or conversely, that a federal court may not afford an equitable remedy not available in a State court. * * * State law cannot define the remedies which a federal court must give simply because a federal court in diversity jurisdiction is available as an alternative tribunal to the State's courts. Contrariwise, a federal court may afford an equitable remedy for a substantive right recognized by a State even though a State court cannot give it. Whatever contradiction or confusion may be produced by a medley of judicial phrases severed from their environment, the body of adjudications concerning equitable relief in diversity cases leaves no doubt that the federal courts enforced State-created substantive rights if the mode of proceeding and remedy were consonant with the traditional body of equitable remedies, practice and procedure, and in so doing they were enforcing rights created by the States and not arising under any inherent or statutory federal law.

* * *

And so this case reduces itself to the narrow question whether, when no recovery could be had in a State court because the action is barred by the statute of limitations, a federal court in equity can take cognizance of the suit because there is diversity of citizenship between the parties. Is the outlawry, according to State law, of a claim created by the States a matter of "substantive rights" to be respected by a federal court of equity when that court's jurisdiction is dependent on the fact that there is a State-created right, or is such statute of "a mere remedial character," * * * which a federal court may disregard?

Matters of "substance" and matters of "procedure" are much talked about in the books as though they defined a great divide cutting across the whole domain of law. But, of course, "substance" and "procedure" are the same keywords to very different problems. Neither "substance" nor "procedure" represents the same invariants. Each implies different variables depending upon the particular problem for which it is used. * * * And the different problems are only distantly related at best, for the terms are in common use in connection with situations turning on such different considerations as those that are relevant to questions pertaining to *ex post facto* legislation, the impairment of the obligations of contract, the enforcement of federal rights in the State courts and the multitudinous phases of the conflict of laws. * * *

Here we are dealing with a right to recover derived not from the United States but from one of the States. When, because the plaintiff happens to be a non-resident, such a right is enforceable in a federal as well as in a State court, the forms and mode of enforcing the right may at times, naturally enough, vary because the two judicial systems are not identical. But since a federal court adjudicating a State-created right solely because of the diversity of citizenship of the parties is for that purpose, in effect, only another court of the State, it cannot afford recovery if the right to recover is made unavailable by the State nor can it substantially affect the enforcement of the right as given by the State.

And so the question is not whether a statute of limitations is deemed a matter of "procedure" in some sense. The question is whether such a statute concerns merely the manner and the means by which a right to recover, as recognized by the State, is enforced, or whether such statutory limitation is a matter of substance in the aspect that alone is relevant to our problem, namely, does it significantly affect the result of a litigation for a federal court to disregard a law of a State that would be controlling in an action upon the same claim by the same parties in a State court?

It is therefore immaterial whether statutes of limitation are characterized either as "substantive" or "procedural" in State court opinions in any use of those terms unrelated to the specific issue before us. Erie R. Co. v. Tompkins was not an endeavor to formulate scientific legal terminology. It expressed a policy that touches vitally the proper distribution of judicial power between State and federal courts. In essence, the intent of that decision was to insure that, in all cases where a federal court is exercising jurisdiction solely because of the diversity of citizenship of the parties, the outcome of the litigation in the federal court should be substantially the same, so far as legal rules determine the outcome of a litigation, as it would be if tried in a State court. The nub of the policy that underlies Erie R. Co. v. Tompkins is that for the same transaction the accident of a suit by a non-resident litigant in a federal court instead of in a State court a block away should not lead to a substantially different result. * * * A policy so important to our federalism must be kept free from entanglements with analytical or terminological niceties.

Plainly enough, a statute that would completely bar recovery in a suit if brought in a State court bears on a State-created right vitally and not merely formally or negligibly. As to consequences that so intimately affect recovery or non-recovery a federal court in a diversity case should follow State law. * * *

Diversity jurisdiction is founded on assurance to non-resident litigants of courts free from susceptibility to potential local bias. The Framers of the Constitution, according to Marshall, entertained "apprehensions" lest distant suitors be subjected to local bias in State courts, or, at least, viewed with "indulgence the possible fears and apprehensions" of such suitors. Bank of the United States v. Deveaux, 5 Cranch 61, 87, 3 L.Ed. 38. And so Congress afforded out-of-State litigants another tribunal, not another body of law. The operation of a double system of conflicting laws in the same State is plainly hostile to the reign of law. Certainly, the fortuitous circumstance of residence out of a State of one of the parties to a litigation ought not to give rise to a discrimination against others equally concerned but locally resident. The source of substantive rights enforced by a federal court under diversity jurisdiction, it cannot be said too often, is the law of the States. * * *

The judgment is reversed and the case is remanded for proceedings not inconsistent with this opinion.

So ordered.

JUSTICE ROBERTS and JUSTICE DOUGLAS took no part in the consideration or decision of this case.

JUSTICE RUTLEDGE dissented in an opinion in which JUSTICE MURPHY joined.

* * * [T]he decision of today does not in so many words rule that Congress could not authorize the federal courts to administer equitable relief in accordance with the substantive rights of the parties, notwithstanding state courts had been forbidden by local statutes of limitations to do so. Nevertheless the implication to that effect seems strong, in view of the reliance upon Erie R. Co. v. Tompkins. * * * In any event, the question looms more largely in the issues than the Court's opinion appears to make it. For if legislative acquiescence in long-established judicial construction can make it part of a statute, it has done so in this instance. More is at stake in the implications of the decision, if not in the words of the opinion, than simply bringing federal and local law into accord upon matters clearly and exclusively within the constitutional power of the state to determine. It is one thing to require that kind of an accord in diversity cases when the question is merely whether the federal court must follow the law of the state as to burden of proof, * * * contributory negligence, * * * or perhaps in application of the so-called parol evidence rule. These ordinarily involve matters of substantive law, though nominated in terms of procedure. But in some instances their application may lie along the border between procedure or remedy and substance, where the one may or may not be in fact but another name for the other. It is exactly in this borderland, where procedural or remedial rights may or may not have the effect of determining the substantive ones completely, that caution is required in extending the rule of the Erie case by the very rule itself.

The words "substantive" and "procedural" or "remedial" are not talismanic. Merely calling a legal question by one or the other does not resolve it otherwise than as a purely authoritarian performance. * * * But they have come to designate in a broad way large and distinctive legal domains within the greater one of the law and to mark, though often indistinctly or with overlapping limits, many divides between such regions.

* * * The large division between adjective law and substantive law still remains, to divide the power of Congress from that of the states and consequently to determine the power of the federal courts to apply federal law or state law in diversity matters.

This division, like others drawn by the broad allocation of adjective or remedial and substantive, has areas of admixture of these two aspects of the law. In these areas whether a particular situation or issue presents one aspect or the other depends upon how one looks at the matter. * * *

Whenever this integration or admixture prevails in a substantial measure, so that a clean break cannot be made, there is danger either of nullifying the power of Congress to control not only how the federal courts may act, but what they may do by way of affording remedies, or of usurping that function, if the Erie doctrine is to be expanded judicially to include such situations to the utmost extent.

It may be true that if the matter were wholly fresh the barring of rights in equity by statutes of limitation would seem to partake more of the substantive than of the remedial phase of law. But the matter is not fresh and it is not without room for debate. A long tradition, in the states and here, as well as in the common law which antedated both state and federal law, has emphasized the remedial character of statutes of limitations, more especially in application to equity causes, on many kinds of issues requiring differentiation of such matters from more clearly and exclusively substantive ones. * * * The tradition now in question is equally long and unvaried. I cannot say the tradition is clearly wrong in this case more than in that. Nor can I say, as was said in the Erie case, that the matter is beyond the power of Congress to control. If that be conceded, I think Congress should make the change if it is to be made. The Erie decision was rendered in 1938. Seven years have passed without action by Congress to extend the rule to these matters. That is long enough to justify the conclusion that Congress also regards them as not governed by Erie and as wishing to make no change. This should be reason enough for leaving the matter at rest until it decides to act. * * *

Applicable statutes of limitations in state tribunals are not always the ones which would apply if suit were instituted in the courts of the state which creates the substantive rights for which enforcement is sought. The state of the forum is free to apply its own period of limitations, regardless of whether the state originating the right has barred suit upon it. Whether or not the action will be held to be barred depends therefore not upon the law of the state which creates the substantive right, but upon the law of the state where suit may be brought. This in turn will depend upon where it may be possible to secure service of process, and thus jurisdiction of the person of the defendant. It may be therefore that because of the plaintiff's inability to find the defendant in the jurisdiction which creates his substantive right, he will be foreclosed of remedy by the sheer necessity of going to the haven of refuge within which the defendant confines its "presence" for jurisdictional purposes. The law of the latter may bar the suit even though suit still would be allowed under the law of the state creating the substantive right.

NOTES AND QUESTIONS

1. What purposes do statutes of limitations serve? Are these purposes "substantive"? Procedural? Consider the following comment:

> Limitations law is famously a body of rules that are neither grass nor hay, being at once both substantive and procedural. In one sense, limitations law is clearly procedural—a sibling or at least a cousin to summary judgment. It is a means of clearing dockets, of protecting both the court and the defendant from waste, and of protecting the defendant from the unjust coercion that can result simply from the threat of waste. It is also a crude means of evaluating proof, a device to protect fact finders from being beguiled by stale and, therefore, suspect proof. * * * They are a tool of judicial administration and an allocation of scarce judicial resources, and thus in classical American conflicts dogma are characterized as procedural.
>
> In another sense, however, limitations law is substantive. Repose is a social and political value with economic consequences. Limitations law is thus a means of healing and stabilizing relationships. It reduces the general level of stress and anxiety, protecting even plaintiffs from the self-injuries that result when resentments are nourished for too long. Limitations "quicken diligence by making it in some measure equivalent to right." * * * They also facilitate and induce economic planning and development. These effects of limitations law occur outside the courthouse and have no bearing on the quality or accuracy of judicial proceedings. To the extent that these considerations are paramount, limitations law can be characterized as substantive.

Carrington, *"Substance" and "Procedure" in the Rules Enabling Act*, 1989 Duke L.J. 281, 290 (1989).

2. If a New York State equity court would not have granted a remedy to York for whatever reason, should a federal court sitting in diversity nevertheless grant a remedy? In answering this question, consider Justice Frankfurter's discussion of the difference between recognizing a state-created right and providing a remedy for infringement of that right. Could it not be argued that available remedies actually define the scope of the underlying rights?

3. To what extent does *York* require the displacement of a Federal Rule of Civil Procedure in favor of a contrary state practice? Consider the following cases:

Shortly after *York,* the Supreme Court considered a trio of cases all decided by the Court on the same day. RAGAN v. MERCHANTS TRANSFER & WAREHOUSE CO., 337 U.S. 530, 69 S.Ct. 1233, 93 L.Ed. 1520 (1949), grew out of a highway accident that occurred on October 1, 1943. On September 4, 1945, Ragan filed a diversity action in a federal court in Kansas. However, service was not made on the defendant until December 28. Kansas had a two-year statute of limitations on tort claims. Ragan claimed that according to Rule 3 of the Federal Rules, the suit was commenced (and hence the statute tolled) by the filing of the complaint. The defendant countered that Kansas law dictated that service had to have been made within the two-year period. The Supreme Court held that state law would determine in diversity when the statute was tolled.

In COHEN v. BENEFICIAL INDUSTRIAL LOAN CORP., 337 U.S. 541, 69 S.Ct. 1221, 93 L.Ed. 1528 (1949), the Court held that a federal court must apply a New Jersey statute requiring a plaintiff in a shareholder derivative suit to post a security-for-expenses bond—even though what is now Federal Rule 23.1, which ostensibly governs such cases, did not require a bond. The Court found that whether the New Jersey statute was classified as procedural or substantive, it created substantive liabilities for expenses. In the Court's view, Rule 23.1 did not contradict the New Jersey statute, but was addressed to independent concerns.

And, finally, in WOODS v. INTERSTATE REALTY CO., 337 U.S. 535, 69 S.Ct. 1235, 93 L.Ed. 1524 (1949), the Court held that a Tennessee corporation that had not qualified to do business in Mississippi could not maintain a diversity action in a federal court in that state if, by virtue of its failure to qualify, the Mississippi state courts were closed to it.

4. In what ways can you distinguish the remedial rights at issue in *York*, as well as in the trio discussed in Note 3, from the substantive duty in *Erie*? Consider this comment, published after the close of the Supreme Court's 1948 Term:

> If indeed the [*Erie*] doctrine rests on constitutional principles, its eventual limits will be governed by the powers granted to Congress in Article I. However, the remedial rights involved in the more recent cases, applying the "outcome" test, are distinguishable from the "substantive" duty of care which was the specific basis of Erie R.R. v. Tompkins. This distinction suggests that the rule, at least as presently applied, is one of administration only, and that Congress and the Supreme Court have the power to control the extent to which diversity jurisdiction can be further curtailed by state action. The Court, at least, is likely to sanction the continued expansion of the *Erie* doctrine until convinced that suits brought in the federal courts merely to evade state rules of law have been substantially eliminated.

The Supreme Court, 1948 Term, 63 Harv.L.Rev. 119, 127 (1949).

5. Almost any legal rule, whether labeled procedural or substantive, has the potential to affect the outcome of litigation. Does this mean that, after *York,* a federal court in a diversity case must apply every state legal rule that, if enforced, would affect the outcome of litigation? Does this include housekeeping rules like rules about the size of briefs or the color of paper used? Did Justice Frankfurter mean any rule that could affect the outcome, or would he say that only rules that influence a lawyer's choice of forum at the time she is choosing a forum are "outcome determinative"?

6. Evaluate the following passage:

> The *York* case, of necessity, spelled death to the hope for a completely uniform federal procedure. When its doctrine is logically applied, each important step in a diversity action must be examined in the light of two systems of law—first, under the Federal Rules, and then under the law of the state in which the federal court sits. In one state, a particular Rule might not clash with a local law or decision which significantly bears upon the outcome of a litigation. Under such circumstances, the Rule should prevail, although the determination as to its applicability is actually made under state law. In another state, the same Rule might conflict in some substantial way with that state's policy or law. In such

instances, state law, and not the Rule, will govern a federal court's decision.

Merrigan, Erie *to* York *to* Ragan—*A Triple Play on the Federal Rules*, 3 Vand.L.Rev. 711, 717 (1950).

7. Justice Rutledge dissented in *York*, as well as in the trio discussed in Note 3. What is the basis for Justice Rutledge's dissent? A prominent scholar characterized Justice Rutledge as

> a lonely but persistent critic of the gloss that the federal court is "merely another court of the state in which it sits," which was written into the *Erie* doctrine in the [*York*] case. Fortunately, the Court has retreated substantially from the illogical and unworkable test announced in [*York*], and now takes a view similar to that Mr. Justice Rutledge championed.

Wright, *Book Review—Justice Rutledge and the Bright Constellation*, 79 Harv.L.Rev. 212, 219 (1965).

BYRD v. BLUE RIDGE RURAL ELECTRIC COOPERATIVE, INC.

Supreme Court of the United States, 1958.
356 U.S. 525, 78 S.Ct. 893, 2 L.Ed.2d 953.

Certiorari to the United States Court of Appeals for the Fourth Circuit.

MR. JUSTICE BRENNAN delivered the opinion of the Court.

This case was brought in the District Court for the Western District of South Carolina. Jurisdiction was based on diversity of citizenship. * * * The petitioner, a resident of North Carolina, sued respondent, a South Carolina corporation, for damages for injuries allegedly caused by the respondent's negligence. He had judgment on a jury verdict. The Court of Appeals for the Fourth Circuit reversed and directed the entry of judgment for the respondent. * * *

The respondent is in the business of selling electric power to subscribers in rural sections of South Carolina. The petitioner was employed as a lineman in the construction crew of a construction contractor. The contractor, R.H. Bouligny, Inc., held a contract with the respondent * * * for the building of some * * * power lines, the reconversion to higher capacities of * * * existing lines, and the construction of 2 new substations and a breaker station. The petitioner was injured while connecting power lines to one of the new substations.

One of respondent's affirmative defenses was that under the South Carolina Workmen's Compensation Act, the petitioner—because the work contracted to be done by his employer was work of the kind also done by the respondent's own construction and maintenance crews—had the status of a statutory employee of the respondent and was therefore barred from suing the respondent at law because obliged to accept statutory compensation benefits as the exclusive remedy for his injuries. Two questions concerning this defense are before us: (1) whether the Court of

Appeals erred in directing judgment for respondent without a remand to give petitioner an opportunity to introduce further evidence; and (2) whether petitioner, state practice notwithstanding, is entitled to a jury determination of the factual issues raised by this defense.

* * *

[The Supreme Court initially decided to remand the case to the trial court to provide the petitioner an opportunity to introduce evidence on the question of whether the respondent was a statutory employer.]

A question is also presented as to whether on remand the factual issue is to be decided by the judge or by the jury. The respondent argues on the basis of the decision of the Supreme Court of South Carolina in Adams v. Davison–Paxon Co., 230 S.C. 532, 96 S.E.2d 566, that the issue of immunity should be decided by the judge and not by the jury. That was a negligence action brought in the state trial court against a store owner by an employee of an independent contractor who operated the store's millinery department. The trial judge denied the store owner's motion for a directed verdict made upon the ground that [South Carolina Code, 1952] § 72–111 barred the plaintiff's action. The jury returned a verdict for the plaintiff. The South Carolina Supreme Court reversed, holding that it was for the judge and not the jury to decide on the evidence whether the owner was a statutory employer, and that the store owner had sustained his defense. * * *

The respondent argues that this state-court decision governs the present diversity case and "divests the jury of its normal function" to decide the disputed fact question of the respondent's immunity under § 72–111. This is to contend that the federal court is bound under Erie R. Co. v. Tompkins * * * to follow the state court's holding to secure uniform enforcement of the immunity created by the State.

First. It was decided in Erie R. Co. v. Tompkins that the federal courts in diversity cases must respect the definition of state-created rights and obligations by the state courts. We must, therefore, first examine the rule in Adams v. Davison–Paxon Co. to determine whether it is bound up with these rights and obligations in such a way that its application in the federal court is required. * * *

The Workmen's Compensation Act is administered in South Carolina by its Industrial Commission. The South Carolina courts hold that, on judicial review of actions of the Commission under § 72–111, the question whether the claim of an injured workman is within the Commission's jurisdiction is a matter of law for decision by the court, which makes its own findings of fact relating to that jurisdiction. The South Carolina Supreme Court states no reasons in Adams v. Davison–Paxon Co. why, although the jury decides all other factual issues raised by the cause of action and defenses, the jury is displaced as to the factual issue raised by the affirmative defense under § 72–111. * * * A State may, of course, distribute the functions of its judicial machinery as it sees fit. The decisions relied upon, however, furnish no reason for selecting the judge rather than the jury to decide this single affirmative defense in the negligence action. They simply reflect a policy * * * that administrative determination of "jurisdictional facts" should not be final but subject to judicial review. The conclusion is inescapable that the Adams holding is grounded in the practical consideration that the question had theretofore come before the South Carolina courts from the Industrial Commission and the courts had become accustomed to deciding the factual issue of immunity without the aid of juries. We find nothing to suggest that this rule was announced as an integral part of the special relationship created by the statute. Thus the requirement appears to be merely a form and mode of enforcing the immunity * * * and not a rule intended to be bound up with the definition of the rights and obligations of the parties. * * *

Second. But cases following *Erie* have evinced a broader policy to the effect that the federal courts should conform as near as may be—in the absence of other considerations—to state rules even of form and mode where the state rules may bear substantially on the question whether the litigation would come out one way in the federal court and another way in the state court if the federal court failed to apply a particular local rule. E.g., Guaranty Trust Co. of New York v. York, * * *; [p. 416, supra,] Bernhardt v. Polygraphic Co., 350 U.S. 198, 76 S.Ct. 273, 100 L.Ed. 199. Concededly the nature of the tribunal which tries issues may be important in the enforcement of the parcel of rights making up a cause of action or defense, and bear significantly upon achievement of uniform enforcement of the right. It may well be that in the instant personal-injury case the outcome would be substantially affected by whether the issue of immunity is decided by a judge or a jury. Therefore, were "outcome" the only consideration, a strong case might appear for saying that the federal court should follow the state practice.

But there are affirmative countervailing considerations at work here. The federal system is an independent system for administering justice to litigants who properly invoke its jurisdiction. An essential characteristic of that system is the manner in which, in civil common-law actions, it distributes trial functions between judge and jury and, under the influence—if not the command—of the Seventh Amendment, assigns the decisions of disputed questions of fact to the jury. * * * The policy of uniform enforcement of state-created rights and obligations * * * cannot in every case exact compliance with a state rule—not bound up with rights and obligations—which disrupts the federal system of allocating functions between judge and jury. * * * Thus the inquiry here is whether the federal policy favoring jury decisions of disputed fact questions should yield to the state rule in the interest of furthering the objective that the litigation should not come out one way in the federal court and another way in the state court.

We think that in the circumstances of this case the federal court should not follow the state rule. It cannot be gainsaid that there is a strong federal policy against allowing state rules to disrupt the judge-jury relationship in the federal courts. In Herron v. Southern Pacific Co., [283 U.S. 91, 51 S.Ct. 383, 75 L.Ed. 857 (1931),] * * * the trial judge in a personal-injury negligence action brought in the District Court for Arizona on diversity grounds directed a verdict for the defendant when it appeared as a matter of law that the plaintiff was guilty of contributory negligence. The federal judge refused to be bound by a provision of the Arizona Constitution which made the jury the sole arbiter of the question of contributory negligence. This Court sustained the action of the trial judge, holding that "state laws cannot alter the essential character or function of a federal court" because that function "is not in any sense a local matter, and state statutes which would interfere with the appropriate performance of that function are not binding upon the federal court under either the Conformity Act or the 'Rules of Decision' Act." * * * Perhaps even more clearly in light of the influence of the Seventh Amendment, the function assigned to the jury "is an essential factor in the process for which the Federal Constitution provides." * * * Concededly the *Herron* case was decided before Erie R. Co. v. Tompkins, but even when Swift v. Tyson * * * was governing law and allowed federal courts sitting in diversity cases to disregard state decisional law, it was never thought that state statutes or constitutions were similarly to be disregarded. * * * Yet *Herron* held that state statutes and constitutional provisions could not disrupt or alter the essential character or function of a federal court.[14]

Third. We have discussed the problem upon the assumption that the outcome of the litigation may be substantially affected by whether the issue of immunity is decided by a judge or a jury. But clearly there is not present here the certainty that a different result would follow * * * or even the strong possibility that this would be the case * * *. There are factors present here which might reduce that possibility. The trial judge in the federal system has powers denied the judges of many States to comment on the weight of evidence and credibility of witnesses, and discretion to grant a new trial if the verdict appears to him to be against the weight of the evidence. We do not think the likelihood of a different result is so strong as to require the federal practice of jury determination of disputed factual issues to yield to the state rule in the interest of uniformity of outcome.[15]

* * *

---

14. Diederich v. American News Co., 10 Cir., 128 F.2d 144, decided after Erie R. Co. v. Tompkins, held that an almost identical provision of the Oklahoma Constitution, art. 23, § 6, O.S.1951 was not binding on a federal judge in a diversity case.

15. Stoner v. New York Life Ins. Co., 311 U.S. 464, 61 S.Ct. 336, 85 L.Ed. 284, is not contrary. It was there held that the federal court should follow the state rule defining the evidence sufficient to raise a jury question whether the state-created right was established. But the state rule did not have the effect of nullifying the function of the federal judge to control a jury submission as did the Arizona constitutional provision which was denied effect in *Herron*. The South Carolina rule here involved affects the jury function as the Arizona provision affected the function of the judge: The rule entirely displaces the jury without regard to the sufficiency of the evidence to support a jury finding of immunity.

Reversed and remanded.

* * *

[JUSTICE WHITTAKER concurred in Part I of the Court's opinion but dissented from Part II on the ground that the South Carolina rule requiring "its courts—not juries—to determine whether jurisdiction over the subject matter of cases like this is vested in its Industrial Commission" should be honored by a federal court. JUSTICE FRANKFURTER and JUSTICE HARLAN dissented on the ground that the evidence required the district court to direct a verdict for the respondent.]

NOTES AND QUESTIONS

1. The Seventh Amendment provides a right to a jury trial in certain civil cases. Unlike other provisions of the Bill of Rights, this amendment does not apply to the states through operation of the Fourteenth Amendment. See Minneapolis & St. Louis R.R. Co. v. Bombolis, 241 U.S. 211, 36 S.Ct. 595, 60 L.Ed. 961 (1916). At the time the Fourteenth Amendment was adopted, Louisiana was the only State without a state constitutional guarantee to a civil jury trial. See Calabresi & Agudo, *Individual Rights Under State Constitutions When the Fourteenth Amendment Was Ratified in 1868: What Rights Are Deeply Rooted in American History and Tradition?*, 87 Texas L. Rev. 7, 77 (2008).

2. What does Justice Brennan mean when he writes that "the influence if not the command of the Seventh Amendment" determined the result in *Byrd*? If the Seventh Amendment provides a rule of decision for *Byrd,* isn't the Rules of Decision Act inapplicable by its own terms? Indeed, if the Seventh Amendment "commands" that a federal court utilize a jury to decide who is a statutory employee, could the Rules of Decision Act dictate a contrary result? On the other hand, if the Seventh Amendment does not "command" the result in *Byrd,* why should it "influence" the result?

In this light, consider the following excerpt from SIMLER v. CONNER, 372 U.S. 221, 222, 83 S.Ct. 609, 610–11, 9 L.Ed.2d 691, 693 (1963):

> The federal policy favoring jury trials is of historic continuing strength. * * * Only through a holding that the jury-trial right is to be determined according to federal law can the uniformity in its exercise which is demanded by the Seventh Amendment be achieved. In diversity cases, of course, the substantive dimension of the claim asserted finds its source in state law, * * * but the characterization of that state-created claim as legal or equitable for purposes of whether a right to jury trial is indicated must be made by recourse to federal law.

3. Do you agree with Justice Brennan's assertion that the South Carolina rule at issue in *Byrd* is "merely a form and mode of enforcing the immunity * * * and not a rule intended to be bound up with the definition of the rights and obligations of the parties"? Most states have adopted their worker compensation schemes only after carefully balancing the equities involved in the typical workplace accident. These statutes are complex and detailed and often are the result of a political compromise. Does it seem likely,

then, that South Carolina randomly would have appropriated to the judge the function of defining a statutory employee?

4. In *Byrd,* Justice Brennan proposes what appears to be a balancing test for determining *Erie* questions. Does the balancing test in *Byrd* replace the outcome-determinative test of *York*? Whether it replaces the outcome-determinative test or not, how does Justice Brennan's balancing test work? If a state rule is "bound up with the definition of the rights and obligations of the parties," does a federal court still engage in balancing? How does a court determine whether a state rule is "bound up with the definition of the rights and obligations of the parties"?

5. Once it begins to engage in the balancing process dictated in *Byrd,* how does a federal court identify and then weigh the competing state and federal policies? What sources should it examine in pursuing this inquiry? In ALLSTATE INS. CO. v. CHARNESKI, 286 F.2d 238 (7th Cir.1960), the court dismissed an action for a judgment declaring an insurance company's nonliability. The court, after reviewing the major *Erie*-doctrine cases and concluding that a Wisconsin court would dismiss the declaratory-judgment action before it, employed the following reasoning:

> First, as to the State of Wisconsin. This is not a case where a federal declaratory judgment action is filed in a state which has no statute providing for such relief. Wisconsin has passed a general statute providing declaratory relief. However, this statute was held not applicable * * * [by the Wisconsin Supreme Court] because it conflicted with the Wisconsin state policy of providing direct actions against insurance companies. This is a declaration of the *substantive* law of Wisconsin. The Wisconsin Supreme Court held that to allow declaratory relief in such circumstances would undercut its policy of direct actions against an insurance company and thereby concluding the action—defining the rights of the insurer, the insured, and the injured party—in a single suit. This holding represents a legitimate and proper implementation of Wisconsin policy. * * *
>
> The federal interest to be served here is slight. There is the general interest of a court controlling its own procedure. There is the general policy evidenced by the federal Declaratory Judgments Act. However, no right to jury trial, guaranteed by the Seventh Amendment, is involved here, as in Byrd. The cause of action arising from the accident, the issue of coverage of the policy, and the rights of the insured, the insurer and the injured parties are intimately connected with Wisconsin law and have no connection with the federal government except that the latter provides a fair and orderly forum in which to try the diversity case. Finally, relief under the Federal act is expressly discretionary. Such relief is permissive and not absolute. Declaratory relief "may" be granted, and need not be when it would create an unnecessary federal-state conflict.

Id. at 244. Is the court's analysis of the Wisconsin and federal policies adequate? Is it persuasive?

6. In BERNHARDT v. POLYGRAPHIC CO. OF AMERICA, INC., 350 U.S. 198, 203, 76 S.Ct. 273, 276, 100 L.Ed. 199, 205 (1956), plaintiff brought an action in a Vermont state court for damages resulting from his discharge by defendant. Defendant removed the action to a federal district court and

moved for a stay pending arbitration in New York pursuant to the contract. The District Court denied the stay, ruling that under *Erie* the arbitration provision was governed by Vermont law, which permitted revocation of an agreement to arbitrate any time before an award was made. The Second Circuit reversed on the ground that arbitration merely relates to the form of the trial. The Supreme Court disagreed and reversed and remanded, stating:

> * * * If the federal court allows arbitration where the state court would disallow it, the outcome of litigation might depend on the courthouse where suit is brought. For the remedy by arbitration, whatever its merits or shortcomings, substantially affects the cause of action created by the State. The nature of the tribunal where suits are tried is an important part of the parcel of rights behind a cause of action. The change from a court of law to an arbitration panel may make a radical difference in ultimate result. Arbitration carries no right to trial by jury that is guaranteed both by the Seventh Amendment and by Ch. 1, Art. 12th, of the Vermont Constitution. Arbitrators do not have the benefit of judicial instruction on the law; they need not give their reasons for their results; the record of their proceedings is not as complete as it is in a court trial; and judicial review of an award is more limited than judicial review of a trial * * *.

After *Byrd,* would *Bernhardt* be decided the same way? Is state law governing arbitration bound up with the definition of the parties' rights and obligations?

7. In light of the federal interest in "an independent system for administering justice to litigants who properly invoke its jurisdiction," should a federal court in a diversity action employ a federal or state standard to determine the existence or nonexistence of in personam jurisdiction over a foreign corporation? Over the years, the post-*Byrd* cases appear to have opted for the state standard. E.g., Arrowsmith v. United Press Int'l, 320 F.2d 219 (2d Cir.1963) (en banc), apparently overruling a contrary two-to-one decision in Jaftex Corp. v. Randolph Mills, Inc., 282 F.2d 508 (2d Cir.1960). See 4 Wright & Miller, Federal Practice and Procedure: Civil 3d § 1075; 19 Wright, Miller & Cooper, Federal Practice and Procedure: Jurisdiction and Related Matters 2d § 4510.

If *Erie* is constitutionally based, does Congress or do the federal courts have the power to establish jurisdictional standards for diversity actions? Putting the question another way, are jurisdictional rules substantive or procedural within the meaning of *Erie* and *York* or don't they fall entirely within either category? Would a federal test for personal jurisdiction promote or discourage forum-shopping? Assuming federal power, has either Congress or the federal courts established a clear test for amenability to suit in a federal court? Is the standard in International Shoe Co. v. Washington, p. 85, supra, relevant? What about Federal Rule 4 or 28 U.S.C. §§ 1391, 1693?

In 1934, Congress passed 28 U.S.C. § 2072, commonly known as the Rules Enabling Act. Read the current version of this Act, which is in the Supplement.

HANNA v. PLUMER

Supreme Court of the United States, 1965.
380 U.S. 460, 85 S.Ct. 1136, 14 L.Ed.2d 8.

Certiorari to the United States Court of Appeals for the First Circuit.

MR. CHIEF JUSTICE WARREN delivered the opinion of the Court.

The question to be decided is whether, in a civil action where the jurisdiction of the United States District Court is based upon diversity of citizenship between the parties, service of process shall be made in the manner prescribed by state law or that set forth in Rule 4(d)(1) of the Federal Rules of Civil Procedure. [Rule 4, and particularly Rule 4(d)(1), has been amended several times since 1965. Most recently, this provision was renumbered as Rule 4(e)(2).]

On February 6, 1963, petitioner, a citizen of Ohio, filed her complaint in the District Court for the District of Massachusetts, claiming damages in excess of $10,000 for personal injuries resulting from an automobile accident in South Carolina, allegedly caused by the negligence of one Louise Plumer Osgood, a Massachusetts citizen deceased at the time of the filing of the complaint. Respondent, Mrs. Osgood's executor and also a Massachusetts citizen, was named as defendant. On February 8, service was made by leaving copies of the summons and the complaint with respondent's wife at his residence, concededly in compliance with Rule 4(d)(1) * * *. Respondent filed his answer on February 26, alleging, *inter alia,* that the action could not be maintained because it had been brought "contrary to and in violation of the provisions of Massachusetts General Laws (Ter.Ed.) Chapter 197, Section 9." That section provides:

> Except as provided in this chapter, an executor or administrator shall not be held to answer to an action by a creditor of the deceased which is not commenced within one year from the time of his giving bond for the performance of his trust, or to such an action which is commenced within said year unless before the expiration thereof the writ in such action has been served by delivery in hand upon such executor or administrator or service thereof accepted by him or a notice stating the name of the estate, the name and address of the creditor, the amount of the claim and the court in which the action has been brought has been filed in the proper registry of probate. * * *

On October 17, 1963, the District Court granted respondent's motion for summary judgment, citing Ragan v. Merchants Transfer & Warehouse Co. * * * and Guaranty Trust Co. of New York v. York * * * in support of its conclusion that the adequacy of the service was to be measured by § 9, with which, the court held, petitioner had not complied. On appeal, petitioner * * * argued that Rule 4(d)(1) defines the method by which service of process is to be effected in diversity actions. The Court of Appeals for the First Circuit, finding that "[r]elatively recent amendments [to § 9] evince a clear legislative purpose to require personal notification within the year,"[1] concluded that the conflict of state and federal rules was over "a substantive rather than a procedural matter," and unanimously affirmed. * * *

We conclude that the adoption of Rule 4(d)(1), designed to control service of process in diversity actions, neither exceeded the congressional mandate embodied in the Rules Enabling Act nor transgressed constitutional bounds, and that the Rule is therefore the standard against which the District Court should have measured the adequacy of the service. Accordingly, we reverse the decision of the Court of Appeals.

* * * Under the cases construing the scope of the Enabling Act, Rule 4(d)(1) clearly passes muster. Prescribing the manner in which a defendant is to be notified that a suit has been instituted against him, it relates to the "practice and procedure of the district courts." * * *

> The test must be whether a rule really regulates procedure,—the judicial process for enforcing rights and duties recognized by substantive law and for justly administering remedy and redress for disregard or infraction of them. Sibbach v. Wilson & Co., [p. 439, infra] * * *.

In Mississippi Pub. Corp. v. Murphree, 326 U.S. 438, 66 S.Ct. 242, 90 L.Ed. 185, this Court upheld Rule 4(f) [now Rule 4(e)], which permits service of a summons anywhere within the State (and not merely the district) in which a district court sits:

> We think that Rule 4(f) is in harmony with the Enabling Act * * *. Undoubtedly most alterations of the rules of practice and procedure may and often do affect the rights of litigants. Congress' prohibition of any alteration of substantive rights of litigants was obviously not addressed to such incidental effects as necessarily attend the adoption of the prescribed new rules of procedure upon the rights of litigants who, agreeably to rules of practice and procedure, have been brought before a court authorized to determine their rights. * * * The fact that the application of Rule 4(f) will operate to subject petitioner's rights to adjudication by the district court for northern Mississippi will undoubtedly affect those rights. But it does not operate to abridge, enlarge or modify the rules of decision by which that court will adjudicate its rights. Id., at 445–446, 66 S.Ct. at 246.

---

1. Section 9 is in part a statute of limitations, providing that an executor need not "answer to an action * * * which is not commenced within one year from the time of his giving bond * * *." This part of the statute, the purpose of which is to speed the settlement of estates, * * * is not involved in this case, since the action clearly was timely commenced. (Respondent filed bond on March 1, 1962; the complaint was filed February 6, 1963; and the service—the propriety of which is in dispute—was made on February 8, 1963.) * * *

Section 9 also provides for the manner of service. Generally, service of process must be made by "delivery in hand." * * * The purpose of this part of the statute, which *is* involved here, is, as the court below noted, to insure that executors will receive actual notice of claims. * * * Actual notice is of course also the goal of Rule 4(d)(1); however, the Federal Rule reflects a determination that this goal can be achieved by a method less cumbersome than that prescribed in § 9. In this case the goal seems to have been achieved; although the affidavit filed by respondent in the District Court asserts that he had neither been served in hand nor accepted service, it does not allege lack of actual notice.

Thus were there no conflicting state procedure, Rule 4(d)(1) would clearly control. National Equipment Rental, Ltd. v. Szukhent, * * * [p. 221, supra]. However, respondent, focusing on the contrary Massachusetts rule, calls to the Court's attention another line of cases, a line which—like the Enabling Act—had its birth in 1938. Erie R. Co. v. Tompkins, * * * overruling Swift v. Tyson, * * * held that federal courts sitting in diversity cases, when deciding questions of "substantive" law, are bound by state court decisions as well as state statutes. The broad command of *Erie* was therefore identical to that of the Enabling Act: federal courts are to apply state substantive law and federal procedural law. However, as subsequent cases sharpened the distinction between substance and procedure, the line of cases following *Erie* diverged markedly from the line construing the Enabling Act. * * *

Respondent, by placing primary reliance on *York* and *Ragan*, suggests that the *Erie* doctrine acts as a check on the Federal Rules of Civil Procedure, that despite the clear command of Rule 4(d)(1), *Erie* and its progeny demand the application of the Massachusetts rule. Reduced to essentials, the argument is: (1) *Erie*, as refined in *York*, demands that federal courts apply state law whenever application of federal law in its stead will alter the outcome of the case. (2) In this case, a determination that the Massachusetts service requirements obtain will result in immediate victory for respondent. If, on the other hand, it should be held that Rule 4(d)(1) is applicable, the litigation will continue, with possible victory for petitioner. (3) Therefore, *Erie* demands application of the Massachusetts rule. The syllogism possesses an appealing simplicity, but is for several reasons invalid.

In the first place, it is doubtful that, even if there were no Federal Rule making it clear that in hand service is not required in diversity actions, the *Erie* rule would have obligated the District Court to follow the Massachusetts procedure. "Outcome determination" analysis was never intended to serve as a talisman. Byrd v. Blue Ridge Rural Elec. Cooperative * * *. Indeed, the message of *York* itself is that choices between state and federal law are to be made not by application of any automatic, "litmus paper" criterion, but rather by reference to the policies underlying the *Erie* rule. Guaranty Trust Co. of New York v. York * * *.

The *Erie* rule is rooted in part in a realization that it would be unfair for the character or result of a litigation materially to differ because the suit had been brought in a federal court. * * * The decision was also in part a reaction to the practice of "forum-shopping" which had grown up in response to the rule of Swift v. Tyson. * * * That the *York* test was an attempt to effectuate these policies is demonstrated by the fact that the opinion framed the inquiry in terms of "substantial" variations between state and federal litigation. * * * Not only are nonsubstantial, or trivial, variations not likely to raise the sort of equal protection problems which troubled the Court in *Erie*; they are also unlikely to influence the choice of a forum. The "outcome-determination" test therefore cannot be read without reference to the twin aims of the *Erie* rule: discouragement of forum-shopping and avoidance of inequitable administration of the laws.[9]

The difference between the conclusion that the Massachusetts rule is applicable, and the conclusion that it is not, is of course at this point "outcome-determinative" in the sense that if we hold the state rule to apply, respondent prevails, whereas if we hold that Rule 4(d)(1) governs, the litigation will continue. But in this sense *every* procedural variation is "outcome-determinative." For example, having brought suit in a federal court, a plaintiff cannot then insist on the right to file subsequent pleadings in accord with the time limits applicable in state courts, even though enforcement of the federal timetable will, if he continues to insist that he must meet only the state time limit, result in determination of the controversy against him. So it is here. Though choice of the federal or state rule will at this point have a marked effect upon the outcome of the litigation, the difference between the two rules would be of scant, if any, relevance to the choice of a forum. Petitioner, in choosing her forum, was not presented with a situation where application of the state rule would wholly bar recovery; rather, adherence to the state rule would have resulted only in altering the way in which process was served.[11] Moreover, it is difficult to argue that permitting service of defendant's wife to take the place of in hand service of defendant himself alters the mode of enforcement of state-created rights in a fashion sufficiently "substantial" to raise the sort of equal protection problems to which the *Erie* opinion alluded.

There is, however, a more fundamental flaw in respondent's syllogism: the incorrect assumption that the rule of Erie R. Co. v. Tompkins constitutes the appropriate test of the validity and therefore the applicability of a Federal Rule of Civil Procedure. The *Erie* rule has never been invoked to void a Federal Rule. It is true that there have been cases where this Court has held applicable a state rule in the face of an argument that the situation was governed by one of the Federal Rules. But the holding of each such case was not that *Erie* commanded displacement of a Federal

9. The Court of Appeals seemed to frame the inquiry in terms of how "important" Section 9 is to the State. In support of its suggestion that Section 9 serves some interest the State regards as vital to its citizens, the court noted that something like Section 9 has been on the books in Massachusetts a long time, that Section 9 has been amended a number of times, and that Section 9 is designed to make sure that executors receive actual notice. * * * The apparent lack of relation among these three observations is not surprising, because it is not clear to what sort of question the Court of Appeals was addressing itself. One cannot meaningfully ask how important something is without first asking "important for what purpose?" *Erie* and its progeny make clear that when a federal court sitting in a diversity case is faced with a question of whether or not to apply state law, the importance of a state rule is indeed relevant, but only in the context of asking whether application of the rule would make so important a difference to the character or result of the litigation that failure to enforce it would unfairly discriminate against citizens of the forum State, or whether application of the rule would have so important an effect upon the fortunes of one or both of the litigants that failure to enforce it would be likely to cause a plaintiff to choose the federal court.

11. * * * We cannot seriously entertain the thought that one suing an estate would be led to choose the federal court because of a belief that adherence to Rule 4(d)(1) is less likely to give the executor actual notice than Section 9, and therefore more likely to produce a default judgment. Rule 4(d)(1) is well designed to give actual notice, as it did in this case. * * *

Rule by an inconsistent state rule, but rather that the scope of the Federal Rule was not as broad as the losing party urged, and therefore, there being no Federal Rule which covered the point in dispute, *Erie* commanded the enforcement of state law. * * * (Here, of course, the clash is unavoidable; Rule 4(d)(1) says—implicitly, but with unmistakable clarity—that in hand service is not required in federal courts.) At the same time, in cases adjudicating the validity of Federal Rules, we have not applied the *York* rule or other refinements of *Erie*, but have to this day continued to decide questions concerning the scope of the Enabling Act and the constitutionality of specific Federal Rules in light of the distinction set forth in *Sibbach*. * * *

Nor has the development of two separate lines of cases been inadvertent. The line between "substance" and "procedure" shifts as the legal context changes. * * * It is true that both the Enabling Act and the *Erie* rule say, roughly, that federal courts are to apply state "substantive" law and federal "procedural" law, but from that it need not follow that the tests are identical. For they were designed to control very different sorts of decisions. When a situation is covered by one of the Federal Rules, the question facing the court is a far cry from the typical, relatively unguided *Erie* choice: the court has been instructed to apply the Federal Rule, and can refuse to do so only if the Advisory Committee, this Court, and Congress erred in their prima facie judgment that the Rule in question transgresses neither the terms of the Enabling Act nor constitutional restrictions.

We are reminded by the *Erie* opinion that neither Congress nor the federal courts can, under the guise of formulating rules of decision for federal courts, fashion rules which are not supported by a grant of federal authority contained in Article I or some other section of the Constitution; in such areas state law must govern because there can be no other law. But the opinion in *Erie*, which involved no Federal Rule and dealt with a question which was "substantive" in every traditional sense * * *, surely neither said nor implied that measures like Rule 4(d)(1) are unconstitutional. For the constitutional provision for a federal court system (augmented by the Necessary and Proper Clause) carries with it congressional power to make rules governing the practice and pleading in those courts, which in turn includes a power to regulate matters which, though falling within the uncertain area between substance and procedure, are rationally capable of classification as either. * * * Neither *York* nor the cases following it ever suggested that the rule there laid down for coping with situations where no Federal Rule applies is coextensive with the limitation on Congress to which *Erie* had adverted. Although this Court has never before been confronted with a case where the applicable Federal Rule is in direct collision with the law of the relevant State, courts of appeals faced with such clashes have rightly discerned the implications of our decisions.

> "One of the shaping purposes of the Federal Rules is to bring about uniformity in the federal courts by getting away from local rules. This is especially true of matters which relate to the administration of legal

proceedings, an area in which federal courts have traditionally exerted strong inherent power, completely aside from the powers Congress expressly conferred in the Rules. The purpose of the *Erie* doctrine, even as extended in *York* and *Ragan*, was never to bottle up federal courts with 'outcome-determinative' and 'integral-relations' stoppers when there are 'affirmative countervailing [federal] considerations' and when there is a Congressional mandate (the Rules) supported by constitutional authority." Lumbermen's Mutual Casualty Co. v. Wright, 322 F.2d 759, 764 (C.A.5th Cir. 1963).

Erie and its offspring cast no doubt on the long-recognized power of Congress to prescribe housekeeping rules for federal courts even though some of those rules will inevitably differ from comparable state rules. * * * Thus, though a court, in measuring a Federal Rule against the standards contained in the Enabling Act and the Constitution, need not wholly blind itself to the degree to which the Rule makes the character and result of the federal litigation stray from the course it would follow in state courts, * * * it cannot be forgotten that the *Erie* rule, and the guidelines suggested in *York*, were created to serve another purpose altogether. To hold that a Federal Rule of Civil Procedure must cease to function whenever it alters the mode of enforcing state-created rights would be to disembowel either the Constitution's grant of power over federal procedure or Congress' attempt to exercise that power in the Enabling Act. Rule 4(d)(1) is valid and controls the instant case.

Reversed.

MR. JUSTICE BLACK concurs in the result.

MR. JUSTICE HARLAN, concurring.

* * *

Erie was something more than an opinion which worried about "forum-shopping and avoidance of inequitable administration of the laws," * * * although to be sure these were important elements of the decision. I have always regarded that decision as one of the modern cornerstones of our federalism, expressing policies that profoundly touch the allocation of judicial power between the state and federal systems. *Erie* recognized that there should not be two conflicting systems of law controlling the primary activity of citizens, for such alternative governing authority must necessarily give rise to a debilitating uncertainty in the planning of everyday affairs. And it recognized that the scheme of our Constitution envisions an allocation of law-making functions between state and federal legislative processes which is undercut if the federal judiciary can make substantive law affecting state affairs beyond the bounds of congressional legislative powers in this regard. * * *

The shorthand formulations which have appeared in some past decisions are prone to carry untoward results that frequently arise from oversimplification. The Court is quite right in stating that the "outcome-determinative" test of Guaranty Trust Co. of New York v. York * * * if taken literally, proves too much, for any rule, no matter how clearly "procedural," can affect the outcome of litigation if it is not obeyed. In turning from the "outcome" test of *Guaranty* back to the unadorned forum-shopping rationale of *Erie*, however, the Court falls prey to like oversimplification, for a simple forum-shopping rule also proves too much; litigants often choose a federal forum merely to obtain what they consider the advantages of the Federal Rules of Civil Procedure or to try their cases before a supposedly more favorable judge. To my mind the proper line of approach in determining whether to apply a state or a federal rule, whether "substantive" or "procedural," is to stay close to basic principles by inquiring if the choice of rule would substantially affect those primary decisions respecting human conduct which our constitutional system leaves to state regulation. If so, *Erie* and the Constitution require that the state rule prevail, even in the face of a conflicting federal rule.

The Court weakens, if indeed it does not submerge, this basic principle by finding, in effect, a grant of substantive legislative power in the constitutional provision for a federal court system * * *, and through it, setting up the Federal Rules as a body of law inviolate. * * * So long as a reasonable man could characterize any duly adopted federal rule as "procedural," the Court, unless I misapprehend what is said, would have it apply no matter how seriously it frustrated a State's substantive regulation of the primary conduct and affairs of its citizens. Since the members of the Advisory Committee, the Judicial Conference, and this Court who formulated the Federal Rules are presumably reasonable men, it follows that the integrity of the Federal Rules is absolute. Whereas the unadulterated outcome and forum-shopping tests may err too far toward honoring state rules, I submit that the Court's "arguably procedural, *ergo* constitutional" test moves too fast and far in the other direction.

The courts below relied upon this Court's decisions in Ragan v. Merchants Transfer & Warehouse Co. * * * and Cohen v. Beneficial Indus. Loan Corp. * * *. Those cases deserve more attention than this Court has given them, particularly *Ragan* which, if still good law, would in my opinion call for affirmance of the result reached by the Court of Appeals. * * *

* * * I think that the [*Ragan*] decision was wrong. At most, application of the Federal Rule would have meant that potential Kansas tort defendants would have to defer for a few days the satisfaction of knowing that they had not been sued within the limitations period. The choice of the Federal Rule would have had no effect on the primary stages of private activity from which torts arise, and only the most minimal effect on behavior following the commission of the tort. In such circumstances the interest of the federal system in proceeding under its own rules should have prevailed.

* * * [A statute like the one in *Cohen*] is not "outcome determinative"; the plaintiff can win with or without it. The Court now rationalizes the case on the ground that the statute might affect the plaintiff's choice

of forum * * * but as has been pointed out, a simple forum-shopping test proves too much. The proper view of *Cohen* is in my opinion, that the statute was meant to inhibit small stockholders from instituting "strike suits," and thus it was designed and could be expected to have a substantial impact on private primary activity. Anyone who was at the trial bar during the period when *Cohen* arose can appreciate the strong state policy reflected in the statute. I think it wholly legitimate to view Federal Rule 23 [now Rule 23.1] as not purporting to deal with the problem. But even had the Federal Rules purported to do so, and in so doing provided a substantially less effective deterrent to strike suits, I think the state rule should still have prevailed. * * *

It remains to apply what has been said to the present case. * * * The evident intent of [the Massachusetts] statute is to permit an executor to distribute the estate which he is administering without fear that further liabilities may be outstanding for which he could be held personally liable. If the Federal District Court in Massachusetts applies Rule 4(d)(1) of the Federal Rules of Civil Procedure instead of the Massachusetts service rule, what effect would that have on the speed and assurance with which estates are distributed? As I see it, the effect would not be substantial. It would mean simply that an executor would have to check at his own house or the federal courthouse as well as the registry of probate before he could distribute the estate with impunity. As this does not seem enough to give rise to any real impingement on the vitality of the state policy which the Massachusetts rule is intended to serve, I concur in the judgment of the Court.

NOTES AND QUESTIONS

1. The Rules Enabling Act is said to codify an "ideal of nationally uniform procedural rules promulgated by the Supreme Court after consideration by expert committees * * *." Bone, *The Process of Making Process: Court Rulemaking, Democratic Legitimacy, and Procedural Efficacy*, 87 Geo. L.J. 887, 888 (1999). Professor Bone explains this rulemaking process as follows:

> * * * The Supreme Court has the power to "prescribe general rules of practice and procedure" for the federal courts, and the Judicial Conference of the United States has the authority to recommend rule changes to the Supreme Court. The Judicial Conference in turn oversees a committee structure that includes a Standing Committee on Rules of Practice and Procedure appointed by the Chief Justice of the Supreme Court and various advisory committees accountable to the Standing Committee. The Advisory Committee on Civil Rules, which consists of judges, lawyers, and legal academics, is responsible for the Federal Rules of Civil Procedure.
>
> There are several stages in the rulemaking process. A proposed rule is first considered by the Advisory Committee. If the Advisory Committee approves the proposal, it is then reviewed by the Standing Committee and finally by the Judicial Conference before being forwarded to the Supreme Court. If the Supreme Court concurs, the proposal is transmitted to

> Congress, which then has roughly seven months to exercise a veto. In the absence of a veto, the proposed rule goes into effect.

Id. at 892 (footnotes omitted).

2. Reread the Rules Enabling Act and the Rules of Decision Act. How do these statutes interact? Are they consistent? If not, how can the inconsistencies be resolved? Upon which of these two statutes is the holding in *Hanna* based?

3. The distinction between substance and procedure is important in both the Rules Enabling Act and the Rules of Decision Act. The second sentence of the Rules Enabling Act says that no Federal Rule may "abridge, enlarge, or modify any substantive right," and of course the distinction between substance and procedure is at the core of the line of cases interpreting the Rules of Decision Act. How does Chief Justice Warren treat the distinction between substance and procedure in *Hanna*? How does he define that distinction for purposes of the Rules Enabling Act? For purposes of the Rules of Decision Act? Are the definitions the same?

In SIBBACH v. WILSON & CO., 312 U.S. 1, 61 S.Ct. 422, 85 L.Ed. 479 (1941), plaintiff sued defendant in an Illinois federal district court for damages inflicted in Indiana. The Supreme Court affirmed the District Court's order that plaintiff undergo a physical examination pursuant to Federal Rule 35, despite an Illinois policy forbidding compulsory physical examinations. The Court concluded that the promulgation of Rule 35 was within the ambit of congressional power, since Rule 35 does not "abridge, enlarge, [or] modify substantive rights, in the guise of regulating procedure." Moreover, the Court rejected plaintiff's argument that a rule regulating procedure still could so affect a substantial personal right as to violate the Rules Enabling Act. In an opinion written by Justice Roberts, the Court held:

> * * * If we were to adopt the suggested criterion of the importance of the alleged right we should invite endless litigation and confusion * * *. The test must be whether a rule really regulates procedure—the judicial process for enforcing rights and duties recognized by substantive law and for justly administering remedy and redress for disregard or infraction of them. That the rules in question are such is admitted.

In dissent, Justice Frankfurter maintained that Rule 35, which provides for "the invasion of the person," is quite different from other rules of procedure. He noted, furthermore, that the Rules are effective automatically absent a veto by Congress.

> * * * [T]o draw any inference of tacit approval from non-action by Congress is to appeal to unreality. And so I conclude that to make the drastic change that Rule 35 sought to introduce would require explicit legislation.

Is the distinction in *Sibbach* usable to interpret the distinction between substance and procedure as that distinction is embodied in the Rules of Decision Act?

4. After *Hanna,* what consideration should be given to *York*'s "outcome determinative" and *Byrd*'s multi-step balancing tests? Has the test enunciat-

ed in *Hanna* rendered the earlier tests obsolete, or is the entire discussion of the *Erie* question in *Hanna* merely dictum?

5. Justice Harlan's approach "inquir[es] if the choice of rule would substantially affect those primary decisions respecting human conduct which our constitutional system leaves to state regulation," p. 437, supra. What does he mean by "primary" decisions of conduct? As Justice Harlan understands the majority opinion in *Hanna,* any "arguably procedural" rule would apply "no matter how seriously it frustrated a State's substantive regulation of the primary conduct and affairs of its citizens." Although Justice Harlan thinks the "outcome determinative" test in *York* "may err too far toward honoring state rules," p. 437, supra, he criticizes the *Hanna* majority as not giving enough weight to state interests. By what metric should state interests be measured?

6. Justice Harlan called *Erie* "one of the modern cornerstones of our federalism," p. 436, supra. Federalism is a term that embraces a number of values, including "freedom to experiment," "flexibility in tailoring regulation to local needs," "decentralization as a strategy to minimize factional control," "independence as a source of strengthened protection of rights," and "the superior democratic pedigree that comes from closer contact with the citizenry." Kramer, *The Lawmaking Power of the Federal Courts*, 12 Pace L. Rev. 263, 295–96 (1992). How does *Erie* serve these values? How does *Hanna*? What other values do you associate with federalism?

7. Chief Justice Warren asserted that "the *Erie* rule is rooted in part in a realization that it would be unfair for the character or result of a litigation materially to differ because the suit had been brought in federal court [and] in part a reaction to the practice of forum-shopping," p. 433, supra. Has he abandoned part of Justice Brandeis's argument in *Erie*? Was not *Erie* based in important part on notions of state and federal relations?

8. What is the effect of *Hanna* on state statutes that close the doors of the state courts to suits by foreign corporations that have not registered to do business in the state? Can the Diversity Clause in Article III of the Constitution be said to exude a federal policy that there be a forum in every state for the protection of foreign corporations? Does anything turn on the nature of the policies underlying the state statute? See Szantay v. Beech Aircraft Corp., 349 F.2d 60 (4th Cir.1965). Compare the earlier decisions in Angel v. Bullington, 330 U.S. 183, 67 S.Ct. 657, 91 L.Ed. 832 (1947), and Woods v. Interstate Realty Co., p. 423, supra.

Since *Hanna,* commentators have been attempting to define precisely the test to be used to answer *Erie* questions. Consider the following:

> * * * [T]he indiscriminate mixture of all questions respecting choices between federal and state law in diversity cases, under the single rubric of "the Erie doctrine" or "the Erie problem," has served to make a major mystery out of what are really three distinct and rather ordinary problems of statutory and constitutional interpretation. Of course there will be occasions with respect to all three on which

> reasonable persons will differ, but that does not make the problems mysterious or even very unusual. The United States Constitution, I shall argue, constitutes the relevant text only where Congress has passed a statute creating law for diversity actions, and it is in this situation alone that *Hanna*'s "arguably procedural" test controls. Where a nonstatutory rule is involved, the Constitution necessarily remains in the background, but it is functionally irrelevant because the applicable statutes are significantly more protective of the prerogatives of state law. Thus, where there is no relevant Federal Rule of Civil Procedure or other Rule promulgated pursuant to the Enabling Act and the federal rule in issue is therefore wholly judge-made, whether state or federal law should be applied is controlled by the Rules of Decision Act, the statute construed in *Erie* and *York*. Where the matter in issue is covered by a Federal Rule, however, the Enabling Act—and not the Rules of Decision Act itself or the line of cases construing it—constitutes the relevant standard. To say that, however, and that is one of the things *Hanna* said, is by no means to concede the validity of all Federal Rules, for the Enabling Act contains significant limiting language of its own. The Court has correctly sensed that that language cannot be construed to protect state prerogatives as strenuously as the Rules of Decision Act protects them in the absence of a Federal Rule. However, the Court's recent appreciation that the Enabling Act constitutes the only check on the Rules—that "Erie" does not stand there as a backstop—should lead it in an appropriate case to take the Act's limiting language more seriously than it has in the past.

Ely, *The Irrepressible Myth of* Erie, 87 Harv.L.Rev. 693, 697–98 (1974).

Compare Professor Ely's analysis with the following:

> If a valid and pertinent federal rule exists, then of course it applies, notwithstanding any state rule to the contrary. The supremacy clause says so. The real task under *Erie,* therefore, is not to choose between federal law and state law, but rather to decide if there really is a valid federal rule on the issue. * * * [T]he Rules of Decision Act is an explicit grant of authority: It directs the federal courts to apply state law with regard to any issue that is not governed by a pertinent and valid federal rule. It reminds the federal courts that if a valid federal rule exists—whether constitutional, statutory, or judge-made—the federal rule shall govern. * * *
>
> To understand how *Erie* operates in diversity cases, it is important to distinguish between the *pertinence* of federal rules and their *validity*. To say a federal rule is "pertinent" means that it was intended or designed to govern the issue at hand—that the rule's purposes would be served by applying it. To say a rule is "valid" means that it has been adopted in conformity with the legal norms controlling the creation of federal law—that it is consistent with the Constitution and other organic statutes regulating the formation of federal law. These

combined qualities of pertinence and validity are necessary and sufficient for the proper application of a federal rule: If either quality is absent, a federal rule cannot be lawfully applied; if both are present, the federal rule must be applied.

* * *

Federal rules of civil procedure should be analyzed in the same way as federal statutes, except the rules must satisfy an additional standard of validity. The pertinence analysis is precisely the same for rules as it is for other laws. The court must determine whether the framers of a rule intended that it govern the issue at hand; if so (and if the rule is valid), the rule applies; if not, state law applies.

Westen & Lehman, *Is There Life for* Erie *After the Death of Diversity?*, 78 Mich.L.Rev. 311, 314–15, 342, 359 (1980).

WALKER v. ARMCO STEEL CORP.

Supreme Court of the United States, 1980.
446 U.S. 740, 100 S.Ct. 1978, 64 L.Ed.2d 659.

Certiorari to the United States Court of Appeals for the Tenth Circuit.

JUSTICE MARSHALL delivered the opinion for a unanimous Court.

This case presents the issue whether in a diversity action the federal court should follow state law or, alternatively, Rule 3 of the Federal Rules of Civil Procedure in determining when an action is commenced for the purpose of tolling the state statute of limitations.

I

According to the allegations of the complaint, petitioner, a carpenter, was injured on August 22, 1975, in Oklahoma City, Okla., while pounding a Sheffield nail into a cement wall. Respondent was the manufacturer of the nail. Petitioner claimed that the nail contained a defect which caused its head to shatter and strike him in the right eye, resulting in permanent injuries. The defect was allegedly caused by respondent's negligence in manufacture and design.

Petitioner is a resident of Oklahoma, and respondent is a foreign corporation having its principal place of business in a State other than Oklahoma. Since there was diversity of citizenship, petitioner brought suit in the United States District Court for the Western District of Oklahoma. The complaint was filed on August 19, 1977. Although summons was issued that same day, service of process was not made on respondent's authorized service agent until December 1, 1977. On January 5, 1978, respondent filed a motion to dismiss the complaint on the ground that the action was barred by the applicable Oklahoma statute of limitations.

Although the complaint had been filed within the 2–year statute of limitations, * * * state law does not deem the action "commenced" for purposes of the statute of limitations until service of the summons on the defendant, Okla.Stat., Tit. 12, § 97 (1971). If the complaint is filed within the limitations period, however, the action is deemed to have commenced from that date of filing if the plaintiff serves the defendant within 60 days, even though that service may occur outside the limitations period. * * * In this case, service was not effectuated until long after this 60–day period had expired. Petitioner in his reply brief to the motion to dismiss admitted that his case would be foreclosed in state court, but he argued that Rule 3 of the Federal Rules of Civil Procedure governs the manner in which an action is commenced in federal court for all purposes, including the tolling of the state statute of limitations.

The District Court dismissed the complaint as barred by the Oklahoma statute of limitations. * * * The court concluded that Okla.Stat., Tit. 12, § 97 (1971) was "an integral part of the Oklahoma statute of limitations," and therefore under Ragan v. Merchants Transfer & Warehouse Co., * * * [p. 422, supra], state law applied. The court rejected the argument that *Ragan* had been implicitly overruled in Hanna v. Plumer * * *.

The United States Court of Appeals for the Tenth Circuit affirmed. * * * That court concluded that Okla.Stat., Tit. 12, § 97 (1971), was in "direct conflict" with Rule 3. * * * However, the Oklahoma statute was "indistinguishable" from the statute involved in *Ragan,* and the court felt itself "constrained" to follow *Ragan.* * * *

We granted certiorari * * * because of a conflict among the Courts of Appeals. We now affirm.

II

The question whether state or federal law should apply on various issues arising in an action based on state law which has been brought in federal court under diversity of citizenship jurisdiction has troubled this Court for many years. [The Court discussed Guaranty Trust Co. v. York, p. 416, supra, emphasizing its focus on whether or not applying state law could substantially affect the outcome.]

The decision in *York* led logically to our holding in Ragan v. Merchants Transfer & Warehouse Co. * * *. In *Ragan,* the plaintiff had filed his complaint in federal court on September 4, 1945, pursuant to Rule 3 of the Federal Rules of Civil Procedure. The accident from which the claim arose had occurred on October 1, 1943. Service was made on the defendant on December 28, 1945. The applicable statute of limitations supplied by Kansas law was two years. Kansas had an additional statute [regarding tolling that was essentially identical to the Oklahoma statute at issue in this case]. The defendant moved for summary judgment on the ground that the Kansas statute of limitations barred the action since service had not been made within either the 2–year period or the 60–day period. It was conceded that had the case been brought in Kansas state court it would have been barred. Nonetheless, the District Court held that the statute had been tolled by the filing of the complaint. The Court of Appeals reversed * * *.

We affirmed, relying on *Erie* and *York*. "We cannot give [the cause of action] longer life in the federal court than it would have had in the state court without adding something to the cause of action. We may not do that consistently with Erie R. Co. v. Tompkins." * * * We rejected the argument that Rule 3 of the Federal Rules of Civil Procedure governed the manner in which an action was commenced in federal court for purposes of tolling the state statute of limitations. Instead, we held that the service of summons statute controlled because it was an integral part of the state statute of limitations, and under *York,* that statute of limitations was part of the state-law cause of action.

Ragan was not our last pronouncement in this difficult area, however. In 1965 we decided Hanna v. Plumer * * *, holding that in a civil action where federal jurisdiction was based upon diversity of citizenship, Rule 4(d)(1) [now Rule (4)(e)(2)] * * *, rather than state law, governed the manner in which process was served. * * *

The Court in *Hanna* * * * concluded that the *Erie* doctrine was simply not the appropriate test of the validity and applicability of one of the Federal Rules * * *. The Court cited *Ragan* as one of the examples of this proposition * * *. The Court explained that where the Federal Rule was clearly applicable, as in *Hanna,* the test was whether the Rule was within the scope of the Rules Enabling Act, 28 U.S.C. § 2072, and if so, within a constitutional grant of power such as the Necessary and Proper Clause of Art. I. * * *

III

The present case is indistinguishable from *Ragan*. The statutes in both cases require service of process to toll the statute of limitations, and in fact the predecessor to the Oklahoma statute in this case was derived from the predecessor to the Kansas statute in *Ragan*. * * * Here, as in *Ragan,* the complaint was filed in federal court under diversity jurisdiction within the 2-year statute of limitations, but service of process did not occur until after the 2-year period and the 60-day service period had run. In both cases the suit would concededly have been barred in the applicable state court, and in both instances the state service statute was held to be an integral part of the statute of limitations by the lower court more familiar than we with state law. Accordingly, as the Court of Appeals held below, the instant action is barred by the statute of limitations unless *Ragan* is no longer good law.

Petitioner argues that the analysis and holding of *Ragan* did not survive our decision in *Hanna*.[8] Petitioner's position is that Okla.Stat.,

8. Mr. Justice Harlan in his concurring opinion in *Hanna* concluded that *Ragan* was no longer good law. * * *

Tit. 12, § 97 (1971), is in direct conflict with the Federal Rule. Under *Hanna,* petitioner contends, the appropriate question is whether Rule 3 is within the scope of the Rules Enabling Act and, if so, within the constitutional power of Congress. In petitioner's view, the Federal Rule is to be applied unless it violates one of those two restrictions. * * *

We note at the outset that the doctrine of *stare decisis* weighs heavily against petitioner in this case. Petitioner seeks to have us overrule our decision in *Ragan.* * * *

This Court in *Hanna* distinguished *Ragan* rather than overruled it, and for good reason. Application of the *Hanna* analysis is premised on a "direct collision" between the Federal Rule and the state law. * * * In *Hanna* itself the "clash" between Rule 4(d)(1) and the state in-hand service requirement was "unavoidable." * * * The first question must therefore be whether the scope of the Federal Rule in fact is sufficiently broad to control the issue before the Court. It is only if that question is answered affirmatively that the *Hanna* analysis applies.[9]

As has already been noted, we recognized in *Hanna* that the present case is an instance where "the scope of the Federal Rule [is] not as broad as the losing party urge[s], and therefore, there being no Federal Rule which cover[s] the point in dispute, *Erie* command[s] the enforcement of state law." * * * Rule 3 simply states that "[a] civil action is commenced by filing a complaint with the court." There is no indication that the Rule was intended to toll a state statute of limitations,[10] much less that it purported to displace state tolling rules for purposes of state statutes of limitations. In our view, in diversity actions[11] Rule 3 governs the date

9. This is not to suggest that the Federal Rules of Civil Procedure are to be narrowly construed in order to avoid a "direct collision" with state law. The Federal Rules should be given their plain meaning. If a direct collision with state law arises from that plain meaning, then the analysis developed in *Hanna v. Plumer* applies.

10. "Rule 3 simply provides that an action is commenced by filing the complaint and has as its primary purpose the measuring of time periods that begin running from the date of commencement; the rule does not state that filing tolls the statute of limitations." 4 C. Wright & A. Miller, Federal Practice and Procedure § 1057, p. 191 (1969) * * *. The Note of the Advisory Committee on the Rules states:

> "When a Federal or State statute of limitations is pleaded as a defense, a question may arise under this rule whether the mere filing of the complaint stops the running of the statute, or whether any further step is required, such as, service of the summons and complaint or their delivery to the marshal for service. The answer to this question may depend on whether it is competent for the Supreme Court, exercising the power to make rules of procedure without affecting substantive rights, to vary the operation of statutes of limitations. The requirement of Rule 4(a) that the clerk shall forthwith issue the summons and deliver it to the marshal for service will reduce the chances of such a question arising." * * * [Rule 4(a) no longer mentions marshals.]

This Note establishes that the Advisory Committee predicted the problem which arose in *Ragan* and arises again in the instant case. It does not indicate, however, that Rule 3 was *intended* to serve as a tolling provision for statute of limitations purposes; it only suggests that the Advisory Committee thought the Rule *might* have that effect.

11. The Court suggested in *Ragan* that in suits to enforce rights under a federal statute Rule 3 means that filing of the complaint tolls the applicable statute of limitations. * * * We do not here address the role of Rule 3 as a tolling provision for a statute of limitations, whether set by federal law or borrowed from state law, if the cause of action is based on federal law.

from which various timing requirements of the Federal Rules begin to run, but does not affect state statutes of limitations. * * *

In contrast to Rule 3, the Oklahoma statute is a statement of a substantive decision by that State that actual service on, and accordingly actual notice by, the defendant is an integral part of the several policies served by the statute of limitations. * * * The statute of limitations establishes a deadline after which the defendant may legitimately have peace of mind; it also recognizes that after a certain period of time it is unfair to require the defendant to attempt to piece together his defense to an old claim. A requirement of actual service promotes both of those functions of the statute. * * * As such, the service rule must be considered part and parcel of the statute of limitations. Rule 3 does not replace such policy determinations found in state law. Rule 3 and Okla.Stat., Tit. 12, § 97 (1971), can exist side by side, therefore, each controlling its own intended sphere of coverage without conflict.

Since there is no direct conflict between the Federal Rule and the state law, the *Hanna* analysis does not apply. Instead, the policies behind *Erie* and *Ragan* control the issue. * * * [A]lthough in this case failure to apply the state service law might not create any problem of forum shopping, the result would be an "inequitable administration" of the law. Hanna v. Plumer * * *. There is simply no reason why, in the absence of a controlling federal rule, an action based on state law which concededly would be barred in the state courts by the state statute of limitations should proceed through litigation to judgment in federal court solely because of the fortuity that there is diversity of citizenship between the litigants. The policies underlying diversity jurisdiction do not support such a distinction between state and federal plaintiffs, and *Erie* and its progeny do not permit it.

The judgment of the Court of Appeals is affirmed.

NOTES AND QUESTIONS

1. Rule 3 states that "[a] civil action is commenced by filing a complaint with the court," but does not specify for what purpose the action is commenced. Two arguments were thus available for the Court in *Walker* to find that Rule 3 did not operate to toll the Oklahoma statute of limitations. First, the Court could have held that Rule 3 applies only to time requirements in other Federal Rules of Civil Procedure, tolling neither state nor federal statutes of limitations. Alternatively, the Court could have found that Rule 3 tolls federal but not state statutes of limitations.

Which argument is more persuasive? Which does the Court make in *Walker*? Note that there was abundant authority, cited in footnote 9 in *Walker* of the Court's opinion (including a dictum in *Ragan*), suggesting that Rule 3 does operate to toll federal statutes of limitations. *Walker* reserves this question, holding that, even if Rule 3 governs federal statutes of limitations, it does not apply to state statutes. But if Rule 3 does not toll federal statutes of limitations, what does?

2. Can you reconcile the Court's interpretation of Rule 3 in *Walker* with its interpretation of Rule 4 in *Hanna*? Rule 4 says simply that service may be made by leaving a copy of the summons and complaint at the defendant's home; it does not qualify this permission in any way or say anything about federal-question cases or diversity cases. Therefore, the *Hanna* Court concluded, Rule 4 says "implicitly, but with unmistakable clarity" that in-hand service is not required in either type of case. Rule 3 is equally plain: it says simply that an action is commenced in federal court by filing the complaint. Yet the *Walker* Court assumes, contrary to the apparent intent of the Advisory Note (quoted in footnote 10), that Rule 3 may toll federal but not state statutes of limitations. Why is Rule 4 read broadly, making a clash with state law "unavoidable," while Rule 3 is read to incorporate an implied exception for state statutes? Is the difference that Oklahoma's tolling provision serves a substantive purpose while the Massachusetts service rule in *Hanna* is purely procedural in nature? And what do you make of the statement in footnote 9 in *Walker* that Federal Rules are not "to be narrowly construed in order to avoid a 'direct collision' with state law"? See p. 445, supra. Isn't that exactly what the Court does in *Walker?*

3. In BURLINGTON NORTHERN R. CO. v. WOODS, 480 U.S. 1, 107 S.Ct. 967, 94 L.Ed.2d 1 (1987), Woods had obtained a jury verdict against Burlington Northern in a personal injury action prosecuted in an Alabama federal district court. After the verdict had been affirmed on appeal without modification, the Court of Appeals assessed the penalty (10% of the damages) prescribed by Alabama law for all unsuccessful appeals of money judgments. Burlington Northern objected, arguing that Rule 38 of the Federal Rules of Appellate Procedure controlled the case—and that, under Rule 38, penalties were appropriate only if, in the judgment of the appellate court, the appeal was frivolous.

The Supreme Court held that Rule 38 controlled. Justice Marshall, writing for the Court, reasoned:

> In *Hanna* * * * we set forth the appropriate test for resolving conflicts between state law and Federal Rules. The initial step is to determine whether, when fairly construed, the scope of Federal Rule 38 is "sufficiently broad" to cause a "direct collision" with the state law or, implicitly, to "control the issue" before the court, thereby leaving no room for the operation of that law. * * * The Rule must then be applied if it represents a valid exercise of Congress' rulemaking authority, which originates in the Constitution and has been bestowed on this Court by the Rules Enabling Act * * *.
>
> * * * Rule 38 affords a court of appeals plenary discretion to assess "just damages" in order to penalize an appellant who takes a frivolous appeal and to compensate the injured appellee for the delay and added expense of defending the district court's judgment. Thus, the Rule's discretionary mode of operation unmistakably conflicts with the mandatory provision of Alabama's affirmance penalty statute. Moreover, the purposes underlying the Rule are sufficiently coextensive with the asserted purposes of the Alabama statute to indicate that the Rule occupies the statute's field of operation so as to preclude its application in federal diversity actions.

> Respondents argue that, because Alabama has a similar Appellate Rule which may be applied in state court alongside the affirmance penalty statute, * * * a federal court sitting in diversity could impose the mandatory penalty and likewise remain free to exercise its discretionary authority under Federal Rule 38. This argument, however, ignores the significant possibility that a court of appeals may, in any given case, find a limited justification for imposing penalties in an amount *less than* 10% of the lower court's judgment. Federal Rule 38 adopts a case-by-case approach to identifying and deterring frivolous appeals; the Alabama statute precludes any exercise of discretion within its scope of operation. Whatever circumscriptive effect the mandatory affirmance penalty statute may have on the state court's exercise of discretion under Alabama's Rule 38, that Rule provides no authority for defining the scope of discretion allowed under Federal Rule 38.
>
> Federal Rule 38 regulates matters which can reasonably be classified as procedural, thereby satisfying the constitutional standard for validity. Its displacement of the Alabama statute also satisfies the statutory constraints of the Rules Enabling Act. The choice made by the drafters of the Federal Rules in favor of a discretionary procedure affects only the process of enforcing litigants' rights and not the rights themselves.

Id. at 4–8, 107 S.Ct. at 969–71, 94 L.Ed.2d at 7–9. Is the Alabama penalty substantive or procedural law? What purpose is served by interpreting Rule 38 to displace this Alabama rule in a diversity case?

STEWART ORGANIZATION, INC. v. RICOH CORP.

Supreme Court of the United States, 1988.
487 U.S. 22, 108 S.Ct. 2239, 101 L.Ed.2d 22.

Certiorari to the United States Court of Appeals for the Eleventh Circuit.

JUSTICE MARSHALL delivered the opinion of the Court.

This case presents the issue whether a federal court sitting in diversity should apply state or federal law in adjudicating a motion to transfer a case to a venue provided in a contractual forum-selection clause.

I

The dispute underlying this case grew out of a dealership agreement that obligated petitioner company, an Alabama corporation, to market copier products of respondent, a nationwide manufacturer with its principal place of business in New Jersey. The agreement contained a forum-selection clause providing that any dispute arising out of the contract could be brought only in a court located in Manhattan. Business relations between the parties soured under circumstances that are not relevant here. In September 1984, petitioner brought a complaint in the United States District Court for the Northern District of Alabama. The core of the complaint was an allegation that respondent had breached the dealership agreement, but petitioner also included claims for breach of warranty, fraud, and antitrust violations.

Relying on the contractual forum-selection clause, respondent moved the District Court either to transfer the case to the Southern District of New York under 28 U.S.C. § 1404(a) or to dismiss the case for improper venue under 28 U.S.C. § 1406. The District Court denied the motion. * * * It reasoned that the transfer motion was controlled by Alabama law and that Alabama looks unfavorably upon contractual forum-selection clauses. The court certified its ruling for interlocutory appeal, * * * and the Court of Appeals for the Eleventh Circuit accepted jurisdiction.

On appeal, a divided panel of the Eleventh Circuit reversed the District Court. The panel concluded that questions of venue in diversity actions are governed by federal law, and that the parties' forum-selection clause was enforceable as a matter of federal law. * * * The panel therefore reversed the order of the District Court and remanded with instructions to transfer the case to a Manhattan court. After petitioner successfully moved for rehearing en banc, * * * the full Court of Appeals proceeded to adopt the result, and much of the reasoning, of the panel opinion. * * * We now affirm under somewhat different reasoning.

II

Both the panel opinion and the opinion of the full Court of Appeals referred to the difficulties that often attend "the sticky question of which law, state or federal, will govern various aspects of the decisions of federal courts sitting in diversity." * * * A district court's decision whether to apply a federal statute such as § 1404(a) in a diversity action, however, involves a considerably less intricate analysis than that which governs the "relatively unguided *Erie* choice." * * * Our cases indicate that when the federal law sought to be applied is a congressional statute, the first and chief question for the district court's determination is whether the statute is "sufficiently broad to control the issue before the Court." * * * This question involves a straightforward exercise in statutory interpretation to determine if the statute covers the point in dispute.[14]

If the district court determines that a federal statute covers the point in dispute, it proceeds to inquire whether the statute represents a valid exercise of Congress' authority under the Constitution. * * * If Congress intended to reach the issue before the district court, and if it enacted its intention into law in a manner that abides with the Constitution, that is the end of the matter; "[f]ederal courts are bound to apply rules enacted by Congress with respect to matters * * * over which it has legislative

14. Our cases at times have referred to the question at this stage of the analysis as an inquiry into whether there is a "direct collision" between state and federal law. * * * Logic indicates, however, and a careful reading of the relevant passages confirms, that this language is not meant to mandate that federal law and state law be perfectly coextensive and equally applicable to the issue at hand; rather, the "direct collision" language, at least where the applicability of a federal statute is at issue, expresses the requirement that the federal statute be sufficiently broad to cover the point in dispute. * * * It would make no sense for the supremacy of federal law to wane precisely because there is no state law directly on point.

power" * * *.[6] Thus, a district court sitting in diversity must apply a federal statute that controls the issue before the court and that represents a valid exercise of Congress' constitutional powers.

III

* * *

B

* * * Under the analysis outlined above, we first consider whether [Section 1404(a)] is sufficiently broad to control the issue before the court. That issue is whether to transfer the case to a court in Manhattan in accordance with the forum-selection clause. We believe that the statute, fairly construed, does cover the point in dispute.

Section 1404(a) is intended to place discretion in the district court to adjudicate motions for transfer according to an "individualized, case-by-case consideration of convenience and fairness." * * * A motion to transfer under § 1404(a) thus calls on the district court to weigh in the balance a number of case-specific factors. The presence of a forum-selection clause such as the parties entered into in this case will be a significant factor that figures centrally in the district court's calculus. In its resolution of the § 1404(a) motion in this case, for example, the District Court will be called on to address such issues as the convenience of a Manhattan forum given the parties' expressed preference for that venue, and the fairness of transfer in light of the forum-selection clause and the parties' relative bargaining power. The flexible and individualized analysis Congress prescribed in § 1404(a) thus encompasses consideration of the parties' private expression of their venue preferences.

Section 1404(a) may not be the only potential source of guidance for the District Court to consult in weighing the parties' private designation of a suitable forum. The premise of the dispute between the parties is that Alabama law may refuse to enforce forum-selection clauses providing for out-of-state venues as a matter of state public policy. If that is so, the District Court will have either to integrate the factor of the forum-selection clause into its weighing of considerations as prescribed by Congress, or else to apply, as it did in this case, Alabama's categorical policy disfavoring forum-selection clauses. Our cases make clear that, as between these two choices in a single "field of operation," * * * the instructions of Congress are supreme. * * *

It is true that § 1404(a) and Alabama's putative policy regarding forum-selection clauses are not perfectly coextensive. Section 1404(a) directs a district court to take account of factors other than those that bear solely on the parties' private ordering of their affairs. The district

6. If no federal statute or Rule covers the point in dispute, the district court then proceeds to evaluate whether application of federal judge-made law would disserve the so-called "twin aims of the *Erie* rule: discouragement of forum-shopping and avoidance of inequitable administration of the laws." * * * If application of federal judge-made law would disserve these two policies, the district court should apply state law. * * *

court also must weigh in the balance the convenience of the witnesses and those public-interest factors of systemic integrity and fairness that, in addition to private concerns, come under the heading of "the interest of justice." It is conceivable in a particular case, for example, that because of these factors district court acting under § 1404(a) would refuse to transfer a case notwithstanding the counterweight of a forum-selection clause, whereas the coordinate state rule might dictate the opposite result. * * * But this potential conflict in fact frames an additional argument for the supremacy of federal law. Congress has directed that multiple considerations govern transfer within the federal court system, and a state policy focusing on a single concern or a subset of the factors identified in § 1404(a) would defeat that command. Its application would impoverish the flexible and multifaceted analysis that Congress intended to govern motions to transfer within the federal system. The forum-selection clause, which represents the parties' agreement as to the most proper forum, should receive neither dispositive consideration (as respondent might have it) nor no consideration (as Alabama law might have it), but rather the consideration for which Congress provided in § 1404(a). * * * This is thus not a case in which state and federal rules "can exist side by side * * * each controlling its own intended sphere of coverage without conflict." * * *

Because § 1404(a) controls the issue before the District Court, it must be applied if it represents a valid exercise of Congress' authority under the Constitution. The constitutional authority of Congress to enact § 1404(a) is not subject to serious question. As the Court made plain in *Hanna,* "the constitutional provision for a federal court system * * * carries with it congressional power to make rules governing the practice and pleading in those courts, which in turn includes a power to regulate matters which, though falling within the uncertain area between substance and procedure, are rationally capable of classification as either." * * * Section 1404(a) is doubtless capable of classification as a procedural rule, and indeed, we have so classified it in holding that a transfer pursuant to § 1404(a) does not carry with it a change in the applicable law. * * * It therefore falls comfortably within Congress' powers under Article III as augmented by the Necessary and Proper Clause. * * *

We hold that federal law, specifically 28 U.S.C. § 1404(a), governs the District Court's decision whether to give effect to the parties' forum-selection clause and transfer this case to a court in Manhattan. * * * The case is remanded so that the District Court may determine in the first instance the appropriate effect under federal law of the parties' forum-selection clause on respondent's § 1404(a) motion.

It is so ordered.

JUSTICE KENNEDY, with whom JUSTICE O'CONNOR joins, concurring.

I concur in full. I write separately only to observe that enforcement of valid forum-selection clauses, bargained for by the parties, protects their legitimate expectations and furthers vital interests of the justice system.

Although our opinion in The Bremen v. Zapata Off–Shore Co., 407 U.S. 1, 10, 92 S.Ct. 1907, 1913, 32 L.Ed.2d 513 (1972), involved a Federal District Court sitting in admiralty, its reasoning applies with much force to federal courts sitting in diversity. The justifications we noted in The Bremen to counter the historical disfavor forum-selection clauses had received in American courts, * * *, should be understood to guide the District Court's analysis under § 1404(a).

* * * Courts should announce and encourage rules that support private parties who negotiate such clauses. Though state policies should be weighed in the balance, the authority and prerogative of the federal courts to determine the issue, as Congress has directed by § 1404(a), should be exercised so that a valid forum-selection clause is given controlling weight in all but the most exceptional cases. * * *

JUSTICE SCALIA, dissenting.

* * *

When a litigant asserts that state law conflicts with a federal procedural statute or formal Rule of Procedure, a court's first task is to determine whether the disputed point in question in fact falls within the scope of the federal statute or Rule. In this case, the Court must determine whether the scope of § 1404(a) is sufficiently broad to cause a direct collision with state law or implicitly to control the issue before the Court, i.e., validity between the parties of the forum-selection clause, thereby leaving no room for the operation of state law. * * * I conclude that it is not.

Although the language of § 1404(a) provides no clear answer, in my view it does provide direction. The provision vests the district courts with authority to transfer a civil action to another district "[f]or the convenience of parties and witnesses, in the interest of justice." This language looks to the present and the future. As the specific reference to convenience of parties and witnesses suggests, it requires consideration of what is likely to be just in the future, when the case is tried, in light of things as they now stand. Accordingly, the courts in applying § 1404(a) have examined a variety of factors, each of which pertains to facts that currently exist or will exist * * *. In holding that the validity between the parties of a forum-selection clause falls within the scope of § 1404(a), the Court inevitably imports, in my view without adequate textual foundation, a new retrospective element into the court's deliberations, requiring examination of what the facts were concerning, among other things, the bargaining power of the parties and the presence or absence of overreaching at the time the contract was made. * * *

* * *

II

Since no federal statute or Rule of Procedure governs the validity of a forum-selection clause, the remaining issue is whether federal courts may fashion a judge-made rule to govern the question. If they may not, the Rules of Decision Act, 28 U.S.C. § 1652, mandates use of state law. * * * Whatever the scope of the federal courts' authority to create federal common law in other areas, it is plain that the mere fact that petitioner company here brought an antitrust claim, * * * does not empower the federal courts to make common law on the question of the validity of the forum-selection clause. * * * The federal courts do have authority, however, to make procedural rules that govern the practice before them. * * * In deciding what is substantive and what is procedural for these purposes, we have adhered to a functional test based on the "twin aims of the Erie rule: discouragement of forum-shopping and avoidance of inequitable administration of the laws." * * *

Under the twin-aims test, I believe state law controls the question of the validity of a forum-selection clause between the parties. The Eleventh Circuit's rule clearly encourages forum shopping. Venue is often a vitally important matter, as is shown by the frequency with which parties contractually provide for and litigate the issue. Suit might well not be pursued, or might not be as successful, in a significantly less convenient forum. Transfer to such a less desirable forum is, therefore, of sufficient import that plaintiffs will base their decisions on the likelihood of that eventuality when they are choosing whether to sue in state or federal court. * * *

I believe creating a judge-made rule fails the second part of the twin-aims test as well, producing inequitable administration of the laws. * * * It is difficult to imagine an issue of more importance, other than one that goes to the very merits of the lawsuit, than the validity of a contractual forum-selection provision. * * *

For the reasons stated, I respectfully dissent.

NOTES AND QUESTIONS

1. After *Stewart*, can a federal court exercising diversity jurisdiction ground its refusal to hear a case on the doctrine of forum non conveniens, if sitting in a state that would not apply the doctrine?

> While *Stewart* authorized the federal courts to ignore state law that refused to enforce forum selection clauses in the context of a section 1404(a) transfer, the case does not resolve whether state law must be followed in the absence of section 1404(a). Thus, an open *Erie* question remains in cases where the contractually stipulated forum is outside of the federal system, or where a defendant moves to dismiss for improper venue rather than to transfer to the contractually stipulated forum.

Stein, Erie *and Court Access*, 100 Yale L.J. 1935, 1981 (1991). What is the source of a federal court's power to develop rules of forum non conveniens? Professor Barrett points out that although the Court in *Gulf Oil*, p. 391, supra, recognized a federal doctrine of forum non conveniens, it "did not point to any specific statutory or constitutional provision that granted federal courts the power to dismiss suits on this basis, nor did it identify the principle that generally empowered it to create procedural common law, of which forum non conveniens is but a part.'' Barrett, *Procedural Common Law*, 94 Va. L. Rev. 813, 826–27 (2008). How would you resolve this question?

2. In analyzing Justice Kennedy's concurrence, p. 451, supra, consider the fact that a federal court sitting in admiralty is ''free to create a common-law rule governing the enforceability of forum selection clauses.'' Buckingham, *Stewart Organization v. Ricoh Corp.: Judicial Discretion in Forum Selection*, 41 Rutgers L. Rev. 1379, 1387 (1989). Thus, in *Carnival Cruise*, p. 189, supra, the Court relied on federal law to determine the enforceability of the forum-selection clause that was at issue in that case. Do you agree with the concurrence's view that Congress, by enacting 28 U.S.C. § 1404, has given the federal courts ''the authority and prerogative * * * to determine'' whether a forum-selection clause is valid, p. 452, supra, even when the court is sitting in diversity?

3. Professor Rowe says that *Stewart* ''provided strong support for the view that the Court would read federal statutes and Rules with no deference to state law * * *.'' Rowe, *Not Bad for Government Work: Does Anyone Else Think the Supreme Court Is Doing a Halfway Decent Job in Its* Erie–Hanna *Jurisprudence*?, 73 Notre Dame L. Rev. 963, 994 (1998). Why might a state not want to give effect to a forum-selection clause? Do you agree that the Court paid insufficient attention in *Stewart* to legitimate state regulatory interests? Is it appropriate to make this assessment on a case-by-case basis, or should it be decided as a general matter through the rulemaking process? See Dudley, Jr. & Rutherglen, *Deforming the Federal Rules: An Essay on What's Wrong with the Recent* Erie *Decisions*, 92 Va. L. Rev. 707, 738–47 (2006).

GASPERINI v. CENTER FOR HUMANITIES, INC.

Supreme Court of the United States, 1996.
518 U.S. 415, 116 S.Ct. 2211, 135 L.Ed.2d 659.

Certiorari to the United States Court of Appeals for the Second Circuit.

JUSTICE GINSBURG delivered the opinion of the Court.

Under the law of New York, appellate courts are empowered to review the size of jury verdicts and to order new trials when the jury's award ''deviates materially from what would be reasonable compensation.'' N. Y. Civ. Prac. Law and Rules (CPLR) § 5501(c) * * *. Under the Seventh Amendment, which governs proceedings in federal court, but not in state court, ''the right of trial by jury shall be preserved, and no fact tried by a jury, shall be otherwise re-examined in any Court of the United States, than according to the rules of the common law.'' The compatibility of these provisions, in an action based on New York law but tried in federal court by reason of the parties' diverse citizenship, is the issue we confront in this case. * * *

We hold that New York's law controlling compensation awards for excessiveness or inadequacy can be given effect, without detriment to the Seventh Amendment, if the review standard set out in CPLR § 5501(c) is applied by the federal trial court judge, with appellate control of the trial court's ruling limited to review for "abuse of discretion."

I

Petitioner William Gasperini, a journalist for CBS News and the Christian Science Monitor, began reporting on events in Central America in 1984. * * * During the course of his seven-year stint in Central America, Gasperini took over 5,000 slide transparencies, depicting active war zones, political leaders, and scenes from daily life. In 1990, Gasperini agreed to supply his original color transparencies to The Center for Humanities, Inc. (Center) for use in an educational videotape, Conflict in Central America. Gasperini selected 300 of his slides for the Center; its videotape included 110 of them. The Center agreed to return the original transparencies, but upon the completion of the project, it could not find them.

Gasperini commenced suit in the United States District Court for the Southern District of New York, invoking the court's diversity jurisdiction * * *. The Center conceded liability for the lost transparencies and the issue of damages was tried before a jury.

At trial, Gasperini's expert witness testified that the "industry standard" within the photographic publishing community valued a lost transparency at $1,500. * * *

After a three-day trial, the jury awarded Gasperini $450,000 in compensatory damages. This sum, the jury foreperson announced, "is [$]1500 each, for 300 slides." Moving for a new trial under Federal Rule of Civil Procedure 59, the Center attacked the verdict on various grounds, including excessiveness. Without comment, the District Court denied the motion. * * *

The Court of Appeals for the Second Circuit vacated the judgment entered on the jury's verdict. * * * Mindful that New York law governed the controversy, the Court of Appeals endeavored to apply CPLR § 5501(c), which instructs that, when a jury returns an itemized verdict, as the jury did in this case, the New York Appellate Division "shall determine that an award is excessive or inadequate if it deviates materially from what would be reasonable compensation." The Second Circuit's application of § 5501(c) as a check on the size of the jury's verdict followed Circuit precedent elaborated two weeks earlier * * *. Surveying Appellate Division decisions that reviewed damage awards for lost transparencies, the Second Circuit concluded that testimony on industry standard alone was insufficient to justify a verdict; prime among other factors warranting consideration were the uniqueness of the slides' subject matter and the photographer's earning level.

Guided by Appellate Division rulings, the Second Circuit held that the $450,000 verdict "materially deviates from what is reasonable compensation." * * * [T]he Second Circuit set aside the $450,000 verdict and ordered a new trial, unless Gasperini agreed to an award of $100,000.

* * *

II

Before 1986, state and federal courts in New York generally invoked the same judge-made formulation in responding to excessiveness attacks on jury verdicts: courts would not disturb an award unless the amount was so exorbitant that it "shocked the conscience of the court." * * *

In both state and federal courts, trial judges made the excessiveness assessment in the first instance, and appellate judges ordinarily deferred to the trial court's judgment. * * *

In 1986, as part of a series of tort reform measures, New York codified a standard for judicial review of the size of jury awards. Placed in CPLR § 5501(c), the prescription reads:

> "In reviewing a money judgment . . . in which it is contended that the award is excessive or inadequate and that a new trial should have been granted unless a stipulation is entered to a different award, the appellate division shall determine that an award is excessive or inadequate if it deviates materially from what would be reasonable compensation." * * *

* * * New York state-court opinions confirm that § 5501(c)'s "deviates materially" standard calls for closer surveillance than "shock the conscience" oversight. * * *

Although phrased as a direction to New York's intermediate appellate courts, § 5501(c)'s "deviates materially" standard, as construed by New York's courts, instructs state trial judges as well. * * * Application of § 5501(c) at the trial level is key to this case.

To determine whether an award "deviates materially from what would be reasonable compensation," New York state courts look to awards approved in similar cases. * * *

III

In cases like Gasperini's, in which New York law governs the claims for relief, does New York law also supply the test for federal-court review of the size of the verdict? The Center answers yes. The "deviates materially" standard, it argues, is a substantive standard that must be applied by federal appellate courts in diversity cases. The Second Circuit agreed. * * * Gasperini, emphasizing that § 5501(c) trains on the New York Appellate Division, characterizes the provision as procedural, an allocation of decisionmaking authority regarding damages, not a hard cap on the amount recoverable. Correctly comprehended, Gasperini urges, § 5501(c)'s direction to the Appellate Division cannot be given effect by federal appellate courts without violating the Seventh Amendment's Reexamination Clause.

As the parties' arguments suggest, CPLR § 5501(c), appraised under *Erie R. Co. v. Tompkins* * * * and decisions in *Erie*'s path, is both "substantive" and "procedural": "substantive" in that § 5501(c)'s "deviates materially" standard controls how much a plaintiff can be awarded; "procedural" in that § 5501(c) assigns decisionmaking authority to New York's Appellate Division. Parallel application of § 5501(c) at the federal appellate level would be out of sync with the federal system's division of trial and appellate court functions, an allocation weighted by the Seventh Amendment. The dispositive question, therefore, is whether federal courts can give effect to the substantive thrust of § 5501(c) without untoward alteration of the federal scheme for the trial and decision of civil cases.

A

* * *

Classification of a law as "substantive" or "procedural" for *Erie* purposes is sometimes a challenging endeavor.[7] *Guaranty Trust Co. v. York*, * * * an early interpretation of *Erie*, propounded an "outcome-determination" test: "[D]oes it significantly affect the result of a litigation for a federal court to disregard a law of a State that would be controlling in an action upon the same claim by the same parties in a State court?" * * * A later pathmarking case, qualifying *Guaranty Trust*, explained that the "outcome-determination" test must not be applied mechanically to sweep in all manner of variations; instead, its application must be guided by "the twin aims of the *Erie* rule: discouragement of forum shopping and avoidance of inequitable administration of the laws." *Hanna v. Plumer* * * *.

* * * [W]e address the question whether New York's "deviates materially" standard, codified in CPLR § 5501(c), is outcome affective in this sense: Would "application of the [standard] ... have so important an effect upon the fortunes of one or both of the litigants that failure to [apply] it would [unfairly discriminate against citizens of the forum State, or] be likely to cause a plaintiff to choose the federal court"? * * *[8]

We start from a point the parties do not debate. Gasperini acknowledges that a statutory cap on damages would supply substantive law for *Erie* purposes. * * * Although CPLR § 5501(c) is less readily classified, it was designed to provide an analogous control.

* * *

It thus appears that if federal courts ignore the change in the New York standard and persist in applying the "shock the conscience" test to

---

7. Concerning matters covered by the Federal Rules of Civil Procedure, the characterization question is usually unproblematic: It is settled that if the Rule in point is consonant with the Rules Enabling Act, 28 U.S.C. § 2072, and the Constitution, the Federal Rule applies regardless of contrary state law. See *Hanna v. Plumer*, * * * *Burlington Northern R. Co. v. Woods* * * *. Federal courts have interpreted the Federal Rules, however, with sensitivity to important state interests and regulatory policies. * * *

8. *Hanna* keyed the question to *Erie*'s "twin aims" * * *.

damage awards on claims governed by New York law, " 'substantial' variations between state and federal [money judgments]" may be expected. * * * We therefore agree with the Second Circuit that New York's check on excessive damages implicates what we have called "twin aims." * * * Just as the *Erie* principle precludes a federal court from giving a state-created claim "longer life . . . than [the claim] would have had in the state court," * * * so *Erie* precludes a recovery in federal court significantly larger than the recovery that would have been tolerated in state court.

B

CPLR § 5501(c) * * * is phrased as a direction to the New York Appellate Division. Acting essentially as a surrogate for a New York appellate forum, the Court of Appeals reviewed Gasperini's award to determine if it "deviate[d] materially" from damage awards the Appellate Division permitted in similar circumstances. The Court of Appeals performed this task without benefit of an opinion from the District Court, which had denied "without comment" the Center's Rule 59 motion. Concentrating on the authority § 5501(c) gives to the Appellate Division, Gasperini urges that the provision shifts fact finding responsibility from the jury and the trial judge to the appellate court. Assigning such responsibility to an appellate court, he maintains, is incompatible with the Seventh Amendment's Reexamination Clause, and therefore, Gasperini concludes, § 5501(c) cannot be given effect in federal court. Although we reach a different conclusion than Gasperini, we agree that the Second Circuit did not attend to "an essential characteristic of [the federal-court] system," * * * when it used § 5501(c) as "the standard for [federal] appellate review." * * *

* * *

The Seventh Amendment, which governs proceedings in federal court, but not in state court, bears not only on the allocation of trial functions between judge and jury, the issue in *Byrd*; it also controls the allocation of authority to review verdicts, the issue of concern here. * * *

Byrd involved the first Clause of the Amendment, the "trial by jury" Clause. This case involves the second, the "Reexamination" Clause. In keeping with the historic understanding, the Reexamination Clause does not inhibit the authority of trial judges to grant new trials "for any of the reasons for which new trials have heretofore been granted in actions at law in the courts of the United States." That authority is large. * * * "The trial judge in the federal system," we have reaffirmed, "has . . . [in original] discretion to grant a new trial if the verdict appears to [the judge] to be against the weight of the evidence." * * * This discretion includes overturning verdicts for excessiveness and ordering a new trial without qualification, or conditioned on the verdict winner's refusal to agree to a reduction (remittitur). * * *

In contrast, appellate review of a federal trial court's denial of a motion to set aside a jury's verdict as excessive is a relatively late, and less secure, development. Such review was once deemed inconsonant with the Seventh Amendment's Reexamination Clause. * * *

As the Second Circuit explained, appellate review for abuse of discretion is reconcilable with the Seventh Amendment as a control necessary and proper to the fair administration of justice: "We must give the benefit of every doubt to the judgment of the trial judge; but surely there must be an upper limit, and whether that has been surpassed is not a question of fact with respect to which reasonable men may differ, but a question of law." [citations omitted] * * * We now approve this line of decisions, and thus make explicit what Justice Stewart thought implicit in our * * * disposition [in an earlier case]: "[N]othing in the Seventh Amendment . . . precludes appellate review of the trial judge's denial of a motion to set aside [a jury verdict] as excessive." * * *

C

In *Byrd*, the Court faced a one-or-the-other choice: trial by judge as in state court, or trial by jury according to the federal practice. In the case before us, a choice of that order is not required, for the principal state and federal interests can be accommodated. The Second Circuit correctly recognized that when New York substantive law governs a claim for relief, New York law and decisions guide the allowable damages. * * *

New York's dominant interest can be respected, without disrupting the federal system, once it is recognized that the federal district court is capable of * * * apply[ing] the State's "deviates materially" standard in line with New York case law evolving under CPLR § 5501(c).[22] * * *

Within the federal system, practical reasons combine with Seventh Amendment constraints to lodge in the district court, not the court of appeals, primary responsibility for application of § 5501(c)'s "deviates materially" check. Trial judges have the "unique opportunity to consider the evidence in the living courtroom context," * * * while appellate judges see only the "cold paper record."

District court applications of the "deviates materially" standard would be subject to appellate review under the standard the Circuits now employ when inadequacy or excessiveness is asserted on appeal: abuse of discretion. * * * In light of *Erie*'s doctrine, the federal appeals court must be guided by the damage-control standard state law supplies, but as the Second Circuit itself has said: "If we reverse, it must be because of an

---

22. Justice SCALIA finds in Federal Rule of Civil Procedure 59 a "federal standard" for new trial motions in " 'direct collision' " with, and " 'leaving no room for the operation of,' " a state law like CPLR § 5501(c). * * * The relevant prescription, Rule 59(a), has remained unchanged since the adoption of the Federal Rules by this Court in 1937. Rule 59(a) is as encompassing as it is uncontroversial. It is indeed "Hornbook" law that a most usual ground for a Rule 59 motion is that "the damages are excessive." See C. Wright, Law of Federal Courts 676–677 (5th ed. 1994). Whether damages are excessive for the claim-in-suit must be governed by some law. And there is no candidate for that governance other than the law that gives rise to the claim for relief—here, the law of New York. * * *

abuse of discretion.... The very nature of the problem counsels restraint.... We must give the benefit of every doubt to the judgment of the trial judge."

IV

It does not appear that the District Court checked the jury's verdict against the relevant New York decisions demanding more than "industry standard" testimony to support an award of the size the jury returned in this case. As the Court of Appeals recognized, * * * the uniqueness of the photographs and the plaintiff's earnings as photographer—past and reasonably projected—are factors relevant to appraisal of the award. * * * Accordingly, we vacate the judgment of the Court of Appeals and instruct that court to remand the case to the District Court so that the trial judge, revisiting his ruling on the new trial motion, may test the jury's verdict against CPLR § 5501(c)'s "deviates materially" standard.

It is so ordered.

JUSTICE STEVENS, dissenting.

* * *

I

* * *

The District Court had its opportunity to consider the propriety of the jury's award, and it erred. The Court of Appeals has now corrected that error after "drawing all reasonable inferences in favor of" petitioner. * * * As there is no reason to suppose that the Court of Appeals has reached a conclusion with which the District Court could permissibly disagree on remand, I would not require the District Court to repeat a task that has already been well performed by the reviewing court. I therefore would affirm the judgment of the Court of Appeals.

* * *

III

* * * I agree with the majority that the Reexamination Clause does not bar federal appellate courts from reviewing jury awards for excessiveness. I confess to some surprise, however, at its conclusion that " 'the influence—if not the command—of the Seventh Amendment,' " * * * requires federal courts of appeals to review district court applications of state-law excessiveness standards for an "abuse of discretion." * * *

Certainly, our decision in *Byrd* does not make the Clause relevant. There, we considered only whether the Seventh Amendment's first clause should influence our decision to give effect to a state-law rule denying the right to a jury altogether. * * * That holding in no way requires us to consult the Amendment's second clause to determine the standard of review for a district court's application of state substantive law.

My disagreement is tempered, however, because the majority carefully avoids defining too strictly the abuse-of-discretion standard it announces. To the extent that the majority relies only on "practical reasons" for its conclusion that the Court of Appeals should give some weight to the District Court's assessment in determining whether state substantive law has been properly applied, * * * I do not disagree with its analysis.

* * *

In the end, therefore, my disagreement with the label that the majority attaches to the standard of appellate review should not obscure the far more fundamental point on which we agree. Whatever influence the Seventh Amendment may be said to exert, Erie requires federal appellate courts sitting in diversity to apply "the damage-control standard state law supplies." * * *

IV

Because I would affirm the judgment of the Court of Appeals, and because I do not agree that the Seventh Amendment in any respect influences the proper analysis of the question presented, I respectfully dissent.

JUSTICE SCALIA, with whom the CHIEF JUSTICE and JUSTICE THOMAS join, dissenting.

* * *

I

* * *

A

* * * [T]he practice of *federal* appellate reexamination of facts found by a jury is precisely what the People of the several States considered *not* to be good legal policy in 1791. Indeed, so fearful were they of such a practice that they constitutionally prohibited it by means of the Seventh Amendment.

* * *

* * * The Reexamination Clause put to rest "apprehensions" of "new trials by the appellate courts," by adopting, in broad fashion, "the rules of the common law" to govern federal-court interference with jury determinations. The content of that law was familiar and fixed. * * * It quite plainly barred reviewing courts from entertaining claims that the jury's verdict was contrary to the evidence.

At common law, review of judgments was had only on writ of error, limited to questions of law. * * *

Nor was the common-law proscription on reexamination limited to review of the correctness of the jury's determination of liability on the facts. No less than the existence of liability, the proper measure of damages "involves only a question of fact," * * * as does a "motion for a new trial based on the ground that the damages . . . are excessive." * * * As appeals from denial of such motions necessarily pose a factual question, courts of the United States are constitutionally forbidden to entertain them.

* * *

B

* * *

I am persuaded that our prior cases were correct that, at common law, "reexamination" of the facts found by a jury could be undertaken only by the trial court, and that appellate review was restricted to writ of error which could challenge the judgment only upon matters of law. * * * Cases of this Court reaching back into the early 19th century establish that the Constitution forbids federal appellate courts to "reexamine" a fact found by the jury at trial; and that this prohibition encompasses review of a district court's refusal to set aside a verdict as contrary to the weight of the evidence.

C

* * *

* * * The cases upon which the Court relies neither affirmed nor rejected the practice of appellate weight-of-the-evidence review that has been adopted by the courts of appeals—a development that, in light of our past cases, amounts to studied waywardness by the intermediate appellate bench. * * *

In any event, it is not *this* Court's statements that the Court puts forward as the basis for dispensing with our prior cases. Rather, it is the Courts of Appeals' unanimous "agree[ment]" [in original] that they may review trial-court refusals to set aside jury awards claimed to be against the weight of the evidence. * * * This current unanimity is deemed controlling, notwithstanding the "relatively late" origin of the practice, * * * and without any inquiry into the reasoning set forth in those Court of Appeals decisions. * * *

The Court's only suggestion as to what rationale might underlie approval of abuse-of-discretion review is to be found in a quotation * * * to the effect that review of denial of a new trial motion, if conducted under a sufficiently deferential standard, poses only " 'a question of law.' " * * * But that is not the test that the Seventh Amendment sets forth. Whether or not it is possible to characterize an appeal of a denial of new trial as raising a "legal question," it is not possible to review such a claim without engaging in a "reexamin[ation]" [in original] of the "facts tried by the jury" in a manner "otherwise" than allowed at common law. Determining whether a particular award is excessive requires that one first determine the nature and extent of the harm—which undeniably requires reviewing the facts of the case. That the court's review also entails application of a legal standard (whether "shocks the conscience," "deviates materially," or some other) makes no difference, for what is necessarily *also* required is *reexamination of facts* found by the jury.

* * *

II

The Court's holding that federal courts of appeals may review district court denials of motions for new trials for error of fact is not the only novel aspect of today's decision. The Court also directs that the case be remanded to the District Court, so that it may "test the jury's verdict against CPLR § 5501(c)'s 'deviates materially' standard." * * * This disposition contradicts the principle that "the proper role of the trial and appellate courts in the federal system in reviewing the size of jury verdicts is . . . a matter of federal law." * * *

* * * The Court approves the "accommodat[ion]" [in original] achieved by having district courts review jury verdicts under the "deviates materially" standard, because it regards that as a means of giving effect to the State's purposes "without disrupting the federal system." * * * But changing the standard by which trial judges review jury verdicts *does* disrupt the federal system, and is plainly inconsistent with the "strong federal policy against allowing state rules to disrupt the judge-jury relationship in the federal court." * * *

* * *

* * * It seems to me quite wrong to regard [Section 5501(c)] as a "substantive" rule for *Erie* purposes. The "analog[y]" to "a statutory cap on damages" * * * fails utterly. There is an absolutely fundamental distinction between a *rule of law* such as that, which would ordinarily be imposed upon the jury in the trial court's instructions, and a *rule of review*, which simply determines how closely the jury verdict will be scrutinized for compliance with the instructions. A tighter standard for reviewing jury determinations can no more plausibly be called a "substantive" disposition than can a tighter appellate standard for reviewing trial-court determinations. The one, like the other, provides additional assurance *that the law has been complied with*; but the other, like the one, *leaves the law unchanged*.

The Court commits the classic *Erie* mistake of regarding whatever changes the outcome as substantive * * *. * * * Outcome-determination "was never intended to serve as a talisman," and * * * does not have the power to convert the most classic elements of the process of assuring that the law is observed into the substantive law itself. The right to have a jury make the findings of fact, for example, is generally thought to favor plaintiffs, and that advantage is often thought significant enough to be the basis for forum selection. But no one would argue that *Erie* confers a right to a jury in federal court wherever state courts would provide it; or that, were it not for the Seventh Amendment, *Erie* would require federal courts to dispense with the jury whenever state courts do so.

In any event, the Court exaggerates the difference that the state standard will make. It concludes that different outcomes are likely to ensue depending on whether the law being applied is the state "deviates materially" standard of § 5501(c) or the "shocks the conscience" standard. * * * Of course, it is not the federal *appellate* standard but the federal *district-court* standard for granting new trials that must be compared with the New York standard to determine whether substantially different results will obtain—and it is far from clear that the district-court standard *ought* to be "shocks the conscience." * * * What seems to me far more likely to produce forum shopping is the consistent difference between the state and federal *appellate* standards, which the Court leaves untouched. * * * The only result that would produce the conformity the Court erroneously believes *Erie* requires is the one adopted by the Second Circuit and rejected by the Court: *de novo* federal appellate review under the § 5501(c) standard.

To say that application of § 5501(c) in place of the federal standard will not consistently produce disparate results is not to suggest that the decision the Court has made today is not a momentous one. The *principle* that the state standard governs is of great importance, since it bears the potential to destroy the uniformity of federal practice and the integrity of the federal court system. Under the Court's view, a state rule that directed courts "to determine that an award is excessive or inadequate if it deviates *in any degree* from *the proper measure of compensation*" would have to be applied in federal courts, effectively requiring federal judges to determine the amount of damages de novo, and effectively taking the matter away from the jury entirely. * * * Or consider a state rule that allowed the defendant a second trial on damages, with judgment ultimately in the amount of the lesser of two jury awards. * * * Under the reasoning of the Court's opinion, even such a rule as that would have to be applied in the federal courts.

The foregoing describes why I think the Court's *Erie* analysis is flawed. But in my view, one does not even reach the *Erie* question in this case. The standard to be applied by a district court in ruling on a motion for a new trial is set forth in Rule 59 of the Federal Rules of Civil Procedure, which provides that "[a] new trial may be granted . . . for any of the reasons for which new trials have heretofore been granted in actions at law *in the courts of the United States*" (emphasis added). [The language of Rule 59(a) was altered nonsubstantively in 2007.] That is undeniably a federal standard.[12] Federal district courts in the Second Circuit have interpreted that standard to permit the granting of new trials

12. I agree with the Court's entire progression of reasoning in its footnote * * *, leading to the conclusion that state law must determine "whether damages are excessive." But the question whether damages are excessive is quite separate from the question of when a jury award may be set aside for excessiveness. * * * It is the latter that is governed by Rule 59 * * *.

where " 'it is quite clear that the jury has reached a seriously erroneous result' " and letting the verdict stand would result in a " 'miscarriage of justice.' " * * * Assuming (as we have no reason to question) that this is a correct interpretation of what Rule 59 requires, it is undeniable that the Federal Rule is " 'sufficiently broad' to cause a 'direct collision' with the state law or, implicitly, to 'control the issue' before the court, thereby leaving no room for the operation of that law." * * * It is simply not possible to give controlling effect both to the federal standard and the state standard in reviewing the jury's award. That being so, the court has no choice but to apply the Federal Rule, which is an exercise of what we have called Congress's "power to regulate matters which, though falling within the uncertain area between substance and procedure, are rationally capable of classification as either * * *."

* * * I respectfully dissent.

NOTES AND QUESTIONS

1. The first part of the Court's decision in *Gasperini* revived a *York*-style outcome-determinative approach to determining the applicable law. After *Byrd* and *Hanna*, although *York* had not been overruled, its influence had waned, and the Court surprised many observers in *Gasperini* by abandoning the balancing approach established by these later cases. What role do the "twin aims" of *Erie* continue to play in determining the applicable law? It remains unclear how courts should determine the applicable law in diversity cases that do not involve a Federal Rule or some other element of federal law.

2. *Gasperini* did not discuss *Byrd* until it already had determined the applicable law. Why not? Like *Byrd*, *Gasperini* involved the division of trial functions between judge and jury. Although in *Byrd* the Court ultimately declined to apply state law, one commentator has suggested it need not have reached the same result in *Gasperini*:

> [T]he state practice in *Byrd* allocated responsibilities based only on a "practical consideration" that was not "bound up with the definition of the rights and obligations of the parties." In contrast, the New York legislature wanted to enact a substantive damage limitation when it enacted 5501(c). The *Gasperini* Court could easily have found the state interest to outweigh the federal interest under *Byrd*, then performed an identical Seventh Amendment analysis, and reached the same result. It simply chose not to do so.

Leading Cases, 110 Harv.L.Rev. 135, 265 (1996). In *Byrd*, the Court held that South Carolina's division between judge and jury was not "bound up" with the substantive rights of the parties. In *Gasperini*, however, the Court found that New York's damage award rule is substantive. Does *Gasperini* provide a new approach that replaces *Byrd,* or can the two decisions be reconciled?

3. The majority in *Gasperini* claimed that Federal Rule 59(a)(1) did not apply. Is this correct? In Atlas Food Sys. & Servs. v. Crane Nat'l Vendors, Inc., 99 F.3d 587 (4th Cir.1996), the court held that although state law supplies the framework for damage awards, the judgment a jury makes as to

the damage amount is reviewed by federal courts under the Rule less deferentially than are factual findings. If the Federal Rules should be "interpreted with sensitivity to important state interests and regulatory policies," as the Court suggested in footnote 7, then perhaps Rule 59 should be interpreted narrowly to avoid a conflict with the substantive purposes of New York's Legislature. See Freer, *Some Thoughts on the State of* Erie *After* Gasperini, 76 Texas L.Rev. 1637 (1998).

SECTION B. THE PROBLEM OF ASCERTAINING STATE LAW

1. DETERMINING WHICH STATE'S LAW GOVERNS

In *Erie,* the parties—and the courts—appear to have assumed that if state law applied, Pennsylvania tort law would govern—even though the action was being tried in a federal court in New York. Why did they make this assumption? Was the federal court free to choose the most appropriate state law to govern the dispute? Or was it that New York's choice-of-law rules pointed to an application of Pennsylvania law?

KLAXON CO. v. STENTOR ELECTRIC MFG. CO., 313 U.S. 487, 61 S.Ct. 1020, 85 L.Ed. 1477 (1941). The Supreme Court held that in order to promote the desired uniform application of substantive law within a state, federal courts must apply the conflicts-of-law rules of the states in which they sit. The Court explained:

> * * * Whatever lack of uniformity this may produce between federal courts in different states is attributable to our federal system, which leaves to a state, within the limits permitted by the Constitution, the right to pursue local policies diverging from those of its neighbors. It is not for the federal courts to thwart such local policies by enforcing an independent "general law" of conflict of laws. * * * [T]he proper function of [a] federal court is to ascertain what the state law is, not what it ought to be.

Id. at 496–97, 61 S.Ct. at 1022, 85 L.Ed. at 1480–81.

NOTES AND QUESTIONS

1. The Supreme Court reaffirmed the *Klaxon* rule in Day & Zimmermann, Inc. v. Challoner, 423 U.S. 3, 96 S.Ct. 167, 46 L.Ed.2d 3 (1975). Plaintiff filed a diversity action in Texas federal court seeking damages for death and personal injury resulting from the premature explosion of a 105–mm. howitzer round in Cambodia. The Court of Appeals declined to apply Texas choice-of-law rules, which it believed required application of the law of Cambodia. The Supreme Court vacated and remanded the judgment, empha-

sizing that "the conflict-of-law rules to be applied by a federal court in Texas must conform to those prevailing in the Texas state court" and that a diversity court "is not free to engraft onto those state rules exceptions or modifications which * * * have not commended themselves to the State in which the federal court sits." Id. at 5, 96 S. Ct. at 168, 46 L. Ed. 2d at 5.

2. Could Congress enact a statute specifying choice-of-law rules for federal courts in diversity cases? In answering this question, remember that, although it is true today that every state contains at least one federal judicial district, there is no constitutional provision that compels this. What if Congress had established only regional courts? Under such a scheme, would Congress or the courts have been forced to establish their own choice-of-law rules?

3. The states have been allowed great leeway in establishing choice-of-law rules. In ALLSTATE INSURANCE CO. v. HAGUE, Note 4, p. 104, supra, the Supreme Court held that a state could apply its substantive law in a case, so long as the state had significant contacts or a significant aggregation of contacts with the parties and the transaction. See also Phillips Petroleum Co. v. Shutts, 472 U.S. 797, 105 S.Ct. 2965, 86 L.Ed.2d 628 (1985), p. 786, infra. Doesn't *Hague* encourage plaintiffs to forum shop and *Klaxon* seal the defendant's fate?

4. If a diversity case is transferred under 28 U.S.C. § 1404(a), what law should the transferee court apply? See p. 389, infra. Does it matter whether the plaintiff or the defendant moved to transfer? In VAN DUSEN v. BARRACK, 376 U.S. 612, 639, 84 S.Ct. 805, 820, 821, 11 L.Ed.2d 945, 962–63 (1964), defendants sought to transfer the action from federal court in Pennsylvania to federal court in Massachusetts, where the state law was more favorable to their case. The Supreme Court rejected a wooden reading of *Erie,* which would require the transferee court to apply the law of the state in which it sits—that is, Massachusetts law. Rather, the Court determined that the "critical identity" is between the federal court that decides the case and the courts of the state in which the action was filed. According to the Court: "A change of venue under § 1404(a) generally should be, with respect to state law, but a change of courtrooms." It appears that *Van Dusen* makes it possible for a suit to be filed in federal court in one state and then transferred to a different state with the result that the law applied will differ from the law that would have applied if the suit had been filed initially in the transferee court. Is the real policy behind *Van Dusen* simply to prevent the defendant from forum shopping? See Maloy, *Forum Shopping? What's Wrong with That?*, 24 Quinnipiac L. Rev. 25 (2005).

5. How does the Class Action Fairness Act of 2005 ("CAFA") affect choice-of-law considerations? CAFA extends a federal forum to large-stakes class actions on a theory of minimal diversity, see p. 276, supra. Professor Woolley argues that CAFA does not authorize federal courts to adopt their own choice-of-law rules; to the contrary, "federal courts remain rigidly bound by state choice-of-law rules in diversity actions." Woolley, Erie *and Choice of Law After the Class Action Fairness Act*, 80 Tul. L. Rev. 1723 (2006). Professor Nagareda foresees a "coming clash" between CAFA and the *Klaxon* rule, Nagareda, *Aggregation and Its Discontents: Class Settlement Pressure,*

Class–Wide Arbitration, and CAFA, 106 Colum. L. Rev. 1872, 1876–78 (2006), but argues that it "would be quite peculiar if the federal courts after CAFA were to refrain from application of a distinctively federal methodology for choice of law." Nagareda, *Bootstrapping in Choice of Law After the Class Action Fairness Act*, 74 UMKC L. Rev. 661, 684 (2006). Professor Sherry goes even further, and argues that "CAFA should be read as overruling *Erie* * * *, at least for the national-market cases that it places within federal court jurisdiction." Sherry, *Overruling* Erie*: Nationwide Class Actions and National Common Law*, 156 U. Pa. L. Rev. 2135, 2136 (2008). But see Burbank, *Aggregation on the Couch: The Strategic Uses of Ambiguity and Hypocrisy*, 106 Colum. L. Rev. 1924, 1943 (2006) ("[T]here is evidence that in enacting CAFA, Congress did not intend to alter the ordering of federal and state lawmaking authority established by *Erie* * * *."). Is the *Klaxon* rule constitutionally compelled? Is it required by the Rules of Decision Act?

2. ASCERTAINING THE STATE LAW

MASON v. AMERICAN EMERY WHEEL WORKS

United States Court of Appeals, First Circuit, 1957.
241 F.2d 906.

MAGRUDER, CHIEF JUDGE. Whit Mason, a citizen of Mississippi, filed his complaint in the United States District Court for the District of Rhode Island against The American Emery Wheel Works, a Rhode Island corporation. The case was one in tort for personal injuries alleged to have been suffered by the plaintiff in Mississippi as a result of negligent misfeasance by the defendant in putting out in commerce without adequate care and inspection, a dangerously defective emery wheel. According to the allegations of the complaint, at some time prior to the date of the accident defendant negligently manufactured, inspected and tested a certain emery wheel designed for attachment to a bench grinder; that due to such negligence the emery wheel was not reasonably fit for the use for which it was intended, but on the contrary subjected to a risk of personal injury all persons lawfully using a bench grinder with the emery wheel attached * * *.

On the face of the complaint it did not specifically appear that plaintiff was not in privity of contract with defendant. The answer of defendant, in addition to denying negligence, and denying that it had manufactured the particular emery wheel which had caused plaintiff's injuries, also set forth as a "First Defense" that the complaint failed to state a claim upon which relief might be granted, and as a "Fourth Defense" that defendant "owed no duty to the said plaintiff as there is no privity of contract between the plaintiff and the defendant."

* * * Plaintiff's evidence tended to show that a certain emery wheel * * * was purchased by the Hoover Company, a New Jersey corporation, from the defendant for attachment to a bench grinding machine made by the Hoover Company; that the Hoover Company affixed to the said bench grinding machine, with emery wheel attached, a label indicating that the

bench grinder had been manufactured by Miller Falls Company, a Massachusetts corporation; that said bench grinder * * * was successively sold by the Hoover Company to Miller Falls Company, by the latter to Komp Equipment Company, and finally by Komp Equipment Company to T.H. Pearce Company, the plaintiff's employer; * * * that while plaintiff was using it in the ordinary and proper manner the emery wheel disintegrated and exploded in plaintiff's face, causing the injuries complained of.

At the conclusion of the plaintiff's case defendant made an oral motion to dismiss the complaint under Rule 41(b) * * *. This motion to dismiss was granted by the district court, and an order was entered dismissing the complaint, from which the present appeal was taken.

Since the injury was inflicted in Mississippi, the district court, no doubt correctly under now familiar authorities, deemed itself to be obliged to apply the Mississippi local law to determine the tort liability, if any, of a manufacturer to one not in privity of contract with him. * * * The district court came to the conclusion "reluctantly" that it was bound by the Mississippi law as declared in Ford Motor Co. v. Myers, 1928, 151 Miss. 73, 117 So. 362; that the "harsh rule" of Mississippi as so declared, "contrary to the great weight of authority" elsewhere, was that a manufacturer was not liable for negligence in the manufacture of appliances which could and would become highly dangerous when put to the uses for which they are intended, where there is no privity of contract between the user and the manufacturer.

Ford Motor Co. v. Myers, supra, was the only Mississippi case relied upon, or even referred to, by the district court. In that case the Supreme Court of Mississippi, in a half-page opinion, did in fact apply what was at one time the prevailing rule, in holding that Ford Motor Company as the manufacturer of a truck owed no duty of care to a remote subvendee of the truck who was injured when the truck collapsed and plunged into a ditch because of a defect which could have been detected by reasonable inspection by the manufacturer before the vehicle left the factory.

* * *

MacPherson v. Buick Motor Co., [217 N.Y. 382, 111 N.E. 1050 (1916)], * * * started a new trend in this particular field of the law, and its substantive result has found favor in § 395 of the * * * Restatement of Torts. If the Supreme Court of Mississippi had recently reconsidered the rule it applied in Ford Motor Co. v. Myers, supra, and had decided to adhere to it on the ground of stare decisis, no doubt the federal courts would have had to accept the local law as so declared. But it would be gratuitous and unwarranted to assume that the Supreme Court of Mississippi would now so hold, when we bear in mind the readiness of other courts, in conservative jurisdictions at that, to overrule their earlier holdings and to bring their jurisprudence into accord with what is now the overwhelming weight of authority. * * * In Anderson v. Linton, 7 Cir., 1949, 178 F.2d 304, the court of appeals declined to accept as the local law of Iowa what it narrowly construed to be a dictum of the Supreme Court of Iowa enunciating the old ruling of nonliability in Larrabee v. Des Moines Tent & Awning Co., 1920, 189 Iowa 319, 178 N.W. 373. * * *

Of course it is not necessary that a case be explicitly overruled in order to lose its persuasive force as an indication of what the law is. A decision may become so overloaded with illogical exceptions that by erosion of time it may lose its persuasive or binding force even in the inferior courts of the same jurisdiction. And where, as in Ford Motor Co. v. Myers, the Supreme Court of Mississippi, twenty or thirty years ago, applied an old rule which has since been generally discredited elsewhere, it is relevant to consider what the Supreme Court of Mississippi has subsequently said on the point. * * * We think that appellant herein rightly stresses the importance of E.I. Du Pont De Nemours & Co. v. Ladner, 1954, 221 Miss. 378, 73 So.2d 249. In that very recent case, the Supreme Court of Mississippi was able to dispose of the particular issue on another ground without the necessity of expressly overruling its earlier decision in Ford Motor Co. v. Myers. But the court did take occasion, in a long and careful opinion, to indicate its awareness of the modern trend in the area * * *. And it quoted, with apparent approval, many more recent authorities in support of the "modern doctrine." * * * We think it is fair to infer from this latest expression by the Supreme Court of Mississippi that it is prepared to reconsider and revise the rule it applied in Ford Motor Co. v. Myers whenever it may have before it a case that squarely presents the issue. We have no doubt that when this occasion does come to pass, the Supreme Court of Mississippi will declare itself in agreement with the more enlightened and generally accepted modern doctrine.

A judgment will be entered vacating the order of the District Court, dismissing the complaint and remanding the case to the District Court for further proceedings not inconsistent with this opinion.

HARTIGAN, CIRCUIT JUDGE (concurring).

I concur in the opinion of the court but I am constrained to comment briefly. We were informed in oral argument by counsel for the appellee that the district court in deciding this case had before it both the Ford and the Du Pont decisions. Moreover, the district court knew from the official Mississippi report that the MacPherson case, then approximately twelve years old, had been considered and rejected by the Mississippi Supreme Court sitting in the Ford case. Therefore, "reluctantly" Judge Day adopted the Ford holding since it, as the only binding and conclusive statement of Mississippi law on the issue, had not been expressly modified or overruled. * * *

We, however, have inferred from pure dicta in the Du Pont case and from the status of the law elsewhere on this issue that Mississippi is prepared to discard the Ford rule and adopt the modern rule. I believe this is a sound inference since the dicta in the Du Pont case though not expressly mentioning Ford, is sufficiently clear and the Ford rule is sufficiently outdated. Yet, in doing so I realize that we present a difficult problem for district judges when they must apply the Erie doctrine to situations wherein the considerations as between conflicting holdings and dicta are not as clearly defined as they are here. The question of how clear dicta must be to prevail over a prior controlling decision does not lend itself to easy solution.

NOTES AND QUESTIONS

1. The history of the privity rule in Mississippi following *Mason* is interesting. Relying heavily on Judge Magruder's opinion, the Fifth Circuit held in Grey v. Hayes–Sammons Chem. Co., 310 F.2d 291 (5th Cir.1962), that under Mississippi law a lack of privity was not a bar to a claim by a Mississippi consumer against a manufacturer of a cotton spray. The Fifth Circuit reached similar conclusions in Necaise v. Chrysler Corp., 335 F.2d 562 (5th Cir.1964), and Putman v. Erie City Mfg. Co., 338 F.2d 911 (5th Cir.1964). Finally, the Mississippi Supreme Court, in State Stove Mfg. Co. v. Hodges, 189 So.2d 113 (Miss.1966), certiorari denied Yates v. Hodges, 386 U.S. 912, 87 S.Ct. 860, 17 L.Ed.2d 784 (1967), reconsidered the privity question and overruled its decision in Ford Motor Co. v. Myers. In doing so, however, the court did not cite either the First Circuit's decision in *Mason* or the series of decisions in the Fifth Circuit.

2. How difficult is it for a diversity court to ascertain the content of state law? Consider the following:

> Identification of state law is easy only in the presence of an on-point statute or law "declared . . . by its highest court in a decision." In all other circumstances, federal courts must act as "another court of the State" and choose from a variety of sources, including high court dicta and lower court rulings. The situation is further complicated when these sources are in conflict, or when the vitality of older precedents is questioned by more recent pronouncements, creating uncertainty as to which should be followed. Worse yet, there may be no relevant precedent at all, requiring the federal court to make an "informed prophecy" of how the state high court would rule.

Kaye & Weissman, *Interactive Judicial Federalism: Certified Questions in New York*, 69 Fordham L. Rev. 373, 376–77 (2000) (citations omitted).

3. How should a diversity court ascertain the content of state law when the state's highest court has not addressed the question at issue? In McKENNA v. ORTHO PHARMACEUTICAL CORP., 622 F.2d 657 (3d Cir.), certiorari denied 449 U.S. 976, 101 S.Ct. 387, 66 L.Ed.2d 237 (1980), the Court of Appeals, trying to avoid "speculative crystal-ball gazing," posited that the process of ascertaining the content of state law

> requires an examination of all relevant sources of that state's law in order to isolate those factors that would inform its decision. * * * In the absence of authority directly on point, decisions by that court in analogous cases provide useful indications of the court's probable disposition of a particular question of law. * * * Considered dicta by the state's highest court may also provide a federal court with reliable indicia of how the state tribunal might rule on a particular question.

Id. at 660–62.

4. Faced with state-law uncertainty, is it ever appropriate for a diversity court to decline to exercise jurisdiction? In MEREDITH v. CITY OF WINTER HAVEN, 320 U.S. 228, 234–35, 64 S.Ct. 7, 11, 88 L.Ed. 9, 14 (1943), Chief Justice Stone stated:

> The diversity jurisdiction was not conferred for the benefit of the federal courts or to serve their convenience. Its purpose was generally to afford to suitors an opportunity in such cases, at their option, to assert their rights in the federal rather than in the state courts. In the absence of some recognized public policy or defined principle guiding the exercise of the jurisdiction conferred, which would in exceptional cases warrant its non-exercise, it has from the first been deemed to be the duty of the federal courts, if their jurisdiction is properly invoked, to decide questions of state law whenever necessary to the rendition of a judgment. * * * When such exceptional circumstances are not present, denial of that opportunity by the federal courts merely because the answers to the questions of state law are difficult or uncertain or have not yet been given by the highest court of the state, would thwart the purpose of the jurisdictional act.

In LOUISIANA POWER & LIGHT CO. v. CITY OF THIBODAUX, 360 U.S. 25, 29, 79 S.Ct. 1070, 1073, 3 L.Ed.2d 1058, 1062 (1959), the District Court, sitting in diversity, on its own motion stayed its proceedings to permit Louisiana's highest court an opportunity to interpret a state expropriation statute. The Supreme Court upheld this exercise of equitable discretion:

> The special nature of eminent domain justifies a district judge, when his familiarity with the problems of local law so counsels him, to ascertain the meaning of a disputed state statute from the only tribunal empowered to speak definitively—the courts of the State under whose statute eminent domain is sought to be exercised—rather than himself make a dubious and tentative forecast. This course does not constitute abnegation of judicial duty. On the contrary, it is a wise and productive discharge of it. There is only postponement of decision for its best fruition. Eventually the District Court will award compensation if the taking is sustained.

Justice Brennan dissented, contending that abstention in diversity cases can be justified by only "one of two important countervailing interests: either the avoidance of a premature and perhaps unnecessary decision of a serious federal constitutional question, or the avoidance of the hazard of unsettling some delicate balance in the area of federal-state relationships." Id. at 32, 79 S.Ct. at 1074, 3 L.Ed.2d at 1064.

Some commentators have urged eliminating judicial discretion to abstain from hearing diversity cases. "Critics contend that so long as diversity jurisdiction continues to exist, federal courts must decide such cases that are properly before them. The argument is that abstention is inconsistent with the very rationale behind diversity jurisdiction: the importance of proving a neutral forum when litigants are from different states." Chemerinsky, Federal Jurisdiction § 12.2.2 (5th ed. 2005).

5. Certification provides another method of ascertaining state law. Certification is a procedure that allows the court of one system to petition the

court of another for the answer to an unresolved legal question. In 1945, Florida became the first state to adopt such a procedure, which now is available in 45 states, the District of Columbia, and Puerto Rico .. In all states that permit certification, the state's highest court accepts questions from the United States Supreme Court and from federal courts of appeal. Thirty-six states also accept questions from federal district courts. See Kaye & Weissman, Note 2, p. 471, supra, at 396 & Appendix A (collecting statutory provisions). In Arizonans for Official English v. Arizona, 520 U.S. 43, 76, 117 S.Ct. 1055, 1073, 137 L.Ed.2d 170, 199 (1997), involving a challenge to a state law making English the state's official language, the Supreme Court underscored the importance of certification procedure in allowing "a federal court faced with a novel state-law question to put the question directly to the State's highest court, reducing the cost, and increasing the assurance of gaining an authoritative response."

6. Both abstention and certification may cause delay that can harm the interests of one or both of the parties. In TUNICK v. SAFIR, 228 F.3d 135 (2d Cir. 2000), a photographer challenged the locality's refusal to grant him a permit to conduct a photo shoot of 75 to 100 nude models configured "in an abstract formation" on a residential street in New York City. Tunick claimed that his planned event was exempt from a New York statute that bans public nudity except for "any person entertaining or performing in a play, exhibition, show or entertainment." The Court of Appeals petitioned New York's highest court to resolve the scope of the public nudity ban, emphasizing the need for expedition given the important First Amendment rights at stake. 209 F.3d 67 (2d Cir.2000). However, the New York court declined to answer the certified questions, emphasizing, that "even with an expedited schedule for new briefing, argument and deliberation, this Court's necessary decisional process would add some months to the life of this case." 94 N.Y.2d 709, 709 N.Y.S.2d 881, 731 N.E.2d 597 (2000).

7. One commentator suggests that if the content of state law is unclear or unresolved, "then arguably there is simply no law to apply * * * and federal courts should rule against the party who bears the burden of persuasion on the question at issue. * * * This static approach alleviates the judicial federalism concerns * * * because federal courts cannot be charged with usurping the lawmaking power of the states." Clark, *Ascertaining the Laws of the Several States: Positivism and Judicial Federalism After* Erie, 145 U.Pa. L.Rev. 1459, 1461–64 (1997). Does this approach promote *Erie*'s twin aims of discouraging forum shopping and avoiding inequitable administration of the law?

8. Does the difficulty of having to ascertain unsettled state law create new opportunities for forum shopping? Judge Calabresi of the Second Circuit Court of Appeals warns:

> * * * [F]ederal courts often get state law wrong because federal judges don't know state law and are not the ultimate decisionmakers on it. Inevitably, this leads to considerable forum shopping of just the sort that Erie sought to avoid. One party or the other tries to get into federal courts because it hopes that the federal courts will get the law wrong. I could give you any number of examples. For instance, the concept of duty

> in the tort law of New York is virtually unique to New York and is very complicated. As a result, federal judges who deal with the concept of duty in a New York tort case frequently get it wrong. They may be right in thinking that what they hold is what New York law ought to be, but it ain't New York law!

Calabresi, *Federal and State Courts: Restoring a Workable Balance*, 78 N.Y.U. L. Rev. 1293, 1300 (2003). He suggests that a federal appellate court, when faced with uncertain state law, should write an opinion stating what it thinks "that law ought to be," and then certify the question to the state's highest court. The state court would be free to decline the certification, but the federal court could then claim "authority to impose" its view "provisionally, until the highest court of the state decides to resolve the question." Id. at 1302. Does this approach solve the problem of delay?

9. Federal judges have expressed divergent attitudes toward the task of ascertaining the content of state law. In POMERANTZ v. CLARK, 101 F.Supp. 341, 345–46 (D.Mass.1951), a diversity action by policyholders against directors of an insurance company to retrieve for the company certain sums allegedly improvidently and illegally loaned, Judge Wyzanski held that no action was maintainable under Massachusetts law and stated:

> In considering whether * * * [to create] an exception to the Massachusetts rule that before bringing a derivative suit a member must first lay his case before the body of members, the never-to-be-forgotten caution is that this Court is not free to render such decision as seems to it equitable, just and in accordance with public policy and responsive to all those jurisprudential criteria which so often enter into what Justice Cardozo called "The Nature of the Judicial Process." A federal judge sitting in a diversity jurisdiction case has not a roving commission to do justice or to develop the law according to his, or what he believes to be the sounder, views. His problem is less philosophical and more psychological. His task is to divine the views of the state court judges. * * *
>
> The eminence of the Massachusetts Supreme Judicial Court, an eminence not surpassed by any American tribunal, is in large measure due to its steadiness, learning and understanding of the durable values long prized in this community. Subtle variations and blurred lines are not characteristic of that court. Principles are announced and adhered to in broad magisterial terms. The emphasis is on precedent and adherence to the older ways, not on creating new causes of action or encouraging the use of novel judicial remedies that have sprung up in less conservative communities. Here abides the ancient faith in the right of men to choose their own associates, make their own arrangements, govern themselves and thus grow in responsibility without much in the way of either hindrance or help from the state. This basic philosophy permeates the Massachusetts rules governing derivative suits * * *.

Compare Judge Friendly's observation in Nolan v. Transocean Air Lines, 276 F.2d 280, 281 (2d Cir.1960): "Our principal task, in this diversity of citizenship case, is to determine what the New York courts would think the California courts would think on an issue about which neither has thought."

10. In FACTORS ETC., INC. v. PRO ARTS, INC., 652 F.2d 278 (2d Cir.1981), certiorari denied 456 U.S. 927, 102 S.Ct. 1973, 72 L.Ed.2d 442 (1982), a federal court sitting in New York was required to apply Tennessee law to the question of whether Elvis Presley's right of publicity survived his death. Tennessee state courts never had addressed that issue, but the Sixth Circuit (the circuit encompassing Tennessee) had decided a similar case. The Second Circuit held that the District Court, in such a circumstance, was bound by the Sixth Circuit's view of Tennessee law. The court reasoned that the Sixth Circuit was more familiar with Tennessee law since it frequently was required to interpret Tennessee law.

The dissent argued that there was no reason to follow the Sixth Circuit's views when they were not derived from the laws or decisions of the state. Since the Sixth Circuit was only espousing what it considered the preferable common-law rule, its decision should be accorded no greater deference than that given to any circuit court's views. The dissent also pointed out that, considering the physical size of the circuit and the relatively small number of diversity cases appealed to the court, the Sixth Circuit was unlikely to have any special familiarity with Tennessee law.

Which position is correct? Or are both incorrect in that the relevant question is not what Tennessee's law is, but, rather, what would a New York state court think what Tennessee's law is? By the time the District Court heard the case on remand from the Second Circuit, a Tennessee court had addressed the issue. Accordingly, the District Court applied the Tennessee court's holding to the facts of the case. See 562 F.Supp. 304 (S.D.N.Y.1983).

11. Does the sometimes erroneous interpretation of state law by federal diversity courts provide an argument for abolishing diversity jurisdiction? Consider the following:

> Until corrected by the state supreme court, such incorrect predictions inevitably skew the decisions of persons and businesses who rely on them and inequitably affect the losing federal litigant who cannot appeal the decision to the state supreme court; they may even mislead lower state courts that may be inclined to accept federal predictions as applicable precedent. * * *
>
> When federal judges make state law—and we do, by whatever euphemism one chooses to call it—judges who are not selected under the state's system and who are not answerable to its constituency are undertaking an inherent state court function. * * * [T]here is no longer any valid basis to justify the fundamental incompatibility of diversity jurisdiction with the most basic principles of federalism.

Sloviter, *A Federal Judge Views Diversity Jurisdiction Through the Lens of Federalism*, 78 Va.L.Rev. 1671, 1681–82, 1684, 1687 (1992). Or, does the risk of error argue for greater use of certification to enable state courts to interpret their own state's laws? See Nash, *The Uneasy Case for Transjurisdictional Adjudication*, 94 Va. L. Rev. 1869 (2008).

SECTION C. FEDERAL "COMMON LAW"

Although *Erie* held that "[t]here is no federal general common law," p. 410, supra, the federal courts retain power to create federal common law, typically defined as "federal judge-made law—that is, rules of decision adopted and applied by federal courts that have the force and effect of positive federal law, but whose content cannot be traced by traditional methods of interpretation to federal or constitutional command." Clark, *Federal Common Law: A Structural Reinterpretation*, 144 U. Pa. L. Rev. 1245, 1247 (1996) (internal citations omitted). Commentators diverge on the scope and legitimacy of this power:

MELTZER, STATE COURT FORFEITURES OF FEDERAL RIGHTS, 99 Harv.L.Rev. 1128, 1167–71 (1986):

Despite *Erie*'s declaration that "[t]here is no federal general common law," courts have fashioned what Judge Friendly has termed "specialized federal common law" to govern a broad range of areas. Unlike the "spurious" federal common law of the era of Swift v. Tyson, this new federal common law is binding under the supremacy clause in the state courts.

The proper scope of federal common lawmaking is a matter of considerable uncertainty. If *Erie* held that federal court jurisdiction does not in itself provide the power to fashion common law, then some more specialized source must be found for each example of judicial lawmaking. The lawmaking power of federal courts has been viewed as far more limited than that of Congress, for two reasons extrapolated from the constitutional structure. The first is the idea of separation of powers and the supremacy (in matters not governed by the Constitution) of Congress. But perhaps more important is the view that federal law is and should be interstitial, operating against a background of existing bodies of state law. Restricted federal common lawmaking reduces the number of agencies broadly fashioning federal rules of decision, and preserves the primary role for Congress, in which the interests of the states are more strongly represented—and in which inertia is more powerful. Hence, state law is presumptively operative, and if it is to be displaced, ordinarily it must be Congress that does so.

But these structural concerns do not indicate whether federal common law should be considered altogether illegitimate or simply restricted in scope. And important countervailing arguments support the existence of some common law power in the federal courts. Numerous cases raise issues implicating important federal interests that are not specifically governed by a statutory or constitutional rule. Congress could have enacted a rule governing the issue, but may not have done so, because it lacked time, foresight, or a political consensus. The Court has, accordingly, recognized that federal common law may be a " 'necessary expedient.' " Nor does Congress's failure to specify a view on a particular subject indicate that Congress preferred that state rules be followed. Here, as elsewhere, congressional inaction is hardly a clear-cut guide for determining congressional intent, and a failure by a court to make law is itself an important and controversial decision.

Thus, legislative inertia and the political safeguards of federalism are ultimately a double-edged sword. They help explain why the authority to make federal common law is nowhere near so broad as congressional authority to legislate, but also argue that federal common lawmaking may be necessary to fill in the interstices of congressional and constitutional mandates or otherwise to deal with matters of important national concern. Despite extensive discussion in the cases and commentary, no clear standard for judging the appropriateness of federal common law has emerged. [Nonetheless, some general points are] * * * accepted by most cases and commentators.

To begin with, there must be a strong need for the formulation of federal common law in order to justify displacing otherwise operative state rules. Moreover, federal common law, perhaps even more than federal law generally, should be interstitial, building upon the total "corpus juris" of the states. Federal common law fits most easily when it supplements federal constitutional or statutory provisions, providing rules of decision that implement or safeguard the norms embodied in such provisions.

Even where federal interests are implicated, it is often possible, and desirable, to rely upon extant state law for the rule of decision. Such reliance eliminates the need for (and possible difficulties in) fashioning a new rule from scratch, and also promotes intrastate uniformity, which may be of great value. Thus, the decision to formulate federal common law is one of judicial policy, in which a court must find that the advantages of borrowing state law are outweighed by either the need for national uniformity or the inconsistency of state law (either of states generally or of the particular state involved) with federal interests.

FIELD, SOURCES OF LAW: THE SCOPE OF FEDERAL COMMON LAW, 99 Harv.L.Rev. 881, 883–92 (1986).

* * *

The received academic tradition on federal common law assumes that there are particular enclaves in which federal common law is in fact appropriate, but that after Erie, federal common law power is the exception, not the rule. * * *

* * *

I suggest that judicial power to act is not limited to particular enclaves and that it is much broader than the usual references to judicial power would suggest. As I shall develop, the only limitation on courts' power to create federal common law is that the court must point to a federal enactment, constitutional or statutory, that it interprets as authorizing the federal common law rule. * * *

* * * I will use "federal common law" to refer to any rule of federal law created by a court (usually but not invariably a federal court) when the substance of that rule is not clearly suggested by federal enactments—constitutional or congressional.

KRAMER, THE LAWMAKING POWER OF THE FEDERAL COURTS, 12 Pace L. Rev. 263, 267–71 (1992).

* * * [L]awmaking in a democracy is supposed to be done by politically accountable, representative institutions, whereas courts operate on principles other than political accountability. That being so, why let courts make law? Why isn't the whole notion of common law undemocratic and hence improper?

Before proceeding further, let me clarify what I mean by "common law." Following other writers, my definition is a broad one: the common law includes any rule articulated by a court that is not easily found on the face of an applicable statute. This definition is designed to include exercises of judicial creativity and is made deliberately broad to minimize the unavoidable line-drawing problems that arise as interpretation shades imperceptibly into judicial lawmaking.

* * *

With these points in mind, return to the question deferred above: why let courts make common law in a representative democracy? In part, the answer must be that judge-made law is unavoidable. That is, courts must make a certain amount of common law simply because there is no clear line between "making" and "applying" law, between commands that are clear on the face of a statute and those made through an exercise of judgment and creativity. Deciding individual cases thus generates some common law because the process of adjudication necessarily entails articulating rules to elaborate and clarify the meaning and operation of statutory texts.

Nor would we want it otherwise. After all, if one function of independent adjudication is to relieve legislators of having to anticipate and deal with every possible contingency, it hardly makes sense to require courts to return every uncertainty to the legislature. The power to clarify legislation through interstitial lawmaking is thus an implicit but important part of the judicial function.

Federal common law has developed in several broad situations. For example, federal common law is used to resolve cases involving important federal interests. These strong federal interests have emerged in several contexts, termed "enclaves." When interstate disputes have erupted, federal common law has been adopted where it would be unfair to apply the statutes or decisional law from either state. See, e.g., Hinderlider v. La Plata River & Cherry Creek Ditch Co., 304 U.S. 92, 58 S.Ct. 803, 82 L.Ed. 1202 (1938) (dispute over the apportionment of the water of an interstate stream). Similarly, federal common law has become firmly established in the admiralty and maritime contexts, because the desire for a uniform body of substantive law has long been considered of primary importance. See, e.g., Kossick v. United Fruit Co., 365 U.S. 731, 81 S.Ct. 886, 6 L.Ed.2d 56 (1961). And, cases implicating the international relations of the United States have provided another occasion for resort to federal common law, including cases involving commercial disputes between United States citizens and foreign parties. See, e.g., Banco Nacional de Cuba v. Sabbatino, 376 U.S. 398, 84 S.Ct. 923, 11 L.Ed.2d 804 (1964). One of the most challenging contexts of federal common lawmaking involves statutes that express national policy in a particular area but leave one or more of the specifics to be developed by the federal courts. Two questions typically arise in these cases. First, is the particular statutory gap at issue one that the federal courts should fill? If the answer is yes, on what sources should a federal court rely in order to derive the law? The answers to these questions can be crucial in shaping the overall national policy involved in the statute. See, e.g., Lampf, Pleva, Lipkind, Prupis & Petigrow v. Gilbertson, 501 U.S. 350, 111 S.Ct. 2773, 115 L.Ed.2d 321 (1991). The various facets of federal common law are discussed in 19 Wright, Miller & Cooper, Federal Practice and Procedure: Jurisdiction and Related Matters 2d §§ 4514–4519.

An important use of federal common law occurs in cases involving the legal activities of the United States. These cases often invoke issues concerning the federal government's contract rights, tort liabilities, rights to collect loans and proceeds due to it, or the management of United States bonds and securities.

CLEARFIELD TRUST CO. v. UNITED STATES

Supreme Court of the United States, 1943.
318 U.S. 363, 63 S.Ct. 573, 87 L.Ed. 838.

Certiorari to the Circuit Court of Appeals for the Third Circuit.

MR. JUSTICE DOUGLAS delivered the opinion of the Court.

[A check issued by the United States had been mailed, but was not received by its intended recipient. An unknown person, who presumably had stolen the check, cashed it at a J.C. Penney store by signing the name of the intended recipient. J.C. Penney in turn endorsed the check to Clearfield Trust, which accepted it. Clearfield then endorsed the check with a guaranty of all prior endorsements, collected the amount of the check from the Federal Reserve and paid it to J.C. Penney. Neither Penney nor Clearfield had suspected forgery. Federal officials did not inform any of the interested parties of the forgery until eight months after they had learned that the intended recipient had not received the check.

The United States sued Clearfield on Clearfield's express guaranty of prior endorsements. The District Court held that the rights of the parties were to be determined by the law of Pennsylvania. Since the United States had unreasonably delayed giving notice of the forgery, it was barred from recovery under Pennsylvania law and the District Court dismissed the complaint. The Court of Appeals for the Third Circuit reversed.]

* * *

We agree with the Circuit Court of Appeals that the rule of Erie R. Co. v. Tompkins * * * does not apply to this action. The rights and duties of the United States on commercial paper which it issues are governed by federal rather than local law. When the United States disburses its funds or pays its debts, it is exercising a constitutional function or power. This check was issued for services performed under the Federal Emergency Relief Act of 1935 * * *. The authority to issue the check had its origin in the Constitution and the statutes of the United States and was in no way dependent on the laws of Pennsylvania or of any other state. * * * The duties imposed upon the United States and the rights acquired by it as a result of the issuance find their roots in the same federal sources.[19] * * * In absence of an applicable Act of Congress it is for the federal courts to fashion the governing rule of law according to their own standards. * * *

In our choice of the applicable federal rule we have occasionally selected state law. * * * But reasons which may make state law at times the appropriate federal rule are singularly inappropriate here. The issuance of commercial paper by the United States is on a vast scale and transactions in that paper from issuance to payment will commonly occur in several states. The application of state law, even without the conflict of laws rules of the forum, would subject the rights and duties of the United States to exceptional uncertainty. It would lead to great diversity in results by making identical transactions subject to the vagaries of the laws of the several states. The desirability of a uniform rule is plain. And while the federal law merchant developed for about a century under the regime of Swift v. Tyson * * * represented general commercial law rather than a choice of a federal rule designed to protect a federal right, it nevertheless stands as a convenient source of reference for fashioning federal rules applicable to these federal questions.

United States v. National Exchange Bank, 214 U.S. 302, 29 S.Ct. 665, 53 L.Ed. 1006 * * * falls in that category. The Court held that the United States could recover as drawee from one who presented for payment a pension check on which the name of the payee had been forged, in spite of

19. Various Treasury Regulations govern the payment and endorsement of government checks and warrants and the reimbursement of the Treasurer of the United States by Federal Reserve banks and member bank depositories on payment of checks or warrants bearing a forged endorsement. * * * Forgery of the check was an offense against the United States. * * *

a protracted delay on the part of the United States in giving notice of the forgery. * * *

The *National Exchange Bank* case went no further than to hold that prompt notice of the discovery of the forgery was not a condition precedent to suit. It did not reach the question whether lack of prompt notice might be a defense. We think it may. If it is shown that the drawee on learning of the forgery did not give prompt notice of it and that damage resulted, recovery by the drawee is barred. * * * The fact that the drawee is the United States and the laches those of its employees are not material. * * * The United States as drawee of commercial paper stands in no different light than any other drawee. As stated in United States v. National Exchange Bank * * *, "The United States does business on business terms." It is not excepted from the general rules governing the rights and duties of drawees "by the largeness of its dealings and its having to employ agents to do what if done by a principal in person would leave no room for doubt." * * * But the damage occasioned by the delay must be established and not left to conjecture. Cases * * * place the burden on the drawee of giving prompt notice of the forgery—injury to the defendant being presumed by the mere fact of delay. * * * But we do not think that he who accepts a forged signature of a payee deserves that preferred treatment. It is his neglect or error in accepting the forger's signature which occasions the loss. * * * He should be allowed to shift that loss to the drawee only on a clear showing that the drawee's delay in notifying him of the forgery caused him damage. * * * No such damage has been shown by Clearfield Trust Co. who so far as appears can still recover from J.C. Penney Co. The only showing on the part of the latter is contained in the stipulation to the effect that if a check cashed for a customer is returned unpaid or for reclamation a short time after the date on which it is cashed, the employees can often locate the person who cashed it. It is further stipulated that when J.C. Penney Co. was notified of the forgery in the present case none of its employees was able to remember anything about the transaction or check in question. The inference is that the more prompt the notice the more likely the detection of the forger. But that falls short of a showing that the delay caused a manifest loss. * * * It is but another way of saying that mere delay is enough.

Affirmed.

MR. JUSTICE MURPHY and MR. JUSTICE RUTLEDGE did not participate in the consideration or decision of this case.

NOTES AND QUESTIONS

1. Why doesn't the *Clearfield* Court mention the Rules of Decision Act?

2. The *Clearfield* decision has been criticized for adopting federal common law in a situation in which there were insufficient considerations to justify a uniform federal rule. As one commentator explains, the presence of a

federal function, the issuance of commercial paper, merely signals that federal law may be appropriate. Note, *Federal Common Law*, 82 Harv.L.Rev. 1512, 1530–31 (1969). Should a need for uniformity be a requisite for the creation of a federal common law rule? In UNITED STATES v. KIMBELL FOODS, INC., 440 U.S. 715, 99 S.Ct. 1448, 59 L.Ed.2d 711 (1979), the question arose whether federal or state rules should be used for Small Business Administration and Farmers Home Administration loans in order to determine whether the federal government or a private creditor would be able to collect first on a loan. In addressing this issue, the Court embarked upon a two-step analysis. First, the Court broadly interpreted *Clearfield* as permitting federal courts to develop federal law for "questions involving the rights of the United States arising under nationwide federal programs." Having decided that federal law controlled, the Court turned to the second and more challenging task of determining the content of the federal law.

> Controversies directly affecting the operations of federal programs, although governed by federal law, do not inevitably require resort to uniform federal rules. * * * Whether to adopt state law or to fashion a nationwide federal rule is a matter of judicial policy "dependent upon a variety of considerations always relevant to the nature of the specific governmental interests and to the effects upon them of applying state law." * * *
>
> * * * Apart from considerations of uniformity, we must also determine whether application of state law would frustrate specific objectives of the federal programs. If so, we must fashion special rules solicitous of those federal interests. Finally, our choice-of-law inquiry must consider the extent to which application of a federal rule would disrupt commercial relationships predicated on state law. * * *

Id. at 727–30, 99 S.Ct. at 1458–59, 59 L.Ed.2d at 723–25. After weighing these factors with respect to priority rules for the SBA and FHA loans, the Court held that there was no need for an independent federal rule. Thus, the Court chose to adopt the state rule as federal law rather than to develop a separate federal rule.

3. Courts have not perceived a need for federal common law in every case involving commercial paper on which the United States may be liable, particularly in lawsuits involving only private parties. BANK OF AMERICA NATIONAL TRUST & SAVINGS ASSOCIATION v. PARNELL, 352 U.S. 29, 77 S.Ct. 119, 1 L.Ed.2d 93 (1956), involved the question of whether defendants had taken bearer bonds, guaranteed by the United States, in good faith, without knowledge or notice of their defects in title. In declining to endorse a federal common-law rule of liability, the Supreme Court explained:

> Securities issued by the Government generate immediate interests of the Government. * * * But they also radiate interests in transactions between private parties. The present litigation is purely between private parties and does not touch the rights and duties of the United States. The only possible interest of the United States in a situation like the one here, exclusively involving the transfer of Government paper between private persons, is that the floating of securities of the United States might

> somehow or other be adversely affected by the local rule of a particular State regarding the liability of a converter. * * *
>
> We do not mean to imply that litigation with respect to Government paper necessarily precludes the presence of a federal interest, to be governed by federal law, in all situations merely because it is a suit between private parties, or that it is beyond the range of federal legislation to deal comprehensively with Government paper. * * *

Id. at 33–34, 77 S.Ct. at 121–22, 1 L.Ed.2d at 96–97.

The majority view did not go unchallenged. Justices Black and Douglas dissented:

> We believe that the "federal law merchant," which Clearfield Trust Co. v. United States * * * held applicable to transactions in the commercial paper of the United States, should be applicable to all transactions in that paper. * * * Not until today has a distinction been drawn between suits by the United States on that paper and suits by other parties to it. But the Court does not stop there. Because this is "essentially a private transaction," it is to be governed by local law. Yet the nature of the rights and obligations created by commercial paper of the United States Government is said to be controlled by federal law. Thus, federal law is to govern some portion of a dispute between private parties, while that portion of the dispute which is "essentially of local concern" is to be governed by local law. The uncertainties which inhere in such a dichotomy are obvious. * * *

Id. at 34, 77 S.Ct. at 122, 1 L.Ed.2d at 97–98.

MIREE v. DeKALB COUNTY

Supreme Court of the United States, 1977.
433 U.S. 25, 97 S.Ct. 2490, 53 L.Ed.2d 557.

Certiorari to the United States Court of Appeals for the Fifth Circuit.

MR. JUSTICE REHNQUIST delivered the opinion of the Court.

These consolidated cases arise out of the 1973 crash of a Lear Jet shortly after takeoff from the DeKalb–Peachtree Airport. The United States Court of Appeals for the Fifth Circuit, en banc, affirmed the dismissal of petitioners' complaint against respondent DeKalb County (hereafter respondent), holding that principles of federal common law were applicable to the resolution of petitioners' breach-of-contract claim. We granted certiorari to consider whether federal or state law should have been applied to that claim; we conclude that the latter should govern.

I

Petitioners are, respectively, the survivors of deceased passengers, the assignee of the jet aircraft owner, and a burn victim. They brought separate lawsuits, later consolidated, against respondent in the United States District Court for the Northern District of Georgia. The basis for federal jurisdiction was diversity of citizenship, 28 U.S.C. § 1332, and the complaints asserted that respondent was liable on three independent theories: negligence, nuisance, and breach of contract. The District Court granted respondent's motion to dismiss each of these claims. The courts below have unanimously agreed that the negligence and nuisance theories are without merit; only the propriety of the dismissal of the contract claims remains in the cases.

Petitioners seek to impose liability on respondent as third-party beneficiaries of contracts between it and the Federal Aviation Administration (FAA). Their complaints allege that respondent entered into six grant agreements with the FAA. * * * Under the terms of the contracts respondent agreed to take action to restrict the use of land adjacent to or in the immediate vicinity of the Airport to activities and purposes compatible with normal airport operations including landing and takeoff of aircraft. * * *

Petitioners assert that respondent breached the FAA contracts by owning and maintaining a garbage dump adjacent to the airport, and that the cause of the crash was the ingestion of birds swarming from the dump into the jet engines of the aircraft.

Applying Georgia law, the District Court found that petitioners' claims as third-party beneficiaries under the FAA contracts were barred by the county's governmental immunity, and dismissed the complaints under Fed. Rule Civ.Proc. 12(b)(6). A divided panel of the Court of Appeals decided that under state law petitioners could sue as third-party beneficiaries and that governmental immunity would not bar the suit. * * * The dissenting judge argued that the court should have applied federal rather than state law; he concluded that under the principles of federal common law the petitioners in this case did not have standing to sue as third-party beneficiaries of the contracts. Sitting en banc, the Court of Appeals reversed the panel on the breach-of-contract issue and adopted the panel dissent on this point as its opinion. * * * Judge Morgan, who had written the panel opinion, argued for five dissenters that there was no identifiable federal interest in the outcome of this diversity case, and thus that federal common law had no applicability.

II

Since the only basis of federal jurisdiction alleged for petitioners' claim against respondent is diversity of citizenship, the case would unquestionably be governed by Georgia law, Erie R. Co. v. Tompkins, * * * but for the fact that the United States is a party to the contracts in question, entered into pursuant to federal statute. * * * The en banc majority of the Court of Appeals adopted, by reference, the view that, given these factors, application of federal common law was required * * *.

We do not agree with the conclusion of the Court of Appeals. The litigation before us raises no question regarding the liability of the United States or the responsibilities of the United States under the contracts. The relevant inquiry is a narrow one: whether petitioners as third-party beneficiaries of the contracts have standing to sue respondent. While federal common law may govern even in diversity cases where a uniform national rule is necessary to further the interests of the Federal Government, Clearfield Trust Co. v. United States * * *, the application of federal common law to resolve the issue presented here would promote no federal interests even approaching the magnitude of those found in *Clearfield Trust*. * * *

* * * [I]n this case, the resolution of petitioners' breach-of-contract claim against respondent will have no direct effect upon the United States or its Treasury. The Solicitor General, waiving his right to respond in these cases, advised us [that the United States' "interests would not be directly affected" by the resolution of these issues] * * *. The operations of the United States in connection with FAA grants such as these are undoubtedly of considerable magnitude. However, we see no reason for concluding that these operations would be burdened or subjected to uncertainty by variant state-law interpretations regarding whether those with whom the United States contracts might be sued by third-party beneficiaries to the contracts. Since only the rights of private litigants are at issue here, we find the *Clearfield Trust* rationale inapplicable.

* * *

The parallel between *Parnell* and these cases is obvious. The question of whether petitioners may sue respondent does not require decision under federal common law since the litigation is among private parties and no substantial rights or duties of the United States hinge on its outcome. On the other hand, nothing we say here forecloses the applicability of federal common law in interpreting the rights and duties of the United States under federal contracts.

Nor is the fact that the United States has a substantial interest in regulating aircraft travel and promoting air travel safety sufficient, given the narrow question before us, to call into play the rule of *Clearfield Trust*. * * * The question of whether private parties may, as third-party beneficiaries, sue a municipality for breach of the FAA contracts involves this federal interest only insofar as such lawsuits might be thought to advance federal aviation policy by inducing compliance with FAA safety provisions. However, even assuming the correctness of this notion, we adhere to the [view] that the issue of whether to displace state law on an issue such as this is primarily a decision for Congress. Congress has chosen not to do so in this case.[5] * * *

Although we have determined that Georgia law should be applied to the question raised by respondent's motion to dismiss, we shall not undertake to decide the correct outcome under Georgia law. * * * We therefore vacate the judgment and remand to the Court of Appeals for consideration of the claim under applicable Georgia law.

* * *

5. The Congress has considered, but not passed, a bill to provide for a federal cause of action arising out of aircraft disasters. * * *

[CHIEF JUSTICE BURGER concurred in the judgment.]

BOYLE v. UNITED TECHNOLOGIES CORP.

Supreme Court of the United States, 1988.
487 U.S. 500, 108 S.Ct. 2510, 101 L.Ed.2d 442.

Certiorari to the United States Court of Appeals for the Fourth Circuit.

JUSTICE SCALIA delivered the opinion of the Court.

This case requires us to decide when a contractor providing military equipment to the Federal Government can be held liable under state tort law for injury caused by a design defect.

I

On April 27, 1983, David A. Boyle, a United States Marine helicopter copilot, was killed when the CH–53D helicopter in which he was flying crashed off the coast of Virginia Beach, Virginia, during a training exercise. Although Boyle survived the impact of the crash, he was unable to escape from the helicopter and drowned. Boyle's father, petitioner here, brought this diversity action in Federal District Court against the Sikorsky Division of United Technologies Corporation (Sikorsky), which built the helicopter for the United States.

At trial, petitioner presented two theories of liability under Virginia tort law that were submitted to the jury. First, petitioner alleged that Sikorsky had defectively repaired a device called the servo in the helicopter's automatic flight control system, which allegedly malfunctioned and caused the crash. Second, petitioner alleged that Sikorsky had defectively designed the copilot's emergency escape system: the escape hatch opened out instead of in (and was therefore ineffective in a submerged craft because of water pressure), and access to the escape hatch handle was obstructed by other equipment. The jury returned a general verdict in favor of petitioner and awarded him $725,000. The District Court denied Sikorsky's motion for judgment notwithstanding the verdict.

The Court of Appeals reversed and remanded with directions that judgment be entered for Sikorsky. 792 F.2d 413 (CA4 1986). It found, as a matter of Virginia law, that Boyle had failed to meet his burden of demonstrating that the repair work performed by Sikorsky, as opposed to work that had been done by the Navy, was responsible for the alleged malfunction of the flight control system. Id., at 415–416. It also found, as a matter of federal law, that Sikorsky could not be held liable for the allegedly defective design of the escape hatch because, on the evidence presented, it satisfied the requirements of the "military contractor defense," which the court had recognized the same day in Tozer v. LTV Corp., 792 F.2d 403 (CA4 1986)[,] 792 F.2d, at 414–415.

Petitioner sought review here, challenging the Court of Appeals' decision on three levels: First, petitioner contends that there is no justification in federal law for shielding Government contractors from liability for design defects in military equipment. Second, he argues in the alternative that even if such a defense should exist, the Court of Appeals' formulation of the conditions for its application is inappropriate. Finally, petitioner contends that the Court of Appeals erred in not remanding for a jury determination of whether the elements of the defense were met in this case. We granted certiorari * * *.

II

Petitioner's broadest contention is that, in the absence of legislation specifically immunizing Government contractors from liability for design defects, there is no basis for judicial recognition of such a defense. We disagree. * * * [W]e have held that a few areas, involving "uniquely federal interests," * * * are so committed by the Constitution and laws of the United States to federal control that state law is pre-empted and replaced, where necessary, by federal law of a content prescribed (absent explicit statutory directive) by the courts—so-called "federal common law." * * *

The dispute in the present case borders upon two areas that we have found to involve such "uniquely federal interests." We have held that obligations to and rights of the United States under its contracts are governed exclusively by federal law. * * * The present case does not involve an obligation to the United States under its contract, but rather liability to third persons. That liability may be styled one in tort, but it arises out of performance of the contract—and traditionally has been regarded as sufficiently related to the contract that until 1962 Virginia would generally allow design defect suits only by the purchaser and those in privity with the seller. * * *

Another area that we have found to be of peculiarly federal concern, warranting the displacement of state law, is the civil liability of federal officials for actions taken in the course of their duty. We have held in many contexts that the scope of that liability is controlled by federal law. * * * The present case involves an independent contractor performing its obligation under a procurement contract, rather than an official performing his duty as a federal employee, but there is obviously implicated the same interest in getting the Government's work done.

We think the reasons for considering these closely related areas to be of "uniquely federal" interest apply as well to the civil liabilities arising out of the performance of federal procurement contracts. * * *

Moreover, it is plain that the Federal Government's interest in the procurement of equipment is implicated by suits such as the present one—even though the dispute is one between private parties. * * * The imposition of liability on Government contractors will directly affect the terms of Government contracts: either the contractor will decline to manufacture the design specified by the Government, or it will raise its price. Either way, the interests of the United States will be directly affected.

That the procurement of equipment by the United States is an area of uniquely federal interest does not, however, end the inquiry. That merely establishes a necessary, not a sufficient, condition for the displacement of state law. * * * Displacement will occur only where, as we have variously described, a "significant conflict" exists between an identifiable "federal policy or interest and the [operation] of state law," * * * or the application of state law would "frustrate specific objectives" of federal legislation * * *.

In *Miree*, [p. 483, supra], the suit was not seeking to impose upon the person contracting with the Government a duty contrary to the duty imposed by the Government contract. Rather, it was the contractual duty itself that the private plaintiff (as third-party beneficiary) sought to enforce. Between *Miree* and the present case, it is easy to conceive of an intermediate situation, in which the duty sought to be imposed on the contractor is not identical to one assumed under the contract, but is also not contrary to any assumed. If, for example, the United States contracts for the purchase and installation of an air conditioning-unit, specifying the cooling capacity but not the precise manner of construction, a state law imposing upon the manufacturer of such units a duty of care to include a certain safety feature would not be a duty identical to anything promised the Government, but neither would it be contrary. The contractor could comply with both its contractual obligations and the state-prescribed duty of care. No one suggests that state law would generally be pre-empted in this context.

The present case, however, is at the opposite extreme from *Miree*. Here the state-imposed duty of care that is the asserted basis of the contractor's liability (specifically, the duty to equip helicopters with the sort of escape-hatch mechanism petitioner claims was necessary) is precisely contrary to the duty imposed by the Government contract (the duty to manufacture and deliver helicopters with the sort of escape-hatch mechanism shown by the specifications). Even in this sort of situation, it would be unreasonable to say that there is always a "significant conflict" between the state law and a federal policy or interest. If, for example, a federal procurement officer orders, by model number, a quantity of stock helicopters that happen to be equipped with escape hatches opening outward, it is impossible to say that the Government has a significant interest in that particular feature. That would be scarcely more reasonable than saying that a private individual who orders such a craft by model number cannot sue for the manufacturer's negligence because he got precisely what he ordered.

* * *

There is * * * a statutory provision that demonstrates the potential for, and suggests the outlines of, "significant conflict" between federal interests and state law in the context of Government procurement. In the

[Federal Tort Claim Act], Congress authorized damages to be recovered against the United States for harm caused by the negligent or wrongful conduct of Government employees, to the extent that a private person would be liable under the law of the place where the conduct occurred. 28 U.S.C. § 1346(b). It excepted from this consent to suit, however,

> "[a]ny claim ... based upon the exercise or performance or the failure to exercise or perform a discretionary function or duty on the part of a federal agency or an employee of the Government, whether or not the discretion involved be abused." 28 U.S.C. § 2680(a).

We think that the selection of the appropriate design for military equipment to be used by our Armed Forces is assuredly a discretionary function within the meaning of this provision. It often involves not merely engineering analysis but judgment as to the balancing of many technical, military, and even social considerations, including specifically the trade-off between greater safety and greater combat effectiveness. And we are further of the view that permitting "second-guessing" of these judgments, * * * through state tort suits against contractors would produce the same effect sought to be avoided by the FTCA exemption. The financial burden of judgments against the contractors would ultimately be passed through, substantially if not totally, to the United States itself, since defense contractors will predictably raise their prices to cover, or to insure against, contingent liability for the Government-ordered designs. To put the point differently: It makes little sense to insulate the Government against financial liability for the judgment that a particular feature of military equipment is necessary when the Government produces the equipment itself, but not when it contracts for the production. In sum, we are of the view that state law which holds Government contractors liable for design defects in military equipment does in some circumstances present a "significant conflict" with federal policy and must be displaced. * * *

* * *

Accordingly the judgment is vacated and the case is remanded.

So ordered.

JUSTICE BRENNAN, with whom JUSTICE MARSHALL and JUSTICE BLACKMUN join, dissenting.

* * * We may assume, for purposes of this case, that Lt. Boyle was trapped under water and drowned because respondent United Technologies negligently designed the helicopter's escape hatch. We may further assume that any competent engineer would have discovered and cured the defects, but that they inexplicably escaped respondent's notice. Had respondent designed such a death trap for a commercial firm, Lt. Boyle's family could sue under Virginia tort law and be compensated for his tragic and unnecessary death. But respondent designed the helicopter for the Federal Government, and that, the Court tells us today, makes all the difference: Respondent is immune from liability so long as it obtained approval of "reasonably precise specifications"—perhaps no more than a

rubber stamp from a federal procurement officer who might or might not have noticed or cared about the defects, or even had the expertise to discover them.

If respondent's immunity "bore the legitimacy of having been prescribed by the people's elected representatives," we would be duty bound to implement their will, whether or not we approved. * * * Congress, however, has remained silent—and conspicuously so, having resisted a sustained campaign by Government contractors to legislate for them some defense. * * * The Court—unelected and unaccountable to the people—has unabashedly stepped into the breach to legislate a rule denying Lt. Boyle's family the compensation that state law assures them. This time the injustice is of this Court's own making.

Worse yet, the injustice will extend far beyond the facts of this case, for the Court's newly discovered Government contractor defense is breathtakingly sweeping. It applies not only to military equipment like the CH–53D helicopter, but (so far as I can tell) to any made-to-order gadget that the Federal Government might purchase after previewing plans—from NASA's Challenger space shuttle to the Postal Service's old mail cars. The contractor may invoke the defense in suits brought not only by military personnel like Lt. Boyle, or Government employees, but by anyone injured by a Government contractor's negligent design, including, for example, the children who might have died had respondent's helicopter crashed on the beach. It applies even if the Government has not intentionally sacrificed safety for other interests like speed or efficiency, and, indeed, even if the equipment is not of a type that is typically considered dangerous; thus, the contractor who designs a Government building can invoke the defense when the elevator cable snaps or the walls collapse. And the defense is invocable regardless of how blatant or easily remedied the defect, so long as the contractor missed it and the specifications approved by the Government, however unreasonably dangerous, were "reasonably precise." * * *

In my view, this Court lacks both authority and expertise to fashion such a rule, whether to protect the Treasury of the United States or the coffers of industry. Because I would leave that exercise of legislative power to Congress, where our Constitution places it, I would reverse the Court of Appeals and reinstate petitioner's jury award.

* * *

IV

At bottom, the Court's analysis is premised on the proposition that any tort liability indirectly absorbed by the Government so burdens governmental functions as to compel us to act when Congress has not. That proposition is by no means uncontroversial. The tort system is premised on the assumption that the imposition of liability encourages actors to prevent any injury whose expected cost exceeds the cost of prevention. If the system is working as it should, Government contractors will design equipment to avoid certain injuries (like the deaths of soldiers or Government employees), which would be certain to burden the Government. The Court therefore has no basis for its assumption that tort liability will result in a net burden on the Government (let alone a clearly excessive net burden) rather than a net gain.

Perhaps tort liability is an inefficient means of ensuring the quality of design efforts, but "[w]hatever the merits of the policy" the Court wishes to implement, "its conversion into law is a proper subject for congressional action, not for any creative power of ours." [*United States v.*] *Standard Oil* [*Co. of Calif.*], 332 U.S. [301], at 314–315, 67 S.Ct. [1604], at 1611[, 91 L.Ed. 2067, 2075 (1947)]. * * * If Congress shared the Court's assumptions and conclusion it could readily enact "A BILL [t]o place limitations on the civil liability of government contractors to ensure that such liability does not impede the ability of the United States to procure necessary goods and services," H.R. 4765, 99th Cong., 2d Sess. (1986); see also S. 2441, 99th Cong., 2d Sess. (1986). It has not.

Were I a legislator, I would probably vote against any law absolving multibillion dollar private enterprises from answering for their tragic mistakes, at least if that law were justified by no more than the unsupported speculation that their liability might ultimately burden the United States Treasury. Some of my colleagues here would evidently vote otherwise (as they have here), but that should not matter here. We are judges not legislators, and the vote is not ours to cast.

I respectfully dissent.

JUSTICE STEVENS, dissenting.

When judges are asked to embark on a lawmaking venture, I believe they should carefully consider whether they, or a legislative body, are better equipped to perform the task at hand. There are instances of so-called interstitial lawmaking that inevitably become part of the judicial process. * * * But when we are asked to create an entirely new doctrine—to answer "questions of policy on which Congress has not spoken," United States v. Gilman, 347 U.S. 507, 511, 74 S.Ct. 695, 697, 98 L.Ed. 898 (1954)—we have a special duty to identify the proper decisionmaker before trying to make the proper decision.

When the novel question of policy involves a balancing of the conflicting interests in the efficient operation of a massive governmental program and the protection of the rights of the individual—whether in the social welfare context, the civil service context, or the military procurement context—I feel very deeply that we should defer to the expertise of the Congress. * * *

NOTES AND QUESTIONS

1. Professors Green and Matasar argue that the *Boyle* majority should have based the federal common law defense "entirely on the sole federal interest implicated—protection of government decisionmaking. The Court then could have crafted a rule narrowly tailored to further that interest."

Green & Matasar, *The Supreme Court and the Products Liability Crisis: Lessons from* Boyle's *Government Contractor Defense*, 63 S. Cal. L. Rev. 637, 642 (1989–1990). How would this approach have affected the result in *Boyle*? Would this approach be more respectful of state interests?

2. How broad is the *Boyle* defense? Does it apply only to military contractors? To any contractor that provides goods and services to the United States? Compare *In re Hawaii Federal Asbestos Cases*, 960 F.2d 806 (9th Cir. 1992) (declining to apply the *Boyle* defense in a products liability suit brought on behalf of individuals exposed to asbestos dust while serving in the United States Navy), with *Silverstein v. Northrop Grumman Corp.*, 367 N.J.Super. 361, 842 A.2d 881 (Ct. App. Div. 2004) (holding that the manufacturer of a postal vehicle could raise the *Boyle* defense in a products liability suit filed by a postal worker injured when the vehicle rolled over in an accident). In confining the *Boyle* defense only to military equipment manufactured for the United States, the Ninth Circuit explained:

> That *Boyle* speaks of the military contractor defense as immunizing contractors only with respect to the military equipment they produce for the United States is consistent with the purposes the Court ascribes to that defense. The Boyle Court noted that the military makes highly complex and sensitive decisions regarding the development of new equipment for military usage. Allowing the contractors who are hired to manufacture that equipment to be sued for the injuries caused by it would impinge unduly on the military's decisionmaking process. The contractors would either refuse to produce the military equipment for the Government or would raise their prices to insure against the potential liability for the Government's design. * * *
>
> These same concerns do not exist in respect to products readily available on the commercial market. The fact that the military may order such products does not make them "military equipment." The products have not been developed on the basis of involved judgments made by the military but in response to the broader needs and desires of end-users in the private sector. The contractors, furthermore, already will have factored the costs of ordinary tort liability into the price of their goods. That they will not enjoy immunity from tort liability with respect to the goods sold to one of their customers, the Government is unlikely to affect their marketing behavior or their pricing.

In re Hawaii Federal Asbestos Cases, 960 F.2d at 811. See Bellia, Jr., *State Courts and the Making of Federal Common Law*, 153 U. Pa. L. Rev. 825, 846–49 (2005).

3. In 1979, Viet Nam veterans, their spouses, and their children filed a federal lawsuit in the Eastern District of New York alleging injury from the veterans' exposure to Agent Orange, a phenoxy herbicide that the military used in South East Asia. Defendants were private companies alleged to have designed, manufactured, or marketed the chemical. The lawsuit was consolidated for pretrial purposes with six hundred similar cases filed nationwide. See *Procedural History of the Agent Orange Product Liability Litigation*, 52 Brooklyn L. Rev. 335 (1986). The trial court denied a motion to dismiss for lack of subject-matter jurisdiction, finding that plaintiffs' claims arose under

federal common law and so federal question jurisdiction was available. The Second Circuit reversed, finding no "identifiable" federal policy, and so no basis for fashioning a federal common law rule of decision. In re Agent Orange Product Liability Litigation, 506 F.Supp. 737, 741–42 (E.D.N.Y.1979), reversed, 635 F.2d 987, 995 (2d Cir.1980), certiorari denied 454 U.S. 1128, 102 S.Ct. 980, 71 L.Ed.2d 116 (1981). The case went forward on the basis of diversity jurisdiction, and the court later considered which state's law to apply to the dispute. In IN RE "AGENT ORANGE" PRODUCT LIABILITY LITIGATION, 580 F.Supp. 690 (E.D.N.Y.1984), the District Court explained that any state presented with the question of what law to apply to plaintiffs' claims would seek to determine "federal or national consensus substantive law," rather than simply apply the law of its own forum:

> * * * [A] state court passing on the claims of an individual or a group of veterans might well recognize the unfairness in treating differently legally identical claims involving servicemen who fought a difficult foreign war shoulder-to-shoulder and were exposed to virtually identical risks. As the Supreme Court stated in a related context, because "the Armed Services perform a unique, nationwide function in protecting the security of the United States," it makes "little sense for the Government's liability to members of the Armed Services [to be] dependent on the fortuity of where the soldier happened to be stationed at the time of his injury." * * *
>
> It quickly becomes apparent that it is impossible through sensible application of Restatement (Second) choice of law doctrine or analysis to identify the interest of any one state as being sufficiently greater than that of any others to a degree sufficient to justify the application of that state's law in resolving the issues in this litigation. * * * A state court * * *, because of its inability to identify and select any other state's law to be applied as the rule of decision and because of the need for uniformity across the country, would seek to divine what the national rule of decision with regard to product liability law would be so that such law would appropriately reflect the national and international characteristics of this case. * * *

Id. at 703. Was the District Court's approach faithful to *Klaxon*, p. 466, supra? Would *Boyle*, p. 486, supra, alter the District Court's analysis? See In re Agent Orange Product Liability Litigation, 517 F.3d 76 (2d Cir.2008) (affirming district court's dismissal of plaintiffs' claims as barred under the government contractor defense).

4. Does the availability of federal common law influence your view on whether disputes under the Class Action Fairness Act ("CAFA"), p. 276, supra, are to be decided by state law? Professor Hazard provocatively calls CAFA "a congressional pronouncement implying that the *Erie* Doctrine is seriously erroneous." Hazard, Jr., *Has the* Erie *Doctrine Been Repealed by Congress?*, 156 U. Pa. L. Rev. 1629 (2008).

NOTE ON FEDERAL COMMON LAW AND FEDERAL RULES OF PRECLUSION

Federal common law plays an important role in determining the preclusive effect of a federal judgment. Although the question in the past has been in doubt, it is now settled that the preclusive effect of a federal judgment "is not directly governed by the text of either the Constitution or the provisions of [28 U.S.C.] § 1738." Shapiro, Civil Procedure: Preclusion in Civil Actions 144–45 (2001). See generally 18B Wright, Miller & Cooper, Federal Practice and Procedure: Federal Jurisdiction and Related Matters § 4468. Instead, as the Supreme Court made clear in Semtek International Inc. v. Lockheed Martin Corp., 531 U.S. 497, 121 S.Ct. 1021, 149 L.Ed.2d 32 (2001), p. 1348, infra, the preclusive effect of a federal judgment, even when the federal court sits in diversity, is governed by federal common law. See *Leading Cases*, 115 Harv. L. Rev. 467 (2001). In determining the content of the federal rule of preclusion, the federal court may choose to borrow a state rule. See Burbank, Semtek, *Forum Shopping, and Federal Common Law*, 77 Notre Dame L. Rev. 1027 (2002). *Semtek* illustrates a federal common law of procedure. See Burbank, *Interjurisdictional Preclusion, Full Faith and Credit and Federal Common Law: A General Approach*, 71 Cornell L. Rev. 733, 737 (1986). Other examples of procedural common law include the doctrines of abstention and forum non conveniens. See Barrett, *Procedural Common Law*, 94 Va. L. Rev. 813 (2008). Why is the creation of a federal common law rule of preclusion consistent with the Rules of Decision Act? See Degnan, *Federalized Res Judicata*, 85 Yale L.J. 741 (1976). Does the Rules Enabling Act authorize the Court to adopt a federal rule of preclusion? Is such a rule essential to the integrity of the federal judicial system? Is it true that preclusion rules have only an incidental effect on substantive rights? See Woolley, *The Sources of Federal Preclusion Law After* Semtek, 72 U. Cin. L. Rev. 527 (2003).

SECTION D. FEDERAL LAW IN THE STATE COURTS

State courts often are called upon to construe and apply federal law. Indeed, Congress has created a number of statutory causes of action, such as actions under the Federal Employers' Liability Act, that can be asserted by plaintiff in either a state or federal court but which defendant cannot remove from a state court. When a state attempts to adjudicate such a right, the Supremacy Clause, U.S. Const. Art. VI, requires the application of federal law. See Ward v. Board of County Com'rs of Love County, 253 U.S. 17, 40 S.Ct. 419, 64 L.Ed. 751 (1920). A federally created right also may become germane to a state-court action when it is interposed as a defense to a claim based on state law. For example, in an action for royalties due under a contract licensing the use of a copyright or patent, defendant commonly will assert that the copyright or patent is invalid under the substantive tests established by the Copyright or Patent Act or that the copyright or patent has been used in violation of the federal antitrust laws. See, e.g., Sola Elec. Co. v. Jefferson Elec. Co., 317 U.S. 173, 63 S.Ct. 172, 87 L.Ed. 165 (1942). By way of further example, federal law may become relevant to a state lawsuit because of the presence of some federal interest or policy, which often springs out of its proprietary or governmental activities, or because one of the parties asserts a right protected by the United States Constitution. Finally, federal decisional law may come into play because it provides precedents bearing on issues being litigated before the state court in a nonfederal action.

DICE v. AKRON, CANTON & YOUNGSTOWN R. CO.

Supreme Court of the United States, 1952.
342 U.S. 359, 72 S.Ct. 312, 96 L.Ed. 398.

Certiorari to the Supreme Court of Ohio.

Opinion of the Court by MR. JUSTICE BLACK, announced by MR. JUSTICE DOUGLAS.

Petitioner, a railroad fireman, was seriously injured when an engine in which he was riding jumped the track. Alleging that his injuries were due to respondent's negligence, he brought this action for damages under the Federal Employers' Liability Act, 35 Stat. 65, 45 U.S.C. § 51 et seq., in an Ohio court of common pleas. Respondent's defenses were (1) a denial of negligence and (2) a written document signed by petitioner purporting to release respondent in full for $924.63. Petitioner admitted that he had signed several receipts for payments made him in connection with his injuries but denied that he had made a full and complete settlement of all his claims. He alleged that the purported release was void because he had signed it relying on respondent's deliberately false statement that the document was nothing more than a mere receipt for back wages.

After both parties had introduced considerable evidence the jury found in favor of petitioner and awarded him a $25,000 verdict. The trial judge later entered judgment notwithstanding the verdict. In doing so he reappraised the evidence as to fraud, found that petitioner had been "guilty of supine negligence" in failing to read the release, and accordingly held that the facts did not "sustain either in law or equity the allegations of fraud by clear, unequivocal and convincing evidence." This judgment notwithstanding the verdict was reversed by the Court of Appeals of Summit County, Ohio, on the ground that under federal law, which controlled, the jury's verdict must stand because there was ample evidence to support its finding of fraud. The Ohio Supreme Court, one judge dissenting, reversed the Court of Appeals' judgment and sustained the trial court's action, holding that: (1) Ohio, not federal, law governed; (2) under that law petitioner, a man of ordinary intelligence who could read, was bound by the release even though he had been induced to sign it by the deliberately false statement that it was only a receipt for back wages; and (3) under controlling Ohio law factual issues as to fraud in the execution of this release were properly decided by the judge rather than by the jury. * * *

First. We agree with the Court of Appeals of Summit County, Ohio, and the dissenting judge in the Ohio Supreme Court and hold that validity of releases under the Federal Employers' Liability Act raises a federal question to be determined by federal rather than state law. Congress in § 1 of the Act granted petitioner a right to recover against his employer for damages negligently inflicted. State laws are not controlling in determining what the incidents of this federal right shall be. * * * Manifestly the federal rights affording relief to injured railroad employees under a federally declared standard could be defeated if states were permitted to have the final say as to what defenses could and could not be properly interposed to suits under the Act. Moreover, only if federal law controls can the federal Act be given that uniform application throughout the country essential to effectuate its purposes. * * * Releases and other devices designed to liquidate or defeat injured employees' claims play an important part in the federal Act's administration. * * * Their validity is but one of the many interrelated questions that must constantly be determined in these cases according to a uniform federal law.

Second. In effect the Supreme Court of Ohio held that * * * the negligence of an innocent worker is sufficient to enable his employer to benefit by its deliberate fraud. Application of so harsh a rule to defeat a railroad employee's claim is wholly incongruous with the general policy of the Act to give railroad employees a right to recover just compensation for injuries negligently inflicted by their employers. And this Ohio rule is out of harmony with modern judicial and legislative practice to relieve injured persons from the effect of releases fraudulently obtained. * * * We hold that the correct federal rule is that * * * a release of rights under the Act is void when the employee is induced to sign it by the deliberately false and material statements of the railroad's authorized representatives made to deceive the employee as to the contents of the release. The trial court's charge to the jury correctly stated this rule of law.

Third. Ohio provides and has here accorded petitioner the usual jury trial of factual issues relating to negligence. But Ohio treats factual questions of fraudulent releases differently. It permits the judge trying a negligence case to resolve all factual questions of fraud "other than fraud in the factum." The factual issue of fraud is thus split into fragments, some to be determined by the judge, others by the jury.

It is contended that since a state may consistently with the Federal Constitution provide for trial of cases under the Act by a nonunanimous verdict, Minneapolis & St. Louis R. Co. v. Bombolis, 241 U.S. 211, 36 S.Ct. 595, 60 L.Ed. 961, Ohio may lawfully eliminate trial by jury as to one phase of fraud while allowing jury trial as to all other issues raised. The *Bombolis* case might be more in point had Ohio abolished trial by jury in all negligence cases including those arising under the federal Act. But Ohio has not done this. It has provided jury trials for cases arising under the federal Act but seeks to single out one phase of the question of fraudulent releases for determination by a judge rather than by a jury. * * *

We have previously held that "The right to trial by jury is 'a basic and fundamental feature of our system of federal jurisprudence' " and that it is "part and parcel of the remedy afforded railroad workers under the Employers' Liability Act." Bailey v. Central Vermont R. Co., 319 U.S. 350, 354, 63 S.Ct. 1062, 1064, 87 L.Ed. 1444. We also recognized in that case that to deprive railroad workers of the benefit of a jury trial where there is evidence to support negligence "is to take away a goodly portion of the relief which Congress has afforded them." It follows that the right to trial by jury is too substantial a part of the rights accorded by the Act to permit it to be classified as a mere "local rule of procedure" for denial in the manner that Ohio has here used. * * *

Reversed and remanded with directions.

MR. JUSTICE FRANKFURTER, whom MR. JUSTICE REED, MR. JUSTICE JACKSON and MR. JUSTICE BURTON join, concurring for reversal but dissenting from the Court's opinion.

Ohio, as do many other States, maintains the old division between law and equity as to the mode of trying issues, even though the same judge administers both. * * * [I]n all cases in Ohio, the judge is the trier of fact on this issue of fraud, rather than the jury. It is contended that the Federal Employers' Liability Act requires that Ohio courts send the fraud issue to a jury in the cases founded on that Act. To require Ohio to try a particular issue before a different fact-finder in negligence actions brought under the Employers' Liability Act from the fact-finder on the identical issue in every other negligence case disregards the settled distribution of judicial power between Federal and State courts where Congress authorizes concurrent enforcement of federally-created rights.

* * *

In 1916 the Court decided without dissent that States in entertaining actions under the Federal Employers' Liability Act need not provide a jury system other than that established for local negligence actions. States are not compelled to provide the jury required of Federal courts by the Seventh Amendment. Minneapolis & St. L.R. Co. v. Bombolis * * *. In the thirty-six years since this early decision after the enactment of the Federal Employers' Liability Act * * *, the *Bombolis* case has often been cited by this Court but never questioned. Until today its significance has been to leave to States the choice of the fact-finding tribunal in all negligence actions, including those arising under the Federal Act. * * *

Although a State must entertain negligence suits brought under the Federal Employers' Liability Act if it entertains ordinary actions for negligence, it need conduct them only in the way in which it conducts the run of negligence litigation. The *Bombolis* case directly establishes that the Employers' Liability Act does not impose the jury requirements of the Seventh Amendment on the States *pro tanto* for Employers' Liability litigation. If its reasoning means anything, the *Bombolis* decision means that, if a State chooses not to have a jury at all, but to leave questions of fact in all negligence actions to a court, certainly the Employers' Liability Act does not require a State to have juries for negligence actions brought under the Federal Act in its courts. Or, if a State chooses to retain the old double system of courts, common law and equity * * *, surely there is nothing in the Employers' Liability Act that requires traditional distribution of authority for disposing of legal issues as between common law and chancery courts to go by the board. * * * So long as all negligence suits in a State are treated in the same way, by the same mode of disposing equitable, non-jury, and common law, jury issues, the State does not discriminate against Employers' Liability suits nor does it make any inroad upon substance.

Ohio and her sister States with a similar division of functions between law and equity are not trying to evade their duty under the Federal Employers' Liability Act * * *. The States merely exercise a preference in adhering to historic ways of dealing with a claim of fraud; they prefer the traditional way of making unavailable through equity an otherwise valid defense. The State judges and local lawyers who must administer the Federal Employers' Liability Act in State courts are trained in the ways of local practice; it multiplies the difficulties and confuses the administration of justice to require, on purely theoretical grounds, a hybrid of State and Federal practice in the State courts as to a single class of cases. Nothing in the Employers' Liability Act or in the judicial enforcement of the Act for over forty years forces such judicial hybridization upon the States. The fact that Congress authorized actions under the Federal Employers' Liability Act to be brought in State as well as in Federal courts seems a strange basis for the inference that Congress overrode State procedural arrangements controlling all other negligence suits in a State * * *. Such an inference is admissible, so it seems to me, only on the theory that Congress included as part of the right created by the Employers' Liability Act an assumed likelihood that trying all issues to juries is more favorable to plaintiffs. * * *

Even though the method of trying the equitable issue of fraud which the State applies in all other negligence cases governs Employers' Liability cases, two questions remain for decision: Should the validity of the release be tested by a Federal or a State standard? And if by a Federal one, did the Ohio courts in the present case correctly administer the standard? If the States afford courts for enforcing the Federal Act, they must enforce the substance of the right given by Congress. They cannot depreciate the legislative currency issued by Congress—either expressly or by local methods of enforcement that accomplish the same result. * * * In order to prevent diminution of railroad workers' nationally-uniform right to recover, the standard for the validity of a release of contested liability must be Federal. * * *

NOTES AND QUESTIONS

1. In what ways is the question of what law governs the right to jury trial in *Dice* the same or distinguishable from the question of the governing law in *Byrd*, see p. 424, supra? Under what circumstances might a state court ignore federal law when it deems it to be inconsistent with its own law or policy? By what method is uniform construction and application of federal law by state courts assured?

2. Why might a state court or legislature voluntarily incorporate or apply federal law to a state-created right? Would such an incorporation or application present a federal question for purposes of original jurisdiction in the federal district courts or appellate jurisdiction in the United States Supreme Court? See generally Hart, *The Relations Between State and Federal Law,* 54 Colum.L.Rev. 489, 536–38 (1954); Note, *Supreme Court Review of State Interpretations of Federal Law Incorporated by Reference,* 66 Harv. L.Rev. 1498 (1953). Are the federal courts bound by the state construction of the incorporated federal law?

3. In BROWN v. WESTERN RY. OF ALABAMA, 338 U.S. 294, 70 S.Ct. 105, 94 L.Ed. 100 (1949), respondent demurred to petitioner's complaint in an action brought in a Georgia state court under the Federal Employers' Liability Act. The theory of the demurrer was that the complaint failed to "set forth a cause of action and is otherwise insufficient in law." The Georgia courts sustained the demurrer on the basis of a state practice rule requiring pleading allegations to be construed "most strongly against the pleader." The Supreme Court reversed, stating in part:

> It is contended that this construction of the complaint is binding on us. The argument is that while state courts are without power to detract from "substantive rights" granted by Congress in FELA cases, they are free to follow their own rules of "practice" and "procedure." To what extent rules of practice and procedure may themselves dig into "substantive rights" is a troublesome question at best * * *. [C]ases in this Court point up the impossibility of laying down a precise rule to distinguish "substance" from "procedure." Fortunately, we need not attempt to do so. A long series of cases previously decided, from which we see no reason to depart, makes it our duty to construe the allegations of this complaint ourselves in order to determine whether petitioner has been denied a right of trial granted him by Congress. This federal right cannot be defeated by the forms of local practice. * * *
>
> Strict local rules of pleading cannot be used to impose unnecessary burdens upon rights of recovery authorized by federal laws. * * * Should this Court fail to protect federally created rights from dismissal because of over-exacting local requirements for meticulous pleadings, desirable uniformity in adjudication of federally created rights could not be achieved.

Id. at 296, 298–99, 70 S.Ct. at 106, 108, 94 L.Ed. at 102–04. Of what relevance is the presence or absence under Georgia practice of a right to replead following a demurrer?

4. Is the process of applying federal law in a state court identical to the process of applying state law in a federal court under the *Erie* doctrine? How does a state court ascertain federal law? Suppose, for example, that there is a conflict between the federal courts of appeals over what a statute means, or over an issue of federal common law. Is the state court free to adopt any position it wishes? What if the federal courts never have ruled on the issue? Should the state court try to figure out how the federal courts might rule? Which federal court? How does a state court determine which aspects of federal law it must apply? See Clermont, *Reverse*–Erie, 82 Notre Dame L. Rev. 1 (2006).

5. May the federal government require state courts to apply the Federal Rules in order to ensure that a federally created right is enforced with procedures which the federal government approves? Should the federal government do so? In FEDERAL ENERGY REGULATORY COMMISSION v. MISSISSIPPI, 456 U.S. 742, 102 S.Ct. 2126, 72 L.Ed.2d 532 (1982), the Supreme Court upheld provisions of the Public Utilities Regulatory Policies Act of 1978 (PURPA) which required state public utility commissions to observe certain federal procedures in regulating energy usage. Justice Powell, concurring in part of the judgment and dissenting in part, wrote:

> "The general rule, bottomed deeply in belief in the importance of state control of state judicial procedure, is that federal law takes the state courts as it finds them." Hart, The Relations Between State and Federal Law, 54 Colum.L.Rev. 489, 508 (1954). I believe the same principle must apply to other organs of state government. It may be true that the procedural provisions of the PURPA may not effect dramatic changes in the laws and procedures of some States. But I know of no other attempt by the Federal Government to supplant state-prescribed procedures that in part define the nature of their administrative agencies. If Congress may do this, presumably it has the power to pre-empt state-court rules of civil procedure and judicial review in classes of cases found to affect commerce.

Id. at 774, 102 S.Ct. at 2145, 72 L.Ed.2d at 556–57.

6. The question of federal control over state procedures when a state court is adjudicating a federal cause of action is discussed in Bellia, *Federal Regulation of State Court Procedures*, 110 Yale L.J. 947, 958–63 (2001). The author recognizes that "state courts do enforce federal procedures that are part of the substance of federal claims," but argues that requiring state courts to enforce a state claim using federal procedure raises "cause for concern." Id. at 994.

CHAPTER 7

THE DEVELOPMENT OF MODERN PROCEDURE

■ ■ ■

In this Chapter, we examine the historical foundations of the modern system of pleading, from the development of the writ and forms of action during the reign of Henry II in twelfth-century England, to the adoption of the Federal Rules of Civil Procedure in 1938. Encompassing ornate distinctions such as that between trespass and case, the recognition of indebitatus assumpsit, and the emergence of the action of trover, the materials carry more than simply antiquarian appeal. Rather, they are critical to an understanding of the ways in which substantive law develops in relation to procedure—in the famous words of Sir Henry Maine, how substantive law appears "secreted in the interstices of Procedure." Maine, Early Law and Custom 389 (1886). Even after eight centuries of common law development, it remains true, as Oliver Wendell Holmes observed, that "whenever we trace a leading doctrine of substantive law far enough back, we are very likely to find some forgotten circumstance of procedure at its source." Koffler & Reppy, Handbook of Common Law Pleading xi (1969). The materials in this Chapter also are important for examining many legal arguments that continue to have currency (for example, the view that the grant of federal diversity jurisdiction does not include domestic-relations cases relies on notions of ecclesiastical law that date to mediaeval times). As you consider these materials, reflect on the ways in which historical arguments affect current understandings of procedure and also how the categories of substance and procedure interact and evolve.

SECTION A. COMMON-LAW PLEADING

STEPHEN, THE PRINCIPLES OF PLEADING IN CIVIL ACTIONS 37, 147–50 (Tyler ed. 1882):[a]

In the course of administering justice between litigating parties there are two successive objects: to ascertain the subject for decision, and to decide. It is evident that, towards the attainment of the first of these

a. This edition is based upon Stephen's own second edition of 1827, which is the last of his editions before the reform of common-law pleading in England in 1834.

results, there is, in a *general* point of view, only one satisfactory mode of proceeding; and that this consists in making each of the parties state his own case, and collecting, from the opposition of their statements, the points of the legal controversy. Thus far, therefore, the course of every system of judicature is the same. It is common to them all to require, on behalf of each contending party, before the decision of the cause, a statement of his case. But from this point the coincidence naturally ceases. * * *

The manner of allegation in our courts may be said to have been first methodically formed and cultivated as a science in the reign of Edward I [1272–1307]. From this time the judges began systematically to prescribe and enforce certain *rules of statement* * * *. None of them seem to have been originally of legislative enactment, or to have had any authority except usage or judicial regulation; but, from the general perception of their wisdom and utility, they acquired the character of fixed and positive institutions, and grew up into an entire and connected *system of pleading.* * * *

As the object of all pleading or judicial allegation is to ascertain the subject for decision, so the main object of that system of pleading established in the common law of England is to ascertain it by the production of an *issue;* and this appears to be peculiar to that system. * * *

The author is of opinion that this peculiarity of coming to issue took its rise in the practice of *oral* pleading. It seems a natural incident of that practice, to compel the pleaders to short and terse allegations, applying to each other by way of answer, in somewhat of a logical form, and at length reducing the controversy to a precise point. For while the pleading was *merely* oral, * * * the court and the pleaders would have to rely exclusively on their memory for retaining the tenor of the discussion; and the development of some precise question or issue would then be a very convenient practice, because it would prevent the necessity of reviewing the different statements, and leave no burden on the memory but that of retaining the question itself so developed. And even after the practice of recording was introduced, the same brief and logical forms of allegation would naturally continue to be acceptable, while the pleadings were still *viva voce* * * *.

A co-operative reason for coming to issue was the variety of the modes of decision which the law assigned to different kinds of question. * * * As questions of law were decided by the *court,* and matters of fact referred to other kinds of investigation, it was, in the first place, necessary to settle whether the question in the cause or issue was a matter of *law* or *fact.* Again, if it happened to be a matter of fact, it required to be developed in a form sufficiently specific to show what was the method of trial appropriate to the case. And, unless the state of the question were thus adjusted between the parties, it is evident that they would not have known whether they were to put themselves on the judgment of the court or to go to trial; nor, in the latter case, whether they were to prepare themselves for trial by jury or for one of the other various modes of deciding [the] matter of fact.

NOTES

1. The change from oral to written pleadings cannot be dated precisely. The shift began in the late fourteenth century and extended into the second half of the sixteenth. Predictably the change increased the rigor and technicality of the pleading rules.

> * * * [T]his system of oral pleading had one great advantage over the later system of written pleadings. It made for far greater freedom in the statement of the case. * * * [W]hen all objections to the writ and process had been disposed of * * * the debate between the opposing counsel, carried on subject to the advice or the rulings of the judge, allowed the parties considerable latitude in pleading to the issue. Suggested pleas will, after a little discussion, be seen to be untenable; a proposition to demur will, after a few remarks by the judge, be obviously the wrong move. The counsel feel their way towards an issue which each can accept and allow to be enrolled. * * *

3 Holdsworth, A History of English Law 635 (4th ed. 1935). Milsom, Historical Foundations of the Common Law 28–37, 39–40 (1969), contains a good description of oral pleadings as well as an excellent explanation of the Yearbooks, from which most of our knowledge of early pleading is derived; this book is a particularly valuable reference for most of the matters covered in this Chapter.

2. In this discussion we are concerned with pleading in the royal courts. It should be noted that at the time of the Norman Conquest (1066) and for a century or more afterward the ordinary recourse of suitors was not to the royal courts but to local, or communal, courts and to feudal courts in which a lord heard cases involving his tenants. The royal courts existed primarily to try offenses against the king's laws and to hear cases involving his tenants-in-chief, which came before the king in his capacity as a feudal lord. Gradually, however, these royal courts began to absorb business from the communal and feudal courts.

A person with a grievance against another sought justice from the king, and the king issued a *writ,* ordering the sheriff to bring the other person before the king's judges to answer the complaint. In the course of the twelfth century this pattern became standardized. When it became established that the king's courts would hear a particular kind of case—for example, an action for assault, an action for debt, an action for the possession of land—the complainant in such a case could obtain a writ from the king's chief minister, the chancellor, as a matter of course. See Milsom, Historical Foundations of the Common Law 22–25 (1969).

The writ, strictly speaking, was simply the document that commenced the action, similar in function to the modern summons; but each writ came to embody a *form of action,* a concept that governed the method of commencing the suit, the substantive requirements of the case, the manner of trial, and the type of sanction that would attend the eventual judgment. See pp. ___–

514, infra. For the present it is enough to say that there was a writ for each type of case—or form of action—that the royal courts would hear; thus, for example, there was a writ of trespass, a writ of debt, and a writ of nuisance. If plaintiff selected a writ that did not fit the case, the action would fail. If there was no writ that fit the case, and the chancellor would not draw up a new one, plaintiff could obtain no relief in the royal courts.

3. The "modes of decision" for issues of fact, referred to in the extract from Stephen, were, at an early date, "trial" by ordeal, by combat, and by oath. These were not trials in the sense in which we now understand and use that term; rather they were proofs undertaken by one of the parties (or both in the case of combat) at the direction of the court. Ordeal—proof by carrying a red-hot iron unscathed or by sinking when thrown into a pool of water[b]—disappeared in England after it was proscribed by the Lateran Council in 1215. Combat—waged by champions of the parties—was resisted as a Norman importation, and during the reign of Henry II (1154–1189) an early form of jury began to supplant it, although it was not formally abolished until 1819.

For our purpose the most important of these early methods of proof was that by oath, or as more generally known, *wager of law* or *compurgation*. It required one of the parties to swear to his case with strict and elaborate formalities, accompanied by a number of "oath-helpers," usually twelve, who swore to the truthfulness of the party's oath, or in later periods to their belief in its truth. If all went as prescribed, he prevailed; but if the party or any of the "helpers" made an error by using a wrong word, that party lost.

> It is hard for us to say how this ancient procedure worked in practice, hard to tell how easy it was to get oath-helpers who would swear falsely, hard to tell how much risk there was in an ordeal. The rational element of law must, it would seem, have asserted itself in the judgment which decided how and by whom the proof should be given; the jurisprudence of the old courts must have been largely composed of the answers to this question; * * * for example, we can see that even before the Norman Conquest the man who has been often accused has to go to the ordeal instead of being allowed to purge himself with oath-helpers.

Maitland, Equity, Also the Forms of Action at Common Law 310 (1909).

The importance of this procedure in legal history lies in the fact that a right to wage one's law was firmly established in certain classes of cases by the last half of the twelfth century, long before the jury began to emerge as an instrument for fact-determination. In its original form the jury, developed as a body for valuing property for taxes, decided cases on its own knowledge rather than after hearing witnesses. Even in this form suitors saw in the jury a more rational mode of trial, and sought to use forms of action such as trespass, which having developed at a relatively late period did not provide a right to wager of law.[c] Thus, as we shall see in Section B of this Chapter, judicial

b. See Lea, Superstition and Force 252, 279 (3d ed. 1878). In ordeal by water, it was thought that the water would reject the evildoer; a rope was tied to the person making the proof in the hope that if proved innocent he could be kept from drowning.

c. A similar desire to avoid trial by combat was among the causes for the desuetude of the writ of right, once the most important action. Preference for jury trial also encouraged the development of the law for four-and-a-half centuries was channeled and motivated to a substantial degree by increasingly successful attempts to avoid the older modes of trial.[d]

1. A BRIEF OVERVIEW OF COMMON-LAW PLEADING

The basic structure of common-law pleading was simple and well-calculated to bring the parties to an issue of law or of fact. It was based on the following analysis. A substantive response to a claim—other than an expression of total agreement—will fall into one of three categories: (1) A party can deny that the alleged facts, even if true, give the claimant any legal right; (2) a party can deny that the alleged facts are true; or (3) a party can say that even if the alleged facts are true and taken alone would establish a right, additional facts not mentioned by the claimant negate that right. Responses (1) and (2) raise issues of law and of fact respectively. Response (3) does not itself raise a contested issue; there is as yet no necessary disagreement between the parties. To raise the necessary issue the claimant must respond to the response, and this response also may fall into any of the three categories. If this response is again of type (3) no issue will have been raised and the process must continue. (How do the Federal Rules avoid the necessity for further pleading after a type (3) response? See Federal Rules 7(a) and 8(b)(6).)

Of course the real process was more complex than this. Plaintiff's claim was set forth in the *declaration.* This document had to meet many formal requirements that might differ from one type of case to another. But stripped of much verbiage, and stated in modern English, it might have said: "Defendant promised to deliver a horse to plaintiff and plaintiff promised to pay 100 dollars for it, but defendant has refused to deliver the horse."

At this point, defendant had to *demur* or *plead.* A demurrer would challenge the legal sufficiency of the declaration. Thus prior to STRANGBOROUGH & WARNERS CASE, 4 Leon. 3, 74 Eng.Rep. 686 (K.B. 1589), the modern language declaration set out above would have failed on demurrer, because a promise was not regarded as good consideration for a promise until that decision. A demurrer also would succeed if plaintiff had chosen the wrong writ (or form of action). There were also a great many technical sins that the declaration might commit, but by statute, 27 Eliz. 1, c. 5, § 1 (1585) and 4 Anne, c. 16, § 1 (1705), unless these defects were raised by a *special demurrer,* which precisely spelled out the faults, they were waived. If a demurrer was sustained, plaintiff was out of court,

---

expanding jurisdiction of royal courts at the expense of the feudal courts since the jury was found only in the former.

d. For a time in the fourteenth century it seemed that wager of law might be denied when the facts were well known to witnesses, but this development aborted. Fifoot, History and Sources of the Common Law—Tort and Contract 28–29 (1949). By the last quarter of the sixteenth century, however, "a defendant proposing to wage his law was somehow examined and admonished." Milsom, Historical Foundations of the Common Law 292–93 (1969).

although he generally was free to begin again if he could correct the mistake, as by suing in another form of action if the original form was incorrect. If the demurrer was quashed, judgment was entered for plaintiff.

If defendant did not demur, he responded to the declaration in a *plea*. Pleas were of two types, *dilatory* and *peremptory*. Dilatory pleas did not deny the merits of plaintiff's claim, but challenged plaintiff's right to have the court hear the case; they included pleas to the jurisdiction of the court, pleas of a variance between the declaration and the writ, and pleas that the case must be suspended (when, for example, one of the parties was under age at the time of suit). A peremptory plea, or *plea in bar,* was on the merits. If defendant denied that he had promised to sell the horse, the plea was a *traverse;* a traverse terminated the pleadings and the case would go to trial to dispose of the issue raised by plaintiff's allegation and defendant's denial. But suppose defendant wanted to allege that at the time of the purported contract he was a minor; defendant would then plead by *confession and avoidance,* that is, admit the allegations of the declaration and seek to avoid them by pleading minority. If defendant followed this course, no issue would have been reached, and plaintiff would have to respond.

Plaintiff's response might be a demurrer to defendant's plea, which would raise the question whether minority was a defense to the agreement he had pleaded and defendant had confessed.[e] Or plaintiff might plead in a *replication,* either traversing defendant's allegation of his age, or confessing it, and alleging that defendant had lied about his age when making the contract. If plaintiff pleaded in confession and avoidance, defendant would again have to respond, by demurrer or by *rejoinder.* The pleas in confession and avoidance theoretically might go on indefinitely, and in some of the cases we read of a *surrejoinder,* a *rebutter,* and a *surrebutter.* Lack of formal names beyond that point suggests that even the ingenuity of the common-law pleader may have had its limits.

The common-law pleading system may seem ornate to you, even after only the brief description on the preceding pages. Yet bear in mind that this is only a skeletal outline. When the outline is filled in with special instances, inexplicable exceptions, arbitrary rules, and untraversable fictions, the result is one of the most complex and snare-ridden creations ever devised by man. Let us look at a common-law record and decision. (The reporter of the case, it should be noted, is the victorious lawyer, Saunders.)

VEALE v. WARNER

Court of King's Bench, 1670.
1 Wms. Saund. 323, 326, 85 Eng.Rep. 463, 468.

Be it remembered that * * * before our lord the King at Westminster came Thomas Veale Esquire * * * and brought here * * * his certain bill

e. After a successful demurrer to a dilatory plea, judgment was not entered for plaintiff, but by an order *respondeat ouster,* defendant was directed to plead over.

against William Warner, * * * in the custody of the marshal, & c. of a plea of debt: and there are pledges of prosecution, to wit, John Doe and Richard Roe; which said bill follows in these words, * * * [Veale] complains of [Warner] * * * that he render to him 2000l., of lawful money of England, which he owes to, and unjustly detains from him; for that whereas the said William, * * * at London aforesaid, to wit, in the parish of St. Mary-le Bow in the ward of Cheap, by his certain writing obligatory, sealed * * * and to the Court of our said lord the King now here shewn, * * * acknowledged himself to be held and firmly bound to * * * [Veale] in the said 2000l. to be paid to the said Thomas when he should be thereunto requested. Nevertheless, the said William (although often requested) hath not yet paid the said 2000l. to the said Thomas, but to pay the same to him hath hitherto altogether refused, and yet refuses, to the damage of him the said Thomas of 100l.: and therefore he brings suit, & c.

And [Warner] * * * comes and defends the wrong and injury when, & c. and prays oyer of the said writing obligatory, and it is read to him, & c. He also prays oyer of the condition of the said writing, & c. and it is read to him in these words, to wit: "The condition of this obligation is such, that if * * * [Warner] shall and do in all things well and truly stand to, obey, abide, perform, fulfil, and keep the award * * * of John Coggs, gent. and John Foxwell, arbitrators * * * to arbitrate * * * and determine of and concerning all and all manner of action and actions, cause and causes of actions, suits, bills, bonds, specialties, judgments, executions, extents, quarrels, controversies, trespasses, damages, and demands whatsoever, at any time heretofore had, made, moved, brought, commenced, sued, prosecuted, done, suffered, committed, or depending by or between the said parties, * * * then this obligation to be void and of none effect, or else to remain in full force and virtue." Which being read and heard, the said William saith, that * * * [Veale] ought not to have his aforesaid action against him, because he saith that * * * the arbitrators in the said condition named, * * * made their award * * * that [Warner] * * * should satisfy, content, and pay to [Veale] * * * the full sum of 3169l. 16s. and 3d. of lawful money of England. And they further awarded that [Warner] * * * should seal, and as his deed deliver to [Veale] * * * a full and general release and discharge of all and all manner of actions, and causes of actions, suits, bills, bonds, specialties, judgments, executions, extents, quarrels, controversies, trespasses, damages, and demands whatsoever, at any time before the date of the bond brought here into Court had, made, moved, commenced, sued, prosecuted, committed, or depending by or between the said parties. And * * * [Warner] further saith, that he the said William * * * paid to * * * [Veale] the said sum * * * and also, then and there did seal, and as his deed deliver to * * * [Veale] the said full release * * * and this he is ready to verify: wherefore he prays judgment if the said Thomas ought to have or maintain his said action thereof against him & c.

And * * * [Veale] saith, that he by any thing by * * * [Warner] above in pleading alleged, ought not to be barred from having his said action thereof against the said William, because he saith that * * * [Warner] did not pay the said sum * * * as the said William hath above thereof in pleading alleged; and this he prays may be inquired of by the country, & c.

And * * * [Warner] saith that * * * [Veale] ought not to be admitted to say that he the said William hath not paid the said sum * * * because he saith that he the said Thomas, * * * by his certain writing acknowledged that he the said William had paid the said sum to the said Thomas * * * and this he is ready to verify: wherefore he prays judgment if the said Thomas ought to be admitted, against his own acknowledgment, to say, that he the said William hath not paid the said sum of money, & c.

Demurrer and joinder in demurrer.

* * *

And now in this term the plaintiff moved to have judgment. And Saunders for the defendant objected that the plaintiff could not have judgment, because it appeared by the record that the award was void, being all to be performed by the defendant and nothing by the plaintiff: and, therefore, if the award is void, it is not material whether the defendant has performed it or not, although he has pleaded a performance of it. And now he has acknowledged the contrary by his waiver of the issue offered by the plaintiff and pleading a bad rejoinder. And the plaintiff and defendant have both agreed, that the award pleaded by the defendant was the true award made by the arbitrators, which is altogether vicious. But if the plaintiff would have helped himself, he ought to have shewn the other part of the award before he assigned the breach, which he has not done here; and therefore he cannot have judgment.

And of such opinion was the whole Court clearly. But they would not give judgment for the defendant, because they conceived it was a trick in pleading; but they gave the plaintiff leave to discontinue on payment of costs. And Kelynge Chief Justice, reprehended Saunders for pleading so subtly on purpose to trick the plaintiff by the omission of the other part of the award. But it was a case of the greatest hardship on the defendant; for the bond of submission was only in the penalty of 2000l., and the arbitrators had awarded him to pay 3100l., being 1100l. more than the real penalty of the bond; when in truth there was nothing at all due to the plaintiff, but he was indebted to the defendant. And afterwards the defendant exhibited an English bill in the Exchequer, disclosing bad practice of the plaintiff with the arbitrators, and had relief against the bond: and so this matter was at rest. * * *

NOTES AND QUESTIONS

1. "[B]efore our lord the King at Westminster." Veale v. Warner was brought in the Court of King's Bench, one of the three royal common-law courts, maintaining separate existence until merged in the High Court of Justice in 1873. The others were the Court of Common Pleas and the Court of Exchequer. All three developed out of the *Curia Regis* (the King's Court),

which at the time of the Norman Conquest and for a period thereafter performed administrative and judicial functions in conjunction with the king. The first offshoot was Exchequer, which originally was charged with the collection and administration of the king's finances, but by 1250 had acquired full judicial jurisdiction. Next to develop separate status was Common Pleas, established by Henry II as the primary tribunal to hear cases not involving the crown. The remaining part of the King's Court supervised Common Pleas through the writ of error, and heard matters particularly touching the king's interests, such as criminal actions and cases involving his tenants in chief; it developed into King's Bench, but the fiction was maintained that hearings before that tribunal were before the king himself. See Plucknett, A Concise History of the Common Law 143–51 (5th ed. 1956).

2. "[H]is * * * bill against William Warner, * * * in the custody of the marshal, & c." Common Pleas was supposed to have exclusive jurisdiction over actions of debt, such as Veale v. Warner. But the judges and lawyers of each common-law court zealously sought to expand the jurisdiction of their tribunal, and Veale v. Warner illustrates one method by which King's Bench accomplished this. Not all common-law proceedings were commenced by writ; to an undefined extent each court could proceed on a *bill,* which was a complaint addressed directly to the court. See 2 Holdsworth, A History of English Law 339 (3d ed. 1923). One instance in which a court clearly could proceed on a bill was an action against one of the court's officers or a person within its custody, and such a bill might be brought on a cause of action that ordinarily was not within the jurisdiction of the court. Thus, a plaintiff who desired to bring an action of debt in King's Bench would first charge defendant with trespass, and by a "bill of Middlesex" that court would order the sheriff of Middlesex to arrest defendant and deliver him to the custody of the marshal of the Marshalsea—the court's prison; once defendant was within the custody of King's Bench, plaintiff could proceed against him by bill in the action of debt. Predictably, the arrest and commitment eventually became wholly fictitious, but defendant was not permitted to challenge the allegation that they had occurred. A similar device used to expand the jurisdiction of Exchequer was the writ of *quo minus,* by which a debtor to the crown could bring suit in that court on the theory that anyone withholding money from the debtor was rendering him unable to pay what was owed the king; in time, the allegation of plaintiff's debt to the king also became untraversable. See Plucknett, op. cit. supra at 161, 387; Milsom, Historical Foundations of the Common Law 53–59 (1969).

3. "[P]ledges of prosecution." The original writ in a lawsuit directed the sheriff, to whom it was addressed, to take some action, conditioned on plaintiff's "mak[ing] you secure of prosecuting his claim." Thus plaintiff had to furnish sureties, who would be liable to pay a fine that was imposed upon unsuccessful claimants. As the names of the pledges in the case suggest, the requirement became a sham.

4. "[I]n the parish of St. Mary-le Bow in the ward of Cheap." As the jury originally decided cases on its own knowledge, it was necessary that jurors be drawn from the vicinity in which a transaction had occurred; the action therefore had to be brought near the place at which it arose, and the declaration had to show this. Since an English court could not summon jurors

from abroad, technically it would have been impossible to bring an action on a contract made outside England. In such cases, however, plaintiff made an untraversable allegation that the contract had been made in the aforesaid parish and ward of the city of London. See Sack, Conflict of Laws in the History of English Law, *in* 3 Law: A Century of Progress 342, 370 (1937). Some cases actually must have arisen there, but you cannot tell from the records which they are.

5. "[T]o the Court * * * now here shewn"; "prays oyer." A plaintiff suing upon a deed or a bond made profert of the document—that is, the plaintiff formally tendered it to the court, although it was strictly speaking not a part of the pleading. If defendant wanted to get the document in the pleadings in order to raise a question of law about it, she had to demand oyer of it, which meant that defendant was entitled to read it and copy as much of it as she chose into the plea. At this point you might conclude that if defendant demurred, she would be demurring to her own pleading, but even though the document was set out in the plea, it was treated as if it were a part of the declaration. See Sutton, Personal Actions at Common Law 103 (1929), which is a particularly valuable introduction to common-law pleading. In what way does this process resemble the modern motion for summary judgment? See pp. 958–87, infra.

6. "[W]herefore he prays judgment if the said Thomas ought to have or maintain his said action." This is the standard conclusion of a pleading in confession and avoidance. Compare the conclusion of plaintiff's replication in the next paragraph of the report of the case. Why was defendant's allegation that he had performed the bond treated as a matter of confession and avoidance?

7. "[W]herefore he prays judgment if the said Thomas ought to be admitted, against his own acknowledgment, to say." Plaintiff in his replication had traversed defendant's claim of payment. Thus the replication already had created an issue, and defendant's rejoinder could not be one of the three responses described in the Overview of Common–Law Pleading, pp. 505–06, supra; it is a plea of estoppel, and as stated in Saunders' argument waives the issue created by the traverse in plaintiff's replication. Why was this rejoinder "bad"? Did it allege that the award had been paid?

8. Why did Saunders, a thoroughly capable lawyer, file what he knew was an inadequate rejoinder? The answer lies in a peculiar facet of the demurrer:

> * * * *[O]n demurrer the court will consider the whole record, and give judgment for the party, who on the whole, appears to be entitled to it.* Thus, on demurrer to the replication, if the court think the replication bad, but perceive a substantial fault in the *plea,* they will give judgment, not for the defendant, but the plaintiff, provided the *declaration* be good; but if the declaration also be bad in substance, then, upon the same principle, judgment would be given for the defendant.

Stephen, The Principles of Pleading in Civil Actions 160 (Tyler ed. 1882). Thus, by making a rejoinder that he knew plaintiff would demur to, Saunders baited the trap he had set in his plea.

9. "[A]n English bill in the Exchequer." That part of the report of Veale v. Warner beginning, "But it was a case of the greatest hardship * * * " is not a part of the record, but is simply the reporter's justification of his own tactics. An English bill was a bill in equity, so-called because it was written in English rather than in the Latin of the common-law courts. As we will see, many instances of fraud and overreaching did not constitute defenses at law, but when such factors were established equity would enjoin a victorious plaintiff from enforcing the judgment at law. See p. 540, infra. But how could such relief be obtained in Exchequer, which was a common-law court? The answer is that Exchequer had an equity side.

2. THE QUEST FOR A SINGLE ISSUE: PATHS AND PITFALLS

The principal aim of common-law pleading was the production of a single issue; in many ways, the most serious problems in common-law pleading grew out of this persistent drive. To achieve the goal of singleness of issue, it was necessary to prohibit *duplicity* in pleading. That term did not connote fraud, but simply meant raising more than one issue in a pleading. Thus, in our example concerning the sale of the horse, defendant might wish to deny that he had made any promise *and* to assert that he was a minor at the time *and* to contend that a promise was not good consideration for another promise. There would be nothing devious or inconsistent in claiming all three defenses, but he was not permitted to do so. The traverse, the plea in confession and avoidance, and the demurrer were mutually exclusive.

A procedure was available that, in effect, permitted a party to delay the "demurrer." After trial and verdict for plaintiff, defendant could *move to arrest the judgment,* thereby raising the question whether the pleadings could support the judgment. In the case of a verdict for defendant, plaintiff's equivalent motion was for *judgment notwithstanding the verdict*—a term that has now come to identify a motion on a quite different theory. See p. 1070, infra. By following this procedure, however, a party could not escape the expense of trial (costs not being awarded to the prevailing party on such a motion), and that party assumed the risk that the defect in a pleading might be cured by a later pleading or aided by the verdict; in any event, a fault that required the use of a special demurrer would not support such a delayed motion. Nonetheless, the practice became very popular.

No such procedure was available to the party who wanted to deny his adversary's allegations and at the same time advance affirmative allegations of his own. For the plea in confession and avoidance had to give *color.* "As a term of pleading, * * * ['color'] signifies an apparent or prima facie right; and the meaning of the rule, that every pleading in confession and avoidance must give color, is, that it must admit an apparent right in the opposite party, and rely, therefore, on some new matter by which that apparent right is defeated." Stephen, The Principles of Pleading in Civil

Actions 206–07 (Tyler ed. 1882). A plea in confession and avoidance that failed to give color was doomed, even though it revealed a defense that could have been raised by traverse. In GIBBONS v. PEPPER, 1 Ld.Raym. 38, 91 Eng.Rep. 922 (K.B. 1695), an action for running down plaintiff, defendant admitted the trespass but pleaded that his horse had become so frightened he could not control it; on demurrer the court ordered judgment for plaintiff, holding that if defendant's facts were true there had been no battery at all and the plea should have been a traverse.

Out of this rule that a party could not plead new matter without confessing the opposing party's prima-facie right grew one of the weirder formulae of common-law pleading—the giving of *express color*. Today, we mercifully are spared the necessity of learning the hoary details that surrounded this device, but a brief look at it will illustrate the complexities of the system that lay beneath the surface of our original simple outline.

Suppose that plaintiff had brought an action of trespass against defendant for entering on plaintiff's land, and that the only genuine issue in the case was the title to the land, defendant contending that although plaintiff had been in possession of the land, defendant was the true owner. If defendant denied the trespass by a traverse, she would be permitted to establish her own title as a defense. However, even if the only issue concerning her title was a question of law, there would have to be a full trial and the case would be decided by a jury under the guidance of the judge. Trial could not be avoided unless defendant somehow could introduce the new matter—her claim of title—into the pleadings and thereby permit it to be made the subject of a demurrer. Yet under the rule that required a plea in confession and avoidance to give color to plaintiff's claim, defendant could not assert new matter without confessing plaintiff's apparent right. The solution of express color was for defendant to confess the existence of a plausible, but imperfect, title in plaintiff, and then to assert her own title by way of avoidance. Having done this, plaintiff could not traverse the confession—even though it was the sheerest fiction—for that would leave two issues in the case; he had to respond to the matter pleaded in avoidance, and when the validity of defendant's claim turned on a question of law, the appropriate response would be a demurrer. You should note, however, that although giving express color enabled defendant to introduce her claim of title into the case, defendant was not able at the same time to deny that she had entered the land at all.

The insistence on arriving at a single issue also prohibited raising more than one issue of fact in a pleading. The fault could be challenged only by a special demurrer, and over a long period the strictness of the prohibition against multiple issues was relaxed, but it never ceased to pose a problem for the pleader. Originally a declaration could not state more than one cause of action; at an early date, however, plaintiffs were permitted to join causes of action arising under the same writ, and, as long as they were stated in separate counts, different versions of the same cause of action could be pleaded.[f] Defendant was permitted to plead separately to each count, and indeed might demur to one, traverse a second, and confess and avoid a third. But defendant could not plead two or more defenses to a single count and the ability to deny more than one of its allegations was severely restricted. By a statute, 4 Anne, c. 16, § 4 (1705), this was changed to allow more than one plea to a count with the court's permission, but as long as common-law pleading survived there could be no more than one replication to a plea.

As a consequence of these rules, a defendant who did not demur was safest if he could make a defense under a plea of the *general issue,* which challenged plaintiff's whole case.[g] This plea spared defendant the necessity of spelling out his defense, which meant that he did not have to divulge it to plaintiff or run the risk of misstating it. More importantly, the general issue in effect permitted defendant to traverse a number of plaintiff's allegations and, in addition, to raise defenses that ordinarily would be matters of confession and avoidance. Of course not all defenses could be raised under the general issue, and knowing which defenses had to be specially pleaded in particular forms of action was a matter of subtle learning. Although the whole theoretical structure of common-law pleading and its quest for a single issue was threatened by the general issue, inexorable pressures—particularly in the eighteenth century—gradually expanded its scope and availability. In conjunction with the common counts—a particularly cryptic form of declaration in contract, see p. 532, infra—the plea of the general issue permitted some cases to come to trial with the issues not only unnarrowed, but indeed undisclosed. A good example of the problem was stated by Henry Brougham in a seminal speech to Parliament on law reform:

> * * * The plaintiff declares, that the defendant, being indebted to him for so much money had and received to the use of the said plaintiff * * * undertook and faithfully promised to pay it, but broke his engagement; and the count is thus framed, the self-same terms being invariably used, whatever be the cause of action which can be brought into Court under this head. * * * In the first place, such is the declaration for money paid by one individual to another, for the use and benefit of the plaintiff; this is what alone the words of the count imply, but to express this they are rarely, indeed, made use of. 2dly, The self-same terms are used on suing for money received on a

---

f. This privilege was widely used because of the strictness of the rule against *variances* between pleading and proof. A good example of the prohibition on variances is Latham v. Rutley, 2 B. & C. 20, 107 Eng.Rep. 290 (K.B. 1823). Plaintiff who had pleaded breach of a contract to carry and deliver goods safely was nonsuited because he proved a contract to carry and deliver goods safely, fire and robbery excepted, even though the verdict established that the loss was not caused by either fire or robbery.

g. Plaintiff's equivalent to the plea of the general issue, the replication *de injuria,* was less frequently available, and in most cases plaintiff was permitted to seize on only one facet of the plea. The most famous illustration is Crogate's Case, 8 Coke 66b, 77 Eng.Rep. 574 (K.B. 1608), which forms the basis for a brilliant satire on the common-law system. Hayes, *Crogate's Case: A Dialogue in Ye Shades on Special Pleading,* in 9 Holdsworth, A History of English Law 417 (2d ed. 1938).

consideration that fails, and used in the same way to describe all the endless variety of cases which can occur of such failure * * *. 3dly, The same words are used * * * to recover money paid under mistake of fact. 4thly, To recover money paid by one person to a stakeholder, in consideration of an illegal contract made with another person. 5thly, Money paid to revenue officers for releasing the goods illegally detained, of the person paying. 6thly, To try the right to any office, instead of bringing an assize. 7thly, To try the liability of the landlord for rates levied on his tenant. What information, then, does such a declaration give?

* * *

In the [form of action of] *indebitatus assumpsit,* from which I took my first example, * * * under [a plea of the general issue] no less than eight different defences may be set up; as, for instance, a denial of the contract, payment, usury, gaming, infancy, coverture, accord and satisfaction, release.

Brougham, Present State of the Law 70–71, 73 (1828).

Thus the pleadings in the English common-law courts immediately preceding the period of reform that began in 1825 presented a strange potpourri of ornate and sinuous paths toward an elusive single issue, side by side with a series of pleading rules that fostered abstract and unilluminating statements of dispute.

SECTION B. THE FORMS OF ACTION

1. THE DEVELOPMENT OF THE FORMS— CHIEFLY OF TRESPASS

MAITLAND, EQUITY, ALSO THE FORMS OF ACTION AT COMMON LAW 296, 298–99, 304–05, 314–15, 332, 335, 342–47, 359–61 (1909):

Let it be granted that one man has been wronged by another; the first thing that he or his advisers have to consider is what form of action he shall bring. * * * This choice is not merely a choice between a number of queer technical terms, it is a choice between methods of procedure adapted to cases of different kinds.

* * * '[A] form of action' has implied a particular original process, a particular mesne process, a particular final process, a particular mode of pleading, of trial, of judgment. But further to a very considerable degree the substantive law administered in a given form of action has grown up independently of the law administered in other forms. Each procedural pigeon-hole contains its own rules of substantive law, and it is with great caution that we may argue from what is found in one to what will probably be found in another; each has its own precedents. It is quite possible that a litigant will find that his case will fit some two or three of these pigeon-holes. If that be so he will have a choice, which will often be a

choice between the old, cumbrous, costly, on the one hand, the modern, rapid, cheap, on the other. Or again he may make a bad choice, fail in his action, and take such comfort as he can from the hints of the judges that another form of action might have been more successful. * * * Lastly he may find that, plausible as his case may seem, it just will not fit any one of the receptacles provided by the courts and he may take to himself the lesson that where there is no remedy there is no wrong.

* * * So long as the forms of action were still in use, it was difficult to tell the truth about their history. * * * But now, * * * the truth might be discovered and be told, and one part of the truth is assuredly this that throughout the early history of the forms of action there is an element of struggle, of struggle for jurisdiction. In order to understand them we must not presuppose a centralized system of justice * * *; rather we must think that the forms of action, the original writs, are the means whereby justice is becoming centralized, whereby the king's court is drawing away business from other courts.

* * * I shall attempt a sketch in brief outline of the order in which the different forms of action are developed. * * *

I. 1066–1154. The first [period] * * * would end with the great reforms of Henry II. Litigation of an ordinary kind still takes place chiefly in the communal and feudal courts; even the king's court may be considered as a feudal court, a court of and for the king's tenants in chief. * * * His court is concerned chiefly with (1) the pleas of the crown, i.e. cases in which royal rights are concerned, (2) litigation between the king's tenants in chief—for such tenants it is the proper feudal court, (3) complaints of default of justice in lower courts. * * *

II. 1154–1189. The legislative activity of Henry II's reign marks a second period. Under Henry II the exceptional becomes normal. He places royal justice at the disposal of anyone who can bring his case within a certain formula. From the end of his reign we have Glanvill's book, and we see already a considerable apparatus of writs * * *; they have assumed distinct forms, forms which they will preserve until the nineteenth century * * *; each writ is the beginning of a particular form of action. * * *

As regards those claims which in after days give rise to the personal actions, those actions which, as we say, are founded on contract or founded on tort, Glanvill has but little to tell us; they are seldom prosecuted in the king's court. But the action of Debt is known there. * * *

III. 1189–1272. This, our third period, extending from the death of Henry II to the accession of Edward I, is a period of rapid growth * * *. New writs are freely invented, though towards the end of Henry III's reign this gives rise to murmurs * * *. There is now a large store of original writs which are writs of course (*brevia de cursu*), that is to say, they may be obtained from the subordinate officers of the royal chancery * * *.

Meanwhile the actions which came to be known as personal make their appearance. The oldest seems to be 'Debt–Detinue' * * *. Gradually this action divides itself into two, Detinue for a specific chattel, Debt for a sum of money—this differentiation takes place early in the thirteenth century. As in Detinue the judgment given for the plaintiff awards him either the chattel itself, or its value; and, as the defendant thus has the option of giving back the chattel or paying its value, Bracton is led to make the important remark that there is no real action for chattels—an important remark, for it is the foundation of all our talk about real and personal property. To Debt and Detinue we must now add Replevin, the action for goods unlawfully taken in distress. * * * Covenant also has appeared * * *. Gradually the judges came to the opinion that the only acceptable evidence of a covenant is a sealed writing, and one of the foundations of our law of contract is thus laid. * * *

But the most important phenomenon is the appearance of Trespass—that fertile mother of actions. Instances of what we can not but call actions of trespass are found even in John's reign, but I think it clear that the writ of trespass did not become a writ of course until very late in Henry III's reign. Now trespass * * * has its roots in criminal law * * *. The old criminal action (yes, action) was the Appeal of Felony * * *. It was but slowly supplanted by indictment—the procedure of the common accuser set going by Henry II, the appeal on the other hand being an action brought by a person aggrieved by the crime.

* * * The new phenomenon appears about the year 1250, it is an action which might be called an attenuated appeal based on an act of violence. * * * The action of trespass is founded on a breach of the king's peace:—with force and arms the defendant has assaulted and beaten the plaintiff, broken the plaintiff's close, or carried off the plaintiff's goods; he is sued for damages. The plaintiff seeks not violence but compensation, but the unsuccessful defendant will also be punished and pretty severely. In other actions the unsuccessful party has to pay an amercement for making an unjust, or resisting a just claim; the defendant found guilty of trespass is fined and imprisoned. What is more, the action for trespass shows its semi-criminal nature in the process that can be used against a defendant who will not appear—if he will not appear, his body can be seized and imprisoned; if he can not be found, he may be outlawed. We thus can see that the action of trespass is one that will become very popular with plaintiffs because of the stringent process against defendants. I very much doubt whether in Henry III's day the action could as yet be used save where there really had been what we might fairly call violence and breach of the peace; but gradually the convenience of this new action showed itself. In order to constitute a case for 'Trespass *vi et armis*,' it was to the last necessary that there should be some wrongful application of physical force to the defendant's lands or goods or person—but a wrongful step on his land, a wrongful touch to his person or chattels

was held to be force enough and an adequate breach of the king's peace. This action then has the future before it.

* * *

IV. 1272–1307. The reign of 'the English Justinian' may be treated as a period by itself—a period of statutory activity. Statutes made by king and parliament now interfere with many details both of substantive law and of procedure. * * * The whole system stiffens. Men have learnt that a power to invent new remedies is a power to create new rights and duties, and it is no longer to be suffered that the chancellor or the judges should wield this power. How far the process of crystallisation had gone, how rigid the system was becoming, we learn from a section of the Statute of Westminster II, 13 Edw. I c. 24 (1285). Men have been obliged to depart from the Chancery without getting writs, because there are none which will exactly fit their cases, although these cases fall within admitted principles. It is not to be so for the future * * *. 'And whensoever from henceforth it shall fortune in the Chancery, that in one case a writ is found, and in a like case falling under like law, and requiring like remedy, is found none, the clerks of the Chancery shall agree in making the writ; or * * * let the cases be written in which they can not agree, and let them refer them until the next Parliament, and by consent of men learned in the law, a writ shall be made, lest it might happen after that the court should long time fail to minister justice unto complainants.' * * * [W]hen we say that but little use was made of this Statute there is one great exception. It is regarded as the statutory warrant for the variation of the writs of trespass so as to suit special cases, until at length—about the end of the Middle Ages—lawyers perceive that they have a new form 'Trespass upon the special case' or 'Case.' * * * It is worth noting that a writ issued by the Chancery is not necessarily a good writ. The justices may quash it as contrary to law, and in the later Middle Ages the judges are conservative * * *. At any rate the tale of common law (*i.e.* non-statutory) actions was now regarded as complete. The king's courts had come to be regarded as omnicompetent courts, they had to do all the important civil justice of the realm and to do it with the limited supply of forms of action which had been gradually accumulated in the days when feudal justice and ecclesiastical justice were serious competitors with royal justice.

V. 1307–1833 * * *

From Edward I's day onwards trespass *vi et armis* is a common action. We may notice three main varieties—unlawful force has been used against the body, the goods, the land of the plaintiff; so we have trespass in assault and battery, trespass *de bonis asportatis, trespass quare clausum fregit.* * * *

I have already said that the writ-making power wielded by the king and his Chancellor was gradually curbed by our parliamentary constitution, and in Edward I's day it has become necessary to tell the Chancery that it is not to be too pedantic, but may make variations in the old formulas when a new case falls under an old rule. * * * [T]he most important use made of this liberty consisted in some extensions of the action of trespass. Gradually during Edward III's reign we find a few writs occurring which in form are extremely like writs of trespass—and they are actually called writs of trespass—but the wrong complained of does not always consist of a direct application of unlawful physical force * * *; sometimes the words *vi et armis* do not appear. Sometimes there is no mention of the king's peace. Still they are spoken of as writs of trespass * * *. The plaintiff is said to bring an action upon his case, or upon the special case, and gradually it becomes apparent that really a new and a very elastic form of action has thus been created. I think that lawyers were becoming conscious of this about the end of the fourteenth century. Certain procedural differences have made their appearance—when there is *vi et armis* in the writ, then the defendant if he will not appear may be taken by *capias ad respondendum* or may be outlawed—this can not be if there is no talk of force and arms or the king's peace. Thus Case falls apart from Trespass—during the fifteenth century the line between them becomes always better marked. * * *

Case becomes a sort of general residuary action; much, particularly, of the modern law of negligence developed within it. Sometimes it is difficult to mark off case from trespass.

NOTES AND QUESTIONS

1. Case developed into a remedy not only for wrongs that were similar to those governed by trespass, but for wrongs that were much more similar to those for which the action of debt was appropriate. Yet case never lost its roots in trespass. Why didn't actions of debt on the case develop? See Kiralfy, The Action on the Case 3, 44 (1951).

2. Maitland's conclusions that trespass grew out of the appeal of felony and that case drew its authority from the Statute of Westminster II are debatable. Others have found the root of trespass in the assize of novel disseisin, in the proceedings of local courts, and in *queralae* ("innominate" actions without writ frequently found in the records of royal courts throughout the thirteenth century). The diversity of opinion is comprehensively reported in Fifoot, History and Sources of the Common Law—Tort and Contract 44–56, 66–74 (1949), a book of very great value in the study of the forms. See also Milsom, Historical Foundations of the Common Law 244–70 (1969).

3. In England's American colonies, the distinctions between the forms of action, although recognized, were not enforced with the rigor that characterized the procedure of the mother country. For example, there are instances of the use of both trespass and case for the specific recovery of chattels and real property, and trover and assumpsit frequently were not distinguished from case. Ejectment, when it was still regarded as a modern improvement in England, was unused in New England because of its technicalities. See Morris, Studies in the History of American Law 46–59 (2d ed. 1959). Since law books were scarce in the colonies, and many of the judges were laymen, these developments were to be expected. The most technical applications of the

forms of action in this country came during the first half of the nineteenth century after the bar had grown in influence, and texts such as Blackstone had become available. See, e.g., Adams v. Hemmenway, 1 Mass. 145 (1804); Wilson v. Smith, 10 Wend. 324 (N.Y.1833).

2. THE LINES BLUR

A. TRESPASS OR CASE?

SCOTT, AN INFANT, BY HIS NEXT FRIEND v. SHEPHERD, AN INFANT, BY GUARDIAN

Court of Common Pleas, 1773.
2 Wm.Bl. 892, 96 Eng.Rep. 525.

Trespass and assault * * *. On not guilty pleaded, the cause came on to be tried before Nares, J., * * * when the jury found a verdict for the plaintiff with 100£. damages, subject to the opinion of the Court on this case: * * * [D]efendant threw a lighted squib, made of gunpowder, & c. from the street into the market-house, * * * where a large concourse of people were assembled; which lighted squib, * * * fell upon the standing of one Yates, who sold gingerbread, & c. That one Willis instantly, and to prevent injury to himself and the said wares of the said Yates, took up the said lighted squib from off the said standing, and then threw it across the said market-house, when it fell upon another standing there of one Ryal, * * * who instantly, and to save his own goods from being injured, took up the said lighted squib from off the said standing, and then threw it to another part of the said market-house, and, in so throwing it, struck the plaintiff * * * in the face therewith, and the combustible matter then bursting, put out one of the plaintiff's eyes. Qu. If this action be maintainable?

* * *

NARES, J., was of opinion, that trespass would well lie in the present case. That the natural and probable consequence of the act done by the defendant was injury to somebody, and therefore the act was illegal at common law. * * * Being therefore unlawful, the defendant was liable to answer for the consequences, be the injury mediate or immediate. * * * The principle I go upon is what is laid down in *Reynolds and Clark,* Stra. 634, that if the act in the first instance be unlawful, trespass will lie. Wherever therefore an act is unlawful at first, trespass will lie for the consequences of it. * * * [Defendant] * * * is the person, who, in the present case, gave the mischievous faculty to the squib. That mischievous faculty remained in it till the explosion. No new power of doing mischief was communicated to it by Willis or Ryal. It is like the case of a mad ox turned loose in a crowd. The person who turns him loose is answerable in trespass for whatever mischief he may do. The intermediate acts of Willis and Ryal will not purge the original tort in the defendant. * * *

BLACKSTONE, J., was of opinion, that an action of trespass did not lie for Scott against Shepherd upon this case. He took the settled distinction to be, that where the injury is immediate, an action of trespass will lie; where it is only consequential, it must be an action on the case: *Reynolds and Clarke,* Lord Raym. 1401. * * * The lawfulness or unlawfulness of the original act is not the criterion; though something of that sort is put into Lord Raymond's mouth in Stra. 635 * * *. But this cannot be the general rule; for it is held by the Court in the same case, that if I throw a log of timber into the highway, (which is an unlawful act), and another man tumbles over it, and is hurt, an action on the case only lies, it being a consequential damage; but if in throwing it I hit another man, he may bring trespass, because it is an immediate wrong. Trespass may sometimes lie for the consequences of a lawful act. If in lopping my own trees a bough accidentally falls on my neighbour's ground, and I go thereon to fetch it, trespass lies. * * * But then the entry is of itself an immediate wrong. And case will sometimes lie for the consequence of an unlawful act. If by false imprisonment I have a special damage, as if I forfeit my recognizance thereby, I shall have an action on the case. * * * Yet here the original act was unlawful, and in the nature of trespass. So that lawful or unlawful is quite out of the case; the solid distinction is between direct or immediate injuries on the one hand, and mediate or consequential on the other. And trespass never lay for the latter. If this be so, the only question will be, whether the injury which the plaintiff suffered was immediate, or consequential only; and I hold it to be the latter. The original act was, as against Yates, a trespass; not as against Ryal, or Scott. The tortious act was complete when the squib lay at rest upon Yates's stall. He, or any bystander, had, I allow, a right to protect themselves by removing the squib, but should have taken care to do it in such a manner as not to endamage others. But Shepherd, I think, is not answerable in an action of trespass and assault for the mischief done by the squib in the new motion impressed upon it, and the new direction given it, by either Willis or Ryal; who both were free agents, and acted upon their own judgment. This differs it from the cases put of turning loose a wild beast or a madman. They are only instruments in the hand of the first agent. Nor is it like diverting the course of an enraged ox, or of a stone thrown, or an arrow glancing against a tree; because there the original motion, the vis impressa, is continued, though diverted. Here the instrument of mischief was at rest, till a new impetus and a new direction are given it, not once only, but by two successive rational agents. But it is said that the act is not complete, nor the squib at rest, till after it is spent or exploded. It certainly has a power of doing fresh mischief, and so has a stone that has been thrown against my windows, and now lies still. Yet if any person gives that stone a new motion, and does farther mischief with it, trespass will not lie for that against the original thrower. No doubt but Yates may maintain trespass against Shepherd. And, according to the doctrine contended for, so may Ryal and Scott. Three actions for one single act! nay, it may be extended in infinitum. If a man tosses a football into the street, and after being kicked about by one hundred people, it at last breaks a tradesman's windows; shall he have trespass against the man who first produced it? Surely only against the man who gave it that mischievous direction. But it is said, if Scott has no action against Shepherd, against whom must he seek his remedy? I give no opinion whether case would lie against Shepherd for the consequential damage; though, as at present advised, I think, upon the circumstances, it would. But I think, in strictness of law, trespass would lie against Ryal, the immediate actor in this unhappy business. * * * The throwing it across the market-house, instead of brushing it down, or throwing [it] out of the open sides into the street, (if it was not meant to continue the sport, as it is called), was at least an unnecessary and incautious act. * * * And I admit that the defendant is answerable in trespass for all the direct and inevitable effects caused by his own immediate act. * * * But he is not responsible for the acts of other men. * * * In our case the verdict is suspended till the determination of the Court. And though after verdict the Court will not look with eagle's eyes to spy out a variance, yet, when a question is put by the jury upon such a variance, and it is made the very point of the cause, the Court will not wink against the light, and say that evidence, which at most is only applicable to an action on the case, will maintain an action of trespass. * * * The same evidence that will maintain trespass, may also frequently maintain case, but not e converso. Every action of trespass with a "per quod" includes an action on the case. I may bring trespass for the immediate injury, and subjoin a "per quod" for the consequential damages;—or may bring case for the consequential damages, and pass over the immediate injury * * *. But if I bring trespass for an immediate injury, and prove at most only a consequential damage, judgment must be for the defendant * * *.

GOULD, J., was of the same opinion with Nares, J., that this action was well maintainable.—The whole difficulty lies in the form of the action, and not in the substance of the remedy. The line is very nice between case and trespass upon these occasions: I am persuaded there are many instances wherein both or either will lie. I agree with brother Nares, that wherever a man does an unlawful act, he is answerable for all the consequences; and trespass will lie against him, if the consequence be in nature of trespass. But, exclusive of this, I think the defendant may be considered in the same view as if he himself had personally thrown the squib in the plaintiff's face. The terror impressed upon Willis and Ryal excited self-defence, and deprived them of the power of recollection. * * *

DE GREY, C.J. * * * I agree with my brother Blackstone as to the principles he has laid down, but not in his application of those principles to the present case. The real question certainly does not turn upon the lawfulness or unlawfulness of the original act; for actions of trespass will lie for legal acts when they become trespasses by accident * * *. They may also not lie for the consequences even of illegal acts, as that of casting a log in the highway, & c.—But the true question is, whether the injury is the direct and immediate act of the defendant; and I am of opinion, that in this case it is. The throwing the squib was an act unlawful and tending to affright the bystanders. So far, mischief was originally intended; not any particular mischief, but mischief indiscriminate and wanton. Whatever mischief therefore follows, he is the author of it * * *. Every one who does an unlawful act is considered as the doer of all that follows. * * * I look upon all that was done subsequent to the original throwing as a continuation of the first force and first act, which will continue till the squib was spent by bursting. And I think that any innocent person removing the danger from himself to another is justifiable; the blame lights upon the first thrower. * * * It has been urged, that the intervention of a free agent will make a difference: but I do not consider Willis and Ryal as free agents in the present case, but acting under a compulsive necessity for their own safety and self-preservation. * * *

Postea to the plaintiff.

NOTES AND QUESTIONS

1. In what ways does Justice Blackstone differ from Chief Justice De Grey? From Justice Nares? On what facts might Chief Justice De Grey and Justice Nares reach a different result? Chief Justice De Grey and Justice Gould? Since Justice Blackstone believes an action in case would lie against Shepherd, is there really any substantive difference between him and his brethren? Would they have agreed with him that Scott could have maintained an action against Ryal? What would have been the nature of that action? In light of Gibbons v. Pepper, p. 512, supra, would actions of trespass lie against both Shepherd and Ryal?

2. Trials ordinarily were held at common law before a single judge and a jury. After verdict, if the losing party wanted the judgment of the entire court on a question of law that was involved in the case, that party asked for a rule *nisi*. A hearing before the court *en banc* was then held, and if that court sustained the rulings of the trial judge it denied the rule; otherwise, it made the rule *absolute*. When a verdict was taken subject to the opinion of the court *en banc*, as in Scott v. Shepherd, the ordinary procedure of applying for a rule *nisi* was unnecessary. Therefore, instead of denying a rule or making it absolute, the order of the court *en banc* was in the form of a *postea* to the prevailing party, which authorized the entry of judgment.

B. CASE CAPTURES NEGLIGENCE

The close of the eighteenth century brought before the judges a great number of cases of a kind theretofore little known but which ever since have glutted our courts: running-down accidents and vehicular collisions. Echoes of Lord Raymond's distinction in Reynolds v. Clarke were less frequently heard, but the categories of direct and indirect injuries became mixed with those of wilful and negligent conduct, often in a context complicated by the involvement of servants. Matters would not stay within the simple confines that Justice Blackstone envisioned.

DAY v. EDWARDS, 5 T.R. 648, 101 Eng.Rep. 361 (K.B.1794), was an action in case against a defendant who had driven his cart "so furiously, negligently and improperly" that it "struck with great force and violence * * * against plaintiff's carriage." Plaintiff's lawyer touched on all the elements that had been or would become significant—legality, indirectness, negligence; the "act of driving * * * in consequence of which the injury arose, was a legal one in itself, although negligently exercised," he said. But Lord Kenyon merely repeated the immediate injury-consequential injury distinction, found that plaintiff "complains of the immediate act," and gave judgment for defendant.

One year later in MORLEY v. GAISFORD, 2 H.Bl. 441, 126 Eng.Rep. 639 (C.P.1795), Common Pleas held case was proper when defendant's servant was alleged to have "badly, ignorantly, and negligently" driven a cart against plaintiff's chaise, saying "it was difficult to put a case where the master could be considered as a trespasser for an act of his servant, which was not done at his command."

The *Morley* holding clearly turned on the issue of a master's liability in trespass, but when plaintiffs brought an action of case against defendants for having "so incautiously, carelessly, negligently, and inexpertly managed, steered and directed" their ship that it collided with plaintiffs' vessel, their counsel relied upon *Morley* solely for the proposition that trespass lay for wilful conduct and case for negligence, and two of the three judges accepted it. OGLE v. BARNES, 8 T.R. 188, 101 Eng.Rep. 1338 (K.B.1799). Lord Kenyon continued to insist upon the distinction between an immediate and a consequential injury, but he agreed that case was proper, since the charge was that by reason of defendants' negligence, their ship sailed against plaintiffs' vessel.

By 1803, we find defendant in LEAME v. BRAY, 3 East 593, 102 Eng.Rep. 724 (K.B.), challenging an action of trespass for a highway collision on the ground that the evidence showed his conduct to be negligent only, and that the action should therefore have been case. The court, however, reaffirmed its position in Day v. Edwards, that trespass lay for an immediate injury. Justice Lawrence, who had sat in *Ogle*, explained now that "what I principally relied on there was, that it did not appear that the mischief happened from the personal acts of the defendants: it might have happened from the operation of the wind and tide counteracting their personal efforts at the time: or indeed they might not even have been on board."

Common Pleas, which now clearly favored case for these actions, twice suggested that *Leame* be reconsidered, but King's Bench under Lord Ellenborough stood fast. In HALL v. PICKARD, 3 Camp. 187, 170 Eng. Rep. 1350 (K.B.1812), however, he raised the question whether it "may * * * be worthy of consideration, whether, in those instances where trespass may be maintained, the party may not waive the trespass, and proceed for the tort?" Later cases built on this suggestion until at last WILLIAMS v. HOLLAND, 10 Bing. 112, 131 Eng.Rep. 848 (C.P.1833), was accepted as settling the matter:

The declaration * * * states the ground of action to be an injury occasioned by the carelessness and negligence of the Defendant in driving his own gig; * * * and the jury have found in the very terms of the declaration, that the jury [sic] was so occasioned. Under such a form of action, therefore, and with such a finding by the jury, the present objection ought not to prevail, unless some positive and inflexible rule of law, or some authority too strong to be overcome, is brought forward in its support. * * *

But upon examining the cases cited in argument, both in support of, and in answer to, the objection, we cannot find one in which it is distinctly held, that the present form of action is not maintainable under the circumstances of this case.

* * * [T]he late case of Moreton v. Hardern [4 B. & C. 223, 107 Eng.Rep. 1042 (K.B.1825)], appears to us to go the full length of deciding, that * * * where the injury is occasioned by the carelessness and negligence of the Defendant, the Plaintiff is at liberty to bring an action on the case, notwithstanding the act is immediate, so long as it is not a wilful act * * *.

3. THE LOSS AND DETENTION OF PERSONAL PROPERTY

The writ of detinue lay when defendant had possession of plaintiff's personal property and refused to relinquish it. The writ would lie, for example, against a bailee who refused to redeliver bailed goods or an executor who withheld the title-deed to an heir's real property. Although the gist of the action was wrongful detention, rather than wrongful taking, detinue would lie against a thief. But in this type of case trespass *de bonis asportatis* was preferred because detinue had several drawbacks: Defendant had a right to wage his law, and could deliver up the property in lieu of paying damages, even though it was damaged, for detinue did not lie for mere harm to goods.

Not surprisingly, plaintiffs began to try to substitute an action on the case in circumstances that seemed to call for detinue. They succeeded, first in the situation in which detinue was clearly inadequate—when the goods had spoiled—and then in situations in which its remedy might be appropriate but its mode of trial was unsatisfactory. See Fifoot, History and Sources of the Common Law—Tort and Contract 102–04 (1949). By 1500, case was essentially an alternative to detinue, and in the course of the sixteenth century a distinct species of case developed—the action of trover. The form of this new action was predicated upon a fiction—plaintiff alleged that he had lost goods, that they had been found by defendant and were now in that party's possession, and that defendant refused to deliver them upon request. Loss and finding soon became recognized as formal allegations only, but the allegations concerning the request for return of the goods and defendant's refusal to deliver retained some significance; after all, your bailee cannot be considered to have committed a tort if you have not asked for your goods back. What might constitute a legitimate, conditional refusal to deliver—as in the case of a finder who wished to check the credentials of a claimant—became an important issue. Apart from the fact that defendant was not entitled to wage his law, trover differed from detinue in this respect: Plaintiff was under no obligation to take back the goods, and in an action against a thief was under no obligation to demand them. The essence of trover was the conversion of the goods.

What is a conversion? The term has troubled the courts for several hundred years, but the most famous definition is that of Chief Justice Holt, in BALDWIN v. COLE, 6 Mod. 212, 87 Eng.Rep. 964 (K.B.1705): "[W]hat is a conversion, but an assuming upon one's self the property and right of disposing another's goods; and he that takes upon himself to detain another man's goods from him without cause, takes upon himself the right of disposing of them * * *." Is this really helpful? Consider the following case.

BUSHEL v. MILLER

Court of King's Bench, 1718.
1 Strange 128, 93 Eng.Rep. 428.

Upon the Custom–House quay there is a hut, where particular porters put in small parcels of goods, if the ship is not ready to receive them when they are brought upon the quay. The porters, who have a right in this hut, have each particular boxes or cupboards, and as such the defendant had one. The plaintiff being one of the porters puts in goods belonging to A and lays them so that the defendant could not get to his chest without removing them. He accordingly does remove them about a yard from the place where they lay, towards the door, and without returning them into their place goes away, and the goods are lost. The plaintiff satisfies A of the value of the goods, and brings trover against the defendant. And upon the trial two points were ruled by the C.J.

1. That the plaintiff having made satisfaction to A for the goods, had thereby acquired a sufficient property in them to maintain trover.

2. That there was no conversion in the defendant. The plaintiff by laying his goods where they obstructed the defendant from going to his chest, was in that respect a wrong-doer. The defendant had a right to remove the goods, so that thus far he was in no fault. Then as to the not returning the goods to the place where he found them; if this were an action of trespass, perhaps it might be a doubt; but he was clear it could not amount to a conversion.

NOTES AND QUESTIONS

1. Plaintiff's goods were delivered by a ship's captain to defendant wharfingers to be held for plaintiff. The goods were then lost or stolen from defendants. Could defendants be said to have converted them? In ROSS v.

JOHNSON, 5 Burrow 2825, 98 Eng.Rep. 483 (K.B.1772), Lord Mansfield said case, not trover, was the only remedy: "[I]n order to maintain trover, there must be an injurious conversion. This is not to be deemed a refusal to deliver the goods. They can't deliver them: it is not in their power to do it. It is a bare omission."

2. If defendant so negligently kept twenty barrels of plaintiff's butter that "they were become of little value," would trover lie? See Walgrave v. Ogden, 1 Leon. 224, 74 Eng.Rep. 205 (K.B.1590).

GORDON v. HARPER

Court of King's Bench, 1796.
7 T.R. 9, 101 Eng.Rep. 828.

In trover for certain goods, being household furniture * * *. [Plaintiff leased a house with the goods in question to A for a term still extant at the time of trial. While A was in possession under the lease, defendant sheriff seized the goods in execution of a judgment against B, who had sold the furniture to plaintiff sometime before the lease. Defendant after the seizure sold the goods.]

LORD KENYON, CH. J. The only point for the consideration of the Court in the case of Ward v. Macauley [4 T.R. 489, 100 Eng.Rep. 1135 (K.B. 1791)] was, whether in a case like the present, the landlord could maintain an action of trespass against the sheriff for seizing goods, let with a house, under an execution against the tenant; and it was properly decided that no such action could be maintained. What was said further by me in that case, that trover was the proper remedy, was an extrajudicial opinion, to which upon further consideration I cannot subscribe. The true question is, whether when a person has leased goods in a house to another for a certain time, whereby he parts with the right of possession during the term to the tenant, and has only a reversionary interest, he can notwithstanding recover the value of the whole property pending the existence of the term in an action of trover. The very statement of the proposition affords an answer to it. If, instead of household goods, the goods here taken had been machines used in manufacture, which had been leased to a tenant, no doubt could have been made but that the sheriff might have seized them under an execution against the tenant, and the creditor would have been entitled to the beneficial use of the property during the term: the difference of the goods then cannot vary the law. * * * I forbear to deliver any opinion as to what remedy the landlord has in this case, not being at present called upon so to do: but it is clear that he cannot maintain trover.

ASHHURST, J. I have always understood the rule of law to be, that in order to maintain trover the plaintiff must have a right of property in the thing, and a right of possession, and that unless both these rights concur, the action will not lie. * * *

GROSE, J. The only question is whether trover will lie where the plaintiff had neither the actual possession of the goods taken at the time, nor the right of possession. * * * Where goods are delivered to a carrier, the owner has still a right of possession as against a tort-feasor, and the carrier is no more than his servant. But here it is clear that the plaintiff had no right of possession; and he would be a trespasser if he took the goods from the tenant: then by what authority can he recover them from any other person during the term? * * *

LAWRENCE, J. * * *. Now here if the taking of the goods by the sheriff determined the interest of the tenant in them, and revested it in the landlord, I admit that the latter might maintain trover for them * * *: but it is clearly otherwise; for here the tenant's property and interest did not determine by the sheriff's trespass, and the tenant might maintain trespass against the wrong-doer, and recover damages. * * *

Postea to the defendant.

NOTES AND QUESTIONS

1. Plaintiff pawned a jeweled hatband to X for 25 pounds with no certain time fixed for redemption. X delivered it to defendant, and then died. Plaintiff tendered 25 pounds to the executrix, who refused it, and then demanded the hatband of defendant. Would trover lie? See Ratcliff v. Davies, Croke Jac. 244, 79 Eng.Rep. 210 (K.B.1611).

2. Plaintiff leased a farm with cattle to Y for one year. After a few months, Y sold the cattle to defendant and absconded. What theory might be used to allow plaintiff to bring trover against defendant? See Swift v. Moseley, 10 Vt. 208 (1838).

4. THE CREATION OF CONTRACT LAW

A. SPECIAL ASSUMPSIT

Glanvill said, shortly before 1200: "[I]t is not the custom of the court of the lord king to protect private agreements, nor does it concern itself with such contracts as can be considered to be like private agreements." The treatise on the laws and customs of the realm of England commonly called Glanvill, Bk. X [18] (Hall ed. 1965). By the middle of the fourteenth century, there remained a good deal of truth in this. Two forms of action, each with significant shortcomings, lay for breach of contract—the writs of covenant and debt. Covenant required a sealed instrument and did not lie when debt was available. Debt lay only when an agreement had been fully performed by one party and he was entitled to a sum certain, and as in the case of detinue, defendant was entitled to wage his law, unless the agreement was sealed. Again, plaintiffs resorted to case as a safety valve for the deficiencies of covenant and debt, but progress was slower than it had been in the evasion of detinue, perhaps because the effort was not so much to avoid a particular writ as to create a new area of substantive law.

By 1400, plaintiff could maintain case against a defendant who had carried out his promise so badly that plaintiff was in a worse position than before defendant made his promise. Thus in 1370 case was held to lie against a defendant who having undertaken to cure plaintiff's horse, treated it so negligently that it died. WALDON v. MARSHALL, Y.B.Mich. 43 Ed. 3, f. 33, pl. 38. Chief Justice Cavendish, in an action against a surgeon for maiming plaintiff while trying to cure him, said "this action of covenant of necessity is maintained without specialty, since for every little thing a man cannot always have a Clerk to make a specialty for him." THE SURGEON'S CASE, Y.B.Hil. 48 Ed. 3, f. 6, pl. 11 (K.B.1375). But case did not lie for nonfeasance. Through the fifteenth century there were occasional departures, but the courts seemed always to return to this rule. Then suddenly it was abandoned for good, and a new form of action developed from case and received judicial acceptance—special assumpsit. No single case seems to have established assumpsit as a remedy for nonperformance of a promise, but shortly after 1500 it had become the accepted view.

B. GENERAL ASSUMPSIT

Special assumpsit filled a major gap left by the action of debt, but it did not take the place of debt, as trover substantially had taken the place of detinue. For another century, argument flared on the question whether assumpsit would lie for a debt. Gradually it was established that if a person, who already was indebted to another, made a fresh promise to pay the debt, assumpsit would lie for a breach of that promise, even though it would not have lain for the debt itself. The question then arose whether the fresh promise actually had to be made, or assumpsit would lie even when the promise was a fiction. In part, the answer lay in the desires of two courts to draw business to themselves; debt was the exclusive province of Common Pleas, while assumpsit with its background in trespass could be brought there or in King's Bench. For thirty years they squabbled over the matter.

SLADE'S CASE

Court of Exchequer Chamber, 1602.
4 Co.Rep. 92b, 76 Eng.Rep. 1074.

John Slade brought an action on the case in the King's Bench against Humphrey Morley * * * and declared, that whereas the plaintiff * * * was possessed of a close of land * * * and being so possessed, the plaintiff * * * the said close had sowed with wheat and rye, which wheat and rye * * * were grown into blades, the defendant, in consideration that the plaintiff, at the special instance and request of the said Humphrey, had bargained and sold to him the said blades of wheat and rye growing upon the said close, * * * assumed and promised the plaintiff to pay him 16l. * * *: and for non-payment thereof * * * the plaintiff brought the said action: the defendant pleaded *non assumpsit modo et forma;* and on the trial of this issue the jurors gave a special verdict, *sc.* that the defendant bought of the plaintiff the wheat and rye in blades growing upon the said close * * * and further found, that between the plaintiff and the defendant there was no other promise or assumption but only the said bargain * * *. And for the honour of the law, and for the quiet of the subject in the appeasing of such diversity of opinions * * * the case was openly argued before all the Justices of England, and Barons of the Exchequer, * * * and after many conferences between the justices and Barons, it was resolved, that the action was maintainable, and that the plaintiff should have judgment. And in this case these points were resolved:—1. That although an action of debt lies upon the contract, yet the bargainor may have an action on the case, or an action of debt at his election * * *. 3. It was resolved, that every contract executory imports in itself an *assumpsit,* for when one agrees to pay money, or to deliver anything, thereby he assumes or promises to pay, or deliver it, and therefore when one sells any goods to another, and agrees to deliver them at a day to come, and the other in consideration thereof agrees to pay so much money as such a day, in that case both parties may have an action of debt, or an action on the case on *assumpsit,* for the mutual executory agreement of both parties imports in itself reciprocal actions upon the case, as well as actions of debt * * *. 4. It was resolved, that the plaintiff in this action on the case on assumpsit should not recover only damages for the special loss (if any be) which he had, but also for the whole debt, so that a recovery or bar in this action would be a good bar in an action of debt brought upon the same contract * * *. And as to the objection which has been made, that it would be mischievous to the defendant that he should not wage his law, forasmuch as he might pay it in secret: to that it was answered, that it should be accounted his folly that he did not take sufficient witnesses with him to prove the payment he made: but the mischief would be rather on the other party, for now experience proves that men's consciences grow so large that the respect of their private advantage rather induces men (and chiefly those who have declining estates) to perjury * * *.

NOTE

You should remember in considering the demise of wager of law that at this time, and for two centuries more, parties were incompetent to testify at a trial. The enactment of the Statute of Frauds, 29 Charles 2, c. 3 (1677), which required several kinds of contracts to be in writing, is attributed by many to the problem of proof posed by the result in Slade's Case. See, e.g., Plucknett, A Concise History of the Common Law 648 (5th ed. 1956).

The recognition of *indebitatus assumpsit* (literally, "being indebted, he promised"), or *general assumpsit,* did more than deliver the quietus to debt. The contract-like sanction it imposed upon an obligation that did not really arise out of an actual promise provided the structure for wholly new developments. When A has delivered goods to B or has performed services for the latter, it may be presumed that A expects payment and B expects to pay; but the common law had furnished no remedy in the absence of an actual agreement. Now a new action of quantum meruit developed based upon an implied promise to pay the reasonable value of the goods or services, not unlike the imputed promise to pay the debt that furnished the basis for Slade's Case. Even more significant was the extension of this same formula into circumstances in which a promise to pay was the last thing in defendant's mind.

LAMINE v. DORRELL

Court of Queen's Bench, 1705.
2 Ld.Raym. 1216, 92 Eng.Rep. 303.

In an indebitatus assumpsit for money received by the defendant to the use of the plaintiff as administrator of J.S. on non assumpsit pleaded, upon evidence the case appeared to be, that J.S. died intestate possessed of certain Irish debentures; and the defendant pretending to a right to be administrator, got administration granted to him, and by that means got these debentures into his hands, and disposed of them: then the defendant's administration was repealed, and administration granted to the plaintiff, and he brought this action against the defendant for the money he sold the debentures for. And it being objected upon the evidence, that this action would not lie, because the defendant sold the debentures as one that claimed a title and interest in them, and therefore could not be said to receive the money for the use of the plaintiff, which indeed he received to his own use; but the plaintiff ought to have brought trover or detinue for the debentures: the point was saved to the defendant, and now the Court was moved, and the same objection made.

POWELL JUSTICE. It is clear the plaintiff might have maintained detinue or trover for the debentures * * *. But the plaintiff may dispense with the wrong, and suppose the sale made by his consent, and bring an action for the money they were sold for, as money received to his use. * * *

HOLT CHIEF JUSTICE. These actions have crept in by degrees. * * * So the defendant in this case pretending to receive the money the debentures were sold for in the right of the intestate, why should he not be answerable for it to the intestate's administrator? If an action of trover should be brought by the plaintiff for these debentures after judgment in this indebitatus assumpsit, he may plead this recovery in bar of the action of trover, in the same manner as it would have been a good plea in bar for the defendant to have pleaded to the action of trover, that he sold the debentures, and paid to the plaintiff in satisfaction. * * * This recovery may be given in evidence upon not guilty in the action of trover, because by this action the plaintiff makes and affirms the act of the defendant in the sale of the debentures to be lawful, and consequently the sale of them is no conversion.

* * *

MOSES v. MacFERLAN, 2 Burrow 1005, 97 Eng.Rep. 676 (K.B.1760). Plaintiff had endorsed four promissory notes to defendant under a written agreement that he should not be liable thereon; in defendant's suit in a Court of Conscience (a small claims court), however, the agreement was not recognized, and plaintiff was found liable for six pounds, which he paid. (On these facts, would Lamine v. Dorrell support an action for money had and received?) Lord Mansfield said:

> 2d objection.—"That no assumpsit lies, except upon an express or implied contract: but here it is impossible to presume any contract to refund money, which the defendant recovered by an adverse suit."
>
> Answer. If the defendant be under an obligation, from the ties of natural justice, to refund; the law implies a debt, and gives this action, founded in the equity of the plaintiff's case, as it were upon a contract ("quasi ex contractu," as the Roman law expresses it).
>
> * * *
>
> Money may be recovered by a right and legal judgment; and yet the iniquity of keeping that money may be manifest, upon grounds which could not be used by way of defence against the judgment.
>
> * * *
>
> Suppose a man recovers upon a policy for a ship presumed to be lost, which afterwards comes home;—or upon the life of a man presumed to be dead, who afterwards appears;—or upon a representation of a risque deemed to be fair, which comes out afterwards to be grossly fraudulent.
>
> * * *
>
> One great benefit, which arises to suitors from the nature of this action, is, that the plaintiff needs not state the special circumstances from which he concludes "that, ex aequo & bono, the money received by the defendant, ought to be deemed as belonging to him:" he may declare generally, "that the money was received to his use;" and make out his case, at the trial.
>
> * * *
>
> This kind of equitable action to recover back money, which ought not in justice to be kept, is very beneficial, and therefore much encouraged. It lies only for money which, ex aequo et bono, the defendant ought to refund: it does not lie for money paid by the plaintiff, which is claimed of him as payable in point of honor and honesty, although it could not have been recovered from him by any course of law; as in payment of a debt barred by the Statute of Limitations, or contracted during his infancy, or to the extent of principal and legal interest upon an usurious contract, or, for money fairly lost at play: because in all these cases, the defendant may retain it with a safe conscience, though by positive law he was barred from recovering.

An important procedural result of the development of indebitatus assumpsit was a new manner of pleading contract actions. The declaration in money had and received, as Lord Mansfield noted in his opinion in Moses v. MacFerlan, was broad in the extreme. The declarations in other actions derived from indebitatus assumpsit were equally broad. Pleaders seized upon this liberality to develop what became known as the "common counts," standardized allegations concealing virtually all of the particulars of an action. The principal common counts were for money had and received, for goods sold and delivered, for work done, for money lent, for money paid by plaintiff to the use of defendant, and for money due on an account stated. See Fifoot, History and Sources of the Common Law—Tort and Contract 369–70, 393–94 (1949).

SECTION C. THE OTHER SYSTEM: EQUITY

1. THE RISE OF CHANCERY

MAITLAND, EQUITY, ALSO THE FORMS OF ACTION AT COMMON LAW 2–10 (1909):

In Edward I's day, at the end of the thirteenth century, three great courts have come into existence * * *.

One of the three courts, namely, the Exchequer, is more than a court of law. From our modern point of view it is not only a court of law but a 'government office'. * * * What we should call the 'civil service' of the country is transacted by two great offices or 'departments'; there is the Exchequer which is the fiscal department, there is the Chancery which is the secretarial department, while above these there rises the king's permanent Council. At the head of the Chancery stands the Chancellor, usually a bishop; he is we may say the king's secretary of state for all departments, he keeps the king's great seal and all the already great mass of writing that has to be done in the king's name has to be done under his supervision.

He is not as yet a judge, but already he by himself or his subordinates has a great deal of work to do which brings him into a close connexion with the administration of justice. One of the duties of that great staff of clerks over which he presides is to draw up and issue those writs whereby actions are begun in the courts of law—such writs are sealed with the king's seal. * * *

But by another route the Chancellor is brought into still closer contact with the administration of justice. Though these great courts of law have been established there is still a reserve of justice in the king. Those who can not get relief elsewhere present their petitions to the king and his council praying for some remedy. * * * In practice a great share of this labour falls on the Chancellor. He is the king's prime minister, he is a member of the council, and the specially learned member of the council. It is in dealing with these petitions that the Chancellor begins to develop his judicial powers.

* * * Very often the petitioner requires some relief at the expense of some other person. He complains that for some reason or another he can not get a remedy in the ordinary course of justice and yet he is entitled to a remedy. He is poor, he is old, he is sick, his adversary is rich and powerful, will bribe or will intimidate jurors, or has by some trick or some accident acquired an advantage of which the ordinary courts with their formal procedure will not deprive him. The petition is often couched in piteous terms, the king is asked to find a remedy for the love of God and in the way of charity. Such petitions are referred by the king to the Chancellor. Gradually in the course of the fourteenth century petitioners, instead of going to the king, will go straight to the Chancellor * * *. Now one thing that the Chancellor may do in such a case is to invent a new writ and so provide the complainant with a means of bringing an action in a court of law. But in the fourteenth century the courts of law have become very conservative and are given to quashing writs which differ in material points from those already in use. But another thing that the Chancellor can do is to send for the complainant's adversary and examine him concerning the charge that has been made against him. Gradually a procedure is established. The Chancellor having considered the petition, or 'bill' as it is called, orders the adversary to come before him and answer the complaint. The writ whereby he does this is called a subpoena—because it orders the man to appear upon pain of forfeiting a sum of money * * *. It is very different from the old writs whereby actions are begun in the courts of law. They tell the defendant what is the cause of action against him * * *. The subpoena, on the other hand, will tell him merely that he has got to come before the Chancellor and answer complaints made against him by A.B. Then when he comes before the Chancellor he will have to answer on oath, and sentence by sentence, the bill of the plaintiff. * * *

I do not think that in the fourteenth century the Chancellors considered that they had to administer any body of substantive rules that differed from the ordinary law of the land. * * * The complaints that come before them are in general complaints of indubitable legal wrongs * * * of which the ordinary courts take cognizance, wrongs which they ought to redress. * * * However this sort of thing can not well be permitted. * * * And so the Chancellor is warned off the field of common law—he is not to hear cases which might go to the ordinary courts, he is not to make himself a judge of torts and contracts, of property in lands and goods.

But then just at this time it is becoming plain that the Chancellor is doing some convenient and useful works that could not be done, or could not easily be done by the courts of common law. He has taken to enforcing uses or trusts. * * * No doubt they were troublesome things, things that might be used for fraudulent purposes, and statutes were passed against those who employed them for the purpose of cheating their creditors or evading the law of mortmain. But I have not a doubt that they were very popular, and I think we may say that had there been no Chancery, the old courts would have discovered some method of enforcing these fiduciary obligations. That method however must have been a clumsy one. A system of law which will never compel, which will never even allow, the defendant to give evidence, a system which sends every question of fact to a jury, is not competent to deal adequately with fiduciary relationships. On the other hand the Chancellor had a procedure which was very well adapted to this end.

* * * And then there were some other matters that were considered to be fairly within his jurisdiction. An old rhyme allows him 'fraud, accident, and breach of confidence'—there were many frauds which the stiff old procedure of the courts of law could not adequately meet, and 'accident,' in particular the accidental loss of a document, was a proper occasion for the Chancellor's interference.

* * * In James I's day occurred the great quarrel between Lord Chancellor Ellesmere and Chief Justice Coke which finally decided that the Court of Chancery was to have the upper hand over the courts of law. If the Chancery was to carry out its maxims about trust and fraud it was essential that it should have a power to prevent men from going into the courts of law and to prevent men from putting in execution the judgments that they had obtained in courts of law. In fraud or in breach of trust you obtain a judgment against me in a court of law; I complain to the Chancellor, and he after hearing what you have to say enjoins you not to put in force your judgment, says in effect that if you do put your judgment in force you will be sent to prison. Understand well that the Court of Chancery never asserted that it was superior to the courts of law; it never presumed to send to them such mandates as the Court of King's Bench habitually sent to the inferior courts, telling them that they must do this or must not do that or quashing their proceedings * * *. It was addressed not to the judges, but to the party. * * * For all this, however, it was natural that the judges should take umbrage at this treatment of their judgments. Coke declared that the man who obtained such an injunction was guilty of the offence denounced by the Statutes of Praemunire, that of calling in question the judgments of the king's courts in other courts (these statutes had been aimed at the Papal curia). King James had now a wished-for opportunity of appearing as supreme over all his judges, and all his courts * * *.

ARGUMENTS PROVING FROM ANTIQUITY THE DIGNITY, POWER, AND JURISDICTION OF THE COURT OF CHANCERY

1 Chan.Rep. (App.) 1, 20, 23–24, 49–50, 21 Eng.Rep. 576, 581–82, 588 (1616).

* * *

His said Majesty being informed of this Difference between his two Courts of Chancery and King's Bench, * * * directed, That his Attorney General, calling to him the Rest of his Learned Counsel, should peruse the

* * * Precedents, and certify his Majesty the Truth thereof with their Opinions.

* * *

And afterwards a Case was presented to his Majesty as followeth.

The Case.

A. hath a Judgment and Execution in the King's Bench or Common Pleas against B. in an Action of Debt of £1000, and in an *Ejectione Firmae* of the Manor of D. B. complains in the Chancery to be relieved against these Judgments according to Equity and Conscience, allowing the Judgment to be lawful and good by the Rigour and strict Rules of the Law, and the Matter in Equity to be such, as the Judges of the Common Law being no Judges of Equity, but bound by their Oaths to do the Law, cannot give any Remedy or Relief for the same, either by Error or Attaint, or by any other Means.

Question.

Whether the Chancery may relieve B. in this or such like Cases, or else leave him utterly remediless and undone? And if the Chancery be restrained herein by any Statute of Praemunire, then by what Statute, and by what Words in any Statute is the Chancery so restrained, and Conscience and Equity excluded, banished and damned?

Which Case his Majesty referred again to his said Attorney and Learned Counsel * * *.

* * *

Upon which Certificate the King gave his Judgment as followeth.

Forasmuch as Mercy and Justice be the true Supporters of our Royal Throne, and that it properly belongeth unto us in our Princely Office to take Care and provide, that our Subjects have equal and indifferent Justice ministered unto them: And that where their Case deserveth to be relieved in Course of Equity by Suit in our Court of Chancery, they should not be abandoned and exposed to perish under the Rigor and Extremity of our Laws, We in our Princely Judgment * * * do approve, ratify and confirm, * * * the Practice of our Court of Chancery * * *. And do will and command that our Chancellor, or Keeper of the Great Seal for the Time being, shall not hereafter desist to give unto our Subjects, * * * such Relief in Equity (notwithstanding any Proceedings at the Common Law against them) as shall stand with the Merit and Justice of their Cause, and with the former, ancient and continued Practice and Presidency of our Chancery have done. * * *

BEALE, EQUITY IN AMERICA, 1 Cambridge L.J. 21, 22–23 (1921):

At about the time of the English Revolution colonies came to be more rigorously governed. Most of the old charters were forfeited, and a new provincial form of government was established; and from that time the Judges were appointed, through the royal governors, by the Crown, and they came to be regarded, naturally, as the enemies of popular rights and as creatures of the Crown. The situation at about the time of the American Revolution was that Judges in the North were still regarded as tools of the King and as enemies of the popular will. * * *

In the South conditions were very different. The ruling class was well satisfied with the condition of affairs in England, and, although there were popular uprisings in some parts of the South, notably in Virginia and Maryland, the power of the aristocracy on the whole was never shaken. They determined the laws, they had no distrust of Judges, and in those States there was no desire to hamper a Judge or to exalt the jury at his expense. * * *

We should not be surprised, therefore, to find that in the North at least the people were very jealous of giving any jurisdiction to the Court of Equity, there being no jury in that Court. Equity seemed to the people of America, a hundred years ago even, as a non-popular method of applying law, which it was the duty of the people alone to deal with. The Courts administering equity were, so to speak, royalist persons administering the law of an effete monarchy which had never taken foothold in the democratic part of America. The consequence was that in New England there was no equity jurisdiction and very little admixture of equity in the law. The law administered was the strictly legal portion of the law; and the books cited, when they came to cite books, were the reports of the common law Courts. In New York there was a Chancellor from the time of the original constitution; but that Chancellor was not supposed to be a Judge who administered the English system of equity. * * *

Pennsylvania never had any Court of equity. The law, however, had more of what they regarded as equitable doctrines in it than the law of Massachusetts * * *. In New Jersey and Delaware, however, and throughout the South, there was set up at the time of our Revolution a separate Court of Chancery, sitting beside the Common Law Court and administering the principles of English equity.

2. PROCEDURE IN EQUITY

BOWEN, PROGRESS IN THE ADMINISTRATION OF JUSTICE DURING THE VICTORIAN PERIOD, 1 Select Essays in Anglo–American Legal History 516, 524–27 (1907):

* * * A bill in a Chancery suit was a marvellous document, which stated the plaintiff's case at full length and three times over. There was first the part in which the story was circumstantially set forth. Then came the part which "charged" its truth against the defendant—or, in other words, which set it forth all over again in an aggrieved tone. Lastly came

the interrogating part, which converted the original allegations into a chain of subtly framed inquiries addressed to the defendant, minutely dovetailed and circuitously arranged so as to surround a slippery conscience and to stop up every earth. No layman, however intelligent, could compose the "answer" without professional aid. It was inevitably so elaborate and so long, that the responsibility for the accuracy of the story shifted, during its telling, from the conscience of the defendant to that of his solicitor and counsel, and truth found no difficulty in disappearing during the operation. * * * [The form of the answer] often rendered necessary a re-statement of the plaintiff's whole position, in which case an amended bill was drawn requiring another answer, until at last the voluminous pleadings were completed and the cause was at issue. By a system which to lawyers in 1887 appears to savour of the Middle Ages, the evidence for the hearing was thereupon taken by interrogatories written down beforehand upon paper and administered to the witnesses in private before an examiner or commissioner. At this meeting none of the parties were allowed to be present, either by themselves or their agents, and the examiner himself was sworn to secrecy. If cross-examined at all (for cross-examination under such conditions was of necessity somewhat of a farce), the witnesses could only be cross-examined upon written inquiries prepared equally in advance by a counsel who had never had the opportunity of knowing what had been said during the examination-in-chief. * * * On the day of the publication of the depositions copies were furnished to the parties at their own expense; but, from that moment, no further evidence was admissible, nor could any slip in the proofs be repaired, except by special permission of the court, when, if such leave was granted, a fresh commission was executed with the same formalities and in the same secret manner as before. The expense of the pleadings, of the preparation for the hearing, and of the other stages of the litigation may be imagined, when we recollect that it was a necessary maxim of the Court of Chancery that all parties interested in the result must be parties to the suit. If, for example, relief was sought against a breach of trust, all who were interested in the trust estate had to be joined, as well as all who had been privy to the breach of trust itself. During the winding journey of the cause towards its termination, whenever any death occurred, bills of review or supplemental suits became necessary to reconstitute the charmed circle of litigants which had been broken. On every such catastrophe the plaintiff had again to begin wearily to weave his web, liable on any new death to find it unravelled and undone. It was satirically observed that a suit to which fifty defendants were necessary parties (a perfectly possible contingency) could never hope to end at all, since the yearly average of deaths in England was one in fifty, and a death, as a rule, threw over the plaintiff's bill for at least a year. The hearing in many cases could not terminate the cause. Often inquiries or accounts were necessary, and had still to be taken under the supervision of a master. Possibly some issue upon the disputed facts required to be sent for trial at the assizes, or a point of law submitted to a common law court. In such cases, the verdict of the jury, or the opinions of the court so taken, in no way concluded the conscience of the Court of Chancery. It resumed charge of the cause again, when the intermediate expedition to the common law was over, and had the power, if it saw fit, to send the same issue to a new trial, or to disregard altogether what had been the result. * * * When a cause had reached its final stage—when all inquiries had been made, all parties represented, all accounts taken, all issues tried—justice was done with vigour and exactitude. Few frauds ever in the end successfully ran the gauntlet of the Court of Chancery. But the honest suitor emerged from the ordeal victorious rather than triumphant, for too often he had been ruined by the way.

NOTES AND QUESTIONS

1. What differences do you find between procedure at common law and procedure in equity as it is described by Bowen? What are the differences in pleading, the manner of receiving evidence, the attitude toward singleness of issue, and the determination of questions of fact? The rules of evidence, which are chiefly concerned with the exclusion of testimony of doubtful value, were developed in the common-law courts and were never strictly applied in equity. How is this fact related to the differences in equity and common-law procedures?

2. Although the division between law and equity in the federal courts never took the form of separate courts or judges of law and equity, the two were separately administered in the federal system until 1938. From the beginning, procedure at law was conformed to that of the state in which the court was held, but—due in part to the fact that some states had no system of equity in 1789—equity procedure in the federal courts was governed by statutes of Congress and rules promulgated by the Supreme Court. In 1915, Congress provided that when "a suit at law should have been brought in equity or a suit in equity should have been brought at law, the court shall order any amendments to the pleadings which may be necessary to conform them to the proper practice," and that in "all actions at law equitable defenses may be interposed by answer, plea, or replication without the necessity of filing a bill on the equity side of the court." 38 Stat. 956.

The elements of procedure in equity discussed in the foregoing materials are significant because of their impact on the substantive and remedial doctrines of equity. Together with the method of enforcing equity decrees, which is discussed below, these elements largely determined the type of case that equity would hear and the disposition it would order. As you read the materials that follow, ask yourself how these differences between law and equity may explain the particular equitable approach in question.

3. THE UNIQUE CHARACTER OF EQUITABLE RELIEF

A. SPECIFIC RELIEF

The ordinary judgment of a common-law court consisted of a declaration of a legal relationship. When plaintiff prevailed in the action, this declaration in all but rare instances was that plaintiff was entitled to a sum of money from defendant. Even this declaration was not an order that defendant pay the sum; if defendant did not pay, plaintiff had to take further steps to execute the judgment. The decree in equity, on the other hand, was an order directed at defendant; imprisonment and fines were used not only to coerce compliance, but to punish disobedience. This difference between the remedies in the two systems of courts was summed up in the maxim that equity acts in personam and not in rem. The primary means by which equity acted in personam was the injunction—an order directing defendant to perform or to stop performing an act.

The injunction and other forms of specific relief shaped the substantive doctrines of equity. But it affected the common law as well in at least three important ways. First, the availability of specific relief through the injunction or specific performance when compensatory relief through a judgment for damages would be inadequate was the chief basis for drawing common-law causes into equity. As a result equity now dominates many areas of controversy originally governed by the common law, because damages are an impotent remedy in such cases; a good example is nuisance. Similarly the enforcement of contracts for the sale of real property has become principally a concern of equity, because specific performance is ordered as a matter of course. Second, the availability of specific relief in equity effectively has dampened pressures to develop common-law remedies in that direction. Third, the injunction was the means by which equity imposed its substantive doctrines on the common-law courts. As noted in the extract from Maitland, if the chancellor found that a common-law judgment had been obtained by fraud, the equity court did not purport to negate it; the chancellor simply took the equally effective step of threatening the judgment creditor with jail if the latter sought to enforce it. In similar fashion equity enjoined the bringing of suits in inconvenient fora and compelled interpleader and class actions in multiparty suits.

A plaintiff who sought specific relief also might have sustained an injury that an injunction could not cure. But there was no necessity for choosing between equitable relief and compensatory damages. A "clean-up" doctrine gave Chancery authority to accord full relief in any case of which it had cognizance even though giving such relief might mean redressing injuries for which there was an adequate remedy at law. See pp. 1001–02, infra.

B. AVAILABILITY OF RELIEF

You must not think that the doctrine of the adequate remedy at law was the only restriction on the use of equitable remedies. Equity carefully husbanded its power. It was reluctant to issue orders that it might not be able to enforce or that might involve it in detailed supervision of a transaction. Traditionally, equity would not direct a party to take action outside its territorial jurisdiction or order specific performance of a building or personal services contract. For other reasons, activity that might be criminal ordinarily would not be enjoined. While the Court of Star Chamber flourished there was no call for criminal jurisdiction in equity, and after that court was abolished in 1642, Chancery, perhaps for fear of meeting a similar fate, refrained from encroaching on this particular domain of the common-law courts. What aspects of Chancery procedure might have seemed particularly odious in criminal cases to people who celebrated the common law as the palladium of their liberty?

The availability of equitable relief also was hedged by doctrines of fairness and justice. Thus the opinions of the chancellor continually repeat that he who seeks equity must do equity, that he must come into equity with "clean hands," that equity abhors a forfeiture, and that equity will not protect one who sleeps on his rights. Is there any reason why these ideas should have been applied only in equity?

C. FRAUD

Fraud often is spoken of as a fount of equitable jurisdiction. Yet the common law also permitted actions for fraud, and defenses as well. Why was protection against fraud thought to be a peculiarly equitable concern? For at least two reasons. For one thing, it was a function of equity's getting there first and going further. The common law would not recognize fraud as a defense to an action on a sealed instrument. Thus, before the rise of assumpsit, at a time when most of the agreements that were enforced by the courts were under seal, equity furnished the only remedy for fraud in the great bulk of cases. When simple contracts—to which fraud was a common-law defense—became enforceable, Chancery sustained its lead by developing the doctrine of constructive fraud, a doctrine in which the rigid technicalities of the common-law fraud concept played little part.

The second reason lay in equity's procedure. Equity implemented its concern with fraud in two ways. First, by denying its own relief to fraudulent complainants, and second, by enjoining legal suitors from pressing their claims or enforcing their judgments. The fraud concept in the latter case has come to be known as an "equitable defense," together with such doctrines as accident, undue influence, and estoppel. Of course, the term "equitable defense" does not indicate a defense in an equity suit, but connotes an effective—if not technical—defense to an action at law.

D. DISCOVERY

Equity and the common law should not be thought of as conflicting systems. In many respects the relationship was one of cooperation, especially after the confrontation of 1616. The most important aspect of this mutual assistance, for our purposes, was discovery, by which a party at law might obtain through equity information for his case. The procedure and the limitations are set forth by Lord Chief Baron Abinger:

> * * * A party has a right to compel the production of a document in which he has an equal interest, though not equal in degree, yet to a certain extent equal, with the party who detains it from him. In that case he may file a bill of discovery, in order to have the possession of it, and the inspection of it. A party has also a right to file a bill of discovery for the purpose of obtaining such facts as may tend to prove his case; and if those facts are either in possession of the other party, or, if they consist of documents in possession of the other party, in which he either has an interest, or which tend to prove his case, and have no relation to the case of the other party, he has a right to have them produced, and he may file a bill of discovery, in order to aid him in law or in equity, to exhibit those documents in evidence, or compel a statement of those facts. * * * Has he a right, as against the defendant, to discover the defendant's case? * * * The ground on which he files his bill, is to make the defendant discover what is material to his (the plaintiff's) case; but he has no right to say to the defendant, "Tell me what your title is—tell me what your case is—tell me how you mean to prove it—tell me the evidence you have to support it—disclose the documents you mean to make use of in support of it—tell me all these things, that I may find a flaw in your title." Surely that is not the principle of a bill of discovery.

COMBE v. CITY OF LONDON, 4 Y. & C.Ex. 139, 154, 160 Eng.Rep. 953, 959 (Exch.1840). What aspects of equitable procedure explain the availability of discovery in equity? In this connection, reread those portions of Maitland and Bowen in this Section dealing with the pleadings and the taking of evidence in equity.

SECTION D. REFORM: NEW PLEADING, ABOLITION OF THE FORMS, AND THE MERGER OF LAW AND EQUITY

1. THE EMERGENCE OF CODE PROCEDURE

The first significant reform in procedure occurred in England in the period between 1825 and 1834. Chancery practice was substantially reformed during these years. One form of writ was adopted for all three common-law courts. All but three real actions were abolished. Debt and detinue were reshaped. Wager of law was ended.

The capstone of the reform was a body of new rules of pleading, drafted by a committee that included Henry Stephen, author of the treatise cited earlier in this Chapter, and Sir James Parke, who, as a judge of the Court of Exchequer, was to become the foremost expositor of the new rules. Many of their recommendations were distinct improvements on existing practice; one—not accepted—would have permitted the joinder of counts in trespass and case, and amendments from the one form of action to the other. The principal defect the commissioners found in the existing system of pleading, however, was the ubiquitous availability of the general issue. The commissioners attributed to pleas of the general issue "the unnecessary accumulation of proof," the failure to raise questions of law by demurrer, the imposition of the duty to separate law and fact upon the busy *nisi prius* judge, and the proliferation of new trials. This position was reflected by the new rules announced under the authority of an Act of Parliament by the judges of all three common-law courts at Hilary Term, 1834, and known as the Hilary Rules; the defenses that could be proved under a plea of the general issue were greatly reduced, and special pleading was substantially restored. 2 C. & M. 1–30, 149 Eng.Rep. 651–63 (1834).

The result was a disaster. "Under the common-law system the matter was bad enough with a pleading question decided in every sixth case. But under the Hilary Rules it was worse. Every fourth case decided a question on the pleadings. Pleading ran riot." Whittier, *Notice Pleading,* 31 Harv. L.Rev. 501, 507 (1918). Fortunately, corrective action was not long in coming. The Common Law Procedure Acts of 1852, 1854, and 1860 weakened the forms of action, expanded joinder, and liberalized pleading. Finally, the Judicature Acts of 1873 and 1875 combined Chancery and the common-law courts into one Supreme Court of Judicature, fused law and equity, and abolished the forms of action. See 15 Holdsworth, A History of English Law 104–38 (Goodhart & Hanbury ed. 1965).

Meanwhile in the United States,[h] a new constitution in New York in 1846 abolished the Court of Chancery and directed the legislature to provide for the appointment of commissioners to "revise, reform, simplify, and abridge" the civil procedure of the state. N.Y. Const. 1846 Art. VI, § 24. The legislature implemented this directive in 1847 and expressly charged the newly appointed commissioners to "provide for the abolition of the present forms of actions and pleadings in cases at common law; for a uniform course of proceeding in all cases whether of legal or equitable cognizance, and for the abandonment * * * of any form and proceeding not necessary to ascertain or preserve the rights of the parties." N.Y.Laws 1847, c. 59, § 8.

FIRST REPORT OF THE COMMISSIONERS ON PRACTICE AND PLEADINGS (New York) 73–74, 87, 123–24, 137–38, 140–41, 144 (1848):

The history of jurisprudence, both in this state and in England, * * * affords a most convincing proof of the wisdom of the measure adopted by the people of this state, in abolishing the distinction between law and

h. The textual discussion is limited to states with a common-law heritage. Louisiana had adopted a system based on Spanish law with only one form of action by 1812, the year it was admitted to the Union. Texas experimented briefly with separate systems but by 1845 had a unitary system based on Spanish–Mexican jurisprudence.

equity tribunals. Notwithstanding their separate existence, they had, under the institutions of this state, but one common object, the administration of justice—depending not upon the mere discretion of the court, but ascertained by fixed and certain rules of law. And yet, while they were kept distinct, though their jurisdictions continually encroached upon each other, there were certain rules, not well defined, but yet existing, by which their powers were distinguished. It is, therefore, no matter of surprise, that the books are filled with cases, in which the injustice has been imposed upon parties, of suffering the loss of a substantial right, because of a mistake in the choice of a forum, before which its enforcement was sought. * * *

From the period [in which the forms of action developed] * * *—a period comparatively benighted and ignorant, in all that is valuable in science—to the present, these forms have been adhered to with a sort of bigoted devotion. While the principles of legal science have expanded and adapted themselves to the exigencies of each successive age, through which they have passed, we find ourselves met with the standing argument against improvement, that the time-honored institutions of ages must be held sacred, and that these forms, which may have been well suited to the age in which they originated, must be left untouched.

* * * It seems to us, clear, that neither the forms of remedies, nor the mode in which they are stated, require the complexity, in which both are now enveloped. The embarrassments, to which they have given rise, have resulted from no difficulty in determining the real rights of parties, but simply in the means of enforcing them; and in this respect, we feel no hesitation in recommending, that the retention of forms, which serve no valuable purpose, should no longer constitute a portion of the remedial law of this state. * * *

The rules respecting parties in the courts of law, differ from those in the courts of equity. The blending of the jurisdictions makes it necessary to revise these rules, to some extent. In doing so, we have had a three-fold purpose in view: first, to do away with the artificial distinctions existing in the courts of law, and to require the real party in interest to appear in court as such: second, to require the presence of such parties as are necessary to make an end of the controversy: and third, to allow otherwise great latitude in respect to the number of parties who may be brought in.

* * *

The courts of law generally administer justice betweee [sic] those parties only who stand in the same relation to * * * [each] other; while courts of equity bring before them various parties, standing in different relations, that the whole controversy may be settled, if possible, in one suit, and others avoided. This reasonable and just rule, we would adopt for all actions. * * *

As has been already remarked, the change in the mode of pleading is the key of the reform which we propose. Without this, we should despair of any substantial and permanent improvement in our modes of legal controversy. * * *

The pleadings, we have said, are the written allegations of the parties of the cause of action on one side, and the defence on the other. Their object is three-fold: to present the facts on which the court is to pronounce the law; to present them in such a manner, as that the precise points in dispute shall be perceived, to which the proofs may be directed; and to preserve the record of the rights determined. Not one of these objects is gained by the law of pleading as it now exists in this state.

* * *

There are many treatises and books of forms, indispensable to the lawyer, on the mode of pleading and the forms of the allegations. The rules and the commentaries upon them, form one of the most technical and abstruse branches of the law * * *. We are * * * disposed to pronounce it a system of dialectics, very fit for the schoolmen with whom it originated, but unfit for the practical business of life.

So unfit has it been found, that in instances almost numberless, the legislature and the courts have departed from it and gone to the other extreme. * * * A form of plea was devised which in many cases would virtually deny every material allegation of the declaration without disclosing any particular defence. The courts from time to time have admitted new defences under these general issues, and still further to encourage them, a statute has been passed allowing the defendant to plead the general issue, and with it give notice of any defence, which he could not otherwise introduce under such issue. * * *

Besides the general issues, we have general declarations, or in technical language, common counts. These have been so contrived as to give no information of the particular demand. They also have been encouraged by the courts and numberless demands allowed to be proven under them. * * *

In truth the arguments of those who defend the present system destroy each other. One is the advantage of having the question of fact drawn out so precisely, that the court and jury may see what they have to try, and the parties be prepared with their proofs; the other is the advantage of having the facts stated in so general a form, that the allegations shall cover any state of facts that may appear on the trial, or in other words, the advantage of having no question of fact drawn out by the pleadings at all.

* * *

Disentangling the questions and separating those of fact and of law, is rarely effected by the present system of pleading at common law. * * * This is necessarily so, so long as the pleadings state the conclusions of fact, instead of the facts themselves. * * *

Following the report of the commissioners, the New York legislature enacted a Code of Civil Procedure, commonly called the Field Code after David Dudley Field, the most influential of the commissioners. N.Y.Laws 1848, c. 379. This Code proved to be the prototype for numerous state codes—at one time more than one-half the states had codes patterned to some degree after the Field Code—and the precursor of the Federal Rules. Among its most important provisions were the following:

§ 69. [§ 62][i] The distinction between actions at law and suits in equity, and the forms of all such actions and suits, heretofore existing, are abolished; and, there shall be in this state, hereafter, but one form of action, for the enforcement or protection of private rights and the redress of private wrongs, which shall be denominated a civil action.

§ 140. [§ 118] All the forms of pleading heretofore existing, inconsistent with the provisions of this act, are abolished * * *.

§ 142. [§ 120] The complaint shall contain:

1. * * *

2. A statement of the facts constituting the cause of action, in ordinary and concise language, without repetition, and in such a manner as to enable a person of common understanding to know what is intended;

3. A demand of the relief, to which the plaintiff supposes himself entitled. If the recovery of money be demanded, the amount thereof shall be stated.

§ 156. [§ 132] No other pleading shall be allowed than the complaint, answer, reply and demurrers.

§ 159. [§ 136] In the construction of a pleading, for the purpose of determining its effect, its allegations shall be liberally construed, with a view to substantial justice between the parties.

§ 176. [§ 151] The court shall, in every stage of an action, disregard any error, or defect in the pleadings or proceedings, which shall not affect the substantial rights of the adverse party; and no judgment shall be reversed or affected by reason of such error or defect.

NOTE

In 1851 the New York legislature amended Section 142(2) to read: "A plain and concise statement of the facts constituting a cause of action without unnecessary repetition." N.Y.Laws 1851, c. 479, § 1.

---

i. The New York legislature added several sections to the Code in 1849, and renumbered the provisions first enacted in 1848 with some very slight changes in language. N.Y.Laws 1849, c. 438. Because the 1849 version became the best known, it is used here. Section numbers in brackets refer to the sections of the 1848 Code.

2. SOME OLD PROBLEMS PERSIST

Could it have been reasonably expected that the transition from the common-law system of procedure to the code system would represent a clean break with the past? Consider the following factors:

(a) The substantive law was supposed to remain unaltered, yet the substantive law had been intimately tied to the older mode of procedure. Moreover, certain procedural institutions—notably trial by jury—had acquired the character of substantive rights.

(b) The most fundamental aspects of procedure—such as the necessity of striking a balance between the function of pleading as setting the limits of the controversy and the function of trial as determining the true merits of the case—are not created by a particular system of procedure but are an integral part of an adjudicative process based upon a theory of party-presentation. Indeed it is rare that any system of procedure attempts by rigid rule to settle these issues definitively. Much will depend on the attitudes, experiences, and predispositions of those who are called upon to apply the rules.

(c) The problems presented by the change in procedure confronted a profession that had traditionally chosen precedent as its polestar, a profession comprised of people who might feel they had an interest in their established ways of proceeding and who in any event were trained in analysis under the older system. The judges who were called upon to interpret the new provisions were of course established members of this profession; indeed, if the methods of judicial selection were effective, they were lawyers who had performed quite competently under the older procedure and they understandably may have been a little impatient with complaints that this procedure was replete with snares and absurdities.

Whatever the reasons, it is clear that many courts did not view the new codes as having been written on a clean slate. Even today concepts of the common-law system occasionally seem to assume a significant role in the decision of pleading and procedure questions. We will see more of this in the next Chapter. For the present we will look at one aspect of the perseverance of common-law notions—the "theory of the pleading" doctrine and related questions.

JONES v. WINSOR

Supreme Court of South Dakota, 1908.
22 S.D. 480, 118 N.W. 716.

CORSON, J. This is an appeal by the defendant from an order overruling his demurrer to the complaint.

It is alleged in the complaint, in substance: That on or about the 1st of April, 1907, the plaintiffs, being desirous of securing a franchise for a city railway system in the city of Sioux Falls, employed the defendant to act as an attorney for them in securing or attempting to secure an ordinance from the city council granting the plaintiffs such license; that carrying out their purpose, * * * it became necessary for the plaintiffs to make a deposit with the city treasurer, and on said day the plaintiffs delivered to the defendant the sum of $2,500 to be by him deposited with the said treasurer of the city, and which money was so deposited * * *; that on or about the 4th day of April the defendant received a further sum of $130, which was to be used by the defendant for these plaintiffs in securing or attempting to secure the said franchise; that the said franchise which plaintiffs were attempting to secure from said city was not granted to these plaintiffs, and thereupon, about the 17th day of April, the city treasurer returned to the defendant the said sum of $2,500 "as money belonging to these plaintiffs and for their use and benefit"; that on or about the same day the said defendant rendered to these plaintiffs an account of all moneys received by him for and on account of these plaintiffs, with an itemized statement of all disbursements, and in connection therewith a pretended charge for his services or fee of $1,250, and with said account was a draft drawn in favor of the plaintiffs for $1,012.25; that the pretended charge of the defendant of the sum of $1,250 as shown upon said account and alleged to be for services rendered by him is unjust, unlawful, and fraudulent, and the reasonable value of the services rendered by the defendant was not and is not of the value of more than $250; that of the moneys so received by the defendant for and on behalf of these plaintiffs and for their use and benefit there remains in his hands the sum of $1,000, which he has refused and still refuses to pay over to these plaintiffs, although frequently requested so to do, and "he has wrongfully and fraudulently converted to his own use the said sum of $1,000"; that on or about the 10th day of September, 1907, the plaintiffs demanded of the said defendant payment * * * "but the said defendant then and there refused and still refuses to pay the same or any part thereof to the plaintiffs and has wrongfully converted the same to his own use." Wherefore "plaintiffs demand judgment against the said defendant for the sum of $1,000 and interest thereon from the 17th day of April, 1907, for the wrongful conversion of said property and for the costs of this action." * * *

It is contended by the appellant that the complaint does not state facts sufficient to constitute a cause of action in trover or conversion, for the reason that the complaint nowhere alleges ownership by the plaintiffs of the property alleged to have been converted at the time the action was brought; nor does it allege ownership or possession of the property in the plaintiffs at the time it is alleged to have been converted which is absolutely essential in the form of action. Assuming that the complaint in this case was intended to state an action for the conversion of this money by the defendant, it is clearly insufficient in not alleging that the plaintiffs, at the time the defendant is charged with having converted it, were the owners or in possession of the money so alleged to have been converted. * * * But it is somewhat difficult to determine from the complaint whether the plaintiffs intended that their action should be for a tort or one ex contractu, as the complaint seems to have been framed with a double aspect. Taking a general view of the allegations of the complaint, it would seem that the pleaders intended to state a cause of action as for money had and received; but looking at the complaint in another aspect, and giving effect to some of the allegations therein, it would seem that the pleaders intended it as an action in conversion, in the nature of the old action of trover.

It is contended by the respondent, in support of the ruling of the court below upon the demurrer, that the action is to recover money had and received by the plaintiffs, and that the allegations contained in the complaint alleged [sic] the fraudulent conversion of the property, etc., may be treated as surplusage. Such a complaint, framed with a double aspect or to unite distinct and incongruous causes of actions, cannot be sustained on demurrer. While our Code has abolished forms of pleading, and only requires that the facts shall be stated in a plain and concise manner without unnecessary repetition, still the distinctions between actions as they formerly existed cannot be entirely ignored. In Pierce v. Carey, 37 Wis. 232, * * * Chief Justice Ryan, quotes with approval * * * Supervisors of Kewaunee County v. Decker, 30 Wis. 624, as follows: "Dixon, C.J. It would certainly be a most anomalous and hitherto unknown condition of the laws of pleading, were it established that the plaintiff in a civil action could file and serve a complaint, the particular nature and object of which no one could tell, but which might and should be held good, as a statement of two or three or more different and inconsistent causes of action, as one in tort, one upon money demand on contract, and one in equity, all combined or fused and moulded into one count or declaration, so that the defendant must await the accidents and events of trial, and until the plaintiff's proofs are all in, before being informed with any certainty or definiteness, what he was called upon to meet. The proposition that a complaint, or any single count of it, may be so framed with a double, treble, or any number of aspects looking to so many distinct and incongruous causes of action, in order to hit the exigencies of the plaintiff's case or any possible demands of his proofs at the trial, we must say, strikes us as something exceedingly novel in the rules of pleading. We do not think it is the law * * *."

As before stated, it is contended by the respondents that these allegations for conversion, etc., may be treated as surplusage, and the complaint held good as an action in assumpsit for money had and received; but in our opinion we would not be justified in holding that these allegations constitute mere surplusage and might be disregarded by the court. To so hold would introduce into the law too much uncertainty and ambiguity in pleading which would have a tendency to mislead the courts and the opposing party. A complaint should be framed upon the theory that it is either a complaint in tort or one ex contractu, and the two theories cannot be combined in one action; neither can an action at law and an action in equity be combined in one count in the same action. As was stated in the headnote in the case of Supervisors of Kewaunee County v. Decker, supra: "* * * On demurrer to a complaint, or any count thereof, the court must determine what cause of action such complaint or count is designed to state, and then whether it states facts sufficient to constitute such a cause of action; and, if not, the demurrer must be sustained, though facts may be stated sufficient to show that plaintiff has a cause of action of a different character."

* * *

The order of the circuit court overruling the demurrer is reversed.

NOTES AND QUESTIONS

1. Reread the provision of the Field Code, p. 545, supra, that tells what a complaint shall contain. Is there language in that provision that lends support to the decision in the principal case?

2. Is it appropriate for a court to insist that plaintiff's complaint is based on a theory that is not supported by the alleged facts, as in Jones v. Winsor, especially when the facts are adequate to support a different theory? Would your answer be different if the facts in the complaint were adequate to sustain either theory but the less apparent theory was the only one proved at trial? Is the result in *Jones* consistent with Section 159 of the Field Code, which is set out on p. 545, supra?

CONAUGHTY v. NICHOLS, 42 N.Y. 83 (1870). Plaintiff alleged that he had consigned goods to defendants for sale, that they had been sold for $690.82, and that after deducting the expenses of the sale there was due to plaintiff $618.43, that defendants had refused to pay this amount over to plaintiff and "have converted the same to their own use." After trial, plaintiff moved to amend the complaint by striking the allegation of conversion, but this motion was denied by the referee who then nonsuited plaintiff "on the ground that the cause of action stated in the complaint was for a tort, and the proof established a cause of action upon contract." The General Term reversed the judgment, and the Court of Appeals affirmed:

> * * * If the words "and have converted the same to their own use" had been omitted in the complaint, it could not reasonably be contended, that the same was not adapted to the cause of action established by the evidence. The case, therefore, seems to be reduced to the proposition, whether the plaintiff, having alleged facts constituting a cause of action, and having sustained them by proof upon the trial, should have been nonsuited, because the pleading contained an allegation adapted to a complaint in an action *ex delicto,* and which was unnecessary to be stated or proved, to justify a recovery on contract. We are of opinion that no such rigid rule of construction in regard to pleading should prevail under the liberal system introduced by the Code.

> * * * If the complaint in question had merely stated facts sufficient to authorize a recovery for a wrongful detention of the money, and upon the trial, the plaintiff had applied to amend by inserting facts appropriate to a cause of action on contract, and thereby changing the form and character of the action, the application should have been denied. That, however, was not the case, as the facts were fully stated, and the defendants apprized of what they were to meet upon the trial, and there was no pretense that they were surprised. If they chose to accept the complaint without moving to strike out any portion of it, or to compel the plaintiff to make it more definite, or to elect in regard to the form of action, they should not, upon the trial, have been allowed to prevent a recovery by the plaintiff of a judgment for the amount of his demand. * * * It is quite probable that the plaintiff intended, down to the trial, to recover against the defendants for a wrongful conversion of the proceeds of the sale of the property consigned to them, and doubtless the mistake should have been fatal but for the ample statement of facts contained in the complaint, which justified a recovery on contract for the amount of his demand. It does not follow that, because the parties go down to the trial upon a particular theory, which is not supported by the proof, the cause is to be dismissed, when there are facts alleged in the complaint, and sustained by the evidence, sufficient to justify a recovery upon a different theory or form of action. * * *

NOTE AND QUESTION

Is *Conaughty* consistent with Jones v. Winsor? "The reasoning of the Court in Conaughty v. Nichols that where the pleading is misleading the defendant should move to make it definite or to have the pleader elect between the possible theories, and that if he proceeds without doing so he is to be taken as fully understanding the pleading, seems very weak." Whittier, *The Theory of a Pleading*, 8 Colum.L.Rev. 523, 534 (1908). Why? If you were preparing a complaint in New York after *Conaughty,* what moral would you draw from the opinion in that case?

GARRITY v. STATE BOARD OF ADMINISTRATION

Supreme Court of Kansas, 1917.
99 Kan. 695, 162 P. 1167.

PORTER, J. * * * A demurrer to the petition was sustained; plaintiff elected to stand upon the petition and appeals.

The petition charges that in July, 1911, the board of regents of the state university, by its assistant curator of mammals, wrongfully and without plaintiff's knowledge or consent, entered upon his farm in Wallace county and removed therefrom a large and valuable fossil, the property of plaintiff, and wrongfully converted it to the use and benefit of the board of regents and its successors, depositing the fossil in the museum of the university for exhibition and scientific purposes; that the fossil was of the value of $2,500, and plaintiff had received no compensation therefor. It is alleged that the board of administration is a board created by law for the government, management, and control of the university of Kansas, * * * and is the successor of the board of regents, subrogated to the rights, duties, and responsibilities of the board of regents, and subject to its obligations and liable for its debts and contracts. * * *

1. It is the defendants' contention that both the original and the amended petition were subject to demurrer because, if they stated a cause of action at all, it was barred by the statute of limitations; that the action is one sounding in tort, and therefore barred by the two-year statute * * *. On the other hand the plaintiff claims the right to waive the tort and recover upon an implied promise to pay what the fossil is worth. We think, if [the] petition stated a cause of action against defendants, it must be held that sufficient facts were stated to authorize plaintiff to waive the tort and rely upon an implied promise to pay the value of the property converted. * * *

The two-year statute of limitations was therefore no bar to the action.

* * *

3. The principal question raised by the appeal is whether the action can be maintained against the board of administration, the original defendant. Prior to 1913 the state university was managed and controlled by a board of regents which was a body corporate created by the Legislature. It went out of existence when the act of 1913 placed the state educational institutions in control of the state board of administration, which was not made a body corporate. The act * * * provided that the board shall manage and control the property of the educational institutions named, including the state university, and conferred upon the board power "to execute trusts or other obligations now or hereafter committed to any of the said institutions * * *." The power "to execute trusts or other obligations now or hereafter committed to any of * * * said institutions" cannot be construed so as to make either the board of administration or its members liable for a tort committed by the board of regents; and the plaintiff cannot, by waiving the tort, make either the board or its members liable upon the theory of an implied promise.

* * *

The judgment is affirmed. All the Justices concurring.

NOTES AND QUESTIONS

1. Is *Garrity,* in either its statute-of-limitations aspect or its liability aspect, concerned with the theory of the pleading? In what way, if any, is the problem in *Garrity* different?

2. Why did the court hold that the action was in contract for purposes of the statute of limitations but in tort for purposes of deciding whether the Board was liable for the Regents' action?

3. Governments generally are immune from suit except as their immunity has been expressly waived by statute. Suits in contract are more commonly consented to than suits in tort. See 3 Davis, Administrative Law Treatise § 25.01 (1958). Under a statute consenting to suit in contract only, should a plaintiff be permitted to "waive" a tort and sue in "assumpsit"?

4. In a contract action, may a claim for money had and received based upon a conversion be brought as a counterclaim under a statute that provides that "in an action on contract, any other cause of action on contract" may be brought as a counterclaim? See Manhattan Egg Co. v. Seaboard Terminal & Refrig. Co., 137 Misc. 14, 242 N.Y.S. 189 (N.Y.City Ct.1929).

3. THE ARRIVAL OF MODERN PROCEDURE

Modern procedure arrived on September 16, 1938, when the Federal Rules of Civil Procedure came into effect. The adoption of the Federal Rules followed an extended period of agitation for uniform procedural rules in the federal district courts and for uniting the procedure of law and equity under one form of action. In 1934, Congress passed the Rules Enabling Act, 28 U.S.C. § 2072, authorizing the United States Supreme Court to promulgate rules of procedure for the district courts. On June 3, 1935, the Supreme Court appointed an Advisory Committee of distinguished lawyers and law professors to prepare and submit a draft of unified rules. The Committee prepared and received public comments on two published drafts. It submitted its final report to the Supreme Court in November 1937. The Supreme Court carefully reviewed and made a number of changes in the rules recommended by the Committee. The rules as adopted by the Court on December 20, 1937, were transmitted to the Attorney General and were submitted by him to the 75th Congress on January 3, 1938. Pursuant to the terms of the Rules Enabling Act, the rules came into effect when the Congress adjourned without taking action to postpone their effective date. See generally Burbank, *The Rules Enabling Act of 1934*, 130 U.Pa.L.Rev. 1015 (1982).

The chief characteristics of the Federal Rules are common sense, simplicity, and flexibility of procedure. Rule 1 states the purpose of the rules is "to secure the just, speedy, and inexpensive determination of every action and proceeding." Some of the major aspects in which the Rules advanced federal practice were the union of law and equity as one form of action, the simplification of pleadings and issues, pretrial procedure, discovery, and trial reforms. All of these subjects are developed in the succeeding Chapters of this book.

NOTE

The Federal Rules of Civil Procedure have had a strong impact on court procedures in most of the states. Nonetheless, state rules of civil procedure still vary greatly. Some states had adopted code systems similar to New York's Field Code, others modeled their rules after the Federal Rules, and others maintained common-law rules. Most states have been influenced by two or more of these models and have adopted elements of each. For example, some states, such as Delaware and New Jersey, have maintained separate court systems for law and for equity, yet they have abandoned common-law pleading. For a state-by-state discussion, see Oakley, *A Fresh Look at the Federal Rules in State Courts, 3 Nev. L.J. 354 (2003)*; and Oakley & Coon, *The Federal Rules in State Courts: A Survey of State Court Systems of Civil Procedure*, 61 Wash.L.Rev. 1367 (1986).

CHAPTER 8

MODERN PLEADING

■ ■ ■

In this Chapter, we explore modern pleading rules and how they relate to other procedural devices. Traditionally, pleading rules served four functions: (1) providing notice of the nature of a claim or defense; (2) identifying baseless claims; (3) setting each party's view of the facts; and (4) narrowing the issues. Modern pleading rules generally are not calculated to perform the last three of these functions. Instead, the framers of the Federal Rules were satisfied that the need to deter baseless claims that may clog a court's calendar could be achieved by requiring a short and plain statement of the claim showing that the plaintiff is entitled to relief, together with a certification that the pleadings are not frivolous (Rule 11), and by establishing other provisions designed expressly to screen claims on the merits (most notably, the motion for summary judgment under Rule 56). The Federal Rules also create a wide array of discovery devices that obviate the need for the parties to provide a detailed statement of the facts at the pleading stage. An important question about modern pleading is whether it generates excessive costs by allowing the filing of baseless suits that require discovery and court time. As you work through this Chapter, consider the implications of revising the pleading rules to make it more difficult to bring suit generally, or whether possible amendments should be applicable only to particular issues or claims.

SECTION A. THE COMPLAINT

1. DETAIL REQUIRED UNDER THE CODES

The Field Code, adopted by New York in 1848, p. 545, supra, became the model for states that adopted code pleading. "Code pleading required plaintiffs to state factual support for all elements of each cause of action. Compliance with these requirements was intended not only to flesh out the extent of the pleader's knowledge of the facts underlying the claim, but also to determine the legitimacy of the claim itself." Main, *Procedural Uniformity and the Exaggerated Role of Rules: A Survey of Intra-State Uniformity in Three States That Have Not Adopted the Federal Rules of Civil Procedure*, 46 Vill. L. Rev. 311, 327 (2001). Even today, some states persist in retaining code pleading and continue to require a "statement of facts" constituting a "cause of action"; others specify a "statement of facts" demonstrating a "right to relief." Is there an important difference between these formulations? Some state provisions specifically call for a statement of "ultimate facts." A number of these code states soften any harsh results of technical enforcement by stating that a pleading is satisfactory if it gives "fair notice" to the opposing party.

GILLISPIE v. GOODYEAR SERVICE STORES, 258 N.C. 487, 128 S.E.2d 762 (1963). Plaintiff alleged:

> [T]he defendants, without cause or just excuse and maliciously came upon and trespassed upon the premises occupied by the plaintiff as a residence, and by the use of harsh and threatening language and physical force directed against the plaintiff assaulted the plaintiff and placed her in great fear, and humiliated and embarrassed her by subjecting her to public scorn and ridicule, and caused her to be seized and exhibited to the public as a prisoner, and to be confined in a public jail, all to her great humiliation, embarrassment and harm.

Under the North Carolina code then in force, plaintiff was required to make a "plain and concise statement of the facts constituting a cause of action." North Carolina cases interpreting the pleading standard had stated that the complaint must "disclose the issuable facts" and allege "the material, essential and ultimate facts upon which plaintiff's right of action is based." The court held that the allegations were insufficient, noting that the pleading was necessary not only to enable the opposing party to respond but also to enable the court to declare the law upon the facts stated. The court could not do so if "a mere legal conclusion" such as "assault" or "trespass" is stated. The court concluded:

> The complaint states no facts upon which * * * legal conclusions may be predicated. Plaintiff's allegations do not disclose *what* occurred, *when* it occurred, *where* it occurred, *who* did *what*, the relationships between defendants and plaintiff or of defendants *inter se*, or any other factual data that might identify the occasion or describe the circumstances of the alleged wrongful conduct of defendants.

Id. at 490, 128 S.E.2d at 766.

The court also discussed the sufficiency of pleadings in other types of cases:

> When a complaint alleges defendant is indebted to plaintiff in a certain amount and such debt is due, but does not allege in what manner or for what cause defendant became indebted to plaintiff, it is demurrable for failure to state facts sufficient to constitute a cause of action. * * *
>
> "In an action or defense based upon negligence, it is not sufficient to allege the mere happening of an event of an injurious

> nature and call it negligence on the part of the party sought to be charged. This is necessarily so because negligence is not a fact in itself, but is the legal result of certain facts. Therefore, the facts which constitute the negligence charged and also the facts which establish such negligence as the proximate cause, or as one of the proximate causes, of the injury must be alleged." Shives v. Sample, 238 N.C. 724, 79 S.E.2d 193.

Id. at 489–90, 128 S.E.2d at 765.

NOTES AND QUESTIONS

1. Is the court in *Gillispie* legitimately concerned with the inability of defendants to ascertain the claims against them in order that they might answer and prepare their defenses? Can it be said that the pleading in *Gillispie* is unsatisfactory because the trial judge will not know what evidence is or is not relevant?

2. To what extent might the court in *Gillispie* have been motivated by the notion that a detailed account of the facts might well show that plaintiff did not have a valid claim for relief? Is it significant that at the time of the *Gillispie* decision North Carolina did not have a provision for summary judgment that allows a party to challenge an opponent's pleadings which have no basis in fact? Has the North Carolina court simply followed a hard and fast line concerning the "fact" pleading requirement, thereby undermining its basic purpose as a device for pretrial communication?

3. Plaintiff was given leave to amend the complaint after the *Gillispie* decision. Suppose that plaintiff's amended complaint also is deficient. Will she be given leave to amend again? How should the right to amend affect the question of whether or not a pleading is or is not satisfactory?

4. In ROBINSON v. BOARD OF COUNTY COMMISSIONERS, 262 Md. 342, 278 A.2d 71 (1971), plaintiff alleged that defendants "did then and there falsely, maliciously, and without just cause * * * arrest [plaintiff] * * * on charge[s] of disorderly conduct and resisting arrest, * * * [they took him] to the police station where he was forceably imprisoned, kept, detained and restrained of his liberty * * * [but upon trial he] was acquitted * * *. [Defendants] well knew that the prosecution was false, groundless, and without probable cause * * *." The court held that this passage stated facts sufficient to constitute a cause of action. Compare this pleading with that in *Gillispie*. Is one of the pleadings more informative than the other?

COOK, STATEMENTS OF FACT IN PLEADING UNDER THE CODES, 21 Colum.L.Rev. 416, 416–19, 423 (1921):

In * * * [California Packing Corp. v. Kelly Storage & Distributing Co., 228 N.Y. 49, 126 N.E. 269 (1920)] the plaintiff alleged in his complaint that the promise for the breach of which he was suing was made in exchange for "a valuable consideration." The case went to the

Court of Appeals upon the question whether this allegation is a "statement of fact" or a "conclusion of law." [The court held it was the former.] * * * An examination of the authorities in [New York and] other code jurisdictions reveals a conflict of authority. * * *

* * *

[Upon careful analysis] * * * it will appear at once that there is no logical distinction between statements which are grouped by the courts under the phrases "statements of fact" and "conclusions of law." It will also be found that many, although by no means all, pleadings held bad because they are said to plead "evidence" rather than "the facts constituting the cause of action" or defense really do nevertheless "state" the operative facts which the pleader will have to prove at the trial, but in a form different from that to which courts and lawyers are accustomed to recognize as a proper method of pleading.

* * *

The facts of life which compose the group of "operative facts" to which the law attaches legal consequences are always *specific* and not *generic.* * * * [I]n an action on the case for, let us say, negligently injuring the plaintiff by the operation of an automobile, the "operative" or "ultimate" facts proved at the trial will always be specific. It will appear that the defendant was driving a particular kind of automobile at some particular rate of speed, *etc., etc.* If now a plaintiff were to state the facts thus specifically in his complaint he would doubtless be told by the average court that he had "pleaded his evidence" and not the "facts constituting the cause of action." This would of course be erroneous. What is according to accepted notions the proper way to plead is merely a mode of stating the facts generically rather than specifically.

It must of course be recognized that at times a pleader really does err by "pleading evidence," i.e., by stating, generically or specifically, facts which do not form part of the group of operative facts, but are merely facts from which by some process of logical inference the existence of the operative facts can be inferred. More often, however, the "error" consists merely in pleading the operative facts more specifically than is usual.

* * * Let us now examine "conclusions of law." The first thing noticed upon analysis is that a so-called "conclusion of law" is a generic statement which can be made only after some legal rule has been applied to some specific group of operative facts. Consider, for example, a statement in a pleading that "defendant owes plaintiff $500." Standing by itself in a pleading this is usually treated as a mere "conclusion of law." It can, however, be made only when one knows certain facts and also the applicable legal rule. It is, in fact, the conclusion of a logical argument: Whenever certain facts, a, b, c, *etc.*, exist, B (defendant) owes A (plaintiff) $500; facts a, b, c, *etc.*, exist; therefore B owes A $500. This being so, when the bare statement is made that "B owes A $500" we may, if we wish, regard it as a statement in generic form that all the facts necessary to

create the legal duty to pay money described by the word "owe" are true as between A and B. In dealing, for example, with misrepresentation, such statements are more often than otherwise regarded in exactly this way. The same statement may, however, under proper circumstances be merely a statement as to the law applicable to facts given or known, and so be purely a statement of a "conclusion of law." * * *

* * * How specific or how generic statements in a pleading may and must be can obviously not be settled by mere logic, but according to notions of fairness and convenience. The pleading should give the adversary and the court reasonable notice of the real nature of the claim or defense; nothing more should be required.

NOTES AND QUESTIONS

1. "Quite commonly an allegation has been held bad as a statement of law only. The stating of evidence, while subject to criticism, is not so often held to render the pleading bad, since the court itself will draw the ultimate conclusion where it is the one necessarily following from the allegations made." Clark, Code Pleading § 38, at 228 (2d ed. 1947). When does the ultimate conclusion "necessarily follow"? Compare Robinson v. Meyer, 135 Conn. 691, 693–94, 68 A.2d 142, 143 (1949), in which the court inferred title by adverse possession on the basis of allegations of "all the facts necessary to establish ouster," with O'Regan v. Schermerhorn, 25 N.J.Misc. 1, 50 A.2d 10 (Sup.Ct.1946), in which the court refused to infer the defense of truth in a defamation suit when defendant alleged he believed the statement to be true and further alleged the facts on which that belief was based.

2. The Principles of Transnational Civil Procedure, issued by the American Law Institute together with the International Institute for the Unification of Private Law, require that pleadings "be in detail with particulars as to the basis of claim and that the particulars reveal a set of facts that, if proved, would entitle the claimant to a judgment." Hazard, Taruffo, Sturner & Gidi, *Introduction to the Principles and Rules of Transnational Civil Procedure*, 33 N.Y.U. J. Int'l L. & Pol. 769, 775 (2001). The transnational principles thus reject notice pleading in favor "of a fuller statement of the facts and evidence supporting the claim," an approach that more closely approximates code pleading. Sherman, *Transnational Perspectives Regarding the Federal Rules of Civil Procedure*, 56 J. Legal Educ. 510, 515 (2006). Do you see any problems with this approach? Any advantages?

2. DETAIL REQUIRED UNDER THE FEDERAL RULES

Read Federal Rules of Civil Procedure 8(a) and 12(b) in the Supplement.

DIOGUARDI v. DURNING

United States Circuit Court of Appeals, Second Circuit, 1944.
139 F.2d 774.

CLARK, CIRCUIT JUDGE. In his complaint, obviously home drawn, plaintiff attempts to assert a series of grievances against the Collector of Customs at the Port of New York growing out of his endeavors to import merchandise from Italy "of great value," consisting of bottles of "tonics." We may pass certain of his claims as either inadequate or inadequately stated and consider only these two: (1) that on the auction day, October 9, 1940, when defendant sold the merchandise at "public custom," "he sold my merchandise to another bidder with my price of $110, and not of his price of $120," and (2) "that three weeks before the sale, two cases, of 19 bottles each case, disappeared." Plaintiff does not make wholly clear how these goods came into the collector's hands, since he alleges compliance with the revenue laws; but he does say he made a claim for "refund of merchandise which was two-thirds paid in Milano, Italy," and that the collector denied the claim. These and other circumstances alleged indicate (what, indeed, plaintiff's brief asserts) that his original dispute was with his consignor as to whether anything more was due upon the merchandise, and that the collector, having held it for a year (presumably as unclaimed merchandise under 19 U.S.C.A. § 1491), then sold it, or such part of it as was left, at public auction. For his asserted injuries plaintiff claimed $5,000 damages, together with interest and costs, against the defendant individually and as collector. This complaint was dismissed by the District Court, with leave, however, to plaintiff to amend, on motion of the United States Attorney, appearing for the defendant, on the ground that it "fails to state facts sufficient to constitute a cause of action."

Thereupon plaintiff filed an amended complaint, wherein, with an obviously heightened conviction that he was being unjustly treated, he vigorously reiterates his claims, including those quoted above and now stated as that his "medicinal extracts" were given to the Springdale Distilling Company "with my betting [bidding?] price of $110: and not their price of $120," and "It isn't so easy to do away with two cases with 37 bottles of one quart. Being protected, they can take this chance." An earlier paragraph suggests that defendant had explained the loss of the two cases by "saying that they had leaked, which could never be true in the manner they were bottled." On defendant's motion for dismissal on the same ground as before, the court made a final judgment dismissing the complaint, and plaintiff now comes to us with increased volubility, if not clarity.

It would seem, however, that he has stated enough to withstand a mere formal motion, directed only to the face of the complaint, and that here is another instance of judicial haste which in the long run makes waste. Under the new rules of civil procedure, there is no pleading requirement of stating "facts sufficient to constitute a cause of action," but only that there be "a short and plain statement of the claim showing that the pleader is entitled to relief," * * * rule 8(a) * * *; and the motion for dismissal under Rule 12(b) is for failure to state "a claim upon which relief can be granted." The District Court does not state why it concluded that the complaints showed no claim upon which relief could be granted; and the United States Attorney's brief before us does not help us, for it is limited to the prognostication—unfortunately ill founded so far as we are concerned—that "the most cursory examination" of them will show the correctness of the District Court's action.

We think that, however inartistically they may be stated, the plaintiff has disclosed his claims that the collector has converted or otherwise done away with two of his cases of medicinal tonics and has sold the rest in a manner incompatible with the public auction he had announced—and, indeed, required by 19 U.S.C.A. § 1491, above cited, and the Treasury Regulations promulgated under it * * *. As to this latter claim, it may be that the collector's only error is a failure to collect an additional ten dollars from the Springdale Distilling Company; but giving the plaintiff the benefit of reasonable intendments in his allegations (as we must on this motion), the claim appears to be in effect that he was actually the first bidder at the price for which they were sold, and hence was entitled to the merchandise. Of course, defendant did not need to move on the complaint alone; he could have disclosed the facts from his point of view, in advance of a trial if he chose, by asking for a pre-trial hearing or by moving for a summary judgment with supporting affidavits. But, as it stands, we do not see how the plaintiff may properly be deprived of his day in court to show what he obviously so firmly believes and what for present purposes defendant must be taken as admitting. * * *

On remand, the District Court may find substance in other claims asserted by plaintiff, which include a failure properly to catalogue the items (as the cited Regulations provide), or to allow plaintiff to buy at a discount from the catalogue price just before the auction sale (a claim whose basis is not apparent), and a violation of an agreement to deliver the merchandise to the plaintiff as soon as he paid for it, by stopping the payments. In view of plaintiff's limited ability to write and speak English, it will be difficult for the District Court to arrive at justice unless he consents to receive legal assistance in the presentation of his case. The record indicates that he refused further help from a lawyer suggested by the court, and his brief (which was a recital of facts, rather than an argument of law) shows distrust of a lawyer of standing at this bar. It is the plaintiff's privilege to decline all legal help * * *; but we fear that he will be indeed ill advised to attempt to meet a motion for summary judgment or other similar presentation of the merits without competent advice and assistance.

Judgment is reversed and the action is remanded for further proceedings not inconsistent with this opinion.

NOTES AND QUESTIONS

1. Dioguardi's amended complaint read as follows:

UNITED STATES DISTRICT COURT

SOUTHERN DISTRICT OF NEW YORK

JOHN DIOGUARDI

Plaintiff,

-against-

HARRY M. DURNING Individually and as Collector of Customs at the Port of New York

Defendant

Plaintiff, as and for his bill of amended complaint the defendant, respectfully alleges:

FIRST: I want justice done on the basis of my medicinal extracts which have disappeared saying that they had leaked, which could never be true in the manner they were bottled.

SECOND: Mr. E.G. Collord Clerk in Charge, promised to give me my merchandise as soon as I paid for it. Then all of a sudden payments were stopped.

THIRD: Then, he didn't want to sell me my merchandise at catalogue price with the 5% off, which was very important to me, after I had already paid $5,000 for them, beside a few other expenses.

FOURTH: Why was the medicinaly given to the Springdale Distilling Co. with my betting price of $110; and not their price of $120.

FIFTH: It isn't so easy to do away with two cases with 37 bottles of one quart. Being protected, they can take this chance.

SIXTH: No one can stop my rights upon my merchandise, because of both the duly and the entry.

WHEREFORE: Plaintiff demands judgment against the defendant, individually and as Collector of Customs at the Port of New York, in the sum of Five Thousand Dollars ($5,000) together with interest from the respective dates of payment as set forth herein, together with the costs and disbursements of this action.

2. The *Dioguardi* decision was sharply criticized in McCaskill, *The Modern Philosophy of Pleading: A Dialogue Outside the Shades*, 38 A.B.A.J. 123 (1952), and became a focal point of opposition to the notice pleading introduced by the Federal Rules. How would the *Dioguardi* case have been decided in a jurisdiction that requires a statement of "facts constituting a cause of action"?

In CONLEY v. GIBSON, 355 U.S. 41, 78 S.Ct. 99, 2 L.Ed.2d 80 (1957), the Supreme Court cited *Dioguardi* and expressed its views on the degree of detail required by Rule 8(a):

> * * * In appraising the sufficiency of the complaint we follow, of course, the accepted rule that a complaint should not be dismissed for failure to state a claim unless it appears beyond doubt that the plaintiff can prove no set of facts in support of his claim which would entitle him to relief. * * *
>
> * * * [T]he Federal Rules of Civil Procedure do not require a claimant to set out in detail the facts upon which he bases his claim. To the contrary, all the Rules require is "a short and plain statement of the claim" that will give the defendant fair notice of what the plaintiff's claim is and the grounds upon which it rests. The illustrative forms appended to the Rules plainly demonstrate this. Such simplified "notice pleading" is made possible by the liberal opportunity for discovery and the other pretrial procedures established by the Rules to disclose more precisely the basis of both claim and defense and to define more narrowly the disputed facts and issues.

NOTES AND QUESTIONS

1. Examples of the simplicity of pleading under Rule 8(a) are found in the Appendix of Forms, which are set out in the Supplement following the Federal Rules of Civil Procedure; in particular see Forms 11 and 15. Note that in 1946, Rule 84 was amended to clarify that the Forms were not mere guides but rather suffice "under the rules." Judge Clark, one of the drafters of the Federal Rules, called the Forms "the most important part of the rules" because they illustrate with models how much detail is needed to survive a motion to dismiss. Clark, *Pleading Under the Federal Rules*, 12 Wyo.L.J. 177, 181 (1958).

2. Consider which, if any, of the following pleadings would, in itself, be sufficient to state a claim under Federal Rule 8(a)(2). Does Form 11 provide a benchmark for judging any of these? Which are too vague? Which are too specific?

(a) D is legally liable to P for damages.

(b) D negligently caused P's injury.

(c) D negligently caused P's injuries on July 4, 2009, at Dreamworld Amusement Park.

(d) D negligently operated a roller coaster ride on which P was a passenger on July 4, 2009, at Dreamworld Amusement Park. As a result of this negligence, P suffered a broken arm and was otherwise injured, and P incurred hospital and other medical expenses, and was prevented from transacting business, resulting in damages of $500,000.

(e) D negligently operated a roller coaster ride on which P was a passenger on July 4, 2009, at Dreamworld Amusement Park. D was negligent because it was operating the roller coaster at excessive speed and the ride was improperly maintained. As a result of this negligence, P suffered a broken arm and was otherwise injured, and P incurred hospital and other medical expenses, and was prevented from transacting business, resulting in damages of $500,000.

(f) D negligently operated a roller coaster ride on which P was a passenger on July 4, 2009, at Dreamworld Amusement Park. D was negligent because it was operating the roller coaster at excessive speed (the roller coaster was traveling at a speed of 32 mph, exceeding the safe speed by 5 mph) and the ride was improperly maintained. As a result of this negligence, P suffered a broken arm and was otherwise injured and P incurred hospital and other medical expenses, and was prevented from transacting business, resulting in damages of $500,000.

(g) D negligently operated a roller coaster ride on which P was a passenger on July 4, 2009, at Dreamworld Amusement Park. D was negligent because it was operating the roller coaster at excessive speed (the roller coaster was traveling at a speed of 32 mph, exceeding the safe speed by 5 mph), and the ride was improperly maintained. P was not contributorily negligent. As a result of this negligence, P suffered a broken arm and was otherwise injured and P incurred hospital and other medical expenses, and was prevented from transacting business, resulting in damages of $500,000.

With the exception of actions based on fraud or mistake, that are dealt with in Rule 9(b), and actions for securities fraud that are governed by a special federal statute, both of which are discussed in section 4 of this Chapter, p. 586, infra, there are no provisions, other than Rule 8(a), regarding pleading requirements in the federal courts. That has not deterred defendants, with some success, from seeking imposition of heightened pleading requirements in a variety of different types of actions, including civil rights claims, complex litigation cases, and antitrust suits. See Marcus, *The Puzzling Persistence of Pleading Practice*, 76 Texas L. Rev. 1749 (1998); see also Fairman, *The Myth of Notice Pleading*, 45 Ariz. L. Rev. 987, 1002 (2003) ("Frequently, courts use the language of Rule 8 and notice pleading yet still impose higher pleading requirements.").

NOTES AND QUESTIONS

1. In LEATHERMAN v. TARRANT COUNTY NARCOTICS INTELLIGENCE & COORDINATION UNIT, 507 U.S. 163, 113 S.Ct. 1160, 122 L.Ed.2d 517 (1993), a unanimous Supreme Court held that a federal court may not apply a more stringent pleading standard in civil rights cases alleging municipal liability under 42 U.S.C. § 1983.

The phenomenon of litigation against municipal corporations based on claimed constitutional violations by their employees dates from our decision in [Monell v. New York City Dep't of Soc. Servs., 436 U.S. 658, 98 S.Ct. 2018, 56 L.Ed.2d 611 (1978)], where we for the first time construed § 1983 to allow such municipal liability. Perhaps if Rules 8 and 9 were rewritten today, claims against municipalities under § 1983 might be subjected to the added specificity requirement of Rule 9(b). But that is a result which must be obtained by the process of amending the Federal Rules, and not by judicial interpretation. In the absence of such an amendment, federal courts and litigants must rely on summary judgment and control of discovery to weed out unmeritorious claims sooner rather than later.

Id. at 168–69, 113 S.Ct. at 1163, 122 L.Ed.2d at 524. *Leatherman* left open whether lower courts may impose heightened pleading requirements on plaintiffs bringing civil rights claims against government officials who claim qualified immunity.

2. In BAUTISTA v. LOS ANGELES COUNTY, 216 F.3d 837 (9th Cir.2000), a federal civil rights action, the trial court dismissed plaintiffs' second amended complaint with prejudice. On appeal, three distinguished Court of Appeals judges wrote separate opinions. Judge Schwarzer, writing for the court, summarized the complaint as follows:

The first claim, on behalf of twenty of the named plaintiffs, alleges that they were over the age of forty [which brings them within the scope of the federal statute prohibiting discrimination on the basis of age] and were denied employment by defendant in favor of younger employees. The second claim, on behalf of fifty-one named plaintiffs, alleges that defendant discriminated against them on account of their race, national origin and ancestry by denying them employment while employing less qualified Anglo employees. The third claim, on behalf of three named plaintiffs, alleges that plaintiff discriminated against them on the basis of their physical disabilities while employing less qualified employees.

Id. at 840. Judge Schwarzer found these allegations to be insufficient under Rule 8 because each individual plaintiff did not set out a claim that "he or she is a member of a particular protected class, was qualified and applied for the position he or she sought, and was rejected on a prohibited ground." Id. However, Judge Schwarzer voted to reverse the trial court on the ground that the latter abused its discretion by failing to give plaintiffs guidance as to how the defects in the complaint could have been cured and a chance to cure them.

Judge Reinhardt concurred but on the entirely different ground that the existing complaint met the requirements of Rule 8: "True, the complaint states the relevant facts at a high level of generality. But that is the point of notice pleading * * *. * * * [T]o the extent that a complaint lacks detail that the defendants believe they need * * * they can obtain such detail readily through interrogatories or early depositions. Surely Judge Schwarzer does not intend to say that each plaintiff in a multi-plaintiff action must plead separately each element of his or her claim in repetitious separate paragraphs." Id. at 843.

Judge O'Scannlain dissented. He agreed with Judge Schwarzer that the complaint was deficient, but he rejected the notion that the trial judge abused his discretion by not giving plaintiffs and their "experienced counsel" guidance on how to plead their case. Id. at 844.

Which of these positions makes the most sense? Which ensures that defendant has notice of the basis of plaintiff's claim? Compare Sparrow v. United Air Lines, Inc., 216 F.3d 1111, 1115 (D.C. Cir.2000) (complaint is sufficient if it alleges "I was turned down for a job because of my race").

3. In SWIERKIEWICZ v. SOREMA N. A., 534 U.S. 506, 122 S.Ct. 992, 152 L.Ed.2d 1 (2002), the Supreme Court rebuffed yet another opportunity to impose a heightened pleading requirement on civil rights claims, this time in a case involving alleged employment discrimination in violation of federal law. Justice Thomas delivered the opinion for a unanimous Court:

> This case presents the question whether a complaint in an employment discrimination lawsuit must contain specific facts establishing a prima facie case of discrimination * * *. We hold that an employment discrimination complaint need not include such facts and instead must contain only "a short and plain statement of the claim showing that the pleader is entitled to relief." Fed. Rule Civ. Proc. 8(a)(2).
>
> Petitioner Akos Swierkiewicz is a native of Hungary, who at the time of his complaint was 53 years old. * * * In April 1989, petitioner began working for respondent Sorema N. A., a reinsurance company headquartered in New York and principally owned and controlled by a French parent corporation. Petitioner was initially employed in the position of senior vice president and chief underwriting officer (CUO). Nearly six years later, Francois M. Chavel, respondent's Chief Executive Officer, demoted petitioner to a marketing and services position and transferred the bulk of his underwriting responsibilities to Nicholas Papadopoulo, a 32–year–old who, like Mr. Chavel, is a French national. About a year later, Mr. Chavel stated that he wanted to "energize" the underwriting department and appointed Mr. Papadopoulo as CUO. Petitioner claims that Mr. Papadopoulo had only one year of underwriting experience at the time he was promoted, and therefore was less experienced and less qualified to be CUO than he, since at that point he had 26 years of experience in the insurance industry.
>
> Following his demotion, petitioner contends that he "was isolated by Mr. Chavel . . . [and] excluded from business decisions and meetings and denied the opportunity to reach his true potential at SOREMA." * * * Petitioner unsuccessfully attempted to meet with Mr. Chavel to discuss his discontent. Finally, in April 1997, petitioner sent a memo to Mr. Chavel outlining his grievances and requesting a severance package. Two weeks later, respondent's general counsel presented petitioner with two options: He could either resign without a severance package or be dismissed. Mr. Chavel fired petitioner after he refused to resign.
>
> Petitioner filed a lawsuit alleging that he had been terminated on account of his national origin in violation of Title VII of the Civil Rights Act of 1964, 78 Stat. 253, as amended, 42 U.S.C. § 2000e et seq. (1994 ed. and Supp. V), and on account of his age in violation of the Age Discrimination in Employment Act of 1967 (ADEA), 81 Stat. 602, as amended, 29 U.S.C. § 621 et seq. (1994 ed. and Supp. V). * * * The United States District

Court for the Southern District of New York dismissed petitioner's complaint because it found that he "ha[d] not adequately alleged a prima facie case, in that he ha[d] not adequately alleged circumstances that support an inference of discrimination." * * * The * * * Second Circuit affirmed * * *. We granted certiorari, * * * and now reverse.

Applying Circuit precedent, the Court of Appeals required petitioner to plead a prima facie case of discrimination in order to survive respondent's motion to dismiss. * * * In the Court of Appeals' view, petitioner was thus required to allege in his complaint: (1) membership in a protected group; (2) qualification for the job in question; (3) an adverse employment action; and (4) circumstances that support an inference of discrimination. * * *

The prima facie case * * *, however, is an evidentiary standard, not a pleading requirement. * * * [T]his Court has reiterated that the prima facie case relates to the employee's burden of presenting evidence that raises an inference of discrimination. * * * [The Court further explained that the prima facie case in an employment-discrimination case sets forth "the basic allocation of burdens and order of presentation of proof" * * *.]

This Court has never indicated that the requirement for establishing a prima facie case * * * also apply to the pleading standard that plaintiffs must satisfy in order to survive a motion to dismiss. * * *

* * * [U]nder a notice pleading system, it is not appropriate to require a plaintiff to plead facts establishing a prima facie case because * * * [this] framework does not apply in every employment discrimination case. For instance, if a plaintiff is able to produce direct evidence of discrimination, he may prevail without proving all the elements of a prima facie case. * * * Under the Second Circuit's heightened pleading standard, a plaintiff without direct evidence of discrimination at the time of his complaint must plead a prima facie case of discrimination, even though discovery might uncover such direct evidence. It thus seems incongruous to require a plaintiff, in order to survive a motion to dismiss, to plead more facts than he may ultimately need to prove to succeed on the merits if direct evidence of discrimination is discovered.

* * * Given that the prima facie case operates as a flexible evidentiary standard, it should not be transposed into a rigid pleading standard for discrimination cases.

Furthermore, imposing the Court of Appeals' heightened pleading standard in employment discrimination cases conflicts with Federal Rule of Civil Procedure 8(a)(2), which provides that a complaint must include only "a short and plain statement of the claim showing that the pleader is entitled to relief." * * * Such a statement must simply "give the defendant fair notice of what the plaintiff's claim is and the grounds upon which it rests." [Conley v. Gibson, p. 562, supra.] This simplified notice pleading standard relies on liberal discovery rules and summary judgment motions to define disputed facts and issues and to dispose of unmeritorious claims. * * *

[The Court then explained that "Rule 8(a)'s simplified pleading standard applies to all civil actions, with limited exceptions," and that "[o]ther provisions of the Federal Rules * * * are inextricably linked" to this simplified pleading standard.]

Applying the relevant standard, petitioner's complaint easily satisfies the requirements of Rule 8(a) because it gives respondent fair notice of the basis for petitioner's claims. Petitioner alleged that he had been terminated on account of his national origin in violation of Title VII and on account of his age in violation of the ADEA. * * * His complaint detailed the events leading to his termination, provided relevant dates, and included the ages and nationalities of at least some of the relevant persons involved with his termination. * * * These allegations give respondent fair notice of what petitioner's claims are and the grounds upon which they rest. * * * In addition, they state claims upon which relief could be granted under Title VII and the ADEA.

Respondent argues that allowing lawsuits based on conclusory allegations of discrimination to go forward will burden the courts and encourage disgruntled employees to bring unsubstantiated suits. * * * Whatever the practical merits of this argument, the Federal Rules do not contain a heightened pleading standard for employment discrimination suits. * * * Furthermore, Rule 8(a) establishes a pleading standard without regard to whether a claim will succeed on the merits. "Indeed it may appear on the face of the pleadings that a recovery is very remote and unlikely but that is not the test." Scheuer [v. Rhodes], 416 U.S. [232], at 236, 94 S.Ct. 1683[, 1686, 40 L.Ed. 2 90, 96 (1974)].

* * *

Complex litigation, such as antitrust disputes, is another area in which some federal courts have considered the imposition of special, heightened pleading requirements. The heavy costs of litigating such cases have been a concern when it does not appear from the pleadings that plaintiff has a strong case. The Supreme Court has weighed in on this problem in *Bell Atlantic Corp. v. Twombly*, the case that follows.

Read the complaint in *Twombly* which is reproduced in the Supplement and focus carefully on ¶ 51.

BELL ATLANTIC CORP. v. TWOMBLY

Supreme Court of the United States, 2007.
550 U.S. 544, 127 S.Ct. 1955, 167 L.Ed.2d 929.

Certiorari to the United States Court of Appeals for the Second Circuit.

JUSTICE SOUTER delivered the opinion of the Court.

* * *

I

* * *

[Plaintiffs, subscribers to local telephone services, filed a class action against the major telephone companies in the United States [hereinafter ILECs], alleging that they had violated Section 1 of the Sherman Antitrust Act through efforts (1) to inhibit the growth of local phone companies [hereinafter CLEC's] and (2) to eliminate competition among themselves in territories where any one was dominant.]

* * *

The United States District Court for the Southern District of New York dismissed the complaint for failure to state a claim upon which relief can be granted. The District Court acknowledged that "plaintiffs may allege a conspiracy by citing instances of parallel business behavior that suggest an agreement," but emphasized that "while '[c]ircumstantial evidence of consciously parallel behavior may have made heavy inroads into the traditional judicial attitude toward conspiracy[, . . .] "conscious parallelism" has not yet read conspiracy out of the Sherman Act entirely.' " 313 F.Supp.2d 174, 179 (2003) * * * ([citation omitted]; alterations in original). Thus, the District Court understood that allegations of parallel business conduct, taken alone, do not state a claim under § 1; plaintiffs must allege additional facts that "ten[d] to exclude independent self-interested conduct as an explanation for defendants' parallel behavior." * * * The District Court found plaintiffs' allegations of parallel ILEC actions to discourage competition inadequate because "the behavior of each ILEC in resisting the incursion of CLECs is fully explained by the ILEC's own interests in defending its individual territory." * * * As to the ILECs' supposed agreement against competing with each other, the District Court found that the complaint does not "alleg[e] facts . . . suggesting that refraining from competing in other territories as CLECs was contrary to [the ILECs'] apparent economic interests, and consequently [does] not rais[e] an inference that [the ILECs'] actions were the result of a conspiracy." * * *

The Court of Appeals for the Second Circuit reversed, holding that the District Court tested the complaint by the wrong standard. It held that "plus factors are not *required* to be pleaded to permit an antitrust claim based on parallel conduct to survive dismissal." 425 F.3d 99, 114 (2005) (emphasis in original). Although the Court of Appeals took the view that plaintiffs must plead facts that "include conspiracy among the realm of 'plausible' possibilities in order to survive a motion to dismiss," it then said that "to rule that allegations of parallel anticompetitive conduct fail to support a plausible conspiracy claim, a court would have to conclude that there is no set of facts that would permit a plaintiff to demonstrate that the particular parallelism asserted was the product of collusion rather than coincidence." *Ibid.*

We granted certiorari to address the proper standard for pleading an antitrust conspiracy through allegations of parallel conduct * * * and now reverse.

II

A

Because § 1 of the Sherman Act "does not prohibit [all] unreasonable restraints of trade . . . but only restraints effected by a contract, combination, or conspiracy," * * * "[t]he crucial question" is whether the challenged anticompetitive conduct "stem[s] from independent decision or from an agreement, tacit or express," * * *. While a showing of parallel "business behavior is admissible circumstantial evidence from which the fact finder may infer agreement," it falls short of "conclusively establish[ing] agreement or . . . itself constitut[ing] a Sherman Act offense." * * * Even "conscious parallelism," a common reaction of "firms in a concentrated market [that] recogniz[e] their shared economic interests and their interdependence with respect to price and output decisions" is "not in itself unlawful." * * *

* * *

B

This case presents the antecedent question of what a plaintiff must plead in order to state a claim under § 1 of the Sherman Act. Federal Rule of Civil Procedure 8(a)(2) requires only "a short and plain statement of the claim showing that the pleader is entitled to relief," in order to "give the defendant fair notice of what the . . . claim is and the grounds upon which it rests," *Conley v. Gibson,* 355 U.S. 41, 47, 78 S.Ct. 99, 2 L.Ed.2d 80 (1957). While a complaint attacked by a Rule 12(b)(6) motion to dismiss does not need detailed factual allegations * * *, a plaintiff's obligation to provide the "grounds" of his "entitle[ment] to relief" requires more than labels and conclusions, and a formulaic recitation of the elements of a cause of action will not do, see *Papasan v. Allain,* 478 U.S. 265, 286, 106 S.Ct. 2932, 92 L.Ed.2d 209 (1986) (on a motion to dismiss, courts "are not bound to accept as true a legal conclusion couched as a factual allegation"). Factual allegations must be enough to raise a right to relief above the speculative level, see 5 C. Wright & A. Miller, Federal Practice and Procedure § 1216, pp. 235–236 (3d ed.2004) (hereinafter Wright & Miller)

("[T]he pleading must contain something more . . . than . . . a statement of facts that merely creates a suspicion [of] a legally cognizable right of action"),[3] on the assumption that all the allegations in the complaint are true (even if doubtful in fact), see, *e.g.*, *Swierkiewicz v. Sorema N. A.*, * * *.

In applying these general standards to a § 1 claim, we hold that stating such a claim requires a complaint with enough factual matter (taken as true) to suggest that an agreement was made. Asking for plausible grounds to infer an agreement does not impose a probability requirement at the pleading stage; it simply calls for enough fact to raise a reasonable expectation that discovery will reveal evidence of illegal agreement. And, of course, a well-pleaded complaint may proceed even if it strikes a savvy judge that actual proof of those facts is improbable, and "that a recovery is very remote and unlikely." *Ibid.* In identifying facts that are suggestive enough to render a § 1 conspiracy plausible, we have the benefit of the prior rulings and considered views of leading commentators, already quoted, that lawful parallel conduct fails to bespeak unlawful agreement. It makes sense to say, therefore, that an allegation of parallel conduct and a bare assertion of conspiracy will not suffice. Without more, parallel conduct does not suggest conspiracy, and a conclusory allegation of agreement at some unidentified point does not supply facts adequate to show illegality. Hence, when allegations of parallel conduct are set out in order to make a § 1 claim, they must be placed in a context that raises a suggestion of a preceding agreement, not merely parallel conduct that could just as well be independent action.

* * *

We alluded to the practical significance of the Rule 8 entitlement requirement in *Dura Pharmaceuticals, Inc. v. Broudo,* 544 U.S. 336, 125 S.Ct. 1627, 161 L.Ed.2d 577 (2005), when we explained that something beyond the mere possibility of loss causation must be alleged, lest a plaintiff with " 'a largely groundless claim' " be allowed to " 'take up the time of a number of other people, with the right to do so representing an *in terrorem* increment of the settlement value.' " *Id.,* at 347, 125 S.Ct. 1627 * * *. * * *

Thus, it is one thing to be cautious before dismissing an antitrust complaint in advance of discovery * * * but quite another to forget that proceeding to antitrust discovery can be expensive. As we indicated over 20 years ago * * *,"a district court must retain the power to insist upon

3. The dissent greatly oversimplifies matters by suggesting that the Federal Rules somehow dispensed with the pleading of facts altogether. * * * While, for most types of cases, the Federal Rules eliminated the cumbersome requirement that a claimant "set out *in detail* the facts upon which he bases his claim," *Conley v. Gibson* * * * (emphasis added), Rule 8(a)(2) still requires a "showing," rather than a blanket assertion, of entitlement to relief. Without some factual allegation in the complaint, it is hard to see how a claimant could satisfy the requirement of providing not only "fair notice" of the nature of the claim, but also "grounds" on which the claim rests. See 5 Wright & Miller § 1202, at 94, 95 (Rule 8(a) "contemplate[s] the statement of circumstances, occurrences, and events in support of the claim presented" and does not authorize a pleader's "bare averment that he wants relief and is entitled to it").

some specificity in pleading before allowing a potentially massive factual controversy to proceed." * * * That potential expense is obvious enough in the present case: plaintiffs represent a putative class of at least 90 percent of all subscribers to local telephone or high-speed Internet service in the continental United States, in an action against America's largest telecommunications firms (with many thousands of employees generating reams and gigabytes of business records) for unspecified (if any) instances of antitrust violations that allegedly occurred over a period of seven years.

It is no answer to say that a claim just shy of a plausible entitlement to relief can, if groundless, be weeded out early in the discovery process through "careful case management," * * * given the common lament that the success of judicial supervision in checking discovery abuse has been on the modest side. See, *e.g.*, Easterbrook, Discovery as Abuse, 69 B.U.L.Rev. 635, 638 (1989) ("Judges can do little about impositional discovery when parties control the legal claims to be presented and conduct the discovery themselves"). And it is self-evident that the problem of discovery abuse cannot be solved by "careful scrutiny of evidence at the summary judgment stage," much less "lucid instructions to juries"; * * * the threat of discovery expense will push cost-conscious defendants to settle even anemic cases before reaching those proceedings. Probably, then, it is only by taking care to require allegations that reach the level suggesting conspiracy that we can hope to avoid the potentially enormous expense of discovery in cases with no " 'reasonably founded hope that the [discovery] process will reveal relevant evidence' " to support a § 1 claim. * * *[6]

Plaintiffs do not, of course, dispute the requirement of plausibility and the need for something more than merely parallel behavior * * *, and their main argument against the plausibility standard at the pleading stage is its ostensible conflict with an early statement of ours construing Rule 8. Justice Black's opinion for the Court in *Conley v. Gibson* spoke not

6. The dissent takes heart in the reassurances of plaintiffs' counsel that discovery would be " ' "phased" ' " and "limited to the existence of the alleged conspiracy and class certification." * * * But determining whether some illegal agreement may have taken place between unspecified persons at different ILECs (each a multibillion dollar corporation with legions of management level employees) at some point over seven years is a sprawling, costly, and hugely time-consuming undertaking not easily susceptible to the kind of line drawing and case management that the dissent envisions. Perhaps the best answer to the dissent's optimism that antitrust discovery is open to effective judicial control is a more extensive quotation of the authority just cited, a judge with a background in antitrust law. Given the system that we have, the hope of effective judicial supervision is slim: "The timing is all wrong. The plaintiff files a sketchy complaint (the Rules of Civil Procedure discourage fulsome documents), and discovery is launched. A judicial officer does not know the details of the case the parties will present and in theory *cannot* know the details. Discovery is used to find the details. The judicial officer always knows less than the parties, and the parties themselves may not know very well where they are going or what they expect to find. A magistrate supervising discovery does not-cannot-know the expected productivity of a given request, because the nature of the requester's claim and the contents of the files (or head) of the adverse party are unknown. Judicial officers cannot measure the costs and benefits to the requester and so cannot isolate impositional requests. Requesters have no reason to disclose their own estimates because they gain from imposing costs on rivals (and may lose from an improvement in accuracy). The portions of the Rules of Civil Procedure calling on judges to trim back excessive demands, therefore, have been, and are doomed to be, hollow. We cannot prevent what we cannot detect; we cannot detect what we cannot define; we cannot define 'abusive' discovery except in theory, because in practice we lack essential information." Easterbrook, Discovery as Abuse, 69 B.U.L.Rev. 635, 638–639 (1989).

only of the need for fair notice of the grounds for entitlement to relief but of "the accepted rule that a complaint should not be dismissed for failure to state a claim unless it appears beyond doubt that the plaintiff can prove no set of facts in support of his claim which would entitle him to relief." * * * This "no set of facts" language can be read in isolation as saying that any statement revealing the theory of the claim will suffice unless its factual impossibility may be shown from the face of the pleadings; and the Court of Appeals appears to have read *Conley* in some such way when formulating its understanding of the proper pleading standard * * *.

On such a focused and literal reading of *Conley's* "no set of facts," a wholly conclusory statement of claim would survive a motion to dismiss whenever the pleadings left open the possibility that a plaintiff might later establish some "set of [undisclosed] facts" [in original] to support recovery. So here, the Court of Appeals specifically found the prospect of unearthing direct evidence of conspiracy sufficient to preclude dismissal, even though the complaint does not set forth a single fact in a context that suggests an agreement. * * * It seems fair to say that this approach to pleading would dispense with any showing of a " 'reasonably founded hope' " that a plaintiff would be able to make a case * * *. Mr. Micawber's optimism would be enough.

Seeing this, a good many judges and commentators have balked at taking the literal terms of the *Conley* passage as a pleading standard. [Several citations omitted.] * * *

* * * [A]fter puzzling the profession for 50 years, this famous observation has earned its retirement. The phrase is best forgotten as an incomplete, negative gloss on an accepted pleading standard: once a claim has been stated adequately, it may be supported by showing any set of facts consistent with the allegations in the complaint. * * * *Conley,* then, described the breadth of opportunity to prove what an adequate complaint claims, not the minimum standard of adequate pleading to govern a complaint's survival.

III

When we look for plausibility in this complaint, we agree with the District Court that plaintiffs' claim of conspiracy in restraint of trade comes up short. To begin with, the complaint leaves no doubt that plaintiffs rest their § 1 claim on descriptions of parallel conduct and not on any independent allegation of actual agreement among the ILECs. * * * Although in form a few stray statements speak directly of agreement, on fair reading these are merely legal conclusions resting on the prior allegations. * * * The nub of the complaint, then, is the ILECs' parallel behavior, consisting of steps to keep the CLECs out and manifest disinterest in becoming CLECs themselves, and its sufficiency turns on the suggestions raised by this conduct when viewed in light of common economic experience.

* * * [T]here is no reason to infer that the companies had agreed among themselves to do what was only natural anyway; so natural, in fact, that if alleging parallel decisions to resist competition were enough to imply an antitrust conspiracy, pleading a § 1 violation against almost any group of competing businesses would be a sure thing.

Plaintiffs' second conspiracy theory rests on the competitive reticence among the ILECs themselves * * *.

But * * * [such a lack of competition is] not suggestive of conspiracy, not if history teaches anything. In a traditionally unregulated industry with low barriers to entry, sparse competition among large firms dominating separate geographical segments of the market could very well signify illegal agreement, but here we have an obvious alternative explanation. * * * [Historically] monopoly was the norm in telecommunications, not the exception. * * * The ILECs were born in that world, doubtless liked the world the way it was, and surely knew the adage about him who lives by the sword. Hence, a natural explanation for the noncompetition alleged is that the former Government-sanctioned monopolists were sitting tight, expecting their neighbors to do the same thing.

* * *

Plaintiffs say that our analysis runs counter to *Swierkiewicz v. Sorema N. A.,* [p. 565 supra] * * *. Even though Swierkiewicz's pleadings "detailed the events leading to his termination * * *," the Court of Appeals dismissed his complaint for failing to allege certain additional facts that Swierkiewicz would need at the trial stage to support his claim in the absence of direct evidence of discrimination * * *. We reversed on the ground that the Court of Appeals had impermissibly applied what amounted to a heightened pleading requirement by insisting that Swierkiewicz allege "specific facts" beyond those necessary to state his claim and the grounds showing entitlement to relief. * * *

Here, in contrast, we do not require heightened fact pleading of specifics, but only enough facts to state a claim to relief that is plausible on its face. Because the plaintiffs here have not nudged their claims across the line from conceivable to plausible, their complaint must be dismissed.

* * *

The judgment of the Court of Appeals for the Second Circuit is reversed, and the cause is remanded for further proceedings consistent with this opinion.

It is so ordered.

JUSTICE STEVENS, with whom JUSTICE GINSBURG joins except as to Part IV, dissenting.

* * *

* * * [T]his is a case in which there is no dispute about the substantive law. If the defendants acted independently, their conduct was perfect-

ly lawful. If, however, that conduct is the product of a horizontal agreement among potential competitors, it was unlawful. Plaintiffs have alleged such an agreement and, because the complaint was dismissed in advance of answer, the allegation has not even been denied. Why, then, does the case not proceed? Does a judicial opinion that the charge is not "plausible" provide a legally acceptable reason for dismissing the complaint? I think not.

Respondents' amended complaint describes a variety of circumstantial evidence and [¶ 51 of the complaint]* * * allege[s] that petitioners entered into an agreement that has long been recognized as a classic *per se* violation of the Sherman Act. See Report of the Attorney General's National Committee to Study the Antitrust Laws 26 (1955).

* * *

The Court and petitioners' legal team are no doubt correct that the parallel conduct alleged is consistent with the absence of any contract, combination, or conspiracy. But that conduct is also entirely consistent with the *presence* of the illegal agreement alleged in the complaint. And the charge that petitioners "agreed not to compete with one another" is not just one of "a few stray statements," * * * it is an allegation describing unlawful conduct. As such, the Federal Rules of Civil Procedure, our longstanding precedent, and sound practice mandate that the District Court at least require some sort of response from petitioners before dismissing the case.

Two practical concerns presumably explain the Court's dramatic departure from settled procedural law. Private antitrust litigation can be enormously expensive, and there is a risk that jurors may mistakenly conclude that evidence of parallel conduct has proved that the parties acted pursuant to an agreement when they in fact merely made similar independent decisions. Those concerns merit careful case management, including strict control of discovery, careful scrutiny of evidence at the summary judgment stage, and lucid instructions to juries; they do not, however, justify the dismissal of an adequately pleaded complaint without even requiring the defendants to file answers denying a charge that they in fact engaged in collective decisionmaking. More importantly, they do not justify an interpretation of Federal Rule of Civil Procedure 12(b)(6) that seems to be driven by the majority's appraisal of the plausibility of the ultimate factual allegation rather than its legal sufficiency.

I

* * *

Under the relaxed pleading standards of the Federal Rules, the idea was not to keep litigants out of court but rather to keep them in. The merits of a claim would be sorted out during a flexible pretrial process and, as appropriate, through the crucible of trial. See *Swierkiewicz* * * * ("The liberal notice pleading of Rule 8(a) is the starting point of a simplified pleading system, which was adopted to focus litigation on the merits of a claim"). * * *

II

It is in the context of this history that *Conley v. Gibson* * * * must be understood. * * *

Consistent with the design of the Federal Rules, *Conley's* "no set of facts" formulation permits outright dismissal only when proceeding to discovery or beyond would be futile. Once it is clear that a plaintiff has stated a claim that, if true, would entitle him to relief, matters of proof are appropriately relegated to other stages of the trial process. Today, however, in its explanation of a decision to dismiss a complaint that it regards as a fishing expedition, the Court scraps *Conley's* "no set of facts" language. Concluding that the phrase has been "questioned, criticized, and explained away long enough," * * * the Court dismisses it as careless composition.

If *Conley's* "no set of facts" language is to be interred, let it not be without a eulogy. That exact language, which the majority says has "puzzl[ed] the profession for 50 years," * * * has been cited as authority in a dozen opinions of this Court and four separate writings. In not one of those 16 opinions was the language "questioned," "criticized," or "explained away." Indeed, today's opinion is the first by any Member of this Court to express *any* doubt as to the adequacy of the *Conley* formulation. Taking their cues from the federal courts, 26 States and the District of Columbia utilize as their standard for dismissal of a complaint the very language the majority repudiates: whether it appears "beyond doubt" that "no set of facts" in support of the claim would entitle the plaintiff to relief.

Petitioners have not requested that the *Conley* formulation be retired, nor have any of the six *amici* who filed briefs in support of petitioners. I would not rewrite the Nation's civil procedure textbooks and call into doubt the pleading rules of most of its States without far more informed deliberation as to the costs of doing so. Congress has established a process—a rulemaking process—for revisions of that order. * * *

* * *

* * * *Conley's* statement that a complaint is not to be dismissed unless "no set of facts" in support thereof would entitle the plaintiff to relief is hardly "puzzling." * * * It reflects a philosophy that, unlike in the days of code pleading, separating the wheat from the chaff is a task assigned to the pretrial and trial process. *Conley's* language, in short, captures the policy choice embodied in the Federal Rules and binding on the federal courts.

We have consistently reaffirmed that basic understanding of the Federal Rules in the half century since *Conley*. * * *

* * *

Everything today's majority says would therefore make perfect sense if it were ruling on a Rule 56 motion for summary judgment and the evidence included nothing more than the Court has described. But it should go without saying * * * that a heightened production burden at the summary judgment stage does not translate into a heightened pleading burden at the complaint stage. The majority rejects the complaint in this case because—in light of the fact that the parallel conduct alleged is consistent with ordinary market behavior—the claimed conspiracy is "conceivable" but not "plausible." * * * But even if the majority's speculation is correct, its "plausibility" standard is irreconcilable with Rule 8 and with our governing precedents. * * * [F]ear of the burdens of litigation does not justify factual conclusions supported only by lawyers' arguments rather than sworn denials or admissible evidence.

* * *

III

* * * [T]he theory on which the Court permits dismissal is that, so far as the Federal Rules are concerned, no agreement has been alleged at all. This is a mind-boggling conclusion.

* * * I am * * * willing to entertain the majority's belief that any agreement among the companies was unlikely. But the plaintiffs allege in three places in their complaint, * * * that the ILECs did in fact agree both to prevent competitors from entering into their local markets and to forgo competition with each other. And as the Court recognizes, at the motion to dismiss stage, a judge assumes "that all the allegations in the complaint are true (even if doubtful in fact)." * * *

The majority circumvents this obvious obstacle to dismissal by pretending that it does not exist. The Court admits that "in form a few stray statements in the complaint speak directly of agreement," but disregards those allegations by saying that "on fair reading these are merely legal conclusions resting on the prior allegations" of parallel conduct. * * * The Court's dichotomy between factual allegations and "legal conclusions" is the stuff of a bygone era * * *. That distinction was a defining feature of code pleading * * *, but was conspicuously abolished when the Federal Rules were enacted in 1938. * * * "Defendants entered into a contract" is no more a legal conclusion than "defendant negligently drove," see [Federal Rules] Form 9 * * * [now Federal Form 11]. Indeed it is less of one.

To be clear, if I had been the trial judge in this case, I would not have permitted the plaintiffs to engage in massive discovery based solely on the allegations in this complaint. On the other hand, I surely would not have dismissed the complaint without requiring the defendants to answer the charge that they "have agreed not to compete with one another and otherwise allocated customers and markets to one another." Even a sworn denial of that charge would not justify a summary dismissal without giving the plaintiffs the opportunity to take depositions from * * * at least one responsible executive representing each of the * * * defendants.

* * *

IV

* * *

The transparent policy concern that drives the decision is the interest in protecting antitrust defendants—who in this case are some of the wealthiest corporations in our economy—from the burdens of pretrial discovery. * * * Even if it were not apparent that the legal fees petitioners have incurred in arguing the merits of their Rule 12(b) motion have far exceeded the cost of limited discovery, or that those discovery costs would burden respondents as well as petitioners, that concern would not provide an adequate justification for this law-changing decision. For in the final analysis it is only a lack of confidence in the ability of trial judges to control discovery, buttressed by appellate judges' independent appraisal of the plausibility of profoundly serious factual allegations, that could account for this stark break from precedent.

* * *

Accordingly, I respectfully dissent.

NOTES AND QUESTIONS

1. Does the *Twombly* case, with its harsh attack on Conley v. Gibson and the "no set of facts" standard, imply that there is a new heightened pleading requirement for all actions in the federal courts, in that any stated claim for relief must be "plausible"? In ERICKSON v. PARDUS, 551 U.S. 89, 127 S.Ct. 2197, 167 L.Ed.2d 1081 (2007), which was decided less than one month after *Twombly*, the Supreme Court again examined the Rule 8(a) pleading requirement. In that case plaintiff, a federal prisoner, filed a pro se lawsuit, alleging that he had been denied proper treatment for a case of hepatitis C, placing his life in jeopardy. The trial court dismissed the action under Rule 12(b)(6) on the ground that the prisoner had failed to plead that he had suffered substantial harm, and the Court of Appeals affirmed on the ground the petitioner had made "only conclusionary allegations to the effect that he ha[d] suffered a cognizable independent harm as a result" of defendant's actions. Erickson v. Pardus, 198 Fed.Appx. 694, 698 (10th Cir.2006). In a per curiam opinion the Supreme Court reversed, stating:

> Federal Rule of Civil Procedure 8(a)(2) requires only "a short and plain statement of the claim showing that the pleader is entitled to relief." Specific facts are not necessary; the statement need only " 'give the defendant fair notice of what the . . . claim is and the grounds on which it rests.' " *Bell Atlantic v. Twombly* * * * (quoting *Conley v. Gibson*, 355 U.S. 41, 47 * * *).

In light of the *Erickson* decision, along with its quotation from *Conley*, just where does the Court stand with regard to pleading standards? Did it backtrack on its holding in *Twombly*? Should *Erickson* be read as bending over backwards for a pro se plaintiff? For a thorough analysis of *Twombly*, and whether *Erickson* ought to be read to limit its scope, see Ides, Bell Atlantic *and the Principle of Substantive Sufficiency Under Federal Rule of Civil Procedure 8(a)(2): Toward a Structured Approach to Federal Pleading Practice*, 243 F.R.D. 604 (2006). A copy of the *Erickson* complaint appears in the Supplement.

2. In ASHCROFT v. IQBAL, 556 U.S. ___, 129 S.Ct. 1937, ___ L.Ed.2d ___ (2009), a discrimination case filed by a Pakistani Muslim man who had been detained in the aftermath of the September 11, 2001 attacks, the Court clarified that its decision in *Twombly* "expounded the pleading standard" for all civil actions, but that "[d]etermining whether a complaint states a plausible claim for relief will * * * be a context-specific task that requires the reviewing court to draw on its judicial experience and common sense." Even before *Iqbal*, the federal appellate courts had invoked *Twombly's* "plausibility" language in cases on a wide variety of non-antitrust topics ranging from religious discrimination, Watts v. Florida Int'l Univ., 495 F.3d 1289 (11th Cir. 2007)), to Fair Housing Act violations, Boykin v. Keycorp, 521 F.3d 202 (2d Cir. 2008)), to employment discrimination claims, Tamayo v. Blagojevich, 526 F.3d 1074 (7th Cir. 2008)).

3. What problems might flow from a system in which pleading rules differ depending on the category of the lawsuit? Should the requirements of a procedural system be uniform regardless of the character of the claim? Should courts retain discretion to adapt general pleading rules in specific cases? See Subrin, *Fudge Points and Thin Ice in Discovery Reform and the Case for Selective Substance–Specific Procedure*, 46 Fla. L. Rev. 27, 28 (1994).

4. Can *Twombly* be read to make the required level of pleading in an action dependent on the cost of discovery should the pleading be upheld? Professor Epstein has argued that *Twombly* correctly recognizes that "as the costs of discovery mount, the case for terminating litigation earlier in the cycle gets ever stronger," and that early termination is particularly appropriate "in those cases where the plaintiff relies on public information, easily assembled and widely available, that can be effectively rebutted by other public evidence." Epstein, *Bell Atlantic v. Twombly: How Motions To Dismiss Become (Disguised) Summary Judgments*, 25 Wash. U. J. L. & Pol'y 61, 66–67 (2007). For a critical comment on that aspect of *Twombly*, see *Leading Cases*, 121 Harv. L. Rev. 305, 309–15 (2007).

5. State courts, when deciding a motion to dismiss under state law, are not required to follow either the Federal Rules or federal judicial standards governing the sufficiency of a complaint. Justice Stevens points out in his dissent that about half of the states did, in fact, follow the *Conley* "no set of facts" standard. See p. 562, supra. State courts so far have not unanimously retreated from *Conley* and embraced the *Twombly* plausibility standard. Compare Sisney v. Best Inc., 754 N.W.2d 804 (S.D. 2008) (adopting *Twombly* pleading standard for state court pleadings), with Colby v. Umbrella, Inc., 955 A.2d 1082 (Vt. 2008) (rejecting *Twombly* and retaining *Conley* standard for state court pleadings) and Cullen v. Auto–Owners Insurance Co., 218 Ariz. 417, 189 P.3d 344 (2008) (rejecting both *Twombly* and *Conley* standards and retaining unique Arizona state pleading requirements). See Chen, Note—

Following the Leader: Twombly, *Pleading Standards, and Procedural Uniformity*, 108 Colum. L. Rev. 1431 (2008).

6. *Twombly* provides a window into a fascinating debate about judicial case management as an alternative to stricter pleading standards. The *Twombly* majority commented that "the success of judicial supervision in checking discovery abuse has been on the modest side," p. 571, supra, citing a 1989 law review article that contended the trial courts are impotent to control abuse. Since 1983, the Federal Rules have been amended in important ways to curb litigation expense and to increase the court's managerial authority. See Cavanagh, Twombly, *the Federal Rules of Civil Procedure and the Courts*, 82 St. John's L. Rev. 877 (2008). Justice Stevens, in his dissent, underscored that "[t]he Court vastly underestimates a district court's case-management arsenal," 550 U.S. at 595 n. 13, 127 S.Ct. at 1988 n. 13, 167 L.Ed.2d at 964 n. 13, and a respected district court judge has sharply questioned this aspect of the majority's decision. See McMahon, *The Law of Unintended Consequences: Shockwaves in the Lower Courts After* Bell Atlantic Corp. v. Twombly, 41 Suffolk U. L. Rev. 851, 869–70 (2008). Keep an open mind on these issues until you have studied such topics as sanctions, see pp. 635–51, infra; discovery case plans and other discovery controls, see Chapter 11, infra; case management, see Chapter 12, infra; and summary judgment, see Chapter 13, infra.

Reread Federal Rule of Civil Procedure 8(a)(2) in the Supplement.

Under the Federal Rules, can a court reject a pleading for including too much information? See Trudeau v. FTC, 456 F.3d 178, 193 (D.C. Cir. 2006) (noting that it "is possible for a plaintiff to plead too much: that is, to plead himself out of court by alleging facts that render success on the merits impossible") (citation omitted). In Deyo v. Internal Revenue Service, 2002 WL 1482517 (D.Conn. 2002), the District Court conditionally dismissed a pro se complaint, pointing to the fact that the pleading was "neither short nor plain," and instead ran for 43 pages and included "verbatim dialogue from such things as telephone conversations."

GARCIA v. HILTON HOTELS INTERNATIONAL, INC.

United States District Court, District of Puerto Rico, 1951.
97 F.Supp. 5.

ROBERTS, DISTRICT JUDGE. The action here is for damages for defamation brought by plaintiff, a citizen and resident of Puerto Rico, against defendant, a Delaware corporation, in the District Court of Puerto Rico and removed to this Court by defendant corporation. The complaint sets forth two causes of action and the paragraphs considered herein are identical in each cause. Defendant has moved to dismiss the complaint for failure to state a claim upon which relief can be granted and, in the alternative, to strike Paragraphs 5, 6, 7 and 8 and for a more definite statement.

In * * * [support] of its motion to dismiss, defendant contends that no publication of the alleged slanderous statement is alleged and that the complaint, therefore, fails to state a cause of action. This contention will be considered first with respect to Paragraph 4 of the complaint, which reads as follows: "4. On August 22, 1950, the plaintiff was violently discharged by the defendant, being falsely and slanderously accused of being engaged in bringing women from outside the Hotel and introducing them into the rooms thereof for the purpose of developing prostitution in the Hotel and that such women brought by him from outside the Hotel and introduced therein carried on acts of prostitution in said Hotel."

* * *

The controlling question here, with respect to the motion to dismiss, is whether the allegations of Paragraph 4 of the complaint, state a claim upon which relief can be granted. An examination of the authorities is persuasive that [it] does. It is settled, with respect to motions to dismiss for insufficiency of statement, that the complaint is to be construed in the light most favorable to the plaintiff with all doubts resolved in his favor and the allegations accepted as true. If, when a complaint is so considered, it reasonably may be anticipated that plaintiff, on the basis of what has been alleged, could make out a case at trial entitling him to some relief, the complaint should not be dismissed. * * *

In the instant case, it is true that Paragraph 4, of the complaint, fails to state, in so many words, that there was a publication of the alleged slanderous utterance and, to that extent, the cause of action is defectively stated. However, it does not follow that the allegations do not state a claim upon which relief can be granted. It is alleged that plaintiff was "violently discharged" and was "falsely and slanderously accused" of procuring for prostitution. While in a technical sense, this language states a conclusion, it is clear that plaintiff used it intending to charge publication of the slanderous utterance and it would be unrealistic for defendant to claim that it does not so understand the allegations. * * * Clearly, under such allegations it reasonably may be conceived that plaintiff, upon trial, could adduce evidence tending to prove a publication. * * *

In further support of its motion to dismiss, defendant contends that the alleged slanderous utterance was conditionally privileged. Conceding that to be so does not require that a different conclusion be reached with respect to the motion to dismiss. Rule 12(b) requires that every defense in law or fact be asserted in a responsive pleading when one is required or permitted under the rules. The rule, however, enumerates certain defenses which may be asserted by motion to dismiss, all of which go to the jurisdiction except that of failure to state a claim upon which relief can be granted, rule 12(b)(6). And this latter defense may be asserted successfully by a motion prior to responsive pleading only when it appears to a certainty that plaintiff would be entitled to no relief under any state of fact which could be proved in support of the claim asserted by him. * * *

The conclusiveness of privilege as a defense depends upon whether the privilege involved [is] absolute or conditional. When the privilege involved is absolute, it constitutes a finally determinative or conclusive defense to an action based on the utterance. Consequently, when it appears from a complaint that absolute privilege exists, the defense of failure to state a claim properly may be asserted to accomplish a dismissal on motion under rule 12(b). It is for the court to determine the existence of privilege and when absolute privilege is found, it constitutes an unassailable defense and, clearly, in such a case, the claim stated is one upon which relief cannot be granted.

But conditional privilege is not a conclusive defense to an action based on a slanderous utterance. It is but a qualified defense which may be lost to the defendant if plaintiff can prove abuse of the privilege or actual malice. * * * When from the allegations contained therein, a complaint indicates the availability of the defense of conditional privilege, it cannot be held therefrom as a matter of law, that there has been a failure to state a claim upon which relief can be granted, such as will warrant dismissal of the complaint on motion under rule 12(b)(6), for the factual question remains whether defendant abused the privilege or made the communication maliciously. * * *

As has been noted, on motion to dismiss for failure to state a claim [the] complaint must be construed in the light most favorable to plaintiff with all doubts resolved in his favor and the allegation taken as true. That being so, when allegations are sufficient to sustain the defense of conditional privilege they will be, generally, sufficient to permit the introduction of evidence tending to prove abuse of the privilege or actual malice. Save in some extraordinary situation, allegations which are adequate for the admission of evidence to prove the defense of qualified privilege are adequate for the admission of evidence to negative that defense. It appears from the complaint in the instant case that defendant is entitled to raise the defense of conditional privilege. But this defense may be lost to it if plaintiff proves abuse of the privilege or actual malice. And, clearly, plaintiff may introduce evidence under the allegations for the purpose of proving abuse of the privilege or actual malice. Therefore, it is concluded that defendant's motion to dismiss the complaint for failure to state a claim upon which relief can be granted should be denied.

The conclusion to deny defendant's motion to dismiss requires that consideration be given its alternative motion to strike Paragraphs 5, 6, 7 and 8 of the complaint. It is alleged in these paragraphs, in substance, that upon being discharged, plaintiff made claim with the Labor Department of Puerto Rico for severance pay and overtime as is provided for by law (Section 20, Organic Act of Labor Department of Puerto Rico, approved April 14, 1931); that during a hearing on such claim held by the Labor Department, defendant, falsely and slanderously, repeated its charge that plaintiff had been engaged in procuring for prostitution; and, that, after said hearing defendant had compromised plaintiff's claim for severance pay and overtime. As respects defendant's motion to strike, the controlling allegations are contained in Paragraph 7 of this complaint.

Section 4 of "An Act Authorizing Civil Actions to recover Damages for Libel and Slander," enacted by the Legislature of Puerto Rico and approved on February 19, 1902, (Code of Civil Procedure of Puerto Rico, Ed. 1933, page 309) provides in part as follows: "Section 4. A publication or communication shall not be held or deemed malicious when made in any legislative or judicial proceeding or in any other proceeding authorized by law. * * * "

The effect of the above quoted portions of the statute is to confer absolute privilege upon any communication made in any of the proceedings contemplated therein. If the hearing held by the Labor Department on plaintiff's claim for severance pay and overtime, referred to in Paragraph 7 of the complaint, is a proceeding within the meaning of the phrase "or any other proceeding authorized by law" as used in said Section 4 of the Act of February 19, 1902, the utterance was absolutely privileged and such privilege constitutes a conclusive defense in an action based on that utterance.

It appears that the hearing on plaintiff's claim by the Labor Department, referred to in Paragraph 7 of the complaint, is a proceeding "authorized by law" within the meaning of Section 4 of the Act of February 19, 1902. The Labor Department is authorized to hold such a hearing by Act No. 122 of the Legislature of Puerto Rico, approved April 27, 1949, which statute requires the Commissioner of Labor to enforce labor protecting laws. * * *

It appears, upon examination, that this Statute (Act No. 122) has for its purpose the protection of the welfare of the workman and the furtherance of the public good, and that when hearings are held pursuant to its terms it is necessary, if those purposes are to be effectuated, that those called upon to give evidence therein must be protected against liability, civil or criminal, for communications given in evidence at such hearings. And this without regard for the motives of the witness or the truth or falsity of his statements. For otherwise, the giving of full, free and honest testimony, essential to the enforcement of such laws, will be discouraged. Therefore, communications made by witnesses in the course of such hearings, should be absolutely privileged in the same manner and to like extent as those made in the course of a judicial proceeding.

* * *

Clearly, then, the utterance of the defendant made during the Labor Department hearing referred to in Paragraph 7 of the complaint was absolutely privileged and that Paragraph 7 is, therefore, redundant in that it fails to state a claim upon which relief can be granted. It appears then, that defendant's motion to strike Paragraphs 5, 6, 7 and 8 should be granted.

The parties have agreed on hearing in open court that Paragraph 9 of the complaint should be stricken. And this Court being of the opinion that Paragraphs 5, 6, 7 and 8 should be stricken as redundant, defendant's motion for a more definite statement need be considered only with respect to the allegations of Paragraph 4 of the complaint.

As has been noted herein, conditional privilege is an affirmative defense which properly should be raised by its assertion in a responsive pleading. Consequently, when it appears from a complaint that the defense of conditional privilege may be available to a defendant, the allegations thereof should be reasonably adequate to permit the preparation of a responsive pleading asserting such defense. But when, in an action for slander, the complaint fails to set out substantially the utterance alleged to have been slanderously made or the facts relied upon to establish a publication of such utterance, such omission constitutes vagueness such as is a ground for granting a motion for more definite statement within the contemplation of rule 12(e). Obviously, when such material allegations are insufficient, it would be unreasonable to require the defendant to prepare a responsive pleading without a more definite statement of the pertinent facts.

Considering the allegations of Paragraph 4 of the complaint, * * * [they] suffer from vagueness with respect to the utterance alleged to have been slanderously made and the facts relied upon to establish a publication of the utterance. It is concluded that the defendant here is entitled to a more definite statement setting forth substantially the words alleged to have been slanderously uttered and the facts relied upon to establish a publication thereof.

Defendant's motion to dismiss the complaint for failure to state a claim upon which relief can be granted is denied. Defendant's motion to strike Paragraphs 5, 6, 7 and 8 of the complaint is granted. Defendant's motion for a more definite statement with respect to the matters prescribed in this opinion, is granted. Paragraph 9 of the complaint is ordered stricken. The decisions herein reached are hereby made applicable to the second cause of action set out in the complaint.

NOTES AND QUESTIONS

1. In current practice, Rule 12(e) motions are disfavored. Given the theory of notice pleading, a motion under it will be denied when the information sought by the moving party is available through discovery. See generally 5C Wright & Miller, Federal Practice and Procedure: Civil 3d §§ 1376–77. To what extent could plaintiff in *Garcia* have phrased the complaint to avoid the granting of defendant's motions? How should plaintiff alter the complaint to satisfy the court's order for a more definite statement? Can he merely eliminate some of the allegations that gave rise to the conditional privilege?

2. Suppose defendant's motion under Rule 12(e) had been denied by the court. What other means might it have used to learn the details of the alleged defamatory publication? What advantage, if any, is there to a motion under Federal Rule 12(e) as opposed to these other means?

3. Assume plaintiff in *Garcia* had not included any facts in the complaint indicating either a conditional or absolute privilege. How could defendant have raised these issues? See Federal Rule 8(c). Since privilege is obviously a matter of defense, why should it be significant whether plaintiff raises it in the complaint? Shouldn't these matters simply be ignored unless defendant pursues them in the answer?

3. THE BURDEN OF PLEADING AND THE BURDEN OF PRODUCTION

The burden of pleading an issue usually is assigned to the party who has the burden of producing evidence on that issue at trial, although "the burden of pleading need not coincide with the burden of producing evidence." Hamabe, *Functions of Rule 12(b)(6) in the Federal Rules of Civil Procedure: A Categorization Approach*, 15 Campbell L. Rev. 119, 172 (1993). Typically, plaintiff must put forth evidence on certain matters basic to the claim for relief or he cannot prevail. In a slander action, for example, plaintiff must introduce evidence that the remarks were made, that they were published, and that he was injured thereby. If plaintiff rests his case without producing evidence on any one of these issues, the court will dismiss the action and enter judgment for defendant. Therefore plaintiff must plead those matters he must prove. The rationale for the rule is simple. If plaintiff cannot legitimately allege the existence of each of the basic elements of his claim, it may be assumed that he could not introduce evidence on them at trial.

On the other hand, plaintiff normally does not have to plead matters on which defendant must introduce proof. If plaintiff were required to plead the nonexistence of every defense, not only would the pleading be long, complex, and fraught with danger for a plaintiff who omitted a remote possibility, but also the pleadings would not reveal, in any direct way, precisely upon which defenses defendant actually intended to rely. By placing the burden of pleading defenses on defendant, the court and parties know exactly on which of the many possible defenses he intends to introduce evidence, thus making preparation for trial and the actual work at trial more manageable. Once defendant has established a defense at trial, plaintiff will then have a second burden of production, this time to introduce evidence as to facts that will avoid defendant's defense. For example, if defendant proves that allegedly slanderous statements were made to plaintiff's prospective employer under conditions that rendered the statements privileged, plaintiff then must carry the burden of producing evidence showing that the statements were made maliciously and solely with intent to injure plaintiff, thereby vitiating the defense. Obviously, plaintiff is not required to plead, in the original complaint, matters to avoid defenses, since he cannot tell which defenses will be raised until the answer is filed. In some jurisdictions plaintiff is required to set forth matters that avoid the defendant's defenses in a second pleading, which serves as a reply to the answer; in other jurisdictions the decision whether to require a reply is left to the trial court's discretion. Matters of avoidance are limited and well recognized so that a reply is most often unnecessary.

Other Considerations in Allocating the Burden of Pleading

Sometimes plaintiff also is required to plead in the complaint the nonexistence of certain defenses upon which defendant has the burden of proof, although as we have seen, such a requirement is technically illogical. The reason for these special rules is a combination of the historical and practical. Consider, for example, a case in which plaintiff sues defendant on an overdue note. Payment of a note traditionally has been considered a defense to be proved by defendant, who by virtue of having a receipt usually is in a better position to put in evidence on the issue. Nevertheless, plaintiff, as part of the claim, must allege nonpayment. Without such an allegation the complaint would really say nothing justifying legal action; it simply would set forth the existence of the note without mentioning the nature of the breach of its terms. To inform the court and defendant as to the basis of the complaint, an allegation of nonpayment is essential. It is only when a defense, such as payment, goes to the very heart of the action, so that plaintiff should, in order to state a claim, be required to face the issue and allege in good faith that such defense does not exist, that the burden of pleading and the burden of producing evidence need not coincide. Another example occurs in the slander context in which some courts consider the truth of the remarks an absolute defense. In some of these jurisdictions, although not all, falsity is thought to be so much a part of the basic action, that plaintiff must plead it, even though defendant has the burden of introducing evidence of truth. The rule that a plaintiff must plead an issue that is "essential" has been criticized as "meaningless" and "circular." Lee, *Pleading and Proof: The Economics of Legal Burdens*, 1997 B.Y.U. L. Rev. 1, 1.

Because of the technical imbalance in cases in which plaintiff must plead the nonexistence of a defense in order to state a claim, some courts require defendant to raise the defense specially in the answer, rather than by simply denying plaintiff's allegation, if defendant really intends to pursue it; otherwise the defense will be waived. Thus before such an issue actually is tried, it will be pleaded both in the complaint and in the answer.

Allocation of the pleading burden sometimes is specified by rules or statutes that set forth matters that are to be considered defenses and contained in the answer. See, e.g., Federal Rule 8(c) in which the enumerated matters usually are those that traditionally have been treated as defenses both as to the burden of pleading and the burden of proof. Not all jurisdictions have adhered to these traditional views, however. For example, contributory negligence historically was treated as a defense, but today, in a number of jurisdictions, plaintiff, in order to prevail in a negligence case, must prove his own due care. If the pleading rule in these jurisdictions deems the issue of plaintiff's negligence to be a defense, it creates a serious anomaly, since defendant must raise the issue even though plaintiff is required to prove it. Furthermore, since a defense is waived if defendant does not plead it, the failure of defendant to raise the matter in the answer seems to obviate any need for plaintiff to prove the matter, thus thwarting the express policy of the jurisdiction requiring plaintiff to prove his own due care.

Statutes, too, may cause uncertainty about which party must carry the burden. In SCHAFFER ex rel. SCHAFFER v. WEAST, 546 U.S. 49, 126 S.Ct. 528, 163 L.Ed.2d 387 (2005), the Supreme Court was divided on a burden of proof issue. Under a federal statute the parents of a child with learning disabilities may challenge the propriety of the individual educational program that the school is required to prepare for the child. The question for the Court was whether the parents must carry the burden of showing that the plan is defective or whether the school district must show that it is appropriate. The statute did not mention the matter. The majority of the Court applied the "ordinary default rule," that the party seeking relief, and thus the one who must raise the issue in its pleading, must also carry the burden of proof, and that would be true whether the parents challenged the plan or whether the school district itself brought an action regarding the plan. The Court acknowledged that very rare exceptions exist, usually when the statute in question clearly indicates such a result. Justice Ginsburg dissented on the ground that an exception to the "ordinary default" rule may exist in special circumstances when the defending party is one with vastly superior means to determine the issue. In *Schaffer*, the school district's ability to establish the validity of the plan, with its array of psychiatrists and other professionals, far outstripped the resources available to the parents for their challenge.

4. PLEADING SPECIAL MATTERS

Read Federal Rule of Civil Procedure 9 and the related materials in the Supplement.

DENNY v. CAREY

United States District Court, Eastern District of Pennsylvania, 1976.
72 F.R.D. 574.

JOSEPH S. LORD, III, CHIEF JUDGE.

Plaintiff brings this proposed class action on behalf of himself and other purchasers of First Pennsylvania Corporation ("First Penn") securities alleging violation of federal and state securities laws. * * * Defendants have not answered the complaint, but have moved to dismiss pursuant to Fed.R.Civ.P. 12(b)(6) on the ground that plaintiff's allegations fail to state the circumstances constituting the alleged fraud with sufficient particularity as required by Fed.R.Civ.P. 9(b). * * *

On information and belief, plaintiff alleges that from January 1, 1974 to January 28, 1976 defendants conspired to conceal the true picture of First Penn's financial condition by issuing false and fraudulent statements which unreasonably avoided recognition and accrual of losses and inadequately provided for loan losses and total reserves, thereby inflating First Penn's equity and net income. * * *

Specifically, plaintiff alleges, *inter alia,* that First Penn: (1) improperly included as income accruals of interest where the borrower had already defaulted; (2) engaged in sales of foreclosed properties on terms which would not have been made in good faith with arm's length bargaining ("paper sales") to avoid showing substantial losses; (3) inadequately provided for loan losses by not accounting for expected uncollectibles in real estate loans where the mortgage loans constituted a high percentage of the total cost of projects undertaken by borrowers; and (4) concealed the default of loans by entering into extensions, modifications and other arrangements with defaulting borrowers. * * *

Defendants contend that these allegations fail to state the circumstances constituting fraud with sufficient particularity to comply with Fed.R.Civ.P. 9(b), and hence, do not state a claim upon which relief can be granted. Defendants also assert that plaintiff's allegations are "conclusory"—that they are "neutral," simply track the statutory language and fail to delineate the underlying acts and transactions. * * * Defendants state that plaintiff's deficiency is exacerbated by the fact that all of the operative allegations are made on information and belief without a statement of the facts upon which plaintiff's belief is founded. * * *

Defendants believe that plaintiff's burden of pleading fraud with particularity is a "rigorous" one. They point to several rationales given for Rule 9(b) which they believe support this position. Defendants state that since fraud is easily charged and such allegations of moral turpitude may at times be advanced only for their nuisance or settlement value, Rule 9(b) serves to protect defendants. * * * Defendants also argue that Rule 9(b) shields defendants, especially accountants and other professional defendants, from lawsuits which wrongfully damage their reputations. * * *

Defendants are incorrect when they argue that Rule 9(b) places a "rigorous" burden of pleading on plaintiff. A court may become too demanding if it unduly focuses on potential harm to defendants' reputations or the possibility of a "strike" or nuisance suit. "[R]ule 9(b) does not insulate professionals from claims of fraud where a complaint alleges the fraudulent acts with particularity * * *." Felton v. Walston and Co., [508 F.2d 577, 581–82 (2d Cir.1974)] * * *. "A strict application of Rule 9(b) in class action securities fraud cases could result in substantial unfairness to persons who are the victims of fraudulent conduct." In re Caesars Palace Securities Litigation, 360 F.Supp. 366, 388 (S.D.N.Y.1973). This is especially true where many of the matters are peculiarly within the knowledge of defendants. * * * Certainly in such cases, once plaintiff has satisfied the minimum burden of Rule 9(b), plaintiff should be allowed to flesh out the allegations in the complaint through discovery. * * *

Fed.R.Civ.P. 8 requires a short and plain statement of the claim which is simple, concise and direct. Rule 9(b) must be harmonized with the notice pleading mandate of Rule 8. * * * "Rule 9(b) does not require nor make legitimate the pleading of detailed evidentiary matter." *Moore* ¶ 9.03 at 1930 * * *.

Since fraud embraces a wide variety of potential misconduct, *Wright & Miller* § 1296 at 400, Rule 9(b) requires slightly more notice than would be forthcoming under Rule 8.[5] * * * But the requirement of Rule 9(b) is met when there is sufficient identification of the circumstances constituting fraud so that the defendant can prepare an adequate answer to the allegations. * * *

We find that the complaint [though not a model of perfect pleading] satisfies the requirement of Rule 9(b). * * * Before discovery, any stricter application of Rule 9(b) is especially inappropriate in a case such as this where the matters alleged are peculiarly within the knowledge of defendants. * * *

NOTES AND QUESTIONS

1. DENNY v. BARBER, 576 F.2d 465 (2d Cir.1978), was a case remarkably similar to Denny v. Carey. Both were brought by the same plaintiff, represented by the same counsel, and the same public accounting firm was one of the defendants in each case. The complaint alleged, inter alia, that defendants fraudulently had concealed defendant Chase Manhattan Corporation's true financial picture by not revealing that the corporation had made "risky and speculative" investments without providing adequate reserves for losses and had delayed in writing off uncollectible loans. The court held that Rule 9(b) had not been satisfied:

> Plaintiff's counsel has called our attention to a number of district court decisions * * * [including Denny v. Carey] which are alleged to have

5. *Wright & Miller* § 1300 at 425 points out: "the notion that Rule 9(b) does not actually require significantly more particularity than Rule 8 seems to be supported by the text of Official Form 13 [now, Form 21], which contains little more than a general allegation of fraud."

> sustained complaints no more specific than this. * * * We see no profit in attempting to analyze these decisions, which may or may not be consistent and each of which necessarily rests on its particular facts. * * * [There] must be more than vague allegations that, as shown by subsequent developments, the corporation's true financial picture was not so bright in some respects as its annual reports had painted and that the defendants knew, or were reckless in failing to know, this. The admission in [plaintiff's] counsel's * * * statement [that he could provide no further facts] * * * in the absence of discovery is significant. The Supreme Court has admonished that to the extent that such discovery "permits a plaintiff with a largely groundless claim to simply take up the time of a number of other people, with the right to do so representing an *in terrorem* increment of the settlement value, rather than a reasonably founded hope that the process will reveal relevant evidence, it is a social cost rather than a benefit."

Id. at 465. The trend of decision is that of *Barber*. For a criticism of Rule 9 as failing to provide "a uniform approach for those cases that clearly fall within its ambit," see Robins, *The Resurgence and Limits of the Demurrer*, 27 Suffolk U. L. Rev. 637, 713 (1993).

2. Why should Rule 9(b) single out fraud and mistake for heightened pleading? See Richman, Lively & Mell, *The Pleading of Fraud: Rhymes Without Reason*, 60 S.Cal.L.Rev. 959 (1987). Four policies are typically put forward for requiring the pleader to allege these claims with particularity: "protection of reputation, deterrence of frivolous or strike suits, defense of completed transactions, and providing adequate notice." Fairman, *Heightened Pleading*, 81 Texas L. Rev. 551, 563 (2002). What are the costs of imposing a heightened requirement?

3. Fraud involves some aspect of concealment by defendant. Yet some courts in construing the particularity requirement demand that the plaintiff specify "the who, what, when, where and how" of defendant's acts. Fairman, Note 2, p. 589, supra, at 565–66. But see Jairett v. First Montauk Secs. Corp., 203 F.R.D. 181, 186 (2001) (stating that "[i]n assessing fraud claims under Rule 9(b), the Court of Appeals for the Third Circuit has held that plaintiffs need not plead the 'date, place or time' of the fraud, so long as they use an 'alternative means of injecting precision and some measure of substantiation into their allegations of fraud' ") (citation omitted). Without discovery, how likely is a plaintiff to have access to information setting out the details of the alleged fraud? Is the particularity requirement of Rule 9(b) justified as a way to shield defendants from the expense of burdensome discovery requests in lawsuits that appear to be marginal? Would a better solution be to shift the expense of discovery in fraud cases? See Sovern, *Reconsidering Federal Civil Rule 9(b): Do We Need Particularized Pleading Requirements in Fraud Cases?*, 104 F.R.D. 143 (1985).

Congress became particularly dissatisfied with the application of Rule 9(b) in securities fraud cases and, in response, enacted the Private

Securities Litigation Reform Act (PSLRA) of 1995, Pub. L. No. 104–67, 109 Stat. 737 (1995). The PSLRA imposes a "super-heightened pleading standard" on such lawsuits. Miller, *The Pretrial Rush to Judgment: Are the "Litigation Explosion," "Liability Crisis," and Efficiency Clichés Eroding Our Day in Court and Jury Trial Commitments?*, 78 N.Y.U. L. Rev. 982, 1012 (2003). Professor Miller explains:

> The statute requires that the complaint specify each statement alleged to have been misleading and give the reason or reasons why each is misleading. In addition, if an allegation is made on information and belief, all facts on which that belief is formed must be stated with particularity. * * * Finally, facts giving rise to a "strong inference" that the defendant acted with scienter must be stated with particularity.

Id. The act also stays discovery until after the motion to dismiss has been decided.

Unfortunately, the PSLRA left ambiguous just what a plaintiff must allege to survive a motion to dismiss, and pleading standards have diverged from circuit to circuit. See Pritchard & Sale, *What Counts as Fraud? An Empirical Study of Motions to Dismiss Under the Private Securities Litigation Reform Act*, 2 J. Empirical Legal Stud. 125, 142 (2005). The Supreme Court, in 2007, attempted to clarify one of the most controversial of those pleading requirements. As you read the following decision, consider how *Twombly*, p. 568, supra, might affect interpretation of the PSLRA's requirements.

TELLABS, INC. v. MAKOR ISSUES & RIGHTS, LTD.

Supreme Court of the United States.
551 U.S. 308, 127 S.Ct. 2499, 168 L.Ed.2d 179 (2007).

Certiorari to the United States Court of Appeals for the Seventh Circuit.

JUSTICE GINSBURG delivered the opinion of the Court.

* * *

Exacting pleading requirements are among the control measures Congress included in the PLSRA. The Act requires plaintiffs to state with particularity both the facts constituting the alleged violation, and the facts evidencing scienter, *i.e.*, the defendant's intention "to deceive, manipulate, or defraud." *Ernst & Ernst v. Hochfelder*, 425 U.S. 185, 194, and n.12, 96 S.Ct. 1375 [, 1381 n.12], 47 L.Ed.2d 668 [, 677 n.12] (1976) * * *. This case concerns the latter requirement. [The Act requires that] plaintiffs must "state with particularity facts giving rise to a strong inference that the defendant acted with the required state of mind." * * *

Congress left the key term "strong inference" undefined, and Courts of Appeals have divided on its meaning. In the case before us, the Court of

Appeals for the Seventh Circuit held that the "strong inference" standard would be met if the complaint "allege[d] facts from which, if true, a reasonable person could infer that the defendant acted with the required intent." 437 F.3d 588, 602 (2006). That formulation, we conclude, does not capture the stricter demand Congress sought to convey * * *. Rather, to determine whether a complaint's scienter allegations can survive threshold inspection for sufficiency, a court * * * must engage in a comparative evaluation; it must consider, not only inferences urged by the plaintiff, as the Seventh Circuit did, but also competing inferences rationally drawn from the facts alleged. An inference of fraudulent intent may be plausible, yet less cogent than other, nonculpable explanations for the defendant's conduct. To qualify as "strong" we hold an inference of scienter must be more than merely plausible or reasonable—it must be cogent and at least as compelling as any opposing inference of nonfraudulent intent.

* * *

* * * Prior to the enactment of the PSLRA, the sufficiency of a complaint for securities fraud was governed not by Rule 8, but by the heightened pleading standard set forth in Rule 9(b). * * *

* * *

Setting a uniform pleading standard for * * * [federal securities fraud] actions was among Congress' objectives when it enacted the PSLRA. * * *

* * *

* * * With no clear guide from Congress other than its "inten[tion] [in original] to strengthen the pleading requirements," H.R. Conf. Rep., p. 41, Courts of Appeals have diverged again, this time in construing the term "strong inference." * * * Our task is to prescribe a workable construction of the "strong inference" standard, a reading geared to the PSLRA's twin goals: to curb frivolous, lawyer-driven litigation, while preserving investors' ability to recover on meritorious claims.

* * *

We establish the following prescriptions: *First*, faced with a Rule 12(b)(6) motion to dismiss * * * courts must * * * accept all factual allegations in the complaint as true. * * *

Second, courts must consider the complaint in its entirety, as well as other sources courts ordinarily examine when ruling on Rule 12(b)(6) motions to dismiss, in particular, documents incorporated into the complaint by reference, and matters of which a court may take judicial notice. * * * The inquiry * * * is whether *all* of the facts alleged, taken collectively, give rise to a strong inference of scienter, not whether any individual allegation, scrutinized in isolation, meets that standard. * * *

Third, in determining whether the pleaded facts give rise to a "strong" inference of scienter, the court must take into account plausible opposing inferences. The Seventh Circuit expressly declined to engage in such a comparative inquiry. * * *

The strength of an inference cannot be decided in a vacuum. The inquiry is inherently comparative: How likely is it that one conclusion, as compared to others, follows from the underlying facts? * * * A complaint will survive, we hold, only if a reasonable person would deem the inference of scienter cogent and at least as compelling as any opposing inference one could draw from the facts alleged. * * *

* * *

While we reject the Seventh Circuit's approach * * *, we do not decide whether, under the standard we have described, * * * [plaintiff's] allegations warrant "a strong inference that * * * [defendants] acted with the required state of mind" * * *. Neither the District Court nor the Court of Appeals had the opportunity to consider the matter in light of the prescriptions we announce today. We therefore vacate the Seventh Circuit's judgment so that the case can be reexamined in accord with our construction * * *.

It is so ordered.

* * *

[JUSTICE SCALIA and JUSTICE ALITO, in separate concurring opinions, each argued that the majority's test is flawed. To establish the "strong inference" required by the PSLRA, they expressed the belief that the inference of scienter must be more plausible than any opposing inference, not just equal to it and "means an inference that is more likely than not correct." 551 U.S. at ___, 127 S.Ct. at 2516, 168 L.Ed.2d at ___.]

NOTES AND QUESTIONS

1. In DURA PHARMACEUTICALS, INC. v. BROUDO, 544 U.S. 336, 125 S.Ct. 1627, 161 L.Ed.2d 577 (2005), cited in *Twombly*, p. 568, supra, the Supreme Court, reversing a decision of the Ninth Circuit, addressed whether a securities fraud class action should be dismissed if the complaint fails to allege an economic loss caused by defendant's misrepresentation. Justice Breyer wrote the opinion for a unanimous Court.

> A private plaintiff who claims securities fraud must prove that the defendant's fraud caused an economic loss. * * * We consider a Ninth Circuit holding that a plaintiff can satisfy this requirement—a requirement that courts call "loss causation"—simply by alleging in the complaint and subsequently establishing that "the price" of the security "*on the date of purchase* was inflated because of the misrepresentation." * * * In our view the Ninth Circuit is wrong * * *.

* * *

> [The Private Securities Litigation Reform Act] makes clear Congress' intent to permit private securities fraud actions for recovery where, but only where, plaintiffs adequately allege and prove the traditional elements of causation and loss. By way of contrast, the Ninth Circuit's approach would allow recovery where a misrepresentation leads to an inflated purchase price but nonetheless does not proximately cause any economic loss. That is to say, it would permit recovery where these two traditional elements in fact are missing.
>
> * * *
>
> Our holding about plaintiffs' need to *prove* proximate causation and economic loss leads us also to conclude that the plaintiffs' complaint here failed adequately to *allege* these requirements. We concede that the Federal Rules of Civil Procedure require only "a short and plain statement of the claim showing that the pleader is entitled to relief." Fed. Rule Civ. Proc. 8(a)(2). And we assume, at least for argument's sake, that neither the Rules nor the securities statutes impose any special further requirement in respect to the pleading of proximate causation or economic loss. * * *
>
> * * * [P]laintiffs' lengthy complaint contains only one statement that we can fairly read as describing the loss caused by the defendants' * * * misrepresentations. That statement says that the plaintiffs "paid artificially inflated prices for Dura's securities" and suffered "damage[s]." * * * The statement implies that the plaintiffs' loss consisted of the "artificially inflated" purchase "prices." The complaint's failure to claim that Dura's share price fell significantly after the truth became known suggests that the plaintiffs considered the allegation of purchase price inflation alone sufficient. The complaint contains nothing that suggests otherwise.
>
> * * * [T]he "artificially inflated purchase price" is not itself a relevant economic loss. And the complaint nowhere else provides the defendants with notice of what the relevant economic loss might be or of what the causal connection might be between that loss and the misrepresentation * * *.
>
> We concede that ordinary pleading rules are not meant to impose a great burden upon a plaintiff. * * * But it should not prove burdensome for a plaintiff who has suffered an economic loss to provide a defendant with some indication of the loss and the causal connection that the plaintiff has in mind. * * *

Id. at 338–47, 125 S.Ct. at 1633–34, 161 L.Ed.2d at 586–88.

2. Congress changed the pleading standard for securities fraud claims in order to deter the filing of frivolous cases. See Perino, *Did the Private Securities Litigation Reform Act Work?*, 2003 U. Ill. L. Rev. 913, 913 (2003). However, some commentators warn that the Act "may also work to chill meritorious litigation" by making it too expensive "to pursue even claims that may turn out to be meritorious." Choi, *The Evidence on Securities Class Actions*, 57 Vand. L. Rev. 1465, 1472–73 (2004). See also Spindler, *Why Shareholders Want Their CEOs To Lie More After* Dura Pharmaceuticals, 95

Geo. L. J. 653, 657, 691 (2007) (arguing that *Dura* encourages corporate fraud by effectively immunizing it from judicial review). Do you expect *Twombly* to make it even more difficult to file some claims that might be meritorious? What kinds of claims?

5. ALTERNATIVE AND INCONSISTENT ALLEGATIONS

Read Federal Rule of Civil Procedure 8(d) and the related materials in the Supplement.

Under the original common-law rules, pleadings were designed to reduce every controversy to a single issue of law or fact. Alternative and hypothetical allegations would have made the search for the single issue impossible and therefore they were forbidden. See generally McDonald, *Alternative Pleading: I,* 48 Mich.L.Rev. 311 (1950). Despite occasional statements indicating that inconsistent allegations are improper, see, e.g., Sinclair v. Fotomat Corp., 140 Cal.App.3d 217, 189 Cal.Rptr. 393, 399 (1983)(a case involving verified pleadings), virtually all courts today permit inconsistent allegations, whether separately pleaded or not, if they are made in good faith. One commentary compares the philosophy of alternative pleading to a famous saying by Yogi Berra: "When you come to the fork in the road, take it." See 39 Authors, *The Jurisprudence of Yogi Berra*, 46 Emory L.J. 697, 775–77 (1997).

The Separate–Statement Requirement

Rules permitting parties to plead in the alternative usually are coupled with provisions requiring each separate cause of action or defense to be separately stated. See the state provisions set out in connection with Federal Rule 10(b) in the Supplement. Federal Rule 10(b) does not contain a formal separate-statement requirement, although the Rule does express the hope that "as far as practicable" each paragraph will be limited "to a single set of circumstances." See 5A Wright & Miller, Federal Practice and Procedure: Civil 3d § 1324. The Rule also requires separation of claims founded on different transactions "if doing so would promote clarity," and some courts interpret Rule 10(b) "to require a separate count for each distinctive statutory and constitutional claim." E.g., Casler v. Janus, 1998 WL 151811 (N.D. Ill.1998). When a party violates the separate-statement requirement, the appropriate corrective procedure may be a motion to compel separate statements, or a motion to strike, or a special preliminary objection. In any case, the party will be allowed to amend his pleading to conform to the rules. If a plaintiff refuses to amend, should the case be dismissed? See Bautista v. Los Angeles County, Note 2, p. 564, supra (federal courts have power to order separate statements and to dismiss if party fails to comply).

6. PLEADING DAMAGES

Reread Federal Rule of Civil Procedure 9(g) in the Supplement.

ZIERVOGEL v. ROYAL PACKING CO.

St. Louis Court of Appeals, Missouri, 1949.
225 S.W.2d 798.

MCCULLEN, JUDGE. This action was brought by respondent as plaintiff against appellant as defendant to recover damages for injuries plaintiff alleged she sustained as a result of a collision between an automobile driven by her and a motor vehicle (tractor-trailer, also referred to as truck) operated by defendant's employee. A trial before the court and a jury resulted in a verdict and judgment in favor of plaintiff against defendant in the sum of $2000.00. After an unavailing motion for a new trial defendant appealed.

* * * Describing her injuries plaintiff alleged in her petition that "Plaintiff sustained injuries to her neck, back, spine and nervous system and was otherwise injured and her earning capacity has been permanently impaired."

* * *

For its first point defendant contends that the trial court erred in permitting plaintiff's counsel in his opening statement, over defendant's objection, to state to the jury that plaintiff's blood pressure had increased by the accident and in refusing to declare a mistrial on defendant's motion because of such statement and in permitting plaintiff to introduce evidence over defendant's objection of plaintiff's increased blood pressure and in refusing to declare a mistrial on defendant's motion because of the introduction of such evidence and also in permitting [plaintiff] over defendant's objection to present evidence of an injury to her shoulder. Defendant points out that plaintiff's petition does not allege that she was caused to develop high blood pressure or that such an existing condition was aggravated by the accident. Defendant further contends that the evidence does not establish that a continuing elevation in blood pressure is an inevitable or necessary result of the injuries averred and that the evidence of such condition was, therefore, inadmissible. In support of these contentions defendant cites a number of cases which apply the principle of law that before a plaintiff can recover for a physical condition claimed to have resulted from the negligence of another, such condition must be pleaded or the evidence must establish the condition as being the inevitable or necessary result of injuries which are particularly set out in the petition. The reason underlying such decisions is that it would be unjust to permit a plaintiff to take advantage of a defendant at the trial by presenting evidence of injuries of which the defendant did not have the kind of notice required by law, namely, through allegations in plaintiff's petition.

It is true the evidence in this case does show, as plaintiff contends, that defendant had actual notice before trial of plaintiff's increased blood pressure, which she claimed was a result of the collision, through a statement made by plaintiff to that effect to the Claim Agent of defendant's insurer and through an examination of plaintiff made by defendant's doctor, Dr. Leo A. Will, and reported by him to said Claim Agent as well as through plaintiff's deposition which was taken by defendant. However, we are of the opinion that although it cannot be said that defendant was "surprised" when plaintiff presented evidence at the trial relating to the condition of her blood pressure, defendant nevertheless had the right to object to such evidence on the ground that it related to "special damages" which were not pleaded in plaintiff's petition. Although defendant could not have claimed "surprise" upon the introduction of such evidence, it was not required to do so and its objections at the trial to such evidence in the absence of proper allegations thereon in plaintiff's petition should have been sustained. No such special damages were pleaded by plaintiff, nor did plaintiff ask leave to amend her petition to include such special damages which she could have done on such terms, at that stage of the proceedings, as the court should order. However, plaintiff did not amend her petition, nor ask leave to amend, and defendant had the right to object to the evidence in question.

* * * [Missouri Rule of Civil Procedure 55.19] expressly provides: "When items of special damage are claimed, they shall be specifically stated." * * *

It has been held by our Supreme Court that a specific personal injury which is not the necessary or inevitable result of an injury alleged in the petition constitutes an element of "special damage" which must be specifically pleaded before evidence thereof is admissible. See State ex rel. Grisham v. Allen, 344 Mo. 66, 124 S.W.2d 1080. * * *

In the case at bar the only allegations in plaintiff's petition with respect to the injuries she suffered as the result of the collision were as follows: "Plaintiff sustained injuries to her neck, back, spine and nervous system and was otherwise injured and her earning capacity has been permanently impaired." It will be observed that not only is there no mention of increased blood pressure but no injuries are alleged from which it can reasonably be said that an increase in blood pressure was an inevitable or necessary result. Nor was there any evidence to show that the increased blood pressure was the necessary or inevitable result of the injuries alleged in the petition.

* * *

What we have said herein with respect to the evidence of plaintiff's increase of blood pressure applies with equal force to the evidence of the injury to plaintiff's shoulder. In the absence of any allegation in plaintiff's petition relating to that injury, it was error for the court to admit such evidence.

* * *

On Motion for Rehearing or, in the Alternative, to Transfer to Supreme Court.

McCULLEN, JUDGE. Plaintiff has filed an extended motion for rehearing in which she earnestly argues that this court committed error in holding that the trial court erred in permitting plaintiff to introduce evidence of her high blood pressure when no such damage was pleaded in plaintiff's petition. * * *

It is contended by plaintiff that [the Missouri rule] * * *, which provides that when "items of special damage" are claimed "they shall be specifically stated," having been copied verbatim from Rule 9(g) of the Federal Rules * * *, the "construction" given said Rule 9(g) by the Federal Courts must be given to [the Missouri rule as well] * * *. [The language of Rule 9(g) was altered slightly in 2007.]

* * *

In the lengthy argument of plaintiff she repeatedly refers to the "construction" given to Federal Rule 9(g) but nowhere is there cited any authority showing what such "construction" was in any kind of a case. * * * Plaintiff evidently has found no case in point on the facts of this case (just as we have found none) because, as we see it, the words of both Federal Rule 9(g) and the state [rule] * * * are so simple, plain and unambiguous that no one has even heretofore contended in a court of last resort that a party could plead only "general" damages and recover for "special" damages.

* * *

[Motion denied.]

NOTES AND QUESTIONS

1. Federal Rule 9(g) "maintains the traditional distinction between general damages, which can be alleged without particularity, and special damages, which require the pleading of considerable detail." 5A Wright & Miller, Federal Practice and Procedure: Civil 3d § 1310. Did plaintiff's lawyer in *Ziervogel* hurt his client's case by pleading too much? See generally 5 Wright & Miller, Federal Practice and Procedure: Civil 3d § 1259.

2. Should medical bills incurred as a result of personal injuries be considered special damages requiring special pleading or should they be provable as a logical and necessary result of the injuries themselves? See Sossamon v. Nationwide Mut. Ins. Co., 243 S.C. 552, 135 S.E.2d 87 (1964), which held a general allegation of damages sufficient to permit proof of doctor and hospital bills. In Estate of Coggins v. Wagner Hopkins, Inc., 183 F. Supp.2d 1126 (W.D. Wis. 2001), plaintiff sought to recover unpaid health insurance benefits. The District Court found it was sufficient for plaintiff to have alleged a "list of denied benefits" without indicating a "monetary value for each of the allegedly denied benefits." However, in Hogan v. Wal–Mart Stores, Inc., 167 F.3d 781, 783 (2d Cir. 1999), the court held that under New York law, "aggravation of a pre-existing condition is an element of special damages which must be specially pleaded and proved before recovery therefor can be allowed [internal citations omitted]."

3. Elements of special damages that must be pleaded if proof of them is to be allowed at trial also may appear in actions other than personal injury. In contract actions, for example, special damages are those that normally would not be foreseen as the consequence of defendant's breach." Bibeault v. Advanced Health Corp., 2002 WL 24305 (S.D.N.Y. 2002). Special damages can be recovered in contract actions from a defaulting party who was informed that they might result from a breach. See Bumann v. Maurer, 203 N.W.2d 434, 440–41 (N.D.1972).

4. Although the normal consequence of failing to plead special damages is being barred from proving them at trial, it is important to note that with regard to a few types of cases the existence of special damages is an integral part of the claim, and the failure to plead them renders the complaint subject to a demurrer or motion to dismiss. See, e.g., Paine–Erie Hosp. Supply, Inc. v. Lincoln First Bank, 82 Misc.2d 432, 370 N.Y.S.2d 370 (Sup.Ct.1975). Should the degree of specificity required in pleading special damages be the same in all cases or should it depend on whether the special damages simply are added elements of injury or are an integral part of the claim? Does the fact that a distinction along these lines is drawn by the courts of the state in which the federal court is sitting have any relevance to a federal court's construction of Federal Rule 9(g)?

7. THE PRAYER FOR RELIEF

Read Federal Rules of Civil Procedure 8(a)(3) and 54(c) in the Supplement.

BAIL v. CUNNINGHAM BROTHERS, INC.

United States Court of Appeals, Seventh Circuit, 1971.
452 F.2d 182.

PELL, CIRCUIT JUDGE. * * * The final contention raised by defendant on this appeal is that the judgment against defendant should be remitted from $135,000 to $85,000.

Plaintiff's original complaint sought damages in the amount of $100,000. On the morning the trial was to begin, plaintiff presented a motion to amend the complaint requesting that the ad damnum clause in the complaint against defendant be increased from $100,000 to $250,000. The district judge denied this motion "* * * for the reason that the case is at issue, it is set for trial this date, and the defendant was not given notice of the filing of the motion."

The jury notwithstanding the complaint-contained limitation of $100,000 returned a verdict for the higher figure of $150,000. In a post-trial motion Bail sought and was granted leave to amend the complaint by increasing the ad damnum clause to $150,000. Bail had received $15,000 from another defendant originally named in the complaint in return for "a covenant not to pursue." This payment had been set off, leaving the final judgment of $135,000. It has been said that the office of the ad damnum in a pleading is to fix the amount beyond which a party may not recover on the trial of his action. Gable v. Pathfinder Irrigation District, 159 Neb. 778, 68 N.W.2d 500, 506 (1955). However, an examination of the cases reveals that the rule thus enunciated, if indeed it still be a rule, has flexibility to the virtual point of nonexistence. Thus, in *Gable* the court pointed out that there was also a general rule that amendment may be made to a pleading which did not change the issues or affect the quantum of proof as to a material fact and that no good reason was apparent for not applying this privilege of amendment to the ad damnum clause. Id. at 506.

In the case before us, even though it is a diversity case, a matter of procedure is involved and governed, therefore, entirely by the federal rules. Riggs, Ferris & Geer v. Lillibridge, 316 F.2d 60, 62 (2d Cir.1963).

* * *

There is substantial authority for the proposition that pursuant to Rule 54(c) a claimant may be awarded damages in excess of those demanded in his pleadings. * * *

Cunningham, however, contends that the authority is not all one way * * * [citing, inter alia,] the case of Wyman v. Morone, 33 A.D.2d 168, 306 N.Y.S.2d 115 (1969), to the effect that under New York law the granting of the motion to increase the amount sued for, after a jury has rendered its verdict, is an abuse of discretion. We, of course, in view of Rule 54(c) are not in any way bound by the interpretation of this lower court of New York as to the law of that state but do observe that there apparently was some significance attached to the extended delay in moving to amend and in any event feel that the dissenting opinion in *Wyman* swims with the main current of judicial thinking in this particular area as opposed to the contrary movement of the majority opinion.

The difficulty, if any there be, posed here, however, lies in the fact that Bail attempted to amend the ad damnum clause in advance of trial and the right of amendment was denied by the court. In this respect the case would seem to be one of first impression as no case involving this exact factual situation has been brought to our attention. It appears to us that the motion to amend, even though on the morning of the trial, should have been granted. It not having been granted, our inquiry must be as to whether the normal rule prevailing under 54(c) should be varied. In our opinion, it should not be.

On oral argument, inquiry was directed to counsel for Cunningham as to how the conduct of the trial would have differed if the pretrial motion to amend had been granted. The thought was ventured that the attorneys might have tried the case differently, that they might have argued damages to the jury (which subject they conspicuously avoided in final argument) or they might have cross-examined more extensively. With hindsight, they may well think that they should have argued damages even if no post-trial amendment were to be permitted and the limitation on recovery were left at $100,000. In essence, however, we cannot see that the quantum of proof as to any material fact varied or that any change of issues resulted, or would have resulted, from an amendment of the ad damnum clause. Counsel competently and vigorously defended on the theory of no liability whatsoever, and we can find no basis for an assumption that $100,000 is such an insignificant amount that counsel somehow would try harder if they knew that the exposure might be $250,000.

No doubt if the ad damnum had sought some insignificant amount such as $1,000, the case would not have received the attention from trial counsel that it did. In the case before us, however, defense counsel were never confronted with an insignificant amount.

It perhaps is unfortunate that the district court did not permit the amendment as requested in advance of trial so as to eliminate the claim that the defendant somehow was prejudiced in relying on this. Finding, however, no real prejudice we will follow the rule generally prevailing to the effect that even though the party was not successful in demanding such relief in his pleadings, he was entitled thereto under the evidence. At least the jury thought that he was so entitled, and we find no basis for upsetting their determination irrespective of whether we would have reached this exact amount in assessing damages. Further, the district court who heard the evidence on a front line basis was satisfied that the amendment should be allowed on a post-trial motion.

Although Bail's counsel under the constraint of the court's ruling did confine his final argument to an amount within the unamended ad damnum clause, it is not entirely unreasonable to assume that he and his client would have been well satisfied with a verdict of $100,000 and, indeed, it does not stretch the imagination too far to conceive that a settlement could have been arrived at for less than that figure if the general practical pattern of settlements in personal injury cases had had any application here. Nevertheless, the case was not settled and inasmuch as the damages cannot be shown to be excessive, nor to have been dictated by passion and prejudice, the verdict will stand. While Cunningham finds some source of complaint in the fact that plaintiff's counsel himself argued less than $100,000 and while it may not now be much solace to Cunningham, nevertheless there was the trial advantage to the defense that plaintiff was precluded from arguing a larger sum.

What we have had to say with regard to the ad damnum clause is indicative of the anachronistic character of the clause. Indeed, there is a well publicized school of thought that it should be done away with altogether. * * * It is true that in some suits it is necessary to allege a jurisdictional amount, but ordinarily this is far less than the ad damnum prayer and can be gleaned in most instances from the pleadings and discovery procedures.

As a matter of fact in the case before us it appears from the record that the jury was in no way aware of the amount of the ad damnum in the complaint and, therefore, clearly their verdict did not reflect a conscious arrival at a figure in excess of the ad damnum.

* * *

Affirmed.

NOTES AND QUESTIONS

1. Is the damage prayer anachronistic as the court in *Bail* suggests? Should it be abolished? What problems would that create? Would elimination of the ad damnum clause have avoided the uncertainty upon which defendant in *Bail* based the claim of prejudice?

2. Federal Rule 54(c) limits relief in default cases to the ad damnum clause. Why should a defendant who defaults be protected by a cap on damages, but a defendant who participates be exposed to damages greater than those pleaded by the plaintiff? See 10 Wright, Miller & Kane, Federal Practice and Procedure: Civil 3d § 2663.

3. In ANHEUSER–BUSCH, INC. v. JOHN LABATT LTD., 89 F.3d 1339, 1349 (8th Cir.1996), certiorari denied 519 U.S. 1109, 117 S.Ct. 944, 136 L.Ed.2d 833 (1997), plaintiff failed to mention punitive damages in its pleadings or answers to interrogatories. Plaintiff did plead a valid claim for injurious falsehood under state law and requested instructions on punitive damages a week prior to the trial. Over defendant's objection the matter was presented to the jury, which awarded punitive damages in the amount of $5 million. The trial court struck the punitive damage award on the ground that plaintiff had not given sufficient notice of its intent to seek punitive damages. The appellate court affirmed. It did not cite Federal Rules 8(a)(3), 9(g), or

54(c). Should it have been unnecessary for plaintiff to specify punitive damages in its demand for relief so long as the alleged facts would justify such an award?

SECTION B. RESPONDING TO THE COMPLAINT

1. THE TIME PERMITTED FOR A RESPONSE

Read Rule 12(a) and the accompanying materials in the Supplement.

Rule 12(a) gives most defendants twenty days from the service of the complaint to respond either by a motion pursuant to Rule 12 or by answering the complaint. In reality, defense counsel routinely requests, and plaintiff's counsel routinely consents to, an extension of the defendant's time to answer. These agreements generally are considered a matter of courtesy among counsel, and Rule 6(b) authorizes the court to grant these extensions. Although practices vary, most judges will order an extension based upon a written stipulation of the attorneys.

2. MOTIONS TO DISMISS

Read Federal Rules of Civil Procedure 12(b), 12(c), 12(d), and 12(f) and the materials accompanying them in the Supplement.

A. HISTORICAL ANTECEDENTS

Any discussion of the sufficiency of the pleadings necessarily involves some consideration of the methods by which pleadings are attacked. At common law, a party who faced a complaint could either answer, responding to each of the claims, or demur. If the defendant demurred, he was not allowed to contest the complaint's facts if the demurrer was overruled. On the other hand, if the demurrer was sustained, the plaintiff had no right to replead or amend her complaint. Later, these harsh rules were modified to allow a party to proceed to the merits if the demurrer was overruled and to allow the plaintiff to amend her complaint if the demurrer was sustained. The common-law demurrer was incorporated into code pleading. In most code states, a complaint could be dismissed on the pleadings for failure to state facts sufficient to constitute a cause of action, absence of subject-matter jurisdiction, and deficiencies in the form of the pleading.

The demurrer and its code equivalents elevated the importance of technicalities and produced considerable delay and dissatisfaction. See Pike, *Objections to Pleadings Under the New Federal Rules of Civil Procedure,* 47 Yale L.J. 50, 51 (1937).

B. THE MOTION TO DISMISS FOR FAILURE TO STATE A CLAIM

AMERICAN NURSES' ASSOCIATION v. ILLINOIS

United States Court of Appeals, Seventh Circuit, 1986.
783 F.2d 716.

POSNER, CIRCUIT JUDGE.

The class action charges the State of Illinois with sex discrimination in employment, in violation of Title VII of the Civil Rights Act of 1964, 42 U.S.C. § 2000e, and the equal protection clause of the Fourteenth Amendment. * * * The precise allegations of the complaint will require our careful attention later, but for now it is enough to note that they include as an essential element the charge that the state pays workers in predominantly male job classifications a higher wage not justified by any difference in the relative worth of the predominantly male and the predominantly female jobs in the state's roster.

* * * [T]he district judge dismissed the complaint under Fed.R.Civ.P. 12(b)(6) * * * [on the ground] that the complaint pleaded a comparable worth case and that a failure to pay employees in accordance with comparable worth does not violate federal antidiscrimination law. The plaintiffs appeal. They argue that their case is not (or perhaps not just) a comparable worth case and that in characterizing the complaint as he did the district judge terminated the lawsuit by a semantic manipulation. * * *

* * * [A]s we understand the plaintiffs' position it is not that a mere failure to rectify traditional wage disparities between predominantly male and predominantly female jobs violates federal law. The circuits that have considered this contention have rejected it. * * *

The * * * question is whether a failure to achieve comparable worth—granted that it would not itself be a violation of law—might permit an inference of deliberate and therefore unlawful discrimination, as distinct from passive acceptance of a market-determined disparity in wages. * * *

* * *

* * * Knowledge of a disparity is not the same thing as an intent to cause or maintain it; if for example the state's intention was to pay market wages, its knowledge that the consequence would be that men got higher wages on average than women and that the difference might exceed any premium attributable to a difference in relative worth would not make it guilty of intentionally discriminating against women. Similar-

ly, even if the failure to act on the comparable worth study could be regarded as "reaffirming" the state's commitment to pay market wages, this would not be enough to demonstrate discriminatory purpose. To demonstrate such a purpose the failure to act would have to be motivated at least in part by a desire to benefit men at the expense of women.

* * *

So if all that the plaintiffs in this case are complaining about is the State of Illinois' failure to implement a comparable worth study, they have no case and it was properly dismissed. We must therefore consider what precisely they are complaining about. * * *

* * *

The key paragraph of the complaint is paragraph 9:

> Defendants State of Illinois, its Departments and other Agencies subject to the State Personnel Code, and State Officials, have intentionally discriminated and continue to intentionally discriminate against female state employees in the terms and conditions of their employment because of their sex and because of their employment in historically female-dominated sex-segregated job classifications. Defendants have intentionally discriminated and continue to discriminate against male state employees because of their employment in historically female-dominated sex-segregated job classifications. The acts, practices and policies of discrimination for which defendants are responsible include, but are not limited to, the following:
>
> (a) Use of a sex-biased system of pay and classification which results in and perpetuates discrimination in compensation against women employed in historically female-dominated sex-segregated job classifications;
>
> (b) Use of a sex-biased system of pay and classification which, because it results in and perpetuates discrimination in compensation against women employed in historically female-dominated sex-segregated job classifications, adversely affects males employed in such historically female-dominated sex-segregated job classifications;
>
> (c) Compensation at lower rates of pay of female employees in historically female-dominated sex-segregated job classifications which are or have been evaluated as being of comparable, equal, or greater worth than historically male-dominated sex-segregated job classifications which receive higher rates of pay;
>
> (d) Compensation at lower rates of pay of male employees in historically female-dominated sex-segregated job classifications which are or have been evaluated as being of comparable, equal, or greater worth than historically male sex-segregated job classifications which receive higher rates of pay;

(e) Compensation at lower rates of pay of female employees than male employees performing work of equal skill, effort and responsibility under similar working conditions;

(f) More favorable treatment in compensation of male state employees than of similarly situated female employees;

(g) Discrimination in classification.

If this were the entire charging part of the complaint, there would be no question of dismissing it for failure to state a claim.

The paragraph initially charges the state with intentional discrimination against its female employees, because of their sex; and this, standing alone, would be quite enough to state a claim under Title VII. It continues, "and because of their employment in historically female-dominated sex-segregated job classifications," and then adds a claim on behalf of male employees in those classifications. The continuation could be interpreted as an allegation that the state's failure to adopt a wage scale based on the principle of comparable worth violates Title VII, and if so fails to state a claim. But the mention of "sex-segregated" blurs the picture. If the state has deliberately segregated jobs by sex, it has violated Title VII. Anyway a complaint cannot be dismissed merely because it includes invalid claims along with a valid one. Nothing is more common.

Subparagraphs (a) through (g) present a list of particular discriminatory practices; and since they are merely illustrative ("not limited to"), the complaint would not fail even if none of them were actionable. Some are, some aren't. * * * [If subparagraph (a)] means to allege that the state has departed from the market measure on grounds of sex—not only paying higher than market wages in predominantly male job classifications and only market wages in predominantly female classifications, but keeping women from entering the predominantly male jobs ("sex-segregated")—it states a claim. Subparagraph (b) adds nothing. If the state is discriminating against women by maintaining unwarranted wage differentials between predominantly male and predominantly female jobs, any men who happen to find themselves in predominantly female jobs will be, as it were, dragged down with the women—will be incidental victims of a discrimination targeted against others.

Subparagraph (c) is an effort to fit the case to the mold of * * * [County of Washington v. Gunther, 452 U.S. 161, 101 S.Ct. 2242, 68 L.Ed.2d 751 (1981)]. * * * But as we said earlier, the failure to accept the recommendations in a comparable worth study is not actionable. Paragraph 9(c) thus fails to state a claim—as does (d), which is the same as (c) except that it, like subparagraph (b), complains on behalf of male occupants of predominantly female jobs.

Subparagraphs (e) and (f) are inscrutable. If they complained about payment of unequal pay for the same work they would state a claim under the Equal Pay Act. But that Act is not cited in the complaint, perhaps deliberately, and the substitution of "work of equal skill" etc. for "equal work [* * *] of equal skill" etc. may also be deliberate. The intention may be to claim that different pay for different *but comparable* work violates Title VII—and if so this is a comparable worth claim by a different name, and fails. However, when a defendant is unclear about the meaning of a particular allegation in the complaint, the proper course is not to move to dismiss but to move for a more definite statement. * * *

That leaves subparagraph (g)—"Discrimination in classification." This could be a reprise of the comparable worth allegations or it could mean that in classifying jobs for pay purposes the responsible state officials had used the fraction of men in each job as a factor in deciding how high a wage to pay—which would be intentional discrimination.

Maybe the allegations in paragraph 9 are illuminated by subsequent paragraphs of the complaint. Paragraph 10, after summarizing the comparable worth study, says, "Defendants knew or should have known of the historical and continuing existence of patterns and practices of discrimination in compensation and classification, as documented at least in part by the State of Illinois Study." All that the study "documents," however, is that 28 percent of the employees subject to the state's personnel code are employed in 24 job classifications, in each of which at least 80 percent of the employees are of the same sex, and that based on the principles of comparable worth the 12 predominantly female job classifications are underpaid by between 29 and 56 percent. * * * These disparities are consistent, however, with the state's paying market wages, and of course the fact that the state knew that market wages do not always comport with the principles of comparable worth would not make a refusal to abandon the market actionable under Title VII. But at the very end of paragraph 10 we read, "Moreover, defendants have knowingly and *willfully* failed to take any action to correct such discrimination" (emphasis added), and in the word "willfully" can perhaps be seen the glimmerings of another theory of violation that could survive a motion to dismiss. Suppose the state has declined to act on the results of the comparable worth study not because it prefers to pay (perhaps is forced by labor-market or fiscal constraints to pay) market wages but because it thinks men deserve to be paid more than women. * * * This would be the kind of deliberate sex discrimination that Title VII forbids, once the statute is understood to allow wage disparities between dissimilar jobs to be challenged * * *.

"Willfully" is, however, a classic legal weasel word. Sometimes it means with wrongful intent but often it just means with knowledge of something or other. Willful evasion of taxes means not paying when you know you owe tax. After reading the comparable worth study the responsible state officials knew that the state's compensation system might not be consistent with the principles of comparable worth ("might" because there has been no determination that the comparable worth study is valid even on its own terms—maybe it's a lousy comparable worth study). But it would not follow that their failure to implement the study was willful in a sense relevant to liability under Title VII. They may have decided not to implement it because implementation would cost too much or lead to excess demand for some jobs and insufficient demand for others. The only thing that would make the failure a form of intentional and therefore actionable sex discrimination would be if the motivation for not implementing the study was the sex of the employees—if for example the officials thought that men ought to be paid more than women even if there is no difference in skill or effort or in the conditions of work. * * *

We have said that a plaintiff can plead himself right out of court. But the court is not to pounce on the plaintiff and by a crabbed and literal reading of the complaint strain to find that he has pleaded facts which show that his claim is not actionable, and then dismiss the complaint on the merits so that the plaintiff cannot replead. (The dismissal would preclude another suit based on any theory that the plaintiff could have advanced on the basis of the facts giving rise to the first suit.) * * * The district judge did not quite do that here, because this complaint can easily be read to allege a departure from the principles of comparable worth, and no more. But that reading is not inevitable, and the fact that it is logical and unstrained is not enough to warrant dismissal. * * * A complaint that alleges intentional sex discrimination * * * cannot be dismissed just because one of the practices, indeed the principal practice, instanced as intentional sex discrimination—the employer's failure to implement comparable worth—is lawful.

Furthermore, a complaint is not required to allege all, or any, of the facts logically entailed by the claim. If Illinois is overpaying men relative to women, this must mean—unless the market model is entirely inapplicable to labor markets—that it is paying women at least their market wage (and therefore men more), for women wouldn't work for less than they could get in the market; and if so the state must also be refusing to hire women in the men's jobs, for above-market wages in those jobs would be a magnet drawing the women from their lower-paying jobs. Maybe the references in the complaint to the segregation of jobs by sex are meant to allege such refusals but if not this pleading omission would not be critical. A plaintiff does not have to plead evidence. If these plaintiffs admitted or the defendants proved that there was no steering or other method of segregating jobs by sex, the plaintiffs' theory of discrimination might be incoherent, and fail. But a complaint does not fail to state a claim merely because it does not set forth a complete and convincing picture of the alleged wrongdoing. So the plaintiffs do not have to allege steering even if it is in some sense implicit in their claim.

* * * We do not want to arouse false hopes; the plaintiffs have a tough row to hoe. They may lose eventually on summary judgment if discovery yields no more evidence than is contained in the unsupported assertions and stale and seemingly isolated incidents in the plaintiffs' exhibits. But the plaintiffs are entitled to make additional efforts to prove a case of intentional discrimination within the boundaries sketched in this opinion.

Reversed and remanded.

NOTES AND QUESTIONS

1. Rule 12(b)(6), the federal system's counterpart to the common-law demurrer, comprises one of a number of procedural devices, together with summary judgment and partial summary judgment, directed verdict, and judgment notwithstanding the verdict (all of which are discussed later), designed to screen out frivolous and nonmeritorious cases.

> The Federal Rules permit an early challenge to the legal sufficiency of the allegations of a claim under Rule 12(b)(6) and (c).* * * When a defendant challenges the plaintiff's legal entitlement to the relief demanded, even if all well-pleaded facts are taken in the light most favorable to the plaintiff, Rule 12(b)(6) permits a judgment as a matter of law in favor of the defendant. Such motions challenge the plaintiff[']s pleading of the required legal elements of the claim—as one court recently put it, "Like a battlefield surgeon sorting the hopeful from the hopeless, a motion to dismiss invokes a form of legal triage, a paring of viable claims from those doomed by law." * * *

Davis, *Summary Adjudication Methods in United States Civil Procedure*, 46 Am. J. Comp. L. 229, 247 (1998).

2. Under the *Conley* "no set of facts" rule, p. 562, supra, federal courts hesitated before dismissing a complaint on a Rule 12(b)(6) motion, taking as the standard "* * * whether the claimant is entitled to offer evidence to support the claims." SCHEUER v. RHODES, 416 U.S. 232, 236, 94 S.Ct. 1683, 1686, 40 L.Ed.2d 90, 96 (1974). However, even before *Twombly*, p. 568, supra, courts showed an increasing willingness to dismiss an action at the threshold stage. Compare these two statements by Professor Miller, the first made in 1984, and the second in 2003:

> [R]ule 12(b)(6), the vaunted motion to dismiss for failure to state a claim upon which relief can be granted * * *, is a wonderful tool on paper, but * * * it was last effectively used during the McKinley Administration.

Miller, The August 1983 Amendments to the Federal Rules of Civil Procedure: Promoting Effective Case Management and Lawyer Responsibility 7–8 (Fed.Jud.Center 1984).

> * * * [I]n In re MCI Worldcom, Inc. Securities Litigation, * * * [191 F.Supp.2d 778 (S.D.Miss.2002),] the plaintiff class complaint alleged in great detail material misrepresentations and omissions in violation of the Securities Exchange Act. The district court granted the defendants motion to dismiss, which almost seems whimsical given more recent public revelations about the company apparently burying billions of dollars of costs with accounting machinations to create a false picture of the company's profits and sales. * * * At one point in the opinion the plaintiffs are faulted for not presenting any "direct evidence," which is not required on a motion challenging the sufficiency of a pleading; elsewhere the court draws inferences against the plaintiffs, again contrary to the well-established rules of pleading construction on a Rule 12(b)(6) motion. * * * Also striking is that the dismissal was with

prejudice, the judge denying a request for leave to replead. In practical effect, the court seems to have demanded that the plaintiffs establish their case at the pleading stage.

Miller, *The Pretrial Rush to Judgment: Are the "Litigation Explosion," "Liability Crisis," and Efficiency Clichés Eroding Our Day in Court and Jury Trial Commitments?*, 78 N.Y.U. L. Rev. 982, 1073 (2003).

3. Would the appellate court's decision in *American Nurses* be the same after *Twombly*? A commentator notes that the dismissal rate of civil rights cases "spiked" in the four months after *Twombly* was decided. See Hannon, *Note—How Much Ado About* Twombly*? A Study on the Impact of Bell Atlantic Corp. v. Twombly on 12(b)(6) Motions*, 83 Notre Dame L. Rev. 1811, 1815 (2008). What factors might explain this trend?

4. How does *Twombly* affect the standard that a court should use to resolve mixed questions of fact and law when deciding a Rule 12(b)(6) motion? Does this question implicate the historic allocation of decision-making authority between the judge and jury? In HARTFORD ACCIDENT & INDEMNITY CO. v. MERRILL LYNCH, PIERCE, FENNER & SMITH, INC., 74 F.R.D. 357 (W.D.Okl.1976), plaintiff sued defendant for negligently failing to inform a bank that its employee was investing with defendant in margin accounts. The employee had forged signatures on certain certificates of deposit drawn from that bank that he had used as collateral to procure personal loans from other banks. When the employee defaulted, the lending banks recovered their losses from plaintiff under plaintiff's blanket fidelity bond. Plaintiff alleged that defendant's failure to inform was the proximate cause of its loss. The court dismissed plaintiff's claim, treating the question of proximate cause as "a question of law for the Court":

> * * * In considering the allegations of the Complaint, the Court finds that the facts contained therein are insufficient to show any causal connection between the alleged negligent acts of Merrill Lynch in failing to advise Conine's employer and obtaining said employer's permission for him to engage in trading on margin accounts and the loss sustained by Plaintiff on its banker's fidelity bond. The Complaint fails to show the required proximate cause between the negligence alleged and the injuries complained of as a matter of law.

Id. at 358. Does the *Erie* doctrine require a federal court sitting in diversity to follow the Oklahoma courts' declaration that under proper circumstances the existence of proximate cause is a question of law?

5. What is the effect of a successful Rule 12(b)(6) motion? Normally plaintiff will be given one opportunity to amend the complaint. But suppose leave to amend is denied. Can the plaintiff modify the complaint and re-serve it as a new action, or do principles of res judicata bar that? In SHAW v. MERRITT–CHAPMAN & SCOTT CORP., 554 F.2d 786 (6th Cir.1977), certiorari denied 434 U.S. 852, 98 S.Ct. 167, 54 L.Ed.2d 122 (1977), the court held that absent specific language to the contrary by the district court, a Rule 12(b)(6) motion constitutes an adjudication on the merits, and so further actions on the same claim are barred. Is this result too harsh? Does it provide the plaintiff with adequate notice of preclusion? Would it be better to convert the motion to dismiss into a motion for summary judgment? See 5B Wright & Miller, Federal Practice and Procedure: Civil 3d § 1357.

NOTE ON THE "SPEAKING DEMURRER"

At common law and under the codes, the "speaking demurrer," a demurrer that attempted to introduce material outside the pleadings, was not permitted. Technically this is still the rule even in most modern jurisdictions. However, in most courts today a motion for summary judgment is available to challenge the factual basis of a pleading that on its face is sufficient to state a claim or defense. Under the Federal Rules and comparable state rules, the distinction between a pleading challenge and a motion for summary judgment is blurred, since a pleading challenge simply is treated as a motion for summary judgment if outside matter is introduced. The Rules were amended in 1948 to provide an express basis for courts to treat motions under Rules 12(b)(6) and 12(c) as motions for summary judgment when matters outside the pleadings are considered. See also Federal Rule 12(d).

NOTE ON RULE 12(b) AND THE COMMON-LAW PLEA OF ABATEMENT

In addition to a Rule 12(b)(6) motion to dismiss for failure to state a claim, Rule 12(b) provides the pleader with the option of raising six other defenses by motion prior to service of a responsive pleading. The defenses in Rules 12(b)(1) through 12(b)(5) and 12(b)(7) are essentially modern counterparts to the common-law pleas of abatement. There never was any doubt as to the court's considering extra-pleading material on these motions, and so, although Rule 12(b) as amended in 1948 expressly permits the use of extraneous matters on a Rule 12(b)(6) motion only, the practice before (and since) the amendment allows "speaking motions" in connection with these other defenses. Their validity rarely is apparent on the face of the pleadings, and motions raising them generally require referral to matters outside the pleadings.

Of the six defenses, which, if any, may a party who makes a motion to dismiss under Rule 12(b) waive by not raising it in the motion? Which may a party waive by failing to raise it either by motion under Rule 12(b) or by the party's answer? When, if ever, is it too late to challenge a pleading for failure to state a claim or defense?

Although the seven motions specifically enumerated in Rule 12(b) are theoretically the only motions that can be made prior to a responsive pleading, in fact the preliminary motion practice in the federal courts has a much broader compass. For example, although affirmative defenses under Rule 8(c) probably were intended to be raised only by responsive pleading, it is now common to allow an affirmative defense to be asserted by a motion under Rule 12(b)(6) when the validity of that defense is apparent from the face of the pleading. A complaint showing that the statute of limitations has run on the claim is the most common situation in which the affirmative defense appears on the face of the pleading. Moreover, the procedure in Rule 12(b) for converting the motion into a Rule 56 motion for summary judgment by presenting matters outside the pleadings, and the possibility of defendant moving for summary judgment prior to serving his responsive pleading, have the effect of allowing the early assertion of defenses other than those specifically enumerated in Rule 12(b).

3. OTHER MOTIONS ATTACKING PLEADINGS

When a party has included "scandalous," "impertinent," or "irrelevant" matter in a pleading, traditionally, the remedy afforded is a motion to strike. See, e.g., Federal Rule 12(f); N.Y.C.P.L.R. 3024(b). On occasion some parties have attempted to utilize this motion to destroy or undercut their opponents' statements of valid claims or defenses. As held in GATEWAY BOTTLING, INC. v. DAD'S ROOTBEER CO., 53 F.R.D. 585, 588 (W.D.Pa.1971): "To strike material as scandalous it must be obviously false and unrelated to the subject matter of the action. * * * The facts here may be unpleasant for plaintiff to have on the record and they certainly contain charges of reprehensible conduct but the same is true of many facts of life which are entitled to be pleaded as relevant to a cause of action or defense."

COBELL v. NORTON, 224 F.R.D. 1 (D.C. Cir. 2004), involved a lawsuit against the Secretary of the Interior and other federal officials for alleged mismanagement of moneys held in trust for members of Indian tribes. In earlier proceedings, defendants were held in civil contempt for failing to produce documents in violation of a discovery order and lying about their maintenance and destruction of trust records. Plaintiffs later filed an Emergency Notice to halt further "destruction and damage to individual Indian trust records," and defendants sought to strike portions of the papers as immaterial under Rule 12(f). The court rejected defendants' arguments:

> Under Rule 12(f) "immaterial" matter consists of statements and averments bearing no essential or important relationship to the claim for relief or the defenses being pled. * * * As stated, [the challenged Notice and supporting documents] detail incidents whereby trust records vital to individual Indian beneficiaries were placed in jeopardy and/or destroyed. To find these averments "immaterial" or "legally impertinent" would be tantamount to ruling that the destruction of trust information bears no essential or important relationship to the plaintiffs' claim for relief. Nothing could be further from the truth. Retention and preservation of document and trust information is at the core of this litigation * * *.

Id. at 3. Both because striking a portion of a pleading is a drastic remedy and because it often is sought by the movant simply as a dilatory tactic, motions under Rule 12(f) are viewed with disfavor and infrequently granted. The question whether allegations really are prejudicial seems to turn on whether the contents of the pleadings will be disclosed to the jury. In some instances pleadings themselves can become part of the evidence in the case and then, of course, the jury will be able to see and use them. There also is another group of cases in which an entire pleading is challenged, either because it was filed too late, or necessary court approval had not been obtained, or other rules or orders have not been satisfied.

Traditionally, this type of defect is reached by a motion to strike the pleading or to dismiss the claims that it contains.

4. ANSWERING THE COMPLAINT

A. DENIALS

Rule 8 requires a defendant to make one of three responses to the contents of plaintiff's complaint. Defendant may admit, deny, or plead insufficient information in response to each allegation. In answering, it is not sufficient for defendant to claim that "the documents 'speak for themselves.'" Kortum v. Raffles Holdings, Ltd. 2002 WL 31455994, *4 (N.D. Ill. 2002). Rule 8(b)(6) provides that all averments to which defendant does not specifically respond are deemed admitted. To avoid an unintended admission, defendants often add an all-inclusive paragraph in their answers denying each and every averment of the complaint unless otherwise admitted.

A defendant under Rule 8 and most state rules also may deny generally the entire complaint, but general denials tend to defeat the purpose of pleading as a means of narrowing and focusing the issues in controversy. For this reason, the Federal Rules discourage the use of the general denial, which must be made in good faith and only in situations in which everything in the complaint can be denied legitimately. Using a general denial can be risky. If a court decides that a general denial does not "fairly respond to the substance of the allegation," it may deem defendant to have admitted plaintiff's specific averments. In addition, a general denial does not put in issue such matters as capacity or conditions precedent, which under Rule 9 must be challenged specifically by defendant. See 5 Wright & Miller, Federal Practice and Procedure: Civil 3d § 1265.

ZIELINSKI v. PHILADELPHIA PIERS, INC.

United States District Court, Eastern District of Pennsylvania, 1956.
139 F.Supp. 408.

VAN DUSEN, DISTRICT JUDGE. Plaintiff requests a ruling that, for the purposes of this case, the motor-driven fork lift operated by Sandy Johnson on February 9, 1953, was owned by defendant and that Sandy Johnson was its agent acting in the course of his employment on that date. The following facts are established by the pleadings, interrogatories, depositions and uncontradicted portions of affidavits:

1. Plaintiff filed his complaint on April 28, 1953, for personal injuries received on February 9, 1953, while working on Pier 96, Philadelphia, for J.A. McCarthy, as a result of a collision of two motor-driven fork lifts.

2. Paragraph 5 of this complaint stated that "a motor-driven vehicle known as a fork lift or chisel, owned, operated and controlled by the defendant, its agents, servants and employees, was so negligently and

carelessly managed * * * that the same * * * did come into contact with the plaintiff causing him to sustain the injuries more fully hereinafter set forth."

3. The "First Defense" of the Answer stated "Defendant * * * denies the averments of paragraph 5 * * *."

4. The motor-driven vehicle known as a fork lift or chisel, which collided with the McCarthy fork lift on which plaintiff was riding, had on it the initials "P.P.I."

5. On February 10, 1953, Carload Contractors, Inc. made a report of this accident to its insurance company, whose policy No. CL 3964 insured Carload Contractors, Inc. against potential liability for the negligence of its employees contributing to a collision of the type described in paragraph 2 above.

6. By letter of April 29, 1953, the complaint served on defendant was forwarded to the above-mentioned insurance company. This letter read as follows:

Gentlemen:

* * *

> We find that a fork lift truck operated by an employee of Carload Contractors, Inc. also insured by yourselves was involved in an accident with another chisel truck, which, was alleged, did cause injury to Frank Zielinski, and same was reported to you by Carload Contractors, Inc. at the time, and you assigned Claim Number OL 0153–94 to this claim.
>
> Should not this Complaint in Trespass be issued against Carload Contractors, Inc. and not Philadelphia Piers, Inc.?
>
> We forward for your handling.

7. Interrogatories * * * and the answers thereto, which were sworn to by defendant's General Manager on June 12, 1953, and filed on June 22, 1953, read as follows:

> 1. State whether you have received any information of an injury sustained by the plaintiff on February 9, 1953, South Wharves. If so, state when and from whom you first received notice of such injury. A. We were first notified of this accident on or about February 9, 1953 by Thomas Wilson.
>
> 2. State whether you caused an investigation to be made of the circumstances of said injury and if so, state who made such investigation and when it was made. A. We made a very brief investigation on February 9, 1953 and turned the matter over to (our insurance company) for further investigation.

* * *

8. At a deposition taken August 18, 1953, Sandy Johnson testified that he was the employee of defendant on February 9, 1953, and had been their employee for approximately fifteen years.

9. At a pre-trial conference held on September 27, 1955,[3] plaintiff first learned that over a year before February 9, 1953, the business of moving freight on piers in Philadelphia, formerly conducted by defendant, had been sold by it to Carload Contractors, Inc. and Sandy Johnson had been transferred to the payroll of this corporation without apparently realizing it, since the nature or location of his work had not changed.

* * *

11. Defendant now admits that on February 9, 1953, it owned the fork lift in the custody of Sandy Johnson and that this fork lift was leased to Carload Contractors, Inc. It is also admitted that the pier on which the accident occurred was leased by defendant.

12. There is no indication of action by either party in bad faith and there is no proof of inaccurate statements being made with intent to deceive. Because defendant made a prompt investigation of the accident (see answers to Interrogatories 1, 2, * * *), its insurance company has been representing the defendant since suit was brought, and this company insures Carload Contractors, Inc. also, requiring defendant to defend this suit, will not prejudice it.

Under these circumstances, and for the purposes of this action, it is ordered that the following shall be stated to the jury at the trial:

> It is admitted that, on February 9, 1953, the towmotor or fork lift bearing the initials "P.P.I." was owned by defendant and that Sandy Johnson was a servant in the employ of defendant and doing its work on that date.

This ruling is based on the following principles:

1. Under the circumstances of this case, the answer contains an ineffective denial of that part of paragraph 5 of the complaint which alleges that "a motor driven vehicle known as a fork lift or chisel (was) owned, operated and controlled by the defendant, its agents, servants and employees." [See] F.R.Civ.P. 8(b) * * *.

For example, it is quite clear that defendant does not deny the averment in paragraph 5 that the fork lift came into contact with plaintiff, since it admits * * * that an investigation of an occurrence of the accident had been made and that a report dated February 10, 1953, was sent to its insurance company stating "While Frank Zielinski was riding on bumper of chisel and holding rope to secure cargo, the chisel truck collided with another chisel truck operated by Sandy Johnson causing injuries to Frank Zielinski's legs and hurt head of Sandy Johnson." Compliance with the above-mentioned rule required that defendant file a more specific answer

3. The applicable statute of limitations prevented any suit against Carload Contractors, Inc. after February 9, 1955, 12 P.S. § 34.

than a general denial. A specific denial of parts of this paragraph and specific admission of other parts would have warned plaintiff that he had sued the wrong defendant.

* * *

Under circumstances where an improper and ineffective answer has been filed, the Pennsylvania courts have consistently held that an allegation of agency in the complaint requires a statement to the jury that agency is admitted where an attempt to amend the answer is made after the expiration of the period of limitation. * * * Although the undersigned has been able to find no federal court decisions on this point, he believes the principle of these Pennsylvania appellate court decisions may be considered in view of all the facts of this case, where jurisdiction is based on diversity of citizenship, the accident occurred in Pennsylvania, and the federal district court is sitting in Pennsylvania. * * *

2. Under the circumstances of this case, principles of equity require that defendant be estopped from denying agency because, otherwise, its inaccurate statements and statements in the record, which it knew (or had the means of knowing within its control) were inaccurate, will have deprived plaintiff of his right of action.

If Interrogatory 2 had been answered accurately by saying that employees of Carload Contractors, Inc. had turned the matter over to the insurance company, it seems clear that plaintiff would have realized his mistake. The fact that if Sandy Johnson had testified accurately, the plaintiff could have brought its action against the proper party defendant within the statutory period of limitations is also a factor to be considered, since defendant was represented at the deposition and received knowledge of the inaccurate testimony.

At least one appellate court has stated that the doctrine of equitable estoppel will be applied to prevent a party from taking advantage of the statute of limitations where the plaintiff has been misled by conduct of such party. * * *

* * *

Since this is a pre-trial order, it may be modified at the trial if the trial judge determines from the facts which then appear that justice so requires. * * *

NOTES AND QUESTIONS

1. A motion to strike, pursuant to Rule 12(f), is the mechanism for challenging the substantive sufficiency of defenses raised in an adversary's answer or other responsive pleading. A motion for judgment on the pleadings, pursuant to Rule 12(c), is a method of attacking the substantive sufficiency of an opposing party's pleading after all the pleadings have been completed. Both motions raise the same issues raised by a motion under Rule 12(b), and are dealt with by the courts in the same manner.

2. In BIGGS v. PUBLIC SERVICE COORDINATED TRANSPORT, 280 F.2d 311, 313–14 (3d Cir.1960), a diversity-of-citizenship case, the defendant generally denied plaintiff's jurisdictional allegations, including an express claim that defendant was a New Jersey corporation. The court stated:

> We cannot for a moment believe that defendant's counsel was denying in good faith that his client was a New Jersey corporation. We think the only fair interpretation of the pleading in this case is that the denial does not run to the allegation of defendant's citizenship. Therefore, that allegation must be deemed to be admitted.

In the *Biggs* case defendant, in addition to the general denial, had specifically denied the allegation that the amount in controversy exceeded the minimum jurisdictional amount required in diversity cases. Does this help to explain the decision?

3. Should a defendant who joins general and special denials in the answer be permitted to rely upon a general denial to put in issue those allegations by plaintiff that have not been specially denied? In Ways v. City of Lincoln, 2002 WL 1742664, *23 (D. Neb. 2002), affirmed 331 F.3d 596 (8th Cir. 2003), the District Court carefully analyzed the answer to determine whether allegations had been admitted because of defendant's failure to put in a special denial:

> The plaintiff claims that he is entitled to judgment on Count X because the defendants have admitted the allegations contained in paragraphs 67–69. * * * It is true that the defendants' answer fails to specifically address paragraphs 67–69 of the amended complaint. * * * However, the answer does state that the defendants "[d]eny that Plaintiff is entitled to any relief at law or in equity as alleged in the Complaint," and that they "[d]eny each and every other allegation contained in Plaintiff's Amended Complaint except those specifically admitted herein. . . ." * * * Federal Rule of Civil Procedure 8(b) [now renumbered as Rule 8(b)(3)] allows defendants to "generally deny all the averments except such designated averments or paragraphs as the pleader expressly admits." * * * In this case, the defendants have included such a denial in paragraph 58 of their answer to the amended complaint. * * * Since the defendants have not expressly admitted the allegations set forth in paragraph 69 of the amended complaint, I find that they have been denied.

4. To what extent should defendant be permitted to respond that "he neither admits nor denies" plaintiff's allegations? Should it make any difference whether or not a general denial is allowed? In many jurisdictions statutes specifically prohibit "evasive denials." E.g., Conn. Gen. Stat. Ann. § 10–47, Practice Book 1998, Ct. R. Super. Ct. Civ. § 10–47 ("where any matter of fact is alleged with diverse circumstances, some of which are untruly stated, it shall not be sufficient to deny it as alleged, but so much as is true and material should be stated or admitted, and the rest only denied"). Compare the language of Federal Rule 8(b).

5. In California, if a complaint is verified, the answer cannot contain a general denial. See Cal.Code Civ.Proc. § 431.30(d)(1986 Amendment). What justification is there for this provision?

IMPROPER FORMS OF DENIAL

1. Denials for Lack of Information—Under Federal Rule 8(b)(5) a party may deny an allegation on the ground that it "lacks knowledge or information sufficient to form a belief about the truth" of the allegation. Similar provisions exist under state codes. But there are limits on the use of this form of denial. In OLIVER v. SWISS CLUB TELL, 222 Cal.App.2d 528, 35 Cal.Rptr. 324 (1963), defendant denied for lack of information its existence as an unincorporated association. This was held to be an admission of defendant's status, since the matter was "presumptively within defendant's knowledge." The consequences of the admission were ameliorated, however, because the issue apparently subsequently was inserted, perhaps inadvertently, in a pretrial order. What other facts are "presumptively within the knowledge" of a defendant?

2. "Negative Pregnant" Denials—Suppose plaintiff alleges that defendant owes her $89,000 under a contract. Defendant denies "that he owes plaintiff $89,000." In some state courts this type of denial has been referred to as a "negative pregnant," and it results in an admission that defendant owes plaintiff one cent less than the specified $89,000. These technical decisions are not very common today. "Even when a negative pregnant in an answer renders it so ambiguous that a court-ordered reply cannot be framed, the proper corrective procedure is an order under Rule 12(e) for a more definite statement rather than dismissal." 5 Wright & Miller, Federal Practice and Procedure: Civil 3d § 1267.

3. Conjunctive Denials—In JANEWAY & CARPENDER v. LONG BEACH PAPER & PAINT CO., 190 Cal. 150, 211 P. 6 (1922), plaintiff alleged that defendant "made, executed, and delivered its contract for goods to the plaintiff." Defendant denied the allegation specifically, using the identical words of the complaint. The court held that this denial was evasive and therefore admitted the existence of a contract. This type of pleading defect is termed a "conjunctive denial." To what extent does it differ from a "negative pregnant"?

B. AFFIRMATIVE DEFENSES

Read Federal Rule of Civil Procedure 8(c) in the Supplement.

Rule 8(c) lists nineteen affirmative defenses that must be raised specifically. An affirmative defense is defined as encompassing "two types of pleadings: ones that admit the allegations of the complaint but suggest some other reason why there is no right of recovery, and ones that concern allegations outside of the plaintiff's prima facie case that the defendant therefore cannot raise by a simple denial in the answer." 5 Wright & Miller, Federal Practice and Procedure: Civil 3d § 1271. The function of Rule 8(c) is to provide notice to plaintiff of the possible existence of the defenses and defendant's intention to advance them. In determining whether a defense not listed in Rule 8(c) must be raised affirmatively, courts look to federal statutes in federal question cases, and to state practice in diversity cases.

INGRAHAM v. UNITED STATES

United States Court of Appeals, Fifth Circuit, 1987.
808 F.2d 1075.

POLITZ, CIRCUIT JUDGE:

The appellees in these consolidated cases sued the United States, under the Federal Tort Claims Act, for severe injuries caused by the negligence of government physicians. In each case, after entry of adverse judgment the government moved for relief from the judgment to the extent that the damages exceeded the limit imposed on medical malpractice awards by the Medical Liability and Insurance Improvement Act of Texas * * *. The respective district courts denied these post-trial motions. Concluding that the government did not raise the issue timely before the trial courts, [and] that the issues were not preserved for appeal, * * * we affirm both judgments.

Background

In 1977, in response to what was perceived to be a medical malpractice crisis, the Legislature of Texas, like several other state legislatures, adopted certain limitations on damages to be awarded in actions against health care providers, for injuries caused by negligence in the rendering of medical care and treatment. Of particular significance to these appeals is the $500,000 cap placed on the *ex delicto* recovery, not applicable to past and future medical expenses.

On February 12, 1979, Dwight L. Ingraham was operated on by an Air Force surgeon. During the back surgery a drill was negligently used and Ingraham's spinal cord was damaged, causing severe and permanent injuries. The court awarded Ingraham judgment for $1,264,000. This total included $364,000 for lost wages and $900,000 for pain, suffering, and disability. There is no reference to the Medical Liability and Insurance Improvement Act of Texas in the pleadings, nor was any reference made to the Act during the trial. After entry of judgment, the United States filed a notice of appeal. Thereafter, urging the Act's limitations, the government sought relief from judgment under Fed.R.Civ.P. 60(b). The district court denied that motion. * * *

Similarly, in March of 1979, Jocelyn and David Bonds, and their infant daughter Stephanie, were victims of the negligent performance by an Air Force physician. Because of the mismanagement of the 43rd week of Jocelyn Bonds's first pregnancy, and the negligent failure to perform timely a caesarian section delivery, Stephanie suffered asphyxiation *in utero*. The loss of oxygen caused extensive brain damage, resulting in spastic quadriparesis, cortical blindness, seizures, and mental retardation. In their FTCA action the court awarded Stephanie $1,814,959.70 for medical expenses and $1,675,595.90 for the other losses. Jocelyn Bonds was awarded $750,000 for her losses, including loss of the society of her daughter. As in the Ingraham case, the government did not invoke the Texas malpractice limitation in pleading or at trial. Post judgment the government filed a motion to amend the judgment under Fed.R.Civ.P. 59, but, again, there was no mention of the limitations Act. Subsequently, three months after entry of the judgment, the government filed a pleading entitled "Motion for Reconsideration," in which it advanced the malpractice Act. That motion was denied. * * *

These appeals do not challenge the courts' findings of liability, but object only to quantum, contending that damages are limited by the Medical Liability and Insurance Improvement Act * * *.

Analysis

Appellees maintain that we should not consider the statutory limitation of liability invoked on appeal because it is an affirmative defense under Rule 8(c) * * *, and the failure to raise it timely constitutes a waiver. We find this argument persuasive.

Rule 8(c) first lists 19 specific affirmative defenses, and concludes with the residuary clause "any other matter constituting an avoidance or affirmative defense." [This provision has been renumbered as 8(c)(1) and the language altered without any change in substance.] In the years since adoption of the rule, the residuary clause has provided the authority for a substantial number of additional defenses which must be timely and affirmatively pleaded. These include: exclusions from a policy of liability insurance; breach of warranty; concealment of an alleged prior undissolved marriage; voidable preference in bankruptcy; noncooperation of an insured; statutory limitation on liability; the claim that a written contract was incomplete; judgment against a defendant's joint tortfeasor; circuity of action; discharge of a contract obligation through novation or extension; re[s]cission or mutual abandonment of a contract; failure to mitigate damages; adhesion contract; statutory exemption; failure to exhaust state remedies; immunity from suit; good faith belief in lawfulness of action; the claim that a lender's sale of collateral was not commercially reasonable; a settlement agreement or release barring an action; and custom of trade or business. * * *

Determining whether a given defense is "affirmative" within the ambit of Rule 8(c) is not without some difficulty. We find the salient comments of Judge Charles E. Clark, Dean of the Yale Law School, later

Chief Judge of the United States Second Circuit Court of Appeals, and the principal author of the Federal Rules to be instructive:

> [J]ust as certain disfavored allegations made by the plaintiff * * * must be set forth with the greatest particularity, so like disfavored defenses must be particularly alleged by the defendant. These may include such matters as fraud, statute of frauds * * *, statute of limitations, truth in slander and libel * * * and so on. In other cases the mere question of convenience may seem prominent, as in the case of payment, where the defendant can more easily show the affirmative payment at a certain time than the plaintiff can the negative of nonpayment over a period of time. Again it may be an issue which may be generally used for dilatory tactics, such as the question of the plaintiff's right to sue * * * a vital question, but one usually raised by the defendant on technical grounds. These have been thought of as issues "likely to take the opposite party by surprise," which perhaps conveys the general idea of fairness or the lack thereof, though there is little real surprise where the case is well prepared in advance.

Clark, *Code Pleading*, 2d ed. 1947, § 96, at 609–10 * * *.

Also pertinent to the analysis is the logical relationship between the defense and the cause of action asserted by the plaintiff. This inquiry requires a determination (1) whether the matter at issue fairly may be said to constitute a necessary or extrinsic element in the plaintiff's cause of action; (2) which party, if either, has better access to relevant evidence; and (3) policy considerations: should the matter be indulged or disfavored? * * *

Central to requiring the pleading of affirmative defenses is the prevention of unfair surprise. A defendant should not be permitted to "lie behind a log" and ambush a plaintiff with an unexpected defense. * * * The instant cases illustrate this consideration. Plaintiffs submit that, had they known the statute would be applied, they would have made greater efforts to prove medical damages which were not subject to the statutory limit. In addition, plaintiffs maintain that they would have had an opportunity and the incentive to introduce evidence to support their constitutional attacks on the statute.

This distinction separates the present cases from our recent decision in Lucas v. United States, 807 F.2d 414 (5th Cir.1986). In *Lucas,* although the limitation of recovery issue was not pleaded, it was raised at trial. We held that the trial court was within its discretion to permit the defendant to effectively amend its pleadings and advance the defense. The treatment we accorded this issue in *Lucas* is consistent with long-standing precedent of this and other circuits that " 'where [an affirmative defense] is raised in the trial court in a manner that does not result in unfair surprise, * * * technical failure to comply with Rule 8(c) is not fatal.' " * * *

We view the limitation on damages as an "avoidance" within the intendment of the residuary clause of 8(c). Black's Law Dictionary * * * defines an avoidance in pleadings as "the allegation or statement of new matter, in opposition to a former pleading, which, admitting the facts alleged in such former pleading, shows cause why they should not have their ordinary legal effect." Applied to the present discussion, a plaintiff pleads the traditional tort theory of malpractice and seeks full damages. The defendant responds that assuming recovery is in order under the ordinary tort principles, because of the new statutory limitation, the traditional precedents "should not have their ordinary legal effect."

Considering these factors, against the backdrop and with the illumination provided by other applications of Rule 8(c), we conclude that the Texas statutory limit on medical malpractice damages is an affirmative defense which must be pleaded timely and that in the cases at bar the defense has been waived.

* * *

TAYLOR v. UNITED STATES, 821 F.2d 1428 (9th Cir.1987), certiorari denied 485 U.S. 992, 108 S.Ct. 1300, 99 L.Ed.2d 510 (1988). The United States appealed from a decision of the Northern District of California, awarding a patient's wife $500,000 in damages for loss of consortium and emotional distress, after the patient sustained permanent brain damage while receiving medical treatment at an army hospital. After the District Court awarded the damages, the government moved, pursuant to Federal Rules 59(a), 59(e), and 60(b), for a reduction in damages to $250,000 under California Civil Code § 3333.2, as incorporated by the Federal Tort Claims Act. Section 3333.2 limits recovery for noneconomic injuries in actions based on professional negligence to $250,000. The Ninth Circuit reversed the lower court's decision over objections that the government had waived the protection afforded by Section 3333.2 by failing to raise the issue before judgment.

> Section 3333.2 is a limitation of liability, not an affirmative defense. Unlike affirmative defenses listed in Fed.R.Civ.Proc. 8(c), § 3333.2 limits, but does not bar recovery for noneconomic damages. If the Federal Rules do not require plaintiffs to plead the extent of damages sought, defendants should not be required to plead the limitation of damages prescribed by § 3333.2. A contrary characterization of § 3333.2 would require defendants to anticipate an award of noneconomic damages in excess of $250,000—a requirement which is unrealistic and inconsistent with the practical notions underlying notice pleading. * * *
>
> Furthermore, Rule 8(d) [now Rule 8(b)(6)] specifies that averments as to the amount of damage which defendant does not deny in his answer are not deemed admitted. This provision indicates that the Federal Rules do not consider limitations of damages affirmative defenses, which, by contrast, must be pleaded. Accordingly, the government was not required to raise § 3333.2 in its answer.

> We recognize, however, that application of § 3333.2 may in some instances require resolution of factual issues. In such cases, plaintiffs may be prejudiced if defendants do not raise § 3333.2 prior to judgment. We need not decide the question in this case because application of § 3333.2 here requires no additional factual inquiry on our part. * * *

Id. at 1433. How can *Taylor* be reconciled with the holding in *Ingraham* that a limitation of damages is an affirmative defense under the residuary clause in Rule 8(c)? Which court makes the better argument? Should it matter that the limitation of damages was not raised until the appeal? Is it relevant that, under California state law, Section 3333.2 is an affirmative defense?

* * *

NOTES AND QUESTIONS

1. In an action for breach of contract, must defendant affirmatively plead a clause of the contract that provides a defense to the claim? See PYCA Industries, Inc. v. Harrison County Waste Water Management Dist., 177 F.3d 351, 362–63 (5th Cir.1999).

2. Must defendant affirmatively plead a state statutory bar to non-economic damages or waive the defense? See Sanderson–Cruz v. United States, 88 F.Supp.2d 388 (E.D.Pa.2000).

3. Can the court, *sua sponte*, consider a defense that defendant has failed affirmatively to plead? See Acosta v. Artuz, 221 F.3d 117, 122–23 (2d Cir.2000).

SECTION C. THE REPLY

Read Federal Rule of Civil Procedure 7(a) and the accompanying materials in the Supplement.

NOTES AND QUESTIONS

1. The common-law practice required pleadings to continue back and forth between plaintiff and defendant until disputed issues were isolated. Federal Rule 7 "* * * unceremoniously abolishes a great deal of ancient procedural dogma that has little place in a streamlined litigation system." 5 Wright & Miller, Federal Practice and Procedure: Civil 3d § 1181.

2. Is Federal Rule 7(a), when read in conjunction with Rule 8(b)(6), consistent with Federal Rule 8(b)(1)–(5), which requires a defendant to answer plaintiff's allegations specifically?

3. A plaintiff must reply to an answer that contains counterclaims; otherwise, a reply is within the discretion of the court. See Federal Rule 7(a). Why, given liberal discovery rules, should it ever be necessary to order a reply? Might a reply be helpful in laying the foundation for a motion to dismiss? See 5 Wright & Miller, Federal Practice and Procedure: Civil 3d § 1185.

4. Allegations to which a reply is not required are considered avoided or denied and plaintiff may controvert them at trial. See Federal Rule 8(b)(6); N.Y.C.P.L.R. 3018(a). Conversely, matters requiring a responsive pleading are taken as admitted if not denied in the reply or if a reply is not filed. See Federal Rule 8(b)(6).

SECTION D. AMENDMENTS

Read Federal Rule of Civil Procedure 15 and the accompanying materials in the Supplement.

> Rule 15 reflects two of the most important policies of the federal rules. First, the rule's purpose is to provide maximum opportunity for each claim to be decided on its merits rather than on procedural technicalities. This is demonstrated by the emphasis Rule 15 places on the permissive approach that the district courts are to take to amendment requests, no matter what their character may be; the rule is in sharp contrast to the common law and code restriction that amendments could not change the original cause of action. * * *
>
> Second, Rule 15 reflects the fact that the federal rules assign the pleadings the limited role of providing the parties with notice of the nature of the pleader's claim or defense and the transaction, event, or occurrence that has been called into question; they no longer carry the burden of fact revelation and issue formulation, which now is discharged by the discovery process, or control the trial phase of the action. * * *

6 Wright, Miller & Kane, Federal Practice and Procedure: Civil 2d § 1471.

BEECK v. AQUASLIDE 'N' DIVE CORP.

United States Court of Appeals, Eighth Circuit, 1977.
562 F.2d 537.

BENSON, DISTRICT JUDGE.

* * *

This case is an appeal from the trial court's exercise of discretion on procedural matters in a diversity personal injury action.

Jerry A. Beeck was severely injured on July 15, 1972, while using a water slide. He and his wife, Judy A. Beeck, sued Aquaslide 'N' Dive Corporation (Aquaslide), a Texas corporation, alleging it manufactured the slide involved in the accident, and sought to recover substantial damages on theories of negligence, strict liability and breach of implied warranty.

Aquaslide initially admitted manufacture of the slide, but later moved to amend its answer to deny manufacture; the motion was resisted. The district court granted leave to amend. On motion of the defendant, a separate trial was held on the issue of "whether the defendant designed, manufactured or sold the slide in question." This motion was also resisted by the plaintiffs. The issue was tried to a jury, which returned a verdict for the defendant, after which the trial court entered summary judgment of dismissal of the case. Plaintiffs took this appeal, and stated the issues presented for review to be:

1. Where the manufacturer of the product, a water slide, admitted in its Answer and later in its Answer to Interrogatories both filed prior to the running of the statute of limitations that it designed, manufactured and sold the water slide in question, was it an abuse of the trial court's discretion to grant leave to amend to the manufacturer in order to deny these admissions after the running of the statute of limitations?

* * *

I. Facts

* * *

In 1971 Kimberly Village Home Association of Davenport, Iowa, ordered an Aquaslide product from one George Boldt, who was a local distributor handling defendant's products. The order was forwarded by Boldt to Sentry Pool and Chemical Supply Co. in Rock Island, Illinois, and Sentry forwarded the order to Purity Swimming Pool Supply in Hammond, Indiana. A slide was delivered from a Purity warehouse to Kimberly Village, and was installed by Kimberly employees. On July 15, 1972, Jerry A. Beeck was injured while using the slide at a social gathering sponsored at Kimberly Village by his employer, Harker Wholesale Meats, Inc. Soon after the accident investigations were undertaken by representatives of the separate insurers of Harker and Kimberly Village. On October 31, 1972, Aquaslide first learned of the accident through a letter sent by a representative of Kimberly's insurer to Aquaslide * * *. Aquaslide forwarded this notification to its insurer. Aquaslide's insurance adjuster made an on-site investigation of the slide in May, 1973, and also interviewed persons connected with the ordering and assembly of the slide. An inter-office letter dated September 23, 1973, indicates that Aquaslide's insurer was of the opinion the "Aquaslide in question was definitely manufactured by our insured." The complaint was filed October 15, 1973. Investigators for three different insurance companies, representing Harker, Kimberly and the defendant, had concluded that the slide had been manufactured by Aquaslide, and the defendant, with no information to the contrary, answered the complaint on December 12, 1973, and admitted that it "designed, manufactured, assembled and sold" the slide in question.

The statute of limitations on plaintiff's personal injury claim expired on July 15, 1974. About six and one-half months later Carl Meyer, president and owner of Aquaslide, visited the site of the accident prior to the taking of his deposition by the plaintiff. From his on-site inspection of the slide, he determined it was not a product of the defendant. Thereafter, Aquaslide moved the court for leave to amend its answer to deny manufacture of the slide.

II. Leave to Amend

* * *

In Foman v. Davis, 371 U.S. 178, 83 S.Ct. 227, 9 L.Ed.2d 222 (1962), the Supreme Court had occasion to construe * * * Rule 15(a) * * *:

> Rule 15(a) declares that leave to amend "shall be freely given when justice so requires," this mandate is to be heeded. * * * [This provision was renumbered as Rule 15(a)(2) and the language was altered by the 2007 restyling of the Federal Rules. These changes are not substantive.] If the underlying facts or circumstances relied upon by a plaintiff may be a proper subject of relief, he ought to be afforded an opportunity to test his claim on the merits. In the absence of any apparent or declared reason—such as undue delay, bad faith or dilatory motive on the part of the movant, repeated failure to cure deficiencies by amendments previously allowed, undue prejudice to the opposing party by virtue of allowance of the amendment, futility of amendment, etc.—the leave sought should, as the rules require, be "freely given." Of course, the grant or denial of an opportunity to amend is within the discretion of the District Court * * *.

371 U.S. at 182, 83 S.Ct. at 230. * * *

This Court in Hanson v. Hunt Oil Co., 398 F.2d 578, 582 (8th Cir.1968), held that "[p]rejudice *must be shown.*" (Emphasis added). The burden is on the party opposing the amendment to show such prejudice. In ruling on a motion for leave to amend, the trial court must inquire into the issue of prejudice to the opposing party, in light of the particular facts of the case. * * *

Certain principles apply to appellate review of a trial court's grant or denial of a motion to amend pleadings. First, as noted in Foman v. Davis, allowance or denial of leave to amend lies within the sound discretion of the trial court, * * * and is reviewable only for an abuse of discretion. * * * The appellate court must view the case in the posture in which the trial court acted in ruling on the motion to amend. * * *

It is evident from the order of the district court that in the exercise of its discretion in ruling on defendant's motion for leave to amend, it searched the record for evidence of bad faith, prejudice and undue delay which might be sufficient to overbalance the mandate of Rule 15(a) * * * and Foman v. Davis, that leave to amend should be "freely given." Plaintiffs had not at any time conceded that the slide in question had not been manufactured by the defendant, and at the time the motion for leave to amend was at issue, the court had to decide whether the defendant should be permitted to litigate a material factual issue on its merits.

In inquiring into the issue of bad faith, the court noted the fact that the defendant, in initially concluding that it had manufactured the slide, relied upon the conclusions of three different insurance companies, each of which had conducted an investigation into the circumstances surrounding the accident. This reliance upon investigations of three insurance companies, and the fact that "no contention has been made by anyone that the defendant influenced this possibly erroneous conclusion," persuaded the court that "defendant has not acted in such bad faith as to be precluded from contesting the issue of manufacture at trial." The court further found "[t]o the extent that 'blame' is to be spread regarding the original identification, the record indicates that it should be shared equally."

In considering the issue of prejudice that might result to the plaintiffs from the granting of the motion for leave to amend, the trial court held that the facts presented to it did not support plaintiffs' assertion that, because of the running of the two year Iowa statute of limitations on personal injury claims, the allowance of the amendment would sound the "death knell" of the litigation. In order to accept plaintiffs' argument, the court would have had to assume that the defendant would prevail at trial on the factual issue of manufacture of the slide, and further that plaintiffs would be foreclosed, should the amendment be allowed, from proceeding against other parties if they were unsuccessful in pressing their claim against Aquaslide. On the state of the record before it, the trial court was unwilling to make such assumptions, and concluded "[u]nder these circumstances, the Court deems that the possible prejudice to the plaintiffs is an insufficient basis on which to deny the proposed amendment." The court reasoned that the amendment would merely allow the defendant to contest a disputed factual issue at trial, and further that it would be prejudicial to the defendant to deny the amendment.

The court also held that defendant and its insurance carrier, in investigating the circumstances surrounding the accident, had not been so lacking in diligence as to dictate a denial of the right to litigate the factual issue of manufacture of the slide.

On this record we hold that the trial court did not abuse its discretion in allowing the defendant to amend its answer.

NOTES AND QUESTIONS

1. Parties may amend their complaints before trial and during trial. In *Beeck*, defendant initially moved to amend before the trial took place. Should the court have granted the motion then?

2. Rule 15(a) allows for the automatic amendment of a pleading before a response has been served, or within twenty-one days of the service of the original pleading if no response is required. After that, an amending party must obtain the leave of the court or the consent of the opposing party. In ADAMS v. QUATTLEBAUM, 219 F.R.D. 195 (D.D.C.2004), a pro se litigant sought to amend her civil-rights complaint after defendant already had moved to dismiss. The District Court treated plaintiff's motion as a Rule 15(a) request: "* * * under Rule 15(a), the plaintiff enjoys an 'absolute right' to amend the complaint once at any time prior to a responsive pleading or the granting of a motion to dismiss. * * * Because the defendant has filed a motion to dismiss and not a responsive pleading, the court grants the plaintiff's proposed amendment as of right."

3. During the trial, parties may amend their pleadings, with leave of the court, to conform to issues raised by unexpected evidence. See Rule 15(b). They also may add supplemental pleadings to their original pleadings to cover events that occur after the original pleading. See Rule 15(d). In MOORE v. MOORE, 391 A.2d 762 (D.C. Ct. App. 1978), a father brought suit for custody. After trial, the mother filed a motion to conform the pleadings to the evidence, as well as a motion for award of counsel fees. The court granted her motion and then awarded her custody:

* * *

> Appellant now asserts, as he did at trial, that because appellee requested no affirmative relief in pretrial pleadings the court erred in affording her any relief. It is one thing, he argues, to deny his claim for custody; it is another to award custody to appellee, as well as child support, separate maintenance, and attorneys' fees. He essentially contends, therefore, that the court abused its discretion in permitting the post-trial pleading amendment under Super.Ct.Dom.Rel.R. 15(b), since he was unaware at trial that the matters ultimately stated in appellee's counterclaim were at stake; he was not prepared, nor given an adequate opportunity, to contest them.
>
> Our treatment of this argument must begin with Rule 15(b), which is identical to Fed.R.Civ.Pro. 15(b). Our analysis is accordingly aided by authorities which have interpreted the federal rule. * * * If issues not raised in pleadings are tried by express consent of the parties, there can be no question about the propriety of permitting amendment. The difficult issue arises when, as in most Rule 15(b) cases, "implied consent" is asserted.
>
> Whether parties have impliedly contested a matter—i.e., whether parties recognize that an issue not stated by the pleadings entered the case * * *—is determined by searching the trial record for indications that the party contesting the amendment received actual notice of the injection of the unpleaded matters, as well as an adequate opportunity to litigate such matters and to cure any surprise from their introduction. * * *
>
> The clearest indications of a party's implied consent to try an issue lie in the failure to object to evidence, or in the introduction of evidence which

is clearly apposite to the new issue but not to other matters specified in the pleadings. * * *

A. Custody

Although at the time of trial only appellant, and not his wife, had filed an action for custody, we conclude—without difficulty—that appellant was on timely notice that the court would decide not merely whether he was entitled to custody but, more broadly, would determine *who* was entitled to custody. Mrs. Moore asserted in her answer to appellant's complaint that "the best interests of the child" would be served by the child's being in her custody. Moreover, both parties introduced evidence supporting their respective qualifications for custodian. * * *

* * *

B. Child Support

The pretrial pleadings do not include a claim for child support. Our determination, therefore, again must be whether the issue was litigated by implied consent. For two reasons we find that it was.

First, and most germane, we believe that the resolution of child support inheres in a custody battle where the best interests of the child are the focal concern. * * * The trial judge recognized this relationship when she opined that a grant of support was required by the court's duty to afford complete relief. Second, our conclusion is bolstered by appellee's introduction of evidence of the financial needs of the child. As appellee points out, this evidence was not contested on relevance grounds; it served to put appellant on notice. * * *

* * *

C. Visitation Rights and Bond

Appellant does not dispute that visitation rights are a proper subject for determination as part of the overall custody question. In her Rule 15(b) motion, appellee did not request imposition of a bond covering her husband's visits with Jessica. However, because trial courts are given broad discretion in resolving custody cases, * * * and ought to fashion relief to foster and safeguard a child's best interests, * * * we find no fault with the imposition of a bond upon a parent whose history reflected a capacity for absconding with the child. * * *

D. Attorneys' Fees

This court has determined that even though there is no specific statutory authorization for attorneys' fees awards in child custody cases, courts are empowered to award them to a parent who has enlisted legal assistance to protect the interests of the child. * * *

* * *

E. Separate Maintenance

> The grant of spousal support is a different matter. The initial pleadings did not mention a claim for separate maintenance, which is not customarily a part of a child custody suit between parents whose marital relationship had not been—and was not being—litigated. While evidence of Mrs. Moore's financial needs was admitted without objection relatively late in the proceedings, we cannot conclude that this evidence was so uniquely pertinent to her support alone, in contrast with the custody or the child support issues, that it justifies our concluding that appellant had adequate, timely notice of, and an opportunity to contest, a claim by his wife for her own support. We find no other indication of record that appellant impliedly consented to try his wife's support claim, Rule 15(b), nor can we conclude that the award was a proper, supportable element of full relief in the child custody action. Rule 54(b) [sic]. We therefore find an abuse of trial court discretion in permitting amendment of the pleadings to include separate maintenance and, thereafter, in making such an award.
>
> * * *

Id. at 768–70. Do you agree with the result? Why or why not?

4. Notice the tactical dilemma faced by the plaintiff in a case like *Moore* when the opposition seeks to introduce evidence at trial on an issue that clearly is not within the pleadings. The litigant may object and keep the evidence out, but this will induce the other side to request leave to amend, perhaps even to add an issue of which the party seeking amendment previously was not aware. On the other hand, a failure to object may be taken as implied consent to try the issue, thus permitting an amendment to conform to the proof. Whenever a party fails to object in this situation a second dilemma must be faced—whether or not to produce evidence on the point in question.

5. Should the implied consent rule ever be applied in a case like *Moore* when relief is sought by a defendant who failed to file a counterclaim asking for any relief whatsoever? How important was it that the action involved child custody?

6. "Delay, standing alone, is an insufficient basis for denying leave to amend, and this is true no matter how long the delay." Wallace Hardware Co. v. Abrams, 223 F.3d 382, 409 (6th Cir.2000). Does that statement go too far? Even if the opposing party shows no prejudice, are there reasons for denying leave to amend at some point? Is a trial judge obligated to instruct a litigant as to how it may amend its pleading to state a valid claim or defense and then permit it to do so?

7. Rule 15(c) was amended in 1991 and provides that when an original pleading is amended, the new pleading "relates back to the date of the original pleading," if certain conditions are met. Relation back allows an amended pleading to be treated as if it had been pled in the initial pleading. If the statute of limitations expired between the original pleading and the amendment, the party still may be allowed to raise the claim. Consider how this rule applies to the following case.

WORTHINGTON v. WILSON

United States Court of Appeals, Seventh Circuit, 1993.
8 F.3d 1253.

MANION, CIRCUIT JUDGE:

In his 42 U.S.C. § 1983 complaint, Richard Worthington claimed that while being arrested the arresting officers purposely injured him. When he filed suit on the day the statute of limitations expired, he named "three unknown named police officers" as defendants. Worthington later sought to amend the complaint to substitute police officers Dave Wilson and Jeff Wall for the unknown officers. The district court concluded that the relation back doctrine of Fed.R.Civ.P. 15(c) did not apply, and dismissed the amended complaint. *Worthington v. Wilson,* 790 F.Supp. 829 (C.D.Ill. 1992). We affirm.

I.

On February 25, 1989, Richard Worthington was arrested by a police officer in the Peoria Heights Police Department. At the time of his arrest, Worthington had an injured left hand, and he advised the arresting officer of his injury. According to Worthington's complaint, the arresting officer responded by grabbing Worthington's injured hand and twisting it, prompting Worthington to push the officer away and tell him to "take it easy." A second police officer arrived at the scene, and Worthington was wrestled to the ground and handcuffed. The police officers then hoisted Worthington from the ground by the handcuffs, which caused him to suffer broken bones in his left hand.

Exactly two years later, on February 25, 1991, Worthington filed a five-count complaint in the Circuit Court of Peoria County, Illinois, against the Village of Peoria Heights and "three unknown named police officers," stating the above facts and alleging that he was deprived of his constitutional rights in violation of 42 U.S.C. § 1983. Counts one through three of the complaint named the police officers in their personal and official capacities, and alleged a variety of damages. * * *

* * * [The action was removed to federal court, and plaintiff obtained leave to file an amended complaint.]

On June 17, 1991, Worthington filed an amended complaint in which he substituted as the defendants Dave Wilson and Jeff Wall, two of the twelve or so members of the Peoria Heights Police Department, for the "unknown named police officers" who arrested him on February 25, 1989. Wilson and Wall moved to dismiss the amended complaint primarily on grounds that Illinois' two-year statute of limitations expired, Ill.Ann.Stat. ch. 735, ¶ 5/13–202 (Smith–Hurd 1993), and that the amendment did not relate back to the filing of the original complaint under Rule 15(c). Worthington responded to this motion, and a hearing was conducted before a magistrate judge on October 31, 1991.

* * * On March 17, 1992, the district judge held a hearing on the objections to the magistrate judge's recommendations. Prior to the hearing, the district judge notified the parties that Rule 15(c), on which Wilson and Wall based their argument, had been amended effective December 1, 1991, and asked them to address the effect of this amendment on the motion to dismiss.

On April 27, 1992, the district judge granted Wilson's and Wall's motion to dismiss the amended complaint under revised Rule 15(c) * * *. Worthington appeals this dismissal. * * *

II.

Rule 15(c) was amended to provide broader "relation back" of pleadings when a plaintiff seeks to amend his complaint to change defendants. [The decision recites the amended rule, in pertinent part.] Prior to this amendment, the standard for relation back under Rule 15(c) was set out in *Schiavone v. Fortune,* 477 U.S. 21, 106 S.Ct. 2379, 91 L.Ed.2d 18 (1986):

> * * * (1) the basic claim must have arisen out of the conduct set forth in the original pleading; (2) the party to be brought in must have received such notice that it will not be prejudiced in maintaining its defense; (3) that party must or should have known that, but for a mistake concerning identity, the action would have been brought against it; and (4) the second and third requirements must have been fulfilled within the proscribed limitations period.

Id. at 29, 106 S.Ct. at 2384 [, 91 L.Ed.2d at 27].[a]

The Advisory Committee Notes to amended Rule 15(c) indicate that the amendment repudiates the holding in *Schiavone* that notice of a lawsuit's pendency must be given within the applicable statute of limitations period. The Advisory Committee stated:

> An intended defendant who is notified of an action within the period allowed by [Rule 4(m)] for service of a summons and complaint may not under the revised rule defeat the action on account of a defect in the pleading with respect to the defendant's name, provided that the requirements of clauses (A) and (B) have been met. If the notice requirement is met within the [Rule 4(m)] period, a complaint may be amended at any time to correct a formal defect such as a misnomer or misidentification.

* * *

In this case, Wilson and Wall did not know of Worthington's action before the limitations period expired, as was required by *Schiavone,* but

a. In *Schiavone*, plaintiffs mistakenly failed to name the correct defendant in the original complaint. Plaintiffs meant to sue the owners of *Fortune* magazine; however, instead of naming "Time, Incorporated," they named "Fortune," which is not a legal entity. Plaintiffs were unable to serve "Fortune," so they amended their complaint to name "Time, Incorporated." Both the amendment and service of process on "Time, Incorporated" took place after the statute of limitations had run.

they were aware of its pendency within the extra 120 days provided by new Rule 15(c). *Worthington,* 790 F.Supp. at 833. Since the amendment was decisive to the issue of "notice," the district judge retroactively applied new Rule 15(c), finding it "just and practicable" to do so. *Id.* at 833–34. We have no need to consider the retroactivity of amended Rule 15(c) as it might apply in this case because Worthington's amended complaint did not relate back under either the old or new version of Rule 15(c).

Both versions of Rule 15(c) require that the new defendants "knew or should have known that, but for a mistake concerning the identity of the proper party, the action would have been brought against the party." In *Wood v. Worachek,* 618 F.2d 1225 (7th Cir.1980), we construed the "mistake" requirement of Rule 15(c):

> A plaintiff may usually amend his complaint under Rule 15(c) to change the theory or statute under which recovery is sought; or to correct a misnomer of plaintiff where the proper party plaintiff is in court; or to change the capacity in which the plaintiff sues; or to substitute or add as plaintiff the real party interest; or to add additional plaintiffs where the action, as originally brought, was a class action. Thus, amendment with relation back is generally permitted in order to correct a misnomer of a defendant where the proper defendant is already before the court and the effect is merely to correct the name under which he is sued. But a new defendant cannot normally be substituted or added by amendment after the statute of limitations has run.
>
> * * * * * * [asterisks in original]
>
> Rule 15(c)(2) [current Rule 15(c)(3)] permits an amendment to relate back only where there has been an error made concerning the identity of the proper party and where that party is chargeable with knowledge of the mistake, but it does not permit relation back where, as here, there is a lack of knowledge of the proper party. Thus, in the absence of a mistake in the identification of the proper party, it is irrelevant for the purposes of Rule 15(c)(2) [current Rule 15(c)(3)] whether or not the purported substitute party knew or should have known that the action would have been brought against him.

Id. at 1229 & 1230 (citation omitted). * * * The record shows that there was no mistake concerning the identity of the police officers. At oral argument, counsel for Worthington indicated that he did not decide to file suit until one or two days before the statute of limitations had expired. At that point, neither Worthington nor his counsel knew the names of the two police officers who allegedly committed the offense. Thus, the complaint was filed against "unknown police officers." Because Worthington's failure to name Wilson and Wall was due to a lack of knowledge as to their identity, and not a mistake in their names, Worthington was prevented from availing himself of the relation back doctrine of Rule 15(c).

Worthington argues that the amended complaint should relate back based on the district judge's proposed reading of Rule 15(c) as not having a separate "mistake" requirement. The district judge construed the word "mistake" to mean "change the party or the naming of the party." *Worthington,* 790 F.Supp. at 835. This construction, however, ignores the continuing vitality of *Wood*'s holding which interprets the "mistake" requirement under the old version of Rule 15(c). That holding remains unaffected by the 1991 amendment to Rule 15(c).

Worthington argues alternatively that equitable tolling should bar Wilson and Wall from asserting a statute of limitations defense because the officers fraudulently concealed their identity from him. * * * Worthington concedes that he only mentioned the tolling argument obliquely in his pleadings. The district judge raised the tolling argument *sua sponte* at the hearing on the motion to dismiss. This appeal is the first time that the parties have had an opportunity to fully brief the tolling argument, so it is not waived. * * *

Under Illinois law, a plaintiff who alleges fraudulent concealment to toll the statute of limitations must set forth affirmative acts or words by the defendants which prevented him from discovering their identity. * * * Worthington states that he "was in too much pain to think clearly and seek the names of the officers immediately"; that "law enforcement avoided revealing the names of the arresting officers by offering [him] a very generous plea bargain before the discovery process even began"; that he accepted the plea bargain, "[c]onfident that the names could be learned by other means"; and, that the " 'other means' turned out to be completely fruitless" because the police department "completely stonewalled" his attempts to uncover Wilson's and Wall's names. These statements negate any claim of fraudulent concealment. They do not establish that either Wilson or Wall concealed his identity from Worthington. Nor do they establish that the Peoria Heights Police Department engaged in any conduct designed to deceive Worthington. The statements suggest that the failure to name Wilson and Wall was due to Worthington's own lack of diligence in learning their identity.

* * *

III.

We conclude that the amendment adding Wilson and Wall failed to satisfy the "mistake" requirement of Rule 15(c). As a result, relation back was precluded, and Worthington's complaint was time-barred under Illinois law. * * *

Affirmed.

NOTES AND QUESTIONS

1. Before Rule 15(c) was amended there was disagreement among the circuits about whether relation back is "substantive" or "procedural." In

SCHIAVONE v. FORTUNE, described at p. 631, supra, a diversity case, the Supreme Court applied Rule 15(c) instead of New Jersey's more liberal relation-back rule because the plaintiffs had conceded in the District Court that the New Jersey rule governing relation back was procedural only. Does the subsequent revision of Rule 15 obviate the need for an *Erie* analysis? Does Rule 15(c)(1)(A) incorporate state relation-back law into the Federal Rules?

2. Should a federal court apply Rule 15(c)(1)(A) or Rule 15(c)(1)(C) when it confronts a state relation-back rule that is more restrictive than Rule 15(c)(1)(C)? Would this present an *Erie* problem? Note that subdivisions (c)(1)(A), (c)(1)(B), and (c)(1)(C) are alternative methods of relation back. Whose rights are impaired if Rule 15(c)(1)(A) is applied? If Rule 15(c)(1)(C) is applied? Whenever state relation-back law is different from Rule 15(c)(1)(C), is it a zero-sum game in terms of abridging state-created rights?

3. In *Schiavone,* p. 631, supra, Justice Blackmun concluded that for relation-back law "[t]he linchpin is notice, and notice within the limitations period." 477 U.S. at 31, 106 S.Ct. at 2385, 91 L.Ed.2d at 29. How much "notice" is required to satisfy Rule 15(c)(1)(C)(i)? What if plaintiff does not know defendant's name and instead uses a "John Doe" designation? One commentator posits:

> Notice demands that the trial court, in deciding whether to permit an amended pleading to relate back, engage in a discretionary, fact-intensive inquiry as to what the intended defendant knew about the filing of the lawsuit and his potential role in that lawsuit and when he knew it. * * * Notice in turn demands that the plaintiff plead the John Doe defendant with some level of specificity, describing who the individuals were, what they did, and the time, place, and manner in which events occurred. * * *

Wasserman, *Civil Rights Plaintiffs and John Doe Defendants: A Study in Section 1983 Procedure*, 25 Cardozo L. Rev. 793, 843 (2003). Do you agree?

4. Does the Seventh Circuit in *Worthington* interpret too narrowly the "mistake" requirement in Rule 15(c)(1)(C)(ii)? If the primary concern is notice to defendant, why should plaintiff's state of mind matter? Is there a danger that a plaintiff can circumvent the Seventh Circuit's bar on replacing fictitious defendants with actual defendants by naming random defendants? See Engrav, *Relation Back of Amendments Naming Previously Unnamed Defendants under Federal Rule of Civil Procedure 15(c)*, 89 Cal. L. Rev. 1549 (2001). Would that practice violate Federal Rule 11, p. 640, infra?

SECTION E. SUPPLEMENTAL PLEADINGS

Read Federal Rules of Civil Procedure 7(a) and 15(d) in the Supplement.

NOTES AND QUESTIONS

1. Federal Rule 15(d) provides that the court may allow the filing of a supplemental pleading "setting out any transaction, occurrence, or event that happened after the date of the pleading to be supplemented." A supplemental pleading can be used to cure defects in the original pleading, to add new claims, or to provide additional facts that update the complaint. See 6A Wright, Miller & Kane, Federal Practice and Procedure: Civil 2d § 1504. In the lower federal courts, there is substantial authority for the proposition that Rule 15(d) permits even the bringing of new claims in a supplemental complaint, because it "promote[s] the economical and speedy disposition of the controversy." Keith v. Volpe, 858 F.2d 467, 473 (9th Cir.1988).

2. Compare Rule 15(d) with the traditional scope of a supplemental pleading: "The office of a supplemental complaint is to aid the cause of action already averred, not to enable the plaintiff to recover upon a cause of action which has accrued since the action was commenced." HALSTED v. HALSTED, 7 Misc. 23, 27 N.Y.S. 408 (Com.Pl.1894). What reason, if any, is there for prohibiting a "new cause of action" in a supplemental pleading?

3. Note that Rule 13(e) permits defendants to use a supplemental pleading to assert counterclaims that arise after filing an answer. What policy reasons would justify treating plaintiffs differently than defendants? Why should a plaintiff's right to file a supplemental pleading under Rule 15(d) be narrower than a defendant's right under Rule 13(e)?

4. Are supplemental pleadings governed by the same relation-back analysis as amended pleadings? One view is reflected in DAVIS v. PIPER AIRCRAFT CORP., 615 F.2d 606, 609 n.3 (4th Cir.1980). In that case, the plaintiff moved to amend his complaint pursuant to Rule 15(a)(1) to reflect his new capacity as ancillary administrator of an estate, which allowed him to go forward with a wrongful death action filed nine months earlier. The Court of Appeals noted that:

> Technically this was more properly an attempt to file a supplemental pleading under Fed.R.Civ.P. 15(d) than an amended pleading under Fed.R.Civ.P. 15(a) [now Rule 15(a)(1)] because the new matter occurred after rather than before the original complaint was filed. For relation back purposes, the technical distinction between the two is not of critical importance, and is frequently simply disregarded by courts * * *. So long as the test of Fed.R.Civ.P. 15(c) is met, a supplemental pleading should ordinarily be given the same relation back effect as an amended pleading. * * * On that basis, our analysis will treat Fed.R. 15(c) as applying to the supplemental pleading actually attempted here. * * *

SECTION F. PROVISIONS TO DETER FRIVOLOUS PLEADINGS

Read Federal Rules of Civil Procedure 11 and 23.1 and related materials in the Supplement.

SUROWITZ v. HILTON HOTELS CORP.

Supreme Court of the United States, 1966.
383 U.S. 363, 86 S.Ct. 845, 15 L.Ed.2d 807.

Certiorari to the United States Court of Appeals for the Seventh Circuit.

MR. JUSTICE BLACK delivered the opinion of the Court.

[Petitioner, Dora Surowitz, a stockholder in Hilton Hotels Corporation, filed a derivative action on behalf of herself and other stockholders charging that the officers and directors of the corporation had defrauded it of several million dollars in violation of the Securities Act of 1933, the Securities Exchange Act of 1934, and the Delaware General Corporation Law. The complaint was 60 printed pages and signed by petitioner's counsel in compliance with Rule 11 of the Federal Rules which, at the time, provided that "The signature of an attorney constitutes a certificate by him that he has read the pleading; that to the best of his knowledge, information, and belief there is good ground to support it; and that it is not interposed for delay."[b] Petitioner also verified the complaint pursuant to Rule 23(b) [now Rule 23.1], stating that some of the allegations in the complaint were true and that she "on information and belief" thought that all the other allegations were true. The district court, before requiring defendants to answer, granted their motion to depose petitioner.]

---

* * * In this examination Mrs. Surowitz showed in her answers to questions that she did not understand the complaint at all, that she could not explain the statements made in the complaint, that she had a very small degree of knowledge as to what the lawsuit was about, that she did not know any of the defendants by name, that she did not know the nature of their alleged misconduct, and in fact that in signing the verification she had merely relied on what her son-in-law had explained to her about the facts in the case. On the basis of this examination, defendants moved to dismiss the complaint, alleging that "1. It is a sham pleading, and 2. Plaintiff, Dora Surowitz, is not a proper party plaintiff. * * * " In response, Mrs. Surowitz's lawyer, in an effort to cure whatever

---

b. The language of both Rule 11 and Rule 23 have been altered since the publication of this opinion, most recently in 2007. These changes are not substantive for the purposes of this Chapter.

infirmity the court might possibly find in Mrs. Surowitz's verification in light of her deposition, filed two affidavits which shed much additional light on an extensive investigation which had preceded the filing of the complaint. Despite these affidavits the District Judge dismissed the case holding that Mrs. Surowitz's affidavit was "false," that being wholly false it was a nullity, that being a nullity it was as though no affidavit had been made in compliance with Rule 23, that being false the affidavit was a "sham" and Rule 23(b) required that he dismiss her case, and he did so, "with prejudice."

The Court of Appeals affirmed the District Court's dismissal * * * despite the fact that the charges made against the defendants were viewed as very serious and grave charges of fraud and that "many of the material allegations of the complaint are obviously true and cannot be refuted." 342 F.2d, at 607. We cannot agree with either of the courts below and reverse their judgments. * * *

Mrs. Surowitz, the plaintiff and petitioner here, is a Polish immigrant with a very limited English vocabulary and practically no formal education. For many years she has worked as a seamstress in New York where by reason of frugality she saved enough money to buy some thousands of dollars worth of stocks. She was of course not able to select stocks for herself with any degree of assurance of their value. Under these circumstances she had to receive advice and counsel and quite naturally she went to her son-in-law, Irving Brilliant. Mr. Brilliant had graduated from the Harvard Law School, possessed a master's degree in economics from Columbia University, was a professional investment advisor, and in addition to his degrees and his financial acumen, he wore a Phi Beta Kappa key. In 1957, six years before this litigation began, he bought some stock for his mother-in-law in the Hilton Hotels Corporation, paying a little more than $2,000 of her own money for it. * * *

About December 1962, Mrs. Surowitz received through the mails a notice from the Hilton Hotels Corporation announcing its plan to purchase a large amount of its own stock. Because she wanted it explained to her, she took the notice to Mr. Brilliant. Apparently disturbed by it, he straightway set out to make an investigation. Shortly thereafter he went to Chicago, Illinois, where Hilton Hotels has its home office and talked the matter over with Mr. Rockler. Mr. Brilliant and Mr. Rockler had been friends for many years. * * * The two decided to investigate further, and for a number of months both pursued whatever avenues of information that were open to them. By August of 1963 on the basis of their investigation, both of them had reached the conclusion [that defendants were engaged in a fraudulent scheme, and Mr. Brilliant explained this to Mrs. Surowitz]. * * *

* * * When, on the basis of this conversation, Mrs. Surowitz stated that she agreed that suit be filed in her name, Mr. Rockler prepared a formal complaint which he mailed to Mr. Brilliant. Mr. Brilliant then, according to both his affidavit and Mrs. Surowitz's testimony, read and explained the complaint to his mother-in-law before she verified it. Her limited education and her small knowledge about any of the English language, except the most ordinarily used words, probably is sufficient

guarantee that the courts below were right in finding that she did not understand any of the legal relationships or comprehend any of the business transactions described in the complaint. She did know, however, that she had put over $2,000 of her hard-earned money into Hilton Hotels stock, that she was not getting her dividends, and that her son-in-law who had looked into the matter thought that something was wrong. She also knew that her son-in-law was qualified to help her and she trusted him. It is difficult to believe that anyone could be shocked or harmed in any way when, in the light of all these circumstances, Mrs. Surowitz verified the complaint, not on the basis of her own knowledge and understanding, but in the faith that her son-in-law had correctly advised her either that the statements in the complaint were true or to the best of his knowledge he believed them to be true.

* * * Rule 23(b) was not written in order to bar derivative suits. Unquestionably it was originally adopted and has served since in part as a means to discourage "strike suits" by people who might be interested in getting quick dollars by making charges without regard to their truth so as to coerce corporate managers to settle worthless claims in order to get rid of them. * * *

When the record of this case is reviewed in the light of the purpose of Rule 23(b)'s verification requirement, there emerges the plain, inescapable fact that this is not a strike suit or anything akin to it. Mrs. Surowitz was not interested in anything but her own investment made with her own money. Moreover, there is not one iota of evidence that Mr. Brilliant, her son-in-law and counselor, sought to do the corporation any injury in this litigation. In fact his purchases for the benefit of his family of more than $50,000 of securities in the corporation, including a $10,000 debenture, all made years before this suit was brought, manifest confidence in the corporation, not a desire to harm it in any way. The Court of Appeals in affirming the District Court's dismissal, however, indicated that whether Mrs. Surowitz and her counselors acted in good faith and whether the charges they made were truthful were irrelevant once Mrs. Surowitz demonstrated in her oral testimony that she knew nothing about the content of the suit. * * *

We cannot construe Rule 23 or any other one of the Federal Rules as compelling courts to summarily dismiss, without any answer or argument at all, cases like this where grave charges of fraud are shown by the record to be based on reasonable beliefs growing out of careful investigation. The basic purpose of the Federal Rules is to administer justice through fair trials, not through summary dismissals as necessary as they may be on occasion. These rules were designed in large part to get away from some of the old procedural booby traps which common-law pleaders could set to prevent unsophisticated litigants from ever having their day in court. If rules of procedure work as they should in an honest and fair judicial system, they not only permit, but should as nearly as possible guarantee that bona fide complaints be carried to an adjudication on the merits. Rule 23(b), like the other civil rules, was written to further, not defeat the ends of justice. The serious fraud charged here, which of course has not been proven, is clearly in that class of deceitful conduct which the federal securities laws were largely passed to prohibit and protect against. There is, moreover, not one word or one line of actual evidence in this record indicating that there has been any collusive conduct or trickery by those who filed this suit except through intimations and insinuations without any support from anything any witness has said. The dismissal of this case was error. It has now been practically three years since the complaint was filed and as yet none of the defendants have even been compelled to admit or deny the wrongdoings charged. They should be. The cause is reversed and remanded to the District Court for trial on the merits.

Reversed and remanded.

MR. JUSTICE HARLAN, concurring.

Rule 23(b) directs that in a derivative suit "the complaint shall be verified by oath" but nothing dictates that the verification be that of the plaintiff shareholder. * * * In the present circumstances, it seems to me the affidavit of Walter J. Rockler, counsel for Mrs. Surowitz, amounts to an adequate verification by counsel, which I think is permitted by a reasonable interpretation of the Rule at least in cases such as this. On this premise, I agree with the decision of the Court.

NOTES AND QUESTIONS

1. Why does Rule 23.1 require verification? Why doesn't the Rule 11 procedure suffice? Should the verification requirement be limited to particular allegations? See Comment, *Verification of Complaint in Stockholders' Derivative Suits under Rule 23(b)*, 114 U. Pa. L. Rev. 614 (1966).

2. In those state courts in which fact pleadings generally do not have to be verified, there are certain exceptions. Some of the typical ones found in state practice are: petitions for divorce; petitions brought by the state to enjoin a nuisance; and complaints to obtain support of an illegitimate child. E.g., Iowa Code Ann. § 600–.13. What makes these actions sufficiently distinctive to require verification?

3. Compare Roussel v. Tidelands Capital Corp., 438 F.Supp. 684, 688 (N.D.Ala.1977), reaffirming the dismissal of an action under Rule 23.1, because, among other things, plaintiff admitted he verified the pleading without reading it, and thus had demonstrated he was not likely to represent the shareholders fairly and adequately. Why is a dismissal ever an appropriate way of enforcing the verification provision of Rule 23.1? Shouldn't plaintiff be prosecuted for the crime of perjury instead? Of what significance is it that any recovery in a suit under Rule 23.1 goes directly to the corporation, not to plaintiff? Suppose the statute of limitations on the claim runs just before the dismissal. What additional problems would this raise?

NOTE ON FEDERAL RULE 11

Permissive pleading rules such as those embodied in the Federal Rules and comparable state systems provide an opportunity for abuse. For example, is it appropriate for a party to institute a colorable claim with the sole intention of pressuring another party into settling? Or would it be right for a party who has been sued on a legitimate claim to interpose a counterclaim on a questionable legal theory—simply to induce plaintiff to drop the suit? However, the ease of pleading is also an important vehicle for enforcing social norms and achieving regulatory compliance. Pleading rules therefore must strike a balance between competing goals.

Federal Rule 11 attempts to curb abuse of the federal pleading rules by imposing affirmative duties on attorneys and by raising the possibility of sanctions for failure to discharge them. As is clear from *Surowitz,* the pre–1983 incarnation of Rule 11 employed a subjective standard to assess attorney conduct—so long as attorneys acted in good faith, they were not subject to sanctions even if it later became clear that their legal theory was faulty or that the facts did not support their claims.

> Rule 11, as originally adopted in 1937, * * * provided that an attorney's signature on a pleading certified that there was good ground to support the pleading and that it was not interposed for delay. The rule also stated that a pleading signed "with intent to defeat the purpose of the rule . . . may be stricken [and that] [f]or a willful violation of this rule an attorney may be subjected to appropriate disciplinary action." * * * During the succeeding forty-five years, the Rule proved to be ineffective and little used.

Schwarzer, *Rule 11: Entering a New Era,* 28 Loy. L.A. L. Rev. 7, 7–8 (1994). One study reveals that, between 1938 and 1976, there were only twenty-three reported cases in which a party invoked Rule 11 to strike a pleading and only nine cases in which violations were found. See Risinger, *Honesty in Pleading and its Enforcement: Some "Striking" Problems with Federal Rule of Civil Procedure 11*, 61 Minn.L.Rev. 1 (1976).

The 1983 amendment to Rule 11 made several important changes to overcome the reluctance of courts to impose sanctions and to ensure that attorneys would "stop and think" before filing papers. One commentary explains: "The 1983 amendment required lawyers and litigants to conduct reasonable prefiling factual and legal inquiries, while certifying that their papers were factually well grounded and legally warranted. The 1983 revision to Rule 11 also mandated that judges levy sanctions on counsel and parties who did not discharge these responsibilities." Sanner & Tobias, *Rule 11 and Rule Revision*, 37 Loy. L.A. L. Rev. 573, 575 (2004).

The number of Rule 11 motions increased dramatically after the 1983 amendment. By 1991, over 3,000 proceedings dealing with Rule 11 had been reported. See Vairo, *Rule 11: Where We Are and Where We Are Going,* 60 Fordham L.Rev. 475, 480 (1991). And, as one court recognized, "[t]he large number of reported opinions can only be a fraction of the large number of instances in which sanctions have been imposed under" Rule 11. Zaldivar v.

City of Los Angeles, 780 F.2d 823, 829 (9th Cir.1986). Between 1989 and 1992, Rule 11 was the subject of five Supreme Court decisions.

One study of Rule 11 under the 1983 amendment revealed that it had a significant impact on the behavior of attorneys even when no sanctions were awarded. See Kritzer, Marshall & Zemans, *Rule 11: Moving Beyond the Cosmic Anecdote*, 75 Judicature 269 (1992). In the twelve months preceding the study, 24.5 percent of lawyers had experienced an in-court reference to Rule 11, and 30.3 percent had experienced out-of-court references to Rule 11. More than one-third of the lawyers surveyed said that a fear of sanctions resulted in "extra pre-filing review of pleadings, motions, or other documents subject to Rule 11," lending credence to the notion that it was encouraging lawyers to "stop and think" before acting, as it was intended to do.

An irony of practice under the 1983 amendment was that Rule 11 itself became a source of tactical litigation. According to some, it was used as a "hardball" technique to intimidate and harass opponents by many of the very attorneys whose abusive behavior Rule 11 was meant to control. See Gaiardo v. Ethyl Corp., 835 F.2d 479, 484–85 (3d Cir.1987); Cole, *Rule 11 Now*, 17 Litigation 10 (1991). Other practices included "bloated requests" for attorney's fees. See Frantz v. United States Powerlifting Fed'n, 836 F.2d 1063, 1066 (7th Cir.1987).

In addition, commentators expressed concern that Rule 11 was having a chilling effect on legitimate, but disfavored, categories of lawsuits such as civil rights claims. One commentary notes that under the 1983 version, "Rule 11 motions were filed and granted against civil rights plaintiffs more frequently than any other class of litigant, and numerous judges vigorously enforced the provision against the plaintiffs, levying large sanctions on them." Tobias, *The 1993 Revision to Federal Rule 11*, 70 Ind. L.J. 171, 171 (1994).

In 1989, the Advisory Committee on the Federal Rules of Civil Procedure began to review the 1983 version of Rule 11. It gathered comments and proposed another set of amendments, which the Supreme Court adopted and which became effective in 1993. See Willging, *Past and Potential Uses of Empirical Research in Civil Rulemaking*, 77 Notre Dame L. Rev. 1121, 1147–53 (2002). The 1993 amendment preserved the "stop and think" objective of the 1983 version of the Rule, but tried to avoid any "chilling effect" on counsel's advancing novel legal theories. The amendment also eliminated the compensatory character that Rule 11 had acquired as a result of courts almost routinely imposing monetary sanctions for violations of the Rule. See Nelken, *Has the Chancellor Shot Himself in the Foot? Looking for Middle Ground on Rule 11 Sanctions*, 41 Hastings L.J. 383 (1990).

The current Rule is simpler, allows more court discretion in the imposition of monetary sanctions, and has added a twenty-one day "safe harbor" during which the filing party may withdraw the challenged paper without censure. Furthermore, the 1993 amendment changes the requirement that an attorney have a "good faith" motive for an argument for a change in law to a requirement that the argument be nonfrivolous, and adds a clause for the establishment of new law. The current version of the Rule also applies to all representations to the court, including the later advocacy of a previously presented position. Finally, present Rule 11 also allows sanctions against the law firms or parties responsible for violations, as well as against the signer of the document.

In dissenting from the adoption of the 1993 amendment Justice Scalia wrote:

> The proposed revision would render the Rule toothless, by allowing judges to dispense with sanction, by disfavoring compensation for litigation expenses, and by providing a 21–day "safe harbor". * * * The Rules should be solicitous of the abused (the courts and the opposing party), and not of the abuser. Under the revised Rule, parties will be able to file thoughtless, reckless, and harassing pleadings, secure in the knowledge that they have nothing to lose: If objection is raised, they can retreat without penalty. The proposed revision contradicts what this court said only three years ago: "Baseless filing puts the machinery of justice in motion, burdening courts and individuals alike with needless expense and delay." Cooter & Gell v. Hartmarx Corp., 496 U.S. 384, 398, 110 S.Ct. 2447, 110 L.Ed.2d 359 (1990).

Order of the Supreme Court Amending the Federal Rules of Civil Procedure (April 22, 1993), reprinted in 146 F.R.D. 404, 507 (1993) (Scalia, J., dissenting). For an analysis of the impact of the 1993 version of Rule 11, see Yablon, *Hindsight, Regret, and Safe Harbors in Rule 11 Litigation*, 37 Loy. L. A. L. Rev. 599, 605 (2004).

HADGES v. YONKERS RACING CORP.

United States Court of Appeals, Second Circuit, 1995.
48 F.3d 1320, 30 Fed.R.Serv.3d 1165.

[Hadges, a harness racehorse driver, trainer, and owner had been licensed by the New York State Racing Board in 1972. The license was suspended and revoked in 1974, reissued in 1976, and suspended for a six-month period in 1989.

Hadges was denied the ability to work at a number of racetracks following the 1989 reinstatement of his license. He sued Yonkers Racing Corporation ("YRC") in both state and federal court for barring him from working at Yonkers Raceway. The federal claim, based on a denial of due process, was dismissed because the court found no state action; the court noted however, that had other tracks (including the Meadowlands in New Jersey) "followed YRC's decision" state action could have been established. (Based partially on an affidavit that so asserted, it was the court's understanding that Hadges could work at other tracks in the region.) In his state case, which alleged that he had been blackballed by New York State tracks, the state court ruled against Hadges on all claims.

In 1992 Hadges brought suit in federal district court against the Meadowlands Raceway (a state agency) based on the same claim as in the YRC case. The case settled; before the settlement, however, the Meadowlands' General Manager submitted an affidavit that, pursuant to a 1992 resolution, the YRC ban would provide a basis for a Meadowlands ban.

Hadges appealed the New York state court decision, and filed a Rule 60(b) motion in the New York federal action requesting that the original decision against him be vacated because the affidavit which had claimed he could work at other tracks was fraudulent. With the Rule 60(b) motion, Hadges and his attorney, William Kunstler, signed statements saying that Hadges had not worked in over four years; neither mentioned the state appeal.

In reply to the Rule 60(b) motion, YRC presented evidence that showed Hadges had raced at Monticello five times in 1991 and seven times in 1993. YRC moved for dismissal and requested that the court impose sanctions on Hadges and possibly Kunstler "for misrepresentation and for failing to disclose the state court action to the district court." Hadges admitted that he had raced at Monticello but offered the excuse that he had only made a total of $100 from the 12 races together. Hadges also submitted a "scratch" sheet that he claimed documented the fact that the New York State Racing Board scratched him (barred him) from a race in 1989 following the re-issuance of his license. YRC later demonstrated, however, that the sheet was from a November 1987 race.

The district court denied the Rule 60(b) motion, but found that it was "not so frivolous as to warrant Rule 11 sanctions." The court did ask, however, that Hadges and Kunstler submit papers arguing against the imposition of sanctions for misrepresentation of Hadges's racing history. Hadges claimed that the erroneous submission of the sheet was a mistake, and that the 1989 scratching incident was a separate one for which he submitted proof in the form of an affidavit. Kunstler claimed that he did not know that the sheet was from 1987, but that the date was irrelevant because the sheet was useful as evidence anyway.]

* * *

Thereafter, in the second ruling on appeal to us, the judge imposed a Rule 11 sanction of $2,000 on Hadges as an appropriate sanction for his misrepresentations. The judge also censured Kunstler under Rule 11 for failing to make adequate inquiry as to the truth of Hadges's affidavits and for failing to inform the court of the pending state court litigation. In the course of his opinion, the judge stated:

> Mr. Kunstler is apparently one of those attorneys who believes that his sole obligation is to his client and that he has no obligations to the court or to the processes of justice. Unfortunately, he is not alone in this approach to the practice of law, which may be one reason why the legal profession is held in such low esteem by the public at this time.

Kunstler responded in a letter to the court, in which he argued that the court erred in sanctioning his client $2,000 and in censuring him. In particular, he objected to the court's characterization of him as an attorney "who believes that his sole obligation is to his client," and he objected to the court's charge that his approach to law practice was in part responsible for the low public esteem for the legal profession. Kunstler went on to state his opinion that the court's comment was "generated by an animus toward activist practitioners who, like myself, have, over the years, vigorously represented clients wholly disfavored by the establishment."

The court treated the letter as an application to reargue the sanction issues. Its order denying the application is the third ruling on appeal to us. In that order, the court quoted at length from a recent New York state court opinion criticizing Kunstler's law partner, Ronald L. Kuby in an entirely unrelated case. * * * The judge's order further reprimanded Kunstler stating:

> Finally, Mr. Kunstler claims that he is entitled to "consideration" because of his representation of unpopular clients. Undoubtedly an attorney who assumes or is assigned the defense of an unpopular case or client and does so at risk to his practice or standing in the community (such as the fictional attorney Atticus Finch in Harper Lee's "To Kill a Mockingbird") is entitled to some consideration. However, an attorney who aggressively and repeatedly seeks to represent unpopular causes or questionable clients for personal reasons of his own is not deserving of any particular consideration. And an attorney who places himself and his causes above the interests of justice is entitled to none.

This appeal from the judgment for YRC in the Rule 60(b) action and from the two April 1994 rulings on sanctions followed.

II. Discussion

* * *

[In Part A the court upheld the district court's denial of Rule 60(b) relief.]

* * *

B. Rule 11 sanctions

As we have already noted, not only did the district court rule against Hadges regarding his claims of fraud on the court in *Hadges I*, but it went on to impose Rule 11 sanctions on both Hadges and Kunstler for their own misrepresentations and omissions. This determination was based on two principal grounds: (1) misstatement of the date of the alleged "scratching" incident and (2) misstatement regarding Hadges's lack of work in the years since the YRC ban. In addition, the court based Kunstler's censure on his failure to inform the court of the state court action. * * *

* * *

1. Hadges's sanction

Hadges argues that the district court abused its discretion in imposing sanctions on him. YRC argues that the sanctions were justified. We believe that Hadges is correct.

In imposing sanctions, the district court apparently did not take into account YRC's failure to comply with the revised procedural requirements of Rule 11. In this case, YRC did not submit the sanction request separately from all other requests, and there is no evidence in the record indicating that YRC served Hadges with the request for sanctions 21 days before presenting it to the court. Thus, YRC denied Hadges the "safe-harbor" period that the current version of the Rule specifically mandates. * * *

If Hadges had received the benefit of the safe-harbor period, the record indicates that he would have "withdrawn or appropriately corrected" his misstatements, thus avoiding sanctions altogether. Hadges did in fact correct one of his misstatements by admitting in an affidavit, sworn to on December 28, 1993, just 12 days after YRC asked for sanctions, that he had raced at Monticello in 1991 and 1993. Thus, this misstatement is not sanctionable.

Hadges also explained and corrected his misstatement about the 1989 date of the first scratching incident and described another scratching incident in 1989 involving another horse (Dazzling GT). This correction was supported by his own affidavit sworn to on March 17, 1994, and the affidavit of Erik Schulman, sworn to on March 16, 1994. Both were filed with the district court on March 21, 1994, just one week after the court issued its order stating that it was considering imposition of sanctions. Apparently, YRC had not previously requested sanctions on the basis of the scratching incident. Although YRC subsequently questioned whether the Dazzling GT incident described by Hadges and Schulman had taken place, the district court did not rely on this as a basis for imposing sanctions. We note that Kunstler also filed an affidavit making similar retractions.

* * *

Rule 11 also provides that a court may impose sanctions on its own initiative. * * * If a court wishes to exercise its discretion to impose sanctions sua sponte, it must "enter an order describing the specific conduct that appears to violate subdivision (b) and directing an attorney, law firm, or party to show cause why it has not violated subdivision (b) with respect thereto." [The language of this provision has been altered without any change in substance.] * * * In this case, the court indicated that it was imposing sanctions in response to YRC's request and did not state that it was imposing sanctions on Hadges sua sponte. We doubt that sua sponte sanctions would have been justified here. The advisory committee note on the 1993 amendment specifically states that such sanctions "will ordinarily be [imposed] only in situations that are akin to a contempt of court." Hadges's conduct did not rise to that level.

Thus, under all the circumstances, particularly the failure to afford Hadges the 21-day safe-harbor period provided by revised Rule 11, we believe that the sanction of Hadges should be reversed.

2. *Kunstler's censure*

Like Hadges, Kunstler did not receive the benefit of the safe-harbor period. The district court imposed sanctions on Kunstler for failing to adequately investigate the truth of Hadges's representations prior to submitting them to the court and for failing to disclose that Hadges had brought an action against YRC in New York state court. Kunstler argues that the court's censure of him was an abuse of discretion because the court was motivated by a personal or political animus against him and because his conduct was not sufficiently egregious to justify imposition of sanctions.

In our decisions concerning the former version of Rule 11 we have had occasion to address the reasonableness of an attorney's reliance on information provided by a client. In *Kamen v. American Tel. & Tel. Co.,* 791 F.2d 1006 (2d Cir.1986), the plaintiff brought suit against her employer and supervisors under the Rehabilitation Act of 1973 and state law. Employers are not liable under the Rehabilitation Act unless they receive "[f]ederal financial assistance." 29 U.S.C. § 794. The employer sent letters to the plaintiff's attorney asserting that it did not receive federal financial assistance, but her attorney persisted in prosecuting the Rehabilitation Act suit. The district court agreed with the employer and dismissed the claims. Although plaintiff's attorney had submitted an affirmation stating that his client had advised him that the employer received federal grants, the district court imposed sanctions. We found that the district court abused its discretion because the attorney's reliance on his client's statements was reasonable. * * *

A few years later, we relied on *Kamen* in holding that "[a]n attorney is entitled to rely on his or her client's statements as to factual claims when those statements are objectively reasonable." *Calloway v. Marvel Entertainment Group,* 854 F.2d 1452, 1470 (2d Cir.1988), rev'd in part on other grounds sub nom. *Pavelic & LeFlore v. Marvel Entertainment Group,* 493 U.S. 120, 110 S.Ct. 456, 107 L.Ed.2d 438 (1989). This interpretation is in keeping with the advisory committee notes on former Rule 11, which indicates that the reasonableness of an inquiry depends upon the surrounding circumstances, including

> such factors as how much time for investigation was available to the signer; whether he had to rely on a client for information as to the facts underlying the pleading . . .; or whether he depended on forwarding counsel or another member of the bar.

Advisory committee note on 1983 amendment to Fed.R.Civ.P. 11.

In *Calloway,* at least one of the plaintiff's claims "was never supported by any evidence at any stage of the proceeding," and we affirmed the district court's imposition of sanctions. * * * However, we went on to set forth a procedure for district courts to follow in analyzing whether an attorney has conducted a reasonable inquiry into the facts underlying a party's position.

> In considering sanctions regarding a factual claim, the initial focus of the district court should be on whether an objectively reasonable evidentiary basis for the claim was demonstrated in pretrial proceedings or at trial. Where such a basis was shown, no inquiry into the adequacy of the attorney's pre-filing investigation is necessary.

* * *

The new version of Rule 11 makes it even clearer that an attorney is entitled to rely on the objectively reasonable representations of the client. No longer are attorneys required to certify that their representations are "well grounded in fact." * * * The current version of the Rule requires only that an attorney conduct "an inquiry reasonable under the circumstances" into whether "factual contentions have evidentiary support." * * * Thus, the new version of Rule 11 is in keeping with the emphasis in *Calloway* on looking to the record before imposing sanctions.

In its first sanction decision in April 1994, the district court here stated:

> With respect to plaintiff's counsel, William M. Kunstler, the situation is not quite as clear. There is nothing to indicate that, on the serious factual misrepresentations made in plaintiff's papers, Mr. Kunstler had independent knowledge of their falsity. However, it is equally clear that he made no attempt to verify the truth of the plaintiff's representations prior to submitting them to the court.

Apparently, the district court did not focus, as Rule 11 now requires, on whether the pretrial proceedings provided "evidentiary support" for the factual misrepresentations with which the court was concerned.

It is clear that the record before the district court contained evidentiary support for Kunstler's incorrect statements. As to the scratching incident, the record included a sworn statement by Hadges describing an October 1989 incident in which he claimed to have been scratched from driving the horse "Me Gotta Bret." A scratch sheet, which did not reveal the year in which it was made out, was also part of the record. Kunstler later submitted an affidavit admitting the error and stating that he had no idea that the 1989 date was wrong. He further maintained that regardless of its date, the scratch sheet was relevant to show collaboration between the Racing Board and YRC in 1987, which would subject the latter to § 1983 liability. Moreover, it appears to be undisputed that most of the evidence YRC produced to persuade the court that the event had taken place in 1987 was within its possession, not Hadges's. See *Kamen,* 791 F.2d at 1012 (noting reasonableness of relying on client representations where "the relevant information [is] largely in the control of the defendants").

We also believe that the record contained evidentiary support for the claim that Hadges had not worked for four years. At the time the district court granted YRC summary judgment in Hadges's Rule 60(b) action, it had before it Hadges's affidavit asserting that he had written to racetrack

General Managers asking for driving privileges and had not received any replies. The record also contained attorney Faraldo's affidavit asserting that Hadges had followed his advice in writing these letters. Moreover, Kunstler represented Hadges in the Meadowlands suit in which Meadowlands admitted banning Hadges based upon the YRC ban. We believe that in light of his familiarity with the Meadowlands litigation and the sworn statements of his client and another attorney, Kunstler had sufficient evidence to support a belief that Hadges had not participated in harness horseracing in New York since the YRC ban. * * *

The district court also believed that censure of Kunstler was justified because "he had to be aware of the recent state court litigation, still on appeal, but made no mention of it in his initial papers." Kunstler concedes that he was aware of this litigation but maintains that he did not believe that it was necessary to bring the proceedings to the court's attention because the New York Supreme Court had not ruled on the merits of the state law blackballing claim. As noted above, we agree with the view that the state court opinion was not a decision on the merits of that issue. Even if it were, there would be no tactical advantage in not mentioning the state court ruling to the district court since YRC was a party to both actions (indeed, it was represented by the same law firm and the same attorney in both actions) and could be expected to inform the district court of the state court action if it were helpful.

Moreover, the portion of the court's opinion in the Rule 60(b) action that listed the possible bases for imposition of sanctions omitted any reference to Kunstler's nondisclosure of the state court action. Rule 11 specifically requires that those facing sanctions receive adequate notice and the opportunity to respond. * * * Although YRC had requested sanctions on this ground, as discussed above, that request was procedurally improper. Thus, although Kunstler would have been wiser to alert the court to the state court proceedings, the nondisclosure was not a proper ground for sanctioning him.

* * *

Finally, the remarks of the district court, which we have quoted in substantial part above, contribute to our conclusion that the sanction of Kunstler was unjustified. These remarks have the appearance of a personal attack against Kunstler, and perhaps more broadly, against activist attorneys who represent unpopular clients or causes. We find the court's criticism of Kunstler's law partner, Ronald L. Kuby, for his activities in *another* case, especially unwarranted. For all these reasons, we reverse the imposition of the sanction of censure on Kunstler.

* * *

NOTES AND QUESTIONS

1. Compare the *Hadges* court's definition of what is reasonable under the 1993 version of Rule 11 to the Supreme Court's under the 1983 version in

BUSINESS GUIDES, INC. v. CHROMATIC COMMUNICATIONS ENTERPRISES, INC., 498 U.S. 533, 111 S.Ct. 922, 112 L.Ed.2d 1140 (1991). Business Guides, Inc. sought a temporary restraining order through its law firm against the publication of a directory by Chromatic Communications Enterprises, Inc., on the ground that Chromatic had copied the listings from the Business Guides, Inc. guide. Business Guides claimed to know of the copying because Chromatic had "reprinted" ten seeded listings, i.e. listings that were deliberately printed incorrectly in order to be able to prove such copying. When the judge's law clerk asked to check the listings, however, Business Guides retracted its claim that three of the ten listings were seeds. The clerk, after calling the numbers, discovered that nine of the ten supposedly incorrect listings were actually valid numbers and thus were not valid proof of copying. Although Chromatic did not in the end pursue sanctions against the law firm because the firm had become insolvent, a magistrate recommended that both Business Guides and the law firm be sanctioned (the firm for not investigating further when the first three listings were retracted by Business Guides) and the Supreme Court upheld the sanctions imposed against Business Guides. The Court equated the standards applicable to attorneys with those of represented parties and wrote that "*any party* who signs a pleading, motion or other paper * * * [has] an affirmative duty to conduct a reasonable inquiry into the facts and the law before filing." (emphasis added) What are the advantages and disadvantages of the pre–1993 standard? Would the 1993 amendment have affected the decision in *Business Guides*? See Vairo, *Rule 11 and the Profession*, 67 Fordham L. Rev. 589, 617 (1998) (explaining that under the 1993 version of Rule 11, "the certification has less to do with whether the facts themselves are true. Rather, it has to do with whether there is objectively reasonable evidence from which an attorney could suggest that a trier of fact could find that the facts are true").

2. The 1993 amendment marks a shift away from monetary sanctions and what had become a compensatory focus in the 1983 version. "In ordering sanctions the courts are encouraged to consider a sliding scale, ordering only those sanctions necessary to achieve deterrence, thereby protecting the courts with the least adverse possible consequence of the litigants." Armour, *Practice Makes Perfect: Judicial Discretion and the 1993 Amendments to Rule 11*, 24 Hofstra L. Rev. 677, 771 (1996). Sanctions that have been imposed include requiring the errant attorney to circulate the court's opinion finding him in violation of Rule 11 to every member of his firm; suspension or disbarment from practice; judicial reprimands in open court or through publication of a critical opinion; or requiring him to take continuing legal education courses.

3. How extensive an inquiry into the law underlying a cause of action must an attorney undertake to satisfy the Rule's requirement that the claim is "warranted by existing law"? In GOLDEN EAGLE DISTRIBUTING CORP. v. BURROUGHS CORP., 103 F.R.D. 124 (N.D.Cal.1984), reversed 801 F.2d 1531 (9th Cir.1986), rehearing denied with a dissenting opinion 809 F.2d 584 (9th Cir.1987), plaintiff's counsel cited a 1965 California Supreme Court case supporting its argument but had not cited a 1979 California Supreme Court opinion that was inconsistent with the 1965 case. Counsel distinguished the later case in its reply brief after it had been cited by the opposition, arguing that the 1965 case had not been overruled. Counsel did not address

two intermediate court opinions that discussed the effect of the 1979 opinion on the 1965 opinion. The District Court held that Rule 11 sanctions were appropriate for counsel's failing to cite adverse authority. On appeal, the Ninth Circuit unanimously reversed. The court conceded that Rule 11 was designed to create an affirmative duty of investigation, both as to law and as to fact, before motions are filed. But the court went on to say that in order to avoid chilling creative advocacy, courts should be careful not to hold lawyers to a standard measured by what the judge later decides. Would the 1993 amendment have changed the analysis?

4. The Private Securities Litigation Reform Act, see p. 589, supra, creates sanctions for actions within the ambit of the statute that are similar to the 1983 version of Rule 11 and eliminates the district court's discretion in imposing such sanctions. The Prison Litigation Reform Act of 1996, Pub.L. No. 104–134, Title VIII, § 804(a), (c)–(e), 110 Stat. 1321–73, 1321–74, 1321–75, creates special rules for lawsuits filed by prisoners, making it more difficult for a plaintiff to amend a complaint and less difficult for a court to dismiss the lawsuit on the view that it is frivolous. See Bloom & Hershkoff, *Federal Courts, Magistrate Judges, and the Pro Se Plaintiff*, 16 Notre Dame J. of Law, Ethics & Pub. Pol'y 475, 487 (2002). Does it make sense to have tougher sanction rules in certain substantive contexts?

5. Rule 11 is not the only sanctioning provision available to the federal courts. The most notable other provision is 28 U.S.C. § 1927, which gives courts authority to impose excess costs against attorneys who have "unreasonably and vexatiously" increased the costs of litigation by "multipl[ying] the proceeding." The statute requires a determination of bad faith. See Salovaara v. Eckert, 222 F.3d 19, 35 (2d Cir.2000). Other statutes authorize courts in specific kinds of actions to award attorney's fees to a prevailing defendant if the plaintiff's claim is frivolous, unreasonable, or groundless. See, e.g., § 706(k) of Title VII of the Civil Rights Act of 1964, 42 U.S.C. § 2000e–5(k)(1988)(employment discrimination actions).

Courts also have an "inherent power" to sanction parties. In CHAMBERS v. NASCO, INC., 501 U.S. 32, 111 S.Ct. 2123, 115 L.Ed.2d 27 (1991), the Supreme Court held, 5–4, in an opinion by Justice White, that the District Court had properly used its "inherent power" to sanction a party's bad-faith conduct. Justice White explained that federal courts have an "inherent power" to punish conduct that abuses the judicial process and discretion to fashion an appropriate sanction. He reasoned that neither Section 1927, Rule 11, nor other Federal Rules displace a court's inherent power to impose attorney's fees as a sanction for bad-faith conduct. Justice Kennedy dissented and severely criticized the ruling: "By inviting district courts to rely on inherent authority as a substitute for attention to the careful distinctions contained in the rules and statutes, today's decision will render these sources of authority superfluous in many instances." Id. at 67, 111 S.Ct. at 2144, 115 L.Ed.2d at 59.

A recent analysis finds that "while Rule 11 use appears to be declining in the federal courts after the 1993 amendments to the Rule, imposing of sanctions under § 1927 and the court's inherent power may be increasing"; moreover, federal courts appear to be using their inherent power "to circumvent the procedural requirements of Rule 11 when those procedural requirements have not been or could not be met." Hart, *And the Chill Goes On—Federal Civil Rights Plaintiffs Beware: Rule 11 vis-à-vis 28 U.S.C. § 1927 and the Court's Inherent Power*, 37 Loy. L.A. L. Rev. 645, 647–48 (2004). The commentator also reports that despite the 1993 amendments, "[c]ivil rights plaintiffs are still targeted for Rule 11 sanctions more frequently than other litigants in the federal courts, and they are actually sanctioned at a much higher rate than any other category of litigant." Hart, *Still Chilling After All These Years: Rule 11 of the Federal Rules of Civil Procedure and Its Impact on Federal Civil Rights Plaintiffs After the 1993 Amendments*, 37 Val. U.L. Rev. 1, 2 (2002).

Chapter 9

Joinder of Claims and Parties: Expanding the Scope of the Civil Action

■ ■ ■

In this Chapter, we examine procedures that allow litigants to combine claims and parties in one lawsuit. The simplest form of lawsuit is bi-polar: one plaintiff asserts one claim against one defendant. Although the equity courts were more flexible, the common-law courts, with their emphasis on the unitary civil action, rarely deviated from this model, and joinder was permitted only along strict and formalistic lines. See Sunderland, *Joinder of Actions,* 18 Mich.L.Rev. 571 (1920). As the complexity of society increased and more intricate disputes were generated, the need for avoiding piecemeal litigation became widely recognized. The most obvious method of accomplishing this objective was by permitting the scope of the civil action to expand beyond the bi-polar model. Broadly speaking, joinder rules today fall into one of two categories: permissive rules, which give a litigant the option of joining parties and claims in a single lawsuit; and mandatory rules, which require a litigant to do so. It is important to remember that the question of joinder is separate from whether the court may exercise jurisdiction over the claim or party to be joined. See Federal Rule 82. The materials in this Chapter, together with Chapter 10 on class actions, focus on some of the most innovative and controversial features of civil procedure today.

SECTION A. JOINDER OF CLAIMS

1. HISTORICAL LIMITATIONS ON THE PERMISSIVE JOINDER OF CLAIMS

HARRIS v. AVERY

Supreme Court of Kansas, 1869.
5 Kan. 146.

VALENTINE, J. This action was brought in the court below by Avery * * *. The petition states two causes of action,—false imprisonment and slander,—and alleges that both arose out of the same transaction. Harris demurred to this petition, on the ground "that it appears on the face of the petition that several causes of action are improperly joined." The district court overruled the demurrer, and this ruling is assigned as error. The petition shows that the two causes of action are founded upon the following facts: Harris met Avery in the city of Fort Scott, and, in the presence of several other persons, called Avery a thief; said he had a stolen horse; took the horse from Avery, and kept the horse for four or five days; arrested Avery, and confined him in the county jail with felons four or five days. We think these facts, as detailed in the petition, constitute only one transaction, * * * and whether they constitute more than one cause of action, under our Code practice, may be questionable. * * * But as we have not been asked to decide the latter question, we will pass it over and treat the case as though the facts stated constitute two causes of action.

Section 89 of the Code (Comp.Laws, 138,) provides "that the plaintiff may unite several causes of action in the same petition, whether they be such as have heretofore been denominated legal or equitable, or both, when they are included in either one of the following classes: First, *the same transaction* or transactions connected with the same subject of action." This differs in many respects from the common-law rule. At common law, "where the same form of action may be adopted for several distinct injuries, the plaintiff may, in general, proceed for all in one action, though the several rights affected were derived from different titles," (1 Chit.Pl. 201; Tidd, Pr. 11;) and different forms of action may be united, "where the same plea may be pleaded and the same judgment given on all the counts of the declaration, or whenever the counts are of the same nature, and the same judgment is to be given on them, although the pleas be different." 1 Chit.Pl. 200.

In the action at bar, if Harris had arrested Avery on a warrant, which Harris had maliciously and without probable cause obtained from a court of competent jurisdiction, and had also converted the horse to his own use, then at common law Avery would have had three distinct causes of action, which he could unite in one suit: *First,* an action for the false imprisonment or malicious prosecution; *second,* an action of slander for the words spoken; and, *third,* an action of trover for the conversion of the horse. These may all be united in an action on the case, * * * trover being a species of case. Avery might, also, at common law unite with these causes of action as many other causes of action as he might have, for malicious prosecution, slander, trover, criminal conversation, nuisance, and other causes of action which may be sued in an action on the case, and although they each may have arisen out of a different transaction, and at a different time, and in a different place. But if Harris arrested Avery without any process—which was the fact in this case—and in an entirely irregular manner, then the two causes of action for false imprisonment and slander could not at common law be united, as the first would have to be sued in an action of trespass and the second in an action on the case, and it would make no difference whether they both arose out of the same transaction or not. Our Code has abolished all the common-law forms of action * * *. It follows the rules of equity more closely than it does those of the common law, one object seeming to be to avoid the multiplicity of suits, and to settle in one action, as equity did, as far as practicable, the whole subject-matter of a controversy. * * * It is probably true that the two causes of action for false imprisonment and slander cannot, under our Code, be united, unless both arise out of the same transaction, one being an injury to the person and the other being an injury to the character; but we do not know of any reason why they should not be united when both do arise out of the same transaction. * * *

The order of the district court overruling the demurrer to the petition is affirmed.

NOTE AND QUESTIONS

At common law, a plaintiff could join claims in a single lawsuit only if they were a part of the same writ and so belonged to the same form of action. See Chapter 7, supra. The typical code provision authorized joinder of claims when they fell within one of several statutory classes, which generally included the following:

(a) Contracts, express or implied;

(b) Injuries to the person;

(c) Injuries to character;

(d) Injuries to property;

(e) Actions to recover real property, with or without damages;

(f) Actions to recover chattels, with or without damages; and

(g) Actions arising out of the same transaction or transactions connected with the same subject of the action.

In what ways do these categories differ from the use of the common-law forms of action as guidelines for the joinder of claims? What is the logic of each of these classes? Is the code approach to joinder of claims as described in *Harris* any less formalistic than the common-law theory? Joinder at common law and under the codes is discussed in Blume, *A Rational Theory for Joinder of Causes of Action and Defences, and for the Use of Counterclaims,* 26 Mich.L.Rev. 1 (1927).

2. PERMISSIVE JOINDER OF CLAIMS BY PLAINTIFFS UNDER FEDERAL RULE OF CIVIL PROCEDURE 18

Read Federal Rule of Civil Procedure 18 in the Supplement.

M.K. v. TENET

United States District Court, District of Columbia, 2002.
216 F.R.D. 133.

URBINA, DISTRICT JUDGE:

[The action was filed by six former employees against the Central Intelligence Agency, its Director, and others alleging that defendants violated the Privacy Act of 1974, as amended, 5 U.S.C. § 552, and various constitutional rights by obstructing plaintiffs' access to counsel. In a proposed second amended complaint, plaintiffs added nine named plaintiffs and provided information about existing claims to cure deficiencies in the original complaint. Defendants moved to sever the claims of the initial six plaintiffs under Federal Rule of Civil Procedure 21.]

* * *

The court now addresses the defendants' instant motion to sever. In the defendants' view, the plaintiffs' obstruction-of-counsel claim consists of "a series of unrelated, isolated grievances, unique to each plaintiff, each of which would have to be decided on its own set of law and facts, and each potentially presenting a 'novel' constitutional claim." * * * Thus, the defendants ask this court to sever the claims of the six existing plaintiffs * * * under Federal Rule of Civil Procedure 21. * * * By the same token, the defendants ask the court to deny the plaintiffs' proposed Rule 20 joinder of the nine new plaintiffs and the 30 new "Doe" defendants. * * *

The plaintiffs, however, argue that the court should not sever the six existing plaintiffs because both prongs of the Rule 20(a) [now Rule 20(a)(1)] joinder requirement are satisfied. The court need not extensively address the joinder of the six existing plaintiffs' new claims because the court is convinced that under the unrestricted joinder provision of Federal Rule of Civil Procedure 18, such joinder of new claims is possible. * * * [For the court's discussion of the Rule 20 joinder issue, see p. 682, infra.]

* * *

NOTES AND QUESTIONS

1. Federal Rule 18 removes all obstacles to joinder of claims and permits the joinder of both legal and equitable actions; the only restriction on the claims that may be joined is imposed by subject-matter jurisdiction requirements. What are the advantages of permitting the liberal joinder of claims? Are there any disadvantages? How much credence should we give to the efficiency rationale? If each claim is different, are there material efficiency gains?

In SPORN v. HUDSON TRANSIT LINES, 265 A.D. 360, 38 N.Y.S.2d 512 (1st Dep't 1942), the court had before it an attempt to join five causes of action for negligence resulting in personal injuries with one cause of action for malicious prosecution. It stated:

> The causes of action for negligence and for malicious prosecution are essentially different in nature; each type involves different rules of law;

> each requires different testimony to establish a case and each carries a different measure of damages. If a single jury were to try both types of action at the one time, there is a strong likelihood that confusion would exist in the minds of the jurors as to the rules of law to be applied to the respective actions and they would undoubtedly entertain much difficulty in applying the various parts of testimony introduced to the appropriate cause of action.

Id. at 361–62, 38 N.Y.S.2d at 514. Would the result in *Sporn* have been different if the action had been brought in a federal court? Read Federal Rule 42. Does the availability of severance of claims eliminate all of the objections to permitting unrestricted joinder of claims as an initial matter? To what extent does the court's power to sever claims prevent the system from achieving the objectives of a liberal joinder rule?

2. Federal Rule 18 only describes the claims that a plaintiff may assert against defendant; it does not require plaintiff to join all such claims in a single action. Should there be compulsory joinder of all related claims existing between a plaintiff and a defendant? See Friedenthal, *Joinder of Claims, Counterclaims and Cross–Complaints: Suggested Revision of the California Provisions*, 23 Stan.L.Rev. 1, 11–17 (1970); and Greenbaum, *Jacks or Better to Open: Procedural Limitations on Co–Party and Third–Party Claims*, 74 Minn. L. Rev. 507, 535–37 (1990). Michigan's joinder provision, Michigan Court Rule 2.203, which is in the Supplement following Federal Rule 18, is unusual in that it provides for the compulsory joinder of certain claims. See 6A Wright, Miller & Kane, Federal Practice and Procedure: Civil 2d § 1582.

3. Even though the joinder of claims by plaintiffs in the federal courts is permissive, the principles of res judicata, which prohibit the splitting of a cause of action into two or more lawsuits, often have the effect of compelling plaintiff to join all related claims. See generally Blume, *Required Joinder of Claims,* 45 Mich.L.Rev. 797 (1947). Thus, for example, if A and B are involved in an automobile accident in which A suffers both bodily injury and damage to her automobile, the risk of res judicata typically will lead A to join both claims in one action, even though Federal Rule 18 does not require her to do so. We take up the topic of preclusion in Chapter 17, infra.

4. Notice how Rule 18, regarding the joinder of claims, works in tandem with Rule 15, the amendment of pleadings, and Rule 20, joinder of parties. Commentators collectively refer to these rules as "packaging devices." Professor Freer writes:

> The primary packaging tools * * * are the joinder provisions of the Federal Rules of Civil procedure. As originally promulgated in 1938, they abandoned the narrow and occasionally mystical notions of common law and code pleading in favor of unlimited claim joinder and expanded party joinder. * * * They thus proposed a return to equity's emphasis on trial convenience and efficiency. * * * Several of the party joinder rules were amended in 1966 to emphasize their relatedness * * * and to root out remnants of the old formalistic approach that had crept into application of the 1938 rules. * * * The revisions kept intact the original version's emphasis on claim joinder based upon transactional relatedness. * * *

Freer, *Avoiding Duplicative Litigation: Rethinking Plaintiff Autonomy and the Court's Role in Defining the Litigative Unit*, 50 U. Pitt. L. Rev. 809, 815–16 (1989).

SECTION B. ADDITION OF CLAIMS BY DEFENDANT

1. COUNTERCLAIMS

The counterclaim in its present form did not exist at common law, although it has well-recognized precursors in set-off and recoupment and in equity practice. The philosophy underlying set-off and recoupment was the common sense view that someone should not be compelled to pay one moment what he will be entitled to recover back the next. Judge Clark outlined the development and theory of set-off and recoupment as follows:

> * * * At first * * * [recoupment] was limited to a showing of payment, or of former recovery. Later, recoupment was developed so as to allow a defendant to show for the purpose of reducing the plaintiff's recovery any facts arising out of the transaction sued upon or connected with the subject thereof, which facts might have founded an independent action in favor of the defendant against the plaintiff. * * * It was not necessary that the opposing claims be liquidated, or that they be of the same character; i.e., a claim in "tort" could be set off against one in "contract." It was essential, however, that the claims of both plaintiff and defendant involve the same "subject-matter," or arise out of the "same transaction" * * *.
>
> But where the defendant's claims arose out of a transaction different from that sued upon, the common-law recoupment was unavailable. The defendant, therefore, was compelled to bring a separate suit in order to satisfy his claim against the plaintiff. Equity, at an early date, relieved the defendant of this hardship by allowing a set-off of claims [growing out of a transaction different from the plaintiff's claim] * * *.
>
> Under the set-off * * *, it was necessary that the demands either be liquidated, or arise out of contract or judgment. It was necessary, also, that the demands be due the defendant in his own right against the plaintiff, or his assignor, and be not already barred by the statute of limitations * * *.

Clark, Code Pleading § 100, at 634–36 (2d ed. 1947). The utility of the common-law recoupment and set-off practice was limited because in the former situation defendant was not permitted to recover affirmative relief; the claim could be used only to reduce or "net out" plaintiff's recovery. In the case of set-off the claim had to be for a liquidated amount.

The movement for procedural reform in the mid-nineteenth century gave passing attention to the problem of defendant's claims against plaintiff; the original New York Field Code of 1848 made no provision for counterclaims. Amendments in 1852 corrected this omission and permitted as a counterclaim:

1. A cause of action arising out of the contract or transaction set forth in the complaint, as the foundation of the plaintiff's claim, or connected with the subject of the action; and

2. In an action arising on contract, any other cause of action arising on contract, and existing at the commencement of the action.

See Blume, *A Rational Theory for Joinder of Causes of Action and Defences, and for the Use of Counterclaims*, 26 Mich.L.Rev. 1, 48 (1927).

The English Judicature Act of 1873 eliminated the historic limitations on defendant's ability to assert claims against plaintiff. Then, at the beginning of this century, a number of states amended their codes to adopt the English practice. Note that the text of Federal Rule 13(a) goes beyond the English and code practice by *requiring* defendant to assert certain claims. Is this step desirable? Why? See generally Kennedy, *Counterclaims Under Federal Rule 13*, 11 Houston L.Rev. 255 (1974).

Read Federal Rules of Civil Procedure 13(a)–(f) and the accompanying material in the Supplement.

UNITED STATES v. HEYWARD–ROBINSON CO.

United States Court of Appeals, Second Circuit, 1970.
430 F.2d 1077.

FREDERICK VAN PELT BRYAN, DISTRICT JUDGE.*

This is an appeal from a judgment for the plaintiff entered in the United States District Court for the District of Connecticut * * *.

The action involves two subcontracts for excavation work between D'Agostino Excavators, Inc. (D'Agostino) and The Heyward–Robinson Company, Inc. (Heyward) as prime contractor on two construction jobs in Connecticut. One of the prime contracts, for the construction of barracks at the Naval Submarine Base in New London, Groton, was with the federal government (the Navy job). The other, a non-federal job, was for the construction of a plant for Stelma, Inc. at Stamford (the Stelma job).

D'Agostino brought this action against Heyward and its surety, Maryland Casualty Company (Maryland) under the Miller Act * * * to recover payments alleged to be due on the Navy job. Heyward answered, denying liability on the Navy job and counterclaiming for alleged overpayments and extra costs of completing both the Navy job and the Stelma job. In

* Of the Southern District of New York, sitting by designation.

reply, D'Agostino denied liability on the Heyward counterclaims and interposed a reply counterclaim to recover from Heyward monies alleged to be due on the Stelma job.

At the trial, the two subcontracts in suit were treated together. D'Agostino claimed that Heyward had breached both subcontracts by failing to make progress payments as required and that substantial sums were owing to it from Heyward on both jobs. Heyward claimed that D'Agostino had breached both subcontracts by permitting its compensation and employee liability insurance to lapse; that, as a result, Heyward on October 19, 1965 had terminated both; and that D'Agostino was liable for overpayments and costs of completion on both.

The issue as to whether Heyward had breached the subcontracts prior to October 19, 1965, when Heyward claimed to have terminated them, was submitted to the jury as a special question. The jury found that Heyward had breached the subcontracts prior to that date.

After amendment of the complaint by D'Agostino to allege a claim in quantum merit for the work performed on both jobs, special questions then were submitted to the jury as to the reasonable value of the work performed by D'Agostino on each project and the net amount owed by Heyward to D'Agostino on both. The jury found, in answer to these questions, that the net amount owed by Heyward to D'Agostino on both jobs was $63,988.36. Judgment against Heyward was rendered accordingly. Under a formula agreed to by the parties, it was determined that the amount due to D'Agostino on the Navy job was $40,771.46 and judgment was entered against Maryland in that sum.

* * *

I.

Appellants' initial contention is that the District Court had no jurisdiction over the counterclaims on the Stelma job. They therefore contend that the Stelma claims must be dismissed and that since D'Agostino's claims on the Navy and Stelma jobs were presented to the jury as inseparable, the judgment below must be reversed.

Appellants urge that the Stelma counterclaims are not compulsory counterclaims over which the federal court acquired jurisdiction ancillary to the jurisdiction which it had over D'Agostino's Miller Act claim stated in the complaint. They say that these are permissive counterclaims over which the court had no ancillary jurisdiction and which lacked the required independent basis of federal jurisdiction.

This jurisdictional issue is raised for the first time in this Court. In the Court below appellants affirmatively urged that the Stelma counterclaims were compulsory. Nevertheless, it is well settled that lack of federal jurisdiction may be raised for the first time on appeal, even by a party who originally asserted that jurisdiction existed or by the court sua sponte. * * * We turn, then, to the jurisdictional issue.

It is apparent from the record that there is no independent basis of federal jurisdiction over the Stelma counterclaims. Both D'Agostino and Heyward are New York corporations with offices in New York. There is thus no diversity jurisdiction. Clearly there is no jurisdiction under the Miller Act over these counterclaims since the Stelma contract did not involve public work for the federal government.

The question is whether the Stelma counterclaims are compulsory or are permissive. Under the rule in this circuit, if they are permissive there is no Federal jurisdiction over them unless they rest on independent jurisdictional grounds. * * * On the other hand, if they are compulsory counterclaims, they are ancillary to the claim asserted in the complaint and no independent basis of Federal jurisdiction is required * * *.

* * * In United Artists Corp. v. Masterpiece Productions, Inc., 221 F.2d 213 (2d Cir.1955) * * *, Chief Judge Clark said:

> In practice this criterion has been broadly interpreted to require not an absolute identity of factual backgrounds for the two claims, but only a logical relationship between them. Lesnik v. Public Industrials Corp., 2 Cir., 144 F.2d 968, 975, citing and quoting, inter alia, Moore v. New York Cotton Exchange, 270 U.S. 593, 610, 46 S.Ct. 367, 371, 70 L.Ed. 750, thus: " 'Transaction' is a word of flexible meaning. It may comprehend a series of many occurrences, depending not so much upon the immediateness of their connection as upon their logical relationship."

Thus " * * * [in original] courts should give the phrase 'transaction or occurrence that is the subject matter' of the suit a broad realistic interpretation in the interest of avoiding a multiplicity of suits." [citing 3 J. Moore, Federal Practice ¶ 13.13 at 33–36 (2d ed. 1969)]. * * * As the Supreme Court [has] said * * *:

> The requirement that counterclaims arising out of the same transaction or occurrence as the opposing party's claim "shall" be stated in the pleadings was designed to prevent multiplicity of actions and to achieve resolution in a single lawsuit of all disputes arising out of common matters. [Southern Construction Co. v. Pickard,] 371 U.S. [57,] at 60, 83 S.Ct. [108,], at 110 [, 9 L.Ed.2d 31, at 34].

In the case at bar the counterclaims were compulsory within the meaning of Rule 13(a). There was such a close and logical relationship between the claims on the Navy and Stelma jobs that the Stelma counterclaims arose out of the same "transaction or occurrence" as those terms are now broadly defined. Both subcontracts were entered into by the same parties for the same type of work and carried on during substantially the same period. Heyward had the right to terminate both subcontracts in the event of a breach by D'Agostino of either. Heyward also had the right to withhold monies due on one to apply against any damages suffered on the other. Progress payments made by Heyward were not allocated as between jobs and were made on a lump sum basis for both as though for a single account.

A single insurance policy covered both jobs. The letters of Heyward to D'Agostino of October 8 and 19, 1965 threatening termination and terminating both jobs, allegedly because of the cancellation by D'Agostino of this joint insurance coverage and failure to properly man both projects, treated both jobs together. These letters formed the basis of one of Heyward's major claims at the trial.

The controversy between the parties which gave rise to this litigation was with respect to both jobs and arose from occurrences affecting both. Indeed, it would seem to have been impossible for Heyward to have fully litigated the claims against it on the Navy job without including the Stelma job, because the payments it made to D'Agostino could not be allocated between the two jobs.

As the appellants themselves point out in their brief, the "Stelma and Navy claims were so interwoven at the trial that they are now absolutely incapable of separation." The proof as to payments and alleged defaults in payments was made without any differentiation between the two claims and neither of the parties was able to offer any evidence of apportionment. Finally, the evidence as to the breaches of contract claimed by the respective parties related in the main to both contracts rather than to one or the other.

The jurisdictional question so belatedly raised by the appellants must be viewed in light of the record as a whole. So viewed, it is plain that the Stelma counterclaims bare [sic] a logical and immediate relationship to the claims on the Navy job. Thus they arose out of the "transaction or occurrence which is the subject matter" of the suit instituted by D'Agostino on the Navy job and are compulsory counterclaims under Rule 13(a). The Stelma counterclaims were thus ancillary to the claims asserted in the complaint over which the Federal Court had acquired jurisdiction under the Miller Act, and there is jurisdiction over them. * * * To require that the closely related Navy and Stelma claims must be litigated separately would result in fragmentation of litigation and multiplicity of suits contrary to one of the major purposes of Rule 13(a). * * *

* * *

The judgment below is affirmed.

FRIENDLY, CIRCUIT JUDGE (concurring).

I cannot agree that, as maintained in Part I of the majority opinion, the counterclaim relating to the Stelma job was compulsory * * *. Of course, it is tempting to stretch a point when a jurisdictional objection is so belatedly raised by the very party who clamored for the exercise of jurisdiction until the decision went against it. But we must consider the question as if Heyward had not pleaded the Stelma counterclaim and proceeded to sue D'Agostino in some other court for failure to perform that subcontract, and D'Agostino then claimed that Heyward's failure to bring the Stelma transaction into this Miller Act suit barred the later action. Despite the desirability of requiring that all claims which in fact arise "out of the transaction or occurrence that is the subject of the opposing party's claim" be litigated in a single action, courts must be wary of extending these words in a way that could cause unexpectedly harsh results.

Even on a liberal notion of "logical relation," * * * I am unable to perceive how Heyward's claim for breach of the Stelma subcontract arose "out of the transaction or occurrence" to wit, the Navy subcontract, that was the subject matter of D'Agostino's Miller Act claim. Whatever historical interest there may be in the circumstances that the two subcontracts were entered into between the same parties for the same type of work and were carried on during substantially the same period, these facts seem to me to be lacking in legal significance. So likewise do D'Agostino's having furnished a single insurance policy to cover both jobs and Heyward's having cancelled the subcontracts in one letter rather than two. The boiler-plate in each subcontract, whereby "if one or more other contracts, now or hereafter, exist between the parties," a breach of any such contract by D'Agostino might, at Heyward's option be considered a breach of the contract at issue and Heyward might terminate any or all contracts so breached and withhold moneys due on any contract and apply these to damages on any other, might meet the test if Heyward had availed itself of these rights, but it did not.

All that is left is that, as the trial proceeded, it turned out that some of Heyward's payments were not earmarked as between the two subcontracts. However, the determination whether a counterclaim is compulsory must be made at the pleading stage. The complaint was specific on how much Heyward owed on the Navy subcontract, and the counterclaims were equally so on how much D'Agostino owed for failure to complete this and how much it owed for failure to complete the Stelma subcontract. To say that the failure to earmark some payments made it impossible to try the claims separately ignores the law on application of payments. If Heyward did not specify the application of its payments, as it could, and D'Agostino had not made an application of them, as it could in default of specification by Heyward, the court would do this. * * *

* * *

[Although Judge Friendly disagreed with the majority's holding that the counterclaims were compulsory, he nevertheless argued that they should not be dismissed on the ground that permissive counterclaims need not have an independent jurisdictional basis.]

NOTES AND QUESTIONS

1. Federal Rule 13 draws a distinction between counterclaims that are compulsory and those that are permissive. The distinction turns on the definition of a transaction or occurrence. See McFarland, *In Search of the Transaction or Occurrence: Counterclaims*, 40 Creighton L. Rev. 699, 699 (2007). The classic definition is found in MOORE v. NEW YORK COTTON

EXCHANGE, 270 U.S. 593, 46 S.Ct. 367, 70 L.Ed. 750 (1926). Plaintiff sought to compel defendant to install a price quotation ticker in plaintiff's place of business. Defendant counterclaimed for damages, alleging that although plaintiff had been denied permission to use quotations from defendant's exchange, plaintiff "was purloining them and giving them out." In the course of holding defendant's counterclaim compulsory under former Equity Rule 30, the Court said:

> * * * "Transaction" is a word of flexible meaning. It may comprehend a series of many occurrences, depending not so much upon the immediateness of their connection as upon their logical relationship. The refusal to furnish the quotations is one of the links in the chain which constitutes the transaction upon which appellant here bases its cause of action. It is an important part of the transaction constituting the subject-matter of the counterclaim. It is the one circumstance without which neither party would have found it necessary to seek relief. Essential facts alleged by appellant enter into and constitute in part the cause of action set forth in the counterclaim. That they are not precisely identical, or that the counterclaim embraces additional allegations, as, for example, that appellant is unlawfully getting the quotations, does not matter. To hold otherwise would be to rob this branch of the rule of all serviceable meaning, since the facts relied upon by the plaintiff rarely, if ever, are in all particulars, the same as those constituting the defendant's counterclaim. * * *

Id. at 610, 46 S.Ct. at 371, 70 L.Ed. at 757.

2. Courts use at least four different tests in determining whether claims arise out of the same transaction or occurrence for the purpose of characterizing a counterclaim as compulsory or permissive:

(a) Are the issues of fact and law raised by the claim and counterclaim largely the same?

(b) Would res judicata bar a subsequent suit on defendant's claim absent the compulsory counterclaim rule?

(c) Will substantially the same evidence support or refute plaintiff's claim as well as defendant's counterclaim?

(d) Is there any logical relation between the claim and the counterclaim?

See Kane, *Original Sin and the Transaction in Federal Civil Procedure*, 76 Texas L.Rev. 1723 (1998). What are the strengths and weaknesses of each of these tests? See 6 Wright, Miller & Kane, Federal Practice and Procedure: Civil 2d § 1410.

3. Before the enactment of 28 U.S.C. § 1367, a compulsory counterclaim fell within the ancillary jurisdiction of the federal court and so did not require an independent basis of subject-matter jurisdiction. See 6 Wright, Miller & Kane, Federal Practice and Procedure: Civil 2d § 1414. As the Third Circuit explained in Great Lakes Rubber Corp. v. Herbert Cooper Co., 286 F.2d 631, 633–34 (3d Cir.1961),

> [T]he issue of the existence of ancillary jurisdiction and the issue as to whether a counterclaim is compulsory are to be answered by the same

test. * * * The tests are the same because Rule 13(a) [this provision has been renumbered Rule 13(a)(1)(A) by the 2007 restyling of the Federal Rules] and the doctrine of ancillary jurisdiction are designed to abolish the same evil, viz., piecemeal litigation in the federal courts.

Currently, Section 1367(a) provides for supplemental jurisdiction over claims that are part of "the same case or controversy under Article III of the Constitution" as claims before the district court and within its "original jurisdiction." Is the requirement of Section 1367 that claims be "so related" broader than the requirement of Rule 13 that claims arise out of the same "transaction and occurrence" for purposes of distinguishing compulsory from permissive counterclaims? If it is broader, does Section 1367(a) allow for the exercise of supplemental jurisdiction over some permissive counterclaims or exclude some compulsory counterclaims? See Notes 1 and 2, pp. 336–37, supra. Should this approach to Section 1367 also apply to a defendant's compulsory counterclaim?

4. The states do not have identical rules for compulsory counterclaims. The Minnesota compulsory-counterclaim rule, for example, is virtually identical to Federal Rule 13(a)(1)(A), except that the reference to "occurrence" is omitted, which has led that state's courts to read the Rule restrictively. In HOUSE v. HANSON, 245 Minn. 466, 72 N.W.2d 874 (1955), the Minnesota Supreme Court held that "Rule 13.01 was approved by this court with the express understanding and intent that the omission therefrom of the word 'occurrence' would insure that tort counterclaims would not be compulsory."

NOTE ON CONSEQUENCES OF FAILING TO PLEAD A COUNTERCLAIM

Rule 13(a) is silent on the effect of failing to plead a compulsory counterclaim. It seems clear that an unasserted compulsory counterclaim cannot be raised in a subsequent suit in a federal court, see, e.g., Twin Disc, Inc. v. Lowell, 69 F.R.D. 64 (E.D.Wis.1975), although courts differ as to the proper theory for reaching this conclusion. Some apply a res judicata principle; others use waiver; and yet another group relies on estoppel. See Scott, *Collateral Estoppel by Judgment*, 56 Harv.L.Rev. 1 (1942) (res judicata theory); Wright, *Estoppel by Rule: The Compulsory Counterclaim Under Modern Pleading*, 38 Minn.L.Rev. 423 (1954) (estoppel). Does it make any difference which theory is used? Do you agree that a defendant who defaults and fails to file an answer to a complaint ought to be barred from later filing a transactionally related claim as a separate action? For a critical view, see Peterson, *The Misguided Law of Compulsory Counterclaims in Default Cases*, 50 Ariz. L. Rev. 1107 (2008).

Under what circumstances should the liberal amendment policy of Federal Rule 13(f) be used to permit the tardy assertion of a compulsory counterclaim? "In assessing what constitutes 'excusable neglect' under Rule 13(f), the lower courts have looked, *inter alia*, to the good faith of the claimant, the extent of the delay, and the danger of prejudice to the opposing party." Pioneer Inv. Servs. Co. v. Brunswick Assocs. Ltd., 507 U.S. 380, 392 n.10, 113 S.Ct. 1489, 1497 n.10, 123 L.Ed.2d 74, 88 n.10 (1993). See Safeway Trails, Inc. v. Allentown & Reading Transit Co., 185 F.2d 918 (4th Cir.1950), in which leave to amend was granted when the excuse for failing to plead an omitted counterclaim was that defendant's lawyer had not read the Federal Rules! For a strict application of the barring effect of a failure to assert a compulsory counterclaim, see Schneeberger v. Hoette Concrete Constr. Co., 680 S.W.2d 301 (Mo.App.1984). If the statute of limitations has run on a counterclaim between the filing of the original action and defendant's motion under Rule 13(f), so that the claim would be barred if asserted independently, does the filing of the counterclaim relate back to the filing of the original action under Rule 15(c)(1)? Should the result depend on whether the counterclaim is compulsory or permissive? See Conway, *Narrowing the Scope of Rule 13(a)*, 60 U. Chi. L. Rev. 141, 144–45 (1993).

Hypothesize an action in a federal court in which defendant fails to raise a compulsory counterclaim. Does the failure to bring the claim in federal court prevent defendant from raising it in a subsequent state court action? What if defendant brings suit on the unasserted claim in a state court before the federal action is terminated? Should the state court hearing the alleged counterclaim grant a motion to dismiss based on the assertion that Federal Rule 13(a) barred the state action? What other action might it take? Is this an instance in which a reverse-*Erie* approach should apply? Should the federal court hearing plaintiff's suit restrain further proceedings in the state court?

> The answer * * * depends upon a determination of whether or not Congress intended in adopting Rule 13(a) to create another statutory exception to its policy of Federal Courts' non-interference with State Court actions. [See 28 U.S.C. § 2283.] Insofar as the effect of a party's failure to plead a compulsory counterclaim * * * in a Federal action is concerned the Congressional intent is clear—said party is thereafter barred from pleading same on the ground that it is res judicata. However, insofar as the effect of such failure on a State Court action is concerned the Congressional intent is not so clear; thus, in the absence of a clearer expression than is contained in Rule 13(a) we are unwilling to say that Congress * * * intended to grant Federal Courts the authority to enjoin State Court actions * * *.

FANTECCHI v. GROSS, 158 F.Supp. 684, 687 (E.D.Pa.1957), appeal dismissed 255 F.2d 299 (3d Cir.1958).

Are the considerations any different when the situation is reversed and the first action is brought in a state court in which a compulsory-counterclaim rule is in effect and the second case is in a federal court? Can plaintiff in the state proceeding ask the state court to enjoin the parties to a federal court action from litigating what should have been a compulsory counterclaim in the state court? Should the federal court grant a motion to dismiss? Cf. Donovan v. City of Dallas, 377 U.S. 408, 84 S.Ct. 1579, 12 L.Ed.2d 409 (1964). Should one state be required to give full faith and credit to another state's compulsory-counterclaim rule?

How does the analysis change if defendant fails to plead a permissive counterclaim? By definition, a permissive counterclaim is not compulsory. However, would it be fair to permit a subsequent pleading of even a permissive counterclaim if its effect is to nullify a judgment that plaintiff won in the initial lawsuit? See Clermont, *Common–Law Compulsory Counterclaim Rule:*

Creating Effective and Elegant Res Judicata Doctrine, 79 Notre Dame L. Rev. 1745 (2004).

NOTES AND QUESTIONS

1. In SOUTHERN CONSTRUCTION CO. v. PICKARD, 371 U.S. 57, 83 S.Ct. 108, 9 L.Ed.2d 31 (1962), the Southern Construction Company was the prime contractor on contracts with the United States for the rehabilitation of certain barracks at Fort Campbell, Tennessee, and Fort Benning, Georgia. The plumbing and heating subcontractor on both projects was the respondent Samuel J. Pickard, doing business as Pickard Engineering Company. Pickard's primary supplier on both projects was the Atlas Supply Company.

Pickard filed suit against Southern in district courts in both Georgia and Tennessee under the Miller Act for amounts due on the contracts. Defendant elected to assert its counterclaim for the amount paid in settlement to Atlas in the Tennessee suit, the second of the two suits commenced. Pickard answered that the counterclaim was barred for failure to raise it in the first suit as a compulsory counterclaim.

The Supreme Court accepted the District Court's ruling that the $35,000 settlement had not been allocated as between the Tennessee and Georgia projects and that it therefore could have been asserted in either action. It stated, however, that Rule 13(a) does not operate to prohibit its use in the later Tennessee action. The Court found the policy of preventing multiplicity of actions and achieving resolution in a single lawsuit of all disputes arising out of common matters to be inapplicable in these circumstances:

> * * * The Rule was particularly directed against one who failed to assert a counterclaim in one action and then instituted a second action in which that counterclaim became the basis of the complaint. * * *
>
> It is readily apparent that this policy has no application here. In this instance, the plaintiff-respondent, who originally sought to combine all his claims in a single suit, correctly concluded that he was required by statute to split those claims and to bring two separate actions in two different districts. The fragmentation of these claims, therefore, was compelled by federal law, and the primary defendant in both actions was thus for the first time confronted with the choice of which of the two pending suits should be resorted to for the assertion of a counterclaim common to both. Under these circumstances, we hold that Rule 13(a) did not compel this counterclaim to be made in whichever of the two suits the first responsive pleading was filed. Its assertion in the later suit, to which Southern, not without reason, considered it more appurtenant * * * by no means involved the circuity of action that Rule 13(a) was aimed at preventing. * * *

Id. at 60, 83 S.Ct. at 110, 9 L.Ed.2d at 34–35. Should the "common-law" exception to Rule 13(a) invoked by the Supreme Court in *Pickard* be limited to the situation in which the governing substantive law requires plaintiff to bring related claims in separate districts?

2. Several exceptions to the compulsory-counterclaim rule are set out in the text of Rule 13(a) itself. Consider their relevance to the following situations:

(a) In UNION PAVING CO. v. DOWNER CORP., 276 F.2d 468 (9th Cir.1960), the court discussed the passage in Rule 13(a)(2)(A) providing that waiver will not result from the failure to assert a counterclaim that already is the subject of litigation pending in another court:

> * * * The purpose of this exception is seemingly to prevent one party from compelling another to try his cause of action in a court not of the latter's choosing when the same cause of action is already the subject of pending litigation in another forum, one which was probably chosen by the owner of the cause of action concerned. * * *

Id. at 470–71.

(b) If defendant has a claim that arises out of the same transaction or occurrence as plaintiff's claim but it can be brought only against plaintiff and a third person who is a "required party" under Federal Rule 19 and over whom defendant cannot obtain jurisdiction, is assertion of the claim mandatory? We take up the topic of Rule 19 required parties on p. 693, infra.

(c) If five days after defendant serves her answer she becomes the assignee of a claim against plaintiff and if the assigned claim arose out of the same transaction or occurrence as plaintiff's claim against defendant, must defendant amend her answer and assert it? Cf. Federal Rule 13(e). What if the counterclaim is acquired during the trial?

(d) If defendant is sued in one capacity (e.g., as an administrator in an action based on the negligence of an intestate) and has a counterclaim in another capacity (e.g., as a beneficiary in a wrongful-death action) that arises out of the same transaction or occurrence, is it compulsory? See Newton v. Mitchell, 42 So.2d 53 (Fla.1949).

3. Assume plaintiff commences an action within the appropriate statute of limitations and defendant has a compulsory counterclaim that would be barred by the statute of limitations if asserted in an independent action. Should the claim be permitted? Compare Minex Resources, Inc. v. Morland, 467 N.W.2d 691 (N.D.1991), with Imbesi v. Carpenter Realty Corp., 357 Md. 375, 744 A.2d 549 (2000). Does it make any difference if defendant's claim was not time-barred when plaintiff commenced the suit but became so before defendant was required to answer? Assuming that the claim would be barred if asserted as a counterclaim, should it be permitted if it otherwise qualifies as a common-law recoupment or set-off? See American Law Institute, Study of the Division of Jurisdiction Between State and Federal Courts 258 (1969).

4. If defendant's answer contains a counterclaim, must plaintiff assert a compulsory counterclaim to defendant's counterclaim? Does it matter whether defendant's counterclaim is compulsory or permissive? Is a counterclaim to a counterclaim likely to be so confusing that it will prevent the orderly disposition of the case? Would it make any difference if plaintiff amended the complaint to include the claim rather than asserting it as a counterclaim? See Millar, *Counterclaim Against Counterclaim*, 48 Nw.U.L.Rev. 671, 690 (1954).

5. What is the relation between a compulsory counterclaim and the amount-in-controversy requirement for purposes of diversity jurisdiction? See p. 285, supra. Should a district court be able to assert supplemental jurisdiction over a compulsory counterclaim that would lack an independent jurisdictional basis if filed as a separate claim? In SPECTACOR MANAGEMENT GROUP v. BROWN, 131 F.3d 120, 121 (3d Cir.1997), certiorari denied 523 U.S. 1120, 118 S.Ct. 1799, 140 L.Ed.2d 939 (1998), defendant elected not to file a motion to dismiss for lack of jurisdiction, but instead asserted a compulsory counterclaim in response to the complaint. The Third Circuit held that the amount of that counterclaim should be considered in determining whether the amount-in-controversy threshold had been met by the plaintiff. Is that result proper? Is it within the contemplation of the supplemental jurisdiction statute, 28 U.S.C. § 1367? See p. 38, supra.

2. CROSS–CLAIMS

Read Federal Rules of Civil Procedure 13(g) and (h) and the accompanying material in the Supplement.

LASA PER L'INDUSTRIA DEL MARMO SOCIETA PER AZIONI v. ALEXANDER

United States Court of Appeals, Sixth Circuit, 1969.
414 F.2d 143.

[This controversy arose out of the construction of the Memphis, Tennessee City Hall. Southern Builders, a Tennessee corporation, was retained by the City as the principal contractor. Southern Builders' performance was secured by a bond, with Continental Casualty as surety. Southern Builders subcontracted with Alexander Marble and Tile Co., a partnership comprised of Tennessee residents, and Marble International, Inc., a Texas corporation, to supply and install some marble in the new City Hall. Alexander then contracted with LASA, an Italian corporation, to supply it with marble.

LASA alleged that it had fully performed its contract with Alexander and that Alexander owed it $127,240.80 out of the $468,641.26 contract price. It sued Alexander, Marble International, Southern Builders, Continental Casualty, and the City for the balance due.

Alexander filed an answer and counterclaim in which it alleged that LASA had breached the contract by not shipping the marble on time, by shipping marble of the wrong type, by shipping damaged marble, and by failing to ship all the marble it was obligated to ship. Alexander further alleged that the contract price was only $265,050.00. It sought restitution of the amount it overpaid LASA plus damages resulting from LASA's breach of contract.

Southern Builders filed an answer and counterclaim. In its counterclaim, Southern Builders alleged that LASA failed to ship marble as agreed to Alexander, and claimed damages resulting from that breach by LASA.

Alexander filed a cross-claim against Southern Builders, Continental Casualty, and the City for money alleged to be due on its contract with Southern Builders. Southern Builders and Continental Casualty filed answers and Southern Builders filed a cross-claim against Alexander for breach of contract.

Alexander filed third-party complaints against A.L. Aydelott and Associates, Inc. and against Aydelott individually alleging that they, as architects on the project, negligently supervised the project, wrongfully required Alexander to install marble in inclement weather, wrongfully directed Southern Builders to terminate its contract with Alexander, willfully refused to approve Alexander's estimates for work done, and wrongfully and maliciously injured Alexander's business reputation. Alexander sought unliquidated actual and punitive damages as well as treble damages, under a Tennessee statute, for inducing Southern Builders to breach the subcontract.

Alexander also sued Southern Builders for actual and punitive damages resulting from the wrongful termination of its contract and for injury to the business reputation of Alexander.]

PHILLIPS, CIRCUIT JUDGE.

* * * The confusion in pleadings that can arise out of cross-claims, counterclaims and a third-party complaint, all involving the same construction project, is demonstrated by the present appeal.

* * *

Among the pleadings were a cross-claim filed by the defendant subcontractor, Alexander, against the prime contractor, its surety and the City of Memphis; a counterclaim filed by the prime contractor against Alexander; and a third-party complaint filed by Alexander against the architect. The third-party complaint was treated by the District Court as a cross-claim against the architect as was the counterclaim of the prime contractor against Alexander.

Construing Rules 13(g) and 13(h) * * *, the District Court dismissed the two cross-claims and the third-party complaint, holding that they do not arise out of the same transaction or occurrence that is the subject matter of the original action or of a counterclaim therein.

We reverse.

* * *

Under the Federal Rules of Civil Procedure the rights of all parties generally should be adjudicated in one action. Rules 13 and 14 are remedial and are construed liberally. Both Rules 13 and 14 are "intended to avoid circuity of action and to dispose of the entire subject matter arising from one set of facts in one action, thus administering complete and evenhanded justice expeditiously and economically." Blair v. Cleveland Twist Drill Co., 197 F.2d 842, 845 (7th Cir.). The aim of these rules "is facilitation not frustration of decisions on the merits." Frommeyer v. L. & R. Construction Co., 139 F.Supp. 579, 585 (D.N.J.).

A decision involving jurisdiction over cross-claims in litigation growing out of a construction project similar in some respects to the issues presented on this appeal is Glens Falls Indemnity Co. v. United States, 229 F.2d 370 (9th Cir.). In that case the Court said:

> It is well settled that a grant of jurisdiction over particular subject matter includes the power to adjudicate all matters ancillary to the particular subject matter. * * * Therefore, if either a cross-claim under Rule 13 or a third-party claim under Rule 14 does arise out of the subject matter of the original action and involves the same persons and issues, the claim is ancillary to the original action. In such cases, if the court has jurisdiction to entertain the original action, no independent basis of jurisdiction for the cross-claim or third-party claim need be alleged or proved. 229 F.2d at 373–374.

* * *

The District Court held that no part of Alexander's cross-claim against the prime contractor, his third-party complaint against the architect or of the prime contractor's cross-claim against Alexander for breach of contract arose out of the transaction or occurrence that is the subject matter of the original action or the two counterclaims. With deference to the well-written opinion of the District Judge, we disagree.

* * *

The words "transaction or occurrence" are given a broad and liberal interpretation in order to avoid a multiplicity of suits. * * *

Our reading of the pleadings in this case convinces us that there is a "logical relationship" between the cross-claims (including the third party complaint against the architect) and the "transaction or occurrence" that is the subject matter of the complaint and the two pending counterclaims. Although different subcontracts are involved, along with the prime contract and specifications, all relate to the same project and to problems arising out of the marble used in the erection of the Memphis City Hall. The recurring question presented by the various pleadings is directed to the principal issue of who is responsible for the marble problems which arose on this job. Blame is sought to be placed upon plaintiff as furnisher of the marble, upon Alexander as subcontractor, upon the prime contractor and upon the architect. Many of the same or closely related factual and legal issues necessarily will be presented under the complaint, counterclaims and cross-claims in the resolution of these issues. It seems apparent that some of the same evidence will be required in the hearing on the cross-claims and in the hearing or hearings with respect to the complaint and the two pending counterclaims.

We understand it to be the purpose of Rule 13 and the related rules that all such matters may be tried and determined in one action and to make it possible for the parties to avoid multiplicity of litigation. The intent of the rules is that all issues be resolved in one action, with all parties before one court, complex though the action may be.

In support of the decision of the District Court it is argued that, since a jury trial has been demanded, the complications and confusions of the cross-claims are such that it would be impossible to try the numerous issues before the jury in an orderly manner. The short answer to this contention is that the District Judge is authorized by Rule 42(b) to order separate trials on any cross-claim, counterclaim, other claim or issues. If on the trial of this case the District Court concludes that separate trials on one or more of the counterclaims, cross-claims or issues would be conducive to expedition and economy, Rule 42(b) provides a practical solution to this problem.

Reversed and remanded for further proceedings not inconsistent with this opinion.

MCALLISTER, SENIOR CIRCUIT JUDGE (dissenting).

* * *

The questions of fact or law involved in the original suit filed by LASA, and the counterclaim for overpayment filed by Alexander, are totally different from Alexander's claim against Southern Builders, claiming damages on the ground that Southern Builders wrongfully prevented and obstructed Alexander from performing its duties; wrongfully forced Alexander off the job; wrongfully brought in an outside subcontractor to complete the job at a highly inflated price, all of which was wrongfully and illegally charged to the account of Alexander—as well as Alexander's allegation in its same cross-claim against Southern Builders charging that Southern Builders and Aydelott entered upon a course of action wrongfully injuring the business reputation of Alexander for which it claimed $250,000 in punitive damages.

Alexander's cross-claim against Aydelott for treble damages in the amount of $750,000 for wrongfully and maliciously damaging Alexander's business reputation by abuse, harassment and public blame, and wrongfully and illegally inducing and procuring by inducement, persuasion or insistence, the breach and violation of Alexander's contract with Southern Builders, was an action in tort.

* * *

* * * Alexander's cross-claim against Aydelott does not arise out of the transaction or occurrence that is the subject matter of the original action—it does not arise out of the transaction or occurrence upon which LASA's suit is based. Nor does it arise out of "a counter-claim *therein*"—that is, out of a counterclaim in LASA's suit.

* * *

* * * [W]e are of the opinion that the cross-claims are not related to the original claim and the counterclaims, and that there is no identity of the many factual issues involved in the original claim and counterclaims, and in the cross-claims.

The proofs in LASA's suit and in Alexander's and Southern Builders' counterclaims against LASA would be entirely different from the proofs in Alexander's cross-claim against Southern Builders and its cross-claim against Aydelott.

* * *

The only claims in this case that arise out of the transaction or occurrence that is the subject matter of the original action *for balance due on a contract* are the counterclaims filed against LASA by Alexander and Southern Builders, *claiming breach of that contract*—not Alexander's two cross-claims against Southern Builders and Aydelott for their claimed deliberately malicious, tortious, and damaging conduct, for which Alexander claimed damages of several hundred thousand dollars.

In accordance with the foregoing, in my opinion, the judgments of the District Court should be affirmed in accordance with the opinion of Chief Judge Bailey Brown.

NOTES AND QUESTIONS

1. What standard does Federal Rule 13(g) set forth for claims between coplaintiffs and codefendants?

2. Is the reasoning of the majority or dissenting opinion more persuasive? Should the fact that different subcontracts were involved, which arguably meant that different transactions were before the court, be determinative? What ways other than dismissal could be employed to deal with the complexity of the litigation or to avoid confusion?

3. Should transactionally related cross-claims be compulsory? Generally speaking, cross-claims are permissive, and the failure to raise them does not bar suit in a subsequent action. Why should this be so? Doesn't this lead to a multiplicity of suits? Isn't judicial economy fostered by hearing all transactionally related claims in one suit? Or, is it unfair to force defendants to file cross-claims in a forum not of their own choosing merely because of the actions of the plaintiff? How would the concept of a compulsory cross-claim have changed the reasoning of both the majority and the dissent in *LASA*?

4. Wisconsin once only permitted a defendant to file a cross-claim against a codefendant, when the relief requested was shown to "involve or in some manner affect the contract, transaction or property, which is the subject-matter of the action." See LIEBHAUSER v. MILWAUKEE ELEC. RY. & LIGHT CO., 180 Wis. 468, 193 N.W. 522 (1923). Plaintiff-passenger sued to recover for personal injuries allegedly sustained while a passenger on one of defendant-railway company's street cars when it collided with an automobile owned and driven by defendant Kroscher. Kroscher cross-claimed against the railway company alleging that the collision was due solely to the negligence of

the company and seeking $150 for damages to his automobile. The court, construing that statute, dismissed the cross-claim, saying:

> * * * The subject-matter of the action * * * in this case is the plaintiff's right to have the defendants exercise the required degree of care in respect to her. Manifestly, the relief demanded by Kroscher in his cross-complaint against the company in no way involves or affects the plaintiff's main primary right. * * *
>
> The mere fact that the two occurrences were nearly contemporaneous in time in no manner affects the question. * * *
>
> * * * Plaintiff should have a right to bring her action and obtain an adjudication of her rights without being compelled to become a mere observer in a contest between two defendants which in no way whatever concerns her.

Id. at 473–74, 475–76, 481–82, 193 N.W. at 524–25, 527. Wisconsin has since amended its statute to delete the term "subject-matter." See 3 Wis. Prac., Civil Procedure § 207.3 (3d ed.), Author's Comments (2003). What are the advantages and disadvantages of the earlier approach?

5. Who counts as a "coparty" for purposes of Federal Rule 13(g)? In EARLE M. JORGENSON CO. v. T.I. UNITED STATES, LTD., 133 F.R.D. 472 (E.D.Pa.1991), plaintiff filed suit to recover cleanup costs and other damages arising from environmental contamination of real property. T.I. United States, one of seven defendants, impleaded a third-party defendant, Tosti. Another one of the original defendants, Reed, then cross-claimed against Tosti for indemnity and contribution. Tosti moved to dismiss, arguing that he as a third-party defendant and Reed as an original defendant were not "coparties" under Rule 13(g). The court found that Reed and Tosti were coparties, not opposing parties, and thus, the original defendant could cross-claim against Tosti for indemnity and contribution. The court defined "opposing parties" as "parties that formally oppose each other on a pleaded claim, such as plaintiffs and original defendants, or third-party plaintiffs and the third-party defendants they have joined." Id. at 475. But see Murray v. Haverford Hosp. Corp., 278 F.Supp. 5, 6 (E.D.Pa.1968) (defining coparties as "parties having like status, such as, co-defendants"). See Bessler, *Note—Defining "Co–Party" Within Federal Rule of Civil Procedure 13(g): Are Cross–Claims Between Original Defendants and Third–Party Defendants Allowable?*, 66 Ind. L.J. 549 (1991).

6. Can a party plaintiff cross-claim against a coplaintiff? If so, under what circumstances? In DANNER v. ANSKIS, 256 F.2d 123 (3d Cir.1958), the driver and passenger of one car sued the driver of a second car for damages arising out of a two-car collision. The passenger-plaintiff also attempted to cross-claim for her injuries against the driver-plaintiff. The trial court's dismissal of the cross-claim was affirmed:

> The purpose of Rule 13(g) is to permit a defendant to state as a cross-claim a claim against a co-defendant growing out of the same transaction or occurrence that is the subject matter of the original action * * *, and to permit a plaintiff against whom a defendant has filed a counterclaim to state as a cross-claim against a co-plaintiff a claim growing out of the

> transaction or occurrence that is the subject matter of the counterclaim. * * * In other words, a cross-claim is intended to state a claim which is ancillary to a claim stated in a complaint or counterclaim which has previously been filed against the party stating the cross-claim. * * * Unless so limited the rule could have the effect of extending the jurisdiction of the district court to controversies not within the federal judicial power. * * * Accordingly, Rule 13(g) does not authorize a plaintiff to state as a cross-claim against a co-plaintiff a claim arising out of the transaction or occurrence which is also the subject matter of their common complaint against the defendant. * * *

Id. at 124. Is the court's approach to the question of cross-claims between coplaintiffs sound? How is the *Danner* court defining "transaction"? Harrison v. M.S. Carriers, Inc., 1999 WL 195539, at *1 (E.D.La.1999) disagreed with the Third Circuit's analysis and allowed such a cross-claim: "The Fifth Circuit has explained that Rule 13(g) 'states two prerequisites for a cross-claim: (1) that it be a claim by one party against a co-party and (2) that the claim arise out of the same transaction or occurrence as the original counterclaim.' "

7. Federal Rule 13(h) is used to add parties not already in the suit. In order to invoke Rule 13(h), a party must be asserting a Rule 13(a), 13(b), or 13(g) claim against someone who already is a party. Note that this differs from claims under Rule 14. In *LASA,* Alexander's claim against the architect, Aydelott, originally was pleaded as a Rule 14 claim. The District Court and the Sixth Circuit treated it as if it were a motion to bring in an additional cross-defendant under Rule 13(h); the courts thus viewed Aydelott as a codefendant on the cross-claims against Southern Builders and the others. Isn't it true, therefore, that Rule 14 claims can be transformed into Rule 13(h) motions whenever defendant can assert a cross-claim against a party? Is there any tactical advantage in doing so? Are the additional party's rights different if it is brought in under Rule 13(h) rather than Rule 14? See 6 Wright, Miller & Kane, Federal Practice and Procedure: Civil 2d § 1435.

8. Federal courts are allowed to assert supplemental jurisdiction over Rule 13(g) cross-claims, but may a court assert such jurisdiction over Rule 13(h) parties joined to a compulsory counterclaim? Recall that supplemental jurisdiction, as codified in 28 U.S.C. § 1367, is available for all related claims that form part of the same case or controversy as the original claims. Section 1367(a) expressly provides that "such supplemental jurisdiction shall include claims that involve the joinder or intervention of additional parties." Review pp. 336–38, supra.

SECTION C. IDENTIFYING PARTIES WHO MAY SUE AND BE SUED

Read Federal Rule of Civil Procedure 17 in the Supplement.

ELLIS CANNING CO. v. INTERNATIONAL HARVESTER CO.

Supreme Court of Kansas, 1953.
174 Kan. 357, 255 P.2d 658.

PARKER, JUSTICE. * * *

In its petition plaintiff alleged that in furnishing service on its tractor defendant negligently started a fire in that vehicle resulting in damage amounting to $479.79; that plaintiff was insured in The Potomac Insurance Company against the loss, under a policy containing a subrogation clause; that it had been paid in full for the amount of its loss; and that it had commenced and was maintaining the action to recover such amount in its own name for the use and benefit of the insurance company.

Defendant's amended answer denied *seriatim* all acts of negligence * * *; admitted all allegations of that pleading respecting insurance, the amount of the loss, and the fact such loss had been fully paid by the insurance company; and then, in the third paragraph thereof, * * * alleged and charged, that since plaintiff was seeking to recover the amount paid to it by the insurer as full compensation for the loss of the tractor, the insurance company was the real party in interest and plaintiff had no legal right to maintain the action.

Plaintiff's motion to strike paragraph three of the answer and its demurrer to the same paragraph of that pleading * * * were overruled by the trial court. This appeal followed.

The appellant insists, the appellee concedes, and we agree, the sole question involved is whether the insured (appellant), after having been paid the full amount of its loss, is a real party in interest and legally entitled to maintain this action, for the use and benefit of the insurer, to recover such loss from the party (appellee), whose negligence is alleged to be responsible therefore. The question thus raised is not new in this jurisdiction and we frankly concede is one on which there is apparent conflict in our decisions.

Subject to certain exceptions, not here involved, our statute, G.S.1949, 60–401, requires that "Every action must be prosecuted in the name of the real party in interest." Given its common and accepted meaning, particularly where—as here—it must be conceded the appellant is no longer directly interested in the subject matter of the litigation, it would seem that, in and of itself, language of the statute would compel a negative answer to the question now under consideration. * * *

Notwithstanding, earlier decisions * * * holding that in the situation disclosed by the pleadings in the case at bar, the insurer is the real and only party in interest and must undertake the maintenance of the action for his reimbursement, it must and should be frankly admitted that in * * * [two decisions], as appellant contends, we held the insured might maintain the action in his own name for the use and benefit of the insurer. Be that as it may it must be conceded, that fully aware of the rule announced in those cases, we have repudiated what was there said and held with respect to such rule and now recognize and adhere to the doctrine that under the facts and circumstances disclosed by such pleadings an insured who has been fully paid for his loss is not the real party in interest * * * and hence cannot maintain an action to recover the amount of such loss in his own name for the use and benefit of the insurer. Conversely stated, the rule now recognized and applied is, that under the confronting conditions and circumstances the right of action against the alleged wrongdoer vests wholly in the insurer who * * * may, and indeed must, bring the action as the real and only party in interest if one is to be maintained. * * *

The judgment is affirmed.

NOTES AND QUESTIONS

1. "The purpose of requiring the real party in interest to prosecute a lawsuit is to avoid prejudice and the possibility of duplicate lawsuits. * * * [Rule 17(a)] also exists to allow a defendant to set out all of its defenses in one action." Verizon New Jersey, Inc. v. Ntegrity Telecontent Servs., Inc., 219 F.Supp.2d 616, 635 (D.N.J. 2002). Another court identifies the rule's "preeminent concern * * * [as] whether the suing party has sufficient legal rights to ensure that the outcome of the case will be *res judicata* * * *. The Ezra Charitable Trust v. Rent–Way, Inc., 136 F.Supp.2d 435, 443 (W.D. Pa. 2001). Is Rule 17 necessary? See Entman, *More Reasons for Abolishing Federal Rule of Civil Procedure 17(a): The Problem of the Proper Plaintiff and Insurance Subrogation*, 68 N.C.L.Rev. 893 (1990).

2. A person is injured due to the negligence of another. She receives payment from an insurance company. The insurance company persuades the insured to sue the negligent party in her name in state court rather than the insurance company pursuing the action itself. Why would the insurance company wish to do this? Consider the following reasons:

(a) The insurance company thinks that a jury might be more sympathetic to an injured individual than to a large company.

(b) The injured party and the negligent party are not diverse. Had the insurance company pursued the action, the parties would have been diverse and the defendant (if not a citizen of the forum state) could have removed the action to federal court. The insurance company wanted the action to remain in state court, where it thought it could get a higher award.

3. Can there be more than one real party in interest to a suit? Suppose, for example, that an injured party is only partly covered by insurance. Can she sue the negligent party? Can the insurance company? Or, must the two sue jointly? In PINEWOOD GIN CO. v. CAROLINA POWER & LIGHT CO., 41 F.R.D. 221 (D.S.C.1966) the court held that the parties should be made to sue jointly, but that each had an interest in the outcome. Is it appropriate to use Rule 17(a) as a rule of compulsory joinder?

4. Is the real party in interest to be determined using a federal standard, or would a federal court adjudicating a state-based claim be bound by the rule of the state in which it sits? In R.J. REYNOLDS TOBACCO CO. v. LANEY & DUKE STORAGE WAREHOUSE CO., 39 F.R.D. 607 (M.D.Fla. 1966), the court held that a Florida rule allowing only the insured to enforce a claim against a tortfeasor, even after payment by an insurer, was procedural and not substantive. Since it did not feel bound to follow Florida law on the matter, the court felt comfortable holding that under Rule 17(a)(1) the insurer and not the insured was the real party in interest. The court distinguished this state procedural rule, however, from a rule that determined whether a subrogee had a right to receive the proceeds of a recovery in a tort action. According to the court, this latter rule was substantive, and thus the state rule had to be applied.

5. Generally, courts have held that diversity of citizenship is to be determined by the citizenship of the real party in interest. Does this invite maneuvers designed to create or destroy diversity jurisdiction? Suppose, for example, that a nondiverse party wishes to sue in federal court. Can she assign her claim to another party so that complete diversity would exist? Alternatively, can a party assign a claim so as to defeat diversity? When assignments or appointments are used to create diversity, 28 U.S.C. § 1359, see Note 9, p. 284, supra, appears to be relevant. Federal courts generally have permitted assignments or appointments to destroy diversity—in large part because of the absence of a statute like Section 1359 dealing with attempts to destroy diversity. See Conley, *Will the Real Party in Interest Please Stand Up? Applying the Capacity to Sue Rule in Diversity Cases*, 65 Wash. & Lee L. Rev. 675 (2008).

6. If the party designated in the original complaint is not the real party in interest, should a substitution of the proper party be given retroactive effect to the date of the original complaint for statute-of-limitations purposes? Federal Rule 17(a) was amended in 1966 to add the provision that no action shall be dismissed because it was not prosecuted in the name of the real party in interest until a reasonable time has been allowed for substitution. In 2007, this provision was moved to Rule 17(a)(3) and now reads: "The court may not dismiss an action for failure to prosecute in the name of the real party in interest until, after an objection, a reasonable time has been allowed for the real party in interest to ratify, join, or be substituted into the action." The Advisory Committee's Notes to Rule 17, which appear in the Supplement, specifically limit the application of this passage to cases in which the proper party to sue is difficult to ascertain or when an excusable mistake has been made. What is the relation between this rule and Rule 15? See p. 623, supra.

NOTE ON CAPACITY, STANDING, AND REAL PARTY IN INTEREST

In addition to the rules on real party in interest, two other concepts are relevant to determining who may sue or be sued—"capacity" and "standing." It is useful to contrast the three issues of capacity, real party in interest, and standing to show how they operate together.

Capacity refers to the ability of an individual or corporation to enforce rights or to be sued by others. Many states, for example, have special rules to deal with suits by or against minors and mental incompetents. See Federal Rules 17(b) and 17(c). Capacity rules are designed to protect a party by ensuring that she is represented adequately. So, a representative will be appointed to advance the interests of a minor or a mental incompetent, who might not be able to understand fully the nature of the issues involved in the lawsuit. Real-party-in-interest rules serve to protect the opposing party's interests by ensuring that only the litigant who has a true stake in the outcome can sue or be sued. This prevents situations in which a person first might be sued by the person who holds the nominal title to a claim, and after successfully defending that claim, is subjected to a second action by the real party in interest. See Commonwealth of Puerto Rico v. Cordeco Dev. Corp., 534 F.Supp. 612, 614 (D.Puerto Rico 1982).

Standing is a related concept that conserves judicial resources by ensuring that the parties before the court have a bona fide dispute and will vigorously argue the legal claims at issue. In the federal system, standing requirements are said to derive from Article III of the federal Constitution and so to protect separation-of-powers concerns. Federal standing rules are treated in detail in a course on Federal Courts or Constitutional Law. Only summary treatment may be given in a Civil Procedure course. Current standing doctrine requires a plaintiff to "allege personal injury fairly traceable to the defendant's allegedly unlawful conduct and likely to be redressed by the requested relief." Allen v. Wright, 468 U.S. 737, 751, 104 S.Ct. 3315, 3324, 82 L.Ed.2d 556, 569 (1984). See Chemerinsky, Federal Jurisdiction § 2.3 (5th ed. 2007).

It is possible, therefore, to have a case in which a real party in interest (the beneficiary of a will, for example) lacks capacity to sue (perhaps because the party is a minor). Moreover, even if this hypothetical beneficiary had capacity to sue, standing to raise particular claims might be lacking. So, for example, the beneficiary of the will might not be able to bring an action against the government on the ground that the estate tax is used for illegal purposes by the government since the injury suffered is of a general nature, not particular to the litigant, and hence the beneficiary lacks standing to sue.

SECTION D. CLAIMS INVOLVING MULTIPLE PARTIES

1. PERMISSIVE JOINDER OF PARTIES

A. HISTORICAL LIMITATIONS ON PERMISSIVE JOINDER OF PARTIES

Joinder of parties at common law was controlled by the substantive rules of law, often as reflected in the forms of action, rather than by notions of judicial economy and trial convenience. Plaintiffs who were asserting joint rights were compelled by these principles to join their respective claims in a single action; permissive joinder of plaintiffs, in the sense of plaintiffs having an option to join their claims when they were not joint, did not exist. The common-law rules governing joinder of defendants were slightly more flexible: joint tortfeasors and defendants whose contract obligations were both joint and several could be joined at the plaintiff's option.

The equity courts adopted a more flexible approach to permissive joinder of parties than prevailed in the common-law courts. They allowed all persons having an interest in the subject matter of the action or in the relief demanded to join in a single proceeding. The early codes adopted the equity rule as a general provision governing joinder of parties. See Bone, *Mapping the Boundaries of the Dispute: Conceptions of Ideal Lawsuit Structure from the Field Code to the Federal Rules*, 89 Colum. L. Rev. 1 (1989). Many state courts read this language as imposing a two-part requirement for joinder of plaintiffs, however. As a result, joinder of plaintiffs was restricted to those cases in which all plaintiffs were interested in both the subject matter of the action and all the relief demanded. Joinder of defendants was even more restricted by code provisions relating to joinder of causes of action, which typically required all parties to be interested in each of the joined causes.

For a history of American joinder rules, see 7 Wright, Miller & Kane, Federal Practice and Procedure: Civil 3d § 1651; Blume, *Free Joinder of Parties, Claims, and Counterclaims,* 2 F.R.D. 250 (1943); *Legislation: Recent Trends in Joinder of Parties, Causes, and Counterclaims,* 37 Colum.L.Rev. 462 (1937). For an early comparative view, see Millar, *The Joinder of Actions in Continental Civil Procedure,* 28 Ill.L.Rev. 26, 177 (1933).

RYDER v. JEFFERSON HOTEL CO.

Supreme Court of South Carolina, 1922.
121 S.C. 72, 113 S.E. 474.

MARION, J. The complaint in this action * * * alleges in substance that the plaintiff Charles A. Ryder and the plaintiff Edith C. Ryder are husband and wife; that [they] * * * became guests of the defendant Jefferson Hotel Company * * *; that thereafter, during the night * * *, the defendant S.J. Bickley, acting as the servant and agent of the defendant Jefferson Hotel Company, roused the plaintiffs by rapping upon their room door, and in a rude and angry manner insulted the plaintiff Edith C. Ryder; that as a result of the insults * * * the plaintiffs were compelled to give up the accommodations due them and leave the said hotel, and were forced at midnight and at great inconvenience and uncertainty to seek another lodging place; that by reason of such high-handed, malicious, and willful conduct, on the part of the said hotel and its servant and agent, the plaintiffs were greatly injured in their reputations, credit, and business, and that the plaintiff Charles A. Ryder has suffered great loss of custom and has been deprived of great gains and profits * * *; and that * * * the plaintiffs have been damaged in the sum of $10,000.

Defendants separately demurred to the complaint upon the ground that it appeared upon the face thereof that several causes of action had been improperly united therein, for the reason that the several causes of action united do not affect all the parties to the action. From an order overruling the demurrer, defendants appeal.

The sole question for determination is: Does the complaint contain two causes of action which may be joined in the same complaint? It is apparent, as appellants suggest, that the complaint alleges a cause of action by Charles A. Ryder against the defendants for a personal tort—that is, for a breach of duty growing out of the relationship existing between the parties, to wit, innkeeper and guest—and also a cause of action by Edith C. Ryder against the defendants for a tortious breach of duty growing out of the same relationship. It is also apparent that both of these alleged causes of action arose out of the same transaction, in the sense that the injury to each of the plaintiffs was caused by the same delict. But appellants contend that it is equally apparent from the allegations of the complaint that the rights invaded and the injuries sustained are necessarily several, and that plaintiffs cannot maintain a joint action and recover joint damages therefor. We think that contention must be sustained.

Section 218 of the Code of Procedure (1912), classifying the various causes of action which may be united in the same complaint, contains this proviso:

> But the causes of action, so united, must all belong to one of these classes, and, except in actions for the foreclosure of mortgages, must affect all the parties to the action, and not require different places of trial, and must be separately stated.

The rule applicable is thus stated by Judge Pomeroy in his work on Code Remedies (4th Ed.) p. 215:

> When a tort of a personal nature * * * is committed upon two or more, the right of action must, except in a very few special cases, be several. In order that a joint action may be possible, there must be some prior bond of legal union between the persons injured—such as partnership relation—of such a nature that the tort interferes with it, *and by virtue of that very interference* produces a wrong and consequent damage common to all. It is not every prior existing legal relation between the parties that will impress a joint character upon the injury and damage. Thus, if a husband and wife be libeled, or slandered, or beaten, although there is a close legal relation between the parties, it is not one which can be affected by such a wrong, and no joint cause of action will arise. * * *

That the rights infringed and the injuries suffered by the two plaintiffs in the case at bar are several, and not joint, would not seem open to question. To illustrate: If the two plaintiffs, husband and wife, occupying the same berth in a sleeping car, had both been physically injured in a wreck of the train, it would scarcely be contended that they could properly bring a joint action for the damages sustained by each on account of the carrier's delict. The complaint here does not state a cause of action for injuries to the wife alone * * *. Neither is the husband's alleged cause of action based upon loss of consortium and expenses incurred on behalf of the wife. The wife's cause of action as alleged does not "affect" the husband, and the husband's cause of action does not "affect" the wife, in the sense that the Code of Procedure (section 218) requires that the causes of action joined in the same complaint "must affect all parties to the action." Neither has a legal interest in the pecuniary recovery of the other, and in contemplation of law there can be no joint and common damage to both resulting from a wrong which gives rise to separate and distinct rights personal to each. * * *

At common law it seems that even the husband's cause of action for the loss of the wife's services and companionship and expenses incurred by him on account of injury to the wife could not be joined with the cause of action for injuries personal to the wife. * * * In the case at bar not only are the parties plaintiff different, and the potential elements of damage recoverable by the parties different, but neither party has the right to sue for the benefit of the other * * *.

The order of the circuit court is reversed.

GARY, C.J., and COTHRAN, J., concur.

FRASER, J. (dissenting). * * * The plaintiffs * * * were expelled from the hotel, under the allegation that they were not husband and wife. It was a denial of the joint relationship that caused the trouble.

It seems to me that the illustrations used are not appropriate to the case. When a husband and wife are injured in one railroad accident, the injuries are individual, and not joint. It seems to me that the case is somewhat like an injury to a copartnership. I do not think that it will be doubted that the copartnership can bring an action for injury to the copartnership, although the injury to the two copartners may not be the same. * * * In the joint action the other copartner may not be able to recover for the injury peculiar to himself; but the injury to the copartnership is a joint injury, and for this injury it may recover. Here the offense was against the husband and wife and affected their relation as husband and wife. This is manifestly a joint injury. * * *

For these reasons I dissent.

NOTE AND QUESTION

Does *Ryder* make ineffective the concept of permissive joinder by allowing joinder only when the parties are "united in interest"? If the parties are united in interest, should they be *compelled* to join in the action? In this connection consider the court's reliance on Pomeroy's statement that "although there is a close legal relation between the parties, it is not one which can be *affected* by such a wrong, and no joint cause of action will arise." (Emphasis added.) If the injury *affected* a relationship, should the parties be required to join in the action? Is the joint-interest standard consistent with the objectives of permissive joinder? Reconsider these questions after completing the material on mandatory joinder, pp. 688–704, infra.

B. PERMISSIVE JOINDER UNDER FEDERAL RULE OF CIVIL PROCEDURE 20

Read Federal Rules of Civil Procedure 20, 21, and 42(a) in the Supplement.

M.K. v. TENET

United States District Court, District of Columbia, 2002.
216 F.R.D. 133.

URBINA, DISTRICT JUDGE.

[Reread M.K. v. Tenet, p. 655, supra. The court then turned to the Rule 20 joinder issue.]

* * *

The plaintiffs cite to the first prong of Rule 20(a) [now Rule 20(a)(1)(A)], also known as the "transactional test," and argue that the defendants' acts and omissions pertaining to the plaintiffs' obstruction-of-counsel claims are "logically related" events that the court can regard as "arising out of the same transaction, occurrence or series of transactions or occurrences." * * * The court agrees with the plaintiffs' assertion that "logically related" events may consist of an alleged "consistent pattern of . . . obstruction of security-cleared counsel by [the] [d]efendants." * * * Specifically, each of the existing plaintiffs allege that they were injured by the defendants through employment-related matters, such as retaliation, discrimination, and the denial of promotions and overseas assignments. * * * After each employment dispute began, each of the plaintiffs or the plaintiffs' counsel sought access to employee and agency records. * * * The defendants, however, denied and continue to deny the plaintiffs and/or their counsel access to the plaintiffs' requested information. * * * As such, without this relevant information, the plaintiffs cannot effectively prepare or submit administrative complaints to the defendants or attempt to seek legal recourse through the applicable Title VII discrimination, Privacy Act, or First, Fifth, and Seventh Amendment claims.* * * The court concludes that the alleged repeated pattern of obstruction of counsel by the defendants against the plaintiffs is "logically related" as "a series of transactions or occurrences" that establishes an overall pattern of policies and practices aimed at denying effective assistance of counsel to the plaintiffs. * * * In this case, each plaintiff alleges that the defendants' policy and practice of obstruction of counsel has damaged the plaintiffs. * * * Further, each plaintiff requests declaratory and injunctive relief. * * * Thus, the court determines that each plaintiff in this case has satisfied the first prong of Rule 20(a). * * *

Turning to the second prong of Rule 20(a) [now Rule 20(a)(1)(B)], the plaintiffs aver that each of their claims are related by a common question of law or fact. * * * Specifically, one question of law or fact that is common to each of the six existing plaintiffs is whether the defendants' September 4, 1998 notice restricting the plaintiffs' counsel from accessing records intruded on the plaintiffs' substantial interest in freely discussing their legal rights with their attorneys. * * * Indeed, the question of law or fact that is common to all may be whether the "defendants have engaged in a common scheme or pattern of behavior" that effectively denies the plaintiffs' legal right to discuss their claims with their counsel. * * * The plaintiffs also allege that the defendants' policy or practice of obstruction of counsel "is implemented through [a] concert of action among CIA management and the Doe Defendants," who are now named in the second amended complaint. * * * In light of the aforementioned common questions of law and fact, the court concludes that the plaintiffs meet the second prong of Rule 20(a). * * *

The court need not stop here in its Rule 20(a) analysis. Indeed, it appears that there exists a further basis supporting the plaintiffs' position challenging severance * * *[.] Each plaintiff alleges common claims under the Privacy Act. * * * Specifically, the plaintiffs' second amended complaint alleges that the defendants "maintained records about the plaintiffs in unauthorized systems of records in violation of § 552a(e)(4) of the Privacy Act" and that the defendants "failed to employ proper physical safeguards for records in violation of § 552a(e)(10) of the Privacy Act." * * * The plaintiffs also allege that the defendants wrongfully denied the plaintiffs and plaintiffs' counsel access to records in violation of § 552a(d)(1) of the Privacy Act and "illegally maintained specific records describing their First Amendment activities in violation of § 552a(e)(7) of the Privacy Act." * * * Furthermore, the plaintiffs' first amended complaint contains similar allegations. Through their alleged Privacy Act violations, the plaintiffs are united by yet another "question of law or fact" that is common to each of them. * * * Accordingly, the court concludes that the plaintiffs satisfy the second prong of Rule 20(a) and, thus, the court denies the defendants' motion to sever.

On a final note, in denying the defendants' motion to sever, the court defers to the policy underlying Rule 20, which is to promote trial convenience, expedite the final determination of disputes, and prevent multiple lawsuits. * * * Indeed, the Supreme Court addressed this important policy in United Mine Workers of America v. Gibbs, * * * [p. 325, supra,] stating that "[u]nder the rules, the impulse is toward entertaining the broadest possible scope of action consistent with fairness to the parties; joinder of claims, parties, and remedies is strongly encouraged." Id. at 724, 86 S.Ct. 1130. In accordance with Gibbs, the court believes that the joinder or non-severance of the six existing plaintiffs and their new claims under Rule 20(a) will promote trial convenience, expedite the final resolution of disputes, and act to prevent multiple lawsuits, extra expense to the parties, and loss of time to the court and the litigants in this case. Gibbs

* * *. For this added reason, the court denies the defendants' motion to sever.

IV. Conclusion

For all of the foregoing reasons, the court grants the plaintiffs' motion to amend and denies the defendants' motion to sever. * * *

NOTES AND QUESTIONS

1. How would *Ryder*, p. 679, supra, have been decided under Federal Rule 20? What are the factors that should be weighed under Rule 20 in deciding a permissive-joinder question? One commentary notes:

> Instead of developing one generalized test for ascertaining whether a particular factual situation constitutes a single transaction or occurrence for purposes of Rule 20, the courts seem to have adopted a case-by-case approach. * * * As a result, it is necessary to extrapolate from the decided cases what is likely to qualify as a single "transaction or occurrence" in a particular case.

7 Wright, Miller & Kane, Federal Practice and Procedure: Civil 3d § 1653.

2. Many of the tactical factors that must be considered before attempting to join multiple defendants are discussed in Friedenthal, *Whom to Sue—Multiple Defendants,* in 5 Am.Jur. Trials 1–25 (1966).

3. Federal Rule 20 describes the parties that may be joined in a litigation; it does not require their joinder. New Jersey adopted, but then abandoned, a mandatory party rule that required joinder "of all persons who have a material interest in the controversy." Erichson, *Of Horror Stories and Happy Endings: The Rise and Fall of Preclusion–Based Compulsory Party Joinder Under the New Jersey Entire Controversy Doctrine*, 9 Seton Hall Const. L.J. 757 (1999). What problems do you foresee with this approach? Any advantages?

4. In GEORGE v. SMITH, 507 F.3d 605 (7th Cir. 2007), a prisoner was barred under Rule 20 from suing two dozen defendants in one lawsuit, all of whom were alleged to have violated his Eighth Amendment rights, whether by "failing to provide medical care," "censoring his mail," "mishandling his applications for parole," and so on. Judge Easterbrook explained: "[M]ultiple claims against a single party are fine, but Claim A against Defendant 1 should not be joined with unrelated Claim B against Defendant 2. Unrelated claims against different defendants belong in different suits * * *." The court found support for this view in the Prison Litigation Reform Act, 28 U.S.C. § 1915(g), which limits the number of lawsuits that a prisoner may file without payment of a fee. The court also emphasized that plaintiff "did not make any effort to show that the 24 defendants he named had participated in the same transaction or series of transactions or that a question of fact is 'common to all defendants.'" Id. at 607–08. Do you agree with the court's implicit definition of "transaction" under Rule 20? Has the court read the Prison Reform Litigation Act to carve out prisoner cases from Rule 20's broad approach to permissive party joinder? See Genetin, *Expressly Repudiating*

Implied Repeals Analysis: A New Framework for Resolving Conflicts Between Congressional Statutes and Federal Rules, 51 Emory L.J. 677 (2002). Does this approach undermine the Federal Rule's goal of providing a uniform set of rules for all cases? See p. 25, supra. See generally Rubenstein, *The Concept of Equality in Civil Procedure*, 23 Cardozo L. Rev. 1865 (2002).

TANBRO FABRICS CORP. v. BEAUNIT MILLS, INC.

Supreme Court of New York, Appellate Division, First Department, 1957.
4 A.D.2d 519, 167 N.Y.S.2d 387.

BREITEL, JUSTICE. * * *

The underlying business dispute spawned three lawsuits. In the first action * * *, the seller, Beaunit, sought to recover the purchase price of goods sold and delivered to Tanbro. The buyer, Tanbro, counterclaimed for breach of warranty for improper manufacture, as a result of which the goods were subject to "yarn slippage." The seller replied to the counterclaim by denying that the slippage was due to improper manufacture. A portion of the goods still being in the hands of the processor, Tanbro initiated another action * * *, in replevin, to recover these goods. The processor, Amity, counterclaimed for its charges and asserted its claim to the goods under an artisan's lien. In the exchanges that preceded and attended the bringing of these lawsuits, the buyer Tanbro received Beaunit's assertion that the yarn slippage was caused by the processor's improper handling, while with equal force the processor charged the same defect to Beaunit as a consequence of its improper manufacture.

At this juncture, Tanbro, the buyer, brought the third lawsuit * * * against Beaunit and Amity, charging the goods were defective because of yarn slippage and that such slippage was caused by either the seller, Beaunit, or alternatively the processor, Amity, or both. This is the main action before the court.

At Special Term, the buyer Tanbro moved to consolidate the three actions. Beaunit and Amity separately cross-moved to dismiss the complaint in the buyer's main action on the ground that there were prior actions pending between the parties with respect to the same cause of action. The motion to consolidate was denied and Beaunit's cross-motion to dismiss the complaint as against it was granted.

* * *

Both the seller and the processor resist consolidation. They do so on the ground that each had a separate and different relationship to the buyer, and that each was involved in a separate and independent contract. Therefore, they say, there is not involved the "same transaction or occurrence," nor any common question of law or fact to sustain either a joinder of parties or a consolidation of the actions. They stress that the buyer Tanbro wishes to pit against each other the seller and the processor on the issue of responsibility for the alleged defect, while the buyer sits back free from the obligation to prove a full case, as it would otherwise have to do in separate actions against the seller and the processor. The buyer, on the other hand, argues that what is identical to the cases are the goods and the defect, with the common question of who is responsible for the defect. The buyer concedes that it would have to prove the defect, and also prove that the defect must have been caused by either the seller or the processor or both of them; that, therefore, this involves a single transaction or occurrence and involves a common question of fact.

The controlling statute is Section 212 of the Civil Practice Act. * * * The portion pertinent to the joinder of defendants reads as follows:

> 2. All persons may be joined in one action as defendants if there is asserted against them jointly, severally, or in the alternative, any right to relief in respect of or arising out of the same transaction, occurrence, or series of transactions or occurrences and if any question of law or fact common to all of them would arise in the action. * * *

A reading of the section by itself would suggest little or no difficulty in permitting a joinder of parties in the buyer's main action or a consolidation of the three actions. However, the section has a history, which has created some confusion as to the meaning and application of the section.

The seller and the processor rely heavily on Ader v. Blau, 241 N.Y. 7, 148 N.E. 771, 41 A.L.R. 1216. The case arose under the predecessor statute permitting joinder * * *. In that case the plaintiff sought to join in one death action the person charged with having caused the accident resulting in the injuries ending in death and a treating physician who, it was charged, by his incompetence, was the cause of the decedent's death. The Court of Appeals * * * [held] that Section 258 of the Civil Practice Act, since repealed, albeit a restriction on joinder of causes of action in pleading, was a limiting factor in permitting joinder of parties. Applying the statute, it held the joinder impermissible.

In reaction to this decision * * * Section 258 was repealed in favor of a broad pleading section * * *. In making the recommendation, the Judicial Council referred to the *Ader* case, supra, and the fact that the court had regarded the area of joinder of parties limited by the pleading restrictions of Section 258. It added, "Complete freedom should be allowed in the joinder of causes of action as in the joinder of parties, and it is submitted that the correct approach to the joinder both of parties and of causes of action is the English one: May the matters conveniently be tried together? The problem is to combine as many matters as possible to avoid multiplicity and at the same time not unduly complicate the litigation for the jury."

The full effect of the repealer of old Section 258 has, however, not been left to speculation. The Court of Appeals, in Great Northern Telegraph Company v. Yokohama Specie Bank, 297 N.Y. 135, 76 N.E.2d 117, discussed the question frontally. It held that the *Ader* case, supra, was a result of the pleading limitation contained in the old, and now repealed, Section 258. * * * And in the *Great Northern* case, itself, joinder was allowed plaintiff against the Superintendent of Banks for payments due plaintiff, on which claim the Superintendent was asserting as a bar a time limitation provided by statute, and a correspondent Bank, which plaintiff asserted owed a duty to plaintiff to file the claim promptly with the Superintendent of Banks, in the event that it should be held that the claim was barred by lapse of time.

Notably, in the *Great Northern Telegraph* case, and in the English cases relied upon therein, there were joined, as defendants, parties that owed to plaintiff obligations under independent and separate contracts and in independent and separate relationships. In none of the cases was the "same transaction or occurrence" construed to require an identity of duty and relationship. * * *

This then is the background for the present section 212 of the Civil Practice Act. It should be beyond argument, by now, that it is no longer a bar to joinder, and, by parallel reasoning, *a fortiori,* to consolidation, that there is not an identity of duty or contract upon which to assert alternative liability. It is still necessary, of course, that there be a finding that the alternative liability arises out of a common transaction or occurrence involving common questions of fact and law. But this is not a rigid test. It is to be applied with judgment and discretion, in the balancing of convenience and justice between the parties involved * * *. Indeed, the buyer's situation prompted Special Term to comment that the buyer, Tanbro, "is in the unenviable position of not knowing possibly which of its contracting parties is responsible and in separate actions may find itself confronted with defeat in each event though the product as finally delivered may be defective."

* * *

The right of joinder and the privilege to obtain consolidation is always counterbalanced, of course, by the power of the court to grant a severance, or to deny a consolidation, if prejudice or injustice appear. In this case, the danger of separate trials, leading, perhaps, to an unjust and illogical result, is a possibility well worth avoiding. The buyer is entitled to a less hazardous adjudication of his dispute, so long as he is able to make out a prima facie case of alternative liability.

Accordingly, the order of Special Term insofar as it granted the cross motion to dismiss the complaint in the first described action as against the defendant Beaunit and denied the buyer Tanbro's motion to consolidate the three actions should be modified to deny the cross motion and to grant the motion to consolidate, and otherwise should be affirmed * * *.

All concur.

NOTES AND QUESTIONS

1. Consider the following:

   Where one of two persons are liable but the plaintiff is not certain he can make out a case against either, the opportunity to join them as

> defendants is of great tactical importance. The court should not dismiss after the close of plaintiff's case merely because the plaintiff has not shown which of the two defendants is responsible if he has shown that one of them must have been. It is not unfair to require each of the defendants to assume the risk of a failure to show that he was not responsible. Some attorneys sometimes fail to recognize that evidence supplied by one co-defendant may be used against another to support the plaintiff's case. * * * Even if the court might feel that a prima facie case has not been made out against one of the co-defendants, it should at least reserve decision on the motion to dismiss until after the defendants rest.

2 Weinstein, Korn & Miller, New York Civil Practice ¶ 1002.08. See also 7 Wright, Miller & Kane, Federal Practice and Procedure: Civil 3d § 1654.

In *Tanbro,* the buyer's motion was for consolidation. The court's opinion might convey the impression that the court assumed the New York standard for consolidation was identical to that for joinder. In fact, however, the New York consolidation provision is much broader than the New York joinder provision. The text of both have been set out in the Supplement—the former under Federal Rule 42(a) and the latter under Federal Rule 20. In comparing the Federal Rules with the New York provisions note that the Federal Rules also differentiate between joinder and consolidation. Can a discrepancy between the availability of joinder and consolidation be justified?

2. Notice that Federal Rule 20 sets out a different standard for the joinder of parties than that of Federal Rule 18 for joinder of claims. How do you explain the difference between the rules? One commentator says that "Rule 20 is only slightly more demanding than Rule 18." Oakley, *Joinder and Jurisdiction in the Federal District Courts: The State of the Union of Rules and Statutes,* 69 Tenn. L. Rev. 35, 35–36 (2001). Do you agree with that analysis?

2. MANDATORY JOINDER OF PERSONS

A. THE TRADITIONAL CONCEPT OF "INDISPENSABLE" PARTIES

BANK OF CALIFORNIA NAT. ASS'N v. SUPERIOR COURT

Supreme Court of California, 1940.
16 Cal.2d 516, 106 P.2d 879.

GIBSON, CHIEF JUSTICE. * * *

Sara M. Boyd * * * died testate in June, 1937, leaving an estate valued at about $225,000. On July 8, 1937, * * * her will was admitted to probate, and petitioner, Bank of California, was appointed executor. The will left individual legacies and bequests amounting to $60,000 to a large number of legatees, * * * some residing in other states and in foreign countries. Petitioner, St. Luke's Hospital, was named residuary legatee and devisee, and thereby received the bulk of the estate.

On October 14, 1937, Bertha M. Smedley, a niece and legatee, brought an action to enforce the provisions of an alleged contract by which decedent agreed to leave her entire estate to the plaintiff. The complaint named as parties defendant the executor and all of the beneficiaries under the will, and prayed for a decree adjudging that plaintiff is, by virtue of the agreement, the owner of the entire estate of the decedent after payment of debts and expenses. It was further prayed that plaintiff's title to the property be quieted * * *.

Summons was served only upon petitioners, the executor and the residuary legatee. No other defendants were served, and none appeared. * * * [At trial] petitioners made a motion * * * for an order to bring in the other defendants, and to have summons issued and served upon them. The motion was made on the ground that all of the other defendants were "necessary and indispensable parties" to the action, and that the court could not proceed without them. The motion was denied by respondent court. Petitioners then applied for a writ of prohibition to restrain the trial until these other parties should be brought in.

In support of their application, petitioners point out that the complaint challenges the right of every legatee and devisee to share in the estate, and prays for an award of the entire property to plaintiff. It is contended that a trial and judgment without the absent defendants would adversely affect the rights of such parties, would result in a multiplicity of suits, and would subject the petitioning executor to inconvenience, expense and the burden of future litigation.

* * * [T]he precise issue is * * * whether the absent defendants are not only proper parties but "indispensable parties" in the sense that service upon them or their appearance is essential to the jurisdiction of the court to proceed in the action. * * *

At common law, joinder of plaintiffs was compulsory where the parties under the substantive law, were possessed of joint rights. * * * Equity courts developed another theory of compulsory joinder, to carry out the policy of avoiding piecemeal litigation and multiplicity of suits. Those persons necessary to a complete settlement of the controversy were usually required to be joined, in order that the entire matter might be concluded by a single suit. Obviously, this theory of joinder covered many situations where the substantive rights were not joint, and accordingly joinder would not have been required in an action at law. * * * Generally speaking, the modern rule under the codes carries out the established equity doctrine. Thus, section 389 of the Code of Civil Procedure states: "The court may determine any controversy between parties before it, when it can be done without prejudice to the rights of others, or by saving their rights; but when a complete determination of the controversy cannot be had without the presence of other parties, the court must then order them to be brought in * * *." * * *

But the equity doctrine as developed by the courts is loose and ambiguous in its expression and uncertain in its application. Sometimes it is stated as a mandatory rule, and at other times as a matter of discretion, designed to reach an equitable result if it is practicable to do so. * * * Bearing in mind the fundamental purpose of the doctrine, we should, in dealing with "necessary" and "indispensable" parties, be careful to avoid converting a discretionary power or a rule of fairness in procedure into an arbitrary and burdensome requirement which may thwart rather than accomplish justice. These two terms have frequently been coupled together as if they have the same meaning; but there appears to be a sound distinction, both in theory and practice, between parties deemed "indispensable" and those considered merely "necessary." * * * "* * * While necessary parties are so interested in the controversy that they should normally be made parties in order to enable the court to do complete justice, yet if their interests are separable from the rest and particularly where their presence in the suit cannot be obtained, they are not indispensable parties. The latter are those without whom the court cannot proceed." (Clark[,] Code Pleading, p. 245, note 21, * * *.)

First, then, what parties are indispensable? There may be some persons whose interests, rights, or duties will inevitably be affected by any decree which can be rendered in the action. Typical are the situations where a number of persons have undetermined interests in the same property, or in a particular trust fund, and one of them seeks, in an action, to recover the whole, to fix his share, or to recover a portion claimed by him. The other persons with similar interests are indispensable parties. The reason is that a judgment in favor of one claimant for part of the property or fund would necessarily determine the amount or extent which remains available to the others. Hence, any judgment in the action would inevitably affect their rights. Thus, in an action by one creditor against assignees for the benefit of creditors, seeking an accounting and payment of his share of the assets, the other creditors were held indispensable * * *. * * * Where, also, the plaintiff seeks some other type of affirmative relief which, if granted, would injure or affect the interests of a third person not joined that third person is an indispensable party. Thus, in an action by a lessor against a sublessee to forfeit a parent lease because of acts of the sublessee, the sublessors (original lessees) were indispensable parties, since a decree of forfeiture would deprive them of their lease. * * *

All of these persons are, of course, "necessary" parties, but the decisions show that they come within a special classification of necessary parties, to which the term "indispensable" seems appropriate. An attempt to adjudicate their rights without joinder is futile. Many cases go so far as to say that the court would have no jurisdiction to proceed without them, and that its purported judgment would be void and subject to collateral attack. The objection being so fundamental, it need not be raised by the parties themselves; the court may, of its own motion, dismiss the proceedings, or refuse to proceed, until these indispensable parties are brought in. * * *

The other classification includes persons who are interested in the sense that they might possibly be affected by the decision, or whose interests in the subject matter or transaction are such that it cannot be finally and completely settled without them; but nevertheless their interests are so separable that a decree may be rendered between the parties before the court without affecting those others. These latter may perhaps be "necessary" parties to a complete settlement of the entire controversy or transaction, but are not "indispensable" to any valid judgment in the particular case. They should normally be joined, and the court, following the equity rule, will usually require them to be joined, in order to carry out the policy of complete determination and avoidance of multiplicity of suits. But, since the rule itself is one of equity, it is limited and qualified by considerations of fairness, convenience, and practicability. Where, for example, it is impossible to find these other persons or impracticable to bring them in, the action may proceed as to those parties who are present.

* * *

The action in these cases is against the distributee personally, and not against the estate; and it is independent of the will and the probate proceeding. Each distributee is individually held as a constructive trustee solely of the property which came to him, and none is interested in the granting or denial of similar relief as to any other. Where there are a number of legatees and devisees, they would all appear to be "necessary" parties in the sense that the main issue, the validity of the testamentary disposition of the property of decedent, affects their property interests, and the entire matter, the disposition of all of the decedent's property, cannot be finally settled without a binding adjudication for or against every legatee or devisee. Hence, the court will usually order them served and brought in unless there is some good reason for not doing so. But the absent defendants in such a case are not indispensable parties. Unlike the situations discussed above, in which any judgment would necessarily affect the rights of the absent persons, the case here is one where plaintiff may litigate her claim against the appearing defendants alone and obtain a decree which binds them alone. The absent defendants, not being before the court, will not be bound by the judgment, whether favorable or unfavorable, and their property interests will not be affected.

* * *

Only brief mention need be made of the contention that the prosecution of the action against less than all of the distributees will cause inconvenience and multiplicity of suits to the injury of the executor. These are all matters within the discretion of the court to consider in connection with its policy to settle the entire controversy in one proceeding, if possible. * * *

We have refrained from discussing the question whether the lower court's denial of the motion to bring in the absent defendants was, under the circumstances, an abuse of discretion. If they were readily available and could have been brought in without serious difficulty, it may well be that the motion should have been granted. On the other hand, if, as is asserted by respondents, many reside outside the state or the country, great difficulty might be encountered in any attempt to bring them in, and the trial might be indefinitely delayed, to the detriment of the present parties. The fact that the interests of the absent defendants are trivial as compared with that of the residuary legatee, which received over seventy-five percent of the estate, is perhaps some indication of the reason why plaintiff chose to go to trial against the latter alone. All these considerations, however, were for the trial court in the first instance, and its determination, though reviewable in the proper manner, cannot be attacked on an application for writ of prohibition.

The alternative writ, heretofore issued, is discharged, and the peremptory writ is denied.

NOTES AND QUESTIONS

1. Before the adoption of Federal Rule 19, the principle of mandatory joinder was a judicially created doctrine. SHIELDS v. BARROW, 58 U.S. (17 How.) 130, 15 L.Ed. 158 (1854), established the notion that parties could be classified as necessary or indispensable depending on the nature of their substantive rights ("joint" or "severable"). The consequences of this classification were extremely important. If an absent party who was not subject to the jurisdiction of the court or whose joinder would destroy the pre-existing diversity of citizenship was labeled indispensable, the entire action had to be dismissed. On the other hand, if the absentee merely was necessary, the court might exercise its discretion in determining whether or not to continue without that person. Because a plaintiff might have been deprived of any remedy if a party was found to be indispensable, courts often strained to avoid that conclusion. As might be suspected, this method had a debilitating effect on the standard for classification. See Comment, *The Litigant and the Absentee in Federal Multiparty Practice*, 116 U. Pa. L. Rev. 531 (1968).

2. WARNER v. PACIFIC TEL. & TEL. CO., 121 Cal.App.2d 497, 263 P.2d 465 (2d Dist.1953), involved the following three successive telephone book listings: (1) Warner, Caryl atty, 639 S Spring—TUkr 9171 Woodland Hills Office, 21042 Rios—DIamnd 85761; (2) Warner, Caryl Mrs. 1600 Westrly Ter—NOrmndy 22011; and (3) Warner, Caryl Mrs. Warner Caryl atty 21042 Rios Wdlnd Hills—DIamnd 85761. The "Mrs. Caryl Warner" in the second listing was the first wife of Caryl Warner; the "Mrs. Caryl Warner" in the third listing was Caryl Warner's wife at the time of the lawsuit. After the telephone company refused to delete or change the second listing, the present Mrs. Warner brought suit against the company for damages on the ground that the existing listings injured her reputation in the community and caused her "emotional distress, humiliation, fear, vexation, annoyance, scorn and ridicule as to her marital status, rendering her sick, with recurrent asthma attacks, to her damage." Plaintiff also asserted that she owned the title "Mrs. Caryl Warner," that the name has acquired a secondary meaning by reason of the professional and social standing of Caryl Warner, that her prestige and

dignity were being depreciated, that the telephone listings constitute an invasion of privacy because they depict plaintiff as a party to a bigamous marriage, and that the telephone company knew or should have known that its maintenance of the listings would cause damage to plaintiff. The telephone company demurred to plaintiff's third amended and supplemental complaint on the ground, *inter alia,* that plaintiff had failed to join an indispensable party—the first Mrs. Caryl Warner. In light of the *Bank of California* case, p. 688, supra, should the California Court of Appeals affirm or reverse the lower court's grant of the demurrer? Why?

3. Is prejudice to defendant and the possibility of inconsistent adjudications only a factor to be weighed as part of a balancing of competing interests or should the threat of multiple liability be elevated to a constitutional level? Is the failure to join an indispensable party really a jurisdictional defect as the *Bank of California* case suggests? See Hazard, *Indispensable Party: The Historical Origin of a Procedural Phantom*, 61 Colum.L.Rev. 1254, 1255–56 (1961).

B. REQUIRED JOINDER OF PERSONS UNDER FEDERAL RULE 19

Read Federal Rule of Civil Procedure 19 and the accompanying material in the Supplement (keep in mind that until 2007, Rule 19 used the common law term "indispensable" to refer to parties who are required to be joined).

PROVIDENT TRADESMENS BANK & TRUST CO. v. PATTERSON

Supreme Court of the United States, 1968.
390 U.S. 102, 88 S.Ct. 733, 19 L.Ed.2d 936.

Certiorari to the Circuit Court of Appeals for the Third Circuit.

MR. JUSTICE HARLAN delivered the opinion of the Court.

This controversy, involving in its present posture the dismissal of a declaratory judgment action for nonjoinder of an "indispensable" party, began nearly 10 years ago with a traffic accident. An automobile owned by Edward Dutcher, who was not present when the accident occurred, was being driven by Donald Cionci, to whom Dutcher had given the keys. John Lynch and John Harris were passengers. The automobile crossed the median strip of the highway and collided with a truck being driven by Thomas Smith. Cionci, Lynch, and Smith were killed and Harris was severely injured.

Three tort actions were brought. Provident Tradesmens Bank, the administrator of the estate of passenger Lynch and petitioner here, sued the estate of the driver, Cionci, in a diversity action. Smith's administratrix, and Harris in person, each brought a state-court action against the estate of Cionci, Dutcher, the owner, and the estate of Lynch. These Smith and Harris actions, for unknown reasons, have never gone to trial and are still pending. The Lynch action against Cionci's estate was settled for $50,000, which the estate of Cionci, being penniless, has never paid.

Dutcher, the owner of the automobile and a defendant in the as yet untried tort actions, had an automobile liability insurance policy with Lumbermens Mutual Casualty Company, a respondent here. That policy had an upper limit of $100,000 for all claims arising out of a single accident. This fund was potentially subject to two different sorts of claims by the tort plaintiffs. First, Dutcher himself might be held vicariously liable as Cionci's "principal"; the likelihood of such a judgment against Dutcher is a matter of considerable doubt and dispute. Second, the policy by its terms covered the direct liability of any person driving Dutcher's car with Dutcher's "permission."

The insurance company had declined, after notice, to defend in the tort action brought by Lynch's estate against the estate of Cionci, believing that Cionci had not had permission and hence was not covered by the policy. The facts allegedly were that Dutcher had entrusted his car to Cionci, but that Cionci had made a detour from the errand for which Dutcher allowed his car to be taken. The estate of Lynch, armed with its $50,000 liquidated claim against the estate of Cionci, brought the present diversity action for a declaration that Cionci's use of the car had been "with permission" of Dutcher. The only named defendants were the company and the estate of Cionci. The other two tort plaintiffs were joined as plaintiffs. Dutcher, a resident of the State of Pennsylvania as were all the plaintiffs, was not joined either as plaintiff or defendant. The failure to join him was not adverted to at the trial level.

The major question of law contested at trial was a state-law question. * * * The District Court * * * directed verdicts in favor of the two estates. * * * The jury * * * found that Cionci had had permission, and hence awarded a verdict to Harris also.

Lumbermens appealed the judgment to the Court of Appeals for the Third Circuit, raising various state-law questions.[1] The Court of Appeals did not reach any of these issues. Instead, after reargument *en banc,* it decided, 5–2, to reverse on two alternative grounds neither of which had been raised in the District Court or by the appellant.

The first of these grounds was that Dutcher was an indispensable party. The court held that the "adverse interests" that had rendered Dutcher incompetent to testify under the Pennsylvania Dead Man Rule also required him to be made a party. The court did not consider whether the fact that a verdict had already been rendered, without objection to the nonjoinder of Dutcher, affected the matter. Nor did it follow the provision of Rule 19 of the Federal Rules of Civil Procedure that findings of

1. Appellants challenged the District Court's ruling on the Dead Man issue that Dutcher was incompetent to testify under Pennsylvania law against an estate if he had an adverse interest to that of the estate, the fairness of submitting the question as to Harris to a jury that had been directed to find in favor of the two estates whose position was factually indistinguishable, and certain instructions.

"indispensability" must be based on stated pragmatic considerations. It held, to the contrary, that the right of a person who "may be affected" by the judgment to be joined is a "substantive" right, unaffected by the federal rules; that a trial court "may not proceed" in the absence of such a person; and that since Dutcher could not be joined as a defendant without destroying diversity jurisdiction the action had to be dismissed.

* * * Concluding that the inflexible approach adopted by the Court of Appeals in this case exemplifies the kind of reasoning that the Rule was designed to avoid, we reverse.

I.

* * *

We may assume, at the outset, that Dutcher falls within the category of persons who, under [Rule 19] (a), should be "joined if feasible." The action was for an adjudication of the validity of certain claims against a fund. Dutcher, faced with the possibility of judgments against him, had an interest in having the fund preserved to cover that potential liability. Hence there existed, when this case went to trial, at least the possibility that a judgment might impede Dutcher's ability to protect his interest, or lead to later relitigation by him.

The optimum solution, an adjudication of the permission question that would be binding on all interested persons, was not "feasible," however, for Dutcher could not be made a defendant without destroying diversity. Hence the problem was the one to which Rule 19(b) appears to address itself: in the absence of a person who "should be joined if feasible," should the court dismiss the action or proceed without him? Since this problem emerged for the first time in the Court of Appeals, there were also two subsidiary questions. First, what was the effect, if any, of the failure of the defendants to raise the matter in the District Court? Second, what was the importance, if any, of the fact that a judgment, binding on the parties although not binding on Dutcher, had already been reached after extensive litigation? The three questions prove, on examination, to be interwoven.

We conclude, upon consideration of the record and applying the "equity and good conscience" test of Rule 19(b), that the Court of Appeals erred in not allowing the judgment to stand.

Rule 19(b) suggests four "interests" that must be examined in each case to determine whether, in equity and good conscience, the court should proceed without a party whose absence from the litigation is compelled. Each of these interests must, in this case, be viewed entirely from an appellate perspective since the matter of joinder was not considered in the trial court. First, the plaintiff has an interest in having a forum. Before the trial, the strength of this interest obviously depends upon whether a satisfactory alternative forum exists. On appeal, if the plaintiff has won, he has a strong additional interest in preserving his judgment. Second, the defendant may properly wish to avoid multiple litigation, or inconsistent relief, or sole responsibility for a liability he shares with another. After trial, however, if the defendant has failed to assert this interest, it is quite proper to consider it foreclosed.

Third, there is the interest of the outsider whom it would have been desirable to join. Of course, since the outsider is not before the court, he cannot be bound by the judgment rendered. This means, however, only that a judgment is not *res judicata* as to, or legally enforceable against, a nonparty. It obviously does not mean either (a) that a court may never issue a judgment that, in practice, affects a nonparty or (b) that (to the contrary) a court may always proceed without considering the potential effect on nonparties simply because they are not "bound" in the technical sense. Instead, as Rule 19(a) expresses it, the court must consider the extent to which the judgment may "as a practical matter impair or impede his ability to protect" his interest in the subject matter [this provision is now Rule 19(a)(1)(B)(i) and the language has been altered]. When a case has reached the appeal stage the matter is more complex. The judgment appealed from may not in fact affect the interest of any outsider even though there existed, before trial, a possibility that a judgment affecting his interest would be rendered. When necessary, however, a court of appeals should, on its own initiative, take steps to protect the absent party, who of course had no opportunity to plead and prove his interest below.

Fourth, there remains the interest of the courts and the public in complete, consistent, and efficient settlement of controversies. We read the Rule's third criterion, whether the judgment issued in the absence of the nonjoined person will be "adequate," to refer to this public stake in settling disputes by wholes, whenever possible, for clearly the plaintiff, who himself chose both the forum and the parties defendant, will not be heard to complain about the sufficiency of the relief obtainable against them. After trial, considerations of efficiency of course include the fact that the time and expense of a trial have already been spent.

Rule 19(b) also directs a district court to consider the possibility of shaping relief to accommodate these four interests. Commentators had argued that greater attention should be paid to this potential solution to a joinder stymie, and the Rule now makes it explicit that a court should consider modification of a judgment as an alternative to dismissal. Needless to say, a court of appeals may also properly require suitable modification as a condition of affirmance.

Had the Court of Appeals applied Rule 19's criteria to the facts of the present case, it could hardly have reached the conclusion it did. We begin with the plaintiffs' viewpoint. It is difficult to decide at this stage whether they would have had an "adequate" remedy had the action been dismissed before trial for nonjoinder: we cannot here determine whether the plaintiffs could have brought the same action, against the same parties plus Dutcher, in a state court. After trial, however, the "adequacy" of this hypothetical alternative, from the plaintiffs' point of view, was obviously greatly diminished. Their interest in preserving a fully litigated judgment should be overborne only by rather greater opposing considerations than would be required at an earlier stage when the plaintiffs' only concern was for a federal rather than a state forum.

Opposing considerations in this case are hard to find. The defendants had no stake, either asserted or real, in the joinder of Dutcher. They showed no interest in joinder until the Court of Appeals took the matter into its own hands. This properly forecloses any interest of theirs, but for purposes of clarity we note that the insurance company, whose liability was limited to $100,000, had or will have full opportunity to litigate each claim on that fund against the claimant involved. Its only concern with the absence of Dutcher was and is to obtain a windfall escape from its defeat at trial.

The interest of the outsider, Dutcher, is more difficult to reckon. The Court of Appeals, concluding that it should not follow Rule 19's command to determine whether, as a practical matter, the judgment impaired the nonparty's ability to protect his rights, simply quoted the District Court's reasoning on the Dead Man issue as proof that Dutcher had a "right" to be joined:

> The subject matter of this suit is the coverage of Lumbermens' policy issued to Dutcher. Depending upon the outcome of this trial, Dutcher may have the policy all to himself or he may have to share its coverage with the Cionci Estate, thereby extending the availability of the proceeds of the policy to satisfy verdicts and judgments in favor of the two Estate plaintiffs. Sharing the coverage of a policy of insurance with finite limits with another, and thereby making that policy available to claimants against that other person is immediately worth less than having the coverage of such policy available to Dutcher alone. By the outcome in the instant case, to the extent that the two Estate plaintiffs will have the proceeds of the policy available to them in their claims against Cionci's estate, Dutcher will lose a measure of protection. Conversely, to the extent that the proceeds of this policy are not available to the two Estate plaintiffs Dutcher will gain. * * * It is sufficient for the purpose of determining adversity [of interest] that it appears clearly that the measure of Dutcher's protection under this policy of insurance is dependent upon the outcome of this suit. That being so, Dutcher's interest in these proceedings is adverse to the interest of the two Estate plaintiffs, the parties who represent, on this record, the interests of the deceased persons in the matter in controversy.[11]

There is a logical error in the Court of Appeals' appropriation of this reasoning for its own quite different purposes: Dutcher had an "adverse" interest (sufficient to invoke the Dead Man Rule) because he would have been *benefited* by a ruling *in favor of* the insurance company; the question

11. 218 F.Supp. 802, 805–806, quoted at 365 F.2d, at 805.

before the Court of Appeals, however, was whether Dutcher was *harmed* by the judgment *against* the insurance company.

The two questions are not the same. If the three plaintiffs had lost to the insurance company on the permission issue, that loss would have ended the matter favorably to Dutcher. If, as has happened, the three plaintiffs obtain a judgment against the insurance company on the permission issue, Dutcher may still claim that as a nonparty he is not estopped by that judgment from relitigating the issue. At that point it might be argued that Dutcher should be bound by the previous decision because, although technically a nonparty, he had purposely bypassed an adequate opportunity to intervene. We do not now decide whether such an argument would be correct under the circumstances of this case. If, however, Dutcher is properly foreclosed by his failure to intervene in the present litigation, then the joinder issue considered in the Court of Appeals vanishes, for any rights of Dutcher's have been lost by his own inaction.

If Dutcher is not foreclosed by his failure to intervene below, then he is not "bound" by the judgment in favor of the insurance company and, in theory, he has not been harmed. There remains, however, the practical question whether Dutcher is likely to have any need, and if so will have any opportunity, to relitigate. The only possible threat to him is that if the fund is used to pay judgments against Cionci the money may in fact have disappeared before Dutcher has an opportunity to assert his interest. Upon examination, we find this supposed threat neither large nor unavoidable.

The state-court actions against Dutcher had lain dormant for years at the pleading stage by the time the Court of Appeals acted. Petitioner asserts here that under the applicable Pennsylvania vicarious liability law there is virtually no chance of recovery against Dutcher. We do not accept this assertion as fact, but the matter could have been explored below. Furthermore, even in the event of tort judgments against Dutcher, it is unlikely that he will be prejudiced by the outcome here. The potential claimants against Dutcher himself are identical with the potential claimants against Cionci's estate. Should the claimants seek to collect from Dutcher personally, he may be able to raise the permission issue defensively, making it irrelevant that the actual monies paid from the fund may have disappeared: Dutcher can assert that Cionci did not have his permission and that therefore the payments made on Cionci's behalf out of Dutcher's insurance policy should properly be credited against Dutcher's own liability. Of course, when Dutcher raises this defense he may lose, either on the merits of the permission issue or on the ground that the issue is foreclosed by Dutcher's failure to intervene in the present case, but Dutcher will not have been prejudiced by the failure of the District Court here to order him joined.

If the Court of Appeals was unconvinced that the threat to Dutcher was trivial, it could nevertheless have avoided all difficulties by proper phrasing of the decree. The District Court, for unspecified reasons, had refused to order immediate payment on the Cionci judgment. Payment could have been withheld pending the suits against Dutcher and relitigation (if that became necessary) by him. In this Court, furthermore, counsel for petitioners represented orally that they, the tort plaintiffs, would accept a limitation of all claims to the amount of the insurance policy. Obviously such a compromise could have been reached below had the Court of Appeals been willing to abandon its rigid approach and seek ways to preserve what was, as to the parties, subject to the appellants' other contentions, a perfectly valid judgment.

The suggestion of potential relitigation of the question of "permission" raises the fourth "interest" at stake in joinder cases—efficiency. It might have been preferable, at the trial level, if there were a forum available in which both the company and Dutcher could have been made defendants, to dismiss the action and force the plaintiffs to go elsewhere. Even this preference would have been highly problematical, however, for the actual threat of relitigation by Dutcher depended on there being judgments against him and on the amount of the fund, which was not revealed to the District Court. By the time the case reached the Court of Appeals, however, the problematical preference on efficiency grounds had entirely disappeared: there was no reason then to throw away a valid judgment just because it did not theoretically settle the whole controversy.

II.

Application of Rule 19(b)'s "equity and good conscience" test for determining whether to proceed or dismiss would doubtless have led to a contrary result below. The Court of Appeals' reasons for disregarding the Rule remain to be examined. The majority of the court concluded that the Rule was inapplicable because "substantive" rights are involved, and substantive rights are not affected by the Federal Rules. Although the court did not articulate exactly what the substantive rights are, or what law determines them, we take it to have been making the following argument: (1) there is a category of persons called "indispensable parties"; (2) that category is defined by substantive law and the definition cannot be modified by rule; (3) the right of a person falling within that category to participate in the lawsuit in question is also a substantive matter, and is absolute.

With this we may contrast the position that is reflected in Rule 19. Whether a person is "indispensable," that is, whether a particular lawsuit must be dismissed in the absence of that person, can only be determined in the context of particular litigation. There is a large category, whose limits are not presently in question, of persons who, in the Rule's terminology, should be "joined if feasible," and who, in the older terminology, were called either necessary or indispensable parties. Assuming the existence of a person who should be joined if feasible, the only further question arises when joinder is not possible and the court must decide whether to dismiss or to proceed without him. To use the familiar but confusing terminology, the decision to proceed is a decision that the absent person is merely "necessary" while the decision to dismiss is a decision that he is "indispensable." The decision whether to dismiss (i.e., the decision whether the person missing is "indispensable") must be based on factors varying with the different cases, some such factors being substantive, some procedural, some compelling by themselves, and some subject to balancing against opposing interests. Rule 19 does not prevent the assertion of compelling substantive interests; it merely commands the courts to examine each controversy to make certain that the interests really exist. To say that a court "must" dismiss in the absence of an indispensable party and that it "cannot proceed" without him puts the matter the wrong way around: a court does not know whether a particular person is "indispensable" until it has examined the situation to determine whether it can proceed without him.

The Court of Appeals concluded, although it was the first court to hold, that the 19th century joinder cases in this Court created a federal, common-law, substantive right in a certain class of persons to be joined in the corresponding lawsuits. At the least, that was not the way the matter started. The joinder problem first arose in equity and in the earliest case giving rise to extended discussion the problem was the relatively simple one of the inefficiency of litigation involving only some of the interested persons. [Elmendorf v. Taylor, 23 U.S. (10 Wheat.) 152, 6 L.Ed. 289 (1825).] * * *

Following this case there arose three cases, also in equity, that the Court of Appeals here held to have declared a "substantive" right to be joined. It is true that these cases involved what would now be called "substantive" rights. This substantive involvement of the absent person with the controversy before the Court was, however, in each case simply an inescapable fact of the situation presented to the Court for adjudication. The Court in each case left the outsider with no more "rights" than it had already found belonged to him. The question in each case was simply whether, given the substantive involvement of the outsider, it was proper to proceed to adjudicate as between the parties.

* * *

The most influential of the cases in which this Court considered the question whether to proceed or dismiss in the absence of an interested but not joinable outsider is Shields v. Barrow, 17 How. 130, 15 L.Ed. 158, referred to in the opinion below. There the Court attempted, perhaps unfortunately, to stage general definitions of those persons without whom litigation could or could not proceed. In the former category were placed

> Persons having an interest in the controversy, and who ought to be made parties, in order that the court may act on that rule which requires it to decide on, and finally determine the entire controversy, and do complete justice, by adjusting all the rights involved in it. These persons are commonly termed necessary parties; but if their interests are separable from those of the parties before the court, so that the court can proceed to a decree, and do complete and final

> justice, without affecting other persons not before the court, the latter are not indispensable parties.

The persons in the latter category were

> Persons who not only have an interest in the controversy, but an interest of such a nature that a final decree cannot be made without either affecting that interest, or leaving the controversy in such a condition that its final termination may be wholly inconsistent with equity and good conscience.

These generalizations are still valid today, and they are consistent with the requirements of Rule 19, but they are not a substitute for the analysis required by that Rule. Indeed, the second *Shields* definition states, in rather different fashion, the criteria for decision announced in Rule 19(b). One basis for dismissal is prejudice to the rights of an absent party that "*cannot*" be avoided in issuance of a final decree. Alternatively, if the decree can be so written that it protects the interests of the absent persons, but as so written it leaves the controversy so situated that the outcome may be inconsistent with "equity and good conscience," the suit should be dismissed.

The majority of the Court of Appeals read Shields v. Barrow to say that a person whose interests "may be affected" by the decree of the court is an indispensable party, and that all indispensable parties have a "substantive right" to have suits dismissed in their absence. We are unable to read *Shields* as saying either. It dealt only with persons whose interests must, unavoidably, be affected by a decree and it said nothing about substantive rights. Rule 19(b), which the Court of Appeals dismissed as an ineffective attempt to change the substantive rights stated in *Shields,* is, on the contrary, a valid statement of the criteria for determining whether to proceed or dismiss in the forced absence of an interested person. It takes, for aught that now appears, adequate account of the very real, very substantive claims to fairness on the part of outsiders that may arise in some cases. This, however, simply is not such a case.

* * *

The judgment is vacated and the case is remanded to the Court of Appeals * * *.

NOTES AND QUESTIONS

1. *Provident Tradesmens* interpreted the amended version of Federal Rule 19, which was promulgated in 1966. Examine the Advisory Committee's Note to Rule 19, which is set out in the Supplement. What impact does the amendment have on the distinction between "persons required to be joined if feasible," of Rule 19(a), and "a person who is required to be joined if feasible cannot be joined," of Rule 19(b)? Given the amendment, what is the purpose of Rule 12(b)(7)? Of Rule 12(h)? For a negative appraisal of the amended text, see Fink, *Indispensable Parties and the Proposed Amendment to Federal Rule 19*, 74 Yale L.J. 403 (1965). For a discussion urging further reform of Federal

Rule 19, see Freer, *Rethinking Compulsory Joinder: A Proposal to Restructure Federal Rule 19*, 60 N.Y.U. L. Rev. 1061 (1985).

2. What was the basis of the Court's finding in *Provident Tradesmens* with regard to prejudice for purposes of Rule 19(b) if Dutcher was not joined? Consider the following comments in an article written shortly after the Third Circuit decision dismissing the action and before the Supreme Court's decision:

> * * * How has Dutcher been affected? The judgment declaring that Cionci was driving with permission does not bind Dutcher legally, since he was not a party. Dutcher is free to contest the point with all, including the insurer. Be it noted that although he testified in the action, Dutcher made no attempt to intervene; as the minority suggests, he might have reasonably preferred to stay out of the action. Whereas a judgment declaring Cionci to be an insured did not bind Dutcher, a judgment the other way would very likely have inured to Dutcher's benefit * * *.

Kaplan, *Continuing Work of the Civil Committee: 1966 Amendments of the Federal Rules of Civil Procedure (I)*, 81 Harv.L.Rev. 356, 373 (1967).

In what ways might the court shape relief in order to lessen any prejudice? Is the court free simply to grant a remedy other than the one originally requested—for example, by awarding money damages when specific performance might have a detrimental impact on the absentee? Of what importance is the availability of another forum in determining whether the action must be dismissed in the absence of someone whose joinder is not feasible? For a case in which the court determined that it was impossible to shape the relief so as to avoid prejudice to absent parties, see Wichita & Affiliated Tribes of Oklahoma v. Hodel, 788 F.2d 765, 776 (D.C.Cir.1986).

3. What weight should be given to the various factors listed in Federal Rule 19? Because there is no precise formula for determining whether a particular nonparty must be joined under Rule 19(a), the decision has to be made in light of the general policies of the Rule. Can you articulate what those policies are? For example, what is the difference between the Rule 19(a)(1)(A) standard that in the absence of the nonparty "the court cannot accord complete relief among existing parties," and the factor listed in Rule 19(b)(3), "whether a judgment rendered in the person's absence would be adequate"? The test set out in Rule 19(a)(1)(B) focuses on the prejudicial effect of not joining the absentee. What type of prejudice must be shown to meet this requirement? See generally Tobias, *Rule 19 and the Public Rights Exception to Party Joinder*, 65 N.C.L.Rev. 745 (1987).

4. Should a court dismiss an action because of the plaintiff's failure to join a required party plaintiff, even though the defendant can join the missing party as a Rule 13(h) party to a compulsory counterclaim? In ASSOCIATED DRY GOODS CORP. v. TOWERS FINANCIAL CORP., 920 F.2d 1121, 1124 (2d Cir.1990), the defendant, a commercial subtenant, sought to dismiss the tenant's action for payment of rent because the tenant had failed to join the building's owner, 417 Fifth, as an indispensable party plaintiff. The plaintiff did not join the building owner because he was nondiverse, which would strip the court of subject-matter jurisdiction. The District Court dismissed the action pursuant to Rule 19(b). The Second Circuit reversed:

The drafters of Rule 19(b) did not assign relative weight to each of the factors enumerated in the Rule. Instead, the Rule allows courts themselves to determine the emphasis to be placed on each consideration according to "the facts of [the] given case and in light of the governing equity-and-good-conscience test." * * * In this case, we view as dispositive Towers' ability to avoid all prejudice to itself by asserting a compulsory counterclaim against Associated pursuant to Rule 13(a) and adding 417 Fifth as a party to the counterclaim under Rule 13(h). * * *

5. What should the result be when plaintiff, a citizen of state A, sues defendant, a citizen of state B, in a federal district court in state B, and, on defendant's motion, the court requires that X, a citizen of state A, be joined as a defendant in the action? See 7 Wright, Miller & Kane, Federal Practice and Procedure: Civil 3d § 1611; Steinman, *Postremoval Changes in the Party Structure of Diversity Cases: The Old Law, the New Law, and Rule 19*, 38 U. Kan. L. Rev. 863 (1990).

6. REPUBLIC OF THE PHILIPPINES v. PIMENTEL, ___ U.S. ___, 128 S.Ct. 2180, 171 L.Ed.2d 131 (2008), concerned the application of Rule 19 to a foreign government that claimed sovereign immunity from suit. The case involved competing claims to $35 million that had been deposited illegally into a New York bank on behalf of Ferdinand Marcos while he was President of the Republic of the Philippines. The New York bank holding the assets filed a federal interpleader action in the District of Hawaii to resolve rival claims by the Republic of the Philippines, a special Philippine Commission investigating the former President's alleged misuse of office, and victims of human rights abuses. On a parallel track, the Republic and the Commission filed an action in a special Philippines court to recover the assets; they moved to dismiss the federal interpleader action on the ground that they were entitled to sovereign immunity and that in their absence the interpleader action could not go forward under Federal Rule 19. The Ninth Circuit held that the interpleader action could go forward even if the foreign entities were absent, finding that their claims were time barred, and affirmed the District Court's award of the contested assets to the human rights victims (known as the "Pimental class"). The United States Supreme Court granted certiorari, and ordered dismissal of the interpleader action on the ground that the federal appellate court erred in giving insufficient weight to the assertion of sovereign immunity and to the prejudice that the foreign parties [collectively, the "Republic"] would suffer if the interpleader action were to go forward in their absence.

In applying Rule 19(b), the majority emphasized that joinder decisions "can be complex, and determinations are case specific." Looking to the first Rule 19(b) factor, the Court held that the decision to proceed in the absence of the Republic ignored the substantial prejudice that the absent party would suffer, given the Republic's "unique interest in resolving the ownership" issues "and in determining if, and how, the assets should be used to compensate those persons who suffered grievous injury under Marcos. There is a comity interest in allowing a foreign state to use its own courts for a dispute if it has a right to do so." Id. at ___, 128 S.Ct. at 2190, 171 L.Ed.2d at 145–46. Turning to Rule 19(b)(2), the Court concluded that prejudice could not be lessened through the design of alternative remedies. As to Rule 19(b)(3), the appeals court "understood 'adequacy' to refer to satisfaction of the Pimentel class' claims." Id. at ___, 128 S.Ct. at 2193171 L.Ed.2d at 148. However, "adequacy refers to the 'public stake in settling disputes by wholes, whenever possible.' * * * [citing *Provident Tradesmens*, p. 693 supra]." Allowing the federal interpleader action to go forward without the Republic would not, in the Court's view, "further the public interest in settling the dispute as a whole" because the Republic "would not be bound by the judgment * * *." Id. Finally, the Court clarified that under Rule 19(b)(4), the question of plaintiff's adequacy of remedy refers to the stakeholder, not the tort victims. Dismissing the interpleader action would protect the New York bank by providing "an effective defense against piecemeal litigation and inconsistent, conflicting judgments," and, in any event, any prejudice to the stakeholder "is outweighed by prejudice to the absent entities invoking sovereign immunity." Id. at ___, 128 S.Ct. at 2193, 171 L.Ed.2d at 149. The Court concluded:

> The Court of Appeals' failure to give sufficient weight to the likely prejudice to the Republic and the Commission should the interpleader proceed in their absence would, in the usual course, warrant reversal and remand for further proceedings. In this case, however, that error and our further analysis under the additional provisions of Rule 19(b) lead us to conclude the action must be dismissed. This leaves the Pimentel class, which has waited for years now to be compensated for grievous wrongs, with no immediate way to recover on its judgment against Marcos. And it leaves * * * [the stakeholder] without a judgment.
>
> The balance of equities may change in due course. One relevant change may occur if it appears that the Sandiganbayan [the Philippines court hearing the Republic's claim] cannot or will not issue its ruling within a reasonable period of time. Other changes could result when and if there is a ruling. * * * We do note that if [the stakeholder] * * *, or other parties, elect to commence further litigation in light of changed circumstances, it would not be necessary to file the new action in the District Court where this action arose, provided venue and jurisdictional requirements are satisfied elsewhere. The present action, however, may not proceed."

Id. at ___, 128 S.Ct. at 2193, 171 L.Ed.2d at 149–50. Justice Stevens in part dissented. He criticized the majority for taking "a more 'inflexible approach' than the Rule contemplates * * * [citing *Provident Tradesmens*, p. 693, supra]" and for ignoring the interest of all parties "in the prompt resolution" of claims to the disputed assets. Id. at ___, 128 S.Ct. at 2197, 171 L.Ed.2d at 153.

SECTION E. IMPLEADER

1. THE HISTORICAL USE OF IMPLEADER

When *A* sues *B*, there is often a third party, *C*, who may ultimately be liable to *B* for all or some part of the damages which *A* might recover. This liability over may be based on such legal relationships as those which arise from a contract of indemnity for loss or liability or a right to contribution from a joint tortfeasor. If it were necessary for *B* to

> institute a separate action to recover reimbursement from *C*, the issue of *B*'s liability to *A* would often have to be relitigated between *B* and *C*, since *C*, not a party to the original litigation, would generally not be bound by the prior determination. * * * Even if *B* could obtain a wholly consistent result against *C*, the courts would have been burdened by two trials and *B* might have been seriously handicapped by having to satisfy *A*'s judgment long before his recovery over from *C*.* * *
>
> * * * [Federal Rule 14(a)] has its roots in the common-law procedure of "vouching to warranty," whereby a person whose title to land had been attacked could notify his vendor of the attack if the latter had warranted the title. The vendor, whether or not he chose to participate, would then be bound by the prior determination in a subsequent suit by his vendee. * * *

Developments in the Law—Multiparty Litigation in the Federal Courts, 71 Harv.L.Rev. 877, 907 (1958). See also Neiderman & Reed, *Vouching In Under the U.C.C.: Its History, Modern Use, and Questions About Its Continued Viability,* 23 J.L. & Com. 1, 1 (2003); Degnan & Barton, *Vouching to Quality Warranty: Case Law and Commercial Code,* 51 Calif.L.Rev. 471 (1963).

2. THIRD–PARTY PRACTICE UNDER FEDERAL RULE 14

Read Federal Rule of Civil Procedure 14 and the material accompanying it in the Supplement.

JEUB v. B/G FOODS, INC.

United States District Court, District of Minnesota, 1942.
2 F.R.D. 238.

NORDBYE, DISTRICT JUDGE. The facts are briefly these: The complainants seek to recover damages from the defendant, B/G Foods, Inc., on the grounds that, in one of the restaurants operated by this defendant, they were served with certain ham which was contaminated, unwholesome, and deleterious to the health, causing complainants to become sick and distressed to their damage. * * * Prior to the service of the answer, on application of the defendant, an ex parte order was obtained, making Swift and Company a third-party defendant. The third-party complaint set forth that the ham served was canned "Swift Premium Ham", a product of Swift and Company, and purchased in a sealed can by B/G Foods the day preceding the serving of the ham to the complainants. It is asserted that B/G Foods was entirely free from any blame or negligence in connection therewith. It is further alleged in the third-party complaint that "if any of said ham was unwholesome, poisonous, deleterious or otherwise in any way unfit for human consumption, such condition was caused solely and entirely by negligence and carelessness and unlawful conduct on the part of Swift and Company." Further, that "Swift and Company is liable to indemnify and reimburse B/G Foods, Inc., for the whole amount of any recovery made by plaintiff, * * * against B/G Foods, Inc., on account of said ham being served to her in its food shop. * * * " Judgment is prayed that any recovery be against Swift and Company and not B/G Foods, Inc., and that B/G Foods, Inc., have judgment against Swift and Company for any and all sums which may be adjudged against B/G Foods, Inc., in favor of the plaintiff.

The motion to vacate the order is based on the showing that plaintiffs have not amended, and have refused to amend, their complaints to state any cause of action against Swift and Company. It is therefore the position of the third-party defendant that no relief can be granted against it in this proceeding; that [Federal] Rule 14 * * * is merely procedural and does not create any substantive rights; that no right of contribution or indemnity exists under the Minnesota law merely because a suit has been commenced; and that the party must have suffered some loss or paid more than his share of the loss before any rights will inure. It is pointed out that, as yet, the B/G Foods has suffered no loss and has made no payment growing out of the incident in question.

That the rights over and against Swift and Company, which B/G Foods may have by reason of any loss sustained by it, must be governed by the substantive laws of this State is entirely clear. The invoking of the third-party procedural practice must not do violence to the substantive rights of the parties. However, an acceleration or an expedition of the presentation of such rights does not conflict with any Minnesota law. [Federal] Rule 14 * * * permits the impleader of a party "who is or may be liable." [This provision has been renumbered as Rule 14(a)(1) by the 2007 restyling of the Federal Rules.] The fact that an independent action for money recovery could not be brought at this time does not militate against B/G Foods' right to invoke a procedure which will determine rights of the parties concurrently with that of the basic proceeding, and if and when any loss has been sustained as to which Swift and Company is liable over, the laws of this State in regard thereto may be made effective. * * * Rule 14 is not restricted to the rights of indemnity or contribution which are presently enforcible [sic] * * *.

The apparent purpose of Rule 14 is to provide suitable machinery whereby the rights of all parties may be determined in one proceeding. Manifestly if Swift and Company is liable over to B/G Foods, Inc., for any or all damages sustained by reason of the tortious act alleged, no cogent reason is suggested why the original defendant should not avail itself of this rule. Otherwise, B/G Foods, Inc., would be required to await the outcome of the present suit, and then if plaintiffs recover, to institute an independent action for contribution or indemnity. The rule under consideration was promulgated to avoid this very circuity of proceeding. Neither is any good reason suggested why the determination of the entire controversy in one proceeding will prejudice the rights of any of the parties. Certainly, plaintiffs cannot complain. They have not availed themselves of the opportunity to join Swift and Company as a party defendant. To require the same jury to determine the controversy between the third-party plaintiff and third-party defendant will not harm or jeopardize their rights or position before these triers of fact. The rights of Swift and Company are likewise not prejudiced by being made a third-party defendant. If it is liable over, it is concerned with the payment by B/G Foods, Inc., of any loss or damage obtained by these plaintiffs. However, the recognition or preservation of that right presents no particular difficulty. Any judgment against it by way of contribution or indemnity may be stayed until the judgment in the original proceeding against the B/G Foods, Inc., is paid or satisfied. One jury impaneled to determine the entire controversy may not only save time and expense, but it is fair to assume that the ends of justice will be served by disposition of the entire matter through the facilities of one jury. * * *

The motion, therefore, to vacate the order making Swift and Company a third-party defendant in each of the above-entitled cases, is denied. * * *

TOO, INC. v. KOHL'S DEPARTMENT STORES, INC.

United States District Court, Southern District of New York, 2003.
213 F.R.D. 138.

MARRERO, DISTRICT JUDGE:

Plaintiff Too, Inc., ("Too") brought this action alleging copyright infringement, trademark infringement and unfair competition. Defendant Windstar Apparel, Inc. ("Windstar") has moved the Court, pursuant to Fed.R.Civ.P. 14(a) [now Rule 14(a)(1)], for leave to file a third-party complaint seeking contribution and indemnification from two of Windstar's former employees, Mia DeCaro ("DeCaro") and Paula Abraham ("Abraham"). For the reasons set forth below, the motion is granted in part and denied in part.

I. Background

* * *

Windstar, which is engaged in the production and sale of apparel, hired DeCaro and Abraham in or about November, 2000. DeCaro and Abraham were employed to start up a girls sleep-wear division. Specifically, DeCaro was employed as Head Designer for Windstar and Abraham was the Windstar salesperson in charge of the Kohl's Department Stores, Inc. ("Kohl's") account, responsible for all sales to Kohl's. Windstar alleges that DeCaro represented to Jae C. Han ("Han"), Windstar's production manager, that she had created each of the designs Too alleges infringed their copyrights and trademarks and that she knew her designs were to be sold by Windstar to third party retailers, including Kohl's. Similarly, Windstar implicates Abraham for potential contribution by alleging that she proceeded to sell girls sleep-wear with the alleged infringing copyright and trademarks, knowing the sleep-wear to contain designs that allegedly infringed Too's copyrights and trademarks.

* * *

II. Discussion

A. *Standard of Review*

* * * Unless the third-party plaintiff files the third-party complaint within ten days of serving the original answer, the third-party plaintiff must seek leave from the court to file the third-party complaint. * * * Impleader is appropriate when the third-party defendant's liability to the third-party plaintiff is "dependent upon the outcome of the main claim" or the third-party defendant is "potentially secondarily liable as a contributor to the defendant." * * * The purpose of this rule is to promote judicial efficiency by eliminating the necessity for the defendant to bring a separate cause of action against a third-party for contribution. * * *

The district court has considerable discretion in deciding whether to permit a third-party complaint. * * * Upon determination that a third-party complaint would be appropriate and foster the interest of judicial economy, the factors to be considered in determining whether to grant leave to implead a third-party defendant are: (i) whether the movant deliberately delayed or was derelict in filing the motion; (ii) whether impleading would unduly delay or complicate the trial; (iii) whether impleading would prejudice the third-party defendant; and (iv) whether the third-party complaint states a claim upon which relief can be granted. * * * " 'The court must balance the benefits derived from impleader—that is, the benefits of settling related matters in one suit—against the potential prejudice to the plaintiff and third-party defendants.' " * * *

C. [sic] Contribution

There can be no dispute that the third-party complaint for contribution proposed by Windstar arises from the "same aggregate core of facts which is determinative [of] the plaintiff's claim". * * * DeCaro and Abraham would be potentially liable for contribution if, and only if, Windstar were found liable on Too's cause of action against it, and DeCaro and Abraham's potential liability is derivative of Windstar's liability. * * * Furthermore, DeCaro and Abraham are material witnesses in the main cause of action. * * * If the third-party complaint is not allowed, Windstar would have to start a separate action, and repeat much of the proceedings and discovery that has already occurred in the case brought by Too against Windstar. Thus, the purpose of judicial economy would be served by allowing the third-party complaint for contribution. * * *

The question here is whether the benefits of judicial economy at this stage of the case are outweighed by the various concerns Too raises. * * *

Under New York law, "two or more persons who are subject to liability for damages for the same personal injury, injury to property or wrongful death, may claim contribution among them whether or not an action has been brought or a judgment has been rendered against the person from whom contribution is sought." N.Y. Civil Practice Law and Rules * * * § 1401. * * *

* * * In order to find that a party contributed to infringement, it is required that the third-party plaintiff demonstrate that the third-party defendant either had knowledge, or "reason to know" of the infringing activity. * * *

Windstar does state a claim upon which relief can be granted. In Windstar's proposed Third Party Complaint * * * Windstar alleges that DeCaro and Abraham had knowledge of the alleged infringing activity and materially contributed to the alleged infringement. * * *

* * *

The Court may consider the merits of a proposed third-party claim at this stage of the proceedings to the extent that the third-party complaint "would foster an obviously unmeritorious claim." * * * However, such an obviously unmeritorious claim is not present here. * * *

Finally, the Court must consider whether the third-party complaint for contribution would unduly prejudice the third-party defendants or unduly delay the proceedings. The Court finds that, under the circumstances of this case, neither concern is grave enough to sufficiently outweigh the interest of judicial economy.

Windstar does not foresee the Proposed Complaint creating any need for further discovery since the depositions of DeCaro and Abraham have already been taken. * * *

Too also asserts that impleading DeCaro and Abraham will cause the third-party defendants great prejudice. However, the specific reasons for the prejudice that they cite, that the need for DeCaro and Abraham to obtain legal counsel is burdensome and that their testimony will be chilled, are not persuasive. The need for legal counsel would present itself at a later time, in any event, in a potential suit by Windstar for contribution from DeCaro and Abraham, and such representation would likely be more costly, since discovery and other proceedings would have to be repeated. * * *

* * * Given the interest in judicial economy and the other factors discussed above, the untimeliness should not prevent the filing of the third-party complaint for contribution. Moreover, the accusation made by Too that the delay was intentional and meant to harass are not sufficient-

ly supported to convince this Court that leave to file the third-party complaint should be denied.

D. Indemnification

Windstar's request to file a third-party complaint against DeCaro and Abraham for indemnification must be denied because it is clearly without merit. Windstar admits that since it has no contractual claim for indemnification, the basis for its indemnification claim is the common law. Under New York law, however, "common-law indemnity is barred altogether where the party seeking indemnification was itself at fault, and both tortfeasors violated the same duty to the plaintiff . . ." * * *.

In this case, if Windstar were found to have infringed Too's copyrights, trademarks and/or to have engaged in unfair competition, attributing to it also liability from Defendants Han and Park, it is highly unlikely to be found blameless, with all fault lying on DeCaro and Abraham.* * * Han, as the production manager, whether or not he forged DeCaro's signature as she alleges, was ultimately responsible for filing the alleged infringing copyrights and was the manager in charge of producing the alleged infringing sleep-wear. Certainly Park, and likely Han as well, in their roles at Windstar, were responsible for policing the conduct of DeCaro and Abraham, even if the latter individuals were the primary infringers. * * *

Here, Windstar could not escape all liability by relegating to Abraham and DeCaro the entire responsibility for any alleged wrongdoing on its part. Windstar does not even so plead in the Proposed Complaint or in its Memoranda of Law. Therefore, based on the dubious merit of the indemnification claim, this Court can not accept such an unlikely a third-party claim, in particular in light of Windstar's delay in filing discussed above, at this stage in the proceedings. Accordingly, Windstar's request to add a third-party claim for indemnification, for which it offers absolutely no legal support, is denied.

* * *

NOTES AND QUESTIONS

1. Federal Rule 14 was amended in 1963 "to permit a third party to be impleaded without leave of court if the third-party complaint is filed not later than ten days after defendant's original answer is served." 6 Wright, Miller & Kane, Federal Practice and Procedure: Civil 2d § 1443. The original version of the rule limited the availability of third-party practice:

> Permission to the defendant to implead a person, not originally a party, asserted to be liable to the defendant for all or part of the plaintiff's claim against the defendant, was something of an innovation when it was brought into the civil practice on a general basis in 1938. Perhaps by reason of its novelty, this 'third-party practice' of rule 14 was closely guarded. The defendant seeking impleader had always to apply to the

> court for leave: he might move ex parte if he had not yet served his answer; after answer, the more common case, he was obliged to give notice to the plaintiff.

Kaplan, *Amendments of the Federal Rules of Civil Procedure, 1961–1963 (II)*, 77 Harv. L. Rev. 801, 801 (1964). Rule 14(a)(1) now requires that "the third party-plaintiff must, by motion, obtain the court's leave if it files the third-party complaint more than 10 days after serving its original answer."

2. Note that in *Jeub* the applicable state law recognized a substantive right of action but merely failed to provide a procedural device for the acceleration or concurrent determination of the liability as part of the principal lawsuit. In a diversity case in a state that adheres to the common-law rule prohibiting contribution among joint tortfeasors, must a federal court deny impleader of a joint tortfeasor? How might the court shape the relief on an accelerated or contingent claim to reflect the limitations of substantive state law?

3. "In exercising its discretion the court should endeavor to effectuate the purpose of Rule 14, which means that impleader is to be allowed if it will avoid circuity of action and eliminate duplication of suits based on closely related matters." 6 Wright, Miller & Kane, Federal Practice and Procedure: Civil 2d § 1443. How was this purpose carried out in *Too*? Is it appropriate to order separate trials if the litigation becomes too complex?

4. Rule 14 does not allow a defendant to implead an existing defendant. See Horton v. Continental Can Co., 19 F.R.D. 429 (D.Neb.1956). But there are at least two other possible procedures for a defendant to assert its claims against an existing defendant. What are they? What difference does it make if a defendant's claim is brought under Rule 14 or some "other appropriate procedure"? What is the logic of Rules 13(a), (b), and (g) permitting or requiring counterclaims and cross-claims to be asserted against persons who already are parties and Rule 14(a) denying impleader in that context?

5. 28 U.S.C. § 1367 provides for supplemental jurisdiction over additional claims so long as they are part of the same case or controversy as the action over which the court has original jurisdiction. See pp. 336–38, supra. This standard encompasses impleader claims and additional related claims asserted by the third-party plaintiff against the third-party defendant. See Washington Hosp. Center National Rehabilitation Hosp. v. Collier, 947 F.2d 1498, 1501 (D.C.Cir.1991). However, when a federal court's subject-matter jurisdiction is based solely on diversity, Section 1367(b) withholds supplemental jurisdiction from claims asserted by plaintiff against parties joined pursuant to Rule 14. See Viacom Int'l, Inc. v. Kearney, 212 F.3d 721, 727 (2d Cir. 2000). For a discussion of whether in diversity cases Section 1367 should be read to bar supplemental jurisdiction over plaintiff's compulsory counterclaims against third parties impleaded by defendant, see Oakley, Kroger *Redux*, 51 Duke L.J. 663, 665 (2001).

6. According to the existing case law, the statutory venue limitations have no application to Rule 14 claims even if they would require the third-party proceeding to be heard in another district had it been brought as an independent action. How should jurisdiction and venue be treated in the context of a claim by the third-party defendant against the original plaintiff?

See generally 6 Wright, Miller & Kane, Federal Practice and Procedure: Civil 2d § 1445.

7. Are there any limitations on the third-party defendant's ability to assert a claim against the third-party plaintiff? Against the original plaintiff? In HEINTZ & CO. v. PROVIDENT TRADESMENS BANK & TRUST CO. v. KERR, 30 F.R.D. 171 (E.D.Pa.1962), plaintiff alleged that defendant negligently permitted Kerr to open a bank account in plaintiff's name and to draw checks without plaintiff's permission. Defendant impleaded Kerr. Kerr then filed a claim against plaintiff for services rendered and materials furnished to plaintiff in connection with the establishment of a branch office managed by Kerr. The court found Kerr's claim within Rule 14 because it arose out of the same transaction as the original suit. "The only distinction between a counterclaim under Rule 13(a) and the sort of claim we have before us under Rule 14 is that defendant 'must' plead his counterclaim under Rule 13(a) if it grows out of the same transaction or occurrence, whereas under Rule 14, the third party 'may' plead his claim for relief." Calling this "a distinction without a difference," the court emphasized that the nature of the claim is to be determined "by its relation to the transaction that is the subject of the main suit." Id. at 174. If the original plaintiff has a counterclaim arising out of the same transaction as the claim asserted by the third-party defendant, is it compulsory? Can the original plaintiff assert a permissive counterclaim against the third-party defendant?

8. States take a variety of approaches to third-party practice. Many of the reasons for this difference in practice are described in Friedenthal, *The Expansion of Joinder in Cross–Complaints by the Erroneous Interpretation of Section 442 of the California Code of Civil Procedure*, 51 Calif.L.Rev. 494 (1963). Some states place time-limits on third-party practice as of right. Pennsylvania, for example allows a defendant to join a third party as of right for sixty days after service of process, but then only with leave of court. A commentary warns that joinder in this situation "may have the effect of requiring the defendant to pay more than its judicially allocated share of damages":

> * * * A defendant faced with the sixty-day time limit for joinder who, in the exercise of diligence, joins an additional party at the outset of litigation likely becomes forever stuck with the joined party. The defendant likely will be prevented from later discontinuing its claims against the joined party, regardless of whether the joined party's presence will prejudice the defendant at trial. * * * When the additional defendant turns out to be judgment-proof, plaintiffs can capitalize on a quickly forced joinder decision that only later, in light of discovery, proves to be improvident.

Goetz & Flannery, *Traps for the Unwary: Why Counsel Should Think Twice Before Joining Additional Parties in Civil Litigation*, 36 Duq. L. Rev. 521, 525–28 (1998).

SECTION F. INTERPLEADER

Read Federal Rule of Civil Procedure 22, 28 U.S.C. §§ 1335, 1397, and 2361, and the accompanying material in the Supplement.

Interpleader is a device designed to enable a party who might be exposed to multiple claims to money or property under her control to settle the controversy in a single proceeding. For example, if two people claim that each is the sole beneficiary of a life insurance policy, the insurance company, in the absence of a joinder device such as interpleader, would be required to defend against both in two actions. Not only would the company be forced to incur the expense of additional litigation, but it would be faced with the possibility that, in separate lawsuits, *both* claimants might win. See 7 Wright, Miller & Kane, Federal Practice and Procedure: Civil 3d § 1702.

1. HISTORICAL LIMITATIONS ON THE USE OF INTERPLEADER

HANCOCK OIL CO. v. INDEPENDENT DISTRIBUTING CO.

Supreme Court of California, 1944.
24 Cal.2d 497, 150 P.2d 463.

EDMONDS, JUSTICE. * * *

According to the complaint [filed by two corporate lessees of certain real property], in 1936 W.L. Hopkins and Gertrude Ann Hopkins, his wife, leased certain real property to Hancock Oil Company of California and R.R. Bush Oil Company. Landowner's royalties of approximately $1,500 have accrued. It is also alleged that in 1941, Independent Distributing Co., a copartnership composed of Merritt Bloxom, Eugene E. Olwell and Murray M. Olwell, brought an action asserting that W.L. Hopkins, Gertrude Ann Hopkins, and two persons sued by fictitious names, hold the real property described in the lease in trust for them. The relief sought in the suit of Independent Distributing Co. was an accounting of the rents of the land.

The copartnership and the copartners, together with W.L. Hopkins and Gertrude Ann Hopkins, H. James Hopkins and W.L. Hopkins, trustees of Wilbur T. Hopkins Trust, and H. James Hopkins and W.L. Hopkins, trustees of the H. James Hopkins Trust, are named as the defendants in the present suit, the charge of the complaint being that the copartnership and the copartners claim to be the owners of the land described in the lease and entitled to all of the landowner's royalties accrued and to accrue under that agreement. A further assertion of the complaint is that the defendants other than the copartnership and the copartners also claim the same royalties and by reason of these conflicting claims the lessees cannot safely determine to whom the rent should be paid. * * *

To this complaint Merritt Bloxom, Eugene E. Olwell, Murray M. Olwell and Independent Distributing Co. filed an answer alleging that they are the owners of the property and entitled to all of the rents and profits from it. They also assert that the defendants named Hopkins are holding title to the property in trust for them. The defendants other than the copartners and the copartnership interposed a general demurrer and a special demurrer upon the ground of uncertainty. Each demurrer was sustained without leave to amend and the corporations' appeal is from the judgment which followed that order.

From an opinion of the trial judge, it appears that the demurrers were sustained upon the sole ground that a tenant may not question the title of his landlord at the date of the lease; accordingly, a suit by a tenant to interplead his landlord and one who claims the rent agreed to be paid in accordance with the terms of the lease by which he holds possession of the real property is in violation of this fundamental principle. The appellants assert that a suit in interpleader does not constitute a denial of the landlord's title but is simply a means by which the tenant may discharge his obligation to pay rent under the lease without becoming involved in the conflict between different claimants to the amount due and unpaid. * * *

The common law bill of interpleader had four essential elements: (1) The same thing, debt, or duty must be claimed by both or all the parties against whom the relief is demanded; (2) all of the adverse titles or claims must be dependent, or be derived from a common source; (3) the one seeking the relief must not have nor claim any interest in the subject matter; and (4) he must have incurred no independent liability to either of the claimants. See 4 Pomeroy's Equity Jurisprudence, 5th Ed.1941, § 1322, p. 906.

These requirements have been termed historical limitations upon this otherwise expeditious equitable proceeding * * *, and in 1881 section 386 of the Code of Civil Procedure was amended to broaden the remedy. The statute * * * declares * * *: "And whenever conflicting claims are or may be made upon a person for or relating to personal property, or the performance of an obligation, or any portion thereof, such person may bring an action against the conflicting claimants to compel them to interplead and litigate their several claims among themselves. The order of substitution may be made and the action of interpleader may be maintained, and the applicant or plaintiff be discharged from liability to all or any of the conflicting claimants, although their titles or claims have not a common origin, or are not identical, but are adverse to and independent of one another." The provision of this enactment, that interpleader lies "although their titles or claims have not a common origin * * * but are adverse to and independent of one another," directly abrogates the common law requirement that all the adverse titles or claims must be dependent or be derived from a common source, and it is therefore clear that privity between the conflicting claimants need not be shown to invoke the remedy under the code. * * *

Early in the history of interpleader, it was held that one who sought to maintain such a suit must show outstanding claims, identical in every respect and without the slightest degree of variation, to the same thing, debt or duty. In the case of conflicting claims to specific personal property, this rigid formalism did not seriously interfere with the effectiveness of the proceeding. But where, as is generally the situation modernly, the subject matter of the conflicting claims was an obligation, a debt or a duty, the requirement as to the identity of the defendant's demands very often prevented a stakeholder from using interpleader where he was doubly vexed with respect to one liability. For example, under the narrow rule of the common law, if one person claimed all of the fund held by a bank and another person asserted the right to only a portion of that fund, the bank could not secure a determination of its liability by means of the equitable proceeding. The Legislature has removed this restriction, yet the very rationale of interpleader compels the conclusion that the amendment does not allow the remedy where each of the claimants asserts the right to a different debt, claim or duty. If the conflicting claims are mutually exclusive, interpleader cannot be maintained, but the fact that an identical right is not asserted by each of the claimants does not preclude the use of the remedy. * * *

In the present case, the plaintiffs have alleged that each of the two groups against whom interpleader is sought claims the right to receive the rents and royalties reserved in the lease. If Independent Distributing Co. and the members of that copartnership should assert that they are entitled to the reasonable value of the use and occupation of the land leased to the plaintiffs, together with the mesne profits or damages for waste, the trial court would be required to deny the plaintiffs the right to interplead those parties with their lessors. Under such circumstances the claims of the parties would not relate to the same obligation. But as the appellants' complaint pleads that there are conflicting claims concerning their obligation to pay the rents and royalties reserved by the lease, the lessors and the third parties must answer and, if each of them agrees that his claim concerns the right to those rents and royalties, the lessees should be discharged from liability upon payment of their obligations under the lease.

As to the remaining common law principles governing a suit of interpleader, the appellants' complaint conforms with the requirement that the plaintiff in such a proceeding must stand in the position of a disinterested stakeholder. However, much of the present controversy centers about the last element which is specified as essential. Although the complaint discloses no obligation of the appellants other than under the lease, the respondents assert that the obligation to pay rent constitutes an independent liability and bars the remedy of interpleader.

* * * The rule concerning independent liability is stated in Corpus Juris as follows: "Interpleader will not lie if the stakeholder has incurred some personal obligation to either of the claimants, independent of the title or the right to possession, because such claimant would in that event have a claim against him which could not be settled in a litigation with the other claimant." 33 C.J. 439. * * * The Supreme Court of Maine put the matter most convincingly when it said: "The mere fact that a contractual relation exists between plaintiff and one of the defendants, under which the fund is required to be paid to such claimant, does not of itself defeat the right of interpleader. * * * If such were the law, it would be difficult to conceive of any set of facts which would enable a bank, a trustee, or other custodian of funds, or even a bailee, to maintain interpleader. The obligation referred to in the rule must be independent of the title or right of possession of the fund or property in question. * * *" First National Bank v. Reynolds, 127 Me. 340, 143 A. 266, 268, 60 A.L.R. 712. * * *

Although Professor Pomeroy declares that an independent liability "arises from the very nature of the original relation subsisting between" the landlord and tenant, he states that such a suit is proper whenever there is some privity between the claimant and the lessor, as, for example, when the relation of trustee and *cestui que trust* has been created between them. It seems, therefore, that the reason why the author asserts that the relationship of the landlord and tenant precludes interpleader by the tenant is not that, under the lease, there is an independent liability but because there is no privity between the landlord and the one joined with him as a defendant. * * *

From what has been said, then, it is clear that, in the present case, as according to the facts alleged in the complaint, the relations inter se of the respondents and the copartners are such that the decision will determine the liability of the lessees to each of them, there is no independent liability which will bar the remedy of interpleader; accordingly the appellants' complaint is sufficient with respect to those of the four common law requirements for interpleader not abolished or modified by the amendment in 1881 to section 386 of the Code of Civil Procedure. * * *

[The court went on to consider the effect of the common-law rule that a tenant may not dispute the title of his landlord at the time of the commencement of the relation.]

Notwithstanding the strict common law limitation on interpleader in landlord-tenant cases which is justified by an ancient rule of real property, the code provision concerning the remedy must be liberally construed. A remedial statute, its purpose is to avoid a multiplicity of suits and prevent vexatious litigation. * * *

* * * [I]n the absence of the right to interplead the landlord and the adverse claimant to the rent, the tenant is faced with the unfortunate

alternative of forfeiting his lease or possibly paying twice. * * * And there is no action at law adequate to shield him from vexation by multiple litigation over the obligation for rent, against the risk of double liability upon the same obligation, and against insecurity of tenancy.

Furthermore, interpleader is not only of importance to the tenant; it is also of advantage to the third party claimant. If the tenant may not interplead his landlord and another under the common law rule, the third party must establish his right to rent in a separate action. During the progress of this litigation the tenant would pay the rents to the landlord. It is entirely conceivable that before judgment was rendered the tenant might become insolvent, leaving the third party without recourse, or because of financial difficulties overtaking the landlord, the tenant would be required to pay his obligation twice.

Unquestionably the landlord may suffer some disadvantage in being forced to defend a suit in interpleader. While the litigation continues the rent is withheld from him without interest. But the tenant may not maintain such a suit upon the mere pretext or suspicion of double vexation; he must allege facts showing a reasonable probability of double vexation. Without accurately appraising the rationale of interpleader, by some decisions this court has mentioned as an additional requirement that the plaintiff must allege facts showing a doubt as to which claimant he can safely pay. * * * However, to demand from a plaintiff that he express a doubt as to which adverse claimant he is liable is an admission that the basis upon which the right to interpleader rests is the avoidance of double liability. "The right to the remedy by interpleader is founded, however, not on the consideration that a man may be subjected to double liability, but on the fact that he is threatened with double vexation in respect to one liability." Pfister v. Wade, * * * 56 Cal. at page 47 * * *.

The complaint therefore states a cause of action against a general demurrer and denial of leave to amend was an abuse of discretion even if the special demurrer was well taken. * * *

The judgment is reversed.

[The dissenting opinion of JUSTICE CARTER has been omitted.]

NOTES AND QUESTIONS

1. The California Supreme Court states in *Hancock* that interpleader would have been denied if Independent Oil Company had asserted a claim for profits and damages. In such a situation, the court reasoned, "the claims of the parties [Independent and Hopkins] would not relate to the same obligation." What does the court mean by "the same obligation"? Consider the probable content of the allegations if Independent had asserted a claim for profits and damages and Hopkins had asserted a claim for the rents; would the claims have been mutually exclusive?

2. Historically, the typical interpleader suit has two stages. The first determines whether interpleader is proper; in it, the controversy is between

the stakeholder on one side and all the claimants on the other. If interpleader is granted, the first stage ends with a decree allowing the stakeholder to withdraw from the case and enjoining the claimants from taking any further proceedings against the stakeholder. Before retiring, however, the stakeholder is required to deposit the money or property involved in the dispute with the court, generally less court costs and attorney's fees. In the second stage, the contest is among the claimants to determine their respective rights to the property or fund deposited in court. See McClintock, Equity § 188 (2d ed. 1948); 4 Pomeroy, Equity Jurisprudence § 1320 (5th ed. 1941).

3. The third requirement for interpleader mentioned in *Hancock* is that the party seeking interpleader must neither have nor claim any interest in the subject matter. The first case in which the requirement appeared, Mitchell v. Hayne, 2 Simons & Stuart 63, 57 Eng.Rep. 268 (Ch.1824), cites no authority and gives no reasons for its adoption. For this requirement's early history, see Hazard & Moskovitz, *An Historical and Critical Analysis of Interpleader*, 52 Calif.L.Rev. 706, 744–47 (1964). At the time *Hancock* was decided, this requirement was still in full force in California. However, in 1951, Section 386 of California's Code of Civil Procedure, which is set out in the Supplement under Federal Rule 22, was amended to permit a defendant to interpose a claim to a portion of the property or money in dispute. For a sharp attack on the no-interest-in-the-subject-matter requirement, see Chafee, *Modernizing Interpleader*, 30 Yale L.J. 814, 840–42 (1921).

4. The fourth historical requirement—that the stakeholder must not have incurred any independent liability with regard to the stake of either of the claimants—derived from the principle that the stakeholder should retire from the case once interpleader was allowed. By way of illustration, assume that a bailee who is subject to conflicting claims to the bailed article has expressly acknowledged the title of one of the claimants to it. Interpleader could not be granted because a decision awarding ownership to the other claimant might not terminate the controversy concerning the bailed item; the losing claimant still might have a cause of action against the stakeholder based on the latter's acknowledgment of title, and the stakeholder could not withdraw from the litigation at the end of the first stage of the suit. What underlies the principle that the stakeholder must be neutral, disinterested, and withdraw permanently from the suit when interpleader is allowed?

2. JURISDICTIONAL LIMITATIONS AND PASSAGE OF THE FEDERAL INTERPLEADER ACT

The historic territorial approach to jurisdiction over the person raised a number of peculiar problems in the interpleader context. Occasionally, the stakeholder was not able to obtain in personam jurisdiction over all of the claimants in any one state because of the limitations imposed by the Due Process Clause of the Fourteenth Amendment. To overcome this difficulty, courts often characterized interpleader as an in rem or quasi-in-rem proceeding and predicated jurisdiction on the presence of the stake within the territorial reach of the court. In New York Life Ins. Co. v.

Dunlevy, which follows, the Supreme Court was faced with the question of whether to treat a debt as an in rem or quasi-in-rem base for interpleader.

NEW YORK LIFE INSURANCE CO. v. DUNLEVY

Supreme Court of the United States, 1916.
241 U.S. 518, 36 S.Ct. 613, 60 L.Ed. 1140.

Certiorari to the Circuit Court of Appeals for the Ninth Circuit.

MR. JUSTICE MCREYNOLDS delivered the opinion of the court:

Respondent, Effie J. Gould Dunlevy, instituted this suit in the Superior Court, Marin county, California, January 14, 1910, against petitioner and Joseph W. Gould, her father, to recover $2,479.70, the surrender value of a policy on his life which she claimed had been assigned to her in 1893, and both were duly served with process while in that state. It was removed to the United States District Court, February 16, 1910, and there tried by the judge in May, 1912, a jury having been expressly waived. Judgment for amount claimed was affirmed by the Circuit Court of Appeals. * * *

The insurance company by an amended answer filed December 7, 1911, set up in defense * * * that Mrs. Dunlevy was concluded by certain judicial proceedings in Pennsylvania wherein it had been garnished and the policy had been adjudged to be the property of Gould. * * *

In 1907 Boggs & Buhl recovered a valid personal judgment by default, after domiciliary service, against Mrs. Dunlevy, in the Common Pleas Court at Pittsburgh, where she then resided. During 1909, "the tontine dividend period" of the life policy having expired, the insurance company became liable for $2,479.70, and this sum was claimed both by Gould, a citizen of Pennsylvania, and his daughter, who had removed to California. In November, 1909, Boggs & Buhl caused issue of an execution attachment on their judgment, and both the insurance company and Gould were summoned as garnishees. He appeared, denied assignment of the policy, and claimed the full amount due thereon. On February 5, 1910,—after this suit was begun in California,—the company answered, admitted its indebtedness, set up the conflicting claims to the fund, and prayed to be advised as to its rights. At the same time it filed a petition asking for a rule upon the claimants to show cause why they should not interplead and thereby ascertain who was lawfully entitled to the proceeds, and, further, that it might be allowed to pay amount due into court for benefit of proper party. An order granted the requested rule, and directed that notice be given to Mrs. Dunlevy in California. This was done, but she made no answer and did not appear. Later the insurance company filed a second petition, and, upon leave obtained thereunder, paid $2,479.70 into court, March 21, 1910. All parties except Mrs. Dunlevy having appeared, a feigned issue was framed and tried to determine validity of alleged transfer of the policy. The jury found, October 1, 1910, there was no valid assignment, and thereupon, under an order of court, the fund was paid over to Gould.

Beyond doubt, without the necessity of further personal service of process upon Mrs. Dunlevy, the Court of Common Pleas at Pittsburgh had ample power through garnishment proceedings to inquire whether she held a valid claim against the insurance company, and, if found to exist, then to condemn and appropriate it so far as necessary to discharge the original judgment. Although herself outside the limits of the state, such disposition of the property would have been binding on her. * * * But the interpleader initiated by the company was an altogether different matter. This was an attempt to bring about a final and conclusive adjudication of her personal rights, not merely to discover property and apply it to debts. And unless in contemplation of law she was before the court, and required to respond to that issue, its orders and judgments in respect thereto were not binding on her. Pennoyer v. Neff * * *.

Counsel maintain that having been duly summoned in the original suit instituted by Boggs & Buhl in 1907, and notwithstanding entry of final judgment therein, "Mrs. Dunlevy was in the Pennsylvania court and was bound by every order that court made, whether she remained within the jurisdiction of that court after it got jurisdiction over her person or not;" and hence, the argument is, "When the company paid the money into court where she was, it was just the same in legal effect as if it had paid it to her." This position is supposed to be supported by our opinion in Michigan Trust Co. v. Ferry, 228 U.S. 346, 57 L.Ed. 867, 33 S.Ct. 550, where it is said: "If a judicial proceeding is begun with jurisdiction over the person of the party concerned, it is within the power of a state to bind him by every subsequent order in the cause. * * * This is true not only of ordinary actions, but of proceedings like the present. It is within the power of a state to make the whole administration of the estate a single proceeding, to provide that one who has undertaken it within the jurisdiction shall be subject to the order of the court in the matter until the administration is closed by distribution, and, on the same principle, that he shall be required to account for and distribute all that he receives, by the order of the probate court."

Of course the language quoted had reference to the existing circumstances, and must be construed accordingly. The judgment under consideration was fairly within the reasonable anticipation of the executor when he submitted himself to the probate court. But a wholly different and intolerable condition would result from acceptance of the theory that, after final judgment, a defendant remains in court and subject to whatsoever orders may be entered under title of the cause. * * * The interpleader proceedings were not essential concomitants of the original action by Boggs & Buhl against Dunlevy, but plainly collateral; and, when summoned to respond in that action, she was not required to anticipate them. * * *

The established general rule is that any personal judgment which a state court may render against one who did not voluntarily submit to its jurisdiction, and who is not a citizen of the state, nor served with process within its borders, no matter what the mode of service, is void, because the court had no jurisdiction over his person. * * *

We are of opinion that the proceedings in the Pennsylvania court constituted no bar to the action in California, and the judgment below is accordingly affirmed.

NOTES AND QUESTIONS

1. Consider the following:

> The Dunlevy decision had the effect of rendering interpleader unavailable in the federal courts in most cases which the claimants were of diverse citizenship. In the absence of a federal statute extending the jurisdictional reach of the district courts in interpleader actions, the prevailing territorial limitations on personal jurisdiction effectively barred the courts from offering relief when one of the claimants was from a state other than the forum. As a result, businesses engaged in interstate commerce that were confronted by conflicting claims to a particular fund often found themselves unavoidably defending several suits in different states. The situation was particularly troublesome for insurance companies due to the frequency with which multiple claims to the proceeds of an insurance policy arose.

7 Wright, Miller & Kane, Federal Practice and Procedure: Civil 3d § 1701.

2. Partially in response to the *Dunlevy* decision, Congress passed the Federal Interpleader Act in 1917. The statute was successively broadened in 1926 and 1936 and was reconstituted in 1948 as part of the United States Judicial Code. It now appears as 28 U.S.C. §§ 1335, 1397, 2361. The present Interpleader Act manifests a congressional intent to avoid a repetition of the *Dunlevy* decision in an action arising in a federal court. Section 1397 permits venue to be laid in any judicial district in which one or more of the claimants reside and Section 2361 permits nationwide service of process in order to reach all of the claimants. Further recognition of the interstate quality of interpleader and the need for the exercise of federal judicial power in this context is the provision in Section 1335 permitting the federal courts to assert jurisdiction when the stake is worth as little as $500. Where there is diversity of citizenship between or among "[t]wo or more adverse claimants." The federal statutes on interpleader are analyzed in a series of articles by their principal proponent, Professor Chafee: *Interstate Interpleader,* 33 Yale L.J. 685 (1924); *Interpleader in the United States Courts,* 41 Yale L.J. 1134 (1932), 42 Yale L.J. 41 (1932); *The Federal Interpleader Act of 1936*, 45 Yale L.J. 963, 1161 (1936); *Federal Interpleader Since the Act of 1936*, 49 Yale L.J. 377 (1940).

3. Interpleader under the Federal Interpleader Act is referred to as "statutory interpleader." Interpleader under Federal Rule 22, known as "rule interpleader," is somewhat different. Although the fourfold requirements of the old equitable remedy are not necessary, the usual jurisdictional, venue,

and process limitations still apply. For a discussion of the differences between the two interpleader devices, see Doernberg, *What's Wrong with this Picture?: Rule Interpleader, the Anti-Injunction Act, In Personam Jurisdiction, and M.C. Escher*, 67 U. Colo. L. Rev. 551 (1996).

3. INTERPLEADER IN THE FEDERAL COURTS

Reread 28 U.S.C. §§ 1335, 1397, and 2361 and Federal Rule of Civil Procedure 22.

PAN AMERICAN FIRE & CASUALTY CO. v. REVERE

United States District Court, Eastern District of Louisiana, 1960.
188 F.Supp. 474.

WRIGHT, DISTRICT JUDGE. On February 3, 1960, a * * * large tractor and trailer collided head-on with a bus carrying school children. The bus driver and three of the children were killed and 23 others were injured, some very seriously. A few moments later, compounding the disaster, another collision occurred between two cars following the bus. * * *

Alleging that three suits against it have already been filed and that numerous other claims have been made, the tractor's liability insurer has instituted this interpleader action, citing all potential claimants. It asks that they be enjoined from initiating legal proceedings elsewhere or further prosecuting the actions already filed and that they be directed to assert their claims in the present suit. Plaintiff has deposited a bond in the full amount of its policy limits, $100,000, and avers that "it has no interest" in these insurance proceeds, being merely "a disinterested stakeholder." On the other hand, the Company denies liability toward any and all claimants. This apparently contradictory position is explained by the statement of its counsel, incorporated in the record as an amendment to the complaint, that plaintiff "has no further claim" on the sum deposited with the court, but cannot technically admit "liability" since that would amount to a concession that its assured was negligent and expose him to a deficiency judgment.

The only question presented at this stage of the proceeding is whether, under the circumstances outlined, the remedy of interpleader is available to the insurer. * * *

1. *Jurisdiction.* * * *

[The court concluded that the jurisdictional amount and diversity requirements of the Interpleader Act and Federal Rule 22 had been satisfied.]

2. *Strict Interpleader or Bill in the Nature of Interpleader.* Apparently of the opinion that the answer may affect the availability of the remedy sought here, the parties have debated the question whether this is a case for "true," "strict," or "pure" interpleader or whether the present facts support only an action "in the nature of interpleader." The difference between the two is that in strict interpleader the plaintiff is a disinterested stakeholder while in the action in the nature of interpleader he is himself a claimant, whether directly or by denying the validity of some or all of the other claims. * * * Thus, if the casualty insurer had brought in the claimants and said to them: "Gentlemen, I put before you the full amount of the policy which those of you who prove your claims must divide between you, but I deny that any of you is entitled to any portion of the fund and pray that all your demands be rejected and that the deposit be returned to me in due course," clearly this would not be a true interpleader but an action in the nature of interpleader. The problem here is whether the allegation of disinterestedness already noted changes the character of the action to one of strict interpleader. * * *

But does it matter how the action is characterized? It would seem to make no difference since both Rule 22 and the Interpleader Act expressly provide for actions in the nature of interpleader as well as strict bills, the drafters in each case voicing their intent to erase the distinction. But before so concluding, we must dispose of an old rule of equity that gave importance to the difference between "pure" and "impure" bills of interpleader.

3. *Special Equitable Ground for Bill in the Nature of Interpleader.* Though apparently known to the early common law, modern interpleader developed in the chancery courts and is today considered an equitable remedy. Hence, in theory at least, the resort to equity must be justified by the absence of an adequate remedy at law. One might suppose that exposure to unnecessary vexation by a multiplicity of suits on the same obligation were a sufficient ground for equitable relief. And so it is if the conditions of strict interpleader are met. But, for reasons that no one bothered to explain, the rule was otherwise when the plaintiff was not a mere stakeholder. It was laid down that a bill in the nature of interpleader would not lie unless supported by some special equity besides double vexation. Thus, a suit like this one which has no independent equitable basis could not be maintained unless it could be characterized as a true bill of interpleader.

Though it was perhaps more honored in the breach than the observance, such was the rule. But, inherently weak, it could not long survive the liberalizing force of the Interpleader Act of 1936 and the Rules of Civil Procedure promulgated in 1938. Indeed, once the difference between strict bills and bills in the nature of interpleader was eliminated, there remained no basis for distinguishing the requirements and demanding special equities for the action in the nature of interpleader. Henceforth, it could be assumed that the prerequisites of interpleader were the same whether the plaintiff were interested or not, and that these conditions were spelled out in the written provisions. The point was forcibly made by Judge Chesnut whose celebrated opinion in John Hancock Mut. Life Ins. Co. v. Kegan, * * * [22 F.Supp. 326 (D.Md.1938)], noted the absurdity of distinguishing between the equities required for "pure" and "impure" interpleader and held that exposure to undue harassment by a multiplicity of suits was a sufficient ground to maintain a bill in the nature of interpleader. * * *

The present law, then, is that the only equitable ground necessary for interpleader, whether the plaintiff is a disinterested stakeholder or not, is exposure to double or multiple vexation. But, of course, this does not mean that every person threatened with a multiplicity of suits is entitled to interplead. The function of interpleader is to rescue a debtor from *undue* harassment when there are several claims made against the *same fund.* It is because the aggregate demands exceed the insurer's contractual obligation that the condition is here satisfied.

4. *Exposure to Multiple Liability.* Though the Interpleader Act makes no such requirement, Rule 22 apparently permits interpleader only if the claims "may expose a plaintiff to double or multiple *liability.*" (Emphasis added.) In theory at least, this is not necessarily the same thing as exposure to double or multiple *vexation* on a single obligation. There may be situations in which the debtor, though harassed by many suits on account of one transaction, is never in danger of being compelled to pay the same debt twice. Indeed, here, the argument is advanced that because it has fixed the limits of its liability in its policy, the insurer is not exposed to multiple liability no matter how many claims are filed, and, therefore, is not entitled to maintain interpleader, at least under the Rule.

But the requirement is not a strict one. * * * The key to the clause requiring exposure to "double or multiple liability" is in the word "may." The danger need not be immediate; any possibility of having to pay more than is justly due, no matter how improbable or remote, will suffice. At least, it is settled that an insurer with limited contractual liability who faces claims in excess of his policy limits is "exposed" within the intendment of Rule 22, and we need go no further to find the requirement satisfied here.

5. *Adversity of Claimants.* In a somewhat overlapping objection, it is said that the present claims are not characterized by that "adversity" to one another which is a prerequisite of interpleader. It is of course true that they are identical neither in origin nor in amount and that they are, in some degree at least, independent demands. But, despite the objection of purists who would retain the old doctrine of complete "mutual exclusiveness," both Rule 22 and the Interpleader Act now expressly provide that this is no bar to the remedy. On the other hand, there remains a requirement that the claimants be "adverse" in some way. The question is whether that requirement is met when, as here, the claimants, though in theory indifferent toward each other, are in fact competing for a fund which is not large enough to satisfy them all. The answer is clear. As Judge Thompson said in Fidelity & Deposit Co. of Maryland v. A.S. Reid &

Co., D.C.E.D.Pa., 16 F.2d 502, 504: "In that situation it is to the interest of its claimant to reduce or defeat altogether the claim of every other claimant. * * * "

6. *Fault of Plaintiff.* * * *

[The court held that the plaintiff was not guilty of "unclean hands," which would have barred equitable relief.]

7. *Unliquidated Tort Claims as Justifying Interpleader.* Over and above the technical objections already disposed of, the argument is advanced that interpleader is not an appropriate method of adjudicating unliquidated tort claims. Such a bald proposition might be rejected summarily were it not for the startling fact that there appears to be no precedent in the federal courts for granting interpleader in the present situation. * * *

At the outset, it seems clear that interpleader will lie when there are several tort claimants who have obtained judgments which aggregate more than the amount of the policy. Indeed, in that case it can make no difference whether the claims originated in tort or contract. Moreover, it is settled that interpleader is available to an insurer whose policy is insufficient to satisfy contract claims, though they have not been reduced to judgment. Why, then, should the remedy be denied to a blameless insurer faced with excessive tort claims? Three reasons have been suggested: (1) As to quantum, at least, tort claims are more conjectural than contract claims; (2) since it is not directly liable to the claimants, the insurer's exposure as to tort claims is "remote" until they have been reduced to judgment; and (3) tort claims "are peculiarly appropriate for jury trial," which would have to be denied under the equitable practice of interpleader.

The effect of the first objection is only this: that it is more difficult in the case of tort claims to determine whether the aggregate will exceed the policy limits so as to render the claimants "adverse" and expose the insurer to "multiple liability." It may be that there are few cases in which this result can be reasonably anticipated, but, clearly, this is one of them.

The second objection, though it forms the basis of the only reported decision denying interpleader to an automobile liability insurer,[36] is no better. Indeed, under the "may expose" clause of Rule 22 and the "may claim" clause of the Interpleader Act, it would not seem to matter how remote the danger might be. But, in any event, prematurity is no defense under the peculiar Louisiana law which allows a direct action against the automobile liability insurer.

8. *Jury Trial.* On the theory that the resort to equity defeats the right of trial by jury, it has been said that once interpleader is granted all issues in the case must be tried to the judge alone. There is, however, eminent authority to the contrary, including Judge Learned Hand, Professor Chafee, and Professor Moore, who hold that legal issues arising in an

36. American Indemnity Co. v. Hale, D.C.W.D.Mo., 71 F.Supp. 529, 533–534.

interpleader action can be tried before a jury. Whatever may be the right solution in another case, here it seems clear that the questions of liability and damages ought to be put to a jury. * * * Nothing in Rule 22 or the Interpleader Act opposes such a procedure. Indeed, the provision of the Federal Rules which permits separate trial of distinct issues invites this solution. * * * Each claimant can be given a full opportunity to prove his case before a jury, reserving to the court only the task of apportioning the fund between those who are successful if the aggregate of the verdicts exceeds the amount of the insurance proceeds.

9. *Enjoining of Other Proceedings.* Usually interpleader will not be really effective unless all claimants are brought before the same court in one proceeding and restricted to that single forum in the assertion of their claims. * * * Immediately, the question arises whether Section 2283 of Title 28 of the Code presents an obstacle to enjoining state court proceedings.

As amended in 1948, that section prohibits a federal court from interfering with a pending state court action except in three situations: (1) Where such a course is "expressly authorized by Act of Congress"; (2) where the issuance of an injunction by the federal court is "necessary in aid of its jurisdiction"; and (3) where the court's action is required "to protect or effectuate its judgments." Clearly, the first exception is applicable to a suit brought under the Interpleader Act since that statute expressly empowers the court to enjoin the claimants "from instituting or prosecuting any proceeding in any State or United States court affecting the property, instrument or obligation involved in the interpleader action * * *." But the exception does not apply to an action under Rule 22, for the quoted provision authorizing stay orders is restricted to statutory interpleader. If state court proceedings can be enjoined when interpleader is brought under the Rule it must be by virtue of the second exception in Section 2283.

The question whether the court entertaining a non-statutory interpleader suit may enjoin state court proceedings on the same issues on the theory that it is "necessary in aid of its jurisdiction" is not free from doubt. * * * But * * * every indication is that, regardless of the Interpleader Act, the power of a federal court to enjoin pending state court proceedings in a case like this one will be sustained. Certainly that result is desirable, if not indispensable. * * *

10. *Venue and Service of Process.* * * * [T]here are two procedural limitations on actions under the Rule which become important whenever the claimants are not all within the territorial jurisdiction of the district court. The first is that the only proper venue for the suit when the defendants do not all reside in the same state is the residence of the plaintiff; the second, that process cannot run beyond the boundaries of the state in which the court sits. These restrictions are of course waivable, but if objection is raised by the affected defendant, they usually form an absolute bar to the action. Thus, here, if Rule 22 alone were applicable,

absent a waiver of venue by Wells [a passenger in one of the cars following the bus], the suit would have to be instituted at the plaintiff's domicile in Texas, and none of the defendants could be validly served unless they were found in that state.

But the situation is different when jurisdiction exists under the statute, for the Interpleader Act specially provides that the action may be commenced in any district where one defendant resides and that process will run throughout the United States. Unfortunately, these exceptional rules apply only to statutory interpleader. The present suit, then, is maintainable only under the Interpleader Act unless the Wisconsin defendant waives venue and voluntarily appears or is found in Louisiana.

11. *Conclusion.* * * * [T]he prayer for interpleader will be granted, without, however, discharging the plaintiff who is contractually bound to resist the demands. Injunctions will issue restraining all parties from further prosecuting any pending suits against plaintiff or its assured on account of the accident described, or from instituting like proceedings before this or any other court. All defendants will be required to enter their claims by way of answer in this action within thirty days from notice of this judgment. Thereafter, upon timely demand by any one of the parties, the court will order a joint jury trial of all the claims upon the issues of liability and damages. In the event the aggregate of the verdicts should exceed the amount of plaintiff's liability, the court reserves unto itself the task of apportioning the insurance proceeds in such manner as it deems just.

The motion to dismiss will be denied.

NOTE AND QUESTIONS

If an insurance company faced with the *Pan American* situation pays the full amount of the policy to certain claimants, either by way of settlement or in satisfaction of a judgment, can it defend later actions by unpaid claimants by arguing that it has already exhausted the policy? To what extent is the answer to this question relevant in determining whether interpleader should be granted?

STATE FARM FIRE & CASUALTY CO. v. TASHIRE

Supreme Court of the United States, 1967.
386 U.S. 523, 87 S.Ct. 1199, 18 L.Ed.2d 270.

[This case arose out of a collision between a Greyhound bus and a pickup truck in Shasta County, California in September, 1964. Two of the bus passengers were killed and 33 others were injured, as were the bus driver, the driver of the truck, and its passenger. One of the dead and 10 of the injured passengers were Canadians; the rest of the individuals were citizens of five American states.

Four of the injured passengers filed suit in California state courts seeking damages in excess of $1,000,000 and naming as defendants:

Greyhound Lines, Inc.; Nauta, the bus driver; Clark, the driver of the truck; and Glasgow, the truck passenger who apparently was its owner. Each of the individual defendants was a citizen of Oregon; Greyhound was a California corporation. Before the California cases came to trial and before any other suits were filed, petitioner, State Farm Fire & Casualty Company, an Illinois corporation, brought this action in the nature of interpleader in the United States District Court for the District of Oregon.

State Farm asserted that at the time of the collision it had in force an insurance policy covering Clark, the driver of the truck, for bodily injury liability up to $10,000 per person and $20,000 per occurrence. State Farm further asserted that the aggregate damages sought in actions already filed in California and other anticipated actions far exceeded the amount of its maximum liability under the policy. Accordingly, it paid into court the sum of $20,000 and asked the court (1) to require all claimants to establish their claims against Clark and his insurer in the Oregon proceeding and in no other action, and (2) to discharge State Farm from all further obligations under its policy. Alternatively, State Farm requested a decree that the insurer owed no duty to Clark and was not liable on the policy, and asked the court to refund the $20,000 deposit. State Farm joined as defendants Clark, Glasgow, Nauta, Greyhound, and each of the prospective claimants. Jurisdiction was predicated both upon the Federal Interpleader Act and general diversity of citizenship. Personal service was effected on each of the American defendants and registered mail was employed to give notice to the 11 Canadian claimants.

The Oregon District Court issued an order requiring each of the defendants to show cause why he should not be restrained from filing or prosecuting any proceeding affecting the property or obligation involved in the interpleader action. In response, several of the defendants contended that the policy did cover the accident and advanced various arguments for the position that interpleader was inappropriate.

When a temporary injunction along the lines sought by State Farm issued, the respondents moved to dismiss and, in the alternative, sought a change of venue to the district in which the collision had occurred. After a hearing, the District Court declined to dissolve the temporary injunction but continued the motion for a change of venue. Later, the temporary injunction was broadened so that all suits against Clark, State Farm, Greyhound, and Nauta had to be prosecuted in the interpleader proceeding.

On interlocutory appeal, the Ninth Circuit reversed on the ground that in states, such as Oregon, that do not permit a "direct action" against an insurance company until a judgment is obtained against the insured, State Farm could not invoke federal interpleader until the claims against the insured had been reduced to judgment. The Court of Appeals held that prior to that time claimants with unliquidated tort claims are not "claimants" within the meaning of Section 1335 of Title 28 and are not "persons having claims against the plaintiff" within the meaning of

Federal Rule 22. [The language has been altered without any substantive change.] The Ninth Circuit directed that the temporary injunction be dissolved and the action be dismissed. The Supreme Court granted certiorari.]

Certiorari to the United States Court of Appeals for the Ninth Circuit.

MR. JUSTICE FORTAS delivered the opinion of the Court.

* * *

I.

Before considering the issues presented by the petition for certiorari, we find it necessary to dispose of a question neither raised by the parties nor passed upon by the courts below. Since the matter concerns our jurisdiction, we raise it on our own motion. * * * The interpleader statute * * * has been uniformly construed to require only "minimal diversity," that is, diversity of citizenship between two or more claimants, without regard to the circumstance that other rival claimants may be co-citizens. The language of the statute, the legislative purpose broadly to remedy the problems posed by multiple claimants to a single fund, and the consistent judicial interpretation tacitly accepted by Congress, persuade us that the statute requires no more. There remains, however, the question whether such a statutory construction is consistent with Article III of our Constitution * * *. In Strawbridge v. Curtiss, * * * [p. 272, supra], this Court held that the diversity of citizenship statute required "complete diversity": where co-citizens appeared on both sides of a dispute, jurisdiction was lost. But Chief Justice Marshall there purported to construe only "The words of the act of Congress," not the Constitution itself. And in a variety of contexts this Court and the lower courts have concluded that Article III poses no obstacle to the legislative extension of federal jurisdiction, founded on diversity, so long as any two adverse parties are not co-citizens. Accordingly, we conclude that the present case is properly in the federal courts.

II.

We do not agree with the Court of Appeals that, in the absence of a state law or contractual provision for "direct action" suits against the insurance company, the company must wait until persons asserting claims against its insured have reduced those claims to judgment before seeking to invoke the benefits of federal interpleader. That may have been a tenable position under the 1926[8] and 1936 interpleader statutes.[9] These statutes did not carry forward the language in the 1917 Act authorizing interpleader where adverse claimants "may claim" benefits as well as

8. 44 Stat. 416 (1926), which added casualty companies to the enumerated categories of plaintiffs able to bring interpleader, and provided for the enjoining of proceedings in other courts.

9. 49 Stat. 1096 (1936), which authorized "bill[s] in the nature of interpleader," meaning those in which the plaintiff is not wholly disinterested with respect to the fund he has deposited in court. * * *

where they "are claiming" them.[10] In 1948, however, in the revision of the Judicial Code, the "may claim" language was restored.[11] Until the decision below, every court confronted by the question has concluded that the 1948 revision removed whatever requirement there might previously have been that the insurance company wait until at least two claimants reduced their claims to judgments. The commentators are in accord.

Considerations of judicial administration demonstrate the soundness of this view which, in any event, seems compelled by the language of the present statute, which is remedial and to be liberally construed. Were an insurance company required to await reduction of claims to judgment, the first claimant to obtain such a judgment or to negotiate a settlement might appropriate all or a disproportionate slice of the fund before his fellow claimants were able to establish their claims. The difficulties such a race to judgment pose for the insurer, and the unfairness which may result to some claimants, were among the principal evils the interpleader device was intended to remedy.

III.

The fact that State Farm had properly invoked the interpleader jurisdiction under § 1335 did not, however, entitle it to an order both enjoining prosecution of suits against it outside the confines of the interpleader proceeding and also extending such protection to its insured, the alleged tortfeasor. Still less was Greyhound Lines entitled to have that order expanded so as to protect itself and its driver, also alleged to be tortfeasors, from suits brought by its passengers in various state or federal courts. Here, the scope of the litigation, in terms of parties and claims, was vastly more extensive than the confines of the "fund," the deposited proceeds of the insurance policy. In these circumstances, the mere existence of such a fund cannot, by use of interpleader, be employed to accomplish purposes that exceed the needs of orderly contest with respect to the fund.

There are situations, of a type not present here, where the effect of interpleader is to confine the total litigation to a single forum and proceeding. One such case is where a stakeholder, faced with rival claims to the fund itself, acknowledges—or denies—his liability to one or the other of the claimants. In this situation, the fund itself is the target of the claimants. It marks the outer limits of the controversy. It is, therefore, reasonable and sensible that interpleader, in discharge of its office to protect the fund, should also protect the stakeholder from vexatious and multiple litigation. In this context, the suits sought to be enjoined are squarely within the language of 28 U.S.C. § 2361 * * *.

---

10. 39 Stat. 929 (1917). See Klaber v. Maryland Cas. Co., 69 F.2d 934, 938–939, 106 A.L.R. 617 (C.A.8th Cir.1934), which held that the omission in the 1926 Act of the earlier statute's "may claim" language required the denial of interpleader in the face of unliquidated claims (alternative holding).

11. * * * [I]t was widely assumed that restoration of the "may claim" language would have the effect of overruling the holding in *Klaber,* supra, that one may not invoke interpleader to protect against unliquidated claims. * * *

But the present case is another matter. Here, an accident has happened. Thirty-five passengers or their representatives have claims which they wish to press against a variety of defendants: the bus company, its driver, the owner of the truck, and the truck driver. The circumstance that one of the prospective defendants happens to have an insurance policy is a fortuitous event which should not of itself shape the nature of the ensuing litigation. * * * [A]n insurance company whose maximum interest in the case cannot exceed $20,000 and who in fact asserts that it has no interest at all, should not be allowed to determine that dozens of tort plaintiffs must be compelled to press their claims—even those claims which are not against the insured and which in no event could be satisfied out of the meager insurance fund—in a single forum of the insurance company's choosing. There is nothing in the statutory scheme, and very little in the judicial and academic commentary upon that scheme, which requires that the tail be allowed to wag the dog in this fashion.

State Farm's interest in this case * * * receives full vindication when the court restrains claimants from seeking to enforce against the insurance company any judgment obtained against its insured, except in the interpleader proceeding itself. To the extent that the District Court sought to control claimants' lawsuits against the insured and other alleged tortfeasors, it exceeded the powers granted to it by the statutory scheme.

We recognize, of course, that our view of interpleader means that it cannot be used to solve all the vexing problems of multiparty litigation arising out of a mass tort. But interpleader was never intended to perform such a function, to be an all-purpose "bill of peace." Had it been so intended, careful provision would necessarily have been made to insure that a party with little or no interest in the outcome of a complex controversy should not strip truly interested parties of substantial rights—such as the right to choose the forum in which to establish their claims, subject to generally applicable rules of jurisdiction, venue, service of process, removal, and change of venue. None of the legislative and academic sponsors of a modern federal interpleader device viewed their accomplishment as a "bill of peace," capable of sweeping dozens of lawsuits out of the various state and federal courts in which they were brought and into a single interpleader proceeding. And only in two reported instances has a federal interpleader court sought to control the underlying litigation against alleged tortfeasors as opposed to the allocation of a fund among successful tort plaintiffs. See Commercial Union Ins. Co. of New York v. Adams, 231 F.Supp. 860 (D.C.S.D.Ind.1964) (where there was virtually no objection and where all of the basic tort suits would in any event have been prosecuted in the forum state), and Pan American Fire & Cas. Co. v. Revere * * *.

In light of the evidence that federal interpleader was not intended to serve the function of a "bill of peace" in the context of multiparty litigation arising out of a mass tort, of the anomalous power which such a construction of the statute would give the stakeholder, and of the thrust of the statute and the purpose it was intended to serve, we hold that the interpleader statute did not authorize the injunction entered in the present case. Upon remand, the injunction is to be modified consistently with this opinion.

IV.

The judgment of the Court of Appeals is reversed * * *.

[JUSTICE DOUGLAS dissented on the ground that the litigants were not "claimants" to the fund as required by the Federal Interpleader Act. He pointed out that the insurance policy specifically provided that no action could be brought against the company until the insured's obligation was determined. Furthermore, he argued, both California and Oregon law did not permit a direct action against the insurer until after final judgment against the insured. The Justice also took issue with the majority's construction of the words "may claim" in the Federal Interpleader Act.]

NOTES AND QUESTIONS

1. In TREINIES v. SUNSHINE MINING CO., 308 U.S. 66, 60 S.Ct. 44, 84 L.Ed. 85 (1939), the Supreme Court held that a federal court could constitutionally assert jurisdiction under the Federal Interpleader Act despite the cocitizenship of the stakeholder and one of the claimants. In arriving at this conclusion, the Court said that the stakeholder's "disinterestedness as between the claimants and as to the property in dispute" was demonstrated by his deposit of the fund in the court, and his discharge, which left the dispute to be ironed out between the "adverse claimants." Id. at 72, 60 S.Ct. at 48, 84 L.Ed. at 90. Was it realistic for the Court to treat the stakeholder as a nominal party for diversity purposes?

2. In *Tashire*, on what basis does the Supreme Court decide that cocitizenship between adverse claimants does not destroy diversity jurisdiction? Would the result have been different had there been a lack of diversity between State Farm and the named defendants and an absence of "complete diversity" among all of the claimants? For a discussion of jurisdiction and interpleader, see 14 Wright, Miller & Cooper, Federal Practice and Procedure: Jurisdiction and Related Matters 3d § 3636.

3. Consider the statement in *Tashire* that "our view of interpleader means that it cannot be used to solve all the vexing problems of multiparty litigation arising out of a mass tort." 386 U.S. at 535, 87 S.Ct. at 1206, 18 L.Ed.2d at 278. Does this prohibit cross-claims between interpleader claimants, the assertion of an unrelated claim by a disinterested stakeholder against a claimant, and a counterclaim by a claimant against the stakeholder? See generally 7 Wright, Miller & Kane, Federal Practice and Procedure: Civil 3d § 1715.

Applicable Law in Federal Interpleader Cases

In GRIFFIN v. McCOACH, 313 U.S. 498, 61 S.Ct. 1023, 85 L.Ed. 1481 (1941), the Supreme Court held that in a statutory interpleader suit based on diversity jurisdiction a federal court is bound by the *Erie* doctrine to apply the conflict-of-law rules of the state in which it sits. The case was decided on the same day as Klaxon Co. v. Stentor Electric Mfg. Co., p. 466, supra. Yet, in certain statutory interpleader actions, the courts of the forum state might never have been able to hear a comparable case due to Fourteenth Amendment limitations on their personal jurisdiction. See Hofmann, *Blurring Lines: How Supplemental Jurisdiction Unknowingly Gave the World Ancillary Personal Jurisdiction*, 38 U.S.F. L. Rev. 809 (2004). For a compelling argument that federal courts should develop their own conflicts rules when a federal act extends service of process beyond what is permitted a state by the Constitution, see *Developments in the Law—Multiparty Litigation in the Federal Courts,* 71 Harv.L.Rev. 877, 924–26 (1958). Are there any other arguments to suggest the inapplicability of *Erie* and *Klaxon* in statutory interpleader cases? Can a federal court grant interpleader under Federal Rule 22 when the state courts would deny interpleader because the stakeholder alleges a personal interest in the outcome of the case?

SECTION G. INTERVENTION

As discussed earlier in this Chapter, through devices such as Federal Rules 19 and 20, the parties may add additional parties to the lawsuit under certain circumstances. These Rules, however, are devices at the disposal of parties already in the lawsuit. But suppose a person learns of a lawsuit, the result of which might affect her. Should she be allowed to enter it as an additional party? Rule 24, which governs intervention, allows a third person to interject himself into a lawsuit, cutting against the grain of the traditional notion that a plaintiff is allowed to control his suit. See 7C Wright, Miller & Kane, Federal Practice and Procedure: Civil 3d § 1901. Consider the following:

> A civil action, in the Anglo–American tradition, has usually been thought of as a private controversy between plaintiff and defendant. Although outsiders were sometimes permitted to take part in order to protect their interests, they were more often regarded by the court and the parties as undesired intermeddlers who would be required to protect themselves—if they could—by bringing a lawsuit of their own. Indeed after courts of admiralty, and later of equity, recognized intervention as a proper means of asserting an interest in property in the custody of the court, there remained considerable uncertainty for many years about whether, and to what extent, intervention could be permitted in a routine action at law.
>
> But in recent decades the increased complexity of litigation and the growing number of cases involving the public interest or a wide variety of private interests have been accompanied by a steady change in the attitude toward intervention. Both intervention of right and permissive intervention were given new vitality in the federal system by adoption of [R]ule 24 of the Federal Rules of Civil Procedure in 1938, and subsequent amendments have broadened their scope.

Shapiro, *Some Thoughts on Intervention before Courts, Agencies, and Arbitrators*, 81 Harv. L. Rev. 721, 721–22 (1968) (footnotes omitted).

Read Federal Rule of Civil Procedure 24 in the Supplement.

SMUCK v. HOBSON

United States Court of Appeals, District of Columbia Circuit, 1969.
132 U.S.App.D.C. 372, 408 F.2d 175.

[In Hobson v. Hansen, 269 F.Supp. 401 (D.D.C.1967), a class action brought on behalf of Black and poor children, the court found that the plaintiffs were being denied their constitutional rights to equal educational opportunities because the District of Columbia schools were being operated on a basis that was racially and economically discriminatory. The Board of Education voted not to appeal and ordered Dr. Carl Hansen, the Superintendent of Schools, not to appeal. Nonetheless, Dr. Hansen and Carl Smuck, one of the dissenting Board members, filed notices of appeal. In addition, motions to intervene were made in the District Court and in the Court of Appeals by Dr. Hansen and twenty parents who said they "dissent from" the court's decision. The Court of Appeals decided to hold the direct appeals in abeyance and remanded the intervention motions for a hearing. The District Court granted the motions to intervene, even though neither Hansen nor the parents had shown a substantial interest that could be protected only through intervention, "in order to give the Court of Appeals an opportunity to pass on the intervention questions raised here, and the questions to be raised by the appeal on the merits * * *." Hobson v. Hansen, 44 F.R.D. 18, 33 (D.D.C.1968). The Court of Appeals then considered the matter *en banc.*]

BAZELON, CHIEF JUDGE.

* * * These appeals challenge the findings of the trial court that the Board of Education has in a variety of ways violated the Constitution in administering the District of Columbia schools. Among the facts that distinguish this case from the normal grist of appellate courts is the absence of the Board of Education as an appellant. Instead, the would-be appellants are Dr. Carl F. Hansen, the resigned superintendent of District schools, who appeals in his former official capacity and as an individual; Carl C. Smuck, a member of the Board of Education, who appeals in that capacity; and the parents of certain school children who have attempted to intervene in order to register on appeal their "dissent" from the order below.

* * * Whatever standing he might have possessed to appeal as a named defendant in the original suit * * * disappeared when Dr. Hansen left his official position. Presumably because he was aware of this, he subsequently moved to intervene under Rule 24(a) [now Rule 24(a)(2)] of the Rules of Civil Procedure in order to appeal as an individual. * * * He does not claim that a reversal or modification of the order by this Court

would make his return to office likely. Consequently, the supposed impact of the decision upon his tenure is irrelevant insofar as an appeal is concerned, since a reversal would have no effect. Dr. Hansen thus has no "interest relating to the property or transaction which is the subject of the action" sufficient for Rule 24(a), and intervention is therefore unwarranted.

We also find that Mr. Smuck has no appealable interest as a member of the Board of Education. While he was in that capacity a named defendant, the Board of Education was undeniably the principal figure and could have been sued alone as a collective entity. Appellant Smuck had a fair opportunity to participate in its defense, and in the decision not to appeal. Having done so, he has no separate interest as an individual in the litigation. The order directs the board to take certain actions. But since its decisions are made by vote as a collective whole, there is no apparent way in which Smuck as an individual could violate the decree and thereby become subject to enforcement proceedings.

The motion to intervene by the parents presents a more difficult problem requiring a correspondingly more detailed examination of the requirements for intervention of right.

* * *

The phrasing of Rule 24(a)(2) as amended parallels that of Rule 19(a)(2) [now Rule 19(a)(1)(B)] concerning joinder. But the fact that the two rules are entwined does not imply that an "interest" for the purpose of one is precisely the same as for the other. The occasions upon which a petitioner should be allowed to intervene under Rule 24 are not necessarily limited to those situations when the trial court should compel him to become a party under Rule 19. And while the division of Rule 24(a) and (b) into "Intervention of Right" and "Permissible Intervention" might superficially suggest that only the latter involves an exercise of discretion by the court, the contrary is clearly the case.

The effort to extract substance from the conclusory phrase "interest" or "legally protectable interest" is of limited promise. Parents unquestionably have a sufficient "interest" in the education of their children to justify the initiation of a lawsuit in appropriate circumstances, as indeed was the case for the plaintiff-appellee parents here. But in the context of intervention the question is not whether a lawsuit should be begun, but whether already initiated litigation should be extended to include additional parties. The 1966 amendments to Rule 24(a) have facilitated this, the true inquiry, by eliminating the temptation or need for tangential expeditions in search of "property" or someone "bound by a judgment." It would be unfortunate to allow the inquiry to be led once again astray by a myopic fixation upon "interest." Rather, as Judge Leventhal recently concluded for this Court, "[A] more instructive approach is to let our construction be guided by the policies behind the 'interest' requirement. * * * [T]he 'interest' test is primarily a practical guide to disposing of lawsuits by involving as many apparently concerned persons as is compatible with efficiency and due process."[12]

The decision whether intervention of right is warranted thus involves an accommodation between two potentially conflicting goals: to achieve judicial economies of scale by resolving related issues in a single lawsuit, and to prevent the single lawsuit from becoming fruitlessly complex or unending. Since this task will depend upon the contours of the particular controversy, general rules and past decisions cannot provide uniformly dependable guides. The Supreme Court, in its only full-dress examination of Rule 24(a) since the 1966 amendments, found that a gas distributor was entitled to intervention of right although its only "interest" was the economic harm it claimed would follow from an allegedly inadequate plan for divestiture approved by the Government in an antitrust proceeding.[14] While conceding that the Court's opinion granting intervention in Cascade Natural Gas Corp. v. El Paso Natural Gas Co. "is certainly susceptible of a very broad reading," the trial judge here would distinguish the decision on the ground that the petitioner "did show a strong direct economic interest, for the new company [to be created by divestiture] would be its sole supplier." Yet while it is undoubtedly true that "*Cascade* should not be read as a carte blanche for intervention by anyone at any time," there is no apparent reason why an "economic interest" should always be necessary to justify intervention. The goal of "disposing of lawsuits by involving as many apparently concerned persons as is compatible with efficiency and due process" may in certain circumstances be met by allowing parents whose only "interest" is the education of their children to intervene. In determining whether such circumstances are present, the first requirement of Rule 24(a)(2), that of an "interest" in the transaction, may be a less useful point of departure than the second and third requirements, that the applicant may be impeded in protecting his interest by the action and that his interest is not adequately represented by others.

This does not imply that the need for an "interest" in the controversy should or can be read out of the rule. But the requirement should be viewed as a prerequisite rather than relied upon as a determinative criterion for intervention. If barriers are needed to limit extension of the right to intervene, the criteria of practical harm to the applicant and the adequacy of representation by others are better suited to the task. If those requirements are met, the nature of his "interest" may play a role in determining the sort of intervention which should be allowed—whether, for example, he should be permitted to contest all issues, and whether he should enjoy all the prerogatives of a party litigant.

Both courts and legislatures have recognized as appropriate the concern for their children's welfare which the parents here seek to protect by intervention. While the artificiality of an appeal without the Board of Education cannot be ignored, neither can the importance of the constitu-

12. Nuesse v. Camp, 128 U.S.App.D.C. 172, 385 F.2d 694, 700 (1967).

14. Cascade Natural Gas Corp. v. El Paso Natural Gas Co., 386 U.S. 129, 132–136, 87 S.Ct. 932, 17 L.Ed.2d 814 (1967).

tional issues decided below. The relevance of substantial and unsettled questions of law has been recognized in allowing intervention to perfect an appeal. And this Court has noted repeatedly, "obviously tailored to fit ordinary civil litigation, [the provisions of Rule 24] require other than literal application in atypical cases."[20] We conclude that the interests asserted by the intervenors are sufficient to justify an examination of whether the two remaining requirements for intervention are met.

* * *

[The court then determined that the disposition of the action might impair the applicants' ability to protect their interests if they were not allowed to intervene.]

The remaining requirement for intervention is that the applicant not be adequately represented by others. No question is raised here but that the Board of Education adequately represented the intervenors at the trial below; the issue rather is whether the parents were adequately represented by the school board's decision not to appeal. The presumed good faith of the board in reaching this decision is not conclusive. * * * As the conditional wording of Rule 24(a)(2) suggests in permitting intervention "unless the applicant's interest is adequately represented by existing parties," "the burden [is] on those opposing intervention to show the adequacy of the existing representation." In this case, the interests of the parents who wish to intervene in order to appeal do not coincide with those of the Board of Education. The school board represents all parents within the District. The intervening appellants may have more parochial interests centering upon the education of their own children. While they cannot of course ask the Board to favor their children unconstitutionally at the expense of others, they like other parents can seek the adoption of policies beneficial to their own children. Moreover, considerations of publicity, cost, and delay may not have the same weight for the parents as for the school board in the context of a decision to appeal. And the Board of Education, buffeted as it like other school boards is by conflicting public demands, may possibly have less interest in preserving its own untrammeled discretion than do the parents. It is not necessary to accuse the board of bad faith in deciding not to appeal or of a lack of vigor in defending the suit below in order to recognize that a restrictive court order may be a not wholly unwelcome haven.

* * *

Our holding that the appellants would be practically disadvantaged by a decision without appeal in this case and that they are not otherwise adequately represented necessitates a closer scrutiny of the precise nature of their interest and the scope of intervention that should accordingly be granted. The parents who seek to appeal do not come before this court to

20. Textile Workers Union, etc. v. Allendale Co., 96 U.S.App.D.C. 401, 403, 226 F.2d 765, 767 (1955) (en banc), cert. denied, Allendale Co. v. Mitchell, 351 U.S. 909, 76 S.Ct. 699, 100 L.Ed. 1444 (1956), cited in Nuesse v. Camp, 128 U.S.App.D.C. 172, 385 F.2d 694, 700 (1967).

protect the good name of the Board of Education. Their interest is not to protect the board, or Dr. Hansen, from an unfair finding. Their asserted interest is rather the freedom of the school board—and particularly the new school board recently elected—to exercise the broadest discretion constitutionally permissible in deciding upon educational policies. Since this is so, their interest extends only to those parts of the order which can fairly be said to impose restraints upon the Board of Education. And because the school board is not a party to this appeal, review should be limited to those features of the order which limit the discretion of the old or new board.

* * *

[A partial concurring opinion by JUDGE MCGOWAN and dissenting opinions by JUDGES DANAHER and BURGER are omitted.]

NOTES AND QUESTIONS

1. In addition to the reasons offered in *Smuck,* typical grounds for the assertion of inadequacy of representation for purposes of intervening as of right under Rule 24(a)(2) are: the applicant's interests are not represented at all, Purnell v. City of Akron, 925 F.2d 941 (6th Cir.1991); the applicant and the attorney who supposedly represents his interest are antagonistic, United States v. C.M. Lane Lifeboat Co., 25 F.Supp. 410 (E.D.N.Y.1938), but see Stadin v. Union Elec. Co., 309 F.2d 912 (8th Cir.1962), certiorari denied 373 U.S. 915, 83 S.Ct. 1298, 10 L.Ed.2d 415 (1963); and there is collusion between the representative and the adverse parties, Commonwealth of Virginia v. Westinghouse Elec. Corp., 542 F.2d 214 (4th Cir.1976). It often is held that the United States adequately represents the public interest in antitrust suits and intervention in those cases is denied absent a clear showing to the contrary. Is this approach justifiable? How does the Department of Justice determine what the public interest is?

2. What factors affect the standard for adequate representation? In NATURAL RESOURCES DEFENSE COUNCIL, INC. v. NEW YORK STATE DEPARTMENT OF ENVIRONMENTAL CONSERVATION, 834 F.2d 60 (2d Cir.1987), the American Petroleum Institute (API) appealed a District Court order denying its motion to intervene in a "citizen suit" brought by the Natural Resources Defense Council, Inc. and other groups concerned with air pollution against the New York State Department of Environmental Conservation, the United States Environmental Protection Agency, and the administrators of both agencies. The Court of Appeals affirmed:

> * * * API contends that in this suit it too has an interest different from that of New York. API's interest, it urges, is economic, whereas the State's interest is governmental.
>
> We think API misperceives the concept of an interest "adequately represented" within the meaning of Rule 24. A putative intervenor does not have an interest not adequately represented by a party to a lawsuit simply because it has a motive to litigate that is different from the motive of an existing party. So long as the party has demonstrated sufficient

> motivation to litigate vigorously and to present all colorable contentions, a district judge does not exceed the bounds of discretion by concluding that the interests of the intervenor are adequately represented. * * *
>
> * * *

Id. Is this case consistent with *Smuck*? Why do you think the two come out differently? See Vreeland, *Public Interest Groups, Public Law Litigation, and Federal Rule 24(a)*, 57 U. Chi. L. Rev. 279 (1990).

3. Should there be a different standard for an intervenor to take an appeal than for a party who seeks to intervene in the original action? Should the original party's motive in deciding not to appeal be a relevant consideration? In the Seventh Circuit, "intervention to take an appeal is permissible only if the original parties' decision to discontinue the battle reflects 'gross negligence or bad faith' * * *." United States v. Chicago, 897 F.2d 243, 244 (7th Cir.1990), citing United States v. South Bend Community School Corp., 692 F.2d 623, 627 (7th Cir.1982).

4. An example of a federal statute that permits intervention is Section 902 of the Civil Rights Act of 1964, 42 U.S.C. § 2000h–2, which gives the United States an unconditional right to intervene in actions seeking relief against a denial of equal protection of the laws under the Fourteenth Amendment on account of race, color, religion, sex, or national origin. See Lemon v. Bossier Parish School Bd., 240 F.Supp. 709 (W.D.La.1965), affirmed 370 F.2d 847 (5th Cir.1967), certiorari denied 388 U.S. 911, 87 S.Ct. 2116, 18 L.Ed.2d 1350 (1967). Perhaps the single most important statutory provision permitting intervention by the United States is Section 2403(a) of the Judicial Code, which applies to actions challenging the constitutionality of an act of Congress. This provision has even enabled the United States to intervene to show that a case should be decided on nonconstitutional grounds. See Smolowe v. Delendo Corp., 36 F.Supp. 790 (S.D.N.Y.1940), affirmed on other grounds 136 F.2d 231 (2d Cir.), certiorari denied 320 U.S. 751, 64 S.Ct. 56, 88 L.Ed. 446 (1943). The government also has used it to show that the suit is collusive and there is no case or controversy before the court. See United States v. Johnson, 319 U.S. 302, 63 S.Ct. 1075, 87 L.Ed. 1413 (1943). See 7C Wright, Miller & Kane, Federal Practice and Procedure: Civil 3d § 1906, for a discussion of other statutes conferring an unconditional right to intervene. 28 U.S.C. § 2403(b) extends the intervention right to states in actions involving the constitutionality of state statutes.

5. Both Rule 24(a) and Rule 24(b) require that an application to intervene be "timely." As the court noted in *Smuck*, intervention after judgment will be allowed only in unique situations. One court has stated:

> The rationale which seems to underlie this general principle * * * is the assumption that allowing intervention after judgment will either (1) prejudice the rights of the existing parties to the litigation or (2) substantially interfere with the orderly processes of the court.

McDONALD v. E.J. LAVINO CO., 430 F.2d 1065, 1072 (5th Cir.1970).

What factors should the court consider when determining whether a motion to intervene is timely? Should a different standard be used for deciding the timeliness of motions to intervene permissively as opposed to motions to intervene as of right? If so, why? Sullivan, *Enforcement of Government Antitrust Decrees by Private Parties: Third Party Beneficiary Rights and Intervenor Status*, 123 U.Pa.L.Rev. 822, 873–92 (1975), explores the possibility of post-judgment intervention in government antitrust suits in order to enforce the judgment.

6. Must an intervenor present an independent basis for subject-matter jurisdiction? Before Congress enacted 28 U.S.C. § 1367, as a general rule, if the applicant had a right to intervene under Rule 24(a), no independent basis for jurisdiction was required. See Lenz v. Wagner, 240 F.2d 666 (5th Cir. 1957). An independent basis for jurisdiction was required for permissive actions. See, e.g., Reedsburg Bank v. Apollo, 508 F.2d 995 (7th Cir.1975). When subject-matter jurisdiction for the original action is based on diversity, what effect does Section 1367(b) have on non-diverse plaintiffs seeking to intervene under Rule 24(a)? Can an intervenor assert additional claims, counterclaims, cross-claims, or third-party claims in the lawsuit? Should your answer depend upon whether the intervention was discretionary or as of right? Does the answer turn on the nature of the claim: compulsory or permissive? See 7C Wright, Miller & Kane, Federal Practice and Procedure: Civil 3d § 1917.

7. Rule 24 treats intervention as a permissive joinder device, so that the "outsider" to the litigation has the option of joining the lawsuit or not. Should a court ever require a potential party to intervene in a lawsuit? The Supreme Court considered and rejected this position in MARTIN v. WILKS, 490 U.S. 755, 109 S.Ct. 2180, 104 L.Ed.2d 835 (1989). The case involved a challenge by white firefighters to hiring decisions taken by the City of Birmingham pursuant to consent decrees that had been entered in federal civil rights suits on behalf of black individuals who allegedly had been denied employment or promotion on the basis of their race. The District Court dismissed the white firefighters' lawsuit on the ground, among others, that the plaintiffs had not intervened in the prior cases and therefore could not collaterally challenge the consent decrees. The Supreme Court, 5–4, held that "[k]nowledge of a lawsuit" does not obligate a party to intervene in a lawsuit; "a party seeking a judgment binding on another cannot obligate that person to intervene; he must be joined." Id. at 763–65, 109 S.Ct. 2185–86, 104 L.Ed.2 at 846–47. Justice Stevens, in a dissent, underscored that "in complex litigation this Court has squarely held that a sideline-sitter may be bound as firmly as an actual party if he had adequate notice and a fair opportunity to intervene and if the judicial interest in finality is sufficiently strong." Id. at 793, 109 S.Ct. at 2200–01, 104 L.Ed.2d at 863. Why did Federal Rule 19 not require the joinder of the white firefighters in the earlier discrimination suits? Are you persuaded that permissive party-initiated joinder is a better approach than a rule of mandatory intervention? See Brunet, *The Triumph of Efficiency and Discretion Over Competing Complex Litigation Policies*, 10 Rev. Litig. 273 (1991).

CHAPTER 10

CLASS ACTIONS

■ ■ ■

This Chapter explores class action practice under Federal Rule 23. A noted commentator says: "Perhaps the most dramatic development in civil procedure in recent decades has been the growth of interest in the class action as an actual and potential means of resolving a wide range of disputes." Shapiro, *Class Actions: The Class as Party and Client*, 73 Notre Dame L. Rev. 913, 913 (1998). Probably no procedural device more often finds itself at the center of political controversy, or is as frequently featured in a newspaper headline, as that of the class action. The materials are designed to introduce you to this complex yet fascinating topic through an examination of the history of the class action device, the operation of Federal Rule 23, the problems that have developed with different kinds of class actions, and the policy questions that this practice raises. The class action, like all of the Federal Rules, continues to be a work in progress. The Advisory Committee on Civil Rules of the United States Judicial Conference, with the aid of numerous lawyers and academics, frequently considers whether Rule 23 is in need of revision and, if so, what shape any changes should take. As you progress through this Chapter, put yourself in role as a member of the Committee and ask what amendments, if any, that you would make.

SECTION A. OVERVIEW AND THEMES

Class action practice developed to address situations in which it is not feasible for a plaintiff to sue individually or for all of those relevant to a dispute to be joined in a single action. The procedure allows a single plaintiff to represent similarly situated persons and to advance their claims. By its very structure, the class action device presents concerns about the due process rights of absent class members and the proper application of the rules of finality. See generally Issacharoff, *Governance and Legitimacy in the Law of Class Actions*, 1999 Sup.Ct.Rev. 337 (1999). Each decision about whether to proceed on a class basis obliges a judge to balance the advantages of a single adjudication with notions of fairness to absent people whose claims may be extinguished by the action.

The class action device can be viewed simply as another joinder device, or it can be viewed as something different—a representational device that empowers the named class representative to act on behalf of others similarly situated whether they could have sued independently, or even wanted to do so. See Hutchinson, *Class Actions: Joinder or Representational Device?*, 1984 Sup.Ct.Rev. 459. Although the 1966 amendments to Rule 23 moved in the direction of the representational model, courts (including the Supreme Court) have vacillated between these two views of the procedure. Is the class action only a procedural convenience that goes slightly beyond Rule 20, or is the device completely different from other approaches to aggregate litigation? For discussions of this issue, see Silver, *Comparing Class Actions and Consolidations*, 10 Rev. Litig. 495 (1991); Cabraser, *The Class Action Counterreformation*, 57 Stan. L. Rev. 1475 (2005).

One other general issue should engage your attention. The rules governing class actions depart from the traditional adversarial notion that individuals can be bound by a court judgment only when they themselves have had a day in court. See Bone, *Rethinking the "Day in Court" Ideal and Nonparty Preclusion*, 67 N.Y.U. L. Rev. 193 (1992). What justifies this departure? What is there about the procedures that have been developed around the class action device that makes it possible and fair to bind a party who has not made an appearance in court? As you consider these questions, pay special attention to the connections among the doctrines governing notice, adequate representation, and res judicata (studied in more detail in Chapter 17, p. 1249, infra). See generally Redish & Larsen, *Class Actions, Litigant Autonomy, and the Foundations of Procedural Due Process*, 95 Cal. L. Rev. 1573 (2007).

Read Federal Rule of Civil Procedure 23 and the material accompanying it in the Supplement.

SECTION B. HISTORY OF THE CLASS ACTION

The class action procedure can be traced to the English "bill of peace" in the seventeenth century, a procedural device utilized by the Courts of Chancery. The "bill" allowed an action to be brought by or against representative parties when (1) the number of persons involved was too large to permit joinder, (2) all the members of the group possessed a joint interest in the question being adjudicated, and (3) the named parties adequately represented the interests of those who were not present. If these three conditions were met, the judgment that ultimately was entered was binding on all the members of the represented group. An excellent summary of the history of class actions can be found in Yeazell, From Medieval Group Litigation to the Modern Class Action (1987).

Since then, the class action procedure has undergone substantial development. The evolution of the rules governing class actions in part parallels an evolution in society and in society's understanding of the role of courts and of individual rights. As two early commentators on the Federal Rules put it:

> Modern society seems increasingly to expose men to * * * group injuries for which individually they are in a poor position to seek legal redress, either because they do not know enough or because such redress is disproportionately expensive. If each is left to assert his rights alone if and when he can, there will at best be a random and fragmentary enforcement, if there is any at all. This result is not only unfortunate in the particular case, but it will operate seriously to impair the deterrent effect of the sanctions which underlie much contemporary law. The problem of fashioning an effective and inclusive group remedy is thus a major one.

Kalven & Rosenfield, *The Contemporary Function of a Class Suit,* 8 U.Chi.L.Rev. 684, 686 (1941).

Provisions for class actions based upon the English procedure existed in various state codes and the Federal Equity Rules. Federal Rule 23, as originally adopted in 1938, marked "a bold * * * attempt to encourage more frequent use of class actions," making the device available in both legal and equitable actions in the federal courts. 7A Wright, Miller & Kane, Federal Practice and Procedure: Civil 3d § 1752. The original rule, however, proved very confusing to apply, and in 1966 the Advisory Committee rewrote Rule 23 to provide a functional test for class certification and to provide some procedural guidance for the courts with regard to handling class actions. The amendments also made clear that a judgment in a class action is binding on all class members, except in those cases in which the right to opt-out applies and has been exercised.

Class action practice greatly expanded after the 1966 amendments to Federal Rule 23. However, at the time of their adoption, the mass tort phenomenon—"in those days often called 'mass accidents' "—had not yet developed. Resnik, *Aggregation, Settlement, and Dismay*, 80 Cornell L. Rev. 918, 922 (1995). Indeed, the Advisory Committee that drafted the 1966 amendments sounded a note of caution that one accident would affect different parties in different ways raising different factual and legal issues—a feature it saw as incompatible with unitary adjudication. Since then, attitudes have changed, and in recent years mass tort class actions have become relatively common, although fraught with controversy. Some commentators view mass tort class actions as efficient vehicles for resolving disputes by multiple litigants who have similar claims against the same defendant, particularly when practical considerations make individual lawsuits unlikely or impossible. However, as will be seen below, the use of class actions in this context has posed numerous and complex procedural questions. Some commentators have criticized these suits for generating unwarranted legal fees, for causing inflated product prices, for contributing to corporate bankruptcies, and for raising due process concerns because of the lack of plaintiff autonomy. On the other hand, commentators have emphasized that mass tort class actions are critical for securing judicial access, for promoting efficiency, and for creating incentives that deter institutional wrongdoing. See generally Coffee, Jr., *Class Wars: The Dilemma of the Mass Tort Class Action*, 95 Colum. L. Rev. 1343 (1995).

The 1966 amendments also expanded the use of class actions in public-law cases involving civil rights and such issues as desegregation, affirmative action, and voter registration. Some commentators regard class actions as an essential form of First Amendment expression that provides a critical bulwark against executive and legislative abuse. However, questions also have been raised whether it is appropriate to use class-action litigation to overturn legislative decisions that have been reached by democratic majorities. See Redish, *Class Actions and the Democratic Difficulty: Rethinking the Intersection of Private Litigation and Public Goals*, 2003 U. Chi. Legal F. 71 (2003).

MILLER, *OF FRANKENSTEIN MONSTERS AND SHINING KNIGHTS: MYTH, REALITY, AND THE "CLASS ACTION PROBLEM,"* 92 Harv.L.Rev. 664, 665–66 (1979) (footnotes omitted):

* * * Opinions regarding the effect of the [1966] revision [to Federal Rule 23] range over an amazing gamut. Class action adherents would have us believe it is a panacea for a myriad of social ills, which deters unlawful conduct and compensates those injured by it. Catch phrases such as "therapeutic" or "prophylactic" and "[taking] care of the smaller guy" are frequently trumpeted. Its opponents have rallied around characterizations of the procedure as a form of "legalized blackmail" or a "Frankenstein Monster." They also have charged widespread abuse of the rule by lawyers and litigants on both sides of the "v.," including unprofessional practices relating to attorneys' fees, "sweetheart" settlement deals, dilatory motion practice, harassing discovery, and misrepresentations to judges. Finally, some have questioned the wisdom of imposing the burdens of class actions on an already overtaxed federal judiciary. They assert that many Rule 23 cases are unmanageable and inordinately protracted by opposing counsel, creating a certain millstone or dinosaur character that diverts federal judges from matters more worthy of their energies.

* * *

Eight years after Professor Miller wrote his *Harvard Law Review* article, he served as the Reporter for a study of complex litigation for the American Law Institute. In it, he wrote:

> Class actions have proven to be the most effective legal technique for avoiding piecemeal litigation and preserving legal resources. Nevertheless, the class action suit continues to be eyed with suspicion by many courts. In complex cases, the goals of the class action device have been frustrated by strict adherence to the requirements of Rule 23. Often, complex multiparty, multiforum cases are denied class action treatment. Certification of large scale tort action classes is rare. Courts deny certification based on decisions that the commonality of interest requirement is not satisfied and based on fear that the size of the class would make the litigation unwieldy and inefficient.
>
> Generally, present treatment of class action suits begins with an initial skepticism towards the class. Cases that involve incidents of personal injury occurring in a series of related events that may be separated by time or geography are usually denied certification. In the case of property damage, the class may receive certification but courts are wary that the litigation may degenerate into individual suits over specific pieces of property. Courts are split as to whether mass tort cases should be certified as * * * cases [in which litigants are not permitted to opt-out of the class]. Proponents argue that certification is more beneficial when total damages requested exceeds defendant's net worth. Detractors are concerned that such certification is merely a shortcut around notice and opt-out requirements. * * *
>
> The usefulness of the class action device for future complex litigation raises two issues concerning the suitability of class actions to modern litigation needs. The first issue is whether the scope of the class action should be broadened to include more types of litigation. The second is whether courts should increase the frequency with which they certify mandatory classes. Presently, class actions are used relatively infrequently in many multiparty, multiforum litigation contexts. With some adjustments the class action device could be made a valuable litigation tool.

American Law Institute, Preliminary Study of Complex Litigation, Report, 61–70 (1987). The Preliminary Study was followed by a comprehensive exploration of the subject, which led to the American Law Institute's formal approval of Complex Litigation: Statutory Recommendations and Analysis (1994). In 2003, the American Law Institute began a major reexamination of the class action in the context of an assessment of aggregate litigation. See American Law Institute, Principles of the Law of Aggregate Litigation, Council Draft No. 2, Nov. 18, 2008.

Questions about the use and abuse of class action procedure have generated a great deal of discussion and research. In 1996, the Research Division of the Federal Judicial Center conducted an empirical study of the use of Rule 23 in four federal districts. Willging, Hooper & Niemic, *An Empirical Analysis of Rule 23 to Address the Rulemaking Challenges*, 71

N.Y.U. L. Rev. 74 (1996). It was a surprise to some that the study found that not all applications of Rule 23 are difficult; indeed, there are significant numbers of "routine" class actions, particularly in the securities and civil rights contexts. The study also seemed to demonstrate that attorney's fees were not disproportionate to class recoveries. As with most civil litigation, class actions follow the general pattern of settlement in lieu of trial. Although anecdotes abound that the mere instigation of a class action suit or at least its certification coerces settlements even in frivolous cases, the study seemed to belie that notion because the certified cases that settled had survived motions to dismiss or motions for summary judgment. See also Silver, *"We're Scared to Death": Class Certification and Blackmail*, 78 N.Y.U. L. Rev. 1357 (2003).

Although Rule 23 retains "the basic architecture" of the 1966 version, it also has undergone some important changes. See Bronsteen & Fiss, *The Class Action Rule*, 78 Notre Dame L. Rev. 1419, 1420 (2003). First, amendments to Rule 23 have brought more demanding requirements for notice, the availability of interlocutory appeals, and opportunities for greater judicial supervision of class counsel and their fees in an effort to afford better protection to absent class members. See pp. 768–77, infra. Second, Congress has made a federal forum available for most large stakes, interstate, state-law class actions on the basis of minimal diversity jurisdiction. See Class Action Fairness Act of 2005, amending 28 U.S.C. §§ 1332, 1453. See pp. 276–78, infra. Finally, Congress has changed the rules of class action practice for particular areas of law. See Leubsdorf, *Class Actions at the Cloverleaf*, 39 Ariz. L. Rev. 453, 454 (1997). See also Sanderson III, *Note—Congressional Involvement in Class Action Reform: A Survey of Legislative Proposals Past and Present*, 2 N.Y.U. J. Legis. & Pub. Pol'y 315, 317 (1998–99). These areas include:

> Securities Fraud. Congress has enacted specific additional requirements for securities fraud class actions filed under federal law. See The Private Securities Litigation Reform Act of 1995 (PSLRA), codified in scattered sections of Title 15 of the United States Code. See Miller, *The Pretrial Rush to Judgment: Are the "Litigation Explosion," "Liability Crisis," and Efficiency Clichés Eroding Our Day in Court and Jury Trial Commitments?*, 78 N.Y.U. L. Rev. 982, 1000–01 (2003). In 1998, Congress passed the Securities Litigation Uniform Standards Act of 1998 which preempts certain state law securities class action claims. See 15 U.S.C. § 78bb(f)(1).
>
> Immigration. Congress has restricted class-wide relief in certain immigration cases. See The Omnibus Consolidated Appropriations Act of 1997, Pub. L. No. 104–208 § 306(a)(2), 110 Stat. 3009–610 (1996). See generally Volpp, *Court–Stripping and Class–Wide Relief: A Response to Judicial Review in Immigration Cases after AADC*, 14 Geo. Immigr. L.J. 463, 465–77 (2000).
>
> Legal Services. Congress has barred indigent litigants, represented by lawyers in organizations that receive any money from the federally

funded Legal Services Corporation, from participating in class action lawsuits, unless the organizations establish privately financed physically and legally separate affiliate organizations through which to do this work. See The Legal Services Corporation Act, 88 Stat. 378, 42 U.S.C. § 2996e(d)(5); Omnibus Consolidated Rescissions and Appropriations Act of 1996, Pub. L. No. 104–134, § 504(a)(7), 110 Stat. 1321–53. See generally Bornstein, *From the Viewpoint of the Poor: An Analysis of the Constitutionality of the Restriction on Class Action Involvement by Legal Services Attorneys*, 2003 U. Chi. Legal F. 693 (2003); Luban, *Taking Out the Adversary: The Assault on Progressive Public–Interest Lawyers*, 91 Cal. L. Rev. 209 (2003).

As you read the materials that follow, consider the different goals that class actions are expected to serve and how effective the practice has been in different legal contexts.

Note on Class Actions From an International Perspective

Commentators frequently point to the class action as "a uniquely American procedural device." Sherman, *Group Litigation Under Foreign Legal Systems: Variations and Alternatives to American Class Actions*, 52 DePaul L. Rev. 401, 401 (2002). English group litigation orders are far more limited than representative actions in the United States, and it has long been assumed that civil law systems are resistant to the class action. See Andrews, *Multi–Party Proceedings in England: Representative and Group Actions*, 11 Duke J. Comp. & Int'l L. 249 (2001); Rowe, *Debates over Group Litigation in Comparative Perspective: What Can We Learn from Each Other?*, 11 Duke J. Comp. & Int'l L. 157, 158 (2001). However, international interest in the class action, or at least in aggregative mechanisms that allow for group or representative litigation, seems to be on the upsurge. Professor Gidi writes: "Despite initial skepticism and strong academic opposition, good sense has suggested and experience proven, that class actions are compatible with civil law systems." Gidi, *Class Actions in Brazil—A Model for Civil Law Countries*, 51 Am. J. Comp. L. 311, 313 (2003). Professor Nagareda likewise has pointed to "greater receptiveness" among foreign countries toward aggregate litigation, although he emphasizes that these trends so far have stopped short of adopting American-style class actions. See Nagareda, *Aggregate Litigation Across the Atlantic and the Future of American Exceptionalism*, 62 Vand. L. Rev. 1 (2009). For illustrative examples, see Chung, *Note—Introduction to South Korea's New Securities–Related Class Action*, 30 J. Corp. L. 165 (2004); Lindblom, *Individual Litigation and Mass Justice: A Swedish Perspective and Proposal on Group Actions in Civil Procedure*, 45 Am. J. Comp. L. 805 (1997). In addition, Germany has adopted aggregative procedures for securities cases. See Act on the Initiation of Model Case Proceedings in Respect of Investors in the Capital Markets, http://www.bmj.bund.de/files/-/1110/KapMuG_english.odf (site last visited April 15, 2009). For an overview of current developments, see Chase, Hershkoff, Silberman, Taniguchi, Varano & Zuckerman, Civil Litigation in Comparative Context 390–423 (Chase & Hershkoff eds. 2007). What do you think accounts for these changing attitudes toward collective litigation?

SECTION C. OPERATION OF THE CLASS ACTION DEVICE

1. INTRODUCTION

Federal Rule 23, which has had a significant impact on state class action procedures, provides a paradigm that can be used to study the operation of class-action provisions generally. Although there are defendant class actions, the plaintiff class action (which is far more common) will be the model used in this discussion.

2. THE INITIATION OF CLASS ACTIONS

Class action lawsuits are commenced in the same way as other lawsuits, namely by the filing of a complaint and the service of a summons. The difference, however, is that a class action lawsuit is filed in a representative capacity on behalf of persons who are similarly situated to the named plaintiff. These represented parties are said to be "absent" and probably do not even know that a lawsuit is being filed. See Fiss, *The Political Theory of the Class Action*, 53 Wash. & Lee L. Rev. 21, 25 (1996). The caption specifies the name of the representative plaintiff and also indicates that the lawsuit is being filed in a representative capacity. The class-action complaint typically alleges the claims of the named plaintiff and also sets forth classwide allegations of the unnamed putative class members.

In practice, attorneys often play a critical role in causing class suits to be brought. Sometimes, attorneys simply persuade individuals who have a legal problem that the best way to obtain a remedy is by filing a class action embracing the claims of others who are similarly situated. Other times, attorneys actually solicit clients for class suits. See Coffee, Jr., *Understanding the Plaintiff's Attorney: The Implications of Economic Theory for Private Enforcement of Law through Class and Derivative Actions*, 86 Colum. L. Rev. 669 (1986). In what some think is a modern version of ambulance chasing, a lawyer, upon hearing of a disaster, may contact one of the victims and offer to serve as counsel in a class action. The Supreme Court has held that this form of solicitation—for the lawyer's personal gain—is prohibited by legal ethical rules. See Ohralik v. Ohio State Bar Ass'n, 436 U.S. 447, 98 S.Ct. 1912, 56 L.Ed.2d 444 (1978). But there are other examples in which the solicitation of clients for class suits is permissible and indeed an important part of democratic life. For instance, during the 1960's and 1970's NAACP lawyers went to the South to inform minorities of their legal rights and to offer themselves as counsel to those who decided to bring suit. The Supreme Court has held that offers of legal services in this context are a form of political expression, and that prohibitions against solicitation are invalid on First Amendment grounds. See In re Primus, 436 U.S. 412, 98 S.Ct. 1893, 56 L.Ed.2d 417 (1978).

3. CERTIFICATION

A. FEDERAL RULE 23(a): "PREREQUISITES"

A plaintiff seeking to file a class action complaint in federal court does not need permission from the court. However, the court will not certify the lawsuit as a class action unless various prerequisites are satisfied. The plaintiff bringing the action has the burden to meet each of these requirements. Rule 23(c)(1)(A) obliges the court to "determine by order" whether to certify the class "[a]t an early practicable time."

1. *The Requirement of a Class.* Conceptually, the first requirement plaintiff must meet is that there be a class. This may sound self-evident, but the 1966 amendment to Rule 23 did not specify this requirement and the condition was only judicially-created. Rule 23 has been amended to require the court that issues the certification order "to define the class and the class claims, issues, or defenses." Federal Rule 23(c)(1)(B). Because a classwide judgment will have profound effects on unnamed class members, definition of the class is important in order to specify which individuals will be affected by the lawsuit and which will not.

Although there is no hard-and-fast rule governing definition of the class, courts generally require that a proposed class definition "be precise, objective, and presently ascertainable," and also that it "not depend on subjective criteria or the merits of the case or require extensive factual inquiry to determine who is a class member." In re Copper Antitrust Litigation, 196 F.R.D. 348 (W.D. Wis.2000) (citations omitted); see generally 7A Wright, Miller & Kane, Federal Practice and Procedure: Civil 3d § 1760. Class definitions may fail if they are too broad (e.g., "all learning disabled children in the state of Texas"); too specific (e.g., "all people with Spanish surnames having Spanish, Mexican, or Indian ancestry who spoke Spanish as a primary or secondary language"); too vague (e.g., "all users of drug X who suffered medical problems"); or too amorphous (e.g., "all recipients of unsolicited SPAM messages"). In Rink v. Cheminova, Inc., 203 F.R.D. 648 (M.D.Fla.2001), the court rejected, as lacking "sufficient precision or specificity," a proposed subclass consisting of all persons living or employed in certain Florida counties from June 1997 through October 1998 and who were exposed to malathion-based insecticide during the class period. What was the problem with this class definition?

2. *The Class Representative Must Be a Member of the Class.* The second requirement is that the class representative must be a member of the class. This requirement, grounded in the language of Rule 23(a) that "[o]ne or more members of a class may sue or be sued as representative parties," is sometimes analogized to that of a standing requirement. See Lee v. Washington, 390 U.S. 333, 88 S.Ct. 994, 19 L.Ed.2d 1212 (1968). Gratz v. Bollinger, 539 U.S. 244, 123 S.Ct. 2411, 156 L.Ed.2d 257 (2003), involved a challenge to a public university's use of racial criteria in the selection of its students for admission. The Supreme Court held that

plaintiff, a transfer student, had standing to represent absent class members challenging the university's freshman admission policy, because the university used the same criteria in selecting freshmen and transfer students.

A problem may arise if the claim of a named plaintiff is resolved before the class is certified. In that event, the action may be dismissed as moot even though a live controversy remains as to other class members. See Bradley v. Housing Auth., 512 F.2d 626 (8th Cir.1975). However, if the matter at issue is such that the class representative's individual interest, in the normal course of events, will expire before a ruling can be made on class certification (such as pretrial detention without a probable cause hearing), the class may be certified despite the mootness of the named plaintiff's claim. See Gerstein v. Pugh, 420 U.S. 103, 110–11 n.11, 95 S.Ct. 854, 861 n.11, 43 L.Ed.2d 54, 63 n.11 (1975). See also United States Parole Comm'n v. Geraghty, 445 U.S. 388, 100 S.Ct. 1202, 63 L.Ed.2d 479 (1980) (named plaintiff may appeal denial of class certification even if individual claim has become moot). Moreover, a class action generally is not rendered moot if the named plaintiff's claim becomes moot after class certification. See Sosna v. Iowa, 419 U.S. 393, 95 S.Ct. 553, 42 L.Ed.2d 532 (1975).

3. *Joinder of All Members Is "Impracticable"*: Rule 23(a)(1) requires that the class be so numerous that joinder of all members is "impracticable." In most instances this requirement is mechanical. In Dukes v. Wal–Mart Stores, Inc., 222 F.R.D. 137 (N.D. Cal. 2004), affirmed 474 F.3d 1214 (9th Cir.), opinion withdrawn and superseded on denial of rehearing 509 F.3d 1168 (9th Cir. 2007), and rehearing en banc granted 556 F.3d 919 (9th Cir. 2009), an employment discrimination case under Title VII of the Civil Rights Act of 1964, the court found it "beyond dispute that joinder would be impracticable" when the class was alleged to include "at least 1.5 million women who have been employed over the past five years at roughly 3,400 stores." However, classes with far fewer members satisfy the Rule 23(a)(1) perquisite. If a class has more than forty members, numerosity usually is met; if the class numbers less than twenty-five, numerosity usually is lacking. When the class is between twenty-five and forty members, variables such as the geographic dispersion of class members and the size of their individual claims become important. Why might joinder be considered impracticable if the monetary value of the individual claims is small?

4. *"Questions of Law or Fact Common to the Class"*: Rule 23(a)(2), the "commonality" requirement, mandates that the action raise questions of law or fact common to the class. Courts tend to give this requirement a "permissive application so that common questions have been found to exist in a wide range of contexts" and even one significant common question is sometimes sufficient. 7A Wright, Miller & Kane, Federal Practice and Procedure: Civil 3d § 1763. The critical question is whether "differences in the factual background of each claim will affect the outcome of the legal issue." Califano v. Yamasaki, 442 U.S. 682, 99 S.Ct.

2545, 61 L.Ed.2d 176 (1979). In some cases the existence of discrete, individualized injuries has been held to defeat a finding of commonality. In Donaldson v. Microsoft Corp., 205 F.R.D. 558, 565 (W.D. Wash.2001), an employment discrimination case, plaintiff alleged "individualized discrimination on the basis of race, coupled with proof that other people of color work in the same environment." The court declined to find commonality. How would you amend the complaint to satisfy the commonality requirement? Is the defect a matter of law or of fact? Would it be sufficient to allege discrimination on the basis of a "system-wide practice or policy that affects all of the putative class members"? Armstrong v. Davis, 275 F.3d 849 (9th Cir.2001).

5. *The Representative Claims or Defenses "Are Typical" of the Class*: Rule 23(a)(3) requires that the claims or defenses of the representative party be typical of those of the class. Some commentators question whether this requirement serves any independent purpose since any objective it might serve already will be achieved by the commonality requirement and by the adequacy requirement of Rule 23(a)(4), discussed below. Typicality usually is found "when each class member's claim arises from the same course of events, and each class member makes similar legal arguments to provide the defendant's liability." Marisol A. v. Giuliani, 126 F.3d 372, 376 (2d Cir. 1997). The goal is to ensure that "the named plaintiff's claim and the class claims are so interrelated that the interests of the class members will be fairly and adequately protected in their absence." Id.

GENERAL TELEPHONE CO. v. FALCON, 457 U.S. 147, 102 S.Ct. 2364, 72 L.Ed.2d 740 (1982). Mariano Falcon was passed over for a promotion to field inspector at the same time several white employees with less seniority were granted promotions. He filed charges with the Equal Employment Opportunity Commission (EEOC), stating his belief that he had been denied promotion because of his national origin and that General Telephone's promotion policy operated against Mexican–Americans as a class. The EEOC issued a right-to-sue letter, and Falcon instituted an action under Title VII of the Civil Rights Act of 1964.

Falcon's complaint alleged that General Telephone maintained a policy of discriminating against Mexican–Americans with respect to compensation and conditions of employment and a policy of subjecting Mexican–Americans to continuous employment discrimination. He claimed that as a result of this policy less qualified whites with lower evaluation scores than his and those of other Mexican–Americans had been promoted more rapidly. The complaint contained no factual allegations concerning General Telephone's hiring practices.

Falcon moved to certify a class of "all hourly Mexican–American employees who had been employed, were employed, or who were to apply for employment, or who had applied or who would have applied had not petitioner practiced racial discrimination in its employment practices." Without conducting an evidentiary hearing, the court certified a class including Mexican–American employees and Mexican–American applicants who had not been hired in the division of the company in which Falcon was employed. The court denied two decertification motions made by General Telephone.

At trial, the District Court found that General Telephone had not discriminated against Falcon in hiring, but that it did discriminate against him in its promotion practices. As to the class, the court found no discrimination in promotion, but did conclude General Telephone had discriminated against Mexican–Americans in its hiring practices. Relief ultimately was awarded to 13 Mexican–Americans who had applied for employment.

The Fifth Circuit rejected Falcon's claim that the class should be broadened to include employees and job applicants at all of General Telephone's plants. It concurrently rejected General Telephone's claim that the class was too broad. On the merits, the Fifth Circuit upheld Falcon's claim of disparate treatment in promotion, but held that the District Court's findings relating to disparate impact in hiring were insufficient to support recovery on behalf of the class. The Supreme Court reversed the Fifth Circuit's affirmance of the certification order:

> We have repeatedly held that "a class representative must be part of the class and 'possess the same interest and suffer the same injury' as the class members." * * *
>
> * * * We * * * [recognize] the theory behind the Fifth Circuit's across-the-board rule, noting our awareness "that suits alleging racial or ethnic discrimination are often by their very nature class suits, involving classwide wrongs," and that "[c]ommon questions of law or fact are typically present." * * * In the same breath, however, we reiterated that "careful attention to the requirements of Fed.Rule Civ.Proc. 23 remains nonetheless indispensable" and that the "mere fact that a complaint alleges racial or ethnic discrimination does not in itself ensure that the party who has brought the lawsuit will be an adequate representative of those who may have been the real victims of that discrimination." * * *
>
> We cannot disagree with the proposition underlying the across-the-board rule—that racial discrimination is by definition class discrimination. But the allegation that such discrimination has occurred neither determines whether a class action may be maintained in accordance with Rule 23 nor defines the class that may be certified. Conceptually, there is a wide gap between (a) an individual's claim that he has been denied a promotion on discriminatory grounds, and his otherwise unsupported allegation that the company has a policy of discrimination, and (b) the existence of a class of persons who have suffered the same injury as that individual, such that the individual's claim and the class claims will share common questions of law or fact

> and that the individual's claim will be typical of the class claims. For respondent to bridge that gap, he must prove much more than the validity of his own claim. Even though evidence that he was passed over for promotion when several less deserving whites were advanced may support the conclusion that respondent was denied the promotion because of his national origin, such evidence would not necessarily justify the additional inferences (1) that this discriminatory treatment is typical of petitioner's promotion practices, (2) that petitioner's promotion practices are motivated by a policy of ethnic discrimination that pervades petitioner's Irving division, or (3) that this policy of ethnic discrimination is reflected in petitioner's other employment practices, such as hiring, in the same way it is manifested in the promotion practices. These additional inferences demonstrate the tenuous character of any presumption that the class claims are "fairly encompassed" within respondent's claim.
>
> Respondent's complaint provided an insufficient basis for concluding that the adjudication of his claim of discrimination in promotion would require the decision of any common question concerning the failure of petitioner to hire more Mexican–Americans. Without any specific presentation identifying the questions of law or fact that were common to the claims of respondent and of the members of the class he sought to represent, it was error for the District Court to presume that respondent's claim was typical of other claims against petitioner by Mexican–American employees and applicants.

Id. at 156–59, 102 S.Ct. at 2370–71, 72 L.Ed.2d at 749–51.

Falcon can be understood as requiring only greater specificity in pleading, and merely holding that the pleadings must show a clear and specific link between the individual and class claims. The Court, after all, did conclude the "[t]he District Court's error in this case, and the error inherent in the across-the-board rule, is the failure to evaluate carefully the legitimacy of the named plaintiff's plea that he is a proper class representative under Rule 23(a)." Id. at 160, 102 S.Ct. at 2372, 72 L.Ed.2d at 752. On the other hand, *Falcon* can be read to be in tension with the notion that some differences among class members are permissible in assessing commonalty and typicality under Rules 23(a)(2) and 23(a)(3).

---

6. *"Fairly and Adequately Protect the Interests of the Class"*: Rule 23(a)(4), that the representative party "will fairly and adequately protect the interests of the class," derives its importance from two factors. First, Rule 23(a)(4) reflects the due process concern that a class action judgment ought not to bind parties who have not *literally* had their "day in court" unless, as members of a defined group with similar claims and proper

representation, they have had a *figurative* day in court. Rule 23(a)(4) ensures the quality of the representation that due process requires. Second, a defect in the adequacy of representation in an action might leave the judgment vulnerable to collateral attack. See p. 819, infra. It would be an extremely wasteful expenditure of time and effort to go through the certification process, complete extensive discovery, negotiate and approve a settlement or actually adjudicate the merits of the case, and draft and enter a judgment, only to have everything unraveled years later by someone who does not want to be bound by the result and claims that the adequacy requirement was not met. Rule 23(a)(4) focuses on the adequacy of the representative plaintiff; an amendment to Rule 23 adopted in 2003 establishes a separate inquiry into the adequacy of class counsel. See Fed. R Civ. P. 23(g). Some commentators question whether an adequate representative plaintiff is necessary if class counsel assumes the laboring oar in representing the interests of the class. See Burns, *Decorative Figureheads: Eliminating Class Representatives in Class Actions*, 42 Hastings L.J. 165 (1990).

In AMCHEM PRODUCTS, INC. v. WINDSOR, 521 U.S. 591, 117 S.Ct. 2231, 138 L.Ed.2d 689 (1997), p. 796, infra, a settlement class involving current and future asbestos-related claims, the Supreme Court explained the purpose of the adequacy requirement as serving "to uncover conflicts of interest between named parties and the class they seek to represent." The Court found that the adequacy requirement had not been met. The Court underscored the fact that

> * * * named parties with diverse medical conditions sought to act on behalf of a single giant class rather than on behalf of discrete subclasses. In significant respects, the interests of those within the single class are not aligned. Most saliently, for the currently injured, the critical goal is generous immediate payments. That goal rubs against the interest of exposure-only plaintiffs in ensuring an ample, inflation-protected fund for the future.

See p. 806, infra. An absent party whose interests have not been adequately represented will be permitted to collaterally attack the class action judgment. See Stephenson v. Dow Chemical Co., 273 F.3d 249 (2d Cir. 2001), affirmed in part by an equally divided court and vacated in part 539 U.S. 111, 123 S.Ct. 2161, 156 L.Ed.2d 106 (2003).

Courts recognize that adequacy of representation cannot be determined by assessing only the named litigant's financial stake in the litigation, although "financial resources of the representatives may be pertinent." 7A Wright, Miller & Kane, Federal Practice and Procedure: Civil 3d § 1767. Nor will "every variation" between the interests of the class representative and the unnamed class members defeat a showing of adequacy of representation. The inquiry focuses "on whether the interests of the class are compatible" and not divergent or antagonistic. See Wolfert v. Transamerica Home First, Inc., 439 F.3d 165, 173 (2d Cir. 2006).

Some critics have argued that courts are not sufficiently vigorous in their assessment of adequacy of representation. One empirical study of adequacy determinations concluded that courts failed to consider "legitimate grounds for attacking unqualified representatives" and that they ignored such factors as honesty and knowledge about the case. See Klonoff, *The Judiciary's Flawed Application of Rule 23's "Adequacy of Representation" Requirement*, 2004 Mich. St. L. Rev. 671, 673 (2004). What factors are relevant in assessing adequacy of representation? For different perspectives on this question, see Woolley, *The Availability of Collateral Attack for Inadequate Representation in Class Suits*, 79 Texas L. Rev. 383, 387 (2000); Bassett, *When Reform Is Not Enough: Assuring More than Merely "Adequate" Representation in Class Actions*, 38 Ga. L. Rev. 927 (2004); Dana, *Adequacy of Representation After* Stephenson: *A Rawlsian/Behavioral Economics Approach to Class Action Settlements*, 55 Emory L.J. 279 (2006).

NOTE ON SELECTION OF THE "LEAD PLAINTIFF" IN SECURITIES-FRAUD CASES

In 1995, Congress passed the Private Securities Litigation Reform Act which, among other things, requires the court to appoint a "lead plaintiff" in securities class actions. The PSLRA establishes "a presumption that the individual so selected should be the one with the largest financial interest in the relief sought by the class." 7A Wright, Miller & Kane, Federal Practice and Procedure: Civil 3d § 1767. The requirement responds to concerns that class actions are "lawyer driven" and subject to collusion and unfairness. By creating incentives for shareholders with large financial stakes to assume a leadership position in the litigation, the PSLRA strives to create incentives for monitoring attorney performance. See Seligman, *Rethinking Private Securities Litigation*, 73 U. Cin. L. Rev. 95, 105 (2004); Fisch, *Class Action Reform: Lessons from Securities Litigation*, 39 Ariz. L.Rev. 533 (1997). A leading commentary has justified this approach by pointing to the "knowledge and financial sophistication" of institutional investors, their financial incentive in the outcome of the class action "to do * * * [the] job well," and the legitimacy that a major financial institution, rather than a figurehead plaintiff, lends to a class action. Weiss & Beckerman, *Let the Money Do the Monitoring: How Institutional Investors Can Reduce Agency Costs in Securities Class Actions*, 104 Yale. L.J. 2053, 2126–27 (1995). For a study of how the PSLRA has affected class action lawyers, see Choi & Thompson, *Securities Litigation and Its Lawyers: Changes During the First Decade After the PSLRA,* 106 Colum L. Rev. 1489 (2006).

The Courts of Appeal have divided on how the lead-plaintiff requirement of the PSLRA affects the Rule 23(a)(4) adequacy determination. The Fifth Circuit has held that the Act "raises the standard adequacy threshold" by directing district courts to appoint as lead plaintiff "the most sophisticated investor available * * *." Berger v. Compaq Computer Corp., 257 F.3d 475

(5th Cir.2001), rehearing denied 279 F.3d 313 (5th Cir.2002), The Ninth Circuit takes a different approach:

> The Reform Act provides a simple three-step process for identifying the lead plaintiff pursuant to * * * criteria [set out in Rule 23]. The first step consists of publicizing the pendency of the action, the claims made and the purported class period. * * * The first plaintiff to file an action covered by the Reform Act must post this notice "in a widely circulated national business-oriented publication or wire service." * * * The notice must also state that "any member of the purported class may move the court to serve as lead plaintiff." * * *
>
> In step two, the district court must consider the losses allegedly suffered by the various plaintiffs before selecting as the "presumptively most adequate plaintiff" * * *—and hence the presumptive lead plaintiff—the one who "has the largest financial interest in the relief sought by the class" and "otherwise satisfies the requirements of Rule 23 * * *." * * * In other words, the district court must compare the financial stakes of the various plaintiffs and determine which one has the most to gain from the lawsuit.[4] It must then focus its attention on that plaintiff and determine, based on the information he has provided in his pleadings and declarations, whether he satisfies the requirements of Rule 23(a), in particular those of "typicality" and "adequacy." * * * If the plaintiff with the largest financial stake in the controversy provides information that satisfies these requirements, he becomes the presumptively most adequate plaintiff. If the plaintiff with the greatest financial stake does not satisfy the Rule 23(a) criteria, the court must repeat the inquiry, this time considering the plaintiff with the next-largest financial stake, until it finds a plaintiff who is both willing to serve and satisfies the requirements of Rule 23.
>
> The third step of the process is to give other plaintiffs an opportunity to rebut the presumptive lead plaintiff's showing that it satisfies Rule 23's typicality and adequacy requirements. * * * In seeking evidence that could rebut the presumptive lead plaintiff's showing on these points, other plaintiffs may be allowed to conduct discovery if they "demonstrate[ ] a reasonable basis for a finding that the presumptively most adequate plaintiff is incapable of adequately representing the class." * * *
>
> * * *
>
> * * * Once [the district court] * * * determines which plaintiff has the biggest stake, the court must appoint that plaintiff as lead, unless it finds that he does not satisfy the typicality or adequacy requirements.
>
> * * *

4. To make this comparison, the district court must calculate each potential lead plaintiff's financial interest in the litigation. In so doing, the court may select accounting methods that are both rational and consistently applied. Because the calculation is not in dispute here, we need not decide the scope of the district court's discretion in determining which plaintiff has the greatest financial interest in the litigation.

> The district court has latitude as to what information it will consider in determining typicality and adequacy. The presumptive lead plaintiff's choice of counsel and fee arrangements may be relevant in ensuring that the plaintiff is not receiving preferential treatment through some back-door financial arrangement with counsel, or proposing to employ a lawyer with a conflict of interest. But this is not a beauty contest; the district court has no authority to select for the class what it considers to be the best possible lawyer or the lawyer offering the best possible fee schedule. Indeed, the district court does not select class counsel at all. Rather, such information is relevant only to determine whether the presumptive lead plaintiff's choice of counsel is so irrational, or so tainted by self-dealing or conflict of interest, as to cast genuine and serious doubt on that plaintiff's willingness or ability to perform the functions of lead plaintiff. * * *

In re Cavanaugh, 306 F.3d 726, 729–33 (9th Cir.2002). Should the investor with the largest financial stake in a class action always represent the interests of the class members? Do you see problems with this approach? Can you suggest a solution? For a comprehensive discussion of the special procedures governing lead plaintiffs in securities class actions and whether they can be expected to curb abusive practice, see 7B Wright, Miller & Kane, Federal Practice and Procedure: Civil 3d § 1806. See also Coffee, Jr., *Accountability and Competition in Securities Class Actions: Why "Exit" Works Better than "Voice,"* 30 Cardozo L. Rev. 407 (2008).

B. FEDERAL RULE 23(b): THE TYPES OF CLASS ACTIONS

After the district judge has determined that the suit satisfies the six prerequisites already discussed, she must decide that it falls within one of the three categories of class actions enumerated in Rule 23(b).

1. *"Prejudice Class Actions" under Rule 23(b)(1)*: Both clauses of this provision ask whether individual actions might cause prejudice that can be avoided by using the class-action device. Certification under this provision is said to create a "mandatory" class action: the absentee cannot opt-out of the class.

Subdivision (A) looks for prejudice to the nonclass party; subdivision (B) inquires into prejudice to members of the class. Subdivision (A) deals with the risk that individual actions would create "incompatible standards of conduct" for the party opposing the class. It is important to note that the Rule does *not* refer to the situation in which the defendant in a series of actions would have to pay damages to some claimants but not to others. Rather, the Rule applies when different results in individual actions would place the nonclass party in a position of total uncertainty, not knowing how to treat the class as a whole. For example, consider a voting rights dispute involving a question of eligibility for registration. If applicants sue individually, some may win and others may lose. The election board then would be in the position of not knowing whether to register all the individuals similarly situated who have not brought suit. If a class action is brought, the judgment will bind all of the class members, and the board can take appropriate action. A similar logic applies in cases involving rate-making proceedings or riparian rights.

Subdivision (B) of Rule (23)(b)(1) contemplates that individual actions "would be dispositive of the interests" or "substantially impair or impede" the ability of nonparties to protect their interests. The classic example is a case in which there are multiple claimants to a limited fund, such as the proceeds of an insurance policy. If litigants are allowed to proceed individually, there is a risk that those who sue first will deplete the fund and leave nothing for the latecomers; thus, the latter group would "as a practical matter" be prejudiced by individual actions. See generally 7AA Wright, Miller & Kane, Federal Practice and Procedure: Civil 3d § 1772.

2. *Injunctive and Declaratory Relief under Rule 23(b)(2)*: More class action cases have been brought under this provision than under Rules 23(b)(1) or 23(b)(3). Its primary application is in injunction suits such as civil rights, employment discrimination, consumer, or environmental cases in which the goal is to change defendant's behavior or policy prospectively and not to provide individual compensation to class members for injuries they suffered in the past. On the theory that an injunctive class is cohesive, notice is not deemed essential in such cases. See Wetzel v. Liberty Mutual Ins. Co., 508 F.2d 239, certiorari denied 421 U.S. 1011, 95 S.Ct. 2415, 44 L.Ed.2d 679 (1975). Note that for an action to fall within Rule 23(b)(2), the defendant's conduct need only be "generally applicable" to the class; there is no requirement that the conduct be damaging or offensive to every class member. Thus, a suit to enjoin the enforcement of a school dress code can be instituted under Rule 23(b)(2) even though a majority of the students are not offended by the code and are willing to comply with it, since the school, by trying to enforce the code, acts in a manner generally applicable to the entire student body.

3. *Damage Class Actions under Rule 23(b)(3)*: This provision, the category most often used in adjudicating a wide range of damage actions, including mass torts, allows the certification of a class when the tie among the members is that they claim to have been injured in the same way by defendant. Two special prerequisites govern the application of this provision. First, questions of law or fact common to the class members must "predominate" over any questions affecting only individual class members. Second, the court must find that a "class action is superior to other available methods for fairly and efficiently adjudicating the controversy." These special requirements are designed to ensure that the efficiency and economy objectives of Rule 23(b)(3) are met. Given the non-natural character of the group that comprises a class under subdivision (b)(3), Rule 23 requires additional procedural protection for the absent class members in the form of mandatory notice and the right to opt-out of the class. See Eisenberg & Miller, *The Role of Opt–Outs and Objectors in Class Action Litigation: Theoretical and Empirical Issues*, 57 Vand.L.Rev. 1529 (2004).

Rule 23(b)(3) outlines four factors that the court should consider in deciding the superiority and predominance questions. The fourth one mentioned, difficulties likely to be encountered in the management of a class action, generally is viewed as key. Matters such as the size or contentiousness of the class, the number of class members who seek to intervene and participate in the action, or the onerousness of the Rule 23(c)(2) notice requirement are to be considered when deciding if the class action is manageable. Although it is easy to state the Rule 23(b)(3) tests, the district courts have not applied them with a great deal of uniformity. Questions of predominance and superiority have become instead highly individualistic and fact dependent. In determining "predominance," it remains unclear whether the district judge is to count the issues and see whether a majority are common, or to evaluate the issues and see if the most important are common. Furthermore, in some cases common and individual issues seem to be in equilibrium no matter which method of determining predominance is followed. The key to resolving this difficulty lies in ascertaining whether the efficiency and economy of common adjudication outweigh the interest each class member may have in an individual adjudication. The "superiority" prerequisite thus obliges the court to compare the class action with other adjudicative possibilities. The most obvious include leaving the disputants to individual actions, administrative proceedings, or an agreement to be bound by the result in a single "test" case. Another option is the availability for consolidation of multidistrict cases under 28 U.S.C. § 1407. See p. 391, supra. Consider the questions associated with the "superiority" prerequisite as you read the following case.

CASTANO v. AMERICAN TOBACCO CO.

United States Court of Appeals, Fifth Circuit, 1996.
84 F.3d 734.

SMITH, CIRCUIT JUDGE.

In what may be the largest class action ever attempted in federal court, the district court in this case embarked "on a road certainly less traveled, if ever taken at all," * * * and entered a class certification order. The court defined the class as:

(a) All nicotine-dependent persons in the United States . . . who have purchased and smoked cigarettes manufactured by the defendants;

(b) the estates, representatives, and administrators of these nicotine-dependent cigarette smokers; and

(c) the spouses, children, relatives and "significant others" of these nicotine-dependent cigarette smokers as their heirs or survivors.

Concluding that the district court abused its discretion in certifying the class, we reverse.

I.

A. The Class Complaint

The plaintiffs filed this class complaint against the defendant tobacco companies and the Tobacco Institute, Inc., seeking compensation solely for the injury of nicotine addiction. The gravamen of their complaint is the novel and wholly untested theory that the defendants fraudulently failed to inform consumers that nicotine is addictive and manipulated the level of nicotine in cigarettes to sustain their addictive nature. * * *

* * *

B. The Class Certification Order

* * * [T]he district court granted, in part, plaintiffs' motion for class certification, concluding that the prerequisites of FED.R.CIV.P. 23(a) had been met. * * *

The court * * * grant[ed] the plaintiffs' motion to certify the class under FED.R.CIV.P. 23(b)(3), organizing the class action issues into four categories: (1) core liability; (2) injury-in-fact, proximate cause, reliance and affirmative defenses; (3) compensatory damages; and (4) punitive damages. * * * It then analyzed each category to determine whether it met the predominance and superiority requirements of rule 23(b)(3). Using its power to sever issues for certification under FED.R.CIV.P. 23(c)(4), the court certified the class on core liability and punitive damages, and certified the class conditionally pursuant to FED.R.CIV.P. 23(c)(1).

* * *

The district court erred in its analysis in two distinct ways. First, it failed to consider how variations in state law affect predominance and superiority. Second, its predominance inquiry did not include consideration of how a trial on the merits would be conducted.

Each of these defects mandates reversal. Moreover, at this time, while the tort is immature, the class complaint must be dismissed as class certification cannot be found to be a superior method of adjudication.

A. Variations in State Law

* * *

A district court's duty to determine whether the plaintiff has borne its burden on class certification requires that a court consider variations in state law when a class action involves multiple jurisdictions. * * *

* * *

A thorough review of the record demonstrates that, in this case, the district court did not properly consider how variations in state law affect predominance. * * *

The district court's review of state law variances can hardly be considered extensive; it conducted a cursory review of state law variations and gave short shrift to the defendants' arguments concerning variations. * * *

* * *

The court also failed to perform its duty to determine whether the class action would be manageable in light of state law variations. The court's only discussion of manageability is a citation and the claim that "[w]hile manageability of the liability issues in this case may well prove to be difficult, the Court finds that any such difficulties pale in comparison to the specter of thousands, if not millions, of similar trials of liability proceeding in thousands of courtrooms around the nation." * * *

* * *

* * * [W]hether the specter of millions of cases outweighs any manageability problems in this class is uncertain when the scope of any manageability problems is unknown. Absent considered judgment on the manageability of the class, a comparison to millions of individual trials is meaningless.

B. Predominance

The district court's second error was that it failed to consider how the plaintiffs' addiction claims would be tried, individually or on a class basis. * * * The district court * * * believed that it could not go past the pleadings for the certification decision. The result was an incomplete and inadequate predominance inquiry.

* * *

A district court certainly may look past the pleadings to determine whether the requirements of rule 23 have been met. Going beyond the pleadings is necessary, as a court must understand the claims, defenses, relevant facts, and applicable substantive law in order to make a meaningful determination of the certification issues. * * *

The district court * * * just assumed that because the common issues would play a part in every trial, they must be significant. The court's [approach] * * * would write the predominance requirement out of the rule, and any common issue would predominate if it were common to all the individual trials. * * *

The court's treatment of the fraud claim also demonstrates the error inherent in its approach. * * * [A] fraud class action cannot be certified when individual reliance will be an issue. * * *

The problem with the district court's approach is that after the class trial, it might have decided that reliance must be proven in individual trials. The court then would have been faced with the difficult choice of decertifying the class * * * and wasting judicial resources, or continuing with a class action that would have failed the predominance requirement of rule 23(b)(3). * * *

III.

In addition to the reasons given above, regarding the district court's procedural errors, this class must be decertified because it independently fails the superiority requirement of rule 23(b)(3). In the context of mass tort class actions, certification dramatically affects the stakes for defendants. Class certification magnifies and strengthens the number of unmeritorious claims. * * * Aggregation of claims also makes it more likely that a defendant will be found liable and results in significantly higher damage awards. * * *

In addition to skewing trial outcomes, class certification creates insurmountable pressure on defendants to settle, whereas individual trials would not. * * * The risk of facing an all-or-nothing verdict presents too high a risk, even when the probability of an adverse judgment is low. * * * These settlements have been referred to as judicial blackmail.

It is no surprise then, that historically, certification of mass tort litigation classes has been disfavored. The traditional concern over the rights of defendants in mass tort class actions is magnified in the instant case. Our specific concern is that a mass tort cannot be properly certified without a prior track record of trials from which the district court can draw the information necessary to make the predominance and superiority analysis required by rule 23. This is because certification of an immature tort results in a higher than normal risk that the class action may not be superior to individual adjudication.

* * * The court acknowledged the extensive manageability problems with this class. Such problems include difficult choice of law determinations, subclassing of eight claims with variations in state law, *Erie* guesses, notice to millions of class members, further subclassing to take account of transient plaintiffs, and the difficult procedure for determining who is nicotine-dependent. Cases with far fewer manageability problems have given courts pause. * * *

The district court's rationale for certification in spite of such problems—i.e., that a class trial would preserve judicial resources in the millions of inevitable individual trials—is based on pure speculation. * * *

What the district court failed to consider, and what no court can determine at this time, is the very real possibility that the judicial crisis may fail to materialize. The plaintiffs' claims are based on a new theory of liability and the existence of new evidence. Until plaintiffs decide to file individual claims, a court cannot, from the existence of injury, presume that all or even any plaintiffs will pursue legal remedies. * * *

As he stated in the record, plaintiffs' counsel in this case has promised to inundate the courts with individual claims if class certification is denied. Independently of the reliability of this self-serving promise, there is reason to believe that individual suits are feasible. First, individual damage claims are high, and punitive damages are available in most states. The expense of litigation does not necessarily turn this case into a negative value suit, in part because the prevailing party may recover attorneys' fees under many consumer protection statutes. * * *

* * *

The remaining rationale for superiority—judicial efficiency—is also lacking. In the context of an immature tort, any savings in judicial resources is speculative, and any imagined savings would be overwhelmed by the procedural problems that certification of a *sui generis* cause of action brings with it.

* * *

The district court's predominance inquiry, or lack of it, squarely presents the problems associated with certification of immature torts. Determining whether the common issues are a "significant" part of each individual case has an abstract quality to it when no court in this country has ever tried an injury-as-addiction claim. * * *

Yet, an accurate finding on predominance is necessary before the court can certify a class. * * * Premature certification deprives the defendant of the opportunity to present that argument to any court and risks decertification after considerable resources have been expended.

* * *

The plaintiffs' final retort is that individual trials are inadequate because time is running out for many of the plaintiffs. They point out that prior litigation against the tobacco companies has taken up to ten years to wind through the legal system. * * *

* * * [T]he plaintiffs' claim that time is running out ignores the reality of the class action device. In a complicated case involving multiple jurisdictions, the conflict of law question itself could take decades to work its way through the courts. Once that issue has been resolved, discovery, subclassing, and ultimately the class trial would take place. Next would come the appellate process. After the class trial, the individual trials and appeals on comparative negligence and damages would have to take place. The net result could be that the class action device would lengthen, not shorten, the time it takes for the plaintiffs to reach final judgment.

* * *

* * * For the forgoing reasons, we REVERSE and REMAND with instructions that the district court dismiss the class complaint.

NOTES AND QUESTIONS

1. The Fifth Circuit decertified a class that was estimated to include fifty million nicotine-dependent tobacco users. 84 F.3d at 737; see Castano v. American Tobacco Co., 160 F.R.D. 544, at 548–50 (E.D. La. 1995). In reaching

its decision, the court emphasized that the class action complaint alleged an "immature tort" in the sense that no tobacco suit ever had been filed based on the *Castano* plaintiff's theory. See 84 F.3d at 749. Plaintiffs claimed that defendants had failed to inform consumers of the addictive nature of nicotine and that defendants had manipulated cigarette nicotine levels to sustain smokers' addiction. The court asserted that these theories had not been litigated sufficiently in the context of individual tobacco cases to assess whether a class action would be a superior way to adjudicate such claims. Is the court's point valid? What is "immature" about a tort that alleges a company's failure to warn of a product's defects or of its injurious character, especially when defendant allegedly manufactured the product knowing it would have the injurious effect? Other courts of appeal also have looked to the maturity of the tort in determining whether class certification or other aggregative techniques are appropriate. See In re Chevron U.S.A., 109 F.3d 1016 (5th Cir. 1997); In re Rhone–Poulenc Rorer, Inc., 51 F.3d 1293 (7th Cir. 1995). How long must the class action be held in abeyance before the plaintiff's theory is thought "mature" enough? See Walker v. Liggett Group, Inc., 175 F.R.D. 226 (S.D.W.Va.1997) (class of tobacco smokers in a lawsuit against Liggett Group, the smallest of the big five tobacco companies, not certified, following the *Castano* rationale).

2. After the *Castano* class failed and legislative reform of the tobacco industry proved unlikely, over forty states filed lawsuits against tobacco companies to recover expenditures made for tobacco-related illnesses. See Player, Note—*After the Fall: The Cigarette Papers, the Global Settlement, and the Future of Tobacco Litigation*, 49 S.C. L. Rev. 311 (1998). The companies negotiated a settlement with the Attorneys General of these states, and in November 1998, the settlement was accepted by forty-six states, the District of Columbia, and five territories. This settlement included payments to the states totaling $206 billion to be paid over the next twenty-five years. Additional settlement provisions included prohibiting tobacco companies from targeting youth in their advertising, using cartoon characters to sell cigarettes, and giving out free samples of tobacco products except in adult establishments. The tobacco companies also were directed to make available to the public all of their research on tobacco. See Dagan & White, *Governments, Citizens, and Injurious Industries*, 75 N.Y.U. L. Rev. 354 (2000).

Considering the terms of this settlement, do you agree that the state governments adequately represented the interests of individual smokers? In what ways might the government's collective interest have diverged from those of individual smokers? See Bianchini, *The Tobacco Agreement that Went Up in Smoke: Defining the Limits of Congressional Intervention into Ongoing Mass Tort Litigation*, 87 Calif. L. Rev. 703, 728–34 (1999). Is it significant that the state governments' settlement did not extinguish the claims of individual smokers against the tobacco companies? The failure of *Castano*, a federal court class action, led some plaintiffs to seek relief in state court, with mixed results. See Ieyoub & Eisenberg, *Class Actions in the Gulf South Symposium: State Attorney General Actions, the Tobacco Litigation, and the Doctrine of Parens Patriae*, 74 Tul. L.Rev. 1859 (2000).

In Florida, a jury verdict for $145 billion in punitive damages to the class was reversed on appeal to the District Court of Appeal with instructions to decertify the class. See Liggett Group Inc. v. Engle, 853 So.2d 434 (Fl.2003). The Supreme Court of Florida approved in part, quashed in part, and remanded. See Engle v. Liggett Group, Inc., 945 So.2d 1246 (Fl. 2006), certiorari denied R.J. Reynolds Tobacco Co. v. Engle, ___ U.S. ___, 128 S.Ct. 96, 169 L.Ed.2d 244, rehearing denied ___ U.S. ___, 128 S.Ct. 694, 169 L.Ed.2d 541 (2007).

In Louisiana, a class action judgment held that defendants had concealed negative information about smoking from the public and also breached an assumed duty to disclose such information. The court ordered the establishment of a ten-year smoking cessation program funded by a $600 million jury award, and the judgment was affirmed in part on appeal. See Scott v. American Tobacco Co., Inc., 949 So.2d 1266 (La.App.2007), certiorari denied Philip Morris USA Inc. v. Jackson, ___ U.S. ___, 128 S.Ct. 2908, 171 L.Ed.2d 842 (2008).

Smokers also filed individual state law actions. In Florida, a jury entered a verdict of more than $500,000, and the verdict was affirmed on a theory of strict liability design defect. See Liggett Group, Inc. v. Davis, 973 So.2d 467 (Fl. 2007), review dismissed 997 So.2d 400 (Fl. 2008). In Oregon, a jury entered a verdict of $821,485 in compensatory and $79.5 million in punitive damages for the smoking-related death of plaintiff's husband. See Williams v. Philip Morris, Inc., 182 Ore. App. 44, 48 P.3d 824 (2002). The Supreme Court vacated and remanded, holding that a punitive damage award based in part on the jury's desire to punish the tobacco company for harm to nonparties violated the Due Process Clause. 549 U.S. 346, 127 S.Ct. 1057, 166 L.Ed.2d 940 (2007). On remand, the Oregon appeals court adhered to its prior decision, 344 Or. 45, 176 P.3d 1255, and the Supreme Court granted certiorari in part ___ U.S. ___, 128 S.Ct. 2904, 171 L.Ed.2d 840 (2008), and dismissed the writ as improvidently granted. 556 U.S. ___, 129 S.Ct. 1436, 173 L.Ed.2d 346 (2009). How do you think *Philip Morris* will affect future mass tort actions? See Stier, *Now It's Personal: Punishment and Mass Tort Litigation after Philip Morris v. Williams*, 2 Charleston L. Rev. 433 (2008); Cabraser & Nelson, *Class Action Treatment of Punitive Damages Issues After Philip Morris v. Williams: We Can Get There From Here*, 2 Charleston L. Rev. 407 (2008).

Smokers also sought relief in federal court relying on theories of relief different from that put forward in *Castano*. In Altria Group, Inc. v. Good, ___ U.S. ___, 129 S.Ct. 538, ___ L.Ed.2d. ___ (2008), the Supreme Court held that plaintiffs' claim that tobacco companies misrepresented the health consequences of "light' cigarettes in violation of a state law that requires truth in labeling was not preempted by federal law. The District Court had stayed decision on plaintiffs' class certification motion pending resolution of the preemption issue on summary judgment. How would you decide the Rule 23(a) certification question?

NOTE ON "HYBRID" CLASS ACTIONS

How hermetic are the three categories of class actions created by Rule 23(b)? Is it appropriate to certify an action as a (b)(2) class if plaintiffs seek damages in addition to injunctive and declaratory relief? The Advisory Committee Note to Rule 23(b)(2) states that it "does not extend to cases in which the appropriate final relief relates exclusively or predominantly to money damages." In JOHNSON v. GENERAL MOTORS CORP., 598 F.2d 432 (5th Cir.1979), plaintiffs alleged claims of racial discrimination. In an earlier racial discrimination class suit involving the same factory, plaintiffs had sought both injunctive and compensatory relief. The injunction was granted, and damages were awarded to the class representatives, but not to the absent class members. Plaintiff in the subsequent suit, Johnson, claimed that he had not received notice of the first suit, and attempted to prosecute his own suit for damages. The Fifth Circuit panel said:

> In light of these developments, we have previously suggested that when both monetary and injunctive relief are sought in an action certified under Rule 23(b)(2), notice may be mandatory if absent class members are to be bound. * * * [But w]hen only equitable relief is sought in an action involving a cohesive plaintiff group such as a class of black employees at an assembly plant, the due process interests of absent members will usually be safeguarded by adequate representation alone. As the Advisory Committee on Rule 23 stated, "[i]n the degree that there is cohesiveness or unity in the class and the representation is effective, the need for notice to the class will tend toward a minimum." * * * Where, however, individual monetary claims are at stake, the balance swings in favor of the provision of some form of notice. It will not always be necessary for the notice in such cases to be equivalent to that required in (b)(3) actions. * * * In some cases it may be proper to delay notice until a more advanced stage of the litigation; for example, until after class-wide liability is proven. * * * Before an absent class member may be forever barred from pursuing an individual damage claim, however, due process requires that he receive some form of notice that the class action is pending and that his damage claims may be adjudicated as part of it.

Id. at 437–38. Do you agree with this reasoning? In DUKES v. WAL–MART STORES, INC., 509 F.3d 1168 (9th Cir. 2007), the appellate court affirmed class certification under Federal Rule 23(b)(2) in an employment discrimination case, finding that plaintiff's claim for monetary relief, including back pay and punitive damages, did not predominate over claims for injunctive or declaratory relief. The courts of appeal differ in their approach to hybrid cases. The Sixth Circuit has held that individual compensatory claims never can be brought in a class action certified under Rule 23(b)(2) because damage claims always predominate over injunctive or declaratory relief. See Coleman v. General Motors Acceptance Corp., 296 F.3d 443 (6th Cir. 2002). The Second Circuit will certify hybrid classes under Rule 23(b)(2), see Robinson v. Metro–North Commuter R.R., 267 F.3d 147 (2d Cir. 2001), certiorari denied 535 U.S. 951, 122 S.Ct. 1349, 152 L.Ed.2d 251 (2002), but district courts have required notice and opt-out procedures as a condition of doing so. See Matyasovszky v. Housing Auth. of the City of Bridgeport, 226 F.R.D. 35 (D. Conn. 2005). See 7AA Wright, Miller & Kane, Federal Practice and Procedure: Civil 3d § 1784.1. Would the absence of these procedural protections raise due process problems? In Ticor Title Ins. Co. v. Brown, 511 U.S. 117, 114 S.Ct. 1359, 128 L.Ed.2d 33 (1994), the Supreme Court suggested that there is "at least a substantial possibility" that in actions seeking monetary damages, classes can be certified only under Rule 23(b)(3), which permits opt-out, and not under Rule 23(b)(1) and (b)(2), which do not. Id. at 121, 114 S.Ct. at 1361, 128 L.Ed. 2 at 38. A similar cautionary note was raised in Ortiz v. Fibreboard Corp., 527 U.S. 815, 119 S.Ct. 2295, 144 L.Ed.2d 715 (1999), see p. 811, infra.

C. RULE 23(c) CERTIFICATION DECISIONS

The district court must issue its certification order "[a]t an early practicable time" and retains authority to change the order any time "before final judgment." Rule 23(c)(1)(A), (C). The court's ongoing authority is regarded as "critical, because the scope and contour of a class may change radically as discovery progresses and more information is gathered about the nature of the putative class members' claims." Prado–Steiman v. Bush, 221 F.3d 1266, 1273 (11th Cir.2000). See 7AA Wright, Miller & Kane, Federal Practice and Procedure: Civil 3d § 1785.4.

The Rule 23(c) certification order defines the substantive claims, issues, or defenses the suit will consider. See Fed. R. Civ. P. 23(c)(1)(B). For instance, a class suit might entertain a broad range of issues (such as allegations of company-wide gender discrimination in hiring, promotion, and pay, as well as allegations of sexual harassment by foremen in all of the company's factories), or it might take a more narrow approach (limiting the class issues to allegations of gender discrimination in a single plant's promotion decisions). A judge may decide to certify a "partial class action"—that is, considering on a class basis only a limited number of factual issues relevant to a larger cause of action. For example, although controversial, a judge in a products liability suit, could create a "partial class action" by certifying only the issue of whether a pharmaceutical manufacturer knew of a drug's potentially lethal side effects before introducing it on the market. In such a case, individual suits, litigated simultaneously or subsequently, would be pursued on the other issues. Finally, the certification addresses the notice that is to be given to the absent class members and appoints class counsel under Rule 23(g). These requirements are discussed in the sections that follow.

4. RULE 23(c) AND THE REQUIREMENT OF NOTICE

The question of notice to absent class members has tremendous theoretical and practical importance to class actions. Until this point in the action, the absent class members, whose rights stand to be adjudicated and precluded by the court, have not yet been formally told that a lawsuit is going forward on their behalf. As a matter of due process, see Chapter 3, p. 199, supra, a party must receive notice and be afforded an opportunity to be heard before rights are extinguished. Provision of adequate notice thus is an essential requisite to the binding effect of a class action judgment. Commentators see the notice requirement as serving two related purposes: "One is to check on the adequacy of representation being provided to the class, and the other is to render viable the right of unnamed class members to take certain protective measures, specifically to intervene or to opt out of the lawsuit." Bronsteen & Fiss, *The Class Action Rule*, 78 Notre Dame L. Rev. 1419, 1435 (2003).

A. THE COURT'S ROLE

Whether the court directs that notice be given to the absent class members depends on the kind of class action that has been certified. Notice to class members is not expressly required by the Rule in so-called mandatory class actions (those certified as a "prejudice" class under Rule 23(b)(1) or as an "injunctive" class under Rule 23 (b)(2)). See Rule 23(c)(2)(A). Do you agree that a presumption of class coherence in these cases is sufficient to avoid the need for notice? See Rule 23 Advisory Committee Note to the 1963 Amendment. A leading commentary recommends that provision of some notice "probably is the best practice in most cases." 7B Wright, Miller & Kane, Federal Practice and Procedure: Civil 3d § 1793. Notice to class members is required in a damages class action under subdivision (b)(3).

B. THE CONTENT OF NOTICE AND WHO SHOULD RECEIVE NOTICE

The content of the notice provided likewise depends on the category of class that has been certified. Courts have tremendous discretion on this score in mandatory class actions. However, Rule 23(c)(2)(B) prescribes "the best notice that is practicable under the circumstances, including individual notice to all members who can be identified through reasonable effort." What is the reason for this approach? Under Rule 23(c)(2)(B), if the class member does nothing, he or she is automatically deemed a part of the lawsuit; any judgment that is entered will bar the absentee's future relitigation of claims. If the class member does not want to be a part of the class action, he or she can "opt-out" and file an independent lawsuit. What information must the notice include? See Federal Rule 23(c)(2)(B)(i)–(vii).

If notice is to serve its function, it must be intelligible to the person who receives it. See Federal Rule 23(c)(2)(B) (requiring "plain easily understood language"). Only then can a potential class member make an informed decision about opting out of the class. Is it likely that nonlawyers will understand the notice they receive? Is the possibility that the notice will not be understood likely to be greatest in those cases in which class members are most in need of protection? See Hilsee, Wheatman & Intrepido, *Do You Really Want Me To Know My Rights? The Ethics*

Behind Due Process in Class Action Notice Is More than Just Plain Language: A Desire To Actually Inform, 18 Geo. J. Legal Ethics 1359 (2005). Consider the following responses received to a notice advising members of a class of antibiotics purchasers that they had the right to opt-out of antitrust litigation seeking damages from several major drug companies:

Dear Sir:

> I received your pamphlet on drugs, which I think will be of great value to me in the future.
>
> Due to circumstances beyond my control I will not be able to attend this class at the time prescribed on your letter due to the fact that my working hours are from 7:00 until 4:30.

Dear Sir:

> Our son is in the Navy, stationed in the Caribbean some place. Please let us know exactly what kind of drugs he is accused of taking.
>
> From a mother who will help if properly informed.

A worried mother,

Jane Doe

Dear Attorney General:

> * * * I received a card from you and I don't understand it, and my husband can't read his. Most of the time all I buy is olive oil for healing oil after praying over it, it is anointed with God's power and ain't nothing like dope.

Rhode, *Class Conflicts in Class Actions,* 34 Stan.L.Rev. 1183, 1235 (1982).

To address concerns about the quality, accuracy, and intelligibility of notices provided to absent class members, the Federal Judicial Center has designed and made available illustrative proposed notices that may be adapted in specific class action lawsuits. See *The Federal Judicial Center's "Illustrative" Forms of Class Action Notices*, SJ069 ALI–ABA 73 (2003). Consider the following proposed notice for use in an employment discrimination suit:

UNITED STATES DISTRICT COURT
FOR THE DISTRICT OF STATE

If you are a woman and are or were employed by MNO, a class action lawsuit may affect your rights.

A court authorized this notice. This is not a solicitation from a lawyer.

- Female employees have sued MNO, Inc., alleging discrimination against women.
- The Court has allowed the lawsuit to be a class action on behalf of all women employed by MNO as account executives at any time from June 6, 1996, through July 15, 2003.
- The Court has not decided whether MNO did anything wrong. There is no money available now, and no guarantee there will be. However, your legal rights are affected, and you have a choice to make now:

YOUR LEGAL RIGHTS AND OPTIONS IN THIS LAWSUIT

DO NOTHING	Stay in this lawsuit. Await the outcome. Give up certain rights. By doing nothing, you keep the possibility of getting money or benefits that may come from a trial or a settlement. But, you give up any rights to sue MNO separately about the same legal claims in the lawsuit.
ASK TO BE EXCLUDED	Get out of this lawsuit. Get no benefits from it. Keep rights. If you ask to be excluded and money or benefits are later awarded, you won't share in those. But, you keep any rights to sue MNO separately about the same legal claims in this lawsuit.

What other information might the notice include? If you received the notice, what questions would you have?

The provision of adequate notice raises other questions of practical and constitutional significance. Is it sufficient for notice to be sent to a class member's last known address? What if the notice is returned? How does the Supreme Court's decision in *Flowers*, p. 209, supra, affect your answer? In the aftermath of Hurricane Katrina, class action lawsuits were filed on behalf of individuals evacuated from New Orleans. Given the uncertain circumstances of the class members' lives, what kind of notice efforts would be required to satisfy Rule 23 and due process? See Hilsee, Intrepido & Wheatman, *Hurricanes, Mobility, and Due Process: The Desire-to-Inform Requirement for Effective Class Action Notice Is Highlighted by Katrina*, 80 Tul. L. Rev. 1771 (2006).

C. COSTS

The Supreme Court has held that the costs of providing notice must be borne by the party seeking class treatment. See EISEN v. CARLISLE &

JACQUELIN, 417 U.S. 156, 94 S.Ct. 2140, 40 L.Ed.2d 732 (1974). If the class suit is successful, the costs of sending notice may be subtracted from the class recovery, thus making each class member share the costs on a pro-rata basis. The costs of producing a mailing list often constitute a large part of the overall expense of providing notice. In some class actions defendant's records will be the best, if not the only, source of information from which a list can be constructed. In the past, some litigants sought to use the discovery process to obtain a plaintiff-class mailing list. This shifted to defendant a major portion of the expenses of providing notice, because in federal discovery practice the party that must comply with a discovery request must bear the costs of production. The Supreme Court disapproved this practice in OPPENHEIMER FUND, INC. v. SANDERS, 437 U.S. 340, 98 S.Ct. 2380, 57 L.Ed.2d 253 (1978), but did not prohibit the representative from requesting certain business records of defendant that might aid in preparing the class mailing list. Allocating the costs of notice also is affected by the timing of its provision. If notice is provided after defendant's liability has been determined, which party ought to bear the cost of its provision? Compare Macarz v. Transworld Sys., Inc., 201 F.R.D. 54, 58 (D.Conn.2001); Hartman v. Wick, 678 F.Supp. 312, 328–29 (D.D.C.1988), with Larsen v. JBC Legal Group, 235 F.R.D. 191 (E.D.N.Y. 2006).

5. RULE 23(g) ORDERS APPOINTING CLASS COUNSEL

The traditional conception of the attorney-client relation assumes that (1) the attorney gives advice to the client and the client makes final decisions about litigation strategy, and (2) the attorney acts with virtually unmitigated loyalty to the client's best interest. Class action litigation strains both of these notions. Class action attorneys exercise unusually significant control over decisions made on behalf of the class, but it is difficult to define "loyalty to the client" when it is not clear who the "client" is. Should the attorney give complete loyalty to the interests and wishes of the class representative? To those of each member of the class? To the attorney's conception of the best interests of the class as a whole? See Shapiro, *Class Actions: The Class as Party and Client*, 73 Notre Dame L. Rev. 913 (1998). These questions are difficult ones, and current ethical rules offer attorneys little help in resolving them. Another complication is that class actions may involve a large number of independent lawyers or legal teams representing interests that might be in tension even if not in conflict. See Kane, *Of Carrots and Sticks: Evaluating the Role of the Class Action Lawyer,* 66 Texas L.Rev. 385, 390 (1987). Class members may not be in a strong position to monitor the performance of class counsel, even though the lawyers' interests are not inevitably aligned with those of the clients. Compare Coffee, Jr., *Class Action Accountability: Reconciling Exit, Voice, and Loyalty in Representative Litigation*, 100 Colum.L.Rev. 370 (2000), with Gilles & Friedman, *Exploding the Class Action Agency Costs*

Myth: The Social Utility of Entrepreneurial Lawyers, 155 U. Pa.L.Rev. 103 (2006).

Rule 23, which originally did not address questions about class counsel, was amended in 2003 to deal with these and other perceived problems. What requirements does Rule 23(g) impose on the district court as a condition of the certification order? Are these the only factors that you think relevant to a decision appointing class counsel? See Manesh, *The New Class Action Rule: Procedural Reforms in an Ethical Vacuum*, 18 Geo. J. Legal Ethics 923, 929–31 (2005). Why is it important for the court to have authority to appoint interim counsel before issuing its certification order? See 7B Wright, Miller & Kane, Federal Practice and Procedure: Civil 3d § 1802.3. What is the relationship between the court's determination of adequacy of representation under Rule 23(a)(4) and the duty to appoint class counsel under Rule 23(g)?

6. INTERLOCUTORY APPEALS FROM CERTIFICATION ORDERS

Certification is among the most critical stages in the life of a class action. The papers, hearings, and discovery that inevitably are generated force the court to analyze the nature of the parties and the issues involved in the case. The certification process is even more critical from the parties' point of view. Most importantly, the certification decision dictates the relative leverage that the parties can bring to settlement negotiations. The value of settlement leverage cannot be underestimated, because most class suits are settled before trial. Moreover, for the party opposing the class, a certification order means more than a loss of leverage; the threat that a class may be certified may be a danger in itself in terms of unfavorable publicity and other reputational effects.

Given the tactical importance of the certification stage, Rule 23 was amended in 1998 to add a provision allowing interlocutory appeal from an order granting or denying class certification. The Advisory Committee Note accompanying Rule 23(f) explains:

> * * * [M]any suits with class-action allegations present familiar and almost routine issues that are not more worthy of immediate appeal than many other interlocutory rulings. Yet several concerns justify expansion of present opportunities to appeal. An order denying certification may confront the plaintiff with a situation in which the only sure path to appellate review is by proceeding to final judgment on the merits of an individual claim that, standing alone, is far smaller than the costs of litigation. An order granting certification, on the other hand, may force a defendant to settle rather than incur the costs of defending a class action and run the risk of potentially ruinous liability.

See also Solimine & Hines, *Deciding To Decide: Class Action Certification and Interlocutory Review by the United States Courts of Appeals under*

Rule 23(f), 41 Wm. & Mary L. Rev. 1531 (2000). The circuit courts have taken different approaches to appeals under Rule 23(f). The First Circuit suggests:

> * * * First, an appeal ordinarily should be permitted when a denial of class status effectively ends the case (because, say, the named plaintiff's claim is not of a sufficient magnitude to warrant the costs of stand-alone litigation). Second, an appeal ordinarily should be permitted when the grant of class status raises the stakes of the litigation so substantially that the defendant likely will feel irresistible pressure to settle. Third, an appeal ordinarily should be permitted when it will lead to clarification of a fundamental issue of law.

Waste Management Holdings, Inc. v. Mowbray, 208 F.3d 288, 293 (1st Cir.2000). The Eleventh Circuit expresses "caution against routinely granting appellate review" under Rule 23(f), out of concern that the district court "may feel constrained from revisiting the issue and thereby potentially triggering a new round of appellate proceedings with the inevitable delay and effort of such proceedings." Prado–Steiman v. Bush, 221 F.3d 1266, 1272–73 (11th Cir.2000). See generally p. 1206, infra.

7. RULE 23(d) ORDERS REGULATING THE CONDUCT OF PRETRIAL AND TRIAL PROCEEDINGS

Rule 23(d) authorizes the district court to issue orders regulating the conduct of class action proceedings. For example, the court may create a timetable for discovery and for the presentation of issues at trial; set time limits on oral presentations made by counsel; establish a committee of counsel (consisting of the attorneys representing various members of the class) to make decisions about the prosecution of the class case; and, regulate the substantive aspects of discovery (for example, by determining the parties from whom discovery may be sought and the items which may be requested). Frequently, courts will issue the management orders after they have held a pretrial conference. Because the class representative, in practice, may be only an incomplete proxy for the absentees' interests, the court sometimes must supplement treatment of the class representative's claims with proceedings designed to evaluate some aspect of each class member's individual claims.

The necessity of these supplementary proceedings to "individualize" aspects of a class suit may vary with the relief sought. Some class-wide injunctions may resemble individual suits for injunctive relief closely in the sense that the problems involved in proving the defendant's liability, of determining the proper relief, and of administering relief are all quite difficult, but are not increased materially by class treatment. Class-wide requests for mandatory injunctions, for example, to desegregate a school system or to secure reapportionment of an electoral district, may present more formidable questions that require additional judicial management.

See Garth, *Conflict and Dissent in Class Actions: A Suggested Perspective*, 77 Nw.U.L. Rev. 492, 518–20 (1982). Class-wide suits for damages inevitably create problems that are not present in traditional binary litigation. The court in these damage class actions must complete three analytically separate tasks: it must determine if defendant is liable; it must calculate the amount of damages to the class; and, it must distribute the proper share of the award to individual class members. Often, one or more of these tasks demands fragmentation or "individualization" of the class. See Rosenberg, *Individual Justice and Collectivizing Risk-Based Claims in Mass–Exposure Cases*, 71 N.Y.U. L. Rev. 210 (1996); Edelman, Nagareda & Silver, *The Allocation Problem in Multiple–Claimant Representations*, 14 Sup. Ct. Econ. Rev. 95 (2006).

Courts have approached the task of individualization in different ways and are continuing to develop judicial techniques to assure efficiency and fairness. One approach is to use a single trial to determine defendant's liability (if any) and the amount of damages. These determinations are based on the representative's individual claims, which in some cases are supplemented by statistics and expert testimony. When liability and the amount of damages are set, the court determines how to distribute the class award among individual class members. Another approach is that of the bifurcated trial. The first trial considers only the issue of liability, using the same evidence techniques as would be used in an ordinary proceeding. The second trial, which occurs only if defendant is found liable, addresses the amount of damages. This second proceeding may be a highly individualized one (involving, for example, mini-trials on individual damages claims, or administrative proceedings on individual claims), or it may be a general proceeding designed to calculate the damages to the class as a whole. A third approach, known as "sampling," involves the judge selecting some individual cases at random to adjudicate, and then combining the outcomes of these sample cases to yield results for the larger class population. The sample cases receive their actual awards, but the others all receive the statistically determined sum. For discussions of different judicial techniques, see Bone, *Statistical Adjudication: Rights, Justice, and Utility in a World of Process Scarcity,* 46 Vand.L.Rev. 561 (1993); Fallon, Grabill & Wynne, *Bellwether Trials in Multidistrict Litigation*, 82 Tul. L. Rev. 2323 (2008).

In cases in which the costs of identifying and distributing the award exceed the award due each class member, or when the amount of money that can be distributed to class members does not exhaust the amount of the defendant's liability as determined at trial, courts sometimes utilize a fourth approach—the "fluid class recovery." In such cases, the class award is used to provide a general benefit to class members rather than to compensate them individually. For example, in DAAR v. YELLOW CAB CO., 67 Cal.2d 695, 63 Cal.Rptr. 724, 433 P.2d 732 (1967), a class action was brought against a taxi company to recover alleged overcharges to customers. Since it was impossible to identify each person who had been overcharged, the court ordered defendant to lower its prices to all riders for a certain period of time. The fluid class recovery is used to ensure that the damage award is spread evenly and benefits all the members of the class. In SHAW v. TOSHIBA AMERICA INFORMATION SYSTEMS, INC., 91 F.Supp.2d 942 (E.D.Tex. 2000), a class action alleging the manufacture of faulty computer disks, the court approved a settlement valued at $2.1 billion. The settlement agreement provided:

> If the cash fund is not exhausted by claims from class members, the remaining funds will be distributed to a charity which will use the funds to purchase Toshiba laptop and desktop computers and distribute them in the United States to schools, churches, non-profit organizations, libraries, hospitals, and the poor. No portion will revert to Toshiba.

Id. at 981. Unclaimed funds of about $350 million were used to establish a charity that funds efforts to defeat the digital divide through the creation of technology centers in schools and community-based organizations. See Beaumont Foundation of America, 2003 Annual Report (2003).

8. SETTLEMENT

Rule 23(e) imposes a virtually unique obligation on the district court to approve any decision to settle, dismiss, or compromise a class action. Rule 23(e) reflects the same philosophical concerns that already have been discussed in connection with adequacy of representation. See pp. 753–55, supra. First, due process demands that the absent class members be protected from an unfair settlement made because the representative parties have lost their enthusiasm for the litigation or are themselves receiving a substantial benefit at the expense of the absentees. In addition, the efficiency and economy objectives of Rule 23 would be subverted if the judgment produced by the settlement proves to be vulnerable to collateral attack, a situation that might arise if the settlement does not take proper account of the rights of the absent class members. What requirements does Rule 23(e) impose in terms of notice and an opportunity to be heard? What is the significance of providing class members a second chance at opting out of any proposed settlement? See Federal Rule 23(e)(4). See also Rutherglen, *Better Late Than Never: Notice and Opt Out at the Settlement Stage of Class Actions*, 71 N.Y.U. L. Rev. 258 (1996); Rubenstein, *The Fairness Hearing: Adversarial and Regulatory Approaches,* 53 UCLA L. Rev. 1435 (2006).

What factors ought to guide a court in deciding that a settlement proposal is fair, reasonable, and in the best interests of the individuals who will be affected by it? Proponents of a settlement have the burden of satisfying Rule 23(e)(2). Whether the class as a whole favors the proposed settlement is an extremely important consideration in the court's assessment. The preference of any particular class member, however, is not dispositive. Settlements can be approved over the objections of the class representatives, as well as those of absent class members who have received and responded to the settlement notice. Objecting class members are free to appeal the court's decision approving the settlement when a judgment based on it is entered. Concerns about the class action settlement process remain one of the most controversial features of Rule 23 practice.

The Class Action Fairness Act, 28 U.S.C. § 1712, imposes special requirements on the district court to assess the fairness, reasonableness, and adequacy of settlements that rely on "coupons." Coupons typically permit the class members to purchase goods at a discount from defendant. See, for example, In re Domestic Air Transportation Antitrust Litigation, 148 F.R.D. 297 (N.D. Ga. 1993), an antitrust suit against the airline industry, in which the settlement resulted in the distribution of discount flight coupons to be used for future travel by class members. SYNFUEL TECHNOLOGIES, INC. v. DHL EXPRESS (USA), 463 F.3d 646 (7th Cir. 2006), involved a suit against a package delivery company for allegedly overcharging customers. The District Court approved a settlement that provided class members with the choice of accepting a number of prepaid shipping envelopes or thirty dollars cash, in addition to injunctive relief that prospectively changed defendant's billing practices. The Court of Appeals vacated the judgment, finding that the District Court had not assessed the fairness of the settlement adequately. Although CAFA did not govern the lawsuit, the Seventh Circuit pointed to Congress's requirement under that statute of heightened judicial scrutiny of coupon settlements; moreover, although pre-paid envelopes are not coupons, the appeals court drew the analogy that "they are a form of in-kind compensation that shares some characteristics of coupons, including forced future business with the defendant * * *." Id. at 654. See generally Leslie, *The Need To Study Coupon Settlements in Class Action Litigation*, 18 Geo. J. Legal Ethics 1395 (2005). Why should a settlement's reliance on coupons raise special concerns for the judiciary's fairness inquiry?

9. ATTORNEY'S FEES

Federal Rule 23(h), adopted in 2003, authorizes the court to award a reasonable attorney's fee in any action certified as a class action. Long before the amendment made this power explicit, courts routinely awarded such fees to the attorney for the successful representative party. The rationale for this practice was that since counsel's representation on behalf of the named plaintiffs conferred a benefit on all the class members, fairness demanded that compensation be awarded out of any fund ordered for the class. In some contexts, a "reasonable" fee is awarded pursuant to a specific statutory provision designed to provide an incentive for lawyers to act in the public interest as "private attorneys general." This is manifest in numerous substantive statutes that provide for fees for the prevailing party's attorney when a violation of the statute is established. In other contexts, courts have awarded attorney's fees out of the common fund created by the recovery from defendant. The Supreme Court has rejected the argument that fee awards are prohibited by the traditional American rule that the losing party shall not be forced to bear the winning parties' legal expenses. Boeing Co. v. Van Gemert, 444 U.S. 472, 100 S.Ct. 745, 62 L.Ed.2d 676 (1980).

Courts use different approaches in setting the amount of class action attorney's fees. See generally Resnik, Curtis & Hensler, *Individuals within the Aggregate: Relationships, Representation, and Fees*, 71 N.Y.U. L. Rev. 296 (1996). In a case that produces a common fund recovered for the class, the court may apply a percentage to the fund to determine the amount that should be awarded for attorney's fees. See, e.g., Camden I Condominium Ass'n v. Dunkle, 946 F.2d 768, 774 (11th Cir.1991). For a discussion of this approach that has influenced judicial practice, see *Court Awarded Attorney Fees, Report of the Third Circuit Task Force*, 108 F.R.D. 237 (1985). An alternative approach, referred to as the "lodestar," looks to the number of hours expended by each lawyer on the case, multiplied by a "normal billing rate," and adjusted, up or down, for discretionary factors such as the riskiness of the lawsuit and the quality of the attorney's performance. The Supreme Court has discouraged the use of risk multipliers in lawsuits involving statutory fee provisions. See PENNSYLVANIA v. DELAWARE VALLEY CITIZENS' COUNCIL, 483 U.S. 711, 107 S.Ct. 3078, 97 L.Ed.2d 585 (1987); CITY OF BURLINGTON v. DAGUE, 505 U.S. 557, 112 S.Ct. 2638, 120 L.Ed.2d 449 (1992). Fee awards in class actions have generated extensive media attention because the amount of the award exceeds the benefit accorded any individual member of the class. For example, a fee award in a Texas tobacco case was $3.4 billion. See, e.g., Gold, *Tobacco Suit Attorneys Land $3.4 Billion in Fees,* Sun–Sentinel, Dec. 12, 1998, at A–1. However, the award is payable over a period of decades and at present value equals about one-tenth the awarded sum. See Texas v. Real Parties in Interest, 259 F.3d 387 (5th Cir.2001). Empirical studies suggest that court awarded class action attorney's fees are lower than the standard contingency fee awarded in individual lawsuits. See Willging, Hooper & Niemic, *An Empirical Analysis of Rule 23 To Address the Rulemaking Challenges*, 71 N.Y.U. L. Rev. 74 (1996); Eisenberg & Miller, *Attorney Fees in Class Action Settlements: An Empirical Study*, 1 J. Empirical Legal Stud. 27 (2004).

SECTION D. DUE PROCESS CONSIDERATIONS

HANSBERRY v. LEE

Supreme Court of the United States, 1940.
311 U.S. 32, 61 S.Ct. 115, 85 L.Ed. 22.

[This suit was brought in an Illinois state court on behalf of a class of landowners to enforce a racially restrictive covenant involving land in the City of Chicago. The covenant provided that it was not effective unless signed by the "owners of 95 per centum of the frontage." Plaintiff alleged that Hansberry, a black man, had purchased some of the restricted land from an owner who had signed the agreement and that suit was being brought to enjoin the sale as a breach of the covenant. He further alleged that the binding effect of the covenant had been established in an earlier Illinois state court action holding that 95 percent of all the landowners involved had signed the agreement. In response, defendants pleaded that they were not bound by the res judicata effect of the earlier judgment as they had not been parties to that suit and were not successors in interest or in privity with any of the parties to that action. Thus they argued it would be a denial of due process to hold them to the first decree.

The Illinois Circuit Court held that the issue whether the covenant was valid was res judicata, even though it found that only about 54 percent of the owners actually had signed the agreement and that the previous judgment rested on a "false and fraudulent" stipulation of the parties. The Supreme Court of Illinois affirmed. It found that although the stipulation was untrue it was not fraudulent or collusive. The Illinois court then went on to conclude that the first action had been a "class" or "representative" suit, that as such it was binding on all the class members unless reversed or set aside on direct proceedings, and that Hansberry and the persons who had sold the land to him were members of the class represented in the first action and consequently were bound by the decree in that suit.]

Certiorari to the Supreme Court of the State of Illinois.

MR. JUSTICE STONE delivered the opinion of the Court.

* * *

* * * [W]hen the judgment of a state court, ascribing to the judgment of another court the binding force and effect of *res judicata*, is challenged for want of due process it becomes the duty of this Court to examine the course of procedure in both litigations to ascertain whether the litigant whose rights have thus been adjudicated has been afforded such notice and opportunity to be heard as are requisite to the due process which the Constitution prescribes. * * *

It is a principle of general application in Anglo–American jurisprudence that one is not bound by a judgment *in personam* in a litigation in which he is not designated as a party or to which he has not been made a party by service of process. Pennoyer v. Neff, * * * [p. 71, supra]. A judgment rendered in such circumstances is not entitled to the full faith and credit which the Constitution and statute of the United States * * * prescribe * * * and judicial action enforcing it against the person or property of the absent party is not that due process which the Fifth and Fourteenth Amendments requires. * * *

To these general rules there is a recognized exception that, to an extent not precisely defined by judicial opinion, the judgment in a "class" or "representative" suit, to which some members of the class are parties, may bind members of the class or those represented who were not made parties to it. * * *

The class suit was an invention of equity to enable it to proceed to a decree in suits where the number of those interested in the subject of the litigation is so great that their joinder as parties in conformity to the usual rules of procedure is impracticable. Courts are not infrequently called upon to proceed with causes in which the number of those interested in the litigation is so great as to make difficult or impossible the joinder of all because some are not within the jurisdiction or because their whereabouts is unknown or where if all were made parties to the suit its continued abatement by the death of some would prevent or unduly delay a decree. In such cases where the interests of those not joined are of the same class as the interests of those who are, and where it is considered that the latter fairly represent the former in the prosecution of the litigation of the issues in which all have a common interest, the court will proceed to a decree. * * *

It is evident that the considerations which may induce a court thus to proceed, despite a technical defect of parties, may differ from those which must be taken into account in determining whether the absent parties are bound by the decree or, if it is adjudged that they are, in ascertaining whether such an adjudication satisfies the requirements of due process and of full faith and credit. Nevertheless there is scope within the framework of the Constitution for holding in appropriate cases that a judgment rendered in a class suit is *res judicata* as to members of the class who are not formal parties to the suit. * * * With a proper regard for divergent local institutions and interests * * *, this Court is justified in saying that there has been a failure of due process only in those cases where it cannot be said that the procedure adopted, fairly insures the protection of the interests of absent parties who are to be bound by it. * * *

It is familiar doctrine of the federal courts that members of a class not present as parties to the litigation may be bound by the judgment where they are in fact adequately represented by parties who are present, or where they actually participate in the conduct of the litigation in which members of the class are present as parties * * * or where the interest of the members of the class, some of whom are present as parties, is joint, or where for any other reason the relationship between the parties present and those who are absent is such as legally to entitle the former to stand in judgment for the latter. * * *

In all such cases, * * * we may assume for present purposes that such procedure affords a protection to the parties who are represented though absent, which would satisfy the requirements of due process and full faith and credit. * * * Nor do we find it necessary for the decision of this case to say that, when the only circumstance defining the class is that the determination of the rights of its members turns upon a single issue of fact or law, a state could not constitutionally adopt a procedure whereby some of the members of the class could stand in judgment for all, provided that the procedure were so devised and applied as to insure that those present are of the same class as those absent and that the litigation is so conducted as to insure the full and fair consideration of the common issue. * * * We decide only that the procedure and the course of litigation sustained here by the plea of res judicata do not satisfy these requirements.

The restrictive agreement did not purport to create a joint obligation or liability. If valid and effective its promises were the several obligations of the signers and those claiming under them. The promises ran severally to every other signer. It is plain that in such circumstances all those alleged to be bound by the agreement would not constitute a single class in any litigation brought to enforce it. Those who sought to secure its benefits by enforcing it could not be said to be in the same class with or represent those whose interest was in resisting performance, for the agreement by its terms imposes obligations and confers rights on the owner of each plot of land who signs it. If those who thus seek to secure the benefits of the agreement were rightly regarded by the state Supreme Court as constituting a class, it is evident that those signers or their successors who are interested in challenging the validity of the agreement and resisting its performance are not of the same class in the sense that their interests are identical so that any group who had elected to enforce rights conferred by the agreement could be said to be acting in the interest of any others who were free to deny its obligation.

Because of the dual and potentially conflicting interests of those who are putative parties to the agreement in compelling or resisting its performance, it is impossible to say, solely because they are parties to it, that any two of them are of the same class. Nor without more, and with the due regard for the protection of the rights of absent parties which due process exacts, can some be permitted to stand in judgment for all.

It is one thing to say that some members of a class may represent other members in a litigation where the sole and common interest of the class in the litigation, is either to assert a common right or to challenge an asserted obligation. * * * It is quite another to hold that all those who are free alternatively either to assert rights or to challenge them are of a single class, so that any group, merely because it is of the class so constituted, may be deemed adequately to represent any others of the class in litigating their interests in either alternative. Such a selection of representatives for purposes of litigation, whose substantial interests are not necessarily or even probably the same as those whom they are deemed to represent, does not afford that protection to absent parties which due process requires. The doctrine of representation of absent parties in a class suit has not hitherto been thought to go so far. * * * Apart from the opportunities it would afford for the fraudulent and collusive sacrifice of the rights of absent parties, we think that the representation in this case no more satisfies the requirements of due process than a trial by a judicial officer who is in such situation that he may have an interest in the outcome of the litigation in conflict with that of the litigants. * * *

The plaintiffs in the [first] case sought to compel performance of the agreement in behalf of themselves and all others similarly situated. They did not designate the defendants in the suit as a class or seek any injunction or other relief against others than the named defendants, and the decree which was entered did not purport to bind others. In seeking to enforce the agreement the plaintiffs in that suit were not representing the petitioners here whose substantial interest is in resisting performance. The defendants in the first suit were not treated by the pleadings or decree as representing others or as foreclosing by their defense the rights of others, and even though nominal defendants, it does not appear that their interest in defeating the contract outweighed their interest in establishing its validity. For a court in this situation to ascribe to either the plaintiffs or defendants the performance of such functions on behalf of petitioners here, is to attribute to them a power that it cannot be said that they had assumed to exercise, and a responsibility which, in view of their dual interests it does not appear that they could rightly discharge.

Reversed.

NOTES AND QUESTIONS

1. For an account of the history surrounding Hansberry v. Lee, including efforts to desegregate Chicago, and noting that the Hansberrys' daughter is the author Lorraine Hansberry, of *Raisin in the Sun* fame, see Kamp, *The History Behind Hansberry v. Lee*, 20 U.C. Davis L.Rev. 481 (1987). See also Tidmarsh, *The Story of* Hansberry*: The Rise of Modern Class Actions*, in Civil Procedure Stories 233–94 (Clermont ed.) (2d ed. 2008).

2. In what ways does the Due Process Clause affect the legitimacy of a class action? In earlier cases that you have studied, due process has required the provision of notice and an opportunity to be heard to a defendant in a lawsuit. See, e.g., Fuentes v. Shevin, p. 240, supra. In *Hansberry,* the Supreme Court shifted its attention to the protection of plaintiffs, and focused on the adequacy of representation. See 7A Wright, Miller & Kane, Federal Practice and Procedure: Civil 3d § 1765.

3. At what point in a proceeding does a court evaluate the adequacy of class action representation? GONZALES v. CASSIDY, 474 F.2d 67 (5th Cir.1973), concerned the effect of a class action that successfully challenged the constitutionality of a Texas statute requiring uninsured motorists to post security when sued for a car accident or else have their drivers' licenses suspended. Class-action relief was applied retroactively to the representative plaintiff and prospectively to all other class members. In *Gonzales*, plaintiff alleged that the class representative was inadequate for having failed to appeal on the issue of retroactivity. The Fifth Circuit outlined a two-part test for reviewing whether the named plaintiff has represented the class adequately as to make the judgment in the suit binding on the absent class members:

> * * * (1) Did the trial court in the first suit correctly determine, initially, that the representative would adequately represent the class? and (2) Does it appear, after the termination of the suit, that the class representative adequately protected the interest of the class? * * *

Id. at 72. The court held that the original plaintiff's failure to appeal the initial judgment rendered him an inadequate representative of the class, since "he was representing approximately 150,000 persons, who, although having had their licenses and registration receipts suspended without due process, were denied any relief by the * * * [trial] court's prospective * * * application of its decision." Id. at 76. The court remanded the case to the District Court for reconsideration of the retroactivity question. Implicit in the two prongs of *Gonzales* is the notion that adequacy of representation may be examined more than once and by different courts: first by the court certifying the class; second by an appellate court; third by a court called upon to evaluate the binding effect of the class action on a class member who seeks to litigate in a later action. See p. 819, infra.

4. If the adequacy of representation provided by class representation is important to safeguarding the due process rights of class members, courts must be vigilant in examining potential conflicts of interest among class members. The conflict of interest in *Hansberry* unquestionably was enough to preclude a finding of adequate representation. In other cases, however, the conflict of interest may be less sharply defined.

Consider whether, as a trial court judge, you would certify the following proposed classes:

(a) The complaint alleges discrimination in hiring, promotion, and conditions of employment; the proposed class includes current minority employees, minorities whose employment applications were denied, and future minority applicants and employees; the sole class representative is a current employee of the company.

(b) Would your answer to (a) be any different if there were a second class representative whom the defendant arguably had failed to hire because of discrimination?

(c) An airline has a practice of discharging flight attendants who become pregnant. A suit for injunctive relief is brought on behalf of female airline cabin attendants, including those stewardesses who still are employed. Reinstatement of the former stewardesses, with no loss of seniority, would leapfrog them over the less senior stewardesses who still are actively employed.

(d) Members of the proposed class in a products-liability suit reside in all parts of the nation, and there are significant differences in the products-liability laws of the various states. Should the class be certified as a single class? Suppose the injured parties can be divided into two groups for whom the applicable laws are substantially the same? What if four groupings are needed? Sixteen? At what point would this subclassing create intolerable management problems?

5. In RICHARDS v. JEFFERSON COUNTY, ALABAMA, 517 U.S. 793, 116 S.Ct. 1761, 135 L.Ed.2d 76 (1996), the Court further elaborated the due-process requirements recognized in *Hansberry*. Petitioners brought a class action on behalf of all nonfederal employees challenging a state employment tax. Their claims were dismissed as barred under a court's earlier judgment that the tax was constitutional. The earlier case had been litigated by the

acting director of finance for a city and the city itself, and had been consolidated with a separate suit brought by three state taxpayers. The United States Supreme Court reversed. In its decision, the Court relied on a number of grounds to explain why the interests of the petitioners in *Richards* were not adequately represented in the prior litigation and so could not be barred from pressing their constitutional claims in a separate action. First, plaintiffs in the first action had not given petitioners notice of their lawsuit; second, the taxpayer-plaintiffs in the first action had not sued on behalf of a class and the judgment did not purport to bind nonparties; third, the government-plaintiffs had not purported to represent the pecuniary interests of petitioners, who were county and not city taxpayers; and the first action was not a special proceeding designed to be brought on behalf of the public. The Court stated:

> Even assuming that our opinion in *Hansberry* may be read to leave open the possibility that in some class suits adequate representation might cure a lack of notice * * *, it may not be read to permit the application of res judicata here. Our opinion explained that a prior proceeding, to have binding effect on absent parties, would at least have to be "so devised and applied as to insure that those present are of the same class as those absent and that the litigation is so conducted as to insure the full and fair consideration of the common issue." * * * It is plain that the * * * prior action * * * does not fit such a description.

Id. at 801, 116 S.Ct. at 1767, 135 L.Ed.2d at 86.

6. Professor Coffee has argued that a court's inquiry into adequacy of representation should be guided by principles of exit, loyalty, and voice. See Coffee, *Class Action Accountability: Reconciling Exit, Voice, and Loyalty in Representative Litigation*, 100 Colum.L.Rev. 370 (2000). What do these terms mean in the class action context? The Supreme Court has focused on loyalty as a way to ensure class cohesion. Might there be a danger that this approach will generate internecine division of warring subclasses, and ultimately may weaken the claim that the class action is superior to adjudication of individual claims? On the other hand, increasing voice may not be appropriate for class actions, either, because class representatives actually play a very small role in the development of a large class action. Is the best solution the enhancement of class members' exit opportunities at all stages of the litigation? Is this suggestion feasible?

SECTION E. CLASS ACTIONS AND JURISDICTION

1. SUBJECT-MATTER JURISDICTION

A class action based upon a federal question usually does not raise any special problems of subject-matter jurisdiction. A class action based upon diversity, however, does raise two special questions: first, to which class members should the court look in determining whether there is diversity of citizenship and, second, to which class members should the court look in calculating the jurisdictional-amount requirement? In addition, the Class Action Fairness Act alters the jurisdictional rules for class actions that come within its provisions.

In SUPREME TRIBE OF BEN–HUR v. CAUBLE, 255 U.S. 356, 41 S.Ct. 338, 65 L.Ed. 673 (1921), the Supreme Court held that determinations of diversity of citizenship in class actions should be based on the citizenship of the named parties only. See generally 7A Wright, Miller & Kane, Federal Practice and Procedure: Civil 3d § 1755. How does this rule apply to a class action brought by an unincorporated association? A court usually looks to the citizenship of each member of the association to determine whether there is diversity of citizenship. Examine 28 U.S.C. § 1332 (c)(1). How does CAFA change this rule for class actions that come within its terms?

In SNYDER v. HARRIS, 394 U.S. 332, 89 S.Ct. 1053, 22 L.Ed.2d 319 (1969), Snyder, a shareholder of Missouri Fidelity Union Trust Life Insurance Co., brought suit in federal court against members of the company's board of directors. Since petitioner's allegations showed that she sought for herself only $8,740 in damages, respondent moved to dismiss on the ground that the matter in controversy did not exceed $10,000 (the requisite jurisdictional amount at the time). Petitioner contended that her claim should be aggregated with those of the other members of her class, approximately 4,000 shareholders of the company stock. If all 4,000 potential claims were aggregated, the amount in controversy would be approximately $1,200,000. The Supreme Court held that separate and distinct claims could not be aggregated. It noted that "[a]ggregation has been permitted only (1) in cases in which a single plaintiff seeks to aggregate two or more of his claims against a single defendant and (2) in cases where two or more plaintiffs unite to enforce a single title or right in which they have a common or undivided interest." 394 U.S. at 335, 89 S.Ct. at 1056, 22 L.Ed.2d at 323.

In ZAHN v. INTERNATIONAL PAPER CO., 414 U.S. 291, 94 S.Ct. 505, 38 L.Ed.2d 511 (1973), petitioners, owners of property fronting on Lake Champlain in Orwell, Vermont, brought a diversity action seeking damages from International Paper Co., a New York corporation, for allegedly polluting the waters of the lake and damaging the value and utility of the surrounding properties. The claims of each of the named plaintiffs were found to satisfy the $10,000 jurisdictional amount, but the District Court was convinced "to a legal certainty" that not every individual owner in the class had suffered pollution damages in excess of $10,000. The Supreme Court held that each plaintiff in a Rule 23(b)(3) class action must satisfy the jurisdictional-amount requirement. Again, the majority opinion rested on the traditional rules that courts had used for aggregating claims.

In EXXON MOBIL CORP. v. ALLAPATTAH SERVICES, INC., 545 U.S. 546, 125 S.Ct. 2611, 162 L.Ed.2d 502 (2005), the Supreme Court held, five-to-four, that the 1990 enactment of the supplemental jurisdiction statute, 28 U.S.C. § 1367, overruled *Zahn*. See p. 338, supra. The Court explained that when the complaint includes "at least one claim that satisfies the amount-in-controversy requirement, and there are no other relevant jurisdictional defects, the district court, beyond all question, has original jurisdiction over that claim," and that the court then "can turn to the question whether it has a constitutional and statutory basis for exercising supplemental jurisdiction over the other claims in the action." The Court found "[n]othing in the text of § 1367(b)" that could be read to withhold "supplemental jurisdiction over the claims of plaintiffs certified as class-action members pursuant to Rule 23." Id. at 559–60, 125 S.Ct. at 2620–21, 162 L.Ed.2d at 521–22.

NOTE ON THE CLASS ACTION FAIRNESS ACT OF 2005

The Class Action Fairness Act, adopted in 2005, authorizes federal jurisdiction on the basis of minimal diversity for any interstate class action that comes within its terms. See Chapter 4, p. 276, supra. Examine the language of Section 1332(d). What is the required amount in controversy for a class action under CAFA? Does the court look to the named plaintiff to determine whether the jurisdictional amount is satisfied? How is minimal diversity determined? Can class actions that meet the jurisdictional requirements of CAFA be removed to federal court? See 28 U.S.C. § 1453. CAFA excludes various categories of class actions from the statute's scope. What are those exceptions? See 28 U.S.C. § 1332(d)(5)(A) (primary defendants are States, State officials, or other governmental entities); Section 1332 (d)(5)(B) (the class contains "less than 100" members); and Section 1332(d)(9)(A)–(B) (the action "solely involves a claim" involving certain securities and corporate governance issues). Finally, the district court has discretion to decline jurisdiction under CAFA based on an assessment of six enumerated factors. See 28 U.S.C. § 1332(d)(3)(A)–(F). "No guidance is given as to how the court is to weigh or balance those factors." 7A Wright, Miller & Kane, Federal Practice and Procedure: Civil 3d § 1756.2.

One commentator calls CAFA "the most significant change in class action practice since the federal class action rule was amended in 1996." Sherman, *Class Actions after the Class Action Fairness Act of 2005*, 80 Tul. L. Rev. 1593 (2006). CAFA's impact on class action practice is not yet clear. See Marcus, *Modes of Procedural Reform*, 31 Hastings Int'l & Comp. L. Rev. 157, 184 (2008). In the short run, CAFA has increased the number of diversity class actions in the federal courts, and these cases largely involve contracts, torts, consumer protection, fraud, and property damage. See Lee & Willging, The Impact of the Class Action Fairness Act of 2005 on the Federal Courts: Fourth Interim Report to the Judicial Conference Advisory Committee on Civil Rules 1–2 (Federal Judicial Center, April 2008). How these cases are affecting the federal judicial workload remains to be seen. Professor Nagareda warns that channeling state law class actions to federal court will cause a "backdoor" revision of state-law substantive rights. See Nagareda, *Aggregation and Its Discontents: Class Settlement Pressure, Class–Wide Arbitration, and CAFA*, 106 Colum. L. Rev. 1872, 1876 (2006). Is that result consistent with *Erie*? See p. 408, supra.

2. PERSONAL JURISDICTION

Class actions raise interesting problems related to personal jurisdiction. Must the requirements of *International Shoe*, p. 85, supra, be satisfied in order for the class action judgment to bind a particular member of a defendant class? Similarly, must the due process requirements of personal jurisdiction be met before a court can bind any individual member of a plaintiff class? Do the traditional doctrines of personal jurisdiction apply to absentee class members who are beyond the court's jurisdiction? The following case addresses that question.

PHILLIPS PETROLEUM CO. v. SHUTTS

Supreme Court of the United States, 1985.
472 U.S. 797, 105 S.Ct. 2965, 86 L.Ed.2d 628.

[During the 1970's, Phillips Petroleum produced or purchased natural gas from leased land located in 11 states. Shutts and several other royalty owners possessing rights to leases from which Phillips Petroleum produced the gas brought a class action against the company in a Kansas state court, seeking to recover interest on royalty payments that had been delayed. The trial court certified a class consisting of 33,000 royalty owners. The class representative provided each class member with a notice by first-class mail describing the action and informing each member that he could appear in person or by counsel, that otherwise he would be represented by the named royalty owners, and that class members would be included in the class and bound by the judgment unless they "opted out" of the action by returning a "request for exclusion." The final class consisted of some 28,100 members, who resided in all 50 states, the District of Columbia, and several foreign countries. Notwithstanding that over 99% of the gas leases in question and some 97% of the plaintiff class members had no apparent connection to Kansas except for the lawsuit, the trial court applied Kansas contract and equity law to every claim and found Phillips Petroleum liable for interest on the suspended royalties to all class members. The Kansas Supreme Court affirmed over the company's contentions that the Due Process Clause of the Fourteenth Amendment prevented Kansas from adjudicating the claims of all the class members, and that the Due Process Clause and the Full Faith and Credit Clause prohibited application of Kansas law to all of the transactions between it and the class members.]

Certiorari to the Supreme Court of Kansas.

JUSTICE REHNQUIST delivered the opinion of the Court.

* * *

I

* * *

* * * As a class-action defendant petitioner is in a unique predicament. If Kansas does not possess jurisdiction over this plaintiff class, petitioner will be bound to 28,100 judgment holders scattered across the globe, but none of these will be bound by the Kansas decree. Petitioner could be subject to numerous later individual suits by these class members because a judgment issued without proper personal jurisdiction over an absent party is not entitled to full faith and credit elsewhere and thus has no res judicata effect as to that party. Whether it wins or loses on the merits, petitioner has a distinct and personal interest in seeing the entire plaintiff class bound by res judicata just as petitioner is bound. The only way a class action defendant like petitioner can assure itself of this binding effect of the judgment is to ascertain that the forum court has jurisdiction over every plaintiff whose claim it seeks to adjudicate, sufficient to support a defense of res judicata in a later suit for damages by class members.

While it is true that a court adjudicating a dispute may not be able to predetermine the res judicata effect of its own judgment, petitioner has alleged that it would be obviously and immediately injured if this class-action judgment against it became final without binding the plaintiff class. We think that such an injury is sufficient to give petitioner standing on its own right to raise the jurisdiction claim in this Court.

* * *

II

Reduced to its essentials, petitioner's argument is that unless out-of-state plaintiffs affirmatively consent, the Kansas courts may not exert jurisdiction over their claims. Petitioner claims that failure to execute and return the "request for exclusion" provided with the class notice cannot constitute consent of the out-of-state plaintiffs; thus Kansas courts may exercise jurisdiction over these plaintiffs only if the plaintiffs possess the sufficient "minimum contacts" with Kansas as that term is used in cases involving personal jurisdiction over out-of-state defendants. * * * Since Kansas had no prelitigation contact with many of the plaintiffs and leases involved, petitioner claims that Kansas has exceeded its jurisdictional reach and thereby violated the due process rights of the absent plaintiffs.

In *International Shoe* we were faced with an out-of-state corporation which sought to avoid the exercise of personal jurisdiction over it as a defendant by Washington state court. We held that the extent of the defendant's due process protection would depend "upon the quality and nature of the activity in relation to the fair and orderly administration of the laws * * *." We noted that the Due Process Clause did not permit a State to make a binding judgment against a person with whom the State had no contacts, ties, or relations. * * * If the defendant possessed certain minimum contacts with the State, so that it was "reasonable and just, according to our traditional conception of fair play and substantial justice" for a State to exercise personal jurisdiction, the State could force the defendant to defend himself in the forum, upon pain of default, and could bind him to a judgment. * * *

The purpose of this test, of course, is to protect a defendant from the travail of defending in a distant forum, unless the defendant's contacts with the forum make it just to force him to defend there. As we explained in *Woodson* * * *, [p. 105, supra,] the defendant's contacts should be such that "he should reasonably anticipate being haled" into the forum. * * * In Insurance Corp. of Ireland v. Compagnie des Bauxites de Guinee, [p. 114, supra,] * * * we explained that the requirement that a court have personal jurisdiction comes from the Due Process Clause's protection of the defendant's personal liberty interest, and said that the requirement "represents a restriction on judicial power not as a matter of sovereignty, but as a matter of individual liberty." * * *

Although the cases like *Shaffer* [, p. 161 supra,] and *Woodson* which petitioner relies on for a minimum contacts requirement all dealt with out-of-state defendants or parties in the procedural posture of a defendant, * * * petitioner claims that the same analysis must apply to absent class-action plaintiffs. In this regard petitioner correctly points out that a chose in action is a constitutionally recognized property interest possessed by each of the plaintiffs. * * * An adverse judgment by Kansas courts in this case may extinguish the chose in action forever through res judicata. Such an adverse judgment, petitioner claims, would be every bit as onerous to an absent plaintiff as an adverse judgment on the merits would be to a defendant. Thus, the same due process protections should apply to absent plaintiffs: Kansas should not be able to exert jurisdiction over the plaintiffs' claims unless the plaintiffs have sufficient minimum contacts with Kansas.

We think petitioner's premise is in error. The burdens placed by a State upon an absent class-action plaintiff are not of the same order or magnitude as those it places upon an absent defendant. An out-of-state defendant summoned by a plaintiff is faced with the full powers of the forum State to render judgment *against* it. The defendant must generally hire counsel and travel to the forum to defend itself from the plaintiff's claim, or suffer a default judgment. The defendant may be forced to participate in extended and often costly discovery, and will be forced to respond in damages or to comply with some other form of remedy imposed by the court should it lose the suit. The defendant may also face liability for court costs and attorney's fees. These burdens are substantial, and the minimum contacts requirement of the Due Process Clause prevents the forum State from unfairly imposing them upon the defendant.

A class-action plaintiff, however, is in quite a different posture. The Court noted this difference in Hansberry v. Lee * * *, [p. 777, supra,] which explained that a "class" or "representative" suit was an exception to the rule that one could not be bound by judgment *in personam* unless one was made fully a party in the traditional sense. * * * As the Court pointed out in *Hansberry,* the class action was an invention of equity to enable it to proceed to a decree in suits where the number of those interested in the litigation was too great to permit joinder. The absent parties would be bound by the decree so long as the named parties adequately represented the absent class and the prosecution of the litigation was within the common interest. * * *

Modern plaintiff class actions follow the same goals, permitting litigation of a suit involving common questions when there are too many plaintiffs for proper joinder. Class actions also may permit the plaintiffs to pool claims which would be uneconomical to litigate individually. For example, this lawsuit involves claims averaging about $100 per plaintiff; most of the plaintiffs would have no realistic day in court if a class action were not available.

In sharp contrast to the predicament of a defendant haled into an out-of-state forum, the plaintiffs in this suit were not haled anywhere to defend themselves upon pain of a default judgment. As commentators have noted, from the plaintiffs' point of view a class action resembles a "quasi-administrative proceeding, conducted by the judge." * * *

A plaintiff class in Kansas and numerous other jurisdictions cannot first be certified unless the judge, with the aid of the named plaintiffs and defendant, conducts an inquiry into the common nature of the named plaintiffs' and the absent plaintiffs' claims, the adequacy of representation, the jurisdiction possessed over the class, and any other matters that will bear upon proper representation of the absent plaintiffs' interest. * * * Unlike a defendant in a civil suit, a class-action plaintiff is not required to fend for himself. * * * The court and named plaintiffs protect his interests. Indeed, the class-action defendant itself has a great interest in ensuring that the absent plaintiffs' claims are properly before the forum. In this case, for example, the defendant sought to avoid class certification by alleging that the absent plaintiffs would not be adequately represented and were not amenable to jurisdiction. * * *

The concern of the typical class-action rules for the absent plaintiffs is manifested in other ways. Most jurisdictions, including Kansas, require that a class action, once certified, may not be dismissed or compromised without the approval of the court. In many jurisdictions such as Kansas the court may amend the pleadings to ensure that all sections of the class are represented adequately. * * *

Besides this continuing solicitude for their rights, absent plaintiff class members are not subject to other burdens imposed upon defendants. They need not hire counsel or appear. They are almost never subject to counterclaims or cross-claims, or liability for fees or costs. Absent plaintiff class members are not subject to coercive or punitive remedies. Nor will an adverse judgment typically bind an absent plaintiff for any damages, although a valid adverse judgment may extinguish any of the plaintiff's claim which was litigated.

Unlike a defendant in a normal civil suit, an absent class-action plaintiff is not required to do anything. He may sit back and allow the litigation to run its course, content in knowing that there are safeguards provided for his protection. In most class actions an absent plaintiff is provided at least with an opportunity to "opt out" of the class, and if he takes advantage of that opportunity he is removed from the litigation entirely. This was true of the Kansas proceedings in this case. The Kansas procedure provided for the mailing of a notice to each class member by first-class mail. The notice, as we have previously indicated, described the action and informed the class member that he could appear in person or by counsel, in default of which he would be represented by the named plaintiffs and their attorneys. The notice further stated that class members would be included in the class and bound by the judgment unless they "opted out" by executing and returning a "request for exclusion" that was included in the notice.

Petitioner contends, however, that the "opt out" procedure provided by Kansas is not good enough, and that an "opt in" procedure is required to satisfy the Due Process Clause of the Fourteenth Amendment. Insofar as plaintiffs who have no minimum contacts with the forum State are concerned, an "opt in" provision would require that each class member affirmatively consent to his inclusion within the class.

Because States place fewer burdens upon absent class plaintiffs than they do upon absent defendants in nonclass suits, the Due Process Clause need not and does not afford the former as much protection from state-court jurisdiction as it does the latter. The Fourteenth Amendment does protect "persons," not "defendants," however, so absent plaintiffs as well as absent defendants are entitled to some protection from the jurisdiction of a forum State which seeks to adjudicate their claims. In this case we hold that a forum State may exercise jurisdiction over the claim of an absent class-action plaintiff, even though that plaintiff may not possess the minimum contacts with the forum which would support personal jurisdiction over a defendant. If the forum State wishes to bind an absent plaintiff concerning a claim for money damages or similar relief at law,[3] it must provide minimal procedural due process protection. The plaintiff must receive notice plus an opportunity to be heard and participate in the litigation, whether in person or through counsel. The notice must be the best practicable, "reasonably calculated, under all the circumstances, to apprise interested parties of the pendency of the action and afford them an opportunity to present their objections." * * * The notice should describe the action and the plaintiffs' rights in it. Additionally, we hold that due process requires at a minimum that an absent plaintiff be provided with an opportunity to remove himself from the class by executing and returning an "opt out" or "request for exclusion" form to the court. Finally, the Due Process Clause of course requires that the named

3. Our holding today is limited to those class actions which seek to bind known plaintiffs concerning claims wholly or predominately for money judgments. We intimate no view concerning other types of class action lawsuits, such as those seeking equitable relief. Nor, of course, does our discussion of personal jurisdiction address class actions where the jurisdiction is asserted against a *defendant* class.

plaintiff at all times adequately represent the interests of the absent class members. * * *

We reject petitioner's contention that the Due Process Clause of the Fourteenth Amendment requires that absent plaintiffs affirmatively "opt in" to the class, rather than be deemed members of the class if they do not "opt out." We think that such a contention is supported by little, if any precedent, and that it ignores the differences between class action plaintiffs, on the one hand, and defendants in non-class civil suits on the other. Any plaintiff may consent to jurisdiction. * * * The essential question, then, is how stringent the requirement for a showing of consent will be.

We think that the procedure followed by Kansas, where a fully descriptive notice is sent first-class mail to each class member, with an explanation of the right to "opt out," satisfies due process. Requiring a plaintiff to affirmatively request inclusion would probably impede the prosecution of those class actions involving an aggregation of small individual claims, where a large number of claims are required to make it economical to bring suit. * * * The plaintiff's claim may be so small, or the plaintiff so unfamiliar with the law, that he would not file suit individually, nor would he affirmatively request inclusion in the class if such a request were required by the Constitution. If, on the other hand, the plaintiff's claim is sufficiently large or important that he wishes to litigate it on his own, he will likely have retained an attorney or have thought about filing suit, and should be fully capable of exercising his right to "opt out."

In this case over 3,400 members of the potential class did "opt out," which belies the contention that "opt out" procedures result in guaranteed jurisdiction by inertia. Another 1,500 were excluded because the notice and "opt out" form was undeliverable. We think that such results show that the "opt out" procedure provided by Kansas is by no means *pro forma,* and that the Constitution does not require more to protect what must be the somewhat rare species of class member who is unwilling to execute an "opt out" form, but whose claim is nonetheless so important that he cannot be presumed to consent to being a member of the class by his failure to do so. Petitioner's "opt in" requirement would require the invalidation of scores of state statutes and of the class-action provision of the Federal Rules of Civil Procedure, and for the reasons stated we do not think that the Constitution requires the State to sacrifice the obvious advantages in judicial efficiency resulting from the "opt out" approach for the protection of the *rara avis* portrayed by petitioner.

We therefore hold that the protection afforded the plaintiff class members by the Kansas statute satisfies the Due Process Clause. The interests of the absent plaintiffs are sufficiently protected by the forum State when those plaintiffs are provided with a request for exclusion that can be returned within a reasonable time to the court. * * * Both the Kansas trial court and the Supreme Court of Kansas held that the class received adequate representation, and no party disputes that conclusion here. We conclude that the Kansas court properly asserted personal jurisdiction over the absent plaintiffs and their claims against petitioner.

III

The Kansas courts applied Kansas contract and Kansas equity law to every claim in this case, notwithstanding that over 99% of the gas leases and some 97% of the plaintiffs in the case had no apparent connection to the State of Kansas except for this lawsuit. Petitioner protested that the Kansas courts should apply the laws of the States where the leases were located, or at least apply Texas and Oklahoma law because so many of the leases came from those States. The Kansas courts disregarded this contention and found petitioner liable for interest on the suspended royalties as a matter of Kansas law, and set the interest rates under Kansas equity principles.

Petitioner contends that total application of Kansas substantive law violated the constitutional limitations on choice of law mandated by the Due Process Clause of the Fourteenth Amendment and the Full Faith and Credit Clause of Article IV, § 1. We must first determine whether Kansas law conflicts in any material way with any other law which could apply. There can be no injury in applying Kansas law if it is not in conflict with that of any other jurisdiction connected to this suit.

Petitioner claims that Kansas law conflicts with that of a number of States connected to this litigation, especially Texas and Oklahoma. These putative conflicts range from the direct to the tangential, and may be addressed by the Supreme Court of Kansas on remand under the correct constitutional standard. * * *

* * *

The conflicts on the applicable interest rates, alone—which we do not think can be labeled "false conflicts" without a more thorough-going treatment than was accorded them by the Supreme Court of Kansas—certainly amounted to millions of dollars in liability. We think that the Supreme Court of Kansas erred in deciding on the basis that it did that the application of its laws to all claims would be constitutional.

Four Terms ago we addressed a similar situation in Allstate Ins. Co. v. Hague [, p. 104 supra] * * *. In that case we were confronted with two conflicting rules of state insurance law. Minnesota permitted the "stacking" of separate uninsured motorist policies while Wisconsin did not. Although the decedent lived in Wisconsin, took out insurance policies and was killed there, he was employed in Minnesota and after his death his widow moved to Minnesota for reasons unrelated to the litigation, and was appointed personal representative of his estate. She filed suit in Minnesota courts, which applied the Minnesota stacking rule.

The plurality in *Allstate* noted that a particular set of facts giving rise to litigation could justify, constitutionally, the application of more than one jurisdiction's laws. The plurality recognized, however, that the Due

Process Clause and the Full Faith and Credit Clause provided modest restrictions on the application of forum law. These restrictions required "that for a State's substantive law to be selected in a constitutionally permissible manner, that State must have a significant contact or significant aggregation of contacts, creating state interests, such that choice of its law is neither arbitrary nor fundamentally unfair." * * * The dissenting Justices were in substantial agreement with this principle. * * *

The plurality in *Allstate* affirmed the application of Minnesota law because of the forum's significant contacts to the litigation which supported the State's interest in applying its law. * * * Kansas' contacts to this litigation, as explained by the Kansas Supreme Court, can be gleaned from the opinion below.

Petitioner owns property and conducts substantial business in the State, so Kansas certainly has an interest in regulating petitioner's conduct in Kansas. * * * Moreover, oil and gas extraction is an important business to Kansas, and although only a few leases in issue are located in Kansas, hundreds of Kansas plaintiffs were affected by petitioner's suspension of royalties; thus the court held that the State has a real interest in protecting "the rights of these royalty owners both as individual residents of [Kansas] and as members of this particular class of plaintiffs." * * *

* * *

Kansas must have a "significant contact or aggregation of contacts" to the claims asserted by each member of the plaintiff class, contacts "creating state interests" in order to ensure that the choice of Kansas law is not arbitrary or unfair. * * * Given Kansas' lack of "interest" in claims unrelated to that State, and the substantive conflict with jurisdictions such as Texas, we conclude that application of Kansas law to every claim in this case is sufficiently arbitrary and unfair as to exceed constitutional limits.

When considering fairness in this context, an important element is the expectation of the parties. There is no indication that when the leases involving land and royalty owners outside of Kansas were executed, the parties had any idea that Kansas law would control. Neither the Due Process Clause nor the Full Faith and Credit Clause requires Kansas "to substitute for its own [laws], applicable to persons and events within it, the conflicting statute of another state," * * * but Kansas "may not abrogate the rights of parties beyond its borders having no relation to anything done or to be done within them." * * *

Here the Supreme Court of Kansas took the view that in a nationwide class action where procedural due process guarantees of notice and adequate representation were met, "the laws of the forum should be applied unless compelling reasons exist for applying a different law." * * * Whatever practical reasons may have commended this rule to the Supreme Court of Kansas, for the reasons already stated we do not believe that it is consistent with the decisions of this Court. We make no effort to determine for ourselves which law must apply to the various transactions involved in this lawsuit, and we reaffirm our observation in *Allstate* that in many situations a state court may be free to apply one of several choices of law. But the constitutional limitations laid down in cases such as *Allstate* * * * must be respected even in a nationwide class action.

We therefore affirm the judgment of the Supreme Court of Kansas insofar as it upheld the jurisdiction of the Kansas courts over the plaintiff class members in this case, and reverse its judgment insofar as it held that Kansas law was applicable to all of the transactions which it sought to adjudicate. We remand the case to that court for further proceedings not inconsistent with this opinion.

JUSTICE POWELL took no part in the decision of this case.

[JUSTICE STEVENS wrote an opinion concurring in Parts I and II of the Court's opinion and dissenting from Part III.]

NOTES AND QUESTIONS

1. On remand to the Kansas courts after the Supreme Court's decision in *Shutts,* Phillips Petroleum continued to press the argument that the laws of five states (Louisiana, New Mexico, Oklahoma, Texas, and Wyoming) differed in important respects from the law of Kansas—in particular on the issue of liability for interest on suspended royalties and on the issue of the applicable interest rate where liability is found. These two issues constituted the heart of the legal controversy in the case, and the five identified states embraced 97 percent of the leases involved. In addressing this argument, the Kansas Supreme Court first analyzed the Supreme Court's decision in *Shutts*:

> * * * As to the choice of law question, however, it was ruled the application of Kansas law to all of the investors' claims for interest violated the due process and full faith and credit clauses. In its analysis, the Court first noted that if the law of Kansas was not in conflict with any of the other jurisdictions connected to the suit, then there would be no injury in applying the law of Kansas. * * * The Court then cited differences in the laws of Kansas, Texas, and Oklahoma which Phillips *contended* existed. It appears, however, no analysis was made by the Court to determine whether these differences existed in fact. * * *

Shutts v. Phillips Petroleum Co., 240 Kan. 764, 767, 732 P.2d 1286, 1291 (1987), certiorari denied 487 U.S. 1223, 108 S.Ct. 2883, 101 L.Ed.2d 918 (1988) (emphasis in original). The Kansas court then examined the laws of the five states—only to conclude that *none* of the five was in conflict with the law of Kansas. It therefore entered a new judgment reflecting no change in the original outcome of the case regarding liability and the applicable prejudgment interest rate. See generally Miller & Crump, *Jurisdiction and Choice of Law in Multistate Class Actions After Phillips Petroleum Co. v. Shutts*, 96 Yale L.J. 1 (1986).

2. In the wake of *Shutts,* should choice-of-law practice move toward the application of a single substantive law in complex litigation, whether it

requires choosing the law of one particular state or developing a body of uniform federal law? See, e.g., Nafziger, *Choice of Law in Air Disaster Cases: Complex Litigation Rules and the Common Law*, 54 La.L.Rev. 1001 (1994). One commentator has resisted this trend, arguing that applying a single substantive law in a complex case would be neither efficient nor fair. See Kramer, *Choice of Law in Complex Litigation*, 71 N.Y.U. L. Rev. 547 (1996). Recall that in *Castano*, p. 759, differences in state law were a ground for decertification of the class.

The Class Action Fairness Act, p. 276, supra, has further complicated the choice-of-law analysis. See Chapter 6, Note 5, p. 467, supra. Do you agree that courts hearing interstate class actions under CAFA have authority "to apply a single state's law (or that of a limited number of states) when that seems appropriate"? Miller, *Reliving and Reflecting on* Shutts, 74 UMKC L. Rev. 505, 510 (2006). See also Issacharoff, *Settled Expectations in a World of Unsettled Law: Choice of Law After the Class Action Fairness Act*, 106 Colum. L. Rev. 1839, 1844 (2006) (urging the crafting of a choice-of-law rule that looks to the law of the primary place of business).

3. In Shaffer v. Heitner, p. 161, supra, the Supreme Court stated that "all assertions of state-court jurisdiction must be evaluated according to the standards set forth in *International Shoe* and its progeny." Does *Shutts* mean that class plaintiffs are not entitled to this protection? Or is *Shutts* based upon the inference of consent from a class member's failure to opt-out of the class? Rule 23 imposes notice and opt-out requirements only in subdivision (b)(3) class actions. Does the concept, articulated in *Shutts,* that the right to opt-out is a fundamental due process requirement mean that there is a constitutional right to opt-out of class suits brought as Rule 23 (b)(1) or (b)(2) class actions? Footnote 3 in the *Shutts* opinion, p. 790, supra, implies that the ruling is not limited to subdivision (b)(3) class actions but applies—at a minimum—to claims "wholly or predominately for monetary judgments." This has caused some confusion about what to do when there is a hybrid class action for both equitable and monetary relief. See p. 766, supra. The Supreme Court has twice heard arguments on the applicability of *Shutts* to Rule 23(b)(1) and (b)(2) classes, but dismissed both cases on the ground that certiorari had been improperly granted. See Ticor Title Ins. Co. v. Brown, 511 U.S. 117, 114 S.Ct. 1359, 128 L.Ed.2d 33 (1994), and Adams v. Robertson, 520 U.S. 83, 117 S.Ct. 1028, 137 L.Ed.2d 203 (1997). See Mullenix, *Gridlaw: The Enduring Legacy of Phillips Petroleum v. Shutts*, 74 UMKC L. Rev. 651 (2006). Does CAFA affect your response to this question? See Andrews, *The Personal Jurisdiction Problem Overlooked in the National Debate About "Class Action Fairness,"* 58 SMU L. Rev. 1313 (2005).

4. What are the implications of *Shutts* for transnational class actions in which class members reside abroad? Foreign class members have become common in securities cases. One commentator has argued that such cases require heightened protection for class members and that Rule 23 should require "an affirmative opt-in procedure in order to bind non-U.S. claimants to a U.S. class judgment." See Bassett, *Implied "Consent" to Personal Jurisdiction in Transnational Class Litigation*, 2004 Mich. St. L. Rev. 619 (2004). Do you agree?

3. VENUE

In applying venue rules to class actions, should courts look to the residence of every member of the class, including absent class members? Or should courts look to the residence of the class representatives alone? Are there advantages to having the rules for venue resemble those for personal jurisdiction? Only the residences of the class representatives are important for purposes of venue; the residences of absent class members and intervenors are irrelevant. See 7A Wright, Miller & Kane, Federal Practice and Procedure: Civil 3d § 1757.

SECTION F. SETTLEMENT CLASSES

A mass tort class action suit may involve millions of individual claims and expose the parties to large and unpredictable transaction costs. These actions thus create significant economic incentives for settlement. Would it be appropriate to certify an action that is filed only for the purposes of settlement, if plaintiff has no intention of ever litigating the claims? Why might defendant agree to such a result? Why might the class representatives also want to accept an early negotiated deal? The possibility of settlement class actions brings to the foreground questions about the adequacy of representation, as well as the role of class actions as an instrument of social policy. Not surprisingly, the settlement of mass tort class actions presents one of the most controversial procedural issues of the day.

AMCHEM PRODUCTS, INC. v. WINDSOR

Supreme Court of the United States, 1997.
521 U.S. 591, 117 S.Ct. 2231, 138 L.Ed.2d 689.

Certiorari to the United States Court of Appeals for the Third Circuit.

JUSTICE GINSBURG delivered the opinion of the Court.

This case concerns the legitimacy under Rule 23 * * * of a class-action certification sought to achieve global settlement of current and future asbestos-related claims. The class proposed for certification potentially encompasses hundreds of thousands, perhaps millions, of individuals tied together by this commonality: Each was, or some day may be, adversely affected by past exposure to asbestos products manufactured by one or more of 20 companies. Those companies, defendants in the lower courts, are petitioners here.

* * *

I

A

* * *

[The Panel on Multidistrict Litigation] * * * transferred all asbestos cases then filed, but not yet on trial in federal courts to a single district * * * for pretrial proceedings * * *. The order aggregated pending cases only; no authority resides in the MDL Panel to license for consolidated proceedings claims not yet filed.

B

After the consolidation, attorneys for plaintiffs and defendants formed separate steering committees and began settlement negotiations. [These negotiations included efforts to resolve future as well as pending cases.] * * *

* * *

Settlement talks thus concentrated on devising an administrative scheme for disposition of asbestos claims not yet in litigation. In these negotiations, counsel for masses of [plaintiffs who had filed suit also] * * * endeavored to represent the interests of the anticipated future claimants, although those lawyers then had no attorney-client relationship with such claimants.

* * *

[An agreement was then reached with regard to the claims that had been filed and the lawyers then] launched this case, exclusively involving persons outside the MDL Panel's province—plaintiffs without already pending lawsuits. * * *

C

The class action thus instituted was not intended to be litigated. Rather, within the space of a single day, January 15, 1993, the settling parties * * * presented to the District Court a complaint, an answer, a proposed settlement agreement, and a joint motion for conditional class certification. * * *

The complaint identified nine lead plaintiffs, designating them and members of their families as representatives of a class comprising all persons who had not filed an asbestos-related lawsuit against a * * * [member of the defendant group (hereinafter referred to as a CCR defendant)] as of the date the class action commenced, but who (1) had been exposed—occupationally or through the occupational exposure of a spouse or household member—to asbestos or products containing asbestos attributable to a CCR defendant, or (2) whose spouse or family member had been so exposed. * * * Untold numbers of individuals may fall within this description. All named plaintiffs alleged that they or a member of their family had been exposed to asbestos-containing products of CCR defendants. More than half of the named plaintiffs alleged that they or their family members had already suffered various physical injuries as a result of the exposure. The others alleged that they had not yet manifested any asbestos-related condition. The complaint delineated no subclasses;

all named plaintiffs were designated as representatives of the class as a whole.

The complaint invoked the District Court's diversity jurisdiction and asserted various state-law claims for relief, including (1) negligent failure to warn, (2) strict liability, (3) breach of express and implied warranty, (4) negligent infliction of emotional distress, (5) enhanced risk of disease, (6) medical monitoring, and (7) civil conspiracy. Each plaintiff requested unspecified damages in excess of $100,000. CCR defendants' answer denied the principal allegations of the complaint and asserted 11 affirmative defenses.

A stipulation of settlement accompanied the pleadings; it proposed to settle, and to preclude nearly all class members from litigating against CCR companies, all claims not filed before January 15, 1993, involving compensation for present and future asbestos-related personal injury or death. An exhaustive document exceeding 100 pages, the stipulation presents in detail an administrative mechanism and a schedule of payments to compensate class members who meet defined asbestos-exposure and medical requirements. * * *

For each qualifying disease category, the stipulation specifies the range of damages CCR will pay to qualifying claimants. Payments under the settlement are not adjustable for inflation. * * *

* * *

Compensation above the fixed ranges may be obtained for "extraordinary" claims. But the settlement places both numerical caps and dollar limits on such claims. * * * The settlement also imposes "case flow maximums," which cap the number of claims payable for each disease in a given year.

Class members are to receive no compensation for certain kinds of claims, even if otherwise applicable state law recognizes such claims. Claims that garner no compensation under the settlement include claims by family members of asbestos-exposed individuals for loss of consortium, and claims by so-called "exposure-only" plaintiffs for increased risk of cancer, fear of future asbestos-related injury, and medical monitoring. "Pleural" claims, which might be asserted by persons with asbestos-related plaques on their lungs but no accompanying physical impairment, are also excluded. Although not entitled to present compensation, exposure-only claimants and pleural claimants may qualify for benefits when and if they develop a compensable disease and meet the relevant exposure and medical criteria. Defendants forgo defenses to liability, including statute of limitations pleas.

Class members, in the main, are bound by the settlement in perpetuity, while CCR defendants may choose to withdraw from the settlement after ten years. A small number of class members—only a few per year—may reject the settlement and pursue their claims in court. Those permitted to exercise this option, however, may not assert any punitive damages claim or any claim for increased risk of cancer. Aspects of the administration of the settlement are to be monitored by the AFL–CIO and class counsel. Class counsel are to receive attorneys' fees in an amount to be approved by the District Court.

D

On January 29, 1993, as requested by the settling parties, the District Court conditionally certified, under Federal Rule * * * 23(b)(3), an encompassing opt-out class. The certified class included persons occupationally exposed to defendants' asbestos products, and members of their families, who had not filed suit as of January 15. Judge Weiner appointed * * * class counsel, noting that "[t]he Court may in the future appoint additional counsel if it is deemed necessary and advisable." Record, Doc. 11, p. 3 (Class Certification Order). * * * [The class was never divided into subclasses.] In a separate order, Judge Weiner assigned to Judge Reed, also of the Eastern District of Pennsylvania, "the task of conducting fairness proceedings and of determining whether the proposed settlement is fair to the class." See [Georgine v. Amchen Products, Inc.,] 157 F.R.D., [246] at 258 [(E.D.Pa.1994)]. Various class members raised objections to the settlement stipulation, and Judge Weiner granted the objectors full rights to participate in the subsequent proceedings. * * *

* * *

Objectors raised numerous challenges * * *. They urged that the settlement unfairly disadvantaged those without currently compensable conditions in that it failed to adjust for inflation or to account for changes, over time, in medical understanding. They maintained that compensation levels were intolerably low in comparison to awards available in tort litigation or payments received by the inventory plaintiffs. And they objected to the absence of any compensation for certain claims, for example, medical monitoring, compensable under the tort law of several States. Rejecting these and all other objections, Judge Reed concluded that the settlement terms were fair and had been negotiated without collusion. * * * He also found that adequate notice had been given to class members, and that final class certification under Rule 23(b)(3) was appropriate * * *.

* * *

Strenuous objections had been asserted regarding the adequacy of representation, a Rule 23(a)(4) requirement. * * * Objectors maintained that class counsel and class representatives had disqualifying conflicts of interests. In particular, objectors urged, claimants whose injuries had become manifest and claimants without manifest injuries should not have common counsel and should not be aggregated in a single class. Furthermore, objectors argued, lawyers representing inventory plaintiffs should not represent the newly formed class.

Satisfied that class counsel had ably negotiated the settlement in the best interests of all concerned, and that the named parties served as adequate representatives, the District Court rejected these objections. * * * Subclasses were unnecessary, the District Court held, bearing in mind the added cost and confusion they would entail and the ability of class members to exclude themselves from the class during the three-month opt-out period. * * * [The objectors appealed. The Court of Appeals for the Third Circuit vacated the certification. See Georgine v. Amchem Products, Inc., 83 F.3d 610 (3d Cir. 1996).]

* * *

E

* * *

* * * While stating that the requirements of Rule 23(a) and (b)(3) must be met "without taking into account the settlement," 83 F.3d, at 626, the Court of Appeals in fact closely considered the terms of the settlement as it examined aspects of the case under Rule 23 criteria. * * *

The Third Circuit recognized that Rule 23(a)(2)'s "commonality" requirement is subsumed under, or superseded by, the more stringent Rule 23(b)(3) requirement that questions common to the class "predominate over" other questions. The court therefore trained its attention on the "predominance" inquiry. * * * The harmfulness of asbestos exposure was indeed a prime factor common to the class, the Third Circuit observed. * * * But uncommon questions abounded.

In contrast to mass torts involving a single accident, class members in this case were [in original exposed to different asbestos-containing products, in different ways, over different periods, and for different amounts of time; some suffered no physical injury, others suffered disabling or deadly diseases. * * * "These factual differences," the Third Circuit explained, "translate[d] [in original] into significant legal differences." Id., at 627. State law governed and varied widely on such critical issues as "viability of [exposure-only] claims [and] availability of causes of action for medical monitoring, increased risk of cancer, and fear of future injury [in original]." * * * "[T]he number of uncommon issues in this humongous class action," the Third Circuit concluded, * * * barred a determination, under existing tort law, that common questions predominated * * * [in original].

The Court of Appeals next found that "serious intra-class conflicts preclude[d] th[e] class from meeting the adequacy of representation requirement" of Rule 23(a)(4) [in original]. * * * Adverting to, but not resolving charges of attorney conflict of interests, the Third Circuit addressed the question whether the named plaintiffs could adequately advance the interests of all class members. The Court of Appeals acknowledged that the District Court was certainly correct to this extent: " '[T]he members of the class are united in seeking the maximum possible recovery for their asbestos-related claims.' " * * * "But the settlement does more than simply provide a general recovery fund," the Court of Appeals immediately added; "[r]ather, it makes important judgments on how recovery is to be allocated among different kinds of plaintiffs, decisions that necessarily favor some claimants over others." 83 F.3d, at 630.

In the Third Circuit's view, the "most salient" divergence of interests separated plaintiffs already afflicted with an asbestos-related disease from plaintiffs without manifest injury (exposure-only plaintiffs). The latter would rationally want protection against inflation for distant recoveries. * * * They would also seek sturdy back-end opt-out rights and "causation provisions that can keep pace with changing science and medicine, rather than freezing in place the science of 1993." * * * Already injured parties, in contrast, would care little about such provisions and would rationally trade them for higher current payouts. * * * These and other adverse interests, the Court of Appeals carefully explained, strongly suggested that an undivided set of representatives could not adequately protect the discrete interests of both currently afflicted and exposure-only claimants.

The Third Circuit next rejected the District Court's determination that the named plaintiffs were "typical" of the class, noting that this Rule 23(a)(3) inquiry overlaps the adequacy of representation question: "both look to the potential for conflicts in the class." *Id.*, at 632. Evident conflict problems, the court said, led it to hold that "no set of representatives can be 'typical' of this class." *Ibid.*

The Court of Appeals similarly rejected the District Court's assessment of the superiority of the class action. The Third Circuit initially noted that a class action so large and complex "could not be tried." * * * The court elaborated most particularly, however, on the unfairness of binding exposure-only plaintiffs who might be unaware of the class action or lack sufficient information about their exposure to make a reasoned decision whether to stay in or opt out. * * * "A series of statewide or more narrowly defined adjudications, either through consolidation under Rule 42(a) or as class actions under Rule 23, would seem preferable," the Court of Appeals said. *Id.*, at 634.

The Third Circuit, after intensive review, ultimately ordered decertification of the class and vacation of the District Court's antisuit injunction. * * *

We granted certiorari * * * and now affirm.

II

* * *

III

* * *

In the 1966 class-action amendments, Rule 23(b)(3), the category at issue here, was "the most adventuresome" innovation. See Kaplan, A Prefatory Note, 10 B.C. Ind. & Com. L.Rev. 497, 497 (1969) (hereinafter

Kaplan, Prefatory Note). Rule 23(b)(3) added to the complex-litigation arsenal class actions for damages designed to secure judgments binding all class members save those who affirmatively elected to be excluded. See 7A Charles Alan Wright, Arthur R. Miller, & Mary Kay Kane, Federal Practice and Procedure § 1777, p. 517 (2d ed.1986) (hereinafter Wright, Miller, & Kane); * * *. Rule 23(b)(3) "opt-out" class actions superseded the former "spurious" class action, so characterized because it generally functioned as a permissive joinder ("opt-in") device. See 7A Wright, Miller, & Kane § 1753, at 28–31, 42–44 * * *.

Framed for situations in which "class-action treatment is not as clearly called for" as it is in Rule 23(b)(1) and (b)(2) situations, Rule 23(b)(3) permits certification where class suit "may nevertheless be convenient and desirable." Adv. Comm. Notes, 28 U.S.C.App., p. 697. * * * In adding "predominance" and "superiority" to the qualification-for-certification list, the Advisory Committee sought to cover cases "in which a class action would achieve economies of time, effort, and expense, and promote . . . uniformity of decision as to persons similarly situated, without sacrificing procedural fairness or bringing about other undesirable results." * * * [Those who drafted the provision were] * * * [s]ensitive to the competing tugs of individual autonomy for those who might prefer to go it alone or in a smaller unit, on the one hand, and systemic efficiency on the other * * *.

Rule 23(b)(3) includes a nonexhaustive list of factors pertinent to a court's "close look" at the predominance and superiority criteria * * *.

* * *

While the text of Rule 23(b)(3) does not exclude from certification cases in which individual damages run high, the Advisory Committee had dominantly in mind vindication of "the rights of groups of people who individually would be without effective strength to bring their opponents into court at all." Kaplan, Prefatory Note 497. * * *

[To protect the rights of individuals, they must be sent notice of their right to opt out and, if they choose to remain without the class, the action may not be dismissed or compromised without notice to them and subsequent court approval.] * * *

* * *

In the decades since the 1966 revision of Rule 23, class-action practice has become ever more "adventuresome" as a means of coping with claims too numerous to secure their "just, speedy, and inexpensive determination" one by one. See Fed. Rule Civ. Proc. 1. The development reflects concerns about the efficient use of court resources and the conservation of funds to compensate claimants who do not line up early in a litigation queue. * * *

* * *

IV

We granted review to decide the role settlement may play, under existing Rule 23, in determining the propriety of class certification. The Third Circuit's opinion stated that each of the requirements of Rule 23(a) and (b)(3) "must be satisfied without taking into account the settlement." 83 F.3d, at 626 * * * That statement, petitioners urge, is incorrect.

We agree with petitioners to this limited extent: Settlement is relevant to a class certification. The Third Circuit's opinion bears modification in that respect. But, as we earlier observed * * *, the Court of Appeals in fact did not ignore the settlement; instead, that court homed in on settlement terms in explaining why it found the absentees' interests inadequately represented. * * * The Third Circuit's close inspection of the settlement in that regard was altogether proper.

Confronted with a request for settlement-only class certification, a district court need not inquire whether the case, if tried, would present intractable management problems, see Fed. Rule Civ. Proc. 23(b)(3)(D), for the proposal is that there be no trial. But other specifications of the Rule—those designed to protect absentees by blocking unwarranted or overbroad class definitions—demand undiluted, even heightened, attention in the settlement context. Such attention is of vital importance, for a court asked to certify a settlement class will lack the opportunity, present when a case is litigated, to adjust the class, informed by the proceedings as they unfold. See Rule 23(c), (d). * * *

* * *

* * * Subdivisions (a) and (b) focus court attention on whether a proposed class has sufficient unity so that absent members can fairly be bound by decisions of class representatives. That dominant concern persists when settlement, rather than trial, is proposed.

The safeguards provided by the Rule 23(a) and (b) class-qualifying criteria, we emphasize, are not impractical impediments—checks shorn of utility—in the settlement-class context. First, the standards set for the protection of absent class members serve to inhibit appraisals of the chancellor's foot kind—class certifications dependent upon the court's gestalt judgment or overarching impression of the settlement's fairness.

Second, if a fairness inquiry under Rule 23(e) controlled certification, eclipsing Rule 23(a) and (b), and permitting class designation despite the impossibility of litigation, both class counsel and court would be disarmed. Class counsel confined to settlement negotiations could not use the threat of litigation to press for a better offer, see Coffee, *Class Wars: The Dilemma of the Mass Tort Class Action*, 95 Colum.L.Rev. 1343, 1379–1380 (1995), and the court would face a bargain proffered for its approval without benefit of adversarial investigation, see, e.g., Kamilewicz v. Bank of Boston Corp., 100 F.3d 1348, 1352 (7th Cir.1996) (Easterbrook, J., dissenting from denial of rehearing en banc) (parties "may even put one over on the court, in a staged performance"), cert. denied, 520 U.S. 1204, 117 S.Ct. 1569, 137 L.Ed.2d 714 (1997).

Federal courts, in any case, lack authority to substitute for Rule 23's certification criteria a standard never adopted—that if a settlement is "fair," then certification is proper. Applying to this case criteria the rulemakers set, we conclude that the Third Circuit's appraisal is essentially correct. Although that court should have acknowledged that settlement is a factor in the calculus, a remand is not warranted on that account. The Court of Appeals' opinion amply demonstrates why—with or without a settlement on the table—the sprawling class the District Court certified does not satisfy Rule 23's requirements. * * *

A

We address first the requirement of Rule 23(b)(3) that "[common] questions of law or fact . . . [in original] predominate over any questions affecting only individual members." The District Court concluded that predominance was satisfied based on two factors: class members' shared experience of asbestos exposure and their common "interest in receiving prompt and fair compensation for their claims, while minimizing the risks and transaction costs inherent in the asbestos litigation process as it occurs presently in the tort system." 157 F.R.D., at 316. The settling parties also contend that the settlement's fairness is a common question, predominating over disparate legal issues that might be pivotal in litigation but become irrelevant under the settlement.

The predominance requirement stated in Rule 23(b)(3), we hold, is not met by the factors on which the District Court relied. The benefits asbestos-exposed persons might gain from the establishment of a grand-scale compensation scheme is a matter fit for legislative consideration, * * * but it is not pertinent to the predominance inquiry. That inquiry trains on the legal or factual questions that qualify each class member's case as a genuine controversy, questions that preexist any settlement.[18]

The Rule 23(b)(3) predominance inquiry tests whether proposed classes are sufficiently cohesive to warrant adjudication by representation. See 7A Wright, Miller, & Kane 518–519. * * * The inquiry appropriate under Rule 23(e), on the other hand, protects unnamed class members "from unjust or unfair settlements affecting their rights when the representatives become fainthearted before the action is adjudicated or are able to secure satisfaction of their individual claims by a compromise." See 7B Wright, Miller, & Kane § 1797, at 340–341. But it is not the mission of Rule 23(e) to assure the class cohesion that legitimizes representative action in the first place. If a common interest in a fair compromise could

18. In this respect, the predominance requirement of Rule 23(b)(3) is similar to the requirement of Rule 23(a)(3) that "claims or defenses" of the named representatives must be "typical of the claims or defenses of the class." The words "claims or defenses" in this context—just as in the context of Rule 24(b)(2) [now, Rule 24(b)(1)(B)] governing permissive intervention—"manifestly refer to the kinds of claims or defenses that can be raised in courts of law as part of an actual or impending law suit." Diamond v. Charles, 476 U.S. 54, 76–77, 106 S.Ct. 1697, 1711, 90 L.Ed.2d 48 (1986) (O'CONNOR, J., concurring in part and concurring in judgment).

satisfy the predominance requirement of Rule 23(b)(3), that vital prescription would be stripped of any meaning in the settlement context.

The District Court also relied upon this commonality: "The members of the class have all been exposed to asbestos products supplied by the defendants.... [in original]" §§ 157 F.R.D., at 316. Even if Rule 23(a)'s commonality requirement may be satisfied by that shared experience, the predominance criterion is far more demanding. * * * Given the greater number of questions peculiar to the several categories of class members, and to individuals within each category, and the significance of those uncommon questions, any overarching dispute about the health consequences of asbestos exposure cannot satisfy the Rule 23(b)(3) predominance standard.

The Third Circuit highlighted the disparate questions undermining class cohesion in this case:

* * *

> "The [exposure-only] [in original] plaintiffs especially share little in common, either with each other or with the presently injured class members. It is unclear whether they will contract asbestos-related disease and, if so, what disease each will suffer. They will also incur different medical expenses because their monitoring and treatment will depend on singular circumstances and individual medical histories." [83 F.3d at 626.] * * *

Differences in state law, the Court of Appeals observed, compound these disparities. * * *

No settlement class called to our attention is as sprawling as this one. * * * Predominance is a test readily met in certain cases alleging consumer or securities fraud or violations of the antitrust laws. * * * Even mass tort cases arising from a common cause or disaster may, depending upon the circumstances, satisfy the predominance requirement. The Advisory Committee for the 1966 revision of Rule 23, it is true, noted that "mass accident" cases are likely to present "significant questions, not only of damages but of liability and defenses of liability, ... affecting the individuals in different ways." * * * And the Committee advised that such cases are "ordinarily not appropriate" for class treatment. * * * But the text of the Rule does not categorically exclude mass tort cases from class certification, and District Courts, since the late 1970's, have been certifying such cases in increasing number. * * * The Committee's warning, however, continues to call for caution when individual stakes are high and disparities among class members great. As the Third Circuit's opinion makes plain, the certification in this case does not follow the counsel of caution. That certification cannot be upheld, for it rests on a conception of Rule 23(b)(3)'s predominance requirement irreconcilable with the Rule's design.

B

Nor can the class approved by the District Court satisfy Rule 23(a)(4)'s requirement that the named parties "will fairly and adequately protect the interests of the class." The adequacy inquiry under Rule 23(a)(4) serves to uncover conflicts of interest between named parties and the class they seek to represent. * * *

As the Third Circuit pointed out, named parties with diverse medical conditions sought to act on behalf of a single giant class rather than on behalf of discrete subclasses. In significant respects, the interests of those within the single class are not aligned. Most saliently, for the currently injured, the critical goal is generous immediate payments. That goal tugs against the interest of exposure-only plaintiffs in ensuring an ample, inflation-protected fund for the future. * * *

The disparity between the currently injured and exposure-only categories of plaintiffs, and the diversity within each category are not made insignificant by the District Court's finding that petitioners' assets suffice to pay claims under the settlement. * * * Although this is not a "limited fund" case certified under Rule 23(b)(1)(B), the terms of the settlement reflect essential allocation decisions designed to confine compensation and to limit defendants' liability. For example, as earlier described, * * * the settlement includes no adjustment for inflation; only a few claimants per year can opt out at the back end; and loss-of-consortium claims are extinguished with no compensation.

The settling parties, in sum, achieved a global compromise with no structural assurance of fair and adequate representation for the diverse groups and individuals affected. Although the named parties alleged a range of complaints, each served generally as representative for the whole, not for a separate constituency. * * *

The Third Circuit found no assurance here—either in the terms of the settlement or in the structure of the negotiations—that the named plaintiffs operated under a proper understanding of their representational responsibilities. * * * That assessment, we conclude, is on the mark.

* * *

C

* * *

V

The argument is sensibly made that a nationwide administrative claims processing regime would provide the most secure, fair, and efficient means of compensating victims of asbestos [exposure] * * *. Congress, however, has not adopted such a solution. And Rule 23, which must be interpreted with fidelity to the Rules Enabling Act and applied with the interests of absent class members in close view, cannot carry the large load CCR, class counsel, and the District Court heaped upon it. As this case exemplifies, the rulemakers' prescriptions for class actions may be endangered by "those who embrace [Rule 23] * * * too enthusiastically just as [they are by] those who approach [the Rule] * * * with distaste [in original]." C. Wright, Law of Federal Courts 508 (5th ed.1994); cf. 83 F.3d, at 634 (suggesting resort to less bold aggregation techniques, including more narrowly defined class certifications).

* * *

For the reasons stated, the judgment of the Court of Appeals for the Third Circuit is

Affirmed.

JUSTICE O'CONNOR took no part in the consideration or decision of this case.

JUSTICE BREYER, with whom JUSTICE STEVENS joins, concurring in part and dissenting in part.

Although I agree with the Court's basic holding that "[s]ettlement is relevant to a class certification," * * * I find several problems in its approach that lead me to a different conclusion. First, I believe that the need for settlement in this mass tort case, with hundreds of thousands of lawsuits, is greater than the Court's opinion suggests. Second, I would give more weight than would the majority to settlement-related issues for purposes of determining whether common issues predominate. Third, I am uncertain about the Court's determination of adequacy of representation, and do not believe it appropriate for this Court to second-guess the District Court on the matter without first having the Court of Appeals consider it. Fourth, I am uncertain about the tenor of an opinion that seems to suggest the settlement is unfair. And fifth, in the absence of further review by the Court of Appeals, I cannot accept the majority's suggestions that "notice" is inadequate.

These difficulties flow from the majority's review of what are highly fact-based, complex, and difficult matters, matters that are inappropriate for initial review before this Court. The law gives broad leeway to district courts in making class certification decisions, and their judgments are to be reviewed by the court of appeals only for abuse of discretion. * * * Indeed, the District Court's certification decision rests upon more than 300 findings of fact reached after five weeks of comprehensive hearings. Accordingly, I do not believe that we should in effect set aside the findings of the District Court. That court is far more familiar with the issues and litigants than is a court of appeals or are we, and therefore has "broad power and discretion ... [in original] with respect to matters involving the certification" of class actions. Reiter v. Sonotone Corp., 442 U.S. 330, 345, 99 S.Ct. 2326, 2334, 60 L.Ed.2d 931 (1979). * * *

I do not believe that we can rely upon the Court of Appeals' review of the District Court record, for that review, and its ultimate conclusions, are infected by a legal error. * * * There is no evidence that the Court of Appeals at any point considered the settlement as something that would help the class meet Rule 23. I find, moreover, the fact-related issues presented here sufficiently close to warrant further detailed appellate court review under the correct legal standard. * * *

I

First, I believe the majority understates the importance of settlement in this case. Between 13 and 21 million workers have been exposed to asbestos in the workplace—over the past 40 or 50 years—but the most severe instances of such exposure probably occurred three or four decades ago. * * * This exposure has led to several hundred thousand lawsuits, about 15% of which involved claims for cancer and about 30% for asbestosis. * * * About half of the suits have involved claims for pleural thickening and plaques—the harmfulness of which is apparently controversial. (One expert below testified that they "don't transform into cancer" and are not "predictor[s] of future disease," App. 781.) Some of those who suffer from the most serious injuries, however, have received little or no compensation. * * * These lawsuits have taken up more than 6% of all federal civil filings in one recent year, and are subject to a delay that is twice that of other civil suits. * * *

Delays, high costs, and a random pattern of noncompensation led the Judicial Conference Ad Hoc Committee on Asbestos Litigation to transfer all federal asbestos personal-injury cases to the Eastern District of Pennsylvania in an effort to bring about a fair and comprehensive settlement. * * *

Although the transfer of the federal asbestos cases did not produce a general settlement, it was intertwined with and led to a lengthy year-long negotiation between the cochairs of the Plaintiff's Multi–District Litigation Steering Committee (elected by the Plaintiff's Committee Members and approved by the District Court) and the 20 asbestos defendants who are before us here. Georgine v. Amchem Products, Inc., 157 F.R.D. 246, 266–267 (E.D.Pa. 1994) * * *. * * * In the end, the negotiations produced a settlement that, the District Court determined based on its detailed review of the process, was "the result of arms-length adversarial negotiations by extraordinarily competent and experienced attorneys." *Id.*, at 335.

The District Court, when approving the settlement, concluded that it improved the plaintiffs' chances of compensation and reduced total legal fees and other transaction costs by a significant amount. Under the previous system, according to the court, "[t]he sickest of victims often go uncompensated for years while valuable funds go to others who remain unimpaired by their mild asbestos disease." *Ibid.* The court believed the settlement would create a compensation system that would make more money available for plaintiffs who later develop serious illnesses.

I mention this matter because it suggests that the settlement before us is unusual in terms of its importance, both to many potential plaintiffs and to defendants, and with respect to the time, effort, and expenditure that it reflects. All of which leads me to be reluctant to set aside the District Court's findings without more assurance than I have that they are wrong. I cannot obtain that assurance through comprehensive review of the record because that is properly the job of the Court of Appeals and that court, understandably, but as we now hold, mistakenly, believed that settlement was not a relevant (and, as I would say, important) consideration.

Second, the majority, in reviewing the District Court's determination that common "issues of fact and law predominate," says that the predominance "inquiry trains on the legal or factual questions that qualify each class member's case as a genuine controversy, questions that preexist any settlement." * * * I find it difficult to interpret this sentence in a way that could lead me to the majority's conclusion. If the majority means that these pre-settlement questions are what matters, then how does it reconcile its statement with its basic conclusion that "settlement is relevant" to class certification, or with the numerous lower court authority that says that settlement is not only relevant, but important? * * *

Nor do I understand how one could decide whether common questions "predominate" in the abstract—without looking at what is likely to be at issue in the proceedings that will ensue, namely, the settlement. Every group of human beings, after all, has some features in common, and some that differ. How can a court make a contextual judgment of the sort that Rule 23 requires without looking to what proceedings will follow? * * *

The majority may mean that the District Court gave too much weight to the settlement. But I am not certain how it can reach that conclusion. It cannot rely upon the Court of Appeals, for that court gave no positive weight at all to the settlement. * * *

The settlement is relevant because it means that these common features and interests are likely to be important in the proceeding that would ensue—a proceeding that would focus primarily upon whether or not the proposed settlement fairly and properly satisfied the interests class members had in common. That is to say, the settlement underscored the importance of (a) the common fact of exposure, (b) the common interest in receiving some compensation for certain rather than running a strong risk of no compensation, and (c) the common interest in avoiding large legal fees, other transaction costs, and delays. * * *

Of course, as the majority points out, there are also important differences among class members. * * * The relevant question, however, is *how much* these differences matter in respect to the legal proceedings that lie ahead. Many, if not all, toxic tort class actions involve plaintiffs with such differences. And the differences in state law are of diminished importance in respect to a proposed settlement in which the defendants have waived all defenses and agreed to compensate all those who were injured. * * *

These differences might warrant subclasses * * *. Or these differences may be too serious to permit an effort at group settlement. This kind of determination, as I have said, is one that the law commits to the discretion of the district court—reviewable for abuse of discretion by a court of appeals. I believe that we are far too distant from the litigation itself to reweigh the fact-specific Rule 23 determinations and to find them erroneous without the benefit of the Court of Appeals first having restudied the matter with today's legal standard in mind.

Third, the majority concludes that the "representative parties" will not "fairly and adequately protect the interests of the class." Rule 23(a)(4). It finds a serious conflict between plaintiffs who are now injured and those who may be injured in the future because "for the currently injured, the critical goal is generous immediate payments," a goal that "tugs against the interest of exposure-only plaintiffs in ensuring an ample, inflation-protected fund for the future." * * *

I agree that there is a serious problem, but it is a problem that often exists in toxic tort cases. * * * And it is a problem that potentially exists whenever a single defendant injures several plaintiffs, for a settling plaintiff leaves fewer assets available for the others. With class actions, at least, plaintiffs have the consolation that a district court, thoroughly familiar with the facts, is charged with the responsibility of ensuring that the interests of no class members are sacrificed.

But this Court cannot easily safeguard such interests through review of a cold record. "What constitutes adequate representation is a question of fact that depends on the circumstances of each case." 7A Wright, Miller, & Kane, Federal Practice and Procedure § 1765, at 271. * * * The majority's use of the lack of an inflation adjustment as evidence of inadequacy of representation for future plaintiffs * * * is one example of this difficulty. An inflation adjustment might not be as valuable as the majority assumes if most plaintiffs are old and not worried about receiving compensation decades from now. There are, of course, strong arguments as to its value. But that disagreement is one that this Court is poorly situated to resolve.

Further, certain details of the settlement that are not discussed in the majority opinion suggest that the settlement may be of greater benefit to future plaintiffs than the majority suggests. The District Court concluded that future plaintiffs receive a "significant value" from the settlement due to a variety of its items that benefit future plaintiffs, such as: (1) tolling the statute of limitations so that class members "will no longer be forced to file premature lawsuits or risk their claims being time-barred"; (2) waiver of defenses to liability; (3) payment of claims, if and when members become sick, pursuant to the settlement's compensation standards, which avoids "the uncertainties, long delays and high transaction costs [including attorney's fees] of the tort system"; (4) "some assurance that there will be funds available if and when they get sick," based on the finding that each defendant "has shown an ability to fund the payment of all qualifying claims" under the settlement; and (5) the right to additional compensation if cancer develops (many settlements for plaintiffs with noncancerous conditions bar such additional claims). 157 F.R.D., at 292. For these reasons, and others, the District Court found that the distinction between present and future plaintiffs was "illusory." Id., at 317–318.

I do not know whether or not the benefits are more or less valuable than an inflation adjustment. But I can certainly recognize an argument that they are. * * * The difficulties inherent in both knowing and understanding the vast number of relevant individual fact-based determinations here counsel heavily in favor of deference to district court decisionmaking in Rule 23 decisions. Or, at the least, making certain that appellate court review has taken place with the correct standard in mind.

Fourth, I am more agnostic than is the majority about the basic fairness of the settlement. * * * The District Court's conclusions rested upon complicated factual findings that are not easily cast aside. It is helpful to consider some of them, such as its determination that the settlement provided "fair compensation ... [in original] while reducing the delays and transaction costs endemic to the asbestos litigation process" and that "the proposed class action settlement is superior to other available methods for the fair and efficient resolution of the asbestos-related personal injury claims of class members." 157 F.R.D., at 316 (citation omitted) * * *. Indeed, the settlement has been endorsed as fair and reasonable by the AFL–CIO (and its Building and Construction Trades Department), which represents a " 'substantial percentage' " of class members, 157 F.R.D., at 325, and which has a role in monitoring implementation of the settlement, *id.*, at 285. I do not intend to pass judgment upon the settlement's fairness, but I do believe that these matters would have to be explored in far greater depth before I could reach a conclusion about fairness. And that task, as I have said, is one for the Court of Appeals.

* * *

In ORTIZ v. FIBREBOARD CORP., 527 U.S. 815, 119 S.Ct. 2295, 144 L.Ed.2d 715 (1999), the Supreme Court again faced the propriety of a settlement class and again decertified. Fibreboard was and is the subject of many personal injury lawsuits arising from exposure to its asbestos products. It already had settled some 45,000 claims, when it decided with its insurers and a group of plaintiffs' lawyers on a plan to effect a "Global Settlement" of the majority of its remaining liability. Under the plan, Fibreboard and its insurers would put up $1.535 billion for asbestos claimants who would file a Rule 23(b)(1)(B) class action, based on the notion that there was a "limited fund" to pay members of the class.

At the time of the settlement talks, litigation was pending in California state court concerning the scope of Fibreboard's insurance coverage for plaintiffs' claims. As a condition of the Global Settlement, plaintiffs' counsel insisted that Fibreboard and two of its insurers settle the coverage dispute by separate agreement. The resulting "Trilateral Settlement Agreement" required the insurers to create a $2 billion fund for damage payments to plaintiffs should the Global Settlement not receive judicial approval. Plaintiffs then filed a class action lawsuit in federal court in the Eastern District of Texas.

The Global Settlement required Fibreboard and its insurers to place the agreed upon amount in a trust. Individual claimants were provided with a process for settling their claims with the trust. If no settlement could be reached, claimants were required to engage in mediation, arbitration, and a mandatory settlement conference. After exhausting that process a claimant could bring a court proceeding against the trust, but there would be a $500,000 limit on recovery, and punitive damages and prejudgment interest would be barred. The class did not cover all claimants. Some 45,000 individuals who had settled their claims were excluded, along with some 53,000 individuals with pending lawsuits. The trial court, after extensive hearings, found that the class action met the requirements of Rule 23(a), and fell within the "limited fund" provision of Rule 23(b)(1)(B). It determined that the plan provided a "fair, reasonable, and adequate" settlement under Rule 23(e). On appeal the Fifth Circuit affirmed both the certification of the class and the adequacy of the settlement.

Justice Souter, writing for the Court, reversed:

* * *

> The inherent tension between representative suits and the day-in-court ideal is only magnified if applied to damage claims gathered in a mandatory class. Unlike Rule 23(b)(3) class members, objectors to the collectivism of a mandatory subdivision (b)(1)(B) action have no inherent right to abstain. The legal rights of absent class members (which in a class like this one would include claimants who by definition may be unidentifiable when the class is certified) are resolved regardless either of their consent, or, in a class with objectors, their express wish to the contrary. * * *And in settlement-only class actions the procedural protections built into the Rule to protect the rights of absent class members during litigation are never invoked in an adversarial setting * * *.

* * *

> The record on which the District Court rested its certification of the class for the purpose of the global settlement did not support the essential premises of mandatory limited fund actions. It failed to demonstrate that the fund was limited except by the agreement of the parties, and it showed exclusions from the class and allocations of assets at odds with the concept of limited fund treatment and the structural protections of Rule 23(a) explained in *Amchem*.

* * *

The defect of certification going to the most characteristic feature of a limited fund action was the uncritical adoption by both the District Court and the Court of Appeals of figures agreed upon by the parties in defining the limits of the fund and demonstrating its inadequacy. When a district court, as here, certifies for class action settlement only, the moment of certification requires "heightene[d] attention," *Amchem*, * * *, to the justifications for binding the class members. * * * Thus, in an action such as this the settling parties must present not only their agreement, but evidence on which the district court may ascertain the limit and the insufficiency of the fund, with support in findings of fact following a proceeding in which the evidence is subject to challenge * * *.

We have already alluded to the difficulties facing limited fund treatment of huge numbers of actions for unliquidated damages arising from mass torts, the first such hurdle being a computation of the total claims. It is simply not a matter of adding up the liquidated amounts, as in the models of limited fund actions. Although we might assume arguendo that prior judicial experience with asbestos claims would allow a court to make a sufficiently reliable determination of the probable total, the District Court here apparently thought otherwise, concluding that "there is no way to predict Fibreboard's future asbestos liability with any certainty." * * * Nothing turns on this conclusion, however, since there was no adequate demonstration of the second element required for limited fund treatment, the upper limit of the fund itself, without which no showing of insufficiency is possible.

The "fund" in this case comprised both the general assets of Fibreboard and the insurance assets provided by the two policies * * *. As to Fibreboard's assets exclusive of the contested insurance, the District Court and the Fifth Circuit concluded that Fibreboard had a then-current sale value of $235 million that could be devoted to the limited fund. While that estimate may have been conservative, * * *at least the District Court heard evidence and made an independent finding at some point in the proceedings. The same, however, cannot be said for the value of the disputed insurance. * * *

* * *

We do not, of course, know exactly what an independent valuation of the limit of the insurance assets would have shown. * * * [O]bjecting and unidentified class members alike are entitled to have the issue settled by specific evidentiary findings independent of the agreement of defendants and conflicted class counsel.

* * *

The explanation of need for independent determination of the fund has necessarily anticipated our application of the requirement of equity among members of the class. There are two issues, the inclusiveness of the class and the fairness of distributions to those within it. On each, this certification for settlement fell short.

The definition of the class excludes myriad claimants with causes of action, or foreseeable causes of action, arising from exposure to Fibreboard asbestos. While the class includes those with present claims never filed, present claims withdrawn without prejudice, and future claimants, it fails to include those who had previously settled with Fibreboard while retaining the right to sue again "upon development of an asbestos related malignancy," plaintiffs with claims pending against Fibreboard at the time of the initial announcement of the Global Settlement Agreement, and the plaintiffs in the "inventory" claims settled as a supposedly necessary step in reaching the global settlement * * *. The number of those outside the class who settled with a reservation of rights may be uncertain, but there is no such uncertainty about the significance of the settlement's exclusion of the 45,000 inventory plaintiffs and the plaintiffs in the unsettled present cases, estimated by the Guardian Ad Litem at more than 53,000 as of August 27, 1993 * * *. It is a fair question how far a natural class may be depleted by prior dispositions of claims and still qualify as a mandatory limited fund class, but there can be no question that such a mandatory settlement class will not qualify when in the very negotiations aimed at a class settlement, class counsel agree to exclude what could turn out to be as much as a third of the claimants that negotiators thought might eventually be involved, a substantial number of whom class counsel represent * * *.

Might such class exclusions be forgiven if it were shown that the class members with present claims and the outsiders ended up with comparable benefits? * * * As for the settled inventory claims, their plaintiffs appeared to have obtained better terms than the class members. They received an immediate payment of 50 percent of a settlement higher than the historical average, and would get the remainder if the global settlement were sustained (or the coverage litigation resolved, as it turned out to be by the Trilateral Settlement Agreement); the class members, by contrast, would be assured of a 3–year payout for claims settled, whereas the unsettled faced a prospect of mediation followed by arbitration as prior conditions of instituting suit, which would even then be subject to a recovery limit, a slower payout and the limitations of the trust's spendthrift protection. * * * Finally, as discussed below, even ostensible parity between settling nonclass plaintiffs and class members would be insufficient to overcome the failure to provide the structural protection of independent representation as for subclasses with conflicting interests.

On the second element of equity within the class, the fairness of the distribution of the fund among class members, the settlement certification is likewise deficient. Fair treatment in the older cases was characteristically assured by straightforward pro rata distribution of the limited fund. * * * While equity in such a simple sense is unattainable in a settlement covering present claims not specifically proven and claims not even due to arise, if at all, until some future time, at the least such a settlement must seek equity by providing for procedures to resolve the difficult issues of treating such differently situated claimants with fairness as among themselves.

First, it is obvious after *Amchem* that a class divided between holders of present and future claims (some of the latter involving no physical injury and to claimants not yet born) requires division into homogeneous subclasses under Rule 23(c)(4)(B) [now Rule 23(c)(5)], with separate representation to eliminate conflicting interests of counsel. * * * No such procedure was employed here, and the conflict was as contrary to the equitable obligation entailed by the limited fund rationale as it was to the requirements of structural protection applicable to all class actions under Rule 23(a)(4).

Second, the class included those exposed to Fibreboard's asbestos products both before and after 1959. The date is significant, for that year saw the expiration of Fibreboard's insurance policy with Continental, the one which provided the bulk of the insurance funds for the settlement. Pre–1959 claimants accordingly had more valuable claims than post–1959 claimants * * *, the consequence being a second instance of disparate interests within the certified class. While at some point there must be an end to reclassification with separate counsel, these two instances of conflict are well within the requirement of structural protection recognized in *Amchem*.

* * *

* * * Here, just as in the earlier case, the proponents of the settlement are trying to rewrite Rule 23; each ignores the fact that Rule 23 requires protections under subdivisions (a) and (b) against inequity and potential inequity at the pre-certification stage, quite independently of the required determination at postcertification fairness review under subdivision (e) that any settlement is fair in an overriding sense. A fairness hearing under subdivision (e) can no more swallow the preceding protective requirements of Rule 23 in a subdivision (b)(1)(B) action than in one under subdivision (b)(3). * * *

* * *

A third contested feature of this settlement certification that departs markedly from the limited fund antecedents is the ultimate provision for a fund smaller than the assets understood by the Court of Appeals to be available for payment of the mandatory class members' claims; most notably, Fibreboard was allowed to retain virtually its entire net worth. Given our treatment of the two preceding deficiencies of the certification, there is of course no need to decide whether this feature of the agreement would alone be fatal to the Global Settlement Agreement. To ignore it entirely, however, would be so misleading that we have decided simply to identify the issue it raises, without purporting to resolve it at this time.

Fibreboard listed its supposed entire net worth as a component of the total (and allegedly inadequate) assets available for claimants, but subsequently retained all but $500,000 of that equity for itself. * * * On the face of it, the arrangement seems irreconcilable with the justification of necessity in denying any opportunity for withdrawal of class members whose jury trial rights will be compromised, whose damages will be capped, and whose payments will be delayed. With Fibreboard retaining nearly all its net worth, it hardly appears that such a regime is the best that can be provided for class members. Given the nature of a limited fund and the need to apply its criteria at the certification stage, it is not enough for a District Court to say that it "need not ensure that a defendant designate a particular source of its assets to satisfy the class' claims; [but only that] the amount recovered by the class [be] fair." * * *

The District Court in this case seems to have had a further point in mind, however. One great advantage of class action treatment of mass tort cases is the opportunity to save the enormous transaction costs of piecemeal litigation, an advantage to which the settlement's proponents have referred in this case. * * *Although the District Court made no specific finding about the transaction cost saving likely from this class settlement, estimating the amount in the "hundreds of millions" * * *, it did conclude that the amount would exceed Fibreboard's net worth as the Court valued it * * * (Fibreboard's net worth of $235 million "is considerably less than the likely savings in defense costs under the Global Settlement"). If a settlement thus saves transaction costs that would never have gone into a class member's pocket in the absence of settlement, may a credit for some of the savings be recognized in a mandatory class action as an incentive to settlement? It is at least a legitimate question, which we leave for another day.

* * *

NOTES AND QUESTIONS

1. Following the decertification of the settlement classes in *Amchem* and *Ortiz*, there was disagreement on the effect these decisions would have on future mass tort class action settlements. Do the Supreme Court decisions suggest that certain mass tort claims are not appropriate for class action certification, or simply that when a large number of claimants are involved and a settlement extinguishes their causes of action without each individual's express consent, the court should pay particular attention to the circumstances in which the settlement was reached, as well as its substantive fairness? What should be the criteria?

2. Chief Justice Rehnquist concurred in *Ortiz,* stating that the problem "cries out for a legislative solution." Justice Ginsburg, writing for the Court

in Norfolk & Western Ry. Co. v. Ayers, 538 U.S. 135, 166, 123 S.Ct. 1210, 1229, 155 L.Ed.2d 261, 187 (2003), echoed this view. Congress has considered legislation addressing compensation for asbestos injuries since at least 1977; most recently the Senate failed to approve asbestos legislation that would have established a national fund mandating compensation to asbestos victims, while requiring claimants to waive rights to sue in court. See Stengel, *The Asbestos End–Game*, 62 N.Y.U. Ann. Surv. Am L. 223 (2006). Professor Carrington locates the asbestos cases in larger questions of administrative regulation, social policy, and judicial authority:

> America's experience with asbestos litigation should teach us to appreciate both the merits and the limits of our system of ex post regulation of business. The civil trial is an important social and political institution on which the public depends for the protection of consumers, workers, and the environment. Even Corporate America cannot long do without it. But civil courts are not a system and cannot be made into a system fit to deal with individual matters as monstrously complex as the scientific issues to be resolved in asbestos cases. Nor can courts usefully try cases before they arise; premature resolution invites the filing of dubious claims. If legislatures insist on leaving such proliferations of complex disputes for the courts, they should be expected to provide enough judges, courtrooms, and juries to timely resolve disputes on their merits for the parties involved. Finally, it is long past the time to reconsider a health care system that is heavily dependent on litigation as the path to medical treatment of sickness and injury.

Carrington, *Asbestos Lessons: The Consequences of Asbestos Litigation*, 26 Rev. Litig. 583, 611–12 (2007). Do you agree with his conclusions? For a discussion of the role of courts and class actions in addressing complex policy questions, compare Barnes, *Defense of Asbestos Tort Litigation: Rethinking Legal Process Analysis in a World of Uncertainty, Second Bests, and Shared Policy–Making Responsibility*, 34 L. & Soc. Inquiry 5 (2009), with Redish & Kastanek, *Settlement Class Actions, The Case-or-Controversy Requirement, and the Nature of the Adjudicatory Process*, 73 U.Chi.L.Rev. 545 (2006).

3. In decertifying the settlement class in *Ortiz*, the Supreme Court criticized Fibreboard's "constructive bankruptcy" (remember that the defendant is still a solvent corporation) because it allowed the defendant corporation to circumvent state law and procedural requirements by treating it as though it were in bankruptcy proceedings. Fibreboard, like any corporate bankrupt, was able to create a fund limited to its insurance coverage to satisfy all of its tort creditors. However, since the Bankruptcy Code did not actually apply, the defendant did not have to accord all its creditors equal treatment. The defendant was able to place its shareholders ahead of its tort creditors. Thus, Fibreboard was required only to contribute a small sum ($10 million) in comparison to the insurers' contributions to the fund. Bear in mind that it is the creation of this limited fund that qualified Fibreboard for Rule 23(b)(1) certification, making the class mandatory. The dramatic increase in the company's stock price that followed the announcement of the settlement terms suggests that the gains conferred upon its stockholders were substantial.

A more common practice has been for corporations to use bankruptcy proceedings as a way of avoiding extensive future litigation. See, e.g., In re Johns–Manville Corp., 78 F.3d 764 (2d Cir.1996). Under this approach, the corporation reorganizes its assets to create a trust for which all claimants compete on equal footing. As a result, the shareholders' claims are satisfied only after the tort creditor's claims; the value of the shareholders' equity interest is likely to drop significantly. However, this approach is not without its problems; settlement funds may be depleted by present claimants entirely, leaving future claimants without recovery.

4. Subsequent to *Amchem* and *Ortiz*, a settlement class of individuals who took the diet drugs Fenfluramine and Dexfenfluramine, which were found to cause a heart valve abnormality in some patients, was approved in IN RE DIET DRUGS (PHENTERMINE, FENFLURAMINE, DEXFENFLURAMINE) PRODUCTS LIABILITY LITIGATION, 2000 WL 1222042 (E.D.Pa 2000). There were approximately six million individuals in the United States who had been prescribed one of these drugs between 1995 and 1997. Plaintiffs were divided into subclasses depending on the length of time they took the drugs and the severity of their symptoms, and each subclass was assigned separate counsel. Benefits of the settlement included medical monitoring, reimbursement of the purchase price of the drugs, and additional payments depending on the severity of a class member's symptoms, with annual increases in payments for inflation. Claimants had the opportunity to opt-out at four different times during the benefit period, including a back-end opt-out for individuals who developed more severe symptoms within fifteen years of the settlement date. There was a matrix for determining the amount of an individual's recovery that included not only severity of illness, but also personal and environmental factors that could have contributed to an individual plaintiff's illness. What administrative difficulties do you foresee in managing a settlement of this size? See Hensler, *Has the Fat Lady Sung? The Future of Mass Toxic Torts*, 26 Rev. Litig. 883, 920 (2007).

5. Several class action lawsuits have been filed in recent years on behalf of victims of Nazi persecution during World War II. The Eastern District of New York approved a $1.25 billion settlement in one class action for targets of racial persecution and their heirs against two leading Swiss banks. IN RE HOLOCAUST VICTIM ASSETS LITIGATION, 105 F.Supp.2d 139 (E.D.N.Y. 2000). The class was made up of an estimated 1.4 million potential class members, who sought to recover deposited assets, looted assets, profits made by Swiss and foreign corporations through slave labor, and damages from denial of entry into Switzerland for refugees who tried to escape the Nazis. The class was divided into five subclasses, and a Special Master was appointed to allocate the settlement proceeds among the subgroups. Identifying and contacting potential class members was problematic. The events that formed the basis of the claims had occurred over sixty years ago. Many of the victims had died in the Holocaust or the year thereafter. Documentation of bank accounts, property, and other assets was limited. Moreover, some heirs and even the victims themselves did not know that they were entitled to recovery under the settlement. Is it true, as the majority in *Amchem* suggests, that even if the problems of commonality and adequate representation are overcome through the creation of subclasses, it will be impossible to provide

adequate notice when potential class members cannot be identified? In certifying the class, the court stated that the concerns about adequate representation that befell *Amchem* and *Ortiz* were not relevant in this case because each subclass had separate counsel and a Special Master allocate funds among the subclasses. Did the court merely delay an inevitable conflict among the subclasses over the distribution of the settlement?

The Southern District of New York approved an analogous settlement in a class action against Austrian banks by Holocaust victims based on a finding that (1) it was produced through arm's length negotiation, (2) the substantive nature of the settlement seemed fair, and (3) there were no objections that indicated to the court that the settlement was unfair or inadequate. In re Austrian & German Bank Holocaust Litigation, 80 F.Supp.2d 164 (S.D.N.Y. 2000), affirmed D'Amato v. Deutsche Bank, 236 F.3d 78 (2d Cir.2001).

Finally, a number of class actions were filed against German (and several American) corporations that had profited during World War II by using uncompensated forced and slave laborers, many of whom were "borrowed" from the concentration camps with the aid of the SS, a volunteer, elite unit of the German army. The suits sought the disgorgement of profits made by the corporations and the value of the work performed by class members. These suits were a great embarrassment to defendants, some of whom are now very active participants in the United States marketplace. With the intercession of several governments, the lawsuits were settled on condition that defendants establish a charitable foundation on behalf of the class. See Neuborne, *Preliminary Reflections on Aspects of Holocaust–Era Litigation in American Courts*, 80 Wash.U.L.Q. 795 (2002).

SECTION G. THE PRECLUSIVE EFFECT OF A CLASS ACTION JUDGMENT

The topic of the binding effect of judgments is studied in Chapter 17, p. 1249, infra. This section raises some of the questions concerning preclusion that recur in the class action context.

COOPER v. FEDERAL RESERVE BANK OF RICHMOND

Supreme Court of the United States, 1984.
467 U.S. 867, 104 S.Ct. 2794, 81 L.Ed.2d 718.

Certiorari to the United States Court of Appeals for the Fourth Circuit.

JUSTICE STEVENS delivered the opinion of the Court.

The question to be decided is whether a judgment in a class action determining that an employer did not engage in a general pattern or practice of racial discrimination against the certified class of employees precludes a class member from maintaining a subsequent civil action alleging an individual claim of racial discrimination against the employer.

I

On March 22, 1977, the Equal Employment Opportunity Commission commenced a civil action against respondent, the Federal Reserve Bank of Richmond. Respondent operates a branch in Charlotte, N.C. (the Bank), where during the years 1974–1978 it employed about 350–450 employees in several departments. The EEOC complaint alleged that the Bank was violating § 703(a) of Title VII of the Civil Rights Act of 1964 by engaging in "policies and practices" that included "failing and refusing to promote *blacks* because of race." * * *

Six months after the EEOC filed its complaint, four individual employees were allowed to intervene as plaintiffs. * * * In due course, the District Court entered an order conditionally certifying the following class pursuant to Federal Rules of Civil Procedure 23(b)(2) and (3):

> "All black persons who have been employed by the defendant at its Charlotte Branch Office at any time since January 3, 1974 * * * who have been discriminated against in promotion, wages, job assignments and terms and conditions of employment because of their race."

After certifying the class, the District Court ordered that notice be published in the Charlotte newspapers and mailed to each individual member of the class. The notice described the status of the litigation, and plainly stated that members of the class "will be bound by the judgment or other determination" if they did not exclude themselves by sending a written notice to the Clerk. * * * Among the recipients of the notice were Phyllis Baxter and five other individuals employed by the Bank. * * * It is undisputed that these individuals—the Baxter petitioners—are members of the class represented by the intervening plaintiffs and that they made no attempt to exclude themselves from the class.

At the trial the intervening plaintiffs, as well as the Baxter petitioners, testified. The District Court found that the Bank had engaged in a pattern and practice of discrimination from 1974 through 1978 by failing to afford black employees opportunities for advancement and assignment equal to opportunities afforded white employees in pay grades 4 and 5. Except as so specified, however, the District Court found that "there does not appear to be a pattern and practice of discrimination pervasive enough for the court to order relief." * * * Finally, the court somewhat cryptically stated that although it had an opinion about "the entitlement to relief of some of the class members who testified at trial," it would defer decision of such matters to a further proceeding. * * *

Thereafter, on March 24, 1981, the Baxter petitioners moved to intervene, alleging that each had been denied a promotion for discriminatory reasons. * * * The District Court stated: "The court has found no proof of any classwide discrimination above grade 5 and, therefore, they are not entitled to participate in any Stage II proceedings in this case."

* * * The court added that it could "see no reason why, if any of the would be intervenors are actively interested in pursuing their claims, they cannot file a Section 1981 suit next week...." [in original] * * *

A few days later the Baxter petitioners filed a separate action against the Bank alleging that each of them had been denied a promotion because of their race in violation of 42 U.S.C. § 1981. The Bank moved to dismiss the complaint on the ground that each of them was a member of the class that had been certified in the Cooper litigation, that each was employed in a grade other than 4 or 5, and that they were bound by the determination that there was no proof of any classwide discrimination above grade 5. The District Court denied the motion to dismiss, but certified its order for interlocutory appeal under 28 U.S.C. § 1292(b). The Bank's interlocutory appeal from the order was then consolidated with the Bank's pending appeal in the Cooper litigation.

The United States Court of Appeals for the Fourth Circuit reversed the District Court's judgment on the merits in the Cooper litigation, concluding that (1) there was insufficient evidence to establish a pattern or practice of racial discrimination in grades 4 and 5, and (2) two of the intervening plaintiffs had not been discriminated against on account of race. EEOC v. Federal Reserve Bank of Richmond, 698 F.2d 633 (4th Cir.1983). The court further held that under the doctrine of res judicata, the judgment in the Cooper class action precluded the Baxter petitioners from maintaining their individual race discrimination claims against the Bank. The court thus reversed the order denying the Bank's motion to dismiss in the Baxter action, and remanded for dismissal of the Baxter complaint. We granted certiorari to review that judgment * * *, and we now reverse.

II

Claims of two types were adjudicated in the Cooper litigation. First, the individual claims of each of the four intervening plaintiffs have been finally decided in the Bank's favor. * * * Those individual decisions do not, of course, foreclose any other individual claims. Second, the class claim that the Bank followed "policies and practices" of discriminating against its employees has also been decided. * * * It is that decision on which the Court of Appeals based its res judicata analysis.

There is of course no dispute that under elementary principles of prior adjudication a judgment in a properly entertained class action is binding on class members in any subsequent litigation. * * * Basic principles of res judicata (merger and bar or claim preclusion) and collateral estoppel (issue preclusion) apply. A judgment in favor of the plaintiff class extinguishes their claim, which merges into the judgment granting relief. A judgment in favor of the defendant extinguishes the claim, barring a subsequent action on that claim. A judgment in favor of either side is conclusive in a subsequent action between them on any issue actually litigated and determined, if its determination was essential to that judgment.

III

* * *

The crucial difference between an individual's claim of discrimination and a class action alleging a general pattern or practice of discrimination is manifest. The inquiry regarding an individual's claim is the reason for a particular employment decision, while "at the liability stage of a pattern-or-practice trial the focus often will not be on individual hiring decisions, but on a pattern of discriminatory decisionmaking." * * *

This distinction was critical to our holding in General Telephone Co. of Southwest v. Falcon, [p. 751, supra,] * * * that an individual employee's claim that he was denied a promotion on racial grounds did not necessarily make him an adequate representative of a class composed of persons who had allegedly been refused employment for discriminatory reasons. * * *

Falcon thus holds that the existence of a valid individual claim does not necessarily warrant the conclusion that the individual plaintiff may successfully maintain a class action. It is equally clear that a class plaintiff's attempt to prove the existence of a companywide policy, or even a consistent practice within a given department, may fail even though discrimination against one or two individuals has been proved. The facts of this case illustrate the point.

The District Court found that two of the intervening plaintiffs, Cooper and Russell, had both established that they were the victims of racial discrimination but, as the Court of Appeals noted, they were employed in grades higher than grade 5 and therefore their testimony provided no support for the conclusion that there was a practice of discrimination in grades 4 and 5. * * * Given the burden of establishing a prima facie case of a pattern or practice of discrimination, it was entirely consistent for the District Court simultaneously to conclude that Cooper and Russell had valid individual claims even though it had expressly found no proof of any classwide discrimination above grade 5. It could not be more plain that the rejection of a claim of classwide discrimination does not warrant the conclusion that no member of the class could have a valid individual claim. "A racially balanced work force cannot immunize an employer from liability for specific acts of discrimination." Furnco Construction Corp. v. Waters, 438 U.S., at 579, 98 S.Ct., at 2950–2951.

* * *

The Court of Appeals was correct in generally concluding that the Baxter petitioners, as members of the class represented by the intervening plaintiffs in the Cooper litigation, are bound by the adverse judgment in that case. The court erred, however, in the preclusive effect it attached to that prior adjudication. That judgment (1) bars the class members from bringing another class action against the Bank alleging a pattern or practice of discrimination for the relevant time period and (2) precludes the class members in any other litigation with the Bank from relitigating the question whether the Bank engaged in a pattern and practice of discrimination against black employees during the relevant time period. The judgment is not, however, dispositive of the individual claims the Baxter petitioners have alleged in their separate action. Assuming they establish a prima facie case of discrimination * * *, the Bank will be required to articulate a legitimate reason for each of the challenged decisions, and if it meets that burden, the ultimate questions regarding motivation in their individual cases will be resolved by the District Court. Moreover, the prior adjudication may well prove beneficial to the Bank in the Baxter action: the determination in the Cooper action that the Bank had not engaged in a general pattern or practice of discrimination would be relevant on the issue of pretext. * * *

The Bank argues that permitting the Baxter petitioners to bring separate actions would frustrate the purposes of Rule 23. We think the converse is true. The class-action device was intended to establish a procedure for the adjudication of common questions of law or fact. If the Bank's theory were adopted, it would be tantamount to requiring that every member of the class be permitted to intervene to litigate the merits of his individual claim.

* * *

The judgment of the Court of Appeals is reversed, and the case is remanded for further proceedings consistent with this opinion.

It is so ordered.

JUSTICE MARSHALL concurs in the judgment.

JUSTICE POWELL took no part in the decision of this case.

NOTES AND QUESTIONS

1. Should a class action judgment be given collateral estoppel effect in favor of a plaintiff who elected to opt-out of the class action and file an individual lawsuit? If allowed, wouldn't this practice enable plaintiff to benefit from a favorable judgment but not to be barred by an unfavorable judgment—even as to the very matter determined in the class action itself? Would this undermine the opt-out procedure? See 7B Wright, Miller & Kane, Federal Practice and Procedure: Civil 3d § 1789; Wolff, *Preclusion in Class Action Litigation*, 105 Colum.L.Rev. 717 (2005).

2. What is the preclusive effect of a state court class action settlement upon a second suit brought by the same parties in federal court raising exclusively federal questions? Although such federal claims cannot be brought in state court, the Supreme Court has held that, in accordance with full faith and credit under 28 U.S.C. § 1738, the state judgment may resolve claims within the exclusive jurisdiction of the federal courts and bar their subsequent litigation in a federal court. MATSUSHITA ELECTRIC INDUSTRIAL CO. v. EPSTEIN, 516 U.S. 367, 116 S.Ct. 873, 134 L.Ed.2d 6 (1996).

3. The Court considered the preclusive effect of a class action judgment in STEPHENSON v. DOW CHEMICAL CO., 273 F.3d 249 (2d Cir.2001), affirmed by an equally divided Court, in part, and vacated on other grounds, in part 539 U.S. 111, 123 S.Ct. 2161, 156 L.Ed.2d 106 (2003). In 1983, the

Eastern District of New York certified a plaintiff class consisting of "all persons who were in the United States, New Zealand or Australian Armed Forces at any time from 1962 to 1971 who were injured in or near Vietnam by exposure to Agent Orange or other phenoxy herbicides, [including] spouses, parents and children of veterans born before January 1, 1984, directly or derivatively injured as a result of the exposure." The class included 15,000 named plaintiffs and nearly 2.5 million potential class members. See In re Agent Orange Product Liability Litigation, 100 F.R.D. 718 (E.D.N.Y.1983), affirmed 818 F.2d 145 (2d Cir.1987), certiorari denied 484 U.S. 1004, 108 S.Ct. 695, 98 L.Ed.2d 648 (1988). The next year, the case settled and defendants agreed to establish a $180 million fund to make payments to individual class members and to agencies that serve Vietnam veterans. In approving the settlement, the district judge declined to appoint counsel for a subclass of veterans whose injuries might be latent and so who might need to file future claims, but stated that he was taking their interests into account. For a discussion of the District Court proceedings, see Rubenstein, *Finality in Class Action Litigation: Lessons from Habeas*, 82 N.Y.U. L. Rev. 790, 801–04 (2007). Fifteen years later, Stephenson, a Vietnam veteran who had not opted-out of the court-approved settlement, was diagnosed with cancer. He believed that his condition was caused by his exposure to Agent Orange during his years of military service. However, the Agent Orange compensation fund had been depleted. Stephenson filed an individual action, which was dismissed as precluded by the settlement. On appeal, the Second Circuit reversed, holding that the interests of future claimants had not been represented adequately and therefore could not be precluded by the settlement The Supreme Court affirmed by an equally divided court without opinion. On remand, the District Court dismissed the claim. See Isaacson v. Dow Chem. Co. (In re "Agent Orange" Product Liability Litigation), 304 F. Supp.2d 404 (E.D.N.Y. 2004), stay lifted 344 F. Supp.2d 873 (E.D.N.Y. 2004). *Stephenson* leaves open important questions about assessing adequacy of representation and the availability of collateral challenges to class action settlements. See Nagareda, *Administering Adequacy in Class Representation*, 82 Texas L. Rev. 287 (2003); Wirt, *Missed Opportunity: Stephenson v. Dow Chemical Co. and the Finality of Class Action Settlements*, 109 Penn. St. L. Rev. 1297 (2005).

SECTION H. THE PROBLEM OF THE MASS TORT CASE

Perhaps the best way to explore the complexities of class action practice is to apply Rule 23 to a concrete example. To that end, consider the consequences of certifying a class in the following action. Questions to think about include how the class is to be managed, what possible intra-class conflicts might develop, and how the court might best protect the interests of the absentees. Keep in mind procedural possibilities other than the class action, such as using the principles of former adjudication and interpleader.

In 1970, the A.H. Robins Company placed the Dalkon Shield, an intra-uterine contraceptive device, on the market. Approximately 2.2 million of these devices were purchased by women in the United States, and many women who used the device developed an infection that caused infertility or sustained other injuries. Some evidence existed that A.H. Robins knew that the device would have these effects. By May 31, 1981, approximately 3,258 actions related to the Dalkon Shield had been filed, and 1,573 suits, in which compensatory damages of well over $500 million and punitive damages in excess of $2.3 billion were claimed, were pending. Against the objections of many of the plaintiffs and all the defendants, a District Court in California certified a nationwide class. The Ninth Circuit reversed on the ground that the prevalence of individual issues outweighed any efficiency the class action device might have brought. Which court was correct? Do the inevitable differences in the plaintiffs' medical and sexual histories affect your decision? How should punitive damages be handled? Should they be awarded to one plaintiff or divided amongst them? See In re Northern District of California, Dalkon Shield IUD Products Liability Litigation, 693 F.2d 847 (9th Cir.1982), certiorari denied 459 U.S. 1171, 103 S.Ct. 817, 74 L.Ed.2d 1015 (1983).

In 1989, in a separate action against the manufacturer's liability insurance company, the Fourth Circuit certified a class that sought recovery against the insurer. See In re A.H. Robins Co., 880 F.2d 709 (4th Cir. 1989). The class was certified under Rule 23(b)(1)(A) on the issue of the insurance company's liability as a joint tortfeasor, because it would pose a substantial burden on the company to have to litigate its liability separately with each plaintiff. The class also was certified under Rule 23(b)(1)(B) with respect to the company's contractual liability under its insurance policy provided to A.H. Robins.

CHAPTER 11

PRETRIAL DEVICES FOR OBTAINING INFORMATION: DEPOSITIONS AND DISCOVERY

■ ■ ■

In this Chapter, we examine procedures that allow, and in some situations require, the parties to exchange information during the pretrial stage of a litigation. American discovery, said to be of "constitutional foundation," Hazard, *From Whom No Secrets Are Hid*, 76 Texas L. Rev. 1665, 1694 (1998), is regarded as exceptional from the perspective of practice abroad. See Subrin, *Discovery in Global Perspective: Are We Nuts?*, 52 DePaul L. Rev. 299 (2002). The practice is of recent vintage. Discovery did not exist at common law, and equity allowed for only a limited disclosure of information. The Federal Rules' approach to discovery ushered in a "revolution" that radically altered litigation practice. Subrin, *Fishing Expeditions Allowed: The Historical Background of the 1938 Federal Discovery Rules*, 39 B.C. L. Rev. 691, 738 (1998). Over the years, the federal discovery rules have been amended numerous times to deal with a broad array of issues such as delay, cost, and technological change. Although discovery is an intensely practical topic, it also is among "the most debated, and in some cases the most fractious and vexing, aspect of litigation today." Beckerman, *Confronting Civil Discovery's Fatal Flaws*, 84 Minn. L. Rev. 505, 505 (2000).

SECTION A. THE GENERAL SCOPE OF DISCOVERY

Read Federal Rule of Civil Procedure 26 in the Supplement.

Modern discovery serves a number of purposes that are important to individual litigants and to the civil justice system as a whole.

From the private perspective, the first, and least controversial, purpose of discovery is the preservation of relevant information that might not be available at trial. Basically, this objective relates to the testimony of witnesses who are aged or ill or who will be out of the jurisdiction at the time the trial commences. The earliest discovery procedures in the federal courts were designed primarily for this purpose. See *Developments in the Law—Discovery,* 74 Harv.L.Rev. 940, 949 (1961). The second purpose is to ascertain and isolate those issues that actually are in controversy between the parties. There is little dispute that it is appropriate for one party to ask whether another party contests the existence or nonexistence of a fact that the pleadings formally have put in issue. A third purpose of discovery is to find out what testimony and other evidence is available on each of the disputed factual issues. Prior to discovery, a party could ascertain these matters only through private investigation; if, for example, a witness refused to discuss a matter with a party, there was no way to learn the substance of that witness's testimony in advance of trial. As a result, cases often turned on the parties' relative access to the facts and their ability to keep certain matters secret until the trial. Views about discovery reflect a division between those who favor broad discovery to obviate all traces of surprise and those who allege the need for privacy of investigation and adversarial development of evidence.

From the public perspective, discovery helps to promote transparency by making information about government and corporate practice available to a broader set of individuals than just the parties to a lawsuit. Discovery also promotes the work of "private attorney generals" who help to enforce the law through the filing of lawsuits. Professor Carrington explains:

> Private litigants do in America much of what is done in other industrial states by public officers working within an administrative bureaucracy. Every day, hundreds of American lawyers caution their clients that an unlawful course of conduct will be accompanied by serious risk of exposure at the hands of some hundreds of thousands of lawyers, each armed with a subpoena power by which misdeeds can be uncovered. Unless corresponding new powers are conferred on public officers, constricting discovery would diminish the disincentives for lawless behavior across a wide spectrum of forbidden conduct.

Carrington, *Renovating Discovery*, 49 Ala. L. Rev. 51, 54 (1997). See also Higginbotham, *Foreword*, 49 Ala. L. Rev. 1, 4–5 (1997) ("Congress has elected to use the private suit, private attorneys-general as an enforcing mechanism for the anti-trust laws, the securities laws, environmental laws, civil rights and more. In the main, the plaintiff in these suits must discover his evidence from the defendant. Calibration of discovery is calibration of the level of enforcement of the social policy set by Congress.").

NOTES AND QUESTIONS

1. One major reason for permitting widespread discovery of the facts before trial is the elimination of surprise. See Klonoski v. Mahlab, 156 F.3d 255, 271 (1st Cir.1998), condemning "trial by ambush." Does full knowledge

by one party of all the evidence to be presented by the opposing party lead to a more accurate result at trial, or can justice sometimes be better served if a litigant is surprised by the evidence presented at trial? For a discussion of surprise from an economic perspective, see Hay, *Civil Discovery: Its Effects and Optimal Scope*, 23 J. Legal Stud. 481 (1994).

2. There is a lively debate about the existence and extent of discovery abuse. How would you define discovery abuse? As a failure to cooperate? As seeking unnecessary evidence? As using the discovery process for inappropriate reasons? Does the adversary system create incentives for discovery abuse? If discovery abuse is pervasive, can its extent perhaps be attributed to such practices as the "American" rule for attorney compensation and the use of hourly billing by one attorney with the other attorney dependent upon contingent compensation? See Sofaer, *Sanctioning Attorneys for Discovery Abuse Under the New Federal Rules: On the Limited Utility of Punishment*, 57 St. John's L. Rev. 680 (1983). Judge Easterbrook has argued that discovery abuse does not stem from deficiencies in the discovery rules and, therefore, that changes in the rules cannot prevent such abuse. See Easterbrook, *Discovery as Abuse*, 69 B.U.L.Rev. 635 (1989). However, empirical studies suggest that discovery "operates effectively in most lawsuits," Tobias, *The 2000 Federal Civil Rules Revisions*, 38 San Diego L. Rev. 875, 884 (2001), with abuse confined to complex cases that involve high stakes damage awards. See Mullenix, The *Pervasive Myth of Pervasive Discovery Abuse: The Sequel*, 39 B.C. L. Rev. 683, 684 (1998). Unquestionably, anecdotal evidence about discovery abuse tends to grab the headlines and often frames public discussion of the issues. Professor Yablon reports:

> In a defamation action brought by Philip Morris Company against the American Broadcasting Company, lawyers for ABC alleged Philip Morris had produced twenty-five boxes containing approximately one million documents. These were the "critically sensitive flavoring documents" relating to ABC's charge that Philip Morris spiked its cigarettes with nicotine. The documents had been transferred onto a special dark red paper with squiggly lines, which made them hard to read and impossible to photocopy. ABC's lawyers alleged that the paper gave off noxious fumes that made it "difficult to work with the altered copies for extended periods of time." The smelly paper was reported to have nauseated one partner and given someone a headache. The extent to which these documents were truly nauseating (that is, more nauseating than any other million documents that have to be reviewed) remains in dispute. Nonetheless, counsel for Philip Morris * * * agreed to produce some of the documents on non-odiferous paper.

Yablon, *Stupid Lawyer Tricks: An Essay on Discovery Abuse*, 96 Colum. L. Rev. 1618, 1618–19 (1996).

3. Even if discovery abuse is not pervasive, the belief that discovery can be burdensome is invoked frequently—summarized in the metaphor of the "fishing expedition." See Thornburg, *Just Say "No Fishing": The Lure of Metaphor*, 40 U. Mich. J.L. Reform 1 (2006). To what extent was the Court influenced by fears of discovery abuse in its decision to abandon the *Conley* "no facts" standard for pleading in favor of *Twombly*'s tougher plausibility

standard, p. 568, supra? See Hoffman, *Burn up the Chaff with Unquenchable Fire: What Two Doctrinal Intersections Can Teach Us About Judicial Power over Pleadings*, 88 B.U. L. Rev. 1217 (2008). What evidence would be relevant in assessing whether the discovery rules are in need of amendment? If research indicates that discovery tends to be a problem in particular kinds of disputes, would it be better to adopt special procedures for those types of cases?

4. "The conventional wisdom that sophisticated parties want to 'discover everything and disclose nothing' assumes that a trial is a realistic possibility. But spending the money and time to discover everything makes little sense in the typical case [in which early settlement is likely]." Subrin & Main, *The Integration of Law and Fact in an Uncharted Parallel Procedural Universe*, 79 Notre Dame L. Rev. 1981, 2016 (2004). How do you think the possibility of settlement affects discovery practice?

Read Federal Rule of Civil Procedure 27 in the Supplement.

---

1. DISCOVERY PRIOR TO COMMENCING A LAWSUIT

IN RE PETITION OF SHEILA ROBERTS FORD

United States District Court, Middle District of Alabama, 1997.
170 F.R.D. 504.

THOMPSON, CHIEF JUDGE.

* * *

On November 15, 1996, Ford filed, through counsel, her petition pursuant to [Federal] Rule [of Civil Procedure] 27. In the petition, Ford asks "for leave to proceed with the deposition of Elmore County Sheriff Bill Franklin." She alleges that she "expects to be a party to an action in the United States District Court for the Middle District of Alabama, Northern Division, but is presently unable to bring said action"; that the "anticipated action surrounds the shooting death of Fred William Roberts by law-enforcement officers of Elmore County on November 8, 1996"; that she "is the Administratrix of the Estate of Fred William Roberts"; that she "intends to establish who the appropriate party defendants to the anticipated action are through the testimony of Elmore County Sheriff Bill Franklin"; that she "is unable to determine the appropriate party defendants and the basic facts surrounding the death of Fred William Roberts without the testimony of Sheriff Franklin" and "needs to establish an accurate account of the events that took place . . . before the memories of those involved fade or become dist[or]ted by publicity"; and that she is "requesting the deposition of . . . Franklin" because he "was the commanding officer of the Elmore County deputies believed to be involved in the shooting of ... Roberts" and he "is expected to identify the facts involved in Mr. Roberts' shooting death as well as the identity of the law enforcement officers involved." Ford also gave the names, addresses, and descriptions of the persons she expected to be adverse parties.

* * *

A hearing was held on the petition on December 13. At the hearing, Sheriff Franklin appeared through counsel and stated that he opposed the petition because it was not authorized by Rule 27. Ford responded by reaffirming that she needed to take Sheriff Franklin's deposition in order "to determine ... the basic facts surrounding the death of Fred William Roberts." Without this information, she said, she could not determine whom to sue. She did not know whether Sheriff Franklin or one of his deputies shot Roberts and whether the shooting was justified.

II. Discussion

* * *

Admittedly, Ford * * * asserts in her petition a desire to preserve testimony; she states that she "needs to establish an accurate account of the events that took place ... before the memories of those involved fade or become dist[or]ted by publicity." This reason is not credible, however. Ford can do this by simply filing suit today. She presented no evidence that Sheriff Franklin's testimony is in imminent danger of being lost because he is gravely ill or about to leave the country. Ford therefore wishes only to discover or uncover what happened on November 8. The simple question for the court is whether Rule 27 authorizes such relief.

* * * [T]he first and obvious place to look to determine whether Rule 27 authorizes pre-complaint discovery is the language of the rule itself. If the language of the rule is unambiguous and dispositive and is reasonable within its context, then the court should go no further and simply should enforce the language. Here, Rule 27 meets this straightforward test.

Subsection (a)(1) of Rule 27 provides, as stated, that "A person who desires to *perpetuate* testimony regarding any matter that may be cognizable in any court of the United States may file a verified petition." (Emphasis added.) Subsection (a)(3) then provides that an order allowing examination may be entered only "If the court is satisfied that the *perpetuation* of the testimony may prevent a failure or delay of justice." (Emphasis added.) [The language of these provisions has been altered by the 2007 restyling of the Federal Rules. These changes are not substantive.] Rule 27's coverage therefore extends only to the "perpetuation" of testimony. The term "perpetuate" is defined as "to make perpetual," "preserve from extinction," or "cause to last indefinitely." Webster's Third International Dictionary, unabridged 1685 (1976); see also Black's

Law Dictionary 1027 (5th ed. 1979) ("perpetuating testimony" is a "means ... for *preserving* the testimony of witness, which might otherwise be lost before the trial in which it is intended to be used") (emphasis added). Here, Ford seeks to discover or uncover testimony, not to perpetuate it. She seeks pre-complaint discovery of evidence, not pre-complaint perpetuation of it. There is nothing before the court to indicate that Sheriff Franklin's testimony is in imminent danger of being lost. Rather, Ford simply wants to know who shot Roberts and why. Rule 27 simply does not provide for such discovery.

* * *

Ford also argues that Rule 27 should be read in conjunction with Rule 11 * * *. The problem, however, is that Rule 27 is not a vehicle for compliance with Rule 11. As stated, the language in Rule 27 is clear that the rule authorizes the perpetuation of evidence, not the discovery or uncovering of it. * * *

To be sure, the court in In the Matter of Alpha Industries, 159 F.R.D. 456 (S.D.N.Y. 1995), reached a contrary understanding of the relationship between Rule 11 and Rule 27. There, as explained by the district court, * * * "[I]n the case at bar, *the fact that petitioner must delay bringing suit until receiving the information sought is a sufficient showing to allow the use of Rule 27 to perpetuate respondent's testimony.*" Alpha Industries, 159 F.R.D. at 457 * * * (emphasis added).

This court disagrees with Alpha Industries * * *.

The court is not without sympathy for Ford. She is understand[ably] deeply troubled by and concerned about the shooting death of her father. If a law enforcement officer was at fault she desires to have him or her held accountable in a court of law. But, under Rule 11, she cannot file suit against any one without first having uncovered some "evidentiary support" for holding the person liable or having obtained some preliminary evidence that there is likely to be some "evidentiary support after a reasonable opportunity for further investigation or discovery." [The language as changed now appears in Rule 11(b)(3).] Similarly, the defense of qualified immunity protects law enforcement officials from federal suit in the absence of detailed factual allegations of a violation of a clearly established federal right. * * * However, without the discovery incident to litigation, Ford is without the means to uncover whether her father was a victim of foul play in violation of a clearly established federal right. Her predicament is a "Catch 22." Indeed, she must feel that, under the rules established by our civil justice system, a law enforcement officer can get away with murder. This court has no answer for her, however, other than that Rule 27 does not offer an avenue of relief.

* * *

It is further ORDERED that costs are taxed against petitioner Ford, for which execution may issue.

NOTES AND QUESTIONS

1. What are the advantages and disadvantages of a provision permitting a prospective plaintiff to discover facts to aid in deciding whether or not a legal action is justified and in ascertaining against whom it should be brought? How should the costs of such a procedure be allocated between the prospective plaintiff and the prospective defendant? Does the Supreme Court's establishment of a "plausibility" standard for pleading, p. 568, supra, affect your view on this subject? For a discussion of Rule 27, arguing that courts should allow pre-complaint discovery "both to preserve evidence and to help frame a complaint," see Kronfeld, Note—*The Preservation and Discovery of Evidence Under Federal Rule of Civil Procedure 27*, 78 Geo.L.J. 593 (1990).

2. Texas, among a small number of states, allows a private individual to take a presuit deposition in order to investigate a potential claim. Texas Rule 202 provides that a person "may petition the court for an order authorizing the taking of a deposition on oral examination or written questions either: (a) to perpetuate or obtain the person's own testimony or that of any other person for use in an anticipated suit; or (b) to investigate a potential claim or suit." Tex. R. Civ. P. 202.1 (a)–(b). In order to prevent abuse of the rule, what should a court require the petitioner to demonstrate? See Hoffman, *Access to Information, Access to Justice: The Role of Presuit Investigatory Discovery*, 40 U. Mich. J.L. Reform 217 (2007).

2. THE SCOPE OF DISCOVERY: RELEVANCE

KELLY v. NATIONWIDE MUTUAL INSURANCE CO.

Ohio Court of Common Pleas, Ashtabula County, 1963.
23 Ohio Op.2d 29, 188 N.E.2d 445.

PONTIUS, JUDGE. Plaintiff sued to recover damages to a motor vehicle under the terms of a comprehensive insurance policy, claiming that the damages arose because someone put sugar in the fuel tank of plaintiff's truck "during the latter part of April, 1961." The defendant denies that such an insurance policy was in effect on April 19, 1961 and otherwise its answer amounts to a general denial. To defendant's answer was attached a list of forty-two interrogatories directed to plaintiff. Plaintiff answered the interrogatories but defendant moved to require more complete answers by plaintiff.

The issue presented by defendant's motion brings into question the proper use by a defendant of interrogatories under R.C. § 2309.43, which reads as follows:

> A party may annex to his pleading, other than a demurrer, interrogatories pertinent to the issue made in the pleadings, which interrogatories, if not demurred to, shall be plainly and fully answered under oath by the party to whom they are propounded, or if such party is a corporation, by the president, secretary, or other officer thereof, as the party propounding requires.

Although the old Common Law Bill in Equity for discovery has been largely supplanted in Ohio by this code section as well as R.C. § 2317.07, the question still remains as to whether some of the equitable principles are still in force. * * *

Defendant's answer sets up no affirmative defense. The defendant therefore has assumed no burden of proof. The issue at first instance, at least, would seem to be narrowed to the question, may a defendant who has pleaded only a general denial attach to his answer and have answered by the plaintiff interrogatories which only pry into the evidence by which the plaintiff may sustain his own case, as distinguished from inquiring for ultimate facts within plaintiff's own knowledge which may be pertinent to the issue. In other words, does the plaintiff have to reveal to the defendant in advance of trial evidence which plaintiff hopes to establish in support of his own case?

In some of the older cases in Ohio, trying to interpret this section (R.C. § 2309.43) there seems to have been established the principle that the general purpose of the discovery procedure was to aid a plaintiff in *establishing his case* or a defendant to *establish his defense.* * * *

* * *

Likewise, it has been held that interrogatories are not proper where the information sought is not within the personal knowledge of the other party and is not pertinent to an issue raised by the pleading of the inquirer. * * * It has been held that interrogatories are not proper where the answer calls for mere opinion of the party, * * * nor where the information sought is not within the personal knowledge of the party interrogated. * * *

* * * In more recent cases it has been held that this statute and likewise its counterpart must be liberally construed and that interrogatories are proper if they are designed to seek information *pertinent to the action* as distinguished from being merely *pertinent to an issue* raised by the *pleading of the inquirer*. See Sloan v. S.S. Kresge Company, Ohio Com.Pl., 97 N.E.2d 238 [(1958);] * * * Feinstein v. Cleveland, 67 Ohio Law Abst. 518 [(1953)], "Interrogatories may seek information relevant to any *issue of the action* and to all sides of the case." (Italics supplied [in original].)

Parenthetically, it also may be observed that this same philosophy is to prevail when the information is sought by way of deposition and the inspection and production of documents is sought under R.C. § 2317.32. * * * Many states have liberalized their statutory procedure, pointing toward, if not actually adopting, the very extreme liberal rules of discovery as provided by rules 26 through 37 of the Federal Rules of Civil Procedure. * * *

* * *

This Court is inclined to the more liberal and later construction of the Ohio statutes as disclosed by Sloan v. S.S. Kresge, rather than the older rule indicated in such cases as * * * Ward v. Mutual Trucking Company; and this Court holds to the view that interrogatories, whether filed with a pleading under favor of R.C. § 2309.43 or separately under R.C. § 2317.07, are proper when:

1. Relevant to an *issue in the action* as distinguished from merely being relevant to an *issue in the pleading* of the inquirer,

2. They do not seek privileged information,

3. The information sought would also be admissible as evidence in the action.

The rule is limited, however, by the further rule that interrogatories may not seek discovery of the manner whereby the opponent's case is to be established nor evidence which relates exclusively to his case, nor to what his witnesses will testify.

In this Court's opinion, there is a marked distinction between records kept by a party in the regular course of his business operations and those amassed by him only after an incident has arisen out of which his lawsuit or defense arises. The former may be ordered produced, if pertinent to an issue in the action; the latter may not. * * *

With these rules in mind further inquiry directed toward the interrogatories of defendant and answers by plaintiff must be made.

The issue in the case as presented by the petition and the answer as distinguished from issues in only one pleading or the other would seem to be:

1. Did the plaintiff hold a comprehensive insurance policy issued by the defendant, which policy was in force in the latter part of April, 1961?

2. Did the policy cover a 1955 White tractor (owned by plaintiff)?

3. Was sugar placed in the mechanism of this tractor?

4. Was the tractor damaged thereby and if so, to what extent?

Defendant's interrogatory number 2 calls upon plaintiff to state whether she was the sole proprietor of a trucking business or whether same was a partnership or corporation at the time of plaintiff's claim. This interrogatory has a direct bearing on the question of truck ownership and policy coverage. The plaintiff's answer to the interrogatory is equivocal. The plaintiff therefore will be directed to answer the interrogatory fully and completely, stating whether she owned the business as a sole proprietor or as a member of a partnership and if so, the other members thereof, or whether the business was incorporated.

Interrogatory number 6 calls for plaintiff to state where the truck was at the time the sugar allegedly got into the mechanism of the truck. The answer given is "Don't personally know." Bearing in mind that previous interrogatories and answers thereto reveal the fact that the truck in question was under the care and custody of someone else other than plaintiff, it would seem as though plaintiff's answer to this interrogatory is full and complete. The motion with respect to interrogatory and answer number 6 is therefore overruled.

Interrogatories numbers 10, 12, and 15 through 33 all deal with matters arising at the time of or after plaintiff's alleged claim arose. None deal with information or records maintained in the normal operation of plaintiff's business. On the contrary, they call for information as to the manner in which the plaintiff may attempt to establish her cause of action and do not countenance information presumably within plaintiff's own personal knowledge. They call for information which plaintiff may or may not be able to produce through testimony of witnesses upon trial. In other words, they call for hearsay or mere opinion evidence if plaintiff's answer of "Don't personally know" is true. Certainly upon trial if plaintiff were so inquired of and should so answer the same or similar interrogatories, she could not then be called upon to give her opinion or an answer which was obviously mere hearsay.

The same objection is true with interrogatories 36 and 37 and the answers given thereto; and likewise interrogatories 39 through 42 and Plaintiff's answers thereto. An additional objection to interrogatory number 42 exists, namely, assuming that a record of a test was made, it calls for the furnishing of information solely in support of plaintiff's cause of action and obviously arises after the claim arose and in connection with plaintiff's preparation for presentation of her claim and her lawsuit. This last mentioned objection is likewise true with many of the other interrogatories heretofore above covered.

Defendant's motion therefore will be overruled in all respects except with reference to the answer given by plaintiff to interrogatory number 2, and plaintiff is directed to file a complete answer as above indicated.

* * *

NOTES AND QUESTIONS

1. *Kelly* illustrates differing approaches to the concept of relevance. In 1970, seven years after *Kelly* was decided, Ohio adopted a set of discovery regulations with a scope almost identical to that of the Federal Rules at the time. That year, Rule 26(b)(1) was amended to permit discovery, without a court order, of any information, not privileged, relevant to the subject matter of the lawsuit, whether or not admissible at trial, provided the information is reasonably calculated to lead to the discovery of admissible evidence. How would the 1970 amendment change the analysis in *Kelly*?

2. In LINDBERGER v. GENERAL MOTORS CORP., 56 F.R.D. 433 (W.D. Wis. 1972), plaintiff alleged "personal injuries proximately caused by the negligence of the defendants in manufacturing and designing a front end loader which was sold to the plaintiff's employer." Defendants refused to answer an interrogatory requesting "whether any changes have been made,

and if so to describe such changes, subsequent to the date when the loader in question was produced, in either the design of the braking system or in the warning system for brake malfunctions." Evidence of subsequent repairs normally is inadmissible at trial. In granting plaintiff's motion to compel, the court explained:

> * * * It is clear that the information sought in the challenged interrogatories is relevant to the subject-matter of this action. The feasibility of the installation of a better brake system and of more adequate warning systems for brake malfunctions may be significant with respect to * * * [defendants' liability]. Furthermore, the knowledge of the defendants about the adequacy of the design of the loader as well as any information on this subject which may have been passed to the employer of the plaintiff may be relevant on the issues of negligence and contributory negligence.

Id. at 435.

3. Rule 26(b) was amended in 2000 and now limits discovery requests to material "relevant to any party's claim or defense." However, "[f]or good cause," the court may order further discovery "of any matter relevant to the subject matter involved in the action," which returns discovery to its prior scope. The Advisory Committee Note to the changes in Rule 26(b)(1) explains:

> The Committee intends that the parties and the court focus on the actual claims and defenses involved in the action. The dividing line between information relevant to the claims and defenses and that relevant only to the subject matter of the action cannot be defined with precision. A variety of types of information not directly pertinent to the incident in suit could be relevant to the claims or defenses raised in a given action. For example, other incidents of the same type, or involving the same product could be properly discoverable under the revised standard. Information about organizational arrangements or filing systems of a party could be discoverable if likely to yield or lead to the discovery of admissible information. Similarly, information that could be used to impeach a likely witness, although not otherwise relevant to the claims or defenses, might be properly discoverable. * * *

Would the result in *Lindberger* be changed by the 2000 amendment? In *Kelly*? Pretrial practice before the 2000 discovery amendment is important because a majority of states have modeled their rules on the earlier federal approach. See Oakley, *A Fresh Look at the Federal Rules in State Courts*, 3 Nev.L.J. 354 (2002/2003).

4. In WORLD WRESTLING FEDERATION ENTERTAINMENT, INC. v. WILLIAM MORRIS AGENCY, INC., 204 F.R.D. 263 (S.D.N.Y. 2001), a breach of contract action, the court refused to allow plaintiff to discover defendant's contractual agreements with third parties, explaining that the " 'treatment of one contracting party in the entertainment field does not really illuminate or is not really relevant to how another party in the entertainment field is treated.' " Is this ruling consistent with the Advisory Committee Note discussed in Note 3, above? For an analysis of decisions interpreting the new claim-or-defense relevance standard, see Rowe, *A Square Peg in a Round Hole? The 2000 Limitation on the Scope of Federal Civil Discovery*, 69 Tenn. L.Rev. 13 (2001).

5. Courts are still developing how best to effectuate the new claim-and-defense approach to relevance. What do you think of a test that looks to the "logical relationship between the information sought and possible proof or refutation of the claim or defense at trial"? What are its advantages and disadvantages? See Stempel & Herr, *Applying Amended Rule 26(b)(1) in Litigation: The New Scope of Discovery*, 199 F.R.D. 396 (2001).

3. THE CONCEPT OF PROPORTIONALITY AND DISCRETIONARY LIMITS ON DISCOVERY

Relevance under the Federal Rules is limited by the concept of proportionality, introduced by amendment in 1983 and currently set out in Rule 26(b)(2)(C). The goal of proportionality is "to promote judicial limitation of the amount of discovery on a case-by-case basis to avoid abuse or overuse of discovery * * *." 8 Wright, Miller & Marcus, Federal Practice and Procedure: Civil 2d § 2008.1. The reporter to the Advisory Committee that first adopted proportionality as a limitation on discovery called it a "180–degree shift" in discovery philosophy. See Miller, The August 1983 Amendments to the Federal Rules of Civil Procedure: Promoting Effective Case Management and Lawyer Responsibility 32–33 (Fed.Jud.Center 1984). However, in practice, the amendment has "created only a ripple" in the case law, and in 2000 the rules were amended again to underscore this limitation. 8 Wright, Miller & Marcus, Federal Practice and Procedure: Civil 2d § 2008.1. In 2006, amendments to Rule 26(b)(2)(C) imposed specific limitations on the discovery of electronically stored information, see p. 874, infra.

MARRESE v. AMERICAN ACADEMY OF ORTHOPAEDIC SURGEONS

United States Court of Appeals, Seventh Circuit, 1984 (en banc).
726 F.2d 1150, reversed on other grounds 470 U.S. 373,
105 S.Ct. 1327, 84 L.Ed.2d 274 (1985).

[Two orthopaedic surgeons initially sued in state court alleging that they were refused membership in the Academy without a hearing. Although membership in the Academy is not necessary to practice as an orthopaedic surgeon, it was alleged to confer some degree of professional advantage. Finding membership in the Academy was not an "economic necessity," the state court dismissed the complaint on the ground that no valid state law claim was stated. Plaintiffs then sued in federal court, alleging violations of the antitrust laws. In the course of discovery, plaintiffs demanded that the Academy produce correspondence and other documents relating to denials of membership applications between 1970 and 1980. The court ordered the Academy to produce the documents pursuant to an order protecting their confidentiality. The Academy refused to comply with the order and was held in criminal contempt and fined $10,000. It appealed.]

POSNER, CIRCUIT JUDGE.

* * *

A motion under Rule 26(c) to limit discovery requires the district judge to compare the hardship to the party against whom discovery is sought, if discovery is allowed, with the hardship to the party seeking discovery if discovery is denied. He must consider the nature of the hardship as well as its magnitude and thus give more weight to interests that have a distinctively social value than to purely private interests; and he must consider the possibility of reconciling the competing interests through a carefully crafted protective order. He must go through the same analysis under Rule 26(d) except that an order merely postponing a particular discovery request obviously should be granted more freely than one denying the request altogether.

* * *

* * * [T]here is in this case, if not a First Amendment right, at least a First Amendment interest, which the discovery sought by the plaintiffs would impair and which differentiates this case from the usual antitrust case, where discovery is sought of invoices or salesmen's reports or the minutes of a board of directors' meeting. * * *

* * * [O]ne does not have to be a student of Aristotle and de Tocqueville to know that voluntary associations are important to many people, Americans in particular, and that voluntary professional associations are important to American professionals (the premise of the plaintiffs' antitrust suit, as it was of their Illinois suits). Since an association would not be genuinely voluntary if the members were not allowed to consider applications for new members in confidence, the involuntary disclosure of deliberations on membership applications cannot but undermine the voluntary character of an association and therefore harm worthy interests, whether or not those interests derive any additional dignity from the First Amendment. The threat to such interests is more than speculative in this case. Dr. Marrese's counsel said at the rehearing en banc that he wants to use the membership files as a source of names of Academy members to depose in an effort to find out the motives behind their opposition to his client's application. It is hard to believe that after members of the Academy find themselves deposed for this purpose they will still be willing to offer candid evaluations of prospective members.

The other side of the coin is that barring the plaintiffs or their counsel from all access to the membership files would probably make it impossible for them to prove their antitrust case. But there were various devices that the district judge could have used to reconcile the parties' competing needs. For example, he could have examined the membership files himself *in camera*, a procedure described by the Supreme Court in a related context as "a relatively costless and eminently worthwhile method to insure that the balance between petitioners' claims of irrelevance and privilege and plaintiffs' asserted need for the documents is correctly struck." Kerr v. United States District Court, 426 U.S. 394, 405, 96 S.Ct. 2119, 2125, 48 L.Ed.2d 725 (1976). We are told the membership files may be voluminous. No doubt the files in *all* cases between 1970 and 1980 where applications for membership in the Academy were refused are voluminous, but the place to start an *in camera* examination would be with the files on Drs. Marrese and Treister. If the judge found no evidence in those files of any anticompetitive purpose attributable to the Academy, he would not have to look at any other files. This is not a class action; the plaintiffs are not suing as the representatives of other orthopaedic surgeons who have been denied membership in the Academy.

Better yet, the judge might have followed the procedure discussed in this court's recent decision in EEOC v. University of Notre Dame Du Lac, 715 F.2d 331, 338–39 (7th Cir.1983). There we ordered the files of faculty tenure deliberations edited ("redacted") to remove the names of the deliberating faculty members and any other information that might enable them to be identified, and we directed that on remand the redaction be reviewed *in camera* by the district judge, who would have the originals before him to compare with (and thereby assure the accuracy of) the redactions. Had the same procedure been followed here, the plaintiffs' counsel would have been able to read the files personally. If the files had turned out to contain evidence or leads to evidence of anticompetitive conduct, the plaintiffs' counsel could then have requested the judge to order names revealed to counsel so that the relevant individuals could be deposed. We do not think that only universities should be entitled to such consideration.

The protective order that the judge did enter ("which draws on each party's submission but parallels neither," in his words) was not well designed to protect the privacy of the Academy's members. It not only allowed the plaintiffs themselves—two disappointed applicants for membership—to read the files on their own applications; it allowed the plaintiffs' counsel "to discuss with plaintiffs the general contents" of all of the other files and to depose anyone whose name they found in the files. The order was not calculated to allay the Academy's justifiable anxiety for the confidentiality of its membership deliberations.

Rule 26(d) (control of the sequence and timing of discovery) provided another method of accommodating the competing interests here with minimal damage to either. If there is other discovery that a plaintiff must complete in order to be able to resist a motion by the defendant for summary judgment, and thus a significant probability that his case will fail regardless of what the internal files he is seeking may show, the district judge has the power under Rule 26(d) to require the plaintiff to complete the other, nonsensitive discovery first. See Wright & Miller, *Federal Practice and Procedure* 2040, 2047. And in an appropriate case he has the duty. "As a threshold matter, the court should be satisfied that a claim is not frivolous, a pretense for using discovery powers in a fishing expedition. In this case, plaintiff should show that it can establish jury issues on the essential elements of its case not the subject of the contested discovery." Bruno & Stillman, Inc. v. Globe Newspaper Co., 633 F.2d 583, 597 (1st Cir.1980). * * *

Of course, if the plaintiffs do not need anything beyond the contents of the Academy's membership files to prove their case, they cannot be asked to do any other discovery before getting access to the files. At oral argument we asked Dr. Marrese's counsel whether his discovery would be complete after he saw the membership files and followed up any leads the files contained. He answered that at that point he would file a motion for summary judgment arguing that the Academy had committed a per se violation of the Sherman Act, but that if the motion was denied he would conduct additional discovery, which he admitted would be necessary to prove a Rule of Reason violation. It is unlikely that the district judge would allow him to proceed in so piecemeal a fashion. The judge probably would tell him to complete discovery before moving for summary judgment. See 10 Wright, Miller & Kane, *Federal Practice and Procedure* § 2717 at p. 666. Assuming discovery would not be at an end when the files were turned over and any leads contained in them were tracked down, Rule 26(d) could have been used to schedule the sensitive discovery last.

We do not hold that all files of all voluntary associations are sacrosanct; we do not even hold that the membership files of an association of medical professionals are sacrosanct. They are discoverable in appropriate circumstances, subject to appropriate safeguards. But we may not ignore as judges what we know as lawyers—that discovery of sensitive documents is sometimes sought not to gather evidence that will help the party seeking discovery to prevail on the merits of his case but to coerce his opponent to settle regardless of the merits rather than have to produce the documents. * * *

* * * There is at least a hint of predatory discovery in this case in the fact that the plaintiffs did not seek access to the federal court system with its liberal discovery rules till after they had lost their state-court suit, and in the determination expressed by Dr. Marrese's counsel to use the Academy's membership files as the basis for deposing the individuals who voted against his client's membership application.

There are so many ways in which Judge Shadur could have prevented the plaintiffs from abusing the discovery process, without denying them any information essential to developing their case, that we are left with the firm conviction that the discovery order he issued, when he issued it, was erroneous. Our conclusion is consistent with the evolving concept of the district judge's managerial responsibility in complex litigation. Although amended Fed.R.Civ.P. 26(b)(1), which expands that responsibility, did not take effect until August 1, 1983, after the discovery order in issue here was issued, the Advisory Committee's Note indicates that the purpose of the amended rule is in part to remind federal district judges of their broad powers—and, we believe, correlative responsibilities—under Rule 26.

* * *

HARLINGTON WOOD, JR., CIRCUIT JUDGE, with whom CUMMINGS, CHIEF JUDGE, and CUDAHY, CIRCUIT JUDGE, join, dissenting.

* * *

Judge Posner's opinion now finds fault in the district court's failure to incorporate other protective devices for resolving the discovery dispute, such as an in camera inspection of the Academy's files or production of a redacted version of the files. I, too, believe that the trial judge could have improved on his discovery order. First, he could have been well-served by taking a look in camera at the Academy files on plaintiffs to see whether the files contained what plaintiffs claimed to need so badly, and whether the Academy had good reason to fight so desperately to keep the files out of sight.

The Supreme Court has commended an in camera view of documents in a discovery dispute to insure the striking of a proper balance between the interests in confidentiality and disclosure. Kerr v. United States District Court, * * *. Failure to make an in camera inspection, however, is not in itself an abuse of discretion. While the district court did not view the Academy's files, it apparently was aware that the state trial court had conducted an in camera inspection of the files in the earlier state court litigation between the same parties. After viewing the files, the state court ordered production over the Academy's objections. * * * Thus, one judge had viewed these materials and determined that the contents were relevant and disclosure was appropriate. We should not ignore the state court's first-hand determination. Further, the Academy has maintained that an in camera inspection would not improve the discovery order. In the Academy's view, as I understand it, an in camera inspection could lead to a discovery order which, even if including redaction of the files, would be an abuse of discretion at this stage of the litigation.

The propriety of the district court's order to produce the unredacted files also must be considered in light of the surrounding circumstances. In the early stages of this litigation, plaintiffs expressed their willingness to accept a redacted version of the Academy's files, at least as the first phase of discovery. The Academy refused plaintiffs' early offer to enter a redaction agreement, and plaintiffs later rescinded the offer. Both sides submitted proposed protective orders to the district court; apparently neither provided for redaction.

The Academy's participation in later court proceedings suggested its general approval of the protective order as it was developing. However, the Academy meanwhile continued to press its effort to avoid any discovery of its files. At oral argument, counsel for Dr. Treister stated that his client now would accept a redaction order if this would not limit the right to seek sanctions against the Academy. The Academy's position at oral argument was that any disclosure of its files, even after excision of names and other identifying information, would enable plaintiffs to determine the source of comments, thereby chilling participation in the Academy's admissions process. The Academy steadfastly maintained that no modification of the district court's protective order would be acceptable to it, and any forced disclosure of confidential information prior to the establishment of a jury issue on antitrust injury would be an abuse of discretion. Although the Academy's stonewalling now has paid off, I do not find an abuse of discretion in the district court's failure to order redaction under these circumstances.

Judge Posner's opinion suggests that the district court should have used its Rule 26(d) powers to control the sequence of discovery in this case. Discovery usually may proceed in any sequence, but the court upon motion, for the convenience of parties and in the interests of justice, may schedule the order of discovery on different issues. Fed.R.Civ.P. 26(d). Judge Posner's opinion correctly notes that the district court's power to order sequential discovery may rise to a duty in some cases, citing Bruno & Stillman, Inc. v. Globe Newspaper Co., 633 F.2d 583 (1st Cir.1980), a reporter's privilege case. The present case does not begin to fit into the *Bruno & Stillman* mold. The interests in the confidentiality of the Academy's files do not require such delicate treatment as do those involved in the case of a reporter seeking to protect confidential news sources from discovery. The district court considered and rejected the Academy's motion to bifurcate discovery. The court was satisfied that plaintiffs' claim was not frivolous, having withstood a motion to dismiss once, and again upon reconsideration. The Academy's proposal for sequential discovery would have required piecemeal discovery, which the district court found would burden plaintiffs unnecessarily since the Academy's confidentiality interests could be preserved adequately through a protective order. I would hold that the district court did not abuse its discretion by refusing to order sequential discovery.

Judge Posner's opinion discusses the misuse of discovery tools to coerce settlement, and apparently concludes that the district court's discovery order failed to prevent plaintiffs from abusing the discovery process. The opinion finds two "hints" of predatory discovery here: first, that plaintiffs sought access to federal court—and its liberal discovery rules—only after losing in the state court; and further, that plaintiffs planned to use information from the Academy's files as the basis for further discovery. The first hint merely returns us to the res judicata issue in the context of a dual court system. The second hint, plaintiffs' plan to follow up leads found in the files, is one of the conventional purposes of discovery.

Upon questioning at oral argument, counsel for the Academy labeled plaintiffs' suit a "fishing expedition," an attempt to gain access to otherwise unavailable information. Under the circumstances, however, plaintiffs' pursuit of the files and plan to seek further discovery using leads from the files were within the bounds of appropriate discovery. The discovery record in this case evidences not the slightest abuse, harassment, or coercion to pressure a settlement. Judicial concern about discovery abuse is always legitimate, but such arguments are gratuitous in the context of this case. The abuse of discovery here instead is the Academy's obstinate defiance of the trial court, which now is sanctioned by this court.

Although not condemning any one omission as an abuse of discretion, the discovery majority is left with the "firm conviction" that the district court's discovery order was erroneous. I am not. The district court sought and received proposed protective orders from the parties, and mediated negotiations on this issue. Bifurcation of discovery was not mandatory in this case, and the court reasonably provided for the Academy's confidentiality concerns through the protective order. The Academy should not now reap a windfall from reversal of the discovery order because the order did not incorporate certain provisions that the Academy still would refuse to accept. The Academy treated the trial judge's reasonable discovery order with contempt and its contempt should be recognized by this court.

* * *

Although the discovery order could have been improved, the district court's fashioning of the terms was not an abuse of discretion under the circumstances of this case. What the merits of this case would have turned out to be, we now will never know; but we must not let a prejudgment on the merits cloud our review of the discovery order. Plaintiffs * * * deserve the opportunity within reasonable limits to develop their case, and then the opportunity to try it before a judge and jury. I would affirm the district court's contempt holding, but on remand I would direct the court to view the Academy's files in camera and to consider possible redaction before actually enforcing the discovery order. * * *

NOTES AND QUESTIONS

1. A district court's discovery rulings are reviewed typically only after entry of final judgment for abuse of discretion, a standard that gives the trial court a great deal of leeway. As the Tenth Circuit has explained:

> In the discovery context, the range of permissible choices available to the district court is notably broad. This is so because discovery decisions necessarily involve an assessment of the anticipated burdens and benefits of particular discovery requests in discrete factual settings, while at the same time also requiring the trial judge to take account of the amount in controversy, the parties' resources, the importance of the issues at stake in the action, and the ability of the proposed discovery to shed light on those issues, among many other things. [Citations omitted.] * * * [F]ew discovery matters are case dispositive and * * * there is more than one way to skin the discovery cat * * *.

Regan–Touhy v. Walgreen Co., 526 F.3d 641, 647 (10th Cir. 2008). Should a party challenging a trial court's discovery ruling have to show prejudice to overturn a particular order? How can prejudice be shown?

2. Some commentators have criticized Rule 26(b)(2) for taking a cost-benefit approach to discovery that restricts disclosure "when the dollar amount or values at stake are low":

> A potential difficulty with this approach is in finding principled criteria for differentiating between various types of cases. What values should be used in deciding whether, for example, the plaintiff in a $10,000 personal injury case should be limited in the number of depositions he may take, or the plaintiff seeking reinstatement in an employment discrimination case should be prohibited from discovering documents only tangentially related to the claim, or the defendant in a $10,000,000 product liability case should be allowed to require answers to voluminous interrogatories involving the most searching details of the plaintiff's past life? Where, one may ask, are judges expected to find the criteria and analytical structure for making such judgments?

Sherman & Kinnard, *Federal Court Discovery in the 80's—Making the Rules Work*, 95 F.R.D. 245, 276 (1983). How might you respond to this criticism?

3. What weight should a court give to a party's individual resources in setting limits on discovery? Is a discovery request that otherwise would be barred or disproportionate to the needs of a case permissible simply because the party from which the discovery is sought has a "deep pocket"? On the other hand, should a relatively wealthy litigant be able to buy additional discovery by offering to pay the expenses of a financially weak litigant? Should relatively wealthy antagonists be permitted to stipulate to unlimited discovery?

4. *Twombly* may be read as suggesting that the cost of discovery is a factor to be considered in deciding a motion to dismiss, p. 568, supra. To what extent should the court's assessment of the likelihood of a party's prevailing on the merits enter, if at all, into a decision about the scope of discovery? In a case that pre-dates *Twombly*, CABLE ELECTRIC PRODUCTS, INC. v. GENMARK, INC., 586 F.Supp. 1505 (N.D.Cal.1984), vacated on other grounds 770 F.2d 1015 (Fed.Cir.1985), the court granted summary judgment to defendant in an unfair-competition action brought by the manufacturer of a light-sensitive "night light." It rejected plaintiff's request that the court not rule on the motion until it had the opportunity to complete discovery concerning actual confusion that may have been occurring in the marketplace as a result of alleged similarities in labeling and packaging the products, since the court thought that the probability was "vanishingly small" that plaintiff could uncover such evidence. If Rule 26(b)(2)(C)(iii) had been in effect when *Cable Electric Products* was decided, could the decision have been supported on the ground that "the burden or expense of the proposed discovery outweighs its likely benefit"? See generally Note, *Summary Judgment Before the Completion of Discovery: A Proposed Revision of Federal Rule of Civil Procedure 56(f)*, 24 U.Mich.J.L.Ref. 253 (1990).

SEATTLE TIMES CO. v. RHINEHART

Supreme Court of the United States, 1984.
467 U.S. 20, 104 S.Ct. 2199, 81 L.Ed.2d 17.

[Rhinehart and the Aquarian Foundation, a religious group of which he was spiritual leader, brought an action for defamation and invasion of privacy in a Washington state court against the publishers and authors of several critical articles. Pursuant to state discovery rules modeled on the Federal Rules, the trial court issued an order compelling plaintiffs to identify donors and the amounts each contributed and to produce a list of the foundation's members. However, the court also issued a protective order prohibiting defendants from publishing the information or otherwise using it except as necessary to prepare for and try the case. Plaintiffs had submitted affidavits showing that public release of donor and membership lists would adversely affect foundation membership and subject its members to harassment. Both sides appealed and the Washington Supreme Court affirmed both orders. The state Supreme Court held that the protective order served the interest of the judiciary in protecting the integrity of its discovery processes, an interest sufficient to sustain it against the claim that it infringed on First Amendment rights.]

Certiorari to the Supreme Court of Washington.

JUSTICE POWELL delivered the opinion of the Court.

* * *

* * * The Washington Civil Rules enable parties to litigation to obtain information "relevant to the subject matter involved" that they believe will be helpful in the preparation and trial of the case. Rule 26, however, must be viewed in its entirety. Liberal discovery is provided for the sole purpose of assisting in the preparation and trial, or the settlement, of litigated disputes. Because of the liberality of pretrial discovery permitted by Rule 26(b)(1), it is necessary for the trial court to have the authority to issue protective orders conferred by Rule 26(c). It is clear from experience that pretrial discovery by depositions and interrogatories has a significant potential for abuse. This abuse is not limited to matters of delay and expense; discovery also may seriously implicate privacy interests of litigants and third parties. The Rules do not distinguish between public and private information. Nor do they apply only to parties to the litigation, as relevant information in the hands of third parties may be subject to discovery.

There is an opportunity, therefore, for litigants to obtain—incidentally or purposefully—information that not only is irrelevant but if publicly released could be damaging to reputation and privacy. The government clearly has a substantial interest in preventing this sort of abuse of its processes. * * * The prevention of the abuse that can attend the coerced production of information under a State's discovery rule is sufficient justification for the authorization of protective orders.[22]

We also find that the provision for protective orders in the Washington Rules requires, in itself, no heightened First Amendment scrutiny. To be sure, Rule 26(c) confers broad discretion on the trial court to decide when a protective order is appropriate and what degree of protection is required. The Legislature of the State of Washington, following the example of the Congress in its approval of the Federal Rules of Civil Procedure, has determined that such discretion is necessary, and we find no reason to disagree. The trial court is in the best position to weigh fairly the competing needs and interests of parties affected by discovery.[23] The unique character of the discovery process requires that the trial court have substantial latitude to fashion protective orders.

The facts in this case illustrate the concerns that justifiably may prompt a court to issue a protective order. As we have noted, the trial court's order allowing discovery was extremely broad. It compelled respondents—among other things—to identify all persons who had made donations over a 5-year period to Rhinehart and the Aquarian Foundation, together with the amounts donated. In effect the order would compel disclosure of membership as well as sources of financial support. The Supreme Court of Washington found that dissemination of this information would "result in annoyance, embarrassment and even oppression." * * * It is sufficient for purposes of our decision that the highest court in the State found no abuse of discretion in the trial court's decision to issue a protective order pursuant to a constitutional state law. We therefore hold that where, as in this case, a protective order is entered on a showing of good cause as required by Rule 26(c), is limited to the context of pretrial civil discovery, and does not restrict the dissemination of the information if gained from other sources, it does not offend the First Amendment.

The judgment accordingly is

Affirmed.

[The concurring opinion of JUSTICE BRENNAN, with whom JUSTICE MARSHALL joined, is omitted.]

---

22. The Supreme Court of Washington properly emphasized the importance of ensuring that potential litigants have unimpeded access to the courts: "[A]s the trial court rightly observed, rather than expose themselves to unwanted publicity, individuals may well forego the pursuit of their just claims. The judicial system will thus have made the utilization of its remedies so onerous that the people will be reluctant or unwilling to use it, resulting in frustration of a right as valuable as that of speech itself." 654 P.2d, at 689. * * *

23. In addition, heightened First Amendment scrutiny of each request for a protective order would necessitate burdensome evidentiary findings and could lead to time-consuming interlocutory appeals, as this case illustrates. * * *

NOTES AND QUESTIONS

1. What is "good cause" for a protective order under Rule 26(c)? The courts generally have required the moving party to demonstrate that "disclosure will work a clearly defined and very serious injury." Publicker Indus., Inc. v. Cohen, 733 F.2d 1059, 1071 (3d Cir.1984). The movant must make a showing "by specific examples or articulated reasoning," Cipollone v. Liggett Group, Inc., 785 F.2d 1108, 1121 (3d Cir.1986), certiorari denied 484 U.S. 976, 108 S.Ct. 487, 98 L.Ed.2d 485 (1987), and cannot rely on "stereotyped and conclusory statements." General Dynamics Corp. v. Selb Mfg. Co., 481 F.2d 1204, 1212 (8th Cir.1973). Courts then use a balancing test to determine whether the protective order should issue. Pansy v. Borough of Stroudsburg, 23 F.3d 772, 787 (3d Cir.1994). What factors ought the court weigh? Does a balancing test of this character make application of the discovery rules unpredictable and uneven?

2. Do additional factors come into play when a party seeks discovery from a top government official? Federal appellate courts generally permit discovery of such officials only in "extraordinary circumstances." Arnold v. Pennsylvania, Dept. of Transp., 477 F.3d 105, 423 (3d Cir. 2007). However, in rare cases, even Presidents "have responded to written interrogatories, given depositions and provided videotaped trial testimony." Clinton v. Jones, 520 U.S. 681, 691 n.14, 117 S.Ct. 1636, 1643 n.14, 137 L.Ed.2d 945, 959 n.14 (1997). What factors ought to guide the District Court's approach to discovery in these circumstances? Of what significance are case management techniques that allow the court to cabin discovery in ways that minimize its potentially disruptive effect on executive function? See Ashcroft v. Iqbal, 556 U.S. ___, 129 S.Ct. 1937, ___ L.Ed.2d ___ (2009).

3. To what extent is it relevant that a suit is chiefly brought for the purpose of obtaining private information about the defendant for purposes of disclosing it publicly? Suppose a third person, desirous of obtaining such private information, finances plaintiff's suit?

4. Should the court have issued an order denying or compelling discovery in each of these cases:

(a) MUTUAL OF OMAHA INSURANCE CO. v. GARRIGAN, 31 Ohio Misc. 1, 4, 285 N.E.2d 395, 396–97 (Com.Pl.1971). Plaintiff insurance company brought an action against the widow of its insured, asking for a declaration that the insured's death by carbon monoxide poisoning had not been accidental and hence was not covered by the policy. The company sought to discover the corpse, which would have required disinterment.

(b) WILLIAMS v. THOMAS JEFFERSON UNIVERSITY, 343 F.Supp. 1131, 1132 (E.D.Pa.1972). Plaintiff, in a medical malpractice action involving abortion, sought to discover the names of women who previously had abortions at defendant hospital. The stated purpose was to gather evidence to impeach testimony expected to be given by defendant doctor.

(c) RASMUSSEN v. SOUTH FLORIDA BLOOD SERVICE, INC., 500 So.2d 533 (Fla.1987), and SNYDER v. MEKHJIAN, 125 N.J. 328, 593 A.2d 318 (1991). In both of these cases, persons who claimed to have received an

HIV-positive blood transfusion sought discovery from a blood bank as to the identity of the blood donor.

(d) BUCHER v. RICHARDSON HOSPITAL AUTHORITY, 160 F.R.D. 88 (N.D. Tex. 1994). Parents sued a hospital alleging that their daughter was abused sexually while she was a patient there receiving treatment. Defendant sought to depose the minor. In support of the motion to quash, a psychiatrist testified that the minor "has an impulse control disorder and is a suicide risk if deposed."

5. It has become commonplace in large cases for parties to stipulate to protective orders negotiated by opposing counsel. And judges generally assent to these agreements, in large part to move cases along and avoid controversy. The stipulations typically provide for "umbrella" protection for confidential information, which is defined as any information that is designated "confidential" by the producing party. The result of these orders is that virtually all nonpublic documents are designated confidential without any individualized review. See Moskowitz, *Discovering Discovery: Non–Party Access to Pretrial Information in the Federal Courts 1938–2006*, 78 U. Colo. L. Rev. 817 (2007). Why have these orders become so common? What is the strategic significance for a defendant of a confidentiality order? Does disclosure to third persons open the door to misuse of the court system for blackmail or extortion through the threat of suits involving sensitive issues? What does a plaintiff's attorney gain by agreeing to a broad protective order? Are these orders consistent with the Supreme Court's analysis in *Seattle Times*? Or is some degree of judicial review necessary? Should umbrella orders be enforced as written? What standard should a court apply if asked to modify an existing protective order to permit the disclosure of discovered material to non-parties? Is it relevant that the matter shielded from public view by the protective order is alleged to impact on the public health and safety? For a discussion of these issues, see Miller, *Confidentiality, Protective Orders, and Public Access to the Courts*, 105 Harv.L.Rev. 427 (1991). On protective orders generally, see Friedenthal, *Secrecy and Confidentiality in Civil Litigation: Discovery and Party Agreements*, 9 J. of L. & Pol'y 61 (2000). For a range of views on the subject, see *Symposium: Secrecy in Litigation*, 81 Chi.–Kent L. Rev. 305 (2006).

SECTION B. MANDATORY DISCLOSURE AND THE DISCOVERY PLAN

1. MANDATORY DISCLOSURE

Read Federal Rule of Civil Procedure 26(a) in the Supplement.

CUMMINGS v. GENERAL MOTORS CORP.

United States Court of Appeals, Tenth Circuit, 2004.
365 F.3d 944.

KELLY, JR., CIRCUIT JUDGE.

Gregory and Tracey Cummings brought this suit against General Motors Corporation ("GM") to recover for injuries Mrs. Cummings sustained in an automobile accident * * *. A jury returned a verdict in favor of GM, and the Cummings appeal, asserting that the court should have directed a verdict in their favor based on the evidence, and that the district court abused its discretion with regard to several discovery rulings.* * * [We affirm in all respects.]

Background

Gregory and Tracey Cummings were involved in a car accident on the evening of September 13, 1998 in rural Carter County, Oklahoma. Mr. Cummings was driving a 1995 Pontiac Grand Am with his wife, Tracey, in the front passenger seat. Their children were in the back seat, with the three-month-old in a car seat behind Mrs. Cummings. Mr. Cummings ran a "partially obscured" stop sign at a T-type intersection and drove off the road, through a ditch, and into a field. * * * Although the other passengers sustained only minor injuries, Mrs. Cummings sustained a compression fracture of the third vertebra resulting in paraplegia. * * *

The Cummings brought this suit against GM, asserting that Mrs. Cummings sustained such severe injuries as a result of the design of the seat belt and the seat, as well as GM's failure to warn. Prior to trial, the parties engaged in multiple discovery disputes, including disputes over the adequacy of responses to requests for production, expert witness designations, depositions, and electronic discovery. * * * These disputes resulted in three motions to compel by the Cummings and several motions for protective orders by GM. The magistrate judge addressed the majority of these disputes in an order dated June 18, 2002, in which the judge denied Plaintiffs' motions, granted Defendant's motions for protective orders, and granted Defendant's [sic] their attorney's fees and costs. * * * The district court reviewed the Plaintiffs' motions de novo and affirmed the magistrate's findings in all respects. * * *

At trial, GM countered the Cummings' claims with evidence that there was no defect in either the seat, the seat belt system, or the warning. * * * GM contended that Mrs. Cummings's injuries resulted not from any defect, but rather from a combination of the forces exerted on her during the accident and her position and posture at the time of the accident. Although the Cummings offered evidence that Mrs. Cummings had her seat angled back approximately 25 degrees, * * * GM's experts testified that she was most likely reclined at 40–45 degrees at the time of the accident * * *; sitting slouched in the seat * * *; and/or turned to attend to the children in the back seat * * *. The Cummings argued that such a conclusion was impossible because there was a rear-facing child safety seat located behind Mrs. Cummings that prevented her from reclining her seat. GM offered evidence that the child seat was actually installed in a forward-facing direction at the time of the accident, thus allowing the front passenger seat to recline.

At the close of all the evidence, out of the presence and hearing of the jury, both the Cummings and GM moved for judgment as a matter of law. * * * GM made its motion first, moving for judgment as a matter of law with regard to all claims, including the alleged defective seat, seat belt, failure to warn, and punitive damages claims. The Cummings responded to GM's contentions, and then the court directed them to make their motion for judgment as a matter of law. Counsel for the Cummings stated:

> Your Honor, I would move for judgment as a matter of law on the foreseeable misuse or the so-called misuse defense. Throughout the trial we have had to listen to [General Motors] accuse Mrs. Cummings of reclining the seat. * * * Your Honor knows foreseeable misuse is not a defense. No one denies that this is foreseeable misuse of a seat. No one denies that they built the capability into the seat to do it. They knew the risk, that they knew people would be injured if they did that. No one whatsoever denies that in this trial. This jury should be instructed that reclining the seat is not a defense, and that if this Defendant built a recliner seat that is dangerous, this Defendant should be held legally responsible for the consequences. That's the law in Oklahoma.

* * * The court denied both motions.

The jury returned a verdict for GM, finding GM not liable for any design defect or failure to warn. * * * The Cummings failed to make any motions following the return of the verdict. * * * The Cummings filed a timely appeal, asserting that (1) they were entitled to judgment as a matter of law with regard to liability, and (2) the trial court abused its discretion in its rulings on various discovery motions.

One month after the verdict, and after filing the appeal, the Cummings discovered six videos of child safety seat acceleration tests conducted by GM and produced by GM in an unrelated trial. The videos show tests by GM involving child-sized dummies in forward-facing child car seats placed in the back seat. In the videos, the children are thrown from the car seat during various accident simulations. The Cummings argue the tests fall within their prior requests for production and would have demonstrated that it was impossible for Mrs. Cummings to have her seat fully reclined at the time of the accident, as their child would have been injured had the child been in a forward-facing child restraint.

The Cummings did not immediately move for relief upon discovery of the videos. Instead, they waited seven months to file a motion for relief under Federal Rule * * * 60(b). The district court, finding the motion both untimely and lacking in support, denied the motion, and the Cummings appeal. The appeals have been consolidated and are addressed jointly below.

Discussion

* * *

B. Discovery Rulings

* * *

The Cummings' reliance on Rule 26 is * * * misplaced. The magistrate ruled the newest version of Rule 26 would govern in this case, including the 2000 amendments, * * * and the Cummings did not object to this holding. Under the 2000 amendments, a party's "initial disclosure obligation . . . has been narrowed." * * * Under this rule, a party is not obligated "to disclose witnesses or documents, whether favorable or unfavorable, that it does not intend to use." * * * *see Gluck v. Ansett Austl. Ltd.*, 204 F.R.D. 217, 221–22 (D.D.C. 2001) (holding under the new version of Rule 26 that the opposing party was not required to produce information with regard to potential witnesses because "the essential inquiry is whether the disclosing party intends to use the witness.").

* * *

Failure to disclose information requested during discovery may constitute "misconduct" under Rule 60(b)(3). * * *

We * * * find lacking the Cummings' argument that GM was required to disclose the video tapes under Federal Rule of Civil Procedure 26. To the extent the Cummings argue GM is required to automatically produce any document "relevant" to the disputed facts at issue in this case, * * * their reference to the prior version of the rule is inappropriate. Rule 26(a)(1) requires that parties make initial disclosures of "all documents, data compilations, and tangible things that are in the possession, custody, or control of the party and that the disclosing party may use to support its claim or defenses, unless solely for impeachment." * * * [This provision has been renumbered as Rule 26(a)(1)(A)(ii) and its language has been altered without any change in substance.] Under the applicable version of the rule, GM was not required to automatically disclose documents that it did not intend to use. * * *

NOTES AND QUESTIONS

1. The Federal Rules were amended in 1993 to require the parties to transmit information "without awaiting a discovery request." Fed. R. Civ. P. 26(a)(1)(A). The proposal to establish a duty of mandatory disclosure generated intense controversy among judges, practitioners, and legal scholars, and the Supreme Court divided, 6–3, in its support of the provision. Arguments against mandatory disclosure focused on its inconsistency with adversarial principles and concerns that it would increase expense and cause delay.

Huang, *Mandatory Disclosure: A Controversial Device with No Effects*, 21 Pace L. Rev. 203, 205 (2000). See also Sorenson, *Disclosure Under Federal Rule of Civil Procedure 26(a)—'Much Ado About Nothing?'*, 46 Hastings L.J. 679 (1995). Although early commentators expressed concern that mandatory disclosure would decrease the likelihood of settlement, see Issacharoff & Loewenstein, *Unintended Consequences of Mandatory Disclosure*, 73 Texas L. Rev. 753 (1995), more recent analysis suggests that mandatory disclosure, because it equalizes the availability of credible information, reduces the number of disputes that proceed to trial. See Farmer & Pecorino, *Civil Litigation with Mandatory Discovery and Voluntary Transmission of Private Information,* 34 J. Legal Stud. 137 (2005).

2. *Cummings* focuses on that part of the 2000 amendment to Rule 26(a)(1) that requires a party, as part of its initial disclosure, to produce only information that will "support its claims and defenses." Previously, each party had to provide information "relevant to disputed facts alleged with particularity in the pleadings." The 2000 amendment also exempts from mandatory initial and pretrial disclosures information to be used "solely for impeachment." What is the purpose of the exemption? What type of information is "solely for impeachment"?

3. What does mandatory disclosure require in terms of actual production of documents? In COMAS v. UNITED TELEPHONE CO. OF KANSAS, 1995 WL 476691 (D. Kan. 1995), the Magistrate Judge explained:

> Initial disclosures may be made by describing or categorizing potentially relevant materials so that the opposing party may "make an informed decision regarding which documents might need to be examined." Fed. R.Civ.P. 26(a)(1) Advisory Committee's Notes (1993 Am.). The rule does not require that either party produce documents at this initial stage. If only a description or categorization is provided, "the other part[y] [is] expected to obtain the documents desired by proceeding under Rule 34 or through informal requests."
>
> Rule 26(a)(1) allows initial disclosures to be made by producing copies of the relevant documents. Parties, therefore, may agree to produce all relevant documents without discovery requests. Production at this stage speeds the discovery process.

4. As adopted in 1993, mandatory disclosure applied to every type of case. In 2000, the amendment added a new provision, Rule 26(a)(1)(B), excluding eight types of cases in which there is little need for discovery or in which a party is likely to be conducting his or her own case. Is it appropriate in this circumstance to depart from the rule of uniform rule making? Should the court have discretion to order mandatory disclosure? See Subrin, *Uniformity in Procedural Rules and the Attributes of a Sound Procedural System: The Case for Presumptive Limits*, 49 Ala. L. Rev. 79 (1997).

5. *Cummings* focuses on the initial stage of mandatory disclosure. Rule 26(a) also contemplates mandatory disclosure later in a litigation regarding expert reports and identification of trial witnesses and documents. See p. 917, infra.

6. Some states have amended their civil procedure rules to mandate disclosure of information without a party request. For the experience in Texas, Arizona, Illinois, and Colorado, see Moskowitz, *Rediscovering Discovery: State Procedural Rules and the Level Playing Field*, 54 Rutgers L. Rev. 595 (2002).

NOTE ON DISCOVERY OF A PARTY'S FINANCIAL WORTH AND INSURANCE COVERAGE

Should a party be able to discover her opponent's financial worth or learn whether the adversary is covered by liability insurance? As amended in 1970, Rule 26 permits discovery of insurance agreements, despite the fact that such materials are not admissible at trial. The justification was that disclosure of insurance coverage "will enable counsel for both sides to make the same realistic appraisal of the case, so that settlement and litigation strategy are based on knowledge and not speculation." Proposed Amendments to the Federal Rules of Civil Procedure Relating to Discovery, reprinted at 48 F.R.D. 487, 499 (1969–70). Rule 26 was further amended in 1993 and Rule 26(a)(1)(A)(iv) now includes insurance agreements among the mandated initial disclosures. Is it appropriate to single out insurance agreements from other information bearing on a party's wealth? See 8 Wright, Miller & Marcus, Federal Practice and Procedure: Civil 2d § 2010. Under what circumstances will a party's financial worth be relevant to a lawsuit? See Powell & Leiferman, *Results Most Embarrassing: Discovery and Admissibility of Net Worth of the Defendant*, 40 Baylor L. Rev. 527 (1988).

2. THE DISCOVERY PLAN

Read Federal Rule of Civil Procedure 26(f) in the Supplement.

NOTES AND QUESTIONS

1. An important part of the judicial response to concerns about discovery abuse is reflected in the series of amendments to Rules 16 and 26 to encourage active judicial supervision of the discovery process. In 1980, Rule 26(f) was adopted to provide for a discovery conference among the parties and the court, but it was not contemplated as a routine procedure. Then, in 1983, Rule 16 was amended to encourage district courts to schedule early pretrial conferences and required them, after consultation with the parties by pretrial conference or otherwise, to issue scheduling orders limiting the time for the parties, among other things, to complete discovery. In 1993, Rule 26(f) was altered and harmonized with Rule 16. Rule 26(f) was amended to require the parties to meet by themselves to arrange for mandatory disclosures under Rule 26(a)(1) and to develop a comprehensive proposed discovery plan that

they then present to the court prior to the time the court's scheduling order is due under Rule 16(b). However, courts were free to issue standing orders that exempted all, or certain types of cases, from the Rule 26(f) requirements. In 2000, Rule 26(f) was amended once again. First, it eliminated the need of the parties to "meet," instead allowing them to "confer" to avoid logistical problems that sometimes sent litigants to court for relief. Second, it eliminated standing exemption orders but left intact the power of the court to exempt or alter the requirements for any particular case before it. (The amended rule does exempt those special cases that are exempted from mandatory disclosure under Rule 26(a)(1).) These Rules are designed to counter the procrastination and delay that is natural to busy lawyers and to give the courts ample control over the discovery process. Rule 26(f) also expects the parties, when conferring, to consider "the possibilities for promptly settling or resolving the case." How does the early exchange of information promote that goal?

2. Taking guidance from federal practice, some states now authorize or require the parties to meet and plan discovery as part of pretrial preparation. One commentary reports:

> Adoptions generally follow two different models. Like the federal courts, a half-dozen make planning meetings mandatory in all cases. In these states, as in the federal courts, absent a court order, discovery may not occur prior to the planning meeting. More states, however, make the planning meetings optional unless ordered by the courts either sua sponte or after motion. In some of these states, the meetings can become required if either party requests one.

Weber, *Potential Innovations in Civil Discovery: Lessons for California from the State and Federal Courts*, 32 McGeorge L. Rev. 1051, 1064 (2001).

SECTION C. THE MECHANICS OF REQUESTED DISCOVERY

1. DEPOSITIONS

Read Federal Rules of Civil Procedure 26(d), 30, and 31 in the Supplement.

An oral deposition allows a party to question any person (the "deponent"), whether a party or not, under oath. The Federal Rules spell out in detail when, how, before whom, and on what notice as to time and place a deposition may be taken (see Federal Rules 28, 29, 30, 31, and 32(d)). Invariably, the parties designate as officer the reporter who records the questions, the answers, and any objections made by the parties or by the witness. Under Federal Rule 30(d)(1), "a deposition is limited to 1 day of 7 hours," but the court may authorize additional time "if needed to fairly examine the deponent or if the deponent, another person, or any other circumstance impedes or delays the examination." When the deposition is concluded, the reporter prepares a transcript, which the deponent then is called upon to sign. Federal Rule 30(a)(2)(A)(i) sets a presumptive limit of ten depositions for each party.

An attorney schedules a deposition merely by serving a notice on the opposing attorney. The notice must include the name and address of the deponent, if known, and the date, time, and place of the deposition. If the deponent is a party, the notice is sufficient to require the party's appearance, and a subpoena is unnecessary. The notice may include a demand that the party produce documents and other items of evidence at the deposition, in which case the procedure of Rule 34 applies.

Under Federal Rule 30(b)(6) an attorney may notice the deposition of a corporation or association, requiring the latter to produce the person or persons having knowledge of the subject matter upon which the deposition is to be taken. Of course, the party seeking the information must detail the issues that are to be explored in order that the organization can ascertain which of its personnel has the relevant knowledge. This form of corporate deposition is useful particularly when the party taking the deposition is unaware of which individual or individuals within a large organization has the information that is needed.

If the deponent is not a party, the notice of deposition will not be sufficient to compel the nonparty's appearance. There is no requirement that a nonparty be subpoenaed to a deposition. However, a nonparty is not subject to any sanction if he is not subpoenaed and does not appear, or if he appears but fails to bring requested documents or other items. A person who fails to respond to a subpoena will be subject to a citation for contempt of court. In addition, if a party notices a deposition but does not subpoena the witness and the witness fails to appear, that party may be ordered to pay the reasonable expenses, including attorneys' fees, of any other party for wasting time appearing at the place where the deposition was to be taken. Thus, unless full cooperation of the nonparty witness is certain, the use of a subpoena is advisable. Finally, the presumptive seven-hour limit on a deposition may be ineffective to protect a nonparty from a long, intense session because the parties can agree among themselves to a longer deposition for a nonparty.

The usual expectation is that a deposition will proceed without court involvement. The deponent usually will answer even those questions to which counsel object, unless the deponent's counsel instructs him not to answer. Counsel interpose objections at depositions to preserve their right to object to another party's use of the deposition's transcript at trial. Counsel must object at the deposition if the ground for the objection is one that might be corrected at the time. Under Rule 30(c)(2), a deponent may be instructed not to answer only when necessary "to preserve a privilege, to enforce a limitation ordered by the court, or to present a motion under Rule 30(d)(3)" to terminate or limit an examination that is oppressive or conducted in bad faith. Moreover, Rule 30(d)(2) authorizes the imposition of costs and attorney's fees to sanction any culpable individual who "impedes, delays, or frustrates the fair examination of the deponent."

POLYCAST TECHNOLOGY CORP. v. UNIROYAL, INC.

United States District Court, Southern District of New York, 1990.
1990 WL 138968.

FRANCIS, UNITED STATES MAGISTRATE.

In October, 1986, Uniroyal, Inc. ("Uniroyal") sold its wholly-owned subsidiary, Uniroyal Plastics Company, Inc. ("Plastics") to Polycast Technology Corporation ("Polycast"). In this action, Polycast alleges that it entered into this transaction on the basis of misleading financial information that Uniroyal provided about Plastics. * * *

* * *

The parties to this action have taken substantial discovery from a non-party, Deloitte & Touche ("Deloitte"). In its incarnation as Deloitte Haskins & Sells, Deloitte had performed auditing services for both Uniroyal and Polycast prior to the sale of Plastics. After the transaction was completed, Deloitte continued as Polycast's independent auditors, reviewing Plastics' operations.

* * *

Durant Deposition

The second pending discovery issue concerns the proposed deposition of Gregory Durant, a Deloitte employee who was the on-site manager of an audit of Plastics that commenced immediately after the acquisition of that entity by Uniroyal on October 31, 1986. Deloitte now seeks a protective order barring Mr. Durant's deposition on the grounds that the information obtained would not be relevant and that it would, in any event, be duplicative of the deposition testimony of Michael Bowman, Deloitte's engagement partner on the audit.

Orders barring the taking of * * * depositions altogether are both unusual and disfavored. * * * On the other hand, non-party witnesses may be subject to somewhat greater protection against costly but marginally relevant discovery than are the parties. * * *

However, even if some heightened consideration should be paid to Deloitte as a non-party witness, it would still be inappropriate to foreclose the deposition of Mr. Durant. Polycast alleges that it bought Plastics in reliance on a representation in October, 1986, that the year-end earnings of Plastics would be approximately $13.3 million. According to Polycast, the actual 1986 earnings for Plastics were $5.25 million, and Polycast therefore contends that it paid an inflated price for Plastics based on

Uniroyal's misrepresentations. Uniroyal argues, however, that Polycast has understated the actual earnings of Plastics for 1986. Since the $5.5 million figure is derived at least in part from the audit conducted by Deloitte for the first ten months of that year, that audit is an entirely proper subject of inquiry. Moreover, the fact that Mr. Bowman has provided substantial deposition testimony about the audit does not relieve Deloitte of the obligation of producing Mr. Durant for examination. There were some gaps in Mr. Bowman's testimony, attributable to a quite understandable inability to recall every detail of the audit process. More significantly, Mr. Durant was present at the location where the audit was conducted and is in a better position to describe the workings of the audit team and its interactions with Plastics' employees. His deposition will therefore go forward.

At the same time, Uniroyal has already obtained from other Deloitte witnesses as well as from discovery of the parties substantial evidence concerning the audit. Mr. Durant's role will largely be to fill in the interstices in a picture that should otherwise be substantially complete. Accordingly, the parties' examination of him shall be limited to one full day of deposition.

Conclusion

* * * Deloitte's request for a protective order barring the deposition of Gregory Durant is denied, but that deposition shall be limited to one day.

NOTES AND QUESTIONS

1. The oral deposition has been called "[t]he most important of the discovery devices":

> It is the only significant discovery device that may be directed against any person, and is not confined to parties to the action. It is the only discovery device that permits examination and cross-examination of a live witness by counsel, where there is no opportunity to reflect and carefully shape the information given. Thus, despite its expense, it is the most valuable device if the deponent has important information.

Wright & Kane, Law of Federal Courts § 84 (6th ed. 2002). For a careful assessment of the costs and benefits of deposition practice, see Legg, *The United States Deposition—Time for Adoption in Australian Civil Procedure?*, 31 Melb. U. L. Rev. 146 (2007).

2. Under the 1938 version of Federal Rule 30, the parties competed to take the first deposition, in an attempt to pin down an opponent before submitting himself or his own witnesses to the discovery process. How does the 1938 version differ from present deposition practice? Have amendments, including mandatory disclosure and the discovery conference, altered the parties' strategic approach to priority? See 8 Wright, Miller & Marcus, Federal Practice and Procedure: Civil 2d §§ 2045–47; *Developments in the Law—Discovery*, 74 Harv.L.Rev. 940, 954–58 (1961).

3. What if a corporate party whose deposition is noted under Rule 30(b)(6) deliberately selects a person to testify who appears for the deposition but who lacks information sufficient to respond to the questions asked? Can the court order sanctions under Rule 37(d) without first issuing an order to compel discovery and giving the deponent an opportunity to comply? For a rejection of the literal reading of the Rule, see Black Horse Lane Assoc., L.P. v. Dow Chem. Corp., 228 F.3d 275 (3d Cir. 2000) (a lack of knowledge by the selected deponent is tantamount to a failure to appear under Rule 37(d)).

4. When the Federal Rules were first adopted, depositions typically were recorded by court reporters using stenography. In 1970, the rules were amended to allow for the taking of videotaped depositions by stipulation of the parties or by court order. The 1993 amendment gives the party noticing the deposition a right to choose how the deposition will be memorialized. What are the advantages and disadvantages of videotaping a deposition? Why might a written transcript be useful? See Henke & Margolis, *The Taking and Use of Video Depositions: An Update*, 17 Rev. Litig. 1 (1998). One commentator suggests that the introduction of the right to take videotaped depositions is "a harbinger of something that could arrive with the computer revolution—the virtual courtroom. * * * [W]ith the advent of teleconferencing, one could adapt depositions to avoid costly travel, and perhaps to produce digital output that one could use to create a video trial product that would supersede the contemporary trial." Marcus, *Confronting the Future: Coping with Discovery of Electronic Material*, 64–SUM Law & Contemp. Probs. 253, 271–72 (2001).

5. The question of whether plaintiff could videotape defendants' depositions arose in WILSON v. OLATHE BANK, 184 F.R.D. 395 (D. Kan. 1999), a class action under the federal racketeering statute filed on behalf of individuals who had invested in distributorships to get the rights to sell Disney merchandise or cigars on carousels. The District Court rejected defendants' motion for a protective order to block the videotaping of their depositions:

> Plaintiffs submit that Fed.R.Civ.P. 30(b)(2) [This provision has been renumbered as Rule 30(b)(3) and the language has been altered.] permits depositions to be videotaped. They contend, furthermore, that videotaping will facilitate the ability of the court to rule on possible claims that counsel or witnesses have violated the specific code of conduct required by Judge Marten at depositions. They further argue that videotaping is necessary, if the court orders separate trials for some 700 plaintiffs. They contend that no defendant is required to bear any additional expense. They deny any impracticality of videotaping.
>
> * * * [Rule 30(b)(3)] specifically permits depositions to be recorded by nonstenographic means, unless the court orders otherwise. No party suggests that the court has disallowed videotaped depositions. * * * The notes of the advisory committee recognize that circumstances may warrant objections to the nonstenographic recording of a deposition. *Id.* Fed.R.Civ.P. 26(c) provides a proper procedure to present such objections to the court. That Rule authorizes a protective order against annoyance, embarrassment, oppression, and undue burden or expense.
>
> Movants object to videotaping their depositions, because there is no indication that they will be unavailable for trial. * * * [Rule 30(b)(3)]

> contains no requirement regarding the availability of the witness for trial. The objection shows no annoyance, embarrassment, oppression, or undue burden or expense. The court overrules the objection.
>
> Movants further argue that it is more expensive to videotape a deposition than to record it stenographically. * * * [Rule 30(b)(3)] provides that "the party taking the deposition shall bear the cost of the recording." Thus, the only expense which might be borne by movants is the purchase of a copy of the videotape. * * * Nothing requires movants * * * to purchase a copy of the video.
>
> Movants also argue that they may face increased taxable costs as well. * * * The speculative possibility that a party may incur increased taxable costs constitutes no good cause to prohibit videotaping. * * * The court does not find that increased taxable costs necessarily equates with undue expense within the meaning of Fed.R.Civ.P. 26(c).
>
> * * *
>
> Movants lastly argue that it is impractical to videotape the depositions, due to the number of parties and attorneys in this case. Movants provide no showing of annoyance, embarrassment, oppression, or undue burden or expense to support the argument. They have thus provided no basis to prohibit the chosen method of recording. The court knows of no principle which the number of parties and attorneys who attend a deposition determines whether it may be videotaped.

Id. at 395–99.

2. DEPOSITION UPON WRITTEN QUESTIONS

Rule 31 authorizes the taking of depositions upon written questions from parties and nonparties. The answers are given orally after the "officer" puts the questions to the deponent. In practice, written depositions are rarely used. 8A Wright, Miller & Marcus, Federal Practice and Procedure: Civil 2d § 2131.

WATSON v. LOWCOUNTRY RED CROSS, 974 F.2d 482 (4th Cir. 1992), involved a wrongful death action on behalf of an infant who died from HIV following a blood transfusion. Defendants were the Red Cross and a local hospital. Plaintiff, alleging that the Red Cross negligently screened the donor who had supplied blood for the decedent infant, sought discovery from the donor. The court permitted plaintiff to propound interrogatories, to which the Red Cross could object. "The approved questions would then be given to the donor's lawyer to forward to his client, and the answers (with the donor's verification redacted) would then be delivered to the parties." Id. at 484. The court noted: "Because these 'interrogatories' are directed at a non-party, they are more properly characterized as 'depositions upon written questions' * * *." Id. at 484 n.3. Questions included:

1. On how many occasions in your life have you donated blood?

2. Thinking back now to February 26 or 27, 1985, to the best of your recollection, were you aware at that time that donated blood can sometimes transmit disease to a patient who receives that blood in a transfusion?

* * *

5. When you gave blood on February 26 or 27, 1985, were you asked about any diseases or behaviors or experiences that put you at risk for these diseases?

* * *

8. Were you at all concerned on February 26 or 27, 1985 that you might be at risk for HIV infection (infection with Human Immunodeficiency Virus) or AIDS?

9. On February 26 or 27, 1985, in the course of your preparing to give blood, did the Red Cross staff or volunteers give you any written or verbal information about AIDS risks?

* * *

13. On February 26 & 27, 1985 could you read?

* * *

16. On February 26 or 27, 1985, did the American Red Cross staff provide you with a private place so you could tell them in privacy any concerns you had about your donating blood?

17. Why did you proceed to donate blood on February 26, or February 27, 1985?

(Check any that apply.)

______ I did not know that I was in a high risk group for AIDS.

______ I was not provided private area to confidentially disclose being in high risk group for AIDS.

______ I thought it would be [sic] opportunity to be tested for AIDS.

______ I knew I was in a high risk group for AIDS but had a great desire to donate blood.

______ I did not know blood would be used for blood transfusion into a patient.

______ Others (please specify).

18. Had you ever been an inmate in a state prison or local jail prior to 2/27/85?

Id. at 490–91.

NOTE AND QUESTION

Why might defendant's counsel have found a written deposition more useful in *Watson* than an oral one? Why was this approach preferable to Rule 33 interrogatories? See Schmertz, *Written Depositions Under the Federal and State Rules as Cost–Effective Discovery at Home and Abroad,* 16 Villa.L.Rev. 7 (1970).

3. INTERROGATORIES TO PARTIES

Read Federal Rule of Civil Procedure 33 in the Supplement.

Written interrogatories allow one party to send to another a series of questions to be answered under oath within a specific time. The procedure is extremely simple. No court order is required and no officers need be appointed; the entire exchange is accomplished by mail. If a question is thought to be improper, the responding party may say so rather than answering. The interrogating party then has the option of seeking a court order requiring an answer. An important advantage of interrogatories exists to the extent that a party has a duty to respond to interrogatories not only on the basis of her own knowledge but also with regard to the knowledge of other persons, including her lawyers, employees, and other agents, that reasonably can be obtained through investigation. Under Rule 33(b)(1)(B) such an obligation clearly exists for a party who is a public or private corporation, an association, or a government entity. Unfortunately, however, the language of Rule 33(b)(1)(A) is unclear as to an individual party, even one who operates a large sole proprietorship. On its face, and contrasted with Rule 33(b)(1)(B), it appears to require such a party to respond only on the basis of her personal knowledge. Prior to the amendment, that was altered solely for style, the Rule could have been read to require all parties to respond on the basis of their investigations and it seems likely that that will be the way in which the courts will interpret the current rule.

Interrogatories had been cited as the most abused of the available discovery devices and the Federal Rules have been amended a number of times to police the process. In 1980, then Rule 33(c) (now Rule 33(d)) was amended to require a party exercising the option to produce its business records to specify the records from which the answer can be found in sufficient detail to permit the interrogating party to locate and to identify them as readily as can the party served. The clarification sought to prevent the party served with interrogatories from directing the party who propounded them to a mass of business records or by offering to make all their records available.

IN RE AUCTION HOUSES ANTITRUST LITIGATION

United States District Court, Southern District of New York, 2000.
190 F.R.D. 444.

KAPLAN, DISTRICT JUDGE.

[The lawsuit involved a class-action challenge to an alleged price-fixing conspiracy by companies "in the business of providing auction services of fine and applied arts, furniture, antiques, automobiles, collectibles and other items." In re Auction Houses Antitrust Litigation, 193 F.R.D. 162, 163 (2000). The discovery dispute concerned efforts to obtain information about the auction houses' dealings outside the United States.]

* * *

Christie's has produced handwritten notes from the files of its former chief executive officer, Christopher Davidge (the "Davidge Documents"), which apparently are important evidence of the alleged conspiracy. Defendant A. Alfred Taubman, former chairman of Sotheby's, served interrogatories on Christie's by which it sought a great many details concerning the Davidge Documents, including such details as their authors, the meaning of abbreviations used in them, the antecedents of pronouns (e.g., "our," "her," etc.) and the like. Christie's objected to substantially all of these interrogatories, principally on the ground that they "seek[ ] information that is not in [its] possession, custody, or control." * * * In conversations among counsel, Christie's has taken the position that it cannot answer these interrogatories because the person with knowledge is Davidge, whom it allegedly no longer controls. Taubman disputes this assertion and seeks an order compelling Christie's to respond fully, including in its response information it contends is available to it from Davidge.

In late December 1999, Christie's International PLC entered into an agreement with Davidge concerning the termination of his employment (the "Agreement"). The Agreement provides for the payment by Christie's to Davidge of £5 million of which at least £2 million has not yet been paid. Christie's obligation to pay it is conditioned upon Davidge's performance of his contractual obligations. Further, paragraph 14 of the Agreement states:

> "You [i.e., Davidge] undertake promptly to provide all such information to the Company [Christie's] or its advisers or agents as is within your knowledge that may from time to time be required by the Company, in the discretion of the board of directors of the Company, in relation to the business of any Group Company during the period of your employment and to provide to the Company details of all matters, including all actual or potential transactions in respect of which the Company's knowledge rests solely or principally with you. You undertake further to co-operate promptly and fully in any ongoing investigations or enquiries relating to the business of any Group

Company, subject to any reasonable objection raised by your legal advisers . . . [alterations in original]."

Following the commencement of most of these actions, Christie's and Davidge entered into a so-called Indemnification and Joint Defence Agreement (the "Defence Agreement") whereby, broadly speaking, Christie's agreed to indemnify Davidge with respect to defense costs, fines, and liability in these cases as well as the pending grand jury investigation and actions arising therefrom in exchange for Davidge's cooperation. Paragraph 2 of the Defence Agreement provides in relevant part as follows:

> "Davidge agrees that, as part of his obligations of cooperation under the Termination Agreement, he will comply with such reasonable requests as shall be made of him by Christie's with respect to any matters concerning the Civil Litigation [i.e., those of these cases already pending] or Future Proceeding [which includes the *Kruman* action] including the conduct, defense or settlement of the Civil Litigation or Future Proceeding as well as, meeting with and providing information to such parties to the litigation as Christie's shall request . . . [alterations in original]."

* * *

* * * Christie's * * * is obliged to respond to the interrogatories not only by providing the information it has, but also the information within its control or otherwise obtainable by it. Taubman maintains that information known to Davidge is available to Christie's by virtue of these agreements and that it therefore should be compelled to provide the information in Davidge's hands.

Christie's resists such relief. It says that it has requested Davidge to furnish the information and that Davidge has declined to do so, ostensibly on the ground that he fears that he might waive his privilege against self-incrimination by doing so. But Christie's does not say that it has done anything more than request Davidge to provide the information necessary to enable it to give complete and responsive answers to the interrogatories, this despite the fact that Davidge's reported refusal arguably breaches the agreements. So far as Christie's has indicated, it has not threatened to cease payments to him and his counsel or to consider its indemnification obligation as unenforceable in light of Davidge's position. Thus, it certainly has not exhausted the means at its disposal to procure a response from Davidge. Indeed, there is reason to suppose that Davidge's reticence is in Christie's interests. Yet Christie's argues the Court should not order it to respond with information known only to Davidge because it somehow would be unfair, or less than sporting, to place it in a position in which it might feel compelled to exert pressure on Davidge to provide the necessary information. But this is decidedly unpersuasive.

Davidge agreed to provide Christie's with information in his possession. He was not coerced to do so, except in the sense that the enormously valuable economic consideration that he stands to receive under the agreements of course might be expected to have had a certain persuasive force. By entering into those agreements, he knowingly and voluntarily subjected himself to the risk that a failure to provide information requested by Christie's might be a material breach of the agreements and excuse Christie's from any further obligation to perform, i.e., any obligation to pay or indemnify him. As he is reaping the benefits of his agreements with Christie's, it is far from clear that there is any reason why he should not be pressed to bear the burdens. And surely there is no reason for saying that Christie's should not be given a substantial incentive to seek his cooperation. In fact, the situation is somewhat analogous to that frequently encountered in respect of blocking statutes.

Many foreign countries have enacted statutes that prohibit their citizens and, often, persons subject to their jurisdiction from complying with discovery requests in U.S. litigation. Companies subject both to U.S. discovery demands and to foreign blocking statutes barring compliance often have invoked such statutes in resisting motions for orders compelling them or those subject to their control to produce information covered by the statutes. And while courts have taken different approaches to this question, the modern trend holds that the mere existence of foreign blocking statutes does not prevent a U.S. court from ordering discovery although it may be more important to the question of sanctions in the event that a discovery order is disobeyed by reason of a blocking statute. * * * In determining whether to enter an order compelling discovery, courts typically consider, among other factors, the national interests of the nations involved, the nature and extent of the hardship that would be imposed upon the discovery target if the two countries took inconsistent positions, the good faith or lack thereof of the party resisting the order, and whether a discovery order reasonably can be expected to achieve compliance.

Here there is no countervailing United Kingdom governmental interest to be taken into account. Nor would Christie's be faced with serious adverse consequences in the United Kingdom if it were to take a firm position opposite Davidge. The worst that might happen is that Davidge could sue Christie's for breach of contract in the event it stops paying and indemnifying him, in which case Christie's would have the opportunity to defend on the ground that Davidge himself had breached the agreements by failing without reasonable excuse to provide the requested information. Indeed, given the lack of any obviously substantial cost to Christie's in pressing Davidge to respond, there is genuine ground to suspect Christie's good faith here. * * *

NOTES AND QUESTIONS

1. How extensive should the duty of investigation be under Rule 33? Should a corporate party be charged with the responsibility of finding out what is known by each of its employees regardless of the size and nature of the business? Should the duty extend to information known to employees of

subsidiary corporations that are not parties? See Sol S. Turnoff Drug Distributors Inc. v. N.V. Nederlandsche Combinatie Voor Chemische Industrie, 55 F.R.D. 347 (E.D.Pa.1972). To what extent should the duty include former employees? Would the result be different in *In re Auction Houses* had the former employee's severance package not required him to provide information to the company?

2. In 1993, Rule 33(a) was amended to impose a presumptive limit of 25 interrogatories, including all discrete parts, that a party may serve. The Notes of the Advisory Committee indicate that although parties cannot evade the limitation "through the device of joining as 'subparts' questions that seek information about discrete separate subjects," nevertheless "a question asking about communications of a particular type should be treated as a single interrogatory" even though it asks for a number of specific details regarding the particular communication. See WILLIAMS v. BOARD OF COUNTY COMMISSIONERS, 192 F.R.D. 698, 701–02 (D.Kan. 2000) (finding that seven interrogatories containing 117 subparts "exceeded the maximum number of interrogatories allowed"). What other ways are there to define a single interrogatory for purposes of the Rule? See Yoo, *Rule 33(a)'s Interrogatory Limitation: By Party or by Side?*, 75 U. Chi. L. Rev. 911 (2008).

3. May a party use an interrogatory to probe an adversary's legal theories or a question of law? See Johnston & Johnston, *Contention Interrogatories in Federal Court*, 148 F.R.D. 441 (1993). Rule 33(a)(2) provides that an interrogatory "* * * is not objectionable merely because it asks for an opinion or contention that relates to fact or the application of law to fact * * *." The following case explores the appropriate boundaries to this Rule.

IN RE CONVERGENT TECHNOLOGIES SECURITIES LITIGATION

United States District Court, Northern District of California, 1985.
108 F.R.D. 328.

BRAZIL, MAGISTRATE JUDGE.

The principal issue in this discovery dispute can be simply framed: *when* (at which juncture in the pretrial period) should plaintiffs answer "contention" interrogatories served by defendants. The parties do *not* disagree about *whether* the questions should be answered. The sole question is when. * * *

* * *

I. General Principles

* * *

At the outset I point out that the phrase "contention interrogatory" is used imprecisely to refer to many different kinds of questions. Some people would classify as a contention interrogatory any question that asks another party to indicate *what* it contends. Some people would define contention interrogatories as embracing only questions that ask another party *whether* it makes some specified contention. Interrogatories of this kind typically would begin with the phrase "Do you contend that...." Another kind of question that some people put in the category "contention interrogatory" asks an opposing party to state all the *facts* on which it *bases* some specified contention. Yet another form of this category of interrogatory asks an opponent to state all the *evidence* on which it *bases* some specified contention. Some contention interrogatories ask the responding party to take a position, and then to explain or defend that position, with respect to *how the law applies to facts*. A variation on this theme involves interrogatories that ask parties to spell out the *legal basis* for, or theory behind, some specified contention.

It is not uncommon for a set of "contention interrogatories" to include *all* of these kinds of questions. * * *

* * *

Despite assertions to the contrary by defendants, no party has an absolute right to have answers to contention interrogatories, or to any kind of interrogatory. * * * After 1983, a court can determine whether any given interrogatory is "otherwise proper" only after considering, among other things, whether it is interposed for any improper purpose, and whether it is "unreasonable or unduly burdensome or expensive, given the needs of the case, the discovery already had in the case, the amount in controversy, and the importance of the issues at stake in the litigation." If it were clear, for example, that by using some other discovery tool a party could acquire information of comparable quality while imposing less of a burden on an opponent, a court would be constrained to rule that a contention interrogatory need not be answered, regardless of when in the pretrial period it was served. * * *

* * *

* * * [T]here is considerable recent authority for the view that the wisest general policy is to defer propounding and answering contention interrogatories until near the end of the discovery period. On the other hand,* * * there may be situations in which this general policy should give way to showings, in specific factual settings, that important interests would be advanced if answers were provided early to at least some contention interrogatories. * * *

* * * First, defendants argue that by helping clarify what the issues in the case are, early answers to contention interrogatories can help parties improve the focus of their discovery and can equip courts to more reliably contain discovery excesses. * * *

Defendants further argue that in the process of crafting answers to contention interrogatories parties can be forced to systematically assess their positions earlier than they might if left to their own devices—and that such early systematic assessments might persuade parties to abandon tenuous causes of action, or to dismiss opponents as to whom proof problems seem very substantial. A systematic assessment also might persuade a litigant that the *cost* of developing the evidence to support a particular claim outweighs whatever benefits might be achieved by prevailing on it. Early answers to interrogatories seeking the factual or evidentiary bases for contentions also might serve as predicates for successful motions for summary judgment on part or all of a suit. * * *

Because the benefits that can flow from clarifying and narrowing the issues in litigation *early* in the pretrial period are potentially significant * * *, it would be unwise to create a rigid rule, even if applicable to only certain categories of cases, that would always protect parties from having to answer contention interrogatories until some predetermined juncture in the pretrial period.

On the other hand, there is substantial reason to believe that the *early* knee jerk filing of sets of contention interrogatories that systematically track all the allegations in an opposing party's pleadings is a serious form of discovery abuse. * * *

This follows in part from the court's skepticism about the *quality* of the information that *early* responses to contention interrogatories are likely to contain. Counsel drafting responses to these kinds of interrogatories early in the pretrial period may fear being boxed into a position * * * or that might be used to try to limit the subject areas of their subsequent discovery. Lawyers generally attempt to maximize and preserve their options while providing as little tactical help to their opponents as possible * * *.

* * *

The court concludes that the following procedure is appropriate with respect to contention interrogatories filed before most other discovery has been completed. The propounding party must craft specific, limited (in number) questions. The responding party must examine such questions in good faith and, where it appears that answering them would materially contribute to any of the goals discussed in this opinion, must answer the interrogatories. If answering some, but not all, of the questions would materially contribute to any of the goals described above, the responding party must answer those questions. Where the responding party feels, in good faith, that providing early answers would not contribute enough to justify the effort involved, that party should telephone or write opposing counsel to explain the basis for his position. If opposing counsel continues to press for early answers, the responding party should enter objections * * * or seek permission from the Court to file an objection to the interrogatories as a group. Thereafter, the burden would fall on the propounding party to seek an order compelling answers. In seeking such an order, the propounding party would bear the burden of justification described above. To the extent, if any, that this procedure modifies the way burdens might be allocated with respect to other kinds of discovery disputes, this court believes that the problems associated with the early filing of contention interrogatories, discussed above, justify the different treatment. * * *

The sections that follow help clarify how this court will apply these general principles.

II. Application of Principles to Motions as Presented

* * *

D. Defendant Burroughs Contention Interrogatories

Defendant Burroughs Corporation has filed a set of 15 interrogatories which, counting subparts, add up to at least 52 questions, many of which are compound and expansive, in part because the allegations against Burroughs in plaintiffs' Complaint are more than occasionally compound and expansive. * * *

* * *

* * * The court fails to see how substantial interests of Burroughs will be harmed it if is forced to wait until no more than 60 days after completion of [certain relevant] * * * document production for answers to its interrogatories. If, prior to the time plaintiffs are required by this order to respond to Burroughs' contention interrogatories, plaintiffs seek to obtain additional discovery from Burroughs, and thus to impose costs on Burroughs that it feels it cannot be fairly asked to incur, Burroughs may approach the court for a protective order.

E. Other Purported Justifications for Compelling Answers To Contention Interrogatories Prior to Substantial Completion of Document Productions by Defendants

* * * The court alludes here * * * to the defendants' arguments that prompt answers to their contention interrogatories might expose grounds for a statute of limitations defense to the Section 11 claims, or might establish a basis for striking from the case the plaintiffs' allegations that Convergent's accounting treatment of certain warrants was unlawful. To put the matter simply, defendants have failed to show, by carefully developing the applicable law, and by applying that law to the facts as alleged by plaintiffs or as supported in competent declarations or documentary evidence from defendants, that there is a real likelihood that *early* answers from plaintiffs to questions in these areas will result in a significant re-shaping of the litigation or a significant savings to one or more of the defendants. * * *

Defendants also argued at the hearing on these motions that early answers to their contention interrogatories would materially help their economic experts develop their analysis of the plaintiffs' fraud on the market theory. Defendants argued generally that answers to their interrogatories would help them ascertain what information was in the market at what junctures, and that it takes experts a great deal of time to conduct the kind of examination of the fraud on the market theory that is necessary either to set the stage for serious settlement negotiations or to conduct final preparations for trial. * * * But it is not clear why defendants should be permitted to press plaintiffs, *early* in the discovery period, *through this problematic type of interrogatory,* for help developing affirmative defenses. It is not clear how defendants would be substantially better off if they had answers to these questions now instead of within 60 days after substantially completing their document production. * * * Defendants already have taken many of the plaintiffs' depositions. Thus defendants already have access to information about the bases on which many of the plaintiffs made their decisions to buy and sell, and about whether plaintiffs would have made their purchases even if they had known about the alleged material misrepresentations and omissions in Convergent's communications to the public. * * * It is not obvious why plaintiffs would have better access than defendants to evidence about how the information Convergent made public got into the market place. Convergent presumably knows what information it published and through which channels. Convergent thus would seem to be in a better position than plaintiffs to begin examining how, and to what extent, that information penetrated the marketplace. Plaintiffs, we must recall, are individuals who purchased shares of Convergent stock during a specified time period. * * * Thus it appears that the real target of defendants' interrogatories in this subject area, as in others, is the information that has been developed by plaintiffs' counsel * * *.

In sum, the court denies defendants' motions to compel except to the limited extents set forth above * * *.

NOTES AND QUESTIONS

1. In ZINSKY v. NEW YORK CENTRAL RAILROAD CO., 36 F.R.D. 680 (N.D.Ohio 1964), plaintiff brought suit under the Federal Employers' Liability Act, alleging that his duties were in furtherance of interstate commerce. Defendant denied all allegations in the complaint. Plaintiff then sent the following interrogatory to defendant: "At the time of the accident, was the plaintiff engaged in duties which were in furtherance of interstate commerce or which directly and substantially affected interstate commerce?" The court upheld defendant's objection that the question improperly called for "a legal analysis of one of the factual issues" in the case, quoting United States v. Selby, 25 F.R.D. 12, 14 (N.D. Ohio 1960), as follows: "The assertion and discussion of legal theories, and the classification of facts in support thereof, should be by the lawyers at trial and in whatever pre-trial procedures the court may require."

The *Zinsky* case was decided prior to the 1970 amendment to Federal Rule 33, which added what is now Rule 33(a)(2). Would *Zinsky* have been decided any differently under the amended rule?

2. To what extent should a party's ability to discover the contentions of an adversary be affected by federal decisions upholding as a sufficient plead-

ing under Rule 8 any statement that possibly can be read to state a valid claim for relief or a defense? For example, in a negligence case in which only general allegations of negligence have been made, is it proper to inquire as to the specific acts or omissions upon which the allegations are based? How might the claim-and-defense approach to relevance under Rule 26 affect the analysis?

4. DISCOVERY AND PRODUCTION OF PROPERTY

Read Federal Rules of Civil Procedure 34 and 45 in the Supplement.

Rule 34 and its state counterparts allow a party to request other parties to produce documents, electronically stored information, and tangible things in their possession or control. How does Rule 34 define electronically stored information? The Rule also allows a party entry to the other parties' land or property for such activities as inspection, survey, or measurement. What are the first steps a party must take in order to make a document request? See Federal Rules 26(d)(1) and (f). What kind of notice must then be served on the opponent? See Federal Rule 34(b).

A request for information must describe the items to be discovered "with reasonable particularity," a standard that varies with circumstances. Most courts allow discovery of general categories of items if the description is easily understood (e.g., all written communications between plaintiff and defendant between July 1 and September 1, 2005). Many attorneys combine Rule 33 interrogatories that ask the opposing party to identify documents with a Rule 34 request that the party produce "all documents identified" in the opposing party's answers to the interrogatories. Although the standard for requesting documents is a flexible one, the writing of a request calls for a great deal of precision.

A request must specify a reasonable time, place, and manner for the inspection. The time usually is set at least thirty days after service of the request because the opposing party generally has at least thirty days to respond. The place typically designated for production of documents is the office of the requesting party's attorney, unless it is more convenient to examine the documents where they are kept or to have them copied at some other place. The manner depends on the kind of items requested. In practice, attorneys negotiate these matters.

The party that receives a request serves a written response on the requesting party, as well as any other parties to the lawsuit, within the time specified by the Rule. The response states the responding party's objections, if any, to part or all of the requested production or inspection. Absent objection, the responding party must produce the documents as requested, or admit counsel to its premises for the scheduled inspection.

In 1980, Rule 34(b) was amended to deal with the problem of a litigant who responds to a request by producing a large number of unsorted documents, some of which are unrelated to the case. A leading commentary explains:

> * * * [T]he problem addressed in the 1980 amendment was the shifting of materials from the sequence in which they were ordinarily kept to somewhere else, perhaps intended to make them hard to find. For instance, a critical internal memorandum might be taken from the memoranda file and buried among mounds of invoices. The amendment forbids the producing party from thus making it harder to find such items. Similarly, the producing party does have a burden to select and produce the items requested rather than simply dumping large quantities of unrequested materials onto the discovering party along with the items actually sought under Rule 34.

8A Wright, Miller & Marcus, Federal Practice and Procedure: Civil 2d § 2213.

Although Rule 34 is limited to parties, amendments to Rule 45 (adopted in 1991) allow a "virtually identical procedure to obtain material from nonparties." Id. at § 2204. If the request for production of documents or inspection of premises is addressed to a nonparty, the litigant must serve a subpoena pursuant to Rule 45. Under former Rule 45, it was not possible to make use of a subpoena to obtain documents or inspect property. Rather, the litigant had to take the nonparty's deposition and in connection with the deposition serve a subpoena ordering the nonparty to bring the designated items to the deposition. In the alternative, the litigant could bring a separate action against the nonparty to obtain discovery. The necessity of using these cumbersome procedures was eliminated when Rule 45 was amended in 1991. The amended Rule now provides that an attorney may issue a subpoena commanding any person to give testimony, to produce and permit inspection and copying of designated records or other tangible objects, or to permit inspection of premises.

NOTES AND QUESTIONS

1. Originally, Federal Rule 34 production was limited to documents and things "material to any matter involved in the action" and only on a showing of "good cause." 8A Wright, Miller & Marcus, Federal Practice and Procedure: Civil 2d § 2201. Does it make sense to apply the same standard of relevance to document production as to the other discovery rules? Why or why not?

2. Rule 34 allows discovery of documents and things in the "possession, custody, or control" of a party, and courts treat this limitation in a "highly fact-specific" manner. 8A Wright, Miller & Marcus, Federal Practice and Procedure: Civil 2d § 2210. Does defendant have "control" over requested documents in the following circumstances?

(a) Defendant has given the documents to his insurer;

(b) The documents are in the custody of defendant's wholly-owned subsidiary;

(c) The documents are in the custody of defendant's former corporate employee; or

(d) The documents are in the custody of a foreign-based subsidiary.

Should the touchstone be legal control over the custodian of the documents or some other factor?

3. How specifically must a party designate requested documents? *Cummings*, see p. 849, supra, involved a product defect action against a car manufacturer for an allegedly flawed seat belt and seat design. One month after the jury returned a verdict for defendant, plaintiff learned that the company had failed to disclose "six videos of child safety acceleration tests" that it had conducted and produced "in an unrelated trial." The Tenth Circuit rejected plaintiffs' argument that defendant had engaged in misconduct in failing to produce the videos:

> Even assuming the videos were relevant, GM was under no duty to produce the videos given the requests for production in this case. Plaintiffs offer various requests for production and a subpoena duces tecum, arguing the tests fall within the requested documents. However, the requests are either overly broad or focus solely on the "seat, shoulder anchorages, seat bottom/pan, the seat back, the seat belt anchorages and seat belt angles." * * * The Cummings have failed to point to any discovery requests that would encompass the videos in question.

365 F.3d at 956. How might a party sequence its use of discovery to ensure that document requests are made with the requisite specificity?

NOTE ON DISCOVERY OF ELECTRONIC DATA

The Federal Rules were adopted before the fax machine or laptop computer came into existence. They have, however, been adapted periodically to meet changes in technology that have affected litigation practice. In 1970, for example, Federal Rule 34 was amended to include "data compilations from which information can be obtained" as among the documents that can be requested under the rule. Since then, computers have dramatically increased the volume of electronically stored information that lawyers and their clients generate in the course of business and other activity:

> In 2000, fewer than 10 billion e-mail messages were sent per day worldwide. By 2005, the number of e-mails sent per day [was] projected to surpass 35 billion * * *. According to a 2003 survey by the Meta Group, 80 percent of business people say e-mail is more valuable than the telephone. More than 7 billion office documents are produced each year, and a recent study from the University of California, Berkeley, concluded that as much as 93% of it is in digital format. Office workers are estimated to be involved in at least 30 e-mail communications per work day and to create about 300 megabytes of electronic documents per year.

Shapiro & Kilpatrick, *E–Mail Discovery and Privilege*, 23 Corp. Counsel Rev. 203, 203 (2004).

Electronically stored information ("ESI") presents challenges that are not raised by the discovery of paper documents. A number of factors deserve mention. The sheer volume of ESI and the ease with which it can be duplicated has increased exponentially the amount of information that may be discovered. In addition, ESI possesses the quality of "persistence," in the sense that it cannot simply be shredded and discarded. ESI likewise has a "dynamic, changeable content" that may transform without any targeted or intentional activity by the user (for example, booting up a computer may change the content of data). Moreover, ESI, unlike paper documents, contains metadata, defined as "information about the document or file that is recorded by the computer to assist the computer and often the user in storing and retrieving the document or file at a later date." The challenges of discovering ESI are compounded by its "environment-dependence," in the sense that ESI "may be incomprehensible when separated from its environment," and by the periodic obsolescence of computer systems. Finally, ESI may be dispersed in different archival media, making it difficult to determine the origin of ESI, yet ESI can often be searched with relative ease. See The Sedona Principles: Best Practices Recommendations & Principles for Addressing Electronic Document Production, SK071 ALI–ABA 363, 373 (2004).

In 2006—following a decade of study by the Advisory Committee on Civil Rules, Discovery Subcommittee—amendments to the Federal Rules on electronic discovery took effect. The amendments in part adapted existing language to include electronic discovery. Federal Rule 34 was amended to change the term documents and data compilations from the 1970 version to "documents and electronically stored information." The hope is that this broader term will allow the rule to adapt alongside constantly changing information technology. Rule 34 also now provides a procedure for producing electronically stored information: unless otherwise requested pursuant to Rule 34, the responding party must produce electronically stored information in the form in which it is ordinarily maintained or in a form that is reasonably useful. Further, Rule 34 allows a party to avoid production of information in separate forms; a party need not provide duplicate physical and electronic copies of a document. The 2006 amendments also make clear that Rule 16 (pretrial conferences), p. 927, supra, Rule 26 (mandatory disclosure, relevance, and proportionality), p. 848, supra, Rule 33 (interrogatories), p. 861, supra, Rule 37 (sanctions), p. 920, infra, and Rule 45 (subpoenas) encompass the discovery of electronically stored information.

Issues concerning the limits and costs of discovering electronic information have generated complicated questions for courts. The amended rules seek to limit the burden of electronic discovery by identifying a category of information that is "not reasonably accessible." Federal Rule 26 (b)(2)(c). How does a court determine if an electronic discovery request is reasonable? How do you think the costs of electronic discovery should be allocated between the parties? What, if any, sanctions should be imposed when a party fails to comply with proper electronic discovery requests? If sanctions are appropriate, what form should they take? Who should be sanctioned? The two Sections that follow focus on these issues.

A. DISCOVERY OF REASONABLY ACCESSIBLE ELECTRONICALLY STORED INFORMATION OR LIMITATIONS ON ELECTRONIC DISCOVERY

The potentially enormous costs of electronic discovery may make it impossible for less affluent litigants to stand up to wealthier opponents. According to one knowledgeable source, the cost of electronic consulting fees begins at $275 per hour and the cost of collecting, reviewing, and producing just one e-mail runs between $2.60 and $4.00. See Fort, *Rising Costs of E–Discovery Requirements Impacting Litigants*, Fulton County Daily Report, March 20, 2007. A widely quoted study by Barry Murphy of Forrestor Research predicts that more than $4.8 billion annually will be spent on e-discovery by the year 2011. The Advisory Committee's Note to the 2006 amendments explains:

> The decision whether to require a responding party to search for and produce information that is not reasonably accessible depends not only on the burdens and costs of doing so, but also on whether those burdens and costs can be justified in the circumstances of the case. Appropriate considerations may include: (1) the specificity of the discovery request; (2) the quantity of information available from other and more easily accessed sources; (3) the failure to produce relevant information that seems likely to have existed is no longer available on more easily accessed sources; (4) the likelihood of finding relevant, responsive information that cannot be obtained from other, more easily accessed sources; (5) predictions as to the importance and usefulness of the further information; (6) the importance of the issues at stake in the litigation; and (7) the parties' resources.

Advisory Committee Note to the 2006 Amendments to Rule 26(b), which appears in the Supplement. See Noyes, *Good Cause is Bad Medicine for the New E–Discovery Rules*, 21 Harv. J.L. & Tech. 49 (2007). In developing a factor approach, the Advisory Committee drew guidance from the District Court's decision in ZUBULAKE v. UBS WARBURG LLC, 217 F.R.D. 309 (S.D.N.Y. 2003), an employment discrimination suit. Plaintiff sought discovery of emails exchanged by defendants' employees that were stored on backup tapes and optical disks. Employees received about 200 emails a day, and, under federal securities law, defendant was required to preserve all communications for a fixed number of years. Defendant resisted producing the materials, arguing that "restoring those e-mails would cost approximately $175,000.00, exclusive of attorney time in reviewing the e-mails":

> Discovery in this action commenced on or about June 3, 2002, when Zubulake served UBS with her first document request. At issue here is request number twenty-eight, for "[a]ll documents concerning any communication by or between UBS employees concerning Plaintiff." * * * The term document in Zubulake's request "includ[es], without limitation, electronic or computerized data compilations." On July 8, 2002, UBS responded by producing approximately 350 pages of docu-

ments, including approximately 100 pages of e-mails. UBS also objected to a substantial portion of Zubulake's requests. * * *

On September 12, 2002—after an exchange of angry * * * letters and a conference before United States Magistrate Judge Gabriel W. Gorenstein—the parties reached an agreement * * *. With respect to document request twenty-eight, * * * [the agreement was, in part, as follows]:

Defendants will [ ] ask UBS about how to retrieve e-mails that are saved in the firm's computer system *and will produce responsive e-mails if retrieval is possible* and Plaintiff names a few individuals. * * *

* * * UBS agreed unconditionally to produce responsive e-mails from the accounts of five individuals named by Zubulake * * *. UBS was to produce such e-mails sent between August 1999 (when Zubulake was hired) and December 2001 (one month after her termination), to the extent possible.

UBS, however, produced no additional e-mails and insisted that its initial production (the 100 pages of e-mails) was complete. As UBS's opposition to the instant motion makes clear—although it remains unsaid—UBS never searched for responsive e-mails on any of its backup tapes. To the contrary, UBS informed Zubulake that the cost of producing e-mails on backup tapes would be prohibitive (estimated at the time at approximately $300,000.00). * * *

Zubulake, believing that the * * * Agreement included production of e-mails from backup tapes, objected to UBS's nonproduction. In fact, Zubulake *knew* that there were additional responsive e-mails that UBS had failed to produce because she herself had produced approximately 450 pages of e-mail correspondence. Clearly, numerous responsive e-mails had been created and deleted[19] at UBS, and Zubulake wanted them.

On December 2, 2002, the parties again appeared before Judge Gorenstein, who ordered UBS to produce for deposition a person with knowledge of UBS's e-mail retention policies in an effort to determine whether the backup tapes contained the deleted e-mails and the burden of producing them. In response, UBS produced Christopher Behny, Manager of Global Messaging, who was deposed on January

19. The term "deleted" is sticky in the context of electronic data. " 'Deleting' a file does not actually erase that data from the computer's storage devices. Rather, it simply finds the data's entry in the disk directory and changes it to a 'not used' status—thus permitting the computer to write over the 'deleted' data. Until the computer writes over the 'deleted' data, however, it may be recovered by searching the disk itself rather than the disk's directory. Accordingly, many files are recoverable long after they have been deleted—even if neither the computer user nor the computer itself is aware of their existence. Such data is referred to as 'residual data.' " Shira A. Scheindlin & Jeffrey Rabkin, *Electronic Discovery in Federal Civil Litigation: Is Rule 34 Up to the Task?*, 41 B.C. L.Rev. 327, 337 (2000) (footnotes omitted). Deleted data may also exist because it was backed up before it was deleted. Thus, it may reside on backup tapes or similar media. Unless otherwise noted, I will use the term "deleted" data to mean residual data, and will refer to backed-up data as "backup tapes."

> 14, 2003. Mr. Behny testified to UBS's e-mail backup protocol, and also to the cost of restoring the relevant data.

Id. at 312–13. The District Court rejected defendant's argument that because it already had produced 100 pages of emails plaintiff was not entitled to additional discovery:

> * * * This argument is unpersuasive for two reasons. *First,* because of the way that UBS backs up its e-mail files, it clearly could not have searched all of its e-mails without restoring the ninety-four backup tapes (which UBS admits that it has not done). UBS therefore cannot represent that it has produced all responsive e-mails. *Second,* Zubulake herself has produced over 450 pages of relevant e-mails, including e-mails that would have been responsive to her discovery requests but were never produced by UBS. These two facts strongly suggest that there are e-mails that Zubulake has not received that reside on UBS's backup media.[41]

Id. at 317. The more complicated question concerned defendants' request that the court shift the cost of production to plaintiff:

> * * * [W]hether production of documents is unduly burdensome or expensive turns primarily on whether it is kept in an *accessible or inaccessible* format (a distinction that corresponds closely to the expense of production). * * *
>
> Whether electronic data is accessible or inaccessible turns largely on the media on which it is stored. Five categories of data, listed in order from most accessible to least accessible, are described in the literature on electronic data storage: * * * [The different categories are: 1. *Active, online data;* 2. *Near-line data;* 3. *Offline storage/archives;* 4. *Backup tapes;* and 5. *Erased, fragmented or damaged data.*]
>
> * * *
>
> The case at bar is a perfect illustration of the range of accessibility of electronic data. As explained above, UBS maintains e-mail files in three forms: (1) active user e-mail files; (2) archived e-mails on optical disks; and (3) backup data stored on tapes. The active (HP OpenMail) data is obviously the most accessible: it is online data that resides on an active server, and can be accessed immediately. The optical disk (Tumbleweed) data is only slightly less accessible, and falls into either the second or third category. The e-mails are on optical disks that need to be located and read with the correct hardware, but the system is configured to make searching the optical disks simple and automated once they are located. For these sources of e-mails—active mail files and e-mails stored on optical disks—it would be wholly inappro-

41. UBS insists that "[f]rom the time Plaintiff commenced her EEOC action in August 2001 . . . UBS collected and produced all existing responsive e-mails sent or received between 1999 and 2001 from these and other employees' computers." Def. Mem. at 6. Even if this statement is completely accurate, a simple search of employees' computer files would not have turned up e-mails deleted prior to August 2001. Such deleted documents exist *only* on the backup tapes and optical disks, and their absence is precisely why UBS's production is not complete.

priate to even consider cost-shifting. UBS maintains the data in an accessible and usable format, and can respond to Zubulake's request cheaply and quickly. Like most typical discovery requests, therefore, the producing party should bear the cost of production.

E-mails stored on backup tapes (via NetBackup), however, are an entirely different matter. Although UBS has already identified the ninety-four potentially responsive backup tapes, those tapes are not currently accessible. In order to search the tapes for responsive e-mails, UBS would have to engage in the costly and time-consuming process detailed above. It is therefore appropriate to *consider* cost shifting.

Id. at 318–29. The District Court identified seven factors to consider in assessing whether to shift the costs of discovery:

1. The extent to which the request is specifically tailored to discover relevant information;
2. The availability of such information from other sources;
3. The total cost of production, compared to the amount in controversy;
4. The total cost of production, compared to the resources available to each party;
5. The relative ability of each party to control costs and its incentive to do so;
6. The importance of the issues at stake in the litigation; and
7. The relative benefits to the parties of obtaining the information.

Id. at 322. What other factors would you consider? See Grimm, Berman, Crowley & Wharton, *Proportionality in the Post-hoc Analysis of Pre–Litigation Preservation Decisions*, 37 U. Balt. L. Rev. 381 (2008).

B. SANCTIONS FOR VIOLATIONS OR ABUSE OF ELECTRONIC DISCOVERY REGULATIONS

QUALCOMM INC. v. BROADCOM CORP., 2008 WL 66932 (S.D.Cal. 2008). In this patent law case, plaintiff Qualcomm turned over voluminous emails, yet withheld 46,000 others that were highly relevant to a major issue in the case. Had those documents been turned over to defendant, it is highly unlikely that the case would have proceeded to trial and surely the cost of the litigation would have been reduced substantially. The trial court, after a decision for defendant on the merits, referred the matter to a magistrate judge to determine what sanctions, if any, should be imposed on Qualcomm or its attorneys. After a detailed analysis showing a failure to act in good faith, Qualcomm was ordered to pay to defendant an $8.5 million sanction. The names of the attorneys allegedly responsible for the failure were to be reported to the California State Bar for possible disciplinary action, and the corporation's legal department was required to undertake an internal "Case Review and Enforcement of Discovery Obligations" program and submit to on-going case management supervision. A magistrate judge's sanctions are subject to review by the trial judge, and the District Court modified in part and remanded, relying on the self-defense exception to the attorney-client privilege. 2008 WL 638108 (S.D.Cal. 2008).

NOTES AND QUESTIONS

The information regarding the withheld emails in *Qualcomm* was not revealed until after the decision on the merits. What action might the court have taken had it learned of the failure to disclose before the trial had commenced? See PLASSE v. TYCO ELECTRONICS CORP., 448 F.Supp.2d 302 (D.Mass.2006), a wrongful termination of employment case in which plaintiff's case was dismissed on the merits for deliberate misconduct by destroying or concealing electronic information. Compare TEAGUE v. TARGET CORP., 2007 WL 1041191 (W.D.N.C.2007), an employee's suit to obtain back pay. Plaintiff was requested to produce relevant files from her computer. She claimed she was unable to do so, because, well after her case was filed, her computer "crashed" and she simply threw it out. The court declined to dismiss plaintiff's case, finding it could not establish that she had acted in bad faith, but as a sanction it gave an instruction to the jury that it could draw an adverse inference against plaintiff due to her destruction of significant evidence. When would dismissal be appropriate? What if defendant deliberately fails to produce requested electronic information? Should the court be able to enter a default judgment? See Federal Rule 37(b)(2)(A)(v). For a discussion of this issue, see Tew, *Electronic Discovery Misconduct in Litigation: Letting the Punishment Fit the Crime*, 61 U. Miami L. Rev. 289 (2007).

5. PHYSICAL AND MENTAL EXAMINATIONS

Read Federal Rule of Civil Procedure 35 in the Supplement.

In many lawsuits, a party will need to have its own medical professionals physically examine an adverse party whose condition is in controversy. However, a compelled medical examination involves an intrusion on a person's privacy, and some medical tests can entail discomfort and pain. Rule 35 requires a court order for an examination and imposes strict standards. A court can force a party to submit to examination or to make persons under their legal custody or control available for examination. But the person's physical or mental condition must be in controversy, and the movant must show "good cause" to compel the examination. The determination of good cause involves weighing the pain, danger, or intrusiveness of the examination against the need for, or usefulness of, the information to be gained.

In practice, most physical and mental examinations occur as a result of agreements between attorneys. The primary effect of Rule 35 is to encourage parties to stipulate to examinations. Examinations are routine in personal injury actions, as well as in litigation involving issues of paternity, incompetence, and undue influence. Of course, the Rule is available in those cases in which the parties cannot agree. Stipulations typically address questions concerning the time and place of the examination, and the procedures to be used. Rule 35 gives the examined party the right to a copy of the examiner's report, even if he or she submitted to an examination without the compulsion of a court order.

SCHLAGENHAUF v. HOLDER

Supreme Court of the United States, 1964.
379 U.S. 104, 85 S.Ct. 234, 13 L.Ed.2d 152.

Certiorari to the United States Court of Appeals for the Seventh Circuit.

MR. JUSTICE GOLDBERG delivered the opinion of the Court.

This case involves the validity and construction of Rule 35(a) of the Federal Rules of Civil Procedure as applied to the examination of a defendant in a negligence action. * * *

An action based on diversity of citizenship was brought in the District Court seeking damages arising from personal injuries suffered by passengers of a bus which collided with the rear of a tractor-trailer. The named defendants were The Greyhound Corporation, owner of the bus; petitioner, Robert L. Schlagenhauf, the bus driver; Contract Carriers, Inc., owner of the tractor; Joseph L. McCorkhill, driver of the tractor; and National Lead Company, owner of the trailer. Answers were filed by each of the defendants denying negligence.

Greyhound then cross-claimed against Contract Carriers and National Lead for damage to Greyhound's bus, alleging that the collision was due solely to their negligence in that the tractor-trailer was driven at an unreasonably low speed, had not remained in its lane, and was not equipped with proper rear lights. Contract Carriers filed an answer to this cross-claim denying its negligence and asserting "[t]hat the negligence of the driver of the * * * bus [petitioner Schlagenhauf] proximately caused and contributed to * * * Greyhound's damages."

* * *

Contract Carriers and National Lead then petitioned the District Court for an order directing petitioner Schlagenhauf to submit to both mental and physical examinations by one specialist in each of the following fields:

(1) Internal medicine;

(2) Ophthalmology;

(3) Neurology; and

(4) Psychiatry.

For the purpose of offering a choice to the District Court of one specialist in each field, the petition recommended two specialists in internal medicine, ophthalmology, and psychiatry, respectively, and three specialists in neurology—a total of nine physicians. The petition alleged that the mental and physical condition of Schlagenhauf was "in controversy" as it had been raised by Contract Carriers' answer to Greyhound's cross-claim. This was supported by a brief of legal authorities and an affidavit of Contract Carriers' attorney stating that Schlagenhauf had seen red lights 10 to 15 seconds before the accident, that another witness had seen the rear lights of the trailer from a distance of three-quarters to one-half mile, and that Schlagenhauf had been involved in a prior accident.

* * *

While disposition of this petition was pending, National Lead filed its answer to Greyhound's cross-claim and itself "cross-claimed" against Greyhound and Schlagenhauf for damage to its trailer. * * *

The District Court, on the basis of the petition filed by Contract Carriers, and without any hearing, ordered Schlagenhauf to submit to nine examinations—one by each of the recommended specialists—despite the fact that the petition clearly requested a total of only four examinations.

Petitioner applied for a writ of mandamus in the Court of Appeals against the respondent, the District Court Judge, seeking to have set aside the order requiring his mental and physical examinations. The Court of Appeals denied mandamus, one judge dissenting * * *.

We granted certiorari to review undecided questions concerning the validity and construction of Rule 35. * * *

Rule 35 on its face applies to all "parties," which under any normal reading would include a defendant. Petitioner contends, however, that the application of the Rule to a defendant would be an unconstitutional invasion of his privacy, or, at the least, be a modification of substantive rights existing prior to the adoption of the Federal Rules of Civil Procedure and thus beyond the congressional mandate of the Rules Enabling Act.

These same contentions were raised [and rejected] in Sibbach v. Wilson & Co., [Note 3, p. 439, supra,] * * * by a plaintiff in a negligence action who asserted a physical injury as a basis for recovery. * * * Petitioner does not challenge the holding in *Sibbach* as applied to plaintiffs. He contends, however, that it should not be extended to defendants. We can see no basis * * * for such a distinction. * * * Issues cannot be resolved by a doctrine of favoring one class of litigants over another.

We recognize that, insofar as reported cases show, this type of discovery in federal courts has been applied solely to plaintiffs, and that some early state cases seem to have proceeded on a theory that a plaintiff who seeks redress for injuries in a court of law thereby "waives" his right to claim the inviolability of his person.

* * * [The Court then rejected the "waiver" theory on the basis of language in the *Sibbach* case.] The chain of events leading to an ultimate determination on the merits begins with the injury of the plaintiff, an involuntary act on his part. Seeking court redress is just one step in this chain. If the plaintiff is prevented or deterred from this redress, the loss is thereby forced on him to the same extent as if the defendant were prevented or deterred from defending against the action.

* * *

Petitioner contends that even if Rule 35 is to be applied to defendants, which we have determined it must, nevertheless it should not be applied to him as he was not a party in relation to Contract Carriers and National Lead—the movants for the mental and physical examinations—at the time the examinations were sought. * * * While it is clear that the person to be examined must be a party to the case,[12] we are of the view that * * * Rule 35 only requires that the person to be examined be a party to the "action," not that he be an opposing party *vis-à-vis* the movant. There is no doubt that Schlagenhauf was a "party" to this "action" by virtue of the original complaint. * * * Insistence that the movant have filed a pleading against the person to be examined would have the undesirable result of an unnecessary proliferation of cross-claims and counterclaims and would not be in keeping with the aims of a liberal, nontechnical application of the Federal Rules. * * *

While the Court of Appeals held that petitioner was not a party *vis-à-vis* National Lead or Contract Carriers at the time the examinations were first sought, it went on to hold that he had become a party *vis-à-vis* National Lead by the time of a second order entered by the District Court and thus was a party within its rule. This second order, identical in all material respects with the first, was entered on the basis of supplementary petitions filed by National Lead and Contract Carriers. These petitions gave no new basis for the examinations, except for the allegation that petitioner's mental and physical condition had been additionally put in controversy by the National Lead answer and cross-claim, which had been filed subsequent to the first petition for examinations. Although the filing of the petition for mandamus intervened between these two orders, we accept, for purposes of this opinion, the determination of the Court of Appeals that this second order was the one before it and agree that petitioner was clearly a party at this juncture under any test.

Petitioner next contends that his mental or physical condition was not "in controversy" and "good cause" was not shown for the examinations, both as required by the express terms of Rule 35.

* * *

12. Although petitioner was an agent of Greyhound, he was himself a party to the action. He is to be distinguished from one who is not a party but is, for example, merely the agent of a party. * * *

It is notable * * * that in none of the other discovery provisions is there a restriction that the matter be "in controversy," and only in Rule 34 is there Rule 35's requirement that the movant affirmatively demonstrate "good cause."[a]

This additional requirement of "good cause" was reviewed by Chief Judge Sobeloff in Guilford National Bank of Greensboro v. Southern Ry. Co., 297 F.2d 921, 924 (C.A.4th Cir.), in the following words:

> * * * The specific requirement of good cause would be meaningless if good cause could be sufficiently established by merely showing that the desired materials are relevant, for the relevancy standard has already been imposed by Rule 26(b). Thus, by adding the words "* * * good cause * * *," the Rules indicate that there must be greater showing of need under Rules 34 and 35 than under the other discovery rules.

The courts of appeals in other cases have also recognized that Rule 34's good-cause requirement is not a mere formality, but is a plainly expressed limitation on the use of that Rule. This is obviously true as to the "in controversy" and "good cause" requirements of Rule 35. They are not met by mere conclusory allegations of the pleadings—nor by mere relevance to the case—but require an affirmative showing by the movant that each condition as to which the examination is sought is really and genuinely in controversy and that good cause exists for ordering each particular examination. Obviously, what may be good cause for one type of examination may not be so for another. The ability of the movant to obtain the desired information by other means is also relevant.

Rule 35, therefore, requires discriminating application by the trial judge, who must decide, as an initial matter in every case, whether the party requesting a mental or physical examination or examinations has adequately demonstrated the existence of the Rule's requirements of "in controversy" and "good cause," which requirements, as the Court of Appeals in this case itself recognized, are necessarily related. 321 F.2d, at 51. * * *

Of course, there are situations where the pleadings alone are sufficient to meet these requirements. A plaintiff in a negligence action who asserts mental or physical injury * * * places that mental or physical injury clearly in controversy and provides the defendant with good cause for an examination to determine the existence and extent of such asserted injury. This * * * applies equally to a defendant who asserts his mental or physical condition as a defense to a claim, such as, for example, where insanity is asserted as a defense to a divorce action. * * *

Here, however, Schlagenhauf did not assert his mental or physical condition either in support of or in defense of a claim. His condition was sought to be placed in issue by other parties. Thus, under the principles discussed above, Rule 35 required that these parties make an affirmative

a. The "good cause" requirement was eliminated from Rule 34 in 1970.

showing that petitioner's mental or physical condition was in controversy and that there was good cause for the examinations requested. This, the record plainly shows, they failed to do.

The only allegations in the pleadings relating to this subject were the general conclusory statement in Contract Carriers' answer to the cross-claim that "Schlagenhauf was not mentally or physically capable of operating" the bus at the time of the accident and the limited allegation in National Lead's cross-claim that, at the time of the accident, "the eyes and vision of * * * Schlagenhauf was [sic] impaired and deficient."

The attorney's affidavit attached to the petition for the examinations provided:

> That * * * Schlagenhauf, in his deposition * * * admitted that he saw red lights for 10 to 15 seconds prior to a collision with a semi-tractor trailer unit and yet drove his vehicle on without reducing speed and without altering the course thereof.
>
> The only eye-witness to this accident known to this affiant * * * testified that immediately prior to the impact between the bus and truck that he had also been approaching the truck from the rear and that he had clearly seen the lights of the truck for a distance of three-quarters to one-half mile to the rear thereof.
>
> * * * Schlagenhauf has admitted in his deposition * * * that he was involved in a [prior] similar type rear end collision. * * *

This record cannot support even the corrected order which required one examination in each of the four specialties of internal medicine, ophthalmology, neurology, and psychiatry. Nothing in the pleadings or affidavit would afford a basis for a belief that Schlagenhauf was suffering from a mental or neurological illness warranting wide-ranging psychiatric or neurological examinations. Nor is there anything stated justifying the broad internal medicine examination.

The only specific allegation made in support of the four examinations ordered was that the "eyes and vision" of Schlagenhauf were impaired. Considering this in conjunction with the affidavit, we would be hesitant to set aside a visual examination if it had been the only one ordered. However, as the case must be remanded to the District Court because of the other examinations ordered, it would be appropriate for the District Judge to reconsider also this order in light of the guidelines set forth in this opinion.

* * *

Accordingly, the judgment of the Court of Appeals is vacated and the case remanded to the District Court to reconsider the examination order in light of the guidelines herein formulated and for further proceedings in conformity with this opinion.

Vacated and remanded.

MR. JUSTICE BLACK, with whom MR. JUSTICE CLARK joins, concurring in part and dissenting in part.

* * *

In a collision case like this one, evidence concerning very bad eyesight or impaired mental or physical health which may affect the ability to drive is obviously of the highest relevance. It is equally obvious, I think, that when a vehicle continues down an open road and smashes into a truck in front of it although the truck is in plain sight and there is ample time and room to avoid collision, the chances are good that the driver has some physical, mental or moral defect. When such a thing happens twice, one is even more likely to ask, "What is the matter with that driver? Is he blind or crazy?" Plainly the allegations of the other parties were relevant and put the question of Schlagenhauf's health and vision "in controversy." * * *

MR. JUSTICE DOUGLAS, dissenting in part.

* * * When the defendant's doctors examine plaintiff, they are normally interested only in answering a single question: did plaintiff in fact sustain the specific injuries claimed? But plaintiff's doctors will naturally be inclined to go on a fishing expedition in search of *anything* which will tend to prove that the defendant was unfit to perform the acts which resulted in the plaintiff's injury. And a doctor for a fee can easily discover something wrong with any patient—a condition that in prejudiced medical eyes might have caused the accident. Once defendants are turned over to medical or psychiatric clinics for an analysis of their physical well-being and the condition of their psyche, the effective trial will be held there and not before the jury. There are no lawyers in those clinics to stop the doctor from probing this organ or that one, to halt a further inquiry, to object to a line of questioning. And there is no judge to sit as arbiter. The doctor or the psychiatrist has a holiday in the privacy of his office. The defendant is at the doctor's (or psychiatrist's) mercy; and his report may either overawe or confuse the jury and prevent a fair trial.

* * *

Neither the Court nor Congress up to today has determined that any person whose physical or mental condition is brought into question during some lawsuit must surrender his right to keep his person inviolate. Congress did, according to *Sibbach*, require a plaintiff to choose between his privacy and his purse; but before today it has not been thought that any other "party" had lost this historic immunity. Congress and this Court can authorize such a rule. But a rule suited to purposes of discovery against defendants must be carefully drawn in light of the great potential of blackmail.

* * *

[JUSTICE HARLAN'S dissenting opinion is omitted.]

NOTES AND QUESTIONS

1. What kinds of diagnostic tests may be ordered under Rule 35? In STORMS v. LOWE'S HOME CENTERS, INC., 211 F.R.D. 296 (W.D. Va. 2002), the District Court declined to order "a mere vocational assessment not connected with any physical or mental examination * * *." The court explained that although the 1991 amendment to Rule 35 "explicitly expanded the scope of *examiners* to be covered, it did not expand the scope of *examinations* available under the Rule." Id. at 298.

2. In WINTERS v. TRAVIA, 495 F.2d 839 (2d Cir.1974), the court refused to order plaintiff to submit to a physical or mental examination. Plaintiff was a Christian Scientist seeking damages on the ground that forced medication administered to her during involuntary hospitalization violated her right to freedom of religion. The court ruled that her present condition was not in controversy since plaintiff was willing to abandon any claim that any present or anticipated physical or mental disability or condition was caused by the medical treatment on which the case was based.

3. In ABDULWALI v. WASHINGTON METRO AREA TRANSIT AUTHORITY, 193 F.R.D. 10 (D.D.C.2000), plaintiff sued for negligent infliction of emotional distress resulting from the witnessing of of her child being killed in a subway train accident. Defendant sought a psychiatric examination of plaintiff, who requested the court to permit her attorney to attend the examination and to have the examination recorded. She also requested that she receive any notes made by the psychiatrist during the examination and that the examination be limited to three hours duration. The court rejected all of plaintiff's requests, noting that the greater weight of federal authority favors the exclusion of a party's attorney.

What arguments could each of the parties make to support their positions? Would it make a difference if plaintiff was seeking damages for physical injuries and the examination was not being conducted by a psychiatrist? Suppose plaintiff was seeking to have her own physician present, rather than her lawyer? Should she be able to have her husband or her mother attend? Are there special times when attendance by another person or a recording of the examination should be permitted or not permitted? See Wyatt & Bales, *The Presence of Third Parties at Rule 35 Examinations*, 71 Temp. L. Rev. 103 (1998).

6. REQUESTS TO ADMIT

Read Federal Rule of Civil Procedure 36 in the Supplement.

Rule 36 authorizes a party to serve on another party written requests to admit the truth of certain matters of fact or of the application of law to fact, or the genuineness of a document or other evidence that may be used at trial. Rule 36 is not a true discovery device since it does not require the responding party to disclose information. Requests for admissions are used to shape information already known into statements that expedite the trial by limiting the issues in dispute and by obviating some of the formalities that control the introduction of evidence at trial. Although responses to other discovery devices are not conclusive proof and may be contradicted at trial, responses to Rule 36 requests constitute conclusive evidence, unless withdrawn, and cannot be contradicted at trial. However, requests for admissions may function as a discovery device if a party uses them early enough in the litigation to help identify the issues not in dispute and to target the remaining issues for discovery.

A request for admission may be served without the necessity of a court order at any time after the parties have conferred in accordance with Rule 26(d), although usually not later than thirty days before a fixed trial date. Rule 36 provides that each matter of admission must be set forth separately, but says nothing else about the format for requests. However, Form 51 appended to the Federal Rules of Civil Procedure, which is reproduced in the Supplement, provides an illustration of a request for admissions.

The party who receives a request to admit must respond under oath and in timely fashion, admitting or denying each matter for which an admission is requested, or providing a detailed explanation why it cannot admit or deny the matter. The responding party also may object to a request because improperly phrased (as "vague," "ambiguous," "a compound sentence," or otherwise defectively drafted), or because it seeks privileged or protected information. The responding party may request a court to extend its time to respond. (Rule 29 provides that counsel may stipulate to extend the time limits set forth in Rule 36 unless the stipulation would "interfere with the time set for completing discovery, for hearing a motion, or for trial.")

If the party who receives a request to admit does nothing, the matter in the request is deemed admitted. The effects of Rule 36, unlike other discovery rules, are self-executing. Once the time to respond has passed, the requesting party can rely on the matters admitted and take no further discovery on those issues. If a party serves a late response, and the opponent refuses to accept it, a court may excuse the party's failure to respond in a timely manner. Likewise, a court may permit a party to withdraw or modify an admission in a timely response. In either situation, the court's decision turns on the degree of prejudice the requesting party will suffer because of its reliance on the admission. Because courts so frequently granted a responding party's request for relief from its failure to respond, leaving requesting parties uncertain about the validity of the admission, and, hence, the necessity of developing evidence for trial, Rule 36(a) was amended in 1970 to permit a requesting party to move for an order deeming the matter to be admitted. Thus, a litigant takes a serious risk by failing to respond to Requests for Admissions. The court may well find that the failure was not justified, that the admissions have been made, and that, as a result, summary judgment is appropriate. See, e.g., Jones v. Sweeney, 2000 WL 1611129 (N.D.Ind.2000).

Although Rule 36 and its state counterparts can be enormously useful, in practice requests for admissions are the least used of the discovery devices. See Connolly, Holleman & Kuhlman, Judicial Controls and the Civil Litigation Process: Discovery 28 (1978). Attorneys tend to think of requests to admit as part of trial preparation, not discovery. They postpone their use to the very end, and frequently fail to file requests before the time fixed by the court to complete discovery runs out. Dombroff, Discovery 260 (1986).

NOTES AND QUESTIONS

1. Rule 36 formerly limited requests for admissions to matters of "fact." The Rule was amended in 1970 and now permits requests for admissions to inquire into matters relating to "facts, the application of law to fact, or opinions about either; and the genuineness of any described documents." Does the amended provision authorize requests for admissions of law unrelated to the facts of the case? See 8A Wright, Miller & Marcus, Federal Practice and Procedure: Civil 2d §§ 2254–56.

Is there any justification for holding improper requests to admit facts that are "in controversy" or that are the ultimate facts in issue? Doesn't it make more sense to permit the request to admit to be made so that the responding party can deny it, if untrue? See Comment, *The Dilemma of Federal Rule 36,* 56 Nw.U.L.Rev. 679, 684–85 (1961).

2. What is a "reasonable inquiry" and when is information not "readily obtainable" by an answering party? In LUMPKIN v. MESKILL, 64 F.R.D. 673 (D.Conn.1974), the court held that the defendants in a school desegregation case were required to admit or deny the accuracy of statistics concerning the racial composition of schools that were derived from the random sampling techniques used by the plaintiff's expert. Note that under Rule 33(b)(2)(B) a corporate or government party has a duty to investigate to ascertain and disclose information that is not within its personal knowledge but reasonably within its power to obtain. Should the standards for investigation be as extensive under Rule 36?

3. Is a party required to admit a matter he believes to be true? Suppose an individual sues a corporation for injuries sustained in a motor vehicle accident, allegedly caused by the negligent driving of defendant's employee. The employee, apparently the only eyewitness, when asked, states that she unlawfully went through a traffic signal. Must the corporate defendant, if requested to do so, admit the unlawful act, even though it suspects that its employee, motivated by compassion for the victim, might not be telling the truth? Suppose that ten impartial witnesses all tell the same story as the employee. Could defendant legitimately deny the request to admit on the theory that all of them could possibly be lying or mistaken? See generally Finman, *The Request for Admissions in Federal Civil Procedure*, 71 Yale L.J. 371, 404–09 (1962); Shapiro, *Some Problems of Discovery in an Adversary System,* 63 Minn.L.Rev. 1055, 1078–92 (1979).

4. If a party serves a denial of the matters in the request to admit and at trial the matter is proved by the party requesting the admission, then Rule 37(c) provides that the latter may collect from the other party the reasonable expenses incurred in making the proof. How useful is this sanction? How can a party show that a given matter has been "proved"? See Board of Directors, Water's Edge v. Anden Group, 136 F.R.D. 100 (E.D.Va.1991). Why isn't a more serious sanction available for a deliberately false denial?

7. THE DUTY TO SUPPLEMENT RESPONSES

Read Federal Rule of Civil Procedure 26(e) and the accompanying Advisory Committee's Notes in the Supplement.

Rule 26(e), adopted in 1970 and amended in 1993, was designed to eliminate inconsistent decisions regarding the existence and scope of the duty to update discovery answers. The 1993 amendments to Rule 26(e) broadened the obligation to supplement discovery responses, requiring that disclosures and responses to interrogatories, requests for production, and requests for admissions be supplemented "if the party learns that in some material respect the disclosure or response is incomplete or incorrect" and if the updated information has not otherwise been made known to the other parties. Note that the Rule is not all-encompassing. What information obtained subsequent to the original responses is not covered by it?

What is the appropriate sanction for a breach of a duty to supplement answers? Consider the following:

> The court necessarily has wide discretion in fashioning a proper sanction response to failure to supplement. * * *
>
> The court should consider the explanation, if any, for the failure to identify a witness or other evidence, the importance of the testimony of the witness, the need for time to prepare to meet the newly-disclosed evidence, and the possibility of a continuance. In addition, a pattern of misconduct by counsel may provide a basis for imposing a severe sanction. In the light of all these factors the court may then determine to permit the witness to testify or the evidence to be introduced, or it may exclude the testimony, or it may grant a continuance so that the other side may take the deposition of the witness or otherwise prepare to meet the testimony.

8 Wright, Miller & Marcus, Federal Practice and Procedure: Civil 2d § 2050.

8. USE OF DISCOVERY AT TRIAL

Read Federal Rules of Civil Procedure 32, 33(c), and 36(b) in the Supplement.

Attorneys can use the discovery devices simply to find out information, but commonly they anticipate using an adversary's or a witness's answers at trial: as admissions, to refresh a witness's recollection, or to provide a basis for cross-examination or impeachment. And sometimes a response to discovery can be used in lieu of or in addition to live testimony. The use of discovery responses at trial is governed by two sets of rules: the rules of procedure and the rules of evidence. As you read the following material, consider how the possibility that discovery responses may be used at trial should affect the conduct of discovery before trial. Are there circumstances in which the objective of obtaining discovery and the objective of using discovery responses at trial conflict?

BATTLE v. MEMORIAL HOSPITAL AT GULFPORT

United States Court of Appeals, Fifth Circuit, 2000.
228 F.3d 544.

PARKER, CIRCUIT JUDGE.

Daniel Battle, Jr. ("Daniel"), a minor, his mother Zeta Battle ("Mrs. Battle"), and his father Daniel Battle, Sr. ("Mr. Battle") brought suit alleging that negligent medical treatment by David L. Reeves, M.D., Dennis W. Aust, M.D. and Emergency Care Specialists of Mississippi, Ltd. resulted in injuries to Daniel Battle, Jr. * * * Defendants prevailed on all claims and Plaintiffs appeal. We affirm in part, vacate in part and remand for further proceedings.

I. Facts

In December 1994, fifteen-month-old Daniel suffered from viral encephalitis, an inflammation of the brain, which resulted in extensive neurological injury. Daniel, now six years old, was characterized at trial as "about as damaged as a human being can be and still be alive."

Daniel, born on September 8, 1993, was healthy and normal until December 22, 1994, when he developed a fever and sores on his tongue. Mrs. Battle took Daniel to his pediatrician, Dr. Reeves, who diagnosed an ear infection and tonsillitis and prescribed a course of antibiotics. Daniel's condition did not improve. Shortly before midnight on December 24, 1994, Mrs. Battle called and left a message with Dr. Reeves's answering service because Daniel's jaws were snapping shut. Mrs. Battle then called 911 because Daniel's face began to twitch and his eyes rolled back. When Dr. Reeves called back, the paramedics had arrived and they informed him that Daniel had seizures, fever and that one hand and his face were twitching.

Daniel was taken to Memorial Hospital and seen in the emergency room by Dr. Graves and Dr. Sheffield. Dr. Sheffield performed a lumbar puncture, which Dr. Graves interpreted as normal. After x-rays and some blood work, Daniel was diagnosed with febrile seizures, pneumonia and an ear infection. He was discharged and went home with a new set of antibiotics.

In the afternoon of December 25, Mrs. Battle called Dr. Reeves again and told him that Daniel was continuing to have seizures. Dr. Reeves instructed her to take Daniel back to the Memorial Hospital emergency room where he was seen by Dr. Aust. On this second trip, Mrs. Battle put "self-pay" on the emergency room paper work. Dr. Aust diagnosed Daniel with "seizure disorder" and pneumonia and administered Dilantin for the seizures. As Mrs. Battle took Daniel home with a prescription for additional Dilantin, Dr. Aust instructed her to "not bring that child right back in here because Dilantin takes time to work."

When the Dilantin wore off, Daniel's seizures returned and continued on and off throughout the day on December 26. That afternoon, Mrs. Battle called Dr. Reeves again. Dr. Reeves instructed her to take Daniel to Memorial Hospital and have him admitted, which she did. Drs. Aust and Reeves ordered a CT scan, without contrast, which was read as negative. They also ordered an EEG, which was not read until seven days later. When read, it was grossly abnormal.

At 9:00 p.m. on December 26, Dr. Reeves saw Daniel for the first time since December 22. Daniel's condition continued to deteriorate. At 5:00 p.m. on December 27, Dr. Reeves's partner, Dr. Akin, saw Daniel. She diagnosed viral encephalitis, possibly the rare and dangerous herpes simplex encephalitis ("HSE"), and initiated treatment with Acyclovir, a drug that can halt the progression of HSE in some patients. She then arranged for a helicopter to transport Daniel to Tulane Medical Center where he could receive care from an infectious disease specialist. When Daniel arrived at Tulane around midnight of December 27, health care personnel immediately did a lumbar puncture which was grossly abnormal. They also performed a CT scan, with and without contrast, and an MRI. All the tests revealed abnormal results consistent with HSE.

A positive diagnosis of HSE requires a brain biopsy or a DNA test called PCR ("polymerase chain reaction"). Daniel's spinal fluid, obtained from the lumbar puncture on December 27, 1994, was tested at Tulane as well as being sent to the Whitley laboratory at the University of Alabama, which specializes in HSE research. Tulane's test was negative for HSE. On January 19, 1995, Dr. Fred Lakeman in the Whitley lab obtained a positive result on the PCR test, indicating that Daniel had HSE.

Despite the fact that the suspicion of HSE was unconfirmed until January 19, Daniel remained on Acyclovir throughout his treatment at Tulane. Daniel was discharged from Tulane on February 1, 1995, in a near vegetative state. He will require 24–hour–a–day care for the rest of his life.

II. Procedural History

* * *

* * * After extensive discovery, the case was set for trial on September 14, 1998.

Prior to trial, the district court granted summary judgment for Memorial Hospital on Plaintiffs' state law claims, finding that the claims had not been filed within the controlling Mississippi one-year statute of limitations.

Approximately three weeks prior to trial, Plaintiffs informed Defendants that expert witness Lowell Young, M.D., would not be available for trial and noticed the videotape deposition of Dr. Young for September 3, 1998, in San Francisco, California. On September 2, 1998, Plaintiffs moved for a continuance based on the unavailability for trial of another expert, Dr. Richard Whitley. On September 3, 1998, Plaintiffs noticed the deposition of Whitley for September 9, 1998. The district court granted Plaintiffs' motion for continuance and reset the trial for January 25, 1999.

* * * [T]he parties consented to trial before Chief Magistrate Judge John Roper. Before trial, Magistrate Judge Roper * * * prohibited Plaintiffs from introducing into evidence the deposition of Plaintiffs' expert Dr. Fred Lakeman. Dr. Young's video deposition was admitted, but Plaintiffs were not allowed to call him live. Plaintiffs challenge each of these rulings on appeal.

* * *

III. Analysis

A. Evidentiary Rulings

Plaintiffs assign as error three evidentiary rulings and argue that the cumulative impact of these errors resulted in prejudice and requires reversal of the judgment for Defendants.

* * *

[Initially the court held that the magistrate judge did not err in refusing to exclude evidence of past criminal acts by a non-family member who sought damages in connection with the infant's treatment.]

2. Exclusion of Lakeman's deposition

Fred Lakeman, a Ph.D. microbiomedical researcher and virologist who runs the Whitley lab at the University of Alabama, has done extensive research on HSE. Lakeman was responsible for HSE testing at the Whitley lab in 1994–95, although the record is not clear whether Lakeman personally ran Daniel's test or had it run by an assistant under his supervision. One critical issue at trial was Defendants' contention that Daniel did not have HSE. This point is material because HSE is the only form of encephalitis treatable by Acyclovir. Plaintiffs' claims hinge on their contention that delay in administering Acyclovir was the cause of Daniel's injuries. The evidence showed that Lakeman's test of Daniel's cerebral spinal fluid ("CSF") extracted on December 27, 1994, was positive for HSE, while Tulane's test on the same sample of CSF was negative. To prevail, Plaintiffs needed to convince the jury that Lakeman's positive result was accurate and Tulane's negative result was erroneous.

Counsel for Defendant Aust noticed Lakeman's deposition "pursuant to Rule 30, * * * and other applicable provisions of said Rules." During the deposition Defendants posited an objection, taking the position that the deposition could be used for "discovery purposes only." Plaintiffs countered that they intended to use it "for all purposes allowed by the Federal Rules * * *." Subsequently, Plaintiffs listed Lakeman in the pretrial order as a "may call" witness, as well as a "may call by deposition" witness. Defendants objected in the pretrial order "to the use of depositions of Defendants and other witnesses available live. Most of these depositions are hearsay and do not meet criteria necessary to substitute for live testimony." At a hearing just before trial started, Defendants submitted that the purpose of Lakeman's deposition was to develop Plaintiffs' expert's opinion and discover the basis of that opinion. Defendants contended that they asked open-ended questions to produce answers to submit to their own experts for review and that they were not prepared and did not cross-examine the witness to challenge or discredit any of his opinions. Defendants further asserted that Lakeman was under Plaintiffs' control and that Plaintiffs did not demonstrate that he was unavailable. The magistrate judge held that because Plaintiffs had not demonstrated that Lakeman was unavailable and had not noticed a "trial" deposition of Lakeman, the "discovery" deposition of Lakeman was not admissible during Plaintiffs' case-in-chief.

On appeal, Plaintiffs challenge the distinction between trial and discovery depositions. * * * This court has held that nothing prohibits the use of a discovery deposition at trial, particularly against the party who conducted it. * * *

Dr. Aust defends the trial/discovery dichotomy used by the trial court by reference to Rule 26(b)(4) * * *. We venture no opinion concerning whether Rule 26 supports the distinction between trial and discovery depositions of experts made by the trial court because that distinction simply does not apply in this case to Lakeman, who, because he was a fact witness as well as an expert, must be treated as an ordinary witness for purposes of Rule 26 analysis.

Dr. Reeves takes a different tack on appeal, arguing that the deposition was properly excluded because it was inadmissible hearsay. * * *

Dr. Reeves contends that Defendants did not have the requisite similar motive to develop Lakeman's testimony as would be the case at trial. Defendants argued to the trial court that the deposition was taken for the limited purpose of developing the expert's opinion and its basis. Defendants asked open ended questions to produce answers to submit to their own experts for review and were neither prepared for, nor did they attempt, cross-examination. Finally, Defendants asserted that Plaintiffs had not demonstrated that Lakeman was unavailable. Magistrate Judge Roper concurred with that position and excluded the deposition, but made no specific finding concerning similar motive.

There is no dispute that Lakeman was more than 100 miles from the place of trial. * * * [The issue then is whether in this case Federal Rule of Evidence 804(b)(1) provides an exception to the hearsay rule to allow admission of former testimony, including testimony in a deposition. Rule 804(b)(1) requires that a party against whom former testimony is offered "had an opportunity and similar motive," at the time the testimony was taken, "to develop the testimony by direct, cross, or redirect examination."] Because similar motive does not mean identical motive, the similar-motive inquiry is inherently a factual inquiry, depending in part on the similarity of the underlying issues and on the context of the questioning. * * *. Moreover, like other inquiries involving the admission of evidence, the similar-motive inquiry appropriately reflects narrow concerns of ensuring the reliability of evidence admitted at trial. * * *

The Fifth Circuit has not addressed how a court is to determine similarity of motive * * *. The Second Circuit has held that the test must turn not only on whether the questioner is on the same side of the same issue at both proceedings, but also on whether the questioner had a substantially similar interest in asserting and prevailing on the issue. * * * The availability of cross-examination opportunities that were forgone is one factor to be considered, but is not conclusive because examiners will virtually always be able to suggest lines of questioning that were not pursued at a prior proceeding. * * * We find this fact-specific test for determining similar motive valuable.

Defendants in this case were clearly on the same side of the same issues at the deposition and at the trial and had the same interest in asserting and prevailing on those issues. The core of their argument is that they did not aggressively test Lakeman's answers with cross-examination type questions. They claim their deposition questions were motivated only by the desire to understand Plaintiffs' case, not to test it with cross examination. Defendants posit no argument that Lakeman's deposition testimony lacked reliability. They do not suggest a single question or line of questioning that would have added reliability to the deposition. In fact, they characterize Lakeman's deposition testimony as cumulative of Whitley's testimony which was admitted at trial. Based on the foregoing, we conclude that Defendants' motive in questioning Lakeman at his deposition was similar to their motive at trial and consequently, Lakeman's deposition was admissible pursuant to Rule 804.

Defendants next argue that if the exclusion of Lakeman's testimony was error, it was harmless error. Lakeman tested Daniel's CSF under the auspices of Whitley's research facility. Defendants contend that Whitley's testimony regarding the lab, the testing procedures and the results covered similar ground, and because Lakeman's deposition added nothing essential, its exclusion does not rise to the level of affecting Plaintiffs' substantial rights. * * * We disagree.

Dr. Whitley testified summarily that Tulane's PCR test was done using a "different set of primers and a different essay [sic], by a laboratory that doesn't have experience doing it." Lakeman, on the other hand, went into great detail about the differences between the practices of the two laboratories, identifying three variables that could account for the different results, all of which indicated that the Whitley lab result was correct. First, he explained that Tulane used an extraction technique that could fail to pick up all the nucleic acid in a particular sample, while the Whitley lab used the straight spinal fluid. Second, he discussed dangers that arose from the handling of the sample. If the specimen was improperly stored, the target breaks down and yields a false negative. On the other hand, if the specimen was contaminated by the introduction of herpes simplex it would yield a false positive. However, although herpes is a rather common virus, the number of people who are capable of transmitting herpes simplex for such a contamination at a given time is very small. Third, he explained at length the controls his lab used to guard against false positives and negatives.

Much was made at trial of the fact that the PCR test was not licensed for diagnosing HSE. Lakeman testified that marketing drives the licensing process much more than science. Although the HSE test is as reliable as HIV testing, for example, there is little market for a HSE test, because the disease is so rare. Whitley testified summarily on this point as well, stating only that the PCR test is the diagnostic method of choice, but that licensure has not been pursued "because of the difficulty required."

Given these differences, we conclude that Lakeman's testimony was not merely cumulative of Whitley's deposition. In fact, it added information that, if the jurors found it credible, might have been determinative of the question of whether Daniel had HSE. Therefore, the exclusion of Lakeman's deposition testimony was not harmless error.

7. *Live Testimony of Dr. Young*

On November 21, 1997, the district court set this case for trial on its September 1998 calendar. On August 26, 1998, Plaintiff noticed the video deposition of an expert witness, Dr. Lowell Young, in San Francisco, California, due to his unavailability for trial. Defendants objected and the court ruled that Dr. Young's trial deposition should be taken in the interest of justice.

On September 2, 1998, one day before Dr. Young's scheduled deposition, Plaintiffs filed a motion for continuance of the trial, citing the unavailability of Dr. Whitley, another expert, for trial or deposition. Defense counsel objected to revealing their cross-examination strategy if Dr. Young was deposed and later allowed to testify live. The court held a hearing on the motion for continuance by telephone conference call on September 3, 1998, just prior to the start of Dr. Young's deposition, but no record was made of the hearing. On September 9, 1998, the court entered an order finding Plaintiffs' actions dilatory, granting the motion to continue, resetting the trial for January 25, 1999, and ruling that Dr. Young's testimony could be presented only by his video deposition taken on September 3, 1998.

On appeal, Plaintiffs contend that the district court abused its discretion in requiring Dr. Young's testimony to be presented by video deposition rather than live. Plaintiffs rely on *Jauch v. Corley,* 830 F.2d 47 (5th Cir.1987), which held that a trial court erred in allowing the introduction of a witness's deposition when the record showed that the witness worked less than a mile from the courthouse, because "a deposition is an acceptable substitute for oral testimony when in-court observation of the witness is extremely difficult or virtually impossible." * * *

Defendants respond that Dr. Young lives and works more than 100 miles from the location of the trial, thus satisfying Rule 32(a)(3)(B)'s unavailability requirement and rebutting the preference for live testimony over deposition. [This provision has been renumbered as Rule 32(a)(4)(B).] There is nothing in the record to otherwise establish his availability. Defendants also point out that the preference for live testimony over depositions is strongest when the deposition is presented to the jury in the form of a cold transcript. A videotaped deposition, on the other hand, allows jurors to gauge the witness's attitude reflected by his motions, facial expressions, demeanor and voice inflections. * * *

* * * [W]e conclude that the district court did not abuse its discretion in requiring Plaintiffs to use the video deposition rather than live testimony in this case. The district court attempted to balance the competing interests of Defendants in protecting their cross examination strategy against Plaintiffs' need for Dr. Young's testimony in light of Plaintiffs' dilatory tactics. * * *

* * *

C. *Cumulative Effect of Trial Errors*

Finding merit in two of Plaintiffs' grounds of error—the exclusion of Lakeman's deposition and error in jury argument—we conclude that the substantial rights of Plaintiffs were affected. Therefore, judgment for Defendants must be vacated and this case remanded for further proceedings.

* * *

NOTES AND QUESTIONS

1. Why didn't the court in *Battle* simply rely on the terms of Federal Rule 32 to find the deposition to be admissible? Rule 32 seems inconsistent with Federal Evidence Rule 804(b)(1). Can they be reconciled?

2. Assume that a party, pursuant to its duty to update responses under Federal Rule 26(e), sends a supplementary set of answers much more favorable to itself than the original replies to deposition questions. May the adverse party introduce the original replies at trial? The court in MANGUAL v. PRUDENTIAL LINES, INC., 53 F.R.D. 301 (E.D.Pa.1971), held "yes," in accordance with normal evidence rules, which allow an adverse party to utilize any statement of its opponent. The court in *Mangual* went on to hold, however, that the party who made the responses was entitled to put in its subsequent answers, arguing that this was consistent with the policy of Rule 32(a)(6) providing that if only part of a deposition is introduced, the court, in the interests of justice, may order other portions to be introduced as well. Is the court's analogy a sound one?

3. Rule 36(b) was amended in 1970 to make clear that admissions under that Rule are conclusive for purposes of the pending action unless the court, on motion, permits the admission to be withdrawn or amended. Should the application of Rule 36(b) be automatic or should it apply only when the party who wishes to rely on an admission offers it into evidence? See National Bank of Georgia v. Hill, 148 Ga.App. 688, 252 S.E.2d 192 (1979) (court will ignore admission not offered into evidence).

4. Federal Rule 33 contains no provision comparable to Rule 36(b). Should an answer to an interrogatory also be binding at trial? How does Federal Rule 26(e), which deals with the duty to supplement responses, affect your answer?

SECTION D. SPECIAL PROBLEMS REGARDING THE SCOPE OF DISCOVERY

1. MATERIALS PREPARED IN ANTICIPATION OF TRIAL

Read Federal Rule of Civil Procedure 26(b)(3) and the related materials in the Supplement.

HICKMAN v. TAYLOR

Supreme Court of the United States, 1947.
329 U.S. 495, 67 S.Ct. 385, 91 L.Ed. 451.

Certiorari to the Circuit Court of Appeals for the Third Circuit.

MR. JUSTICE MURPHY delivered the opinion of the Court.

This case presents an important problem under the Federal Rules * * * as to the extent to which a party may inquire into oral and written statements of witnesses, or other information, secured by an adverse party's counsel in the course of preparation for possible litigation after a claim has arisen. Examination into a person's files and records, including those resulting from the professional activities of an attorney, must be judged with care. It is not without reason that various safeguards have been established to preclude unwarranted excursions into the privacy of a man's work. At the same time, public policy supports reasonable and necessary inquiries. Properly to balance these competing interests is a delicate and difficult task.

On February 7, 1943, the tug "J.M. Taylor" sank while engaged in helping to tow a car float of the Baltimore & Ohio Railroad across the Delaware River at Philadelphia. The accident was apparently unusual in nature, the cause of it still being unknown. Five of the nine crew members were drowned. Three days later the tug owners and the underwriters employed a law firm, of which respondent Fortenbaugh is a member, to defend them against potential suits by representatives of the deceased crew members and to sue the railroad for damages to the tug.

A public hearing was held on March 4, 1943, before the United States Steamboat Inspectors, at which the four survivors were examined. This testimony was recorded and made available to all interested parties. Shortly thereafter, Fortenbaugh privately interviewed the survivors and took statements from them with an eye toward the anticipated litigation; the survivors signed these statements on March 29. Fortenbaugh also interviewed other persons believed to have some information relating to the accident and in some cases he made memoranda of what they told him. At the time when Fortenbaugh secured the statements of the survivors, representatives of two of the deceased crew members had been in communication with him. Ultimately claims were presented by representatives of all five of the deceased; four of the claims, however, were settled without litigation. The fifth claimant, petitioner herein, brought suit in a federal court under the Jones Act on November 26, 1943, naming as defendants the two tug owners, individually and as partners, and the railroad.

One year later, petitioner filed 39 interrogatories directed to the tug owners. The 38th interrogatory read: "State whether any statements of the members of the crews of the Tugs 'J.M. Taylor' and 'Philadelphia' or of any other vessel were taken in connection with the towing of the car float and the sinking of the Tug 'John M. Taylor'. Attach hereto exact copies of all such statements if in writing, and if oral, set forth in detail the exact provisions of any such oral statements or reports."

Supplemental interrogatories asked whether any oral or written statements, records, reports or other memoranda had been made concerning any matter relative to the towing operation, the sinking of the tug, the salvaging and repair of the tug, and the death of the deceased. If the answer was in the affirmative, the tug owners were then requested to set forth the nature of all such records, reports, statements or other memoranda.

The tug owners, through Fortenbaugh, answered all of the interrogatories except No. 38 and the supplemental ones just described. While admitting that statements of the survivors had been taken, they declined to summarize or set forth the contents. They did so on the ground that such requests called "for privileged matter obtained in preparation for litigation" and constituted "an attempt to obtain indirectly counsel's private files." It was claimed that answering these requests "would involve practically turning over not only the complete files, but also the telephone records and, almost, the thoughts of counsel."

In connection with the hearing on these objections, Fortenbaugh made a written statement and gave an informal oral deposition explaining the circumstances under which he had taken the statements. But he was not expressly asked in the deposition to produce the statements. The District Court for the Eastern District of Pennsylvania, sitting en banc, held that the requested matters were not privileged. 4 F.R.D. 479. The court then decreed that the tug owners and Fortenbaugh, as counsel and agent for the tug owners forthwith "Answer Plaintiff's 38th interrogatory and supplemental interrogatories; produce all written statements of witnesses obtained by Mr. Fortenbaugh, as counsel and agent for Defendants; state in substance any fact concerning this case which Defendants learned through oral statements made by witnesses to Mr. Fortenbaugh whether or not included in his private memoranda and produce Mr. Fortenbaugh's memoranda containing statements of fact by witnesses or to submit these memoranda to the Court for determination of those portions which should be revealed to Plaintiff." Upon their refusal, the court adjudged them in contempt and ordered them imprisoned until they complied.

The Third Circuit Court of Appeals, also sitting en banc, reversed the judgment of the District Court. 153 F.2d 212. It held that the information here sought was part of the "work product of the lawyer" and hence privileged from discovery under the Federal Rules of Civil Procedure. The importance of the problem, which has engendered a great divergence of views among district courts, led us to grant certiorari. * * *

There is an initial question as to which of the deposition-discovery rules is involved in this case. Petitioner, in filing his interrogatories, thought that he was proceeding under Rule 33.

* * * [I]t does not appear from the record that petitioner filed a motion under Rule 34 for a court order directing the production of the documents in question. Indeed, such an order could not have been entered as to Fortenbaugh since Rule 34, like Rule 33, is limited to parties to the proceeding, thereby excluding their counsel or agents.

Thus to the extent that petitioner was seeking the production of the memoranda and statements gathered by Fortenbaugh in the course of his activities as counsel, petitioner misconceived his remedy. Rule 33 did not permit him to obtain such memoranda and statements as adjuncts to the interrogatories addressed to the individual tug owners. A party clearly cannot refuse to answer interrogatories on the ground that the information sought is solely within the knowledge of his attorney. But that is not this case. Here production was sought of documents prepared by a party's attorney after the claim has arisen. Rule 33 does not make provision for such production, even when sought in connection with permissible interrogatories. Moreover, since petitioner was also foreclosed from securing them through an order under Rule 34, his only recourse was to take Fortenbaugh's deposition under Rule 26 and to attempt to force Fortenbaugh to produce the materials by use of a subpoena *duces tecum* in accordance with Rule 45. * * * But despite petitioner's faulty choice of action, the District Court entered an order, apparently under Rule 34, commanding the tug owners and Fortenbaugh, as their agent and counsel, to produce the materials in question. Their refusal led to the anomalous result of holding the tug owners in contempt for failure to produce that which was in the possession of their counsel and of holding Fortenbaugh in contempt for failure to produce that which he could not be compelled to produce under either Rule 33 or Rule 34.

But under the circumstances we deem it unnecessary and unwise to rest our decision upon this procedural irregularity, an irregularity which is not strongly urged upon us and which was disregarded in the two courts below. * * * [T]he basic question at stake is whether any of those devices may be used to inquire into materials collected by an adverse party's counsel in the course of preparation for possible litigation. The fact that the petitioner may have used the wrong method does not destroy the main thrust of his attempt. * * * [I]n the present circumstances, for the purposes of this decision, the procedural irregularity is not material. * * *

In urging that he has a right to inquire into the materials secured and prepared by Fortenbaugh, petitioner emphasizes that the deposition-discovery portions of the Federal Rules of Civil Procedure are designed to enable the parties to discover the true facts and to compel their disclosure wherever they may be found. It is said that inquiry may be made under these rules, epitomized by Rule 26, as to any relevant matter which is not privileged; and since the discovery provisions are to be applied as broadly and liberally as possible, the privilege limitation must be restricted to its narrowest bounds. On the premise that the attorney-client privilege is the one involved in this case, petitioner argues that it must be strictly confined to confidential communications made by a client to his attorney.

And since the materials here in issue were secured by Fortenbaugh from third persons rather than from his clients, the tug owners, the conclusion is reached that these materials are proper subjects for discovery under Rule 26.

As additional support for this result, petitioner claims that to prohibit discovery under these circumstances would give a corporate defendant a tremendous advantage in a suit by an individual plaintiff. Thus in a suit by an injured employee against a railroad or in a suit by an insured person against an insurance company the corporate defendant could pull a dark veil of secrecy over all the pertinent facts it can collect after the claim arises merely on the assertion that such facts were gathered by its large staff of attorneys and claim agents. At the same time, the individual plaintiff, who often has direct knowledge of the matter in issue and has no counsel until some time after his claim arises could be compelled to disclose all the intimate details of his case. By endowing with immunity from disclosure all that a lawyer discovers in the course of his duties, it is said, the rights of individual litigants in such cases are drained of vitality and the lawsuit becomes more of a battle of deception than a search for truth.

But framing the problem in terms of assisting individual plaintiffs in their suits against corporate defendants is unsatisfactory. Discovery concededly may work to the disadvantage as well as to the advantage of individual plaintiffs. Discovery, in other words, is not a one-way proposition. It is available in all types of cases at the behest of any party, individual or corporate, plaintiff or defendant. The problem thus far transcends the situation confronting this petitioner. And we must view that problem in light of the limitless situations where the particular kind of discovery sought by petitioner might be used.

We agree, of course, that the deposition-discovery rules are to be accorded a broad and liberal treatment. No longer can the time-honored cry of "fishing expedition" serve to preclude a party from inquiring into the facts underlying his opponent's case. Mutual knowledge of all the relevant facts gathered by both parties is essential to proper litigation. To that end, either party may compel the other to disgorge whatever facts he has in his possession. The deposition-discovery procedure simply advances the stage at which the disclosure can be compelled from the time of trial to the period preceding it, thus reducing the possibility of surprise. But discovery, like all matters of procedure, has ultimate and necessary boundaries. As indicated by Rules 30(b) and (d) and 31(d), limitations inevitably arise when it can be shown that the examination is being conducted in bad faith or in such a manner as to annoy, embarrass or oppress the person subject to the inquiry. [These matters are now covered by Rule 26(c).] And as Rule 26(b) provides, further limitations come into existence when the inquiry touches upon the irrelevant or encroaches upon the recognized domains of privilege.

We also agree that the memoranda, statements and mental impressions in issue in this case fall outside the scope of the attorney-client privilege and hence are not protected from discovery on that basis. * * *

But the impropriety of invoking that privilege does not provide an answer to the problem before us. Petitioner has made more than an ordinary request for relevant, non-privileged facts in the possession of his adversaries or their counsel. He has sought discovery as of right of oral and written statements of witnesses whose identity is well known and whose availability to petitioner appears unimpaired. He has sought production of these matters after making the most searching inquiries of his opponents as to the circumstances surrounding the fatal accident, which inquiries were sworn to have been answered to the best of their information and belief. Interrogatories were directed toward all the events prior to, during and subsequent to the sinking of the tug. Full and honest answers to such broad inquiries would necessarily have included all pertinent information gleaned by Fortenbaugh through his interviews with the witnesses. Petitioner makes no suggestion, and we cannot assume, that the tug owners or Fortenbaugh were incomplete or dishonest in the framing of their answers. In addition, petitioner was free to examine the public testimony of the witnesses taken before the United States Steamboat Inspectors. We are thus dealing with an attempt to secure the production of written statements and mental impressions contained in the files and the mind of the attorney Fortenbaugh without any showing of necessity or any indication or claim that denial of such production would unduly prejudice the preparation of petitioner's case or cause him any hardship or injustice. For aught that appears, the essence of what petitioner seeks either has been revealed to him already through the interrogatories or is readily available to him direct from the witnesses for the asking.

* * *

In our opinion, neither Rule 26 nor any other rule dealing with discovery contemplates production under such circumstances. That is not because the subject matter is privileged or irrelevant, as those concepts are used in these rules. Here is simply an attempt, without purported necessity or justification, to secure written statements, private memoranda and personal recollections prepared or formed by an adverse party's counsel in the course of his legal duties. As such, it falls outside the arena of discovery and contravenes the public policy underlying the orderly prosecution and defense of legal claims. Not even the most liberal of discovery theories can justify unwarranted inquiries into the files and the mental impressions of an attorney.

Historically, a lawyer is an officer of the court and is bound to work for the advancement of justice while faithfully protecting the rightful interests of his clients. In performing his various duties, however, it is essential that a lawyer work with a certain degree of privacy, free from unnecessary intrusion by opposing parties and their counsel. Proper preparation of a client's case demands that he assemble information, sift what he considers to be the relevant from the irrelevant facts, prepare his legal theories and plan his strategy without undue and needless interference. That is the historical and the necessary way in which lawyers act within the framework of our system of jurisprudence to promote justice and to protect their clients' interests. This work is reflected, of course, in interviews, statements, memoranda, correspondence, briefs, mental impressions, personal beliefs, and countless other tangible and intangible ways—aptly though roughly termed by the Circuit Court of Appeals in this case (153 F.2d 212, 223) as the "work product of the lawyer." Were such materials open to opposing counsel on mere demand, much of what is now put down in writing would remain unwritten. An attorney's thoughts, heretofore inviolate, would not be his own. Inefficiency, unfairness and sharp practices would inevitably develop in the giving of legal advice and in the preparation of cases for trial. The effect on the legal profession would be demoralizing. And the interests of the clients and the cause of justice would be poorly served.

We do not mean to say that all written materials obtained or prepared by an adversary's counsel with an eye toward litigation are necessarily free from discovery in all cases. Where relevant and non-privileged facts remain hidden in an attorney's file and where production of those facts is essential to the preparation of one's case, discovery may properly be had. Such written statements and documents might, under certain circumstances, be admissible in evidence or give clues as to the existence or location of relevant facts. Or they might be useful for purposes of impeachment or corroboration. And production might be justified where the witnesses are no longer available or can be reached only with difficulty. Were production of written statements and documents to be precluded under such circumstances, the liberal ideals of the deposition-discovery portions of the Federal Rules * * * would be stripped of much of their meaning. But the general policy against invading the privacy of an attorney's course of preparation is so well recognized and so essential to an orderly working of our system of legal procedure that a burden rests on the one who would invade that privacy to establish adequate reasons to justify production through a subpoena or court order. That burden, we believe, is necessarily implicit in the rules as now constituted.

Rule 30(b), as presently written, gives the trial judge the requisite discretion to make a judgment as to whether discovery should be allowed as to written statements secured from witnesses. But in the instant case there was no room for that discretion to operate in favor of the petitioner. No attempt was made to establish any reason why Fortenbaugh should be forced to produce the written statements. There was only a naked, general demand for these materials as of right and a finding by the District Court that no recognizable privilege was involved. That was insufficient to justify discovery under these circumstances and the court should have sustained the refusal of the tug owners and Fortenbaugh to produce.

But as to oral statements made by witnesses to Fortenbaugh, whether presently in the form of his mental impressions or memoranda, we do not believe that any showing of necessity can be made under the circumstances of this case so as to justify production. Under ordinary conditions, forcing an attorney to repeat or write out all that witnesses have told him and to deliver the account to his adversary gives rise to grave dangers of inaccuracy and untrustworthiness. No legitimate purpose is served by such production. The practice forces the attorney to testify as to what he remembers or what he saw fit to write down regarding witnesses' remarks. Such testimony could not qualify as evidence; and to use it for impeachment or corroborative purposes would make the attorney much less an officer of the court and much more an ordinary witness. The standards of the profession would thereby suffer.

Denial of production of this nature does not mean that any material, nonprivileged facts can be hidden from the petitioner in this case. He need not be unduly hindered in the preparation of his case, in the discovery of facts or in his anticipation of his opponents' position. Searching interrogatories directed to Fortenbaugh and the tug owners, production of written documents and statements upon a proper showing and direct interviews with the witnesses themselves all serve to reveal the facts in Fortenbaugh's possession to the fullest possible extent consistent with public policy. Petitioner's counsel frankly admits that he wants the oral statements only to help prepare himself to examine witnesses and to make sure that he has overlooked nothing. That is insufficient under the circumstances to permit him an exception to the policy underlying the privacy of Fortenbaugh's professional activities. If there should be a rare situation justifying production of these matters, petitioner's case is not of that type.

We fully appreciate the wide-spread controversy among the members of the legal profession over the problem raised by this case. It is a problem that rests on what has been one of the most hazy frontiers of the discovery process. But until some rule or statute definitely prescribes otherwise, we are not justified in permitting discovery in a situation of this nature as a matter of unqualified right. When Rule 26 and the other discovery rules were adopted, this Court and the members of the bar in general certainly did not believe or contemplate that all the files and mental processes of lawyers were thereby opened to the free scrutiny of their adversaries. And we refuse to interpret the rules at this time so as to reach so harsh and unwarranted a result.

We therefore affirm the judgment of the Circuit Court of Appeals.

Affirmed.

MR. JUSTICE JACKSON, concurring.

* * *

To consider first the most extreme aspect of the requirement in litigation here, we find it calls upon counsel, if he has had any conversations with any of the crews of the vessels in question or of any other, to "set forth in detail the exact provision of any such oral statements or reports." Thus the demand is not for the production of a transcript in existence but calls for the creation of a written statement not in being. But the statement by counsel of what a witness told him is not evidence when written. Plaintiff could not introduce it to prove his case. What, then, is the purpose sought to be served by demanding this of adverse counsel?

Counsel for the petitioner candidly said on argument that he wanted this information to help prepare himself to examine witnesses, to make sure he overlooked nothing. He bases his claim to it in his brief on the view that the Rules were to do away with the old situation where a law suit developed into "a battle of wits between counsel." But a common law trial is and always should be an adversary proceeding. Discovery was hardly intended to enable a learned profession to perform its functions either without wits or on wits borrowed from the adversary.

The real purpose and the probable effect of the practice ordered by the district court would be to put trials on a level even lower than a "battle of wits." I can conceive of no practice more demoralizing to the Bar than to require a lawyer to write out and deliver to his adversary an account of what witnesses have told him. Even if his recollection were perfect, the statement would be his language permeated with his inferences. Every one who has tried it knows that it is almost impossible so fairly to record the expressions and emphasis of a witness that when he testifies in the environment of the court and under the influence of the leading question there will not be departures in some respects. Whenever the testimony of the witness would differ from the "exact" statement the lawyer had delivered, the lawyer's statement would be whipped out to impeach the witness. Counsel producing his adversary's "inexact" statement could lose nothing by saying, "Here is a contradiction, gentlemen of the jury. I do not know whether it is my adversary or his witness who is not telling the truth, but one is not." Of course, if this practice were adopted, that scene would be repeated over and over again. The lawyer who delivers such statements often would find himself branded a deceiver afraid to take the stand to support his own version of the witness's conversation with him, or else he will have to go on the stand to defend his own credibility—perhaps against that of his chief witness, or possibly even his client.

Every lawyer dislikes to take the witness stand and will do so only for grave reasons. This is partly because it is not his role; he is almost invariably a poor witness. But he steps out of professional character to do it. He regrets it; the profession discourages it. But the practice advocated here is one which would force him to be a witness, not as to what he has seen or done but as to other witnesses' stories, and not because he wants to do so but in self-defense.

And what is the lawyer to do who has interviewed one whom he believes to be a biased, lying or hostile witness to get his unfavorable statements and know what to meet? He must record and deliver such statements even though he would not vouch for the credibility of the witness by calling him. Perhaps the other side would not want to call him either, but the attorney is open to the charge of suppressing evidence at the trial if he fails to call such a hostile witness even though he never regarded him as reliable or truthful.

Having been supplied the names of the witnesses, petitioner's lawyer gives no reason why he cannot interview them himself. If an employee-witness refuses to tell his story, he, too, may be examined under the Rules. He may be compelled on discovery as fully as on the trial to disclose his version of the facts. But that is his own disclosure—it can be used to impeach him if he contradicts it and such a deposition is not useful to promote an unseemly disagreement between the witness and the counsel in the case.

It is true that the literal language of the Rules would admit of an interpretation that would sustain the district court's order. * * * But all such procedural measures have a background of custom and practice which was assumed by those who wrote and should be by those who apply them. * * * Certainly nothing in the tradition or practice of discovery up to the time of these Rules would have suggested that they would authorize such a practice as here proposed.

The question remains as to signed statements or those written by witnesses. Such statements are not evidence for the defendant. * * * Nor should I think they ordinarily could be evidence for the plaintiff. But such a statement might be useful for impeachment of the witness who signed it, if he is called and if he departs from the statement. There might be circumstances, too, where impossibility or difficulty of access to the witness or his refusal to respond to requests for information or other facts would show that the interests of justice require that such statements be made available. Production of such statements are governed by Rule 34 and on "Showing good cause therefore" the court may order their inspection, copying or photographing. No such application has here been made; the demand is made on the basis of right, not on showing of cause. [The requirement of "good cause" was removed by the 1970 amendment to Rule 34.]

I agree to the affirmance of the judgment of the Circuit Court of Appeals which reversed the district court.

MR. JUSTICE FRANKFURTER joins in this opinion.

NOTES AND QUESTIONS

1. In 1970, Federal Rule 26(b)(3) was added specifically to deal with the discovery of work product. In what ways does the work-product doctrine in the Rule differ from that stated in *Hickman*? Does *Hickman* survive the codification of the work-product doctrine in the Rule in any way? See Clermont, *Surveying Work Product,* 68 Cornell L.Rev. 755 (1983).

2. Does Rule 26(b)(3) protect documents containing the results of a party's investigations made prior to hiring an attorney or the initiation of litigation? Does it protect material prepared as part of an organization's normal course of business even if the probability of litigation is overwhelming? Should protection cover the following circumstances?

a) A company prepares a memorandum about a contemplated transaction recognizing that the transaction may result in litigation;

b) A company is engaged in merger discussions with another company, which requests a candid assessment of the likelihood of success in pending litigations; or

c) A company prepares financial statements for its executives, including reserves for projected litigation.

See United States v. Adlman, 134 F.3d 1194 (2d Cir.1998) (providing a comprehensive discussion of the different positions).

3. What circumstances constitute a sufficient showing of necessity to overcome work-product protection under Rule 26(b)(3)? In SNEAD v. AMERICAN EXPORT–ISBRANDTSEN LINES, INC., 59 F.R.D. 148, 151 (E.D.Pa. 1973), plaintiff, who had brought suit to recover for personal injuries, moved for a court order requiring defendant to answer interrogatories as to whether defendant had possession of any secret motion pictures taken of plaintiff that would tend to bear on the scope of plaintiff's injuries. The court held as follows:

> * * * The only time there will be a substantial need to know about surveillance pictures will be in those instances where there would be a major discrepancy between the testimony the plaintiff will give and that which the films would seem to portray. By the same token this would be the only instance where there is a substantial need to withhold that information from plaintiff's counsel. If the discrepancy would be the result of the plaintiff's untruthfulness, the substantial need for his counsel to know of the variance can hardly justify making the information available to him. On the other hand, if the discrepancy would result from misleading photography, the necessary background information should be made available to the plaintiff's attorney so the fraud can be exposed. It goes without saying that the means to impeach should not be the exclusive property of the defense. * * *
>
> I conclude these purposes can best be achieved by requiring the defense to disclose the existence of surveillance films or be barred from showing them at trial. If the defense has films and decides it wants to use them, they should be exhibited to the plaintiff and his counsel. * * *
>
> Before any of these disclosures, however, the defense must be given an opportunity to depose the plaintiff fully as to his injuries, their effects, and his present disabilities. Once his testimony is memorialized in deposition, any variation he may make at trial to conform to the surveillance films can be used to impeach his credibility, and his knowledge at deposition that the films may exist should have a salutary effect on any tendency to be expansive. * * *

Isn't it true that whenever a document or other item is to be introduced into evidence by one party, there will be a need for discovery, at least for the purpose of determining whether such an item has been forged, distorted, or altered in some way?

Is the *Snead* court's view as to the relevance of surveillance films too narrow? Impeachment is solely for the purpose of casting doubt on the veracity of a witness. But films of a party's physical condition also may be direct evidence of the condition itself. Certainly evidence that bears directly on the facts at issue in the case cannot be kept hidden until trial and then held to be admissible. The vast majority of courts thus permit discovery of such evidence if it is to be used at trial, regardless of its intended purpose. See Gutshall v. New Prime, Inc., 196 F.R.D. 43 (W.D.Va.2000). Suppose in *Snead* the motion pictures strongly supported plaintiff's case and would not have been introduced at trial by defendant. Should they be protected from discovery by plaintiff? See Fisher v. National R.R. Passenger Corp., 152 F.R.D. 145 (S.D. Ind.1993).

4. How can Rule 26(b)(3)(B), which provides protection "against disclosure of the mental impressions, conclusions, opinions or legal theories of a party's attorney or other representative concerning litigation," be harmonized with Rules 33(c) and 36(a), which allow interrogatories and requests for admissions involving opinions or contentions that relate to fact or the application of law to fact? Consider these problems:

(a) Should a party have to disclose the selection of documents made by counsel to prepare a witness for deposition?

(b) Can a party depose the opposing party's attorney to determine whether discovery production has been complete?

For a discussion of these and other problems, see Waits, *Opinion Work Product: A Critical Analysis of Current Law and a New Analytical Framework*, 73 Ore. L. Rev. 385 (1994).

5. Rule 26(b)(3)(C) excludes from protection a party's own prior statement concerning the action. Why? See the Advisory Committee's Note to Rule 26(b)(3) set out in the Supplement. The Rule also permits a nonparty witness to obtain a copy of his statement upon request. Are the reasons for allowing a witness to obtain his own statement the same for a nonparty as they are for a party? Might a court usefully postpone release of the statement of a witness until after she has been deposed? See 8 Wright, Miller & Marcus, Federal Practice and Procedure: Civil 2d § 2028.

2. PRIVILEGES AND WORK PRODUCT— THE EXTENT OF PROTECTION

Rule 26(b)(1) limits discovery to "any nonprivileged matter," and the usual view has been that the same rules of privilege apply to discovery as apply at the trial. A privilege rule gives a person a right to refuse to disclose information that he otherwise would be required to provide. It also may give a person the right to prevent someone else from disclosing information, or it may give its possessor a right to refuse to become a witness. A rule of privilege is a counterweight to the general power of courts to compel testimony. Modern pretrial discovery involves an extension of the judicial power to compel disclosure and has been met by the expansion of old privileges and the creation of new ones that will check this power.

One rule of privilege that all American courts recognize is the attorney-client privilege. They also agree on its basic contours. For the privilege to attach to a communication, four elements must be present:

> (1) [T]he asserted holder of the privilege is or sought to be a client; (2) the person to whom the communication was made (a) is a member of the bar of a court, or his subordinate and (b) in connection with this communication is acting as a lawyer; (3) the communication relates to a fact of which the attorney was informed (a) by his client (b) without the presence of strangers (c) for the purpose of securing primarily either (i) an opinion on law or (ii) legal services or (iii) assistance in some legal proceeding, and not (d) for the purpose of committing a crime or tort; and (4) the privilege has been (a) claimed and (b) not waived by the client.

United States v. United Shoe Machinery Corp., 89 F.Supp. 357, 358–59 (D.Mass.1950).

Because the attorney-client privilege results in the suppression of relevant facts, courts tend to construe it narrowly and to resolve doubtful cases against a finding of privilege. One observer has said that "[w]hile often unexpressed, the crucial factor limiting the privilege's availability is not the past law of the privilege but the developing rules of liberal discovery. * * * At least when precedent is not absolutely clear, whether a party can assert the privilege will often depend less on the jurisdiction's law of privilege than on the particular judge's attitude toward liberal discovery." Bartell, "The Attorney–Client Privilege and the Work–Product Doctrine," in *ALI–ABA* Civil Procedure and Litigation in Federal and State Courts, vol. I, at 507 (1987).

UPJOHN CO. v. UNITED STATES

Supreme Court of the United States, 1981.
449 U.S. 383, 101 S.Ct. 677, 66 L.Ed.2d 584.

Certiorari to the United States Court of Appeals for the Sixth Circuit.

JUSTICE REHNQUIST delivered the opinion of the Court.

We granted certiorari in this case to address important questions concerning the scope of the attorney-client privilege in the corporate context and the applicability of the work-product doctrine in proceedings to enforce tax summonses. * * * With respect to the privilege question the parties and various *amici* have described our task as one of choosing between two "tests" which have gained adherents in the courts of appeals. We are acutely aware, however, that we sit to decide concrete cases and not abstract propositions of law. We decline to lay down a broad rule or series of rules to govern all conceivable future questions in this area, even were we able to do so. We can and do, however, conclude that the attorney-client privilege protects the communications involved in this case from compelled disclosure and that the work-product doctrine does apply in tax summons enforcement proceedings.

I

Petitioner Upjohn Co. manufactures and sells pharmaceuticals here and abroad. In January 1976 independent accountants conducting an audit of one of Upjohn's foreign subsidiaries discovered that the subsidiary made payments to or for the benefit of foreign government officials in order to secure government business. The accountants so informed Mr. Gerard Thomas, Upjohn's Vice President, Secretary, and General Counsel. * * * He consulted with outside counsel and R.T. Parfet, Jr., Upjohn's Chairman of the Board. It was decided that the company would conduct an internal investigation of what were termed "questionable payments." As part of this investigation the attorneys prepared a letter containing a questionnaire which was sent to "All Foreign General and Area Managers" over the Chairman's signature. The letter began by noting recent disclosures that several American companies made "possibly illegal" payments to foreign government officials and emphasized that the management needed full information concerning any such payments made by Upjohn. The letter indicated that the Chairman had asked Thomas, identified as "the company's General Counsel," "to conduct an investigation for the purpose of determining the nature and magnitude of any payments made by the Upjohn Company or any of its subsidiaries to any employee or official of a foreign government." The questionnaire sought detailed information concerning such payments. Managers were instructed to treat the investigation as "highly confidential" and not to discuss it with anyone other than Upjohn employees who might be helpful in providing the requested information. Responses were to be sent directly to Thomas. Thomas and outside counsel also interviewed the recipients of the questionnaire and some 33 other Upjohn officers or employees as part of the investigation.

On March 26, 1976, the company voluntarily submitted a preliminary report to the Securities and Exchange Commission on Form 8BK disclosing certain questionable payments. A copy of the report was simultaneously submitted to the Internal Revenue Service, which immediately began an investigation to determine the tax consequences of the payments. Special agents conducting the investigation were given lists by Upjohn of all those interviewed and all who had responded to the questionnaire. On November 23, 1976, the Service issued a summons pursuant to 26 U.S.C. § 7602 demanding production of:

> All files relative to the investigation conducted under the supervision of Gerard Thomas to identify payments to employees of foreign governments and any political contributions made by the Upjohn Company or any of its affiliates since January 1, 1971 and to deter-

> mine whether any funds of the Upjohn Company had been improperly accounted for on the corporate books during the same period.
>
> The records should include but not be limited to written questionnaires sent to managers of the Upjohn Company's foreign affiliates, and memoranda or notes of the interviews conducted in the United States and abroad with officers and employees of the Upjohn Company and its subsidiaries. App. 17a–18a.

The company declined to produce the documents specified in the second paragraph on the grounds that they were protected from disclosure by the attorney-client privilege and constituted the work product of attorneys prepared in anticipation of litigation. On August 31, 1977, the United States filed a petition seeking enforcement of the summons under 26 U.S.C. §§ 7402(b) and 7604(a) in the United States District Court for the Western District of Michigan. That court adopted the recommendation of a magistrate who concluded that the summons should be enforced. Petitioners appealed to the Court of Appeals for the Sixth Circuit which rejected the Magistrate's finding of a waiver of the attorney-client privilege, * * * but agreed that the privilege did not apply "[t]o the extent that the communications were made by officers and agents not responsible for directing Upjohn's actions in response to legal advice * * * for the simple reason that the communications were not the 'client's.' " * * * The court reasoned that accepting petitioner's claim for a broader application of the privilege would encourage upper-echelon management to ignore unpleasant facts and create too broad a "zone of silence." Noting that Upjohn's counsel had interviewed officials such as the Chairman and President, the Court of Appeals remanded to the District Court so that a determination of who was within the "control group" could be made. In a concluding footnote the court stated that the work-product doctrine "is not applicable to administrative summonses issued under 26 U.S.C. § 7602." * * *

II

Federal Rule of Evidence 501 provides that "the privilege of a witness * * * shall be governed by the principles of the common law as they may be interpreted by the courts of the United States in light of reason and experience." The attorney-client privilege is the oldest of the privileges for confidential communications known to the common law. 8 Wigmore, Evidence § 2290 (McNaughton rev. 1961). Its purpose is to encourage full and frank communication between attorneys and their clients and thereby promote broader public interests in the observance of law and administration of justice. The privilege recognizes that sound legal advice or advocacy serves public ends and that such advice or advocacy depends upon the lawyer's being fully informed by the client. * * * Admittedly complications in the application of the privilege arise when the client is a corporation, which in theory is an artificial creature of the law, and not an individual; but this Court has assumed that the privilege applies when the client is a corporation * * *.

The Court of Appeals, however, considered the application of the privilege in the corporate context to present a "different problem," since the client was an inanimate entity and "only the senior management, guiding and integrating the several operations, ... [omission in original] can be said to possess an identity analogous to the corporation as a whole." * * * Such a view, we think, overlooks the fact that the privilege exists to protect not only the giving of professional advice to those who can act on it but also the giving of information to the lawyer to enable him to give sound and informed advice. * * * The first step in the resolution of any legal problem is ascertaining the factual background and sifting through the facts with an eye to the legally relevant. * * *

In the case of the individual client the provider of information and the person who acts on the lawyer's advice are one and the same. In the corporate context, however, it will frequently be employees beyond the control group as defined by the court below—"officers and agents ... [omission in original] responsible for directing [the company's] actions in response to legal advice"—who will possess the information needed by the corporation's lawyers. Middle-level—and indeed lower-level—employees can, by actions within the scope of their employment, embroil the corporation in serious legal difficulties, and it is only natural that these employees would have the relevant information needed by corporate counsel if he is adequately to advise the client with respect to such actual or potential difficulties. * * *

The control group test adopted by the court below thus frustrates the very purpose of the privilege by discouraging the communication of relevant information by employees of the client to attorneys seeking to render legal advice to the client corporation. The attorney's advice will also frequently be more significant to noncontrol group members than to those who officially sanction the advice, and the control group test makes it more difficult to convey full and frank legal advice to the employees who will put into effect the client corporation's policy. * * *

The narrow scope given the attorney-client privilege by the court below not only makes it difficult for corporate attorneys to formulate sound advice when their client is faced with a specific legal problem but also threatens to limit the valuable efforts of corporate counsel to ensure their client's compliance with the law. In light of the vast and complicated array of regulatory legislation confronting the modern corporation, corporations, unlike most individuals, "constantly go to lawyers to find out how to obey the law[.]" * * * [I]f the purpose of the attorney-client privilege is to be served, the attorney and client must be able to predict with some degree of certainty whether particular discussions will be protected. An uncertain privilege, or one which purports to be certain but results in widely varying applications by the courts, is little better than no privilege at all. The very terms of the test adopted by the court below suggest the unpredictability of its application. The test restricts the availability of the privilege to those officers who play a "substantial role" in deciding and directing a corporation's legal response. * * *

The communications at issue were made by Upjohn employees to counsel for Upjohn acting as such, at the direction of corporate superiors in order to secure legal advice from counsel. * * * Information, not available from upper-echelon management, was needed to supply a basis for legal advice concerning compliance with securities and tax laws, foreign laws, currency regulations, duties to shareholders, and potential litigation in each of these areas. The communications concerned matters within the scope of the employees' corporate duties, and the employees themselves were sufficiently aware that they were being questioned in order that the corporation could obtain legal advice. The questionnaire identified Thomas as "the company's General Counsel" and referred in its opening sentence to the possible illegality of payments such as the ones on which information was sought. * * * A statement of policy accompanying the questionnaire clearly indicated the legal implications of the investigation. The policy statement was issued "in order that there be no uncertainty in the future as to the policy with respect to the practices which are the subject of this investigation." It began "Upjohn will comply with all laws and regulations," and stated that commissions or payments "will not be used as a subterfuge for bribes or illegal payments" and that all payments must be "proper and legal." Any future agreements with foreign distributors or agents were to be approved "by a company attorney" and any questions concerning the policy were to be referred "to the company's General Counsel." * * * This statement was issued to Upjohn employees worldwide, so that even those interviewees not receiving a questionnaire were aware of the legal implications of the interviews. Pursuant to explicit instructions from the Chairman of the Board, the communications were considered "highly confidential" when made, * * * and have been kept confidential by the company. Consistent with the underlying purposes of the attorney-client privilege, these communications must be protected against compelled disclosure.

The Court of Appeals declined to extend the attorney-client privilege beyond the limits of the control group test for fear that doing so would entail severe burdens on discovery and create a broad "zone of silence" over corporate affairs. Application of the attorney-client privilege to communications such as those involved here, however, puts the adversary in no worse position than if the communications had never taken place. The privilege only protects disclosure of communications; it does not protect disclosure of the underlying facts by those who communicated with the attorney * * *. Here the Government was free to question the employees who communicated with Thomas and outside counsel. Upjohn has provided the IRS with a list of such employees, and the IRS has already interviewed some 25 of them. While it would probably be more convenient for the Government to secure the results of petitioner's internal investigation by simply subpoenaing the questionnaires and notes taken by petitioner's attorneys, such considerations of convenience do not overcome the policies served by the attorney-client privilege. As Justice Jackson noted in his concurring opinion in Hickman v. Taylor * * *: "Discovery was hardly intended to enable a learned profession to perform its functions ... [omission in original] on wits borrowed from the adversary."

* * *

III

Our decision that the communications by Upjohn employees to counsel are covered by the attorney-client privilege disposes of the case so far as the responses to the questionnaires and any notes reflecting responses to interview questions are concerned. * * * To the extent that the material subject to the summons is not protected by the attorney-client privilege as disclosing communications between an employee and counsel, we must reach the ruling by the Court of Appeals that the work-product doctrine does not apply to summonses issued under 26 U.S.C. § 7602.[6]

The Government concedes, wisely, that the Court of Appeals erred and that the work-product doctrine does apply to IRS summonses. * * * This doctrine was announced by the Court over 30 years ago in Hickman v. Taylor * * *. In that case the Court rejected "an attempt, without purported necessity or justification, to secure written statements, private memoranda and personal recollections prepared or formed by an adverse party's counsel in the course of his legal duties." * * * The Court noted that "it is essential that a lawyer work with a certain degree of privacy" * * *. The "strong public policy" underlying the work-product doctrine * * * has been substantially incorporated in Federal Rule * * * 26(b)(3).

* * * Nothing in the language of the IRS summons provisions or their legislative history suggests an intent on the part of Congress to preclude application of the work-product doctrine. Rule 26(b)(3) codifies the work-product doctrine, and the Federal Rules of Civil Procedure are made applicable to summons enforcement proceedings by Rule 81(a)(3) [now Rule 81(a)(5)]. * * * While conceding the applicability of the work-product doctrine, the Government asserts that it has made a sufficient showing of necessity to overcome its protections. * * * The Government stresses that interviewees are scattered across the globe and that Upjohn has forbidden its employees to answer questions it considers irrelevant. The above-quoted language from *Hickman,* however, did not apply to "oral statements made by witnesses ... [omission in original] whether presently in the form of [the attorney's] mental impressions or memoranda." * * * As to such material the Court did "not believe that any showing of necessity can be made under the circumstances of this case so as to justify production * * *." * * * Forcing an attorney to disclose notes and memoranda of witnesses' oral statements is particularly disfavored because it tends to reveal the attorney's mental processes * * *.

Rule 26 accords special protection to work product revealing the attorney's mental processes. The Rule permits disclosure of documents

6. The following discussion will also be relevant to counsels' notes and memoranda of interviews with the seven former employees should it be determined that the attorney-client privilege does not apply to them. * * *

and tangible things constituting attorney work product upon a showing of substantial need and inability to obtain the equivalent without undue hardship. * * * Rule 26 goes on, however, to state that "[i]n ordering discovery of such materials when the required showing has been made, the court shall protect against disclosure of the mental impressions, conclusions, opinions or legal theories of an attorney or other representative of a party concerning the litigation." [This language has been altered but its substance has not been changed.] Although this language does not specifically refer to memoranda based on oral statements of witnesses, the *Hickman* court stressed the danger that compelled disclosure of such memoranda would reveal the attorney's mental processes. It is clear that this is the sort of material the draftsmen of the Rule had in mind as deserving special protection. * * *

* * * It is clear that the Magistrate applied the wrong standard when he concluded that the Government had made a sufficient showing of necessity to overcome the protections of the work-product doctrine. The Magistrate applied the "substantial need" and "without undue hardship" standard articulated in the first part of Rule 26(b)(3). The notes and memoranda sought by the Government here, however, are work product based on oral statements. If they reveal communications, they are, in this case, protected by the attorney-client privilege. To the extent they do not reveal communications, they reveal the attorneys' mental processes in evaluating the communications. As Rule 26 and *Hickman* make clear, such work product cannot be disclosed simply on a showing of substantial need and inability to obtain the equivalent without undue hardship.

While we are not prepared at this juncture to say that such material is always protected by the work-product rule, we think a far stronger showing of necessity and unavailability by other means than was made by the Government or applied by the Magistrate in this case would be necessary to compel disclosure. * * *

Accordingly, the judgment of the Court of Appeals is reversed, and the case remanded for further proceedings.

[The concurring opinion of CHIEF JUSTICE BURGER is omitted.]

NOTES AND QUESTIONS

1. In state courts, the attorney-client privilege is a creation of state law (state common law or statute), not of federal law. For state courts, therefore, the *Upjohn* decision is not binding authority, and several have not found its reasoning to be persuasive. See, e.g., Consolidation Coal Co. v. Bucyrus–Erie Co., 89 Ill.2d 103, 59 Ill.Dec. 666, 432 N.E.2d 250 (1982) (rejecting *Upjohn* and adopting the "control group" test).

In federal courts, the privilege is solely a matter of federal law, except that Federal Rule of Evidence 501 directs a federal district court sitting in a diversity case to apply the privilege law that would be applied by the courts of the state in which the federal court sits. When federal and state law claims are joined, federal law may govern the attorney-client privilege, Valente v. Pepsico, Inc., 68 F.R.D. 361, 366 n.10 (D.Del.1975), unless the allegedly privileged communication relates solely to the state law claims.

2. The *Upjohn* opinion did not announce a set of rules controlling the attorney-client privilege. How, then, can a corporation predict whether or not a communication will be found to be privileged? It has been suggested that the following rules underlie the *Upjohn* analysis: 1) the communication must be one that would not have been made but for the contemplation of legal services; 2) the content of the communication must relate to the legal services being rendered; 3) the information-giver must be an employee, agent, or independent contractor with a significant relationship to the corporation and the corporation's involvement in the transaction that is the subject of legal services; 4) the communication must be made in confidence; and 5) the privilege may be asserted either by the corporation or by the information-giver. See Sexton, *A Post–*Upjohn *Consideration of the Corporate Attorney–Client Privilege*, 57 N.Y.U. L. Rev. 443, 487 (1982). Do you agree?

3. Does the employee or the former employee who speaks to the corporation's attorney enjoy the protection of the attorney-client privilege? Suppose, for example, that a corporation conducts an internal investigation concerning its accounting practices and an employee or a former employee, in the course of describing how sloppy the practices are, admits to embezzling funds. Can the employee invoke the attorney-client privilege to prevent disclosure of the admission? Can the corporation authorize its attorney to disclose the admission? How far must a corporation's attorney go to make clear to an employee the nature of their relationship, and to warn the employee of the risks of using counsel for the corporation as the employee's personal counsel?

4. Historically, the attorney-client privilege and the work-product protection were waived if the protected communication was voluntarily disclosed. Once waived the party could be forced to disclose not only the specific communication but all communications involving the same subject matter. See Duplan Corp. v. Deering Milliken, Inc., 397 F.Supp. 1146 (D.S.C.1974). Given the breadth of modern discovery of documents and electronically stored information, the danger of an inadvertent disclosure of protected materials resulting in a waiver has become significant. The costs of discovery have escalated in a number of cases in which individuals are hired to scan every document or piece of information before turning it over to an opposing party. Concern over the injustice that this can cause has been addressed in Rule 26(b)(5)(B) and by enactment of Federal Rule of Evidence 502 that provides relief in federal courts from waiver in cases of inadvertent disclosure or when disclosure occurred despite reasonable efforts to prevent it. It is important to note, however, that the protection afforded by these rules applies only when materials are turned over in the course of a formal proceeding or to a governmental agency. Revealing the contents to a prospective witness or to an expert or to a nonparty is likely to result in a waiver. When protected information is formally sought, the responding party must assert the grounds of the privilege or protection; it cannot selectively reveal a portion of a communication and maintain the privilege for the remainder. Nguyen v. Excel Corp., 197 F.3d 200, 206 (5th Cir.1999).

5. The attorney-client privilege is an example of an "absolute" privilege. If the privilege attaches to a communication, a court cannot compel its disclosure no matter how compelling the adversary's need for the information.

Some privileges are "qualified." How might this difference affect the courts' handling of the two types of privileges?

6. The attorney-client privilege is just one of the privileges that affect the scope of discovery. The Constitution is the source of several privileges—for example, the Fifth Amendment privilege against self-incrimination. Other privileges are founded on common law and statutes. Among the widely recognized privileges are the privileges for communications between husband and wife, priest and penitent, and physician and patient. Other privileges struggle for recognition—for example, a privilege for communications between accountants and their clients. See generally *Developments in the Law—Privileged Communications*, 98 Harv.L.Rev. 1450 (1985).

7. The 1993 amendments to the Federal Rules added a new Rule 26(b)(5), which requires that a claim of privilege or work product be made expressly and that the nature of the items withheld be described in a manner that enables other parties to assess the applicability of the privilege. Failure to comply will result in a loss of protection. In MOLONEY v. UNITED STATES, 204 F.R.D. 16 (D. Mass.2001), a medical malpractice action, plaintiff deposed the attending physician and asked questions about the doctor's conversations about plaintiff's treatment. During the deposition, the following colloquy occurred:

> [Plaintiff's counsel] * * *: Tell me how you came to speak to Dr. Barrett * * * about * * * [plaintiff]?
>
> [Defendant's counsel] * * *: I'm going to object at this point. I think that this conversation may be privileged and so I'm going to assert the objection with respect to privilege. I think you can ascertain the chronology of the conversation, but with respect to the subject, at this point in time I'm going to object and instruct her not to answer as to substance. We may change the position but at this point in time, I believe that this conversation is privileged.
>
> [Plaintiff's counsel]* * *: Privileged on what grounds?
>
> [Defendant's counsel] * * *: Attorney/client and work product privilege in anticipation of litigation. * * *

Id. at 18. Later in the deposition, the colloquy resumed:

> [Plaintiff's counsel] * * *: I just [want] to be clear for the record, Mary, that your position is that these are privileged under the attorney/client privilege and the work product privilege?
>
> [Defendant's counsel] * * *: At this time that's my position.
>
> * * *
>
> [Plaintiff's counsel] * * *: Again, your position on those is they're privileged by virtue of the attorney/client privilege or the attorney work product privilege?
>
> [Defendant's counsel] * * *: At this time, yes, that's my assertion.
>
> [Plaintiff's counsel] * * *: Just so you'll know, I'm going to move to compel these. Obviously if you don't agree that they're not privileged—well, I'm going to expect more than a telephone deposition. I mean, I

really don't think that's an acceptable way, at least from my point of view. I want a witness to talk about these things. I think this could be absolutely critical in my preparation of this case.

[Defendant's counsel] * * *: We'll talk about that. * * *

Id. at 19. Plaintiff later moved to compel production, and defendant resisted, claiming protection under the federal self-critical analysis privilege, federal medical peer review privilege, and state statutory privilege, but not work-product protection or attorney-client privilege. The District Court ordered production, explaining: "[I]t defies logic to permit counsel to assert one privilege so as to preclude testimony at a deposition, but thereafter research and claim an entirely different privilege in response to a motion to compel. Such conduct most assuredly circumvents both the letter and the spirit of Rules 26(b)(5) and 30(d)(1) [now Rule 30(c)(2)]." Did defendant's counsel provide sufficient information? What more could she have done?

3. EXPERT INFORMATION

Read Federal Rule of Civil Procedure 26(a)(2) and 26(b)(4) in the Supplement.

KRISA v. EQUITABLE LIFE ASSURANCE SOCIETY

United States District Court, Middle District of Pennsylvania, 2000.
196 F.R.D. 254.

This case concerns Equitable's decision to deny Krisa's application for disability benefits under insurance policies issued to Krisa by Equitable. * * *

A. The Production of Draft Expert Reports and Written Analyses Prepared by Testifying Experts

Krisa seeks production of preliminary reports and other documents created by Equitable's experts in connection with this litigation. Equitable responds that it need not produce the draft reports and written analyses generated by its experts because such documents are protected by the work product doctrine codified in Rule 26(b)(3) * * *. Equitable's argument disregards the fact that the protection afforded by Rule 26(b)(3) is subject to Rule 26(b)(4), which generally authorizes discovery of testifying expert witnesses. * * * [T]he structure of Rule 26 and the Advisory Committee Notes that accompanied the authorization of expert witness discovery in 1970 suggest the conclusion that documents prepared by expert witnesses are not within the ambit of the work product doctrine. * * * [T]he Rules plainly contemplate discovery of not only the opinions the testifying experts intend to advance at trial, but also preliminary or tentative opinions expressed by the testifying experts that may be in conflict with their final opinions. * * *

The conclusion that draft reports and other documents prepared by Equitable's witnesses in this case are not covered by the work product privilege is consistent with the policy considerations underlying the privilege. The work product privilege is based upon "the general policy against invading the privacy of an attorney's course of preparation." Bogosian v. Gulf Oil Corp., 738 F.2d 587, 592 (3d Cir.1984) * * *. * * * Equitable's representations indicate that counsel's mental processes and opinions are not contained in the expert's draft reports. Thus, requesting production of these documents will not invade the privacy to be accorded Equitable's trial counsel in developing litigation strategies and theories. Moreover, Krisa could be deprived of information that would be material to effective cross-examination of Equitable's experts if deprived of the expression of the evolution of the experts' opinions.

B. Communications From Equitable's Counsel to Testifying Expert Witnesses

There has been a significant split among courts that have addressed whether core attorney work product shared with a party's expert is discoverable. * * *

* * *

* * * Our Court of Appeals addressed this issue in *Bogosian*, 738 F.2d at 595, and held that core work product generated by an attorney was shielded from discovery even if disclosed to an expert. * * *

Although courts have noted that "the reasoning of those cases interpreting the Rule prior to 1993 [when the Rule was amended] * * * is probably obsolete," they have remained divided on whether attorney work product is discoverable when given to an expert.

Several courts have held that the 1993 Amendments to Rule 26(a)(2) were "designed to mandate full disclosure of those materials reviewed by an expert witness, regardless of whether they constitute opinion work product." Karn [v. Ingersoll–Rand Co., 168 F.R.D. 633, 637 (N.D.Ind. 1996)]. * * * Those courts that have favored the disclosure of attorney work product argue that their "bright-line" interpretation "makes good sense on several policy grounds: effective cross-examination of expert witnesses will be enhanced; the policies underlying the work product doctrine will not be violated; and, finally, litigation certainty will be achieved–counsel will know exactly what documents will be subject to disclosure and can react accordingly." Karn, 168 F.R.D. at 639.

However, other courts have rejected the reasoning of Karn [and other cases]. * * * In Haworth, [Inc. v. Herman Miller, Inc., 162 F.R.D. 289 (W.D.Mich.1995)] the court stated that "for the high privilege accorded attorney opinion work product not to apply would require clear and unambiguous language...." Id. at 295. * * *

The policy reason apparently given the most weight by courts in favor of the "bright-line" rule for production of materials disclosed to an expert is that an expert cannot be properly impeached without knowledge of all the relevant materials that shaped the expert's opinion. *E.g.*, Karn, 168 F.R.D. at 639. In Begosian, however, our Court of Appeals noted that "the marginal value on cross-examination that the expert's view may have originated with an attorney's opinion or theory does not warrant overriding the strong policy against disclosure of documents consisting of core attorney's work product." 738 F.2d at 595. The Third Circuit recognized that even where an expert's opinion originated with the attorney, the most effective way to discredit an opposing expert is the presentation of one's own credible expert. * * *

Adoption of a "bright-line" rule in favor of mandating production of attorney work product, while increasing the potential for a party to effectively cross-examine an opponent's expert, abridges the attorney work product privilege without specific authority to do so. * * *

Only one document sent by Equitable's counsel to an expert contains attorney work product, and only one document prepared by an expert witness * * * embodies core work product. * * * Equitable will not be compelled to produce those documents.

NOTES AND QUESTIONS

1. Until 1993, discovery regarding the information of experts who were called to testified was limited to interrogatories unless the District Court otherwise provided. That year, the Federal Rules were amended to include a requirement of mandatory disclosure, which affects the exchange of information about expert witnesses. See Fed. R. Civ. P. 26(a)(2)(A)–(C). In addition, Rule 26(e)(1) imposes a duty to supplement the mandatory disclosures, and this obligation extends to an expert's responses during a deposition. The Advisory Committee note to the 1993 amendment of Rule 26(a)(2)(A), referred to in *Krisa*, provides:

> The report is to disclose the data and other information considered by the expert and any other exhibits or charts that summarize or support the expert's opinions. Given this obligation of disclosure, litigants should no longer be able to argue that materials furnished to their experts to be used in forming their opinions—whether or not ultimately relied upon by the expert—are privileged or otherwise protected from disclosure when such persons are testifying or being deposed.

Do you agree with the District Court's decision in *Krisa*? In *Krisa*, the documents were not cited by the expert in his report, and arguably were not relied on by the expert in forming his opinion. What if the expert not only relied on the documents, but also specifically cited them in his report? See Doe v. Luzerne County, 2008 WL 2518131 (N.D. Pa. 2008).

2. Rule 26(b)(4)(B) permits discovery of facts and opinions from an expert employed in anticipation of trial and who will not be called to testify,

but only upon a showing of special circumstances. What circumstances justify discovery under this provision? See Disidore v. Mail Contractors of America, Inc., 196 F.R.D. 410, 415–19 (D.Kan.2000). What if an expert who will not testify at trial develops materials that are then provided to another expert for the party who will testify? Should work-product protection apply to those materials that the expert states did not form a basis for his conclusions? See Mickum, *Guise, Contrivance, or Artful Dodging? The Discovery Rules Governing Testifying Employee Experts*, 24 Rev. Litig. 301 (2005).

SECTION E. SANCTIONS AND JUDICIAL SUPERVISION OF DISCOVERY

Read Federal Rules of Civil Procedure 26(c) and 37 in the Supplement.

CINE FORTY–SECOND STREET THEATRE CORP. v. ALLIED ARTISTS PICTURES CORP.

United States Court of Appeals, Second Circuit, 1979.
602 F.2d 1062.

IRVING R. KAUFMAN, CHIEF JUDGE.

* * *

I

Appellee Cine * * * has operated a movie theater in New York City's Times Square area since July 1974. It alleges that those owning neighboring theaters on West Forty–Second Street * * * entered into a conspiracy with certain motion picture distributors to cut off its access to first-run, quality films. Bringing suit on August 1, 1975, Cine claimed $3,000,000 in treble damages under the antitrust laws, and sought an injunction against the defendants' alleged anticompetitive practices.

On November 6, 1975, the eleven defendants served plaintiff with a set of consolidated interrogatories. Cine thereupon secured its adversaries' consent to defer discovery on the crucial issue of damages until it could retain an expert to review the rival exhibitors' box office receipts. Not until four months after the deadline upon which the parties had agreed, however, did Cine file its first set of answers to the remaining interrogatories. Moreover, even casual scrutiny reveals the patent inadequacy of these responses. Many were bare, ambiguous cross-references to general answers elsewhere in the responses. Highly specific questions concerning the design of Cine's theater were answered with architectural drawings that did not even purport to show the dimensions requested.

Although Cine now complains bitterly that these interrogatories amounted to pure harassment, it never moved to strike them as irrelevant or as harassing. Rather, it filed supplemental answers, which were similarly deficient, and then failed to obey two subsequent orders from Magistrate Gershon compelling discovery. At a hearing in October of 1977, the magistrate found Cine's disobedience to have been willful, and assessed $500 in costs against it. Soon afterwards, she further warned plaintiff that any further noncompliance would result in dismissal.

By the summer of 1978, as this conflict was coming to a head, Cine had still not retained the expert it claimed was necessary to respond to the damages interrogatories. Magistrate Gershon quite reasonably and leniently ordered Cine merely to produce a plan to answer, but this yielded no result. The magistrate then directed Cine to answer the damages interrogatories, admonishing its counsel that future nonfeasance would be viewed in light of past derelictions. Cine did file two sets of answers, one over two months late and both seriously deficient.

* * *

At a formal hearing on October 19, 1978, * * * after noting plaintiff's history of disobedience in the face of her own repeated warnings, the magistrate concluded that Cine's present non-compliance was willful. "[T]he plaintiff," she stated, "has decided when it will be cooperative and when it will not be cooperative, and that it does not have any right to do." She thereupon recommended to the district court that Cine be precluded from introducing evidence with respect to damages. This sanction was, of course, tantamount to a dismissal of Cine's damage claim, but left standing its claim for injunctive relief.

Judge Goettel, the district judge to whom Magistrate Gershon's order was submitted for approval, reacted to Cine's behavior as did Magistrate Gershon. He wrote, "[i]f there were ever a case in which drastic sanctions were justified, this is it." But Judge Goettel could not fully accept the magistrate's finding of willfulness. * * * [He] apparently believed it possible that Cine's counsel, confused as to the precise terms of Magistrate Gershon's oral orders, could have thought in good faith that the answers were not due. Action taken upon that baseless belief, however, was, at the very least, grossly negligent. The district court "regretfully" concluded that under Flaks v. Koegel, 504 F.2d 702 (2d Cir.1974), it lacked the power, absent a finding of willfulness, to impose the extreme sanction recommended by the magistrate. Instead, the court merely assessed costs in the amount of $1,000.[6] But, recognizing that he might have "misperceive[d] the controlling law of this circuit," Judge Goettel certified this interlocutory appeal on his own motion under 28 U.S.C. § 1292(b).

* * *

6. Defendants estimate that their actual costs in seeking to compel discovery total at least $50,000.

II

The question before us is whether a grossly negligent failure to obey an order compelling discovery may justify the severest disciplinary measures available under Fed.R.Civ.P. 37. This rule provides a spectrum of sanctions[8] * * * [that] serve a threefold purpose. Preclusionary orders ensure that a party will not be able to profit from its own failure to comply. * * * Rule 37 strictures are also specific deterrents and, like civil contempt, they seek to secure compliance with the particular order at hand. * * * Finally, although the most drastic sanctions may not be imposed as "mere penalties," Hammond Packing Co. v. Arkansas, 212 U.S. 322, 29 S.Ct. 370, 53 L.Ed. 530 (1909) * * *, courts are free to consider the general deterrent effect their orders may have on the instant case and on other litigation, provided that the party on whom they are imposed is, in some sense, at fault. National Hockey League v. Metropolitan Hockey Club, Inc., 427 U.S. 639, 96 S.Ct. 2778, 49 L.Ed.2d 747 (1976) (per curiam); Societé Internationale Pour Participations Industrielles Et Commerciales v. Rogers, 357 U.S. 197, 78 S.Ct. 1087, 2 L.Ed.2d 1255 (1958).

Where the party makes good faith efforts to comply, and is thwarted by circumstances beyond his control—for example, a foreign criminal statute prohibiting disclosure of the documents at issue—an order dismissing the complaint would deprive the party of a property interest without due process of law. See *Societé Internationale,* supra, 357 U.S. at 212, 78 S.Ct. 1087. It would, after all, be unfair and irrational to prevent a party from being heard solely because of a nonculpable failure to meet the terms of a discovery order. * * *

* * * Judge Goettel apparently believed that Cine's counsel simply did not understand the exact requirements of the magistrate's unwritten order compelling discovery. If so, Cine's failure to answer the damages interrogatories might not rise to the level of "willfulness" or "bad faith" for both of these conditions imply a deliberate disregard of the lawful orders of the court. * * * The question, then, is whether gross negligence amounting to a "total dereliction of professional responsibility," but not a conscious disregard of court orders, is properly embraced within the "fault" component of *Societé Internationale's* triple criterion.

Fault, of course, is a broad and amorphous concept, and the Courts of Appeals have had considerable difficulty construing it in this context. Indeed, one court defined "fault" by the apparent oxymoron "intentional negligence." *Bon Air Hotel, Inc.,* * * * 376 F.2d at 120. Thus, commentators have opined that an element of willfulness or conscious disregard of the court's orders is a prerequisite to the harsher categories of Rule 37 sanctions. * * * But the appellate cases commonly cited for this proposi-

8. Rule 37 was amended in 1970 to permit the imposition of a broader range of sanctions. By deleting the word "wilfully" from subsection (d) of the Rule, the drafters intended "that wilfullness [be] relevant only to the selection of sanctions, if any, to be imposed." Advisory Committee Note * * *.

tion hold only that dismissal is an abuse of discretion where failure to comply was not the result of the fault of any party. * * *

Unless we are to assume that the Court chose its words carelessly, we must accord the term "fault" a meaning of its own within the *Societé Internationale* triad. And plainly, if "fault" has any meaning not subsumed by "willfulness" and "bad faith," it must at least cover gross negligence of the type present in this case. The holding in Edgar v. Slaughter, 548 F.2d 770, 773 (8th Cir.1977), which contains the apparent suggestion that dismissal is appropriate only for actions taken "deliberately or in bad faith," does not conflict with this conclusion. Counsel's action in that case at worst amounted to simple negligence and indeed may have been partially excusable, id. at 773 n. 4. Flagrant negligence of the type involved in the case at bar was simply not at issue.

In the only case that actually presented the question now before us, Affanato v. Merrill Bros., 547 F.2d 138 (1st Cir.1977), the First Circuit implicitly adopted the view we have expressed. There, the district court had entered a default judgment after what the appellant court characterized as "a series of episodes of nonfeasance which amounted, in sum, to a near total dereliction of professional responsibility" on the part of defendant's counsel. Id. at 141. The Court of Appeals affirmed, noting that counsel's failures "went well beyond ordinary negligence"—but without finding willfulness or bad faith. Id.

In the final analysis, however, this question cannot turn solely upon a definition of terms. We believe that our view advances the basic purposes of Rule 37, while respecting the demands of due process. The principal objective of the general deterrent policy of *National Hockey* is strict adherence to the "responsibilities counsel owe to the Court and to their opponents," 427 U.S. at 640, 96 S.Ct. at 2780. Negligent, no less than intentional, wrongs are fit subjects for general deterrence * * *. And gross professional incompetence no less than deliberate tactical intransigence may be responsible for the interminable delays and costs that plague modern complex lawsuits. An undertaking on the scale of the large contemporary suit brooks none of the dilation, posturing, and harassment once expected in litigation. * * * The parties, and particularly their lawyers, must rise to the freedom granted by the Rules and cooperate in good faith both in question and response.

Considerations of fair play may dictate that courts eschew the harshest sanctions provided by Rule 37 where failure to comply is due to a mere oversight of counsel amounting to no more than simple negligence * * *. But where gross professional negligence has been found—that is, where counsel clearly should have understood his duty to the court—the full range of sanctions may be marshaled. Indeed, in this day of burgeoning, costly and protracted litigation courts should not shrink from imposing harsh sanctions where, as in this case, they are clearly warranted.

A litigant chooses counsel at his peril, Link v. Wabash Railroad Co., 370 U.S. 626, 82 S.Ct. 1386, 8 L.Ed.2d 734 (1962), and here, as in countless other contexts, counsel's disregard of his professional responsibilities can lead to extinction of his client's claim. * * *

Plaintiff urges that because it has at last filed answers to the damage interrogatories, it should be permitted to prove its losses at trial. But it forgets that sanctions must be weighed in light of the full record in the case * * *. Furthermore, "[i]f parties are allowed to flout their obligations, choosing to wait to make a response until a trial court has lost patience with them, the effect will be to embroil trial judges in day-to-day supervision of discovery, a result directly contrary to the overall scheme of the federal discovery rules," *Dellums* [*v. Powell*], * * * 184 U.S.App.D.C. at 343–44, 566 F.2d at 235–36. Moreover, as we have indicated, compulsion of performance in the particular case at hand is not the sole function of Rule 37 sanctions. Under the deterrence principle of *National Hockey,* plaintiff's hopelessly belated compliance should not be accorded great weight. Any other conclusion would encourage dilatory tactics, and compliance with discovery orders would come only when the backs of counsel and the litigants were against the wall.

In light of the fact that plaintiff, through its undeniable fault, has frozen this litigation in the discovery phase for nearly four years, we see no reason to burden the court below with extensive proceedings on remand. Judge Goettel's opinion makes it abundantly clear that but for his misinterpretation of the governing law in this circuit, he would have wholeheartedly adopted Magistrate Gershon's original recommendation. Accordingly, the judge's order declining to adopt the magistrate's recommendation that proof of damages be precluded is reversed.

OAKES, CIRCUIT JUDGE (concurring):

I concur in the result. It may be that the fault for the inexcusable delays in compliance with the discovery requests and orders lay with the client or with the complexity of the interrogatories and requests of opposing counsel. If the latter, remedy lay with an application under Fed.R.Civ.P. 26(c). If the former, then the magistrate's recommendation of preclusion strikes at the proper party. It would be with the greatest reluctance, however, that I would visit upon the client the sins of counsel, absent client's knowledge, condonation, compliance, or causation.

NOTES AND QUESTIONS

1. Although the Federal Rules went into effect in 1938, judges until relatively recently were extremely reluctant to apply available sanctions to curb violations of the discovery rules.

> The typical pattern of sanctioning that emerges from the reported cases is one in which the delay, obfuscation, contumacy, and lame excuses on the part of litigants and their attorneys are tolerated without any measured remedial action until the court is provoked beyond endurance. At that point the court punishes one side or the other with a swift and final termination of the lawsuit by dismissal or default. This "all or nothing"

approach to sanctions results in considerable laxity in the day-to-day application of the rules. Attorneys are well aware that sanctions will be imposed only in the most flagrant situations.

Rodes, Ripple & Mooney, Sanctions Imposable for Violations of the Federal Rules of Civil Procedure 85 (Fed.Jud.Center 1981). Spurred in part by the Supreme Court's opinions in NATIONAL HOCKEY LEAGUE v. METROPOLITAN HOCKEY CLUB, INC., 427 U.S. 639, 96 S.Ct. 2778, 49 L.Ed.2d 747 (1976), and ROADWAY EXPRESS, INC. v. PIPER, 447 U.S. 752, 100 S.Ct. 2455, 65 L.Ed.2d 488 (1980), which strongly supported the use of sanctions, judges increasingly have applied and upheld sanctions in a much wider variety of situations. See American Bar Association, Sanctions: Rule 11 and Other Powers 34–36, 46–48, 61–70, 79–82, 97–101, 115–16, 128–29, 138–42, 158–60, 170, 175–77, 182, 186–87 (2d ed. 1988) (surveying recent decisions); see also American Law Institute–American Bar Association, Sanctions in Civil Litigation: A Review of Sanctions by Rule, Statute, and Inherent Power (2007). A survey of decisions involving the discovery of electronic information before the 2006 amendments found that courts granted sanctions in about two-thirds of the cases, most often when a party had willfully destroyed documents in violation of a court order or caused prejudice to the opposing party. See Scheindlin & Wangkeo, *Electronic Discovery Sanctions in the Twenty–First Century*, 11 Mich. Telecomm. & Tech. L. Rev. 71, 73 (2004). What other factors might account for this tougher approach to sanctions?

2. How do discovery disputes get to court? How does the Rule 26(c) route differ from that of Rule 37(a)? Under both, the parties must first confer to try to resolve their differences. What other potential sanction does Rule 26(g) add? How do these three provisions differ from Rule 11?

3. Rule 37 was revised in 1993 to reflect the addition of the mandatory disclosure provision in Rule 26(a), by providing a means to compel that disclosure. What happens if a party fails to disclose information in accordance with Rule 26(a) then seeks to introduce the information as evidence at trial?. In this circumstance, must the opposing party move to block introduction of the evidence?

4. The district courts have broad discretion in devising sanctions to remedy discovery abuse. See In re Phenylpropanolamine (PPA) Prods. Liab. Litig., 460 F.3d 1217, 1226–32 (9th Cir. 2006). The most severe sanction that a court can impose is dismissal of plaintiff's complaint or ordering the entry of judgment against defendant. See Chrysler Corp. v. Carey, 186 F.3d 1016, 1020–22 (8th Cir.1999) (affirming entry of judgment of liability against defendants). This extreme sanction is disfavored because the courts are reluctant to deny a litigant her day in court. An appellate court will scrutinize the decision closely to ensure that the determination is within the proper bounds of the trial court's discretion, but can affirm even if a more modest sanction is available. See Everyday Learning Corp. v. Larson, 242 F.3d 815 (8th Cir. 2001). Other possible sanctions include the imposition of costs, attorney's fees, and expenses, see, e.g., Legault v. Zambarano, 105 F.3d 24, 28 (1st Cir. 1997) (imposing on client and lawyer monetary sanction equal to cost of fees reasonably expended by opposing party), as well as reprimands and

censure. See Slawotsky, *Rule 37 Discovery Sanctions—The Need for Supreme Court Ordered National Uniformity*, 104 Dick. L. Rev. 471, 479–80 (2000).

5. The courts also have obligations if the discovery process is to work appropriately. The failure of a trial court to take charge of a case and issue timely rulings on matters of substantive law—for example, the proposed dismissal of one of plaintiff's set of allegations that fails to state a claim for relief—can confuse defendant as to its obligations to comply with discovery orders and requests related to the challenged claim. In that situation, if the trial judge imposes severe sanctions on defendant for failure to comply with court ordered discovery, to what extent should the court of appeals become involved? See Chudasama v. Mazda Motor Corp., 123 F.3d 1353 (11th Cir. 1997).

CHAPTER 12

CASE MANAGEMENT

■ ■ ■

In this Chapter, we examine the history, theory, and practice of case management. Case management is a catchall phrase encompassing the idea that a judge serves not only as a detached decision maker, but also as an engaged supervisor, responsible for encouraging, facilitating, and even pressuring the parties to resolve their disputes. The rise of case management techniques, including the centrality of the Rule 16 pretrial conference, marks a sharp contrast to the adversarial system's emphasis on party autonomy and the traditional view of the judicial role. Rising caseloads, increased costs, and shifting attitudes toward civil litigation have contributed to a reliance on case management as way to enhance the efficiency of dispute resolution. What other values ought to inform the disposition of a case?

SECTION A. RULE 16 AND THE DEVELOPMENT OF CASE MANAGEMENT TECHNIQUES

MILLER, THE PRETRIAL RUSH TO JUDGMENT: ARE THE "LITIGATION EXPLOSION," "LIABILITY CRISIS," AND EFFICIENCY CLICHÉS ERODING OUR DAY IN COURT AND JURY TRIAL COMMITMENTS?, 78 N.Y.U. L. Rev. 982, 1003 (2003) (footnotes omitted):

Federal district judges began utilizing management techniques on an ad hoc basis in the years following the Second World War. These experimental procedures were organized under the aegis of the Handbook of Recommended Procedure for the Trial of Protracted Cases and then the Manual on Complex Litigation, which first appeared in the 1960s. Their principles were given greater prominence and officially sanctioned in 1983, and then embellished further in 1993 by amendments to Rule 16; prior to these amendments the Rule described a discretionary and rather simple eve-of-trial conference. Given that by the early 1980s only an estimated six percent of cases actually reached trial and the lion's share of resource expenditures occurred pretrial, the Rule was of little help in reducing the institution-to-termination litigation timeframe, let alone achieving any systemic economy. Recognizing that judicial intervention should occur shortly after commencement, Rule 16 was transformed into a provision that encouraged—and in time effectively mandated—judicial management throughout the pretrial proceedings.

SHAPIRO, FEDERAL RULE 16: A LOOK AT THE THEORY AND PRACTICE OF RULEMAKING, 137 U. Pa. L. Rev. 1969, 1977, 1980–84 (1989) (footnotes omitted):

* * * Rule [16 was] designed to substitute for formal pleadings the less formal processes of discussion and exchange as ways of narrowing issues for trial and of expediting proof. But because flexibility and discretion were the watchwords, judges were not instructed to do anything; they would only be encouraged to act. At the same time, they were not given express power to act coercively in any way not authorized by other, more formal procedures, and the comments of several important figures in the drafting of the rules left little doubt of their resistance to the coercive use of the conference.

* * *

* * * [A]n extraordinary range of practices * * * developed within the framework of the Rule [as promulgated in 1938]. While in some districts judges made relatively little use of the Rule, and seldom required pretrial conferences, other districts promulgated elaborate local rules that required pretrial conferences in most or all cases and/or imposed heavy burdens on counsel to confer in advance and to prepare detailed pretrial orders for the judge's consideration. Some judges held pretrial conferences early and often, and were encouraged to do so in complex cases by the Manual for Complex Litigation. Some judges saw the pretrial conference as the chance to compel the parties to produce information that had not been (and perhaps could not be) sought in routine pretrial discovery; others saw the occasion as an opportunity to rid the case of frivolous or insubstantial issues of fact or law, whether or not requested to do so by one of the parties in an appropriate motion; still others saw the conference as a device to facilitate settlement, and saw the judge as a major player in that process.

* * *

At a more general level, the major development during this period was a sea-change in the attitude of many, perhaps most, judges toward their role in the pretrial period—a change that occurred with surprisingly little concern for the purposes and limitations of Rule 16. Judges began to see themselves less as neutral adjudicators—deciding what the parties brought to them for decision and proceeding at a pace to be determined by the parties—and more as managers of a costly and complicated process.

Many district courts began to assign judges to a case from the beginning, and many judges, encouraged by this system and by the increased availability of magistrates and other support staff, began to manage their cases with a firm hand. Crowded dockets, costly discovery, and delay were seen as problems not just for the litigants but for the system, and even the litigants were thought of as frequent victims of their lawyers' self-interest. The role of the judge, then, was to keep cases moving at a reasonable pace, and to see that cases not be needlessly tried. Indeed, the concept of disposition without trial began to embrace a variety of inventive techniques other than simple mediation and settlement.

* * *

The purposes of the [1983] amended Rule have been described in the Advisory Committee's Note and in comments by its Reporter, Arthur Miller. A major purpose was to recognize, and indeed to embrace, the strong trend toward increased judicial management of litigation from an early stage of the lawsuit. Among the means of expressing this purpose were the authorization of an early scheduling conference at which various deadlines would be established and further conferences agreed upon, and the inclusion among the subjects to be discussed of a number of matters relating not to the trial itself but to the pretrial period.

* * *

NOTES AND QUESTIONS

1. For a discussion of the early operation and significance of Rule 16, see Rosenberg, The Pretrial Conference and Effective Justice (1964); Flanders, *Blind Umpires—A Response to Professor Resnik,* 35 Hastings L.J. 505 (1984); Peckham, *The Federal Judge as Case Manager: The New Role in Guiding a Case from Filing to Disposition,* 69 Calif.L.Rev. 770 (1981); Richey, *Rule 16 Revisited: Reflections for the Benefit of Bench and Bar,* 139 F.R.D. 525 (1991).

2. Case management responds to concerns that "the adversary system as we know it has become too costly and inefficient a device for resolving civil disputes." Miller, *The Adversary System: Dinosaur or Phoenix,* 69 Minn. L.Rev. 1, 20 (1984). Nevertheless, commentators question whether Rule 16, in practice, cuts against the grain of adversarial justice: "[J]udges are not supposed to have an involvement or interest in the controversies they adjudicate. Disengagement and dispassion supposedly enable judges to decide cases fairly and impartially." Resnik, *Managerial Judges,* 96 Harv.L.Rev. 374, 376–78 (1982) (footnotes omitted).

Some commentators argue that case management as it has developed gives the judge unchecked authority that dilutes the jury and undermines litigant autonomy. See Tornquist, *The Active Judge in Pre-trial Settlement: Inherent Authority Gone Awry,* 25 Willamette L.Rev. 743 (1989); see also Vorrasi, Note—*England's Reform To Alleviate the Problems of Civil Process:*

A Comparison of Judicial Case Management in England and the United States, 30 J. Legis. 361 (2003–2004) (emphasizing that case management "shifts * * * power from the parties to judges throughout pretrial process").

Other commentators caution that managerial judging emphasizes efficiency and speed to the exclusion of other values. See Tigar, *Pretrial Case Management under the Amended Rules: Too Many Words for a Good Idea*, 14 Rev. Litig. 137 (1994). One respected federal judge recommended that instead of case management, judges ought to engage in judging and its associated duties of "care and control, stewardship over the trial, superintendence, * * * direction and leadership." See Keeton, *Time Limits as Incentives in an Adversary System*, 137 U. Pa. L. Rev. 2053, 2057 (1989). From a different perspective, some commentators express skepticism that case management can control litigation abuse. See p. 571 n.6, supra.

As you read the cases in this section, consider whether Rule 16 promotes or threatens litigant autonomy, procedural fairness, uniformity, and public accountability.

3. On what basis should managerial judging be assessed? Professor Resnik underscores the difficult valuation questions that the claim "the more dispositions, the better" raises:

> On any given day, are four judges who speak with parties to sixteen lawsuits and report that twelve of those cases ended without trial more "productive" than four judges who preside at four trials? Is it relevant to an assessment of "productivity" that * * * in the one case tried to conclusion, the judge writes a forty-page opinion on a novel point of law that is subsequently affirmed by the Supreme Court and thereafter affects thousands of litigants?

Resnik, Note 2, p. 929, supra, at 422. Empirical studies show that use of case management techniques positively affect such quantifiable factors as length of disposition, waiting periods, and cost. See, e.g, Kakalik, Dunworth, Hill, McCaffrey, Oshiro, Pace & Vaiana, *Just, Speedy, and Inexpensive? An Evaluation of Judicial Case Management under the Civil Justice Reform Act*, 49 Ala. L. Rev. 17 (1997). What else would you want to know about Rule 16 to determine its effectiveness?

4. Case management practices vary from state to state, and different techniques are used for complex cases and in courts of specialized jurisdiction. See, e.g., King, *Judicious Intervention: What One California Judge Has Done To Expedite Settlement*, 19 Fam. Advoc. 22 (Spring 1997) (describing case management programs in California family court); Schaller, *Managerial Judging: A Principled Approach To Complex Cases in State Court*, 68 Conn. B.J. 77 (1994); Paetty, *Classless Not Clueless: A Comparison of Case Management Mechanisms for Non–Class–Based Complex Litigation in California and Federal Courts*, 41 Loy. L.A. L. Rev. 845 (2008). For a survey of state Rule 16–analogues, see Oakley, *A Fresh Look at the Federal Rules in State Courts*, 3 Nev. L.J. 354 (2002/03). See also Hanson & Rottman, *United States: So Many States, So Many Reforms*, 20 Just. Sys. J. 121 (1999); Walker & Weirman, *Pretrial Rules and Procedures in State Courts*, 41 La. B.J. 232 (1993); *Note, Pretrial Conference Procedures*, 26 S.C.L.Rev. 481 (1974).

5. In the late 1960s a committee of federal judges, known as the Coordinating Committee for Multiple Litigation of the United States District Courts, together with legal scholars and representatives of the bar, drafted a manual of suggested procedures for dealing with the so-called "big case." This manual, which has been revised and updated from time to time, and is now the Manual for Complex Litigation (Fourth) (Fed.Jud. Center 2004), traces its origins to the Handbook of Recommended Procedures for the Trial of Protracted Cases, 25 F.R.D. 351 (1960), and also to the Prettyman Report on Procedure in Antitrust and Other Protracted Cases, 13 F.R.D. 62 (1951). See Simons, *The Manual for Complex Litigation: More Rules or Mere Recommendations*, 62 St. John's L. Rev. 493 (1988). The Manual deals with many contemporary procedural devices that are now also used in less complex cases. For an early analysis of the successes and problems faced by the courts in cases in which some of the manual's procedures have been utilized, see Note, *The Judicial Panel and the Conduct of Multidistrict Litigation*, 87 Harv. L.Rev. 1001 (1974).

SECTION B. THE OPERATION OF RULE 16

Read Federal Rule of Civil Procedure 16 and the sample pretrial scheduling order set out in the Supplement.

Rule 16 was amended in 1993 to strengthen the trial judge's authority to manage the litigation and facilitate disposition of the case. The Rule provides deadlines for specific litigation activities, makes explicit and expands the topics to be discussed at the pretrial conference, provides for greater supervision of discovery, allows for earlier consideration of Rule 56 motions, and confirms the judge's authority to encourage settlement by ordering the parties to be present at pretrial conferences. Rule 16 also clarifies the scope of trial court discretion to impose sanctions on the parties for such dereliction as failing to comply with a scheduling order or absence from, or lack of preparation for, a pretrial conference. The 2006 amendment to Rule 16(b) makes clear that the scheduling order can address the discovery or disclosure of electronically stored information.

For discussion of Rule 16 by an experienced trial judge who urged greater use of case management techniques, see Richey, *Rule 16 Revised, and Related Rules: Analysis of Recent Developments for the Benefit of Bench and Bar*, 157 F.R.D. 69 (1994). See also Kelleher, *The December 1993 Amendments to the Federal Rules of Civil Procedure—A Critical Analysis*, 12 Touro L. Rev. 7, 80 (1995).

VELEZ v. AWNING WINDOWS, INC.

United States Court of Appeals, First Circuit, 2004.
375 F.3d 35.

SELYA, CIRCUIT JUDGE.

This appeal tells a cautionary tale of the risks run by parties who adopt a laissez-faire attitude toward court-imposed deadlines. The defendants in this case * * * acted in that fashion. The district court, after patiently granting several extensions and issuing pointed warnings, finally decided that enough was enough. It held the defendants to the deadlines previously announced, denied certain of their motions for noncompliance with the court's scheduling order, disregarded the defendants' tardy opposition to a motion for partial summary judgment, took the proffer of plaintiff * * * (Velez) as true, and resolved the issue of liability in Velez's favor. A jury thereafter awarded Velez nearly three-quarters of a million dollars in damages. The defendants appeal. Discerning no semblance of error, we affirm.

* * *

[Plaintiff engaged in an adulterous affair with her employer. After she ended the relationship, she was allegedly sexually harassed and terminated from employment. She filed an employment discrimination lawsuit raising federal and state claims.]

As this appeal turns largely on the * * * procedural history of the case, * * * we set out a procedural chronology (each date refers to the time when the filing in question was entered on the district court's docket).

1. **March 26, 2002.** The plaintiff instituted the action.

2. **April 30, 2002.** The plaintiff moved for the entry of default, see Fed.R.Civ.P. 55(a), because the defendants failed to answer or otherwise plead within the allotted twenty-day period.

3. **May 3, 2002.** The district court ordered the defendants to show cause, on or before May 15, why a default should not be entered.

4. **May 22, 2002.** The plaintiff renewed her motion for entry of default, noting that neither defendant had responded to the show-cause order.

5. **May 31, 2002.** The district court defaulted both defendants.

6. **June 6, 2002.** Citing Nieves's sudden death in a helicopter accident on May 25, AWI asked the district court to set aside the default and afford the defendants forty-five additional days within which to answer the complaint.

7. **June 24, 2002.** The district court granted the plaintiff's request to substitute the Estate in Nieves's stead as a party defendant. See Fed.R.Civ.P. 25(a)(1). The court also granted AWI's request to set

aside the default and ordered the defendants to answer or otherwise plead by July 19. The court warned that failure to comply "on or before the aforementioned date SHALL result in the Court re-entering default and proceeding with a Damages Hearing."

8. **July 11, 2002.** The defendants answered the plaintiff's complaint. Discovery then ensued.

9. **November 15, 2002.** The plaintiff moved for partial summary judgment on the issue of liability.

10. **December 2, 2002.** The defendants' opposition to the motion for partial summary judgment was due, but none was filed.

11. **December 5, 2002.** The district court granted the defendants until December 13 to submit their opposition.

12. **December 13, 2002.** Instead of filing their opposition by the extended deadline, the defendants moved for a further extension.

13. **December 17, 2002.** The district court held an omnibus scheduling conference (the OSC).

14. **December 20, 2002.** The court entered an order that, inter alia, directed the defendants to file (i) no later than January 7, 2003, answers to the plaintiff's interrogatories; (ii) no later than January 17, 2003, a legal memorandum, concerning the "admissibility of hearsay and other evidence" following a party's death prior to discovery; and (iii) no later than January 17, 2003, a memorandum detailing AWI's finances and the Estate's assets. The court admonished that the defendants' failure to comply with any of these directives would "result in sanctions including ... elimination of all defenses set forth in their answer to the complaint."

In tandem with these orders, the court further extended the time for filing an opposition to the plaintiff's motion for partial summary judgment. The court fixed February 20 as the due date for the opposition, warned the defendants that "[n]o extensions will be given," and advised them that, should they "fail to file an opposition on or before the aforementioned date the Court SHALL consider Plaintiff's motion as unopposed."

15. **January 7, 2003.** The defendants served their answers to interrogatories.

16. **January 15, 2003.** The defendants filed a motion to dismiss, alleging that the plaintiff did not have a cause of action against Nieves (and, therefore, could not sue the Estate) because supervisors are not personally liable under Title VII.

17. **January 17, 2003.** The defendants moved for an extension of time, up to and including February 4, 2003, within which to file the hearsay memorandum and comply with the remaining commands of the OSC. Although the court took no immediate action on this motion, the defendants failed to make the required filings.

18. **February 5, 2003.** Citing the plaintiff's delay in completing her deposition and answers to interrogatories, the defendants moved to extend the deadline for filing an opposition to the motion for partial summary judgment from February 20 to February 28.

19. **February 20, 2003.** (This was the date set by the district court for the filing of the opposition to the motion for partial summary judgment.) Although the court had not yet ruled on their last previous motion for an extension, the defendants asked for another extension, this time to March 3, for the filing of their opposition.

20. **March 18, 2003.** The defendants made multiple submissions: (i) they finally filed their opposition to the plaintiff's motion for partial summary judgment; (ii) in the same memorandum, doubling in brass as a motion to dismiss, they claimed for the first time that the plaintiff had failed to file a timely administrative complaint with the Equal Employment Opportunity Commission (the EEOC) and that, as a consequence, her action should be jettisoned for want of subject-matter jurisdiction; and (iii) in a separate memorandum, they addressed the district court's hearsay concerns.

21. **March 20, 2003.** Faithful to its earlier warning that no extensions of time would be countenanced, the district court disregarded the defendants' out-of-time filings, denied their sundry extension requests, and deemed the plaintiff's motion for partial summary judgment unopposed. As a sanction for the defendants' failure to comply with the court's earlier order to submit both a legal memorandum anent hearsay evidence (which had been filed over two months late) and a memorandum detailing the defendants' financial resources (which had not been filed at all), the court denied the defendants' motion to dismiss the supervisory liability claim.

22. **March 23, 2003.** The district court refused to dismiss the case for lack of subject-matter jurisdiction.

23. **March 25, 2003.** The district court handed down an opinion in which it granted the plaintiff's motion for partial summary judgment. * * * That decision resolved the issue of liability.

24. **July 22–24, 2003.** The district court convened a damages hearing before a jury and, pursuant to the jury's verdict, entered final judgment for the plaintiff in the sum of $740,000.

25. **August 15, 2003.** The defendants filed a timely notice of appeal.

* * *

The defendants' principal complaint is that the district court erred in granting the plaintiff's motion for partial summary judgment without considering their late-filed opposition. * * *

We agree with the defendants that trial courts should refrain from entertaining summary judgment motions until after the parties have had a sufficient opportunity to conduct necessary discovery. * * * A party who legitimately requires more time to oppose a motion for summary judgment has a corollary responsibility to make the court aware of its plight.

Typically, this is accomplished by way of either a Rule 56(f) motion or its functional equivalent. * * * The record on appeal contains nothing of the sort: the defendants neither invoked nor substantially complied with Rule 56(f). To benefit from the protections of Rule 56(f), a litigant ordinarily must furnish the nisi prius court with a timely statement—if not by affidavit, then in some other authoritative manner—that (i) explains his or her current inability to adduce the facts essential to filing an opposition, (ii) provides a plausible basis for believing that the sought-after facts can be assembled within a reasonable time, and (iii) indicates how those facts would influence the outcome of the pending summary judgment motion. * * * Such a litigant also must have exercised "due diligence both in pursuing discovery before the summary judgment initiative surfaces and in pursuing an extension of time thereafter." * * *

The defendants' motions to extend time, filed on February 5 and February 20, do not satisfy these criteria. * * * Neither motion identifies a single sought-after fact. Neither motion indicates whether the desired information can be gathered within a reasonable interval. And neither motion relates how that information, if unearthed, would influence the outcome of the pending summary judgment motion.

What the February motions do attempt to provide are reasons why an extension should be granted. The defendants attribute their predicament to a week-long delay in the taking of the plaintiff's deposition, a week-long delay in the plaintiff's service of answers to interrogatories, and defense counsel's professed "need" to travel to Florida "in matters regarding to [sic] [in original] our legal profession." These are more excuses than reasons. The deposition was completed a full two weeks before the court-appointed deadline for filing an opposition, and the plaintiff answered the interrogatories in approximately the same time frame. Last—but far from least—the fact that counsel may have bitten off more than he could chew does not exempt him from meeting court-appointed deadlines. * * *

The defendants now try to rectify some of their earlier omissions. In this court, they attribute the need for a further extension to a motley of events, including Nieves's untimely demise, a switch in counsel resulting from his death, and the fact that the plaintiff's attorneys closed their offices for two weeks. These importunings are too little and too late. A party who seeks to be relieved from a court-appointed deadline has an obligation, at a bare minimum, to present his arguments for relief to the ordering court. An unexcused failure to do so constitutes a waiver. * * *

Here, moreover, the defendants' proffered reasons are less than compelling. Nieves died on May 25, 2002—almost nine months before the due date for the defendants' opposition. The switch in counsel occurred in that same time frame—and in any event, a party's decision to discharge one lawyer and retain another does not serve as a free pass to ignore court-appointed deadlines. Finally, the relevance of the office closing is less than obvious, and the defendants do nothing to enlighten us.

To cinch matters, it would strain credulity to characterize the defendants' pretrial discovery efforts in this case as duly diligent. As the chronology indicates, * * * the defendants dragged their feet from the very inception of the action. * * *

Appellate review of a district court's case-management decisions is solely for abuse of discretion. * * * Given the circumstances at hand, the district court plainly did not abuse its discretion * * *.

The defendants have a fallback position: they claim that genuine issues of material fact existed in the record and that the plaintiff was not entitled to a liability finding as a matter of law. We review the merits of the entry of partial summary judgment de novo. * * *

Because the defendants failed to file an opposition to the motion for partial summary judgment by the court-appointed deadline * * *, the district judge was entitled to consider the motion as unopposed * * *. * * * In the same vein, the court was obliged to take the plaintiff's statement of uncontested facts as true. * * *

* * *

The district court denied both of the defendants' motions to dismiss in the course of sanctioning them for their noncompliance with the OSC order. * * *

* * *

[The court considered and rejected defendants' argument that they "substantially complied" with the requirements of the order and that the timetable was too "rigorous."]

In an effort to alter this conclusion, the defendants point out that the March 18 motion to dismiss implicated the court's subject-matter jurisdiction. * * * It follows, they say, that federal courts are precluded from sanctioning litigants by refusing to consider their motions to dismiss for lack of subject-matter jurisdiction.

That proposition is true as far as it goes, but it does not take the defendants very far. The March 18 motion was premised on the plaintiff's supposed failure to file timely charges with the EEOC. Over two decades ago, the Supreme Court held that "filing a timely charge of discrimination with the EEOC is not a jurisdictional prerequisite to suit in federal court, but a requirement that, like a statute of limitations, is subject to waiver, estoppel, and equitable tolling." * * * That the defendants improperly classified this motion as raising a lack of subject-matter jurisdiction does not change its real nature. Consequently, the district court was free to consider the denial of the motion as a sanction.

* * *

The defendants expend considerable energy calumnizing the district court's method of handling the potential hearsay evidence issue in this case. * * *

* * * The record reflects that they arrived at the OSC unprepared to participate effectively in the proceedings. There is no indication that they objected when the district court afforded them approximately one month within which to file "a memorandum concerning the admissibility of hearsay and other evidence in the occasion when a party has died prior to having given a deposition and/or prior to trial." Nor is any basis for an objection apparent. The January 17 deadline fixed by the court gave the defendants ample time within which to research the hearsay issue. Yet January 17 came and went without the filing of the requisite memorandum.

Courts are entitled—indeed, they should be encouraged—to ask counsel for input on legal issues that seem likely to arise in the course of trial. Here, the defendants squandered what should have been a welcome opportunity to persuade the court that hearsay evidence should be liberally admitted in view of Nieves's demise. * * * We cannot say that the court below abused its discretion when it precluded certain hearsay testimony as a sanction for the defendants' protracted delay in submitting the memorandum in question. * * *

NOTES AND QUESTIONS

1. What standard applies when a party seeks to amend its pleadings after the scheduling order deadline has expired? In KASSNER v. 2nd AVENUE DELICATESSEN, INC., 496 F.3d 229 (2d Cir. 2007), an employment discrimination action, plaintiff moved to amend the complaint before defendant had filed an answer, but one month after the date specified in the Rule 16(b) scheduling order as the final date for the amendment of the pleadings. The Court of Appeals held that Rule 16(b), and not Rule 15(a), applied:

> * * * Although the Rule 16(b) scheduling order, in the district court's discretion, may impose various time limits for pre-trial proceedings * * *, amendment of the pleadings is one of four time limits that the trial court generally must include in a Rule 16(b) scheduling order. * * * The advisory committee notes [to the 1983 amendments] provide that "[i]tem (1) assures that at some point both the parties and the pleadings will be fixed, by setting a time within which joinder of parties shall be completed and the pleadings amended." * * * This objective would be frustrated by an interpretation of the first sentence of Rule 15(a) that precludes a district court from exercising any discretion to specify the time period during which a party may effect the first amendment of its complaint prior to the serving of a responsive pleading. Rule 16(b), in allowing modifications of scheduling orders only for good cause, provides the district courts discretion to ensure that limits on time to amend pleadings do not result in prejudice or hardship to either side. * * *

* * *

> On remand, the district court must exercise its discretion under Rule 16(b) to determine whether the scheduling order should be modified so as to allow an amended complaint. * * * [T]he primary consideration is whether the moving party can demonstrate diligence. It is not, however, the only consideration. The district court * * * also may consider other relevant factors including, in particular, whether allowing the amendment of the pleading at this stage of the litigation will prejudice defendants. * * *

Id. at 243–44.

2. What counts as "good cause" to modify a pretrial scheduling order? In FAHIM v. MARRIOTT HOTEL SERVICES, INC., 551 F.3d 344, 348 (5th Cir. 2008), the Court of Appeals relied on a four-factor test in affirming denial of a belated motion to amend a pleading: "(1) the explanation for the failure to timely move for leave to amend; (2) the importance of the amendment; (3) potential prejudice in allowing the amendment; and (4) the availability of a continuance to cure such prejudice." The Eleventh Circuit applied a similar test in Millennium Partners v. Colmar Storage, 494 F.3d 1293 (11th Cir. 2007), affirming denial of defendant's motion to amend affirmative defenses to add an anti-subrogation defense. Defendant's lack of knowledge of plaintiff's insurance was rejected as good cause; "with some investigation," the court explained, defendant could have timely learned of the possible defense. Id. at 1299.

3. Will noncompliance with a scheduling order block a party from presenting expert testimony at trial? In deciding whether to amend the scheduling order, courts generally rely on the factors discussed in *Fahim*, Note 2, supra, but ascribe varying weights. Compare POTOMAC ELECTRIC POWER CO. v. ELECTRIC MOTOR SUPPLY, INC., 190 F.R.D. 372 (D.Md. 1999) (permitting belated amendment more than two months after the deadline for designating witnesses, but imposing a modest financial sanction), with FRANCOIS v. McDONALD, 2000 WL 1528083 (E.D. La. 2000) (denying amendment 31 days after the deadline for exchange of expert reports). *Potomac Electric* has been criticized as inconsistent with Rule 16(b). See, e.g., Excelsior College v. Frye, 2005 WL 5994158 (S.D.Cal.2005).

4. In CONNOLLY v. NATIONAL SCHOOL BUS SERVICE, INC., 177 F.3d 593 (7th Cir.1999), the District Court ordered the parties to mediate a fee dispute and delegated to his law clerk responsibility to conduct the mediation. When an attorney refused to attend the conference, the court reduced the award of fees. The Court of Appeals reversed, finding it an abuse of discretion for a judge to delegate his case management authority to his law clerk. "Law clerks serve as judicial adjuncts," the court explained. "Their duties and responsibilities are to assist the judge in this work, not to be the judge. A judge's law clerk may therefore properly assist the judge in the judge's settlement efforts, but to allow the clerk rather than the judge to conduct a settlement conference is to confuse the adjunct with the judge." Id. at 598.

5. Rule 16 anticipates that the judge will play an energetic role in encouraging the parties to settle their dispute. Until the 1993 amendments, it was not clear whether the court's power to order a litigant to be present at a

conference or available by telephone to discuss settlement was a matter of inherent authority or authorized under the rule. See G. HEILEMAN BREWING CO. v. JOSEPH OAT CORP., 871 F.2d 648 (7th Cir.1989) (en banc). What if a party and its attorney appear at a settlement conference as ordered, but announce that the client's policy is never to settle a case and refuse to discuss any compromise? See Shedden v. Wal–Mart Stores, Inc., 196 F.R.D. 484 (E.D.Mich.2000). Is it appropriate to impose settlement on a party that has a viable claim? See Resnik, *Mediating Preferences: Litigant Preferences for Process and Judicial Preferences for Settlement,* 2002 J. Disp. Resol. 155 (2002).

6. Does Rule 16 authorize a district judge to order insurers and other interested parties to attend a settlement conference? See Parness & Walker, *Thinking Outside the Civil Case Box: Reformulating Pretrial Conference Laws*, 50 U. Kan. L. Rev. 347 (2002). What problems do you see with allowing nonparties to attend such a discussion? See Parness, *Civil Claim Settlement Talks Involving Third Parties and Insurance Company Adjusters: When Should Lawyer Conduct Standards Apply?*, 77 St. John's L. Rev. 603 (2003).

7. Does judicial participation in settlement discussion—even if only as a facilitator—inevitably undermine the judge's ability to preside as a neutral umpire in the dispute should the case proceed to trial? Does your answer depend on whether the trial is to a jury or to the bench? Would it be preferable to refer all settlement discussions to a magistrate, master, or other third party? See Adams, *Let's Make a Deal: Effective Utilization of Judicial Settlement in State and Federal Courts*, 73 Oregon L.Rev. 427 (1993). Is it appropriate to have the same magistrate judge who conducts a settlement conference preside at a hearing to enforce the settlement agreement? See Omega Engineering, Inc. v. Omega, S.A., 432 F.3d 437 (2d Cir. 2005).

SECTION C. EXTRAJUDICIAL PERSONNEL: MAGISTRATE JUDGES AND MASTERS

Read Federal Rules of Civil Procedure 53, 72, and 73, the material accompanying Rule 53 in the Supplement, and 28 U.S.C. §§ 631–39.

---

1. MAGISTRATE JUDGES

ROELL v. WITHROW

Supreme Court of the United States, 2003.
538 U.S. 580, 123 S.Ct. 1696, 155 L.Ed.2d 775.

Certiorari to the United States Court of Appeals for the Fifth Circuit.

JUSTICE SOUTER delivered the opinion of the Court.

The Federal Magistrate Act of 1979 (Federal Magistrate Act or Act) expanded the power of magistrate judges by authorizing them to conduct "any or all proceedings in a jury or nonjury civil matter and order the entry of judgment in the case," as long as they are "specially designated ... by the district court" [in original] and are acting "[u]pon the consent of the parties." 28 U.S.C. § 636(c)(1). The question is whether consent can be inferred from a party's conduct during litigation, and we hold that it can be.

I

[Respondent is a Texas state prisoner who filed a civil rights action alleging that members of the prison's medical staff disregarded his medical needs in violation of the Eighth Amendment to the United States Constitution.] * * * During a preliminary hearing before a Magistrate Judge to determine whether the suit could proceed *in forma pauperis* * * * the Magistrate Judge told Withrow that he could choose to have her rather than the District Judge preside over the entire case. * * * Withrow agreed orally * * * and later in writing * * *. A lawyer from the Texas attorney general's office who attended the hearing, but was not permanently assigned to Withrow's case, indicated that she would have to "talk to the attorneys who have been assigned the case to see if [petitioners] will execute consent forms." * * *

Without waiting for the petitioners' decision, the District Judge referred the case to the Magistrate Judge for final disposition, but with the caveat that "all defendants [would] be given an opportunity to consent to the jurisdiction of the magistrate judge," and that the referral order would be vacated if any of the defendants did not consent. * * * The Clerk of Court sent the referral order to the petitioners along with a summons directing them to include "[i]n their answer or in a separate pleading ... [in original] a statement that 'All defendants consent to the jurisdiction of a United States Magistrate Judge' or 'All defendants do not consent to the jurisdiction of a United States Magistrate Judge.'" * * * The summons advised them that "[t]he court shall not be told which parties do not consent." * * * Only [one of the defendants] * * *, who was represented by private counsel, gave written consent to the referral; [the other defendants,] Roell and Garibay, who were represented by an assistant in the attorney general's office, filed answers but said nothing about the referral. * * *

The case nevertheless proceeded in front of the Magistrate Judge, all the way to a jury verdict and judgment for the petitioners. When Withrow appealed, the Court of Appeals *sua sponte* remanded the case to the District Court to "determine whether the parties consented to proceed before the magistrate judge and, if so, whether the consents were oral or written." * * * It was only then that Roell and Garibay filed a formal letter of consent with the District Court, stating that "they consented to all proceedings before this date before the United States Magistrate Judge, including disposition of their motion for summary judgment and trial." * * *

The District Court nonetheless referred the Court of Appeals's enquiry to the same Magistrate Judge who had conducted the trial, who reported that "by their actions [Roell and Garibay] [addition in original] clearly implied their consent to the jurisdiction of a magistrate." * * * She was surely correct, for the record shows that [these defendants] * * * voluntarily participated in the entire course of proceedings before the Magistrate Judge, and voiced no objection when, at several points, the Magistrate Judge made it clear that she believed they had consented.[1] The Magistrate Judge observed, however, that under the Circuit's precedent "consent cannot be implied by the conduct of the parties," * * * and she accordingly concluded that the failure of Roell and Garibay to give express consent before sending their postjudgment letter to the District Court meant that she had lacked jurisdiction to hear the case * * *. The District Court adopted the report and recommendation over the petitioners' objection. * * *

The Court of Appeals affirmed the District Court * * *. We granted certiorari * * * and now reverse.

II

* * * Unlike nonconsensual referrals of pretrial but case-dispositive matters under § 636(b)(1), which leave the district court free to do as it sees fit with the magistrate judge's recommendations, a § 636(c)(1) referral gives the magistrate judge full authority over dispositive motions, conduct of trial, and entry of final judgment, all without district court review. A judgment entered by "a magistrate judge designated to exercise civil jurisdiction under [§ 636(c)(1)]" is to be treated as a final judgment of the district court, appealable "in the same manner as an appeal from any other judgment of a district court." § 636(c)(3).[2]

Section 636(c)(2) establishes the procedures for a § 636(c)(1) referral. "If a magistrate judge is designated to exercise civil jurisdiction under [§ 636(c)(1)], the clerk of court shall, at the time the action is filed, notify the parties of the availability of a magistrate judge to exercise such jurisdiction." § 636(c)(2). Within the time required by local rule, "[t]he decision of the parties shall be communicated to the clerk of court." *Ibid.* Federal Rule * * * 73(b) specifies that the parties' election of a magistrate judge shall be memorialized in "a joint form of consent or separate forms of consent setting forth such election," see Fed. Rules Civ. Proc. Form 34, and that neither the magistrate nor the district judge "shall ... be informed of a party's response to the clerk's notification, unless all parties

---

1. On at least three different occasions, counsel for Roell and Garibay was present and stood silent when the Magistrate Judge stated that they had consented to her authority. * * *

2. Prior to the 1996 amendments to the Act, see Federal Courts Improvement Act of 1996, Pub.L. 104–317, § 207(1)(B), 110 Stat. 3850, parties could also elect to appeal to "a judge of the district court in the same manner as on an appeal from a judgment of the district court to a court of appeals." 28 U.S.C. § 636(c)(4) (1994 ed.) (repealed 1996). If the latter course was pursued, the court of appeals could grant leave to appeal the district court's judgment. § 636(c)(5) (same). In all events, whether the initial appeal was to the court of appeals under § 636(c)(3) or to the district court under § 636(c)(4), the parties retained the right to seek ultimate review from this Court. § 636(c)(5) (same).

have consented to the referral of the matter to a magistrate judge." * * * [These procedures envision] advance, written consent communicated to the clerk, the point being to preserve the confidentiality of a party's choice, in the interest of protecting an objecting party against any possible prejudice at the magistrate judge's hands later on. * * *

Here, of course, § 636(c)(2) was honored in the breach, by a referral before Roell and Garibay gave their express consent, without any statement from them, written or oral, until after judgment. * * * Nonetheless, Roell and Garibay "clearly implied their consent" by their decision to appear before the Magistrate Judge, without expressing any reservation, after being notified of their right to refuse and after being told that she intended to exercise case-dispositive authority. Ibid.* * * The only question is whether consent so shown can count as conferring "civil jurisdiction" under § 636(c)(1), or whether adherence to the letter of § 636(c)(2) is an absolute demand.

* * * [T]he font of a magistrate judge's authority, § 636(c)(1), speaks only of "the consent of the parties," without qualification as to form, and § 636(c)(3) similarly provides that "[t]he consent of the parties allows" a full-time magistrate judge to enter a final, appealable judgment of the district court. These unadorned references to "consent of the parties" contrast with the language in § 636(c)(1) covering referral to certain part-time magistrate judges, which requires not only that the parties consent, but that they do so by "specific written request." * * * A distinction is thus being made between consent simple, and consent expressed in a "specific written request." And although the specific referral procedures in 28 U.S.C. § 636(c)(2) and Federal Rule * * * 73(b) are by no means just advisory, the text and structure of the section as a whole suggest that a defect in the referral to a full-time magistrate judge under § 636(c)(2) does not eliminate that magistrate judge's "civil jurisdiction" under § 636(c)(1) so long as the parties have in fact voluntarily consented. * * *

These textual clues are complemented by a good pragmatic reason to think that Congress intended to permit implied consent. In giving magistrate judges case-dispositive civil authority, Congress hoped to relieve the district courts' "mounting queue of civil cases" and thereby "improve access to the courts for all groups." * * * At the same time, though, Congress meant to preserve a litigant's right to insist on trial before an Article III district judge insulated from interference with his obligation to ignore everything but the merits of a case. * * * It was thus concern about the possibility of coercive referrals that prompted Congress to make it clear that "the voluntary consent of the parties is required before a civil action may be referred to a magistrate for a final decision." * * *

When, as here, a party has signaled consent to the magistrate judge's authority through actions rather than words, the question is what outcome does better by the mix of congressional objectives. On the one hand, the virtue of strict insistence on the express consent requirement * * * is simply the value of any bright line: here, absolutely minimal risk of compromising the right to an Article III judge. But there is another risk, and insisting on a bright line would raise it: the risk of a full and complicated trial wasted at the option of an undeserving and possibly opportunistic litigant. This risk is right in front of us in this case. Withrow consented orally and in writing to the Magistrate Judge's authority following notice of his right to elect trial by an Article III district judge; he received the protection intended by the statute, and deserves no boon from the other side's failure to cross the bright line. In fact, there is even more to Withrow's unworthiness, since under the local rules of the District Court, it was Withrow's unmet responsibility as plaintiff to get the consent of all parties and file the completed consent form with the clerk. * * * In another case, of course, the shoe might be on the other foot; insisting on the bright line would allow parties in Roell's and Garibay's position to sit back without a word about their failure to file the form, with a right to vacate any judgment that turned out not to their liking.

The bright line is not worth the downside. We think the better rule is to accept implied consent where, as here, the litigant or counsel was made aware of the need for consent and the right to refuse it, and still voluntarily appeared to try the case before the Magistrate Judge. Inferring consent in these circumstances thus checks the risk of gamesmanship by depriving parties of the luxury of waiting for the outcome before denying the magistrate judge's authority. Judicial efficiency is served; the Article III right is substantially honored. * * *

III

Roell's and Garibay's general appearances before the Magistrate Judge, after they had been told of their right to be tried by a district judge, supply the consent necessary for the Magistrate Judge's "civil jurisdiction" under § 636(c)(1). * * * We reverse the judgment of the Court of Appeals and remand the case for proceedings consistent with this opinion.

It is so ordered.

[The dissenting opinion of JUSTICE THOMAS, with whom JUSTICE STEVENS, JUSTICE SCALIA, and JUSTICE KENNEDY join, is omitted.]

NOTES AND QUESTIONS

1. The modern office of magistrate judge dates to the 1968 enactment of the Federal Magistrates Act which abolished the United States commissioner system. Amendments to the statute have expanded the magistrate judge's authority and assigned the office additional responsibilities. Magistrate judges work within the Article III courthouse; the statute does not create a separate court system. See Conetta v. National Hair Care Centers, 236 F.3d 67, 73 (1st Cir. 2001).

> * * * The purpose behind the Act was "to help relieve the burgeoning caseloads of the United States District Courts and the corresponding

> burdens on federal trial judges[,]" and its effect was to broaden greatly the jurisdiction of magistrates.
>
> The Act * * * authorized magistrates to conduct trials of "minor" criminal cases; to assist district judges in civil and criminal pretrial and discovery proceedings; and to carry out "such additional duties as are not inconsistent with the Constitution and laws of the United States."
>
> In 1976, in response to several restrictive court decisions, Congress amended the Act to give magistrates the authority to act as special masters in civil cases and further granted magistrate judges the authority to hear and determine "any pretrial matter" except for eight dispositive matters. Three years later, Congress passed the Federal Magistrate Act of 1979, which authorized magistrates, upon written consent of the parties, to conduct civil trials and to enter final judgments. Following the 1979 amendments to the Act, drafts of proposed new Rules 72 through 76 were circulated. These new rules took effect in 1983.
>
> In 1990, Congress changed the title of magistrate to " 'United States magistrate judge' to reflect more accurately the responsibilities and duties of the office" [citation omitted]. These amendments, particularly the 1976 and 1979 amendments, have greatly expanded the role of magistrate judges.
>
> Magistrate judges are judicial officers appointed by the judges of the district in which they sit, with the assistance of a citizen merit selection panel. Although they perform many of the same functions as district judges, unlike Article III judges, they do not serve for life. Instead, their term of office is eight years. The duties of magistrate judges are established by the rules of the district court in which they serve. Their salary is protected by statute from reduction, and they can be removed by the district judge of that court "only for incompetency, misconduct, neglect of duty, or physical or mental disability."

Bell, *The Power To Award Sanctions: Does It Belong In the Hands of Magistrate Judges?*, 61 Alb. L. Rev. 433, 437–40 (1997); see also Foschio, *A History of the Development of the Office of United States Commissioner and Magistrate Judge System*, 1999 Fed. Cts. L. Rev. 4 (1999).

2. The Anglo–American legal system long has used extrajudicial personnel to help process disputes. See generally Silberman, *Masters and Magistrates, Part I: The English Model,* 50 N.Y.U. L. Rev. 1070 (1975); Silberman, *Masters and Magistrates, Part II: The American Analogue,* 50 N.Y.U. L. Rev. 1297 (1975). Their use in civil cases, however, traditionally was disfavored. It was believed that resort to such personnel merely increased costs and created delays without producing any measurable improvement in the quality of adjudication. Although some contemporary commentators still question the use of extrajudicial personnel, crowded dockets and complex cases have led to greater willingness to employ them in civil disputes.

> Beginning in the 1980s, attention turned to whether adding magistrates could suffice in lieu of requesting more life-tenured judgeships and to whether some life-tenured positions could be decommissioned. * * * During the following decade, the number of full-time magistrate judges

> rose from 307 to 447; by 1999 in ten districts, the number of magistrate judges was greater than the number of life-tenured judges. Some districts also put magistrate judges "on the wheel," assigned directly to civil cases, as are district judges.
>
> A preference for magistrate judges can be explained by considering the comparative "prices" of a life-tenured judgeship and of a magistrate judgeship. Not only are Article III judges more expensive in dollar terms, they also create possibilities for party patronage and for conflicts between Congress and the Executive. Further, Article III judgeships typically require lag time from judicial request to congressional authorization and executive appointment. In contrast, magistrate judge lines can be created directly by the judiciary which remains dependent on Congress for funding but not for appointing or allocating positions.

Resnik, *Trial as Error, Jurisdiction as Injury, Transforming the Meaning of Article III,* 113 Harv. L. Rev. 924, 989 (2000).

3. A magistrate judge lacks the protection of life tenure that federal judges enjoy under Article III of the Constitution. Nevertheless, courts have upheld the exercise of judicial authority by magistrate judges on the theory that an Article III judge "firmly" controls each magistrate. See e.g., Orsini v. Wallace, 913 F.2d 474, 477–79 (8th Cir.1990), certiorari denied 498 U.S. 1128, 111 S.Ct. 1093, 112 L.Ed.2d 1197 (1991). Is this an example of "the Article III right * * * [being] substantially honored" while "[j]udicial efficiency is served"? See Roell v. Withrow, p. 943, supra. Justice Thomas, in his dissent in *Withrow*, argued that "litigants' rights under Article III are either protected or they are not," 538 U.S. at 597, 123 S.Ct. at 1707, 155 L.Ed.2d at 790. What is your response to that concern? In what ways might a judge's life tenure affect the quality and impartiality of his or her decision making? See Carroll, *The Possible Impact of Article I Judges: Collective Analyses of Judicial Decision Making Between Article I and Article III Judges*, 15 Trinity L. Rev. 50 (2008).

4. What are the procedures for objecting to a magistrate judge's decision? See 12 Wright, Miller & Marcus, Federal Practice and Procedure: Civil 2d §§ 3077.1–80.

5. For an interesting critique of the use of magistrates in the United States District Courts for the Southern and Eastern Districts of New York, see Report on Magistrates by the Committee on the Federal Courts of the New York County Lawyers' Association, 136 F.R.D. 193 (1990). On the special use of magistrates to handle pro se cases, see Bloom & Hershkoff, *Federal Courts, Magistrate Judges, and the Pro Se Plaintiff*, 16 Notre Dame J. L., Ethics & Pub. Pol'y 475 (2002). General discussions include: 12 Wright, Miller & Marcus, Federal Practice and Procedure: Civil 2d §§ 3066–73; Dessem, *The Role of the Federal Magistrate Judge in Civil Justice Reform*, 67 St. John's L. Rev. 799 (1993); Weinstein & Wiener, *Of Sailing Ships and Seeking Facts: Brief Reflections on Magistrates and the Federal Rules of Civil Procedure*, 62 St. John's L. Rev. 429 (1988).

2. MASTERS

Read Federal Rule of Civil Procedure 53.

IN RE PETERSON

Supreme Court of the United States, 1920.
253 U.S. 300, 40 S.Ct. 543, 64 L.Ed. 919.

Petition for Writ of Mandamus and/or Writ of Prohibition to the District Court for the Southern District of New York.

JUSTICE BRANDEIS delivered the opinion of the Court.

[Petitioner challenged the authority of the District Court to appoint an auditor to conduct a preliminary hearing to determine amounts due for coal sold and delivered, and to tax the auditor's expenses as costs. Petitioner also claimed that the appointment of the auditor violated his jury trial right under the Seventh Amendment.]

* * *

The order expressly declared that the auditor should not "finally determine any of the issues in this action, the final determination of all issues of fact to be made by the jury at the trial"; but it did not provide affirmatively what use should be made of the report at the trial. It may be assumed that, if accepted by the court, the report would be admitted at the trial before the jury as prima facie evidence both of the evidentiary facts and of the conclusions of fact therein set forth. * * * A more intelligent consideration of the issues submitted to the jury for final determination would result.

* * * Prior to the adoption of the federal Constitution there did not exist in England, or so far as appears in any of the colonies, any officer, permanent or temporary, who, in connection with trials by jury, exercised the powers of an auditor above described. * * *

The office of auditor, with functions and powers like those here in question, was apparently invented in Massachusetts. It was introduced there by chapter 142 of the Acts of the Legislature of the year 1818, and as a part of the judicial machinery it has received the fullest development in that state. No act of Congress has specifically authorized the adoption of the practice in the federal courts. * * *

* * * The command of the Seventh Amendment * * * does not prohibit the introduction of new methods for determining what facts are actually in issue, nor does it prohibit the introduction of new rules of evidence. * * * New devices may be used to adapt the ancient institution to present needs * * *.

In so far as the task of the auditor is to define and simplify the issues, his function is, in essence, the same as that of pleading. The object of each is to concentrate the controversy upon the questions which should control the result.* * * [I]t cannot be deemed an undue obstruction of the right to a jury trial to require a preliminary hearing before an auditor.

* * *

* * * There being no constitutional obstacle to the appointment of an auditor in aid of jury trials, it remains to consider whether Congress has conferred upon District Courts power to make the order. There is here, * * * no legislation of Congress which directly or by implication forbids the court to provide for such preliminary hearing and report. But, on the other hand, there is no statute which expressly authorizes it. The question presented is, therefore, whether the court possesses the inherent power to supply itself with this instrument for the administration of justice when deemed by it essential.

Courts have (at least in the absence of legislation to the contrary) inherent power to provide themselves with appropriate instruments required for the performance of their duties. * * * This power includes authority to appoint persons unconnected with the court to aid judges in the performance of specific judicial duties, as they may arise in the progress of a cause. * * * Whether such aid shall be sought is ordinarily within the discretion of the trial judge; but this court has indicated that where accounts are complex and intricate, or the documents and other evidence voluminous, or where extensive computations are to be made, it is the better practice to refer the matter to a special master or commissioner than for the judge to undertake to perform the task himself. * * *

* * *

* * * As Congress * * * has made no provision for paying from public funds either the fees of auditors or the expense of the stenographer, the power to make the appointment without consent of the parties is practically dependent upon the power to tax the expense as costs. May the compensation of auditor and stenographer be taxed as costs; and, if so, may the expense be imposed in the discretion of the trial court upon either party?

Federal trial courts have, sometimes by general rule, sometimes by decision upon the facts of a particular case, included in the taxable costs expenditures incident to the litigation which were ordered by the court because deemed essential to a proper consideration of the case by the court or the jury. * * *

The allowance of costs in the federal courts rests, not upon express statutory enactment by Congress, but upon usage long continued and confirmed by implication from provisions in many statutes. * * *

* * * As there is no statute, federal or state, and no rule of court excluding auditors' fees and the expense of his stenographer from the

items taxable as costs, no reason appears why they may not be included, like other expenditures ordered by the court with a view to securing an intelligent consideration of a case.

Denied.

[JUSTICES MCKENNA, PITNEY, and MCREYNOLDS dissented.]

NOTES AND QUESTIONS

1. Before the adoption of Federal Rule 53 in 1938, the Supreme Court recognized that in "exceptional circumstances" a court had authority to appoint a master "to aid judges in the performance of specific judicial duties, as they may arise in the progress of a cause." LA BUY v. HOWES LEATHER CO., 352 U.S. 249, 256, 77 S.Ct. 309, 313, 1 L.Ed.2d 290, 297 (1957) (internal citations omitted). What circumstances ought to count as "exceptional?"

2. What is the scope of a master's role under Federal Rule 53? Would the accounting matter at issue in In Re Peterson be exempt from the "exceptional condition" requirement of the rule? Courts adhered initially to a strict reading of Rule 53, and refused to treat either the complexity of a lawsuit or docket congestion as exceptional conditions warranting a master's appointment. See Kaufman, *Masters in the Federal Courts: Rule* 53, 58 Colum.L.Rev. 452 (1958). Amendments adopted in 2003 are aimed at making the appointment of a master less unusual. See Fellows & Hardock, *Federal Court Special Masters: A Vital Resource in the Era of Complex Litigation*, 31 Wm. Mitchell L. Rev. 1269, 1272–73 (2005); and Scheindlin & Redgrave, *The Evolution and Impact of the New Federal Rule Governing Special Masters*, 51 Fed. Law. 34 (2004).

3. What are the key differences between a magistrate judge and a special master?

4. Special masters have been appointed to assist in complex litigation such as antitrust and civil rights. See Brazil, *Special Masters in Complex Cases: Extending the Judiciary or Reshaping Adjudication?*, 53 U. Chi. L. Rev. 394 (1986); Fiss, *The Supreme Court 1978 Term—Foreword: The Forms of Justice*, 93 Harv.L.Rev. 1 (1979). For examples, see Goldberg, *Cleaning Labor's House: Institutional Reform Litigation in the Labor Movement*, 1989 Duke L.J. 903, 929 (1989) (union reform); Berger, *Away From the Courthouse and Into the Field: The Odyssey of a Special Master,* 78 Colum.L.Rev. 707 (1978) (school desegregation); Brazil, Hazard & Rice, Managing Complex Litigation: A Practical Guide to the Use of Special Masters (1983) (antitrust).

5. Special masters also have been appointed to facilitate and supervise the settlement of a lawsuit. See Feinberg, *Creative Use of ADR: The Court–Appointed Special Settlement Master*, 59 Alb. L. Rev. 881 (1996). In re Holocaust Victim Assets Litigation, 105 F.Supp.2d 139 (E.D.N.Y.2000), involved claims by World War II concentration-camp survivors seeking restitution of wrongfully withheld property by Swiss banks. As part of a major settlement, the court appointed a master to "develop a proposed plan of

allocation and distribution of the Settlement Fund, employing open and equitable procedures to ensure fair consideration of all proposals." Id. at 149.

6. Special masters similarly oversee discovery disputes, coordinate litigation, serve as an expert advisor, monitor compliance, assist the jury, and provide notice in class actions. See, e.g., In re "Agent Orange" Product Liability Litigation, 94 F.R.D. 173 (E.D.N.Y.1982). See McGovern, Appointing Special Masters and Other Judicial Adjuncts: A Handbook for Judges (ALI–ABA, 2007). For a discussion of the special master's potential role in disputes involving electronic discovery, see Scheindlin & Redgrave, *Special Masters and E-Discovery: The Intersection of Two Recent Revisions of the Federal Rules of Civil Procedure*, 30 Cardozo L. Rev. 347 (2008).

7. In NILSSEN v. MOTOROLA, INC., 2001 WL 883696 (N.D. Ill. 2001), a patent infringement case, the District Court rejected plaintiff's objection to the appointment of a special master, despite the fact that the appointee, a lawyer, was a member of a law firm that represented defendant's subsidiary and was "courting" defendant as a client. The court explained that "strict standards of impartiality" would make the appointment of a master "an impossibility," given the small number of individuals with the requisite expertise, relying on decisions from the First, Second, Fourth, and District of Columbia Circuits. Is this decision consistent with Rule 53(a)(2)?

SECTION D. THE FINAL PRETRIAL ORDER

PAYNE v. S.S. NABOB

United States Court of Appeals, Third Circuit, 1962.
302 F.2d 803.

McLAUGHLIN, CIRCUIT JUDGE.

In this personal injury admiralty action libellant filed a pretrial memorandum stating that he was relying upon the condition of a winch to prove his cause of action. The judge's pretrial report noted that. Sometime later the suit went to trial. Libellant's attorney included in his opening the fact that the loading had been handled improperly as an important element of his proof of unseaworthiness. The impleaded stevedore employer objected as it was outside the scope of the pretrial memorandum and report. The trial court sustained the objection. Two witnesses on behalf of the libellant, not listed in his pretrial memorandum, were not allowed to testify. Libellant's attorney moved for a continuance and this was denied.

* * *

Appellant * * * would have it that the Standing Order [local rule adopting Rule 16] did not furnish any ground for the court's barring of the unseaworthy allegation and of the witnesses not mentioned in the appellant's pretrial memorandum or the court's pretrial report. This seems to be founded on the thought that a pretrial memorandum is merely preparatory to the conference and that the court's pretrial order is the sole proof of the results of the pretrial procedure. In this instance, goes the contention, the function of appellant's memorandum was exhausted at the conference and since no pretrial "order" was made there were no binding results of the pretrial steps. [Padovani v. Bruchhausen, 293 F.2d 546 (2d Cir.1961)] * * * is cited for this, where it states:

> "Nothing in the rule [16] affords basis for clubbing the parties into admissions they do not willingly make; but it is a way of advancing the trial ultimately to be had by setting forth points on which the parties are agreed after a conference directed by a trained judge."

Appellant was not clubbed into admissions he did not willingly make. It was his own voluntary statement of the basis of his claim that was included in the pretrial report of the judge. The report was never objected to as incorrectly outlining appellant's pretrial statement.

The position now taken that the pretrial report of the trial judge because it is not titled as an "order" does not comply with Rule 16 is without merit. Appellant's pretrial memorandum was filed. In accordance with the Standing Order it contained a "brief summary statement of both the facts of this case and counsel's contention as to the liability of defendant." It also contained "The names and addresses of all witnesses (except rebuttal) whom the plaintiff expects to call to testify at the time of trial." The pretrial conference was held in due course and attended by the attorneys for the parties. Based on the pretrial memoranda and the conference, the district judge drew and filed his report. There was no complaint concerning it or any part of it down to and including the trial until libellant's attorney was stopped in his opening as he went beyond his pretrial outline of alleged liability. The pretrial "report"[2] drawn, signed and filed by the pretrial judge properly and fully (having the particular litigation and its requirements in mind) complies with the requirements of

---

2. "Pre–Trial Report of Judge Van Dusen

Date Pre–Trial Held: 9/21/59 No. on Consolidated List: 2109 303 of 1958 in Admiralty

Case Title: Hosea Payne v. S.S. Nabob & North German Lloyd v. Lavino Shipping Co.

1. Trial Counsel: LCPhilip Dorfman, Esq. & Saul C. Waldbaum, Esq.

R—Robert A. Hauslohner, Esq. (T. Mount will try)

IR—F. Hastings Griffin, Jr., Esq. (P. Price will try)

2. Amendments: If IR wishes to amend pre-trial memo, notice to be given to undersigned.

3. Discovery: Respondent will answer impleaded respondent's interrogatories (unexecuted copies to be furnished counsel by September 23).

4. L's Claim: Ship unseaworthy due to improper port winch on after side at #2 hatch. Brakes would not hold when set in neutral. Port winch on house-fall did not work from early hours of morning. See pre-trial memo.

5. R's Claim: Sole cause of injuries was L's negligence and that of his fellow workmen. Two men pushed draft into L and 2 other men said nothing was defective in winches. See pre-trial memo. IR's position—see pre-trial memo.

6. Stipulations:

7. Issues:

8. Legal Issues:

9. Trial Time: 6 days

Francis L. Van Dusen, J."

Rule 16. It, including its references to the pretrial memoranda, succinctly fulfilled the letter and spirit of pretrial. It reduced the action to essentials, eliminated surplusage, enabled the parties and the court to prepare for a trial of stated issues, named witnesses and contained no hidden charms. The argument to the contrary, depending as it does on a quibble over the word "report", is rootless.

It is asserted on behalf of the appellant that the Standing Order can only be construed as a request to stipulate, that counsel had no intention of stipulating and that no warning or notice was given by the Standing Order that failure to list the requirements ordered would constitute a stipulation or a waiver of all other theories. Rule 16 gives as the first purpose of pretrial "The simplification of issues". [This language has been altered without any substantive change.] Under the Standing Order counsel were asked to furnish "A brief summary of both the facts of the case and counsel's contentions as to the liability of the defendant." That was done. Libellant's contentions as to the liability of the defendant were inserted into the Court's Report with the note "See pre-trial memo". The Report was filed September 28, 1959. The trial did not commence until March 14, 1960, a five and a half months interval during which no effort was made to change the signed and filed contentions of the libellant regarding the liability of the defendant or to add names of witnesses. The facts that the situation was plain on its face and that the practice was well settled by then, (the Standing Order having been in effect since October 23, 1958), set the tone for this contention on behalf of appellant. Krieger v. Ownership Corporation, 270 F.2d 265 (3 Cir.1959), relied upon by appellant is inapposite. We there held that disputed issues of fact *actually raised* at the pretrial stage could not be resolved by the trial court on motion for summary judgment. It has long been the law that attorneys at the pretrial stage "owe a duty to the court and opposing counsel to make a full and fair disclosure of their views as to what the real issues at the trial will be." Cherney v. Holmes, 185 F.2d 718, 721 (7th Cir.1950) * * *. It is through such disclosure at pretrial that trial prejudice can be avoided. The awareness of appellant's attorney to the trial situation is apparent in his request for a continuance when he told the court "I think under the circumstances I would move for a continuance of the case to give *the other side* ample time, because actually this is a question of surprise." * * * [Emphasis supplied in original.]

It is argued also that the court abused its discretion by refusing to permit amendment of the pretrial memorandum. This was not an easy decision for the trial judge. His inclination clearly, as is habitual with judges, was to help. And help he would have if, in his opinion, he could have done so fairly. But he was confronted with the realization that if he granted the request or allowed a continuance of the trial he was repudiating the whole pretrial theory and system as understood and followed in the Eastern District at a crucial period of its existence. Pretrial was finally on a firm foundation there. The judges had all given it generous and complete attention. This, with the gradual realization of the bar that pretrial was here to stay as a vital element of litigation practice and its resultant full cooperation, had made pretrial procedure routine in the Eastern District. One consequence was that directly and indirectly enormous relief was given the badly clogged trial list. It was admittedly vitally important to make sure that pretrial procedure would continue to function properly. One necessary phase of attaining that objective was, as expressed by the trial judge, "We have come to the point of enforcing it very strictly." In the circumstances he considered himself obliged to deny the motions to amend the pretrial memorandum with respect to liability allegations and witnesses. The refusal of appellant's motion for a continuance is in the same category.

Beyond all doubt the judge acted entirely within his discretion. It was difficult for him, it took courage but it was what this sound, experienced judge had to do as he saw it, in accordance with his judicial obligation.

The decree of the district court will be affirmed.

NOTES AND QUESTIONS

1. Courts generally treat the final pretrial order, including the stipulations, agreements, and statements of counsel made at the final pretrial conference, as binding for purposes of trial. Kona Technology Corp. v. Southern Pacific Transportation Co., 225 F.3d 595, 604 (5th Cir.2000). Many of the benefits associated with the use of the pretrial order depend upon its binding effect. But given the exigencies that are an inevitable part of litigation, particularly at the trial level, is strict finality reasonable?

2. What happens if a claim is included in a complaint but omitted from a pretrial order? Conversely, if a claim is included in a pretrial order that does not appear in the complaint, is it necessary to amend the pleading? Does Rule 16(d) provide an answer? The pretrial order sometimes has been used to widen consideration of issues beyond those listed in the pleadings. In Howard v. Kerr Glass Mfg. Co., 699 F.2d 330 (6th Cir.1983), the Sixth Circuit ruled that the final pretrial order prevailed over the original pleadings and that the trial judge had erred in refusing to admit evidence on issues included in the final pretrial order but not in the pleadings. But omission of an issue from a pretrial order can prove fatal. In McLean Contracting Co. v. Waterman S.S. Corp., 277 F.3d 477 (4th Cir. 2002), plaintiff had made it clear that defendant's liability depended upon the fact that a third company had acted as defendant's agent. Defendant intended to dispute the agency but failed to have it included as an issue in the pretrial order. The appellate court held it was not an abuse of discretion to refuse defendant's evidence on the issue.

SECTION E. CASE MANAGEMENT SANCTIONS

NICK v. MORGAN'S FOODS, INC.

United States Court of Appeals, Eighth Circuit, 2001.
270 F.3d 590.

MCMILLIAN, CIRCUIT JUDGE.

[The District Court imposed a monetary sanction on defendant and its counsel for failing to participate in good faith in court-ordered alternative dispute resolution in an effort to settle the lawsuit.]

* * *

* * * Nick filed suit against appellant on June 15, 1998, alleging sexual harassment and retaliation in violation of Title VII of the Civil Rights Act of 1964, as amended, 42 U.S.C. § 2000e et seq. At that time, appellant was represented by outside counsel Robert Seibel, but all business decisions were made by appellant's in-house counsel Barton Craig. Pursuant to Fed.R.Civ.P. 16(f) [now, Rule 16(b)(1)(B)], a pretrial scheduling conference was held on May 20, 1999. The parties consented to ADR with a court-appointed mediator pursuant to E.D.Mo.L.R. 6.01—6.05 ("the local rules"), and agreed to report back to the district court with the results of the ADR by September 30, 1999. On August 2, 1999, the district court issued an Order Referring Case to Alternate Dispute Resolution ("Referral Order") mandating that the ADR process be conducted in compliance with the local rules and listing other specific requirements. * * * These requirements included, inter alia, that, at least seven days before the first ADR conference, each party shall supply the mediator with a memorandum presenting a summary of the disputed facts and its position on liability and damages; that all parties, counsel, corporate representatives and claims professionals with settlement authority shall attend all mediation conferences and participate in good faith; and that noncompliance with any court deadline could result in the imposition of sanctions against the appropriate party or parties.

On appellant's request, the district court agreed to postpone the first ADR conference until October 18, 1999. Appellant did not file the memorandum that was required to be filed at least seven days before the first ADR conference. In attendance at the conference on October 18, 1999 was the court-appointed mediator; Nick; Nick's counsel; appellant's outside counsel, Seibel; and a corporate representative of appellant who had no independent knowledge of the facts of the case and had permission to settle only up to $500. Any settlement offer over $500 had to be relayed by telephone to Craig, who chose not to attend the ADR conference on the advice of outside counsel Seibel. During the ADR conference, Nick twice made offers of settlement that were rejected without a counteroffer by appellant. The ADR conference ended shortly thereafter without a settlement having been reached.

After the ADR conference, the mediator informed the district court of appellant's minimal level of participation, and the district court issued an order directing appellant to show cause why it should not be sanctioned for its failure to participate in good faith in the court-ordered ADR process. In an October 29, 1999 response, appellant asserted that the Referral Order was only a set of nonbinding guidelines and admitted that it decided not to comply with the guidelines because doing otherwise would be a waste of time and money. On the same day, Nick moved to sanction appellant for failing to participate in good faith in the ADR process and requested attorneys' fees and costs arising out of her participation in the mediation.

The district court held a hearing on its show cause order and Nick's motion for sanctions on December 1, 1999, at which time Seibel confirmed that appellant's corporate representative at the ADR conference had only $500 settlement authority; that any change in appellant's position could only be made by Craig, who was not present but available by telephone; and that counsel had indeed failed to file the pre-ADR conference memorandum. After hearing argument by both parties, the district court concluded that appellant failed to participate in good faith in the court-ordered ADR process and sanctioned appellant $1,390.63 and appellant's outside counsel $1,390.62. These sanctions were calculated to cover the cost of the ADR conference fees ($506.25) and Nick's attorneys' fees ($2,275.00). The court also ordered appellant to pay a $1,500.00 fine to the Clerk of the District Court as a sanction for failing to prepare the required memorandum and for its decision to send a corporate representative with limited authority to settle to the ADR conference. The district court ordered appellant and appellant's outside counsel each to pay $30.00 to Nick for the costs she incurred attending the ADR conference.

On December 20, 1999, appellant filed a Motion for Reconsideration and Vacation of the Court's Order Granting Plaintiff's Motion for Sanctions (motion for reconsideration). The district court denied the motion for reconsideration and imposed additional sanctions against appellant and appellant's counsel in the amount of $1,250.00 each to be paid to the Clerk of the District Court for vexatiously increasing the costs of litigation by filing a frivolous motion. This appeal followed. Appellant appeals the sanctions levied against it that are to be paid to the Clerk of the District Court; Appellant does not contest the sanctions levied against it that are to be paid to Nick and her counsel.

* * *

Appellant argues that, whereas Rule 11 * * * authorizes monetary fines payable to the court, Rule 16 does not. * * * Rule 16(f) expressly permits a judge to impose any other sanction the judge deems appropriate in addition to, or in lieu of, reasonable expenses. * * * Here, the district court judge acted well within his discretion by imposing a monetary fine payable to the Clerk of the District Court as a sanction for failing to prepare the required memorandum, deciding to send a corporate representative with limited authority to the ADR conference, and for vexatiously increasing the costs of litigation by filing a frivolous motion for reconsideration.

* * *

Appellant urges that the "uncontroverted facts on the record conclusively establish that all of the conduct which irritated the Trial Court was the exclusive product of Appellant's trial lawyer and unknown to Appellant." * * * Appellant argues that the affidavits of Craig and Seibel establish that it had no knowledge that its conduct was sanctionable and that its outside counsel was solely responsible for the noncompliance. * * * Appellant claims that Seibel did not pass along to Craig the necessity for a memorandum, and that, although Seibel advised Craig of the district court's Referral Order and the relevant local rules, Craig read neither and relied instead on the advice of Seibel. * * * Appellant further claims that Seibel advised Craig that his attendance at the ADR conference was not necessary. * * * For this reason, appellant argues that the district court abused its discretion in imposing the sanctions against it and not solely against its outside counsel.

It is undisputed that appellant did not provide the court-ordered memorandum to the mediator because appellant's outside counsel considered it unnecessary and duplicative, and thus too costly. * * * It is further undisputed that appellant's corporate representative at the ADR conference had settlement authority limited to $500 * * *, and that any settlement offer over $500 could only be considered by Craig, who was not present and only available by telephone. * * * Appellant argues that its counsel, Seibel, failed to inform appellant that Craig was required to attend the mediation and instead erroneously assured appellant that sending its highest ranking manager in Missouri was sufficient. * * * This argument incorrectly frames the issue because the problem was not the rank of the corporate representative but the corporate representative's ability to meaningfully participate in the ADR conference and to reconsider the company's position on settlement at that conference.

It is a well-established principle in this Circuit that a party may be held responsible for the actions of its counsel. * * * While forcing parties to answer for their attorneys' behavior may seem harsh * * * litigants who are truly misled and victimized by their attorneys have recourse in malpractice actions. * * * [T]he sanction imposed by the district court need only be proportionate to the litigant's transgression. * * *

* * *

In sum, we hold that the district court did not abuse its discretion in imposing monetary sanctions against appellant for its lack of good faith participation in the ADR process, for its failure to comply with the district court's August 2, 1999, Referral Order, and for vexatiously increasing the costs of litigation by filing a frivolous motion for reconsideration. The order of the district court is affirmed.

NOTES AND QUESTIONS

1. How should courts penalize the failure to cooperate in the pretrial process? Should the failure to abide by a pretrial order ever result in dismissal of the suit, or in summary judgment? Compare Barreto v. Citibank, N.A., 907 F.2d 15 (1st Cir.1990), with John v. Louisiana, 828 F.2d 1129 (5th Cir.1987). Does Rule 41(b) provide an answer to this question? When would a lesser remedy—such as preclusion of an issue or exclusion of evidence—be appropriate? Consider this question in the light of *Payne* p. 949, supra. Are monetary sanctions preferable to the relatively drastic remedy of dismissal?

2. Is it an abuse of discretion to impose Rule 16 monetary sanctions on a corporate defendant that accidentally fails to produce documents until after the deadline has expired? In TRACINDA CORP. v. DAIMLERCHRYSLER AG, 502 F.3d 212 (3d Cir. 2007), the appeals court affirmed a discovery sanction of $556,061 for defendant's failing to produce 61 pages of documents until a year after discovery had closed and on the eve of the last day of trial, in a case in which defendant already had produced 250,000 documents. A Special Master found no evidence of bad faith or intentional misconduct, and instead attributed the failure to the negligence of a third party vendor that had copied the documents. Nevertheless, the appeals court upheld the sanction against charges that it was "unjust," underscoring the prejudicial effect and the substantial costs that the discovery failure imposed on the opposing party. The court rejected out of hand defendant's suggestion that the sanction would create perverse incentives for parties to correct good faith litigation mistakes:

> Production errors discovered at the pre-trial stage of litigation will result in little, if any, expense or prejudice to the opposing party and therefore are not likely to warrant the imposition of sanctions under Rule 16(f). On the other hand, if a litigant knows that even inadvertent failure to produce relevant documents may result in a sanction when the existence of the documents is discovered during trial, the litigant may exercise more care in ensuring that all relevant documents are produced.
>
> DaimlerChrysler * * * argues that our holding will have the effect of deterring future litigants from admitting and rectifying discovery errors. However, * * * the obligation on parties and counsel to come forward with relevant documents not produced during discovery is "absolute." Indeed, the failure to do so can result in penalties more severe than monetary sanctions including dismissal of the case. We are not concerned about chilling conduct that is compulsory and required by law.

Id at 243. Is it appropriate to review a Rule 16 monetary sanction under the abuse-of-discretion standard?

3. Is the remedy of monetary penalties preferable to the relatively drastic remedy of dismissal? Is Rule 16 intended as a compensatory remedy, designed to deter and to reimburse the opposing party and the court for the cost of any deviations from a pretrial order made by a party; or as a punitive remedy designed to encourage compliance with a court order? See Brazil, *Improving Judicial Controls over the Pretrial Development of Civil Actions:*

Model Rules for Case Management and Sanctions, 1981 Am.B.Found.Research J. 873, 921–55; Peckham, *The Federal Judge as Case Manager: The New Role of Guiding a Case from Filing to Disposition*, 69 Calif.L.Rev. 770, 800–04 (1981).

4. How do Rule 16 sanctions differ from those that may be imposed under Rule 11?

5. In TORRES v. COMMONWEALTH OF PUERTO RICO, 485 F.3d 5 (1st Cir.2007), the First Circuit affirmed the District Court's denial of a potentially dispositive but belated pretrial motion asserting sovereign and qualified immunity. The court emphasized: "Whatever the merits of the excuse, trial courts are not required to accept at face value litigants' reasons for their failure to meet deadlines." Id. at 10–11. Should the result be the same if defendant files a motion to dismiss for lack of subject-matter jurisdiction after the date set out in the pretrial order?

6. Is the practice of managerial judging reshaping American courts in the image of the civil law? Some commentators point to an increasing convergence of American judicial practice with that of European "inquisitorial" judges. See, e.g., Rowe, Jr., *Authorized Managerialism Under the Federal Rules—and the Extent of Convergence with Civil–Law Judging*, 36 Sw. U. L. Rev. 191 (2007); Hazard, *Responsibilities of Judges and Advocates in Civil and Common Law: Some Lingering Misconceptions Concerning Civil Lawsuits*, 39 Cornell Int'l L.J. 59 (2006); and Sherman, *The Evolution of American Civil Trial Process Towards Greater Congruence with Continental Practice*, 7 Tul. J. Int'l & Comp. L. 125 (1999). Are there dangers in transplanting legal procedures from civil law systems to the American system? What are the benefits in learning from practices abroad?

CHAPTER 13

ADJUDICATION WITHOUT TRIAL OR BY SPECIAL PROCEEDING

■ ■ ■

In this Chapter, we examine summary procedures that allow a court to dispose of an action without a full-blown trial. The main focus is Federal Rule 56, which permits a court to enter judgment if a material issue of fact is not in dispute and the movant is entitled to judgment as a matter of law. See 10A Wright, Miller & Kane, Federal Practice and Procedure: Civil 3d § 2712. "Simply stated, a material fact is one which will affect the outcome of the case, and a material fact raises a genuine issue if a reasonable jury could reach different conclusions concerning that fact." Gordillo, *Summary Judgment and Problems in Applying the Celotex Trilogy Standard*, 42 Clev.St.L.Rev. 263, 263–64 (1994). When the rule was first promulgated, courts used Rule 56 sparingly, "to weed out frivolous and sham cases, and cases for which the law had a quick and definitive answer." Wald, *Summary Judgment at Sixty*, 76 Texas L. Rev. 1897 (1998). However, an emphasis on efficiency has led to an increased reliance on summary judgment, and this trend coincides with a decline in the number of cases that proceed to trial. See Mollica, *Federal Summary Judgment at High Tide*, 84 Marq. L. Rev. 141, 141 (2000). The percentage of cases disposed of by Rule 56 motions doubled between 1975 and 2000, see Coleman, *The* Celotex *Initial Burden Standard and an Opportunity to "Revivify" Rule 56*, 32 S. Ill. U. L.J. 295, 295 (2008), and some commentators now warn that the "hyperactive" use of summary judgment and other pretrial motions "threatens longstanding constitutional values." Miller, *The Pretrial Rush to Judgment: Are the "Litigation Explosion," "Liability Crisis," and Efficiency Clichés Eroding Our Day in Court and Jury Trial Commitments?*, 78 N.Y.U. L. Rev. 982, 2093 (2003). The materials in this Chapter thus raise important questions about the current nature of civil litigation and the values that ought to inform procedural reform.

SECTION A. SUMMARY JUDGMENT

Read Federal Rule of Civil Procedure 56 and the accompanying materials in the Supplement.

Summary Judgment: A Short History

FRIEDENTHAL & GARDNER, JUDICIAL DISCRETION TO DENY SUMMARY JUDGMENT IN THE ERA OF MANAGERIAL JUDGING, 31 Hofstra L. Rev. 91, 96 (2002) (footnotes omitted):

Modern summary judgment has its root in nineteenth century English law. Both the 1855 Summary Procedure on Bills of Exchange Act, more commonly known as Keating's Act, and the Judicature Act of 1873 allowed plaintiffs summary adjudication in their collection of liquidated claims when they demonstrated no dispute as to the terms of an agreement to provide goods or services, the actual provision of those goods or services, and nonpayment. The purpose of these acts was to "reduce delay and expense resulting from frivolous defenses." Although forms of summary proceedings existed in the United States as early as 1769, several states enacted summary judgment statutes based on the English model in the late 1800s. These American statutes were similar to the English Acts in that they were limited to use by plaintiffs and could only be used for claims appropriately resolved by documentary proof. Initially, judges expressed reluctance in granting summary judgment motions, viewing summary judgment as a drastic remedy. Yet by the mid–1920s, judges granted more than half of such motions before them.

For a discussion of the civil law roots of summary judgment, see Millar, *Three American Ventures in Summary Civil Procedure*, 38 Yale L.J. 193, 193–95 (1928).

NOTES AND QUESTIONS

1. Summary proceedings and other "shortcuts" to judgment often are characterized as devices to reduce cost and to avoid delay. Not all commentators agree, however, that summary judgment practice is efficient. To the contrary, a recent study concludes: "In some courts and types of cases, it may be a useful tool for avoiding costly trials, but in others, it may be wasting resources and imposing delay." Rave, Note—*Questioning the Efficiency of Summary Judgment*, 81 N.Y.U. L. Rev. 875, 909 (2006). Can summary procedure be justified by any value other than efficiency?

2. Does a district court's dismissal of a case on summary judgment undermine the constitutional commitment to trial by jury, at least in those cases in which the Seventh Amendment would afford such a right? Given the constitutional dimension of the issue, is it ever appropriate for a court to use Federal Rule 56 as a docket-clearing device? Compare Thomas, *Why Summary*

Judgment Is Unconstitutional, 93 Va. L. Rev. 139 (2007), with Nelson, *Summary Judgment and the Progressive Constitution*, 93 Iowa L. Rev. 1653 (2008); and Brunet, *Summary Judgment Is Constitutional*, 93 Iowa L. Rev. 1625 (2008).

Early Debates about the Use of Federal Rule 56

MILLER, THE PRETRIAL RUSH TO JUDGMENT: ARE THE "LITIGATION EXPLOSION," "LIABILITY CRISIS," AND EFFICIENCY CLICHÉS ERODING OUR DAY IN COURT AND JURY TRIAL COMMITMENTS?, 78 N.Y.U. L. Rev. 982, 1019–23 (2003) (footnotes omitted):

Since its promulgation, Rule 56 has been the subject of periodic debate, as first exemplified in the 1940s by the opinions of two extremely distinguished Second Circuit judges, Charles E. Clark and Jerome N. Frank, in Arnstein v. Porter, [154 F.2d 464 (2d Cir. 1946),] an action charging one of America's greatest songwriters with the infringement of musical copyrights of an apparently litigious plaintiff. Judge Frank, writing for the majority, decided against summary judgment and in favor of trial, stating that the "[p]laintiff must not be deprived of the invaluable privilege of cross-examining the defendant—the 'crucial test of credibility'—in the presence of the jury." Although finding composer Ira Arnstein's theory about Cole Porter's plagiarism to be highly implausible, Judge Frank held that it raised a credibility question requiring a jury's determination, and that summary judgment should not be granted when there was the "slightest doubt as to the facts." He was concerned that liberal utilization of the motion would allow judges to usurp the role of juries, and would "favor unduly the party with the more ingenious and better paid lawyer." Judge Frank viewed trial by paper to be retrogressive, reminiscent of the abolished equity practice of relying on written testimony, and sought to interpret Rule 56 * * * so that all testimony on the motion would be taken in open court absent exceptional circumstances. He also expressed the sentiment that use of summary procedures in the name of clearing crowded dockets unjustly deprived litigants of their day in court.

Conversely, Judge Clark argued that summary judgment was "more necessary in the system of simple pleading now enforced in the federal courts" to avoid useless and unnecessary trials. He disagreed with an across-the-board limitation on summary judgment that would prevent it from being granted whenever credibility issues were crucial, and he accused his colleague of judicially amending the Rules, stating that "the clear-cut provisions of F.R. 56 conspicuously do not contain either a restriction on the kinds of actions to which it is applicable (unlike most state summary procedures) or any presumption against its use." He also mounted a vigorous assault on Judge Frank's "slightest doubt" standard, commenting in a later writing that "a slight doubt can be developed as to practically all things human." A narrow construction of the Rule, in his view, would encourage trials for the purpose of harassment and mean that the federal courts were endorsing the "obvious tendency to force settlement of the claim not because it is just, but because contesting it has become too costly or too inconvenient."

* * * The Supreme Court seemed to adopt Judge Frank's philosophy of discouraging summary judgment by urging courts to apply it cautiously, keeping in mind the importance of jury trial, and calling for even greater restraint in lawsuits involving state-of-mind questions and complex issues. The paradigm case, Poller v. CBS, Inc. [, 368 U.S. 464, 82 S.Ct. 486, 71 L.Ed.2d 458 (1962)], involved a private antitrust action brought against CBS alleging conspiracy to restrain and monopolize trade in violation of the Sherman Act by canceling its affiliation with a UHF station to drive the plaintiff out of business. The District of Columbia District Court granted the defendant's summary judgment motion alleging lack of the illicit motive required to prove a Sherman Act violation [, 174 F.Supp. 802, 804–05 (D.D.C. 1959)]. The Court of Appeals for the District of Columbia affirmed, [284 F.2d 599 (D.C. Cir. 1960),] but the Supreme Court reversed, with Justice Clark writing that:

> [S]ummary procedures should be used sparingly in complex antitrust litigation where motive and intent play leading roles, the proof is largely in the hands of the alleged conspirators, and hostile witnesses thicken the plot. It is only when the witnesses are present and subject to cross-examination that their credibility and the weight to be given their testimony can be appraised. Trial by affidavit is no substitute for trial by jury which so long has been the hallmark of "even handed justice."

[368 U.S. at 473, 82 S.Ct. at 491, 7 L.Ed.2d at 464 (footnote omitted).]

* * * Poller had a decidedly dampening effect on summary judgment in the federal courts; indeed, the reported decisions reveal few cases of any complexity adjudicated under Rule 56 during the succeeding two decades [footnotes omitted].

LUNDEEN v. CORDNER

United States Court of Appeals, Eighth Circuit, 1966.
354 F.2d 401.

GIBSON, CIRCUIT JUDGE. * * *

Appellant, plaintiff below, (hereinafter referred to as plaintiff) is a former wife of one Joseph Cordner, deceased. During their marriage two children were born, Maureen Joan Cordner and Michael Joseph Cordner. Prior to the time of his death Joseph Cordner was working in Libya. Mr. Cordner's employer Socony Mobil Oil Company, Inc. (Socony) carried a group life insurance contract with Metropolitan Life Insurance Company, (Metropolitan) under which Mr. Cordner as the insured had in 1956 designated his children, Maureen and Michael, as equal beneficiaries. In 1958 Joseph Cordner, having been divorced by plaintiff, married intervener, France Jeanne Cordner. In April 1960 a child was born of this second marriage. On October 3, 1962 Joseph Cordner died. During all periods above mentioned Mr. Cordner was in the employ of Socony stationed in Libya. The insurance policy and the annuity were in effect and due proof of loss was made. The contest for the proceeds arises between adverse claimants; the original designated beneficiaries, Maureen Joan and Michael Joseph Cordner; and France Jeanne Cordner, the second wife of assured, and Northwestern, as Trustee under the Last Will and Testament of Joseph F. Cordner, deceased.

On November 5, 1963, plaintiff as guardian and on behalf of her two children Maureen and Michael Cordner, the named beneficiaries, sued the insurer, Metropolitan, to recover the proceeds of the policy. Metropolitan answered that there were adverse claims to the policy benefits. Thereafter, Northwestern as the Trustee under the Last Will and Testament of the deceased, Joseph Cordner, was interpleaded as an additional defendant. Appellee, France J. Cordner, then intervened in the action. Both intervener and Northwestern allege that sometime in 1961 the decedent effected a change of beneficiaries [in favor of intervener]. * * *

It is clear that the first two children of decedent, Maureen and Michael, are the named beneficiaries. However, it is asserted that Joseph Cordner did everything within his power to effect a change of beneficiaries as alleged by intervener. Intervener presented affidavits and exhibits in support of her position and moved for summary judgment. The motion was granted and plaintiff contests this ruling on the ground that a summary judgment is not proper at this point in the litigation and that there remains a genuine issue on a material fact. It is now our task to determine if the summary judgment was properly granted.

* * * Plaintiff accepts as controlling the general rule of law that an insured's attempt to change his beneficiary will be given effect if all that remains to be done is a ministerial duty on the part of the insurer. * * *

Therefore, if deceased completed all the necessary steps required of him to change the beneficiary in his policy, intervener would be entitled to judgment. Furthermore, if intervener can demonstrate this fact so clearly that there is no longer a genuine issue of fact, summary judgment may be properly granted under provisions of Rule 56(c)* * *.

We are of the opinion that the affidavits and exhibits introduced by intervener clearly and undeniably indicate that deceased made a change in his policy's beneficiaries. First, it appears that after deceased's marriage in 1958 to intervener he amended his group hospitalization and employee savings plan to include intervener. Furthermore, certain correspondence conclusively indicates that a change in the life insurance was actually made.

Mr. Iten, an employee of Socony in Libya, whose duties included administration of company benefit plans, * * * prepared a letter to the New York office, dated April 19, 1961, stating that Joseph Cordner desired information as to who were his present beneficiaries under the company benefit plans and that Mr. Cordner had married for a second time and was not certain whether he had changed his beneficiary. * * *

Mr. Iten was transferred from Libya shortly thereafter and his duties were assumed by Mr. Burks. Burks by affidavit stated that early in 1961 Mr. Cordner came to him with a request to change his beneficiaries; that Burks issued the necessary forms to Cordner and gave him instructions on how to complete the forms, at which time Cordner produced a copy of his Will made in North Dakota while vacationing from Libya in 1960. They discussed the form of beneficiary designation which might be appropriate under the terms of the Will. Mr. Cordner personally completed the forms, endorsed the beneficiary changes he wished to make on the back of each form, signed the forms in Burks' presence, (the latter acting as a witness to the signature) and then left the completed forms with Burks for transmittal. Since Burks was unfamiliar with the type of beneficiary changes endorsed on the forms he made a thermofax copy of Cordner's Will and sent this reproduction together with the completed change of beneficiary forms to the New York office in a letter dated May 11, 1961, which letter in part reads as follows:

> Please review the enclosed employee change of beneficiary forms and advise us if this designation is acceptable under the plan.
>
> The Home Office responded by stating in a letter dated June 1, 1961:
>
> We are processing the Change of Beneficiary forms completed by the above employee [J.F. Cordner] and forwarded to us. * * * We see no reason why the designation will not be acceptable.

Mr. Burks in his earlier affidavit of March 30, 1963 states that to the best of his recollection the change of beneficiary requested by Cordner was as follows:

> "One-fourth of the proceeds to my wife France Jeanne Cordner and the balance to the Northwestern National Bank of Minneapolis, Minnesota in trust for the uses and purposes set forth in my Last Will and Testament."

Burks in his second affidavit prepared for the purpose of the summary judgment proceeding confirmed the factual statements in his earlier affidavit and detailed the discussion and the procedures employed in the requested change of beneficiary by Cordner. He further stated that since the New York office had the Certificate for endorsement and since the Home Office stated in its letter of June 1, 1961 that they were processing the change of beneficiary forms he had no reason to believe that the processing of the changes had not proceeded to completion in the normal course. He was in the New York office at the time when a search of the files was made for the change of beneficiary forms, which, of course, they were unable to locate. When he returned to Tripoli, with instructions from the New York office to continue the search and to forward to New York all company papers having to do with Mr. Cordner's employment, he found a copy of a letter addressed to Cordner by his attorney suggesting the form of beneficiary designation required to effect the provisions of his Will. Burks then recalled that Mr. Cordner had referred to this same letter when discussing beneficiary changes in 1961 and that Cordner had used the suggested language in completing his change of beneficiary forms. After stating that he cannot restate from memory the text of the changes, he said that "I can and do reconfirm, upon my own direct knowledge and positive recollection that beneficiary changes so made by Joseph Franklin Cordner were in the form suggested by his attorney's letter and quoted verbatim from that letter in my prior affidavit."

Further correspondence indicates that the change of beneficiary forms were forwarded to the employer's Annuity and Insurance Department. A search of the department, however, never uncovered the form or the exact language used therein. It also appears by affidavit that all of the above related correspondence was properly identified and was prepared, mailed, received and kept as part of the business records of the company.

Plaintiff presents no counter evidence nor in any way indicates that intervener's evidence is not worthy of belief. Therefore, we believe there is no genuine issue of fact on this point. It is clear that Joseph Cordner actually made a change in the beneficiaries of his life insurance policy.

However, to entitle intervener to summary judgment, it must not only be clear that a change was made, but the wording of that change must be shown beyond any reasonable and genuine dispute. This point, too, was well covered in intervener's supporting papers.

* * *

From the affidavit of the attorney concerning the discussion of deceased's desires, from the letter written by the attorney explaining how the beneficiaries should be changed to effectuate these desires, and from the wording of the Last Will and Testament it is clear that Joseph Cordner intended to change the beneficiaries of his insurance policy by giving one-fourth to intervener and the balance to Northwestern in trust. We can presume that this intent remained with Mr. Cordner during the intervening ten months between the Will's execution and the date of the beneficiary change. * * *

However, in addition to this presumption we have the uncontested affidavits of a non-interested third party who was in a position to be aware of the actual wording of the change. The affiant, Mr. Harold Burks, was a fellow employee of Mr. Cordner in Libya, and supervised Mr. Cordner in filling out the required change of beneficiary forms. Mr. Burks is probably the only person that was in a position to be aware of the wording of the document. His affidavits are entitled to considerable weight in determining the merits of a summary judgment motion, especially where there is no indication of any counter-evidence. Moreover, Mr. Burks' assistance in processing the change in beneficiary was done in the regular course of business of Socony, and pursuant to his assigned duties. It has been held that the clear affidavits from the only persons in a position to be aware of a factual situation can well serve as the basis for a summary judgment. Dyer v. MacDougall, 201 F.2d 265 (2 Cir.1952).

* * *

So, in support of intervener's claim there is undisputed proof that Mr. Cordner had manifested an intent to give intervener one-fourth of his insurance proceeds with the balance going into the trust established by his Will. It is likewise clear beyond any shadow of doubt that Mr. Cordner subsequently made a change in his insurance beneficiaries. The logical conclusion is clear. He made the change in accordance with his prior expressed intent. This presumption is supported by the two affidavits of Mr. Burks which recite from direct and positive recollection that the beneficiary changes were copied from Mr. Cordner's letter from his attorney and were in form exactly as alleged by intervener.

In response to the overwhelming documentary evidence supported by affidavits all of which consistently showed that Cordner had requested a change of beneficiary in accordance with his lawyer's letter and his own Last Will and Testament, the plaintiff submitted her own counter-affidavit to the effect that Mr. Cordner was very much interested in the welfare of his first two children (the named beneficiaries) and was aware of the future financial difficulties they would face. No further information was offered. The Court, therefore, was not presented with a situation where it was asked to weigh conflicting affidavits. The problem was only, did the affidavits and exhibits of intervener sustain the necessary burden in order to allow a summary judgment? The trial court felt the burden was sustained, and from the above related facts we agree with the trial court's conclusion. * * *

We are of the opinion that if this information were presented at trial, intervener would be entitled to a directed verdict in her favor, and it has been said that if the information presented entitles one to a directed verdict, a summary judgment is in order. * * * Intervener having made a sufficient showing, it then rests upon the plaintiff to specify at least some evidence which could be produced at trial. * * * Plaintiff apparently is of the opinion that, since she makes a prima facie case by merely introducing the Certificate showing her children as designated beneficiaries, she is entitled to a trial on the issue of (1) whether any change of beneficiary was made, and (2) if so, what changes were actually made. This we do not feel is a correct view of the law.

The counter-affidavit of the plaintiff does not meet the issues raised and supported by the intervener. This leaves no genuine issue as to any material fact, and presents a predicate for a summary judgment under Rule 56(c)* * *.

* * *

The real gravamen of plaintiff's objection is not that there is conflicting evidence but rather that the summary judgment rests upon the affidavits of Harold Burks. His testimony being so vital to intervener's cause, it is asserted that the case should proceed to trial in order that the demeanor of the witness could be observed and his testimony subjected to the test of cross-examination.

In passing on this contention it might be well to make four preliminary observations. First, affiant Burks appears to be an unbiased witness. He has no financial or personal interest in the outcome of this litigation. Second, there is no doubt but what his testimony is competent both in regard to his mental capacity and his being in a position to directly observe the facts related in his affidavits. Third, his participation in the change of beneficiaries was in the regular course of his duties with Socony. Finally, both affidavits are positive, internally consistent, unequivocal, and in full accord with the documentary exhibits. Therefore, even though cross-examination is a trial right which must be carefully protected, in this case, unlike many others there is no obvious advantage to be gained from a cross-examination. If there were, a summary judgment might arguably be improper. But where there is no indication that the affiant was biased, dishonest, mistaken, unaware or unsure of the facts, the cases declaring that cross-examination is necessary when one of the above is present, have no application here. There being no positive showing that this witness's testimony could be impeached or that he might have additional testimony valuable to plaintiff, summary judgment was properly granted. The opposing party cannot as a matter of course force a trial merely in order to cross-examine such an affiant, nor must the Court deny the motion for summary judgment on the basis of a vague supposition that something might turn up at the trial. * * *

There is absolutely no showing that a trial would produce any different or additional evidence. It appears that Burks is now stationed in Singapore, far beyond the subpoena powers of the trial court. Neither party would be able to compel his attendance before the trial court. Since this witness is out of the jurisdiction, any of the parties, on the other hand, would be free to introduce Burks' testimony by use of a deposition. Therefore, in all likelihood Burks would never have to appear in open court. What would plaintiff have to gain by forcing a trial under these circumstances? We feel very little, if anything. A full trial would not give plaintiff an opportunity to cross-examine Burks in open court, nor would it unveil his demeanor to the trier of fact.

In the event of a trial plaintiff would only be free to obtain Burks' sworn testimony by deposition or upon written interrogatories pursuant to Rule 28(b) or Rule 31 * * * and by 28 U.S.C.A. § 1783(a)(1). Plaintiff, however, was free to take this action even prior to the present motion for summary judgment but chose not to do so. When the motion for summary judgment was presented, plaintiff, if she felt Burks had information valuable to her cause, was again free to move for a delay in judgment and secure Burks' deposition. Again plaintiff took no action. Apparently plaintiff felt she had nothing to gain by a deposition, yet under the circumstances of this case that is probably the most she could expect even if this case went to trial. Therefore, we do not feel that plaintiff is in a position at this time to force a trial. A trial would not secure Burks' presence, it would only force the taking of his deposition, a course previously open to plaintiff which she elected not to pursue.

* * *

The position declaring that a party opposed to a summary judgment based upon affidavits must assume some initiative in showing that a factual issue actually exists is perfectly sound in the light of Rule 56 * * *, which specifically allows the use of affidavits in summary judgment proceedings. For if plaintiff's position is correct that an affiant's credibility is always an issue for the trial court, then the granting of a summary judgment would be virtually impossible when it is based in any way upon an affidavit. Rule 56 would be nullified by the prevailing party's use of one affidavit and the bald objection by the opposing party to the affiant's credibility. The reference in this rule to "affidavits" would therefore be of no effect.

This does not mean that an affiant's credibility cannot properly be put in issue by a litigant, but in doing so specific facts must be properly produced. At this point the 1963 amendment to Rule 56(e)(2) comes into play requiring the opposing party to respond or suffer the fate of a summary judgment, if otherwise appropriate. Plaintiff failed to respond to the adequate and substantial showing of intervener, so the trial court properly granted the summary judgment. Keeping in mind that the purpose of the summary judgment is to avoid useless trials, from the circumstances of this case we believe a trial would indeed be a useless waste of time and expense to the parties as well as a needless inconvenience to the Court.

* * *

Judgment affirmed.

NOTES AND QUESTIONS

1. Of what consequence is it that at trial the intervenor would have had the burden of persuading the trier of fact that it was more probable than not that decedent had changed the names of the beneficiaries? Did the appellate court erroneously assume that the burden was on plaintiff to show that the beneficiaries had not been changed? If so, should the decision below have been reversed? Would the result have changed had plaintiff deposed defendant's affiant and shown that there were valid reasons in the record not to believe the witness? See Friedenthal, *Cases on Summary Judgment: Has There Been a Material Change in Standards?*, 63 Notre Dame L. Rev. 770, 774 (1988).

2. In CROSS v. UNITED STATES, 336 F.2d 431 (2d Cir. 1964), the Court of Appeals reversed the District Court's granting of plaintiff's summary judgment motion in an income tax refund suit that turned on whether plaintiff, a professor of romance languages, was entitled to various deductions for summer travel. The court explained: "While there was no dispute that

Professor Cross was a teacher of languages and that he traveled abroad, many of the facts remain largely within his own knowledge and the Government should have the opportunity to test his credibility on cross-examination." Id. at 433. The Court continued:

> * * * In 1954 Professor Cross was an Assistant Professor at City College in New York where he taught French, Spanish and romance linguistics (described by him as the study of the development of Latin into the romance languages, the study of the various dialects and the historic stages of those dialects). He, his wife and a pet dog sailed from New York on June 30, 1954 aboard a French freighter. The ship put in briefly in Portugal, Morocco, Tangiers, Oran, Algiers, Naples and Genoa and appellees spent a day or so in each place. When the freighter arrived at Marseilles, twenty-one days after leaving New York, appellees separated. Mrs. Cross joined a friend and continued touring while Professor Cross and their pet dog travelled to Paris. Although he did not pursue a formal course of study or engage in research, Professor Cross did visit schools, courts of law, churches, book publishers, theaters, motion pictures, restaurants, cafes and other places of amusement, read newspapers, listen to radio broadcasts, converse with students and teachers and attend political meetings. He rejoined his wife in this country on September 23, 1954 after his return aboard a French passenger liner.
>
> Section 162(a), Int.Rev.Code of 1954 permits a deduction for "all the ordinary and necessary expenses paid or incurred * * * in carrying on any trade or business * * *." The Regulations promulgated under that section * * * state:
>
> Expenses for education—(a) Expenditures made by a taxpayer for his education are deductible if they are for education (including research activities) undertaken primarily for the purpose of:
>
> (1) Maintaining or improving skills required by the taxpayer in his employment or trade or business * * *.
>
> * * *
>
> Whether or not education is of the type referred to in subparagraph (1) of this paragraph shall be determined upon the basis of all the facts of each case. If it is customary for other established members of the taxpayer's trade or business to undertake such education, the taxpayer will ordinarily be considered to have undertaken this education for the purposes described in subparagraph (1) of this paragraph.
>
> * * *
>
> (c) In general, a taxpayer's expenditures for travel (including travel while on sabbatical leave) as a form of education shall be considered as primarily personal in nature and therefore not deductible.
>
> Appellees claim, and the district court held, that all of Professor Cross's expenses are deductible. Professor Cross asserted in his deposition, which was taken for discovery purposes and did not include cross-examination,

> My purpose [in making the trip] was to maintain my contacts with my foreign languages for the purpose of maintaining and improving my skill as a linguist and teacher of languages, and to make my general teaching more effective, and to extend my contacts with foreign culture which I have to teach in connection with my teaching of foreign languages per se, and this can be done effectively and properly only by going into a foreign language area.

The Government disputes this explanation. It contends that all or at least part of Professor Cross's travel was a vacation and thus a personal living expense for which a deduction is not allowed under Section 162 * * *.

The essentially factual character of the issue is particularly apparent here, where the ultimate facts were warmly contested. * * *. Summary judgment is particularly inappropriate where "the inferences which the parties seek to have drawn deal with questions of motive, intent and subjective feelings and reactions." Empire Electronics Co. v. United States, 311 F.2d 175, 180 (2d Cir.1962) * * *. " 'A judge may not, on a motion for summary judgment, draw fact inferences. * * * Such inferences may be drawn only on a trial.' " Bragen v. Hudson County News Co., 278 F.2d 615, 618 (3d Cir.1960).

Who can doubt that the alert American trial lawyer as a part of a summer vacation might not profit greatly by spending some time at the Old Bailey listening to British barristers exhibit their skills. The surgeon, too, might be benefitted in his profession by observing some delicate operation conducted by a European surgeon of renown. Yet it is questionable whether such tangible evidences of constant interest in one's profession entitle a taxpayer to deduct all his summer vacation expenses.

In addition to determining whether the trip was devoted in whole or in part to educational advancement, the trier of the facts will have to ascertain such amounts as are to be attributed to such purpose. Were the preliminary twenty-one days prior to the Marseilles landing all part of an educational program? What part, if any, was allocable to Mrs. Cross? What charges were incurred by the dog? Although probably *de minimis,* the Treasury frequently watches every penny and might not be generously inclined even though the dog were a French poodle.

The district court reasoned that summary judgment should be granted because the Government did not adduce facts to refute Professor Cross's claims as to the purpose of his trip, and that the Government had an opportunity to cross-examine when taking his deposition. The "right to use depositions for discovery * * * does not mean that they are to supplant the right to call and examine the adverse party * * * before the jury. * * * '[W]e cannot very well overestimate the importance of having the witness examined and cross-examined in presence of the court and jury.' " Arnstein v. Porter, 154 F.2d 464, 470 (2d Cir.1946). By the same process, Professor Cross will have an opportunity to show with greater particularity that his more modern approach to the problem of linguistic improvement is far superior to the old-fashioned classroom lecture method.

Id. at 432–34. Why wasn't the government at least required to cross-examine Professor Cross at the deposition as to the truth of his assertions?

3. How far can the trial court go in finding support for a party so as to deny summary judgment even though no witnesses will testify in his favor? In DYER v. MacDOUGALL, 201 F.2d 265, 268–69 (2d Cir.1952), plaintiff brought suit for slander; defendant was granted summary judgment on the basis of the affidavits of all the persons present when the slanderous statements allegedly had been made. All of the affidavits denied plaintiff's allegations. The appellate court affirmed:

> * * * [A]lthough it is therefore true that in strict theory a party having the affirmative might succeed in convincing a jury of the truth of his allegations in spite of the fact that all the witnesses denied them, we think it plain that a verdict would nevertheless have to be directed against him. This is owing to the fact that otherwise in such cases there could not be an effective appeal from the judge's disposition of a motion for a directed verdict. He, who has seen and heard the "demeanor" evidence, may have been right or wrong in thinking that it gave rational support to a verdict; yet, since that evidence has disappeared, it will be impossible for an appellate court to say which he was. Thus, he would become the final arbiter in all cases where the evidence of witnesses present in court might be determinative.

4. Suppose A and B were killed in an automobile accident, and A's executor brings suit against B's executor alleging wrongful death. Plaintiff moves for summary judgment on the basis of a deposition of an impartial eyewitness who testified that B drove through a red light. Defendant counters with an affidavit of a police officer who avers that at the scene, shortly after the accident, another impartial eyewitness, now deceased, informed the officer that it was A rather than B who had disobeyed the traffic signal. Should any attention be paid to defendant's affidavit? Should a different test be applied to affidavits on a Rule 56 motion in a case that will be tried by a court than in one that will be heard by a jury?

ADICKES v. S.H. KRESS & CO., 398 U.S. 144, 90 S.Ct. 1598, 26 L.Ed.2d 142 (1970), involved a civil rights claim filed by a white New York City school teacher who had volunteered to teach at a "Freedom School" in Hattiesburg, Mississippi during the summer of 1964. The District Court found the following undisputed facts:

> On August 14, 1964, plaintiff and six Negro students sought to integrate the Hattiesburg Public Library, but were refused the use of its facilities and shortly thereafter the library was closed by the Chief of Police of Hattiesburg. On leaving the library, plaintiff and the six students proceeded to a Woolworth store for the purposes of eating lunch and, on the way, plaintiff observed policemen following them. Since the Woolworth store was crowded, the plaintiff and her group went to defendant's store and sat down in two lunch booths and ordered lunch. The waitress took the orders of the six Negroes, but

> refused to take plaintiff's order. The six Negroes refused to eat unless plaintiff was served. They left the store and had proceeded only a short distance when a police officer, previously observed by plaintiff, arrested her for vagrancy.

Adickes v. S. H. Kress & Co., 252 F.Supp. 140, 142 (S.D.N.Y. 1966). Plaintiff's complaint raised two counts: first, that the denial of restaurant service violated her civil rights; and second, that the refusal to serve and her subsequent arrest were the result of a conspiracy between defendant and the town police.

Kress moved for summary judgment, and supported its motion with affidavits from the store manager, the chief of police, and the arresting officers denying the existence of a pre-arranged scheme to arrest Adickes after she was denied service. The store manager's affidavit also stated that he arranged for Adickes not to be served because he believed a riot would otherwise take place. In opposing the motion, Adickes responded by pressing her circumstantial case. She noted the allegation in the complaint that the policeman who arrested her had earlier been in the store, and pointed out that defendant had failed to dispute this allegation. She adduced her sworn deposition testimony that "one of [her] students saw a policeman come in," and she offered an unsworn statement by a Kress employee (given by Kress to Adickes in discovery) stating that the officer who arrested Adickes once she was outside the restaurant had been in the store before she was refused service. Adickes also submitted an affidavit disputing the store manager's statement that serving her would have created a riot.

The District Court denied the motion with respect to the first count, but granted summary judgment on the second, finding that there was "no evidence in the complaint or in the affidavits and other papers from which a 'reasonably-minded person' might draw an inference of conspiracy." Id. at 144, and the court of appeals affirmed, 409 F.2d 121, 126–27 (2d Cir. 1968). The Supreme Court reversed, finding that the movant had not met its procedural burden "of showing the absence of any disputed material fact." 398 U.S. at 148, 90 S.Ct. at 1603, 26 L.Ed. at 149.

> * * * [Kress] did not carry its burden because of its failure to foreclose the possibility that there was a policeman in the Kress store while petitioner was awaiting service, and that this policeman reached an understanding with some Kress employee that petitioner not be served.
>
> It is true that * * * [the store manager] claimed in his deposition that he had not seen or communicated with a policeman prior to his tacit signal to * * * the supervisor of the food counter [not to serve Adickes]. But respondent did not submit any affidavits from * * * [the supervisor of the food counter], or from * * * the waitress who actually refused petitioner service, either of whom might well have seen and communicated with a policeman in the store. Finally, we find it particularly noteworthy that the two officers involved in the

> arrest each failed in his affidavit to foreclose the possibility (1) that he was in the store while petitioner was there; and (2) that, upon seeing petitioner with Negroes, he communicated his disapproval to a Kress employee, thereby influencing the decision not to serve petitioner.
>
> Given these unexplained gaps in the materials submitted by respondent, we conclude that respondent failed to fulfill its initial burden of demonstrating what is a critical element in this aspect of the case—that there was no policeman in the store. If a policeman were present, we think it would be open to a jury, in light of the sequence that followed, to infer from the circumstances that the policeman and a Kress employee had a "meeting of the minds" and thus reached an understanding that petitioner should be refused service. Because "[o]n summary judgment the inferences to be drawn from the underlying facts contained in [the moving party's] materials must be viewed in the light most favorable to the party opposing the motion," * * * we think respondent's failure to show there was no policeman in the store requires reversal.

Id. at 158, 90 S.Ct. at 1609, 26 L.Ed.2d at 159.

The Court rejected Kress's argument that because the form of plaintiff's evidence did not satisfy Rule 56(e)—for example, the deposition was hearsay and the waitress's statement was unsworn—plaintiff could not avoid summary judgment.

> If respondent had met its initial burden by, for example, submitting affidavits from the policemen denying their presence in the store at the time in question, Rule 56(e) would then have required petitioner to have done more than simply rely on the contrary allegation in her complaint. To have avoided conceding this fact for purposes of summary judgment, petitioner would have had to come forward with either (1) the affidavit of someone who saw the policeman in the store or (2) an affidavit under Rule 56(f) explaining why at that time it was impractical to do so. Even though not essential here to defeat respondent's motion, the submission of such an affidavit would have been the preferable course for petitioner's counsel to have followed. * * *

Id. at 159–60, 90 S.Ct. at 1609–10, 26 L.Ed.2d at 155–56.

NOTES AND QUESTIONS

1. Under *Adickes*, can a defendant who moves for summary judgment meet its initial burden only by disproving the existence of all material facts? Does this mean that the movant must "negate the nonmovant's allegations," or is the burden less than that? Miller, *The Pretrial Rush to Judgment: Are the "Litigation Explosion," "Liability Crisis," and Efficiency Clichés Eroding Our Day in Court and Jury Trial Commitments?*, 78 N.Y.U. L. Rev. 982, 1027 (2003). Professors Issacharoff and Loewenstein point out that the Court in *Adickes* "did not address what evidence, short of Kress's satisfying its complete burden of proof of negating the existence of issues in dispute, might

suffice to shift the burden of production to the plaintiff to establish the viability of her case." Issacharoff & Loewenstein, *Second Thoughts About Summary Judgment*, 100 Yale L.J. 73, 80 (1990). Would reading *Adickes* to impose a "foreclose the possibility" standard on a defendant who moves for summary judgment impermissibly shift plaintiff's burden of proof at trial to the defendant at the Rule 56 stage of the proceeding? See Louis, *Federal Summary Judgment: A Critical Analysis*, 83 Yale L.J. 745, 751–53 (1974).

2. Plaintiff in *Adickes* alleged a conspiracy between the restaurant owner and the local police. Does the question of the existence of a conspiracy, which turns on the state of mind of the participants, inevitably depend on credibility issues that ought to be decided by the jury?

CELOTEX CORP. v. CATRETT

Supreme Court of the United States, 1986.
477 U.S. 317, 106 S.Ct. 2548, 91 L.Ed.2d 265.

Certiorari to the United States Court of Appeals for the District of Columbia Circuit.

JUSTICE REHNQUIST delivered the opinion of the Court.

* * *

Respondent commenced this lawsuit in September 1980, alleging that the death in 1979 of her husband, Louis H. Catrett, resulted from his exposure to products containing asbestos manufactured or distributed by 15 named corporations. Respondent's complaint sounded in negligence, breach of warranty, and strict liability.

* * *

Petitioner's summary judgment motion, which was first filed in September 1981, argued that summary judgment was proper because respondent had "failed to produce evidence that any [Celotex] product * * * was the proximate cause of the injuries alleged within the jurisdictional limits of [the District] Court." In particular, petitioner noted that respondent had failed to identify, in answering interrogatories specifically requesting such information, any witnesses who could testify about the decedent's exposure to petitioner's asbestos products. In response to petitioner's summary judgment motion, respondent then produced three documents which she claimed "demonstrate that there is a genuine material factual dispute" as to whether the decedent had ever been exposed to petitioner's asbestos products. The three documents included a transcript of a deposition of the decedent, a letter from an official of one of the decedent's former employers whom petitioner planned to call as a trial witness, and a letter from an insurance company to respondent's attorney, all tending to establish that the decedent had been exposed to petitioner's asbestos products in Chicago during 1970–1971. Petitioner, in turn, argued that the three documents were inadmissible hearsay and thus could not be considered in opposition to the summary judgment motion.

In July 1982, almost two years after the commencement of the lawsuit, the District Court granted [the motion] * * * because "there [was] no showing that the plaintiff was exposed to the defendant Celotex's product in the District of Columbia or elsewhere within the statutory period." * * * Respondent appealed * * *. The majority of the Court of Appeals held that petitioner's summary judgment motion was rendered "fatally defective" by the fact that petitioner "made no effort to adduce *any* evidence, in the form of affidavits or otherwise, to support its motion." * * * According to the majority, Rule 56(e) * * *, and this Court's decision in Adickes v. S.H. Kress & Co., * * * establish that "the party opposing the motion for summary judgment bears the burden of responding *only after* the moving party has met its burden of coming forward with proof of the absence of any genuine issues of material fact." * * * [The Rule's language has been altered without any changes in substance.] The majority therefore declined to consider petitioner's argument that none of the evidence produced by respondent in opposition to the motion for summary judgment would have been admissible at trial. * * *

We think that the position taken by the majority of the Court of Appeals is inconsistent with the standard for summary judgment set forth in Rule 56(c)* * *. In our view, the plain language of Rule 56(c) mandates the entry of summary judgment, after adequate time for discovery and upon motion, against a party who fails to make a showing sufficient to establish the existence of an element essential to that party's case, and on which that party will bear the burden of proof at trial. * * *

Of course, a party seeking summary judgment always bears the initial responsibility of informing the district court of the basis for its motion, and identifying those portions of "the pleadings, depositions, answers to interrogatories, and admissions on file, together with the affidavits, if any," which it believes demonstrate the absence of a genuine issue of material fact. But unlike the Court of Appeals, we find no express or implied requirement in Rule 56 that the moving party support its motion with affidavits or other similar materials *negating* the opponent's claim. On the contrary, Rule 56(c), which refers to "the affidavits, *if any*" (emphasis added), suggests the absence of such a requirement. And if there were any doubt about the meaning of Rule 56(c) in this regard, such doubt is clearly removed by Rules 56(a) and (b), which provide that claimants and defendants, respectively, may move for summary judgment "*with or without supporting affidavits*" (emphasis added). The import of these subsections is that, regardless of whether the moving party accompanies its summary judgment motion with affidavits, the motion may, and should, be granted so long as whatever is before the district court demonstrates that the standard for the entry of summary judgment, as set forth in Rule 56(c), is satisfied. One of the principal purposes of the summary judgment rule is to isolate and dispose of factually unsupported claims or defenses, and we think it should be interpreted in a way that allows it to accomplish this purpose.

Respondent argues, however, that Rule 56(e), by its terms, places on the nonmoving party the burden of coming forward with rebuttal affidavits, or other specified kinds of materials, only in response to a motion for summary judgment "made and supported as provided in this rule." According to respondent's argument, since petitioner did not "support" its motion with affidavits, summary judgment was improper in this case. But as we have already explained, a motion for summary judgment may be made pursuant to Rule 56 "with or without supporting affidavits." In cases like the instant one, where the nonmoving party will bear the burden of proof at trial on a dispositive issue, a summary judgment motion may properly be made in reliance solely on the "pleadings, depositions, answers to interrogatories, and admissions on file." Such a motion, whether or not accompanied by affidavits, will be "made and supported as provided in this rule," and Rule 56(e) therefore requires the nonmoving party to go beyond the pleadings and by her own affidavits, or by the "depositions, answers to interrogatories, and admissions on file," designate "specific facts showing that there is a genuine issue for trial." * * *

The Court of Appeals in this case felt itself constrained, however, by language in our decision in Adickes v. S.H. Kress & Co. * * *. In the course of its opinion, the *Adickes* Court said that "both the commentary on and the background of the 1963 Amendment conclusively show that it was not intended to modify the burden of the moving party * * * to show initially the absence of a genuine issue concerning any material fact." * * * We think that this statement is accurate in a literal sense, since we fully agree with the *Adickes* Court that the 1963 Amendment to Rule 56(e) was not designed to modify the burden of making the showing generally required by Rule 56(c). It also appears to us that, on the basis of the showing before the Court in *Adickes,* the motion for summary judgment in that case should have been denied. But we do not think the *Adickes* language quoted above should be construed to mean that the burden is on the party moving for summary judgment to produce evidence showing the absence of a genuine issue of material fact, even with respect to an issue on which the nonmoving party bears the burden of proof. Instead, as we have explained, the burden on the moving party may be discharged by "showing"—that is, pointing out to the District Court—that there is an absence of evidence to support the nonmoving party's case.

The last two sentences of Rule 56(e) were added, as this Court indicated in *Adickes,* to disapprove a line of cases allowing a party opposing summary judgment to resist a properly made motion by reference only to its pleadings. While the *Adickes* Court was undoubtedly correct in concluding that these two sentences were not intended to *reduce* the burden of the moving party, it is also obvious that they were not adopted to *add to* that burden. Yet that is exactly the result which the reasoning of the Court of Appeals would produce; in effect, an amendment to Rule 56(e) designed to *facilitate* the granting of motions for summary judgment would be interpreted to make it *more difficult* to grant such motions. Nothing in the two sentences themselves requires this result, for the reasons we have previously indicated, and we now put to rest any inference that they do so.

* * *

Respondent commenced this action in September 1980, and petitioner's motion was filed in September 1981. The parties had conducted discovery, and no serious claim can be made that respondent was in any sense "railroaded" by a premature motion for summary judgment. Any potential problem with such premature motions can be adequately dealt with under Rule 56(f), which allows a summary judgment motion to be denied, or the hearing on the motion to be continued, if the nonmoving party has not had an opportunity to make full discovery.

In this Court, respondent's brief and oral argument have been devoted as much to the proposition that an adequate showing of exposure to petitioner's asbestos products was made as to the proposition that no such showing should have been required. But the Court of Appeals declined to address either the adequacy of the showing made by respondent in opposition to petitioner's motion for summary judgment, or the question whether such a showing, if reduced to admissible evidence, would be sufficient to carry respondent's burden of proof at trial. We think the Court of Appeals with its superior knowledge of local law is better suited than we are to make these determinations in the first instance.

The Federal Rules of Civil Procedure have for more than 50 years authorized motions for summary judgment upon proper showings of the lack of a genuine, triable issue of material fact. Summary judgment procedure is properly regarded not as a disfavored procedural shortcut, but rather as an integral part of the Federal Rules as a whole, which are designed "to secure the just, speedy and inexpensive determination of every action." * * * Before the shift to "notice pleading" accomplished by the Federal Rules, motions to dismiss a complaint or to strike a defense were the principal tools by which factually insufficient claims or defenses could be isolated and prevented from going to trial with the attendant unwarranted consumption of public and private resources. But with the advent of "notice pleading," the motion to dismiss seldom fulfills this function any more, and its place has been taken by the motion for summary judgment. Rule 56 must be construed with due regard not only for the rights of persons asserting claims and defenses that are adequately based in fact to have those claims and defenses tried to a jury, but also for the rights of persons opposing such claims and defenses to demonstrate in the manner provided by the Rule, prior to trial, that the claims and defenses have no factual basis.

The judgment of the Court of Appeals is accordingly reversed, and the case is remanded for further proceedings consistent with this opinion.

It is so ordered.

JUSTICE WHITE, concurring.

I agree that the Court of Appeals was wrong in holding that the moving defendant must always support his motion with evidence or affidavits showing the absence of a genuine dispute about a material fact. I also agree that the movant may rely on depositions, answers to interrogatories and the like to demonstrate that the plaintiff has no evidence to prove his case and hence that there can be no factual dispute. But the movant must discharge the burden the rules place upon him: It is not enough to move for summary judgment without supporting the motion in any way or with a conclusory assertion that the plaintiff has no evidence to prove his case.

* * *

Petitioner Celotex does not dispute that if respondent has named a witness to support her claim, summary judgment should not be granted without Celotex somehow showing that the named witness' possible testimony raises no genuine issue of material fact. * * * It asserts, however, that respondent has failed on request to produce any basis for her case. Respondent, on the other hand, does not contend that she was not obligated to reveal her witnesses and evidence but insists that she has revealed enough to defeat the motion for summary judgment. Because the Court of Appeals found it unnecessary to address this aspect of the case, I agree that the case should be remanded for further proceedings.

JUSTICE BRENNAN, with whom THE CHIEF JUSTICE and JUSTICE BLACKMUN join, dissenting.

This case requires the Court to determine whether Celotex satisfied its initial burden of production in moving for summary judgment on the ground that the plaintiff lacked evidence to establish an essential element of her case at trial. I do not disagree with the Court's legal analysis. The Court clearly rejects the ruling of the Court of Appeals that the defendant must provide affirmative evidence disproving the plaintiff's case. Beyond this, however, the Court has not clearly explained what is required of a moving party seeking summary judgment on the ground that the nonmoving party cannot prove its case. This lack of clarity is unfortunate: district courts must routinely decide summary judgment motions, and the Court's opinion will very likely create confusion. For this reason, even if I agreed with the Court's result, I would have written separately to explain more clearly the law in this area. However, because I believe that Celotex did not meet its burden of production under Federal Rule * * * 56, I respectfully dissent from the Court's judgment.

I

* * * The burden of establishing the nonexistence of a "genuine issue" is on the party moving for summary judgment. * * * This burden has two distinct components: an initial burden of production, which shifts to the nonmoving party if satisfied by the moving party; and an ultimate burden of persuasion, which always remains on the moving party. * * * The court need not decide whether the moving party has satisfied its

ultimate burden of persuasion unless and until the court finds that the moving party has discharged its initial burden of production.

* * *

The manner in which this showing can be made depends upon which party will bear the burden of persuasion on the challenged claim at trial. If the *moving* party will bear the burden of persuasion at trial that party must support its motion with credible evidence—using any of the material specified in Rule 56(c)—that would entitle it to a directed verdict if not controverted at trial. * * * Such an affirmative showing shifts the burden of production to the party opposing the motion and requires that party either to produce evidentiary materials that demonstrate the existence of a "genuine issue" for trial or to submit an affidavit requesting additional time for discovery. * * *

If the burden of persuasion at trial would be on the *non-moving* party, the party moving for summary judgment may satisfy Rule 56's burden of production in either of two ways. First, the moving party may submit affirmative evidence that negates an essential element of the nonmoving party's claim. Second, the moving party may demonstrate to the Court that the nonmoving party's evidence is insufficient to establish an essential element of the nonmoving party's claim. * * * If the nonmoving party cannot muster sufficient evidence to make out its claim, a trial would be useless and the moving party is entitled to summary judgment as a matter of law. * * *

Where the moving party adopts this second option and seeks summary judgment on the ground that the nonmoving party—who will bear the burden of persuasion at trial—has no evidence, the mechanics of discharging Rule 56's burden of production are somewhat trickier. Plainly, a conclusory assertion that the nonmoving party has no evidence is insufficient. * * * Such a "burden" of production is no burden at all and would simply permit summary judgment procedure to be converted into a tool for harassment. * * * Rather, as the Court confirms, a party who moves for summary judgment on the ground that the nonmoving party has no evidence must affirmatively show the absence of evidence in the record. * * * This may require the moving party to depose the nonmoving party's witnesses or to establish the inadequacy of documentary evidence. If there is literally no evidence in the record, the moving party may demonstrate this by reviewing for the court the admissions, interrogatories and other exchanges between the parties that are in the record. Either way, however, the moving party must affirmatively demonstrate that there is no evidence in the record to support a judgment for the nonmoving party.

If the moving party has not fully discharged this initial burden of production, its motion for summary judgment must be denied, and the Court need not consider whether the moving party has met its ultimate burden of persuasion. Accordingly, the nonmoving party may defeat a motion for summary judgment that asserts that the nonmoving party has no evidence by calling the Court's attention to supporting evidence already in the record that was overlooked or ignored by the moving party.

* * *

II

I do not read the Court's opinion to say anything inconsistent with or different than the preceding discussion. My disagreement with the Court concerns the application of these principles to the facts of this case.

* * *

On these facts, there is simply no question that Celotex failed to discharge its initial burden of production. Having chosen to base its motion on the argument that there was no evidence in the record to support plaintiff's claim, Celotex was not free to ignore supporting evidence that the record clearly contained. Rather, Celotex was required, as an initial matter, to attack the adequacy of this evidence. Celotex' failure to fulfill this simple requirement constituted a failure to discharge its initial burden of production under Rule 56, and thereby rendered summary judgment improper.

* * *

[A dissenting opinion by JUSTICE STEVENS is omitted.]

NOTES AND QUESTIONS

1. On remand to the Court of Appeals, a divided panel found that the plaintiff had produced sufficient evidence of exposure and, therefore, that summary judgment was still inappropriate. Catrett v. Johns–Manville Sales Corp., 826 F.2d 33 (D.C.Cir.1987), certiorari denied 484 U.S. 1066, 108 S.Ct. 1028, 98 L.Ed.2d 992 (1988). The majority opinion on remand described the three documents on which plaintiff Catrett based her argument—a transcript of Louis Catrett's testimony in a workmen's compensation claim, in which he indicated his exposure to a product called "Firebar" while working for a company named Anning–Johnson; a letter from T.R. Hoff, the Assistant Secretary of Anning–Johnson, to an Aetna insurance agent reporting on Mr. Catrett's employment with Anning–Johnson; and a letter from the Aetna agent to Mrs. Catrett's counsel essentially restating the contents of Hoff's letter. Catrett argued that, since Celotex supplied the asbestos used by Anning–Johnson, all three documents tended to establish exposure to defendant's product. Celotex countered that the three documents were inadmissible hearsay, out-of-court statements that are inadmissible at trial, and thus should not be considered on the Rule 56 motion. Judge Starr, writing for the majority, stated:

> In the circumstances of this case, we believe that the Hoff letter [a potentially damning piece of evidence] should be considered. The inadmissibility of the letter, despite Celotex's contention to the contrary, is by no means obvious (although we need not and do not pass judgment on its admissibility). Mrs. Catrett argues that the letter is admissible * * * as

falling within the business records exception to the hearsay rule. See Fed.R.Evid. 803(6). *More importantly, Celotex never objected to the District Court's consideration of the Hoff letter.* * * * Since it is well established that "inadmissible documents may be considered by the court if not challenged [at trial]," * * * we are satisfied that the Hoff letter is properly (at this stage) to be considered in assessing whether a genuine issue of fact exists.

[Moreover, i]n her supplemental interrogatory responses, Mrs. Catrett listed Hoff as a witness. There can, of course, be no doubt that this response is properly considered in ruling on a summary judgment motion. * * * Taking this response together with the Hoff letter, the record, dispassionately viewed, reflects the existence of a witness who can testify with respect to Mr. Catrett's exposure to Firebar. Thus, even if the Hoff letter itself would not be admissible at trial, Mrs. Catrett has gone on to indicate that the substance of the letter is reducible to admissible evidence in the form of trial testimony. * * *

Id. at 37–38 (emphasis in original).

Judge Bork, in dissent, wrote:

* * * [P]laintiff has not identified "specific facts" that would indicate such exposure occurred, and I certainly think that plaintiff has not made the kind of showing necessary to defeat a directed verdict motion. I would therefore grant defendant's motion for summary judgment.

* * * [T]he mere listing of a potential witness, without more, does not constitute setting forth specific facts. Here plaintiff has never claimed that Mr. Hoff has any personal knowledge that her husband was exposed to asbestos during his year of work at this company, and indeed did not specify the grounds of his possible testimony at all, except to say that he would be able to testify about "facts relevant to the subject matter of this lawsuit." * * * On the other hand, plaintiff has failed ever to answer interrogatories served by defendant that asked for a variety of specific items of information she might have about her husband's possible exposure to asbestos on any occasion. * * *

The majority concludes, however, that we should interpret plaintiff's listing of Mr. Hoff as a witness in light of his letter to the insurance company, thereby finding enough evidence to stave off the equivalent of a motion for directed verdict on causation. This conclusion is incorrect for two reasons. First, the sum total of all this "evidence" falls far short of showing, or even suggesting, that anyone has been identified who can testify from personal knowledge about any asbestos exposure. That lack alone requires that defendant's motion for summary judgment be granted.

In addition, and also dispositive, the letter itself is inadmissible as evidence and thus cannot be considered by this court in evaluating the summary judgment motion. * * * It is settled law that the judge may consider only these specific materials or other evidence that would be admissible at trial. Inadmissible evidence is not to be considered unless, like an affidavit, it is "otherwise provided for" in Rule 56.

Id. at 41.

2. Is the decision in *Celotex* consistent with *Adickes*? Consider the following:

> * * * [A] party may satisfy the standard for summary judgment by one or both of two methods. First, the movant may, by submitting affirmative evidence, negate an element essential to the opposing party's claim or defense. Second, the movant may show that the opposing party lacks sufficient evidence to establish an essential element of its claim or defense. *Celotex* involved the second method exclusively; *Adickes*, arguably, involved a combination of the two methods. The defendant in *Adickes* offered affirmative evidence in the form of the deposition of the store manager and affidavits from the involved officers. In addition, the defendant pointed to statements in the plaintiff's deposition that the plaintiff lacked any knowledge of communications between the police and Kress employees. The inadequacy of Kress's motion was not its failure to offer affirmative evidence, but rather that the affirmative evidence it offered was insufficient to establish the absence of a genuine issue of a material fact. *Adickes*, therefore, should not be read as requiring the moving party to negate an essential element of the opposing party's case by affirmative evidence in every instance. Rather, the decision may be viewed as stating the proposition that the moving party is required to sustain its burden of proving the absence of a genuine issue of a material fact by affirmative evidence only if it must utilize the first method, or a combination of the two methods, of obtaining summary judgment. If the moving party is able to use the second method exclusively, it is only required to show that the opposing party has failed to establish sufficient evidence of an essential element of its claim or defense. Celotex, viewed in this light, is therefore consistent with the *Adickes* decision. By failing to fully explain this distinction, however, Justice Rehnquist's statements, while correct in the context of the *Celotex* decision, appear to eviscerate *Adickes* and may promote rather than resolve doctrinal confusion.

Foremaster, *The Movant's Burden in a Motion for Summary Judgment*, 1987 Utah L. Rev. 731, 748–49.

3. Examine the language of Rule 56(e)(1), which deals with the character and content of the affidavits required to support or oppose summary judgment. Should a federal court, in ruling upon a Rule 56 motion, be required to disregard completely all affidavits containing only hearsay or other matters to which the affiant would not be permitted to testify at trial? Does *Celotex* authorize the district court to consider evidence that would be inadmissible at trial? Compare Steinman, *The Irrepressible Myth of* Celotex: *Reconsidering Summary Judgment Burdens Twenty Years After the Trilogy*, 63 Wash. & Lee L. Rev. 81 (2006), with Shannon, *Responding to Summary Judgment*, 91 Marq. L. Rev. 815 (2008).

SCOTT v. HARRIS, 550 U.S. 372, 127 S.Ct. 1769, 167 L.Ed.2d 686 (2007). This case raises the issue, as a follow-up to Justice Brennan's dictum in *Celotex*, as to when a party with the burden of proof on an issue nevertheless might argue successfully for a summary judgment in its favor. In the action, plaintiff Harris suffered severe personal injuries when his vehicle, engaged in a police chase, was forced off of the road by defendant Scott, a deputy police officer. Plaintiff sued Scott, alleging that the latter had used excessive force in violation of Harris' Fourth Amendment rights. Defendant Scott moved for summary judgment on the basis of qualified immunity. The District Court denied the motion and the Court of Appeals for the Eleventh Circuit affirmed.

The Supreme Court reversed as follows:

> [Harris'] * * * version of events (unsurprisingly) differs substantially from Scott's version. When things are in such a posture courts are required to view the facts and draw reasonable inferences "in the light most favorable to the party opposing the [summary judgment] motion." *United States* v. *Diebold, Inc.*, 369 U.S. 654, 655, 82 S.Ct. 993, 8 L.Ed.2d 176 (1962). * * * In qualified immunity cases, this usually means adopting (as the Court of Appeals did here) the plaintiff's version of the facts.
>
> There is, however, an added wrinkle in this case: the existence in the record of a videotape capturing the events in question. There are no allegations or indications that this videotape was doctored or altered in any way, nor any contention that what it depicts differs from what actually happened. The videotape quite clearly contradicts the version of the story told by * * * [Harris] and adopted by the Court of Appeals. * * * Indeed, reading the lower court's opinion, one gets the impression that * * * [Harris], rather than fleeing from police, was attempting to pass his driving test * * *.
>
> The videotape tells quite a different story. * * * Far from [Harris] being the cautious and controlled driver the lower court depicts, what we see on the video more closely resembles a Hollywood-style car chase of the most frightening sort, placing police officers and innocent bystanders alike at great risk of serious injury.
>
> At the summary judgment stage, facts must be viewed in the light most favorable to the nonmoving party only if there is a "genuine" dispute as to those facts. Fed. Rule Civ. Proc. 56(c). As we have emphasized, "[w]hen the moving party has carried its burden under Rule 56(c) its opponent must do more than show that there is some metaphysical doubt as to the material facts.... Where the record taken as a whole could not lead a rational trier of fact to find for the nonmoving party, there is no 'genuine issue for trial' " *Matsushita Elec. Industrial Co.* v. *Zenith Radio Corp.*, 475 U.S. 574, 586–587, 106 S.Ct. 1348, 89 L.Ed.2d 538 (1986). * * * When opposing parties tell two different stories, one of which is blatantly contradicted by the record, so that no reasonable jury could believe it, a court should not adopt that version of the facts for purposes of ruling on a motion for summary judgment. * * * The Court of Appeals should not have

> relied on such visible fiction; it should have viewed the facts in the light depicted by the videotape.
>
> * * *
>
> The car chase that * * * [Harris] initiated in this case posed a substantial and immediate risk of serious physical injury to others; no reasonable jury could conclude otherwise. Scott's attempt to terminate the chase by forcing respondent off the road was reasonable, and Scott is entitled to summary judgment.

Id. at 378–86, 127 S.Ct. at 1774–76, 1779, 167 L.Ed.2d at 692–95, 697.

NOTES AND QUESTIONS

1. What if there had been no videotape available in *Scott*? Could Scott have presented affidavits or other evidence in order to secure a summary judgment? Suppose Scott presented affidavits of witnesses which, if true, would have established his defense of immunity. Could Harris decline to introduce contrary affidavits and yet avoid summary judgment merely by arguing that a jury would be entitled to disbelieve Scott's witnesses when they testified at trial?

2. The Supreme Court uploaded to its website the video at issue in *Scott*, see http://www.supremecourtus.gov/opinions/video/scott_v_harris.rmvb. After viewing the video, do you agree with the Court's conclusion that "no reasonable juror" could find that the driver's flight did not pose a danger to the public? A study based on a sample of 1350 viewers of the video found that although a "fairly substantial majority did interpret the facts the way the Court did," "members of various subcommunities did not. African Americans, low-income workers, and residents of the Northeast, for example, tended to form more pro-plaintiff views of the facts than did the Court. So did individuals who characterized themselves as liberals and Democrats." Based on these findings, the authors criticize the Court's approach in *Scott* for its characterizing as "unreasonable" the views of those who drew different inferences from the videotaped evidence:

> * * * Although an admitted minority of American society, citizens disposed to see the facts differently from the *Scott* majority share a perspective founded on common experiences and values. By insisting that a case like *Scott* be decided summarily, the Court not only denied those citizens an opportunity, in the context of jury deliberations, to inform and possibly change the view of citizens endowed with a different perspective. It also needlessly bound the result in the case to a process of decisionmaking that deprived the decision of any prospect of legitimacy in the eyes of that subcommunity whose members saw the facts differently.

Kahan, Hoffman & Braman, *Whose Eyes Are You Going To Believe? Scott v. Harris and the Perils of Cognitive Illiberalism*, 122 Harv. L. Rev. 837, 841–42 (2009). Is this concern unique to summary judgment cases that involve videotaped evidence? See Schneider, *The Dangers of Summary Judgment: Gender and Federal Litigation*, 59 Rutgers L.Rev. 705 (2007).

ANDERSON v. LIBERTY LOBBY, INC., 477 U.S. 242, 106 S.Ct. 2505, 91 L.Ed.2d 202 (1986). Willis Carto, a right-wing publisher, and Liberty Lobby, the organization he headed, filed a libel suit against *The Investigator* magazine, its president and its publisher, columnist Jack Anderson, for articles that portrayed plaintiffs as neo-Nazi, anti-Semitic, racist, and fascist. Following discovery, defendants moved for summary judgment on the ground that plaintiffs could not prove by clear and convincing evidence that defendants acted with actual malice—with knowledge that the statements were false or with reckless disregard of whether they were true or false—the standard required by New York Times Co. v. Sullivan, 376 U.S. 254, 84 S.Ct. 710, 11 L.Ed.2d 686 (1964), and its progeny for libel suits brought by public figures. In support of the motion, defendants submitted an affidavit from Charles Bermant, the employee who had written the allegedly libelous articles, stating that he had spent a substantial amount of time researching and writing the articles. His affidavit also detailed the sources for each of the statements in the article, and affirmed that he believed the facts he reported to be true. Plaintiffs responded to the motion by pointing to numerous claimed inaccuracies in the articles. On the issue of malice, plaintiffs showed that one of Bermant's sources was a twelve-year-old article published in *Time* magazine that had been the subject of an earlier libel suit by plaintiff, which resulted in a settlement under which *Time* paid Carto a sum of money and published a favorable article about Liberty Lobby, and that one of the co-authors of the *Time* article was an editor of *The Investigator*. Plaintiffs also showed that another source was a freelance journalist whom Bermant never met and who was not asked to, and never identified, his sources. Finally, they showed that another editor of *The Investigator* had told the magazine's president that the articles were "terrible" and "ridiculous."

The District Court granted the motion for summary judgment. The Court of Appeals reversed, ruling that it was irrelevant on a motion for summary judgment that the standard for proving actual malice was clear and convincing evidence, rather than a preponderance of evidence. In an opinion written by Justice White, the Court reversed:

> * * * [I]n ruling on a motion for summary judgment, the judge must view the evidence presented through the prism of the substantive evidentiary burden. This conclusion is mandated by the nature of this determination. The question here is whether a jury could reasonably find *either* that the plaintiff proved his case by the quality and quantity of evidence required by the governing law *or* that he did not. Whether a jury could reasonably find for either party, however, cannot be defined except by the criteria governing what evidence would enable the jury to find for either the plaintiff or the defendant: It makes no sense to say that a jury could reasonably find for either party without some benchmark as to what standards govern its deliberations and within what boundaries its ultimate decision must

> fall, and these standards and boundaries are in fact provided by the applicable evidentiary standards.
>
> Our holding that the clear-and-convincing standard of proof should be taken into account does not denigrate the role of the jury. It by no means authorizes trial on affidavits. Credibility determinations, the weighing of the evidence, and the drawing of legitimate inferences from the facts are jury functions, not those of a judge, whether he is ruling on a motion for summary judgment or for a directed verdict. The evidence of the non-movant is to be believed, and all justifiable inferences are to be drawn in his favor. * * * Neither do we suggest that the trial courts should act other than with caution in granting summary judgment or that the trial court may not deny summary judgment in a case where there is reason to believe that the better course would be to proceed to a full trial. * * *

Id. at 254–56, 106 S.Ct. at 2513–14, 91 L.Ed.2d 215–16.

NOTES AND QUESTIONS

1. Is *Anderson* consistent with Rule 56 as construed and applied in *Lundeen* and *Cross*?

2. Is it appropriate to define the burden of production in terms of the burden of persuasion? See pp. 1063–64, infra. In answering this question, should any weight be given to the "* * * difference between prejudging whether an item of evidence will be admissible in trial and on the other hand ruling contemporaneously at trial on the same question"? Kennedy, *Federal Summary Judgment: Reconciling Celotex v. Catrett with Adickes v. Kress and the Evidentiary Problem Under Rule 56*, 6 Rev. Litig. 227, 232–33 (1987).

3. The law distinguishes between two types of evidence: direct and indirect. A witness's statement that "I saw the light and it was green" is direct evidence that the light was green. The inferences required to credit the testimony are that the witness is speaking honestly and accurately recalls the incident. A witness's statement that "I saw the car in the next lane go through the intersection without slowing down" is indirect or circumstantial evidence that the light was green, but is also consistent with the conclusion that "the car in the next lane also ran the red light." The inferences required to believe that the light was green depend not only on the assumption that the witness is worthy of belief, but also on some implicit generalizations about how well drivers obey the law and the probability of two drivers simultaneously running a red light. These examples are taken from Collins, Note—*Summary Judgment and Circumstantial Evidence*, 40 Stan. L. Rev. 491, 493 (1988). In *Anderson*, the parties presented indirect evidence that was in conflict. By requiring the Rule 56 decision to take account of plaintiff's trial burden, did the Court impermissibly authorize the trial court to weigh the evidence? If not, how does *Anderson* affect the standard a judge must use in deciding a motion for summary judgment?

MATSUSHITA ELECTRIC INDUSTRIAL CO. v. ZENITH RADIO CORP., 475 U.S. 574, 106 S.Ct. 1348, 89 L.Ed.2d 538 (1986). Plaintiffs, a group of American television manufacturers, alleged that a group of twenty-one Japanese manufacturers and distributors conspired to fix prices in an effort to monopolize the American market. The trial court granted defendant's motion for summary judgment, but the Third Circuit reversed, arguing that a genuine issue for trial existed because "there is both direct evidence of certain kinds of concert of action and circumstantial evidence having some tendency to suggest that other kinds of concert of action may have occurred," so that "a reasonable factfinder could find a conspiracy to depress prices in the American market in order to drive out American competitors, which conspiracy was funded by excess profits obtained in the Japanese market." Id. at 581, 106 S.Ct. at 1352–53, 89 L.Ed.2d at 548–49. The Supreme Court reversed, finding that the Court of Appeals had made two errors. First, "the 'direct evidence' on which the court relied had little, if any, relevance to the alleged predatory pricing conspiracy"; and second, "the court failed to consider the absence of a plausible motive to engage in predatory pricing." Id. at 595, 106 S.Ct. at 1360, 89 L.Ed.2d at 558. The Supreme Court underscored that an absence of plausible motive for the conspiracy "is highly relevant to whether a 'genuine issue for trial' exists within the meaning of Rule 56(e)":

> Lack of motive bears on the range of permissible conclusions that might be drawn from ambiguous evidence: if petitioners had no rational economic motive to conspire, and if their conduct is consistent with other, equally plausible explanations, the conduct does not give rise to an inference of conspiracy. * * * In sum, in light of the absence of any rational motive to conspire, neither petitioner's (respondent's) pricing practices, nor their conduct in the Japanese market, nor their agreements respecting prices and distribution in the American market, suffice to create a "genuine issue for trial." * * *

Id. at 595–96, 106 S.Ct. at 1360–61, 89 L.Ed.2d at 558–59.

NOTES AND QUESTIONS

1. The Supreme Court in *Matsushita* stated that on remand the Court of Appeals could find predatory pricing only if the evidence would tend " 'to exclude the possibility' that petitioners underpriced respondents to compete for business rather than to implement an economically senseless conspiracy." Id. at 597–98, 106 S.Ct. at 1362, 89 L.Ed.2d at 559. Under this standard, is the trier of fact permitted to select between competing inferences from the undisputed evidence if the inferences seem equally plausible? What is the relation between the Rule 56 standard and the requirement of plausibility at the pleading stage? See p. 568, supra. Should summary judgment be granted on the following undisputed facts?

(a) Two cars enter an intersection at right angles and strike one another killing both drivers and all passengers. There are no eyewitnesses to the accident. The only evidence available is that there was a working traffic light; thus one of the drivers, but only one, had to go through a red light.

(b) X must take a certain pill once a day to remain alive. The pill is highly toxic. To take two within 24 hours is fatal. X is found dead in his bedroom and the evidence is clear that he took two pills that day. If X died by accident, his estate will receive a large sum of insurance money; if he committed suicide, the amount will be substantially reduced. Several hours before his death, X made out a new will, substantially different from the one previously in force. It also shows that at about the same time, X made plans to accompany several friends on a fishing trip on the following day.

Problems adapted from: Friedenthal, *Cases on Summary Judgment: Has There Been a Material Change in Standards?*, 63 Notre Dame L. Rev. 770, 784–86 (1988).

2. For a comprehensive discussion of the Court's changing approach to summary judgment, see Miller, *The Pretrial Rush to Judgment: Are the "Litigation Explosion," "Liability Crisis," and Efficiency Clichés Eroding Our Day in Court and Jury Trial Commitments?*, 78 N.Y.U. L. Rev. 982 (2003).

NOTE ON PARTIAL SUMMARY JUDGMENT

Rules and statutes permitting summary judgment normally provide that in circumstances in which judgment cannot be granted on the entire action, the court at least may withdraw from trial those aspects of the case that are established in the summary-judgment proceeding. See, e.g., Federal Rule 56(d). Furthermore, in a substantial number of jurisdictions the trial court may enter judgment with regard to any single claim that has been fully determined. See, e.g., Federal Rule 54(b). A major question remains, however, whether a party may secure the entry of summary judgment as to part of a claim that has not been fully adjudicated. For example, if plaintiff salesperson alleges that defendant employer owes him five items of back salary, and plaintiff conclusively establishes a right to two of those items, should plaintiff be entitled to a judgment on the amount of the two items in order to collect immediately from defendant? Do Federal Rules 56(a) and 56(b) answer the problem? A number of federal courts have denied relief by reading Rule 56(a) in light of Rule 54(b) or Rule 56(d). What justification, if any, exists for these decisions? See 10B Wright, Miller & Kane, Federal Practice and Procedure: Civil 3d § 2737.

SECTION B. DISMISSAL OF ACTIONS

Read Federal Rule of Civil Procedure 41 and the materials accompanying it in the Supplement.

---

1. VOLUNTARY DISMISSAL

The voluntary dismissal allows the moving party to extricate himself from the lawsuit without affecting his legal rights before significant judicial and litigant resources are expended. Generally, a voluntary dismissal places the parties in the positions they occupied before the lawsuit began; it does not, in general, have the effect of an adjudication on the merits. Because voluntary dismissal might be used to harass defendants, if a party attempts to dismiss after previously doing so with respect to the same cause of action, the dismissal is granted, but is viewed as being an adjudication on the merits. See 9 Wright & Miller, Federal Practice and Procedure: Civil 3d §§ 2361–68. What effect does a voluntary dismissal have on the statute of limitations? Is the statute tolled while the initial complaint is active? Or does the notion that the dismissal returns the parties to the position they occupied before the action require the court to refuse to consider the previous action for purposes of applying the statute of limitations?

McCANTS v. FORD MOTOR CO., 781 F.2d 855 (11th Cir.1986). Johnny McCants, a member of the United States Army Reserve on a two-week active duty training mission, was killed while riding in a military jeep built by Ford. His administratrix commenced a wrongful death suit in federal district court in Alabama. After discovery proceeded for about a year, interrogatories were served and answered, and defendant had moved for summary judgment based on Alabama's one-year general statute of limitations, the plaintiff moved for an order pursuant to Rule 41(a)(2) for voluntary dismissal of the action without prejudice. The plaintiff sought to dismiss the suit so that she could file a new suit in Mississippi, where the controlling statute of limitations had not expired. The District Court granted the motion to dismiss, and simultaneously denied Ford's motion for summary judgment.

WOJTAS v. CAPITAL GUARDIAN TRUST CO., 477 F.3d 924 (7th Cir. 2007). Plaintiff, the owner of an Individual Retirement Account, instructed the custodian to roll over the investment into a new IRA managed by a successor custodian. An employee at the successor custodian converted the funds and later was convicted of mail fraud. Plaintiff sued the original custodian for breach of fiduciary duty and negligence, alleging that defendant had failed to verify that the successor custodian was legally qualified. Defendant answered and moved for judgment on the pleadings, arguing that both claims were time-barred under Wisconsin's two-year statute of limitations, and, in the alternative, that plaintiff failed to state a claim upon which relief could be granted. Plaintiff responded to the latter argument but also moved for a voluntary dismissal without prejudice, in order to refile the action in Illinois, where the controlling statute of limitations was longer. The District Court denied the motion for voluntary dismissal and granted the motion for judgment on the pleadings. The Court of Appeals affirmed, finding that the plaintiff's failure to respond to the statute of limitations argument constituted a waiver, and further, that it would be an abuse of the District Court's discretion to permit voluntary dismissal "where the defendant would suffer 'plain legal prejudice' as a result.'" Id. at 927.

NOTES AND QUESTIONS

1. At common law, plaintiff was permitted, at any time prior to judgment, to dismiss a case voluntarily and without prejudice to refiling the action. Today the right to dismiss voluntarily generally is governed by a rule or statute that typically permits a dismissal before "trial" or "commencement" of trial. These provisions have raised many problems of interpretation regarding the meaning of the words "trial" and "commencement." A few courts have held that "before trial" means at any time prior to submission of the case to the jury or court for decision. See generally Annot., 1 A.L.R.3d 711 (1965). What justification is there for this construction?

2. In ESPOSITO v. PIATROWSKI, 223 F.3d 497 (7th Cir. 2000), plaintiff voluntarily dismissed his initial case against defendant. Plaintiff was ordered to reimburse defendant the costs of that proceeding. Subsequently plaintiff sued on the same cause, joining other defendants with the original defendant. Because plaintiff never did comply with the order to pay costs, the trial court, under Rule 41(b), dismissed the second case, not only against the original defendant but against all the defendants. The court of appeals affirmed. Is the decision consistent with the spirit of Rule 41(d)? The Sixth Circuit in Rogers v. Wal–Mart Stores, Inc., 230 F.3d 868 (6th Cir. 2000), certiorari denied 532 U.S. 953, 121 S.Ct. 1428, 149 L.Ed.2d 367 (2001), refused to award attorney's fees on the ground that Rule 41(d) "does not explicitly provide for them." Professor Southard recommends that the rule be amended to make explicit the court's power to award attorney's fees, observing that the "amendment's likely effect will be to dissuade repetitive filings of identical lawsuits and thereby reduce the negative cost impact such filings have on litigation in federal courts." Southard, *Increasing the "Costs" Nonsuit: A Proposed Clarifying Amendment to Federal Rule of Civil Procedure 41(d)*, 32 Seton Hall L. Rev. 367, 370 (2002). Under the proposed amendment, would it have been appropriate to award fees against the *McCants* plaintiff? Required?

3. In *McCants,* plaintiff moved to dismiss after defendant had made a motion for summary judgment. Could any plaintiff simply move to dismiss before losing such a motion and refile in another, possibly more sympathetic, court? Could plaintiff do this repeatedly? Is the power of unilateral dismissal under Rule 41(a) "an anachronism in an age of managerial judging"? Solimine & Lippert, *Deregulating Voluntary Dismissals*, 36 U. Mich. J.L. Reform 367, 367 (2003) (suggesting reform of the rule).

2. DISMISSAL FOR FAILURE TO PROSECUTE

Courts long have been regarded as possessing inherent discretionary power to dismiss an action if plaintiff does not proceed to trial with "due diligence." Exactly when this power should be invoked has been a matter about which judges have disagreed. Should simple delay by plaintiff be sufficient to justify dismissal, or should prejudice to defendant also be required? In MESSENGER v. UNITED STATES, 231 F.2d 328, 331 (2d Cir.1956), the court said: "The operative condition of the Rule is lack of due diligence on the part of the plaintiff—not a showing by the defendant that it will be prejudiced by denial of its motion. * * * It may well be that the latter factor may be considered by the court, especially in cases of moderate or excusable neglect, in the formulation of its discretionary ruling." Does this standard make sense? Does it have any practical utility as a guide for the trial judge? What is its effect on appellate-court review of the trial court's exercise of discretion?

Some jurisdictions control dismissals for want of prosecution by statute. In the federal system, Rule 41(b) "allows dismissal for the plaintiff's failure to prosecute, [and] is intended as a safeguard against delay in litigation and harassment of a defendant." 9 Wright & Miller, Federal Practice and Procedure: Civil 3d § 2370. In view of the fact that, by definition, cases in which there is a failure to prosecute are not consuming judicial time or energy, why is a formal dismissal procedure necessary?

LINK v. WABASH RAILROAD CO., 370 U.S. 626, 629–30, 633–34, 82 S.Ct. 1386, 1388, 1390–91, 8 L.Ed.2d 734, 737–38, 739–40 (1962). Petitioner appealed a *sua sponte* dismissal of his diversity negligence action after petitioner and his counsel failed to attend a pretrial conference. The trial date had been set some six years after the action had been commenced, during which two other fixed trial dates had been postponed. The Seventh Circuit affirmed, after which the Supreme Court, in an opinion by Justice Harlan, affirmed, holding:

> The authority of a federal trial court to dismiss a plaintiff's action with prejudice because of his failure to prosecute cannot seriously be doubted. The power to invoke this sanction is necessary in order to prevent undue delays in the disposition of pending cases and to avoid congestion in the calendars of the District Courts. The power is of ancient origin, having its roots in judgments of *nonsuit* and *non prosequitur* entered at common law, e.g., 3 Blackstone, Commentaries (1768), 295–296, and dismissals for want of prosecution of bills in equity * * *. It has been expressly recognized in Federal Rule of Civil Procedure 41(b) * * *.

* * *

> Accordingly, when circumstances make such action appropriate, a District Court may dismiss a complaint for failure to prosecute even without affording notice of its intention to do so or providing an adversary hearing before acting. Whether such an order can stand on appeal depends not on power but on whether it was within the permissible range of the court's discretion.
>
> On this record we are unable to say that the District Court's dismissal of this action for failure to prosecute, as evidenced only partly by the failure of petitioner's counsel to appear at a duly scheduled pretrial conference, amounted to an abuse of discretion. * * *
>
> There is certainly no merit to the contention that dismissal of petitioner's claim because of his counsel's unexcused conduct imposes an unjust penalty on the client. Petitioner voluntarily chose this attorney as his representative in the action, and he cannot now avoid the consequences of the acts or omissions of this freely selected agent. Any other notion would be wholly inconsistent with our system of representative litigation, in which each party is deemed bound by the acts of his lawyer-agent and is considered to have "notice of all facts, notice of which can be charged upon the attorney." * * *
>
> We need not decide whether unexplained absence from a pretrial conference would *alone* justify a dismissal with prejudice if the record showed no other evidence of dilatoriness on the part of the plaintiff. For the District Court in this case relied on *all* the circumstances that were brought to its attention, including the earlier delays.

In his dissent, Justice Black argued that it was unfair to impose such a harsh penalty upon plaintiff for the misconduct of his or her attorney. The Justice suggested that numerous other sanctions were available in this instance that could have served the purpose of penalizing the attorney without resorting to a dismissal of the action, thus barring forever the plaintiff's right to recovery for his injuries.

NOTES AND QUESTIONS

1. If the court has power under Rule 41(b) to dismiss the action, does it have an implied authority to fashion other, less onerous sanctions? In J.M. CLEMINSHAW CO. v. CITY OF NORWICH, 93 F.R.D. 338, 355 (D.Conn. 1981), the court said:

> Fines may be imposed upon offending attorneys under Rule 41(b) even though that rule, by its terms, specifically provides only for the sanction of dismissal of the action. Indeed, fines are an appropriate sanction under Rule 41(b) precisely because dismissal is the only sanction specified by that rule. That is, the district courts have been directed to avoid the harsh result of dismissal in cases where the delays or disobedience have been the fault of counsel rather than their clients. In these cases, the courts may draw on their inherent authority to control the course of litigation to impose on counsel the less severe sanction of a fine. * * * Cf.

Schwarz v. United States, 384 F.2d 833, 836 (2d Cir.1967) (affirming dismissal pursuant to Rule 41(b); "suggest[ing] that the [district] court keep in mind the possibility, in future cases of inexcusable neglect by counsel, of imposing substantial costs and attorney's fees payable by offending counsel personally to the opposing party, as an alternative to the drastic remedy of dismissal.") * * *.

2. Lengthy delays do not necessarily lead to a dismissal for failure to prosecute. For example, in GCIU EMPLOYER RETIREMENT FUND v. CHICAGO TRIBUNE, 8 F.3d 1195 (7th Cir.1993), the Court held that a dismissal with prejudice for failure to prosecute was improper, despite a twenty-two month delay between judicial proceedings, because during that period the litigants were actively negotiating. What other factors ought a court to consider? Is the district court required to warn the plaintiff before dismissing the case? See Aura Lamp & Lighting, Inc. v. Int'l Trading Corp., 325 F.3d 903, 908 (7th Cir. 2003) ("A judge is not obliged to treat lawyers like children.") (citation and internal quotation omitted). Is it appropriate to dismiss a claim because of the lawyer's failure to meet court deadlines? See Note, *Dismissal With Prejudice For Failure To Prosecute: Visiting the Sins of the Attorney Upon the Client*, 22 Ga.L.Rev. 195 (1987).

SECTION C. DEFAULT JUDGMENT

Read Federal Rule of Civil Procedure 55 and the accompanying materials in the Supplement.

COULAS v. SMITH

Supreme Court of Arizona, 1964.
96 Ariz. 325, 395 P.2d 527.

UDALL, CHIEF JUSTICE. This is an appeal from an order of the Superior Court of Pima County, denying a motion to set aside a judgment entered against the appellant.

* * *

The plaintiff filed a complaint against the defendant and cross-claimant on two counts. The first count was for $669.32 on an open account. The second count was on a promissory note upon which $3,666.67 was alleged to be due. The cross-claimant answered individually by his attorney and denied any liability to the plaintiff on either count and thereafter filed a cross-claim against the defendant in which he sought judgment against the defendant for any sums or amounts which the plaintiff may obtain against him by virtue of the judgment; for the sum of $4,000 on a debt alleged to be owed by the defendant to him, and $500 attorney's fees. The defendant appeared individually by his attorneys and answered the complaint of the plaintiff, answered the cross-claim of the cross-claimant, and counterclaimed against the plaintiff, seeking damages in the sum of $18,000. The plaintiff replied to the defendant's counterclaim.

On July 11, 1958, the lower court made an order setting the case for trial on October 10, 1958. All counsel were notified by the clerk of the court. On October 6, 1958, counsel for the plaintiff and counsel for the cross-claimant stipulated that the trial be set for December 10, 1958. The lower court ordered that the prior trial date be vacated and the case be reset for trial on December 10, 1958. All counsel were regularly notified by the clerk of the new trial setting. The defendant's counsel was not present before the court on October 6, 1958, and did not participate in the stipulation vacating the original trial setting and resetting the case for trial on December 10, 1958. The defendant and defendant's counsel deny ever receiving any notice from the clerk concerning the new trial date.

On December 10, 1958, the new trial date, the case came on regularly to be heard. The defendant did not appear either in person or by counsel. The court made the following minute entry during the course of the trial:

* * *

> The plaintiff Smith and the defendant Bray announce ready for trial.
>
> William J. Bray is sworn, cross-examined, and examined.
>
> Plaintiff's Exhibit 1, being a promissory note in the sum of $4,000.00 dated February 14, 1955, is marked for identification and admitted in evidence.
>
> Nicholas Coulas having failed to appear at this time either in person or by counsel, and it further appearing that this case was previously set for trial both as to the issues framed by the complaint and answer thereto of the defendant Nicholas Coulas and as to the cross-claim filed by the defendant William J. Bray, Jr., against the defendant Nicholas Coulas,
>
> IT IS HEREBY ORDERED that the default of the said defendant Nicholas Coulas be entered as to said complaint and as to said cross-claim and the court proceeding to hear evidence pertaining to said complaint and cross-claim and being fully advised in the premises,
>
> IT IS THEREFORE ORDERED that judgment is hereby rendered * * * against the defendant Nicholas Coulas * * *.

The plaintiff obtained judgment against the defendant on both counts and against the cross-claimant as to count two (the promissory note). The cross-claimant obtained judgment against the defendant on the promissory note. The judgment was entered on December 11, 1958.

On October 29, 1960, nearly two years later, the defendant filed a motion to set aside and vacate the judgment. The trial court denied this motion. * * *

The defendant subsequently filed this appeal.

The defendant contends that the "default" judgment entered against him was void, since he did not receive 3 days' notice of the application for judgment by default pursuant to Rule 55(b) of the Arizona Rules of Civil Procedure * * *. The defendant's contention would be valid if the judgment below was a judgment by default. A default judgment obtains when a defendant fails to plead or otherwise defend. Rule 55. If he has made an appearance in the case, he must be given 3 days' notice of application for judgment by default. * * *

However, the defendant's contention is invalid here since the judgment below was not a default judgment. It should be noted that the defendant did plead to the merits. He answered the complaint and filed a counterclaim. He then failed to appear at the trial in person or by counsel. The trial proceeded, evidence was heard, and a judgment on the merits of the plaintiff's and counter-claimant's claims was entered. The judgment was not by default within the meaning of Rule 55. Therefore Rule 55(b) with its 3–day notice requirement is not applicable. In fact, the trial court would have erred if a default was entered, since the case was at issue. Bass v. Hoagland, 172 F.2d 205 (5th Cir.1949), cert. denied, 338 U.S. 816, 70 S.Ct. 57, 94 L.Ed. 494 (1949) * * *.

The following language is from Bass v. Hoagland * * * concerning the applicability of Rule 55:

> "Rule 55(a) authorizes the clerk to enter a default * * *. This does not require that to escape default the defendant must not only file a sufficient answer to the merits, but must also have a lawyer or be present in court when the case is called for a trial. The words 'otherwise defend' refer to attacks on the service, or motions to dismiss, or for better particulars, and the like, which may prevent default without presently pleading to the merits. *When Bass by his attorney filed a denial of the plaintiff's case neither the clerk nor the judge could enter a default against him. The burden of proof was put on the plaintiff in any trial. When neither Bass nor his attorney appeared at the trial, no default was generated;* the case was not confessed. The plaintiff might proceed, but he would have to prove his case." 172 F.2d p. 210 (emphasis added).

* * *

* * * It should * * * be stated that once an answer on the merits is filed and the case is at issue, a default judgment is not proper, and if the defendant fails to appear at the trial a judgment on the merits may be entered against him upon proper proof.

* * *

The contention of the defendant that he did not receive notice of the new trial date is not substantiated by the minutes. The record indicates that the clerk of the superior court notified all counsel of all of the orders and judgment pursuant to Rule 77(h) * * *. It is well settled that in the absence of a showing to the contrary a public officer, such as the clerk of the court in this case, is presumed to have performed the duty imposed upon him by law. * * * In addition, if the defendant's counsel did not receive the notice of the change of the trial date to December 10, 1958, he certainly would have learned of the change in the trial date when he appeared for trial on the earlier date, October 10, 1958.

Since the judgment of the lower court is merely voidable, at most, Rule 60(c) * * * prevents the defendant from attacking the judgment more than six months after it was entered. The defendant attempted to attack the judgment nearly two years after it was entered. * * * The lower court properly denied defendant's motion to set aside and vacate the judgment.

Judgment affirmed.

NOTES AND QUESTIONS

1. In BASS v. HOAGLAND, which is relied upon in *Coulas,* a default judgment was rendered in favor of plaintiff after defendant's counsel, who had filed an answer, had withdrawn from the case. The judgment recited that defendant had been informed of the withdrawal. Defendant did not appeal but collaterally attacked the judgment when enforcement was sought against him in another jurisdiction. Defendant claimed that he did not know of the counsel's withdrawal from the case and was not aware that the adverse judgment had been rendered. A majority of the Fifth Circuit held that, since an answer had been filed, defendant was not in default under Rule 55, that the entry of judgment without trial by jury, which had been demanded, was a violation of the Due Process Clause of the Fifth Amendment, and that the judgment was void. The court indicated that even if the case fell within Rule 55, the failure to give notice under Rule 55(b)(2) might render the judgment void, although in that event no jury trial would be required. The dissenting judge took the position that defendant, by not attending trial, was in default, no jury trial was required and therefore the decision was not void and not subject to collateral attack. See Note, *Extending Collateral Attack: An Invitation to Repetitious Litigation*, 59 Yale L.J. 345 (1950). Compare Sheepscot Land Corp. v. Gregory, 383 A.2d 16, 22 (Me.1978) (failure of defendant to appear for trial justifies default even though answer was filed).

2. Federal Rule 54(c) provides that plaintiff may recover all the relief to which he is entitled except that plaintiff is limited to the amount prayed for in the case of a default judgment. Suppose at trial in Coulas v. Smith plaintiff's evidence showed that defendant was liable for $10,000, although only $4,000 had been claimed. Would the court have been justified in awarding plaintiff the full amount?

3. What activities by defendant, short of a formal challenge to the jurisdiction or the pleadings, constitute an "appearance" within the meaning of Federal Rule 55(b)(2)? In RHODES v. RHODES, 3 Mich.App. 396, 142 N.W.2d 508 (1966), plaintiff, in a divorce action, obtained a default judgment against defendant without giving the notice required by the then applicable Michigan General Court Rule 520.2(2), which was analogous to Federal Rule 55(b)(2). Defendant claimed that by signing a property settlement agreement

and stipulating that it be incorporated in the divorce judgment, he "appeared" in the action. The court held that defendant had not shown that these acts were intended to constitute an "appearance" and refused to set aside the judgment. For differing views as to what constitutes an appearance, see Wilson v. Moore & Associates, Inc., 564 F.2d 366 (9th Cir.1977), and Petty v. Weyerhaeuser Co., 272 S.C. 282, 251 S.E.2d 735 (1979).

4. It is important to recognize that although relief-from-judgment rules, such as Federal Rule 60(b), do not distinguish between default and other judgments, the courts clearly disfavor default judgments, and, in exercising discretion, are far more willing to set aside default judgments in order that cases may be decided on their merits. See Glist, *Enforcing Courtesy: Default Judgments and the Civility Movement*, 69 Fordham L. Rev. 757 (2000). This is often the case when the default is due to the carelessness of counsel. Why shouldn't the default judgment be left unopened and the losing party be remitted to a negligence action against a careless attorney? To what extent should a client be required to ensure that its attorney is properly handling the client's case? It is exceedingly rare that an appellate court will find that a trial court has abused its discretion in setting aside a default judgment. Nevertheless such decisions are reached from time to time.

5. A special type of default judgment is one that is imposed on a party who has appeared and contested the matters at issue but has willfully violated the rules of procedure or disobeyed an order of the court. Such a "penalty" is invoked normally against parties who are defending claims; if the complaining party is guilty of comparable violations, the most typical remedy is to dismiss the case with prejudice. See, e.g., Federal Rule 41(b). The penalty default most frequently is rendered in cases in which a defending party willfully refuses to comply with orders for pretrial discovery. Federal Rules 37(b)(2)(A) and 37(d) and their state counterparts specifically permit default judgments in these situations. Should "penalty" defaults fall within the scope of Federal Rule 55? Are "penalty" defaults subject to the limitation on recovery in Federal Rule 54(c)? In TRANS WORLD AIRLINES, INC. v. HUGHES, 32 F.R.D. 604, 607–08 (S.D.N.Y.1963), modified 332 F.2d 602 (2d Cir.1964), certiorari dismissed 380 U.S. 248, 85 S.Ct. 934, 13 L.Ed.2d 817 (1965), the court, after granting plaintiff's motion for entry of a default judgment on the ground of defendant's failure to produce the owner of 100% of its stock for a deposition, held:

> That branch of the [plaintiff's] motion seeking to increase the *ad damnum* clause from $105,000,000 to $135,000,000 is granted. This is not a case where a party has defaulted in appearance. Here issue was joined and adversary proceedings continued in the pretrial stages of this litigation. The damages originally asserted were unliquidated and TWA is entitled to recover for whatever damage it can show it suffered. Furthermore, Toolco [a defendant] will be represented at the hearings necessary to assess damages under rule 55(b)(2).

Compare Fong v. United States, 300 F.2d 400, 412–13 (9th Cir.), certiorari denied 370 U.S. 938, 82 S.Ct. 1584, 8 L.Ed.2d 807 (1962). Suppose TWA's suit had been on a contract and the damages were for a liquidated sum that plaintiff had erroneously understated in its complaint. Would the result have been different?

CHAPTER 14

TRIAL

■ ■ ■

In prior Chapters we have explored the ways in which litigants initiate actions, prepare for trial, and avoid trial when possible. But trials do take place, and it is important to discuss and analyze how they proceed, how decisions ultimately are reached, and whether the process is a fair one. We begin with a discussion of jury trial, both when a right to a jury exists and the way in which it is implemented. The latter encompasses the way in which we inform jurors about their duties, the types of questions that they must decide as distinguished from those that the judge determines, and situations in which, for lack of a true factual dispute or misconduct, we do not allow or heed a jury decision. We also discuss the nature of the trial when the judge hears the case without a jury. And finally we explore the ways in which errors, omissions, and improper tactics may result in overturning a decision and ordering a new trial. Primarily we discuss matters in the context of federal courts. There are several reasons. First, each state has its own rules and procedures and it would be impossible to deal with each of them in any meaningful detail. Second, the federal system is a sound prototype for study since most states, generally speaking, employ procedures that follow those of the federal courts. In studying these matters it is important to consider the efficacy of the rules and regulations as they are now implemented and to decide if they should be altered to reflect changes in our society. Is the current drive to eliminate trials through summary procedure, settlement, and methods of alternative dispute resolution the result of antiquated trial procedures or a misguided emphasis on efficiency at the expense of other values?

SECTION A. TRIAL BY JURY

1. THE INSTITUTION OF TRIAL BY JURY

During its formative period the jury was an activist group that not only judged the evidence but also acquired much of it through its own investigation. An example of this drawn from twelfth-century English history is the "jury" used to compile the famous Domesday Book, which contained an inventory of William the Conqueror's realm. The Domesday "jury" viewed the land and formed its own judgments without using witnesses. Today, of course, the jury is a passive, disinterested body that renders its decisions on the basis of the information placed before it.

The revered status of jury trial at common law is evidenced by Blackstone's statement that the right "has been, and I trust ever will be, looked upon as the glory of the English law * * * and * * * that it is the most transcendent privilege which any subject can enjoy or wish for, that he not be affected either in his property, his liberty, or his person, but by unanimous consent of twelve of his neighbors and equals." 3 Blackstone, Commentaries *378. Yet, in modern English practice, trial by jury in civil actions has been abandoned except in rare cases.

In this country the jury system often has been eulogized, see for example, SIOUX CITY & PACIFIC RAILROAD CO. v. STOUT, 84 U.S. (17 Wall.) 657, 664, 21 L.Ed. 745, 749 (1873). Recently, however, the jury system has come under increasing attack from commentators claiming that the system is expensive and slow and that juries cannot understand the complex cases that, today, comprise a large part of courts' dockets. Chief Justice Burger listed the following problems associated with jury trials in civil cases:

> *First,* do we really have truly representative juries? Experienced business executives, bankers, professional people, accountants, professors of economics, statisticians, teachers, and others arguably more competent than most to cope with complex economic or scientific questions, rarely survive to sit in the box. Peremptory challenges in the jury selection process eliminate them and more often they are excused for cause, including the cause that they are too busy! We must stop deluding ourselves. The juries actually selected in most protracted cases are rarely true cross-sections, as we are so fond of repeating.
>
> * * *
>
> *Second,* the factual issues in protracted cases are often of enormous complexity. The analysis of documents, of expert testimony, of charts, graphs and other visual aids, and the comprehension of such evidence, present problems which often only a sophisticated business executive, an economist, or another expert could grasp; some cases would baffle even them.
>
> *Third,* the legal issues, which must be explained to jurors by the trial judge, may take not hours, but a whole day or several days, by way of instructions.
>
> *Fourth,* there is a limit to the capacity of any of us—jurors or judges—to understand and remember the mass of complicated transactions, documents, and legal principles usually described in the course of a long trial.
>
> *Fifth,* quite apart from these considerations, there is an enormous—and inordinate—impact on the life of each of twelve jurors, and alternate jurors, thrust for months into a totally strange environment,

and then confronted with the burden of decisions in areas in which few, if any of them, have any experience.

Burger, *Thinking the Unthinkable,* 31 Loyola L.Rev. 205, 210–11 (1985). For a comprehensive analysis of modern methods for the restriction of the jury trial right, see Miller, *The Pretrial Rush to Judgment: Are the "Litigation Explosion," "Liability Crisis," and Efficiency Clichés Eroding Our Day in Court and Jury Trial Commitments?*, 78 N.Y.U. L. Rev. 982, 1074–1134 (2003).

Excellent historical material on the jury can be found in 1 Holdsworth, A History of English Law 298–350 (7th ed. 1956); 1 Pollock & Maitland, The History of English Law 138–49 (2d ed. 1911); 2 id. 616–32, 641–59: Thayer, *The Jury and Its Development*, 5 Harv. L.Rev. 249, 295, 357 (1892), substantially reprinted in A Preliminary Treatise on Evidence at the Common Law 47–182 (1898). For discussions of civil jury trial in other countries, see Devlin, Trial by Jury (3d imp. 1966); Smith, *Civil Jury Trial: A Scottish Assessment*, 50 Va. L. Rev. 1076 (1964). For a thoughtful general analysis of jury trial in the United States, see Abramson, We, The Jury (2000).

2. THE RIGHT TO A JURY TRIAL

A. THE NATURE OF THE RIGHT UNDER THE UNITED STATES CONSTITUTION

Examine the Seventh Amendment to the United States Constitution and the state jury-trial guarantees in the Supplement. In what ways are the guarantees substantively different from one another? What reasons underlie these differences?

The federal Constitution and most state constitutions do not "create" a right to jury trial. Rather, they "preserve" the right as it existed at common law, either in 1791, the date of the Seventh Amendment's ratification, or, in the case of some states, as of the time the state constitution was adopted. Because the Seventh Amendment was assumed to incorporate the jury-trial practice as of 1791, federal judges frequently have been called upon to determine the actual availability of jury trial as of that date.

> * * * The Amendment frequently is said to articulate a "historical test" for determining when the jury right attaches to a cause of action. If the issue in the context in which it arises would have been heard at common law in 1791, when the Seventh Amendment was adopted, or, "according to some judge," in 1938 when law and equity were merged, it is now triable of right to a jury * * *. There is no right to jury trial if viewed historically the issue would have been tried in the courts of equity or if otherwise it would have been tried without a jury.

* * *

> [The historical test] * * * proved difficult to apply, particularly for a generation to which the distinctions between law and equity are ancient, and largely unlearned, history. Even if the history were known, it often could shed but dim light as novel kinds of actions were developed and as modern procedure permitted a hybrid form of lawsuit that could never have existed in the ancient days. A vast and controversial literature developed as scholars sought to solve what were essentially insoluble problems. * * * Courts have complained of being held in "historical bondage" and have apologized for an analysis that "may seem to reek unduly of the study."

9 Wright & Miller, Federal Practice and Procedure: Civil 3d § 2302. For a scholarly analysis taking the view that the framers of the Bill of Rights intended that Congress would have complete power to decide what types of matters were to be tried before a jury, and that therefore much of the Supreme Court's subsequent analyses regarding "suits at common law" has been based upon incorrect assumptions, see Krauss, *The Original Understanding of the Seventh Amendment Right to Jury Trial*, 33 U. Rich. L. Rev. 407 (1999).

B. THE EFFECT OF FEDERAL RULE 2 (THE SINGLE FORM OF ACTION) AND OTHER MODERN–DAY PROCEDURAL DEVELOPMENTS ON THE RIGHT TO TRIAL BY JURY IN FEDERAL COURTS

The formal elimination under Federal Rule 2 of separate actions in law and equity and other procedural innovations have raised a number of challenging issues regarding the historic right to a trial by jury:

(1) What remains of the law-equity distinction that governed the right to a jury in 1791?

(2) What happens when parties seek both legal and equitable remedies in the same case?

(3) What is the situation when a party makes a claim in court, pursuant to a statute or common-law development that was unknown in 1791?

(4) What is the situation when vindication of a claim is taken out of the jurisdiction of the courts and placed in an administrative tribunal?

(5) What is the nature of the right to a jury when a party initiates a claim, normally cognizable only at law, but historically brought in courts of equity because of the status of the party?

As we will see, the answers to these questions, at least as determined by the United States Supreme Court, have not been self-evident.

C. THE IMPLEMENTATION OF THE RIGHT TO JURY TRIAL IN FEDERAL COURTS

(I) MAINTENANCE OF THE LAW–EQUITY DISTINCTION

It is important to recognize that cases at law—those that were brought in the courts of law in 1791—continue to carry the right to trial by jury in cases in federal courts whereas suits in equity, historically decided by the chancellor, continue to be decided by judges, although they can, in their discretion, employ an advisory jury. See Federal Rule 39(c).

The distinction is based primarily on the nature of the relief sought. Relief at law is limited in general to compensatory damages along with the ejectment of a defendant who wrongfully is in occupation of plaintiff's land. Equity provides remedies when the law does not, and thus covers a "waterfront" of potential redress, from injunctions, to restitution, rescission, and reformation of contracts. In simple cases, therefore, a plaintiff, by designating the right to relief sought, is able to control whether or not a jury trial is required.

(II) CASES INVOLVING BOTH EQUITABLE AND LEGAL RELIEF

Professor Chafee, in a famous statement in an unpublished lecture, characterized jury trial as "the sword in the bed that prevents the complete fusion of law and equity." See Fredal v. Forster, 9 Mich.App. 215, 228, 156 N.W.2d 606, 612 (1967). In many ways merger actually has complicated the application of the jury-trial right because a party now may enter a single court with both legal and equitable claims, and even if a plaintiff brings claims of only one type, a defendant, by way of counterclaim, may introduce the other type.

The "mixed" remedies case was not completely unknown in 1791. Long before merger, equity developed the so-called clean-up doctrine as a partial response to the problems of the bifurcation of law and equity. Under this doctrine, once an equity court obtained jurisdiction of a suit primarily of an equitable character, the court could decide any incidental legal issues that arose in the course of the litigation.

> Sound considerations of policy lay behind * * * [the] "clean-up" rule, considerations which loom large and real against the background of two entirely independent systems of trial courts. The plaintiff entitled to both legal and equitable remedies needed relief from the burden of two days in court. Even worse was the plight of the litigant who had legitimately but vainly sought the chancellor's aid. The statute of limitations threatened him with total loss of remedy on an admittedly valid claim. It was the more dangerous a choice when crowded dockets and cumbersome procedure made the equitable process less than speedy. In any event, the dangers of a wrong choice of forum involved delay and all-consuming expense of litigation.

> Here then was plaintiff's dilemma: to turn first to law might, as a simple matter of res judicata, lose him the more-desired chancellor's remedy; to turn to equity would often invite decision by an unpredictable conscience and perhaps the loss of all remedy. Equities had to be weighed on an imprecise balance and hardships measured by a rule the fine divisions of which were often known only to the chancellor himself. Small wonder then that the clean-up rule, the disposition of incidental questions legal in nature, was often applied even where all equitable relief was denied.
>
> The cost of this efficiency was, however, substantial, for it involved the denial of trial by jury on all legal issues so adjudicated. In some situations this price was considered too heavy to pay for the trial convenience achieved. In others, where equity viewed a plaintiff's conduct as sufficiently reprehensible, the chancellor was pleased not to afford him aid by rapid disposition of a remaining issue.

Levin, *Equitable Clean-up and the Jury: A Suggested Orientation,* 100 U. Pa. L.Rev. 320, 320–21 (1951).

BEACON THEATRES, INC. v. WESTOVER

Supreme Court of the United States, 1959.
359 U.S. 500, 79 S.Ct. 948, 3 L.Ed.2d 988.

Certiorari to the United States Court of Appeals for the Ninth Circuit.

MR. JUSTICE BLACK delivered the opinion of the Court.

Petitioner, Beacon Theatres, Inc., sought by mandamus to require a district judge in the Southern District of California to vacate certain orders alleged to deprive it of a jury trial of issues arising in a suit brought against it by Fox West Coast Theatres, Inc. The Court of Appeals for the Ninth Circuit refused the writ, holding that the trial judge had acted within his proper discretion in denying petitioner's request for a jury. * * *

Fox had asked for declaratory relief against Beacon alleging a controversy arising under the Sherman Antitrust Act, 26 Stat. 209, as amended, 15 U.S.C. §§ 1, 2, and under the Clayton Act, 38 Stat. 731, 15 U.S.C. § 15, which authorizes suits for treble damages against Sherman Act violators. According to the complaint Fox operates a movie theatre in San Bernardino, California, and has long been exhibiting films under contracts with movie distributors. These contracts grant it the exclusive right to show "first run" pictures in the "San Bernardino competitive area" and provide for "clearance"—a period of time during which no other theatre can exhibit the same pictures. After building a drive-in theatre about 11 miles from San Bernardino, Beacon notified Fox that it considered contracts barring simultaneous exhibitions of first-run films in the two theatres to be overt acts in violation of the antitrust laws. Fox's complaint alleged that this notification, together with threats of treble damage suits against Fox and its distributors, gave rise to "duress and coercion" which deprived Fox of a valuable property right, the right to negotiate for exclusive first-run contracts. Unless Beacon was restrained, the complaint continued, irreparable harm would result. Accordingly, while its pleading was styled a "Complaint for Declaratory Relief," Fox prayed both for a declaration that a grant of clearance between the Fox and Beacon theatres is reasonable and not in violation of the antitrust laws, and for an injunction, pending final resolution of the litigation, to prevent Beacon from instituting any action under the antitrust laws against Fox and its distributors arising out of the controversy alleged in the complaint. Beacon filed an answer, a counterclaim against Fox, and a cross-claim against an exhibitor who had intervened. These denied the threats and asserted that there was no substantial competition between the two theatres, that the clearances granted were therefore unreasonable, and that a conspiracy existed between Fox and its distributors to manipulate contracts and clearances so as to restrain trade and monopolize first-run pictures in violation of the antitrust laws. Treble damages were asked.

Beacon demanded a jury trial of the factual issues in the case as provided by Federal Rule * * * 38(b). The District Court, however, viewed the issues raised by the "Complaint for Declaratory Relief," including the question of competition between the two theatres, as essentially equitable. Acting under the purported authority of Rules 42(b) and 57, it directed that these issues be tried to the court before jury determination of the validity of the charges of antitrust violations made in the counterclaim and cross-claim. A common issue of the "Complaint for Declaratory Relief," the counterclaim, and the cross-claim was the reasonableness of the clearances granted to Fox, which depended, in part, on the existence of competition between the two theatres. Thus the effect of the action of the District Court could be, as the Court of Appeals believed, "to limit the petitioner's opportunity fully to try to a jury every issue which has a bearing upon its treble damage suit," for determination of the issue of clearances by the judge might "operate either by way of res judicata or collateral estoppel so as to conclude both parties with respect thereto at the subsequent trial of the treble damage claim." * * *

The District Court's finding that the Complaint for Declaratory Relief presented basically equitable issues draws no support from the Declaratory Judgment Act, 28 U.S.C. §§ 2201, 2202; Fed.Rules Civ.Proc. 57. * * * That statute, while allowing prospective defendants to sue to establish their nonliability, specifically preserves the right to jury trial for both parties. It follows that if Beacon would have been entitled to a jury trial in a treble damage suit against Fox it cannot be deprived of that right merely because Fox took advantage of the availability of declaratory relief to sue Beacon first. Since the right to trial by jury applies to treble damage suits under the antitrust laws, and is, in fact, an essential part of the congressional plan for making competition rather than monopoly the rule of trade * * *, the Sherman and Clayton Act issues * * * were essentially jury questions.

Nevertheless the Court of Appeals * * * held that the question of whether a right to jury trial existed was to be judged by Fox's complaint read as a whole. In addition to seeking a declaratory judgment, the court said, Fox's complaint can be read as making out a valid plea for injunctive relief, thus stating a claim traditionally cognizable in equity. A party who is entitled to maintain a suit in equity for an injunction, said the court, may have all the issues in his suit determined by the judge without a jury regardless of whether legal rights are involved. The court then rejected the argument that equitable relief, traditionally available only when legal remedies are inadequate, was rendered unnecessary in this case by the filing of the counterclaim and cross-claim which presented all the issues necessary to a determination of the right to injunctive relief. Relying on American Life Ins. Co. v. Stewart, 300 U.S. 203, 215, 57 S.Ct. 377, 380, 81 L.Ed. 605, decided before the enactment of the Federal Rules * * *, it invoked the principle that a court sitting in equity could retain jurisdiction even though later a legal remedy became available. In such instances the equity court had discretion to enjoin the later lawsuit in order to allow the whole dispute to be determined in one case in one court. Reasoning by analogy, the Court of Appeals held it was not an abuse of discretion for the district judge, acting under Federal Rule * * * 42(b), to try the equitable cause first even though this might, through collateral estoppel, prevent a full jury trial of the counterclaim and cross-claim which were as effectively stopped as by an equity injunction.[6]

Beacon takes issue with the holding of the Court of Appeals that the complaint stated a claim upon which equitable relief could be granted. As initially filed the complaint alleged that threats of lawsuits by petitioner against Fox and its distributors were causing irreparable harm to Fox's business relationships. The prayer for relief, however, made no mention of the threats but asked only that pending litigation of the claim for declaratory judgment, Beacon be enjoined from beginning any lawsuits under the antitrust laws against Fox and its distributors arising out of the controversy alleged in the complaint. Evidently of the opinion that this prayer did not state a good claim for equitable relief, the Court of Appeals construed it to include a request for an injunction against threats of lawsuits. * * * But this fact does not solve our problem. Assuming that the pleadings can be construed to support such a request and assuming additionally that the complaint can be read as alleging the kind of harassment by a multiplicity of lawsuits which would *traditionally* have justified equity to take jurisdiction and settle the case in one suit, we are nevertheless of the opinion that, under the Declaratory Judgment Act and the Federal Rules * * *, neither claim can justify denying Beacon a trial by jury of all the issues in the antitrust controversy.

---

6. 252 F.2d at page 874. In Ettelson v. Metropolitan Life Ins. Co., 317 U.S. 188, 192, 63 S.Ct. 163, 164, 87 L.Ed. 176, this Court recognized that orders enabling equitable causes to be tried before legal ones had the same effect as injunctions. In City of Morgantown, W.Va. v. Royal Ins. Co., 337 U.S. 254, 69 S.Ct. 1067, 93 L.Ed. 1347, the Court denied at least some such orders the status of injunctions for the purposes of appealability. It did not, of course, imply that when the orders came to be reviewed they would be examined any less strictly than injunctions. * * *

The basis of injunctive relief in the federal courts has always been irreparable harm and inadequacy of legal remedies. At least as much is required to justify a trial court in using its discretion under the Federal Rules to allow claims of equitable origins to be tried ahead of legal ones, since this has the same effect as an equitable injunction of the legal claims. And it is immaterial, in judging if that discretion is properly employed, that before the Federal Rules and the Declaratory Judgment Act were passed, courts of equity, exercising a jurisdiction separate from courts of law, were, in some cases, allowed to enjoin subsequent legal actions between the same parties involving the same controversy. This was because the subsequent legal action, though providing an opportunity to try the case to a jury, might not protect the right of the equity plaintiff to a fair and orderly adjudication of the controversy. * * * Under such circumstances the legal remedy could quite naturally be deemed inadequate. Inadequacy of remedy and irreparable harm * * * today must be determined, not by precedents decided under discarded procedures, but in the light of the remedies now made available by the Declaratory Judgment Act and the Federal Rules.

Viewed in this manner, the use of discretion by the trial court under Rule 42(b) to deprive Beacon of a full jury trial on its counterclaim and cross-claim, as well as on Fox's plea for declaratory relief, cannot be justified. Under the Federal Rules the same court may try both legal and equitable causes in the same action. * * *

Thus any defenses, equitable or legal, Fox may have to charges of antitrust violations can be raised either in its suit for declaratory relief or in answer to Beacon's counterclaim. On proper showing, harassment by threats of other suits, or other suits actually brought, involving the issues being tried in this case, could be temporarily enjoined pending the outcome of this litigation. Whatever permanent injunctive relief Fox might be entitled to on the basis of the decision in this case could, of course, be given by the court after the jury renders its verdict. In this way the issues between these parties could be settled in one suit giving Beacon a full jury trial of every antitrust issue. * * * By contrast, the holding of the court below while granting Fox no additional protection unless the avoidance of jury trial be considered as such, would compel Beacon to split his antitrust case, trying part to a judge and part to a jury. Such a result, which involves the postponement and subordination of Fox's own legal claim for declaratory relief as well as of the counterclaim which Beacon was compelled by the Federal Rules to bring, is not permissible.

Our decision is consistent with the plan of the Federal Rules and the Declaratory Judgment Act to effect substantial procedural reform while retaining a distinction between jury and nonjury issues and leaving substantive rights unchanged. Since in the federal courts equity has always acted only when legal remedies were inadequate, the expansion of adequate legal remedies provided by the Declaratory Judgment Act and the Federal Rules necessarily affects the scope of equity. Thus, the justification for equity's deciding legal issues once it obtains jurisdiction, and refusing to dismiss a case, merely because subsequently a legal remedy becomes available, must be re-evaluated in the light of the liberal joinder provisions of the Federal Rules which allow legal and equitable causes to be brought and resolved in one civil action. Similarly the need for, and therefore, the availability of such equitable remedies as Bills of Peace, *Quia Timet* and Injunction must be reconsidered in view of the existence of the Declaratory Judgment Act as well as the liberal joinder provision of the Rules. * * *

If there should be cases where the availability of declaratory judgment or joinder in one suit of legal and equitable causes would not in all respects protect the plaintiff seeking equitable relief from irreparable harm while affording a jury trial in the legal cause, the trial court will necessarily have to use its discretion in deciding whether the legal or equitable cause should be tried first. Since the right to jury trial is a constitutional one, however, while no similar requirement protects trials by the court, that discretion is very narrowly limited and must, wherever possible, be exercised to preserve jury trial. * * * [O]nly under the most imperative circumstances, circumstances which in view of the flexible procedures of the Federal Rules we cannot now anticipate, can the right to a jury trial of legal issues be lost through prior determination of equitable claims. * * *

As we have shown, this is far from being such a case.

* * *

The judgment of the Court of Appeals is reversed.

Reversed.

MR. JUSTICE FRANKFURTER took no part in the consideration or decision of this case.

MR. JUSTICE STEWART, with whom MR. JUSTICE HARLAN and MR. JUSTICE WHITTAKER concur, dissenting.

* * *

I.

The Court suggests that "the expansion of adequate legal remedies provided by the Declaratory Judgment Act * * * necessarily affects the scope of equity." Does the Court mean to say that the mere availability of an action for a declaratory judgment operates to furnish "an adequate remedy at law" so as to deprive a court of equity of the power to act? That novel line of reasoning is at least implied in the Court's opinion. But the Declaratory Judgment Act did not "expand" the substantive law. That Act merely provided a new statutory remedy, neither legal nor equitable, but available in the areas of both equity and law. When declaratory relief is sought, the right to trial by jury depends upon the basic context in which the issues are presented. * * * If the basic issues in an action for declaratory relief are of a kind traditionally cognizable in equity, e.g., a suit for cancellation of a written instrument, the declaratory judgment is not a "remedy at law." If, on the other hand, the issues arise in a context traditionally cognizable at common law, the right to a jury trial of course remains unimpaired, even though the only relief demanded is a declaratory judgment.

Thus, if in this case the complaint had asked merely for a judgment declaring that the plaintiff's specified manner of business dealings with distributors and other exhibitors did not render it liable to Beacon under the antitrust laws, this would have been simply a "juxtaposition of parties" case in which Beacon could have demanded a jury trial. But the complaint * * * presented issues of exclusively equitable cognizance, going well beyond a mere defense to any subsequent action at law. Fox sought from the court protection against Beacon's allegedly unlawful interference with its business relationships—protection which this Court seems to recognize might not have been afforded by a declaratory judgment, unsupplemented by equitable relief. The availability of a declaratory judgment did not, therefore, operate to confer upon Beacon the right to trial by jury with respect to the issues raised by the complaint.

II.

* * * [T]he Court holds, quite apart from its reliance upon the Declaratory Judgment Act, that Beacon by filing its counterclaim and cross-claim acquired a right to trial by jury of issues which otherwise would have been properly triable to the court. Support for this position is found in the principle that, "in the federal courts equity has always acted only when legal remedies were inadequate. * * *" Yet that principle is not employed in its traditional sense as a limitation upon the exercise of power by a court of equity. This is apparent in the Court's recognition that the allegations of the complaint entitled Fox to equitable relief—relief to which Fox would not have been entitled if it had had an adequate remedy at law. Instead, the principle is employed today to mean that because it is possible under the counterclaim to have a jury trial of the factual issue of substantial competition, that issue must be tried by a jury, even though the issue was primarily presented in the original claim for equitable relief. This is a marked departure from long-settled principles.

It has been an established rule "that equitable jurisdiction existing at the filing of a bill is not destroyed because an adequate legal remedy may have become available thereafter." American Life Ins. Co. v. Stewart * * *. It has also been long settled that the District Court in its discretion may order the trial of a suit in equity in advance of an action at law between the same parties, even if there is a factual issue common to both. * * *

III.

The Court today sweeps away these basic principles as "precedents decided under discarded procedures." It suggests that the Federal Rules * * * have somehow worked an "expansion of adequate legal remedies" so as to oust the District Courts of equitable jurisdiction, as well as to deprive them of their traditional power to control their own dockets. But obviously the Federal Rules could not and did not "expand" the substantive law one whit.

Like the Declaratory Judgment Act, the Federal Rules preserve inviolate the right to trial by jury in actions historically cognizable at common law, as under the Constitution they must. They do not create a right of trial by jury where that right "does not exist under the Constitution or statutes of the United States." Rule 39(a) [comparable language now found in Rule 38(a)]. Since Beacon's counterclaim was compulsory under the Rules, see Rule 13(a), it is apparent that by filing it Beacon could not be held to have waived its jury rights. * * * But neither can the counterclaim be held to have transformed Fox's original complaint into an action at law. * * *

The Rules make possible the trial of legal and equitable claims in the same proceeding, but they expressly affirm the power of a trial judge to determine the order in which claims shall be heard. Rule 42(b). Certainly the Federal Rules were not intended to undermine the basic structure of equity jurisprudence, developed over the centuries and explicitly recognized in the United States Constitution.

For these reasons I think the petition for a writ of mandamus should have been dismissed.

NOTES AND QUESTIONS

1. Consider the relevance of *Beacon Theatres* to the jury-trial right in the following situations:

(a) An action in which plaintiff seeks redress for a single wrong but asks for both legal and equitable relief. An example would be a copyright infringement action in which damages for past infringement (legal) and injunctive relief against future infringement (equitable) are sought. See Bruckman v. Hollzer, 152 F.2d 730 (9th Cir.1946). Suppose that the defendant in addition to denying infringement, puts forward a number of affirmative defenses, some of which pertain only to the demand for legal relief. After the presentation of evidence in the case, the jury renders a general verdict for the defendant. Under what circumstances may the trial judge thereafter enter a judgment for plaintiff for equitable relief? See Ag Servs. of America v. Nielsen, 231 F.3d 737 (10th Cir.2000).

(b) A situation in which plaintiff is entitled to either legal or equitable relief but not both. For example, a breach of contract action in which plaintiff sues for specific performance or damages in the alternative. If plaintiff demands a jury, will the resolution of the question depend on which relief he prefers and on the extent of the common issues? See Ford v. C.E. Wilson & Co., 30 F.Supp. 163 (D.Conn.1939), affirmed 129 F.2d 614 (2d Cir.1942). If defendant demands a jury trial and plaintiff opposes it, does this mean that plaintiff elects equitable relief?

(c) A case in which a legal counterclaim is asserted against a claim for equitable relief or an equitable counterclaim is asserted against a legal claim. Compare Bendix Aviation Corp. v. Glass, 81 F.Supp. 645 (E.D.Pa. 1948), with Liberty Oil Co. v. Condon Nat. Bank, 260 U.S. 235, 43 S.Ct. 118, 67 L.Ed. 232 (1922). Should the permissive or compulsory nature of the counterclaim be relevant in determining whether there is a jury-trial right?

(d) A situation in which an issue that was determined without a jury in an equitable proceeding arises in a subsequent action at law under circumstances in which the doctrine of collateral estoppel (or issue preclusion, as it is now called) normally would bar relitigation. See pp. 1272–92, infra. How should the court rule if one of the parties demands a jury trial in the second action? See Parklane Hosiery Co. v. Shore, p. 1313, infra.

For an excellent analysis of many *Beacon Theatres* problems, see McCoid, *Procedural Reform and the Right to Jury Trial*, 116 U. Pa. L. Rev. 1 (1967).

2. Because of the crowded condition of jury dockets in many parts of the country, application of the *Beacon Theatres* decision may delay the adjudication of cases that would progress more rapidly on a nonjury docket. The delay may cause commercial injury to the litigants. For example, in the *Beacon Theatres* context some parties might hesitate to deal with Fox pending the outcome of the litigation, thereby adversely affecting Fox's commercial relationships during a potentially long period. This problem partially is alleviated by Rule 57, which permits the trial court to advance all declaratory-judgment actions on the calendar for speedy determination. Can the procedure in Rule 42(b) be used to mitigate some of the detrimental effects of the litigation on the parties?

3. Think about the crucial role the court's grant of a preliminary injunction might play in many cases. See pp. 1166–67, infra. It freezes the status quo during the case without taking the ultimate fact-finding role away from the jury. Is it possible that a preliminary injunction would so strongly affect the litigants' behavior that it would be the de facto end of the case?

DAIRY QUEEN, INC. v. WOOD, 369 U.S. 469, 82 S.Ct. 894, 8 L.Ed.2d 44 (1962), arose out of a licensing agreement entered into by respondents, owners of the trademark "DAIRY QUEEN," under which petitioner agreed to pay $150,000 for the exclusive right to use that trademark in certain parts of Pennsylvania. The contract provided for a small initial payment, with the remaining payments to be made at the rate of 50% of all amounts received by petitioner on sales and franchises to deal with the trademark; minimum annual payments were to be made regardless of petitioner's receipts. In August, 1960, respondents wrote petitioner a letter in which they claimed that the latter had committed "a material breach of that contract" by defaulting on the contract's payment provisions and notified petitioner that the contract would be terminated unless the claimed default was remedied immediately. When petitioner continued to deal with the trademark, respondents brought an action for breach of contract praying for: (1) temporary and permanent injunctions to restrain petitioner from any future use of or dealing in the franchise and the trademark; (2) an accounting to determine the exact amount of money owed by petitioner and a judgment for that amount; and (3) an injunction pending an accounting to prevent petitioner from collecting any money from "Dairy Queen" stores in the territory.

The Eastern District of Pennsylvania granted a motion to strike petitioner's demand for a jury trial on the alternative grounds that either the action was "purely equitable" or, if not purely equitable, the legal issues were "incidental" to equitable issues, and, in either case, no right to trial by jury existed. The Third Circuit refused to mandamus the district judge to vacate this order. The Supreme Court reversed.

The Court first disposed of the District Court's conclusion that there is no right to jury trial on legal issues that are "incidental" to equitable issues.

> * * * The holding in *Beacon Theatres* * * * applies whether the trial judge chooses to characterize the legal issues presented as "incidental" to equitable issues or not. Consequently, * * * *Beacon Theatres* requires that any legal issues for which a trial by jury is timely and properly demanded be submitted to a jury. * * *

Id. at 472–73, 82 S.Ct. at 897, 8 L.Ed.2d at 48.

As to the lower court's conclusion that the action was "purely equitable," the Court said:

> * * * The most natural construction of the respondents' claim for a money judgment would seem to be that it is a claim that they are entitled to recover whatever was owed them under the contract as of the date of its purported termination plus damages for infringement of their trademark since that date. * * * As an action on a debt allegedly due under a contract, it would be difficult to conceive of an action of a more traditionally legal character. And as an action for damages based upon a charge of trademark infringement, it would be no less subject to cognizance by a court of law.
>
> The respondents' contention that this money claim is "purely equitable" is based primarily upon the fact that their complaint is cast in terms of an "accounting," rather than in terms of an action for "debt" or "damages." But the constitutional right to trial by jury cannot be made to depend upon the choice of words used in the pleadings. The necessary prerequisite to the right to maintain a suit for an equitable accounting, like all other equitable remedies, is, as we pointed out in *Beacon Theatres*, the absence of an adequate remedy at law. Consequently, in order to maintain such a suit on a cause of action cognizable at law, as this one is, the plaintiff must be able to show that the "accounts between the parties" are of such a "complicated nature" that only a court of equity can satisfactorily unravel

> them. In view of the powers given to District Courts by Federal Rule * * * 53(b) to appoint masters to assist the jury in those exceptional cases where the legal issues are too complicated for the jury adequately to handle alone, the burden of such a showing is considerably increased and it will indeed be a rare case in which it can be met. * * * A jury, under proper instructions from the court, could readily determine the recovery, if any, to be had here, whether the theory finally settled upon is that of breach of contract, that of trademark infringement, or any combination of the two. * * *

Id. at 476–79, 82 S.Ct. at 899–900, 8 L.Ed.2d at 50–52.

ROSS v. BERNHARD, 396 U.S. 531, 90 S.Ct. 733, 24 L.Ed.2d 729 (1970). Plaintiffs brought a derivative suit in federal court against the directors of a closed-end investment company of which they were shareholders and joined the company's brokers, alleging that the company had been charged excessive brokerage fees. Plaintiffs' demand for jury trial, granted by the trial court but set aside by the Second Circuit, was upheld by the Supreme Court in a five-to-three decision:

> The common law refused * * * to permit stockholders to call corporate managers to account in actions at law. * * * Early in the 19th century, equity provided relief both in this country and in England. * * * The remedy made available in equity was the derivative suit, viewed in this country as a suit to enforce a *corporate* cause of action against officers, directors, and third parties. As elaborated in the cases, one precondition for the suit was a valid claim on which the corporation could have sued; another was that the corporation itself had refused to proceed after suitable demand, unless excused by extraordinary conditions. Thus the dual nature of the stockholder's action: first, the plaintiff's right to sue on behalf of the corporation and, second, the merits of the corporation's claim itself.
>
> Derivative suits posed no Seventh Amendment problems where the action against the directors and third parties would have been by a bill in equity had the corporation brought the suit. Our concern is with cases based upon a legal claim of the corporation against directors or third parties. Does the trial of such claims at the suit of a stockholder and without a jury violate the Seventh Amendment?
>
> * * * The heart of the action is the corporate claim. If it presents a legal issue, one entitling the corporation to a jury trial under the Seventh Amendment, the right to a jury is not forfeited merely because the stockholder's right to sue must first be adjudicated as an equitable issue triable to the court. *Beacon* and *Dairy Queen* require no less.
>
> If under older procedures, now discarded, a court of equity could properly try the legal claims of the corporation presented in a deriva-

tive suit, it was because irreparable injury was threatened and no remedy at law existed as long as the stockholder was without standing to sue and the corporation itself refused to pursue its own remedies. * * *

* * * Actions are no longer brought as actions at law or suits in equity. Under the Rules there is only one action—a "civil action"—in which all claims may be joined and all remedies are available. Purely procedural impediments to the presentation of any issue by any party, based on the difference between law and equity, were destroyed. In a civil action presenting a stockholder's derivative claim, the court after passing upon the plaintiff's right to sue on behalf of the corporation is now able to try the corporate claim for damages with the aid of a jury. * * * The "expansion of adequate legal remedies provided by * * * the Federal Rules necessarily affects the scope of equity." Beacon Theatres, Inc. v. Westover, 359 U.S., at 509.

Thus, for example, before-merger class actions were largely a device of equity, and there was no right to a jury even on issues that might, under other circumstances, have been tried to a jury. * * * [I]t now seems settled in the lower federal courts that class action plaintiffs may obtain a jury trial on any legal issues they present. * * *

JUSTICE STEWART, dissenting, responded:

* * * Since, as the Court concedes, a shareholder's derivative suit could be brought only in equity, it would seem to me to follow by the most elementary logic that in such suits there is no constitutional right to trial by jury. * * *

* * * [T]he Court's effort to force the facts of this case into the mold of *Beacon Theatres* and *Dairy Queen* simply does not succeed. Those cases involved a combination of historically separable suits, one in law and one in equity. * * *

But the present case is not one involving traditionally equitable claims by one party, and traditionally legal claims by the other. Nor is it a suit in which the plaintiff is asserting a combination of legal and equitable claims. For, as we have seen, a derivative suit has always been conceived of as a single, unitary, equitable cause of action. It is for this reason, and not because of "procedural impediments," that the courts of equity did not transfer derivative suits to the law side. * * *

If history is to be so cavalierly dismissed, the derivative suit can, of course, be artificially broken down into separable elements. But so then can any traditionally equitable cause of action, and the logic of the Court's position would lead to the virtual elimination of all equity jurisdiction. An equitable suit for an injunction, for instance, often involves issues of fact which, if damages had been sought, would have been triable to a jury. Does this mean that in a suit asking only for injunctive relief these factual issues *must* be tried to the jury, with the

> judge left to decide only whether, given the jury's findings, an injunction is the appropriate remedy? * * *

Id. at 534–35, 539–41, 544, 549–50, 90 S.Ct. at 736, 738–39, 741, 743–44, 24 L.Ed.2d at 733–34, 736–37, 739, 742.

NOTES AND QUESTIONS

1. A footnote in the majority opinion in *Ross* provides some guidance regarding the categorization of issues as legal or equitable for Seventh Amendment purposes:

> As our cases indicate, the "legal" nature of an issue is determined by considering, first, the pre-merger custom with reference to such questions; second, the remedy sought; and, third, the practical abilities and limitations of juries. * * *

396 U.S. at 538 n.10, 90 S.Ct. at 738 n.10, 24 L.Ed.2d at 736 n.10. The significance of the third factor mentioned by the Court—the practical abilities and limitations of juries—is unclear. Should it give the trial judge discretion to limit the jury trial right to issues that are well suited for lay jury determination? Or should it be construed to deny a jury trial on complex issues or whenever there is community bias? Or is it merely a reformulation of the traditional basis for equity jurisdiction—absence of an adequate remedy at law? Kane, *Civil Jury Trial: The Case for Reasoned Iconoclasm*, 28 Hastings L.J. 1, 11, 34 (1976), sees the third factor as representing "a movement toward a truly functional jury trial test":

> The language and purpose of the seventh amendment does not prevent the Supreme Court from adopting a functional, nonhistorical approach both to expand and to contract the right to a civil jury trial. The right to a civil jury symbolizes, among other things, notions of fair trial. The decision whether an action falls within the language of the constitutional guarantee may depend upon whether jury trial provides an adequate legal remedy. Thus, if the seventh amendment is read as a rigid historical rule, it not only may be dysfunctional, but in some instances it actually may pose a threat to justice.

But compare Redish, *Seventh Amendment Right to Jury Trial: A Study in the Irrationality of Rational Decision Making*, 70 Nw.U.L.Rev. 486 (1975).

2. Some lower federal courts have read the third "consideration" mentioned in the *Ross* footnote, Note 1, above, as a basis for denying a jury trial in cases in which the number of parties, complexity of the issues, or conceptual sophistication of the evidence and applicable substantive law support a finding that a jury would not be a rational and capable fact-finder. In re Japanese Electronic Prods. Antitrust Litigation, 631 F.2d 1069 (3d Cir.1980), affirmed in part and reversed in part on other grounds following summary judgment 723 F.2d 238, 319 (3d Cir.1983), reversed on other grounds Matsushita Elec. Indus. Co. v. Zenith Radio Corp., 475 U.S. 574, 106 S.Ct. 1348, 89 L.Ed.2d 538 (1986). Other federal courts have rejected this approach as too great an incursion on the Seventh Amendment. See, e.g., In re United States Financial Secs. Litigation, 609 F.2d 411 (9th Cir.1979), certiorari denied 446

U.S. 929, 100 S.Ct. 1866, 64 L.Ed.2d 281 (1980), overruling In re United States Fin. Secs. Litig. 75 F.R.D. 702 (S.D. Cal. 1977). This issue has arisen in major securities and antitrust suits, which present questions of a technical and esoteric nature arguably outstripping the capacity of even the most well-educated jurors.

The argument for the "complexity exception" is threefold. First, because this exception was recognized at common law at the time of the drafting and adoption of the Seventh Amendment, it is said to be consistent with the Constitution. See Arnold, *A Historical Inquiry into the Right to Trial by Jury in Complex Civil Litigation*, 128 U.Pa.L.Rev. 829 (1980); Campbell & Poidevin, *Complex Cases and Jury Trials: A Reply to Professor Arnold*, 128 U.Pa.L.Rev. 965 (1980); Arnold, *A Modest Replication to a Lengthy Discourse*, 128 U.Pa.L.Rev. 986 (1980). Second, because there are practical limitations on jurors' knowledge, experience, and ability, it is argued that complex and esoteric cases, such as *Japanese Electronic* or *U.S. Financial Securities,* are best entrusted to the fact-finding capacity of an experienced trial judge. Third, it is contended that to submit to a jury issues exceeding its capacity for rational and sound decisionmaking constitutes a denial of the litigants' due process rights.

In *U.S. Financial Securities,* the District Court on its own motion struck the demands for jury trial because of the complexity of the factual and legal issues involved, the daunting bulk of the evidence; and the expectation that the trial would last for two years. On interlocutory appeal, the Ninth Circuit rejected all three proffered justifications for the complexity exception.

In *Japanese Electronic,* the Third Circuit reversed the District Court's decision to reject the parties' motions to strike demands for jury trial. See Zenith Radio Corp. v. Matsushita Elec. Industrial Co., 478 F.Supp. 889 (E.D.Pa.1979). The court rejected the historical justification and the "juror capacity" argument for the complexity exception, although tentatively accepting the due process argument. The Third Circuit maintained that if a jury could not rationally reach a verdict because of the complexity of the case, a court should balance the interests protected by the Fifth and Seventh Amendments. A court then would be justified in finding, as the Third Circuit did in this case, that considerations of procedural due process outweigh the constitutional right to a jury trial.

Judge Gibbons dissented in *Japanese Electronic*, pointing out that, even though the case was complex, its complexity was "for the most part products of the liberal joinder rules of the Federal Rules * * * and of the district court's ruling consolidating two multi-count cases for trial"; none of these rules is constitutionally required. The solution, Judge Gibbons maintained, is to use the provisions of the Federal Rules providing for separate trials to reduce the case to a form that jurors can understand. Therefore, a plaintiff who requests a jury trial cannot liberally join parties and claims if these actions contribute to the overly complex nature of the case. Similarly, a defendant who demands a jury trial must seek to prevent a plaintiff from joining many separate claims and creating a complex lawsuit. Judge Gibbons concluded that his difference with the majority was based in part on differing perceptions "of the nature of the judicial process and the role of juries in that process." Id. As he explained, because the jury performs a critical role in the legitimizing of the legal system, "any erosion of citizen participation in [that] system is in the long run likely * * * to result in a reduction in the moral authority that supports the process."

The court in *Japanese Electronic* suggested the use of "special trial techniques to increase a jury's capabilities." What techniques might a court employ? See pp. 1094–1107, infra. The 2005 American Bar Association publication, Principles for Juries and Jury Trials, encourages the use of juror note-taking, permitting interim and on-going discussion of complicated evidence, and making available juror "notebooks" to enhance understanding of complicated material. See also Hans, *Judges, Juries, and Scientific Evidence*, 16 J. L. & Pol'y 19 (2007) (discussing techniques). Similarly, a number of states have identified techniques that could improve juror decision making. See Krauss, *Jury Trial Innovations in New York State*, 77 N.Y. St. B.J. 22 (May 2005). Would it be constitutional, in complex cases, to require a trial by a jury of highly educated intellectuals? What are the practical problems with this suggestion? See Fisher, *Going for the Blue Ribbon*, 2 Colum. Sci. & Tech. L. Rev. 1 (2001).

3. Do you see a relation between the complexity exception to the jury trial right and the Supreme Court's increasing tendency to dispose of discovery-rich cases on motions to dismiss and summary judgment? See pp. 568–79; 973–81, supra. These developments coincide with a drop in the number of jury trials overall. See Ellis, *Saving the Jury Trial*, 34 Brief 15 (Summer 2005). Consider Professor Miller's analysis of these trends:

> The less confident a court is in a jury's ability to comprehend, retain, and apply quantities of technical, scientific, and economic information, or to distinguish intertwined legal and factual issues, the more disposed it may be to use the occasion of a summary judgment motion to decide mixed law and fact questions and those it labels "beyond dispute." Thus the court may tend to believe that its own determination will be more rational than that of a jury. However, jurors should not be assumed incompetent or unable to comprehend issues posed by difficult cases. In fact, the ability to employ court-appointed experts or masters under Rule 53 to assist a jury when issues are complex exhibits the Rules' presumption of juror competence.

Miller, *The Pretrial Rush to Judgment: Are the "Litigation Explosion," "Liability Crisis," and Efficiency Clichés Eroding Our Day in Court and Jury Trial Commitments?*, 78 N.Y.U. L. Rev. 982, 1108–09 (2003).

4. Is there a constitutional right to a nonjury trial on issues that historically were considered equitable and therefore were tried by the chancellor? What is the significance of the statement in *Beacon Theatres* that "the right to jury trial is a constitutional one * * * while no similar requirement protects trials by the court"? In MICHAELSON v. UNITED STATES ex rel. CHICAGO, ST. P., M. & O. R. CO., 291 Fed. 940, 946 (7th Cir.1923), the court remarked that "Congress cannot constitutionally deprive the parties in an equity court of the right of trial by the chancellor." The Supreme Court

reversed on other grounds, 266 U.S. 42, 45 S.Ct. 18, 69 L.Ed. 162 (1924), and simply acknowledged the importance of the question.

Courts in a few states have declared that there is a constitutional right to a nonjury trial. The judicial reasoning is described in Van Hecke, *Trial by Jury in Equity Cases*, 31 N.C.L.Rev. 157, 173 (1953), as follows:

> The courts which have asserted that there is a constitutional right in equity cases to a trial of the facts by the judge alone, appear to have been motivated by (a) tradition, (b) respect for the chancellor's professional skill as a trier of facts, (c) a consciousness that the need for a court of equity had arisen in part from the limitation that jury trial had imposed upon the adequacy of various common-law actions, (d) an over-literal application of state constitutional provisions relating to the structure of state courts, (e) unsympathetic reaction to early legislative attempts to fuse the administration of law and equity into one procedural system, and (f) an uninformed fear of how jury trial would work in equity cases.

Are any of these reasons of sufficient magnitude to counter the policy in favor of jury trials apparent in *Ross, Beacon Theatres,* and *Dairy Queen?*

(III) NEWLY ESTABLISHED COURT–BASED RIGHTS TO RELIEF

CURTIS v. LOETHER

Supreme Court of the United States, 1974.
415 U.S. 189, 94 S.Ct. 1005, 39 L.Ed.2d 260.

Certiorari to the United States Court of Appeals for the Seventh Circuit.

MR. JUSTICE MARSHALL delivered the opinion of the Court.

Section 812 of the Civil Rights Act of 1968, 82 Stat. 88, 42 U.S.C. § 3612, authorizes private plaintiffs to bring civil actions to redress violations of Title VIII, the fair housing provisions of the Act * * *. The question presented in this case is whether the Civil Rights Act or the Seventh Amendment requires a jury trial upon demand by one of the parties in an action for damages and injunctive relief under this section.

Petitioner, a Negro woman, brought this action under § 812, claiming that respondents, who are white, had refused to rent an apartment to her because of her race * * *. In her complaint she sought only injunctive relief and punitive damages; a claim for compensatory damages was later added. After an evidentiary hearing, the District Court granted preliminary injunctive relief, enjoining the respondents from renting the apartment in question to anyone else pending the trial on the merits. This injunction was dissolved some five months later with the petitioner's consent, after she had finally obtained other housing, and the case went to trial on the issues of actual and punitive damages.

Respondents made a timely demand for jury trial in their answer. The District Court * * * denied the jury request. * * * After trial on the merits, the District Judge found that respondents had in fact discriminated against petitioner on account of her race. Although he found no actual damages, * * * he awarded $250 in punitive damages, denying petitioner's request for attorney's fees and court costs.

The Court of Appeals reversed on the jury trial issue. * * * In view of the importance of the jury trial issue in the administration and enforcement of Title VIII and the diversity of views in the lower courts on the question, we granted certiorari * * *. We affirm.

The legislative history on the jury trial question is sparse, and what little is available is ambiguous. There seems to be some indication that supporters of Title VIII were concerned that the possibility of racial prejudice on juries might reduce the effectiveness of civil rights damages actions. On the other hand, one bit of testimony during committee hearings indicates an awareness that jury trials would have to be afforded in damages actions under Title VIII. Both petitioner and respondents have presented plausible arguments from the wording and construction of § 812. We see no point to giving extended consideration to these arguments, however, for we think it is clear that the Seventh Amendment entitles either party to demand a jury trial in an action for damages in the federal courts under § 812.

* * * Although the thrust of the Amendment was to preserve the right to jury trial as it existed in 1791, it has long been settled that the right extends beyond the common-law forms of action recognized at that time. * * *

Petitioner nevertheless argues that the Amendment is inapplicable to new causes of action created by congressional enactment. As the Court of Appeals observed, however, we have considered the applicability of the constitutional right to jury trial in actions enforcing statutory rights "as a matter too obvious to be doubted." * * * Although the Court has apparently never discussed the issue at any length, we have often found the Seventh Amendment applicable to causes of action based on statutes. * * * Whatever doubt may have existed should now be dispelled. The Seventh Amendment does apply to actions enforcing statutory rights, and requires a jury trial upon demand, if the statute creates legal rights and remedies, enforceable in an action for damages in the ordinary courts of law.

NLRB v. Jones & Laughlin Steel Corp., 301 U.S. 1, 57 S.Ct. 615, 81 L.Ed. 893 (1937), relied on by petitioner, lends no support to her statutory-rights argument. The Court there upheld the award of back pay without jury trial in an NLRB unfair labor practice proceeding, rejecting a Seventh Amendment claim on the ground that the case involved a "statutory proceeding" and "not a suit at common law or in the nature of such a suit." Id. at 48, 57 S.Ct. at 629. *Jones & Laughlin* merely stands for the proposition that the Seventh Amendment is generally inapplicable in administrative proceedings, where jury trials would be incompatible with the whole concept of administrative adjudication and would substantially interfere with the NLRB's role in the statutory scheme. * * * These cases uphold congressional power to entrust enforcement of statutory rights to an administrative process or specialized court of equity free from the strictures of the Seventh Amendment. But when Congress provides for enforcement of statutory rights in an ordinary civil action in the district courts, where there is obviously no functional justification for denying the jury trial right, a jury trial must be available if the action involves rights and remedies of the sort typically enforced in an action at law.

We think it is clear that a damages action under § 812 is an action to enforce "legal rights" within the meaning of our Seventh Amendment decisions. See, e.g., Ross v. Bernhard * * *; Dairy Queen, Inc. v. Wood, * * *. A damages action under the statute sounds basically in tort—the statute merely defines a new legal duty, and authorizes the courts to compensate a plaintiff for the injury caused by the defendant's wrongful breach. As the Court of Appeals noted, this cause of action is analogous to a number of tort actions recognized at common law.[10] More important, the relief sought here—actual and punitive damages—is the traditional form of relief offered in the courts of law.

We need not, and do not, go so far as to say that any award of monetary relief must necessarily be "legal" relief. * * * A comparison of Title VIII with Title VII of the Civil Rights Act of 1964, where the courts of appeals have held that jury trial is not required in an action for reinstatement and back pay, is instructive, although we of course express no view on the jury trial issue in that context. In Title VII cases the courts of appeals have characterized back pay as an integral part of an equitable remedy, a form of restitution. But the statutory language on which this characterization is based—

> [T]he court may enjoin the respondent from engaging in such unlawful employment practice, and order such affirmative action as may be appropriate, which may include, but is not limited to, reinstatement or hiring of employees, with or without back pay * * *, or any other equitable relief as the court deems appropriate, 42 U.S.C. § 2000e–5(g) (1970 ed., Supp. II)—

contrasts sharply with § 812's simple authorization of an action for actual and punitive damages. In Title VII cases, also, the courts have relied on the fact that the decision whether to award back pay is committed to the discretion of the trial judge. There is no comparable discretion here: if a plaintiff proves unlawful discrimination and actual damages, he is entitled to judgment for that amount. Nor is there any sense in which the award here can be viewed as requiring the defendant to disgorge funds wrongful-

10. For example, the Court of Appeals recognized that Title VIII could be viewed as an extension of the common-law duty of innkeepers not to refuse temporary lodging to a traveler without justification, a duty enforceable in a damages action triable to a jury, to those who rent apartments on a long-term basis. See 467 F.2d at 1117. An action to redress racial discrimination may also be likened to an action for defamation or intentional infliction of mental distress. * * *

ly withheld from the plaintiff. Whatever may be the merit of the "equitable" characterization in Title VII cases, there is surely no basis for characterizing the award of compensatory and punitive damages here as equitable relief.

We are not oblivious to the force of petitioner's policy arguments. Jury trials may delay to some extent the disposition of Title VIII damages actions. But Title VIII actions seeking only equitable relief will be unaffected, and preliminary injunctive relief remains available without a jury trial even in damages actions, Dairy Queen, Inc. v. Wood * * *. Moreover, the statutory requirement of expedition of § 812 actions * * * applies equally to jury and nonjury trials. We recognize, too, the possibility that jury prejudice may deprive a victim of discrimination of the verdict to which he or she is entitled. Of course, the trial judge's power to direct a verdict, to grant judgment notwithstanding the verdict, or to grant a new trial provides substantial protection against this risk, and respondents' suggestion that jury trials will expose a broader segment of the populace to the example of the federal civil rights laws in operation has some force. More fundamentally, however, these considerations are insufficient to overcome the clear command of the Seventh Amendment. The decision of the Court of Appeals must be affirmed.

Affirmed.

NOTES AND QUESTIONS

1. In a case decided the same term as *Curtis,* PERNELL v. SOUTHALL REALTY, 416 U.S. 363, 94 S.Ct. 1723, 40 L.Ed.2d 198 (1974), the Court, again speaking through Justice Marshall, decided that because a landlord's right to recover possession of real property was a right protected at common law, the Seventh Amendment jury trial guarantee applies in a summary process action for repossession under the District of Columbia Code.

2. The principal case referred to in the opinion as denying jury trial in actions for reinstatement with back pay under Title VII is Johnson v. Georgia Highway Express, Inc., 417 F.2d 1122 (5th Cir.1969). See also cases cited in Ochoa v. American Oil Co., 338 F.Supp. 914, 923 n. 6 (S.D.Tex.1972), a scholarly opinion that quarrels with the ruling of the Fifth Circuit in *Johnson,* although adhering to it, and Note, *Is There a Jury Trial Right in Title VII Actions?*, 33 Ariz.L.Rev. 655 (1991).

3. In 1991 Congress enacted 42 U.S.C. § 1981a(a), (c) of the Civil Rights Act, covering claims alleging that a defendant employer unlawfully "intentionally" discriminated against plaintiff employee (but excluding cases alleging unlawful discrimination based solely upon disparate impact). The statute provides for a right to jury trial in cases brought under the Act. It permits assessment of both compensatory and punitive damages, but specifically excludes back pay and "other equitable relief," which can be sought from the court under the prior existing provisions of Title VII.

4. Given the result in *Curtis,* what techniques might be available to Congress to diminish the availability of jury trials?

TULL v. UNITED STATES, 481 U.S. 412, 107 S.Ct. 1831, 95 L.Ed.2d 365 (1987), further answered the question of just how a federal court should go about deciding whether a modern-day statutory action is or is not entitled to a trial by jury. In *Tull* the Government sued in federal court to impose a statutory monetary penalty on defendant for alleged violations of the Clean Water Act. Defendant demanded a jury trial, arguing that the action was akin to an historical action in debt decided by the law courts. The Government countered with arguments that the action was basically one in equity to abate a nuisance. The Supreme Court noted that in making its decision it first must "compare the statutory action to 18th–century actions brought in the courts of England prior to the merger of the courts of law and equity * * * [and then] examine the remedy sought and determine whether it is legal or equitable in nature." However, the Court went on to state "that characterizing the relief sought is '[m]ore important' than finding a precisely analogous common law cause of action in determining whether the Seventh Amendment guarantees a jury trial." The court then found that a civil penalty was a remedy enforced by the law courts and thus entitled to a trial by jury.

NOTES AND QUESTIONS

Does the Court's two-part "test" make any sense? If the nature of the remedy is "more important" than the characterization of the action, what is the value of the latter determination? See the concurring opinion of Justice Brennan in Chauffers, Teamsters & Helpers, Local 391 v. Terry, pp. 1030–32, infra.

(IV) DECISIONS BY SPECIAL TRIBUNALS

ATLAS ROOFING CO. v. OCCUPATIONAL SAFETY & HEALTH REVIEW COMMISSION, 430 U.S. 442, 97 S.Ct. 1261, 51 L.Ed.2d 464 (1977). Petitioners were cited for violations of the Occupational Safety and Health Act (OSHA) and fines were imposed on them after hearings before administrative law judges of the Occupational Safety and Health Review Commission (OSHRC). Two Courts of Appeals upheld the Commission's orders and rejected the petitioners' claim that the enforcement scheme violated the Seventh Amendment. In an opinion by Justice White, the Supreme Court affirmed:

> * * * At least in cases in which "public rights" are being litigated—e.g., cases in which the Government sues in its sovereign capacity to enforce public rights created by statutes within the power of Congress

to enact—the Seventh Amendment does not prohibit Congress from assigning the factfinding function and initial adjudication to an administrative forum with which the jury would be incompatible.

* * * [Petitioners also argue] that the right to jury trial was never intended to depend on the identity of the forum to which Congress has chosen to submit a dispute; otherwise, it is said, Congress could utterly destroy the right to a jury trial by always providing for administrative rather than judicial resolution of the vast range of cases that now arise in the courts. The argument is well put, but it overstates the holdings of our prior cases and is in any event unpersuasive. Our prior cases support administrative factfinding in only those situations involving "public rights," e.g., where the Government is involved in its sovereign capacity under an otherwise valid statute creating enforceable public rights. Wholly private tort, contract, and property cases, as well as a vast range of other cases, are not at all implicated.

More to the point, it is apparent from the history of jury trial in civil matters that factfinding, which is the essential function of the jury in civil cases, * * * was never the exclusive province of the jury under either the English or American legal systems at the time of the adoption of the Seventh Amendment; and the question whether a fact would be found by a jury turned to a considerable degree on the nature of the forum in which a litigant found himself. * * * The question whether a particular case was to be tried in a court of equity—without a jury—or a court of law—with a jury—did not depend on whether the suit involved factfinding or on the nature of the facts to be found. * * * Rather, as a general rule, the decision turned on whether courts of law supplied a cause of action and an adequate remedy to the litigant. If it did, then the case would be tried in a court of law before a jury. * * * Thus, suits for damages for breach of contract, for example, were suits at common law with the issues of the making of the contract and its breach to be decided by a jury; but specific performance was a remedy unavailable in a court of law and where such relief was sought the case would be tried in a court of equity with the facts as to making and breach to be ascertained by the court.

The Seventh Amendment * * * did not purport to require a jury trial where none was required before. Moreover, it did not seek to change the factfinding mode in equity or admiralty or to freeze equity jurisdiction * * *, preventing it from developing new remedies where those available in courts of law were inadequate. Ross v. Bernhard, * * * [p. 1011, supra,] held that a jury trial is required in stockholder derivative suits where * * * a jury trial would have been available to the corporation. It is apparent, however, that prior to the 1938 Federal Rules of Civil Procedure merging the law and equity functions of the federal courts, the very suit involved in *Bernhard* would have been in a court of equity sitting without a jury, not because the underlying issue was any different at all from the issue the corporation would have presented had it sued, but because the stockholder plaintiff who was denied standing in a court of law to sue on the issue was enabled in proper circumstances, starting in the early part of the 19th century, to sue in equity on behalf of the company.

The point is that the Seventh Amendment was never intended to establish the jury as the exclusive mechanism for factfinding in civil cases. It took the existing legal order as it found it, and there is little or no basis for concluding that the Amendment should now be interpreted to provide an impenetrable barrier to administrative factfinding under otherwise valid federal regulatory statutes. We cannot conclude that the Amendment rendered Congress powerless—when it concluded that remedies available in courts of law were inadequate to cope with a problem within Congress' power to regulate—to create new public rights and remedies by statute and commit their enforcement, if it chose, to a tribunal other than a court of law—such as an administrative agency—in which facts are not found by juries. * * *

* * * [H]istory and our cases support the proposition that the right to a jury trial turns not solely on the nature of the issue to be resolved but also on the forum in which it is to be resolved. Congress found the common-law and other existing remedies for work injuries resulting from unsafe working conditions to be inadequate to protect the Nation's working men and women. It created a new cause of action, and remedies therefor, unknown to the common law, and placed their enforcement in a tribunal supplying speedy and expert resolutions of the issues involved. The Seventh Amendment is no bar to the creation of new rights or to their enforcement outside the regular courts of law.

* * *

Id. at 450, 457–61, 97 S.Ct. at 1266, 1270–72, 51 L.Ed.2d at 472, 476–79.

NOTES AND QUESTIONS

1. Does *Atlas* only create a "public rights" exception to the jury trial guarantee? Justice White relied on a number of prior cases, including Justice Marshall's dicta in *Curtis* and *Pernell* interpreting NLRB v. Jones & Laughlin Steel Corp., 301 U.S. 1, 57 S.Ct. 615, 81 L.Ed. 893 (1937), as support for the proposition that Congress may avoid the jury-trial guarantee by entrusting enforcement of statutory rights to administrative proceedings in which the Seventh Amendment generally is inapplicable. But neither of those cases indicated that there are any limits on Congress' power to replace common-law actions with statutory actions and assign their adjudication to administrative tribunals, as was done with OSHA and workers' compensation. Could the

legislature provide that ordinary personal-injury actions be decided by such a tribunal?

GRANFINANCIERA, S.A. v. NORDBERG, 492 U.S. 33, 109 S.Ct. 2782, 106 L.Ed.2d 26 (1989). Nordberg, the bankruptcy trustee for the debtor, Chase & Sanborn Corporation, filed a claim against Granfinanciera to recover funds fraudulently transferred to it from the debtor's estate. Granfinanciera's request for a jury trial was denied on the ground that the bankruptcy courts were, like administrative agencies, outside the Seventh Amendment. The Supreme Court disagreed:

> The form of our analysis is familiar. "First, we compare the statutory action to 18th–century actions brought in the courts of England prior to the merger of the courts of law and equity. Second, we examine the remedy sought and determine whether it is legal or equitable in nature." *Tull v. United States* * * *. The second stage of this analysis is more important than the first. * * * If, on balance, these two factors indicate that a party is entitled to a jury trial under the Seventh Amendment, we must decide whether Congress may assign and has assigned resolution of the relevant claim to a non-Article III adjudicative body that does not use a jury as factfinder.

Id. at 42, 109 S.Ct. at 2790, 106 L.Ed.2d at 41.

The Court then performed the analysis, and determined that the recovery of a fraudulent conveyance is an action in which a jury trial is available. The Court then considered the "public rights" exception:

> In *Atlas Roofing,* we noted that "when Congress creates new statutory 'public rights,' it may assign their adjudication to an administrative agency with which a jury trial would be incompatible, without violating the Seventh Amendment's injunction that jury trial is to be 'preserved' in 'suits at common law.' " We emphasized, however, that Congress' power to block application of the Seventh Amendment to a cause of action has limits. Congress may only deny trials by jury in actions at law, we said, in cases where "public rights" are litigated: "Our prior cases support administrative factfinding in only those situations involving 'public rights,' e.g., where the Government is involved in its sovereign capacity under an otherwise valid statute creating enforceable public rights. Wholly private tort, contract, and property cases, as well as a vast range of other cases, are not at all implicated." * * *
>
> We adhere to that general teaching. * * * Congress may devise novel causes of action involving public rights free from the strictures of the Seventh Amendment if it assigns their adjudication to tribunals without statutory authority to employ juries as factfinders. But it lacks the power to strip parties contesting matters of private right of their constitutional right to a trial by jury. * * *

In certain situations, of course, Congress may fashion causes of action that are closely *analogous* to common-law claims and place them beyond the ambit of the Seventh Amendment by assigning their resolution to a forum in which jury trials are unavailable. * * * Congress' power to do so is limited, however, just as its power to place adjudicative authority in non-Article III tribunals is circumscribed.

* * * If a statutory right is not closely intertwined with a federal regulatory program Congress has power to enact, and if the right neither belongs to nor exists against the Federal Government, then it must be adjudicated by an Article III court. If the right is legal in nature, then it carries with it the Seventh Amendment's guarantee of a jury trial.

The Court then considered the bankruptcy courts in specific:

* * * Although the issue admits of some debate, a bankruptcy trustee's right to recover a fraudulent conveyance under 11 U.S.C. 548(a)(2) seems to us more accurately characterized as a private rather than a public right as we have used those terms in our Article III decisions. * * * There can be little doubt that fraudulent conveyance actions by bankruptcy trustees * * * are quintessentially suits at common law that more nearly resemble state-law contract claims brought by a bankrupt corporation to augment the bankruptcy estate than they do creditors' hierarchically ordered claims to a pro rata share of the bankruptcy res. They therefore appear matters of private rather than public right. * * *

* * * It may be that providing jury trials in some fraudulent conveyance actions—if not in this particular case, because respondent's suit was commenced after the bankruptcy court approved the debtor's plan of reorganization—would impede swift resolution of bankruptcy proceedings and increase the expense of Chapter 11 reorganizations. But "these considerations are insufficient to overcome the clear command of the Seventh Amendment." * * *

Id. at 55–63, 109 S.Ct. at 2797–802, 106 L.Ed.2d at 49–54.

NOTES AND QUESTIONS

1. In footnote 4 of the majority opinion in *Granfinanciera,* Justice Brennan commented:

This quite distinct inquiry into whether Congress has permissibly entrusted the resolution of certain disputes to an administrative agency or specialized court of equity, and whether jury trials would impair the functioning of the legislative scheme, appears to be what the Court contemplated when, in Ross v. Bernhard, * * * it identified "the practical abilities and limitations of juries" as an additional factor to be consulted in determining whether the Seventh Amendment confers a jury trial right. * * *

Justice Brennan seems to be suggesting that the third prong of the test advanced in *Ross* has resurfaced in *Atlas Roofing* as the "public rights" exception. Does this mean that the complexity of the issues in a case only can lead to a denial of the Seventh Amendment right to a jury trial when Congress has created an administrative agency to provide a forum for the resolution of public rights' disputes? How does this affect the Court of Appeals decisions in *Japanese Electronic* and *U.S. Financial Securities?* Reread Note 2, pp. 1013–15, supra.

2. Does the ruling in *Granfinanciera* mean that a bankruptcy judge can empanel a jury and conduct a trial, or does the Seventh Amendment require an Article III judge to administer the proceedings?

3. In KATCHEN v. LANDY, 382 U.S. 323, 86 S.Ct. 467, 15 L.Ed.2d 391 (1966), petitioner filed two claims in bankruptcy for sums allegedly due him from an insolvent corporation. The trustee in bankruptcy responded by asserting that certain payments from corporate assets to petitioner and others were "voidable preferences" under the Bankruptcy Act and could be recouped by the trustee in summary bankruptcy proceedings. Despite petitioner's objections, judgment was rendered for the trustee on the preferences and it was ordered that petitioner's claims remain unpaid until after the judgment in favor of the trustee had been satisfied. The Tenth Circuit affirmed.

In the Supreme Court, petitioner argued that a creditor who has received a preference can hold the property under a substantial adverse claim without filing a claim in the bankruptcy proceeding, thereby forcing the trustee to recover the preference by a plenary action under Section 60 of the Act, 11 U.S.C. § 96; in such a plenary action the creditor could demand a jury trial. Petitioner also contended that the situation is the same when a creditor files a claim and the trustee not only objects to its allowance but also demands surrender of the preference; petitioner's theory was that the Bankruptcy Act does not give the bankruptcy court summary jurisdiction to order the preferences surrendered; petitioner contended that if it did, it would violate the Seventh Amendment.

After an extensive analysis of the "structure and purpose" of the Bankruptcy Act, the Court held that the Act does confer summary jurisdiction to compel a claimant to surrender preferences. As to the jury-trial issue, the Court said:

> * * * [A]lthough petitioner might be entitled to a jury trial on the issue of preference if he presented no claim in the bankruptcy proceeding and awaited a federal plenary action by the trustee * * *, when the same issue arises as part of the process of allowance and disallowance of claims, it is triable in equity. The Bankruptcy Act, * * * converts the creditor's legal claim into an equitable claim to a pro rata share of the *res* * * *, a share which can neither be determined nor allowed until the creditor disgorges the alleged voidable preference he has already received. * * * As bankruptcy courts have summary jurisdiction to adjudicate controversies relating to property over which they have actual or constructive possession * * * and as the proceedings of bankruptcy courts are inherently proceedings in equity * * * there is no Seventh Amendment right to a jury trial for determination of objections to claims * * *.
>
> Petitioner's final reliance is on the doctrine of Beacon Theatres v. Westover * * * and Dairy Queen v. Wood * * *.

> The argument here is that the same issues—whether the creditor has received a preference and, if so, its amount—may be presented either as equitable issues in the bankruptcy court or as legal issues in a plenary suit and that the bankruptcy court should stay its own proceedings and direct the bankruptcy trustee to commence a plenary suit so as to preserve petitioner's right to a jury trial. * * *
>
> * * * [P]etitioner's argument would require that in every case where a [trustee claims that a creditor holds a preference that is void or voidable and when the creditor denies the existence of such a preference] and a jury trial is demanded the proceedings on allowance of claims must be suspended and a plenary suit initiated, with all the delay and expense that course would entail. Such a result is not consistent with the equitable purposes of the Bankruptcy Act nor with the rule of *Beacon Theatres* and *Dairy Queen* * * *. In neither *Beacon Theatres* nor *Dairy Queen* was there involved a specific statutory scheme contemplating the prompt trial of a disputed claim without the intervention of a jury. We think Congress intended the trustee's § 57g objection to be summarily determined * * *. Both *Beacon Theatres* and *Dairy Queen* recognize that there might be situations in which the Court could proceed to resolve the equitable claim first even though the results might be dispositive of the issues involved in the legal claim. * * *

Id. at 336–40, 86 S.Ct. at 476–78, 15 L.Ed.2d at 401–03. Justice Black and Justice Douglas dissented for the reasons stated in the dissenting opinion of Judge Phillips in the Court of Appeals. 336 F.2d 535, 540 (10th Cir.1964).

Is *Katchen* a retreat from *Beacon Theatres* and *Dairy Queen?* Would the plaintiff in *Katchen* be entitled to a jury trial under *Granfinanciera?*

(V) THE MODERN EFFECT OF HISTORICAL EQUITY JURISDICTION BASED ON A PARTY'S LEGAL STATUS

CHAUFFEURS, TEAMSTERS AND HELPERS LOCAL 391 v. TERRY

Supreme Court of the United States, 1990.
494 U.S. 558, 110 S.Ct. 1339, 108 L.Ed.2d 519.

Certiorari to the United States Court of Appeals for the Fourth Circuit.

JUSTICE MARSHALL delivered the opinion of the Court except as to Part III–A.

This case presents the question whether an employee who seeks relief in the form of backpay for a union's alleged breach of its duty of fair representation has a right to trial by jury. We hold that the Seventh Amendment entitles such a plaintiff to a jury trial.

I

McLean Trucking Company and the Chauffeurs, Teamsters, and Helpers Local Union No. 391 were parties to a collective-bargaining agreement that governed the terms and conditions of employment at McLean's terminals. The 27 respondents were employed by McLean as truckdrivers in bargaining units covered by the agreement, and all were members of the Union.

* * * Claiming a violation of their seniority rights, respondents filed a * * * grievance with the Union, but the Union declined to refer the charges to a grievance committee on the ground that the relevant issues had been determined in * * * prior proceedings.

In July 1983, respondents filed an action in District Court, alleging * * * that the Union had violated its duty of fair representation * * * [and] sought, *inter alia,* compensatory damages for lost wages and health benefits. * * *

Respondents had requested a jury trial in their pleadings. The Union moved to strike the jury demand on the ground that no right to a jury trial exists in a duty of fair representation suit. The District Court denied the motion to strike. After an interlocutory appeal, the Fourth Circuit affirmed the trial court, holding that the Seventh Amendment entitled respondents to a jury trial of their claim for monetary relief. 863 F.2d 334 (1988). We granted the petition for certiorari to resolve a circuit conflict on this issue * * * and now affirm the judgment of the Fourth Circuit.

II

The duty of fair representation is inferred from unions' exclusive authority under the National Labor Relations Act, 49 Stat. 449, 29 U.S.C. § 159(a) (1982 ed.), to represent all employees in a bargaining unit. * * * The duty requires a union "to serve the interests of all members without hostility or discrimination toward any, to exercise its discretion with complete good faith and honesty, and to avoid arbitrary conduct." * * *

III

* * *

To determine whether a particular action will resolve legal rights, we examine both the nature of the issues involved and the remedy sought. "First, we compare the statutory action to 18th-century actions brought in the courts of England prior to the merger of the courts of law and equity. Second, we examine the remedy sought and determine whether it is legal or equitable in nature." *Tull* * * *. The second inquiry is the more important in our analysis. *Granfinanciera.*

A

An action for breach of a union's duty of fair representation was unknown in 18th-century England; in fact, collective bargaining was unlawful. * * * We must therefore look for an analogous cause of action that existed in the 18th century to determine whether the nature of this duty of fair representation suit is legal or equitable.

The Union contends that this duty of fair representation action resembles a suit brought to vacate an arbitration award because respondents seek to set aside the result of the grievance process. In the 18th century, an action to set aside an arbitration award was considered equitable. * * *

The arbitration analogy is inapposite, however, to the Seventh Amendment question posed in this case. No grievance committee has considered respondents' claim that the Union violated its duty of fair representation; the grievance process was concerned only with the employer's alleged breach of the collective-bargaining agreement. Thus, respondents' claim against the Union cannot be characterized as an action to vacate an arbitration award * * *.

The Union next argues that respondents' duty of fair representation action is comparable to an action by a trust beneficiary against a trustee for breach of fiduciary duty. Such actions were within the exclusive jurisdiction of courts of equity. * * * This analogy is far more persuasive than the arbitration analogy. Just as a trustee must act in the best interests of the beneficiaries, * * * a union, as the exclusive representative of the workers, must exercise its power to act on behalf of the employees in good faith * * *. Moreover, just as a beneficiary does not directly control the actions of a trustee, * * * an individual employee lacks direct control over a union's actions taken on his behalf * * *.

The trust analogy extends to a union's handling of grievances. In most cases, a trustee has the exclusive authority to sue third parties who injure the beneficiaries' interest in the trust, * * * including any legal claim the trustee holds in trust for the beneficiaries, * * *. The trustee then has the sole responsibility for determining whether to settle, arbitrate, or otherwise dispose of the claim. * * * Similarly, the union typically has broad discretion in its decision whether and how to pursue an employee's grievance against an employer. * * * Just as a trust beneficiary can sue to enforce a contract entered into on his behalf by the trustee only if the trustee "improperly refuses or neglects to bring an action against the third person," * * * so an employee can sue his employer for a breach of the collective-bargaining agreement only if he shows that the union breached its duty of fair representation in its handling of the grievance * * *.

Respondents contend that their duty of fair representation suit is less like a trust action than an attorney malpractice action, which was historically an action at law * * *.

The attorney malpractice analogy is inadequate in several respects. Although an attorney malpractice suit is in some ways similar to a suit alleging a union's breach of its fiduciary duty, the two actions are fundamentally different. The nature of an action is in large part controlled by the nature of the underlying relationship between the parties. Unlike employees represented by a union, a client controls the significant decisions concerning his representation. Moreover, a client can fire his attorney if he is dissatisfied with his attorney's performance. This option is not available to an individual employee who is unhappy with a union's representation, unless a majority of the members of the bargaining unit share his dissatisfaction. * * * Thus, we find the malpractice analogy less convincing than the trust analogy.

Nevertheless, the trust analogy does not persuade us to characterize respondents' claim as wholly equitable. The Union's argument mischaracterizes the nature of our comparison of the action before us to 18th–century forms of action. As we observed in *Ross v. Bernhard* * * *, "The Seventh Amendment question depends on the nature of the *issue* to be tried rather than the character of the overall action." * * * [T]o recover from the Union here, respondents must prove both that McLean violated § 301 by breaching the collective-bargaining agreement and that the Union breached its duty of fair representation. When viewed in isolation, the duty of fair representation issue is analogous to a claim against a trustee for breach of fiduciary duty. The § 301 issue, however, is comparable to a breach of contract claim—a legal issue.

Respondents' action against the Union thus encompasses both equitable and legal issues. The first part of our Seventh Amendment inquiry, then, leaves us in equipoise as to whether respondents are entitled to a jury trial.

B

Our determination under the first part of the Seventh Amendment analysis is only preliminary. Granfinanciera * * *. In this case, the only remedy sought is a request for compensatory damages representing backpay and benefits. Generally, an action for money damages was "the traditional form of relief offered in the courts of law." Curtis v. Loether * * *. This Court has not, however, held that "any award of monetary relief must *necessarily* be 'legal' relief." *Ibid.* (emphasis added). * * * Nonetheless, because we conclude that the remedy respondents seek has none of the attributes that must be present before we will find an exception to the general rule and characterize damages as equitable, we find that the remedy sought by respondents is legal.

First, we have characterized damages as equitable where they are restitutionary, such as in "action[s] for disgorgement of improper profits," *Tull* * * *. * * * The backpay sought by respondents is not money wrongfully held by the Union, but wages and benefits they would have received from McLean had the Union processed the employees' grievances properly. Such relief is not restitutionary.

Second, a monetary award "incidental to or intertwined with injunctive relief" may be equitable. *Tull* * * *. * * * Because respondents seek only money damages, this characteristic is clearly absent from the case.[8]

8. Both the Union and the dissent argue that the backpay award sought here is equitable because it is closely analogous to damages awarded to beneficiaries for a trustee's breach of trust.

The Union argues that the backpay relief sought here must nonetheless be considered equitable because this Court has labeled backpay awarded under Title VII, 42 U.S.C. § 2000e *et seq.* (1982 ed.), as equitable. * * *

The Court has never held that a plaintiff seeking backpay under Title VII has a right to a jury trial. See Lorillard v. Pons, 434 U.S. 575, 581–582, 98 S.Ct. 866, 870–871, 55 L.Ed.2d 40 (1978). Assuming, without deciding, that such a Title VII plaintiff has no right to a jury trial, the Union's argument does not persuade us that respondents are not entitled to a jury trial here. Congress specifically characterized backpay under Title VII as a form of "equitable relief." * * * Congress made no similar pronouncement regarding the duty of fair representation. Furthermore, the Court has noted that backpay sought from an employer under Title VII would generally be restitutionary in nature, see Curtis v. Loether * * *, in contrast to the damages sought here from the union. Thus, the remedy sought in this duty of fair representation case is clearly different from backpay sought for violations of Title VII.

* * *

We hold, then, that the remedy of backpay sought in this duty of fair representation action is legal in nature. Considering both parts of the Seventh Amendment inquiry, we find that respondents are entitled to a jury trial on all issues presented in their suit.

* * *

It is so ordered.

JUSTICE BRENNAN, concurring in part and concurring in the judgment.

I agree with the Court that respondents seek a remedy that is legal in nature and that the Seventh Amendment entitles respondents to a jury trial on their duty of fair representation claims. * * * I do not join that part of the opinion which reprises the particular historical analysis this Court has employed to determine whether a claim is a "Suit at common law" under the Seventh Amendment, * * *, because I believe the historical test can and should be simplified.

The current test, first expounded in Curtis v. Loether * * *, requires a court to compare the right at issue to 18th–century English forms of action to determine whether the historically analogous right was vindicated in an action at law or in equity, and to examine whether the remedy

* * *. Such damages were available only in courts of equity because those courts had exclusive jurisdiction over actions involving a trustee's breach of his fiduciary duties. * * *

The Union's argument, however, conflates the two parts of our Seventh Amendment inquiry. Under the dissent's approach, if the action at issue were analogous to an 18th–century action within the exclusive jurisdiction of the courts of equity, we would necessarily conclude that the remedy sought was also equitable because it would have been unavailable in a court of law. This view would, in effect, make the first part of our inquiry dispositive. We have clearly held, however, that the second part of the inquiry—the nature of the relief—is more important to the Seventh Amendment determination. * * * The second part of the analysis, therefore, should not replicate the "abstruse historical" inquiry of the first part, *Ross* * * *, but requires consideration of the general types of relief provided by courts of law and equity.

sought is legal or equitable in nature. However, this Court, in expounding the test, has repeatedly discounted the significance of the analogous form of action for deciding where the Seventh Amendment applies. I think it is time we dispense with it altogether. I would decide Seventh Amendment questions on the basis of the relief sought. If the relief is legal in nature, *i.e.*, if it is the kind of relief that historically was available from courts of law, I would hold that the parties have a constitutional right to a trial by jury—unless Congress has permissibly delegated the particular dispute to a non-Article III decisionmaker and jury trials would frustrate Congress' purposes in enacting a particular statutory scheme.

I believe that our insistence that the jury trial right hinges in part on a comparison of the substantive right at issue to forms of action used in English courts 200 years ago needlessly convolutes our Seventh Amendment jurisprudence. For the past decade and a half, this Court has explained that the two parts of the historical test are not equal in weight, that the nature of the remedy is more important than the nature of the right. * * * Since the existence of a right to jury trial therefore turns on the nature of the remedy, absent congressional delegation to a specialized decisionmaker, there remains little purpose to our rattling through dusty attics of ancient writs. The time has come to borrow William of Occam's razor and sever this portion of our analysis.

We have long acknowledged that, of the factors relevant to the jury trial right, comparison of the claim to ancient forms of action, "requiring extensive and possibly abstruse historical inquiry, is obviously the most difficult to apply." Ross v. Bernhard * * *. Requiring judges, with neither the training nor time necessary for reputable historical scholarship, to root through the tangle of primary and secondary sources to determine which of a hundred or so writs is analogous to the right at issue has embroiled courts in recondite controversies better left to legal historians. * * *

To rest the historical test required by the Seventh Amendment solely on the nature of the relief sought would not, of course, offer the federal courts a rule that is in all cases self-executing. Courts will still be required to ask which remedies were traditionally available at law and which only in equity. But this inquiry involves fewer variables and simpler choices, on the whole, and is far more manageable than the scholasticist debates in which we have been engaged. Moreover, the rule I propose would remain true to the Seventh Amendment, as it is undisputed that, historically, "[j]urisdictional lines [between law and equity] were primarily a matter of remedy." McCoid, Procedural Reform and the Right to Jury Trial: A Study of *Beacon Theaters, Inc. v. Westover,* 116 U.Pa.L.Rev. 1 (1967). * * *

This is not to say that the resulting division between claims entitled to jury trials and claims not so entitled would exactly mirror the division between law and equity in England in 1791. But it is too late in the day for this Court to profess that the Seventh Amendment preserves the right to jury trial only in cases that would have been heard in the British law courts of the 18th century. See, e.g., * * * Ross v. Bernhard * * *.

We can guard * * * [the jury trial] right and save our courts from needless and intractable excursions into increasingly unfamiliar territory simply by retiring that prong of our Seventh Amendment test which we have already cast into a certain doubt. If we are not prepared to accord the nature of the historical analog sufficient weight for this factor to affect the outcome of our inquiry, except in the rarest of hypothetical cases, what reason do we have for insisting that federal judges proceed with this arduous inquiry? It is time we read the writing on the wall, especially as we ourselves put it there.

JUSTICE STEVENS, concurring in part and concurring in the judgment.

Because I believe the Court has made this case unnecessarily difficult by exaggerating the importance of finding a precise common-law analogue to the duty of fair representation, I do not join Part III–A of its opinion. * * *

* * * Duty of fair representation suits are for the most part ordinary civil actions involving the stuff of contract and malpractice disputes. There is accordingly no ground for excluding these actions from the jury right.

In my view, the evolution of this doctrine through suits tried to juries, the useful analogy to common-law malpractice cases, and the well-recognized duty to scrutinize any proposed curtailment of the right to a jury trial "with the utmost care," * * * provide a plainly sufficient basis for the Court's holding today. * * *

JUSTICE KENNEDY, with whom JUSTICE O'CONNOR and JUSTICE SCALIA join, dissenting.

* * *

I disagree with the analytic innovation of the Court that identification of the trust action as a model for modern duty of fair representation actions is insufficient to decide the case. The Seventh Amendment requires us to determine whether the duty of fair representation action "is more similar to cases that were tried in courts of law than to suits tried in courts of equity." Tull v. United States. Having made this decision in favor of an equitable action, our inquiry should end. Because the Court disagrees with this proposition, I dissent.

* * *

II

The Court relies on two lines of precedents to overcome the conclusion that the trust action should serve as the controlling model. The first consists of cases in which the Court has considered simplifications in litigation resulting from modern procedural reforms in the federal courts. Justice Marshall asserts that these cases show that the Court must look at the character of individual issues rather than claims as a whole. * * *. The second line addresses the significance of the remedy in determining the equitable or legal nature of an action for the purpose of choosing the most appropriate analogy. Under these cases, the Court decides that the respondents have a right to a jury because they seek money damages. * * * These authorities do not support the Court's holding.

A

In * * * [*Beacon Theatres*, *Dairy Queen*, and *Ross*] we have found a right to trial by jury where there are legal claims that, for procedural reasons, a plaintiff could have or must have raised in the courts of equity before the systems merged. * * *

These three cases responded to the difficulties created by a merged court system. * * * They stand for the proposition that, because distinct courts of equity no longer exist, the possibility or necessity of using former equitable procedures to press a legal claim no longer will determine the right to a jury. Justice Marshall reads these cases to require a jury trial whenever a cause of action contains legal issues and would require a jury trial in this case because the respondents must prove a breach of the collective-bargaining agreement as one element of their claim. * * *

I disagree. The respondents, as shown above, are asserting an equitable claim. Having reached this conclusion, the *Beacon, Dairy Queen,* and *Ross* cases are inapplicable. Although we have divided self-standing legal claims from equitable declaratory, accounting, and derivative procedures, we have never parsed legal elements out of equitable claims absent specific procedural justifications. Actions which, beyond all question, are equitable in nature may involve some predicate inquiry that would be submitted to a jury in other contexts. For example, just as the plaintiff in a duty of fair representation action against his union must show breach of the collective-bargaining agreement as an initial matter, in an action against a trustee for failing to pursue a claim the beneficiary must show that the claim had some merit. * * * But the question of the claim's validity, even if the claim raises contract issues, would not bring the jury right into play in a suit against a trustee.

* * *

B

The Court also rules that, despite the appropriateness of the trust analogy as a whole, the respondents have a right to a jury trial because they seek money damages. * * * The nature of the remedy remains a factor of considerable importance in determining whether a statutory action had a legal or equitable analog in 1791, but we have not adopted a rule that a statutory action permitting damages is by definition more analogous to a legal action than to any equitable suit. In each case, we look to the remedy to determine whether, taken with other factors, it places an action within the definition of "suits at common law."

In *Curtis* * * *, for example, we ruled that the availability of actual and punitive damages made a statutory antidiscrimination action resemble a legal tort action more than any equitable action. We made explicit that we did not "go so far as to say that any award of monetary relief must necessarily be 'legal' relief." * * * Although monetary damages might cause some statutory actions to resemble tort suits, the presence of monetary damages in this duty of fair representation action does not make it more analogous to a legal action than to an equitable action. Indeed, as shown above, the injunctive and monetary remedies available make the duty of fair representation suit less analogous to a malpractice action than to a suit against a trustee.

* * *

III

The Court must adhere to the historical test in determining the right to a jury because the language of the Constitution requires it. The Seventh Amendment "preserves" the right to jury trial in civil cases. We cannot preserve a right existing in 1791 unless we look to history to identify it. * * *

I would hesitate to abandon or curtail the historical test out of concern for the competence of the Court to understand legal history. We do look to history for the answers to constitutional questions. * * * Although opinions will differ on what this history shows, the approach has no less validity in the Seventh Amendment context than elsewhere.

If Congress has not provided for a jury trial, we are confined to the Seventh Amendment to determine whether one is required. Our own views respecting the wisdom of using a jury should be put aside. Like Justice Brennan, I admire the jury process. Other judges have taken the opposite view. * * * But the judgment of our own times is not always preferable to the lessons of history. Our whole constitutional experience teaches that history must inform the judicial inquiry. Our obligation to the Constitution and its Bill of Rights, no less than the compact we have with the generation that wrote them for us, do not permit us to disregard provisions that some may think to be mere matters of historical form.

NOTES AND QUESTIONS

1. In footnote 8 of his opinion in *Terry*, p. 1029, supra, does Justice Marshall provide an adequate explanation for continuing to employ a two-prong test that values the second prong more than the first? Or does the historical analysis "needlessly convolute our Seventh Amendment jurisprudence," as Justice Brennan argues? Justices Marshall and Stevens and the dissenters all disagree on the appropriate historical model for a "duty of fair representation" action. Is this disagreement evidence in favor of severing the historical analysis from the Seventh Amendment test, or is it evidence in favor of keeping the analysis as it is?

2. The Supreme Court's analysis of the scope of the right to jury trial under the Seventh Amendment remains ongoing. In CITY OF MONTEREY v. DEL MONTE DUNES, 526 U.S. 687, 119 S.Ct. 1624, 143 L.Ed.2d 882 (1999), damages were sought under the Civil Rights Acts, 42 U.S.C. § 1983, on the ground that the city had taken defendant's property without just compensation. The Court rendered three opinions, holding by a 5 to 4 majority, that a jury trial was proper. The four dissenting Justices argued that the case was at heart a condemnation action under the Fifth Amendment to the Constitution for which there is no right to trial by jury. Four Justices disagreed, noting that a condemnation action historically is one brought by the government conceding that it owes compensation to the owner of the property and seeking a fair evaluation of its worth. In *Del Monte Dunes*, the property owner initiated the suit, arguing that the actions of the county with regard to zoning deprived the owner of the value of the property. The four Justices held that such a case is akin historically to a tort action for damages, and thus carries the right to a jury trial under the Seventh Amendment. Justice Scalia concurred with them on the ground that Section 1983 itself, when an action is brought to recover damages, provides for a jury trial, regardless of the nature of the underlying cause.

D. THE RIGHT TO JURY TRIAL IN THE STATE COURTS

In some states there is a right to jury trial in equity cases, which eliminates the problem presented by *Beacon Theatres* and *Dairy Queen*. In most states that have merged law and equity, however, issues similar to those in the federal courts have arisen since the adoption of the codes.

The Commissioners who prepared the original New York Code of Procedure (1848) were aware of the problem presented by abolishing the distinction between law and equity at a time when that state's constitution continued to guarantee "trial by jury in all cases in which it has been heretofore used." This language appeared in the New York Constitutions of 1777, 1821, 1846, and 1894. Because it was interpreted to mean that each successive constitution guaranteed jury trial in any case to which it had been extended by the legislature since the adoption of the preceding constitution, it was changed in the constitution of 1938 to guarantee jury trial only "in all cases in which it has heretofore been guaranteed by constitutional provision." N.Y. Const. Art. I, § 2. But they may have underestimated the difficulty. Not content to leave the issue solely one of constitutional interpretation as it has been in the federal courts, they attempted to solve it by specific provisions, N.Y. Code of Proc. §§ 208–09 (1848):

> § 208. Whenever, in an action for the recovery of money only, or of specific real or personal property, there shall be an issue of fact, it must be tried by a jury, unless a jury trial be waived * * *.
>
> § 209. Every other issue is triable by the court, which, however, may order the whole issue, or any specific question of fact involved therein, to be tried by a jury * * *.

These provisions were copied in a great many states. But "in most jurisdictions * * * the courts, while occasionally giving the statute some weight, have regarded it generally as merely restating the law-equity dichotomy, and have proceeded to make their determination on historical grounds." Note, *The Right to Jury Trial Under Merged Procedures,* 65 Harv.L.Rev. 453, 454 (1952). In civil actions in which damages alone are sought, there has been little difficulty in finding that a jury is required, and of course in traditional equity cases, such as those involving trusts or injunctions, no jury has been allowed. In most states, there has been a reluctance to allow a mixed form of trial, with some issues being tried by the court and some by a jury. When there have been "legal" and "equitable" issues in the same case, the tendency has been to find one or the other the "predominant" concern and try the case accordingly. Perhaps most frequently the decision has been to find the case "predominantly" equitable, with jury trial denied on the "legal" issues on the grounds that they are "incidental," or that a jury trial is waived by joining a legal claim in an equitable action. Id. at 454–55. For a classic example, see Hiatt v. Yergin, 152 Ind.App. 497, 284 N.E.2d 834 (1972).

The Supreme Court's decisions, from *Beacon Theatres* through *Del Monte Dunes,* have not had a broad impact on the state courts and, in the state opinions in which these cases have been discussed, the reception has been mixed. For state court opinions that have looked at the *Beacon Theatres*-line approvingly, see, e.g., Onvoy, Inc. v. ALLETE, Inc., 736 N.W.2d 611 (Minn. 2007); Perilli v. Board of Educ. Monongalia County, 182 W.Va. 261, 387 S.E.2d 315 (1989); Bendick v. Cambio, 558 A.2d 941 (R.I.1989); Higgins v. Barnes, 310 Md. 532, 530 A.2d 724 (1987); Benson v. City of Nenana, 725 P.2d 490 (Alaska 1986). See also McDaniel, Jr., Case Note—*First National Bank of Dewitt v. Cruthis: An Analysis of the Right to a Jury Trial in Arkansas after the Merger of Law and Equity*, 60 Ark. L. Rev. 563 (2007).

3. THE PROVINCE OF JUDGE AND JURY

There is substantial evidence that during the colonial period and the first part of the nineteenth century the jury determined questions of law in some jurisdictions, see Georgia v. Brailsford, 3 U.S. (3 Dall.) 1, 1 L.Ed. 483 (1794), and that the law-fact dichotomy was a later development. See Scott, *Trial by Jury and the Reform of Civil Procedure,* 31 Harv.L.Rev. 669, 675–78 (1918); Note, *The Changing Role of the Jury in the Nineteenth Century,* 74 Yale L.J. 170 (1964); Harrington, *The Law–Finding Function of the American Jury*, 1999 Wis. L. Rev. 377. Differing views on the modern-day distinction between the roles of the judge and the jury are set out below.

SLOCUM v. NEW YORK LIFE INSURANCE CO., 228 U.S. 364, 382, 33 S.Ct. 523, 530, 57 L.Ed. 879, 888 (1913):

In the trial by jury * * * both the court and the jury are essential factors. To the former is committed a power of direction and superintendence, and to the latter the ultimate determination of the issues of fact. Only through the cooperation of the two, each acting within its appropriate sphere, can the constitutional right be satisfied. And so, to dispense with either, or to permit one to disregard the province of the other, is to impinge on that right.

JERKE v. DELMONT STATE BANK, 54 S.D. 446, 456–59, 223 N.W. 585, 589–90 (1929):

* * * We frequently see the phrase, "It is for the jury to say what the facts are." Historically speaking, this may have been true in the sixteenth century, but it has long since ceased to be true. The power and right and duty of the jury is not "to *say* what the facts are," but to adjudge and determine what the facts are by the usual and ordinary intellectual processes; that is, by applying the thinking faculties of their minds to the evidence received and the presumptions existing in the case, if any, and thereby forming an opinion or judgment. * * *

Jurors do not determine all questions of ultimate fact, even in jury cases. They determine the existence or nonexistence of those facts, and those only, with reference to the existence of which the judgment of reasonable men might differ as a result of the application of their intellectual faculties to the evidence. If the proof offered by the party having the burden in support of the existence of ultimate issuable facts is so meager that a reasonable mind could not therefrom arrive at the existence of such ultimate fact, there is nothing for the jury, and the judge not only may, but should, direct a verdict against the party having the burden of proof. * * *

WEINER, THE CIVIL JURY AND THE LAW–FACT DISTINCTION, 54 Calif.L.Rev. 1867, 1867–68 (1966):

The categories of "questions of law" and "questions of fact" have been the traditional touchstones by which courts have purported to allocate decision-making between judge and jury. * * * Many statutes in effect today echo * * * [the] dichotomy, utilizing the law and fact terminology to identify the respective provinces of the judge and the jurors in a civil case. None of these statutes, however, attempts to define what is meant by a question of law or a question of fact. Nor have the courts shown any inclination to fashion definitions which can serve as useful guidelines. Indeed, when faced with a dispute as to whether a specific issue should be resolved by the judge or the jury, the typical appellate opinion today does no more than label the question as one of law or of fact, perhaps citing some authorities which are equally devoid of any more detailed consideration of the point. * * * A question of law or a question of fact is a mere synonym for a judge question or a jury question.

MARKMAN v. WESTVIEW INSTRUMENTS, INC.

Supreme Court of the United States, 1996.
517 U.S. 370, 116 S.Ct. 1384, 134 L.Ed.2d 577.

Certiorari to the United States Court of Appeals for the Federal Circuit

JUSTICE SOUTER delivered the opinion of the Court.

The question here is whether the interpretation of a so-called patent claim, the portion of the patent document that defines the scope of the patentee's rights, is a matter of law reserved entirely for the court, or subject to a Seventh Amendment guarantee that a jury will determine the meaning of any disputed term of art about which expert testimony is offered. We hold that the construction of a patent, including terms of art within its claim, is exclusively within the province of the court.

[The dispute involved competing claims to a patent used to monitor clothing in a dry-cleaning establishment. Both systems used a keyboard and data processor and generated records including bar codes. Respondent argued that petitioner's patent was not infringed by Westview's because the latter only records an inventory of receivables by tracking invoices, rather than an inventory of articles of clothing.]

* * * Part of the dispute hinges upon the meaning of the word "inventory," a term found in Markman's independent claim 1, which states that Markman's product can "maintain an inventory total" and "detect and localize spurious additions to inventory." The case was tried before a jury, which heard, among others, a witness produced by Markman who testified about the meaning of the claim language.

After the jury compared the patent to Westview's device, it found an infringement of Markman's claim 1 * * *. The District Court nevertheless granted Westview's deferred motion for judgment as a matter of law, one of its reasons being that the term "inventory" in Markman's patent encompasses "both cash inventory and the actual physical inventory of articles of clothing." * * * Under the trial court's construction of the patent, the production, sale, or use of a tracking system for dry cleaners would not infringe Markman's patent unless the product was capable of tracking articles of clothing throughout the cleaning process and generating reports about their status and location. Since Westview's system cannot do these things, the District Court directed a verdict * * *.

Markman appealed, arguing it was error for the District Court to substitute its construction of the disputed claim term "inventory" for the construction the jury had presumably given it. The United States Court of Appeals for the Federal Circuit affirmed, holding the interpretation of claim terms to be the exclusive province of the court and the Seventh Amendment to be consistent with that conclusion. * * * Markman sought our review on each point, and we granted certiorari. * * *

* * *

III

Since evidence of common law practice at the time of the Framing does not entail application of the Seventh Amendment's jury guarantee to the construction of the claim document, we must look elsewhere to characterize this determination of meaning in order to allocate it as between court or jury. We accordingly consult existing precedent and consider both the relative interpretive skills of judges and juries and the statutory policies that ought to be furthered by the allocation.

A.

* * * [The Court examined the few cases that were alleged to be relevant and found them to be inconclusive. The Court indicated that, if anything, they supported the view that a jury determination of the issue was not required.]

B.

Where history and precedent provide no clear answers, functional considerations also play their part in the choice between judge and jury to define terms of art. We said in *Miller v. Fenton*, 474 U.S. 104, 114, 106 S.Ct. 445, 451, 88 L.Ed.2d 405 (1985), that when an issue "falls somewhere between a pristine legal standard and a simple historical fact, the fact/law distinction at times has turned on a determination that, as a matter of sound administration of justice, one judicial actor is better positioned than another to decide the issue in question." So it turns out here, for judges, not juries, are the better suited to find the acquired meaning of patent terms.

The construction of written instruments is one of those things that judges often do and are likely to do better than jurors unburdened by training in exegesis. Patent construction in particular "is a special occupation, requiring, like all others, special training and practice. The judge, from his training and discipline, is more likely to give a proper interpretation to such instruments than a jury, and he is, therefore, more likely to be right, in performing such a duty, than a jury can be expected to be." *Parker v. Hulme*, 18 F. Cas., at 1140. Such was the understanding nearly a century and a half ago, and there is no reason to weigh the respective strengths of judge and jury differently in relation to the modern claim; quite the contrary, for "the claims of patents have become highly technical in many respects as the result of special doctrines relating to the proper form and scope of claims that have been developed in the courts and the Patent Office." Woodward, Definiteness and Particularity in Patent Claims, 46 Mich. L.Rev. 755, 765 (1948).

Markman would trump these considerations with his argument that a jury should decide a question of meaning peculiar to a trade or profession simply because the question is a subject of testimony requiring credibility determinations, which are the jury's forte. It is, of course, true that credibility judgments have to be made about the experts who testify in patent cases, and in theory there could be a case in which a simple credibility judgment would suffice to choose between experts whose testimony was equally consistent with a patent's internal logic. But our own experience with document construction leaves us doubtful that trial courts will run into many cases like that. In the main, we expect, any credibility determinations will be subsumed within the necessarily sophisticated analysis of the whole document, required by the standard construction rule that a term can be defined only in a way that comports with the instrument as a whole. * * * Thus, in these cases a jury's capabilities to evaluate demeanor, * * * to sense the "mainsprings of human conduct," * * * or to reflect community standards, * * * are much less significant than a trained ability to evaluate the testimony in relation to the overall structure of the patent. The decisionmaker vested with the task of construing the patent is in the better position to ascertain whether an expert's proposed definition fully comports with the specification and claims and so will preserve the patent's internal coherence. We accordingly think there is sufficient reason to treat construction of terms of art like many other responsibilities that we cede to a judge in the normal course of trial, notwithstanding its evidentiary underpinnings.

C

Finally, we see the importance of uniformity in the treatment of a given patent as an independent reason to allocate all issues of construction to the court. As we noted in *General Elec. Co. v. Wabash Appliance Corp.*, 304 U.S. 364, 369, 58 S.Ct. 899, 902, 82 L.Ed. 1402 (1938), "[t]he limits of a patent must be known for the protection of the patentee, the encouragement of the inventive genius of others and the assurance that the subject of the patent will be dedicated ultimately to the public." Otherwise, a "zone of uncertainty which enterprise and experimentation may enter only at the risk of infringement claims would discourage invention only a little less than unequivocal foreclosure of the field," *United Carbon Co. v. Binney & Smith Co.*, 317 U.S. 228, 236, 63 S.Ct. 165, 170, 87 L.Ed. 232 (1942), and "[t]he public [would] be deprived of rights supposed to belong to it, without being clearly told what it is that limits these rights." *Merrill v. Yeomans*, 94 U.S. 568, 573, 24 L.Ed. 235 (1877). * * *

Uniformity would, however, be ill served by submitting issues of document construction to juries. Making them jury issues would not, to be sure, necessarily leave evidentiary questions of meaning wide open in every new court in which a patent might be litigated, for principles of issue preclusion would ordinarily foster uniformity. * * * But whereas issue preclusion could not be asserted against new and independent infringement defendants even within a given jurisdiction, treating interpretive issues as purely legal will promote (though it will not guarantee) intrajurisdictional certainty through the application of stare decisis on those questions not yet subject to interjurisdicitional uniformity under the authority of the single appeals court.

* * *

Accordingly, we hold that the interpretation of the word "inventory" in this case is an issue for the judge, not the jury, and affirm the decision of the Court of Appeals for the Federal Circuit.

It is so ordered.

NOTES AND QUESTIONS

1. Is *Markman* consistent with prior decisions that leave construction of a contract to the jury?

In DOBSON v. MASONITE CORP., 359 F.2d 921 (5th Cir.1966), plaintiff brought suit for breach of an oral agreement by which he was to clear timber from defendant's lands, sell it, pay a set amount of the money received to defendant, and retain the rest as compensation for his work. There was no dispute about the existence of the contract or its terms. The sole question was whether such an oral agreement was enforceable under the state Statute of Frauds. If the contract was interpreted as one for services, it would be enforceable; if it was found to be a contract for the sale of timber, recovery would be barred. The issue was presented to a jury on a special interrogatory. It determined that the contract was for services and rendered a verdict for plaintiff. The trial court disagreed with the jury's determination, finding that as a matter of law the contract was one for the sale of timber, and held for defendant. On appeal the decision was reversed, the Fifth Circuit stating:

> The district court, apparently because there was no dispute regarding the existence of the oral contract or its terms, felt that only a legal question, what was the effect of the contract, was involved. But "legal effect" is the result of applying rules of law to the facts; necessarily this determination must await a determination of all the facts. And, as we have stated, deciding what is the meaning of the contract is a question of fact.

Id. at 923–24.

In RANKIN v. FIDELITY INSURANCE, TRUST & SAFE DEPOSIT CO., 189 U.S. 242, 23 S.Ct. 553, 47 L.Ed. 792 (1903), the existence or nonexistence of a contract depended upon the effect given to a series of letters that were contradictory in many respects. The Supreme Court held that the question whether a contract existed was for the jury subject to the court's instruction. But in HOLTMAN v. BUTTERFIELD, 51 Cal.App. 89, 196 P. 85 (1st Dist.1921), in which plaintiff alleged that an undisputed unambiguous letter constituted a contract, the court held that there being no contradictory evidence, the question was for the court. Can the two cases be harmonized? In what way is it relevant that in *Dobson* the contract was oral? What difficulties in differentiating questions of law from questions of fact do these cases suggest? Shifting to another context, should the interpretation of the words of an unambiguous contract be left to the jury or to the court?

2. Can *Markman* be reconciled with the decision in Byrd v. Blue Ridge Rural Electric Cooperative, Inc., p. 424, supra? Recall that in *Byrd*, a diversity-of-citizenship case, the Court upheld the right to trial by jury on the issue whether plaintiff was an employee of defendant under the terms of the state worker's compensation act even though, on that single issue, state court judges, rather than juries, would make that determination.

3. What about the issue of negligence? Should a court or jury decide whether undisputed conduct was or was not negligent? See the classic discussion in Holmes, The Common Law 123–26 (1881). See also Gergen, *The Jury's Role in Deciding Normative Issues in the American Common Law*, 68 Fordham L.Rev. 407 (1999).

4. To what extent should the categorization of a particular issue as one of fact or law depend, as it did in part in *Markman*, on whether the question should be decided with reference to a fixed standard that applies to all members of the community impartially or as an ad hoc matter in particular cases? When an issue is classified as one of "law," the rule binds litigants in subsequent cases. Of course, the crucial question is: When is the need for a precise legal standard sufficient to justify withdrawing the matter from the jury? In many contexts the answer depends on whether the system has accumulated enough experience on the issue to justify announcing a standard that will be binding in future cases. Another basis for differentiation is whether the issue involves a sensitive area that warrants a "popular" or "communal" judgment. Consider, for example, the case of a prosecution of a publisher for distributing an allegedly obscene book. Shouldn't the decision to give the question of obscenity to a judge or a jury depend on whether the need for certainty on that issue outweighs the desirability of a judgment by the community as reflected by several juries passing on the question in different locales? For a discussion of the issues raised by *Markman*, see Miller, *The Pretrial Rush to Judgment: Are the "Litigation Explosion," "Liability Crisis," and Efficiency Clichés Eroding Our Day in Court and Jury Trial Commitments?*, 78 N.Y.U. L. Rev. 982, 1094–1126 (2003).

5. Preliminary questions such as those involving personal or subject-matter jurisdiction, or venue, often require resolution of factual disputes. In the ordinary course, these determinations are considered "legal" and thus not subject to jury trial. But what happens when the factual question on such a preliminary matter also is an issue regarding the right to relief? Thus when a nonresident defendant is sued in a state based on an allegation that he negligently caused plaintiff an injury in that state, the defendant's claim that plaintiff has sued the wrong defendant and that defendant never has been in the forum state goes both to the question of personal jurisdiction as well as to substantive liability. Does the analysis in the *Beacon Theatres* case require that the jury determine the matter?

4. TACTICAL CONSIDERATIONS IN DECIDING BETWEEN TRIAL BY JUDGE OR BY JURY

As will be discussed later, the right to trial by jury may be waived. Unless the right is invoked properly by one of the parties, the case can be decided by the trial judge sitting alone, as are cases in which the right does not exist. In many jurisdictions the judge has the power in a nonjury case or when a jury-trial right is waived to impanel an advisory jury whose verdict the court has discretion either to embrace or ignore. See, e.g., Federal Rule 39(c).

A. INSTITUTIONAL FACTORS

Even when an attorney feels that a client's chances of winning on the merits are the same whether the case is tried by judge or by jury, there may be a decided tactical advantage in choosing one form of trial over another. Suppose, for example, that plaintiff in a personal-injury action is in serious financial difficulty. Obviously she will want to pursue the fastest litigation route possible in order to obtain a recovery at an early date. In many jurisdictions there is a substantial backlog of cases on the jury-trial calendar and a long wait is inevitable, whereas the judge-trial calendar is practically current and the case may be heard within a few months. If the suit has been brought in a jurisdiction in which this type of imbalance between the jury and nonjury calendars exists, plaintiff probably will waive the jury. On the other hand, a defendant who knows plaintiff's plight will demand a jury trial, hoping to force plaintiff into a quick settlement favorable to defendant.

Similar considerations exist when time may ameliorate the extent of plaintiff's injuries. For example, if a young unmarried girl is injured seriously in an accident so that her physician will testify that there is a chance she may never be able to have children, a substantial verdict is likely. But she will be awarded far less if her case is not heard for a number of years and she has married and had a family in the interim. In cases of serious injury defendant usually has little to lose and much to gain by delay, except when the injuries are of a degenerative nature.

Also significant is the difference in cost between a jury and nonjury trial. On the average, a jury trial takes considerably more time than does a court trial. Jurors must be selected and instructed, more witnesses are called to testify, final arguments are longer, and more recesses are required. The result usually is higher counsel fees, more extensive payments to experts, and increased trial costs in the form of fees for jurors and witnesses. Although the witness fees often ultimately will be paid by the losing party, jury trial increases the financial gamble by a party who is uncertain as to his chances for success. Still another factor to be considered in an era of extensive scientific development is the complexity of the case and the ability of jurors to digest the evidence to be presented.

B. PSYCHOLOGICAL FACTORS

When is a jury more likely to give a favorable verdict than a judge? Are there substantial differences between judge and jury attitudes on questions of liability? On measuring damages? Every trial lawyer has a number of personal theories regarding these matters. For a discussion of empirical studies on this issue, see Hans & Albertson, *Empirical Research and Civil Jury Reform*, 78 Notre Dame L. Rev. 1497 (2003). As to the question of liability, the statistics indicate that plaintiffs win more often in trial before judges (65.1 percent) than they do in trials before juries (52.6 percent). On the other hand, juries tend to award greater damages than do judges. Cohen & Smith, *Civil Trial Cases and Verdicts in Large Counties, 2001*, at 3–7, in Bureau of Statistics Bulletin, U.S. Department of Justice, Office of Justice Programs, April 2004. Commentary is split on whether juries tend to award higher levels of punitive damages than do judges. Compare Hersch & Viscusi, *Punitive Damages: How Judges and Juries Perform*, 33 J. Legal Stud. 1 (2004) (stating that juries "are significantly more likely to award punitive damages than are judges and award higher levels of punitive damages"), with Eisenberg, LaFountain, Ostrom, Rottman & Wells, *Juries, Judges, and Punitive Damages: An Empirical Study*, 87 Cornell L. Rev. 743 (2002) (reporting "the absence of evidence that judges and juries behave substantially differently"). See also Hensler, *Jurors in the Material World: Putting Tort Verdicts in Their Social Context*, 13 Roger Williams L. Rev. 8 (2008).

In making the choice between judge and jury, a lawyer has much more to go on in the context of a particular case than these generalized comparisons between judge and jury trials. An attorney will consider the nature of the case, the characteristics of the parties and the witnesses, the passions that may surround the trial, the type of jurors who are likely to be chosen, and the background and predilections of the trial judge, if the judge's identity is known in advance, which often is not the case. Each of these factors is important in deciding whether the judge or the jury is most likely to identify with and be sympathetic to a lawyer's client. For an interesting empirical study regarding jury attitudes toward various types of witnesses, attorneys, and parties, see Sonaike, *The Influence of Jury Deliberation on Juror Perception of Trial, Credibility, and Damage Awards*, 1978 B.Y.U.L.Rev. 889. See generally Green & Bornstein, Determining Damages: The Psychology of Jury Awards (2003).

Finally, the decision to demand a jury may depend on counsel's assessment of whether he is more effective in a judge or jury trial. In presenting a case to jurors the attorney must be a bit of a showman; he must be entertaining or their attention will wander; he must know how to excite their interest so that the presentation of crucial testimony appears as a triumphant climax; and he must establish rapport with each and every juror, taking pains not to antagonize any of them by his actions or his appearance. By contrast, a lawyer in a nonjury trial need not concentrate heavily on the form of presentation since the judge will look for and pick out the significant aspects of the testimony even if they are not presented dramatically.

Rarely during the course of a jury case will an attorney have any clear sense of his success or failure in convincing the jury. He only can follow the planned presentation and hope that it was properly conceived. A sudden shift of tactics or a change of emphasis will tend to confuse and alienate the jurors. On the other hand, in a nonjury case, the judge, through statements during conferences, questions from the bench, and rulings on minor points, is constantly supplying the lawyers with clues as to her impressions of the case and the testimony. A sensitive attorney, upon detecting that things are not going well, may be able to salvage the case by changing the focus or direction of the testimony. For an interesting discussion of the different levels of involvement in the trial process as between the judge, sitting as a trier of fact, and the jury, see Wolf, *Trial by Jury: A Sociological Analysis,* 1966 Wis.L.Rev. 820. For an excellent debate on the choice of judge or jury, see Clermont & Eisenberg, *Trial by Jury or Judge: Transcending Empiricism,* 77 Cornell L.Rev. 1124 (1992), and Gross, *Settling for a Judge: A Comment on Clermont & Eisenberg,* 77 Cornell L.Rev. 1178 (1992).

5. DEMAND AND WAIVER OF TRIAL BY JURY

Read Federal Rules of Civil Procedure 38 and 39 in the Supplement.

In BERESLAVSKY v. CAFFEY, 161 F.2d 499 (2d Cir.), certiorari denied 332 U.S. 770, 68 S.Ct. 82, 92 L.Ed. 355 (1947), plaintiff sought an injunction against patent infringement. Subsequently he amended the complaint by striking the request for equitable relief and asking for money damages. The court held that plaintiff was entitled to trial by jury even though the Rule 38(b) time period had expired. The court reasoned that although the original complaint carried no right to jury trial, a later amendment changing the claim from equitable to legal relief renewed the right and gave plaintiff an additional ten days to demand a jury. A contrary decision was reached in AMERICAN HOME PRODUCTS CORP. v. JOHNSON & JOHNSON, 111 F.R.D. 448 (S.D.N.Y. 1986), on the ground that by requesting only equitable relief in its initial complaint when it could have also asked for legal relief at that time, the plaintiff had irrevocably waived the right to trial by jury.

What should a court do when an amendment is sought to change a claim for legal relief, on which jury trial has been demanded, to a claim for equitable relief? In ruling on the motion to amend, should the court take into account that the opposing party wants to retain a jury trial?

The "discretion" given the district court by Federal Rule 39(b) to permit a jury trial despite the absence of a demand is exercised sparingly. Does the following passage from BECKSTROM v. COASTWISE LINE, 14 Alaska 190, 13 F.R.D. 480, 483 (D.Alaska 1953), explain why?

> * * * For more than two years past, the Court has uniformly denied such requests by reason of the volume of litigation—more than 850 cases a year—coming before this Court for determination. This is more than three times the average number of cases per judge in the 86 * * * District Courts of the United States. The granting of trials by jury in such cases, where demand is not seasonably made, inevitably results in further delay and consequent further "denial of justice" to other litigants, who are presumed to have equally meritorious causes. Until an additional judge is authorized and appointed for this Division the practice will be adhered to. * * *

Is the attitude expressed in *Beckstrom* consistent with this country's commitment to jury trial? Should a constitutional right be used as a pawn in a struggle for more adequately staffed courts?

Contrast the decision in BATTEAST CONSTRUCTION CO. v. HENRY COUNTY BOARD OF COMMISSIONERS, 196 F.R.D. 543 (S.D.Ind. 2000):

> In exercising discretion, "the district court ought to approach each application under Rule 39(b) with an open mind * * * rather than with a fixed policy." * * * As a guide to inquiry, other district courts in the Seventh Circuit have considered five factors * * * (1) whether the issues involved are best tried before a jury; (2) whether the court's schedule or that of the adverse party will be disrupted; (3) the degree of prejudice to the opposing party; (4) the length of the delay; and (5) the reason for the moving party's tardiness in demanding a jury trial.

The *Batteast* court went on to allow a jury trial because (1) the case turned on witness credibility, a matter well suited for juries, (2) the trial was set for nearly a year later and thus no schedules would be disrupted, (3) the opposing party could give no examples of how it would conduct the litigation differently without a jury and why it would be prejudiced, (4) the three-month delay in requesting a jury was not excessive. The court noted that the requesting party had no sound excuse for failing to request a jury on time, but held that was outweighed by the other factors.

So far we have looked at a waiver of the jury right that is made after the filing of the complaint in an action. A party also can waive the jury right before litigation begins and, indeed, before a dispute even arises. A waiver of this sort can take the form of a contract clause that explicitly waives the jury right. It also can take the form of an agreement to arbitrate a dispute that might later develop.

Waiver of a constitutional right usually requires a voluntary, intentional, and knowing decision. Can a jury waiver that is made before a dispute arises meet this standard? Compare National Equip. Rental, Ltd. v. Hendrix, 565 F.2d 255 (2d Cir. 1977), with Bank South, N.A. v. Howard, 264 Ga. 339, 444 S.E.2d 799 (1994). What about an arbitration clause that does not mention the jury right? The Federal Arbitration Act, 9 U.S.C. § 1, enacted in 1925, authorizes federal courts to uphold predispute arbitration agreements that do not violate law or public policy. Is it relevant that the arbitration clause appears in a form contract, rather than as the result of an arms-length negotiation? See Sternlight, *Mandatory Binding Arbitration and the Demise of the Seventh Amendment Right to a Jury Trial*, 16 Ohio St. J. Disp. Resol. 669 (2001). The topic has generated considerable debate. Compare Ware, *Arbitration Clauses, Jury-Waiver Clauses, and Other Contractual Waivers of Constitutional Rights*, 67 Law & Contemp. Probs. 167 (2004), with Kepper, *Contractual Waiver of Seventh Amendment Rights: Using the Public Rights Doctrine to Justify a Higher Standard of Waiver for Jury Waiver Clauses than for Arbitration Clauses*, 91 Iowa L. Rev. 1345 (2006).

6. SELECTION AND COMPOSITION OF THE JURY

A. SIZE

In PATTON v. UNITED STATES, 281 U.S. 276, 288, 50 S.Ct. 253, 254, 74 L.Ed. 854, 858 (1930), a criminal case, the Court said that the phrase "trial by jury"

> includes all the essential elements as they were recognized in this country and England when the Constitution was adopted * * *. Those elements were: (1) That the jury should consist of twelve men, neither more nor less; (2) that the trial should be in the presence and under the superintendence of a judge having power to instruct them as to the law and advise them in respect of the facts; and (3) that the verdict should be unanimous.

But in WILLIAMS v. FLORIDA, 399 U.S. 78, 90 S.Ct. 1893, 26 L.Ed.2d 446 (1970), the Court held that a state constitutionally might use a jury with six (or perhaps fewer) members in a criminal case. Because the Court had held in DUNCAN v. LOUISIANA, 391 U.S. 145, 88 S.Ct. 1444, 20 L.Ed.2d 491 (1968), that the Sixth Amendment guarantee of jury trial in criminal cases applied to the states through "incorporation" in the Fourteenth Amendment, the result in *Williams* required the Court to recognize that such a jury also would satisfy the constitutional guarantee in federal criminal cases, a recognition it made explicit. See Miller, *Six of One Is Not a Dozen of the Other: A Reexamination of Williams v. Florida and the Size of State Criminal Juries*, 146 U. Pa. L. Rev. 621 (1998); Smith & Saks, *The Case for Overturning Williams v. Florida and the Six–Person Jury: History, Law, and Empirical Evidence*, 60 Fla. L. Rev. 441 (2008).

Seizing upon the holding in *Williams* and transferring its analysis to the civil-jury guarantee in the Seventh Amendment, numerous federal district courts in the years following *Williams* used their Rule 83 power to promulgate local rules to provide that ordinary civil actions shall be tried by six-member juries.

COLGROVE v. BATTIN, 413 U.S. 149, 93 S.Ct. 2448, 37 L.Ed.2d 522 (1973). Petitioner sought mandamus to compel a federal district judge to impanel a twelve-member jury, notwithstanding Local Rule 13(d)(1) of the District Court for the District of Montana, which provided for a six-member jury in all civil cases. Petitioner argued that the Local Rule violated the Seventh Amendment, the Enabling Act, 28 U.S.C. § 2072, and Federal Rule 48. The Ninth Circuit denied mandamus, and the Supreme Court affirmed, five to four:

> * * * [T]he historical setting in which the Seventh Amendment was adopted highlighted a controversy that was generated not by concern for preservation of jury characteristics at common law but by fear that the civil jury itself would be abolished unless protected in express words. * * *
>
> * * * We can only conclude, therefore, that by referring to the "common law," the Framers of the Seventh Amendment were concerned with preserving the *right* of trial by jury in civil cases where it existed at common law, rather than the various incidents of trial by jury. In short, what was said in *Williams* with respect to the criminal jury is equally applicable here: constitutional history reveals no intention on the part of the Framers "to equate the constitutional and common-law characteristics of the jury." * * *
>
> * * * In *Williams,* we rejected the notion that "the reliability of the jury as a factfinder * * * [is] a function of its size," * * * and nothing has been suggested to lead us to alter that conclusion. * * *
>
> * * * Significantly, our determination that there was "no discernible difference between the results reached by the two different-sized juries" * * * drew largely upon the results of studies of the operations of juries of six in civil cases. * * * Thus, while we express no view as to whether any number less than six would suffice, we conclude that a jury of six satisfies the Seventh Amendment's guarantee of trial by jury in civil cases.

Id. at 152, 155–56, 157, 158–60, 93 S.Ct. at 2450, 2452, 2453–54, 37 L.Ed.2d at 526, 528, 529, 530–31.

The Court further found that the Montana Local Rule did not violate the Enabling Act, since it concluded that the Congress in saying that the rules "shall preserve the right of trial by jury as at common law and as declared by the Seventh Amendment" had not intended to go beyond the Seventh Amendment guarantee itself. Finally, it held that the Local Rule was not in conflict with Federal Rule 48, saying that the latter only was concerned with numbers stipulated by the parties, and was inapplicable when a number was imposed regardless of the parties' consent.

NOTES

1. The majority and dissenting opinions in *Colgrove* cite a number of studies of the six-member jury, including Devitt, *The Six–Man Jury in the*

Federal Court, 53 F.R.D. 273 (1971), and Zeisel, *And Then There Were None: The Diminution of the Federal Jury*, 38 U.Chi.L.Rev. 710 (1970), which are two excellent presentations of opposing views. For a critique of the Court's use of empirical data in *Colgrove,* see Zeisel & Diamond, "*Convincing Empirical Evidence" on the Six Member Jury*, 41 U.Chi.L.Rev. 281 (1974). See also Sperlich, * * * *And Then There Were Six: The Decline of the American Jury*, 63 Judicature 262 (1980). For more recent empirical data, see Chud & Berman, *Six–Member Juries: Does Size Really Matter?*, 67 Tenn. L. Rev. 743 (2000); Devine, Clayton, Dunford, Seying & Pryce, *Jury Decision Making*, 7 Psychol. Pub. Pol'y & L. 622 (2001); Miller & Kazmar, *Psychology Research and Public Opinion Do Not Support Proposed Changes to the Jury System*, 30 Hamline L. Rev. 285 (2007).

2. In 1991, Federal Rule 48 was amended to permit a court to decide the size of the jury so long as it consists of no fewer than six and no more than twelve members. Prior to the amendment, the Rule merely allowed parties to stipulate that the jury could consist of any number less than twelve. Note that the local court rule at issue in *Colgrove* predated this amendment and arguably was inconsistent with the Federal Rules as they existed at the time. See Resnik, *Changing Practices, Changing Rules: Judicial and Congressional Rulemaking on Civil Juries, Civil Justice, and Civil Judging*, 49 Ala. L. Rev. 133 (1997). In 1996 the Advisory Committee recommended the restoration of the twelve-person jury. The proposal was rejected by the Judicial Conference of the United States.

3. In some states, juries of less than six members are permitted in civil trials. See Rottman, Flango, Cantrell, Hansen & LaFountain, State Court Organization 1998 tbl 42 (2000) (stating jury size requirements for all states). Reread Virginia Code § 8.01–359 in the Supplement, following Federal Rule 48. In Virginia, three-person juries are an option if the parties consent, and some Virginia judges consider a three-member jury to be a superior trier of fact. See Painter v. Fred Whitaker Co., 235 Va. 631, 369 S.E.2d 191 (1988).

B. EMPANELING THE JURY

Jury selection is a two-stage process. First, a list of potential jurors, the venire, is compiled and they are assembled. A number of them, equal to the number who will serve, usually twelve or six, are then selected at random to sit as a tentative jury. Second, these tentative jurors are questioned by the judge and/or by the attorneys to determine whether each of them can decide the case fairly and appropriately. This questioning is called "*voir dire.*" If one of them is dismissed, his or her place is taken by another member of the venire, selected at random, who is in turn subject to questioning. This process continues until the final panel is in place. For a summary of the empirical literature about *voir dire*, see Zalman & Tsoudis, *Plucking Weeds from the Garden: Lawyers Speak About Voir Dire*, 51 Wayne L. Rev. 163 (2005).

THIEL v. SOUTHERN PACIFIC CO., 328 U.S. 217, 66 S.Ct. 984, 90 L.Ed. 1181 (1946). Plaintiff, in an action for negligence, moved to strike the jury panel on the ground that it had been unfairly selected. The clerk of the court and the jury commissioner testified that they deliberately and intentionally had excluded from the jury lists all persons who work for a daily wage. They noted that in the past, because of the financial hardship imposed by jury service, those workers inevitably were excused by the judge. Workers who were paid by the week or the month, as well as the wives of daily wage earners were included on the jury lists. The Court held that such an exclusion cannot be justified "without doing violence to the democratic nature of the jury system. Were we to sanction an exclusion of this nature * * * we would breathe life into any latent tendencies to establish the jury as an instrument of the economically and socially privileged." Id. at 223–24, 66 S.Ct. at 987, 90 L.Ed. at 1186. Although the judge can excuse individuals for whom jury service would be a financial hardship, that cannot justify the exclusion of all daily wage earners regardless of whether an actual hardship is involved. The dissent noted that the matter was one of judicial administration, and that no constitutional issue was at stake. It took the position that selection of jurors from a jury pool that contained weekly wage earners and wives of daily workers was sufficient to avoid reversal of a judgment otherwise untainted by error.

NOTES AND QUESTIONS

1. Read 28 U.S.C. §§ 1861–66 in the Supplement. The Report of the Committee on the Operation of the Jury System of the Judicial Conference of the United States, on which the present federal jury-selection statute is based, appears at 42 F.R.D. 353 (1967). How representative of the community is a federal jury in view of the substantial classes of people who are exempt or may be exempted under Section 1863(b)(6) or who may be excused under Section 1863(b)(5)? Qualifications for jury service vary from state to state and include such factors as citizenship, local residence, ownership of property, health, and payment of taxes. See Rottman, Flango, Cantrell, Hansen & LaFountain, State Court Organization 1998 tbls 39–40 (2000) (stating jury qualifications, source lists, exemptions, excusals, and fees for all states).

2. A guarantee of accessible jury service derives from both the Americans with Disabilities Act, 42 U.S.C. § 12101, enacted in 1990, and Section 504 of the Rehabilitation Act of 1973, 29 U.S.C. § 794. See Bleyer, McCarty & Wood, *Access to Jury Service for Persons with Disabilities*, 19 Mental & Physical Disability L. Rep. 249 (1995). In GALLOWAY v. SUPERIOR COURT, 816 F.Supp. 12 (D.D.C.1993), the court held that blind persons cannot automatically be excluded. "[P]laintiff has offered uncontradicted evidence that blind individuals, like cited jurors, weigh the content of the testimony given and examine speech patterns, intonation, and syntax in assessing credibility." Id. at 16. The court went on to note that with reasonable accommodation, a juror who otherwise might not be able to serve in a case may be qualified to do so. See Dickhute, *Jury Duty for the Blind in*

the Time of Reasonable Accommodations: The ADA's Interface with a Litigant's Right to a Fair Trial, 32 Creighton L.Rev. 849 (1999); Blanck, Wilichowski & Schmeling, *Disability Civil Rights Law and Policy: Accessible Courtroom Technology*, 12 Wm. & Mary Bill Rts. J. 825 (2004).

3. The most common method for creating jury lists is by relying on voter registration records. 28 U.S.C. § 1863(b)(2) requires federal jury lists to be based on these records, with the use of supplemental sources when that is necessary to promote the interests of fair representation, as described in 28 U.S.C. §§ 1861 and 1862. Supplemental sources can include driver's license or public utilities lists, state tax rolls, or telephone lists. Exclusive reliance on voter registration lists has been much criticized. Because of the underrepresentation of minority and low-income persons in voter registration records, as well as the low percentage of voters overall, many have argued that use of multiple lists should be constitutionally compelled. See generally King, *Racial Jurymandering: Cancer or Cure? A Contemporary Review of Affirmative Action in Jury Selection*, 68 N.Y.U. L. Rev. 707 (1993); Note, *Jury Source Lists: Does Supplementation Really Work?*, 82 Cornell L.Rev. 390 (1997); Note, *Jury Source Representativeness and the Use of Voter Registration Lists*, 65 N.Y.U. L. Rev. 590 (1990).

4. The special or "blue ribbon" jury, which is composed of people who are specially selected because of their level of education, is an attempt to meet the contention that the ordinary juror is incompetent to deal with the complex problems of modern litigation. See Strier, *The Educated Jury: A Proposal for Complex Litigation*, 47 DePaul L. Rev. 49 (1997). In FAY v. NEW YORK, 332 U.S. 261, 67 S.Ct. 1613, 91 L.Ed. 2043 (1947), the Supreme Court upheld the constitutionality of a New York statute that gave the trial court discretion to empanel a "blue ribbon" jury upon application of either party. Would the Supreme Court uphold a federal statute that provided for "blue ribbon" juries in federal courts? Are "blue ribbon" juries consistent with the Seventh Amendment or the idea that a person should be "judged by peers" or by a group that represents a cross-section of society? See Oldham, *Origins of the Special Jury*, 50 U.Chi.L.Rev. 137 (1983).

5. The use of questionnaires, personal interviews, and psychological tests has been suggested for ascertaining the competence of prospective jurors. See Note, *Psychological Tests and Standards of Competence for Selecting Jurors*, 65 Yale L.J. 531, 541 (1956). Wouldn't psychological testing of jurors result in the erosion of our traditional views of jury composition? Would they be permissible under *Thiel*? See generally Cecil, Hans & Wiggins, *Citizen Comprehension of Difficult Issues: Lesson from Civil Jury Trials*, 40 Am. U. L. Rev. 727 (1991).

6. Do large-scale national cases, such as inter-state class actions, require special juries? Should the jury in such cases be drawn from a national, rather than a state or local, pool? See Dooley, *National Juries for National Cases: Preserving Citizen Participation in Large–Scale Litigation*, 83 N.Y.U. L. Rev. 411 (2008). What problems do you foresee in assembling a jury pool on a national scale?

C. CHALLENGING INDIVIDUAL JURORS

Challenges to individual jurors—sometimes called challenges to the polls—are of two kinds: for cause and peremptory. Challenges for cause permit a prospective juror to be rejected when partiality can be shown. Peremptory challenges permit rejection of jurors without any statement of reason and usually are based on an assumed partiality that may not be susceptible of proof.

An unlimited number of challenges for cause are permitted each party. These challenges are determined by the trial judge, although some states have experimented with so-called "triers"—independent officials who have the responsibility of determining challenges for cause. The number of peremptory challenges allowed each side varies among the states. The general range is from two to six. See Rottman, Flango, Cantrell, Hansen & LaFountain, State Court Organization 1998 tbl 41 (2000) (stating number of peremptory challenges permitted in all states). In the federal courts each side is permitted three. See 28 U.S.C. § 1870. Should the number be increased if there are multiple parties on one or both sides? Since the number of peremptory challenges is limited, they usually are husbanded carefully. Can the use of the peremptory challenge be reconciled with the principle that a jury should be composed of a representative sampling of the community?

The process of trying to eliminate people who will not be favorable jurors is extremely complex. Not only is it important to assess the way in which each individual juror is likely to view the case, but it also is necessary to analyze what effect each juror may have on the others during the course of deliberations. For example, one study indicates that as to issues involving scientific or technical information, a juror who has some relevant expertise wields considerable influence over the other jurors and often may control the verdict. Broeder, *Occupational Expertise and Bias as Affecting Juror Behavior: A Preliminary Look,* 40 N.Y.U. L. Rev. 1079 (1965). See also Bevan, Albert, Loiseaux, Mayfield & Wright, *Jury Behavior as a Function of the Prestige of the Foreman and the Nature of His Leadership,* 7 J.Pub.L. 419 (1958). For a review of forty-five years of empirical research on the subject, see Devine, Clayton, Dunford, Seying & Pryce, *Jury Decision Making*, 7 Psychol. Pub. Pol'y & L. 622 (2001).

As a general rule a lawyer will seek jurors who will identify and sympathize with his client. Consider, for example, a case brought by a young mother for the wrongful death of her husband. One would think that her attorney would be overjoyed if the jury contained a woman who also had been widowed and left with small children to raise. But the lawyer would not be pleased to learn that the juror in question, after a short period of mourning, had remarried happily, since that would greatly affect her attitude as to the proper amount of damages. Even if the juror had not remarried, her presence would be less desirable if her own marriage had been so unhappy that she preferred her present status. In an earlier period, the lawyer only could guess at an individual juror's biases and hostilities. But see Suggs & Sales, *Using Communication Clues To Evaluate Prospective Jurors During the Voir Dire,* 20 Ariz.L.Rev. 629 (1978). See also Broeder, *Plaintiff's Family Status as Affecting Jury Behavior: Some Tentative Insights,* 14 J.Pub.L. 131 (1965); Zeigler, *Young Adults as a Cognizable Group in Jury Selection,* 76 Mich.L.Rev. 1045 (1978). Social science research over the last thirty years has attempted to make more systematic the process of jury selection through the use of questionnaires, survey research, and statistical analysis that depend on research methodology and social science theory, rather than on lawyer intuition. How candid do you think potential jurors are in their responses to questions attempting to uncover their unconscious biases?

On what grounds should a juror be challenged for cause? Can the judge disqualify a prospective juror on the court's own motion or must he wait for a motion from one of the parties? May jurors be interrogated as to possible racial, religious, economic, or political prejudice? Is it relevant that the plaintiff or defendant is an individual or an organization espousing an unpopular viewpoint or cause? What if plaintiff or defendant merely happens to be a member of a group of this type? May jurors be excluded because of their race, gender, or disability? Consider these questions as you read the three cases that follow.

FLOWERS v. FLOWERS

Court of Civil Appeals of Texas, 1965.
397 S.W.2d 121.

CHAPMAN, JUSTICE.

The subject matter of this suit involves a question of the disqualification of a juror in a child custody contest tried to a jury * * *.

This case was tried in a town and county of very small population where the record shows many members of the jury panel had heard what they referred to as gossip or rumors concerning the case. The parties to the suit are Billie Charlene Flowers, plaintiff below, the mother; and R.A. Flowers, Jr., the father. The victims of the unfortunate broken home are three little girls ranging in ages from two to ten at the time of the filing of divorce by their mother in January 1964.

* * *

The jurors were told on voir dire examination that the evidence would show that plaintiff drank some socially and on one or two occasions had consumed alcoholic beverages to excess. They were questioned as to whether that fact standing alone would prejudice them against her as a fit and proper person to have custody of the children.

The record preserved upon examination of Mrs. Schmidt as a prospective juror shows that she first testified she was well acquainted with the Flowers family, belonged to the same Baptist church they did in the little town of Miami, and that she had no opinion formed in the case at all. Then when counsel said to her the evidence will show "that Billie does drink upon social occasions with the crowd at a dance, or something of that sort, she would have a highball or cocktail, and it will show on one occasion that she had too much, or two times had too much, what is your attitude—," she answered:

A. I am against drinking in any manner, any kind.

Q. Any way or any fashion at all?

A. Any type.

Q. Mrs. Schmidt, that would definitely affect your judgment in the case wouldn't it?

A. If the evidence was true.

Q. Could you enter the—you would take a seat as a juror with a positive feeling that any drinking whatsoever is wrong, and it is bad so far as the mother of these little girls is concerned,—

A. Anybody else.

Q. If the evidence shows Billie has had one drink or two—drinks at a social occasion, you would hold that against her?

A. I don't approve.

The court then took over the examination and asked her a number of questions, one of which was:

Q. Well, are you saying by that, Mrs. Schmidt, that you wouldn't grant either party to this law suit custody of their children if they drank?

A. I am.

The court then turned to leading questions to the juror as to her attitude about passing upon whether the mother was a fit person to have the custody of the girls, saying:

Q. Dependent upon the testimony you hear in a trial; the mere fact that she got drunk a few times and threw a conniption fit or something, you wouldn't hold that against her and think she wasn't—

A. Not especially.

The court then overruled the challenge of the juror for cause.

The record also shows by affidavit of a lady juror panelist who sat next to Mrs. Schmidt during voir dire examination that Mrs. Schmidt stated "* * * she felt sorry for R.A. Flowers, Jr. and that you had to admire a man that would go on to Sunday School and church after what had happened to him." Mrs. Philpot's affidavit also affirmed that Mrs. Schmidt made a statement to one of the other prospective jurors sitting next to her before the jury was selected that Billie Flowers had run off and left R.A. Flowers, Jr. once before and that both of such statements were made before she was selected and sworn to serve as a juror.

At both the motion for mistrial and motion for new trial based partly upon the proceedings just related, the court declined to hear Mrs. Philpot's tendered testimony as a witness in support of her affidavit. Upon the hearing of the motion for new trial Mrs. Flowers' attorney testified there were eleven jurors, including Mrs. Schmidt, who were undesirable to the plaintiff and that if Mrs. Schmidt on voir dire had correctly stated her attitude reflected by Mrs. Philpot's affidavit, they would have exercised a peremptory challenge as to her rather than as to some other juror. * * *

Article 2134, Vernon's Ann.Tex.Civ.St., provides as one of the disqualifications: "Any person who has a bias or prejudice in favor of or against either of the parties."

This disqualification for bias or prejudice extends not only to the parties personally, but also to the subject matter of the litigation. * * * Compton v. Henrie, Tex., 364 S.W.2d 179.

In defining the terms "bias" and "prejudice" as used in Article 2134 our Supreme Court in the HENRIE case just cited has said:

> Bias, in its usual meaning, is an inclination toward one side of an issue rather than to the other, but to disqualify, it must appear that the state of mind of the juror leads to the natural inference that he will not or did not act with impartiality. Prejudice is more easily defined for it means pre-judgment, and consequently embraces bias; the converse is not true. * * *

Mrs. Schmidt's statements indicate to us both bias and prejudice factually and such a prejudgment of the case as to indicate she could not have acted with impartiality. If we are correct in this factual conclusion then under the authorities just cited her disqualification is not a matter of discretion with the trial court but a matter of law. * * *

Even if we are in error in our pronouncements in the preceding paragraphs, it cannot be gainsaid that the record shows bias and prejudice on the part of Mrs. Schmidt toward plaintiff and toward her alcoholic consumption her attorney admitted would be shown before the examination of the jury on voir dire. From the viewpoint of this writer, such feelings on the part of Mrs. Schmidt are to her credit even if it did disqualify her as a juror. But even if under the facts of this case bias or prejudice was a fact to be determined by the trial court, those feelings having been clearly established, her answer of "Yes, sir" to a leading question to the effect that she would be able to decide the case on the evidence submitted, should be disregarded. * * * In any event we believe the court abused its discretion in refusing to hold the juror disqualified.

* * *

The judgment of the trial court is reversed and remanded for a new trial.

———

EDMONSON v. LEESVILLE CONCRETE COMPANY, INC.

Supreme Court of the United States, 1991.
500 U.S. 614, 111 S.Ct. 2077, 114 L.Ed.2d 660.

Certiorari to the United States Court of Appeals for the Fifth Circuit.

MR. JUSTICE KENNEDY delivered the opinion of the Court.

We must decide in the case before us whether a private litigant in a civil case may use peremptory challenges to exclude jurors on account of their race. * * * This civil case originated in a United States District Court, and we apply the equal protection component of the Fifth Amendment's Due Process Clause. * * *

I

Thaddeus Donald Edmonson, a construction worker, was injured in a job-site accident at Fort Polk, Louisiana, a federal enclave. Edmonson sued Leesville Concrete Company for negligence in the United States District Court for the Western District of Louisiana, claiming that a Leesville employee permitted one of the company's trucks to roll backward and pin him against some construction equipment. Edmonson invoked his Seventh Amendment right to a trial by jury.

During voir dire, Leesville used two of its three peremptory challenges authorized by statute to remove black persons from the prospective jury. Citing our decision in Batson v. Kentucky, 476 U.S. 79, 106 S.Ct. 1712, 90 L.Ed.2d 69 (1986), Edmonson, who is himself black, requested that the District Court require Leesville to articulate a race-neutral explanation for striking the two jurors. The District Court denied the request on the ground that Batson does not apply in civil proceedings. As impaneled, the jury included 11 white persons and 1 black person. The jury rendered a verdict for Edmonson, assessing his total damages at $90,000. It also attributed 80% of the fault to Edmonson's contributory negligence, however, and awarded him the sum of $18,000.

Edmonson appealed, and a divided en banc panel affirmed * * *. We granted certiorari, and now reverse the Court of Appeals.

II

A

In Powers v. Ohio, 499 U.S. 400, 111 S.Ct. 1364, 113 L.Ed.2d 411 (1991), we held that a criminal defendant, regardless of his or her race, may object to a prosecutor's race-based exclusion of persons from the petit jury. Our conclusion rested on a two-part analysis. First, following our opinions in *Batson* and in Carter v. Jury Commission of Greene County, 396 U.S. 320, 90 S.Ct. 518, 24 L.Ed.2d 549 (1970), we made clear that a prosecutor's race-based peremptory challenge violates the equal protection rights of those excluded from jury service. * * * Second, we relied on well-established rules of third-party standing to hold that a defendant may raise the excluded jurors' equal protection rights. * * *

That an act violates the Constitution when committed by a government official, however, does not answer the question whether the same act offends constitutional guarantees if committed by a private litigant or his attorney. The Constitution's protections of individual liberty and equal protection apply in general only to action by the government. * * * Racial discrimination, though invidious in all contexts, violates the Constitution only when it may be attributed to state action. * * * Thus, the legality of the exclusion at issue here turns on the extent to which a litigant in a civil case may be subject to the Constitution's restrictions. * * *

The trial judge exercises substantial control over voir dire in the federal system. See Fed.Rule Civ.Proc. 47. The judge determines the range of information that may be discovered about a prospective juror, and so affects the exercise of both challenges for cause and peremptory challenges. In some cases, judges may even conduct the entire voir dire by themselves, a common practice in the District Court where the instant case was tried. See Louisiana Rules of Court, Local Rule W.D.La. 13.02 (1990). The judge oversees the exclusion of jurors for cause, in this way determining which jurors remain eligible for the exercise of peremptory strikes. In cases involving multiple parties, the trial judge decides how peremptory challenges shall be allocated among them. 28 U.S.C. § 1870. When a lawyer exercises a peremptory challenge, the judge advises the juror he or she has been excused. * * *

The principle that the selection of state officials, other than through election by all qualified voters, may constitute state action applies with even greater force in the context of jury selection through the use of peremptory challenges. Though the motive of a peremptory challenge may be to protect a private interest, the objective of jury selection proceedings is to determine representation on a governmental body. Were it not for peremptory challenges, there would be no question that the entire process of determining who will serve on the jury constitutes state action. The fact that the government delegates some portion of this power to private litigants does not change the governmental character of the power exercised. * * *

Here, as in most civil cases, the initial decision whether to sue at all, the selection of counsel, and any number of ensuing tactical choices in the course of discovery and trial may be without the requisite governmental character to be deemed state action. That cannot be said of the exercise of peremptory challenges, however; when private litigants participate in the selection of jurors, they serve an important function within the government and act with its substantial assistance. If peremptory challenges based on race were permitted, persons could be required by summons to be put at risk of open and public discrimination as a condition of their participation in the justice system. The injury to excluded jurors would be the direct result of governmental delegation and participation.

Finally, we note that the injury caused by the discrimination is made more severe because the government permits it to occur within the courthouse itself. Few places are a more real expression of the constitutional authority of the government than a courtroom, where the law itself unfolds. Within the courtroom, the government invokes its laws to determine the rights of those who stand before it. In full view of the public, litigants press their cases, witnesses give testimony, juries render verdicts, and judges act with the utmost care to ensure that justice is done.

Race discrimination within the courtroom raises serious questions as to the fairness of the proceedings conducted there. Racial bias mars the integrity of the judicial system and prevents the idea of democratic government from becoming a reality. * * * In the many times we have addressed the problem of racial bias in our system of justice, we have not "questioned the premise that racial discrimination in the qualification or selection of jurors offends the dignity of persons and the integrity of the courts." *Powers* * * *. To permit racial exclusion in this official forum compounds the racial insult inherent in judging a citizen by the color of his or her skin. * * *

III

It remains to consider whether a prima facie case of racial discrimination has been established in the case before us, requiring Leesville to offer race-neutral explanations for its peremptory challenges. In *Batson*, we held that determining whether a prima facie case has been established requires consideration of all relevant circumstances, including whether there has been a pattern of strikes against members of a particular race. * * * The same approach applies in the civil context, and we leave it to the trial courts in the first instance to develop evidentiary rules for implementing our decision.

The judgment is reversed, and the case is remanded for further proceedings consistent with our opinion.

It is so ordered.

JUSTICE O'CONNOR, with whom THE CHIEF JUSTICE and JUSTICE SCALIA join, dissenting.

* * * As an initial matter, the judge does not "encourage" the use of a peremptory challenge at all. The decision to strike a juror is entirely up to the litigant, and the reasons for doing so are of no consequence to the judge. It is the attorney who strikes. The judge does little more than acquiesce in this decision by excusing the juror. In point of fact, the government has virtually no role in the use of peremptory challenges. Indeed, there are jurisdictions in which, with the consent of the parties, voir dire and jury selection may take place in the absence of any court personnel. * * *

Whatever reason a private litigant may have for using a peremptory challenge, it is not the government's reason. The government otherwise establishes its requirements for jury service, leaving to the private litigant the unfettered discretion to use the strike for any reason. This is not part of the government's function in establishing the requirements for jury service. * * *

Racism is a terrible thing. It is irrational, destructive, and mean. Arbitrary discrimination based on race is particularly abhorrent when manifest in a courtroom, a forum established by the government for the resolution of disputes through "quiet rationality." * * *. But not every opprobrious and inequitable act is a constitutional violation. The Fifth Amendment's Due Process Clause prohibits only actions for which the Government can be held responsible. The Government is not responsible for everything that occurs in a courtroom. The Government is not responsible for a peremptory challenge by a private litigant. I respectfully dissent.

In J.E.B. v. ALABAMA EX REL. T.B., 511 U.S. 127, 114 S.Ct. 1419, 128 L.Ed.2d 89 (1994), the State of Alabama, on behalf of the mother of a minor child, brought suit in a state court against the defendant for paternity and child support. The state used nine of its ten peremptory challenges to remove male jurors, with the result that the jury consisted solely of women. The Alabama courts rejected the defendant's objection that the use of peremptory challenges solely to exclude persons on the basis of gender violated the Fourteenth Amendment's Equal Protection Clause. A divided Supreme Court, noting that both federal and state courts were in disagreement on the matter, reversed. Justice Blackmun, writing for himself and three others, stated:

> Discrimination in jury selection, whether based on race or on gender, causes harm to the litigants, the community and the individual jurors who are wrongfully excluded from participation in the judicial process. * * *
>
> * * * All persons, when granted the opportunity to serve on a jury, have the right not to be excluded summarily because of discriminatory and stereotypical presumptions that reflect and reinforce patterns of historical discrimination. Striking individual jurors on the assumption that they hold particular views simply because of their gender is "practically a brand upon them, affixed by the law, an assertion of their inferiority." *Strauder v. West Virginia*, 100 U.S. at 308, 25 L.Ed. 6664 (1880).
>
> Our conclusion that litigants may not strike potential jurors solely on the basis of gender does not imply the elimination of all peremptory challenges. * * * Parties still may remove jurors who they feel might be less acceptable than others on the panel; gender simply may not serve as a proxy for bias. * * * Even strikes based on characteristics that are disproportionately associated with one gender [e.g. employ-

> ment in the military or as nurses] could be appropriate, absent a showing of pretext.

Id. at 140–43, 114 S.Ct. at 1427–29, 128 L.Ed.2d at 104–06.

Justice Kennedy concurred in a separate opinion strongly supporting the notion that sex discrimination in the courts could not be tolerated. Justice O'Connor also concurred in a separate opinion. She wrote:

> Today's decision severely limits a litigant's ability to act on * * * intuition, for the import of our holding is that any correlation between a juror's gender and attitudes is irrelevant as a matter of constitutional law. * * * [T]o say that gender makes no difference as a matter of law is not to say that gender makes no difference as a matter of fact. * * * In extending [our holdings on race] * * * to gender we have * * * taken a step closer to eliminating the peremptory challenge, and diminishing the ability of litigants to act on sometimes accurate gender-based assumptions about juror attitudes.
>
> * * *
>
> Accordingly, I adhere to my position that the Equal Protection Clause does not limit the exercise of peremptory challenges by private civil litigants * * *. This case itself presents no state action dilemma for here the State of Alabama itself filed the paternity suit. * * * But what of the next case? Will we, in the name of fighting gender discrimination, hold that the battered wife—on trial for wounding her abusive husband—is a state actor? Will we preclude her from using her peremptory challenges to ensure that the jury of her peers contains as many women members as possible? I assume we will, but I hope we will not.

Id. at 149–51, 114 S.Ct. at 1432–33, 128 L.Ed.2d at 109–10.

Justice Scalia, writing for himself and two other Justices, dissented. Essentially he agreed with Justice O'Connor's assessment of the importance of the peremptory challenge system and argued that it did not deny anyone the equal protection of the laws even in the case before the Court.

NOTES AND QUESTIONS

1. The Seventh Amendment does not apply to civil cases in state courts. On what basis did the Court in *J.E.B.* extend its reasoning in *Edmonson* to encompass state jury trials?

2. After *Batson, Edmonson*, and *J.E.B.*, should it be considered forbidden to exercise peremptory challenges on the basis of religion or political affiliation? In this regard, do religion and politics differ from race and gender? See Gendleman, *The Equal Protection Clause, the Free Exercise Clause and Religion–Based Peremptory Challenges,* 63 U. Chi. L. Rev. 1639 (1996); Waggoner, *Peremptory Challenges and Religion: the Unanswered Prayer for a Supreme Court Opinion,* 36 Loy. U. Chi. L.J. 285 (2004). What about disability? Age? Sexual orientation?

D. CONDUCTING THE *VOIR DIRE*

Rules concerning the extent to which the judge or the lawyers conduct *voir dire* vary among jurisdictions. See Hans & Jehle, *Avoid Bald Men and People with Green Socks? Other Ways To Improve the Voir Dire Process in Jury Selection*, 78 Chi.–Kent L. Rev. 1179 (2003). Federal Rule 47(a) leaves the matter entirely in the district judge's discretion. No uniform approach exists among the states. In Massachusetts, for example, the judge controls questioning of the potential jurors, see Mass. Gen. Laws ch. 234, § 28; in New York, the lawyers do, see N.Y. Ct. Rules § 202.33. Some states have held it error not to allow each juror to be examined by counsel prior to the exercise of challenges. E.g., Whitlock v. Salmon, 104 Nev. 24, 752 P.2d 210 (1988). In *Whitlock* the court underscored that trial counsel are likely to know their case better than the judge and therefore are more aware of what areas to probe in order to ascertain a juror's bias or antagonism, and that jurors may be less candid in answering questions regarding their biases when asked by the trial judge. Do you agree? See Jones, *Judge–Versus Attorney–Conducted Voir Dire: An Empirical Investigation of Juror Candor*, 11 Law & Human Behav. 131 (1987). See generally Babcock, *Voir Dire: Preserving Its Wonderful Power*, 27 Stan. L.Rev. 545 (1975).

NOTES AND QUESTIONS

1. How far can an attorney go in relating the *voir dire* examination to the lawsuit that the jury will hear? Would it be prejudicial for the lawyer to set out a hypothetical situation based on his view of the facts in the particular case and to ask questions as to how the jurors would react to those facts or how the jurors would apply certain legal principles to those facts?

2. How about questions on *voir dire* regarding the fact that the defendant is insured for the liability the plaintiff seeks to impose? Should the plaintiff's counsel be barred from mentioning insurance? Should either counsel be able to ask whether jurors or relatives work for or own stock in an insurance company? Many defense lawyers ask jurors: "Can you be fair even though you know that a verdict that must be paid by an insurance company ultimately might result in a raise in your own premiums?" See King v. Westlake, 264 Ark. 555, 572 S.W.2d 841 (1978). For a colorful debate on questions about insurance on *voir dire*, read the four opinions in Fosness v. Panagos, 376 Mich. 485, 138 N.W.2d 380 (1965).

SECTION B. THE SCOPE AND ORDER OF TRIAL

1. SETTING THE CASE FOR TRIAL

Trial will take place only after one of the parties or the court takes steps to have the case placed on the appropriate trial calendar and the court disposes of all the cases previously on that calendar. The technique for placing a case on a waiting list for trial will vary from jurisdiction to jurisdiction and from one judge to another. The Federal Rules contemplate that the trial judge, after consulting the parties, may schedule the date of trial. See, e.g., Federal Rule 16(b)(3)(B)(v) and (c)(2)(G). How is it possible to know when the previous cases assigned to a trial judge will be completed so that he and his courtroom will be available? Can one be certain that the lawyers will be free of other pressing obligations, or that crucial witnesses will not be indisposed? The answer, of course, is that there is no such certainty, but case management techniques and computers have helped to rationalize the flow of business through the courts and to increase predictability. See Nihan, *A Study in Contrasts: The Ability of the Federal Judiciary to Change Its Adjudicative and Administrative Structures*, 44 Am.U.L.Rev. 1693 (1995); Michels, *Case Management Techniques Work*, 18 Just. Sys. J. 75 (1995). For a description of a federal district judge's use of a running calendar technique to manage his civil jury docket, see Young, *Vanishing Trials, Vanishing Juries, Vanishing Constitution*, 40 Suffolk U. L. Rev. 67, 90 (2006).

Delay nevertheless persists in the scheduling of civil jury trials, despite a decline in the number of trials overall. See Shuman, *When Time Does Not Heal: Understanding the Importance of Avoiding Unnecessary Delay in the Resolution of Tort Cases*, 6 Psychol. Pub. Pol'y & L. 880, 895 (2000). In the federal system, litigants may try to expedite the scheduling of a jury trial by selecting a magistrate judge, p. 939, supra. See Murtha, *Why Do Lawyers Elect, or Not Elect, To Have Magistrate Judges Conduct Their Civil Trials*, 15–July Nev. Law. 32 (2007). Do you see problems with this approach?

What accounts for delay in the scheduling of civil jury trials? Some commentators emphasize that a lack of adequate funding may make it difficult for courts to pay jury fees or jury expenses. See Bunge, *Congressional Underappropriation for Civil Juries: Responding to the Attack on a Constitutional Guarantee*, 55 U. Chi. L. Rev. 237 (1988); DeBeneictis, *Tight Budget Squeezes Courts*, ABA Journal (Dec. 1992), at 22; *Even Jury Hiring is Frozen*, L.A. Times (Dec. 22, 2008), at 22. Others underscore the constitutional priority given to criminal trials. See generally Frase, *The Speedy Trial Act of 1974*, 43 U. Chi. L. Rev. 667 (1976). What other factors seem relevant?

2. ORDER OF TRIAL

Trial courts have the ability to split cases into discrete portions, trying claims or issues separately whenever that is convenient, economical, or avoids prejudice to a party or parties. See Federal Rules 42(b) and 16(c)(2)(M), and (O).

A. JURY CASES

When a particular case or aspect of a case comes before a jury, the court invariably has discretion to determine the order of trial, but a judge usually will not deviate from standard practice, which is as follows:

1. Plaintiff's opening statement
2. Defendant's opening statement
3. Plaintiff's presentation of direct evidence
4. Defendant's presentation of direct evidence
5. Plaintiff's presentation of rebuttal evidence
6. Defendant's presentation of rebuttal evidence
7. Opening final argument by plaintiff
8. Defendant's final argument
9. Closing final argument by plaintiff
10. Giving instructions to the jury.

B. NONJURY CASES

Although jury and nonjury cases generally are handled in the same way, there are a number of significant differences in scope. For example, the court often will dispense with the opening statement and the closing argument, and, of course, there is never a need to give instructions. Some jurisdictions provide that an attorney has an absolute right to argue, even in nonjury cases. Rarely will that right be exercised, however, if the judge, as is often the situation, makes clear that she believes an argument to be unnecessary.

3. THE BURDEN OF PROOF

A. BURDEN OF PRODUCTION

The term "burden of proof" usually refers to two different burdens: the burden of production and the burden of persuasion. The burden of production, sometimes called the burden of going forward, usually is placed on the plaintiff in civil actions. This means that the plaintiff is responsible for "producing" a certain threshold amount of evidence to raise a claim. However, defendant must normally meet the burden of production with respect to affirmative defenses. The threshold is defined as the minimum amount of evidence needed to satisfy the standard or proof and, thus, win the case. Put another way, one has met the burden of production if he has produced enough evidence for a reasonable jury to decide in his favor. Therefore, one can meet the burden of production even if all the evidence produced is refuted by the opposing party.

Meeting the burden of production does not ensure victory—one must still "persuade" the fact finder—but failing to meet it will ensure defeat. If the party charged with the burden of production has failed to adduce enough evidence, a summary judgment motion (prior to trial) or a motion for judgment as a matter of law (at trial) will be granted. The burden of production must be met if the case is to be decided by the trier of fact.

B. THE BURDEN OF PERSUASION

If the burden of production is met, the case can move forward to the stage of persuasion. Once there is enough evidence for the plaintiff to win, the defendant will try to cast doubt on the credibility or reliability of that evidence, in addition to bringing forth evidence of his own. Each party will try to persuade the trier of fact that its evidence is more weighty than the other's. If the plaintiff has the burden of persuasion, and does not convince the jury (or judge, in a bench trial) by the standard of proof required, the jury must rule for the defendant. Even if the plaintiff has satisfied the burden of production and the defendant brings forth no evidence of his own, if the jury is not persuaded that the plaintiff's evidence is sufficiently reliable or credible, the defendant must prevail.

C. STANDARDS FOR MEETING THE BURDEN OF PERSUASION

The standard for meeting the burden of persuasion represents the quantity and quality of evidence a party must produce at trial to prevail. The three most common standards are (1) preponderance of the evidence, (2) clear and convincing evidence, and (3) beyond a reasonable doubt. These standards usually are not defined any more specifically than their plain meaning suggests, although a "preponderance" is considered to be "more than fifty percent," and the clear and convincing standard lies somewhere between a preponderance and "beyond a reasonable doubt."

In most civil cases, the party bearing the burden of persuasion must prove by a preponderance of the evidence that she is entitled to the relief requested. In some civil actions, such as libel and slander and child custody proceedings, the clear-and-convincing-evidence standard often is used. And in all criminal cases, the prosecution must prove its case beyond a reasonable doubt.

D. SHIFTING BURDENS

The burdens of production and persuasion usually fall on same party at trial, either plaintiff or defendant. But there are times when the burden of production is placed on one party and the burden of persuasion on the other. In these cases, once the burden of production is satisfied, the burden of persuasion "shifts" to the other party.

One example of a type of action in which the burden shifts is an employment discrimination action alleging disparate impact or systemic disparate treatment under Title VII of the Civil Rights Act of 1964. In proceedings under this statute, the employee must make out a prima facie case (meet the burden of production) that there was discrimination. At that point, the burden of persuasion falls on the employer, who must prove by clear and convincing evidence that the firing was not race related. If the employee fails to meet the burden of production, she will lose the case. But once she meets that burden, it is the employer who must persuade the jury or else lose. See Texas Dep't of Comm'y Affairs v. Burdine, 450 U.S. 248, 101 S.Ct. 1089, 67 L.Ed.2d 207 (1981).

4. TACTICAL CONSIDERATIONS REGARDING THE OPENING STATEMENT

Normally, a case begins with plaintiff's opening statement. In the rare situation in which defendant has the burden of proof on *all* issues, such as when defendant admits plaintiff's allegations and goes to trial solely on his own affirmative defenses, the position of the parties is reversed throughout the trial and defendant has the right to open. Most lawyers regard the right to deliver the opening statement as so important that when they represent plaintiff they include some allegations in the complaint that defendant must deny in order to preserve the right. The reasons for viewing the right to open as substantial are fairly obvious. At the outset of the case the jurors are fresh, attentive, and impressionable. A carefully constructed statement laying out plaintiff's case in a positive, coherent fashion can convince the jurors that plaintiff's version of the facts is the correct one, which will force defendant to fight an uphill battle to offset plaintiff's initial advantage. On experimental studies of the advantages in order of argument and proof, see Walker, Thibaut & Andreoli, *Order of Presentation at Trial,* 82 Yale L.J. 216 (1972). See also Lawson, *Order of Presentation as a Factor in Jury Presentation,* 56 Ky.L.J. 523 (1968).

At common law, defendant did not make his opening statement until plaintiff had presented the affirmative case. Today, in most jurisdictions, however, defendant has the option of making an opening statement immediately after plaintiff has done so. Most trial lawyers recommend that defendant open at the earliest opportunity. If defendant waits, the initial impression created by plaintiff's opening statement may be so fortified by the opening evidence that the case is lost by the time defendant begins presenting the opposing evidence. Defendant may be able to neutralize plaintiff's initial advantage if the former immediately sets out a contrary version of the facts. For an opposite view, see Stramondo & Goodspeed, *Defendant's Presentation,* 57 Mass.L.Q. 179 (1972), in which the authors take the position that defendant's opening argument is more effective when it refutes plaintiff's evidence.

One of the most difficult tactical questions regarding the opening argument is whether or not a party should avoid mentioning an important issue or a dramatic piece of evidence in the hope of gaining an advantage through surprise. With the availability of modern discovery techniques, including provisions for required disclosures, updates for newly found materials, and an early planning conference as required under sections (a), (e), and (f), of Rule 26, it has become increasingly difficult to surprise one's opponent; moreover opposing counsel, by raising and disposing of the issue in his own opening argument, will insulate the jury from a dramatic shock. Nevertheless, with some items of evidence, with respect to their impact on the jury, the less said about them in advance the better. This occurs, for example, in cases in which defendant suddenly displays a movie of plaintiff, alleged to have suffered permanent leg injuries as a result of defendant's negligence, finishing a marathon run on the day before trial. However, since most items of evidence are not of such caliber, it generally is considered unsound to keep them secret, because doing so weakens the effectiveness of the opening statement and gives significant advantage to the opposition. For some interesting views on the tactics and style of opening argument, see Melilli, *Succeeding in the Opening Statement*, 28 Am. J. Trial Advoc. 525 (2006); Powell, *Opening Statements: The Art of Storytelling*, 31 Stetson L.Rev. 89 (2001); Fuchsberg, *Opening Statements—Plaintiff's View,* in 5 Am.Jur. Trials 285 (1966); Stern, *Opening Statements—Defense View,* in 5 Am.Jur. Trials 305 (1966).

Just as an attorney's opening statement may advance a client's cause, it also may reveal fatal flaws in the claim or defense. If this occurs, in most jurisdictions the opposing party may move immediately for the entry of a judgment. The theory of this motion is the same as the philosophy underlying the demurrer and summary judgment—the court is not required to try a case once it becomes clear that one of the parties *must* prevail. See Lucas, *Opening Statement,* 13 U. Haw. L. Rev. 349, 359 (1991).

5. THE PRESENTATION OF EVIDENCE

A. THE PROBLEMS OF ADMISSIBILITY

The admissibility of evidence at trial is determined by a large and complex set of rules. Each lawyer must plan carefully and in advance of trial to make certain that the evidence considered to be important will be accepted. Often, if an item of evidence cannot be admitted under one rule, it can come in under another. Moreover, except in rare circumstances, no proffered item of evidence will be excluded unless the opposing party objects to its introduction. As a result, an attorney often will offer otherwise inadmissible evidence in the hope that it will not be challenged. A lawyer must be careful, however, not to do this unsuccessfully too often as it may antagonize the judge or jury. Similarly, in many circumstances the opposing party will be well advised not to challenge inadmissible evidence that is not seriously prejudicial. An attorney who constantly objects may antagonize the jury by appearing to be an obstructionist. Even if the objections are sustained, the jurors may begin to believe something is being hidden from them, and will assume that the answers, had they been permitted, would have been unfavorable to the lawyer's client.

In some situations, even the most diligent attorney is powerless to keep inadmissible, highly prejudicial statements from the jurors. For example, a witness simply may blurt out such a statement voluntarily without having been asked a question pertaining to it. In such cases, the court has a choice. It may admonish the jury not to consider the evidence or it may declare a mistrial. In the latter case the jury is dismissed and the trial must begin anew before an entirely different panel. Obviously such drastic action is taken only when the error is severely prejudicial. Yet, is it realistic to expect jurors to ignore completely something they have heard and are told to forget? Do you think judges would be any better at ignoring relevant but inadmissible information? See Wistrich, Guthrie & Rachlinski, *Can Judges Ignore Inadmissible Information? The Difficulty of Deliberately Disregarding*, 153 U. Pa.L.Rev. 1251 (2005).

B. THE TECHNIQUE OF PRESENTATION

Much has been written concerning the way in which evidence should be presented. Most of this commentary can be distilled into one basic observation: the better the preparation before trial, the better the presentation.

Usually most evidence is presented at trial through the examination and cross-examination of witnesses. A party should call witnesses in a logical order so that the jury will know, at every step of the way, what part of the case is being explored. Usually the most important witnesses are called first to put the jurors in a favorable frame of mind. The testimony of less important witnesses will then be understood by the jury as backing and fortifying that party's version of the facts. There are, of course, many factors that interfere with a planned presentation. First, the opposition, through cross-examination, will attempt to upset the pattern not only by raising questions as to the witnesses' accuracy but also by injecting new considerations that tend to confuse the jurors. Second, a party who wishes to stay on the good side of witnesses, particularly experts, may be forced to accommodate their interests by calling them when it is convenient for them to testify rather than at the most logical point in the trial. Finally, no matter how fine the preparation, every trial produces a number of surprises to which the lawyer must react immediately. If, for example, during cross-examination of an opposition witness, the interrogating attorney receives a surprise favorable response, he must press forward on the issue immediately, before the witness and the opposing attorney have the time and opportunity to soften the impact by planning an explanation.

Cross-examination is a potent trial weapon. With it a clever attorney can raise doubts concerning the accuracy of even the most accomplished and prepared witness, let alone an unsophisticated witness who actually is trying to cover up the facts. Consider, for example, the effect on the trier of fact of the following exchange from an actual cross-examination of a woman as reported in *Saturday Review*, August 19, 1967, p. 12, col. 2:

Q: Did you ever stay all night with this man in New York?

A: I refuse to answer that question.

Q: Did you ever stay all night with this man in Chicago?

A: I refuse to answer that question.

Q: Did you ever stay all night with this man in Miami?

A: No.

There are two ways to minimize the effects of cross-examination. The first is to make certain that the witness is clear as to the story and is telling the truth. This requires the attorney and the witness to go over the facts in detail shortly before the trial begins. Even after this precaution the excitement of the trial may so unnerve the witness that he forgets even the most basic facts. Consider the following actual exchange (with the names changed), again as reported in *Saturday Review,* August 19, 1967, p. 12, col. 2:

Q: What is your brother-in-law's name?

A: Borofkin.

Q: What's his first name?

A: I can't remember.

Q: He's been your brother-in-law for forty-five years and you can't remember his first name?

A: No, I tell you I'm too excited! (Rising from the witness chair and pointing to Borofkin.) Nathan, for God's sake tell them your first name!

The second method of limiting the effectiveness of cross-examination is for the attorney on direct examination to raise and dispense with any matter that might cast doubt on a witness' veracity if it were raised for the first time on cross-examination. For example, in most jurisdictions an attorney may impugn the credibility of an opposition witness by introducing evidence showing that the witness previously has been convicted of a felony. If the fact that the witness had once been convicted of a felony is raised at the very beginning of his testimony by the attorney who called him, the jury will tend to think of the witness as a person willing to suffer embarrassment to tell the truth; but if the matter is first raised on cross-examination, the jurors may tend to consider the witness a person who is trying to hide important facts.

C. THE ROLE OF THE TRIAL JUDGE IN THE PRESENTATION OF EVIDENCE

Suppose that an attorney's presentation of a case appears inadequate. To what extent should the trial judge take over the trial by interrogating the witness herself and perhaps by calling new witnesses she believes should be heard? Does it make a difference if the case is before a jury? See Blanck, *Calibrating the Scales of Justice: Studying Judges' Behavior in Bench Trials*, 68 Ind. L.J. 1119 (1993). These questions raise some fundamental considerations regarding the role of the trial judge: Is the court a mere umpire who must stand aloof except when called upon to make decisions or a participant with the right to supervise the conduct of the trial to help ensure a just result?

Although there is general agreement that judges do have some power to call and interrogate witnesses, there is considerable controversy as to the extent of the power. For example, in some jurisdictions it has been held that a case may be reversed if the trial judge frequently interrupts counsel's presentation or engages in extensive examination of the witnesses. See Laub, *Trial and Submission of a Case From a Judge's Standpoint,* 34 Temple L.Q. 1, 5–6 (1960). In other jurisdictions, however, the power apparently is unlimited and the only question is how it is to be exercised. See Gitelson & Gitelson, *A Trial Judge's Credo Must Include*

His Affirmative Duty to Be an Instrumentality of Justice, 7 Santa Clara L. Rev. 7 (1966). In recent years judges generally have tended to increase their active participation in the trial process. Do you think a judge ought to be required to take a hand when the failure to do so will result in a miscarriage of justice? Does the judge owe a special responsibility to a pro se litigant?

D. THE POWER OF JURORS TO QUESTION WITNESSES

What if a juror is dissatisfied with the evidence? Should he be permitted to ask a witness questions that were not asked by the attorneys? Would it be feasible, tactically, for an attorney to object to the question if it called for inadmissible evidence? Is there some means by which this latter problem could be avoided? Would it be preferable to permit the juror to submit written questions to witnesses? See ABA Civil Trial Practice Standards (2007); ABA Principles for Juries and Jury Trials, Principle 13(c) (2005).

6. THE CLOSING ARGUMENT

A. THE NATURE OF THE ARGUMENT

Closing argument is important because it is the only time when the attorneys can organize the evidence in the case for the trier of fact in a coherent fashion, without interruption, and when the logical implications of the evidence can be spelled out in detail.

Normally, final argument is in three parts, with plaintiff having the benefit of speaking both first and last. If, however, the only issues in the case are those upon which defendant has the burden of proof, the roles of the parties are reversed and defendant speaks first and last. Often the court will limit the amount of time available to each party. See Annot., 71 A.L.R.4th 130 (1989). Whether or not such limits are imposed, the arguments should be brief, concise, sincere, and easily understood, and they should emphasize the vital points of the case. See Comment, *Understatement and Overstatement in Closing Arguments,* 51 La.L.Rev. 651 (1991).

B. PROPER VERSUS IMPROPER ARGUMENT

A proper argument is one that follows from the facts of the case as supported by the evidence or inferences that properly can be drawn from the evidence. An argument is improper when it is based upon matters not in evidence, or appeals to irrational passion that distorts the evidence in order to arrive at unjustified inferences. In practice, lawyers are permitted considerable leeway in argument, with limitations being imposed only in certain easily defined circumstances. It often is difficult to detect an improper argument that is introduced subtly. Consider, for example, a case in which plaintiff, injured in a hit-and-run auto collision, is attempting to prove that defendant was the driver of the other car. Plaintiff's only evidence is that the accident occurred on Sunday and that the other car involved belonged to a neighbor of defendant who had permitted defendant to borrow it every Sunday for several months prior to the collision. In trying to convince the jury of the importance of this circumstantial evidence, plaintiff's attorney might say: "Suppose I were to tell you that defendant's fresh fingerprints were found on the steering wheel of the car shortly after the accident and that defendant's sweater was found near the accident. Surely there would be no doubt in your minds after that as to who was driving, even though no one saw defendant." Obviously such an argument, though proper on its face, should not be permitted, since members of the jury might well believe that the fingerprints and the sweater were indeed found at the scene, although nothing in the evidence so indicates. See Levin & Levy, *Persuading the Jury with Facts Not in Evidence: The Fiction–Science Spectrum,* 105 U.Pa.L.Rev. 139 (1956); Montz, *Why Lawyers Continue To Cross the Line in Closing Argument: An Examination of Federal and State Cases*, 28 Ohio N.U. L. Rev. 67 (2001).

SECTION C. TAKING THE CASE FROM THE JURY—MOTIONS FOR JUDGMENT AS A MATTER OF LAW, FORMERLY DIRECTED VERDICTS AND JUDGMENTS NOTWITHSTANDING THE VERDICT

Read Federal Rule of Civil Procedure 50 in the Supplement.

Various procedural devices enable a judge to ensure that the jury carries out its functions. Rule 50(a) permits the judge, after the witnesses have testified and the evidence has been presented, to withhold the case from the jury and instead to enter judgment as a matter of law if the facts are sufficiently clear to require a particular result under the governing law (until 1991, this procedure was known as a "directed verdict"). Rule 50(b) authorizes a similar procedure for cases that have been submitted to the jury once the jurors have already reached a verdict. If the judge in this situation decides that judgment as a matter of law should have been granted, the court may set aside the verdict and enter judgment (until 1991, this procedure was known as a "judgment notwithstanding the verdict").

The Advisory Committee specifically noted that the 1991 language change did not alter the standards governing Rule 50(a) and Rule 50(b) motions. The Committee stated that the purpose of the amendment was to show that directed verdicts and judgments notwithstanding the verdict should be governed by identical standards, and that a motion under Rule 56 for summary judgment is to be governed by the same standard as well.

Thus it is important to reconsider the standards discussed in Chapter 13, pp. 984–85, supra. Is the time when they are made the only significant difference among motions under Rule 50(a), Rule 50(b), and Rule 56? For the view that because of the difference in timing, summary judgment should be accorded different treatment from motions for judgment as a matter of law, see Miller, *The Pretrial Rush to Judgment: Are the "Litigation Explosion," "Liability Crisis," and Efficiency Clichés Eroding Our Day in Court and Jury Trial Commitments?*, 78 N.Y.U. L. Rev. 982, 1057–62 (2003).

1. THE CONSTITUTIONAL ISSUES

In GALLOWAY v. UNITED STATES, 319 U.S. 372, 63 S.Ct. 1077, 87 L.Ed. 1458 (1943), the Supreme Court faced directly the charge that taking a case away from a jury on the ground that a plaintiff had not met its burden of production at trial was a violation of the Seventh Amendment right to a trial by jury. The Court held as follows:

> If the intention is to claim generally that the Amendment deprives the federal courts of power to direct a verdict for insufficiency of evidence, the short answer is the contention has been foreclosed by repeated decisions made here consistently for nearly a century. More recently the practice has been approved explicitly in the promulgation of the Federal Rules of Civil Procedure. * * * The objection therefore comes too late.
>
> Furthermore, the argument from history is not convincing. It is not that "the rules of the common law" in 1791 deprived trial courts of power to withdraw cases from the jury, because not made out, or appellate courts of power to review such determinations. The jury was not absolute master of fact in 1791. Then as now courts excluded evidence for irrelevancy and relevant proof for other reasons. The argument concedes they weighed the evidence, not only piecemeal but *in toto* for submission to the jury, by at least two procedures, the demurrer to the evidence and the motion for a new trial. The objection is not therefore to the basic thing, which is the power of the court to withhold cases from the jury or set aside the verdict for insufficiency of the evidence. It is rather to incidental or collateral effects, namely, that the directed verdict as now administered differs from both those procedures because, on the one hand, allegedly higher standards of proof are required and, on the other, different consequences follow as to further maintenance of the litigation. Apart from the standards of proof, the argument appears to urge that in 1791, a litigant could challenge his opponent's evidence, either by the demurrer, which when determined ended the litigation, or by motion for a new trial which, if successful, gave the adversary another chance to prove his case; and therefore the Amendment excluded any challenge to which one or the other of these consequences does not attach.

> The Amendment did not bind the federal courts to the exact procedural incidents or details of jury trial according to the common law in 1791, any more than it tied them to the common-law system of pleading or the specific rules of evidence then prevailing. Nor were "the rules of the common law" then prevalent, including those relating to the procedure by which the judge regulated the jury's role on questions of fact, crystalized in a fixed and immutable system. On the contrary, they were constantly changing and developing during the late eighteenth and early nineteenth centuries. In 1791 this process already had resulted in widely divergent common-law rules on procedural matters among the states, and between them and England. * * *
>
> This difficulty, no doubt, accounts for the amorphous character of the objection now advanced, which insists, not that any single one of the features criticized, but that the cumulative total or the alternative effect of all, was embodied in the Amendment. The more logical conclusion, we think, and the one which both history and the previous decisions here support, is that the Amendment was designed to preserve the basic institution of jury trial in only its most fundamental elements, not the great mass of procedural forms and details, varying even then so widely among common-law jurisdictions.
>
> * * *
>
> Finally, the objection appears to be directed generally at the standards of proof judges have required for submission of evidence to the jury. But standards, contrary to the objection's assumption, cannot be framed wholesale for the great variety of situations in respect to which the question arises. * * * The matter is essentially one to be worked out in particular situations and for particular types of cases. Whatever may be the general formulation, the essential requirement is that mere speculation be not allowed to do duty for probative facts, after making due allowance for all reasonably possible inferences favoring the party whose case is attacked. The mere difference in labels used to describe this standard * * * cannot amount to a departure from "the rules of the common law" which the Amendment requires to be followed. * * *

Id. at 389–95, 63 S.Ct. at 1086–89, 87 L.Ed. at 1470–73.

Justice Black, with whom Justices Douglas and Murphy concurred, wrote a dissenting opinion as follows:

> The Court here re-examines testimony offered in a common law suit, weighs conflicting evidence, and holds that the litigant may never take this case to a jury. * * * Today's decision marks a continuation of the gradual process of judicial erosion which in one hundred fifty years has slowly worn away a major portion of the essential guarantee of the Seventh Amendment.

I.

Alexander Hamilton in The Federalist emphasized his loyalty to the jury system in civil cases and declared that jury verdicts should be re-examined, if at all, only "by a second jury, either by remanding the cause to the court below for a second trial of the fact, or by directing an issue immediately out of the Supreme Court."

* * * The first Congress expected the Seventh Amendment to meet the objections of men like Patrick Henry to the Constitution itself. Henry, speaking in the Virginia Constitutional Convention, had expressed the general conviction of the people of the Thirteen States when he said, " * * * We are told that we are to part with that trial by jury with which our ancestors secured their lives and property. * * * I hope we shall never be induced, by such arguments, to part with that excellent mode of trial. No appeal can now be made as to fact in common law suits. *The unanimous verdict of impartial men cannot be reversed.*" * * *

* * *

As Hamilton had declared in The Federalist, the basic judicial control of the jury function was in the court's power to order a new trial. In 1830, this Court said: "The only modes known to the common law to re-examine such facts, are the granting of a new trial by the court where the issue was tried, or to which the record was properly returnable; or the award of a venire facias de novo, by an appellate court, for some error of law which intervened in the proceedings." Parsons v. Bedford, * * * 3 Pet. at page 448, 7 L.Ed. 732. * * *

A long step toward the determination of fact by judges instead of by juries was the invention of the directed verdict. In 1850, what seems to have been the first directed verdict case considered by this Court, Parks v. Ross, 11 How. 362, 374, 13 L.Ed. 730, was presented for decision. The Court held that the directed verdict serves the same purpose as the demurrer to the evidence, and that since there was "no evidence whatever" on the critical issue in the case, the directed verdict was approved. The decision was an innovation, a departure from the traditional rule restated only fifteen years before in Greenleaf v. Birth, 1835, 9 Pet. 292, 299, 9 L.Ed. 132, in which this Court had said: "Where there is no evidence tending to prove a particular fact, the court[s] are bound so to instruct the jury, when requested; but they cannot legally give any instruction which shall take from the jury the right of weighing the evidence and determining what effect it shall have."

This new device contained potentialities for judicial control of the jury which had not existed in the demurrer to the evidence. In the first place, demurring to the evidence was risky business, for in so doing the party not only admitted the truth of all the testimony against him but also all reasonable inferences which might be drawn from it; and upon joinder in demurrer the case was withdrawn from the jury while the court proceeded to give final judgment either for or against the demurrant. * * * Imposition of this risk was no mere technicality; for by making withdrawal of a case from the jury dangerous to the moving litigant's cause, the early law went far to assure that facts would never be examined except by a jury. * * * The litigant not only takes no risk by a motion for a directed verdict, but in making such a motion gives himself two opportunities to avoid the jury's decision; for under the federal variant of judgment notwithstanding the verdict, the judge may reserve opinion on the motion for a directed verdict and then give judgment for the moving party after the jury was formally found against him. In the second place, under the directed verdict practice the courts soon abandoned the "admission of all facts and reasonable inferences" standard referred to, and created the so-called "substantial evidence" rule which permitted directed verdicts even though there was far more evidence in the case than a plaintiff would have needed to withstand a demurrer.

The substantial evidence rule did not spring into existence immediately upon the adoption of the directed verdict device. For a few more years federal judges held to the traditional rule that juries might pass finally on facts if there was "any evidence" to support a party's contention. The rule that a case must go to the jury unless there was "no evidence" was completely repudiated in Schuylkill and Dauphin Improvement Co. v. Munson, 1871, 14 Wall. 442, 447, 448, 20 L.Ed. 867, upon which the Court today relies in part. There the Court declared that "some" evidence was not enough—there must be evidence sufficiently persuasive to the judge so that he thinks "a jury can properly proceed." The traditional rule was given an ugly name, "the scintilla rule", to hasten its demise. * * * The same transition from jury supremacy to jury subordination through judicial decisions took place in State courts.

Later cases permitted the development of added judicial control. * * * [J]ury verdicts on disputed facts have been set aside or directed verdicts authorized so regularly as to make the practice commonplace while the motion for directed verdict itself has become routine. * * * Today the Court comes dangerously close to weighing the credibility of a witness and rejecting his testimony because the majority do not believe it.

* * *

The call for the true application of the Seventh Amendment is not to words, but to the spirit of honest desire to see that Constitutional right preserved. Either the judge or the jury must decide facts and to the extent that we take this responsibility, we lessen the jury function. Our duty to preserve this one of the Bill of Rights may be peculiarly difficult, for here it is our own power which we must restrain. * * * As for myself, I believe that a verdict should be directed, if at all, only when, without weighing the credibility of the witnesses, there is in the evidence no room whatever for honest difference of opinion over the factual issue in controversy. * * *

* * *

Id. at 397–407, 63 S.Ct. at 1089–96, 87 L.Ed. 1474–81.

NEELY v. MARTIN K. EBY CONSTRUCTION CO., 386 U.S. 317, 87 S.Ct. 1072, 18 L.Ed.2d 75 (1967). Plaintiff brought a wrongful death action against defendant, claiming that defendant's negligent construction, maintenance, and supervision of a missile silo proximately caused the death of plaintiff's father, who died when he fell from a platform while working at the silo. At the close of plaintiff's case and again at the close of all the evidence, defendant moved unsuccessfully for a directed verdict. The jury returned a $25,000 verdict for plaintiff, and the trial judge entered judgment for plaintiff after denying defendant's Rule 50(b) motion or, alternatively, its motion for a new trial.

On appeal, the Court of Appeals for the Tenth Circuit found the evidence insufficient to establish negligence or proximate cause, and reversed the District Court's ruling on defendant's Rule 50(b) motion. Plaintiff appealed to the Supreme Court, arguing that she had had no opportunity to raise claims for a new trial, and therefore an appellate court could not dismiss the case without running afoul of the Seventh Amendment jury trial right. Justice White wrote:

> * * * The question here is whether the Court of Appeals, after reversing the denial of a defendant's Rule 50(b) motion * * *, may itself order dismissal or direct entry of judgment for defendant. As far as the Seventh Amendment's right to jury trial is concerned, there is no greater restriction on the province of the jury when an appellate court enters judgment n.o.v. than when a trial court does; consequently, there is no constitutional bar to an appellate court granting judgment n.o.v. * * *
>
> In our view, therefore, Rule 50(d) [now, Rule 50(e)] makes express and adequate provision for the opportunity—which the plaintiff-appellee had without this rule—to present his grounds for a new trial in the event his verdict is set aside by the court of appeals. If he does so in his brief—or in a petition for rehearing if the court of appeals has directed entry of judgment for appellant—the court of appeals may make final disposition of the issues presented, except those which in its informed discretion should be reserved for the trial court. If appellee presents no new trial issues in his brief or in a petition for rehearing, the court of appeals may, in any event, order a new trial on its own motion or refer the question to the district court, based on factors encountered in its own review of the case.

* * *

In the case before us, petitioner won a verdict in the District Court which survived respondent's n.o.v. motion. In the Court of Appeals the issue was the sufficiency of the evidence and that court set aside the verdict. Petitioner, as appellee, suggested no grounds for a new trial in the event her judgment was reversed, nor did she petition for rehearing in the Court of Appeals, even thought that court had directed a dismissal of her case. Neither was it suggested that the record was insufficient to present any new trial issues or that any other reason required a remand to the District Court. Indeed, in her brief in the Court of Appeals, petitioner stated, "this law suit was fairly tried and the jury was properly instructed." It was, of course, incumbent on the Court of Appeals to consider the new trial question in the light of its own experience with the case. But we will not assume that the court ignored its duty in this respect, although it would have been better had its opinion expressly dealt with the new trial question.

NOTE AND QUESTION

In WEISGRAM v. MARLEY CO., 528 U.S. 440, 120 S.Ct. 1011, 145 L.Ed.2d 958 (2000), a product liability action, plaintiff introduced expert testimony over defendant's objection and won a jury verdict. On appeal, the Eighth Circuit held that the District Court erred in admitting the expert testimony, and found that the remainder of the evidence in the record was insufficient to support the verdict. Under *Neely,* may the court of appeals instruct the entry of judgment as a matter of law for defendant, or must it remand the case? See Mollica, *Federal Summary Judgment at High Tide*, 84 Marq. L. Rev. 141, 205–06 (2000).

2. STANDARDS FOR MOTIONS FOR JUDGMENT AS A MATTER OF LAW (FORMERLY DIRECTED VERDICT AND JUDGMENT NOTWITHSTANDING THE VERDICT)

DENMAN v. SPAIN

Supreme Court of Mississippi, 1961.
242 Miss. 431, 135 So.2d 195.

LEE, PRESIDING JUSTICE.

Betty Denman, a minor, * * * sued * * * [the] executrix of the estate of Joseph A. Ross, deceased, to recover damages for personal injuries sustained by her, allegedly resulting from the negligence of the decedent in the operation of an automobile. The issue was submitted to a jury on the evidence for the plaintiff—no evidence being offered for the defendant—and there was a verdict and judgment for the plaintiff in the sum of $5,000. However, on motion of the defendant, a judgment *non obstante* *veredicto* * * * was sustained and entered. From that action, the plaintiff has appealed.

* * *

The appellant contends that the evidence offered by her, together with the reasonable inferences therefrom, was sufficient to make an issue for the jury as to whether the alleged negligence of the deceased driver, Ross, proximately caused or contributed to the collision and the consequent damage * * *.

A careful scrutiny and analysis of the evidence is therefore necessary:

Sunday, March 23, 1958, was a rainy, foggy day. About six o'clock that afternoon, at dusk, Mrs. Eva B. Denman, accompanied by her granddaughter, Betty, the plaintiff, was driving her Ford car southward on U.S. Highway 49E. At that time, Joseph A. Ross, accompanied by Miss Euna Tanner and Mrs. J.L. Haining, was driving his Plymouth car northward on said highway. Just south of the Town of Sumner, the cars collided. Mrs. Denman, Miss Tanner and Ross were killed. Betty, nearly seven years of age at the time, and Mrs. Haining were injured. Neither had any recollection of what had happened at the time of the collision. * * *

Plaintiff's father, Stuart Denman, who went to the scene shortly after the collision, described the situation substantially as follows: The Ford car was about seven yards off the paved surface on the east side in a bar pit "heading back towards the railroad track, which is in an easterly direction." The engine and transmission were on the opposite side of the road, out of the car and about fifty yards apart. The Plymouth was also on the east side, facing west, about fifteen yards north of the Ford.

No proof was offered as to skid marks, or other evidence to show the point of contact between these two vehicles. Eleven photographs of the damaged Plymouth, taken from various positions, and thirteen pictures of the damaged Ford, also taken from various positions, other than being mute evidence of a terrible tragedy, depict no reasonable or plausible explanation as to why this collision occurred, or who was responsible for it. * * *

Over objection by the defendant, John Barnett testified that he was driving a Dodge pickup north of [sic] highway 49E on his way to Tutwiler; that he was traveling at a speed of fifty or fifty-five miles per hour; that the Plymouth, which was in the wreck, passed him about three-fourths of a mile south of where the collision occurred, going at a speed of about seventy miles per hour; that when it passed, it got back in its lane, and neither wavered nor wobbled thereafter; that he followed and observed it for a distance of forty or fifty yards, and that it stayed in its proper lane as long as he saw it. Although another car was on the road ahead of him, he could have seen as far as the place of the accident except for the rain and fog.

Over objection by the defendant, Hal Buckley, a Negro man, testified that he was also traveling north on 49E on his way to Tutwiler at a speed of forty to fifty miles per hour. About two hundred yards south of the place where the collision occurred, a light green Plymouth, which he later saw at the scene of the accident, passed him at a speed of seventy-five or eighty miles an hour. He could see its taillights after it passed, and "he was just steady going; he wasn't doing no slowing up." He saw it until it ran into the other car. On cross-examination, he said that, after this car passed him, it got back on its side of the road, drove straight, and he did not notice that it ever went back over the center. Also on cross-examination, in an effort at impeachment, a part of the transcript in [an earlier] * * * trial [brought unsuccessfully against the estate of plaintiff's grandmother] containing this question and answer, was read to him as follows: "What do you estimate the speed of that car was when it passed you—the one that was going the same direction that you were?," and the answer was: "Well, I don't have no idea." * * * He then admitted that when the car passed him, it got back on its side and drove straight ahead, and that he could see the accident, but he could not tell anything about it or on which side of the road it happened. He also did not notice the other car, which came from the other direction.

Since Barnett did not see the car any more after it had gone forty or fifty yards beyond him, and his knowledge of speed was based on what he saw about three-fourths of a mile south of the place where the collision occurred, this evidence was inadmissible * * *. On the contrary, since Buckley testified the speed of this car, when it passed him, was seventy-five to eighty miles an hour and that it did not slow down in the remaining distance of two hundred yards before the collision, such evidence was competent and admissible * * *. The attempted impeachment went to its credibility and not its admissibility.

From this evidence, the plaintiff reasons that the jury could, and did, find that the Ross car was being operated, under inclement weather conditions, at an unlawful and negligent rate of speed, and that, if Ross had had his car under adequate and proper control, in all probability the collision could have been avoided. She voices the opinion that the physical facts, including the pictures of the wrecked vehicles, indicated that the Ford car was probably across the highway at an angle of perhaps forty-five degrees at the time of the collision.

But the testimony of Buckley showed only that the Plymouth was being operated at an excessive and negligent rate of speed. It otherwise showed that the car was in its proper lane. He did not notice it go over the center at any time, but it was driven straight down the road. No eyewitness claimed to have seen what happened. There was no evidence to indicate the place in the road where the vehicles came in contact with each other. There was no showing as to the speed of the Ford, whether fast or slow; or as to whether it was traveling on the right or wrong side of the road; or as to whether it slid or was suddenly driven to the wrong side of the road into the path of the Plymouth. The cars were so badly damaged that the pictures afford no reasonable explanation as to what person or persons were legally responsible for their condition. In other words, just how and why this grievous tragedy occurred is completely shrouded in mystery.

The burden was on the plaintiff to prove by a preponderance of the evidence, not only that the operator of the Plymouth was guilty of negligence but also that such negligence proximately caused or contributed to the collision and consequent damage. By the use of metaphysical learning, speculation and conjecture, one may reach several possible conclusions as to how the accident occurred. However such conclusions could only be classed as possibilities; and this Court has many times held that verdicts cannot be based on possibilities. At all events, there is no sound or reasonable basis upon which a jury or this Court can say that the plaintiff met that burden.

The judgment must be affirmed.

Affirmed.

NOTES AND QUESTIONS

1. At this point I am going to say something which you may find very shocking. [The judge] * * * is supposed to submit an issue to the jury if, as the judges say, the jury can decide reasonably either way. But to say that I can decide an issue of fact reasonably either way is to say, I submit, that I cannot, by the exercise of reason, decide the question. That means that the issue which we typically submit to juries is an issue which the jury cannot decide by the exercise of its reason.

   The decision of an issue of fact in cases of closely balanced probabilities, therefore, must, in the nature of things, be an emotional rather than a rational act * * *.

Michael, *The Basic Rules of Pleading*, 5 Record of N.Y.C.B.A. 175, 199–200 (1950). Do you agree with Professor Michael? What is the relevance of this comment to the opinion in the *Denman* case?

2. Do you believe a jury properly could have found for plaintiff in the *Denman* case? What inferences would have to be drawn from the evidence to reach such a conclusion? How would you support the proposition that these inferences reasonably could be found to be stronger than other inferences that would not lead to a verdict for plaintiff?

3. Is the *Denman* case contrary to Lavender v. Kurn, p. 57, supra? In PLANTERS MANUFACTURING. CO. v. PROTECTION MUTUAL INSURANCE CO., 380 F.2d 869 (5th Cir.1967), the Court of Appeals concluded that the two cases are inconsistent, and thus had to confront squarely the question whether a state standard for directing a verdict is controlling under *Erie,* a question the United States Supreme Court has found unnecessary to answer in two cases that raised it. Dick v. New York Life Ins. Co., 359 U.S. 437, 79 S.Ct. 921, 3 L.Ed.2d 935 (1959), and Mercer v. Theriot, 377 U.S. 152, 84 S.Ct. 1157, 12 L.Ed.2d 206 (1964). To what extent, if any, does Gasperini v. Center for Humanities, Inc., p. 454, supra, help settle the dispute? For a discussion of

this and related jury issues, see Woolhandler & Collins, *The Article III Jury*, 87 Va. L. Rev. 587, 694–96 (2001).

4. Cases like *Denman,* which involve head-on vehicular collisions, present a difficult problem with regard to the control of jury verdicts. The circumstances of these collisions ordinarily suggest that at least one driver was negligent but may not indicate which driver it was, and direct evidence often is lacking because all witnesses are dead. See Annot., 77 A.L.R.2d 580 (1961). Can you suggest a solution to the problem?

5. In KIRCHER v. ATCHISON, TOPEKA & SANTA FE RY. CO., 32 Cal.2d 176, 195 P.2d 427 (1948), plaintiff sued for the loss of a hand, which had been run over by defendant's train. A judgment for plaintiff was affirmed. Justice Carter, for the court, said:

> * * * In the light of all the circumstances * * * it cannot be held as a matter of law, that plaintiff's version was such as to contravene the laws of nature, or as to render the jury's acceptance of it unreasonable. * * * Although he stated quite frankly that he was unable to explain with certainty the manner in which his left hand came to be placed on the east rail * * *, the jury had before it evidence indicating that * * * there was a hole in the depot platform * * * and the ultimate fact that defendant's train ran over his hand at the time and place in question. In these circumstances the jury was not compelled to find against him because he could not with certainty relate the exact manner in which his left hand came to be on the east rail. It could reasonably have inferred that his failure to explain this circumstance was due to the fact that in the critical few minutes he was under the train he was unconscious, or substantially so, from the blow on his head as the outcome of stepping into the hole.

Id. at 184, 195 P.2d at 433.

Justice Traynor, dissenting, said:

> It is my opinion that although the accident as described by plaintiff is not outside the realm of possibility, his version, which is that of an interested and impeached witness, involves so extraordinary and improbable a sequence of events that without corroboration it does not warrant belief by a reasonable jury.

Id. at 189, 195 P.2d at 436.

Does the *Kircher* case present the same kind of issue as the *Denman* case? Should a verdict ever be directed for the party having the burden of producing evidence on an issue when the evidence in that party's favor is testimonial rather than documentary? Hearsay evidence sometimes is excluded on objection because it is not regarded as a reliable basis for a jury's decision. If hearsay evidence comes in without objection, and the party against whom that evidence militates subsequently moves for a directed verdict, should the hearsay evidence be taken into account in determining whether there is sufficient evidence to support a jury verdict for the other party?

ROGERS v. MISSOURI PACIFIC RAILROAD CO.

Supreme Court of the United States, 1957.
352 U.S. 500, 77 S.Ct. 443, 1 L.Ed.2d 493.

Certiorari to the Supreme Court of Missouri.

MR. JUSTICE BRENNAN delivered the opinion of the Court.

A jury in the Circuit Court of St. Louis awarded damages to the petitioner in this action under the Federal Employers' Liability Act. The Supreme Court of Missouri reversed upon the ground that the petitioner's evidence did not support the finding of respondent's liability. * * *

Petitioner was a laborer in a section gang, working on July 17, 1951, along a portion of respondent's double-track line which, near Garner, Arkansas, runs generally north and south. The tracks are on ballast topping the surface of a dirt "dump" with sloping sides, and there is a path about a yard wide bordering each side of the surface between the crest of the slope and the edge of the ballast. Weeds and vegetation, killed chemically preparatory to burning them off, covered the paths and slopes. Petitioner's foreman assigned him to burn off the weeds and vegetation—the first time he was given that task in the two months he had worked for the respondent. He testified that it was customary to burn off such vegetation with a flame thrower operated from a car running on the tracks. Railroad witnesses testified, however, that the respondent discontinued the use of flame throwers at least a year earlier because the fires started by them sometimes spread beyond the railroad right of way.

Petitioner was supplied with a crude hand torch and was instructed to burn off the weeds and vegetation along the west path and for two or three feet down the west slope. The events leading to his mishap occurred after he proceeded with the work to a point within thirty to thirty-five yards of a culvert adjoining the path.

Petitioner testified, without contradiction, that the foreman instructed him and other members of the section gang to stop what they were doing when a train passed and to take positions off the tracks and ties to observe the journals of the passing train for hot boxes. The instructions were explicit not to go on either of the tracks or to stand on or near the ends of the ties when a train was passing on a far track. This was a safety precaution because "the sound of one train would deaden the sound of another one that possibly would come from the other way."

On this day, petitioner heard the whistle of a train which was approaching from behind him on the east track. He promptly "quit firing" and ran north to a place on the path near the mentioned culvert. He was standing a few feet from the culvert observing the train for hotboxes when he became enveloped in smoke and flames. The passing train had fanned the flames of the burning vegetation and weeds, carrying the fire to the vegetation around his position. He threw his arm over his face, retreated quickly back on the culvert and slipped and fell from the top of the culvert, suffering the serious injuries for which he sought damages in this suit.

* * *

We think that the evidence was sufficient to support the jury finding for the petitioner. The testimony that the burning off of weeds and vegetation was ordinarily done with flame throwers from cars on the tracks and not, as here, by a workman on foot using a crude hand torch, when that evidence is considered with the uncontradicted testimony that the petitioner was where he was on this narrow path atop the dirt "dump" in furtherance of explicit orders * * *, supplied ample support for a jury finding that respondent's negligence played a part in the petitioner's injury. These were probative facts from which the jury could find that respondent was or should have been aware of conditions which created a likelihood that petitioner, in performing the duties required of him, would suffer just such an injury as he did. Common experience teaches both that a passing train will fan the flames of a fire, and that a person suddenly enveloped in flames and smoke will instinctively react by retreating from the danger and in the process pay scant heed to other dangers which may imperil him. In this view, it was an irrelevant consideration whether the immediate reason for his slipping off the culvert was the presence of gravel negligently allowed by respondent to remain on the surface, or was some cause not identified from the evidence.

The Missouri Supreme Court based its reversal upon its finding of an alleged admission by the petitioner that he knew it was his primary duty to watch the fire. From that premise the Missouri court reasoned that petitioner was inattentive to the fire and that the emergency which confronted him "was an emergency brought about by himself." It said that if, as petitioner testified, the immediate cause of his fall was that loose gravel on the surface of the culvert rolled out from under him, yet it was his inattention to the fire which caused it to spread and obliged petitioner "to move blindly away and fall," and this was "something extraordinary, unrelated to, and disconnected from the incline of the gravel at the culvert."

We interpret the foregoing to mean that the Missouri court found as a matter of law that the petitioner's conduct was the sole cause of his mishap. But when the petitioner agreed that his primary duty was to watch the fire he did not also say that he was relieved of the duty to stop to watch a passing train for hotboxes. Indeed, no witness testified that the instruction was countermanded. At best, uncertainty as to the fact arises from the petitioner's testimony, and in that circumstance not the court, but the jury, was the tribunal to determine the fact.

We may assume that the jury could properly have reached the court's conclusion. But, as the probative facts also supported with reason the verdict favorable to the petitioner, the decision was exclusively for the jury to make. The jury was instructed to return a verdict for the respondent if it was found that negligence of the petitioner was the sole cause of his mishap. We must take it that the verdict was obedient to the trial judge's charge and that the jury found that such was not the case but that petitioner's injury resulted at least in part from the respondent's negligence.

The opinion may also be read as basing the reversal on another ground, namely, that it appeared to the court that the petitioner's conduct was at least as probable a cause for his mishap as any negligence of the respondent, and that in such case there was no case for the jury. But that would mean that there is no jury question in actions under this statute, although the employee's proofs support with reason a verdict in his favor, unless the judge can say that the jury may exclude the idea that his injury was due to causes with which the defendant was not connected, or, stated another way, unless his proofs are so strong that the jury, on grounds of probability, may exclude a conclusion favorable to the defendant. That is not the governing principle defining the proof which requires a submission to the jury in these cases. The Missouri court's opinion implies its view that this is the governing standard by saying that the proofs must show that "the injury would not have occurred but for the negligence" of his employer, and that "[t]he test of whether there is causal connection is that, absent the negligent act the injury would not have occurred." * * *

Under this statute the test of a jury case is simply whether the proofs justify with reason the conclusion that employer negligence played any part, even the slightest, in producing the injury or death for which damages are sought. It does not matter that, from the evidence, the jury may also with reason, on grounds of probability, attribute the result to other causes, including the employee's contributory negligence. Judicial appraisal of the proofs to determine whether a jury question is presented is narrowly limited to the single inquiry whether, with reason, the conclusion may be drawn that negligence of the employer played any part at all in the injury or death. Judges are to fix their sights primarily to make that appraisal and, if that test is met, are bound to find that a case for the jury is made out whether or not the evidence allows the jury a choice of other probabilities. The statute expressly imposes liability upon the employer to pay damages for injury or death due "in whole or *in part*" to its negligence. (Emphasis added.)

* * *

The Congress when adopting the law was particularly concerned that the issues whether there was employer fault and whether that fault played any part in the injury or death of the employee should be decided by the jury whenever fair-minded men could reach these conclusions on the evidence. Originally, judicial administration of the 1908 Act substantially limited the cases in which employees were allowed a jury determination. That was because the courts developed concepts of assumption of risk and of the coverage of the law, which defeated employee claims as a matter of law. Congress corrected this by the 1939 amendments and removed the fetters which hobbled the full play of the basic congressional intention to leave to the fact-finding function of the jury the decision of the primary question raised in these cases—whether employer fault played any part in the employee's mishap. * * *

The judgment is reversed. * * *

MR. JUSTICE BURTON concurs in the result.

MR. JUSTICE REED would affirm the judgment of the Supreme Court of Missouri.

[Dissenting opinions of JUSTICE FRANKFURTER and JUSTICE HARLAN are omitted.]

NOTES AND QUESTIONS

1. Is the nature of the issue that the Court said should have been left to the jury in *Rogers* different from that in *Lavender, Denman,* and *Kircher?* If so, is the difference significant to the formulation of a standard? Might a judgment as a matter of law be sustained more readily on one type of issue than the other?

2. A municipal ordinance permitted an authorized emergency vehicle to proceed past a stop signal or exceed the speed limit "when the driver of such vehicle sounds a siren, bell or exhaust whistle to the extent reasonably necessary." A police car in rush-hour traffic, on call to a robbery then in progress, proceeded at excessive speed through a red light, and struck plaintiff. In LO CICERO v. COLUMBIA CASUALTY CO., 268 F.2d 440 (5th Cir.), certiorari denied 361 U.S. 917, 80 S.Ct. 261, 4 L.Ed.2d 187 (1959), the court held that the jury should have been instructed that the policeman was negligent as a matter of law in failing to sound the siren. Is this distinguishable from entering a judgment as a matter of law on the issue of negligence when no statute is involved?

3. For a criticism of *Galloway* and other Supreme Court cases upholding procedures that affect the jury trial right, see Thomas, *The Seventh Amendment, Modern Procedure, and the English Common Law*, 82 Wash. U.L.Q. 687 (2004).

The Supreme Court denied certiorari in two cases involving the nature of the evidence to be considered when deciding whether a judgment as a matter of law is appropriate. Schwimmer dba Supersonic Electronics Co. v. Sony Corp., and Venture Technology, Inc. v. National Fuel Gas Distribution Corp., 459 U.S. 1007, 103 S.Ct. 362, 74 L.Ed.2d 398 (1982). Justice White dissented from the denial of certiorari as follows:

> [A conflict in the Circuits concerns] * * * the portion of the evidence a court is to consider in ruling upon a motion for judgment notwithstanding the verdict. These cases indicated that it is the Second Circuit's practice to examine all of the evidence in a manner most favorable to the non-moving party. This is also the position of at least

the Fifth and Seventh Circuits. * * * In the Eighth Circuit, however, it appears that only evidence which supports the verdict winner is to be considered. * * * The first and Third Circuits follow a middle ground: the reviewing court may consider uncontradicted, unimpeached evidence from disinterested witnesses.* * * Thus, the Federal Courts of Appeals follow three different approaches to determining whether evidence is sufficient to create a jury issue. * * * Because the scope of review will often be influential, if not dispositive of a motion for judgment n.o.v., this disagreement among the Federal courts of Appeals is of far more than academic interest.

Consider this disagreement as you read the decision that follows.

REEVES v. SANDERSON PLUMBING PRODUCTS, INC.

Supreme Court of the United States, 2000.
530 U.S. 133, 120 S.Ct. 2097, 147 L.Ed.2d 105.

Certiorari to the United States Court of Appeals for the Fifth Circuit.

JUSTICE O'CONNOR delivered the opinion of the Court.

This case concerns the kind and amount of evidence necessary to sustain a jury's verdict that an employer unlawfully discriminated on the basis of age. Specifically, we must resolve whether a defendant is entitled to judgment as a matter of law when the plaintiff's case consists exclusively of a prima facie case of discrimination and sufficient evidence for the trier of fact to disbelieve the defendant's legitimate, nondiscriminatory explanation for its action. * * *

I

[Petitioner was 57–years–old and had been employed for forty years by respondent as an attendance monitor in a production department known as the "Hinge Room." Petitioner's supervisor found that "production was down" in the Hinge Room, and believed that workers were often absent or leaving early, but these practices were not recorded in the attendance records maintained by petitioner. The supervisor investigated petitioner's work practices, recommended that he be fired, and the company acted on that recommendation. Petitioner then filed suit in the Northern District of Mississippi contending that he had been fired on the basis of his age in violation of the Age Discrimination in Employment Act of 1967.]

* * * At trial, respondent contended that it had fired petitioner due to his failure to maintain accurate attendance records, while petitioner attempted to demonstrate that respondent's explanation was pretext for age discrimination. * * * Petitioner introduced evidence that he had accurately recorded the attendance and hours of the employees under his supervision, and that [his supervisor] * * * [who was described by anoth-

er witness] as wielding "absolute power" within the company, * * * had demonstrated age-based animus in his dealings with petitioner. * * *

During the trial, the District Court twice denied oral motions by respondent for judgment as a matter of law under [Federal] Rule 50 * * *, and the case went to the jury. * * * The court instructed the jury that "[i]f the plaintiff fails to prove age was a determinative or motivating factor in the decision to terminate him, then your verdict shall be for the defendant." * * * So charged, the jury returned a verdict in favor of petitioner, * * *.

The Court of Appeals for the Fifth Circuit reversed, holding that petitioner had not introduced sufficient evidence to sustain the jury's finding of unlawful discrimination. * * * After noting respondent's proffered justification for petitioner's discharge, the court acknowledged that petitioner "very well may" have offered sufficient evidence for "a reasonable jury [to] have found that [respondent's] explanation for its employment decision was pretextual." * * * The court explained, however, that this was "not dispositive" of the ultimate issue—namely, "whether Reeves presented sufficient evidence that his age motivated [respondent's] employment decision." * * * Addressing this question, the court weighed petitioner's additional evidence of discrimination against other circumstances surrounding his discharge. * * * Specifically, the court noted that * * * [the supervisor's] age-based comments "were not made in the direct context of Reeves's termination"; there was no allegation that the two other individuals who had recommended that petitioner be fired * * * were motivated by age; two of the decisionmakers involved in petitioner's discharge * * * were over the age of 50; all three of the Hinge Room supervisors were accused of inaccurate recordkeeping; and several of respondent's management positions were filled by persons over age 50 when petitioner was fired. * * * On this basis, the court concluded that petitioner had not introduced sufficient evidence for a rational jury to conclude that he had been discharged because of his age. * * *

* * *

II

Under the ADEA, it is "unlawful for an employer . . . to fail or refuse to hire or to discharge any individual or otherwise discriminate against any individual with respect to his compensation, terms, conditions, or privileges of employment, because of such individual's age." * * *. When a plaintiff alleges disparate treatment, "liability depends on whether the protected trait (under the ADEA, age) actually motivated the employer's decision." * * * That is, the plaintiff's age must have "actually played a role in [the employer's decisionmaking] process and had a determinative influence on the outcome." * * *

* * * [In age discrimination cases, the Courts of Appeals generally first require the plaintiff to establish a prima facia case of discrimination, and then the burden of production shifts to the defendant to present

evidence supporting a legitimate, nondiscriminatory reason for the job action. Petitioner satisfied this burden, and the burden shifted to respondent.] Respondent met this burden by offering admissible evidence sufficient for the trier of fact to conclude that petitioner was fired because of his failure to maintain accurate attendance records. * * * Accordingly, * * * the sole remaining issue was "discrimination *vel non,*" * * *.

Although intermediate evidentiary burdens shift back and forth under this framework, "[t]he ultimate burden of persuading the trier of fact that the defendant intentionally discriminated against the plaintiff remains at all times with the plaintiff." * * * And in attempting to satisfy this burden, the plaintiff—once the employer produces sufficient evidence to support a nondiscriminatory explanation for its decision—must be afforded the "opportunity to prove by a preponderance of the evidence that the legitimate reasons offered by the defendant were not its true reasons, but were a pretext for discrimination." * * * That is, the plaintiff may attempt to establish that he was the victim of intentional discrimination "by showing that the employer's proffered explanation is unworthy of credence." * * * Moreover, although the presumption of discrimination "drops out of the picture" once the defendant meets its burden of production, * * * the trier of fact may still consider the evidence establishing the plaintiff's prima facie case "and inferences properly drawn therefrom ... [omission in original] on the issue of whether the defendant's explanation is pretextual," * * *.

In this case, the evidence supporting respondent's explanation for petitioner's discharge consisted primarily of testimony by [the supervisor and others] * * * of petitioner's alleged "shoddy record keeping." * * *

Petitioner, however, made a substantial showing that respondent's explanation was false. First, petitioner offered evidence that he had properly maintained the attendance records. Most of the timekeeping errors cited by respondent involved employees who were not marked late but who were recorded as having arrived at the plant at 7 a.m. for the 7 a.m. shift. * * * Respondent contended that employees arriving at 7 a.m. could not have been at their workstations by 7 a.m., and therefore must have been late. * * * But both petitioner and * * * [another witness] testified that the company's automated timeclock often failed to scan employees' timecards, so that the timesheets would not record any time of arrival. * * * On these occasions, petitioner and * * * [the other witness] would visually check the workstations and record whether the employees were present at the start of the shift. * * * They stated that if an employee arrived promptly but the timesheet contained no time of arrival, they would reconcile the two by marking "7 a.m." as the employee's arrival time, even if the employee actually arrived at the plant earlier. * * * On cross-examination, [the supervisor] * * * acknowledged that the timeclock sometimes malfunctioned, and that if "people were there at their work station[s]" at the start of the shift, the supervisor "would write in seven o'clock." * * * Petitioner also testified that when employees arrived before or stayed after their shifts, he would assign them additional work so they would not be overpaid. * * *

Petitioner similarly cast doubt on whether he was responsible for any failure to discipline late and absent employees. Petitioner testified that his job only included reviewing the daily and weekly attendance reports, and that disciplinary writeups were based on the monthly reports, which were reviewed by [a different employee.] * * * [The company admitted that petitioner was not responsible for disciplining employees, and conceded that there had never been a union grievance or employee complaint about petitioner's recordkeeping, and there was testimony about the absence of overpayments.]

Based on this evidence, the Court of Appeals concluded that petitioner "very well may be correct" that "a reasonable jury could have found that [respondent's] explanation for its employment decision was pretextual." * * * Nonetheless, the court held that this showing, standing alone, was insufficient to sustain the jury's finding of liability: "We must, as an essential final step, determine whether Reeves presented sufficient evidence that his age motivated [respondent's] employment decision." * * * And in making this determination, the Court of Appeals ignored the evidence supporting petitioner's prima facie case and challenging respondent's explanation for its decision. * * * The court confined its review of evidence favoring petitioner to that evidence showing that * * * [the supervisor] had directed derogatory, age-based comments at petitioner, and that * * * [the supervisor] had singled out petitioner for harsher treatment than younger employees. * * * It is therefore apparent that the court believed that only this additional evidence of discrimination was relevant to whether the jury's verdict should stand. That is, the Court of Appeals proceeded from the assumption that a prima facie case of discrimination, combined with sufficient evidence for the trier of fact to disbelieve the defendant's legitimate, nondiscriminatory reason for its decision, is insufficient as a matter of law to sustain a jury's finding of intentional discrimination.

In so reasoning, the Court of Appeals misconceived the evidentiary burden borne by plaintiffs who attempt to prove intentional discrimination through indirect evidence. * * * [T]he factfinder's rejection of the employer's legitimate, nondiscriminatory reason for its action does not *compel* judgment for the plaintiff. * * *

* * * [H]owever, * * * it is *permissible* for the trier of fact to infer the ultimate fact of discrimination from the falsity of the employer's explanation. * * *

Proof that the defendant's explanation is unworthy of credence is simply one form of circumstantial evidence that is probative of intentional discrimination, and it may be quite persuasive. * * * In appropriate circumstances, the trier of fact can reasonably infer from the falsity of the explanation that the employer is dissembling to cover up a discriminatory purpose. * * * Moreover, once the employer's justification has been eliminated, discrimination may well be the most likely alternative explanation, especially since the employer is in the best position to put forth the actual reason for its decision. * * * Thus, a plaintiff's prima facie case, combined with sufficient evidence to find that the employer's asserted justification is false, may permit the trier of fact to conclude that the employer unlawfully discriminated.

This is not to say that such a showing by the plaintiff will *always* be adequate to sustain a jury's finding of liability. Certainly there will be instances where, although the plaintiff has established a prima facie case and set forth sufficient evidence to reject the defendant's explanation, no rational factfinder could conclude that the action was discriminatory. For instance, an employer would be entitled to judgment as a matter of law if the record conclusively revealed some other, nondiscriminatory reason for the employer's decision, or if the plaintiff created only a weak issue of fact as to whether the employer's reason was untrue and there was abundant and uncontroverted independent evidence that no discrimination had occurred. * * *

Whether judgment as a matter of law is appropriate in any particular case will depend on a number of factors. Those include the strength of the plaintiff's prima facie case, the probative value of the proof that the employer's explanation is false, and any other evidence that supports the employer's case and that properly may be considered on a motion for judgment as a matter of law. * * * For purposes of this case, we need not—and could not—resolve all of the circumstances in which such factors would entitle an employer to judgment as a matter of law. It suffices to say that, because a prima facie case and sufficient evidence to reject the employer's explanation may permit a finding of liability, the Court of Appeals erred in proceeding from the premise that a plaintiff must always introduce additional, independent evidence of discrimination.

III

A

The remaining question is whether, despite the Court of Appeals' misconception of petitioner's evidentiary burden, respondent was nonetheless entitled to judgment as a matter of law [under Federal Rule 50]. * * * The Courts of Appeals have articulated differing formulations as to what evidence a court is to consider in ruling on a Rule 50 motion. * * * Some decisions have stated that review is limited to that evidence favorable to the nonmoving party, * * * while most have held that review extends to the entire record, drawing all reasonable inferences in favor of the nonmovant, * * *.

On closer examination, this conflict seems more semantic than real. Those decisions holding that review under Rule 50 should be limited to evidence favorable to the nonmovant appear to have their genesis in *Wilkerson v. McCarthy,* 336 U.S. 53, 69 S.Ct. 413, 93 L.Ed. 497 (1949). * * * In *Wilkerson,* we stated that "in passing upon whether there is sufficient evidence to submit an issue to the jury we need look only to the evidence and reasonable inferences which tend to support the case of" the nonmoving party. * * * But subsequent decisions have clarified that this passage was referring to the evidence to which the trial court should *give credence,* not the evidence that the court should *review.* In the analogous context of summary judgment under Rule 56, we have stated that the court must review the record "taken as a whole." *Matsushita* * * * [, p. 986, supra]. And the standard for granting summary judgment "mirrors" the standard for judgment as a matter of law, such that "the inquiry under each is the same." *Anderson v. Liberty Lobby* * * * [, p. 984, supra]; see also *Celotex* * * *[, p. 973, supra]. It therefore follows that, in entertaining a motion for judgment as a matter of law, the court should review all of the evidence in the record.

In doing so, however, the court must draw all reasonable inferences in favor of the nonmoving party, and it may not make credibility determinations or weigh the evidence. * * *. "Credibility determinations, the weighing of the evidence, and the drawing of legitimate inferences from the facts are jury functions, not those of a judge." * * * Thus, although the court should review the record as a whole, it must disregard all evidence favorable to the moving party that the jury is not required to believe. See [9a Wright & Miller, Federal Practice and Procedure: Civil 2d § 2529, at] 299. That is, the court should give credence to the evidence favoring the nonmovant as well as that "evidence supporting the moving party that is uncontradicted and unimpeached, at least to the extent that that evidence comes from disinterested witnesses." Id. at 300.

B

Applying this standard here, it is apparent that respondent was not entitled to judgment as a matter of law. In this case, in addition to establishing a prima facie case of discrimination and creating a jury issue as to the falsity of the employer's explanation, petitioner introduced additional evidence that * * * [the supervisor] was motivated by age-based animus and was principally responsible for petitioner's firing. Petitioner testified that * * * [the supervisor] had told him that he "was so old [he] must have come over on the Mayflower" and, on one occasion when petitioner was having difficulty starting a machine, that he "was too damn old to do [his] job." * * * According to petitioner, * * * [the supervisor] would regularly "cuss at me and shake his finger in my face." * * * [Another witness], roughly 24 years younger than petitioner, corroborated that there was an "obvious difference" in how * * * [the supervisor] treated them. * * * Petitioner also demonstrated that, according to company records, he and [another employee responsible for monitoring attendance] had nearly identical rates of productivity in 1993. * * * Yet respondent conducted an efficiency study of * * * petitioner, and placed only petitioner on probation. * * *

Further, petitioner introduced evidence that [the supervisor] was the actual decisionmaker behind his firing. * * *

* * * Again, the court disregarded critical evidence favorable to petitioner * * *. The court also failed to draw all reasonable inferences in favor of petitioner. For instance, while acknowledging "the potentially damning nature" of * * * [the supervisor's] age-related comments, the court discounted them on the ground that they "were not made in the direct context of Reeves's termination." * * * And the court discredited petitioner's evidence that * * * [the supervisor] was the actual decision-maker by giving weight to the fact that there was "no evidence to suggest that any of the other decision makers were motivated by age." * * * In concluding that these circumstances so overwhelmed the evidence favoring petitioner that no rational trier of fact could have found that petitioner was fired because of his age, the Court of Appeals impermissibly substituted its judgment concerning the weight of the evidence for the jury's.

* * * Given the evidence in the record supporting petitioner, we see no reason to subject the parties to an additional round of litigation before the Court of Appeals rather than to resolve the matter here. * * * Given that petitioner established a prima facie case of discrimination, introduced enough evidence for the jury to reject respondent's explanation, and produced additional evidence of age-based animus, there was sufficient evidence for the jury to find that respondent had intentionally discriminated. The District Court was therefore correct to submit the case to the jury, and the Court of Appeals erred in overturning its verdict.

For these reasons, the judgment of the Court of Appeals is reversed.

It is so ordered.

[A concurring opinion of JUSTICE GINSBURG is omitted.]

NOTES AND QUESTIONS

1. Does *Reeves* adequately answer Justice White's concern? What standard did the *Reeves* Court adopt?

2. Suppose the issue is whether defendant paid plaintiff $100 that was owed to the latter. Plaintiff is dead, and the lawsuit is brought by plaintiff's estate. Defendant is the only witness in the case and testified that she paid. Defendant moves for a judgment as a matter of law. Suppose defendant has the burden of persuasion. Will the motion be granted? Now suppose, instead, that plaintiff has the burden. Can plaintiff get to the jury solely on the possibility that the jury could disbelieve the other side's witnesses?

3. How might *Reeves* affect summary judgment? Would it ever be appropriate for the court to rest summary judgment against plaintiff on an affidavit from the corporate defendant's chief operating officer that the company did not engage in any of the alleged statutory violations? See Mollica, *Federal Summary Judgment at High Tide*, 84 Marq. L. Rev. 141, 207 (2000). See also Childress, *Taking Jury Verdicts Seriously*, 54 SMU L. Rev. 1739 (2001). Can a court revisit the strength of plaintiff's prima facie case and decide that the evidence is not strong enough to avoid summary judgment? See Hayes, *That Pernicious Pop–Up, the Prima Facie Case*, 39 Suffolk U. L. Rev. 343 (2006).

3. THE MOTION FOR JUDGMENT AS A MATTER OF LAW AFTER THE VERDICT (J.N.O.V.)

Why is there a need for a judgment as a matter of law after the jury has rendered its verdict? If a case has not been made during the presentation of the evidence, shouldn't the court have dismissed the case without submission to the jury? In fact, it is extremely rare that a court will grant a motion for judgment as a matter of law at the end of all of the evidence. Instead it will wait until after the jury has made its decision. Why is this so? In this context consider the situation if the trial judge is held to be incorrect in granting the motion and the appellate court reverses. What is the posture of the case at that point? Do the same considerations obtain when the court grants such a motion at an earlier time, e.g., at the end of the plaintiff's case?

BALTIMORE & CAROLINA LINE, INC. v. REDMAN, 295 U.S. 654, 656, 658–60, 55 S.Ct. 890, 891–93, 79 L.Ed. 1636, 1637–40 (1935) (opinion by Justice Van Devanter):

This was an action in a federal court in New York to recover damages for personal injuries allegedly sustained by the plaintiff through the defendant's negligence. The issues were tried before the court and a jury. At the conclusion of the evidence, the defendant moved for a dismissal of the complaint because the evidence was insufficient to support a verdict for the plaintiff, and also moved for a directed verdict in its favor on the same ground. The court reserved its decision on both motions, submitted the case to the jury subject to its opinion on the questions reserved, and received from the jury a verdict for the plaintiff. No objection was made to the reservation or this mode of proceeding. Thereafter the court held the evidence sufficient and the motions ill grounded, and accordingly entered a judgment for the plaintiff on the verdict.

The defendant appealed to the Circuit Court of Appeals, which held the evidence insufficient and reversed the judgment with a direction for a new trial. The defendant urged that the direction be for a dismissal of the complaint. But the Court of Appeals ruled that under our decision in Slocum v. New York Life Insurance Company [228 U.S. 364, 33 S.Ct. 523, 57 L.Ed. 879] the direction must be for a new trial. * * *

In Slocum * * * a jury trial in a federal court resulted in a general verdict for the plaintiff over the defendant's request that a verdict for it be directed. Judgment was entered on the verdict for the plaintiff and the defendant obtained a review in the court of appeals. That court examined the evidence, concluded that it was insufficient to support the verdict, and on that basis reversed the judgment given to the plaintiff on the verdict, and directed that judgment be entered for the defendant. The question presented to us was whether, in the situation disclosed, the direction for a judgment for the defendant was an infraction of the Seventh Amendment. We held it was and that the direction should be for a new trial.

It therefore is important to have in mind the situation to which our ruling applied. In that case the defendant's request for a directed verdict was denied without any reservation of the question of the sufficiency of the evidence or of any other matter; and the verdict for the plaintiff was taken unconditionally, and not subject to the court's opinion on the sufficiency of the evidence. * * *

A very different situation is disclosed in the present case. The trial court expressly reserved its ruling on the defendant's motions to dismiss and for a directed verdict, both of which were based on the asserted insufficiency of the evidence to support a verdict for the plaintiff. Whether the evidence was sufficient or otherwise was a question of law to be resolved by the court. The verdict for the plaintiff was taken pending the court's rulings on the motions and subject to those rulings. No objection was made to the reservation or this mode of proceeding, and they must be regarded as having the tacit consent of the parties. * * *

At common law there was a well-established practice of reserving questions of law arising during trials by jury and of taking verdicts subject to the ultimate ruling on the questions reserved; and under this practice the reservation carried with it authority to make such ultimate disposition of the case as might be made essential by the ruling under the reservation, such as nonsuiting the plaintiff where he had obtained a verdict, entering a verdict or judgment for one party where the jury had given a verdict to the other, or making other essential adjustments.

Fragmentary references to the origin and basis of the practice indicate that it came to be supported on the theory that it gave better opportunity for considered rulings, made new trials less frequent, and commanded such general approval that parties litigant assented to its application as a matter of course. But whatever may have been its origin or theoretical basis, it undoubtedly was well established when the Seventh Amendment was adopted, and therefore must be regarded as a part of the common-law rules to which resort must be had in testing and measuring the right of trial by jury as preserved and protected by that amendment.

NOTES AND QUESTIONS

1. Note that the Seventh Amendment provides that "no fact tried by a jury, shall be otherwise re-examined in any Court of the United States, other than according to the rules of the common law." It was in that regard that the Supreme Court in SLOCUM v. NEW YORK LIFE INSURANCE CO., 228 U.S. 364, 33 S.Ct. 523, 57 L.Ed. 879 (1913), held that once the trial court has denied a defendant's directed verdict motion and allowed the case to go to the jury, the court could not order a judgment contrary to the jury verdict, but could only order a new trial. In *Redman,* the Court distinguished *Slocum* because the judge had reserved ruling on the directed verdict, so that the jury

verdict was taken subject to his decision on the motion. Note that since the adoption of the Federal Rules, this procedure no longer is necessary. Under Rule 50(b), even if a preverdict motion for judgment as a matter of law is denied, there is an automatic reservation of decision by the court.

2. Initially, Rule 50(b) appeared to authorize a court to grant a motion for judgment as a matter of law after a jury verdict only if a motion for a directed verdict had been made "at the close of all of the evidence." Some courts had read this strictly to bar the later motion if the motion for a directed verdict had originally been made only at the end of the plaintiff's case. The current Rule 50(a)(1) would allow a renewed motion for judgment as a matter of law on an issue so long as the initial motion was made after the party against whom it was requested had "been fully heard" on the issue during the trial. It is important to note that a party has ten days after an adverse verdict to file a motion to renew the party's motion for judgment as a matter of law. Otherwise such a motion will not be entertained. See Unitherm Food Sys., Inc. v. Swift–Eckrich, Inc., 546 U.S. 394, 126 S.Ct. 980, 163 L.Ed.2d 974 (2006), p. 1150, infra.

3. What are the purposes of Rule 50(b) other than to satisfy the requirements of *Redman*? Suppose a party who has moved for a judgment as a matter of law at the end of all the evidence solely on the ground that one element of the case has not been proven, argues that the evidence was insufficient to establish a different element when the motion is renewed after the jury verdict? Should the new ground be considered? See Sweeney v. Westvaco Co., 926 F.2d 29 (1st Cir.1991); Affiliated FM Ins. Co. v. Neosho Constr. Co., 192 F.R.D. 662, 667–68 (D.Kan.2000).

SECTION D. INSTRUCTIONS AND VERDICTS

1. INSTRUCTIONS TO THE JURY

Read Federal Rule of Civil Procedure 51 and the accompanying materials in the Supplement.

A. REQUESTS FOR AND OBJECTIONS TO INSTRUCTIONS

Before it retires to deliberate and decide, the court instructs the jury as to the law to be applied and the manner in which it is to reach a decision. The most significant legal controversy regarding the proper sequence of this phase of a jury trial is whether the instructions should come *before* or *after* the final arguments by counsel. In most jurisdictions, the courts take the position that the judge, as the impartial umpire in the case, should have the last word in order that partisan appeals by counsel will be tempered by a dispassionate statement of the law to be applied. Look at the comparative state provisions that are reprinted in the Supplement. Those who favor instructions prior to argument ask: "How can any rational argument be made if the jurors have not yet been told about the law they must apply?" Can this question be satisfactorily answered? Note that Federal Rule 51 was amended in 1987 to give the judge the option to instruct the jury before or after closing arguments, or both. See 9C Wright & Miller, Federal Practice and Procedure: Civil 3d § 2551. It also might be argued that the jury cannot properly understand the opening statements of counsel or evaluate evidence as it is introduced unless they have prior knowledge of the legal significance of the facts presented. Why then are the instructions not given by the court at the beginning rather than at the end of trial? Would it make sense to give two sets of instructions, one at the beginning of trial and the other at the end? How might instructions be devised to ensure that the court "vigorously promote" "juror comprehension"? The ABA Principles for Juries and Jury Trials, Principles 13 and 14 (2005). See Grenig, *The Civil Jury in America: Improving the Jury's Understanding of a Case,* 24 Am. J. Trial Advoc. 93 (2000).

Normally, the court requires the attorneys to submit proposed instructions at some point during the trial, usually after the evidence has been completed. The court then determines which of these instructions to give and which of its own to add. Under the rules of most jurisdictions, a party cannot appeal the failure to give an instruction that he did not request or the giving of an erroneous instruction to which he made no immediate objection. What is the purpose of rules such as these? Why should an instruction be requested or challenged prior to the time the jury commences its deliberations? See Alexander v. Kramer Bros. Freight Lines, Inc., p. 45, supra.

From a tactical point of view, the drafting of proposed instructions poses a serious dilemma. On the one hand, every attorney wants a set of instructions that is as favorable to his client as possible. On the other hand, the more slanted the instructions proposed, the less likely they are to be given and the more probable the judge will be antagonized by them since they will be of little assistance. Moreover, there is always the danger that the judge will accept an instruction so prejudicial that a judgment based upon it will be reversed on appeal. This not only is against the interests of the client but also harms the reputation of the attorney in the eyes of the trial judge who will hesitate to trust the attorney in future cases. See generally Powers, *Requests for Instructions,* 28 F.R.D. 239 (1960). Even if the instructions are favorable in substance, they will be ignored totally if they are so long and technical that the jurors cannot understand them. Thus an attorney often is wise to seek a simple, favorable instruction on a point, even though a more complex charge might be framed in much more favorable terms. For examples of state practice, see Bissett & Margi, *State Jury Instructions on the Web*, 81 Mich. B.J. 46 (Dec. 2002) (identifying print and Web sources for jury instructions for all states).

KENNEDY v. SOUTHERN CALIFORNIA EDISON CO.

United States Court of Appeals, Ninth Circuit, 2000.
219 F.3d 988, withdrawn 268 F.3d 763 (2001), certiorari denied
535 U.S. 1079, 122 S.Ct. 1964, 152 L.Ed.2d 1024 (2002).[a]

[Plaintiffs brought a wrongful death action for the death of their wife and mother from a rare form of cancer, allegedly caused by exposure to nuclear radiation from nuclear rods defectively manufactured in defendant's plant referred to as "SONGS." The applicable California law for such cases was established in Rutherford v. Owens–Illinois, Inc., 16 Cal.4th 953, 67 Cal.Rptr.2d 16, 941 P.2d 1203 (1997), which held that a jury must be instructed that "plaintiff may meet the burden of proving that exposure to defendant's product was a substantial factor causing the illness by showing that in reasonable medical probability it was a substantial factor contributing to the plaintiff's or decedent's risk of developing cancer." The trial court did not give this instruction and the jury found for defendant. Plaintiffs appealed.]

HAWKINS, CIRCUIT JUDGE:

* * *

Having held that a *Rutherford* instruction was required, we now turn to the specific instruction proffered by Kennedy. At oral argument, appellees argued that the requested instruction was not a proper *Rutherford* instruction. We agree.

On two occasions, Kennedy proposed the following instruction * * *:

> In order to prove that radiation from the nuclear power plant was a substantial factor, Plaintiffs do not need to prove that it actually contributed to the development of Ellen Marie Kennedy's cancer. If exposure to radiation from the nuclear power plant in reasonable medical probability contributed to her risk of developing cancer then such exposure was a substantial factor in causing her cancer.

The proposed instruction leaves out a small, but critical, phrase. It states that radiation from SONGS need only have "contributed" to Mrs. Kennedy's risk of developing cancer. We read *Rutherford* to require more. Kennedy's burden is not to show that exposure to radiation in reasonable medical probability "contributed" to a risk of cancer. Rather, it is to demonstrate that the exposure in reasonable medical probability was "*a substantial factor*" in contributing to the risk of cancer. The omission of this modifier is essential to a proper *Rutherford* instruction.

* * *

---

a. This opinion was issued by the Ninth Circuit Court of Appeals at 219 F.3d 988 (9th Cir.2000). It was withdrawn in 2001 and a new opinion was issued at 268 F.3d 763 (9th Cir.2001). The court in the latter case based its decision on entirely different grounds than the decision printed here and was not required to, and did not, discuss the obligations of a trial court to issue a proper instruction when not specifically requested to do so.

That the proposed instructions were not entirely correct under *Rutherford* is insufficient to affirm the district court's refusal to instruct the jury properly. Ordinarily, a district court does not err in refusing to give incorrect or misleading instructions. * * *

A district court, however, may have an obligation to correctly instruct the jury even after being presented with an arguably improper instruction that nonetheless directs its attention to an important issue. While this issue has not been expressly decided in this circuit, several of our sister circuits have held that such an obligation does exist. * * *

In *Ursich v. da Rosa*, 328 F.2d 794, 797 (9th Cir.1964), we held that a district court "was under no obligation to redraw" an incorrect, yet otherwise applicable jury instruction for the requesting party. The holding of *Ursich* was limited by its circumstances. We specifically noted that the requested instruction concerned an "old rule," the doctrine of res ipsa loquitor, and that we "expect[ed] counsel to be aware of it and to frame proper instructions...." *Id.* n. 1. The instant case however, presents a much different scenario. Kennedy requested an instruction based on a "new rule" of state law, one that was only a few months old and had yet to be interpreted or applied by any other court.

Moreover, in a case subsequent to *Ursich*, we implicitly recognized that a trial court may have the obligation to correct improperly requested jury instructions. In *Washington State Bowling Proprietors Ass'n v. Pacific Lanes, Inc.*, 356 F.2d 371, 376–77 (9th Cir.1966), we stated that "we do not suggest a trial court is under no obligation to charge on a material issue after requested to do so, even if the instructions as proposed are faulty...."[6]

Today we make explicit what *Pacific Lanes* suggested, and align this circuit with the majority of our sister circuits. We hold that when the district court is presented with an applicable instruction that raises an important issue of law or directs the court's attention to a point upon which an instruction to the jury would be important, it is not relieved from the responsibility of giving a proper instruction simply because the party making the request has proposed an instruction that does not completely comply with the relevant law.

C. Harmless Error Analysis

Harmless-error review applies to jury instructions in a civil case. * * * This review is "less stringent" than review for harmless error in a criminal case, but "more stringent" than review for sufficiency of the evidence. * * * In review of civil jury instructions for harmless error, unlike review under sufficiency of the evidence, the "prevailing party is *not* entitled to have disputed factual issues resolved in his favor because the jury's verdict may have resulted from a misapprehension of the law

6. Our decision to uphold the district court's refusal to give the proffered instructions was based on the fact that the appellants had failed to resubmit the instructions after the trial judge pointed out the errors, and that the evidence did not support the contention that the requested instruction was on a material issue. * * *

rather than from factual determinations in favor of the prevailing party." * * *

We hold the district court's failure to give a proper *Rutherford* instruction was *not* harmless error. "An error in a trial court's jury instructions relating to the parties' respective burdens of proof ordinarily [requires] reversal." *Larez v. Holcomb*, 16 F.3d 1513, 1518 (9th Cir.1994). *But see Mockler v. Multnomah County*, 140 F.3d 808, 812–814 (9th Cir.1998) (improper instruction on plaintiff's burden of proof held harmless when evidence would support verdict for plaintiff in any event).

* * *

The decision of the district court is REVERSED, and the case is REMANDED for a new trial consistent with this opinion.

NOTES AND QUESTIONS

1. Suppose plaintiffs in *Kennedy* had failed to request any *Rutherford* instruction. The standard notion is that a party waives any objection based on the trial court's failure to give an instruction unless the matter was properly raised below. How strict should courts be in that regard? See TURNER CONSTRUCTION CO. v. HOULIHAN, 240 F.2d 435, 439 (1st Cir.1957):

> The first sentence of Rule 51 permits, but does not require, the filing of requests for instructions. If none are filed, the court must nevertheless charge the jury on the broad general fundamental rules of law applicable to the principal issues of fact in the case. * * * If, however, counsel want the jury instructed specifically on particular matters, requests for such instructions must be filed.

2. Compare *Kennedy* with ROMANO v. U–HAUL INTERNATIONAL, 233 F.3d 655, 663 (1st Cir.2000), a case in which the trial court failed to give an instruction submitted initially by the plaintiff who thereafter did not object to its absence from either the list of instructions to be given or the instructions that were in fact given, to the jury.

> An awareness by the parties and the district court [of an issue in the case] * * * is not sufficient to excuse appellants obligation to object to the jury instructions under Rule 51. The requirement that the grounds for objecting to a jury instruction must be distinctly stated is treated seriously by this Court. * * * We will not excuse appellant's failure to argue * * * [that the instruction should have been given] based on a purely speculative claim that the district court has some awareness that [such an instruction would have been appropriate].

3. Would it be more sensible to be lenient with an attorney who fails to request a vital instruction than with one who sits back and permits an erroneous instruction to be given? Consider Fisher v. Ford Motor Co., 224 F.3d 570, 576 (6th Cir.2000), in which the court stated that it reviews *de novo* the accuracy of instructions that were given, whereas it reviews a trial court's decision not to give a requested instruction only for an abuse of discretion.

Does this distinction make any sense? See also WIRTZ v. INTERNATIONAL HARVESTER CO., 331 F.2d 462 (5th Cir.), certiorari denied 379 U.S. 845, 85 S.Ct. 36, 13 L.Ed.2d 50 (1964), in which the court reversed a judgment on the ground that a vital instruction, not challenged below, clearly was incorrect. The appellate court stated that *both* parties have a duty to ensure that important instructions are phrased properly, not just the party who would be injured if the improper instruction were to be given. Reversals on the basis of improper jury instructions without objections by the parties are rare, although more numerous when "plain error" is found.

4. Why shouldn't instructions be the sole responsibility of the trial judge? Federal Rule 51 and its state counterparts usually are justified on the ground that a court should be told of its errors and omissions in time to correct them in order to avoid the costs and delays of a new trial. Is there some other reason? Note that Rule 51 requires the trial judge to inform the lawyers prior to their closing arguments as to what instructions will be given. Objections are then to be made before the jury retires but out of its hearing. What purpose do these provisions serve?

5. The precise wording of jury instructions are a matter of concern because technical inaccuracies may lead to reversal on appeal. But the jury's capacity to deliberate and reach sound results also may be compromised by instructions that are written in abstruse terms and read by the judge in a nearly inaudible monotone without regard for the fact that the statements are nearly incomprehensible. A noted federal judge pointed to serious problems in the instruction process:

> Prevailing practices of instructing juries are often so archaic and unrealistic that even in relatively simple cases what the jurors hear is little more than legal mumbo jumbo to them. Responsibility for the shortcomings of present practices must be shared by lawyers, trial courts, and appellate courts—lawyers for submitting self-serving, excessively long and argumentative instructions, trial judges for adhering to archaic practices out of fear of being reversed, and appellate courts for elevating legal abstractions over juror understanding.

Schwartzer, *Communicating with Juries: Problems and Remedies,* 69 Cal. L. Rev. 731, 732 (1981).

In the more than twenty-five years since Judge Schwartzer made his comments, steps have been taken to change instructions in order to improve juror comprehension. See Dumas, *Jury Trials: Lay Jurors, Pattern Jury Instructions, and Comprehension Issues*, 67 Tenn. L. Rev. 701 (2000) (providing an overview of the social science research on which reforms are based); Lieberman & Sales, *What Social Science Teaches Us About the Jury Instruction Process*, 3 Psychol. Pub. Pol'y & L. 589 (1997). However, many reforms still need to be implemented. See Marder, *Bringing Jury Instructions into the Twenty–First Century,* 81 Notre Dame L. Rev. 449 (2006). What institutional barriers do you see to this reform effort?

6. The most significant value of the jury may lie in the fact that it does not, and should not be expected to, apply the law in strict fashion. Juries frequently have been accused of invading the province of the judge by

ignoring its instructions, fabricating their own rules of law, and applying them to the facts. E.g., Frank, Courts on Trial 110–11 (1949). Consider the following excerpt in terms of whether the jury really is abusing its function:

> Some might view the jury's * * * [ability to ignore the law] as a disadvantage of the jury. However it does ensure that the process of adjudication is democratic and allows for flexibility from the potentially rigid application of rules of law that do not countenance novel situations or fact patterns. Furthermore, the actions of the jury in importing community values into the adjudicatory process are incremental in the sense that a single jury can act only in the case before it based on the facts presented to it. * * * The ability of the jury to import community values into the process of adjudication is also what allows it to function as a "bulwark of liberty" and to resist abusive exercise of governmental power against the citizenry. * * *

Smith, *Structural and Functional Aspects of the Jury: Comparative Analysis and Proposals for Reform*, 48 Ala.L.Rev. 441, 473–74 (1997). See also James, *Functions of Judge and Jury in Negligence Cases*, 58 Yale L.J. 667 (1949); Kalven, *The Dignity of the Civil Jury*, 50 Va.L.Rev. 1055, 1062–68 (1964). Does the fact that the law often lags behind social reality justify the jury stepping outside its historical bounds and "taking the law into its own hands"? Is the jury's invasion of the court's province and its knocking "off many rough edges of the law" likely to inhibit change in the law by making legislative and judicial innovation "unnecessary"?

B. COMMENTING ON THE EVIDENCE BY JUDGES

NUNLEY v. PETTWAY OIL CO., 346 F.2d 95 (6th Cir.1965). Plaintiff brought suit for personal injuries received when a truck fell off a grease rack in a gas station. The jury found plaintiff to be a licensee rather than an invitee at the time of the accident, and, applying the applicable law, the court entered judgment for defendant. On appeal plaintiff contended that the court had commented improperly to the jury on the licensee-invitee question. During their initial deliberations the jurors were unable to agree on this issue. The judge then called them into the courtroom and urged them to try to arrive at a decision as follows:

> Now, the jury of course is the sole and exclusive judge of the facts in this lawsuit. It is appropriate that the Court in an effort to be possibly of some help to the jury may comment upon the evidence. I refrain from doing that and have refrained until this time from doing it in this case. However, in an effort to be of some possible assistance to you I think that I should under these circumstances make some comment upon the evidence upon this issue of invitee-licensee. I want you to understand, however, that in making these comments that you are not in any degree, in any respect, obligated to receive or accept or agree with what I may say. It is your duty to accept what I say with regard to the law in the case, but it is not your duty to accept any comment that I may make or any evaluation that I may make or conclusion that I might reach on the evidence. That is solely your

> responsibility and solely your duty. *But, with that understanding, it is the opinion of the Court in this case that, from all the evidence upon the issue of invitee or licensee, that the evidence will establish that at the time and place of the accident the plaintiff was a licensee and not an invitee.* Now, I say that just for the purpose, as I say, of possibly being of some help to you, but I want you to understand that in making that comment you are not obligated whatsoever to accept that comment as your comment or as your opinion in the case, because it is your job and your responsibility to resolve that issue. I only make that with the thought and the hope that it may be of some possible assistance to you. At any rate, I want to ask you once again to retire and consider your verdict and see if you cannot come to some agreement, some verdict that will reflect the views of all of the jurors. * * *

Id. at 98. The Court of Appeals reversed, stating:

> We recognize that the right of a District Judge to comment on the evidence is firmly established in the federal system. See Quercia v. United States, 289 U.S. 466, 53 S.Ct. 698, 77 L.Ed. 1321 (1933) * * *.
>
> Nonetheless, we believe that under the circumstances enumerated, the trial judge's opinion on the licensee-invitee issue was an opinion on an ultimate fact question peculiarly for jury consideration and amounted to an instructed verdict as to defendant Pettway Oil Company.
>
> In Quercia v. United States, supra, Chief Justice Hughes commented:
>
> This privilege of the judge to comment on the facts has its inherent limitations. His discretion is not arbitrary and uncontrolled, but judicial, to be exercised in conformity with the standards governing the judicial office. In commenting upon testimony he may not assume the role of a witness. He may analyze and dissect the evidence, but he may not either distort it or add to it. His privilege of comment in order to give appropriate assistance to the jury is too important to be left without safeguards against abuses.
>
> * * *
>
> Nor do we think that the error was cured by the statement of the trial judge that his opinion of the evidence was not binding on the jury and that if they did not agree with it they should find the defendant not guilty. His definite and concrete assertion of fact, which he had made with all the persuasiveness of judicial utterance, as to the basis of his opinion, was not withdrawn. * * *

Id. at 98–99.

NOTES AND QUESTIONS

1. In *Quercia,* a *criminal* case, the Supreme Court reversed a conviction because the following charge was given to the jury:

> And now I am going to tell you what I think of the defendant's testimony. You may have noticed, Mr. Foreman and gentlemen, that he wiped his hands during his testimony. It is rather a curious thing, but that is almost always an indication of lying. Why it should be so we don't know, but that is the fact. I think that every single word that man said, except when he agreed with the Government's testimony, was a lie.
>
> Now, that opinion is an opinion of evidence and is not binding on you, and if you don't agree with it, it is your duty to find him not guilty.

Id. at 468–69, 53 S.Ct. at 698, 77 L.Ed. at 1324. Is the court in *Nunley* justified in relying on *Quercia*? Aren't there substantial differences between the two cases?

2. In light of the decision in *Nunley,* what is the meaning of the court's statement: "We recognize that the right of a District Judge to comment on the evidence is firmly established in the federal system"? The trial judge's common-law power to comment on the evidence includes the power to express an opinion regarding both evidentiary issues and the credibility of witnesses. Those federal decisions that appear to limit the common-law practice are in line with limitations in a majority of states, which take two basic forms: (1) the trial judge is confined to a statement of the applicable law and deprived of power even to mention the evidence (see Colorado Rule of Civil Procedure 51), or (2) the court is limited to presenting an impartial summary of the evidence. Is the latter approach feasible? See Wright, *Instructions to the Jury: Summary Without Comment*, 1954 Wash.U.L.Q. 177.

3. The *Nunley* opinion emphasizes that the judge's comment was on an "ultimate fact question." The Fifth Circuit holds that comments are proper on "evidentiary matters," but not on "ultimate factual issues." Travelers Ins. Co. v. Ryan, 416 F.2d 362, 364 (5th Cir.1969). Is there any sound basis for this distinction?

4. What are the arguments for and against allowance of a broad judicial power to comment on the evidence? Professor Wigmore passionately advocated restoration of the broad power, and severely criticized the federal approach exemplified in *Quercia*. 9 Wigmore on Evidence § 2551 (Chadbourn rev. 1981). See also Weinstein, *The Power and Duty of Federal Judges to Marshall and Comment on the Evidence in Jury Trials and Some Suggestions on Charging Juries*, 118 F.R.D. 161 (1988); Lerner, *The Transformation of the American Civil Trial: The Silent Judge*, 42 Wm. & Mary L. Rev. 195 (2000).

5. Jurisdiction in the *Nunley* case was based on diversity of citizenship. Suppose that the law of the state permits the trial judge to express an opinion as to whether the evidence is sufficient to establish the ultimate facts in the case. To what extent is the federal court allowed to follow the state practice? See *Byrd*, p. 424, supra.

2. PERMITTING INSTRUCTIONS TO BE TAKEN INTO THE JURY ROOM; NOTE-TAKING AND JUROR DISCUSSIONS DURING TRIAL

SECURITIES AND EXCHANGE COMMISSION v. KOENIG

United States Court of Appeals, Seventh Circuit, 2009.
557 F.3d 736.

EASTERBROOK, CHIEF JUDGE.

Waste Management, Inc., grew at an average annual rate of 26% from 1979 through 1991. When growth fell off, James Koenig, its Chief Financial Officer, decided to improve appearances. He devised several accounting strategies that a jury found to be fraudulent. The district judge imposed a civil penalty of about $2.1 million and ordered Koenig to disgorge the bonuses he received in 1992, 1994, and 1995 ($831,500, plus more than $1.2 million in prejudgment interest). Bonuses depended on Waste Management's profits. If its profits had been stated correctly, the judge concluded, Koenig would not have received these bonuses. The court also enjoined Koenig from again serving as a director or top manager of a public company.

* * *

Several of Koenig's arguments [on appeal] concern trial management. * * *

After learning that Koenig planned to pitch his defense on the theory that Waste Management's new management had taken an "earnings bath" to make its own performance look good by comparison, the SEC filed a motion in limine asking the district court to exclude all evidence related to this theme. The right question, the SEC insisted, was whether Koenig intentionally made (or caused Waste Management to make) materially misleading statements * * *. According to the SEC, the motive of anyone other than Koenig was irrelevant. Indeed, Koenig's motive also was irrelevant; * * *. The plaintiff in a securities-fraud suit must show intentional deceit * * *; the motive for that deceit is beside the point.

The district court should have granted the SEC's motion. Instead the judge denied the motion, while warning Koenig that if motive became an issue he would allow the SEC to introduce its own evidence (much of which was sure to be hearsay) about why people acted as they did. Koenig then presented his defense, the SEC responded in kind, hearsay became rampant, and the trial dragged on and on, lasting a total of 12 weeks.

A good deal of research shows that 20 days is about the longest trial any jury can comprehend fully; the longer the trial goes, the more the jury forgets and the less accurate the decision becomes. See, e.g., Richard Lempert, *Civil Juries and Complex Cases: Taking Stock After Twelve Years* 20 (Center for Research on Social Organization Working Paper

Series #488, Nov. 1992); *A Handbook of Jury Research* § 3.02(c) at 3–6 (Walter F. Abbott & John Batt eds.1999); Joe S. Cecil et al., *Jury Service in Lengthy Civil Trials* 1, 9, 11–13, 28 (tab.7), 33 (tab.8) (Fed. Judicial Center 1987); Patrick E. Longan, *The Shot Clock Comes to Trial: Time Limits for Federal Civil Trials,* 35 Ariz. L.Rev. 663, 703–07 (1993). No wonder the ABA strongly recommends short trials. "Principle 12: Courts Should Limit the Length of Jury Trials Insofar As Justice Allows, and Jurors Should Be Fully Informed of the Trial Schedule Established," in American Bar Association, *Principles of Juries and Jury Trials* (Aug. 2005). Koenig does not complain about the trial's length; perhaps he was hoping that jurors would lose focus. (A 12–week trial *about accounting!* Sounds like material for Jay Leno.) * * *

* * *

* * * Principle 13(C) of the ABA's American Jury Project recommends that judges permit jurors to ask questions of witnesses. The Final Report of the Seventh Circuit's American Jury Project 15–24 (Sept.2008) concurs, with the proviso that jurors should submit their questions to the judge, who will edit them and pose appropriate, non-argumentative queries. District judges throughout the Seventh Circuit participated in that project. The judges, the lawyers for the winning side, and, tellingly, the lawyers for the losing side, all concluded (by substantial margins) that when jurors were allowed to ask questions, their attention improved, with benefits for the overall quality of adjudication. Keeping the jurors' minds on their work is an especially vital objective during a long trial about a technical subject, such as accounting. The district judge in this case permitted jurors to submit questions to him. Some were asked; others were reformulated and asked; some were not asked, when the judge thought them inappropriate or repetitive.

Koenig contends that permitting the jurors to participate in this fashion is a reversible error. That can't be because any statute or rule of procedure bans the process. There is no such statute or rule. Nor has any court of appeals forbidden the judge to ask questions submitted by the jurors. * * * The ABA and Seventh Circuit jury projects found benefits; so have scholars. See, e.g., Shari Seidman Diamond, Mary R. Rose, Beth Murphy & Sven Smith, *Juror Questions During Trial: A Window into Juror Thinking,* 59 Vand. L.Rev.1927 (2006); Nicole L. Mott, *The Current Debate on Juror Questions,* 78 Chi.–Kent L.Rev. 1099 (2003).

In opposition to these studies, Koenig has only occasional judicial skepticism. For example, we said more than a decade ago that questions from jurors are "fraught with risks". * * * Similar [judicial] statements are easy to find * * * [citations to federal appellate decisions omitted]. These expressions reflect concern that allowing jurors to ask questions will lead them to take positions too early in the trial, emulating the advocates by choosing sides and becoming argumentative rather than reflective. The jury projects and other studies were designed to find out whether these risks are realized so frequently that they overcome the benefits, such as keeping jurors alert and focused. Now that several studies have concluded that the benefits exceed the costs, there is no reason to disfavor the practice. Like other issues of trial management—may jurors take notes? should written jury instructions and copies of exhibits be sent to the jury room during deliberations?—whether to allow the jurors to pose questions is a topic committed to the sound discretion of the judge. That discretion was not abused in this case; to the contrary, the judge's decision, like his supervision of the questioning process, was well considered and sensible.

Koenig contends that the judge should have limited the jurors to "clarifying" questions, but jurors' perspectives are so different from those of lawyers that it is difficult to see how such a limit could be enforced (or why it would be appropriate). Testimony that seems clear to a specialist in accounting or securities law may be confusing to a juror encountering these subjects for the first time, so a juror may see as "clarifying" a question that the lawyer sees as unnecessary or obtuse. A judge should serve as a filter for questions and eliminate or rephrase those that are irrelevant or disguised argument (as the judge at this trial did); more than that a court of appeals cannot sensibly demand.

That some glitches occurred in the process-the judge forgot to ask some of the jurors' questions for some witnesses, and he failed to call back one witness when the jurors wanted to ask additional questions-is neither surprising nor a ground for concern. Trials are complex proceedings, and a judge must concentrate attention on what is most pressing. Jurors were told not to draw inferences from the judge's decision not to ask particular questions; there is little reason to think that jurors would have held against Koenig the judge's failure (even if inadvertent) to ask any particular question. Nor does it strike us as unusual or a source of concern that three jurors collectively asked about two-thirds of the 127 total questions submitted by the panel; some people are more voluble than others. That the panel had members of different interests and proclivities is a strength rather than a weakness of the system. (Note that 127 questions is roughly two per trial day; this litigation was not taken over by the jury.)

Koenig sees in some of the proposed questions (principally those filtered out by the judge) signs that a few jurors had made up their minds or taken an adversarial position in mid-trial. It is dangerous to draw such inferences from questions; judges often ask pointed questions of both sides, and it would be a mistake to infer from these questions that the judge was leaning against *both* litigants. No matter. Koenig's position seems to be that ignorance is bliss: if some jurors have reached a tentative conclusion in mid-trial, it is best not to know it. Why? Jurors must be impartial, but like everyone else they respond to evidence and may think that they know enough even when lawyers want to feed them more. (We've already said that this trial lasted far too long; it is no surprise that some jurors thought they knew enough to decide even while the trial was ongoing.) Lawyers should want to *know* when some jurors are tending the other side's way, so that they can make adjustments to their presentations in an effort to supply whatever proof the jurors think vital, but missing. Just as questions from the bench can supply insight that helps lawyers make a stronger case, so questions from jurors can help lawyers tailor their presentations. Keeping jurors silent won't prevent them from reacting to the evidence; it will just make it harder for lawyers to know how things are going. It is a lot easier (and more reliable) to read jurors' questions than to read the expressions on their faces.

* * *

Koenig's other arguments have been considered but do not require discussion. The judgment is affirmed except with respect to the calculation of Koenig's bonuses [relevant to the District Court's disgorgement remedy] * * *, and the case is remanded for further proceedings consistent with this opinion.

NOTES AND QUESTIONS

The *Koenig* decision reflects recent efforts to enhance juror performance through various procedural reforms. In addition to permitting jurors to ask questions, reforms include providing jurors with a written copy of instructions, permitting jurors to take notes, and allowing interim discussion.

Written Instructions: Courts follow different practices in requiring or permitting the judge to give written instructions to the jury that jurors may take into the jury room. Some courts provide the jury with only a single copy of the instructions which the jurors must share. See Mize, Hannaford–Agor & Waters, The State-of-the States Survey of Jury Improvement Efforts: A Compendium Report (2007). See also Hannaford–Agor *Judicial Nullification? Judicial Compliance and Non–Compliance with Jury Improvement Efforts*, 28 N. Ill. U.L. Rev. 407 (2008). Other courts have provided an audiotape or videotape of the judge reading the instructions. See Marder, *Bringing Jury Instructions into the Twenty–First Century*, 81 Notre Dame L. Rev. 449, 500–01 (2006).

As early study of the merits of providing written instructions found it to be "hardly reasonable to suppose that the jury, composed as it is of persons unfamiliar with either law or legal language and having heard the instructions but once as given orally by the court, will be able to remember them in detail as it ponders the matters committed to it for decision." California Law Revision Commission, Recommendation and Study Relating to Taking Instructions into the Jury Room, pp. C–15–C–17 (1956) (Tabular Summary of the Law of Other States). Later empirical studies associate written jury instructions with improved juror performance. See, e.g., Heuer & Penrod, *Instructing Jurors: A Field Experiment with Written and Preliminary Instructions*, 13 Law & Hum. Behav. 409 (1989). Does Federal Rule 51 mandate the practice?

Are there any effective arguments against allowing the jury to possess written instructions during its deliberations? Might the possession of written instructions unduly influence the jury's discussion? Does possession of written instructions tend to affect the amount of influence some jurors have on the rest of the panel?

Juror Note–Taking: In many jurisdictions jurors are permitted and even encouraged to take notes throughout the trial for use during the deliberations, and empirical research supports the practice as a way to enhance juror performance. See Hans, *Empowering the Active Jury: A Genuine Tort Reform,* 13 Roger Williams U.L. Rev. 39, 50–52 (2008) (reporting survey data that jurors could take notes in more than 70 per cent of state and federal civil trials). Empirical research supports the practice as a way to enhance juror performance. The ABA Principles, referred to in *Koenig*, recommend the practice in Principle 13. Is there a danger that note-taking will distract the juror from listening to the evidence? Will jurors tend to give excessive weight to their notes, even if taken in error? Does the ability to take notes quickly give untoward influence to some jurors?

Early Juror Discussion: Jurors almost always are warned that they are not to discuss the case with anyone, even the other jurors until the case is submitted to them at the close of the trial. What dangers do you see if jurors were to be permitted to discuss the case at an earlier stage? The Arizona judiciary, a leader among the states in studying jury practices and implementing reforms, has adopted a rule permitting jurors to discuss the case among themselves during the course of trial, but only if all jurors are present in the room. What are the potential advantages of the Arizona rule? Is it ever possible to reserve judgment on complicated issues while engaged in an active discussion? See Strier, *Making Jury Trials More Truthful,* 30 U.C. Davis L. Rev. 95, 140–41 (1996). For a study of the participants' views of the Arizona experiment, see Hans, Hannaford & Munsterman, *The Arizona Jury Reform Permitting Civil Jury Trial Discussions: The Views of Trial Participants, Judges, and Jurors*, 32 U.Mich.J.L.F. 349 (1999). See also Diamond, Vidmar, Rose, Ellis & Murphy, *Juror Discussions During Civil Trials: Studying an Arizona Innovation*, 45 Ariz. L. Rev. 1 (2003).

3. VERDICTS

A. SUBMISSION OF THE CASE TO THE JURY

After final arguments are completed and the instructions given, the jurors are placed in the custody of a bailiff or similar court official who guards them during deliberations. It is the bailiff's duty to make certain that the jurors remain together and have no contact with other persons except by court order.

In some cases the jurors will find it difficult to agree on a verdict. If this is due to uncertainty as to the content of the instructions, they may ask the court to reread the instructions, and, if necessary, to augment them. See, e.g., Diniero v. United States Lines Co., p. 48, supra. If the major difficulty is due to disagreement as to what one or more of the witnesses said, the jurors may request that the testimony of those witnesses be read to them. Whenever the jury reenters the courtroom, whether for further instructions or for the reading of testimony, it is wise to notify both parties and their attorneys in advance. Otherwise the verdict may be subject to reversal on appeal. What is the purpose of a rule requiring notice? How rigidly should it be enforced?

Suppose after lengthy deliberations the jurors still are unable to agree. How long may they be kept in session? At what point does a court abuse its discretion by forcing them to continue their discussions? When a court does order an end to a session, must it then dismiss the jury and order a new trial? If not, must the jurors be locked up, free from all contact with outsiders, or should they be allowed to go home until such time as they are ordered to reassemble? See Kramer v. Kister, p. 1126, infra; Annot. 19 A.L.R.5th 622 (1994), for detailed discussion of these matters.

At some point, of course, if the jurors continue to be unable to agree, they will have to be discharged and a mistrial declared. Courts are extremely reluctant to discharge a jury without its having reached a verdict because of the cost and delay of a new trial. Thus, a court often will urge a stalemated jury to make a further attempt to arrive at a verdict. Although some jurisdictions still require the traditional unanimous jury verdict, a substantial number have tried to cut down the number of stalemates by permitting a verdict to be based on something less than unanimity in civil cases. Does a requirement of unanimity promote or deter the quality of deliberations and the accuracy of decisions? For a discussion of current research on the topic, see Diamond, *Revisiting the Unanimity Requirement: The Behavior of the Non–Unanimous Civil Jury,* 100 Nw. U. L. Rev. 201 (2006).

In some cases the jury is able to arrive at a verdict almost immediately. Indeed, it may be possible for the jurors to agree without even leaving the jury box. Should a verdict in a complex case ever be subject to attack because it was rendered quickly?

B. THE FORM OF THE VERDICTS

Read Federal Rule of Civil Procedure 49 in the Supplement.

The traditional form of the jury decision, used almost exclusively in the great majority of courts, is the general verdict. No matter how complex the case and how long and involved the instructions were, all a jury need do to render a general verdict is to announce which party wins, and, if it is plaintiff, the amount that should be recovered. This type of verdict has two major deficiencies. First, there is no way to tell how the jurors decided specific issues, which, in turn, can result in the unnecessary retrial of the entire case. For example, suppose defendant raises a number of defenses, any one of which, if established, would require a verdict for defendant. Then the court, in an otherwise faultless charge, erroneously instructs the jury on one of these defenses in a manner detrimental to plaintiff, after which the jury finds for defendant. On appeal, the court will be required to reverse, since it has no way of telling whether the verdict was based solely on the tainted defense. If, however, the jury had been required to render a separate verdict on each one of the defenses, the court would know at once the bases of the jury decision and whether the error in the instruction was harmless. The second major drawback to the general verdict is the fact that there is no way of knowing whether the jury actually focused its attention on every major aspect of the case as required by the instructions, or whether it ignored the instructions altogether and rendered a decision based solely on sentiment, public opinion, bias, or similar emotion.

To avoid these objections, many writers have advocated use of the special verdict, which requires the jury to answer a series of questions regarding each facet of the case but not to enter a verdict stating who wins. For example, in Frank, Courts on Trial 141–42 (1950), the following argument is advanced:

> A special verdict would seem to do away with some of the most objectionable features of trial by jury. The division of functions between jury and judge is apparently assured, the one attending to the facts alone, the other to the legal rules alone. The jury seems, by this device, to be shorn of its power to ignore the rules or to make rules to suit itself. As one court said, special verdicts "dispel * * * the darkness visible of general verdicts." The finding of facts, says Sunderland, "is much better done by means of the special verdict. Every advantage which the jury is popularly supposed to have over the [judge] as a trier of facts is retained, with the very great additional advantage that the analysis and separation of the facts in the case which the court and the attorney must necessarily effect in employing the special verdict, materially reduce the chance of error. It is easy to make mistakes in dealing at large with aggregates of facts. The special verdict compels detailed consideration. But above all it enables the public, the parties and the court to see what the jury has really done * * *. The morale of the jury also is aided by throwing off the cloak of secrecy, for only through publicity is there developed the proper feeling of responsibility in public servants. So far, then, as the facts go, they can be much more effectively, conveniently, and usefully tried by abandoning the general verdict * * *." [Sunderland, *Verdicts General and Special,* 29 Yale L.J. 253 (1920).]
>
> * * * It is suggested, too, that a special verdict "searches the conscience of the individual juror, as a general verdict does not," because "such are the contradictions in human nature that many a man who will unite in a general verdict for a large and unwarranted sum of money will shrink from a specific finding against his judgment of

> right and wrong." [Clementson, *Special Verdicts and Special Findings by Juries* 15 (1905).]

This view has been strongly opposed on the ground that the special verdict improperly subverts the fundamental nature of the jury decision. See 9B Wright & Miller, Federal Practice and Procedure: Civil 3d § 2503:

> Not all would agree that * * * [making jury decisions more scientific and trustworthy] is desirable, even if it were assumed that it is possible. Little is gained by making the law more scientific if, in the process, it becomes harder to achieve substantial justice. Some of the most famous students of the judicial process have argued that one of the purposes of the jury system is to permit the jury to temper strict rules of law by the demands and necessities of substantial justice and changing social conditions, thereby adding a much needed element of flexibility. Those who share this conception of the role of the jury rightly fear that it will be limited or defeated by the restraints imposed by the special verdict practice, and thus oppose widespread use of it.

These very concerns induced Justices Black and Douglas to issue the following statement in connection with the Court's 1963 amendment of Rule 49, at 374 U.S. 865, 867–68, 83 S.Ct. 43, 44–45 (1963):

> * * * Rule 49 should be repealed. * * * Such devices are used to impair or wholly take away the power of a jury to render a general verdict. One of the ancient, fundamental reasons for having general jury verdicts was to preserve the right of trial by jury as an indispensable part of a free government. Many of the most famous constitutional controversies in England revolved around litigants' insistence, particularly in seditious libel cases, that a jury had the right to render a general verdict without being compelled to return a number of subsidiary findings to support its general verdict. Some English jurors had to go to jail because they insisted upon their right to render general verdicts over the repeated commands of tyrannical judges not to do so. Rule 49 is but another means utilized by courts to weaken the constitutional power of juries and to vest judges with more power to decide cases according to their own judgments.

For a comprehensive discussion of the special verdict procedure, see Kotler, *Reappraising the Jury's Role as Finder of Fact*, 20 Ga.L.Rev. 123 (1985); Larsen, *Specificity and Juror Agreement in Civil Cases*, 69 U. Chi. L. Rev. 379 (2002).

One reason why judges are reluctant to utilize the special verdict procedure is the fact that it is difficult to form appropriate questions that will cover the significant elements of the case yet avoid ambiguities that can lead to a reversal on appeal. Does it make sense to require the jury to answer questions about particular details as to what occurred (For example: Did defendant fall asleep at the wheel of his vehicle?) or questions of ultimate fact (For example: Was defendant negligent in the operation of his vehicle?)? See Ginsburg, *Special Findings and Jury Unanimity in the*

Federal Courts, 65 Colum. L. Rev. 256 (1965) (setting out history of the forms of jury verdict and raising questions about the unanimity requirement in cases in which an ultimate issue is supported by separate fact theories).

A third form of verdict, an intermediate approach, is the general verdict with answers to interrogatories, which requires the jury to give a general verdict but also requires it to provide answers to a series of questions that usually are less extensive than those used with the special verdict. Although this form alleviates some of the concerns about the general verdict, problems arise when the answers to the interrogatories are inconsistent with the general verdict or with each other.

NOLLENBERGER v. UNITED AIR LINES, INC.

United States District Court, Southern District of California, 1963.
216 F.Supp. 734, vacated 335 F.2d 379 (9th Cir.), certiorari dismissed 379 U.S. 951, 85 S.Ct. 452, 13 L.Ed.2d 549 (1964).

HALL, CHIEF JUDGE.

[This is a wrongful-death action in which the jury, pursuant to Rule 49(b), rendered a general verdict accompanied by interrogatories. The plaintiffs allege that the answers to the interrogatories are inconsistent with the general verdict. They request that the court either submit additional interrogatories to the jury, or calculate the verdict on the basis of the answers to the questions given, or grant a new trial.]

* * *

The first task of the Court is to determine whether or not the Findings of Fact in the answers, given by the jury to the special interrogatories, are consistent with each other and whether one or more, if consistent with each other, are inconsistent with the general verdict fixing the total sum of damages to the plaintiffs resulting from the death of the decedent. And in doing so, Gallick v. Baltimore & Ohio R.R. Co., 372 U.S. 108, 83 S.Ct. 659, 9 L.Ed.2d 618 (1963), "it is the duty of the courts to attempt to harmonize the answers, if it is possible under a fair reading of them * * *."

The text of the special verdict on damages in the Nollenberger case is as follows:

We, the Jury in the above entitled case, unanimously find as follows:

QUESTIONS	ANSWERS
1. Which one of the following named persons, viz.: William Edward Nollenberger, 45 years of age on April 21, 1958; Catherine B. Nollenberger, his widow, age 47 on April 21, 1958; William Edward Nollenberger, Jr., son, age 20 on April 21, 1958; Lawrence P. Nollenberger, son, age 11 on April 21, 1958; had the shortest life expectancy?	Wm. E. Nollenberger

QUESTIONS	ANSWERS
	(Name)
2. How many years was that life expectancy on April 21, 1958?	25 (Total number of years)
3. How many years was decedent's work and earning expectancy from and after April 21, 1958?	15 yrs (Total number of years)
4. From and after April 21, 1958, what total sum of money do you find the decedent would have earned during the period of his work and earning expectancy stated in your answer to No. 3 above?	$235,210 (Total)
5. From and after the end of his work and earning expectancy, and during the remainder of his life, if any such remained, what total sum of money do you find decedent would have received as a result of his government employment?	$100,200 (Total sum)
6. What is the total reasonable value of services susceptible of being furnished by others which you find it was reasonably probable that decedent would have provided under my instructions to you to the plaintiffs during his lifetime?	$25,000 (Total value)
7. What percentage of his annual earnings, had he lived, from and after April 21, 1958, would have been used by decedent for his own personal expenses which were eliminated by his death?	25% (Percentage of annual earnings)
8. What percentage of his income would be paid as annual income tax had he lived after April 21, 1958?	15%
9. What percentage of the income from the award will be paid by plaintiffs as income tax?	11%
10. In determining the present reasonable value of services as defined in No. 6 above, what annual rate of inflation, if any, do you find should be allowed?	1%
11. What discount rate should be applied in arriving at the total sum of general damages?	4% (Discount rate)

QUESTIONS	ANSWERS
12. What sum of money do you find plaintiffs' general damages to be which you assess against Defendant United Air Lines?	$114,655.00

DATED: At Los Angeles, California, January 16, 1963.

S/Burford A. Reynold

Foreman

The answers to the Special Interrogatories No. 1 to No. 11 are plainly consistent with each other and are amply supported by the evidence.

But, in repeated efforts to "harmonize" and "reconcile" the answers to the 11 special interrogatories with the general verdict of $114,655.00, I have been unable to do so. And hence I must and do conclude that they are not harmonious or reconcilable.

While Rule 49(b) * * * under such circumstances permits, as one of three alternatives, the Court to re-submit the matter to the jury for further consideration, the plaintiffs desire the Court to go further and to submit additional interrogatories * * *. [H]ad it been the intention to permit *additional interrogatories* to be submitted *after* the general verdict and answers to the special interrogatories submitted with the verdict, the rule would have so provided, and the rule would not have contained the restrictive language of the second sentence of Rule 49(b) [the substance of which now appears in Rule 49(b)(1)] that the Court "* * * shall direct the jury both to make written answers and to render a general verdict," or the language * * * of Rule 49(b) [now contained in substance in Rule 49(b)(3)(B)] (applicable here) that the Court, as one alternative, "* * * may return the jury for *further consideration of its answers and verdict.*"

It could be argued from the portion of the rule last quoted that if that procedure were followed the jury could change both its answers and general verdict, or only the answers and not the general verdict. * * * That such action by the jury was not intended by the Rule is evidenced from the citation in the note to Rule 49 by the Advisory Committee of the case of Victor–American Fuel Co. v. Peccarich (C.C.A.1913) 209 F. 568, cert. den. 232 U.S. 727, 34 S.Ct. 603, 58 L.Ed. 817. In that case the Court stated, at page 571: "* * * these special findings must control when they clearly compel a different judgment from that which would follow the general verdict" * * *.

I conclude (1) that the findings of fact of the jury in answer to special interrogatories control over the general verdict; (2) that it is not within the power of the court under F.R.Civ.P. 49(b) to submit additional interrogatories after the jury has returned its verdict answering special interrogatories and at the same time returned a general verdict; (3) that in * * * Nollenberger * * * the answers to the special interrogatories are consistent with each other and inconsistent with and cannot be reconciled or harmonized with the general verdict; (4) that before granting a new trial, it is the duty of the Court to make calculations from the special interrogatories, and enter a judgment thereon. Which latter, I shall now do.

[The court then calculated the damages at $171,702.00 and entered judgment for that amount.]

* * *

NOTES AND QUESTIONS

1. In overturning the *Nollenberger* decision, the Court of Appeals held as follows (335 F.2d at 407–09):

> The district court stated that after repeated efforts, by mathematical calculation, to harmonize and reconcile the answers to the eleven special interrogatories with the general verdict, no harmony resulted. This may be so. But nothing in the law compelled the jury to calculate its damage awards according to a fixed mathematical formula using only the factors contained in the eleven special findings. * * *
>
> The jury was admonished to award damages in accordance with all the instructions of the court. No party specifies as error the giving of any of the instructions set forth in the margin.[43]
>
> * * * Suffice it to say that the answers to the eleven special interrogatories do not exhaust all of the factors of damage included within the instructions, and therefore no square conflict exists between the answers and the general verdict. We are not called upon to consider either whether the jury should not have been permitted to consider one or more of the italicized factors or whether the damage awards manifest such passion or prejudice as would render them inadequate. We hold that the court's utilization of the provisions of Rule 49(b) did not render proper its increase of damages in accordance with mathematical computations based upon the special findings.

2. Is the appellate decision in *Nollenberger* realistic? If so, what possible justification was there for the trial court's decision to present the jury with special interrogatories? The appellate court gave plaintiff the option of accepting the jury's general verdict or of having the case returned to the trial court for a ruling on plaintiff's motion for a new trial. Should the Court of Appeals

---

43. * * *

"You should award the plaintiffs herein such sum as, *under all of the circumstances of the case, may be fair and just compensation* for the pecuniary loss which the [widow and child(ren)] have suffered by reason of the death of [decedent].

"* * *

"In weighing these matters, you may consider * * * *the disposition of the deceased, whether it was kindly, affectionate or otherwise; whether or not he showed an inclination to contribute to the support of the plaintiffs or any of them;* the earning capacity of the deceased; and *such other facts shown by the evidence as throw light upon the pecuniary value of the support, society, care, comfort and protection* other than the loss of consortium between husband and wife, which the plaintiffs reasonably might have expected to receive from the deceased had he lived. * * *" (Emphasis added [in original].)

itself have decided whether there should be a new trial in the event that plaintiff decided not to accept the jury award?

3. Just how far should a court go in attempting to reconcile a jury's answers to specific interrogatories, either among themselves or with a general verdict? In POPHAM v. CITY OF KENNESAW, 820 F.2d 1570 (11th Cir. 1987), plaintiff sued to recover for violations of his civil rights alleging that the police used excessive force to arrest him, falsely arrested him, and arrested him in order to deprive him of his First Amendment rights. The trial court submitted special interrogatories, including one asking whether the police used excessive force and another asking whether the officers held qualified immunity. The jury answered both in the affirmative, yet awarded damages to plaintiff. The Court of Appeals, in upholding the jury verdict, held that the trial judge had an obligation to interpret apparently conflicting interrogatories so as to sustain the jury's general verdict. Applying the principle to the facts of the case, the court found that the jury's answer about immunity was made only with respect to the false arrest and First Amendment claims, citing the trial judge's instructions as support for its holding.

4. FINDINGS AND CONCLUSIONS IN NONJURY CASES

Read Federal Rule of Civil Procedure 52 in the Supplement.

ROBERTS v. ROSS

United States Court of Appeals, Third Circuit, 1965.
344 F.2d 747.

MARIS, CIRCUIT JUDGE.

The plaintiff, Herbert J. Roberts, appeals from a judgment entered in the District Court of the Virgin Islands dismissing his action brought to recover the sum of $3,087.50 which he alleged the defendant Norman M. Ross, Jr. promised to pay him for services rendered in producing a buyer for a dwelling house which the defendant had built in St. Thomas. The defendant answered, denying any such promise and, subsequently, with leave of court, he filed an amended answer in which he interposed the special defense of the Statute of Frauds.

* * *

On December 30, 1963, the trial judge entered an order stating that he had found for the defendant on the issues presented and directing counsel for the defendant within 10 days to file proposed findings of fact, conclusions of law and draft of judgment. Counsel for the plaintiff was given leave within 10 days thereafter to file objections thereto, which he did. On January 14, 1964 the findings of fact, conclusions of law, and judgment prepared and filed by counsel for the defendant were signed by the trial judge without change. It was concluded as a matter of law that "plaintiff has failed to prove by a preponderance of the evidence that the sale of said property by the defendant was procured through the agency of plaintiff," and that "in any event, said alleged promise not being in writing is within the Statute of Frauds." The plaintiff appealed from the judgment entered thereon dismissing his complaint.

* * *

The defendant * * * argues that * * * the plaintiff failed to prove the alleged agreement by a preponderance of the evidence, and the trial judge was accordingly justified in concluding that any discussion relating to compensating plaintiff for alleged sale of the property was at most the offer of a gratuity on the part of the defendant not specifically enforceable for indefiniteness. The fallacy in defendant's argument is that the trial judge failed to make any such findings. There is no finding as to whether the defendant agreed to pay the plaintiff a commission for producing a customer for the sale of the property—a question which was the crucial issue in the case. And there is no support in the record for the conclusion as a matter of law that "plaintiff has failed to prove by a preponderance of the evidence that the sale of said property by the defendant was procured through the agency of plaintiff." For it was undisputed that the plaintiff brought [the buyer] * * * to the property and introduced him to the defendant as a prospective purchaser. Perhaps the term "agency" in the quoted conclusion is intended to mean that the plaintiff, in doing so, did not act as agent for the defendant, thus possibly implying that the defendant did not agree to pay plaintiff a commission if he producd [sic] a buyer for the property. The trial judge's conclusion is, however, so inadequate as to afford this court no indication of the legal standard under which the evidence was considered.

This Court has had occasion to point out that [Federal] Rule 52(a) * * * requires the trier of the facts to find the facts specially and state his conclusions of law thereon with clarity. The findings of fact and conclusions of law must be sufficient to indicate the bases of the trial judge's decision. * * * The findings and conclusions in the present case do not meet this requirement.

Moreover we have observed in this case and in a number of others which have been brought here from the district court for review that the judge of the court has followed the practice of announcing his decision for the plaintiff or the defendant substantially in the form of a general verdict, either in a written order or by communication to counsel, and of thereupon directing counsel for the prevailing party to prepare and submit findings of fact, conclusions of law and a form of judgment. The trial judge's order has not been accompanied by an opinion setting out, even summarily, the facts and legal conclusions which have brought him to his decision. Obviously the judge must have dealt with the questions of fact and law involved in the case in the course of the reasoning by which he has reached his ultimate conclusion, even though his reasoning has not been articulated and put on paper. But counsel who is called upon to articulate and write out the findings and conclusions must do so without any knowledge of the fact findings and reasoning processes through which the judge has actually gone in reaching his decision.

We strongly disapprove this practice. For it not only imposes a well-nigh impossible task upon counsel but also flies in the face of the spirit and purpose, if not the letter, of Rule 52(a). The purpose of that rule is to require the trial judge to formulate and articulate his findings of fact and conclusions of law in the course of his consideration and determination of the case and as a part of his decision making process, so that he himself may be satisfied that he has dealt fully and properly with all the issues in the case before he decides it and so that the parties involved and this court on appeal may be fully informed as to the bases of his decision when it is made. Findings and conclusions prepared ex post facto by counsel, even though signed by the judge, do not serve adequately the function contemplated by the rule. At most they provide the judge with an opportunity to reconsider the bases of his original decision but without affording the parties any information as to what those bases were or which of them are being reconsidered. At worst they are likely to convict the judge of error because, as here, they are inadequate to support his decision or because, as we have observed in other cases, they are loaded down with argumentative over-detailed partisan matter much of which is likely to be of doubtful validity or even wholly without support in the record.

* * * We * * * do not * * * mean to suggest that a trial judge should not have the right to invite counsel for both parties to submit to him proposed findings of fact and conclusions of law, accompanied by briefs if he desires them, to assist him in formulating his own findings and conclusions and reaching his decision. In the process of studying the facts and the law, findings and conclusions formulated and proposed by the parties may be most helpful to the judge in sharpening the issues and may serve a very useful purpose in aiding him in drafting his own findings and conclusions. In most cases it will appear that many of the findings proposed by one or the other of the parties are fully supported by the evidence, are directed to material matters and may be adopted verbatim and it may even be that in some cases the findings and conclusions proposed by a party will be so carefully and objectively prepared that they may all properly be adopted by the trial judge without change. But it should be remembered that findings and conclusions prepared by a party and adopted by the trial judge without change are likely to be looked at by the appellate court more narrowly and given less weight on review than if they are the work product of the judge himself or at least bear evidence that he has given them careful study and revision. For the latter procedure would assure the appellate court, as Judge Wisdom pointed out in Louis Dreyfus & Cie. v. Panama Canal Company, 5 Cir., 1962, 298 F.2d 733, 738, "that the trial judge did indeed consider all the factual questions thoroughly and would guarantee that each word in the finding is impar-

tially chosen." It has been the general practice of the district judges of the Third Circuit in the past under Rule 52(a) to formulate their findings of fact and conclusions of law in the course of and as a part of their decision-making process and to articulate and file them at the time of announcing the decision, either in an opinion if filed at that time or in a separate document. * * * [W]e strongly approve this practice and direct it to be followed * * * by the court below.

* * *

NOTES AND QUESTIONS

1. Roberts v. Ross is discussed in 51 Cornell L.Q. 567 (1966), in which it is noted that on remand, the trial court, without a new hearing, reversed its earlier decision, and entered judgment for the party against whom it ruled initially.

2. In LEIGHTON v. ONE WILLIAM STREET FUND, INC., 343 F.2d 565, 567 (2d Cir.1965), the court discussed Federal Rule 52(a) as follows:

> The purpose of Rule 52(a), as it is applied to a non-jury case, is usually stated to be three-fold: (1) to aid the appellate court by affording it a clear understanding of the ground or the basis of the decision of the trial court; (2) to make definite just what is decided by the case to enable the application of *res judicata* and estoppel principles to subsequent decisions; and (3) to evoke care on the part of the trial judge in ascertaining the facts.

Which of the listed purposes of Rule 52(a) do you find most important? How detailed must the findings and conclusions be to satisfy these purposes?

3. Rule 52(a) was amended in 1987 to include the phrase "whether based on oral or documentary evidence," and currently refers to "oral or other evidence." Federal Rule 52(a)(6). The amendment responded to confusion among the courts concerning whether the same standard of review existed for findings of fact based on credibility evidence and those based on documentary evidence. Prior to the amendment, the Supreme Court addressed the issue in ANDERSON v. CITY OF BESSEMER CITY, 470 U.S. 564, 105 S.Ct. 1504, 84 L.Ed.2d 518 (1985), although the holding is somewhat cloudy. Justice White, speaking for the majority, explains:

> [The clearly erroneous standard applies] * * * even when the district court's findings do not rest on credibility determinations, but are based instead on physical or documentary evidence or inferences from other facts. * * *
>
> The rationale for deference of the original finder of fact is not limited to the superiority of the trial judge's position to make determinations of credibility. The trial judge's major role is the determination of fact, and with experience in fulfilling that role comes expertise. Duplication of the trial judge's efforts in the court of appeals would very likely contribute only negligibly to the accuracy of fact determination at a huge cost in diversion of judicial resources. In addition, the parties to a case on appeal have already been forced to concentrate their energies and resources on

> persuading the trial judge that their account of the facts is the correct one; requiring them to persuade three more judges at the appellate level is requiring too much. * * * For these reasons, review of factual findings under the clearly-erroneous standard—with its deference to the trier of fact—is the rule, not the exception.
>
> When findings are based on determinations regarding the credibility of witnesses, Rule 52(a) demands even greater deference to the trial court's findings; for only the trial judge can be aware of the variations in demeanor and tone of voice that bear so heavily on the listener's understanding of and belief in what is said. * * * This is not to suggest that the trial judge may insulate his findings from review by denominating them credibility determinations, for factors other than demeanor and inflection go into the decision whether or not to believe a witness. Documents or objective evidence may contradict the witness' story; or the story itself may be so internally inconsistent or implausible on its face that a reasonable factfinder would not credit it. Where such factors are present, the court of appeals may well find clear error even in a finding purportedly based on a credibility determination. * * * But when a trial judge's finding is based on his decision to credit the testimony of one of two or more witnesses, each of whom has told a coherent and facially plausible story that is not contradicted by extrinsic evidence, that finding, if not internally inconsistent, can virtually never be clear error.

Id. at 574, 105 S.Ct. at 1511–12, 84 L.Ed.2d at 528–30. What standard did the Supreme Court adopt? See Childress, *"Clearly Erroneous": Judicial Review Over District Courts in the Eighth Circuit and Beyond*, 51 Mo.L.Rev. 93 (1986); Adamson, *Federal Rule of Civil Procedure 52(a) as an Ideological Weapon?*, 34 Fla. St. U. L Rev.1025 (2007).

SECTION E. CHALLENGING ERRORS: NEW TRIAL

1. THE NATURE AND THE SCOPE OF THE POWER TO GRANT A NEW TRIAL

Read Federal Rules of Civil Procedure 59 and 61 and the accompanying materials in the Supplement. Note particularly the grounds for new trial listed in Minnesota Rule of Civil Procedure 59.01.

NOTE ON THE RANGE OF THE TRIAL COURT'S DISCRETION

1. Errors committed during the course of a trial may be categorized as follows: (i) those that would result in reversal if the case were to be appealed; (ii) those that may have had an impact on the verdict, but do not justify reversal of the case on appeal, and (iii) those that did not significantly affect

the outcome. Obviously errors that do not have any impact on the decision are harmless and it would be an abuse of discretion for the trial court to predicate a new trial on them. On the other hand, errors that would justify a reversal by an appellate court demand remedial measures at the trial level. A judge should not force a litigant to pay the costs of prosecuting an appeal as well as the costs of the new trial to which he is entitled.

2. Theoretically, it is only with regard to errors that affect the result in the case but would not lead to reversal on appeal that the trial court has discretion to decide whether or not a new trial is appropriate. As a practical matter, however, the almost unlimited power of the court with regard to the granting of new trials is far greater than it might otherwise seem to be. First, an aggrieved litigant may decide to stand or fall on the motion for new trial since the case simply may not be worth the added cost of an appeal or the litigant may not have sufficient funds to continue fighting. Second, in many jurisdictions, the grant of a new trial, not being a final judgment, cannot be appealed. Thus the cost of a new trial will have to be absorbed before an appeal is even possible. Third, the very question of what constitutes reversible error on appeal often is affected by the ruling of the trial judge on the motion for new trial. In those jurisdictions in which a motion for a new trial is a prerequisite for appeal, the denial of a new trial certainly will influence the appellate court in deciding whether the error is harmless for purposes of appeal if the effect of the error in question can better be determined by the trial judge. Even when a motion for a new trial is not required, and when, theoretically, the appellate court should not penalize a litigant for having so moved, knowledge that the trial judge has rejected the alleged error as harmless may have an impact on the appellate-court decision. Finally, in some jurisdictions the trial judge may grant a new trial without specifying or without actually relying on any precise grounds. Obviously this narrows the scope of review of such decisions.

GINSBERG v. WILLIAMS, 270 Minn. 474, 135 N.W.2d 213 (1965). Plaintiff brought suit for damages received in an automobile accident. The jury rendered a verdict for defendant and plaintiff moved for a new trial. The court granted the motion "in the interests of justice," giving no other basis for its ruling. Defendant sought a writ of prohibition to restrain enforcement of the ruling, claiming that the trial court is empowered to grant a new trial only for one of the grounds specifically set forth in Rule 59.01 of the Minnesota Rules of Civil Procedure. The Minnesota Supreme Court granted the writ, holding as follows:

> * * * The causes enumerated in Rule 59.01 are so comprehensive that they include every conceivable reason for which a new trial ought to be ordered. Those causes requiring the exercise of discretion, such as 59.01(1) (irregularities depriving the moving party of a fair trial) and 59.01(8) (insufficiency of the evidence), vest the broadest possible discretionary power in the trial court. To permit granting a new trial "in the interests of justice" would invite an arbitrary exercise of

> power over which appellate review is not now available. Even if it were, it would be difficult to fashion any effective rules to control arbitrary action since the basis for such an order would necessarily be subjective, varying from judge to judge. Further, each of the causes enumerated is designed to promote justice and prevent injustice. It is one thing to order a new trial "on the ground that on the evidence substantial justice has not been done" or in the interest of justice on the ground that the evidence does not justify the verdict, and quite another thing to order a new trial simply "in the interests of justice." It is difficult to conceive how such a general ground would anything to the grounds enumerated in our rules unless it is desirable to restore the common-law power of granting a new trial when the judge is personally dissatisfied with the verdict.

Id. at 483–84, 135 N.W.2d at 220.

NOTES AND QUESTIONS

1. In COPPO v. VAN WIERINGEN, 36 Wash.2d 120, 123–24, 217 P.2d 294, 297 (1950), the court stated:

> One of the reasons assigned by the trial judge in the instant cases for granting new trials is that "substantial justice has not been done." The statutes which enumerate the grounds on which new trials may be granted * * * make no mention of such a ground for a new trial; but we have always upheld the right of the trial judge to grant a new trial when he is convinced that substantial justice has not been done, on the theory that it is an exercise of the trial court's inherent power. * * *
>
> Actually, of course, when a trial judge says that "substantial justice has not been done," he is stating a conclusion for which there must be a reason or reasons. * * * The reason we have barred any review of an order granting a new trial based on this conclusion * * * was expressed by the supreme court of Wisconsin in the case of McLimans v. City of Lancaster, 57 Wis. 297, 15 N.W. 194, 195: "The judge before whom the cause was tried heard the testimony, observed the appearance and bearing of the witnesses and their manner of testifying, and was much better qualified to pass upon the credibility and weight of their testimony than this court can be. *There are many comparatively trifling appearances and incidents, lights and shadows, which are not preserved in the record, which may well have affected the mind of the judge as well as the jury in forming opinions of the weight of the evidence, the character and credibility of the witnesses, and of the very right and justice of the case.* These considerations cannot be ignored in determining whether the judge exercised a reasonable discretion or abused his discretion in granting or refusing a motion for a new trial." (Italics ours.)

2. Suppose a party moves for a new trial based on a number of specific errors, no one of which alone would be sufficiently prejudicial to justify a new trial. May the court under Ginsberg v. Williams grant the motion on the ground that all of the errors, taken together, deprived the losing party of a fair trial?

3. To what extent does the decision in *Ginsberg* provide significant appellate-court control over the "arbitrary exercise" of power by the trial judge? What more can the exercise of discretion mean than that the trial judge can decide that errors, trivial in appearance, have resulted in manifest injustice to the party seeking a new trial because of "lights and shadows which are not preserved in the record"?

2. INCOHERENT JURY VERDICTS

MAGNANI v. TROGI

Appellate Court of Illinois, Second District, 1966.
70 Ill.App.2d 216, 218 N.E.2d 21.

CORYN, PRESIDING JUSTICE. * * *

Plaintiff's complaint states two separate causes of action. In Count I she seeks recovery of $30,000.00, as Administratrix, for the wrongful death of her decedent, pursuant to the Wrongful Death Act (Ill.Rev.Stats., ch. 70, §§ 1 & 2). By the second count of the complaint she seeks reimbursement, in her individual capacity, for medical and funeral expenses necessarily incurred by her as the result of the injury and death to her husband, pursuant to the Family Expense Statute (Ill.Rev.Stats., ch. 68, § 15).

The Wrongful Death Act provides that any recovery thereunder shall be distributed by the court in which the cause was heard to the widow and next of kin of the decedent, in proportion, as determined by the trial court, "that the percentage of dependency of each such person upon the deceased person bears to the sum of the percentages of dependency of all such persons upon the deceased person." Here, any award of the jury, for a wrongful death, would be apportioned by the trial court to the widow and minor son of decedent. There would be no apportionment of any award made under the provisions of the Family Expense Statute.

* * *

In the instant case, there can be no doubt that the recovery sought under each count of plaintiff's complaint was based on separate causes of action, that is, one action for wrongful death, and the other under the Family Expense Statute. Unfortunately, neither party to this suit tendered separate forms of verdict for each of these counts. Rather, a single form of verdict was submitted by the court to the jury without objection from plaintiff or defendant. Using this form the jury returned the following verdict: "We, the jury, find in favor of the plaintiff and against the defendant. We assess the damages in the sum of $19,000.00." The trial judge, in his memorandum of opinion allowing a new trial, properly expressed the dilemma this verdict created for him by stating: "In the case at bar, there were two counts. Does the single verdict all apply to just one count, or to both counts? It might be that the verdict was all for the wrongful death action, and non-liability as to the medical expense cause of action." After making this observation, the trial judge then concluded that the verdict must be set aside and a new trial ordered as to both the liability and damage aspects of the case. Although other points have been raised in this appeal, we believe the determinative issue to be whether the trial judge, when faced with this situation, abused his discretion by granting a new trial.

The purpose of vesting the trial judge with power to grant a new trial is to permit him, before losing jurisdiction of the case, to correct errors that he or the jury might have made during the course of the trial. Courts of review have repeatedly stated that they will not disturb the decision of a trial court on a motion for new trial unless a clear abuse of discretion is affirmatively shown. The reason for this rule is that the trial court has had the opportunity to consider the conduct of the trial as a whole, and therefore is in a superior position to consider the effects of errors which occurred, the fairness of the trial to all parties, and whether substantial justice was accomplished. * * * Greater latitude is allowed a trial court in granting a new trial than in denying a new trial. * * *

Plaintiff argues that defendant has waived his right to complain of the form of verdict because he did not object to the giving of this form to the jury, but raised the issue for the first time in his post-trial motion. In most instances this would be a valid argument. Here, however, because of the single form of verdict, the jury's determination of liability and damages on each of the two causes of action was not made known. It appears that the jury found liability against the defendant on the wrongful death action, but any conclusion about what the jury's verdict was regarding liability on the family expense action is pure conjecture. Also, the language of the verdict returned gives no indication of the jury's determination as to what portion of the total verdict of $19,000.00 it attributed to damages for wrongful death, and what portion, if any, to damages for medical and funeral expenses. The determination of liability and damages, in the first instance, is to be made by the jury.

The jury returned its verdict on December 21, 1962, and the defendant filed his post-trial motion on January 15, 1963, thereby raising this issue for the first time. It was impossible, then, for the court to reassemble the jury and instruct them to correct the error in the form of verdict. * * * We are not holding, by this opinion, that the failure to submit to the jury separate forms of verdict in cases involving multiple causes of action should, in every instance, result in the granting of a new trial, but rather, that in the situation presented here it was not an abuse of discretion for the trial judge to grant a new trial.

The order of the Circuit Court of Lake County, granting defendant's motion for new trial, vacating and setting aside the verdict and judgment, and denying defendant's motion for judgment notwithstanding the verdict, is affirmed.

Affirmed.

STOUDER, JUSTICE (dissenting). * * * The record before us clearly shows that Plaintiff waived any individual interest in the verdict. The verdict, then being within the range of the evidence and the law, any possible dilemma facing the trial court was thereby solved.

As was succinctly stated in Hall v. Chicago and Northwestern Ry. Company, 349 Ill.App. 175, 110 N.E.2d 654 "We are not unmindful of the rule and cases which hold that the trial judge is allowed broad discretion in granting motions for a new trial, and that his actions will not be reversed on appeal except in cases of clear abuse of such discretion; but this rule, like all others, has its limitations. A judge is not empowered to set aside a verdict in any case simply because he does not agree with it. * * *" In the instant case the trial court's granting of a new trial was based upon a finding that the forms of verdict submitted to the jury were improper. It therefore should be our duty to examine the propriety of this finding in order to determine the limits which were self-imposed upon the discretion of the trial court.

Upon thorough examination of the record before us I am unable to find that Defendant made any objection to the forms of verdict at the conference on instructions or at any time prior to his post-trial motion. * * * Defendant's failure to object to the forms at the proper time as well as his later failure to show that he was in fact prejudiced compels me in the instant case to find that the trial court's finding was erroneous and Defendant's motion for a new trial should have been denied.

* * *

ROBB v. JOHN C. HICKEY, INC.

Circuit Court of New Jersey, Morris County, 1941.
19 N.J.Misc. 455, 20 A.2d 707.

LEYDEN, JUDGE.

The issues presented by the pleadings were the negligence of the defendants and the contributory negligence of the plaintiff's decedent. The jury was instructed concerning the applicable principles of law, in the course of which it was pointed out that if contributory negligence upon the part of the plaintiff's decedent had been established, the comparative degrees of the negligence of the parties was immaterial.

The jury returned a verdict in the absence of the judge and it was recorded at the clerk's desk as follows: "The jury finds that there was negligence on the part of both parties involved—The evidence shown is that the defendant was more negligent than the plaintiff—We therefore recommend an award of $2,000.00 to the plaintiff Clyde J. Robb and against the defendants John C. Hickey, Inc., a New Jersey Corporation and Roger W. King."

Both parties are dissatisfied with the verdict; the plaintiff with its substance and the defendants with its form. Plaintiff has a rule to set aside the verdict upon the ground that it is ambiguous, inconsistent, inadequate and contrary to the charge of the court. Defendants, upon notice, move to mould the verdict into one in favor of the defendants and against the plaintiff, urging that it is merely informal and the intent of the jury to find for the defendants is clearly indicated * * *.

It is true that a verdict must be responsive to the issues and recommendations of the jury dehors the issues submitted by the court, such as the suggestion of the equal division of another fund between the parties * * * or the amount claimed in the suit be donated to the American Red Cross * * * or each party (plaintiff being unsuccessful) pay his own cost * * * or of leniency in a criminal case * * * may be treated as surplusage and properly disregarded.

However, such is not the situation in the instant case. Here the verdict finds both parties guilty of negligence, erroneously compares the degrees of their negligence and recommends an award of $2,000 in favor of the plaintiff and against both defendants. What then did the jury agree upon and intend? Did it find in favor of the defendants as is legally indicated by the first sentence, or in favor of plaintiff in the sum of $2,000 as is clearly indicated by the last sentence? The recommendation of an award to the plaintiff is pertinent to the issues, for basically the liability of defendants to plaintiff in damages was in question. It cannot be treated as surplusage and disregarded. Reading the verdict as a whole, it is self-contradictory, inconsistent and ambiguous. One is left to conjecture and surmise as to the real purpose of the jury. It is defective in substance, not merely in form.

The court may, in fact should, mould an informal verdict to render it formal, effective and to coincide with the substance of the verdict as agreed upon and intended by the jury, but this power is only exercised where the real purpose and intent of the jury clearly, sufficiently and convincingly appears. * * * Where, as here, the verdict is uncertain or ambiguous, it cannot be moulded. The court will not substitute its verdict in place thereof. * * *

This leads to the denial of defendants' motion to mould and is also dispositive of the plaintiff's rule. The latter will be made absolute and a new trial granted.

NOTES AND QUESTIONS

1. Why is the verdict in *Robb* different from a verdict that recommends that the amount claimed be donated to the American Red Cross? Can't a strong argument be made in favor of a new trial in the latter situation? See Rusidoff v. DeBolt Transfer, Inc., 251 Pa.Super. 208, 380 A.2d 451 (1977), in which the trial judge's denial of a new trial was reversed when the jury verdict for defendant was rendered "with reservations due to the evidence provided."

2. Suppose plaintiff brings suit for injuries suffered in an accident allegedly due to defendant's negligence. The jury renders a verdict in favor of plaintiff but assesses damages at zero, although it is clear from the evidence that plaintiff has been badly hurt. May the judge enter judgment on the

verdict? See Wingerter v. Maryland Cas. Co., 313 F.2d 754 (5th Cir.1963), and Pitcher v. Rogers, 259 F.Supp. 412 (N.D.Miss.1966), in which the courts answered "yes." Can these decisions be reconciled with *Robb*? To what extent does the answer depend upon the nature of the evidence regarding the causation of damages? See, e.g., Fugitt v. Jones, 549 F.2d 1001 (5th Cir.1977).

3. How far should a trial court go in attempting to ascertain the "true intent" of the jury in order to be able to "mould" a verdict? Should the court be permitted to ask the jurors what they intended? Why shouldn't all but the clearest cases be returned for a new trial? Is there any way to avoid the costs and delays of a new trial if the verdict cannot be moulded?

KRAMER v. KISTER, 187 Pa. 227, 233–36, 40 A. 1008, 1008–10 (1898):

[The jury agreed to a sealed verdict and separated. When the verdict was opened the next morning, one juror dissented from it; the jury was sent out again and returned shortly with the same verdict, which was entered.]

* * * At common law the jury were kept together from the time they were sworn, as is still the general rule in criminal cases involving life. After they had retired to consider their verdict, they were kept without food, drink, fire, or light until they agreed; and Blackstone says, "It has been held that, if the jurors do not agree in their verdict before the judges are about to leave the town, though they are not to be threatened or imprisoned, the judges are not bound to wait for them, but may carry them round the circuit, from town to town, in a cart." 3 Bl.Comm. 376. From the manner of this mention, it is to be inferred that this latter practice was at least unusual in Blackstone's day; and he says expressly that the deprivation of food, fire, and light was subject to the indulgence of the court. * * * With the prolongation of trials in the more complicated issues of modern times, and especially with the amelioration of manners, the treatment of jurors has gradually become less harsh, and changes of practice have been made in their relief. It is no longer the custom to keep them together and secluded during the whole trial, though I apprehend that the judge may do so in any case where public excitement or other exceptional reason may make it advisable, in the interest of the proper administration of justice, to do so * * *. After the retirement of the jury to consider their verdict, this indulgence terminates, and they are kept together and apart from others until verdict rendered. But, if the adjournment of the court is to such time or under such circumstances as seem likely to lead to serious inconvenience to the jurors, the practice of allowing them to seal a verdict grew up. * * * When a juror dissents from a sealed verdict, there is a necessary choice of evils,—a mistrial, or a verdict finally delivered under circumstances that justly subject it to suspicion of coercion or improper influences. * * * If the dissenting juror was honest in his declaration that he had not agreed to the first verdict,

except because he thought he was obliged to, then his agreement to the second without having been instructed as to his rights cannot be freed from a well-founded appearance of coercion. If, on the other hand, the second verdict had been for the defendant, contrary to the first, the inference could hardly have been escaped that the change was produced by new evidence, or information illegally acquired by the dissenting juror, or by even more reprehensible means. The only safe way out of such a situation is to treat it as a mistrial, and discharge the jury. * * *

DUK v. MGM GRAND HOTEL, INC.

United States Court of Appeals for the Ninth Circuit, 2003.
320 F.3d 1052.

HAWKINS, CIRCUIT JUDGE.

Fernando Duk ("Duk") appeals the judgment arising from a defense verdict in favor of MGM Grand Hotel, Inc. ("MGM") in Duk's personal injury action in which there were two trials and three verdicts. MGM cross-appeals the district court's decision to resubmit the first verdict to the jury for clarification. Because we find that the court was within its discretion in resubmitting the first verdict, but erred in ordering a new trial upon receipt of the second verdict, we reverse and remand with instructions to enter judgment in Duk's favor consistent with the first jury's second verdict.

* * *

[Plaintiff spent a night of drinking and gambling at defendant's casino. He became "quite drunk" and engaged in "disruptive behavior, banging on the wooden dividers between booths and blowing kisses * * *." Defendant's security guards requested that plaintiff leave, and when he refused, they made a citizen's arrest. Security took plaintiff to a detention room prior to his transport to a Las Vegas city jail. Plaintiff's wife contacted security and informed them that plaintiff is an insulin-dependent diabetic. After being in the detention room for twenty minutes, plaintiff complained of lung pain. Defendant's security guards called for an ambulance and medics examined plaintiff. At trial, plaintiff presented evidence that he also had complained of chest pain, but that defendant failed to communicate this information to the medics. More than two hours later, plaintiff was taken to jail. He was released the next morning and went to a local hospital, where it was determined that he had suffered a heart attack, leading to massive damage to the left ventricle of the heart, and requiring a heart transplant.]

* * * Duk filed suit against MGM, claiming damages for medical expenses, pain and suffering, and economic damages suffered because of his inability to work following the transplant. The first jury trial was held in 1998. Because Nevada's comparative negligence scheme awards dam-

ages only to those plaintiffs who are found to be 50% negligent or less, the jury was presented with a special verdict form in which it was asked to determine the relative negligence of each party. Nev.Rev.Stat. § 41.141. Question 5 of the verdict form asked the jury to allot a percentage of the total negligence to the plaintiff and to the defendant. Following question 5, the jury was instructed that if it found the plaintiff to be more than 50% negligent, it should "sign and return [the] [in original] verdict" and judgment would be entered for the defendant. However, if in question 5 the jury found the plaintiff's negligence to be 50% or less, it was instructed to answer question 6, which asked for a determination of damages. Despite these instructions, the verdict form returned by the jury ("the first verdict") attributed 65% of the negligence to Duk and 35% to MGM, but still went on to award Duk $3.3 million in damages.

The district court reviewed the first verdict and, before announcing it, resubmitted the verdict form to the jury, informing the jury that the verdict contained an inconsistency and asking it to "continue [its] deliberations." Following 20 minutes of deliberation, the jury returned with a new verdict ("the second verdict"), apportioning 51% of the fault to MGM and 49% to Duk, but leaving the award of damages the same. The court granted MGM's subsequent motion for a new trial based on the inconsistency between the two verdicts.

* * *

At the second trial, the jury returned a verdict for MGM. Duk appeals the new trial grant and the judgment based upon the MGM verdict in the second trial, claiming that the second verdict was legitimate. * * * MGM cross-appeals, claiming that the trial court should not have resubmitted the original inconsistent verdict, but should have discarded the damages award and entered judgment for MGM. In the alternative, MGM argues that a new trial was properly ordered. * * *

* * *

* * * Although Rule 49(a), dealing with special verdicts such as this one, does not explicitly provide for resubmission in case of an inconsistency, we have held that, because the rule does not prohibit it, special verdicts are also subject to the practice. * * *

* * * [E]mbrace of the practice is based on the notion that resubmission "promotes both fairness and efficiency." * * * That principle was reaffirmed in *Larson v. Neimi,* 9 F.3d 1397 (9th Cir.1993), when we held that the resubmission of an inconsistent special verdict to a jury, with a request for clarification, was within the district court's discretion. * * * *Id.* at 1402. Larson had brought a 42 U.S.C. § 1983 damage action arising out of his allegedly wrongful arrest. The jury returned a special verdict form in which it found that the arresting officer had qualified immunity, but nonetheless proceeded to award damages to Larson. *Id.* at 1398. The trial judge, with approval from the parties, resubmitted the verdict to the jury, and the jury changed the verdict to say the officer did not have

qualified immunity. *Id.* We approved the district court's actions, and held that "[w]here the district judge does not push the jury in one direction or another, resubmission is a most sensible solution." *Id.* at 1401. * * * [W]e endorsed the policy underlying the practice of resubmission, noting that "when the very body that issued the ambiguous or inconsistent verdict is still available to clarify its meaning, a request that it do so comports with common sense as well as efficiency and fairness." *Id.* at 1402.

Here, the inconsistency arose when the jury awarded damages to Duk, even though it found him more than 50% responsible for his own injuries. MGM argues that the jury contravened the verdict form's instructions to "sign and return [the] verdict" if Duk were found to be more than 50% negligent and, as a result, resubmission was barred by *Floyd v. Laws,* 929 F.2d 1390, 1397 (9th Cir.1991) (responses in special verdict given in violation of a "stop here" instruction should be disregarded).

Floyd involved a 42 U.S.C. § 1983 suit and pendent state tort claims brought by a mother and her children against a municipality and its police chief. *Id.* at 1392. The jury was given a special verdict form addressing each of the claims, and found the police chief liable for assault and false imprisonment. *Id.* However, after the jury had been discharged, the defendant's counsel pointed out that the jury's answers to two of the questions were apparently inconsistent with one another. The jury answered "no" to question 13, which asked whether the plaintiffs were damaged as a result of the chief's actions. Following question 13 was an instruction which read: "If your answer to question 13 is 'No,' do not answer any further questions, but proceed to the end of this form and sign the verdict. If you answered 'Yes' to question 13, proceed to question 14." *Id.* at 1392–93. Question 14 asked the jury to award damages, which it did, awarding the plaintiffs $7,500. *Id.* at 1393. The trial court declared the answer to question 14 to be surplusage and entered judgment for the defendants. *Id.*

We upheld the trial court's decision, holding that, "as in the case of parenthetical comments, special findings issued in violation of the trial court's express instructions do not constitute legitimate or viable findings of fact." *Id.* at 1397. Because the trial court was "bound by law to disregard any answer to question 14 as surplusage," the damages award "never became a part of the special verdict, and the trial court was faced with no apparent inconsistency." *Id.* at 1399–1400.

Floyd, however, does not address the situation where the jury is still available when the inconsistency is recognized. *Id.* at 1392. * * * Because the jury had already been dismissed, the trial court in *Floyd* was left with the option of either disregarding the jury's answers following the "stop here" instruction or ordering a new trial. Thus, we had no occasion to consider whether resubmission, if it were possible, would *also* be within a trial court's discretion.

Here, unlike in *Larson,* the verdict form did contain a "stop here" instruction. * * * We now hold that where the jury is still available, a district court's decision to resubmit an inconsistent verdict for clarification is within its discretion.

* * *

* * * [W]hen the jury is still available, resubmitting an inconsistent verdict best comports with the fair and efficient administration of justice. Allowing the jury to correct its own mistakes conserves judicial resources and the time and convenience of citizen jurors, as well as those of the parties. It also allows for a resolution of the case according to the intent of the original fact-finder, while that body is still present and able to resolve the matter. An entirely different situation is present where the jury has been dismissed. There, dismissal of surplusage * * * makes sense. It is certainly preferable to ordering a new trial, and is very probably the best available instrument to determine the jury's intent.

Resubmission, of course, leaves open the possibility that the jury will reach an improper "compromise" verdict. * * * However, we presume that citizen jurors will properly perform the duties entrusted them and will not construe resubmission as an invitation to subvert the law and contort findings of fact in favor of a desired result.

* * *

A trial court is rarely entitled to disregard jury verdicts that are supported by substantial evidence. The Supreme Court has held that a trial court has a duty to attempt to harmonize seemingly inconsistent answers to special verdict interrogatories, "if it is possible under a fair reading of them." *Gallick* * * *, [p. 1111, supra]. A court may not disregard a jury's verdict and order a new trial until it "attempt[s] to reconcile the jury's findings, by exegesis if necessary." *Id.* * * *

[T]here is little authority addressing the question whether harmonization is required *across different verdicts,* where a verdict has been resubmitted for clarification. Indeed, resubmission necessarily means that there might well be a difference between the first verdict and that reached after resubmission. Such an "inconsistency" will usually be considered a proper correction of a mistake in the original verdict. However, even if the second verdict appears to the trial court to be an improper compromise, the Seventh Amendment requires the court to seek a legitimate explanation for a verdict that is not contrary to the weight of the evidence.* * * Further, verdicts rendered pursuant to resubmission are readily amenable to the harmonization requirement. In this case, the second verdict is flatly inconsistent with the first because it apportions liability differently. However, this discrepancy is easily explained by the process of redeliberation.

* * *

Resubmission of an inconsistent verdict is done with the sole purpose of allowing a jury to reconcile inconsistencies. This process is not simply restricted to correcting transcription errors, but also envisions a process of redeliberation. * * * Such a result is possible only where the jury is allowed to resume its deliberations. Some inconsistencies may only be resolved if the jury reconsiders its answers in light of the instructions given to determine how its legally inconsistent answers can be properly reconciled according to its view of the facts.

Once this premise is accepted, it becomes clear that a post-resubmission verdict can easily be harmonized with its earlier counterpart by reference to a wholly proper process of redeliberation. In this case, the second verdict was not internally inconsistent. The only reason the district court expressed in finding that a new trial was required was that the second verdict was the product of a "manipulation of negligence percentages." The court did not consider the possibility that the jury came to a different conclusion as to the facts because it engaged in further deliberations and legitimately came to new findings of fact. This is precisely what the trial court instructed the jury to do. When the court resubmitted the verdict to the jury, it twice instructed the jurors to "continue [their] deliberations."

In deeming the jury's second verdict an improper manipulation, the district court [relied on a decision of the Third Circuit Court of Appeals, holding that a new trial was necessary because the jury's deliberations appeared result-oriented and the court had "no rational reason" to accept the second verdict over the first]. * * *

* * * Here, however, the amount of damages remained unchanged from the first verdict to the second. Therefore, it is still quite plausible that the jury changed the apportionment of liability because it redeliberated and either changed its mind or clarified its thinking. It cannot be said here that the jury was clearly seeking a predetermined result. * * * As we have stated, the trial court has a duty to reconcile the verdicts "on *any reasonable theory* consistent with the evidence." * * *. Because it is possible to explain the inconsistency in a way that comports with the law, the district court's decision to disregard the second verdict and order a new trial was an abuse of discretion.

* * *

The trial court did not abuse its discretion in ordering resubmission of the first verdict. Because the second verdict was reconcilable with the first, the Seventh Amendment dictates that the second verdict was valid, and the court abused its discretion when it ordered a new trial. We order reinstatement of the second verdict and entry of judgment for the plaintiff, including such interest thereon as calculated by the district court.

NOTES AND QUESTIONS

1. One of the practical difficulties of resubmission is the fact that very few jurisdictions require jurors to remain together constantly once the case has been submitted to them. However, before allowing the jurors to separate,

the court normally will warn them not to discuss the case with anyone outside the jury room and not to inspect sites referred to in the testimony or otherwise to obtain evidence. See Steckler, *Management of the Jury*, 28 F.R.D. 190, 191 (1960). Can we really expect jurors not to have some discussions of a case with other jurors or with their families? What should the court do if it learns that discussions have occurred?

2. Do you agree with the reasoning of the court in *Kramer* as to why the resubmission was improper? To what extent does the case turn upon the time at which the resubmission was made? Suppose, for example, that the original verdict had been an oral one, rendered at the end of the deliberations. Would an immediate resubmission have been justifiable? If so, in light of modern practice permitting jurors to separate during their deliberations, isn't *Kramer* outmoded? Do you agree that the validity of resubmission in part depends on whether the jury has been discharged from the case?

3. To what extent may a court resubmit a verdict for defects other than the lack of unanimity or a proper majority? What if the error is one that the court could correct itself by moulding a proper verdict? What if the error was similar to that in Robb v. John C. Hickey, Inc., p. 1124, supra, in which the court held that it could not correct the verdict itself. Would a resubmission to the jury have been improper? See generally Martin, *Rationalizing the Irrational: The Treatment of Untenable Federal Civil Jury Verdicts*, 28 Creighton L. Rev. 683 (1995).

3. JURY MISCONDUCT AND THE INTEGRITY OF THE VERDICT

Should a juror be permitted to impeach his own verdict? Lord Mansfield's rule traditionally has barred courts from relying on jurors' affidavits to revisit a verdict. See Vaise v. Delaval, 1 Term r. 11, 99 Eng. Rep. 944 (K.B. 1785). However, the rule has been subject to criticism for more than a century. In 1866, the Iowa Supreme Court became the first state to deviate from the Mansfield rule, holding that "affidavits of jurors may be received for the purpose of avoiding a verdict, to show any matter occurring during the trial or in the jury room, which does not essentially inhere in the verdict." Wright v. Illinois & Mississippi Telegraph Co., 20 Iowa 195, 210 (1866). See also Woodward v. Leavitt, 107 Mass. 453 (1871).

Almost one hundred years later, in SOPP v. SMITH, 59 Cal.2d 12, 27 Cal.Rptr. 593, 377 P.2d 649 (1963), the majority's adherence to the Mansfield rule provoked a strong dissent from Justice Peters. Justice Peters acknowledged four reasons for adhering to "the strict rule of exclusion":

> (1) The need for stability of verdicts; (2) the need to protect jurors from fraud and harassment by disappointed litigants; (3) the desire to prevent prolonged litigation; (4) the need to prevent verdicts from being set aside because of the subsequent doubts or change of attitude by a juror; (5) the concept of the sanctity of the jury room.

But he saw the Iowa alternative as a better way to protect the integrity of the verdict without unduly intruding on jury deliberations:

> The Iowa rule is based upon the distinction between extrinsic or overt acts which may be corroborated or disproved, such as access to improper matter or an illegal method of reaching a verdict, and intrinsic matters which "inhere in the verdict itself" and hence are known only to the individual juror, such as misunderstanding or prejudice. Because matters which "inhere" in the verdict, including the thought processes and motives of the juror in reaching his decision, are not readily capable of being either corroborated or disproved they should be excluded.

Id. at 15–20, 27 Cal.Rptr. at 595–98, 377 P.2d at 651–54. In 1969 the California Supreme Court in PEOPLE v. HUTCHINSON, 71 Cal.2d 342, 78 Cal.Rptr. 196, 455 P.2d 132 (1969), reversed its prior stance and accepted Justice Peters' position that juror affidavits may be used in appropriate circumstances to impeach the verdict. Can you explain the distinction between extrinsic and intrinsic matters?

For an example of the difficulties that can arise when the court accepts affidavits of dissenting jurors alleging misconduct of the majority (when only a majority verdict is required), see Johns v. City of Los Angeles, 78 Cal.App.3d 983, 144 Cal.Rptr. 629 (2d Dist.1978) (hearing denied by 4–3 vote of the California Supreme Court). For developments in other states, see, e.g., Mudd, *Note—Liberalizing the Mansfield Rule in Missouri: Making Sense of the Extraneous Evidence Exception After Travis v. Stone*, 69 Mo. L. Rev. 779 (2004); Gallagher, *Pennsylvania's Exception to the No–Impeachment Rule Regarding Jury Deliberations Affected by Extraneous Information: Pratt v. St. Christopher's Hospital*, 44 Duq. L. Rev. 575 (2006).

NOTES AND QUESTIONS

1. Examine the language of Federal Rule of Evidence 606(b)(1), set out below.

> Upon an inquiry into the validity of a verdict or indictment, a juror may not testify as to any matter or statement occurring during the course of the jury's deliberations or to the effect of anything upon that or any other juror's mind or emotions as influencing the juror to assent to or dissent from the verdict or indictment or concerning the juror's mental processes in connection therewith. But a juror may testify about (1) whether extraneous prejudicial information was improperly brought to the jury's attention, (2) whether any outside influence was improperly brought to bear upon any juror, or (3) whether there was a mistake in entering the verdict onto the verdict form. A juror's affidavit or evidence of any statement by the juror may not be received on a matter about which the juror would be precluded from testifying.

Does Rule 606(b)(1) follow the Mansfield or the Iowa rule? See *Juror Impeachment of Verdicts*, 101 Harv. L. Rev. 250 (1987). For discussion of the problems raised by impeachment of verdicts through the use of juror testimony or affidavits, see Cammack, *The Jurisprudence of Jury Trials: The No Impeachment Rule and the Conditions for Legitimate Legal Decisionmaking*, 64 U. Colo. L. Rev. 57 (1993).

2. Suppose the jurors agree upon a verdict but through the mistake of the jury foreman, judge, or court clerk a different verdict is entered. Should affidavits of jurors be admissible to correct the error? Is this "impeachment" within the meaning of the common law? If so, would the case fall within the exceptions permitted by the Iowa rule? See FORD MOTOR CREDIT CO. v. AMODT, 29 Wis.2d 441, 139 N.W.2d 6 (1966), in which the court refused to accept affidavits of eight of twelve jurors to the effect that a "No" rather than a "Yes" answer had been reported improperly as to a crucial interrogatory.

3. May affidavits be used when a verdict for plaintiff was rendered, but the amount of damages found was omitted? See Hodgkins v. Mead, 119 N.Y. 166, 23 N.E. 559 (1890).

4. HUKLE v. KIMBLE, 172 Kan. 630, 243 P.2d 225 (1952), involved a damage action for injuries suffered "when plaintiff was caught between a truck driven by one of defendants and a pillar in the driveway of an elevator where plaintiff was employed." The jury rendered a verdict for plaintiff, and defendants appealed from the judgment:

> Defendants * * * argue that the trial court erred in overruling their motion for a new trial. One of the grounds of this motion was misconduct of the jury. On the hearing of the motion for a new trial testimony of various members of the jury was heard on the question of whether the verdict was a quotient verdict. One of the jurors testified as follows:
>
> > Q. Without giving any of the other deliberations—in other words, without telling what was in your mind—I would like to ask you how this verdict was arrived at, the amount of this verdict? A. Mr. Brann was the foreman of the jury and he asked that—or suggested that if the—there was a judgment, which he thought there should be, if we would all put down an amount on a piece of paper, which we did, then someone in the group added it up and divided it by 12 and arrived at the $5,208.33, and then Mr. Brann said, "Is there anyone that feels this is an unfair amount? Is this the amount that all of us wish, if you don't feel that way why speak up now," and we all agreed that that would be the amount that we felt was right.
> >
> > Q. And there had been something said before the quotient was taken, before you divided by 12 to do that to arrive at a verdict? A. I think so. I think it was. I think it was agreed that, before we wrote down those amounts that that would be the fair way, if one person said one amount and someone else said something higher and not knowing any better way, we agreed that an average would be right, and we discussed the average after we took it.
>
> The foreman of the jury testified as follows:
>
> > Q. You have heard the testimony of these two other jurors? A. Yes, sir.
> >
> > Q. Is that what occurred there at the time? A. That is correct.

Q. Do you have anything to add to it at all? A. I don't know as there is anything I could. I thought it was fair and square.

Q. You suggested that you add their respective figures together and then divide the sum by 12 and that that would be adopted as the verdict; is that right? A. Well, yes.

Plaintiff realizes the potency of this evidence and seeks to counteract it by claiming that on cross-examination these jurors testified that they were asked after the quotient had been reached whether they believed the amount to be fair and all the jury members said it was. The fact remains, however, that the evidence is uncontradicted, that the jury members all agreed that the quotient would be the verdict and it was. * * * The result is the trial court erred in overruling the defendant's motion for a new trial.

Id. at 630–39, 243 P.2d at 225–31.

As a practical matter does reversal in the *Hukle* case make any sense? Is the quotient verdict really all that evil? Would it be of significance if the jurors had taken a quotient verdict before deliberating the question of liability? What difference, if any, would it have made had the jury, after arriving at the quotient figure, discussed at length its propriety in light of the evidence? In SCHULZ v. CHADWELL, 558 S.W.2d 183, 186 (Ky.App.1977), the jurors used the quotient method to set an amount for each element of the claimed damage. The court rejected the appellant's claim that the verdict was thus an invalid quotient verdict: "The average of the jurors' views was obtained merely as a basis for further deliberation."

5. There are many forms of jury misconduct, as mentioned in Chapter One, see p. 53, supra. See also O'Malley, *Impeaching a Jury Verdict, Juror Misconduct, and Related Issues: A View from the Bench*, 33 J. Marshall L. Rev. 145 (1999). Often the question is not whether the conduct was improper but whether the error is so serious that the verdict must be overturned. Assuming that a trial court has before it the following sets of facts, what rulings should it make on motions for a new trial?

(a) The jury, after deliberation, was deadlocked seven to five for defendant, but because, during trial, one juror had learned of the death of a son and wished to return home, the jurors agreed to abide by the vote of the majority, and therefore, without further discussion, rendered a verdict for defendant. See Jorgensen v. York Ice Mach. Corp., 160 F.2d 432 (2d Cir.), certiorari denied 332 U.S. 764, 68 S.Ct. 69, 92 L.Ed. 349 (1947). Suppose the jury, although properly instructed, erroneously believed that a majority verdict was all that was necessary? Cf. Hoffman v. French, Ltd., 394 S.W.2d 259, 266 (Tex.Civ.App.1965).

(b) After the case was submitted to the jury and the jury deliberated for more than an hour without reaching a verdict the bailiff, on instruction of the court, took the jurors to lunch in a local hotel and supplied them with alcoholic beverages in moderate amounts. Shortly thereafter the jurors returned to the court and, after a half hour of deliberation, rendered a verdict. See Kealoha v. Tanaka, 45 Haw. 457, 370 P.2d 468 (1962) (denial of new trial affirmed by 3–2 decision). What difference would it make if one juror had become intoxicated?

(c) During a court recess plaintiff entered an elevator containing three jurors on their way to lunch. Plaintiff initiated a friendly conversation with one of the jurors regarding the fact that some of plaintiff's relatives lived in the area where the juror owned and operated a drugstore. The conversation was short and nothing was said about the case. See United States v. Harry Barfield Co., 359 F.2d 120 (5th Cir.1966) (denial of new trial reversed by a 2–to–1 decision).

There are many cases in which jurors have been charged with misconduct for holding unauthorized conversations concerning the case. Most of the decisions turn on the nature of the conversation regarding the case and the extent to which the juror might have been influenced in his decision. See, e.g., Adams v. Davis, 578 S.W.2d 899 (Ky.App.1979). Does it make sense to presume prejudice conclusively in contexts such as United States v. Harry Barfield Co., above? Should every contact between a juror and a party or attorney, or between a juror and a witness, be considered prejudicial? See Printed Terry Finishing Co. v. City of Lebanon, 247 Pa.Super. 277, 299–300, 372 A.2d 460, 469 (1977) (unexplained contact requires new trial).

In McDONOUGH POWER EQUIPMENT, INC. v. GREENWOOD, 464 U.S. 548, 104 S.Ct. 845, 78 L.Ed.2d 663 (1984), the respondent was injured in an accident involving a power mower manufactured by the petitioner. During the *voir dire* before the empaneling of the six-member jury, the respondents' attorney asked prospective jurors whether they or any member of their immediate family had sustained any severe injury. The jury ultimately found for the petitioner. After judgment was entered for the petitioner, the respondents' attorney questioned the jurors and discovered that the son of the foreman of the jury had been injured some time before by the explosion of a truck tire, sustaining a broken leg. During the post-judgment interview, the foreman said that "having accidents are [sic] a part of life," and that "all his children have been involved in accidents." Id. at 553 n. 3, 104 S.Ct. at 848 n. 3, 78 L.Ed.2d at 669 n. 3. The District Court, which did not have these details before it, refused the respondents' motion for a new trial. The Tenth Circuit held (based in part on the information quoted above but not presented to the District Court) that the juror's failure to respond to the question during the *voir dire* proceeding constituted juror misconduct requiring a new trial. The Supreme Court reversed:

> To invalidate the result of a 3–week trial because of a juror's mistaken, though honest, response to a question, is to insist on something closer to perfection than our judicial system can be expected to give. A trial represents an important investment of private and social resources, and it ill serves the important end of finality to wipe the slate clean simply to recreate the peremptory challenge process because

> counsel lacked an item of information which objectively he should have obtained from a juror on *voir dire* examination. * * * We hold that to obtain a new trial in such a situation, a party must first demonstrate that a juror failed to answer honestly a material question on *voir dire,* and then further show that a correct response would have provided a valid basis for a challenge for cause. The motives for concealing information may vary, but only those reasons that affect a juror's impartiality can truly be said to affect the fairness of a trial.

Id. at 555–56, 104 S.Ct. at 849–50, 78 L.Ed.2d at 671.

Justice Blackmun, joined by Justices Stevens and O'Connor, concurred, stressing that the decision should not be understood as "foreclos[ing] the normal avenue of relief available to a party who is asserting that he did not have the benefit of an impartial jury." Id. at 556, 104 S.Ct. at 850, 78 L.Ed.2d at 672. Justice Brennan, joined by Justice Marshall, concurred in the judgment, proposing a different legal standard:

> * * * In my view, the proper focus when ruling on a motion for new trial in this situation should be on the bias of the juror and the resulting prejudice to the litigant. More specifically, to be awarded a new trial, a litigant should be required to demonstrate that the juror incorrectly responded to a material question on *voir dire,* and that, under the facts and circumstances surrounding the particular case, the juror was biased against the moving litigant. * * *
>
> * * * [F]or a court to determine properly whether bias exists, it must consider at least two questions: are there any facts in the case suggesting that bias should be conclusively presumed; and, if not, is it more probable than not that the juror was actually biased against the litigant. Whether the juror answered a particular question on *voir dire* honestly or dishonestly, or whether an inaccurate answer was inadvertent or intentional, are simply factors to be considered in this latter determination of actual bias. * * *

Id. at 557–58, 104 S.Ct. at 851, 78 L.Ed.2d at 672–73.

NOTE AND QUESTIONS

Suppose that a finance company is a party in a case and its attorney asks each potential juror if he or she has ever applied unsuccessfully for a loan from the company. One juror falsely and deliberately answers "no." At what point must the finance company object to the juror's participation in the case? Should the answer depend upon how easy it would be for the company to ascertain the name of all unsuccessful loan applicants from the company's files? See Tidewater Finance Co. v. Fiserv Solutions, Inc., 192 F.R.D. 516, 519–20 (E.D.Va.2000).

---

4. NEW TRIAL BECAUSE THE VERDICT IS AGAINST THE WEIGHT OF THE EVIDENCE

Read Federal Rule of Civil Procedure 59.

AETNA CASUALTY & SURETY CO. v. YEATTS

United States Circuit Court of Appeals, Fourth Circuit, 1941.
122 F.2d 350.

PARKER, CIRCUIT JUDGE.

This is the second appeal in a suit originally instituted to obtain a declaratory judgment with respect to the coverage of a policy of indemnity insurance. * * * The company denied liability on the ground that the defendant Yeatts was engaged in the performance of a criminal abortion at the time he incurred the liability for which the recovery was had against him, and that such liability was expressly excluded from the coverage of the policy. The question as to whether the defendant Yeatts was engaged in such criminal conduct was submitted to the jury, and from verdict and judgment in his favor the plaintiff brings this appeal.

There was testimony below from which the jury would have been amply justified in finding in favor of the plaintiff insurance company on the issue submitted; but the defendant himself was examined as a witness and, if his testimony is believed, he was guilty of no criminal act. No motion for directed verdict was made by the plaintiff, nor was the sufficiency of the evidence to sustain a finding in favor of the defendant challenged in any other way before verdict. After verdict, plaintiff moved for judgment non obstante veredicto and also for a new trial, on the ground that the verdict was contrary to the credible evidence in the case; and exceptions directed to denial of these motions constitute the only points presented by the appeal.

Even if a motion for directed verdict had been made by plaintiff, it is clear that same should have been denied as should also, any motion for judgment non obstante veredicto based thereon * * *.

The motion to set aside the verdict and grant a new trial was a matter of federal procedure, governed by Rule * * * 59 and not subject in any way to the rules of state practice. On such a motion it is the duty of the judge to set aside the verdict and grant a new trial, if he is of opinion that the verdict is against the clear weight of the evidence, or is based upon evidence which is false, or will result in a miscarriage of justice, even though there may be substantial evidence which would prevent the direction of a verdict. The exercise of this power is not in derogation of the right of trial by jury but is one of the historic safeguards of that right.

* * * The matter was well put by Mr. Justice Mitchell, speaking for the Supreme Court of Pennsylvania in Smith v. Times Publishing Co., * * * [178 Pa. 481, 501, 36 A. 296, 298], as follows: "The authority of the common pleas in the control and revision of excessive verdicts through the means of new trials was firmly settled in England before the foundation of this colony, and has always existed here without challenge under any of our constitutions. It is a power to examine the whole case on the law and the evidence, with a view to securing a result, not merely legal, but also not manifestly against justice,—a power exercised in pursuance of a sound judicial discretion, *without which the jury system would be a capricious and intolerable tyranny,* which no people could long endure. This court has had occasion more than once recently to say that it was *a power the courts ought to exercise unflinchingly.*" (Italics supplied [in original]).

In the same case, Mr. Justice Williams, in a concurring opinion, traces the history of the exercise of this power and sums up his conclusion as follows:

* * *

> As early * * * as 1665, the courts at Westminster did precisely what we have done in this case, and for the same reason. The right of trial by jury was not then supposed to give to a successful party the right to insist on an advantage due to the mistake or the willful misconduct of the jury, no matter how grossly unjust and oppressive the result might be; but the supervisory control of the court in banc, sitting as a court of review, was promptly exercised to relieve against the miscarriage of justice. The exercise of this power was then thought to be in aid of trial by jury. * * *

[Id. at 508–09, 36 A. at 309.]

* * *

The distinction between the rules to be followed in granting a new trial and directing a verdict were stated by us with some care in Garrison v. United States, 4 Cir., 62 F.2d 41, 42, * * * as follows: "Where there is substantial evidence in support of plaintiff's case, the judge may not direct a verdict against him, even though he may not believe his evidence or may think that the weight of the evidence is on the other side; for, under the constitutional guaranty of trial by jury, it is for the jury to weigh the evidence and pass upon its credibility. He may, however, set aside a verdict supported by substantial evidence where in his opinion it is contrary to the clear weight of the evidence, or is based upon evidence which is false; for, even though the evidence be sufficient to preclude the direction of a verdict, it is still his duty to exercise his power over the proceedings before him to prevent a miscarriage of justice. * * *"

It is equally well settled, however, that the granting or refusing of a new trial is a matter resting in the sound discretion of the trial judge, and that his action thereon is not reviewable upon appeal, save in the most exceptional circumstances. * * * The rule and the reason therefor is thus stated by Mr. Justice Brandeis in Fairmount Glass Works v. Cub Fork Coal Co., * * * [287 U.S. 474, 481, 53 S.Ct. 252, 254, 77 L.Ed. 439, 443]: "The rule that this Court will not review the action of a federal trial court in granting or denying a motion for a new trial for error of fact has been settled by a long and unbroken line of decisions * * *. The rule precludes likewise a review of such action by a Circuit Court of Appeals. Its early formulation by this Court was influenced by the mandate of the Judiciary Act of 1789, which provided in section 22 that there should be 'no reversal in either (circuit or Supreme) court on such writ of error * * * for any error in fact.' Sometimes the rule has been rested on that part of the Seventh Amendment which provides that 'no fact tried by a jury, shall be otherwise reexamined in any court of the United States than according to the rules of the common law'. More frequently the reason given for the denial of review is that the granting or refusing of a motion for a new trial is a matter within the discretion of the trial court."

While an examination of the record has led us to the conclusion that the trial judge might very properly have granted the motion for new trial, we cannot say that his denial of the motion amounted to an abuse of discretion on his part or that there are present any of the special circumstances which would subject his action to review by this court. The judgment appealed from will accordingly be affirmed.

Affirmed.

NOTES AND QUESTIONS

1. In MARSH v. ILLINOIS CENT. R. CO., 175 F.2d 498, 500 (5th Cir.1949), the district judge had granted judgment notwithstanding the verdict, but had denied an alternative motion for new trial, saying: "It is my judgment that the evidence was insufficient to go to the jury, but if I am wrong in that, then I do not think a new trial should be granted as there were no other errors of law." The Court of Appeals reversed:

> * * * While it is not our function to weigh the evidence, we do agree with the trial judge's first expressed opinion that the weight of the evidence is "overwhelmingly against the plaintiff". But we do not agree that the grant of a judgment notwithstanding the verdict was therefore justified. There was evidence of the appellant, not very explicit or positive, which if believed might authorize a jury to conclude he was hurt in the manner he claims. Because the trial judge does not believe it, because of appellant's own contradictions and conduct and of opposing evidence which seem to overwhelm it, is not ground for a judgment notwithstanding the verdict, and we must reverse that judgment. * * *
>
> But it is ground for the trial judge to grant a new trial, though the trial was free of other error. He has in strong terms disapproved the verdict as contrary to the evidence * * *. We have reversed the entering of a final judgment, but it is evident that the new trial ought to be granted and would have been except for the misconception that absence of other error prevented it. The full discretion vested in the trial judge not having been

exercised, we will remand the case with direction to the judge to grant a new trial * * * if he continues to think the verdict to be against the overwhelming weight of the evidence.

2. In cases such as Lavender v. Kurn, p. 57, supra, and Denman v. Spain, p. 1076, supra, when there is a lack of proof of what happened rather than a conflict of proof, would the grant of a new trial be any more appropriate than the direction of a verdict?

3. In DYER v. MacDOUGALL, 201 F.2d 265, 271 (2d Cir.1952), Judge Frank, concurring, said:

> * * * The well-settled rule is that, in passing on a motion for a directed verdict, the trial judge always must utterly disregard his own views of witnesses' credibility, and therefore of their demeanor; that he believes or disbelieves some of the testimony is irrelevant. When asked to direct a verdict for the defendant, the judge must assume that, if he lets the case go to the jury, the jurymen will believe all evidence—including "demeanor evidence"—favorable to the plaintiff. In other words, the judge must not deprive plaintiff of any advantage that plaintiff might derive from having the jury pass upon the oral testimony. Indeed, the important difference between a trial judge's power on a motion for a new trial and on a motion for a directed verdict is precisely that on a new-trial motion he may base his action on his belief or disbelief in some of the witnesses, while on a directed-verdict motion he may not.

See also BOWDITCH v. CITY OF BOSTON, 101 U.S. (11 Otto) 16, 18, 25 L.Ed. 980, 980–81 (1879): "It is now a settled rule in the courts of the United States that whenever, in the trial of a civil case, it is clear that the state of the evidence is such as not to warrant a verdict for a party, and that if such a verdict were rendered the other party would be entitled to a new trial, it is the right and duty of the judge to direct the jury to find according to the views of the court." The *Bowditch* case is but one of many with language of this kind. On this distinction, also consider the scholarly opinion of Judge (later Justice) Lurton, in Mt. Adams & E.P. Inclined Ry. Co. v. Lowery, 74 F. 463 (6th Cir.1896).

4. Suppose a verdict has been set aside and a new trial granted. If the jury in the second trial returns a verdict similar to the one rendered in the first action, may the court again order a new trial on the ground that the verdict is against the weight of the evidence? Compare Palmer v. Miller, 60 F.Supp. 710 (W.D.Mo.1945) (yes), with Mo.Stat. Ann. § 510.330, which appears in the Supplement following Federal Rule 59. See Friedenthal, Kane & Miller, Civil Procedure § 12.4 at 592 (4th ed. 2005): "[A] series of new trial orders in jury cases in which the judge's view of the result does not comport with the jury verdicts would be inappropriate. To order repeated new trials could be an intrusion on the institution of jury trial. The right to jury trial would be meaningless if verdicts could stand only if the judge would reach the same result."

DYER v. HASTINGS, 87 Ohio App. 147, 149–50, 94 N.E.2d 213, 215 (1950):

No judgment may be vacated or set aside and new trial granted upon the ground that the verdict is against the weight of the evidence except as a matter of law; and a judgment will not be vacated or set aside and a new trial granted upon such ground where the verdict is supported by competent, substantial and apparently credible evidence which goes to all the essential elements of the case. * * *

In formulating this rule the word, "substantial," modifying the word, "evidence," is used in the sense of "constituting more than a scintilla of," and the word, "apparently," as used to modify the word "credible," is used to indicate that the court does not undertake to judge the credibility of the evidence, but only to judge whether it has the semblance of credibility.

The evidence in the instant case is in direct and sharp conflict on many essential elements of the case and is such that a verdict for either party would be supported by competent, substantial and apparently credible evidence.

In this situation it was the sole function of the jury to determine the credibility of the evidence, which it did by returning a verdict in favor of the defendant.

IN RE GREEN'S ESTATE, 25 Cal.2d 535, 542–43, 154 P.2d 692, 695–96 (1944):

It is next contended by contestant that the court erred in granting proponent's motion for a new trial on the ground "that the evidence as a whole was insufficient as a matter of law to support a verdict for respondents." The rules of law applicable to an appeal from an order of the trial court granting a motion for a new trial on the ground of the insufficiency of the evidence are well settled and, as stated in one of our most recent decisions, are as follows: " * * * When the motion is granted, as here, for insufficiency of the evidence, it is only in rare cases showing abuse of discretion that an appellate court will interfere because the trial judge must weigh all the evidence and determine the just conclusion to be drawn therefrom. * * * It cannot be held that a trial court has abused its discretion where there is a conflict in the evidence or where there is any evidence which would support a judgment in favor of the moving party." Hames v. Rust, 14 Cal.2d 119, 123, 124, 92 P.2d 1010, 1012 (1939).

* * *

We may not agree with the determination reached by the trial judge or with any of his conclusions. That is not the question before us. It is his duty to weigh the evidence and to pass upon any and all conflicts existing therein. * * * If after such an examination of the evidence he concludes that it is insufficient to support the verdict, his duty is to grant the motion and a reviewing court may not set aside his conclusion unless a showing of abuse of discretion is made out by appellant. * * * As we have seen, if there is any substantial evidence in the case supporting the trial court's action, then we should not interfere with its order granting said motion.

NOTES AND QUESTIONS

1. In *In re Green's Estate*, is the California Supreme Court discussing a standard for granting the motion for a new trial or a standard for reviewing the grant of the motion?

2. Professor James has underscored the difficulty of comparing the test for a judgment notwithstanding the verdict with that for a new trial:

> As for equating the test for directing a verdict to that for setting aside a verdict and granting a new trial, the matter is complicated by the wide range among the tests used in different jurisdictions for setting a verdict aside. * * * [T]he equation is more nearly valid in some jurisdictions than it is in others, but the differences are rather because of variations in the new trial test than because of any variation in the directed verdict test.

James, *Sufficiency of the Evidence and Jury–Control Devices Available Before Verdict*, 47 Va.L.Rev. 218, 233–34 (1961). Indeed, it also is difficult to ascertain the standard for granting a new trial in a particular jurisdiction and to compare it with the standard applied in another jurisdiction because of peculiarities regarding the appealability, reviewability, and scope of review of a decision on a motion for a new trial. In many jurisdictions the grant of a new trial may be unappealable because it is not a "final order"; even if appealable, a grant or denial of the motion may not be disturbed on appeal except upon a showing of an abuse of discretion by the trial court, which rarely is found. The result is that the new-trial standard actually is formulated and controlled by trial judges, not appellate courts; inasmuch as the standard is shaped by courts whose opinions often are not reported and therefore will not provide a guideline for other courts, or establish a body of precedent, the standard may vary widely from case to case.

3. Should an appeals court be more likely to uphold a trial judge's decision to grant a new trial than a decision to deny a new trial? Isn't the trial judge in the best position to have seen errors that may have occurred at trial and to gauge whether those errors may have affected the fairness of the first trial? For a full discussion of the weight-of-the evidence standard and its relation to the judge's discretion to grant a new trial, see Robertson, *Judging Jury Verdicts*, 83 Tul. L. Rev. 157 (2008).

4. In a diversity-of-citizenship case in federal court, is the judge bound to apply the standard for new trial that would be applied in the courts of the state in which it sits? Review *Gasperini*, p. 454, supra.

5. THE POWER TO GRANT CONDITIONAL AND PARTIAL NEW TRIALS

FISCH v. MANGER

Supreme Court of New Jersey, 1957.
24 N.J. 66, 130 A.2d 815.

JACOBS, J.

The plaintiff suffered serious injuries in an automobile accident and, after trial, received a jury verdict in the sum of $3,000. He applied for a new trial because of the inadequacy of the verdict but his application was denied when the defendants consented that the damages awarded to the plaintiff be increased to the sum of $7,500. The plaintiff appealed and we thereafter certified on our own motion.

* * *

The plaintiff's actual expenditures to doctors and nurses and for drugs and hospitalization exceeded $2,200. And although he received most of his normal earnings despite his temporary incapacity, there was a loss of wages approximating $620. While the jury's verdict of $3,000 just about took care of the plaintiff's actual monetary losses, it awarded substantially nothing for his suffering and permanent injuries. Its gross inadequacy was recognized by the trial judge who pointed out that "there was no dispute but that the plaintiff suffered excruciating pain, and was rendered totally helpless for a considerable period of time." On June 28, 1956 the trial judge wrote to the parties advising that unless the defendants filed a consent in writing that the verdict be increased from $3,000 to $7,500, "then the verdict heretofore rendered will be set aside and a new trial granted limited to damages only." The consent was filed by the defendants and on June 30, 1956 a formal order was entered dismissing the plaintiff's motion for a new trial. * * *

The first point which he urges in support of his appeal is that once the trial court had concluded that the damages awarded by the verdict were inadequate it had no legal power whatever to condition the grant of a new trial upon the defendants' failure to consent to a prescribed increase in the verdict. * * * The term *remittitur* is used to describe an order denying the defendant's application for new trial on condition that the plaintiff consent to a specified reduction in the jury's award, whereas the term *additur* is used to describe an order denying the plaintiff's application for a new trial on condition that the defendant consent to a specified increase in the jury's award. While it is now recognized that the two practices are logically and realistically indistinguishable, *remittiturs* have been recognized almost everywhere, whereas *additurs* are still outlawed in some, though by no means all, of the states. * * *

The English precedents prior to the American Revolution are somewhat obscure and they are discussed in the majority and minority opinions in Dimick v. Schiedt, 293 U.S. 474, 55 S.Ct. 296, 302, 79 L.Ed. 603 (1935). There Justice Sutherland, speaking for a majority of five (with Justice Stone, joined by Chief Justice Hughes and Justices Brandeis and Cardozo, dissenting) held that although *remittitur* is permissible in the federal courts, *additur* is prohibited by * * * the Seventh Amendment * * *. Justice Sutherland in the Dimick case * * * declined to upset the *remittitur* practice, first approved by Justice Story in Blunt v. Little, 3 Fed.Cas. 760, No. 1,578 (C.C.Mass.1822), and since reaffirmed in many federal decisions. * * *

In his dissenting opinion in the Dimick case, Justice Stone pointed out that the Seventh Amendment was concerned with substance rather than form and that the Supreme Court had often declined to construe it as perpetuating in changeless form the minutiae of trial practice as it existed in the English courts in 1791; he referred to the many jury procedures unknown to the common law but now well established in federal practice; he considered wholly impersuasive the suggested differentiation between the settled *remittitur* practice which the majority continued and the *additur* practice which it rejected; and he concluded with the following remarks * * *:

> To me it seems an indefensible anachronism for the law to reject the like principle of decision, in reviewing on appeal denials of motions for new trial, where the plaintiff has consented to decrease the judgment or the defendant has consented to increase it by the proper amount, or to apply it in the one case and reject it in the other. It is difficult to see upon what principle the denial of a motion for a new trial, which for centuries has been regarded as so much a matter of discretion that it is not disturbed when its only support may be a bad or inadequate reason, may nevertheless be set aside on appeal when it is supported by a good one: That the defendant has bound himself to pay an increased amount of damages which the court judicially knows is within the limits of a proper verdict.

The majority opinion in Dimick has been the subject of much criticism and it is doubtful whether the Supreme Court would still subscribe to it; in any event, the Seventh Amendment differs somewhat from our constitutional provision and has no application to proceedings in our state courts. * * * We must look primarily to our own history and precedents in ascertaining whether the highly desirable practices of *remittitur* and *additur* may be adhered to in our State * * *.

The *remittitur* practice has been recognized in New Jersey since early days. * * * [In 1917] the Court of Errors and Appeals had occasion to deal with a negligence case in which the practice of *additur* had been invoked. * * * Chancellor Walker, speaking for the entire court, had this to say ([Gaffney v. Illingsworth,] 90 N.J.L. at page 492, 101 A. at page 243):

> The power of the court in granting a new trial upon the ground that the damages are *excessive,* upon terms that a new trial shall be had unless the plaintiff will accept a certain sum named, less than that

awarded by a verdict, is too well established to be questioned. It would seem to follow, by parity of reasoning, that when a new trial is granted because the damages are inadequate, the court may impose like terms, that is, terms to the effect that if the defeated party will pay a certain sum, greater than that awarded by the verdict, the rule will be discharged, subject, doubtless, to the power of an appellate court to vacate any such terms when they appear to be an abuse of discretion. * * *

* * *

* * *[W]e are satisfied that the practices of *remittitur* and *additur* violate none of our constitutional interdictions and, if fairly invoked, serve the laudable purpose of avoiding a further trial where substantial justice may be attained on the basis of the original trial. * * * Accordingly, we reject the first point urged by the plaintiff and come now to his meritorious contention that, in any event, the prescribed increase to $7,500 was "grossly inadequate and should be set aside." * * * In the instant matter, we believe that the trial judge had a mistaken notion of the evidence which led to his prescribing the scanty sum of $7,500. He stated that the plaintiff was not entitled to a "great sum, because he certainly did have a back condition before this accident occurred"; but the evidence in the record points to the view that whatever "back condition" the plaintiff had as a result of the 1950 accident had cleared up and had no relation to the very severe injuries resulting from the 1953 accident. Under these highly special circumstances, we believe that the trial court's action should not be permitted to stand and that the interests of justice will best be served by permitting a second jury to pass on the issue of damages. The separable issue of liability was clearly and properly decided against the defendants; under the evidence it could hardly have been determined otherwise and need not be submitted for redetermination. * * *

Reversed, with direction for a new trial on the issue of damages.

HEHER, J. (concurring in result). * * *

As is shown by Justice Sutherland's analysis of the case history in Dimick v. Schiedt * * *, there was no power in the English courts at the time of the adoption of the New Jersey Constitution of 1776 to increase, either absolutely or conditionally, the damages fixed by a jury in a case such as this. * * *

* * * Justice Sutherland concluded, and with unquestionable authority, that "while there was some practice to the contrary in respect of *decreasing* damages, the established practice and the rule of the common law, as it existed in England at the time of the adoption of the Constitution, forbade the court to *increase* the amount of damages awarded by a jury in actions such as that here under consideration." He observed that "this court in a very special sense is charged with the duty of construing and upholding the Constitution; and in the discharge of that important duty, it ever must be alert to see that a doubtful precedent [involving

remittitur] be not extended by mere analogy to a different case if the result will be to weaken or subvert what it conceives to be a principle of the fundamental law of the land"; and that "the power to conditionally increase the verdict of a jury does not follow as a necessary corollary from the power to conditionally decrease it," since in the case of a conditional *remittitur* "a jury has already awarded a sum in excess of that fixed by the court as a basis for a *remittitur,* which at least finds some support in the early English practice, while in the second case, no jury has ever passed on the increased amount, and the practice has no precedent according to the rules of the common law."

The "controlling distinction between the power of the court and that of the jury," said Justice Sutherland, "is that the former is the power to determine the law and the latter to determine the facts," and while the *remittitur* practice in the case of an excessive verdict "is not without plausible support in the view that what remains is included in the verdict along with the unlawful excess,—in the sense that it has been found by the jury,—and that the *remittitur* has the effect of merely lopping off an excrescence," yet where an inadequate verdict is increased by the court there is a "bald addition of something which in no sense can be said to be included in the verdict," and if that be done with the consent of the defendant alone, the plaintiff is compelled to forego his "constitutional right to the verdict of a jury and accept 'an assessment partly made by a jury which has acted improperly, and partly by a tribunal which has no power to assess.' "

* * *

POWERS v. ALLSTATE INSURANCE CO., 10 Wis.2d 78, 102 N.W.2d 393 (1960). Plaintiff received a jury award for permanent injuries in the amount of $5,000. The award was excessive and called for a remittitur. The question before the state supreme court was what standard should determine the amount to which the damages should be reduced. The court noted that since its decision in Heimlich v. Tabor, 123 Wis. 565, 102 N.W. 10 (1905), Wisconsin judges had been required to set damages at the lowest amount that a reasonable jury could have awarded. This rule was contrary to the practice in most jurisdictions, in which "the courts follow the practice of allowing the plaintiff the option of avoiding a new trial by remission of the excess above an amount which the court considers reasonable." The court went on to point out that the Wisconsin rule tended to limit the effectiveness of the remittitur practice.

> * * * We are firmly of the opinion that if the plaintiff were granted the option of accepting a reasonable amount as determined by the trial or appellate court, instead of the least amount that an unprejudiced jury properly instructed might award, the number of instances

in which the plaintiff would be likely to refuse such option and elect a new trial would be greatly reduced.

The court then specifically overruled *Heimlich* and adopted the standard rule.

NOTES AND QUESTIONS

1. For an argument that the practice of remittitur is not constitutional under the Seventh Amendment, see Thomas, *Re–Examining the Constitutionality of Remittitur Under the Seventh Amendment*, 64 Ohio St.L.J. 731 (2003).

2. Should a trial court have discretion to set a reasonable remittitur figure somewhere between the highest and lowest possible verdicts? Would it make more sense to require, as the alternative to a new trial, the highest amount an unprejudiced jury properly could have awarded plaintiff?

3. Suppose the federal courts had adopted the rule in the *Heimlich* case, which was overruled in *Powers*. Would application of an analogous rule to additur have permitted its use without violation of the Seventh Amendment?

4. In an action under the Federal Employers' Liability Act, 45 U.S.C. § 51, the California Supreme Court held that the trial court could order an additur. Jehl v. Southern Pac. Co., 66 Cal.2d 821, 59 Cal.Rptr. 276, 427 P.2d 988 (1967). In light of *Dimick,* is this holding consistent with *Dice*, p. 495, supra?

DOUTRE v. NIEC

Michigan Court of Appeals, 1965.
2 Mich.App. 88, 138 N.W.2d 501.

Defendants operate a beauty shop in Flint. On April 19, 1962 plaintiff was given a bleach and color treatment by defendants without a pretreatment patch test. Plaintiff received head and facial injuries as a result of the treatment and sued for damages.

During the trial defendants were not allowed to testify as to the standard of care observed by beauty shops in the Flint area when administering such treatment. The jury awarded plaintiff $10,000. Defendants filed a motion for a new trial. Such motion was granted and a new trial ordered but limited to the question of liability.

Both parties appeal.

The plaintiff alleges error in granting the new trial as to liability on the theory that the court was correct in the first place when he ruled at the trial that the proffered testimony on the standard of care was not admissible. The defendants allege the court erred in limiting the new trial to the issue of liability on the theory that the questions of liability and damages are so closely intertwined that they should be tried together.

As to the plaintiff's claim we find little merit. His objection is based on the theory that the defendants could know of the practices of the trade in Flint only by hearsay. This is not supported by the record.

The record shows that one of the defendants had been in the business for 24 years and the other for 14 years; they had attended conventions of beauticians and observed their practices and said they were abreast of the practices of other beauticians in Genesee County.

We agree with the trial court's last ruling that these witnesses should have been allowed to testify and that to exclude their testimony was error requiring a new trial. Such testimony is admissible because no one is held to a higher standard of care than the average in the industry. * * *

The limitation of the trial to the issue of liability only poses a more difficult problem.

It has long been recognized that the questions of liability and damages are so closely intertwined that they may not usually be separated. The only exception the Michigan Supreme Court has so far recognized is in the case wherein "liability is clear" a retrial of the issue of damage alone may be permitted. Trapp v. King (1965), 374 Mich. 608, 132 N.W.2d 640.

In this case the court reiterated its position that despite the court rule authorizing it (GCR 1963, 527.1), limited new trials are not favored.

No compelling reason moves us to extend the rule.

The trial judge's opinion states: "This ruling (on the evidentiary question) may have materially influenced the jury on the liability issue. It could not, however, by any stretch of the imagination have affected the issue of damages." This bespeaks an assurance we do not share.

In the case before us the damages are not liquidated and the liability was determined pursuant to a trial in which an admitted error touching on liability was committed.

Under these circumstances it seems to us that justice requires that the jury which determines the liability or lack of it should have the responsibility for measuring any damages.

The trial court's order for a new trial shall be extended to all of the issues.

Costs are awarded defendants.

NOTES AND QUESTIONS

1. Compare the dissenting opinion of Judge Freedman in HUTTON v. FISHER, 359 F.2d 913, 920 (3d Cir.1966):

> * * * [A]s a matter of practical justice the damage verdict should not be permitted to stand where the question of liability is to be retried. It is the great and saving virtue of the jury system in accident cases that it permits laymen guided by the courts on questions of law to work out in a

worldly way an accommodation between the strict requirements of law and their everyday view of justice. That a defendant therefore suffers disadvantage when a trial is limited to damages and liability is conceded is a fact of life, acknowledged everywhere but in courtrooms. * * * The limitation of a new trial by excluding some of the issues decided is exceptional, and the power to grant a partial new trial must be "exercised with caution." Geffen v. Winer, 100 U.S.App.D.C. 286, 244 F.2d 375, 376 (1957). A retrial of liability will be less than the full relief the defendants are entitled to have, for its effect will be insulated from the damage question into which it ordinarily percolates.

See also Vizzini v. Ford Motor Co., 569 F.2d 754, 760 (3d Cir.1977) (reversing decision to limit new trial to amount of damages).

2. To what extent should the court, in deciding whether to grant a partial new trial, consider the extra cost to the court and the parties of a new trial on all of the issues?

6. REQUIREMENT AND TIMELINESS OF REQUESTS FOR NEW TRIAL

UNITHERM FOOD SYSTEMS, INC. v. SWIFT–ECKRICH INC., 546 U.S. 394, 126 Sup. Ct. 980, 163 L.Ed.2d 974 (2006). Under Rule 50(a), defendant moved for judgment as a matter of law at the end of the evidence. The motion was denied, and the case was submitted to the jury, which found for plaintiff. Defendant failed either to renew the motion for judgment as a matter of law or to move for a new trial. The Court of Appeals held that although the failure to file a renewed motion for judgment as a matter of law precluded a court from entering judgment as a matter of law, an appeals court nevertheless could grant a new trial as long as a preverdict motion for judgment as a matter of law had been filed.

The Supreme Court reversed as follows:

* * * The text of Rule 50(b) confirms that respondent's preverdict Rule 50(a) motion did not present the District Court with the option of granting a new trial. That text provides that a district court may only order a new trial on the basis of issues raised in a preverdict 50(a) motion when "ruling on a renewed motion" under Rule 50(b). Accordingly, even if the District Court was inclined to grant a new trial on the basis of arguments raised in respondents's preverdict motion, it was without the power to do so under Rule 50(b) absent a postverdict motion pursuant to that Rule. Consequently the Court of Appeals was similarly powerless.

* * * [T]he District Court's denial of respondent's preverdict motion cannot form the basis of respondent's appeal, because the denial of that motion was not in error. It was merely an exercise of the District Court's discretion, in accordance with the text of the Rule and the accepted practice of permitting the jury to make an initial judgment about the sufficiency of the evidence. The only error here was counsel's failure to file a post-verdict motion pursuant to Rule 50(b).

Justice Stevens, in his dissent, emphasized that counsel's error did not oust the appellate court of its authority to correct plain error:

> Murphy's law applies to trial lawyers as well as pilots. Even an expert will occasionally blunder. For that reason Congress has preserved the federal appeals courts' power to correct plain error, even though trial counsel's omission will ordinarily give rise to a binding waiver. This is not a case, in my view, in which the authority of the appellate court is limited by an explicit statute or controlling rule. The spirit of the Federal Rules * * * favors preservation of a court's power to avoid manifestly unjust results in exceptional cases.

Id. at 407, 126 S.Ct. at 988, 163 L.Ed.2d at 987. See Eanes, *Federal Rule 50: Medium Rare Application? Unitherm Food Systems, Inc v. Swift–Eckrich, Inc.*, 58 Mercer L. Rev. 1069 (2007). Do you agree that an appeals court retains inherent power to correct procedural lapses that cause a waiver of the jury right? See Childress, *Revolving Trapdoors: Preserving Sufficiency Review of the Civil Jury After* Unitherm *and Amended Rule 50*, 26 Rev. Litig. 239 (2007).

HULSON v. ATCHISON, TOPEKA & SANTA FE RAILWAY, 289 F.2d 726 (7th Cir.), certiorari denied 368 U.S. 835, 82 S.Ct. 61, 7 L.Ed.2d 36 (1961). On June 7, 1960, the trial court entered judgment for defendant based on a jury verdict. On June 17, 1960, plaintiffs' attorney orally moved the court for an order extending the time in which to file plaintiffs' motions for a judgment n.o.v. or a new trial. Defendant's attorney was present and made no objection to an extension so long as argument would not interfere with his calendar. Later that day the court granted plaintiffs' counsel a ten-day extension. On June 27, 1960, counsel filed the motion. On July 15, 1960, defendant moved to strike the motion because it had not been filed within the 10 day limits prescribed by Rule 50(b) and Rule 59(b), (d), and (e). The motion to strike was granted and plaintiffs' motion for relief under Rule 60(b) was denied. The trial judge stated that if he had the power to do so, he would have granted the motion for a new trial. The appeals court affirmed, stating as follows:

> Under Rule 6(b) the trial court "may not extend the time for taking any action under rules * * * 50(b), * * * 59(b)[and others] * * *. If the motion for a new trial is untimely, the trial court has no choice but to deny the motion. * * *
>
> Plaintiffs candidly admit that they were mistaken in understanding the requirements of the rules, but urge that counsel for all parties and the trial judge in good faith believed at the time that granting the extension of time was proper and permissible under the rules. Ignorance of the rules resulting in an agreement for an unauthorized extension of time cannot serve to furnish grounds for relief under Rule 60(b), under the facts before us in this appeal.

NOTES AND QUESTIONS

1. Under Federal Rule 7(b) a motion in the federal courts normally must be in writing and state the grounds on which it is based. Suppose a party files a timely motion for new trial but fails to specify a ground upon which he intends to rely. May he amend his motion subsequent to the ten-day period?

2. Rule 59(d) provides that a court may order a new trial on its own initiative, but again, there is a ten-day limit. Suppose a party files a timely motion but fails to include as a ground an error that the court believes should result in a new trial. May the court order a new trial on such a ground subsequent to the ten-day period? Prior to the 1966 amendment to Federal Rule 59(d) the answer was generally held to be "no." The amendment, adding what is now the second sentence of that Rule, was designed specifically to give the trial courts such power. As a practical matter does this amendment take the sting out of the rule that a party cannot amend a motion once the ten-day period has elapsed? The Advisory Committee, concerned that the ten-day period is insufficient for a litigant to prepare a thoughtful motion after a complicated trial, has proposed extending the period to thirty days. See Report of the Committee on Rules of Practice and Procedure of the Judicial Conference of the United States (2006).

7. THE POWER TO SET ASIDE A JUDGMENT ON GROUNDS DISCOVERED AFTER IT WAS RENDERED

Read Federal Rule of Civil Procedure 60 in the Supplement.

A. MISTAKE AND EXCUSABLE NEGLECT

BRIONES v. RIVIERA HOTEL & CASINO, 116 F.3d 379 (9th Cir. 1997). Plaintiff sued his former employer for unlawful discharge. Defendant filed a Federal Rule 12 (b) motion to dismiss to which plaintiff failed to respond. The court thus granted the motion. Plaintiff, who was appearing *pro se* and was not proficient in English, moved for relief under Federal Rule 60(b)(1) on the ground that the court had never informed him that his case might be dismissed and he had failed to notify his translator and typist of the deadline for filing his opposition papers. The trial court denied the Rule 60(b) motion. At that time case law had seemed to establish as a *per se* rule that a motion under Rule 60(b) could not be utilized to cure a failure to comply with court rules. See, e.g., Hulson v. Atchison, Topeka & Santa Fe Ry., p. 1151, supra. However the appeals court noted the Supreme Court's decision in Pioneer Inv. Servs. Co. v. Brunswick Associates Ltd. Partnership, 507 U.S. 380, 113 S.Ct. 1489, 123 L.Ed.2d 74 (1993), that analyzed the term "excusable neglect" in a number of different contexts, including Rule 60(b). Although the Supreme Court was dealing with a case under the Bankruptcy Act, it referred directly to Rules 6(b) and 60(b) as follows:

> Although inadvertence, ignorance of the rules, or mistakes construing the rules do not usually constitute "excusable" neglect, it is clear the "excusable neglect" under Rule 6(b) is a somewhat "elastic concept" and is not limited strictly to omissions caused by circumstances beyond the control of the movant. * * * [A]t least for purposes of Rule 60(b), "excusable neglect" is understood to encompass situations in which the failure to comply with a filing deadline is attributable to negligence.

The Supreme Court listed four factors to be considered in deciding if neglect was "excusable" in the bankruptcy case: (1) the danger of prejudice to the opposing party, (2) the length of the delay and its potential impact on the judicial proceedings, (3) the reason for the delay, and (4) whether the moving party acted in good faith. In view of the *Pioneer* opinion, the *Briones* court remanded the case to the trial court to determine whether or not plaintiff's negligence was "excusable" under all the circumstances.

NOTES AND QUESTIONS

1. Even with a more flexible approach to the use of Rule 60(b)(1), cases in which negligence is held to be excusable are likely to be quite rare. Nearly all of the cases in which relief has been granted involve situations in which a party was prevented from obtaining any trial whatsoever, such as a default judgment, see Rooks v. American Brass Co., 263 F.2d 166 (6th Cir.1959) (defendant's illness prevented a proper defense), an erroneous stipulation by counsel that resulted in a summary judgment against the client, see Griffin v. Kennedy, 344 F.2d 198 (D.C.Cir.1965), or a dismissal for failure of plaintiff to prosecute the action, see Leong v. Railroad Transfor Serv., Inc., 302 F.2d 555 (7th Cir.1962). Should the Rule specifically be limited to such matters of default? That the courts generally disfavor default judgments and readily set them aside is abundantly clear. See, e.g., Wong v. Partygaming Ltd., 2008 WL 1995369 (N.D. Ohio 2008) ("matters involving large sums of money should not be determined by default judgments if it can be reasonably avoided") (citing *Rooks*, 263 F.2d at 169).

2. The proper scope of Rule 60(b)(6) has been the subject of considerable litigation. It frequently has been stated that the Rule must have been intended to cover only matters outside the scope of Rules 60(b)(1)–(5). E.g., Pioneer Inv. Servs. Co. v. Brunswick Associates Ltd. Partnership, 507 U.S. 380, 393–94, 113 S.Ct. 1489, 123 L.Ed.2d 74 (1993). Otherwise the specific time limits on motions under Rules 60(b)(1), (2), and (3) would be meaningless. But it is the existence of these very limits that have pressured courts, in the interests of justice, to find that errors ostensibly falling within Rules 60(b)(1), (2), or (3) are somehow so special that they come within Rule 60(b)(6) and hence are not subject to a specific time limitation. Can a strained interpretation of Rule 60(b) be justified by the fact that otherwise few if any

cases would fall within Rule 60(b)(6)? For a comprehensive analysis of Rule 60(b)(6), see Kane, *Relief from Federal Judgments: A Morass Unrelieved by a Rule*, 30 Hastings L.J. 41 (1978). Should the errors of counsel be attributed to the client? See Meadows, *Rule 60(b)(6): Whether "Tapping the Grand Reservoir of Equitable Power" Is Appropriate To Right an Attorney's Wrong*, 88 Marq. L. Rev. 997 (2005).

B. NEWLY DISCOVERED EVIDENCE; FRAUD

PATRICK v. SEDWICK, 413 P.2d 169 (Alaska 1966). Plaintiff brought an action for medical malpractice, alleging permanent physical injuries. The case was tried in October 1961 without a jury. In February 1962, the trial judge rendered findings on the issues of liability. These findings were subject to a lengthy appeal and it was not until more than two years later that the appellate court directed the trial court to enter findings for plaintiff on all issues of liability and to proceed to determine damages. The trial judge fixed the amount of damages on the basis of the evidence that had been presented at the trial and entered judgment on January 12, 1965. On January 22, 1965, defendant moved for a new trial on the ground that in 1963 a Dr. Robert Lewy had devised a new treatment that would ameliorate plaintiff's injuries and therefore should reduce his damages. The trial court denied the motion. The judge rejected the significance of the new treatment since there was no assurance that any improvement it might bring would be permanent.

The appellate court affirmed the denial of a new trial with the following explanation:

> * * * [A] motion for new trial on the grounds of newly discovered evidence must meet the following requirements before it [can] be granted:
>
> (1) must be such as would probably change the result on a new trial; (2) must have been discovered since the trial; (3) must be of such a nature that it could not have been discovered before trial by due diligence; (4) must be material; (5) must not be merely cumulative or impeaching.
>
> In addition to the foregoing requirements, it is established that for any evidence to come within the category of "newly discovered" such evidence must relate to facts which were in existence at the time of the trial. * * *
>
> We hold, under the authorities referred to, that the trial court did not abuse its discretion in denying appellee's motion for a new trial on the grounds of newly discovered evidence. It is clear from the record that Dr. Lewy's discovery of the Teflon technique did not occur until a considerable period of time had elapsed after the case was tried in October 1961. Thus, the Lewy technique was not in existence at the time the trial took place and under the above authorities would not qualify as newly discovered evidence.

Id. at 177.

NOTE AND QUESTION

To what extent, if any, should Rule 60(b) permit a case to be reopened for consideration of a change in the applicable law? In TITLE v. UNITED STATES, 263 F.2d 28, 31 (9th Cir.), certiorari denied 359 U.S. 989, 79 S.Ct. 1118, 3 L.Ed.2d 978 (1959), appellant sought to set aside a judgment of denaturalization on the ground that some two years thereafter the United States Supreme Court, in a different case, interpreted the immigration act in such a way as to demonstrate that the original decision in *Title* was erroneous. Appellant relied on Rules 60(b)(4) and (5). The trial court denied the motions and the Court of Appeals affirmed: "Rule 60(b) was not intended to provide relief for error on the part of the court or to afford a substitute for appeal. * * * Nor is a change in the judicial view of applicable law after a final judgment sufficient basis for vacating such judgment entered before announcement of the change." See also Carlson v. Hyundai Motor Co., 222 F.3d 1044 (8th Cir.2000). Assume that the change in the law is announced after the trial court has rendered judgment but before the time for appeal has run? Should it be open to a party to seek relief under Rule 60(b) in that case?

In HAZEL–ATLAS GLASS CO. v. HARTFORD–EMPIRE CO., 322 U.S. 238, 245–46, 64 S.Ct. 997, 1001, 88 L.Ed. 1250, 1255–56 (1944), plaintiff brought an action in the Court of Appeals to set aside a judgment rendered against it some nine years earlier. The first action had turned on the validity of a patent held by defendant. Both the issuance of that patent by the Patent Office and the determination of its validity by the federal Court of Appeals for the Third Circuit in the prior action had been affected by an article offered by defendant, ostensibly written by a disinterested expert, but actually prepared by defendant's own officials, to the effect that the machine under patent was a "revolutionary device." One of the attorneys who presented defendant's case in the first action also had participated in the scheme to prepare and publish the fraudulent article. The Court of Appeals refused to set aside the judgment; the Supreme Court reversed:

> Every element of the fraud here disclosed demands the exercise of the historic power of equity to set aside fraudulently begotten judgments. This is not simply a case of a judgment obtained with the aid of a witness who, on the basis of after-discovered evidence, is believed possibly to have been guilty of perjury. Here, even if we consider nothing but Hartford's sworn admissions, we find a deliberately planned and carefully executed scheme to defraud not only the Patent Office but the Circuit Court of Appeals. * * *
>
> The Circuit Court did not hold that Hartford's fraud fell short of that which prompts equitable intervention, but thought Hazel had not exercised proper diligence in uncovering the fraud and that this should stand in the way of its obtaining relief. We cannot easily

understand how, under the admitted facts, Hazel should have been expected to do more than it did to uncover the fraud. But even if Hazel did not exercise the highest degree of diligence, Hartford's fraud cannot be condoned for that reason alone. This matter does not concern only private parties. There are issues of great moment to the public in a patent suit. * * * Furthermore, tampering with the administration of justice in the manner indisputably shown here involves far more than an injury to a single litigant. It is a wrong against the institutions set up to protect and safeguard the public, institutions in which fraud cannot complacently be tolerated consistently with the good order of society. Surely it cannot be that preservation of the integrity of the judicial process must always wait upon the diligence of litigants. The public welfare demands that the agencies of public justice be not so impotent that they must always be mute and helpless victims of deception and fraud.

NOTES AND QUESTIONS

1. Does *Hazel–Atlas* stand for the proposition that a court on its own motion may set aside a judgment obtained by fraud on the court? Was it proper for the Court to find that there had been a fraud on the lower court? If so, wouldn't ordinary perjury also qualify? Should the notion of fraud on the court apply only to situations such as bribery or corruption of a member of the court or jury?

2. In PEACOCK RECORDS, INC. v. CHECKER RECORDS, INC., 365 F.2d 145, 147 (7th Cir.1966), certiorari denied 385 U.S. 1003, 87 S.Ct. 707, 17 L.Ed.2d 542 (1967), the court reversed as an abuse of discretion a denial of a Rule 60(b) motion:

> * * * We hold that where it appears that perjured testimony may have played some part in influencing the court to render a judgment, the perjury will not be *weighed,* on a motion to set aside the judgment. This seems self evident. * * * [If the judgment was obtained in part by the use of perjury] then it was clearly the duty of the district court to set aside the judgment, because poison had permeated the fountain of justice.

In BROWN v. PENNSYLVANIA RAILROAD CO., 282 F.2d 522 (3d Cir.1960), certiorari denied 365 U.S. 818, 81 S.Ct. 690, 5 L.Ed.2d 696 (1961), plaintiff brought suit under the Federal Employers' Liability Act against the railroad, his employer. Plaintiff's doctor testified that plaintiff's condition was such as to make it increasingly difficult if not impossible for him to work in the future. Defendant's medical witnesses testified that plaintiff had fully recovered from any injuries received in the accident. A verdict was rendered for plaintiff, but in an amount less than had been sought. Shortly after the trial, defendant discharged plaintiff, relying on the testimony given by plaintiff's doctor at the trial. Plaintiff moved for a new trial on damages under Rule 60(b)(3). The motion was denied and the appellate court affirmed. Is the decision sound? Is it consistent with the *Peacock Records* case?

3. Many jurisdictions, including the federal courts under Rule 60(b), permit an independent action in equity to set aside a judgment, which is

discussed after these Notes. Fraud is one of the substantive grounds upon which relief may be granted in such an action. Suppose that instead of putting forth false information, a party merely conceals facts of which she has direct knowledge that would have a definite bearing on the outcome of the case. Does this constitute fraud?

C. THE INDEPENDENT ACTION TO OBTAIN RELIEF FROM A PRIOR JUDGMENT

Reread Federal Rule of Civil Procedure 60(d).

MARCELLI v. WALKER

United States Court of Appeals for the Sixth Circuit, 2009.
2009 WL 415998.

COLE, CIRCUIT JUDGE.

This case arises from an appeal from the district court's denial of Plaintiff–Appellant Tony Marcelli's ("Marcelli") motion to reopen a closed case. * * *

* * *

[The dispute concerned an indemnification agreement in connection with municipal construction projects. The Oakland County Circuit Court ruled against plaintiff and awarded damages. The Michigan Supreme Court denied review, and plaintiff filed a second suit in Oakland County Circuit Court, asking the court to set aside the previous judgment. The circuit court granted summary judgment against plaintiff on grounds of res judicata, and the Michigan Court of Appeals affirmed. Plaintiff then filed a federal court action alleging fraud, conspiracy, legal malpractice, violation of the Racketeer Influenced and Corrupt Organizations Act, as well as violations of due process and equal protection rights under the Fifth and Fourteenth Amendments against multiple defendants. The District Court ordered plaintiff to provide "a Case Statement to assure compliance" with Federal Rule 11.]

* * *

On February 7, 2007, Michael Reynolds, counsel for Plaintiffs, filed Plaintiffs' Response in Lieu of Case Statement, stating:

1. This action was filed on December 11, 2006 in the erroneous belief that the pleading satisfied the requirements of Rule 11 in all its particulars.
2. Through collegial conversation with one of defense counsel, plaintiffs' counsel became aware that the *action could not be maintained in good faith* and commenced the process of

negotiating dismissal of the action *with his clients* and all counsel of record.

3. A stipulation to entry of an order of dismissal by all counsel of record was finally completed and submitted to the court with a proposed form of order.

4. Plaintiffs entered voluntary dismissals against the remaining defendants with proof of service.

5. The foregoing steps were taken in recognition of Plaintiff[s'] counsel's error to minimize or mitigate harm caused by the error to the parties.

* * *

Wherefore, Plaintiffs request that [the] Court accept the foregoing statement as substitute for the Case Statement and enter the proposed consent dismissal Order.

* * * Thereafter, on February 13, 2007, the district court entered an order dismissing Plaintiffs' claims with prejudice under stipulation of counsel.

Sixteen months later, on June 10, 2008, Marcelli filed an Affidavit with the district court, requesting that the court reopen his case because his attorney had allegedly acted without his consent. On June 12, 2008, the district court interpreted Marcelli's Affidavit as a motion to reopen, and denied his motion.

Marcelli then filed an application to proceed In Forma Pauperis, which the district court denied on July 7, 2008, stating "Plaintiff Tony Marcelli has failed to present an actionable claim. Thus, any appeal from this decision would be frivolous." * * *

On July 11, 2008, Marcelli appealed the district court's June 12, 2008 Order to this Court. In September 2008, Marcelli also filed a "Motion for Reinstating my Case that was Wrongfully Dismissed with Prejudice by my Former Attorney" with this Court. He has also filed two Addenda to that motion.

* * *

Marcelli claims that the district court abused its discretion by denying his June 10, 2008, motion to reopen. Marcelli argues that his attorney improperly dismissed his lawsuit in the district court without his permission. He seeks relief under * * * [Federal Rule 60(d)].

* * *

While Rule 60(b) is generally a party's exclusive avenue when seeking relief from a final judgment or order, *see United States v. Beggerly,* 524 U.S. 38, 46 (1998), Rule 60(d) provides a "savings clause, preserving the law before its enactment in 1946, that allows judgments to be attacked without regard to the passage of time[.]" * * *

* * *

Independent actions for relief under this section "must, if Rule 60(b) is to be interpreted as a coherent whole, be reserved for those cases of 'injustice which, in certain instances, are deemed sufficiently gross to demand a departure' from rigid adherence to the doctrine of *res judicata.*" *Beggerly,* 524 U.S. at 46 (quoting *Hazel–Atlas Glass Co. v. Hartford–Empire Co.,* 322 U.S. 238, 244 (1944))

We have set forth the elements of such an independent cause of action as:

> (1) a judgment which ought not, in equity and good conscience, to be enforced; (2) a good defense to the alleged cause of action on which the judgment is founded; (3) fraud, accident, or mistake which prevented the defendant in the judgment from obtaining the benefit of his defense; (4) the absence of fault or negligence on the part of the defendant; and (5) the absence of any adequate remedy at law.

* * * Relief through an independent action is available only in cases "of unusual and exceptional circumstances." * * *

We find that the district court did not abuse its discretion in denying Marcelli Rule 60(d) relief. Marcelli's effort to reopen his district court case fails to meet the standards for an independent action under the Rules. Marcelli has not filed an independent action under Rule 60(d), nor has he presented good cause for the stipulated dismissal to be overturned. Moreover, it appears from the record that Marcelli had more than an adequate opportunity to be heard on his claims.

NOTES AND QUESTIONS

1. What circumstances would be so exceptional as to warrant relief under Federal Rule 60(d)(1)? What are the countervailing interests in finality?

2. Suppose a party brings an action in a federal court, based on diversity-of-citizenship jurisdiction, to set aside a judgment rendered in a state court. If the state itself would provide a means of challenging the judgment, should the federal court refuse to hear the case? If the federal court does hear the case, what law should it apply in determining whether relief is appropriate?

CHAPTER 15

SECURING AND ENFORCING JUDGMENTS

■ ■ ■

In this Chapter, we discuss the procedures that are available to secure and enforce a judgment. The commencement of a lawsuit or, for that matter, even the entry of a judgment, does not mean that plaintiff actually will achieve the goals of the action. A victorious plaintiff's ability to collect a judgment depends primarily on the defendant's capacity and willingness to pay at the time the award is made and secondarily on the effectiveness of the court's judgment-enforcement procedures in the event the judgment debtor is capable of paying but is being recalcitrant. Plaintiff's efforts may be frustrated if the defendant has become insolvent during the litigation or has secreted his assets or fraudulently conveyed them to third persons. In short, the arduous litigation process often proves to be a preliminary to the equally protracted travail of collecting the award. Many of the procedures studied in this Chapter trace their origins to medieval times, but their contemporary application is restrained by the federal Due Process Clause and its requirement of notice and an opportunity to be heard. The materials in this Chapter raise questions of strategic and constitutional significance.

SECTION A. INTRODUCTION

The attempts to enforce a libel judgment against a well-known New York Congressman, Adam Clayton Powell, illustrate some of the problems that often face a judgment creditor. In the case of Powell, the creditor was Ethel James whose efforts to claim her due are a study in the breakdown of the enforcement process. James originally was awarded a $46,000 libel judgment in April, 1963 and that judgment was affirmed by the New York Court of Appeals in July, 1964. Employing a number of tactics, including transfers of property to relatives and invocations of congressional immunity from arrest and process, Powell avoided collection for 32 months. His maneuvers frustrated James's attempts to discover Powell's assets in New York and Puerto Rico and resulted in her bringing suit against the Congressman again, basing her claim on the little used common-law tort of evasion of a judgment. After Powell failed to appear for examination in the second suit, his answer was stricken and compensatory damages were set at $75,000 and punitive damages were assessed at $500,000. These were reduced to $56,000 and $100,000 respectively in James v. Powell, 26 A.D.2d 525, 270 N.Y.S.2d 789 (1st Dep't 1966). Pursuit of Powell continued into 1967, but so did his appeals and in early March, 1967, the New York Court of Appeals reversed the verdict in the evasion-of-judgment suit because Puerto Rican law should have been applied to the compensatory-damage claim and New York law, which governed the remainder of the claim, apparently did not permit punitive damages under the circumstances of the case. 19 N.Y.2d 249, 279 N.Y.S.2d 10, 225 N.E.2d 741 (1967). Thus, Mrs. James was left with the original libel judgment and a cause of action under Puerto Rican law. See "No Home in the House," *Time,* March 10, 1967.

At one point Powell was paying off James's libel judgment through the proceeds from a long-playing album, "Keep the Faith, Baby," part of which was recorded live at his Caribbean island retreat on Bimini. James, apparently disillusioned by the entire episode, decided there must be a better way to make a living than collecting judgments. She followed Powell's example and recorded an album of her own. Fittingly, in some eyes at least, one number on that album exclaims:

> There was once a man who said that he
> Would like to retire to Bimini
> But that was before he broke the law,
> And now the people are going haw-haw-haw.

Who had the last laugh is not clear, but it certainly was not the courts. Other reports of the pursuit of the Congressman include "Hooking a Catfish," *Newsweek,* December 27, 1965; "Man May Come and Man May Go (But Powell Goes on Forever)," *National Review,* June 29, 1965; and "Monstrous Mackerel," *Time,* December 24, 1965.

NOTES AND QUESTIONS

1. Most of the material in this Chapter focuses on the enforcement of money judgments and the availability of provisional remedies in private disputes that do not involve the government. However, the procedures studied also play an important role in public law cases seeking to enforce constitutional rights and statutory protections against public officials. For example, the ability to obtain injunctive relief can be critical in lawsuits involving elections. During the Civil Rights Era of the 1960s, the United States sometimes sought preliminary injunctive relief to protect state voter-registration efforts. See, e.g., United States v. Wood, 295 F.2d 772 (5th Cir.1961). See generally Garrow, Protest at Selma: Martin Luther King, Jr. and the Voting Rights Act of 1965 (1978). More recently, the Supreme Court's decision in litigation involving the 2000 presidential election to stay voter recount efforts (a stay is similar to a preliminary injunction and requires a showing of irreparable injury) proved dispositive of the questions raised. See Bush v. Gore, 531 U.S. 1046, 121 S.Ct. 512, 148 L.Ed.2d 553 (2000). See also Fischer, *"Preliminarily" Enjoining Elections: A Tale of Two Ninth Circuit Panels*, 41 San Diego L. Rev. 1647, 1691 (2004).

2. Provisional remedies prominently figure in "end-of-life" cases concerning whether to withhold or to provide life-sustaining medical treatment. Mack v. Mack, 329 Md. 188, 618 A.2d 744 (1993), involved an effort by a wife, opposed by her in-laws, to withdraw artificial nutrition and hydration from her husband, who for the previous decade had been in a persistently vegetative state. See Allen, *Life, Death, and Advocacy: Rules of Procedure in the Contested End-of-Life Case*, 34 Stetson L. Rev. 55, 66 (2004). See also In re Guardianship of Schiavo, 792 So.2d 551 (Fla. 2d Dist. App. 2001) (deciding motion for preliminary injunctive relief in end-of-life case).

3. Provisional remedies offer an important vehicle for enforcing federal regulatory statutes involving such matters as antitrust, intellectual property, and securities. The United States, in a much publicized antitrust lawsuit, sought preliminary injunctive relief against Microsoft requiring it to "unbundle" Windows 95 from Internet Explorer in order to prevent monopolization of the market. See United States v. Microsoft Corp., 980 F.Supp. 537, 544 (D.D.C. 1997). The Court of Appeals reversed, in part, because the preliminary injunction was issued without adequate notice. See United States v. Microsoft Corp., 147 F.3d 935 (D.C. Cir. 1998).

4. In WINTER v. NATURAL RESOURCES DEFENSE COUNCIL, ___ U.S. ___, 129 S.Ct. 365, 172 L.Ed.2d 249 (2008), a coalition of environmental groups sued the United States Navy to halt Naval training activities involving sonar testing that might injure dolphins, whales, sea lions, and other marine mammals that live in waters in Southern California. The District Court granted plaintiff's request for a preliminary injunction, but the Ninth Circuit, after first issuing an emergency stay, reversed and remanded, requiring the District Court to tailor the injunctive relief. The District Court entered a revised preliminary injunction that required the Navy to shut down sonar whenever a marine mammal came within 2,200 yards of a vessel. The Ninth Circuit affirmed, finding that the 2,200–yard shutdown zone would not affect naval operations. The Supreme Court reversed: "We do not discount the importance of plaintiff's ecological, scientific, and recreational interests in marine mammals," the Court stated. "Those interests, however, are plainly outweighed by the Navy's need to conduct realistic training exercises to ensure that it is able to neutralize the threat posed by enemy submarines." Id. at ___, 129 S.Ct. at 382, 172 L.Ed.2d at 269. At oral argument, plaintiffs acknowledged that the preliminary injunction was "the whole ball game." Id. at ___, 129 S.Ct. at 381–82, 172 L.Ed.2d at 268. See Burke, *Green Peace? Protecting Our National Treasures While Providing for Our National Security*, 32 Wm. & Mary Envtl. L. & Pol'y Rev. 803 (2008). What factors ought to govern the granting of preliminary injunctive relief? See p. 1166, infra.

SECTION B. PROVISIONAL REMEDIES AND THE DUE PROCESS CLAUSE

1. FEDERAL RULE 64 AND THE AVAILABILITY OF STATE PROVISIONAL REMEDIES

By virtue of Federal Rule 64, a federal court may use the provisional remedies available to the courts of the state in which it is sitting to the extent that these state remedies are not inconsistent with any other federal rule or statute. See 11A Wright, Miller & Kane, Federal Practice and Procedure: Civil 2d §§ 2931–36. Provisional remedies primarily are a creature of statute and their character and effectiveness vary considerably from state to state. For a general discussion of provisional remedies, see Millar, Civil Procedure of the Trial Court in Historical Perspective 481–515 (1952). For an illustrative example of state practice, see Articles 60 through 65 of New York's Civil Practice Law and Rules, which provide a claimant with the remedies of attachment and garnishment of property and debts, injunction, receivership, and notice of pendency. See 12 & 13 Weinstein, Korn & Miller, New York Civil Practice ¶¶ 6001.01–6515.07 (2d ed. 2004). (New York abolished the provisional remedy of civil arrest in 1979.) The next section explains each of these provisional remedies in greater detail.

2. THE EFFECT OF THE DUE PROCESS CLAUSE

Provisional remedies are subject to the constraints of the Due Process Clause, which requires notice and an opportunity to be heard before property is taken or its use is limited. See Countryman, *The Bill of Rights and the Bill Collector,* 15 Ariz.L.Rev. 521 (1973). In SNIADACH v. FAMILY FINANCE CORP., p. 249, supra, the Supreme Court invalidated the Wisconsin prejudgment garnishment procedure, which authorized a summons to issue at the request of the creditor's lawyer who served the garnishee to freeze the debtor's wages during the period before trial of the main suit without the wage earner having any opportunity to be heard. Initially, the effect of *Sniadach* on other provisional remedies was unclear. However, in FUENTES v. SHEVIN, p. 240, supra, the Court held unconstitutional state statutes providing for the replevin of chattels without a prior opportunity to be heard. State courts applying *Sniadach* also have invalidated statutes permitting the prejudgment garnishment of accounts receivable without notice and a statute permitting a prejudgment writ of immediate possession by a landlord pending a hearing on the merits. See generally Clark & Landers, *Sniadach, Fuentes and Beyond: The Creditor Meets the Constitution,* 59 Va.L.Rev. 355 (1973); Note, *Procedural Due Process—The Prior Hearing Rule and the Demise of Ex Parte Remedies,* 53 B.U.L.Rev. 41 (1973).

Uncertainty about the requirements of due process surfaced again after the Court in MITCHELL v. W.T. GRANT CO., p. 249, supra, upheld the Louisiana sequestration statute permitting the creditor to obtain the writ on an ex parte application without giving the debtor either notice or a prior opportunity for a hearing. The Court reasoned that the risk of a wrongful taking was minimized by the creditor's interest in the property prior to the lawsuit, the judicial authorization of the writ, and the immediate availability of a post-seizure hearing. Then, in NORTH GEORGIA FINISHING, INC. v. DI-CHEM, INC., p. 252, supra, the Court relied on *Fuentes* to invalidate the Georgia garnishment statute, which permitted the writ to be issued on the basis of conclusory allegations by the plaintiff without providing the defendant with an opportunity for an "early" hearing "or other safeguard against mistaken repossession." The opinion for the Court stressed the need for statutes to guard against the risk of initial error resulting in irreparable injury to the defendant even when the debt arises in a commercial context between parties of equal bargaining power, two corporations in this case.

More recently, in CONNECTICUT v. DOEHR, p. 254, supra, the Court invalidated a Connecticut statute pursuant to which a judge could allow the prejudgment attachment of real estate, without prior notice or hearing, merely upon the plaintiff's assertion under oath that there is probable cause to sustain the validity of his claims. The Court indicated that there must be either a preattachment hearing, a showing of some exigent circumstance, or both, before an order of attachment may issue. Four Justices stated that, in their view, due process also requires the plaintiff to post a bond or some other security. Lower courts have diverged in their application of these principles. The Second Circuit has held that "a security bond need not be posted in connection with a prejudgment attachment in order to satisfy the requirements of due process." British Int'l Ins. Co. v. Seguros La Republica, S.A., 212 F.3d 138 (2d Cir.) (internal quotations omitted), certiorari denied 531 U.S. 1010, 121 S.Ct. 564, 148 L.Ed.2d 484 (2000). By contrast, the Ninth Circuit, in Tri–State Dev., Ltd. v. Johnston, 160 F.3d 528 (9th Cir.1998), invalidated the state of Washington's attachment statute, which included a creditor bond but did not afford a preattachment hearing. See also Hartford Acc. & Indem. Co. v. Ace American Reinsur. Co., 103 Conn.App. 319, 950 A.2d 701 (2007) (whether to require prepleading security). See generally Beale, *Note—Connecticut v. Doehr and Procedural Due Process Values: The* Sniadach *Tetrad Revisited*, 79 Cornell L. Rev. 1603 (1994); Vandevelde, *Ideology, Due Process and Civil Procedure*, 67 St. John's L. Rev. 265, 317–24 (1993); Alderman, *Default Judgments and Prejudgment Remedies Meet the Constitution: Effectuating* Sniadach *and Its Progeny,* 65 Geo.L.J. 1 (1976).

NOTE AND QUESTION

Provisional remedies may raise constitutional concerns that go beyond the Due Process Clause. Temporary restraining orders, for example, present special problems when used to restrain speech that is protected by the First Amendment. As the Supreme Court has explained: "[A] system of prior restraints of expression comes * * * bearing a heavy presumption against its constitutional validity." Carroll v. President & Commissioners of Princess Anne, 393 U.S. 175, 181, 89 S.Ct. 347, 351, 21 L.Ed.2d 325, 331 (1968). See also Procter & Gamble Co. v. Bankers Trust Co., 78 F.3d 219, 224–25 (6th Cir.1996). Can you describe any other potential constitutional problems with provisional remedies?

SECTION C. METHODS OF SECURING THE JUDGMENT—PROVISIONAL REMEDIES

1. ATTACHMENT

Attachment is a provisional remedy that prevents defendant from selling or otherwise disposing of any real or personal property that has been taken into the custody of the attaching officer. Attachment deprives defendant of the use and enjoyment of property long before liability is established (and, of course, in many cases no liability will be found). Regarded as "harsh" and "drastic," the granting of an attachment is discretionary. Elliott Associates, L.P. v. Republic of Peru, 948 F.Supp. 1203, 1211 (S.D.N.Y.1996). Even if the statutory requirements for attachment are met and even if plaintiff is willing to post a bond to protect defendant, a court still may deny the attachment if it believes that the harm to defendant outweighs the risk that plaintiff's judgment will be unenforceable. Thus when the value of the property sought to be attached is significantly greater than defendant's potential liability or when the property is part of an ongoing business, the remedy may be denied. See Interpetrol Bermuda Ltd. v. Trinidad & Tobago Oil Co., 135 Misc.2d 160, 167–69, 513 N.Y.S.2d 598, 603–05 (Sup.Ct.1987).

New York's attachment statute, N.Y.C.P.L.R. 6201, permits prejudgment attachment (1) when the defendant is a nondomiciliary residing outside the state or an unlicensed foreign corporation, (2) when the defendant is within the state but diligent efforts to serve her personally have failed, or (3) when the defendant's conduct in connection with the property indicates her intent to defraud creditors or frustrate the enforcement of a potentially unfavorable judgment. When the purpose of the attachment is security and not jurisdiction, New York courts require the movant to show "that something, whether it is a defendant's financial position or past and present conduct, poses a real risk of the enforcement of a future judgment." Bank of China v. NBM L.L.C., 192 F. Supp.2d 183, 188 (S.D.N.Y. 2002) (citation and internal quotation omitted). The mere "possibility" that defendants will remove their assets out of the state is considered to be "too remote" to justify an order of attachment. Id. (citation and internal quotation omitted). In *Bank of China*, plaintiff documented the need for the levy by showing that defendants had attempted repeatedly to remove their assets through such devices as issuing payments on transactions that had not taken place, submitting fake bills of lading, trying to sell real estate that served as collateral on a bank loan, and by attempting to transfer more than $1 million to the Cayman Islands using a forged hypothecation agreement. See also Monteleone v. Leverage Group, 2008 WL 4541124, *7 (E.D.N.Y. 2008) ("Plaintiffs need not show actual proof of disposition or secretion of property. * * * It is enough to show the transfer or disappearance of an abnormal amount of property, although the burden is on the plaintiff to show the defendant has begun removing its assets.").

All nonexempt tangible and intangible property in which defendant has a recognizable interest is subject to attachment for purposes of securing the enforcement of the prospective judgment. New York permits the attachment of income, whether already earned or to be earned in the future, claims under insurance policies, bank accounts, and assignable choses in action and judgments. Certain property is exempt from attachment in order to permit defendant to maintain his standard of living during the pendency of the action. The elaborate, and somewhat archaic, New York exemptions are set out in N.Y.C.P.L.R. 5205–06. Finally, when property of or a debt owed to defendant is in the hands of a third person, that person (the garnishee) may be prohibited from selling, assigning, or interfering with any property in which defendant has an interest or from paying or discharging any debt except as directed by the sheriff or a court order. The garnishee also may be ordered to turn the property or proceeds of the debt over to the court at the conclusion of the action for application to the final judgment.

2. PRELIMINARY INJUNCTIONS AND TEMPORARY RESTRAINING ORDERS

A. PRELIMINARY INJUNCTIONS

Federal Rule 65 authorizes the issuance of a preliminary injunction by a federal court. "Defined broadly, a preliminary injunction is an injunction that is issued by the court to protect plaintiff from irreparable injury and to preserve the court's power to render a meaningful decision after a trial on the merits." 11A Wright, Miller & Kane, Federal Practice and Procedure: Civil 2d § 2947. Since a preliminary injunction is granted before there has been a trial on the merits and it often has the same effect as the ultimate relief requested by plaintiff, it may have an extremely adverse impact on defendant; as a result, the courts use preliminary injunctions only on notice to the defendant and in the most necessary circumstances.

Federal Rule 65 does not prescribe the standard for issuing a preliminary injunction. The Supreme Court has set out a four-part test for a preliminary injunction: "[a] plaintiff * * * must establish that he is likely to succeed on the merits, that he is likely to suffer irreparable harm in the absence of preliminary relief, that the balance of equities tips in his favor, and that an injunction is in the public interest." Winter, Note 4, p. 1162, supra. The goal of the relief is to preserve the status quo, on the view that without the injunction, "it becomes difficult, and sometimes virtually impossible, for a court to 'unscramble the eggs.'" Sonesta Int'l Hotels Corp. v. Wellington Assocs., 483 F.2d 247, 250 (2d Cir.1973). Is this balancing technique objectionable because it amounts to a trial on the merits and thus is wasteful of judicial time? Are there ways of avoiding this duplication? See Federal Rule 65(a), which allows for the consolidation of a hearing on the preliminary injunction with the trial on the merits. What protection does Federal Rule 65(c) extend to a defendant who might be "wrongfully enjoined"? See 11A Wright, Miller & Kane, Federal Practice and Procedure: Civil 2d §§ 2947–50; Leubsdorf, *The Standard for Preliminary Injunctions,* 91 Harv.L.Rev. 525 (1978); Rendleman, *Inadequate Remedy at Law Prerequisite for an Injunction,* 33 U.Fla. L.Rev. 346 (1981).

B. TEMPORARY RESTRAINING ORDERS

Federal Rule 65 also authorizes the issuance of a temporary restraining order. A "TRO," which is issued ex parte, is appropriate only when the threat of irreparable injury is immediate and the need to preserve the status quo is urgent. Unlike the preliminary injunction, an application for a restraining order is sought when time considerations do not permit the giving of formal notice. Because of a concern over the potential unfairness of ex parte proceedings, a number of special conditions, such as those set out in Federal Rule 65(b), usually are imposed. Indeed, courts are reluctant to issue TRO's without notice and tend to proceed ex parte only when there is "no reasonable alternative." American Can Co. v. Mansukhani, 742 F.2d 314, 322 (7th Cir.1984). See generally 11A Wright, Miller & Kane, Federal Practice and Procedure: Civil 2d §§ 2951–53.

Are temporary restraining orders consistent with the *Sniadach* requirements of notice and an opportunity to defend? See p. 249, supra. To what extent does the imposition of special conditions such as those described in Rule 65(b) satisfy due process considerations? A temporary restraining order generally will remain effective only for a relatively brief period or until a hearing is held on plaintiff's request for a preliminary injunction. Does that temporal limitation afford adequate protection? In Commodity Futures Trading Comm'n v. Lake Shore Asset Mgt. Ltd., 496 F.3d 769, 771–72 (7th Cir. 2007), the Seventh Circuit vacated an ex parte TRO that had remained in force for longer than twenty days, explaining that continuation of the order "would pose serious constitutional problems. It would allow a business to be destroyed without giving the affected party any opportunity to present evidence."

NOTES AND QUESTIONS

1. Despite the judicial hesitancy in issuing preliminary injunctions and temporary restraining orders, these remedies are among the most useful weapons in the procedural arsenal. Injunctions are extremely flexible and can be molded to restrain or compel the performance of a wide variety of acts. Because the primary purpose of these orders is to preserve the status quo pending a full hearing on the merits, they usually will be negative or prohibitory in character and restrain defendant from acting in a particular fashion. On the other hand, when property must be maintained or a course of conduct continued in order to preserve the status quo or prevent irreparable injury, the court will grant a request that defendant undertake or continue certain activities or honor a given standard of care. Such an order generally is referred to as mandatory or affirmative. See RoDa Drilling Co. v. Siegal, 552

F.3d 1203, 1209–09 (10th Cir. 2009). A classic discussion of mandatory injunctions appears in then-Judge William Howard Taft's opinion in TOLEDO, A.A. & N.M. RY. v. PENNSYLVANIA CO., 54 Fed. 730, 741 (C.C.N.D.Ohio), appeal dismissed 150 U.S. 393, 14 S.Ct. 123, 37 L.Ed. 1120 (1893):

> The office of a preliminary injunction is to preserve the status quo until, upon final hearing, the court may grant full relief. Generally this can be accomplished by an injunction prohibitory in form, but it sometimes happens that the status quo is a condition not of rest, but of action, and the condition of rest is exactly what will inflict the irreparable injury upon complainant, which he appeals to a court of equity to protect him from. In such a case courts of equity issue mandatory writs before the case is heard on its merits. * * *

2. In addition to the requirement that defendant's conduct violate plaintiff's rights and tend to render the ultimate judgment ineffectual, the act to be restrained must affect the subject matter of the action. Thus, a preliminary injunction or temporary restraining order relating to defendant's conduct is unavailable in an ordinary tort or contract action for money damages, since money is not considered the "subject" of the action. The objective of the relief must be the preservation or a change in the status of property or a right. See Credit Agricole Indosuez v. Rossiyskiy Kredit Bank, 94 N.Y.2d 541, 729 N.E.2d 683, 708 N.Y.S.2d 26 (N.Y. 2000); Eastern Rock Prods., Inc. v. Natanson, 239 A.D. 529, 269 N.Y.S. 435 (3d Dep't 1933). Further, the equitable remedy of a preliminary injunction is unavailable when the plaintiff's claim is essentially a claim at law. See Rosen v. Cascade Int'l, 21 F.3d 1520, 1527–29 (11th Cir.1994) (overturning district court's grant of preliminary injunction freezing defendant's assets in securities fraud case since plaintiff's action was one at law).

3. Even if a preliminary injunction is warranted, the court may lack the power to issue it. In GRUPO MEXICANO DE DESARROLLO, S.A. v. ALLIANCE BOND FUND, INC., 527 U.S. 308, 119 S.Ct. 1961, 144 L.Ed.2d 319 (1999), a divided Supreme Court held that a district court exceeded its authority when it entered a preliminary injunction freezing defendants' use of their assets pending adjudication of plaintiffs' right to a lien. Writing for the majority, Justice Scalia concluded that an injunction of this sort is beyond the equitable powers of the Article III courts. For a sympathetic account of the decision, see Burbank, *The Bitter with the Sweet: Tradition, History, and Limitations on Federal Judicial Power—A Case Study*, 75 Notre Dame L. Rev. 1291 (2000). "Freezing" injunctions are available in the common law courts of England in which their use is subject to important procedural safeguards. See Capper, *The Need for* Mareva *Injunctions Reconsidered*, 73 Fordham L. Rev. 2161 (2005). What kind of showing would you require before issuing a prejudgment freezing injunction?

4. Preliminary injunctions and temporary restraining orders usually bind not only the parties to the action, but also their agents, servants, and anyone acting in collusion with or for the benefit of a party. Must the district court hold a hearing to determine who is bound by the order? Is it appropriate to bind an individual because he or she is a member of a group or an

unincorporated association that has been enjoined by the court?. Should the court inquire into the association's control over its members as an aid in determining whether or not individual members should be bound by an order issued against the group? See Rendleman, *Beyond Contempt: Obligors to Injunctions*, 53 Texas L.Rev. 873 (1975).

5. A particularly difficult question arises when a party seeks a preliminary injunction or temporary restraining order to prohibit parties from commencing or continuing an action in another court or from enforcing a judgment issued by another court. The traditional view, as expressed in MERRITT–CHAPMAN & SCOTT CORP. v. MUTUAL BENEFIT LIFE INS. CO., 237 App.Div. 70, 73, 260 N.Y.S. 374, 378 (1st Dep't 1932), is that a court would not interfere with an action in another court "unless it has a clear priority of jurisdiction, or exceptional circumstances are shown to exist which require such drastic remedy." See McClintock, Equity § 37 (2d ed. 1948). For an historical survey of the issue, see Moore, *Conflict of Jurisdiction*, 23 La.L.Rev. 29 (1962).

The problem of inter-court injunctions is bound up with questions of federalism, jurisdiction, and conflict of laws. See generally 17A Wright, Miller, Cooper & Amar, Federal Practice and Procedure: Jurisdiction and Related Matters 3d §§ 4211, 4221; 17B Wright, Miller, Cooper & Amar, Federal Practice and Procedure: Jurisdiction & Related Matters 3d § 4251. What factors are relevant when a federal court is asked to enjoin parties from proceeding in a state-court action? See Younger v. Harris, 401 U.S. 37, 91 S.Ct. 746, 27 L.Ed.2d 669 (1971); Huffman v. Pursue, Ltd., 420 U.S. 592, 95 S.Ct. 1200, 43 L.Ed.2d 482 (1975); Pennzoil Co. v. Texaco, Inc., 481 U.S. 1, 107 S.Ct. 1519, 95 L.Ed.2d 1 (1987). How does the analysis change when a state court is asked to enjoin proceedings in a federal or in another state court? See Donovan v. City of Dallas, 377 U.S. 408, 84 S.Ct. 1579, 12 L.Ed.2d 409 (1964). Should a federal court sitting in diversity under the Class Action Fairness Act, p. 276, supra, have the power to enjoin a parallel or overlapping class action filed in state court? For an analysis that precedes the enactment of CAFA, see Miller, *Overlapping Class Actions*, 71 N.Y.U. L. Rev. 514 (1996). What added complications are there when a federal court is asked to enjoin a foreign defendant from prosecuting a similar action in a foreign country? See Kaepa, Inc. v. Achilles Corp., 76 F.3d 624 (5th Cir.1996). See Teitz, *Both Sides of the Coin: A Decade of Parallel Proceedings and Enforcement of Foreign Judgments in Transnational Litigation*, 10 Roger Williams U.L. Rev. 1 (2004).

3. RECEIVERSHIP

The appointment of receivers in the federal courts is governed by Federal Rule 66. Section 959(b) of Title 28 of the United States Code defines the receiver's substantive rights, duties, and liabilities. See 12 Wright, Miller & Marcus, Federal Practice and Procedure: Civil 2d §§ 2981–86, for a discussion of federal receivers. Should federal or state law govern when the court sits in diversity? See Canada Life Assur. Co. v. LaPeter, 2009 WL 530935 (9th Cir.) (holding that federal law governs).

Historically receivers were appointed by equity courts to manage property that plaintiff feared would be squandered, destroyed, or otherwise diminished in value during the course of litigation. Because the remedy originated in equity and therefore can be characterized as "extraordinary," a number of courts refuse to appoint a receiver to act as a custodian or manager of disputed property pendente lite whenever the movant is shown to have an adequate remedy at law or an alternative remedy. See, e.g., State ex rel. Larry C. Iverson, Inc. v. District Court, 146 Mont. 362, 406 P.2d 828 (1965). The appointment of a receiver is subject to an abuse-of-discretion standard on appeal. See Fulp v. Holt, 284 Ga. 751, 670 S.E.2d 785 (2008) affirming appointment of receiver to oversee proceedings dissolving partnership). Receivership is also available post-judgment in aid of execution. See First Nat'l State Bank v. Kron, 190 N.J.Super. 510, 464 A.2d 1146 (App.Div.), certification denied 95 N.J. 204, 470 A.2d 424 (1983).

Courts typically consider a number of factors in deciding whether to appoint a receiver, including the existence of "a valid claim by the party seeking the appointment; the probability that fraudulent conduct has occurred or will occur to frustrate that claim; imminent danger that property will be concealed, lost, or diminished in value; inadequacy of legal remedies; lack of a less drastic equitable remedy; and likelihood that appointing the receiver will do more good than harm." In Aviation Supply Corp. v. R.S.B.I. Aerospace, Inc., 999 F.2d 314, 316–17 (8th Cir.1993). Although no factor is dispositive, defendant's actual or potential insolvency usually is the primary reason for the appointment of a receiver. See Resolution Trust Corp. v. Fountain Circle Assocs., 799 F.Supp. 48 (N.D. Ohio 1992). Receivers also are appointed to preserve property pending litigation when there is a substantial danger that the property will be removed from the state, lost, materially injured, or destroyed.

In SECURITIES & EXCHANGE COMMISSION v. MADOFF, Case No. 08 Civ. 10791 (S.D.N.Y. Dec. 11, 2008), the Securities and Exchange Commission filed an emergency application to the court for the appointment of a receiver for defendants' assets. The SEC alleged that defendant was engaged in a gigantic "Ponzi" scheme estimated at $50 billion through his investment advisor activities. For the background to the litigation, see Securities Investor Protection Corp. v. Bernard L. Madoff Investment Secs., ___ B.R. ___, 2009 WL 458770 (Bktcy.S.D.N.Y.2009) The court granted the motion, finding the appointment of the receiver necessary to preserve the status quo, to prevent dissipation of assets, to determine defendant's financial condition, and to file responses to investor inquiries. See also Donell v. Kowell, 533 F.3d 762 (9th Cir. 2008) (receiver appointed to recover monies lost by Ponzi-scheme investors had authority to recover moneys from innocent investor).

In most states, only plaintiff can secure the appointment of a receiver and the receivership extends only to property actually involved in the litigation. New York, however, gives its courts the power to appoint a receiver upon the motion of any person having an "apparent interest" in the property. N.Y.C.P.L.R. 6401. What possible justification is there for such a provision? New York practice also requires any person who moves for the appointment of a receiver to be joined as a party, thereby permitting the movant to protect her interest in the property in the previously commenced action; of course, this practice occasionally may prove burdensome to the person seeking the appointment of the receiver. See 13 Weinstein, Korn & Miller, New York Civil Practice ¶ 6401.14. Does this practice unnecessarily complicate the litigation?

A temporary receiver must be disinterested and give primary allegiance to the appointing court and not to the parties or the person who sought the appointment. See Jacynicz v. 73 Seaman Associates, 270 A.D.2d 83, 704 N.Y.S.2d 68 (1st Dep't 2000). Because of this status, virtually all of a receiver's official acts are subject to the approval of the appointing court. Moreover, when the debtor requests the appointment of a receiver, the court will look to see whether the debtor is manipulating the receivership to hinder and delay recovery by the creditors. See Shapiro v. Wilgus, 287 U.S. 348, 53 S.Ct. 142, 77 L.Ed. 355 (1932). In order to prevent dereliction in the performance of his duties, a temporary receiver normally is required to execute and file an undertaking before any official duties are initiated. The undertaking protects the integrity of the court and the litigants by guaranteeing that injuries caused by any defalcation by the receiver can be indemnified.

A temporary receiver's powers are limited by the statute or rule authorizing the appointment or in the court order naming the receiver and are only those expressly authorized by the court. See Security Pacific Mortgage & Real Estate Servs., Inc. v. Republic of the Philippines, 962 F.2d 204 (2d Cir.1992). Typically the receiver takes possession of the property as soon as possible after the appointing order has been entered. In VANDER VORSTE v. NORTHWESTERN NATIONAL BANK, 81 S.D. 566, 138 N.W.2d 411 (1965), the basic obligation of a receiver is described as the duty of preserving and protecting the property and assets of the estate that have been placed in protective custody. Although the receiver is not given title to the property, he generally is given the responsibility of managing or disposing of the property and the power to take any action necessary to maintain or improve it. See City of Santa Monica v. Gonzalez, 43 Cal.4th 905, 182 P.3d 1027, 76 Cal.Rptr.3d 483 (2008) (receiver appointed to oversee residential rental properties that presented serious health and safety violations with power, among others, to rehabilitate or demolish the property).

4. CIVIL ARREST

The provisional remedy of civil arrest had its genesis in the common-law practice of commencing an action by taking into custody and imprisoning defendant until judgment was rendered or bail was posted. Although incarceration effectively prevented defendant from rendering the potential judgment unenforceable, its Draconian quality made it a frequent source of abuse. The debtor's prison strikingly portrayed by Charles Dickens in the *Pickwick Papers* illustrates the unpleasant consequences of the remedy. Consequently, courts and legislatures have sharply restricted the availability of civil arrest in most jurisdictions. For an historical discussion of the development and use of civil arrest, see Freedman, *Imprisonment for Debt,* 2 Temple L.Q. 330 (1928). See also Morris & Wiener, *Civil Arrest: A Medieval Anachronism,* 43 Brooklyn L.Rev. 383 (1976).

The availability of civil arrest varies widely from state to state. Some state constitutions prohibit imprisonment for debt and thus render civil arrest unavailable; a number of states simply have not enacted legislation authorizing civil arrest, although their constitutions would not prohibit use of the remedy. For a comprehensive collection of state constitutional provisions concerning "imprisonment for debt," see Vogt, *Note—State v. Allison: Imprisonment for Debt in South Dakota*, 46 S.D. L. Rev. 334, 368 n. 9 (2001). See also Shatz v. Paul, 7 Ill.App.2d 223, 129 N.E.2d 348 (1st Dist.1955), which contains an excellent historical discussion of the use of arrest. For a discussion of the due process implications of civil arrest, see In re Harris, 69 Cal.2d 486, 72 Cal.Rptr. 340, 446 P.2d 148 (1968). Since *Harris,* California has severely restricted the use of civil arrest. See Cal.Civ.Proc. Code § 501 (1995) (noting persons may not be imprisoned in a civil action, whether before or after judgment, with a possible exception if one violates a court order).

Even when civil arrest has been authorized by statute, certain public policy exemptions generally have limited its application. For example, some courts have exempted all public servants from civil arrest. States granting immunity from service of process to nonresident witnesses also generally extend that immunity to cover civil arrest. Traditionally, women were exempted from civil arrest in many states. In 1976, New York modified its statute by deleting the word "women" and substituting the language "parent, guardian or other person * * * whose principal responsibility is * * * the daily care and supervision of [a child under sixteen or an incompetent of any age] * * *." After further restricting the availability of civil arrest, the 1978 amendment eliminated the exemption altogether. N.Y.C.P.L.R. 6101. New York abolished the remedy of civil arrest in 1979.

A motion for civil arrest is addressed to the court's discretion, which, in view of the severity of the remedy, is exercised with a great degree of caution. See SUMMERS v. DISTRICT COURT, 68 Nev. 99, 108, 227 P.2d 201, 205 (1951). Furthermore, plaintiff usually must file an "undertaking" guaranteeing the payment of any legal costs and damages that defendant may sustain if the arrest proves to have been wrongful. The undertaking protects defendant and insures that those thinking about invoking the remedy will "look before they leap." An arrested defendant will be released if bail is posted in an amount designated by the court; the bail then serves as security for any judgment plaintiff ultimately may recover. See Massey, *The Excessive Fines Clause and Punitive Damages:*

Some Lessons from History, 40 Vand. L. Rev. 1233 (1987). Bail usually is set high enough to cover the prospective judgment, although the court will avoid setting bail at a figure that makes it impossible for defendant to secure his release.

NOTES AND QUESTIONS

1. Civil arrest can be used for purposes that do not relate to the enforcement of judgments. For example, arrest and detention can be made in connection with immigration deportation proceedings, and because they are characterized as civil, rather than as criminal, they do not trigger the protections of the Speedy Trial Act, 18 U.S.C. § 3161(b). See United States v. Pasillas–Castanon, 525 F.3d 994 (10th Cir. 2008). However, the federal courts have recognized a "ruse exception" for cases in which civil arrest or detention "amount[] to nothing but a cover for criminal detention." United States v. Rodriguez–Amaya, 521 F.3d 437, 441 (4th Cir. 2008). Why should the purpose of the arrest affect the protections given to the arrestee? See Kuckes, *Civil Due Process, Criminal Due Process*, 25 Yale L. & Pol'y Rev. 1 (2006).

2. In STATE v. ALLISON, 2000 S.D. 21, 607 N.W.2d 1 (2000), a former member of the South Dakota National Guard was charged with failing to return $650 worth of clothing, footwear, and assorted equipment following the end of his service and was indicted for grand theft. The lower court dismissed the indictment on the ground that failure to return the items created a debt for which imprisonment was barred under the state constitution. The South Dakota Supreme Court reversed, rejecting the characterization of defendant's contractual obligation to return property as a debt. A spirited dissent emphasized the availability of less intrusive civil remedies, such as replevin, specific performance, or an action to collect a debt, to obtain the unpaid sum.

5. NOTICE OF PENDENCY

Although not strictly a provisional remedy, the notice of pendency is included in this discussion because of its similarity to the other provisional remedies already described. Notice of pendency traces back to the common-law doctrine of *lis pendens,* which sought to guarantee the effectiveness of a judgment in an action involving specific tangible property by charging any purchaser or encumbrancer of the property with knowledge that an action involving it had been instituted. Thus, the prospective purchaser or encumbrancer not only had to check all of the conveyance records to be certain of the vendor's good title but also had to investigate whether the vendor was involved in any pending litigation that might affect the property—often a practical impossibility. The statutory notice of pendency is designed to protect prospective purchasers and encumbrancers by requiring plaintiff to file a notice of the litigation before the protection of constructive notice can be claimed. Thus, if plaintiff fails to file a notice of pendency and properly index it, he will not be protected against a purchaser or encumbrancer who does not have actual knowledge of the litigation involving the property. Statutory notice of pendency differs from other provisional remedies because it usually does not involve judicial discretion; the right to file a notice is absolute in any litigation falling within the classes enumerated in the notice-of-pendency statute.

NOTE AND QUESTIONS

How can the *lis pendens* procedure be justified in light of the cases discussed pp. 240–65, supra, which invalidated statutes providing for the attachment of a defendant's property without probable cause or a hearing? Is it significant that the notice of pendency does not deprive anyone of the use or enjoyment of property, but merely gives notice to third parties of the pendency of litigation? Isn't it possible that the filing of the notice will exert financial pressure on the owner of property by rendering the property "unmarketable and unsuitable as security for a loan"? Kirkeby v. Superior Court of Orange County, 33 Cal.4th 642, 651, 15 Cal.Rptr.3d 805, 93 P.3d 395, 401 (Sup. Ct. 2004) (internal citations omitted). Compare Kukanskis v. Griffith, 180 Conn. 501, 430 A.2d 21 (1980) (finding Connecticut's *lis pendens* statute violative of due process requirements because it failed to provide for a hearing) and New Destiny Dev. Corp. v. Piccione, 802 F.Supp. 692 (D. Conn.1992) (reaffirming the constitutionality of Connecticut's lis pendens statute even after *Doehr*, p. 254, supra), with Chrysler Corp. v. Fedders Corp., 670 F.2d 1316 (3d Cir.1982) (upholding New Jersey's *lis pendens* statute) and Diaz v. Paterson, 547 F.3d 88 (2d Cir. 2008) (upholding New York's *lis pendens* statute).

6. A POSTSCRIPT

Despite their obvious practical importance to the proper functioning of a judicial system, little effort has been devoted to the rationalization of provisional remedies and their integration into the total procedural picture. Indeed many practitioners are ill-informed as to the availability and operation of provisional remedies in their jurisdiction and often miss an opportunity to protect their clients against debilitating and frustrating post-judgment enforcement procedures. Do you agree that the Federal Rules should rely exclusively on state provisional remedy practice? Would it be preferable to design a provisional remedies rule for the federal courts? With the goals and the structure of federal procedure as a background, see if you can formulate a comprehensive provisional-remedies rule for the federal courts; make certain that it will be consistent with contemporary notions of due process as set forth in the United States Supreme Court cases described on pages 240–65, supra. In what ways does the availability of post-judgment enforcement techniques affect the framing of a provisional-remedies rule? Reconsider this question after studying the remaining materials in this Chapter.

SECTION D. METHODS OF COLLECTING AND ENFORCING THE JUDGMENT

1. EXECUTION

GRIGGS v. MILLER

Supreme Court of Missouri, 1963.
374 S.W.2d 119.

WALTER H. BOHLING, SPECIAL COMMISSIONER.

Bill Griggs, on January 19, 1961, sued W. A. Brookshire in ejectment for the possession of a 322 acre farm in Boone County, Missouri, and for damages for withholding possession. Plaintiff had purchased the farm for $20,600 on January 16, 1961, at a public sale under a general execution against defendant. * * * Defendant's answer was a general denial, and his counterclaim sought to set aside the sheriff's execution sale and deed. * * * The cause was considered and treated by the parties and the court "as one of 'equitable cognizance.'" The court found the issues for the plaintiff and against the defendant on plaintiff's petition; for the plaintiff and the third-party defendant [the sheriff] on defendant's counterclaim; and that plaintiff was entitled to $2,483.24 damages by reason of defendant's withholding of possession of said farm from January 18, 1961, to November 15, 1961, the date of said judgment and decree, and that plaintiff recover $250 per month from and after November 15, 1961, for so long as defendant withheld possession from plaintiff. Defendant Brookshire, after filing his notice of appeal, was incarcerated in the Missouri Penitentiary. * * * Miller was appointed trustee of the Estate of W. A. Brookshire, and substituted as a party litigant for said Brookshire.

* * *

Ray Crouch recovered a judgment against W. A. Brookshire, defendant, in the Circuit Court of Henry County, Missouri, on July 15, 1959, for $1,966.69. Said judgment was affirmed on December 5, 1960 * * *. The right to an execution follows immediately upon the rendition of a judgment. * * * No supersedeas bond was given to stay an execution. * * * A general execution was issued on said judgment to the Sheriff of Boone County on December 10, 1960. The Sheriff levied on defendant's 322 acre farm December 14, 1960, filed a notice of his levy in the office of the Recorder of Deeds of Boone County, and advertised and sold said real estate at public sale on January 16, 1961.

Dorothy Contestible, Administratrix of the Estate of Ralph Burton Collings, Deceased, recovered a judgment of $17,000 against William Albert Brookshire, defendant, in a wrongful death action in the Circuit Court of Audrain County, Missouri, on July 29, 1960. A general execution issued on said $17,000 judgment to the Sheriff of Boone County on December 23, 1960. This execution was mailed to Mrs. Contestible's attorneys in Columbia and was delivered to Sheriff Powell January 10, 1961. He levied upon defendant's 322 acres under said execution on January 11, 1961.

Defendant contends it was error to sell his 322 acre farm without attempting to make the judgment debt, interest and costs out of a portion of said farm.

* * * [A] judgment debtor is to be afforded reasonable protection in levying on and selling his property under execution. Civil Rule 76.21 (§ 513.095) [amended in 1993 and recodified as 31 Mo. Prac., Civil Rules Handbook Rule 76.11 (2004 ed.)], provides in effect that if a judgment debtor gives the officer a list of his property sufficient to satisfy the execution, "the officer shall levy upon the property and, no other, if in his opinion it is sufficient; if not, then upon such additional property as shall be sufficient."

Civil Rule 76.24 (§ 513.210) [recodified as 31 Mo. Prac., Civil Rules Handbook Rule 76.12 (2004 ed.)] provides: "When an execution shall be levied upon real estate, the officer levying the same shall divide such property, if susceptible of division, and sell so much thereof as will be sufficient to satisfy such execution, unless the debtor in the execution shall desire the whole of any tract or lot of land to be sold together, in which case it shall be sold accordingly."

And Rule 76.25 (§ 513.100) provides: "The person whose goods, chattels and real estate are taken in execution may elect what part thereof shall be first sold; and if he shall deliver to the officer having charge thereof a statement, in writing, of such election, three days before the day appointed for the sale, stating specifically what goods, chattels and real estate he desires to be first sold, and so on, until the execution be satisfied, the officer shall proceed according to such election, until sufficient money shall be made to satisfy the amount in the execution specified and costs."

It is stated in 21 Am.Jur., Execution, § 380, that an execution is not "leviable upon all the debtor's property, but only upon sufficient property owned by the debtor within the jurisdiction to satisfy the debt, interest, and costs"; and, while the officer is left to his own judgment, he "must exercise the care and discretion which a reasonably prudent man would exercise under like conditions and circumstances." And, with respect to the property to be sold when more than enough to satisfy the debt is seized, it is stated in § 384: "The general rule is that the execution officer may make a division of the property, if that is practicable, and sell only so much of it as is necessary to satisfy the debt." * * * A failure to divide real estate and sell only enough to satisfy the execution [has been] considered an abuse of discretion * * * and a constructive fraud * * *.

* * *

Defendant wrote Sheriff Powell under date of January 11, 1961, re the Crouch judgment, levy and sale, stating, among other things, that his land was worth in excess of $100 an acre; and: "I am restricting the amount which you can sell to the northeast 40 acres of said tract of land. This land is clear. There is no mortgage or encumbrance of any kind against it."

Defendant protested the execution sale to those assembled for the sale and stated in effect that the judgment involved had been obtained in Henry County and the case was on appeal and the judgment was not final; that: "After the judgment becomes final it will be paid"; that Crouch had in his possession cattle belonging to defendant worth $10,000 against which there was no lien; that "I have notified the sheriff that this farm is clear of any mortgages whatsoever; that it is worth approximately $50,000.00; that one forty acre sold would be more than adequate. I have pointed out the forty acres * * * to be sold"; that he was certain the $17,000 judgment against him in the Contestible case would be reversed; that a supersedeas bond would be given; that this sale would be illegal and whoever bought the farm would buy a law suit. (The Contestible judgment, however, was affirmed January 8, 1962, in Contestible v. Brookshire, Mo., 355 S.W.2d 36.)

Sheriff Powell, who had been sheriff for about twenty years, admitted 40 acres of defendant's farm "might have been" worth far in excess of $2,000. Asked why he had not told defendant the 40 acres would not be sufficient, he would take 80 acres, Sheriff Powell answered: "I didn't intend to take 80 acres." He testified he had levied on and held three or four execution sales of defendant's 322 acre farm. He stated he did not know it was illegal to sell $50,000 worth of property to satisfy a $2,000 judgment; and there was testimony he had levied on the 322 acres to collect a $13.00 judgment, and to collect a $600 judgment. He stated "I checked the record and there was several thousand dollars" against all of the farm, and that is why "I levied on all of it." He also stated "I never checked the records." He did not levy on personal property because "It was much easier to do it this way." He knew defendant had stocks in various corporations and had more than 200 head of Hereford cattle on the farm; that they might have sold for at least $200 a head on the market and as registered cattle would have brought more, and that 20 head of the cattle "might have" been sufficient to more than pay the Crouch judgment, interest and costs.

Ray Crouch, the judgment creditor, testified he wanted to and asked his attorney to levy on defendant's farm, and that he knew defendant had collateral * * * to take care of the Crouch judgment. Sheriff Powell testified that Crouch had told him defendant had deposited sufficient collateral with the Hartford Insurance Company to take care of the Crouch judgment.

* * *

A sheriff conducting an execution sale is the agent of the property owner and the judgment creditor, and his duty is to protect the interests of both and to see that the property is not sacrificed. * * * Forced sales of property usually do not bring full value.

Sheriff Powell's advertisement of the sale of defendant's 322 acre farm was to "sell all of said real estate or as much thereof as *it* be necessary to pay the judgment of $1,966.69," in the Henry County Circuit Court, which, with interest and costs, amounted to $2,308.16 on the day of sale.

Defendant's farm was never advertised for sale under the Audrain County (Contestible) execution. Defendant first knew of the levy on his farm under the $17,000 Audrain County judgment about 30 minutes before its sale under the Crouch judgment. Sheriff Powell testified that he sold under the Henry County, and not under the Audrain County, execution.

Defendant's 322 acres was not divided for the purpose of selling but was sold as a whole to plaintiff for $20,600.00. The only bidders were Ed Orr, one of the attorneys for Mrs. Contestible, and Ralph Alexander, a bondsman and attorney for the sheriff. Plaintiff Griggs testified he heard the farm would bring enough to satisfy the two judgments about 15 or 20 minutes before the sale; that about 5 or 10 minutes before it was sold he decided to buy it because "it didn't bring any more than it did," and that he asked Mr. Alexander to bid for him. * * *

It is not questioned but that this 322 acre farm, consisting of approximately eight forties, could have been offered for sale in parcels. Rule 76.24 (§ 513.210) contemplates that the officer "divide such property, if susceptible of division, and sell so much thereof as will be sufficient to satisfy such execution." This was not done, and we hold that it should have been so divided. In Brookshire v. Powell, Mo., 335 S.W.2d 176, 181, the disparity between the market value of this farm and a bid of $2,300 was considered so great as to require setting aside that execution sale and sheriff's deed. In the case at bar the Henry County judgment, interest and costs amounted to $2,308.16; and for that amount under said execution and the constructive levy of the Audrain County execution, but without an advertisement for sale under Rule 76.36, supra, under said Audrain County execution, it is sought to justify this forced sale for $20,600 of property valued at about $46,000. This record calls for the result reached in Brookshire v. Powell * * *.

Defendant is entitled to relief upon doing equity. * * * Accordingly, if defendant will, within thirty days, deposit in this court, for the use and benefit of those entitled thereto, the sum of $20,600 with interest at the rate of 6% per annum from the date of sale until the same is paid, the decree appealed from will be reversed and the cause remanded with directions to cancel the sheriff's sale and the sheriff's deed to plaintiff made pursuant thereto; otherwise the decree will stand affirmed. In either event the costs are assessed against the estate of defendant Brookshire.

PER CURIAM. The foregoing opinion by BOHLING, Special Commissioner, is adopted as the opinion of the court.

All of the Judges concur.

[The court's opinion on a motion to modify and for a rehearing and the court's supplemental opinion are omitted.]

NOTES AND QUESTIONS

1. Execution is the traditional method of enforcing a money judgment. It applies to both personal and real property. Various factors tend to influence the effectiveness of the device, including: the territorial reach of an execution; the order in which various types of property are levied upon and sold by the officer to whom the execution is delivered; and the determination of priorities as between competing executions.

2. Federal Rule 69 provides that the procedures of the state in which the federal court is sitting are to be followed in enforcing federal-court judgments, but "a federal statute governs to the extent it applies." In Coonts v. Potts, 316 F.3d 745 (8th Cir. 2003), the federal court relied on the Missouri law discussed in *Griggs* to determine whether an execution constituted an unreasonable seizure. In addition, a federal court retains jurisdiction to enforce its own judgments even if the applicable state law seems to require that proceedings to enforce judgments be brought in a specified state court. See Duchek v. Jacobi, 646 F.2d 415 (9th Cir.1981). The Supreme Court discussed the availability (or not) of federal ancillary jurisdiction to enforce settlement agreements that result in a stipulation of dismissal in Kokkonen v. Guardian Life Ins. Co. of America, 511 U.S. 375, 114 S.Ct. 1673, 128 L.Ed.2d 391 (1994). See p. 349, supra.

3. State law may exempt various types of real and personal property from execution. Exemptions are designed to ensure that the affected litigant can meet "essential needs" and to prevent the need for "public relief." SCHLAEFER v. SCHLAEFER, 112 F.2d 177, 185 (D.C.Cir.1940). See also Woliner v. Woliner, 148 N.J.Super. 510, 372 A.2d 1170 (1977). The exemptions also promote long-term investment and encourage family stability. However, commentators warn that debtors may abuse the exemptions by trying to shield their assets from execution. See Corbit, *Montana Should Raise Homestead Exemption*, 32 Mont. Law. 36 (March 2007).

4. Exempt property typically is defined by dollar amount and type of property, both of which vary greatly from state to state. See, e.g., Laurence, *Mobile Homesteads, and in Particular the Exempt Status of Mobile Homes Located on Rented Lots: The Laws of Arkansas, Mississippi, Nebraska, and Utah Compared and the Principle of the Liberal Construction of Exemption Statutes* Analyzed, 57 Ark. L. Rev. 221 (2004); Peterson, *Note—Exemption Stacking in Montana Bankruptcies—"Windfall" or "Fresh Start"?*, 64 Mont. L.Rev. 543 (2003). The system of exemptions is said to reflect a balance between "the traditional state legislative prerogative to adjust exemptions to local economic conditions" and an interest in both "federal uniformity" and "conceptions of national equity." In re Davis, 170 F.3d 475, 478 (5th Cir.),

certiorari denied 528 U.S. 822, 120 S.Ct. 67, 145 L.Ed.2d 57 (1999). See Rivera, *State Homestead Exemptions and Their Effect on Federal Bankruptcy Laws*, 39 Real Prop. Prob. & Tr. J. 71 (2004).

5. Perhaps the most important exemption is the homestead exemption. For a history of the homestead exemption, see Morantz, *There's No Place Like Home: Homestead Exemption and Judicial Constructions of Family in Nineteenth Century America,* 24 Law & Hist. Rev. 245 (2006). In most states, the exemption protects the family house up to a certain dollar amount. As of 2005, 45 states subjected the homestead exemption to a dollar cap, and the exemption was unlimited in Florida, Texas, Iowa, Kansas, and South Dakota. See Coveny, *Saying Goodbye to Texas's Homestead Protection: One Step Toward Economic Efficiency with the Bankruptcy Abuse Prevention and Consumer Protection Act of 2005*, 44 Hous. L. Rev. 433 (2007) (discussing the preemptive effect of federal bankruptcy law on state homestead exemptions).

By way of illustration, see the lists of property exempted from execution by Section 5205 (personal) and Section 5206 (real) of New York's Civil Practice Law and Rules. The failure to revise these statutes over long periods of time has led to some incredibly outdated provisions. For example, New York exempts from execution a lot of land that is being used as the principal residence, but for many years, the exemption was limited to $2,000. See Dean, *Economic Relations Between Husband and Wife in New York*, 41 Cornell L.Q. 175, 213–14 (1956). In 2005 the exemption was raised to $50,000. See 2005 N.Y. A.B. 7939 (May 3, 2005). Compare In re Betz, 273 B.R. 313 (Bkrtcy. D.Mass.2002) (Massachusetts homestead exemption increased in 1991 from $100,000 to $300,000).

6. Garnishment is a controversial form of execution used to attach intangible property. The most common subject is wages, although bank accounts also may be garnished. State law generally exempts part of the judgment debtor's income from enforcement procedures such as execution and garnishment. The percentage of income exempted from execution has varied state to state, from little or nothing to a high of 90%. The Consumer Credit Protection Act of 1968 establishes a nationwide limit on the amount of an employee's wages that are subject to garnishment and affords an employee protection against being fired because of a garnishment. See 15 U.S.C. §§ 1673–74 (1988). However, in some states, wages that are exempt under the Act lose their exemption once they are deposited in a bank. See Walker, *Wyoming's Statutory Exemption on Wage Garnishment: Should It Include Deposited Wages?*, 6 Wyo. L. Rev. 53 (2006); Bernard, *Garnishing the Congressional Intent: Protecting Debtor Wages in Bank Accounts Under the Federal and Louisiana Wage Garnishment Exemption Statutes*, 66 La. L. Rev. 233 (2005). How would you justify this result? One study suggests that the rate of garnishment has dropped over time, but the percentage of garnished debtors who are women may have risen. See Hynes, *Bankruptcy and State Collections: The Case of the Missing Garnishments*, 91 Cornell L. Rev. 603, 638 (2006). For a historical critique of garnishment, see Brunn, *Wage Garnishment in California: A Study and Recommendations*, 53 Calif.L.Rev. 1214 (1965); see also Abrahams & Feldman, *The Exemption of Wages from Garnishment: Some Comparisons and Comments*, 3 De Paul L.Rev. 153 (1954).

7. Execution may also be critical in securing payment of child support by a noncustodial parent. See Swank, *The National Child Non–Support Epidemic*, 2003 Mich. St. DCL L. Rev. 357 (2003). In 1950, the federal government entered the field of child support enforcement. See id. That same year, the National Conference of Commissioners on Uniform State Laws adopted the Uniform Reciprocal Enforcement of Support Act to reduce the cost of enforcement. The Act was amended in 1968. In 1992, it was replaced by the Uniform Interstate Family Support Act, 9 U.L.A. 229 (1993).

8. What if a federal judgment is rendered in one judicial district, but the defendant's assets are located in another district? Under 28 U.S.C. § 1963, the judgment may be registered in any other district by filing a certified copy with that district. It then may be enforced in the same manner as any judgment of the court in which it is registered. A 1988 amendment to the statute provides for the registration of a judgment even before it becomes final "when ordered by the court that entered the judgment for good cause shown." For a discussion of the meaning of "good cause" in this context, see Garden State Tanning, Inc. v. Mitchell Mfg. Group Inc., 2000 WL 1201372 (E.D.Pa.2000); Associated Bus. Telephone Sys. Corp. v. Greater Capital Corp., 128 F.R.D. 63 (D.N.J.1989). See generally Registration in Federal District Court of Judgment of Another Federal Court Under 28 U.S.C.A. § 1963, 194 A.L.R. Fed. 531 (2004)

2. SUPPLEMENTARY PROCEEDINGS

Supplementary proceedings allow a judgment creditor "to reach 'equitable' assets beyond the scope of legal execution, and * * * to uncover property owned by the judgment debtor but deviously concealed and 'transferred.' " Cohen, *Collection of Money Judgments in New York: Supplementary Proceedings*, 35 Colum.L.Rev. 1007, 1012 (1935). The procedure has its origins in the common law but the enforcement process today is a creature of statute and varies from state to state. For a discussion of an illustrative state practice, see Lippman, *Proceedings Supplementary and Uniform Fraudulent Transfer Act: Dual Remedies to Execute Against a Judgment Debtor's Transferred Assets*, Florida Bar. J. (1996). See also Note, *Supplementary Proceedings in Illinois: The Uncertain Remedy*, 1979 U.Ill.L.F. 241. Because discovery within the execution process now is more widely available than it once was, judgment creditors have less occasion to resort to supplementary proceedings. Federal Rule 60 permits broad discovery in aid of execution. Additionally, of the many states that have loosened or eliminated restrictions on pre-execution discovery of assets, most have followed the pattern of Federal Rule 69.

NOTES AND QUESTIONS

1. Should supplementary proceedings be treated as a separate action or merely as an adjunct to the action in which the judgment was recovered? What turns on the answer to this question?

2. Suppose A recovers a judgment from B and during supplementary proceedings B claims that C is in possession of property belonging to B. When

A attempts to have the property applied to the judgment, C contests B's interest. How is the dispute between B and C as to the ownership of the property to be determined? If the supplementary proceeding is under the control of a judge, can the court determine the dispute between B and C and, if it finds in B's favor, apply the property to the satisfaction of A's judgment? What objections are there to the judge making such a determination? Compare Letz v. Letz, 123 Mont. 494, 215 P.2d 534 (1950), with Exceletech, Inc. v. Williams, 597 So.2d 275 (Fla.1992).

3. CONTEMPT AND BODY EXECUTION

REEVES v. CROWNSHIELD

Court of Appeals of New York, 1937.
274 N.Y. 74, 8 N.E.2d 283.

FINCH, JUDGE.

The uncollectibility of money judgments has ever been a subject of concern to bench and bar. A large part of the statute law of this state is designed to enable a judgment creditor to obtain satisfaction upon his money judgment. That a large percentage of these money judgments have remained uncollectible has been confirmed by statistical surveys. Johns Hopkins University Institute of Law, Survey of Litigation in New York (1931). Many debtors who were in a position to pay have evaded their legal obligations by unlawful and technical means. Discontent with this situation resulted in agitation for reform in collection procedure. * * * Finally, in 1935, upon the recommendation of the Judicial Council, a law was enacted creating a new mode of enforcing the payment of judgments. * * *

Section 793 of the Civil Practice Act [currently N.Y.C.P.L.R. 5226] now provides that, in addition to the garnishee provisions of the old law, the court may make an order directing a judgment debtor to make payments in installments out of the income which he receives. Such orders must be made upon notice to the judgment debtor and after he has had an opportunity to show inability to pay, and with due regard to the reasonable requirements of the judgment debtor and his family, as well as of payments required to be made by him to other creditors. Section 801 of the Civil Practice Act [now found in N.Y.C.P.L.R. 5251] provides that refusal to pay after such an order of the court is punishable as a contempt. * * *

This new procedure was invoked against the appellant, in an attempt to collect a judgment for approximately $400. The examination in supplementary proceedings disclosed that he was employed by the Federal Government as a steamship inspector at a salary of $230 per month, less a small pension deduction. He has no children, and the whereabouts of his wife are unknown. Aside from $48 a month paid as rent and his living expenses, he has no financial obligations. The court ordered the appellant to pay installments of $20 per month until the judgment was satisfied.

Upon his failure to pay, he was held in contempt and fined the sum of $20, commitment being provided for in default of payment.

An appeal was taken directly to this court from the City Court of New York City on the ground that a constitutional question was involved.

* * *

The judgment debtor challenges the constitutionality of section 793 and section 801 on the ground that in effect they provide for imprisonment for debt. It is admitted that neither the State nor the Federal Constitutions contain provisions expressly prohibiting imprisonment for debt, and that the statutory provision forbidding imprisonment for debt found in section 21 of the New York Civil Rights Law excepts cases otherwise specially prescribed by law. It is asserted, however, that imprisonment for debt is barred by the due process clauses of the State and Federal Constitutions (Const.N.Y. art. 1, § 6; Const.U.S. Amend. 14). No cases so holding are cited * * *. Whatever doubt there may exist as to whether imprisonment for debt without regard to ability to pay may be treated as a deprivation of liberty without due process of law * * *, there can be no doubt that imprisonment for failure to obey an order of a court to make payment out of income, which order is made with due regard to the needs of the debtor and his family, is not violative of the due process clause.

* * *

In the case at bar the judgment debtor has not complained that the order directing the payment of $20 per month is unjust, inequitable, or harsh. His position is an arbitrary refusal to pay. It is based upon the ground that the courts are powerless to compel him to pay out of his income an amount fixed after deducting the sum necessary for his reasonable needs.

The Legislature has seen fit to provide a creditor with a direct remedy for the collection of his just debts. A refusal to recognize such an order by the judgment debtor entitles the creditor to move to have him punished for contempt. Without this right, there would be no power in the court to enforce its order. To compel the judgment debtor to obey the order of the court is not imprisonment for debt, but only imprisonment for disobedience of an order with which he is able to comply. His refusal is contumacious conduct, the same as a refusal to obey any other lawful order of the court.

It also is asserted that the application of this law to the appellant is unconstitutional, since it interferes with the operation of a federal instrumentality. To sustain this contention, reference is made to the cases declaring State laws taxing the salaries of federal officers unconstitutional. * * * Analysis shows that these cases are not in point. The true basis for declaring a state tax on the salaries of federal officers unconstitutional is that since the Federal Government presumably finds it necessary to pay its officers a salary based upon the value of their services, the state should not be permitted to tax the salaries thereby reducing the compensation and making it necessary for the Federal Government to increase the salaries paid by it.

* * *

It is true that the wages of a federal employee cannot be garnisheed, but once his wage has been paid to him a state is not prohibited from ordering him to apply a portion of such income towards the payment of his just debts. The moment the salary is received it becomes a part of the general income of the owner. If he should therewith purchase property the property could be taken under execution for the payment of a judgment against the owner. No reason appears for exempting the income while still held as money and not exempting it when it has been converted into property. * * *

* * *

Orders affirmed.

NOTES AND QUESTIONS

1. Compare the principal case with PEOPLE EX REL. SARLAY v. POPE, 230 A.D. 649, 650, 246 N.Y.S. 414, 416 (3d Dep't 1930), in which the court said that the "imprisonment of the defendants until the payment of a fine in the amount of the judgment recovered in the contract action would be, in effect, imprisonment for a civil debt." In the absence of an express constitutional provision forbidding imprisonment for debt, is there any theory under which it can be held unconstitutional? See Kinsey v. Preeson, 746 P.2d 542 (Colo.1987). If contempt or body execution is aimed at the recalcitrant or dilatory judgment debtor, how is the good faith, but penniless, debtor protected against being caught in the contempt trap? Is it sufficient simply to require that the judgment debtor's failure be "willful" in order to punish for contempt? See Note, *Body Attachment and Body Execution: Forgotten But Not Gone*, 17 Wm. & Mary L.Rev. 543 (1976).

2. The use of imprisonment to collect debts dates back 3000 years. Ford, *Imprisonment for Debt*, 25 Mich.L.Rev. 24 (1926–1927). The American practice traces its genesis to Acts of Parliament adopted in England during the thirteenth century:

> Under this system, arrest of the alleged debtor was accomplished via a series of writs. For example, the *Writ of Capias ad Respondendum* (alternatively, termed the process of a "Mesne"), obtained at the inception of a suit, allowed arrest to prevent the debtor from fraudulently hiding assets or fleeing. The arrested debtor could obtain freedom by turning over the disputed property he was alleged to be concealing and/or posting bail to assure he would not flee. The *Writ of Capias ad Satisfaciendum*, on the other hand, was meant to insure collection of the debt once the court determined the debt was valid. Thus, the debtor sat in prison until he, family, or friends came forth to pay. It was not unheard

of for low-income debtors to die in prison when family and friends could not help.

Debtor's prison, and the accompanying legal writs of *Capias ad Respondendum* (Mesne) and *Capias ad Satisfaciendum*, came to America with the colonists. Long after the ratification of our Constitution, there existed a federal debtor's prison. In contrast to the separate English debtor's prisons, debtors in the United States were generally thrown into the same jails with criminals. In fact, in 1830s Massachusetts, New York, Pennsylvania, and Maryland, three to five times as many persons were imprisoned for debt as for crime.

Lest you think all this was part of a long ago, more primitive time, the threat of jail as a means of encouraging payment for private debt in America coexisted with remote-controlled color TV's. While by the 1920s every state abolished imprisonment for debt by Constitution or statute, well into the 1960s there existed a great variety of approaches for the use of Mesne in tort and fraud cases. Thus, pleadings could be crafted to plead a contract claim (for which Mesne was not permitted) as fraud in the inducement (for which Mesne could be employed under law). By such framing of the pleadings, creditor's counsel thus would raise the spectre of bodily arrest, thereby coercing the alleged debtor to settle rather than face arrest and jail.

Mitchell & Kunsch, *Of Driver's Licenses and Debtor's Prison*, 4 Seattle J. for Soc. Just. 439, 445–46 (2005) (internal quotation and citations omitted).

3. The Fair Debt Collection Act, which was amended in 2006, regulates the collection of consumer debts. The statute forbids a debt collector from representing or implying "that nonpayment of any debt will result in the arrest or imprisonment of any person or the seizure, garnishment, attachment, or sale of any property or wages of any person unless such action is lawful and the debt collector or creditor intends to take such action." 15 U.S.C. § 1692e(4). Guidry v. Clare, 442 F. Supp.2d 282 (E.D. Va. 2006) affirmed the right of debt collectors to file criminal complaints that might lead to the arrest or imprisonment of the debtor. See Young & McIntyre, *Developments Under the Fair Debt Collection Practices Act (FDCPA)*, 27(2) Banking & Fin. Services Pol'y Rep. 18 (2008). Writing a check on a bank account with insufficient funds can be criminally punished in every one of the fifty states, and some states impose strict liability so that the prosecutor does not need to prove intent to defraud. See Sanders, Jr., *Time to Close the Collection Agency: Addressing the Abuse of Bad Check Laws*, 2 Charleston L. Rev. 215, 217–18 (2007). Doesn't this permit the state in some situations to imprison an individual for debt?

4. What are the differences between body execution and contempt? Should courts in jurisdictions that have prohibited or severely limited body execution be able to use contempt proceedings to circumvent the restrictions on body execution? See Marshall v. Matthei, 327 N.J.Super. 512, 525 744 A.2d 209, 217 (2000); Zeitinger v. Mitchell, 244 S.W.2d 91 (Mo.1951).

4. LIENS AND PRIORITIES

Lien and priority-of-lien problems are among the most complex in the law of judgment enforcement. The traditional "lien" situation involves the judgment creditor's right to a particular piece of property as against the judgment debtor or someone claiming under the latter, such as an assignee or purchaser of the property. The judgment creditor's rights against a transferee are based on the purchaser's or assignee's having actual or constructive notice of the creditor's rights in the property. Questions of priority of liens involve a dispute between two or more judgment creditors over the debtor's property. As a general rule, the rights of one creditor *vis à vis* another are based on the equitable principle of "diligence," which seeks to prevent a creditor from refraining from enforcing a judgment while maintaining priority of lien. What factors should determine whether one judgment creditor is more "diligent" than another? Because courts often confuse "priority-of-lien" and "lien" situations, the line between the two has been somewhat obscured. The New York practice is analyzed in 11 Weinstein, Korn & Miller, New York Civil Practice ¶ 5202.02 (2d ed. 2005). On what basis did the Supreme Court uphold the constitutionality of the lien in *Doehr*, p. 254, supra? For a discussion of the social consequences of liens and priorities, see Warren, *What Is a Women's Issue? Bankruptcy, Commercial Law, and Other Gender–Neutral Topics*, 25 Harv. Women's L.J. 19 (2002).

CHAPTER 16

APPELLATE REVIEW

■ ■ ■

In this Chapter, we consider appellate review on a number of levels. First there is the question of timing. When can an aggrieved party obtain review of a court order? Must he or she await a final decision in the action or may the matter be reviewed at once? For an historical analysis of how the final judgment rule developed, see Crick, *The Final Judgment as a Basis for Appeal*, 41 Yale L.J. 539, 541–50 (1932). As we shall see, the basic rule limiting appeals to final judgments has a number of exclusions and exceptions. Second there is the question of what decisions of the court are reviewable on their merits. To what extent, for example, should a person who prevailed in a case be able to appeal an adverse determination of the court, one made along the way, that could have an impact on future cases?

SECTION A. THE PRINCIPLE OF FINALITY

1. APPLICATION OF THE BASIC CONCEPT

Read 28 U.S.C. §§ 1291 and 1292 in the Supplement.

COOPER, EXTRAORDINARY WRIT PRACTICE IN CRIMINAL CASES: ANALOGIES FOR THE MILITARY COURTS, 98 F.R.D. 593, 594–96 (1983):

A truly final judgment is one that marks the completion of all the events that will occur in a trial court. Nothing more remains to be done, unless it be execution of a judgment against the defendant.

The advantages that may be gained by deferring appeals until entry of a truly final judgment are familiar, and can be summarized in short order. Immediate review of every ruling made by a trial court could not be tolerated. Repeated interruptions and delays could put the trial process beyond any reasonable control, even if appeals were taken only when there was a good faith and reasonable belief that the court was wrong. The opportunities for less honorable delay and harassment of an adversary also would not go entirely unexploited. More limited opportunities for interlocutory review would not be so disastrous, but would carry some part of the same costs. The possible advantages to be set against these costs arise from the opportunity to correct a wrong ruling. These advantages, however, are reduced by the prospects that most trial court rulings are correct; that wrong rulings often are corrected by the trial court; and that uncorrected wrong rulings will not, in the end, taint the final judgment.

The price that is paid for a final judgment rule, however, can be high. An erroneous ruling may taint everything that follows. If appeal must be delayed until final judgment, it may become necessary to repeat the entire trial proceeding. The costs of repeating the trial go beyond the obvious costs of expense and anxiety. The further proceedings will be held later, and may suffer from lapses of memory, inconsequential inconsistencies that are blown into exaggerated importance, and actual loss of evidence. Beyond these defects, the retrial proceedings often will be affected by lessons learned at the first trial. * * * The problem is more than one of boredom; strategies have been revealed and must be revised, opportunities to sustain truth by impeachment are diminished, and so on.

* * *

Beyond the impact on individual cases, loss of the opportunity for interlocutory review means that some areas of law must develop without much opportunity for appellate guidance. Questions of discovery, for example, may confuse and divide trial courts for years without the guidance and uniformity that appeals could provide.

LIBERTY MUTUAL INSURANCE CO. v. WETZEL

Supreme Court of the United States, 1976.
424 U.S. 737, 96 S.Ct. 1202, 47 L.Ed.2d 435.

Certiorari to the United States Court of Appeals for the Third Circuit.

MR. JUSTICE REHNQUIST delivered the opinion of the Court.

Respondents filed a complaint in the United States District Court for the Western District of Pennsylvania in which they asserted that petitioner's employee insurance benefits and maternity leave regulations discriminated against women in violation of Title VII of the Civil Rights Act of 1964 * * *. The District Court ruled in favor of respondents on the issue of petitioner's liability under that Act, and petitioner appealed to the Court of Appeals for the Third Circuit. That court held that it had jurisdiction of petitioner's appeal under 28 U.S.C. § 1291, and proceeded to affirm on the merits the judgment of the District Court. We granted certiorari * * * and heard argument on the merits. Though neither party has questioned the jurisdiction of the Court of Appeals to entertain the appeal, we are obligated to do so on our own motion if a question thereto exists. * * *

Respondents' complaint, after alleging jurisdiction and facts deemed pertinent to their claim, prayed for a judgment against petitioner embodying the following relief:

(a) requiring that defendant establish non-discriminatory hiring, payment, opportunity, and promotional plans and programs;

(b) enjoining the continuance by defendant of the illegal acts and practices alleged herein;

(c) requiring that defendant pay over to plaintiffs and to the members of the class the damages sustained by plaintiffs and the members of the class by reason of defendant's illegal acts and practices, including adjusted backpay, with interest, and an additional equal amount as liquidated damages, and exemplary damages;

(d) requiring that defendant pay to plaintiffs and to the members of the class the costs of this suit and a reasonable attorneys' fee, with interest; and

(e) such other and further relief as the Court deems appropriate. App. 19.

After extensive discovery, respondents moved for partial summary judgment only as to the issue of liability. * * * The District Court * * *, finding no issues of material fact in dispute, entered an order to the effect that petitioner's pregnancy-related policies violated Title VII of the Civil Rights Act of 1964. It also ruled that Liberty Mutual's hiring and promotion policies violated Title VII. Petitioner thereafter filed a motion for reconsideration which was denied by the District Court. * * *

It is obvious from the District Court's order that respondents, although having received a favorable ruling on the issue of petitioner's liability to them, received none of the relief which they expressly prayed for in the portion of their complaint set forth above. They requested an injunction, but did not get one; they requested damages, but were not awarded any; they requested attorneys' fees, but received none.

Counsel for respondents when questioned during oral argument in this Court suggested that at least the District Court's order of February 20 amounted to a declaratory judgment on the issue of liability pursuant to the provisions of 28 U.S.C. § 2201. Had respondents sought *only* a declaratory judgment, and no other form of relief, we would of course have a different case. But even if we accept respondents' contention that the District Court's order was a declaratory judgment on the issue of liability, it nonetheless left unresolved respondents' requests for an injunction, for compensatory and exemplary damages, and for attorneys' fees. It finally disposed of none of respondents' prayers for relief.

The District Court and the Court of Appeals apparently took the view that because the District Court made the recital required by Fed.Rule

Civ.Proc. 54(b) that final judgment be entered on the issue of liability, and that there was no just reason for delay, the orders thereby became appealable as a final decision pursuant to 28 U.S.C. § 1291. We cannot agree with this application of the Rule and statute in question.

Rule 54(b) "does not apply to a single claim action * * *. It is limited expressly to multiple claims actions in which 'one or more but less than all' of the multiple claims have been finally decided and are found otherwise to be ready for appeal." Sears, Roebuck & Co. v. Mackey, 351 U.S. 427, 435, 76 S.Ct. 895, 899, 100 L.Ed. 1297, 1306 (1956). Here, however, respondents set forth but a single claim: that petitioner's employee insurance benefits and maternity leave regulations discriminated against its women employees in violation of Title VII of the Civil Rights Act of 1964. They prayed for several different types of relief in the event that they sustained the allegations of their complaint * * *, but their complaint advanced a single legal theory which was applied to only one set of facts. Thus, despite the fact that the District Court undoubtedly made the findings required under the Rule had it been applicable, those findings do not in a case such as this make the order appealable pursuant to 28 U.S.C. § 1291. * * *

We turn to consider whether the District Court's order might have been appealed by petitioner to the Court of Appeals under any other theory. The order, viewed apart from its discussion of Rule 54(b), constitutes a grant of partial summary judgment limited to the issue of petitioner's liability. Such judgments are by their terms interlocutory, see Fed. Rule Civ.Proc. 56(c) [now, Rule 56(d)(2)], and where assessment of damages or awarding of other relief remains to be resolved have never been considered to be "final" within the meaning of 28 U.S.C. § 1291. * * * Thus the only possible authorization for an appeal from the District Court's order would be pursuant to the provisions of 28 U.S.C. § 1292.

If the District Court had granted injunctive relief but had not ruled on respondents' other requests for relief, this interlocutory order would have been appealable under § 1292(a)(1). But, as noted above, the court did not issue an injunction. It might be argued that the order of the District Court, insofar as it failed to include the injunctive relief requested by respondents, is an interlocutory order refusing an injunction within the meaning of § 1292(a)(1). But even if this would have allowed *respondents* to then obtain review in the Court of Appeals, there was no denial of any injunction sought by *petitioner* and it could not avail itself of that grant of jurisdiction.

Nor was this order appealable pursuant to 28 U.S.C. § 1292(b). Although the District Court's findings made with a view to satisfying Rule 54(b) might be viewed as substantial compliance with the certification requirement of that section, there is no showing in this record that petitioner made application to the Court of Appeals within the 10 days therein specified. And that court's holding that its jurisdiction was pursuant to § 1291 makes it clear that it thought itself obliged to consider on the merits petitioner's appeal. There can be no assurance that had the other requirements of § 1292(b) been complied with, the Court of Appeals would have exercised its discretion to entertain the interlocutory appeal.

Were we to sustain the procedure followed here, we would condone a practice whereby a district court in virtually any case before it might render an interlocutory decision on the question of liability of the defendant, and the defendant would thereupon be permitted to appeal to the court of appeals without satisfying any of the requirements that Congress carefully set forth. We believe that Congress, in enacting present §§ 1291 and 1292 of Title 28, has been well aware of the dangers of an overly rigid insistence upon a "final decision" for appeal in every case, and has in those sections made ample provision for appeal of orders which are not "final" so as to alleviate any possible hardship. We would twist the fabric of the statute more than it will bear if we were to agree that the District Court's order of February 20, 1974, was appealable to the Court of Appeals.

The judgment of the Court of Appeals is therefore vacated, and the case is remanded with instructions to dismiss the petitioner's appeal.

It is so ordered.

MR. JUSTICE BLACKMUN took no part in the consideration or decision of this case.

JETCO ELECTRONIC INDUSTRIES, INC. v. GARDINER, 473 F.2d 1228 (5th Cir.1973). Plaintiff Jetco filed suit against three defendants, ETL, Gardiner, and Gardiner Electronics. The trial court granted ETL's motion to dismiss for lack of personal jurisdiction and for failure to state a claim for relief, and an appeal was taken by Jetco from that order. Several months after the order involving ETL, the trial court entered a second order disposing of Jetco's claims against Gardiner and Gardiner Electronics. On ETL's motion to dismiss the appeal, the Court of Appeals held:

> The March order dismissing appellants' suit against ETL * * * said nothing about appellants' rights as against the other two defendants, Gardiner and Gardiner Electronics * * *. That order is thus not a final judgment * * *. Nor was the later order entering an agreed judgment disposing of appellants' claim against Gardiner and Gardiner Electronics a final judgment [since] * * * it did not adjudicate appellants' rights as against ETL. Nevertheless, these two orders, considered together, terminated this litigation just as effectively as would have been the case had the district judge gone through the motions of entering a single order formally reciting the substance of the earlier two orders. Mindful of the Supreme Court's command that practical, not technical, considerations are to govern the application of principles of finality * * * we decline appellee's invitation to exalt form over substance by dismissing this appeal. We hold that the

> March order dismissing appellants' suit against ETL is, under the circumstances of this case, within our appellate jurisdiction. * * *

Id. at 1231.

NOTES AND QUESTIONS

1. *Liberty Mutual* illustrates the proposition that the question whether a court may hear an appeal—with its constituent issues of finality, timeliness, and mode—is almost without exception viewed as involving "jurisdiction over the subject matter." See also Firestone Tire & Rubber Co. v. Risjord, 449 U.S. 368, 101 S.Ct. 669, 66 L.Ed.2d 571 (1981); Collins v. Miller, 252 U.S. 364, 40 S.Ct. 347, 64 L.Ed. 616 (1920); United States v. Girault, 52 U.S. (11 How.) 22, 13 L.Ed. 587 (1851). All the doctrinal overtones of that concept are present. For example, a lower appellate court's decision will be reversed for lack of appellate jurisdiction and the appeal will be ordered dismissed even though the issue of the propriety of the appeal was not raised in the lower court; the parties may not waive the requirements for an appeal; neither the trial nor appellate court can supply the defects or depart from the rigid rules of law regarding appeals. What are the reasons for this approach? Are the same dangers present when an appellate court conducts a premature review as when a trial court hears a cause that is not within its competence? See 15A Wright, Miller & Cooper, Federal Practice and Procedure: Jurisdiction and Related Matters 2d § 3905.

2. Does the *Jetco* decision represent a departure from the traditional approach discussed in Note 1 above? Would your answer be different if the trial court's second order, dismissing the case against Gardiner and Gardiner Electronics, had been rendered prior to the time Jetco's appeal was filed? Compare Oak Constr. Co. v. Huron Cement Co., 475 F.2d 1220 (6th Cir.1973) (subsequent trial-court action cannot save appeal that was inappropriate at the time it was filed). Should Jetco be free to file a separate appeal challenging the court's second order?

3. Suppose plaintiff brings an action against defendant alleging two related claims and the trial court makes a final ruling dismissing one of them. If plaintiff then voluntarily dismisses the second claim without prejudice, should plaintiff be permitted to appeal on the ground that the court's decision is final under Section 1291? See CSX Transp., Inc. v. City of Garden City, 235 F.3d 1325 (11th Cir.2000).

4. Commentators point to the following justifications for maintaining an appellate system: "(1) to correct errors committed by the tribunal from which the appeal is taken; (2) to have a consistent, uniform declaration of what the law is, not only in the case on appeal, but also as it will be applied to similar cases in the future; and (3) to satisfy the public's demand for justice, which includes a demand that important grievances be heard and resolved by the highest possible governmental authority." See Kelso, *A Report on the California Appellate System*, 45 Hastings L.J. 433, 434–35 (1994) (citations omitted). To these traditional purposes commentators also point to the appellate court's lawmaking function, as well as its role in error prevention. See Shavell, *The*

Appeals Process as a Means of Error Correction, 24 J. Legal Stud. 379, 379–80, 416, 425–26 (1995). How does finality promote these purposes?

2. THE NEW YORK APPROACH

New York has taken a different approach than that followed by the federal courts, allowing appeals to the state's intermediate appellate court—the Appellate Division—in a great many situations in which no final judgment has been rendered. Read the New York provision, N.Y.C.P.L.R. 5701, which is found in the Supplement following 28 U.S.C. § 1292. What benefits and burdens does the New York system contain that the federal system does not?

KORN, CIVIL JURISDICTION OF THE NEW YORK COURT OF APPEALS AND APPELLATE DIVISIONS, 16 Buffalo L.Rev. 307, 332 (1967):

Today * * * it is well known that there is hardly a question of practice that cannot be appealed; and, if a matter is said to be addressed to the court's discretion or favor, this may mean a more limited scope of review but will rarely affect appealability. Appeals on practice matters are legion, ranging far and wide over questions of venue, parties, consolidation and joint trial, pleading and pre-trial disclosure. The only meaningful method of inquiry as to the content of the present standards is to examine the types of orders that have been held *not* to involve some part of the merits or affect a substantial right.

NOTES AND QUESTIONS

1. What are the advantages of freely allowing appeals from interlocutory orders? The disadvantages? Is it better to resolve the question of allowing an interlocutory appeal by weighing these advantages and disadvantages against each other in the abstract or by considering them as they apply in each case? See Scheffel, *Interlocutory Appeals in New York—Time Has Come for a More Efficient Approach*, 16 Pace L. Rev. 607 (1996).

2. In refusing to allow an appeal from an interlocutory order, an unnecessary appellate hearing may be avoided; in allowing an appeal, an unnecessary trial may be avoided, either by disposing of the case at that stage or by correcting in advance of trial an error that might otherwise require a new trial. Is there any basis for supposing that the appellate hearing is more likely to prove unnecessary than the trial? Is it relevant that the trial judge, hopefully, will be correct in his rulings more often than he is wrong?

Even if it is assumed that a reversal of the trial court's order by the appellate court is as probable as its affirmance and consideration is taken of the possibility that trial may demand more time of lawyers and judges than an appeal, does it follow that interlocutory appeals should be freely allowed?

Consider the effect of the following factors. (1) In the course of a single lawsuit there may be many interlocutory orders from which one of the parties would like to appeal; thus, if finality is required, several appeals may be saved for every trial that would be saved under the other approach. (2) Not every reversal of an interlocutory order will terminate the case without trial. (3) The number of appellate courts cannot be increased as readily as can the number of trial courts in order to take care of heavier calendars. There will be a serious problem as long as it is the function of appellate courts not only to review trial-court decisions but to establish and maintain a degree of uniformity in the law.

Is the trial judge's independence and discretion threatened by too frequent a review? Is a party who has been ordered to answer questions in a deposition interested in obtaining immediate review solely in order to save time or money? Moreover, the debate over the relative merits of a final-judgment rule and an interlocutory-appeal system is intertwined with the larger problem of court congestion at the appellate level. The attention given to crowding at the trial level has obscured the fact that a comparable problem exists in many reviewing courts.

3. Preparation of an appeal demands a substantial amount of a lawyer's time, and, even with technological advances, the duplication of a trial record can be costly. Some commentators have argued that the expense of taking an appeal may present a strategic opportunity to one of the parties, who might use the appeal for purely tactical reasons. See Willcox, Karlen & Roemer, *Justice Lost—By What Appellate Papers Cost,* 33 N.Y.U. L. Rev. 934 (1958). Other commentators have insisted that appeals are not that costly, see Clermont & Eisenberg, *Litigation Realities*, 88 Cornell L. Rev. 119, 152 (2002), but for that reason appeals likewise may present a strategic opportunity to one of the parties. Is there any effective sanction against the use of an appeal for purely tactical reasons? Examine Appellate Rule 38, as well as 28 U.S.C. § 1912 and § 1927. How extensive is the federal appeals court's power to impose sanctions on a frivolous appeal? See Kravitz, *Unpleasant Duties: Imposing Sanctions for Frivolous Appeals*, 4 J. App. Prac. & Process 335 (2002). Should it be sufficient for the imposing of a sanction to show that the appeal was filed in bad faith, or simply that it is "without merit"? See Wilton Corp. v. Ashland Castings Corp., 188 F.3d 670, 677 (6th Cir. 1999).

3. DEPARTURES FROM THE FINAL JUDGMENT RULE IN THE FEDERAL COURTS

A. DEFINING "FINALITY"

(I) CASES INVOLVING MULTIPLE CLAIMS

Read Federal Rule of Civil Procedure 54(b) in the Supplement, with the accompanying material.

SEARS, ROEBUCK & CO. v. MACKEY, 351 U.S. 427, 76 S.Ct. 895, 100 L.Ed. 1297 (1956). Mackey brought suit for damages against Sears, Roebuck under the Sherman Antitrust Act (Counts I and II) and under common law for unlawfully inducing a breach of contract (Count III) and unfair competition and patent infringement (Count IV). The District Court dismissed only those claims presented in Counts I and II. On appeal to the Court of Appeals for the Seventh Circuit, the court upheld its appellate jurisdiction under 28 U.S.C. § 1291. The Supreme Court affirmed.

The Court noted that before the promulgation of the Federal Rules, no appeal would have been allowed from the final determination of Counts I and II since the District Court's judgment was not a final decision of the whole case. However, with the adoption of the Federal Rules and the subsequent increase in multiple-claim actions, the promulgators recognized the need to ameliorate the standard that "*all* claims had to be finally decided before an appeal could be entertained from a final decision upon any of them." Id. at 434, 76 S.Ct. at 899, 100 L.Ed. at 1305. Consequently, Rule 54(b) was adopted.

> * * * [Rule 54(b), as amended in 1946,] does not relax the finality required of each decision, as an individual claim, to render it appealable, but it does provide a practical means of permitting an appeal to be taken from one or more final decisions on individual claims, in multiple claims actions, without waiting for final decisions to be rendered on *all* the claims in the case. * * *
>
> To meet the demonstrated need for flexibility, the District Court is used as a "dispatcher." It is permitted to determine, in the first instance, the appropriate *time when each "final decision"* upon "one or more but less than all" of the claims in a multiple claims action is ready for appeal. This arrangement already has lent welcome certainty to the appellate procedure. Its "negative effect" has met with uniform approval. The effect so referred to is the rule's specific requirement that for "one or more but less than all" multiple claims to become appealable, the District Court must make both "an express determination that there is no just reason for delay" and "an express direction for the entry of judgment." A party adversely affected by a final decision thus knows that his time for appeal will *not* run against him until this certification has been made.
>
> * * *
>
> In the case before us, there is no doubt that each of the claims dismissed is a "claim for relief" within the meaning of Rule 54(b), or that their dismissal constitutes a "final decision" on individual claims. Also, it cannot well be argued that the claims stated in Counts I and II are so inherently inseparable from, or closely related to, those stated in Counts III and IV that the District Court has abused its

> discretion in certifying that there exists no just reason for delay. They certainly *can* be decided independently of each other.
>
> * * *
>
> * * * The District Court *cannot,* in the exercise of its discretion, treat as "final" that which is not "final" within the meaning of § 1291. But the District Court *may,* by the exercise of its discretion in the interest of sound judicial administration, release for appeal final decisions upon one or more, but less than all, claims in multiple claims actions. The timing of such a release is, with good reason, vested by the rule primarily in the discretion of the District Court as the one most likely to be familiar with the case and with any justifiable reasons for delay. * * *
>
> * * * [Rule 54] does not supersede any statute controlling appellate jurisdiction. It scrupulously recognizes the statutory requirement of a "final decision" under § 1291 as a basic requirement for an appeal to the Court of Appeals. It merely administers that requirement in a practical manner in multiple claims actions and does so by rule instead of by judicial decision. By its negative effect, it operates to restrict in a valid manner the number of appeals in multiple claims actions.
>
> We reach a like conclusion as to the validity of the amended rule where the District Court acts affirmatively and thus assists in properly timing the release of final decisions in multiple claims actions. The amended rule adapts the single judicial unit theory so that it better meets the current needs of judicial administration. Just as Rule 54(b), in its original form, resulted in the release of some decisions on claims in multiple claims actions before they otherwise would have been released, so amended Rule 54(b) now makes possible the release of more of such decisions subject to judicial supervision. The amended rule preserves the historic federal policy against piecemeal appeals in many cases more effectively than did the original rule.

Id. at 435–38, 76 S.Ct. at 899–901, 100 L.Ed. at 1306–07 (emphasis in original).

On the same day it decided *Mackey,* the Supreme Court in COLD METAL PROCESS CO. v. UNITED ENGINEERING & FOUNDRY CO., 351 U.S. 445, 76 S.Ct. 904, 100 L.Ed. 1311 (1956), held that an appeal by defendant was appropriate under Section 1291 and Rule 54(b) even though a counterclaim arising out of the same transaction had not yet been decided. Justice Frankfurter, who concurred in *Mackey,* dissented in *Cold Metal*:

> * * * The Court does not * * * indicate what standards the district courts and the courts of appeals are now to apply in determining when a decision is final. It leaves this problem in the first instance to

the district courts, subject to review by the courts of appeals for an abuse of discretion.

* * *

* * * The expansion by the Federal Rules of the allowable content of a proceeding and the range of a litigation inevitably enlarged the occasions for severing one aspect or portion of a litigation from what remains under the traditional test of a "final decision." On the basis of prior cases, we held that it was not a departure from the policy against piecemeal appeals to permit an appeal with respect to that part of a multiple claims litigation based on a set of facts separate and independent from the facts on which the remainder of the litigation was based. * * *

The principles which this Court has heretofore enunciated over a long course of decisions under § 1291 furnish ready guides for deciding the appealability of the certified parts of the litigation in the two cases now before the Court. Count II in Sears, Roebuck & Co. v. Mackey * * * is appealable since the transactions and occurrences involved in it do not involve any of those embraced in Counts III and IV. Count I involves at least two transactions which are also the subject matter of Counts III and IV but is appealable under § 1292(1) as an interlocutory order denying an injunction. In *Cold Metal* * * * the counterclaim, even if not compulsory, is based in substantial part on the transactions involved in the main litigation and hence not appealable.

Id. at 439–40, 442–43, 76 S.Ct. at 902–04, 100 L.Ed. at 1308–10.

NOTES AND QUESTIONS

1. In CURTISS–WRIGHT CORP. v. GENERAL ELECTRIC CO., 446 U.S. 1, 100 S.Ct. 1460, 64 L.Ed.2d 1 (1980), Curtiss–Wright brought a diversity action, seeking damages and reformation with regard to a series of contracts between it and General Electric. General Electric counterclaimed. As to one of Curtiss–Wright's affirmative claims—for $19 million due on the contracts already performed—the District Court granted summary judgment for Curtiss–Wright. When Curtiss–Wright requested certification of this judgment as a final judgment under Rule 54(b), the court granted the motion—after determining, as required by the Rule, that there was "no just reason for delay." The Third Circuit reversed on the ground that the existence of a nonfrivolous counterclaim limited the power of the District Court to enter a final judgment on the original claim. In the view of the Court of Appeals, the District Court had abused its discretion by granting the Rule 54(b) certification.

The Supreme Court agreed with the District Court:

* * * The mere presence of [nonfrivolous counterclaims] * * * does not render a Rule 54(b) certification inappropriate. If it did, Rule 54(b) would lose much of its utility. * * * [C]ounterclaims, whether compulsory or permissive, present no special problems for Rule 54(b) determinations;

> counterclaims are not to be evaluated differently from other claims. * * * Like other claims, their significance for Rule 54(b) purposes turns on their interrelationship with the claims on which certification is sought. Here, the District Judge determined that General Electric's counterclaims were severable from the claims which had been determined in terms of both the factual and the legal issues involved. The Court of Appeals did not conclude otherwise.
>
> What the Court of Appeals found objectionable about the District Judge's exercise of discretion was the assessment of the equities involved. The Court of Appeals concluded that the possibility of a setoff required that the status quo be maintained unless petitioner could show harsh or unusual circumstances; it held that such a showing had not been made in the District Court.
>
> This holding reflects a misinterpretation of the standard of review for Rule 54(b) certifications and a misperception of the appellate function in such cases. * * *
>
> There are thus two aspects to the proper function of a reviewing court in Rule 54(b) cases. The court of appeals must, of course, scrutinize the district court's evaluation of such factors as the interrelationship of the claims so as to prevent piecemeal appeals in cases which should be reviewed only as single units. But once such juridical concerns have been met, the discretionary judgment of the district court should be given substantial deference, for that court is "the one most likely to be familiar with the case and with any justifiable reasons for delay." * * * The reviewing court should disturb the trial court's assessment of the equities only if it can say that the judge's conclusion was clearly unreasonable. Plainly, sound judicial administration does not require that Rule 54(b) requests be granted routinely. That is implicit in commending them to the sound discretion of a district court. Because this discretion "is, with good reason, vested by the rule primarily" in the district courts, * * * and because the number of possible situations is large, we are reluctant either to fix or sanction narrow guidelines for the district courts to follow. We are satisfied, however, that on the record here the District Court's assessment of the equities was reasonable.

Id. at 9–11, 100 S.Ct. at 1465–66, 64 L.Ed.2d at 11–13.

2. If the trial judge determines that there is no reason for delay and orders judgment entered on a separate claim, and no immediate appeal is taken from that order, may the judgment on the separate claim be attacked on an appeal from the final judgment on the entire case? May the propriety of entering judgment on the separate claim be challenged at that time?

3. If the trial judge, in accordance with Rule 54(b), directs entry of judgment on a separate claim that "certainly *can* be decided independently," may the court of appeals nonetheless refuse to hear the appeal? In PANICHELLA v. PENNSYLVANIA RAILROAD CO., 252 F.2d 452 (3d Cir.1958), the court held that the district judge had abused his discretion in directing the separate entry of judgment against defendant on his claim against an impleaded third party, because (1) the whole matter would be moot if defendant prevailed against plaintiff, (2) the legal effect of the same release was in

question both on the third-party claim and the principal claim and thus would have to be determined twice by the Court of Appeals if this appeal were allowed, and (3) the claimed advantage of allowing the appeal—that the two claims could be tried together if the appeal were successful—would necessitate delaying the trial of the principal claim. Does the fact that a third-party claim was involved affect the weight to be given the court's third point?

(II) DECISIONS INVOLVING "COLLATERAL ORDERS"

In COHEN v. BENEFICIAL INDUSTRIAL LOAN CORP., 337 U.S. 541, 69 S.Ct. 1221, 93 L.Ed. 1528 (1949), Cohen brought a shareholder's derivative suit in a New Jersey federal court. The District Court denied Beneficial's motion to require Cohen to post security for costs pursuant to a New Jersey statute, holding the statute inapplicable to an action in a federal court. The Court of Appeals reversed, and the Supreme Court affirmed that decision. The Justices addressed the question of appealability in the following passage:

> * * * Appeal gives the upper court a power of review, not one of intervention. So long as the matter remains open, unfinished or inconclusive, there may be no intrusion by appeal. But the District Court's action upon this application was concluded and closed and its decision final in that sense before the appeal was taken.
>
> Nor does the statute permit appeals, even from fully consummated decisions, where they are but steps towards final judgment in which they will merge. The purpose is to combine in one review all stages of the proceeding that effectively may be reviewed and corrected if and when final judgment results. But this order of the District Court did not make any step toward final disposition of the merits of the case and will not be merged in final judgment. When that time comes, it will be too late effectively to review the present order and the rights conferred by the statute, if it is applicable, will have been lost, probably irreparably. We conclude that the matters embraced in the decision appealed from are not of such an interlocutory nature as to affect, or to be affected by, decision of the merits of this case.
>
> This decision appears to fall in that small class which finally determine claims of right separable from, and collateral to, rights asserted in the action, too important to be denied review and too independent of the cause itself to require that appellate consideration be deferred until the whole case is adjudicated. The Court has long given this provision of the statute this practical rather than a technical construction. * * *
>
> We hold this order appealable because it is a final disposition of a claimed right which is not an ingredient of the cause of action and does not require consideration with it. * * * Here it is the right to security that presents a serious and unsettled question. If the right were admitted or clear and the order involved only an exercise of

discretion as to the amount of security, a matter the statute makes subject to reconsideration from time to time, appealability would present a different question.

Id. at 545, 69 S.Ct. at 1225, 93 L.Ed. at 1536.

WILL v. HALLOCK

Supreme Court of the United States, 2006.
546 U.S. 345, 126 S.Ct. 952, 163 L.Ed.2d 836.

Certiorari to the United States Court of Appeals for the Second Circuit.

JUSTICE SOUTER delivered the opinion of the Court.

[Agents of the United States Customs Service, acting on a warrant, seized computer equipment at plaintiff's home. No charges were brought and the equipment was returned, albeit in severely damaged condition, resulting in serious financial loss to plaintiff. Plaintiff brought suit against the United States under the Federal Tort Claims Act, alleging negligence of the agents. While that action was pending, plaintiff filed a separate negligence suit against the agents. The action against the United States was dismissed after which the agents moved to dismiss the second suit on the ground that a federal statute, 28 U.S.C. § 2676, barred the action against them once the first case was dismissed. The trial court denied the agents' motion on the ground that the statute did not apply. On appeal the Court of Appeals for the Second Circuit held that the "collateral order" doctrine justified the appeal despite the lack of a final judgment and upheld the trial court's decision.]

* * *

The collateral order doctrine, identified with *Cohen*, * * * [p. 1199, supra,] is "best understood not as an exception to the 'final decision' rule laid down by Congress in § 1291, but as a 'practical construction' of it." * * * [T]he collateral order doctrine accommodates a "small class" of rulings, not concluding the litigation, but conclusively resolving "claims of right separable from, and collateral to, rights asserted in the action" * * *. The claims are "too important to be denied review and too independent of the cause itself to require that appellate consideration be deferred until the whole case is adjudicated." *Cohen* * * *.

The requirements for collateral order appeal have been distilled down to three conditions: that an order " '[1] conclusively determine the disputed question, [2] resolve an important issue completely separate from the merits of the action, and [3] be effectively unreviewable on appeal from a final judgment.' " * * *. The conditions are "stringent," * * * and unless they are kept so, the underlying doctrine will overpower the substantial finality interests § 1291 is meant to further: judicial efficiency, for example, and the "sensible policy 'of avoid[ing] the obstruction to just claims that would come from permitting the harassment and cost of a succession of separate appeals from the various rulings to which a litigation may give rise.' " * * *

* * * [A]lthough the Court has been asked many times to expand the "small class" of collaterally appealable orders, we have instead kept it narrow and selective in its membership.

A

Prior cases mark the line between rulings within the class and those outside. On the immediately appealable side are orders rejecting absolute immunity, * * * and qualified immunity * * *. A State has the benefit of the doctrine to appeal a decision denying its claim to Eleventh Amendment immunity, * * * and a criminal defendant may collaterally appeal an adverse ruling on a defense of double jeopardy * * *.

The examples admittedly raise the lawyer's temptation to generalize. In each case, the collaterally appealing party was vindicating or claiming a right to avoid trial, in satisfaction of the third condition: unless the order to stand trial was immediately appealable, the right would be effectively lost. * * * But * * * [such a] generalization is too easy to be sound and, if accepted, would leave the final order requirement of § 1291 in tatters. * * *

* * *

B

Since only some orders denying an asserted right to avoid the burdens of trial qualify, then, as orders that cannot be reviewed "effectively" after a conventional final judgment, the cases have to be combed for some further characteristic that merits appealability under *Cohen;* and * * * that something further boils down to "a judgment about the value of the interests that would be lost through rigorous application of a final judgment requirement." * * *

* * *

In each case [in which immediate appeal has been permitted], some particular value of a high order was marshaled in support of the interest in avoiding trial: honoring the separation of powers, preserving the efficiency of government and the initiative of its officials, respecting a State's dignitary interests, and mitigating the government's advantage over the individual. That is, it is not mere avoidance of a trial, but avoidance of a trial that would imperil a substantial public interest, that counts when asking whether an order is "effectively" unreviewable if review is to be left until later. * * *

C

Does the claim of the customs agents in this case serve such a weighty public objective that the judgment bar [of the dismissal of the case against the United States] should be treated as an immunity demanding the protection of a collateral order appeal? * * * Qualified immunity is not the law simply to save trouble for the Government and its employees; it is recognized because the burden of trial is unjustified in the face of a colorable claim that the law on point was not clear when the official took action, and the action was reasonable in light of the law as it was. The nub of qualified immunity is the need to induce officials to show reasonable initiative when the relevant law is not "clearly established," * * * a quick resolution of a qualified immunity claim is essential.

There is, however, no such public interest at stake simply because the judgment bar is said to be applicable. It is not the preservation of initiative [of public officials] but the avoidance of litigation for its own sake that supports the judgment bar, and if simply abbreviating litigation troublesome to Government employees were important enough for *Cohen* treatment, collateral order appeal would be a matter of right whenever the Government lost a motion to dismiss under the Tort Claims Act. * * *

Another difference between qualified immunity and the judgment bar lies in the bar's essential procedural element. While a qualified immunity claim is timely from the moment an official is served with a complaint, the judgment bar can be raised only after a case under the Tort Claims Act has been resolved in the Government's favor. * * * In the present case, if [plaintiff] * * * had brought * * * action [only against the agents] * * *, the agents could not possibly have invoked the judgment bar in claiming a right to be free of trial. The closer analogy to the judgment bar, then, is not immunity but the defense of claim preclusion, or res judicata.

* * *

The judgment bar at issue in this case has no claim to greater importance than the typical defense of claim preclusion; and we hold true to form in deciding * * * that an order rejecting the defense of judgment bar under 28 U.S.C. § 2676 cries for no immediate appeal of right as a collateral order.

We vacate the judgment of the Court of Appeals and remand with instructions to dismiss the appeal for lack of jurisdiction.

NOTES AND QUESTIONS

1. There are numerous other examples of situations in which a party's interlocutory appeal based on the collateral order doctrine has been rejected despite hardship for the appealing party and the potential waste of resources:

(a) In LAURO LINES S.R.L. v. CHASSER, 490 U.S. 495, 109 S.Ct. 1976, 104 L.Ed.2d 548 (1989), defendant argued that the case, brought in a United States court, should have been filed in Italy in accordance with a contract between plaintiffs and defendant. The Supreme Court held that the issue would be reviewable at the end of the case.

(b) In VAN CAUWENBERGHE v. BIARD, 486 U.S. 517, 108 S.Ct. 1945, 100 L.Ed.2d 517 (1988), defendant, who had been extradited to the United

States, argued that he was immune from civil process. Again, the Supreme Court held that the issue would be reviewable at the end of the civil case.

(c) In RICHARDSON–MERRELL, INC. v. KOLLER, 472 U.S. 424, 105 S.Ct. 2757, 86 L.Ed.2d 340 (1985), the Supreme Court held that an order to disqualify a party's attorney is not subject to immediate appeal regardless of how difficult and costly it might be for a substitute attorney to "catch up."

(d) In DIGITAL EQUIP. CORP. v. DESKTOP DIRECT, INC., 511 U.S. 863, 114 S.Ct. 1992, 128 L.Ed.2d 842 (1994), the Supreme Court held that immediate review was not available from an order rejecting a party's claim to immunity from suit under a private settlement agreement.

(e) In CUNNINGHAM v. HAMILTON COUNTY, 527 U.S. 198, 119 S.Ct. 1915, 144 L.Ed.2d 184 (1999), the Supreme Court held that an order imposing sanctions for discovery violations under Federal Rule 37 on an attorney who no longer represented the client in the on-going matter could not be immediately appealed.

In such cases, if all parties to the action agree that an immediate appeal is in everyone's interest, should a joint request for immediate appeal be honored?

2. On the other hand, the Supreme Court has stated that when a party refuses to obey a court order and has been held in criminal contempt, the issue is so distinct from the underlying case, and so important, that an appeal will be permitted. See, e.g., United States v. Ryan, 402 U.S. 530, 91 S.Ct. 1580, 29 L.Ed.2d 85 (1971). Indeed the Court went even further in UNITED STATES v. NIXON, 418 U.S. 683, 690–92, 94 S.Ct. 3090, 3098–99, 41 L.Ed.2d 1039, 1053–55 (1974), when the President of the United States had been ordered to produce certain tape recordings for examination by a federal judge. The Court found that an appeal was appropriate even though the President had not refused to comply and thus had not been held in contempt. It explained that "the traditional contempt avenue to immediate appeal is peculiarly inappropriate due to the unique setting in which the question arises. To require a President of the United States to place himself in the posture of disobeying an order of a court merely to trigger the procedural mechanism for review of the ruling would be unseemly, and would present an unnecessary occasion for constitutional confrontation between two branches of Government."

3. If an order satisfies the requirements of the collateral order doctrine, does the court have discretion to decline review? Are you influenced by the fact that the Supreme Court has construed *Cohen* and the collateral order doctrine as being best understood "not as an exception to the 'final decision' rule laid down by Congress in Section 1291, but as a 'practical construction' of it"? *Digital Equipment*, Note 1(d), p. 1203, supra. See Steinman, *Reinventing Appellate Jurisdiction*, 48 B.C. L. Rev. 1237, 1251, 1256–57 (2007).

(III) DECISIONS BASED ON "PRAGMATIC FINALITY"

In BROWN SHOE CO. v. UNITED STATES, 370 U.S. 294, 82 S.Ct. 1502, 8 L.Ed.2d 510 (1962), the District Court found defendant had violated the antitrust laws and directed divestiture of a subsidiary, but it reserved its ruling on a specific plan of divestiture. On a direct appeal by the shoe company under the Expediting Act, 15 U.S.C. § 29, the Supreme Court held the divestiture decree was sufficiently final to be appealable even though a specific plan had not been formulated. Its own past practice, said the Court, had been to hear such appeals in antitrust cases; the substantive aspects of the case had been fully determined and to delay decision on the merits would chill the "careful, and often extended, negotiation and formulation" of the final divestiture order. Id. at 309, 82 S.Ct. at 1515, 8 L.Ed.2d at 526.

NOTES AND QUESTIONS

1. In BUDINICH v. BECTON DICKINSON & CO., 486 U.S. 196, 108 S.Ct. 1717, 100 L.Ed.2d 178 (1988), the Supreme Court addressed the issue of whether a decision on the merits is final when the recoverability or amount of attorney's fees remains to be determined. Citing, among other cases, *Brown Shoe,* the Court found that "[a] question remaining to be decided after an order ending the litigation on the merits does not prevent finality if its resolution will not alter the order or moot or revise decisions embodied in the order." Id. at 199, 108 S.Ct. at 1720, 100 L.Ed.2d at 183. In the interest of providing a uniform rule, attorney's fees were held not to be part of the merits:

> We are not inclined to adopt a disposition that requires the merits or nonmerits status of each attorney's fee provision to be clearly established before [finality can be determined]. Courts and litigants are best served by the bright-line rule, which accords with traditional understanding, that a decision on the merits is a "final decision" for purposes of § 1291 whether or not there remains for adjudication a request for attorney's fees attributable to the case.

Id. at 202, 108 S.Ct. at 1722, 100 L.Ed.2d at 185. See also Forgay v. Conrad, 47 U.S. (6 How.) 201, 203, 12 L.Ed. 404, 405 (1848), in which the Supreme Court upheld an appeal of an order that property be delivered to an assignee in bankruptcy even though an accounting of the bankrupt estate before a special master had not yet been completed. The Court was concerned that the assignee was free to sell or otherwise alienate the property while the accounting was still in progress.

2. Does the justification for the decisions in *Brown Shoe* and *Budinich* differ from that for *Cohen?* Should the pragmatic finality doctrine require a lesser showing of harm from delay than the collateral order doctrine? See Redish, *The Pragmatic Approach to Appealability in the Federal Courts*, 75 Colum. L. Rev. 89, 112 (1975).

GILLESPIE v. UNITED STATES STEEL CORP.

Supreme Court of the United States, 1964.
379 U.S. 148, 85 S.Ct. 308, 13 L.Ed.2d 199.

Certiorari to the United States Court of Appeals for the Sixth Circuit.

MR. JUSTICE BLACK delivered the opinion of the Court.

The petitioner, administratrix of the estate of her son Daniel Gillespie, brought this action in federal court against the respondent shipowner-employer to recover damages for Gillespie's death, which was alleged to have occurred when he fell and was drowned while working as a seaman on respondent's ship docked in Ohio. She claimed a right to recover for the benefit of herself and of the decedent's dependent brother and sisters under the Jones Act, which subjects employers to liability if by negligence they cause a seaman's injury or death. She also claimed a right of recovery under the Ohio wrongful death statute because the vessel allegedly was not seaworthy as required by the "general maritime law." The complaint in addition sought damages for Gillespie's pain and suffering before he died, based on the Jones Act and the general maritime law, causes of action which petitioner said survived Gillespie's death by force of the Jones Act itself and the Ohio survival statute, respectively. The District Judge, holding that the Jones Act supplied the exclusive remedy, on motion of respondent struck all parts of the complaint which referred to the Ohio statutes or to unseaworthiness. He also struck all reference to recovery for the benefit of the brother and sisters of the decedent, who respondent had argued were not beneficiaries entitled to recovery under the Jones Act while their mother was living.

Petitioner immediately appealed to the Court of Appeals. Respondent moved to dismiss the appeal on the ground that the ruling appealed from was not a "final" decision of the District Court * * *. [D]eciding the "close" question of appealability, the Court of Appeals proceeded to determine the controversy "on the merits * * *"; this the court said it felt free to do since its resolution of the merits did not prejudice respondent in any way, because it sustained respondent's contentions by * * * affirming the District Court's order. * * *

In this Court respondent joins petitioner in urging us to hold that 28 U.S.C. § 1291 does not require us to dismiss this case * * *. We agree. * * * [A]s this Court often has pointed out, a decision "final" within the meaning of § 1291 does not necessarily mean the last order possible to be made in a case. * * * It is true that the review of this case by the Court of Appeals could be called "piecemeal"; but it does not appear that the inconvenience and cost of trying this case will be greater because the Court of Appeals decided the issues raised instead of compelling the parties to go to trial with them unanswered. * * * And it seems clear now that the case is before us that the eventual costs, as all the parties recognize, will certainly be less if we now pass on the questions presented here rather than send the case back with those issues undecided. Moreover, delay of perhaps a number of years in having the brother's and sisters' rights determined might work a great injustice on them, since the claims for recovery for their benefit have been effectively cut off so long as the District Judge's ruling stands. And while their claims are not formally severable so as to make the court's order unquestionably appealable as to them, * * * there certainly is ample reason to view their claims as severable in deciding the issue of finality, particularly since the brother and sisters were separate parties in the petition for extraordinary relief. * * *. * * * Furthermore, in United States v. General Motors Corp., 323 U.S. 373, 377, 65 S.Ct. 357, 359, 89 L.Ed. 311, this Court contrary to its usual practice reviewed a trial court's refusal to permit proof of certain items of damages in a case not yet fully tried, because the ruling was "fundamental to the further conduct of the case." * * * We think that the questions presented here are equally "fundamental to the further conduct of the case." It is true that if the District Judge had certified the case to the Court of Appeals under 28 U.S.C. § 1292(b), the appeal unquestionably would have been proper; in light of the circumstances we believe that the Court of Appeals properly implemented the same policy Congress sought to promote in § 1292(b) by treating this obviously marginal case as final and appealable * * *.

[The opinion of JUSTICE GOLDBERG, concurring in part and dissenting in part, is omitted.]

MR. JUSTICE HARLAN, dissenting.

* * * The Court substantially affirms the judgment of the Court of Appeals and the parties are remanded to a trial on the merits, but only after they have incurred needless delay and expense in consequence of the loose practices sanctioned by the Court of Appeals and in turn by this Court. This case thus presents a striking example of the vice inherent in a system which permits piecemeal litigation of the issues in a lawsuit.

* * * The justifications given by the Court for tolerating the lower court's departure from the requirements of § 1291 are, with all respect, unsatisfactory.

NOTES AND QUESTIONS

1. In COOPERS & LYBRAND v. LIVESAY, 437 U.S. 463, 98 S.Ct. 2454, 57 L.Ed.2d 351 (1978), the Court was called upon to determine whether or not a district court's decision not to certify an action as a class action under Federal Rule 23 was a "final decision" within the meaning of 28 U.S.C. § 1291 and therefore appealable as a matter of right. The Court of Appeals had held that the decision was "final," even though the case technically remained intact to be pursued by the named plaintiffs for themselves alone, because the latters' individual damages were insufficient to justify a continuation of the case. The decision not to allow the case to go forward on behalf of the class was said to be its "death knell." The Supreme Court reversed. First it objected to the decision below because it turned on a determination of

whether the named plaintiff would or would not continue to go forward with the case. "The potential waste of judicial resources is plain. The district court must take evidence, entertain argument, and make findings; and the court of appeals must review that record and those findings simply to determine whether a discretionary class determination is subject to appellate review." Id. at 473, 98 S.Ct. at 2460, 57 L.Ed.2d at 361.

Second, the Court noted that the appellate court decision undercut Section 1292(b) that had been enacted to meet the need for immediate review of certain nonfinal orders. Such a review can occur only in limited situations when the trial judge approves and the appeals court agrees to accept the case, and the latter can refuse "for any reason, including docket congestion." Third, the "death knell" doctrine would provide a one-sided ability to review, available only to plaintiffs, even though a decision to certify "a large class may so increase the defendant's potential damages liability and litigation costs that he may find it economically prudent to settle and abandon a meritorious defense." Finally,

> allowing appeals of right from nonfinal orders that turn on the facts of a particular case thrusts appellate courts indiscriminately into the trial process and thus defeats one vital purpose of the final-judgment rule—"that of maintaining the appropriate relationship between the respective courts.... This goal, in the absence of the most compelling reasons to the contrary, is very much worth preserving."

Id. at 476, 98 S.Ct. at 2462, 57 L.Ed.2d at 362–63 (footnote omitted).

2. In 1998, the Supreme Court promulgated Rule 23(f), which permits plaintiffs or defendants to petition the Court of Appeals to review a grant or denial of class certification. See p. 772, supra. Under what circumstances should such a petition be granted? Why was Rule 23(f) needed? Couldn't the occasional desirability of an appeal have been met by 28 U.S.C. § 1292(b), enacted in 1958 to allow discretionary appeals from interlocutory orders that raise a "controlling question of law" if both the trial and appellate courts agree? See pp. 1216–19, infra.

3. Is *Gillespie* still good law after *Coopers & Lybrand*? See Anderson v. City of Boston, 244 F.3d 236, 241 (1st Cir.2001): "Numerous courts have agreed that *Gillespie*, in itself, does not provide appellate review unless another exception to the final judgment rule is available. * * * Apart from established exceptions, this Court has indicated that appellate jurisdiction does not exist in the absence of finality, and that cases in the 'twilight zone' of finality, such as *Gillespie*, are only addressable via mandamus upon a showing of palpable error and irreparable harm." Should *Gillespie* be confined to cases in which the issue of appellate jurisdiction does not arise until the case is already in the appeals court and when remand would only result in a waste of resources? See Service Employees Int'l Union, Local 102 v. County of San Diego, 60 F.3d 1346, 1349–50 (9th Cir. 1994), certiorari denied 516 U.S. 1072, 116 S.Ct. 774, 133 L.Ed.2d 726 (1996).

The Judicial Improvements Act of 1990 added subdivision (c) to Section 2072, which allows the Supreme Court to define, by rule, "when a ruling of a district court is final for the purposes of appeal under section 1291 * * *." The Federal Courts Study Committee, which was charged with the task of studying the federal courts and making recommendations, explained the need for that authority as follows:

> The state of the law on when a district court ruling is appealable because it is "final," or is an appealable interlocutory action, strikes many observers as unsatisfactory in several respects. The area has produced much purely procedural litigation. Courts of appeals often dismiss appeals as premature. Litigants sometimes face the possibility of waiving their right to appeal when they fail to seek timely review because it is unclear when a decision is "final" and the time for appeal begins to run. Decision doctrines—* * * especially the "collateral order" rule—blur the edges of the finality principle, require repeated attention from the Supreme Court, and may in some circumstances restrict too sharply the opportunity for interlocutory review.
>
> We propose that Congress consider permitting the rulemaking process to refine and supplement definitions of appellate jurisdiction under the Rules Enabling Act, 28 U.S.C. § 2072, which, we emphasize, includes the constraint that "[s]uch rules shall not abridge, enlarge or modify any substantive right." * * * Favorable experience under this limited rulemaking authority over appellate jurisdiction might later support a broader delegation of power to treat the entire area of appealability from federal district courts by rule rather than statute.

Report of the Federal Courts Study Committee 95–96 (1990).

In 1992, Congress amended Section 1292(e) of the Judicial Code to authorize the Supreme Court to prescribe rules providing for appeals of interlocutory decisions not otherwise covered by that statute. As of this writing, the Supreme Court has promulgated only one new provision, Rule 23(f), under either Section 2072(c) or Section 1292(e). See Note 2, at page 1219, supra.

B. AVOIDANCE OR EVASION OF THE BASIC CONCEPT—MANDAMUS

Read 28 U.S.C. § 1651(a) in the Supplement.

LA BUY v. HOWES LEATHER CO.

Supreme Court of the United States, 1957.
352 U.S. 249, 77 S.Ct. 309, 1 L.Ed.2d 290.

Certiorari to the United States Court of Appeals for the Seventh Circuit.

MR. JUSTICE CLARK delivered the opinion of the Court.

These two consolidated cases present a question of the power of the Courts of Appeals to issue writs of mandamus to compel a District Judge to vacate his orders entered under Rule 53(b) * * * referring antitrust cases for trial before a master. The petitioner, a United States District Judge * * *, contends that the Courts of Appeals have no such power and that, even if they did, these cases were not appropriate ones for its exercise. The Court of Appeals for the Seventh Circuit has decided unanimously that it has such power and, by a divided court, that the circumstances surrounding the references by the petitioner required it to issue the mandamus about which he complains. * * *

History of the Litigation.—These petitions for mandamus * * * arose from two antitrust actions instituted in the District Court in 1950. Rohlfing involves 87 plaintiffs * * * [and] six named defendants * * *. Shaffer involves six plaintiffs * * * and six defendants * * *.

The record indicates that the cases had been burdensome to the petitioner. In Rohlfing alone, 27 pages of the record are devoted to docket entries reflecting that petitioner had conducted many hearings on preliminary pleas and motions. * * * It is reasonable to conclude that much time would have been saved at the trial had petitioner heard the case because of his familiarity with the litigation.

* * * The cases were called on February 23, 1955, on a motion to reset them for trial. * * * The petitioner announced that "it has taken a long time to get this case at issue. I remember hearing more motions, I think, in this case than any case I have ever sat on in this court." The plaintiffs estimated that the trial would take six weeks, whereupon petitioner stated he did not know when he could try the case "if it is going to take this long." He asked if the parties could agree "to have a Master hear" it. The parties ignored this query and at a conference in chambers the next day petitioner entered the orders of reference *sua sponte*. The orders declared that the court was "confronted with an extremely congested calendar" and that "exception [*sic*] conditions exist for this reason" requiring the references. The cases were referred to the master "to take evidence and to report the same to this Court, together with his findings of fact and conclusions of law." * * *

Upon petitioner's refusal to vacate the references, these mandamus actions were filed in the Court of Appeals seeking the issuance of writs ordering petitioner to do so. These applications were grounded on 28 U.S.C. § 1651(a), the All Writs Act. * * * Declaring that the references amounted to * * * "a refusal on his [petitioner's] part, as a judge, to try the causes in due course," the Court of Appeals concluded that "in view of the extraordinary nature of these causes" the references must be vacated "if we find that the orders were beyond the court's power under the pertinent rule." * * * And, it being so found, the writs issued under the authority of the All Writs Act. * * *

The Power of the Courts of Appeals.—Petitioner contends that the power of the Courts of Appeals does not extend to the issuance of writs of mandamus to review interlocutory orders except in those cases where the review of the case on appeal after final judgment would be frustrated. * * * The question of naked power has long been settled by this Court. As late as Roche v. Evaporated Milk Association, 1943, 319 U.S. 21, 25, 63 S.Ct. 938, 941, 87 L.Ed. 1185, Mr. Chief Justice Stone reviewed the decisions and, in considering the power of Courts of Appeals to issue writs of mandamus, the Court held that "the common-law writs, like equitable remedies, may be granted or withheld in the sound discretion of the court." * * * Since the Court of Appeals could at some stage of the antitrust proceedings entertain appeals in these cases, it has power in proper circumstances, as here, to issue writs of mandamus reaching them. * * *

The Discretionary Use of the Writs.—It appears from the docket entries to which we heretofore referred that the petitioner was well informed as to the nature of the antitrust litigation * * *. Nevertheless, he referred both suits to a master on the general issue. Furthermore, neither the existence of the alleged conspiracy nor the question of liability *vel non* had been determined in either case. These issues, as well as the damages, if any, and the question concerning the issuance of an injunction, were likewise included in the references. Under all of the circumstances, we believe the Court of Appeals was justified in finding the orders of reference were an abuse of the petitioner's power under Rule 53(b). They amounted to little less than an abdication of the judicial function depriving the parties of a trial before the court on the basic issues involved in the litigation.

The use of masters is "to aid judges in the performance of specific judicial duties, as they may arise in the progress of a cause," Ex parte Peterson, [p. 946, supra] * * *, and not to displace the court. The exceptional circumstances here warrant the use of the extraordinary remedy of mandamus. * * *

It is also contended that the Seventh Circuit has erroneously construed the All Writs Act as "conferring on it a 'roving commission' to supervise interlocutory orders of the District Courts in advance of final decision." Our examination of its opinions in this regard leads us to the conclusion that the Court of Appeals has exercised commendable self-restraint. It is true that mandamus should be resorted to only in extreme cases, since it places trial judges in the anomalous position of being litigants without counsel other than uncompensated volunteers. However, there is an end of patience and it clearly appears that the Court of Appeals has [since 1938] * * * admonished the trial judges of the Seventh Circuit that the practice of making references "does not commend itself" and "* * * should seldom be made, and if at all only when unusual circumstances exist." * * * Still the Court of Appeals did not disturb the reference practice by reversal or mandamus until this case was decided in October 1955. * * * The record does not show to what extent references are made by the full bench of the District Court in the Northern District; however, it does reveal that petitioner has referred 11 cases to masters in the past 6 years. But even "a little cloud may bring a flood's downpour" if we approve the practice here indulged, particularly in the face of presently congested dockets, increased filings, and more extended trials. * * * [B]e that as it may, congestion in itself is not such an exceptional circumstance as to warrant a reference to a master. If such were the test, present congestion would make references the rule rather than the exception. Petitioner realizes this, for in addition to calendar congestion he alleges that the cases referred had unusual complexity of issues of both fact and law. But most litigation in the antitrust field is complex. It does not follow that antitrust litigants are not entitled to a trial before a court. On the contrary, we believe that this is an impelling reason for trial before a regular, experienced trial judge rather than before a temporary substitute appointed on an *ad hoc* basis and ordinarily not experienced in judicial work. * * * We agree that the detailed accounting required in order to determine the damages suffered by each plaintiff might be referred to a master after the court has determined the over-all liability of defendants, provided the circumstances indicate that the use of the court's time is not warranted in receiving the proof and making the tabulation.

* * *

Affirmed.

MR. JUSTICE BRENNAN, with whom MR. JUSTICE FRANKFURTER, MR. JUSTICE BURTON and MR. JUSTICE HARLAN join, dissenting.

* * * The case before the Court of Appeals was "not a case where a court has exceeded or refused to exercise its jurisdiction * * *." Rule 53(b) * * * vested Judge La Buy with discretionary power to make a reference if he found, and he did, that "some exceptional condition" required the reference. * * * If Judge La Buy erred in finding that there was an "exceptional condition" requiring the reference or did not give proper weight to the caveat of the Rule that a "reference to a master shall be the exception and not the rule," that was mere error "in ruling on matters within [the District Court's] jurisdiction." * * *

But, regrettable as is this Court's approval of what I consider to be a clear departure by the Court of Appeals from the settled principles governing the issuance of the extraordinary writs, what this Court says in reaching its result is reason for particularly grave concern. I think this Court has today seriously undermined the long-standing statutory policy against piecemeal appeals. My brethren say: "Since the Court of Appeals could at some stage of the antitrust proceedings entertain appeals in these cases, it has power in proper circumstances, as here, to issue writs of mandamus reaching them. * * * " I understand this to mean that proper circumstances are present for the issuance of a writ in this case because, if the litigants are not now heard, the Court of Appeals will not have an opportunity to relieve them of the burden of the added expense and delay of decision alleged to be the consequence of the reference. But that bridge was crossed by this Court in *Roche* * * *.

What this Court is saying, therefore, is that the All Writs Act confers an independent appellate power in the Courts of Appeals to review interlocutory orders. I have always understood the law to be precisely to the contrary. * * *

The power of the Courts of Appeals to issue extraordinary writs stems from § 14 of the Judiciary Act of 1789. Chief Judge Magruder, in In re Josephson, 1 Cir., 218 F.2d 174, provides us with an invaluable history of this power and of the judicial development of its scope. He demonstrates most persuasively that "[t]he all writs section does not confer an independent appellate power; the power is strictly of an auxiliary nature, in aid of a jurisdiction granted in some other provision of law * * *."

The focal question posed for a Court of Appeals by a petition for the issuance of a writ is whether the action of the District Court tends to frustrate or impede the ultimate exercise by the Court of Appeals of its appellate jurisdiction granted in some other provision of the law. The answer is clearly in the affirmative where, for example, the order of the District Court transfers a cause to a District Court of another circuit for decision. That was Josephson, where * * * "the effect of the order is that the district judge has declined to proceed with the determination of a case which could eventually come to this court by appeal from a 'final decision'." * * * In contrast, a District Court order denying a transfer would not come under the umbrella of power under the All Writs Act, since retention of the cause by the District Court can hardly thwart or tend to defeat the power of the Court of Appeals to review that order after final decision of the case. * * *

The view now taken by this Court that the All Writs Act confers an independent appellate power, although not so broad as "to authorize the indiscriminate use of prerogative writs as a means of reviewing interlocutory orders," in effect engrafts upon federal appellate procedure a standard of interlocutory review never embraced by the Congress throughout our history, although it is written into the English Judicature Act and is followed in varying degrees in some of the States. That standard allows interlocutory appeals by leave of the appellate court. * * *

NOTES AND QUESTIONS

1. In SCHLAGENHAUF v. HOLDER, 379 U.S. 104, 85 S.Ct. 234, 13 L.Ed.2d 152 (1964), the substantive aspects of which are set out at p. 879,

supra, the Court upheld the use of mandamus to review an order requiring a defendant to submit to a physical and mental examination:

> It is, of course, well settled that the writ is not to be used as a substitute for appeal * * * even though hardship may result from delay and perhaps unnecessary trial * * *. The writ is appropriately issued, however, when there is "usurpation of judicial power" or a clear abuse of discretion * * *.
>
> [T]he challenged order * * * appears to be the first of its kind in any reported decision in the federal courts under Rule 35 * * *.
>
> * * * It is thus appropriate for us to determine on the merits the issues presented and to formulate the necessary guidelines in this area. * * * This is not to say, however, that following the setting of guidelines in this opinion, any future allegation that the District Court was in error in applying these guidelines to a particular case makes mandamus an appropriate remedy.

Id. at 110–12, 85 S.Ct. at 238–39, 13 L.Ed.2d at 156–60.

2. Do the decisions in *LaBuy* and *Schlagenhauf* give sufficient guidance as to when mandamus is an appropriate means of review? Note that both cases involve significant problems regarding application of the Federal Rules. It has been suggested that the *LaBuy* holding might "possibly be limited to issues of judicial administration which have broad significance beyond the particular case." Note, *Appealability in the Federal Courts,* 75 Harv.L.Rev. 351, 377 (1961). Many of the Supreme Court's decisions regarding mandamus concern discovery disputes. Compare WILL v. UNITED STATES, 389 U.S. 90, 88 S.Ct. 269, 19 L.Ed.2d 305 (1967), a criminal case in which the government sought mandamus to overturn a District Court order granting discovery for the defendant. The Court of Appeals granted the writ. The Supreme Court reversed, stating that the facts did not reveal an extraordinary situation for which the writs must be reserved. The Court did not discuss the fact that without mandamus the government cannot obtain guidance on discovery matters since it cannot appeal an acquittal.

Relying heavily on *Will,* the Supreme Court in KERR v. UNITED STATES DISTRICT COURT, 426 U.S. 394, 96 S.Ct. 2119, 48 L.Ed.2d 725 (1976), affirmed a denial of mandamus by a court of appeals in a civil case in which the trial judge had ordered defendants, state correction officers, to turn over to plaintiff a number of prisoner personnel files. Defendants argued that such discovery should be compelled only after a determination by the trial judge that plaintiff's need for the information outweighs its confidentiality. The Court reiterated the reasons for limiting use of writs to avoid piecemeal appeals and also recognized that restricting the use of writs to matters of "jurisdiction" in the technical sense would be too narrow. The Court "assumed" that the trial judge would now accept its "suggestion" to review each of the personnel files *in camera* to determine if discovery should be permitted, thus making a writ unnecessary.

In NIXON v. SIRICA, 487 F.2d 700, 707 (D.C.Cir.1973), a district judge ordered the President of the United States to produce certain tape recordings for the judge's inspection prior to a determination whether the recordings were subject to a grand jury subpoena. The President petitioned for a writ of mandamus, and the Court of Appeals, although denying the petition on the merits, held that mandamus was an appropriate mode of review "particularly in light of the great public interest in prompt resolution of the issues * * *."

3. In CHENEY v. UNITED STATES DISTRICT COURT, 542 U.S. 367, 124 S.Ct. 2576, 159 L.Ed.2d 459 (2004), the then-Vice President sought a writ of mandamus to halt discovery of the National Energy Policy Development Group, an Executive Branch task force charged with making policy recommendations to the President. The Court of Appeals declined to issue the writ because, relying on *Nixon*, it regarded the possible assertion of executive privilege as an available avenue of relief. The Supreme Court reversed, holding that it was error to treat the assertion of the privilege as a "necessary precondition" to mandamus, and remanded to permit the appeals court to consider whether the writ should issue. In *Cheney*, the Supreme Court set out a three-part test for issuance of the writ of mandamus: there must be "no other adequate means" to attain the relief sought; the movant bears the burden of showing that the right to relief is clear and indisputable"; and the issuing court in its discretion "must be satisfied that the writ is appropriate under the circumstances." Id. at 380–81, 124 S.Ct. at 2587, 159 L.Ed.2d at 477–78 (internal quotations and citations omitted). Why does the issuance of mandamus to resolve a discovery dispute ever meet this test? See Fullerton, *Exploring the Far Reaches of Mandamus*, 49 Brooklyn L. Rev. 1131, 1152 (1983). For a discussion of this issue in the context of privilege claims, see Robertson, *Appellate Review of Discovery Orders in Federal Court: A Suggested Approach for Handling Privilege Claims*, 81 Wash. L. Rev. 733, 756–58 (2006).

Before *Cheney*, federal appeals courts had articulated various multi-factor tests for determining whether the writ should issue. In IN RE CEMENT ANTITRUST LITIGATION, 688 F.2d 1297 (9th Cir.1982), the Ninth Circuit refused to issue a writ of mandamus compelling the district judge to revoke his order granting the defendants' motion that the judge recuse himself, relying on a flexible "analytic framework":

> In order to confine the use of mandamus to its proper office, we enunciated five general guidelines * * * to assist in the determination of whether mandamus is the appropriate remedy in a particular case. The guidelines are: (1) whether the party seeking the writ has no other adequate means, such as direct appeal, to attain the relief he desires; (2) whether the petitioner will be damaged or prejudiced in a way that is not correctable on appeal; (3) whether the district court's order is clearly erroneous as a matter of law; (4) whether the district court's order is an oft repeated error or manifests persistent disregard for the federal rules; and (5) whether the district court's order raises new and important problems or issues of law of first impression. * * * Related considerations include: whether the injury alleged by petitioners, although not correctable on appeal, is the kind that justifies invocation of our mandamus authority; whether the petition presents an issue of law which may repeatedly evade appellate review; and whether there are other compelling factors relating to the efficient and orderly administration of the district courts.

Id. at 1301. How do these factors compare to *Cheney*'s three-part approach? Although the Ninth Circuit held that the exercise of supervisory mandamus authority was appropriate in this case because the issue raised was an important issue of first impression capable of evading review because of its collateral nature, it also held that the grant of the recusal motion was not erroneous and that, even if erroneous, it was harmless error. Because only five Justices of the Supreme Court were not disqualified from hearing the appeal, a quorum of the Court did not exist and the Ninth Circuit's decision was affirmed summarily under 28 U.S.C. § 2109. Arizona v. United States District Court, 459 U.S. 1191, 103 S.Ct. 1173, 75 L.Ed.2d 425 (1983).

4. For an example of the traditional principle that mandamus is available when a court exceeds its jurisdiction, consider MALLARD v. UNITED STATES DISTRICT COURT, 490 U.S. 296, 109 S.Ct. 1814, 104 L.Ed.2d 318 (1989), in which the District Court assigned an unwilling lawyer to represent an indigent inmate under 28 U.S.C. § 1915(d). "[T]he District Court plainly acted beyond its 'jurisdiction' * * *," the Supreme Court explained, "for * * * § 1915(d) does not authorize coercive appointments of counsel." Id. at 309, 109 S.Ct. at 1822, 104 L.Ed.2d at 331. The Court underscored that petitioner had no alternative remedy, that issuance of the writ would not produce the inefficiency of piecemeal litigation, and that relief did not require joining the district judge as a party.

In THERMTRON PRODUCTS, INC. v. HERMANSDORFER, 423 U.S. 336, 96 S.Ct. 584, 46 L.Ed.2d 542 (1976), the Supreme Court considered whether mandamus is available to review the remand of a properly removed diversity case where the district court had issued the order to relieve docket congestion. Section 1447(d) bars appellate review of a remand under Section 1447(c) where the removal was done "improvidently and without jurisdiction." The District Court did not rely on Section 1447(c) and instead remanded for a reason not within the statute. The Court held that mandamus was available "to prevent nullification of the removal statutes by remand orders resting on grounds having no warrant in the law. Id. at 353, 96 S.Ct. at 594, 46 L.Ed.2d. at 555. Does *Thermtron Products* illustrate a court acting outside its jurisdiction or some other defect? Two years later, in WILL v. CALVERT FIRE INSURANCE CO., 437 U.S. 655, 98 S.Ct. 2552, 57 L.Ed.2d 504 (1978), the Supreme Court reversed the Court of Appeal's issuance of mandamus ordering a district judge "to proceed immediately" in a federal securities action even though a substantially identical case was pending in state court between the same parties. "So far as appears," the Court explained, "the delay in adjudicating the damages claim is simply a product of the normal excessive load of business in the District Court," and therefore not an extraordinary circumstances warranting mandamus relief. Id. at 667, 98 S.Ct. at 2559, 57 L.Ed.2d at 514.

5. In LYONS v. WESTINGHOUSE ELECTRIC CORP., 222 F.2d 184 (2d Cir.), certiorari denied 350 U.S. 825, 76 S.Ct. 52, 100 L.Ed. 737 (1955), the district judge had stayed an antitrust case pending the determination of a related state-court action. The Court of Appeals held that if a state judgment would have a collateral estoppel effect on the federal action, it would not,

> literally speaking, end the jurisdiction of the district court; but it will do so in substance, if it is an estoppel at all, for it will conclude any further consideration of the existence of the conspiracy, and on that all else depends. For this reason, we hold * * * that the question whether a final judgment will be an estoppel so nearly touches the jurisdiction of the district court, as to make it proper for us to entertain the petition for mandamus.

Id. at 186.

In light of the court's holding on the merits that the state-court judgment "can have no effect upon the decision of the action at bar," was the court justified in directing the District Court to vacate the stay? What would the court have directed if it had ruled the other way on the merits? The Court of Appeals did not in fact issue a writ of mandamus. Its order reads: "Writ of mandamus to go thirty days after the filing of this opinion * * * unless [the stay] * * * has been vacated theretofore." Such conditional orders are common in mandamus cases. Why?

C. DISPLACEMENT OF THE BASIC CONCEPT—DISCRETIONARY APPEALS

Read 28 U.S.C. §§ 1292(b) and 1292(e) in the Supplement.

ATLANTIC CITY ELECTRIC CO. v. GENERAL ELECTRIC CO.

United States Court of Appeals, Second Circuit, 1964.
337 F.2d 844.

PER CURIAM. The district court has certified pursuant to section 1292(b) * * * that its order, sustaining objections to interrogatories designed to discover whether damages were actually sustained by plaintiffs who may have shifted such damages, if any, to their customers of electricity, involves a controlling question of law in these litigations and that there is substantial ground for differences of opinion. * * *

In sustaining the objections to the interrogatories posed, the district court has, in effect, foreclosed defendants from pre-trial discovery of facts relating to a defense that plaintiffs have "passed-on" to their customers any damages incurred by plaintiffs and hence are not entitled to recover to the extent that defendants can prove such passing-on.

Upon this application for leave to appeal it would not be appropriate to isolate and endeavor to decide before an appeal from any final judgment this particular question of law. Pre-trial leave to appeal applications must be decided against the background of the entire case. Many important questions of law will undoubtedly arise in these cases but the problem now confronting us is the feasibility and advisability of trying to decide this particular question in advance of trial.

If pre-trial discovery were allowed as defendants request it could easily develop into a multitude of full scale rate cases which could dwarf in time and testimony the already extensive pre-trial proceedings. If the district court is in error * * * defendants will have full opportunity in the event of an adverse judgment, if based in whole or in part upon this error, to have it corrected upon appeal together with any other errors which may be urged. It is doubtful that any discoveries or hearings required to establish the extent of any damages, if the passing-on-doctrine applies, would be more burdensome then than now. Since defendants' rights to this defense are not being taken away or prejudiced on any ultimate appeal by denial of the pre-trial appeal now sought, we believe that the ultimate disposition of these cases would be delayed rather than advanced by granting this application.

Application denied.

NOTES AND QUESTIONS

1. In COMMONWEALTH EDISON CO. v. ALLIS–CHALMERS MANUFACTURING CO., 335 F.2d 203 (7th Cir.1964), having accepted an appeal under Section 1292(b) on the same issue involved in the principal case, the Seventh Circuit held that the passing-on defense was not available, and hence affirmed an order sustaining objections to similar interrogatories. Which of the courts of appeals followed the sounder procedure? Should the Second Circuit have ruled differently if the district judge had directed plaintiffs to answer the interrogatories?

2. Under Section 1292(b), must the appeals court limit its review to the question of law identified by the district court? YAMAHA MOTOR CORP. v. CALHOUN, 516 U.S. 199, 116 S.Ct. 619, 133 L.Ed.2d 578 (1996), involved the death of a young girl in territorial waters off Puerto Rico while riding a jet ski manufactured by petitioner. The District Court certified the question of whether particular items of damage are available under the federal maritime wrongful death action. The Third Circuit granted interlocutory review, but then considered the antecedent question of whether state remedies remain available in maritime accidents of this sort. The Supreme Court held that appellate jurisdiction under Section 1292(b) is limited to the order certified by the district court, "and is not tied to the particular question formulated by the district court." Rather, "the appellate court may address any issue fairly included within the certified order," because it is the order—and not the controlling question—that is appealable. Id. at 205, 116 S.Ct. at 623, 133 L.Ed.2d at 585.

Earlier, the Supreme Court had appeared to take a narrower approach to the scope of review under Section 1292(b) in UNITED STATES v. STANLEY, 483 U.S. 669, 107 S.Ct. 3054, 97 L.Ed.2d 550 (1987), a damage action brought by a former serviceman. In 1958, respondent volunteered to participate in an Army program described to him as testing the effectiveness of protective clothing against chemical warfare. Afterwards, respondent suffered severe mental disturbance leading to his discharge from the Army and the breakup of his marriage. In 1975, respondent learned that during the testing program, the government had secretly administered doses of lysergic acid diethylamide (LSD) to test the drug's effect on human beings. Respondent's federal court action spanned many years and included multiple interlocutory appeals to the Eleventh Circuit. Early in the litigation, the District Court dismissed respondent's statutory claim. In later proceedings, the District Court declined to dismiss constitutional claims that respondent included in his amended complaint, but certified questions about the scope of the claims to the Court of Appeals. The Eleventh Circuit affirmed the District Court's denial of the government's summary judgment motion on the constitutional claim, and also remanded to permit respondent to replead the statutory claim in the light of recent precedent indicating that the claim might be viable. The Supreme Court reversed, holding that appellate jurisdiction under Section 1292(b) is limited to the certified order, and does not reach "any other orders that may have been entered in the case." Id. at 677, 107 S.Ct. at 3060, 97 L.Ed.2d at 563.

3. UNITED STATES v. PHILIP MORRIS USA INC., 396 F.3d 1190 (D.C. Cir.), certiorari denied 546 U.S. 960, 126 S.Ct. 478, 163 L.Ed.2d 363 (2005), involved a lawsuit under the federal Racketeer Influenced and Corrupt Organizations Act (RICO) by the federal government against a group of cigarette manufacturers. The government sought disgorgement of defendant's illegal profits in order to recover public expenditures for tobacco-related illnesses. The District Court denied defendant's motion for summary judgment and certified the question of whether disgorgement is permissible only if it will "prevent and restrain" future RICO violations. The District of Columbia Circuit construed its appellate jurisdiction to reach the question of whether disgorgement is an available remedy under the statute. Answering that question in the negative, the appeals court reversed and granted summary judgment for appellant on the disgorgement claim. Judge Tatel, in dissent, argued that the appeals court could review only the certified question, underscoring that the broader issue of whether disgorgement is available as a statutory remedy was "not briefed in the motion leading up to the certified order," was "not decided in the district court's opinion accompanying the certified order"; was "not raised by Philip Morris in its request for certification"; was "not discussed in the order granting certification"; was "not raised by Philip Morris in its section 1292(b) petition"; and was "decided in an entirely different order which Philip Morris could at any time have asked the district court to certify." Id. at 1211. Does *Yamaha Motors* support the majority's approach? Does *Stanley*? Does the majority's approach undermine the District Court's discretionary role in certifying questions for review? Should the court of appeals be given power to hear appeals from orders fulfilling the requirements described in Section 1292(b) without the certificate of the district judge? Compare Leasco Data Processing Equip. Corp. v. Maxwell, 468 F.2d 1326, 1344 (2d Cir.1972) (court of appeals cannot order trial court to issue certificate).

4. Section 1292(b) provides no guidance on what it means for a question of law to be "controlling" or subject to a "substantial ground for disagreement." Must the issue be "dispositive" of the lawsuit in order to be consid-

ered controlling? Is it sufficient that the issue could produce "reversible error" on final appeal? Does the party's "strong disagreement" with the district court's ruling deserve any weight? For a discussion of these questions, see Best Western Int'l, Inc. v. Govan, 2007 WL 1545776 (D. Ariz.2007).

5. Since 1992 the Supreme Court has had the power pursuant to Section 1292(e) to promulgate rules permitting interlocutory appeals from any orders that it deems appropriate. As previously noted, the Court has used the power only once, to add Federal Rule 23(f). Are there other areas that call for such a special provision? In California the grant of a new trial is an appealable order. West's Cal.Code Civ.Proc. § 904.1(a)(4). What is the justification for such a provision? For a comprehensive analysis of Section 1292(b), see *Note—Interlocutory Appeals in the Federal Courts Under 28 U.S.C. § 1292(b),* 88 Harv. L.Rev. 607 (1975).

D. AN HISTORICAL FOOTNOTE TO THE BASIC CONCEPT—INJUNCTIONS

Read 28 U.S.C. § 1292(a)(1) and Federal Rules of Civil Procedure 65(a) and (b) in the Supplement.

SMITH v. VULCAN IRON WORKS, 165 U.S. 518, 525, 17 S.Ct. 407, 410, 41 L.Ed. 810, 812 (1897):

The manifest intent of this provision, read in the light of the previous practice in the courts of the United States, contrasted with the practice in courts of equity of the highest authority elsewhere, appears to this court to have been, not only to permit the defendant to obtain immediate relief from an injunction, the continuance of which throughout the progress of the cause might seriously affect his interests, but also to save both parties from the expense of further litigation, should the appellate court be of opinion that the plaintiff was not entitled to an injunction because his bill had no equity to support it.

NOTES AND QUESTIONS

1. Is the Supreme Court's ruling that an appeal under the predecessor of Section 1292(a)(1) allows the reviewing court to consider not only the question whether the injunction should have been issued, but the merits of the whole case, supported by the traditional doctrines regarding the character of equitable relief? Is it consistent with *Stanley*, p. 1217, supra? What accounts for the difference?

2. What are the reasons for allowing appeals from interlocutory orders granting or refusing injunctions? Do these reasons apply to orders granting or denying preliminary, as opposed to permanent, injunctions? Could these reasons be served as well by relegating the parties to discretionary appeals under Section 1292(b)?

3. Is the grant or denial of a temporary restraining order, see Federal Rule 65(b), appealable under Section 1292(a)(1)? Are the differences between preliminary injunctions and temporary restraining orders relevant to the question whether appeal should be permitted in the case of the former and not permitted in the case of the latter? In close cases it may be difficult to tell the difference between a preliminary injunction and a temporary restraining order.

In UNITED STATES v. WOOD, 295 F.2d 772 (5th Cir.1961), certiorari denied 369 U.S. 850, 82 S.Ct. 933, 8 L.Ed.2d 9 (1962), a black man who was active in voter registration in Mississippi was arrested for disturbing the peace and ordered to trial in fifteen days. Two days before trial, the United States, moving under 42 U.S.C. § 1971 and alleging that the prosecution would intimidate African–Americans in the exercise of their voting rights, brought suit to restrain the criminal action. A temporary restraining order was denied and the Government appealed. The Court of Appeals held that it had jurisdiction under Section 1291. Inasmuch as the case would quickly become moot if the restraining order was not issued, the court said, its denial was "a final disposition of the * * * claimed right. * * * [T]o call this de facto dismissal a nonappealable interlocutory order is to preclude review altogether."

In SAMPSON v. MURRAY, 415 U.S. 61, 94 S.Ct. 937, 39 L.Ed.2d 166 (1974), the respondent, a probationary federal employee, filed an action to enjoin temporarily her dismissal pending her pursuit of an administrative appeal to the Civil Service Commission. The District Court granted the temporary restraining order and, after an adversary hearing, extended the interim relief until the respondent's supervisor testified about the reasons for her dismissal. The appeals court for the District of Columbia Circuit affirmed. The Supreme Court reversed, holding that the Court of Appeals had correctly treated the extension order as a preliminary injunction, but that the order in question failed to meet the standards for such injunctions set by Rule 65. In the Court's view, the respondent had failed to demonstrate irreparable harm justifying the granting of a preliminary injunction. Justices Marshall and Brennan, in dissent, argued that the order was not appealable. In their view, because the temporary restraining order at issue did not meet any of the requirements for interlocutory injunctions set forth in Rule 52(a), "no valid preliminary injunction was ever issued." Thus, it did not make sense for the Court to review the District Court's order as the grant of a preliminary injunction. Id. at 99–100, 94 S.Ct. at 957, 39 L.Ed.2d at 191–92.

4. In GULFSTREAM AEROSPACE CORP. v. MAYACAMAS CORP., 485 U.S. 271, 108 S.Ct. 1133, 99 L.Ed.2d 296 (1988), the Supreme Court was faced with the question whether a decision to stay or not to stay a federal action when a similar state case is pending constitutes a decision on an injunction allowing an immediate appeal under Section 1291(a)(1). In several previous cases the Court had answered the question in the affirmative on the ground that historically such a stay resulted from an injunction by an equity court issued to a court of law. However, the Court noted that with the merger of law and equity into a single federal court, the classical analogy no longer fit. A judge in deciding such a question is not determining whether or not to enjoin herself, but merely determining when the action should go forward.

5. Does Section 1292(a)(1) apply to an order denying a motion for summary judgment in an action in which a permanent injunction is sought? This question, which had plagued the courts of appeals for years, was resolved in SWITZERLAND CHEESE ASSOCIATION, INC. v. E. HORNE'S MARKET, INC., 385 U.S. 23, 25, 87 S.Ct. 193, 195, 17 L.Ed.2d 23, 25 (1966):

> * * * [T]he denial of a motion for summary judgment because of unresolved issues of fact does not settle or even tentatively decide anything about the merits of the claim. It is strictly a pre-trial order that decides only one thing—that the case should go to trial. Orders that in no way touch on the merits of the claim but only relate to pre-trial procedures are not in our view "interlocutory" within the meaning of § 1292(a)(1). We see no other way to protect the integrity of the congressional policy against piecemeal appeals.

6. In CARSON v. AMERICAN BRANDS, INC., 450 U.S. 79, 101 S.Ct. 993, 67 L.Ed.2d 59 (1981), petitioners brought a class action against the respondent employers, charging violations of Title VII of the Civil Rights Act of 1964 and seeking injunctive and declaratory relief and damages. The parties settled and together moved for entry of a proposed consent decree enjoining further discrimination and implementing an affirmative action plan for hiring and seniority preferences. The District Court denied the motion, holding that, since there was no showing of present or past discrimination, the proposed decree illegally granted racial preferences to the petitioner class and also illegally provided relief to all present and future black employees rather than only to the actual victims of the alleged discrimination. The Fourth Circuit dismissed the petitioners' appeal for want of jurisdiction, holding that the District Court's order was not appealable under Section 1292(a)(1). The Supreme Court unanimously reversed, holding that the order, although not explicitly refusing an injunction, had the practical effect of doing so.

SECTION B. THE TIME TO APPEAL

Read Federal Rule of Civil Procedure 58 and Rules 3, 4, and 5 of the Federal Rules of Appellate Procedure.

The time limit for appeal is treated as a matter of jurisdiction and cannot be altered by consent of the parties. See 16A Wright, Miller, Cooper & Struve, Federal Practice and Procedure: Jurisdiction and Related Matters 4th § 3949.6. It may be extended by the district court only, not by an appellate court, for thirty days upon a showing of "excusable neglect." The time limitation is triggered when the district court clerk enters a judgment conforming to the requirements of Federal Rule 58. The clerk is required to mail notice of entry of judgment to the parties but a party may elect to serve notice formally on his opponent. Federal Rule 77(d).

In PINCAY, JR. v. ANDREWS, 389 F.3d 853 (9th Cir. 2004), defendant lost its case trial and sought to appeal. Defense counsel relied on paralegal's research to determine when an appeal had to be filed. The paralegal misread Federal Appellate Rule 4(a) to allow 60 days rather than 30 days from the date of the judgment for the filing of a notice of appeal. Defendant successfully moved the trial court under Federal Appellate Rule 4(a)(5) for an extension of 30 days based on a showing of excusable neglect Plaintiff appealed the granting of the extension. A three-judge panel of the Ninth Circuit, by a two-to-one vote, held that the extension was improper because reliance on a paralegal's research was "inexcusable as a matter of law." 351 F.3d 947, 951–52 (9th Cir. 2003). The Ninth Circuit, sitting en banc, held that the question of whether the error was inexcusable was a matter of discretion for the trial judge and that the rigid rule was improper, although it recognized that the misreading of the Rule "* * * was egregious, and the lawyer undoubtedly should have checked the Rule itself before relying on the paralegal's reading. Both the paralegal and the lawyer were negligent." 389 F.3d at 858. The en banc court relied on the Supreme Court's decision in Pioneer Inv. Servs. Co. v. Brunswick Assocs. Ltd. Partnership, 507 U.S. 380, 113 S.Ct. 1489, 123 L.Ed.2d 74 (1993), that had dealt with a similar issue under the bankruptcy laws. The Supreme Court provided four factors to be considered in such a case: (1) the danger of prejudice to the nonmoving party, (2) the length of delay and its potential impact on the judicial proceedings, (3) the reasons for the delay, and (4) whether the moving party had acted in good faith. The majority of the en banc court held that the trial judge had properly considered the four factors in making its decision. In a dissent, Judge Kozinski noted that in almost every case the key factor will be the third, focusing on the nature of the reasons for the failure to file the appeal on time. In the present case, the court had simply relied on the defendant's carelessness, which he said was not sufficient.

> [E]xcusable neglect must be neglect [but] it must also be excusable. * * * In this case, the district court found that there was no prejudice to [plaintiff] * * *, the delay was short and there was no bad faith. Thus, defendants need not have offered a terribly good countervailing reason to make their neglect excusable.
>
> But they needed to show *something*. Was this a class action that bristled with client "consultation difficulties"? * * * Was the client distracted by a divorce and job change, and had he lost his lawyer to boot? * * * Was the rule confusing or notice of the deadline unusual? * * * No, no and no. * * *
>
> * * *

> I would hold that error here—whether made by the lawyer, the calendaring clerk or the candlestick maker—is inexcusable and dismiss the appeal as untimely.

389 F.3d 862–64.

NOTES AND QUESTIONS

1. The question of when a judgment is deemed entered has plagued the federal courts and would-be appellants over the years. See, e.g., United States v. F. & M. Schaefer Brewing Co., 356 U.S. 227, 78 S.Ct. 674, 2 L.Ed.2d 721 (1958). In 1963 and again in 2002, Federal Rule 58 was amended to clarify just when a judgment was to be considered entered and thus when the time for appeal begins to run.

2. Rule 4(a)(4)(A) of the Federal Rules of Appellate Procedure provides that the time for filing an appeal will be extended if a party moves for certain orders challenging a judgment. They include motions for judgment as a matter of law under Rule 50(b), requesting new or amended findings under Rule 52(b), requesting a new trial or an altered judgment under Rule 59, and for relief under Rule 60(b) if requested within ten days of the entry of judgment.

3. Federal Rules of Appellate Procedure 4(a)(2) and 4(a)(4)(B)(1) eliminate the danger of losing the appeal for an appellant who files a premature notice of appeal after the court announces a decision or order but before the judgment or order has been formally entered. The notice is treated as taking effect on the date of the entry. However, the Supreme Court in FIRSTIER MORTGAGE CO. v. INVESTORS MORTGAGE INSURANCE CO., 498 U.S. 269, 111 S.Ct. 648, 112 L.Ed.2d 743 (1991), issued a note of explanation and caution in interpreting such a provision:

> This is not to say that Rule 4(a)(2) permits a notice of appeal from a clearly interlocutory decision * * * to serve as a notice of appeal from the final judgment. * * * In our view, Rule 4(a)(2) permits a notice of appeal from a nonfinal decision to operate as a notice of appeal from the final judgment only when a district court announces a decision that would be appealable if immediately followed by the entry of judgment. In these instances, a litigant's confusion is understandable, and permitting the notice of appeal to become effective when judgment is entered does not catch the appellee by surprise. * * *

How should the appellate court treat a notice of appeal filed from an order that leaves open the calculation of interest? What about a notice of appeal filed from an order dismissing all claims but counterclaims remain? For a discussion of how the appeals courts have treated these and related questions, see Afrasiabi, *The Growing Split Over Whether Premature Notices of Appeal Preserve Appellate Review*, 55 Fed.Law. 42 (July 2008).

4. If an appeal is not taken from an interlocutory order that is made appealable by Section 1292(a)(1), are matters adjudged therein foreclosed on

an appeal from the final judgment? See Victor Talking Mach. Co. v. George, 105 F.2d 697 (3d Cir.), certiorari denied 308 U.S. 611, 60 S.Ct. 176, 84 L.Ed. 511 (1939).

SECTION C. THE AMBIT OF REVIEW

1. ISSUES SUBJECT TO REVIEW

There are a number of well-defined limits on the scope of appellate review. First, the alleged errors must appear in the trial court record. Thus it is vital during the course of pretrial preparation as well as during trial itself that an attorney make certain that all rulings and evidence that might form the basis for an appeal be formally recorded. Second, an aggrieved party must have objected promptly to the trial court regarding rulings or events that the judge could have corrected or ameliorated. Normally an error is waived unless a proper objection was taken. Third, even if the issue that the appellant seeks to have reviewed has been presented properly below and has not been waived, it must not constitute "harmless error"—that is, it must have affected substantial rights. Finally, an alleged error must be presented to the appellate court in appellant's brief and the relevant portions of the trial court record must be brought to the appellate court's attention.

J.F. WHITE CONTRACTING CO. v. NEW ENGLAND TANK INDUSTRIES OF NEW HAMPSHIRE, INC.

United States Court of Appeals, First Circuit, 1968.
393 F.2d 449.

COFFIN, CIRCUIT JUDGE.

This appeal concerns a contract to build oil tanker dock facilities on the Piscataqua river. Appellant, J.F. White Contracting Co. (White) agreed to build the dock, consisting of four cylindrical metal cells filled with sand and gravel, connected with each other and with the shore by catwalks. Appellee, New England Tank Industries of New Hampshire, Inc. (Tank), owner of the premises, sues for defective workmanship. Unlike the Piscataqua itself, the case meandered interminably for five years before a jury trial was finally reached. From an adverse verdict in the amount of $20,000 White takes this appeal.

* * *

Appellant * * * [contends] that recovery is barred by a contract provision which stipulated that approval of invoices by Tank's engineer was "final, conclusive, and binding on both parties". Without saying what effect we would give to such a provision under the factual circumstances of this case, we merely observe that we cannot consider this issue on appeal since appellant neither pleaded it as an affirmative defense nor had it "raised, considered nor passed upon in the district court." * * *

* * * White argues alternatively that it was error to have allowed the question of one of the cells being "out of round" to go to the jury. This cell had been struck in the process of installation by a ship and knocked "out of round". White undertook to repair it. This damage, being above the waterline, was visible and much less hidden or latent than the underwater ruptures.

Even if the fact that the dented cell was located some four hundred feet from shore constituted enough evidence of latency for the jury, and even if Tank had received something less than the cylindrical cell it had bargained for, there was no evidence of the extent to which it was damaged. There was no evidence that the utility or longevity of the cell was affected, nor does there seem to have been sufficient evidence regarding the cost of repairing the dent. The underwater inspection report of the diver Howard B. Pratt did mention that cell 3 was "noticeably out of round" and his original estimate of repairs to cell 3 "as per our drawing" was $43,150. This figure might conceivably be considered some evidence of the cost to repair the dented cell. Without more, however, it would seem to be an insufficient basis for the jury to make any rational determination.

While the court's action in submitting the "out-of-roundness" issue to the jury was error, we are not persuaded that there was even a remote possibility that this error affected the verdict or "the substantial rights of the parties". Fed.R.Civ.P. 61 * * * [the rule currently refers to "any party's substantial rights"]. Nor does appellant assert that it did. Briefs of both sides argue the adequacy of damages issue by reference solely to testimony of cost of repairs and value addressed to the ruptures. Counsel for Tank did not argue the issue at all to the jury while counsel for White made it clear that it ought not be considered. Finally, the court's instructions on damages were proper and emphasized that only evidence of value, which included evidence of cost of repairs, could be considered. There is no reason to suspect that the jury did not follow these instructions.

* * *

Affirmed.

NOTES AND QUESTIONS

1. What justification is there for a rule that a party may not raise an issue on appeal that was not raised in the trial court? Is it fair to penalize the party for what is likely a lawyer's error? Note that under Rule 60(b) a party may ask a district court to reopen a judgment on the basis of newly discovered facts.

2. If a party has presented undisputed facts or facts necessarily determined at trial for that party which sustain a claim or defense on a theory not argued at trial, should the appellate court be permitted to make its determination on the basis of the newly raised theory?

3. What underlies a rule that an error, if "harmless," will not provide a basis for reversal? Is it possible for an appellate court to determine what

would have affected a jury's determination? Does this rule give the appellate court broad latitude to disregard error below, undermining the appellate system's error-correction function? Or does the rule make it possible for an appellate court to instruct lower courts without needlessly incurring the costs of a new trial?

Even when the issues have been preserved properly in the trial court and presented to the appellate court for review, there is another aspect of the scope of appellate review that must be considered—whether, and in what circumstances, an appellate court may entertain an appeal by the party who, at least ostensibly, won below.

ELECTRICAL FITTINGS CORP. v. THOMAS & BETTS CO.

Supreme Court of the United States, 1939.
307 U.S. 241, 59 S.Ct. 860, 83 L.Ed. 1263.

Certiorari to United States Circuit Court of Appeals for the Second Circuit.

MR. JUSTICE ROBERTS delivered the opinion of the Court.

This was a suit in equity by the respondents for alleged infringement of a patent. The District Court held claim 1 valid but not infringed and claim 2 invalid. Instead of dismissing the bill without more, it entered a decree adjudging claim 1 valid but dismissing the bill for failure to prove infringement.

The respondents did not appeal, but filed in the Patent Office a disclaimer of claim 2. The petitioners appealed to the Circuit Court of Appeals from so much of the decree as adjudicated claim 1 valid. The appeal was dismissed on the ground that the petitioners had been awarded all the relief to which they were entitled, the litigation having finally terminated in their favor. The court was of opinion that the decree would not bind the petitioners in subsequent suits on the issue of the validity of claim 1.

* * * A party may not appeal from a judgment or decree in his favor, for the purpose of obtaining a review of findings he deems erroneous which are not necessary to support the decree. But here the decree itself purports to adjudge the validity of claim 1, and though the adjudication was immaterial to the disposition of the cause, it stands as an adjudication of one of the issues litigated. We think the petitioners were entitled to have this portion of the decree eliminated, and that the Circuit Court of Appeals had jurisdiction * * * to entertain the appeal, not for the purpose of passing on the merits, but to direct the reformation of the decree.

* * *

Reversed and remanded.

NOTES AND QUESTIONS

1. NEW YORK TELEPHONE CO. v. MALTBIE, 291 U.S. 645, 645, 54 S.Ct. 443, 443, 78 L.Ed. 1041, 1042 (1934) (per curiam):

> The District Court * * * permanently enjoined, as confiscatory, the enforcement of the rate orders which are the subject of this suit. The injunction is unqualified. Appellant, having obtained this relief, is not entitled to prosecute an appeal from the decree in its favor, for the purpose of reviewing the portions of the decree fixing the value of appellant's property as of the years 1924, 1926, and 1928, and the rate of return to be allowed. The matters set forth in these portions of the decree are not to be regarded as res judicata in relation to subsequent legislative action by the Public Service Commission in fixing rates for the future or in any judicial proceeding relating to such rates.

2. Would the decree in *Electrical Fittings* have been res judicata of the validity of claim 1 of the patent? Why else might petitioners in that case have been concerned about the decree? The Declaratory Judgment Act, 28 U.S.C. §§ 2201–2202, was not in force at the time of the *Electrical Fittings* decision. Had it been, might it have been possible to treat the District Court's decree as a declaratory judgment with respect to claim 1 and consider it as having been entered under the authority of Rule 54(c)?

3. In PARTMAR CORP. v. PARAMOUNT PICTURES THEATRES CORP., 347 U.S. 89, 74 S.Ct. 414, 98 L.Ed. 532 (1954), plaintiff leased its theater to, and entered into a franchise agreement with, defendant; the lease was to be terminable at plaintiff's option if the franchise agreement were terminated. Plaintiff sued to regain possession of the theater, alleging that it was entitled to terminate the lease because the franchise agreement was invalid under the antitrust laws; defendant counterclaimed for damages under the antitrust laws. The trial court denied plaintiff's claim, holding that the franchise agreement was not invalid because no conspiracy in violation of the antitrust laws had been established; it also dismissed the counterclaims. Defendant appealed from the dismissal of its counterclaims. The Supreme Court upheld the dismissal on the ground that the trial court's decision on the plaintiff's claim that there was no unlawful antitrust conspiracy was binding on the counterclaim. Could the defendant have appealed the decision of the trial court on the plaintiff's claim, despite the fact that it had been decided in defendant's favor? In a footnote, a majority of the Supreme Court, citing *New York Tel. Co.*, p. 1227, supra, and *Electrical Fittings,* p. 1226, supra, said "yes." In effect, the Court took the position that the defendant was a "winner" on the plaintiff's claim, but a "loser" on the counterclaim and could therefore appeal any issue that directly affected the counterclaim. See id. at 99 n.6, 74 S.Ct. at 420 n.6, 98 L.Ed. at n.6.

Chief Justice Warren, in dissent, took the position that defendant could not have appealed the trial court's decision on the claim, arguing that the adverse finding that there was no conspiracy had not been included in the decree, thus distinguishing *Electrical Fittings,* see p. 1226, supra. Under those circumstances defendant need not have appealed because the decision on the plaintiff's claim should not have been held to have had a binding effect on the counterclaim.

4. A related question is whether a nonparty to an action may appeal a decision. As noted in 15A Wright, Miller & Cooper, Federal Practice and Procedure: Jurisdiction and Related Matters 2d § 3902.1.

> The basic rule that a nonparty cannot appeal the judgment in an action between others seems obviously sensible. Yet complications arise in dealing with appeals by persons who present plausible arguments that they should be treated for this purpose as if they had been parties. * * * The courts have not yet worked out entirely clear standards governing nonparty appeals, nor have they established clear procedural routines. Appeal is likely to be available, however, if the would-be appellant can show significant involvement with the judgment, plausible reasons for not becoming involved earlier, a risk that its interests will not be adequately protected by the parties, and a lack of untoward interference in the affairs of the parties.

See generally Steinman, *Shining a Light in a Dim Corner: Standing to Appeal and the Right to Defend a Judgment in the Federal Courts,* 38 Ga. L. Rev. 813 (2004).

INTERNATIONAL ORE & FERTILIZER CORP. v. SGS CONTROL SERVICES, INC.

United States Court of Appeals, Second Circuit, 1994.
38 F.3d 1279.

WINTER, CIRCUIT JUDGE.

[Defendant agreed to transport a cargo of fertilizer for plaintiff to a buyer in New Zealand. Defendant's ship had not been cleaned sufficiently with the result that the cargo was contaminated and the purchaser refused delivery, resulting in damages to plaintiff. Plaintiff sued defendant both for breach of contract and for negligent misrepresentation of the condition of its ship. After evidence was presented, the trial judge rejected the contract claim, but upheld the claim of negligent misrepresentation and awarded damages. Defendant appealed. The appellate court held that the negligent misrepresentation claim should have been dismissed and determined that the contract claim, which would have justified a larger damage award to plaintiff, should have been upheld. However, the court was faced with the argument that it could not rule on the contract claim because plaintiff had not filed a cross-appeal.]

The general rule in a case in which a party fails to cross-appeal * * * and an appellate court would otherwise have held in its favor is that [that party]:

> * * * cannot be heard in opposition thereto when the case is brought here by the appeal of the adverse party. In other words, the appellee may not attack the decree with a view either to enlarging his own rights thereunder or of lessening the rights of his adversary, whether what he seeks is to correct an error or to supplement the decree with

respect to a matter not dealt with below. But it is likewise settled that the appellee may, without taking a cross-appeal, urge in support of a decree any matter appearing in the record, although his argument may involve an attack upon the reasoning of the lower court or an insistence upon matter overlooked or ignored by it. * * *

This rule has been modified in some circuits by treating the requirement of a cross-appeal as one of practice rather than jurisdiction, allowing the court to use its discretion to consider unappealed grounds so as to exercise its "broad power 'to make such a disposition . . . as justice requires.'" * * * Generally, however, these cases have involved multiple parties where only one of several plaintiffs or defendants failed to cross-appeal. In each case, the court included the non-cross-appellant in the amended judgment so as to preserve "fairness."

Several of our recent decisions have referred without elaboration to the discretionary nature of our power to disregard the cross-appeal requirement. * * * These cases conform to the general rule that the appellee may seek to sustain a judgment on any grounds with support in the record * * * This rule applies even when the alternative grounds were not asserted until the court's questioning at oral argument. * * * We may, therefore, uphold the finding of liability on a breach of contract theory.

We do not believe, however, that given the present procedural circumstances, * * * [plaintiff] is entitled to its full damages. Although an appellee who has not cross-appealed may urge alternative grounds for affirmance, it may not seek to enlarge its rights under the judgment by enlarging the amount of damages or scope of equitable relief. * * * We may therefore uphold the present judgment but we may not enlarge it to award * * * [plaintiff] its full contract damages.

* * *

Read Rules 3 and 4 of the Federal Rules of Appellate Procedure in the Supplement.

NOTES AND QUESTIONS

1. In TORRES v. OAKLAND SCAVENGER Co., 487 U.S. 312, 108 S.Ct. 2405, 101 L.Ed.2d 285 (1988), the Supreme Court interpreted Federal Rule of Appellate Procedure 3, governing the contents of the Notice of Appeal, as a jurisdictional requirement. Rule 3(c) requires, among other things, that the notice name each appellant or otherwise make clear who is appealing. Note that the Rule does not require that the appellees be designated. Should an exception be recognized in the cross-appeal situation?

2. In SMITH v. BARRY, 502 U.S. 244, 112 S.Ct. 678, 116 L.Ed.2d 678 (1992), appellant, a prisoner appearing pro se, filed a premature notice of appeal.

> * * * Although the Fourth Circuit's jurisdiction had not been properly invoked, its Clerk responded to the notice of appeal by sending all of the parties copies of the "informal brief" the court uses in pro se appeals and an order explaining the court's procedures. The briefing forms asked the parties to answer six questions about their legal positions. Under its Rules, the Fourth Circuit reviews these responses and the record to determine whether appointment of counsel and/or oral argument are warranted. * * * [Petitioner] returned his informal brief to the Court of Appeals * * * within the deadline for filing a notice of appeal.
>
> After appointment of appellate counsel, the fourth Circuit dismissed Smith's appeal for want of jurisdiction.

Id. at 246–47, 112 S.Ct. at 681, 116 L.Ed.2d at 684. The Supreme Court reversed, holding that the brief was the functional equivalent of a notice to appeal, and that it was the contents of the notice, and not the litigant's motivation, that determined if the notice was sufficient under Federal Appellate Rule 3. Justice Scalia, in a concurrence, rejected the "functional equivalent" doctrine and relied instead on the language of Federal Appellate Rule 3(c)(4). What documents might be considered to be a "functional equivalent" to the formal notice of appeal?

3. In BOWLES v. RUSSELL, 551 U.S. 205, 127 S.Ct. 2360, 168 L.Ed.2d 96 (2007), an inmate who had been imprisoned for life for his involvement in the beating death of an individual, unsuccessfully challenged his conviction on habeas corpus and failed to file a timely notice of appeal. The District Court granted petitioner's motion to reopen the period in which he could appeal and extended the time by seventeen days, although fourteen days is the period set out in statute. Relying on the District Court's order, petitioner filed a notice of appeal within the period set out in the judicial order. The Court of Appeals dismissed the appeal for lack of jurisdiction, and the Supreme Court affirmed, holding that timely filing is jurisdictional and that a court lacks power to create equitable exceptions. Justice Souter, in dissent, stated that it is "intolerable for the judicial system to treat people this way, and there is not even a technical justification for condoning this bait and switch," insisting that the timely notice requirement for appellate review is not jurisdictional. Id. at ___, 127 S.Ct. at 2368, 168 L.Ed.2d at 107. Which of the purposes of appeal, p. 1192, supra, does the *Bowles* decision promote? *Bowles* has generated a provocative discussion, compare Dodson, *Jurisdictionality and Bowles v. Russell*, 102 Nw. U. L. Rev. Colloquy 42 (2007), with Burch, *Nonjurisdictionality or Inequity*, 102 Nw. U. L. Rev. Colloquy 64 (2007). Review the material on timeliness of appeal, see p. 1221, supra.

2. SCOPE OF REVIEW OF FACTS

A. THE POWER TO ORDER A NEW TRIAL IN A CASE DECIDED BY A JURY

CORCORAN v. CITY OF CHICAGO

Supreme Court of Illinois, 1940.
373 Ill. 567, 27 N.E.2d 451.

MURPHY, JUSTICE. John F. Corcoran * * * began a suit * * * against the city of Chicago * * * to recover damages for personal injuries alleged to have been caused by the negligent acts of the defendant. The cause was tried with a jury and resulted in a verdict for the plaintiff for $5,000. A motion for new trial was overruled and judgment entered on the verdict. On appeal, the Appellate Court for the First District reversed the judgment and remanded the cause for another trial. The plaintiff filed a motion in the Appellate Court asking that the remanding part of the order be stricken [in order that on appeal to the state Supreme Court, that court could then order that the initial verdict be reinstated]. * * * The motion was granted * * *.

The negligence charged was that defendant had carelessly and negligently permitted certain streets to be and remain in an unsafe condition for travel * * *. The evidence was conflicting. The Appellate Court found the verdict was against the manifest weight of the evidence and reversed the judgment for that reason.

It is conceded the power which the Appellate Court assumed to exercise in reviewing the evidence and setting aside the verdict is found in section 92(3b) of the Civil Practice Act * * * which provides that Appellate Courts may review "error of fact, in that the judgment, decree or order appealed from is not sustained by the evidence or is against the weight of the evidence." Plaintiff's position is that such provision, as applied to facts found by a jury upon conflicting evidence, as in the instant case, is unconstitutional, in that the findings of the Appellate Court * * * take from him the right to a trial by jury as guaranteed by section 5 of article 2 of the [Illinois] Constitution * * *.

* * *

Prior to 1837, the law of this state was that the granting or refusal of a motion for a new trial rested in the sound discretion of the trial court and the ruling thereon could not be urged as error in the court of review. * * * In 1837, an act was passed which provided "exceptions taken to opinions or decisions of circuit court overruling motions in arrest of judgment, motions for new trials and for continuance of causes shall hereafter be allowed and the party excepting may assign for error any opinion so excepted to, any usage to the contrary notwithstanding." The substance of the act * * * has been the statutory law of this state since 1837.

* * *

The effect of the operation of the statute was considered in Chicago & Rock Island Railroad Co. v. McKean, 40 Ill. 218, a case where the trial court had overruled a motion for new trial and error was assigned on such ruling. Mr. Justice Breese, speaking for the court, said: "An appellate court was, before the passage of that act, judge of the law only * * *. The old and honored maxim once was, 'the judges respond to the law, the jury to the facts,' but now, by this innovation, the judges of an appellate court have as much power over the facts as the jury had in the first instance, for it is undeniable this court may set aside a verdict if the facts fail to satisfy it of its propriety. * * * "

Plaintiff contends that on all questions of fact where the evidence is conflicting the verdict of the jury can not be set aside as being against the weight of the evidence except by the court that tried the case, and asserts that such was the practice at common law. * * *

* * *

From the authorities cited and others which have been examined, we conclude that there was a practice at common law which authorized courts exercising appellate jurisdiction to set aside verdicts on the grounds the findings of fact were not supported by the evidence. * * *

Judgment affirmed.

NOTES AND QUESTIONS

1. In 1957, Professor Charles Alan Wright stated "that, so far as I can find, there is not a single case in which a federal appellate court has ever reversed and ordered a new trial on the ground that the trial court did abuse its discretion in denying a motion [for a new trial on the weight of the evidence] * * *." Wright, *The Doubtful Omniscience of Appellate Courts,* 41 Minn.L.Rev. 751, 760 (1957). At the time he was criticizing a dictum of the Court of Appeals for the District of Columbia Circuit claiming the existence of the power to reverse; but, he observed, "today's dictum claiming extended power for appellate courts is frequently the prelude to tomorrow's holding to that effect." Id. at 763.

Two years later, a court of appeals acted as Professor Wright prophesied, see Georgia–Pac. Corp. v. United States, 264 F.2d 161 (5th Cir.1959), but cases following suit remain "extremely few." 11 Wright, Miller & Kane, Federal Practice and Procedure: Civil 2d § 2819. Is there a significant difference between an appellate court's reversing a trial court's order denying a new trial and an appellate court's ordering a new trial because the trial court has erroneously denied a motion for a directed verdict as in Slocum v. New York Life Ins. Co., Note 1, p. 1093, supra? Is there really a difference between reversing an order denying a new trial and reversing an order granting a new trial? See Carrington, *The Power of District Judges and the Responsibility of Courts of Appeals*, 3 Ga. L. Rev. 507 (1969); Schnapper, *Judges Against Juries—Appellate Review of Federal Civil Jury Verdicts*, 1989 Wis. L. Rev. 237, 298–313.

2. The power to reverse denials of new trials on the ground that the verdict is excessive or to condition affirmance upon a remittitur is not precluded by the Seventh Amendment, see Gasperini v. Center for Humanities, Inc., 518 U.S. 415, 116 S.Ct. 2211, 135 L.Ed.2d 659 (1996), p. 454, supra, in spite of the extremely strong doubts thrown on the subject by Justice Brandeis's opinion in FAIRMOUNT GLASS WORKS v. CUB FORK COAL CO., 287 U.S. 474, 53 S.Ct. 252, 77 L.Ed. 439 (1933). Why should this power be more commonly found than the power discussed in Note 1, above?

B. THE POWER TO SET ASIDE A TRIAL JUDGE'S FINDINGS IN A NON-JURY CASE—RULE 52(a)

Federal Rule 52(a) was amended in 1985 to apply the "clearly erroneous" standard to a trial court's findings of fact, even if they are based on documentary evidence. The logic of the change also would apply to other situations in which the findings do not involve the credibility of witnesses. What is the justification for the amendment? If an appeals court is in the same position as the trial court to ascertain the facts, why isn't a de novo review appropriate? See Wright, *The Doubtful Omniscience of Appellate Courts*, 41 Minn.L.Rev. 751, 782 (1957).

PULLMAN–STANDARD v. SWINT

Supreme Court of the United States, 1982.
456 U.S. 273, 102 S.Ct. 1781, 72 L.Ed.2d 66.

Certiorari to the United States Court of Appeals for the Fifth Circuit.

JUSTICE WHITE delivered the opinion of the Court.

Respondents were black employees at the Bessemer, Alabama plant of petitioner, Pullman–Standard (the "company"), a manufacturer of railway freight cars and parts. They brought suit against the company and the union petitioners * * * alleging violations of Title VII of the Civil Rights Act of 1964 * * *. As they come here, these cases involve only the validity, under Title VII, of a seniority system maintained by the Company and USW [the United Steel Workers of America]. The District Court found "that the differences in terms, conditions or privileges of employment resulting [from the seniority system] are 'not the result of an intention to discriminate' because of race or color," * * * and held, therefore, that the system satisfied the requirements of § 703(h) of the Act. The Court of Appeals for the Fifth Circuit reversed:

> Because we find that the differences in the terms, conditions and standards of employment for black workers and white workers at Pullman–Standard resulted from an intent to discriminate because of race, we hold that the system is not legally valid under section 703(h) of Title VII, 42 U.S.C. 2000e–2(h). * * *

We granted the petitions for certiorari * * * limited to the first question presented in each petition: whether a Court of Appeals is bound by the "clearly erroneous" rule of Fed.Rules Civ.Proc. 52(a) in reviewing a District Court's findings of fact, arrived at after a lengthy trial, as to the motivation of the parties who negotiated a seniority system; and whether the court below applied wrong legal criteria in determining the *bona fides* of the seniority system. We conclude that the Court of Appeals erred in the course of its review and accordingly reverse its judgment and remand for further proceedings.

* * *

In connection with its assertion that it was convinced that a mistake had been made, the Court of Appeals, in a footnote, referred to the clearly erroneous standard of Rule 52(a). * * * It pointed out, however, that if findings "are made under an erroneous view of controlling legal principles, the clearly erroneous rule does not apply, and the findings may not stand." Finally, quoting from East v. Romine, Inc., 518 F.2d 332, 339 (C.A.5 1975), the Court of Appeals repeated the following view of its appellate function in Title VII cases where purposeful discrimination is at issue:

> Although discrimination *vel non* is essentially a question of fact it is, at the same time, the ultimate issue for resolution in this case, being expressly proscribed by 42 U.S.C.A. § 2000e–2(a). As such, a finding of discrimination or nondiscrimination is a finding of ultimate fact. * * * In reviewing the district court's findings, therefore, we will proceed to make an independent determination of appellant's allegations of discrimination, though bound by findings of subsidiary fact which are themselves not clearly erroneous.

* * * Petitioners submit that the Court of Appeals made an independent determination of discriminatory purpose, the "ultimate fact" in this case, and that this was error under Rule 52. We agree with petitioners that if the Court of Appeals followed what seems to be the accepted rule in that circuit, its judgment must be reversed.

Rule 52 broadly requires that findings of fact not be set aside unless clearly erroneous. It does not make exceptions or purport to exclude certain categories of factual findings from the obligation of a Court of Appeals to accept a district court's findings unless clearly erroneous. It does not divide facts into categories; in particular, it does not divide findings of fact into those that deal with "ultimate" and those that deal with "subsidiary" facts.

The rule does not apply to conclusions of law. The Court of Appeals, therefore, was quite right in saying that if a District Court's findings rest on an erroneous view of the law, they may be set aside on that basis. But here the District Court was not faulted for misunderstanding or applying an erroneous definition of intentional discrimination. It was reversed for arriving at what the Court of Appeals thought was an erroneous finding as to whether the differential impact of the seniority system reflected an intent to discriminate on account of race. That question, as we see it, is a pure question of fact, subject to Rule 52's clearly erroneous standard. It is not a question of law and not a mixed question of law and fact.

* * * Rule 52 does not furnish particular guidance with respect to distinguishing law from fact. Nor do we yet know of any other rule or principle that will unerringly distinguish a factual finding from a legal conclusion. For the reasons that follow, however, we have little doubt about the factual nature of § 703(h)'s requirement that a seniority system be free of an intent to discriminate.

* * *

* * * It would make no sense to say that the intent to discriminate required by § 703(h) may be presumed from such an impact. As § 703(h) was construed in * * * [International Broth. of Teamsters v. United States, 431 U.S. 324, 97 S.Ct. 1843, 52 L.Ed.2d 396 (1977)] there must be a finding of actual intent to discriminate on racial grounds on the part of those who negotiated or maintained the system. That finding appears to us to be a pure question of fact.

This is not to say that discriminatory impact is not part of the evidence to be considered by the trial court in reaching a finding on whether there was such a discriminatory intent as a factual matter. We do assert, however, that under § 703(h) discriminatory intent is a finding of fact to be made by the trial court; it is not a question of law and not a mixed question of law and fact of the kind that in some cases may allow an appellate court to review the facts to see if they satisfy some legal concept of discriminatory intent. Discriminatory intent here means actual motive; it is not a legal presumption to be drawn from a factual showing of something less than actual motive. Thus, a court of appeals may only reverse a district court's finding on discriminatory intent if it concludes that the finding is clearly erroneous under Rule 52(a). Insofar as the Fifth Circuit assumed otherwise, it erred.

Appellees do not directly defend the Fifth Circuit rule that a trial court's finding on discriminatory intent is not subject to the clearly erroneous standard of Rule 52. Rather, among other things, they submit that the Court of Appeals recognized and, where appropriate, properly applied Rule 52 in setting aside the findings of the District Court. This position has force, but for two reasons it is not persuasive.

First, although the Court of Appeals acknowledged and correctly stated the controlling standard of Rule 52, the acknowledgement came late in the court's opinion. The court had not expressly referred to or applied Rule 52 in the course of disagreeing with the District Court's resolution of the factual issues * * *. Furthermore, the paragraph in which the court finally concludes that the USW seniority system is unprotected by § 703(h) strongly suggests that the outcome was the product of the court's independent consideration of the totality of the circumstances it found in the record.

Second and more fundamentally, when the court stated that it was convinced that a mistake had been made, it then not only identified the mistake but also the source of that mistake. The mistake of the District

Court was that on the record there could be no doubt about the existence of a discriminatory purpose. * * *

When an appellate court discerns that a district court has failed to make a finding because of an erroneous view of the law, the usual rule is that there should be a remand for further proceedings to permit the trial court to make the missing findings * * *. Likewise, where findings are infirm because of an erroneous view of the law, a remand is the proper course unless the record permits only one resolution of the factual issue. All of this is elementary. Yet the Court of Appeals, after holding that the District Court had failed to consider relevant evidence and indicating that the District Court might have come to a different conclusion had it considered that evidence, failed to remand for further proceedings * * *. Instead, the Court of Appeals made its own determination [and findings] * * * and apparently concluded that the foregoing was sufficient to remove the system from the protection of § 703(h).

Proceeding in this manner seems to us incredible unless the Court of Appeals construed its own well-established Circuit rule with respect to its authority to arrive at independent findings on ultimate facts free of the strictures of Rule 52 also to permit it to examine the record and make its own independent findings with respect to those issues on which the district court's findings are set aside for an error of law. As we have previously said, however, the premise for this conclusion is infirm: whether an ultimate fact or not, discriminatory intent under § 703(h) is a factual matter subject to the clearly erroneous standard of Rule 52. It follows that when a district court's finding on such an ultimate fact is set aside for an error of law, the court of appeals is not relieved of the usual requirement of remanding for further proceedings to the tribunal charged with the task of fact-finding in the first instance.

* * *

[JUSTICE STEVENS concurred in part; JUSTICE MARSHALL and BLACKMUN dissented, primarily on the ground that the evidence was documentary and thus the appellate court was in an equally good position to determine the facts as was the trial judge. Note that it was some three years later that the Court amended Rule 52(a) and specifically undercut the dissenters' position.]

INWOOD LABORATORIES, INC. v. IVES LABORATORIES, INC., 456 U.S. 844, 102 S.Ct. 2182, 72 L.Ed.2d 606 (1982). In a patent infringement suit brought by Ives Laboratories against Inwood Laboratories, the District Court entered judgment for Inwood, finding that Ives had not made the necessary factual showings. The Court of Appeals reversed, making its own review of the evidence, and concluding that the District Court did not give enough weight to the evidence offered by Ives. The court held that the evidence was clearly sufficient to establish a Section 32 violation. The Supreme Court reversed:

> In reviewing the factual findings of the District Court, the Court of Appeals was bound by the "clearly erroneous" standard of Rule 52(a). * * * That Rule recognizes and rests upon the unique opportunity afforded the trial court judge to evaluate the credibility of witnesses and to weigh the evidence. * * * Because of the deference due the trial judge, unless an appellate court is left with the "definite and firm conviction that a mistake has been committed," * * * it must accept the trial court's findings.
>
> * * *
>
> Each of [the Second Circuit's] conclusions is contrary to the findings of the District Court. An appellate court cannot substitute its interpretation of the evidence for that of the trial court simply because the reviewing court "might give the facts another construction, resolve the ambiguities differently, and find a more sinister cast to actions which the District Court apparently deemed innocent." * * *
>
> The Court of Appeals erred in setting aside findings of fact that were not clearly erroneous. Accordingly, the judgment of the Court of Appeals that the petitioners violated § 32 of the Lanham Act is reversed.

Id. at 855–59, 102 S.Ct. at 2186–87, 72 L.Ed.2d at 616–18. Justices White and Marshall concurred in the result only, maintaining that the Rule 52(a) issue had not been properly presented to the Court.

BOSE CORP. v. CONSUMERS UNION OF UNITED STATES, INC., 466 U.S. 485, 104 S.Ct. 1949, 80 L.Ed.2d 502 (1984). Bose, a manufacturer of stereo loudspeaker systems, sued Consumers Union for product disparagement based on statements contained in an article evaluating a loudspeaker system manufactured by Bose. The District Court found that Bose was a "public figure" under the standard of New York Times Co. v. Sullivan, 376 U.S. 254, 84 S.Ct. 710, 11 L.Ed.2d 686 (1964), and its progeny, and therefore held that Bose was required to prove by clear and convincing evidence that the respondent made a false disparaging statement with "actual malice." The trial court found "actual malice," and entered judgment for Bose. The Court of Appeals reversed, holding that its review of the "actual malice" determination was not limited by the "clearly erroneous" standard of Rule 52(a) and that it must perform a de novo review of the record to evaluate the District Court's application of the governing constitutional standard.

The Supreme Court affirmed. Writing for the Court, Justice Stevens noted that the Rule's command of deference to findings of fact made by trial courts seems to conflict with the requirement, embodied in the *New*

York Times case, that appellate courts conduct a complete examination of the trial record to measure the judgment by the constitutional protection afforded by the First Amendment. He continued:

> Rule 52(a) applies to findings of fact, including those described as "ultimate facts" because they may determine the outcome of litigation. See Pullman–Standard v. Swint, [p. 1233, supra] * * *. But Rule 52(a) does not inhibit an appellate court's power to correct errors of law, including those that may infect a so-called mixed finding of law and fact, or a finding of fact that is predicated on a misunderstanding of the governing rule of law. * * * Nor does Rule 52(a) "furnish particular guidance with respect to distinguishing law from fact." Pullman–Standard v. Swint * * *.
>
> In a consideration of the possible application of the distinction to the issue of "actual malice," at least three characteristics of the rule enunciated in the *New York Times* case are relevant. First, the common law heritage of the rule itself assigns an especially broad role to the judge in applying it to specific factual situations. Second, the content of the rule is not revealed simply by its literal text, but rather is given meaning through the evolutionary process of common law adjudication; though the source of the rule is found in the Constitution, it is nevertheless largely a judge-made rule of law. Finally, the constitutional values protected by the rule make it imperative that judges—and in some cases judges of this Court—make sure that it is correctly applied. * * *
>
> * * *
>
> The requirement of independent appellate review reiterated in New York Times v. Sullivan is a rule of federal constitutional law. It emerged from the exigency of deciding concrete cases; it is law in its purest form under our common law heritage. It reflects a deeply held conviction that judges—and particularly members of this Court—must exercise such review in order to preserve the precious liberties established and ordained by the Constitution. The question whether the evidence in the record in a defamation case is of the convincing clarity required to strip the utterance of First Amendment protection is not merely a question for the trier of fact. * * *
>
> * * * We hold that the clearly erroneous standard of Rule 52(a) * * * does not prescribe the standard of review to be applied in reviewing a determination of actual malice in a case governed by New York Times v. Sullivan. Appellate judges in such a case must exercise independent judgment and determine whether the record establishes actual malice with convincing clarity.

Id. at 514, 104 S.Ct. at 1967, 80 L.Ed.2d at 525–26. Chief Justice Burger concurred in the result. Justices White, Rehnquist, and O'Connor dissented.

NOTES AND QUESTIONS

1. Is *Bose* consistent with *Pullman–Standard* and *Inwood Labs*? Do you accept Justice Stevens' identification and resolution of the conflict between the "independent review" requirement of *New York Times* and the "clearly erroneous" standard embodied in Rule 52(a)?

2. Can you identify any other constitutional mandates that would conflict with the "clearly erroneous" standard? What of the argument that the Civil Rights Act of 1964 is the statutory embodiment of the constitutional commands on civil rights embodied in the Fourteenth Amendment? Is there a clash between the constitutional requirements and Rule 52(a) that the majority disregarded in *Pullman–Standard*?

3. In ANDERSON v. CITY OF BESSEMER, 470 U.S. 564, 105 S.Ct. 1504, 84 L.Ed.2d 518 (1985), an employment discrimination case, the Supreme Court clarified the *Swint* standard and held that the Rule 52(a) clearly erroneous test applies even to findings of historical fact—"physical or documentary evidence or inferences from other facts—that do not depend on the credibility of witnesses. The Supreme Court emphasized:

> The trial judge's major role is the determination of fact, and with experience in fulfilling that role comes expertise. Duplication of the trial judge's efforts in the court of appeals would very likely contribute only negligibly to the accuracy of fact determination at a huge cost in diversion of judicial resources. In addition, the parties to a case on appeal have already been forced to concentrate their energies and resources on persuading the trial judge that their account of the facts is the correct one; requiring them to persuade three more judges at the appellate level is requiring too much.

Id. at 575, 105 S.Ct. at 1512, 84 L.Ed.2d at 529.

4. The standard of review in a case in which the trial court has issued a preliminary injunction is that of abuse of discretion. But application of that standard has been hotly debated. In ROLAND MACHINERY CO. v. DRESSER INDUSTRIES, INC., 749 F.2d 380 (7th Cir. 1984), writing for the court that overturned an injunction in an action under the Clayton Act, Judge Posner set out a multi-factor test for determining the propriety of granting a preliminary injunction, and questioned whether a district court's decision to grant or deny a preliminary injunction involves a discretionary judgment in the relevant sense "that either the need for or the feasibility of appellate review is very limited"

> * * * [T]he analytical procedure for deciding whether to grant or deny a motion for preliminary injunction * * * constitutes a true legal standard. It does not call for a discretionary—in the sense of standardless or intuitive—judgment, or for a consideration of numerous factors none enjoying any particular weight, or for an evaluation of factors inaccessible to a reviewing court * * *. The factors to be considered are few and definite; they are * * * spread out on a record; and they are to be compared in a particular sequence and in accordance with a specific formula which requires first deciding whether the plaintiff has crossed

> specified thresholds and then weighting the parties' likely harms from the grant and denial of the preliminary judgment, respectively, by the strength of the plaintiff's case.
>
> Although there is a sense in which equitable relief is inherently discretionary because historically, and still to a large extent, there is no absolute right to an equitable remedy * * * this is a different meaning of discretion, one that actually cuts against a highly deferential standard of review when as in this case the district court *grants* the preliminary injunction.

Id. at 385–91.

Judge Swygert dissented:

> * * * I believe that the majority's discussion of the standard of review represents a fundamental misunderstanding of the role of preliminary injunctive relief in our legal system and the role of the district courts in dispensing that relief. I endorse the four-part test set forth by the majority for determining the propriety of granting a preliminary injunction. I believe, however, that the formulation of that or any other test cannot replace the role of discretion in the decision to grant or deny a preliminary injunction. I further believe that the discretion that inheres in the decision whether to grant a preliminary injunction cannot rest with the reviewing court but must lie in the district court. First, it must be remembered that the district court has the responsibility for making a final determination on the merits of the case. * * * Second, given the flexibility of the standard for preliminary injunctive relief and the necessity for discretionary judgments, two courts could easily arrive at different although equally viable conclusions. Refusal to defer to the decision of the lower court in the first instance frequently will result in a substitution of the judgment of the reviewing court for that of the district court. This is a poor use of judicial resources. * * * Finally, and most importantly, if discretionary judgments must be made * * * in deciding to grant or deny preliminary injunctive relief, the trial court with its greater knowledge of the case and the parties * * * is in a better position than a reviewing court to make those judgments. * * *

Id. at 396–99. Who has the better argument, Judge Posner or Judge Swygert? Isn't Judge Posner actually arguing in favor of *de novo* review? See generally Kim, *Lower Court Discretion*, 82 N.Y.U. L. Rev. 383 (2007).

5. In the declaratory judgment context, an appellate court may make two inquiries. It may determine whether the trial court abused its discretion by making an arbitrary choice to hear a claim for declaratory judgment. Additionally it may determine that, even if the action is properly a declaratory judgment action, the lower court's opinion was nevertheless erroneous. In other words, the appellate court may engage in *de novo* review. What is it about declaratory judgments that justifies *de novo* review?

6. Suppose that neither of the parties, nor the trial court, refers to a precedent that would have altered the judgment rendered. If the party who lost below appeals, should the appellate court consider the precedent even though appellant did not refer to it below? In Elder v. Holloway, 510 U.S. 510,

114 S.Ct. 1019, 127 L.Ed.2d 344 (1994), the Court held that the precedent should be considered.

7. Appellate courts often are not as deferential to trial court findings as the standards or the case law normally would indicate. See Goettel, *Appellate Fact Finding—and Other Atrocities,* 13 Litig. 7 (Fall 1986). In fact, Judge Goettel notes that "[t]rial judges often can barely recognize their cases in appellate opinions, so convoluted have the facts become. With the facts so extensively revamped, reversal becomes inevitable." Id. at 7. See generally Sward, *Appellate Review of Judicial Fact–Finding,* 40 U. Kan. L.Rev. 1 (1991).

SECTION D. THE VIEW AT THE TOP—COURTS ABOVE APPELLATE COURTS

Read 28 U.S.C. §§ 1251, 1253–54, 1257 in the Supplement and all the accompanying material.

1. REVIEW AS OF RIGHT

In the federal courts and in the judicial systems of more than three-quarters of the states, intermediate appellate courts are interposed between the trial courts of general jurisdiction and the highest court. See Najam, Jr., *Caught in the Middle: The Role of State Intermediate Appellate Courts*, 35 Ind. L. Rev. 329 (2002). The principal purpose in creating intermediate appellate courts has been to relieve the pressure of burgeoning appellate litigation on the highest court, leaving that tribunal free to concentrate on deciding important and novel questions of law and on maintaining uniformity in the law applied by the lower courts. To achieve this purpose fully, two conditions must be met. Most appeals must begin and end in the intermediate appellate courts, but the possibility of review by the highest court must be open in every case.

Both conditions would be satisfied if the intermediate courts heard every appeal in the first instance and the highest court had complete discretion to review the decisions of those courts. But no American system seems to have fully adopted this approach. In every state that has intermediate appellate courts, as well as in the federal courts, some matters are reviewable directly by the highest court, and, in most systems, some matters, decided in the first instance by the intermediate courts, are appealable as of right to the highest court. The systems differ markedly, however, both in the extent to which the intermediate appellate courts are bypassed and in the amount of discretion given to the highest court to choose the cases it hears.

NOTES AND QUESTIONS

1. Compare the provisions for direct appeal to the Supreme Court of California and the Court of Appeals of New York that are set out in the Supplement following 28 U.S.C. § 1254. What is the reason for each of these provisions? Which set of state provisions seems most appropriate?

2. Prior to 1988, when it repealed 28 U.S.C. § 1252, Congress had provided for direct appeal to the Supreme Court of the United States from any decision of a federal district court "holding an Act of Congress unconstitutional in any civil action * * * to which the United States or any of its agencies [or employees] * * * is a party." What might have led Congress to repeal this provision? See Brown Shoe Co. v. United States, 370 U.S. 294, 355, 364, 82 S.Ct. 1502, 1541, 1546, 8 L.Ed.2d 510, 557, 562 (1962) (sharp criticisms by Justice Clark and Justice Harlan of direct appeals). Direct appeals still are available under 28 U.S.C. § 1253. What is the justification for such a provision? Note that the Supreme Court can effect a direct appeal in any case in which certiorari would lie by taking up the case as soon as it is docketed in the court of appeals and before that court considers it, but this power rarely has been exercised. One case in which it was employed was United States v. Nixon, referred to in Note 2, p. 1023, supra. Do the state courts mentioned in Note 1, above, possess comparable authority?

3. For many years, Congress had provided in 28 U.S.C. §§ 1254 and 1257 that the Supreme Court was *required* to review certain decisions of the federal courts of appeals and of state courts in situations involving the validity of state laws under the Constitution, treaties, or laws of the United States. In fact, the requirement was somewhat illusory because the Court took the position that it had jurisdiction only if the case involved a "substantial federal question." Zucht v. King, 260 U.S. 174, 43 S.Ct. 24, 67 L.Ed. 194 (1922). Many such appeals therefore were dismissed because the issue was considered remote or already well-settled. In 1988, Congress amended Sections 1254 and 1257 to provide that such decisions receive no special treatment, but shall be reviewed, as are most others, only if the Supreme Court, in its discretion, grants a petition for a writ of certiorari. See the section entitled Discretionary Review, p. 1243, infra.

4. The most important restriction on Supreme Court review of state court decisions is that a federal question have been presented to the highest court that could consider the question, the state judgment is final, and the state determination not rest on an independent and adequate state ground. See MICHIGAN v. LONG, 463 U.S. 1032, 103 S.Ct. 3469, 77 L.Ed.2d 1201 (1983). Should review be denied if the state court decision rests upon alternative grounds, one federal and one state? See Zacchini v. Scripps–Howard Broadcasting Co., 433 U.S. 562, 568, 97 S.Ct. 2849, 2853–54, 53 L.Ed.2d 965, 971–72 (1977). Suppose that the highest state court, in deciding how to interpret its own law, feels bound by federal law. In such cases Supreme Court review is permitted. Why?

5. Appeals from courts of inferior jurisdiction, such as justice-of-the-peace courts, probate courts, and municipal courts, frequently lie to the trial

courts of general jurisdiction. The organization of inferior courts differs so widely from state to state that few generalizations can be drawn. Typically, however, the jurisdictional provisions call for a *de novo* hearing in the court of general jurisdiction and, in the case of very small claims, make the determination of the latter court final and unreviewable.

2. DISCRETIONARY REVIEW

Review 28 U.S.C. §§ 1254(1), 1257(a) in the Supplement.

DICK v. NEW YORK LIFE INSURANCE CO., 359 U.S. 437, 448–55, 79 S.Ct. 921, 928–31, 3 L.Ed.2d 935, 943–47 (1959). Justice Frankfurter, dissenting:

> Establishment of intermediate appellate courts in 1891 was designed by Congress to relieve the overburdened docket of the Court. The Circuit Courts of Appeals were to be equal in dignity to the Supreme Courts of the several States. The essential purpose of the Evarts Act was to enable the Supreme Court to discharge its indispensable functions in our federal system by relieving it of the duty of adjudication in cases that are important only to the litigants. * * * The Act provided, therefore, that in diversity cases "the judgments or decrees of the circuit courts of appeals shall be final." * * * [However], this Court was given the discretionary power to grant certiorari in these cases, to be exercised if some question of general interest, outside the limited scope of an ordinary diversity litigation, was also involved.
>
> * * *
>
> Time and again in the years immediately following the passage of the Evarts Act this Court stated that it was only in cases of "gravity and general importance" or "to secure uniformity of decision" that the certiorari power should be exercised. * * *
>
> These considerations have led the Court in scores of cases to dismiss the writ of certiorari even after oral argument when it became manifest that the writ was granted under a misapprehension of the true issues. * * *
>
> To strengthen further this Court's control over its docket and to avoid review of cases which in the main raise only factual controversies, Congress in 1916 made cases arising under the Federal Employers' Liability Act * * * final in the Courts of Appeals, reviewable by this Court only when required by the guiding standards for exercising its certiorari jurisdiction.

In 1925 Congress enacted the "Judges' Bill," called such because it was drafted by a committee of this Court composed of Van Devanter, McReynolds, and Sutherland, JJ. At the hearings on the bill * * * Mr. Chief Justice Taft said:

> No litigant is entitled to more than two chances, namely, to the original trial and to a review, and the intermediate courts of review are provided for that purpose. When a case goes beyond that, it is not primarily to preserve the rights of the litigants. The Supreme Court's function is for the purpose of expounding and stabilizing principles of law for the benefit of the people of the country, passing upon constitutional questions and other important questions of law for the public benefit. It is to preserve uniformity of decision among the intermediate courts of appeal.

* * *

Questions of fact have traditionally been deemed to be the kind of questions which ought not to be recanvassed here unless they are entangled in the proper determination of constitutional or other important legal issues. * * * The proper use of the discretionary certiorari jurisdiction was on a later occasion thus expounded by Mr. Chief Justice Hughes:

> Records are replete with testimony and evidence of facts. But the questions on certiorari are questions of law. * * * It is only when the facts are interwoven with the questions of law which we should review that the evidence must be examined and then only to the extent that it is necessary to decide the questions of law. * * *

HARRIS v. PENNSYLVANIA RAILROAD CO., 361 U.S. 15, 17–19, 80 S.Ct. 22, 24–25, 4 L.Ed.2d 1, 3–4 (1959). Justice Douglas, concurring:

> It is suggested that the Court has consumed too much of its time in reviewing these FELA cases. An examination of the 33 cases in which the Court has granted certiorari during the period [1949–1959] * * * reveals that 16 of these cases were summarily reversed without oral argument and without full opinions. Only 17 cases were argued during this period of more than a decade and, of these, 5 were disposed of by brief *per curiam* opinions. Only 12 cases in over 10 years were argued, briefed and disposed of with full opinions by the Court. We have granted certiorari in these cases on an average of less than 3 per year and have given plenary consideration to slightly more than 1 per year. Wastage of our time is therefore a false issue.
>
> The difference between the majority and minority of the Court in our treatment of FELA cases concerns the degree of vigilance we should exercise in safeguarding the jury trial—guaranteed by the Seventh

Amendment and part and parcel of the remedy under this Federal Act when suit is brought in state courts. * * * Whether that right has been impaired in a particular instance often produces a contrariety of views. Yet the practice of the Court in allowing four out of nine votes to control the certiorari docket is well established and of long duration. Without it, the vast discretion which Congress allowed us in granting or denying certiorari might not be tolerable. Every member of the Court has known instances where he has strongly protested the action of the minority in bringing a case or type of case here for adjudication. He may then feel that there are more important and pressing matters to which the Court should give its attention. That is, however, a price we pay for keeping our promise to Congress[1] to let the vote of four Justices bring up any case here on certiorari.

NOTES AND QUESTIONS

1. In the early 1970s, the sharp increase in the number of petitions for review filed with the Supreme Court led some commentators to conclude that the Court was being strangled by its workload. Some of these commentators proposed the creation of a new federal appellate court, positioned between the Supreme Court and the present courts of appeals—the so-called National Court of Appeals. See, e.g., Report of the Study Group on the Caseload of the Supreme Court (1972), reprinted at 57 F.R.D. 573 (1972); Commission on Revision of the Federal Court Appellate System Structure and Internal Procedures: Recommendations for Change (1975), reprinted at 67 F.R.D. 195 (1975). Finally, in the early 1980s, Chief Justice Burger endorsed these proposals and considerable interest in them was generated. In 1987, the Senate and the House of Representatives conducted hearings on bills that would have created a temporary, experimental National Court of Appeals or Intercircuit Tribunal. The Supreme Court would have referred cases to this new court for resolution, but would have retained power of ultimate review by writ of certiorari. The results of the experiment would have been assessed at the end of five years, at which time the court could be made permanent or abolished. The legislation failed.

At the time, scholars questioned whether the Supreme Court inevitably must face more cases demanding its attention than it can handle, and they have challenged the premise upon which the case for a national court of appeals is most often made. See Estreicher & Sexton, *A Managerial Theory of the Supreme Court's Responsibilities: An Empirical Study*, 59 N.Y.U. L. Rev. 681 (1984), in which the authors examine the history and the contours of the debate over the Court's "workload problem," offer a theory of the Court's role

---

1. The "rule of four" was given as one of the reasons why the Congress thought that the increase of our discretionary jurisdiction was warranted. The House Report stated:

* * *

"'* * * We always grant the petition when as many as four think that it should be granted and sometimes when as many as three think that way. We proceed upon the theory that, if that number out of the nine are impressed with the thought that the case is one that ought to be heard and decided by us, the petition should be granted.'"

H.R.Rep. No. 1075, 68th Cong., 2d Sess., p. 3.

in the federal judicial system, and present a detailed examination of the case selection process as it operated in the October 1982 Term. Their study concludes that the unfocused nature of the criteria for case selection presented in what was then Supreme Court Rule 17 caused the Court to "overgrant," thereby creating the illusion of overload. The authors argued that revision of these criteria and other minor procedural changes would dispose of the need for a new federal appellate court.

2. Beginning in the late 1980s, the number of cases disposed of by the Supreme Court began to decline to a significant extent, despite an increase in the number of cases seeking review. See Hellman, *The Shrunken Docket of the Rehnquist Court*, 1996 Sup. Ct. Rev. 403 (1996); George & Solimine, *Supreme Court Monitoring of the United States Courts of Appeals En Banc*, 9 Sup. Ct. Econ. Rev. 171, 172 (2001).

THE SUPREME COURT AND ITS DOCKET: 1926–2005[a]

Term	Total Number of Cases on the Docket	Number of Cases Disposed of by Signed Opinion	Percent of Cases Disposed of by Signed Opinion
1926	1,183	223	18.9 %
1935	1,092	187	17.1 %
1945	1,460	170	11.6 %
1955	1,849	103	5.6 %
1965	3,256	120	3.7 %
1975	4,761	160	3.4 %
1985	5,158	161	3.1 %
1995	7,565	87	1.2 %
2004	8,593	85	1.0 %

Is this decline in cases healthy? Commentators point to various explanations for the trend. See Cordray & Cordray, *The Supreme Court's Plenary Docket*, 58 Wash. & Lee L. Rev. 737 (2001); Scott, *Shaping the Supreme Court's Federal Certiorari Docket*, 27 Just. Sys. J. 191 (2006).

3. Compare United States Supreme Court Rule 10, which replaced Supreme Court Rule 17, with California Appellate Rule 28(b), both of which are set out in the Supplement following 28 U.S.C. § 1254. What considerations should govern the highest court of a state in deciding whether to hear a case within its discretionary jurisdiction? See Cuomo, *The New York Court of Appeals: A Practical Perspective*, 34 St. John's L.Rev. 197, 201 (1960); Poulos & Varner, *Review of Intermediate Appellate Court Decisions in California*, 15 Hastings L.J. 11, 15 (1963). Should these considerations be any different from those followed by the Supreme Court of the United States in ruling on a petition for a writ of certiorari? For a critical discussion of Supreme Court certiorari procedure, see Thompson & Wachtell, *An Empirical Analysis of Supreme Court Certiorari Petition Procedures: The Call for Response and the Call for the Views of the Solicitor General*, 16 Geo. Mason L. Rev. 237 (2009).

a. Table adapted from information set out in Starr, *The Supreme Court and Its Shrinking Docket: The Ghost of William Howard Taft*, 90 Minn. L. Rev. 1363, 1368 nn.24–27 (2006).

3. THE FINAL JUDGMENT REQUIREMENT UNDER SECTION 1257

Section 1257 limits Supreme Court review to "final judgments of the highest state court in which a decision could be had." Should determinations as to what is final under Section 1257 be influenced by decisions as to what is final under Section 1291? See pp. 1187–93, 1206–08, supra. In COX BROADCASTING CORP. v. COHN, 420 U.S. 469, 95 S.Ct. 1029, 43 L.Ed.2d 328 (1975), plaintiff brought suit for damages in a state court against the owner of a television station, alleging that the station had wrongfully invaded his privacy by revealing that his daughter had been the victim of rape and murder. Defendant claimed the broadcast was privileged under the First and Fourteenth Amendments to the federal Constitution. The trial judge granted partial summary judgment for plaintiff on liability. The state supreme court overturned the summary judgment, but held that the federal Constitution did not necessarily rule out the possibility of liability and returned the case to the trial court for further proceedings. On appeal, the Supreme Court, noting that the requirement of finality under Section 1257 has been applied in a "pragmatic" rather than in a "mechanical fashion," upheld immediate appeal since the state decision was final as to the federal issue, a vital issue that should be decided as soon as possible so that broadcasters would know what they could or could not publish without fear of a lawsuit. The Court cited Gillespie v. United States Steel Corp., set out at p. 1205, supra, accepting its approach even though it had been decided under Section 1291. Justice Rehnquist dissented, arguing that the policies underlying Sections 1257 and 1291 differ substantially.

NOTES AND QUESTIONS

1. Does the Supreme Court's decision in Coopers & Lybrand v. Livesay, see Note 1, p. 1206, supra, undermine the *Cox* decision?

2. Even if the policies behind Sections 1257 and 1291 differ, should that impact the interpretation given to the word "final" in each? Aren't the reasons for avoiding appeals of interlocutory orders applicable under both provisions? Shouldn't it be up to Congress to create exceptions to Section 1257 as it has with regard to Section 1291?

3. The Court in *Cox* listed four situations in which a technical definition of "final" may give way to "pragmatic" considerations:

(1) When the decision is final from a practical point of view—for example, when the interlocutory decision clearly dictates the final result.

(2) When the federal issue necessarily would survive no matter how the state courts would rule in subsequent proceedings.

(3) When, under state law, subsequent review could be prohibited—for example, in criminal or certain administrative-law cases in which an acquittal or decision against the government would not be appealable.

(4) When important federal rights are involved and when delay would erode federal policy.

How much emphasis should be placed on the last situation? Suppose in *Cox* the state supreme court merely had vacated the summary judgment and returned the case to the trial court with the admonition, "study anew the defenses based on the federal Constitution which were originally treated summarily and without adequate briefing from counsel." Should an immediate appeal to the Supreme Court be permitted to avoid leaving local broadcasters uncertain about their rights? For a comprehensive review of *Cox* and of the final judgment rule under Section 1257, see Note, *The Finality Rule for Supreme Court Review of State Court Orders*, 91 Harv.L.Rev. 1004 (1978).

CHAPTER 17

THE BINDING EFFECT OF PRIOR DECISIONS: RES JUDICATA AND COLLATERAL ESTOPPEL

■ ■ ■

In this Chapter, we focus on the twin doctrines of res judicata and collateral estoppel—now known as claim preclusion and issue preclusion—to explore the binding effect of prior judgments. We look at the history, the doctrine, and the policies that support the concept of finality. "Courts can only do their best to determine the truth on the basis of the evidence, and the first lesson one must learn on the subject of res judicata is that judicial findings must not be confused with absolute truth." Currie, *Mutuality of Collateral Estoppel: Limits of the Bernhard Doctrine,* 9 Stan.L.Rev. 281, 315 (1957). The Chapter opens by examining the reach of claim and issue preclusion within a single court system and closes by widening the scope to the inter-system effects of a judgment, which is surely one of the most difficult and vexing questions in the entire Procedure course. As you study these materials, notice how attitudes toward this defense have changed over the years and consider how preclusion rules might best be adapted to balance competing values of efficiency, repose, deterrence, dignity, and compensation.

SECTION A. TERMINOLOGY

Although the doctrine of former adjudication is complex, four common sense principles explain it. First, a party ordinarily gets only one chance to litigate a "claim"; if a party litigates only a portion of a claim the first time around, she risks losing the chance to litigate the rest. Second, a party ordinarily gets only one chance to litigate a factual or a legal "issue"; once litigated, she cannot ask a second court to decide it differently later. Third, a party is entitled to at least one "full and fair" chance to litigate before being precluded. And fourth, preclusion may be waived unless it is claimed at an early stage of the litigation.

The effects of a former adjudication have been discussed in varying and occasionally conflicting terminology. Although the time has not yet come when courts will use a single vocabulary, substantial progress has been made toward a convention.

> "Res judicata" has been used * * * as a general term referring to all of the ways in which one judgment will have a binding effect on another. That usage is and doubtless will continue to be common, but it lumps under a single name two quite different effects of judgments. The first is the effect of foreclosing any litigation of matters that never have been litigated, because of the determination that they should have been advanced in an earlier suit. The second is the effect of foreclosing relitigation of matters that have once been litigated and decided. The first of these, preclusion of matters that were never litigated, has gone under the name, "true res judicata," or the names, "merger and bar." The second doctrine, preclusion of matters that have once been decided, has usually been called "collateral estoppel."

Wright & Kane, Law of Federal Courts § 100A (6th ed.2002) (footnotes omitted).

Another useful summary is the following:

> * * * "Res judicata" is the term traditionally used to describe two discrete effects: (1) what we now call claim preclusion (a valid final adjudication of a claim precludes a second action on that claim or any part of it), see Restatement (Second) of Judgments §§ 17–19 (1982); and (2) issue preclusion, long called "collateral estoppel" (an issue of fact or law, actually litigated and resolved by a valid final judgment, binds the parties in a subsequent action, whether on the same or a different claim), see *id.*, at § 27.

Baker v. General Motors Corp., 522 U.S. 222, 233 n.5, 118 S.Ct. 657, 664 n.5, 139 L.Ed.2d 580, 592 n.5 (1998). For excellent and comprehensive discussions of claim preclusion, see 18 Wright, Miller & Cooper, Federal Practice and Procedure: Jurisdiction and Related Matters 2d §§ 4401–15; Shapiro, Civil Procedure: Preclusion in Civil Actions (2001).

SECTION B. CLAIM AND DEFENSE PRECLUSION

It is difficult to give a precise definition of the doctrine of claim preclusion, but it is possible to sketch its general form. One formulation is: In certain circumstances, when a second suit is brought, the judgment from a prior suit will be considered conclusive, both on the parties to the judgment and on those in privity with them, as to matters that actually were litigated or should have been litigated in the first suit. Justice Field has provided a more detailed formulation of the same basic rule:

> * * * [A] judgment, if rendered upon the merits, constitutes an absolute bar to a subsequent action. It is a finality as to the claim or demand in controversy, concluding parties and those in privity with them, not only as to every matter which was offered and received to sustain or defeat the claim or demand, but as to any other admissible matter which might have been offered for that purpose. Thus, for example, a judgment rendered upon a promissory note is conclusive as

to the validity of the instrument and the amount due on it, although it be subsequently alleged that perfect defences actually existed, of which no proof was offered, such as forgery, want of consideration, or payment. * * * The judgment is as conclusive, so far as future proceedings at law are concerned, as though the defences never existed. * * *

CROMWELL v. COUNTY OF SAC, 94 U.S. (4 Otto) 351, 352–53, 24 L.Ed. 195, 197–98 (1876), p. 1273, infra.

Another helpful explanation is the following:

> * * * [T]he preclusive scope of a judgment * * * depends on defining the breadth of the claim or cause of action hazarded in the first suit. If the plaintiff wins, the entire claim is merged in the judgment; the plaintiff cannot bring a second independent action for additional relief, and the defendant cannot avoid the judgment by offering new defenses. If the plaintiff loses, the entire claim is barred by the judgment, even as to evidence, theories, arguments, and remedies that were not advanced in the first litigation. The process of defining the claim or cause of action is thus aimed at defining the matters that both might and *should* have been advanced in the first litigation. * * * If the second lawsuit involves a new claim or cause of action, the parties may raise assertions or defenses that were omitted from the first lawsuit even though they were equally relevant to the first cause of action. * * *

18 Wright, Miller & Cooper, Federal Practice and Procedure: Jurisdiction and Related Matters 2d § 4406 (emphasis in original).

For claim preclusion to operate, three elements must be present. First, only judgments that are "final," "valid," and "on the merits" have preclusive effect. Second, the parties in the subsequent action must be identical to those in the first. This requirement is one of the most important distinctions between claim preclusion and its sister doctrine, issue preclusion. And third, the claim in the second suit must involve matters properly considered included in the first action. Clearly, this last requirement turns on what the first action decided or should have decided.

1. CLAIM PRECLUSION

RUSH v. CITY OF MAPLE HEIGHTS

Supreme Court of Ohio, 1958.
167 Ohio St. 221, 147 N.E.2d 599,
certiorari denied 358 U.S. 814, 79 S.Ct. 21, 3 L.Ed.2d 57.

[Plaintiff was injured in a fall from a motorcycle. She brought an action in the Municipal Court of Cleveland for damage to her personal property; that court found that defendant city was negligent in maintaining its street and that this negligence was the proximate cause of plaintiff's damages, which were fixed at $100. Defendant appealed and the judgment was affirmed by the Ohio Court of Appeals and Supreme Court. Plaintiff also brought this action in the Court of Common Pleas of Cuyahoga County for personal injuries she incurred in the same accident; her motion to set trial on the issue of damages alone was granted on the ground that the issue of negligence was barred by res judicata because of the Municipal Court action; judgment was entered on a verdict for $12,000, and the Court of Appeals affirmed.]

HERBERT, JUDGE. The eighth error assigned by the defendant is that "the trial and appellate courts committed error in permitting plaintiff to split her cause of action * * *."

In the case of Vasu v. Kohlers, Inc., 145 Ohio St. 321, 61 N.E.2d 707, 709, 166 A.L.R. 855, plaintiff operating an automobile came into collision with defendant's truck, in which collision he suffered personal injuries and also damage to his automobile. At the time of collision, plaintiff had coverage of a $50 deductible collision policy on his automobile. The insurance company paid the plaintiff a sum covering the damage to his automobile, whereupon, in accordance with a provision of the policy, the plaintiff assigned to the insurer his claim for such damage.

In February 1942, the insurance company commenced an action * * * against Kohlers, Inc., * * * to recoup the money paid by it to cover the damage to Vasu's automobile.

In August 1942, Vasu commenced an action in the same court against Kohlers, Inc., to recover for personal injuries which he suffered in the same collision.

In March 1943, in the insurance company's action, a verdict was rendered in favor of the defendant, followed by judgment.

Two months later an amended answer was filed in the Vasu case, setting out as a bar to the action * * * the judgment rendered in favor of defendant in the insurance company case. A motion to strike that defense * * * [was] sustained * * *. A trial of the action resulted in a verdict for plaintiff, upon which judgment was entered.

On appeal to the Court of Appeals the defendant claimed that the Court of Common Pleas erred in sustaining plaintiff's motion to strike from the defendant's answer the defense of *res judicata* claimed to have arisen by reason of the judgment in favor of the defendant in the action by the insurance company.

The Court of Appeals reversed the judgment of the Court of Common Pleas and entered final judgment in favor of defendant.

This court reversed the judgment of the Court of Appeals, holding in the syllabus, in part, as follows:

* * *

4. Injuries to both person and property suffered by the same person as a result of the same wrongful act are infringements of different

rights and give rise to distinct causes of action, with the result that the recovery or denial of recovery of compensation for damages to the property is no bar to an action subsequently prosecuted for the personal injury, unless by an adverse judgment in the first action issues are determined against the plaintiff which operate as an estoppel against him in the second action.

* * *

6. Where an injury to person and to property through a single wrongful act causes a prior contract of indemnity and subrogation as to the injury to property to come into operation for the benefit of the person injured, the indemnitor may prosecute a separate action against the party causing such injury for reimbursement for indemnity monies paid under such contract.

7. Parties in privy, in the sense that they are bound by a judgment, are those who acquired an interest in the subject matter after the beginning of the action or the rendition of the judgment; and if their title or interest attached before that fact, they are not bound unless made parties.

8. A grantor or assignor is not bound, as to third persons, by any judgment which such third persons may obtain against his grantee or assignee adjudicating the title to or claim for the interest transferred unless he participated in the action in such manner as to become, in effect, a party.

* * * The sixth, seventh and eighth paragraphs deal with the factual situation which existed in the Vasu case, i.e., a prior contract of indemnity and subrogation. Although, as discussed infra, it was not actually necessary to the determination of the issue in that case, attention centers on the fourth paragraph.

* * * [Subsequent] cases, distinguishing and explaining the Vasu case, have not changed the rule established in paragraph four of the syllabus * * *.

However, it is contended here that that rule is in conflict with the great weight of authority in this country and has caused vexatious litigation. * * *

Upon examination of decisions of courts of last resort, we find that the majority rule is followed in the following cases in each of which the action was between the person suffering injury and the person committing the tort, and where insurers were not involved, as in the case here. * * * [The court cited cases from 20 states forming the majority and 5 states forming the minority.]

The reasoning behind the majority rule seems to be well stated in the case of Mobile & Ohio Rd. Co. v. Matthews * * * [115 Tenn. 172, 91 S.W. 194 (1906)], as follows:

> The negligent action of the plaintiff in error constituted but one tort. The injuries to the person and property of the defendant in error were the several results and effects of one wrongful act. A single tort can be the basis of but one action. It is not improper to declare in different counts for damages to the person and property when both result from the same tort, and it is the better practice to do so where there is any difference in the measure of damages, and all the damages sustained must be sued for in one suit. This is necessary to prevent multiplicity of suits, burdensome expense, and delays to plaintiffs, and vexatious litigation against defendants. * * *

The minority rule would seem to stem from the English case of Brunsden v. Humphrey (1884), 14 Q.B. 141. The facts in that case are set forth in the opinion in the Vasu case * * * concluding with the statement:

> The Master of the Rolls, in his opinion, stated that the test is "whether the same sort of evidence would prove the plaintiff's case in the two actions," and that, in the action relating to the cab, "it would be necessary to give evidence of the damage done to the plaintiff's vehicle. In the present action it would be necessary to give evidence of the bodily injury occasioned to the plaintiff, and of the sufferings which he has undergone, and for this purpose to call medical witnesses. This one test shows that the causes of action as to the damage done to the plaintiff's cab, and as to the injury occasioned to the plaintiff's person, are distinct."

The fallacy of the reasoning in the English court is best portrayed in the dissenting opinion of Lord Coleridge, as follows:

> * * * [I]t seems to me a subtlety not warranted by law to hold that a man cannot bring two actions, if he is injured in his arm and in his leg, but can bring two, if besides his arm and leg being injured, his trousers which contain his leg, and his coat-sleeve which contains his arm, have been torn.

There appears to be no valid reason in these days of code pleading to adhere to the old English rule as to distinctions between injuries to the person and damages to the person's property resulting from a single tort. It would seem that the minority rule is bottomed on the proposition that the right of bodily security is fundamentally different from the right of security of property and, also, that, in actions predicated upon a negligent act, damages are a necessary element of each independent cause of action and no recovery may be had unless and until actual consequential damages are shown.

Whether or not injuries to both person and property resulting from the same wrongful act are to be treated as injuries to separate rights or as separate items of damage, * * * a plaintiff may maintain only one action to enforce his rights existing at the time such action is commenced.

The decision of the question actually in issue in the Vasu case is found in paragraphs six, seven and eight of the syllabus, as it is quite apparent from the facts there that the first judgment, claimed to be *res judicata* in Vasu's action against the defendant, was rendered against Vasu's insurer in an action initiated by it after having paid Vasu for the damages to his automobile. * * *

Upon further examination of the cases from other jurisdictions, it appears that in those instances where the courts have held to the majority rule, a separation of causes of action is almost universally recognized where an insurer has acquired by an assignment or by subrogation the right to recover for money it has advanced to pay for property damage.

* * *

In the light of the foregoing, it is the view of this court that the so-called majority rule conforms much more properly to modern practice, and that the rule declared in the fourth paragraph of the syllabus in the Vasu case, on a point not actually at issue therein, should not be followed.

* * *

Judgment reversed and final judgment for defendant.

STEWART, JUDGE (concurring). * * * If it had been necessary [in *Vasu*] to decide the question whether a single tort gives rise to two causes of action as to the one injured by such tort, I would be reluctant to disturb that holding. However, neither the discussion in the Vasu case as to whether a single or double cause of action arises from one tort nor the language of the fourth paragraph of the syllabus was necessary to decide the issue presented in the case, and obviously both such language and such paragraph are obiter dicta and, therefore, are not as persuasive an authority as if they had been appropriate to the question presented.

* * *

ZIMMERMAN, JUDGE (dissenting). I am not unalterably opposed to upsetting prior decisions of this court where changing conditions and the lessons of experience clearly indicate the desirability of such course, but, where those considerations do not obtain, established law should remain undisturbed in order to insure a stability on which the lower courts and the legal profession generally may rely with some degree of confidence.

* * *

NOTES AND QUESTIONS

1. The *Rush* case provides an illustration of an important concept with which you are already familiar: *stare decisis*. Although neither party in *Rush* had been a party to Vasu v. Kohler's, Inc., both of the lower Ohio courts as well as the dissenting judge in the Supreme Court of Ohio regarded that case as controlling in *Rush*. Of course, as the *Rush* case itself demonstrates, the binding force of *stare decisis* is not absolute, and the parties to a later action are free to argue that the law announced in an earlier case should be changed. But a court will not lightly depart from precedent even though the parties

who are before it were not represented in the case that established the precedent.

Stare decisis is a self-governing principle that helps the judiciary carry out the sensitive and difficult task of fashioning and preserving a system of laws based upon rational principle and not arbitrary discretion. The Supreme Court has explained:

> The obligation to follow precedent begins with necessity, and a contrary necessity marks its outer limit. With Cardozo, we recognize that no judicial system could do society's work if it eyed each issue afresh in every case that raised it. See B. Cardozo, The Nature of the Judicial Process 149 (1921). Indeed, the very concept of the rule of law underlying our own Constitution requires such continuity over time that a respect for precedent is, by definition, indispensable. * * * At the other extreme, a different necessity would make itself felt if a prior judicial ruling should come to be seen so clearly as error that its enforcement was for that very reason doomed.

PLANNED PARENTHOOD OF SOUTHEASTERN PENNSYLVANIA v. CASEY, 505 U.S. 833, 854, 112 S.Ct. 2791, 2808, 120 L.Ed.2d 674, 699–700 (1992). Justice Frankfurter, in HELVERING v. HALLOCK, 309 U.S. 106, 119, 60 S.Ct. 444, 451, 84 L.Ed. 604, 612 (1940), emphasized that "*stare decisis* is a principle of policy and not a mechanical formula of adherence to the latest decision * * *." Should the role of *stare decisis* be different when the Court is interpreting the Constitution, rather than a statute or an administrative regulation? Why or why not?

2. *Rush* illustrates two additional ways in which adjudication in one action may affect a subsequent lawsuit: through the doctrines of claim and issue preclusion introduced in Section A. How does *stare decisis* differ from these concepts? We will explore issue preclusion in Section C, p. 1272, infra. For now, consider what its effect would have been if the Ohio court had not found claim preclusion in *Rush*. Note that both lower courts in *Rush* held that the only issue open in plaintiff's suit for her personal injuries was the amount of her damages, because the issues of negligence, proximate cause, and contributory negligence all had been determined conclusively by her judgment in the earlier action for property damage.

3. The results of res judicata sometimes may seem harsh, but the doctrine is supported by a number of important policy goals: "res judicata and collateral estoppel relieve parties of the cost and vexation of multiple lawsuits, conserve judicial resources, and, by preventing inconsistent decisions, encourage reliance on adjudication." Allen v. McCurry, 449 U.S. 90, 94, 101 S.Ct. 411, 415, 66 L.Ed.2d 308, 313 (1980). Why are these goals so important? What effect would eliminating res judicata have on the judicial system?

4. Was the critical language in *Vasu* a holding or dictum? Consider the following:

> "It is often difficult to determine whether statements in a court's opinion constitute an alternative ground for the decision or merely dicta." * * * Black's Law Dictionary defines "obiter dictum" as a statement "made during the course of delivering a judicial opinion, but one that is unneces-

> sary to the decision in the case and therefore not precedential (though it may be considered persuasive.)." * * * However, "where a decision rests on two or more grounds, none can be relegated to the category of obiter dictum."

Best Life Assur. Co. of California v. Comm'r of Internal Revenue, 281 F.3d 828, 833–34 (9th Cir. 2002) (internal citations omitted). Professors Abramowicz and Stearns offer the following distinction between a holding and a dictum: "A holding consists of those propositions along the chosen decisional path or paths of reasoning that (1) are actually decided, (2) are based upon the facts of the case, and (3) lead to the judgment. If not a holding, a proposition stated in a case counts as dicta." Abramowicz & Stearns, *Defining Dicta*, 57 Stan. L.Rev. 953, 961 (2005). See also Dorf, *Dicta and Article III*, U. Pa. L. Rev. 1997 (1994); Leval, *Judging Under the Constitution: Dicta About Dicta*, 81 N.Y.U. L. Rev. 1249 (2006).

5. What reasons might plaintiff in *Rush* have had for wishing to sue first on the claim for property damage and then separately for the personal injuries?

6. In making his decision, Judge Herbert in *Rush* applied the "transactional" test to determine whether plaintiff's claim was barred by the previous litigation. The transactional test currently is the most commonly used test for determining the preclusive effect of a prior judgment.

> * * * Under that test, the preclusive effect of a prior judgment extends to all rights the original plaintiff had "with respect to all or any part of the transaction, or series of connected transactions, out of which the [original] action arose." * * * What factual grouping constitutes a "transaction", and what groupings constitute a "series", are to be determined pragmatically, giving weight to such considerations as whether the facts are related in time, space, origin, or motivation, whether they form a convenient trial unit, and whether their treatment as a unit conforms to the parties' expectations or business understanding or usage. * * * "[T]he critical issue is whether the two actions under consideration are based on the *same nucleus of operative facts.*" * * *

Petro–Hunt, L.L.C. v. United States, 365 F.3d 385, 395–96 (5th Cir.2004) (internal citations omitted). The factors relied on in applying the transaction test are set out in Restatement (Second), Judgments § 24, comment *a* (1982).

7. The tests for determining the scope of claim preclusion have undergone a significant development since the beginning of the century. The Restatement (Second) of Judgments summarizes this transition:

> * * * In defining claim to embrace all the remedial rights of the plaintiff against the defendant growing out of the relevant transaction (or series of connected transactions), * * * [Section 24 of the Restatement (Second)] responds to modern procedural ideas which have found expression in the Federal Rules of Civil Procedure and other procedural systems.
>
> "Claim," in the context of res judicata, has never been broader than the transaction to which it related. But in the days when civil procedure still bore the imprint of the forms of action and the division between law and equity, the courts were prone to associate claim with a single theory of

> recovery, so that, with respect to one transaction, a plaintiff might have as many claims as there were theories of the substantive law upon which he could seek relief against the defendant. Thus, defeated in an action based on one theory, the plaintiff might be able to maintain another action based on a different theory, even though both actions were grounded upon the defendant's identical act or connected acts forming a single life-situation. In those earlier days there was also some adherence to a view that associated claim with the assertion of a single primary right as accorded by the substantive law, so that, if it appeared that the defendant had invaded a number of primary rights conceived to be held by the plaintiff, the plaintiff had the same number of claims, even though they all sprang from a unitary occurrence. There was difficulty in knowing which rights were primary and what was their extent, but a primary right and the corresponding claim might turn out to be narrow. Thus it was held by some courts that a judgment for or against the plaintiff in an action for personal injuries did not preclude an action by him for property damage occasioned by the same negligent conduct on the part of the defendant—this deriving from the idea that the right to be free of bodily injury was distinct from the property right. Still another view of claim looked to sameness of evidence; a second action was precluded where the evidence to support it was the same as that needed to support the first. Sometimes this was made the sole test of identity of claim; sometimes it figured as a positive but not as a negative test; that is, in certain situations a second action might be precluded although the evidence material to it varied from that in the first action. Even so, claim was not coterminous with the transaction itself.
>
> The present trend is to see claim in factual terms and to make it coterminous with the transaction regardless of the number of substantive theories, or variant forms of relief flowing from those theories, that may be available to the plaintiff; regardless of the number of primary rights that may have been invaded; and regardless of the variations in the evidence needed to support the theories or rights. The transaction is the basis of the litigative unit or entity which may not be split.

Restatement (Second), Judgments § 24, comment *a* (1982).

8. A party may waive the benefits of preclusion by failing to raise it as an affirmative defense in the second suit. Given the systemic interest in preclusion, should a court be able to raise preclusion on its own initiative? Would this be feasible?

MATHEWS v. NEW YORK RACING ASSOCIATION, INC.

United States District Court, Southern District of New York, 1961.
193 F.Supp. 293.

MACMAHON, DISTRICT JUDGE. Defendants move for summary judgment, pursuant to Rule 56(b), Federal Rules on [sic] Civil Procedure, on the ground that a judgment in a prior action in this court is res judicata as to the claim alleged in the complaint.

New York Racing Association Inc. is a New York corporation which operates Jamaica Race Track. It employs defendant Thoroughbred Racing

Protective Association Inc., a private detective agency, for security purposes.

Plaintiff brings this action against the Association and Thoroughbred alleging that on April 4, 1958, at Jamaica Race Track, he was "assaulted," "kidnapped," "falsely arrested," and "falsely imprisoned" by employees of Thoroughbred. He further alleges that the defendants charged him with disorderly conduct and maliciously caused him to be prosecuted and convicted in the Magistrate's Court of the City of New York on April 10, 1958. He prays for relief in the form of money damages and an injunction restraining the defendants from interfering with his attendance at race tracks, from publication of libelous statements, and from acting as peace officers.

The prior judgment on which defendants rely was entered in this court on June 30, 1960 following a trial before Judge Palmieri sitting without a jury. The complaint in that action alleged, among other matters, that plaintiff was assaulted by the defendant's private investigators at Jamaica Race Track on April 4, 1958. It also alleged that the employees of the defendants had made libelous statements concerning the plaintiff on several occasions, including plaintiff's trial for disorderly conduct on April 10, 1958. The relief prayed for in that action was also money damages and an injunction from further interference with plaintiff's attendance at race tracks within the United States. The earlier action named three individuals as defendants. The only two properly served were employees of the defendants named in the present suit.

* * *

* * * [T]he question is whether the claim alleged in this complaint is the same as that in the suit concluded earlier. The term "claim" refers to a group of facts limited to a single occurrence or transaction without particular reference to the resulting legal rights. It is the facts surrounding the occurrence which operate to make up the claim, not the legal theory upon which a plaintiff relies. * * *

* * *

The facts relevant to [plaintiff's current lawsuit] * * * along with three other separate claims based on different facts, were tried to a conclusion in the earlier suit. There, the plaintiff relied on the acts of the agents occurring on April 4, 1958 as the basis of a claim against them on the theory of assault. Now, he asserts these same acts as the basis of a claim against the agents' principals on the theory of false arrest. In the earlier action, plaintiff relied on the statements of the agents made on April 10, 1958 as the basis of a claim against them on the theory of libel. Now, he asserts those same statements as the basis of a claim against their principals on the theory of malicious prosecution. Clearly, any liability of the defendants for the acts or statements of their agents must be predicated upon the familiar principle of respondeat superior. Thus, if the agents committed no actionable wrong against the plaintiff, neither did their principals. * * *

* * *

The plaintiff cannot be permitted to splinter his claim into a multiplicity of suits and try them piecemeal at his convenience. * * * "The plaintiff having alleged operative facts which state a cause of action because he tells of defendant's misconduct and his own harm has had his day in court. He does not get another day after the first lawsuit is concluded by giving a different reason than he gave in the first for recovery of damages for the same invasion of his rights. The problem of his rights against the defendant based upon the alleged wrongful acts is fully before the court whether all the reasons for recovery were stated to the court or not." * * *

* * *

The court is cognizant of the fact that plaintiff appears pro se, but as the law provides a beginning for litigation, it must also provide an end. * * *

NOTES AND QUESTIONS

1. How would the different tests for determining a claim, see Note 7, p. 1257, supra, affect the reasoning in *Mathews*?

2. *Rush* and *Mathews* illustrate one of the primary purposes of the claim preclusion doctrine: to prevent the splitting of a single claim into two separate suits. In *Rush,* the plaintiff won her first suit for property damage, and the court held that any claims she had for personal injuries were "merged"—in other words, extinguished—in the first suit. In *Mathews,* the plaintiff had lost the first suit. Since the basic factual setting of the claim in the second suit was the same as in the first, the court held that the allegations were "barred" by the earlier judgment. By using a different definition of a "claim," could you make an argument that the second suit should not have been precluded?

3. *Rush* and *Mathews* used the transaction approach to determine the scope of the first suit's preclusive effect. One of the greatest advantages of this test is its flexibility. Yet, flexibility comes at a price. Because a court may interpret the claim presented in the first lawsuit more broadly than a litigant does, the litigant unknowingly may forfeit parts of his action by failing to raise them. For this reason litigants will learn "by trial and error in the harsh school of experience" of the need to raise all possibly connected allegations in the first proceeding. Cleary, *Res Judicata Reexamined*, 57 Yale L.J. 339, 340 (1948). This well may mean that they will advance claims that they otherwise might not have brought to court. Recall that in *Mathews*, the plaintiff was appearing pro se. Should the sophistication of the litigant be considered in deciding issues of claim preclusion?

4. In the federal system, the transaction test governs whether counterclaims are compulsory and whether supplemental jurisdiction may be exer-

cised. See p. 658 and p. 336, supra. Is the concept of a "transaction" the same in these two contexts? In defining what a transaction is, should it matter whether a judge is using supplemental jurisdiction to open the court to litigants, or invoking compulsory counterclaim and preclusion rules to shut litigants out of court?

5. Consider how the transaction test would affect the preclusive effect of a judgment in the following situations:

(a) An abused spouse sues for divorce. Does the divorce judgment bar her from filing a later tort action for spousal abuse? Should it matter whether the abuse was claimed as the basis for the divorce in the earlier suit? Compare McCoy v. Cooke, 165 Mich.App. 662, 419 N.W.2d 44 (Mich.Ct.App. 1988), with Shelar v. Shelar, 910 F.Supp. 1307 (N.D. Ohio 1995). See Dalton, *Domestic Violence, Domestic Torts and Divorce: Constraints and Possibilities*, 31 New Engl. L. Rev. 319, 378–94 (1997).

(b) An individual who was exposed to toxic chemicals sues for damages and seeks reimbursement for the expense of on-going medical monitoring. Years later, plaintiff learns that she has suffered greater physical injury than initially anticipated or diagnosed. Can she bring a new lawsuit? See In re St. Jude Medical, Inc. Silzone Heart Valves Prods. Liability Litigation, 2004 WL 45504 (D. Minn.2004). For a discussion of the impact of the transaction approach in cases of latent medical injury, see Note, *Claim Preclusion in Modern Latent Disease Cases: A Proposal for Allowing Second Suits*, 103 Harv.L.Rev.1989 (1990); Comment, *Medical Monitoring Plaintiffs and Subsequent Claims for Disease*, 66 U.Chi.L.Rev. 969 (1999).

FEDERATED DEPARTMENT STORES, INC. v. MOITIE, 452 U.S. 394, 101 S.Ct. 2424, 69 L.Ed.2d 103 (1981). Respondents Moitie and Brown were two of seven plaintiffs to file separate antitrust actions against petitioner (*Moitie I* and *Brown I*). The actions were consolidated in the District Court after which they were dismissed for failure to allege an "injury" to their "business or property" within the meaning of Section 4 of the Clayton Act. The other five plaintiffs appealed to the Ninth Circuit. Moitie and Brown, however, did not appeal, but, instead, refiled their actions in state court (*Moitie II* and *Brown II*). The actions were removed to federal court and then dismissed on res judicata grounds. Meanwhile, the five appeals cases were reversed and remanded to the District Court to be reconsidered in light of an intervening Supreme Court opinion. When *Moitie II* and *Brown II* reached the Ninth Circuit on appeal, the court held that, although a strict application of res judicata would preclude the second action, an exception should be made when the dismissal rested on a case that had been effectively overruled. The Supreme Court disagreed:

> The Court of Appeals * * * rested its opinion in part on what it viewed as "simple justice." But we do not see the grave injustice which would be done by the application of accepted principles of res judicata. "Simple justice" is achieved when a complex body of law

> developed over a period of years is evenhandedly applied. The doctrine of res judicata serves vital public interests beyond any individual judge's ad hoc determination of the equities in a particular case. There is simply "no principle of law or equity which sanctions the rejection by a federal court of the salutary principle of *res judicata.*" * * * The Court of Appeals' reliance on "public policy" is similarly misplaced. This Court has long recognized that "[p]ublic policy dictates that there be an end of litigation; that those who have contested an issue shall be bound by the result of the contest, and that matters once tried shall be considered forever settled as between the parties." Baldwin v. Traveling Men's Association, 283 U.S. 522, 525, 51 S.Ct. 517, 518, 75 L.Ed. 1244 (1931). We have stressed that "[the] doctrine of *res judicata* is not a mere matter of practice or procedure inherited from a more technical time than ours. It is a rule of fundamental and substantial justice, 'of public policy and of private peace,' which should be cordially regarded and enforced by the courts * * *." Hart Steel Co. v. Railroad Supply Co., 244 U.S. 294, 299, 37 S.Ct. 506, 507, 61 L.Ed. 1148 (1917). * * *

Id. at 401–02, 101 S.Ct. at 2429–30, 69 L.Ed.2d at 110–11.

NOTES AND QUESTIONS

1. In spite of the harsh language of *Moitie,* there are situations in which considerations of justice and fairness dictate that prior judgments not be given preclusive effect. When the prior judgment was obtained by the use of fraud, courts generally will not consider it binding. See, e.g., McCarty v. First of Georgia Ins. Co., 713 F.2d 609 (10th Cir.1983). Similarly, when there was a clear and fundamental jurisdictional defect that should have prevented the first court from hearing the suit, courts often will hold that the judgment has no preclusive effect.

2. What impact should an appeal have on the preclusive effect of a trial court's judgment? See, e.g., Crawford v. Chabot, 202 F.R.D. 223 (W.D. Mich. 1998), affirmed without opinion 229 F.3d 1151 (6th Cir.2000). Federal courts grant preclusion pending appeal of an underlying judgment, but state rules vary. Suppose the appeals court remands the initial judgment for retrial. Does the initial judgment retain any preclusive effect? What if the appellate opinion overrules the legal basis underlying the initial judgment? See Federal Rule 60(b)(5); 18A Wright, Miller & Cooper, Federal Practice and Procedure: Jurisdiction and Related Matters 2d § 4433.

3. In *Moitie*, the defendants removed the actions to federal court on the basis of federal question jurisdiction, and the cases subsequently were dismissed due to the preclusive effect of the prior judgment. In a similar case, Rivet v. Regions Bank, 522 U.S. 470, 118 S.Ct. 921, 139 L.Ed.2d 912 (1998), the dispute involved only state issues, but the defendants, relying on *Moitie*, sought to remove the case to federal court on the ground that the plaintiff's action was precluded by a prior federal judgment. The United States Supreme Court rejected this interpretation of *Moitie*, holding that claim preclusion does not create an exception to the rule that a defendant cannot remove on the

basis of a federal defense under Section 1441(b). On *Moitie*, see generally Miller, *Artful Pleading: A Doctrine in Search of Definition*, 76 Texas L. Rev. 1781 (1998).

JONES v. MORRIS PLAN BANK OF PORTSMOUTH

Supreme Court of Appeals of Virginia, 1937.
168 Va. 284, 191 S.E. 608.

GREGORY, JUSTICE.

William B. Jones instituted an action for damages against the Morris Plan Bank of Portsmouth for the conversion of his automobile. * * *

After the plaintiff had introduced all of his evidence and before the defendant had introduced any evidence on its behalf, the latter's counsel moved to strike the evidence of the plaintiff and the court sustained the motion. A verdict for the defendant resulted.

The facts are that the plaintiff purchased from J.A. Parker, a dealer in automobiles, a Plymouth sedan, agreeing to pay therefor $595. He paid a part of the purchase price by the delivery of a used car to Parker of the agreed value of $245 and after crediting that amount on the purchase price and adding a finance charge of $78.40, there remained an unpaid balance due the dealer of $428. This latter amount was payable in 12 monthly installments of $35.70 each and evidenced by one note in the principal sum of $428.40. The note contained this provision: "The whole amount of this note (less any payments made hereon) becomes immediately due and payable in the event of nonpayment at maturity of any installment thereof." The note was secured by the usual conditional sales contract * * * in which it was agreed that the title to the car would be retained by the dealer until the entire purchase price was paid in full. * * * [T]he contract was assigned to the defendant * * * and the note was indorsed by Parker and delivered to the defendant at the same time.

Installment payments due on the note for May and June were not made when payable and for them an action was instituted in the civil and police court of the city of Suffolk. No appearance was made by the defendant (Jones) in that action and judgment was obtained against him for the two payments. Execution issued upon the judgment and it was satisfied * * * by Jones * * *.

Later the defendant instituted another action against Jones in the same court for the July installment which had become due and was unpaid, and to that action Jones filed a plea of res adjudicata, whereupon the * * * [Bank] took a nonsuit.

* * * [T]he defendant * * * took possession of the automobile without the consent of the plaintiff and later sold it and applied the proceeds upon the note.

Afterwards, the plaintiff instituted the present action for conversion to recover damages for the loss of the automobile. His action in the court below was founded upon the theory that when the May and June installments became due and were unpaid, then under the acceleration clause in the note, the entire balance due thereon matured and at once became due and the defendant having elected to sue him for only two installments instead of the entire amount of the note, and having obtained a judgment for the two installments and satisfaction of the execution issued thereon, it waived its right to collect the balance. He also contends that the note was satisfied in the manner narrated and that the conditional sales contract, the sole purpose of which was to secure the payment of the note, served its purpose and ceased to exist, and, therefore, the title to the automobile was no longer retained, but upon the satisfaction of the note, passed to the plaintiff and was his property when the agent of the defendant removed it and converted it to its own use.

The position of the defendant is that * * * the title to the automobile, which was the subject of the alleged conversion, was not vested in the plaintiff at the time of the action, nor since, because the condition in the contract was that the title should be retained by the seller (whose rights were assigned to the defendant) until the entire purchase price was paid, and that the purchase price had never been paid * * *.

The defendant also contends that the note and conditional sales contract were divisible; that successive actions could be brought upon the installments as they matured; and that it was not bound, at the risk of waiving its right to claim the balance, to sue for all installments in one action.

* * *

We decide that under the unconditional acceleration provision in the note involved here and in the absence of the usual optional provision reserved to the holder, the entire amount due upon the note became due and payable when default was made in paying an installment. * * *

Was it essential that the defendant here institute an action for all of the installments then due, or could it institute its action for only two of the installments and later institute another action for other installments? The answer to that question depends upon the nature of the transaction. If a transaction is represented by one single and indivisible contract and the breach gives rise to one single cause of action, it cannot be split into distinct parts and separate actions maintained for each.

On the other hand, if the contract is divisible giving rise to more than one cause of action, each may be proceeded upon separately.

Was the contract here single and indivisible or was it divisible? Our answer is that the note and conditional sales contract constituted one single contract. The sole purpose of the conditional sales contract was to retain the title in the seller until the note was paid. When that condition was performed, the contract ended.

One of the principal tests in determining whether a demand is single and entire, or whether it is several, so as to give rise to more than one cause of action, is the identity of facts necessary to maintain the action. If the same evidence will support both actions, there is but one cause of action.

In the case at bar, all of the installments were due. The evidence essential to support the action on the two installments for which the action was brought would be the identical evidence necessary to maintain an action upon all of the installments. All installments having matured at the time the action was begun, under well-settled principles, those not embraced in that action are now barred.

* * * At the time the defendant lost its right to institute any action for the remaining installments, the title to the automobile passed to the plaintiff. He was the owner at the time the agent of the defendant took possession of it and exposed it to sale.

It follows that the judgment of the court below will be reversed, and the case will be remanded for the sole purpose of determining the quantum of damages.

Reversed and remanded.

NOTES AND QUESTIONS

1. In AIGLON ASSOCIATES, LTD. v. ALLAN, 248 Va. 150, 445 S.E.2d 138 (1994), the Virginia Supreme Court considered the question of whether an acceleration clause in a lease required the plaintiff to claim all future rent payments due in the first suit or be barred by res judicata. The relevant portions of the lease agreement read as follows:

> SECTION 22.01: *Right to Reenter*. In the event of any failure of Tenant to pay any rental due hereunder . . . the Tenant shall be in default of this Lease, and the Landlord, besides other rights or remedies it may have, shall have the immediate right of reentry * * *.
>
> SECTION 22.02: *Right to Relet*. Should the Landlord elect to reenter * * * *it may either terminate this Lease or it* . . . may relet the leased premises * * *. *No such reentry or taking possession of the leased premises by Landlord shall be construed as an election on its part to terminate this Lease unless a written notice of such intention be given to Tenant* * * *. Should Landlord at any time terminate this Lease for any breach * * * it may recover from Tenant all damages it may incur by reason of such breach, including * * * the amount of rent and charges equivalent to rent reserved in this Lease for the remainder of the stated term * * *.

Id. at 150, 445 S.E.2d at 139 (emphasis in original). The court held the mandatory acceleration clause applied only upon termination of the lease, so a second suit on these facts was not barred. The court remanded to the trial court for the purpose of determining damages. In *Jones* and in *Aiglon*, why did the court remand only for the purpose of determining damages rather than order a new trial?

2. When a debt is secured by a series of notes or when a bond includes a number of interest coupons, an action on one of the notes or coupons, even

though others are due, does not bar a subsequent action on those others. Restatement, Judgments § 62, comment i (1942); Restatement (Second), Judgments § 24, comment d (1982). Cf. NESBIT v. RIVERSIDE INDEPENDENT DISTRICT, 144 U.S. 610, 619, 12 S.Ct. 746, 748, 36 L.Ed. 562, 565 (1892):

> Each matured coupon is a separable promise, and gives rise to a separate cause of action. It may be detached from the bond and sold by itself. Indeed, the title to several matured coupons of the same bond may be in as many different persons, and upon each a distinct and separate action be maintained. So, while the promises of the bond and of the coupons in the first instance are upon the same paper, and the coupons are for interest due upon the bond, yet the promise to pay the coupon is as distinct from that to pay the bond as though the two promises were placed in different instruments, upon different paper.

3. It is difficult to define the scope of a prior judgment in controversies involving continuing or renewed conduct. The Restatement (Second) of Judgments lists some considerations relevant to determining whether a factual grouping constitutes a single transaction, and suggests evaluating "whether the facts are related in time, space, origin, or motivation, whether they form a convenient trial unit, and whether their treatment as a unit conforms to the parties' expectations or business understanding or usage." See Restatement (Second), Judgments § 24 (1982).

There are some other useful rules of thumb to be used in cases of continuing or renewed conduct. For example, if the conduct that is the subject of the first action continues after judgment in the first action, claim preclusion would not prevent a second suit. Issue preclusion may apply, however, to matters of status or to issues of fact resolved in the first action. When the purpose of the first suit is to establish general rules of legality, such as when the first suit is a declaratory judgment action, subsequent claims involving the same conduct are precluded.

Nuisance suits commonly involve continuing conduct. Judgments involving "permanent" nuisances are considered to have full preclusive effect; those involving "temporary" nuisances are not considered to preclude later litigation involving the same behavior. Courts are not always consistent in their classification of nuisances. For a further discussion of claims that involve continuing and renewed conduct, see 18 Wright, Miller & Cooper, Federal Practice and Procedure: Jurisdiction and Related Matters 2d § 4409.

4. As the previous Notes suggest, often the underlying substantive law will affect the definition of the claim for the purposes of preclusion. For example, if one party to a contract commits a material breach that is neither accompanied nor followed by a repudiation, the law of contracts teaches that the other party is free, on the one hand, to treat the contract as binding and sue for the damages or, on the other hand, to treat the contract as ended. If the aggrieved party chooses the former option and then suffers further material breaches, she will not be barred from suing for damages not sought in the first suit. See Restatement (Second), Judgments § 26, comment g (1982).

The expectations of the parties also may be decisive in determining the scope of the prior judgment. Imagine that a wholesale distributor regularly ships goods to a retailer on credit. If the parties conceive of their relationship as a series of discrete transactions, a suit by the creditor seeking to recover any one of the payments would not bar subsequent suits for other payments. If, however, the parties believe they have a single running account, the creditor would have to seek to recover the entire balance then due.

2. DEFENSE PRECLUSION

Thus far we have looked at claim preclusion from the perspective of the plaintiff. However, defendants also need to take the doctrine into account, typically in one of three situations:

> The first two situations involve a second action in which a former defendant seeks to advance a claim against the original plaintiff. In one, the claim involves matters that were not advanced in the first action; in the other, the claim involves matters that were advanced in the first action but are not foreclosed by issue preclusion. The third situation involves a second action by the original plaintiff in which the defendant seeks to raise defenses that were equally available in the first action but were not advanced there.

18 Wright, Miller & Cooper, Federal Practice and Procedure: Jurisdiction and Related Matters 2d § 4414. "The third situation" is referred to as "defense preclusion," and the scope of the doctrine is implicated in the case that follows.

MITCHELL v. FEDERAL INTERMEDIATE CREDIT BANK

Supreme Court of South Carolina, 1932.
165 S.C. 457, 164 S.E. 136.

[An action for an accounting against defendant bank for proceeds of a crop of potatoes. Plaintiff alleged that in order to obtain loans from defendant he had—at the behest of defendant's agent—sold his potatoes through a growers' association and assigned the proceeds as security for two notes, totaling $9,000, which had been discounted with defendant; that the potatoes had netted $18,000, but that he had never received any of this, and that the proceeds had been received by defendant or an agent of defendant. In a previous action by defendant on the notes, plaintiff had pleaded in the answer the same facts now the basis of an affirmative claim, but had not counterclaimed or asked relief; judgment had been for him in that action. In the present suit, defendant contended that plaintiff's claim was merged in the earlier judgment. This contention was upheld by the trial court.]

STABLER, J. * * *

We now come to the main question presented by the appeal, namely, Was the circuit judge in error in sustaining the plea in bar to plaintiff's action? Turning to appellant's answer in the federal court case * * * we find that the facts there pleaded by him as a defense to the bank's recovery on its notes are the same as those set out by him in his complaint as the basis of his action in the case at bar, it being alleged that the total amount paid to the bank was in excess of all sums advanced to him on the notes or otherwise, and as a result of the transaction the notes sued upon were fully paid and discharged. In addition, we find in the record of the case before us the following statement by appellant as an admission of fact on his part: "* * * The indebtedness of the bank to Mitchell arising from the embezzlement of the proceeds of the crop was used pro tanto as an offset to the claim of the bank in the Federal Court. The case at bar seeks recovery of the surplusage, over the offset, of the proceeds of the same crop lost by the same embezzlement. The appellant, however, is not seeking to recover in this action the same money that has already been used as an offset."

* * *

In support of his position * * * appellant cites certain decisions of this court, which he claims to be conclusive of the issue, relying especially upon Kirven v. Chemical Co., 77 S.C. 493, 58 S.E. 424, 426.

* * * [T]he record shows that Kirven had bought from the Chemical Company $2,228 worth of fertilizers and had given his note for that amount. The company, upon maturity of the note, brought action against him on his obligation. He at first filed an answer setting up three defenses, the third of which was that the fertilizers furnished were deleterious and destructive to the crops, and that there was an entire failure of consideration for the note. Later, he was permitted to file a supplemental answer in which he withdrew the third defense. On trial in the federal court, the jury rendered a verdict for the Chemical Company. Thereafter, Kirven brought an action against the company * * * alleging that the defendant caused damage to his crop in the sum of $1,995 by reason of the deleterious effect of the fertilizers furnished. The company set up the defense that the issues in this action were or could have been adjudicated in the [first] suit * * *. A verdict was given Kirven in the amount prayed for, and on appeal * * * it was pointed out that the question raised in the state court was not *actually* litigated and determined in the federal action, and it appears that the court, for that reason, took the view that a bar or estoppel did not exist. Mr. Justice Woods, in his concurring opinion, took the view that, as Kirven elected not to use, as a defense, the fact of *worthlessness,* which might have been available in the action of the company against him, "he was not precluded from using the very different facts of deleteriousness and positive injury caused by appellant's alleged negligence in the manufacture of the fertilizer as the basis of an independent cause of action."

We think the facts of the case at bar, however, present a different situation. * * *

O'Connor v. Varney, 10 Gray (Mass.) 231, was an action on contract to recover damages for Varney's failure to build certain additions to a house according to the terms of a written agreement between the parties. The defendant set up as a defense "a judgment recovered by O'Connor in an action brought by Varney against him on that contract to recover the price therein agreed to be paid for the work, in defence of which O'Connor relied on the same nonperformance by Varney, and in which an auditor to whom the case was referred * * * found that Varney was not entitled to recover under the agreement," as the work had been so imperfectly done that it would require a greater sum than the amount sued for to make it correspond with the contract. At the trial of the second action, the trial judge ruled that the judgment in the first suit was a bar, and directed a verdict for the defendant. The plaintiff O'Connor thereupon appealed.

Chief Justice Shaw, who rendered the opinion of the court, said: "The presiding judge rightly ruled that the former judgment was a bar to this action. A party against whom an action is brought on a contract has two modes of defending himself. He may allege specific breaches of the contract declared upon, and rely on them in defence. But if he intends to claim, by way of damages for nonperformance of the contract, more than the amount for which he is sued, he must not rely on the contract in defence, but must bring a cross action, and apply to the court to have the cases continued so that the executions may be set off. He cannot use the same defence, first as a shield, and then as a sword. * * *"

It will be noted that Varney was not entitled to recover in the first suit because his dereliction amounted to more than he sued for. This would seem to be exactly the situation in the case at bar.

* * * When the bank sued * * * [Mitchell] on his two notes, amounting to about $9,000, he had the option to interpose his claim as a defense to that suit or to demand judgment against the bank, by way of counterclaim, for the amount owing him by it. * * * The transaction out of which the case at bar arises is the same transaction that Mitchell pleaded as a defense in the federal suit. He might, therefore, "have recovered in that action, upon the same allegations and proofs which he there made, the judgment which he now seeks, if he had prayed for it." He did not do this, but attempted to split his cause of action, and to use one portion of it for defense in that suit and to reserve the remainder for offense in a subsequent suit, which, under applicable principles, could not be done. * * *

The judgment of the circuit court is affirmed.

NOTES AND QUESTIONS

1. The federal courts and all but nine states require a party to include a compulsory counterclaim in the answer. See Federal Rule 13(a); Peterson, *The Misguided Law of Compulsory Counterclaims in Default Cases*, 50 Ariz. L. Rev. 1107, 1108–09 (2008). Can a party raise the omitted claim in a separate

action? Professor Wright has written that "it has never been doubted in any of the jurisdictions which have adopted such a rule that the pleader who fails to comply therewith is prohibited from subsequent assertion of his claim." Wright, *Estoppel by Rule: The Compulsory Counterclaim Under Modern Pleading*, 38 Minn. L. Rev. 423, 449 n.121 (1954). See, e.g., May v. Exxon Corp., 256 Ark. 865, 867, 512 S.W.2d 11, 12 (1974) ("Failure to plead the counterclaim is res judicata."). Is the preclusion a result of waiver or res judicata?

2. At common law, would Mitchell's defense in the first action have been in the nature of a recoupment or a set-off? Consider the following definitions:

> At common law the term "recoupment" described a claim that defendant could assert against plaintiff only if it arose from the same transaction as plaintiff's claim. It was purely defensive in its character and could be used only to defeat or diminish plaintiff's recovery; recoupment could not be the basis for affirmative relief. "Setoff," on the other hand, referred to a claim by defendant that was unrelated to plaintiff's claim. Moreover, unlike recoupment, setoff permitted defendant to assert an affirmative claim for relief. But the utility of setoff was limited by the requirement that the claim either be for a liquidated amount or arise out of a contract of judgment.

6 Wright, Miller & Kane, Federal Practice and Procedure: Civil 2d § 1401. Assuming that the defense would have been one or the other, would this have made a difference as to Mitchell's right to bring a later suit for the excess?

LINDERMAN MACHINE CO. v. HILLENBRAND CO., 75 Ind.App. 111, 127 N.E. 813 (1920). L sold H a machine, and subsequently sued to recover the purchase price. H answered that the contract had been obtained by fraudulent representations as to the machine's capacity to do H's work, that the machine did not perform as represented, and that H had notified L to remove the machine. Judgment was rendered against L. Subsequently H sued L to recover damages for fraud, alleging that H had incurred great expense in transporting, installing, attempting to operate, and removing the machine. L answered that the action was barred by the judgment in the first suit. The court held for H:

> It is true that a party, when sued, must interpose all defenses which he has, and as to them, whether pleaded or not, the judgment is conclusive; but it is not conclusive as to an affirmative right or cause of action which he may have against the plaintiff, and of which he could have taken advantage by way of cross-complaint. He is not compelled to file his cross-complaint, and, on his failure to do so, his rights with reference thereto will not be adjudged. * * *
>
> There was no issue in the action brought by [L] to recover the purchase price * * * as to the right of [H] to recover the expenses which it had been put to in installing the machinery, and without

> such issue therein, [L] is not in position now to invoke against [H] the doctrine of res adjudicata.

Id. at 118, 127 N.E. at 815.

NOTES AND QUESTIONS

1. Is *Linderman* consistent with *Mitchell*? Notice that generally defendant's failure to raise a counterclaim that is not compulsory does not preclude a later action. See Harrison v. Springdale Water & Sewer Commission, 780 F.2d 1422 (8th Cir.1986). However, the rule is more complicated when the claim that defendant seeks to assert would undermine the basis of a prior judgment. In these cases, some federal courts apply a judicially created rule of preclusion "to protect the repose established by the original judgment against effective destruction in a later action by the former defendant." 18 Wright, Miller & Cooper, Federal Practice and Procedure: Jurisdiction and Related Matters 2d § 4414. As the Seventh Circuit explained in RUDELL v. COMPREHENSIVE ACCOUNTING CORP., 802 F.2d 926 (7th Cir.1986), certiorari denied 480 U.S. 907, 107 S.Ct. 1351, 94 L.Ed.2d 521 (1987):

> * * * The long-standing principles of *res judicata* establish a narrowly defined class of "common law compulsory counterclaims," and in limited circumstances failure to raise such counterclaims or related defenses in previous proceedings *does* constitute a bar to related claims being raised later. * * *
>
> *Both precedent and policy require that res judicata bar a counterclaim when its prosecution would nullify rights established by the prior action.* Judicial economy is not the only basis for the doctrine of res judicata. Res judicata also preserves the integrity of judgments and protects those who rely on them.

Id. at 928 (internal quotations omitted) (emphasis in original). See also International Ambassador Programs, Inc. v. Archexpo, 68 F.3d 337 (9th Cir.1995), certiorari denied 517 U.S. 1167, 116 S.Ct. 1567, 134 L.Ed.2d 666 (1996). For a comprehensive discussion, see Clermont, *Common-Law Compulsory Counterclaim Rule: Creating Effective and Elegant Res Judicata*, 79 Notre Dame L. Rev. 1745 (2004).

2. The common law compulsory counterclaim rule also applies in state systems. Consider JACOBSON v. MILLER, 41 Mich. 90, 1 N.W. 1013 (1879). A landlord brought and prevailed on an action to recover unpaid installments of rent. Subsequently, the landlord brought another suit to recover later unpaid installments. Although he had made no mention of a defense in the initial proceeding, the tenant sought to defend the second suit by alleging that he had never executed the lease. Should the court have permitted the defense to be made? Remember that if the defendant had raised this claim in the first action successfully, the landlord could have taken affirmative steps to remedy the problem, and perhaps even could have found a new tenant. See generally 18 Wright, Miller & Cooper, Federal Practice and Procedure: Jurisdiction and Related Matters 2d § 4414; Restatement (Second), Judgments § 22 (1982).

3. Section 20(1) of Restatement (Second) of Judgments sets forth certain valid and final judgments that are not preclusive: (a) dismissal for lack of jurisdiction, dismissal for improper venue, dismissal for nonjoinder or misjoinder of parties; and (b) election or direction of a nonsuit. The list set out in Section 20(1) is not exhaustive. How should dismissals that are not expressly listed be treated? Should a dismissal be considered an adjudication on the merits if the "defendant must incur the inconvenience of preparing to meet the merits because there is no initial bar to the Court's reaching them"? Costello v. United States, 365 U.S. 265, 287, 81 S.Ct. 534, 545, 5 L.Ed.2d 551, 565 (1961). For instance, in RINEHART v. LOCKE, 454 F.2d 313 (7th Cir.1971), the Seventh Circuit concluded that a dismissal for failure to state a claim precluded a subsequent suit on the claim plaintiff apparently "was attempting to state." This conclusion places upon plaintiff the burden of either persuading the district court to allow an amendment to the complaint or appealing the district court's judgment. Do you think this is an appropriate rule?

SECTION C. ISSUE PRECLUSION

One of the most frequently quoted descriptions of what once was called collateral estoppel and is now referred to as issue preclusion was provided by the first Justice Harlan in SOUTHERN PACIFIC RAILROAD CO. v. UNITED STATES, 168 U.S. 1, 48–49, 18 S.Ct. 18, 27, 42 L.Ed. 355, 377 (1897):

> The general principle announced in numerous cases is that a right, question, or fact distinctly put in issue and directly determined by a court of competent jurisdiction, as a ground of recovery, cannot be disputed in a subsequent suit between the same parties or their privies; and, even if the second suit is for a different cause of action, the right, question, or fact once so determined must, as between the same parties or their privies, be taken as conclusively established, so long as the judgment in the first suit remains unmodified.

As this passage reveals, there is a critical difference between claim preclusion and issue preclusion. Under the doctrine of claim preclusion, a claim may be "merged" or "barred" by a party's failure to raise the claim in a prior action. Issue preclusion, however, applies only to matters argued and decided in an earlier lawsuit.

For issue preclusion to exist, a proceeding must involve the same issue as a previous suit. The term "issue," like the term "transaction" in the context of claim preclusion, is ambiguous and subject to manipulation. And, the application *vel non* of doctrines of issue preclusion sometimes will turn on the ability of advocates to manipulate the definition of this crucial term.

To trigger the doctrine of issue preclusion, however, more than a mere duplication of issues is required. It is necessary to examine the nature of the first action and the treatment that the issue received in it. Just as for claim preclusion, the judgment in the first action must have been of a certain "quality"—that is, it must have been valid, final, and on the merits (the "on the merits" requirement does not apply if the issue being precluded is exclusively a procedural issue). Moreover, the issue raised in a second suit actually must have been litigated in the first action, and must have been decided by the first court. And, determination of that issue must have been necessary to the court's judgment.

Some courts require still more before they will allow a party to invoke issue preclusion. For example, some demand that the issue have occupied a high position in the hierarchy of legal rules applied in the first action—that it was important. Others require "mutuality"—that is, that the party invoking preclusion would have been bound by an unfavorable judgment in the first suit. Fewer and fewer courts now impose these latter two conditions, however, and the mutuality requirement in particular is now widely disregarded.

Issue preclusion can be used in a variety of ways. It can be invoked offensively, when the plaintiff in the second action seeks to preclude litigation of an issue that was decided favorably to him in a prior action. Or, it can be used defensively, when the defendant in the second suit seeks to preclude relitigation of an issue that was decided in his favor in a prior suit. Some courts and commentators further distinguish between "direct" and "collateral" preclusion or estoppel—depending upon whether the second proceeding involves the same cause of action as the first. When the two suits involve the same cause of action, issue preclusion sometimes is referred to as direct estoppel. When the second suit involves a new claim or cause of action, issue preclusion sometimes is referred to as collateral estoppel.

1. ACTUALLY LITIGATED

CROMWELL v. COUNTY OF SAC

Supreme Court of the United States, 1876.
94 U.S. (4 Otto) 351, 24 L.Ed. 195.

Error to the Circuit Court of the United States for the District of Iowa.

MR. JUSTICE FIELD delivered the opinion of the court.

This was an action on four bonds * * * each for $1,000, and four coupons for interest, attached to them, each for $100. The bonds were issued in 1860, and were made payable to bearer, in the city of New York, in the years 1868, 1869, 1870, and 1871, respectively, with annual interest at the rate of ten per cent a year.

To defeat this action, the defendant relied upon the estoppel of a judgment rendered in favor of the county in a prior action brought by one Samuel C. Smith upon certain earlier maturing coupons on the same bonds, accompanied with proof that the plaintiff Cromwell was at the time the owner of the coupons in that action, and that the action was prosecuted for his sole use and benefit.

* * *

In considering the operation of this judgment, it should be borne in mind * * * that there is a difference between the effect of a judgment as a bar or estoppel against the prosecution of a second action upon the same claim or demand, and its effect as an estoppel in another action between the same parties upon a different claim or cause of action. In the former case, the judgment, if rendered upon the merits, constitutes an absolute bar to a subsequent action. [The Court's description of claim preclusion appears at pp. 1250–51, supra.] * * * The language * * * which is so often used, that a judgment estops not only as to every ground of recovery or defence actually presented in the action, but also as to every ground which might have been presented, is strictly accurate, when applied to the demand or claim in controversy. * * *

But where the second action between the same parties is upon a different claim or demand, the judgment in the prior action operates as an estoppel only as to those matters in issue or points controverted, upon the determination of which the finding or verdict was rendered. In all cases, therefore, where it is sought to apply the estoppel of a judgment rendered upon one cause of action to matters arising in a suit upon a different cause of action, the inquiry must always be as to the point or question actually litigated and determined in the original action, not what might have been thus litigated and determined. Only upon such matters is the judgment conclusive in another action.

The difference in the operation of a judgment in the two classes of cases mentioned is seen through all the leading adjudications upon the doctrine of estoppel. Thus, in the case of Outram v. Morewood, 3 East, 346, the defendants were held estopped from averring title to a mine, in an action of trespass for digging out coal from it, because, in a previous action for a similar trespass, they had set up the same title, and it had been determined against them. In commenting upon a decision cited in that case, Lord Ellenborough, in his elaborate opinion, said: "It is not the recovery, but the matter alleged by the party, and upon which the recovery proceeds, which creates the estoppel. The recovery of itself in an action of trespass is only a bar to the future recovery of damages for the same injury; but the estoppel precludes parties and privies from contending to the contrary of that point or matter of fact, which, having been once distinctly put in issue by them, or by those to whom they are privy in estate or law, has been, on such issue joined, solemnly found against them."

* * *

Various considerations, other than the actual merits, may govern a party in bringing forward grounds of recovery or defence in one action, which may not exist in another action upon a different demand, such as the smallness of the amount or the value of the property in controversy, the difficulty of obtaining the necessary evidence, the expense of the litigation, and his own situation at the time. A party acting upon considerations like these ought not to be precluded from contesting in a subsequent action other demands arising out of the same transaction. * * *

If, now, we consider the main question presented for our determination * * * its solution will not be difficult. It appears from the findings in the original action of Smith, that the county of Sac, by a vote of its people, authorized the issue of bonds to the amount of $10,000, for the erection of a court-house; that bonds to that amount were issued by the county judge, and delivered to one Meserey, with whom he had made a contract for the erection of the court-house; that immediately upon receipt of the bonds the contractor gave one of them as a gratuity to the county judge; and that the court-house was never constructed by the contractor, or by any other person pursuant to the contract. It also appears that the plaintiff had become, before their maturity, the holder of twenty-five coupons, which had been attached to the bonds, but there was no finding that he had ever given any value for them. * * * The case coming here on writ of error, this court held that the facts disclosed by the findings were sufficient evidence of fraud and illegality in the inception of the bonds to call upon the holder to show that he had given value for the coupons; and, not having done so, the judgment was affirmed. Reading the record of the lower court by the opinion and judgment of this court, it must be considered that the matters adjudged in that case were these: that the bonds were void as against the county in the hands of parties who did not acquire them before maturity and give value for them, and that the plaintiff, not having proved that he gave such value, was not entitled to recover upon the coupons. * * * The finding and judgment upon the invalidity of the bonds, as against the county, must be held to estop the plaintiff here from averring to the contrary. But as the bonds were negotiable instruments * * * they would be held as valid obligations against the county in the hands of a *bona fide* holder taking them for value before maturity * * *. If, therefore, the plaintiff received the bond and coupons in suit before maturity for value, as he offered to prove, he should have been permitted to show that fact. There was nothing adjudged in the former action in the finding that the plaintiff had not made such proof in that case which can preclude the present plaintiff from making such proof here. The fact that a party may not have shown that he gave value for one bond or coupon is not even presumptive, much less conclusive, evidence that he may not have given value for another and different bond or coupon. The exclusion of the evidence offered by the plaintiff was erroneous * * *.

Judgment reversed, and cause remanded for a new trial.

[The dissenting opinion of JUSTICE CLIFFORD is omitted.]

NOTES AND QUESTIONS

1. Section 27 of the Restatement (Second) of Judgments (1982) adopts the actually litigated requirement. What are the reasons supporting this approach? Are you persuaded that these justifications are sound? Consider this criticism of the doctrine:

> * * * [One argument made in favor of the actually litigated requirement is] that an action may involve "so small an amount that litigation of the issue may cost more than the value of the lawsuit." [Restatement (Second), Judgments § 27, comment *e* (1982).] * * * This is a rather curious rationale. It does not support the "actually litigated" requirement; rather it supports a rejection of issue preclusion under any circumstances. If there is insufficient incentive to litigate a matter, then there should be no issue preclusion. Litigation in small claims courts or prosecutions for misdemeanors cannot give rise to issue preclusion because often those actions provide litigants with inadequate incentive to litigate. Although the line is not clearly defined, it seems reasonable to conclude that prosecutions for felonies and civil litigation involving substantial amounts will give rise to issue preclusion. The burden properly falls on the presumably precluded party to show why issue preclusion should not apply.
>
> * * * [A second argument used to justify the actually litigated requirement is] that "the forum may be an inconvenient one in which to produce the necessary evidence or in which to litigate at all." [Id.] If a valid judgment is going to be handed down, then this forum must have jurisdiction over the defendant and it is the forum of choice of the plaintiff. As the forum of choice of the plaintiff, it is proper to hold that the plaintiff should be bound by any adverse decision reached by the court. It is only in the case of the defendant that he might be able to assert that he should not be bound because it is inconvenient.
>
> In light of (a) the present constitutional limitations on the exercise of jurisdiction over defendants, (b) the fact that the suit by definition involves a substantial interest, and (c) the availability of procedures to get and present the relevant evidence, this justification is not very persuasive. Would it not be better to hold for issue preclusion, and then permit the apparently precluded party to explain why preclusion should not apply?
>
> The [Restatement's] Comment also gives as a reason for the "actually litigated" rule that a rule to the contrary "might serve to discourage compromise, to decrease the likelihood that the issues in an action would be narrowed by stipulation, and thus to intensify litigation." Id. This litigation, where there is the incentive to litigate, must involve substantial interests on the part of the parties. The issue preclusion that may flow from the judgment does not change the suit from unimportant to important. The suit is, by definition, important. If a compromise is going to be discouraged, it probably will be by the size of the present suit. If there is going to be a refusal to stipulate and thus narrow issues, in all

> probability it will be because of the importance of the instant suit and not because of the issue preclusion that may flow from the decision.

Vestal, *The Restatement (Second) of Judgments: A Modest Dissent,* 66 Cornell L.Rev. 464, 473–74 (1981).

2. Should an issue be considered actually litigated simply because it is included in the pleadings? Consider this analysis:

> A good case can be made for saying that if a matter is distinctly put in issue and formally admitted, the party making the admission should be bound by it in subsequent litigation. This was the old formulation of the rule of "judicial estoppel," as it was then called: "The former verdict is conclusive only as to facts directly and distinctly put in issue * * *." But how can a matter be "directly and distinctly put in issue"? Obviously, by actual litigation. Another way is through pleadings. In a pleading system where matters are "distinctly put in issue," it makes sense to say that if a proposition is clearly asserted, and if a party is called upon solemnly to admit or deny the proposition, and if the stakes are high enough to assure that the party is serious in dealing with the issue, and if the party then admits or fails to deny the proposition, then he ought to be estopped from controverting it on some other occasion, particularly if that other occasion involves essentially the same transaction. The clearest case for such an estoppel is where a defendant pleads guilty to a substantial criminal charge and then seeks in civil litigation concerning the same transaction to assert that he did not commit the criminal act. Particularly galling is the situation where a criminal convicted on his own guilty plea seeks as plaintiff in a subsequent civil action to claim redress based on a repudiation of the confession. * * *
>
> The same principle could apply when an issue is put forward and admitted "distinctly"—that is, clearly and solemnly—in a civil case. It is therefore appropriate to impose an estoppel based on a formal admission in a civil case, and the law of evidence does so. A judicial admission is considered in subsequent litigations as prima facie evidence that the admitted matter is true.
>
> * * *
>
> Professor Vestal says there should be an estoppel because, where there is an incentive to deny, failure to deny constitutes an admission. This turns the notion of incentive to litigate on its head. The "incentive to litigate" formula, as used in most of the cases and in the *Restatement Second,* allows a party who *did* litigate an issue to relitigate it if the party can show that the original litigation was a side show rather than a struggle to the finish. [See *Restatement (Second), Judgments* § 28, comment *j* (1982).] The *Restatement Second* allows a party to rebut the inference naturally drawn from the fact that the issue was actually litigated—the inference that the party had treated the issue with entire seriousness in the first litigation. In Professor Vestal's system, however, "incentive to litigate" allows a court to conjecture that the party probably had reason to litigate the issue in the first action, and to conjecture further that the failure to litigate is an admission of a proposition not litigated. Professor

> Vestal's "opportunity" theory allows the court to infer that the issue was important to a party whose behavior indicates he thought the issue was unimportant, and, having done that, to convict the party by his silence.
> * * *

Hazard, *Revisiting the Second Restatement of Judgments: Issue Preclusion and Related Problems*, 66 Cornell L.Rev. 564, 577–79, 584 (1981).

3. What is the preclusive effect of a guilty plea in a subsequent civil lawsuit? Not surprisingly, Professor Vestal argues that a guilty plea should be given preclusive effect unless the defendant can show that he lacked an adequate opportunity or incentive to litigate. However, the Restatement contains no exception from the actually litigated requirement for guilty pleas and, thus, concludes that issue preclusion is inapplicable. Restatement (Second), Judgments § 85, comment b (1982). But see Allen v. McCurry, pp. 1341–45, infra, in which a guilty plea had preclusive effect because the defendant had an evidentiary hearing regarding a motion to suppress. The Restatement does note that guilty pleas are admissible into evidence in later civil suits. Despite the Restatement's position, some courts, without always setting forth a clear rationale, have granted preclusive effect to guilty pleas in subsequent suits involving the essential elements of the crime. See Shapiro, *Should a Guilty Plea Have Preclusive Effect?*, 70 Iowa L.Rev. 27 (1984).

4. How should a court go about determining what was decided in a prior litigation? Will the difficulty of this task be affected by whether the case was tried to a judge or to a jury? Are there any procedural rules that can play a role in defining what a suit has decided? Consider, in particular, Rule 49 and Rule 52. When the prior decision is ambiguous on what it actually decided, doubts should be resolved against the party seeking to assert preclusion. But it sometimes will be necessary to conduct a hearing to determine what was decided. Is it possible to use the record of the prior trial to help ascertain what issues actually were decided? Is it permissible to introduce extrinsic evidence to prove what issues were litigated? There is some authority for permitting both of these methods of proof. How should the court determine whether an issue was actually litigated in the following situations?

(a) In the course of a divorce proceeding, the court determines that a child has been born of the marriage and orders the husband to pay child support. Does the decree collaterally estop the child when she seeks to litigate the question of paternity? If paternity is disproved, does the divorce decree issue preclude the husband from seeking reimbursement for child support payments already made? See Tedford v. Gregory, 125 N.M. 206, 959 P.2d 540 (Ct. App. 1998). What additional information would you want to know about the divorce proceeding?

(b) In the course of a "*Markman*" proceeding, see p. 1038, supra, the court construes the meaning of a patent claim. Is the trial court's construction binding on the patent holder in a subsequent infringement suit? See In re Freeman, 30 F.3d 1459 (Fed. Cir. 1994). See Van Over, *Collateral Estoppel and* Markman *Rulings: The Call for Uniformity*, 45 St. Louis U. L.J. 1151 (2001).

For a general discussion of this topic, see 18 Wright, Miller & Cooper, Federal Practice and Procedure: Jurisdiction and Related Matters 2d § 4420. See also

Heiser, *California's Confusing Collateral Estoppel (Issue Preclusion) Doctrine*, 35 San Diego L. Rev. 509, 535–58 (1998).

2. NECESSARILY DECIDED

RUSSELL v. PLACE

Supreme Court of the United States, 1876.
94 U.S. (4 Otto) 606, 24 L.Ed. 214.

Appeal from the Circuit Court of the United States for the Northern District of New York.

MR. JUSTICE FIELD delivered the opinion of the court.

This is a suit for an infringement of a patent to the complainant for an alleged new and useful improvement in the preparation of leather * * *.

The bill of complaint sets forth the invention claimed, the issue of a patent for the same, its surrender for alleged defective and insufficient description of the invention, its reissue with an amended specification, and the recovery of judgment against the defendants for damages in an action at law for a violation of the exclusive privileges secured by the patent.

The bill then alleges the subsequent manufacture, use, and sale by the defendants, without the license of the patentee, of the alleged invention and improvement, and prays that they may be decreed to account for the gains and profits thus acquired by them, and be enjoined from further infringement.

The answer admits the issue of the patent, its surrender and reissue, and, as a defence to this suit, sets up in substance the want of novelty in the invention, its use by the public for more than two years prior to the application for the patent, and that the reissue, so far as it differs from the original patent, is not for the same invention. * * *

The action at law was brought * * * in the ordinary form of such actions for infringement of the privileges secured by a patent. The defendants pleaded the general issue, and set up, by special notice under the act of Congress, the want of novelty in the invention, and its use by the public for more than two years prior to the application for a patent. The plaintiff obtained a verdict for damages, upon which the judgment mentioned was entered; and this judgment, it is now insisted, estops the defendants in this suit from insisting upon the want of novelty in the invention patented, and its prior use by the public, and also from insisting upon any ground going to the validity of the patent which might have been availed of as a defence in that action, and, of course, upon the want of identity in the invention covered by the reissue with that of the original patent.

It is undoubtedly settled law that a judgment of a court of competent jurisdiction, upon a question directly involved in one suit, is conclusive as to that question in another suit between the same parties. But to this operation of the judgment it must appear, either upon the face of the record or be shown by extrinsic evidence, that the precise question was raised and determined in the former suit. If there be any uncertainty on this head in the record—as, for example, if it appear that several distinct matters may have been litigated, upon one or more of which the judgment may have passed, without indicating which of them was thus litigated, and upon which the judgment was rendered—the whole subject-matter of the action will be at large, and open to a new contention, unless this uncertainty be removed by extrinsic evidence showing the precise point involved and determined. * * *

Tested by these views, the question presented * * * is of easy solution. The record of that action does not disclose the nature of the infringement for which damages were recovered. The declaration only avers * * * as the infringement complained of, that the defendants have made and used the invention, and have caused others to make and use it. The patent contains two claims: one for the use of fat liquor generally in the treatment of leather, and the other for a process of treating bark tanned lamb or sheep skin by means of a compound composed and applied in a particular manner. Whether the infringement for which the verdict and judgment passed consisted in the simple use of fat liquor in the treatment of leather, or in the use of the process specified, does not appear from the record. A recovery for an infringement of one claim of the patent is not of itself conclusive of an infringement of the other claim, and there was no extrinsic evidence offered to remove the uncertainty upon the record * * *. The verdict may have been for an infringement of the first claim; it may have been for an infringement of the second; it may have been for an infringement of both. The validity of the patent was not necessarily involved, except with respect to the claim which was the basis of the recovery. A patent may be valid as to a single claim and not valid as to the others. The record wants, therefore, that certainty which is essential to its operation as an estoppel, and does not conclude the defendants from contesting the infringement or the validity of the patent in this suit.

The record is not unlike a record in an action for money had and received to the plaintiff's use. It would be impossible to affirm from such a record, with certainty, for what moneys thus received the action was brought, without extrinsic evidence showing the fact; and, of course, without such evidence the verdict and judgment would conclude nothing, except as to the amount of indebtedness established.

* * *

Decree affirmed.

MR. JUSTICE CLIFFORD dissented.

NOTES AND QUESTIONS

1. Plaintiff brings an action against defendant for personal injuries arising out of a collision of their automobiles. Defendant answers, denying

negligence and affirmatively pleading contributory negligence. Evidence is presented on both issues, and there is a general verdict for defendant. If defendant subsequently sues plaintiff for his own injuries arising out of the same accident, may defendant rely upon the first judgment as establishing any part of the case? See *Developments in the Law—Res Judicata*, 65 Harv.L.Rev. 818, 845–46 (1952).

2. In KELLEY v. CURTISS, 16 N.J. 265, 273, 108 A.2d 431, 435 (1954), the New Jersey Supreme Court said: "The case against [defendant] having been submitted to the jury with instructions that he was entitled to a verdict of no cause of action if the jury found either that he was not negligent or that [plaintiff] was guilty of contributory negligence, the general verdict is to be considered as determining both grounds in [defendant's] favor." Is this holding consistent with Russell v. Place? If not, which case advances the better rule?

3. Should the principles embodied in *Russell* call for a different result if the jury in the first action makes specific findings of fact on each of the alternative grounds? What if the first action is a bench trial and the judge specifically discussed her findings on each of the alternative grounds? In Malloy v. Trombley, 50 N.Y.2d 46, 427 N.Y.S.2d 969, 405 N.E.2d 213 (1980), issue preclusion was allowed, even though the issue had been treated as an alternative ground in the earlier action. The *Malloy* court's holding was based, in part, on the fact that the judge in the earlier action had provided a complete discussion of his holding on each ground. See also National Satellite Sports, Inc. v. Eliadis, Inc., 253 F.3d 900 (6th Cir.2001).

4. What should be the outcome if an appellate court, faced with alternative determinations by the trial court, affirms on only one ground? If conservation of judicial resources is the ultimate goal, why should anything short of reversal on appeal strip a conclusive determination of its preclusive effect? See generally Lucas, *The Direct and Collateral Estoppel Effects of Alternative Holdings*, 50 U.Chi.L.Rev. 701 (1983).

RIOS v. DAVIS

Court of Civil Appeals of Texas, Eastland, 1963.
373 S.W.2d 386.

COLLINGS, JUSTICE.

Juan C. Rios brought this suit against Jessie Hubert Davis in the District Court to recover damages * * * alleged to have been sustained as a result of personal injuries received * * * in an automobile collision. Plaintiff alleged that his injuries were proximately caused by negligence on the part of the defendant. The defendant answered alleging that Rios was guilty of contributory negligence. Also, among other defenses, the defendant urged a plea of res judicata and collateral estoppel based upon the findings and the judgment entered * * * in a suit between the same parties in the County Court at Law of El Paso County. The plea of res judicata was sustained and judgment was entered in favor of the defendant * * *.

It is shown by the record that * * * Popular Dry Goods Company brought suit against appellee Davis * * * seeking to recover for damages to its truck in the sum of $443.97, alleged to have been sustained in the same collision here involved. Davis answered alleging contributory negligence on the part of Popular and joined appellant Juan C. Rios as a third party defendant and sought to recover from Rios $248.50, the alleged amount of damages to his automobile. The jury * * * found that Popular Dry Goods Company and Rios were guilty of negligence proximately causing the collision. However, the jury also found that Davis was guilty of negligence proximately causing the collision, and judgment was entered * * * denying Popular Dry Goods any recovery against Davis and denying Davis any recovery against Rios.

Appellant Rios in his third point contends that the District Court erred in sustaining appellee's plea of res judicata based upon the judgment of the County Court at Law because the findings on the issues regarding appellant's negligence and liability * * * were immaterial because the judgment entered in that case was in favor of appellant. We sustain this point. * * * The sole basis for the judgment * * * as between Rios and Davis was the findings concerning the negligence of Davis. The finding that Rios was negligent was not essential or material to the judgment and the judgment was not based thereon. On the contrary, the finding * * * that Rios was negligent proximately causing the accident would, if it had been controlling, led [sic] to a different result. Since the judgment was in favor of Rios he had no right or opportunity to complain of or to appeal from the finding that he was guilty of such negligence even if such finding had been without any support whatever in the evidence. The right of appeal is from a judgment and not from a finding. * * * In the case of Word v. Colley, Tex.Civ.App., 173 S.W. 629, at page 634 of its opinion (Error Ref.), the court stated as follows:

> It is the judgment, and not the verdict or the conclusions of fact, filed by a trial court which constitutes the estoppel, and a finding of fact by a jury or a court which does not become the basis or one of the grounds of the judgment rendered is not conclusive against either party to the suit.

* * *

The judgment is, therefore, reversed, and the cause is remanded.

NOTES AND QUESTIONS

1. The verdict in the earlier action in *Rios* reflects the consistent practice, utilized in some states, of submitting a case to the jury on "special issues." Does *Rios* offer a reason for special verdicts to be used more frequently?

2. In *Russell,* there was no issue preclusion because the jury gave a general verdict. In *Rios,* even though the jury gave a special verdict, certain issues were not given preclusive effect because the outcome did not depend

upon those findings. However, multiple findings have been found preclusive when the jury could not have arrived at the same judgment without each of those findings. See, e.g., Patterson v. Saunders, 194 Va. 607, 74 S.E.2d 204 (1953).

3. The court in *Rios* held that the judgment in the earlier case did not estop Rios from denying his own negligence. Should the earlier judgment estop Davis from denying his own negligence?

4. Suppose Davis had not cross-claimed against Rios, but had merely impleaded the latter on a contingent claim for contribution; that Popular had then made a claim against Rios; that at trial Davis and Rios each had argued the other was solely negligent; and that the jury had found for Popular against both of them. In a subsequent suit by Rios against Davis, would the earlier finding that each had been negligent estop Rios from denying negligence? Compare Byrum v. Ames & Webb, Inc., 196 Va. 597, 85 S.E.2d 364 (1955) (no), with Stangle v. Chicago, R. I. & P. R. Co., 295 F.2d 789 (7th Cir.1961) (yes). In both of these cases, the parties in the later action had been named as codefendants by the plaintiff in the earlier action; should it make any difference if one of them had brought the other in by impleader? Should it make any difference if, in the earlier case, the jury had found one of them negligent, and the other not negligent?

Generally, a judgment does not act as collateral estoppel between coparties unless they are adversaries, and they are considered adversaries only if there is a claim for relief by one coparty against the other. The fact that their interests clash and that they are on opposite sides of every issue does not make them adversaries for this purpose in the absence of such a claim.

5. The court in *Rios* supports its view by noting that Rios could not appeal the finding of his negligence in the earlier action. See also Restatement (Second), Judgments § 28(1) (1982). Should the prevailing party in the earlier action be permitted in a later action to attack a finding that was necessary to the judgment in the earlier action? Such a situation will not be common.

6. *Rios* should be compared with HOME OWNERS FEDERAL SAVINGS & LOAN ASSOCIATION v. NORTHWESTERN FIRE & MARINE INSURANCE CO., 354 Mass. 448, 238 N.E.2d 55 (1968), in which the majority opinion states, in what may well be dictum, that "certain findings not strictly essential to the final judgment in the prior action * * * may be relied upon if it is clear that the issues underlying them were treated as essential to the prior case by the court and the party to be bound." Three of the seven justices dissented. What advantages does this test have over the *Rios* approach? What disadvantages?

7. How would you justify each of these statements?

(a) When a judgment is supported by multiple independent grounds, all of the grounds may be relitigated. See Halpern v. Schwartz, 426 F.2d 102, 106 (2d Cir. 1970).

(b) When a judgment is supported by multiple independent grounds, none of the grounds may be relitigated. See In re Westgate–California Corp., 642 F.2d 1174 (9th Cir. 1981).

(c) When a judgment is supported by multiple independent grounds, the primary issue may not be relitigated, but secondary issues are not barred. See National Satellite Sports, Inc. v. Eliadis, Inc., 253 F.3d 900 (6th Cir. 2001).

For a full discussion of each approach, see Brownewell, *Note—Rethinking the Restatement View (Again!): Multiple Independent Holdings and the Doctrine of Issue Preclusion*, 37 Val. U. L. Rev. 879 (2003).

3. DEFINING AND CHARACTERIZING THE ISSUE

UNITED STATES v. MOSER, 266 U.S. 236, 45 S.Ct. 66, 69 L.Ed. 262 (1924). Moser was a captain when he retired from the Navy. In his first action, he won a ruling that service as a Naval Academy cadet during the Civil War constituted service during the war that entitled him to be retired with the rank and three-fourths of the sea pay of the next higher grade. Although the Court of Claims changed its mind about the interpretation of the pension statutes, he won his next two actions for later installments of his pay on the basis of res judicata. In his fourth action for still later installments, the Court of Claims ruled both that its initial interpretation of the statute had been correct and that in any event he was entitled to rely on res judicata. The Supreme Court affirmed solely on the res judicata ground:

> * * * The question expressly and definitely presented in this suit is the same as that definitely and actually litigated and adjudged in favor of the claimant in the three preceding suits, viz. whether he occupied the status of an officer who had served during the Civil War.
>
> The contention of the government seems to be that the doctrine of res judicata does not apply to questions of law; and, in a sense, that is true. It does not apply to unmixed questions of law. Where, for example, a court in deciding a case has enunciated a rule of law, the parties in a subsequent action upon a different demand are not estopped from insisting that the law is otherwise, merely because the parties are the same in both cases. But a *fact, question* or *right* distinctly adjudged in the original action cannot be disputed in a subsequent action, even though the determination was reached upon an erroneous view or by an erroneous application of the law. That would be to affirm the principle in respect of the thing adjudged but, at the same time, deny it all efficacy by sustaining a challenge to the grounds upon which the judgment was based. * * *

Id. at 241–42, 45 S.Ct. at 67, 69 L.Ed. at 264.

COMMISSIONER OF INTERNAL REVENUE v. SUNNEN

Supreme Court of the United States, 1948.
333 U.S. 591, 68 S.Ct. 715, 92 L.Ed. 898.

Certiorari to the United States Circuit Court of Appeals for the Eighth Circuit.

MR. JUSTICE MURPHY delivered the opinion of the Court.

[Under a series of agreements, a taxpayer had licensed a corporation, which he controlled, to use his patents in exchange for payment of a 10% royalty. At various times, the taxpayer assigned his interest in these agreements to his wife without consideration. Income from these agreements was reported on her income tax returns, and these taxes were paid. The Commissioner contended that the income was taxable to the taxpayer himself and a deficiency was assessed against him.]

* * * [T]he Tax Court held that, with one exception, all the royalties paid to the wife from 1937 to 1941 were part of the taxable income of the taxpayer. * * * The one exception concerned the royalties of $4,881.35 paid in 1937 under the 1928 agreement. In an earlier proceeding in 1935, the Board of Tax Appeals dealt with the taxpayer's income tax liability for the years 1929–1931; it concluded that he was not taxable on the royalties paid to his wife during those years under the 1928 license agreement. This prior determination by the Board caused the Tax Court to apply the principle of *res judicata* to bar a different result as to the royalties paid pursuant to the same agreement during 1937.

The Tax Court's decision was affirmed in part and reversed in part by the Eighth Circuit Court of Appeals. * * * Approval was given to the Tax Court's application of the *res judicata* doctrine to exclude from the taxpayer's income the $4,881.35 in royalties paid in 1937 under the 1928 agreement. But to the extent that the taxpayer had been held taxable on royalties paid to his wife during the taxable years of 1937–1941, the decision was reversed on the theory that such payments were not income to him. * * *

If the doctrine of *res judicata* is properly applicable so that all the royalty payments made during 1937–1941 are governed by the prior decision of the Board of Tax Appeals, the case may be disposed of without reaching the merits of the controversy. * * *

* * * [The concepts of res judicata and collateral estoppel] are applicable in the federal income tax field. Income taxes are levied on an annual basis. Each year is the origin of a new liability and of a separate cause of action. Thus if a claim of liability or non-liability relating to a particular tax year is litigated, a judgment on the merits is *res judicata* as to any subsequent proceeding involving the same claim and the same tax year. But if the later proceeding is concerned with a similar or unlike claim relating to a different tax year, the prior judgment acts as a collateral estoppel only as to those matters in the second proceeding which were actually presented and determined in the first suit. Collateral estoppel operates, in other words, to relieve the government and the taxpayer of "redundant litigation of the identical question of the statute's application to the taxpayer's status." Tait v. Western Md. R. Co., 289 U.S. 620, 624, 53 S.Ct. 706, 707, 77 L.Ed. 1405.

But collateral estoppel is a doctrine capable of being applied so as to avoid an undue disparity in the impact of income tax liability. A taxpayer may secure a judicial determination of a particular tax matter, a matter which may recur without substantial variation for some years thereafter. But a subsequent modification of the significant facts or a change or development in the controlling legal principles may make that determination obsolete or erroneous, at least for future purposes. If such a determination is then perpetuated each succeeding year as to the taxpayer involved in the original litigation, he is accorded a tax treatment different from that given to other taxpayers of the same class. As a result, there are inequalities in the administration of the revenue laws, discriminatory distinctions in tax liability, and a fertile basis for litigious confusion. * * * Such consequences, however, are neither necessitated nor justified by the principle of collateral estoppel. That principle is designed to prevent repetitious lawsuits over matters which have once been decided and which have remained substantially static, factually and legally. It is not meant to create vested rights in decisions that have become obsolete or erroneous with time, thereby causing inequities among taxpayers.

And so where two cases involve income taxes in different taxable years, collateral estoppel must be used with its limitations carefully in mind so as to avoid injustice. It must be confined to situations where the matter raised in the second suit is identical in all respects with that decided in the first proceeding and where the controlling facts and applicable legal rules remain unchanged. * * * As demonstrated by Blair v. Commissioner, 300 U.S. 5, 9, 57 S.Ct. 330, 331, 81 L.Ed. 465, a judicial declaration intervening between the two proceedings may so change the legal atmosphere as to render the rule of collateral estoppel inapplicable. But the intervening decision need not necessarily be that of a state court, as it was in the Blair case. While such a state court decision may be considered as having changed the facts for federal tax litigation purposes, a modification or growth in legal principles as enunciated in intervening decisions of this Court may also effect a significant change in the situation. Tax inequality can result as readily from neglecting legal modulations by this Court as from disregarding factual changes wrought by state courts. In either event, the supervening decision cannot justly be ignored by blind reliance upon the rule of collateral estoppel. * * * It naturally follows that an interposed alteration in the pertinent statutory provisions or Treasury regulations can make the use of that rule unwarranted. * * *

Of course, where a question of fact essential to the judgment is actually litigated and determined in the first tax proceeding, the parties are bound by that determination in a subsequent proceeding even though the cause of action is different. * * * And if the very same facts and no others are involved in the second case, a case relating to a different tax year, the prior judgment will be conclusive as to the same legal issues which appear, assuming no intervening doctrinal change. But if the relevant facts in the two cases are separable, even though they be similar or identical, collateral estoppel does not govern the legal issues which recur in the second case. Thus the second proceeding may involve an instrument or transaction identical with, but in a form separable from, the one dealt with in the first proceeding. In that situation, a court is free in the second proceeding to make an independent examination of the legal matters at issue. It may then reach a different result or, if consistency in decision is considered just and desirable, reliance may be placed upon the ordinary rule of *stare decisis*. Before a party can invoke the collateral estoppel doctrine in these circumstances, the legal matter raised in the second proceeding must involve the same set of events or documents and the same bundle of legal principles that contributed to the rendering of the first judgment. * * *

It is readily apparent in this case that the royalty payments growing out of the license contracts which were not involved in the earlier action before the Board of Tax Appeals and which concerned different tax years are free from the effects of the collateral estoppel doctrine. That is true even though those contracts are identical in all important respects with the 1928 contract, the only one that was before the Board, and even though the issue as to those contracts is the same as that raised by the 1928 contract. * * *

A more difficult problem is posed as to the $4,881.35 in royalties paid to the taxpayer's wife in 1937 under the 1928 contract. Here there is complete identity of facts, issues and parties as between the earlier Board proceeding and the instant one. The Commissioner claims, however, that legal principles developed in various intervening decisions of this Court have made plain the error of the Board's conclusion in the earlier proceeding, thus creating a situation like that involved in Blair v. Commissioner, supra. * * *

The principles which have * * * been recognized and developed by * * * [Helvering v. Clifford, 309 U.S. 331, 60 S.Ct. 554, 84 L.Ed. 788 (1940), and Helvering v. Horst, 311 U.S. 112, 61 S.Ct. 144, 85 L.Ed. 75, 131 A.L.R. 655 (1940)] are directly applicable to the transfer of patent license contracts between members of the same family. They are guideposts for those who seek to determine in a particular instance whether such an assignor retains sufficient control over the assigned contracts or over the receipt of income by the assignee to make it fair to impose income tax liability on him.

Moreover, the clarification and growth of these principles through the Clifford–Horst line of cases constitute, in our opinion, a sufficient change in the legal climate to render inapplicable in the instant proceeding, the doctrine of collateral estoppel relative to the assignment of the 1928 contract. True, these cases did not originate the concept that an assignor is taxable if he retains control over the assigned property or power to defeat the receipt of income by the assignee. But they gave much added emphasis and substance to that concept, making it more suited to meet the "attenuated subtleties" created by taxpayers. So substantial was the amplification of this concept as to justify a reconsideration of earlier Tax Court decisions reached without the benefit of the expanded notions, decisions which are now sought to be perpetuated regardless of their present correctness. Thus in the earlier litigation in 1935, the Board of Tax Appeals was unable to bring to bear on the assignment of the 1928 contract the full breadth of the ideas enunciated in the Clifford–Horst series of cases. And, as we shall see, a proper application of the principles as there developed might well have produced a different result, such as was reached by the Tax Court in this case in regard to the assignments of the other contracts. Under those circumstances collateral estoppel should not have been used by the Tax Court in the instant proceeding to perpetuate the 1935 viewpoint of the assignment.

* * *

The judgment below must therefore be reversed and the case remanded for such further proceedings as may be necessary in light of this opinion.

Reversed.

MR. JUSTICE FRANKFURTER and MR. JUSTICE JACKSON believe the judgment of the Tax Court is based on substantial evidence and is consistent with the law, and would affirm that judgment * * *.

NOTES AND QUESTIONS

1. How might you reconcile *Sunnen* and *Moser*? Both opinions, in a sense, seek to determine if the subsequent suit concerns facts that are separable from those of the first suit. What is the proper test for this separability? Is it whether historically distinct facts are at issue? Is it whether the facts in the subsequent suit legally are indistinguishable from those of the earlier suit?

2. Is the outcome in the *Sunnen* case consistent with the underlying goals of res judicata? Does its holding undermine the sense of reliance that judgments should foster? After all, if *Sunnen* had lost the first litigation, he probably would not have renewed the contract assigning income to his wife.

3. *Moser* held that "unmixed questions of law" are not subject to issue preclusion. More recently, however, the Supreme Court has recognized that "the purpose underlying the exception for 'unmixed questions of law' in successive actions on unrelated claims is far from clear." UNITED STATES v. STAUFFER CHEMICAL CO., 464 U.S. 165, 172, 104 S.Ct. 575, 579, 78 L.Ed.2d 388, 394 (1984). Rather than engaging in the virtually impossible task of delineating the boundary between an issue of fact, law, or mixed fact and law, the Court adopted the more pragmatic approach suggested in Restatement (Second), Judgments § 28, comment b (1982):

> When the claims in two separate actions between the same parties are the same or are closely related * * * it is not ordinarily necessary to characterize an issue as one of fact or of law for purposes of issue preclusion. * * * In such a case, it is unfair to the winning party and an unnecessary burden on the courts to allow repeated litigation of the same issue in what is essentially the same controversy, even if the issue is regarded as one of "law."

4. As *Sunnen* and *Moser* illustrate, the careful "delineation" of questions of pure law, and their exemption from issue preclusion, may be important especially when the government is a party. "Decisions of law in cases involving [a public agency] generally have significance beyond their immediate impact * * *. [A] 'repeat' litigant, particularly the government, ordinarily should be free to relitigate a legal issue in subsequent litigation that could result in appeal to a higher level of authority in the legal system." Hazard, *Preclusion as to Issues of Law: The Legal System's Interest*, 70 Iowa L.Rev. 81, 92 (1984).

5. When a court makes a determination on a mixed question of law and fact, how should subsequent changes in the relevant substantive law influence whether preclusive effect is given to those determinations? The *Sunnen* opinion helps answer this question. When new historic facts are the basis of the second suit and there has been a change in legal regime since the prior suit was adjudicated, the first judgment will not preclude the second litigation. See, e.g., Spradling v. City of Tulsa, 198 F.3d 1219, 1223 (10th Cir.2000); Bingaman v. Dep't of the Treasury, 127 F.3d 1431, 1438 (Fed.Cir.1997).

In some situations it is easy to determine when this exception is invoked properly. When a new statute or new regulation has been enacted, or when a controlling Supreme Court precedent has been altered, the exception's application is indisputable. In other situations it is not so clear that a change in substantive law should prevent preclusion. Should preclusion be allowed if there is an inconsistent decision by the same court on similar facts? Should a "change in legal atmosphere" count as an intervening "change in controlling legal principles"? See Charter Fed. Savs. Bank v. United States, 54 Fed.Cl. 120, 127 (Fed.Cl.2002).

6. The frequent changes in tax law arguably prevent any individual from developing much of a sense of repose in tax decisions, and there is a particularly urgent need to treat similarly situated taxpayers alike. These factors suggest that a narrow definition of "issue" may be appropriate in cases involving tax law. However, in tax, as in other areas, the policy considerations that underlie substantive law still must be balanced against the strong individual interests in repose and reliance that particular fact patterns may exhibit. See Webster, *The Limits of Collateral Estoppel in Tax Court Litigation*, 8 B.U.J. Tax Law 43 (1990).

THE EVERGREENS DOCTRINE. In addition to limiting collateral estoppel to identical issues, courts sometimes have distinguished between "ultimate" and "mediate" facts when determining whether issues decided in one suit will be viewed as preclusive in a later one. The most influential explanation of this distinction is found in Judge Learned Hand's opinion in THE EVERGREENS v. NUNAN, 141 F.2d 927 (2d Cir.), certiorari denied 323 U.S. 720, 65 S.Ct. 49, 89 L.Ed. 579 (1944). The gist of the doctrine is simple: imagine a lawsuit as a logical structure resembling a pyramid. At its base are the facts introduced into evidence. From these facts are drawn conclusions that, when combined with other deductions or evidence, lead eventually to "ultimate facts" that establish a legal right, duty, or status. The ultimate facts are the summit of the structure; all that supports them are "mediate data." *The Evergreens* held that only matters constituting ultimate facts in the second action are subject to preclusion by collateral estoppel.

The controversy in *The Evergreens* turned on the value for tax purposes of cemetery lots appropriated by the City of New York. The lots were of two kinds, improved and unimproved. An earlier proceeding had determined the value of the improved lots, and that determination was accepted in the later action without dispute. The earlier proceeding also had fixed the cost of upgrading the unimproved lots to "improved" status. The plaintiff maintained that these two findings taken together should determine the value of the unimproved lots: the uncontested value of the improved lots minus the cost of improving them should be taken as the value of the unimproved lots.

The Second Circuit rejected this argument, relying on the distinction between ultimate and mediate facts. Judge Hand first noted that authorities differed concerning whether mediate facts or only ultimate facts in the first suit are decided conclusively by the judgment. The question presented, however, was whether a determination, either mediate or ultimate in the first suit, could establish a mediate fact in the second suit. On this question, authority was silent; Judge Hand decided that collateral estoppel could not be used.

This determination was based on the notion that the consequences that would result if estoppel were to apply might be both unintended and unjust as a given fact can lead to unpredictable deductions. Restricting the use of collateral estoppel to ultimate issues in the second suit attempts to ensure that the consequences of issues decided by the first judgment are plainly visible when that judgment was entered.

> What jural relevance facts may acquire in the future it is often impossible even remotely to anticipate. Were the law to be recast, it would therefore be a pertinent inquiry whether the conclusiveness * * * might not properly be limited to future controversies which could be thought reasonably in prospect when the first suit was tried. That is, of course, not the law as it stands * * *.

Id. at 929.

NOTES AND QUESTIONS

1. Commentators have criticized the mediate and ultimate fact terminology as difficult to understand and even more difficult to apply. See Heckman, *Collateral Estoppel as the Answer to Multiple Litigation Problems in Federal Tax Law: Another View of* Sunnen *and* The Evergreens, 19 Case W.Res.L.Rev. 230 (1967); Polasky, *Collateral Estoppel—Effects of Prior Litigation*, 39 Iowa L.Rev. 217 (1954). Moreover, some courts have rejected the analysis set out in *The Evergreens* as inconsistent with the purposes of collateral estoppel:

> [Criticism of *The Evergreens* rule] is based primarily upon the difficulty in administering a distinction between ultimate and mediate facts, and the lack of correspondence of such a distinction to any intelligible reasons for limiting preclusion. * * *
>
> [E]ven though a fact may be regarded in theory as less than an ultimate fact, the parties may have expended great effort in proving whether or not that fact existed, and the fact may even have been regarded by everyone involved in the litigation as the key issue in a dispute. In these circumstances, * * * the rule is at odds with the purposes of the doctrine of issue preclusion: the conservation of judicial resources and the fostering of reliance on prior judicial action by minimizing the possibility of inconsistent decisions and by protecting a prevailing party from vexatious litigation. * * *
>
> On this basis, many courts * * * have ignored the *Evergreens* rule, and they have measured the scope of preclusion, not by a distinction between ultimate and mediate facts, but rather by focusing more directly on the quality and extensiveness of litigation in the first action. For that reason too, the *Restatement (Second) of Judgments* § 27 comment j has rejected the distinction between ultimate and evidentiary facts, instead according preclusive effect to determinations that are essential or necessary to the judgment.
>
> * * *
>
> Accordingly, we hold, following the Restatement, that preclusive effect may be accorded to a decision on an issue if that issue was "actually recognized by the parties as important and by the trier of fact as necessary to the first judgment." *Restatement (Second) of Judgments* § 27 comment j.

SYNANON CHURCH v. UNITED STATES, 820 F.2d 421, 426–27 (D.C.Cir. 1987).

2. A second part of Judge Hand's analysis in *The Evergreens*—which looks to the role that the issue will play in the second litigation—seems to embody legitimate concerns, but they have been well concealed in Judge Hand's formulation. The following excerpt may help cast some light on the purposes that underlie *The Evergreens* rule:

> The valid core of the Evergreens rule might be preserved by expanding the requirement that the first action afford a full and fair opportunity to litigate the common issue. Substantial changes in the legal context or the consequences of the issue, particularly, could support the conclusion that the initial opportunity was not sufficient to support preclusion. It would be more difficult to consider the need to retry related issues on substantially the same evidence through the full and fair opportunity test. Reliance on the full and fair opportunity test would also work against relitigation because of a common reluctance to challenge directly the adequacy of a prior action. Wise administration of the full and fair opportunity test can go far; it may not go far enough.
>
> In the end, the question can be simply put. There are strong reasons to adopt a general rule that issue preclusion is defeated by substantial

changes in the legal context in which the issue arises, by substantial changes in the consequences it may entail, or by the need to retry related issues. A general rule framed in these terms would force attention to the real sources of concern. It seems likely that such a general rule would not defeat issue preclusion in any substantial portion of the cases that satisfy all of the other requirements. Even when the result is to deny preclusion, there may be little injury to the values generally served by preclusion. Nonetheless, the price might prove too high. Federal courts have not yet spun any such rule out of the Evergreens decision, and any proof of its value must await the effort and the experience.

18 Wright, Miller & Cooper, Federal Practice and Procedure: Jurisdiction and Related Matters 2d § 4424.

SECTION D. THE REQUIRED QUALITY OF JUDGMENT

Only judgments of a certain quality will give rise to preclusion. For the most part, this Chapter's discussion of preclusion doctrine has assumed thus far that the prior judgment satisfied that requirement. It will now be examined in greater detail.

The traditional words used to describe a judgment of sufficient quality to create preclusion are that the judgment must be valid, final, and on the merits. These terms are not unambiguous, however; indeed, they are somewhat misleading. Courts often enter judgments that are considered "on the merits," despite the fact that the judgment resulted from less than a full adjudicatory proceeding. In addition, courts increasingly are faced with the prior determinations of state or federal administrative agencies that act in a quasi-judicial capacity. This Section is designed to highlight some of the difficult questions the "quality of judgment" requirement raises.

1. JUDGMENTS OF JUDICIAL TRIBUNALS

HANOVER LOGANSPORT, INC. v. ROBERT C. ANDERSON, INC.

Court of Appeals of Indiana, Third District, 1987.
512 N.E.2d 465.

STATON, JUDGE.

[Hanover Logansport, Inc. ("Hanover") and Robert C. Anderson, Inc. ("Anderson") entered into an agreement pursuant to which Hanover agreed to lease certain property to Anderson for use as a liquor store. Hanover failed to deliver the premises on the agreed upon date, and Anderson filed suit for breach of the lease. Before trial, Hanover offered to deliver the real estate to Anderson, and Anderson accepted with the following reservation: "[T]he offer is only accepted for purposes of mitigation of damages and not in settlement of damages arising to Plaintiff caused by Defendants' breach of contract."

The parties filed a stipulation that "the judgment as stipulated to by the Defendants herein should be recorded of record in the judgment record book of the County of St. Joseph." Anderson took possession of the premises, and, after several months, Hanover moved to dismiss the earlier breach action. The trial court denied the motion, and Hanover appealed, arguing that the prior consent judgment precluded any further litigation based on the same cause of action.]

* * *

Hanover makes the following argument:

1. The complaint seeks specific performance of the lease or *in the alternative* money damages for loss of profits *over the term of the lease.*

2. Hanover made an offer of real estate pursuant to [Indiana Trial Rule 68] consistent with one of the alternatives—specific performance—in the complaint.[a]

3. Anderson accepted the offer.

4. Under T.R. 68, the clerk is required to enter judgment.

5. Anderson took possession of the real estate.

6. By accepting the offer of real estate and taking possession of the premises, Anderson chose its remedy and is now barred by law from continuing the litigation.

Anderson argues that (1) an offer of judgment under T.R. 68 may be in part or in whole; and (2) both Hanover and the trial court were on notice that the offer of judgment did not address and dispose of the whole of its claim. Anderson points to the portion of its acceptance which states: "* * * Further, the offer is only accepted for purposes of mitigation of damages and not in settlement of damages arising to Plaintiff caused by Defendants' breach of contract." In its brief, Anderson states: "The acceptance of said offer specifically states that the lease between the parties would be as contracted, subject to the conditions in the lease, but that the Plaintiff did not waive damages for breach of contract which arose due to the failure of Defendant to honor its contract *between the date the offer was signed and the date the Court entered an Order approving the settlment [sic]* [in original] *as to possession.*" (Emphasis added [in original].)

Thus, we address the following issue: Whether, by law, a plaintiff, who accepts an offer of judgment which conforms to one of the alternative prayers for relief contained in his complaint, may then seek additional damages arising from the same cause of action.

* * *

A consent judgment has a dual aspect. It represents an agreement between the parties settling the underlying dispute and providing for the

---

a. Indiana Rules of Procedure, Trial Rule 68, is similar to Federal Rule 68, and is set out in the Supplement.

entry of judgment in a pending or contemplated action. See James, Consent Judgments as Collateral Estoppel, 108 U.Pa.L.Rev. 173, 175 (1959). It also represents the entry of such a judgment by a court—with all that this means in the way of committing the force of society to implement the judgment of its courts. Id.

As a result of this dual aspect, some courts and commentators focus on the contractual aspect of a consent judgment, thus determining whatever its preclusive effect may be by ascertaining the intent of the parties—in the same way courts construe other agreements. * * *

Yet, other courts and commentators focus on the entry of a consent judgment by a court and argue that such a judgment possesses the same force with regard to *res judicata* and collateral estoppel as a judgment entered after a trial on the merits. * * *

Proponents of the consent-judgment-as-contract theory argue that if consent judgments are given preclusive effect regardless of the intent of the parties, such a rule would lessen the chance of compromise between them. This, they argue, is true for two reasons. First, in many cases, the application of such a rule (at least in regard to the collateral estoppel aspect of the rule) would be unforeseeable—it would reach into all possible future disputes among the parties, no matter how hard it may be to predict them at the outset of the first litigation. Second, if all issues and claims must be negotiated and dealt with in a consent judgment or foregone forever, parties will be reluctant to enter into such an agreement for fear that they will "miss" something.

But, proponents of the consent-judgment-as-final judgment theory counter that the preclusive effect of a consent judgment serves several objectives. Among them, economy is achieved in the use of judicial resources, the harassment of parties avoided, and the possibility of inconsistent results is eliminated. * * *

* * *

We note that T.R. 68 is intended to encourage settlements, discourage vexatious suits, and avoid protracted litigation. See 12 Wright & Miller, *Federal Practice and Procedure,* § 3001. Therefore, the result we reach should serve those purposes.

Because we agree that if all issues and claims must be negotiated and dealt with in a consent judgment or foregone forever, parties will be reluctant to enter into such agreements, we adopt the consent-judgment-as-contract theory and hold that the preclusive effect of a consent judgment must be measured by the intent of the parties. However, it must be clear that *both* parties have agreed to reserve an issue or claim. *And,* it must be precisely stated what issues or claims are being reserved.

* * *

[I]n order to insure that both parties have agreed to reserve a claim or issue[9] and that the reserved claim or issue is clearly apparent to both parties, we hold that (1) the reservation must be incorporated into the offer of judgment itself and (2) it must be an inherent part of the original complaint. Thus, for example, before a party may reserve an additional cause of action in a consent judgment, that cause of action must have been originally set out on the face of the complaint. Because Anderson did not include a claim for damages for delay in tendering the real estate in its Complaint, it is precluded from reserving such a claim in the consent judgment.[10] * * *

[T]his rule will avoid protracted litigation, since it requires plaintiffs to reserve a claim or issue both in the complaint and in the consent judgment. If we were to require such a reservation only in the consent judgment (as Anderson asks us to do here), the potential for protracted litigation would be too great. For example, in a situation where A and B have entered a consent judgment and B thinks the controversy has ended, such a rule would allow A: (1) to argue that it had no intention of ending the controversy and (2) to proceed on the alleged balance of its claim. This could potentially allow the litigation to continue on and on through the years.

But, under the rule we have set forth here, A would not be allowed to make such a claim unless it was shown that a reservation was made in A's complaint and in the consent judgment. In this way, courts can be assured it was also B's intention to continue the litigation.

Therefore, we reverse and remand to the trial court, with instructions to enter a judgment on the offer of judgment and to grant Hanover's motion to dismiss.

Reversed and remanded.

NOTES AND QUESTIONS

1. Should the agreement between Hanover and Anderson be considered a court judgment, or is it more properly characterized as a contract? If it is merely a contract, should the intent of the parties as to its preclusive effect be dispositive? Did the parties require the approval of the court in the form of a judgment to make a new contract? Do you agree that a rule that did not make the intent of the parties dispositive would have the effect of discouraging

---

9. Here, we are dealing with the reservation of a claim for damages. However, there may be cases where a party desires to reserve an issue or another cause of action. The same rule would apply in those situations.

10. Indiana Rules of Procedure, Trial Rule 12(B) states, in part:

"* * * When a motion to dismiss is sustained for failure to state a claim under subdivision (B)(6) of this rule the pleading may be amended once as of right pursuant to Rule 15(A) within ten [10] days after service of notice of the court's order sustaining the motion and thereafter with permission of the court pursuant to such rule. * * *"

However, Anderson may not take advantage of this rule by amending the complaint, then arguing it has met the requirements set out by this opinion. Obviously, the claim or issue must be in the complaint at the time the parties reach an agreement or enter a judgment.

consent judgments? For a discussion of consent judgments, see Easterbrook, *Justice and Contract in Consent Judgments*, 1987 U. Chi. Legal F. 19.

2. Even if a consent decree has claim preclusive effect, should it also have issue preclusive effect? Doesn't collateral estoppel doctrine require that an issue be "actually litigated"? In ARIZONA v. CALIFORNIA, 530 U.S. 392, 120 S.Ct. 2304, 147 L.Ed.2d 374 (2000), the Supreme Court explained:

> * * * [S]ettlements ordinarily occasion no *issue preclusion* (sometimes called collateral estoppel), unless it is clear * * * that the parties intend their agreement to have such an effect. * * * "In most circumstances, it is recognized that consent agreements ordinarily are intended to preclude any further litigation on the claim presented but are not intended to preclude further litigation on any of the issues presented. Thus consent judgments ordinarily support claim preclusion but not issue preclusion." * * * This differentiation is grounded in basic res judicata doctrine. It is the general rule that issue preclusion attaches only "[w]hen an issue of fact or law is actually litigated and determined by a valid and final judgment, and the determination is essential to the judgment." Restatement (Second) of Judgments, § 27 * * * (1982). "In the case of a judgment entered by confession, consent, or default, none of the issues is actually litigated. * * *."

Id. at 414, 120 S.Ct. at 2319, 147 L.Ed.2d at 395–96 (internal citation omitted).

3. Should a final judgment be stripped of its preclusive effect if both parties consent to that result on appeal? A stipulated reversal allows parties seeking to facilitate settlement during the pendency of an appeal to join in asking the appellate court to set aside a trial court judgment, rather than dismissing the appeal, thereby avoiding the preclusive effect of a final judgment. In U.S. BANCORP MORTGAGE CO. v. BONNER MALL PARTNERSHIP, 513 U.S. 18, 115 S.Ct. 386, 130 L.Ed.2d 233 (1994), the Supreme Court unanimously denied petitioner's motion to vacate a judgment of a court of appeals in a case that had become moot by reason of settlement after certiorari was sought, but the Court recognized that vacatur could be granted in "extraordinary circumstances." Id. at 29, 115 S.Ct. at 393, 130 L.Ed.2d at 244. What circumstances might count as "extraordinary"?

Two years earlier, in NEARY v. REGENTS OF THE UNIVERSITY OF CALIFORNIA, 3 Cal.4th 273, 10 Cal.Rptr.2d 859, 834 P.2d 119 (1992), the California Supreme Court had held that stipulated reversals are consistent with the policy in favor of peaceful settlements and should be granted *absent* a showing of extraordinary circumstances warranting an exception to this general rule. What did the California court mean by "extraordinary circumstances"? Why is it appropriate to permit a losing defendant to cloak himself against collateral estoppel in later cases, thereby denying subsequent plaintiffs the benefit of having complex liability issues resolved in the initial litigation? The California legislature during its 1999–2000 session modified California Code of Civil Procedure § 128(a)(8) to provide that an appellate court shall not permit a stipulated reversal

> unless the court finds both of the following: (a) there is no reasonable possibility that the interests of nonparties or the public will be adversely

affected by the reversal; and (b) that the reasons of the parties for requesting reversal outweigh the erosion of public trust that may result from the nullification of a judgment and the risk that the availability of stipulated reversal will reduce the incentive for pretrial settlement.

See Martin & Shatz, *Reverse Course*, 25 L.A. Law. 24 (Feb. 2003) (discussing trend in denial of stipulated reversal requests post-amendment of Section 128(a)(8)).

For a discussion of *Bancorp* and *Neary*, see Resnik, *Whose Judgment? Vacating Judgments, Preferences for Settlement, and the Role of Adjudication at the Close of the Twentieth Century*, 41 UCLA L. Rev. 1471 (1994).

4. Suppose that rather than settling the dispute in *Hanover*, the parties merely stipulated most of the material facts concerning the lease agreement. The case went to trial, further factual findings were made, and a decision was rendered for Hanover against Anderson. Should the admissions in those stipulations be available in a subsequent suit between the parties? What if the suit is between another plaintiff and Hanover, and the complaint is based upon the same alleged breach of the lease? What light does the last sentence of Rule 36(b) shed on this problem? Do stipulated facts constitute an "adjudication on the merits"?

5. Modern rules of procedure allow courts to dismiss an action and enter judgment at various stages of a litigation prior to a final verdict. See, e.g., Federal Rule 12. These dismissals are not based upon the agreement of the parties, and, indeed, usually are opposed vigorously. Should a judgment consented to by the parties be considered more "on the merits" than an involuntary dismissal or judgment? Why?

HOUSING AUTHORITY FOR LA SALLE COUNTY v. YOUNG MEN'S CHRISTIAN ASSOCIATION OF OTTAWA, 101 Ill.2d 246, 78 Ill.Dec. 125, 461 N.E.2d 959 (1984). In 1932, the federal government sought to condemn easements over certain property for the purpose of constructing a system of locks and dams on the Illinois River. Seventy parties were summoned to court to adjudicate the title to the property so the government would know who was entitled to compensation as a result of the condemnation. With respect to a certain parcel of land, the government's petition pointed to a conflict over the title between Ella E. Deenis and The First Trust Company of Ottawa, Illinois ("First Trust"). Deenis failed to appear after being served properly with summons, resulting in a default judgment in favor of First Trust. The judgment determined that First Trust owned the property in question, and First Trust was awarded $650 as compensation for the easements.

The second suit arose over fifty years later between the parties' successors in interest to the property. The Housing Authority for La Salle County, Deenis' successor in interest, sought an injunction prohibiting the Young Men's Christian Association of Ottawa ("YMCA"), First Trust's successor in interest, from constructing a parking lot on the real estate.

The YMCA asserted the earlier judgment in the condemnation action as collateral estoppel with respect to the title to the property. The court decided that the case was governed by the principles of res judicata rather than collateral estoppel, but nonetheless held that the earlier judgment was conclusive as to the parties' rights:

> * * * When Deenis defaulted and the court entered a judgment finding First Trust to be the fee owner of the property, the title dispute was resolved and the doctrine of *res judicata* applied to bar any relitigation of that claim.
>
> Although the judgment against Deenis was by default, it is entitled to the same preclusive effect under the doctrine of *res judicata* as any other judgment. Some courts have held that default judgments have limited preclusive effects under the doctrine of collateral estoppel. * * * However, default judgments are always *res judicata* on the ultimate claim or demand presented in the complaint.
>
> * * *
>
> The housing authority argues that Deenis lacked sufficient incentive to litigate the issue of title in the condemnation proceeding and, therefore, it is inequitable to accord the judgment in that proceeding preclusive effect as having determined the ownership of the disputed parcel. This argument is unpersuasive. Under special circumstances, the absence of an incentive to litigate might be relevant in the application of collateral estoppel (Restatement (Second) of Judgments sec. 28(5)(c) (1982)), but no authority suggests that it is relevant when the doctrine to be applied is *res judicata.*

Id. at 253, 78 Ill.Dec. at 129, 461 N.E.2d at 963.

NOTES AND QUESTIONS

1. Suppose a small Massachusetts computer company contracts with a large California microchip supplier. The computer company refuses to pay for a shipment, alleging that a large percentage of the chips are defective. The supplier files suit in California to recover $2,000, the balance due on the contract. The computer company chooses not to defend the action because the liability isn't large enough to justify the cost of litigation, and a default judgment is entered against it. Subsequently, the computer company is sued for $1,000,000 by a customer whose computer exploded due to a defective chip. The computer company impleads the supplier, seeking indemnification. But the supplier argues that the judgment in the California suit determined that it had delivered chips produced to specifications. Should the default judgment be given preclusive effect in these circumstances? Is the supplier seeking claim or issue preclusion? Should the absence of incentive to litigate be treated differently where issue preclusion, rather than claim preclusion, is sought?

2. How should the dismissal of a prior action on the ground that it was barred by a statute of limitations be treated in a subsequent suit on the same

matter? Suppose a discharged employee brings a sex-discrimination suit against her employer, but the case is dismissed because it was filed after the limitations period had expired. The employee then files a second suit based on breach of contract, a cause of action that would not be barred by the statute of limitations. Is the second action precluded?

3. How should prior criminal proceedings affect subsequent civil litigation? Suppose that upon trial in federal court a criminal defendant, who asserted the defense of entrapment, was acquitted of charges of knowingly engaging in the business of dealing in firearms without a license, and that the government then instituted an in rem action for forfeiture of the firearms involved, pursuant to a federal statute which authorizes forfeiture of firearms used or intended to be used in violation of federal law. Can the defendant argue that the in rem proceeding is precluded by the prior acquittal? Are you influenced by the fact that the acquittal reflected only the existence of a reasonable doubt about the defendant's guilt as the jury did not find that it was more probable than not that the defendant did not have possession of the firearms with an intent to violate federal law? See United States v. One Assortment of 89 Firearms, 465 U.S. 354, 104 S.Ct. 1099, 79 L.Ed.2d 361 (1984).

2. JUDGMENTS OF NONJUDICIAL TRIBUNALS

HOLMBERG v. STATE, DIVISION OF RISK MANAGEMENT

Supreme Court of Alaska, 1990.
796 P.2d 823.

MOORE, JUSTICE.

Karen Holmberg asks us to reverse the Alaska Workers' Compensation Board ("AWCB") decision denying her permanent total disability benefits on the ground that a later decision of the Public Employees Retirement Board ("PERB") conclusively determined that she was not physically able to perform her duties as an employee of the State of Alaska. * * *

* * *

I.

Karen Holmberg began working for the State of Alaska, Division of Risk Management ("Risk Management") in 1979. She has a history of back injuries dating to the early 1960s. * * *

* * *

* * * On February 18, 1988, AWCB awarded Holmberg temporary total disability benefits, but denied her claim for permanent total disability benefits. Holmberg appealed AWCB's denial of permanent total disability benefits to the superior court in March 1988.

Holmberg also sought disability benefits from [the Public Employees Retirement System ("PERS")]. The Division of Retirement and Benefits

("Retirement and Benefits"), which administers PERS, awarded her non-occupational disability benefits. However, the Disability Review Board denied her claim for occupational disability benefits. Holmberg appealed this initial decision to PERB. On April 20, 1988, after AWCB had denied her claim for permanent total disability benefits, PERB found that Holmberg was permanently and totally disabled as a result of accidents at work, and accordingly, awarded her occupational disability benefits.

Holmberg supplemented the record in her appeal from the prior AWCB decision with the new PERB decision. In the proceedings before the superior court, Holmberg argued that the AWCB decision should be reversed because of the preclusive effect of the later PERB decision. The superior court affirmed the AWCB decision and Holmberg appealed.

II.

Holmberg's primary contention is that PERB's factual determination that she was physically unable to perform her duties at Risk Management should be given binding effect in this appeal of the AWCB decision against her.[2] * * *

* * *

Although res judicata principles were developed in judicial settings, they "may be applied to adjudicative determinations made by administrative agencies." Jeffries v. Glacier State Tel. Co., 604 P.2d 4, 8 (Alaska 1979) * * *. Of course, "[a]n administrative decision commands preclusive effects only if it resulted from a procedure that seems an adequate substitute for judicial procedure." * * * [18 Wright, Miller and Cooper, Federal Practice and Procedure § 4475].

Recently, we held that AWCB decisions may have preclusive effect. * * * We see no reason why PERB decisions should not also be given preclusive effect. First, like AWCB proceedings, PERB hearings include many of the procedural safeguards of a judicial hearing including the right to introduce evidence, call witnesses, and cross-examine opposing witnesses. * * * Second there is no indicating in the PERS enabling statute * * * that a PERB determination should not preclude an independent judicial determination.

The state does not contend that PERB decisions should not be given preclusive effect. Rather, the state argues that preclusive effect should not be given to PERB determinations in AWCB proceedings. We have not addressed the question how res judicata principles apply between different agencies. The Supreme Court has held that litigation conducted before one agency or official is generally binding on another agency or official of the

2. * * * Holmberg recognizes that the question whether she was disabled for purposes of PERS is not the same question as whether she was disabled for purposes of the Alaska Workers' Compensation Act. * * * Holmberg limits her collateral estoppel claim to the narrower factual question whether she was physically able to work at Risk Management. However, she maintains that the resolution of this factual issue in her favor is tantamount to a finding that she was permanently and totally disabled for purposes of workers' compensation because the state conceded as much in the AWCB proceeding.

same government because officers of the same government are in privity with each other. *Sunshine Anthracite Coal Co. v. Adkins,* 310 U.S. 381, 402–03, 60 S.Ct. 907, 916–17, 84 L.Ed. 1263 (1940). The Court stated that "[t]he crucial point is whether or not in the earlier litigation the representative of the United States had authority to represent its interests in a final adjudication of the issue in controversy." 310 U.S. at 403, 60 S.Ct. at 917. * * *

The United States Court of Appeals has applied this authority principle in appropriate cases. In *Safir v. Gibson,* 432 F.2d 137 (2d Cir.), *cert. denied,* 400 U.S. 850, 91 S.Ct. 57, 27 L.Ed.2d 88 (1970), the court relied on the authority principle in holding that the Federal Maritime Commission's determination that the rates of a conference of common carriers were unfair and unjustly discriminatory precluded the independent Maritime Administration from relitigating the issue. * * * In *Porter & Dietsch, Inc. v. FTC,* 605 F.2d 294 (7th Cir.1979), *cert. denied,* 445 U.S. 950, 100 S.Ct. 1597, 63 L.Ed.2d 784 (1980), the court refused to give preclusive effect to a Postal Service factual determination concerning the safety of a diet pill in a Federal Trade Commission proceeding. The court found that there was "a clear and convincing need for a new determination of the issue ... because of the potential impact of the determination on the public interest or the interests of persons not themselves parties to the initial action." 605 F.2d at 300.

The court's holding in *Porter & Dietsch* illustrates the principle that preclusion may be defeated by finding such an important difference in the functions of different agencies that one does not have authority to represent the interests of the other. * * *

* * *

In this case, it does not appear that PERB has any more expertise than AWCB in making factual determinations of a person's physical ability to work at a particular job. Therefore, there is no affirmative reason why the PERB decision should be given preclusive effect as * * * [the agency's] decision was in *Safir*. The state makes several arguments why granting PERB determinations preclusive effect in AWCB proceedings would be inconsistent with the Alaska Workers Compensation Act * * * [but this argument] stems from the false premise that Holmberg seeks to preclude AWCB's ultimate disability determination instead of its factual determination that Holmberg was physically able to perform her job duties.[3]

The state argues that the different functions of the workers compensation system and PERS prevent the application of collateral estoppel. * * * [The court noted that the disability standards for PERB and AWCB

3. For example, the State's argument that collateral estoppel is not properly invoked between two independent tribunals which have statutory discretion to fashion separate remedies confuses issue preclusion with claim preclusion. * * * AWCB's authority to fashion a separate remedy is no argument against precluding the relitigation of identical factual issues decided in an earlier PERB proceeding. * * *

decisions differ, but went on to state] * * * they provide no substantial reason why AWCB should be allowed to relitigate the narrow factual question whether Holmberg is physically able to continue performing her job with Risk Management. Although the value of collateral estoppel may be low in light of the [different] * * * disability inquiry under AWCA, that is not a substantial reason to allow relitigation.* * *

* * *

III.

[The court then determined whether the two agencies are in privity with each other as to allow issue preclusion against a nonparty to a judgment.]

* * *

A.

* * * Privity exists between different agencies of the same government unless "there are important differences in the authority of the respective agencies." Briggs v. State, 732 P.2d 1078, 1082 (Alaska 1987). This is the same test that determines whether the decision of one agency binds another agency. In the privity context, however, the question is not whether the forum agencies are in privity, but whether the agencies appearing before them are. * * *

* * * Holmberg * * * argues that Retirement and Benefits is in privity with Risk Management because "the interests of the two agencies are virtually identical for purposes of [her] claims, and Retirement and Benefits had every incentive to vigorously defend the PERS claim."

Holmberg's error is in identifying Retirement and Benefits as the party against which PERB entered judgment. Retirement and Benefits is charged with administrative responsibility for PERS. The significance of this is that when Retirement and Benefits appears before PERB, it represents the interests of PERS, not the interests of the state. Thus, while Retirement and Benefits contested Holmberg's claim before PERB, the state is correct in saying that the party against which PERB entered judgment is the system itself.

* * *

* * * PERS is not a state agency but an independent retirement plan in which public employees are members and in which their employers participate. * * * While a state agency administers PERS and represents it during appeals, the state as employer is just one participant. The state treasury is affected by a benefit determination only insofar as the state is an employer participant. * * *

* * * The question is not whether PERS is bound by an AWCB decision against one of its members, but whether one of its members is bound by a decision against PERS. The questions are not symmetrical.

The PERS constituency is not represented at all in a workers' compensation proceeding. The employer-participant, however, is at least nominally represented in the PERS proceeding to the extent that it has an interest in the PERS fund. At the same time, this nominal representation is not sufficient to assure that the participant has had adequate notice and opportunity to be heard and that its rights and interests have been protected. We therefore hold that the state as a participant in PERS is not in privity with PERS.

B.

Our holding that the state is not in privity with PERS is sufficient to deny affording any preclusive effect to the PERB decision as against the state. However, even if the state and PERS were in privity, the PERB decision would not preclude any issues raised in the earlier AWCB proceeding because the PERB decision was not the first final judgment addressing those issues. Holmberg observes that "[t]his case presents the collateral estoppel issue in a somewhat unusual procedural context." AWCB reached its decision first. While that decision was on appeal, PERB entered a contrary decision which was not appealed. Holmberg argues that the PERB decision was the first final judgment for the res judicata purposes and therefore precludes AWCB's contrary decision because the AWCB decision was appealed.

We disagree. A final judgment retains all of its res judicata effects pending resolution of an appeal of the judgment. * * * This rule respects the principle of repose inherent in the doctrine of res judicata. If a judgment was denied its res judicata effects merely because an appeal was pending, a litigant could refile an identical case in another trial court creating duplicative litigation. This case well illustrates the point. Having lost on the issue whether she was physically able to perform her job duties in the AWCB proceeding, Holmberg appealed the decision and then successfully relitigated the issue before PERB. Retirement and Benefits did not argue that PERB was precluded from relitigating the issue that AWCB already had decided. Now Holmberg asks us to reverse the earlier AWCB determination simply because of the later PERB determination. * * * To reward relitigation of an issue by reversing the original determination is completely at odds with the purpose of collateral estoppel to prevent relitigation of issues that already have been decided.

* * *

In this case, the AWCB decision was the first final judgment even though it was appealed. The later PERB determination that Holmberg was not physically able to perform her duties at Risk Management cannot preclude AWCB's earlier contrary determination. Indeed, if the other requirements of collateral estoppel were satisfied, Retirement and Benefits could have precluded Holmberg from relitigating the issue already decided by AWCB.

* * *

The decision of the superior court is AFFIRMED.

NOTE AND QUESTIONS

1. In evaluating whether to give preclusive effect to the PERB judgment, the *Holmberg* court examined whether the adjudication was sufficiently judicial to warrant issue preclusion. What factors are significant to this assessment? In *Holmberg*, the court focused on the availability of procedural protections. The same considerations are present in inter-system preclusion, for example, when a court in the federal system considers the preclusive effect of a determination of a state nonjudicial tribunal. See University of Tennessee v. Elliott, p. 1355, supra.

2. Ratemaking proceedings are conducted by administrative agencies with special expertise to assess economic and other conditions. The proceedings often involve the calling of witnesses, the availability of cross-examination, and other adjudicative protections. Should issue preclusion attach to ratemaking determinations, or are they really legislative decisions? See Allied Chem., An Operating Unit of Allied Corp. v. Niagara Mohawk Power Corp., 72 N.Y.2d 271, 278, 528 N.E.2d 153, 156 (1988), in which the New York Court of Appeals explained that "[b]ecause a ratemaking agency must be free to reassess the reasonableness of rates, it would be illogical, and inconsistent with the agency's function, to give preclusive effect to a prior ratemaking determination * * *."

3. What role did privity play in the court's decision? Privity recognizes that certain substantive relationships justify extending the preclusive effect of a judgment to a nonparty. These relationships include that of a partnership and its members, successors in interest to property, and a corporation and its officers. Restatement (Second) of Judgments §§ 41, 54, 59–60 (1982). Privity has been criticized as an "elusive" concept that is more conclusory than explanatory:

> * * * [T]he term privity in itself does not state a reason for either including or excluding a person from the binding effect of a prior judgment, but rather it represents a legal conclusion that the relationship between the one who is a party on the record and the non-party is sufficiently close to afford application of the principle of preclusion.

Southwest Airlines Co. v. Texas Int'l Airlines, 546 F.2d 84, 95 (5th Cir.), certiorari denied 434 U.S. 832, 98 S.Ct. 117, 54 L.Ed.2d 93 (1977) (citation omitted). See also 18A Wright, Miller & Cooper, Federal Practice and Procedure: Jurisdiction and Related Matters § 4449. What factors were significant in *Holmberg* in determining whether the two government agencies were in privity? Are these the same factors you would consider in determining whether two individuals are in privity? See deJesus, *Interagency Privity and Claim Preclusion,* 57 U. Chi. L. Rev. 195 (1990).

SECTION E. PERSONS BENEFITTED AND PERSONS BOUND BY PRECLUSION

1. THE TRADITIONAL MODEL

The traditional rule of issue preclusion was that persons benefitted from a prior judgment only if they also were bound by it. "This rule, known as the rule of mutuality, established a pleasing symmetry—a judgment was binding only on parties and persons in privity with them, and a judgment could be invoked only by parties and their privies." 18A Wright, Miller & Cooper, Federal Practice and Procedure: Jurisdiction and Related Matters 2d § 4463. The modern trend has been an erosion in the requirement of mutuality—"followed more recently by second thoughts about whether the erosion is sufficiently justified." Shapiro, Civil Procedure: Preclusion in Civil Actions 102–03 (2001).

Indemnification relations provided the earliest basis for an exception from the rule of mutuality. See First Nat. Bank v. City Nat. Bank, 182 Mass. 130, 65 N.E. 24 (1902). The policy rationale was rooted in the indemnification obligation:

> * * * [D]enial of preclusion would force an impossible choice between unacceptable alternatives. If a second action can be maintained against the indemnitee, either the indemnitee must be allowed to assert his right of indemnification or the right must be defeated by the judgment in favor of the indemnitor. To allow the right of indemnification would be to destroy the victory won by the indemnitor in the first action. To deny the right of indemnification would be to destroy the indemnitee's right by the result of an action in which he took no part.

18A Wright, Miller & Cooper, Federal Practice and Procedure: Jurisdiction and Related Matters 2d § 4463. As you read the remainder of this Section, consider whether it is appropriate to allow a nonparty to take advantage of a favorable judgment when that nonparty would not have been subject to preclusion if the prior judgment had been unfavorable to him. Courts have shown an increasing willingness to permit preclusion (often referred to as nonmutual estoppel) in such circumstances. Also consider whether it is appropriate to bind nonparties by an unfavorable judgment. A limited number of courts have shown a willingness to permit exceptions to the traditional rule that an individual can be bound by a court decision only when he has had his "day in court."

NOTES AND QUESTIONS

1. How would the rule of mutuality affect the analysis in the following situations?

(a) A, an employee acting within the scope of his employment and driving the employer's, B's, car, collides with a car driven by C. C sues A, and judgment is for A. Subsequently B sues C for damages to the car. What effect should the earlier judgment for A have in B's suit against C?

(b) Suppose on the facts of Question (a) that C had first sued B, and judgment had been for B, and C had then sued A. What effect should the earlier judgment for B have in C's suit against A? Would your answer be different if the second suit had been by A against C?

(c) Suppose that in the first action, A, a real-estate broker, had sued the seller of property, B, for commissions. The trial court dismissed A's action after trial on the ground that A had not produced the person, C, who ultimately had purchased B's property and therefore was not entitled to a brokerage commission. In the second action A sues C for inducing B to breach the brokerage contract causing a loss of the commission. Can C successfully rely on the decision against A in the first action as a bar to A's action against him?

(d) Suppose a wrongful-death action for the death of a child is brought by a personal representative and judgment was for defendant. Is the mother estopped by the earlier judgment in an action for her personal injuries arising out of the same accident when she would have been one of the beneficiaries if the first action had been successful?

2. THE DECLINE OF THE MUTUALITY DOCTRINE

BERNHARD v. BANK OF AMERICA NAT. TRUST & SAVINGS ASS'N

Supreme Court of California, 1942.
19 Cal.2d 807, 122 P.2d 892.

TRAYNOR, JUSTICE.

In June, 1933, Mrs. Clara Sather, an elderly woman, made her home with Mr. and Mrs. Charles O. Cook in San Dimas, California. Because of her failing health, she authorized Mr. Cook and Dr. Joseph Zeiler to make drafts jointly against her commercial account in the Security First National Bank of Los Angeles. On August 24, 1933, Mr. Cook opened a commercial account at the First National Bank of San Dimas in the name of "Clara Sather by Charles O. Cook." * * * Thereafter, a number of checks drawn by Cook and Zeiler on Mrs. Sather's commercial account in Los Angeles were deposited in the San Dimas account * * *.

On October 26, 1933, a teller from the Los Angeles Bank called on Mrs. Sather at her request to assist in transferring her money from the Los Angeles Bank to the San Dimas Bank. In the presence of this teller, the cashier of the San Dimas Bank, Mr. Cook, and her physician, Mrs. Sather signed by mark an authorization directing the Security First National Bank of Los Angeles to transfer the balance of her savings account in the amount of $4,155.68 to the First National Bank of San Dimas * * * "for credit to the account of Mrs. Clara Sather." The order was credited by the San Dimas Bank to the account of "Clara Sather by Charles O. Cook." Cook withdrew the entire balance from that account and opened a new account in the same bank in the name of himself and his wife. * * *

Mrs. Sather died in November, 1933. Cook qualified as executor of the estate and proceeded with its administration. After a lapse of several years he filed an account at the instance of the probate court accompanied by his resignation. The account made no mention of the money transferred by Mrs. Sather to the San Dimas Bank; and Helen Bernhard * * * [and other] beneficiaries under Mrs. Sather's will, filed objections to the account for this reason. After a hearing on the objections the court settled the account, and as part of its order declared that the decedent during her lifetime had made a gift to Charles O. Cook of the amount of the deposit in question.

After Cook's discharge, Helen Bernhard was appointed administratrix with the will annexed. She instituted this action against defendant, the Bank of America, successor to the San Dimas Bank, seeking to recover the deposit on the ground that the bank was indebted to the estate for this amount because Mrs. Sather never authorized its withdrawal. In addition to a general denial, defendant pleaded two affirmative defenses: (1) That the money on deposit was paid out to Charles O. Cook with the consent of Mrs. Sather and (2) that this fact is res judicata by virtue of the finding of the probate court * * *. The trial court * * * gave judgment for defendant on the ground that Cook's ownership of the money was conclusively established by the finding of the probate court. * * *

Plaintiff contends that the doctrine of res judicata does not apply because the defendant who is asserting the plea was not a party to the previous action nor in privity with a party to that action and because there is no mutuality of estoppel.

* * *

Many courts have stated the facile formula that the plea of res judicata is available only when there is privity and mutuality of estoppel. * * * Under the requirement of privity, only parties to the former judgment or their privies may take advantage of or be bound by it. * * * A party in this connection is one who is "directly interested in the subject matter, and had a right to make defense, or to control the proceeding, and to appeal from the judgment." * * * A privy is one who, after rendition of the judgment, has acquired an interest in the subject matter affected by the judgment through or under one of the parties, as by inheritance, succession, or purchase. * * * The estoppel is mutual if the one taking advantage of the earlier adjudication would have been bound by it, had it gone against him. * * *

The criteria for determining who may assert a plea of res judicata differ fundamentally from the criteria for determining against whom a plea of res judicata may be asserted. The requirements of due process of law forbid the assertion of a plea of res judicata against a party unless he was bound by the earlier litigation in which the matter was decided. * * * He is bound by that litigation only if he has been a party thereto or in privity with a party thereto. * * * There is no compelling reason, however, for requiring that the party asserting the plea of res judicata must have been a party, or in privity with a party, to the earlier litigation.

No satisfactory rationalization has been advanced for the requirement of mutuality. Just why a party who was not bound by a previous action should be precluded from asserting it as res judicata against a party who was bound by it is difficult to comprehend. * * * Many courts have abandoned the requirement of mutuality and confined the requirement of privity to the party against whom the plea of res judicata is asserted. * * * The commentators are almost unanimously in accord. * * * The courts of most jurisdictions have in effect accomplished the same result by recognizing a broad exception to the requirements of mutuality and privity, namely, that they are not necessary where the liability of the defendant asserting the plea of res judicata is dependent upon or derived from the liability of one who was exonerated in an earlier suit brought by the same plaintiff upon the same facts. * * * Typical examples of such derivative liability are master and servant, principal and agent, and indemnitor and indemnitee. Thus, if a plaintiff sues a servant for injuries caused by the servant's alleged negligence within the scope of his employment, a judgment against the plaintiff of [sic] the grounds that the servant was not negligent can be pleaded by the master as res judicata if he is subsequently sued by the same plaintiff for the same injuries. Conversely, if the plaintiff first sues the master, a judgment against the plaintiff on the grounds that the servant was not negligent can be pleaded by the servant as res judicata if he is subsequently sued by the plaintiff. In each of these situations the party asserting the plea of res judicata was not a party to the previous action nor in privity with such a party * * *. Likewise, the estoppel is not mutual since the party asserting the plea, not having been a party or in privity with a party to the former action, would not have been bound by it had it been decided the other way. The cases justify this exception on the ground that it would be unjust to permit one who has had his day in court to reopen identical issues by merely switching adversaries.

In determining the validity of a plea of res judicata three questions are pertinent: Was the issue decided in the prior adjudication identical with the one presented in the action in question? Was there a final judgment on the merits? Was the party against whom the plea is asserted a party or in privity with a party to the prior adjudication?

* * * Since the issue as to the ownership of the money is identical with the issue raised in the probate proceeding, and since the order of the probate court settling the executor's account was a final adjudication of this issue on the merits * * *, it remains only to determine whether the plaintiff in the present action was a party or in privity with a party to the earlier proceeding. The plaintiff has brought the present action in the capacity of administratrix of the estate. In this capacity she represents the very same persons and interests that were represented in the earlier hearing on the executor's account. In that proceeding plaintiff and the other legatees who objected to the executor's account represented the

estate of the decedent. They were seeking not a personal recovery but, like the plaintiff in the present action, as administratrix, a recovery for the benefit of the legatees and creditors of the estate, all of whom were bound by the order settling the account. * * *

The judgment is affirmed.

NOTES AND QUESTIONS

1. In *Bernhard* Justice Traynor mentions that some courts already had recognized that exceptions to the mutuality requirement arise most often in cases involving vicarious liability. Consider these common examples:

(a) A institutes an action for negligence against B, an employee of C, for conduct occurring while B was acting in the scope of employment. If B prevails, C will be able to raise the first judgment in a suit by A to recover against C.

(b) X corporation is a general contractor liable for the proper performance of an entire contract in which Y is a subcontractor. Z, the beneficiary of the contract, sues Y for incomplete performance and loses. If Z brings a suit against X that raises the same claim as the earlier suit, X will be able to invoke the preclusive effects of this prior judgment.

2. In which of the following situations would preclusion be available under *Bernhard*?

(a) Three cars, driven by A, B, and C, respectively, collide in an intersection in a jurisdiction without a compulsory-joinder statute. Driver A, believing that C does not have enough money to satisfy the judgment, institutes a negligence action against B. At trial B is exonerated, the court holding that A's injuries were solely the result of A's own negligence. A then discovers that C actually does have enough money to make him worth suing, and promptly files suit against him. Can C invoke the judgment in A's prior action against B to preclude recovery by A against him?

(b) Assume the same fact pattern as above. Could C assert the judgment in the prior suit as the basis to recover on a counterclaim against A?

(c) A bus owned and driven by D is in an accident. Passenger P1 sues D, alleging that the accident was caused by D's negligent driving. The trial court finds for P1. Passenger P2 files a claim against D, also alleging damages as a result of D's negligence. Is preclusion available to P2? Can you articulate how this fact pattern differs from that of (b)?

(d) What if, on the facts of (c), the bus driver/owner had prevailed in the first suit? When P2 brought the second litigation, could D then use the first suit's judgment as a defense to the second action?

3. *Bernhard* focuses on the question of whether a defendant can prevent a plaintiff from relitgating an issue that previously was decided against the plaintiff. Commentators call this type of estoppel "nonmutual defensive collateral estoppel." For a classic discussion, see Currie, *Civil Procedure: The Tempest Brews*, 53 Calif.L.Rev. 25, 38–46 (1965). See also Currie, *Mutuality of*

Collateral Estoppel—Limits of the Bernhard *Doctrine*, 9 Stan.L.Rev. 281 (1957).

4. In BLONDER–TONGUE LABORATORIES, INC. v. UNIVERSITY OF ILLINOIS FOUNDATION, 402 U.S. 313, 91 S.Ct. 1434, 28 L.Ed.2d 788 (1971), involving a patent infringement action, the Supreme Court first began to abrogate the mutuality requirement for the federal system. The Court expressed the following views on the propriety of nonmutual preclusion:

> The cases and authorities discussed * * * connect erosion of the mutuality requirement to the goal of limiting relitigation of issues where that can be achieved without compromising fairness in particular cases. The courts have often discarded the rule while commenting on crowded dockets and long delays preceding trial. Authorities differ on whether the public interest in efficient judicial administration is a sufficient ground in and of itself for abandoning mutuality, but it is clear that more than crowded dockets is involved. The broader question is whether it is any longer tenable to afford a litigant more than one full and fair opportunity for judicial resolution of the same issue. The question in these terms includes as part of the calculus the effect on judicial administration, but it also encompasses the concern exemplified by Bentham's reference to the gaming table in his attack on the principle of mutuality of estoppel. In any lawsuit where a defendant, because of the mutuality principle, is forced to present a complete defense on the merits to a claim which the plaintiff has fully litigated and lost in a prior action, there is an arguable misallocation of resources. To the extent the defendant in the second suit may not win by asserting, without contradiction, that the plaintiff had fully and fairly, but unsuccessfully, litigated the same claim in the prior suit, the defendant's time and money are diverted from alternative uses—productive or otherwise—to relitigation of a decided issue. And, still assuming that the issue was resolved correctly in the first suit, there is reason to be concerned about the plaintiff's allocation of resources. Permitting repeated litigation of the same issue as long as the supply of unrelated defendants holds out reflects either the aura of the gaming table or "a lack of discipline and of disinterestedness on the part of the lower courts, hardly a worthy or wise basis for fashioning rules of procedure." Kerotest Mfg. Co. v. C–O–Two Co., 342 U.S. 180, 185, 72 S.Ct. 219, 222, 96 L.Ed. 200 (1952). Although neither judges, the parties, nor the adversary system performs perfectly in all cases, the requirement of determining whether the party against whom an estoppel is asserted had a full and fair opportunity to litigate is a most significant safeguard.
>
> Some litigants—those who never appeared in a prior action—may not be collaterally estopped without litigating the issue. They have never had a chance to present their evidence and arguments on the claim. Due process prohibits estopping them despite one or more existing adjudications of the identical issue which stand squarely against their position. * * * Also, the authorities have been more willing to permit a defendant in a second suit to invoke an estoppel against a plaintiff who lost on the same claim in an earlier suit than they have been to allow a plaintiff in the second suit to use offensively a judgment obtained by a different plaintiff in a prior suit against the same defendant. But the case before us involves neither due

> process nor "offensive use" questions. Rather, it depends on the considerations weighing for and against permitting a patent holder to sue on his patent after it has once been held invalid following opportunity for full and fair trial.

Id. at 328–33, 91 S.Ct. at 1442–43, 28 L.Ed.2d at 799–800.

The Court emphasized that the district court retained discretion to accept or reject a plea of collateral estoppel:

> * * * [W]e do not suggest, without legislative guidance, that a plea of estoppel by an infringement or royalty suit defendant must automatically be accepted once the defendant in support of his plea identifies the issue in suit as the identical question finally decided against the patentee or one of his privies in previous litigation. * * * Rather, the patentee-plaintiff must be permitted to demonstrate, if he can, that he did not have "a fair opportunity procedurally, substantively and evidentially to pursue his claim the first time." * * * This element in the estoppel decision will comprehend, we believe, the important concerns about the complexity of patent litigation and the posited hazard that the prior proceedings were seriously defective.
>
> Determining whether a patentee has had a full and fair chance to litigate the validity of his patent in an earlier case is of necessity not a simple matter. In addition to * * * considerations of choice of forum and incentive to litigate * * *, certain other factors immediately emerge. For example, if the issue is nonobviousness, appropriate inquiries would be whether the first validity determination purported to employ the [appropriate legal] standards * * *; whether the opinions filed by the District Court and the reviewing court, if any, indicate that the prior case was one of those relatively rare instances where the courts wholly failed to grasp the technical subject matter and issues in suit; and whether without fault of his own the patentee was deprived of crucial evidence or witnesses in the first litigation. But as so often is the case, no one set of facts, no one collection of words or phrases will provide an automatic formula for proper rulings on estoppel pleas. In the end, decision will necessarily rest on the trial courts' sense of justice and equity.

Id. at 332–34, 91 S.Ct. at 1445, 28 L.Ed.2d at 802.

The Court underscored that relaxing the mutuality requirement in patent cases would produce cost savings for the federal courts:

> * * *[A]lthough patent trials are only a small portion of the total amount of litigation in the federal courts, they tend to be of disproportionate length. * * *
>
> * * * [I]t is clear that abrogation of [the mutuality rule in patent cases] * * * will save *some* judicial time if even a few relatively lengthy patent suits may be fairly disposed of on pleas of estoppel. More fundamentally, while the cases do discuss reduction in dockets as an effect of elimination of the mutuality requirement, they do not purport to hold that predictions about the actual amount of judicial time that will be saved under such a holding control decision of that question.

Id. at 348–49, 91 S.Ct. at 1452–53, 28 L.Ed.2d at 810–11.

NOTES AND QUESTIONS

1. Do you find the justification for relaxing the mutuality requirement in patent cases persuasive? Doesn't the *Blonder–Tongue* rule "merely shift the focus of litigation from the merits of the dispute to the question whether the party to be estopped had a full and fair opportunity to litigate his claim in the first action"? *Blonder–Tongue*, id. at 347, 91 S.Ct. at 1452, 28 L.Ed.2d at 810.

2. Although *Blonder–Tongue* could be read as limited to patent actions, lower courts freely cite to it as authority for nonmutual preclusion in all types of substantive claims. Is it clear that relaxing the mutuality requirement in these other cases will produce cost savings?

3. Is it feasible or fair to require extensive party joinder in a single lawsuit? Is it possible that the presence of too many defendants in an action will undermine the quality of decision making in the first action? See 18A Wright, Miller & Cooper, Federal Practice and Procedure: Jurisdiction and Related Matters 2d § 4464.

4. Does the *Bernhard* test for nonmutual collateral estoppel differ from that of the Supreme Court in *Blonder–Tongue*? In what ways? Which test is preferable?

5. In both *Bernhard* and *Blonder–Tongue* the party that was precluded in the second action was the party that had instituted the first action. Should this be an important factor in determining whether nonmutual preclusion is appropriate? Or should the only relevant consideration be whether the party against whom preclusion is being asserted had a full and fair opportunity to litigate? See Zdanok v. Glidden Co., 327 F.2d 944 (2d Cir.) (Friendly, J.), certiorari denied 377 U.S. 934, 84 S.Ct. 1338, 12 L.Ed.2d 298 (1964). See generally Waggoner, *Fifty Years of* Bernhard v. Bank of America *Is Enough: Collateral Estoppel Should Require Mutuality But Res Judicata Should Not*, 12 Rev. Litig. 391 (1993), who argues:

> That nonmutual collateral estoppel is unfair emerges from the fact that litigation involves a substantial element of chance * * *.
>
> The risk in litigation is much like the risk in a coin flip, even though the court system by a variety of mechanisms tries to resolve disputes accurately, and even though each side tries by retention of skilled counsel and by diligent preparation to make the odds as much as possible favor it. In such a coin flip you put up your money and you abide by the result, win or lose. That seems fair. Now suppose a bystander who has watched the coin flip but who has not risked his cash were to approach the loser and say, "Pay me, too." Such a demand would be laughed away, it is so obviously unfair. Yet such demands are now commonly enforced under the doctrine of nonmutual collateral estoppel.

Id. at 416.

PARKLANE HOSIERY CO. v. SHORE

Supreme Court of the United States, 1979.
439 U.S. 322, 99 S.Ct. 645, 58 L.Ed.2d 552.

Certiorari to the United States Court of Appeals for the Second Circuit.

MR. JUSTICE STEWART delivered the opinion of the Court.

* * *

The respondent brought this stockholder's class action against the petitioners in a federal district court. The complaint alleged that the petitioners * * * had issued a materially false and misleading proxy statement in connection with a merger. * * * The complaint sought damages, rescission of the merger, and recovery of costs.

Before this action came to trial, the SEC filed suit against the same defendants in a federal district court, alleging that the proxy statement that had been issued by Parklane was materially false and misleading in essentially the same respects as those that had been alleged in the respondent's complaint. Injunctive relief was requested. After a four-day trial, the District Court found that the proxy statement was materially false and misleading in the respects alleged, and entered a declaratory judgment to that effect. * * * The Court of Appeals for the Second Circuit affirmed * * *.

The respondent in the present case then moved for partial summary judgment against the petitioners, asserting that the petitioners were collaterally estopped from relitigating the issues that had been resolved against them in the action brought by the SEC. The District Court denied the motion on the ground that such an application of collateral estoppel would deny the petitioners their Seventh Amendment right to a jury trial. The Court of Appeals for the Second Circuit reversed * * *. Because of an intercircuit conflict,[3] we granted certiorari.

I

The threshold question to be considered is whether, quite apart from the right to a jury trial under the Seventh Amendment, the petitioners can be precluded from relitigating facts resolved adversely to them in a prior equitable proceeding with another party under the general law of collateral estoppel. Specifically, we must determine whether a litigant who was not a party to a prior judgment may nevertheless use that judgment "offensively" to prevent a defendant from relitigating issues resolved in the earlier proceeding.[4]

* * *

3. The position of the Court of Appeals for the Second Circuit is in conflict with that taken by the Court of Appeals for the Fifth Circuit in Rachal v. Hill, 435 F.2d 59.

4. In this context, offensive use of collateral estoppel occurs when the plaintiff seeks to foreclose the defendant from litigating an issue the defendant has previously litigated unsuccess-

B

The *Blonder–Tongue* case involved defensive use of collateral estoppel * * *. The present case, by contrast, involves offensive use of collateral estoppel—a plaintiff is seeking to estop a defendant from relitigating the issues which the defendant previously litigated and lost against another plaintiff. In both the offensive and defensive use situations, the party against whom estoppel is asserted has litigated and lost in an earlier action. Nevertheless, several reasons have been advanced why the two situations should be treated differently.

First, offensive use of collateral estoppel does not promote judicial economy in the same manner as defensive use does. Defensive use of collateral estoppel precludes a plaintiff from relitigating identical issues by merely "switching adversaries." * * * Thus defensive collateral estoppel gives a plaintiff a strong incentive to join all potential defendants in the first action if possible. Offensive use of collateral estoppel, on the other hand, creates precisely the opposite incentive. Since a plaintiff will be able to rely on a previous judgment against a defendant but will not be bound by that judgment if the defendant wins, the plaintiff has every incentive to adopt a "wait and see" attitude, in the hope that the first action by another plaintiff will result in a favorable judgment. * * * Thus offensive use of collateral estoppel will likely increase rather than decrease the total amount of litigation, since potential plaintiffs will have everything to gain and nothing to lose by not intervening in the first action.[13]

A second argument against offensive use of collateral estoppel is that it may be unfair to a defendant. If a defendant in the first action is sued for small or nominal damages, he may have little incentive to defend vigorously, particularly if future suits are not foreseeable. * * * Allowing offensive collateral estoppel may also be unfair to a defendant if the judgment relied upon as a basis for the estoppel is itself inconsistent with one or more previous judgments in favor of the defendant. Still another situation where it might be unfair to apply offensive estoppel is where the second action affords the defendant procedural opportunities unavailable in the first action that could readily cause a different result.[15]

---

fully in an action with another party. Defensive use occurs when a defendant seeks to prevent a plaintiff from asserting a claim the plaintiff has previously litigated and lost against another defendant.

13. The *Restatement (Second) of Judgments* (Tent. Draft No. 2, 1975) § 88(3), provides that application of collateral estoppel may be denied if the party asserting it "could have effected joinder in the first action between himself and his present adversary."

15. If, for example, the defendant in the first action was forced to defend in an inconvenient forum and therefore was unable to engage in full scale discovery or call witnesses, application of offensive collateral estoppel may be unwarranted. Indeed, differences in available procedures may sometimes justify not allowing a prior judgment to have estoppel effect in a subsequent action even between the same parties, or where defensive estoppel is asserted against a plaintiff who has litigated and lost. The problem of unfairness is particularly acute in cases of offensive estoppel, however, because the defendant against whom estoppel is asserted typically will not have chosen the forum in the first action. See *Restatement (Second) of Judgments* (Tentative Draft No. 2, 1975) § 88(2) and Comment *d*.

C

We have concluded that the preferable approach for dealing with these problems in the federal courts is not to preclude the use of offensive collateral estoppel, but to grant trial courts broad discretion to determine when it should be applied. The general rule should be that in cases where a plaintiff could easily have joined in the earlier action or where, either for the reasons discussed above or for other reasons, the application of offensive estoppel would be unfair to a defendant, a trial judge should not allow the use of offensive collateral estoppel.

In the present case, however, none of the circumstances that might justify reluctance to allow the offensive use of collateral estoppel is present. The application of offensive collateral estoppel will not here reward a private plaintiff who could have joined in the previous action, since the respondent probably could not have joined in the injunctive action brought by the SEC even had he so desired.[17] Similarly, there is no unfairness to the petitioners in applying offensive collateral estoppel in this case. First, in light of the serious allegations made in the SEC's complaint against the petitioners, as well as the foreseeability of subsequent private suits that typically follow a successful government judgment, the petitioners had every incentive to litigate the SEC lawsuit fully and vigorously. Second, the judgment in the Commission action was not inconsistent with any previous decision. Finally, there will in the respondent's action be no procedural opportunities available to the petitioner that were unavailable in the first action of a kind that might be likely to cause a different result.[19]

We conclude, therefore, that none of the considerations that would justify a refusal to allow the use of offensive collateral estoppel is present in this case. Since the petitioners received a "full and fair" opportunity to litigate their claims in the SEC action, the contemporary law of collateral estoppel leads inescapably to the conclusion that the petitioners are collaterally estopped from relitigating the question of whether the proxy statements were materially false and misleading.

II

The question that remains is whether, notwithstanding the law of collateral estoppel, the use of offensive collateral estoppel in this case would violate the petitioners' Seventh Amendment right to a jury trial.

17. SEC v. Everest Management Corp., 475 F.2d 1236, 1240 (CA2) ("[T]he complicating effect of the additional issues and the additional parties outweighs any advantage of a single disposition of the common issues"). Moreover, consolidation of a private action with one brought by the SEC without its consent is prohibited by statute. 15 U.S.C. § 78u(g).

19. It is true, of course, that the petitioners in the present action would be entitled to a jury trial of the issues bearing on whether the proxy statement was materially false and misleading had the SEC action never been brought—a matter to be discussed in Part II of this opinion. But the presence or absence of a jury as factfinder is basically neutral, quite unlike, for example, the necessity of defending the first lawsuit in an inconvenient forum.

A

* * *

Recognition that an equitable determination could have collateral estoppel effect in a subsequent legal action was the major premise of this Court's decision in Beacon Theatres v. Westover, [p. 1002, supra] * * *.

It is clear that the Court in the *Beacon Theatres* case thought that if an issue common to both legal and equitable claims was first determined by a judge, relitigation of the issue before a jury might be foreclosed by res judicata or collateral estoppel. * * *

B

* * * The petitioners contend that since the scope of the Amendment must be determined by reference to the common law as it existed in 1791, and since the common law permitted collateral estoppel only where there was mutuality of parties, collateral estoppel cannot constitutionally be applied when such mutuality is absent.

The petitioners have advanced no persuasive reason, however, why the meaning of the Seventh Amendment should depend on whether or not mutuality of parties is present. A litigant who has lost because of adverse factual findings in an equity action is equally deprived of a jury trial whether he is estopped from relitigating the factual issues against the same party or a new party. In either case, the party against whom estoppel is asserted has litigated questions of fact, and has had the facts determined against him in an earlier proceeding. In either case there is no further factfinding function for the jury to perform, since the common factual issues have been resolved in the previous action. * * *

The Seventh Amendment has never been interpreted in the rigid manner advocated by the petitioners. On the contrary, many procedural devices developed since 1791 that have diminished the civil jury's historic domain have been found not to be inconsistent with the Seventh Amendment. * * *

The law of collateral estoppel, like the law in other procedural areas defining the scope of the jury's function, has evolved since 1791. * * * [T]hese developments are not repugnant to the Seventh Amendment simply for the reason that they did not exist in 1791. Thus if, as we have held, the law of collateral estoppel forecloses the petitioners from relitigating the factual issues determined against them in the SEC action, nothing in the Seventh Amendment dictates a different result, even though because of lack of mutuality there would have been no collateral estoppel in 1791.

The judgment of the Court of Appeals is

Affirmed.

MR. JUSTICE REHNQUIST, dissenting.

It is admittedly difficult to be outraged about the treatment accorded by the federal judiciary to petitioners' demand for a jury trial in this lawsuit. Outrage is an emotion all but impossible to generate with respect to a corporate defendant in a securities fraud action, and this case is no exception. But the nagging sense of unfairness as to the way petitioners have been treated, engendered by the *imprimatur* placed by the Court of Appeals on respondent's "heads I win, tails you lose" theory of this litigation, is not dispelled by this Court's antiseptic analysis of the issues in the case. It may be that if this Nation were to adopt a new Constitution today, the Seventh Amendment guaranteeing the right of jury trial in civil cases in federal courts would not be included among its provisions. But any present sentiment to that effect cannot obscure or dilute our obligation to enforce the Seventh Amendment, which *was* included in the Bill of Rights in 1791 and which has not since been repealed in the only manner provided by the Constitution for repeal of its provisions.

* * *

The Seventh Amendment requires that the right of trial by jury be "preserved." Because the Seventh Amendment demands preservation of the jury trial right, our cases have uniformly held that the content of the right must be judged by historical standards. * * * If a jury would have been impaneled in a particular kind of case in 1791, then the Seventh Amendment requires a jury trial today, if either party so desires.

* * *

To say that the Seventh Amendment does not tie federal courts to the exact procedure of the common law in 1791 does not imply, however, that any nominally "procedural" change can be implemented, regardless of its impact on the functions of the jury. * * *

Judged by the foregoing principles, I think it is clear that petitioners were denied their Seventh Amendment right to a jury trial in this case. Neither respondents nor the Court doubt that at common law as it existed in 1791, petitioners would have been entitled in the private action to have a jury determine whether the proxy statement was false and misleading in the respects alleged. The reason is that at common law in 1791, collateral estoppel was permitted only where the parties in the first action were identical to, or in privity with, the parties to the subsequent action. * * * [D]evelopments in the judge-made doctrine of collateral estoppel, however salutary, cannot, consistent with the Seventh Amendment, contract in any material fashion the right to a jury trial that a defendant would have enjoyed in 1791. * * *

* * * [T]he Court seems to suggest that the offensive use of collateral estoppel in this case is permissible under the limited principle set forth above that a mere procedural change that does not invade the province of the jury and a defendant's right thereto to a greater extent than authorized by the common law is permissible. But the Court's actions today constitute a far greater infringement of the defendant's rights than it ever

before has sanctioned. * * * The procedural devices of summary judgment and directed verdict are direct descendants of their common-law antecedents. They accomplish nothing more than could have been done at common law, albeit by a more cumbersome procedure. * * *

By contrast, the development of nonmutual estoppel is a substantial departure from the common law and its use in this case completely deprives petitioners of their right to have a jury determine contested issues of fact. * * *

Even accepting, *arguendo,* the majority's position that there is no violation of the Seventh Amendment here, I nonetheless would not sanction the use of collateral estoppel in this case. * * * In my view, it is "unfair" to apply offensive collateral estoppel where the party who is sought to be estopped has not had an opportunity to have the facts of his case determined by a jury. Since in this case petitioners were not entitled to a jury trial in the Securities and Exchange Commission (SEC) lawsuit, I would not estop them from relitigating the issues determined in the SEC suit before a jury in the private action. I believe that several factors militate in favor of this result.

First, the use of offensive collateral estoppel in this case runs counter to the strong federal policy favoring jury trials, even if it does not, as the majority holds, violate the Seventh Amendment. * * *

Second, I believe that the opportunity for a jury trial in the second action could easily lead to a different result from that obtained in the first action before the court and therefore that it is unfair to estop petitioners from relitigating the issues before a jury. * * *

The ultimate irony of today's decision is that its potential for significantly conserving the resources of either the litigants or the judiciary is doubtful at best. That being the case, I see absolutely no reason to frustrate so cavalierly the important federal policy favoring jury decisions of disputed fact questions. The instant case is an apt example of the minimal savings that will be accomplished by the Court's decision. As the Court admits, even if petitioners are collaterally estopped from relitigating whether the proxy was materially false and misleading they are still entitled to have a jury determine whether respondents were injured by the alleged misstatements and the amount of damages, if any, sustained by respondents. * * * Thus, a jury must be impaneled in this case in any event. The time saved by not trying the issue of whether the proxy was materially false and misleading before the jury is likely to be insubstantial.[24] It is just as probable that today's decision will have the result of coercing defendants to agree to consent orders, or settlements in agency enforcement action in order to preserve their right to jury trial in the private actions. In that event, the Court, for no compelling reason, will

---

24. Much of the delay in jury trials is attributed to the jury selection, *voir dire* and the charge. See H. Zeisel, H. Kalven, & B. Buchholtz, Delay in the Court 79 (1959). None of these delaying factors will be avoided by today's decision.

have simply added a powerful club to the administrative agencies' arsenals that even Congress was unwilling to provide them.

NOTES AND QUESTIONS

1. Offensive nonmutual collateral estoppel is the term used to describe a case in which "a plaintiff seeks to preclude a defendant from relitigating an issue which the defendant previously litigated and lost against a different plaintiff." 47 Am Jur.2d Judgments § 647 (2d ed. 2004). How does this situation differ from the defensive use of collateral estoppel in *Bernhard* and *Blonder–Tongue*?

2. *Parklane* permits the offensive use of nonmutual issue preclusion by a nonparty against a party, but limits its application. One limitation involves prior judgments that are inconsistent with each other. See Hynes, *Inconsistent Verdicts, Issue Preclusion, and Settlement in the Presence of Judicial Bias*, 2 U. Chi. L. Sch. Roundtable 663, 664 (1995). Consider the justification for this limitation in the context of the following problem: A train accident injures fifty passengers. Each of these passengers files a separate negligence action against the railroad. The railroad prevails in the first twenty-five suits to reach judgment, but loses the twenty-sixth. How should the twenty-sixth judgment affect the remaining suits? See Currie, *Mutuality of Collateral Estoppel: The Limits of the* Bernhard *Doctrine*, 9 Stan.L.Rev. 281 (1957).

How might your answer to this question change if the prior twenty-five cases all had been litigated in a court of limited jurisdiction, such as a small-claims court, and if the twenty-sixth judgment was rendered by a court of general jurisdiction? How does this variation on the hypothetical differ from the issue of whether a judgment by a court of limited jurisdiction should itself preclude the relitigation of certain issues?

Currie's hypothetical was designed to highlight the aberrant quality of the twenty-sixth judgment. Yet there is no reason that this "aberrant" result might not have been reached in the first trial rather than the twenty-sixth. If the holding against the railroad had been rendered in the first case, nonmutual estoppel would have been available to the remaining forty-nine passengers. In short, although any single decision may be an anomaly, a single decision still can have preclusive effect. See, e.g., Harrison v. Celotex Corp., 583 F.Supp. 1497 (E.D. Tenn.1984).

3. What factors other than a prior inconsistent judgment might persuade a court not to accept a plea of offensive nonmutual issue preclusion?

(a) What if before a case settles it yields a judicial finding that conflicts with a prior adjudication of the same issue? Such a finding may result, for example, when a motion to dismiss is denied before a settlement is reached. Can that finding create sufficient inconsistency to block offensive issue preclusion? See Jack Faucett Assocs. v. American Telephone & Telegraph Co., 744 F.2d 118 (D.C.Cir.1984), certiorari denied 469 U.S. 1196, 105 S.Ct. 980, 83 L.Ed.2d 982 (1985).

(b) What if a prior judgment has been affirmed on appeal, but in the course of its affirmance, the Circuit Court has held that one of the trial judge's evidentiary rulings had been erroneous, although harmless. Should the presence of even "harmless" error in the rulings upon whose findings a second court was being urged to rely be an obstacle to offensive issue preclusion? See *Jack Faucett*, Note 3(a), p. 1319, supra, at 128–29.

(c) What if before the parties settle a lawsuit, the court makes an in limine ruling on an issue that arises in a different lawsuit against the same defendant? In GARCIA v. GENERAL MOTORS CORP., 195 Ariz. 510, 990 P.2d 1069 (Ct.App.1999), the plaintiffs attempted to use a prior Idaho ruling that prohibited General Motors from using seatbelt evidence in defending a products liability suit. *Garcia* concerned Arizona residents who were injured in Idaho while going on a church camping trip in a General Motors van. The passengers were not wearing seatbelts. One of the injured campers immediately sued in federal court in Idaho and subsequently settled with General Motors and the other defendants before trial. Meanwhile, the rest of the passengers brought suit regarding the same accident in an Arizona state court. They sought to use the Idaho ruling to preclude General Motors from using their failure to wear seatbelts as a defense. Does this ruling deserve preclusive effect when mutuality is not present? Does it deserve any preclusive effect at all?

(d) What if the prior judgment is a guilty verdict? Obviously, since plaintiff in a subsequent civil action did not have the opportunity to join in the criminal case, the concern that plaintiff will bring repetitious litigation is not present. On the other hand, are the issues necessary to resolve the civil case the same as those that are central to the criminal case? Does the criminal defendant have the same range of discovery as a civil litigant?

(e) What if the prior judgment reflects a compromise verdict? For example, in TAYLOR v. HAWKINSON, 47 Cal.2d 893, 306 P.2d 797 (1957), the California Supreme Court, in an opinion by Justice Traynor, held that the *Bernhard* rule should not be applied due to evidence of a compromise verdict. Id. at 896–97, 306 P.2d at 799. Should the court hold a hearing to determine whether a prior judgment reflects a compromise verdict? In KATZ v. ELI LILLY & CO., 84 F.R.D. 378 (E.D.N.Y.1979), plaintiff sued a drug manufacturer for the wrongful death of her child who had ingested defendant's drug during the mother's pregnancy. A similar action by a different party resulted in a verdict against the drug manufacturer, and plaintiff sought to use that judgment to issue preclude defendant. Defendant, noticing signs that the earlier verdict may have been a compromise, subpoenaed two members of the jury in the prior case. Plaintiff moved to quash the subpoenas on the ground that the testimony of jurors may not be used to impeach a verdict. The court denied the motion to quash. Can you justify the court's refusal? See p. 1132, supra. At what point does the effort involved in evaluating the prior verdict outweigh the effort saved in not relitigating the substantive issues at stake in the suit?

4. Suits against the federal government represent an important exception to the extension of offensive nonmutual collateral estoppel. See United States v. Mendoza, 464 U.S. 154, 104 S.Ct. 568, 78 L.Ed.2d 379 (1984). What are the policy reasons for not applying offensive nonmutual issue preclusion

against the government? Should the government be able to invoke offensive nonmutual issue preclusion against a private party?

3. BINDING NONPARTIES

In MONTANA v. UNITED STATES, 440 U.S. 147, 99 S.Ct. 970, 59 L.Ed.2d 210 (1979), the Supreme Court held that when nonparties assume control over litigation in which they have a direct financial or pecuniary interest, they may be precluded from relitigating issues that the earlier suit resolved. Montana gave contractors different tax treatment depending on whether they contracted to build public or private projects. A contractor on a federal construction project brought a state-court action challenging the constitutionality of this practice. The United States directed and financed the litigation for the contractor, but it also brought a federal court action challenging the practice. After the Montana Supreme Court upheld Montana's system of taxation, the United States continued with its federal action. But Montana argued that the federal government was bound by the state-court judgment. When the case reached the United States Supreme Court, Justice Marshall, writing for the Court, observed that "although not a party, the United States plainly had a sufficient laboring oar in the conduct of the state-court litigation to actuate principles of estoppel." Id. at 154–55, 99 S.Ct. at 974, 59 L.Ed.2d at 217–18.

Montana recognizes an important but somewhat open-ended exception to the rule that a judgment lacks preclusive effect against a nonparty. Does the concept of privity provide a more predictable set of exceptions? Another exception is that by contract, an individual can agree to be bound by a judgment. See Restatement (Second) of Judgments § 40 (1982). For example, an individual might agree to accept a test case as preclusive of further litigation. See Lahav, *Bellwether Trials*, 76 Geo. Wash.L.Rev. 576 (2008). In addition, certain substantive proceedings, such as bankruptcy and probate actions, will bind nonparties. These actions use special procedures to make sure due process is satisfied. See Begleiter, *Serve the Cheerleader—Serve the World: An Analysis of Representation in Estate and Trust Proceedings and Under the Uniform Trust Code and Other Modern Trust Codes*, 43 Real Prop. Tr. & Est. L.J. 311 (2008). Should a nonparty be precluded if he stays on the sidelines of an action but his interests are litigated through an agent or proxy? Does due process require the court to make sure that the nonparty's interests have been represented adequately? What factors are relevant to that assessment?

MARTIN v. WILKS

Supreme Court of the United States, 1989.
490 U.S. 755, 109 S.Ct. 2180, 104 L.Ed.2d 835.

Certiorari to the United States Court of Appeals for the Eleventh Circuit.

CHIEF JUSTICE REHNQUIST delivered the opinion of the Court.

[The City of Birmingham, Alabama ("City") and the Jefferson County Personnel Board ("Board") entered into consent judgments with black firefighters setting goals for hiring blacks as firefighters and for promoting them. White firefighters who were not a party to the prior lawsuits sued the City and the Board alleging that they were being denied promotions illegally on the basis of race. The City and the Board defended on the basis of the consent decrees which mandated the challenged promotion procedures, and argued that these consent decrees precluded the current suit. The District Court held that the earlier consent decrees provided a defense to the reverse discrimination suits, but the Court of Appeals reversed, holding that because the white firefighters were not parties to the earlier litigation, their discrimination claims could not be precluded.]

* * *

* * * All agree that "[i]t is a principle of general application in Anglo–American jurisprudence that one is not bound by a judgment *in personam* in a litigation in which he is not designated as a party or to which he has not been made a party by service of process." * * * This rule is part of our "deep-rooted historic tradition that everyone should have his own day in court." * * * A judgment or decree among parties to a lawsuit resolves issues as among them, but it does not conclude the rights of strangers to those proceedings.[2]

Petitioners argue that, because respondents failed to timely intervene in the initial proceedings, their current challenge to actions taken under the consent decree constitutes an impermissible "collateral attack." They argue that respondents were aware that the underlying suit might affect them and if they chose to pass up an opportunity to intervene, they should not be permitted to later litigate the issues in a new action. The position has sufficient appeal to have commanded the approval of the great majority of the Federal Courts of Appeals, but we agree with the contrary view expressed by the Court of Appeals for the Eleventh Circuit in this case.

* * * [A] party seeking a judgment binding on another cannot obligate that person to intervene; he must be joined. * * * [T]he drafters cast Rule 24, governing intervention [, see p. 733, supra], in permissive terms. * * * They determined that the concern for finality and completeness of judgments would be "better [served] by mandatory joinder procedures." * * * Accordingly, Rule 19(a) provides for mandatory joinder in circumstances where a judgment rendered in the absence of a person may * * *

2. We have recognized an exception to the general rule when, in certain limited circumstances, a person, although not a party, has his interests adequately represented by someone with the same interests who is a party. See Hansberry v. Lee, [p. 777, supra] * * * ("class" or "representative" suits); Fed.Rule Civ.Proc. 23 (same); Montana v. United States, [p. 1321, supra] * * * (control of litigation on behalf of one of the parties in the litigation). Additionally, where a special remedial scheme exists expressly foreclosing successive litigation by nonlitigants, as for example in bankruptcy or probate, legal proceedings may terminate preexisting rights if the scheme is otherwise consistent with due process. See * * * Tulsa Professional Collection Services, Inc., [p. 207 supra] * * * (nonclaim statute terminating unsubmitted claims against the estate). Neither of these exceptions, however, applies in this case.

[produce inconsistent obligations for those who are already parties]. Rule 19(b) sets forth the factors to be considered by a court in deciding whether to allow an action to proceed in the absence of an interested party.

Joinder as a party, rather than knowledge of a lawsuit and an opportunity to intervene, is the method by which potential parties are subjected to the jurisdiction of the court and bound by a judgment or decree. The parties to a lawsuit presumably know better than anyone else the nature and scope of relief sought in the action, and at whose expense such relief might be granted. It makes sense, therefore, to place on them a burden of bringing in additional parties where such a step is indicated, rather than placing on potential additional parties a duty to intervene when they acquire knowledge of the lawsuit. The linchpin of the "impermissible collateral attack" doctrine—the attribution of preclusive effect to a failure to intervene—is therefore quite inconsistent with Rule 19 and Rule 24.

* * *

Petitioners contend that a different result should be reached because the need to join affected parties will be burdensome and ultimately discouraging to civil rights litigation. Potential adverse claimants may be numerous and difficult to identify; if they are not joined, the possibility for inconsistent judgments exists. Judicial resources will be needlessly consumed in relitigation of the same question.

* * *

The difficulties petitioners foresee in identifying those who could be adversely affected by a decree granting broad remedial relief are undoubtedly present, but they arise from the nature of the relief sought and not because of any choice between mandatory intervention and joinder. Rule 19's provisions for joining interested parties are designed to accommodate the sort of complexities that may arise from a decree affecting numerous people in various ways. We doubt that a mandatory intervention rule would be any less awkward. As mentioned, plaintiffs who seek the aid of the courts to alter existing employment policies, or the employer who might be subject to conflicting decrees, are best able to bear the burden of designating those who would be adversely affected if plaintiffs prevail; these parties will generally have a better understanding of the scope of likely relief than employees who are not named but might be affected. Petitioners' alternative does not eliminate the need for, or difficulty of, identifying persons who, because of their interests, should be included in a lawsuit. It merely shifts that responsibility to less able shoulders.

* * *

* * * A voluntary settlement in the form of a consent decree between one group of employees and their employer cannot possibly "settle," voluntarily or otherwise, the conflicting claims of another group of em-

ployees who do not join in the agreement. This is true even if the second group of employees is a party to the litigation:

> "[P]arties who choose to resolve litigation through settlement may not dispose of the claims of a third party * * * without that party's agreement. A court's approval of a consent decree between some of the parties therefore cannot dispose of the valid claims of nonconsenting intervenors." * * *

Insofar as the argument is bottomed on the idea that it may be easier to settle claims among a disparate group of affected persons if they are all before the Court, joinder bids fair to accomplish that result as well as a regime of mandatory intervention.

* * *

Affirmed.

JUSTICE STEVENS, with whom JUSTICE BRENNAN, JUSTICE MARSHALL, and JUSTICE BLACKMUN join, dissenting.

As a matter of law there is a vast difference between persons who are actual parties to litigation and persons who merely have the kind of interest that may as a practical matter be impaired by the outcome of a case. Persons in the first category have a right to participate in a trial and to appeal from an adverse judgment; depending on whether they win or lose, their legal rights may be enhanced or impaired. Persons in the latter category have a right to intervene in the action in a timely fashion, or they may be joined as parties against their will. But if they remain on the sidelines, they may be harmed as a practical matter even though their legal rights are unaffected. One of the disadvantages of sideline-sitting is that the bystander has no right to appeal from a judgment no matter how harmful it may be.

In this case the Court quite rightly concludes that the white firefighters who brought the second series of Title VII cases could not be deprived of their legal rights in the first series of cases because they had neither intervened nor been joined as parties. * * * The consent decrees obviously could not deprive them of any contractual rights, such as seniority, * * * or accrued vacation pay, * * * or of any other legal rights, such as the right to have their employer comply with federal statutes like Title VII, * * *. There is no reason, however, why the consent decrees might not produce changes in conditions at the white firefighters' place of employment that, as a practical matter, may have a serious effect on their opportunities for employment or promotion even though they are not bound by the decrees in any legal sense. The fact that one of the effects of a decree is to curtail the job opportunities of nonparties does not mean that the nonparties have been deprived of legal rights or that they have standing to appeal from that decree without becoming parties.

Persons who have no right to appeal from a final judgment—either because the time to appeal has elapsed or because they never became parties to the case—may nevertheless collaterally attack a judgment on certain narrow grounds. If the court had no jurisdiction over the subject matter, or if the judgment is the product of corruption, duress, fraud, collusion, or mistake, under limited circumstances it may be set aside in an appropriate collateral proceeding. * * * This rule not only applies to parties to the original action, but also allows interested third parties collaterally to attack judgments. In both civil and criminal cases, however, the grounds that may be invoked to support a collateral attack are much more limited than those that may be asserted as error on direct appeal. Thus, a person who can foresee that a lawsuit is likely to have a practical impact on his interests may pay a heavy price if he elects to sit on the sidelines instead of intervening and taking the risk that his legal rights will be impaired.

In this case there is no dispute about the fact that respondents are not parties to the consent decrees. It follows as a matter of course that they are not bound by those decrees. Those judgments could not, and did not, deprive them of any legal rights. The judgments did, however, have a practical impact on respondents' opportunities for advancement in their profession. For that reason, respondents had standing to challenge the validity of the decrees, but the grounds that they may advance in support of a collateral challenge are much more limited than would be allowed if they were parties prosecuting a direct appeal. * * *

* * *

There is nothing unusual about the fact that litigation between adverse parties may, as a practical matter, seriously impair the interests of third persons who elect to sit on the sidelines. Indeed, in complex litigation this Court has squarely held that a sideline-sitter may be bound as firmly as an actual party if he had adequate notice and a fair opportunity to intervene and if the judicial interest in finality is sufficiently strong. * * *

There is no need, however, to go that far in order to agree with the District Court's eminently sensible view that compliance with the terms of a valid decree remedying violations of Title VII cannot itself violate that statute or the Equal Protection Clause. The city of Birmingham, in entering into and complying with this decree, has made a substantial step toward the eradication of the long history of pervasive racial discrimination that has plagued its fire department. The District Court, after conducting a trial and carefully considering respondents' arguments, concluded that this effort is lawful and should go forward. Because respondents have thus already had their day in court and have failed to carry their burden, I would vacate the judgment of the Court of Appeals and remand for further proceedings consistent with this opinion.

NOTES AND QUESTIONS

1. The specific holding of *Martin,* in the Title VII arena, was legislatively overruled by Section 108 of the Civil Rights Act of 1991, Pub.L.No. 102–

166, tit. I, § 108, 105 Stat. 1071, 1076. The 1991 Act prohibits challenges to employment consent decrees by individuals who had actual notice and a reasonable opportunity to intervene, or whose interests were represented adequately. Is this legislative solution consistent with *Blonder–Tongue*, p. 1310, supra?

2. What problems do you see with a rule requiring intervention by persons who are aware of litigation that could potentially affect their interests, see p. 740 supra? Suppose a nonparty becomes aware of litigation that will affect her interests, but the litigation is taking place in a jurisdiction where she would not be subject to in personam jurisdiction. Are there due process concerns? See Bone, *Rethinking the "Day in Court" Ideal and Nonparty Preclusion*, 67 N.Y.U. L. Rev. 193 (1992).

3. The issues addressed in *Martin* have generated much commentary. See Kramer, *Consent Decrees and the Rights of Third Parties*, 87 Mich.L.Rev. 321 (1988); Pielemeier, *Due Process Limitations on the Application of Collateral Estoppel Against Nonparties to Prior Litigation*, 63 B.U.L.Rev. 383 (1983).

TAYLOR v. STURGELL

Supreme Court of the United States, 2008.
___ U.S. ___, 128 S.Ct. 2161, 171 L.Ed.2d 155.

Certiorari to the United States Court of Appeals for the District of Columbia.

JUSTICE GINSBURG delivered the opinion of the Court.

[Petitioner filed a lawsuit under the Freedom of Information Act in the District Court for the District of Columbia seeking documents related to a vintage airplane manufactured by the Fairchild Engine and Airplane Corporation. Greg Herrick, petitioner's friend, had previously filed an unsuccessful suit seeking the same documents. Petitioner and Herrick had no legal relationship, and there was no evidence that petitioner controlled, financed, participated in, or had notice of Herrick's lawsuit. The District Court granted summary judgment to defendants, holding that petitioner was barred by the judgment against Herrick because his interests had been virtually represented by a party. In reaching this result, the District Court relied on the Eighth Circuit's seven-factor test that requires an identity of interests between the nonparty and the party to the judgment, and six other factors that are relevant but not required: (1) a close relationship between the present party and a party to the judgment alleged to be preclusive; (2) participation in the prior litigation by the present party; (3) the present party's apparent acquiescence to the preclusive effect of the judgment; (4) the present party's deliberate maneuvering to avoid the preclusive effect of the prior judgment; (5) adequate representation of the present party by a party to the prior adjudication; and (6) a suit raising a public law (such as a constitutional question) rather than a private law issue. The Eighth Circuit's multifactor balancing test contrasts with the narrower approach used by the Fourth Circuit, which precludes a nonparty only when the court has given tacit approval to a party to act on a nonparty's behalf and the party is accountable to the nonparty.]

* * *

Rejecting both of these approaches, the D.C. Circuit announced its own five-factor test. The first two factors—"identity of interests" and "adequate representation"—are necessary but not sufficient for virtual representation. * * * In addition, at least one of three other factors must be established: "a close relationship between the present party and his putative representative," "substantial participation by the present party in the first case," or "tactical maneuvering on the part of the present party to avoid preclusion by the prior judgment." * * *

Applying this test to the record in Taylor's case, the D.C. Circuit found both of the necessary conditions for virtual representation well met. * * *

We granted certiorari * * * to resolve the disagreement among the Circuits over the permissibility and scope of preclusion based on "virtual representation." * * *

* * *

II

* * *

A person who was not a party to a suit generally has not had a "full and fair opportunity to litigate" the claims and issues settled in that suit. The application of claim and issue preclusion to nonparties thus runs up against the "deep-rooted historic tradition that everyone should have his own day in court." Richards [v. Jefferson County], 517 U.S. * * * 793, 798, 116 S.Ct. 1761 [, 1766, 135 L.Ed.2d 76, 82 (1996)] * * *.

B

Though hardly in doubt, the rule against nonparty preclusion is subject to exceptions. For present purposes, the recognized exceptions can be grouped into six categories. * * *

[The Court summarized the exceptions as: (1) a nonparty may agree to be bound by a judgment; (2) certain substantive relationships, traditionally referred to by the term privity, may justify preclusion of a nonparty; (3) a nonparty may be bound if its interests are represented adequately by a party to the suit, citing as examples class actions and suits by trustees and guardians; (4) a nonparty who has assumed control over a lawsuit, as in *Montana*, p. 1321, supra, may be precluded; (5) a nonparty who has colluded to avoid the preclusive effect of a judgment by litigating through a proxy may be bound; and (6) special statutory schemes, such as bankruptcy, or other suits that are brought "only on behalf of the public at large," see *Richards*, p. 782, supra, may bind a nonparty.]

* * *

III

Reaching beyond these six established categories, some lower courts have recognized a "virtual representation" exception to the rule against nonparty preclusion. * * *

The D.C. Circuit, the FAA, and Fairchild have presented three arguments in support of an expansive doctrine of virtual representation. We find none of them persuasive.

A

[The D.C. Circuit argued that] * * * a person may be bound by a judgment if she was adequately represented by a party to the proceeding yielding that judgment. * * * But the D.C. Circuit's definition of "adequate representation" strayed from the meaning our decisions have attributed to that term.

* * * [Our precedent has] established that representation is "adequate" for purposes of nonparty preclusion only if (at a minimum) one of * * * two circumstances is present. [The Court described the two circumstances as when (1) the court uses "special procedures to protect the nonparties' interests" or (2) "an understanding by the concerned parties that the first suit was brought in a representative capacity.] * * *

* * *

B

Fairchild and the FAA do not argue that the D.C. Circuit's virtual representation doctrine fits within any of the recognized grounds for nonparty preclusion. Rather, they ask us to abandon the attempt to delineate discrete grounds and clear rules altogether. Preclusion is in order, they contend, whenever "the relationship between a party and a non-party is 'close enough' to bring the second litigant within the judgment." * * * Courts should make the "close enough" determination, they urge, through a "heavily fact-driven" and "equitable" inquiry. * * * Only this sort of diffuse balancing, Fairchild and the FAA argue, can account for all of the situations in which nonparty preclusion is appropriate.

We reject this argument for three reasons. First, our decisions emphasize the fundamental nature of the general rule that a litigant is not bound by a judgment to which she was not a party. * * * Accordingly, we have endeavored to delineate discrete exceptions that apply in "limited circumstances." * * * Respondents' amorphous balancing test is at odds with the constrained approach to nonparty preclusion our decisions advance.

* * *

Our second reason for rejecting a broad doctrine of virtual representation rests on the limitations attending nonparty preclusion based on adequate representation. A party's representation of a nonparty is "adequate" for preclusion purposes only if, at a minimum: (1) the interests of the nonparty and her representative are aligned * * * and (2) either the party understood herself to be acting in a representative capacity or the original court took care to protect the interests of the nonparty * * *. In addition, adequate representation sometimes requires (3) notice of the original suit to the persons alleged to have been represented * * *. In the class-action context, these limitations are implemented by the procedural safeguards contained in Federal Rule * * * 23.

An expansive doctrine of virtual representation, however, would "recogniz[e], in effect, a common-law kind of class action." Tice [v. American Airlines, Inc., 162 F.3d 966,] * * * 972 [(7th Cir. 1988)] * * *. That is, virtual representation would authorize preclusion based on identity of interests and some kind of relationship between parties and nonparties, shorn of the procedural protections [that are grounded in due process and] prescribed in *Hansberry*, *Richards*, and Rule 23. * * *

Third, a diffuse balancing approach to nonparty preclusion would likely create more headaches than it relieves. Most obviously, it could significantly complicate the task of district courts faced in the first instance with preclusion questions. An all-things-considered balancing approach might spark wide-ranging, time-consuming, and expensive discovery tracking factors potentially relevant under seven- or five-prong tests. And after the relevant facts are established, district judges would be called upon to evaluate them under a standard that provides no firm guidance. * * * Preclusion doctrine, it should be recalled, is intended to reduce the burden of litigation on courts and parties. * * * "In this area of the law," we agree, " 'crisp rules with sharp corners' are preferable to a round-about doctrine of opaque standards." Bittinger v. Tecumseh Products Co., 123 F.3d 877, 881 (C.A. 6 1997).

C

Finally, * * * the FAA maintains that nonparty preclusion should apply more broadly in "public-law" litigation than in "private-law" controversies. To support this position, the FAA offers two arguments. First, the FAA urges * * * the plaintiff has a reduced interest in controlling the litigation "because of the public nature of the right at issue." * * *

Taylor's FOIA action falls within * * * the [public-law] category * * *, the FAA contends, because "the duty to disclose under FOIA is owed to the public generally." * * * The Act, however, instructs agencies receiving FOIA requests to make the information available not to the public at large, but rather to the "person" making the request. * * * Thus, in contrast to * * * public-law litigation * * *, a successful FOIA action results in a grant of relief to the individual plaintiff, not a decree benefiting the public at large.

Furthermore, * * * States are free to adopt procedures limiting repetitive litigation [of public-law claims]. * * * It hardly follows, however, that *this Court* should proscribe or confine successive FOIA suits by different requesters. Indeed, Congress' provision for FOIA suits with no statutory constraint on successive actions counsels against judicial imposition of constraints through extraordinary application of the common law of preclusion.

But we are not convinced that this risk justifies departure from the usual rules governing nonparty preclusion. First, *stare decisis* will allow courts swiftly to dispose of repetitive suits brought in the same circuit. Second, even when *stare decisis* is not dispositive, "the human tendency not to waste money will deter the bringing of suits based on claims or issues that have already been adversely determined against others." Shapiro [, Civil Procedure: Preclusion in Civil Actions] 97 [(2001)]. This intuition seems to be borne out by experience: The FAA has not called our attention to any instances of abusive FOIA suits in the Circuits that reject the virtual-representation theory respondents advocate here.

IV

For the foregoing reasons, we disapprove the theory of virtual representation on which the decision below rested. * * *

Although references to "virtual representation" have proliferated in the lower courts, our decision is unlikely to occasion any great shift in actual practice. Many opinions use the term "virtual representation" in reaching results at least arguably defensible on established grounds. * * *

In some cases, however, lower courts have relied on virtual representation to extend nonparty preclusion beyond the latter doctrine's proper bounds. We now turn back to Taylor's action to determine whether his suit is such a case, or whether the result reached by the courts below can be justified on one of the recognized grounds for nonparty preclusion.

A

It is uncontested that * * * [there] is no indication that Taylor agreed to be bound by Herrick's litigation, that Taylor and Herrick have any legal relationship, that Taylor exercised any control over Herrick's suit, or that this suit implicates any special statutory scheme limiting relitigation. Neither the FAA nor Fairchild contends otherwise.

It is equally clear that preclusion cannot be justified on the theory that Taylor was adequately represented in Herrick's suit. Nothing in the record indicates that Herrick understood himself to be suing on Taylor's behalf, that Taylor even knew of Herrick's suit, or that the Wyoming District Court took special care to protect Taylor's interests. Under our pathmarking precedent, therefore, Herrick's representation was not "adequate." * * *

That leaves only the * * * [possibility of] preclusion because a nonparty to an earlier litigation has brought suit as a representative or agent of a party who is bound by the prior adjudication. Taylor is not Herrick's legal representative and he has not purported to sue in a representative capacity. He concedes, however, that preclusion would be appropriate if respondents could demonstrate that he is acting as Herrick's "undisclosed agen[t]." * * *

Respondents argue here, as they did below, that Taylor's suit is a collusive attempt to relitigate Herrick's action. * * * The D.C. Circuit considered a similar question in addressing the "tactical maneuvering" prong of its virtual representation test. * * * The Court of Appeals did not, however, treat the issue as one of agency, and it expressly declined to reach any definitive conclusions due to "the ambiguity of the facts." * * * We therefore remand to give the courts below an opportunity to determine whether Taylor, in pursuing the instant FOIA suit, is acting as Herrick's agent. Taylor concedes that such a remand is appropriate. * * *

We have never defined the showing required to establish that a nonparty to a prior adjudication has become a litigating agent for a party to the earlier case. Because the issue has not been briefed in any detail, we do not discuss the matter elaboratively here. We note, however, that courts should be cautious about finding preclusion on this basis. A mere whiff of "tactical maneuvering" will not suffice; instead, principles of agency law are suggestive. They indicate that preclusion is appropriate only if the putative agent's conduct of the suit is subject to the control of the party who is bound by the prior adjudication. * * *

B

On remand, Fairchild suggests, Taylor should bear the burden of proving he is not acting as Herrick's agent. * * *

We reject Fairchild's suggestion. Claim preclusion, like issue preclusion, is an affirmative defense. * * * Ordinarily, it is incumbent on the defendant to plead and prove such a defense, * * * and we have never recognized claim preclusion as an exception to that general rule * * *. We acknowledge that direct evidence justifying nonparty preclusion is often in the hands of plaintiffs rather than defendants. * * * But "[v]ery often one must plead and prove matters as to which his adversary has superior access to the proof." * * * In these situations, targeted interrogatories or deposition questions can reduce the information disparity. We see no greater cause here than in other matters of affirmative defense to disturb the traditional allocation of the proof burden.

* * *

For the reasons stated, the judgment of the United States Court of Appeals for the District of Columbia Circuit is vacated, and the case is remanded for further proceedings consistent with this opinion.

It is so ordered.

NOTES AND QUESTIONS

1. Why might nonparty preclusion apply more broadly in public law cases than in private law cases? Hasn't the law traditionally recognized an exception for certain public law cases by characterizing them as in rem actions? Are there some substantive areas of law in which the need for finality and predictability ought to outweigh an individual's autonomy interests? See Headwaters Inc. v. United States Forest Serv., 399 F.3d 1047 (9th Cir. 2005).

2. So far, issue preclusion has been applied defensively or offensively only against persons who were parties to a litigation. See Tidmarsh & Transgrud, Complex Litigation: Problems in Advanced Civil Procedure 177 (2002). Does *Taylor* bar issue preclusion against a nonparty? In Lynch v. Merrell–National Labs. Div. of Richardson-Merrell, Inc., 646 F.Supp. 856 (D. Mass. 1986), affirmed on other grounds 830 F.2d 1190 (1st Cir. 1987), plaintiff sought damages for injuries sustained by her child's exposure during gestation to a prescription drug manufactured by defendant. Plaintiff had elected not to participate in earlier consolidated trials raising identical claims against the drug company. The court held that plaintiff was issue precluded by the earlier judgment from proving causation. Is *Lynch* at odds with the day-in-court ideal that informs the Court's decision in *Taylor*?

3. Hasn't the day-in-court ideal been compromised by such trends as summary disposition, aggregate litigation, and mass settlement? See Miller, *The Pretrial Rush to Judgment: Are the "Litigation Explosion," "Liability Crisis," and Efficiency Clichés Eroding Our Day in Court and Jury Trial Commitments?*, 78 N.Y.U. L. Rev. 982 (2003). Why draw the line at nonparty preclusion?

SECTION F. INTERSYSTEM PRECLUSION

The preceding discussion of preclusion assumed that both the original and subsequent courts were in the same judicial system. Often, however, questions of preclusion are presented to a court that is part of a different judicial system from the court that rendered the prior judgment. Should this affect the preclusive effect given the prior judgment? The materials in this section are designed to introduce a very complicated area of the law that is a subject of advanced courses on judgments and federal jurisdiction.

Read U.S. Const. Art. IV, § 1 and 28 U.S.C. § 1738 in the Supplement.

---

1. INTERSTATE PRECLUSION

HART v. AMERICAN AIRLINES, INC.

Supreme Court of New York, 1969.
61 Misc.2d 41, 304 N.Y.S.2d 810.

FRANK, JUSTICE.

* * *

The actions all arise out of the crash, in Kentucky on November 8, 1965, of an American Airlines aircraft while the plane was en route from La Guardia Airport, New York to an airport in Covington, Kentucky. The crash resulted in the death of 58 out of the 62 persons aboard and, in addition to the multiple actions pending in this court, comparable actions have been instituted in other States and in various United States District Courts.

Of the various actions instituted as a result of the crash, the first case to be tried to conclusion was that brought in the United States District Court, Northern District of Texas (*Creasy v. American Airlines*), which resulted in a verdict in favor of the plaintiff therein against the defendant American Airlines. * * * [I]t is undisputable from the pleadings and papers herein that the issue of defendant airline's liability in these cases is identical to the issue in that regard determined in the Texas action.

In light of the Texas result which has now been affirmed on appeal, plaintiffs Landano and Kirchstein oppose defendant's motion for a joint trial by cross-moving for summary judgment on the issue of liability which, if granted, would obviate a trial on such issue and necessarily require a denial of defendant's motion.

Plaintiffs contend that while, concededly, they were not parties to the Texas action, nevertheless the determination in that action of defendant's liability for the plane crash of November 8, 1965 is, under the doctrine of collateral estoppel, conclusive on the issue of defendant's liability for such crash in the actions brought by these plaintiffs.

* * * [In order to invoke the doctrine of collateral estoppel:] "There must be an identity of issue which has necessarily been decided in the prior action and is decisive of the present action, and, second, there must have been a full and fair opportunity to contest the decision now said to be controlling."

* * * [S]uch requirements are amply met in the instant cases. As already indicated, the issue of defendant airline's liability for the crash in which plaintiffs' decedents perished is identical to the issue of liability litigated in the Texas action where defendant was similarly charged with responsibility for that same accident. Indeed, in an airplane crash there are absent any of the problems with respect to "identity of issue" on liability which might arise in other types of accidents involving multiple

participants such as automobile accident cases. With respect to the second requirement, it is in no way disputed that defendant had a full and fair opportunity to contest the issue of its liability in the course of the 19–day trial in the Texas action, and in order to defeat collateral estoppel on this ground the burden rests on the defendant to show that it had no such opportunity.

* * *

Defendant's reliance on "full faith and credit" to defeat the application of collateral estoppel herein is misplaced. This is not a situation where the judgment, as such, of the Texas court is sought to be enforced. What is here involved is a policy determination by our courts that " 'One who has had his day in court should not be permitted to litigate the question anew' " (*B.R. De Witt, Inc. v. Hall,* 19 N.Y.2d 141, 144, *supra*), and, further, refusal "to tolerate a condition where, on relatively the same set of facts, one fact-finder, be it court or jury" may find a party liable while another exonerates him leading to the "inconsistent results which are always a blemish on a judicial system" (*Schwartz v. Public Administrator,* 24 N.Y.2d 65, 74, *supra*). * * *

Perhaps the strongest argument for applying the New York doctrine of collateral estoppel herein is the nature of the showing by defendant of the supposed "inequity" that would ensue from such application. There is a belabored emphasis on the merits of "mutuality of estoppel" and its favored status in "a majority of jurisdictions". Such of course wholly ignores the fact that our highest court has resoundingly stated in terms leaving no room for doubt that "the 'doctrine of mutuality' is a dead letter" (*B.R. De Witt, Inc. v. Hall,* 19 N.Y.2d 141, 147, *supra*). * * *

Among the reasons submitted by defendant as to why it should have an opportunity to retry the issue of its liability, notwithstanding its failure to prove its freedom therefrom on the trial in Texas, is the argument that such issue was submitted to the jury under the substantive law of Kentucky which is less favorable to defendant than is the New York law. While one is tempted to wonder what the argument would be if the situation were reversed, such contention is in any event wholly without merit since a New York court would also be obliged to submit the case under the substantive law of Kentucky, the place where the crash occurred. * * *

* * *

Even more interesting is the argument raised by defendant which may be paraphrased in Biblical terms as "hear them not for they know not what they do". Defendant seriously suggests that the determination in the Texas action should not be accorded further conclusive effect because that action involved only a single claimant and the jury's decision as to defendant's negligence is somehow impaired because rendered "without any awareness whatsoever by the jury that its verdict would determine the obligation of the defendant to many other persons not before it". It is apparently defendant's contention that the issue as to whether or not it was negligent in the operation of its aircraft is in some manner dependent upon the number of claims which may ultimately be asserted against it.

* * *

Accordingly, plaintiffs' cross motion for summary judgment is granted and defendant's motion for a joint trial is denied. Settle order providing for an assessment of damages.

NOTES AND QUESTIONS

1. Do the statutory and constitutional provisions require that states give a judgment the same preclusive effect—neither more nor less—as would the courts of the rendering state? Or do the provisions establish a minimum preclusive effect that one state must give another's judgment? What limits does the Due Process Clause place on expanding the preclusive effect accorded a state judgment? How should the foreseeability of the expanded preclusive effect figure into this question? See Shreve, *Preclusion and Federal Choice of Law*, 64 Texas L.Rev. 1209, 1251–63 (1986).

There has been considerable debate over whether a court can rest nonmutual preclusion on the judgment of a court that itself would require mutuality. The more common view appears to be in favor of employing the rules of the rendering court. This approach allows the first court the power to limit the effect of its own proceedings See 18B Wright, Miller & Cooper, Federal Practice and Procedure: Jurisdiction and Related Matters 2d §§ 4467, 4469. The issue is left open in Restatement (Second), Judgments § 86, comment *g* (1982). Nonetheless, some courts have given nonmutual preclusive effect to a judgment that the rendering state's courts would not have treated as preclusive.

In FINLEY v. KESLING, 105 Ill.App.3d 1, 60 Ill.Dec. 874, 433 N.E.2d 1112 (1982), Finley testified in Indiana divorce proceedings that four of his children owned 40% of the stock in a family corporation, and this testimony was accepted as the basis for the division of property. Thereafter he sued his four children in Illinois for a declaration that he was the beneficial owner of the stock. The Illinois court expressed doubt whether Indiana would cling to its traditional mutuality requirement in these circumstances, but concluded that it could apply collateral estoppel without regard to what Indiana might do. In the Illinois court's view, although a second state cannot reduce the effect of a judgment below the level commanded by the law of the judgment state, it can expand its effect. The court, nonetheless, advanced an alternative ground for its decision—that Illinois courts would not permit a party to contradict his sworn testimony in a prior proceeding, and that this is a matter independent of the effect of judgments or full faith and credit requirements.

2. Often a plaintiff may wish to enforce a judgment in a state other than the one that rendered the judgment. The procedures for enforcing an out-of-state judgment vary from state to state. Sometimes it is possible simply to register the existence of the out-of-state judgment with the clerk of the court in which the judgment is to be enforced. Other times the plaintiff must

institute a new suit, which is then subject to abbreviated procedures. What requirements do the constitutional and statutory provisions regarding full faith and credit place on a state's treatment of enforcement proceedings?

The basic implications of full faith and credit are the same for enforcement proceedings as they are for preclusion. There are, however, some exceptions to this general rule. The Supreme Court tackled this issue in BAKER v. GENERAL MOTORS CORP., 522 U.S. 222, 118 S.Ct. 657, 139 L.Ed.2d 580 (1998). The Bakers subpoenaed Elwell, a former GM engineering analyst, to testify in a wrongful-death action brought in Missouri against the automobile company. GM asserted Elwell's testimony was barred by a prior Michigan court settlement and permanent injunction generally prohibiting Elwell from testifying in any litigation involving GM. Reversing the Eighth Circuit, the Supreme Court, in an opinion delivered by Justice Ginsburg, held Elwell may testify "without offense" to the full faith and credit requirement: "Recognition, under full faith and credit, is owed to dispositions Michigan has authority to order. But a Michigan decree cannot command obedience elsewhere on a matter the Michigan court lacks authority to resolve." Id. at 240–41, 118 S.Ct. at 667–68, 139 L.Ed.2d at 597. The Court held that Michigan "lacks authority" to dictate evidentiary issues in courts of other states, in the context of actions brought by strangers to the Michigan litigation. However, the Court noted that this exception is a narrow one: "If the Bakers had been parties to the Michigan proceedings and had actually litigated the privileged character of Elwell's testimony, the Bakers would of course be precluded from relitigating that issue in Missouri." Id. at 239 n.12, 118 S.Ct. at 667 n.12, 139 L.Ed.2d at 596 n.12 (internal citations omitted).

Another example of the limits of full faith and credit is that judgments based on limited forms of judicial jurisdiction—in rem and quasi-in-rem judgments—need not be honored in execution proceedings. Or, a state may refuse to entertain an enforcement proceeding on grounds that its statute of limitations for such enforcement proceedings has run, even though the statute of the rendering state would not have run. And, for a final example, state statutes often specify that certain items of personal property, such as social-security payments and the last $200 of a savings account, cannot be used to satisfy court judgments. It is not a violation of full faith and credit for a state to refuse to enforce a judgment because it would require attachment of exempt property, even though that property would not have been considered exempt in the state rendering the judgment. For more general discussions of full faith and credit, see Nadelmann, *Full Faith and Credit to Judgments and Public Acts*, 56 Mich.L.Rev. 33 (1957); Radin, *The Authenticated Full Faith and Credit Clause: Its History*, 39 Ill.L.Rev. 1 (1994). See also Sterk, *The Muddy Boundaries Between Res Judicata and Full Faith and Credit*, 58 Wash. & Lee L. Rev. 47 (2001).

The substantive areas of matrimonial and custody law present special problems for the application of preclusion.

THOMPSON v. THOMPSON

Supreme Court of the United States, 1988.
484 U.S. 174, 108 S.Ct. 513, 98 L.Ed.2d 512.

Certiorari to the United States Court of Appeals for the Ninth Circuit.

JUSTICE MARSHALL delivered the opinion of the Court.

We granted certiorari in this case to determine whether the Parental Kidnapping Prevention Act of 1980, 28 U.S.C. § 1738A, furnishes an implied cause of action in federal court to determine which of two conflicting state custody decisions is valid.

I

The Parental Kidnapping Prevention Act (PKPA or Act) imposes a duty on the States to enforce a child custody determination entered by a court of a sister State if the determination is consistent with the provisions of the Act. In order for a state court's custody decree to be consistent with the provisions of the Act, the State must have jurisdiction under its own local law and one of five conditions set out in § 1738A(c)(2) must be met. Briefly put, these conditions authorize the state court to enter a custody decree if the child's home is or recently has been in the State, if the child has no home State and it would be in the child's best interest for the State to assume jurisdiction, or if the child is present in the State and has been abandoned or abused. Once a State exercises jurisdiction consistently with the provisions of the Act, no other State may exercise concurrent jurisdiction over the custody dispute, § 1738A(g), even if it would have been empowered to take jurisdiction in the first instance, and all States must accord full faith and credit to the first State's ensuing custody decree.

As the legislative scheme suggests, and as Congress explicitly specified, one of the chief purposes of the PKPA is to "avoid jurisdictional competition and conflict between State courts." Pub.L. 96–611, 94 Stat. 3569, § 7(c)(5), note following 28 U.S.C. § 1738A. This case arises out of a jurisdictional stalemate that came to pass notwithstanding the strictures of the Act. In July 1978, respondent Susan Clay (then Susan Thompson) filed a petition in Los Angeles Superior Court asking the court to dissolve her marriage to petitioner David Thompson and seeking custody of the couple's infant son, Matthew. The court initially awarded the parents joint custody of Matthew, but that arrangement became infeasible when respondent decided to move from California to Louisiana to take a job. The court then entered an order providing that respondent would have sole custody of Matthew once she left for Louisiana. This state of affairs was to remain in effect until the court investigator submitted a report on custody, after which the court intended to make a more studied custody determination. * * *

Respondent and Matthew moved to Louisiana in December 1980. Three months later, respondent filed a petition in Louisiana state court for enforcement of the California custody decree, judgment of custody, and modification of petitioner's visitation privileges. By order dated April 7, 1981, the Louisiana court granted the petition and awarded sole custody of Matthew to respondent. Two months later, however, the California court, having received and reviewed its investigator's report, entered an order awarding sole custody of Matthew to petitioner. Thus arose the current impasse.

In August 1983, petitioner brought this action in the District Court for the Central District of California. Petitioner requested an order declaring the Louisiana decree invalid and the California decree valid, and enjoining the enforcement of the Louisiana decree. Petitioner did not attempt to enforce the California decree in a Louisiana state court before he filed suit in federal court. The District Court granted respondent's motion to dismiss the complaint for lack of subject-matter and personal jurisdiction. * * * The Court of Appeals for the Ninth Circuit affirmed. * * * We granted certiorari * * * and we now affirm.

II

* * *

We examine initially the context of the PKPA with an eye toward determining Congress' perception of the law that it was shaping or reshaping. * * * At the time Congress passed the PKPA, custody orders held a peculiar status under the full faith and credit doctrine, which requires each State to give effect to the judicial proceedings of other States, see U.S. Const., Art. IV, § 1; 28 U.S.C. § 1738. The anomaly traces to the fact that custody orders characteristically are subject to modification as required by the best interests of the child. As a consequence, some courts doubted whether custody orders were sufficiently "final" to trigger full faith and credit requirements, * * * and this Court had declined expressly to settle the question. See *Ford v. Ford,* 371 U.S. 187, 192, 83 S.Ct. 273, 276, 9 L.Ed.2d 240 (1962). Even if custody orders were subject to full faith and credit requirements, the Full Faith and Credit Clause obliges States only to accord the same force to judgments as would be accorded by the courts of the State in which the judgment was entered. Because courts entering custody orders generally retain the power to modify them, courts in other States were no less entitled to change the terms of custody according to their own views of the child's best interest. * * * For these reasons, a parent who lost a custody battle in one State had an incentive to kidnap the child and move to another State to relitigate the issue. This circumstance contributed to widespread jurisdictional deadlocks like this one, and more importantly, to a national epidemic of parental kidnapping. At the time the PKPA was enacted, sponsors of the Act estimated that between 25,000 and 100,000 children were kidnapped by parents who had been unable to obtain custody in a legal forum. See Parental Kidnapping Prevention Act of 1979: Joint Hearing on S. 105 before the Subcommittee on Criminal Justice of the Judiciary Committee and the Subcommittee on Child and Human Development of the Committee on Labor and Human Resources, 96th Cong., 2d Sess., 10 (1980) (hereinafter PKPA Joint Hearing) (statement of Sen. Malcolm Wallop).

A number of States joined in an effort to avoid these jurisdictional conflicts by adopting the Uniform Child Custody Jurisdiction Act (UCCJA), 9 U.L.A. §§ 1–28 (1979). The UCCJA prescribed uniform standards for deciding which State could make a custody determination and obligated enacting States to enforce the determination made by the State with proper jurisdiction. The project foundered, however, because a number of States refused to enact the UCCJA while others enacted it with modifications. In the absence of uniform national standards for allocating and enforcing custody determinations, noncustodial parents still had reason to snatch their children and petition the courts of any of a number of haven States for sole custody.

The context of the PKPA therefore suggests that the principal problem Congress was seeking to remedy was the inapplicability of full faith and credit requirements to custody determinations. Statements made when the Act was introduced in Congress forcefully confirm that suggestion. The sponsors and supporters of the Act continually indicated that the purpose of the PKPA was to provide for nationwide enforcement of custody orders made in accordance with the terms of the UCCJA. As Acting Deputy Attorney General Michel testified:

* * *

> "In essence [the PKPA] would impose on States a Federal duty, under enumerated standards derived from the UCCJA, to give full faith and credit to the custody decrees of other States. Such legislation would, in effect, amount to Federal adoption of key provisions of the UCCJA for all States and would eliminate the incentive for one parent to remove a minor child to another jurisdiction." PKPA Joint Hearing 48.

* * * [T]he [Full Faith and Credit Clause] "only prescribes a rule by which courts, Federal and state, are to be guided when a question arises in the progress of a pending suit as to the faith and credit to be given by the court to the public acts, records, and judicial proceedings of a State other than that in which the court is sitting." [*Minnesota v. Northern Securities Co.,* 194 U.S. 48, 72, 24 S.Ct. 598, 605, 48 L.Ed. 870, 881 (1904)]. Because Congress' chief aim in enacting the PKPA was to extend the requirements of the Full Faith and Credit Clause to custody determinations, the Act is most naturally construed to furnish a rule of decision for courts to use in adjudicating custody disputes and not to create an entirely new cause of action. It thus is not compatible with the purpose and context of the legislative scheme to infer a private cause of action. * * *

The language and placement of the statute reinforce this conclusion. The PKPA, 28 U.S.C. § 1738A, is an addendum to the full faith and credit statute, 28 U.S.C. § 1738. This fact alone is strong proof that the Act is intended to have the same operative effect as the full faith and credit statute.

* * *

In sum, the context, language, and history of the PKPA together make out a conclusive case against inferring a cause of action in federal court to determine which of two conflicting state custody decrees is valid. Against this impressive evidence, petitioner relies primarily on the argument that failure to infer a cause of action would render the PKPA nugatory. We note, as a preliminary response, that ultimate review remains available in this Court for truly intractable jurisdictional deadlocks. In addition, the unspoken presumption in petitioner's argument is that the States are either unable or unwilling to enforce the provisions of the Act. This is a presumption we are not prepared, and more importantly, Congress was not prepared, to indulge. State courts faithfully administer the Full Faith and Credit Clause every day; now that Congress has extended full faith and credit requirements to child custody orders, we can think of no reason why the courts' administration of federal law in custody disputes will be any less vigilant. Should state courts prove as obstinate as petitioner predicts, Congress may choose to revisit the issue. But any more radical approach to the problem will have to await further legislative action; we "will not engraft a remedy on a statute, no matter how salutary, that Congress did not intend to provide." *California v. Sierra Club,* 451 U.S. 287, 297 (1981). The judgment of the Court of Appeals is affirmed.

It is so ordered.

[JUSTICE O'CONNOR concurred in part and concurred in the judgment. JUSTICE SCALIA concurred.]

NOTES AND QUESTIONS

1. Thompson v. Thompson raises the peculiar issue of interstate preclusion when each state retains jurisdiction over a dispute. In the context of custody disputes, a court always can reopen proceedings if it is in the best interests of the child. The ability to reopen the case, then, is actually what is granted preclusive effect.

2. In PARKER v. HOEFER, 2 N.Y.2d 612, 162 N.Y.S.2d 13, 142 N.E.2d 194, certiorari denied 355 U.S. 833, 78 S.Ct. 51, 2 L.Ed.2d 45 (1957), the New York Court of Appeals gave full faith and credit to a Vermont final judgment, notwithstanding that the underlying claim would not be enforceable in New York. In holding that the plaintiff could initiate an enforcement action in New York, the court said:

> * * * [T]he plaintiff is not attempting to enforce in the courts of New York an action for alienation of affections and criminal conversation, which have been abolished in New York but, rather, to enforce a judgment rendered in Vermont as between these parties, which was final and conclusive on the rights litigated. New York cannot retry the case or

> review as on appeal the Vermont judgment. * * * The present suit, then, is upon an entirely different cause of action from that merged in the judgment * * * and may not be called a suit on an action abolished in New York. * * *

Id. at 617, 162 N.Y.S.2d at 17, 142 N.E.2d at 197.

2. STATE–FEDERAL PRECLUSION

Although it is generally agreed that the Full Faith and Credit Clause of the Constitution applies only to state courts, Section 1738 (known as the Full Faith and Credit Statute) imposes the same general principles on the federal courts, requiring them to accord full faith and credit to the judgments of state courts. Because the requirement is statutory and not constitutional, however, it may be supervened. For example, the writ of habeas corpus, 28 U.S.C. §§ 2241–2255, provides a federal forum in which people who have been convicted of crimes in state court may litigate constitutional claims arising out of their prosecutions. Under traditional rules of preclusion, this subsequent action would be prevented.

What other circumstances might justify departing from the usual rules of intersystem preclusion? Consider, for example, cases involving federal issues. Should a federal court give preclusive effect to a state-court determination of federal law? What about circumstances in which the federal claim arises only by way of defense, and thus the original action could not have been removed to federal court? What if the issue was an area, such as copyright, which is within the exclusive jurisdiction of the federal courts?

ALLEN v. McCURRY

Supreme Court of the United States, 1980.
449 U.S. 90, 101 S.Ct. 411, 66 L.Ed.2d 308.

[McCurry was charged with possession of heroin in a state-court proceeding. At a pretrial suppression hearing, the trial judge excluded some of the evidence on the ground that it was the product of an illegal police search, but admitted the drugs and other contraband that the officers had found "in plain view." McCurry subsequently was convicted after a jury trial. McCurry later filed a civil action for damages under 42 U.S.C. § 1983, claiming that Allen and other police officers had unconstitutionally searched his house and seized the property that had been used to convict him. The District Court granted Allen and the other defendants summary judgment, holding that McCurry already had raised the Fourth Amendment issue unsuccessfully in the state-court proceeding. The Court of Appeals reversed, holding that the issue should be allowed to go to trial unencumbered by rules of issue preclusion due to the special role of the federal courts in protecting civil rights.]

Certiorari to the United States Court of Appeals for the Eighth Circuit.

JUSTICE STEWART delivered the opinion of the Court.

* * *

In recent years, this Court has reaffirmed the benefits of collateral estoppel in particular, finding the policies underlying it to apply in contexts not formerly recognized at common law. Thus, the Court has eliminated the requirement of mutuality in applying collateral estoppel to bar relitigation of issues decided earlier in federal-court suits, * * * and has allowed a litigant who was not a party to a federal case to use collateral estoppel "offensively" in a new federal suit against the party who lost on the decided issue in the first case * * *. But one general limitation the Court has repeatedly recognized is that the concept of collateral estoppel cannot apply when the party against whom the earlier decision is asserted did not have a "full and fair opportunity" to litigate that issue in the earlier case. * * *

The federal courts generally have * * * consistently accorded preclusive effect to issues decided by state courts. E.g., Montana v. United States, supra; Angel v. Bullington, 330 U.S. 183, 67 S.Ct. 657, 91 L.Ed. 832. Thus, res judicata and collateral estoppel not only reduce unnecessary litigation and foster reliance on adjudication, but also promote the comity between state and federal courts that has been recognized as a bulwark of the federal system. * * *

Indeed, though the federal courts may look to the common law or to the policies supporting res judicata and collateral estoppel in assessing the preclusive effect of decisions of other federal courts, Congress has specifically required all federal courts to give preclusive effect to state-court judgments whenever the courts of the State from which the judgments emerged would do so * * * [citing 28 U.S.C. § 1738]. It is against this background that we examine the relationship of § 1983 and collateral estoppel, and the decision of the Court of Appeals in this case.

III

This Court has never directly decided whether the rules of res judicata and collateral estoppel are generally applicable to § 1983 actions. But in Preiser v. Rodriguez * * *, the Court noted with implicit approval the view of other federal courts that res judicata principles fully apply to civil rights suits brought under that statute. * * * And the virtually unanimous view of the Courts of Appeals since *Preiser* has been that § 1983 presents no categorical bar to the application of res judicata and collateral estoppel concepts.[10] These federal appellate court decisions have spoken with little explanation or citation in assuming the compatibility of § 1983 and rules of preclusion, but the statute and its legislative history clearly support the courts' decisions.

---

10. * * * A very few courts have suggested that the normal rules of claim preclusion should not apply in § 1983 suits in one peculiar circumstance: Where a § 1983 plaintiff seeks to litigate in federal court a federal issue which he could have raised but did not raise in an earlier state-court suit against the same adverse party. * * * These cases present a narrow question not now before us, and we intimate no view as to whether they were correctly decided.

Because the requirement of mutuality of estoppel was still alive in the federal courts until well into this century, * * * the drafters of the 1871 Civil Rights Act, of which § 1983 is a part, may have had less reason to concern themselves with rules of preclusion than a modern Congress would. Nevertheless, in 1871 res judicata and collateral estoppel could certainly have applied in federal suits following state-court litigation between the same parties or their privies, and nothing in the language of § 1983 remotely expresses any congressional intent to contravene the common-law rules of preclusion or to repeal the express statutory requirements of the predecessor of 28 U.S.C. § 1738 * * *. Section 1983 creates a new federal cause of action. It says nothing about the preclusive effect of state-court judgments.

Moreover, the legislative history of § 1983 does not in any clear way suggest that Congress intended to repeal or restrict the traditional doctrines of preclusion. The main goal of the Act was to override the corrupting influence of the Ku Klux Klan and its sympathizers on the governments and law enforcement agencies of the Southern States, see Monroe v. Pape, 365 U.S. 167, 174, 81 S.Ct. 473, 477, 5 L.Ed.2d 492, and of course the debates show that one strong motive behind its enactment was grave congressional concern that the state courts had been deficient in protecting federal rights * * *. But in the context of the legislative history as a whole, this congressional concern lends only the most equivocal support to any argument that, in cases where the state courts have recognized the constitutional claims asserted and provided fair procedures for determining them, Congress intended to override § 1738 or the common-law rules of collateral estoppel and res judicata. Since repeals by implication are disfavored, * * * much clearer support than this would be required to hold that § 1738 and the traditional rules of preclusion are not applicable to § 1983 suits.

As the Court has understood the history of the legislation, Congress realized that in enacting § 1983 it was altering the balance of judicial power between the state and federal courts. * * * But in doing so, Congress was adding to the jurisdiction of the federal courts, not subtracting from that of the state courts. * * * The debates contain several references to the concurrent jurisdiction of the state courts over federal questions, and numerous suggestions that the state courts would retain their established jurisdiction so that they could, when the then current political passions abated, demonstrate a new sensitivity to federal rights.

To the extent that it did intend to change the balance of power over federal questions between the state and federal courts, the 42d Congress was acting in a way thoroughly consistent with the doctrines of preclusion. In reviewing the legislative history of § 1983, * * * the Court inferred that Congress had intended a federal remedy in three circumstances: where state substantive law was facially unconstitutional, where state procedural law was inadequate to allow full litigation of a constitutional claim, and where state procedural law, though adequate in theory, was inadequate in practice. * * * In short, the federal courts could step in where the state courts were unable or unwilling to protect federal rights. * * * This understanding of § 1983 might well support an exception to res judicata and collateral estoppel where state law did not provide fair procedures for the litigation of constitutional claims, or where a state court failed to even acknowledge the existence of the constitutional principle on which a litigant based his claim. Such an exception, however, would be essentially the same as the important general limit on rules of preclusion that already exists: Collateral estoppel does not apply where the party against whom an earlier court decision is asserted did not have a full and fair opportunity to litigate the claim or issue decided by the first court. * * * But the Court's view of § 1983 in *Monroe* lends no strength to any argument that Congress intended to allow relitigation of federal issues decided after a full and fair hearing in a state court simply because the state court's decision may have been erroneous.

* * *

The actual basis of the Court of Appeals' holding appears to be a generally framed principle that every person asserting a federal right is entitled to one unencumbered opportunity to litigate that right in a federal district court, regardless of the legal posture in which the federal claim arises. But the authority for this principle is difficult to discern. It cannot lie in the Constitution, which makes no such guarantee, but leaves the scope of the jurisdiction of the federal district courts to the wisdom of Congress. And no such authority is to be found in § 1983 itself. For reasons already discussed at length, nothing in the language or legislative history of § 1983 proves any congressional intent to deny binding effect to a state-court judgment or decision when the state court, acting within its proper jurisdiction, has given the parties a full and fair opportunity to litigate federal claims, and thereby has shown itself willing and able to protect federal rights. And nothing in the legislative history of § 1983 reveals any purpose to afford less deference to judgments in state criminal proceedings than to those in state civil proceedings. There is, in short, no reason to believe that Congress intended to provide a person claiming a federal right an unrestricted opportunity to relitigate an issue already decided in state court simply because the issue arose in a state proceeding in which he would rather not have been engaged at all.

* * *

The only other conceivable basis for finding a universal right to litigate a federal claim in a federal district court is hardly a legal basis at all, but rather a general distrust of the capacity of the state courts to render correct decisions on constitutional issues. * * *

The Court of Appeals erred in holding that McCurry's inability to obtain federal habeas corpus relief upon his Fourth Amendment claim renders the doctrine of collateral estoppel inapplicable to his § 1983 suit. Accordingly, the judgment is reversed, and the case is remanded to the Court of Appeals for proceedings consistent with this opinion.

It is so ordered.

JUSTICE BLACKMUN, with whom JUSTICE BRENNAN and JUSTICE MARSHALL join, dissenting.

* * *

The following factors persuade me to conclude that this respondent should not be precluded from asserting his claim in federal court. First, at the time § 1983 was passed, a nonparty's ability, as a practical matter, to invoke collateral estoppel was nonexistent. One could not preclude an opponent from relitigating an issue in a new cause of action, though that issue had been determined conclusively in a prior proceeding, unless there was "mutuality." Additionally, the definitions of "cause of action" and "issue" were narrow. As a result, and obviously, no preclusive effect could arise out of a criminal proceeding that would affect subsequent *civil* litigation. Thus, the 42d Congress could not have anticipated or approved that a criminal defendant, tried and convicted in state court, would be precluded from raising against police officers a constitutional claim arising out of his arrest.

Also, the process of deciding in a state criminal trial whether to exclude or admit evidence is not at all the equivalent of a § 1983 proceeding. The remedy sought in the latter is utterly different. In bringing the civil suit the criminal defendant does not seek to challenge his conviction collaterally. At most, he wins damages. In contrast, the exclusion of evidence may prevent a criminal conviction. A trial court, faced with the decision whether to exclude relevant evidence, confronts institutional pressures that may cause it to give a different shape to the Fourth Amendment right from what would result in civil litigation of a damages claim. Also, the issue whether to exclude evidence is subsidiary to the purpose of a criminal trial, which is to determine the guilt or innocence of the defendant, and a trial court, at least subconsciously, must weigh the potential damage to the truth-seeking process caused by excluding relevant evidence. * * *

NOTES AND QUESTIONS

1. The logic of *Allen* was soon extended by the Supreme Court. In MIGRA v. WARREN CITY SCHOOL DISTRICT BOARD OF EDUCATION, 465 U.S. 75, 104 S.Ct. 892, 79 L.Ed.2d 56 (1984), the Court found that a prior state-court adjudication precluded the plaintiff from bringing a subsequent suit in federal court, even though the later proceeding was based on constitutional issues that the plaintiff failed to raise, but could have raised, in the earlier state action. Justice Blackmun, who dissented in *Allen,* wrote for the Court:

> Petitioner suggests that to give state-court judgments full issue preclusive effect but not claim preclusive effect would enable litigants to bring their state claims in state court and their federal claims in federal court, thereby taking advantage of the relative expertise of both forums. Al-

> though such a division may seem attractive from a plaintiff's perspective, it is not the system established by § 1738. That statute embodies the view that it is more important to give full faith and credit to state-court judgments than to ensure separate forums for federal and state claims. This reflects a variety of concerns, including notions of comity, the need to prevent vexatious litigation, and a desire to conserve judicial resources. In the present litigation, petitioner does not claim that the state court would not have adjudicated her federal claims had she presented them in her original suit in state court. Alternatively, petitioner could have obtained a federal forum for her federal claim by litigating it first in a federal court. Section 1983, however, does not override state preclusion law and guarantee petitioner a right to proceed to judgment in state court on her state claims and then turn to federal court for adjudication of her federal claims. We hold, therefore, that petitioner's state-court judgment in this litigation has the same claim preclusive effect in federal court that the judgment would have in the Ohio state courts.

Id. at 84, 104 S.Ct. at 898, 79 L.Ed.2d at 64.

2. *Allen* and *Migra* held that Section 1983 did not imply an exception to Section 1738. Does a congressional grant of exclusive federal jurisdiction imply such an exception? For example, can an action based upon state antitrust law preclude a later action under the Sherman Antitrust Act, over which federal courts have exclusive jurisdiction? In MARRESE v. AMERICAN ACADEMY OF ORTHOPAEDIC SURGEONS, 470 U.S. 373, 105 S.Ct. 1327, 84 L.Ed.2d 274 (1985), a case arising under the Sherman Act, Justice O'Connor set forth a two-step approach for determining the preclusive effect of a state court judgment in a subsequent suit over which federal courts have exclusive jurisdiction. First, applying the Full Faith and Credit Statute, the federal court must determine whether *state* claim-preclusion law would preclude the federal suit. If not, there is no preclusion. If the state would bar the federal action, then, as a second step, the federal court must determine whether the relevant federal law contains an implied or explicit exception to Section 1738. The *Marrese* Court remanded the case before it for a determination of how Illinois would have treated the second lawsuit, thereby avoiding the issue of whether the Sherman Act creates an exception to Section 1738.

In most cases *Marrese* will prevent preclusion. This is so because virtually every state follows the "prior jurisdictional competency" rule, which prohibits preclusion of a claim beyond the rendering court's jurisdiction. Since state courts cannot hear cases when the federal court's jurisdiction is exclusive, the prior jurisdictional competency rule would prevent a state court from precluding such cases; *Marrese* prohibits federal courts from precluding claims that would not be precluded under state rules.

Marrese does raise the possibility, however, of the application of state issue preclusion rules whenever a congressional grant of exclusive jurisdiction is deemed not to imply an exception to Section 1738. The application of state rules of issue preclusion often will effectively eliminate the federal action. See Murphy v. Gallagher, 761 F.2d 878 (2d Cir.1985) (state rules of issue preclusion apply in later federal securities fraud action, over which federal court has exclusive jurisdiction, even though the result is to dispose of entire federal action). The Supreme Court has since applied the *Marrese* test to a Delaware state court-settlement judgment in a securities class action suit in MATSUSHITA ELECTRIC INDUSTRIAL CO. v. EPSTEIN, 516 U.S. 367, 116 S.Ct. 873, 134 L.Ed.2d 6 (1996). Justice Thomas held that under Section 1738, the Delaware settlement was entitled to full faith and credit even though it included claims within the exclusive subject matter jurisdiction of the federal courts. Writing separately, Justice Ginsburg dissented from part of the Court's opinion because of the due process problems resulting from denying the plaintiffs the opportunity to raise exclusively federal issues. For an analysis of *Matsushita*'s effects on state court global settlements encompassing exclusively federal claims, see Kahan & Silberman, Matsushita *and Beyond: The Role of State Courts in Class Actions Involving Exclusive Federal Claims*, 1996 Sup.Ct.Rev. 219 (1996).

3. In KREMER v. CHEMICAL CONSTRUCTION CORP., 456 U.S. 461, 102 S.Ct. 1883, 72 L.Ed.2d 262 (1982), the Court held that, although plaintiff could have sued in federal court on an employment-discrimination claim initially, once he opted to appeal a state agency determination in state court, he was subject to the usual rules of preclusion. Having litigated in state court, he could only relitigate the issues in federal court if there was reason to doubt the quality, extensiveness, or fairness of the procedures followed in the state-court action. Justice Blackmun, in dissent, argued that the nature of the state-court review was different from the review that a federal district court would give the action. The standard of review in state court was whether the state agency's determination was arbitrary; a federal court would have engaged in a full adjudication on the merits of the employment-discrimination claim.

3. FEDERAL–STATE PRECLUSION

Must a state court grant preclusive effect to a prior federal-court judgment? The general requirement that federal judgments be given full faith and credit in state courts never has been challenged seriously, even though the Full Faith and Credit Clause does not apply to the situation, and even though most courts agree that Section 1738 is inapplicable as well. Commentators invoke various provisions of the Constitution (including the Supremacy Clause and the "case or controversy" doctrine) to support binding state courts to federal-court judgments. The lack of any express provision may reflect the constitutional compromise that relegated to Congress the decision of whether to establish inferior federal courts.

The conclusion that state courts are obliged to grant preclusive effect to federal court judgments does not determine which rules of preclusion the state should apply. There is almost universal agreement that federal preclusion rules usually apply in a state court when the prior federal-court judgment involved a federal question. But should federal preclusion rules define the effect in a subsequent action of a prior federal judgment deciding state-law claims? Arguably, the *Erie* doctrine requires the court to treat a prior federal determination of the claim in the same way that it would treat a prior state determination of the claim; under Section 1738, that would mean the application of the preclusion rules of the state in which the rendering federal court sits.

For many years a lively debate took place among scholars, who reached different conclusions as to a number of the issues. Among the most prominent writings are Burbank, *Interjurisdictional Preclusion, Full Faith and Credit and Federal Common Law: A General Approach*, 71 Cornell L.Rev. 733 (1986) (arguing that Article III is not a grant of power to federal courts as to all matters relating to the preclusive effect of their judgments), and Degnan, *Federalized Res Judicata*, 85 Yale L.J. 741 (1976) (arguing that federal law should define the preclusive effect of all federal judgments). The Restatement of Judgments adopted the position that, although federal law ultimately must control the choice of preclusion rules, federal law should mandate the application of state rules when those rules are important to the effectuation of substantive state policies. Restatement (Second), Judgments § 87 (1982). See also 18B Wright, Miller & Cooper, Federal Practice and Procedure: Jurisdiction and Related Matters 2d §§ 4468, 4472.

SEMTEK INTERNATIONAL INC. v. LOCKHEED MARTIN CORP.

Supreme Court of the United States, 2001.
531 U.S. 497, 121 S.Ct. 1021, 149 L.Ed.2d 32.

Certiorari to the Court of Special Appeals of Maryland.

MR. JUSTICE SCALIA delivered the opinion of the Court

[Petitioner sued respondent in California state court, alleging breach of contract and various business torts. After removal to the United States District Court for the Central District of California on the basis of diversity of citizenship, the action was dismissed "on the merits and with prejudice" because it was barred by California's two-year statute of limitations. The Ninth Circuit affirmed. Petitioner also brought suit against respondent in the Circuit Court for Baltimore City, Maryland, alleging the same causes of action, which were not time barred under Maryland's three-year statute of limitations. Respondent asked the California federal court to enjoin this action; it also removed the Maryland state court action on federal-question grounds (diversity grounds were not available because Lockheed "is a Maryland citizen"). The California federal court denied the requested relief, and the Maryland federal court remanded the case to state court because the federal question arose only by way of defense. The Maryland state court granted Lockheed's motion to dismiss on the ground of res judicata. Petitioner appealed the Maryland trial court's order of dismissal to the Maryland Court of Special Appeals. That court affirmed, holding that, regardless of whether California would have accorded claim-preclusive effect to a statute-of-limitations dismissal by one of its own courts, the dismissal by the California federal court barred the Maryland complaint since the res judicata effect of federal diversity judgments is prescribed by federal law, under which the earlier dismissal was "on the merits" and claim preclusive. The Maryland Court of Appeals declined to review the case.]

* * *

II

Petitioner contends that the outcome of this case is controlled by *Dupasseur v. Rochereau*, 21 Wall. 130, 135 (1874), which held that the res judicata effect of a federal diversity judgment "is such as would belong to judgments of the State courts rendered under similar circumstances," and may not be accorded any "higher sanctity or effect." Since, petitioner argues, the dismissal of an action on statute-of-limitations grounds by a California state court would not be claim preclusive, it follows that the similar dismissal of this diversity action by the California federal court cannot by claim preclusive. While we agree that this would be the result demanded by *Dupasseur*, the case is not dispositive because it was decided under the Conformity Act of 1872, 17 Stat. 196, which required federal courts to apply the procedural law of the forum State in nonequity cases.

Respondent, for its part, contends that the outcome of this case is controlled by Federal Rule * * * 41(b), which provides as follows:

> * * * Unless the court in its order for dismissal otherwise specifies, a dismissal under this subdivision and any dismissal not provided for in this rule, other than a dismissal for lack of jurisdiction, for improper venue, or for failure to join a party under Rule 19, operates as an adjudication upon the merits.

Since the dismissal here did not "otherwise specify" (indeed, it specifically stated that it was "on the merits"), and did not pertain to the excepted subjects of jurisdiction, venue, or joinder, it follows, respondent contends, that the dismissal "is entitled to claim preclusive effect." * * * [The language of the provision quoted throughout the decision has been altered by the 2007 restyling of the Federal Rules. These changes are not substantive.]

Implicit in this reasoning is the unstated minor premise that all judgments denominated "on the merits" are entitled to claim-preclusive effect. That premise is not necessarily valid. The original connotation of an "on the merits" adjudication is one that actually "pass[es] directly on the substance of [a particular] claim" before the court. Restatement § 19, Comment *a*, at 161. That connotation remains common to every jurisdiction of which we are aware. See *ibid.* * * * And it is, we think, the meaning intended in those many statements to the effect that a judgment "on the merits" triggers the doctrine of res judicata or claim preclusion. * * *

But over the years the meaning of the term "judgment on the merits" "has gradually undergone change," R. Marcus, M. Redish, & E. Sherman, Civil Procedure: A Modern Approach 1140–1141 (3d ed. 2000), and it has come to be applied to some judgments (such as the one involved here) that do *not* pass upon the substantive merits of a claim and hence do *not* (in many jurisdictions) entail claim-preclusive effect. * * * That is why the Restatement of Judgments has abandoned the use of the term—"because of its possibly misleading connotations," Restatement § 19, Comment *a*, at 161.

In short, it is no longer true that a judgment "on the merits" is necessarily a judgment entitled to claim-preclusive effect; and there are a number of reasons for believing that the phrase "adjudication upon the merits" does not bear that meaning in Rule 41(b). To begin with, Rule 41(b) sets forth nothing more than a default rule for determining the import of a dismissal (a dismissal is "upon the merits," with the three stated exceptions, unless the court "otherwise specifies"). This would be a highly peculiar context in which to announce a federally prescribed rule on the complex question of claim preclusion, saying in effect, "All federal dismissals (with three specified exceptions) preclude suit elsewhere, unless the court otherwise specifies."

And even apart from the purely default character of Rule 41(b), it would be peculiar to find a rule governing the effect that must be accorded federal judgments by other courts ensconced in rules governing the internal procedures of the rendering court itself. Indeed, such a rule would arguably violate the jurisdictional limitation of the Rules Enabling Act: that the Rules "shall not abridge, enlarge or modify any substantive right" * * *. In the present case, for example, if California law left petitioner free to sue on this claim in Maryland even after the California statute of limitations had expired, the federal court's extinguishment of that right (through Rule 41(b)'s mandated claim-preclusive effect of its judgment) would seem to violate this limitation.

Moreover, as so interpreted, the rule would in many cases violate the federalism principle of *Erie R. Co. v. Tompkins*, [p. 408, supra,] * * * by engendering " 'substantial' variations [in outcomes] between state and federal litigation" which would "likely ... influence the choice of a forum," *Hanna v. Plumer*, [p. 431, supra,] * * *. With regard to the claim-preclusion issue involved in the present case, for example, the traditional rule is that expiration of the applicable statute of limitations merely bars the remedy and does not extinguish the substantive right, so that dismissal on that ground does not have claim-preclusive effect in other jurisdictions with longer, unexpired limitation periods. * * * Out-of-state defendants sued on stale claims in California and in other States adhering to this traditional rule would systematically remove state-law suits brought against them to federal court—where, unless otherwise specified, a statute-of-limitations dismissal would bar suit everywhere.

Finally, if Rule 41(b) did mean what respondent suggests, we would surely have relied upon it in our cases recognizing the claim-preclusive effect of federal judgments in federal-question cases. Yet for over half a century since the promulgation of Rule 41(b), we have not once done so. * * *

We think the key to a more reasonable interpretation of the meaning of "operates as an adjudication upon the merits" in Rule 41(b) is to be found in Rule 41(a), which, in discussing the effect of voluntary dismissal by the plaintiff, makes clear than an "adjudication upon the merits" is the opposite of a "dismissal without prejudice" * * *. * * * The primary meaning of "dismissal without prejudice," we think, is dismissal without barring the defendant from returning later, to the same court, with the same underlying claim. That will also ordinarily (though not always) have the consequence of not barring the claim from *other* courts, but its primary meaning relates to the dismissing court itself. Thus, Black's Law Dictionary (7th ed. 1999) defines "dismissed without prejudice" as "removed from the court's docket in such a way that the plaintiff may refile the same suit on the same claim," * * * and defines "dismissal without prejudice" as "[a] dismissal that does not bar the plaintiff from refiling the lawsuit within the applicable limitations period," *ibid.*

We think, then, that the effect of the "adjudication upon the merits" default provision of Rule 41(b)—and, presumably, of the explicit order in the present case that used the language of that default provision—is simply that, unlike a dismissal "without prejudice," the dismissal in the present case barred refiling of the same claim in the United States District Court for the Central District of California. That is undoubtedly a necessary condition, but it is not a sufficient one, for claim-preclusive effect in other courts.

III

Having concluded that the claim-preclusive effect, in Maryland, of this California federal diversity judgment is dictated neither by *Dupasseur v. Rochereau*, as petitioner contends, nor by Rule 41(b), as respondent contends, we turn to consideration of what determines the issue. Neither the Full Faith and Credit Clause * * * [and] no other federal textual provision, neither of the Constitution nor of any statute, addresses the claim-preclusive effect of a judgment in a federal diversity action.

It is also true, however, that no federal textual provision addresses the claim-preclusive effect of a federal-court judgment in a federal-question case, yet we have long held that States cannot give those judgments merely whatever effect they would give their own judgments, but must accord them the effect that this Court prescribes. * * * The reasoning of that line of cases suggests, moreover, that even when States are allowed to give federal judgments * * * no more than the effect accorded to state judgments, that disposition is by direction of *this* Court, which has the last word on the claim-preclusive effect of *all* federal judgments * * *. In other words, in *Dupasseur* the State was allowed (indeed, required) to give a federal diversity judgment no more effect than it would accord one of its own judgments only because reference to state law was the *federal rule that this Court deemed appropriate.* In short, federal common law governs the claim-preclusive effect of a dismissal by a federal court sitting in diversity. * * *

It is left to us, then, to determine the appropriate federal rule. And despite the sea change that has occurred in the background law since *Dupasseur* was decided * * * we think the result decreed by *Dupasseur* continues to be correct for diversity cases. Since state, rather than federal, substantive law is at issue there is no need for a uniform federal rule. And indeed, nationwide uniformity in the substance of the matter is better served by having the same claim-preclusive rule (the state rule) apply whether the dismissal has been ordered by a state or a federal court. This is, it seems to us, a classic case for adopting, as the federally prescribed rule of decision, the law that would be applied by state courts in the State in which the federal diversity court sits. * * * As we have alluded to above, any other rule would produce the sort of "forum-shopping ... and ... inequitable administration of the laws" that *Erie* seeks to avoid * * * since filing in, or removing to, federal court would be encouraged by the divergent effects that the litigants would anticipate from likely grounds of dismissal. * * *

This federal reference to state law will not obtain, of course, in situations in which the state law is incompatible with federal interests. * * * No such conflict with potential federal interests exists in the present case. Dismissal of this state cause of action was decreed by the California federal court only because the California statute of limitations so required; and there is no conceivable federal interest in giving that time bar more effect in other courts than the California courts themselves would impose.

* * *

Because the claim-preclusive effect of the California federal court's dismissal "upon the merits" of petitioner's action on statute-of-limitations grounds is governed by a federal rule that in turn incorporates California's law of claim preclusion (the content of which we do not pass upon today), the Maryland Court of Special Appeals erred in holding that the dismissal necessarily precluded the bringing of this action in the Maryland courts. The judgment is reversed * * *.

It is so ordered.

NOTES AND QUESTIONS

1. Do you agree with the Court's conclusions regarding the relevance of *Erie* and *Hanna*, the Rules Enabling Act, and federal common law, all subjects you have encountered in Chapter 6, p. 404, supra?

2. The rule in *Semtek* requires courts to apply the law of the forum state of the prior action to determine the preclusive effect of prior diversity actions. Will this rule, as Justice Scalia claims, really reduce forum shopping? The *Semtek* decision, of course, is completely consistent with the principles espoused in *Erie* and *Klaxon*. Although preclusion doctrines vary from state to state, and state preclusion rules are part and parcel of each state's law, note that if the California preclusion rules had been applied by the Maryland court, that court's dismissal on res judicata grounds might well have been sustained. Did the Maryland court's failure to do so justify reversal?

3. Will there be situations in which the Supreme Court might conclude that a federal interest would be "incompatible" with the application of a state standard? What would they be? When could a federal court craft its own rule of federal common law of claim preclusion?

4. What happens if a state court, in attempting to apply federal preclusion rules to a prior federal judgment, makes a mistake? If the parties subsequently return to federal court to correct the error, is the federal court bound under Section 1738 to give preclusive effect to the state court's prior decision on the issue of preclusion?

In PARSONS STEEL, INC. v. FIRST ALABAMA BANK, 474 U.S. 518, 106 S.Ct. 768, 88 L.Ed.2d 877 (1986), the Supreme Court held that a state court's rejection of a claim that an earlier federal judgment precludes the state action is itself res judicata in the context of a later federal action to enjoin the enforcement of the state-court judgment.

5. What rules of preclusion should a diversity court apply to the judgment of a prior diversity court from another state? Again, Professor Degnan argues that federal law should govern the effect of the prior federal judgment, whether or not the prior federal judgment involved a federal question. Degnan, *Federalized Res Judicata*, 85 Yale L.J. 741 (1976). Other commentators argue that rules of preclusion are substantive, since they materially affect the outcome of a case, and that *Erie* therefore mandates the application of the rules the state court would apply. As discussed above, however, Note 2, p. 1352, supra, state courts themselves are undecided as to the proper rules of preclusion to apply to a prior diversity judgment. See Note, *Erie and the Preclusive Effect of Federal Diversity Judgments*, 85 Colum.L.Rev. 1505 (1985).

6. If a plaintiff properly brings an action in federal court and fails to include certain related state claims that may have been heard under pendent jurisdiction, should that plaintiff be permitted to litigate those claims in a subsequent state action? The Restatement (Second) of Judgments recommends that preclusion result if the federal court would have exercised jurisdiction over the claims. See Restatement (Second), Judgments § 25, comment *e* (1982). Yet even assuming that answer, difficult questions remain. How will a court considering such preclusion determine whether the first court would have exercised pendent jurisdiction?

One commentator has suggested that whether the federal court would have invoked pendent jurisdiction can be determined by looking at (1) whether there was a common nucleus of operative fact between the federal and state claims, thus ensuring that the federal court would have had the power to exercise pendent jurisdiction; and (2) looking at how the prior court disposed of the federal claim. Assuming the existence of a common nucleus of operative fact, the court should determine which one of four possible ways the prior court disposed of the federal claim. When the federal claim is decided after a full trial on the merits, or when it is decided by default judgment, the state claims should be precluded from subsequent litigation. When the federal claim is dismissed for lack of jurisdiction, improper venue, or failure to join an indispensable party, preclusion should not attach. Similarly, when the federal claim is dismissed for failure to state a claim on which relief can be granted, the plaintiff should not be precluded from subsequently filing a state suit asserting the state claims.

4. INTERSYSTEM ADMINISTRATIVE PRECLUSION

The Supreme Court has held that Section 1738 is limited in scope to the judgments of courts, and does not apply to the decisions of administrative agencies. Recall the discussion, pp. 1292–1304, supra, regarding the quality of administrative determinations and the preclusive effect accorded to factual and legal decisions of administrative agencies. More and more, states are moving toward giving preclusive effect *within the state court system* to the decisions of state administrative agencies. But what preclusive effect should a federal court give to the determination of a state administrative agency?

The door to administrative preclusion in federal courts was opened by the Supreme Court in UNITED STATES v. UTAH CONSTRUCTION & MINING CO., 384 U.S. 394, 86 S.Ct. 1545, 16 L.Ed.2d 642 (1966), in which the Court said: "When an administrative agency is acting in a judicial capacity and resolves disputed issues of fact properly before it which the parties have had an adequate opportunity to litigate, the courts have not hesitated to apply *res judicata* * * *." Id. at 422, 86 S.Ct. at 1560, 16 L.Ed.2d at 661. What factors should determine when an agency is acting in a "judicial capacity"? Restatement (Second), Judgments § 83(2) (1982) suggests the following:

> (2) An adjudicative determination by an administrative tribunal is conclusive under the rules of res judicata only insofar as the proceeding resulting in the determination entailed the essential elements of adjudication, including:
>
> (a) Adequate notice to persons who are to be bound by the adjudication * * *;
>
> (b) The right on behalf of a party to present evidence and legal argument in support of the party's contentions and fair opportunity to rebut evidence and argument by opposing parties;
>
> (c) A formulation of issues of law and fact in terms of the application of rules with respect to specified parties concerning a specific transaction, situation, or status, or a specific series thereof;
>
> (d) A rule of finality, specifying a point in the proceeding when presentations are terminated and a final decision is rendered; and
>
> (e) Such other procedural elements as may be necessary to constitute the proceeding a sufficient means of conclusively determining the matter in question, having regard for the magnitude and complexity of the matter in question, the urgency with which

the matter must be resolved, and the opportunity of the parties to obtain evidence and formulate legal contentions.

In UNIVERSITY OF TENNESSEE v. ELLIOTT, 478 U.S. 788, 106 S.Ct. 3220, 92 L.Ed.2d 635 (1986), plaintiff was discharged as an employee of the University. He commenced an action in federal court alleging that his racially motivated discharge violated Title VII of the Civil Rights Act of 1964 and 42 U.S.C. § 1983. While the federal lawsuit was pending, a state administrative law judge found that the discharge was not racially motivated, and the University moved for summary judgment in the federal action on the grounds of issue preclusion. The Sixth Circuit denied preclusion on both the Title VII and the Section 1983 claims. The Supreme Court affirmed the Court of Appeals' ruling that the agency's decision did not preclude the Title VII claim, citing a specific congressional intent that state agency findings *not* preclude later Title VII actions on the same facts. However, reversing in part, the Supreme Court found that the agency's ruling did preclude the Section 1983 claim. The Court reasoned that Congress had not expressed a desire that state-agency decisions not preclude Section 1983 claims; therefore, the general principles of Section 1738 applied. The Court conceded that Section 1738 itself did not require preclusion, because it applies only to court judgments. The Justices felt free, however, to promulgate a common-law rule of preclusion requiring federal courts to give preclusive effect to the decisions of state administrative agencies in circumstances where the courts of the agency's state would give their decisions preclusive effect in a subsequent action.

NOTES AND QUESTIONS

1. Once the Supreme Court found, based on legislative intent, that certain claims could not be precluded by state agency findings of fact (Title VII claims) but that others could be precluded (Section 1983 claims), the federal courts were left to decide which federal statutes fell into each category. In ASTORIA FEDERAL SAVINGS & LOAN ASSOCIATION v. SOLIMINO, 501 U.S. 104, 111 S.Ct. 2166, 115 L.Ed.2d 96 (1991), the Supreme Court provided some guidance as to what level of congressional intent is required to defeat the presumption in favor of administrative preclusion. The Court rejected a test that would have required a "clear statement" by Congress, and held that the presumption would apply unless "administrative preclusion would be inconsistent with Congress' intent in enacting the particular statute." The "clear statement" test would have provided more certainty to lower courts trying to determine when administrative preclusion should apply. Why then did the Court reject the "clear statement" test in favor of a less certain test that requires congressional intent to be discerned by inference?

2. *Elliott* addressed the issue preclusive effect accorded to unreviewed state administrative determinations under federal common law. Does it also require a federal court to give the same *claim* preclusive effect to a state administrative agency as would a court of the rendering state? The court addressed this issue in GJELLUM v. CITY OF BIRMINGHAM, 829 F.2d 1056 (11th Cir.1987). Although *Migra,* Note 1, p. 1345, supra, had held that Section

1983 did not create an exception to state claim preclusion laws under the full faith and credit statute, the court in *Gjellum* saw different interests at stake when the administrative determination was not subject to judicial review:

> With respect to the claim preclusive effect of unreviewed state agency rulings, we conclude that the importance of the federal rights at issue, the desirability of avoiding the forcing of litigants to file suit initially in federal court rather than seek relief in an unreviewed administrative proceeding, and the limitations of state agencies as adjudicators of federal rights override the lessened federalism concerns implicated outside the contours of the full faith and credit statute. In addition, claim preclusion, unlike issue preclusion, does not create a risk of inconsistent results in this context after *Elliott* because claim preclusion seeks to prevent litigation of issues that were not adjudicated before the state agency. We hold therefore that, at least in the context of section 1983 suits, the federal common law of preclusion does not require application of state claim preclusion rules to unreviewed state administrative decisions.

Id. at 1064–65. Assume that a state establishes a Personnel Court to decide employment discrimination disputes. Would the fact that the state has characterized the decision maker as a court be dispositive for purposes of Section 1738, or is that a question controlled by federal law? See McInnes v. California, 943 F.2d 1088 (9th Cir. 1991).

3. Arbitration is a form of alternative dispute resolution that engages a third party to make a decision to which the parties agree by contract to be bound. See p. 1367, infra. Arbitration makes use of adversarial procedures, but often is conducted in a more informal way than adjudication. See generally Resnik, Processes of the Law: Understanding Courts and Their Alternatives 101–02 (2004). Should arbitral determinations be given preclusive effect in a judicial proceeding? E.g., Dujardin v. Liberty Media Corp., 359 F.Supp.2d 337 (S.D.N.Y. 2005). See Carlisle, *Getting a Full Bite of the Apple: When Should the Doctrine of Issue Preclusion Make an Administrative or Arbitral Determination Binding in a Court of Law*, 55 Fordham L. Rev. 63 (1986).

CHAPTER 18

ALTERNATIVE DISPUTE RESOLUTION

■ ■ ■

In this Chapter, we examine nonadversarial approaches to dispute resolution and the ways in which they are reshaping civil litigation. Although nonadjudicative processes have existed for centuries, a movement arose in the 1970s to promote "alternative dispute resolution" in place of or as a complement to litigation. "ADR" has become since then not only a common element of most lawyers' practices but also a mandatory feature of many court systems. The materials explore the critiques of adversarial justice, the variety of ADR procedures, their integration into civil litigation, and the advantages and disadvantages of ADR. The institutionalization of ADR means that it no longer can be understood entirely as a voluntary, private, nonlaw-based approach. What are the implications of ADR's constituting both a parallel "private" system of dispute resolution and an integrated element of the public civil dispute resolution system? Are ADR mechanisms qualitatively different from litigation or merely different points on a spectrum of binding civil dispute resolution? To the extent that ADR programs represent instances of state-sponsored dispute resolution, should they be subject to the constitutional guarantees of due process? What new problems, as well as new possibilities, does ADR present for the fair and efficient resolution of disputes?

SECTION A. THE CRITIQUE OF ADVERSARIAL JUSTICE

KRUSE, LEARNING FROM PRACTICE: WHAT ADR NEEDS FROM A THEORY OF JUSTICE, 5 Nev. L.J. 389, 390–92 (2004–05) (citations omitted):

There are two types of critiques of [the] * * * adversary model of justice. One is that the "justice conditions" that define the ideal are rarely, if ever, met. For the adversary system to work according to its ideal, all sides to a dispute must have equally balanced resources, access to zealous representation, and relevant information. The decision maker must also be free of bias and undue influence. However, because resources are not distributed equally among litigants, because lawyers' loyalty and zeal are distorted by self-interested pursuit of profit, and because decision makers are inescapably tainted by bias, the adversary system rarely, if ever, lives up to its ideal.

This first type of critique is essentially practical in nature. It tests the operation of the system against its ideal, showing that the machinery of the adversary system allows—and even encourages—results that are contrary to its goals. Rather than truth and justice, adversary litigation produces obfuscation and strategic manipulation. Lawyers' professional training encourages narrow framing of their clients' interests into "legal issues" that may or may not capture the clients' true wishes, a process that distorts the clients' goals and stunts the lawyers' ability to solve problems creatively. The duty of zealous advocacy deteriorates into excesses of adversarial zeal such as discovery abuse, forum shopping, the filing of frivolous pleadings and motions, and deceptive practices such as witness coaching and manipulative cross-examination that warp the truth. Moreover, lawyers have self-interested reasons for maintaining adversarial excesses, because these excesses require heavy investments of billable hours. However, the existence of poor lawyer-client communication and sharp practices does not necessarily call for the abolishment of the adversary system; it merely suggests avenues for reforming procedures to make them work according to their intended goals, or changing the structures for regulating the behavior of lawyers, or both.

The second type of critique of the adversary model of justice is deeper and more profound, questioning the theoretical efficacy of the adversary system ideal at its core. Drawing on post-modern critiques of objectivity and neutrality, this type of critique suggests that "the truth" and "the facts" are not singular, knowable commodities that can be delivered at the conclusion of any process. Because different people simply view "the facts" differently, there is not a right answer to the question of "what really happened?" that adversary testing can reveal. Because truths are multiple, "truth-finding" is not a viable goal around which to structure the ideal of adversary justice. Under this view, there is no objectively determinable "right result" of dispute resolution proceedings.

* * *

The preceding Chapters focused on one important mode of dispute resolution: civil litigation. As you have seen, courts are highly structured institutions in which technically trained representatives (lawyers) present arguments on behalf of their clients before a fact-finding body (judge and/or jury). And, of course, a court's decisions are enforced by the state. The formality that is characteristic of courts offers many advantages in terms of public accountability, enforcement of rights, and opportunities for individual participation. But formality also carries a number of disadvantages, which have led some to conclude that court-based solutions are not always the best or even an appropriate approach to dispute resolution.

A primary criticism of litigation is that it takes too long and costs too much. See Priest, *Private Litigants and the Court Congestion Problem*, 69 B.U. L. Rev. 527 (1989). As is well known, it sometimes takes years for a case to work its way through the process. Some commentators attribute delay to a dramatic increase in the number of cases filed in recent years. See Posner, The Federal Courts: Crisis and Reform (1985). Judicial administrators have noted with concern the court system's declining ability to manage the growing caseload with which it is burdened, and have attempted to streamline the litigation process. However, the extent and even the existence of a "litigation crisis" remain controversial. See Galanter, *The Day after the Litigation Explosion*, 46 Md. L. Rev. 3 (1986). Professor Miller has warned "that the supposed litigation crisis is the product of assumption; that reliable empirical data is in short supply; and that data exist that support any proposition." Miller, *The Pretrial Rush to Judgment: Are The "Litigation Explosion," "Liability Crisis," and Efficiency Clichés Eroding Our Day in Court and Jury Trial Commitments?*, 78 N.Y.U. L. Rev. 982, 996 (2003); see also Heise, *Justice Delayed?: An Empirical Analysis of Civil Case Disposition Time*, 50 Case W. Res. L. Rev. 813 (2000).

How much delay might be attributable to the rules of procedure, evidence, and appellate review that govern formal adjudication? These rules, while protecting litigants, might invite strategic behavior by lawyers. The extent of strategic behavior might depend on the type of case and litigant. For certain litigants, delay may produce serious injustice—directly, because justice delayed often is justice denied, and indirectly, because the threat of delay may create an artificial pressure on one of the litigants to settle on less than fair terms. In addition, because delay might increase the cost of litigation, some individuals with meritorious claims may perceive them as too small to pursue or may find themselves "out litigated" by an opponent with greater resources and experience.

Commentators also have offered more fundamental criticisms of the desirability of adversarial adjudication as a way to resolve disputes. One criticism is that court-centered dispute resolution removes the parties from direct control of the decision making process and the crafting of solutions, and instead substitutes lawyers and judges who have legal expertise and professional skill. Moreover, instead of providing for maximal disclosure of relevant facts, the litigation process may create incentives for adversaries to hide those facts. Finally, litigation in some settings may tend to polarize the parties, decreasing opportunities for future cooperation and straining the social fabric. This is particularly problematic when disputants have an ongoing relationship, as in the case o neighbors or family members and even in commercial settings. All of thes factors may combine in some situations to obstruct disputants from reaching optimal outcomes.

Another fundamental criticism of adversarial justice is that its law-based focus, which aims at the enforcement of rights and entitlements, may not adequately consider or sufficiently protect the interests that motivate an individual to press a dispute. Professor Menkel–Meadow explains:

> * * * The "culture of adversarialism" and the rules that enforce this culture often (not always) distort how we think about legal and human problem solving by assuming there are only two sides to an issue or question, that "truth" about either what happened factually or what is correct legally can best be resolved by vigorous contestations between two fully armed advocates and decided by a third-party judge who is separate from the parties and appointed by the state. * * * Often, what is most important to parties may be excluded from consideration, as irrelevant or inadmissible, according to our well-worn legal principles, which may protect other important interests (like privileges, trade secrets, bias and prejudice, or constitutional rights).

Menkel–Meadow, *The Lawyer as Problem Solver and Third–Party Neutral: Creativity and Non–Partisanship in Lawyering*, 72 Temple L. Rev. 785, 788–89 (1999) (citations omitted).

NOTES AND QUESTIONS

1. The critique of adversarial justice suggests that certain kinds of disputes ought not to be litigated and instead are better resolved through an alternative process. What factors would you consider in making this assessment? Might these factors include: The likelihood of convincing a jury that the claim is worthy? The availability of a remedy? The litigant's psychic gains from participating in a public proceeding? Costs to reputation? Disruption to family life? See Sternlight, *Separate and Not Equal: Integrating Civil Procedure and ADR in Legal Academia*, 80 Notre Dame L. Rev. 681, 703–04 (2005).

2. Why might disputants choose one mode of dispute resolution rather han another? A classic study of adversarial and inquisitorial process found hat participants consistently favored adjudicative procedure because of its erceived fairness and its related capacity to generate participant satisfaction nd trust. See Thibaut & Walker, Procedural Justice (1975). However, many uestions remain unanswered, and empirical study of the issue has been mited. See Hensler, *Suppose It's Not True: Challenging Mediation Ideology*,)02 J. Disp. Resol. 81. A recent psychological experiment found that partici-ınts favor dispute resolution processes that offer "control": "(a) control over e decision such that a neutral third party would help disputants arrive at eir own resolution; (b) a process that granted disputants control over the esentation of evidence (rather than using a representative to do so); and (c) ther a set of rules that both disputants would have agreed to in advance of t resolution process, or the well-established rules used in a court of law."

The study was limited, however, to "relatively simple civil law issues that may not generalize to high-stake civil disputes or to criminal cases." Shestowsky, *Procedural Preferences in Alternative Dispute Resolution: A Closer, Modern Look at an Old Idea*, 10 Psych., Pub. Pol'y, & L. 211 (2004). What other information would be relevant to designing policy in this area?

3. How might the financial stakes of a dispute affect the parties' preference for different forms of procedure? In the aftermath of the attack on the World Trade Center on September 11, 2001, Congress created a Victim Compensation Fund to ensure the payment of damages to individuals who suffered loss. Compensation was conditioned on the claimant's waiver of any right to bring any claim against anyone for damages associated with the attack. For a description of the establishment of the VCF, see Berkowitz, *The Problematic Role of the Special Master: Undermining the Legitimacy of the September 11th Compensation Fund*, 24 Yale L. & Pol'y Rev. 1, 5–7 (2006). The VCF paid out more than $7.048 billion for about 5,500 claims, and only ninety-five lawsuits were filed on behalf of ninety-six claimants. See In re September 11 Litigation, 600 F.Supp.2d 549, 552 (S.D.N.Y. 2009). These lawsuits were judicially managed to secure a mediated, coordinated settlement, and the aggregate amount that was approved by the District Court totaled $500 million. All but three lawsuits settled. See Report of the Mediator on the Mediation and the Settlement Efforts of the Parties in the Cases Previously Docketed Under 21 MC 97, in id. at *6. The District Court noted the different reasons for the claimants' decision to litigate rather than accept a cash payment from the VCF:

> Some, the successors of victims with very high incomes or income potential, believed that the Fund would not compensate them adequately in relation to lost income, and filed suits instead. Others filed suits to avoid having to deduct their life insurance recoveries and other collateral source payments * * *. Still others wanted to tell their stories, participate in forcing facts into the public domain, or avail themselves of traditional remedies for other reasons. And some could not free themselves from the shadows and despair of the September 11 tragedy to do anything on a timely basis, even though the Special Master [of the VCF] made special efforts to reach such people and relaxed the Fund's requirements to accommodate such claimants.

Id. A study of why victims chose not to participate in the VCF and instead file lawsuits found that respondents framed their decision in the public language of community and citizenship, rather than in the private language of monetary compensation. Those who sued stated that they were motivated to find out why the attack had taken place and which groups ought to be held accountable. Indeed, some respondents stated that they would have pursued a declaratory judgment action, without any money damages, if the legal proceeding could generate public information, encourage government accountability, and trigger necessary change. See Hadfield, *Framing the Choice Between Cash and the Courthouse: Experiences with the 9/11 Victim Compensation Fund*, 42 L. & Soc'y Rev. 645 (2008).

4. One criticism of a formal, rights-based approach to dispute resolution is that it benefits some groups more than others. See Nader, *Controlling*

Processes in the Practice of Law: Hierarchy and Pacification in the Movement to Re–Form Dispute Ideology, 9 Ohio St. J. on Disp. Resol. 1 (1993). What information is needed to assess the merits of this critique? Might ADR, with its emphasis on informal, "normless" decision making, subvert democratic values? See Edwards, *Alternative Dispute Resolution: Panacea or Anathema?*, 99 Harv. L. Rev. 668, 671 (1986). See generally Kovach, *Privatization of Dispute Resolution: In the Spirit of Pound, But Mission Incomplete: Lessons Learned and a Possible Blueprint for the Future*, 48 S. Tex. L. Rev. 1003 (2007).

SECTION B. ALTERNATIVE DISPUTE RESOLUTION PROCESSES

RESNIK, FAILING FAITH: ADJUDICATORY PROCEDURE IN DECLINE, 53 U. Chi. L. Rev. 494, 536–37 (1986) (citations omitted).

The motivations for advocating ADR to judges are as diverse as its champions. * * * For those who offer themselves for hire to perform ADR, there are obvious economic incentives. Others seek shelter in ADR as a means of resolving their disputes safe from public scrutiny. * * * Others simply argue that adjudication is too cumbersome, that it costs too much, that it requires too much counter-productive behavior, and that "mini," "summary," or abbreviated proceedings are better. Yet others have serious quality claims to make affirmatively on behalf of ADR. * * * Some ADR mechanisms are predicated upon the assumption that litigants, and not their lawyers, are the key actors to be engaged in dispute resolution. In contrast to the Federal Rules, which tacitly posit the lawyer as central, some of the ADR procedures are designed to foster direct participation by litigants. In this respect, some ADR mechanisms do not reject the adversarial mode but only question the faith in the lawyer-client unit. Yet other ADR procedures confront the assumptions of the desirability of adversarial approaches and seek to develop a range of more cooperative responses beyond those typically employed in and by courts. * * * Underlying all these diverse views is a shared aversion to adjudication. * * *

* * *

ADR is not a single system but rather a multiplicity of approaches to the problem of how best to resolve disputes. Professor Resnik refers to ADR as "an umbrella term that encompasses a range of processes * * * and of places." See generally Resnik, Processes of the Law: Understanding Courts and Their Alternatives 97 (2004). Others refer to ADR as a continuum or spectrum of processes. E.g., Dessem, Pretrial–Litigation: Law, Policy, and Practice 569 (1991). Most would agree, however, that "there is no comprehensive or widely-accepted system for identifying, describing, or classifying" the different ADR mechanisms. Riskin, *Understanding Mediators' Orientation, Strategies and Techniques: A Grid for* *the Perplexed*, 1 Harv. Negot. L. Rev. 7, 8 (1996). By drawing a contrast between ADR and adjudication, commentators seek to emphasize ADR's "informality, its focus on interpersonal relationships, its low cost or speed, or its ability to foster personal growth and awareness * * *." Sternlight, *Is Binding Arbitration a Form of ADR?: An Argument That the Term "ADR" Has Begun To Outlive Its Usefulness*, 2000 J. Disp. Resol. 97, 99. As you read these materials, consider whether in practice all ADR mechanisms share these qualities.

Some commentators have come to favor the term "appropriate," rather than "alternative," dispute resolution, pointing to "an intertwining" between litigation and other decision making devices. Sternlight, *ADR Is Here: Preliminary Reflections on Where It Fits in a System of Justice*, 3 Nev. L.J. 289, 295 (2002–03). What are the questions a policy maker might need to consider in designing a fair and efficient dispute-resolution system? Some of these questions include:

- **Who resolves the dispute?** Possibilities include: a judge, an officer of the state with professional education in the law; a lawyer with similar professional training; an expert in the field in which the dispute arose with no legal training; a representative of the community; the disputants with the help of a neutral third party; the disputants themselves.
- **What is the source of the standard for resolution?** Possibilities include: rules established by legislatures and courts ("law"); the prior practice of those similarly situated; community values; standards developed by the disputants themselves.
- **Who speaks for the disputants?** Possibilities include: lawyers; persons without professional legal training (including friends, relatives, or neighbors); the disputants themselves.
- **What is the nature and extent of fact-finding and standard-finding?** Possibilities include: no fact finding or standard-finding; monopolization of these tasks by a third-party; the sharing of these tasks by a third-party and the disputants and their representatives; responsibility in the disputants and their representatives alone.
- **Who decides the dispute?** Possibilities include: a third-party privately chosen by the disputants; a third-party mandated by the state; the parties themselves.
- **What is the binding effect of any resolution?** Possibilities include: binding on the parties through coercive sanctions; binding on the parties in an advisory or precatory sense; binding on nonparties; binding on the parties in ways that they decide themselves.

By combining answers to these and other questions in various ways, ADR offers a menu of procedural options that can supplement or supplant litigation. The following description of different ADR processes is designed to introduce you to the basic themes and concepts. However, keep in mind that ADR is in a state of transition, with processes evolving in response to institutional and other pressures.

1. NEGOTIATION

Negotiation is perhaps the most familiar form of dispute resolution. See generally Fischer & Ury, Getting to Yes (1981). In a negotiated settlement, the disputants themselves resolve the conflict under whatever standards they choose. An influential commentary, however, emphasizes the strategic role that legal rules play in negotiation strategy. See Mnookin & Kornhauser, *Bargaining in the Shadow of the Law: The Case of Divorce*, 88 Yale L. J. 950 (1979); Jacob, *The Elusive Shadow of the Law*, 26 L. & Soc'y Rev. 565 (1992). In addition, studies indicate that standards of fairness are important to the success and acceptance of negotiated solutions. See Hollander–Blumoff & Tyler, *Procedural Justice in Negotiation: Procedural Fairness, Outcome Acceptance, and Integrative Potential*, 33 L. & Soc. Inq'y 473 (2008).

Although in the early stages the disputants may represent themselves, once lawyers become involved they tend to handle the negotiations as well. There is no need for fact-finding or standard-finding as such, since the only facts and standards that matter are those that the disputants choose to recognize. One commentator distinguishes between negotiation and adjudication as follows:

> In contrast [to adjudication], the universe and operation of norms in dispute-negotiation is typically open-ended. Thus it is characteristic of dispute-negotiation that when norms collide account is taken of both, although the eventual settlement may reflect an adjustment for relative applicability and weight. Similarly, the parties in dispute-negotiation may accord partial or even full recognition to a norm that is generally deemed subordinate or even legally invalid, so that a negligent plaintiff who has no "right" to prevail in a tort action because of the doctrine of contributory negligence may nevertheless make a favorable settlement by reason of the legally invalid but socially real principle of comparative negligence. Finally, parties to dispute-negotiation can and frequently do take person-oriented norms into account as freely as act-oriented norms.

Eisenberg, *Private Ordering through Negotiation: Dispute–Settlement and Rulemaking*, 89 Harv.L.Rev. 637, 644–45 (1976). Commentary also distinguishes between problem-solving and adversarial negotiation. See Hurder, *The Lawyers Dilemma: To Be or Not To Be a Problem–Solving Negotiator*, 14 Clinical L. Rev. 253 (2007). What do you think are the important differences between these two negotiation approaches?

2. MEDIATION

Mediation is a process in which a neutral third party, who is often but not always a human-relations professional, assists the disputants in reaching a negotiated settlement of their differences. The mediator is not empowered to render a decision. Thus the decision makers are the disputants themselves. Since mediation ultimately seeks agreement between the disputants, a mediator, at least in theory, does not evaluate the strengths and weaknesses of each side's evidence and arguments. Instead, she seeks common ground between the disputants concerning facts and standards. One commentator explains: "[M]ediation goes beyond * * * 'lawyers only' bargaining sessions and brings in a third party with no personal interest in the outcome of the case to serve as a 'neutral'—literally, a go-between for the parties." Tarpley, *ADR, Jurisprudence, and Myth*, 17 Ohio St. J. on Disp. Resol. 113, 116 (2001). See also Daiker, *No J.D. Required: The Critical Role and Contributions of Non–Lawyer Mediators,* 24 Rev. Litig. 499 (2005). There are, however, different forms of mediation, and mediators have differing conceptions of their proper role. Some mediators are simply communication facilitators. Others are more active, suggesting possible grounds for settlement and attempting to persuade the disputants to do so. Mediators of the former type are more likely to conduct all sessions with both disputants present; mediators of the latter type are more likely to conduct both joint sessions and private sessions with each disputant.

Parties in mediation do not have a discovery mechanism to force the opposing side to reveal information (such as financial or mental health information) that may be critical to a full and fair evaluation of the dispute. Although the source of the standard for resolution is the disputants, when a mediator attempts persuasion, other values, such as those of the mediator or the community, also come into play. Disputants often but not always represent themselves; some mediators actively discourage the presence of lawyers and witnesses. Mediation is considered to be most appropriate when the disputants have equal bargaining power. This ordinarily occurs when the conflict is between individuals, rather than a conflict between an individual and a private institution or government. If successful, mediation results in a signed agreement that defines the parties' future behavior. This agreement may be an enforceable contract. Mediation often is used when the disputants have a continuing relationship that is important to preserve. Rather than attempting to assess blame for past conduct, mediation focuses the disputants' attention on the future and the desirability of maintaining an amicable relationship. In its early years, mediation often was seen as appropriate to resolve disputes between neighbors or family members, and mediation programs were established for domestic-relations cases. These programs have evolved from a voluntary court-connected process to one that sometimes is judicially mandated. Mediation is also used for corporate and commercial disputes. See Brazil, *Hosting Mediations as a Representative of the System of Civil Justice*, 22 Ohio St. J. on Disp. Resol. 227 (2007).

3. NEUTRAL FACTFINDING AND OMBUDSPERSONS

Neutral fact-finding is a generic term for the use of a third party to gather information relevant to the settlement of a dispute. One of the most common institutional instances of a neutral fact finder is the ombudsperson. An ombudsperson is a third party who receives and investigates complaints aimed at an institution by its constituents, clients, or employees. She may take actions such as bringing an apparent injustice to the attention of high-level officials, advising the complainant of available options and resources, proposing a settlement of the dispute, or proposing systemic changes in the institution. A neutral fact finder often is employed by the institution against which the complaint is made. In government, an ombudsperson can serve the important function of steering a complaint through a tangled bureaucracy.

Ombudspersons are most likely to be hired in closely regulated institutions, those in which customer satisfaction is critical, and in institutions concerned with resolving disputes internally. Universities frequently use ombudspersons to enforce a set of university rules that may be different from those applicable to people generally. Some independent ombudspersons are employed by local media and use publicity as their major tool. The disputants are responsible for resolving the dispute, although the ombudsperson can pressure them to settle. The source of the standard for resolution is either internal policy or commonly shared values. The ombudsperson acts as representative of the complainant, investigating and presenting the facts for her as well as reminding the high-level officials of the policies they have set or the community's shared values.

4. EARLY NEUTRAL EVALUATION

It has been observed that parties often do not settle at an early stage in the litigation process because they fail to evaluate the case adequately until the trial process requires them to do so. Early neutral evaluation is a mechanism designed to respond to this problem. ENE involves the factual and legal presentation of a dispute to a neutral selected by the parties or a court. On the basis of this presentation the neutral, often an experienced lawyer, arbitrator, or former judge, provides the parties with an open assessment of their respective positions. This can have the effect of encouraging settlement, but at the very least it should help to focus the issues for the litigation process and assist in its efficient management.

5. MINI-TRIALS

Similar to early neutral evaluation, but procedurally more complex, the mini-trial is a privately developed method of helping to bring about a negotiated settlement in lieu of protracted corporate litigation. The procedural contours of mini-trials are tailored individually in accordance with the desires of the disputants. A typical mini-trial is a confidential process that entails a period of limited discovery after which attorneys for each side present an abbreviated version of the case before a panel consisting of managers with authority to settle and a neutral advisor. The neutral advisor is often a retired judge or respected lawyer. The managers then enter settlement negotiations.

Thus the parties resolve the dispute aided by the assessment of the neutral advisor as to the likely outcome should the matter go to court. The advisor's impartial appraisal of the conflict encourages the parties to adopt more realistic goals in negotiating a settlement. The source of the resolution standard is the disputants, despite the presence of the neutral legal advisor. Both sides are represented by lawyers, but the key to the process is that the managers see the other side's best case directly, in addition to the filtered version provided by their own lawyer. Facts and standards are researched and presented by the disputants' lawyers, although in an abbreviated way. Mini-trials have been used successfully in disputes that were bogged down in discovery and motion practice by reconverting what had become a lawyer's problem back into a business problem. See *Recent Developments in Alternative Forms of Dispute Resolution,* 100 F.R.D. 512 (1984).

6. SUMMARY JURY TRIAL

A summary jury trial is similar in some respects to a mini-trial, but is used for cases ready to be tried before a jury. Instead of presenting a formal case before a full jury panel, the lawyers for the parties present an abbreviated case before a panel of six jurors. The presentations usually last less than a week and the resulting "verdict"—although not binding on the parties—provides a basis for settlement. The summary jury trial has proven to be helpful when each party has a very different view regarding the likely outcome of the case, and prior settlement attempts have been unsuccessful. See Posner, *The Summary Jury Trial and Other Alternative Methods of Alternative Dispute Resolution: Some Cautionary Observations,* 53 U.Chi.L.Rev. 366 (1986).

7. ARBITRATION

Arbitration is the method of alternative dispute resolution with which the American legal system has had the longest experience. The parties select an arbitrator or arbitrators, who conduct hearings and then reach a decision. The arbitration hearing is an adversary proceeding, in which each of the parties presents its case, with full opportunity for cross-examination and rebuttal. Lawyers often represent the disputants, and are responsible for gathering and presenting evidence and arguments. Frequently, the decision of the arbitrator, called an "award," is then entered in court, much as a judgment in a formally adjudicated case is entered. In each case, both parties are bound to abide by the award, even though in certain limited circumstances, either or both parties may seek to challenge, modify, or even vacate the award.

As a general matter, arbitration is contractual: either the parties must have agreed in writing, before the dispute in question arose, to submit disagreements to arbitration, or they must have entered into an agreement to submit an existing dispute to arbitration. Arbitration developed first in the commercial context and, in the latter half of the nineteenth century, in the labor-management field, achieving widespread acceptance after World War II. Binding arbitration then extended to areas in which the parties shared roughly equal bargaining power, such as securities broker agreements and construction contracts. More recently, arbitration has become a tool for resolving a broad range of disputes, and binding arbitration clauses are inserted frequently into employment, hospital, and consumer contracts. Federal and state statutes play a significant role in shaping the context in which arbitration occurs. The Federal Arbitration Act, 9 U.S.C. §§ 1 et seq., and Article 75 of New York's Civil Practice Law and Rules are the most notable statutes of this type, and both have served as models for other states' arbitration statutes.

Although arbitration is a form of adversary adjudication, its procedural structure depends largely on the pre-dispositions of the arbitrator or arbitrators conducting a given hearing. The arbitrator is relatively free to shape the hearing as he sees fit. The arbitrator has three broad areas of responsibility: (1) the pre-hearing phase; (2) the hearing; and (3) the award and the opinion (if an opinion is thought necessary). Patterns of practice tend to become associated with particular types of arbitration. For example, commercial arbitrators receive written briefs frequently. By contrast, labor arbitrators tend to discourage them. Pre-hearing discovery is often limited to what the parties voluntarily disclose. However, arbitrators are empowered at the request of either party to subpoena documents and persons for the hearing, and counsel generally can agree on a procedure to review the subpoenaed documents in advance of the hearing. Further, arbitration in the securities industry offers formalized discovery proceedings in the pre-hearing phase that permit the parties themselves to serve written requests for information or documents on other parties to the arbitration. The arbitrator is the sole judge of the relevance and materiality of evidence offered and need not conform to the legal rules of evidence. However, some arbitrators believe that at least some compliance with traditional rules of evidence is both necessary and beneficial. Because the arbitrator has such broad discretion to choose to admit or exclude evidence or to hear or refuse to hear witnesses, his or her power to find facts and decide questions of law virtually is unlimited. The final phase of arbitration produces the award. The arbitrator's award of a dispute need not contain anything more than a statement of the rights and obligations of the parties to that dispute. However, the parties may request a written statement of decision.

In addition to standard arbitration, there are several other forms, including final-offer and one-way arbitration. Final-offer arbitration is much like standard arbitration but is used typically to set the terms of contracts (such as the salaries of major league baseball players and some public employees) rather than to interpret and apply contractual provisions. Each party proposes a final offer of settlement, and the neutral must choose between the two. This process encourages parties to be reasonable in the positions they advocate and is designed to encourage serious negotiation in contexts in which it is important that the disputants' dealings not be interrupted. Fact-finding can be more limited because the arbitrator need only choose between two positions rather than find and justify one particular result out of many that are possible. In one-way arbitration only one party agrees to be bound.

Court-annexed arbitration builds upon the standard model of arbitration described above except that the parties have not previously agreed to arbitrate their dispute. Instead, certain disputes, usually those in which the amount in controversy is less than a certain dollar figure, must be referred to an arbitrator before the court will hear them. The arbitrator thus is less likely to have expertise in the subject area in which the conflict arose. Moreover, since the source of the standard for resolution is the law, the arbitrator typically will be a lawyer. The nature and extent of fact-finding and standard-finding are not substantially different from adjudication, although discovery may be limited and the rules of evidence may be relaxed. If a disputant is dissatisfied with the arbitrator's decision, he can demand a trial *de novo*, but if the disputant fails to obtain a better result at trial, he may be required to pay the costs of the opposing party.

8. PRIVATE JUDGING

Disputants who can afford it may utilize private judging in order to avoid the delays of the court system. The disputants agree, after the dispute has arisen and been filed in court, to hire a private judge. Often a private judge has retired from the public court system. The court then refers the case to that judge.

The source of the standard for resolution is the law and the proceedings are conducted in much the same manner as a bench trial, although in an expedited and simplified manner. Unlike an arbitrator's award, the decision can be appealed as if the court referring it to the private judge had made the decision itself. Thus the disputants can ensure that the resolution will be in accordance with the law, while bypassing the backlog in the trial courts.

NOTE AND QUESTIONS

Each form of dispute resolution has its own strengths and weaknesses. Mediation may provide an excellent forum for dealing with disputes involving an ongoing relationship, but may prove useless in a setting characterized by acute antagonism. Arbitration is designed as a quick and inexpensive method of resolving simple disputes, but may be inappropriate in complex multi-party disputes or when the disputants lack parity of bargaining power. Litigation is well-equipped to deal with complex issues requiring public adjudication, but demands sophisticated knowledge and legal expertise. What principles should guide selecting the best process for resolving a particular dispute?

SECTION C. ADR AND CIVIL LITIGATION

Read Federal Rules of Civil Procedure 16, 54(a), 54(d), and 68 and 28 U.S.C. § 1920 in the Supplement.

At the start of the ADR movement, commentators suggested establishing a Dispute Resolution Center that would match disputes to the decision making mechanism "best suited for the resolution of the particular controversy":

> Take, for example, a case involving a minor assault by one neighbor against another growing out of increasing anger over a trespassing dog. Presently such a dispute would probably wind up in criminal court because that is the tag society has placed on this type of conflict. But since the parties really want help in resolving this interpersonal problem, not a determination of whether A struck B, the case might well be sent to mediation, at least in the first instance. Similar treatment might be accorded to a landlord-tenant dispute over the adequacy of the services provided by the landlord. But if the landlord sought to raise questions about the constitutionality of the rent-control law, then obviously that case would have to be sent to the regular court. * * *
>
> The notion thus is that a sophisticated intake officer would analyze the dispute and refer it to that process, or sequence of processes, most likely to resolve it effectively. The potential benefits of such a multi-faceted mechanism are increased efficiency, possible time and cost savings, and the legitimization of various alternative dispute-resolution processes, thus decreasing citizens' frustration in attempting to locate the most appropriate mechanism. An additional benefit is that it would help us to gain a better understanding of the peculiar advantages and disadvantages of particular dispute-resolution processes for specific types of disputes. Perhaps the intake official could also refer disputants' associated nonlegal problems to appropriate social service agencies.

Sander, Varieties of Dispute Processing, in The Pound Conference: Perspectives on Justice in the Future 65 (Levin & Wheeler eds. 1979); see also

Sander, *The Multidoor Courthouse,* National Forum, Vol. LXIII, No. 4, Fall 1983.

Within twenty years of the "multidoor" suggestion, ADR had become an accepted method of dispute resolution the use of which was encouraged and even required. See Resnik, *Many Doors? Closing Doors? Alternative Dispute Resolution and Adjudication*, 10 Ohio St. J. on Disp. Resol. 211 (1995). Both Congress and the Supreme Court supported this trend.

Faced with concerns about caseload pressure, Congress enacted the Civil Justice Reform Act of 1990, requiring federal courts to consider ADR mechanisms as a way to reduce litigation expense and delay. 28 U.S.C. §§ 471 *et seq.* In 1998, this "invitation" was upgraded to a requirement under the Alternative Dispute Resolution Act, 28 U.S.C. § 651, that federal courts implement ADR programs and mandate participation. In parallel developments, state courts incorporated ADR into their judicial systems. See, e.g., Dana, Jr., *Court–Connected Alternative Dispute Resolution in Maine*, 57 Me. L. Rev. 349 (2005). For a comprehensive assessment of court-annexed ADR, see Shestowsky, *Disputants' Preferences for Court–Connected Dispute Resolution Procedures: Why We Should Care and Why We Know So Little*, 23 Ohio St. J. on Disp. Resol. 549 (2008).

Administrative agencies also established large-scale ADR programs, a development required by Congress through the enactment of the Administrative Dispute Resolution Act, 5 U.S.C. §§ 571–83. See Marcus & Senger, *ADR and the Federal Government: Not Such Strange Bedfellows After All*, 66 Mo. L. Rev. 709 (2001). The private sector's use of ADR also increased dramatically, with corporations and professional associations institutionalizing mediation and arbitration procedures for the resolution of both internal and external disputes. See *Developments—The Paths of Civil Litigation*, 113 Harv. L. Rev. 1851 (2000).

Some have suggested that the "mainstreaming" of ADR, particularly in the context of court-annexed mediation, has subverted ADR's fundamental vision of flexibility, participation, and cooperative resolution. See Menkel–Meadow, *Pursuing Settlement in an Adversary Culture: A Tale of Innovation Co-opted or "The Law of ADR,"* 19 Fla.St.U. L. Rev. 1 (1990). It is argued that ADR has become mass-produced and that it models itself too closely on procedural rules and evidentiary devices usually employed in litigation. These include notice requirements, "information exchanges" (discovery), party submissions to neutrals (briefs, motions), induced attendance of persons and production of things (subpoenas), consolidation, interim relief, and a number of others. See Welsh, *The Thinning Vision of Self–Determination in Court–Connected Mediation: The Inevitable Price of Institutionalization?*, 6 Harv. Negot. L. Rev. 1, 5 (2001); Sabatino, *ADR as "Litigation Lite": Procedural and Evidentiary Norms Embedded Within Alternative Dispute Resolution*, 47 Emory L.J. 1289 (1998). Commentators express concerns that although ADR has become more expensive and complex, it nevertheless fails to provide participants with adequate procedural protection. See generally Reuben, *Public Justice: Toward a State Action Theory of Alternative Dispute Resolution*, 85 Calif. L. Rev. 579 (1997).

Other commentators criticize court-annexed ADR programs as being no more than settlement conferences that push disputants to a quick disposition rather than a consensual working out of grievances. See Brown, *A Community of Court ADR Programs: How Court–Based ADR Programs Help Each Other Survive and Thrive*, 26 Just. Sys. J. 327, 330 (2005). In addition, commentators question whether ADR should ever be mandatory. For example, some states now mandate mediation for domestic disputes, and require mediation before permitting the filing of an action for divorce. Does mandating mediation in this setting violate due process? See King, *Burdening Access to Justice: The Cost of Divorce Mediation on the Cheap*, 73 St. John's L. Rev. 375 (1999).

Questions also are raised as to whether the private sector's increasing trend toward including mandatory ADR clauses in employment and consumer contracts promotes the values that ADR is intended to serve, namely, party control, informality, preservation of relationships, and nonadversarial justice. See Sternlight, *Rethinking the Constitutionality of the Supreme Court's Preference for Binding Arbitration: A Fresh Assessment of Jury Trial, Separation of Powers, and Due Process Concerns*, 72 Tul. L. Rev. 1 (1997). Critics warn that ADR is producing long-term deleterious effects on democratic life, that it is encouraging the elimination of jury trials, and that it is impeding the ability of courts to generate precedent. Is there an inevitable conflict between mandatory ADR and the day-in-court ideal on which American justice is based? See Reuben, *Democracy and Dispute Resolution: The Problem of Arbitration*, 67 Law & Contemp. Probs. 279, 310 (Spring 2004).

---

1. CHANGING ATTITUDES TOWARD ADR: THE EXAMPLE OF BINDING ARBITRATION

Initially, the judicial system viewed arbitration with distrust. For example, in Wilko v. Swan, 346 U.S. 427, 74 S.Ct. 182, 98 L.Ed. 168 (1953), the Supreme Court ruled that claims arising under Section 12(2) of the Securities Act of 1933 were not subject to compulsory arbitration. In recent years, however, the legal system has experienced a dramatic shift from a distrust of and reluctance to enforce arbitration agreements, to a strong presumption in favor of arbitration as a sound, acceptable method of resolving disputes without litigation. See Resnik, *Procedure as Contract*, 80 Notre Dame L. Rev. 593, 620–21 (2005).

One step in this shift was SOUTHLAND CORP. v. KEATING, 465 U.S. 1, 104 S.Ct. 852, 79 L.Ed.2d 1 (1984). In *Southland,* the appellant, the owner and franchisor of 7–Eleven convenience stores, entered into franchise agreements with over 800 franchisees located in California.

Between September 1975 and May 1977, a class of these franchisees as well as several individual appellees sued appellant for breach of contract, fraud, misrepresentation, breach of fiduciary duty, and violations of the California Franchise Investment Law. The California courts consolidated the various actions. Pursuant to the terms of the franchise agreements, appellant sought arbitration of all the claims. However, the California Supreme Court held that appellees' claims under the Franchise Investment Law were not arbitrable under the arbitration clauses. The Court interpreted the California Investment Law to require judicial consideration of claims brought under the statute and concluded that the California statute did not contravene Section 2 of the Federal Arbitration Act, which provides that an arbitration provision relating to a transaction involving commerce "shall be valid, irrevocable, and enforceable, save upon such grounds as exist at law or in equity for the revocation of any contract."

The Supreme Court reversed, holding that "in enacting Section 2 of the federal Act, Congress declared a national policy favoring arbitration and withdrew the power of the states to require a judicial forum for the resolution of claims which the contracting parties agreed to resolve by arbitration. * * * Congress has thus mandated the enforcement of arbitration agreements." The Court rejected the argument advanced in dissent by Justices O'Connor and Rehnquist that Congress intended the Act to be a procedural restraint only on federal courts; writing for the Court, Chief Justice Burger maintained that the possibility of forum-shopping by litigants militated in favor of reading the statute as a source of substantive law binding both federal and state courts.

In SHEARSON/AMERICAN EXPRESS, INC. v. McMAHON, 482 U.S. 220, 107 S.Ct. 2332, 96 L.Ed.2d 185 (1987), the Court upheld compulsory arbitration under the Federal Arbitration Act of claims alleging violation of Section 10(b) of the Securities Exchange Act of 1934 and the Racketeer Influenced and Corrupt Organizations Act (RICO). The arbitration clause appeared in predispute brokerage customer agreements. Although a section of the Securities Exchange Act provided that "[t]he district courts of the United States * * * shall have exclusive jurisdiction" over violations of the Act, and another section declared void any agreement "to waive compliance with any provision" of the Act, the Court interpreted these provisions to prohibit only a waiver of compliance with the substantive provisions of the Act. Noting that the arbitration procedures of the various stock exchanges had been specifically approved by the Securities and Exchange Commission, the Court reasoned that arbitration tribunals are "fully capable of handling" claims of Securities Exchange Act violations. Id. at 232–34, 107 S.Ct. at 2341, 96 L.Ed.2d at 198–99. Similarly, the Court rejected the arguments that RICO claims are "too complex to be subject to arbitration," that "the 'overlap' between RICO's civil and criminal provisions" precluded arbitration even of civil RICO claims, and that "the public interest in the enforcement of RICO precludes its submission to arbitration." Id. at 239–40, 107 S.Ct. at 2344, 96 L.Ed.2d at 202.

Two years later, in RODRIGUEZ de QUIJAS v. SHEARSON/AMERICAN EXPRESS, 490 U.S. 477, 109 S.Ct. 1917, 104 L.Ed.2d 526 (1989), the Court held that a predispute agreement to arbitrate claims arising under the Securities Act of 1933 was enforceable. Going one step beyond its decision in the *McMahon* case, the Court concluded "that *Wilko* was incorrectly decided and is inconsistent with the prevailing uniform construction of other federal statutes governing arbitration agreements in the setting of business transactions." Id. at 484, 109 S.Ct. at 1921, 104 L.Ed.2d at 536. In both *McMahon* and *Rodriguez,* Justices Stevens, Brennan, Marshall, and Blackmun dissented, asserting that the policy arguments presented were not sufficient to "overturn an interpretation of an Act of Congress that has been settled for many years." Id. at 487, 109 S.Ct. at 1923, 104 L.Ed.2d at 539.

In GILMER v. INTERSTATE/JOHNSON LANE CORP., 500 U.S. 20, 111 S.Ct. 1647, 114 L.Ed.2d 26 (1991), the Court held that claims arising under the Age Discrimination in Employment Act (ADEA) are subject to compulsory arbitration. The Court explained that the purpose of the Federal Arbitration Act "was to reverse the longstanding judicial hostility to arbitration agreements that had existed at English common law and had been adopted by American courts, and to place arbitration agreements upon the same footing as other contracts." Id. at 24, 111 S.Ct. at 1651, 114 L.Ed.2d at 36. It went on to reject the arguments that arbitration would fail to address the "important social policies" embodied in ADEA and would "undermine the role of the * * * [Equal Employment Opportunity Commission] in enforcing the ADEA." After dismissing a number of arguments directed against the fairness of arbitration proceedings, the Court found that the arbitration agreement in *Gilmer* did not result from "unequal bargaining power between employers and employees." It reasoned that there was no indication "that Gilmer, an experienced businessman, was coerced or defrauded into agreeing to the arbitration clause." Id. at 29–30, 111 S.Ct. at 1656, 114 L.Ed.2d at 41–42.

Justices Stevens and Marshall dissented. They pointed to a provision contained in Section 1 of the Federal Arbitration Act: "Nothing herein contained shall apply to contracts of employment of * * * any * * * class of workers engaged in foreign or interstate commerce." This exclusion, they argued, "should be interpreted to cover any agreements by the employee to arbitrate disputes with the employer arising out of the employment relationship" even where—as was the situation in *Gilmer*—the arbitration agreement was not a part of the contract of employment. Id. at 32, 111 S.Ct. at 1659, 114 L.Ed.2d at 46. The dissenters also contended that compulsory arbitration "conflicts with the statutory purpose animating the ADEA." Id. at 33, 111 S.Ct. at 1660, 114 L.Ed.2d at 47.

In ALLIED–BRUCE TERMINIX COS. v. DOBSON, 513 U.S. 265, 115 S.Ct. 834, 130 L.Ed.2d 753 (1995), the Court held that a predispute agreement to arbitrate trumped a state statute invalidating such agreements. The Court explained that the Federal Arbitration Act's grant of enforcement of written arbitration provisions in contracts "evidencing a transaction involving commerce" extends the Act's federal supremacy to the limits of Congress' Commerce Clause power. Id. at 270–72, 115 S.Ct. at 837–38, 130 L.Ed.2d at 756–57. The Court acknowledged that the statute's basic purpose, to put arbitration provisions on the same footing as a contract's other terms, was consistent with that broad interpretation of the Act's language. Id. at 272–274, 115 S.Ct. at 838–39, 130 L.Ed.2d at 758. Justices Thomas and Scalia dissented, reiterating the view advanced by Justices O'Connor and Rehnquist in dissent in *Southland* that Congress intended that the Act be a procedural restraint only in federal court.

The trend in favor of arbitration continued in GREEN TREE FINANCIAL CORP. v. RANDOLPH, 531 U.S. 79, 121 S.Ct. 513, 148 L.Ed.2d 373 (2000), in which the Court held that an arbitration agreement is not unenforceable merely because it fails to address the question of arbitration costs; arbitral procedures need not "affirmatively protect a party from potentially steep arbitration costs." Id. at 82, 121 S.Ct. at 517, 148 L.Ed.2d at 378. Although recognizing that "the existence of large arbitration costs could preclude a litigant such as * * * [the consumer in this case, the purchaser of a mobile home] from effectively vindicating her federal statutory rights in the arbitral forum," the Court nevertheless held that "the party resisting arbitration bears the burden of proving that the claims at issue are unsuitable for arbitration." Id. at 90–92, 121 S.Ct. at 522–23, 148 L.Ed. 2d at 383–84.

The Court's endorsement of binding arbitration continued in CIRCUIT CITY STORES, INC. v. ADAMS, 532 U.S. 105, 121 S.Ct. 1302, 149 L.Ed.2d 234 (2001), holding that Section 1 of the Federal Arbitration Act, exempting from its scope contracts of employment of workers engaged in interstate or foreign commerce, was intended to apply only to contracts involving transportation workers. Thus other workers would be prohibited from filing a discrimination suit in court and instead would be compelled to submit their claims to binding arbitration.

The Supreme Court also has shown an increasing willingness to accord broad power to arbitral decision making. In GREEN TREE FINANCIAL CORP. v. BAZZLE, 539 U.S. 444, 123 S.Ct. 2402, 156 L.Ed.2d 414 (2003), the Court held that the question whether an arbitration contract forbids class arbitration is one for the arbitrator and not the court to decide. In BUCKEYE CHECK CASHING INC. v. CARDEGNA, 546 U.S. 440, 126 S.Ct. 1204, 163 L.Ed.2d 1038 (2006), the Court held that an arbitrator, and not a federal or a state court, should consider a claim that a contract containing an arbitration provision is void for illegality. The decision in *Buckeye Check Cashing* was followed by the Court in PRESTON v. FERRER, ___ U.S. ___, 128 S.Ct. 978, 169 L.Ed.2d 917 (2008), in which it was held that an agreement between parties to arbitrate all aspects of an employment dispute under the Federal Arbitration Act superseded a state statutory provision requiring the particular dispute to be heard first by a state designed tribunal (in this case, the state Labor commissioner).

In HALL STREET ASSOCIATES v. MATTEL, INC., ___ U.S. ___, 128 S.Ct. 1396, 170 L.Ed.2d 254 (2008), the Court placed limits on the parties' authority to expand by contract the scope of judicial review of arbitral awards, holding that the grounds for prompt vacatur and modification set out in the Federal Arbitration Act may not be supplemented or compromised by contract. However, the decision presents an interesting wrinkle involving the scope of a district court's Federal Rule 16 power to review an award on grounds beyond those in the FAA:

> * * * The Arbitration agreement was entered into in the course of district-court litigation, was submitted to the District Court as a request to deviate from the standard sequence of trial procedure, and was adopted by the District Court as an order. * * * Hence a question raised by this Court at oral argument: should the agreement be treated as an exercise of the District Court's authority to manage its cases under Federal * * * [Rule] 16?

Id. at ___, 128 S.Ct. at 1406, 170 L.Ed.2d at 266. The Supreme Court remanded to allow the Court of Appeals to consider "whether the District Court's authority to manage litigation independently warranted that court's order on the mode of resolving the * * * issues remaining in this case." Id. at ___, 128 S.Ct. at 1408, 170 L.Ed.2d at 268.

Finally, in VADEN v. DISCOVER BANK, ___ U.S. ___, 129 S.Ct. 1262, 173 L.Ed.2d 206 (2009), the Court considered the relation between Section 1331's well-pleaded complaint rule, see p. 299, supra, and the District Court's jurisdiction to hear a petition to compel arbitration of a dispute under Section 4 of the Federal Arbitration Act. Defendant, a credit card company, sued a credit card-holder in state court under state law to recover arrearages. Petitioner answered and alleged counterclaims, styled as class actions, challenging defendant's finance and other charges as violative of state law. Relying on an arbitration provision in the credit card contract, defendant petitioned the District Court to compel arbitration of petitioner's counterclaims, arguing that they were completely preempted by federal banking law. The Fourth Circuit affirmed the District Court's order of arbitration, on the ground that the court has jurisdiction over a petition to arbitrate if the underlying dispute presents a federal question. The Supreme Court reversed, with Justice Ginsburg writing the Court's opinion. Although the Court agreed that a district court may "look through" the petition to determine whether it has Section 1331 jurisdiction to hear the underlying dispute, jurisdiction must be determined by plaintiff's well-pleaded complaint, and cannot rest on counterclaims. In dissent, Chief Justice Roberts, joined by Justice Stevens, Justice Breyer, and Justice Alito, agreed that a district court must "look through" the petition to determine whether Section 1331 jurisdiction exists over the underlying dispute, but insisted that the underlying dispute, includes only the issue that the petition seeks to arbitrate, and not the entire controversy as set out in the state-court complaint.

NOTES AND QUESTION

1. In *Vaden*, Justice Ginsburg noted that petitioner's "preference for court adjudication is unsurprising," underscoring the fact that the arbitration clause that Discover Bank sought to enforce contained language that barred the card-holder from filing any claims as a representative or member of a class. Id. at ___, 129 S.Ct. at 1269 n.2, 173 L.Ed.2d at 215 n.2. Do you agree that a court must enforce a contractual provision that waives the protections of a Federal Rule of Civil Procedure? Compare Sternlight, *As Mandatory Binding Arbitration Meets the Class Action, Will the Class Action Survive?*, 42 Wm. & Mary L. Rev. 1 (2000), with Ware, *The Case for Enforcing Adhesive Arbitration Agreements—With Particular Consideration of Class Actions and Arbitration Fees*, 5 J. Am. Arb. 251 (2006). The circuit courts currently are divided on the answer to this question, as are the state courts. See Rice, *Enforceable or Not: Class Action Waivers in Mandatory Arbitration Clauses and the Need for a Judicial Standard*, 45 Hous. L. Rev. 215 (2008) (collecting cases). What would be the costs and benefits of permitting litigants to design their own procedures for federal court actions, rather than requiring them to conform to the Federal Rules? See Moffitt, *Customized Litigation: The Case for Making Civil Procedure Negotiable*, 75 Geo. Wash. L. Rev. 461 (2007).

2. Arbitrators do not receive any in-depth professional training or briefing on their task. Although they lack the protections of life tenure associated with Article III judges, arbitrators exercise broad discretion in their decision making. Is there a danger that their method of selection might create a potential for bias, particularly among arbitrators who receive repeat appointments by one company or by one segment of a regulated industry? See Rossein & Hope, *Disclosure and Disqualification Standards for Neutral Arbitrators: How Far to Cast the Net and What Is Sufficient to Vacate Award*, 81 St. John's L. Rev. 203 (2007). An empirical study has found a perception of pro-industry bias among securities-industry arbitrators, leading customers to "express a consistently negative impression of the overall arbitration process * * *." Gross, *When Perception Changes Reality: An Empirical Study of Investors' Views of the Fairness of Securities Arbitration*, 2008 J. Disp. Resol. 349, 389 (2008). Is there also a danger that informality will permit gender bias or racial prejudice in arbitral decision making to go unchecked? See Delgado, Dunn, Brown, Lee & Hubbert, *Fairness and Formality: Minimizing the Risk of Prejudice in Alternative Dispute Resolution*, 1985 Wis. L. Rev. 1359. Similar concerns have been raised about other forms of ADR. See, e.g., Bryan, *Women's Freedom to Contract at Divorce: A Mask for Contextual Coercion*, 47 Buffalo L. Rev. 1153 (1999); Lefcourt, *Women, Mediation and Family Law*, Clearinghouse Rev. 266 (July 1984).

3. In reaching her decision, the arbitrator is not required to apply rules of decision derived from federal or state statutes, common-law rules, or even

from the decisions of other arbitrators, although she may draw on such sources for guidance in reaching a decision. For this reason, many commentators refer to arbitration as "lawless." E.g., Black & Gross, *Making It Up As They Go Along: The Role of Law in Securities Arbitration*, 23 Cardozo L. Rev. 991 (2002). Yet it has become common practice for parties to arbitration proceedings to circulate arbitration awards and decisions. Considering the legal system's reluctance to disturb arbitration awards and decisions except in certain narrowly defined circumstances, is this use of arbitration awards and decisions as nonbinding precedent sound? Moreover, might the diversion of disputes to arbitration proceedings make it more difficult for the courts to create precedent in important fields of law? See Scodro, *Note—Arbitrating Novel Legal Questions: A Recommendation for Reform*, 105 Yale L. J. 1927 (1996).

4. How much preclusive effect should be given to an arbitrator's award in subsequent litigation? As to claim preclusion, it seems safe to infer that most agreements to submit disputes to arbitration contemplate that the award will merge or bar all of the claims and defenses involved. Unless the express terms of the agreement or the peculiar custom of a trade dictate otherwise, subsequent judicial proceedings on the same claim or defenses ordinarily should be precluded. Special statutory schemes may provide judicial remedies that are intended to supplement arbitration without regard to the intent of the parties. Thus, the Supreme Court has ruled that grievance arbitration under a collective-bargaining contract does not preclude an employment discrimination claim under Title VII of the Civil Rights Act of 1964; at most, the findings of the arbitrator can be admitted in evidence with such weight as the court may find appropriate. Alexander v. Gardner–Denver Co., 415 U.S. 36, 94 S.Ct. 1011, 39 L.Ed.2d 147 (1974). Recall the questions the *Gilmer* decision raised in the context of statutory discrimination claims. Could overriding public policies make some disputes unfit for arbitration? Should the courts, the legislature, or the arbitrator decide whether a policy is off limits? See generally Lindsay, *"Public" Rights and Private Forums: Predispute Arbitration Agreements and Securities Litigation*, 20 Loy. L.A. L. Rev. 643 (1987).

5. Advocates of arbitration maintain that it is a flexible device capable of resolving disputes that are more complex than conventional two-party claims, but the various structures and rules for arbitration presuppose that the dispute in question will be a two-party dispute. Are the arbitration procedures described in this section as adaptable to multi-party disputes as proponents of arbitration contend? What difficulties would an arbitrator face in adjudicating a multi-party dispute? See Szalai, *The New ADR: Aggregate Dispute Resolution and Green Tree Financial Corp. v. Bazzle*, 41 Cal. W. L. Rev. 1 (2004).

6. Although at first it may appear that issues of notice and service of process do not arise in the context of arbitration, arbitration proceedings may take place *ex parte* if one side doesn't appear. If a party proves that she had no notice of the arbitration, should she be allowed to challenge the award arrived at by the arbitration in the *ex parte* proceeding?

7. The expansion of international trade and commercial transactions in the past fifty years has created a need for private international commercial

dispute resolution. Many commercial parties are uncomfortable adjudicating disputes in foreign court systems because they are unfamiliar with the procedures and law of foreign forums and fear favoritism to nationals. The demand for mechanisms for private commercial dispute resolution has led to the development of international commercial arbitration rules (such as the International Chamber of Commerce (ICC) Rules). These are applied in international arbitration centers around the world. Using these accepted rules and forums, private parties are able to arbitrate and resolve their commercial disputes without submitting the dispute to a foreign forum. Given these resources, why might parties still prefer to resolve their dispute in court? Should an international commercial arbitration decision be enforceable in any forum in the world?

2. ADR AND THE JUDICIAL PREFERENCE FOR SETTLEMENT

DELTA AIR LINES, INC. v. AUGUST, 450 U.S. 346, 101 S.Ct. 1146, 67 L.Ed.2d 287 (1981). Rosemary August filed suit against Delta Air Lines seeking $20,000 in back pay for violation of Title VII of the Civil Rights Act of 1964. Delta made a formal settlement offer of $450, which August rejected. At trial, judgment was for Delta and the District Court directed that each party bear its own costs. The court held that Federal Rule 68, which directs that a plaintiff who rejects a formal settlement offer must pay post-offer costs if the "judgment that the offeree finally obtains is not more favorable than the unaccepted offer," was not applicable since Delta's offer of $450 was not a reasonable, good-faith attempt to settle the case. The Court of Appeals for the Seventh Circuit affirmed on the same grounds.

The Supreme Court affirmed the result, although it rejected the reasoning of the lower courts. In an opinion written by Justice Stevens, the Court held that "the plain language, the purpose, and the history of Rule 68" made clear that the words, in Rule 68 as it then existed, "judgment * * * obtained by the offeree" do not encompass a judgment against the offeree:

> Our interpretation of the Rule is consistent with its purpose. The purpose of Rule 68 is to encourage the settlement of litigation. In all litigation, the adverse consequences of potential defeat provide both parties with an incentive to settle in advance of trial. Rule 68 provides an additional inducement to settle in those cases in which there is a strong probability that the plaintiff will obtain a judgment but the amount of recovery is uncertain. Because prevailing plaintiffs presumptively will obtain costs under Rule 54(d), Rule 68 imposes a special burden on the plaintiff to whom a formal settlement offer is made. If a plaintiff rejects a Rule 68 settlement offer, he will lose some of the benefits of victory if his recovery is less than the offer.

> Because costs are usually assessed against the losing party, liability for costs is a normal incident of defeat. Therefore, a nonsettling plaintiff does not run the risk of suffering additional burdens that do not ordinarily attend a defeat, and Rule 68 would provide little, if any, additional incentive if it were applied when the plaintiff loses.
>
> Defendant argues that Rule 68 does provide such an incentive, because it operates to deprive the district judge of the discretion vested in him by Rule 54(d). According to this reasoning, Rule 68 is mandatory, and a district judge must assess costs against a plaintiff who rejects a settlement offer and then either fails to obtain a judgment or recovers less than the offer. * * *
>
> * * * If, as defendant argues, Rule 68 applies to defeated plaintiffs, any settlement offer, no matter how small, would apparently trigger the operation of the Rule. Thus any defendant, by performing the meaningless act of making a nominal settlement offer, could eliminate the trial judge's discretion under Rule 54(d). We cannot reasonably conclude that the drafters of the Federal Rules intended on the one hand affirmatively to grant the district judge discretion to deny costs to the prevailing party under Rule 54(d) and then on the other hand to give defendants—and only defendants—the power to take away that discretion by performing a token act. Moreover, if the Rule operated as defendant argues, we cannot conceive of a reason why the drafters would have given only defendants, and not plaintiffs, the power to divest the judge of his Rule 54(d) discretion. * * * When Rule 68 is read literally, however, it is evenhanded in its operation. As we have already noted, it does not apply to judgments in favor of the defendant or to judgments in favor of the plaintiff for an amount greater than the settlement offer. In both of those extreme situations the trial judge retains his Rule 54(d) discretion. * * * Thus unless we assume that the Federal Rules were intended to be biased in favor of defendants, we can conceive of no reason why defendants—and not plaintiffs—should be given an entirely risk-free method of denying trial judges the discretion that Rule 54(d) confers regardless of the outcome of the litigation.
>
> The Court of Appeals, perceiving the anomaly of allowing defendants to control the discretion of district judges by making sham offers, resolved the problem by holding that only reasonable offers trigger the operation of Rule 68. But the plain language of the Rule makes it unnecessary to read a reasonableness requirement into the Rule. * * *

Id. at 352–55, 101 S.Ct. at 1150–52, 67 L.Ed.2d at 292–95.

MAREK v. CHESNY, 473 U.S. 1, 105 S.Ct. 3012, 87 L.Ed.2d 1 (1985). Three police officers, in answering a call on a domestic disturbance, shot and killed Alfred Chesny's son. Chesny, on his own behalf and as administrator of his son's estate, filed suit against the officers in federal district court under 42 U.S.C. § 1983 and state tort law. Prior to trial, the police officers made a timely offer of settlement of $100,000, expressly including accrued costs and attorney's fees, but Chesny did not accept the offer. The case went to trial and Chesny was awarded $5,000 on the state-law claim, $52,000 for the Section 1983 violation, and $3,000 in punitive damages. Chesny then filed a request for attorney's fees under 42 U.S.C. § 1988, which provides that a prevailing party in a Section 1983 action may be awarded attorney's fees "as part of the costs." The claimed attorney's fees included fees for work performed subsequent to the settlement offer. The District Court declined to award these latter fees pursuant to Rule 68. The Court of Appeals reversed, but the Supreme Court agreed with the District Court.

The Court held first that the officers' offer was valid under Rule 68. As the Court read it, the Rule does not require that a defendant's offer itemize the respective amounts being tendered for settlement of the underlying substantive claim and for costs. In reaching this result, Chief Justice Burger, writing for the majority, asserted that the drafters' concern was not so much with the particular components of offers, but with the judgments to be allowed against defendants. Whether or not the offer recites that costs are included or specifies an amount for costs, the offer allows judgment to be entered against the defendant both for damages caused by the challenged conduct and for costs. In Chief Justice Burger's view, this construction of Rule 68 furthers its objective of encouraging settlements.

Chief Justice Burger next noted that the drafters of Rule 68 were aware of the various federal statutes that, as an exception to the "American Rule," authorize an award of attorney's fees to prevailing parties as part of the costs in particular cases. From this, he concluded that the term "costs" in the Rule was intended to refer to all costs properly awardable under the relevant substantive statute. Thus, when the underlying statute defines "costs" to include attorney's fees, the fees are to be included as costs for purposes of Rule 68. Since Section 1983 expressly includes attorney's fees as "costs" available to a prevailing plaintiff in a suit under the statute, those fees are subject to the cost-shifting provision of Rule 68. As Chief Justice Burger saw it, rather than "cutting against the grain" of Section 1983, applying Rule 68 in the context of a Section 1983 action is consistent with Section 1988's policies and objectives of encouraging plaintiffs to bring meritorious civil rights suits; Rule 68 simply encourages settlements.

Justice Brennan filed a vigorous dissent for himself and Justices Marshall and Blackmun.

NOTES AND QUESTIONS

1. The majority in *Marek* argues that the effect of Rule 68 is neutral because settlements serve the interest of plaintiffs as well as defendants. But does Rule 68 actually encourage settlements? Or is its primary effect to force plaintiffs to accept a lower settlement amount than would be offered in the absence of the rule? See Miller, *An Economic Analysis of Rule 68*, 15 J.Legal Stud. 93 (1986); Rowe, *Predicting the Effects of Attorney Fee Shifting*, 47 Law & Contemp. Probs. 139 (1984).

2. For a comprehensive discussion of Federal Rule 68, see Bone, *"To Encourage Settlement": Rule 68, Offers of Judgment, and the History of the Federal Rules of Civil Procedure*, 102 Nw. U. L. Rev. 1561 (2008).

3. Implicit in the attempt to encourage settlement is an assumption that a negotiated resolution of a dispute is more desirable than that of a judicial disposition. See Menkel–Meadow, *Whose Dispute Is It Anyway?: A Philosophical and Democratic Defense of Settlement (In Some Cases)*, 83 Geo. L.J. 2663 (1995). Consider the contrary position of Professor Fiss, who has emphasized the public role of litigation as "an institutional arrangement for using state power to bring a recalcitrant reality closer to our chosen ideals":

> * * * I do not believe that settlement as a generic practice is preferable to judgment or should be institutionalized on a wholesale and indiscriminate basis. It should be treated instead as a highly problematic technique for streamlining dockets. Settlement is for me the civil analogue of plea bargaining: Consent is often coerced; the bargain may be struck by someone without authority; the absence of a trial and judgment renders subsequent judicial involvement troublesome; and although dockets are trimmed, justice may not be done. Like plea bargaining, settlement is a capitulation to the conditions of mass society and should be neither encouraged nor praised.

Fiss, *Against Settlement*, 93 Yale L.J. 1073, 1075, 1089 (1984) (citations omitted).

4. Settlement terms may be drafted to protect the privacy of the parties to the contract. Retaining the confidentiality of information may be desirable for the parties, but is it desirable for society as a whole? See Macklin, *Promoting Settlement, Foregoing the Facts*, 14 N.Y.U. Rev. L. & Soc. Change 579 (1986) (stressing the value of judicial fact-finding as "a source of tested facts" for use in public policy discussion and planning).

5. How does judicial participation in the settlement process affect the judge's traditional role as decision maker? Some judges delegate the task of negotiating a settlement to an extrajudicial officer. See p. 948, supra. Other judges may conduct a mediation conference with the goal of settling the dispute. See Brunet, *Judicial Mediation and Signaling*, 3 Nev. L. Rev. 233 (2002–03). Is there a danger that judicial mediation will undermine the judge's ability to be a neutral decision maker? See Shweder, *Judicial Limitations on ADR: The Role and Ethics of Judges Encouraging Settlements*, 20 Geo. J. Legal Ethics 51 (2007).

3. ADR IN THE COURTS

IN RE AFRICAN–AMERICAN SLAVE DESCENDANTS' LITIGATION

United States District Court, Northern District of Illinois, 2003.
272 F.Supp.2d 755.

NORGLE, DISTRICT JUDGE.

Before the court is Plaintiffs' Motion to Appoint a Mediator. For the following reasons, Plaintiffs' motion is denied.

I. Background

Plaintiffs, who identify themselves as both formerly enslaved African–Americans and descendants of formerly enslaved African–Americans, seek monetary and injunctive relief against various corporate Defendants for present and past wrongs in connection with the institution of slavery. Plaintiffs seek, among other remedies, restitution from the named Defendants and other unknown defendants who allegedly profited from the Trans–Atlantic slave trade or the use of slave labor. Plaintiffs claim they have a property right in the fruits of their unpaid ancestor's labor under the theories of unjust enrichment and quasi-contract. Plaintiffs also claim that Defendants are liable under the theory of third-party liability for their participation in the violation of international norms and crimes against humanity. * * *

* * * [T]he court held an initial status conference where all of the parties involved in this multi-district litigation were given an opportunity to be heard. At the initial status conference, Plaintiffs, through their counsel, expressed their intention of filing a motion for the appointment of a special master * * *

* * * [T]wo months beyond the deadline set by the court, Plaintiffs filed their Motion to Appoint a Mediator. Although [Plaintiffs'] motion is styled as "Plaintiffs' Motion to Appoint a Mediator," the court notes that Plaintiffs request the court to "enter an order appointing a mediator or a special master." * * *

II. Discussion

Courts have increasingly relied on mediation and other forms of Alternative Dispute Resolution ("ADR") to reduce the costs of litigation which, in many cases, can become quite burdensome on both the parties and the judicial system. This is particularly true in complex cases involving numerous litigants. * * * The Alternative Dispute Resolution Act of 1998 ("ADR Act") provides, in part:

> [E]ach district court shall, by local rule adopted under section 2071(a), require that litigants in all civil cases consider the use of an alterna-

> tive dispute resolution process at an appropriate stage in the litigation.... Any district court that elects to require the use of alternative dispute resolution in certain cases may do so only with respect to mediation, early neutral evaluation, and, if the parties consent, arbitration.

28 U.S.C. § 652(a).

Where one or both parties do not voluntarily submit to mediation, the court may order mandatory mediation in some instances. The court's authority to order mandatory mediation arises from four potential sources: "(a) the court's local rules; (b) an applicable statute; (c) the Federal Rules of Civil Procedure; and (d) the court's inherent powers." *In re Atlantic Pipe Corp.*, 304 F.3d 135, 140 (1st Cir.2002). * * * Plaintiffs allude to all four sources of judicial authority in support [of] their position that the court can order Defendants to mediate over an objection. The court will now consider whether it has the authority to compel mediation, and if so, whether it will do so in this case.

A. The Local Rules

The Northern District of Illinois has complied with the requirements of § 652 of the ADR Act by implementing its "Voluntary Mediation Program." See Local Rule 16.3. Rule 16.3 provides, in part: "[a] program for voluntary mediation is established for cases arising under the Federal Trademark Act of 1946, 15 U.S.C. §§ 1051–1127 ('the Lanham Act')." * * *

In this case, Plaintiffs' Consolidated Amended Complaint contains no claims which would invoke the court's local rule on mediation. * * * Additionally, the local rule only provides for voluntary mediation, not court ordered mediation. Although § 652 of the ADR Act states that district courts may require mediation in certain cases if it chooses to do so, the Northern District of Illinois' use of the term "voluntary" indicates that the court is not authorized to order mediation in cases where one or both of the parties object. Because Defendants strongly object to mediation at this time, the court cannot compel Defendants to mediate Plaintiffs' claims pursuant to the local rules.

B. Applicable Statute

Plaintiffs cite 28 U.S.C. § 652 of the ADR Act as authority for the court to order Defendants to mediate at this stage of the litigation. Congress enacted the ADR Act to promote the use of alternative dispute resolution methods in the federal courts. The ADR Act specifically promotes the use of mediation, early neutral evaluation, mini-trials and arbitration. 28 U.S.C. § 652(a). Although the ADR Act requires the court to order arbitration only upon the consent of the parties, there is no such provision precluding the district courts from compelling mediation even if one or both of the parties object. * * *

In spite of the ADR Act's broad scope and strong language encouraging district courts to use alternative dispute resolution methods, the Act clearly establishes that each judicial district adopt its own local rules establishing the parameters which outline its alternative dispute resolution procedures. See 28 U.S.C. § 652(a). "In the absence of such local rules, the ADR Act itself does not authorize any specific court to use a particular ADR mechanism." *In re Atlantic Pipe Corp.*, 304 F.3d at 140. Because the Northern District of Illinois has not adopted a local rule giving the court authority to compel mediation on an unwilling litigant, the court cannot, pursuant to the ADR Act, order mediation where one party objects.

C. The Federal Rules of Civil Procedure

Plaintiffs also cite Federal Rule of Civil Procedure 16(c)(9) [now, Rule 16(c)(2)(I)] in support of their motion. * * * The advisory committee's notes to the 1993 Amendments to FRCP 16(c) provide, in part:

> Even if a case cannot immediately be settled, the judge and attorneys can explore possible use of alternative procedures such as mini-trials, summary jury trials, mediation, neutral evaluation, and non-binding arbitration that can lead to consensual resolution of the dispute without a full trial on the merits. The rule acknowledges the presence of statutes and local procedures even when not agreed to by the parties. The rule does not attempt to resolve questions as the extent a court would be authorized to require such proceedings as an exercise of its inherent powers.

* * * Both the express wording of * * * [the rule] and the language in the advisory committee's notes provide limits on the district court's authority to compel mediation. Federal Rule * * * 16(c)(9) [now Federal Rule 16(c)(2)(I)] does not give the court authority to order mediation on unwilling litigants absent a statute or local rule authorizing such a decision. * * *

D. The Court's Inherent Powers

* * * Although the scope of a district court's inherent powers appears broad, it is actually quite limited.

> There are at least four limiting principles. First, inherent powers must be used in a way reasonably suited to the enhancement of the court's processes, including the orderly and expeditious disposition of pending cases. * * * Second, inherent powers cannot be exercised in a manner that contradicts an applicable statute or rule. * * * Third, the use of inherent powers must comport with procedural fairness. * * * And, finally, inherent powers "must be exercised with restraint and discretion." * * *

In re Atlantic Pipe Corp., 304 F.3d at 143.

In this instance, the court does have the inherent power to order the parties to submit to non-binding mediation. However, the issuance of such an order would not facilitate an expeditious end to the litigation. Both parties have different views pertaining to the viability of the claims presented [and all defendants have moved to dismiss the claims]. * * * Defendants have also objected to the imposition of mediation. "When mediation is forced upon unwilling litigants, it stands to reason that the likelihood of settlement is diminished. Requiring parties to invest substantial amounts of time and money in mediation under such circumstances may well be inefficient." *In re Atlantic Pipe Corp.*, 304 F.3d at 143 (citing Cf. Richard A. Posner, The Summary Jury Trial and Other Methods of Alternative Dispute Resolution: Some Cautionary Observations, 53 U. Chi. L. Rev. 366, 369–72 (1986) (offering a model to evaluate ADR techniques in terms of their capacity to encourage settlements)). Arguably, the motion for the appointment of a mediator may be premature.

III. Conclusion

For the foregoing reasons, Plaintiffs' Motion to Appoint a Mediator is denied.

IT IS SO ORDERED.

NOTES AND QUESTIONS

1. Compare *Nick*, p. 953, supra, with *In re African–American Slave Descendants' Litigation,* p. 1383, supra. Should court-annexed ADR in the federal system be subject to uniform rules? See Maull, *ADR in the Federal Courts: Would Uniformity Be Better?*, 34 Duq. L. Rev. 245, 253 (1996).

2. Why might plaintiffs in *In re African–American Slave Descendants' Litigation* have desired to engage the defendants in mediation despite the other side's resistance? Could these goals be equally well served in litigation? See Van Schaack, *With All Deliberate Speed: Civil Human Rights Litigation as a Tool for Social Change*, 57 Vand. L. Rev. 2305, 2330 (2004).

3. Mediation is the most frequently used ADR process in the federal courts. Sixty percent of all cases sent to ADR in the federal system during the period 2000–01 were referred to mediation. See Subrin, *A Traditionalist Looks at Mediation: It's Here to Stay and Much Better than I Thought*, 3 Nev. L. J. 196, 229 at Appendix (2002–03). The trend in the state courts is similar. Id. What do you think accounts for the judiciary's preference for mediation as an ADR process?

SECTION D. ASSESSING ADR AND THE ROLE OF CIVIL LITIGATION IN AMERICAN SOCIETY

Does ADR deliver the benefits it promises in terms of speed, cost, participation, and flexibility? Data are limited, show mixed results, and are difficult to assess given the variety of ADR mechanisms. See, e.g., Kakalik, Dunworth, Hill, McCaffrey, Oshiro, Pace & Vaiana, An Evaluation of Mediation and Early Neutral Evaluation Under the Civil Justice

Reform Act (1996); Rosenberg & Folberg, *Alternative Dispute Resolution: An Empirical Analysis*, 46 Stan.L.Rev. 1487 (1994); Federal Judicial Center, Report to the Judicial Conference Committee on Court Administration and Case Management: A Study of the Five Demonstration Programs Established Under the Civil Justice Reform Act of 1990, at 8–10 (1997) (showing some evidence of increased disputant satisfaction and savings of time and money using certain ADR techniques in some jurisdictions). Moreover, because many ADR services are private and the proceedings are closed to the public, it is difficult to obtain information that a proper assessment would require. See Landsman, *ADR and the Cost of Compulsion*, 57 Stan.L.Rev. 1593 (2005). For a summary of available, recent data on mandatory federal court-annexed ADR, see Ward, *Mandatory Court–Annexed Alternative Dispute Resolution in the United States Federal Courts: Panacea or Pandemic?*, 81 St. John's L. Rev. 77 (2007).

In assessing ADR, consider whether its widespread availability, coupled with a trend toward mandatory participation in ADR processes, might affect the traditional role that civil litigation has played in democratic life. Professor Hensler has stated:

> The public spectacle of civil litigation gives life to the "rule of law." * * * In a democracy where many people are shut out of legislative power either because they are too few in number, or too dispersed to elect representatives, or because they do not have the financial resources to influence legislators, collective litigation in class or other mass form provides an alternative strategy for group action. Private individualized dispute resolution extinguishes the possibility of such collective litigation. Conciliation has much to recommend it. But the visible presence of institutionalized and legitimized conflict, channeled productively, teaches citizens that it is not always better to compromise and accept the status quo because, sometimes, great gains are to be had by peaceful contest.

Hensler, *Our Courts, Ourselves: How the Alternative Dispute Resolution Movement Is Re–Shaping Our Legal System*, 108 Pa. St. L. Rev. 165 (2003). In what ways might a parallel system of private justice affect the operation of the public courts? A noted federal judge has expressed these concerns:

> Widespread privatization of dispute resolution has the potential to stunt the common law's development as entire areas of law are removed from the courts; deprive the public of important information, such as news of a product's harmful effects; deny plaintiffs the therapeutic benefit of having their "day in court;" degrade constitutional guarantees of the right to a jury trial; and prevent public debate and consensus-building in cases with national public policy implications.

Weinstein, *Some Benefits and Risks of Privatization of Justice through ADR*, 11 Ohio St. J. on Disp. Resol. 241, 246 (1996). Compare Main, *ADR: The New Equity*, 74 U. Cin. L. Rev. 329 (2005), with Sternlight, *Is*

Alternative Dispute Resolution Consistent with the Rule of Law? Lessons from Abroad, 56 DePaul L. Rev. 569 (2007).

Recall the question posed at the outset of this book: "What is the test of a good system of procedure?" See p. 3, supra. What is the relevance of this question to your assessment of ADR? How has your answer to this question changed over the course of your study of civil procedure?

INDEX

References are to Pages

References are to Pages

References are to Pages

References are to Pages

References are to Pages

†